CORPORATIONS AND OTHER BUSINESS ASSOCIATIONS

STATUTES, RULES AND FORMS

2003 EDITION

Edited By

Jeffrey D. Bauman
Professor of Law
Georgetown University Law Center

THOMSON
WEST

Mat #40150078

610 Opperman Drive
P.O. Box 64526
St. Paul, MN 55164–0526
1–800–328–9352

Printed in the United States of America

ISBN 0–314–14654–7

TEXT IS PRINTED ON 10% POST CONSUMER RECYCLED PAPER

Preface

This book has several goals. First, it is intended to provide students with the statutes, rules and forms to be used in the basic courses in Corporations, Business Organizations and Corporate Finance. There are also materials dealing with the federal securities laws. Although they are not as comprehensive as would be necessary in a full course in Securities Regulation, they are intended to cove those parts of the securities laws that are most likely to be treated in a corporate law context.

The second goal of the book is to provide examples of corporate, partnership and securities documents that reflect the best in current practice. As examples of such documents, this edition contains the corporate governance guidelines for General Electric and Disney and shareholder proposals drawn from the current proxy season. Although prior editions have contained model documents, this edition includes documents provided by practitioners that are drawn from their own files. I have expressed my thanks to them both in the book and below.

Finally, the book is intended to reflect the broad range of sources of corporate law and to emphasize the importance of legal ethics in the practice of business law. Thus there are extensive excerpts from the 2002 version of the American Bar Association's Model Rules of Professional Conduct and the comments thereto as well as from the New York Stock Exchange's current and proposed corporate governance provisions in its listing standards. Future editions will expand this type of material. Some of the materials in this edition are the direct result of suggestions made by users of earlier editions. I invite suggestions for future editions.

I owe thanks to many people for their assistance in preparing this edition. Many of the documents were generously provided by practitioners who spent time making sure they would be useful to a broad range of users. I am particularly grateful to Frederick H. Alexander, Esq., a member of Morris, Nichols, Arsht & Tunnell, Daniel Goelzer, Esq., formerly a member of Baker & Mc Kenzie, Jack Lewis, Esq., a member of Shaw Pittman, Herbert S. Wander, Esq., a member of Katten, Muchin, Zavin & Rosenman, and those others in their firms who assisted them in compiling these documents.

I continue to be grateful to Roxy Birkel at Thomson/West for the substantial assistance she provided in the production of the book. Her good cheer, unflagging patience and keen intelligence under considerable time pressure made the entire production process substantially easier. Thanks also to my assistant, Rada Stojanovich-Hayes for putting disparate documents into usable form for publication.

My greatest debt, however, is to my research assistant, Kimberly Brickell, a student at the Georgetown University Law Center. She spent countless hours collecting and arranging many of the materials and working with the attorneys listed above. It is a commonplace in an acknowledgment for the author or editor to say that the work could not have been done without a particular person. In my case, that would be a gross understatement. She has my thanks for all that she has done and bears no responsibility for whatever errors inevitably may have crept into a book of this size.

JEFFREY D. BAUMAN

June 2003

Table of Contents

CORPORATIONS AND OTHER BUSINESS ASSOCIATIONS

STATUTES, RULES AND FORMS

2003 EDITION

*

I. CORPORATIONS

A. MODEL BUSINESS CORPORATION ACT

(with selected Official Comments)

Contents

CHAPTER 1. GENERAL PROVISIONS

SUBCHAPTER A. SHORT TITLE AND RESERVATION OF POWER

SUBCHAPTER B. FILING DOCUMENTS

SUBCHAPTER C. SECRETARY OF STATE

SUBCHAPTER D. DEFINITIONS

CHAPTER 2. INCORPORATION

SUBCHAPTER D. DISTRIBUTIONS

CHAPTER 7. SHAREHOLDERS

SUBCHAPTER A. MEETINGS

SUBCHAPTER B. VOTING

SUBCHAPTER C. VOTING TRUSTS AND AGREEMENTS

SUBCHAPTER D. DERIVATIVE PROCEEDINGS

CHAPTER 8. DIRECTORS AND OFFICERS

SUBCHAPTER A. BOARD OF DIRECTORS

SUBCHAPTER B. MEETINGS AND ACTION OF THE BOARD

SUBCHAPTER C. STANDARDS OF CONDUCT

SUBCHAPTER D. OFFICERS

SUBCHAPTER E. INDEMNIFICATION

SUBCHAPTER F. DIRECTORS' CONFLICTING INTEREST TRANSACTIONS

CHAPTER 9. DOMESTICATION AND CONVERSION

SUBCHAPTER A. PRELIMINARY PROVISIONS

SUBCHAPTER B. DOMESTICATION

SUBCHAPTER C. NONPROFIT CONVERSION [OMITTED]

SUBCHAPTER D. FOREIGN NONPROFIT DOMESTICATION AND CONVERSION [OMITTED]

SUBCHAPTER E. ENTITY CONVERSION

CHAPTER 10. AMENDMENT OF ARTICLES OF INCORPORATION AND BYLAWS

SUBCHAPTER A. AMENDMENT OF ARTICLES OF INCORPORATION

CHAPTER 1. GENERAL PROVISIONS

SUBCHAPTER A. SHORT TITLE AND RESERVATION OF POWER

§ 1.01 Short Title

This Act shall be known and may be cited as the "[name of state] Business Corporation Act."

§ 1.02 Reservation of Power to Amend or Repeal

The [name of state legislature] has power to amend or repeal all or part of this Act at any time and all domestic and foreign corporations subject to this Act are governed by the amendment or repeal.

SUBCHAPTER B. FILING DOCUMENTS

§ 1.20 Filing Requirements

(a) A document must satisfy the requirements of this section, and of any other section that adds to or varies these requirements, to be entitled to filing by the secretary of state.

(b) This Act must require or permit filing the document in the office of the secretary of state.

(c) The document must contain the information required by this Act. It may contain other information as well.

(d) The document must be typewritten or printed or, if electronically transmitted, it must be in a format that can be retrieved or reproduced in typewritten or printed form.

(e) The document must be in the English language. A corporate name need not be in English if written in English letters or Arabic or Roman numerals, and the certificate of existence required of foreign corporations need not be in English if accompanied by a reasonably authenticated English translation.

(f) The document must be executed:

(1) by the chairman of the board of directors of a domestic or foreign corporation, by its president, or by another of its officers;

(2) if directors have not been selected or the corporation has not been formed, by an incorporator; or

(3) if the corporation is in the hands of a receiver, trustee, or other court-appointed fiduciary, by that fiduciary.

(g) The person executing the document shall sign it and state beneath or opposite his signature his name and the capacity in which he signs. The document may but need not contain a corporate seal, attestation, acknowledgement or verification.

(h) If the secretary of state has prescribed a mandatory form for the document under section 1.21, the document must be in or on the prescribed form.

(i) The document must be delivered to the office of the secretary of state for filing. Delivery may be made by electronic transmission if and to the extent permitted by the secretary of state. If it is filed in typewritten or printed form and not transmitted electronically, the secretary of state may require one exact or conformed copy to be delivered with the document (except as provided in sections 5.03 and 15.09).

(j) When the document is delivered to the office of the secretary of state for filing, the correct filing fee, and any franchise tax, license fee, or penalty required to be paid therewith by this Act or other law must be paid or provision for payment made in a manner permitted by the secretary of state.

(k) Whenever a provision of this Act permits any of the terms of a plan or a filed document to be dependent on facts objectively ascertainable outside the plan or filed document, the following provisions apply:

(1) The manner in which the facts will operate upon the terms of the plan or filed document shall be set forth in the plan or filed document.

(2) The facts may include, but are not limited to:

(i) any of the following that is available in a nationally recognized news or information medium either in print or electronically: statistical or market indices, market prices of any security or group of securities, interest rates, currency exchange rates, or similar economic or financial data;

(ii) a determination or action by any person or body, including the corporation or any other party to a plan or filed document; or

(iii) the terms of, or actions taken under, an agreement to which the corporation is a party, or any other agreement or document.

(3) As used in this subsection:

(i) "filed document" means a document filed with the secretary of state under any provision of this Act except chapter 15 or section 16.21; and

(ii) "plan" means a plan of domestication, nonprofit conversion, entity conversion, merger or share exchange.

(4) The following provisions of a plan or filed document may not be made dependent on facts outside the plan or filed document:

(i) The name and address of any person required in a filed document.

(ii) The registered office of any entity required in a filed document.

(iii) The registered agent of any entity required in a filed document.

(iv) The number of authorized shares and designation of each class or series of shares.

(v) The effective date of a filed document.

(vi) Any required statement in a filed document of the date on which the underlying transaction was approved or the manner in which that approval was given.

(5) If a provision of a filed document is made dependent on a fact ascertainable outside of the filed document, and that fact is not ascertainable by reference to a source described in subsection (k)(2)(i) or a document that is a matter of public record, or the affected shareholders have not received notice of the fact from the corporation, then the corporation shall file with the secretary of state articles of amendment setting forth the fact promptly after the time when the fact referred to is first ascertainable or thereafter changes. Articles of amendment under this subsection (k)(5) are deemed to be authorized by the authorization of the original filed document or plan to which they relate and may be filed by the corporation without further action by the board of directors or the shareholders.

§ 1.21 Forms

(a) The secretary of state may prescribe and furnish on request forms for: (1) an application for a certificate of existence, (2) a foreign corporation's application for a certificate of authority to transact business in this state, (3) a foreign corporation's application for a certificate of withdrawal, and (4) the annual report. If the secretary of state so requires, use of these forms is mandatory.

(b) The secretary of state may prescribe and furnish on request forms for other documents required or permitted to be filed by this Act but their use is not mandatory.

§ 1.22 Filing, Service and Copying Fees

(a) The secretary of state shall collect the following fees when the documents described in this subsection are delivered to him for filing:

	Document	Fee
(1)	Articles of incorporation	$_______.
(2)	Application for use of indistinguishable name	$_______.
(3)	Application for reserved name	$_______.
(4)	Notice of transfer of reserved name	$_______.
(5)	Application for registered name	$_______.
(6)	Application for renewal of registered name	$_______.
(7)	Corporation's statement of change of registered agent or registered office or both	$_______.
(8)	Agent's statement of change of registered office for each affected corporation	$_______.
	not to exceed a total of	$_______.
(9)	Agent's statement of resignation	No fee.
(9A)	Articles of domestication	$_______.
(9B)	Articles of charter surrender	$_______.
(9C)	Articles of nonprofit conversion	$_______.
(9D)	Articles of domestication and conversion	$_______.
(9E)	Articles of entity conversion	$_______.
(10)	Amendment of articles of incorporation	$_______.
(11)	Restatement of articles of incorporation	$_______.
	with amendment of articles	$_______.
(12)	Articles of merger or share exchange	$_______.
(13)	Articles of dissolution	$_______.
(14)	Articles of revocation of dissolution	$_______.
(15)	Certificate of administrative dissolution	No fee.
(16)	Application for reinstatement following administrative dissolution	$_______.
(17)	Certificate of reinstatement	No fee.
(18)	Certificate of judicial dissolution	No fee.
(19)	Application for certificate of authority	$_______.
(20)	Application for amended certificate of authority	$_______.
(21)	Application for certificate of withdrawal	$_______.

	Document	Fee
(21A)	Application for transfer of authority	$______.
(22)	Certificate of revocation of authority to transact business	No fee.
(23)	Annual report	$______.
(24)	Articles of correction	$______.
(25)	Application for certificate of existence or authorization	$______.
(26)	Any other document required or permitted to be filed by this Act.	$______.

(b) The secretary of state shall collect a fee of $______ each time process is served on him under this Act. The party to a proceeding causing service of process is entitled to recover this fee as costs if he prevails in the proceeding.

(c) The secretary of state shall collect the following fees for copying and certifying the copy of any filed document relating to a domestic or foreign corporation:

(1) $______ a page for copying; and

(2) $______ for the certificate.

§ 1.23 Effective Time and Date of Document

(a) Except as provided in subsection (b) and section 1.24(c), a document accepted for filing is effective:

(1) at the date and time of filing , as evidenced by such means as the secretary of state may use for the purpose of recording the date and time of filing; or

(2) at the time specified in the document as its effective time on the date it is filed.

(b) A document may specify a delayed effective time and date, and if it does so the document becomes effective at the time and date specified. If a delayed effective date but no time is specified, the document is effective at the close of business on that date. A delayed effective date for a document may not be later than the 90th day after the date it is filed.

§ 1.24 Correcting Filed Document

(a) A domestic or foreign corporation may correct a document filed by the secretary of state if (1) the document contains an inaccuracy, or (2) the document was defectively executed, attested, sealed, verified or acknowledged, or (3) the electronic transmission was defective.

(b) A document is corrected:

(1) by preparing articles of correction that

(i) describe the document (including its filing date) or attach a copy of it to the articles,

(ii) specify the inaccuracy or defect to be corrected, and

(iii) correct the inaccuracy or defect; and

(2) by delivering the articles to the secretary of state for filing.

(c) Articles of correction are effective on the effective date of the document they correct except as to persons relying on the uncorrected document and adversely affected by the correction. As to those persons, articles of correction are effective when filed.

OFFICIAL COMMENT

Section 1.24 permits making corrections in filed documents without refiling the entire document or submitting formal articles of amendment. This correction procedure has two advantages: (1) filing articles of correction may be less expensive than refiling the document or filing articles of amendment, and (2) articles of correction do not alter the effective date of the underlying document being corrected. Indeed, under section 1.24(c), even the correction relates back to the original effective date of the document except as to persons relying on the original document and adversely affected by the correction. As to these persons, the effective date of articles of correction is the date the articles are filed.

A document may be corrected either because it contains an inaccuracy or because it was defectively executed (including defects in optional forms of execution that do not affect the eligibility of the original document for filing). In addition, the document may be corrected if the electronic transmission was defective. This is intended to cover the situation where an electronic filing is made but, due to a defect in transmission, the filed document is later discovered to be inconsistent with the document intended to be filed. If no filing is made because of a defect in transmission, articles of correction may not be used to make a retroactive filing. Therefore, a corporation making an electronic filing should take steps to confirm that the filing was received by the secretary of state.

A provision in a document setting an effective date (section 1.23) may be corrected under this section, but the corrected effective date must comply with section 1.23 measured from the date of the original filing of the document being corrected, i.e. it cannot be before the date of filing of the document or more than 90 days thereafter.

§ 1.25 Filing Duty of Secretary of State

(a) If a document delivered to the office of the secretary of state for filing satisfies the requirements of section 1.20, the secretary of state shall file it.

(b) The secretary of state files a document by recording it as filed on the date and time of receipt. After filing a document, except as provided in sections 5.03 and 15.10, the secretary of state shall deliver to the domestic or foreign corporation or its representative a copy of the document with an acknowledgement of the date and time of filing.

(c) If the secretary of state refuses to file a document, he shall return it to the domestic or foreign corporation or its representative within five days after the document was delivered, together with a brief, written explanation of the reason for his refusal.

(d) The secretary of state's duty to file documents under this section is ministerial. His filing or refusing to file a document does not:

(1) affect the validity or invalidity of the document in whole or part;

(2) relate to the correctness or incorrectness of information contained in the document;

(3) create a presumption that the document is valid or invalid or that information contained in the document is correct or incorrect.

§ 1.26 Appeal From Secretary of State's Refusal to File Document

(a) If the secretary of state refuses to file a document delivered to his office for filing, the domestic or foreign corporation may appeal the refusal to the [name or describe] court [of the county where the corporations's principal office (or, if none in this state, its registered office) is or will be located] [of $______ county]. The appeal is commenced by petitioning the court to compel filing the document and by attaching to the petition the document and the secretary of state's explanation of his refusal to file.

(b) The court may summarily order the secretary of state to file the document or take other action the court considers appropriate.

(c) The court's final decision may be appealed as in other civil proceedings.

§ 1.27 Evidentiary Effect of Copy of Filed Document

A certificate from the secretary of state delivered with a copy of a document filed by the secretary of state, is conclusive evidence that the original document is on file with the secretary of state.

OFFICIAL COMMENT

The secretary of state may be requested to certify that a specific document has been filed with him upon payment of the fees specified in section 1.22(c). Section 1.27 provides that the certificate is conclusive evidence only that the document is on file. The limited effect of the certificate is consistent with the ministerial filing obligation imposed on the secretary of state under the Model Act. The certificate from the secretary of state, as well as the copy of the document, may be delivered by electronic transmission.

§ 1.28 Certificate of Existence

(a) Anyone may apply to the secretary of state to furnish a certificate of existence for a domestic corporation or a certificate of authorization for a foreign corporation.

(b) A certificate of existence or authorization sets forth:

(1) the domestic corporation's corporate name or the foreign corporation's corporate name used in this state;

(2) that (i) the domestic corporation is duly incorporated under the law of this state, the date of its incorporation, and the period of its duration if less than perpetual; or (ii) that the foreign corporation is authorized to transact business in this state;

(3) that all fees, taxes, and penalties owed to this state have been paid, if (i) payment is reflected in the records of the secretary of state and (ii) nonpayment affects the existence or authorization of the domestic or foreign corporation;

(4) that its most recent annual report required by section 16.22 has been delivered to the secretary of state;

(5) that articles of dissolution have not been filed; and

(6) other facts of record in the office of the secretary of state that may be requested by the applicant.

(c) Subject to any qualification stated in the certificate, a certificate of existence or authorization issued by the secretary of state may be relied upon as conclusive evidence that the domestic or foreign corporation is in existence or is authorized to transact business in this state.

§ 1.29 Penalty for Signing False Document

(a) A person commits an offense if he signs a document he knows is false in any material respect with intent that the document be delivered to the secretary of state for filing.

(b) An offense under this section is a [________] misdemeanor [punishable by a fine of not to exceed $________].

SUBCHAPTER C. SECRETARY OF STATE

§ 1.30 Powers

The secretary of state has the power reasonably necessary to perform the duties required of him by this Act.

SUBCHAPTER D. DEFINITIONS

§ 1.40 Act Definitions

In this Act:

(1) "Articles of incorporation" means the original articles of incorporation, all amendments thereof, and any other documents filed with the secretary of state with respect to a domestic business corporation under any provision of this Act except section 16.21. If

any document filed under this Act restates the articles in their entirety, thenceforth the articles shall not include any prior documents.

(2) "Authorized shares" means the shares of all classes a domestic or foreign corporation is authorized to issue.

(3) "Conspicuous" means so written that a reasonable person against whom the writing is to operate should have noticed it. For example, printing in italics or boldface or contrasting color, or typing in capitals or underlined, is conspicuous.

(4) "Corporation," "domestic corporation" or "domestic business corporation" means a corporation for profit, which is not a foreign corporation, incorporated under or subject to the provisions of this Act.

(5) "Deliver" or "delivery" means any method of delivery used in conventional commercial practice, including delivery by hand, mail, commercial delivery, and electronic transmission.

(6) "Distribution" means a direct or indirect transfer of money or other property (except its own shares) or incurrence of indebtedness by a corporation to or for the benefit of its shareholders in respect of any of its shares. A distribution may be in the form of a declaration or payment of a dividend; a purchase, redemption, or other acquisition of shares; a distribution of indebtedness; or otherwise.

(6A) "Domestic unincorporated entity" means an unincorporated entity whose internal affairs are governed by the laws of this state.

(7) "Effective date of notice" is defined in section 1.41.

(7A) "Electronic transmission" or "electronically transmitted" means any process of communication not directly involving the physical transfer of paper that is suitable for the retention, retrieval, and reproduction of information by the recipient.

(7B) "Eligible entity" means a domestic or foreign unincorporated entity or a domestic or foreign nonprofit corporation.

(7C) "Eligible interests" means interests or memberships.

(8) "Employee" includes an officer but not a director. A director may accept duties that make him also an employee.

(9) "Entity" includes a domestic and foreign business corporation; domestic and foreign nonprofit corporation; estate; trust; domestic and foreign unincorporated entity; and state, United States, and foreign government.

(9A) The phrase "facts objectively ascertainable" outside of a filed document or plan is defined in section 1.20(k).

(9B) "Filing entity" means an unincorporated entity that is created by filing a public organic document.

(10) "Foreign corporation" or "foreign business corporation" means a corporation incorporated under a law other than the law of this state, which would be a business corporation if incorporated under the laws of this state.

(10A) "Foreign nonprofit corporation" means a corporation incorporated under a law other than the law of this state, which would be a nonprofit corporation if incorporated under the laws of this state.

(10B) "Foreign unincorporated entity" means an unincorporated entity whose internal affairs are governed by an organic law of a jurisdiction other than this state.

(11) "Governmental subdivision" includes an authority, county, district, and municipality.

(12) "Includes" denotes a partial definition.

(13) "Individual" means a natural person.

(13A) "Interest" means either or both of the following rights under the organic law of an unincorporated entity:

(i) the right to receive distributions from the entity either in the ordinary course or upon liquidation; or

(ii) the right to receive notice or vote on issues involving its internal affairs, other than as an agent, assignee, proxy or person responsible for managing its business and affairs.

(13B) "Interest holder" means a person who holds of record an interest.

(14) "Means" denotes an exhaustive definition.

(14A) "Membership" means the rights of a member in a domestic or foreign nonprofit corporation.

(14B) "Nonfiling entity" means an unincorporated entity that is not created by filing a public organic document.

(14C) "Nonprofit corporation" or "domestic nonprofit corporation" means a corporation incorporated under the laws of this state and subject to the provisions of the [Model Nonprofit Corporation Act].

(15) "Notice" is defined in section 1.41.

(15A) "Organic document" means a public organic document or a private organic document.

(15B) "Organic law" means the statute governing the internal affairs of a domestic or foreign business or nonprofit corporation or unincorporated entity.

(15C) "Owner liability" means personal liability for a debt, obligation or liability of a domestic or foreign business or nonprofit corporation or unincorporated entity that is imposed on a person:

(i) solely by reason of the person's status as a shareholder, member or interest holder; or

(ii) by the articles of incorporation, bylaws or an organic document pursuant to a provision of the organic law authorizing the articles of incorporation, bylaws or an organic document to make one or more specified shareholders, members or interest holders liable in their capacity as shareholders, members or interest holders for all or specified debts, obligations or liabilities of the entity.

(16) "Person" includes an individual and an entity.

(17) "Principal office" means the office (in or out of this state) so designated in the annual report where the principal executive offices of a domestic or foreign corporation are located.

(17A) "Private organic document" means any document (other than the public organic document, if any) that determines the internal governance of an unincorporated entity. Where a private organic document has been amended or restated, the term means the private organic document as last amended or restated.

(17B) "Public organic document" means the document, if any, that is filed of public record to create an unincorporated entity. Where a public organic document has been amended or restated, the term means the public organic document as last amended or restated.

(18) "Proceeding" includes civil suit and criminal, administrative, and investigatory action.

(19) "Record date" means the date established under chapter 6 or 7 on which a corporation determines the identity of its shareholders and their shareholdings for purposes of this Act. The determinations shall be made as of the close of business on the record date unless another time for doing so is specified when the record date is fixed.

(20) "Secretary" means the corporate officer to whom the board of directors has delegated responsibility under section 8.40(c) for custody of the minutes of the meetings of the board of directors and of the shareholders and for authenticating records of the corporation.

(21) "Share" means the unit into which the proprietary interests in a corporation are divided.

(22) "Shareholder" means the person in whose name shares are registered in the records of a corporation or the beneficial owner of

shares to the extent of the rights granted by a nominee certificate on file with a corporation.

(22A) "Sign" or "signature" includes any manual, facsimile, conformed or electronic signature.

(23) "State," when referring to a part of the United States, includes a state and commonwealth (and their agencies and governmental subdivisions) and a territory, and insular possession (and their agencies and governmental subdivisions) of the United States.

(24) "Subscriber" means a person who subscribes for shares in a corporation, whether before or after incorporation.

(24A) "Unincorporated entity" means an organization or artificial legal person that either has a separate legal existence or has the power to acquire an estate in real property in its own name and that is not any of the following: a domestic or foreign business or nonprofit corporation, an estate, a trust, a state, the United States, or a foreign government. The term includes a general partnership, limited liability company, limited partnership, business trust, joint stock association and unincorporated nonprofit association.

(25) "United States" includes a district, authority, bureau, commission, department, and any other agency of the United States.

(26) "Voting group" means all shares of one or more classes or series that under the articles of incorporation or this Act are entitled to vote and be counted together collectively on a matter at a meeting of shareholders. All shares entitled by the articles of incorporation or this Act to vote generally on the matter are for that purpose a single voting group.

(27) "Voting power" means the current power to vote in the election of directors.

OFFICIAL COMMENT

2. Corporation, Domestic Corporation, Domestic Business Corporation, Foreign Corporation and Foreign Business Corporation

"Corporation," "domestic corporation," "domestic business corporation," "foreign corporation," and "foreign business corporation" are defined in sections 1.40(4) and (10). The word "corporation," when used alone, refers only to domestic corporations. In a few instances, the phrase "domestic corporation" has been used in order to contrast it with a foreign corporation. The phrase "domestic business corporation" has been used on occasion to contrast it with a domestic nonprofit corporation.

* * *

4. Electronic Transmission

"Electronic transmission" or "electronically transmitted" includes both communication systems which in the normal course produce paper, such as telegrams and facsimiles, as well as communication systems which transmit and permit the retention of data which is then subject to subsequent retrieval and reproduction in written form. Electronic transmission is intended to be broadly construed and include the evolving methods of electronic delivery, including electronic transmissions between computers via modem, as well as data stored and delivered on magnetic tapes or computer diskettes. The phrase is not intended to include voice mail and other similar systems which do not automatically provide for the retrieval of data in printed or typewritten form.

5. Entity

The term "entity," defined in section 1.40(9), appears in the definition of "person" in section 1.40(16) and is included to cover all types of artificial persons. Estates and trusts and general partnerships are included even though they may not, in some jurisdictions, be considered artificial persons. "Trust," by itself, means a non-business trust, such as a traditional testamentary or inter vivos trust.

The term "entity" is broader than the term "unincorporated entity" which is defined in section 1.40(24A). See also the definitions of "governmental subdivision" in section 1.40(11), "state" in section 1.40(23), and "United States" in section 1.40(25).

A form of co-ownership of property or sharing of returns from property that is not a partnership under the Uniform Partnership Act (1997) will not be an "unincorporated entity." In that connection, section 202(c) of the Uniform Partnership Act (1997) provides, among other things, that:

> In determining whether a partnership is formed, the following rules apply:
>
> (1) Joint tenancy, tenancy in common, tenancy by the entireties, joint property, common property, or part ownership does not by itself establish a partnership, even if the co-owners share profits made by the use of the property.
>
> (2) The sharing of gross returns does not by itself establish a partnership, even if the persons sharing them have a joint or common right or interest in property from which the returns are derived.

5.1 Membership

"Membership" is defined in section 1.40(14A) for purposes of this Act to refer only to the rights of a member in a nonprofit corporation. Although the owners of a limited liability company are generally referred to as "members," for purposes of this Act they are referred to as "interest holders" and what they own in the limited liability company is referred to in this Act as an "interest."

5.2 Organic Documents, Public Organic Documents, and Private Organic Documents

The term "organic documents" in section 1.40(15A) includes both public organic documents and private organic documents. The term "public organic document" includes such documents as the certificate of limited partnership of a limited partnership, the articles of organization or certificate of formation of a limited liability company, the deed of trust of a business trust and comparable documents, however denominated, that are publicly filed to create other types of unincorporated entities. An election of limited liability partnership status is not of itself a public organic document because it does not create the underlying general or limited partnership filing the election, although the election may be made part of the public organic document of the partnership by its organic law. The term "private organic document" includes such documents as a partnership agreement of a general or limited partnership, an operating agreement of a limited liability company and comparable documents, however denominated, of other types of unincorporated entities.

5.3 Owner Liability

The term "owner liability" is used in the context of provisions in chapters 9 and 11 that preserve the personal liability of shareholders, members, and interest holders when the entity in which they hold shares, memberships or interests is the subject of a transaction under those chapters. The term includes only liabilities that are imposed pursuant to statute on shareholders, members or interest holders. Liabilities that a shareholder, member or interest holder incurs by contract are not included. Thus, for example, if a state's business corporation law were to make shareholders personally liable for unpaid wages, that liability would be an "owner liability." If, on the other hand, a shareholder were to guarantee payment of an obligation of a corporation, that liability would not be an "owner liability." The reason for excluding contractual liabilities from the definition of "owner liability" is because those liabilities are constitutionally protected from impairment and thus do not need to be separately protected in chapters 9 and 11.

5.4 Unincorporated Entity

The term "unincorporated entity" is a subset of the broader term "entity."

There is some question as to whether a partnership subject to the Uniform Partnership Act (1914) is an entity or merely an aggregation of its partners. That question has been resolved by section 201 of the Uniform Partnership Act (1997), which makes clear that a general partnership is an entity with its own separate legal existence. Section 8 of the Uniform Partnership Act (1914) gives partnerships subject to it the power to acquire estates in real property and thus such a partnership will be an "unincorporated entity." As a result, all general partnerships will be "unincorporated entities" regardless of whether the state in which they are organized has adopted the new Uniform Partnership Act (1997).

The term "unincorporated entity" includes limited liability partnerships and limited liability limited partnerships because those entities are forms of general partnerships and limited partnerships, respectively, that have made the additional required election claiming that status.

Section 4 of the Uniform Unincorporated Nonprofit Association Act gives an unincorporated nonprofit association the power to acquire an estate in real property and thus an unincorporated nonprofit association organized in a state that has adopted that act will be an "unincorporated entity." At common law, an unincorporated nonprofit association was not a legal entity and did not have the power to acquire real property. Most states that have not adopted the Uniform Act have nonetheless modified the common law rule, but states that have not adopted the Uniform Act should analyze whether they should modify the definition of "unincorporated entity" to add an express reference to unincorporated nonprofit associations.

"Business trust" includes any trust carrying on a business, such as a Massachusetts trust, real estate investment trust, or other common law or statutory business trust. The term "unincorporated entity" expressly excludes estates and trusts (i.e., trusts that are not business trusts), whether or not they would be considered artificial persons under the governing jurisdiction's law, to make it clear that they are not eligible to participate in a conversion under subchapter E of chapter 9 or a merger or share exchange under chapter 11.

9. Sign

The definition of "sign" or "signature" includes manual, facsimile, conformed or electronic signatures. In this regard, it is intended that any manifestation of an intention to execute or authenticate a document will be accepted. Electronic signatures are expected to encompass any methodology approved by the secretary of state for purposes of verification of the authenticity of the document. This could include a typewritten conformed signature or other electronic entry in the form of a computer data compilation of any characters or series of characters comprising a name intended to evidence authorization and execution of a document.

* * *

12. Voting Power

Under section 1.40(27) the term "voting power" means the current power to vote in the election of directors. Application of this definition turns on whether the relevant shares carry the power to vote in the election of directors as of the time for voting on the relevant transaction. If shares carry the power to vote in the election of directors only under a certain contingency, as is often the case with preferred stock, the shares would not carry voting power within the meaning of section 1.40(27) unless the contingency has occurred, and only during the period when the voting rights are in effect. Shares that carry the power to vote for any directors as of the time to vote on the relevant transaction have the current power to vote in the election of directors within the meaning of section 1.40(27) even if the shares do not carry the power to vote for all directors.

§ 1.41 Notice

(a) Notice under this Act must be in writing unless oral notice is reasonable under the circumstances. Notice by electronic transmission is written notice.

(b) Notice may be communicated in person; by mail or other method of delivery; or by telephone, voice mail or other electronic means. If these forms of personal notice are impracticable, notice may be communicated by a newspaper of general circulation in the area where published, or by radio, television, or other form of public broadcast communication.

(c) Written notice by a domestic or foreign corporation to its shareholder, if in a comprehensible form, is effective (i) upon deposit in the United States mail, if mailed postpaid and correctly addressed to the shareholder's address shown in the corporation's current record of shareholders, or (ii) when electronically transmitted to the shareholder in a manner authorized by the shareholder.

(d) Written notice to a domestic or foreign corporation (authorized to transact business in this state) may be addressed to its registered agent at its registered office or to the corporation or its secretary at its principal office shown in its most recent annual report or, in the case of a foreign corporation that has not yet delivered an annual report, in its application for a certificate of authority.

(e) Except as provided in subsection (c), written notice, if in a comprehensible form, is effective at the earliest of the following:

(1) when received;

(2) five days after its deposit in the United States Mail, if mailed postpaid and correctly addressed;

(3) on the date shown on the return receipt, if sent by registered or certified mail, return receipt requested, and the receipt is signed by or on behalf of the addressee.

(f) Oral notice is effective when communicated if communicated in a comprehensible manner.

(g) If this Act prescribes notice requirements for particular circumstances, those requirements govern. If articles of incorporation or bylaws prescribe notice requirements, not inconsistent with this section or other provisions of this Act, those requirements govern.

§ 1.42 Number of Shareholders

(a) For purposes of this Act, the following identified as a shareholder in a corporation's current record of shareholders constitutes one shareholder:

(1) three or fewer co-owners;

(2) a corporation, partnership, trust, estate, or other entity;

(3) the trustees, guardians, custodians, or other fiduciaries of a single trust, estate, or account.

(b) For purposes of this Act, shareholdings registered in substantially similar names constitute one shareholder if it is reasonable to believe that the names represent the same person.

CHAPTER 2. INCORPORATION

§ 2.01 Incorporators

One or more persons may act as the incorporator or incorporators of a corporation by delivering articles of incorporation to the secretary of state for filing.

§ 2.02 Articles of Incorporation

(a) The articles of incorporation must set forth:

(1) a corporate name for the corporation that satisfies the requirements of section 4.01;

(2) the number of shares the corporation is authorized to issue;

(3) the street address of the corporation's initial registered office and the name of its initial registered agent at that office; and

(4) the name and address of each incorporator.

(b) The articles of incorporation may set forth:

(1) the names and addresses of the individuals who are to serve as the initial directors;

(2) provisions not inconsistent with law regarding:

(i) the purpose or purposes for which the corporation is organized;

(ii) managing the business and regulating the affairs of the corporation;

(iii) defining, limiting, and regulating the powers of the corporation, its board of directors, and shareholders;

(iv) a par value for authorized shares or classes of shares;

(v) the imposition of personal liability on shareholders for the debts of the corporation to a specified extent and upon specified conditions;

(3) any provision that under this Act is required or permitted to be set forth in the bylaws; and

(4) a provision eliminating or limiting the liability of a director to the corporation or its shareholders for money damages for any action taken, or any failure to take any action, as a director, except liability for (A) the amount of a financial benefit received by a director to which he is not entitled; (B) an intentional infliction of harm on the corporation or the shareholders; (C) a violation of section 8.33; or (D) an intentional violation of criminal law.

(5) a provision permitting or making obligatory indemnification of a director for liability (as defined in section 8.50(5)) to any person for any action taken, or any failure to take any action, as director except liability for (A) receipt of a financial benefit to which he is not entitled, (B) an intentional infliction of harm on the corporation or its shareholders, (C) a violation of section 8.33, or (D) an intentional violation of criminal law.

(c) The articles of incorporation need not set forth any of the corporate powers enumerated in this Act.

(d) Provisions of the articles of incorporation may be made dependent upon facts objectively ascertainable outside the articles of incorporation in accordance with section 1.20(k).

§ 2.03 Incorporation

(a) Unless a delayed effective date is specified, the corporate existence begins when the articles of incorporation are filed.

(b) The secretary of state's filing of the articles of incorporation is conclusive proof that the incorporators satisfied all conditions precedent to incorporation except in a proceeding by the state to cancel or revoke the incorporation or involuntarily dissolve the corporation.

§ 2.04 Liability for Preincorporation Transactions

All persons purporting to act as or on behalf of a corporation, knowing there was no incorporation under this Act, are jointly and severally liable for all liabilities created while so acting.

OFFICIAL COMMENT

Earlier versions of the Model Act, and the statutes of many states, have long provided that corporate existence begins only with the acceptance of articles of incorporation by the secretary of state. Many states also have statutes that provide expressly that those who prematurely act as or on behalf of a corporation are personally liable on all transactions entered into or liabilities incurred before incorporation. A review of recent case law indicates, however, that even in states with such statutes courts have continued to rely on common law concepts of de facto corporations, de jure corporations, and corporations by estoppel that provide uncertain protection against liability for preincorporation transactions. These cases caused a review of the underlying policies represented in earlier versions of the Model Act and the adoption of a slightly more flexible or relaxed standard.

Incorporation under modern statutes is so simple and inexpensive that a strong argument may be made that nothing short of filing articles of incorporation should create the privilege of limited liability. A number of situations have arisen, however, in which the protection of limited liability arguably should be recognized even though the simple incorporation process established by modern statutes has not been completed.

(1) The strongest factual pattern for immunizing participants from personal liability occurs in cases in which the participant honestly and reasonably but erroneously believed the articles had been filed. In Cranson v. International Business Machines Corp., 234 Md. 477, 200 A.2d 33 (1964), for example, the defendant had been shown executed articles of incorporation some months earlier before he invested in the corporation and became an officer and director. He was also told by the corporation's attorney that the articles had been filed, but in fact they had not been filed because of a mix-up in the attorney's office. The defendant was held not liable on the "corporate" obligation.

(2) Another class of cases, which is less compelling but in which the participants sometimes have escaped personal liability, involves the defendant who mails in articles of incorporation and then enters into a transaction in the corporate name; the letter is either delayed or the secretary of

state's office refuses to file the articles after receiving them or returns them for correction. E.g., Cantor v. Sunshine Greenery, Inc., 165 N.J.Super. 411, 398 A.2d 571 (1979). Many state filing agencies adopt the practice of treating the date of receipt as the date of issuance of the certificate even though delays and the review process may result in the certificate being backdated. The finding of nonliability in cases of this second type can be considered an extension of this principle by treating the date of original mailing or original filing as the date of incorporation.

(3) A third class of cases in which the participants sometimes have escaped personal liability involves situations where the third person has urged immediate execution of the contract in the corporate name even though he knows that the other party has not taken any steps toward incorporating. E.g., Quaker Hill v. Parr, 148 Colo. 45, 364 P.2d 1056 (1961).

(4) In another class of cases the defendant has represented that a corporation exists and entered into a contract in the corporate name when he knows that no corporation has been formed, either because no attempt has been made to file articles of incorporation or because he has already received rejected articles of incorporation from the filing agency. In these cases, the third person has dealt solely with the "corporation" and has not relied on the personal assets of the defendant. The imposition of personal liability in this class of cases, it has sometimes been argued, gives the plaintiff more than he originally bargained for. On the other hand, to recognize limited liability in this situation threatens to undermine the incorporation process, since one then may obtain limited liability by consistently conducting business in the corporate name. Most courts have imposed personal liability in this situation. E.g., Robertson v. Levy, 197 A.2d 443 (D.C.App.1964).

(5) A final class of cases involves inactive investors who provide funds to a promoter with the instruction, "Don't start doing business until you incorporate." After the promoter does start business without incorporating, attempts have been made, sometimes unsuccessfully, to hold the investors liable as partners. E.g., Frontier Refining Co. v. Kunkels, Inc., 407 P.2d 880 (Wyo.1965). One case held that the language of section 146 of the 1969 Model Act ["*persons who assume to act* as a corporation are liable for preincorporation transactions"] creates a distinction between active and inactive participants, makes only the former liable as partners, and therefore relieves the latter of personal liability. Nevertheless, "active" participation was defined to include all investors who actively participate in the policy and operational decisions of the organization and is, therefore, a larger group than merely the persons who incurred the obligation in question on behalf of the "corporation." Timberline Equipment Co. v. Davenport, 267 Or. 64, 72–76, 514 P.2d 1109, 1113–14 (1973).

After a review of these situations, it seemed appropriate to impose liability only on persons who act as or on behalf of corporations "knowing" that no corporation exists. Analogous protection has long been accorded under the uniform limited partnership acts to limited partners who contribute capital to a partnership in the erroneous belief that a limited partnership certificate has been filed. Uniform Limited Partnership Act § 12 (1916); Revised Uniform Limited Partnership Act § 3.04 (1976). Persons protected under § 3.04 of the latter are persons who "erroneously but in good faith" believe that a limited partnership certificate has been filed. The language of section 2.04 has essentially the same meaning.

While no special provision is made in section 2.04, the section does not foreclose the possibility that persons who urge defendants to execute contracts in the corporate name knowing that no steps to incorporate have been taken may be estopped to impose personal liability on individual defendants. This estoppel may be based on the inequity perceived when persons, unwilling or reluctant to enter into a commitment under their own name, are persuaded to use the name of a nonexistent corporation, and then are sought to be held personally liable under section 2.04 by the party advocating that form of execution. By contrast, persons who knowingly participate in a business under a corporate name are jointly and severally liable on "corporate" obligations under section 2.04 and may not argue that plaintiffs are "estopped" from holding them personally liable because all transactions were conducted on a corporate basis.

§ 2.05 Organization of Corporation

(a) After incorporation:

(1) if initial directors are named in the articles of incorporation, the initial directors shall hold an organizational meeting, at the call of a majority of the directors, to complete the organization of the corporation by appointing officers, adopting bylaws, and carrying on any other business brought before the meeting;

(2) if initial directors are not named in the articles, the incorporator or incorporators shall hold an organizational meeting at the call of a majority of the incorporators:

(i) to elect directors and complete the organization of the corporation; or

(ii) to elect a board of directors who shall complete the organization of the corporation.

(b) Action required or permitted by this Act to be taken by incorporators at an organizational meeting may be taken without a meeting if the action taken is evidenced by one or more written consents describing the action taken and signed by each incorporator.

(c) An organizational meeting may be held in or out of this state.

§ 2.06 Bylaws

(a) The incorporators or board of directors of a corporation shall adopt initial bylaws for the corporation.

(b) The bylaws of a corporation may contain any provision for managing the business and regulating the affairs of the corporation that is not inconsistent with law or the articles of incorporation.

§ 2.07 Emergency Bylaws

(a) Unless the articles of incorporation provide otherwise, the board of directors of a corporation may adopt bylaws to be effective only in an emergency defined in subsection (d). The emergency bylaws, which are subject to amendment or repeal by the shareholders, may make all provisions necessary for managing the corporation during the emergency, including:

(1) procedures for calling a meeting of the board of directors;

(2) quorum requirements for the meeting; and

(3) designation of additional or substitute directors.

(b) All provisions of the regular bylaws consistent with the emergency bylaws remain effective during the emergency. The emergency bylaws are not effective after the emergency ends.

(c) Corporate action taken in good faith in accordance with the emergency bylaws:

(1) binds the corporation; and

(2) may not be used to impose liability on a corporate director, officer, employee, or agent.

(d) An emergency exists for purposes of this section if a quorum of the corporation's directors cannot readily be assembled because of some catastrophic event.

CHAPTER 3. PURPOSES AND POWERS

§ 3.01 Purposes

(a) Every corporation incorporated under this Act has the purpose of engaging in any lawful business unless a more limited purpose is set forth in the articles of incorporation.

(b) A corporation engaging in a business that is subject to regulation under another statute of this state may incorporate under this Act only if permitted by, and subject to all limitations of, the other statute.

§ 3.02 General Powers

Unless its articles of incorporation provide otherwise, every corporation has perpetual duration and succession in its corporate name and has the same powers as an individual to do all things necessary or convenient to carry out its business and affairs, including without limitation power:

(1) to sue and be sued, complain and defend in its corporate name;

(2) to have a corporate seal, which may be altered at will, and to use it, or a facsimile of it, by impressing or affixing it or in any other manner reproducing it;

(3) to make and amend bylaws, not inconsistent with its articles of incorporation or with the laws of this state, for managing the business and regulating the affairs of the corporation;

(4) to purchase, receive, lease, or otherwise acquire, and own, hold, improve, use, and otherwise deal with, real or personal property, or any legal or equitable interest in property, wherever located;

(5) to sell, convey, mortgage, pledge, lease, exchange, and otherwise dispose of all or any part of its property;

(6) to purchase, receive, subscribe for, or otherwise acquire; own, hold, vote, use, sell, mortgage, lend, pledge, or otherwise dispose of; and deal in and with shares or other interests in, or obligations of, any other entity;

(7) to make contracts and guarantees, incur liabilities, borrow money, issue its notes, bonds, and other obligations, (which may be convertible into or include the option to purchase other securities of the corporation), and secure any of its obligations by mortgage or pledge of any of its property, franchises, or income;

(8) to lend money, invest and reinvest its funds, and receive and hold real and personal property as security for repayment;

(9) to be a promoter, partner, member, associate, or manager of any partnership, joint venture, trust, or other entity;

(10) to conduct its business, locate offices, and exercise the powers granted by this Act within or without this state;

(11) to elect directors and appoint officers, employees, and agents of the corporation, define their duties, fix their compensation, and lend them money and credit;

(12) to pay pensions and establish pension plans, pension trusts, profit sharing plans, share bonus plans, share option plans, and benefit or incentive plans for any or all of its current or former directors, officers, employees, and agents;

(13) to make donations for the public welfare or for charitable, scientific, or educational purposes;

(14) to transact any lawful business that will aid governmental policy;

(15) to make payments or donations, or do any other act, not inconsistent with law, that furthers the business and affairs of the corporation.

§ 3.03 Emergency Powers

(a) In anticipation of or during an emergency defined in subsection (d), the board of directors of a corporation may:

(1) modify lines of succession to accommodate the incapacity of any director, officer, employee, or agent; and

(2) relocate the principal office, designate alternative principal offices or regional offices, or authorize the officers to do so.

(b) During an emergency defined in subsection (d), unless emergency bylaws provide otherwise:

(1) notice of a meeting of the board of directors need be given only to those directors whom it is practicable to reach and may be given in any practicable manner, including by publication and radio; and

(2) one or more officers of the corporation present at a meeting of the board of directors may be deemed to be directors for the meeting, in order of rank and within the same rank in order of seniority, as necessary to achieve a quorum.

(c) Corporate action taken in good faith during an emergency under this section to further the ordinary business affairs of the corporation:

(1) binds the corporation; and

(2) may not be used to impose liability on a corporate director, officer, employee, or agent.

(d) An emergency exists for purposes of this section if a quorum of the corporation's directors cannot readily be assembled because of some catastrophic event.

§ 3.04 Ultra Vires

(a) Except as provided in subsection (b), the validity of corporate action may not be challenged on the ground that the corporation lacks or lacked power to act.

(b) A corporation's power to act may be challenged:

(1) in a proceeding by a shareholder against the corporation to enjoin the act;

(2) in a proceeding by the corporation, directly, derivatively, or through a receiver, trustee, or other legal representative, against an incumbent or former director, officer, employee, or agent of the corporation; or

(3) in a proceeding by the Attorney General under section 14.30.

(c) In a shareholder's proceeding under subsection (b)(1) to enjoin an unauthorized corporate act, the court may enjoin or set aside the act, if equitable and if all affected persons are parties to the proceeding, and may award damages for loss (other than anticipated profits) suffered by the corporation or another party because of enjoining the unauthorized act.

CHAPTER 4. NAME

§ 4.01 Corporate Name

(a) A corporate name:

(1) must contain the word "corporation," "incorporated," "company," or "limited," or the abbreviation "corp.," "inc.," "co.," or "ltd.", or words or abbreviations of like import in another language; and

(2) may not contain language stating or implying that the corporation is organized for a purpose other than that permitted by section 3.01 and its articles of incorporation.

(b) Except as authorized by subsections (c) and (d), a corporate name must be distinguishable upon the records of the secretary of state from:

(1) the corporate name of a corporation incorporated or authorized to transact business in this state;

(2) a corporate name reserved or registered under section 4.02 or 4.03;

(3) the fictitious name adopted by a foreign corporation authorized to transact business in this state because its real name is unavailable; and

(4) the corporate name of a not-for-profit corporation incorporated or authorized to transact business in this state.

(c) A corporation may apply to the secretary of state for authorization to use a name that is not distinguishable upon his records from one or more of the names described in subsection (b). The secretary of state shall authorize use of the name applied for if:

(1) the other corporation consents to the use in writing and submits an undertaking in form satisfactory to the secretary of state to change its name to a name that is distinguishable upon the records of the secretary of state from the name of the applying corporation; or

(2) the applicant delivers to the secretary of state a certified copy of the final judgment of a court of competent jurisdiction establishing the applicant's right to use the name applied for in this state.

(d) A corporation may use the name (including the fictitious name) of another domestic or foreign corporation that is used in this state if the other corporation is incorporated or authorized to transact business in this state and the proposed user corporation:

(1) has merged with the other corporation;

(2) has been formed by reorganization of the other corporation; or

(3) has acquired all or substantially all of the assets, including the corporate name, of the other corporation.

(e) This Act does not control the use of fictitious names.

§ 4.02 Reserved Name

(a) A person may reserve the exclusive use of a corporate name, including a fictitious name for a foreign corporation whose corporate name is not available, by delivering an application to the secretary of state for filing. The application must set forth the name and address of the applicant and the name proposed to be reserved. If the secretary of state finds that the corporate name applied for is available, he shall reserve the name for the applicant's exclusive use for a nonrenewable 120–day period.

(b) The owner of a reserved corporate name may transfer the reservation to another person by delivering to the secretary of state a signed notice of the transfer that states the name and address of the transferee.

§ 4.03 Registered Name

(a) A foreign corporation may register its corporate name, or its corporate name with any addition required by section 15.06, if the name is distinguishable upon the records of the secretary of state from the corporate names that are not available under section 4.01(b)(3).

(b) A foreign corporation registers its corporate name, or its corporate name with any addition required by section 15.06, by delivering to the secretary of state for filing an application:

(1) setting forth its corporate name, or its corporate name with any addition required by section 15.06, the state or country and date of its incorporation, and a brief description of the nature of the business in which it is engaged; and

(2) accompanied by a certificate of existence (or a document of similar import) from the state or country of incorporation.

(c) The name is registered for the applicant's exclusive use upon the effective date of the application.

(d) A foreign corporation whose registration is effective may renew it for successive years by delivering to the secretary of state for filing a renewal application, which complies with the requirements of subsection (b), between October 1 and December 31 of the preceding year. The renewal application renews the registration for the following calendar year.

(e) A foreign corporation whose registration is effective may thereafter qualify as a foreign corporation under that name or consent in writing to the use of that name by a corporation thereafter incorporated under this Act or by another foreign corporation thereafter authorized to transact business in this state. The registration terminates when the domestic corporation is incorporated or the foreign corporation qualifies or consents to the qualification of another foreign corporation under the registered name.

CHAPTER 5. OFFICE AND AGENT

§ 5.01 Registered Office and Registered Agent

Each corporation must continuously maintain in this state:

(1) a registered office that may be the same as any of its places of business; and

(2) a registered agent, who may be:

(i) an individual who resides in this state and whose business office is identical with the registered office;

(ii) a domestic corporation or not-for-profit domestic corporation whose business office is identical with the registered office; or

(iii) a foreign corporation or not-for-profit foreign corporation authorized to transact business in this state whose business office is identical with the registered office.

§ 5.02 Change of Registered Office or Registered Agent

(a) A corporation may change its registered office or registered agent by delivering to the secretary of state for filing a statement of change that sets forth:

(1) the name of the corporation,

(2) the street address of its current registered office;

(3) if the current registered office is to be changed, the street address of the new registered office;

(4) the name of its current registered agent;

(5) if the current registered agent is to be changed, the name of the new registered agent and the new agent's written consent (either on the statement or attached to it) to the appointment; and

(6) that after the change or changes are made, the street addresses of its registered office and the business office of its registered agent will be identical.

(b) If a registered agent changes the street address of his business office, he may change the street address of the registered office of any corporation for which he is the registered agent by notifying the corporation in writing of the change and signing (either manually or in facsimile) and delivering to the secretary of state for filing a statement that complies with the requirements of subsection (a) and recites that the corporation has been notified of the change.

§ 5.03 Resignation of Registered Agent

(a) A registered agent may resign his agency appointment by signing and delivering to the secretary of state for filing the signed original and two exact or conformed copies of a statement of resignation. The statement may include a statement that the registered office is also discontinued.

(b) After filing the statement the secretary of state shall mail one copy to the registered office (if not discontinued) and the other copy to the corporation at its principal office.

(c) The agency appointment is terminated, and the registered office discontinued if so provided, on the 31st day after the date on which the statement was filed.

§ 5.04 Service on Corporation

(a) A corporation's registered agent is the corporation's agent for service of process, notice, or demand required or permitted by law to be served on the corporation.

(b) If a corporation has no registered agent, or the agent cannot with reasonable diligence be served, the corporation may be served by registered or certified mail, return receipt requested, addressed to the secretary of the corporation at its principal office. Service is perfected under this subsection at the earliest of:

(1) the date the corporation receives the mail;

(2) the date shown on the return receipt, if signed on behalf of the corporation; or

(3) five days after its deposit in the United States Mail, if mailed postpaid and correctly addressed.

(c) This section does not prescribe the only means, or necessarily the required means, of serving a corporation.

CHAPTER 6. SHARES AND DISTRIBUTIONS

SUBCHAPTER A. SHARES

§ 6.01 Authorized Shares

(a) The articles of incorporation must set forth any classes of shares and series of shares within a class, and the number of shares of each class and series, that the corporation is authorized to issue. If more than one class or series of shares is authorized, the articles of incorporation must prescribe a distinguishing designation for each class or series and must describe, prior to the issuance of shares of a class or series, the terms, including the preferences, rights, and limitations, of that class or series. Except to the extent varied as permitted by this section, all shares of a class or series must have terms, including preferences, rights and limitations, that are identical with those of other shares of the same class or series.

(b) The articles of incorporation must authorize:

(1) one or more classes or series of shares that together have unlimited voting rights, and

(2) one or more classes or series of shares (which may be the same class or classes as those with voting rights) that together are entitled to receive the net assets of the corporation upon dissolution.

(c) The articles of incorporation may authorize one or more classes of shares that:

(1) have special, conditional, or limited voting rights, or no right to vote, except to the extent otherwise provided by this Act;

(2) are redeemable or convertible as specified in the articles of incorporation:

(i) at the option of the corporation, the shareholder, or another person or upon the occurrence of a specified event;

(ii) for cash, indebtedness, securities, or other property; and

(iii) at prices and in amounts specified, or determined in accordance with a formula;

(3) entitle the holders to distributions calculated in any manner, including dividends that may be cumulative, noncumulative, or partially cumulative; or

(4) have preference over any other class or series of shares with respect to distributions, including distributions upon the dissolution of the corporation.

(d) Terms of shares may be made dependent upon facts objectively ascertainable outside the articles of incorporation in accordance with section 1.20(k).

(e) Any of the terms of shares may vary among holders of the same class or series so long as such variations are expressly set forth in the articles of incorporation.

(f) The description of the preferences, rights and limitations of classes or series of shares in subsection (c) is not exhaustive.

§ 6.02 Terms of Class or Series Determined by Board of Directors

(a) If the articles of incorporation so provide, the board of directors is authorized, without shareholder approval, to:

(1) classify any unissued shares into one or more classes or into one or more series within a class,

(2) reclassify any unissued shares of any class into one or more classes or into one or more series within one or more classes, or

(3) reclassify any unissued shares of any series of any class into one or more classes or into one or more series within a class.

(b) If the board of directors acts pursuant to subsection (a), it must determine the terms, including the preferences, rights and limitations, to the same extent permitted under section 6.01, of:

(1) any class of shares before the issuance of any shares of that class, or

(2) any series within a class before the issuance of any shares of that series.

(c) Before issuing any shares of a class or series created under this section, the corporation must deliver to the secretary of state for filing articles of amendment setting forth the terms determined under subsection (a).

§ 6.03 Issued and Outstanding Shares

(a) A corporation may issue the number of shares of each class or series authorized by the articles of incorporation. Shares that are issued are outstanding shares until they are reacquired, redeemed, converted, or cancelled.

(b) The reacquisition, redemption, or conversion of outstanding shares is subject to the limitations of subsection (c) of this section and to section 6.40.

(c) At all times that shares of the corporation are outstanding, one or more shares that together have unlimited voting rights and one or more shares that together are entitled to receive the net assets of the corporation upon dissolution must be outstanding.

§ 6.04 Fractional Shares

(a) A corporation may:

(1) issue fractions of a share or pay in money the value of fractions of a share;

(2) arrange for disposition of fractional shares by the shareholders;

(3) issue scrip in registered or bearer form entitling the holder to receive a full share upon surrendering enough scrip to equal a full share.

(b) Each certificate representing scrip must be conspicuously labeled "scrip" and must contain the information required by section 6.25(b).

(c) The holder of a fractional share is entitled to exercise the rights of a shareholder, including the right to vote, to receive dividends, and to participate in the assets of the corporation upon liquidation. The holder of scrip is not entitled to any of these rights unless the scrip provides for them.

(d) The board of directors may authorize the issuance of scrip subject to any condition considered desirable, including:

(1) that the scrip will become void if not exchanged for full shares before a specified date; and

(2) that the shares for which the scrip is exchangeable may be sold and the proceeds paid to the scripholders.

SUBCHAPTER B. ISSUANCE OF SHARES

§ 6.20 Subscription for Shares Before Incorporation

(a) A subscription for shares entered into before incorporation is irrevocable for six months unless the subscription agreement provides a longer or shorter period or all the subscribers agree to revocation.

(b) The board of directors may determine the payment terms of subscriptions for shares that were entered into before incorporation, unless the subscription agreement specifies them. A call for payment by the board of directors must be uniform so far as practicable as to all shares of the same class or series, unless the subscription agreement specifies otherwise.

(c) Shares issued pursuant to subscriptions entered into before incorporation are fully paid and nonassessable when the corporation receives the consideration specified in the subscription agreement.

(d) If a subscriber defaults in payment of money or property under a subscription agreement entered into before incorporation, the corporation may collect the amount owed as any other debt. Alternatively, unless the subscription agreement provides otherwise, the corporation may rescind the agreement and may sell the shares if the debt remains unpaid more than 20 days after the corporation sends written demand for payment to the subscriber.

(e) A subscription agreement entered into after incorporation is a contract between the subscriber and the corporation subject to section 6.21.

§ 6.21 Issuance of Shares

(a) The powers granted in this section to the board of directors may be reserved to the shareholders by the articles of incorporation.

(b) The board of directors may authorize shares to be issued for consideration consisting of any tangible or intangible property or benefit to the corporation, including cash, promissory notes, services performed, contracts for services to be performed, or other securities of the corporation.

(c) Before the corporation issues shares, the board of directors must determine that the consideration received or to be received for shares to be issued is adequate. That determination by the board of directors is conclusive insofar as the adequacy of consideration for the issuance of shares relates to whether the shares are validly issued, fully paid, and nonassessable.

(d) When the corporation receives the consideration for which the board of directors authorized the issuance of shares, the shares issued therefor are fully paid and nonassessable.

(e) The corporation may place in escrow shares issued for a contract for future services or benefits or a promissory note, or make other arrangements to restrict the transfer of the shares, and may credit distributions in respect of the shares against their purchase price, until the services are performed, the note is paid, or the benefits received. If the services are not performed, the note is not paid, or the benefits are not received, the shares escrowed or restricted and the distributions credited may be cancelled in whole or part.

(f)(1) An issuance of shares or other securities convertible into or rights exercisable for shares, in a transaction or a series of integrated transactions, requires approval of the shareholders, at a meeting at which a quorum consisting of at least a majority of the votes entitled to be cast on the matter exists, if:

(i) the shares, other securities, or rights are issued for consideration other than cash or cash equivalents, and

(ii) the voting power of shares that are issued and issuable as a result of the transaction or series of integrated transactions will comprise more than 20 percent of the voting power of the shares of the corporation that were outstanding immediately before the transaction.

(2) In this subsection:

(i) For purposes of determining the voting power of shares issued and issuable as a result of a transaction or series of integrated transactions, the voting power of shares shall be the greater of (A) the voting power of the shares to be issued, or (B) the voting power of the shares that would be outstanding after giving effect to the conversion of convertible shares and other securities and the exercise of rights to be issued.

(ii) A series of transactions is integrated if consummation of one transaction is made contingent on consummation of one or more of the other transactions.

OFFICIAL COMMENT

The financial provisions of the Model Act reflect a modernization of the concepts underlying the capital structure and limitations on distributions of corporations. This process of modernization began with amendments in 1980 to the 1969 Model Act that eliminated the concepts of "par value" and "stated capital," and further modernization occurred in connection with the development of the revised Act in 1984. Practitioners and legal scholars have long recognized that the statutory structure embodying "par value" and "legal capital" concepts is not only complex and confusing but also fails to serve the original purpose of protecting creditors and senior security holders from payments to junior security holders. Indeed, to the extent security holders are led to believe that it provides this protection, these provisions may be affirmatively misleading. The Model Act has therefore eliminated these concepts entirely and substituted a simpler and more flexible structure that provides more realistic protection to these interests. Major aspects of this new structure are:

(1) the provisions relating to the issuance of shares set forth in this and the following sections;

(2) the provisions limiting distributions by corporations set forth in section 6.40 and discussed in the Official Comment to that section; and

(3) the elimination of the concept of treasury shares described in the Official Comment to section 6.31.

Section 6.21 incorporates not only the elimination of the concepts of par value and stated capital from the Model Act in 1980 but also eliminates the earlier rule declaring certain kinds of property ineligible as consideration for shares. The caption of the section, "Issuance of Shares by the Board of Directors," reflects the change in emphasis from imposing restrictions on the issuance of shares to establishing general principles for their issuance. The section replaces two sections captioned, respectively, "Consideration for Shares" (section 18) and "Payment for Shares" (section 19) in the 1969 Model Act.

Since shares need not have a par value, under section 6.21 there is no minimum price at which specific shares must be issued and therefore there can be no "watered stock" liability for issuing shares below an arbitrarily fixed price. The price at which shares are issued is primarily a matter of concern to other shareholders whose interests may be diluted if shares are issued at unreasonably low prices or for overvalued property. This problem of equality of treatment essentially involves honest and fair judgments by directors and cannot be effectively addressed by an arbitrary doctrine establishing a minimum price for shares such as "par value" provided under older statutes.

Section 6.21(b) specifically validates contracts for future services (including promoters' services), promissory notes, or "any tangible or intangible property or benefit to the corporation," as consideration for the present issue of shares. The term "benefit" should be broadly construed to include, for example, a reduction of a liability, a release of a claim, or benefits obtained by a corporation by contribution of its shares to a charitable organization or as a prize in a promotion. In the realities of commercial life, there is sometimes a need for the issuance of shares for contract rights or such intangible property or benefits. And, as a matter of business economics, contracts for future services, promissory notes, and intangible property or benefits often have value that is as real as the value of tangible property or past services, the only types of property that many older statutes permit as consideration for shares. Thus, only business judgment should determine what kind of property should be obtained for shares, and a determination by the directors meeting the requirements of section 8.30 to accept a specific kind of valuable property for shares should be accepted and not circumscribed by artificial or arbitrary rules.

The issuance of some shares for cash and other shares for promissory notes, contracts for past or future services, or for tangible or intangible property or benefits, like the issuance of shares for an inadequate consideration, opens the possibility of dilution of the interests of other shareholders. For example, persons acquiring shares for cash may be unfairly treated if optimistic values are placed on past or future services or intangible benefits being provided by other persons. The problem is particularly acute if the persons providing services, promissory notes, or property or benefits of debatable value are themselves connected with the promoters of the corporation or with its directors. Protection of shareholders against abuse of the power granted to the board of directors to determine that shares should be issued for intangible property or benefits is provided in part by the requirement that the board must act in accordance with the requirements of section 8.30, and, if applicable, section 8.31, in determining that the consideration received for shares is adequate, and in part by the requirement of section 16.21 that the corporation must inform all shareholders annually of all shares issued during the previous year for promissory notes or promises of future services.

Accounting principles are not specified in the Model Act, and the board of directors is not required by the statute to determine the "value" of noncash consideration received by the corporation (as was the case in earlier versions of the Model Act). In many instances, property or benefit received by the corporation will be of uncertain value; if the board of directors determines that the issuance of shares for the property or benefit is an appropriate transaction that protects the shareholders from dilution, that is sufficient under section 6.21. The board of directors does not have to make an explicit "adequacy" determination by formal resolution; that determination may be inferred from a determination to authorize the issuance of shares for a specified consideration.

Section 6.21 also does not require that the board of directors determine the value of the consideration to be entered on the books of the corporation, though the board of directors may do so if it wishes. Of course, a specific value must be placed on the consideration received for the shares for bookkeeping purposes, but bookkeeping details are not the statutory responsibility of the board of directors. The statute also does not require the board of directors to determine the corresponding entry on the right-hand side of the balance sheet under owner's equity to be designated as "stated capital" or be allocated among "stated capital" and other surplus accounts. The corporation, however, may determine that the shareholders' equity accounts should be divided into these traditional categories if it wishes.

The second sentence of section 6.21(c) describes the effect of the determination by the board of directors that consideration is adequate for the issuance of shares. That determination, without more, is conclusive to the extent that adequacy is relevant to the question whether the shares are validly issued, fully paid, and nonassessable. Section 6.21(c) provides that shares are fully paid and nonassessable when the corporation receives the consideration for which the board of directors authorized their issuance. Whether shares are validly issued may depend on compliance with corporate procedural requirements, such as issuance within the amount authorized in the articles of incorporation or holding a directors' meeting upon proper notice and with a quorum present. The Model Act does not address the remedies that may be available for issuances that are subject to challenge. This somewhat more elaborate clause replaces the provision in earlier versions of the Model Act and many state statutes that the determination by the board of directors of consideration for the issuance of shares was "conclusive in the absence of fraud in the transaction."

Shares issued pursuant to preincorporation subscriptions are governed by section 6.20 and not this section.

The revised Model Act does not address the question whether validly issued shares may thereafter be cancelled on the grounds of fraud or bad faith if the shares are in the hands of the original shareholder or other persons who were aware of the circumstances under which they were issued when they acquired the shares. It also leaves to the Uniform Commercial Code other questions relating to the rights of persons other than the person acquiring the shares from the corporation. See the Official Comment to section 6.22.

Section 6.21(e) permits the board of directors to determine that shares issued for promissory notes or for contracts for future services or benefits be placed in escrow or their transfer otherwise restricted until the services are performed, the benefits received, or the notes are paid. The section also defines the rights of the corporation with respect to these shares. If the shares are issued without being restricted as provided in this subsection, they are validly issued insofar as the adequacy of consideration is concerned. See section 6.22 and its Official Comment.

Section 6.21(a) provides that the powers granted to the board of directors by this section may be reserved to the shareholders by the articles of incorporation. No negative inference should be drawn from section 6.21(a) with respect to the efficacy of similar provisions under other sections of the Model Act.

Section 6.21(f) provides that an issuance of shares or other securities convertible into or rights exercisable for shares, in a transaction or a series of integrated transactions, for consideration other than cash or cash equivalents, requires shareholder approval if either the voting power of the shares to be issued, or the voting power of the shares into which those shares and other securities are convertible and for which any rights to be issued are exercisable, will comprise more than 20 percent of the voting power outstanding immediately before the issuance. Section 6.21(f) is generally patterned on New York Stock Exchange Listed Company Manual Rule 312.03, American Stock Exchange Company Guide Rule 712(b), and NASDAQ Stock Market Rule 4310(c)(25)(H)(i). The calculation of the 20 percent compares the maximum number of votes entitled to be cast by the shares to be issued or that could be outstanding after giving effect to the conversion of convertible securities and the exercise of rights being issued, with the actual number of votes entitled to be cast by outstanding shares before the transaction. The test tends to be conservative: The calculation of one part of the equation, voting power outstanding immediately before the transaction, is based on actual voting power of the shares then outstanding, without giving effect to the possible conversion of existing convertible shares and securities and the exercise of existing rights. In contrast, the calculation of the other part of the equation voting power that is or may be outstanding as a result of the issuance takes into account the possible future conversion of shares and securities and the exercise of rights to be issued as part of the transaction.

In making the 20 percent determination under this subsection, shares that are issuable in a business combination of any kind, including a merger, share exchange, acquisition of assets, or otherwise, on a contingent basis are counted as shares or securities to be issued as a result of the transaction. On the other hand, shares that are issuable under antidilution clauses, such as those designed to take account of future share splits or share dividends, are not counted as shares or securities to be issued as a result of the transaction, because they are issuable only as a result of a later corporate action authorizing the split or dividend. If a transaction involves an earnout provision, under which the total amount of shares or securities to be issued will depend on future earnings or other performance measures, the maximum amount of shares or securities that can be issued under the earnout shall be included in the determination.

If the number of shares to be issued or issuable is not fixed, but is subject to a formula, the application of the test in section 6.21(f)(2)(i) requires a calculation of the maximum amount that could be issued under the formula, whether stated as a range or otherwise, in the governing agreement. Even if ultimate issuance of the maximum amount is unlikely, a vote will be required if the maximum amount would result in an issuance of more than 20 percent of the voting power of shares outstanding immediately before the transaction.

Shares that have or would have only contingent voting rights when issued or issuable are not shares that carry voting power for purposes of the calculation under section 6.21(f).

The vote required to approve issuances that fall within section 6.21(f) is the basic voting rule under the Act, set forth in section 7.25, that more shares must be voted in favor of the issuance than are voted against. This is the same voting rule that applies under chapter 10 for amendments of the articles of incorporation, under chapter 11 for mergers and share exchanges, under chapter 12 for a disposition of assets that requires shareholder approval, and under chapter 14 for voluntary dissolution. The quorum rule under section 6.21(f) is also the same as the quorum rule under chapters 10, 11, 12, and 14: there must be present at the meeting at least a majority of the votes entitled to be cast on the matter.

Section 6.21(f) does not apply to an issuance for cash or cash equivalents, whether or not in connection with a public offering. "Cash equivalents," within the meaning of section 6.21(f), are shortterm investments that are both readily convertible to known amounts of cash and present insignificant risk of changes in interest rates. Generally, only investments with original maturities of three months or less or investments that are highly liquid and can be cashed in at any time on short notice could qualify under these definitions. Examples of cash equivalents are types of Treasury Bills, investment grade commercial paper, and moneymarket funds. Shares that are issued partly for cash or cash equivalents and partly for other consideration are "issued for consideration other than cash or cash equivalents" within the meaning of section 6.21(f).

The term "rights" in section 6.21(f) includes warrants, options, and rights of exchange, whether at the option of the holder, the corporation, or another person. The term "voting power" is defined in section 1.40(27) as the current power to vote in the election of directors. See also the Comment to that subsection. Transactions are integrated within the meaning of section 6.21(f) where consummation of one transaction is made contingent on consummation of one or more of the other transactions. If this test is not satisfied, transactions are not integrated for purposes of section 6.21(f) merely because they are proximate in time or because the kind of consideration for which the corporation issues shares is similar in each transaction.

Section 6.21(f) only applies to issuances for consideration. Accordingly, like the Stock Exchange and NASDAQ rules on which section 6.21(f) is based, section 6.21(f) does not require shareholder approval for share dividends (which includes "splits") or for shareholder rights plans. See section 6.23 and the official Comment thereto.

Illustrations of the application of section 6.21(f) follow:

1. C corporation, which has 2 million shares of Class A voting common stock outstanding (carrying one vote per share), proposes to issue 600,000 shares of authorized but unissued shares of Class B nonvoting common stock in exchange for a business owned by D Corporation. The proposed issuance does not require shareholder approval under section 6.21(f), because the Class B shares do not carry voting power.

2. The facts being otherwise as stated in Illustration 1, C proposes to issue 600,000 additional shares of its Class A voting common stock. The proposed issuance requires shareholder approval under section 6.21(f), because the voting power carried by the shares to be issued will comprise more than 20 percent of the voting power of C's shares outstanding immediately before the issuance.

3. The facts being otherwise as stated in Illustration 1, C proposes to issue 400,000 shares of authorized but unissued voting preferred, each share of which carries one vote and is convertible into 1.5 shares of Class A voting common. The proposed issuance requires shareholder approval under section 6.21(f). Although the voting power of the preferred shares to be issued will not comprise more than 20 percent of the voting power of C's shares outstanding immediately before the issuance, the voting power of the shares issuable upon conversion of the preferred will carry more than 20 percent of such voting power.

4. The facts being otherwise as stated in Illustration 1, C proposes to issue 200,000 shares of its Class A voting common stock, and 100,000 shares of authorized but unissued nonvoting preferred stock, each share of which is convertible into 2.5 shares of C's Class A voting common stock. The proposed issuance requires shareholder approval under section 6.21(f), because the voting power of the Class A shares to be issued, after giving effect to the common stock that is issuable upon conversion of the preferred, would comprise more than 20 percent of the voting power of C's outstanding shares immediately before the issuance.

5. The facts being otherwise as stated in Illustration 4, each share of the preferred stock is convertible into 1.2 shares of the Class A voting common stock. The proposed issuance does not require shareholder approval under section 6.21(f), because neither the voting power of the shares to be issued at the outset (200,000) nor the voting power of the shares that would be outstanding after giving effect to the common issuable upon conversion of the preferred (a total of 320,000) constitutes more than 20 percent of the voting power of C's outstanding shares immediately before the issuance.

6. The facts being otherwise as stated in Illustration 1, C proposes to acquire businesses from Corporations G, H, and I, for 200,000, 300,000, and 400,000 shares of Class A voting common stock, respectively, within a short period of time. None of the transactions is conditioned on the negotiation or completion of the other transactions. The proposed issuance of voting shares does not require shareholder approval, because the three transactions are not integrated within the meaning of section 6.21(f), and none of the transactions individually involves the issuance of more than 20 percent of the voting power of C's outstanding shares immediately before each issuance.

§ 6.22 Liability of Shareholders

(a) A purchaser from a corporation of its own shares is not liable to the corporation or its creditors with respect to the shares except to pay the consideration for which the shares were authorized to be issued (section 6.21) or specified in the subscription agreement (section 6.20).

(b) Unless otherwise provided in the articles of incorporation, a shareholder of a corporation is not personally liable for the acts or debts of the corporation except that he may become personally liable by reason of his own acts or conduct.

OFFICIAL COMMENT

With the elimination of the concepts of par value and watered stock in 1980, the sole obligation of a purchaser of shares from the corporation, as set forth in section 6.22(a), is to pay the consideration established by the board of directors (or the consideration specified in the subscription, in the case of preincorporation subscriptions). The consideration for the shares may consist of promissory notes, contracts for future services, or tangible or intangible property or benefits, and, if the board of directors so decide, the delivery of the notes, contracts, or accrual of the benefits constitute full payment for the shares. See the Official Comment to section 6.21. Upon the transfer to the corporation of the consideration so determined or specified, the shareholder has no further responsibility to the corporation or its creditors "with respect to the shares," though the shareholder may have continuing obligations under a contract or promissory note entered into in connection with the acquisition of shares.

Section 6.22(a) deals only with the responsibility for payment by the purchaser of shares from the corporation. The revised Model Act leaves to the Uniform Commercial Code questions with respect to the rights of subsequent purchasers of shares and the power of the corporation to cancel shares if the consideration is not paid when due. See sections 8–202 and 8–301 of the Uniform Commercial Code.

Section 6.22(b) sets forth the basic rule of nonliability of shareholders for corporate acts or debts that underlies modern corporation law. Unless such liability is provided for in the articles of incorporation, see section 2.02(b)(v), shareholders are not liable for corporate obligations, though the last clause recognizes that such liability may be assumed voluntarily or by other conduct.

§ 6.23 Share Dividends

(a) Unless the articles of incorporation provide otherwise, shares may be issued pro rata and without consideration to the corporation's shareholders or to the shareholders of one or more classes or series. An issuance of shares under this subsection is a share dividend.

(b) Shares of one class or series may not be issued as a share dividend in respect of shares of another class or series unless (1) the articles of incorporation so authorize, (2) a majority of the votes entitled to be cast by the class or series to be issued approve the issue, or (3) there are no outstanding shares of the class or series to be issued.

(c) If the board of directors does not fix the record date for determining shareholders entitled to a share dividend, it is the date the board of directors authorizes the share dividend.

§ 6.24 Share Options

(a) A corporation may issue rights, options, or warrants for the purchase of shares or other securities of the corporation. The board of directors shall determine (i) the terms upon which the rights, options, or warrants are issued and (ii) the terms, including the consideration for which the shares or other securities are to be issued. The authorization by the board of directors for the corporation to issue such rights, options, or warrants constitutes authorization of the issuance of the shares or other securities for which the rights, options or warrants are exercisable.

(b) The terms and conditions of such rights, options or warrants, including those outstanding on the effective date of this section, may include, without limitation, restrictions or conditions that:

(1) preclude or limit the exercise, transfer or receipt of such rights, options or warrants by any person or persons owning or offering to acquire a specified number or percentage of the outstanding shares or other securities of the corporation or by any transferee or transferees of any such person or persons, or

(2) invalidate or void such rights, options or warrants held by any such person or persons or any such transferee or transferees.

OFFICIAL COMMENT

A specific provision authorizing the creation of rights, options and warrants appears in many state business corporation statutes. Even though corporations doubtless have the inherent power to issue these instruments, specific authorization is desirable because of the economic importance of rights, options and warrants, and because it is desirable to confirm the broad discretion of the board of directors in determining the consideration to be received by the corporation for their issuance. The creation of incentive compensation plans for directors, officers, agents, and employees is basically a matter of business judgment. This is equally true for incentive plans that involve the issuance of rights, options or warrants and for those that involve the payment of cash. In appropriate cases incentive plans may provide for exercise prices that are below the current market prices of the underlying shares or other securities.

Section 6.24(a) does not require shareholder approval of rights, options or warrants. Of course, prior shareholder approval may be sought as a discretionary matter, or required in order to comply with the rules of national securities markets (see N.Y.S.E. Listed Company Manual section 309.00), or to acquire the federal income tax benefits conditioned upon shareholder approval of such plans (see section 422(b)(1) of the Internal Revenue Code of 1986, as amended).

Under section 6.24(a), the board of directors may designate the interests issued as options, warrants, rights, or by some other name. These interests may be evidenced by certificates, contracts, letter agreements, or in other forms that are appropriate under the circumstances. Rights, options, or warrants may be issued together with or independently of the corporation's issuance and sale of its shares or other securities.

Some publicly held corporations have delegated administration of programs involving incentive compensation in the form of share rights or options to compensation committees composed of nonmanagement directors, subject to the general oversight of the board of directors.

Section 6.24(b) is intended to clarify that the issuance of rights, options, or warrants as part of a shareholder rights plan is permitted. A number of courts have addressed whether shareholder rights plans are permitted under statutes similar to prior sections 6.01, 6.02, and 6.24. These courts have not agreed on whether provisions similar in language in sections 6.01, 6.02, and 6.24 permit such plans to distinguish between holders of the same class of shares based on the identity of the holder of the shares. However, in each of the states in which a court has interpreted a statute of that state as prohibiting such shareholder rights plans, the legislature has subsequently adopted legislation validating such plans. Section 6.24(b) clarifies that such plans are permitted.

The permissible scope of shareholder rights plans may, however, be limited by the courts. For example, courts have been sensitive to plans containing provisions which the courts perceive as infringing upon the power of the board of directors.

§ 6.25 Form and Content of Certificates

(a) Shares may but need not be represented by certificates. Unless this Act or another statute expressly provides otherwise, the rights and obligations of shareholders are identical whether or not their shares are represented by certificates.

(b) At a minimum each share certificate must state on its face:

(1) the name of the issuing corporation and that it is organized under the law of this state;

(2) the name of the person to whom issued; and

(3) the number and class of shares and the designation of the series, if any, the certificate represents.

(c) If the issuing corporation is authorized to issue different classes of shares or different series within a class, the designations, relative rights, preferences, and limitations applicable to each class and the variations in rights, preferences, and limitations determined for each series (and the authority of the board of directors to determine variations for future series) must be summarized on the front or back of each certificate. Alternatively, each certificate may state conspicuously on its front or back that the corporation will furnish the shareholder this information on request in writing and without charge.

(d) Each share certificate (1) must be signed (either manually or in facsimile) by two officers designated in the bylaws or by the board of directors and (2) may bear the corporate seal or its facsimile.

(e) If the person who signed (either manually or in facsimile) a share certificate no longer holds office when the certificate is issued, the certificate is nevertheless valid.

§ 6.26 Shares Without Certificates

(a) Unless the articles of incorporation or bylaws provide otherwise, the board of directors of a corporation may authorize the issue of some or all of the shares of any or all of its classes or series without certificates. The authorization does not affect shares already represented by certificates until they are surrendered to the corporation.

(b) Within a reasonable time after the issue or transfer of shares without certificates, the corporation shall send the shareholder a written statement of the information required on certificates by section 6.25(b) and (c), and, if applicable, section 6.27.

§ 6.27 Restriction on Transfer or Registration of Shares and Other Securities

Restrictions on Sale of Stock

(a) The articles of incorporation, bylaws, an agreement among shareholders, or an agreement between shareholders and the corporation may impose restrictions on the transfer or registration of transfer of shares of the corporation. A restriction does not affect shares issued before the restriction was adopted unless the holders of the shares are parties to the restriction agreement or voted in favor of the restriction.

(b) A restriction on the transfer or registration of transfer of shares is valid and enforceable against the holder or a transferee of the holder if the restriction is authorized by this section and its existence is noted conspicuously on the front or back of the certificate or is contained in the information statement required by section 6.26(b). Unless so noted, a restriction is not enforceable against a person without knowledge of the restriction.

(c) A restriction on the transfer or registration of transfer of shares is authorized:

(1) to maintain the corporation's status when it is dependent on the number or identity of its shareholders;

(2) to preserve exemptions under federal or state securities law;

(3) for any other reasonable purpose.

(d) A restriction on the transfer or registration of transfer of shares may:

(1) obligate the shareholder first to offer the corporation or other persons (separately, consecutively, or simultaneously) an opportunity to acquire the restricted shares;

(2) obligate the corporation or other persons (separately, consecutively, or simultaneously) to acquire the restricted shares;

(3) require the corporation, the holders of any class of its shares, or another person to approve the transfer of the restricted shares, if the requirement is not manifestly unreasonable;

(4) prohibit the transfer of the restricted shares to designated persons or classes of persons, if the prohibition is not manifestly unreasonable.

(e) For purposes of this section, "shares" includes a security convertible into or carrying a right to subscribe for or acquire shares.

§ 6.28 Expense of Issue

A corporation may pay the expenses of selling or underwriting its shares, and of organizing or reorganizing the corporation, from the consideration received for shares.

SUBCHAPTER C. SUBSEQUENT ACQUISITION OF SHARES BY SHAREHOLDERS AND CORPORATION

§ 6.30 Shareholders' Preemptive Rights

(a) The shareholders of a corporation do not have a preemptive right to acquire the corporation's unissued shares except to the extent the articles of incorporation so provide.

(b) A statement included in the articles of incorporation that "the corporation elects to have preemptive rights" (or words of similar import) means that the following principles apply except to the extent the articles of incorporation expressly provide otherwise:

(1) The shareholders of the corporation have a preemptive right, granted on uniform terms and conditions prescribed by the

board of directors to provide a fair and reasonable opportunity to exercise the right, to acquire proportional amounts of the corporation's unissued shares upon the decision of the board of directors to issue them.

(2) A shareholder may waive his preemptive right. A waiver evidenced by a writing is irrevocable even though it is not supported by consideration.

(3) There is no preemptive right with respect to:

(i) shares issued as compensation to directors, officers, agents, or employees of the corporation, its subsidiaries or affiliates;

(ii) shares issued to satisfy conversion or option rights created to provide compensation to directors, officers, agents, or employees of the corporation, its subsidiaries or affiliates;

(iii) shares authorized in articles of incorporation that are issued within six months from the effective date of incorporation;

(iv) shares sold otherwise than for money.

(4) Holders of shares of any class without general voting rights but with preferential rights to distributions or assets have no preemptive rights with respect to shares of any class.

(5) Holders of shares of any class with general voting rights but without preferential rights to distributions or assets have no preemptive rights with respect to shares of any class with preferential rights to distributions or assets unless the shares with preferential rights are convertible into or carry a right to subscribe for or acquire shares without preferential rights.

(6) Shares subject to preemptive rights that are not acquired by shareholders may be issued to any person for a period of one year after being offered to shareholders at a consideration set by the board of directors that is not lower than the consideration set for the exercise of preemptive rights. An offer at a lower consideration or after the expiration of one year is subject to the shareholders' preemptive rights.

(c) For purposes of this section, "shares" includes a security convertible into or carrying a right to subscribe for or acquire shares.

§ 6.31 Corporation's Acquisition of Its Own Shares

(a) A corporation may acquire its own shares, and shares so acquired constitute authorized but unissued shares.

(b) If the articles of incorporation prohibit the reissue of the acquired shares, the number of authorized shares is reduced by the number of shares acquired.

(c) Articles of amendment may be adopted by the board of directors without shareholder action, shall be delivered to the secretary of state for filing, and shall set forth:

(1) the name of the corporation;

(2) the reduction in the number of authorized shares, itemized by class and series; and

(3) the total number of authorized shares, itemized by class and series, remaining after reduction of the shares.

OFFICIAL COMMENT

Section 6.31 applies only to shares that a corporation acquires for its own account. Shares that a corporation acquires in a fiduciary capacity for the account of others are not considered to be acquired by the corporation for purposes of this section.

Shares that are reacquired by the corporation become authorized but unissued shares under section 6.31(a) unless the articles prohibit reissue, in which event the shares are canceled and the number of authorized shares is reduced as required by section 6.31(b).

If the number of authorized shares of a class is reduced as a result of the operation of section 6.31(b), the board should amend the articles of incorporation under section 10.05(6) to reflect that reduction. If there are no remaining authorized shares in a class as a result of the operation of section 6.31, the board should amend the articles of incorporation under section 10.05(7) to delete the class from the classes of shares authorized by articles of incorporation.

SUBCHAPTER D. DISTRIBUTIONS

§ 6.40 Distributions to Shareholders

(a) A board of directors may authorize and the corporation may make distributions to its shareholders subject to restriction by the articles of incorporation and the limitation in subsection (c).

(b) If the board of directors does not fix the record date for determining shareholders entitled to a distribution (other than one involving a purchase, redemption, or other acquisition of the corporation's shares), it is the date the board of directors authorizes the distribution.

(c) No distribution may be made if, after giving it effect:

(1) the corporation would not be able to pay its debts as they become due in the usual course of business; or

(2) the corporation's total assets would be less than the sum of its total liabilities plus (unless the articles of incorporation permit otherwise) the amount that would be needed, if the corporation were to be dissolved at the time of the distribution, to satisfy the preferential rights upon dissolution of shareholders whose preferential rights are superior to those receiving the distribution.

(d) The board of directors may base a determination that a distribution is not prohibited under subsection (c) either on financial statements prepared on the basis of accounting practices and principles that are reasonable in the circumstances or on a fair valuation or other method that is reasonable in the circumstances.

(e) Except as provided in subsection (g), the effect of a distribution under subsection (c) is measured:

(1) in the case of distribution by purchase, redemption, or other acquisition of the corporation's shares, as of the earlier of (i) the date money or other property is transferred or debt incurred by the corporation or (ii) the date the shareholder ceases to be a shareholder with respect to the acquired shares;

(2) in the case of any other distribution of indebtedness, as of the date the indebtedness is distributed;

(3) in all other cases, as of (i) the date the distribution is authorized if the payment occurs within 120 days after the date of authorization or (ii) the date the payment is made if it occurs more than 120 days after the date of authorization.

(f) A corporation's indebtedness to a shareholder incurred by reason of a distribution made in accordance with this section is at parity with the corporation's indebtedness to its general, unsecured creditors except to the extent subordinated by agreement.

(g) Indebtedness of a corporation, including indebtedness issued as a distribution, is not considered a liability for purposes of determinations under subsection (c) if its terms provide that payment of principal and interest are made only if and to the extent that payment of a distribution to shareholders could then be made under this section. If the indebtedness is issued as a distribution, each payment of principal or interest is treated as a distribution, the effect of which is measured on the date the payment is actually made.

(h) This section shall not apply to distributions in liquidation under chapter 14.

OFFICIAL COMMENT

The reformulation of the statutory standards governing distributions is another important change made by the 1980 revisions to the financial provisions of the Model Act. It has long been recognized that the traditional "par value" and "stated capital" statutes do not provide significant protection against distributions of capital to shareholders. While most of these statutes contained elaborate provisions establishing "stated capital," "capital surplus," and "earned surplus" (and often other types of surplus as well), the net effect of most statutes was to permit the distribution to shareholders of most or all of the corporation's net assets—its capital along with its earnings—if the shareholders wished this to be done. However, statutes also generally imposed an equity insolvency test on distributions that prohibited distributions of assets if the corporation was insolvent or if the distribution had the effect of making the corporation insolvent or unable to meet its obligations as they were projected to arise.

The financial provisions of the revised Model Act, which are based on the 1980 amendments, sweep away all the distinctions among the various types of surplus but retain restrictions on distributions built around both the traditional equity insolvency and balance sheet tests of earlier statutes.

The Scope of Section 6.40

Section 1.40 defines "distribution" to include virtually all transfers of money, indebtedness of the corporation or other property to a shareholder in respect of the corporation's shares. It thus includes cash or property dividends, payments by a corporation to purchase its own shares, distributions of promissory notes or indebtedness, and distributions in partial or complete liquidation or voluntary or involuntary dissolution. Section 1.40 excludes from the definition of "distribution" transactions by the corporation in which only its own shares are distributed to its shareholders. These transactions are called "share dividends" in the revised Model Business Corporation Act. See section 6.23.

Section 6.40 imposes a single, uniform test on all distributions. Many of the old "par value" and "stated capital" statutes provided tests that varied with the type of distribution under consideration or did not cover certain types of distributions at all.

Equity Insolvency Test

As noted above, older statutes prohibited payment of dividends if the corporation was, or as a result of the payment would be, insolvent in the equity sense. This test is retained, appearing in section 6.40(c)(1).

In most cases involving a corporation operating as a going concern in the normal course, information generally available will make it quite apparent that no particular inquiry concerning the equity insolvency test is needed. While neither a balance sheet nor an income statement can be conclusive as to this test, the existence of significant shareholders' equity and normal operating conditions are of themselves a strong indication that no issue should arise under that test. Indeed, in the case of a corporation having regularly audited financial statements, the absence of any qualification in the most recent auditor's opinion as to the corporation's status as a "going concern," coupled with a lack of subsequent adverse events, would normally be decisive.

It is only when circumstances indicate that the corporation is encountering difficulties or is in an uncertain position concerning its liquidity and operations that the board of directors or, more commonly, the officers or others upon whom they may place reliance under section 8.30(b), may need to address the issue. Because of the overall judgment required in evaluating the equity insolvency test, no one or more "bright line" tests can be employed. However, in determining whether the equity insolvency test has been met, certain judgments or assumptions as to the future course of the corporation's business are customarily justified, absent clear evidence to the contrary. These include the likelihood that (a) based on existing and contemplated demand for the corporation's products or services, it will be able to generate funds over a period of time sufficient to satisfy its existing and reasonably anticipated obligations as they mature, and (b) indebtedness which matures in the near-term will be refinanced where, on the basis of the corporation's financial condition and future prospects and the general availability of credit to businesses similarly situated, it is reasonable to assume that such refinancing may be accomplished. To the extent that the corporation may be subject to asserted or unasserted contingent liabilities, reasonable judgments as to the likelihood, amount, and time of any recovery against the corporation, after giving consideration to the extent to which the corporation is insured or otherwise protected against loss, may be utilized. There may be occasions when it would be useful to consider a cash flow analysis, based on a business forecast and budget, covering a sufficient period of time to permit a conclusion that known obligations of the corporation can reasonably be expected to be satisfied over the period of time that they will mature.

In exercising their judgment, the directors are entitled to rely, under section 8.30(b) as noted above, on information, opinions, reports, and statements prepared by others. Ordinarily, they should not be expected to become involved in the details of the various analyses or market or economic projections that may be relevant. Judgments must of necessity be made on the basis of information in the hands of the directors when a distribution is authorized. They should not, of course, be held responsible as a matter of hindsight for unforeseen developments. This is particularly true with respect to assumptions as to the ability of the corporation's business to repay long-term obligations which do not mature for several years, since the primary focus of the directors' decision to make a distribution should normally be on the corporation's prospects and obligations in the shorter term, unless special factors concerning the corporation's prospects require the taking of a longer term perspective.

Relationship to the Federal Bankruptcy Act and Other Fraudulent Conveyance Statutes

The revised Model Business Corporation Act establishes the validity of distributions from the corporate law standpoint under section 6.40 and determines the potential liability of directors for improper distributions under sections 8.30 and 8.33. The federal Bankruptcy Act and state fraudulent conveyance statutes, on the other hand, are designed to enable the trustee or other representative to recapture for the benefit of creditors funds distributed to others in some circumstances. In light of these diverse purposes, it was not thought necessary to make the tests of section 6.40 identical with the tests for insolvency under these various statutes.

Balance Sheet Test

Section 6.40(c)(2) requires that, after giving effect to any distribution, the corporation's assets equal or exceed its liabilities plus (with some exceptions) the dissolution preferences of senior equity securities. Section 6.40(d) authorizes asset and liability determinations to be made for this purpose on the basis of either (1) financial statements prepared on the basis of accounting practices and principles that are reasonable in the circumstances or (2) a fair valuation or other method that is reasonable in the circumstances. The determination of a corporation's assets and liabilities and the choice of the permissible basis on which to do so are left to the judgment of its board of directors. In making a judgment under section 6.40(d), the board may rely under section 8.30 upon opinions, reports, or statements, including financial statements and other financial data prepared or presented by public accountants or others.

Section 6.40 does not utilize particular accounting terminology of a technical nature or specify particular accounting concepts. In making determinations under this section, the board of directors may make judgments about accounting matters, giving full effect to its right to rely upon professional or expert opinion.

In a corporation with subsidiaries, the board of directors may rely on unconsolidated statements prepared on the basis of the equity method of accounting (see American Institute of Certified Public Accountants, *APB Opinion No. 18* (1971)) as to the corporation's investee corporations, including corporate joint ventures and subsidiaries, although other evidence would be relevant in the total determination.

Generally accepted accounting principles

The board of directors should in all circumstances be entitled to rely upon reasonably current financial statements prepared on the basis of generally accepted accounting principles in determining whether or not the balance sheet test of section 6.40(c)(2) has been met, unless the board is then aware that it would be unreasonable to rely on the financial statements because of newly-discovered or subsequently arising facts or circumstances. But section 6.40 does not mandate the use of generally accepted accounting principles; it only requires the use of accounting practices and principles that are reasonable in the circumstances. While publicly-owned corporations subject to registration under the Securities Exchange Act of 1934 must, and many other corporations in fact do, utilize financial statements prepared on the basis of generally accepted accounting principles, a great number of smaller or closely-held corporations do not. Some of these corporations maintain records solely on a tax accounting basis and their financial statements are of necessity prepared on that basis. Others prepare financial statements that substantially reflect generally accepted accounting principles but may depart from them in some respects (e.g., footnote disclosure). These facts of corporate life indicate that a statutory standard of reasonableness, rather than stipulating generally accepted accounting principles as the normative standard, is appropriate in order to achieve a reasonable degree of flexibility and to accommodate the needs of the many different types of business corporations which might be subject to these provisions, including in particular closely-held corporations. Accordingly, the revised Model Business Corporation Act contemplates that generally acceptable accounting principles are always "reasonable in the circumstances" and that other accounting principles may be perfectly acceptable, under a general standard of reasonableness, even if they do not involve the "fair value" or "current value" e also contemplated by section 6.40(d).

Other principles

Section 6.40(d) specifically permits determinations to be made under section 6.40(c)(2) on the basis of a fair valuation or other method that is reasonable in the circumstances. Thus the statute authorizes departures from historical cost accounting and sanctions the use of appraisal and current value methods to determine the amount available for distributions. No particular method of valuation is prescribed in the statute, since different methods may have validity depending upon the circumstances, including the type of enterprise and the purpose for which the determination is made. For example, it is inappropriate to apply a "quick-sale liquidation" method to value an enterprise, particularly with respect to the payment of normal dividends. On the other hand, a "quick-sale liquidation valuation" method might be appropriate in certain circumstances for an enterprise in the course of reducing its asset or business base by a material degree. In most cases, a fair valuation method or a going-concern basis would be appropriate if it is believed that the enterprise will continue as a going concern.

Ordinarily a corporation should not selectively revalue assets. It should consider the value of all of its material assets, whether or not reflected in the financial statements (e.g., a valuable executory contract). Likewise, all of a corporation's material obligations should be considered and revalued to the extent appropriate and possible. In any event, section 6.40(d) calls for the application under section 6.40(c)(2) of a method of determining the aggregate amount of assets and liabilities that is reasonable in the circumstances.

Section 6.40(d) also refers to some "other method that is reasonable in the circumstances." This phrase is intended to comprehend within section 6.40(c)(2) the wide variety of possibilities that might not be considered to fall under a "fair valuation" but might be reasonable in the circumstances of a particular case.

Preferential Dissolution Rights and the Balance Sheet Test

Section 6.40(c)(2) provides that a distribution may not be made unless the total assets of the corporation exceed its liabilities plus the amount that would be needed to satisfy any shareholders' superior preferential rights upon dissolution if the corporation were to be dissolved at the time of the distribution. This requirement in effect treats preferential dissolution rights of shares for distribution purposes as if they were liabilities for the sole purpose of determining the amount available for distributions, and carries forward analogous treatment of shares having preferential dissolution rights from earlier versions of the Model Act. In making the calculation of the amount that must be added to the liabilities of the corporation to reflect the preferential dissolution rights, the assumption should be made that the preferential dissolution rights are to be established pursuant to the articles of incorporation, as of the date of the distribution or proposed distribution. The amount so determined must include arrearages in preferential dividends if the articles of incorporation require that they be paid upon the dissolution of the corporation. In the case of shares having both a preferential right upon dissolution and other nonpreferential rights, only the preferential right should be taken into account. The treatment of preferential dissolution rights of classes of shares set forth in section 6.40(c)(2) is applicable only to the balance sheet test and is not applicable to the equity insolvency test of section 6.40(c)(1). The treatment of preferential rights mandated by this section may always be eliminated by an appropriate provision in the articles of incorporation.

Time of Measurement

Section 6.40(e)(3) provides that the time for measuring the effect of a distribution for compliance with the equity insolvency and balance sheet tests for all distributions not involving the reacquisition of shares or the distribution of indebtedness is the date of authorization, if the payment occurs within 120 days following the authorization; if the payment occurs more than 120 days after the authorization, however, the date of payment must be used. If the corporation elects to make a distribution in the form of its own indebtedness under section 6.40(e)(2), the validity of that distribution must be measured as of the time of distribution unless the indebtedness qualifies under section 6.40(g).

Section 6.40(e)(1) provides a different rule for the time of measurement when the distribution involves a reacquisition of shares. See below, Application to Reacquisition of Shares—Time of measurement.

Record Date

Section 6.40(b) fixes the record date (if the board of directors does not otherwise fix it) for distributions other than those involving a reacquisition of shares as the date the board of directors authorizes the distribution. No record date is necessary for a reacquisition of shares from one or more specific shareholders. The board of directors has discretion to set a record date for a reacquisition if it is to be pro rata and to be offered to all shareholders as of a specified date.

Application to Repurchases or Redemption of Shares

The application of the equity insolvency and balance sheet tests to distributions that involve the purchase, redemption, or other acquisition of shares creates unique problems; section 6.40 provides specific rules for the resolution of these problems as described below.

Time of measurement

Section 6.40(e)(1) provides that the time for measuring the effect of a distribution under section 6.40(c), if shares of the corporation are reacquired, is the earlier of (i) the payment date, or (ii) the date the shareholder ceased to be a shareholder with respect to the shares, except as provided in section 6.40(g).

When tests are applied to redemption-related debt

In an acquisition of its shares, a corporation may transfer property or incur debt to the former holder of the shares. The case law on the status of this debt is conflicting. However, share repurchase agreements involving payment for shares over a period of time are of special importance in closely held corporate enterprises. Section 6.40(e) provides a clear rule for this situation: the legality of the distribution must be measured at the time of the issuance or incurrence of the debt, not at a later date when the debt is actually paid. Of course, this does not preclude a later challenge of a payment on account of redemption-related debt by a bankruptcy trustee on the ground that it constitutes a preferential payment to a creditor.

Priority of debt distributed directly or incurred in connection with a reacquisition of shares

Section 6.40(f) provides that indebtedness created to acquire the corporation's shares or issued as a distribution is on a parity with the indebtedness of the corporation to its general, unsecured creditors, except to the extent subordinated by agreement. General creditors are better off in these situations than they would have been if cash or other property had been paid out for the shares or distributed (which is proper under the statute), and no worse off than if cash had been paid or distributed and then lent back to the corporation, making the shareholders (or former shareholders) creditors. The parity created by section 6.40(f) is logically consistent with the rule established by section 6.40(e) that these transactions should be judged at the time of the issuance of the debt.

Treatment of certain indebtedness

Section 6.40(g) provides that indebtedness need not be taken into account as a liability in determining whether the tests of section 6.40(c) have been met if the terms of the indebtedness provide that payments of principal or interest can be made only if and to the extent that payment of a distribution could then be made under section 6.40. This has the effect of making the holder of the indebtedness junior to all other creditors but senior to the holders of all classes of shares, not only during the time the corporation is operating but also upon dissolution and liquidation. It should be noted that the creation of such indebtedness, and the related limitations on payments of principal and interest, may create tax problems or raise other legal questions.

Although section 6.40(g) is applicable to all indebtedness meeting its tests, regardless of the circumstances of its issuance, it is anticipated that it will be applicable most frequently to permit the reacquisition of shares of the corporation at a time when the deferred purchase price exceeds the net worth of the corporation. This type of reacquisition will often be necessary in the case of businesses in early stages of development or service businesses whose value derives principally from existing or prospective net income or cash flow rather than from net asset value. In such situations, it is anticipated that net worth will grow over time from operations so that when payments in respect of the indebtedness are to be made the two insolvency tests will be satisfied. In the meantime, the fact that the indebtedness is outstanding will not prevent distributions that could be made under subsection (c) if the indebtedness were not counted in making the determination.

Subsection (h) provides that distributions in liquidation under chapter 14 are not subject to the distribution limitations of section 6.40. Chapter 14 provides specifically for payment of creditor claims and distributions to shareholders in liquidation upon dissolution of the corporation. See section 14.09.

CHAPTER 7. SHAREHOLDERS

SUBCHAPTER A. MEETINGS

§ 7.01 Annual Meeting

(a) A corporation shall hold annually at a time stated in or fixed in accordance with the bylaws a meeting of shareholders.

(b) Annual shareholders' meetings may be held in or out of this state at the place stated in or fixed in accordance with the bylaws. If no place is stated in or fixed in accordance with the bylaws, annual meetings shall be held at the corporation's principal office.

(c) The failure to hold an annual meeting at the time stated in or fixed in accordance with a corporation's bylaws does not affect the validity of any corporate action.

§ 7.02 Special Meeting

(a) A corporation shall hold a special meeting of shareholders:

(1) on call of its board of directors or the person or persons authorized to do so by the articles of incorporation or bylaws; or

(2) if shareholders having at least 10 percent of all the votes entitled to be cast on an issue proposed to be considered at the proposed special meeting sign, date, and deliver to the corporation one or more written demands for the meeting describing the purpose or purposes for which it is to be held, provided that the articles of incorporation may fix a lower percentage or a higher percentage not exceeding 25 percent of all the votes entitled to be cast on any issue proposed to be considered. Unless otherwise provided in the articles of incorporation, a written demand for a special meeting may be revoked by a writing to that effect received by the corporation prior to the receipt by the corporation of demands sufficient in number to require the holding of a special meeting.

(b) If not otherwise fixed under sections 7.03 or 7.07, the record date for determining shareholders entitled to demand a special meeting is the date the first shareholder signs the demand.

(c) Special shareholders' meetings may be held in or out of this state at the place stated in or fixed in accordance with the bylaws. If no place is stated or fixed in accordance with the bylaws, special meetings shall be held at the corporation's principal office.

(d) Only business within the purpose or purposes described in the meeting notice required by section 7.05(c) may be conducted at a special shareholders' meeting.

§ 7.03 Court–Ordered Meeting

(a) The [name or describe] court of the county where a corporation's principal office (or, if none in this state, its registered office) is located may summarily order a meeting to be held:

(1) on application of any shareholder of the corporation entitled to participate in an annual meeting if an annual meeting was not held within the earlier of 6 months after the end of the corporation's fiscal year or 15 months after its last annual meeting; or

(2) on application of a shareholder who signed a demand for a special meeting valid under section 7.02 if:

(i) notice of the special meeting was not given within 30 days after the date the demand was delivered to the corporation's secretary; or

(ii) the special meeting was not held in accordance with the notice.

(b) The court may fix the time and place of the meeting, determine the shares entitled to participate in the meeting, specify a record date for determining shareholders entitled to notice of and to vote at the meeting, prescribe the form and content of the meeting notice, fix the quorum required for specific matters to be considered at the meeting (or direct that the votes represented at the meeting constitute a quorum for action on those matters), and enter other orders necessary to accomplish the purpose or purposes of the meeting.

§ 7.04 Action Without Meeting

(a) Action required or permitted by this Act to be taken at a shareholders' meeting may be taken without a meeting if the action is taken by all the shareholders entitled to vote on the action. The action must be evidenced by one or more written consents bearing the date of signature and describing the action taken, signed by all the shareholders entitled to vote on the action, and delivered to the corporation for inclusion in the minutes or filing with the corporate records.

(b) If not otherwise fixed under section 7.03 or 7.07, the record date for determining shareholders entitled to take action without a meeting is the date the first shareholder signs the consent under subsection (a). No written consent shall be effective to take the corporate action referred to therein unless, within 60 days of the earliest date appearing on a consent delivered to the corporation in the manner required by this section, written consents signed by all shareholders entitled to vote on the action are received by the corporation. A written consent may be revoked by a writing to that effect received by the corporation prior to the receipt by the corporation of unrevoked written consents sufficient in number to take corporate action.

(c) A consent signed under this section has the effect of a meeting vote and may be described as such in any document.

(d) If this Act requires that notice of proposed action be given to nonvoting shareholders and the action is to be taken by unanimous consent of the voting shareholders, the corporation must give its nonvoting shareholders written notice of the proposed action at least 10 days before the action is taken. The notice must contain or be accompanied by the same material that, under this Act, would have been required to be sent to nonvoting shareholders in a notice of meeting at which the proposed action would have been submitted to the shareholders for action.

§ 7.05 Notice of Meeting

(a) A corporation shall notify shareholders of the date, time, and place of each annual and special shareholders' meeting no fewer than 10 nor more than 60 days before the meeting date. Unless this Act or the articles of incorporation require otherwise, the corporation is required to give notice only to shareholders entitled to vote at the meeting.

(b) Unless this Act or the articles of incorporation require otherwise, notice of an annual meeting need not include a description of the purpose or purposes for which the meeting is called.

(c) Notice of a special meeting must include a description of the purpose or purposes for which the meeting is called.

(d) If not otherwise fixed under sections 7.03 or 7.07, the record date for determining shareholders entitled to notice of and to vote at an annual or special shareholders' meeting is the day before the first notice is delivered to shareholders.

(e) Unless the bylaws require otherwise, if an annual or special shareholders' meeting is adjourned to a different date, time, or place, notice need not be given of the new date, time, or place if the new date, time, or place is announced at the meeting before adjournment. If a new record date for the adjourned meeting is or must be fixed under section 7.07, however, notice of the adjourned meeting must be given under this section to persons who are shareholders as of the new record date.

§ 7.06 Waiver of Notice

(a) A shareholder may waive any notice required by this Act, the articles of incorporation, or bylaws before or after the date and time stated in the notice. The waiver must be in writing, be signed by the shareholder entitled to the notice, and be delivered to the corporation for inclusion in the minutes or filing with the corporate records.

(b) A shareholder's attendance at a meeting:

(1) waives objection to lack of notice or defective notice of the meeting, unless the shareholder at the beginning of the meeting objects to holding the meeting or transacting business at the meeting;

(2) waives objection to consideration of a particular matter at the meeting that is not within the purpose or purposes described in the meeting notice, unless the shareholder objects to considering the matter when it is presented.

§ 7.07 Record Date

(a) The bylaws may fix or provide the manner of fixing the record date for one or more voting groups in order to determine the shareholders entitled to notice of a shareholders' meeting, to demand a special meeting, to vote, or to take any other action. If the bylaws do not fix or provide for fixing a record date, the board of directors of the corporation may fix a future date as the record date.

(b) A record date fixed under this section may not be more than 70 days before the meeting or action requiring a determination of shareholders.

(c) A determination of shareholders entitled to notice of or to vote at a shareholders' meeting is effective for any adjournment of the meeting unless the board of directors fixes a new record date, which it must do if the meeting is adjourned to a date more than 120 days after the date fixed for the original meeting.

(d) If a court orders a meeting adjourned to a date more than 120 days after the date fixed for the original meeting, it may provide that the original record date continues in effect or it may fix a new record date.

§ 7.08 Conduct of the Meeting

(a) At each meeting of shareholders, a chair shall preside. The chair shall be appointed as provided in the bylaws or, in the absence of such provision, by the board.

(b) The chair, unless the articles of incorporation or bylaws provide otherwise, shall determine the order of business and shall have the authority to establish rules for the conduct of the meeting.

(c) Any rules adopted for, and the conduct of, the meeting shall be fair to shareholders.

(d) The chair of the meeting shall announce at the meeting when the polls close for each matter voted upon. If no announcement is made, the polls shall be deemed to have closed upon the final adjournment of the meeting. After the polls close, no ballots, proxies or votes nor any revocations or changes thereto may be accepted.

OFFICIAL COMMENT

Section 7.08 provides that, at any meeting of the shareholders, there shall be a chair who shall preside over the meeting. The chair is appointed in accordance with the bylaws. Generally, the chair of the board of directors presides over the meeting. However, the bylaws could provide that the chief executive officer, if different than the chair of the board, preside over the meeting and they should provide a means of designating an alternate if that individual is for any reason unable to preside.

Section 7.08(b) gives the chair, unless the articles of incorporation or bylaws provide otherwise, the authority to determine in what order items of business should be discussed and decided. Inherent in the chair's power to establish rules for the conduct of the meeting is the authority to require that the order of business be observed and that any discussion or comments from shareholders or their proxies be confined to the business item under discussion. However, it is also expected that the chair will not misuse the power to determine the order of business and to establish rules for the conduct of the meeting so as to unfairly foreclose the right of shareholders subject to the Act, the articles of incorporation and the bylaws to raise items which are properly a subject for shareholder discussion or action at some point in the meeting prior to adjournment.

The Act provides that only business within the purpose or purposes described in the meeting notice may be conducted at a special shareholders' meeting. See sections 7.02(d) and 7.05(c). In addition, a corporation's articles of incorporation or, more typically, its bylaws, may contain advance notice provisions requiring that shareholder nominations for election to the board of directors or resolutions intended to be voted on at the annual meeting must be made in writing and received by the corporation a prescribed number of days in advance of the meeting. Such advance notice bylaws are permitted provided (1) there is reasonable opportunity for shareholders to comply with them in a timely fashion, and (2) the requirements of the bylaws are reasonable in relationship to corporate needs.

Among the considerations to be taken into account in determining reasonableness are (a) how and with what frequency shareholders are advised of the specific bylaw provisions, and (b) whether the time frame within which director nominations or shareholder resolutions must be submitted is consistent with the corporation's need, if any, (i) to prepare and publish a proxy statement, (ii) to verify that the director nominee meets any established qualifications for director and is willing to serve, (iii) to determine that a proposed resolution is a proper subject for shareholder action under the Act or other state law, or (iv) to give interested parties adequate opportunity to communicate a recommendation or response with respect to such matters, or to solicit proxies. Whether or not an advance notice provision has been adopted, if a public company receives advance notice of a matter to be raised for a vote at an annual meeting, management may exercise its discretionary proxy authority only in compliance with SEC Rule 14a4(c)(1) adopted under the Securities Exchange Act of 1934.

Section 7.08(b) also provides that the chair shall have the authority to establish rules for the conduct of the meeting. Complicated parliamentary rules (such as Robert's Rules of Order) ordinarily are not appropriate for shareholder meetings. The rules may cover such subjects as the proper means for obtaining the floor, who shall have the right to address the meeting, the manner in which shareholders will be recognized to speak, time limits per speaker, the number of times a shareholder may address the meeting, and the person to whom questions should be addressed. The substance of the rules should be communicated to shareholders prior to or at the beginning of the meeting. The chair is entitled to wide latitude in conducting the meeting and, unless inconsistent with a previously prescribed rule, may set requirements, observe practices, and follow customs that facilitate a fair and orderly meeting. Since, absent a modifying bylaw provision, the chair has exclusive authority with respect to the rules for and the conduct of the meeting, rulings by the chair may not be overruled by shareholders. On the other hand, any rule for or conduct of the meeting which does not satisfy the fairness mandate of Section 7.08(c) would be subject to a judicial remedy.

Section 7.08(d) requires that an announcement be made at the meeting of shareholders specifying when the polls will close for each matter voted upon. It also provides that, once the polls close, no ballots, proxies, or votes and no changes thereto may be accepted. This statutory provision eliminates an area of uncertainty which had developed in the relatively sparse case law dealing with the effect of closing the polls, some of which suggested that, notwithstanding the closing of the polls, votes could be changed up until the time that the inspectors of election announced the results. Young v. Jebbett, 211 N.Y.S. 61 (N.Y. App. Div. 1925); State ex rel. David v. Dailey, 168 P.2d 330 (Wash. 1945). Any abusive use of the poll-closing power would be subject to judicial review under subsection (c) as well as under that line of cases requiring that meetings of shareholders be conducted fairly and proscribing inequitable manipulations of the shareholder voting machinery. See, e.g., Duffy v. Loft, Inc., 151 A. 223 (Del. Ch. 1930); Schnell v. Chris Craft Ind., Inc., 285 A.2d 437 (Del. 1971).

SUBCHAPTER B. VOTING

§ 7.20 Shareholders' List for Meeting

(a) After fixing a record date for a meeting, a corporation shall prepare an alphabetical list of the names of all its shareholders who are entitled to notice of a shareholders' meeting. The list must be arranged by voting group (and within each voting group by class or series of shares) and show the address of and number of shares held by each shareholder.

(b) The shareholders' list must be available for inspection by any shareholder, beginning two business days after notice of the meeting is given for which the list was prepared and continuing through the meeting, at the corporation's principal office or at a place identified in the meeting notice in the city where the meeting will be held. A shareholder, his agent, or attorney is entitled on written demand to inspect and, subject to the requirements of section 16.02(c), to copy the list, during regular business hours and at his expense, during the period it is available for inspection.

(c) The corporation shall make the shareholders' list available at the meeting, and any shareholder, his agent, or attorney is entitled to inspect the list at any time during the meeting or any adjournment.

(d) If the corporation refuses to allow a shareholder, his agent, or attorney to inspect the shareholders' list before or at the meeting (or copy the list as permitted by subsection (b)), the [name or describe] court of the county where a corporation's principal office (or, if none in this state, its registered office) is located, on application of the shareholder, may summarily order the inspection or copying at the corporation's expense and may postpone the meeting for which the list was prepared until the inspection or copying is complete.

(e) Refusal or failure to prepare or make available the shareholders' list does not affect the validity of action taken at the meeting.

§ 7.21 Voting Entitlement of Shares

(a) Except as provided in subsections (b) and (c) or unless the articles of incorporation provide otherwise, each outstanding share, regardless of class, is entitled to one vote on each matter voted on at a shareholders' meeting. Only shares are entitled to vote.

(b) Absent special circumstances, the shares of a corporation are not entitled to vote if they are owned, directly or indirectly, by a second corporation, domestic or foreign, and the first corporation owns, directly or indirectly, a majority of the shares entitled to vote for directors of the second corporation.

(c) Subsection (b) does not limit the power of a corporation to vote any shares, including its own shares, held by it in a fiduciary capacity.

(d) Redeemable shares are not entitled to vote after notice of redemption is mailed to the holders and a sum sufficient to redeem the shares has been deposited with a bank, trust company, or other financial institution under an irrevocable obligation to pay the holders the redemption price on surrender of the shares.

§ 7.22 Proxies

(a) A shareholder may vote his shares in person or by proxy.

(b) A shareholder or his agent or attorney-in-fact may appoint a proxy to vote or otherwise act for the shareholder by signing an appointment form, or by an electronic transmission. An electronic transmission must contain or be accompanied by information from which one can determine that the shareholder, the shareholder's agent, or the shareholder's attorney-in-fact authorized the electronic transmission.

(c) An appointment of a proxy is effective when a signed appointment form or an electronic transmission of the appointment is received by the inspector of election or the officer or agent of the corporation authorized to tabulate votes. An appointment is valid for 11 months unless a longer period is expressly provided in the appointment.

(d) An appointment of a proxy is revocable unless the appointment form or electronic transmission conspicuously states that it is irrevocable and the appointment is coupled with an interest. Appointments coupled with an interest include the appointment of: . . . .

(e) The death or incapacity of the shareholder appointing a proxy does not affect the right of the corporation to accept the proxy's authority unless notice of the death or incapacity is received by the secretary or other officer or agent authorized to tabulate votes before the proxy exercises his authority under the appointment.

(f) An appointment made irrevocable under subsection (d) is revoked when the interest with which it is coupled is extinguished.

(g) A transferee for value of shares subject to an irrevocable appointment may revoke the appointment if he did not know of its existence when he acquired the shares and the existence of the irrevocable appointment was not noted conspicuously on the certificate representing the shares or on the information statement for shares without certificates.

(h) Subject to section 7.24 and to any express limitation on the proxy's authority stated in the appointment form or electronic transmission, a corporation is entitled to accept the proxy's vote or other action as that of the shareholder making the appointment.

* * *

§ 7.23 Shares Held by Nominees

(a) A corporation may establish a procedure by which the beneficial owner of shares that are registered in the name of a nominee is recognized by the corporation as the shareholder. The extent of this recognition may be determined in the procedure.

(b) The procedure may set forth:

(1) the types of nominees to which it applies;

(2) the rights or privileges that the corporation recognizes in a beneficial owner;

(3) the manner in which the procedure is selected by the nominee;

(4) the information that must be provided when the procedure is selected;

(5) the period for which selection of the procedure is effective; and

(6) other aspects of the rights and duties created.

§ 7.24 Corporation's Acceptance of Votes

(a) If the name signed on a vote, consent, waiver, or proxy appointment corresponds to the name of a shareholder, the corporation if acting in good faith is entitled to accept the vote, consent, waiver, or proxy appointment and give it effect as the act of the shareholder.

(b) If the name signed on a vote, consent, waiver, or proxy appointment does not correspond to the name of its shareholder, the corporation if acting in good faith is nevertheless entitled to accept the vote, consent, waiver, or proxy appointment and give it effect as the act of the shareholder if:

(1) the shareholder is an entity and the name signed purports to be that of an officer or agent of the entity;

(2) the name signed purports to be that of an administrator, executor, guardian, or conservator representing the shareholder and, if the corporation requests, evidence of fiduciary status acceptable to the corporation has been presented with respect to the vote, consent, waiver, or proxy appointment;

(3) the name signed purports to be that of a receiver or trustee in bankruptcy of the shareholder and, if the corporation requests, evidence of this status acceptable to the corporation has been presented with respect to the vote, consent, waiver, or proxy appointment;

(4) the name signed purports to be that of a pledgee, beneficial owner, or attorney-in-fact of the shareholder and, if the corporation requests, evidence acceptable to the corporation of the signatory's authority to sign for the shareholder has been presented with respect to the vote, consent, waiver, or proxy appointment;

(5) two or more persons are the shareholder as cotenants or fiduciaries and the name signed purports to be the name of at least one of the coowners and the person signing appears to be acting on behalf of all the coowners.

(c) The corporation is entitled to reject a vote, consent, waiver, or proxy appointment if the secretary or other officer or agent authorized to tabulate votes, acting in good faith, has reasonable basis for doubt about the validity of the signature on it or about the signatory's authority to sign for the shareholder.

* * *

(d) The corporation and its officer or agent who accepts or rejects a vote, consent, waiver, or proxy appointment in good faith and in accordance with the standards of this section or section 7.22(b) are not liable in damages to the shareholder for the consequences of the acceptance or rejection.

(e) Corporate action based on the acceptance or rejection of a vote, consent, waiver, or proxy appointment under this section or section 7.22(b) is valid unless a court of competent jurisdiction determines otherwise.

§ 7.25 Quorum and Voting Requirements for Voting Groups

(a) Shares entitled to vote as a separate voting group may take action on a matter at a meeting only if a quorum of those shares exists with respect to that matter. Unless the articles of incorporation or this Act provide otherwise, a majority of the votes entitled to be cast on the matter by the voting group constitutes a quorum of that voting group for action on that matter.

(b) Once a share is represented for any purpose at a meeting, it is deemed present for quorum purposes for the remainder of the meeting and for any adjournment of that meeting unless a new record date is or must be set for that adjourned meeting.

(c) If a quorum exists, action on a matter (other than the election of directors) by a voting group is approved if the votes cast within the voting group favoring the action exceed the votes cast opposing the action, unless the articles of incorporation or this Act require a greater number of affirmative votes.

(d) An amendment of articles of incorporation adding, changing, or deleting a quorum or voting requirement for a voting group greater than specified in subsection (b) or (c) is governed by section 7.27.

(e) The election of directors is governed by section 7.28.

§ 7.26 Action by Single and Multiple Voting Groups

(a) If the articles of incorporation or this Act provide for voting by a single voting group on a matter, action on that matter is taken when voted upon by that voting group as provided in section 7.25.

(b) If the articles of incorporation or this Act provide for voting by two or more voting groups on a matter, action on that matter is taken only when voted upon by each of those voting groups counted separately as provided in section 7.25. Action may be taken by one voting group on a matter even though no action is taken by another voting group entitled to vote on the matter.

§ 7.27 Greater Quorum or Voting Requirements

(a) The articles of incorporation may provide for a greater quorum or voting requirement for shareholders (or voting groups of shareholders) than is provided for by this Act.

(b) An amendment to the articles of incorporation that adds, changes, or deletes a greater quorum or voting requirement must meet the same quorum requirement and be adopted by the same vote and voting groups required to take action under the quorum and voting requirements then in effect or proposed to be adopted, whichever is greater.

§ 7.28 Voting for Directors; Cumulative Voting

(a) Unless otherwise provided in the articles of incorporation, directors are elected by a plurality of the votes cast by the shares entitled to vote in the election at a meeting at which a quorum is present.

(b) Shareholders do not have a right to cumulate their votes for directors unless the articles of incorporation so provide.

(c) A statement included in the articles of incorporation that "[all] [a designated voting group of] shareholders are entitled to cumulate their votes for directors" (or words of similar import) means that the shareholders designated are entitled to multiply the number of votes they are entitled to cast by the number of directors for whom they are entitled to vote and cast the product for a single candidate or distribute the product among two or more candidates.

(d) Shares otherwise entitled to vote cumulatively may not be voted cumulatively at a particular meeting unless:

(1) the meeting notice or proxy statement accompanying the notice states conspicuously that cumulative voting is authorized; or

(2) a shareholder who has the right to cumulate his votes gives notice to the corporation not less than 48 hours before the time set for the meeting of his intent to cumulate his votes during the meeting, and if one shareholder gives this notice all other shareholders in the same voting group participating in the election are entitled to cumulate their votes without giving further notice.

§ 7.29 Inspectors of Election

(a) A corporation having any shares listed on a national securities exchange or regularly traded in a market maintained by one or more members of a national or affiliated securities association shall, and any other corporation may, appoint one or more inspectors to act at a meeting of shareholders and make a written report of the inspectors's determinations. Each inspector shall take and sign an oath faithfully to execute the duties of inspector with strict impartiality and according to the best of the inspector's ability.

(b) The inspectors shall

(1) ascertain the number of shares outstanding and the voting power of each;

(2) determine the shares represented at a meeting;

(3) determine the validity of proxies and ballots;

(4) count all votes; and

(5) determine the result.

(c) An inspector may be an officer or employee of the corporation.

OFFICIAL COMMENT

Section 7.29(a) requires that, if a corporation has shares which are listed on a national securities exchange or regularly traded in a market maintained by one or more members of a national or affiliated securities association, one or more inspectors of election must be appointed to act at each meeting of shareholders and make a written report of the determinations made pursuant to section 7.29(b). It is contemplated that the selection of inspectors would be made by responsible officers or by the directors, as authorized either generally or specifically in the corporation's bylaws. Alternate inspectors could also be designated to replace any inspector who fails to act. The requirement of a written report is to facilitate judicial review of determinations made by inspectors.

Section 7.29(b) specifies the duties of inspectors of election. If no challenge of a determination by the inspectors within the authority given them under this section is timely made, such determination shall be conclusive. In the event of a challenge of any determination by the inspectors in a court of competent jurisdiction, the court should give such weight to determinations of fact by the inspectors as it shall deem appropriate, taking into account the relationship of the inspectors, if any, to the management of the company and other persons interested in the outcome of the vote, the evidence available to the inspectors, whether their determinations appear to be reasonable, and such other circumstances as the court shall regard as relevant. The court should review de novo all determinations of law made implicitly or explicitly by the inspectors.

Normally, in making the determinations contemplated by section 7.29(b), the only facts before the inspectors should be appointment forms and electronic transmissions (or written evidence thereof), envelopes submitted with appointment forms, ballots and the regular books and records of the corporation, including lists of holders obtained from depositories. However, inspectors may consider other reliable information for the limited purpose of reconciling appointment forms, electronic transmissions, and ballots submitted by or on behalf of banks, brokers, their nominees, and similar persons which represent more votes than the holder of a proxy is authorized by the record owner to cast or more votes than the shareholder holds of record. If the inspectors do consider such other information, it should be specifically referred to in their written report, including the person or persons from whom they obtained the information, when the information was obtained, the means by which the information was obtained, and the basis for the inspectors' belief that such information is accurate and reliable.

Section 7.29(c) provides that an inspector may be an officer or employee of the corporation. However, in the case of publicly-held corporations, good corporate practice suggests that such inspectors should be independent persons who are neither employees nor officers if there is a contested matter or a shareholder proposal to be considered. Not only will the issue of independent inspectors enhance investor perception as to the fairness of the voting process, but also the report of independent inspectors can be expected to be given greater evidentiary weight by any court reviewing a contested vote.

SUBCHAPTER C. VOTING TRUSTS AND AGREEMENTS

§ 7.30 Voting Trusts

(a) One or more shareholders may create a voting trust, conferring on a trustee the right to vote or otherwise act for them, by signing an agreement setting out the provisions of the trust (which may include anything consistent with its purpose) and transferring their shares to the trustee. When a voting trust agreement is signed, the trustee shall prepare a list of the names and addresses of all owners of beneficial interests in the trust, together with the number and class of shares each transferred to the trust, and deliver copies of the list and agreement to the corporation's principal office.

(b) A voting trust becomes effective on the date the first shares subject to the trust are registered in the trustee's name. A voting trust is valid for not more than 10 years after its effective date unless extended under subsection (c).

(c) All or some of the parties to a voting trust may extend it for additional terms of not more than 10 years each by signing an extension agreement and obtaining the voting trustee's written consent to the extension. An extension is valid for 10 years from the date the first shareholder signs the extension agreement. The voting trustee must deliver copies of the extension agreement and list of beneficial owners to the corporation's principal office. An extension agreement binds only those parties signing it.

X

§ 7.31 Voting Agreements

(a) Two or more shareholders may provide for the manner in which they will vote their shares by signing an agreement for that purpose. A voting agreement created under this section is not subject to the provisions of section 7.30.

(b) A voting agreement created under this section is specifically enforceable.

X

§ 7.32 Shareholder Agreements

(a) An agreement among the shareholders of a corporation that complies with this section is effective among the shareholders and the corporation even though it is inconsistent with one or more other provisions of this Act in that it:

(1) eliminates the board of directors or restricts the discretion or powers of the board of directors;

(2) governs the authorization or making of distributions whether or not in proportion to ownership of shares, subject to the limitations in section 6.40;

(3) establishes who shall be directors or officers of the corporation, or their terms of office or manner of selection or removal;

(4) governs, in general or in regard to specific matters, the exercise or division of voting power by or between the shareholders and directors or by or among any of them, including use of weighted voting rights or director proxies;

(5) establishes the terms and conditions of any agreement for the transfer or use of property or the provision of services between the corporation and any shareholder, director, officer or employee of the corporation or among any of them;

(6) transfers to one or more shareholders or other persons all or part of the authority to exercise the corporate powers or to manage the business and affairs of the corporation, including the resolution of any issue about which there exists a deadlock among directors or shareholders;

(7) requires dissolution of the corporation at the request of one or more of the shareholders or upon the occurrence of a specified event or contingency; or

(8) otherwise governs the exercise of the corporate powers or the management of the business and affairs of the corporation or the relationship among the shareholders, the directors and the corporation, or among any of them, and is not contrary to public policy.

(b) An agreement authorized by this section shall be:

(1) set forth (A) in the articles of incorporation or bylaws and approved by all persons who are shareholders at the time of the agreement or (B) in a written agreement that is signed by all persons who are shareholders at the time of the agreement and is made known to the corporation;

(2) subject to amendment only by all persons who are shareholders at the time of the amendment, unless the agreement provides otherwise; and

(3) valid for 10 years, unless the agreement provides otherwise.

(c) The existence of an agreement authorized by this section shall be noted conspicuously on the front or back of each certificate for outstanding shares or on the information statement required by section 6.26(b). If at the time of the agreement the corporation has shares outstanding represented by certificates, the corporation shall recall the outstanding certificates and issue substitute certificates that comply with this subsection. The failure to note the existence of the agreement on the certificate or information statement shall not affect the validity of the agreement or any action taken pursuant to it. Any purchaser of shares who, at the time of purchase, did not have knowledge of the existence of the agreement shall be entitled to rescission of the purchase. A purchaser shall be deemed to have knowledge of the existence of the agreement if its existence is noted on the certificate or information statement for the shares in compliance with this subsection and, if the shares are not represented by a certificate, the information statement is delivered to the purchaser at or prior to the time of purchase of the shares. An action to enforce the right of rescission authorized by this subsection must be commenced within the earlier of 90 days after discovery of the existence of the agreement or two years after the time of purchase of the shares.

(d) An agreement authorized by this section shall cease to be effective when shares of the corporation are listed on a national securities exchange or regularly traded in a market maintained by one or more members of a national or affiliated securities association. If the agreement ceases to be effective for any reason, the board of directors may, if the agreement is contained or referred to in the corporation's articles of incorporation or bylaws, adopt an amendment to the articles of incorporation or bylaws, without shareholder action, to delete the agreement and any references to it.

(e) An agreement authorized by this section that limits the discretion or powers of the board of directors shall relieve the directors of, and impose upon the person or persons in whom such discretion or powers are vested, liability for acts or omissions imposed by law on directors to the extent that the discretion or powers of the directors are limited by the agreement.

(f) The existence or performance of an agreement authorized by this section shall not be a ground for imposing personal liability on any shareholder for the acts or debts of the corporation even if the agreement or its performance treats the corporation as if it were a partnership or results in failure to observe the corporate formalities otherwise applicable to the matters governed by the agreement.

(g) Incorporators or subscribers for shares may act as shareholders with respect to an agreement authorized by this section if no shares have been issued when the agreement is made.

OFFICIAL COMMENT

Shareholders of closely-held corporations, ranging from family businesses to joint ventures owned by large public corporations, frequently enter into agreements that govern the operation of the enterprise. In the past, various types of shareholder agreements were invalidated by courts for a variety of reasons, including so-called "sterilization" of the board of directors and failure to follow the statutory norms of the applicable corporation act. See, e.g., Long Park, Inc. v. Trenton–New Brunswick Theatres Co., 297 N.Y. 174, 77 N.E.2d 633 (1948). The more modern decisions reflect a greater willingness to uphold shareholder agreements, See, e.g., Galler v. Galler, 32 Ill.2d 16, 203 N.E.2d 577 (1964). In addition, many state corporation acts now contain provisions validating shareholder agreements. Heretofore, however, the Model Act has never expressly validated shareholder agreements.

Rather than relying on further uncertain and sporadic development of the law in the courts, section 7.32 rejects the older line of cases. It adds an important element of predictability currently absent from the Model Act and affords participants in closely-held corporations greater contractual freedom to tailor the rules of their enterprise.

Section 7.32 is not intended to establish or legitimize an alternative form of corporation. Instead, it is intended to add, within the context of the traditional corporate structure, legal certainty to shareholder agreements that embody various aspects of the business arrangement established by the shareholders to meet their business and personal needs. The subject matter of these arrangements includes governance of the entity, allocation of the economic return from the business, and other aspects of the relationships among shareholders, directors, and the corporation which are part of the business arrangement. Section 7.32 also recognizes that many of the corporate norms contained in the Model Act, as well as the corporation statutes of most states, were designed with an eye towards public companies, where management and share ownership are quite distinct. Cf. 1 O'Neal & Thompson, O'Neal's Close Corporations, section 5.06 (3d ed.). These functions are often conjoined in the close corporation. Thus, section 7.32 validates for nonpublic corporations various types of agreements among shareholders even when the agreements are inconsistent with the statutory norms contained in the Act.

Importantly, section 7.32 only addresses the parties to the shareholder agreement, their transferees, and the corporation, and does not have any binding legal effect on the state, creditors, or other third persons.

Section 7.32 supplements the other provisions of the Model Act. If an agreement is not in conflict with another section of the Model Act, no resort need be made to section 7.32, with its requirement of unanimity. For example, special provisions can be included in the articles of incorporation or bylaws with less than unanimous shareholder agreement so long as such provisions are not in conflict with other provisions of the Act. Similarly, section 7.32 would not have to be relied upon to validate typical buy-sell agreements among two or more shareholders or the covenants and other terms of a stock purchase agreement entered into in connection with the issuance of shares by a corporation.

The types of provisions validated by section 7.32 are many and varied. Section 7.32(a) defines the range of permissible subject matter for shareholder agreements largely by illustration, enumerating seven types of agreements that are expressly validated to the extent they would not be valid absent section 7.32. The enumeration of these types of agreements is not exclusive; nor should it give rise to a negative inference that an agreement of a type that is or might be embraced by one of the categories of section 7.32(a) is, ipso facto, a type of agreement that is not valid unless it complies with section 7.32. Section 7.32(a) also contains a "catch all" which adds a measure of flexibility to the seven enumerated categories.

Omitted from the enumeration in section 7.32(a) is a provision found in the Close Corporation Supplement and in the statutes of many of the states, broadly validating any arrangement the effect of which is to treat the corporation as a partnership. This type of provision was considered to be too elastic and indefinite, as well as unnecessary in light of the more detailed enumeration of permissible subject areas contained in section 7.32(a). Note, however, that under section 7.32(f) the fact that an agreement authorized by section 7.32(a) or its performance treats the corporation as a partnership is not a ground for imposing personal liability on the parties if the agreement is otherwise authorized by subsection (a).

1. Section 7.32(a)

Subsection (a) is the heart of section 7.32. It states that certain types of agreements are effective among the shareholders and the corporation even if inconsistent with another provision of the Model Act. Thus, an agreement authorized by section 7.32 is, by virtue of that section, "not inconsistent with law" within the meaning of sections 2.02(b)(2) and 2.06(b) of the Act. In contrast, a shareholder agreement that is not inconsistent with any provisions of the Model Act is not subject to the requirements of section 7.32.

The range of agreements validated by section 7.32(a) is expansive though not unlimited. The most difficult problem encountered in crafting a shareholder agreement validation provision is to determine the reach of the provision. Some states have tried to articulate the limits of a shareholder agreement validation provision in terms of negative grounds, stating that no shareholder agreement shall be invalid on certain specified grounds. See, e.g., Del.Code Ann. tit. 8, sections 350, 354 (1983); N.C.Gen.Stat. section 55–73(b) (1982). The deficiency in this type of statute is the uncertainty introduced by the ever present possibility of articulating another ground on which to challenge the validity of the agreement. Other states have provided that shareholder agreements may waive or alter all provisions in the corporation act except certain enumerated provisions that cannot be varied. See, e.g., Cal.Corp.Code section 300(b)–(c) (West 1989 and Supp.1990). The difficulty with this approach is that any enumeration of the provisions that can never be varied will almost inevitably be subjective, arbitrary, and incomplete.

The approach chosen in section 7.32 is more pragmatic. It defines the types of agreements that can be validated largely by illustration. The seven specific categories that are listed are designed to cover the most frequently used arrangements. The outer boundary is provided by section 7.32(a)(8), which provides an additional "catch all" for any provisions that, in a manner inconsistent with any other provision of the Model Act, otherwise govern the exercise of the corporate powers, the management of the business and affairs of the corporation, or the relationship between and among the shareholders, the directors, and the corporation or any of them. Section 7.32(a) validates virtually all types of shareholder agreements that, in practice, normally concern shareholders and their advisors.

Given the breadth of section 7.32(a), any provision that may be contained in the articles of incorporation with a majority vote under sections 2.02(b)(2)(ii) and (iii), as well as under section 2.02(b)(4), may also be effective if contained in a shareholder agreement that complies with section 7.32.

The provisions of a shareholder agreement authorized by section 7.32(a) will often, in operation, conflict with the literal language of more than one section of the Act, and courts should in such cases construe all related sections of the Act flexibly and in a manner consistent with the underlying intent of the shareholder agreement. Thus, for example, in the case of an agreement that provides for weighted voting by directors, every reference in the Act to a majority or other proportion of directors should be construed to refer to a majority or other proportion of the votes of the directors.

While the outer limits of the catch-all provision of subsection 7.32(a)(8) are left uncertain, there are provisions of the Model Act that cannot be overridden by resort to the catch-all. Subsection (a)(8), introduced by the term "otherwise," is intended to be read in context with the preceding seven subsections and to be subject to a *ejusdem generis* rule of construction. Thus, in defining the outer limits, courts should consider whether the variation from the Model Act under consideration is similar to the variations permitted by the first seven subsections. Subsection (a)(8) is also subject to a public policy limitation, intended to give courts express authority to restrict the scope of the catch-all where there are substantial issues of public policy at stake. For example, a shareholder agreement that provides that the directors of the corporation have no duties of care or loyalty to the corporation or the shareholders would not be within the purview of section 7.32(a)(8), because it is not sufficiently similar to the types of arrangements suggested by the first seven subsections of section 7.32(a) and because such a provision could be viewed as contrary to a public policy of substantial importance. Similarly, a provision that exculpates directors from liability more broadly than permitted by section 2.02(b)(4) likely would not be validated under section 7.32, because, as the Official Comment to section 2.02(b)(4) states, there are serious public policy reasons which support the few limitations that remain on the right to exculpate directors from liability. Further development of the outer limits is left, however, for the courts.

As noted above, shareholder agreements otherwise validated by section 7.32 are not legally binding on the state, on creditors, or on other third parties. For example, an agreement that dispenses with the need to make corporate filings required by the Act would be ineffective. Similarly, an agreement among shareholders that provides that only the president has authority to enter into contracts for the corporation would not, without more, be binding against third parties, and ordinary principles of agency, including the concept of apparent authority, would continue to apply.

2. Section 7.32(b)

Section 7.32 minimizes the formal requirements for a shareholder agreement so as not to restrict unduly the shareholders' ability to take advantage of the flexibility the section provides. Thus, unlike comparable provisions in special close corporation legislation, it is not necessary to "opt in" to a special class of close corporations in order to obtain the benefits of section 7.32. An agreement can be validated under section 7.32 whether it is set forth in the articles of incorporation, the bylaws or in a separate agreement, and whether or not section 7.32 is specifically referenced in the agreement. The principal requirements are simply that the agreement be in writing and be approved or agreed to by all persons who are then shareholders. Where the corporation has a single shareholder, the requirement of an "agreement among the shareholders" is satisfied by the unilateral action of the shareholder in establishing the terms of the agreement, evidenced by provisions in the articles or by-laws, or in a writing signed by the sole shareholder. Although a writing signed by all the shareholders is not required where the agreement is contained in articles of incorporation or bylaws unanimously approved, it may be desirable to have all the shareholders actually sign the instrument in order to establish unequivocally their agreement. Similarly, while transferees are bound by a valid shareholder agreement, it may be desirable to obtain the affirmative written assent of the transferee at the time of the transfer. Subsection (b) also establishes and permits amendments by less than unanimous agreement if the shareholder agreement so provides.

Section 7.32(b) requires unanimous shareholder approval regardless of entitlement to vote. Unanimity is required because an agreement authorized by section 7.32 can effect material organic changes in the corporation's operation and structure, and in the rights and obligations of shareholders.

The requirement that the shareholder agreement be made known to the corporation is the predicate for the requirement in subsection (c) that share certificates or information statements be legended to note the existence of the agreement. No specific form of notification is required and the agreement need not be filed with the corporation. In the case of shareholder agreements in the articles or bylaws, the corporation will necessarily have notice. In the case of shareholder agreements outside the articles or bylaws, the requirement of signatures by all of the shareholders will in virtually all cases be sufficient to constitute notification to the corporation, as one or more signatories will normally also be a director or an officer.

3. Section 7.32(c)

Section 7.32(c) addresses the effect of a shareholder agreement on subsequent purchasers or transferees of shares. Typically, corporations with shareholder agreements also have restrictions on the transferability of the shares as authorized by section 6.27 of the Model Act, thus lessening the practical effects of the problem in the context of voluntary transferees. Transferees of shares without knowledge of the agreement or those acquiring shares upon the death of an original participant in a close corporation may, however, be heavily impacted. Weighing the burdens on transferees against the burdens on the remaining shareholders in the enterprise, section 7.32(c) affirms the continued validity of the shareholder agreement on all transferees, whether by purchase, gift, operation of law, or otherwise. Unlike restrictions on transfer, it may be impossible to enforce a shareholder agreement against less than all of the shareholders. Thus, under section 7.32, one who inherits shares subject to a shareholder agreement must continue to abide by the agreement. If that is not the desired result, care must be exercised at the initiation of the shareholder agreement to ensure a different outcome, such as providing for a buy-back upon death.

Where shares are transferred to a purchaser without knowledge of a shareholder agreement, the validity of the agreement is similarly unaffected, but the purchaser is afforded a rescission remedy against the seller. The term "purchaser" imports consideration. Under subsection (c) the time at which notice to a purchaser is relevant for purposes of determining entitlement to rescission is the time when a purchaser acquires the shares rather than when a commitment is made to acquire the shares. If the purchaser learns of the agreement after he is committed to purchase but before he acquires the shares, he should not be permitted to proceed with the purchase and still obtain the benefits of the remedies in section 7.32(c). Moreover, under contract principles and the securities laws a failure to disclose the existence of a shareholder agreement would in most cases constitute the omission of a material fact and may excuse performance of the commitment to purchase. The term purchaser includes a person acquiring shares upon initial issue or by transfer, and also includes a pledgee, for whom the time of purchase is the time the shares are pledged.

Section 7.32 addresses the underlying rights that accrue to shares and shareholders and the validity of shareholder action which redefines those rights, as contrasted with questions regarding entitlement to ownership of the security, competing ownership claims, and disclosure issues. Consistent with this dichotomy, the rights and remedies available to purchasers under section 7.32(c) are independent of those provided by contract law, article 8 of the Uniform Commercial Code, the securities laws, and other law outside the Model Act. With respect to the related subject of restrictions on transferability of shares, note that section 7.32 does not directly address or validate such restrictions, which are governed instead by section 6.27 of the Act. However, if such restrictions are adopted as a part of a shareholder agreement that complies with the requirements of section 7.32, a court should construe broadly the concept of reasonableness under section 6.27 in determining the validity of such restrictions.

Section 7.32(c) contains an affirmative requirement that the share certificate or information statement for the shares be legended to note the existence of a shareholder agreement. No specified form of legend is required, and a simple statement that "[t]he shares represented by this certificate are subject to a shareholder agreement" is sufficient. At that point a purchaser must obtain a copy of the shareholder agreement from his transferor or proceed at his peril. In the event a corporation fails to legend share certificates or information statements, a court may, in an appropriate case, imply a cause of action against the corporation in favor of an injured purchaser without knowledge of a shareholder agreement. The circumstances under which such a remedy would be implied, the proper measure of damages, and other attributes of and limitations on such an implied remedy are left to development in the courts.

If the purchaser has no actual knowledge of a shareholder agreement, and is not charged with knowledge by virtue of a legend on the certificate or information statement, he has a rescission remedy against his transferor (which would be the corporation in the case of a new issue of shares). While the statutory rescission remedy provided in subsection (c) is nonexclusive, it is intended to be a purchaser's primary remedy.

If the shares are certificated and duly-legended, a purchaser is charged with notice of the shareholder agreement even if the purchaser never saw the certificate. Thus, a purchaser is exposed to risk if he does not ask to see the certificate at or prior to the purchase of the shares. In the case of uncertificated shares, however, the purchaser is not charged with notice of the shareholder agreement unless a duly-legended information statement is delivered to the purchaser at or prior to the time of purchase. This different rule for uncertificated shares is intended to provide an additional safeguard to protect innocent purchasers, and is necessary because section 6.26(b) of the Act and section 8–408 of the U.C.C. permit delivery of information statements after a transfer of shares.

4. Section 7.32(d)

Section 7.32(d) contains a self-executing termination provision for a shareholder agreement when the shares of the corporation become publicly held. The statutory norms in the Model Act become more necessary and appropriate as the number of shareholders increases, as there is greater opportunity to acquire or dispose of an investment in the corporation, and as there is less opportunity for negotiation over the terms under which the enterprise will be conducted. Given that section 7.32 requires unanimity, however, in most cases a practical limit on the availability of a shareholder agreement will be reached before a public market develops. Subsection (d), coupled with a parallel change in section 8.01, rejects the use of an absolute number of shareholders in determining when the shelter of section 7.32 is lost.

5. Miscellaneous Provisions

Sections 7.32(c) through (g) contain a number of technical provisions. Subsection (c) provides a shift of liability from the directors to any person or persons in whom the discretion or powers otherwise exercised by the board of directors are vested. A shareholder agreement which provides for such a shift of responsibility, with the concomitant shift of liability provided by subsection (e), could also provide for exculpation from that liability to the extent otherwise authorized by the Act. The transfer of liability provided by subsection (e) covers liabilities imposed on directors "by law," which is intended to include liabilities arising under the Act, the common law, and statutory law outside the Act. Nevertheless, there could be cases where subsection (e) is ineffective and where a director is exposed to liability *qua* director, even though under a shareholder agreement he may have given up some or all of the powers normally exercised by directors.

Subsection (f), based on the Close Corporation Supplement and the Texas statute, narrows the grounds for imposing personal liability on shareholders for the liabilities of a corporation for acts or omissions authorized by a shareholder agreement validated by section 7.32. Subsection (g) addresses shareholder agreements for corporations that are in the process of being organized and do not yet have shareholders.

The Model Act does not, of course, address the tax status of a corporation formed under the Act. When an unorthodox arrangement is established pursuant to a shareholder agreement authorized by section 7.32, the corporation could in some circumstances be deemed a partnership for tax purposes, an issue to which counsel should be attuned, but which is not addressed in the Model Act. See Treas.Reg. section 301.7701–1 (as amended in 1977); Rev.Rul. 88–76, 1988–2 C.B. 360 (company organized pursuant to a Wyoming statute for "limited liability companies" classified for federal tax purposes as a partnership).

SUBCHAPTER D. DERIVATIVE PROCEEDINGS

INTRODUCTORY COMMENT

Subchapter D deals with the requirements applicable to shareholder derivative suits. A great deal of controversy has surrounded the derivative suit, and widely different perceptions as to the value and efficacy of this litigation continue to exist. On the one hand, the derivative suit has historically been the principal method of challenging allegedly illegal action by management. On the other hand, it has long been recognized that the derivative suit may be instituted more with a view to obtaining a settlement resulting in fees to the plaintiff's attorney than to righting a wrong to the corporation (the so-called "strike suit").

Subchapter D replaces section 7.40 of the Revised Model Business Corporation Act which at the time of its adoption was stated to reflect a reappraisal of the various procedural devices designed to control abuses of the derivative suit "in light of major developments in corporate governance, the public demand for corporate accountability, and the corporate response in the form of greater independence and sense of responsibility in boards of directors."

Subchapter D reflects a further reappraisal of the requirements for a derivative suit particularly in the light of the large number of judicial decisions dealing with (a) whether demand upon the board of directors is required and (b) the power of independent directors to dismiss a derivative suit. The first of these issues was dealt with indirectly in former section 7.40 by requiring that the complaint state whether demand was made and, if not, why not; the second issue was not covered at all.

Section 7.42 of subchapter D requires a demand on the corporation in all cases. The demand must be made at least 90 days before commencement of suit unless irreparable injury to the corporation would result. It is believed that this provision will eliminate the often excessive time and expense for both litigants and the court in litigating the question whether demand is required but at the same time will not unduly restrict the legitimate derivative suit.

Section 7.44 expressly requires the dismissal of a derivative suit if independent directors have determined that the maintenance of the suit is not in the best interests of the corporation. This section confirms the basic principle that a derivative suit is an action on behalf of the corporation and therefore should be controlled by those directors who can exercise an independent business judgment with respect to its continuance. At the same time, the court is required to assess the independence and good faith of the directors and the reasonableness of their inquiry and, if a majority of the board is not independent, the burden is placed on the corporation to prove each of these elements.

Section 7.44 also provides a procedure for the determination to be made by a panel appointed by the court.

§ 7.40 Subchapter Definitions

In this subchapter:

(1) "Derivative proceeding" means a civil suit in the right of a domestic corporation or, to the extent provided in section 7.47, in the right of a foreign corporation.

(2) "Shareholder" includes a beneficial owner whose shares are held in a voting trust or held by a nominee on the beneficial owner's behalf.

OFFICIAL COMMENT

The definition of "derivative proceeding" makes it clear that the subchapter applies to foreign corporations only to the extent provided in section 7.47. Section 7.47 provides that the law of the jurisdiction of incorporation governs except for sections 7.43 (stay of proceedings), 7.45 (discontinuance or settlement) and 7.46 (payment of expenses). See the Official Comment to section 7.47.

The definition of "shareholder," which applies only to subchapter D, includes all beneficial owners and therefore goes beyond the definition in section 1.40(22) which includes only record holders and beneficial owners who are certified by a nominee pursuant to the procedure specified in section 7.23. Similar definitions are found in section 13.01 (dissenters' rights) and section 16.02(f) (inspection of records by a shareholder). In the context of subchapter D, beneficial owner means a person having a direct economic interest in the shares. The definition is not intended to adopt the broad definition of beneficial ownership in SEC Rule 13d–2 under the Securities Exchange Act of 1934, 17 C.F.R. § 240.13d–2, which includes persons with the right to vote or dispose of the shares even though they have no economic interest in them.

§ 7.41 Standing

A shareholder may not commence or maintain a derivative proceeding unless the shareholder:

(1) was a shareholder of the corporation at the time of the act or omission complained of or became a shareholder through transfer by operation of law from one who was a shareholder at that time; and

(2) fairly and adequately represents the interests of the corporation in enforcing the right of the corporation.

OFFICIAL COMMENT

The Model Act and the statutes of many states have long imposed a "contemporaneous ownership" rule, i.e., the plaintiff must have been an owner of shares at the time of the transaction in question. This rule has been criticized as being unduly narrow and technical and unnecessary to prevent the transfer or purchase of lawsuits. A few states, particularly California, Cal.Corp. Code § 800(B) (West 1977 & Supp.1989), have relaxed this rule in order to grant standing to some subsequent purchasers of shares in limited circumstances.

The decision to retain the contemporaneous ownership rule in section 7.41(1) was based primarily on the view that it was simple, clear, and easy to apply. In contrast, the California approach might encourage the acquisition of shares in order to bring a lawsuit, resulting in litigation on peripheral issues such as the extent of the plaintiff's knowledge of the transaction in question when the plaintiff acquired the shares. Further, there has been no persuasive showing that the contemporaneous ownership rule has prevented the litigation of substantial suits, at least with respect to publicly held corporations where there are many persons who might qualify as plaintiffs to bring suit even if subsequent purchasers are disqualified.

Section 7.41 requires the plaintiff to be a shareholder and therefore does not permit creditors or holders of options, warrants or conversion rights to commence a derivative proceeding.

Section 7.41(2) follows the requirement of Federal Rule of Civil Procedure 23.1 with the exception that the plaintiff must fairly and adequately represent the interests of *the corporation* rather than *shareholders similarly situated* as provided in the rule. The clarity of the rule's language in this regard has been questioned by the courts. See Nolen v. Shaw–Walker Company, 449 F.2d 506, 508 n. 4 (6th Cir.1971). Furthermore, it is believed that the reference to the corporation in section 7.41(2) more properly reflects the nature of the derivative suit.

The introductory language of section 7.41 refers both to the commencement and maintenance of the proceeding to make it clear that the proceeding should be dismissed if, after commencement, the plaintiff ceases to be a shareholder or a fair and adequate representative. The latter would occur, for example, if the plaintiff were using the proceeding for personal advantage. If a plaintiff no longer has standing, courts have in a number of instances provided an opportunity for one or more other shareholders to intervene.

§ 7.42 Demand

No shareholder may commence a derivative proceeding until:

(1) a written demand has been made upon the corporation to take suitable action; and

(2) 90 days have expired from the date the demand was made unless the shareholder has earlier been notified that the demand has been rejected by the corporation or unless irreparable injury to the corporation would result by waiting for the expiration of the 90 day period.

OFFICIAL COMMENT

Section 7.42 requires a written demand on the corporation in all cases. The demand must be made at least 90 days before commencement of suit unless irreparable injury to the corporation would result. This approach has been adopted for two reasons. First, even though no director may be independent, the demand will give the board of directors the opportunity to reexamine the act complained of in the light of a potential lawsuit and take corrective action. Secondly, the provision eliminates the time and expense of the litigants and the court involved in litigating the question whether demand is required. It is believed that requiring a demand in all cases does not impose an onerous burden since a relatively short waiting period of 90 days is provided and this period may be shortened if irreparable injury to the corporation would result by waiting for the expiration of the 90 day period. Moreover, the cases in which demand is excused are relatively rare. Many plaintiffs' counsel as a matter of practice make a demand in all cases rather than litigate the issue whether demand is excused.

1. Form of Demand

Section 7.42 specifies only that the demand shall be in writing. The demand should, however, set forth the facts concerning share ownership and be sufficiently specific to apprise the corporation of the action sought to be taken and the grounds for that action so that the demand can be evaluated. See Allison v. General Motors Corp., 604 F.Supp. 1106, 1117 (D.Del.1985). Detailed pleading is not required since the corporation can contact the shareholder for clarification if there are any questions. In keeping with the spirit of this section, the specificity of the demand should not become a new source of dilatory motions.

2. Upon Whom Demand Should Be Made

Section 7.42 states that demand shall be made upon the corporation. Reference is not made specifically to the board of directors as in previous section 7.40(b) since there may be instances, such as a decision to sue a third party for an injury to the corporation, in which the taking of, or refusal to take, action would fall within the authority of an officer of the corporation. Nevertheless, it is expected that in most cases the board of directors will be the appropriate body to review the demand.

To ensure that the demand reaches the appropriate person for review, it should be addressed to the board of directors, chief executive officer or corporate secretary of the corporation at its principal office.

3. The 90 Day Period

Section 7.42(2) provides that the derivative proceeding may not be commenced until 90 days after demand has been made. Ninety days has been chosen as a reasonable minimum time within which the board of directors can meet, direct the necessary inquiry into the charges, receive the results of the inquiry and make its decision. In many instances a longer period may be required. See, e.g., Mozes v. Welch, 638 F.Supp. 215 (D.Conn.1986) (eight month delay in responding to demand not unreasonable). However, a fixed time period eliminates further litigation over what is or is not a reasonable time. The corporation may request counsel for the shareholder to delay filing suit until the inquiry is completed or, if suit is commenced, the corporation can apply to the court for a stay under section 7.43.

Two exceptions are provided to the 90 day waiting period. The first exception is the situation where the shareholder has been notified of the rejection of the demand prior to the end of the 90 days. The second exception is where irreparable injury to the corporation would otherwise result if the commencement of the proceeding is delayed for the 90 day period. The standard to be applied is intended to be the same as that governing the entry of a preliminary injunction. Compare Gimbel v. Signal Cos., 316 A.2d 599 (Del.Ch.1974) with Gelco Corp. v. Coniston Partners, 811 F.2d 414 (8th Cir.1987). Other factors may also be considered such as the possible expiration of the statute of limitations although this would depend on the period of time during which the shareholder was aware of the grounds for the proceeding.

It should be noted that the shareholder bringing suit does not necessarily have to be the person making the demand. Only one demand need be made in order for the corporation to consider whether to take corrective action.

4. Response by the Corporation

There is no obligation on the part of the corporation to respond to the demand. However, if the corporation, after receiving the demand, decides to institute litigation or, after a derivative proceeding has commenced, decides to assume control of the litigation, the shareholder's right to commence or control the proceeding ends unless it can be shown that the corporation will not adequately pursue the matter. As stated in Lewis v. Graves, 701 F.2d 245, 247–48 (2d Cir.1983):

> The [demand] rule is intended "to give the derivative corporation itself the opportunity to take over a suit which was brought on its behalf in the first place, and thus to allow the directors the chance to occupy their normal status as conductors of the corporation's affairs." Permitting corporations to assume control over shareholder derivative suits also has numerous practical advantages. Corporate management may be in a better position to pursue alternative remedies, resolving grievances without burdensome and expensive litigation. Deference to directors' judgments may also result in the termination of meritless actions brought solely for their settlement or harassment value. Moreover, where litigation is appropriate, the derivative corporation will often be in a better position to bring or assume the suit because of superior financial resources and knowledge of the challenged transactions. [Citations omitted.]

§ 7.43 Stay of Proceedings

If the corporation commences an inquiry into the allegations made in the demand or complaint, the court may stay any derivative proceeding for such period as the court deems appropriate.

OFFICIAL COMMENT

Section 7.43 provides that if the corporation undertakes an inquiry, the court may in its discretion stay the proceeding for such period as the court deems appropriate. This might occur where the complaint is filed 90 days after demand but the inquiry into the matters raised by the demand has not been completed or where a demand has not been investigated but the corporation commences the inquiry after the complaint has been filed. In either case, it is expected that the court will monitor the course of the inquiry to ensure that it is proceeding expeditiously and in good faith.

§ 7.44 Dismissal

(a) A derivative proceeding shall be dismissed by the court on motion by the corporation if one of the groups specified in subsections (b) or (f) has determined in good faith after conducting a reasonable inquiry upon which its conclusions are based that the maintenance of the derivative proceeding is not in the best interests of the corporation.

(b) Unless a panel is appointed pursuant to subsection (f), the determination in subsection (a) shall be made by:

(1) a majority vote of independent directors present at a meeting of the board of directors if the independent directors constitute a quorum; or

(2) a majority vote of a committee consisting of two or more independent directors appointed by majority vote of independent directors present at a meeting of the board of directors, whether or not such independent directors constituted a quorum.

(c) None of the following shall by itself cause a director to be considered not independent for purposes of this section:

(1) the nomination or election of the director by persons who are defendants in the derivative proceeding or against whom action is demanded;

(2) the naming of the director as a defendant in the derivative proceeding or as a person against whom action is demanded; or

(3) the approval by the director of the act being challenged in the derivative proceeding or demand if the act resulted in no personal benefit to the director.

(d) If a derivative proceeding is commenced after a determination has been made rejecting a demand by a shareholder, the complaint shall allege with particularity facts establishing either (1) that a majority of the board of directors did not consist of independent directors at the time the determination was made or (2) that the requirements of subsection (a) have not been met.

(e) If a majority of the board of directors does not consist of independent directors at the time the determination is made, the corporation shall have the burden of proving that the requirements of subsection (a) have been met. If a majority of the board of directors consists of independent directors at the time the determination is made, the plaintiff shall have the burden of proving that the requirements of subsection (a) have not been met.

(f) The court may appoint a panel of one or more independent persons upon motion by the corporation to make a determination whether the maintenance of the derivative proceeding is in the best interests of the corporation. In such case, the plaintiff shall have the burden of proving that the requirements of subsection (a) have not been met.

OFFICIAL COMMENT

The prior version of the Model Act did not expressly provide what happens when a board of directors properly rejects a demand to bring an action. Judicial decisions indicate that a derivative action should be dismissed in these circumstances. See Aronson v. Lewis, 473 A.2d 805, 813 (Del.1984). The prior version of the Model Act was also silent on the effect of a determination by a special litigation committee of independent directors that a previously commenced derivative action be dismissed. Several state corporation laws have been amended to provide for action by such a committee. Ind.Code Ann. § 23–1–32–4 (Burns 1984 & Supp.1988); N.D.Cent.Code § 10–19.1–49 (1985). Section 7.44(a) specifically provides that the proceeding shall be dismissed if there is a proper determination that the maintenance of the proceeding is not in the best interests of the corporation. This determination can be made prior to commencement of the suit in response to a demand or after commencement upon examination of the allegations of the complaint.

The procedures set forth in section 7.44 are not intended to be exclusive. As noted in the comment to section 7.42, there may be instances where a decision to commence an action falls within the authority of an officer of the corporation depending upon the amount of the claim and the identity of the potential defendants.

1. The Persons Making the Determination

Section 7.44(b) prescribes the persons by whom the determination in subsection (a) may be made. The subsection provides that the determination may be made by a majority vote of independent directors if there is a quorum of independent directors, or by a committee of independent directors. These provisions parallel the mechanics for determining entitlement to indemnification in section 8.55 of the Model Act except that clause (2) provides that the committee of independent directors shall be appointed by a vote of the independent directors only, rather than the entire board. In this respect this clause is an exception to section 8.25 of the Model Act which requires the approval of at least a majority of all the directors in office to create a committee and appoint members. This approach has been taken to respond to the criticism expressed in a few cases that special litigation committees suffer from a structural bias because of their appointment by vote of non-independent directors. See Hasan v. Cleve Trust Realty Investors, 729 F.2d 372, 376–77 (6th Cir.1984).

The decisions which have examined the qualifications of directors making the determination have required that they be both "disinterested" in the sense of not having a personal interest in the transaction being challenged as opposed to a benefit which devolves upon the corporation or all shareholders generally, and "independent" in the sense of not being influenced in favor of the defendants by reason of personal or other relationships. See, e.g., Aronson v. Lewis, 473 A.2d 805, 812–16 (Del.1984). Only the word "independent" has been used in section 7.44(b) because it is believed that this word necessarily also includes the requirement that a person have no interest in the transaction. The concept of an independent director is not intended to be limited to non-officer or "outside" directors but may in appropriate circumstances include directors who are also officers.

Many of the special litigation committees involved in the reported cases consisted of directors who were elected after the alleged wrongful acts by the directors who were named as defendants in the action. Subsection (c)(1) makes it clear that the participation of non-independent directors or shareholders in the nomination or election of a new director shall not prevent the new director from being considered independent. This sentence therefore rejects the concept that the mere appointment of new directors by the non-independent directors makes the new directors not independent in making the necessary determination because of an inherent structural bias. Clauses (2) and (3) also confirm the decisions by a number of courts that the mere fact that a director has been named as a defendant or approved the action being challenged does not cause the director to be considered not independent. See Aronson v. Lewis, 473 A.2d 805, 816 (Del.1984); Lewis v. Graves, 701 F.2d 245 (2d Cir.1983). It is believed that a court will be able to assess any actual bias in deciding whether the director is independent without any presumption arising out of the method of the director's appointment, the mere naming of the director as a defendant or the director's approval of the act where the director received no personal benefit from the transaction.

Subsection (f) also provides for a determination by a panel of one or more independent persons appointed by the court. Cf. Virginia Stock Corp.Act § 13.1–672D (1987) (court may appoint a committee of two or more persons). The subsection provides for the appointment only upon motion by the corporation. This would not, however, prevent the court on its own initiative from appointing a special master pursuant to applicable state rules of procedure.

This procedure may be desirable in a number of circumstances. If there are no independent directors available, the corporation may not wish to enlarge the board to add independent directors or may be unable to find persons willing to serve as independent directors. In addition, if there are independent directors, they may not have the available time to conduct the inquiry in an expeditious manner.

Appointment by the court should also eliminate any question about the independence of the person making the determination. Although the corporation may wish to suggest to the court possible appointees, the court will not be bound by these suggestions and, in any case, will want to satisfy itself with respect to independence at the time the person is appointed. When the court appoints a panel, section 7.44(f) places the burden on the plaintiff to prove that the requirements of section 7.44(a) have not been met.

Although subsection (b)(2) requires a committee of at least two directors, subsection (f) permits the appointment of only one person in recognition of the potentially increased costs to the corporation for the fees and expenses of an outside person.

2. Standard to be Applied

Section 7.44(a) requires that the determination be made by the appropriate persons in good faith after conducting a reasonable inquiry upon which their conclusions are based. The word "inquiry" rather than "investigation" has been used to make it clear that the scope of the inquiry will depend upon the issues raised and the knowledge of the group making the determination with respect to the issues. In some cases, the issues may be so simple or the knowledge of the group so extensive that little additional inquiry is required. In other cases, the group may need to engage counsel and other professionals to make an investigation and assist the group in its evaluation of the issues.

The phrase "in good faith" modifies both the determination and the inquiry. The test, which is also included in sections 8.30 (general standards of conduct for directors) and 8.51 (authority to indemnify), is a subjective one, meaning "honestly or in an honest manner." "The Corporate Director's Guidebook," 33 Bus.Law. 1595, 1601 (1978). As stated in Abella v. Universal Leaf Tobacco Co., 546 F.Supp. 795, 800 (E.D.Va.1982), "the inquiry intended by this phrase goes to the spirit and sincerity with which the investigation was conducted, rather than the reasonableness of its procedures or basis for conclusions."

The phrase "upon which its conclusions are based" requires that the inquiry and the conclusions follow logically. This provision authorizes the court to examine the determination to ensure that it has some support in the findings of the inquiry. The burden of convincing the court about this issue lies with whichever party has the burden under section 7.44(e). This phrase does not require the persons making the determination to prepare a written report that sets forth their determination and the bases therefor, since circumstances will vary as to the need for such a report. There may, however, be many instances where good corporate practice will commend such a procedure.

Section 7.44 is not intended to modify the general standards of conduct for directors set forth in section 8.30 of the Model Act, but rather to make those standards somewhat more explicit in the derivative proceeding context. In this regard, the independent directors making the determination would be entitled to rely on information and reports from other persons in accordance with section 8.30(b).

Section 7.44 is similar in several respects and differs in certain other respects from the law as it has developed in Delaware and been followed in a number of other states. Under the Delaware cases, the role of the court in reviewing the board's determination varies depending upon whether the plaintiff is in a demand required or demand excused situation. Demand is excused only if the plaintiff pleads particularized facts that create a reasonable doubt that a majority of directors at the time demand would be made are independent or disinterested, or alternatively, that the challenged transaction was the product of a valid exercise of business judgment by the approving board. Aronson v. Lewis,

473 A.2d 805, 814 (Del.1984); Pogostin v. Rice, 480 A.2d 619, 624 (Del.1984). If the plaintiff fails to make either of these two showings, demand is required. Since the Aronson requirements are difficult to satisfy, the plaintiff normally must make demand on the board.

In the unusual case where the plaintiff's demand is excused under either of the Aronson tests, the plaintiff has standing to bring the derivative suit. If the corporation seeks to reassert its right to control the litigation, the corporation will form a special litigation committee to determine if the litigation is in the best interests of the corporation. If the corporation files a motion to dismiss the litigation based upon the recommendation of the special committee, Delaware law requires the corporation to bear the burden of proving the independence of the committee, the reasonableness of its investigation, and the reasonableness of the bases of its decision reflected in the motion. Zapata Corp. v. Maldonado, 430 A.2d 779 (Del.1981). Zapata also permits the court a discretionary second step to review the special committee's decision by invoking the court's "independent business judgment." Id. at 789.

In the usual scenario where demand is not excused, the shareholder must demand that the board take action and the Zapata principles do not apply. The board or special committee of independent directors decides whether the corporation should take the action the shareholder requests or respond in some other way. As in the case of all board decisions, the board's response to the shareholder's demand is presumptively protected by the traditional business judgment rule. Allison v. General Motors Corp., 604 F.Supp. 1106, 1122 (D.Del.1985). As a result, the shareholder in filing suit bears the normal burden of creating by particularized pleadings a reasonable doubt that the board's response to the demand was wrongful. Levine v. Smith, C.A. No. 8833, n. 5 (Del.Ch. Nov. 27, 1989) (available on LEXIS). The plaintiff must allege with particularity a lack of good faith, care, independence or disinterestedness by the directors in responding to the demand.

In contrast to Delaware's approach, some jurisdictions have adopted uniform tests to judge both demand required and demand excused situations. For example, in New York judicial review is always limited to an analysis of the independence and good faith of the board or committee and the reasonableness of its investigation; the court does not examine the reasonableness of the bases for the board's decision, nor does the court have the discretionary authority to use its independent business judgment. Auerbach v. Bennett, 47 N.Y.2d 619, 633–34, 419 N.Y.S.2d 920, 928–29, 393 N.E.2d 994, 1002–03 (1979). In contrast, the North Carolina Supreme Court has interpreted that state's statutory provisions on derivative actions as requiring the application of the Zapata criteria in both demand required and demand excused cases. Alford v. Shaw, 358 S.E.2d 323, 327 (N.C.1987).

Since section 7.42 requires demand in all cases, the distinction between demand excused and demand required cases does not apply. Subsections (d) and (e) of section 7.44 carry forward the distinction, however, by establishing pleading rules and allocating the burden of proof depending on whether there is a majority of independent directors. Subsection (d), like Delaware law, assigns the plaintiff the threshold burden of alleging facts establishing that a majority of the board is not independent. If there is an independent majority, the burden remains with the plaintiff to plead and establish that the requirements of section

7.44(a) have not been met. If there is no independent majority, the burden is on the corporation on the issues delineated in section 7.44(a). In this case, the corporation must prove both the independence of the decisionmakers and the propriety of the inquiry and determination.

Subsections (d) and (e) of section 7.44 thus follow the first Aronson standard in allocating the burden of proof depending on whether the majority of the board is independent. The Committee decided, however, not to adopt the second Aronson standard for excusing demand (and thus shifting the burden to the corporation) based on whether the decision of the board that decided the challenged transaction is protected by the business judgment rule. The Committee believes that the only appropriate concern in the context of derivative litigation is whether the board considering the demand has a disabling conflict. See Starrels v. First Nat'l Bank, 870 F.2d 1168, 1172–76 (7th Cir.1989) (Easterbrook, J., concurring).

Thus, the burden of proving that the requirements of section 7.44(a) have not been met will remain with the plaintiff in several situations. First, in subsection (b)(1), the burden of proof will generally remain with the plaintiff since the subsection requires a quorum of independent directors and a quorum is normally a majority. See section 8.24. The burden will also remain with the plaintiff if there is a majority of independent directors which appoints the committee under subsection (b)(2). Under section 7.44(f), the burden of proof also remains with the plaintiff in the case of a determination by a panel appointed by the court.

The burden of proof will shift to the corporation, however, where a majority of directors is not independent, and the determination is made by the group specified in subsection (b)(2). It can be argued that, if the directors making the determination under subsection (b)(2) are independent and have been delegated full responsibility for making the decision, the composition of the entire board is irrelevant. This argument is buttressed by the section's method of appointing the group specified in subsection (b)(2) since subsection (b)(2) departs from the general method of appointing committees and allows only independent directors, rather than a majority of the entire board, to appoint the committee which will make the determination. Nevertheless, despite the argument that the composition of the board is irrelevant in these circumstances, the Committee adopted the provisions of subsections (b)(2) and (e) of section 7.44 to respond to concerns of structural bias.

Finally, section 7.44 does not authorize the court to review the reasonableness of the determination. As discussed above, the phrase in section 7.44(a) "upon which its conclusions are based" limits judicial review to whether the determination has some support in the findings of the inquiry.

3. Pleading

Former section 7.40(b) provided that the complaint in a derivative proceeding must allege with particularity whether demand has been made on the board of directors and the board's response or why demand was excused. This requirement is similar to Rule 23.1 of the Federal Rules of Civil Procedure. Since demand is now required in all cases, this provision is no longer necessary.

Subsection (d) sets forth a modified pleading rule to cover the typical situation where plaintiff makes demand on the board, the board rejects that demand, and the plaintiff commences an action. In that scenario, in order to state a cause of action, subsection (d) requires the complaint to allege facts with particularity demonstrating either (1) that no majority of independent directors exists or (2) why the determination does not meet the standards in subsection (a). Discovery is available to the plaintiff only after the plaintiff has successfully stated a cause of action by making either of these two showings.

§ 7.45 Discontinuance or Settlement

A derivative proceeding may not be discontinued or settled without the court's approval. If the court determines that a proposed discontinuance or settlement will substantially affect the interests of the corporation's shareholders or a class of shareholders, the court shall direct that notice be given to the shareholders affected.

OFFICIAL COMMENT

Section 7.45 follows the Federal Rules of Civil Procedure, and the statutes of a number of states, and requires that all proposed settlements and discontinuances must receive judicial approval. This requirement seems a natural consequence of the proposition that a derivative suit is brought for the benefit of all shareholders and avoids many of the evils of the strike suit by preventing the individual shareholder-plaintiff from settling privately with the defendants.

Section 7.45 also requires notice to all affected shareholders if the court determines that the proposed settlement may substantially affect their interests. This provision permits the court to decide that no notice need be given if, in the court's judgment, the proceeding is frivolous or has become moot. The section also makes a distinction between classes of shareholders, an approach which is not in Federal Rule of Civil Procedure 23.1, but is adapted from the New York and Michigan statutes. This procedure could be used, for example, to eliminate the costs of notice to preferred shareholders where the settlement does not have a substantial effect on their rights as a class, such as their rights to dividends or a liquidation preference.

Unlike the statutes of some states, section 7.45 does not address the issue of which party should bear the cost of giving this notice. That is a matter left to the discretion of the court reviewing the proposed settlement.

§ 7.46 Payment of Expenses

On termination of the derivative proceeding the court may:

(1) order the corporation to pay the plaintiff's reasonable expenses (including counsel fees) incurred in the proceeding if it finds that the proceeding has resulted in a substantial benefit to the corporation;

(2) order the plaintiff to pay any defendant's reasonable expenses (including counsel fees) incurred in defending the proceeding if it finds that the proceeding was commenced or maintained without reasonable cause or for an improper purpose; or

(3) order a party to pay an opposing party's reasonable expenses (including counsel fees) incurred because of the filing of a pleading, motion or other paper, if it finds that the pleading, motion or other paper was not well grounded in fact, after reasonable inquiry, or warranted by existing law or a good faith argument for the extension, modification or reversal of existing law and was interposed for an improper purpose, such as to harass or to cause unnecessary delay or needless increase in the cost of litigation.

OFFICIAL COMMENT

Section 7.46(1) is intended to be a codification of existing case law. See, e.g., Mills v. Electric Auto–Lite Co., 396 U.S. 375 (1970). It provides that the court may order the corporation to pay the plaintiff's reasonable expenses (including counsel fees) if it finds that the proceeding has resulted in a substantial benefit to the corporation. The subsection requires that there be a "substantial" benefit to the corporation to prevent the plaintiff from proposing inconsequential changes in order to justify the payment of counsel fees. While the subsection does not specify the method for calculating attorneys' fees since there is a substantial body of court decisions delineating this issue, it does require that the expenses be reasonable which would include taking into account the amount or character of the benefit to the corporation.

Section 7.46(2) provides that on termination of a proceeding the court may require the plaintiff to pay the defendants' reasonable expenses, including attorneys' fees, if it finds that the proceeding "was commenced or maintained without reasonable cause or for an improper purpose." The phrase "for an improper purpose" has been added to parallel Federal Rule of Civil Procedure 11 as recently amended in order to prevent proceedings which may be brought to harass the corporation or its officers. The test in this section is similar to but not identical with the test utilized in section 13.31, relating to dissenters' rights, where the standard for award of expenses and attorneys' fees is that dissenters "acted arbitrarily, vexatiously or not in good faith" in demanding a judicial appraisal of their shares. The derivative action situation is sufficiently different from the dissenters' rights situation to justify a different and less onerous test for imposing costs on the plaintiff. The test of section 7.46 that the action was brought without reasonable cause or for an improper purpose is appropriate to deter strike suits, on the one hand, and on the other hand to protect plaintiffs whose suits have a reasonable foundation.

Section 7.46(3) has been added to deal with other abuses in the conduct of derivative litigation which may occur on the part of the defendants and their counsel as well as by the plaintiffs and their counsel. The section follows generally the provisions of Rule 11 of the Federal Rules of Civil Procedure. Section 7.46(3) will not be necessary in states which already have a counterpart to Rule 11.

§ 7.47 Applicability to Foreign Corporations

In any derivative proceeding in the right of a foreign corporation, the matters covered by this subchapter shall be governed by the laws of the jurisdiction of incorporation of the foreign corporation except for sections 7.43, 7.45 and 7.46.

OFFICIAL COMMENT

Section 7.47 clarifies the application of the provisions of subchapter D to foreign corporations. Previous section 7.40 referred to proceedings in the right of both domestic and foreign corporations, but neither the section nor the comment discussed the interaction between section 7.40 as it applied to a foreign corporation and the law of its state of incorporation. Under generally prevailing practice, a court will look to the choice-of-law rules of the forum state to determine which law shall apply. If the issue is "procedural", the law of the forum state will apply; if the issue is "substantive", relating to the internal affairs of the corporation, the law of the state of incorporation will apply. See, e.g., Hausman v. Buckley, 299 F.2d 696, 700–06 (2d Cir.1962); Galef v. Alexander, 615 F.2d 51 (2d Cir.1980). Compare Restatement (Second) of Conflict of Laws §§ 302, 303, 304, 306, 309 (1988) (the local law of the state of incorporation will be applied except in the unusual case where, with respect to the particular issue, some other state has a more significant relationship under the principles stated in § 6 of the Restatement to the parties and the corporation or the transaction).

However, the distinction between what is procedural and what is substantive is not clear. See, e.g., Cohen v. Beneficial Indus. Loan Corp., 337 U.S. 541, 555–57 (1949). For example, in Susman v. Lincoln American Corp., 550 F.Supp. 442, 446 n. 6 (N.D.Ill.1982), the court suggested that the standing requirement might be considered a federal procedural question under Federal Rule of Civil Procedure 23.1 and a matter of substantive law under the Delaware statute.

In view of the uncertainties created by these decisions, section 7.47 sets forth a choice of law provision for foreign corporations. It provides, subject to three exceptions, that the matters covered by the subchapter shall be governed by the laws of the jurisdiction of incorporation of the foreign corporation. In this respect, the section is similar to section 901 of the Revised Uniform Limited Partnership Act which provides that the laws of the state under which a foreign limited partnership is organized govern its organization and internal affairs.

The three exceptions to the general rule are areas which are traditionally part of the forum's oversight of the litigation process: section 7.43 dealing with the ability of the court to stay proceedings; section 7.45 setting forth the procedure for settling a proceeding; and section 7.46 providing for the assessment of reasonable expenses (including counsel fees) in certain situations.

CHAPTER 8. DIRECTORS AND OFFICERS

SUBCHAPTER A. BOARD OF DIRECTORS

§ 8.01 Requirements for and Duties of Board of Directors

(a) Except as provided is section 7.32, each corporation must have a board of directors.

(b) All corporate powers shall be exercised by or under the authority of, and the business and affairs of the corporation managed by or under the direction of, its board of directors, subject to any limitation set forth in the articles of incorporation or in an agreement authorized under section 7.32.

OFFICIAL COMMENT

Section 8.01 requires that every corporation have a board of directors except that a corporation with a shareholder agreement authorized by section 7.32 may dispense with or limit the authority of the board of directors.

Obviously, some form of governance is necessary for every corporation. The board of directors is the traditional form of corporate governance but it need not be the exclusive form. Patterns of management may also be tailored to specific needs in connection with family controlled enterprises, wholly or partially owned subsidiaries, or corporate joint ventures through a shareholder agreement under section 7.32.

Under section 7.32, an agreement among all shareholders can provide for a nontraditional form of corporate governance until there is a regular market for the corporation's shares, a change from the 50 or fewer shareholder test in place in section 8.01 prior to 1990. The former standard was determined to be unsatisfactory primarily because it bore too tenuous a relationship to the underlying market reasons for limiting nontraditional governance structures. As the number of shareholders increases and a market for the shares develops, there is (i) an opportunity for unhappy shareholders to dispose of shares—a "market out," (ii) a correlative opportunity for others to acquire shares with related expectations regarding the applicability of the statutory norms of governance, and (iii) no real opportunity to negotiate over the terms upon which the enterprise will be conducted. Moreover, tying the availability of nontraditional governance structures to an absolute number of shareholders at the time of adoption took no account of subsequent events, was overly mechanical, and subject to circumvention. If a corporation does not have a shareholders agreement that satisfies the requirements of section 7.32 or a market exists for its shares as specified in section 7.32, it must adopt the traditional board of directors as its sole form of governance.

Section 8.01(b) states that if a corporation has a board of directors "all corporate powers shall be exercised by or under the authority of, and the business and affairs of the corporation managed by or under the direction of," the board of directors. The phrase "by or under the direction of" was chosen to encompass the varying functions of boards of directors of different corporations. In some corporations, the board of directors may be involved in the day-to-day business and affairs and it may be reasonable to describe management as being "by" the board of directors. But in most corporations, the business and affairs are managed "under the direction of" the board of directors, since the role of the board of directors consists principally of the formulation of policy, the selection of the chief executive officer and other key officers, and the approval of major actions or transactions.

It is generally recognized that the board of directors may delegate to appropriate officers, employees or agents of the corporation authority to exercise powers and perform functions not required by law to be exercised or performed by the board of directors itself. Although delegation does not relieve the board of directors from its responsibilities of oversight, directors should not be held personally responsible for actions or omissions of officers, employees or agents of the corporation so long as the directors have relied reasonably upon these officers, employees or agents. See section 8.31 and its Official Comment. The board of directors generally has the power to probe into day-to-day management to any depth it chooses, but it has the obligation to do so only to the extent that the directors' oversight responsibilities may require.

Section 8.01(b) also recognizes that the powers of the board of directors may be limited by express provisions in the articles of incorporation.

§ 8.02 Qualifications of Directors

The articles of incorporation or bylaws may prescribe qualifications for directors. A director need not be a resident of this state or a shareholder of the corporation unless the articles of incorporation or bylaws so prescribe.

§ 8.03 Number and Election of Directors

(a) A board of directors must consist of one or more individuals, with the number specified in or fixed in accordance with the articles of incorporation or bylaws.

(b) The number of directors may be increased or decreased from time to time by amendment to, or in the manner provided in, the articles of incorporation or the bylaws.

(c) Directors are elected at the first annual shareholders' meeting and at each annual meeting thereafter unless their terms are staggered under section 8.06.

OFFICIAL COMMENT

Section 8.03 prescribes rules for (i) the determination of the size of the board of directors of corporations that have not dispensed with a board of directors under section 7.32(a)(1), and (ii) changes in the number of directors once the board's size has been established.

1. Minimum Number of Directors

Section 8.03(a) provides that the size of the initial board of directors may be "specified in or fixed in accordance with" the articles of incorporation or bylaws. The size of the board of directors may thus be fixed initially in one or more of the fundamental corporate documents, or the decision as to the size of the initial board of directors may be made thereafter in the manner authorized in those documents.

Before 1969 the Model Act required a board of directors to consist of at least three directors. Since then, the Model Act (as well as the corporation statutes of an increasing number of states) has provided that the board of directors may consist of one or more members. A board of directors consisting of one or two individuals may be appropriate for corporations with one or two shareholders, or for corporations with more than two shareholders where in fact the full power of management is vested in only one or two persons. The requirement that every corporation have a board of directors of at least three directors may require the introduction into these closely held corporations of persons with no financial interest in the corporation.

2. Changes in the Size of the Board of Directors

Section 8.03(b) provides a corporation with the freedom to design its articles of incorporation and bylaw provisions relating to the size of the board with a view to achieving the combination of flexibility for the board of directors and protection for shareholders that it deems appropriate. The articles of incorporation could provide for a specified number of directors or a variable range board, thereby requiring shareholder action to change the fixed size of the board, to change the limits established for the size of the variable range board or to change from a variable range board to a fixed board or vice versa. An alternative would be to have the bylaws provide for a specified number of directors or a variable range for the board of directors. Any change would be made in the manner provided by the bylaws. The bylaws could permit amendment by the board of directors or the bylaws could require that any amendment, in whole or in part, be made only by the shareholders in accordance with section 10.20(a). Typically the board of directors would be permitted to change the board size within the established variable range. If a corporation wishes to ensure that any change in the number of directors be approved by shareholders, then an appropriate restriction would have to be included in the articles or bylaws.

The board's power to change the number of directors, like all other board powers, is subject to compliance with applicable standards governing director conduct. In particular, it may be inappropriate to change the size of the board for the primary purpose of maintaining control or defeating particular candidates for the board. See Blasius Industries, Inc. v. Atlas Corp., 564 A.2d 651 (Del. Ch. 1988).

Experience has shown, particularly in larger corporations, that it is desirable to grant the board of directors authority to change its size without incurring the expense of obtaining shareholder approval. In closely held corporations, shareholder approval for a change in the size of the board of directors may be readily accomplished if that is desired. In many closely held corporations a board of directors of a fixed size may be an essential part of a control arrangement. In these situations, an increase or decrease in the size of the board of directors by even a single member may significantly affect control. In order to maintain control arrangements dependent on a board of directors of a fixed size, the power of the board of directors to change its own size must be negated. This may be accomplished by fixing the size of the board of directors in the articles of incorporation or by expressly negating the power of the board of directors to change the size of the board, whether by amendment of the bylaws or otherwise. See section 10.20(a).

3. Annual Elections of Directors

Section 8.03(c) makes it clear that all directors are elected annually unless the board is staggered. See section 8.05 and its Official Comment.

§ 8.04 Election of Directors by Certain Classes of Shareholders

If the articles of incorporation authorize dividing the shares into classes, the articles may also authorize the election of all or a specified number of directors by the holders of one or more authorized classes of shares. Each class (or classes) of shares entitled to elect one or more directors is a separate voting group for purposes of the election of directors.

§ 8.05 Terms of Directors Generally

(a) The terms of the initial directors of a corporation expire at the first shareholders' meeting at which directors are elected.

(b) The terms of all other directors expire at the next annual shareholders' meeting following their election unless their terms are staggered under section 8.06.

(c) A decrease in the number of directors does not shorten an incumbent director's term.

(d) The term of a director elected to fill a vacancy expires at the next shareholders' meeting at which directors are elected.

(e) Despite the expiration of a director's term, he continues to serve until his successor is elected and qualifies or until there is a decrease in the number of directors.

§ 8.06 Staggered Terms for Directors

The articles of incorporation may provide for staggering the terms of directors by dividing the total number of directors into two or three groups, with each group containing one-half or one-third of the total, as near as may be. In that event, the terms of directors in the first group expire at the first annual shareholders' meeting after their election, the terms of the second group expire at the second annual shareholders' meeting after their election, and the terms of the third group, if any, expire at the third annual shareholders' meeting after their election. At each annual shareholders' meeting held thereafter, directors shall be chosen for a term of two years or three years, as the case may be, to succeed those whose terms expire.

OFFICIAL COMMENT

Section 8.06 recognizes the practice of "classifying" the board or "staggering" the terms of directors so that only one-half or one-third of them are elected at each annual shareholders' meeting and directors are elected for two or three-year terms rather than one-year terms.

The traditional purpose of a staggered board has been to assure the continuity and stability of the corporation's business strategies and policies as determined by the board. In recent years the practice has been employed with increasing frequency to ensure that a majority of the board of directors remains in place following a sudden change in shareholdings or a proxy contest. It also reduces the impact of cumulative voting since a greater number of votes is required to elect a director if the board is staggered than is required if the entire board is elected at each annual meeting. A staggered board of directors also can have the effect of making unwanted takeover attempts more difficult, particularly where the articles of incorporation provide that the shareholders may remove directors only with cause or by a supermajority vote, or both.

§ 8.07 Resignation of Directors

(a) A director may resign at any time by delivering written notice to the board of directors, its chairman, or to the corporation.

(b) A resignation is effective when the notice is delivered unless the notice specifies a later effective date.

§ 8.08 Removal of Directors by Shareholders

(a) The shareholders may remove one or more directors with or without cause unless the articles of incorporation provide that directors may be removed only for cause.

(b) If a director is elected by a voting group of shareholders, only the shareholders of that voting group may participate in the vote to remove him.

(c) If cumulative voting is authorized, a director may not be removed if the number of votes sufficient to elect him under cumulative voting is voted against his removal. If cumulative voting is not authorized, a director may be removed only if the number of votes cast to remove him exceeds the number of votes cast not to remove him.

(d) A director may be removed by the shareholders only at a meeting called for the purpose of removing him and the meeting notice must state that the purpose, or one of the purposes, of the meeting is removal of the director.

§ 8.09 Removal of Directors by Judicial Proceeding

(a) The [name or describe] court of the county where a corporation's principal office (or, if none in this state, its registered office) is located may remove a director of the corporation from office in a proceeding commenced by or in the right of the corporation if the court finds that (1) the director engaged in fraudulent conduct with respect to the corporation or its shareholders, grossly abused the position of director, or intentionally inflicted harm on the corporation; and (2) considering the director's course of conduct and the inadequacy of other available remedies, removal would be in the best interest of the corporation.

(b) A shareholder proceeding on behalf of the corporation under subsection (a) shall comply with all of the requirements of subchapter 7D, except 7.41(1).

(c) The court, in addition to removing the director, may bar the director from reelection for a period prescribed by the court.

(d) Nothing in this section limits the equitable powers of the court to order other relief.

OFFICIAL COMMENT

Section 8.09 is designed to operate in the limited circumstance where other remedies are inadequate to address serious misconduct by a director and it is impracticable for shareholders to invoke the usual remedy of removal under section 8.08. In recognition that director election and removal are principal prerogatives of shareholders, section 8.09 authorizes judicial removal of a director who is found to have engaged in serious misconduct as described in subsection (a)(1) if the court also finds that, taking into consideration the director's course of conduct and the inadequacy of other available remedies, removal of the director would be in the best interest of the corporation. Misconduct serious enough to justify the extraordinary remedy of judicial removal does not involve any matter falling within an individual director's lawful exercise of business judgment, no matter how unpopular the director's views may be with the other members of the board. Policy and personal differences among the members of the board of directors should be left to be resolved by the shareholders.

Section 8.09(d) makes it clear that the court is not restricted to the removal remedy in actions under this section but may order any other equitable relief. Where, for example, the complaint concerns an ongoing course of conduct that is harmful to the corporation, the court may enjoin the director from continuing that conduct. In another instance, the court may determine that the director's continuation in office is inimical to the best interest of the corporation. Judicial removal might be the most appropriate remedy in that case if shareholder removal under section 8.08 is impracticable because of situations like the following:

(1) The director charged with serious misconduct personally owns or controls sufficient shares to block removal.

(2) The director was elected by voting group or cumulative voting, and the shareholders with voting power to prevent his removal will exercise that power despite the director's serious misconduct and without regard to what the court deems to be the best interest of the corporation.

(3) A shareholders' meeting to consider removal under section 8.08 will entail considerable expense and a period of delay that will be contrary to the corporation's best interest.

A proceeding under this section may be brought by the board of directors or by a shareholder suing derivatively. If an action is brought derivatively, all of the provisions of subchapter 7D, including dismissal under section 7.44, are applicable to the action with the exception of the contemporaneous ownership requirement of section 7.41(1).

Section 8.09 is designed to interfere as little as possible with the usual mechanisms of corporate governance. Accordingly, except for limited circumstances such as those described above, where shareholders have reelected or declined to remove a director with full knowledge of the director's misbehavior, the court should decline to entertain an action for removal under section 8.09. It is not intended to permit judicial resolution of internal corporate disputes involving issues other than those specified in subsection (a)(1).

§ 8.10 Vacancy on Board

(a) Unless the articles of incorporation provide otherwise, if a vacancy occurs on a board of directors, including a vacancy resulting from an increase in the number of directors:

(1) the shareholders may fill the vacancy;

(2) the board of directors may fill the vacancy; or

(3) if the directors remaining in office constitute fewer than a quorum of the board, they may fill the vacancy by the affirmative vote of a majority of all the directors remaining in office.

(b) If the vacant office was held by a director elected by a voting group of shareholders, only the holders of shares of that voting group are entitled to vote to fill the vacancy if it is filled by the shareholders.

(c) A vacancy that will occur at a specific later date (by reason of a resignation effective at a later date under section 8.07(b) or otherwise) may be filled before the vacancy occurs but the new director may not take office until the vacancy occurs.

§ 8.11 Compensation of Directors

Unless the articles of incorporation or bylaws provide otherwise, the board of directors may fix the compensation of directors.

SUBCHAPTER B. MEETINGS AND ACTION OF THE BOARD

§ 8.20 Meetings

(a) The board of directors may hold regular or special meetings in or out of this state.

(b) Unless the articles of incorporation or bylaws provide otherwise, the board of directors may permit any or all directors to participate in a regular or special meeting by, or conduct the meeting through the use of, any means of communication by which all directors participating may simultaneously hear each other during the meeting. A director participating in a meeting by this means is deemed to be present in person at the meeting.

§ 8.21 Action Without Meeting

(a) Except to the extent that the articles of incorporation or bylaws require that action by the board of directors be taken at a meeting, action required or permitted by this Act to be taken by the board of directors may be taken without a meeting if each director signs a consent describing the action to be taken and delivers it to the corporation.

(b) Action taken under this section is the act of the board of directors when one or more consents signed by all the directors are delivered to the corporation. The consent may specify the time at which the action taken thereunder is to be effective. A director's consent may be withdrawn by a revocation signed by the director and delivered to the corporation prior to delivery to the corporation of unrevoked written consents signed by all the directors.

(c) A consent signed under this section has the effect of action taken at a meeting of the board of directors and may be described as such in any document.

§ 8.22 Notice of Meeting

(a) Unless the articles of incorporation or bylaws provide otherwise, regular meetings of the board of directors may be held without notice of the date, time, place, or purpose of the meeting.

(b) Unless the articles of incorporation or bylaws provide for a longer or shorter period, special meetings of the board of directors must be preceded by at least two days' notice of the date, time, and place of the meeting. The notice need not describe the purpose of the special meeting unless required by the articles of incorporation or bylaws.

§ 8.23 Waiver of Notice

(a) A director may waive any notice required by this Act, the articles of incorporation, or bylaws before or after the date and time stated in the notice. Except as provided by subsection (b), the waiver must be in writing, signed by the director entitled to the notice, and filed with the minutes or corporate records.

(b) A director's attendance at or participation in a meeting waives any required notice to him of the meeting unless the director at the beginning of the meeting (or promptly upon his arrival) objects to holding the meeting or transacting business at the meeting and does not thereafter vote for or assent to action taken at the meeting.

§ 8.24 Quorum and Voting

(a) Unless the articles of incorporation or bylaws require a greater number, a quorum of a board of directors consists of:

(1) a majority of the fixed number of directors if the corporation has a fixed board size; or

(2) a majority of the number of directors prescribed, or if no number is prescribed the number in office immediately before the meeting begins, if the corporation has a variable-range size board.

(b) The articles of incorporation or bylaws may authorize a quorum of a board of directors to consist of no fewer than one-third of the fixed or prescribed number of directors determined under subsection (a).

(c) If a quorum is present when a vote is taken, the affirmative vote of a majority of directors present is the act of the board of directors unless the articles of incorporation or bylaws require the vote of a greater number of directors.

(d) A director who is present at a meeting of the board of directors or a committee of the board of directors when corporate action is taken is deemed to have assented to the action taken unless: (1) he objects at the beginning of the meeting (or promptly upon his arrival) to holding it or transacting business at the meeting; (2) his dissent or abstention from the action taken is entered in the minutes of the meeting; or (3) he delivers written notice of his dissent or abstention to the presiding officer of the meeting before its adjournment or to the corporation immediately after adjournment of the meeting. The right of dissent or abstention is not available to a director who votes in favor of the action taken.

§ 8.25 Committees

(a) Unless this Act, the articles of incorporation or the bylaws provide otherwise, a board of directors may create one or more committees and appoint one or more members of the board of directors to serve on any such committee.

(b) Unless this Act otherwise provides, the creation of a committee and appointment of members to it must be approved by the greater of (1) a majority of all the directors in office when the action is taken or (2) the number of directors required by the articles of incorporation or bylaws to take action under section 8.24.

(c) Sections 8.20 through 8.24 apply both to committees of the board and to their members.

(d) To the extent specified by the board of directors or in the articles of incorporation or bylaws, each committee may exercise the powers of the board of directors under section 8.01.

(e) A committee may not, however:

(1) authorize or approve distributions, except according to a formula or method, or within limits, prescribed by the board of directors;

(2) approve or propose to shareholders action that this Act requires be approved by shareholders;

(3) fill vacancies on the board of directors or, subject to subsection (g), on any of its committees; or

(4) adopt, amend, or repeal bylaws.

(f) The creation of, delegation of authority to, or action by a committee does not alone constitute compliance by a director with the standards of conduct described in section 8.30.

(g) The board of directors may appoint one or more directors as alternate members of any committee to replace any absent or disqualified member during the member's absence or disqualification. Unless the articles of incorporation or the bylaws or the resolution creating the committee provide otherwise, in the event of the absence or disqualification of a member of a committee, the member or members present at any meeting and not disqualified from voting, unanimously, may appoint another director to act in place of the absent or disqualified member.

OFFICIAL COMMENT

Section 8.25 makes explicit the common law power of a board of directors to act through committees of directors and specifies the powers of the board of directors that are nondelegable, that is, powers that only the full board of directors may exercise. Section 8.25 deals only with board committees exercising the powers or performing the functions of the board of directors; the board of directors or management, independently of section 8.25, may establish nonboard committees composed of directors, employees, or others to exercise corporate powers not required to be exercised by the board of directors.

Section 8.25(b) states that, unless this Act otherwise provides, a committee of the board of directors may be created only by the affirmative vote of a majority of the board of directors then in office, or, if greater, by the number of directors required to take action by the articles of incorporation or the bylaws. This supermajority requirement reflects the importance of the decision to invest board committees with power to act under section 8.25. Section 7.44(b) requires that a special litigation committee, to consider whether the maintenance of a derivative action is in the corporation's best interest, be appointed by a majority vote of independent directors present at a meeting of the board. Sections 8.55(b) and 8.62(a), respectively, contain a similar requirement with regard to the appointment of a committee to consider whether indemnification is permissible and the appointment of a committee to consider approval of a director conflicting interest transaction.

Committees of the board of directors are assuming increasingly important roles in the governance of publicly held corporations. See "Corporate Director's Guidebook, 1994 Edition," 49 BUS. LAW. 1243 (1994). Nominating and compensation committees, composed primarily or entirely of nonmanagement directors, are widely used by publicly held corporations. Audit committees perform important review functions assigned to them by the board of directors.

Section 8.25(a) permits a committee to consist of a single director. This accommodates situations in which only one director may be present or available to make a decision on short notice, as well as situations in which it is unnecessary or inconvenient to have more than one member on a committee. Committees also are often employed to decide matters in which other members of the board have a conflict of interest; in such a case, a court will typically scrutinize with care the committee's decision when it is the product of a lone director. See, e.g., Lewis v. Fuqua, 502 A.2d 962, 967 (Del. Ch. 1985). Additionally, various sections of the Model Act require the participation or approval of at least two independent directors in order for the decision of the board or committee to have effect. These include a determination that maintenance of a derivative suit is not in the corporation's best interests (section 7.44(b)(3)), a determination that indemnification is permissible (section 8.55(b)(1)) and an approval of a director conflicting interest transaction (section 8.62(a)).

Section 8.25 limits the role of board committees in light of competing policies: on the one hand, it seems clear that appropriate committee action is not only desirable but is also likely to improve the functioning of larger and more diffuse boards of directors; on the other hand, wholesale delegation of authority to a board committee, to the point of abdication of director responsibility as a board of directors, is manifestly inappropriate and undesirable. Overbroad delegation also increases the potential, where the board of directors is divided, for usurpation of basic board functions by means of delegation to a committee dominated by one faction.

The statement of nondelegable functions set out in section 8.25(e) is based on the principle that prohibitions against delegation to board committees should be limited generally to actions that substantially affect the rights of shareholders or are fundamental to the governance of the corporation. As a result, delegation of authority to committees under section 8.25(e) may be broader than mere authority to act with respect to matters arising within the ordinary course of business.

Section 8.25(e) prohibits delegation of authority with respect to most mergers, sales of substantially all the assets, amendments to articles of incorporation and voluntary dissolution since these require shareholder action. In addition, section 8.25(e) prohibits delegation to a board committee of authority to fill board vacancies, subject to subsection (g), or to amend the bylaws. On the other hand, under section 8.25(e) many actions of a material nature, such as the authorization of long-term debt and capital investment or the issuance of shares, may properly be made the subject of committee delegation. In fact, the list of nondelegable powers has been reduced from the prior formulation of section 8.25(e).

Although section 8.25(e)(1) generally makes nondelegable the decision whether to authorize or approve distributions, including dividends, it does permit the delegation to a committee of power to approve a distribution pursuant to a formula or method or within limits prescribed by the board of directors. Therefore, the board could set a dollar range and timeframe for a prospective dividend and delegate to a committee the authority to determine the exact amount and record and payment dates of the dividend. The board also could establish certain conditions to the payment of a distribution and delegate to a committee the power to determine whether the conditions have been satisfied.

The statutes of several states make nondelegable certain powers not listed in section 8.25(e)for example, the power to change the principal corporate office, to appoint or remove officers, to fix director compensation, or to remove agents. These are not prohibited by section 8.25(e) since the whole board of directors may reverse or rescind the committee action taken, if it should wish to do so, without undue risk that implementation of the committee action might be irrevocable or irreversible.

Section 8.25(f) makes clear that although the board of directors may delegate to a committee the authority to take action, the designation of the committee, the delegation of authority to it, and action by the committee does not alone constitute compliance by a noncommittee board member with the director's responsibility under section 8.30. On the other hand, a noncommittee director also does not automatically incur personal risk should the action of the particular committee fail to meet the standards of conduct set out in section 8.30. The noncommittee member's liability in these cases will depend upon whether the director's conduct was actionable under section 8.31. Factors to be considered in this regard will include the care used in the delegation to and supervision over the committee, and the amount of knowledge regarding the actions being taken by the committee which is available to the noncommittee director. Care in delegation and supervision may be facilitated, in the usual case, by review of minutes and receipt of other reports concerning committee activities. The enumeration of these factors is intended to emphasize that directors may not abdicate their responsibilities and avoid liability simply by delegating authority to board committees. Rather, a director against whom liability is asserted based upon acts of a committee of which the director is not a member avoids liability under section 8.31 by an appropriate measure of monitoring particularly if the director met the standards contained in section 8.30 with respect to the creation and supervision of the committee.

Section 8.25(f) has no application to a member of the committee itself. The standards of conduct applicable to a committee member are set forth in section 8.30.

Section 8.25(g) is a rule of convenience that permits the board or the other committee members to replace an absent or disqualified member during the time that the member is absent or disqualified. Unless otherwise provided, replacement of an absent or disqualified member is not necessary to permit the other committee members to continue to perform their duties.

SUBCHAPTER C. STANDARDS OF CONDUCT

§ 8.30 Standards of Conduct for Directors

(a) Each member of the board of directors, when discharging the duties of a director, shall act: (1) in good faith, and (2) in a manner the director reasonably believes to be in the best interests of the corporation.

(b) The members of the board of directors or a committee of the board, when becoming informed in connection with their decisionmaking function or devoting attention to their oversight function, shall discharge their duties with the care that a person in a like position would reasonably believe appropriate under similar circumstances.

(c) In discharging board or committee duties a director, who does not have knowledge that makes reliance unwarranted, is entitled to rely on the performance by any of the persons specified in subsection (e)(1) or subsection (e)(3) to whom the board may have delegated, formally or informally by course of conduct, the authority or duty to perform one or more of the board's functions that are delegable under applicable law.

(d) In discharging board or committee duties a director, who does not have knowledge that makes reliance unwarranted, is entitled to rely on information, opinions, reports or statements, including financial statements and other financial data, prepared or presented by any of the persons specified in subsection (e).

(e) A director is entitled to rely, in accordance with subsection (c) or (d), on:

(1) one or more officers or employees of the corporation whom the director reasonably believes to be reliable and competent in the functions performed or the information, opinions, reports or statements provided;

(2) legal counsel, public accountants, or other persons retained by the corporation as to matters involving skills or expertise the director reasonably believes are matters (i) within the particular person's professional or expert competence *161 or (ii) as to which the particular person merits confidence; or

(3) a committee of the board of directors of which the director is not a member if the director reasonably believes the committee merits confidence.

OFFICIAL COMMENT

Section 8.30 defines the general standards of conduct for directors. Under subsection (a), each board member must always perform a director's duties in good faith and in a manner reasonably believed to be in the best interests of the corporation. Although each director also has a duty to comply with its requirements, the focus of subsection (b) is on the discharge of those duties by the board as a collegial body. Under subsection (b), the members of the board or a board committee are to perform their duties with the care that a person in a like position would reasonably believe appropriate under similar circumstances. This standard of conduct is often characterized as a duty of care.

Section 8.30 sets forth the standards of conduct for directors by focusing on the manner in which directors perform their duties, not the correctness of the decisions made. These standards of conduct are based on former section 35 of the 1969 Model Act, a number of state statutes and on judicial formulations of the standards of conduct applicable to directors. Section 8.30 should be read in light of the basic role of directors set forth in section 8.01(b), which provides that the "business and affairs of a corporation [shall be] managed by or under the direction of" the board, as supplemented by various provisions of the Act assigning specific powers or responsibilities to the board. Relevant thereto, directors often act collegially in performing their functions and discharging their duties. If the observance of the directors' conduct is called into question, courts will typically evaluate the conduct of the entire board (or committee). Deficient performance of section 8.30 duties on the part of a particular director may be overcome, absent unusual circumstances, by acceptable conduct (meeting, for example, subsection (b)'s standard of care) on the part of other directors sufficient in number to perform the function or discharge the duty in question.

While not thereby remedied, the deficient performance becomes irrelevant in any evaluation of the action taken. (This contrasts with a director's duty of loyalty and fair dealing, which will be evaluated on an individual basis and will also implicate discharge of the director's duties under subsection (a).) Further relevant thereto, the board may delegate or assign to appropriate officers, employees or agents of the corporation the authority or duty to exercise powers that the law does not require it to retain. Since the directors are entitled to rely thereon absent knowledge making reliance unwarranted, deficient performance of the directors' section 8.30 duties will not result from their delegatees' actions or omissions so long as the board complied with the standards of conduct set forth in section 8.30 in delegating responsibility and, where appropriate, monitoring performance of the duties delegated.

In earlier versions of the Model Act the duty of care element was included in subsection (a), with the text reading: "[a] director shall discharge his duties ... with the care an ordinarily prudent person in a like position would exercise under similar circumstances." The use of the phrase "ordinarily prudent person" in a basic guideline for director conduct, suggesting caution or circumspection vis-à-vis danger or risk, has long been problematic given the fact that risk-taking decisions are central to the directors' role. When coupled with the exercise of "care," the prior text had a familiar resonance long associated with the field of tort law. See the Official Comment to section 8.31. The further coupling with the phrasal verb "shall discharge" added to the inference that former section 8.30(a)'s standard of conduct involved a negligence standard, with resultant confusion. In order to facilitate its understanding and analysis, independent of the other general standards of conduct for directors, the duty of care element has been set forth as a separate standard of conduct in subsection (b).

Long before statutory formulations of directors' standards of conduct, courts would invoke the business judgment rule in evaluating directors' conduct and determining whether to impose liability in a particular case. The elements of the business judgment rule and the circumstances for its application are continuing to be developed by the courts. Section 8.30 does not try to codify the business judgment rule or to delineate the differences between that defensive rule and the section's standards of director conduct. Section 8.30 deals only with standards of conduct the level of performance expected of every director entering into the service of a corporation and undertaking the role and responsibilities of the office of director. The section does not deal directly with the liability of a director although exposure to liability will usually result from a failure to honor the standards of conduct required to be observed by subsection (a). See clauses (i) and (ii)(A) of section 8.31(a)(2). The issue of directors' liability is addressed in sections 8.31 and 8.33 of this subchapter. Section 8.30 does, however, play an important role in evaluating a director's conduct and the effectiveness of board action. It has relevance in assessing, under section 8.31, the reasonableness of a direct or's belief. Similarly, it has relevance in assessing a director's timely attention to appropriate inquiry when particular facts and circumstances of significant concern materialize. It serves as a frame of reference for determining, under section 8.33(a), liability for an unlawful distribution. Further, compliance with the section is important under section 8.62 for board action to be effective, under section 8.61(b)(1), to protect (i) a director's conflicting interest transaction, and (ii) the director(s) interested in the transaction. Finally, section 8.30

compliance may have a direct bearing on a court's analysis where transactional justification (e.g., a suit to enjoin a pending merger) is at issue.

A director complying with the standard of care expressed in subsection (b) is entitled to rely (under subsection (c)) upon board functions performed pursuant to delegated authority by, and to rely (under subsection (d)) upon information, opinions, reports or statements, including financial statements and other financial data, provided by, the persons or committees specified in the relevant parts of subsection (e). Within this authorization, the right to rely applies to the entire range of matters for which the board of directors is responsible. However, a director so relying must be without knowledge that would cause that reliance to be unwarranted. Section 8.30 expressly prevents a director from "hiding his or her head in the sand" and relying on the delegation of board functions, or on information, opinions reports or statements, when the director has actual knowledge that makes (or has a measure of knowledge that would cause a person, in a like position under similar circumstances, to undertake reasonable inquiry that would lead to information making) reliance unwarranted.

1. Section 8.30(a)

Section 8.30(a) establishes the basic standards of conduct for all directors. Its command is to be understood as peremptory its obligations are to be observed by every director and at the core of the subsection's mandate is the requirement that, when performing directors' duties, a director shall act in good faith coupled with conduct reasonably believed to be in the best interests of the corporation. This mandate governs all aspects of directors' duties: the duty of care, the duty to become informed, the duty of inquiry, the duty of informed judgment, the duty of attention, the duty of loyalty, the duty of fair dealing and, finally, the broad concept of fiduciary duty that the courts often use as a frame of reference when evaluating a director's conduct. These duties do not necessarily compartmentalize and, in fact, tend to overlap. For example, the duties of care, inquiry, becoming informed, attention and informed judgment all relate to the board's decisionmaking function, whereas the duties of attention, becoming informed and inquiry relate to the board's oversight function.

Two of the phrases chosen to specify the manner in which a director's duties are to be discharged deserve further comment:

(1) The phrase "reasonably believes" is both subjective and objective in character. Its first level of analysis is geared to what the particular director, acting in good faith, actually believes not what objective analysis would lead another director (in a like position and acting in similar circumstances) to conclude. The second level of analysis is focused specifically on "reasonably." While a director has wide discretion in marshalling the evidence and reaching conclusions, whether a director's belief is reasonable (i.e., could not would a reasonable person in a like position and acting in similar circumstances have arrived at that belief) ultimately involves an overview that is objective in character.

(2) The phrase "best interests of the corporation" is key to an explication of a director's duties. The term "corporation" is a surrogate for the business enterprise as well as a frame of reference encompassing the shareholder body. In determining the corporation's "best interests," the director has wide discretion in deciding how to weigh near term opportuni-

ties versus long term benefits as well as in making judgments where the interests of various groups within the shareholder body or having other cognizable interests in the enterprise may differ.

As a generalization, section 8.30 operates as a "baseline" principle governing director conduct "when discharging the [ongoing] duties of a director" in circumstances uncomplicated by self interest taint. The Model Act recognizes, however, that directors' personal interests may not always align with the corporation's best interests and provides procedures by which interest conflict transactions can be processed. See subchapter D (derivative proceedings) of chapter 7 and subchapter E (indemnification) and subchapter F (directors' conflicting interest transactions) of this chapter 8. Those procedures generally contemplate that the interested director will not be involved in taking action on the interest conflict transaction. And the common law has recognized that other interest conflict situations may arise which do not entail a "transaction" by or with the corporation (e.g., the corporate opportunity doctrine). The interested director is relieved of the duty to act in connection with the matter on behalf of the corporation (specifically, the traditional mandate to act in the corporation's best interests), given the inherent conflict. However, the interested director is still expected to act in good faith, and that duty is normally discharged by observing the obligation of fair dealing. In the case of interest conflict transactions, where there is a conflicting interest with respect to the corporation under section 8.60(1), the interested director's conduct is governed by subchapter F of this chapter 8. The duty of fair dealing is embedded in the subsection 8.60(4) provision calling for the interested director to make the required disclosure as to the conflicting interest and the transaction and, if one of the two safe harbor procedures is not properly observed, the interested director must prove the fairness (i.e., procedure, involving good faith among other aspects, as well as price) of the transaction to the corporation. In other cases, Section 8.30's standards of conduct are overlaid by various components of the duty to act fairly, the particular thrusts of which will depend upon the kind of interested director's conduct at issue and the circumstances of the case. As a general rule, the duty of fair dealing is normally discharged by the interested director through appropriate disclosure to the other directors considering the matter followed by abstention from participation in any decisionmaking relevant thereto. If and to the extent that the interested director's action respecting the matter goes further, the reasonableness of the director's belief as to the corporation's best interests, in respect of the action taken, should be evaluated on the basis of not only the director's honest and good faith belief but also on considerations bearing on the fairness of the transaction or conduct to the corporation.

2. Section 8.30(b)

Section 8.30(b) establishes a general standard of care for directors in the context of their dealing with the board's decisionmaking and oversight functions. While certain aspects will involve individual conduct (e.g., preparation for meetings), these functions are generally performed by the board through collegial action, as recognized by the reference in subsection (b) to board and committee "members" and "their duties." In contrast with subsection (a)'s individual conduct mandate, section 8.30(b) has a twofold thrust: it provides a standard of conduct for individual action and, more broadly, it states a conduct obligation"shall discharge their duties" concerning the degree of care to be collegially used by the directors when performing those functions. It provides that directors have a duty to exercise "the care that a person in a like position would reasonably believe appropriate under similar circumstances."

The traditional formulation for a director's standard (or duty) of care has been geared to the "ordinarily prudent person." For example, the Model Act's prior formulation (in former section 8.30(a)(2)) referred to "the care an ordinarily prudent person in a like position would exercise under similar circumstances," and almost all state statutes that include a standard of care reflect parallel language. The phrase "ordinarily prudent person" constitutes a basic frame of reference grounded in the field of tort law and provides a primary benchmark for determining negligence. For this reason, its use in the standard of care for directors, suggesting that negligence is the proper determinant for measuring deficient (and thus actionable) conduct, has caused confusion and misunderstanding. Accordingly, the phrase "ordinarily prudent person" has been removed from the Model Act's standard of care and in its place "a person in a like position" has been substituted. The standard is not what care a particular director might believe appropriate in the circumstances but what a person in a like position and acting under similar circumstances would reasonably believe to be appropriate. Thus, the degree of care that directors should employ, under subsection (b), involves an objective standard.

Some state statutes have used the words "diligence," "care,"and "skill" to define the duty of care. There is very little authority as to what "skill" and "diligence," as distinguished from "care," can be required or properly expected of corporate directors in the performance of their duties. "Skill," in the sense of technical competence in a particular field, should not be a qualification for the office of director. The concept of "diligence" is sufficiently subsumed within the concept of "care." Accordingly, the words "diligence" and "skill" are not used in section 8.30's standard of care.

The process by which a director becomes informed, in carrying out the decisionmaking and oversight functions, will vary. Relevant thereto, the directors' decisionmaking function is established in large part by various sections of the Act: the issuance of shares (6.21); distributions (6.40); dismissal of derivative proceedings (7.44); indemnification (8.55); interested transaction authorization (8.62); articles of incorporation amendments (10.02 and 10.03); bylaw amendments (10.20); mergers (11.01); share exchanges (11.02); asset sales and mortgages (12.01 and 12.02); and dissolution (14.02). In contrast, the Act does not deal directly with the directors' oversight function. That function is established indirectly by section 8.01(b)'s broad provision making the board responsible for the exercise of corporate powers and the direction of how the corporation's business and affairs are managed. In relying on the performance by management of delegated or assigned section 8.01 duties (including, for example, matters of law and legal compliance), as authorized by subsection (c), directors may depend upon the presumption of regularity absent knowledge or notice to the contrary. In discharging the section 8.01 duties associated with the board's oversight function, the standard of care entails primarily a duty of attention. In contrast with the board's decisionmaking function, which generally involves informed action at a point in time, the oversight function is concerned with a continuum and the duty of attention accordingly involves participatory performance over a period of time.

Several of the phrases chosen to define the standard of conduct in section 8.30(b) deserve specific mention:

(1) The phrase "becoming informed," in the context of the decisionmaking function, refers to the process of gaining sufficient familiarity with the background facts and circumstances in order to make an informed judgment. Unless the circumstances would permit a reasonable director to conclude that he or she is already sufficiently informed, the standard of care requires every director to take steps to become informed about the background facts and circumstances before taking action on the matter at hand. The process typically involves review of written materials provided before or at the meeting and attention to/participation in the deliberations leading up to a vote. It can involve consideration of information and data generated by persons other than legal counsel, public accountants, etc., retained by the corporation, as contemplated by subsection (e)(2); for example, review of industry studies or research articles prepared by unrelated parties could be very useful. It can also involve direct communications, outside of the boardroom, with members of management or other directors. There is no one way for "becoming informed," and both the method and measure "how to" and "how much" are matters of reasonable judgment for the director to exercise.

(2) The phrase "devoting attention," in the context of the oversight function, refers to concern with the corporation's information and reporting systems and not to proactive inquiry searching out system inadequacies or noncompliance. While directors typically give attention to future plans and trends as well as current activities, they should not be expected to anticipate the problems which the corporation may face except in those circumstances where something has occurred to make it obvious to the board that the corporation should be addressing a particular problem. The standard of care associated with the oversight function involves gaining assurances from management and advisers that systems believed appropriate have been established coupled with ongoing monitoring of the systems in place, such as those concerned with legal compliance or internal controls followed up with a proactive response when alerted to the need for inquiry.

(3) The reference to "person," without embellishment, is intended to avoid implying any qualifications, such as specialized expertise or experience requirements, beyond the basic director attributes of common sense, practical wisdom, and informed judgment.

(4) The phrase "reasonably believe appropriate" refers to the array of possible options that a person possessing the basic director attributes of common sense, practical wisdom and informed judgment would recognize to be available, in terms of the degree of care that might be appropriate, and from which a choice by such person would be made. The measure of care that such person might determine to be appropriate, in a given instance, would normally involve a selection from the range of options and any choice within the realm of reason would be an appropriate decision under the standard of care called for under subsection (b). However, a decision that is so removed from the realm of reason or so unreasonable as to fall outside the permissible bounds of sound discretion, and thus an abuse of discretion, will not satisfy the standard.

(5) The phrase "in a like position" recognizes that the "care" under consideration is that which would be used by the "person" if he or she were a director of the particular corporation.

(6) The combined phrase "in a like position . . . under similar circumstances" is intended to recognize that (a) the nature and extent of responsibilities will vary, depending upon such factors as the size, complexity, urgency, and location of activities carried on by the particular corporation, (b) decisions must be made on the basis of the information known to the directors without the benefit of hindsight, and (c) the special background, qualifications, and management responsibilities of a particular director may be relevant in evaluating that director's compliance with the standard of care. Even though the combined phrase is intended to take into account the special background, qualifications and management responsibilities of a particular director, it does not excuse a director lacking business experience or particular expertise from exercising the basic director attributes of common sense, practical wisdom, and informed judgment.

3. Section 8.30(c)

The delegation of authority and responsibility under subsection (c) may take the form of (i) formal action through a board resolution, (ii) implicit action through the election of corporate officers (e.g., chief financial officer or controller) or the appointment of corporate managers (e.g., credit manager), or (iii) informal action through a course of conduct (e.g., involvement through corporate officers and managers in the management of a significant 50% owned joint venture). A director may properly rely on those to whom authority has been delegated pursuant to subsection (c) respecting particular matters calling for specific action or attention in connection with the directors' decisionmaking function as well as matters on the board's continuing agenda, such as legal compliance and internal control, in connection with the directors' oversight function. Delegation should be carried out in accordance with the standard of care set forth in section 8.30(b).

By identifying those upon whom a director may rely in connection with the discharge of duties, section 8.30(c) does not limit the ability of directors to delegate their powers under section 8.01(b) except where delegation is expressly prohibited by the Act or otherwise by applicable law (see, e.g., section 8.25(e) and § 11 of the Securities Act of 1933). See section 8.25 and its Official Comment for detailed consideration of delegation to board committees of the authority of the board under section 8.01 and the duty to perform one or more of the board's functions. And by employing the concept of delegation, section 8.30(c) does not limit the ability of directors to establish baseline principles as to management responsibilities. Specifically, section 8.01(b) provides that "all corporate powers shall be exercised by or under the authority of" the board, and a basic board function involves the allocation of management responsibilities and the related assignment (or delegation) of corporate powers. For example, a board can properly decide to retain a third party to assume responsibility for the administration of designated aspects of risk management for the corporation (e.g., health insurance or disability claims). This would involve the directors in the exercise of judgment in connection with the decisionmaking function pursuant to subsection (b) (i.e., the assignment of authority to exercise corporate powers to an agent). See the Official Comment to section 8.01. It would not entail impermissible delegation to a person specified in subsection (e)(2) pursuant to subsection (c)of a board function for which the directors by law have a duty to perform. They have the corporate power (under section 8.01(b)) to perform the task but administration of risk management is not a board function coming within the ambit of directors' duties; together with many similar management responsibilities, they may assign the task in the context of the allocation of corporate powers exercised under the authority of the board. This illustration highlights the distinction between delegation of a board function and assignment of authority to exercise corporate powers.

Although the board may delegate the authority or duty to perform one or more of its functions, reliance on delegation under subsection (c) may not alone constitute compliance with section 8.30 and reliance on the action taken by the delegatee may not alone constitute compliance by the directors or a noncommittee board member with section 8.01 responsibilities. On the other hand, should the board committee or the corporate officer or employee performing the function delegated fail to meet section 8.30's standard of care, noncompliance by the board with section 8.01 will not automatically result. Factors to be considered, in this regard, will include the care used in the delegation to and supervision over the delegatee, and the amount of knowledge regarding the particular matter which is available to the particular director. Care in delegation and supervision includes appraisal of the capabilities and diligence of the delegatee in light of the subject and its relative importance and may be facilitated, in the usual case, by receipt of reports concerning the delegatee's activities. The enumeration of these factors is intended to emphasize that directors may not abdicate their responsibilities and avoid accountability simply by delegating authority to others. Rather, a director charged with accountability based upon acts of others will fulfill the director's duties if the standards contained in section 8.30 are met.

4. Section 8.30(d)

Reliance under subsection (d) on a report, statement, opinion, or other information is permitted only if the director has read the information, opinion, report or statement in question, or was present at a meeting at which it was orally presented, or took other steps to become generally familiar with it. A director must comply with the general standard of care of section 8.30(b) in making a judgment as to the reliability and competence of the source of information upon which the director proposes to rely or, as appropriate, that it otherwise merits confidence.

5. Section 8.30(e)

Reliance on one or more of the corporation's officers or employees, pursuant to the intracorporate frame of reference of subsection (e)(1), is conditioned upon a reasonable belief as to the reliability and competence of those who have undertaken the functions performed or who prepared or communicated the information, opinions, reports or statements presented. In determining whether a person is "reliable," the director would typically consider (i) the individual's background experience and scope of responsibility within the corporation in gauging the individual's familiarity and knowledge respecting the subject matter and (ii) the individual's record and reputation for honesty, care and ability in discharging responsibilities which he or she undertakes. In determining whether a person is "competent," the director would normally take into account the same considerations and, if expertise should be relevant, the director would consider the individual's technical skills as well. Recognition in the statute of the right of one director to rely on the expertise and experience of another director, in the context of board or committee deliberations, is unnecessary, for the group's reliance on shared experience and wisdom is an implicit underpinning of director conduct. In relying on another member of the board, a director would quite properly take advantage of the colleague's knowledge and experience in becoming informed about the matter at hand before taking action; however, the director would be expected to exercise independent judgment when it comes time to vote.

Subsection (e)(2), which has an extra-corporate frame of reference, permits reliance on outside advisers retained by the corporation, including persons specifically engaged to advise the board or a board committee. Possible advisers include not only those in the professional disciplines customarily supervised by state authorities, such as lawyers, accountants, and engineers, but also those in other fields involving special experience and skills, such as investment bankers, geologists, management consultants, actuaries, and real estate appraisers. The adviser could be an individual or an organization, such as a law firm. Reliance on a nonmanagement director, who is specifically engaged (and, normally, additionally compensated) to undertake a special assignment or a particular consulting role, would fall within this outside adviser frame of reference. The concept of "expert competence" embraces a wide variety of qualifications and is not limited to the more precise and narrower recognition of experts under the Securities Act of 1933. In this respect, subsection (e)(2) goes beyond the reliance provision found in many existing state business corporation acts. In addition, a director may also rely on outside advisers where skills or expertise of a technical nature is not a prerequisite, or where the person's professional or expert competence has not been established, so long as the director reasonably believes the person merits confidence. For example, a board might choose to assign to a private investigator the duty of inquiry (e.g., follow up on rumors about a senior executive's "grand lifestyle") and properly rely on the private investigator's report. And it would be entirely appropriate for a director to rely on advice concerning highly technical aspects of environmental compliance from a corporate lawyer in the corporation's outside law firm, without due inquiry concerning that particular lawyer's technical competence, where the director reasonably believes the lawyer giving the advice is appropriately informed by reason of resources known to be available from that adviser's legal organization or through other means and therefore merits confidence.

Subsection (e)(3) permits reliance on a board committee when it is submitting recommendations for action by the full board of directors as well as when it is performing supervisory or other functions in instances where neither the full board of directors nor the committee takes dispositive action. For example, the compensation committee typically reviews proposals and makes recommendations for action by the full board of directors. In contrast, there may be reliance upon an investigation undertaken by a board committee and reported to the full board, which forms the basis for a decision by the board of directors not to take dispositive action. Another example is reliance on a committee of the board of directors, such as a corporate audit committee, with respect to the board's ongoing role of oversight of the accounting and auditing functions of the corporation. In addition, where reliance on information or materials prepared or presented by a board committee is not involved, in connection with board action, a director may properly rely on oversight monitoring or dispositive action by a board committee (of which the director is not a member) empowered to act pursuant to authority delegated under section 8.25 or acting with the acquiescence of the board of directors. See the Official Comment to section 8.25. A director may similarly rely on committees not created under section 8.25 which have nondirector members. In parallel with subsection (e)(2)(ii), the concept of "confidence" is substituted for "competence" in order to avoid any inference that technical skills are a prerequisite. In the usual case, the appointment of committee members or the reconstitution of the membership of a standing committee (e.g., the audit committee), following an annual shareholders' meeting, would alone manifest the noncommittee members' belief that the committee "merits confidence." However, the reliance contemplated by subsection (e)(3) is geared to the point in time when the board takes action or the period of time over which a committee is engaged in an oversight function; consequently, the judgment to be made (i.e., whether a committee "merits confidence") will arise at varying points in time. After making an initial judgment that a committee (of which a director is not a member) merits confidence, the director may depend upon the presumption of regularity absent knowledge or notice to the contrary.

6. Application to Officers

Section 8.30 generally deals only with directors. Section 8.42 and its Official Comment explain the extent to which the provisions of section 8.30 apply to officers.

§ 8.31 Standards of Liability for Directors

(a) A director shall not be liable to the corporation or its shareholders for any decision to take or not to take action, or any failure to take any action, as a director, unless the party asserting liability in a proceeding establishes that:

(1) any provision in the articles of incorporation authorized by section 2.02(b)(4) or the protection afforded by section 8.61 for action taken in compliance with section 8.62 or 8.63, if interposed as a bar to the proceeding by the director, does not preclude liability; and

(2) the challenged conduct consisted or was the result of:

(i) action not in good faith; or

(ii) a decision

(A) which the director did not reasonably believe to be in the best interests of the corporation, or

(B) as to which the director was not informed to an extent the director reasonably believed appropriate in the circumstances; or

(iii) a lack of objectivity due to the director's familial, financial or business relationship with, or a lack of independence due to the director's domination or control by, another person having a material interest in the challenged conduct

(A) which relationship or which domination or control could reasonably be expected to have affected the director's judgment respecting the challenged conduct in a manner adverse to the corporation, and

(B) after a reasonable expectation to such effect has been established, the director shall not have established that the challenged conduct was reasonably believed by the director to be in the best interests of the corporation; or

(iv) a sustained failure of the director to devote attention to ongoing oversight of the business and affairs of the corporation, or a failure to devote timely attention, by making (or causing to be made) appropriate inquiry, when particular facts and circumstances of significant concern materialize that would alert a reasonably attentive director to the need therefor; or

(v) receipt of a financial benefit to which the director was not entitled or any other breach of the director's duties to deal fairly with the corporation and its shareholders that is actionable under applicable law.

(b) The party seeking to hold the director liable:

(1) for money damages, shall also have the burden of establishing that:

(i) harm to the corporation or its shareholders has been suffered, and

(ii) the harm suffered was proximately caused by the director's challenged conduct; or

(2) for other money payment under a legal remedy, such as compensation for the unauthorized use of corporate assets, shall also have whatever persuasion burden may be called for to establish that the payment sought is appropriate in the circumstances; or

(3) for other money payment under an equitable remedy, such as profit recovery by or disgorgement to the corporation, shall also have whatever persuasion burden may be called for to establish that the equitable remedy sought is appropriate in the circumstances.

(c) Nothing contained in this section shall (1) in any instance where fairness is at issue, such as consideration of the fairness of a transaction to the corporation under section 8.61(b)(3), alter the burden of proving the fact or lack of fairness otherwise applicable, (2) alter the fact or lack of liability of a director under another section of this Act, such as the provisions governing the consequences of an unlawful distribution under section 8.33 or a transactional interest under section 8.61, or (3) affect any rights to which the corporation or a shareholder may be entitled under another statute of this state or the United States.

OFFICIAL COMMENT

Subsections (a) and (b) of section 8.30 establish standards of conduct that are central to the role of directors. Section 8.30(b)'s standard of conduct is frequently referred to as a director's duty of care. The employment of the concept of "care," if considered in the abstract, suggests a tort law/negligence-based analysis looking toward a finding of fault and damage recovery where the duty of care has not been properly observed and loss has been suffered. But the Model Act's desired level of director performance, with its objectively based standard of conduct ("the care that a person in a like position would reasonably believe appropriate under similar circumstances"), does not carry with it the same type of result-oriented liability analysis. The courts recognize that boards of directors and corporate managers make numerous decisions that involve the balancing of risks and benefits for the enterprise. Although some decisions turn out to be unwise or the result of a mistake of judgment, it is not reasonable to reexamine an unsuccessful decision with the benefit of hindsight. As observed in Joy v. North, 692 F.2d 880, 885 (2d Cir. 1982): "Whereas an automobile driver who makes a mistake in judgment as to speed or distance injuring a pedestrian will likely be called upon to respond in damages, a corporate [director or] officer who makes a mistake in judgment as to economic conditions, consumer tastes or production line efficiency will rarely, if ever, be found liable for damages suffered by the corporation." Therefore, as a general rule, a director is not exposed to personal liability for injury or damage caused by an unwise decision. While a director is not personally responsible for unwise decisions or mistakes of judgment and conduct conforming with the standards of section 8.30 will almost always be protected a director can be held liable for misfeasance or nonfeasance in performing the duties of a director. And while a director whose performance meets the standards of section 8.30 should have no liability, the fact that a director's performance fails to reach that level does not automatically establish personal liability for damages that the corporation may have suffered as a consequence.

* * *

Note on Directors' Liability

A director's financial risk exposure (e.g., in a lawsuit for money damages suffered by the corporation or its shareholders claimed to have resulted from misfeasance or nonfeasance in connection with the performance of the director's duties) can be analyzed as follows:

1. articles of incorporation limitation. If the corporation's articles of incorporation contain a provision eliminating its directors' liability to the corporation or its shareholders for money damages, adopted pursuant to section 2.02(b)(4), there is no liability unless the director's conduct involves one of the prescribed exceptions that preclude the elimination of liability. See section 2.02 and its Official Comment.

2. director's conflicting interest transaction safe harbor. If the matter at issue involves a director's conflicting interest transaction (as defined in section 8.60(2)) and a safe harbor procedure under section 8.61 involving action taken in compliance with section 8.62 or 8.63 has been properly

implemented, there is no liability for the interested director arising out of the transaction. See subchapter F of this chapter 8.

3. business judgment rule. If an articles of incorporation provision adopted pursuant to section 2.02 or a safe harbor procedure under section 8.61 does not shield the director's conduct from liability, this standard of judicial review for director conduct deeply rooted in the case law presumes that, absent self-dealing or other breach of the duty of loyalty, directors' decisionmaking satisfies the applicable legal requirements. A plaintiff challenging the director's conduct in connection with a corporate decision, and asserting liability by reason thereof, encounters certain procedural barriers. In the first instance, many jurisdictions have special pleading requirements that condition the ability to pursue the challenge on the plaintiff's bringing forward specific factual allegations that put in question the availability of the business judgment presumption. Assuming the suit survives a motion to dismiss for failure to state (in satisfaction of such a condition) an actionable claim, the plaintiff has the burden of overcoming that presumption of regularity.

4. damages and proximate cause. If the business judgment rule does not shield the directors' decisionmaking from liability, as a general rule it must be established that money damages were suffered by the corporation or its shareholders and those damages resulted from and were legally caused by the challenged act or omission of the director.

5. other liability for money payment. Aside from a claim for damages, the director may be liable to reimburse the corporation pursuant to a claim under quantum meruit (the reasonable value of services) or quantum valebant (the reasonable value of goods and materials) if corporate resources have been used without proper authorization. In addition, the corporation may be entitled to short-swing profit recovery, stemming from the director's trading in its securities, under § 16(b) of the Securities Exchange Act of 1934.

6. equitable profit recovery or disgorgement. An equitable remedy compelling the disgorgement of the director's improper financial gain or entitling the corporation to profit recovery, where directors' duties have been breached, may require the payment of money by the director to the corporation.

7. corporate indemnification. If the court determines that the director is liable, the director may be indemnified by the corporation for any payments made and expenses incurred, depending upon the circumstances, if a third-party suit is involved. If the proceeding is by or in the right of the corporation, the director may be reimbursed for reasonable expenses incurred in connection with the proceeding if ordered by a court under section 8.54(a)(3).

8. insurance. To the extent that corporate indemnification is not available, the director may be reimbursed for the money damages for which the director is accountable, together with proceeding related expenses, if the claim/grounds for liability come within the coverage under directors' and

officers' liability insurance that has been purchased by the corporation pursuant to section 8.57.

* * *

Section 8.31 includes steps (1) through (6) in the analysis of a director's liability exposure set forth in the above Note. In establishing general standards of director liability under the Model Act, the section also serves the important purpose of providing clarification that the general standards of conduct set forth in section 8.30 are not intended to codify the business judgment rule a point as to which there has been confusion on the part of some courts (notwithstanding a disclaimer of that purpose and effect in the prior Official Comment to section 8.30). For example, one court viewed the standard of care set forth in Washington's business corporation act (a provision based upon and almost identical to the prior section 8.30(a)which read "A director shall discharge his duties as a director . . .: (1) in good faith; (2) with the care an ordinarily prudent person in a like position would exercise under similar circumstances; and (3) in a manner he reasonably believes to be in the best interests of the corporation") as having codified the business judgment rule. See Seafirst Corp. v. Jenkins, 644 F. Supp. 1152, 1159 (W.D. Wash. 1986). (A later court characterized this view as a mistaken assumption and recognized the disclaimer made in section 8.30's Official Comment. See Shinn v. Thrust IV Inc., 786 P. 2d 285, 290 n.1 (Wash. App. 1990).) Another court declared "Section 309 [a standard of conduct almost identical to the prior section 8.30(a)] codifies California's business judgment rule." See Gaillard v. Natomas Co., 208 Cal. App. 3d 1250, 1264 (1989). The Court of Appeals of New York referred to that state's statutory standard of care for directors, a formulation set forth in NYBCL § 717 that is similar to the prior section 8.30(a), as "New York's business judgment rule." See Lindner Fund, Inc. v. Waldbaum, Inc., 624 N.E. 2d 160, 161 (1993). In contrast, another court considering New York's conduct standard observed:

A board member's obligation to a corporation and its shareholders has two prongs, generally characterized as the duty of care and the duty of loyalty. The duty of care refers to the responsibility of a corporate fiduciary to exercise, in the performance of his tasks, the care that a reasonably prudent person in a similar position would use under similar circumstances. See NYBCL § 717. In evaluating a manager's compliance with the duty of care, New York courts adhere to the business judgment rule, which "bars judicial inquiry into actions of corporate directors taken in good faith and in the exercise of honest judgment in the lawful and legitimate furtherance of corporate purposes." Norlin Corp. v. Rooney, Pace Inc., 744 F.2d 255, 264 (2d Cir. 1984) [quoting Auerbach v. Bennett, 47 N.Y. 2d 619, 629 (1979)].

Sections 8.30 and 8.31 adopt the approach to director conduct and director liability taken in the Norlin decision. See section 8.30 and its Official Comment with respect to the standards of conduct for directors. For a detailed analysis of how and why standards of conduct and standards of liability diverge in corporate law, see Melvin A. Eisenberg, The Divergence of Standards of Conduct and Standards of Review in Corporate Law, 62 Fordham L. Rev. 437 (1993).

The Model Act does not undertake to prescribe detailed litigation procedures. However, it does deal with requirements applicable to shareholder derivative suits (see sections 7.407.47) and section 8.31 builds on those requirements. If either a liability eliminating provision included in the corporation's articles of incorporation, pursuant to section 2.02(b)(4), or protection for a director's conflicting interest transaction afforded by section 8.61(b)(1) or section 8.61(b)(2), is interposed by a defendant director as a bar to the challenge of his or her conduct, the plaintiff's role in satisfying the requirement of subsection (a)(1)i.e., establishing that the articles of incorporation provision or the safe harbor provision interposed does not apply would be governed by the court's procedural rules. Parenthetically, where fairness of a director's conflicting interest transaction can be established, protection from liability is also afforded by section 8.61(b)(3). If it is asserted by a defendant director as a defense, it is important to note that subsection (a)(2)(v) rather than subsection (a)(1) would be implicated and the burden of establishing that the transaction was fair to the corporation and, therefore, no improper financial benefit was received is placed on the interested director under section 8.61(b)(3). Similarly, the local pleading and other rules would govern the plaintiff's effort to satisfy subsection (a)(2)'s requirements. Consistent with the general rules of civil procedure, the plaintiff generally has the burden under subsection (b) of proving that the director's deficient conduct caused harm resulting in monetary damage or calls for monetary reimbursement; in the alternative, the circumstances may justify or require an equitable remedy.

1. Section 8.31(a)

If a provision in the corporation's articles of incorporation (adopted pursuant to section 2.02(b)(4)) shelters the director from liability for money damages, or if a safe harbor provision, under subsection (b)(1) or (b)(2) of section 8.61, shelters the director's conduct in connection with a conflicting interest transaction, there is no need to consider further the application of section 8.31's standards of liability. In either case, the court would presumably grant the defendant director's motion for dismissal or summary judgment (or the equivalent) and the proceeding would be ended. Termination of the proceeding will not automatically follow, however, if the party challenging the director's conduct can assert any of the valid bases for contesting the availability of the liability shelter. In the absence thereof, the relevant shelter provision is self-executing and the individual director's exoneration from liability is automatic. Further, if the shelter provision is section 8.61(b)(1)'s safe harbor, the directors approving the conflicting interest transaction will presumably be protected as well, for compliance with the relevant standards of conduct under section 8.30 is important for their action to be effective and, as noted above, conduct meeting section 8.30's standards will almost always be protected.

If a claim of liability arising out of a challenged act or omission of a director is not resolved and disposed of under subsection (a)(1), subsection (a)(2) provides the basis for evaluating whether the conduct in question can be challenged.

* * *

Note on the Business Judgment Rule

Over the years, the courts have developed a broad common law concept geared to business judgment. In basic principle, a board of directors enjoys a presumption of sound business judgment and its decisions will not be disturbed (by a court substituting its own notions of what is or is not sound business judgment) if they can be attributed to any rational business purpose. See Sinclair Oil Corp. v. Levien, 280 A.2d 717, 720 (Del. 1971). Relatedly, it is presumed that, in making a business decision, directors act in good faith, on an informed basis, and in the honest belief that the action taken is in the best interests of the corporation. See Aronson v. Lewis, 473 A.2d 805, 812 (Del. 1983). When applied, this principle operates both as a procedural rule of evidence and a substantive rule of law, in that if the plaintiff fails to rebut the presumption that the directors acted in good faith, in the corporation's best interest and on an informed basis, the business judgment standard protects both the directors and the decisions they make. See Citron v. Fairchild Camera & Instrument Corp., 569 A. 2d 53, 64 (Del. 1989).

Some have suggested that, within the business judgment standard's broad ambit, a distinction might usefully be drawn between that part which protects directors from personal liability for the decision they make and the part which protects the decision itself from attack. See Revlon, Inc. v. MacAndrews & Forbes Holdings, Inc., 506 A. 2d 173, 180 n.10 (Del. 1986). While these two objects of the business judgment standard's protection are different, and judicial review might result in the decision being enjoined but no personal liability (or vice versa), their operative elements are identical (i.e., good faith, disinterest, informed judgment and "best interests"). As a consequence, the courts have not observed any distinction in terminology and have generally followed the practice of referring only to the business judgment rule, whether dealing with personal liability issues or transactional justification matters.

While, in substance, the operative elements of the standard of judicial review commonly referred to as the business judgment rule have been widely recognized, courts have used a number of different word formulations to articulate the concept. The formulation adopted in § 4.01(c) of The American Law Institute's PRINCIPLES OF CORPORATE GOVERNANCE: ANALYSIS AND RECOMMENDATIONS (1994) provides that a director who makes a business judgment **in good faith** (an obvious prerequisite) fulfills the duty of care standard if the director:

(1) is not interested [as defined] in the subject of the business judgment;

(2) is informed with respect to the subject of the business judgment to the extent the director ... reasonably believes to be appropriate under the circumstances; and

(3) rationally believes that the business judgment is in the best interests of the corporation.

Referring to clause (2) above, the decisionmaking process is to be reviewed on a basis that is to a large extent individualized in nature ("informed ... to the extent the director ... reasonably believes to be appropriate under the circumstances")as contrasted with the traditional objectively based duty of care standard (e.g., the prior section 8.30(a)'s "care ... an ordinarily prudent person ... would exercise"). An "ordinarily prudent person" might do more to become better informed, but if a director believes, in good faith, that the director can make a sufficiently informed business judgment, the director will be protected so long as that belief is within the bounds of reason. Referring to clause (3) above, the phrase "rationally believes" is stated in the PRINCIPLES to be a term having "both an objective and subjective content. A director ... must actually believe that the business judgment is in the best interests of the corporation and that belief must be rational," 1 PRINCIPLES, at 179. Others see that aspect to be primarily geared to the process employed by a director in making the decision as opposed to the substantive content of the board decision made. See Aronson v. Lewis, supra, at 812 ("The business judgment rule is ... a presumption that in making a business decision the directors of a corporation acted on an informed basis, in good faith and in the honest belief that the action taken was in the best interests of the company.... Absent an abuse of discretion, that judgment will be respected by the courts.") In practical application, an irrational belief would in all likelihood constitute an abuse of discretion. Compare In Re Caremark International Inc. Derivative Litigation (September 25, 1996) (1996 Del. Ch. LEXIS 125 at p. 27: "whether a judge or jury considering the matter after the fact ... believes a decision substantively wrong, or degrees of wrong extending through "stupid" to "egregious" or "irrational", provides no ground for director liability, so long as the court determines that the process employed was either rational or employed in a good faith effort to advance corporate interests ... the business judgment rule is process oriented and informed by a deep respect for all good faith board decisions.")

* * *

Section 8.31 does not codify the business judgment rule as a whole. The section recognizes the common law doctrine and provides guidance as to its application in dealing with director liability claims. Because the elements of the business judgment rule and the circumstances for its application are continuing to be developed by the courts, it would not be desirable to freeze the concept in a statute. For example, in recent years the Delaware Supreme Court has established novel applications of the concept to various transactional justification matters, such as the role of special litigation committees and change-of-control situations. See Zapata Corporation v. Maldonado, 430 A. 2d 779 (1981), and Unocal Corp. v. Mesa Petroleum Co., 493 A. 2d 946 (1985), respectively. Under Zapata, a rule that applies where there is no disinterested majority on the board appointing the special litigation committee, there is no presumption of regularity and the corporation must bear the burden of proving the independence of the committee, the reasonableness of its investigation, and the reasonableness of the bases of its determination that dismissal of the derivative litigation is in the best interests of the corporation. Under Unocal, the board must first establish reasonable grounds for believing an unsolicited takeover bid poses a danger to corporate policy and effectiveness, and a reasonable relationship of defensive measures taken to the threat posed, before the board's action will be entitled to the business judgment presumptions. The business judgment concept has been employed in countless legal decisions and is a topic that has received a great deal of scholarly attention. For an exhaustive treatment of the subject, see D. Block, N. Barton & S. Radin, The Business Judgment Rule: Fiduciary Duties of Corporate Directors (4th ed. 1993 & Supp. 1995). While codification of the business judgment rule in section 8.31 is expressly disclaimed, its principal elements, relating to personal liability issues, are embedded in subsection (a)(2).

(a) good faith

The expectation that a director's conduct will be in good faith is an overarching element of his or her baseline duties. Relevant thereto, it has been stated that a lack of good faith is presented where a board "lacked an actual intention to advance corporate welfare" and "bad faith" is presented where "a transaction ... is authorized for some purpose other than a genuine attempt to advance corporate welfare or is known to constitute a violation of applicable positive law." See Gagliardi v. TriFoods Int'l Inc., 683 A.2d 1049 (Del. Ch. 1996). If a director's conduct can be successfully challenged pursuant to other clauses of subsection (a)(2), there is a substantial likelihood that the conduct in question will also present an issue of good faith implicating clause 2(i). Conduct involving knowingly illegal conduct that exposes the corporation to harm will constitute action not in good faith, and belief that decisions made (in connection with such conduct) were in the best interests of the corporation will be subject to challenge as well. If subsection (a)(2) included only clause 2(i), much of the conduct with which the other clauses are concerned could still be considered pursuant to the subsection, on the basis that such conduct evidenced the actor's lack of good faith. Accordingly, the canon of construction known as ejusdem generis has substantial relevance in understanding the broad overlap of the good faith element with the various other subsection (a)(2) clauses. Where conduct has not been found deficient on other grounds, decisionmaking outside the bounds of reasonable judgment an abuse of discretion perhaps explicable on no other basis can give rise to an inference of bad faith. That form of conduct (characterized by the court as "constructive fraud" or "reckless indifference" or "deliberate disregard" in the relatively few case precedents) giving rise to an inference of bad faith will also raise a serious question whether the director could have reasonably believed that the best interests of the corporation would be served. If a director's conflicting interest transaction is determined to be manifestly unfavorable to the corporation, giving rise to an inference of bad faith tainting the directors' action approving the transaction under section 8.62, the safe harbor protection afforded by section 8.61 for both the transaction and the conflicted director would be in jeopardy. See the Official Comment to section 8.61. Depending on the facts and circumstances, the directors who approve a director's conflicting interest transaction that is manifestly unfavorable to the corporation may be at risk under clause (2)(i).

(b) reasonable belief

A director should reasonably believe that his or her decision will be in the best interests of the corporation and a director should become sufficiently informed, with respect to any action taken or not taken, to the extent he or she reasonably believes appropriate in the circumstances. In each case, the director's reasonable belief calls for a subjective belief and, so long as it is his or her honest and good faith belief, a director has wide discretion. However, in the rare case where a decision respecting the corporation's best interests is so removed from the realm of reason (e.g., corporate waste), or a belief as to the sufficiency of the director's preparation to make an informed judgment is so unreasonable as to fall outside the permissible bounds of sound discretion (e.g., a clear case is presented if the director has undertaken no preparation and is woefully uninformed), the director's judgment will not be sustained.

(c) lack of objectivity or independence

If a director has a familial, financial or business relationship with another person having a material interest in a transaction or other conduct involving the corporation, or if the director is dominated or controlled by another person having such a material interest, there is a potential for that conflicted interest or divided loyalty to affect the director's judgment. If the matter at issue involves a director's transactional interest, such as a "director's conflicting interest transaction" (see section 8.60(2)) in which a "related person" (see section 8.60(3)) is involved, it will be governed by section 8.61; otherwise, the lack of objectivity due to a relationship's influence on the director's judgment will be evaluated, in the context of the pending conduct challenge, under section 8.31. If the matter at issue involves lack of independence, the proof of domination or control and its influence on the director's judgment will typically entail different (and perhaps more convincing) evidence than what may be involved in a lack of objectivity case. The variables are manifold, and the facts must be sorted out and weighed on a case-by-case basis. If that other person is the director's spouse or employer, the concern that the director's judgment might be improperly influenced would be substantially greater than if that person is the spouse of the director's stepgrandchild or the director's partner in a vacation timeshare. When the party challenging the director's conduct can establish that the relationship or the domination or control in question could reasonably be expected to affect the director's judgment respecting the matter at issue in a manner adverse to the corporation, the director will then have the opportunity to establish that the action taken by him or her was reasonably believed to be in the best interests of the corporation. The reasonableness of the director's belief as to the corporation's best interests, in respect of the action taken, should be evaluated on the basis of not only the director's honest and good faith belief but also on considerations bearing on the fairness to the corporation of the transaction or other conduct involving the corporation that is at issue.

(d) improper financial benefit

Subchapter F of chapter 8 of the Model Act deals in detail with directors' transactional interests. Its coverage of those interests is exclusive and its safe harbor procedures for directors' conflicting interest transactions (as defined) providing shelter from legal challenges based on interest conflicts, when properly observed will establish a director's entitlement to any financial benefit gained from the transactional event. A director's conflicting interest transaction that is not protected by the fairness standard set forth in section 8.61(b)(3), pursuant to which the conflicted director may establish the transaction to have been fair to the corporation, would often involve receipt of a financial benefit to which the director was not entitled (i.e., the transaction was not "fair" to the corporation). Unauthorized use of corporate assets, such as aircraft or hotel suites, would also provide a basis for the proper challenge of a director's conduct. There can be other forms of improper financial benefit not involving a transaction with the corporation or use of its facilities, such as where a director profits from unauthorized use of proprietary information.

(e) financial benefit and material interest

A director is expected to observe an obligation of undivided loyalty to the corporation and, while the law will not concern itself with trifling deviations (de minimis non curat lex), there is no materiality threshold that applies to a financial benefit to which a director is not properly entitled. The Model Act observes this principle in several places (e.g., the exception to liability elimination prescribed in section 2.02(b)(4)(A) and the indemnification restriction in section 8.51(d)(2), as well as the liability standard in subsection (a)(2)(v)). In contrast, there is a materiality threshold for the interest of another in a transaction or conduct where a director's lack of objectivity or lack of independence has been asserted under subsection (a)(2)(iii). In the typical case, analysis of another's interest would first consider the materiality of the transaction or conduct at issue in most cases, any transaction or other action involving the attention of the board or one of its committees will cross the materiality threshold, but not always and would then consider the materiality of that person's interest therein. The possibility that another's interest in a transaction or conduct that is not material, or that an immaterial interest of another in a transaction or conduct, would adversely affect a director's judgment is sufficiently remote that it should not be made subject to judicial review.

(f) sustained inattention

The director's role involves two fundamental components: the decisionmaking function and the oversight function. In contrast with the decisionmaking function, which generally involves action taken at a point in time, the oversight function under section 8.01(b) involves ongoing monitoring of the corporation's business and affairs over a period of time. This involves the duty of ongoing attention, when actual knowledge of particular facts and circumstances arouse suspicions which indicate a need to make inquiry. As observed by the Supreme Court of New Jersey in Francis v. United Jersey Bank, 432 A.2d 814, 822 (Sup. Ct. 1981):

Directors are under a continuing obligation to keep informed about the activities of the corporation.... Directors may not shut their eyes to corporate misconduct and then claim that because they did not see the misconduct, they did not have a duty to look. The sentinel asleep at his post contributes nothing to the enterprise he is charged to protect.... Directorial management does not require a detailed inspection of day-to-day activities, but rather a general monitoring of corporate affairs and policies.

While the facts will be outcome determinative, deficient conduct involving a sustained failure to exercise oversight where found actionable-has typically been characterized by the courts in terms of abdication and continued neglect of a director's duty of attention, not a brief distraction or temporary interruption. However, embedded in the oversight function is the need to inquire when suspicions are aroused. This duty is not a component of ongoing oversight, and does not entail proactive vigilance, but arises when, and only when, particular facts and circumstances of material concern (e.g., evidence of embezzlement at a high level or the discovery of significant inventory shortages) suddenly surface.

(g) other breaches of a director's duties

Subsection (a)(2)(v) is, in part, a catchall provision that implements the intention to make section 8.31 a generally inclusive provision but, at the same time, to recognize the existence of other breaches of commonlaw duties that can give rise to liability for directors. A doctrine of corporate governance, well established in the case law, is that a director owes a duty of loyalty to the corporation; relatedly, the courts impose a duty of fair dealing on directors when their conduct affects the interests of the corporation. It has long been recognized that a director must first offer a "corporate opportunity" to the corporation before taking advantage of it. The term "corporate opportunity" can be readily stated in principle but, when determining the doctrine's application, the facts will often be outcome determinative. It has been defined in § 5.05(b)(1) of The American Law Institute's PRINCIPLES OF CORPORATE GOVERNANCE: ANALYSIS AND RECOMMENDATIONS (1994) to mean, insofar as a director is concerned:

Any opportunity to engage in a business activity of which a director ... becomes aware, either:

(A) In connection with the performance of functions as a director ... , or under circumstances that should reasonably lead the director ... to believe that the person offering the opportunity expects it to be offered to the corporation; or

(B) Through the use of corporate information or property, if the resulting opportunity is one that the director ... should reasonably be expected to believe would be of interest to the corporation....

The application of the corporate opportunity doctrine, in cases where it is operative, is typically conditioned on the corporation's financial ability to exploit the opportunity, although some courts have held it is up to the corporation to judge that ability and the opportunity should therefore always be offered. Relatedly, a formal offer is not essential, so long as the surrounding circumstances indicate an awareness of, and afford the corporation reasonable access to, the opportunity and there is indicated disinterest, manifested by inaction or due to financial inability. See Broz v. Cellular Information Systems, Inc., 673 A.2d 148 (Del. 1996). Failure to observe this obligation first to refer a corporate opportunity to the corporation results in a breach of a director's duty. A related duty obligates the director to refrain from gaining a pecuniary benefit by engaging in competition with the corporation that would cause reasonably foreseeable harm to it; unless authorized by the corporation, that conduct will constitute a breach of the director's duties.

(h) fairness

Pursuant to section 8.61(b)(3), an interested director (or the corporation, if it chooses) can gain protection for a director's conflicting interest transaction by establishing that it was fair to the corporation. (The concept of "fair" and "fairness," in this and various other contexts, can take into account both fair price and fair dealing on the part of the interested director. See the Official Comment to section 8.61.) Under case law, personal liability as well as transactional justification issues will be subject to a fairness standard of judicial review if the plaintiff makes out a credible claim of breach of the duty of loyalty or if the presumptions of the business judgment standard (e.g., an informed judgment) are overcome, with the burden of proof shifting from the plaintiff to the defendant. In this respect, the issue of fairness is relevant to both subsection (a) and subsection (b). Within the ambit of subsection (a)(2), a director can often respond to the challenge that his or her conduct was deficient by establishing that the transaction or conduct at issue was fair to the corporation. See Kahn v. Lynch Communications Systems, Inc. 669 A.2d 79 (Del. 1995). Cf. Cede & Co. v. Technicolor Inc., 634 A.2d 345 (Del. 1993) (when the business judgment rule is rebutted procedurally the burden shifts to the defendant directors to prove the "entire fairness" of the challenged transaction). It is to be noted, however, that fairness may not be relevant to the matter at issue (see, e.g., clause (iv) of subsection (a)(2)). If the director is successful in establishing fairness, where the issue of fairness is relevant, then it is unlikely that the complainant can establish legal liability or the appropriateness of an equitable remedy under subsection (b).

(i) director conduct

Subsection (a)(2) deals, throughout, with a director's action that is taken or not taken. To the extent that the director's conduct involves a breach of his or her duty of care or duty of attention within the context of collegial action by the board or one of its committees, proper performance of the relevant duty through the action taken by the director's colleagues can overcome the consequences of his or her deficient conduct. For example, where a director's conduct can be challenged under subsection (a)(2)(ii)(B) by reason of having been uninformed about the decision he or she did not read the merger materials distributed prior to the meeting, arrived late at the board meeting just in time for the vote but, nonetheless, voted for the merger solely because the others were in favor the favorable action by a quorum of properly informed directors would ordinarily protect the director against liability. When the director's conduct involves the duty of fair dealing within the context of action taken by the board or one of its committees, the wiser choice will usually be for the director not to participate in the collegial action. That is to say, where a director may have a conflicting interest or a divided loyalty, or even where there may be grounds for the issue to be raised, the better course to follow is usually for the director to disclose the conduct related facts and circumstances posing the possible compromise of his or her independence or objectivity, and then to withdraw from the meeting (or, in the alternative, to abstain from the deliberations and voting). The board members free of any possible taint can then take appropriate action as contemplated by section 8.30. (If a director's conflicting interest transaction is involved, it will be governed by subchapter F of this chapter and the directors' action will be taken pursuant to section 8.62 (or the board can refer the matter for shareholder's action respecting the transaction under section 8.63). In this connection, particular reference is made to the definition of "qualified director" in section 8.62(d).) If this course is followed, the director's conduct respecting the matter in question will in all likelihood be beyond challenge.

2. Section 8.31(b)

After satisfying the burden of establishing that the conduct of the director is challengeable under subsection (a), the plaintiff, in order to hold the director liable for money damages under clause (b)(1), has the further burden of establishing that: (i) harm (measurable in money damages) has been suffered by the corporation or its shareholders and (ii) the director's challenged conduct was the proximate cause of that harm. The concept of "proximate cause" is a term of art that is basic to tort law, and the cases providing content to the phrase represent well developed authority to which a court will undoubtedly refer. A useful approach for the concept's application, for purposes of subsection (b)(1), would be that the challenged conduct must have been a "substantial factor in producing the harm." See Francis v. United Jersey Bank, supra, 432 A.2d at 829. Similarly, the plaintiff has the burden of establishing money payment is due from the director pursuant to clause (b)(2). If, while challengeable, the conduct at issue caused no harm under clause (b)(1) or does not provide the basis for other legal remedy under clause (b)(2), but may provide the basis for an equitable remedy under clause (b)(3), the plaintiff must satisfy whatever further burden of persuasion may be indicated to establish that imposition of the remedy sought is appropriate in the circumstances. In Brophy v. Cities Service Co, 70 A.2d 5, 8 (Del. Ch. 1949), an employee was required to account for profits derived from the use of the corporation's confidential plans to reacquire its securities through open market purchases. Notwithstanding the fact that harm to the corporation had not been established, the Chancellor observed: "[p]ublic policy will not permit an employee occupying a position of trust and confidence toward his employer to abuse that relation to his own profit, regardless of whether his employer suffers a loss." Once actionable conduct that provides the basis for an equitable remedy under clause (b)(3) has been established, its appropriateness will often be clear and, if so, no further advocacy on the part of the plaintiff will be required.

Section 8.31(c)

While section 8.31 addresses director liability to the corporation or its shareholders under the Model Act and related case law dealing with interpretation by the courts of their states' business corporation acts or dealing with corporate governance concepts coming within the common law's ambit it does not limit any liabilities or foreclose any rights expressly provided for under other law. For example, directors can have liability (i) to shareholders (as well as former shareholders), who purchased their shares in a registered public offering, under § 11 of the Securities Act of 1933 and (ii) to the corporation, for short swing profit recovery, under § 16(b) of the Securities Exchange Act of 1934. Subsection (c) merely acknowledges that those rights are unaffected by section 8.31. And directors can have liability to persons other than the corporation and its shareholders, such as (i) employee benefit plan participants and beneficiaries (who may or may not be shareholders), if the directors are determined to be fiduciaries under the Employee Retirement Income Security Act of 1974, 29 U.S.C. pp. 1001–461 (1988 & Supp. IV 1992), (ii) government agencies for regulatory violations or (iii) individuals claiming damages for injury governed by tort law concepts (e.g., libel or slander).

As discussed above in the Official Comment to section 8.31(a), the concept of "fairness" is often relevant to whether a director will have liability if his or her conduct is challenged. Specifically, a director can successfully defend a financial interest in a transaction with the corporation by establishing that it was fair to the corporation. See section 8.61 and its Official Comment. More generally, the courts have resorted to a fairness standard of review where the business judgment rule has been inapplicable. See Weinberger v. UOP, Inc., 457 A.2d 701 (Del. 1983). In the usual case, the defendant seeking to justify challenged conduct, on the basis of fairness, has the burden of proving that it was fair to the corporation. Subsection (c) expressly disclaims any intention to shift the burden of proof otherwise applicable where the question of the fairness of a transaction or other challenged conduct is at issue.

Finally, the Model Act deals expressly with certain aspects of director liability in other sections. For example, a director has a duty to observe the limitations on shareholder distributions set forth in section 6.40 and, if a director votes for or assents to a distribution in violation thereof, the director has personal liability as provided in section 8.33. And section 8.61 channels all directors' transactional interests into the exclusive treatment for directors' conflicting interest transactions that is therein provided, rejecting an award of damages or other sanctions for interests that do not come within its conceptual framework. Subsection (c) expressly acknowledges that the liability standard provided in section 8.33 and the exclusive treatment for directors' transactional interests provided in section 8.61 are unaffected by section 8.31.

§ 8.33 Directors' Liability for Unlawful Distributions

(a) A director who votes for or assents to a distribution in excess of what may be authorized and made pursuant to section 6.40(a) is personally liable to the corporation for the amount of the distribution that exceeds what could have been distributed without violating section 6.40(a) if the party asserting liability establishes that when taking the action the director did not comply with section 8.30.

(b) A director held liable under subsection (a) for an unlawful distribution is entitled to:

(1) contribution from every other director who could be held liable under subsection (a) for the unlawful distribution; and

(2) recoupment from each shareholder of the prorata portion of the amount of the unlawful distribution the shareholder accepted, knowing the distribution was made in violation of section 6.40(a).

(c) A proceeding to enforce:

(1) the liability of a director under subsection (a) is barred unless it is commenced within two years after the date on which the effect of the distribution was measured under section 6.40(e) or (g) or as of which the violation of section 6.40(a) occurred as the consequence of disregard of a restriction in the articles of incorporation; or

(2) contribution or recoupment under subsection (b) is barred unless it is commenced within one year after the liability of the claimant has been finally adjudicated under subsection (a).

OFFICIAL COMMENT

Although the revisions to the financial provisions of the Model Act have simplified and rationalized the rules for determining the validity of distributions (see section 6.40), the possibility remains that a distribution may be made in violation of these rules. Section 8.33 provides that if it is established a director failed to meet the relevant standards of conduct of section 8.30 (e.g., good faith, reasonable care, warranted reliance) and voted for or assented to an unlawful distribution, the director is personally liable for the portion of the distribution that exceeds the maximum amount that could have been lawfully distributed.

A director whose conduct, in voting for or assenting to a distribution, is challenged under section 8.33 will have all defenses which would ordinarily be available, including the common law business judgment rule. Relevant thereto, however, there would be common issues posed by (i) a defense geared to compliance with section 8.30 (e.g., reasonable care under subsection (b) and warranted reliance under subsections (d) and (e)) and, in the alternative, (ii) a defense relying on the business judgment rule's shield (e.g., informed judgment). Thus, section 8.30 compliance will in most cases make resort to the business judgment rule's shield unnecessary.

A director who is compelled to restore the amount of an unlawful distribution to the corporation is entitled to contribution from every other director who could have been held liable for the unlawful distribution. The director may also recover the prorata portion of the amount of the unlawful distribution from any shareholder who accepted the distribution knowing that its payment was in violation of the statute. A shareholder (other than a director) who receives a payment not knowing of its invalidity is not subject to recoupment under subsection (b)(2). Although no attempt has been made in the Model Act to work out in detail the relationship between the right of recoupment from shareholders and the right of contribution from directors, it is expected that a court will equitably apportion the obligations and benefits arising from the application of the principles set forth in this section.

Section 8.33(c) limits the time within which a proceeding may be commenced against a director for an unlawful distribution to two years after the date on which the effect of the distribution was measured or breach of a restriction in the articles of incorporation occurred. Although a statute of limitations provision is a novel concept for the Model Act, a substantial minority of jurisdictions have provisions limiting the time within which an action may be brought on account of an unlawful distribution. Section 8.33(c) also limits the time within which a proceeding for contribution or recoupment may be made to one year after the date on which the liability of the claimant has been finally determined and adjudicated. This one year period specified in clause (2) may end within or extend beyond the two year period specified in clause (1).

SUBCHAPTER D. OFFICERS

§ 8.40 Officers

(a) A corporation has the offices described in its bylaws or designated by the board of directors in accordance with the bylaws.

(b) The board of directors may elect individuals to fill one or more offices of the corporation. An officer may appoint one or more officers if authorized by the bylaws or the board of directors.

(c) The bylaws or the board of directors shall assign to one of the officers responsibility for preparing minutes of the directors' and shareholders' meetings and for maintaining and authenticating the records of the corporation required to be kept under sections 16.01(a) and 16.01(e).

(d) The same individual may simultaneously hold more than one office in a corporation.

OFFICIAL COMMENT

Section 8.40 permits every corporation to designate the offices it wants. The designation may be made in the bylaws or by the board of directors consistently with the bylaws. This is a departure from earlier versions of the Model Act and most state corporation acts, which require certain offices, usually the president, the secretary and the treasurer, and generally authorize the corporation to designate additional offices. Experience has shown, however, that little purpose is served by a statutory requirement that there be certain offices, and statutory requirements may sometimes create problems of apparent authority or confusion with nonstatutory offices the corporation desires to create.

Section 8.40(b) indicates that, while it is generally the responsibility of the board of directors to elect officers, an officer may appoint one or more officers if authorized by the bylaws or the board of directors.

The board of directors, as well as duly authorized officers, employees or agents, may also appoint other agents for the corporation. Nothing in this section is intended to limit the authority of a board of directors to organize its own internal affairs, including designating officers of the board.

The bylaws or the board of directors must assign to an officer the responsibility to prepare minutes and authenticate the corporate records referred to in sections 16.01(a) and (e); the person performing this function is referred to as the "secretary" of the corporation throughout the Model Act. See section 1.40. Under the Act, a corporation may have this and all other corporate functions performed by a single individual.

The person who is designated by the bylaws or the board to have responsibility for preparing minutes of meetings and maintaining the corporate records has authority to bind the corporation by that officer's authentication under this section. This assignment of authority, traditionally vested in the corporate "secretary," allows third persons to rely on authenticated records without inquiry as to their truth or accuracy.

§ 8.41 Duties of Officers

Each officer has the authority and shall perform the duties set forth in the bylaws or, to the extent consistent with the bylaws, the duties prescribed by the board of directors or by direction of an officer authorized by the board of directors to prescribe the duties of other officers.

§ 8.42 Standards of Conduct for Officers

(a) An officer, when performing in such capacity, shall act:

(1) in good faith;

(2) with the care that a person in a like position would reasonably exercise under similar circumstances; and

(3) in a manner the officer reasonably believes to be in the best interests of the corporation.

(b) In discharging those duties an officer, who does not have knowledge that makes reliance unwarranted, is entitled to rely on:

(1) the performance of properly delegated responsibilities by one or more employees of the corporation whom the officer reasonably believes to be reliable and competent in performing the responsibilities delegated; or

(2) information, opinions, reports or statements, including financial statements and other financial data, prepared or presented by one or more employees of the corporation whom the officer reasonably believes to be reliable and competent in the matters presented or by legal counsel, public accountants, or other persons retained by the corporation as to matters involving skills or exper-

tise the officer reasonably believes are matters (i) within the particular person's professional or expert competence or (ii) as to which the particular person merits confidence.

(c) An officer shall not be liable to the corporation or its shareholders for any decision to take or not to take action, or any failure to take any action, as an officer, if the duties of the office are performed in compliance with this section. Whether an officer who does not comply with this section shall have liability will depend in such instance on applicable law, including those principles of § 8.31 that have relevance.

OFFICIAL COMMENT

This section provides that an officer, when performing in such officer's official capacity, shall meet standards of conduct generally similar to those expected of directors under section 8.30. Consistent with the principles of agency, which generally govern the conduct of corporate employees, an officer is expected to observe the duties of obedience and loyalty and to act with the care that a person in a like position would reasonably exercise under similar circumstances. See RESTATEMENT (SECOND) OF AGENCY § 379(1) (1957) ("Unless otherwise agreed, a paid agent is subject to a duty to the principal to act with standard care and with the skill which is standard in the locality for the kind of work which he is employed to perform and, in addition, to exercise any special skill that he has").

An officer's ability to rely on others may be more limited, depending upon the circumstances of the particular case, than the measure and scope of reliance permitted a director under section 8.30, in view of the greater obligation the officer may have to be familiar with the affairs of the corporation. The proper delegation of responsibilities by an officer, separate and apart from the exercise of judgment as to the delegatee's reliability and competence, is concerned with the procedure employed. This will involve, in the usual case, sufficient communication to the end that the delegatee understands the scope of the assignment and, in turn, manifests to the officer a willingness and commitment to undertake its performance. The definition of "employee" in section 1.40(8) includes an officer; accordingly, section 8.42 contemplates the delegation of responsibilities to other officers as well as to nonofficer employees.

It is made clear, in subsection (c), that performance meeting the section's standards of conduct will eliminate an officer's exposure to any liability to the corporation or its shareholders. In contrast, an officer failing to meet its standards will not automatically face liability. Deficient performance of duties by an officer, depending upon the facts and circumstances, will normally be dealt with through intracorporate disciplinary procedures, such as reprimand, compensation adjustment, delayed promotion, demotion or discharge. Such a procedure would be subject to any employment agreement between the corporation and the officer. See section 8.43.

In some cases, failure to observe relevant standards of conduct can give rise to an officer's liability to the corporation or its shareholders. A court review of challenged conduct will involve an evaluation of the particular facts and circumstances in light of applicable law. In this connection, subsection (c) recognizes that relevant principles of section 8.31, such as duties to deal fairly with the corporation and its shareholders and the challenger's burden of establishing proximately caused harm, should be taken into account. In addition, the business judgement rule will normally apply to decisions within an officer's discretionary authority. Liability to others can also arise from an officer's own acts or omissions (e.g., violations of law or tort claims) and, in some cases, an officer with supervisory responsibilities can have risk exposure in connection with the acts or omissions of others.

The Official Comment to section 8.30 supplements this Official Comment to the extent that it can be appropriately viewed as generally applicable to officers as well as to directors.

§ 8.43 Resignation and Removal of Officers

(a) An officer may resign at any time by delivering notice to the corporation. A resignation is effective when the notice is delivered unless the notice specifies a later effective time. If a resignation is made effective at a later time and the board or the appointing officer accepts the future effective time, the board or the appointing officer may fill the pending vacancy before the effective time if the board or the appointing officer provides that the successor does not take office until the effective time.

(b) An officer may be removed at any time with or without cause by: (i) the board of directors; (ii) the officer who appointed such officer, unless the bylaws or the board of directors provide otherwise; or (iii) any other officer if authorized by the bylaws or the board of directors.

(c) In this section, "appointing officer" means the officer (including any successor to that officer) who appointed the officer resigning or being removed.

OFFICIAL COMMENT

Section 8.43(a) is consistent with current practice and declaratory of current law. It recognizes: that corporate officers may resign; that, with the consent of the board of directors or the appointing officer, they may resign effective at a later date; and that a future vacancy may be filled to become effective as of the effective date of the resignation.

In part because of the unlimited power of removal confirmed by section 8.43(b), a board of directors may enter into an employment agreement with the holder of an office that extends beyond the term of the board of directors. This type of contract is binding on the corporation even if the articles of incorporation or bylaws provide that officers are elected for a term shorter than the period of the employment contract. If a later board of directors refuses to reelect that person as an officer, the person has the right to sue for damages but not for specific performance of the contract.

Section 8.43(b) is consistent with current practice and declaratory of current law. It recognizes that the officers of the corporation are subject to removal by the board of directors and, in certain instances, by other officers. It provides the corporation with the flexibility to determine when, if ever, an officer will be permitted to remove another officer. To the extent that the corporation wishes to permit an officer, other than the appointing officer, to remove another officer, the bylaws or a board resolution should set forth clearly the persons having removal authority.

A person may be removed from office irrespective of contract rights or the presence or absence of "cause" in a legal sense. Section 8.44 provides that removal from office of a holder who has contract rights is without prejudice to whatever rights the former officer may assert in a suit for damages for breach of contract.

§ 8.44 Contract Rights of Officers

(a) The appointment of an officer does not itself create contract rights.

(b) An officer's removal does not affect the officer's contract rights, if any, with the corporation. An officer's resignation does not affect the corporation's contract rights, if any, with the officer.

SUBCHAPTER E. INDEMNIFICATION

§ 8.50 Subchapter Definitions

In this subchapter:

(1) "Corporation" includes any domestic or foreign predecessor entity of a corporation in a merger.

(2) "Director" or "officer" means an individual who is or was a director or officer, respectively, of a corporation or who, while a director or officer of the corporation, is or was serving at the corporation's request as a director, officer, partner, trustee, employee, or agent of another domestic or foreign corporation, partnership, joint venture, trust, employee benefit plan, or other entity. A director or officer is considered to be serving an employee benefit plan at the corporation's request if his duties to the corporation also impose duties on, or otherwise involve services by, him to the plan or to participants in or beneficiaries of the plan. "Director" or "officer" includes, unless the context requires otherwise, the estate or personal representative of a director or officer.

(3) "Disinterested director" means a director who, at the time of a vote referred to in section 8.53(c) or a vote or selection referred to in section 8.55(b) or (c), is not (i) a party to the proceeding, or (ii) an individual having a familial, financial, professional, or employment relationship with the director whose indemnification or advance for expenses is the subject of the decision being made, which relationship would, in the circumstances, reasonably be expected to exert an influence on the director's judgment when voting on the decision being made.

(4) "Expenses" includes counsel fees.

(5) "Liability" means the obligation to pay a judgment, settlement, penalty, fine (including an excise tax assessed with respect to an employee benefit plan), or reasonable expenses incurred with respect to a proceeding.

(6) "Official capacity" means: (i) when used with respect to a director, the office of director in a corporation; and (ii) when used with respect to an officer, as contemplated in section 8.56, the office in a corporation held by the officer. "Official capacity" does not include service for any other domestic or foreign corporation or any partnership, joint venture, trust, employee benefit plan, or other entity.

(7) "Party" means an individual who was, is, or is threatened to be made, a defendant or respondent in a proceeding.

(8) "Proceeding" means any threatened, pending, or completed action, suit, or proceeding, whether civil, criminal, administrative, arbitrative, or investigative and whether formal or informal.

§ 8.51 Permissible Indemnification

(a) Except as otherwise provided in this section, a corporation may indemnify an individual who is a party to a proceeding because he is a director against liability incurred in the proceeding if:

(1)(i) he conducted himself in good faith; and

(ii) he reasonably believed:

(A) in the case of conduct in his official capacity, that his conduct was in the best interests of the corporation; and

(B) in all other cases, that his conduct was at least not opposed to the best interests of the corporation; and

(iii) in the case of any criminal proceeding, he had no reasonable cause to believe his conduct was unlawful; or

(2) he engaged in conduct for which broader indemnification has been made permissible or obligatory under a provision of the articles of incorporation (as authorized by section 2.02(b)(5)).

(b) A director's conduct with respect to an employee benefit plan for a purpose he reasonably believed to be in the interests of the participants in, and the beneficiaries of, the plan is conduct that satisfies the requirement of subsection (a)(1)(ii)(B).

(c) The termination of a proceeding by judgment, order, settlement, or conviction, or upon a plea of nolo contendere or its equivalent, is not, of itself, determinative that the director did not meet the relevant standard of conduct described in this section.

(d) Unless ordered by a court under section 8.54(a)(3), a corporation may not indemnify a director:

(1) in connection with a proceeding by or in the right of the corporation, except for reasonable expenses incurred in connection with the proceeding if it is determined that the director has met the relevant standard of conduct under subsection (a); or

(2) in connection with any proceeding with respect to conduct for which he was adjudged liable on the basis that he received a financial benefit to which he was not entitled, whether or not involving action in his official capacity.

OFFICIAL COMMENT

1. Section 8.51(a)

Subsection 8.51(a) permits, but does not require, a corporation to indemnify directors if the standards of subsection (a)(1) or of a provision of the articles referred to in subsection (a)(2) are met. This authorization is subject to any limitations set forth in the articles of incorporation pursuant to section 8.58(c). Absent any such limitation, the standards for indemnification of directors contained in this subsection define the outer limits for which discretionary indemnification is permitted under the Model Act. Conduct which does not meet one of these standards is not eligible for permissible indemnification under the Model Act, although court-ordered indemnification may be available under section 8.54(a)(3). Conduct that falls within these outer limits does not automatically entitle directors to indemnification, although a corporation may obligate itself to indemnify directors to the maximum extent permitted by applicable law. See section 8.58(a). No such obligation, however, may exceed these outer limits. Absent such an obligatory provision, section 8.52 defines much narrower circumstances in which directors are entitled as a matter of right to indemnification.

Some state statutes provide separate, but usually similarly worded, standards for indemnification in third-party suits and indemnification in suits brought by or in the right of the corporation. Section 8.51 makes clear that the outer limits of conduct for which indemnification is permitted should not be dependent on the type of proceeding in which the claim arises. To prevent circularity in recovery, however, section 8.51(d)(1) limits indemnification in connection with suits brought by or in the right of the corporation to expenses incurred and excludes amounts paid to settle such suits or to satisfy judgments. In addition, to discourage wrongdoing, section 8.51(d)(2) bars indemnification where the director has been adjudged to have received a financial benefit to which he is not entitled. Nevertheless, a court may order certain relief from these limitations under section 8.54(a)(3).

The standards of conduct described in subsections (a)(1)(i) and (a)(1)(ii)(A) that must be met in order to permit the corporation to indemnify a director are closely related, but not identical, to the standards of conduct imposed on directors by section 8.30. Section 8.30(a) requires a director acting in his official capacity to discharge his duties in good faith, with due care (i.e., that which an ordinarily prudent person in a like position would exercise under similar circumstances) and in a manner he reasonably believes to be in the corporation's best interests. Unless authorized by a charter provision adopted pursuant to subsection (a)(2), it would be difficult to justify indemnifying a director who has not met any of these standards. It would not, however, make sense to require a director to meet all these standards in order to be indemnified because a director who meets all three of these standards would have no liability, at least to the corporation, under the terms of section 8.30(d).

Section 8.51(a) adopts a middle ground by authorizing discretionary indemnification in the case of a failure to meet the due care standard of section 8.30(a) because public policy would not be well served by an absolute bar. A director's potential liability for conduct which does not on each and every occasion satisfy the due care requirement of section 8.30(a), or which with the benefit of hindsight could be so viewed, would in all likelihood deter qualified individuals from serving as directors and inhibit some who serve from taking risks. Permitting indemnification against such liability tends to counter these undesirable consequences. Accordingly, section 8.51(a) authorizes indemnification at the corporation's option even though section 8.30's due care requirement is not met, but only if the director satisfies the "good faith" and "corporation's best interests" standards. This reflects a judgment that, balancing public policy considerations, the corporation may indemnify a director who does not satisfy the due care test but not one who fails either of the other two standards.

As in the case of section 8.30, where the concept of good faith is also used, no attempt is made in section 8.51 to provide a definition. The concept involves a subjective test, which would permit indemnification for "a mistake of judgment," in the words of the Official Comment to section 8.30, even though made unwisely or negligently by objective standards. Section 8.51 also requires, as does section 8.30, a "reasonable" belief by a director acting in his official capacity that his conduct was in the corporation's best interests. It then adds a provision, not found in section 8.30, relating to criminal proceedings that requires the director to have had no "reasonable cause" to believe that his conduct was unlawful. These both involve objective standards applicable to the director's belief concerning the effect of his conduct. Conduct includes both acts and omissions.

Section 8.51(a)(1)(ii)(B) requires, if a director is not acting in his official capacity, that his action be "at least not opposed to" the corporation's best interests. This standard is applicable to the director when serving another entity at the request of the corporation or when sued simply because of his status as a director. The words "at least" qualify "not opposed to" in order to make it clear that this standard is an outer limit for conduct other than in an official capacity. While this subsection is directed at the interests of the indemnifying (i.e., requesting) corporation, a director serving another entity by request remains subject to the provisions of the law governing his service to that entity, including provisions dealing with conflicts of interest. Compare sections 8.60–8.63. Should indemnification from the requesting corporation be sought by a director for acts done while serving another entity, which acts involved breach of the duty of loyalty owed to that entity, nothing in section 8.51(a)(1)(ii)(B) would preclude the requesting corporation from considering, in assessing its own best interests, whether the fact that its director had engaged in a violation of the duty owed to the other entity was in fact "opposed to" the interests of the indemnifying corporation. Receipt of an improper financial benefit from a subsidiary would normally be opposed to the best interests of the parent.

Section 8.51 also permits indemnification in connection with a proceeding involving an alleged failure to satisfy legal standards other than the standards of conduct in section 8.30, e.g., violations of federal securities laws and environmental laws. It should be noted, however, that the Securities and Exchange Commission takes the position that indemnification against liabilities under the Securities Act of 1933 is against public policy and requires that, as a condition for accelerating the effectiveness of a registration statement under the Act, the issuer must undertake that, unless in the opinion of its counsel the matter has been settled by controlling precedent, it will submit to a court the question whether such indemnification is against public policy as expressed in the Act. 17 C.F.R. § 229.512(h) (1993).

In addition to indemnification under section 8.51(a)(1), section 8.51(a)(2) permits indemnification under the standard of conduct set forth in a charter provision adopted pursuant to section 2.02(b)(5). Based on such a charter provision, section 8.51(a)(2) permits indemnification in connection with claims by third parties and, through section 8.56, applies to officers as well as directors. (This goes beyond the scope of a charter provision adopted pursuant to section 2.02(b)(4), which can only limit liability of directors against claims by the corporation or its shareholders.) Section 8.51(a)(2) is subject to the prohibition of subsection (d)(1) against indemnification of settlements and judgments in derivative suits. It is also subject to the prohibition of subsection (d)(2) against indemnification for receipt of an improper financial benefit; however, this prohibition is already subsumed in the exception contained in section 2.02(b)(5)(A).

Notice of any indemnification under this section (or sections 8.52, 8.53, or 8.54) in a derivative proceeding must be given to the shareholders pursuant to section 16.21(a).

2. Section 8.51(b)

As discussed in the Official Comment to section 8.50(2), ERISA requires that a "fiduciary" (as defined in ERISA) discharge his duties "solely in the interest" of the participants in and beneficiaries of an employee benefit plan. Section 8.51(b) makes clear that a director who is serving as a trustee or fiduciary for an employee benefit plan under ERISA meets the standard for indemnification under section 8.51(a) if he reasonably believes his conduct was in the best interests of the participants in and beneficiaries of the plan.

This standard is arguably an exception to the more general standard that conduct not in an official corporate capacity is indemnifiable if it is "at least not opposed to" the best interests of the corporation. However, a corporation that causes a director to undertake fiduciary duties in connection with an employee benefit plan should expect the director to act in the best interests of the plan's beneficiaries or participants. Thus, subsection (b) establishes and provides a standard for indemnification that is consistent with the statutory policies embodied in ERISA. See Official Comment to section 8.50(2).

3. Section 8.51(c)

The purpose of section 8.51(c) is to reject the argument that indemnification is automatically improper whenever a proceeding has been concluded on a basis that does not exonerate the director claiming indemnification. Even though a final judgment or conviction is not automatically determinative of the issue of whether the minimum standard of conduct was met, any judicial determination of substantive liability would in most instances be entitled to considerable weight. By the same token, it is clear that the termination of a proceeding by settlement or plea of nolo contendere should not of itself create a presumption either that conduct met or did not meet the relevant standard of subsection (a) since a settlement or nolo plea may be agreed to for many reasons unrelated to the merits of the claim. On the other hand, a final determination of non-liability (including one based on a liability-limitation provision adopted under section 2.02(b)(4)) or an acquittal in a criminal case automatically entitles the director to indemnification of expenses under section 8.52.

Section 8.51(c) applies to the indemnification of expenses in derivative proceedings (as well as to indemnification in third-party suits). The most likely application of this subsection in connection with a derivative proceeding will be to a settlement since a judgment or order would normally result in liability to the corporation and thereby preclude indemnification for expenses under section 8.51(d)(1), unless ordered by a court under section 8.54(a)(3). In the rare event that a judgment or order entered against the director did not include a determination of liability to the corporation, the entry of the judgment or order would not be determinative that the director failed to meet the relevant standard of conduct.

4. Section 8.51(d)

This subsection makes clear that indemnification is not permissible under section 8.51 in two situations: (i) a proceeding brought by or in the right of a corporation that results in a settlement or a judgment against the director and (ii) a proceeding that results in a judgment that the director received an improper financial benefit as a result of his conduct.

Permitting indemnification of settlements and judgments in derivative proceedings would give rise to a circularity in which the corporation receiving payment of damages by the director in the settlement or judgment (less attorneys' fees) would then immediately return the same amount to the director (including attorneys' fees) as indemnification. Thus, the corporation would be in a poorer economic position than if there had been no proceeding. This situation is most egregious in the case of a judgment against the director. Even in the case of a settlement, however, prohibiting indemnification is not unfair. Under the revised procedures of section 7.44, upon motion by the corporation, the court must dismiss any derivative proceeding which independent directors (or a court-appointed panel) determine in good faith, after a reasonable inquiry, is not in the best interests of the corporation. Furthermore, under section 2.02(b)(4), the directors have the opportunity to propose to shareholders adoption of a provision limiting the liability of directors in derivative proceedings. In view of these considerations, it is unlikely that directors will be unnecessarily exposed to meritless actions. In addition, if directors were to be indemnified for amounts paid in settlement, the dismissal procedures in section 7.44 might not be fully employed since it could be less expensive for the corporation to indemnify the directors immediately for the amount of the claimed damages rather than bear the expense of the inquiry required by section 7.44. The result could increase the filing of meritless derivative proceedings in order to generate small but immediately paid attorneys' fees. Despite the prohibition on indemnification of a settlement or a judgment in a derivative proceeding, subsection (d)(1) permits indemnification of the related reasonable expenses incurred in the proceeding so long as the director meets the relevant standard of conduct set forth in section 8.51(a). In addition, indemnification of derivative expenses and amounts paid in settlement where the relevant standard was not met may be ordered by a court under section 8.54(a)(3).

If a corporation indemnifies a director in connection with a derivative proceeding, the corporation must report that fact to the shareholders prior to their next meeting. See section 16.21(a).

Indemnification under section 8.51 is also prohibited if there has been an adjudication that a director received an improper financial benefit (i.e., a benefit to which he is not entitled), even if, for example, he acted in a manner not opposed to the best interests of the corporation. For example, improper use of inside information for financial benefit should not be an action for which the corporation may elect to provide indemnification, even if the corporation was not thereby harmed. Given the express language of section 2.02(b)(5) establishing the outer limit of an indemnification provision contained in the articles of incorporation, a director found to have received an improper financial benefit would not be permitted indemnification under subsection (a)(2). Although it is unlikely that a director found to have received an improper financial benefit could meet the standard in subsection (a)(1)(ii)(B); this limitation is made explicit in section 8.51(d)(2). Section 8.54(a)(3) permits a director found liable in a proceeding referred to in subsection (d)(2) to petition a court for a judicial determination of entitlement to indemnification for reasonable expenses. The language of section 8.51(d)(2) is based on section 2.02(b)(4)(A) and, thus, the same standards should be used in interpreting the application of both provisions. Although a settlement may create an obligation to pay money, it should not be construed for purposes of this subchapter as an adjudication of liability.

§ 8.52 Mandatory Indemnification

A corporation shall indemnify a director who was wholly successful, on the merits or otherwise, in the defense of any proceeding to which he was a party because he was a director of the corporation against reasonable expenses incurred by him in connection with the proceeding.

OFFICIAL COMMENT

Section 8.51 determines whether indemnification may be made voluntarily by a corporation if it elects to do so. Section 8.52 determines whether a corporation must indemnify a director for his expenses; in other words, section 8.52 creates a statutory right of indemnification in favor of the director who meets the requirements of that section. Enforcement of this right by judicial proceeding is specifically contemplated by section 8.54(a)(1). Section 8.54(b) gives the director a statutory right to recover expenses incurred by him in enforcing his statutory right to indemnification under section 8.52.

The basic standard for mandatory indemnification is that the director has been "wholly successful, on the merits or otherwise," in the defense of the proceeding. The word "wholly" is added to avoid the argument accepted in Merritt–Chapman & Scott Corp. v. Wolfson, 321 A.2d 138 (Del.1974), that a defendant may be entitled to partial mandatory indemnification if, by plea bargaining or otherwise, he was able to obtain the dismissal of some but not all counts of an indictment. A defendant is "wholly successful" only if the entire proceeding is disposed of on a basis which does not involve a finding of liability. A director who is precluded from mandatory indemnification by this requirement may still be entitled to permissible indemnification under section 8.51(a) or court ordered indemnification under section 8.54(a)(3).

The language in earlier versions of the Model Act and in many other state statutes that the basis of success may be "on the merits or otherwise" is retained. While this standard may result in an occasional defendant becoming entitled to indemnification because of procedural defenses not related to the merits, e.g., the statute of limitations or disqualification of the plaintiff, it is unreasonable to require a defendant with a valid procedural defense to undergo a possibly prolonged and expensive trial on the merits in order to establish eligibility for mandatory indemnification.

If the corporation indemnifies or advances expenses to a director in connection with a derivative proceeding, the corporation must report that fact to the shareholders prior to their next meeting. See section 16.21(a).

§ 8.53 Advance for Expenses

(a) A corporation may, before final disposition of a proceeding, advance funds to pay for or reimburse the reasonable expenses incurred by a director who is a party to a proceeding because he is a director if he delivers to the corporation:

(1) a written affirmation of his good faith belief that he has met the relevant standard of conduct described in section 8.51 or that the proceeding involves conduct for which liability has been eliminated under a provision of the articles of incorporation as authorized by section 2.02(b)(4); and

(2) his written undertaking to repay any funds advanced if he is not entitled to mandatory indemnification under section 8.52 and it is ultimately determined under section 8.54 or section 8.55 that he has not met the relevant standard of conduct described in section 8.51.

(b) The undertaking required by subsection (a)(2) must be an unlimited general obligation of the director but need not be secured and may be accepted without reference to the financial ability of the director to make repayment.

(c) Authorizations under this section shall be made:

(1) by the board of directors:

(i) if there are two or more disinterested directors, by a majority vote of all the disinterested directors (a majority of whom shall for such purpose constitute a quorum) or by a majority of the members of a committee of two or more disinterested directors appointed by such a vote; or

(ii) if there are fewer than two disinterested directors, by the vote necessary for action by the board in accordance with section 8.24(c), in which authorization directors who do not qualify as disinterested directors may participate; or

(2) by the shareholders, but shares owned by or voted under the control of a director who at the time does not qualify as a disinterested director may not be voted on the authorization.

§ 8.54 Court–Ordered Indemnification and Advance for Expenses

(a) A director who is a party to a proceeding because he is a director may apply for indemnification or an advance for expenses to the court conducting the proceeding or to another court of competent jurisdiction. After receipt of an application and after giving any notice it considers necessary, the court shall:

(1) order indemnification if the court determines that the director is entitled to mandatory indemnification under section 8.52;

(2) order indemnification or advance for expenses if the court determines that the director is entitled to indemnification or advance for expenses pursuant to a provision authorized by section 8.58(a); or

(3) order indemnification or advance for expenses if the court determines, in view of all the relevant circumstances, that it is fair and reasonable

(i) to indemnify the director, or

(ii) to advance expenses to the director, even if he has not met the relevant standard of conduct set forth in section 8.51(a), failed to comply with section 8.53 or was adjudged liable in a proceeding referred to in subsection 8.51(d)(1) or (d)(2), but if he was adjudged so liable his indemnification shall be limited to reasonable expenses incurred in connection with the proceeding.

(b) If the court determines that the director is entitled to indemnification under subsection (a)(1) or to indemnification or advance for expenses under subsection (a)(2), it shall also order the corporation to pay the director's reasonable expenses incurred in connection with obtaining court-ordered indemnification or advance for expenses. If the court determines that the director is entitled to indemnification or advance for expenses under subsection (a)(3), it may also order the corporation to pay the director's reasonable expenses to obtain court-ordered indemnification or advance for expenses.

§ 8.55 Determination and Authorization of Indemnification

(a) A corporation may not indemnify a director under section 8.51 unless authorized for a specific proceeding after a determination has been made that indemnification of the director is permissible because he has met the relevant standard of conduct set forth in section 8.51.

(b) The determination shall be made:

(1) if there are two or more disinterested directors, by the board of directors by a majority vote of all the disinterested directors (a majority of whom shall for such purpose constitute a quorum), or by a majority of the members of a committee of two or more disinterested directors appointed by such a vote;

(2) by special legal counsel:

(i) selected in the manner prescribed in subdivision (1); or

(ii) if there are fewer than two disinterested directors, selected by the board of directors (in which selection directors who do not qualify as disinterested directors may participate); or

(3) by the shareholders, but shares owned by or voted under the control of a director who at the time does not qualify as a disinterested director may not be voted on the determination.

(c) Authorization of indemnification shall be made in the same manner as the determination that indemnification is permissible, except that if there are fewer than two disinterested directors or if the determination is made by special legal counsel, authorization of indemnification shall be made by those entitled under subsection (b)(2)(ii) to select special legal counsel.

§ 8.56 Officers

(a) A corporation may indemnify and advance expenses under this subchapter to an officer of the corporation who is a party to a proceeding because he is an officer of the corporation

(1) to the same extent as a director; and

(2) if he is an officer but not a director, to such further extent as may be provided by the articles of incorporation, the bylaws, a resolution of the board of directors, or contract except for (A) liability in connection with a proceeding by or in the right of the corporation other than for reasonable expenses incurred in connection with the proceeding or (B) liability arising out of conduct that constitutes (i) receipt by him of a financial benefit to which he is not entitled, (ii) an intentional infliction of harm on the corporation or the shareholders, or (iii) an intentional violation of criminal law.

(b) The provisions of subsection (a)(2) shall apply to an officer who is also a director if the basis on which he is made a party to the proceeding is an act or omission solely as an officer.

(c) An officer of a corporation who is not a director is entitled to mandatory indemnification under section 8.52, and may apply to a court under section 8.54 for indemnification or an advance for expenses, in each case to the same extent to which a director may be entitled to indemnification or advance for expenses under those provisions.

§ 8.57 Insurance

A corporation may purchase and maintain insurance on behalf of an individual who is a director or officer of the corporation, or who, while a director or officer of the corporation, serves at the corporation's request as a director, officer, partner, trustee, employee, or agent of another domestic or foreign corporation, partnership, joint venture, trust, employee benefit plan, or other entity, against liability asserted against or incurred by him in that capacity or arising from his status as a director or officer, whether or not the corporation would have power to indemnify or advance expenses to him against the same liability under this subchapter.

§ 8.58 Variation by Corporate Action; Application of Subchapter

(a) A corporation may, by a provision in its articles of incorporation or bylaws or in a resolution adopted or a contract approved by its board of directors or shareholders, obligate itself in advance of the act or omission giving rise to a proceeding to provide indemnification in accordance with section 8.51 or advance funds to pay for or reimburse expenses in accordance with section 8.53. Any such obligatory provision shall be deemed to satisfy the requirements for authorization referred to in section 8.53(c) and in section 8.55(c). Any such provision that obligates the corporation to provide indemnification to the fullest extent permitted by law shall be deemed to obligate the corporation to advance funds to pay for or reimburse expenses in accordance with section 8.53 to the fullest extent permitted by law, unless the provision specifically provides otherwise.

(b) Any provision pursuant to subsection (a) shall not obligate the corporation to indemnify or advance expenses to a director of a predecessor of the corporation, pertaining to conduct with respect to the predecessor, unless otherwise specifically provided. Any provision for indemnification or advance for expenses in the articles of incorporation, bylaws, or a resolution of the board of directors or shareholders of a predecessor of the corporation in a merger or in a contract to which the predecessor is a party, existing at the time the merger takes effect, shall be governed by section 11.06(a)(3).

(c) A corporation may, by a provision in its articles of incorporation, limit any of the rights to indemnification or advance for expenses created by or pursuant to this subchapter.

(d) This subchapter does not limit a corporation's power to pay or reimburse expenses incurred by a director or an officer in connection with his appearance as a witness in a proceeding at a time when he is not a party.

(e) This subchapter does not limit a corporation's power to indemnify, advance expenses to or provide or maintain insurance on behalf of an employee or agent.

OFFICIAL COMMENT

Section 8.58(a) authorizes a corporation to make obligatory the permissive provisions of subchapter E in advance of the conduct giving rise to the request for assistance. Many corporations have adopted such provisions, often with shareholder approval. An obligatory provision satisfies the requirements for authorization in subsection (c) of sections 8.53 and 8.55, but compliance would still be required with subsections (a) and (b) of these sections.

Section 8.58(a) further provides that a provision requiring indemnification to the fullest extent permitted by law shall be deemed, absent an express statement to the contrary, to include an obligation to advance expenses under section 8.53. This provision of the statute is intended to avoid a decision such as that of the Delaware Supreme Court in Advanced Mining Systems, Inc. v. Fricke, 623 A.2d 82 (Del. 1992). If a corporation provides for obligatory indemnification and not for obligatory advance for expenses, the provision should be reviewed to ensure that it properly reflects the intent in light of the third sentence of section 8.58(a). Also, a corporation should consider whether obligatory expense advance is intended for direct suits by the corporation as well as for derivative suits by shareholders in the right of the corporation. In the former case, assuming compliance with subsections (a) and (b) of section 8.53, the corporation could be required to fund the defense of a defendant director even where the board of directors has already concluded that he has engaged in significant wrongdoing. See Official Comment to section 8.53.

§ 8.59 Exclusivity of Subchapter

A corporation may provide indemnification or advance expenses to a director or an officer only as permitted by this subchapter.

SUBCHAPTER F. DIRECTORS' CONFLICTING INTEREST TRANSACTIONS

INTRODUCTORY COMMENT

The common law, drawing by analogy on the fiduciary principles of the law of trusts, initially took the position that any transaction between X Co. and a director of X Co. was contaminated by the director's conflicting interest, that the transaction was null and void or voidable and, at least by implication, that the interested director who benefited from the transaction could be required to disgorge any profits and be held liable for any damages. In time, this rule was perceived to be demonstrably unworkable in the real business world and contrary to the best interests of the corporation. Accordingly, some courts modified their initial rigidity and, in addition, corrective legislation was enacted as a part of the business corporation acts.

The new statutory provisions on directors' conflicting interest transactions allowed the courts to develop the substantive content of the duty of loyalty owed by agents to their principals, by employees to their employers, and by directors to their corporations. The statutes themselves concentrated on creating procedures by which interest-conflict transactions between corporations and their directors could be salvaged while, at the same time, corporations and their shareholders could be protected against unfair dealing by self-aggrandizing directors. Section 41 of the 1969 Model Business Corporation Act was such a procedural provision, so was its successor, section 8.31 of the Model Act.

The replacement for section 8.31, now embodied as subchapter F of chapter 8 of the Model Act, is of the same procedural character. But new subchapter F has some important new features.

1. Purposes and Special Characteristics of Subchapter F

Predecessor provisions to subchapter F were sweeping and generalized in character. Subchapter F is not. Its key objectives are to increase predictability and to enhance practical administrability. To that end, the new subchapter spells out a safe harbor procedure more meticulously than its predecessors. To the same end, the subchapter goes further. Earlier statutes left entirely to judicial interpretation—and to the guess of corporate counsel—the central question as to what does and what does not constitute a conflicting interest of a director. Great uncertainty has arisen as to the scope of that concept. Subchapter F takes the new step of spelling out a practical working definition of "conflicting interest" and declares that definition to be exclusive. Circumstances that fall outside the statutory definition of conflicting interest cannot constitute the basis for an attack on a transaction on grounds of a director's interest conflict, although they may, of course, afford basis for legal attack on some other ground. Finally, to a greater degree than its predecessors, the subchapter specifies when judicial intervention is appropriate and when it is not.

In sum, subchapter F is new in that it adopts a "bright-line" statutory approach. An inevitable feature of any bright-line statute or regulation is that, no matter where the line may be set, some situations that fall outside the line will closely resemble other situations that fall inside it. Some observers find that outcome anomalous and argue that a bright-line approach is inferior to a statement of broad principles. But the legislative draftsman who chooses to suppress marginal anomalies by resorting to generalized statements of principle will pay a cost in terms of predictability. The choice between these two drafting approaches is a matter of judgment; an experienced legislative draftsman would never write a bright-line constitutional "due process" clause, nor would he provide, in a business corporation act, for "a reasonable period" of notice for a shareholders' meeting.

For a number of reasons, subchapter F is deliberately weighted towards bright-line specificity and predictability. That there will be imaginable situations at the margin that are similar but yield different results can be anticipated and is accepted.

One consideration arguing for the bright-line approach in subchapter F is that the existing case law governing interest conflicts of directors is in a state of unhealthy uncertainty, reflecting differing judicial attitudes toward and varying levels of comprehension concerning the subject. Equal uncertainty surrounds the working of the procedural machinery for dealing with transactions that involve a director's conflicting interest.

A second consideration arguing for a bright-line approach is that the fundamental perspective of subchapter F is prospective. In the real business world, a decision must be made *now* whether or not to proceed with the transaction and legal counsel's opinion must be delivered *now* as to whether clearance procedures are available and have been complied with. The business executive can accept either "yes" or "no" as an answer but he cannot effectively function in an environment in which the law, lawyers, or the courts say, "Go ahead and I will tell you later—perhaps years later—whether the transaction is vulnerable to attack."

Further, the essential character of interest conflict is often, unfortunately, misunderstood by the public and the media (and sometimes misunderstood, too, by lawyers and judges). Interest conflicts can and often do lead to baneful acts. The law regulates interest conflict transactions because experience shows that people do often yield to the temptation to advance their self-interests and, if they do, other people may be injured. That contingent fear is sufficient reason to warrant caution and to apply special standards and procedures to interest conflict transactions.

Nonetheless, it is important to keep firmly in mind that it is a contingent risk we are dealing with—that an interest conflict is not in itself a crime or a tort or necessarily injurious to others. Contrary to much popular usage, having a "conflict of interest" is not something one is "guilty of"; it is simply a state of affairs. Indeed, in many situations, the corporation and the shareholders may secure major benefits from a transaction despite the presence of a director's conflicting interest. Further, while history is replete with selfish acts, it is also oddly counterpointed by numberless acts taken contrary to self interest.

And, as an additional consideration, while conflicting interests surely carry potential danger, other important social values, such as economic efficiency, predictability and business finality are also at stake and should be accorded heavy countering weight in the law.

One last point. Even if one were to disregard these considerations and draft statutory language governing directors' interest conflicts in the most generalized form in an effort to catch the last malefactor, "anomalous" results still would not be avoided. One reason is that generalized drafting invites varying judicial and practitioner interpretation, as has in fact occurred in the cases on directors' conflicts of interest. But the ultimate unresolvable problem in seeking to regulate interest conflicts is that human beings are motivated by unimaginably varied and indeterminable mixes of ambitions, likes, dislikes, and biases. At the end of the day, who can say in respect of any matter that a particular director was, in a deeper sense, "disinterested" in a particular transaction and acted objectively on the merits? In regulating the conflicting interests of directors, the courts (and pertinent statutes) have limited inquiry to the financial interests of the director and his immediate family and associates. That is the wise course and, indeed, the only practical course. But in adopting that course, one obviously excludes a large fraction of the interests that actually drive the actions of human beings. Thus, the law may preclude a director from voting on a transaction in which he has an economic interest even if, given his resources, the amount at stake will have no real impact upon his decisionmaking, yet the law does not prohibit the same director from voting on a transaction which significantly benefits a religious institution to whose creed he is deeply devoted and that guides his life. Such deeper anomalies cannot be eradicated and the law should not seek to eradicate them. But it is worthwhile to be reminded that they exist, for in this field a degree of anomaly is a condition that must be accepted and lived with.

2. Scope of Subchapter F

The focus of subchapter F is sharply defined and limited.

First, the subchapter is targeted on legal challenges based on interest conflicts only. Subchapter F does not undertake to define, regulate, or provide any form of procedure regarding other possible claims. For example, subchapter F does not address a claim that a controlling shareholder has violated a duty owed to the corporation or minority shareholders.

Second, the subchapter is applicable only when there is a "transaction" by or with the corporation. For purposes of subchapter F, "transaction" generally connotes negotiations or a consensual bilateral arrangement between the corporation and another party or parties that concern their respective and differing economic rights or interests—not simply a unilateral action by the corporation but rather a "deal." See the discussion regarding "transaction" under clause (2) of Section 8.60(2). Whether safe harbor procedures of some kind might be available to the director and the corporation with respect to non-transactional matters is discussed at division 4 of this Introductory Comment.

Third, subchapter F deals with directors only. (The same was true of predecessor section 8.31 and section 41 of the 1969 Model Act.) Conflicts of interest of non-director officers or employees of the corporation are dealt with by the law of agency prescribing loyalty of agent to principal. Moreover, most large corporations today have internal regulations governing the business conduct of all personnel, including loyalty to the employer and avoidance of conflicting personal interests. A corporate employee can also deal with a personal conflict situation by going to his supervisor. Thus the conflict of interest problems of all corporate personnel except directors can be satisfactorily handled by general law, internal rules, and personnel procedures. For the directors, however—those who are ultimately responsible for the corporation—special provision in the business corporation statute is required.

Fourth, it is important to stress that the voting procedures and standards prescribed in subchapter F deal solely with the element of the director's conflicting interest. A transaction that receives a directors' or shareholders' vote that complies with subchapter F may well fail to achieve a different vote or quorum that may be requisite for substantive approval of the transaction under other applicable statutory provisions or under the articles of incorporation, and vice versa. (Under the Model Act, latitude is granted for setting higher voting requirements and different quorum requirements in the articles of incorporation. See sections 7.27 and 2.02(b)(2).)

Fifth, a few corporate transactions or arrangements in which directors inherently have a special personal interest are of a unique character and are regulated by special procedural provisions of the Act. See sections 8.51 and 8.52 dealing with indemnification arrangements and section 7.40 dealing with termination of derivative proceedings by board action. Any corporate transactions or arrangements affecting directors that are governed by such regulatory sections of the Act are not governed by subchapter F.

Subchapter F contemplates deletion of former Model Act section 8.32 dealing specially with loans to directors; a loan to a director is simply a subspecies of directors' conflicting interest transactions and is procedurally governed by subchapter F. See the Note on Fair Transactions in the Official Comment to section 8.61(B).

3. Structure of Subchapter F

The skeleton of subchapter F has only four parts. Definitions are in section 8.60. Section 8.61 prescribes what a court may or may not do in various situations. Section 8.62 prescribes procedures for action by boards of directors regarding a director's conflicting interest transaction. Section 8.63 prescribes corresponding procedures for shareholders. Thus, the most important operative section of the subchapter is section 8.61.

4. Non–Transactional Situations Involving Interest Conflicts

Many situations arise in which a director's personal economic interest is or may be adverse to the economic interest of the corporation, but which do not entail a "transaction" by or with the corporation.

Corporate Opportunity

An authoritative succinct statement of the corporate opportunity doctrine is that "the corporation has a prior claim to opportunities of business and profit which may be regarded as incident to its business. . . ." (*Ballantine on Corporations,* 79). Whether a court will declare a "corporate opportunity" to have been presented has always been wholly dependent on the facts of the case and often difficult to predict. And the scope of the "incident to its business" concept has become ever more murky in an era in which it is not unknown for a manufacturer of electrical equipment to become an investment bank, or a builder of concert pianos to become an insurance underwriter. If, however, one assumes a situation in which the circumstances presented are such that all would agree that it constitutes a corporate opportunity, to what extent are the procedures provided for in subchapter F relevant?

Obviously, the subchapter does not apply by its terms to such a situation since no transaction between the corporation and the director is involved. Yet, on analysis, a director's conflicting interest transaction and a director's corporate opportunity are fundamentally alike. If at the same board meeting the transaction and the opportunity are brought before the board with adequate disclosure of the relevant facts about each and the board, by action of disinterested directors, votes to enter into the transaction and votes to decline the opportunity (which the director then takes up), the integrity of the board's informed decisional process has been satisfied in both instances. The legal outcome should, therefore, be the same in both instances; *i.e.,* the board's action should afford safe harbor protection against later attack.

The procedures of subchapter F, specifically designed for transactions, cannot simply be mechanically transferred and applied to the corporate opportunity situation, however. The reason is that the subchapter's rules declaring which directors are legally qualified to vote are structurally dependent upon the subchapter's basic definition of "conflicting interest"—a definition that has no bearing on a corporate opportunity situation. Thus, the board will have to derive out of general common law the principles for determining which directors are, and which ones are not, to be considered qualified for this purpose. That question will usually not be difficult to resolve, but it is one that is not answered by the subchapter itself. For the corporate opportunity situation, therefore, the subchapter F procedure can be utilized, except for one missing component that in most cases can be readily supplied in the first instance by the board, and if challenged, ultimately determined by the court.

Other Situations

Many other kinds of situations can give rise to a clash of economic interest between a director and the corporation. For example, a director's personal financial interests can be impacted by a non-transactional policy decision of the board—for example where it decides to establish a divisional headquarters in the director's small hometown. In other situations, simple inaction by a board might work to a director's personal advantage. Or a flow of ongoing business relationships between a director and his corporation may, without centering upon any discrete "transaction," raise questions of possible favoritism, unfair dealing, or undue influence. If a director wishes to engage in business activity that directly competes with the corporation's own business, his economic interest in the competing activity ordinarily will conflict with the best interests of the corporation and put in issue the breach of the director's duties to the corporation. Obvious interest-clash can also arise out of a director's personal appropriation of corporate assets or improper use of corporate proprietary or inside information.

The circumstances in which such non-transactional conflict situations should be brought to the board or shareholders for clearance, and the legal effects, if any, of such clearance, are matters for development under the common law and lie outside the ambit of subchapter F. While these non-transactional situations are unaffected one way or the other by the provisions of subchapter F, a court may well recognize the subchapter F procedures as a useful analogy for dealing with such situations. Where similar procedures are followed in such situations, the court may, in its discretion, accord to them the same or similar effect to that provided by subchapter F.

NOTE

In the Official Comments to subchapter F, the director who has a conflicting interest is for convenience referred to as "the director" or "D", the corporation of which he is a director is referred to as "the corporation" or "X Co." Another corporation dealing with X Co. is referred to as "Y Co."

§ 8.60 Subchapter Definitions

In this subchapter:

(1) "Conflicting interest" with respect to a corporation means the interest a director of the corporation has respecting a transac-

tion effected or proposed to be effected by the corporation (or by a subsidiary of the corporation or any other entity in which the corporation has a controlling interest) if

(i) whether or not the transaction is brought before the board of directors of the corporation for action, the director knows at the time of commitment that he or a related person is a party to the transaction or has a beneficial financial interest in or so closely linked to the transaction and of such financial significance to the director or a related person that the interest would reasonably be expected to exert an influence on the director's judgment if he were called upon to vote on the transaction; or

(ii) the transaction is brought (or is of such character and significance to the corporation that it would in the normal course be brought) before the board of directors of the corporation for action, and the director knows at the time of commitment that any of the following persons is either a party to the transaction or has a beneficial financial interest in or so closely linked to the transaction and of such financial significance to the person that the interest would reasonably be expected to exert an influence on the director's judgment if he were called upon to vote on the transaction: (A) an entity (other than the corporation) of which the director is a director, general partner, agent, or employee; (B) a person that controls one or more of the entities specified in subclause (A) or an entity that is controlled by, or is under common control with, one or more of the entities specified in subclause (A); or (C) an individual who is a general partner, principal, or employer of the director.

(2) "Director's conflicting interest transaction" with respect to a corporation means a transaction effected or proposed to be effected by the corporation (or by a subsidiary of the corporation or any other entity in which the corporation has a controlling interest) respecting which a director of the corporation has a conflicting interest.

(3) "Related person" of a director means (i) the spouse (or a parent or sibling thereof) of the director, or a child, grandchild, sibling, parent (or spouse of any thereof) of the director, or an individual having the same home as the director, or a trust or estate of which an individual specified in this clause (i) is a substantial beneficiary; or (ii) a trust, estate, incompetent, conservatee, or minor of which the director is a fiduciary.

(4) "Required disclosure" means disclosure by the director who has a conflicting interest of (i) the existence and nature of his conflicting interest, and (ii) all facts known to him respecting the subject matter of the transaction that an ordinarily prudent person

would reasonably believe to be material to a judgment about whether or not to proceed with the transaction.

(5) "Time of commitment" respecting a transaction means the time when the transaction is consummated or, if made pursuant to contract, the time when the corporation (or its subsidiary or the entity in which it has a controlling interest) becomes contractually obligated so that its unilateral withdrawal from the transaction would entail significant loss, liability, or other damage.

OFFICIAL COMMENT

The definitions set forth in section 8.60 apply to subchapter F only and have no application elsewhere in the Model Act.

1. Conflicting Interest

The definition of conflicting interest requires that the director know of the transaction. More than that, it requires that he know of his interest conflict at the time of the corporation's commitment to the transaction. Absent that knowledge by the director, the risk to the corporation addressed by subchapter F is not present. In a corporation of significant size, routine transactions in the ordinary course of business, involving decisionmaking at lower management levels, will usually not be known to the director and will thus be excluded by the "knowledge" criterion in the definition.

The term "conflicting interest" as defined in subchapter F is never abstract or freestanding; its use must always be linked to a particular director, to a particular transaction and to a particular corporation.

The definition of "conflicting interest" is exclusive. An interest of a director is a conflicting interest *if and only if* it meets the requirements of subdivision (1).

D can have a conflicting interest in only three ways.

First a conflicting interest of D will obviously arise if the transaction is between D and X Co.

A conflicting interest will also arise under subdivision (1)(i) if D is not a party but has a beneficial financial interest in the transaction that is separate from his interest as a director or shareholder and is of such significance to the director that it would reasonably be expected to exert an influence on his judgment if he were called upon to vote on the matter. The personal economic stake of the director must be in or closely linked to the transaction—that is, his gain must hinge directly on the transaction itself. A contingent or remote gain (such as a future reduction in tax rates in the local community) is not enough to give rise to a conflicting interest under subdivision (1)(i). See the discussion of "transaction" under the Official Comment to subdivision (2).

If Y Co. is a party to or interested in the transaction with X Co. and Y Co. is somehow linked to D, the matter is in general governed by subdivision (1)(ii). But D's economic interest in Y Co. could be so substantial and the impact of the transaction so important to Y Co. that D could also have a conflicting interest under subdivision (1)(i).

Note that the basic standard set by subdivision (1)(i) and throughout subchapter F—"would reasonably be expected to exert an influence"—is an objective, not a subjective, criterion.

Second, a conflicting interest of D can arise under subdivision (1)(i) from the involvement in the transaction of a "related person" of D. "Related person" is defined in subdivision (3).

Third, in limited circumstances, subsequently discussed, a conflicting interest of D can arise through the economic involvement of certain other persons specified in subdivision (1)(ii). These are any entity (other than X Co.) of which the director is a director, general partner, agent, or employee; a person that controls, or an entity that is controlled by, or is under common control with one or more of the entities specified in the preceding clause; and any individual who is a general partner, principal, or employer of D.

The terms "principal" and "employer" as used in subdivision (1)(ii) are not separately defined but should be interpreted sensibly in the context of the purpose of the subdivision. The key question is whether D is, by force of an overt or covert tie to an employer or a principal who has a significant stake in the outcome of the transaction, beholden to act in the interest of that outside employer or principal rather than in the interest of X Co.

The "would reasonably be expected" criterion of subdivision (1)(i) applies also to subdivision (1)(ii).

Any director will, of course, have countless relationships and linkages to persons and institutions other than those specified in subdivision (1)(ii) and those defined in subdivision (3) to be related persons. But, for the reasons outlined in the Introduction, the subcategories of persons encompassed by subdivision (1)(ii) are expressly intended to be exclusive and to cover the field for purposes of subchapter F and particularly section 8.61(a). Thus, if, in a case involving a transaction between X Co. and Y Co., a court is presented with the argument that D, a director of X Co., is also a major creditor of Y Co. and that that stake in Y Co. gives D a conflicting interest, the court should reply that D's creditor interest in Y Co. does not fit any subcategory of subdivision (1)(ii) or subdivision (3) and therefore the conflict of interest claim must be rejected by force of section 8.61(a). The result would be otherwise if Y Co.'s debt to D is of such economic significance to D that it would fall under subdivision (1)(i) or put him in control of Y Co. and thus come within subdivision (1)(ii).

Subdivision (1)(ii) has a differentiated threshold keyed to the significance of the transaction. See the Official Comment to subdivision (2).

It is to be noted that under subdivision (1) of Section 8.60, any interest that the director has that meets the criteria set forth is considered a "conflicting interest". If a director has an interest that meets those criteria, subchapter F draws no further distinction between a director's interest that clashes with the interests of the corporation and a director's interest that coincides with or is parallel to the interests of the corporation. If the director's "interest" is present, "conflict" is assumed.

2. Director's Conflicting Interest Transaction

The definition of "director's conflicting interest transaction" in subdivision (2) is the key concept of subchapter F, establishing the area that lies within—and without—the scope of the subchapter's provisions. The definition operates preclusively; it not only designates the area within which the rules of subchapter F are to be applied but also denies the power of the court to act with respect to conflict of interest claims against directors in circumstances that lie outside the statutory definition of "director's conflicting interest transaction." See section 8.61(a).

(1) *Transaction*

To constitute a director's conflicting interest transaction, there must first be a transaction by the corporation, its subsidiary, or controlled entity in which the director has a financial interest. As discussed earlier, the safe harbor provisions provided by subchapter F have no application to circumstances in which there is no "transaction" by the corporation, however apparent the director's conflicting interest. Other strictures of the law prohibit a director from seizing corporate opportunities for himself and from competing against the corporation of which he is a director; subchapter F has no application to such situations. Moreover, a director might personally benefit if the corporation takes no action, as where the corporation decides not to make a bid. Subchapter F has no application to such instances. The limited thrust of the subchapter is to establish procedures which, if followed, immunize a corporate transaction and the interested director against the common law doctrine of voidability grounded on the director's conflicting interest. See the Introductory Comment for further discussion.

However, a policy decision and a transactional decision can blur and overlap. Assume X Co. operates a steel mini-mill that is running at a loss. A real estate developer offers to buy the land on which the mill is located and the X Co. board, having no other use for the the land, accepts the offer. This corporate action can readily be characterized either as a transaction—the sale of the land—or as a business policy decision—to go out of an unprofitable business. If D is a partner of the real estate developer, D has a stake in the sale transaction and subdivisions (1)(i) and (1)(ii) and all of subchapter F apply. But what if D, having no such interest, is in the local trucking business and a predictable consequence of closing the local mini-mill is that D will benefit from a future increase in demand for hauling services to bring in steel from more distant supply sources. An intent of the words "in or so closely linked to the transaction" in subdivisions (1)(i) and (1)(ii) is to focus subchapter F on the transaction itself. D's financial stake as a trucker in this situation lies not in the transaction, which is governed by subchapter F, but in the corporate business decision, which is not; accordingly, section 8.61(a) is inapplicable and imposes no bar to the court's discretion. Board action, though in compliance with section 8.62, will not, ipso facto, yield safe harbor protection for D or the transaction under section 8.61(b). The matter will be treated as provided in paragraph 4 of the Introductory Comment.

As another feature of the key term "transaction", the text of subdivision (1) emphasizes that the term implies and is limited to action by the corporation itself. The language of subchapter F has no application one way or the other to economic actions by the director in which the corporation is not a party or in which the corporation takes no action. Thus, a purchase by the director of the corporation's shares on the open market or from a third party is not a "transaction" within the scope of subchapter F and the subchapter does not govern an attack made on the propriety of such a share purchase.

If the board of directors of X Co. decides to distribute "poison pill" rights in order to fend off a possible takeover, that occurrence does not constitute a "transaction" as contemplated by subchapter F. See the discussion in division 4 of the Introductory Comment as to the character of a "transaction." If, on the other hand, a board of directors commits the corporation to a "crown jewel" option granted to a third party, there would be a "transaction".

But as noted earlier, for the transaction to be covered by subchapter F, the director (or other person designated by Section 8.60(i)) must have a beneficial interest respecting the transaction. Subchapter F would obviously govern such a crown jewel contract if a director was himself (or had a defined relationship to) the third party. But the fact that the crown jewel contract was in part motivated by the directors' desire to keep themselves on the board would not, taken alone, constitute a sufficiently direct interest in the transaction to bring it with subchapter F.

(2) *Party to the Transaction—The Corporation*

Transaction by what entity? In the usual case, the transaction in question would be by X Co. But assume that X Co. is the controlling corporation of S Co. (i.e., it controls the vote for directors of S Co.). D wishes to sell a building he owns to X Co. and X Co. is willing to buy it. As a business matter, it will often make no difference to X Co. whether it takes the title itself or places it with its subsidiary S Co. or another entity that X Co. controls. The applicability of subchapter F cannot be allowed to depend upon that formal distinction. The subchapter therefore includes within its operative framework transactions by a subsidiary or controlled entity of X Co. See the Note on Parent Companies and Subsidiaries below.

(3) *Party to the Transaction—The Director*

Subdivision (1)(i) and subdivision (1)(ii) differ as to the persons covered and as to the threshold of transactional significance. Subdivision (1)(i), addressed to D and related persons of D, includes as directors' conflicting interest transactions *all* transactions that meet the substantive criteria prescribed. By contract, subdivision (1)(ii), addressed to transactions involving other designated persons, excludes from its coverage transactions that are not sufficiently significant to the corporation to warrant decision at the boardroom level.

As a generalization, the linkage between a director and a "related person" is closer than that between the director and those persons and entities specified in subdivision (1)(ii). Correspondingly, the threshold of conflicting interest under subdivision (1)(i) is lower than that set for subdivision (1)(ii). Thus, all routine transactions of X Co. are excluded from the definition of director's conflicting interest transaction unless they fall within subdivision (1)(i). If Y Co., a computer company of which D is also an outside director, sells office machinery to X Co., the transaction will not normally give rise to a conflicting interest for D from the perspective of either company since the transaction is a routine matter that would not come before either board. If, however, the transaction is of such significance to one of the two companies that it would come before the board of that company, then D has a conflicting interest in the transaction with respect to that company.

Implicit in subdivision (1)(ii) is a recognition that X Co. and Y Co., particularly if large enterprises, are likely to have routine, perhaps frequent, business dealings with each other as they buy and sell goods and services in the marketplace. The terms of these dealings are dictated by competitive market forces and the transactions are conducted at personnel levels far below the board room. The fact that D has some relationship with Y Co. is not in itself sufficient reason to open these smaller scale impersonal business transactions to challenge if not passed through the board in accordance with section 8.62 procedures. It would be doubly impractical to do so twice where X Co. and Y Co. have a common director.

Subchapter F takes the practical position. The definition in subdivision (1)(ii) excludes most such transactions both by its "knowledge" requirement and by its higher threshold of economic significance. In almost all cases, any such transaction, if challenged, would be easily defensible as being "fair." In respect of day-to-day business dealings, the main practical risk of impropriety would be that a director having a conflicting interest might seek to exert inappropriate influence upon the interior operations of the enterprise, might try to use his status as a director to pressure lower level employees to divert their business out of ordinary channels to his advantage. But a director's affirmative misconduct goes well beyond a claim that he has a conflicting interest, and judicial action against such improper behavior remains available. See also the Official Comment to section 8.62(b) regarding common directors.

The absence of the significance threshold in subdivision (1)(i) does not impose an inappropriate burden on directors and related persons. The commonplace and oftentimes recurring transaction will involve purchase of the corporation's product line, it will usually not be difficult for D to show that the transaction was on commercial terms and was fair, or indeed, that he had no knowledge of the transaction. As a result, these transactions do not invite harassing lawsuits against the director. A purchase by D of a product of X Co. at a usual "employee's discount," while technically assailable as a conflicting interest transaction, would customarily be viewed as "fair" to the corporation as a routine incident of the office of director. For other transactions between the corporation and the director or those close to him, D can, and should, have the burden of establishing the fairness of the transaction if it is not passed upon by the arm's length review of qualified directors or the holders of qualified shares. If there are any reasons to believe that the terms of the transaction might be questioned as unfair to X Co., D is well advised to pass the transaction through the safe harbor procedures of subchapter F.

Note on Parent Companies and Subsidiaries

If a subsidiary is wholly owned, there is no outside holder of shares of the subsidiary to be injured with respect to transactions between the two corporations.

Transactions between a parent corporation and a partially-owned subsidiary may raise the possibility of abuse of power by a majority shareholder to the disadvantage of a minority shareholder. Subchapter F has no relevance as to how a court should deal with that claim.

If there are not at least two outside directors of the subsidiary, the subsidiary and the board of directors must operate on the basis that any transaction between the subsidiary and the parent that reaches the significance threshold in subdivision (1)(ii) may, as a technical matter, be challengeable by a minority shareholder of the subsidiary on grounds that it is a director's conflicting interest transaction. In that case, the directors of the subsidiary will have to establish the fairness of the transaction to the subsidiary. In practice, however, the case law has dealt with such claims under the rubric of the duties of a majority shareholder and that is, in reality, the better approach. See the Official Comment to section 8.61(b).

3. Related Person

Two subcategories of "related person" of the director are set out in subdivision (3). These subcategories are specified, exclusive, and preemptive.

The first subcategory is made up of closely related family, or near-family, individuals, trusts, and estates as specified in clause (i). The clause is exclusive insofar as family relationships are concerned. The references to a "spouse" are intended to include a common law spouse or unrelated cohabitant.

The second subcategory is made up of persons specified in clause (ii) to whom or which the director is linked in a fiduciary capacity as, for example, in his status as a trustee or administrator. (Note that the definition of "person" in the Model Act includes both individuals and entities. See section 1.40(16).) From the perspective of X Co., D's fiduciary relationships are always a sensitive concern. A conscientious director may be able to control his own greed arising from a conflicting personal interest. And he may resist the temptation to assist his wife or child. But he can never escape his legal obligation to act in the best interests of another person for whom he is a trustee or other fiduciary.

4. Required Disclosure

Two separate elements make up the defined term "required disclosure." They are disclosure of the existence of the conflicting interest and then disclosure of the material facts known to D about the subject of the transaction.

Subdivision (4) calls for disclosure of all facts known to D about the subject of the transaction that an ordinarily prudent person would reasonably believe to be material to a judgment by the person acting for the corporation as to whether to proceed or not to proceed with the transaction. If a director knows that the land the corporation is buying from him is sinking into an abandoned coal mine, he must disclose not only that he is the owner and that he has an interest in the transaction but also that the land is subsiding; as a director of X Co. he may not invoke caveat emptor. But in the same circumstances the director is *not* under an obligation to reveal the price he paid for the property ten years ago, or that he inherited it, since that information is not material to the corporation's business judgment as to whether or not to proceed with the transaction. Further, while material facts that pertain to the *subject* of the transaction must be disclosed, a director is not required to reveal personal or subjective information that bears upon his negotiating position (such as, for example, his urgent need for cash, or the lowest price he would be willing to accept). This is true despite the fact that such information would obviously be relevant to the corporation's decisionmaking in the sense that, if known to the corporation, it could equip the corporation to hold out for terms more favorable to it.

Underlying the definition of the twin components of "required disclosure" is the critically important provision contained in subdivision (1) that a basic precondition for the existence of a "conflicting interest" is that the director *know* of the transaction and also that he *know* of the existence of his conflicting interest.

5. Time of Commitment

The time of the commitment by the corporation (or its subsidiary or other controlled entity) to the transaction is defined in operational terms geared to change of economic position.

§ 8.61 Judicial Action

(a) A transaction effected or proposed to be effected by a corporation (or by a subsidiary of the corporation or any other entity in which the corporation has a controlling interest) that is not a director's conflicting interest transaction may not be enjoined, set aside, or give rise to an award of damages or other sanctions, in a proceeding by a shareholder or by or in the right of the corporation, because a director of the corporation, or any person with whom or which he has a personal, economic, or other association, has an interest in the transaction.

(b) A director's conflicting interest transaction may not be enjoined, set aside, or give rise to an award of damages or other sanctions, in a proceeding by a shareholder or by or in the right of the corporation, because the director, or any person with whom or which he has a personal, economic, or other association, has an interest in the transaction, if:

(1) directors' action respecting the transaction was at any time taken in compliance with section 8.62;

(2) shareholders' action respecting the transaction was at any time taken in compliance with section 8.63; or

(3) the transaction, judged according to the circumstances at the time of commitment, is established to have been fair to the corporation.

OFFICIAL COMMENT

Section 8.61 is the operational section of subchapter F as it prescribes the judicial consequences of the other sections.

Speaking generally:

(i) If the procedure set forth in section 8.62 or in section 8.63 is complied with, or if the transaction is fair to the corporation, then a director's conflicting interest transaction is immune from attack on any ground of a personal interest or conflict of interest of the director. However, the narrow scope of subchapter F must again be strongly emphasized; if the transaction is vulnerable to attack on some other ground, subchapter F does not make it less so for having been passed through the procedures of subchapter F. See, however, paragraph 4 of the Introductory Comment.

(ii) If a transaction is *not* a director's conflicting interest transaction as defined in section 8.60, then the transaction may *not* be enjoined, rescinded, or made the basis of other sanction *on the ground of a conflict of interest of a director, whether or not it went through the procedures of subchapter F.* In that sense, subchapter F is specifically intended to be both comprehensive and exclusive.

(iii) If a transaction that is a director's conflicting interest transaction was not at any time the subject of action taken in compliance with section 8.62 or section 8.63, and it is attacked on grounds of a director's conflicting interest and is not shown to be fair to the corporation, then the court may grant such remedial action as it considers appropriate under the applicable law of the jurisdiction. If the attack is on other grounds, subchapter F has no relevance to the issue(s) before the court.

1. Section 8.61(a)

Section 8.61(a) is a key component in the design of subchapter F. It draws a bright-line circle, declaring that the definitions of section 8.60 wholly occupy and preempt the field of directors' conflicting interest transactions. Of course, outside this circle there is a penumbra of director interests, desires, goals, loyalties, and prejudices that may, in a particular context, run at odds with the best interests of the corporation, but section 8.61(a) forbids a court to ground remedial action on any of them. If a plaintiff charges that a director had a conflict of interest with respect to a transaction of the corporation because the other party was his cousin, the answer of the court should be: "No. A cousin, as such and without more, is not included in section 8.60(3) as a related person—and under section 8.61(a), I have no authority to reach out farther." If a plaintiff contends that the director had a conflict of interest in a corporate transaction because the other party is president of the golf club the director wants desperately to join, the court should respond: "No. The only director's conflicting interest on the basis of which I can set aside a corporate transaction or impose other sanctions is a financial interest as defined in section 8.60." The reasons why subchapter F adopts this bright-line approach are reviewed in the Introductory Comment.

In the real world, however, matters are often not clear, and one cannot always predict with comfort a future judicial response. It must be expected that quite often a director (and his legal/business advisors) may be in doubt as to whether a particular person would or would not be held to fall within a subcategory in section 8.60(3), or whether the economic impact on the director will be considered "in or closely linked" to the transaction, or whether the director is an "agent" or "employee," or whether the scale of the director's interest is large enough to be likely to sway him if brought to a vote. Some directors will wish, too, to make it clear that they are leaning over backwards. In such circumstances, the obvious avenue to follow is to clear the matter with qualified directors under section 8.62 or with the holders of qualified shares under section 8.63. If it is later judicially determined that a conflicting interest of the director did exist, the director will be grateful for the safe harbor protection. If it should be ultimately held that there was no conflicting interest in the transaction as defined by subchapter F, no harm (other than nuisance) has been done by passing the transaction through the procedures of section 8.62 or section 8.63. It may be expected, therefore, that the procedures of section 8.62 (and, to a lesser extent, section 8.63) will be used with regard to many transactions that lie outside the sharp definitions of section 8.60—a result that is healthy and constructive.

Once again, it is important to stress that subchapter F deals only with "transactions." If a non-transactional corporate decision is challenged on the ground that D has a conflicting personal stake in it, subsection 8.61(a) is irrelevant. For a discussion of corporate action that may be considered either a business decision or a transaction, see the Official Comment to section 8.60(1)(ii) and paragraph 4 of the Introductory Comment.

2. Section 8.61(b)

Section 8.61(b) is the heart of subchapter F—the fundamental section that provides for the safe harbor.

Clause (1) of subsection (b) provides that if a director has a conflicting interest respecting a transaction, neither the transaction nor the director is legally vulnerable if the procedures of section 8.62 have been properly followed. Subsection (b)(1) is, however, subject to a critically important predicate condition.

The condition—an obvious one—is that the board's action must comply with the care, best interests and good faith criteria prescribed in section 8.30(a) for all directors' actions. If the directors who voted for the conflicting interest transaction were qualified directors under subchapter F, but approved the transaction merely as an accommodation to the director with the conflicting interest, going through the motions of board action without complying with the requirements of section 8.30(a), the action of the board would not be given effect for purposes of section 8.61(b)(1).

Board action on a director's conflicting interest transaction provides a context in which the function of the "best interests of the corporation" language in section 8.30(a) is brought into clear focus. Consider, for example, a situation in which it is established that the board of a manufacturing corporation approved a cash loan to a director where the duration, security and interest terms of the loan were at prevailing commercial rates, but (i) the loan was not made in the course of the corporation's ordinary business and (ii) the loan required a commitment of limited working capital that would otherwise have been used in furtherance of the corporation's business activities. Such a loan transaction would not be afforded safe-harbor protection by section 8.62(b)(1) since the board did not comply with the requirement in section 8.30(a) that the board's action be, in its reasonable judgment, in the best interests of the corporation—that is, that the action will, as the board judges the circumstances at hand, yield favorable results (or reduce detrimental results) as judged from the perspective of furthering the corporation's business activities.

If a determination is made that the terms of a director's conflicting interest transaction, judged according to the circumstances at the time of commitment, were manifestly unfavorable to the corporation, that determination would be relevant to an allegation that the directors' action was not taken in good faith and therefore did not comply with section 8.30(a).

The Model Act does not undertake to prescribe litigation procedures. If board action under section 8.62(b)(1) is interposed as a bar to a challenge to a director's conflicting interest transaction and the complainant wishes to put in issue an alleged non-compliance with section 8.30(a) by the board, he would do so by proceeding under the same local pleading, presumption and burden of proof rules that would govern any other attack on an action of a board of directors.

Clause (2) of subsection (b) regarding shareholders' approval of the transaction is the matching piece to clause (1) regarding directors' approval.

Clause (3) of subsection (b) provides that a director's conflicting interest transaction will be secure against judicial intervention if the interested director (or the corporation, if it chooses) shows that although neither directors' nor shareholders' action was taken complying with sections 8.62 or 8.63, the transaction was fair to the corporation. The term "fair" accords with traditional language in the cases. But it must be understood that, as used in the context of those cases and of subchapter F, the term has a special, flexible meaning and a wide embrace.

Note on Fair Transactions

(1) *Terms of the Transaction.* If the issue in a transaction is the "fairness" of a price, "fair" is not to be taken to imply that there is a single "fair" price, all others being "unfair." It has long been settled that a "fair" price is any price in that broad range which an unrelated party might have been willing to pay or willing to accept, as the case may be, for the property, following a normal arm's-length business negotiation, in the light of the knowledge that would have been reasonably acquired in the course of such negotiations, any result within that range being "fair." The same statement applies not only to price but to any other key term of the deal.

Although the "fair" criterion applied by the court is a range rather than a point, the width of that range is only a segment of the full spectrum of the directors' discretion associated with the exercise of business judgment under section 8.30(a). That is to say, the scope of decisional discretion that a court would have allowed to the directors if they had acted and had complied with section 8.30(a) is wider than the range of "fairness" contemplated for judicial determination where section 8.61(b)(3) is the governing provision.

(2) *Benefit to the Corporation.* In considering the "fairness" of the transaction, the court will in addition be required to consider not only the market fairness of the terms of the deal, but also, as the board would have been required to do, whether the transaction was one that was reasonably likely to yield favorable results (or reduce detrimental results) from the perspective of furthering the corporation's business activities. Thus, if a manufacturing company that is short of working capital allocates some of its scarce funds to purchase a sailing yacht owned by one of its directors, it will not be easy to persuade the court that the transaction is "fair" in the sense that it was reasonably made to further the business interests of the corporation; the fact that the price paid for the yacht was stipulated to be a "fair" market price will not be enough alone to uphold the transaction. See also the discussion above regarding section 8.30(a).

(3) *Process of Decision.* In some circumstances, the behavior of the director having the conflicting interest can itself affect the finding and content of "fairness." The most obvious illustration of unfair dealing arises out of the director's failure to disclose fully his interest or hidden defects known to him regarding the transaction. Another illustration could be the exertion of improper pressure by the director upon the other directors. When the facts of such unfair dealing become known, the court should offer the corporation its option as to whether to rescind the transaction on grounds of "unfairness" even if it appears that the terms were "fair" by market standards and the corporation profited from it. If the corporation decides not to rescind the transaction because of business advantages accruing to the corporation from it, the court may still find in the director's misconduct a basis for judicially imposed sanction against the

director personally. Thus, the course of dealing—or process—is a key component to a "fairness" determination under subsection (b)(3).

Note on Directors' Compensation

Directors' fees and similar forms of compensation, expense reimbursement practices, directors' and officer's liability insurance and routine incidents of office (such as a privilege to buy the corporation's products at a discount) in the normal course of business are typically set by the board and are specially authorized (though not regulated) by sections 8.11 and 8.57 of the Model Act. These practices obviously involve a conflicting interest on the part of most if not all of the directors and are capable of being abused, although, in the usual case, they fall within normative patterns and fairness can be readily established. While, as a matter of practical necessity, these practices are universally accepted in principle by the law, board action on directors' compensation and benefits would be subject to judicial sanction if not in the circumstances fair to the corporation or favorably acted upon by shareholders pursuant to section 8.63. Sustainable action by the board in this regard must, of course, meet the general criteria for board action prescribed in Section 8.30(a); see the Official Comment to section 8.61(b).

Note on Directors' Personal Liability

At common law, articulation of the legal principles applicable to directors' conflicts of interest typically declare the transaction to be void or (sometimes) voidable. These formulations say little about the liabilities, if any, of the parties to the transaction. It is clear, however, that in some special circumstances a court would hold that the interested director must disgorge the profits he made from the transaction or must respond in damages for injury suffered by the corporation as a result of the transaction. Such sanctions could arise in contexts where the court leaves the transaction itself in place as well as in situations where the court rescinds the transaction. Subchapter F leaves these matters of sanction entirely to the judgment of the court.

In some situations, a transaction will contain an element of conflicting interest on the part of the director but in reality the director himself is a surrogate in the board room and not the real beneficiary of the transaction. Thus, where P Co. is a majority or controlling shareholder in X Co., and some or all of the directors of X Co. are the employees or agents of P Co., there is always a risk that, in a transaction between P Co. and X Co., P Co. may take advantage of its position to press its agents and employees who are on the X Co. board to approve a transaction that is disadvantageous to X Co. but advantageous to P Co. Under subchapter F, if X Co. has directors who are not affiliated with P. Co., action pursuant to section 8.62 is possible. But many less-than-wholly-owned subsidiaries have no unaffiliated directors to pass on a transaction between X Co. and its controlling shareholder P Co. In such a circumstance, the minority shareholders of X Co. are entitled to fair treatment; if they are not treated fairly, the responsibility should, in most cases, be laid at the door of P Co. and not be placed upon P Co.'s agents or employees on the X Co. board.

As a matter of case law, the courts have arrived at that result by treating such cases under the rubric of the duty of fair dealing on the part of the controlling shareholder vis-a-vis the minority shareholders. In so doing, the courts have deliberately skipped over any analytically available alternative approach predicated on a theory of conflicting interest of the X Co. director who is an employee or agent of the controlling shareholder. All rights of minority shareholders against a controlling shareholder are preserved unaffected by subchapter F. All directors of X Co., regardless of their other affiliations, have duties to perform for the benefit of all X Co. shareholders, not just some of them. D is not relieved of those obligations merely because he happens to be an employee of the majority shareholder. At the same time, in these circumstances D often has little real discretion in voting to approve the transaction and the beneficiary of the transaction is not D but P Co., his employer.

In a transaction between P Co. and X Co., if the transaction is important to X Co., if D is an agent or employee of P Co., if the transaction is not protected by the procedures of section 8.62 or section 8.63, and if the transaction is not shown to be fair to X Co., then a court may well set aside the transaction or take other remedial action with regard to P Co., but it would not usually be equitable in such cases to hold D personally liable.

Parallels to this commonplace parent-subsidiary example can also arise under subchapter F out of almost any circumstance that meets the criteria of section 8.60(1)(ii). It is evident that a common director of X Co. and of Y Co. has a degree of conflicting interest in a transaction between the two corporations; but (assuming no valid safe harbor action under subchapter F) the sanction that would be appropriate would in most circumstances be addressed to the transaction itself and to one or both of the companies involved, rather than to D personally. See the Official Comment to section 8.60(2) and section 8.62(d).

§ 8.62 Directors' Action

(a) Directors' action respecting a transaction is effective for purposes of section 8.61(b)(1) if the transaction received the affirmative vote of a majority (but no fewer than two) of those qualified directors on the board of directors or on a duly empowered committee of the board who voted on the transaction after either required disclosure to them (to the extent the information was not known by them) or compliance with subsection (b); provided that action by a committee is so effective only if:

(1) all its members are qualified directors; and

(2) its members are either all the qualified directors on the board or are appointed by the affirmative vote of a majority of the qualified directors on the board.

(b) If a director has a conflicting interest respecting a transaction, but neither he nor a related person of the director specified in section 8.60(3)(i) is a party to the transaction, and if the director has a duty under law or professional canon, or a duty of confidentiality to another person, respecting information relating to the transaction such that the director may not make the disclosure described in section 8.60(4)(ii), then disclosure is sufficient for purposes of subsection (a) if the director (1) discloses to the directors voting on the transaction the existence and nature of his conflicting interest and informs them of the character and limitations imposed by that duty before their vote on the transaction, and (2) plays no part, directly or indirectly, in their deliberations or vote.

(c) A majority (but no fewer than two) of all the qualified directors on the board of directors, or on the committee, constitutes a quorum for purposes of action that complies with this section. Directors' action that otherwise complies with this section is not affected by the presence or vote of a director who is not a qualified director.

(d) For purposes of this section, "qualified director" means, with respect to a director's conflicting interest transaction, any director who does not have either (1) a conflicting interest respecting the transaction, or (2) a familial, financial, professional, or employment relationship with a second director who does have a conflicting interest respecting the transaction, which relationship would, in the circumstances, reasonably be expected to exert an influence on the first director's judgment when voting on the transaction.

OFFICIAL COMMENT

Section 8.62 provides the procedure for action of the board of directors under subchapter F. In the normal course, this section, taken together with section 8.61(b), will be the key provision for dealing with directors' conflicting interest transactions.

All discussion of section 8.62 must be conducted in light of the overarching provisions of section 8.30(a) prescribing the criteria for decisions by directors. Board action that does not comply with the requirements of section 8.30(a) will not, of course, be given effect under section 8.62. See the Official Comment to section 8.61(b).

1. Section 8.62(a)

A transaction in which a director has a conflicting interest is approved under section 8.62 if and only if it is approved by qualified directors, as defined in subsection 8.62(d). Action by the board of directors as a whole is effective if approved by the affirmative vote of a majority (but not less than two) of the qualified directors on the board. Action may also be taken by a duly authorized committee of the board but, to be effective, all members of the committee must be qualified directors and the committee must either contain all of the qualified directors on the board or must have been appointed by the affirmative vote of a majority of the qualified directors on the board. The effect of the limitation on committee action is to make it impossible to handpick as committee members a favorably inclined minority from among the qualified directors.

Except to the limited extent provided in subsection (b), approval by the board or committee must be preceded by required disclosure.

Action complying with subsection 8.62(a) may be taken by the board of directors at any time, before or after the transaction, and may deal with a single transaction or a specified category of similar transactions.

2. Section 8.62(b)

Subsection (b) is a new provision designed to deal, in a practical way, with situations in which a director who has a conflicting interest is not able to comply fully with the disclosure requirement of subsection (a) because of an extrinsic duty of confidentiality. The director may, for example, be prohibited from making full disclosure because of restrictions of law that happen to apply to the transaction (e.g., grand jury seal or national security statute) or professional canon (e.g. lawyers' or doctors' client privilege). The most frequent use of subsection (b), however, will undoubtedly be in connection with common directors who find themselves in a position of dual fiduciary obligations that clash. If D is also a director of Y Co., D may have acquired privileged confidential information from one or both sources relevant to a transaction between X Co. and Y Co. that he cannot reveal to one without violating his fiduciary duty to the other. In such circumstance, subsection (b) makes it possible for such a matter to be brought to the board for consideration under subsection (a) and thus enable X Co. to secure the protection afforded by subchapter F for the transaction despite the fact that D cannot make the full disclosure usually required.

To comply with subsection (b), D must disclose that he has a conflicting interest, inform the directors who vote on the transaction of the nature of his duty of confidentiality (e.g., inform them that it arises out of an attorney-client privilege or his duty as a director of Y Co. that prevents him from making the disclosure called for by clause (ii) of section 8.60(4)), and then play no personal part in the board's deliberations. The point of subsection (b) is simply to make clear that the provisions of subchapter F may be employed with regard to a transaction in circumstances where an interested director cannot, because of enforced fiduciary silence, make disclosure of the facts known to him.[1] Of course, if D invokes subsection (b) and then remains silent before leaving the boardroom, the remaining directors may decline to act on the transaction if troubled by a concern that D knows (or may know) something they do not. On the other hand, if D is subject to an extrinsic duty of confidentiality but has no knowledge of facts that should be disclosed, he would normally so state and disregard subsection (b), and (having disclosed the existence and nature of his conflicting interest) thereby comply with section 8.60(4).

While subchapter F explicitly contemplates the application of subsection (b) to the frequently recurrent problem of common directors and officers, it should not otherwise be read as attempting to define the scope or mandate the consequences of various silence-privileges; that is a topic for local law.

Subsection (b) is not available to D if the transaction is directly between the corporation and D or his related person—if, that is, the director or a related person is a party to the transaction. If D or a related person is a party to the transaction, D's only options are required disclosure on an unqualified basis, abandonment of the transaction, or acceptance of the risk of establishing fairness in a court proceeding if the transaction is challenged.

Whenever D proceeds as provided in subsection 8.62(b), the board should recognize that he may well have information that in usual circumstances he

1. A director could, of course, encounter the same problem of mandated silence with regard to any matter that comes before the board; that is, the problem of forced silence is not linked at all to the problems of transactions involving a conflicting interest of a director. It could easily happen that at the same board meeting of X Co. at which D, the interested director, invokes section 8.62(b) and excuses himself, another director who has absolutely no financial interest in the transaction might conclude that under local law he is bound to silence (because of attorney-client privilege, for example) and would under general principles of sound director conduct withdraw from participation in the board's deliberations and action.

would be required to reveal to the board—information that may well indicate that the transaction is a favorable or unfavorable one for X Co.

3. Section 8.62(c)

Subsection (c) contains technical provisions dealing with quorum and superfluous votes by interested directors.

4. Section 8.62(d)

Obviously, a director's conflicting interest transaction and D cannot be provided safe harbor protection by fellow directors who themselves have conflicting interests, only "qualified directors" can provide such safe harbor protection pursuant to subsection (a). "Qualified director" is defined in subsection (d). The definition is broad. It excludes not only any director who has a conflicting interest respecting the matter, but also—going significantly beyond the persons specified in the subcategories of section 8.60(1)(ii) for purposes of the "conflicting interest" definition—any director whose familial or financial relationship with D or whose employment or professional relationship with D would be likely to influence the director's vote on the transaction.

The determination of whether there is a financial, employment or professional relationship should be based on the practicalities of the situation rather than formalistic circumstances. For example, a director employed by a corporation controlled by D should be regarded as having an employment relationship with D.

§ 8.63 Shareholders' Action

(a) Shareholders' action respecting a transaction is effective for purposes of section 8.61(b)(2) if a majority of the votes entitled to be cast by the holders of all qualified shares were cast in favor of the transaction after (1) notice to shareholders describing the director's conflicting interest transaction, (2) provision of the information referred to in subsection (d), and (3) required disclosure to the shareholders who voted on the transaction (to the extent the information was not known by them).

(b) For purposes of this section, "qualified shares" means any shares entitled to vote with respect to the director's conflicting interest transaction except shares that, to the knowledge, before the vote, of the secretary (or other officer or agent of the corporation authorized to tabulate votes), are beneficially owned (or the voting of which is controlled) by a director who has a conflicting interest respecting the transaction or by a related person of the director, or both.

(c) A majority of the votes entitled to be cast by the holders of all qualified shares constitutes a quorum for purposes of action that complies with this section. Subject to the provisions of subsections (d) and (e), shareholders' action that otherwise complies with this section is not affected by the presence of holders, or the voting, of shares that are not qualified shares.

(d) For purposes of compliance with subsection (a), a director who has a conflicting interest respecting the transaction shall, before the shareholders' vote, inform the secretary (or other office or agent of the corporation authorized to tabulate votes) of the number, and the identity of persons holding or controlling the vote, of all shares that the director knows are beneficially owned (or the voting of which is controlled) by the director or by a related person of the director, or both.

(e) If a shareholders' vote does not comply with subsection (a) solely because of a failure of a director to comply with subsection (d), and if the director establishes that his failure did not determine and was not intended by him to influence the outcome of the vote, the court may, with or without further proceedings respecting section 8.61(b)(3), take such action respecting the transaction and the director, and give such effect, if any, to the shareholders' vote, as it considers appropriate in the circumstances.

OFFICIAL COMMENT

Section 8.63 provides the machinery for shareholder safe harbor of a director's conflicting interest transaction, as section 8.62 provides the machinery for safe harbor by action of directors.

1. Section 8.63(a)

Subsection (a) specifies the procedure required to establish effective safe harbor protection of a director's conflicting interest transaction through vote of shareholders. In advance of the vote, three steps must be taken. Shareholders must be given notice describing the transaction. D must provide the information called for in subsection (d), discussed below. And required disclosure must be made, as defined in section 8.60(4). If, then, a majority of all qualified shares that are entitled to vote on the matter vote favorably, the safe harbor provision of section 8.61(b)(2) becomes effective.

Action that complies with subsection 8.63(a) may be taken at any time, before or after the transaction.

Note that section 8.63 does not contain a provision comparable to section 8.62(b). Thus, the safe harbor protection of subchapter F cannot be made available through shareholder action under section 8.63 in a case where D remains silent because of an extrinsic duty of confidentiality. This is advertent. While it is believed that the section 8.62(b) procedure is workable in the collegial setting of the board room, one must have reservations whether the same is true vis-a-vis the shareholder body, especially in larger corporations where there is heavy reliance upon the proxy mechanic. In most situations no opportunity exists for shareholders to quiz D about his duty and to discuss the implications of acting without the benefit of D's knowledge concerning the transaction. In a case involving a closely-held corporation where section 8.63 procedures are followed, but with D acting as provided in section 8.62(b), a court could, of course, attach significance to a favorable shareholder vote in evaluating the fairness of the transaction to the corporation. See the discussion in paragraph 4 of the Introductory Comment.

2. Section 8.63(b)

Under subsection (a), only "qualified shares" may be counted in the vote for purposes of safe harbor action pursuant to section 8.61(b)(2). Subsection (b) defines "qualified shares" to exclude all shares that, prior to the vote, the secretary or other tabulator of the votes *knows* to be owned or controlled by the director who has the conflicting interest or any related person of that director. It should be stressed that this definition is dependent upon the tabulator's actual knowledge. If the tabulator does not know that certain shares are owned by the director who has the conflicting interest, he cannot be expected to exclude those shares from the vote count. But see the Official Comment to subsection (e).

The category of persons whose shares are excluded from the vote count under subsection (b) is not the same as the category of persons specified in section 8.60(1)(ii) for purposes of defining D's "conflicting interest" and—*importantly*—is not the same as the category of persons excluded for purposes of the definition of non-qualified directors under section 8.62(d). The distinctions among these three categories are deliberate and carefully drawn.

The definition of "qualified shares" excludes shares owned by D or a related person as defined in section 8.60(3). If D is an employee or director of Y Co., Y Co. is *not* prevented by that fact from exercising its usual voting rights as to any shares it may hold in X Co. D's linkage to a related person is close. But the net of section 8.60(1)(ii) specifying other persons and entities for purposes of the "conflicting interest" definition is cast so wide that D will never be able to know whether, nor have a reason to try to monitor whether, some person within those subcategories holds X Co. shares. Typically, moreover, D will have no control over those persons and how they vote their X Co. shares. There is, in reality, no reason to strip those persons of their voting rights as shareholders, for in the usual commercial situation they will vote in accordance with their own interests, which may well not coincide with the personal interest of D.

To illustrate the operation of subsection (b), consider a case in which D is also a director of Y Co., and to his knowledge: thirty percent of Y Co.'s stock is owned by X Co.; D, his wife, a trust of which D is the trustee, and a corporation he controls, together own ten percent of X Co.'s stock but not stock of Y Co.; and X Co. and Y Co. wish to enter into a transaction that is of major significance to both.

From the perspective of X Co., D has a conflicting interest since he is a director of Y Co. If X Co. submits the transaction to a vote of its shareholders under section 8.63, the shares held by D, his wife, the trust of which he is the trustee, and the corporation he controls are not qualified shares and may not be counted in the vote.

From the perspective of Y Co., D has a conflicting interest since he is a director of X Co. If Y Co. submits the transaction to a vote of its shareholders under section 8.63, the thirty percent of Y Co. shares held by X Co. *are* qualified shares and may be counted for purposes of section 8.63. The same would be equally true if X Co. were the majority shareholder of Y Co., but as emphasized elsewhere, the vote under section 8.63 has no effect whatever of exonerating or protecting X Co. if X Co. fails to meet any legal obligation that, as the majority shareholder of Y Co., it may owe to the minority shareholders of Y Co.

3. Section 8.63(c)

Subsection (c) contains administratively useful quorum provisions and provides that superfluous voting of shares that were not qualified to vote does not vitiate the effectiveness of the vote. But see subsection (e).

The fact that certain shares are not qualified and are not countable for purposes of subsection (a) says nothing as to whether they are properly countable for other purposes such as, for example, a statutory requirement that a certain fraction of the total vote or a special majority vote be obtained.

4. Section 8.63(d)

In most circumstances, the secretary of X Co. will have no way to know whether certain of X Co.'s outstanding shares should be excluded from the teller's count because of the identity of the owners or of those persons who control the voting of the shares. Subsection (a) together with subsection (d) therefore impose on a director who has a conflicting interest respecting the transaction, as a prerequisite to safe harbor protection by shareholder vote, the obligation to inform the secretary, or other officer or agent authorized to tabulate votes, of the number and holders of shares known by him to be owned by him or by a related person of his. Thus, a director who has a conflicting interest respecting the transaction, because he stands to make a commission from it, is obligated to report shares owned or the vote of which is controlled by him and by all related persons of his; a director who has a conflicting interest respecting the transaction because his brother stands to make a commission from it has the same reporting obligation. The tabulator may also, of course, have other independent knowledge of shares that are owned or controlled by a related person of the director.

If the tabulator of votes knows that particular shares should be excluded but fails to exclude them from the count and their inclusion in the vote does not affect its outcome, subsection (c) governs and the shareholders' vote stands. If the improper inclusion determines the outcome, the shareholders' vote fails to comply with subsection (a). If the tabulator *does not know* that certain shares are owned or controlled by the director who has the conflicting interest or a related person of his, the shares are "qualified" pursuant to the definition in subsection (b), and the vote cannot be attacked on that ground for failure to comply with subsection (a); but see subsection (e).

5. Section 8.63(e)

If D did not provide the information required under subsection (d), on the face of it shareholders' action is not in compliance with subsection (a) and D has no safe harbor under subsection (a). In the absence of such safe harbor D can be put to the challenge of establishing the fairness of the transaction under section 8.61(b)(3).

That result is the proper one where D's failure to inform was determinative of the vote or, worse, was part of a deliberate effort on D's part to influence the outcome of the vote. But if D's omission was essentially an act of negligence, if the number of unreported shares was not determinative of the outcome of the vote, and if the omission was not motivated by D's effort to influence the integrity of the voting process, the court should be free to fashion an appropriate response to the situation in the light of all the considerations at the time of trial. The court should not be automatically forced by the mechanics of the subchapter to a lengthy and retrospective trial on "fairness." Subsection (e) grants the court that discretion in those circumstances and permits it to accord such effect, if any, to the shareholders' vote, or grant such relief respecting the transaction or D, as the court may find appropriate.

Despite the presumption of regularity customarily accorded the secretary's record, a plaintiff may go behind the secretary's record for purposes of subsection (e).

CHAPTER 9. DOMESTICATION AND CONVERSION

Introductory Official Comment to Chapter 9

This chapter provides a series of procedures by which a domestic business corporation may become a different form of entity or, conversely, an entity that is not a domestic business corporation may become a domestic business corporation. These various types of procedures are as follows:

- *Domestication.* The procedures in subchapter 9B permit a corporation to change its state of incorporation, thus allowing a domestic business corporation to become a foreign business corporation or a foreign business corporation to become a domestic business corporation.

- *Nonprofit Conversion.* The procedures in subchapter 9C permit a domestic business corporation to become either a domestic nonprofit corporation or a foreign nonprofit corporation.

- *Foreign Nonprofit Domestication and Conversion.* The procedures in subchapter 9D permit a foreign nonprofit corporation to become a domestic business corporation.

- *Entity Conversion.* The procedures in subchapter 9E permit a domestic business corporation to become a domestic or foreign unincorporated entity, and also permit a domestic or foreign unincorporated entity to become a domestic business corporation.

Each of the foregoing transactions could previously be accomplished by a merger under chapter 11 with a wholly owned subsidiary of the appropriate type. An important purpose of this chapter is to permit the transactions to be accomplished directly.

The provisions of this chapter apply only if a domestic business corporation is present either immediately before or immediately after a transaction. Some states may wish to generalize the provisions of this chapter so that they are not limited to transactions involving a domestic business corporation, for example, to permit a domestic limited partnership to become a domestic limited liability company. The Model Entity Transactions Act prepared by the Ad Hoc Committee on Entity Rationalization of the Section of Business Law is such a generalized statute.

The procedures of this chapter do not permit the combination of two or more entities into a single entity. Transactions of that type must continue to be conducted under chapters 11 and 12.

SUBCHAPTER A. PRELIMINARY PROVISIONS

§ 9.01 Excluded Transactions

This chapter may not be used to effect a transaction that:

(1) [converts an insurance company organized on the mutual principle to one organized on a stock-share basis];

(2) * * *

(3) * * *

§ 9.02 Required Approvals [Optional]

(a) If a domestic or foreign business corporation or eligible entity may not be a party to a merger without the approval of the [attorney general], the [department of banking], the [department of insurance] or the [public utility commission], the corporation or eligible entity shall not be a party to a transaction under this chapter without the prior written approval of that agency.

(b) Property held in trust or for charitable purposes under the laws of this state by a domestic or foreign eligible entity shall not, by any transaction under this chapter, be diverted from the objects for which it was donated, granted or devised, unless and until the eligible entity obtains an order of [court] [the attorney general] specifying the disposition of the property to the extent required by and pursuant to [cite state statutory cy pres or other nondiversion statute].

SUBCHAPTER B. DOMESTICATION

§ 9.20 Domestication

(a) A foreign business corporation may become a domestic business corporation only if the domestication is permitted by the organic law of the foreign corporation.

(b) A domestic business corporation may become a foreign business corporation if the domestication is permitted by the laws of the foreign jurisdiction. Regardless of whether the laws of the foreign jurisdiction require the adoption of a plan of domestication, the domestication shall be approved by the adoption by the corporation of a plan of domestication in the manner provided in this subchapter.

(c) The plan of domestication must include:

(1) a statement of the jurisdiction in which the corporation is to be domesticated;

(2) the terms and conditions of the domestication;

(3) the manner and basis of reclassifying the shares of the corporation following its domestication into shares or other securi-

ties, obligations, rights to acquire shares or other securities, cash, other property, or any combination of the foregoing; and

(4) any desired amendments to the articles of incorporation of the corporation following its domestication.

(d) The plan of domestication may also include a provision that the plan may be amended prior to filing the document required by the laws of this state or the other jurisdiction to consummate the domestication, except that subsequent to approval of the plan by the shareholders the plan may not be amended to change:

(1) the amount or kind of shares or other securities, obligations, rights to acquire shares or other securities, cash, or other property to be received by the shareholders under the plan;

(2) the articles of incorporation as they will be in effect immediately following the domestication, except for changes permitted by section 10.05 or by comparable provisions of the laws of the other jurisdiction; or

(3) any of the other terms or conditions of the plan if the change would adversely affect any of the shareholders in any material respect.

(e) Terms of a plan of domestication may be made dependent upon facts objectively ascertainable outside the plan in accordance with section 1.20(k).

(f) If any debt security, note or similar evidence of indebtedness for money borrowed, whether secured or unsecured, or a contract of any kind, issued, incurred or executed by a domestic business corporation before [the effective date of this subchapter] contains a provision applying to a merger of the corporation and the document does not refer to a domestication of the corporation, the provision shall be deemed to apply to a domestication of the corporation until such time as the provision is amended subsequent to that date.

OFFICIAL COMMENT

1. Applicability

This subchapter authorizes a foreign business corporation to become a domestic business corporation. It also authorizes a domestic business corporation to become a foreign business corporation. In each case, the domestication is authorized only if the laws of the foreign jurisdiction permit the domestication. Whether and on what terms a foreign business corporation is authorized to domesticate in this state are issues governed by the laws of the foreign jurisdiction, not by this subchapter.

A foreign corporation is not required to have in effect a valid certificate of authority under chapter 15 in order to domesticate in this state.

2. Terms and Conditions of Domestication

This subchapter imposes virtually no restrictions or limitations on the terms and conditions of a domestication, except for those set forth in section 9.20(d) concerning provisions in a plan of domestication for amendment of the plan after it has been approved by the shareholders. Shares of a domestic business corporation that domesticates in another jurisdiction may be reclassified into shares or other securities, obligations, rights to acquire shares or other securities, cash or other property. The capitalization of the corporation may be restructured in the domestication, and its articles of incorporation may be amended by the articles of domestication in any way deemed appropriate. When a foreign business corporation domesticates in this state, the laws of the foreign jurisdiction determine which of the foregoing actions may be taken.

Although this subchapter imposes virtually no restrictions or limitations on the terms and conditions of a domestication, section 9.20(c) requires that the terms and conditions be set forth in the plan of domestication. The plan of domestication is not required to be publicly filed, and the articles of domestication that are filed with the secretary of state by a foreign corporation domesticating in this state are not required to include a plan of domestication. See section 9.22. Similarly, articles of charter surrender that are filed with the secretary of state by a domestic business corporation domesticating in another jurisdiction are not required to include a plan of domestication. See section 9.23.

The list in section 9.20(c) of required provisions in a plan of domestication is not exhaustive and the plan may include any other provisions that may be desired.

3. Amendments of Articles of Incorporation

A corporation's articles of incorporation may be amended in a domestication. Under section 9.20(c)(4), a plan of domestication of a domestic business corporation proposing to domesticate in a foreign jurisdiction may include amendments to the articles of incorporation and should include, at a minimum, any amendments required to conform the articles of incorporation to the requirements for articles of incorporation of a corporation incorporated in the foreign jurisdiction. It is assumed that the foreign jurisdiction will give effect to the articles of incorporation as amended to the same extent that it would if the articles had been independently amended before the domestication.

The laws of the foreign jurisdiction determine whether and to what extent a foreign corporation may amend its articles of incorporation when domesticating in this state. Following the domestication of a foreign corporation in this state, of course, its articles of incorporation may be amended under chapter 10.

4. Adoption and Approval; Abandonment

The domestication of a domestic business corporation in a foreign jurisdiction must be adopted and approved as provided in section 9.21. Under section 9.25, the board of directors of a domestic business corporation may abandon a domestication before its effective date even if the plan of domestication has already been approved by the corporation's shareholders.

5. Appraisal Rights

A shareholder of a domestic business corporation that adopts and approves a plan of domestication has appraisal rights if the shareholder does not receive shares in the foreign corporation resulting from the domestication that have terms as favorable to the shareholder in all material respects, and represent at least the same percentage interest of the total voting rights of the outstanding shares of the corporation, as the shares held by the shareholder before the domestication. See sections 9.24(b) and 13.02(a)(6).

6. Transitional Rule

Because the concept of domestication is new, a person contracting with a corporation or loaning it money who drafted and negotiated special rights relating to the transaction before the enactment of this subchapter should not be charged with the consequences of not having dealt with the concept of domestication in the context of those special rights. Section 9.20(e) accordingly provides a transitional rule that is intended to protect such special rights. If, for example, a corporation is a party to a contract that provides that the corporation cannot participate in a merger without the consent of the other party to the contract, the requirement to obtain the consent of the other party will also apply to the domestication of the corporation in another jurisdiction. If the corporation fails to obtain the consent, the result will be that the other party will have the same rights it would have if the corporation were to participate in a merger without the required consent.

The purpose of section 9.20(e) is to protect the third party to a contract with the corporation, and section 9.20(e) should not be applied in such a way as to impair unconstitutionally the third party's contract. As applied to the corporation, section 9.20(e) is an exercise of the reserved power of the state legislature set forth in section 1.02.

The transitional rule in section 9.20(e) ceases to apply at such time as the provision of the agreement or debt instrument giving rise to the special rights is first amended after the effective date of this subchapter because at that time the provision may be amended to address expressly a domestication of the corporation.

A similar transitional rule governing the application to a domestication of special voting rights of directors and shareholders and other internal corporate procedures is found in section 9.21(7).

§ 9.21 Action on a Plan of Domestication

In the case of a domestication of a domestic business corporation in a foreign jurisdiction:

(1) The plan of domestication must be adopted by the board of directors.

(2) After adopting the plan of domestication the board of directors must submit the plan to the shareholders for their approval. The board of directors must also transmit to the shareholders a recommendation that the shareholders approve the plan, unless the board of directors makes a determination that because of conflicts of interest or other special circumstances it should not make such a recommendation, in which case the board of directors must transmit to the shareholders the basis for that determination.

(3) The board of directors may condition its submission of the plan of domestication to the shareholders on any basis.

(4) If the approval of the shareholders is to be given at a meeting, the corporation must notify each shareholder, whether or not entitled to vote, of the meeting of shareholders at which the plan of domestication is to be submitted for approval. The notice must state that the purpose, or one of the purposes, of the meeting is to consider the plan and must contain or be accompanied by a copy or summary of the plan. The notice shall include or be accompanied by a copy of the articles of incorporation as they will be in effect immediately after the domestication.

(5) Unless the articles of incorporation, or the board of directors acting pursuant to paragraph (3), requires a greater vote or a greater number of votes to be present, approval of the plan of domestication requires the approval of the shareholders at a meeting at which a quorum consisting of at least a majority of the votes entitled to be cast on the plan exists, and, if any class or series of shares is entitled to vote as a separate group on the plan, the approval of each such separate voting group at a meeting at which a quorum of the voting group consisting of at least a majority of the votes entitled to be cast on the domestication by that voting group exists.

(6) Separate voting by voting groups is required by each class or series of shares that:

(i) are to be reclassified under the plan of domestication into other securities, obligations, rights to acquire shares or other securities, cash, other property, or any combination of the foregoing;

(ii) would be entitled to vote as a separate group on a provision of the plan that, if contained in a proposed amendment to articles of incorporation, would require action by separate voting groups under section 10.04; or

(iii) is entitled under the articles of incorporation to vote as a voting group to approve an amendment of the articles.

(7) If any provision of the articles of incorporation, bylaws or an agreement to which any of the directors or shareholders are parties, adopted or entered into before [the effective date of this subchapter], applies to a merger of the corporation and that document does not refer to a domestication of the corporation, the provision shall be deemed to apply to a domestication of the corporation until such time as the provision is amended subsequent to that date.

OFFICIAL COMMENT

1. In General

This section sets forth the rules for adoption and approval of a plan of domestication of a domestic business corporation in a foreign jurisdiction. The manner in which the domestication of a foreign business corporation in this state must be adopted and approved will be controlled by the laws of the foreign jurisdiction. The provisions of this section follow generally the rules in chapter 11 for adoption and approval of a plan of merger or share exchange.

A plan of domestication must be adopted by the board of directors. Although section 9.21(2) permits the board to refrain from making a recommendation to the shareholders that they approve the plan, that does not change the underlying requirement that the board first adopt the plan before it is submitted to the shareholders. Approval by the shareholders of a plan of domestication is always required.

2. Voting by Separate Groups

Section 9.21(6) provides that a class or series has a right to vote on a plan of domestication as a separate voting group if, as part of the domestication, the class or series would be reclassified into other securities, interests, obligations, rights to acquire shares or other securities, cash or other property. A class or series also is entitled to vote as a separate voting group if the class or series would be entitled to vote as a separate group on a provision in the plan that, if contained in an amendment to the articles of incorporation, would require approval by that class or series under section 10.04. In this latter case, a class or series will be entitled to vote as a separate voting group if the terms of that class or series are being changed, or if the shares of that class or series are being reclassified into shares of any other class or series. It is not intended that immaterial changes in the language of the articles of incorporation made to conform to the usage of the laws of the foreign jurisdiction will alone create an entitlement to vote as a separate group.

Under section 10.04, and therefore under section 9.21(6), if a change that requires voting by separate voting groups affects two or more classes or two or more series in the same or a substantially similar way, the relevant classes or series will vote together, rather than separately, on the change. For the mechanics of voting where voting by voting groups is required under section 9.21(6), see sections 7.25 and 7.26.

If a domestication would amend the articles of incorporation to change the voting requirements on future amendments of the articles, the transaction must also be approved by the vote required by section 7.27.

3. Quorum and Voting

Section 9.21(5) provides that approval of a plan of domestication requires approval of the shareholders at a meeting at which there exists a quorum consisting of a majority of the votes entitled to be cast on the plan. Section 9.21(5) also provides that if any class or series of shares are entitled to vote as a separate group on the plan, the approval of each such separate group must be given at a meeting at which there exists a quorum consisting of at least a majority of the votes entitled to be cast on the plan by that class or series. If a quorum is present, then under sections 7.25 and 7.26 the plan will be approved if more votes are cast in favor of the plan than against it by each voting group entitled to vote on the plan.

In lieu of approval at a shareholders' meeting, approval can be given by the consent of all the shareholders entitled to vote on the domestication, under the procedures set forth in section 7.04.

4. Transitional Rule

Because the concept of domestication is new, persons who drafted and negotiated special rights for directors or shareholders before the enactment of this subchapter should not be charged with the consequences of not having dealt with the concept of domestication in the context of those special rights. Section 9.21(7) accordingly provides a transitional rule that is intended to protect such special rights. Other documents, in addition to the articles of incorporation and bylaws, that may contain such special rights include shareholders agreements, voting trust agreements, vote pooling agreements or other similar arrangements. If, for example, the articles of incorporation provide that the corporation cannot participate in a merger without a supermajority vote of the shareholders, that supermajority requirement will also apply to the domestication of the corporation in another jurisdiction.

The purpose of section 9.21(7) is to protect persons who negotiated special rights for directors or shareholders whether in a contract with the corporation or in the articles of incorporation or bylaws, and section 9.21(7) should not be applied in such a way as to impair unconstitutionally the rights of any party to a contract with the corporation. As applied to the corporation, section 9.21(7) is an exercise of the reserved power of the state legislature set forth in section 1.02.

The transitional rule in section 9.21(7) ceases to apply at such time as the provision of the articles of incorporation, bylaws or agreement giving rise to the special rights is first amended after the effective date of this subchapter because at that time the provision may be amended to address expressly a domestication of the corporation.

A similar transitional rule with regard to the application to a domestication of special contractual rights of third parties is found in section 9.20(e).

§ 9.22 Articles of Domestication

(a) After the domestication of a foreign business corporation has been authorized as required by the laws of the foreign jurisdiction, articles of domestication shall be executed by any officer or other duly authorized representative. The articles shall set forth:

(1) the name of the corporation immediately before the filing of the articles of domestication and, if that name is unavailable for use in this state or the corporation desires to change its name in connection with the domestication, a name that satisfies the requirements of section 4.01;

(2) the jurisdiction of incorporation of the corporation immediately before the filing of the articles of domestication and the date the corporation was incorporated in that jurisdiction; and

(3) a statement that the domestication of the corporation in this state was duly authorized as required by the laws of the jurisdiction in which the corporation was incorporated immediately before its domestication in this state.

(b) The articles of domestication shall either contain all of the provisions that section 2.02(a) requires to be set forth in articles of incorporation and any other desired provisions that section 2.02(b) permits to be included in articles of incorporation, or shall have attached articles of incorporation. In either case, provisions that would not be required to be included in restated articles of incorporation may be omitted.

(c) The articles of domestication shall be delivered to the secretary of state for filing, and shall take effect at the effective time provided in section 1.23.

(d) If the foreign corporation is authorized to transact business in this state under chapter 15, its certificate of authority shall be cancelled automatically on the effective date of its domestication.

§ 9.23 Surrender of Charter Upon Domestication

(a) Whenever a domestic business corporation has adopted and approved, in the manner required by this subchapter, a plan of domestication providing for the corporation to be domesticated in a foreign jurisdiction, articles of charter surrender shall be executed on behalf of the corporation by any officer or other duly authorized representative. The articles of charter surrender shall set forth:

(1) the name of the corporation;

(2) a statement that the articles of charter surrender are being filed in connection with the domestication of the corporation in a foreign jurisdiction;

(3) a statement that the domestication was duly approved by the shareholders and, if voting by any separate voting group was required, by each such separate voting group, in the manner required by this Act and the articles of incorporation;

(4) the corporation's new jurisdiction of incorporation.

(b) The articles of charter surrender shall be delivered by the corporation to the secretary of state for filing. The articles of charter surrender shall take effect on the effective time provided in section 1.23.

OFFICIAL COMMENT

The filing of articles of charter surrender makes the domestication of the corporation in its new jurisdiction of incorporation a matter of public record in this state. It also terminates the status of the corporation as a corporation incorporated under the laws of this state. Once the articles of charter surrender have become effective, the corporation will no longer be in good standing in this state. The corporation may, however, apply for a certificate of authority as a foreign corporation under subchapter 15A.

Where a foreign corporation domesticates in this state, the filing required to terminate its status as a corporation incorporated under the laws of the foreign jurisdiction is determined by the laws of that jurisdiction.

The filing requirements for articles of charter surrender are set forth in sections 1.20 and 1.23. Under section 1.23, a document may specify a delayed effective time and date, and if it does so the document becomes effective at the time and date specified, except that a delayed effective date may not be later than the 90th day after the date the document is filed. To avoid any question about a gap in the continuity of its existence, it is recommended that a corporation use a delayed effective date provision in its domestication filings in both this state and the foreign jurisdiction, or otherwise coordinate those filings, so that the filings become effective at the same time.

§ 9.24 Effect of Domestication

(a) When a domestication becomes effective:

(1) the title to all real and personal property, both tangible and intangible, of the corporation remains in the corporation without reversion or impairment;

(2) the liabilities of the corporation remain the liabilities of the corporation;

(3) an action or proceeding pending against the corporation continues against the corporation as if the domestication had not occurred;

(4) the articles of domestication, or the articles of incorporation attached to the articles of domestication, constitute the articles of incorporation of a foreign corporation domesticating in this state;

(5) the shares of the corporation are reclassified into shares, other securities, obligations, rights to acquire shares or other securities, or into cash or other property in accordance with the terms of the domestication, and the shareholders are entitled only to the rights provided by those terms and to any appraisal rights they may have under the organic law of the domesticating corporation; and

(6) the corporation is deemed to:

(i) be incorporated under and subject to the organic law of the domesticated corporation for all purposes;

(ii) be the same corporation without interruption as the domesticating corporation; and

(iii) have been incorporated on the date the domesticating corporation was originally incorporated.

(b) When a domestication of a domestic business corporation in a foreign jurisdiction becomes effective, the foreign business corporation is deemed to:

(1) appoint the secretary of state as its agent for service of process in a proceeding to enforce the rights of shareholders who exercise appraisal rights in connection with the domestication; and

(2) agree that it will promptly pay the amount, if any, to which such shareholders are entitled under chapter 13.

(c) The owner liability of a shareholder in a foreign corporation that is domesticated in this state shall be as follows:

(1) The domestication does not discharge any owner liability under the laws of the foreign jurisdiction to the extent any such owner liability arose before the effective time of the articles of domestication.

(2) The shareholder shall not have owner liability under the laws of the foreign jurisdiction for any debt, obligation or liability of the corporation that arises after the effective time of the articles of domestication.

(3) The provisions of the laws of the foreign jurisdiction shall continue to apply to the collection or discharge of any owner liability preserved by paragraph (1), as if the domestication had not occurred.

(4) The shareholder shall have whatever rights of contribution from other shareholders are provided by the laws of the foreign jurisdiction with respect to any owner liability preserved by paragraph (1), as if the domestication had not occurred.

[(d) A shareholder who becomes subject to owner liability for some or all of the debts, obligations or liabilities of the corporation as a result of its domestication in this state shall have owner liability only for those debts, obligations or liabilities of the corporation that arise after the effective time of the articles of domestication.]

OFFICIAL COMMENT

When a corporation is domesticated in this state under this subchapter, the corporation becomes a domestic business corporation with the same status as if it had been originally incorporated under this Act. Thus, the domesticated corporation will have all of the powers, privileges, and rights granted to corporations originally incorporated in this state and will be subject to all of the duties, liabilities and limitations imposed on domestic business corporations. Except as provided in section 9.24(b), the effect of domesticating a corporation of this state in a foreign jurisdiction is governed by the laws of the foreign jurisdiction. See section 9.20(b).

A domestication is not a conveyance, transfer or assignment. It does not give rise to claims of reverter or impairment of title based on a prohibited conveyance, transfer or assignment. Nor does it give rise to a claim that a contract with the corporation is no longer in effect on the ground of nonassignability, unless the contract specifically provides that it does not survive a domestication.

Section 9.24(a)(1)-(3) and (b) are similar to section 11.07(a)(3)-(5) and (c) with respect to the effects of a merger. Although section 9.24(a)(1)-(3) would be implied by the general rule stated in section 9.24(a)(6) even if not stated expressly, those rules have been included to avoid any question as to whether a different result was intended.

The rule in section 9.24(a)(6)(iii) that the date of incorporation of the foreign corporation remains its date of incorporation after the corporation has been domesticated in this state is a specific application of the general rule in section 9.24(a)(6)(ii). The date of incorporation is required by section 9.22(a)(2) to be set forth in the articles of domestication.

One of the continuing liabilities of the corporation following its domestication in a foreign jurisdiction is the obligation to its shareholders who exercise appraisal rights to pay them the amount, if any, to which they are entitled under chapter 13.

Section 9.24(c) preserves liability only for owner liabilities to the extent they arise before the domestication. Owner liability is not preserved for subsequent changes in an underlying liability, regardless of whether a change is voluntary or involuntary.

Section 9.24(d) is an optional provision that will not be needed in most states. It should be included only when the statutory laws of a state impose personal liability on the shareholders of a corporation, for example, for unpaid wages owed to employees of the corporation.

§ 9.25 Abandonment of a Domestication

(a) Unless otherwise provided in a plan of domestication of a domestic business corporation, after the plan has been adopted and approved as required by this subchapter, and at any time before the domestication has become effective, it may be abandoned by the board of directors without action by the shareholders.

(b) If a domestication is abandoned under subsection (a) after articles of charter surrender have been filed with the secretary of state but before the domestication has become effective, a statement that the domestication has been abandoned in accordance with this section, executed by an officer or other duly authorized representative, shall be delivered to the secretary of state for filing prior to the effective date of the domestication. The statement shall take effect upon filing and the domestication shall be deemed abandoned and shall not become effective.

(c) If the domestication of a foreign business corporation in this state is abandoned in accordance with the laws of the foreign jurisdiction after articles of domestication have been filed with the secretary of state, a statement that the domestication has been abandoned, executed by an officer or other duly authorized representative, shall be delivered to the secretary of state for filing. The statement shall take effect upon filing and the domestication shall be deemed abandoned and shall not become effective.

SUBCHAPTER C. NONPROFIT CONVERSION [OMITTED]

SUBCHAPTER D. FOREIGN NONPROFIT DOMESTICATION AND CONVERSION [OMITTED]

SUBCHAPTER E. ENTITY CONVERSION

§ 9.50 Entity Conversion Authorized; Definitions

(a) A domestic business corporation may become a domestic unincorporated entity pursuant to a plan of entity conversion.

(b) A domestic business corporation may become a foreign unincorporated entity if the entity conversion is permitted by the laws of the foreign jurisdiction.

(c) A domestic unincorporated entity may become a domestic business corporation. If the organic law of a domestic unincorporated entity does not provide procedures for the approval of an entity conversion, the conversion shall be adopted and approved, and the entity conversion effectuated, in the same manner as a merger of the unincorporated entity, and its interest holders shall be entitled to appraisal rights if appraisal rights are available upon any type of merger under the organic law of the unincorporated entity. If the organic law of a domestic unincorporated entity does not provide procedures for the approval of either an entity conversion or a merger, a plan of entity conversion shall be adopted and approved, the entity conversion effectuated, and appraisal rights exercised, in accordance with the procedures in this subchapter and chapter 13. Without limiting the provisions of this subsection, a domestic unincorporated entity whose organic law does not provide procedures for the approval of an entity conversion shall be subject to subsection (e) and section 9.52(7). For purposes of applying this subchapter and chapter 13:

(1) the unincorporated entity, its interest holders, interests and organic documents taken together, shall be deemed to be a domestic business corporation, shareholders, shares and articles of incorporation, respectively and vice versa, as the context may require; and

(2) if the business and affairs of the unincorporated entity are managed by a group of persons that is not identical to the interest holders, that group shall be deemed to be the board of directors.

(d) A foreign unincorporated entity may become a domestic business corporation if the organic law of the foreign unincorporated entity authorizes it to become a corporation in another jurisdiction.

(e) If any debt security, note or similar evidence of indebtedness for money borrowed, whether secured or unsecured, or a contract of any kind, issued, incurred or executed by a domestic business corporation before [the effective date of this subchapter], applies to a merger of the corporation and the document does not refer to an entity conversion of the corporation, the provision shall be deemed to apply to an entity conversion of the corporation until such time as the provision is amended subsequent to that date.

(f) As used in this subchapter:

(1) "Converting entity" means the domestic business corporation or domestic unincorporated entity that adopts a plan of entity conversion or the foreign unincorporated entity converting to a domestic business corporation.

(2) "Surviving entity" means the corporation or unincorporated entity as it continues in existence immediately after consummation of an entity conversion pursuant to this subchapter.

OFFICIAL COMMENT

1. Scope of Subchapter

Subject to certain restrictions which are discussed below, this subchapter authorizes the following types of conversion:

1. a domestic business corporation to a domestic unincorporated entity,
2. a domestic business corporation to a foreign unincorporated entity,
3. a domestic unincorporated entity to a domestic business corporation,
4. a foreign unincorporated entity to a domestic business corporation.

This subchapter provides for the conversion of a domestic unincorporated entity only to a domestic business corporation because the conversion of a domestic unincorporated entity to another form of unincorporated entity or to a foreign business corporation would be outside of the scope of this Act. This subchapter similarly does not provide for the conversion of a foreign corporation or unincorporated entity to a domestic unincorporated entity. States may nonetheless wish to consider generalizing the provisions of this subchapter to authorize those types of conversions.

2. Procedural Requirements

The concept of entity conversion as authorized by this subchapter is not found in many laws governing the incorporation or organization of corporations and unincorporated entities. In recognition of that fact, the rules in this section vary depending on whether the corporation or unincorporated entity desiring to convert pursuant to this subchapter is incorporated or organized under the laws of this state or of some other jurisdiction.

If the organic law of a domestic unincorporated entity does not expressly authorize it to convert to a domestic business corporation, it is intended that the first sentence of subsection (c) will provide the necessary authority. Until such time as the various organic laws of each form of unincorporated entity have been amended to provide procedures for adopting and approving a plan of entity conversion, subsection (c) provides those procedures by reference to the procedures for mergers under the organic law of the unincorporated entity or, if there are no such merger provisions, by reference to the provisions of this subchapter applicable to domestic business corporations.

Subsection (d) provides that a foreign unincorporated entity may convert to a domestic business corporation pursuant to this subchapter only if the law under which the foreign unincorporated entity is organized permits the conversion. This rule avoids issues that could arise if this state authorized a foreign unincorporated entity to participate in a transaction in this state that its home jurisdiction did not authorize. This subchapter does not specify the procedures that a foreign unincorporated entity must follow to authorize a conversion under this subchapter on the assumption that if the organic law of the foreign unincorporated entity authorizes the conversion that law will also provide the applicable procedures and any safeguards considered necessary to protect the interest holders of the unincorporated entity.

3. Transitional Rule

Because the concept of entity conversion is new, a person contracting with a corporation or loaning it money who drafted and negotiated special rights relating to the transaction before the enactment of this subchapter should not be charged with the consequences of not having dealt with the concept of entity conversion in the context of those special rights. Section 9.50(e) accordingly provides a transitional rule that is intended to protect such special rights. If, for example, a corporation is a party to a contract that provides that the corporation cannot participate in a merger without the consent of the other party to the contract, the requirement to obtain the consent of the other party will also apply to the conversion of the corporation to a domestic or foreign unincorporated entity. If the corporation fails to obtain the consent, the result will be that the other party will have the same rights it would have if the corporation were to participate in a merger without the required consent.

The purpose of section 9.50(e) is to protect the third party to a contract with the corporation, and section 9.50(e) should not be applied in such a way as to impair unconstitutionally the third party's contract. As applied to the corporation, section 9.50(e) is an exercise of the reserved power of the state legislature set forth in section 1.02.

The transitional rule in section 9.50(e) ceases to apply at such time as the provision of the agreement or debt instrument giving rise to the special rights is first amended after the effective date of this subchapter because at that time the provision may be amended to address expressly an entity conversion of the corporation.

Section 9.50(e) will also apply in the case of an unincorporated entity whose organic law does not provide procedures for the approval of an entity conversion because section 9.50(c) treats such an unincorporated entity as a business corporation for purposes of section 9.50(e).

A similar transitional rule governing the application to an entity conversion of special voting rights of directors and shareholders and other internal corporate procedures is found in section 9.52(6).

§ 9.51 Plan of Entity Conversion

(a) A plan of entity conversion must include:

(1) a statement of the type of unincorporated entity the surviving entity will be and, if it will be a foreign unincorporated entity, its jurisdiction of organization;

(2) the terms and conditions of the conversion;

(3) the manner and basis of converting the shares of the domestic business corporation following its conversion into interests or other securities, obligations, rights to acquire interests or other securities, cash, other property, or any combination of the foregoing; and

(4) the full text, as they will be in effect immediately following the conversion, of the organic documents of the surviving entity.

(b) The plan of entity conversion may also include a provision that the plan may be amended prior to filing articles of entity conversion, except that subsequent to approval of the plan by the shareholders the plan may not be amended to change:

(1) the amount or kind of shares or other securities, interests, obligations, rights to acquire shares, other securities or interests, cash, or other property to be received under the plan by the shareholders;

(2) the organic documents that will be in effect immediately following the conversion, except for changes permitted by a provision of the organic law of the surviving entity comparable to section 10.05; or

(3) any of the other terms or conditions of the plan if the change would adversely affect any of the shareholders in any material respect.

(c) Terms of a plan of entity conversion may be made dependent upon facts objectively ascertainable outside the plan in accordance with section 1.20(k).

OFFICIAL COMMENT

1. Terms and Conditions of Entity Conversion

This subchapter imposes virtually no restrictions or limitations on the terms and conditions of an entity conversion, except for those set forth in section 9.51(b) concerning provisions in a plan of entity conversion for amendment of the plan after it has been approved by the shareholders. Shares of a domestic business corporation that converts to an unincorporated entity may be reclassified into interests or other securities, obligations, rights to acquire interests or other securities, cash or other property. The capitalization of the entity will need to be restructured in the conversion and its organic documents or articles of incorporation may be amended by the articles of entity conversion in any way deemed appropriate. When a foreign unincorporated entity converts to a domestic business corporation, the laws of the foreign jurisdiction determine which of the foregoing actions may be taken.

Although this subchapter imposes virtually no restrictions or limitations on the terms and conditions of an entity conversion, section 9.51(a) requires that the terms and conditions be set forth in the plan of entity conversion. The plan of entity conversion is not required to be publicly filed, and the articles of entity conversion that are filed with the secretary of state are not required to include a plan of entity conversion. See section 9.53. Similarly, articles of charter surrender that are filed with the secretary of state by a domestic business corporation converting to a foreign unincorporated entity are not required to include the plan of entity conversion. See section 9.54.

The list in section 9.51(a) of required provisions in a plan of entity conversion is not exhaustive and the plan may include any other provisions that may be desired.

2. Adoption and Approval; Abandonment

The conversion of a domestic business corporation to a foreign unincorporated entity must be adopted and approved as provided in section 9.52. Shareholders of a domestic business corporation that adopts and approves a plan of entity conversion have appraisal rights. See chapter 13. Under section 9.55, the board of directors of a domestic business corporation may abandon an entity conversion before its effective date even if the plan of entity conversion has already been approved by the corporation's shareholders.

§ 9.52 Action on a Plan of Entity Conversion

In the case of an entity conversion of a domestic business corporation to a domestic or foreign unincorporated entity:

(1) The plan of entity conversion must be adopted by the board of directors.

(2) After adopting the plan of entity conversion, the board of directors must submit the plan to the shareholders for their approval. The board of directors must also transmit to the shareholders a recommendation that the shareholders approve the plan, unless the board of directors makes a determination that because of conflicts of interest or other special circumstances it should not make such a recommendation, in which case the board of directors must transmit to the shareholders the basis for that determination.

(3) The board of directors may condition its submission of the plan of entity conversion to the shareholders on any basis.

(4) If the approval of the shareholders is to be given at a meeting, the corporation must notify each shareholder, whether or not entitled to vote, of the meeting of shareholders at which the plan of entity conversion is to be submitted for approval. The notice must state that the purpose, or one of the purposes, of the meeting is to consider the plan and must contain or be accompanied by a copy or summary of the plan. The notice shall include or be accompanied by a copy of the organic documents as they will be in effect immediately after the entity conversion.

(5) Unless the articles of incorporation, or the board of directors acting pursuant to paragraph (3), requires a greater vote or a greater number of votes to be present, approval of the plan of entity conversion requires the approval of each class or series of shares of the corporation voting as a separate voting group at a meeting at which a quorum of the voting group consisting of at least a majority of the votes entitled to be cast on the conversion by that voting group exists.

(6) If any provision of the articles of incorporation, bylaws or an agreement to which any of the directors or shareholders are parties, adopted or entered into before [the effective date of this subchapter], applies to a merger of the corporation and the document does not refer to an entity conversion of the corporation, the provision shall be deemed to apply to an entity conversion of the corporation until such time as the provision is subsequently amended.

(7) If as a result of the conversion one or more shareholders of the corporation would become subject to owner liability for the debts, obligations or liabilities of any other person or entity, approval of the plan of conversion shall require the execution, by each such shareholder, of a separate written consent to become subject to such owner liability.

OFFICIAL COMMENT

1. In General

This section sets forth the rules for adoption and approval of a plan of entity conversion by a domestic business corporation. The manner in which the conversion of a foreign unincorporated entity to a domestic business corporation must be adopted and approved will be controlled by the laws of the foreign jurisdiction. The provisions of this section follow generally the rules in chapter 11 for adoption and approval of a plan of merger or share exchange.

A plan of entity conversion must be adopted by the board of directors. Although section 9.52(2) permits the board to refrain from making a recommendation to the shareholders that they approve the plan, that does not change the underlying requirement that the board adopt the plan before it is submitted to the shareholders. Approval by the shareholders of a plan of entity conversion is always required.

2. Quorum and Voting

Section 9.52(5) provides that if the corporation has more than one class or series of shares, approval of an entity conversion requires the approval of each class or series voting as a separate voting group at a meeting at which there exists a quorum consisting of at least a majority of the votes entitled to be cast on the plan by that class or series. If a quorum is present, then under sections 7.25 and 7.26 the plan will be approved if more votes are cast in favor of the plan than against it by each voting group entitled to vote on the plan. If the shares of a corporation are not divided into two or more classes or series, all of the shares together will constitute a single class for purposes of section 9.52(5).

In lieu of approval at a shareholders' meeting, approval can be given by the consent of all the shareholders entitled to vote on the domestication, under the procedures set forth in section 7.04.

3. Transitional Rule

Because the concept of entity conversion is new, persons who drafted and negotiated special rights for directors or shareholders before the enactment of this subchapter should not be charged with the consequences of not having dealt with the concept of entity conversion in the context of those special rights. Section 9.52(7) accordingly provides a transitional rule that is intended to protect such special rights. Other documents, in addition to the articles of incorporation and bylaws, that may contain such special rights include shareholders agreements, voting trust agreements, vote pooling agreements or other similar arrangements. If, for example, the articles of incorporation provide that the corporation cannot participate in a merger without a supermajority vote of the shareholders, that supermajority requirement will also apply to the conversion of the corporation to a domestic or foreign unincorporated entity.

The purpose of section 9.52(6) is to protect persons who negotiated special rights for directors or shareholders whether in a contract with the corporation or in the articles of incorporation or bylaws, and section 9.52(6) should not be applied in such a way as to impair unconstitutionally the rights of any party to a contract with the corporation. As applied to the corporation, section 9.52(6) is an exercise of the reserved power of the state legislature set forth in section 1.02.

The transitional rule in section 9.52(6) ceases to apply at such time as the provision of the articles of incorporation, bylaws or agreement giving rise to the special rights is first amended after the effective date of this subchapter because at that time the provision may be amended to address expressly an entity conversion of the corporation.

Section 9.52(6) will also apply in the case of an unincorporated entity whose organic law does not provide procedures for the approval of an entity conversion because section 9.50(c) treats such an unincorporated entity as a business corporation for purposes of section 9.52(6).

A similar transitional rule with regard to the application to an entity conversion of special contractual rights of third parties is found in section 9.50(e).

§ 9.53 Articles of Entity Conversion

(a) After the conversion of a domestic business corporation to a domestic unincorporated entity has been adopted and approved as required by this Act, articles of entity conversion shall be executed on behalf of the corporation by any officer or other duly authorized representative. The articles shall:

(1) set forth the name of the corporation immediately before the filing of the articles of entity conversion and the name to which the name of the corporation is to be changed, which shall be a name that satisfies the organic law of the surviving entity;

(2) state the type of unincorporated entity that the surviving entity will be;

(3) set forth a statement that the plan of entity conversion was duly approved by the shareholders in the manner required by this Act and the articles of incorporation;

(4) if the surviving entity is a filing entity, either contain all of the provisions required to be set forth in its public organic document and any other desired provisions that are permitted, or have attached a public organic document; except that, in either case, provisions that would not be required to be included in a restated public organic document may be omitted.

(b) After the conversion of a domestic unincorporated entity to a domestic business corporation has been adopted and approved as required by the organic law of the unincorporated entity, articles of entity conversion shall be executed on behalf of the unincorporated entity by any officer or other duly authorized representative. The articles shall:

(1) set forth the name of the unincorporated entity immediately before the filing of the articles of entity conversion and the name to which the name of the unincorporated entity is to be changed, which shall be a name that satisfies the requirements of section 4.01;

(2) set forth a statement that the plan of entity conversion was duly approved in accordance with the organic law of the unincorporated entity;

(3) either contain all of the provisions that section 2.02(a) requires to be set forth in articles of incorporation and any other desired provisions that section 2.02(b) permits to be included in articles of incorporation, or have attached articles of incorporation; except that, in either case, provisions that would not be required to be included in restated articles of incorporation of a domestic business corporation may be omitted.

(c) After the conversion of a foreign unincorporated entity to a domestic business corporation has been authorized as required by the laws of the foreign jurisdiction, articles of entity conversion shall be executed on behalf of the foreign unincorporated entity by any officer or other duly authorized representative. The articles shall:

(1) set forth the name of the unincorporated entity immediately before the filing of the articles of entity conversion and the name to which the name of the unincorporated entity is to be changed, which shall be a name that satisfies the requirements of section 4.01;

(2) set forth the jurisdiction under the laws of which the unincorporated entity was organized immediately before the filing of the articles of entity conversion and the date on which the unincorporated entity was organized in that jurisdiction;

(3) set forth a statement that the conversion of the unincorporated entity was duly approved in the manner required by its organic law; and

(4) either contain all of the provisions that section 2.02(a) requires to be set forth in articles of incorporation and any other desired provisions that section 2.02(b) permits to be included in articles of incorporation, or have attached articles of incorporation; except that, in either case, provisions that would not be required to be included in restated articles of incorporation of a domestic business corporation may be omitted.

(d) The articles of entity conversion shall be delivered to the secretary of state for filing, and shall take effect at the effective time provided in section 1.23. Articles of entity conversion filed under section 9.53(a) or (b) may be combined with any required conversion filing under the organic law of the domestic unincorporated entity if the combined filing satisfies the requirements of both this section and the other organic law.

(e) If the converting entity is a foreign unincorporated entity that is authorized to transact business in this state under a provision of law similar to chapter 15, its certificate of authority or other type of foreign qualification shall be cancelled automatically on the effective date of its conversion.

§ 9.54 Surrender of Charter Upon Conversion

(a) Whenever a domestic business corporation has adopted and approved, in the manner required by this subchapter, a plan of entity conversion providing for the corporation to be converted to a foreign unincorporated entity, articles of charter surrender shall be executed on behalf of the corporation by any officer or other duly authorized representative. The articles of charter surrender shall set forth:

(1) the name of the corporation;

(2) a statement that the articles of charter surrender are being filed in connection with the conversion of the corporation to a foreign unincorporated entity;

(3) a statement that the conversion was duly approved by the shareholders in the manner required by this Act and the articles of incorporation;

(4) the jurisdiction under the laws of which the surviving entity will be organized;

(5) if the surviving entity will be a nonfiling entity, the address of its executive office immediately after the conversion.

(b) The articles of charter surrender shall be delivered by the corporation to the secretary of state for filing. The articles of charter surrender shall take effect on the effective time provided in section 1.23.

§ 9.55 Effect of Entity Conversion

(a) When a conversion under this subchapter becomes effective:

(1) the title to all real and personal property, both tangible and intangible, of the converting entity remains in the surviving entity without reversion or impairment;

(2) the liabilities of the converting entity remain the liabilities of the surviving entity;

(3) an action or proceeding pending against the converting entity continues against the surviving entity as if the conversion had not occurred;

(4) in the case of a surviving entity that is a filing entity, its articles of incorporation or public organic document and its private organic document become effective;

(5) in the case of a surviving entity that is a nonfiling entity, its private organic document becomes effective;

(6) the shares or interests of the converting entity are reclassified into shares, interests, other securities, obligations, rights to acquire shares, interests or other securities, or into cash or other property in accordance with the plan of conversion; and the shareholders or interest holders of the converting entity are entitled only to the rights provided to them under the terms of the conversion and to any appraisal rights they may have under the organic law of the converting entity; and

(7) the surviving entity is deemed to:

(i) be incorporated or organized under and subject to the organic law of the converting entity for all purposes;

(ii) be the same corporation or unincorporated entity without interruption as the converting entity; and

(iii) have been incorporated or otherwise organized on the date that the converting entity was originally incorporated or organized.

(b) When a conversion of a domestic business corporation to a foreign unincorporated entity becomes effective, the surviving entity is deemed to:

(1) appoint the secretary of state as its agent for service of process in a proceeding to enforce the rights of shareholders who exercise appraisal rights in connection with the conversion; and

(2) agree that it will promptly pay the amount, if any, to which such shareholders are entitled under chapter 13.

(c) A shareholder who becomes subject to owner liability for some or all of the debts, obligations or liabilities of the surviving entity shall have owner liability only for those debts, obligations or liabilities of the surviving entity that arise after the effective time of the articles of entity conversion.

(d) The owner liability of an interest holder in an unincorporated entity that converts to a domestic business corporation shall be as follows:

(1) The conversion does not discharge any owner liability under the organic law of the unincorporated entity to the extent any such owner liability arose before the effective time of the articles of entity conversion.

(2) The interest holder shall not have owner liability under the organic law of the unincorporated entity for any debt, obligation or liability of the corporation that arises after the effective time of the articles of entity conversion.

(3) The provisions of the organic law of the unincorporated entity shall continue to apply to the collection or discharge of any owner liability preserved by paragraph (1), as if the conversion had not occurred.

(4) The interest holder shall have whatever rights of contribution from other interest holders are provided by the organic law of the unincorporated entity with respect to any owner liability preserved by paragraph (1), as if the conversion had not occurred.

§ 9.56 Abandonment of an Entity Conversion

(a) Unless otherwise provided in a plan of entity conversion of a domestic business corporation, after the plan has been adopted and approved as required by this subchapter, and at any time before the entity conversion has become effective, it may be abandoned by the board of directors without action by the shareholders.

(b) If an entity conversion is abandoned after articles of entity conversion or articles of charter surrender have been filed with the secretary of state but before the entity conversion has become effective, a statement that the entity conversion has been abandoned in accordance with this section, executed by an officer or other duly authorized representative, shall be delivered to the secretary of state for filing prior to the effective date of the entity conversion. Upon filing, the statement shall take effect and the entity conversion shall be deemed abandoned and shall not become effective.

CHAPTER 10. AMENDMENT OF ARTICLES OF INCORPORATION AND BYLAWS

SUBCHAPTER A. AMENDMENT OF ARTICLES OF INCORPORATION

§ 10.01 Authority to Amend

(a) A corporation may amend its articles of incorporation at any time to add or change a provision that is required or permitted in the articles of incorporation as of the effective date of the amendment or to delete a provision that is not required to be contained in the articles of incorporation.

(b) A shareholder of the corporation does not have a vested property right resulting from any provision in the articles of incorporation, including provisions relating to management, control, capital structure, dividend entitlement, or purpose or duration of the corporation.

OFFICIAL COMMENT

Section 10.01(a) authorizes a corporation to amend its articles of incorporation by adding a new provision to its articles of incorporation, modifying an existing provision, or deleting a provision in its entirety. The sole test for the validity of an amendment is whether the provision could lawfully have been included in (or in the case of a deletion, omitted from) the articles of incorporation as of the effective date of the amendment.

The power of amendment must be exercised pursuant to the procedures set forth in chapter 10. Section 10.03 requires most amendments to be approved by a majority of the votes cast on the proposed amendment at a meeting at which a quorum consisting of at least a majority of the votes entitled to be cast is present. This requirement is supplemented by section 10.04, which governs voting by voting groups on amendments that directly affect a single class or series of shares, and by section 7.27, which governs amendments that change the voting requirements for future amendments.

Section 10.01(b) restates the policy embodied in earlier versions of the Act and in all modern state corporation statutes, that a shareholder "does not have a vested property right" in any provision of the articles of incorporation. Under section 1.02, corporations and their shareholders are also subject to amendments of the governing statute.

Section 10.01 should be construed liberally to achieve the fundamental purpose of this chapter of permitting corporate adjustment and change by majority vote. Section 10.01(b) rejects decisions by a few courts that have applied a vested right or property right doctrine to restrict or invalidate amendments to articles of incorporation because they modified particular rights conferred on shareholders by the original articles of incorporation.

Under general corporation law and under the Act, a provision in the articles of incorporation is subject to amendment under section 10.01 even though the provision is described, referred to, or stated in a share certificate, information statement, or other document issued by the corporation that reflects provisions of the articles of incorporation. The only exception to this unlimited power of amendment is section 6.27, which provides that without the consent of the holder, amendments cannot impose share transfer restrictions on previously issued shares.

However, section 10.01 does not concern obligations of a corporation to its shareholders based upon contracts independent of the articles of incorporation. An amendment permitted by this section may constitute a breach of such a contract or of a contract between the shareholders themselves. A shareholder with contractual rights (or who otherwise is concerned about possible onerous amendments) may obtain complete protection against these amendments by establishing procedures in the articles of incorporation or bylaws that limit the power of amendment without the shareholder's consent. In appropriate cases, a shareholder may be able to enjoin an amendment that constitutes a breach of a contract.

Minority shareholders are protected from the power of the majority to impose onerous or objectionable amendments in several ways. First, such shareholders may have the right to vote on amendments by separate voting groups (section 10.04). Second, a decision by a majority shareholder or a control group to exercise the powers granted by this section in a way that may breach a duty to minority or noncontrolling interests may be reviewable by a court under its inherent equity power to review transactions for good faith and fair dealing to the minority shareholders. McNulty v. W. & J. Sloane, 184 Misc. 835, 54 N.Y.S.2d 253 (Sup. Ct. 1945); Kamena v. Janssen Dairy Corp., 133 N.J. Eq. 214, 31 A.2d 200, 202 (Ch. 1943), aff'd, 134 N.J. Eq. 359, 35 A.2d 894 (1944) (where the court stated that it "is more a question of fair dealing between the strong and the weak than it is a question of percentages or proportions of the votes favoring the plan"). See also Teschner v. Chicago Title & Trust Co., 59 Ill. 2d 452, 322 N.E.2d 54, 57 (1974), where the court, in upholding a transaction that had a reasonable business purpose, relied partially on the fact that there was "no claim of fraud or deceptive conduct ... [or] that the exchange offer was unfair or that the price later offered for the shares was inadequate."

Because of the broad power of amendment contained in this section, it is unnecessary to make any reference to, or reserve, an express power to amend in the articles of incorporation.

§ 10.02 Amendment Before Issuance of Shares

If a corporation has not yet issued shares, its board of directors, or its incorporators if it has no board of directors, may adopt one or more amendments to the corporation's articles of incorporation.

OFFICIAL COMMENT

Section 10.02 provides that, before any shares are issued, amendments may be made by the persons empowered to complete the organization of the corporation. Under section 2.04 the organizers may be either the incorporators or the initial directors named in the articles of incorporation.

§ 10.03 Amendment by Board of Directors and Shareholders

If a corporation has issued shares, an amendment to the articles of incorporation shall be adopted in the following manner:

(a) The proposed amendment must be adopted by the board of directors.

(b) Except as provided in sections 10.05, 10.07, and 10.08, after adopting the proposed amendment the board of directors must submit the amendment to the shareholders for their approval. The board of directors must also transmit to the shareholders a recommendation that the shareholders approve the amendment, unless the board of directors makes a determination that because of conflicts of interest or other special circumstances it should not make such a recommendation, in which case the board of directors must transmit to the shareholders the basis for that determination.

(c) The board of directors may condition its submission of the amendment to the shareholders on any basis.

(d) If the amendment is required to be approved by the shareholders, and the approval is to be given at a meeting, the corporation must notify each shareholder, whether or not entitled to vote, of the meeting of shareholders at which the amendment is to be submitted for approval. The notice must state that the purpose, or one of the purposes, of the meeting is to consider the amendment and must contain or be accompanied by a copy of the amendment.

(e) Unless the articles of incorporation, or the board of directors acting pursuant to subsection (c), requires a greater vote or a greater number of shares to be present, approval of the amendment requires the approval of the shareholders at a meeting at which a quorum consisting of at least a majority of the votes entitled to be cast on the amendment exists, and, if any class or series of shares is entitled to vote as a separate group on the amendment, except as provided in section 10.04(c), the approval of each such separate voting group at a meeting at which a quorum of the voting group consisting of at least a majority of the votes entitled to be cast on the amendment by that voting group exists.

OFFICIAL COMMENT

1. In General

Under section 10.03, if a corporation has issued shares, a proposed amendment to the articles of incorporation must be adopted by the board. Thereafter, the board must submit the amendment to the shareholders for their approval, except as provided in sections 10.05, 10.07, and 10.08.

2. Submission to the Shareholders

Section 10.03 requires the board of directors, after having adopted an amendment, to submit the amendment to the shareholders for approval except as otherwise provided by sections 10.05, 10.07, and 10.08. When submitting the amendment, the board of directors must make a recommendation to the shareholders that the amendment be approved, unless the board of directors makes a determination that because of conflicts of interest or other special circumstances it should make no recommendation. For example, the board of directors may make such a determination where there is not a sufficient number of directors free of a conflicting interest to approve the amendment or because the board of directors is evenly divided as to the merits of an amendment but is able to agree that shareholders should be permitted to consider the amendment. If the board of directors makes such a determination, it must describe the conflict of interest or special circumstances, and communicate the basis for the determination, when submitting the amendment to the shareholders. The exception for conflicts of interest or other special circumstances is intended to be sparingly available. Generally, shareholders should not be asked to act on an amendment in the absence of a recommendation by the board of directors. The exception is not intended to relieve the board of directors of its duty to consider carefully the amendment and the interests of shareholders.

Section 10.03(c) permits the board of directors to condition its submission of an amendment on any basis. Among the conditions that a board might impose are that the amendment will not be deemed approved (i) unless it is approved by a specified vote of the shareholders, or by one or more specified classes or series of shares, voting as a separate voting group, or by a specified percentage of disinterested shareholders, or (ii) if shareholders holding more than a specified fraction of outstanding shares assert appraisal rights. The board of directors is not limited to conditions of these types.

3. Quorum and Voting

Section 10.03(e) provides that approval of an amendment requires approval of the shareholders at a meeting at which a quorum consisting of at least a majority of the votes entitled to be cast on the amendment exists, including, if any class or series of shares is entitled to vote as a separate group on the amendment, the approval of each such separate group, at a meeting at which a similar quorum of the voting group exists. If a quorum exists, then under sections 7.25 and 7.26 the amendment will be approved if more votes are cast in favor of the amendment than against it by the voting group or separate voting groups entitled to vote on the plan. This represents a change from the Act's previous voting rule for amendments, which required approval by a majority of votes cast, with no minimum quorum, for some amendments, and approval by a majority of the votes entitled to be cast by a voting group, for others.

If an amendment would affect the voting requirements on future amendments, it must also be approved by the vote required by section 7.27.

§ 10.04 Voting on Amendments by Voting Groups

(a) If a corporation has more than one class of shares outstanding, the holders of the outstanding shares of a class are entitled to vote as a separate voting group (if shareholder voting is otherwise required by this Act) on a proposed amendment to the articles of incorporation if the amendment would:

(1) effect an exchange or reclassification of all or part of the shares of the class into shares of another class;

(2) effect an exchange or reclassification, or create the right of exchange, of all or part of the shares of another class into shares of the class;

(3) change the rights, preferences, or limitations of all or part of the shares of the class;

(4) change the shares of all or part of the class into a different number of shares of the same class;

(5) create a new class of shares having rights or preferences with respect to distributions or to dissolution that are prior or superior to the shares of the class;

(6) increase the rights, preferences, or number of authorized shares of any class that, after giving effect to the amendment, have rights or preferences with respect to distributions or to dissolution that are prior or superior to the shares of the class;

(7) limit or deny an existing preemptive right of all or part of the shares of the class; or

(8) cancel or otherwise affect rights to distributions that have accumulated but not yet been authorized on all or part of the shares of the class.

(b) If a proposed amendment would affect a series of a class of shares in one or more of the ways described in subsection (a), the holders of shares of that series are entitled to vote as a separate voting group on the proposed amendment.

(c) If a proposed amendment that entitles the holders of two or more classes or series of shares to vote as separate voting groups under this section would affect those two or more classes or series in the same or a substantially similar way, the holders of shares of all the classes or series so affected must vote together as a single voting group on the proposed amendment, unless otherwise provided in the articles of incorporation or required by the board of directors.

(d) A class or series of shares is entitled to the voting rights granted by this section although the articles of incorporation provide that the shares are nonvoting shares.

OFFICIAL COMMENT

Section 10.04(a) requires separate approval by voting groups for certain types of amendments to the articles of incorporation where the corporation has more than one class of shares outstanding. In general, section 10.04 carries forward provisions of the prior Act, but certain changes have been made. Under the prior Act, approval by a class, voting as a separate voting group, was required for an amendment that would increase or decrease the aggregate number of shares of the class. That provision does not appear in the present Act. Also, in the prior Act approval by a class, voting as a separate voting group, was required for an amendment that would create a new class of shares having rights or preferences with respect to dissolution that would be prior, superior, or substantially equal to the class, and for an amendment that would increase the rights, preferences, or number of authorized shares of any class that, after giving effect to the amendment, would have rights or preferences with respect to distributions or dissolution that would be prior, superior, or substantially equal to the shares of the class. Under the present Act, approval by a class, voting as a separate voting group, is required in these cases only when the new or other class would have rights with respect to distributions or dissolution that would be prior or superior to the class, not when the rights would be substantially equal.

Shares are entitled to vote as separate voting groups under this section even though they are designated as nonvoting shares in the articles of incorporation, or the articles of incorporation purport to deny them entirely the right to vote on the proposal in question, or purport to allow other classes or series of shares to vote as part of the same voting group. However, an amendment that does not require shareholder approval does not trigger the right to vote by voting groups under this section. This would include a determination by the board of directors, pursuant to authority granted in the articles of incorporation, of the preferences, limitations and relative rights of any class prior to the issuance of any shares of that class, or of one or more series within a class before the issuance of any shares of that series (see section 6.02(a)).

The right to vote as a separate voting group provides a major protection for classes or series of shares with preferential rights, or classes or series of limited or nonvoting shares, against amendments that are especially burdensome to that class or series. This section, however, does not make the right to vote by separate voting group dependent on an evaluation of whether the amendment is detrimental to the class or series; if the amendment is one of those described in section 10.04(a), the class or series is automatically entitled to vote as a separate voting group on the amendment. The question whether an amendment is detrimental is often a question of judgment, and approval by the affected class or series is required irrespective of whether the board or other shareholders believe it is beneficial or detrimental to the affected class or series.

Under subsection (a)(4), a class is entitled to vote as a separate voting group on an amendment that would change the shares of all or part of the class into a different number of shares of the same class. An amendment that changes the number of shares owned by one of more shareholders of a class into a fraction of a share, through a "reverse split," falls within subsection (a)(4) and therefore requires approval by the class, voting as a separate voting group, whether or not the fractional share is to be acquired for cash under section 6.04.

Sections 7.25 and 7.26 set forth the mechanics of voting by multiple voting groups.

Subsection (b) extends the privilege of voting by separate voting group to a series of a class of shares if the series has financial or voting provisions unique to the series that are affected in one or more of the ways described in subsection (a). Any significant distinguishing feature of a series, which an amendment affects or alters, should trigger the right of voting by separate voting group for that series. However, under subsection (c) if a proposed amendment that entitles two or more classes or series of shares to vote as separate voting groups would affect those classes or series in the same or a substantially similar way, the shares of all the class or series so affected must vote together, as a single voting group, unless otherwise provided in the articles of incorporation or required by the board of directors.

The application of subsections (b) and (c) may best be illustrated by examples.

First, assume there is a class of shares, with preferential rights, comprised of three series, each with different preferential dividend rights. A proposed amendment would reduce the rate of dividend applicable to the "Series A" shares and would change the dividend right of the "Series B" shares from a cumulative to a noncumulative right. The amendment would not affect the preferential dividend right of the "Series C" shares. Both Series A and B would be entitled to vote as separate voting groups on the proposed amendment; the holders of the Series C shares, not directly affected by the amendment, would not be entitled to vote at all, unless otherwise provided, or unless the shares are voting shares under the articles of incorporation, in which case they would not vote as a separate voting group but in the voting group consisting of all shares with general voting rights under the articles of incorporation.

Second, if the proposed amendment would reduce the dividend right of Series A and change the dividend right of both Series B and C from a cumulative to a noncumulative right, the holders of Series A would be entitled to vote as a single voting group, and the holders of Series B and C would be required to vote together as a single, separate voting group.

Third, assume that a corporation has common stock and two classes of preferred stock. A proposed amendment would create a new class of senior preferred that would have priority in distribution rights over both the common stock and the existing classes of preferred stock. Because the creation of the new senior preferred would affect all three classes of stock in the same or a substantially similar way, all three classes would vote together as a single voting group on the proposed amendment.

Under the prior version of section 10.04(c), series that were affected by an amendment in the same or a substantially similar manner were required to vote together, but classes that were affected by an amendment in the same or a substantially similar manner voted separately. Thus under the prior version of section 10.04(c) if, in the second example, the A, B, and C stock had been denominated as classes rather than series, then the A, B, and C holders would have been required to vote separately rather than together. Similarly, in the third example, under the prior version of section 10.04(c) the Common and existing Preferred would have been required to vote separately rather than together, because each was a separate class. The distinction between classes and series for this purpose seems artificial, and therefore has been eliminated in the current version of section 10.04(c).

Section 10.04(d) makes clear that the right to vote by separate voting groups provided by section 10.04 may not be narrowed or eliminated by the articles of incorporation. Even if a class or series of shares is described as "nonvoting" and the articles purport to make that class or series nonvoting "for all purposes," that class or series nevertheless has the voting right provided by this section. No inference should be drawn from section 10.04(d) as to whether other, unrelated sections of the Act may be modified by provisions in the articles of incorporation.

§ 10.05 Amendment by Board of Directors

Unless the articles of incorporation provide otherwise, a corporation's board of directors may adopt amendments to the corporation's articles of incorporation without shareholder approval:

(1) to extend the duration of the corporation if it was incorporated at a time when limited duration was required by law;

(2) to delete the names and addresses of the initial directors;

(3) to delete the name and address of the initial registered agent or registered office, if a statement of change is on file with the secretary of state;

(4) if the corporation has only one class of shares outstanding:

(a) to change each issued and unissued authorized share of the class into a greater number of whole shares of that class; or

(b) to increase the number of authorized shares of the class to the extent necessary to permit the issuance of shares as a share dividend;

(5) to change the corporate name by substituting the word "corporation," "incorporated," "company," "limited," or the abbreviation "corp.," "inc.," "co.," or "ltd.," for a similar word or abbreviation in the name, or by adding, deleting, or changing a geographical attribution for the name;

(6) to reflect a reduction in authorized shares, as a result of the operation of section 6.31(b), when the corporation has acquired its own shares and the articles of incorporation prohibit the reissue of the acquired shares;

(7) to delete a class of shares from the articles of incorporation, as a result of the operation of section 6.31(b), when there are no remaining shares of the class because the corporation has acquired all shares of the class and the articles of incorporation prohibit the reissue of the acquired shares; or

(8) to make any change expressly permitted by section 6.02(a) or (b) to be made without shareholder approval.

OFFICIAL COMMENT

The amendments described in clauses (1) through (8) are so routine and "housekeeping" in nature as not to require approval by shareholders. None affects substantive rights in any meaningful way.

Section 10.05(4)(a) authorizes the board of directors to change each issued and unissued share of an outstanding class of shares into a greater number of whole shares if the corporation has only that class of shares outstanding. All shares of the class being changed must be treated identically under this clause. Section 10.05(4)(b) authorizes the board of directors to increase the number of shares of the class to the extent necessary to permit the issuance of shares as a share dividend, if the corporation has only that one class of stock outstanding.

Amendments provided for in this section may be included in restated articles of incorporation under section 10.07 or in articles of merger under chapter 11.

§ 10.06 Articles of Amendment

After an amendment to the articles of incorporation has been adopted and approved in the manner required by this Act and by the articles of incorporation, the corporation shall deliver to the secretary of state, for filing, articles of amendment, which shall set forth:

(1) the name of the corporation;

(2) the text of each amendment adopted, or the information required by section 1.20(k)(5);

(3) if an amendment provides for an exchange, reclassification, or cancellation of issued shares, provisions for implementing the amendment (if not contained in the amendment itself), which may be made dependent upon facts objectively ascertainable outside the articles of amendment in accordance with section 1.20(k);

(4) the date of each amendment's adoption; and

(5) if an amendment:

(a) was adopted by the incorporators or board of directors without shareholder approval, a statement that the amendment was duly approved by the incorporators or by the board of directors, as the case may be, and that shareholder approval was not required;

(b) required approval by the shareholders, a statement that the amendment was duly approved by the shareholders in the manner required by this Act and by the articles of incorporation; or

(c) is being filed pursuant to section 1.20(k)(5), a statement to that effect.

OFFICIAL COMMENT

Section 10.06(3) requires the articles of amendment to contain a statement of the manner in which an exchange, reclassification, or cancellation of issued shares is to be put into effect if not set forth in the amendment itself. This requirement avoids any possible confusion that may arise as to how the amendment is to be put into effect and also permits the amendment itself to be limited to provisions of permanent applicability, with transitional provisions having no long-range effect appearing only in the articles of amendment.

§ 10.07 Restated Articles of Incorporation

(a) A corporation's board of directors may restate its articles of incorporation at any time, with or without shareholder approval, to consolidate all amendments into a single document.

(b) If the restated articles include one or more new amendments that require shareholder approval, the amendments must be adopted and approved as provided in section 10.03.

(c) A corporation that restates its articles of incorporation shall deliver to the secretary of state for filing articles of restatement setting forth the name of the corporation and the text of the restated articles of incorporation together with a certificate which states that the restated articles consolidate all amendments into a single document and, if a new amendment is included in the restated articles, which also includes the statements required under section 10.06.

(d) Duly adopted restated articles of incorporation supersede the original articles of incorporation and all amendments thereto.

(e) The secretary of state may certify restated articles of incorporation as the articles of incorporation currently in effect, without including the certificate information required by subsection (c).

OFFICIAL COMMENT

Restated articles of incorporation serve the useful purpose of permitting articles of incorporation that have been amended from time to time, or are being concurrently amended, to be consolidated into a single document.

A restatement of a corporation's articles of incorporation is not an amendment of the articles of incorporation, but only a consolidation of amendments into a single document. A corporation that is restating its articles may concurrently amend the articles, and include the new amendments in the restated articles. In such a case, the provisions of this chapter that govern amendments of the articles of incorporation would apply to the new amendments. In case of doubt whether a provision of a restatement of the articles of incorporation might be deemed to be an amendment, rather than a consolidation, the prudent course for the corporation is to treat that provision as an amendment, and follow the procedures that apply to amendments under this chapter.

Where the articles of incorporation are amended at the same time they are restated, a combined articles of amendment and restatement may be filed.

§ 10.08 Amendment Pursuant to Reorganization

(a) A corporation's articles of incorporation may be amended without action by the board of directors or shareholders to carry out a plan of reorganization ordered or decreed by a court of competent jurisdiction under the authority of a law of the United States.

(b) The individual or individuals designated by the court shall deliver to the secretary of state for filing articles of amendment setting forth:

(1) the name of the corporation;

(2) the text of each amendment approved by the court;

(3) the date of the court's order or decree approving the articles of amendment;

(4) the title of the reorganization proceeding in which the order or decree was entered; and

(5) a statement that the court had jurisdiction of the proceeding under federal statute.

(c) This section does not apply after entry of a final decree in the reorganization proceeding even though the court retains jurisdiction of the proceeding for limited purposes unrelated to consummation of the reorganization plan.

OFFICIAL COMMENT

Section 10.08 provides a simplified method of conforming corporate documents filed under state law with the federal statutes relating to corporate reorganization. If a federal court confirms a plan of reorganization that requires articles of amendment to be filed, those amendments may be prepared and filed by the persons designated by the court and the approval of neither the shareholders nor the board of directors is required.

This section applies only to amendments in articles of incorporation approved before the entry of a final decree in the reorganization.

§ 10.09 Effect of Amendment

An amendment to the articles of incorporation does not affect a cause of action existing against or in favor of the corporation, a proceeding to which the corporation is a party, or the existing rights of persons other than shareholders of the corporation. An amendment changing a corporation's name does not abate a proceeding brought by or against the corporation in its former name.

OFFICIAL COMMENT

Under section 10.09, amendments to articles of incorporation do not interrupt the corporate existence and do not abate a proceeding by or against the corporation even though the amendment changes the name of the corporation.

Amendments are effective when filed unless a delayed effective date is elected. See section 1.23.

SUBCHAPTER B. AMENDMENT OF BYLAWS

§ 10.20 Amendment by Board of Directors or Shareholders

(a) A corporation's shareholders may amend or repeal the corporation's bylaws.

(b) A corporation's board of directors may amend or repeal the corporation's bylaws, unless:

(1) the articles of incorporation or section 10.21 reserve that power exclusively to the shareholders in whole or part; or

(2) the shareholders in amending, repealing, or adopting a bylaw expressly provide that the board of directors may not amend, repeal, or reinstate that bylaw.

OFFICIAL COMMENT

The power to amend or repeal bylaws is shared by the board of directors and the shareholders, unless that power is reserved exclusively to the shareholders by an appropriate provision in the articles of incorporation. Section 10.20(b)(1) provides that the power to amend or repeal the bylaws may be reserved to the shareholders "in whole or part." This language permits the reservation of power to be limited to specific articles or sections of the bylaws or to specific subjects or topics addressed in the bylaws.

Section 10.20(b)(2) permits the shareholders to amend, repeal, or adopt a bylaw and reserve exclusively to themselves the power to amend, repeal, or reinstate that bylaw if the reservation is express.

Section 10.21 limits the power of directors to adopt or amend supermajority provisions in bylaws. See section 10.21 and the Official Comment thereto.

§ 10.21 Bylaw Increasing Quorum or Voting Requirement for Directors

(a) A bylaw that increases a quorum or voting requirement for the board of directors may be amended or repealed:

(1) if adopted by the shareholders, only by the shareholders, unless the bylaw otherwise provides;

(2) if adopted by the board of directors, either by the shareholders or by the board of directors.

(b) A bylaw adopted or amended by the shareholders that increases a quorum or voting requirement for the board of directors may provide that it can be amended or repealed only by a specified vote of either the shareholders or the board of directors.

(c) Action by the board of directors under subsection (a) to amend or repeal a bylaw that changes the quorum or voting requirement for the board of directors must meet the same quorum requirement and be adopted by the same vote required to take action under the quorum and voting requirement then in effect or proposed to be adopted, whichever is greater.

OFFICIAL COMMENT

Provisions that increase a quorum or voting requirement for the board over the requirement that would otherwise apply under this Act or that was previously set forth in the bylaws ("supermajority requirements") may be placed in the bylaws of the corporation without specific authorization in the articles of incorporation. See section 8.24(a) and (c). Like other bylaw provisions, they may be adopted either by the shareholders or by the board of directors. See section 10.20. Such provisions may be amended or repealed by the board of directors or shareholders as provided in this section.

Section 10.21(a)(1) provides that if a supermajority requirement is imposed by a bylaw adopted by the shareholders, only the shareholders may amend or repeal it. Under section 10.21(b), such a bylaw may impose restrictions on the manner in which it may be thereafter amended or repealed by the shareholders. If a supermajority requirement is imposed in a bylaw adopted by the board of directors, the bylaw may be amended either by the shareholders or the board of directors (see section 10.21(a)(2)). However, if such an amendment is amended by the board of directors, section 10.21(c) requires approval by the supermajority requirement then in effect or proposed to be adopted, whichever is greater. Compare section 7.27.

CHAPTER 11. MERGER AND SHARE EXCHANGES

§ 11.01 Definitions

As used in this chapter:

(a) "Merger" means a business combination pursuant to section 11.02.

(b) "Party to a merger" or "party to a share exchange" means any domestic or foreign corporation or eligible entity that will either:

(1) merge under a plan of merger;

(2) acquire shares or eligible interests of another corporation or an eligible entity in a share exchange; or

(3) have all of its shares or eligible interests or all of one or more classes or series of its shares or eligible interests acquired in a share exchange.

(c) "Share exchange" means a business combination pursuant to section 11.03.

(d) "Survivor" in a merger means the corporation or eligible entity into which one or more other corporations or eligible entities are merged. A survivor of a merger may preexist the merger or be created by the merger.

OFFICIAL COMMENT

1. In General

The definition of what constitutes an "eligible entity" in section 1.40(7B) determines the kinds of entities, other than corporations, with which a corporation may merge. The definition of "voting power" in section 1.40 also has important substantive implications, because whether shareholder approval is required for a transaction under chapter 11 depends in part on the proportion of voting power that is carried by shares that would be issued and issuable as a result of the transaction.

2. Interests

The term "interests" in section 1.40(13B) includes such interests as general and limited partnership interests in limited partnerships, equity interests in limited liability companies, and any other form of equity or ownership interests in an unincorporated entity, as defined in section 1.40(24A), however denominated. For purposes of this chapter, the definition of "eligible interests" in section 1.40(7C) adds to those types of interests any form of membership in a domestic or foreign nonprofit corporation.

3. Organic Documents

The definition of the term "organic documents" which was previously found in section 11.01(c) is now set forth in section 1.40(15A).

4. Survivor

The term "survivor" is used in chapter 11 as a defined technical term and therefore is not always used in a manner that is equivalent to the ordinary meaning of the term. For example, a corporation may be the "survivor" of a merger within the meaning of section 11.01(g) even if it is created by the merger, and therefore had no existence before the merger.

§ 11.02 Merger

(a) One or more domestic business corporations may merge with one or more domestic or foreign business corporations or eligible entities pursuant to a plan of merger, or two or more foreign business corporations or domestic or foreign eligible entities may merge into a new domestic business corporation to be created in the merger in the manner provided in this chapter.

(b) A foreign business corporation, or a foreign eligible entity, may be a party to a merger with a domestic business corporation, or may be created by the terms of the plan of merger, only if the merger is permitted by the organic law of the foreign business corporation or eligible entity.

(b.1) If the organic law of a domestic eligible entity does not provide procedures for the approval of a merger, a plan of merger may be adopted and approved, the merger effectuated, and appraisal rights exercised in accordance with the procedures in this chapter and chapter 13. For the purposes of applying this chapter and chapter 13:

(1) the eligible entity, its members or interest holders, eligible interests and organic documents taken together shall be deemed to be a domestic business corporation, shareholders, shares and articles of incorporation, respectively and vice versa as the context may require; and

(2) if the business and affairs of the eligible entity are managed by a group of persons that is not identical to the members or interest holders, that group shall be deemed to be the board of directors.

(c) The plan of merger must include:

(1) the name of each domestic or foreign business corporation or eligible entity that will merge and the name of the domestic or foreign business corporation or eligible entity that will be the survivor of the merger;

(2) the terms and conditions of the merger;

(3) the manner and basis of converting the shares of each merging domestic or foreign business corporation and eligible interests of each merging domestic or foreign eligible entity into shares or other securities, eligible interests, obligations, rights to acquire shares, other securities or eligible interests, cash, other property, or any combination of the foregoing;

(4) the articles of incorporation of any domestic or foreign business or nonprofit corporation, or the organic documents of any domestic or foreign unincorporated entity, to be created by the merger, or if a new domestic or foreign business or nonprofit corporation or unincorporated entity is not to be created by the merger, any amendments to the survivor's articles of incorporation or organic documents.

(d) The terms described in subsections (c)(2) and (c)(3) may be made dependent on facts ascertainable outside the plan of merger, provided that these facts are objectively ascertainable. The term "facts" includes, but is not limited to, the occurrence of any event, including a determination or action by any person or body, including the corporation.

(e) The plan of merger may also include a provision that the plan may be amended prior to filing articles of merger, but if the shareholders of a domestic corporation that is a party to the merger are required or permitted to vote on the plan, the plan must provide that subsequent to approval of the plan by such shareholders the plan may not be amended to change:

(1) the amount or kind of shares or other securities, eligible interests, obligations, rights to acquire shares, other securities or

eligible interests, cash, or other property to be received under the plan by the shareholders of or owners of eligible interests in any party to the merger;

(2) the articles of incorporation of any corporation, or the organic documents of any unincorporated entity, that will survive or be created as a result of the merger, except for changes permitted by section 10.05 or by comparable provisions of the organic laws of any such foreign business or nonprofit corporation or domestic or foreign unincorporated entity; or

(3) any of the other terms or conditions of the plan if the change would adversely affect such shareholders in any material respect.

(f) Property held in trust or for charitable purposes under the laws of this state by a domestic or foreign eligible entity shall not be diverted by a merger from the objects for which it was donated, granted or devised, unless and until the eligible entity obtains an order of [court] [the attorney general] specifying the disposition of the property to the extent required by and pursuant to [cite state statutory cy pres or other nondiversion statute].

OFFICIAL COMMENT

1. In General

Section 11.02 authorizes mergers between one or more domestic corporations, or between one or more domestic corporations and one or more foreign corporations or domestic or foreign eligible entities. Upon the effective date of the merger the survivor becomes vested with all the assets of the corporations or eligible entities that merge into the survivor and becomes subject to their liabilities, as provided in section 11.07.

2. Applicability

A merger of a domestic business corporation with a foreign business corporation or a foreign eligible entity is authorized by chapter 11 only if the merger is permitted by the laws under which the foreign business corporation or eligible entity is organized, and in effecting the merger the foreign business corporation or eligible entity complies with such laws. Whether and on what terms a foreign business corporation or a foreign eligible entity is authorized to merge with a domestic business corporation is a matter that is governed by the laws under which that corporation or eligible entity is organized or by which it is governed, not by chapter 11.

Nevertheless, certain provisions of chapter 11 have an indirect effect on a foreign business corporation or foreign eligible entity that proposes to or does merge with a domestic business corporation, because they set conditions concerning the effectiveness and effect of the merger. For example, section 11.02(c) sets forth certain requirements for the contents of a plan of merger. This section is directly applicable only to domestic business corporations, but has an indirect effect on a foreign corporation or eligible entity that is a party to a proposed merger with a domestic business corporation.

In some cases, the impact of chapter 11 on a foreign corporation or eligible entity is more direct. For example, section 11.07(d) provides that upon a merger becoming effective, a foreign corporation or eligible entity that is the survivor of the merger is deemed to appoint the secretary of state as its agent for service of process in a proceeding to enforce the rights of shareholders of each domestic corporation that is a party to the merger to exercise appraisal rights and to agree that it will promptly pay to such shareholders the amount, if any, to which they are entitled under chapter 13.

If the law under which a domestic eligible entity is organized does not expressly authorize it to merge with a domestic business corporation, it is intended that section 11.02(a) will provide the necessary authority. Until such time as the various laws governing the organization of each form of eligible entity have been amended to provide procedures for adopting and approving a plan of merger, section 11.02(b.1) provides those procedures by reference to the provisions of this subchapter applicable to domestic business corporations.

3. Terms and Conditions of Merger

Chapter 11 imposes virtually no restrictions or limitations on the terms or conditions of a merger, except for those set forth in section 11.02(e) concerning provisions in a plan of merger for amendment of the plan after it has been approved by shareholders. Owners of shares or eligible interests in a party to the merger that merges into the survivor may receive shares or other securities of the survivor, shares or other securities of a party other than the survivor, eligible interests, obligations, rights to acquire shares, other securities or eligible interests, cash, or other property. The capitalization of the survivor may be restructured in the merger, and its articles or organic documents may be amended by the articles of merger, in any way deemed appropriate.

Although chapter 11 imposes virtually no restrictions or limitations on the terms or conditions of a merger, section 11.02(c) requires that the terms and conditions be set forth in the plan of merger. The present Act clarifies that the plan of merger need not be set forth in the articles of merger that are to be delivered to the secretary of state for filing after the merger has been adopted and approved. See section 11.06.

Section 11.02(c)(4) provides that a plan of merger must set forth the articles of incorporation of any business or nonprofit corporation, and the organic documents of any unincorporated entity, to be created by the merger, or if a new corporation or unincorporated entity is not to be created by the merger, any amendments to the survivor's articles of incorporation or organic documents. If a domestic corporation is merged into an existing domestic or foreign corporation or eligible entity, section 11.02(c) does not require that the survivor's articles of incorporation or organic documents be included in the plan of merger. However, if approval of the plan of merger by the shareholders of a domestic corporation to be merged into another party to the merger is required under section 11.04, section 11.04(d) requires that the shareholders be furnished with a copy or summary of those articles of incorporation or organic documents in connection with voting on approval of the merger.

The list in section 11.02(c) of required provisions in a plan of merger is not exhaustive and the plan may include any other provisions that may be desired.

4. Amendments of Articles of Incorporation

Under section 11.02, a corporation's articles of incorporation may be amended by a merger. Under section 11.02(c)(4), a plan of merger must include any amendments to the survivor's articles of incorporation or organic documents. If the plan of merger is approved, the amendments will be effective.

5. Adoption and Approval; Abandonment

A merger must be adopted and approved as set forth in sections 11.04 and 11.05. Under section 11.08, the board of directors may abandon a merger before its effective date even if the plan of merger has already been approved by the corporation's shareholders.

6. Effective Date of Merger

A merger takes effect on the date the articles of merger are filed, unless a later date, not more than 90 days after filing, is specified in the articles. See section 11.06 and the Official Comment thereto.

7. Appraisal Rights

Shareholders of a domestic corporation that is a party to a merger may have appraisal rights. See chapter 13.

8. Protection of Restricted Property

This section permits a nonprofit corporation or unincorporated nonprofit association to merge into a for-profit corporation or unincorporated entity. The laws of some states governing the nondiversion of charitable and trust property to other uses may not be worded in a fashion that will cover a merger under section 11.02. To prevent a merger from being used to avoid restrictions on the use of property held by nonprofit entities, optional section 11.02(f) may be used to require approval of mergers by the appropriate arm of government having supervision of nonprofit entities.

§ 11.03 Action on Plan

(a) Through a share exchange:

(1) a domestic business corporation may acquire all of the shares of one or more classes or series of shares of another domestic or foreign business corporation, or all of the eligible interests of one or more classes or series of eligible interests of a domestic or foreign eligible entity, in exchange for shares, other securities, eligible interests, obligations, rights to acquire shares, other securities or eligible interests, cash, other property, or any combination of the foregoing, pursuant to a plan of share exchange, or

(2) all of the shares of one or more classes or series of shares of a domestic business corporation may be acquired by another domestic or foreign business corporation or eligible entity, in exchange for shares, other securities, eligible interests, obligations, rights to acquire shares, other securities or eligible interests, cash, other prop-

erty, or any combination of the foregoing, pursuant to a plan of share exchange.

(b) A foreign corporation or eligible entity may be a party to a share exchange only if the share exchange is permitted by the organic law of the corporation or eligible entity.

(b.1) If the organic law of a domestic eligible entity does not provide procedures for the approval of a share exchange, a plan of share exchange may be adopted and approved, and the share exchange effectuated, in accordance with the procedures, if any, for a merger. If the organic law of a domestic eligible entity does not provide procedures for the approval of either a share exchange or a merger, a plan of share exchange may be adopted and approved, the share exchange effectuated, and appraisal rights exercised, in accordance with the procedures in this chapter and chapter 13. For the purposes of applying this chapter and chapter 13:

(1) the eligible entity, its members or interest holders, eligible interests and organic documents taken together shall be deemed to be a domestic business corporation, shareholders, shares and articles of incorporation, respectively and vice versa as the context may require; and

(2) if the business and affairs of the eligible entity are managed by a group of persons that is not identical to the members or interest holders, that group shall be deemed to be the board of directors.

(c) The plan of share exchange must include:

(1) the name of each corporation or eligible entity whose shares or eligible interests will be acquired and the name of the corporation or eligible entity that will acquire those shares or eligible interests;

(2) the terms and conditions of the share exchange;

(3) the manner and basis of exchanging shares of a corporation or eligible interests in an eligible entity whose shares or eligible interests will be acquired under the share exchange into shares, other securities, eligible interests, obligations, rights to acquire shares, other securities, or eligible interests, cash, other property, or any combination of the foregoing.

(d) The terms described in subsections (c)(2) and (c)(3) may be made dependent on facts ascertainable outside the plan of share exchange, provided that those facts are objectively ascertainable. The term "facts" includes, but is not limited to, the occurrence of any event, including a determination or action by any person or body, including the corporation.

(e) The plan of share exchange may also include a provision that the plan may be amended prior to filing articles of share exchange, but if the shareholders of a domestic corporation that is a party to the share exchange are required or permitted to vote on the plan, the plan must provide that subsequent to approval of the plan by such shareholders the plan may not be amended to change:

(1) the amount or kind of shares, other securities, eligible interests, obligations, rights to acquire shares, other securities or eligible interests, cash, or other property to be issued by the corporation or to be received under the plan by the shareholders of or holders of eligible interests in any party to the share exchange; or

(2) any of the other terms or conditions of the plan if the change would adversely affect such shareholders in any material respect.

(f) Section 11.03 does not limit the power of a domestic corporation to acquire shares of another corporation or eligible interests in an eligible entity in a transaction other than a share exchange.

OFFICIAL COMMENT

1. In General

It is often desirable to structure a corporate combination so that the separate existence of one or more parties to the combination does not cease although another corporation or eligible entity obtains ownership of the shares or eligible interests of those parties. This objective is often particularly important in the formation of insurance and bank holding companies, but is not limited to those contexts. In the absence of the procedure authorized in section 11.03, this kind of result often can be accomplished only by a triangular merger, which involves the formation by a corporation, A, of a new subsidiary, followed by a merger of that subsidiary with another party to the merger, B, effected through the exchange of A's securities for securities of B. Section 11.03 authorizes a more straightforward procedure to accomplish the same result.

Under section 11.03, the acquiring corporation in a share exchange must acquire all of the shares or eligible interests of the class or series of shares or eligible interests that is being acquired. The shares or eligible interests of one or more other classes or series of the acquired corporation or eligible entity may be excluded from the share exchange or may be included on different bases. After the plan of share exchange is adopted and approved as required by section 11.04, it is binding on all holders of the class or series to be acquired. Accordingly, a share exchange may operate in a mandatory fashion on some holders of the class or series of shares or eligible interests acquired.

Section 11.03(f) makes clear that the authorization of share exchange combinations under section 11.03 does not limit the power of corporations to acquire shares or eligible interests without using the share-exchange procedure, either as part of a corporate combination or otherwise.

In contrast to mergers, the articles of incorporation of a party to a share exchange may not be amended by a plan of share exchange. Such an amendment may, however, be effected under chapter 10 as a separate element of a corporate combination that involves a share exchange.

2. Applicability

Whether and on what terms a foreign business corporation or a foreign eligible entity is authorized to enter into a share exchange with a domestic business corporation is a matter that is governed by the laws under which that corporation or eligible entity is organized or by which it is governed, not by chapter 11. Therefore, for example, section 11.04, which governs the manner in which a plan of share exchange must be adopted, applies only to adoption of a plan of share exchange by a domestic business corporation.

Nevertheless, certain provisions of chapter 11 have an indirect effect on a foreign business corporation or foreign eligible entity that proposes to or does engage in a share exchange with a domestic business corporation, because they set conditions concerning the effectiveness and effect of the share exchange. For example, section 11.03(c) sets forth certain requirements for the contents of a plan of share exchange. This section is directly applicable only to domestic corporations, but has an indirect effect on a foreign corporation or eligible entity that is a party to a proposed share exchange with a domestic corporation.

If the law under which a domestic eligible entity is organized does not expressly authorize it to participate in a share (or eligible interest) exchange with a domestic business corporation, it is intended that section 11.03(a) will provide the necessary authority. Until such time as the various laws governing the organization of each form of eligible entity have been amended to provide procedures for adopting and approving a plan of share (or eligible interest) exchange, section 11.03(b.1) provides those procedures by reference to the provisions of this subchapter applicable to domestic business corporations.

3. Terms and Conditions of Share Exchange

Chapter 11 imposes virtually no restrictions or limitations on the terms and conditions of a share exchange, except for those contained in section 11.03(e) concerning provisions in a plan of share exchange for amendment of the plan after it has been approved by shareholders, and the requirement in section 11.03(a) that the acquiring party must acquire all the shares of the acquired class or series of stock or eligible interests. Owners of shares or eligible interests in a party whose shares are acquired under section 11.03(a)(2) may receive securities or eligible interests of the acquiring party, securities or eligible interests of a party other than the acquiring party, or cash or other property.

Although chapter 11 imposes virtually no restrictions or limitations on the terms or conditions of a share exchange, section 11.03(c) requires that the terms and conditions be set forth in the plan of share exchange. The present Act clarifies that the plan of share exchange need not be set forth in the articles of share exchange that are to be delivered to the secretary of state for filing after the share exchange has been adopted and approved. See section 11.06.

The list in section 11.03(c) of required provisions in a plan of share exchange is not exhaustive and the plan may include any other provisions that may be desired.

4. Adoption and Approval; Abandonment

A share exchange must be adopted and approved as set forth in section 11.04. Under section 11.08, the board of directors may abandon a share exchange before its effective date even if the plan of share exchange has already been approved by the corporation's shareholders.

5. Effective Date of Share Exchange

A share exchange takes effect on the date the articles of share exchange are filed, unless a later date, not more than 90 days after filing, is specified in the articles. See section 11.06 and the Official Comment thereto.

6. Appraisal Rights

Holders of a class or series of shares of a domestic corporation that is acquired in a share exchange may have appraisal rights. See chapter 13.

§ 11.04 Action on a Plan of Merger or Share Exchange

In the case of a domestic corporation that is a party to a merger or share exchange:

(a) The plan of merger or share exchange must be adopted by the board of directors.

(b) Except as provided in subsection (g) and in section 11.05, after adopting the plan of merger or share exchange the board of directors must submit the plan to the shareholders for their approval. The board of directors must also transmit to the shareholders a recommendation that the shareholders approve the plan, unless the board of directors makes a determination that because of conflicts of interest or other special circumstances it should not make such a recommendation, in which case the board of directors must transmit to the shareholders the basis for that determination.

(c) The board of directors may condition its submission of the plan of merger or share exchange to the shareholders on any basis.

(d) If the plan of merger or share exchange is required to be approved by the shareholders, and if the approval is to be given at a meeting, the corporation must notify each shareholder, whether or not entitled to vote, of the meeting of shareholders at which the plan is to be submitted for approval. The notice must state that the purpose, or one of the purposes, of the meeting is to consider the plan and must contain or be accompanied by a copy or summary of the plan. If the corporation is to be merged into an existing corporation or eligible entity, the notice shall also include or be accompanied by a copy or summary of the articles of incorporation or organic documents of that corporation or eligible entity. If the corporation is to be merged into a corporation or eligible entity that is to be created pursuant to the merger, the notice shall include or be accompanied by a copy or a summary of the articles of incorporation or organic documents of the new corporation or eligible entity.

(e) Unless the articles of incorporation, or the board of directors acting pursuant to subsection (c), requires a greater vote or a greater number of votes to be present, approval of the plan of merger or share exchange requires the approval of the shareholders at a meeting at which a quorum consisting of at least a majority of the votes entitled to be cast on the plan exists, and, if any class or series of shares is entitled to vote as a separate group on the plan of merger or share exchange, the approval of each such separate voting group at a meeting at which a quorum of the voting group consisting of at least a majority of the votes entitled to be cast on the merger or share exchange by that voting group is present.

(f) Separate voting by voting groups is required:

(1) on a plan of merger, by each class or series of shares that:

(i) are to be converted under the plan of merger into other securities, eligible interests, obligations, rights to acquire shares, other securities or eligible interests, cash, other property, or any combination of the foregoing; or

(ii) would be entitled to vote as a separate group on a provision in the plan that, if contained in a proposed amendment to articles of incorporation, would require action by separate voting groups under section 10.04;

(2) on a plan of share exchange, by each class or series of shares included in the exchange, with each class or series constituting a separate voting group; and

(3) on a plan of merger or share exchange, if the voting group is entitled under the articles of incorporation to vote as a group to approve a plan of merger or share exchange.

(g) Unless the articles of incorporation otherwise provide, approval by the corporation's shareholders of a plan of merger or share exchange is not required if:

(1) the corporation will survive the merger or is the acquiring corporation in a share exchange;

(2) except for amendments permitted by section 10.05, its articles of incorporation will not be changed;

(3) each shareholder of the corporation whose shares were outstanding immediately before the effective date of the merger or share exchange will hold the same number of shares, with identical preferences, limitations, and relative rights, immediately after the effective date of change; and

(4) the issuance in the merger or share exchange of shares or other securities convertible into or rights exercisable for shares does not require a vote under section 6.21(f).

(h) If as a result of a merger or share exchange one or more shareholders of a domestic corporation would become subject to owner liability for the debts, obligations or liabilities of any other person or entity, approval of the plan of merger or share exchange shall require the execution, by each such shareholder, of a separate written consent to become subject to such owner liability.

OFFICIAL COMMENT

1. In General

Under section 11.04, a plan of merger or share exchange must be adopted by the board. Thereafter, the board must submit the plan to the shareholders for their approval, unless the conditions stated in section 11.04(g) or section 11.05 are satisfied. A plan of share exchange must always be approved by the shareholders of the class or series that is being acquired in a share exchange. Similarly, a plan of merger must always be approved by the shareholders of a corporation that is merged into another party in a merger, unless the corporation is a subsidiary and the merger falls within section 11.05. However, under section 11.04(g) approval of a plan of merger or share exchange by the shareholders of a surviving corporation in a merger or of an acquiring corporation in a share exchange is not required if the conditions stated in that section, including the fundamental rule of section 6.21(f), are satisfied.

Section 11.04(f) provides that a class or series has a right to vote on a plan of merger as a separate voting group if, pursuant to the merger, the class or series would be converted into other securities, eligible interests, obligations, rights to acquire shares, other securities or eligible interests, cash, or other property. A class or series also is entitled to vote as a separate voting group if the class or series would be entitled to vote as a separate group on a provision in the plan that, if contained in an amendment to the articles of incorporation, would require approval by that class or series, voting as a separate voting group, under section 10.04. Under this latter requirement, a class or series will be entitled to vote as a separate voting group if the terms of that class or series are being changed or the shares of that class or series are being converted into shares of any other class or series. Where the surviving entity is a foreign business corporation, it is not intended that immaterial changes in the terms of a class or series that conform to the usage of the laws of the foreign jurisdiction will alone create an entitlement to vote as a separate group.

If a merger would amend the articles of incorporation in such a way as to affect the voting requirements on future amendments, the transaction must also be approved by the vote required by section 7.27.

2. Submission to the Shareholders

Section 11.04(b) requires the board of directors, after having adopted the plan of merger or share exchange, to submit the plan of merger or share exchange to the shareholders for approval, except as provided in subsection (g) and section 11.05. When submitting the plan of merger or share exchange the board of directors must make a recommendation to the shareholders that the plan be approved, unless the board of directors makes a determination that because of conflicts of interest or other special circumstances it should make no recommendation. For example, the board or directors may make such a determination where there is not a sufficient number of directors free of a conflicting interest to approve the transaction or because the board of directors is evenly divided as to the merits of a transaction but is able to agree that shareholders should be permitted to consider the transaction. If the board of directors makes such a determination, it must describe the conflict of interest or special circumstances, and communicate the basis for the determination, when submitting the plan of merger or share exchange to the shareholders. The exception for conflicts of interest or other special circumstances is intended to be sparingly available. Generally, shareholders should not be asked to act on a merger or share exchange in the absence of a recommendation by the board of directors. The exception is not intended to relieve the board of directors of its duty to consider carefully the proposed transaction and the interests of shareholders.

Section 11.04(c) permits the board of directors to condition its submission of a plan of merger or share exchange on any basis. Among the conditions that a board might impose are that the plan will not be deemed approved (i) unless it is approved by a specified vote of the shareholders, or by one or more specified classes or series of shares, voting as a separate voting group, or by a specified percentage of disinterested shareholders or (ii) if shareholders holding more than a specified fraction of the outstanding shares assert appraisal rights. The board of directors is not limited to conditions of these types.

Section 11.04(d) provides that if the plan of merger or share exchange is required to be approved by the shareholders, and if the approval is to be given at a meeting, the corporation must notify each shareholder, whether or not entitled to vote, of the meeting of shareholders at which the plan is to be submitted. Requirements concerning the timing and content of a notice of meeting are set out in section 7.05. Section 11.04(d) does not itself require that notice be given to nonvoting shareholders where the merger is approved, without a meeting, by unanimous consent. However, that requirement is imposed by section 7.04(d).

3. Quorum and Voting

Section 11.04(e) provides that approval of a plan of merger or share exchange requires approval of the shareholders at a meeting at which a quorum consisting of a majority of the votes entitled to be cast on the plan exists and, if any class or series of shares are entitled to vote as a separate group on the plan, the approval of each such separate group at a meeting at which a quorum consisting of at least a majority of the votes entitled to be cast on the plan by that class or series exists. If a quorum is present, then under sections 7.25 and 7.26 the plan will be approved if more votes are cast in favor of the plan than against it by the voting group or separate voting groups entitled to vote on the plan. This represents a change from the Act's previous voting rule for mergers and share exchanges, which required approval by a majority of outstanding shares.

In lieu of approval at a shareholders' meeting, approval can be given by the consent of all the shareholders entitled to vote on the merger or share exchange, under the procedures set forth in section 7.04.

4. Abandonment of Merger or Share Exchange

Under section 11.08, the board of directors may abandon a merger or share exchange before its effective date even if the plan of merger or share exchange has already been approved by the corporation's shareholders.

5. Personal Liability of Shareholders

Section 11.04(h) applies only in situations where a shareholder is becoming subject to "owner liability" as defined in section 1.40(15C), for example, where a corporation is merging into a general partnership. Where an unincorporated entity whose interest holders have owner liability, such as a general partnership, is merging into a corporation, the effect of the transaction on the owner liability of the interest holders in the unincorporated entity will be determined by section 11.07(e).

§ 11.05 Merger Between Parent and Subsidiary or Between Subsidiaries

(a) A domestic parent corporation that owns shares of a domestic or foreign subsidiary corporation that carry at least 90 percent of the voting power of each class and series of the outstanding shares of the subsidiary that have voting power may merge the subsidiary into itself or into another such subsidiary, or merge itself into the subsidiary, without the approval of the board of directors or shareholders of the subsidiary, unless the articles of incorporation of any of the corporations otherwise provide, and unless, in the case of a foreign subsidiary, approval by the subsidiary's board of directors or shareholders is required by the laws under which the subsidiary is organized.

(b) If under subsection (a) approval of a merger by the subsidiary's shareholders is not required, the parent corporation shall, within ten days after the effective date of the merger, notify each of the subsidiary's shareholders that the merger has become effective.

(c) Except as provided in subsections (a) and (b), a merger between a parent and a subsidiary shall be governed by the provisions of chapter 11 applicable to mergers generally.

OFFICIAL COMMENT

Under section 11.05, if a parent owns 90 percent of the voting power of each class and series of the outstanding shares of a subsidiary that have voting power, the subsidiary may be merged into the parent or another such subsidiary, or the parent may be merged into the subsidiary, without the approval of the subsidiary's shareholders or board of directors, subject to certain informational and notice requirements. Approval by the subsidiary's shareholders is not required partly because if a parent already owns 90 percent or more of the voting power of each class and series of a subsidiary's shares, approval of a merger by the subsidiary's shareholders would be a foregone conclusion, and partly to facilitate the simplification of corporate structure where only a very small fraction of stock is held by outside shareholders. Approval by the subsidiary's board of directors is not required because if the parent owns 90 percent or more of the voting power of each class and series of the subsidiary's outstanding shares, the subsidiary's directors cannot be expected to be independent of the parent, so that the approval by the subsidiary's board of directors would also be a foregone conclusion. In other respects, mergers between parents and 90 percent owned subsidiaries are governed by the provisions of chapter 11.

Section 11.05 dispenses with approval by the board of directors or the shareholders of a subsidiary that is merged into the parent or another subsidiary if the conditions of the section are met. Section 11.05 does not in itself dispense with approval by the shareholders of the parent. Under section 11.04(g), a merger of the kind described in section 11.05 in which the subsidiary is merged upstream into the parent would usually not require approval of the parent's shareholders, because in such cases the parent's articles of incorporation are usually not affected by the merger and the parent usually does not issue stock carrying more than 20 percent of its voting power. If, however, a parent is merged downstream into the subsidiary, approval by the parent's shareholders would be required under section 11.04.

§ 11.06 Articles of Merger or Share Exchange

(a) After a plan of merger or share exchange has been adopted and approved as required by this Act, articles of merger or share exchange shall be executed on behalf of each party to the merger or share exchange by any officer or other duly authorized representative. The articles shall set forth:

(1) the names of the parties to the merger or share exchange and the date on which the merger or share exchange occurred or is to be effective;

(2) if the articles of incorporation of the survivor of a merger are amended, or if a new corporation is created as a result of a merger, the amendments to the survivor's articles of incorporation or the articles of incorporation of the new corporation;

(3) if the plan of merger or share exchange required approval by the shareholders of a domestic corporation that was a party to the merger or share exchange, a statement that the plan was duly approved by the shareholders and, if voting by any separate voting group was required, by each such separate voting group, in the manner required by this Act and the articles of incorporation;

(4) if the plan of merger or share exchange did not require approval by the shareholders of a domestic corporation that was a party to the merger or share exchange, a statement to that effect; and

(5) as to each foreign corporation or eligible entity that was a party to the merger or share exchange, a statement that the participation of the foreign corporation or eligible entity was duly authorized as required by the organic law of the corporation or eligible entity.

(b) Articles of merger or share exchange shall be delivered to the secretary of state for filing by the survivor of the merger or the acquiring corporation or eligible entity in a share exchange, and shall take effect at the effective time provided in section 1.23. Articles of merger or share exchange filed under this section may be combined with any filing required under the organic law of any domestic eligible entity involved in the transaction if the combined filing satisfies the requirements of both this section and the other organic law.

OFFICIAL COMMENT

The filing of articles of merger or share exchange makes the transaction a matter of public record. The requirements of filing are set forth in section 1.20. The effective date of the articles is the effective date of their filing, unless otherwise specified. Under section 1.23, a document may specify a delayed effective time and date, and if it does so the document becomes effective at the time and date specified, except that a delayed effective date may not be later than the 90th day after the date the document is filed.

If a merger or share exchange involves a domestic eligible entity whose organic law also requires a filing to effectuate the transaction, section 11.06(b) permits the filings under that organic law and this section to be combined so that only one document need be filed with the secretary of state.

§ 11.07 Effect of Merger or Share Exchange

(a) When a merger becomes effective:

(1) the corporation or eligible entity that is designated in the plan of merger as the survivor continues or comes into existence, as the case may be;

(2) the separate existence of every corporation or eligible entity that is merged into the survivor ceases;

(3) all property owned by, and every contract right possessed by, each corporation or eligible entity that merges into the survivor is vested in the survivor without reversion or impairment;

(4) all liabilities of each corporation or eligible entity that is merged into the survivor are vested in the survivor;

(5) the name of the survivor may, but need not be, substituted in any pending proceeding for the name of any party to the merger whose separate existence ceased in the merger;

(6) the articles of incorporation or organic documents of the survivor are amended to the extent provided in the plan of merger;

(7) the articles of incorporation or organic documents of a survivor that is created by the merger become effective; and

(8) the shares of each corporation that is a party to the merger, and the eligible interests in an eligible entity that is a party to a merger, that are to be converted under the plan of merger into shares, eligible interests, obligations, rights to acquire shares, other securities, or eligible interests, cash, other property, or any combination of the foregoing, are converted, and the former holders of such shares or eligible interests are entitled only to the rights provided to them in the plan of merger or to any appraisal rights they may have under chapter 13 or the organic law of the eligible entity.

(b) When a share exchange becomes effective, the shares of each domestic corporation that are to be exchanged for shares, other securities, eligible interests, obligations, rights to acquire shares, other securities, or eligible interests, cash, other property, or any combination of the foregoing, are entitled only to the rights provided to them in the plan of share exchange or to any rights they may have under chapter 13.

(c) A person who becomes subject to owner liability for some or all of the debts, obligations or liabilities of any entity as a result of a merger or share exchange shall have owner liability only to the extent provided in the organic law of the entity and only for those debts, obligations and liabilities that arise after the effective time of the articles of merger or share exchange.

(d) Upon a merger becoming effective, a foreign corporation, or a foreign eligible entity, that is the survivor of the merger is deemed to:

(1) appoint the secretary of state as its agent for service of process in a proceeding to enforce the rights of shareholders of each domestic corporation that is a party to the merger who exercise appraisal rights, and

(2) agree that it will promptly pay the amount, if any, to which such shareholders are entitled under chapter 13.

(e) The effect of a merger or share exchange on the owner liability of a person who had owner liability for some or all of the debts, obligations or liabilities of a party to the merger or share exchange shall be as follows:

(1) The merger or share exchange does not discharge any owner liability under the organic law of the entity in which the person was a shareholder, member or interest holder to the extent any such owner liability arose before the effective time of the articles of merger or share exchange.

(2) The person shall not have owner liability under the organic law of the entity in which the person was a shareholder, member or interest holder prior to the merger or share exchange for any debt, obligation or liability that arises after the effective time of the articles of merger or share exchange.

(3) The provisions of the organic law of any entity for which the person had owner liability before the merger or share exchange shall continue to apply to the collection or discharge of any owner liability preserved by paragraph (1), as if the merger or share exchange had not occurred.

(4) The person shall have whatever rights of contribution from other persons are provided by the organic law of the entity for which the person had owner liability with respect to any owner liability preserved by paragraph (1), as if the merger or share exchange had not occurred.

OFFICIAL COMMENT

Under section 11.07(a), in the case of a merger the survivor and the parties that merge into the survivor become one. The survivor automatically becomes the owner of all real and personal property and becomes subject to all the liabilities, actual or contingent, of each party that is merged into it. A merger is not a conveyance, transfer, or assignment. It does not give rise to claims of reverter or impairment of title based on a prohibited conveyance, transfer or assignment. It does not give rise to a claim that a contract with a party to the merger is no longer in effect on the ground of nonassignability, unless the contract specifically provides that it does not survive a merger. All pending proceedings involving either the survivor or a party whose separate existence ceased as a result of the merger are continued. Under section 11.07(a)(5), the name of the survivor may be, but need not be, substituted in any pending proceeding for the name of a party to the merger whose separate existence ceased as a result of the merger. The substitution may be made whether the survivor is a complainant or a respondent, and may be made at the instance of either the survivor or an opposing party. Such a substitution has no substantive effect, because whether or not the survivor's name is substituted it succeeds to the claims of, and is subject to the liabilities of, any party to the merger whose separate existence ceased as a result of the merger.

In contrast to a merger, a share exchange does not in and of itself affect the separate existence of the parties, vest in the acquiring party the assets of the party whose stock or eligible interests are to be acquired, or render the acquiring party liable for the liabilities of the party whose stock or eligible interests the acquiring party acquires.

Under section 11.07(a)(8), on the effective date of a merger the former shareholders of a corporation that is merged into the survivor are entitled only to the rights provided in the plan of merger (which would include any rights they have as holders of the consideration they acquire) or to any rights they may have under chapter 13. Similarly, under section 11.07(b), on the effective date of a share exchange the former shareholders of a corporation whose shares are acquired are entitled only to the rights provided in the plan of share exchange (which would include any rights they have as holders of the consideration they acquire) or to any rights they may have under chapter 13. These provisions are not intended to preclude an otherwise proper question concerning the merger's validity, or to override or otherwise affect any provisions of chapter 13 concerning the exclusiveness of rights under that chapter.

Under section 11.07(d), when a merger becomes effective a foreign corporation or eligible entity that is the survivor of the merger is deemed to appoint the secretary of state as its agent for service of process in a proceeding to enforce the rights of any shareholders of each domestic corporation that is a party to the merger who exercise appraisal rights, and to agree that is will promptly pay the amount, if any, to which such shareholders are entitled under chapter 13. This result is based on the implied consent of such a foreign corporation or eligible entity to the terms of chapter 11 by virtue of entering into an agreement that is governed by this chapter.

Section 11.07(e) preserves liability only for owner liabilities to the extent they arise before the merger or share exchange. Owner liability is not preserved for subsequent changes in an underlying liability, regardless of whether a change is voluntary or involuntary.

Under section 11.04(h), a merger cannot have the effect of making any shareholder of a domestic corporation subject to owner liability for the debts, obligations or liabilities of any other person or entity unless each such shareholder has executed a separate written consent to become subject to such owner liability.

This section does not address the issue that could arise in a merger where a person who had authority to bind a party to the merger loses that authority because of the merger and yet purports to act to bind the survivor of the merger. For example, in a merger of a general partnership into a corporation, a person who is a general partner but does not become an officer of the corporation will lose the authority of a general partner to bind the business to obligations incurred in the ordinary course, but might purport to commit the corporation to such an obligation in dealing with a person who does not have knowledge of the merger. Instances in which this occurs are rare and, in the limited instances in which it does occur, general principles of agency law are sufficient to resolve the problems created.

§ 11.08 Abandonment of a Merger or Share Exchange

(a) Unless otherwise provided in a plan of merger or share exchange or in the laws under which a foreign business corporation or a domestic or foreign eligible entity that is a party to a merger or a share exchange is organized or by which it is governed, after the plan has been adopted and approved as required by this chapter, and at any time before the merger or share exchange has become effective, it may be abandoned by a domestic business corporation that is a party thereto without action by its shareholders, in accordance with any procedures set forth in the plan of merger or share exchange or, if no such procedures are set forth in the plan, in the manner determined by the board of directors, subject to any contractual rights of other parties to the merger or share exchange.

(b) If a merger or share exchange is abandoned under subsection (a) after articles of merger or share exchange have been filed with the secretary of state but before the merger or share exchange has become effective, a statement that the merger or share exchange has been abandoned in accordance with this section, executed on behalf of a party to the merger or share exchange by an officer or other duly authorized representative, shall be delivered to the secretary of state for filing prior to the effective date of the merger or share exchange. Upon filing, the statement shall take effect and the merger or share exchange shall be deemed abandoned and shall not become effective.

OFFICIAL COMMENT

Under section 11.08, unless otherwise provided in the plan of merger or share exchange, a domestic business corporation that is a party to a merger or share exchange may abandon the transaction without shareholder approval, even though the transaction has been previously approved by the shareholders. The power under section 11.08 to abandon a transaction without shareholder approval does not affect any contract rights that other parties may have. The power of a foreign business corporation or a domestic or foreign eligible entity to abandon a transaction will be determined by the organic law of the corporation or eligible entity, except as provided in sections 11.02(b.1) and 11.03(b.1).

CHAPTER 12. SALE OF ASSETS

§ 12.01 Disposition of Assets Not Requiring Shareholder Approval

No approval of the shareholders of a corporation is required, unless the articles of incorporation otherwise provide:

(1) to sell, lease, exchange, or otherwise dispose of any or all of the corporation's assets in the usual and regular course of business;

(2) to mortgage, pledge, dedicate to the repayment of indebtedness (whether with or without recourse), or otherwise encumber any or all of the corporation's assets, whether or not in the usual and regular course of business;

(3) to transfer any or all of the corporation's assets to one or more corporations or other entities all of the shares or interests of which are owned by the corporation; or

(4) to distribute assets pro rata to the holders of one or more classes or series of the corporation's shares.

OFFICIAL COMMENT

Section 12.01 provides that no approval of the shareholders is required for dispositions of assets of the types described therein, unless the articles of incorporation otherwise provide. Dispositions other than those described in section 12.01 require shareholder approval if they fall within section 12.02.

Under subsection (1), shareholder approval is not required for a disposition of the corporation's assets in the usual and regular course of business, regardless of the size of the transaction. Examples of such dispositions would include the sale of a building that was the corporation's only major asset where the corporation was formed for the purpose of constructing and selling that building, or the sale by a corporation of its only major business where the corporation was formed to buy and sell businesses and the proceeds of the sale are to be reinvested in the purchase of a new business, or an open or closed end investment company whose portfolio turns over many times in short periods.

Subsection (3) provides that no approval of shareholders is required to transfer any or all of the corporation's assets to a wholly owned subsidiary or other entity. This provision may not be used as a device to avoid a vote of shareholders by a multistep transaction.

Subsection (4) provides that no approval of the shareholders is required to distribute assets pro rata to the holders of one or more classes of the corporation's shares. A traditional spinoff that is, a pro rata distribution of the shares of a subsidiary to the holders of one or more classes of shares falls within this subsection. A splitoff that is, a non pro rata distribution of shares of a subsidiary to some or all shareholders in exchange for some of their shares would require shareholder approval if the disposition left the parent without a significant continuing business activity under subsection 12.02(a). A splitup that is, a distribution of the shares of two or more subsidiaries in complete liquidation to shareholders would be governed by section 14.02 (dissolution), not by chapter 12. In each of the foregoing situations, the subsidiary or subsidiaries could be historical or newly created.

§ 12.02 Shareholder Approval of Certain Dispositions

(a) A sale, lease, exchange, or other disposition of assets, other than a disposition described in section 12.01, requires approval of the corporation's shareholders if the disposition would leave the corporation without a significant continuing business activity. If a corporation retains a business activity that represented at least 25 percent of total assets at the end of the most recently completed fiscal year, and 25 percent of either income from continuing operations before taxes or revenues from continuing operations for that fiscal year, in each case of the corporation and its subsidiaries on a consolidated basis, the corporation will conclusively be deemed to have retained a significant continuing business activity.

(b) A disposition that requires approval of the shareholders under subsection (a) shall be initiated by a resolution by the board of directors authorizing the disposition. After adoption of such a resolution, the board of directors shall submit the proposed disposition to the shareholders for their approval. The board of directors shall also transmit to the shareholders a recommendation that the shareholders approve the proposed disposition, unless the board of directors makes a determination that because of conflicts of interest or other special circumstances it should not make such a recommendation, in which case the board of directors shall transmit to the shareholders the basis for that determination.

(c) The board of directors may condition its submission of a disposition to the shareholders under subsection (b) on any basis.

(d) If a disposition is required to be approved by the shareholders under subsection (a), and if the approval is to be given at a meeting, the corporation shall notify each shareholder, whether or not entitled to vote, of the meeting of shareholders at which the disposition is to be submitted for approval. The notice shall state that the purpose, or one of the purposes, of the meeting is to consider the disposition and shall contain a description of the disposition, including the terms and conditions thereof and the consideration to be received by the corporation.

(e) Unless the articles of incorporation or the board of directors acting pursuant to subsection (c) requires a greater vote, or a greater number of votes to be present, the approval of a disposition by the shareholders shall require the approval of the shareholders at a meeting at which a quorum consisting of at least a majority of the votes entitled to be cast on the disposition exists.

(f) After a disposition has been approved by the shareholders under subsection (b), and at any time before the disposition has been consummated, it may be abandoned by the corporation without action by the shareholders, subject to any contractual rights of other parties to the disposition.

(g) A disposition of assets in the course of dissolution under chapter 14 is not governed by this section.

(h) The assets of a direct or indirect consolidated subsidiary shall be deemed the assets of the parent corporation for the purposes of this section.

OFFICIAL COMMENT

1. In General

Section 12.02(a) requires shareholder approval for a sale, lease, exchange or other disposition by a corporation that would leave the corporation without a significant continuing business activity. The test employed in section 12.02(a) for whether a disposition of assets requires shareholder approval differs verbally from the test employed in past versions of the Model Act, which centered on whether a sale involves "all or substantially all" of a corporation's assets. The "all or substantially all" test has also been used in most corporate statutes. In practice, however, courts interpreting these statutes have commonly employed a test comparable to that embodied in 12.02(a). For example, in Gimbel v. Signal Cos., 316 A.2d 599 (Del. Ch.), aff'd, 316 A.2d 619 (Del. 1974), the court stated that "While it is true that [the all or substantially all] test does not lend itself to a strict mathematical standard to be applied in every case, the qualitative factor can be defined to some degree.... If the sale is of assets quantitatively vital to the operation of the corporation and is out of the ordinary [course] and substantially affects the existence and purpose of the corporation then it is beyond the power of the Board of Directors." In Thorpe v. Cerbco, Inc., 676 A.2d 436 (Del. 1996), a major issue was whether the sale by a corporation, CERBCO, of one of its subsidiaries, East, would have been a sale of all or substantially all of the corporation's assets, and therefore would have required shareholder approval under the Delaware statute. The court, quoting Oberly v. Kirby, 592 A.2d 445 (Del. 1991), stated:

> "[T]he rule announced in Gimbel v. Signal Cos., Del. Ch., 316 A.2d 599, aff'd, Del. Supr., 316 A.2d 619 (1974), makes it clear that the need for shareholder ... approval is to be measured not by the size of a sale alone, but also by its qualitative effect upon the corporation. Thus, it is relevant to ask whether a transaction 'is out of the ordinary and substantially affects the existence and purpose of the corporation.' [Gimbel, 316 A.2d] at 606."
>
> In the opinion below, the Chancellor determined that the sale of East would constitute a radical transformation of CERBCO. In addition, CERBCO's

> East stock accounted for 68 [percent] of CERBCO's assets in 1990 and this stock was its primary income generating asset. We therefore affirm the decision that East stock constituted "substantially all" of CERBCO's assets as consistent with Delaware law.

See also Katz v. Bregman, 431 A.2d 1274 (Del. Ch.), appeal refused sub nom. Plant Industries, Inc. v. Katz, 435 A.2d 1044 (Del. 1981); Stiles v. Aluminum Products Co., 338 Ill. App. 48, 86 N.E.2d 887 (1949); Campbell v. Vose, 515 F.2d 256 (10th Cir. 1975); South End Improvement Group, Inc. v. Mulliken, 602 So. 2d 1327 (Fla. App. 1992); Schwadel v. Uchitel, 455 So. 2d 401 (Fla. App. 1984).

Whether a disposition leaves a corporation with a significant continuing business activity, within the meaning of section 12.02(a), depends primarily on whether the corporation will have a remaining business activity that is significant when compared to the corporation's business prior to the disposition. The addition of a safe harbor, embodied in the second sentence of section 12.02(a), under which a significant business activity exists if the continuing business activity represented at least 25 percent of the total assets and 25 percent of either income from continuing operations before income taxes or revenues from continuing operations, in each case of the company and its subsidiaries on a consolidated basis for the most recent full fiscal year, the corporation will conclusively be deemed to have retained a significant continuing business activity, represents a policy judgment that a greater measure of certainty than is provided by interpretations of the current case law is highly desirable. The application of this brightline safe harbor test should, in most cases, produce a reasonably clear result substantially in conformity with the approaches taken in the better case law developing the "quantitative" and "qualitative" analyses. The test is to be applied to assets, revenue, and income for the most recent fiscal year ended immediately before the decision to make the disposition in question.

If a corporation disposes of assets for the purpose of reinvesting the proceeds of the disposition in substantially the same business in a somewhat different form (for example, by selling the corporation's only plant for the purpose of buying or building a replacement plant), the disposition and reinvestment should be treated together, so that the transaction should not be deemed to leave the corporation without a significant continuing business activity.

In determining whether a disposition would leave a corporation without a significant continuing business activity, the term "the corporation" includes subsidiaries that are or should be consolidated with the parent under generally accepted accounting principles. Accordingly, if, for example, a corporation's only significant business is owned by a wholly or almost wholly owned subsidiary, a sale of that business requires approval of the parent's shareholders under section 12.02. See Schwadel v. Uchitel, 455 So. 2d 401 (Fla. App. 1984). Correspondingly, if a corporation owns one significant business directly, and several other significant businesses through one or more wholly or almost wholly owned subsidiaries, a sale by the corporation of the single business it owns directly does not require shareholder approval under section 12.02.

If all or a large part of a corporation's assets are held for investment, the corporation actively manages those assets, and it has no other significant business, for purposes of the statute the corporation should be considered to be in the business of investing in such assets, so that a sale of most of those assets without a reinvestment should be considered a sale that would leave the corporation without a significant continuing business activity. In applying the 25 percent tests of section 12.02(a), an issue could arise if a corporation had more than one business activity, one or more of which might be traditional operating activities such as manufacturing or distribution, and another of which might be considered managing investments in other securities or enterprises. If the activity constituting the management of investments is to be a continuing business activity as a result of the active engagement of the management of the corporation in that process, and the 25 percent tests were met upon the disposition of the other businesses, shareholder approval would not be required.

As under section 6.40(d) (determination of whether a dividend is permissible), and for the same reasons, the board of directors may base a determination that a retained continuing business falls within the 25 percent brightline tests of the safe harbor embodied in the second sentence of section 12.02(a) either on accounting principles and practices that are reasonable in the circumstances or (in applying the asset test) on a fair valuation or other method that is reasonable in the circumstances. See section 6.40(d) and Comment 4 thereto.

The utilization of the term "significant," and the specific 25 percent safe harbor test for purposes of this section, should not be read as implying a standard for the test of significance or materiality for any other purposes under the Act or otherwise.

2. Submission to Shareholders

Section 12.02(b) requires the board of directors, after having adopted a resolution authorizing a disposition that requires shareholder approval, to submit the disposition to the shareholders for approval. When submitting the disposition to the shareholders, the board of directors must make a recommendation to the shareholders that the disposition be approved, unless the board makes a determination that because of conflicts of interests or other special circumstances it should make no recommendation. For example, the board of directors may make such a determination where there is not a sufficient number of directors free of a conflicting interest to approve the transaction or because the board of directors is evenly divided as to the merits of a transaction but is able to agree that shareholders should be permitted to consider the transaction. If the board of directors makes such a determination, it must describe the conflicts of interests or special circumstances, and communicate the basis for the determination, when submitting the disposition to the shareholders. The exception for conflicts of interest or other special circumstances is intended to be sparingly available. Generally, shareholders should not be asked to act on a disposition in the absence of a recommendation by the board of directors. The exception is not intended to relieve the board of directors of its duty to consider carefully the proposed transaction and the interests of shareholders.

Section 12.02(c) permits the board of directors to condition its submission of a proposed disposition to the shareholders. Among the conditions that board might impose are that the disposition will not be deemed approved: (i) unless it is approved by a specified percentage of the shareholders, or by one or more specified classes or series of shares, voting as a separate voting group, or by a specified percentage of disinterested shareholders, or (ii) if shareholders holding more than a specified fraction of the outstanding shares assert appraisal rights. The board of directors is not limited to conditions of these types.

3. Quorum and Voting

Section 12.02(e) provides that approval of a plan of merger or share exchange requires approval of the shareholders at a meeting at which at least a majority of the votes entitled to be cast on the plan is present, including, if any class or series of shares are entitled to vote as a separate group on the plan, the approval of each such separate group at a meeting at which a similar quorum of the voting group exists. If a quorum is present, then under sections 7.25 and 7.26 the plan will be approved if more votes are cast in favor of the plan than against it by the voting group or separate voting groups entitled to vote on the plan. This represents a change from the Act's previous voting rule, which required approval by a majority of outstanding shares.

In lieu of approval at a shareholders' meeting, approval can be given by the consent of all the shareholders entitled to vote on the merger or share exchange, under the procedures set forth in section 7.04.

4. Appraisal Rights

Shareholders of a domestic corporation that engages in a disposition that requires shareholder approval under section 12.02 may have appraisal rights. See chapter 13.

5. Subsidiaries

The term "subsidiary" or "subsidiaries," as used in section 12.02, includes both corporate and noncorporate subsidiaries. Accordingly, for example, a limited liability company or a partnership may be a subsidiary for purposes of section 12.02.

CHAPTER 13. APPRAISAL RIGHTS

SUBCHAPTER A. RIGHT TO APPRAISAL AND PAYMENT FOR SHARES

§ 13.01 Definitions

In this chapter:

(1) "Affiliate" means a person that directly or indirectly through one or more intermediaries controls, is controlled by, or is under common control with another person or is a senior executive thereof For purposes of section 13.02(b)(4), a person is deemed to be an affiliate of its senior executives.

(2) "Beneficial shareholder" means a person who is the beneficial owner of shares held in a voting trust or by a nominee on the beneficial owner's behalf

(3) "Corporation" means the issuer of the shares held by a shareholder demanding appraisal and, for matters covered in sections 13.22–13.31, includes the surviving entity in a merger.

(4) "Fair value" means the value of the corporation's shares determined:

(i) immediately before the effectuation of the corporate action to which the shareholder objects;

(ii) using customary and current valuation concepts and techniques generally employed for similar businesses in the context of the transaction requiring appraisal; and

(iii) without discounting for lack of marketability or minority status except, if appropriate, for amendments to the articles pursuant to section 13.02(a)(5).

(5) "Interest" means interest from the effective date of the corporate action until the date of payment, at the rate of interest on judgments in this state on the effective date of the corporate action.

(6) "Preferred shares" means a class or series of shares whose holders have preference over any other class or series with respect to distributions.

(7) "Record shareholder" means the person in whose name shares are registered in the records of the corporation or the beneficial owner of shares to the extent of the rights granted by a nominee certificate on file with the corporation.

(8) "Senior executive" means the chief executive officer, chief operating officer; chief financial officer; and anyone in charge of a principal business unit or function.

(9) "Shareholder" means both a record shareholder and a beneficial shareholder.

OFFICIAL COMMENT

1. Overview

Chapter 13 deals with the tension between the desire of the corporate leadership to be able to enter new fields, acquire new enterprises, and rearrange investor rights, and the desire of investors to adhere to the rights and the risks on the basis of which they invested. Contemporary corporation statutes in the United States attempt to resolve this tension through a combination of two devices, On the one hand, through their approval of an amendment to the articles of incorporation, a merger; share exchange or disposition of assets, the majority may change the nature and shape of the enterprise and the rights of all its shareholders. On the other hand, shareholders who object to these changes may withdraw the fair value of their investment in cash through their exercise of appraisal rights.

The traditional accommodation has been sharply criticized from two directions. From the viewpoint of investors who object to the transaction, the appraisal process is criticized for providing little help to the ordinary investor because its technicalities make its use difficult, expensive, and risky From the viewpoint of the corporate leadership, the appraisal process is criticized because it fails to protect the corporation from demands that are motivated by the hope of a nuisance settlement or by fanciful conceptions of value. See generally

Bayless Manning, "The Shareholders' Appraisal Remedy: An Essay for Frank Coker," 72 YALE U. 223 (1962).

Chapter 13 is a compromise between these opposing points of view It is designed to increase the frequency with which assertion of appraisal rights leads to economical and satisfying solutions, and to decrease the frequency with which such assertion leads to delay, expense, and dissatisfaction. It seeks to achieve these goals primarily by simplifying and clarifying the appraisal process, as well as by motivating the parties to settle their differences in private negotiations without resort to judicial appraisal proceedings.

Chapter 13 proceeds from the premise that judicial appraisal should be provided by statute only when two conditions co-exist. First, the proposed corporate action as approved by the majority will result in a fundamental change in the shares to be affected by the action. Second, uncertainty concerning the fair value of the affected shares may cause reasonable persons to differ about the fairness of the terms of the corporate action. Uncertainty is greatly reduced, however; in the case of publicly-traded shares. This explains both the market exception described below and the limits provided to the exception.

Appraisal rights in connection with mergers and share exchanges under chapter 11 and dispositions of assets requiring shareholder approval under chapter 12 are provided when these two conditions co-exist. Each of these actions will result in a fundamental change in the shares that a disapproving shareholder may feel was not adequately compensated by the terms approved by the majority. Except for shareholders of a subsidiary corporation that is merged under section 11.05 (the "short-form" merger), only those shareholders who are entitled to vote on a transaction are entitled to appraisal rights. The linkage between voting and appraisal rights is justified because the right to a shareholder vote is a good proxy for assessing the seriousness of the change contemplated by the corporate action. This is especially true where the action triggers group-voting provisions.

Notwithstanding this linkage, amended chapter 13 eliminates appraisal for voting shareholders in several instances where it would have been available under the 1984 Act. Shareholders who are entitled to vote on a corporate action, whether because such shareholders have general voting rights or because group voting provisions are triggered, are not entitled to appraisal if the change will not alter the terms of the class or series of securities that they hold. Thus, statutory appraisal rights are not available for shares of any class of the surviving corporation in a merger or any class of shares that is not included in a share exchange. Appraisal is also not triggered by a voluntary dissolution under chapter 14 because that action does not affect liquidation rights—the only rights that are relevant following a shareholder vote to dissolve.

With the exception of reverse stock splits that result in cashing out some of the shares of a class or series, amended chapter 13 also eliminates appraisal in connection with all amendments to the articles of incorporation. This change in amended chapter 13 does not reflect a judgment that an amendment changing the terms of a particular class or series may not have significant economic effects. Rather; it reflects a judgment that distinguishing among different types of amendments for the purposes of statutory appraisal is necessarily arbitrary and thus may not accurately reflect the actual demand of shareholders for appraisal in specific instances. Instead, amended chapter 13 permits a high degree of private-ordering by delineating a list of transactions for which the corporation may voluntarily choose to provide appraisal and by permitting a provision in the articles of incorporation that eliminates, in whole or in part, statutory appraisal tights for preferred shares.

Chapter 13 also is unique in its approach to appraisal rights for publicly-traded shares; Approximately half of the general corporation statutes in the United States provide exceptions to appraisal for publicly-traded shares, on the theory that it is not productive to expose the corporation to the time, expense and cash drain imposed by appraisal demands when shareholders who are dissatisfied with the consideration offered in an appraisal-triggering transaction could sell their shares and obtain cash from the market. This exception to appraisal is generally known as the "market-out" and is referred to here as the "market exception." Opponents of the market exception argue that it results in unfairness where neither the consideration offered in connection with the transaction nor the market price reflects the fair value of the shares, particularly if the corporate decision-makers have a conflict of interest.

Chapter 13 seeks to accommodate both views by providing a market exception that is limited to those situations where shareholders are likely to receive fair value when they sell their shares in the market after the announcement of an appraisal-triggering transaction. For the market exception to apply under chapter 13, there must first be a liquid market. Second, unique to chapter 13, the market exception does not apply in specified circumstances where the appraisal-triggering action is deemed to be a conflict-of-interest transaction.

2. Definitions

Section 13.01 contains specialized definitions applicable only to chapter 13.

Beneficial shareholder

The definition of "beneficial shareholder" means a person who owns the beneficial interest in shares; "shares" is defined in section 1.40(22) to include, without limitation, a holder of a depository receipt for shares. Similar definitions are found in section 7.40(2) (derivative proceedings) and section 16.02(1) (inspection of records by a shareholder). In the context of chapter 13, beneficial shareholder means a person having a direct economic interest in the shares. The definition is not intended to adopt the broad definition of beneficial ownership in SEC Rule 13d–2, which includes persons with a right to vote or dispose of the shares even though they have no economic interest in them. However; section 13.02(b)(5) includes the concept of the right to vote in determining whether the event represents a conflict transaction that renders the market exception unavailable.

Corporation

The definition of "corporation" in section 13.01(3) includes, for purposes of the post-transaction matters covered in section 13.22 through 13.31, a successor entity in a merger where the corporation is not the surviving entity. The definition does not include a domestic acquiring corporation in a share exchange or disposition of assets because the corporation whose shares or assets were acquired continues in existence in both of these instances and remains responsible for the appraisal obligations. Whether a foreign corporation or other form of domestic or foreign entity is subject to appraisal rights in connection with any of these transactions depends upon the corporation or other applicable law of the relevant jurisdiction.

Fair value

Subsection (i) of the definition of "fair value" in section 13.0 1(4) makes clear that fair value is to be determined immediately before the effectuation of the corporate action, rather than, as is the case under most state.statutes that address the issue, the date of the shareholders' vote. This comports with the purpose of this chapter to preserve the shareholder's prior rights as a shareholder until the effective date of the corporate action, rather than leaving the shareholder in an ambiguous state with neither rights as a shareholder nor perfected appraisal rights. The corporation and, as relevant, its shares are valued as they exist immediately before the effectuation of the corporate action requiring appraisal. Accordingly, section 13.01(4) permits consideration of changes in the market price of the corporation's shares in anticipation of the transaction, to the extent such changes are relevant. Similarly, in a two-step transaction culminating in a merger; the corporation is valued immediately before the second step merger; taking into account any interim changes in value. *Cf Cede & Co. v. Technicolor, Inc.,* 684 A.2d 289 (Del. 1996).

The definition of "fair value" in section 13.01(4) makes several changes from the prior version. The 1984 Model Act's definition of "fair value" was silent on how fair value was to be determined, except for a concluding clause that excluded from the valuation "any appreciation or depreciation in anticipation of the corporate action, unless exclusion would be inequitable." The Official Comment provided that the section left to the courts "the details by which 'fair value' is to be determined within the broad outlines of the definition." While the logic of the prior Official Comment continues to apply, the exclusionary clause in the prior Model Act definition, including the qualification for cases where the exclusion would be inequitable, has been deleted. Those provisions have not been susceptible to meaningful judicial interpretation and have been set aside in favor of the broader concept in subsection (ii).

The new formulation in paragraph (ii), which is patterned on section 7.22 of the Principles of Corporate Governance promulgated by the American Law Institute, directs courts to keep the methodology chosen in appraisal proceedings consistent with evolving economic concepts and adopts that part of section 7.22 which provides that fair value should be determined using "customary valuation concepts and techniques generally employed . . ., for similar businesses in the context of the transaction requiring appraisal." Subsection (ii) adopts the accepted view that different transactions and different contexts may warrant different valuation methodologies. Customary valuation concepts and techniques will typically take into account numerous relevant factors, including assigning a higher valuation to corporate assets that would be more productive if acquired in a comparable transaction but excluding any element of value attributable to the unique synergies of the actual purchaser of the corporation or its assets. For example, if the corporation's assets include undeveloped real estate that is located in a prime commercial area, the court should consider the value that would be attributed to the real estate as commercial development property in a comparable transaction. The court should not, however; assign any additional value based upon the specific plans or special use of the actual purchaser.

Modern valuation methods will normally result in a range of values, not a particular single value. When a transaction falls within that range, "fair value" has been established. Absent unusual circumstances, it is expected that the consideration in an arm's-length transaction will fall within the range of "fair value" for purposes of section 13.01(4). Section 7.22 of the ALI Principles of Corporate Governance also provides that in situations that do not involve certain types of specified conflicts of interest, "the aggregate price accepted by the board of directors of the subject corporation should be presumed to represent the fair value of the corporation, or of the assets sold in the case of an asset sale, unless the plaintiff can prove otherwise by clear and convincing evidence." That presumption has not been included in the definition of "fair value m section 13.01(4) because the framework of defined types of conflict transactions which is a predicate for the ALI's presumption is not contained in the Model Act. Nonetheless, under section 13.01(4), a court determining fair value should give great deference to the aggregate consideration accepted or approved by a disinterested board of directors for an appraisal-triggering transaction.

Subsection (iii) of the definition of "fair value" establishes that valuation discounts for lack of marketability or minority status are inappropriate in most appraisal actions, both because most transactions that trigger appraisal rights affect the corporation as a whole and because such discounts give the majority the opportunity to take advantage of minority shareholders who have been forced against their will to accept the appraisal-triggering transaction. Subsection (iii), in conjunction with the lead-in language to the definition, is also designed to adopt the more modern view that appraisal should generally award a shareholder his or her proportional interest in the corporation after valuing the corporation as a whole, rather than the value of the shareholder's shares when valued alone. If, however; the corporation voluntarily grants appraisal tights for transactions that do not affect the entire corporation—such as certain amendments to the articles of incorporation—the court should use its discretion in applying discounts if appropriate. As the introductory clause of section 13.01 notes, the definition of "fair value" applies only to chapter 13. See the Official Comment to section 14.34 which recognizes that a minority discount may be appropriate under that section.

Interest

The definition of "interest" in section 13.01(5) is included to apprise the parties of their respective rights and obligations. The right to receive interest is based on the elementary consideration that the corporation, rather than the shareholder demanding appraisal, has the use of the shareholder's money from the effective date of the corporate action (when those shareholders who do not demand appraisal rights have the right to receive their consideration from the transaction) until the date of payment. Section 13.01(5) thus requires interest to be paid at the rate of interest on judgments from the effective date of the corporate action until the date of payment. The specification of the rate of interest on judgments, rather than a more subjective rate, eliminates a possible issue of contention and should facilitate voluntary settlements. Each state determines whether interest is compound or simple.

Senior executive

The definition of "senior executive" in section 13.01(8) encompasses the group of individuals in control of corporate information and the day-to-day operations. An employee of a subsidiary organization is a "senior executive" of the parent if the employee is "in charge of a principal business unit or function" of the parent and its subsidiaries on a combined or consolidated basis.

Shareholder

The definition of "shareholder" in section 13.01(9) for purposes of chapter 13 differs from the definition of that term used elsewhere in the Model Act. Section 1.40(21) defines "shareholder" as used generally in the Act to mean only a "record shareholder"; that term is specifically defined in section 13.01(7). Section 13.01(9), on the other hand, defines "shareholder" to include not only a "record shareholder" but also a "beneficial shareholder;" a term that is itself defined in section 13.01(2). The specially defined terms "record shareholder" and "beneficial shareholder" appear primarily in section 13.03, which establishes the manner in which beneficial shareholders, and record shareholders who are acting on behalf of beneficial shareholders, perfect appraisal rights. The word "shareholder" is used generally throughout chapter 13 in order to permit both record and beneficial shareholders to take advantage of the provisions of this chapter; subject to their fulfilling the applicable requirements of this chapter.

§ 13.02 Right to Appraisal

(a) A shareholder is entitled to appraisal tights, and to obtain payment of the fair value of that shareholder's shares, in the event of any of the following corporate actions:

(1) consummation of a merger to which the corporation is a party (i) if shareholder approval is required for the merger by section 11.04 and the shareholder is entitled to vote on the merger; except that appraisal rights shall not be available to any shareholder of the corporation with respect to shares of any class or series that remain outstanding after consummation of the merger; or (ii) if the corporation is a subsidiary and the merger is governed by section 11.05;

(2) consummation of a share exchange to which the corporation is a party as the corporation whose shares will be acquired if the shareholder is entitled to vote on the exchange, except that appraisal rights shall not be available to any shareholder of the corporation with respect to any class or series of shares of the corporation that is not exchanged;

(3) consummation of a disposition of assets pursuant to section 12.02 if the shareholder is entitled to vote on the disposition;

(4) an amendment of the articles of incorporation with respect to a class or series of shares that reduces the number of shares of a class or series owned by the shareholder to a fraction of a share if the corporation has the obligation or right to repurchase the fractional share so created;

(5) any other amendment to the articles of incorporation, merger; share exchange or disposition of assets to the extent provided by

the articles of incorporation, bylaws or a resolution of the board of directors;

(6) consummation of a domestication if the shareholder does not receive shares in the foreign corporation resulting from the domestication that have terms as favorable to the shareholder in all material respects, and represent at least the same percentage interest of the total voting rights of the outstanding shares of the corporation, as the shares held by the shareholder before the domestication;

(7) consummation of a conversion of the corporation to nonprofit status pursuant to subchapter 9C; or

(8) consummation of a conversion of the corporation to an unincorporated entity pursuant to subchapter 9E.

(b) Notwithstanding subsection (a), the availability of appraisal rights under subsections (a)(1), (2), (3), (4), (6) and (8) shall be limited in accordance with the following provisions:

(1) Appraisal rights shall not be available for the holders of shares of any class or series of shares which is:

(i) listed on the New York Stock Exchange or the American Stock Exchange or designated as a national market system security on an interdealer quotation system by the National Association of Securities Dealers, Inc.; or

(ii) not so listed or designated, but has at least 2,000 shareholders and the outstanding shares of such class or series has a market value of at least $20 million (exclusive of the value of such shares held by its subsidiaries, senior executives, directors and beneficial shareholders owning more than 10 percent of such shares).

(2) The applicability of subsection (b)(1) shall be determined as of:

(i) the record date fixed to determine the shareholders entitled to receive notice of and to vote at, the meeting of shareholders to act upon the corporate action requiring appraisal tights; or

(ii) the day before the effective date of such corporate action if there is no meeting of shareholders.

(3) Subsection (b)(1) shall not be applicable and appraisal rights shall be available pursuant to subsection (a) for the holders of any class or series of shares who are required by the terms of the corporate action requiring appraisal rights to accept for such shares anything other than cash. or shares of any class or any series of shares of any corporation, or any other proprietary interest of any

other entity, that satisfies the standards set forth in subsection (b)(1) at the time the corporate action becomes effective.

(4) Subsection (b)(1) shall not be applicable and appraisal rights shall be available pursuant to subsection (a) for the holders of any class or series of shares where:

(i) any of the shares or assets of the corporation are being acquired or converted, whether by merger; share exchange or otherwise, pursuant to the corporate action by a person, or by an affiliate of a person, who:

(A) is, or at any time in the one-year period immediately preceding approval by the board of directors of the corporate action requiring appraisal rights was, the beneficial owner of 20 percent or more of the voting power of the corporation, excluding any shares acquired pursuant to an offer for all shares having voting power if such offer was made within one year prior to the corporate action requiring appraisal rights for consideration of the same kind and of a value equal to or less than that paid in connection with the corporate action; or

(B) directly or indirectly has, or at any time in the one-year period immediately preceding approval by the board of directors of the corporation of the corporate action requiring appraisal rights had, the power; contractually or otherwise, to cause the appointment or election of 25 percent or more of the directors to the board of directors of the corporation; or

(ii) any of the shares or assets of the corporation are being acquired or converted, whether by merger; share exchange or otherwise, pursuant to such corporate action by a person. or by an affiliate of a person, who is, or at any time in the one-year period immediately preceding approval by the board of directors of the corporate action requiring appraisal tights was, a senior executive or director of the corporation or a senior executive of any affiliate thereof, and that senior executive or director will receive, as a result of the corporate action, a financial benefit not generally available to other shareholders as such, other than:

(A) employment, consulting, retirement or similar benefits established separately and not as part of or in contemplation of the corporate action; or

(B) employment, consulting, retirement or similar benefits established in contemplation of; or as part of, the corporate action that are not more favorable than those existing before the corporate action or; if more favorable, that have been approved on behalf of the corporation in the same manner as is provided in section 8.62; or

(C) in the case of a director of the corporation who will, in the corporate action, become a director of the acquiring entity in the corporate action or one of its affiliates, rights and benefits as a director that are provided on the same basis as those afforded by the acquiring entity generally to other directors of such entity or such affiliate.

(5) For the purposes of paragraph (4) only, the term "beneficial owner" means any person who, directly or indirectly, through any contract, arrangement, or understanding, other than a revocable proxy has or shares the power to vote, or to direct the voting of, shares, provided that a member of a national securities exchange shall not be deemed to be a beneficial owner of securities held directly or indirectly by it on behalf of another person solely because such member is the record holder of such securities if the member is precluded by the rules of such exchange from voting without instruction on contested matters or matters that may affect substantially the rights or privileges of the holders of the securities to be voted. When two or more persons agree to act together for the purpose of voting their shares of the corporation, each member of the group formed thereby shall be deemed to have acquired beneficial ownership, as of the date of such agreement, of all voting shares of the corporation beneficially owned by any member of the group.

(c) Notwithstanding any other provision of section 13.02, the articles of incorporation as originally filed or any amendment thereto may limit or eliminate appraisal rights for any class or series of preferred shares, but any such limitation or elimination contained in an amendment to the articles of incorporation that limits or eliminates appraisal rights for any of such shares that are outstanding immediately prior to the effective date of such amendment or that the corporation is or may be required to issue or sell thereafter pursuant to any conversion, exchange or other right existing immediately before the effective date of such amendment shall not apply to any corporate action that becomes effective within one year of that date if such action would otherwise afford appraisal rights.

(d) A shareholder may not challenge a completed corporate action described in subsection (a), other than those described in subsection (b)(3) and (4), unless such corporate action:

(1) was not effectuated in accordance with the applicable provisions of chapters 9, 10, 11 or 12 or the corporation's articles of incorporation, bylaws or board of directors' resolution authorizing the corporate action; or

(2) was procured as a result of fraud or material misrepresentation.

OFFICIAL COMMENT

1. Transactions Requiring Appraisal Rights

Section 13.02(a) establishes the scope of appraisal rights by identifying those transactions which afford this right. In view of the significant degree of private ordering permitted by section 13.02(a)(5), the scope of statutory appraisal provided is somewhat narrower than that provided in the 1984 Model Act. As discussed in the first section of the Official Comment to section 13.01, statutory appraisal is made available only for corporate actions that will result in a fundamental change in the shares to be affected by the action and then only when uncertainty concerning the fair value of the affected shares may cause reasonable differences about the fairness of the terms of the corporate action. The transactions that satisfy both of these criteria are:

(1) A merger pursuant to section 11.04 or a short-form merger pursuant to section 11.05. Holders of any class or series that is to be exchanged or converted in connection with a merger under section 11.04 are entitled both to a vote under section 11.04(f) and to appraisal under section 13.02(a)(1). Although shareholders of a subsidiary that is a party to a merger under section 11.05 are not entitled to a vote, they are entitled to appraisal under 13.02(a)(1) because their interests will be extinguished by the merger. Section 13.02(a)(1)(i) denies appraisal rights to any class or series of shares in the surviving corporation if such class or series remains outstanding.

(2) A share exchange under section 11.03 if the corporation is a party whose shares are being acquired in the exchange. Consistent with the treatment in section 13.02(a)(1) of mergers requiring shareholder approval, subsection (2) provides appraisal only for those shares that will be exchanged.

(3) A disposition of assets requiring shareholder approval under section 12.02. Minimally, shareholders of all classes or series of the corporation that are generally entitled to vote on matters requiring shareholder approval will be entitled to assert appraisal rights. Whether shares of a class or series that do not have general voting rights will be entitled to vote on the asset disposition and thus become entitled to appraisal rights depends on the form of the transaction disposing of the corporation's assets. In the usual form of this transaction, which is governed by chapter 12, the acquirer purchases substantially all of the assets and assumes substantially all of the liabilities of the corporation, which then liquidates pursuant to a plan of dissolution approved by the shareholders as part of the transaction and distributes the consideration received from the acquirer to its shareholders. If the transaction provides a non-voting class of preferred with its liquidation preference, there is no change in the contractual terms of the preferred and it is entitled neither to vote nor to appraisal rights. By the same token, a preferred class cannot be required to accept any consideration different from that called for in its liquidation preference without amending the terms of the class. For example, a plan that called for the preferred to accept securities of the acquirer in lieu of its cash liquidation preference would trigger both group voting and appraisal rights on behalf of the class. In the unusual event that the asset disposition plan contemplated that the corporation would continue

in existence, the terms of a non-voting class would not have been changed as a result of the transaction, and appraisal rights would not be available. As provided in section 12.02(g), a disposition of assets by a corporation in the course of dissolution under chapter 14 is governed by that chapter, not chapter 12, and thus does not implicate appraisal rights.

(4) Amendments to the articles of incorporation that effectuate a reverse stock split which reduces the number of shares that a shareholder owns of a class or series to a fractional share if the corporation has the obligation or right to repurchase the fractional share so created. The reasons for granting appraisal rights in this situation are similar to those granting such rights in cases of cash-out mergers, as both transactions could compel affected shareholders to accept cash for their investment in an amount established by the corporation. Appraisal is afforded only for those shareholders of a class or series whose interest is so affected.

(5) Any other merger; share exchange, disposition of assets or amendment to the articles to the extent the articles, bylaws, or a resolution of the board of directors grants appraisal rights to a particular class or series of stock. A corporation may voluntarily wish to grant to the holders of one or more of its classes or series of shares appraisal rights in connection with these important transactions whenever the Act does not provide statutory appraisal rights. The grant of appraisal rights may satisfy shareholders who might, in the absence of appraisal rights, seek other remedies. Moreover, in situations where the existence of appraisal rights may otherwise be disputed, the voluntary offer of those rights under this section may avoid litigation. Obviously, an express grant of voluntary appraisal tights under section 13.02(a)(5) is intended to override any of the exceptions to the availability of appraisal rights in section 13.02(a). Any voluntary grant of appraisal rights by the corporation to the holders of one or more of its classes or series of shares will thereby automatically make all of the provisions of chapter 13 applicable to the corporation and such holders regarding this corporate action.

(6) A domestication in which the shares held by a shareholder are reclassified in a manner that results in the shareholder holding shares either with terms that are not as favorable in all materials respects or representing a smaller percentage of the total outstanding voting rights in the corporation as those held before the domestication. Appraisal rights are not provided if the shares of a shareholder are otherwise reclassified so long as the foregoing restrictions are satisfied.

(7) A conversion to nonprofit status pursuant to subchapter 9C. Such a conversion involves such a fundamental change in the nature of the corporation that appraisal rights are provided to all of the shareholders.

(8) A conversion of the corporation to an unincorporated entity pursuant to subchapter 9E. As with the previous type of transaction, this form of conversion is so fundamental that appraisal rights are provided to all of the shareholders.

2. Market Exception to Appraisal Rights

Chapter 13 provides a limited exception to appraisal rights for those situations where shareholders can either accept the consideration offered in the appraisal-triggering transaction or can obtain the fair value of their shares by selling them in the market. This provision is predicated on the theory that where an efficient market exists, the market price will be an adequate proxy for the fair value of the corporation's shares, thus making appraisal unnecessary. Furthermore, after the corporation announces an appraisal-triggering action, the market operates at maximum efficiency with respect to that corporation's shares because interested parties and market professionals evaluate the offer and competing offers may be generated if the original offer is deemed inadequate. Moreover, the market exception reflects an evaluation that the uncertainty costs and time commitment involved in any appraisal proceeding are not warranted where shareholders can sell their shares in an efficient, fair and liquid market. For these reasons, approximately half of the states have enacted market exceptions to their appraisal statutes.

For purposes of this chapter; the market exception is provided for a class or series if two criteria are met: the market in which the class or series is traded must be "liquid" and the value of the shares established by the appraisal-triggering event must be "reliable." Liquidity is defined in section 13.02(b)(1) and requires the class or series of stock to satisfy either of two requirements: the class or series is either listed on the New York Stock Exchange or the American Stock Exchange or is designated as a national market system security on an interdealer quotation system by the National Association of Securities Dealers, Inc.; or; although not so listed or designated, the class or series has at least 2,000 record or beneficial shareholders, provided that using both concepts does not result in duplication. In this instance, the outstanding class or series must also have a market value of at least $20 million, excluding the value of shares held by the corporation's subsidiaries, senior executives, directors and beneficial shareholders owning more than 10 percent of the class or series.

Because section 13.02(b)(3) excludes from the market exception those transactions that require shareholders to accept anything other than cash or securities that also meet the liquidity tests of section 13.02(b)(1), shareholders are assured of receiving either appraisal tights, cash from the transaction, or shares or other proprietary interests in the survivor entity that are liquid. Section 13.02(b)(2) provides that the corporation generally must satisfy the requirements of section 13.02(b)(1) on the record date for a shareholder vote on the appraisal-triggering transaction. For purposes of subsection 13.02(a)(1)(ii), the requirements of section 13.02(b)(1) must be met as of the day before the corporate action becomes effective.

3. Appraisal Rights in Conflict Transactions

The premise of the market exception is that the market must be liquid and the valuation assigned to the relevant shares must be "reliable." Section 13.02(b)(1) is designed to assure liquidity. For purposes of these provisions, section 13.02(b)(4) is designed to assure reliability by recognizing that the market price of or consideration for; shares of a corporation that proposes to engage in a section 13.02(a) transaction may be subject to influences where a corporation's management, controlling shareholders or directors have conflicting interests that could, if not dealt with appropriately, adversely affect the consideration that otherwise could have been expected. Section 13.02(b)(4) addresses two groups of conflict transactions: those in clause (i), which involve controlling shareholders; and those in clause (ii), which involve senior executives and directors.

Section 13.02(b)(4)(i) covers two possible conflict situations: subsection (A) covers the acquisition or exchange of shares or assets of the corporation by a shareholder or an affiliate of the shareholder that could be considered controlling by virtue of ownership of a substantial amount of voting stock (20 percent); and subsection (B) covers the acquisition or exchange of shares or assets of the corporation by an individual or group, or by an affiliate of such individual or group, that has the ability to exercise control, through contract, stock ownership, or some other means, over at least one fourth of the board's membership. The definition of "beneficial owner" in section 13.02(b)(5) serves to identify possible conflict situations by deeming each member of a group that agrees to vote in tandem to be a beneficial owner of all the voting shares owned by the group. In contrast, the term "beneficial shareholder;" as defined in section 13.01(2), is used to identify those persons entitled to appraisal tights. The last portion of subsection (A) recognizes that an acquisition effected in two steps (a tender offer followed by a merger) within one year; where the two steps are either on the same terms or the second step is on terms that are more favorable to target shareholders, is properly considered a single transaction for purposes of identifying conflict transactions, regardless of whether the second-step merger is governed by sections 11.04 or 11.05.

Section 13.02(b)(4)(ii) covers the acquisition or exchange of shares or assets of the corporation by a person, or an affiliate of a person, who is, or in the year leading up to the transaction was, a senior executive or director of the corporation. The section eliminates the market exception for management buyouts because participation in the buyout group is itself "a financial benefit not available to other shareholders as such." The market exception is also not available for transactions involving other types of economic benefits (in addition to benefits afforded to shareholders generally, as such) afforded to senior executives (as defined in section 13.01(8)) and directors in specified conflict situations, unless specific objective or procedural standards are met. Section 13.01(1) specially defines the term "affiliate" for purposes of section 13.02(b)(4) to include an entity of which a person is a senior executive. Due to this specialized definition, if a senior executive of the corporation is to continue and is to receive enumerated employment and other financial benefits after the transaction, the availability of the market exception will depend on meeting one of the three conditions specified in clauses (A), (B) and (C) of section 13.02(b)(4)(ii).

First, under section 13.02(b)(4)(ii)(A), the market exception is not lost if financial benefits that result from the transaction consist of employment, consulting, retirement or similar benefits established separately and not in contemplation of the transaction. For example, if an individual has an arrangement under which benefits will be triggered on a "change of control," such as accelerated vesting of options, retirement benefits, deferred compensation and similar items, or is afforded the opportunity to retire or leave the employ of the enterprise with more favorable economic results than would be the case absent a change of control, the existence of these arrangements would not disqualify the transaction from the market exception if the arrangements had been established as a general condition of the individual's employment or continued employment, rather than in contemplation of the particular transaction. Second, under section 13.02(b)(4)(ii)(B), if such arrangements are established as part of; or as a condition of, the transaction, the market exception will not be lost if the arrangements are either not more favorable than those already in existence or; if more favorable, are approved by "qualified" directors *(i.e.,* meeting the standard of independence specified in section 8.62(d)), in the satin-manner as is provided for conflicting interest transactions generally with the corporation under section 8.62. This category would include arrangements with the corporation which have been negotiated as part of; or as a condition of, the transaction or arrangements with the acquiring company or one or more of its other subsidiaries. The third situation, delineated in section 13.02(b)(4)(ii)(C), addresses a person who is a director of the issuer and, in connection with the transaction, is to become a director of the acquiring entity or its parent, or to continue as a director of the corporation when it becomes a subsidiary of the acquiring entity. In this situation, the market exception is not lost as long as that person will not be treated more favorably as a director than are other persons who arc serving in the same director positions.

4. Elimination of Appraisal Rights for Preferred Shares

Section 13.02(c) permits the corporation to eliminate or limit appraisal rights for the holders of one or more series or classes of preferred shares. The operative provisions may be set forth in the corporation's articles of incorporation as originally filed or in any amendment thereto, but any such amendment will not become effective for one year with respect to outstanding shares or shares which the corporation is or may be required to issue or sell at some later date pursuant to any rights outstanding prior to such amendment becoming effective. Shareholders who have not yet acquired, or do not have a right to acquire from the corporation, any shares of preferred stock, should have the ability either not to acquire any shares of preferred stock or to have appraisal rights granted or restored for such shares, if such shareholders so desire, before purchasing them. In contrast, because the terms of common shares are rarely negotiated, section 13.02 does not permit the corporation to eliminate or limit the appraisal rights of common shares.

5. Exclusivity of Appraisal Rights

With three exceptions, section 13.02(d) provides that appraisal is the exclusive remedy for a corporate action that has been completed.

The theory underlying this section is that when a majority of shareholders has approved a corporate change, the corporation should be permitted to proceed even if a minority considers the change unwise or disadvantageous. The very existence of the appraisal remedy recognizes that shareholders may disagree about the financial consequences that a corporate action may have and some may hold such strong views that they will want to vindicate them in a judicial proceeding. Since a judicial proceeding is insulated from the dynamics of an actual negotiation, it is not surprising that the two processes could produce different valuations. Accordingly, if such a proceeding results in an award of additional consideration to the shareholders who pursued appraisal, no inference should be drawn that the judgment of the majority was wrong or that compensation is now owed to shareholders who did not seek appraisal. Thus, an exclusivity principle is generally justified.

Nevertheless, there may be exceptional circumstances where judicial review of a completed transaction is warranted. The same reasoning that supports the provision of appraisal rights for conflict of interest transactions described in section 13.02(b)(3) and (4) supports the decision in the first clause of section 13.02(d) not to preclude judicial review of such transactions for fairness. Similarly, there may be instances where the process by which the corporate action was approved was so flawed that it is appropriate to provide more general relief on behalf of all affected shareholders. Thus section 13.02(d)(1) does not preclude challenges to serious procedural defects in approving the action, such as a failure to obtain the votes required by statute or by the corporation's own articles, bylaws, or board resolution authorizing the transaction. Similarly, subsection (2) creates an exception for cases where fraud or material misrepresentation have affected the shareholder vote to such an extent as to have caused the corporate action to be approved mistakenly. The concept of misrepresentation includes the omission of a material fact necessary to make statements made not misleading.

Although section 13.02(d) does not address the question of remedies, such as injunctive relief; that may be available before the corporate action is effected, it should be noted that a complaint based solely on adequacy of consideration is not actionable unless accompanied by credible allegations of wrongdoing. Since section 13.02(d) is concerned with challenges only to the corporate action, it does not address remedies, if any, that shareholders may have against directors or other persons as a result of the corporate action. See section 8.31 and Official Comment.

§ 13.03 Assertion of Rights by Nominees and Beneficial Owners

(a) A record shareholder may assert appraisal rights as to fewer than all the shares registered in the record shareholder's name but owned by a beneficial shareholder only if the record shareholder objects with respect to all shares of the class or series owned by the beneficial shareholder and notifies the corporation in writing of the name and address of each beneficial shareholder on whose behalf appraisal rights are being asserted. The rights of a record shareholder who asserts appraisal rights for only part of the shares held of record in the record shareholder's name under this subsection shall be determined as if the shares as to which the record shareholder objects and the record shareholder's other shares were registered in the names of different record shareholders.

(b) A beneficial shareholder may assert appraisal fights as to shares of any class or series held on behalf of the shareholder only if such shareholder:

(1) submits to the corporation the record shareholder's written consent to the assertion of such rights no later than the date referred to in section 13.22(b)(2)(ii); and

(2) does so with respect to all shares of the class or series that are beneficially owned by the beneficial shareholder.

OFFICIAL COMMENT

Section 13.03 addresses the relationship between those who are entitled to assert appraisal rights and the widespread practice of nominee or street name ownership of publicly-held shares. Generally, a shareholder must demand appraisal for all the shares of a class or series which the shareholder owns. If a record shareholder is a nominee for several beneficial shareholders, some of whom wish to demand appraisal and some of whom do not, section 13.03(a) permits the record shareholder to assert appraisal rights with respect to a portion of the shares held of record by the record shareholder but only with respect to all the shares beneficially owned by a single person. This limitation is necessary to prevent abuse by a single beneficial shareholder who is not fundamentally opposed to the proposed corporate action but who may wish to speculate on the appraisal process, as to some of that shareholder's shares, on the possibility of a high payment. On the other hand, a shareholder who owns shares in more than one class or series may assert appraisal rights for only some-but not all classes or series that the shareholder owns. This is permitted because fair treatment of one class or series does not guarantee fair treatment of oilier classes or series.

Section 13.03(a) also requires a record shareholder who demands appraisal with respect to a portion of the shares held by the record shareholder to notify the corporation of the name and address of the beneficial owner on whose behalf the record shareholder has demanded appraisal rights.

Section 13.03(b) permits a beneficial shareholder to assert appraisal rights directly if the beneficial shareholder submits the record shareholder's written consent. Although generally the record shareholder is treated as the owner of shares, this section recognizes that sometimes the record shareholders are holding shares on behalf of beneficial shareholders. It would be foreign to the premises underlying nominee and street name ownership to require these record shareholders to forward demands and participate in litigation on behalf of their clients. In order to make appraisal rights effective without burdening record shareholders, beneficial shareholders should be allowed to assert their own claims as provided in this subsection. The beneficial shareholder is required to submit, no later than the date specified in section 13.22(b)(2)(ii), a written consent by the record shareholder to the assertion of appraisal rights to verify the beneficial shareholder's entitlement and to permit the protection of any security interest in the shares. In practice, a broker's customer who wishes to assert appraisal rights may request the broker to supply the customer with the name of the record shareholder (which may be a house nominee or a nominee of the Depository Trust Company), and a form of consent signed by the record shareholder. At the same time, the customer may want to obtain certificates for the shares so that they may be deposited pursuant to section 13.23. After the corporation has received the form of consent, the corporation must deal with the beneficial shareholder.

SUBCHAPTER B. PROCEDURE FOR EXERCISE OF APPRAISAL RIGHTS

§ 13.20 Notice of Appraisal Rights

(a) If proposed corporate action described in section 13.02(a) is to be submitted to a vote at a shareholders' meeting, the meeting notice must state that the corporation has concluded that shareholders are, are not or may be entitled to assert appraisal rights under this chapter. If the corporation concludes that appraisal rights are or may be available, a copy of this chapter must accompany the meeting notice sent to those record shareholders entitled to exercise appraisal rights.

(b) In a merger pursuant to section 11.05, the parent corporation must notify in writing all record shareholders of the subsidiary who are entitled to assert appraisal rights that the corporate action became effective. Such notice must be sent within ten days after the corporate action became effective and include the materials described in section 13.22.

OFFICIAL COMMENT

Before a vote is taken on a corporate action, the corporation is required by section 13.20(a) to notify record shareholders that a transaction is proposed and that the corporation has concluded either that appraisal rights are or are not available; alternatively, if the corporation is unsure about the availability of appraisal rights, it may state that appraisal rights may be available. Notice of appraisal rights is needed because many shareholders do not know what appraisal rights they may have or how to assert them. If the corporation has concluded appraisal rights are or may be available, the notice must be accompanied by a copy of this chapter.

Section 13.20(b) provides that notice be given by the parent corporation within ten days after the effective date of a merger of its subsidiary under section 11.05. This notice may be combined with the notice required by section 13.22.

§ 13.21 Notice of Intent to Demand Payment

(a) If proposed corporate action requiring appraisal rights under section 13.02 is submitted to a vote at a shareholders' meeting, a shareholder who wishes to assert appraisal rights with respect to any class or series of shares:

(1) must deliver to the corporation before the vote is taken written notice of the shareholder's intent to demand payment if the proposed action is effectuated; and

(2) must not vote, or cause or permit to be voted, any shares of such class or series in favor of the proposed action.

(b) A shareholder who does not satisfy the requirements of subsection (a) is not entitled to payment under this chapter.

OFFICIAL COMMENT

Section 13.21 applies to all transactions requiring appraisal, except short-form mergers under section 11.05. In the latter case, shareholders of the subsidiary do not vote on the transaction but are nevertheless entitled to appraisal.

Section 13.21(a) requires the shareholder to give notice of an intent to demand payment before the vote on the corporate action is taken. This notice enables the corporation to determine how much of a cash payment may be required. It also serves to limit the number of persons to whom the corporation must give further notice during the remainder of the appraisal process.

In order for a shareholder to remain eligible to demand payment, section 13.21 (a)(2) mandates that the shareholder must not vote (or, in the case of a beneficial shareholder, cause or permit to be voted) any shares of any class or series *for* which the shareholder is demanding appraisal in favor of the proposal.

§ 13.22 Appraisal Notice and Form

(a) If proposed corporate action requiring appraisal rights under section 13.02(a) becomes effective, the corporation must deliver a written appraisal notice and form required by subsection (b)(1) to all shareholders who satisfied the requirements of section 13.21. In the case of a merger under section 11.05, the parent must deliver a written appraisal notice and form to all record shareholders who may be entitled to assert appraisal rights.

(b) The appraisal notice must be sent no earlier than the date the corporate action became effective and no later than ten days after such date and must:

(1) supply a form that specifies the date of the first announcement to shareholders of the principal terms of the proposed corporate action and requires the shareholder asserting appraisal rights to certify (i) whether or not beneficial ownership of those shares for which appraisal rights are asserted was acquired before that date and (ii) that the shareholder did not vote for the transaction;

(2) state:

(i) where the form must be sent and where certificates for certificated shares must be deposited and the date by which those certificates must be deposited, which date may not be earlier than the date for receiving the required form under subsection (2)(ii);

(ii) a date by which the corporation must receive the form which date may not be fewer than 40 nor more than 60 days after the date the subsection (a) appraisal notice and form arc sent, and state that the shareholder shall have waived the right to demand appraisal with respect to the shares unless the form is received by the corporation by such specified date;

(iii) the corporation's estimate of the fair value of the shares;

(iv) that, if requested in writing, the corporation will provide, to the shareholder so requesting, within ten days after the date specified in subsection (2)(ii) the number of shareholders who return the forms by the specified date and the total number of shares owned by them; and

(v) the date by which the notice to withdraw under section 13.23 must be received, which date must be within 20 days after the date specified in subsection (2)(ii); and

(3) be accompanied by a copy of this chapter.

OFFICIAL COMMENT

The purpose of section 13.22 is to require the corporation to provide shareholders with information and a form for perfecting appraisal rights. The content of this notice and form are spelled out in detail to ensure that they accomplish this purpose.

When an action is submitted to the vote of shareholders, the appraisal notice must be sent only to those persons who gave notice of their intention to demand appraisal under section 13.21 and did not vote (or permit or cause to be voted) such shares in favor of the proposed action. In a short-form merger under section 11.05, the notice must be sent to all persons who may be eligible for appraisal rights no earlier than the effective date of the merger and no later than ten days thereafter. In either case, the notice must be accompanied by a copy of this chapter.

The notice must supply a form to be used by the person asserting appraisal tights in order to complete the exercise of those rights. Under section 13.22(b)(2)(ii), the notice must specify the date by which the shareholder's executed form must be received by the corporation, which date must be at least 40 days but not more than 60 days after the appraisal notice is sent.

Under section 13.22(b)(2)(i), the notice must also specify where and when share certificates must be deposited; the time for deposit may not be set at a date earlier than the date for receiving the required form under section 13.22(b)(2)(ii).

Sections 13.22(b)(1) and (2)(i) require the corporation to specify in the form supplied for demanding payment where the form must be sent as well as the date of the first announcement of the terms of the proposed corporate action. This is the critical date for determining the rights of shareholder-transferees: persons who became shareholders prior to that date are entitled to full appraisal rights, while persons who became shareholders on or after that date are entitled only to the more limited rights provided by section 13.25. See the Official Comments to sections 13.23 and 13.25. The date set forth in the form should be the date the principal terms of the transaction were announced by the corporation to shareholders. This may be the day the terms were communicated directly to the shareholders, included in a public filing with the Securities and Exchange Commission, published in a newspaper of general circulation that can be expected to reach the financial community, or any earlier date on which such terms were first announced by any other person or entity to such persons or sources. Any announcement to news media or to shareholders that relates to the proposed transaction but does not contain the principal terms of the transaction to be authorized at the shareholders' meeting is not considered to be an announcement for the purposes of section 13.22.

Sections 13.22(b)(2)(iii) and (b)(2)(iv) require the corporation to state its estimate of the fair value of the shares and how shareholders may obtain the number of shareholders and number of shares demanding appraisal tights. The information required by sections 13.22(b)(2)(iii) and (b)(2)(iv) is intended to help shareholders assess whether they wish to demand payment or to withdraw their demand for appraisal, but the information under section 13.22(b)(2)(iv) is required to be sent only to those shareholders from whom the corporation has received a written request. If such request is received, the corporation must respond within ten days after forms are due pursuant to section 13.22(b)(2)(ii). Finally, section 13.22(b)(2)(v) requires the corporation to specify the date by which the shareholder's notice to withdraw under section 13.23 must be received.

§ 13.23 Perfection of Rights; Right to Withdraw

(a) A shareholder who receives notice pursuant to section 13.22 and who wishes to exercise appraisal rights must certify on the form Sent by the corporation whether the beneficial owner of such shares acquired beneficial ownership of the shares before the date required to be set forth in the notice pursuant to section 13.22(b)(1). If a shareholder fails to make this certification, the corporation may elect to treat the shareholder's shares as after-acquired shares under section 13.25. In addition, a shareholder who wishes to exercise appraisal rights must execute and return the form and, in the case of certificated shares, deposit the shareholder's certificates in accordance with the terms of the notice by the date referred to in the notice pursuant to section 13.22(b)(2)(ii). Once a shareholder deposits that shareholder's certificates or, in the case of uncertificated shares, returns the executed forms, that shareholder loses all rights as a shareholder, unless the shareholder withdraws pursuant to subsection (b).

(b) A shareholder who has complied with subsection (a) may nevertheless decline to exercise appraisal rights and withdraw from the appraisal process by so notifying the corporation in writing by the date set forth in the appraisal notice pursuant to section 13.22(b)(2)(v). A shareholder who fails to so withdraw from the appraisal process may not thereafter withdraw without the corporation's written consent.

(c) A shareholder who does not execute and return the form and, in the case of certificated shares, deposit that shareholder's share certificates where required, each by the date set forth in the notice described in section 13.22(b), shall not be entitled to payment under this chapter.

OFFICIAL COMMENT

Section 13.23 permits shareholders to perfect their appraisal rights under subsection (a), subject to their right to withdraw under subsection (b). In the case of a transaction involving a vote by shareholders, returning the executed form and, in the case of certificated shares, depositing the shares are the shareholder's confirmation of the shareholder's intention expressed earlier under section 13.21(a) to pursue appraisal rights; in the case of a merger of a subsidiary under section 11.05, it is the shareholder's first statement of this position.

The shareholder should include on the appraisal form a certification as to whether the date on which the beneficial shareholder acquired beneficial ownership of the shares was before (or on or after) the date the transaction was announced. See section 13.22(b)(1). This information permits the corporation to exercise its tight under section 13.25 to defer payment of compensation for certain shares. The corporation may elect to proceed under section 13.25 with respect to those shareholders who fail to make the required certification.

Section 13.23(a) also requires persons with certificated shares who file the required form to deposit their share certificates as directed by the corporation in its appraisal notice. Once a shareholder deposits that shareholder's shares, that shareholder loses all rights as a shareholder unless the shareholder withdraws from the appraisal process pursuant to section 13.23(b).

With respect to certificated shares, this provision differs from many statutes in that the certificates are deposited for retention, rather than "submitted for notation." This difference reflects the requirement in section 13.22(b)(2)(i) for deposit only after the corporate action became effective; in contrast, many state statutes require shareholders to send in their certificates in anticipation of the effectuation of the proposed corporate action.

Alternatively, under section 13.23(b), a shareholder may withdraw from the appraisal process by so notifying the corporation in writing by the deadline set forth in the appraisal notice. After that date, however a shareholder who has complied with the requirements to execute and return the form and, in the case of certificated shares, deposit the share certificates may not withdraw from the process without the corporation's written consent.

Under section 13.23(c), a shareholder who fails to execute and return the form with respect to the shares of a class or series for which the shareholder is demanding appraisal or does not deposit that shareholder's share certificates as required by section 13.23(a) loses all tights to pursue appraisal and obtain payment under this chapter. If a beneficial shareholder wishes to assert appraisal rights in place of the record shareholder, the beneficial shareholder must also comply with section 13.03(b).

§ 13.24 Payment

(a) Except as provided in section 13.25, within 30 days after the form required by section 13.22(b)(2)(ii) is due, the corporation shall pay in cash to those shareholders who complied with section 13.23(a) the amount the corporation estimates to be the fair value of their shares, plus interest.

(b) The payment to each shareholder pursuant to subsection (a) must be accompanied by:

(1) financial statements of the corporation that issued the shares to be appraised, consisting of a balance sheet as of the end of a fiscal year ending not more than 16 months before the date of payment, an income statement for that year; a statement of changes in shareholders' equity for that year; and the latest available interim financial statements, if any;

(2) a statement of the corporation's estimate of the fair value of the shares, which estimate must equal or exceed the corporation's estimate given pursuant to section 13.22(b)(2)(iii);

(3) a statement that shareholders described in subsection (a) have the right to demand further payment under section 13.26 and that if any such shareholder does not do so within the time period specified therein, such shareholder shall be deemed to have accepted such payment in full satisfaction of the corporation's obligations under this chapter.

OFFICIAL COMMENT

Section 13.24 is applicable both to shareholders who have complied with section 13.23(a), as well as to shareholders who are described in section 13.25(a) if the corporation so chooses. The corporation must, however, elect to treat all shareholders described in section 13.25(a) either under section 13.24 or under section 13.25; it may not elect to treat some shareholders from this group under section 13.24 but treat others under section 13.25. Considerations of simplicity and harmony may prompt the corporation to elect to treat all shareholders under section 13.24.

Section 13.24 changes the relative balance between the corporation and shareholders demanding appraisal by requiring the corporation to pay in cash within 30 days after the required form is due the corporation's estimate of the fair value of the stock plus interest. Section 13.24(b)(2) requires that estimate to at least equal the corporation's estimate of fair value given pursuant to section 13.22(b)(2)(iii). Since under section 13.23(a) all rights as a shareholder are terminated with the deposit of that shareholder's shares, the former shareholder should have immediate use of such money A difference of opinion over the total amount to be paid should not delay payment of the amount that is undisputed. Thus, the corporation must pay its estimate of fair value, plus interest from the effective date of the corporate action, without waiting for the conclusion of the appraisal proceeding.

Since the former shareholder must decide whether or not to accept the payment in full satisfaction, the corporation must at this time furnish the former shareholder with the information specified in section 13.24(b), with a reminder of the former shareholder's further rights and liabilities.

§ 13.25 After-acquired Shares

(a) A corporation may elect to withhold payment required by section 13.24 from any shareholder who did not certify that beneficial ownership of all of the shareholder's shares for which appraisal rights are asserted was acquired before the date set forth in the appraisal notice sent pursuant to section 13.22(b)(1).

(b) If the corporation elected to withhold payment under subsection (a), it must, within 30 days after the form required by section 13.22(b)(2)(ii) is due, notify all shareholders who are described in subsection (a):

(1) of the information required by section 13.24(b)(1);

(2) of the corporation's estimate of fair value pursuant to section 13.24(b)(2);

(3) that they may accept the corporation s estimate of fair value, plus interest, in full satisfaction of their demands or demand appraisal under section 13.26;

(4) that those shareholders who wish to accept such offer must so notify the corporation of their acceptance of the corporation's offer within 30 days after receiving the offer; and

(5) that those shareholders who do not satisfy the requirements for demanding appraisal under section 13.26 shall be deemed to have accepted the corporation's offer.

(c) Within ten days after receiving the shareholder's acceptance pursuant to subsection (b), the corporation must pay in cash the amount it offered under subsection (b)(2) to each shareholder who agreed to accept the corporation's offer in full satisfaction of the shareholder's demand.

(d) Within 40 days after sending the notice described in subsection (b), the corporation must pay in cash the amount it offered to pay under subsection (b)(2) to each shareholder described in subsection (b)(5).

OFFICIAL COMMENT

Section 13.25(a) gives the corporation the option to treat differently shares acquired on or after the date of public announcement of the pro. posed corporate action; this date is specified by the corporation in its appraisal notice under section 13.22(b)(1). At the corporation's option. holders of shares acquired on or after this date, or shareholders who fail to certify otherwise under section 13.23(a), are not entitled to immediate payment under section 13.24. Instead, shareholders described in subsection (a) may receive only an offer of payment which is conditioned on their agreement to accept it in full satisfaction of their claim. If the right of unconditional immediate payment were granted as to all after-acquired shares, speculators and others might be tempted to buy shares merely for the purpose of demanding appraisal. Since the function of appraisal rights is to protect investors against unforeseen changes, there is no need to give equally favorable treatment to purchasers who knew or should have known about the proposed changes.

The date used as a cut-off for determining the application of this section is when "the principal terms" of the transaction are first announced to shareholders or to a newspaper of general circulation that can be expected to reach the financial community or included in a public filing with the Securities and Exchange Commission. The cut-off should not be set at an earlier date, such as when the first public statement that the corporate action was under consideration was made, because the goal of this section is to prevent use of appraisal rights as a speculative device after the terms of the transaction are announced. See the Official Comment to section 13.22.

Section 13.25(b) requires the corporation to furnish specified information to all shareholders described in subsection (a) and offer them the option of accepting the corporation's estimate of fair value plus interest, in full satisfaction of their claims, provided that such shareholders so accept and notify the corporation within ten days of receiving this offer. Within ten days after receiving a shareholder's acceptance, the corporation must pay that shareholder in cash the stated fair value plus interest.

A shareholder may accept the offered payment in full satisfaction of that shareholder's claim; alternatively, a shareholder may reject the corporation's offer and demand a judicial determination under section 13.26 and payment of the amount so determined at the termination of the proceeding. A shareholder who does not satisfy the requirements of section 13.26 shall be deemed to have accepted the corporation's offer.

§ 13.26 Procedure if Shareholder Dissatisfied With Payment or Offer

(a) A shareholder paid pursuant to section 13.24 who is dissatisfied with the amount of the payment must notify the corporation in writing of that shareholder's estimate of the fair value of the shares and demand payment of that estimate plus interest (less any payment under section 13.24). A shareholder offered payment under section 13.25 who is dissatisfied with that offer must reject the offer and demand payment of the shareholder's stated estimate of the fair value of the shares plus interest.

(b) A shareholder who fails to notify the corporation in writing of that shareholder's demand to be paid the shareholder's stated estimate of the fair value plus interest under subsection (a) within 30 days after receiving the corporation's payment or offer of payment under section 13.24 or section 13.25, respectively, waives the right to demand payment under this section and shall be entitled only to the payment made or offered pursuant to those respective sections.

OFFICIAL COMMENT

A shareholder who is not content with the corporation's remittance under section 13.24, or offer of remittance under section 13.25, and wishes to pursue appraisal rights further must state m writing the amount the shareholder is willing to accept. A shareholder whose demand is deemed arbitrary unreasonable or not in good faith, however; runs the risk of being assessed litigation expenses under section 13.31. These provisions are designed to encourage settlement without a judicial proceeding.

A shareholder to whom the corporation has made payment (or who has been offered payment under section 13.25) must make a supplemental demand within 30 days after receipt of the payment or offer of payment in order to permit the corporation to make an early decision on initiating appraisal proceedings. A failure to make such demand causes the shareholder to relinquish under section 13.26(b) anything beyond the amount the corporation paid or offered to pay.

SUBCHAPTER C. JUDICIAL APPRAISAL OF SHARES

§ 13.30 Court Action

(a) If a shareholder makes demand for payment under section 13.26 which remains unsettled, the corporation shall commence a proceeding within 60 days after receiving the payment demand and petition the court to determine the fair value of the shares and accrued interest. If the corporation does not commence the proceeding within the 60–day period, it shall pay in cash to each shareholder the amount the shareholder demanded pursuant to section 13.26 plus interest.

(b) The corporation shall commence the proceeding in the appropriate court of the county where the corporation's principal office (or; if none, its registered office) in this state is located. If the corporation is a foreign corporation without a registered office in this state, it shall commence the proceeding in the county in this state where the principal office or registered office of the domestic corporation merged with the foreign corporation was located at the time of the transaction.

(c) The corporation shall make all shareholders (whether or not residents of this state) whose demands remain unsettled parties to the proceeding as in an action against their shares, and all parties must be served with a copy of the petition. Nonresidents may be sewed by registered or certified mail or by publication as provided by law

(d) The jurisdiction of the court in which the proceeding is commenced under subsection (b) is plenary and exclusive. The court may appoint one or more persons as appraisers to receive evidence and recommend a decision on the question of fair value. The appraisers shall have the powers described in the order appointing them, or in any amendment to it. The shareholders demanding appraisal rights are entitled to the same discovery rights as parties in other civil proceedings. There shall be no right to a jury trial.

(e) Each shareholder made a party to the proceeding is entitled to judgment (i) for the amount, if any, by which the court finds the fair value of the shareholder's shares, plus interest, exceeds the amount paid by the corporation to the shareholder for such shares or (ii) for the fair value, plus interest, of the shareholder's shares for which the corporation elected to withhold payment under section 13.25.

OFFICIAL COMMENT

Section 13.30 retains the concept of judicial appraisal as the ultimate means of determining fair value. The proceeding is to be commenced by the corporation within 60 days after a timely demand for payment under section 13.26 was received. If the proceeding is not commenced within this period, the corporation must pay the additional amounts demanded by the shareholders under section 13.26. See the Official Comment to section 13.26.

All demands for payment made under section 13.26 are to be resolved in a single proceeding brought in the county in the state where the corporation's principal office is located or, if it is a foreign corporation, where its registered office is located, or if it has no registered office, where the principal office of the corporation which issued the shares to be appraised was located. All shareholders making section 13.26 demands must be made parties, with service by publication authorized if necessary Appraisers may be appointed within the discretion of the court. Since the nature of the proceeding is similar to a proceeding in equity or for an accounting, section 13.30(d) provides that there is no right to a jury trial. The final judgment establishes not only the fair value of the shares in the abstract but also determines how much each shareholder who made a section 13.26 demand should actually receive.

§ 13.31 Court Costs and Counsel Fees

(a) The court in an appraisal proceeding commenced under section 13.30 shall determine all costs of the proceeding, including the reasonable compensation and expenses of appraisers appointed by the court. The court shall assess the costs against the corporation, except that the court may assess costs against all or some of the shareholders demanding appraisal, in amounts the court finds equitable, to the extent the court finds such shareholders acted arbitrarily, vexatiously, or not in good faith with respect to the rights provided by this chapter.

(b) The court in an appraisal proceeding may also assess the fees and expenses of counsel and experts for the respective parties, in amounts the court finds equitable:

(1) against the corporation and in favor of any or all shareholders demanding appraisal if the court finds the corporation did not substantially comply with the requirements of sections 13.20, 13.22, 13.24 or 13.25; or

(2) against either the corporation or a shareholder demanding appraisal, in favor of any other party? if the court finds that the party against whom the fees and expenses are assessed acted arbitrarily, vexatiously, or not in good faith with respect to the rights provided by this chapter.

(c) If the court in an appraisal proceeding finds that the services of counsel for any shareholder were of substantial benefit to other shareholders similarly situated, and that the fees for those services should not be assessed against the corporation, the court may award to such counsel reasonable fees to be paid out of the amounts awarded the shareholders who were benefitted.

(d) To the extent the corporation fails to make a required payment pursuant to sections 13.24, 13.25, or 13.26, the shareholder may sue directly for the amount owed and, to the extent successful, shall be entitled to recover from the corporation all costs and expenses of the suit, including counsel fees.

OFFICIAL COMMENT

Section 13.31(a) provides a general rule that the costs of the appraisal proceeding should be assessed against the corporation. Nevertheless, the court is authorized to assess these costs, in whole or in part, against all or some of the shareholders demanding appraisal if it concludes they acted arbitrarily, vexatiously, or not in good faith regarding the rights provided by this chapter. Similarly, under section 13.31(b), the court may assess fees and expenses of counsel and experts against the corporation or against all or some of the shareholders demanding appraisal for the reasons stated in this subsection. Under section 13.31(c), if the corporation is not required to pay the counsel fees for the shareholders demanding appraisal, the court may require all shareholders who benefitted from the services of counsel to share in the payment of such fees. The purpose of all these grants of discretion with respect to costs and counsel fees is to increase the incentives of both sides to proceed in good faith under this chapter to attempt to resolve their disagreement without the need of a formal judicial appraisal of the value of shares.

While subsections (a)-(c) allocate costs and expenses m an appraisal proceeding, subsection (d) covers the situation where the corporation was obligated to make payment and did not meet this obligation. In that event, the shareholder may sue the corporation directly for the amount owed. In such an action, subsection (d) requires the court, to the extent the shareholder was successful, to impose all costs and expenses, including counsel fees, on the corporation.

CHAPTER 14. DISSOLUTION

SUBCHAPTER A. VOLUNTARY DISSOLUTION

§ 14.01 Dissolution by Incorporators or Initial Directors

A majority of the incorporators or initial directors of a corporation that has not issued shares or has not commenced business may dissolve the corporation by delivering to the secretary of state for filing articles of dissolution that set forth:

(1) the name of the corporation;

(2) the date of its incorporation;

(3) either (i) that none of the corporation's shares has been issued or (ii) that the corporation has not commenced business;

(4) that no debt of the corporation remains unpaid;

(5) that the net assets of the corporation remaining after winding up have been distributed to the shareholders, if shares were issued; and

(6) that a majority of the incorporators or initial directors authorized the dissolution.

§ 14.02 Dissolution by Board of Directors and Shareholders

(a) A corporation's board of directors may propose dissolution for submission to the shareholders.

(b) For a proposal to dissolve to be adopted:

(1) the board of directors must recommend dissolution to the shareholders unless the board of directors determines that because of conflict of interest or other special circumstances it should make no recommendation and communicates the basis for its determination to the shareholders; and

(2) the shareholders entitled to vote must approve the proposal to dissolve as provided in subsection (e).

(c) The board of directors may condition its submission of the proposal for dissolution on any basis.

(d) The corporation shall notify each shareholder, whether or not entitled to vote, of the proposed shareholders' meeting. The notice must also state that the purpose, or one of the purposes, of the meeting is to consider dissolving the corporation.

(e) Unless the articles of incorporation or the board of directors acting pursuant to subsection (c) require a greater vote, a greater number of shares to be present, or a vote by voting groups, adoption of the proposal to dissolve shall require the approval of the shareholders at a meeting at which a quorum consisting of at least a majority of the votes entitled to be cast exists.

OFFICIAL COMMENT

Section 14.02(b) requires the board of directors, after approving a proposal to dissolve, to submit the proposal to the shareholders for their approval. When submitting the proposal the board of directors must make a recommendation to the shareholders that the plan be approved, unless the board of directors makes a determination that because of conflicts of interest or other special circumstances it should make no recommendation. For example, the board or directors may make such a determination where there is not a sufficient number of directors free of a conflicting interest to approve the proposal or because the board of directors is evenly divided as to the merits of the proposal but is able to agree that shareholders should be permitted to consider dissolution. If the board of directors makes such a determination, it must describe the conflict of interest or special circumstances, and communicate the basis for the determination, when submitting the proposal to dissolve to the shareholders. The exception for conflicts of interest or other special circumstances is intended to be sparingly available. Generally, shareholders should not be asked to act on a proposal for dissolution in the absence of a recommendation by the board of directors. The exception is not intended to relieve the board of directors of its duty to consider carefully the proposed dissolution and the interests of shareholders.

Section 14.02(c) permits the board of directors to condition its submission of a proposal for dissolution on any basis. Among the conditions that a board might impose are that the proposal will not be deemed approved unless it is approved by a specified vote of the shareholders, or by one or more specified classes or series of shares, voting as a separate voting group, or by a specified percentage of disinterested shareholders. The board of directors is not limited to conditions of these types.

Section 14.02(d) provides that if the proposal is required to be approved by the shareholders, and if the approval is to be given at a meeting, the corporation must notify each shareholder, whether or not entitled to vote, of the meeting of shareholders at which the proposal is to be submitted. Requirements concerning the timing and content of a notice of meeting are set out in section 7.05. Section 14.02(d) does not itself require that notice be given to nonvoting shareholders where the proposal is approved, without a meeting, by unanimous consent. However, that requirement is imposed by section 7.04(d).

Section 14.02(e) provides that approval of a proposal for dissolution requires approval of the shareholders at a meeting at which a quorum consisting of a majority of the votes entitled to be cast on the proposal exists. If a quorum is present, then under sections 7.25 and 7.26 the proposal will be approved if more votes are cast in favor of the proposal than against it by the voting group or separate voting groups entitled to vote on the proposal. This represents a change from the Act's previous voting rule for dissolution, which required approval by a majority of outstanding shares.

The Act does not mandate separate voting by voting groups or appraisal rights in relation to dissolution proposals on the theory that, upon dissolution, the rights or all classes or series of shares are fixed by the articles of incorporation. Of course, group voting rights may be conferred by the articles of incorporation or by the board of directors, acting pursuant to subsection (c).

§ 14.03 Articles of Dissolution

(a) At any time after dissolution is authorized, the corporation may dissolve by delivering to the secretary of state for filing articles of dissolution setting forth:

(1) the name of the corporation;

(2) the date dissolution was authorized; and

(3) if dissolution was approved by the shareholders, a statement that the proposal to dissolve was duly approved by the shareholders in the manner required by this Act and by the articles of incorporation.

(b) A corporation is dissolved upon the effective date of its articles of dissolution.

(c) For purposes of this subchapter, "dissolved corporation" means a corporation whose articles of dissolution have become effective and includes a successor entity to which the remaining assets of the corporation are transferred subject to its liabilities for purposes of liquidation.

OFFICIAL COMMENT

If dissolution was approved by the shareholders, the articles of dissolution must state that dissolution was duly approved by the shareholders in the manner required by the Act and the articles of incorporation of the corporation.

§ 14.04 Revocation of Dissolution

(a) A corporation may revoke its dissolution within 120 days of its effective date.

(b) Revocation of dissolution must be authorized in the same manner as the dissolution was authorized unless that authorization permitted revocation by action of the board of directors alone, in which event the board of directors may revoke the dissolution without shareholder action.

(c) After the revocation of dissolution is authorized, the corporation may revoke the dissolution by delivering to the secretary of state for filing articles of revocation of dissolution, together with a copy of its articles of dissolution, that set forth:

(1) the name of the corporation;

(2) the effective date of the dissolution that was revoked;

(3) the date that the revocation of dissolution was authorized;

(4) if the corporation's board of directors (or incorporators) revoked the dissolution, a statement to that effect;

(5) if the corporation's board of directors revoked a dissolution authorized by the shareholders, a statement that revocation was permitted by action by the board of directors alone pursuant to that authorization; and

(6) if shareholder action was required to revoke the dissolution, the information required by section 14.03(a)(3).

(d) Revocation of dissolution is effective upon the effective date of the articles of revocation of dissolution.

(e) When the revocation of dissolution is effective, it relates back to and takes effect as of the effective date of the dissolution and the corporation resumes carrying on its business as if dissolution had never occurred.

§ 14.05 Effect of Dissolution

(a) A dissolved corporation continues its corporate existence but may not carry on any business except that appropriate to wind up and liquidate its business and affairs, including:

(1) collecting its assets;

(2) disposing of its properties that will not be distributed in kind to its shareholders;

(3) discharging or making provision for discharging its liabilities;

(4) distributing its remaining property among its shareholders according to their interests; and

(5) doing every other act necessary to wind up and liquidate its business and affairs.

(b) Dissolution of a corporation does not:

(1) transfer title to the corporation's property;

(2) prevent transfer of its shares or securities, although the authorization to dissolve may provide for closing the corporation's share transfer records;

(3) subject its directors or officers to standards of conduct different from those prescribed in chapter 8;

(4) change quorum or voting requirements for its board of directors or shareholders; change provisions for selection, resignation, or removal of its directors or officers or both; or change provisions for amending its bylaws;

(5) prevent commencement of a proceeding by or against the corporation in its corporate name;

(6) abate or suspend a proceeding pending by or against the corporation on the effective date of dissolution; or

(7) terminate the authority of the registered agent of the corporation.

OFFICIAL COMMENT

Section 14.05 (a) provides that dissolution does not terminate the corporate existence but simply requires the corporation thereafter to devote itself to winding up its affairs and liquidating its assets; after dissolution, the corporation may not carry on its business except as may be appropriate for winding up.

The Model Act uses the term "dissolution" in the specialized sense described above and not to describe the final step in the liquidation of the corporate business. This is made clear by section 14.05 (b), which provides that Chapter 14 dissolution does not have any of the characteristics of common law dissolution, which treated corporate dissolution as analogous to the death of a natural person and abated lawsuits, vested equitable title to corporate property in the shareholders, imposed the fiduciary duty of trustees on directors who had custody of corporate assets, and revoked the authority of the registered agent. Section 14.05(b) expressly reverses all of these common law attributes of dissolution and makes clear that the rights, powers, and duties of shareholders, the directors, and the registered agent are not affected by dissolution and that suits by or against the corporation are not affected in any way.

§ 14.06 Known Claims Against Dissolved Corporation

(a) A dissolved corporation may dispose of the known claims against it by notifying its known claimants in writing of the dissolution at any time after its effective date.

(b) The written notice must:

(1) describe information that must be included in a claim;

(2) provide a mailing address where a claim may be sent;

(3) state the deadline, which may not be fewer than 120 days from the effective date of the written notice, by which the dissolved corporation must receive the claim; and

(4) state that the claim will be barred if not received by the deadline.

(c) A claim against the dissolved corporation is barred:

(1) if a claimant who was given written notice under subsection (b) does not deliver the claim to the dissolved corporation by the deadline; or

(2) if a claimant whose claim was rejected by the dissolved corporation does not commence a proceeding to enforce the claim within 90 days from the effective date of the rejection notice.

(d) For purposes of this section, "claim" does not include a contingent liability or a claim based on an event occurring after the effective date of dissolution.

OFFICIAL COMMENT

Sections 14.06 and 14.07 provide a new and-simplified system for handling known and unknown claims against a dissolved corporation, including claims based on events that occur after the dissolution of the corporation. Section 14.06 deals solely with known claims while section 14.07 deals with unknown or subsequently arising claims. A claim can be a "known" claim even if it is unliquidated; a claim that is contingent or has not yet matured or in certain cases has matured but has not been asserted is not a "known" claim (see section 14.06(c). For example, an unmatured liability under a guarantee, a potential default under a lease, or an unasserted claim based upon a defective product manufactured by the dissolved corporation would not be a "known" claim.

Known claims are handled in section 14.06 through a process of written notice to claimants; the written notice must contain the information described in section 14.06(a). Section 14.06 (b) then provides fixed deadlines by which claims are barred under various circumstances, as follows:

(1) If a claimant was given effective written notice satisfying section 14.06(a) but fails to file the claim by the deadline specified by the dissolved corporation, the claim is barred by section 14.06(b)(1). See section 1.41(e) as to the effectiveness of notice.

(2) If a claimant receives written notice satisfying section 14.06(a) and files the claim as required:

(i) but the dissolved corporation rejects the claim, the claimant must commence a proceeding to enforce the claim within 90 days of the rejection or the claim is barred by section 14.06(b)(2); or

(ii) if the dissolved corporation does not act on the claim or fails to notify the claimant of the rejection, the claimant is not barred by section 14.06(b) until the dissolved corporation notifies the claimant.

(3) If the dissolved corporation publishes notice under section 14.07, a claimant who was not notified in writing is barred unless a proceeding is commenced to enforce the claim within five three years after publication of the notice.

(4) If the dissolved corporation does not publish notice, a claimant who was not notified in writing is not barred by section 14.06(b) from pursuing the his claim.

These principles, it should be emphasized, do not lengthen statutes of limitation applicable under general state law. Thus, claims that are not barred under the foregoing rules—for example, if the corporation does not act on a claim will nevertheless be subject to the general statute of limitations applicable to claims of that type.

Even though the directors are not trustees of the assets of a dissolved corporation (see section 14.05(b)(3)), they must discharge or make provision for discharging the corporation's liabilities before distributing the remaining assets to the shareholders. See section sections 14.09.

§ 14.07 Other Claims Against Dissolved Corporation

(a) A dissolved corporation may also publish notice of its dissolution and request that persons with claims against the dissolved corporation present them in accordance with the notice.

(b) The notice must:

(1) be published one time in a newspaper of general circulation in the county where the dissolved corporation's principal office (or, if none in this state, its registered office) is or was last located;

(2) describe the information that must be included in a claim and provide a mailing address where the claim may be sent; and

(3) state that a claim against the dissolved corporation will be barred unless a proceeding to enforce the claim is commenced within three years after the publication of the notice.

(c) If the dissolved corporation publishes a newspaper notice in accordance with subsection (b), the claim of each of the following claimants is barred unless the claimant commences a proceeding to enforce the claim against the dissolved corporation within three years after the publication date of the newspaper notice:

(1) a claimant who was not given written notice under section 14.06;

(2) a claimant whose claim was timely sent to the dissolved corporation but not acted on;

(3) a claimant whose claim is contingent or based on an event occurring after the effective date of dissolution.

(d) A claim that is not barred by section 14.06(b) or section 14.07(c) may be enforced:

(1) against the dissolved corporation, to the extent of its undistributed assets; or

(2) except as provided in section 14.08(d), if the assets have been distributed in liquidation, against a shareholder of the dissolved corporation to the extent of the shareholder's pro rata share of the claim or the corporate assets distributed to the shareholder in liquidation, whichever is less, but a shareholder's total liability for all claims under this section may not exceed the total amount of assets distributed to the shareholder.

§ 14.08 Court Proceedings

(a) A dissolved corporation that has published a notice under section 14.07 may file an application with the [name or describe] court of the county where the dissolved corporation's principal office (or, if none in this state, its registered office) is located for a determination of the amount and form of security to be provided for payment of claims that are contingent or have not been made known to the dissolved corporation or that are based on an event occurring after the effective date of dissolution but that, based on the facts known to the dissolved corporation, are reasonably estimated to arise after the effective date of dissolution. Provision need not be made for any claim that is or is reasonably anticipated to be barred under section 14.07(c).

(b) Within 10 days after the filing of the application, notice of the proceeding shall be given by the dissolved corporation to each claimant holding a contingent claim whose contingent claim is shown on the records of the dissolved corporation.

(c) The court may appoint a guardian ad litem to represent all claimants whose identities are unknown in any proceeding brought under this section. The reasonable fees and expenses of such guardian, including all reasonable expert witness fees, shall be paid by the dissolved corporation.

(d) Provision by the dissolved corporation for security in the amount and the form ordered by the court under section 14.08(a) shall satisfy the dissolved corporation's obligations with respect to claims that are contingent, have not been made known to the dissolved corporation or are based on an event occurring after the effective date of dissolution, and such claims may not be enforced against a shareholder who received assets in liquidation.

OFFICIAL COMMENT

Section 14.08 adds a provision to the Model Act allowing a dissolved corporation to initiate a proceeding to establish the provision that should be made for unknown or contingent claims before a distribution in liquidation is made to shareholders. Similar proceedings are authorized in several states to remove the risk of director and shareholder liability for inadequate provision for claims.

Section 14.08(a) authorizes the proceeding and specifies that provision for unknown and contingent claims can only be for those claims that are estimated to arise after dissolution that are not expected to be barred by section 14.07(d). The same analysis may be made by the board of directors under section 14.09 if court proceedings are not used. As a result, estimates for unknown or contingent claims, such as product liability injury claims that might arise after dissolution, need only be made for those claims that the court determines are reasonably anticipated to be asserted within three years after dissolution. Such estimates might reasonably be based on the claims experience of the corporation prior to its dissolution.

If the dissolved corporation elects to initiate a proceeding, it must give notice of the proceeding within 10 days after filing the court application to each holder of a contingent claim whose claim is shown on the records of the corporation. Notice to holders of guarantees made by the corporation typically would be required under this subsection.

Subsection (c) allows the court to appoint a guardian ad litem for unknown claimants, but does not make the appointment mandatory. Reasonable fees and expenses of the guardian ad litem are to be paid by the dissolved corporation. Section 14.08 is designed to permit the court to adopt procedures appropriate to the circumstances.

If the proceeding is completed, section 14.08(d) establishes that the dissolved corporation is deemed to have satisfied its obligation to discharge or make provision for discharging its liabilities (see section 14.05(a)(3)). With respect to claims that have not matured, directors are protected from liability by section 14.09(b), and shareholders are protected from claims under section 14.08(d).

If a court determines that the corporation is dissolving for the primary purpose of avoiding anticipated claims of future tort claimants, it is expected that the court will use its general discretionary powers and deny the protections of section 14.08 to the dissolved corporation.

§ 14.09 Director Duties

(a) Directors shall cause the dissolved corporation to discharge or make reasonable provision for the payment of claims and make distributions of assets to shareholders after payment or provision for claims.

(b) Directors of a dissolved corporation which has disposed of claims under sections 14.06, 14.07, or 14.08 shall not be liable for breach of section 14.09(a) with respect to claims against the dissolved corporation that are barred or satisfied under sections 14.06, 14.07, or 14.08.

OFFICIAL COMMENT

New section 14.09(a) establishes the duty of directors to discharge or make provision for claims and to make distributions of the remaining assets to shareholders. The earlier version of chapter 14 inferred the obligation from sections 14.05(3) and (4) concerning the powers of the corporation to pay claims and make distributions upon dissolution. Liability of directors formerly was based on violations of section 6.40 concerning distributions. New section 6.40(h) removed distributions in liquidation from the coverage of section 6.40.

Section 14.09(b) provides that directors of a dissolved corporation that complies with sections 14.06, 14.07, or 14.08 are not liable for breach of section 14.09(a) with respect to claims that are disposed of under those sections. For example, directors need not make provision for claims of known creditors who are barred under section 14.06 for failure to file a claim or commence a proceeding within the specified times, for contingent claimants whose estimated claims are barred by the three-year period after publication, pursuant to section 14.07(c), or for claimants such as guarantors if provision for the claims have been approved by a court under section 14.08(d).

Section 14.09(b) leaves unchanged the section 8.33 provision that director liability is to the corporation. There are, however, cases that under various theories recognize liability directly to creditors for wrongful payments in liquidation. While there might be circumstances under which direct creditor claims are appropriate, the basic approach of chapter 14 is that claims for breach of duty of directors for breach of section 14.09(a) and claims against shareholders for recoupment of amounts improperly distributed in liquidation should be mediated through the corporation.

SUBCHAPTER B. ADMINISTRATIVE DISSOLUTION

§ 14.20 Grounds for Administrative Dissolution

The secretary of state may commence a proceeding under section 14.21 to administratively dissolve a corporation if:

(1) the corporation does not pay within 60 days after they are due any franchise taxes or penalties imposed by this Act or other law;

(2) the corporation does not deliver its annual report to the secretary of state within 60 days after it is due;

(3) the corporation is without a registered agent or registered office in this state for 60 days or more;

(4) the corporation does not notify the secretary of state within 60 days that its registered agent or registered office has been changed, that its registered agent has resigned, or that its registered office has been discontinued; or

(5) the corporation's period of duration stated in its articles of incorporation expires.

§ 14.21 Procedure for and Effect of Administrative Dissolution

(a) If the secretary of state determines that one or more grounds exist under section 14.20 for dissolving a corporation, he shall serve the corporation with written notice of his determination under section 5.04.

(b) If the corporation does not correct each ground for dissolution or demonstrate to the reasonable satisfaction of the secretary of state that each ground determined by the secretary of state does not exist within 60 days after service of the notice is perfected under section 5.04, the secretary of state shall administratively dissolve the corporation by signing a certificate of dissolution that recites the ground or grounds for dissolution and its effective date. The secretary of state shall file the original of the certificate and serve a copy on the corporation under section 5.04.

(c) A corporation administratively dissolved continues its corporate existence but may not carry on any business except that necessary to wind up and liquidate its business and affairs under section 14.05 and notify claimants under sections 14.06 and 14.07.

(d) The administrative dissolution of a corporation does not terminate the authority of its registered agent.

§ 14.22 Reinstatement Following Administrative Dissolution

(a) A corporation administratively dissolved under section 14.21 may apply to the secretary of state for reinstatement within two years after the effective date of dissolution. The application must:

(1) recite the name of the corporation and the effective date of its administrative dissolution;

(2) state that the ground or grounds for dissolution either did not exist or have been eliminated;

(3) state that the corporation's name satisfies the requirements of section 4.01; and

(4) contain a certificate from the [taxing authority] reciting that all taxes owed by the corporation have been paid.

(b) If the secretary of state determines that the application contains the information required by subsection (a) and that the information is correct, he shall cancel the certificate of dissolution and prepare a certificate of reinstatement that recites his determination and the effective date of reinstatement, file the original of the certificate, and serve a copy on the corporation under section 5.04.

(c) When the reinstatement is effective, it relates back to and takes effect as of the effective date of the administrative dissolution and the corporation resumes carrying on its business as if the administrative dissolution had never occurred.

§ 14.23 Appeal From Denial of Reinstatement

(a) If the secretary of state denies a corporation's application for reinstatement following administrative dissolution, he shall serve the corporation under section 5.04 with a written notice that explains the reason or reasons for denial.

(b) The corporation may appeal the denial of reinstatement to the [name or describe] court within 30 days after service of the notice of denial is perfected. The corporation appeals by petitioning the court to set aside the dissolution and attaching to the petition copies of the secretary of state's certificate of dissolution, the corporation's application for reinstatement, and the secretary of state's notice of denial.

(c) The court may summarily order the secretary of state to reinstate the dissolved corporation or may take other action the court considers appropriate.

(d) The court's final decision may be appealed as in other civil proceedings.

SUBCHAPTER C. JUDICIAL DISSOLUTION

§ 14.30 Grounds for Judicial Dissolution

The [name or describe court or courts] may dissolve a corporation:

(1) in a proceeding by the attorney general if it is established that:

(i) the corporation obtained its articles of incorporation through fraud; or

(ii) the corporation has continued to exceed or abuse the authority conferred upon it by law;

(2) in a proceeding by a shareholder if it is established that:

(i) the directors are deadlocked in the management of the corporate affairs, the shareholders are unable to break the deadlock, and irreparable injury to the corporation is threatened or being suffered, or the business and affairs of the corporation can no longer be conducted to the advantage of the shareholders generally, because of the deadlock;

(ii) the directors or those in control of the corporation have acted, are acting, or will act in a manner that is illegal, oppressive, or fraudulent;

(iii) the shareholders are deadlocked in voting power and have failed, for a period that includes at least two consecutive annual meeting dates, to elect successors to directors whose terms have expired; or

(iv) the corporate assets are being misapplied or wasted;

(3) in a proceeding by a creditor if it is established that:

(i) the creditor's claim has been reduced to judgment, the execution on the judgment returned unsatisfied, and the corporation is insolvent; or

(ii) the corporation has admitted in writing that the creditor's claim is due and owing and the corporation is insolvent; or

(4) in a proceeding by the corporation to have its voluntary dissolution continued under court supervision.

OFFICIAL COMMENT

Section 14.30 provides grounds for the judicial dissolution of corporations at the request of the state, a shareholder, a creditor, or a corporation which has commenced voluntary dissolution. This section states that a court "may" order dissolution if a ground for dissolution exists. Thus, there is discretion on the part of the court as to whether dissolution is appropriate even though grounds exist under the specific circumstances.

1. Involuntary Dissolution by State

Section 14.30 (1) preserves long standing and traditional provisions authorizing the state to seek to dissolve involuntarily a corporation by judicial decree. While this power has been exercises only rarely in recent years, this right of the state involves a policing action that provides a means by which the state may ensure compliance with, and nonabuse of, the fundamentals of corporate existence. Section 14.30(1) limits the power of the state in this regard to grounds that are reasonably related to this objective.

The legality of proposed corporations or of proposed actions has sometimes been tested by the secretary of state's refusal to accept documents for filing. The role of the secretary of state in reviewing documents for filing has been restricted by the Model Act (see section 1.25 and its Official Comment). It is intended that suits under this subchapter will replace those actions.

2. Involuntary Dissolution By Shareholders

Section 14.31 (2) provides for involuntary dissolution at the suit of a shareholder under circumstances involving deadlock or significant abuse of power by controlling shareholders or directors.

a. Deadlock

Dissolution because of deadlock is available if there is a deadlock at the directors' level but only if (1) the shareholders are unable to break the deadlock and (2) either "irreparable injury" to the corporation is being threatened or suffered or the business and affairs "can no longer be conducted to the advantage of" the shareholders. This language closely follows the earlier versions of the Model Act except that the requirement of "irreparable injury" has been relaxed to some extent. Dissolution because of deadlock at the director's level is not dependent on the lapse of time during which the deadlock continues.

Dissolution is also available because of deadlock at the shareholders' level if the shareholders are unable to elect directors over a two-year period. This remedy is particularly important in small or family-held corporations in which share ownership may be divided on a 50–50 basis or a supermajority provision (including possibly a requirement of unanimity) may effectively prevent the election of any directors. Dissolution under section 14.30(2)(iii) is not dependent on irreparable injury or misconduct by the directors then in office; if injury or misconduct is present, a deadlocked shareholder may proceed under another clause of section 14.30(2).

b. Abuse of power

A Shareholder may sue for involuntary dissolution upon proof either that those in control of the corporation are acting illegally, oppressively, or fraudulently (section 14.30 (2) (ii)) or that the corporate assets are being misapplied or wasted (section 14.30 (2) (iv)). The application of these grounds for dissolution to specific circumstances obviously involves judicial discretion in the application of a general standard to concrete circumstances. The court should be cautious in the application of these grounds so as to limit them to genuine abuse rather than instances of acceptable tactics in a power struggle for control of a corporation.

3. Dissolution By Creditors

Creditors may obtain involuntary dissolution only when the corporation is insolvent and only in the limited circumstances set forth in section 14.30 (3). Typically, a proceeding under the federal Bankruptcy Act is an alternative in these situations.

4. Dissolution By Corporation

A corporation that has commenced voluntary dissolution may petition a court to supervise its dissolution. Such an action may be appropriate to permit the orderly liquidation of the corporate assets and to protect the corporation from a multitude of creditors' suits or suits by dissatisfied shareholders.

§ 14.31 Procedure for Judicial Dissolution

(a) Venue for a proceeding by the attorney general to dissolve a corporation lies in [name the county or counties]. Venue for a proceeding brought by any other party named in section 14.30 lies in the county where a corporation's principal office (or, if none in this state, its registered office) is or was last located.

(b) It is not necessary to make shareholders parties to a proceeding to dissolve a corporation unless relief is sought against them individually.

(c) A court in a proceeding brought to dissolve a corporation may issue injunctions, appoint a receiver or custodian pendente lite with all powers and duties the court directs, take other action required to preserve the corporate assets wherever located, and carry on the business of the corporation until a full hearing can be held.

(d) Within 10 days of the commencement of a proceeding under section 14.30(2) to dissolve a corporation that has no shares listed on a national securities exchange or regularly traded in a market maintained by one or more members of a national securities exchange, the corporation must send to all shareholders, other than the petitioner, a notice stating that the shareholders are entitled to avoid the dissolution of the corporation by electing to purchase the petitioner's shares under section 14.34 and accompanied by a copy of section 14.34.

§ 14.32 Receivership or Custodianship

(a) A court in a judicial proceeding brought to dissolve a corporation may appoint one or more receivers to wind up and liquidate, or one or more custodians to manage, the business and affairs of the corporation. The court shall hold a hearing, after notifying all parties to the proceeding and any interested persons designated by the court, before appointing a receiver or custodian. The court appointing a receiver or custodian has exclusive jurisdiction over the corporation and all its property wherever located.

(b) The court may appoint an individual or a domestic or foreign corporation (authorized to transact business in this state) as a receiver or custodian. The court may require the receiver or custodian to post bond, with or without sureties, in an amount the court directs.

(c) The court shall describe the powers and duties of the receiver or custodian in its appointing order, which may be amended from time to time. Among other powers:

(1) the receiver (i) may dispose of all or any part of the assets of the corporation wherever located, at a public or private sale, if authorized by the court; and (ii) may sue and defend in his own name as receiver of the corporation in all courts of this state;

(2) the custodian may exercise all of the powers of the corporation, through or in place of its board of directors or officers, to the extent necessary to manage the affairs of the corporation in the best interests of its shareholders and creditors.

(d) The court during a receivership may redesignate the receiver a custodian, and during a custodianship may redesignate the custodian a receiver, if doing so is in the best interests of the corporation, its shareholders, and creditors.

(e) The court from time to time during the receivership or custodianship may order compensation paid and expense disbursements or reimbursements made to the receiver or custodian and his counsel from the assets of the corporation or proceeds from the sale of the assets.

§ 14.33 Decree of Dissolution

(a) If after a hearing the court determines that one or more grounds for judicial dissolution described in section 14.30 exist, it may enter a decree dissolving the corporation and specifying the effective date of the dissolution, and the clerk of the court shall deliver a certified copy of the decree to the secretary of state, who shall file it.

(b) After entering the decree of dissolution, the court shall direct the winding up and liquidation of the corporation's business and affairs in accordance with section 14.05 and the notification of claimants in accordance with sections 14.06 and 14.07.

§ 14.34 Election to Purchase in Lieu of Dissolution

X

(a) In a proceeding under section 14.30(2) to dissolve a corporation that has no shares listed on a national securities exchange or regularly traded in a market maintained by one or more members of a national or affiliated securities association, the corporation may elect or, if it fails to elect, one or more shareholders may elect to purchase all shares owned by the petitioning shareholder at the fair value of the shares. An election pursuant to this section shall be irrevocable unless the court determines that it is equitable to set aside or modify the election.

(b) An election to purchase pursuant to this section may be filed with the court at any time within 90 days after the filing of the petition under section 14.30(2) or at such later time as the court in its discretion may allow. If the election to purchase is filed by one or more shareholders, the corporation shall, within 10 days thereafter, give written notice to all shareholders, other than the petitioner. The notice must state the name and number of shares owned by the petitioner and the name and number of shares owned by each electing shareholder and must advise the recipients of their right to join in the election to purchase shares in accordance with this section. Shareholders who wish to participate must file notice of their intention to join in the purchase no later than 30 days after the effective date of the notice to them. All shareholders who have filed an election or notice of their intention to participate in the election to purchase thereby become parties to ownership of shares as of the date the first election was filed, unless they otherwise agree or the court otherwise directs. After an election has been filed by the corporation or one or more shareholders, the proceeding under section 14.30(2) may not be discontinued or settled, nor may the petitioning shareholder sell or otherwise dispose of his shares, unless the court determines that it would be equitable to the corporation and the shareholders, other than the petitioner, to permit such discontinuance, settlement, sale, or other disposition.

(c) If, within 60 days of the filing of the first election, the parties reach agreement as to the fair value and terms of purchase of the petitioner's shares, the court shall enter an order directing the purchase of petitioner's shares upon the terms and conditions agreed to by the parties.

(d) If the parties are unable to reach an agreement as provided for in subsection (c), the court, upon application of any party, shall stay the section 14.30(2) proceedings and determine the fair value of the petitioner's shares as of the day before the date on which the petition under section 14.30(2) was filed or as of such other date as the court deems appropriate under the circumstances.

(e) Upon determining the fair value of the shares, the court shall enter an order directing the purchase upon such terms and conditions as the court deems appropriate, which may include payment of the purchase price in installments, where necessary in the interests of equity, provision for security to assure payment of the purchase price and any additional costs, fees, and expenses as may have been awarded, and, if the shares are to be purchased by shareholders, the allocation of shares among them. In allocating petitioner's shares among holders of different classes of shares, the court should attempt to preserve the existing distribution of voting rights among holders of different classes insofar as practicable and may direct that holders of a specific class or classes shall not participate in the purchase. Interest may be allowed at the rate and from the date determined by the court to be equitable, but if the court finds that the refusal of the petitioning shareholder to accept an offer of payment was arbitrary or otherwise not in good faith, no interest shall be allowed. If the court finds that the petitioning shareholder had probable grounds for relief under paragraphs (ii) or (iv) of section 14.30(2), it may award to the petitioning shareholder reasonable fees and expenses of counsel and of any experts employed by him.

(f) Upon entry of an order under subsections (c) or (e), the court shall dismiss the petition to dissolve the corporation under section 14.30, and the petitioning shareholder shall no longer have any rights or status as a shareholder of the corporation, except the right to receive the amounts awarded to him by the order of the court which shall be enforceable in the same manner as any other judgment.

(g) The purchase ordered pursuant to subsection (e), shall be made within 10 days after the date the order becomes final unless before that time the corporation files with the court a notice of its intention to adopt articles of dissolution pursuant to sections 14.02 and 14.03, which articles must then be adopted and filed within 50 days thereafter. Upon filing of such articles of dissolution, the corporation shall be dissolved in accordance with the provisions of sections 14.05 through 07, and the order entered pursuant to subsection (e) shall no longer be of any force or effect, except that the court may award the petitioning shareholder reasonable fees and expenses in accordance with the provisions of the last sentence of subsection (e) and the petitioner may continue to pursue any claims previously asserted on behalf of the corporation.

(h) Any payment by the corporation pursuant to an order under subsections (c) or (e), other than an award of fees and expenses pursuant to subsection (e), is subject to the provisions of section 6.40.

SUBCHAPTER D. MISCELLANEOUS

§ 14.40 Deposit With State Treasurer

Assets of a dissolved corporation that should be transferred to a creditor, claimant, or shareholder of the corporation who cannot be found or who is not competent to receive them shall be reduced to cash and deposited with the state treasurer or other appropriate state official for safekeeping. When the creditor, claimant, or shareholder furnishes satisfactory proof of entitlement to the amount deposited, the state treasurer or other appropriate state official shall pay him or his representative that amount.

CHAPTER 15. [FOREIGN CORPORATIONS—OMITTED]

CHAPTER 16. RECORDS AND REPORTS

SUBCHAPTER A. RECORDS

§ 16.01 Corporate Records

(a) A corporation shall keep as permanent records minutes of all meetings of its shareholders and board of directors, a record of all actions taken by the shareholders or board of directors without a meeting, and a record of all actions taken by a committee of the board of directors in place of the board of directors on behalf of the corporation.

(b) A corporation shall maintain appropriate accounting records.

(c) A corporation or its agent shall maintain a record of its shareholders, in a form that permits preparation of a list of the names and addresses of all shareholders, in alphabetical order by class of shares showing the number and class of shares held by each.

(d) A corporation shall maintain its records in written form or in another form capable of conversion into written form within a reasonable time.

(e) A corporation shall keep a copy of the following records at its principal office:

(1) its articles or restated articles of incorporation, all amendments to them currently in effect and any notices to shareholders referred to in section 1.20(k)(5) regarding facts on which a filed document is dependent;

(2) its bylaws or restated bylaws and all amendments to them currently in effect;

(3) resolutions adopted by its board of directors creating one or more classes or series of shares, and fixing their relative rights, preferences, and limitations, if shares issued pursuant to those resolutions are outstanding;

(4) the minutes of all shareholders' meetings, and records of all action taken by shareholders without a meeting, for the past three years;

(5) all written communications to shareholders generally within the past three years, including the financial statements furnished for the past three years under section 16.20;

(6) a list of the names and business addresses of its current directors and officers; and

(7) its most recent annual report delivered to the secretary of state under section 16.22.

§ 16.02 Inspection of Records by Shareholders

(a) Subject to section 16.03(c), a shareholder of a corporation is entitled to inspect and copy, during regular business hours at the corporation's principal office, any of the records of the corporation described in section 16.01(e) if he gives the corporation written notice of his demand at least five business days before the date on which he wishes to inspect and copy.

(b) A shareholder of a corporation is entitled to inspect and copy, during regular business hours at a reasonable location specified by the corporation, any of the following records of the corporation if the shareholder meets the requirements of subsection (c) and gives the corporation written notice of his demand at least five business days before the date on which he wishes to inspect and copy:

(1) excerpts from minutes of any meeting of the board of directors, records of any action of a committee of the board of directors while acting in place of the board of directors on behalf of the corporation, minutes of any meeting of the shareholders, and records of action taken by the shareholders or board of directors without a meeting, to the extent not subject to inspection under section 16.02(a);

(2) accounting records of the corporation; and

(3) the record of shareholders.

(c) A shareholder may inspect and copy the records identified in subsection (b) only if:

(1) his demand is made in good faith and for a proper purpose;

(2) he describes with reasonable particularity his purpose and the records he desires to inspect; and

(3) the records are directly connected with his purpose.

(d) The right of inspection granted by this section may not be abolished or limited by a corporation's articles of incorporation or bylaws.

(e) This section does not affect:

(1) the right of a shareholder to inspect records under section 7.20 or, if the shareholder is in litigation with the corporation, to the same extent as any other litigant;

(2) the power of a court, independently of this Act, to compel the production of corporate records for examination.

(f) For purposes of this section, "shareholder" includes a beneficial owner whose shares are held in a voting trust or by a nominee on his behalf.

§ 16.03 Scope of Inspection Right

(a) A shareholder's agent or attorney has the same inspection and copying rights as the shareholder represented.

(b) The right to copy records under section 16.02 includes, if reasonable, the right to receive copies by xerographic or other means, including copies through an electronic transmission if available and so requested by the shareholder.

(c) The corporation may comply at its expense with a shareholder's demand to inspect the record of shareholders under section 16.02(b)(3) by providing the shareholder with a list of shareholders that was compiled no earlier than the date of the shareholder's demand.

(d) The corporation may impose a reasonable charge, covering the costs of labor and material, for copies of any documents provided to the shareholder. The charge may not exceed the estimated cost of production, reproduction or transmission of the records.

OFFICIAL COMMENT

The right of inspection set forth in section 16.02 includes the general right to copy the documents inspected. Section 16.03 follows precedent established under earlier statutes and extends the right of inspection to an agent or attorney of a shareholder as well as the shareholder. The right to copy means more than a right to copy by longhand and extends to the right to receive copies made by copying machines or through an electronic transmission with the cost of reproduction and transmission being paid by the shareholder. The requirement of availability with respect to electronic transmissions is intended to insure that the corporation can provide the document electronically and that an undue burden is not placed on the corporation to provide copies through an electronic transmission or other similar means.

Section 16.03(c) is designed to give the corporation the option of providing a reasonably current list of its shareholders instead of granting the right of inspection; a "reasonably current" list is defined in section 16.03(c) as one compiled no earlier than the date of the written demand, which under section 16.02(b) must provide at least five days' notice.

Many corporations make available to shareholders without charge some or all of the basic documents described in section 16.01(e). Section 16.03(d) authorizes the corporation to charge a reasonable fee based on reproduction costs (including labor and materials) for providing a copy of any document. The phrase "estimated cost of production, reproduction or transmission of the records" in section 16.03(d) refers to the cost of assembling information and data to meet a demand as well as the cost of reproducing and transmitting documents that are already in existence.

Under applicable law, a list of shareholders generally will include underlying information in the corporation's possession relating to stock ownership, including, where applicable, breakdowns of stock holdings by nominees and nonobjecting beneficial ownership (NOBO) lists. However, a corporation generally is not required to generate this information for the requesting shareholder and is only required to provide NOBO and other similar lists to the extent such information is in the corporation's possession.

Section 7.20 creates a right of shareholders to inspect a list of shareholders in advance of and at a meeting that is independent of the rights of shareholders to inspect corporate records under chapter 16.

§ 16.04 Court–Ordered Inspection

(a) If a corporation does not allow a shareholder who complies with section 16.02(a) to inspect and copy any records required by that subsection to be available for inspection, the [name or describe court] of the county where the corporation's principal office (or, if none in this state, its registered office) is located may summarily order inspection and copying of the records demanded at the corporation's expense upon application of the shareholder.

(b) If a corporation does not within a reasonable time allow a shareholder to inspect and copy any other record, the shareholder who complies with section 16.02(b) and (c) may apply to the [name or describe court] in the county where the corporation's principal office (or, if none in this state, its registered office) is located for an order to permit inspection and copying of the records demanded. The court shall dispose of an application under this subsection on an expedited basis.

(c) If the court orders inspection and copying of the records demanded, it shall also order the corporation to pay the shareholder's costs (including reasonable counsel fees) incurred to obtain the order unless the corporation proves that it refused inspection in good faith because it had a reasonable basis for doubt about the right of the shareholder to inspect the records demanded.

(d) If the court orders inspection and copying of the records demanded, it may impose reasonable restrictions on the use or distribution of the records by the demanding shareholder.

§ 16.05 Inspection of Records by Directors

(a) A director of a corporation is entitled to inspect and copy the books, records and documents of the corporation at any reasonable time to the extent reasonably related to the performance of the director's duties as a director, including duties as a member of a committee, but not for any other purpose or in any manner that would violate any duty to the corporation.

(b) The [name or describe the court] of the county where the corporation's principal office (or if none in this state, its registered office) is located may order inspection and copying of the books, records and documents at the corporation's expense, upon application of a director who has been refused such inspection rights, unless the corporation establishes that the director is not entitled to such inspection rights. The court shall dispose of an application under this subsection on an expedited basis.

(c) If an order is issued, the court may include provisions protecting the corporation from undue burden or expense, and prohibiting the director from using information obtained upon exercise of the inspection rights in a manner that would violate a duty to the corporation, and may also order the corporation to reimburse the director for the director's costs (including reasonable counsel fees) incurred in connection with the application.

OFFICIAL COMMENT

The purpose of subsection 16.05(a) is to confirm the principle that a director always is entitled to inspect books, records and documents to the extent reasonably related to the performance of the director's oversight or decisional duties provided that the requested inspection is not for an improper purpose and the director's use of the information obtained would not violate any duty to the corporation. The statute attempts to reconcile and balance competing principles articulated in the common law which suggest that a director has a nearly "absolute" right to information subject only to limitation if it can be shown that the director has an improper motive or intent in asking for the information or would violate law by receiving the information. In addition, the statutory provision sets forth a remedy for the director in circumstances where the corporation improperly denies the right of inspection.

Under subsection (a), a director typically would be entitled to review books, records and documents relating to matters such as (i) compliance by a corporation with applicable law, (ii) adequacy of the corporation's system of internal controls to provide accurate and timely financial statements and disclosure documents, or (iii) the proper operation, maintenance and protection of the corporation's assets. In addition, a director would be entitled to review records and documents to the extent required to consider and make decisions with respect to matters placed before the Board.

Subsection (b) provides a director with the right to seek on an expedited basis a court order permitting inspection and copying of the books, records and documents of the corporation, at the corporation's expense. There is a presumption that significant latitude and discretion should be granted to the director, and the corporation has the burden of establishing that a director is not entitled to inspection of the documents requested. Circumstances where the director's inspection rights might be denied include requests which (i) are not reasonably related to performance of a director's duties (e.g., seeking a specified confidential document not necessary for the performance of a director's duties), (ii) impose an unreasonable burden and expense on the corporation (e.g., compliance with the request would be duplicative of information already provided or would be unreasonably expensive and time-consuming), (iii) violate the director's duty to the corporation (e.g., the director could reasonably be expected to use or exploit confidential information in personal or third-party transactions), or (iv) violate any applicable law (e.g., the director does not have the necessary governmental security clearance to see the requested classified information).

Section 16.05 does not directly deal with the ability of a director to inspect records of a subsidiary of which he or she is not also a director. A director's ability to inspect records of a subsidiary generally should be exercised through the parent's rights or power and subsection (a) does not independently provide that right or power to a director of the parent. In the case of wholly-owned subsidiaries, a director's ability to inspect should approximate his or her rights with respect to the parent. In the case of a partially-owned subsidiary, the ability of the director to inspect is likely to be influenced by the level of ownership of the parent (this ability can be expected to be greater for a subsidiary which is part of a consolidated group than for a minority-owned subsidiary). In any case, the inspection by a director of the parent will be subject to the parent's fiduciary obligation to the subsidiary's other shareholders.

Subsection (c) provides that the court may place limitations on the use of information obtained by the director and may include in its order other provisions protecting the corporation from undue burden or expense. Further, the court may order the corporation to reimburse the director for costs (including reasonable counsel fees) incurred in connection with the application. The amount of any reimbursement is left in the court's discretion, since it must consider the reasonableness of the expenses incurred, as well as the fact that a director may be only partially successful in the application.

§ 16.06 Exception to Notice Requirements

(a) Whenever notice is required to be given under any provision of this Act to any shareholder, such notice shall not be required to be given if:

(i) Notice of two consecutive annual meetings, and all notices of meetings during the period between such two consecutive annual meetings, have been sent to such shareholder at such shareholder's address as shown on the records of the corporation and have been returned undeliverable; or

(ii) All, but not less than two, payments of dividends on securities during a twelve-month period, or two consecutive payments of dividends on securities during a period of more than twelve months, have been sent to such shareholder at such shareholder's address as shown on the records of the corporation and have been returned undeliverable.

(b) If any such shareholder shall deliver to the corporation a written notice setting forth such shareholder's then-current address, the requirement that notice be given to such shareholder shall be reinstated.

OFFICIAL COMMENT

Section 16.06 balances the requirement that the corporation provide notice to shareholders regarding meetings and the practical need to allow corporations to cease providing notices where notices are being returned undelivered and it is clear that the shareholder no longer is located at the address previously provided to the corporation. Absent such a provision, the corporation technically may be required to continue to attempt to provide a notice to the shareholder in order to satisfy a statutory requirement regarding notices to shareholders or otherwise risk questions concerning the validity of the meeting for which the notice is required. A number of states have adopted statutory provisions eliminating the obligation of the corporation to provide notice under certain circumstances. In addition, the federal proxy rules have adopted a similar provision.

Section 16.06 provides that notice is not required to be given to a shareholder if a notice of two consecutive annual meetings, and all notices required during the period between the meetings, are returned undeliverable. In addition, no notice is required if all dividends required to be paid during a twelve-month period (assuming at least two dividends were payable during that period) or two consecutive payments of dividends during a period of more than twelve months, are returned undeliverable. In both of these instances, written notice is not required, and any meeting which is held will have the same force and effect as if notice had been given. The notice for a particular shareholder is reinstated if a written notice to the corporation setting forth the shareholder's then current address is sent to the corporation.

Based upon these provisions, the corporation generally will be required to continue to provide the notice unless undeliverable items are returned over a period that could not be less than twelve months and could extend for up to twenty-four months. For instance, if the first undeliverable communication were sent to a shareholder six months before the next notice of an annual meeting is required, the corporation would have to wait until the annual meeting notice proves to be undeliverable to commence the nondelivery period, and then would have to wait until the next annual meeting notice after that also proves to be undeliverable before suspending the notification requirement. This amounts to a nondelivery period of eighteen months which could extend to two years under the right circumstances. It is believed that this accomplishes the proper balance between protecting the rights of shareholders and eliminating unnecessary notices.

Section 16.06 only deals with notices and does not have application to payment of dividends or other distributions to shareholders. There is no statutorily mandated practice with respect to payment of dividends. However, a decision by a corporation to withhold dividends pending location of the shareholder will not affect the validity of corporate action. Under state law, dividend payments unclaimed by shareholders eventually will escheat to the state in accordance with applicable statutory provisions.

SUBCHAPTER B. REPORTS

§ 16.20 Financial Statements for Shareholders

(a) A corporation shall furnish its shareholders annual financial statements, which may be consolidated or combined statements of the corporation and one or more of its subsidiaries, as appropriate, that include a balance sheet as of the end of the fiscal year, an income statement for that year, and a statement of changes in shareholders' equity for the year unless that information appears elsewhere in the financial statements. If financial statements are prepared for the corporation on the basis of generally accepted accounting principles, the annual financial statements must also be prepared on that basis.

(b) If the annual financial statements are reported upon by a public accountant, his report must accompany them. If not, the statements must be accompanied by a statement of the president or the person responsible for the corporation's accounting records.

(1) stating his reasonable belief whether the statements were prepared on the basis of generally accepted accounting principles and, if not, describing the basis of preparation; and

(2) describing any respects in which the statements were not prepared on a basis of accounting consistent with the statements prepared for the preceding year.

(c) A corporation shall mail the annual financial statements to each shareholder within 120 days after the close of each fiscal year. Thereafter, on written request from a shareholder who was not mailed the statements, the corporation shall mail him the latest financial statements.

OFFICIAL COMMENT

The requirement that a corporation regularly submit some financial information to shareholders is appropriate considering the relationship between corporate management and the shareholders as the ultimate owners of the enterprise. This requirement was first added as an amendment in 1979 to the 1969 Model Act.

Section 16.20 has its principal impact on small, closely held corporations, since enterprises whose securities are registered under federal statutes are required to supply audited financial statements to shareholders. The securities of the vast majority of corporations in the Untied States are not registered under federal law. It is these corporations that section 16.20 principally affects.

Section 16.20 requires every corporation to prepare and submit to shareholders annual financial statements consisting of a balance sheet as of the end of the fiscal year, an income statement for the year, and a statement of changes in shareholders' equity for the year. The last statement may be omitted if the data that normally appears in that statement appears in the other financial statements or in the notes thereto. Consolidated statements of the corporation and any subsidiary, or subsidiaries, or combined statements for corporations under common control, may be used. Section 16.20 does not require financial statements to be prepared on the basis of generally accepted accounting principles ("GAAP"). May small corporations have never prepared financial statements on the basis of GAAP. "Cash basis" financial statements (often used in preparing the tax returns of small corporations) do not comply with GAAP. Even closely held corporations that keep accrual basis records, and file their federal income tax returns on that basis, frequently do not make the adjustments that may be required to present their financial statements on a GAAP basis. In light of these considerations, it would be too burdensome on some small and closely held corporations to require GAAP statements. Accordingly, internally or externally prepared financial statements prepared on the basis of other accounting practices and principles that are reasonable in the circumstances, including tax returns filed with the Federal Internal Revenue Service (if that is all that is prepared), will suffice for these types of corporations. If a corporation does prepare financial statements on a GAAP basis for any purpose for the particular year, however, it must send those statements to the shareholders as provided by the last sentence of section 16.20(a).

Section 16.20 (b) requires an accompanying report or statement in one of two forms: (1) if the financial statements have been reported upon by a public accountant, his report must be furnished; or (2) in other cases, a statement of the president or the person responsible for the corporation's accounting records must be furnished (i) stating his reasonable belief as to whether the financial statements were prepared on the basis of generally accepted accounting principles, and, if not, describing the basis on which they were prepared, and (ii) describing any respects in which the financial statements were not prepared on a basis of accounting consistent with those prepared for the previous year.

Section 16.20 refers to a "public accountant." The same terminology is used in section 8.30 (standards of conduct for directors) of the Model Act. In various states different terms are employed to identify those persons who are permitted under the state licensing requirements to act as professional accountants. Phrases like "independent public accountant," "certified public accountant," "public accountant," and others may be used. In adopting the term "public accountant," the Model Act uses the words in a general sense to refer to any class or classes of persons who, under the applicable requirements of a particular jurisdiction, are professionally entitled to practice accountancy.

In requiring a statement by the president or person responsible for the corporation's financial affairs, it is recognized that in many cases this person will not be a professionally trained accountant and that he should not be held to the standard required of a professional. To emphasize this difference, section 16.20 requires a "statement" (rather than a "report" or "certificate") and calls for the person to express his "reasonable belief" (rather than "opinion") about whether or not the statements are prepared on the basis of GAAP or, if not, to describe the basis of presentation and any inconsistencies in the basis of the presentation as compared with the previous year. He is not required to describe any inconsistencies between the basis of presentation and GAAP. If the statements are not prepared on a GAAP basis, the description would normally follow guidelines of the accounting profession as to the reporting format considered appropriate for a presentation which departs from GAAP. See, e.g., " 'Statement on Auditing

Standards No. 14" of the American Institute of Certified Public Accountants. For example, the description might state, with respect to a cash basis statement of receipts and disbursements, that the statement was prepared on that basis and that it presents the cash receipts and disbursements of the entity for the period but does not purport to present the results of operations on the accrual basis of accounting.

Section 16.20(c) specifies that annual financial statements are to be mailed to each shareholder within 120 days after the close of each fiscal year, further emphasizing that the statements required to be delivered are annual statements and not interim statements. In addition, if a shareholder was not mailed the corporation's latest annual financial statements, he may obtain them on written request. See also section 16.01 (e)(5).

Failure to comply with the requirements of section 16.20 does not adversely affect the existence or good standing of the corporation. Rather, failure to comply gives an aggrieved shareholder rights to compel compliance or to obtain damages, if they can be established, under general principles of law.

§ 16.21 Other Reports to Shareholders

(a) If a corporation indemnifies or advances expenses to a director under section 8.51, 8.52, 8.53, or 8.54 in connection with a proceeding by or in the right of the corporation, the corporation shall report the indemnification or advance in writing to the shareholders with or before the notice of the next shareholders' meeting.

(b) If a corporation issues or authorizes the issuance of shares for promissory notes or for promises to render services in the future, the corporation shall report in writing to the shareholders the number of shares authorized or issued, and the consideration received by the corporation, with or before the notice of the next shareholders' meeting.

§ 16.22 Annual Report for Secretary of State

(a) Each domestic corporation, and each foreign corporation authorized to transact business in this state, shall deliver to the secretary of state for filing an annual report that sets forth:

(1) the name of the corporation and the state or country under whose law it is incorporated;

(2) the address of its registered office and the name of its registered agent at that office in this state;

(3) the address of its principal office;

(4) the names and business addresses of its directors and principal officers;

(5) a brief description of the nature of its business;

(6) the total number of authorized shares, itemized by class and series, if any, within each class; and

(7) the total number of issued and outstanding shares, itemized by class and series, if any, within each class.

(b) Information in the annual report must be current as of the date the annual report is executed on behalf of the corporation.

(c) The first annual report must be delivered to the secretary of state between January 1 and April 1 of the year following the calendar year in which a domestic corporation was incorporated or a foreign corporation was authorized to transact business. Subsequent annual reports must be delivered to the secretary of state between January 1 and April 1 of the following calendar years.

(d) If an annual report does not contain the information required by this section, the secretary of state shall promptly notify the reporting domestic or foreign corporation in writing and return the report to it for correction. If the report is corrected to contain the information required by this section and delivered to the secretary of state within 30 days after the effective date of notice, it is deemed to be timely filed.

CHAPTER 17. TRANSITION PROVISIONS

§ 17.01 Application to Existing Domestic Corporations

This Act applies to all domestic corporations in existence on its effective date that were incorporated under any general statute of this state providing for incorporation of corporations for profit if power to amend or repeal the statute under which the corporation was incorporated was reserved.

§ 17.02 Application to Qualified Foreign Corporations

A foreign corporation authorized to transact business in this state on the effective date of this Act is subject to this Act but is not required to obtain a new certificate of authority to transact business under this Act.

§ 17.03 Saving Provisions

(a) Except as provided in subsection (b), the repeal of a statute by this Act does not affect:

(1) the operation of the statute or any action taken under it before its repeal;

(2) any ratification, right, remedy, privilege, obligation, or liability acquired, accrued, or incurred under the statute before its repeal;

(3) any violation of the statute, or any penalty, forfeiture, or punishment incurred because of the violation, before its repeal;

(4) any proceeding, reorganization, or dissolution commenced under the statute before its repeal, and the proceeding, reorganization, or dissolution may be completed in accordance with the statute as if it had not been repealed.

(b) If a penalty or punishment imposed for violation of a statute repealed by this Act is reduced by this Act, the penalty or punishment if not already imposed shall be imposed in accordance with this Act.

§ 17.04 Severability

If any provision of this Act or its application to any person or circumstance is held invalid by a court of competent jurisdiction, the invalidity does not affect other provisions or applications of the Act that can be given effect without the invalid provision or application, and to this end the provisions of the Act are severable.

§ 17.05 Repeal

The following laws and parts of laws are repealed: [to be inserted].

§ 17.06 Effective Date

This Act takes effect ______.

B. PRIOR MODEL BUSINESS CORPORATION ACT PROVISIONS

In recent years, the Model Business Corporation Act has been amended in significant respects, although many jurisdictions have not adopted some or all of these amendments. This section contains former provisions of the Act and the relevant Official Comments. The current version of the Act is in Section I–A.

CHAPTER 8

SUBCHAPTER C. STANDARDS OF CONDUCT

§ 8.30 General Standards for Director Conduct

(a) A director shall discharge his duties as a director, including his duties as a member of a committee:

(1) In good faith;

(2) with the care an ordinarily prudent person in a like position would exercise under similar circumstances; and

(3) in a manner he reasonably believes to be in the best interests of the corporation.

(b) In discharging his duties a director is entitled to rely on information, opinions, reports, or statements, including financial statements and other financial data, if prepared or presented by:

(1) one or more officers or employees of the corporation whom the director reasonably believes to be reliable and competent in the matters presented;

(2) legal counsel, public accountants, or other persons as to matters the director reasonably believes are within the person's professional or expert competence; or

(3) a committee of the board of directors of which he is not a member if the director reasonably believes the committee merits confidence.

(c) A director is not acting in good faith if he has knowledge concerning the matter in question that makes reliance otherwise permitted by subsection (b) unwarranted.

(d) A director is not liable for any action taken as a director, or any failure to take any action, if he performed the duties of his office in compliance with this section.

§ 8.31 Director Conflict of Interest

(a) A conflict of interest transaction is a transaction with the corporation in which a director of the corporation has a direct or indirect interest. A conflict of interest transaction is not voidable by the corporation solely because of the director's interest in the transaction if any one of the following is true:

(1) the material facts of the transaction and the director's interest were disclosed or known to the board of directors or a committee of the board of directors and the board of directors or committee authorized, approved, or ratified the transaction;

(2) the material facts of the transaction and the director's interest were disclosed or known to the shareholders entitled to vote and they authorized, approved, or ratified the transaction; or

(3) the transaction was fair to the corporation.

(b) For purposes of this section, a director of the corporation has an indirect interest in a transaction if (1) another entity in which he has a material financial interest or in which he is a general partner is a party to the transaction or (2) another entity of which he is a director, officer, or trustee is a party to the transaction and the transaction is or should be considered by the board of directors of the corporation.

(c) For purposes of subsection (a)(1), a conflict of interest transaction is authorized, approved, or ratified if it receives the affirmative vote of a majority of the directors on the board of directors (or on the committee) who have no direct or indirect interest in the transaction, but a transaction may not be authorized, approved, or ratified under this section by a single director. If a majority of the directors who have no direct or indirect interest in the transaction vote to authorize, approve, or ratify the transaction, a quorum is present for the purpose of taking action under this section. The presence of, or a vote cast by, a director with a direct or indirect interest in the transaction does not affect the validity of any action taken under subsection (a)(1) if the transaction is otherwise authorized, approved, or ratified as provided in that subsection.

(d) For purposes of subsection (a)(2), a conflict of interest transaction is authorized, approved, or ratified if it receives the vote of a majority of the shares entitled to be counted under this subsection. Shares owned by or voted under the control of a director who has a direct or indirect interest in the transaction, and shares owned by or voted under the control of an entity described in subsection (b)(1), may not be counted in a vote of shareholders to determine whether to authorize, approve, or ratify a conflict of interest transaction under subsection (a)(2). The vote of those shares, however, is counted in determining whether the transaction is approved under other sections of this Act. A majority of the shares, whether or not present, that are entitled to be counted in a vote on the transaction under this subsection constitutes a quorum for the purpose of taking action under this section.

OFFICIAL COMMENT

1. Conflict of Interest Transactions in General

Section 8.31 deals only with "conflict of interest" transactions by a director with the corporation, that is, transactions in which the director has an interest either (1) directly or (2) indirectly through an entity in which the director has a financial or managerial interest covered by section 8.31(b). A conflict of interest transaction does not include transactions in which the director participates in the transaction only as a shareholder and receives only a proportionate share of the advantage or benefit of the transaction. Section 8.31 deals only with conflict of interest transactions involving directors; it does not address analogous transactions entered into by officers, employees, or substantial or dominating shareholders unless they are also directors.

Section 8.31 rejects the common law view that all conflict of interest transactions entered into by directors are automatically voidable at the option of the corporation without regard to the fairness of the transaction or the manner in which the transaction was approved by the corporation. Section 8.31(a) makes any automatic rule of voidability inapplicable to transactions that are fair or that have been approved by directors or shareholders in the manner provided by the balance of section 8.31. The approval mechanisms set forth in section 8.31(c) and (d) relate only to the elimination of this automatic rule of voidability and do not address the manner in which the transactions must be approved under other sections of this Act. This is made clear by the express limitations in sections 8.31(c) and (d) that they are applicable only "for the purposes of this section" as well as the language of the second and third sentences of section 8.31(d).

The elimination of the automatic rule of voidability does not mean that all transactions that meet one or more of the tests set forth in section 8.31(a) are automatically valid. These transactions may be subject to attack on a variety of grounds independent of section 8.31—for example, that the transaction constituted waste, that it was not authorized by the appropriate corporate body, that it violated other sections of the Model Business Corporation Act, or that it was unenforceable under other common law principles. The sole purpose of section 8.31 is to sharply limit the common law principle of automatic voidability and in this respect section 8.31 follows earlier versions of the Model Act and the statutes of many states dealing with conflict of interest transactions.

* * *

2. Requirements for Approval of Conflict of Interest Transactions

Sections 8.31(c) and (d) provide special rules for determining whether the board of directors (or a committee thereof) or the shareholders have authorized, approved, or ratified a conflict of interest transaction so as to bring subsections (a)(1) or (a)(2) into play. Basically, these subsections require the transaction in question to be approved by an absolute majority of the directors (on the board of directors, or on the committee, as the case may be) or shares whose votes may be counted in determining whether the transaction should be authorized, approved, or ratified. If these votes are not obtained the transaction is tested under the fairness test of subsection (a)(3). The vote required for authorization, approval, or ratification of a conflict of interest transaction is more onerous than the standard applicable to normal voting requirements for approval of corporate actions—i.e., that a quorum be present and only the votes of directors or shares present or represented at that meeting be considered—because of the importance of assuring that conflict of interest transactions receive as broad consideration within the corporation as possible if independent review on the basis of fairness is to be avoided.

b. Consideration by the shareholders

In some situations, the prohibition of section 8.31(d) will result in the conflict of interest issue being resolved by a majority of a minority of the shares. This will occur, for example, whenever a director who is the majority shareholder of the corporation is interested in a transaction. The vote on the conflict of interest issue under section 8.31, however, must be distinguished from the vote on the approval of the transaction itself under other sections of the Model Act, in which there is no prohibition against the voting of shares owned or controlled by an interested director. For example, if a parent corporation wishes to merge its 60–percent-owned subsidiary into itself, and the majority shareholder of the parent is a director of the subsidiary, the votes of the shares owned by the parent corporation may not be counted under section 8.31(d) (since the shares are owned by an entity which is a party to the transaction and which the director controls). The shares nevertheless may be voted on the merger proposal itself under chapter 11 of the Model Act, and the merger will, of course, normally be approved solely by the vote of the shares owned by the parent corporation. On the other hand, the test of section 8.31(a)(2) is not met unless the transaction is approved by at least a majority of the votes cast by the holders of the 40 percent of the shares not owned by the parent corporation. If this requirement is not met, the transaction may be evaluated under the fairness test of section 8.31(a)(3).

3. Indirect Conflicts of Interest

Section 8.31 is applicable to "indirect" as well as direct conflicts; "indirect" is defined in section 8.31(b) to cover transactions between the corporation and an entity in which the director has a material financial interest or is a general partner. Further, section 8.31(b) covers indirect conflicts where the director is an officer or director of another entity (but does not have a material financial interest in the transaction) if the transaction is of sufficient importance that it is or should be considered by the board of directors of the corporation. The purpose of this last clause is to permit normal business transactions between large business entities that may have a common director to go forward without concern about the technical rules relating to conflict of interest unless the transaction is of such importance that it is or should be considered by the board of directors or the director may be deemed to have a material financial interest in the transaction. Thus, section 8.31 covers transactions between corporations with interlocking or common directors as well as the direct "interested director" transaction.

4. "Fairness" of a Transaction

The fairness of a transaction for purposes of section 8.31 should be evaluated on the basis of the facts and circumstances as they were known or should have been known at the time the transaction was entered into. For example, the terms of a transaction subject to section 8.31 should normally be deemed "fair" if they are within the range that might have been entered into at arm's-length by disinterested persons.

5. An "Interested" Director

The Model Act does not attempt to define precisely when a director should be viewed as "interested" for purposes of participating in the decision to adopt, approve, or ratify a conflict of interest transaction. Section 8.31(b) does, however, define one aspect of this concept—the "indirect" interest. For purposes of section 8.31 a director should normally be viewed as interested in a transaction if he or the immediate members of his family have a financial interest in the transaction or a relationship with the other parties to the transaction such that the relationship might reasonably be expected to affect his judgment in the particular matter in a manner adverse to the corporation.

CHAPTER 10. AMENDMENT OF ARTICLES OF INCORPORATION AND BYLAWS

SUBCHAPTER A. AMENDMENT OF ARTICLES OF INCORPORATION

§ 10.01 Authority to Amend

(a) A corporation may amend its articles of incorporation at any time to add or change a provision that is required or permitted in the articles of incorporation or to delete a provision not required in the articles of incorporation. Whether a provision is required or permitted in the articles of incorporation is determined as of the effective date of the amendment.

(b) A shareholder of the corporation does not have a vested property right resulting from any provision in the articles of incorporation, including provisions relating to management, control, capital structure, dividend entitlement, or purpose or duration of the corporation.

§ 10.02 Amendment by Board of Directors

Unless the articles of incorporation provide otherwise, a corporation's board of directors may adopt one or more amendments to the corporation's articles of incorporation without shareholder action:

(1) to extend the duration of the corporation if it was incorporated at a time when limited duration was required by law;

(2) to delete the names and addresses of the initial directors;

(3) to delete the name and address of the initial registered agent or registered office, if a statement of change is on file with the secretary of state;

(4) to change each issued and unissued authorized share of an outstanding class into a greater number of whole shares if the corporation has only shares of that class outstanding;

(5) to change the corporate name by substituting the word "corporation," "incorporated," "company," "limited," or the abbreviation "corp.," "inc.," "co.," or "ltd.," for a similar word or abbreviation in the name, or by adding, deleting, or changing a geographical attribution for the name; or

(6) to make any other change expressly permitted by this Act to be made without shareholder action.

§ 10.03 Amendment by Board of Directors and Shareholders

(a) A corporation's board of directors may propose one or more amendments to the articles of incorporation for submission to the shareholders.

(b) For the amendment to be adopted:

(1) the board of directors must recommend the amendment to the shareholders unless the board of directors determines that because of conflict of interest or other special circumstances it should make no recommendation and communicates the basis for its determination to the shareholders with the amendment; and

(2) the shareholders entitled to vote on the amendment must approve the amendment as provided in subsection (e).

(c) The board of directors may condition its submission of the proposed amendment on any basis.

(d) The corporation shall notify each shareholder, whether or not entitled to vote, of the proposed shareholders' meeting in accordance with section 7.05. The notice of meeting must also state that the purpose, or one of the purposes, of the meeting is to consider the proposed amendment and contain or be accompanied by a copy or summary of the amendment.

(e) Unless this Act, the articles of incorporation, or the board of directors (acting pursuant to subsection (c)) require a greater vote or a vote by voting groups, the amendment to be adopted must be approved by:

(1) a majority of the votes entitled to be cast on the amendment by any voting group with respect to which the amendment would create dissenters' rights; and

(2) the votes required by sections 7.25 and 7.26 by every other voting group entitled to vote on the amendment.

§ 10.04 Voting on Amendments by Voting Groups

(a) The holders of the outstanding shares of a class are entitled to vote as a separate voting group (if shareholder voting is otherwise required by this Act) on a proposed amendment if the amendment would:

(1) increase or decrease the aggregate number of authorized shares of the class;

(2) effect an exchange or reclassification of all or part of the shares of the class into shares of another class;

(3) effect an exchange or reclassification, or create the right of exchange, of all or part of the shares of another class into shares of the class;

(4) change the designation, rights, preferences, or limitations of all or part of the shares of the class;

(5) change the shares of all or part of the class into a different number of shares of the same class;

(6) create a new class of shares having rights or preferences with respect to distributions or to dissolution that are prior, superior, or substantially equal to the shares of the class;

(7) increase the rights, preferences, or number of authorized shares of any class that, after giving effect to the amendment, have rights or preferences with respect to distributions or to dissolution that are prior, superior, or substantially equal to the shares of the class;

(8) limit or deny an existing preemptive right of all or part of the shares of the class; or

(9) cancel or otherwise affect rights to distributions or dividends that have accumulated but not yet been declared on all or part of the shares of the class.

(b) If a proposed amendment would affect a series of a class of shares in one or more of the ways described in subsection (a), the shares of that series are entitled to vote as a separate voting group on the proposed amendment.

(c) If a proposed amendment that entitles two or more series of shares to vote as separate voting groups under this section would affect those two or more series in the same or a substantially similar way, the shares of all the series so affected must vote together as a single voting group on the proposed amendment.

(d) A class or series of shares is entitled to the voting rights granted by this section although the articles of incorporation provide that the shares are nonvoting shares.

§ 10.05 Amendment Before Issuance of Shares

If a corporation has not yet issued shares, its incorporators or board of directors may adopt one or more amendments to the corporation's articles of incorporation.

§ 10.06 Articles of Amendment

A corporation amending its articles of incorporation shall deliver to the secretary of state for filing articles of amendment setting forth:

(1) the name of the corporation;

(2) the text of each amendment adopted;

(3) if an amendment provides for an exchange, reclassification, or cancellation of issued shares, provisions for implementing the amendment if not contained in the amendment itself;

(4) the date of each amendment's adoption;

(5) if an amendment was adopted by the incorporators or board of directors without shareholder action, a statement to that effect and that shareholder action was not required;

(6) if an amendment was approved by the shareholders:

(i) the designation, number of outstanding shares, number of votes entitled to be cast by each voting group entitled to vote separately on the amendment, and number of votes of each voting group indisputably represented at the meeting;

(ii) either the total number of votes cast for and against the amendment by each voting group entitled to vote separately on the amendment or the total number of undisputed votes cast for the amendment by each voting group and a statement that the number cast for the amendment by each voting group was sufficient for approval by that voting group.

§ 10.09 Effect of Amendment

An amendment to articles of incorporation does not affect a cause of action existing against or in favor of the corporation, a proceeding to which the corporation is a party, or the existing rights of persons other than shareholders of the corporation. An amendment changing a corporation's name does not abate a proceeding brought by or against the corporation in its former name.

SUBCHAPTER B. AMENDMENT OF BYLAWS

§ 10.20 Amendment by Board of Directors or Shareholders

(a) A corporation's board of directors may amend or repeal the corporation's bylaws unless:

(1) the articles of incorporation or this Act reserve this power exclusively to the shareholders in whole or part; or

(2) the shareholders in amending or repealing a particular bylaw provide expressly that the board of directors may not amend or repeal that bylaw.

(b) A corporation's shareholders may amend or repeal the corporation's bylaws even though the bylaws may also be amended or repealed by its board of directors.

OFFICIAL COMMENT

In the absence of a provision in the articles of incorporation, the power to amend or repeal bylaws is shared by the board of directors and shareholders. Amendment of bylaws by the board of directors is often simpler and more convenient than amendment by the shareholders and avoids the expense of calling a shareholders' meeting, a cost that may may be significant in publicly held corporations. As used in this subchapter, "amendment" includes the adoption of a bylaw on a new subject as well as the alteration of existing bylaws.

Section 10.20(a) provides. however. that the power to amend or repeal bylaws may be reserved exclusively to the shareholders by an appropriate provision in the articles of incorporation. This option may appropriately be elected by a closely held corporation—for example,where control arrangements appear in the bylaws but one shareholder or group of shareholders has the power to name a majority of the board of directors. In such a corporation, the control arrangements may alternatively be placed in the articles of incorporation rather than the bylaws if there is no objection to making them a matter of public record.

Section 10.20(a)(1) provides that the power to amend or repeal the bylaws may be reserved to the shareholders "in whole or part." This language permits the reservation of power to be limited to specific articles or sections of the bylaws or to specific subjects or topics addressed in the bylaws. It is important that the areas reserved exclusively to the shareholders be delineated clearly and unambiguously.

Section 10.20(a)(2) permits the shareholders to adopt or amend a bylaw and reserve exclusively to themselves the power to amend or repeal it later. This reservation must be expressed in the action by the shareholders adopting or amending the bylaw. This option is also included for the benefit of closely held corporations.

Section 10.20(b) states that the power of shareholders to amend or repeal bylaws exists even though that power is shared with the board of directors. This section makes inapplicable the holdings of a few cases under differently phrased statutes that shareholders do not have a general or residual power to amend bylaws or that the power to amend bylaws may be vested exclusively in the board of directors. Under the Model Act the shareholders always have the power to amend or repeal the bylaws.

Section 10.21 and 10.22 limit the power of directors to adopt or amend supermajority provisions in bylaws.

§ 10.21 Bylaw Increasing Quorum or Voting Requirement for Shareholders

(a) If authorized by the articles of incorporation, the shareholders may adopt or amend a bylaw that fixes a greater quorum or voting requirement for shareholders (or voting groups of shareholders) than is required by this Act. The adoption or amendment of a bylaw that adds, changes, or deletes a greater quorum or voting requirement for shareholders must meet the same quorum requirement and be adopted by the same vote and voting groups required to take action under the quorum and voting requirement then in effect or proposed to be adopted, whichever is greater.

(b) A bylaw that fixes a greater quorum or voting requirement for shareholders under subsection (a) may not be adopted, amended, or repealed by the board of directors.

OFFICIAL COMMENT

This section permits "supermajority" provisions relating to shareholder meetings to appear in the bylaws if express authorization for the provisions appears in the articles of incorporation.

The Model Act generally requires that supermajority provisions relating to shareholder voting appear in the articles of incorporation where they are a matter of public record. See section 7.27. Section 10.21(a) is consistent with these general principle since it permits a supermajority provision relating to shareholders to appear in the bylaws only if expressly authorized in the articles of incorporation. The option to place shareholder supermajority provisions in the bylaws rather than in the articles is designed primarily for the benefit of closely held corporations. Such a supermajority provision, like supermajority provisions appearing in articles of incorporation (section 7.27), amy be adopted or amended only by the shareholders (section 10.21(b)) and the vote must meet the supermajority requirement then being imposed or amended, whichever is greater (section 10.21(a)). For an example of the application of this language, see the Official Comment to section 7.27.

A supermajority provision in the bylaws relating to shareholder voting that is not expressly authorized by the articles of incorporation is not effective under the Model Act. The Model Act does not, however, address whether such a provision may be binding as a contract upon those shares voting in favor of the bylaw or upon subsequent holders of those shares with knowledge of the bylaw provision.

§ 10.22 Bylaw Increasing Quorum or Voting Requirement for Directors

(a) A bylaw that fixes a greater quorum or voting requirement for the board of directors may be amended or repealed:

(1) if originally adopted by the shareholders, only by the shareholders;

(2) if originally adopted by the board of directors, either by the shareholders or by the board of directors.

(b) A bylaw adopted or amended by the shareholders that fixes a greater quorum or voting requirement for the board of directors may provide that it may be amended or repealed only by a specified vote of either the shareholders or the board of directors.

(c) Action by the board of directors under subsection (a)(2) to adopt or amend a bylaw that changes the quorum or voting requirement for the board of directors must meet the same quorum requirement and be adopted by the same vote required to take action under the quorum and voting requirement then in effect or proposed to be adopted, whichever is greater.

OFFICIAL COMMENT

Supermajority provisions relating to the board of directors may appear in the bylaws of the corporation without specific authorization in the articles of incorporation. See section 8.24(a) and (c). Like other bylaw provisions, they may be adopted either by the board of directors or by the shareholders. See section 10.20. Such provisions, further, may be amended or repealed by the board of directors or shareholders as provided in thus section. This treatment of supermajority provisions for the board of directors should be contrasted with the treatment of analogous provisions for shareholders which must either be set forth in the articles of incorporation, section 7.27, or included in the bylaws when expressly authorized by the articles, section 10.21, and their adoption, amendment, or repeal must be approved by the shareholders by the vote specified in sections 7.27 and 10.21.

Supermajority provisions relating to the board of directors are usually part of control arrangements in closely held corporations, and section 10.22 is designed with this end in view. Its basic purpose is to ensure that control arrangements negotiated by shareholders for their own protection will not be prematurely terminated by a majority vote of the shareholders or the board of directors. Thus, section 10.22(a)(1) provides that if a supermajority requirement is originally imposed by a bylaw adopted by the shareholders, only the shareholders may amend or repeal it. Further, under section 10.22(b), that bylaw may impose restrictions on the manner in which it may be thereafter amended or repealed by the shareholders. On the other hand, if a supermajority requirement is originally imposed in a bylaw adopted by the board of directors, that bylaw may be amended either by the board of directors or shareholders (see section 10.22(a)(2)), but if it is amended by the board of directors, section 10.22(c) requires approval by the supermajority requirement then being imposed or amended, whichever is greater. This requirement is analogous to that imposed or supermajority amendments appearing in the articles of incorporation. See section 7.27. For an example of the application of this language, see the Official Comment to section 7.27.

CHAPTER 11. MERGER AND SHARE EXCHANGE

§ 11.01 Merger

(a) One or more corporations may merge into another corporation if the board of directors of each corporation adopts and its shareholders (if required by section 11.03) approve a plan of merger.

(b) The plan of merger must set forth:

(1) the name of each corporation planning to merge and the name of the surviving corporation into which each other corporation plans to merge;

(2) the terms and conditions of the merger; and

(3) the manner and basis of converting the shares of each corporation into shares, obligations, or other securities of the surviving or any other corporation or into cash or other property in whole or part.

(c) The plan of merger may set forth:

(1) amendments to the articles of incorporation of the surviving corporation; and

(2) other provisions relating to the merger.

OFFICIAL COMMENT

1. Statutory Mergers

Section 11.01(a) authorizes a statutory merger, to be accomplished by the adoption of a plan of merger under section 11.01(b), approval of the transaction by the shareholders (if required by section 11.03), and filing articles of merger under section 11.05. Upon the effective date of the merger, the surviving corporation becomes vested with all the assets of the disappearing corporations and becomes subject to their liabilities.

Under the Model Act there are virtually no restrictions or limitations on the terms of a statutory merger. Shareholders of the disappearing corporations may receive securities of the surviving corporation, securities of a third corporation, e.g., shares issued by the parent of the surviving or disappearing corporation (which may be publicly traded and marketable while the shares of the surviving or disappearing corporation are not), or cash or other property (a "cash" or "cash out" merger). Some of the holders of a single class of shares may be required to accept securities or properties while the remaining holders may be compelled to accept different securities, property, or cash. The capitalization of the surviving corporation may be restructured in the merger, or its articles of incorporation may be amended by the articles of merger in any way deemed appropriate. Any other provisions considered necessary or desirable with respect to the merger may be included in the plan of merger.

Merger transactions may give rise to voting by separate voting groups of shareholders under section 11.03(f), and dissenting shareholders may have dissenters' right under chapter 13.

Courts have held the merger transactions that are formally authorized by the procedures set forth in this chapter may in some circumstances constitute a breach of duty to minority shareholders where the effect of the transaction is to eliminate them from further equity participation in the enterprise. See McBride, "Delaware Corporate Law: Judicial Scrutiny of Mergers—The Aftermath of *Singer v. Magnavox Co.*," 33 BUS. LAW. 2231 (1978). In Delaware, case law establishes that these transactions must be fully disclosed and entirely fair to the minority shareholders. See *Singer v. Magnavox Co.*, 380 A.2d 969 (Del. 1977); *Weinberger v. UOP, Inc.*, 457 A.2d 701 (Del.1983); *Harman v. Mansoneilan International, Inc.*, 442 A.2d 487 (Del. 1982).

2. Equivalent Nonstatutory Transactions

A transaction may have the same economic effect as a statutory merger even though it is cast in the form of a nonstatutory transaction. For example, assets of the disappearing corporations may be sold for consideration in the form of shares of the surviving corporation, followed by the distribution of those shares by the disappearing corporations to their shareholders and their subsequent dissolution. Transactions have sometimes been structured in nonstatutory form for tax reasons or in an effort to avoid some of the consequences of a statutory merger, particularly appraisal rights to dissenting shareholders. Faced with these transactions, a few courts have developed or accepted the "de facto merger" concept which, to some uncertain extent, grants to dissenting shareholders the rights they would have had if the transaction had been structured as a statutory merger. See Folk, "De Facto Mergers in Delaware: Hariton v. Arco Electronics, Inc.," 49 Va.L.Rev. 1261 (1963). These problems should not occur under the Model Act since the procedural requirements for authorization and consequences of various types of transactions are largely standardized. For example, dissenters' rights are granted not only in mergers but also in share exchanges, in sales of all or substantially all the corporate assets, and in amendments to articles of incorporation that significantly affect rights of shareholders.

§ 11.02 Share Exchange

(a) A corporation may acquire all of the outstanding shares of one or more classes or series of another corporation if the board of directors of each corporation adopts and its shareholders (if required by section 11.03) approve the exchange.

(b) The plan of exchange must set forth:

(1) the name of the corporation whose shares will be acquired and the name of the acquiring corporation;

(2) the terms and conditions of the exchange;

(3) the manner and basis of exchanging the shares to be acquired for shares, obligations, or other securities of the acquiring or any other corporation or for cash or other property in whole or part.

(c) The plan of exchange may set forth other provisions relating to the exchange.

(d) This section does not limit the power of a corporation to acquire all or part of the shares of one or more classes or series of another corporation through a voluntary exchange or otherwise.

§ 11.03 Action on Plan

(a) After adopting a plan of merger or share exchange, the board of directors of each corporation party to the merger, and the board of directors of the corporation whose shares will be acquired in the share exchange, shall submit the plan of merger (except as provided in subsection (g)) or share exchange for approval by its shareholders.

(b) For a plan of merger or share exchange to be approved:

(1) the board of directors must recommend the plan of merger or share exchange to the shareholders, unless the board of directors determines that because of conflict of interest or other special circumstances it should make no recommendation and communicates the basis for its determination to the shareholders with the plan; and

(2) the shareholders entitled to vote must approve the plan.

(c) The board of directors may condition its submission of the proposed merger or share exchange on any basis.

(d) The corporation shall notify each shareholder, whether or not entitled to vote, of the proposed shareholders' meeting in accordance with section 7.05. The notice must also state that the purpose, or one of the purposes, of the meeting is to consider the plan of merger or share exchange and contain or be accompanied by a copy or summary of the plan.

(e) Unless this Act, the articles of incorporation, or the board of directors (acting pursuant to subsection (c)) require a greater vote or a vote by voting groups, the plan of merger or share exchange to be authorized must be approved by each voting group entitled to vote separately on the plan by a majority of all the votes entitled to be cast on the plan by that voting group.

(f) Separate voting by voting groups is required:

(1) on a plan of merger if the plan contains a provision that, if contained in a proposed amendment to articles of incorporation, would require action by one or more separate voting groups on the proposed amendment under section 10.04;

(2) on a plan of share exchange by each class or series of shares included in the exchange, with each class or series constituting a separate voting group.

(g) Action by the shareholders of the surviving corporation on a plan of merger is not required i:f

(1) the articles of incorporation of the surviving corporation will not differ (except for amendments enumerated in section 10.02) from its articles before the merger;

(2) each shareholder of the surviving corporation whose shares were outstanding immediately before the effective date of the merger will hold the same number of shares, with identical designations, preferences, limitations, and relative rights, immediately after;

(3) the number of voting shares outstanding immediately after the merger, plus the number of voting shares issuable as a result of the merger (either by the conversion of securities issued pursuant to the merger or the exercise of rights and warrants issued pursuant to the merger), will not exceed by more than 20 percent the total number of voting shares of the surviving corporation outstanding immediately before the merger; and

(4) the number of participating shares outstanding immediately after the merger, plus the number of participating shares issuable as a result of the merger (either by the conversion of securities issued pursuant to the merger or the exercise of rights and warrants issued pursuant to the merger), will not exceed by more than 20 percent the total number of participating shares outstanding immediately before the merger.

(h) As used in subsection (g):

(1) "Participating shares" means shares that entitle their holders to participate without limitation in distributions.

(2) "Voting shares" means shares that entitle their holders to vote unconditionally in elections of directors.

(i) After a merger or share exchange is authorized, and at any time before articles of merger or share exchange are filed, the planned merger or share exchange may be abandoned (subject to any contractual rights), without further shareholder action, in accordance with the procedure set forth in the plan of merger or share exchange or, if none is set forth, in the manner determined by the board of directors.

OFFICIAL COMMENT

1. Introduction

Section 11.03 requires merger or share exchanges to be approved by the shareholders as follows:

In the case of a merger:

(1) the transaction must always be approved by the shareholders of the disappearing corporation; and

(2) the transaction must be approved by the shareholders of the surviving corporation if the number of voting or participating shares is increased by more than 20 percent as a result of the transaction.

In the case of a share exchange:

(1) the transaction must always be approved by the shareholders of the corporation whose shares are being acquired; and

(2) the transaction need not be approved by the shareholders of the corporation acquiring the shares.

Section 11.03 requires the board of directors to propose the plan of merger or sale exchange and then submit the proposal to the shareholders. When proposing a plan of merger or share exchange, the board of directors must make a recommendation to the shareholders that the plan be approved, unless it determines that because of conflict of interest or other special circumstances it should make no recommendation. If the board of directors so determines, it must describe the conflict or circumstances, and communicate the basis for its determination, when presenting the proposed plan of merger or share exchange to the shareholders.

Section 11.03(c) permits the board of directors to condition its submission of a plan of merger or share exchange on any basis; for example, the board may direct that the plan is approved only if it receives a statutory merger have a right to vote if the increase in the number of shares exceeds 20 percent may be avoided by arranging the transaction in the form of a merger involving a subsidiary of the acquiring corporation or as a share exchange under section 11.02, This anomaly reflects a compromise among basically conflicting points of view.

The 20 percent requirement is applicable only if the corporation has available enough authorized shares to permit it to issue the shares without amending its articles of incorporation to increase authorized capital. If it must amend its articles of incorporation to authorize the shares necessary to complete the transaction, a shareholder vote on the amendment will be necessary in all cases. See section 10.03.

* * *

4. Application of the 20-percent requirement

In a merger transaction that involves an increase in shares of more than 20 percent, section 11.03(g) requires a shareholder vote in order to prevent significant dilution without the approval of the shareholders involved. Sections 11.03(g)(3) and (4) separately apply the 20-percent test to increases in the "voting shares" (as defined in section 11.03(h)(2)) and increases in "participating shares" (as defined in section 11.03(h)(1)). If either type of shares is increased by more than 20 percent in the merger transaction, the transaction must be approved by the shareholders.

Under the definitions in subsections (h)(1) and (2), the 20 percent requirement may be applied to shares with preferential rights if they are either voting or fully participating, and to deferred or contingent shares issued as a result of the merger. On the other hand, it is typically not applicable to shares issuable under antidilution clauses to balance share splits or share dividends; these shares would not become issuable "pursuant to the merger," but by virtue of later corporate action authorizing the split or dividends.

Section 11.03(g)(3) and 4 only determine when a shareholders' vote is required; they do not relate to voting by voting groups. Whether or not a class or series of shares is entitled to vote as a separate voting group is determined by section 11.03(f).

§ 11.04 Merger of Subsidiary

(a) A parent corporation owning at least 90 percent of the outstanding shares of each class of a subsidiary corporation may merge the subsidiary into itself without approval of the shareholders of the parent or subsidiary.

(b) The board of directors of the parent shall adopt a plan of merger that sets forth:

(1) the names of the parent and subsidiary; and

(2) the manner and basis of converting the shares of the subsidiary into shares, obligations, or other securities of the parent or any other corporation or into cash or other property in whole or part.

(c) The parent shall mail a copy or summary of the plan of merger to each shareholder of the subsidiary who does not waive the mailing requirement in writing.

(d) The parent may not deliver articles of merger to the secretary of state for filing until at least 30 days after the date it mailed a copy of the plan of merger to each shareholder of the subsidiary who did not waive the mailing requirement.

(e) Articles of merger under this section may not contain amendments to the articles of incorporation of the parent corporation (except for amendments enumerated in section 10.02).

OFFICIAL COMMENT

Section 11.04(a) defines a "parent" corporation as one that owns at least 90 percent of the outstanding shares of each class of another corporation, and a "subsidiary" corporation as one whose shares are so owned. Section 11.04 permits merger of a subsidiary into its parent corporation upon adoption of a plan of merger by the board of directors of the parent alone. Separate action by the board of directors of the subsidiary is unnecessary because the share ownership of the parent corporation is normally sufficient to permit it to elect or remove the subsidiary's board of directors.

Further, the merger transaction need not be approved by the shareholders of either corporation. Approval by the shareholders of the subsidiary is meaningless because the parent's share ownership is sufficient to ensure the plan will be approved. Approval by the parent's shareholders is also unnecessary because the transaction does not materially change their rights: the ownership of the parent corporation is being changed only from 90 percent indirect ownership to 100 percent direct ownership of the same assets, and no significant amendment of the parent's articles of incorporation is being made. For the same reason, shareholders of the parent corporation do not have the right to dissent from the transaction under chapter 13.

Minority shareholders of the subsidiary corporation may receive shares, obligations, or other securities of the parent or any other corporation, or cash or other property in whole or in part in exchange for their shares. These shareholders are entitled to 30 days' notice of the plan of merger before it is effectuated.

Shareholders of the subsidiary corporation have a right to dissent from the merger transaction under chapter 13. * * *

§ 11.05 Articles of Merger or Share Exchange

(a) After a plan of merger or share exchange is approved by the shareholders, or adopted by the board of directors if shareholder approval is not required, the surviving or acquiring corporation shall deliver to the secretary of state for filing articles of merger or share exchange setting forth:

(1) the plan of merger or share exchange;

(2) if shareholder approval was not required, a statement to that effect;

(3) if approval of the shareholders of one or more corporations party to the merger or share exchange was required:

(i) the designation, number of outstanding shares, and number of votes entitled to be cast by each voting group entitled to vote separately on the plan as to each corporation; and

(ii) either the total number of votes cast for and against the plan by each voting group entitled to vote separately on the plan or the total number of undisputed votes cast for the plan separately by each voting group and a statement that the number cast for the plan by each voting group was sufficient for approval by that voting group.

(b) A merger or share exchange takes effect upon the effective date of the articles of merger or share exchange.

§ 11.06 Effect of Merger or Share Exchange

(a) When a merger takes effect:

(1) every other corporation party to the merger merges into the surviving corporation and the separate existence of every corporation except the surviving corporation ceases;

(2) the title to all real estate and other property owned by each corporation party to the merger is vested in the surviving corporation without reversion or impairment;

(3) the surviving corporation has all liabilities of each corporation party to the merger;

(4) a proceeding pending against any corporation party to the merger may be continued as if the merger did not occur or the

surviving corporation may be substituted in the proceeding for the corporation whose existence ceased;

(5) the articles of incorporation of the surviving corporation are amended to the extent provided in the plan of merger; and

(6) the shares of each corporation party to the merger that are to be converted into shares, obligations, or other securities of the surviving or any other corporation or into cash or other property are converted, and the former holders of the shares are entitled only to the rights provided in the articles of merger or to their rights under chapter 13.

(b) When a share exchange takes effect, the shares of each acquired corporation are exchanged as provided in the plan, and the former holders of the shares are entitled only to the exchange rights provided in the articles of share exchange or to their rights under chapter 13.

§ 11.07 Effect of Merger or Share Exchange

(a) When a merger becomes effective:

(1) the corporation or other entity that is designated in the plan of merger as the survivor continues or comes into existence, as the case may be;

(2) the separate existence of every corporation or other entity that is merged into the survivor ceases;

(3) all property owned by, and every contract right possessed by, each corporation or other entity that merges into the survivor is vested in the survivor without reversion or impairment;

(4) all liabilities of each corporation or other entity that is merged into the survivor are vested in the survivor;

(5) the name of the survivor may, but need not be, substituted in any pending proceeding for the name of any party to the merger whose separate existence ceased in the merger;

(6) the articles of incorporation or organizational documents of the survivor are amended to the extent provided in the plan of merger;

(7) the articles of incorporation or organizational documents of a survivor that is created by the merger become effective; and

(8) the shares of each corporation that is a party to the merger, and the interests in an other entity that is a party to a merger, that are to be converted under the plan of merger into shares, interests, obligations, rights to acquire securities, other securities, cash, other property, or any combination of the foregoing, are converted, and the former holders of such shares or interests are entitled only to the rights provided to them in the plan of merger or to any rights they may have under chapter 13.

(b) When a share exchange becomes effective, the shares of each domestic corporation that are to be exchanged for shares or other securities, interests, obligations, rights to acquire shares or other securities, cash, other property, or any combination of the foregoing, are entitled only to the rights provided to them in the plan of share exchange or to any rights they may have under chapter 13.

(c) Any shareholder of a domestic corporation that is a party to a merger or share exchange who, prior to the merger or share exchange, was liable for the liabilities or obligations of such corporation, shall not be released from such liabilities or obligations by reason of the merger or share exchange.

(d) Upon a merger becoming effective, a foreign corporation, or a foreign other entity, that is the survivor of the merger is deemed to:

(1) appoint the secretary of state as its agent for service of process in a proceeding to enforce the rights of shareholders of each domestic corporation that is a party to the merger who exercise appraisal rights, and

(2) agree that it will promptly pay the amount, if any, to which such shareholders are entitled under chapter 13.

OFFICIAL COMMENT

Under section 11.07(a), in the case of a merger the survivor and the parties that merge into the survivor become one. The survivor automatically becomes the owner of all real and personal property and becomes subject to all the liabilities, actual or contingent, of each party that is merged into it. A merger is not a conveyance, transfer, or assignment. It does not give rise to claims of reverter or impairment of title based on a prohibited conveyance or transfer. It does not give rise to a claim that a contract with a party to the merger is no longer in effect on the ground of nonassignability, unless the contract specifically provides that it does not survive a merger. All pending proceedings involving either the survivor or a party whose separate existence ceased as a result of the merger are continued. Under section 11.07(a)(5), the name of the survivor may be, but need not be, substituted in any pending proceeding for the name of a party to the merger whose separate existence ceased as a result of the merger. The substitution may be made whether the survivor is a complainant or a respondent, and may be made at the instance of either the survivor or an opposing party. Such a substitution has no substantive effect, because whether or not the survivor's name is substituted it succeeds to the claims of, and is subject to the liabilities of, any party to the merger whose separate existence ceased as a result of the merger.

In contrast to a merger, a share exchange does not in and of itself affect the separate existence of the parties, vest in the acquiring corporation the assets of the corporation whose stock is to be acquired, or render the acquiring corporation liable for the liabilities of the corporation whose stock the acquiring corporation acquires.

Under section 11.07(a)(8), on the effective date of a merger the former shareholders of a corporation that is merged into the survivor are entitled only to the rights provided in the plan of merger (which would include any rights they have as holders of the consideration they acquire) or to any rights they may have under chapter 13. Similarly, under section 11.07(b), on the effective date of a share exchange the former shareholders of a corporation whose shares are acquired are entitled only to the rights provided in the plan of share exchange (which would include any rights they have as holders of the consideration they acquire) or to any rights they may have under chapter 13. These provisions are not intended to preclude an otherwise proper question concerning the merger's validity, or to override or otherwise affect any provisions of chapter 13 concerning the exclusiveness of rights under that chapter.

Under section 11.07(d), when a merger becomes effective a foreign corporation, or a foreign other entity, that is the survivor of the merger is deemed to appoint the secretary of state as its agent for service of process in a proceeding to enforce the rights of any shareholders of each domestic corporation that is a party to the merger who exercise appraisal rights, and to agree that it will promptly pay the amount, if any, to which such shareholders are entitled under chapter 13. This result is based on the implied consent of such a foreign corporation, or foreign other entity, to the terms of chapter 11 by virtue of entering into an agreement that is governed by this chapter.

Under section 11.04(h), a merger cannot have the effect of making any shareholder of a domestic corporation subject to personal liability for the obligations or liabilities of any other person or entity unless each such shareholder has executed a separate written consent to become subject to such liability.

§ 11.08 Abandonment of a Merger or Share Exchange

(a) Unless otherwise provided in a plan of merger or share exchange or in the laws under which a foreign corporation or a domestic or foreign other entity that is a party to a merger or a share exchange is organized or by which it is governed, after the plan has been adopted and approved as required by this chapter, and at any time before the merger or share exchange has become effective, it may be abandoned by any party thereto without action by the party's shareholders or owners of interests, in accordance with any procedures set forth in the plan of merger or share exchange or, if no such procedures are set forth in the plan, in the manner determined by the board of directors of a corporation, or the managers of an other entity, subject to any contractual rights of other parties to the merger or share exchange.

(b) If a merger or share exchange is abandoned under subsection (a) after articles of merger or share exchange have been filed with the secretary of state but before the merger or share exchange has become effective, a statement that the merger or share exchange has been abandoned in accordance with this section, executed on behalf of a party to the merger or share exchange by an officer or other duly authorized representative, shall be delivered to the secretary of state for filing prior to the effective date of the merger or share exchange. Upon filing, the statement shall take effect and the merger or share exchange shall be deemed abandoned and shall not become effective.

OFFICIAL COMMENT

Under section 11.08, unless otherwise provided in the plan of merger or share exchange, a party to a merger or share exchange may abandon the transaction without shareholder approval, even though the transaction has been previously approved by the party's shareholders or the owners of the party's interests. The power of a party under section 11.08 to abandon a transaction without shareholder approval does not affect any contract rights that other parties may have.

CHAPTER 12. SALE OF ASSETS

§ 12.01 Sale of Assets in Regular Course of Business and Mortgage of Assets

(a) A corporation may, on the terms and conditions and for the consideration determined by the board of directors:

(1) sell, lease, exchange, or otherwise dispose of all, or substantially all, of its property in the usual and regular course of business,

(2) mortgage, pledge, dedicate to the repayment of indebtedness (whether with or without recourse), or otherwise encumber any or all of its property whether or not in the usual and regular course of business, or

(3) transfer any or all of its property to a corporation all the shares of which are owned by the corporation.

(b) Unless the articles of incorporation require it, approval by the shareholders of a transaction described in subsection (a) is not required.

OFFICIAL COMMENT

A sale of "all or substantially all" the corporate assets in the regular course of business is governed by section 12.01. Mortgages of all of the corporation's assets or redeployment of those assets through a wholly owned subsidiary are also covered by section 12.01. All other sales of "all or substantially all" the corporate assets are governed by section 12.02. Dispositions or transfers of property that do not involve "all or substantially all" the property of the corporation are not controlled by statute and may be approved by the board of directors (or authorized corporate officer) in the same manner as any other corporate transaction.

1. The Meaning of "All or Substantially All"

The phrase "all or substantially all," chosen by the draftsmen of the Model Act, is intended to mean what it literally says, "all or substantially all." The phrase "substantially all" is synonymous with "nearly all" and was added merely to make it clear that the statutory requirements could not be avoided by retention of some minimal or nominal residue of the original assets. A sale of all the corporate assets other than cash or cash equivalents is normally the sale of "all or substantially all" of the corporation's property. A sale of several distinct manufacturing lines while retaining one or more lines is normally not a sale of "all or substantially all" even though the lines being sold are substantial and include a significant fraction of the corporation's former business. If the lines retained are viewed only as a temporary operation or as a pretext to avoid the "all or substantially all" requirements, however, the statutory requirements of chapter 12 must be complied with. Similarly, as sale of a plant but retention of operating assets (e.g. machinery and equipment), accounts receivable, good will, and the like with a view toward continuing the operation at another location is not a sale of "all or substantially all" the corporation's property.

Some court decisions have adopted a narrower construction of somewhat similar statutory language. These decisions should be viewed as resting on the diverse statutory language involved in those cases and should not be viewed as illustrating the meaning of "all or substantially all" intended by the draftsmen of the Model Act.

2. Transfers of "All or Substantially All" of a Corporation's Assets That Do Not Require Shareholder Approval

Section 12.01 describes transfers or dispositions of "all or substantially all" the corporate assets that do not require shareholder approval unless the articles of incorporation require it. These transactions consist of (1) mortgages or pledges of all the corporation's property, whether or not the loan they secure is in the ordinary course of business, (2) transactions within the usual and regular course of business, and (3) transfers to wholly owned subsidiaries.

a. Mortgages or pledges

Mortgages or pledges of all the corporate assets may be demanded by lenders. They are essentially and substantively different from a sale or other disposition of assets even though they may take the form of a formal transfer of title to the mortgagee for security purposes, or of a dedication of assets to the repayment of indebtedness, as in the case of oil and gas production payments. The corporation remains in possession of the mortgaged property, may continue to use it for corporate purposes, in most cases must continue to manage the property, and may recover full title to the property by discharging the indebtedness.

b. Sales in the usual and regular course of business

Most transfers of "all or substantially all" the corporate property (as defined above) are, almost be definition, not in the usual and regular course of business; sales by real estate corporations and by corporations organized to liquidate a business are examples of sales that may be included in this part of section 12.01(a). Typically, sales falling within the usual and regular course of business do not involve the sale of the corporate name or good will.

c. Transfers to a subsidiary

Section 12.01 provides that a transfer of property to a wholly owned subsidiary does not require a vote of shareholders. This provision, however, may not be used as a device to avoid a vote of shareholders by a multiple-step transaction.

§ 12.02 Sale of Assets Other Than in Regular Course of Business

(a) A corporation may sell, lease, exchange, or otherwise dispose of all, or substantially all, of its property (with or without the good will), otherwise than in the usual and regular course of business, on the terms and conditions and for the consideration determined by the corporation's board of directors, if the board of directors proposes and its shareholders approve the proposed transaction.

(b) For a transaction to be authorized:

(1) the board of directors must recommend the proposed transaction to the shareholders unless the board of directors determines that because of conflict of interest or other special circumstances it should make no recommendation and communicates the basis for its determination to the shareholders with the submission of the proposed transaction; and

(2) the shareholders entitled to vote must approve the transaction.

(c) The board of directors may condition its submission of the proposed transaction on any basis.

(d) The corporation shall notify each shareholder, whether or not entitled to vote, of the proposed shareholders' meeting in accordance with section 7.05. The notice must also state that the purpose, or one of the purposes, of the meeting is to consider the sale, lease, exchange, or other disposition of all, or substantially all, the property of the corporation and contain or be accompanied by a description of the transaction.

(e) Unless the articles of incorporation or the board of directors (acting pursuant to subsection (c)) require a greater vote or a vote by voting groups, the transaction to be authorized must be approved by a majority of all the votes entitled to be cast on the transaction.

(f) After a sale, lease, exchange, or other disposition of property is authorized, the transaction may be abandoned (subject to any contractual rights) without further shareholder action.

(g) A transaction that constitutes a distribution is governed by section 6.40 and not by this section.

CHAPTER 13. DISSENTERS' RIGHTS

SUBCHAPTER A. RIGHT TO DISSENT AND OBTAIN PAYMENT FOR SHARES

§ 13.01 Definitions

In this chapter:

(1) "Corporation" means the issuer of the shares held by a dissenter before the corporate action, or the surviving or acquiring corporation by merger or share exchange of that issuer.

(2) "Dissenter" means a shareholder who is entitled to dissent from corporate action under section 13.02 and who exercises that right when and in the manner required by sections 13.20 through 13.28.

(3) "Fair value," with respect to a dissenter's shares, means the value of the shares immediately before the effectuation of the corporate action to which the dissenter objects, excluding any appreciation or depreciation in anticipation of the corporate action unless exclusion would be inequitable.

(4) "Interest" means interest from the effective date of the corporate action until the date of payment, at the average rate currently paid by the corporation on its principal bank loans or, if none, at a rate that is fair and equitable under all the circumstances.

(5) "Record shareholder" means the person in whose name shares are registered in the records of a corporation or the beneficial owner of shares to the extent of the rights granted by a nominee certificate on file with a corporation.

(6) "Beneficial shareholder" means the person who is a beneficial owner of shares held in a voting trust or by a nominee as the record shareholder.

(7) "Shareholder" means the record shareholder or the beneficial shareholder.

§ 13.02 Right to Dissent

(a) A shareholder is entitled to dissent from, and obtain payment of the fair value of his shares in the event of, any of the following corporate actions:

(1) consummation of a plan of merger to which the corporation is a party (i) if shareholder approval is required for the merger by section 11.03 or the articles of incorporation and the shareholder is entitled to vote on the merger or (ii) if the corporation is a subsidiary that is merged with its parent under section 11.04;

(2) consummation of a plan of share exchange to which the corporation is a party as the corporation whose shares will be acquired, if the shareholder is entitled to vote on the plan;

(3) consummation of a sale or exchange of all, or substantially all, of the property of the corporation other than in the usual and regular course of business, if the shareholder is entitled to vote on the sale or exchange, including a sale in dissolution, but not including a sale pursuant to court order or a sale for cash pursuant to a

plan by which all or substantially all of the net proceeds of the sale will be distributed to the shareholders within one year after the date of sale;

(4) an amendment of the articles of incorporation that materially and adversely affects rights in respect of a dissenter's shares because it:

(i) alters or abolishes a preferential right of the shares;

(ii) creates, alters, or abolishes a right in respect of redemption, including a provision respecting a sinking fund for the redemption or repurchase, of the shares;

(iii) alters or abolishes a preemptive right of the holder of the shares to acquire shares or other securities;

(iv) excludes or limits the right of the shares to vote on any matter, or to cumulate votes, other than a limitation by dilution through issuance of shares or other securities with similar voting rights; or

(v) reduces the number of shares owned by the shareholder to a fraction of a share if the fractional share so created is to be acquired for cash under section 6.04; or

(5) any corporate action taken pursuant to a shareholder vote to the extent the articles of incorporation, bylaws, or a resolution of the board of directors provides that voting or nonvoting shareholders are entitled to dissent and obtain payment for their shares.

(b) A shareholder entitled to dissent and obtain payment for his shares under this chapter may not challenge the corporate action creating his entitlement unless the action is unlawful or fraudulent with respect to the shareholder or the corporation.

§ 13.03 Dissent by Nominees and Beneficial Owners

(a) A record shareholder may assert dissenters' rights as to fewer than all the shares registered in his name only if he dissents with respect to all shares beneficially owned by any one person and notifies the corporation in writing of the name and address of each person on whose behalf he asserts dissenters' rights. The rights of a partial dissenter under this subsection are determined as if the shares as to which he dissents and his other shares were registered in the names of different shareholders.

(b) A beneficial shareholder may assert dissenters' rights as to shares held on his behalf only if:

(1) he submits to the corporation the record shareholder's written consent to the dissent not later than the time the beneficial shareholder asserts dissenters' rights; and

(2) he does so with respect to all shares of which he is the beneficial shareholder or over which he has power to direct the vote.

SUBCHAPTER B. PROCEDURE FOR EXERCISE OF DISSENTERS' RIGHTS

§ 13.20 Notice of Dissenters' Rights

(a) If proposed corporate action creating dissenters' rights under section 13.02 is submitted to a vote at a shareholders' meeting, the meeting notice must state that shareholders are or may be entitled to assert dissenters' rights under this chapter and be accompanied by a copy of this chapter.

(b) If corporate action creating dissenters' rights under section 13.02 is taken without a vote of shareholders, the corporation shall notify in writing all shareholders entitled to assert dissenters' rights that the action was taken and send them the dissenters' notice described in section 13.22.

§ 13.21 Notice of Intent to Demand Payment

(a) If proposed corporate action creating dissenters' rights under section 13.02 is submitted to a vote at a shareholders' meeting, a shareholder who wishes to assert dissenters' rights (1) must deliver to the corporation before the vote is taken written notice of his intent to demand payment for his shares if the proposed action is effectuated and (2) must not vote his shares in favor of the proposed action.

(b) A shareholder who does not satisfy the requirements of subsection (a) is not entitled to payment for his shares under this chapter.

§ 13.22 Dissenters' Notice

(a) If proposed corporate action creating dissenters' rights under section 13.02 is authorized at a shareholders' meeting, the corporation shall deliver a written dissenters' notice to all shareholders who satisfied the requirements of section 13.21.

(b) The dissenters' notice must be sent no later than 10 days after the corporate action was taken, and must:

(1) state where the payment demand must be sent and where and when certificates for certificated shares must be deposited;

(2) inform holders of uncertificated shares to what extent transfer of the shares will be restricted after the payment demand is received;

(3) supply a form for demanding payment that includes the date of the first announcement to news media or to shareholders of the terms of the proposed corporate action and requires that the person

asserting dissenters' rights certify whether or not he acquired beneficial ownership of the shares before that date;

(4) set a date by which the corporation must receive the payment demand, which date may not be fewer than 30 nor more than 60 days after the date the subsection (a) notice is delivered; and

(5) be accompanied by a copy of this chapter.

§ 13.23 Duty to Demand Payment

(a) A shareholder sent a dissenters' notice described in section 13.22 must demand payment, certify whether he acquired beneficial ownership of the shares before the date required to be set forth in the dissenter's notice pursuant to section 13.22(b)(3), and deposit his certificates in accordance with the terms of the notice.

(b) The shareholder who demands payment and deposits his shares under section (a) retains all other rights of a shareholder until these rights are cancelled or modified by the taking of the proposed corporate action.

(c) A shareholder who does not demand payment or deposit his share certificates where required, each by the date set in the dissenters' notice, is not entitled to payment for his shares under this chapter.

§ 13.24 Share Restrictions

(a) The corporation may restrict the transfer of uncertificated shares from the date the demand for their payment is received until the proposed corporate action is taken or the restrictions released under section 13.26.

(b) The person for whom dissenters' rights are asserted as to uncertificated shares retains all other rights of a shareholder until these rights are cancelled or modified by the taking of the proposed corporate action.

§ 13.25 Payment

(a) Except as provided in section 13.27, as soon as the proposed corporate action is taken, or upon receipt of a payment demand, the corporation shall pay each dissenter who complied with section 13.23 the amount the corporation estimates to be the fair value of his shares, plus accrued interest.

(b) The payment must be accompanied by:

(1) the corporation's balance sheet as of the end of a fiscal year ending not more than 16 months before the date of payment, an income statement for that year, a statement of changes in shareholders' equity for that year, and the latest available interim financial statements, if any;

(2) a statement of the corporation's estimate of the fair value of the shares;

(3) an explanation of how the interest was calculated;

(4) a statement of the dissenter's right to demand payment under section 13.28; and

(5) a copy of this chapter.

§ 13.26 Failure to Take Action

(a) If the corporation does not take the proposed action within 60 days after the date set for demanding payment and depositing share certificates, the corporation shall return the deposited certificates and release the transfer restrictions imposed on uncertificated shares.

(b) If after returning deposited certificates and releasing transfer restrictions, the corporation takes the proposed action, it must send a new dissenters' notice under section 13.22 and repeat the payment demand procedure.

§ 13.27 After–Acquired Shares

(a) A corporation may elect to withhold payment required by section 13.25 from a dissenter unless he was the beneficial owner of the shares before the date set forth in the dissenters' notice as the date of the first announcement to news media or to shareholders of the terms of the proposed corporate action.

(b) To the extent the corporation elects to withhold payment under subsection (a), after taking the proposed corporate action, it shall estimate the fair value of the shares, plus accrued interest, and shall pay this amount to each dissenter who agrees to accept it in full satisfaction of his demand. The corporation shall send with its offer a statement of its estimate of the fair value of the shares, an explanation of how the interest was calculated, and a statement of the dissenter's right to demand payment under section 13.28.

§ 13.28 Procedure if Shareholder Dissatisfied With Payment or Offer

(a) A dissenter may notify the corporation in writing of his own estimate of the fair value of his shares and amount of interest due, and demand payment of his estimate (less any payment under section 13.25), or reject the corporation's offer under section 13.27 and demand payment of the fair value of his shares and interest due, if:

(1) the dissenter believes that the amount paid under section 13.25 or offered under section 13.27 is less than the fair value of his shares or that the interest due is incorrectly calculated;

(2) the corporation fails to make payment under section 13.25 within 60 days after the date set for demanding payment; or

(3) the corporation, having failed to take the proposed action, does not return the deposited certificates or release the transfer restrictions imposed on uncertificated shares within 60 days after the date set for demanding payment.

(b) A dissenter waives his right to demand payment under this section unless he notifies the corporation of his demand in writing under subsection (a) within 30 days after the corporation made or offered payment for his shares.

SUBCHAPTER C. JUDICIAL APPRAISAL OF SHARES

§ 13.30 Court Action

(a) If a demand for payment under section 13.28 remains unsettled, the corporation shall commence a proceeding within 60 days after receiving the payment demand and petition the court to determine the fair value of the shares and accrued interest. If the corporation does not commence the proceeding within the 60–day period, it shall pay each dissenter whose demand remains unsettled the amount demanded.

(b) The corporation shall commence the proceeding in the [name or describe] court of the county where a corporation's principal office (or, if none in this state, its registered office) is located. If the corporation is a foreign corporation without a registered office in this state, it shall commence the proceeding in the county in this state where the registered office of the domestic corporation merged with or whose shares were acquired by the foreign corporation was located.

(c) The corporation shall make all dissenters (whether or not residents of this state) whose demands remain unsettled parties to the proceeding as in an action against their shares and all parties must be served with a copy of the petition. Nonresidents may be served by registered or certified mail or by publication as provided by law.

(d) The jurisdiction of the court in which the proceeding is commenced under subsection (b) is plenary and exclusive. The court may appoint one or more persons as appraisers to receive evidence and recommend decision on the question of fair value. The appraisers have the powers described in the order appointing them, or in any amendment to it. The dissenters are entitled to the same discovery rights as parties in other civil proceedings.

(e) Each dissenter made a party to the proceeding is entitled to judgment (1) for the amount, if any, by which the court finds the fair value of his shares, plus interest, exceeds the amount paid by the corporation or (2) for the fair value, plus accrued interest, of his after-acquired shares for which the corporation elected to withhold payment under section 13.27.

§ 13.31 Court Costs and Counsel Fees

(a) The court in an appraisal proceeding commenced under section 13.30 shall determine all costs of the proceeding, including the reasonable compensation and expenses of appraisers appointed by the court. The court shall assess the costs against the corporation, except that the court may assess costs against all or some of the dissenters, in amounts the court finds equitable, to the extent the court finds dissenters acted arbitrarily, vexatiously, or not in good faith in demanding payment under section 13.28.

(b) The court may also assess the fees and expenses of counsel and experts for the respective parties, in amounts the court finds equitable:

(1) against the corporation and in favor of any or all dissenters if the court finds the corporation did not substantially comply with the requirements of sections 13.20 through 13.28; or

(2) against either the corporation or a dissenter, in favor of any other party, if the court finds that the party against whom the fees and expenses are assessed acted arbitrarily, vexatiously, or not in good faith with respect to the rights provided by this chapter.

(c) If the court finds that the services of counsel for any dissenter were of substantial benefit to other dissenters similarly situated, and that the fees for those services should not be assessed against the corporation, the court may award to these counsel reasonable fees to be paid out of the amounts awarded the dissenters who were benefited.

C. MODEL STATUTORY CLOSE CORPORATION SUPPLEMENT

SUBCHAPTER A. CREATION

SUBCHAPTER B. SHARES

SUBCHAPTER C. GOVERNANCE

SUBCHAPTER D. REORGANIZATION AND TERMINATION

SUBCHAPTER E. JUDICIAL SUPERVISION

SUBCHAPTER F. TRANSITION PROVISIONS

SUBCHAPTER A. CREATION

§ 1. Short Title

This Supplement shall be known and may be cited as the "[name of state] Statutory Close Corporation Supplement."

§ 2. Application of [Model] Business Corporation Act and [Model] Professional Corporation Supplement

(a) The [Model] Business Corporation Act applies to statutory close corporations to the extent not inconsistent with the provisions of this Supplement.

(b) This Supplement applies to a professional corporation organized under the [Model] Professional Corporation Supplement whose articles of incorporation contain the statement required by section 3(a), except insofar as the [Model] Professional Corporation Supplement contains inconsistent provisions.

(c) This Supplement does not repeal or modify any statute or rule of law that is or would apply to a corporation that is organized under the [Model] Business Corporation Act or the [Model] Professional Corporation Supplement and that does not elect to become a statutory close corporation under section 3.

§ 3. Definition and Election of Statutory Close Corporation Status

(a) A statutory close corporation is a corporation whose articles of incorporation contain a statement that the corporation is a statutory close corporation.

(b) A corporation having 50 or fewer shareholders may become a statutory close corporation by amending its articles of incorporation to include the statement required by subsection (a). The amendment must be approved by the holders of at least two-thirds of the votes of each class or series of shares of the corporation, voting as separate voting groups, whether or not otherwise entitled to vote on amendments. If the amendment is adopted, a shareholder who voted against the amendment is entitled to assert dissenters' rights under [MBCA ch. 13].

SUBCHAPTER B. SHARES

§ 10. Notice of Statutory Close Corporation Status on Issued Shares

(a) The following statement must appear conspicuously on each share certificate issued by a statutory close corporation:

> The rights of shareholders in a statutory close corporation may differ materially from the rights of shareholders in other corporations. Copies of the articles of incorporation and bylaws, shareholders' agreements, and other documents, any of which may restrict transfers and affect voting and other rights, may be obtained by a shareholder on written request to the corporation.

(b) Within a reasonable time after the issuance or transfer of uncertificated shares, the corporation shall send to the shareholders a written notice containing the information required by subsection (a).

(c) The notice required by this section satisfies all requirements of this Act and of [MBCA § 6.27] that notice of share transfer restrictions be given.

(d) A person claiming an interest in shares of a statutory close corporation which has complied with the notice requirement of this section is bound by the documents referred to in the notice. A person claiming an interest in shares of a statutory close corporation which has not complied with the notice requirement of this section is bound by any documents of which he, or a person through whom he claims, has knowledge or notice.

(e) A corporation shall provide to any shareholder upon his written request and without charge copies of provisions that restrict transfer or affect voting or other rights of shareholders appearing in articles of incorporation, bylaws, or shareholders' or voting trust agreements filed with the corporation.

§ 11. Share Transfer Prohibition

(a) An interest in shares of a statutory close corporation may not be voluntarily or involuntarily transferred, by operation of law or otherwise, except to the extent permitted by the articles of incorporation or under section 12.

(b) Except to the extent the articles of incorporation provide otherwise, this section does not apply to a transfer:

(1) to the corporation or to any other holder of the same class or series of shares;

(2) to members of the shareholder's immediate family (or to a trust, all of whose beneficiaries are members of the shareholder's immediate family), which immediate family consists of his spouse, parents, lineal descendants (including adopted children and stepchildren) and the spouse of any lineal descendant, and brothers and sisters;

(3) that has been approved in writing by all of the holders of the corporation's shares having general voting rights;

(4) to an executor or administrator upon the death of a shareholder or to a trustee or receiver as the result of a bankruptcy, insolvency, dissolution, or similar proceeding brought by or against a shareholder;

(5) by merger or share exchange [under MBCA ch. II] or an exchange of existing shares for other shares of a different class or series in the corporation;

(6) by a pledge as collateral for a loan that does not grant the pledgee any voting rights possessed by the pledgor;

(7) made after termination of the corporation's status as a statutory close corporation.

§ 12. Share Transfer After First Refusal by Corporation

(a) A person desiring to transfer shares of a statutory close corporation subject to the transfer prohibition of section II must first offer them to the corporation by obtaining an offer to purchase the shares for cash from a third person who is eligible to purchase the shares under subsection (b). The offer by the third person must be in writing and state the offeror's name and address, the number and class (or series) of shares offered, the offering price per share, and the other terms of the offer.

(b) A third person is eligible to purchase the shares if:

(1) he is eligible to become a qualified shareholder under any federal or state tax statute the corporation has adopted and he agrees in writing not to terminate his qualification without the approval of the remaining shareholders; and

(2) his purchase of the shares will not impose a personal holding company tax or similar federal or state penalty tax on the corporation.

(c) The person desiring to transfer shares shall deliver the offer to the corporation, and by doing so offers to sell the shares to the corporation on the terms of the offer. Within 20 days after the corporation receives the offer, the corporation shall call a special shareholders' meeting, to be held not more than 40 days after the call, to decide whether the corporation should purchase all (but not less than all) of the offered shares. The offer must be approved by the affirmative vote of the holders of a majority of votes entitled to be cast at the meeting, excluding votes in respect of the shares covered by the offer.

(d) The corporation must deliver to the offering shareholder written notice of acceptance within 75 days after receiving the offer or the offer is rejected. If the corporation makes a counteroffer, the shareholder must deliver to the corporation written notice of acceptance within 15 days after receiving the counteroffer or the counteroffer is rejected. If the corporation accepts the original offer or the shareholder accepts the corporation's counteroffer, the shareholder shall deliver to the corporation duly endorsed certificates for the shares, or instruct the corporation in writing to transfer the shares if uncertificated, within 20 days after the effective date of the notice of acceptance. The corporation may specifically enforce the shareholder's delivery or instruction obligation under this subsection.

(e) A corporation accepting an offer to purchase shares under this section may allocate some or all of the shares to one or more of its shareholders or to other persons if all the shareholders voting in favor of the purchase approve the allocation. If the corporation has more than one class (or series) of shares, however, the remaining holders of the class (or series) of shares being purchased are entitled to a first option to purchase the shares not purchased by the corporation in proportion to their shareholdings or in some other proportion agreed to by all the shareholders participating in the purchase.

(f) If an offer to purchase shares under this section is rejected, the offering shareholder, for a period of 120 days after the corporation received his offer, is entitled to transfer to the third person offeror all (but not less than all) of the offered shares in accordance with the terms of his offer to the corporation.

§ 13. Attempted Share Transfer in Breach of Prohibition

(a) An attempt to transfer shares in a statutory close corporation in violation of a prohibition against transfer binding on the transferee is ineffective.

(b) An attempt to transfer shares in a statutory close corporation in violation of a prohibition against transfer that is not binding on the transferee, either because the notice required by section 10 was not given or because the prohibition is held unenforceable by a court, gives the corporation an option to purchase the shares from the transferee for the same price and on the same terms that he purchased them. To exercise its option, the corporation must give the transferee written notice within 30 days after they are presented for registration in the transferee's name. The corporation may specifically enforce the transferee's sale obligation upon exercise of its purchase option.

§ 14. Compulsory Purchase of Shares After Death of Shareholder

(a) This section, and sections 15 through 17, apply to a statutory close corporation only if so provided in its articles of incorporation. If these sections apply, the executor or administrator of the estate of a deceased shareholder may require the corporation to purchase or cause to be purchased all (but not less than all) of the decedent's shares or to be dissolved.

(b) The provisions of sections 15 through 17 may be modified only if the modification is set forth or referred to in the articles of incorporation.

(c) An amendment to the articles of incorporation to provide for application of sections 15 through 17, or to modify or delete the provisions of these sections, must be approved by the holders of at least two-thirds of the votes of each class or series of shares of the statutory close corporation, voting as separate voting groups, whether or not otherwise entitled to vote on amendments. If the corporation has no shareholders when the amendment is proposed, it must be approved by at least two-thirds of the subscribers for shares, if any, or, if none, by all of the incorporators.

(d) A shareholder who votes against an amendment to modify or delete the provisions of sections 15 through 17 is entitled to dissenters' rights under [MBCA chapter 13] if the amendment upon adoption terminates or substantially alters his existing rights under these sections to have his shares purchased.

(e) A shareholder may waive his and his estate's rights under sections 15 through 17 by a signed writing.

(f) Sections 15 through 17 do not prohibit any other agreement providing for the purchase of shares upon a shareholder's death, nor do they prevent a shareholder from enforcing any remedy he has independently of these sections.

§ 15. Exercise of Compulsory Purchase Right

(a) A person entitled and desiring to exercise the compulsory purchase right described in section 14 must deliver a written notice to the corporation, within 120 days after the death of the shareholder, describing the number and class or series of shares beneficially owned by the decedent and requesting that the corporation offer to purchase the shares.

(b) Within 20 days after the effective date of the notice, the corporation shall call a special shareholders' meeting, to be held not more than 40 days after the call, to decide whether the corporation should offer to purchase the shares. A purchase offer must be approved by the affirmative vote of the holders of a majority of votes entitled to be cast at the meeting, excluding votes in respect of the shares covered by the notice.

(c) The corporation must deliver a purchase offer to the person requesting it within 75 days after the effective date of the request notice. A purchase offer must be accompanied by the corporation's balance sheet as of the end of a fiscal year ending not more than 16 months before the effective date of the request notice, an income statement for that year, a statement of changes in shareholders' equity for that year, and the latest available interim financial statements, if any. The person must accept the purchase offer in writing within 15 days after receiving it or the offer is rejected.

(d) A corporation agreeing to purchase shares under this section may allocate some or all of the shares to one or more of its shareholders or to other persons if all the shareholders voting in favor of the purchase offer approve the allocation. If the corporation has more than one class or series of shares, however, the remaining holders of the class or series of shares being purchased are entitled to a first option to purchase the shares not purchased by the corporation in proportion to their shareholdings or in some other proportion agreed to by all the shareholders participating in the purchase.

(e) If price and other terms of a compulsory purchase of shares are fixed or are to be determined by the articles of incorporation, bylaws, or a written agreement, the price and terms so fixed or determined govern the compulsory purchase unless the purchaser defaults, in which event the buyer is entitled to commence a proceeding for dissolution under section 16.

§ 16. Court Action to Compel Purchase

(a) If an offer to purchase shares made under section 15 is rejected, or if no offer is made, the person exercising the compulsory purchase right may commence a proceeding against the corporation to compel the purchase in the [name or describe] court of the county where the corporation's principal office (or, if none in this state, its registered office) is located. The corporation at its expense shall notify in writing all of its shareholders, and any other person the court directs, of the commencement of the proceeding. The jurisdiction of the court in which the proceeding is commenced under this subsection is plenary and exclusive.

(b) The court shall determine the fair value of the shares subject to compulsory purchase in accordance with the standards set forth in section 42 together with terms for the purchase. Upon making these determinations the court shall order the corporation to purchase or cause the purchase of the shares or empower the person exercising the compulsory purchase right to have the corporation dissolved.

(c) After the purchase order is entered, the corporation may petition the court to modify the terms of purchase and the court may do so if it finds that changes in the financial or legal ability of the corporation or other purchaser to complete the purchase justify a modification.

(d) If the corporation or other purchaser does not make a payment required by the court's order within 30 days of its due date, the seller may petition the court to dissolve the corporation and, absent a showing of good cause for not making the payment, the court shall do so.

(e) A person making a payment to prevent or cure a default by the corporation or other purchaser is entitled to recover the payment from the defaulter.

§ 17. Court Costs and Other Expenses

(a) The court in a proceeding commenced under section 16 shall determine the total costs of the proceeding, including the reasonable compensation and expenses of appraisers appointed by the court and of counsel and experts employed by the parties. Except as provided in subsection (b), the court shall assess these costs equally against the corporation and the party exercising the compulsory purchase right.

(b) The court may assess all or a portion of the total costs of the proceeding:

(1) against the person exercising the compulsory purchase right if the court finds that the fair value of the shares does not substantially exceed the corporation's last purchase offer made before commencement of the proceeding and that the person's failure to accept the offer was arbitrary, vexatious, or otherwise not in good faith; or

(2) against the corporation if the court finds that the fair value of the shares substantially exceeds the corporation's last sale offer made before commencement of the proceeding and that the offer was arbitrary, vexatious, or otherwise not made in good faith.

SUBCHAPTER C. GOVERNANCE

§ 20. Shareholder Agreements

(a) All the shareholders of a statutory close corporation may agree in writing to regulate the exercise of the corporate powers and the management of the business and affairs of the corporation or the relationship among the shareholders of the corporation.

(b) An agreement authorized by this section is effective although:

(1) it eliminates a board of directors;

(2) it restricts the discretion or powers of the board or authorizes director proxies or weighted voting rights;

(3) its effect is to treat the corporation as a partnership; or

(4) it creates a relationship among the shareholders or between the shareholders and the corporation that would otherwise be appropriate only among partners.

(c) If the corporation has a board of directors, an agreement authorized by this section restricting the discretion or powers of the board relieves directors of liability imposed by law, and imposes that liability on each person in whom the board's discretion or power is vested, to the extent that the discretion or powers of the board of directors are governed by the agreement.

(d) A provision eliminating a board of directors in an agreement authorized by this section is not effective unless the articles of incorporation contain a statement to that effect as required by section 21.

(e) A provision entitling one or more shareholders to dissolve the corporation under section 33 is effective only if a statement of this right is contained in the articles of incorporation.

(f) To amend an agreement authorized by this section, all the shareholders must approve the amendment in writing unless the agreement provides otherwise.

(g) Subscribers for shares may act as shareholders with respect to an agreement authorized by this section if shares are not issued when the agreement was made.

(h) This section does not prohibit any other agreement between or among shareholders in a statutory close corporation.

§ 21. Elimination of Board of Directors

(a) A statutory close corporation may operate without a board of directors if its articles of incorporation contain a statement to that effect.

(b) An amendment to articles of incorporation eliminating a board of directors must be approved by all the shareholders of the corporation, whether or not otherwise entitled to vote on amendments, or if no shares have been issued, by all the subscribers for shares, if any, or if none, by all the incorporators.

(c) While a corporation is operating without a board of directors as authorized by subsection (a):

(1) all corporate powers shall be exercised by or under the authority of, and the business and affairs of the corporation managed under the direction of, the shareholders;

(2) unless the articles of incorporation provide otherwise, (i) action requiring director approval or both director and shareholder approval is authorized if approved by the shareholders and (ii) action requiring a majority or greater percentage vote of the board of directors is authorized if approved by the majority or greater

percentage of the votes of shareholders entitled to vote on the action;

(3) a shareholder is not liable for his act or omission, although a director would be, unless the shareholder was entitled to vote on the action;

(4) a requirement by a state or the United States that a document delivered for filing contain a statement that specified action has been taken by the board of directors is satisfied by a statement that the corporation is a statutory close corporation without a board of directors and that the action was approved by the shareholders;

(5) the shareholders by resolution may appoint one or more shareholders to sign documents as "designated directors."

(d) An amendment to articles of incorporation deleting the statement eliminating a board of directors must be approved by the holders of at least two-thirds of the votes of each class or series of shares of the corporation, voting as separate voting groups, whether or not otherwise entitled to vote on amendments. The amendment must also specify the number, names, and addresses of the corporation's directors or describe who will perform the duties of a board under [MBCA § 8.01].

§ 22. Bylaws

(a) A statutory close corporation need not adopt bylaws if provisions required by law to be contained in bylaws are contained in either the articles of incorporation or a shareholder agreement authorized by section 20.

(b) If a corporation does not have bylaws when its statutory close corporation status terminates under section 31, the corporation shall immediately adopt bylaws under [MBCA § 2.06].

§ 23. Annual Meeting

(a) The annual meeting date for a statutory close corporation is the first business day after May 31st unless its articles of incorporation, bylaws, or a shareholder agreement authorized by section 20 fixes a different date.

(b) A statutory close corporation need not hold an annual meeting unless one or more shareholders deliver written notice to the corporation requesting a meeting at least 30 days before the meeting date determined under subsection (a).

§ 24. Execution of Documents in More Than One Capacity

Notwithstanding any law to the contrary, an individual who holds more than one office in a statutory close corporation may execute, acknowledge, or verify in more than one capacity any document required to be executed, acknowledged, or verified by the holders of two or more offices.

§ 25. Limited Liability

The failure of a statutory close corporation to observe the usual corporate formalities or requirements relating to the exercise of its corporate powers or management of its business and affairs is not a ground for imposing personal liability on the shareholders for liabilities of the corporation.

SUBCHAPTER D. REORGANIZATION AND TERMINATION

§ 30. Merger, Share Exchange, and Sale of Assets

(a) A plan of merger or share exchange:

(1) that if effected would terminate statutory close corporation status must be approved by the holders of at least two-thirds of the votes of each class or series of shares of the statutory close corporation, voting as separate voting groups, whether or not the holders are otherwise entitled to vote on the plan;

(2) that if effected would create the surviving corporation as a statutory close corporation must be approved by the holders of at least two-thirds of the votes of each class or series of shares of the surviving corporation, voting as separate voting groups, whether or not the holders are otherwise entitled to vote on the plan.

(b) A sale, lease, exchange, or other disposition of all or substantially all of the property (with or without the good will) of a statutory close corporation, if not made in the usual and regular course of business, must be approved by the holders of at least two-thirds of the votes of each class or series of shares of the corporation, voting as separate voting groups, whether or not the holders are otherwise entitled to vote on the transaction.

§ 31. Termination of Statutory Close Corporation Status

(a) A statutory close corporation may terminate its statutory close corporation status by amending its articles of incorporation to delete the statement that it is a statutory close corporation. If the statutory close corporation has elected to operate without a board of directors under section 21, the amendment must either comply with [MBCA § 8.01] or delete the statement dispensing with the board of directors from its articles of incorporation.

(b) An amendment terminating statutory close corporation status must be approved by the holders of at least two-thirds of the votes of each class or series of shares of the corporation, voting as separate voting groups, whether or not the holders are otherwise entitled to vote on amendments.

(c) If an amendment to terminate statutory close corporation status is adopted, each shareholder who voted against the amendment is entitled to assert dissenters' rights under [MBCA ch. 13].

§ 32. Effect of Termination of Statutory Close Corporation Status

(a) A corporation that terminates its status as a statutory close corporation is thereafter subject to all provisions of the [Model] Business Corporation Act or, if incorporated under the [Model] Professional Corporation Supplement, to all provisions of that Supplement.

(b) Termination of statutory close corporation status does not affect any right of a shareholder or of the corporation under an agreement or the articles of incorporation unless this Act, the [Model] Business Corporation Act, or another law of this state invalidates the right.

§ 33. Shareholder Option to Dissolve Corporation

(a) The articles of incorporation of a statutory close corporation may authorize one or more shareholders, or the holders of a specified number or percentage of shares of any class or series, to dissolve the corporation at will or upon the occurrence of a specified event or contingency. The shareholder or shareholders exercising this authority must give written notice of the intent to dissolve to all the other shareholders. Thirty-one days after the effective date of the notice, the corporation shall begin to wind up and liquidate its business and affairs and file articles of dissolution under [MBCA sections 14.03 through 14.07].

(b) Unless the articles of incorporation provide otherwise, an amendment to the articles of incorporation to add, change, or delete the authority to dissolve described in subsection (a) must be approved by the holders of all the outstanding shares, whether or not otherwise entitled to vote on amendments, or if no shares have been issued, by all the subscribers for shares, if any, or if none, by all the incorporators.

SUBCHAPTER E. JUDICIAL SUPERVISION

§ 40. Court Action to Protect Shareholders

(a) Subject to satisfying the conditions of subsections (c) and (d), a shareholder of a statutory close corporation may petition the [name or describe] court for any of the relief described in section 41, 42, or 43 if:

(1) the directors or those in control of the corporation have acted, are acting, or will act in a manner that is illegal, oppressive, fraudulent, or unfairly prejudicial to the petition, whether in his capacity as shareholder, director, or officer, of the corporation;

(2) the directors or those in control of the corporation are deadlocked in the management of the corporation's affairs, the shareholders are unable to break the deadlock, and the corporation is suffering or will suffer irreparable injury or the business and affairs of the corporation can no longer be conducted to the advantage of the shareholders generally because of the deadlock; or

(3) there exists one or more grounds for judicial dissolution of the corporation under [MBCA § 14.30].

(b) A shareholder must commence a proceeding under subsection (a) in the [name or describe] court of the county where the corporation's principal office (or, if none in this state, its registered office) is located. The jurisdiction of the court in which the proceeding is commenced is plenary and exclusive.

(c) If a shareholder has agreed in writing to pursue a nonjudicial remedy to resolve disputed matters, he may not commence a proceeding under this section with respect to the matters until he has exhausted the nonjudicial remedy.

(d) If a shareholder has dissenters' rights under this Act or [MBCA ch. 13] with respect to proposed corporate action, he must commence a proceeding under this section before he is required to give notice of his intent to demand payment under [MBCA § 13.21] or to demand payment under [MBCA § 13.23] or the proceeding is barred.

(e) Except as provided in subsections (c) and (d), a shareholder's right to commence a proceeding under this section and the remedies available under sections 41 through 43 are in addition to any other right or remedy he may have.

§ 41. Ordinary Relief

(a) If the court finds that one or more of the grounds for relief described in section 40(a) exist, it may order one or more of the following types of relief:

(1) the performance, prohibition, alteration, or setting aside of any action of the corporation or of its shareholders, directors, or officers of or any other party to the proceeding;

(2) the cancellation or alteration of any provision in the corporation's articles of incorporation or bylaws;

(3) the removal from office of any director or officer;

(4) the appointment of any individual as a director or officer;

(5) an accounting with respect to any matter in dispute;

(6) the appointment of a custodian to manage the business and affairs of the corporation;

(7) the appointment of a provisional director (who has all the rights, powers, and duties of a duly elected director) to serve for the term and under the conditions prescribed by the court;

(8) the payment of dividends;

(9) the award of damages to any aggrieved party.

(b) If the court finds that a party to the proceeding acted arbitrarily, vexatiously, or otherwise not in good faith, it may award one or more other parties their reasonable expenses, including counsel fees and the expenses of appraisers or other experts, incurred in the proceeding.

§ 42. Extraordinary Relief: Share Purchase

(a) If the court finds that the ordinary relief described in section 41(a) is or would be inadequate or inappropriate, it may order the corporation dissolved under section 43 unless the corporation or one or more of its shareholders purchases all the shares of the shareholder for their fair value and on terms determined under subsection (b).

(b) If the court orders a share purchase, it shall:

(1) determine the fair value of the shares, considering among other relevant evidence the going concern value of the corporation, any agreement among some or all of the shareholders fixing the price or specifying a formula for determining share value for any purpose, the recommendations of appraisers (if any) appointed by the court, and any legal constraints on the corporation's ability to purchase the shares;

(2) specify the terms of the purchase, including if appropriate terms for installment payments, subordination of the purchase obligation to the rights of the corporation's other creditors, security for a deferred purchase price, and a covenant not to compete or other restriction on the seller;

(3) require the seller to deliver all his shares to the purchaser upon receipt of the purchase price or the first installment of the purchase price;

(4) provide that after the seller delivers his shares he has no further claim against the corporation, its directors, officers, or shareholders, other than a claim to any unpaid balance of the purchase price and a claim under any agreement with the corporation or the remaining shareholders that is not terminated by the court; and

(5) provide that if the purchase is not completed in accordance with the specified terms, the corporation is to be dissolved under section 43.

(c) After the purchase order is entered, any party may petition the court to modify the terms of the purchase and the court may do so if it finds that changes in the financial or legal ability of the corporation or other purchaser to complete the purchase justify a modification.

(d) If the corporation is dissolved because the share purchase was not completed in accordance with the court's order, the selling shareholder has the same rights and priorities in the corporation's assets as if the sale had not been ordered.

§ 43. Extraordinary Relief: Dissolution

(a) The court may dissolve the corporation if it finds:

(1) there are one or more grounds for judicial dissolution under [MBCA § 14.30]; or

(2) all other relief ordered by the court under section 41 or 42 has failed to resolve the matters in dispute.

(b) In determining whether to dissolve the corporation, the court shall consider among other relevant evidence the financial condition of the corporation but may not refuse to dissolve solely because the corporation has accumulated earnings or current operating profits.

SUBCHAPTER F. TRANSITION PROVISIONS

§ 50. Application to Existing Corporations

(a) This Supplement applies to all corporations electing statutory close corporation status under section 3 after its effective date.

(B) [If Sec. 54 repeals an integrated close corporation statute enacted before this Supplement, this and additional subsections should provide a cutoff date by which corporations qualified under the repealed statute must elect whether to be covered by this Supplement, the procedure for making the election, and the effect of the election on existing agreements among shareholders. Cf. MBCA ch. 17 and Model Professional Corporation Supplement sec. 70.]

§ 51. Reservation of Power to Amend or Repeal

The [name of state legislature] has power to amend or repeal all or part of this Supplement at any time and all corporations subject to this Supplement are governed by the amendment or repeal.

§ 52. Saving Provisions

(a) The repeal of a statute by this Supplement does not affect:

(1) the operation of the statute or any action taken under it before its repeal;

(2) any ratification, right, remedy, privilege, obligation, or liability acquired, accrued, or incurred under the statute before its repeal;

(3) any violation of the statute, or any penalty, forfeiture, or punishment incurred because of the violation, before its repeal;

(4) any proceeding, reorganization, or dissolution commenced under the statute before its repeal, and the proceeding, reorganization, or dissolution may be completed in accordance with the statute as if it had not been repealed.

§ 53. Severability

If any provision of this Supplement or its application to any person or circumstance is held invalid by a court of competent jurisdiction, the invalidity does not affect other provisions or applications of the Supplement that can be given effect without the invalid provision or application, and to this end the provisions of the Supplement are severable.

§ 54. Repeal

The following laws and parts of laws are repealed: ______.

§ 55. Effective Date

This Supplement takes effect ______.

D. CALIFORNIA GENERAL CORPORATION LAW

(Selected Sections)

Contents

CHAPTER 1. GENERAL PROVISIONS AND DEFINITIONS

CHAPTER 2. ORGANIZATION AND BYLAWS

CHAPTER 3. DIRECTORS AND MANAGEMENT

CHAPTER 8. SHAREHOLDER DERIVATIVE ACTIONS

CHAPTER 10. SALES OF ASSETS

CHAPTER 11. MERGER

CHAPTER 12. REORGANIZATIONS

CHAPTER 13. DISSENTERS' RIGHTS

CHAPTER 19. VOLUNTARY DISSOLUTION

CHAPTER 21. FOREIGN CORPORATIONS

CHAPTER 1. GENERAL PROVISIONS AND DEFINITIONS

§ 114. Financial Statements and Accounting Items

All references in this division to financial statements, balance sheets, income statements and statements of changes in financial position of a corporation and all references to assets, liabilities, earnings, retained earnings and similar accounting items of a corporation mean such financial statements or such items prepared or determined in conformity with generally accepted accounting principles then applicable, fairly presenting in conformity with generally accepted accounting principles the matters which they purport to present, subject to any specific accounting treatment required by a particular section of this division. Unless otherwise expressly stated, all references in this division to such financial statements mean, in the case of a corporation which has subsidiaries, consolidated statements of the corporation and such of its subsidiaries as are required to be included in such consolidated statements under generally accepted accounting principles then applicable and all references to such accounting items mean such items determined on a consolidated basis in accordance with such consolidated financial statements. Financial statements other than annual statements may be condensed or otherwise presented as permitted by authoritative accounting pronouncements.

§ 158. Close Corporation

(a) "Close corporation" means a corporation whose articles contain, in addition to the provisions required by Section 202, a provision that all of the corporation's issued shares of all classes shall be held of record by not more than a specified number of persons, not exceeding 35, and a statement "This corporation is a close corporation."

(b) The special provisions referred to in subdivision (a) may be included in the articles by amendment, but if such amendment is adopted after the issuance of shares only by the affirmative vote of all of the issued and outstanding shares of all classes.

(c) The special provisions referred to in subdivision (a) may be deleted from the articles by amendment, or the number of shareholders specified may be changed by amendment, but if such amendment is adopted after the issuance of shares only by the affirmative vote of at least two-thirds of each class of the outstanding shares; provided, however, that the articles may provide for a lesser vote, but not less than a majority of the outstanding shares, or may deny a vote to any class, or both.

(d) In determining the number of shareholders for the purposes of the provision in the articles authorized by this section, a husband and wife and the personal representative of either shall be counted as one regardless of how shares may be held by either or both of them, a trust or personal representative of a decedent holding shares shall be counted as one regardless of the number of trustees or beneficiaries and a partnership or corporation or business association holding shares shall be counted as one (except that any such trust or entity the primary purpose of which was the acquisition or voting of the shares shall be counted according to the number of beneficial interests therein).

(e) A corporation shall cease to be a close corporation upon the filing of an amendment to its articles pursuant to subdivision (c) or if it shall have more than the maximum number of holders of record of its shares specified in its articles as a result of an inter vivos transfer of shares which is not void under subdivision (d) of Section 418, the transfer of shares on distribution by will or pursuant to the laws of descent and distribution, the dissolution of a partnership or corporation or business association or the termination of a trust which holds shares, by court decree upon dissolution of a marriage or otherwise by operation of law. Promptly upon acquiring more than the specified number of holders of record of its shares, a close corporation shall execute and file an amendment to its articles deleting the special provisions referred to in subdivision (a) and deleting any other provisions not permissible for a corporation which is not a close corporation, which amendment shall be promptly approved and filed by the board and need not be approved by the outstanding shares.

(f) Nothing contained in this section shall invalidate any agreement among the shareholders to vote for the deletion from the articles of the special provisions referred to in subdivision (a) upon the lapse of a specified period of time or upon the occurrence of a certain event or condition or otherwise.

(g) The following sections contain specific references to close corporations: 186, 202, 204, 300, 418, 421, 1111, 1201, 1800 and 1904.

§ 160. Control

(a) Except as provided in subdivision (b), "control" means the possession, direct or indirect, of the power to direct or cause the direction of the management and policies of a corporation.

(b) "Control" in Sections 181, 1001 and 1200 means the ownership directly or indirectly of shares or equity securities possessing more than 50 percent of the voting power of a domestic corporation, a foreign corporation, or any other business entity.

§ 163.1 Cumulative Dividends in Arrears

"cumulative dividends in arrears" means only cumulative dividends that have not been paid as required on a scheduled payment date set forth in, or determined pursuant to, the articles of incorporation, regardless of whether those dividends had been declared prior to that scheduled payment date.

§ 166. Distribution to Its Shareholders

"Distribution to its shareholders" means the transfer of cash or property by a corporation to its shareholders without consideration, whether by way of dividend or otherwise, except a dividend in shares of the corporation, or the purchase or redemption of its shares for cash or property, including the transfer, purchase, or redemption by a subsidiary of the corporation. The time of any distribution by way of dividend shall be the date of declaration thereof and the time of any distribution by purchase or redemption of shares shall be the date cash or property is transferred by the corporation, whether or not pursuant to a contract of an earlier date; provided, that where a debt obligation that is a security (as defined in subdivision (1) of Section 8102 of the Commercial Code) is issued in exchange for shares the time of the distribution is the date when the corporation acquires the shares in the exchange. In the case of a sinking fund payment, cash or property is transferred within the meaning of this section at the time that it is delivered to a trustee for the holders of preferred shares to be used for the redemption of the shares or physically segregated by the corporation in trust for that purpose. "Distribution to its shareholders" shall not include (a) satisfaction of a final judgment of a court or tribunal of appropriate jurisdiction ordering the rescission of the issuance of shares, (b) the rescission by a corporation of the issuance of its shares, if the board determines (with any director who is, or would be, a party to the transaction not being entitled to vote) that (1) it is reasonably likely that the holder or holders of the shares in question could legally enforce a claim for the rescission, (2) that the rescission is in the best interests of the corporation, and (3) the corporation is likely to be able to meet its liabilities (except those for which payment is otherwise adequately provided) as they mature, or (c) the repurchase by a corporation of its shares issued by it pursuant to Section 408, if the board determines (with any director who is, or would be, a party to the transaction not being entitled to vote) that (1) the repurchase is in the best interests of the corporation and that (2) the corporation is likely to be able to meet its liabilities (except those for which payment is otherwise adequately provided) as they mature.

§ 172. Liquidation Price; Liquidation Preference

"Liquidation price" or "liquidation preference" means amounts payable on shares of any class upon voluntary or involuntary dissolution, winding up or distribution of the entire assets of the corporation, including any cumulative dividends accrued and unpaid, in priority to shares of another class or classes.

§ 178. Proxy

"Proxy" means a written authorization signed or an electronic transmission authorized by a shareholder or the shareholder's attorney in fact giving another person or persons power to vote with respect to the shares of such shareholder. "Signed" for the purpose of this section means the placing of the shareholder's name or other authorization on the proxy (whether by manual signature, typewriting, telegraphic, or electronic transmission or otherwise) by the shareholder or the shareholder's attorney in fact.

A proxy may be transmitted by an oral telephonic transmission if it is submitted with information from which it may be determined that the proxy was authorized by the shareholder, or his or her attorney in fact.

§ 181. Reorganization

"Reorganization" means:

(a) A merger pursuant to Chapter 11 (commencing with Section 1100) other than a short-form merger (a "merger reorganization");

(b) The acquisition by one corporation, or other business entity in exchange, in whole or in part, for its equity securities (or the equity securities of a domestic corporation, a foreign corporation, or an other business entity which is in control of the acquiring entity) of equity securities of another domestic corporation, foreign corporation, or other business entity if, immediately after the acquisition, the acquiring entity has control of the other entity (an "exchange reorganization").

(c) The acquisition by one domestic corporation, foreign corporation, or other business entity in exchange in whole or in part for its equity securities (or the equity securities of a domestic corporation, a foreign corporation, or an other business entity which is in control of the acquiring entity) or for its debt securities (or debt securities of a domestic corporation, foreign corporation, or other business entity which is in control of the acquiring entity) which are not adequately secured and which have a maturity date in excess of five years after the consummation of the reorganization, or both, of all or substantially all of the assets of another domestic corporation, foreign corporation, or other business entity (a "sale-of-assets reorganization").

§ 183.5 Share Exchange Tender Offer

"Share exchange tender offer" means any acquisition by one corporation in exchange in whole or in part for its equity securities (or the equity securities of a corporation which is in control of the acquiring corporation) or of shareholders of another corporation, other than an exchange reorganization (subdivision (b) of Section 181).

§ 186. Shareholders' Agreement

"Shareholders' agreement" means a written agreement among all of the shareholders of a close corporation, or if a close corporation has only one shareholder between such shareholder and the corporation, as authorized by subdivision (b) of Section 300.

§ 194. Vote

"Vote" includes authorization by written consent, subject to the provisions of subdivision (b) of Section 307 and subdivision (d) of Section 603.

§ 194.5 Voting Power

"Voting power" means the power to vote for the election of directors at the time any determination of voting power is made and does not include the right to vote upon the happening of some condition or event which has not yet occurred. In any case where different classes of shares are entitled to vote as separate classes for different members of the board, the determination of percentage of voting power shall be made on the basis of the percentage of the total number of authorized directors which the shares in question (whether of one or more classes) have the power to elect in an election at which all shares then entitled to vote for the election of any directors are voted.

§ 194.7 Voting Shift

"Voting shift" means a change, pursuant to or by operation of a provision of the articles, in the relative rights of the holders of one or more classes or series of shares, voting as one or more separate classes or series, to elect one or more directors.

CHAPTER 2. ORGANIZATION AND BYLAWS

§ 204. Articles of Incorporation; Optional Provisions

The articles of incorporation may set forth:

(a) Any or all of the following provisions, which shall not be effective unless expressly provided in the articles:

(1) Granting, with or without limitations, the power to levy assessments upon the shares or any class of shares;

(2) Granting to shareholders preemptive rights to subscribe to any or all issues of shares or securities;

(3) Special qualifications of persons who may be shareholders;

(4) A provision limiting the duration of the corporation's existence to a specified date;

(5) A provision requiring, for any or all corporate actions (except as provided in Section 303, subdivision (b) of Section 402.5, subdivision (c) of Section 708 and Section 1900) the vote of a larger proportion or of all of the shares of any class or series, or the vote or quorum for taking action of a larger proportion or of all of the directors, than is otherwise required by this division;

(6) A provision limiting or restricting the business in which the corporation may engage or the powers which the corporation may exercise or both;

(7) A provision conferring upon the holders of any evidences of indebtedness, issued or to be issued by the corporation, the right to vote in the election of directors and on any other matters on which shareholders may vote;

(8) A provision conferring upon shareholders the right to determine the consideration for which shares shall be issued.

(9) A provision requiring the approval of the shareholders (Section 153) or the approval of the outstanding shares (Section 152) for any corporate action, even though not otherwise required by this division.

(10) Provisions eliminating or limiting the personal liability of a director for monetary damages in an action brought by or in the right of the corporation for breach of a director's duties to the corporation and its shareholders, as set forth in Section 309, provided, however, that (A) such a provision may not eliminate or limit the liability of directors (i) for acts or omissions that involve intentional misconduct or a knowing and culpable violation of law, (ii) for acts or omissions that a director believes to be contrary to the best interests of the corporation or its shareholders or that involve the absence of good faith on the part of the director, (iii) for any transaction from which a director derived an improper personal benefit, (iv) for acts or omissions that show a reckless disregard for the director's duty to the corporation or its shareholders in circumstances in which the director was aware, or should have been aware, in the ordinary course of performing a director's duties, of a risk of serious injury to the corporation or its shareholders, (v) for acts or omissions that constitute an unexcused pattern of inattention that amounts to an abdication of the director's duty to the corporation or its shareholders, (vi) under Section 310, or (vii) under Section 316, (B) no such provision shall eliminate or limit the liability of a director for any act or omission occurring prior to the date when the provision becomes effective, and (C) no such provision shall eliminate or limit the liability of an officer for any act or omission as an officer, notwithstanding that the officer is also a director or that his or her actions, if negligent or improper, have been ratified by the directors.

(11) A provision authorizing, whether by bylaw, agreement, or otherwise, the indemnification of agents (as defined in Section 317) in excess of that expressly permitted by Section 317 for those agents of the

corporation for breach of duty to the corporation and its stockholders, provided, however, that the provision may not provide for indemnification of any agent for any acts or omissions or transactions from which a director may not be relieved of liability as set forth in the exception to paragraph (10) or as to circumstances in which indemnity is expressly prohibited by Section 317.

Notwithstanding this subdivision, in the case of a close corporation any of the provisions referred to above may be validly included in a shareholders' agreement. Notwithstanding this subdivision, bylaws may require for all or any actions by the board the affirmative vote of a majority of the authorized number of directors. Nothing contained in this subdivision shall affect the enforceability, as between the parties thereto, of any lawful agreement not otherwise contrary to public policy.

(b) Reasonable restrictions upon the right to transfer or hypothecate shares of any class or classes or series, but no restriction shall be binding with respect to shares issued prior to the adoption of the restriction unless the holders of such shares voted in favor of the restriction.

(c) The names and addresses of the persons appointed to act as initial directors.

(d) Any other provision, not in conflict with law, for the management of the business and for the conduct of the affairs of the corporation, including any provision which is required or permitted by this division to be stated in the bylaws.

§ 204.5 Director Liability; Limiting Provision in Articles; Wording; Disclosure to Shareholders Regarding Provision

(a) If the articles of a corporation include a provision reading substantially as follows: "The liability of the directors of the corporation for monetary damages shall be eliminated to the fullest extent permissible under California law"; the corporation shall be considered to have adopted a provision as authorized by paragraph (10) of subdivision (a) of Section 204 and more specific wording shall not be required.

(b) This section shall not be construed as setting forth the exclusive method of adopting an article provision as authorized by paragraph (10) of subdivision (a) of Section 204.

(c) This section shall not change the otherwise applicable standards or duties to make full and fair disclosure to shareholders when approval of such a provision is sought.

§ 212. Bylaws; Contents

(a) The bylaws shall set forth (unless such provision is contained in the articles, in which case it may only be changed by an amendment of the articles) the number of directors of the corporation; or that the number of directors shall be not less than a stated minimum nor more than a stated maximum (which in no case shall be greater than two times the stated minimum minus one), with the exact number of directors to be fixed, within the limits specified, by approval of the board or the shareholders (Section 153) in the manner provided in the bylaws, subject to paragraph (5) of subdivision (a) of Section 204. The number or minimum number of directors shall not be less than three; provided, however, that (1) before shares are issued, the number may be one, (2) before shares are issued, the number may be two, (3) so long as the corporation has only one shareholder, the number may be one, (4) so long as the corporation has only one shareholder, the number may be two, and (5) so long as the corporation has only two shareholders, the number may be two. After the issuance of shares, a bylaw specifying or changing a fixed number of directors or the maximum or minimum number or changing from a fixed to a variable board or vice versa may only be adopted by approval of the outstanding shares (Section 152); provided, however, that a bylaw or amendment of the articles reducing the fixed number or the minimum number of directors to a number less than five cannot be adopted if the votes cast against its adoption at a meeting or the shares not consenting in the case of action by written consent are equal to more than 16⅔ percent of the outstanding shares entitled to vote.

(b) The bylaws may contain any provision, not in conflict with law or the articles for the management of the business and for the conduct of the affairs of the corporation, including but not limited to:

(1) Any provision referred to in subdivision (b), (c) or (d) of Section 204.

(2) The time, place and manner of calling, conducting and giving notice of shareholders', directors' and committee meetings.

(3) The manner of execution, revocation and use of proxies.

(4) The qualifications, duties and compensation of directors; the time of their annual election; and the requirements of a quorum for directors' and committee meetings.

(5) The appointment and authority of committees of the board.

(6) The appointment, duties, compensation and tenure of officers.

(7) The mode of determination of holders of record of its shares.

(8) The making of annual reports and financial statements to the shareholders.

CHAPTER 3. DIRECTORS AND MANAGEMENT

§ 300. Powers of Board; Delegation; Close Corporations; Shareholders' Agreements; Validity; Liability; Failure to Observe Formalities

(a) Subject to the provisions of this division and any limitations in the articles relating to action required to be approved by the shareholders (Section 153) or by the outstanding shares (Section 152), or by a less than majority vote of a class or series of preferred shares (Section 402.5), the business and affairs of the corporation shall be managed and all corporate powers shall be exercised by or under the direction of the board. The board may delegate the management of the day-to-day operation of the business of the corporation to a management company or other person provided that the business and affairs of the corporation shall be managed and all corporate powers shall be exercised under the ultimate direction of the board.

(b) Notwithstanding subdivision (a) or any other provision of this division, but subject to subdivision (c), no shareholders' agreement, which relates to any phase of the affairs of a close corporation, including but not limited to management of its business, division of its profits or distribution of its assets on liquidation, shall be invalid as between the parties thereto on the ground that it so relates to the conduct of the affairs of the corporation as to interfere with the discretion of the board or that it is an attempt to treat the corporation as if it were a partnership or to arrange their relationships in a manner that would be appropriate only between partners. A transferee of shares covered by such an agreement which is filed with the secretary of the corporation for inspection by any prospective purchaser of shares, who has actual knowledge thereof or notice thereof by a notation on the certificate pursuant to Section 418, is bound by its provisions and is a party thereto for the purposes of subdivision (d). Original issuance of shares by the corporation to a new shareholder who does not become a party to the agreement terminates the agreement, except that if the agreement so provides it shall continue to the extent it is enforceable apart from this subdivision. The agreement may not be modified, extended or revoked without the consent of such a transferee, subject to any provision of the agreement permitting modification, extension or revocation by less than unanimous agreement of the parties. A transferor of shares covered by such an agreement ceases to be a party thereto upon ceasing to be a shareholder of the corporation unless the transferor is a party thereto other than as a shareholder. An agreement made pursuant to this subdivision shall terminate when the corporation ceases to be a close corporation, except that if the agreement so provides it shall continue to the extent it is enforceable apart from this subdivision. This subdivision does not apply to an agreement authorized by subdivision (a) of Section 706.

(c) No agreement entered into pursuant to subdivision (b) may alter or waive any of the provisions of Sections 158, 417, 418, 500, 501, and 1111, subdivision (e) of Section 1201, Sections 2009, 2010, and 2011, or of Chapters 15 (commencing with Section 1500), 16 (commencing with Section 1600), 18 (commencing with Section 1800), and 22 (commencing with Section 2200). All other provisions of this division may be altered or waived as between the parties thereto in a shareholders' agreement, except the required filing of any document with the Secretary of State.

(d) An agreement of the type referred to in subdivision (b) shall, to the extent and so long as the discretion or powers of the board in its management of corporate affairs is controlled by such agreement, impose upon each shareholder who is a party thereto liability for managerial acts performed or omitted by such person pursuant thereto that is otherwise imposed by this division upon directors, and the directors shall be relieved to that extent from such liability.

(e) The failure of a close corporation to observe corporate formalities relating to meetings of directors or shareholders in connection with the management of its affairs, pursuant to an agreement authorized by subdivision (b), shall not be considered a factor tending to establish that the shareholders have personal liability for corporate obligations.

§ 301. Directors; Election; Term

(a) Except as provided in Section 301.5, at each annual meeting of shareholders, directors shall be elected to hold office until the next annual meeting. However, to effectuate a voting shift (Section 194.7) the articles may provide that directors hold office for a shorter term. The articles may provide for the election of one or more directors by the holders of the shares of any class or series voting as a class or series.

(b) Each director, including a director elected to fill a vacancy, shall hold office until the expiration of the term for which elected and until a successor has been elected and qualified.

§ 301.5 Listed Corporations; Classes of Directors; Cumulative Voting; Election of Directors; Amendment of Articles and Bylaws

(a) A listed corporation may, by amendment of its articles or bylaws, adopt provisions to divide the board of directors into two or three classes to serve for terms of two or three years respectively, or to eliminate cumulative voting, or both. After the issuance of shares, a corporation which is not a listed corporation may, by amendment of its articles or bylaws, adopt provisions to be effective when the corporation becomes a listed corporation to divide the board of directors into two or three classes to serve for terms of two or three years respectively, or to eliminate cumulative voting, or both. An article or bylaw amendment providing for division of the board of directors into classes, or any change in the number of classes, or the elimination of cumulative voting may only be adopted by the approval of the board and the outstanding shares (Section 152) voting as a single class, notwithstanding Section 903.

(b) If the board of directors is divided into two classes pursuant to subdivision (a), the authorized number of directors shall be no less than six and one-half of the directors or as close an approximation as possible shall be elected at each annual meeting of shareholders. If the board of directors is divided into three classes, the authorized number of directors shall be no less than nine and one-third of the directors or as close an approximation as possible shall be elected at each annual meeting of shareholders. Directors of a listed corporation may be elected by classes at a meeting of shareholders at which an amendment to the articles or bylaws described in subdivision (a) is approved, but the extended terms for directors are contingent on that approval, and in the case of an amendment to the articles, the filing of any necessary amendment to the articles pursuant to Section 905 or 910.

(c) If directors for more than one class are to be elected by the shareholders at any one meeting of shareholders and the election is by cumulative voting pursuant to Section 708, votes may be cumulated only for directors to be elected within each class.

(d) For purposes of this section, a "listed corporation" means any of the following:

(1) A corporation with outstanding shares listed on the New York Stock Exchange or the American Stock Exchange.

(2) A corporation with outstanding securities listed on the National Market System of the NASDAQ Stock Market (or any successor to that entity).

(e) Subject to subdivision (h), if a listed corporation having a board of directors divided into classes pursuant to subdivision (a) ceases to be a listed corporation for any reason, unless the articles of incorporation or bylaws of the corporation provide for the elimination of classes of directors at an earlier date or dates, the board of directors of the corporation shall cease to be divided into classes as to each class of directors on the date of the expiration of the term of the directors in that class and the term of each director serving at the time the corporation ceases to be a listed corporation (and the term of each director elected to fill a vacancy resulting from the death, resignation, or removal of any of those directors) shall continue until its expiration as if the corporation had not ceased to be a listed corporation.

(f) Subject to subdivision (h), if a listed corporation having a provision in its articles or bylaws elimination cumulative voting pursuant to that subdivision, or both, ceases to be a listed corporation for any reason, the shareholders shall be entitled to cumulate their votes pursuant to Section 708 at any election of directors occurring while the corporation is not a listed corporation notwithstanding that provision in its articles of incorporation or bylaws.

(g) Subject to subdivision (i), if a corporation that is not a listed corporation adopts amendments to its articles of incorporation of bylaws to divide its board of directors into classes or to eliminate cumulative voting, or both, pursuant to subdivision (a) and then becomes a listed corporation, unless the articles of incorporation or bylaws provide for those provisions to become effective at some other time and, in cases where classes directors are provided for, identify the directors who, or the directorships that, are to be in each class or the method by which those directors or directorships are to be identified, the provisions shall become effective for the next election of dimes a listed corporation at which all directors are to be elected.

(h) If a corporation ceases to be a listed corporation on or after the record date for a meeting of shareholders and prior to the conclusion of the meeting, including the conclusion of the meeting after an adjournment or postponement that does not require or result in the setting of a new record date, then, solely for purposes of subdivisions (e) and (f), the corporation shall not be deemed to have ceased to be a listed corporation until the conclusion of the meeting of shareholders.

(i) If a corporation becomes a listed corporation on or after the record date for a meeting of shareholders and prior to the conclusion of the meeting, including the conclusion of the meeting after an adjournment or postponement that does not require or result in the setting of a new record date, then, solely for purposes or subdivision (g), the corporation shall not be deemed to have because of the meeting of shareholders.

(j) If an article amendment referred to in subdivision (a) is adopted by a listed corporation, the certificate of amendment shall include a statement of the facts showing that the corporation is a listed corporation within the meaning of subdivision (d). If an article or bylaw amendment referred to in subdivision (a) is adopted by a corporation which is not a listed corporation, the provision as adopted, shall include the following statement or the substantial equivalent of: "This provision shall become effective only when the corporation becomes a listed corporation within the meaning of Section 301.5 of the Corporations Code."

§ 303. Directors; Removal Without Cause

(a) Any or all of the directors may be removed without cause if the removal is approved by the outstanding shares (Section 152), subject to the following:

(1) Except for a corporation to which paragraph (3) is applicable, no director may be removed (unless the entire board is removed) when the

votes cast against removal, or not consenting in writing to the removal, would be sufficient to elect the director if voted cumulatively at an election at which the same total number of votes were cast (or, if the action is taken by written consent, all shares entitled to vote were voted) and the entire number of directors authorized at the time of the director's most recent election were then being elected.

(2) When by the provisions of the articles the holders of the shares of any class or series, voting as a class or series, are entitled to elect one or more directors, any director so elected may be removed only by the applicable vote of the holders of the shares of that class or series.

(3) A director of a corporation whose board of directors is classified pursuant to Section 301.5 may not be removed if the votes cast against removal of the director, or not consenting in writing to the removal, would be sufficient to elect the director if voted cumulatively (without regard to whether shares may otherwise be voted cumulatively) at an election at which the same total number of votes were cast (or, if the action is taken by written consent, all shares entitled to vote were voted) and either the number of directors elected at the most recent annual meeting of shareholders, or if greater, the number of directors for whom removal is being sought, were then being elected.

(b) Any reduction of the authorized number of directors or amendment reducing the number of classes of directors does not remove any director prior to the expiration of the director's term of office.

(c) Except as provided in this section and Sections 302 and 304, a director may not be removed prior to the expiration of the director's term of office.

§ 307. Board Meetings; Notice; Participation; Use of Conference Telephone Communication Equipment; Quorum; Waiver of Meeting Requirement

(a) Unless otherwise provided in the articles or (subject to paragraph (5) of subdivision (a) of Section 204) in the bylaws:

(1) Meetings of the board may be called by the chairperson of the board or the president or any vice president or the secretary or any two directors.

(2) Regular meetings of the board may be held without notice if the time and place of such meetings are fixed by the bylaws or the board. Special meetings of the board shall be held upon four days' notice by mail or 48 hours' notice delivered personally or by telephone, including a voice messaging system or other system or technology designed to record and communicate messages, telegraph, facsimile, electronic mail, or other electronic means. The articles or bylaws may not dispense with notice of a special meeting. A notice, or waiver of notice, need not specify the purpose of any regular or special meeting of the board.

(3) Notice of a meeting need not be given to any director who signs a waiver of notice or a consent to holding the meeting or an approval of the minutes thereof, whether before or after the meeting, or who attends the meeting without protesting, prior thereto or at its commencement, the lack of notice to such director. All such waivers, consents and approvals shall be filed with the corporate records or made a part of the minutes of the meeting.

(4) A majority of the directors present, whether or not a quorum is present, may adjourn any meeting to another time and place. If the meeting is adjourned for more than 24 hours, notice of any adjournment to another time or place shall be given prior to the time of the adjourned meeting to the directors who were not present at the time of the adjournment.

(5) Meetings of the board may be held at any place within or without the state which has been designated in the notice of the meeting or, if not stated in the notice or there is no notice, designated in the bylaws or by resolution of the board.

(6) Members of the board may participate in a meeting through use of conference telephone or similar communications equipment, as long as all members participating in such meeting can hear one another. Participation in a meeting pursuant to this subdivision constitutes presence in person at such meeting.

(7) A majority of the authorized number of directors constitutes a quorum of the board for the transaction of business. The articles or bylaws may not provide that a quorum shall be less than one-third the authorized number of directors or less than two, whichever is larger, unless the authorized number of directors is one, in which case one director constitutes a quorum.

(8) Every act or decision done or made by a majority of the directors present at a meeting duly held at which a quorum is present is the act of the board, subject to the provisions of Section 310 and subdivision (e) of Section 317. The articles or bylaws may not provide that a lesser vote than a majority of the directors present at a meeting is the act of the board. A meeting at which a quorum is initially present may continue to transact business notwithstanding the withdrawal of directors, if any action taken is approved by at least a majority of the required quorum for such meeting.

(b) Any action required or permitted to be taken by the board may be taken without a meeting, if all members of the board shall individually or collectively consent in writing to such action. Such written consent or consents shall be filed with the minutes of the proceedings of the board. Such action by written consent shall have the same force and effect as a unanimous vote of such directors.

(c) The provisions of this section apply also to committees of the board and incorporators and action by such committees and incorporators, mutatis mutandis.

(d) This section shall become operative on January 1, 2003.

§ 309. Performance of Duties by Director; Liability

(a) A director shall perform the duties of a director, including duties as a member of any committee of the board upon which the director may serve, in good faith, in a manner such director believes to be in the best interests of the corporation and its shareholders and with such care, including reasonable inquiry, as an ordinarily prudent person in a like position would use under similar circumstances.

(b) In performing the duties of a director, a director shall be entitled to rely on information, opinions, reports or statements, including financial statements and other financial data, in each case prepared or presented by any of the following:

(1) One or more officers or employees of the corporation whom the director believes to be reliable and competent in the matters presented,

(2) Counsel, independent accountants or other persons as to matters which the director believes to be within such person's professional or expert competence.

(3) A committee of the board upon which the director does not serve, as to matters within its designated authority, which committee the director believes to merit confidence, so long as, in any such case, the director acts in good faith, after reasonable inquiry when the need therefor is indicated by the circumstances and without knowledge that would cause such reliance to be unwarranted.

(c) A person who performs the duties of a director in accordance with subdivisions (a) and (b) shall have no liability based upon any alleged failure to discharge the person's obligations as a director. In addition, the liability of a director for monetary damages may be eliminated or limited in a corporation's articles to the extent provided in paragraph (10) of subdivision (a) of Section 204.

§ 310. Contracts in Which Director Has Material Financial Interest; Validity

(a) No contract or other transaction between a corporation and one or more of its directors, or between a corporation and any corporation, firm or association in which one or more of its directors has a material financial interest, is either void or voidable because such director or directors or such other corporation, firm or association are parties or because such director or directors are present at the meeting of the board or a committee thereof which authorizes, approves or ratifies the contract or transaction, if

(1) The material facts as to the transaction and as to such director's interest are fully disclosed or known to the shareholders and such contract or transaction is approved by the shareholders (Section 153) in good faith, with the shares owned by the interested director or directors not being entitled to vote thereon, or

(2) The material facts as to the transaction and as to such director's interest are fully disclosed or known to the board or committee, and the board or committee authorizes, approves or ratifies the contract or transaction in good faith by a vote sufficient without counting the vote of the interested director or directors and the contract or transaction is just and reasonable as to the corporation at the time it is authorized, approved or ratified, or

(3) As to contracts or transactions not approved as provided in paragraph (1) or (2) of this subdivision, the person asserting the validity of the contract or transaction sustains the burden of proving that the contract or transaction was just and reasonable as to the corporation at the time it was authorized, approved or ratified.

A mere common directorship does not constitute a material financial interest within the meaning of this subdivision. A director is not interested within the meaning of this subdivision in a resolution fixing the compensation of another director as a director, officer or employee of the corporation, notwithstanding the fact that the first director is also receiving compensation from the corporation.

(b) No contract or other transaction between a corporation and any corporation or association of which one or more of its directors are directors is either void or voidable because such director or directors are present at the meeting of the board or a committee thereof which authorizes, approves or ratifies the contract or transaction, if

(1) The material facts as to the transaction and as to such director's other directorship are fully disclosed or known to the board or committee, and the board or committee authorizes, approves or ratifies the contract or transaction in good faith by a vote sufficient without counting the vote of the common director or directors or the contract or transaction is approved by the shareholders (Section 153) in good faith, or

(2) As to contracts or transactions not approved as provided in paragraph (1) of this subdivision, the contract or transaction is just and reasonable as to the corporation at the time it is authorized, approved or ratified.

This subdivision does not apply to contracts or transactions covered by subdivision (a).

(c) Interested or common directors may be counted in determining the presence of a quorum at a meeting of the board or a committee thereof which authorizes, approves or ratifies a contract or transaction.

§ 313. Instrument in Writing and Assignment or Endorsement Thereof; Signatures; Validity

Subject to the provisions of subdivision (a) of Section 208, any note, mortgage, evidence of indebtedness, contract, share certificate, initial transaction statement or written statement, conveyance or other instrument in writing, and any assignment or endorsement thereof, executed or entered into between any corporation and any other person, when signed by the chairman of the board, the president or any vice president and the secretary, any assistant secretary, the chief financial officer or any assistant treasurer of such corporation, is not invalidated as to the corporation by any lack of authority of the signing officers in the absence of actual knowledge on the part of the other person that the signing officers had no authority to execute the same.

§ 317. Indemnification of Agent of Corporation in Proceedings or Actions

(a) For the purposes of this section, "agent" means any person who is or was a director, officer, employee or other agent of the corporation, or is or was serving at the request of the corporation as a director, officer, employee or agent of another foreign or domestic corporation, partnership, joint venture, trust or other enterprise, or was a director, officer, employee or agent of a foreign or domestic corporation which was a predecessor corporation of the corporation or of another enterprise at the request of such predecessor corporation; "proceeding" means any threatened, pending or completed action or proceeding, whether civil, criminal, administrative or investigative; and "expenses" includes without limitation attorneys' fees and any expenses of establishing a right to indemnification under subdivision (d) or paragraph (4) of subdivision (e).

(b) A corporation shall have power to indemnify any person who was or is a party or is threatened to be made a party to any proceeding (other than an action by or in the right of the corporation to procure a judgment in its favor) by reason of the fact that the person is or was an agent of the corporation, against expenses, judgments, fines, settlements and other amounts actually and reasonably incurred in connection with the proceeding if that person acted in good faith and in a manner the person reasonably believed to be in the best interests of the corporation and, in the case of a criminal proceeding, had no reasonable cause to believe the conduct of the person was unlawful. The termination of any proceeding by judgment, order, settlement, conviction or upon a plea of nolo contendere or its equivalent shall not, of itself, create a presumption that the person did not act in good faith and in a manner which the person reasonably believed to be in the best interests of the corporation or that the person had reasonable cause to believe that the person's conduct was unlawful.

(c) A corporation shall have power to indemnify any person who was or is a party or is threatened to be made a party to any threatened, pending or completed action by or in the right of the corporation to procure a judgment in its favor by reason of the fact that the person is or was an agent of the corporation, against expenses actually and reasonably incurred by that person in connection with the defense or settlement of the action if the person acted in good faith, in a manner the person believed to be in the best interests of the corporation and with such care, including reasonable inquiry, as an ordinarily prudent person in a like position would use under similar circumstances.

No indemnification shall be made under this subdivision for any of the following:

(1) In respect of any claim, issue or matter as to which the person shall have been adjudged to be liable to the corporation in the performance of that person's duty to the corporation and its shareholders, unless and only to the extent that the court in which the proceeding is or was pending shall determine upon application that, in view of all the circumstances of the case, the person is fairly and reasonably entitled to indemnity for the expenses which such court shall determine;

(2) Of amounts paid in settling or otherwise disposing of a threatened or pending action, with or without court approval; or

(3) Of expenses incurred in defending a threatened or pending action which is settled or otherwise disposed of without court approval.

(d) To the extent that an agent of a corporation has been successful on the merits in defense of any proceeding referred to in subdivision (b) or (c) or in defense of any claim, issue or matter therein, the agent shall be indemnified against expenses actually and reasonably incurred by the agent in connection therewith.

(e) Except as provided in subdivision (d), any indemnification under this section shall be made by the corporation only if authorized in the specific case, upon a determination that indemnification of the agent is proper in the circumstances because the agent has met the applicable standard of conduct set forth in subdivision (b) or (c), by:

(1) A majority vote of a quorum consisting of directors who are not parties to such proceeding;

(2) If such a quorum of directors is not obtainable, by independent legal counsel in a written opinion.

(3) Approval of the shareholders (Section 153), with the shares owned by the person to be indemnified not being entitled to vote thereon.

(4) The court in which the proceeding is or was pending upon application made by the corporation or the agent or the attorney or other person rendering services in connection with the defense, whether

or not the application by the agent, attorney or other person is opposed by the corporation.

(f) Expenses incurred in defending any proceeding may be advanced by the corporation prior to the final disposition of the proceeding upon receipt of an undertaking by or on behalf of the agent to repay that amount if it shall be determined ultimately that the agent is not entitled to be indemnified as authorized in this section. The provisions of subdivision (a) of Section 315 do not apply to advances made pursuant to this subdivision.

(g) The indemnification provided by this section shall not be deemed exclusive of any additional rights to indemnification for breach of duty to the corporation and its shareholders while acting in the capacity of a director or officer of the corporation to the extent the additional rights to indemnification are authorized in an article provision adopted pursuant to paragraph (11) of subdivision (a) of Section 204. The indemnification provided by this section for acts, omissions, or transactions while acting in the capacity of, or while serving as, a director or officer of the corporation but not involving breach of duty to the corporation and its shareholders shall not be deemed exclusive of any other rights to which those seeking indemnification may be entitled under any bylaw, agreement, vote of shareholders or disinterested directors, or otherwise, to the extent the additional rights to indemnification are authorized in the articles of the corporation. An article provision authorizing indemnification "in excess of that otherwise permitted by Section 317" or "to the fullest extent permissible under California law" or the substantial equivalent thereof shall be construed to be both a provision for additional indemnification for breach of duty to the corporation and its shareholders as referred to in, and with the limitations required by, paragraph (11) of subdivision (a) of Section 204 and a provision for additional indemnification as referred to in the second sentence of this subdivision. The rights to indemnity hereunder shall continue as to a person who has ceased to be a director, officer, employee, or agent and shall inure to the benefit of the heirs, executors, and administrators of the person. Nothing contained in this section shall affect any right to indemnification to which persons other than the directors and officers may be entitled by contract or otherwise.

(h) No indemnification or advance shall be made under this section, except as provided in subdivision (d) or paragraph (4) of subdivision (e), in any circumstance where it appears:

(1) That it would be inconsistent with a provision of the articles, bylaws, a resolution of the shareholders or an agreement in effect at the time of the accrual of the alleged cause of action asserted in the proceeding in which the expenses were incurred or other amounts were paid, which prohibits or otherwise limits indemnification.

(2) That it would be inconsistent with any condition expressly imposed by a court in approving a settlement.

(i) A corporation shall have power to purchase and maintain insurance on behalf of any agent of the corporation against any liability asserted against or incurred by the agent in that capacity or arising out of the agent's status as such whether or not the corporation would have the power to indemnify the agent against that liability under this section. The fact that a corporation owns all or a portion of the shares of the company issuing a policy of insurance shall not render this subdivision inapplicable if either of the following conditions are satisfied: (1) if the articles authorize indemnification in excess of that authorized in this section and the insurance provided by this subdivision is limited as indemnification is required to be limited by paragraph (11) of subdivision (a) of Section 204; or (2)(A) the company issuing the insurance policy is organized, licensed, and operated in a manner that complies with the insurance laws and regulations applicable to its jurisdiction of organization, (B) the company issuing the policy provides procedures for processing claims that do not permit that company to be subject to the direct control of the corporation that purchased that policy, and (C) the policy issued provides for some manner of risk sharing between the issuer and purchaser of the policy, on one hand, and some unaffiliated person or persons, on the other, such as by providing for more than one unaffiliated owner of the company issuing the policy or by providing that a portion of the coverage furnished will be obtained from some unaffiliated insurer or reinsurer.

(j) This section does not apply to any proceeding against any trustee, investment manager or other fiduciary of an employee benefit plan in that person's capacity as such, even though the person may also be an agent as defined in subdivision (a) of the employer corporation. A corporation shall have power to indemnify such a trustee, investment manager or other fiduciary to the extent permitted by subdivision (f) of Section 207.

CHAPTER 4. SHARES AND SHARE CERTIFICATES

§ 409. Issuance of Shares; Consideration; Liability to Call; Determination by Shareholders; Valuation of Property Other Than Money by Board Resolution

(a) Shares may be issued:

(1) For such consideration as is determined from time to time by the board, or by the shareholders if the articles so provide, consisting of any or all of the following: money paid; labor done; services actually rendered to the corporation or for its benefit or in its formation or reorganization; debts or securities canceled; and tangible or intangible property actually

received either by the issuing corporation or by a wholly owned subsidiary; but neither promissory notes of the purchaser (unless adequately secured by collateral other than the shares acquired or unless permitted by Section 408) nor future services shall constitute payment or part payment for shares of the corporation; or

(2) As a share dividend or upon a stock split, reverse stock split, reclassification of outstanding shares into shares of another class, conversion of outstanding shares into shares of another class, exchange of outstanding shares for shares of another class or other change affecting outstanding shares.

(b) Except as provided in subdivision (d), shares issued as provided in this section or Section 408 shall be declared and taken to be fully paid stock and not liable to any further call nor shall the holder thereof be liable for any further payments under the provisions of this division. In the absence of fraud in the transaction, the judgment of the directors as to the value of the consideration for shares shall be conclusive.

(c) If the articles reserve to the shareholders the right to determine the consideration for the issue of any shares, such determination shall be made by approval of the outstanding shares (Section 152).

(d) A corporation may issue the whole or any part of its shares as partly paid and subject to call for the remainder of the consideration to be paid therefor. On the certificate issued to represent any such partly paid shares or, for uncertificated securities, on the initial transaction statement for such partly paid shares, the total amount of the consideration to be paid therefor and the amount paid thereon shall be stated. Upon the declaration of any dividend on fully paid shares, the corporation shall declare a dividend upon partly paid shares of the same class, but only upon the basis of the percentage of the consideration actually paid thereon.

(e) The board shall state by resolution its determination of the fair value to the corporation in monetary terms of any consideration other than money for which shares are issued. This subdivision does not affect the accounting treatment of any transaction, which shall be in conformity with generally accepted accounting principles.

§ 410. Liability for Full Agreed Consideration; Time of Payment

(a) Every subscriber to shares and every person to whom shares are originally issued is liable to the corporation for the full consideration agreed to be paid for the shares.

(b) The full agreed consideration for shares shall be paid prior to or concurrently with the issuance thereof, unless the shares are issued as partly paid pursuant to subdivision (d) of Section 409, in which case the consideration shall be paid in accordance with the agreement of subscription or purchase.

§ 414. Creditor's Remedy to Reach Liability Due Corporation on Shares

(a) No action shall be brought by or on behalf of any creditor to reach and apply the liability, if any, of a shareholder to the corporation to pay the amount due on such shareholder's shares unless final judgment has been rendered in favor of the creditor against the corporation and execution has been returned unsatisfied in whole or in part or unless such proceedings would be useless.

* * *

CHAPTER 5. DIVIDENDS AND REACQUISITIONS OF SHARES

§ 500. Distributions; Retained Earnings or Assets Remaining After Completion; Exemption of Broker–Dealer Licensee Meeting Certain Net Capital Requirements

Neither a corporation nor any of its subsidiaries shall make any distribution to the corporation's shareholders (Section 166) except as follows:

(a) The distribution may be made if the amount of the retained earnings of the corporation immediately prior thereto equals or exceeds the amount of the proposed distribution.

(b) The distribution may be made if immediately after giving effect thereto:

(1) The sum of the assets of the corporation (exclusive of goodwill, capitalized research and development expenses and deferred charges) would be at least equal to 1 ¼ times its liabilities (not including deferred taxes, deferred income and other deferred credits); and

(2) The current assets of the corporation would be at least equal to its current liabilities or, if the average of the earnings of the corporation before taxes on income and before interest expense for the two preceding fiscal years was less than the average of the interest expense of the corporation for those fiscal years, at least equal to 1 ¼ times its current liabilities; provided, however, that in determining the amount of the assets of the corporation profits derived from an exchange of assets shall not be included unless the assets received are currently realizable in cash; and provided, further, that for the purpose of this subdivision "current assets" may include net amounts which the board has determined in good faith may reasonably be expected to be received from customers during the 12–month period used in calculating current liabilities pursuant to existing contractual relationships obligating those

customers to make fixed or periodic payments during the term of the contract or, in the case of public utilities, pursuant to service connections with customers, after in each case giving effect to future costs not then included in current liabilities but reasonably expected to be incurred by the corporation in performing those contracts or providing service to utility customers. Paragraph (2) of subdivision (b) is not applicable to a corporation which does not classify its assets into current and fixed under generally accepted accounting principles.

(c) The amount of any distribution payable in property shall, for the purposes of this chapter, be determined on the basis of the value at which the property is carried on the corporation's financial statements in accordance with generally accepted accounting principles.

(d) For the purpose of applying this section to a distribution by a corporation of cash or property in payment by the corporation in connection with the purchase of its shares, there shall be added to retained earnings all amounts that had been previously deducted therefrom with respect to obligations incurred in connection with the corporation's repurchase of its shares and reflected on the corporation's balance sheet, but not in excess of the principal of the obligations that remain unpaid immediately prior to the distribution. In addition, there shall be deducted from liabilities all amounts that had been previously added thereto with respect to the obligations incurred in connection with the corporation's repurchase of its shares and reflected on the corporation's balance sheet, but not in excess of the principal of the obligations that will remain unpaid after the distribution, provided that no addition to retained earnings or deduction from liabilities under this subdivision shall occur on account of any obligation that is a distribution to the corporation's shareholders (Section 166) at the time the obligation is incurred.

(e) This section does not apply to a corporation licensed as a broker-dealer under Chapter 2 (commencing with Section 25210) of Part 3 of Division 1 of Title 4, if immediately after giving effect to any distribution the corporation is in compliance with the net capital rules of the Commissioner of Corporations and the Securities and Exchange Commission.

§ 501. Inability to Meet Liabilities as They Mature; Prohibition of Distribution

Neither a corporation nor any of its subsidiaries shall make any distribution to the corporation's shareholders (Section 166) if the corporation or the subsidiary making the distribution is, or as a result thereof would be, likely to be unable to meet its liabilities (except those whose payment is otherwise adequately provided for) as they mature.

§ 502. Distribution to Junior Shares if Excess of Assets Over Liabilities Less Than Liquidation Preference of Senior Shares; Prohibition

Neither a corporation nor any of its subsidiaries shall make any distribution to the corporation's shareholders (Section 166) on any shares of its stock of any class or series that are junior to outstanding shares of any other class or series with respect to distribution of assets on liquidation if, after giving effect thereto, the excess of its assets (exclusive of goodwill, capitalized research and development expenses and deferred charges) over its liabilities (not including deferred taxes, deferred income and other deferred credits) would be less than the liquidation preference of all shares having a preference on liquidation over the class or series to which the distribution is made; provided, however, that for the purpose of applying this section to a distribution by a corporation of cash or property in payment by the corporation in connection with the purchase of its shares, there shall be deducted from liabilities all amounts that had been previously added thereto with respect to obligations incurred in connection with the corporation's repurchase of its shares and reflected on the corporation's balance sheet, but not in excess of the principal of the obligations that will remain unpaid after the distribution; provided, further, that no deduction from liabilities shall occur on account of any obligation that is a distribution to the corporation's shareholders (Section 166) at the time the obligation is incurred.

§ 503. Retained Earnings Necessary to Allow Distribution to Junior Shares

Neither a corporation nor any of its subsidiaries shall make any distribution to the corporation's shareholders (Section 166) on any shares of its stock of any class or series that are junior to outstanding shares of any other class or series with respect to payment of dividends, and as to which senior class or series the corporation has cumulative dividends in arrears unless the amount of the retained earnings of the corporation immediately prior thereto equals or exceeds the amount of the proposed distribution plus the aggregate amount of the cumulative dividends in arrears on all shares having a preference with respect to payment of dividends over the class or series to which the distribution is made; provided, however, that for the purpose of applying this section to a distribution by a corporation of cash or property in payment by the corporation in connection with the purchase of its shares, there shall be added to retained earnings all amounts that had been previously deducted therefrom with respect to obligations incurred in connection with the corporation's repurchase of its shares and reflected on the corporation's balance sheet, but not in excess of the principal of the obligations that remain unpaid immediately prior to the distribution; provided, further, that no addition to retained earnings shall occur on account of any obligation that is a distribution to the corporation's shareholders (Section 166) at the time the obligation is incurred.

§ 506. Receipt of Prohibited Dividend; Liability of Shareholder; Suit by Creditors or Other Shareholders; Fraudulent Transfers

(a) Any shareholder who receives any distribution prohibited by this chapter with knowledge of facts indicating the impropriety thereof is liable to the corporation for the benefit of all of the creditors or shareholders entitled to institute an action under subdivision (b) for the amount so received by the shareholder with interest thereon at the legal rate on judgments until paid, but not exceeding the liabilities of the corporation owed to nonconsenting creditors at the time of the violation and the injury suffered by nonconsenting shareholders, as the case may be. For purposes of this chapter, in the event that any shareholder receives any distribution of the corporation's property that is prohibited by this chapter, the shareholder receiving that illegal distribution shall be liable to the corporation for an amount equal to the fair market value of the property at the time of the illegal distribution plus interest thereon from the date of the distribution at the legal rate on judgments until paid, together with all reasonably incurred costs of appraisal or other valuation, if any, of that property, but not exceeding the liabilities of the corporation owed to nonconsenting creditors at the time of the violation and the injury suffered by nonconsenting shareholders, as the case may be.

(b) Suit may be brought in the name of the corporation to enforce the liability (1) to creditors arising under subdivision (a) for a violation of Section 500 or 501 against any or all shareholders liable by any one or more creditors of the corporation whose debts or claims arose prior to the time of the distribution to shareholders and who have not consented thereto, whether or not they have reduced their claims to judgment, or (2) to shareholders arising under subdivision (a) for a violation of Section 502 or 503 against any or all shareholders liable by any one or more holders of preferred shares outstanding at the time of the distribution who have not consented thereto, without regard to the provisions of Section 800.

(c) Any shareholder sued under this section may implead all other shareholders liable under this section and may compel contribution, either in that action or in an independent action against shareholders not joined in that action.

(d) Nothing contained in this section affects any liability which any shareholder may have under Sections 3439 to 3439.12, inclusive, of the Civil Code.

CHAPTER 6. SHAREHOLDERS' MEETINGS AND CONSENTS

§ 604. Proxies or Written Consents; Contents; Form

(a) Any form of proxy or written consent distributed to 10 or more shareholders of a corporation with outstanding shares held of record by 100 or more persons shall afford an opportunity on the proxy or form of written consent to specify a choice between approval and disapproval of each matter or group of related matters intended to be acted upon at the meeting for which the proxy is solicited or by such written consent, other than elections to office, and shall provide, subject to reasonable specified conditions, that where the person solicited specifies a choice with respect to any such matter the shares will be voted in accordance therewith.

(b) In any election of directors, any form of proxy in which the directors to be voted upon are named therein as candidates and which is marked by a shareholder "withhold" or otherwise marked in a manner indicating that the authority to vote for the election of directors is withheld shall not be voted for the election of a director.

(c) Failure to comply with this section shall not invalidate any corporate action taken, but may be the basis for challenging any proxy at a meeting and the superior court may compel compliance therewith at the suit of any shareholder.

(d) This section does not apply to any corporation with an outstanding class of securities registered under Section 12 of the Securities Exchange Act of 1934 or whose securities are exempted from such registration by Section 12(g)(2) of that act.

CHAPTER 7. VOTING OF SHARES

§ 705. Proxies; Validity; Expiration; Revocation; Irrevocable Proxies

(a) Every person entitled to vote shares may authorize another person or persons to act by proxy with respect to such shares. Any proxy purporting to be executed in accordance with the provisions of this division shall be presumptively valid.

(b) No proxy shall be valid after the expiration of 11 months from the date thereof unless otherwise provided in the proxy. Every proxy continues in full force and effect until revoked by the person executing it prior to the vote pursuant thereto, except as otherwise provided in this section. Such revocation may be effected by a writing delivered to the corporation stating that the proxy is revoked or by a subsequent proxy executed by the person executing the prior proxy and presented to the meeting, or as to any meeting by attendance at such meeting and voting in person by the person executing the proxy. The dates contained on the forms of proxy presumptively determine the order of execution, regardless of the postmark dates on the envelopes in which they are mailed.

(c) A proxy is not revoked by the death or incapacity of the maker unless, before the vote is counted, written notice of such death or incapacity is received by the corporation.

(d) Except when other provision shall have been made by written agreement between the parties, the recordholder of shares which such person holds as pledgee or otherwise as security or which belong to another shall issue to the pledgor or to the owner of such shares, upon demand therefor and payment of necessary expenses thereof, a proxy to vote or take other action thereon.

(e) A proxy which states that it is irrevocable is irrevocable for the period specified therein (notwithstanding subdivision (c)) when it is held by any of the following or a nominee of any of the following:

(1) A pledgee.

(2) A person who has purchased or agreed to purchase or holds an option to purchase the shares or a person who has sold a portion of such person's shares in the corporation to the maker of the proxy.

(3) A creditor or creditors of the corporation or the shareholder who extended or continued credit to the corporation or the shareholder in consideration of the proxy if the proxy states that it was given in consideration of such extension or continuation of credit and the name of the person extending or continuing credit.

(4) A person who has contracted to perform services as an employee of the corporation, if a proxy is required by the contract of employment and if the proxy states that it was given in consideration of such contract of employment, the name of the employee and the period of employment contracted for.

(5) A person designated by or under an agreement under Section 706.

(6) A beneficiary of a trust with respect to shares held by the trust.

Notwithstanding the period of irrevocability specified, the proxy becomes revocable when the pledge is redeemed, the option or agreement to purchase is terminated or the seller no longer owns any shares of the corporation or dies, the debt of the corporation or the shareholder is paid, the period of employment provided for in the contract of employment has terminated, the agreement under Section 706 has terminated, or the person ceases to be a beneficiary of the trust. In addition to the foregoing clauses (1) through (5), a proxy may be made irrevocable (notwithstanding subdivision (c)) if it is given to secure the performance of a duty or to protect a title, either legal or equitable, until the happening of events which, by its terms, discharge the obligations secured by it.

(f) A proxy may be revoked, notwithstanding a provision making it irrevocable, by a transferee of shares without knowledge of the existence of the provision unless the existence of the proxy and its irrevocability appears, in the case of certificated securities, on the certificate representing such shares, or in the case of uncertificated securities, on the initial transaction statement and written statements.

§ 706. Agreement Between Two or More Shareholders of Close Corporation; Voting Trust Agreements

(a) Notwithstanding any other provision of this division, an agreement between two or more shareholders of a corporation, if in writing and signed by the parties thereto, may provide that in exercising any voting rights the shares held by them shall be voted as provided by the agreement, or as the parties may agree or as determined in accordance with a procedure agreed upon by them, and the parties may but need not transfer the shares covered by such an agreement to a third party or parties with authority to vote them in accordance with the terms of the agreement. Such an agreement shall not be denied specific performance by a court on the ground that the remedy at law is adequate or on other grounds relating to the jurisdiction of a court of equity.

(b) Shares in any corporation may be transferred by written agreement to trustees in order to confer upon them the right to vote and otherwise represent the shares for such period of time, not exceeding 10 years, as may be specified in the agreement. The validity of a voting trust agreement, otherwise lawful, shall not be affected during a period of 10 years from the date when it was created or last extended as hereinafter provided by the fact that under its terms it will or may last beyond such 10–year period. At any time within two years prior to the time of expiration of any voting trust agreement as originally fixed or as last extended as provided in this subdivision, one or more beneficiaries under the voting trust agreement may, by written agreement and with the written consent of the voting trustee or trustees, extend the duration of the voting trust agreement with respect to their shares for an additional period not exceeding 10 years from the expiration date of the trust as originally fixed or as last extended as provided in this subdivision. A duplicate of the voting trust agreement and any extension thereof shall be filed with the secretary of the corporation and shall be open to inspection by a shareholder, a holder of a voting trust certificate or the agent of either, upon the same terms as the record of shareholders of the corporation is open to inspection.

(c) No agreement made pursuant to subdivision (a) shall be held to be invalid or unenforceable on the ground that it is a voting trust that does not comply with subdivision (b) or that is a proxy that does not comply with Section 705.

(d) This section shall not invalidate any voting or other agreement among shareholders or any irrevocable proxy complying with subdivision (e) of Section 705, which agreement or proxy is not otherwise illegal.

§ 708. Directors; Cumulative Voting; Election by Ballot

(a) Except as provided in Section 301.5, every shareholder complying with subdivision (b) and entitled to vote at any election of directors may cumulate such shareholder's votes and give one candidate a number of votes equal to the number of directors to be elected multiplied by the number of votes to which the shareholder's shares are normally entitled, or distribute the shareholder's votes on the same principle among as many candidates as the shareholder thinks fit.

(b) No shareholder shall be entitled to cumulate votes (i.e., cast for any candidate a number of votes greater than the number of votes which such shareholder normally is entitled to cast) unless such candidate or candidates' names have been placed in nomination prior to the voting and the shareholder has given notice at the meeting prior to the voting of the shareholder's intention to cumulate the shareholder's votes. If any one shareholder has given such notice, all shareholders may cumulate their votes for candidates in nomination.

(c) In any election of directors, the candidates receiving the highest number of affirmative votes of the shares entitled to be voted for them up to the number of directors to be elected by such shares are elected; votes against the director and votes withheld shall have no legal effect.

(d) Subdivision (a) applies to the shareholders of any mutual water company organized or existing for the purpose of delivering water to its shareholders at cost on lands located within the boundaries of one or more reclamation districts now or hereafter legally existing in this state and created by or formed under the provisions of any statute of this state, but does not otherwise apply to the shareholders of mutual water companies unless their articles or bylaws so provide.

(e) Elections for directors need not be by ballot unless a shareholder demands election by ballot at the meeting and before the voting begins or unless the bylaws so require.

§ 710. Supermajority Vote Requirement; Approval; Duration; Readoption

(a) This section applies to a corporation with outstanding shares held of record by 100 or more persons (determined as provided in Section 605) which files an amendment of articles or certificate of determination containing a "supermajority vote" provision on or after January 1, 1989; provided that this section shall not apply to a corporation which files an amendment of articles or certificate of determination on or after January 1, 1994, if, at the time of filing, the corporation has (1) outstanding shares of more than one class or series of stock; (2) no class of equity securities registered under Section 12(b) or 12(g) of the Securities Exchange Act of 1934; (3) outstanding securities held of record by fewer than 300 persons determined as provided by Section 605; and (4) no supermajority vote provision, and has never had a supermajority vote provision, subject to the requirement of readoption under subdivision (c).

(b) A "supermajority vote" is a requirement set forth in the articles or in a certificate of determination authorized under any provision of this division that specified corporate action or actions be approved by a larger proportion of the outstanding shares than a majority, or by a larger proportion of the outstanding shares of a class or series than a majority, but no supermajority vote which is subject to this section shall require a vote in excess of 66⅔ percent of the outstanding shares or 66⅔ percent of the outstanding shares of any class or series of such shares.

(c) An amendment of the articles or a certificate of determination that includes a supermajority vote requirement shall be approved by at least as large a proportion of the outstanding shares (Section 152) as is required pursuant to that amendment or certificate of determination for the approval of the specified corporate action or actions. The supermajority vote requirement shall cease to be effective two years after the filing of the most recent filing of the amendment or certificate of determination to adopt or readopt the supermajority vote requirement. At any time within one year before the application expiration date, a supermajority vote requirement may be renewed, and at any time after the expiration date, a supermajority vote requirement may again be made effective for another two-year period, by readopting the provision and filing a certificate of amendment pursuant to, and subject to the limitations of, this subdivision. If the provision is not readopted in this manner, then the particular corporate action or actions previously subject to the supermajority vote shall thereafter require a vote of only a majority of either the outstanding shares or the shares of the specified class or series which had previously been subject to the supermajority vote provision, whichever the case may be.

§ 711. Maintenance by Holding Legal Owners and Disclosure to Persons on Whose Behalf Shares Are Voted; Charges; Actions to Enforce Section; Payment of Costs and Attorney's Fees; Commencement of Duties on Jan. 1, 1990

(a) The Legislature finds and declares that:

Many of the residents of this state are the legal and beneficial owners or otherwise the ultimate beneficiaries of shares of stock of domestic and foreign corporations, title to which may be held by a variety of intermediate owners as defined in subdivision (b). The informed and active involvement of such beneficial owners and beneficiaries in holding legal owners and, through them, management, accountable in their exercise of corporate power is essential to the interest of those beneficiaries and beneficial owners and to the economy and well-being of this state.

The purpose of this section is to serve the public interest by ensuring that voting records are maintained and disclosed as provided in this section. In the event that by statute or regulation pursuant to the federal Employee Retirement Income Security Act of 1974 (29 U.S.C. Sec. 1001 et seq.), there are imposed upon investment managers as defined in Sec. 2(38) thereof, duties substantially the same as those set forth in this section, compliance with those statutory or regulatory requirements by persons subject to this section shall be deemed to fulfill the obligations contained in this section.

This section shall be construed liberally to achieve that purpose.

(b) For purposes of this section, a person on whose behalf shares are voted includes, but is not limited to:

(1) A participant or beneficiary of an employee benefit plan with regard to shares held for the benefit of the participant or beneficiary.

(2) A shareholder, beneficiary, or contract owner of any entity (or of any portfolio of any entity) as defined in Section 3(a) of the federal Investment Company Act of 1940 (15 U.S.C. Sec. 80a–1 et seq.), as amended, to the extent the entity (or portfolio) holds the shares for which the record is requested.

(c) For the purposes of this section, a person on whose behalf shares are voted does not include:

(1) A person who possesses the right to terminate or withdraw from the shareholder, contract owner, participant, or beneficiary relationship with any entity (or any portfolio of any entity) defined in subdivision (b). This exclusion does not apply in the event the right of termination or withdrawal cannot be exercised without automatic imposition of a tax penalty. The right to substitute a relationship with an entity or portfolio, the shares of which are voted by or subject to the direction of the investment adviser (as defined in Section 2 of the federal Investment Company Act of 1940 (15 U.S.C. Sec. 80a–1 et seq.), as amended), of the prior entity or portfolio, or an affiliate of the investment adviser, shall not be deemed to be a right of termination or withdrawal within the meaning of this subdivision.

(2) A person entitled to receive information about a trust pursuant to Section 16061 of the Probate Code.

(3) A beneficiary, participant, contract owner, or shareholder whose interest is funded through the general assets of a life insurance company authorized to conduct business in this state.

(d) Every person possessing the power to vote shares of stock on behalf of another shall maintain a record of the manner in which the shares were voted. The record shall be maintained for a period of 12 consecutive months from the effective date of the vote.

(e) Upon a reasonable written request, the person possessing the power to vote shares of stock on behalf of another, or a designated agent, shall disclose the voting record with respect to any matter involving a specific security or securities in accordance with the following procedures:

(1) Except as set forth in paragraph (2), disclosure shall be made to the person making the request. The person making the disclosure may require identification sufficient to identify the person making the request as a person on whose behalf the shares were voted. A request for identification, if made, shall be reasonable, shall be made promptly, and may include a request for the person's social security number.

(2) If the person possessing the power to vote shares on behalf of another holds that power pursuant to an agreement entered into with a party other than the person making the request for disclosure, the person maintaining and disclosing the record pursuant to this section may, instead, make the requested disclosure to that party. Disclosure to that party shall be deemed compliance with the disclosure requirement of this section. If disclosure is made to that party and not to the person making the request, subdivision (i) shall not apply. However, nothing herein shall prohibit that party and the person possessing the power to vote on shares from entering into an agreement between themselves for the payment or assessment of a reasonable charge to defray expenses of disclosing the record.

(f) Where the entity subject to the requirements of this section is organized as a unit investment trust as defined in Section 4(2) of the federal Investment Company Act of 1940 (15 U.S.C. Sec. 80a–1 et seq.), the open-ended investment companies underlying the unit investment trust shall promptly make available their proxy voting records to the unit investment trust upon evidence of a bona fide request for voting record information pursuant to subdivision (e).

(g) Signing a proxy on another's behalf and forwarding it for disposition or receiving voting instructions does not constitute the power to vote. A person forwarding proxies or receiving voting instructions shall disclose the identity of the person having the power to vote shares upon reasonable written request by a person entitled to request a voting record under subdivision (c).

(h) For purposes of this section, if one or more persons has the power to vote shares on behalf of another, unless a governing instrument provides otherwise, the person or persons may designate an agent who shall maintain and disclose the record in accordance with subdivisions (b) and (c).

(i) Except as provided in paragraph (2) of subdivision (e), or as otherwise provided by law or a governing instrument, a person maintaining and disclosing a record pursuant to this section may assess a reasonable charge to the requesting person in order to defray expenses of disclosing the record in accordance with subdivision (e). Disclosure shall be made within a reasonable period after payment is received.

(j) Upon the petition of any person who successfully brings an action pursuant to or to enforce this section, the court may award costs and reasonable attorney's fees if the court finds that the defendant willfully violated this section.

(k) The obligation to maintain and disclose a voting record in accordance with subdivisions (b) and (c) shall commence January 1, 1990.

CHAPTER 8. SHAREHOLDER DERIVATIVE ACTIONS

§ 800. Conditions; Security; Motion for Order; Determination

(a) As used in this section, "corporation" includes an unincorporated association; "board" includes the managing body of an unincorporated association; "shareholder" includes a member of an unincorporated association; and "shares" includes memberships in an unincorporated association.

(b) No action may be instituted or maintained in right of any domestic or foreign corporation by any holder of shares or of voting trust certificates of the corporation unless both of the following conditions exist:

(1) The plaintiff alleges in the complaint that plaintiff was a shareholder, of record or beneficially, or the holder of voting trust certificates at the time of the transaction or any part thereof of which plaintiff complains or that plaintiff's shares or voting trust certificates thereafter devolved upon plaintiff by operation of law from a holder who was a holder at the time of the transaction or any part thereof complained of; provided, that any shareholder who does not meet these requirements may nevertheless be allowed in the discretion of the court to maintain the action on a preliminary showing to and determination by the court, by motion and after a hearing, at which the court shall consider such evidence, by affidavit or testimony, as it deems material, that (i) there is a strong prima facie case in favor of the claim asserted on behalf of the corporation, (ii) no other similar action has been or is likely to be instituted, (iii) the plaintiff acquired the shares before there was disclosure to the public or to the plaintiff of the wrongdoing of which plaintiff complains, (iv) unless the action can be maintained the defendant may retain a gain derived from defendant's willful breach of a fiduciary duty,

and (v) the requested relief will not result in unjust enrichment of the corporation or any shareholder of the corporation; and

(2) The plaintiff alleges in the complaint with particularity plaintiff's efforts to secure from the board such action as plaintiff desires, or the reasons for not making such effort, and alleges further that plaintiff has either informed the corporation or the board in writing of the ultimate facts of each cause of action against each defendant or delivered to the corporation or the board a true copy of the complaint which plaintiff proposes to file.

(c) In any action referred to in subdivision (b), at any time within 30 days after service of summons upon the corporation or upon any defendant who is an officer or director of the corporation, or held such office at the time of the acts complained of, the corporation or the defendant may move the court for an order, upon notice and hearing, requiring the plaintiff to furnish a bond as hereinafter provided. The motion shall be based upon one or both of the following grounds:

(1) That there is no reasonable possibility that the prosecution of the cause of action alleged in the complaint against the moving party will benefit the corporation or its shareholders.

(2) That the moving party, if other than the corporation, did not participate in the transaction complained of in any capacity.

The court on application of the corporation or any defendant may, for good cause shown, extend the 30–day period for an additional period or periods not exceeding 60 days.

(d) At the hearing upon any motion pursuant to subdivision (c), the court shall consider such evidence, written or oral, by witnesses or affidavit, as may be material (1) to the ground or grounds upon which the motion is based, or (2) to a determination of the probable reasonable expenses, including attorneys' fees, of the corporation and the moving party which will be incurred in the defense of the action. If the court determines, after hearing the evidence adduced by the parties, that the moving party has established a probability in support of any of the grounds upon which the motion is based, the court shall fix the amount of the bond, not to exceed fifty thousand dollars ($50,000), to be furnished by the plaintiff for reasonable expenses, including attorneys' fees, which may be incurred by the moving party and the corporation in connection with the action, including expenses for which the corporation may become liable pursuant to Section 317. A ruling by the court on the motion shall not be a determination of any issue in the action or of the merits thereof. If the court, upon the motion, makes a determination that a bond shall be furnished by the plaintiff as to any one or more defendants, the action shall be dismissed as to the defendant or defendants, unless the bond required by the court has been furnished within such reasonable time as may be fixed by the court.

(e) If the plaintiff shall, either before or after a motion is made pursuant to subdivision (c), or any order or determination pursuant to the motion, furnish a bond in the aggregate amount of fifty thousand dollars ($50,000) to secure the reasonable expenses of the parties entitled to make the motion, the plaintiff has complied with the requirements of this section and with any order for a bond theretofore made, and any such motion then pending shall be dismissed and no further or additional bond shall be required.

(f) If a motion is filed pursuant to subdivision (c), no pleadings need be filed by the corporation or any other defendant and the prosecution of the action shall be stayed until 10 days after the motion has been disposed of.

CHAPTER 10. SALES OF ASSETS

§ 1001. Disposition of Substantially All Assets; Approval

(a) A corporation may sell, lease, convey, exchange, transfer, or otherwise dispose of all or substantially all of its assets when the principal terms are approved by the board, and, unless the transaction is in the usual and regular course of its business, approved by the outstanding shares (Section 152), either before or after approval by the board and before or after the transaction.

A transaction constituting a reorganization (Section 181) is subject to the provisions of Chapter 12 (commencing with Section 1200) and not this section (other than subdivision (d)).

(b) Notwithstanding approval of the outstanding shares (Section 152), the board may abandon the proposed transaction without further action by the shareholders, subject to the contractual rights, if any, of third parties.

(c) The sale, lease, conveyance, exchange, transfer or other disposition may be made upon those terms and conditions and for that consideration as the board may deem in the best interests of the corporation. The consideration may be money, securities, or other property.

(d) If the acquiring party in a transaction pursuant to subdivision (a) of this section or subdivision (g) of Section 2001 is in control of or under common control with the disposing corporation, the principal terms of the sale must be approved by at least 90 percent of the voting power of the disposing corporation unless the disposition is to a domestic or foreign corporation or other business entity in consideration of the nonredeemable common shares or nonredeemable equity securities of the acquiring party or its parent.

(e) Subdivision (d) does not apply to any transaction if the Commissioner of Corporations, the Commissioner of Financial Institutions, the

Insurance Commissioner or the Public Utilities Commission has approved the terms and conditions of the transaction and the fairness of such terms and conditions pursuant to Section 25142, Section 696.5 of the Financial Code, Section 838.5 of the Insurance Code or Section 822 of the Public Utilities Code.

CHAPTER 11. MERGER

§ 1101. Agreement of Merger; Approval of Boards; Contents

* * *

Each share of the same class or series of any constituent corporation (other than the cancellation of shares held by a constituent corporation or its parent or a wholly owned subsidiary of either in another constituent corporation) shall, unless all shareholders of the class or series consent and except as provided in Section 407, be treated equally with respect to any distribution of cash, rights, securities, or other property. Notwithstanding subdivision (d), except in a short-form merger, and in the merger of a corporation into its subsidiary in which it owns at least 90 percent of the outstanding shares of each class, the nonredeemable common shares or nonredeemable equity securities of a constituent corporation may be converted only into nonredeemable common shares of the surviving party or a parent party if a constituent corporation or its parent owns, directly or indirectly, prior to the merger shares of another constituent corporation representing more than 50 percent of the voting power of the other constituent corporation prior to the merger, unless all of the shareholders of the class consent and except as provided in Section 407.

CHAPTER 12. REORGANIZATIONS

§ 1200. Approval by Board

A reorganization (Section 181) or a share exchange tender offer (Section 183.5) shall be approved by the board of:

(a) Each constituent corporation in a merger reorganization;

(b) The acquiring corporation in an exchange reorganization;

(c) The acquiring corporation and the corporation whose property and assets are acquired in a sale-of-assets reorganization;

(d) The acquiring corporation in a share exchange tender offer (Section 183.5); and

(e) The corporation in control of any constituent or acquiring domestic or foreign corporation or other business entity under subdivision (a), (b) or (c) and whose equity securities are issued, transferred, or exchanged in the reorganization (a "parent party").

§ 1201. Approval of Shareholders; Board Abandonment

(a) The principal terms of a reorganization shall be approved by the outstanding shares (Section 152) of each class of each corporation the approval of whose board is required under Section 1200, except as provided in subdivision (b) and except that (unless otherwise provided in the articles) no approval of any class of outstanding preferred shares of the surviving or acquiring corporation or parent party shall be required if the rights, preferences, privileges and restrictions granted to or imposed upon such class of shares remain unchanged (subject to the provisions of subdivision (c)). For the purpose of this subdivision, two classes of common shares differing only as to voting rights shall be considered as a single class of shares.

(b) No approval of the outstanding shares (Section 152) is required by subdivision (a) in the case of any corporation if that corporation, or its shareholders immediately before the reorganization, or both, shall own (immediately after the reorganization) equity securities, other than any warrant or right to subscribe to or purchase those equity securities, of the surviving or acquiring corporation or a parent party (subdivision (d) of Section 1200) possessing more than five-sixths of the voting power of the surviving or acquiring corporation or parent party. In making the determination of ownership by the shareholders of a corporation, immediately after the reorganization, of equity securities pursuant to the preceding sentence, equity securities which they owned immediately before the reorganization as shareholders of another party to the transaction shall be disregarded. For the purpose of this section only, the voting power of a corporation shall be calculated by assuming the conversion of all equity securities convertible (immediately or at some future time) into shares entitled to vote but not assuming the exercise of any warrant or right to subscribe to or purchase those shares.

(c) Notwithstanding subdivision (b), the principal terms of a reorganization shall be approved by the outstanding shares (Section 152) of the surviving corporation in a merger reorganization if any amendment is made to its articles which would otherwise require that approval.

(d) Notwithstanding subdivision (b) a reorganization shall be approved by the outstanding shares (Section 152) of any class of a corporation which is a party to a merger or sale-of-assets reorganization if holders of shares of that class receive shares of the surviving or acquiring corporation or parent party having different rights, preferences, privileges or restrictions than those surrendered. Shares in a foreign corporation received in exchange for shares in a domestic corporation have different rights, preferences, privileges and restrictions within the meaning of the preceding sentence.

(e) Notwithstanding subdivisions (a) and (b), the principal terms of a reorganization shall be approved by the affirmative vote of at least two-thirds of each class of the outstanding shares of any close corporation if the reorganization would result in their receiving shares of a corporation which is not a close corporation. However, the articles may provide for a lesser vote, but not less than a majority of the outstanding shares of each class.

(f) Notwithstanding subdivisions (a) and (b), the principal terms of a reorganization shall be approved by the outstanding shares (Section 152) of any class of a corporation which is a party to a merger reorganization if holders of shares of that class receive interests of a surviving other business entity in the merger.

(g) Notwithstanding subdivisions (a) and (b), the principal terms of a reorganization shall be approved by all shareholders of any class or series if, as a result of the reorganization, the holders of that class or series become personally liable for any obligations of a party to the reorganization, unless all holders of that class or series have the dissenters' rights provided in Chapter 13 (commencing with Section 1300).

(h) Any approval required by this section may be given before or after the approval by the board. Notwithstanding approval required by this section, the board may abandon the proposed reorganization without further action by the shareholders, subject to the contractual rights, if any, of third parties.

§ 1201.5 Share Exchange Tender Offers; Approval of Principal Terms

(a) The principal terms of a share-exchange tender offer (Section 183.5) shall be approved by the outstanding shares (Section 152) of each class of the corporation making the tender offer or whose shares are to be used in the tender offer, except as provided in subdivision (b) and except that (unless otherwise provided in the articles) no approval of any class of outstanding preferred shares of either corporation shall be required, if the rights, preferences, privileges, and restrictions granted to or imposed upon that class of shares remain unchanged. For the purpose of this subdivision, two classes of common shares differing only as to voting rights shall be considered as a single class of shares.

(b) No approval of the outstanding shares (Section 152) is required by subdivision (a) in the case of any corporation if the corporation, or its shareholders immediately before the tender offer, or both, shall own (immediately after the completion of the share exchange proposed in the tender offer) equity securities, (other than any warrant or right to subscribe to or purchase the equity securities), of the corporation making the tender offer or of the corporation whose shares were used in the tender offer, possessing more than five-sixths of the voting power of either corporation. In making the determination of ownership by the shareholders of a corporation, immediately after the tender offer, of equity securities pursuant to the preceding sentence, equity securities which they owned immediately before the tender offer as shareholders of another party to the transaction shall be disregarded. For the purpose of this section only, the voting power of a corporation shall be calculated by assuming the conversion of all equity securities convertible (immediately or at some future time) into shares entitled to vote but not assuming the exercise of any warrant or right to subscribe to, or purchase, shares.

§ 1202. Terms of Merger Reorganization or Sale-of-Assets Reorganization; Approval by Shareholders; Foreign Corporations

(a) In addition to the requirements of Section 1201, the principal terms of a merger reorganization shall be approved by all the outstanding shares of a corporation if the agreement of merger provides that all the outstanding shares of that corporation are canceled without consideration in the merger.

(b) In addition to the requirements of Section 1201, if the terms of a merger reorganization or sale-of-assets reorganization provide that a class or series of preferred shares is to have distributed to it a lesser amount than would be required by applicable article provisions, the principal terms of the reorganization shall be approved by the same percentage of outstanding shares of that class or series which would be required to approve an amendment of the article provisions to provide for the distribution of that lesser amount.

(c) If a parent within the meaning of Section 1200 is a foreign corporation (other than a foreign corporation to which subdivision (a) of Section 2115 is applicable), any requirement or lack of a requirement for approval by the outstanding shares of the foreign corporation shall be based, not on the application of Sections 1200 and 1201, but on the application of the laws of the state or place of incorporation of the foreign corporation.

§ 1203. Interested Party Proposal or Tender Offer to Shareholders; Affirmative Opinion; Delivery; Approval; Later Proposal or Tender Offer; Withdrawal of Vote, Consent, or Proxy; Procedures

(a) If a tender offer, including a share exchange tender offer (Section 183.5) or a written proposal for approval of a reorganization subject to Section 1200 or for a sale of assets subject to subdivision (a) of Section 1001 is made to some or all of a corporation's shareholders by an interested party (herein referred to as an "Interested Party Proposal"), an affirmative opinion in writing as to the fairness of the consideration to the shareholders of that corporation shall be delivered as follows:

(1) If no shareholder approval or acceptance is required for the consummation of the transaction, the opinion shall be delivered to the corporation's board of directors not later than the time that consumma-

tion of the transaction is authorized and approved by the board of directors.

(2) If a tender offer is made to the corporation's shareholders, the opinion shall be delivered to the shareholders at the time that the tender offer is first made in writing to the shareholders. However, if the tender offer is commenced by publication and tender offer materials are subsequently mailed or otherwise distributed to the shareholders, the opinion may be omitted in that publication if the opinion is included in the materials distributed to the shareholders.

(3) If a shareholders' meeting is to be held to vote on approval of the transaction, the opinion shall be delivered to the shareholders with the notice of the meeting (Section 601).

(4) If consents of all shareholders entitled to vote are solicited in writing (Section 603), the opinion shall be delivered at the same time as that solicitation.

(5) If the consents of all shareholders are not solicited in writing, the opinion shall be delivered to each shareholder whose consent is solicited prior to that shareholder's consent being given, and to all other shareholders at the time they are given the notice required by subdivision (b) of Section 603.

For purposes of this section, the term "interested party" means a person who is a party to the transaction and (A) directly or indirectly controls the corporation that is the subject of the tender offer or proposal, (B) is, or is directly or indirectly controlled by, an officer or director of the subject corporation, or (C) is an entity in which a material financial interest (subdivision (a) of Section 310) is held by any director or executive officer of the subject corporation. For purposes of the preceding sentence, "any executive officer" means the president, any vice president in charge of a principal business unit, division, or function such as sales, administration, research or development, or finance, and any other officer or other person who performs a policymaking function or has the same duties as those of a president or vice president. The opinion required by this subdivision shall be provided by a person who is not affiliated with the offeror and who, for compensation, engages in the business of advising others as to the value of properties, businesses, or securities. The fact that the opining person previously has provided services to the offeror or a related entity or is simultaneously engaged in providing advice or assistance with respect to the proposed transaction in a manner which makes its compensation contingent on the success of the proposed transaction shall not, for those reasons, be deemed to affiliate the opining person with the offeror. Nothing in this subdivision shall limit the applicability of the standards of review of the transaction in the event of a challenge thereto under Section 310 or subdivision (c) of Section 1312.

This subdivision shall not apply to an Interested Party Proposal if the corporation that is the subject thereof does not have shares held of record by 100 or more persons (determined as provided in Section 605), or if the transaction has been qualified under Section 25113 or 25121 and no order under Section 25140 or subdivision (a) of Section 25143 is in effect with respect to that qualification.

(b) If a tender of shares or a vote or written consent is being sought pursuant to an Interested Party Proposal and a later tender offer or written proposal for a reorganization subject to Section 1200 or sale of assets subject to subdivision (a) of Section 1001 that would require a vote or written consent of shareholders is made to the corporation or its shareholders (herein referred to as a "Later Proposal") by any other person at least 10 days prior to the date for acceptance of the tendered shares or the vote or notice of shareholder approval on the Interested Party Proposal, then each of the following shall apply:

(1) The shareholders shall be informed of the Later Proposal and any written material provided for this purpose by the later offeror shall be forwarded to the shareholders at that offeror's expense.

(2) The shareholders shall be afforded a reasonable opportunity to withdraw any vote, consent, or proxy previously given before the vote or written consent on the Interested Party Proposal becomes effective, or a reasonable time to withdraw any tendered shares before the purchase of the shares pursuant to the Interested Party Proposal. For purposes of this subdivision, a delay of 10 days from the notice or publication of the Later Proposal shall be deemed to provide a reasonable opportunity or time to effect that withdrawal.

CHAPTER 13. DISSENTERS' RIGHTS

§ 1300. Reorganization or Short-Form Merger; Dissenting Shares; Corporate Purchase at Fair Market Value; Definitions

(a) If the approval of the outstanding shares (Section 152) of a corporation is required for a reorganization under subdivisions (a) and (b) or subdivision (e) or (f) of Section 1201, each shareholder of the corporation entitled to vote on the transaction and each shareholder of a subsidiary corporation in a short-form merger may, by complying with this chapter, require the corporation in which the shareholder holds shares to purchase for cash at their fair market value the shares owned by the shareholder which are dissenting shares as defined in subdivision (b). The fair market value shall be determined as of the day before the first announcement of the terms of the proposed reorganization or short-form merger, excluding any appreciation or depreciation in consequence of the proposed action, but adjusted for any stock split, reverse stock split, or share dividend which becomes effective thereafter.

(b) As used in this chapter, "dissenting shares" means shares which come within all of the following descriptions:

(1) Which were not immediately prior to the reorganization or short-form merger either (A) listed on any national securities exchange certified by the Commissioner of Corporations under subdivision (*o*) of Section 25100 or (B) listed on the National Market System of the NASDAQ Stock Market, and the notice of meeting of shareholders to act upon the reorganization summarizes this section and Sections 1301, 1302, 1303 and 1304; provided, however, that this provision does not apply to any shares with respect to which there exists any restriction on transfer imposed by the corporation or by any law or regulation; and provided, further, that this provision does not apply to any class of shares described in subparagraph (A) or (B) if demands for payment are filed with respect to 5 percent or more of the outstanding shares of that class.

(2) Which were outstanding on the date for the determination of shareholders entitled to vote on the reorganization and (A) were not voted in favor of the reorganization or, (B) if described in subparagraph (A) or (B) of paragraph (1) (without regard to the provisos in that paragraph), were voted against the reorganization, or which were held of record on the effective date of a short-form merger; provided, however, that subparagraph (A) rather than subparagraph (B) of this paragraph applies in any case where the approval required by Section 1201 is sought by written consent rather than at a meeting.

(3) Which the dissenting shareholder has demanded that the corporation purchase at their fair market value, in accordance with Section 1301.

(4) Which the dissenting shareholder has submitted for endorsement, in accordance with Section 1302.

(c) As used in this chapter, "dissenting shareholder" means the recordholder of dissenting shares and includes a transferee of record.

§ 1312. Right of Dissenting Shareholder to Attack, Set Aside or Rescind Merger or Reorganization; Restraining Order or Injunction; Conditions

(a) No shareholder of a corporation who has a right under this chapter to demand payment of cash for the shares held by the shareholder shall have any right at law or in equity to attack the validity of the reorganization or short-form merger, or to have the reorganization or short-form merger set aside or rescinded, except in an action to test whether the number of shares required to authorize or approve the reorganization have been legally voted in favor thereof; but any holder of shares of a class whose terms and provisions specifically set forth the amount to be paid in respect to them in the event of a reorganization or short-form merger is entitled to payment in accordance with those terms and provisions or, if the principal terms of the reorganization are approved pursuant to subdivision (b) of Section 1202, is entitled to payment in accordance with the terms and provisions of the approved reorganization.

(b) If one of the parties to a reorganization or short-form merger is directly or indirectly controlled by, or under common control with, another party to the reorganization or short-form merger, subdivision (a) shall not apply to any shareholder of such party who has not demanded payment of cash for such shareholder's shares pursuant to this chapter; but if the shareholder institutes any action to attack the validity of the reorganization or short-form merger or to have the reorganization or short-form merger set aside or rescinded, the shareholder shall not thereafter have any right to demand payment of cash for the shareholder's shares pursuant to this chapter. The court in any action attacking the validity of the reorganization or short-form merger or to have the reorganization or short-form merger set aside or rescinded shall not restrain or enjoin the consummation of the transaction except upon 10–days prior notice to the corporation and upon a determination by the court that clearly no other remedy will adequately protect the complaining shareholder or the class of shareholders of which such shareholder is a member.

(c) If one of the parties to a reorganization or short-form merger is directly or indirectly controlled by, or under common control with, another party to the reorganization or short-form merger, in any action to attack the validity of the reorganization or short-form merger or to have the reorganization or short-form merger set aside or rescinded, (1) a party to a reorganization or short-form merger which controls another party to the reorganization or short-form merger shall have the burden of proving that the transaction is just and reasonable as to the shareholders of the controlled party, and (2) a person who controls two or more parties to a reorganization shall have the burden of proving that the transaction is just and reasonable as to the shareholders of any party so controlled.

CHAPTER 19. VOLUNTARY DISSOLUTION

§ 1900. Election by Shareholders; Required Vote; Election by Board; Grounds

(a) Any corporation may elect voluntarily to wind up and dissolve by the vote of shareholders holding shares representing 50 percent or more of the voting power.

(b) Any corporation which comes within one of the following descriptions may elect by approval by the board to wind up and dissolve:

(1) A corporation as to which an order for relief has been entered under Chapter 7 of the federal bankruptcy law.

(2) A corporation which has disposed of all its assets and has not conducted any business for a period of five years immediately preceding the adoption of the resolution electing to dissolve the corporation.

(3) A corporation which has issued no shares.

CHAPTER 21. FOREIGN CORPORATIONS

§ 2115. Foreign Corporations Subject to Corporate Laws of State; Tests to Determine Subject Corporations; Laws Applicable; Time of Application

(a) A foreign corporation (other than a foreign association or foreign nonprofit corporation but including a foreign parent corporation even though it does not itself transact intrastate business) is subject to the requirements of subdivision (b) commencing on the date specified in subdivision (d) and continuing until the date specified in subdivision (e) if the average of the property factor, the payroll factor and the sales factor (as defined in sections 25129, 25132, and 25134 of the Revenue and Taxation Code) with respect to it is more than 50 percent during its latest full income year and more than one-half of its outstanding voting securities are held of record by persons having addresses in this state appearing on the books of the corporation on the record date for the latest meeting of shareholders held during its latest full income year or, if no meeting was held during that year, on the last day of the latest full income year. The property factor, payroll factor, and sales factor shall be those used in computing the portion of its income allocable to this state in its franchise tax return or, with respect to corporations the allocation of whose income is governed by special formulas or that are not required to file separate or any tax returns, which would have been so used if they were governed by this three-factor formula. The determination of these factors with respect to any parent corporation shall be made on a consolidated basis, including in a unitary computation (after elimination of intercompany transactions) the property, payroll, and sales of the parent and all of its subsidiaries in which it owns directly or indirectly more than 50 percent of the outstanding shares entitled to vote for the election of directors, but deducting a percentage of the property, payroll, and sales of any subsidiary equal to the percentage minority ownership, if any, in the subsidiary. For the purpose of this subdivision, any securities held to the knowledge of the issuer in the names of broker-dealers, nominees for broker-dealers (including clearing corporations), or banks, associations, or other entities holding securities in a nominee name or otherwise on behalf of a beneficial owner (collectively "Nominee Holders"), shall not be considered outstanding. However, if the foreign corporation requests all Nominee Holders to certify, with respect to all beneficial owners for whom securities are held, the number of shares held for those beneficial owners having addresses (as shown on the records of the Nominee Holder) in this state and outside of this state, then all shares so certified shall be considered outstanding and held of record by persons having addresses either in this state or outside of this state as so certified, provided that the certification so provided shall be retained with the record of shareholders and made available for inspection and copying in the same manner as is provided in Section 1600 with respect to that record. A current list of beneficial owners of a foreign corporation's securities provided to the corporation by one or more Nominee Holders or their agent pursuant to the requirements of Rule 14b–1(b)(3) or 14b–2(b)(3) as adopted on January 6, 1992, promulgated under the Securities Exchange Act of 1934, shall constitute an acceptable certification with respect to beneficial owners for the purposes of this subdivision.

(b) Except as provided in subdivision (c), the following chapters and sections of this division shall apply to a foreign corporation as defined in subdivision (a)(to the exclusion of the law of the jurisdiction in which it is incorporated):

Chapter 1 (general provisions and definitions), to the extent applicable to the following provisions;

Section 301 (annual election of directors);

Section 303 (removal of directors without cause);

Section 304 (removal of directors by court proceedings);

Section 305, subdivision (c) (filing of director vacancies where less than a majority in office elected by shareholders);

Section 309 (directors' standard of care);

Section 316 (excluding paragraph (3) of subdivision (a) and paragraph (3) of subdivision (f)) (liability of directors for unlawful distributions);

Section 317 (indemnification of directors, officers and others);

Sections 500 to 505, inclusive (limitations on corporate distributions in cash or property);

Section 506 (liability of shareholder who receives unlawful distribution);

Section 600, subdivisions (b) and (c) (requirement for annual shareholders' meeting and remedy if same not timely held);

Section 708, subdivisions (a), (b) and (c) (shareholder's right to cumulate votes at any election of directors);

Section 710 (supermajority vote requirement);

Section 1001, subdivision (d) (limitations on sale of assets);

Section 1101 (provisions following subdivision (e)) (limitations on mergers);

Chapter 12 (commencing with Section 1200) (reorganizations);

Chapter 13 (commencing with Section 1300) (dissenters' rights);

Sections 1500 and 1501 (records and reports);

Section 1508 (action by Attorney General);

Chapter 16 (commencing with Section 1600) (rights of inspection).

(c) This section does not apply to any corporation (1) with outstanding securities listed on the New York Stock Exchange or the American Stock Exchange, or (2) with outstanding securities designated as qualified for trading on the Nasdaq National Market (or any successor thereto) of the Nasdaq Stock Market operated by the Nasdaq Stock Market, Inc., or (3) if all of its voting shares (other than directors' qualifying shares) are owned directly or indirectly by a corporation or corporations not subject to this section. For purposes of determining the number of holders of a corporation's equity securities under clause (2) of this subdivision, there shall be included, in addition to the number of recordholders reflected on the corporation's stock records, the number of holders of the equity securities held in the name of any Nominee Holder which furnishes the corporation with a certification pursuant to subdivision (a) provided that the corporation retains the certification with the record of shareholders and makes it available for inspection and copying in the same manner as is provided in Section 1600 with respect to that record.

(d) For purposes of subdivision (a), the requirements of subdivision (b) shall become applicable to a foreign corporation only upon the first day of the first income year of the corporation (i) commencing on or after the 135th day of the income year immediately following the latest income year with respect to which the tests referred to in subdivision (a) have been met or(ii) commencing on or after the entry of a final order by a court of competent jurisdiction declaring that those tests have been met.

(e) For purposes of subdivision (a), the requirements of subdivision (b) shall cease to be applicable to a foreign corporation (i) at the end of the first income year of the corporation immediately following the latest income year with respect to which at least one of the tests referred to in subdivision (a) is not met or (ii) at the end of the income year of the corporation during which a final order has been entered by a court of competent jurisdiction declaring that one of those tests is not met, provided that a contrary order has not been entered before the end of the income year.

(f) Any foreign corporation that is subject to the requirements of subdivision (b) shall advise any shareholder of record, any officer, director, employee, or other agent (within the meaning of Section 317) and any creditor of the corporation in writing, within 30 days of receipt of written request for that information, whether or not it is subject to subdivision (b) at the time the request is received. Any party who obtains a final determination by a court of competent jurisdiction that the corporation failed to provide to the party information required to be provided by this subdivision or provided the party information of the kind required to be provided by this subdivision that was incorrect, then the court, in its discretion, shall have the power to include in its judgment recovery by the party from the corporation of all court costs and reasonable attorneys' fees incurred in that legal proceeding to the extent they relate to obtaining that final determination.

E. DELAWARE GENERAL CORPORATION LAW

(Selected Sections)

Contents

---

§ 101. Incorporators; How Corporation Formed; Purposes

(a) Any person, partnership, association or corporation, singly or jointly with others, and without regard to such person's or entity's residence, domicile or state of incorporation, may incorporate or organize a corporation under this chapter by filing with the Division of Corporations in the Department of State a certificate of incorporation which shall be executed, acknowledged and filed in accordance with section 103 of this title.

(b) A corporation may be incorporated or organized under this chapter to conduct or promote any lawful business or purposes, except as may otherwise be provided by the constitution or other law of this State.

(c) Corporations for constructing, maintaining and operating public utilities, whether in or outside of this State, may be organized under this chapter, but corporations for constructing, maintaining and operating public utilities within this State shall be subject to, in addition to the provisions of this chapter, the special provisions and requirements of Title 26 applicable to such corporations.

§ 102. Contents of Certificate of Incorporation

(a) The certificate of incorporation shall set forth:

(1) The name of the corporation, which (i) shall contain 1 of the words "association," "company," "corporation," "club," "foundation," "fund," "incorporated," "institute," "society," "union," "syndicate," or "limited," (or abbreviations thereof, with or without punctuation), or words (or abbreviations thereof, with or without punctuation) of like import of foreign countries or jurisdictions (provided they are written in roman characters or letters); provided, however, that the Division of Corporations in the Department of State may waive such requirement (unless it determines that such name is, or might otherwise appear to be, that of a natural person) if such corporation executes, acknowledges and files with the Secretary of State in accordance with s 103 of this title a certificate stating that its total assets, as defined in subsection (i) of s 503 of this title, are not less than $10,000,000, (ii) shall be such as to distinguish it upon the records in the office of the Division of Corporations in the Department of State from the names on such records of other corporations, partnerships, limited partnerships, limited liability companies or business trusts organized, reserved or registered as a foreign corporation, partnership, limited partnership, limited liability company or business trust under the laws of this State, except with the written consent of such other foreign corporation or domestic or foreign partnership, limited partnership, limited liability company or business trust executed, acknowledged and filed with the Secretary of State in accordance with § 103 of this title and (iii) shall not contain the word "bank," or any variation thereof, except for the name of a bank reporting to and under the supervision of the State Bank Commissioner of this State or a subsidiary of a bank or savings association (as those terms are defined in the Federal Deposit Insurance Act, as amended, at 12 U.S.C. § 1813), or a corporation regulated under the Bank Holding Company Act of 1956, as amended, 12 U.S.C. § 1841 et seq., or the Home Owners'

Loan Act, as amended, 12 U.S.C. § 1461 et seq.; provided, however, that this section shall not be construed to prevent the use of the word "bank," or any variation thereof, in a context clearly not purporting to refer to a banking business or otherwise likely to mislead the public about the nature of the business of the corporation or to lead to a pattern and practice of abuse that might cause harm to the interests of the public or the State as determined by the Division of Corporations in the Department of State;

(2) The address (which shall include the street, number, city and county) of the corporation's registered office in this State, and the name of its registered agent at such address;

(3) The nature of the business or purposes to be conducted or promoted. It shall be sufficient to state, either alone or with other businesses or purposes, that the purpose of the corporation is to engage in any lawful act or activity for which corporations may be organized under the General Corporation Law of Delaware, and by such statement all lawful acts and activities shall be within the purposes of the corporation, except for express limitations, if any;

(4) If the corporation is to be authorized to issue only 1 class of stock, the total number of shares of stock which the corporation shall have authority to issue and the par value of each of such shares, or a statement that all such shares are to be without par value. If the corporation is to be authorized to issue more than 1 class of stock, the certificate of incorporation shall set forth the total number of shares of all classes of stock which the corporation shall have authority to issue and the number of shares of each class and shall specify each class the shares of which are to be without par value and each class the shares of which are to have par value and the par value of the shares of each such class. The certificate of incorporation shall also set forth a statement of the designations and the powers, preferences and rights, and the qualifications, limitations or restrictions thereof, which are permitted by s 151 of this title in respect of any class or classes of stock or any series of any class of stock of the corporation and the fixing of which by the certificate of incorporation is desired, and an express grant of such authority as it may then be desired to grant to the board of directors to fix by resolution or resolutions any thereof that may be desired but which shall not be fixed by the certificate of incorporation. The foregoing provisions of this paragraph shall not apply to corporations which are not to have authority to issue capital stock. In the case of such corporations, the fact that they are not to have authority to issue capital stock shall be stated in the certificate of incorporation. The conditions of membership of such corporations shall likewise be stated in the certificate of incorporation or the certificate may provide that the conditions of membership shall be stated in the bylaws;

(5) The name and mailing address of the incorporator or incorporators;

(6) If the powers of the incorporator or incorporators are to terminate upon the filing of the certificate of incorporation, the names and mailing addresses of the persons who are to serve as directors until the first annual meeting of stockholders or until their successors are elected and qualify.

(b) In addition to the matters required to be set forth in the certificate of incorporation by subsection (a) of this section, the certificate of incorporation may also contain any or all of the following matters:

(1) Any provision for the management of the business and for the conduct of the affairs of the corporation, and any provision creating, defining, limiting and regulating the powers of the corporation, the directors, and the stockholders, or any class of the stockholders, or the members of a nonstock corporation; if such provisions are not contrary to the laws of this State. Any provision which is required or permitted by any section of this chapter to be stated in the bylaws may instead be stated in the certificate of incorporation;

(2) The following provisions, in haec verba, viz:

"Whenever a compromise or arrangement is proposed between this corporation and its creditors or any class of them and/or between this corporation and its stockholders or any class of them, any court of equitable jurisdiction within the State of Delaware may, on the application in a summary way of this corporation or of any creditor or stockholder thereof or on the application of any receiver or receivers appointed for this corporation under § 291 of Title 8 of the Delaware Code or on the application of trustees in dissolution or of any receiver or receivers appointed for this corporation under § 279 of Title 8 of the Delaware Code order a meeting of the creditors or class of creditors, and/or of the stockholders or class of stockholders of this corporation, as the case may be, to be summoned in such manner as the said court directs. If a majority in number representing three fourths in value of the creditors or class of creditors, and/or of the stockholders or class of stockholders of this corporation, as the case may be, agree to any compromise or arrangement and to any reorganization of this corporation as consequence of such compromise or arrangement, the said compromise or arrangement and the said reorganization shall, if sanctioned by the court to which the said application has been made, be binding on all the creditors or class of creditors, and/or on all the stockholders or class of stockholders, of this corporation, as the case may be, and also on this corporation";

(3) Such provisions as may be desired granting to the holders of the stock of the corporation, or the holders of any class or series of a class thereof, the preemptive right to subscribe to any or all additional issues of stock of the corporation of any or all classes or series thereof, or to any securities of the corporation convertible into such stock. No stockholder shall have any preemptive right to subscribe to an additional

issue of stock or to any security convertible into such stock unless, and except to the extent that, such right is expressly granted to such stockholder in the certificate of incorporation. All such rights in existence on July 3, 1967, shall remain in existence unaffected by this paragraph unless and until changed or terminated by appropriate action which expressly provides for the change or termination;

(4) Provisions requiring for any corporate action, the vote of a larger portion of the stock or of any class or series thereof, or of any other securities having voting power, or a larger number of the directors, than is required by this chapter;

(5) A provision limiting the duration of the corporation's existence to a specified date; otherwise, the corporation shall have perpetual existence;

(6) A provision imposing personal liability for the debts of the corporation on its stockholders or members to a specified extent and upon specified conditions; otherwise, the stockholders or members of a corporation shall not be personally liable for the payment of the corporation's debts except as they may be liable by reason of their own conduct or acts;

(7) A provision eliminating or limiting the personal liability of a director to the corporation or its stockholders for monetary damages for breach of fiduciary duty as a director, provided that such provision shall not eliminate or limit the liability of a director: (i) For any breach of the director's duty of loyalty to the corporation or its stockholders; (ii) for acts or omissions not in good faith or which involve intentional misconduct or a knowing violation of law; (iii) under § 174 of this title; or (iv) for any transaction from which the director derived an improper personal benefit. No such provision shall eliminate or limit the liability of a director for any act or omission occurring prior to the date when such provision becomes effective. All references in this paragraph to a director shall also be deemed to refer (x) to a member of the governing body of a corporation which is not authorized to issue capital stock, and (y) to such other person or persons, if any, who, pursuant to a provision of the certificate of incorporation in accordance with § 141(a) of this title, exercise or perform any of the powers or duties otherwise conferred or imposed upon the board of directors by this title.

(c) It shall not be necessary to set forth in the certificate of incorporation any of the powers conferred on corporations by this chapter.

§ 103. Execution, Acknowledgment, Filing, Recording and Effective Date of Original Certificate of Incorporation and Other Instruments; Exceptions

(a) Whenever any instrument is to be filed with the Secretary of State or in accordance with this section or chapter, such instrument shall be executed as follows:

(1) The certificate of incorporation, and any other instrument to be filed before the election of the initial board of directors if the initial directors were not named in the certificate of incorporation, shall be signed by the incorporator or incorporators (or, in the case of any such other instrument, such incorporator's or incorporators' successors and assigns). If any incorporator is not available by reason of death, incapacity, unknown address, or refusal or neglect to act, then any such other instrument may be signed, with the same effect as if such incorporator had signed it, by any person for whom or on whose behalf such incorporator, in executing the certificate of incorporation, was acting directly or indirectly as employee or agent, provided that such other instrument shall state that such incorporator is not available and the reason therefor, that such incorporator in executing the certificate of incorporation was acting directly or indirectly as employee or agent for or on behalf of such person, and that such person's signature on such instrument is otherwise authorized and not wrongful.

(2) All other instruments shall be signed—

(a) By the chairman or vice-chairman of the board of directors, or by the president, or by a vice president, and attested by the secretary or an assistant secretary (or by such officers as may be duly authorized to exercise the duties, respectively, ordinarily exercised by the president or vice president and by the secretary or assistant secretary of a corporation); or

(b) If it shall appear from the instrument that there are no such officers, then by a majority of the directors or by such directors as may be designated by the board; or

(c) If it shall appear from the instrument that there are no such officers or directors, then by the holders of record, or such of them as may be designated by the holders of record, of a majority of all outstanding shares of stock; or

(d) By the holders of record of all outstanding shares of stock.

(b) Whenever any provision of this chapter requires any instrument to be acknowledged, such requirement is satisfied by either:

(1) The formal acknowledgment by the person or 1 of the persons signing the instrument that it is such person's act and deed or the act and deed of the corporation, as the case may be, and that the facts stated therein are true. Such acknowledgment shall be made before a person who is authorized by the law of the place of execution to take acknowledgments of deeds. If such person has a seal of office such person ~~he~~ shall affix it to the instrument.

(2) The signature, without more, of the person or persons signing the instrument, in which case such signature or signatures shall constitute the affirmation or acknowledgment of the signatory, under penalties of perjury, that the instrument is such person's act and deed or the act

and deed of the corporation, as the case may be, and that the facts stated therein are true.

(c) Whenever any instrument is to be filed with the Secretary of State or in accordance with this section or chapter, such requirement means that:

(1) The signed instrument shall be delivered to the office of the Secretary of State.

(2) All taxes and fees authorized by law to be collected by the Secretary of State in connection with the filing of the instrument shall be tendered to the Secretary of State, and

(3) Upon delivery of the instrument, the Secretary of State shall record the date and time of its delivery. Upon such delivery and tender of the required taxes and fees, the Secretary of State shall certify that the instrument has been filed in the Secretary of State's office by endorsing upon the signed instrument the word 'Filed,' and the date and time of its filing. This endorsement is the 'filing date' of the instrument, and is conclusive of the date and time of its filing in the absence of actual fraud. The Secretary of State shall file and index the endorsed instrument. Except as provided in paragraph (4) of this subsection and in subsection (i) of this Section, such filing date of an instrument shall be the date and time of delivery of the instrument.

(4) Upon request made upon or prior to delivery, the Secretary of State may, to the extent deemed practicable, establish as the filing date of an instrument a date and time after its delivery. If the Secretary of State refuses to file any instrument due to an error, omission or other imperfection, the Secretary of State may hold such instrument in suspension, and in such event, upon delivery of a replacement instrument in proper form for filing and tender of the required taxes and fees within five business days after notice of such suspension is given to the filer, the Secretary of State shall establish as the filing date of such instrument the date and time that would have been the filing date of the rejected instrument had it been accepted for filing. The Secretary of State shall not issue a certificate of good standing with respect to any corporation with an instrument held in suspension pursuant to this subsection. The Secretary of State may establish as the filing date of an instrument the date and time at which information from such instrument is entered pursuant to subsection (c)(7) of this Section if such instrument is delivered on the same date and within four hours after such information is entered.

(5) The Secretary of State, acting as agent for the recorders of each of the counties, shall collect and deposit in a separate account established exclusively for that purpose a county assessment fee with respect to each filed instrument and shall thereafter weekly remit from such account to the recorder of each of the said counties the amount or amounts of such fees as provided for in paragraph (c)(6) of this section or

as elsewhere provided by law. Said fees shall be for the purposes of defraying certain costs incurred by the counties in merging the information and images of such filed documents with the document information systems of each of the recorder's offices in the counties and in retrieving, maintaining and displaying such information and images in the offices of the recorders and at remote locations in each of such counties. In consideration for its acting as the agent for the recorders with respect to the collection and payment of the county assessment fees, the Secretary of State shall retain and pay over to the General Fund of the State an administrative charge of 1 percent of the total fees collected.

(6) The assessment fee to the counties shall be $24 for each 1–page instrument filed with the Secretary of State in accordance with this section and $9 for each additional page for instruments with more than 1 page. The recorder's office to receive the assessment fee shall be the recorder's office in the county in which the corporation's registered office in this State is, or is to be, located, except that an assessment fee shall not be charged for either a certificate of dissolution qualifying for treatment under § 391(a)(5)b. of this title or a document filed in accordance with subchapter XV of this chapter.

(7) The Secretary of State shall cause to be entered such information from each instrument as the Secretary deems appropriate into the Delaware Corporation Information System or any system which is a successor thereto in the office of the Secretary of State, and such information and a copy of such information shall be permanently maintained as a public record on a suitable medium. The Secretary of State is authorized to grant direct access to such system to registered agents subject to the execution of an operating agreement between the Secretary of State and such registered agent. Any registered agent granted such access shall demonstrate the existence of policies to ensure that information entered into the system accurately reflects the content of instruments in the possession of the registered agent at the time of entry.

(d) Any instrument filed in accordance with subsection (c) of this section shall be effective upon its filing date. Any instrument may provide that it is not to become effective until a specified time subsequent to the time it is filed, but such time shall not be later than a time on the 90th day after the date of its filing.

(e) If another section of this chapter specifically prescribes a manner of executing, acknowledging, or filing a specified instrument or a time when such instrument shall become effective which differs from the corresponding provisions of this section, then the provisions of such other section shall govern.

(f) Whenever any instrument authorized to be filed with the Secretary of State under any provision of this title has been so filed and is an inaccurate record of the corporate action therein referred to, or was defectively or erroneously executed, sealed or acknowledged, the instrument may be corrected by filing with the Secretary of State a certificate of correction of the instrument which shall be executed, acknowledged, and filed in accordance with this section. [The certificate of correction shall specify the inaccuracy or defect to be corrected and shall set forth the portion of the instrument in corrected form.] In lieu of filing a certificate of correction the instrument may be corrected by filing with the Secretary of State a corrected instrument which shall be executed, acknowledged and filed in accordance with this section. The corrected instrument shall be specifically designated as such in its heading, shall specify the inaccuracy or defect to be corrected, and shall set forth the entire instrument in corrected form. An instrument corrected in accordance with this section shall be effective as of the date the original instrument was filed, except as to those persons who are substantially and adversely affected by the correction and as to those persons the instrument as corrected shall be effective from the filing date.

(g) Notwithstanding that any instrument authorized to be filed with the Secretary of State under any provision of this title is when filed inaccurately, defectively or erroneously executed, sealed or acknowledged, or otherwise defective in any respect, the Secretary of State shall have no liability to any person for the preclearance for filing, the acceptance for filing, or the filing and indexing of such instrument by the Secretary of State.

(h) Any signature on any instrument authorized to be filed with the Secretary of State under any provision of this title may be a facsimile.

(i) If:

(A) together with the actual delivery of an instrument and tender of the required taxes and fees, there is delivered to the Secretary of State a separate affidavit (which in its heading shall be designated as an affidavit of extraordinary condition) attesting, on the basis of personal knowledge of the affiant or a reliable source of knowledge identified in the affidavit, that an earlier effort to deliver such instrument and tender such taxes and fees was made in good faith, specifying the nature, date and time of such good faith effort and requesting that the Secretary of State establish such date and time as the filing date of such instrument; or

(B) upon the actual delivery of an instrument and tender of the required taxes and fees, the Secretary of State in his or her discretion provides a written waiver of the requirement for such an affidavit stating that it appears to the Secretary of State that an earlier effort to deliver such instrument and tender such taxes and fees was made in good faith and specifying the date and time of such effort; and

(C) the Secretary of State determines that an extraordinary condition existed at such date and time, that such earlier effort was unsuccessful as a result of the existence of such extraordinary condition, and that such actual delivery and tender were made within a reasonable period (not to exceed two business days) after the cessation of such extraordinary condition, then the Secretary of State may establish such date and time as the filing date of such instrument. No fee shall be paid to the Secretary of State for receiving an affidavit of extraordinary condition. For purposes of this subsection, an extraordinary condition means: any emergency resulting from an attack on, invasion or occupation by foreign military forces of, or disaster, catastrophe, war or other armed conflict, revolution or insurrection, or rioting or civil commotion in, the United States or a locality in which the Secretary of State conducts its business or in which the good faith effort to deliver the instrument and tender the required taxes and fees is made, or the immediate threat of any of the foregoing; or any malfunction or outage of the electrical or telephone service to the Secretary of State's office, or weather or other condition in or about a locality in which the Secretary of State conducts its business, as a result of which the Secretary of State's office is not open for the purpose of the filing of instruments under this Chapter or such filing cannot be effected without extraordinary effort. The Secretary of State may require such proof as it deems necessary to make the determination required under clause (C) of this subsection, and any such determination shall be conclusive in the absence of actual fraud. If the Secretary of State establishes the filing date of an instrument pursuant to this subsection, the date and time of delivery of the affidavit of extraordinary condition or the date and time of the Secretary of State's written waiver of such affidavit shall be endorsed on such affidavit or waiver and such affidavit or waiver, so endorsed, shall be attached to the filed instrument to which it relates. Such filed instrument shall be effective as of the date and time established as the filing date by the Secretary of State pursuant to this subsection, except as to those persons who are substantially and adversely affected by such establishment and, as to those persons, the instrument shall be effective from the date and time endorsed on the affidavit of extraordinary condition or written waiver attached thereto.

§ 104. Certificate of Incorporation; Definition

The term "certificate of incorporation," as used in this chapter, unless the context requires otherwise, includes not only the original certificate of incorporation filed to create a corporation but also all other certificates, agreements of merger or consolidation, plans of reorganization, or other instruments, howsoever designated, which are filed pursuant to §§ 102, 133–136, 151, 241–243, 245, 251–258, 263–264, 303, or any other section of this title, and which have the effect of amending or supplementing in some respect a corporation's original certificate of incorporation.

§ 105. Certificate of Incorporation and Other Certificates; Evidence

A copy of a certificate of incorporation or restated certificate of incorporation, or of any other certificate which has been filed in the office of the Secretary of State as required by any provision of this title shall, when duly certified by the Secretary of State, be received in all courts, public offices, and official bodies as prima facie evidence of:

(1) due execution, acknowledgment and filing of the instrument;

(2) observance and performance of all acts and conditions necessary to have been observed and performed precedent to the instrument becoming effective; and

(3) any other facts required or permitted by law to be stated in the instrument.

§ 106. Commencement of Corporate Existence

Upon the filing with the Secretary of State of the certificate of incorporation, executed and acknowledged in accordance with section 103, the incorporator or incorporators who signed the certificate, and such incorporator's or incorporators' successors and assigns, shall, from the date of such filing, be and constitute a body corporate, by the name set forth in the certificate, subject to the provisions of section 103(d) of this title and subject to dissolution or other termination of its existence as provided in this chapter.

§ 107. Powers of Incorporators

If the persons who are to serve as directors until the first annual meeting of stockholders have not been named in the certificate of incorporation, the incorporator or incorporators, until the directors are elected, shall manage the affairs of the corporation and may do whatever is necessary and proper to perfect the organization of the corporation, including the adoption of the original by-laws of the corporation and the election of directors.

§ 108. Organization Meeting of Incorporators or Directors Named in Certificate of Incorporation

(a) After the filing of the certificate of incorporation an organization meeting of the incorporator or incorporators, or of the board of directors if the initial directors were named in the certificate of incorporation, shall be held, either within or without this State, at the call of a majority of the incorporators or directors, as the case may be, for the purposes of adopting by-laws, electing directors (if the meeting is of the incorporators) to serve or hold office until the first annual meeting of stockholders or until their successors are elected and qualify, electing officers if the meeting is of the directors, doing any other or further acts to perfect the organization of the corporation, and transacting such other business as may come before the meeting.

(b) The persons calling the meeting shall give to each other incorporator or director, as the case may be, at least 2 days written notice thereof by any usual means of communication, which notice shall state the time, place and purposes of the meeting as fixed by the persons calling it. Notice of the meeting need not be given to anyone who attends the meeting or who signs a waiver of notice either before or after the meeting.

(c) Any action permitted to be taken at the organization meeting of the incorporators or directors, as the case may be, may be taken without a meeting if each incorporator or director, where there is more than one, or sole incorporator or director where there is only one, signs an instrument which states the action so taken.

§ 109. By-Laws

(a) The original or other by-laws of a corporation may be adopted, amended, or repealed by the incorporators, by the initial directors if they were named in the certificate of incorporation, or, before a corporation has received any payment for any of its stock, by its board of directors. After a corporation has received any payment for any of its stock, the power to adopt, amend or repeal by-laws shall be in the stockholders entitled to vote, or, in the case of a nonstock corporation, in its members entitled to vote; provided, however, any corporation may, in its certificate of incorporation, confer the power to adopt, amend, or repeal by-laws upon the directors or, in the case of a non-stock corporation, upon its governing body by whatever name designated. The fact that such power has been so conferred upon the directors or governing body, as the case may be, shall not divest the stockholders or members of the power, nor limit their power to adopt, amend or repeal by-laws.

(b) The by-laws may contain any provision, not inconsistent with law or with the certificate of incorporation, relating to the business of the corporation, the conduct of its affairs, and its rights or powers or the rights or powers of its stockholders, directors, officers or employees.

§ 110. Emergency By-Laws and Other Powers in Emergency

(a) The board of directors of any corporation may adopt emergency by-laws, subject to repeal or change by action of the stockholders, which shall notwithstanding any different provision elsewhere in this chapter or in Chapters 3 and 5 of Title 26, or in Chapter 7 of Title 5, or in the certificate of incorporation or by-laws, be operative during any emergency resulting from an attack on the United States or on a locality in which the corporation conducts its business or customarily holds meetings of its board of directors or its stockholders, or during any nuclear or atomic disaster, or during the existence of any catastrophe, or other similar emergency condition, as a result of which a quorum of the board of directors or a standing committee thereof cannot readily be convened for action. The emergency by-laws may make any provision that may be practical and necessary for the circumstances of the emergency, including provisions that:

(1) A meeting of the board of directors or a committee thereof may be called by any officer or director in such manner and under such conditions as shall be prescribed in the emergency by-laws;

(2) The director or directors in attendance at the meeting, or any greater number fixed by the emergency by-laws, shall constitute a quorum; and

(3) The officers or other persons designated on a list approved by the board of directors before the emergency, all in such order of priority and subject to such conditions and for such period of time (not longer than reasonably necessary after the termination of the emergency) as may be provided in the emergency by-laws or in the resolution approving the list, shall, to the extent required to provide a quorum at any meeting of the board of directors, be deemed directors for such meeting.

(b) The board of directors, either before or during any such emergency, may provide, and from time to time modify, lines of succession in the event that during such emergency any or all officers or agents of the corporation shall for any reason be rendered incapable of discharging their duties.

(c) The board of directors, either before or during any such emergency, may, effective in the emergency, change the head office or designate several alternative head offices or regional offices, or authorize the officers so to do.

(d) No officer, director or employee acting in accordance with any emergency by-laws shall be liable except for willful misconduct.

(e) To the extent not inconsistent with any emergency by-laws so adopted, the by-laws of the corporation shall remain in effect during any emergency and upon its termination the emergency by-laws shall cease to be operative.

(f) Unless otherwise provided in emergency by-laws, notice of any meeting of the board of directors during such an emergency may be given only to such of the directors as it may be feasible to reach at the time and by such means as may be feasible at the time, including publication or radio.

(g) To the extent required to constitute a quorum at any meeting of the board of directors during such an emergency, the officers of the corporation who are present shall, unless otherwise provided in emergency by-laws, be deemed, in order of rank and within the same rank in order of seniority, directors for such meeting.

(h) Nothing contained in this section shall be deemed exclusive of any other provisions for emergency powers consistent with other sections of this title which have been or may be adopted by corporations created under the provisions of this chapter.

§ 121. General Powers

(a) In addition to the powers enumerated in Section 122 of this title, every corporation, its officers, directors, and stockholders shall possess and may exercise all the powers and privileges granted by this chapter or by any other law or by its certificate of incorporation, together with any powers incidental thereto, so far as such powers and privileges are necessary or convenient to the conduct, promotion or attainment of the business or purposes set forth in its certificate of incorporation.

(b) Every corporation shall be governed by the provisions and be subject to the restrictions and liabilities contained in this chapter.

§ 122. Specific Powers

Every corporation created under this chapter shall have power to:

(1) Have perpetual succession by its corporate name, unless a limited period of duration is stated in its certificate of incorporation;

(2) Sue and be sued in all courts and participate, as a party or otherwise, in any judicial, administrative, arbitrative or other proceeding, in its corporate name;

(3) Have a corporate seal, which may be altered at pleasure, and use the same by causing it or a facsimile thereof, to be impressed or affixed or in any other manner reproduced;

(4) Purchase, receive, take by grant, gift, devise, bequest or otherwise lease, or otherwise acquire, own, hold, improve, employ, use and otherwise deal in and with real or personal property, or any interest therein, wherever situated, and to sell, convey, lease, exchange, transfer or otherwise dispose of, or mortgage or pledge, all or any of its property and assets, or any interest therein, wherever situated;

(5) Appoint such officers and agents as the business of the corporation requires and to pay or otherwise provide for them suitable compensation;

(6) Adopt, amend and repeal by-laws;

(7) Wind up and dissolve itself in the manner provided in this chapter;

(8) Conduct its business, carry on its operations, and have offices and exercise its powers within or without this State;

(9) Make donations for the public welfare or for charitable, scientific or educational purposes, and in time of war or other national emergency in aid thereof;

(10) Be an incorporator, promoter, or manager of other corporations of any type or kind;

(11) Participate with others in any corporation, partnership, limited partnership, joint venture, or other association of any kind, or in any transaction, undertaking or arrangement which the participating corporation would have power to conduct by itself, whether or not such participation involves sharing or delegation of control with or to others;

(12) Transact any lawful business which the corporation's board of directors shall find to be in aid of governmental authority;

(13) Make contracts, including contracts of guaranty and suretyship, incur liabilities, borrow money at such rates of interest as the corporation may determine, issue its notes, bonds and other obligations, and secure any of its obligations by mortgage, pledge or other encumbrance of all or any of its property, franchises and income, and make contracts of guaranty and suretyship which are necessary or convenient to the conduct, promotion or attainment of the business of (a) a corporation all of the outstanding stock of which is owned, directly or indirectly, by the contracting corporation, or (b) a corporation which owns, directly or indirectly, all of the outstanding stock of the contracting corporation, or (c) a corporation all of the outstanding stock of which is owned, directly or indirectly, by a corporation which owns, directly or indirectly, all of the outstanding stock of the contracting corporation, which contracts of guaranty and suretyship shall be deemed to be necessary or convenient to the conduct, promotion or attainment of the business of the contracting corporation, and make other contracts of guaranty and suretyship which are necessary or convenient to the conduct, promotion or attainment of the business of the contracting corporation;

(14) Lend money for its corporate purposes, invest and reinvest its funds, and take, hold and deal with real and personal property as security for the payment of funds so loaned or invested;

(15) Pay pensions and establish and carry out pension, profit sharing, stock option, stock purchase, stock bonus, retirement, benefit, incentive and compensation plans, trusts and provisions for any or all of its directors, officers, and employees, and for any or all of the directors, officers, and employees of its subsidiaries;

(16) Provide insurance for its benefit on the life of any of its directors, officers, or employees, or on the life of any stockholder for the purpose of acquiring at such stockholder's ~~his~~ death shares of its stock owned by such stockholder.

(17) Renounce, in its certificate of incorporation or by action of its board of directors, any interest or expectancy of the corporation in, or in

being offered an opportunity to participate in, specified business opportunities or specified classes or categories of business opportunities that are presented to the corporation or one or more of its officers, directors or stockholders.

§ 123. Powers Respecting Securities of Other Corporations or Entities

Any corporation organized under the laws of this State may guarantee, purchase, take, receive, subscribe for or otherwise acquire; own, hold, use or otherwise employ; sell, lease, exchange, transfer, or otherwise dispose of; mortgage, lend, pledge or otherwise deal in and with, bonds and other obligations of, or shares or other securities or interests in, or issued by, any other domestic or foreign corporation, partnership, association, or individual, or by any government or agency or instrumentality thereof. A corporation while owner of any such securities may exercise all the rights, powers and privileges of ownership, including the right to vote.

§ 124. Effect of Lack of Corporate Capacity or Power; Ultra Vires

No act of a corporation and no conveyance or transfer of real or personal property to or by a corporation shall be invalid by reason of the fact that the corporation was without capacity or power to do such act or to make or receive such conveyance or transfer, but such lack of capacity or power may be asserted:

(1) In a proceeding by a stockholder against the corporation to enjoin the doing of any act or acts or the transfer of real or personal property by or to the corporation. If the unauthorized acts or transfer sought to be enjoined are being, or are to be, performed or made pursuant to any contract to which the corporation is a party, the court may, if all of the parties to the contract are parties to the proceeding and if it deems the same to be equitable, set aside and enjoin the performance of such contract, and in so doing may allow to the corporation or to the other parties to the contract, as the case may be, such compensation as may be equitable for the loss or damage sustained by any of them which may result from the action of the court in setting aside and enjoining the performance of such contract, but anticipated profits to be derived from the performance of the contract shall not be awarded by the court as a loss or damage sustained.

(2) In a proceeding by the corporation, whether acting directly or through a receiver, trustee, or other legal representative, or through stockholders in a representative suit, against an incumbent or former officer or director of the corporation, for loss or damage due to such incumbent or former officer's or director's ~~his~~ unauthorized act.

(3) In a proceeding by the Attorney General to dissolve the corporation, or to enjoin the corporation from the transaction of unauthorized business.

* * *

§ 131. Registered Office in State; Principal Office or Place of Business in State

(a) Every corporation shall have and maintain in this State a registered office which may, but need not be, the same as its place of business.

(b) Whenever the term "corporation's principal office or place of business in this State" or "principal office or place of business of the corporation in this State", or other term of like import, is or has been used in a corporation's certificate of incorporation, or in any other document, or in any statute, it shall be deemed to mean and refer to, unless the context indicates otherwise, the corporation's registered office required by this section; and it shall not be necessary for any corporation to amend its certificate of incorporation or any other document to comply with this section.

§ 132. Registered Agent in State; Resident Agent

(a) Every corporation shall have and maintain in this State a registered agent, which agent may be any of (i) the corporation itself, (ii) an individual resident in this State, (iii) a domestic corporation (other than the corporation itself), a domestic limited partnership, a domestic limited liability company or a domestic business trust or (iv) a foreign corporation, a foreign limited partnership or a foreign limited liability company authorized to transact business in this State, in each case, having a business office identical with the office of such registered agent which generally is open during normal business hours to accept service of process and otherwise perform the functions of a registered agent.

(b) Whenever the term "resident agent" or "resident agent in charge of a corporation's principal office or place of business in this State", or other term of like import which refers to a corporation's agent required by statute to be located in this State, is or has been used in a corporation's certificate of incorporation, or in any other document, or in any statute, it shall be deemed to mean and refer to, unless the context indicates otherwise, the corporation's registered agent required by this section; and it shall not be necessary for any corporation to amend its certificate of incorporation or any other document to comply with this section.

§ 133. Change of Location of Registered Office; Change of Registered Agent

Any corporation may, by resolution of its board of directors, change the location of its registered office in this State to any other place in this

State. By like resolution, the registered agent of a corporation may be changed to any other person or corporation including itself. In either such case, the resolution shall be as detailed in its statement as is required by section 102(a)(2) of this title. Upon the adoption of such a resolution, a certificate certifying the change shall be executed, acknowledged, and filed in accordance with section 103 of this title.

§ 134. Change of Address or Name of Registered Agent

(a) A registered agent may change the address of the registered office of the corporation or corporations for which the agent is a registered agent to another address in this State by filing with the Secretary of State a certificate, executed and acknowledged by such registered agent, setting forth the address at which such registered agent has maintained the registered office for each of the corporations for which it is a registered agent, and further certifying to the new address to which each such registered office will be changed on a given day, and at which new address such registered agent will thereafter maintain the registered office for each of the corporations for which it is a registered agent. Thereafter, or until further change of address, as authorized by law, the registered office in this State of each of the corporations for which the agent is a registered agent shall be located at the new address of the registered agent thereof as given in the certificate.

(b) In the event of a change of name of any person or corporation acting as registered agent in this State, such registered agent shall file with the Secretary of State a certificate, executed and acknowledged by such registered agent, setting forth the new name of such registered agent, the name of such registered agent before it was changed, and the address at which such registered agent has maintained the registered office for each of the corporations for which it acts as a registered agent. A change of name of any person or corporation acting as a registered agent as a result of a merger or consolidation of the registered agent, with or into another person or corporation which succeeds to its assets by operation of law, shall be deemed a change of name for purposes of this section.

§ 135. Resignation of Registered Agent Coupled With Appointment of Successor

The registered agent of 1 or more corporations may resign and appoint a successor registered agent by filing a certificate with the Secretary of State, stating the name and address of the successor agent, in accordance with § 102(a)(2) of this title. There shall be attached to such certificate a statement of each affected corporation ratifying and approving such change of registered agent. Each such statement shall be executed and acknowledged in accordance with section 103 of this title. Upon such filing, the successor registered agent shall become the registered agent of such corporations as have ratified and approved such substitution and the successor registered agent's address, as stated in such certificate, shall become the address of each such corporation's registered office in this State. The Secretary of State shall then issue a certificate that the successor registered agent has become the registered agent of the corporations so ratifying and approving such change, and setting out the names of such corporations.

§ 136. Resignation of Registered Agent Not Coupled With Appointment of Successor

(a) The registered agent of 1 or more corporations may resign without appointing a successor by filing a certificate of resignation with the Secretary of State, but such resignation shall not become effective until 30 days after the certificate is filed. The certificate shall be executed and acknowledged by the registered agent, shall contain a statement that written notice of resignation was given to the corporation at least 30 days prior to the filing of the certificate by mailing or delivering such notice to the corporation at its address last known to the registered agent and shall set forth the date of such notice.

(b) After receipt of the notice of the resignation of its registered agent, provided for in subsection (a) of this section, the corporation for which such registered agent was acting shall obtain and designate a new registered agent to take the place of the registered agent so resigning in the same manner as provided in § 133 of this title for change of registered agent. If such corporation, being a corporation of this State, fails to obtain and designate a new registered agent as aforesaid prior to the expiration of the period of 30 days after the filing by the registered agent of the certificate of resignation, the Secretary of State shall declare the charter of such corporation forfeited. If such corporation, being a foreign corporation, fails to obtain and designate a new registered agent as aforesaid prior to the expiration of the period of 30 days after the filing by the registered agent of the certificate of resignation, the Secretary of State shall forfeit its authority to do business in this State.

(c) After the resignation of the registered agent shall have become effective as provided in this section and if no new registered agent shall have been obtained and designated in the time and manner aforesaid, service of legal process against the corporation for which the resigned registered agent had been acting shall thereafter be upon the Secretary of State in accordance with § 321 of this title.

§ 141. Board of Directors; Powers; Number, Qualifications, Terms and Quorum; Committees; Classes of Directors; Non-profit Corporations; Reliance Upon Books; Action Without Meeting; Removal

(a) The business and affairs of every corporation organized under this chapter shall be managed by or under the direction of a board of directors, except as may be otherwise provided in this chapter or in its certificate of incorporation. If any such provision is made in the certificate of incorporation, the powers and duties conferred or imposed upon the board of directors by this chapter shall be exercised or performed to such extent and by such person or persons as shall be provided in the certificate of incorporation.

(b) The board of directors of a corporation shall consist of 1 or more members, each of whom shall be a natural person. The number of directors shall be fixed by, or in the manner provided in, the by-laws, unless the certificate of incorporation fixes the number of directors, in which case a change in the number of directors shall be made only by amendment of the certificate. Directors need not be stockholders unless so required by the certificate of incorporation or the by-laws. The certificate of incorporation or by-laws may prescribe other qualifications for directors. Each director shall hold office until such director's ~~his~~ successor is elected and qualified or until his earlier resignation or removal. Any director may resign at any time upon notice given in writing or by electronic transmission to the corporation. A majority of the total number of directors shall constitute a quorum for the transaction of business unless the certificate of incorporation or the by-laws require a greater number. Unless the certificate of incorporation provides otherwise, the by-laws may provide that a number less than a majority shall constitute a quorum which in no case shall be less than 1/3 of the total number of directors except that when a board of 1 director is authorized under the provisions of this section, then 1 director shall constitute a quorum. The vote of the majority of the directors present at a meeting at which a quorum is present shall be the act of the board of directors unless the certificate of incorporation or the by-laws shall require a vote of a greater number.

(c)(1) All corporations incorporated prior to July 1, 1996, shall be governed by paragraph (1) of this subsection, provided that any such corporation may by a resolution adopted by a majority of the whole board elect to be governed by paragraph (2) of this subsection, in which case paragraph (1) of this subsection shall not apply to such corporation. All corporations incorporated on or after July 1, 1996, shall be governed by paragraph (2) of this subsection. The board of directors may, by resolution passed by a majority of the whole board, designate 1 or more committees, each committee to consist of 1 or more of the directors of the corporation. The board may designate 1 or more directors as alternate members of any committee, who may replace any absent or disqualified member at any meeting of the committee. The bylaws may provide that in the absence or disqualification of a member of a committee, the member or members present at any meeting and not disqualified from voting, whether or not the member or members present constitute a quorum, may unanimously appoint another member of the board of directors to act at the meeting in the place of any such absent or disqualified member. Any such committee, to the extent provided in the resolution of the board of directors, or in the bylaws of the corporation, shall have and may exercise all the powers and authority of the board of directors in the management of the business and affairs of the corporation, and may authorize the seal of the corporation to be affixed to all papers which may require it; but no such committee shall have the power or authority in reference to amending the certificate of incorporation (except that a committee may, to the extent authorized in the resolution or resolutions providing for the issuance of shares of stock adopted by the board of directors as provided in subsection (a) of § 151 of this title, fix the designations and any of the preferences or rights of such shares relating to dividends, redemption, dissolution, any distribution of assets of the corporation or the conversion into, or the exchange of such shares for, shares of any other class or classes or any other series of the same or any other class or classes of stock of the corporation or fix the number of shares of any series of stock or authorize the increase or decrease of the shares of any series), adopting an agreement of merger or consolidation under § 251, § 252, § 254, § 255, § 256, § 257, § 258, § 263 or § 264 of this title, recommending to the stockholders the sale, lease or exchange of all or substantially all of the corporation's property and assets, recommending to the stockholders a dissolution of the corporation or a revocation of a dissolution, or amending the bylaws of the corporation; and, unless the resolution, bylaws or certificate of incorporation expressly so provides, no such committee shall have the power or authority to declare a dividend, to authorize the issuance of stock or to adopt a certificate of ownership and merger pursuant to § 253 of this title.

(2) The board of directors may designate 1 or more committees, each committee to consist of 1 or more of the directors of the corporation. The board may designate 1 or more directors as alternate members of any committee, who may replace any absent or disqualified member at any meeting of the committee. The bylaws may provide that in the absence or disqualification of a member of a committee, the member or members present at any meeting and not disqualified from voting, whether or not such member or members constitute a quorum, may unanimously appoint another member of the board of directors to act at the meeting in the place of any such absent or disqualified member. Any such committee, to the extent provided in the resolution of the board of directors, or in the bylaws of the corporation, shall have and may exercise all the powers and authority of the board of directors in the management of the business and affairs of the corporation, and may authorize the seal of the corporation to be affixed to all papers which may require it; but no such committee shall have the power or authority in reference to the following matter: (i) approving or adopting, or recommending to the stockholders, any action or matter expressly required by this chapter to be submitted to stockholders for approval or (ii) adopting, amending or repealing any bylaw of the corporation.

(3) Unless otherwise provided in the certificate of incorporation, the bylaws or the resolution of the board of directors designating the committee, a committee may create one or more subcommittees, each subcommittee to consist of one or more members of the committee, and delegate to a subcommittee any or all of the powers and authority of the committee.

(d) The directors of any corporation organized under this chapter may, by the certificate of incorporation or by an initial by-law, or by a by-law adopted by a vote of the stockholders, be divided into 1, 2 or 3 classes; the term of office of those of the first class to expire at the annual meeting next ensuing; of the second class 1 year thereafter; of the third class 2 years thereafter; and at each annual election held after such classification and election, directors shall be chosen for a full term, as the case may be, to succeed those whose terms expire. The certificate of incorporation may confer upon holders of any class or series of stock the right to elect one or more directors who shall serve for such term, and have such voting powers as shall be stated in the certificate of incorporation. The terms of office and voting powers of the directors elected in the manner so provided in the certificate of incorporation may be greater than or less than those of any other director or class of directors. If the certificate of incorporation provides that directors elected by the holders of a class or series of stock shall have more or less than 1 vote per director on any matter, every reference in this chapter to a majority or other proportion of directors shall refer to a majority or other proportion of the votes of such directors.

(e) A member of the board of directors, or a member of any committee designated by the board of directors, shall, in the performance of such member's ~~his~~ duties, be fully protected in relying in good faith upon the records of the corporation and upon such information, opinions, reports or statements presented to the corporation by any of the corporation's officers or employees, or committees of the board of directors, or by any other person as to matters the member reasonably believes are within such other person's professional or expert competence and who has been selected with reasonable care by or on behalf of the corporation.

(f) Unless otherwise restricted by the certificate of incorporation or by-laws, any action required or permitted to be taken at any meeting of the board of directors, or of any committee thereof may be taken without a meeting if all members of the board or committee, as the case may be, consent thereto in writing or by electronic transmission, and the writing or writings or electronic transmission or transmissions are filed with the minutes of proceedings of the board, or committee. Such filing shall be in paper form if the minutes are maintained in paper form and shall be in electronic form if the minutes are maintained in electronic form.

(g) Unless otherwise restricted by the certificate of incorporation or by-laws, the board of directors of any corporation organized under this chapter may hold its meetings, and have an office or offices, outside of this State.

(h) Unless otherwise restricted by the certificate of incorporation or by-laws, the board of directors shall have the authority to fix the compensation of directors.

(i) Unless otherwise restricted by the certificate of incorporation or by-laws, members of the board of directors of any corporation, or any committee designated by such board, may participate in a meeting of such board, or committee by means of conference telephone or other communications equipment by means of which all persons participating in the meeting can hear each other, and participation in a meeting pursuant to this subsection shall constitute presence in person at such meeting.

(j) The certificate of incorporation of any corporation organized under this chapter which is not authorized to issue capital stock may provide that less than one-third of the members of the governing body may constitute a quorum thereof and may otherwise provide that the business and affairs of the corporation shall be managed in a manner different from that provided in this section. Except as may be otherwise provided by the certificate of incorporation, the provisions of this section shall apply to such a corporation, and when so applied, all references to the board of directors, to members thereof, and to stockholders shall be deemed to refer to the governing body of the corporation, the members thereof and the members of the corporation, respectively.

(k) Any director or the entire board of directors may be removed, with or without cause, by the holders of a majority of the shares then entitled to vote at an election of directors, except as follows:

(1) Unless the certificate of incorporation otherwise provides, in the case of a corporation whose board is classified as provided in subsection (d) of this section, shareholders may effect such removal only for cause; or

(2) ~~(ii)~~ In the case of a corporation having cumulative voting, if less than the entire board is to be removed, no director may be removed without cause if the votes cast against such director's ~~his~~ removal would be sufficient to elect such director ~~him~~ if then cumulatively voted at an election of the entire board of directors, or, if there be classes of directors, at an election of the class of directors of which such director ~~he~~ is a part.

Whenever the holders of any class or series are entitled to elect 1 ~~one~~ or more directors by the provisions of the certificate of incorporation, the provisions of this subsection shall apply, in respect to the removal without cause of a director or directors so elected, to the vote of the holders of the outstanding shares of that class or series and not to the vote of the outstanding shares as a whole.

§ 142. Officers; Titles; Duties; Selection; Term; Failure to Elect; Vacancies

(a) Every corporation organized under this chapter shall have such officers with such titles and duties as shall be stated in the by-laws or in a resolution of the board of directors which is not inconsistent with the by-laws and as may be necessary to enable it to sign instruments and stock certificates which comply with sections 103(a)(2) and 158 of this chapter. One of the officers shall have the duty to record the proceedings of the meetings of the stockholders and directors in a book to be kept for that purpose. Any number of offices may be held by the same person unless the certificate of incorporation or by-laws otherwise provide.

(b) Officers shall be chosen in such manner and shall hold their offices for such terms as are prescribed by the by-laws or determined by the board of directors or other governing body. Each officer shall hold office until such officer's successor is elected and qualified or until such officer's earlier resignation or removal.

(c) The corporation may secure the fidelity of any or all of its officers or agents by bond or otherwise.

(d) A failure to elect officers shall not dissolve or otherwise affect the corporation.

(e) Any vacancy occurring in any office of the corporation by death, resignation, removal or otherwise, shall be filled as the by-laws provide. In the absence of such provision, the vacancy shall be filled by the board of directors or other governing body.

§ 143. Loans to Employees and Officers; Guaranty of Obligations of Employees and Officers

Any corporation may lend money to, or guarantee any obligation of, or otherwise assist any officer or other employee of the corporation or of its subsidiary, including any officer or employee who is a director of the corporation or its subsidiary, whenever, in the judgment of the directors, such loan, guaranty or assistance may reasonably be expected to benefit the corporation. The loan, guaranty or other assistance may be with or without interest, and may be unsecured, or secured in such manner as the board of directors shall approve, including, without limitation, a pledge of shares of stock of the corporation. Nothing in this section contained shall be deemed to deny, limit or restrict the powers of guaranty or warranty of any corporation at common law or under any statute.

§ 144. Interested Directors; Quorum

(a) No contract or transaction between a corporation and one or more of its directors or officers, or between a corporation and any other corporation, partnership, association, or other organization in which one or more of its directors or officers are directors or officers, or have a financial interest, shall be void or voidable solely for this reason, or solely because the director or officer is present at or participates in the meeting of the board or committee thereof which authorizes the contract or transaction, or solely because any such director's or officer's votes are counted for such purpose, if:

(1) The material facts as to the director's or officer's relationship or interest and as to the contract or transaction are disclosed or are known to the board of directors or the committee, and the board or committee in good faith authorizes the contract or transaction by the affirmative votes of a majority of the disinterested directors, even though the disinterested directors be less than a quorum; or

(2) The material facts as to the director's or officer's relationship or interest and as to the contract or transaction are disclosed or are known to the shareholders entitled to vote thereon, and the contract or transaction is specifically approved in good faith by vote of the shareholders; or

(3) The contract or transaction is fair as to the corporation as of the time it is authorized, approved or ratified, by the board of directors, a committee thereof, or the shareholders.

(b) Common or interested directors may be counted in determining the presence of a quorum at a meeting of the board of directors or of a committee which authorizes the contract or transaction.

§ 145. Indemnification of Officers, Directors, Employees and Agents; Insurance

(a) A corporation shall have power to indemnify any person who was or is a party or is threatened to be made a party to any threatened, pending or completed action, suit or proceeding, whether civil, criminal, administrative or investigative (other than an action by or in the right of the corporation) by reason of the fact that he is or was a director, officer, employee or agent of the corporation, or is or was serving at the request of the corporation as a director, officer, employee or agent of another corporation, partnership, joint venture, trust or other enterprise, against expenses (including attorneys' fees), judgments, fines and amounts paid in settlement actually and reasonably incurred by him in connection with such action, suit or proceeding if he acted in good faith and in a manner he reasonably believed to be in or not opposed to the best interests of the corporation, and, with respect to any criminal action or proceeding, had no reasonable cause to believe his conduct was unlawful. The termination of any action, suit or proceeding by judgment, order, settlement, conviction, or upon a plea of *nolo contendere* or its equivalent, shall not, of itself, create a presumption that the person did not act in good faith and in a manner which he reasonably believed to be in or not opposed to the best interests of the corporation, and, with respect to any criminal action or proceeding, had reasonable cause to believe that his conduct was unlawful.

(b) A corporation may indemnify any person who was or is a party or is threatened to be made a party to any threatened, pending or completed action or suit by or in the right of the corporation to procure a judgment in its favor by reason of the fact that he is or was a director, officer, employee or agent of the corporation, or is or was serving at the request of the corporation as a director, officer, employee or agent of another corporation, partnership, joint venture, trust or other enterprise against expenses (including attorneys' fees) actually and reasonably incurred by him in connection with the defense or settlement of such action or suit if he acted in good faith and in a manner he reasonably believed to be in or not opposed to the best interests of the corporation and except that no indemnification shall be made in respect of any claim, issue or matter as to which such person shall have been adjudged to be liable to the corporation unless and only to the extent that the Court of Chancery or the court in which such action or suit was brought shall determine upon application that, despite the adjudication of liability but in view of all the circumstances of the case, such person is fairly and reasonably entitled to indemnity for such expenses which the Court of Chancery or such other court shall deem proper.

(c) To the extent that a present or former director or officer of a corporation has been successful on the merits or otherwise in defense of any action, suit or proceeding referred to in subsections (a) and (b), or in defense of any claim, issue or matter therein, such person shall be indemnified against expenses (including attorneys' fees) actually and reasonably incurred by such person in connection therewith.

(d) Any indemnification under subsections (a) and (b) (unless ordered by a court) shall be made by the corporation only as authorized in the specific case upon a determination that indemnification of the present or former director, officer, employee or agent is proper in the circumstances because he has met the applicable standard of conduct set forth in subsections (a) and (b) of this section. Such determination shall be made with respect to a person who is a director or officer at the time of such determination, (1) by a majority vote of the directors who are not parties to such action, suit or proceeding, even though less than a quorum, or (2) by a committee of such directors designated by majority vote of such directors, even though less than a quorum, or (3) if there are no such directors, or if such directors so direct, by independent legal counsel in a written opinion, or (4) by the stockholders.

(e) Expenses (including attorneys' fees) incurred by an officer or director in defending any civil, criminal, administrative or investigative action, suit or proceeding may be paid by the corporation in advance of the final disposition of such action, suit or proceeding upon receipt of an undertaking by or on behalf of such director or officer to repay such amount if it shall ultimately be determined that such person is not entitled to be indemnified by the corporation as authorized in this section. Such expenses (including attorneys' fees) incurred by former directors and officers or other employees and agents may be so paid upon such terms and conditions, if any, as the corporation deems appropriate.

(f) The indemnification and advancement of expenses provided by, or granted pursuant to, the other subsections of this section shall not be deemed exclusive of any other rights to which those seeking indemnification or advancement of expenses may be entitled under any bylaw, agreement, vote of stockholders or disinterested directors or otherwise, both as to action in such person's official capacity and as to action in another capacity while holding such office.

(g) A corporation shall have power to purchase and maintain insurance on behalf of any person who is or was a director, officer, employee or agent of the corporation, or is or was serving at the request of the corporation as a director, officer, employee or agent of another corporation, partnership, joint venture, trust or other enterprise against any liability asserted against such person and incurred by such person in any such capacity, or arising out of such person's status as such, whether or not the corporation would have the power to indemnify such person against such liability under the provisions of this section.

(h) For purposes of this section, references to "the corporation" shall include, in addition to the resulting corporation, any constituent corporation (including any constituent of a constituent) absorbed in a consolidation or merger which, if its separate existence had continued, would have had power and authority to indemnify its directors, officers, and employees or agents, so that any person who is or was a director, officer, employee or agent of such constituent corporation, or is or was serving at the request of such constituent corporation as a director, officer, employee or agent of another corporation, partnership, joint venture, trust or other enterprise, shall stand in the same position under the provisions of this section with respect to the resulting or surviving corporation as such person would have with respect to such constituent corporation if its separate existence had continued.

(i) For purposes of this section, references to "other enterprises" shall include employee benefit plans; references to "fines" shall include any excise taxes assessed on a person with respect to an employee benefit plan; and references to "serving at the request of the corporation" shall include any service as a director, officer, employee or agent of the corporation which imposes duties on, or involves services by, such director, officer, employee, or agent with respect to an employee benefit plan, its participants, or beneficiaries; and a person who acted in good faith and in a manner such person reasonably believed to be in the interest of the participants and beneficiaries of an employee benefit plan shall be deemed to have acted in a manner "not opposed to the best interests of the corporation" as referred to in this section.

(j) The indemnification and advancement of expenses provided by, or granted pursuant to, this section shall, unless otherwise provided when authorized or ratified, continue as to a person who has ceased to be a director, officer, employee or agent and shall inure to the benefit of the heirs, executors and administrators of such a person.

(k) The Court of Chancery is hereby vested with exclusive jurisdiction to hear and determine all actions for advancement of expenses or indemnification brought under this section or under any bylaw, agreement, vote of stockholders or disinterested directors, or otherwise. The Court of Chancery may summarily determine a corporation's obligation to advance expenses (including attorneys' fees).

§ 146. [Uncaptioned]

A corporation may agree to submit a matter to a vote of its stockholders whether or not the board of directors determines at any time subsequent to approving such matter that such matter is no longer advisable and recommends that the stockholders reject or vote against the matter.

§ 151. Classes and Series of Stock; Redemption; Rights

(a) Every corporation may issue one or more classes of stock or one or more series of stock within any class thereof, any or all of which classes may be of stock with par value or stock without par value and which classes or series may have such voting powers, full or limited, or no voting powers, and such designations, preferences and relative, participating, optional or other special rights, and qualifications, limitations or restrictions thereof, as shall be stated and expressed in the certificate of incorporation or of any amendment thereto, or in the resolution or resolutions providing for the issue of such stock adopted by the board of directors pursuant to authority expressly vested in it by the provisions of its certificate of incorporation. Any of the voting powers, designations, preferences, rights and qualifications, limitations or restrictions of any such class or series of stock may be made dependent upon facts ascertainable outside the certificate of incorporation or of any amendment thereto, or outside the resolution or resolutions providing for the issue of such stock adopted by the board of directors pursuant to authority expressly vested in it by its certificate of incorporation, provided that the manner in which such facts shall operate upon the voting powers, designations, preferences, rights and qualifications, limitations or restrictions of such class or series of stock is clearly and expressly set forth in the certificate of incorporation or in the resolution or resolutions providing for the issue of such stock adopted by the board of directors. The term "facts," as used in this subsection, includes, but is not limited to, the occurrence of any event, including a determination or action by any person or body, including the corporation. The power to increase or decrease or otherwise adjust the capital stock as provided in this chapter shall apply to all or any such classes of stock.

(b) Any stock of any class or series may be made subject to redemption by the corporation at its option or at the option of the holders of such stock or upon the happening of a specified event; provided, however, that immediately following any such redemption the corporation shall have outstanding 1 or more shares of 1 or more classes or series off stock, which share, or shares together, shall have full voting powers. Notwithstanding the limitation stated in the foregoing proviso:

(1) Any stock of a regulated investment company registered under the Investment Company Act of 1940, as heretofore or hereafter amended, may be made subject to redemption by the corporation at its option or at the option of the holders of such stock.

(2) Any stock of a corporation which holds (directly or indirectly) a license or franchise from a governmental agency to conduct its business or is a member of a national securities exchange, which license, franchise or membership is conditioned upon some or all of the holders of its stock possessing prescribed qualifications, may be made subject to redemption by the corporation to the extent necessary to prevent the loss of such license, franchise or membership or to reinstate it.

Any stock which may be made redeemable under this section may be redeemed for cash, property or rights, including securities of the same or another corporation, at such time or times, price or prices, or rate or rates, and with such adjustments, as shall be stated in the certificate of incorporation or in the resolution or resolutions providing for the issue of such stock adopted by the board of directors pursuant to subsection (a) of this section.

(c) The holders of preferred or special stock of any class or of any series thereof shall be entitled to receive dividends at such rates, on such conditions and at such times as shall be stated in the certificate of incorporation or in the resolution or resolutions providing for the issue of such stock adopted by the board of directors as hereinabove provided, payable in preference to, or in such relation to, the dividends payable on any other class or classes or of any other series of stock, and cumulative or non-cumulative as shall be so stated and expressed. When dividends upon the preferred and special stocks, if any, to the extent of the preference to which such stocks are entitled, shall have been paid or declared and set apart for payment, a dividend on the remaining class or classes or series of stock may then be paid out of the remaining assets of the corporation available for dividends as elsewhere in this chapter provided.

(d) The holders of the preferred or special stock of any class or of any series thereof shall be entitled to such rights upon the dissolution of, or upon any distribution of the assets of, the corporation as shall be stated in the certificate of incorporation or in the resolution or resolutions providing for the issue of such stock adopted by the board of directors as hereinabove provided.

(e) Any stock of any class or of any series thereof may be made convertible into, or exchangeable for, at the option of either the holder or the corporation or upon the happening of a specified event, shares of any other class or classes or any other series of the same or any other class or classes of stock of the corporation, at such price or prices or at such rate or rates of exchange and with such adjustments as shall be stated in the certificate of incorporation or in the resolution or resolutions providing for the issue of such stock adopted by the board of directors as hereinabove provided.

(f) If any corporation shall be authorized to issue more than one class of stock or more than one series of any class, the powers, designations, preferences and relative, participating, optional or other special rights of each class of stock or series thereof and the qualifications, limitations or restrictions of such preferences and/or rights shall be set forth in full or summarized on the face or back of the certificate which the corporation shall issue to represent such class or series of stock, provided that, except as otherwise provided in section 202 of this title, in lieu of the foregoing requirements, there may be set forth on the face or back of the certificate which the corporation shall issue to represent such class or series of stock, a statement that the corporation will furnish without charge to each stockholder who so requests the powers, designations, preferences and relative, participating optional or other special rights of each class of stock or series thereof and the qualifications, limitations or restrictions of such preferences and/or rights. Within a reasonable time after the issuance or transfer of uncertificated stock, the corporation shall send to the registered owner thereof a written notice containing the information required to be set forth or stated on certificates pursuant to this section or § 156, 202(a) or 218(a) of this title or with respect to this section a statement that the corporation will furnish without charge to each stockholder who so requests the powers, designations, preferences and relative participating, optional or other special rights of each class of stock or series thereof and the qualifications, limitations or restrictions of such preferences and/or rights. Except as otherwise expressly provided by law, the rights and obligations of the holders of uncertificated stock and the rights and obligations of the holders of certificates representing stock of the same class and series shall be identical.

(g) When any corporation desires to issue any shares of stock of any class or of any series of any class of which the powers, designations, preferences and relative, participating, optional or other rights, if any, or the qualifications, limitations or restrictions thereof, if any, shall not have been set forth in the certificate of incorporation or in any amendment thereto but shall be provided for in a resolution or resolutions adopted by the board of directors pursuant to authority expressly vested in it by the certificate of incorporation or any amendment thereto, a certificate of designations setting forth a copy of such resolution or resolutions and the number of shares of stock of such class or series as to which the resolution or resolutions apply shall be executed, acknowledged, filed and shall become effective, in accordance with § 103 of this title. Unless otherwise provided in any such resolution or resolutions, the number of shares of stock of any such series to which such resolution or resolutions apply may be increased (but not above the total number of authorized shares of the class) or decreased (but not below the number of shares thereof then outstanding) by a certificate likewise executed, acknowledged, and filed setting forth a statement that a specified increase or decrease therein had been authorized and directed by a resolution or resolutions likewise adopted by the board of directors. In case the number of such shares shall be decreased the number of shares so specified in the certificate shall resume the status which they had prior to the adoption of the first resolution or resolutions. When no shares of any such class or series are outstanding, either because none were issued or because no issued shares of any such class or series remain outstanding, a certificate setting forth a resolution or resolutions adopted by the board of directors that none of the authorized shares of such class or series are outstanding, and that none will be issued subject to the certificate previously filed with respect to such class or series, may be executed, acknowledged, and filed in accordance with § 103 of this title and, when such certificate becomes effective, it shall have the effect of eliminating from the certificate of incorporation all matters set forth in the certificate of designations with respect to such class or series of stock. Unless otherwise provided in the certificate of incorporation, if no shares of stock have been issued of a class or series of stock established by a resolution of the board of directors, the voting powers, designations, preferences and relative, participating, optional or other rights, if any, or the qualifications, limitations or restrictions thereof, may be amended by a resolution or resolutions adopted by the board of directors. A certificate which (1) states that no shares of the class or series have been issued, (2) sets forth a copy of the resolution or resolutions and (3) if the designation of the class or series is being changed, indicates the original designation and the new designation, shall be executed, acknowledged, and filed and shall become effective, in accordance with § 103 of this title. When any certificate filed under this subsection becomes effective, it shall have the effect of amending the certificate of incorporation; except that neither the filing of such certificate nor the filing of a restated certificate of incorporation pursuant to § 245 of this title shall prohibit the board of directors from subsequently adopting such resolutions as authorized by this subsection.

§ 152. Issuance of Stock; Lawful Consideration; Fully Paid Stock

The consideration, as determined pursuant to subsections (a) and (b) of Section 153 of this title, for subscriptions to, or the purchase of, the capital stock to be issued by a corporation shall be paid in such form and in such manner as the board of directors shall determine. In the absence of actual fraud in the transaction, the judgment of the directors as to the value of such consideration shall be conclusive. The capital stock so issued shall be deemed to be fully paid and nonassessable stock, if: (1) the entire amount of such consideration has been received by the corporation in the form of cash, services rendered, personal property, real property, leases of real property, or a combination thereof; or (2) not less than the amount of the consideration determined to be capital pursuant to Section 154 of this title has been received by the corporation in such form and the corporation has received a binding obligation of the subscriber or purchaser to pay the balance of the subscription or purchase price; provided, however, nothing contained herein shall prevent the board of directors from issuing partly paid shares under Section 156 of this title.

§ 153. Consideration for Stock

(a) Shares of stock with par value may be issued for such consideration, having a value not less than the par value thereof, as is determined from time to time by the board of directors, or by the stockholders if the certificate of incorporation so provides.

(b) Shares of stock without par value may be issued for such consideration as is determined from time to time by the board of directors, or by the stockholders if the certificate of incorporation so provides.

(c) Treasury shares may be disposed of by the corporation for such consideration as may be determined from time to time by the board of directors, or by the stockholders if the certificate of incorporation so provides.

(d) If the certificate of incorporation reserves to the stockholders the right to determine the consideration for the issue of any shares, the stockholders shall, unless the certificate requires a greater vote, do so by a vote of a majority of the outstanding stock entitled to vote thereon.

§ 154. Determination of Amount of Capital; Capital, Surplus and Net Assets Defined

Any corporation may, by resolution of its board of directors, determine that only a part of the consideration which shall be received by the corporation for any of the shares of its capital stock which it shall issue from time to time shall be capital; but, in case any of the shares issued shall be shares having a par value, the amount of the part of such consideration so determined to be capital shall be in excess of the aggregate par value of the shares issued for such consideration having a par value, unless all the shares issued shall be shares having a par value, in which case the amount of the part of such consideration so determined to be capital need be only equal to the aggregate par value of such shares. In each such case the board of directors shall specify in dollars the part of such consideration which shall be capital. If the board of directors shall not have determined (1) at the time of issue of any shares of the capital stock of the corporation issued for cash or (2) within 60 days after the issue of any shares of the capital stock of the corporation issued for property other than cash what part of the consideration for such shares shall be capital, the capital of the corporation in respect of such shares shall be an amount equal to the aggregate par value of such shares having a par value, plus the amount of the consideration for such shares without par value. The amount of the consideration so determined to be capital in respect of any shares without par value shall be the stated capital of such shares. The capital of the corporation may be increased from time to time by resolution of the board of directors directing that a portion of the net assets of the corporation in excess of the amount so determined to be capital be transferred to the capital account. The board of directors may direct that the portion of such net assets so transferred shall be treated as capital in respect of any shares of the corporation of any designated class or classes. The excess, if any, at an the net assets of the corporation over the amount so determined to be capital shall be surplus. Net assets means the amount by which total assets exceed total liabilities. Capital and surplus are not liabilities for this purpose.

§ 155. Fractions of Shares

A corporation may, but shall not be required to, issue fractions of a share. If it does not issue fractions of a share, it shall (1) arrange for the disposition of fractional interests by those entitled thereto, (2) pay in cash the fair value of fractions of a share as of the time when those entitled to receive such fractions are determined or (3) issue scrip or warrants in registered form (either represented by a certificate or uncertificated) or in bearer form (represented by a certificate) which shall entitle the holder to receive a full share upon the surrender of such scrip or warrants aggregating a full share. A certificate for a fractional share or an uncertificated fractional share shall, but scrip or warrants shall not unless otherwise provided therein, entitle the holder to exercise voting rights, to receive dividends thereon and to participate in any of the assets of the corporation in the event of liquidation. The board of directors may cause scrip or warrants to be issued subject to the conditions that they shall become void if not exchanged for certificates representing the full shares of uncertificated full shares before a specified date, or subject to the conditions that the shares for which scrip or warrants are exchangeable may be sold by the corporation and the proceeds thereof distributed to the holders of scrip or warrants, or subject to any other conditions which the board of directors may impose.

§ 156. Partly Paid Shares

Any corporation may issue the whole or any part of its shares as partly paid and subject to call for the remainder of the consideration to be paid therefor. Upon the face or back of each stock certificate issued to represent any such partly paid shares, or upon the books and records of the corporation in the case of uncertificated partly paid shares, the total amount of the consideration to be paid therefor and the amount paid thereon shall be stated. Upon the declaration of any dividend on fully paid shares, the corporation shall declare a dividend upon partly paid shares of the same class, but only upon the basis of the percentage of the consideration actually paid thereon.

§ 157. Rights and Options Respecting Stock

(a) Subject to any provisions in the certificate of incorporation, every corporation may create and issue, whether or not in connection with the issue and sale of any shares of stock or other securities of the corporation, rights or options entitling the holders thereof to purchase from the corporation any shares of its capital stock of any class or classes, such rights or options to be evidenced by or in such instrument or instruments as shall be approved by the board of directors.

(b) The terms upon which, including the time or times, which may be limited or unlimited in duration, at or within which, and the price or prices (including a formula by which such price or prices may be determined at which any such shares may be purchased from the corporation upon the exercise of any such right or option, shall be such as shall be stated in the certificate of incorporation, or in a resolution adopted by the board of directors providing for the creation and issue of such rights or options, and, in every case, shall be set forth or incorporated by reference in the instrument or instruments evidencing such rights or options). In the absence of actual fraud in the transaction, the judgment of the directors as to the consideration for the issuance of such rights or options and the sufficiency thereof shall be conclusive.

(c) The board of directors may, by a resolution adopted by the board, authorize one or more officers of the corporation to do one or both of the following: (i) designate officers and employees of the corporation or of any of its subsidiaries to be recipients of such rights or options created by the corporation and (ii) determine the number of such rights or options to be received by such officers and employees; provided, however, that the resolution so authorizing such officer or officers shall specify the total number of rights or options such officer or officers may so award. The board of directors may not authorize an officer to designate himself or herself as a recipient of any such rights or options.

(d) In case the shares of stock of the corporation to be issued upon the exercise of such rights or options shall be shares having a par value, the price or prices so to be received therefor shall not be less than the par value thereof. In case the shares of stock so to be issued shall be shares of stock without par value, the consideration therefor shall be determined in the manner provided in section 153 of this title.

§ 158. Stock Certificates; Uncertificated Shares

The shares of a corporation shall be represented by certificates, provided that the board of directors of the corporation may provide by resolution or resolutions that some or all of any or all classes or series of its stock shall be uncertificated shares. Any such resolution shall not apply to shares represented by a certificate until such certificate is surrendered to the corporation. Notwithstanding the adoption of such a resolution by the board of directors, every holder of stock represented by certificates and upon request every holder of uncertificated shares shall be entitled to have a certificate signed by, or in the name of the corporation by the chairperson or vice-chairperson of the board of directors, or the president or vice-president, and by the treasurer or an assistant treasurer, or the secretary or an assistant secretary of such corporation representing the number of shares registered in certificate form. Any or all the signatures on the certificate may be a facsimile. In case any officer, transfer agent or registrar who has signed or whose facsimile signature has been placed upon a certificate shall have ceased to be such officer, transfer agent or registrar before such certificate is issued, it may be issued by the corporation with the same effect as if such person were such officer, transfer agent or registrar at the date of issue. A corporation shall not have power to issue a certificate in bearer form.

§ 159. Shares of Stock; Personal Property, Transfer and Taxation

The shares of stock in every corporation shall be deemed personal property and transferable as provided in Article 8 of Subtitle I of Title 6. No stock or bonds issued by any corporation organized under this chapter shall be taxed by this State when the same shall be owned by non-residents of this State, or by foreign corporations. Whenever any transfer of shares shall be made for collateral security, and not absolutely, it shall be so expressed in the entry of transfer if, when the certificates are presented to the corporation for transfer or uncertificated shares are requested to be transferred, both the transferor and transferee request the corporation to do so.

§ 160. Corporation's Powers Respecting Ownership, Voting, etc., of Its Own Stock; Rights of Stock Called for Redemption

(a) Every corporation may purchase, redeem, receive, take or otherwise acquire, own and hold, sell, lend, exchange, transfer or otherwise dispose of, pledge, use and otherwise deal in and with its own shares; provided, however, that no corporation shall—

1. Purchase or redeem its own shares of capital stock for cash or other property when the capital of the corporation is impaired or when such purchase or redemption would cause any impairment of the capital of the corporation, except that a corporation may purchase or redeem out of capital any of its own shares which are entitled upon any distribution of its assets, whether by dividend or in liquidation, to a preference over another class or series of its stock if such shares will be retired upon their acquisition and the capital of the corporation reduced in accordance with Sections 243 and 244 of this title. Nothing in this subsection shall invalidate or otherwise affect a note, debenture or other obligation of a corporation given by it as consideration for its acquisition by purchase, redemption or exchange of its shares of stock if at the time such note, debenture or obligation was delivered by the corporation its capital was not then impaired or did not thereby become impaired;

2. Purchase, for more than the price at which they may then be redeemed, any of its shares which are redeemable at the option of the corporation; or,

3. Redeem any of its shares unless their redemption is authorized by Section 151(b) of this title and then only in accordance with such Section and the certificate of incorporation.

(b) Nothing in this section limits or affects a corporation's right to resell any of its shares theretofore purchased or redeemed out of surplus and which have not been retired, for such consideration as shall be fixed by the board of directors.

(c) Shares of its own capital stock belonging to the corporation or to another corporation, if a majority of the shares entitled to vote in the election of directors of such other corporation is held, directly or indirectly, by the corporation, shall neither be entitled to vote nor be counted for quorum purposes. Nothing in this section shall be construed as limiting the right of any corporation to vote stock, including but not limited to its own stock, held by it in a fiduciary capacity.

(d) Shares which have been called for redemption shall not be deemed to be outstanding shares for the purpose of voting or determining the total number of shares entitled to vote on any matter on and after the date on which written notice of redemption has been sent to holders thereof and a sum sufficient to redeem such shares has been irrevocably deposited or set aside to pay the redemption price to the holders of the shares upon surrender of certificates therefor.

§ 161. Issuance of Additional Stock; When and by Whom

The directors may, at any time and from time to time, if all of the shares of capital stock which the corporation is authorized by its certificate of incorporation to issue have not been issued, subscribed for, or otherwise committed to be issued, issue or take subscriptions for additional shares of its capital stock up to the amount authorized in its certificate of incorporation.

§ 162. Liability of Stockholder or Subscriber for Stock Not Paid in Full

(a) When the whole of the consideration payable for shares of a corporation has not been paid in, and the assets shall be insufficient to satisfy the claims of its creditors, each holder of or subscriber for such shares shall be bound to pay on each share held or subscribed for by such holder or subscriber the sum necessary to complete the amount of the unpaid balance of the consideration for which such shares were issued or to be issued by the corporation.

(b) The amounts which shall be payable as provided in subsection (a) of this section may be recovered as provided in section 325 of this title, after a writ of execution against the corporation has been returned unsatisfied as provided in that section.

(c) Any person becoming an assignee or transferee of shares or of a subscription for shares in good faith and without knowledge or notice that the full consideration therefor has not been paid shall not be personally liable for any unpaid portion of such consideration, but the transferor shall remain liable therefor.

(d) No person holding shares in any corporation as collateral security shall be personally liable as a stockholder but the person pledging such shares shall be considered the holder thereof and shall be so liable. No executor, administrator, guardian, trustee or other fiduciary shall be personally liable as a stockholder, but the estate or funds held by such executor, administrator, guardian, trustee or other fiduciary in such fiduciary capacity shall be liable.

(e) No liability under this section or under section 325 of this title shall be asserted more than six years after the issuance of the stock or the date of the subscription upon which the assessment is sought.

(f) In any action by a receiver or trustee of an insolvent corporation or by a judgment creditor to obtain an assessment under this section, any stockholder or subscriber for stock of the insolvent corporation may appear and contest the claim or claims of such receiver or trustee.

§ 163. Payment for Stock Not Paid in Full

The capital stock of a corporation shall be paid for in such amounts and at such times as the directors may require. The directors may, from time to time, demand payment, in respect of each share of stock not fully paid, of such sum of money as the necessities of the business may, in the judgment of the board of directors, require, not exceeding in the whole the balance remaining unpaid on said stock, and such sum so demanded shall be paid to the corporation at such times and by such installments as the directors shall direct. The directors shall give written notice of the time and place of such payments, which notice shall be mailed at least 30 days before the time for such payment, to each holder of or subscriber for stock which is not fully paid at such holder's or subscriber's last known postoffice address.

§ 164. Failure to Pay for Stock; Remedies

When any stockholder fails to pay any installment or call upon such stockholder's stock which may have been properly demanded by the directors, at the time when such payment is due, the directors may collect the amount of any such installment or call or any balance thereof remaining unpaid, from the said stockholder by an action at law, or they shall sell at public sale such part of the shares of such delinquent stockholder as will pay all demands then due from such stockholder with interest and all incidental expenses, and shall transfer the shares so sold to the purchaser, who shall be entitled to a certificate therefor. Notice of the time and place of such sale and of the sum due on each share shall be given by advertisement at least one week before the sale, in a newspaper of the county in this State where such corporation's registered office is located, and such notice shall be mailed by the corporation to such delinquent stockholder at his last known postoffice address, at least 20 days before such sale. If no bidder can be had to pay the amount due on the stock, and if the amount is not collected by an action at law, which may be brought within the county where the corporation has its registered office, within one year from the date of the bringing of such action at law, the said stock and the amount previously paid in by the delinquent stockholder on the stock shall be forfeited to the corporation.

§ 165. Revocability of Preincorporation Subscriptions

Unless otherwise provided by the terms of the subscription, a subscription for stock of a corporation to be formed shall be irrevocable, except with the consent of all other subscribers or the corporation, for a period of 6 months from its date.

§ 166. Formalities Required of Stock Subscriptions

A subscription for stock of a corporation, whether made before or after the formation of a corporation, shall not be enforceable against a subscriber, unless in writing and signed by the subscriber or by such subscriber's agent.

* * *

§ 169. Situs of Ownership of Stock

For all purposes of title, action, attachment, garnishment and jurisdiction of all courts held in this State, but not for the purpose of taxation, the situs of the ownership of the capital stock of all corporations existing under the laws of this State, whether organized under this chapter or otherwise, shall be regarded as in this State.

§ 170. Dividends; Payment; Wasting Asset Corporations

(a) The directors of every corporation, subject to any restrictions contained in its certificate of incorporation, may declare and pay dividends upon the shares of its capital stock, or to its members if the corporation is a nonstock corporation organized for profit, either (1) out of its surplus, as defined in and computed in accordance with §§ 154 and 244 of this title, or (2) in case there shall be no such surplus, out of its net profits for the fiscal year in which the dividend is declared and/or the preceding fiscal year. If the capital of the corporation, computed in accordance with §§ 154 and 244 of this title, shall have been diminished by depreciation in the value of its property, or by losses, or otherwise, to an amount less than the aggregate amount of the capital represented by the issued and outstanding stock of all classes having a preference upon the distribution of assets, the directors of such corporation shall not declare and pay out of such net profits any dividends upon any shares of any classes of its capital stock until the deficiency in the amount of capital represented by the issued and outstanding stock of all classes having a preference upon the distribution of assets shall have been repaired. Nothing in this subsection shall invalidate or otherwise affect a note, debenture or other obligation of the corporation paid by it as a dividend on shares of its stock, or any payment made thereon, if at the time such note, debenture or obligation was delivered by the corporation, the corporation had either surplus or net profits as provided in clause (1) or (2) of this subsection from which the dividend could lawfully have been paid.

(b) Subject to any restrictions contained in its certificate of incorporation, the directors of any corporation engaged in the exploitation of wasting assets (including but not limited to a corporation engaged in the exploitation of natural resources or other wasting assets, including patents, or engaged primarily in the liquidation of specific assets) may determine the net profits derived from the exploitation of such wasting assets or the net proceeds derived from such liquidation without taking into consideration the depletion of such assets resulting from lapse of time, consumption, liquidation or exploitation of such assets.

§ 171. Special Purpose Reserves

The directors of a corporation may set apart out of any of the funds of the corporation available for dividends a reserve or reserves for any proper purpose and may abolish any such reserve.

§ 172. Liability of Directors and Committee Members as to Dividends or Stock Redemption

A member of the board of directors, or a member of any committee designated by the board of directors, shall be fully protected in relying in good faith upon the records of the corporation and upon such information, opinions, reports or statements presented to the corporation by any of its officers or employees, or committees of the board of directors, or by any other person as to matters the director reasonably believes are within such other person's professional or expert competence and who has been selected with reasonable care by or on behalf of the corporation, as to the value and amount of the assets, liabilities and/or net profits of the corporation, or any other facts pertinent to the existence and amount of surplus or other funds from which dividends might properly be declared and paid, or with which the corporation's stock might properly be purchased or redeemed.

§ 173. Declaration and Payment of Dividends

No corporation shall pay dividends except in accordance with this chapter. Dividends may be paid in cash, in property, or in shares of the corporation's capital stock. If the dividend is to be paid in shares of the corporation's theretofore unissued capital stock the board of directors shall, by resolution, direct that there be designated as capital in respect of such shares an amount which is not less than the aggregate par value of par value being declared as a dividend and, in the case of shares without par value shares being declared as a dividend, such amount as shall be determined by the board of directors. No such designation as capital shall be necessary if shares are being distributed by a corporation pursuant to a split-up or division of its stock rather than as payment of a dividend declared payable in stock of the corporation.

§ 174. Liability of Directors for Unlawful Payment of Dividend or Unlawful Stock Purchase or Redemption; Exoneration From Liability; Contribution Among Directors; Subrogation

(a) In case of any willful or negligent violation of the provisions of sections 160 or 173 of this title, the directors under whose administration the same may happen shall be jointly and severally liable, at any time within six years after paying such unlawful dividend or after such unlawful stock purchase or redemption, to the corporation, and to its creditors in the event of its dissolution or insolvency, to the full amount of the dividend unlawfully paid, or to the full amount unlawfully paid for the purchase or redemption of the corporation's stock, with interest from the time such liability accrued. Any director who may have been absent when the same was done, or who may have dissented from the act or resolution by which the same was done, may be exonerated from such liability by causing his or her dissent to be entered on the books containing the minutes of the proceedings of the directors at the time the same was done, or immediately after such director ~~he~~ has notice of the same.

(b) Any director against whom a claim is successfully asserted under this section shall be entitled to contribution from the other directors who voted for or concurred in the unlawful dividend, stock purchase or stock redemption.

(c) Any director against whom a claim is successfully asserted under this section shall be entitled, to the extent of the amount paid by such director as a result of such claim, to be subrogated to the rights of the corporation against stockholders who received the dividend on, or assets for the sale or redemption of, their stock with knowledge of facts indicating that such dividend, stock purchase or redemption was unlawful under this chapter, in proportion to the amounts received by such stockholders respectively.

§ 201. Transfer of Stock, Stock Certificate and Uncertificated Stock

Except as otherwise provided in this chapter, the transfer of stock and the certificates of stock which represent the stock or uncertificated stock shall be governed by Article 8 of Subtitle I of Title 6. To the extent that any provision of this chapter is inconsistent with any provision of subtitle I of Title 6, of this chapter shall be controlling.

§ 202. Restriction on Transfer of Securities

(a) A written restriction on the transfer or registration of transfer of a security of a corporation, if permitted by this section and noted conspicuously on the certificate representing the security or, in the case of uncertificated shares, contained in the notice sent pursuant to subsection (f) of § 151 of this title, may be enforced against the holder of the restricted security or any successor or transferee of the holder including an executor, administrator, trustee, guardian or other fiduciary entrusted with like responsibility for the person or estate of the holder. Unless noted conspicuously on the certificate representing the security or, in the case of uncertificated shares, contained in the notice sent pursuant to subsection (f) of § 151 of this title, a restriction, even though permitted by this section, is ineffective except against a person with actual knowledge of the restriction.

(b) A restriction on the transfer or registration of transfer of securities of a corporation may be imposed either by the certificate of incorporation or by the bylaws or by an agreement among any number of security holders or among such holders and the corporation. No restriction so imposed shall be binding with respect to securities issued prior to the adoption of the restriction unless the holders of the securities are parties to an agreement or voted in favor of the restriction.

(c) A restriction on the transfer of securities of a corporation is permitted by this section if it:

(1) Obligates the holder of the restricted securities to offer to the corporation or to any other holders of securities of the corporation or to any other person or to any combination of the foregoing, a prior opportunity, to be exercised within a reasonable time, to acquire the restricted securities; or

(2) Obligates the corporation or any holder of securities of the corporation or any other person or any combination of the foregoing, to purchase the securities which are the subject of an agreement respecting the purchase and sale of the restricted securities; or

(3) Requires the corporation or the holders of any class of securities of the corporation to consent to any proposed transfer of the restricted securities or to approve the proposed transferee of the restricted securities; or

(4) Prohibits the transfer of the restricted securities to designated persons or classes of persons, and such designation is not manifestly unreasonable.

(d) Any restriction on the transfer of the shares of a corporation for the purpose of maintaining its status as an electing small business corporation under subchapter S of the United States Internal Revenue Code or of maintaining any other tax advantage to the corporation is conclusively presumed to be for a reasonable purpose.

(e) Any other lawful restriction on transfer or registration of transfer of securities is permitted by this section.

§ 203. Business Combinations With Interested Stockholders

(a) Notwithstanding any other provisions of this chapter, a corporation shall not engage in any business combination with any interested stockholder for a period of 3 years following the time that such stockholder became an interested stockholder, unless:

(1) Prior to such time the board of directors of the corporation approved either the business combination or the transaction which resulted in the stockholder becoming an interested stockholder;

(2) Upon consummation of the transaction which resulted in the stockholder becoming an interested stockholder, the interested stock-

holder owned at least 85% of the voting stock of the corporation outstanding at the time the transaction commenced, excluding for purposes of determining the voting stock outstanding (but not the outstanding voting stock owned by the interested stockholder) those shares owned (i) by persons who are directors and also officers and (ii) employee stock plans in which employee participants do not have the right to determine confidentially whether shares held subject to the plan will be tendered in a tender or exchange offer; or

(3) At or subsequent to such time the business combination is approved by the board of directors and authorized at an annual or special meeting of stockholders, and not by written consent, by the affirmative vote of at least 66⅔% of the outstanding voting stock which is not owned by the interested stockholder.

(b) The restrictions contained in this section shall not apply if:

(1) The corporation's original certificate of incorporation contains a provision expressly electing not to be governed by this section;

(2) The corporation, by action of its board of directors, adopts an amendment to its bylaws within 90 days of February 2, 1988, expressly electing not to be governed by this section, which amendment shall not be further amended by the board of directors;

(3) The corporation, by action of its stockholders, adopts an amendment to its certificate of incorporation or bylaws expressly electing not to be governed by this section; provided that, in addition to any other vote required by law, such amendment to the certificate of incorporation or bylaws must be approved by the affirmative vote of a majority of the shares entitled to vote. An amendment adopted pursuant to this paragraph shall be effective immediately in the case of a corporation that both (i) has never had a class of voting stock that falls within any of the three categories set out in subsection (b)(4) hereof, and (ii) has not elected by a provision in its original certificate of incorporation or any amendment thereto to be governed by this section. In all other cases, an amendment adopted pursuant to this paragraph shall not be effective until 12 months after the adoption of such amendment and shall not apply to any business combination between such corporation and any person who became an interested stockholder of such corporation on or prior to such adoption. A bylaw amendment adopted pursuant to this paragraph shall not be further amended by the board of directors;

(4) The corporation does not have a class of voting stock that is: (i) Listed on a national securities exchange; (ii) authorized for quotation on The NASDAQ Stock Market; or (iii) held of record by more than 2,000 stockholders, unless any of the foregoing results from action taken, directly or indirectly, by an interested stockholder or from a transaction in which a person becomes an interested stockholder;

(5) A stockholder becomes an interested stockholder inadvertently and (i) as soon as practicable divests itself of ownership of sufficient shares so that the stockholder ceases to be an interested stockholder; and (ii) would not, at any time within the 3–year period immediately prior to a business combination between the corporation and such stockholder, have been an interested stockholder but for the inadvertent acquisition of ownership;

(6) The business combination is proposed prior to the consummation or abandonment of and subsequent to the earlier of the public announcement or the notice required hereunder of a proposed transaction which (i) constitutes one of the transactions described in the 2nd sentence of this paragraph; (ii) is with or by a person who either was not an interested stockholder during the previous 3 years or who became an interested stockholder with the approval of the corporation's board of directors or during the period described in paragraph (7) of this subsection (b); and (iii) is approved or not opposed by a majority of the members of the board of directors then in office (but not less than 1) who were directors prior to any person becoming an interested stockholder during the previous 3 years or were recommended for election or elected to succeed such directors by a majority of such directors. The proposed transactions referred to in the preceding sentence are limited to (x) a merger or consolidation of the corporation (except for a merger in respect of which, pursuant to § 251(f) of this title, no vote of the stockholders of the corporation is required); (y) a sale, lease, exchange, mortgage, pledge, transfer or other disposition (in 1 transaction or a series of transactions), whether as part of a dissolution or otherwise, of assets of the corporation or of any direct or indirect majority-owned subsidiary of the corporation (other than to any direct or indirect wholly-owned subsidiary or to the corporation) having an aggregate market value equal to 50% or more of either that aggregate market value of all of the assets of the corporation determined on a consolidated basis or the aggregate market value of all the outstanding stock of the corporation; or (z) a proposed tender or exchange offer for 50% or more of the outstanding voting stock of the corporation. The corporation shall give not less than 20 days' notice to all interested stockholders prior to the consummation of any of the transactions in (x) or (y) of the 2nd sentence of this paragraph; or

(7) The business combination is with an interested stockholder who became an interested stockholder at a time when the restrictions contained in this section did not apply by reason of any of paragraphs (1) through (4) of this subsection (b), provided, however, that this paragraph (7) shall not apply if, at the time such interested stockholder became an interested stockholder, the corporation's certificate of incorporation contained a provision authorized by the last sentence of this subsection (b).

Notwithstanding paragraphs (1), (2), (3) and (4) of this subsection, a corporation may elect by a provision of its original certificate of incorporation or any amendment thereto to be governed by this section; provided that any such amendment to the certificate of incorporation shall not apply to restrict a business combination between the corporation and an interested stockholder of the corporation if the interested stockholder became such prior to the effective date of the amendment.

(c) As used in this section only, the term:

(1) "Affiliate" means a person that directly, or indirectly through 1 or more intermediaries, controls, or is controlled by, or is under common control with, another person.

(2) "Associate," when used to indicate a relationship with any person, means: (i) Any corporation, partnership, unincorporated association or other entity of which such person is a director, officer or partner or is, directly or indirectly, the owner of 20% or more of any class of voting stock; (ii) any trust or other estate in which such person has at least a 20% beneficial interest or as to which such person serves as trustee or in a similar fiduciary capacity; and (iii) any relative or spouse of such person, or any relative of such spouse, who has the same residence as such person.

(3) "Business combination," when used in reference to any corporation and any interested stockholder of such corporation, means:

(i) Any merger or consolidation of the corporation or any direct or indirect majority-owned subsidiary of the corporation with (A) the interested stockholder, or (B) with any other corporation, partnership, unincorporated association or other entity if the merger or consolidation is caused by the interested stockholder and as a result of such merger or consolidation subsection (a) of this section is not applicable to the surviving entity;

(ii) Any sale, lease, exchange, mortgage, pledge, transfer or other disposition (in 1 transaction or a series of transactions), except proportionately as a stockholder of such corporation, to or with the interested stockholder, whether as part of a dissolution or otherwise, of assets of the corporation or of any direct or indirect majority-owned subsidiary of the corporation which assets have an aggregate market value equal to 10% or more of either the aggregate market value of all the assets of the corporation determined on a consolidated basis or the aggregate market value of all the outstanding stock of the corporation;

(iii) Any transaction which results in the issuance or transfer by the corporation or by any direct or indirect majority-owned subsidiary of the corporation of any stock of the corporation or of such subsidiary to the interested stockholder, except: (A) Pursuant to the exercise, exchange or conversion of securities exercisable for, exchangeable for or convertible into stock of such corporation or any such subsidiary which securities were outstanding prior to the time that the interested stockholder became such; (B) pursuant to a merger under § 251(g) of this title; (C) pursuant to a dividend or distribution paid or made, or the exercise, exchange or conversion of securities exercisable for, exchangeable for or convertible into stock of such corporation or any such subsidiary which security is distributed, pro rata to all holders of a class or series of stock of such corporation subsequent to the time the interested stockholder became such; (D) pursuant to an exchange offer by the corporation to purchase stock made on the same terms to all holders of said stock; or (E) any issuance or transfer of stock by the corporation; provided however, that in no case under items (C)-(E) of this subparagraph shall there be an increase in the interested stockholder's proportionate share of the stock of any class or series of the corporation or of the voting stock of the corporation;

(iv) Any transaction involving the corporation or any direct or indirect majority-owned subsidiary of the corporation which has the effect, directly or indirectly, of increasing the proportionate share of the stock of any class or series, or securities convertible into the stock of any class or series, of the corporation or of any such subsidiary which is owned by the interested stockholder, except as a result of immaterial changes due to fractional share adjustments or as a result of any purchase or redemption of any shares of stock not caused, directly or indirectly, by the interested stockholder; or

(v) Any receipt by the interested stockholder of the benefit, directly or indirectly (except proportionately as a stockholder of such corporation), of any loans, advances, guarantees, pledges or other financial benefits (other than those expressly permitted in subparagraphs (i)-(iv) of this paragraph) provided by or through the corporation or any direct or indirect majority-owned subsidiary.

(4) "Control," including the terms "controlling," "controlled by" and "under common control with," means the possession, directly or indirectly, of the power to direct or cause the direction of the management and policies of a person, whether through the ownership of voting stock, by contract or otherwise. A person who is the owner of 20% or more of the outstanding voting stock of any corporation, partnership, unincorporated association or other entity shall be presumed to have control of such entity, in the absence of proof by a preponderance of the evidence to the contrary; Notwithstanding the foregoing, a presumption of control shall not apply where such person holds voting stock, in good faith and not for the purpose of circumventing this section, as an agent, bank, broker, nominee, custodian or trustee for 1 or more owners who do not individually or as a group have control of such entity.

(5) "Interested stockholder" means any person (other than the corporation and any direct or indirect majority-owned subsidiary of the corporation) that (i) is the owner of 15% or more of the outstanding voting stock of the corporation, or (ii) is an affiliate or associate of the corporation and was the owner of 15% or more of the outstanding voting

stock of the corporation at any time within the 3–year period immediately prior to the date on which it is sought to be determined whether such person is an interested stockholder; and the affiliates and associates of such person; provided, however, that the term "interested stockholder" shall not include (x) any person who (A) owned shares in excess of the 15% limitation set forth herein as of, or acquired such shares pursuant to a tender offer commenced prior to, December 23, 1987, or pursuant to an exchange offer announced prior to the aforesaid date and commenced within 90 days thereafter and either (I) continued to own shares in excess of such 15% limitation or would have but for action by the corporation or (II) is an affiliate or associate of the corporation and so continued (or so would have continued but for action by the corporation) to be the owner of 15% or more of the outstanding voting stock of the corporation at any time within the 3–year period immediately prior to the date on which it is sought to be determined whether such a person is an interested stockholder or (B) acquired said shares from a person described in item (A) of this paragraph by gift, inheritance or in a transaction in which no consideration was exchanged; or (y) any person whose ownership of shares in excess of the 15% limitation set forth herein is the result of action taken solely by the corporation; provided that such person shall be an interested stockholder if thereafter such person acquires additional shares of voting stock of the corporation, except as a result of further corporate action not caused, directly or indirectly, by such person. For the purpose of determining whether a person is an interested stockholder, the voting stock of the corporation deemed to be outstanding shall include stock deemed to be owned by the person through application of paragraph (9) of this subsection but shall not include any other unissued stock of such corporation which may be issuable pursuant to any agreement, arrangement or understanding, or upon exercise of conversion rights, warrants or options, or otherwise.

(6) "Person" means any individual, corporation, partnership, unincorporated association or other entity.

(7) "Stock" means, with respect to any corporation, capital stock and, with respect to any other entity, any equity interest.

(8) "Voting stock" means, with respect to any corporation, stock of any class or series entitled to vote generally in the election of directors and, with respect to any entity that is not a corporation, any equity interest entitled to vote generally in the election of the governing body of such entity. Every reference to a percentage of voting stock shall refer to such percentage of the votes of such voting stock.

(9) "Owner," including the terms "own" and "owned," when used with respect to any stock, means a person that individually or with or through any of its affiliates or associates:

(i) Beneficially owns such stock, directly or indirectly; or

(ii) Has (A) the right to acquire such stock (whether such right is exercisable immediately or only after the passage of time) pursuant to any agreement, arrangement or understanding, or upon the exercise of conversion rights, exchange rights, warrants or options, or otherwise; provided, however, that a person shall not be deemed the owner of stock tendered pursuant to a tender or exchange offer made by such person or any of such person's affiliates or associates until such tendered stock is accepted for purchase or exchange; or (B) the right to vote such stock pursuant to any agreement, arrangement or understanding; provided, however, that a person shall not be deemed the owner of any stock because of such person's right to vote such stock if the agreement, arrangement or understanding to vote such stock arises solely from a revocable proxy or consent given in response to a proxy or consent solicitation made to 10 or more persons; or

(iii) Has any agreement, arrangement or understanding for the purpose of acquiring, holding, voting (except voting pursuant to a revocable proxy or consent as described in item (B) of subparagraph (ii) of this paragraph), or disposing of such stock with any other person that beneficially owns, or whose affiliates or associates beneficially own, directly or indirectly, such stock.

(d) No provision of a certificate of incorporation or bylaw shall require, for any vote of stockholders required by this section, a greater vote of stockholders than that specified in this section.

(e) The Court of Chancery is hereby vested with exclusive jurisdiction to hear and determine all matters with respect to this section.

§ 211. Meetings of Stockholders

(a)(1) Meetings of stockholders may be held at such place, either within or without this State, as may be designated by or in the manner provided in the certificate of incorporation or bylaws or, if not so designated, as determined by the board of directors. If, pursuant to this paragraph (a)(1) or the certificate of incorporation or the bylaws of the corporation, the board of directors is authorized to determine the place of a meeting of stockholders, the board of directors may, in its sole discretion, determine that the meeting shall not be held at any place, but may instead be held solely by means of remote communication as authorized by paragraph (a)(2) of this Section 211.

(2) If authorized by the board of directors in its sole discretion, and subject to such guidelines and procedures as the board of directors may adopt, stockholders and proxyholders not physically present at a meeting of stockholders may, by means of remote communication:

(A) participate in a meeting of stockholders; and

(B) be deemed present in person and vote at a meeting of stockholders whether such meeting is to be held at a designated place or solely by means of remote communication, provided that (i) the corporation shall implement reasonable measures to verify that each person deemed present and permitted to vote at the meeting by means of remote communication is a stockholder or proxyholder, (ii) the corporation shall implement reasonable measures to provide such stockholders and proxyholders a reasonable opportunity to participate in the meeting and to vote on matters submitted to the stockholders, including an opportunity to read or hear the proceedings of the meeting substantially concurrently with such proceedings, and (iii) if any stockholder or proxyholder votes or takes other action at the meeting by means of remote communication, a record of such vote or other action shall be maintained by the corporation."

(b) Unless directors are elected by written consent in lieu of an annual meeting as permitted by this subsection, an annual meeting of stockholders shall be held for the election of directors on a date and at a time designated by or in the manner provided in the by-laws. Any other proper business may be transacted at the annual meeting.

(c) A failure to hold the annual meeting at the designated time or to elect a sufficient number of directors to conduct the business of the corporation shall not affect otherwise valid corporate acts or work a forfeiture or dissolution of the corporation except as may be otherwise specifically provided in this chapter. If the annual meeting for election of directors is not held on the date designated therefor or action by written consent to elect directors in lieu of an annual meeting has not been taken, the directors shall cause the meeting to be held as soon as is convenient. If there be a failure to hold the annual meeting or to take action by written consent to elect directors in lieu of an annual meeting for a period of thirty days after the date designated for the annual meeting, or if no date has been designated, for a period of 13 months after the latest to occur of the organization of the corporation, its last annual meeting, or the last action by written consent to elect directors in lieu of an annual meeting, the Court of Chancery may summarily order a meeting to be held upon the application of any stockholder or director. The shares of stock represented at such meeting, either in person or by proxy, and entitled to vote thereat, shall constitute a quorum for the purpose of such meeting, notwithstanding any provision of the certificate of incorporation or bylaws to the contrary. The Court of Chancery may issue such orders as may be appropriate, including, without limitation, orders designating the time and place of such meeting, the record date for determination of stockholders entitled to vote, and the form of notice of such meeting.

(d) Special meetings of the stockholders may be called by the board of directors or by such person or persons as may be authorized by the certificate of incorporation or by the by-laws.

(e) All elections of directors shall be by written ballot, unless otherwise provided in the certificate of incorporation; if authorized by the board of directors, such requirement of a written ballot shall be satisfied by a ballot submitted by electronic transmission, provided that any such electronic transmission must either set forth or be submitted with information from which it can be determined that the electronic transmission was authorized by the stockholder or proxy holder.

§ 212. Voting Rights of Stockholders; Proxies; Limitations

(a) Unless otherwise provided in the certificate of incorporation and subject to the provisions of section 213 of this title, each stockholder shall be entitled to one vote for each share of capital stock, voting stock or shares held by such stockholder. If the certificate of incorporation provides for more or less than one vote for any share, on any matter, every reference in this chapter to a majority or other proportion of stock, voting stock or shares shall refer to such majority or other proportion of the votes of such stock, voting stock or shares.

(b) Each stockholder entitled to vote at a meeting of stockholders or to express consent or dissent to corporate action in writing without a meeting may authorize another person or persons to act for such stockholder by proxy, but no such proxy shall be voted or acted upon after three years from its date, unless the proxy provides for a longer period.

(c) Without limiting the manner in which a stockholder may authorize another person or persons to act for such stockholder as proxy pursuant to subsection (b) of this section, the following shall constitute a valid means by which a stockholder may grant such authority.

(1) A stockholder may execute a writing authorizing another person or persons to act for such stockholder as proxy. Execution may be accomplished by the stockholder or such stockholder's HIS authorized officer, director, employee or agent signing such writing or causing such person's signature to be affixed to such writing by any reasonable means including, but not limited to, by facsimile signature.

(2) A stockholder may authorize another person or persons to act for such stockholder as proxy by transmitting or authorizing the transmission of a telegram, cablegram, or other means of electronic transmission to the person who will be the holder of the proxy or to a proxy solicitation firm, proxy support service organization or like agent duly authorized by the person who will be the holder of the proxy to receive such transmission, provided that any such telegram, cablegram or other means of electronic transmission must either set forth or be submitted with information from which it can be determined that the telegram, cablegram or other electronic transmission was authorized by the stockholder. If it is determined that such telegrams, cablegrams or other electronic transmissions are valid, the inspectors or, if there are no

inspectors, such other persons making that determination shall specify the information upon which they relied.

(d) Any copy, facsimile telecommunication or other reliable reproduction of the writing or transmission created pursuant to subsection (c) of this section may be substituted or used in lieu of the original writing or transmission for any and all purposes for which the original writing or transmission could be used, provided that such copy, facsimile telecommunication or other reproduction shall be a complete reproduction of the entire original writing or transmission.

(e) A duly executed proxy shall be irrevocable if it states that it is irrevocable and if, and only as long as, it is coupled with an interest sufficient in law to support an irrevocable power. A proxy may be made irrevocable regardless of whether the interest with which it is coupled is an interest in the stock itself or an interest in the corporation generally.

§ 213. Fixing Date for Determination of Stockholders of Record

(a) In order that the corporation may determine the stockholders entitled to notice of or to vote at any meeting of stockholders or any adjournment thereof, the board of directors may fix a record date, which record date shall not precede the date upon which the resolution fixing the record date is adopted by the board of directors, and which record date shall not be more than sixty nor less than ten days before the date of such meeting. If no record date is fixed by the board of directors, the record date for determining stockholders entitled to notice of or to vote at a meeting of stockholders shall be at the close of business on the day next preceding the day on which notice is given, or, if notice is waived, at the close of business on the day next preceding the day on which the meeting is held. A determination of stockholders of record entitled to notice of or to vote at a meeting of stockholders shall apply to any adjournment of the meeting; provided, however, that the board of directors may fix a new record date for the adjourned meeting.

(b) In order that the corporation may determine the stockholders entitled to consent to corporate action in writing without a meeting, the board of directors may fix a record date, which record date shall not precede the date upon which the resolution fixing the record date is adopted by the board of directors, and which date shall not be more than ten days after the date upon which the resolution fixing the record date is adopted by the board of directors. If no record date has been fixed by the board of directors, the record date for determining stockholders entitled to consent to corporate action in writing without a meeting, when no prior action by the board of directors is required by this chapter, shall be the first date on which a signed written consent setting forth the action taken or proposed to be taken is delivered to the corporation by delivery to its registered office in this State, its principal place of business, or an officer or agent of the corporation having custody of the book in which proceedings of meetings of stockholders are recorded. Delivery made to a corporation's registered office shall be by hand or by certified or registered mail, return receipt requested. If no record date has been fixed by the board of directors and prior action by the board of directors is required by this chapter, the record date for determining stockholders entitled to consent to corporate action in writing without a meeting shall be at the close of business on the day on which the board of directors adopts the resolution taking such prior action.

(c) In order that the corporation may determine the stockholders entitled to receive payment of any dividend or other distribution or allotment of any rights or the stockholders entitled to exercise any rights in respect of any change, conversion or exchange of stock, or for the purpose of any other lawful action, the board of directors may fix a record date, which record date shall not precede the date upon which the resolution fixing the record date is adopted, and which record date shall be not more than sixty days prior to such action. If no record date is fixed, the record date for determining stockholders for any such purpose shall be at the close of business on the day on which the board of directors adopts the resolution relating thereto.

§ 214. Cumulative Voting

The certificate of incorporation of any corporation may provide that at all elections of directors of the corporation, or at elections held under specified circumstances, each holder of stock or of any class or classes or of a series or series thereof shall be entitled to as many votes as shall equal the number of votes which (except for such provision as to cumulative voting) such holder would be entitled to cast for the election of directors with respect to such holder's shares of stock multiplied by the number of directors to be elected by such holder, and that such holder may cast all of such votes for a single director or may distribute them among the number to be voted for, or for any two or more of them as such holder may see fit.

§ 216. Quorum and Required Vote for Stock Corporations

Subject to this chapter in respect of the vote that shall be required for a specific action, the certificate of incorporation or by-laws of any corporation authorized to issue stock may specify the number of shares and/or amount of other securities having voting power the holders of which shall be present or represented by proxy at any meeting in order to constitute a quorum for, and the votes that shall be necessary for, the transaction of any business, but in no event shall a quorum consist of less than one-third of the shares entitled to vote at the meeting, except that, where a separate vote by a class or series or classes or series is required, a quorum shall consist of no less than one-third of the shares of such class or series or classes or series. In the absence of such specification in the certificate of incorporation or by-laws of the corporation:

(1) A majority of the shares entitled to vote, present in person or represented by proxy, shall constitute a quorum at a meeting of stockholders;

(2) In all matters other than the election of directors, the affirmative vote of the majority of shares present in person or represented by proxy at the meeting and entitled to vote on the subject matter shall be the act of the stockholders;

(3) Directors shall be elected by a plurality of the votes of the shares present in person or represented by proxy at the meeting and entitled to vote on the election of directors; and

(4) Where a separate vote by a class or series or classes or series is required, a majority of the outstanding shares of such class or series or classes or series, present in person or represented by proxy, shall constitute a quorum entitled to take action with respect to that vote on that matter and the affirmative vote of the majority of shares of such class or series or classes or series present in person or represented by proxy at the meeting shall be the act of such class or series or classes or series.

§ 217. Voting Rights of Fiduciaries, Pledgors and Joint Owners of Stock

(a) Persons holding stock in a fiduciary capacity shall be entitled to vote the shares so held. Persons whose stock is pledged shall be entitled to vote, unless in the transfer by the pledgor on the books of the corporation such person has expressly empowered the pledgee to vote thereon, in which case only the pledgee, or such person's proxy, may represent such stock and vote thereon.

(b) If shares or other securities having voting power stand of record in the names of two or more persons, whether fiduciaries, members of a partnership, joint tenants, tenants in common, tenants by the entirety or otherwise, or if two or more persons have the same fiduciary relationship respecting the same shares, unless the secretary of the corporation is given written notice to the contrary and is furnished with a copy of the instrument or order appointing them or creating the relationship wherein it is so provided, their acts with respect to voting shall have the following effect:

(1) If only one votes, such person's act binds all;

(2) If more than one vote, the act of the majority so voting binds all;

(3) If more than one vote, but the vote is evenly split on any particular matter, each faction may vote the securities in question proportionally, or any person voting the shares, or a beneficiary, if any, may apply to the Court of Chancery or such other court as may have

jurisdiction to appoint an additional person to act with the persons so voting the shares, which shall then be voted as determined by a majority of such persons and the person appointed by the Court. If the instrument so filed shows that any such tenancy is held in unequal interests, a majority or even-split for the purpose of this subsection shall be a majority or even-split in interest.

§ 218. Voting Trusts and Other Voting Agreements

(a) One stockholder or 2 or more stockholders may by agreement in writing deposit capital stock of an original issue with or transfer capital stock to any person or persons, or entity or entities authorized to act as trustee, for the purpose of vesting in such person or persons, entity or entities, who may be designated voting trustee, or voting trustees, the right to vote thereon for any period of time determined by such agreement, upon the terms and conditions stated in such agreement. The agreement may contain any other lawful provisions not inconsistent with such purpose. After the filing of a copy of the agreement in the registered office of the corporation in this State, which copy shall be open to the inspection of any stockholder of the corporation or any beneficiary of the trust under the agreement daily during business hours, certificates of stock or uncertificated stock shall be issued to the voting trustee or trustees to represent any stock of an original issue so deposited with such voting trustee or trustees, and any certificates of stock or uncertificated stock so transferred to the voting trustee or trustees shall be surrendered and cancelled and new certificates or uncertificated stock shall be issued therefore to the voting trustee or trustees. In the certificate so issued, if any, it shall be stated that it is issued pursuant to such agreement, and that fact shall also be stated in the stock ledger of the corporation. The voting trustee or trustees may vote the stock so issued or transferred during the period specified in the agreement. Stock standing in the name of the voting trustee or trustees may be voted either in person or by proxy, and in voting the stock, the voting trustee or trustees shall incur no responsibility as stockholder, trustee or otherwise, except for his or their own individual malfeasance. In any case where 2 or more persons or entities are designated as voting trustees, and the right and method of voting any stock standing in their names at any meeting of the corporation are not fixed by the agreement appointing the trustees, the right to vote the stock and the manner of voting it at the meeting shall be determined by a majority of the trustees, or if they be equally divided as to the right and manner of voting the stock in any particular case, the vote of the stock in such case shall be divided equally among the trustees.

(b) Any amendment to a voting trust agreement shall be made by a written agreement, a copy of which shall be filed in the registered office of the corporation in this State.

(c) An agreement between 2 or more stockholders, if in writing and signed by the parties thereto, may provide that in exercising any voting rights, the shares held by them shall be voted as provided by the agreement, or as the parties may agree, or as determined in accordance with a procedure agreed upon by them.

(d) This section shall not be deemed to invalidate any voting or other agreement among stockholders or any irrevocable proxy which is not otherwise illegal.

§ 219. List of Stockholders Entitled to Vote; Penalty for Refusal to Produce; Stock Ledger

(a) The officer who has charge of the stock ledger of a corporation shall prepare and make, at least ten days before every meeting of stockholders, a complete list of the stockholders entitled to vote at the meeting, arranged in alphabetical order, and showing the address of each stockholder and the number of shares registered in the name of each stockholder. Nothing contained in this Section shall require the corporation to include electronic mail addresses or other electronic contact information on such list. Such list shall be open to the examination of any stockholder, for any purpose germane to the meeting for a period of at least 10 days prior to the meeting: (i) on a reasonably accessible electronic network, provided that the information required to gain access to such list is provided with the notice of the meeting, or (ii) during ordinary business hours, at the principal place of business of the corporation. In the event that the corporation determines to make the list available on an electronic network, the corporation may take reasonable steps to ensure that such information is available only to stockholders of the corporation. If the meeting is to be held at a place, then the list shall be produced and kept at the time and place of the meeting during the whole time thereof, and may be inspected by any stockholder who is present. If the meeting is to be held solely by means of remote communication, then the list shall also be open to the examination of any stockholder during the whole time of the meeting on a reasonably accessible electronic network, and the information required to access such list shall be provided with the notice of the meeting.

(b) Upon the willful neglect or refusal of the directors to produce such a list at any meeting for the election of directors held at a place, or to open such a list to examination on a reasonably accessible electronic network during any meeting for the election of directors held solely by means of reasonable communication, they shall be ineligible for election to any office at such meeting.

(c) The stock ledger shall be the only evidence as to who are the stockholders entitled by this section or to vote in person or by proxy at any meeting of stockholders.

§ 220. Inspection of Books and Records

(a) As used in this section:

(1) 'Stockholder' means a holder of record of stock in a stock corporation, or a person who is the beneficial owner of shares of such stock held either in a voting trust or by a nominee on behalf of such person, and also a member of a nonstock corporation as reflected on the records of the nonstock corporation.

(2) 'List of stockholders' includes list of members in a nonstock corporation.

(3) 'Under oath' includes statements the declarant affirms to be true under penalty of perjury under the laws of the United States or any State.

(4) 'Subsidiary' means any entity directly or indirectly owned, in whole or in part, by the corporation of which the stockholder is a stockholder and over the affairs of which the corporation directly or indirectly exercises control, and includes, without limitation, corporations, partnerships, limited partnerships, limited liability partnerships, limited liability companies, statutory trusts and/or joint ventures.

(b) Any stockholder, in person or by attorney or other agent, shall, upon written demand under oath stating the purpose thereof, have the right during the usual hours for business to inspect for any proper purpose, and to make copies and extracts from: (1) the corporation's stock ledger, a list of its stockholders, and its other books and records; and (2) a subsidiary's books and records, to the extent that (i) the corporation has actual possession and control of such records of such subsidiary, or (ii) the corporation could obtain such records through the exercise of control over such subsidiary, provided that as of the date of the making of the demand (A) stockholder inspection of such books and records of the subsidiary would not constitute a breach of an agreement between the corporation or the subsidiary and a person or persons not affiliated with the corporation, and (B) the subsidiary would not have the right under the law applicable to it to deny the corporation access to such books and records upon demand by the corporation. In every instance where the stockholder is other than a record holder of stock in a stock corporation or a member of a nonstock corporation, the demand under oath shall state the person's status as a stockholder, be accompanied by documentary evidence of beneficial ownership of the stock, and state that such documentary evidence is a true and correct copy of what it purports to be. A proper purpose shall mean a purpose reasonably related to such person's interest as a stockholder. In every instance where an attorney or other agent shall be the person who seeks the right to inspection, the demand under oath shall be accompanied by a power of attorney or such other writing which authorizes the attorney or other agent to so act on behalf of the stockholder. The demand under oath shall be directed to the corporation at its registered office in this State or at its principal place of business.

(c) If the corporation, or an officer or agent thereof, refuses to permit an inspection sought by a stockholder or attorney or other agent acting for the stockholder pursuant to sub-section (b) or does not reply to the demand within five business days after the demand has been made, the stockholder may apply to the Court of Chancery for an order to compel such inspection. The Court of Chancery is hereby vested with exclusive jurisdiction to determine whether or not the person seeking inspection is entitled to the inspection sought. The Court may summarily order the corporation to permit the stockholder to inspect the corporation's stock ledger, an existing list of stockholders, and its other books and records, and to make copies or extracts therefrom; or the Court may order the corporation to furnish to the stockholder a list of its stockholders as of a specific date on condition that the stockholder first pay to the corporation the reasonable cost of obtaining and furnishing such list and on such other conditions as the Court deems appropriate. Where the stockholder seeks to inspect the corporation's books and records, other than its stock ledger or list of stockholders, such stockholder shall first establish that (1) he, she or it is a stockholder, (2) he, she or it has complied with this section respecting the form and manner of making demand for inspection of such documents; and (3) the inspection such stockholder seeks is for a proper purpose. Where the stockholder seeks to inspect the corporation's stock ledger or list of stockholders and establishes that he, she or it is a stockholder and has complied with this section respecting the form and manner of making demand for inspection of such documents, the burden of proof shall be upon the corporation to establish that the inspection such stockholder seeks is for an improper purpose. The Court may, in its discretion, prescribe any limitations or conditions with reference to the inspection, or award such other or further relief as the court may deem just and proper. The Court may order books, documents and records, pertinent extracts therefrom, or duly authenticated copies thereof, to be brought within this State and kept in this State upon such terms and conditions as the order may prescribe.

(d) Any director (including a member of the governing body of a nonstock corporation) shall have the right to examine the corporation's stock ledger, a list of its stockholders and its other books and records for a purpose reasonably related to his position as a director. The Court of Chancery is hereby vested with the exclusive jurisdiction to determine whether a director is entitled to the inspection sought. The court may summarily order the corporation to permit the director to inspect any and all books and records, the stock ledger and the list of stockholders and to make copies or extracts therefrom. The burden of proof shall be upon the corporation to establish that the inspection such director seeks is for an improper purpose. The Court may, in its discretion, prescribe any limitations or conditions with reference to the inspection, or award such other and further relief as the Court may deem just and proper.

§ 221. Voting, Inspection and Other Rights of Bondholders and Debenture Holders

Every corporation may in its certificate of incorporation confer upon the holders of any bonds, debentures or other obligations issued or to be issued by the corporation the power to vote in respect to the corporate affairs and management of the corporation to the extent and in the manner provided in the certificate of incorporation and may confer upon such holders of bonds, debentures or other obligations the same right of inspection of its books, accounts and other records, and also any other rights, which the stockholders of the corporation have or may have by reason of this chapter or of its certificate of incorporation. If the certificate of incorporation so provides, such holders of bonds, debentures or other obligations shall be deemed to be stockholders, and their bonds, debentures or other obligations shall be deemed to be shares of stock, for the purpose of any provision of this chapter which requires the vote of stockholders as a prerequisite to any corporate action and the certificate of incorporation may divest the holders of capital stock, in whole or in part, of their right to vote on any corporate matter whatsoever, except as set forth in paragraph (2) of subsection (b) of § 242 of this title.

§ 222. Notice of Meetings and Adjourned Meetings

(a) Whenever stockholders are required or permitted to take any action at a meeting, a written notice of the meeting shall be given which shall state the place, if any, date and hour of the meeting, the means of remote communications, if any, by which stockholders and proxy holders may be deemed to be present in person and vote at such meeting, and, in the case of a special meeting, the purpose or purposes for which the meeting is called.

(b) Unless otherwise provided in this chapter, the written notice of any meeting shall be given not less than ten nor more than sixty days before the date of the meeting to each stockholder entitled to vote at such meeting. If mailed, notice is given when deposited in the United States mail, postage prepaid, directed to the stockholder at such stockholder's address as it appears on the records of the corporation. An affidavit of the secretary or an assistant secretary or of the transfer agent or other agent of the corporation that the notice has been given shall, in the absence of fraud, be prima facie evidence of the facts stated therein.

(c) When a meeting is adjourned to another time or place, unless the by-laws otherwise require, notice need not be given of the adjourned meeting if the time, place, if any, thereof, and the means of remote communications, if any, by which stockholders and proxy holders may be deemed to be present in person and vote at such adjourned meeting are announced at the meeting at which the adjournment is taken. At the adjourned meeting the corporation may transact any business which might have been transacted at the original meeting. If the adjournment is for more than thirty days, or if after the adjournment a new record date is fixed for the adjourned meeting, a notice of the adjourned meeting shall be given to each stockholder of record entitled to vote at the meeting.

§ 223. Vacancies and Newly Created Directorships

(a) Unless otherwise provided in the certificate of incorporation or by-laws: (1) Vacancies and newly created directorships resulting from any increase in the authorized number of directors elected by all of the stockholders having the right to vote as a single class may be filled by a majority of the directors then in office, although less than a quorum, or by a sole remaining director; (2) Whenever the holders of any class or classes of stock or series thereof are entitled to elect one or more directors by the provisions of the certificate of incorporation, vacancies and newly created directorships of such class or classes or series may be filled by a majority of the directors elected by such class or classes or series thereof then in office, or by a sole remaining director so elected.

If at any time, by reason of death or resignation or other cause, a corporation should have no directors in office, then any officer or any stockholder or an executor, administrator, trustee or guardian of a stockholder, or other fiduciary entrusted with like responsibility for the person or estate of a stockholder, may call a special meeting of stockholders in accordance with the provisions of the certificate of incorporation or the by-laws, or may apply to the Court of Chancery for a decree summarily ordering an election as provided in section 211 of this title.

(b) In the case of a corporation the directors of which are divided into classes, any directors chosen under subsection (a) of this section shall hold office until the next election of the class for which such directors shall have been chosen, and until their successors shall be elected and qualified.

(c) If, at the time of filling any vacancy or any newly created directorship, the directors then in office shall constitute less than a majority of the whole board (as constituted immediately prior to any such increase), the Court of Chancery may, upon application of any stockholder or stockholders holding at least ten percent of the total number of the shares at the time outstanding having the right to vote for such directors, summarily order an election to be held to fill any such vacancies or newly created directorships, or to replace the directors chosen by the directors then in office as aforesaid, which election shall be governed by the provisions of section 211 of this title as far as applicable.

(d) Unless otherwise provided in the certificate of incorporation or by-laws, when one or more directors shall resign from the board, effective at a future date, a majority of the directors then in office, including those who have so resigned, shall have power to fill such vacancy or vacancies, the vote thereon to take effect when such resignation or resignations shall become effective, and each director so chosen shall hold office as provided in this section in the filling of other vacancies.

§ 224. Form of Records

Any records maintained by a corporation in the regular course of its business, including its stock ledger, books of account, and minute books, may be kept on, or by means of, or be in the form of, any information storage device or method, provided that the records so kept can be converted into clearly legible paper form within a reasonable time. Any corporation shall so convert any records so kept upon the request of any person entitled to inspect such records pursuant to any provision of this chapter. Where records are kept in such manner, a clearly legible paper form produced from or by means of the information storage device or method shall be admissible in evidence and shall be accepted for all other purposes, to the same extent as an original paper record of the same information would have been, when said paper form accurately portrays the record.

§ 225. Contested Election of Directors; Proceedings to Determine Validity

(a) Upon application of any stockholder or director, or any officer whose title to office is contested, or any member of a corporation without capital stock, the Court of Chancery may hear and determine the validity of any election, appointment, removal or resignation of any director, member of the governing body, or officer of any corporation, and the right of any person to hold or continue to hold such office, and, in case any such office is claimed by more than 1 person, may determine the person entitled thereto; and to that end make such order or decree in any such case as may be just and proper, with power to enforce the production of any books, papers and records of the corporation relating to the issue. In case it should be determined that no valid election has been held, the Court of Chancery may order an election to be held in accordance with § 211 or 215 of this title. In any such application, service of copies of the application upon the registered agent of the corporation shall be deemed to be service upon the corporation and upon the person whose title to office is contested and upon the person, if any, claiming such office; and the registered agent shall forward immediately a copy of the application to the corporation and to the person whose title to office is contested and to the person, if any, claiming such office, in a postpaid, sealed, registered letter addressed to such corporation and such person at their post-office addresses last known to the registered agent or furnished to the registered agent by the applicant stockholder. The Court may make such order respecting further or other notice of such application as it deems proper under the circumstances.

(b) Upon application of any stockholder or any member of a corporation without capital stock, the Court of Chancery may hear and determine the result of any vote of stockholders or members, as the case may be, upon matters other than the election of directors, officers or members of the governing body. Service of the application upon the registered agent of the corporation shall be deemed to be service upon the corporation, and no other party need be joined in order for the Court to adjudicate the result of the vote. The Court may make such order respecting notice of the application as it deems proper under the circumstances.

§ 226. Appointment of Custodian or Receiver of Corporation on Deadlock or for Other Cause

(a) The Court of Chancery, upon application of any stockholder, may appoint one or more persons to be custodians, and, if the corporation is insolvent, to be receivers, of and for any corporation when:

(1) At any meeting held for the election of directors the stockholders are so divided that they have failed to elect successors to directors whose terms have expired or would have expired upon qualification of their successors; or

(2) The business of the corporation is suffering or is threatened with irreparable injury because the directors are so divided respecting the management of the affairs of the corporation that the required vote for action by the board of directors cannot be obtained and the stockholders are unable to terminate this division; or

(3) The corporation has abandoned its business and has failed within a reasonable time to take steps to dissolve, liquidate or distribute its assets.

(b) A custodian appointed under this section shall have all the powers and title of a receiver appointed under section 291 of this title, but the authority of the custodian is to continue the business of the corporation and not to liquidate its affairs and distribute its assets, except when the Court shall otherwise order and except in cases arising under subparagraph (a)(3) of this section or section 352(a)(2) of this title.

§ 227. Powers of Court in Elections of Directors

(a) The Court of Chancery, in any proceeding instituted under sections 211, 215 or 225 of this title may determine the right and power of persons claiming to own stock, or in the case of a corporation without capital stock, of the persons claiming to be members, to vote at any meeting of the stockholders or members.

(b) The Court of Chancery may appoint a master to hold any election provided for in sections 211, 215 or 225 of this title under such orders and powers as it deems proper; and it may punish any officer or director for contempt in case of disobedience of any order made by the Court; and, in case of disobedience by a corporation of any order made by the Court, may enter a decree against such corporation for a penalty of not more than $5,000.

§ 228. Consent of Stockholders or Members in Lieu of Meeting

(a) Unless otherwise provided in the certificate of incorporation, any action required by this chapter to be taken at any annual or special meeting of stockholders of a corporation, or any action which may be taken at any annual or special meeting of such stockholders, may be taken without a meeting, without prior notice and without a vote, if a consent or consents in writing, setting forth the action so taken, shall be signed by the holders of outstanding stock having not less than the minimum number of votes that would be necessary to authorize or take such action at a meeting at which all shares entitled to vote thereon were present and voted and shall be delivered to the corporation by delivery to its registered office in this State, its principal place of business, or an officer or agent of the corporation having custody of the bank in which proceedings of meetings of stockholders are recorded. Delivery made to a corporation's registered office shall be by hand or by certified or registered mail, return receipt requested.

(b) Unless otherwise provided in the certificate of incorporation, any action required by this chapter to be taken at a meeting of the members of a non-stock corporation, or any action which may be taken at any meeting of the members of a non-stock corporation, may be taken without a meeting, without prior notice and without a vote, if a consent or consents in writing, setting forth the action so taken, shall be signed by members having not less than the minimum number of votes that would be necessary to authorize or take such action at a meeting at which all members having a right to vote thereon were present and voted and shall be delivered to the corporation by delivery to its registered office in this State, its principal place of business, or an officer or agent of the corporation having custody of the book in which proceedings of meetings of members are recorded. Delivery made to a corporation's registered office shall be by hand or by certified or registered mail, return receipt requested.

(c) Every written consent shall bear the date of signature of each stockholder or member who signs the consent and no written consent shall be effective to take the corporate action referred to therein unless, within sixty days of the earliest dated consent delivered in the manner required by this Section to the corporation, written consents signed by a sufficient number of holders or members to take action are delivered to the corporation by delivery to its registered office in this State, its principal place of business or an officer or agent of the corporation having custody of the book in which proceedings of meetings of stockholders or members are recorded. Delivery made to a corporation's registered office shall be by hand or by certified or registered mail, return receipt requested.

(d)(1) A telegram, cablegram or other electronic transmission consenting to an action to be taken and transmitted by a stockholder, member or proxyholder, or by a person or persons authorized to act for a stockholder, member or proxyholder, shall be deemed to be written, signed and dated for the purposes of this section, provided that any such telegram, cablegram or other electronic transmission sets forth or is delivered with information from which the corporation can determine (A) that the telegram, cablegram or other electronic transmission was transmitted by the member or proxyholder or by a person or persons authorized to act for the member or proxyholder and (B) the date on which such member or proxyholder or authorized person or persons transmitted such telegram, cablegram or electronic transmission. The date on which such telegram, cablegram or electronic transmission is transmitted shall be deemed to be the date on which such consent was signed. No consent given by telegram, cablegram or other electronic transmission shall be deemed to have been delivered until such consent is reproduced in paper form and until such paper form shall be delivered to the corporation by delivery to its registered office in this State, its principal place of business or an officer or agent of the corporation having custody of the book in which proceedings of meetings of stockholders or members are recorded. Delivery made to a corporation's registered office shall be made by hand or by certified or registered mail, return receipt requested. Notwithstanding the foregoing limitations on delivery, consents given by telegram, cablegram or other electronic transmission may be otherwise delivered to the principal place of business of the corporation or to an officer or agent of the corporation having custody of the book in which proceedings of meetings of stockholders or members are recorded if, to the extent and in the manner provided by resolution of the board of directors or governing body of the corporation.

(d)(2) Any copy, facsimile or other reliable reproduction of a consent in writing may be substituted or used in lieu of the original writing for any and all purposes for which the original writing could be used, provided that such copy, facsimile or other reproduction shall be a complete reproduction of the entire original writing.

(e) Prompt notice of the taking of the corporate action without a meeting by less than unanimous written consent shall be given to those stockholders or members, as the case may be, who have not consented in writing. In the event that the action which is consented to is such as would have required the filing of a certificate under any other section of this title, if such action had been voted on by stockholders or by members at a meeting thereof, the certificate filed under such other section shall state, in lieu of any statement required by such section concerning any vote of stockholders or members, that written consent has been given in accordance with the provisions of this section, and that written notice has been given as provided in this section.

§ 229. Waiver of Notice

Whenever notice is required to be given under any provision of this chapter or of the certificate of incorporation or by-laws, a written waiver thereof, signed by the person entitled to notice, or a waiver by electronic transmission by the person entitled to notice, whether before or after the time stated therein, shall be deemed equivalent to notice. Attendance of a person at a meeting shall constitute a waiver of notice of such meeting, except when the person attends a meeting for the express purpose of objecting, at the beginning of the meeting, to the transaction of any business because the meeting is not lawfully called or convened. Neither the business to be transacted at, nor the purpose of, any regular or special meeting of the stockholders, directors, or members of a committee of directors need be specified in any written waiver of notice or any waiver by electronic transmission unless so required by the certificate of incorporation or the by-laws.

§ 230. Exception to Requirements of Notice

(a) Whenever notice is required to be given, under any provision of this chapter or of the certificate of incorporation or by-laws of any corporation, to any person with whom communication is unlawful, the giving of such notice to such person shall not be required and there shall be no duty to apply to any governmental authority or agency for a license or permit to give such notice to such person. Any action or meeting which shall be taken or held without notice to any such person with whom communication is unlawful shall have the same force and effect as if such notice had been duly given. In the event that the action taken by the corporation is such as to require the filing of a certificate under any of the other sections of this title, the certificate shall state, if such is the fact and if notice is required, that notice was given to all persons entitled to receive notice except such persons with whom communication is unlawful.

(b) Whenever notice is required to be given, under any provision of this chapter or the certificate of incorporation or by-laws of any corporation, to any stockholder or, if the corporation is a nonstock corporation, to any member, to whom (i) notice of two consecutive annual meetings, and all notices of meetings or of the taking of action by written consent without a meeting to such person during the period between such two consecutive annual meetings, or (ii) all, and at least two, payments (if sent by first-class mail) of dividends or interest on securities during a 12–month period, have been mailed addressed to such person at such stockholder's ~~his~~ address as shown on the records of the corporation and have been returned undeliverable, the giving of such notice to such person shall not be required. Any action or meeting which shall be taken or held without notice to such person shall have the same force and effect as if such notice had been duly given. If any such person shall deliver to the corporation a written notice setting forth his then current address, the requirement that notice be given to such person shall be reinstated. In the event that the action taken by the corporation is such as to require the filing of a certificate under any of the other sections of this Title, the certificate need not state that notice was not given to persons to whom notice was not required to be given pursuant to this subsection.

(c) The exception in Section 230(b)(1) to the requirement that notice be given shall not be applicable to any notice returned as undeliverable if the notice was given by electronic transmission.

§ 231. Voting Procedures and Inspectors of Elections

(a) The corporation shall, in advance of any meeting of stockholders, appoint 1 or more inspectors to act at the meeting and make a written report thereof. The corporation may designate 1 or more persons as alternate inspectors to replace any inspector who fails to act. If no inspector or alternate is able to act at a meeting of stockholders, the person presiding at the meeting shall appoint 1 or more inspectors to act at the meeting. Each inspector, before entering upon the discharge of the duties of inspector , shall take and sign an oath faithfully to execute the duties of inspector with strict impartiality and according to the best of such inspector's ability.

(b) The inspectors shall:

(1) Ascertain the number of shares outstanding and the voting power of each;

(2) Determine the shares represented at a meeting and the validity of proxies and ballots;

(3) Count all votes and ballots;

(4) Determine and retain for a reasonable period a record of the disposition of any challenges made to any determination by the inspectors; and

(5) Certify their determination of the number of shares represented at the meeting, and their count of all votes and ballots.

The inspectors may appoint or retain other persons or entities to assist the inspectors in the performance of the duties of the inspectors.

(c) The date and time of the opening and the closing of the polls for each matter upon which the stockholders will vote at a meeting shall be announced at the meeting. No ballot, proxies or votes, nor any revocations thereof or changes thereto, shall be accepted by the inspectors after the closing of the polls unless the Court of Chancery upon application by a stockholder shall determine otherwise.

(d) In determining the validity and counting of proxies and ballots, the inspectors shall be limited to an examination of the proxies, any envelopes submitted with those proxies, any information provided in accordance with Section 211(e) or Section 212(c)(2) of this title, or any information provided pursuant to Section 211(a)(2)(B)(i) or (iii), ballots and the regular books and records of the corporation, except that the inspectors may consider other reliable information for the limited purpose of reconciling proxies and ballots submitted by or on behalf of banks, brokers, their nominees or similar persons which represent more votes than the holder of a proxy is authorized by the record owner to cast or more votes than the stockholder holds of record. If the inspectors consider other reliable information for the limited purpose permitted herein, the inspectors at the time they make their certification pursuant to subsection (b)(5) of this section shall specify the precise information considered by them including the person or persons from whom they obtained the information, when the information was obtained, the means by which the information was obtained and the basis for the inspectors' belief that such information is accurate and reliable.

(e) Unless otherwise provided in the certificate of incorporation or bylaws, this section shall not apply to a corporation that does not have a class of voting stock that is:

(1) Listed on a national securities exchange;

(2) Authorized for quotation on an interdealer quotation system of a registered national securities association; or

(3) Held of record by more than 2,000 stockholders.

§ 232. Notice by Electronic Transmission

(a) Without limiting the manner by which notice otherwise may be given effectively to stockholders, any notice to stockholders given by the corporation under any provision of this chapter, the certificate of incorporation, or the bylaws shall be effective if given by a form of electronic transmission consented to by the stockholder to whom the notice is given. Any such consent shall be revocable by the stockholder by written notice to the corporation. Any such consent shall be deemed revoked if (1) the corporation is unable to deliver by electronic transmission two consecutive notices given by the corporation in accordance with such consent and (2) such inability becomes known to the secretary or an assistant secretary of the corporation or to the transfer agent, or other person responsible for the giving of notice; provided, however, the inadvertent failure to treat such inability as a revocation shall not invalidate any meeting or other action.

(b) Notice given pursuant to subsection (a) of this section shall be deemed given: (1) if by facsimile telecommunication, when directed to a number at which the stockholder has consented to receive notice; (2) if by electronic mail, when directed to an electronic mail address at which the stockholder has consented to receive notice; (3) if by a posting on an electronic network together with separate notice to the stockholder of such specific posting, upon the later of (A) such posting and (B) the giving of such separate notice; and (4) if by any other form of electronic transmission, when directed to the stockholder. An affidavit of the secretary or an assistant secretary or of the transfer agent or other agent of the corporation that the notice has been given by a form of electronic transmission shall, in the absence of fraud, be prima facie evidence of the facts stated therein.

(c) For purposes of this chapter, "electronic transmission" means any form of communication, not directly involving the physical transmission of paper, that creates a record that may be retained, retrieved, and reviewed by a recipient thereof, and that may be directly reproduced in paper form by such a recipient through an automated process.

(d) This section shall apply to a corporation organized under this chapter that is not authorized to issue capital stock, and when so applied, all references to stockholders shall be deemed to refer to members of such a corporation.

(e) This section shall not apply to Sections 164, 296, 311, 312, or 324 of this chapter."

§ 233. Notice to Stockholders Sharing an Address

(a) Without limiting the manner by which notice otherwise may be given effectively to stockholders, any notice to stockholders given by the corporation under any provision of this chapter, the certificate of incorporation or the bylaws shall be effective if given by a single written notice to stockholders who share an address if consented to by the stockholders at that address to whom such notice is given. Any such consent shall be revocable by the stockholder by written notice to the corporation.

(b) Any stockholder who fails to object in writing to the corporation, within 60 days of having been given written notice by the corporation of its intention to send the single notice permitted under subsection (a) of this section, shall be deemed to have consented to receiving such single notice.

(c) This section shall apply to a corporation organized under this chapter that is not authorized to issue capital stock, and when so applied, all references to stockholders shall be deemed to refer to members of such a corporation.

(d) This section shall not apply to §§ 164, 296, 311, 312 or 324 of this chapter.

§ 241. Amendment of Certificate of Incorporation Before Receipt of Payment for Stock

(a) Before a corporation has received any payment for any of its stock, it may amend its certificate of incorporation at any time or times, in any and as many respects as may be desired, so long as its certificate of incorporation as amended would contain only such provisions as it would be lawful and proper to insert in an original certificate of incorporation filed at the time of filing the amendment.

(b) The amendment of a certificate of incorporation authorized by this section shall be adopted by a majority of the incorporators, if directors were not named in the original certificate of incorporation or have not yet been elected, or, if directors were named in the original certificate of incorporation or have been elected and have qualified, by a majority of the directors. A certificate setting forth the amendment and certifying that the corporation has not received any payment for any of its stock and that the amendment has been duly adopted in accordance with this section shall be executed, acknowledged, and filed in accordance with section 103 of this title. Upon such filing, the corporation's certificate of incorporation shall be deemed to be amended accordingly as of the date on which the original certificate of incorporation became effective except as to those persons who are substantially and adversely affected by the amendment and as to those persons the amendment shall be effective from the filing date.

§ 242. Amendment of Certificate of Incorporation After Receipt of Payment for Stock; Non-stock Corporations

(a) After a corporation has received payment for any of its capital stock, it may amend its certificate of incorporation, from time to time, in any and as many respects as may be desired, so long as its certificate of incorporation as amended would contain only such provisions as it would be lawful and proper to insert in an original certificate of incorporation filed at the time of the filing of the amendment; and, if a change in stock or the rights of stockholders, or an exchange, reclassification, subdivision, combination or cancellation of stock or rights of stockholders is to be made, such provisions as may be necessary to effect such change, exchange, reclassification, subdivision, combination or cancellation. In particular, and without limitation upon such general power of amendment, a corporation may amend its certificate of incorporation, from time to time, so as:

(1) To change its corporate name; or

(2) To change, substitute, enlarge or diminish the nature of its business or its corporate powers and purposes; or

(3) To increase or decrease its authorized capital stock or to reclassify the same, by changing the number, par value, designations, preferences, or relative, participating, optional, or other special rights of the shares, or the qualifications, limitations or restrictions of such rights, or by changing shares with par value into shares without par value, or shares without par value into shares with par value either with or without increasing or decreasing the number of shares, or by subdividing or combining the outstanding shares of any class or series of a class of shares into a greater or lesser number of outstanding shares; or

(4) To cancel or otherwise affect the right of the holders of the shares of any class to receive dividends which have accrued but have not been declared; or

(5) To create new classes of stock having rights and preferences either prior and superior or subordinate and inferior to the stock of any class then authorized, whether issued or unissued; or

(6) To change the period of its duration.

Any or all such changes or alterations may be effected by 1 certificate of amendment.

(b) Every amendment authorized by subsection (a) of this section shall be made and effected in the following manner:

(1) If the corporation has capital stock, its board of directors shall adopt a resolution setting forth the amendment proposed, declaring its advisability, and either calling a special meeting of the stockholders entitled to vote in respect thereof for the consideration of such amendment or directing that the amendment proposed be considered at the next annual meeting of the stockholders. Such special or annual meeting shall be called and held upon notice in accordance with s 222 of this title. The notice shall set forth such amendment in full or a brief summary of the changes to be effected thereby, as the directors shall deem advisable. At the meeting a vote of the stockholders entitled to vote thereon shall be taken for and against the proposed amendment. If a majority of the outstanding stock entitled to vote thereon, and a majority of the outstanding stock of each class entitled to vote thereon as a class has been voted in favor of the amendment, a certificate setting forth the amendment and certifying that such amendment has been duly adopted in accordance with this section shall be executed, acknowledged and filed and shall become effective in accordance with § 103 of this title.

(2) The holders of the outstanding shares of a class shall be entitled to vote as a class upon a proposed amendment, whether or not entitled to vote thereon by the certificate of incorporation, if the amendment would increase or decrease the aggregate number of authorized shares of such class, increase or decrease the par value of the shares of such class,

or alter or change the powers, preferences, or special rights of the shares of such class so as to affect them adversely. If any proposed amendment would alter or change the powers, preferences, or special rights of 1 or more series of any class so as to affect them adversely, but shall not so affect the entire class, then only the shares of the series so affected by the amendment shall be considered a separate class for the purposes of this paragraph. The number of authorized shares of any such class or classes of stock may be increased or decreased (but not below the number of shares thereof then outstanding) by the affirmative vote of the holders of a majority of the stock of the corporation entitled to vote irrespective of this subsection, if so provided in the original certificate of incorporation, in any amendment thereto which created such class or classes of stock or which was adopted prior to the issuance of any shares of such class or classes of stock, or in any amendment thereto which was authorized by a resolution or resolutions adopted by the affirmative vote of the holders of a majority of such class or classes of stock.

(3) If the corporation has no capital stock, then the governing body thereof shall adopt a resolution setting forth the amendment proposed and declaring its advisability. If a majority of all the members of the governing body shall vote in favor of such amendment, a certificate thereof shall be executed, acknowledged and filed and shall become effective in accordance with § 103 of this title. The certificate of incorporation of any such corporation without capital stock may contain a provision requiring any amendment thereto to be approved by a specified number or percentage of the members or of any specified class of members of such corporation in which event such proposed amendment shall be submitted to the members or to any specified class of members of such corporation without capital stock in the same manner, so far as applicable, as is provided in this section for an amendment to the certificate of incorporation of a stock corporation; and in the event of the adoption thereof by such members, a certificate evidencing such amendment shall be executed, acknowledged and filed and shall become effective in accordance with § 103 of this title.

(4) Whenever the certificate of incorporation shall require for action by the board of directors, by the holders of any class or series of shares or by the holders of any other securities having voting power the vote of a greater number or proportion than is required by any section of this title, the provision of the certificate of incorporation requiring such greater vote shall not be altered, amended or repealed except by such greater vote.

(c) The resolution authorizing a proposed amendment to the certificate of incorporation may provide that at any time prior to the effectiveness of the filing of the amendment with the Secretary of State, notwithstanding authorization of the proposed amendment by the stockholders of the corporation or by the members of a nonstock corporation, the board of directors or governing body may abandon such proposed amendment without further action by the stockholders or members.

§ 243. Retirement of Stock

(a) A corporation, by resolution of its board of directors, may retire any shares of its capital stock that are issued but are not outstanding.

(b) Whenever any shares of the capital stock of a corporation are retired, they shall resume the status of authorized and unissued shares of the class or series to which they belong unless the certificate of incorporation otherwise provides. If the certificate of incorporation prohibits the reissuance of such shares, or prohibits the reissuance of such shares as a part of a specific series only, a certificate stating that reissuance of the shares (as part of the class or series) is prohibited identifying the shares and reciting their retirement shall be executed, acknowledged and filed and shall become effective in accordance with § 103 of this Title. When such certificate becomes effective, it shall have the effect of amending the certificate of incorporation so as to reduce accordingly the number of authorized shares of the class or series to with such shares belong or, if such retired shares constitute all of the authorized shares of the class or series to which they belong, of eliminating from the certificate of incorporation all reference to such class or series of stock.

(c) If the capital of the corporation will be reduced by or in connection with the retirement of shares, the reduction of capital shall be effected pursuant to Section 244 of this Title.

§ 244. Reduction of Capital

(a) A corporation, by resolution of its board of directors, may reduce its capital in any of the following ways:

1. By reducing or eliminating the capital represented by shares of capital stock which have been retired;

2. By applying to an otherwise authorized purchase or redemption of outstanding shares of its capital stock some or all of the capital represented by the shares being purchased or redeemed, or any capital that has not been allocated to any particular class of its capital stock;

3. By applying to an otherwise authorized conversion or exchange of outstanding shares of its capital stock some or all of the capital represented by the shares being converted or exchanged, or some or all of any capital that has not been allocated to any particular class of its capital stock, or both, to the extent that such capital in the aggregate exceeds the total aggregate par value or the stated capital of any previously unissued shares issuable upon such conversion or exchange; or,

4. By transferring to surplus (i) some or all of the capital not represented by any particular class of its capital stock; (ii) some or all of the capital represented by issued shares of its par value capital stock, which capital is in excess of the aggregate par value of such shares; or (iii) some of the capital represented by issued shares of its capital stock without par value.

(b) Notwithstanding the other provisions of this section, no reduction of capital shall be made or effected unless the assets of the corporation remaining after such reduction shall be sufficient to pay any debts of the corporation for which payment has not been otherwise provided. No reduction of capital shall release any liability of any stockholder whose shares have not been fully paid.

§ 245. Restated Certificate of Incorporation

(a) A corporation may, whenever desired, integrate into a single instrument all of the provisions of its certificate of incorporation which are then in effect and operative as a result of there having theretofore been filed with the Secretary of State one or more certificates or other instruments pursuant to any of the sections referred to in § 104 of this title, and it may at the same time also further amend its certificate of incorporation by adopting a restated certificate of incorporation.

(b) If the restated certificate of incorporation merely restates and integrates but does not further amend the certificate of incorporation, as theretofore amended or supplemented by any instrument that was filed pursuant to any of the sections mentioned in § 104 of this title, it may be adopted by the board of directors without a vote of the stockholders, or it may be proposed by the directors and submitted by them to the stockholders for adoption, in which case the procedure and vote required by § 242 of this title for amendment of the certificate of incorporation shall be applicable. If the restated certificate of incorporation restates and integrates and also further amends in any respect the certificate of incorporation, as theretofore amended or supplemented, it shall be proposed by the directors and adopted by the stockholders in the manner and by the vote prescribed by § 242 of this title "or, if the corporation has not received any payment for any of its stock, in the manner and by the vote prescribed by § 241 of this title."

(c) A restated certificate of incorporation shall be specifically designated as such in its heading. It shall state, either in its heading or in an introductory paragraph, the corporation's present name, and, if it has been changed, the name under which it was originally incorporated, and the date of filing of its original certificate of incorporation with the Secretary of State. A restated certificate shall also state that it was duly adopted in accordance with the provisions of this section. If it was adopted by the board of directors without a vote of the stockholders (unless it was adopted pursuant to the provisions of section 241 of this title), it shall state that it only restates and integrates and does not further amend the provisions of the corporation's certificate of incorporation as theretofore amended or supplemented, and that there is no discrepancy between those provisions and the provisions of the restated certificate. A restated certificate of incorporation may omit (a) such provisions of the original certificate of incorporation which named the incorporator or incorporators, the initial board of directors and the original subscribers for shares, and (b) such provisions contained in any amendment to the certificate of incorporation as were necessary to effect a change, exchange, reclassification, subdivision, combination or cancellation of stock, if such change, exchange, reclassification, subdivision, combination or cancellation has become effective. Any such omissions shall not be deemed a further amendment.

(d) A restated certificate of incorporation shall be executed, acknowledged, and filed in accordance with § 103 of this title. Upon its filing with the Secretary of State, the original certificate of incorporation, as theretofore amended or supplemented, shall be superseded; thenceforth, the restated certificate of incorporation, including any further amendments or changes made thereby, shall be the certificate of incorporation of the corporation, but the original date of incorporation shall remain unchanged.

(e) Any amendment or change effected in connection with the restatement and integration of the certificate of incorporation shall be subject to any other provision of this chapter, not inconsistent with this section, which would apply if a separate certificate of amendment were filed to effect such amendment or change.

§ 251. Merger or Consolidation of Domestic Corporations

(a) Any 2 or more corporations existing under the laws of this State may merge into a single corporation, which may be any 1 of the constituent corporations or may consolidate into a new corporation formed by the consolidation, pursuant to an agreement of merger or consolidation, as the case may be, complying and approved in accordance with this section.

(b) The board of directors of each corporation which desires to merge or consolidate shall adopt a resolution approving an agreement of merger or consolidation and declaring its advisability. The agreement shall state: (1) The terms and conditions of the merger or consolidation; (2) the mode of carrying the same into effect; (3) in the case of a merger, such amendments or changes in the certificate of incorporation of the surviving corporation as are desired to be effected by the merger, or, if no such amendments or changes are desired, a statement that the certificate of incorporation of the surviving corporation shall be its certificate of incorporation; (4) in the case of a consolidation, that the certificate of incorporation of the resulting corporation shall be as is set forth in an attachment to the agreement; (5) the manner, if any, of converting the shares of each of the constituent corporations into shares or other securities of the corporation surviving or resulting from the merger or consolidation, or of cancelling some or all of such shares, and, if any shares of any of the constituent corporations are not to remain outstanding, to be converted solely into shares or other securities of the surviving or resulting corporation or to be cancelled, the cash, property, rights or securities of any other corporation or entity which the holders of such shares are to receive in exchange for, or upon conversion of such shares and the surrender of any certificates evidencing them, which cash, property, rights or securities of any other corporation or entity may be in addition to or in lieu of shares or other securities of the surviving or resulting corporation; and (6) such other details or provisions as are deemed desirable, including, without limiting the generality of the foregoing, a provision for the payment of cash in lieu of the issuance or recognition of fractional shares, interests or rights, or for any other arrangement with respect thereto, consistent with § 155 of this title. The agreement so adopted shall be executed and acknowledged in accordance with § 103 of this title. Any of the terms of the agreement of merger or consolidation may be made dependent upon facts ascertainable outside of such agreement, provided that the manner in which such facts shall operate upon the terms of the agreement is clearly and expressly set forth in the agreement of merger or consolidation.

(c) The agreement required by subsection (b) of this section shall be submitted to the stockholders of each constituent corporation at an annual or special meeting for the purpose of acting on the agreement. Due notice of the time, place and purpose of the meeting shall be mailed to each holder of stock, whether voting or nonvoting, of the corporation at his address as it appears on the records of the corporation, at least 20 days prior to the date of the meeting. The notice shall contain a copy of the agreement or a brief summary thereof, as the directors shall deem advisable. At the meeting, the agreement shall be considered and a vote taken for its adoption or rejection. If a majority of the outstanding stock of the corporation entitled to vote thereon shall be voted for the adoption of the agreement, that fact shall be certified on the agreement by the secretary or assistant secretary of the corporation. If the agreement shall be so adopted and certified by each constituent corporation, it shall then be filed and shall become effective, in accordance with § 103 of this title. In lieu of filing the agreement of merger or consolidation required by this section, the surviving or resulting corporation may file a certificate of merger or consolidation, executed in accordance with § 103 of this title, which states:

(1) The name and state of incorporation of each of the constituent corporations;

(2) That an agreement of merger or consolidation has been approved, adopted, certified, executed and acknowledged by each of the constituent corporations in accordance with this section;

(3) The name of the surviving or resulting corporation;

(4) In the case of a merger, such amendments or changes in the certificate of incorporation of the surviving corporation as are desired to be effected by the merger, or, if no such amendments or changes are desired, a statement that the certificate of incorporation of the surviving corporation shall be its certificate of incorporation;

(5) In the case of a consolidation, that the certificate of incorporation of the resulting corporation shall be as set forth in an attachment to the certificate;

(6) That the executed agreement of consolidation or merger is on file at the principal place of business of the surviving corporation, stating the address thereof; and

(7) That a copy of the agreement of consolidation or merger will be furnished by the surviving corporation, on request and without cost, to any stockholder of any constituent corporation.

(d) Any agreement of merger or consolidation may contain a provision that at any time prior to the time that the agreement (or a certificate in lieu thereof) filed with the Secretary of State becomes effective in accordance with § 103 of this title, the agreement may be terminated by the board of directors of any constituent corporation notwithstanding approval of the agreement by the stockholders of all or any of the constituent corporations; in the event the agreement of merger or consolidation is terminated after the filing of the agreement (or a certificate in lieu thereof) with the Secretary of State but before the agreement (or a certificate in lieu thereof) has become effective, a certificate of termination or merger or consolidation shall be filed in accordance with § 103 of this title. Any agreement of merger or consolidation may contain a provision that the boards of directors of the constituent corporations may amend the agreement at any time prior to the time that the agreement (or a certificate in lieu thereof) filed with the Secretary of State becomes effective in accordance with § 103 of this title, provided that an amendment made subsequent to the adoption of the agreement by the stockholders of any constituent corporation shall not (1) alter or change the amount or kind of shares, securities, cash, property and/or rights to be received in exchange for or on conversion of all or any of the shares of any class or series thereof of such constituent corporation, (2) alter or change any term of the certificate of incorporation of the surviving corporation to be effected by the merger or consolidation, or (3) alter or change any of the terms and conditions of the agreement if such alteration or change would adversely affect the holders of any class or series thereof of such constituent corporation; in the event the agreement of merger or consolidation is amended after the filing thereof with the Secretary of State but before the agreement has become effective, a certificate of consolidation shall be filed in accordance with § 103 of this title.

(e) In the case of a merger, the certificate of incorporation of the surviving corporation shall automatically be amended to the extent, if any, that changes in the certificate of incorporation are set forth in the agreement of merger.

(f) Notwithstanding the requirements of subsection (c) of this section, unless required by its certificate of incorporation, no vote of stockholders of a constituent corporation surviving a merger shall be necessary to authorize a merger if (1) the agreement of merger does not amend in any respect the certificate of incorporation of such constituent corporation, (2) each share of stock of such constituent corporation outstanding immediately prior to the effective date of the merger is to be an identical outstanding or treasury share of the surviving corporation after the effective date of the merger, and (3) either no shares of common stock of the surviving corporation and no shares, securities or obligations convertible into such stock are to be issued or delivered under the plan of merger, or the authorized unissued shares or the treasury shares of common stock of the surviving corporation to be issued or delivered under the plan of merger plus those initially issuable upon conversion of any other shares, securities or obligations to be issued or delivered under such plan do not exceed 20% of the shares of common stock of such constituent corporation outstanding immediately prior to the effective date of the merger. No vote of stockholders of a constituent corporation shall be necessary to authorize a merger or consolidation if no shares of the stock of such corporation shall have been issued prior to the adoption by the board of directors of the resolution approving the agreement of merger or consolidation. If an agreement of merger is adopted by the constituent corporation surviving the merger, by action of its board of directors and without any vote of its stockholders pursuant to this subsection, the secretary or assistant secretary of that corporation shall certify on the agreement that the agreement has been adopted pursuant to this subsection and, (1) if it has been adopted pursuant to the first sentence of this subsection, that the conditions specified in that sentence have been satisfied, or (2) if it has been adopted pursuant to the second sentence of this subsection, that no shares of stock of such corporation were issued prior to the adoption by the board of directors of the resolution approving the agreement of merger or consolidation. The agreement so adopted and certified shall then be filed and shall become effective, in accordance with § 103 of this title. Such filing shall constitute a representation by the person who executes the agreement that the facts stated in the certificate remain true immediately prior to such filing.

(g) Notwithstanding the requirements of subsection (c) of this section, unless expressly required by its certificate of incorporation, no vote of stockholders of a constituent corporation shall be necessary to authorize a merger with or into a single direct or indirect wholly-owned subsidiary of such constituent corporation if: (1) such constituent corporation and the direct or indirect wholly-owned subsidiary of such constituent corporation are the only constituent entities to the merger; (2) each share or fraction of a share of the capital stock of the constituent corporation outstanding immediately prior to the effective time of the merger is converted in the merger into a share or equal fraction of share of capital stock of a holding company having the same designations, rights, powers and preferences, and the qualifications, limitations and restrictions thereof, as the share of stock of the constituent corporation being converted in the merger; (3) the holding company and the constituent corporation are corporations of this State and the direct or indirect wholly-owned subsidiary that is the other constituent entity to the merger is a corporation or limited liability company of this State; (4) the certificate of incorporation and by-laws of the holding company immediately following the effective time of the merger contain provisions identical to the certificate of incorporation and by-laws of the constituent corporation immediately prior to the effective time of the merger (other than provisions, if any, regarding the incorporator or incorporators, the corporate name, the registered office and agent, the initial board of directors and the initial subscribers for shares and such provisions contained in any amendment to the certificate of incorporation as were necessary to effect a change, exchange, reclassification, subdivision, combination or cancellation of stock, if such change, exchange, reclassification, subdivision, combination or cancellation has become effective); (5) as a result of the merger the constituent corporation or its successor becomes or remains a direct or indirect wholly-owned subsidiary of the holding company; (6) the directors of the constituent corporation become or remain the directors of the holding company upon the effective time of the merger; (7) the organizational documents of the surviving entity immediately following the effective time of the merger contain provisions identical to the certificate of incorporation of the constituent corporation immediately prior to the effective time of the merger (other than provisions, if any, regarding the incorporator or incorporators, the corporate or entity name, the registered office and agent, the initial board of directors and the initial subscribers for shares, references to members rather than stockholders or shareholders, references to interests, units or the like rather than stock or shares, references to managers, managing members or other members of the governing body rather than directors and such provisions contained in any amendment to the certificate of incorporation as were necessary to effect a change, exchange, reclassification, subdivision, combination or cancellation of stock, if such change, exchange, reclassification, subdivision, combination or cancellation has become effective); provided, however, that (i) if the organizational documents of the surviving entity do not contain the following provisions, they shall be amended in the merger to contain provisions requiring that (A) any act or transaction by or involving the surviving entity, other than the election or removal of directors or managers, managing members or other members of the governing body of the surviving entity, that requires for its adoption under this chapter or its organizational documents the approval of the stockholders or members of the surviving entity shall, by specific reference to this subsection, require, in addition, the approval of the stockholders of the holding company (or any successor by merger), by the same vote as is required by this chapter and/or by the organizational documents of the surviving entity; provided, however, that for purposes of this clause (i)(A), any surviving entity that is not a corporation shall include in such amendment a requirement that the approval of the stockholders of the holding company be obtained for any act or transaction by or involving the surviving entity, other than the election or removal of directors or managers, managing members or other members of the governing body of the surviving entity, which would require the approval of the stockholders of the surviving entity if the surviving entity were a corporation subject to this chapter, (B) any amendment of the organizational documents of a surviving entity that is not a corporation, which amendment would, if adopted by a corporation subject to this chapter, be required to be included in the certificate of incorporation of such corporation, shall, by specific reference to this subsection, require, in addition, the approval of the stockholders of the holding company (or any successor by merger), by the same vote as is required by this chapter and/or by the organizational documents of the surviving entity, and (C) the business and affairs of a surviving entity that is not a corporation shall be managed by or under the direction of a board of directors, board of managers or other governing body consisting of individuals who are subject to the same fiduciary duties applicable to, and who are liable for breach of such duties to the same extent as, directors of a corporation subject to this chapter, and (ii) the organizational documents of the surviving entity may be amended in the merger to reduce the number of classes and shares of capital stock or other equity interests or units that the surviving entity is authorized to issue; and (8) the stockholders of the constituent corporation do not recognize gain or loss for United States federal income tax purposes as determined by the board of directors of the constituent corporation. Neither subsection (g)(7)(i) of this section nor any provision of a surviving entity's organizational documents required by subsection (g)(7)(i) shall be deemed or construed to require approval of the stockholders of the holding company to elect or remove directors or managers, managing members or other members of the governing body of the surviving entity. The term 'organizational documents', as used in subsection (g)(7) and in the preceding sentence, shall, when used in reference to a corporation, mean the certificate of incorporation of such corporation and, when used in reference to a limited liability company, mean the limited liability company agreement of such limited liability company.

As used in this subsection only, the term "holding company" means a corporation which, from its incorporation until consummation of a merger governed on, was at all times a direct or indirect wholly-owned subsidiary of the constituent corporation and whose capital stock is issued in such merger. From and after the effective time of a merger adopted by a constituent corporation by action of its board of directors and without any vote of stockholders pursuant to this subsection: (i) to the extent the restrictions of § 203 of this title applied to the constituent corporation and its stockholders at the effective time of the merger, such restrictions shall apply to the holding company and its stockholders immediately after the effective time of the merger as though it were the constituent corporation, and all shares of stock of the holding company acquired in the merger shall for purposes of § 203 of this title be deemed to have been acquired at the time that the shares of stock of the constituent corporation converted in the merger were acquired, and provided further that any stockholder who immediately prior to the effective time of the merger was not an interested stockholder within the meaning of § 203 of this title shall not solely by reason of the merger become an interested stockholder of the holding company, (ii) if the corporate name of the holding company immediately following the effective time of the merger is the same as the corporate name of the constituent corporation immediately prior to the effective time of the merger, the shares of capital stock of the holding company into which the shares of capital stock of the constituent corporation are converted in the merger shall be represented by the stock certificates that previously represented shares of capital stock of the constituent corporation and (iii) to the extent a stockholder of the constituent corporation immediately prior to the merger had standing to institute or maintain derivative litigation on behalf of the constituent corporation, nothing in this section shall be deemed to limit or extinguish such standing. If an agreement of merger is adopted by a constituent corporation by action of its board of directors and without any vote of stockholders pursuant to this subsection, the secretary or assistant secretary of the constituent corporation shall certify on the agreement that the agreement has been adopted pursuant to this subsection, and that the conditions specified in the first sentence of this subsection have been satisfied. The agreement so adopted and certified shall then be filed and become effective, in accordance with § 103 of this title. Such filing shall constitute a representation by the person who executes the agreement that the facts stated in the certificate remain true immediately prior to such filing.

§ 252. Merger or Consolidation of Domestic and Foreign Corporations; Service of Process Upon Surviving or Resulting Corporation

(a) Any 1 or more corporations of this State may merge or consolidate with 1 or more other corporations of any other state or states of the

United States, or of the District of Columbia if the laws of the other state or states, or of the District permit a corporation of such jurisdiction to merge or consolidate with a corporation of another jurisdiction. The constituent corporations may merge into a single corporation, which may be any 1 of the constituent corporations, or they may consolidate into a new corporation formed by the consolidation, which may be a corporation of the state of incorporation of any 1 of the constituent corporations, pursuant to an agreement of merger or consolidation, as the case may be, complying and approved in accordance with this section. In addition, any 1 or more corporations existing under the laws of this State may merge or consolidate with 1 or more corporations organized under the laws of any jurisdiction other than 1 of the United States if the laws under which the other corporation or corporations are organized permit a corporation of such jurisdiction to merge or consolidate with a corporation of another jurisdiction.

(b) All the constituent corporations shall enter into an agreement of merger or consolidation. The agreement shall state: (1) The terms and conditions of the merger or consolidation; (2) the mode of carrying the same into effect; (3) the manner, if any, of converting the shares of each of the constituent corporations into shares or other securities of the corporation surviving or resulting from the merger or consolidation, or of cancelling some or all of such shares, and, if any shares of any of the constituent corporations are not to remain outstanding, to be converted solely into shares or other securities of the surviving or resulting corporation or to be cancelled, the cash, property, rights or securities of any other corporation or entity which the holders of such shares are to receive in exchange for, or upon conversion of, such shares and the surrender of any certificates evidencing them, which cash, property, rights or securities of any other corporation or entity may be in addition to or in lieu of the shares or other securities of the surviving or resulting corporation; (4) such other details or provisions as are deemed desirable, including, without limiting the generality of the foregoing, a provision for the payment of cash in lieu of the issuance or recognition of fractional shares of the surviving or resulting corporation or of any other corporation the securities of which are to be received in the merger or consolidation, or for some other arrangement with respect thereto consistent with § 155 of this title; and (5) such other provisions or facts as shall be required to be set forth in certificates of incorporation by the laws of the state which are stated in the agreement to be the laws that shall govern the surviving or resulting corporation and that can be stated in the case of a merger or consolidation. Any of the terms of the agreement of merger or consolidation may be made dependent upon facts ascertainable outside of such agreement, provided that the manner in which such facts shall operate upon the terms of the agreement is clearly and expressly set forth in the agreement of merger or consolidation.

(c) The agreement shall be adopted, approved, certified, executed and acknowledged by each of the constituent corporations in accordance with the laws under which it is formed, and, in the case of a Delaware corporation, in the same manner as is provided in § 251 of this title. The agreement shall be filed and shall become effective for all purposes of the laws of this State when and as provided in § 251 of this title with respect to the merger or consolidation of corporations of this State. In lieu of filing the agreement of merger or consolidation, the surviving or resulting corporation may file a certificate of merger or consolidation, executed in accordance with § 103 of this title, which states: (1) The name and state or jurisdiction of incorporation of each of the constituent corporations; (2) That an agreement of merger or consolidation has been approved, adopted, certified, executed and acknowledged by each of the constituent corporations in accordance with this subsection; (3) the name of the surviving or resulting corporation; (4) in the case of a merger, such amendments or changes in the certificate of incorporation of the surviving corporation as are desired to be effected by the merger, or, if no such amendments or changes are desired, a statement that the certificate of incorporation of the surviving corporation shall be its certificate of incorporation; (5) in the case of a consolidation, that the certificate of incorporation of the resulting corporation shall be as is set forth in an attachment to the certificate; (6) That the executed agreement of consolidation or merger is on file at the principal place of business of the surviving corporation and the address thereof; (7) That a copy of the agreement of consolidation or merger will be furnished by the surviving corporation, on request and without cost, to any stockholder of any constituent corporation; (8) if the corporation surviving or resulting from the merger or consolidation is to be a corporation of this State, the authorized capital stock of each constituent corporation which is not a corporation of this State; and (9) The agreement, if any, required by subsection (d) of this section.

(d) If the corporation surviving or resulting from the merger or consolidation is to be governed by the laws of the District of Columbia or any state or jurisdiction other than this State, it shall agree that it may be served with process in this State in any proceeding for enforcement of any obligation of any constituent corporation of this State, as well as for enforcement of any obligation of the surviving or resulting corporation arising from the merger or consolidation, including any suit or other proceeding to enforce the right of any stockholders as determined in appraisal proceedings pursuant to § 262 of this title, and shall irrevocably appoint the Secretary of State as its agent to accept service of process in any such suit or other proceedings and shall specify the address to which a copy of such process shall be mailed by the Secretary of State. In the event of such service upon the Secretary of State in accordance with this subsection, the Secretary of State shall forthwith notify such surviving or resulting corporation thereof by letter, certified mail, return receipt requested, directed to such surviving or resulting corporation at its address so specified, unless such surviving or resulting corporation shall have designated in writing to the Secretary of State a different address for such purpose, in which case it shall be mailed to the last address so designated. Such letter shall enclose a copy of the process and any other papers served on the Secretary of State pursuant to this subsection. It shall be the duty of the plaintiff in the event of such service to serve process and any other papers in duplicate, to notify the Secretary of State that service is being effected pursuant to this subsection and to pay the Secretary of State the sum of $50 for the use of the State, which sum shall be taxed as part of the costs in the proceeding, if the plaintiff shall prevail therein. The Secretary of State shall maintain an alphabetical record of any such service setting forth the name of the plaintiff and the defendant, the title, docket number and nature of the proceeding in which process has been served upon him, the fact that service has been effected pursuant to this subsection, the return date thereof, and the day and hour service was made. The Secretary of State shall not be required to retain such information longer than 5 years from his receipt of the service of process.

(e) The provisions of subsection (d) and the second sentence of subsection (c) of section 251 of this title shall apply to any merger or consolidation under this section; the provisions of subsection (e) of section 251 shall apply to a merger under this section in which the surviving corporation is a corporation of this State; the provisions of subsection (f) of section 251 shall apply to any merger under this section.

§ 253. Merger of Parent Corporation and Subsidiary or Subsidiaries

(a) In any case in which at least 90% of the outstanding shares of each class of the stock of a corporation or corporations (other than a corporation which has in its certificate of incorporation the provision required by subsection (g)(7)(i) of Section 251 of this title) is owned by another corporation and 1 of the corporations is a corporation of this State and the other or others are corporations of this State, or any other state or states, or the District of Columbia and the laws of the other state or states, or the District permit a corporation of such jurisdiction to merge with a corporation of another jurisdiction, the corporation having such stock ownership may either merge the other corporation or corporations into itself and assume all of its or their obligations, or merge itself, or itself and 1 or more of such other corporations, into 1 of the other corporations by executing, acknowledging and filing, in accordance with § 103 of this title, a certificate of such ownership and merger setting forth a copy of the resolution of its board of directors to so merge and the date of the adoption; provided, however, that in case the parent corporation shall not own all the outstanding stock of all the subsidiary corporations, parties to a merger as aforesaid, the resolution of the board of directors of the parent corporation shall state the terms and conditions of the merger, including the securities, cash, property, or rights to be issued, paid, delivered or granted by the surviving corporation upon surrender of each share of the subsidiary corporation or corporations not owned by the parent corporation or the cancellation of some or all of such shares. Any of the terms of the resolution of the board of directors to so merge may be made dependent upon facts ascertainable outside of such resolution, provided that the manner in which such facts shall operate upon the terms of the resolution is clearly and expressly set forth in the resolution. The term "facts," as used in the preceding sentence, includes, but is not limited to, the occurrence of any event including a determination or action by any person or body, including the corporation. If the parent corporation be not the surviving corporation, the resolution shall include provision for the pro rata issuance of stock of the surviving corporation to the holders of the stock of the parent corporation on surrender of any certificates therefor, and the certificate of ownership and merger shall state that the proposed merger has been approved by a majority of the outstanding stock of the parent corporation entitled to vote thereon at a meeting duly called and held after 20 days' notice of the purpose of the meeting mailed to each such stockholder at the stockholder's address as it appears on the records of the corporation if the parent corporation is a corporation of this State or state that the proposed merger has been adopted, approved, certified, executed and acknowledged by the parent corporation in accordance with the laws under which it is organized if the parent corporation is not a corporation of this State. If the surviving corporation exists under the laws of the District of Columbia or any state or jurisdiction other than this State, subsection (d) of § 252 of this title shall also apply to a merger under this section.

(b) If the surviving corporation is a Delaware corporation, it may change its corporate name by the inclusion of a provision to that effect in the resolution of merger adopted by the directors of the parent corporation and set forth in the certificate of ownership and merger, and upon the effective date of the merger, the name of the corporation shall be so changed.

(c) Subsection (d) of § 251 of this title shall apply to a merger under this section, and subsection (e) of § 251 of this title shall apply to a merger under this section in which the surviving corporation is the subsidiary corporation and is a corporation of this State. References to "agreement of merger" in subsections (d) and (e) of § 251 of this title shall mean for purposes of this subsection the resolution of merger adopted by the board of directors of the parent corporation. Any merger which effects any changes other than those authorized by this section or made applicable by this subsection shall be accomplished under § 251 or § 252 of this title. Section 262 of this title shall not apply to any merger effected under this section, except as provided in subsection (d) of this section.

(d) In the event all of the stock of a subsidiary Delaware corporation party to a merger effected under this section is not owned by the parent corporation immediately prior to the merger, the stockholders of the subsidiary Delaware corporation party to the merger shall have appraisal rights as set forth in § 262 of this title.

(e) A merger may be effected under this section although 1 or more of the corporations parties to the merger is a corporation organized under the laws of a jurisdiction other than 1 of the United States; provided that the laws of such jurisdiction permit a corporation of such jurisdiction to merge with a corporation of another jurisdiction.

* * *

§ 259. Status, Rights, Liabilities, etc., of Constituent and Surviving or Resulting Corporations Following Merger or Consolidation

(a) When any merger or consolidation shall have become effective under this chapter, for all purposes of the laws of this State the separate existence of all the constituent corporations, or of all such constituent corporations except the one into which the other or others of such constituent corporations have been merged, as the case may be, shall cease and the constituent corporations shall become a new corporation, or be merged into one of such corporations, as the case may be, possessing all the rights, privileges, powers and franchises as well of a public as of a private nature, and being subject to all the restrictions, disabilities and duties of each of such corporations so merged or consolidated; and all and singular, the rights, privileges, powers and franchises of each of said corporations, and all property, real, personal and mixed, and all debts due to any of said constituent corporations on whatever account, as well for stock subscriptions as all other things in action or belonging to each of such corporations shall be vested in the corporation surviving or resulting from such merger or consolidation; and all property, rights, privileges, powers and franchises, and all and every other interest shall be thereafter as effectually the property of the surviving or resulting corporation as they were of the several and respective constituent corporations, and the title to any real estate vested by deed or otherwise, under the laws of this State, in any of such constituent corporations, shall not revert or be in any way impaired by reason of this chapter; but all rights of creditors and all liens upon any property of any of said constituent corporations shall be preserved unimpaired, and all debts, liabilities and duties of the respective constituent corporations shall thenceforth attach to said surviving or resulting corporation, and may be enforced against it to the same extent as if said debts, liabilities and duties had been incurred or contracted by it.

(b) In the case of a merger of banks or trust companies, without any order or action on the part of any court or otherwise, all appointments, designations, and nominations, and all other rights and interests as trustee, executor, administrator, registrar of stocks and bonds, guardian of estates, assignee, receiver, trustee of estates of persons mentally ill and in every other fiduciary capacity, shall be automatically vested in the corporation resulting from or surviving such merger; provided, however, that any party in interest shall have the right to apply to an appropriate court or tribunal for a determination as to whether the surviving corporation shall continue to serve in the same fiduciary capacity as the merged corporation, or whether a new and different fiduciary should be appointed.

§ 260. Powers of Corporation Surviving or Resulting From Merger or Consolidation; Issuance of Stock, Bonds or Other Indebtedness

When two or more corporations are merged or consolidated, the corporation surviving or resulting from the merger may issue bonds or other obligations, negotiable or otherwise, and with or without coupons or interest certificates thereto attached, to an amount sufficient with its capital stock to provide for all the payment it will be required to make, or obligations it will be required to assume, in order to effect the merger or consolidation. For the purpose of securing the payment of any such bonds and obligations, it shall be lawful for the surviving or resulting corporation to mortgage its corporate franchise, rights, privileges and property, real, personal or mixed. The surviving or resulting corporation may issue certificates of its capital stock or uncertificated stock if authorized to do so and other securities to the stockholders of the constituent corporations in exchange or payment for the original shares, in such amount as shall be necessary in accordance with the terms of the agreement of merger or consolidation in order to effect such merger or consolidation in the manner and on the terms specified in the agreement.

§ 261. Effect of Merger Upon Pending Actions

Any action or proceeding, whether civil, criminal or administrative, pending by or against any corporation which is a party to a merger or consolidation shall be prosecuted as if such merger or consolidation had not taken place, or the corporation surviving or resulting from such merger or consolidation may be substituted in such action or proceeding.

§ 262. Appraisal Rights

(a) Any stockholder of a corporation of this State who holds shares of stock on the date of the making of a demand pursuant to subsection (d) of this section with respect to such shares, who continuously holds such shares through the effective date of the merger or consolidation, who has otherwise complied with subsection (d) of this section and who has neither voted in favor of the merger or consolidation nor consented thereto in writing pursuant to § 228 of this title shall be entitled to an appraisal by the Court of Chancery of the fair value of his shares of stock under the circumstances described in subsections (b) and (c) of this section. As used in this section, the word "stockholder" means a holder of record of stock in a stock corporation and also a member of record of a nonstock corporation; the words "stock" and "share" mean and include what is ordinarily meant by those words and also membership or membership interest of a member of a nonstock corporation; and the words "depository receipt" mean a receipt or other instrument issued by a depository representing an interest in one or more shares, or fractions thereof, solely of stock of a corporation, which stock is deposited with the depository.

(b) Appraisal rights shall be available for the shares of any class or series of stock of a constituent corporation in a merger or consolidation to be effected pursuant to § 251 (other than a merger effected pursuant to subsection (g) of § 251), § 252, § 254, § 257, § 258, § 263 or § 264 of this title:

(1) Provided, however, that no appraisal rights under this section shall be available for the shares of any class or series of stock, which stock, or depository receipts in respect thereof, at the record date fixed to determine the stockholders entitled to receive notice of and to vote at the meeting of stockholders to act upon the agreement of merger or consolidation, were either (i) listed on a national securities exchange or designated as a national market system security on an interdealer quotation system by the National Association of Securities Dealers, Inc. or (ii) held of record by more than 2,000 holders; and further provided that no appraisal rights shall be available for any shares of stock of the constituent corporation surviving a merger if the merger did not require for its approval the vote of the stockholders of the surviving corporation as provided in subsection (f) of § 251 of this title.

(2) Notwithstanding paragraph (1) of this subsection, appraisal rights under this section shall be available for the shares of any class or series of stock of a constituent corporation if the holders thereof are required by the terms of an agreement of merger or consolidation pursuant to §§ 251, 252, 254, 257, 258, 263 and 264 of this title to accept for such stock anything except:

a. Shares of stock of the corporation surviving or resulting from such merger or consolidation, or depository receipts in respect thereof;

b. Shares of stock of any other corporation, or depository receipts in respect thereof, which shares of stock (or depository receipts in respect thereof) or depository receipts at the effective date of the merger or consolidation will be either listed on a national securities exchange or designated as a national market system security on an interdealer quotation system by the National Association of Securities Dealers, Inc. or held of record by more than 2,000 holders;

c. Cash in lieu of fractional shares or fractional depository receipts described in the foregoing subparagraphs a. and b. of this paragraph; or

d. Any combination of the shares of stock, depository receipts and cash in lieu of fractional shares or fractional depository receipts described in the foregoing subparagraphs a., b. and c. of this paragraph.

(3) In the event all of the stock of a subsidiary Delaware corporation party to a merger effected under § 253 of this title is not owned by the parent corporation immediately prior to the merger, appraisal rights shall be available for the shares of the subsidiary Delaware corporation.

(c) Any corporation may provide in its certificate of incorporation that appraisal rights under this section shall be available for the shares of any class or series of its stock as a result of an amendment to its certificate of incorporation, any merger or consolidation in which the corporation is a constituent corporation or the sale of all or substantially all of the assets of the corporation. If the certificate of incorporation contains such a provision, the procedures of this section, including those set forth in subsections (d) and (e) of this section, shall apply as nearly as is practicable.

(d) Appraisal rights shall be perfected as follows:

(1) If a proposed merger or consolidation for which appraisal rights are provided under this section is to be submitted for approval at a meeting of stockholders, the corporation, not less than 20 days prior to the meeting, shall notify each of its stockholders who was such on the record date for such meeting with respect to shares for which appraisal rights are available pursuant to subsection (b) or (c) hereof that appraisal rights are available for any or all of the shares of the constituent corporations, and shall include in such notice a copy of this section. Each stockholder electing to demand the appraisal of such stockholder's ~~his~~ shares shall deliver to the corporation, before the taking of the vote on the merger or consolidation, a written demand for appraisal of such stockholder's shares. Such demand will be sufficient if it reasonably informs the corporation of the identity of the stockholder and that the stockholder intends thereby to demand the appraisal of such stockholder's shares. A proxy or vote against the merger or consolidation shall not constitute such a demand. A stockholder electing to take such action must do so by a separate written demand as herein provided. Within 10 days after the effective date of such merger or consolidation, the surviving or resulting corporation shall notify each stockholder of each constituent corporation who has complied with this subsection and has not voted in favor of or consented to the merger or consolidation of the date that the merger or consolidation has become effective; or

(2) If the merger or consolidation was approved pursuant to § 228 or § 253 of this title, then, either a constituent corporation before the effective date of the merger or consolidation, or the surviving or resulting corporation within ten days thereafter, shall notify each of the holders of any class or series of stock of such constituent corporation who are entitled to appraisal rights of the approval of the merger or consolidation and that appraisal rights are available for any or all shares of such class or series of stock of such constituent corporation, and shall include in such notice a copy of this section. The notice shall be sent by certified or registered mail, return receipt requested, addressed to the stockholder at his address as it appears on the records of the corporation. Any stockholder entitled to appraisal rights may, within 20 days after the date of mailing of the notice, demand in writing from the surviving or resulting corporation the appraisal of his shares. Such demand will be sufficient if it reasonably informs the corporation of the identity of the stockholder and that the stockholder intends thereby to demand the appraisal of his shares.

(e) Within 120 days after the effective date of the merger or consolidation, the surviving or resulting corporation or any stockholder who has complied with subsections (a) and (d) hereof and who is otherwise entitled to appraisal rights, may file a petition in the Court of Chancery demanding a determination of the value of the stock of all such stockholders. Notwithstanding the foregoing, at any time within 60 days after the effective date of the merger or consolidation, any stockholder shall have the right to withdraw such stockholder's ~~his~~ demand for appraisal and to accept the terms offered upon the merger or consolidation. Within 120 days after the effective date of the merger or consolidation, any stockholder who has complied with the requirements of subsections (a) and (d) hereof, upon written request, shall be entitled to receive from the corporation surviving the merger or resulting from the consolidation a statement setting forth the aggregate number of shares not voted in favor of the merger or consolidation and with respect to which demands for appraisal have been received and the aggregate number of holders of such shares. Such written statement shall be mailed to the stockholder within 10 days after such stockholder's written request for such a statement is received by the surviving or resulting corporation or within 10 days after expiration of the period for delivery of demands for appraisal under subsection (d) hereof, whichever is later.

(f) Upon the filing of any such petition by a stockholder, service of a copy thereof shall be made upon the surviving or resulting corporation, which shall within 20 days after such service file in the office of the Register in Chancery in which the petition was filed a duly verified list containing the names and addresses of all stockholders who have demanded payment for their shares and with whom agreements as to the value of their shares have not been reached by the surviving or resulting corporation. If the petition shall be filed by the surviving or resulting corporation, the petition shall be accompanied by such a duly verified list. The Register in Chancery, if so ordered by the Court, shall give notice of the time and place fixed for the hearing of such petition by registered or certified mail to the surviving or resulting corporation and to the stockholders shown on the list at the addresses therein stated. Such notice shall also be given by 1 or more publications at least 1 week before the day of the hearing, in a newspaper of general circulation published in the City of Wilmington, Delaware or such publication as the Court deems advisable. The forms of the notices by mail and by publication shall be approved by the Court, and the costs thereof shall be borne by the surviving or resulting corporation.

(g) At the hearing on such petition, the Court shall determine the stockholders who have complied with this section and who have become entitled to appraisal rights. The Court may require the stockholders who have demanded an appraisal for their shares and who hold stock represented by certificates to submit their certificates of stock to the Register in Chancery for notation thereon of the pendency of the appraisal proceedings; and if any stockholder fails to comply with such direction, the Court may dismiss the proceedings as to such stockholder.

(h) After determining the stockholders entitled to an appraisal, the Court shall appraise the shares, determining their fair value exclusive of any element of value arising from the accomplishment or expectation of the merger or consolidation, together with a fair rate of interest, if any, to be paid upon the amount determined to be the fair value. In determining such fair value, the Court shall take into account all relevant factors. In determining the fair rate of interest, the Court may consider all relevant factors, including the rate of interest which the surviving or resulting corporation would have had to pay to borrow money during the pendency of the proceeding. Upon application by the surviving or resulting corporation or by any stockholder entitled to participate in the appraisal proceeding, the Court may, in its discretion, permit discovery or other pretrial proceedings and may proceed to trial upon the appraisal prior to the final determination of the stockholder entitled to an appraisal. Any stockholder whose name appears on the list filed by the surviving or resulting corporation pursuant to subsection (f) of this section and who has submitted his certificates of stock to the Register in Chancery, if such is required, may participate fully in all proceedings until it is finally determined that such stockholder is not entitled to appraisal rights under this section.

(i) The Court shall direct the payment of the fair value of the shares, together with interest, if any, by the surviving or resulting corporation to the stockholders entitled thereto. Interest may be simple or compound, as the Court may direct. Payment shall be so made to each such stockholder, in the case of holders of uncertificated stock forthwith, and the case of holders of shares represented by certificates upon the surrender to the corporation of the certificates representing such stock.

The Court's decree may be enforced as other decrees in the Court of Chancery may be enforced, whether such surviving or resulting corporation be a corporation of this State or of any state.

(j) The costs of the proceeding may be determined by the Court and taxed upon the parties as the Court deems equitable in the circumstances. Upon application of a stockholder, the Court may order all or a portion of the expenses incurred by any stockholder in connection with the appraisal proceeding, including, without limitation, reasonable attorney's fees and the fees and expenses of experts, to be charged pro rata against the value of all the shares entitled to an appraisal.

(k) From and after the effective date of the merger or consolidation, no stockholder who has demanded appraisal rights as provided in subsection (d) of this section shall be entitled to vote such stock for any purpose or to receive payment of dividends or other distributions on the stock (except dividends or other distributions payable to stockholders of record at a date which is prior to the effective date of the merger or consolidation); provided, however, that if no petition for an appraisal shall be filed within the time provided in subsection (e) of this section, or if such stockholder shall deliver to the surviving or resulting corporation a written withdrawal of such stockholder's demand for an appraisal and an acceptance of the merger or consolidation, either within 60 days after the effective date of the merger or consolidation as provided in subsection (e) of this section or thereafter with the written approval of the corporation, then the right of such stockholder to an appraisal shall cease. Notwithstanding the foregoing, no appraisal proceeding in the Court of Chancery shall be dismissed as to any stockholder without the approval of the Court, and such approval may be conditioned upon such terms as the Court deems just.

(*l*) The shares of the surviving or resulting corporation to which the shares of such objecting stockholders would have been converted had they assented to the merger or consolidation shall have the status of authorized and unissued shares of the surviving or resulting corporation.

§ 264. Merger or Consolidation of Domestic Corporation and Limited Liability Company

(a) Any 1 or more corporations of this State may merge or consolidate with 1 or more limited liability companies, of this State or of any other state or states of the United States, or of the District of Columbia, unless the laws of such other state or states or the District of Columbia forbid such merger or consolidation. Such corporation or corporations and such 1 or more limited liability companies may merge with or into a corporation, which may be any 1 of such corporations, or they may merge with or into a limited liability company, which may be any 1 of such limited liability companies, or they may consolidate into a new corporation or limited liability company formed by the consolidation, which shall be a corporation or limited liability company of this State or any other state of the United States, or the District of Columbia, which permits such merger or consolidation, pursuant to an agreement of merger or consolidation, as the case may be, complying and approved in accordance with this section.

(b) Each such corporation and limited liability company shall enter into a written agreement of merger or consolidation. The agreement shall state: (1) the terms and conditions of the merger or consolidation; (2) the mode of carrying the same into effect; (3) the manner of converting the shares of stock of each such corporation and the limited liability company interests of each such limited liability company into shares, limited liability company interests or other securities of the entity surviving or resulting from such merger or consolidation, and if any shares of any such corporation or any limited liability company interests of any such limited liability company are not to be converted solely into shares, limited liability company interests or other securities of the entity surviving or resulting from such merger or consolidation, the cash, property, rights or securities of any other corporation or entity which the holders of such shares or limited liability company interests are to receive in exchange for, or upon conversion of such shares or limited liability company interests and the surrender of any certificates evidencing them, which cash, property, rights or securities of any other corporation or entity may be in addition to or in lieu of shares, limited liability company interests or other securities of the entity surviving or resulting from such merger or consolidation; and (4) such other details or provisions as are deemed desirable, including, without limiting the generality of the foregoing, a provision for the payment of cash in lieu of the issuance of fractional shares or interests of the surviving or resulting corporation or limited liability company. Any of the terms of the agreement of merger or consolidation may be made dependent upon facts ascertainable outside of such agreement, provided that the manner in which such facts shall operate upon the terms of the agreement is clearly and expressly set forth in the agreement of merger or consolidation.

(c) The agreement required by subsection (b) shall be adopted, approved, certified, executed and acknowledged by each of the corporations in the same manner as is provided in § 251 of this title and, in the case of the limited liability companies, in accordance with their limited liability company agreements and in accordance with the laws of the state under which they are formed, as the case may be. The agreement shall be filed and shall become effective for all purposes of the laws of this State when and as provided in § 251 of this title with respect to the merger or consolidation of corporations of this State. In lieu of filing the agreement of merger or consolidation, the surviving or resulting corporation or limited liability company may file a certificate of merger or consolidation, executed in accordance with § 103 of this title, if the surviving or resulting entity is a corporation, or by an authorized person, if the surviving or resulting entity is a limited liability company, which states:

(1) the name and state of domicile of each of the constituent entities;

(2) that an agreement of merger or consolidation has been approved, adopted, certified, executed and acknowledged by each of the constituent entities in accordance with this subsection;

(3) the name of the surviving or resulting corporation or limited liability company;

(4) in the case of a merger in which a corporation is the surviving entity, such amendments or changes in the certificate of incorporation of the surviving corporation as are desired to be effected by the merger, or, if no such amendments or changes are desired, a statement that the certificate of incorporation of the surviving corporation shall be its certificate of incorporation;

(5) in the case of a consolidation in which a corporation is the resulting entity, that the certificate of incorporation of the resulting corporation shall be as is set forth in an attachment to the certificate;

(6) that the executed agreement of consolidation or merger is on file at the principal place of business of the surviving corporation or limited liability company and the address thereof;

(7) that a copy of the agreement of consolidation or merger will be furnished by the surviving or resulting entity, on request and without cost, to any stockholder of any constituent corporation or any member of any constituent limited liability company; and

(8) the agreement, if any, required by subsection (d) of this section.

(d) If the entity surviving or resulting from the merger or consolidation is to be governed by the laws of the District of Columbia or any state other than this State, it shall agree that it may be served with process in this State in any proceeding for enforcement of any obligation of any constituent corporation or limited liability company of this State, as well as for enforcement of any obligation of the surviving or resulting corporation or limited liability company arising from the merger or consolidation, including any suit or other proceeding to enforce the right of any stockholders as determined in appraisal proceedings pursuant to the provisions of § 262 of this title, and shall irrevocably appoint the Secretary of State as its agent to accept service of process in any such suit or other proceedings and shall specify the address to which a copy of such process shall be mailed by the Secretary of State. In the event of such service upon the Secretary of State in accordance with this subsection, the Secretary of State shall forthwith notify such surviving or resulting corporation or limited liability company thereof by letter, certified mail, return receipt requested, directed to such surviving or resulting corporation or limited liability company at its address so specified, unless such surviving or resulting corporation or limited liability company shall have designated in writing to the Secretary of State a different address for such purpose, in which case it shall be mailed to the last address so designated. Such letter shall enclose a copy of the process and any other papers served on the Secretary of State pursuant to this subsection. It shall be the duty of the plaintiff in the event of such service to serve process and any other papers in duplicate, to notify the Secretary of State that service is being effected pursuant to this subsection and to pay the Secretary of State the sum of $50 for the use of the State, which sum shall be taxed as part of the costs in the proceeding,hall prevail therein. The Secretary of State shall maintain an alphabetical record of any such service setting forth the name of the plaintiff and the defendant, the title, docket number and nature of the proceeding in which process has been served upon the Secretary of State, the fact that service has been effected pursuant to this subsection, the return date thereof, and the day and hour service was made. The Secretary of State shall not be required to retain such information longer than five years from receipt of the service of process.

(e) Sections 251(c) (second sentence) and (d), 251(e), 251(f), 259 through 261 and 328 of this title shall, insofar as they are applicable, apply to mergers or consolidations between corporations and limited liability companies.

§ 271. Sale, Lease or Exchange of Assets; Consideration; Procedure

(a) Every corporation may at any meeting of its board of directors or governing body sell, lease or exchange all or substantially all of its property and assets, including its goodwill and its corporate franchises, upon such terms and conditions and for such consideration, which may consist in whole or in part of money or other property, including shares of stock in, and/or other securities of, any other corporation or corporations, as its board of directors or governing body deems expedient and for the best interests of the corporation, when and as authorized by a resolution adopted by the holders of a majority of the outstanding stock of the corporation entitled to vote thereon or, if the corporation is a nonstock corporation, by a majority of the members having the right to vote for the election of the members of the governing body, at a meeting duly called upon at least 20 days' notice. The notice of the meeting shall state that such a resolution will be considered.

(b) Notwithstanding authorization or consent to a proposed sale, lease or exchange of a corporation's property and assets by the stockholders or members, the board of directors or governing body may abandon such proposed sale, lease or exchange without further action by the stockholders or members, subject to the rights, if any, of third parties under any contract relating thereto.

§ 272. Mortgage or Pledge of Assets

The authorization or consent of stockholders to the mortgage or pledge of a corporation's property and assets shall not be necessary, except to the extent that the certificate of incorporation otherwise provides.

§ 273. Dissolution of Joint Venture Corporation Having Two Stockholders

(a) If the stockholders of a corporation of this State, having only two stockholders each of which own 50% of the stock therein, shall be engaged in the prosecution of a joint venture and if such stockholders shall be unable to agree upon the desirability of discontinuing such joint venture and disposing of the assets used in such venture, either stockholder may file with the Court of Chancery a petition stating that it desires to discontinue such joint venture and to dispose of the assets used in such venture in accordance with a plan to be agreed upon by both stockholders or that, if no such plan shall be agreed upon by both stockholders, the corporation be dissolved. Such petition shall have attached thereto a copy of the proposed plan of discontinuance and distribution and a certificate stating that copies of such petition and plan have been transmitted in writing to the other stockholder and to the directors and officers of such corporation. The petition and certificate shall be executed and acknowledged in accordance with section 103 of this title.

(b) Unless both stockholders file with the Court of Chancery (1) within three months of the date of the filing of such petition, a certificate similarly executed and acknowledged stating that they have agreed on such plan, or a modification thereof, and (2) within one year from the date of the filing of such petition, a certificate similarly executed and acknowledged stating that the distribution provided by such plan has been completed, the Court of Chancery may dissolve such corporation and may by appointment of one or more trustees or receivers with all the powers and title of a trustee or receiver appointed under section 279 of this title, administer and wind up its affairs. Either or both of the above periods may be extended by agreement of the stockholders, evidenced by a certificate similarly executed, acknowledged and filed with the Court of Chancery prior to the expiration of such period.

§ 274. Dissolution Before the Issuance of Shares or Beginning of Business; Procedure

If a corporation has not issued shares or has not commenced the business for which the corporation was organized, a majority of the incorporators, or, if directors were named in the certificate of incorporation or have been elected, a majority of the directors, may surrender all of the corporation's rights and franchises by filing in the office of the

Secretary of State a certificate, executed and acknowledged by a majority of the incorporators or directors, stating that no shares of stock have been issued or that the business or activity for which the corporation was organized has not been begun; that no part of the capital of the corporation has been paid, or, if some capital has been paid, that the amount actually paid in for the corporation's shares, less any part thereof disbursed for necessary expenses, has been returned to those entitled thereto; that if the corporation has begun business but it has not issued shares all debts of the corporation have been paid; that if the corporation has not begun business but has issued stock certificates all issued stock certificates, if any, have been surrendered and cancelled; and that all rights and franchises of the corporation are surrendered. Upon such certificate becoming effective in accordance with section 103 of this title, the corporation shall be dissolved.

§ 275. Dissolution; Procedure

(a) If it should be deemed advisable in the judgment of the board of directors of any corporation that it should be dissolved, the board, after the adoption of a resolution to that effect by a majority of the whole board at any meeting called for that purpose, shall cause notice to be mailed to each stockholder entitled to vote thereon of the adoption of the resolution and of a meeting of stockholders to take action upon the resolution.

(b) At the meeting a vote shall be taken upon the proposed dissolution. If a majority of the outstanding stock of the corporation entitled to vote thereon shall vote for the proposed dissolution, a certification of dissolution shall be filed with the Secretary of State pursuant to subsection (d) of this Section.

(c) Dissolution of a corporation may also be authorized without action of the directors if all the stockholders entitled to vote thereon shall consent in writing and a certificate of dissolution shall be filed with the Secretary of State pursuant to subsection (d) of this Section.

(d) If dissolution is authorized in accordance with this Section, a certificate of dissolution shall be executed, acknowledged and filed, and shall become effective, in accordance with § 103 of this Title. Such certificate of dissolution shall set forth:

(i) the name of the corporation;

(ii) the date dissolution was authorized;

(iii) that the dissolution has been authorized by the board of directors and stockholders of the corporation, in accordance with subsections (a) and (b) of this Section, or that the dissolution has been authorized by all of the stockholders of the corporation entitled to vote on a dissolution, in accordance with subsection (c) of this section; and

(iv) the names and addresses of the directors and officers of the corporation.

(e) The resolution authorizing a proposed dissolution may provide that notwithstanding authorization or consent to the proposed dissolution by the stockholders, or the members of a nonstock corporation pursuant to § 276 of this title, the board of directors or governing body may abandon such proposed dissolution without further action by the stockholders or members.

(f) Upon a certificate of dissolution becoming effective in accordance with § 103 of this title, the corporation shall be dissolved.

* * *

§ 277. Payment of Franchise Taxes Before Dissolution or Merger

No corporation shall be dissolved or merged under this chapter until all franchise taxes due to or assessable by the State including all franchise taxes due or which would be due or assessable for the entire calendar month during which the dissolution or merger becomes effective have been paid by the corporation.

§ 278. Continuation of Corporation After Dissolution for Purposes of Suit and Winding Up Affairs

All corporations, whether they expire by their own limitation or are otherwise dissolved, shall nevertheless be continued, for the term of three years from such expiration or dissolution or for such longer period as the Court of Chancery shall in its discretion direct, bodies corporate for the purpose of prosecuting and defending suits, whether civil, criminal or administrative, by or against them, and of enabling them gradually to settle and close their business, to dispose of and convey their property, to discharge their liabilities, and to distribute to their stockholders any remaining assets, but not for the purpose of continuing the business for which the corporation was organized. With respect to any action, suit or proceeding begun by or against the corporation either prior to or within 3 years after the date of its expiration or dissolution the action shall not abate by reason of the dissolution of the corporation; the corporation shall, solely for the purpose of such action, suit or proceeding, be continued as a body corporate beyond the 3–year period and until any judgments, orders or decrees therein shall be fully executed, without the necessity for any special direction to that effect by the Court of Chancery.

§ 279. Trustees or Receivers for Dissolved Corporations; Appointment; Powers; Duties

When any corporation organized under this chapter shall be dissolved in any manner whatever, the Court of Chancery, on application of any creditor, stockholder or director of the corporation, or any other person who shows good cause therefor, at any time, may either appoint one or more of the directors of the corporation to be trustees, or appoint one or more persons to be receivers, of and for the corporation, to take charge of the corporation's property, and to collect the debts and property due and belonging to the corporation, with power to prosecute and defend, in the name of the corporation, or otherwise, all such suits as may be necessary or proper for the purposes aforesaid, and to appoint an agent or agents under them, and to do all other acts which might be done by the corporation, if in being, that may be necessary for the final settlement of the unfinished business of the corporation. The powers of the trustees or receivers may be continued as long as the Court of Chancery shall think necessary for the purposes aforesaid.

§ 280. Notice to Claimants; Filing of Claims

(a)(1) After a corporation has been dissolved in accordance with the procedures set forth in this chapter, the corporation or any successor entity may give notice of the dissolution, requiring all persons having a claim against the corporation other than a claim against the corporation in a pending action, suit or proceeding to which the corporation is a party to present their claims against the corporation in accordance with such notice. Such notice shall state:

a. That all such claims must be presented in writing and must contain sufficient information reasonably to inform the corporation or successor entity of the identity of the claimant and the substance of the claim;

b. The mailing address to which such a claim must be sent;

c. The date by which such a claim must be received by the corporation or successor entity, which date shall be no earlier than 60 days from the date thereof; and

d. That such claim will be barred if not received by the date referred to in subparagraph c. of this subsection; and

e. That the corporation or a successor entity may make distributions to other claimants and the corporation's stockholders or persons interested as having been such without further notice to the claimant; and

f. The aggregate amount, on an annual basis, of all distributions made by the corporation to its stockholders for each of the 3 years prior to the date the corporation dissolved.

Such notice shall also be published at least once a week for 2 consecutive weeks in a newspaper of general circulation in the county in which the office of the corporation's last registered agent in this State is located and in the corporation's principal place of business and, in the case of a corporation having $10,000,000 or more in total assets at the time of its dissolution, at least once in all editions of a daily newspaper with a national circulation. On or before the date of the first publication of such notice, the corporation or successor entity shall mail a copy of such notice by certified or registered mail, return receipt requested, to each known claimant of the corporation including persons with claims asserted against the corporation in a pending action, suit or proceeding to which the corporation is a party.

(2) Any claim against the corporation required to be presented pursuant to this subsection is barred if a claimant who was given actual notice under this subsection does not present the claim to the dissolved corporation or successor entity by the date referred to in subparagraph (1)c. of this subsection.

(3) A corporation or successor entity may reject, in whole or in part, any claim made by a claimant pursuant to this subsection by mailing notice of such rejection by certified or registered mail, return receipt requested, to the claimant within 90 days after receipt of such claim and, in all events, at least 150 days before the expiration of the period described in § 278 of this title; provided however, that in the case of a claim filed pursuant to § 295 of this title against a corporation or successor entity for which a receiver or trustee has been appointed by the Court of Chancery the time period shall be as provided in § 296 of this title, and the 30–day appeal period provided for in § 296 of this title shall be applicable. A notice sent by a corporation or successor entity pursuant to this subsection shall state that any claim rejected therein will be barred if an action, suit or proceeding with respect to the claim is not commenced within 120 days of the date thereof, and shall be accompanied by a copy of §§ 278–283 of this title and, in the case of a notice sent by a court-appointed receiver or trustee and as to which a claim has been filed pursuant to § 295 of this title, copies of §§ 295 and 296 of this title.

(4) A claim against a corporation is barred if a claimant whose claim is rejected pursuant to paragraph (3) of this subsection does not commence an action, suit or proceeding with respect to the claim no later than 120 days after the mailing of the rejection notice.

(b)(1) A corporation or successor entity electing to follow the procedures described in subsection (a) of this section shall also give notice of the dissolution of the corporation to persons with contractual claims contingent upon the occurrence or nonoccurrence of future events or otherwise conditional or unmatured, and request that such persons present such claims in accordance with the terms of such notice. Provided however, that as used in this section and in § 281 of this title, the term "contractual claims" shall not include any implied warranty as to any product manufactured, sold, distributed or handled by the dissolved corporation. Such notice shall be in substantially the form, and sent and published in the same manner, as described in subsection (a)(1) of this section.

(2) The corporation or successor entity shall offer any claimant on a contract whose claim is contingent, conditional or unmatured such security as the corporation or successor entity determines is sufficient to provide compensation to the claimant if the claim matures. The corporation or successor entity shall mail such offer to the claimant by certified or registered mail, return receipt requested, within 90 days of receipt of such claim and, in all events, at least 150 days before the expiration of the period described in § 278 of this title. If the claimant offered such security does not deliver in writing to the corporation or successor entity a notice rejecting the offer within 120 days after receipt of such offer for security, the claimant shall be deemed to have accepted such security as the sole source from which to satisfy his claim against the corporation.

(c)(1) A corporation or successor entity which has given notice in accordance with subsection (a) of this section shall petition the Court of Chancery to determine the amount and form of security that will be reasonably likely to be sufficient to provide compensation for any claim against the corporation which is the subject of a pending action, suit or proceeding to which the corporation is a party other than a claim barred pursuant to subsection (a) of this section.

(2) A corporation or successor entity which has given notice in accordance with subsections (a) and (b) of this section shall petition the Court of Chancery to determine the amount and form of security that will be sufficient to provide compensation to any claimant who has rejected the offer for security made pursuant to subsection (b)(2) of this section.

(3) A corporation or successor entity which has given notice in accordance with subsection (a) of this section shall petition the Court of Chancery to determine the amount and form of security which will be reasonably likely to be sufficient to provide compensation for claims that have not been made known to the corporation or that have not arisen but that, based on facts known to the corporation or successor entity, are likely to arise or to become known to the corporation or successor entity within 5 years after the date of dissolution or such longer period of time as the Court of Chancery may determine not to exceed 10 years after the date of dissolution. The Court of Chancery may appoint a guardian ad litem in respect of any such proceeding brought under this subsection. The reasonable fees and expenses of such guardian, including all reasonable expert witness fees, shall be paid by the petitioner in such proceeding.

(d) The giving of any notice or making of any offer pursuant to this section shall not revive any claim then barred or constitute acknowledgment by the corporation or successor entity that any person to whom such notice is sent is a proper claimant and shall not operate as a waiver of any defense or counterclaim in respect of any claim asserted by any person to whom such notice is sent.

(e) As used in this section, the term "successor entity" shall include any trust, receivership or other legal entity governed by the laws of this State to which the remaining assets and liabilities of a dissolved corporation are transferred and which exists solely for the purposes of prosecuting and defending suits, by or against the dissolved corporation, enabling the dissolved corporation to settle and close the business of the dissolved corporation, to dispose of and convey the property of the dissolved corporation, to discharge the liabilities of the dissolved corporation and to distribute to the dissolved corporation's stockholders any remaining assets, but not for the purpose of continuing the business for which the dissolved corporation was organized.

(f) The time periods and notice requirements of this section shall, in the case of a corporation or successor entity for which a receiver or trustee has been appointed by the Court of Chancery, be subject to variation by, or in the manner provided in, the Rules of the Court of Chancery.

§ 281. Payment and Distribution to Claimants and Stockholders

(a) A dissolved corporation or successor entity which has followed the procedures described in § 280 of this title:

(1) Shall pay the claims made and not rejected in accordance with § 280(a) of this title,

(2) Shall post the security offered and not rejected pursuant to § 280(b)(2) of this title,

(3) Shall post any security ordered by the Court of Chancery in any proceeding under § 280(c) of this title, and

(4) Shall pay or make provision for all other claims that are mature, known and uncontested or that have been finally determined to be owing by the corporation or such successor entity.

Such claims or obligations shall be paid in full and any such provision for payment shall be made in full if there are sufficient assets. If there are insufficient assets, such claims and obligations shall be paid or provided for according to their priority, and, among claims of equal priority, ratably to the extent of assets legally available therefor. Any remaining assets shall be distributed to the stockholders of the dissolved corporation; provided, however, that such distribution shall not be made before the expiration of 150 days from the date of the last notice of rejections given pursuant to § 280(a)(3) of this title. In the absence of actual fraud, the judgment of the directors of the dissolved corporation or the governing persons of such successor entity as to the provision made for the payment of all obligations under paragraph (4) of this subsection shall be conclusive.

(b) A dissolved corporation or successor entity which has not followed the procedures described in § 280 of this title shall, prior to the expiration of the period described in § 278 of this title, adopt a plan of distribution pursuant to which the dissolved corporation or successor entity (i) shall pay or make reasonable provision to pay all claims and obligations, including all contingent, conditional or unmatured contractual claims known to the corporation or such successor entity, (ii) shall make such provision as will be reasonably likely to be sufficient to provide compensation for any claim against the corporation which is the subject of a pending action, suit or proceeding to which the corporation is a party and (iii) shall make such provision as will be reasonably likely to be sufficient to provide compensation for claims that have not been made known to the corporation or that have not arisen but that, based on facts known to the corporation or successor entity, are likely to arise or to become known to the corporation or successor entity within 10 years after the date of dissolution. The plan of distribution shall provide that such claims shall be paid in full and any such provision for payment made shall be made in full if there are sufficient assets. If there are insufficient assets, such plan shall provide that such claims and obligations shall be paid or provided for according to their priority and, among claims of equal priority, ratably to the extent of assets legally available therefor. Any remaining assets shall be distributed to the stockholders of the dissolved corporation.

(c) Directors of a dissolved corporation or governing persons of a successor entity which has complied with subsection (a) or (b) of this section shall not be personally liable to the claimants of the dissolved corporation.

(d) As used in this section, the term "successor entity" has the meaning set forth in § 280(e) of this title.

(e) The term "priority," as used in this section, does not refer either to the order of payments set forth in subsection (a)(1)-(4) of this section or to the relative times at which any claims mature or are reduced to judgment.

§ 282. Liability of Stockholders of Dissolved Corporations

(a) A stockholder of a dissolved corporation the assets of which were distributed pursuant to § 281(a) or (b) of this title shall not be liable for any claim against the corporation in an amount in excess of such stockholder's pro rata share of the claim or the amount so distributed to such stockholder, whichever is less.

(b) A stockholder of a dissolved corporation the assets of which were distributed pursuant to § 281(a) of this title shall not be liable for any claim against the corporation on which an action, suit or proceeding is not begun prior to the expiration of the period described in § 278 of this title.

(c) The aggregate liability of any stockholder of a dissolved corporation for claims against the dissolved corporation shall not exceed the amount distributed to such stockholder ~~him~~ in dissolution.

§ 283. Jurisdiction

The Court of the Chancery shall have jurisdiction of any application prescribed in this subchapter and of all questions arising in the proceedings thereon, and may make such orders and decrees and issue injunctions therein as justice and equity shall require.

§ 284. Revocation or Forfeiture of Charter; Proceedings

(a) The Court of Chancery shall have jurisdiction to revoke or forfeit the charter of any corporation for abuse, mis-use or non-use of its corporate powers, privileges or franchises. The Attorney General shall, upon the Attorney General's own motion or upon the relation of a proper party, proceed for this purpose by complaint in the County in which the registered office of the corporation is located.

(b) The Court of Chancery shall have power, by appointment of receivers or otherwise, to administer and wind up the affairs of any corporation whose charter shall be revoked or forfeited by any court under any section of this title or otherwise, and to make such orders and decrees with respect thereto as shall be just and equitable respecting its affairs and assets and the rights of its stockholders and creditors.

(c) No proceeding shall be instituted under this section for non-use of any corporation's powers, privileges or franchises during the first two years after its incorporation.

§ 285. Dissolution or Forfeiture of Charter by Decree of Court; Filing

Whenever any corporation is dissolved or its charter forfeited by decree or judgment of the Court of Chancery, the decree or judgment shall be forthwith filed by the Register in Chancery of the county in which the decree or judgment was entered, in the office of the Secretary of State, and a note thereof shall be made by the Secretary of State on the corporation's charter or certificate of incorporation and on the index thereof.

§ 291. Receivers for Insolvent Corporations; Appointment and Powers

Whenever a corporation shall be insolvent, the Court of Chancery, on the application of any creditor or stockholder thereof, may, at any time, appoint one or more persons to be receivers of and for the corporation, to take charge of its assets, estate, effects, business and affairs, and to collect the outstanding debts, claims, and property due and belonging to the corporation, with power to prosecute and defend, in the name of the corporation or otherwise, all claims or suits, to appoint an agent or agents under them, and to do all other acts which might be done by the corporation and which may be necessary or proper. The powers of the receivers shall be such and shall continue so long as the court shall deem necessary.

§ 292. Title to Property; Filing Order of Appointment; Exception

(a) Trustees or receivers appointed by the Court of Chancery of and for any corporation, and their respective survivors and successors, shall, upon their appointment and qualification or upon the death, resignation or discharge of any co-trustee or co-receiver, be vested by operation of law and without any act or deed, with the title of the corporation to all of its property, real, personal or mixed of whatsoever nature, kind, class or description, and wheresoever situate, except real estate situate outside this State.

(b) Trustees or receivers appointed by the Court of Chancery shall, within 20 days from the date of their qualification, file in the office of the Recorder in each county in this State, in which any real estate belonging to the corporation may be situated, a certified copy of the order of their appointment and evidence of their qualification.

(c) This section shall not apply to receivers appointed pendente lite.

§ 293. Notices to Stockholders and Creditors

All notices required to be given to stockholders and creditors in any action in which a receiver or trustee for a corporation was appointed shall be given by the Register in Chancery, unless otherwise ordered by the Court of Chancery.

§ 294. Receivers or Trustees; Inventory; List of Debts and Report

Trustees or receivers shall, as soon as convenient, file in the office of the Register in Chancery of the county in which the proceeding is pending, a full and complete itemized inventory of all the assets of the corporation which shall show their nature and probable value, and an account of all debts due from and to it, as nearly as the same can be ascertained. They shall make a report to the Court of their proceedings, whenever and as often as the Court shall direct.

§ 295. Creditors' Proofs of Claims; When Barred; Notice

All creditors shall make proof under oath of their respective claims against the corporation, and cause the same to be filed in the office of the Register in Chancery of the county in which the proceeding is pending within the time fixed by and in accordance with the procedure established by the Rules of the Court of Chancery. All creditors and claimants failing to do so, within the time limited by this section, or the time prescribed by the order of the Court, may, by direction of the Court, be barred from participating in the distribution of the assets of the corporation. The Court may also prescribe what notice, by publication or otherwise, shall be given to the creditors of the time fixed for the filing and making proof of claims.

§ 296. Adjudication of Claims; Appeal

(a) The Register in Chancery, immediately upon the expiration of the time fixed for the filing of claims, in compliance with the provisions of section 295 of this title, shall notify the trustee or receiver of the filing of the claims, and the trustee or receiver, within 30 days after receiving the notice, shall inspect the claims, and if the trustee or receiver or any creditor shall not be satisfied with the validity or correctness of the same, or any of them, the trustee or receiver shall forthwith notify the creditors whose claims are disputed of his decision. The trustee or receiver shall require all creditors whose claims are disputed to submit themselves to such examination in relation to their claims as the trustee or receiver shall direct, and the creditors shall produce such books and papers relating to their claims as shall be required. The trustee or receiver shall have power to examine, under oath or affirmation, all witnesses produced before such trustee or receiver ~~him~~ touching the claims, and shall pass upon and allow or disallow the claims, or any part thereof, and notify the claimants of such trustee or receiver's ~~his~~ determination.

(b) Every creditor or claimant who shall have received notice from the receiver or trustee that such creditor's or claimant's ~~his~~ claim has been disallowed in whole or in part may appeal to the Court of Chancery within 30 days thereafter. The Court, after hearing, shall determine the rights of the parties.

* * *

§ 303. Reorganization Under a Statute of the United States; Effectuation

(a) Any corporation of this State, a plan of reorganization of which, pursuant to any applicable statute of the United States relating to reorganizations of corporations, has been or shall be confirmed by the decree or order of a court of competent jurisdiction, may put into effect and carry out the plan and the decrees and orders of the court or judge relative thereto and may take any proceeding and do any act provided in the plan or directed by such decrees and orders, without further action by its directors or stockholders. Such power and authority may be exercised, and such proceedings and acts may be taken, as may be directed by such decrees or orders, by the trustee or trustees of such corporation appointed in the reorganization proceedings (or a majority thereof), or if none be appointed and acting, by designated officers of the corporation, or by a Master or other representative appointed by the court or judge, with like effect as if exercised and taken by unanimous action of the directors and stockholders of the corporation.

(b) Such corporation may, in the manner provided in subsection (a) of this section, but without limiting the generality or effect of the foregoing, alter, amend, or repeal its bylaws; constitute or reconstitute and classify or reclassify its board of directors, and name, constitute or appoint directors and officers in place of or in addition to all or some of the directors or officers then in office; amend its certificate of incorporation, and make any change in its capital or capital stock, or any other amendment, change, or alteration, or provision, authorized by this chapter; be dissolved; transfer all or part of its assets, merge or consolidate as permitted by this chapter, in which case, however, no stockholder shall have any statutory right of appraisal of such stockholder's ~~his~~ stock; change the location of its registered office, change its registered agent, and remove or appoint any agent to receive service of process; authorize and fix the terms, manner and conditions of, the issuance of bonds, debentures or other obligations, whether or not convertible into stock of any class, or bearing warrants or other evidences of optional rights to purchase or subscribe for stock of any class; or lease its property and franchises to any corporation, if permitted by law.

(c) A certificate of any amendment, change or alteration, or of dissolution, or any agreement of merger or consolidation, made by such corporation pursuant to the foregoing provisions, shall be filed with the Secretary of State in accordance with § 103 of this title, and, subject to subsection (d) of said § 103, shall thereupon become effective in accordance with its terms and the provisions thereof. Such certificate, agreement of merger or other instrument shall be made, executed and acknowledged, as may be directed by such decrees or orders, by the trustee or trustees appointed in the reorganization proceedings (or a majority thereof), or, if none be appointed and acting, by the officers of the corporation, or by a Master or other representative appointed by the court or judge, and shall certify that provision for the making of such certificate, agreement or instrument is contained in a decree or order of a court or judge having jurisdiction of a proceeding under such applicable statute of the United States for the reorganization of such corporation.

(d) This section shall cease to apply to such corporation upon the entry of a final decree in the reorganization proceedings closing the case and discharging the trustee or trustees, if any.

(e) On filing any certificate, agreement, report or other paper made or executed pursuant to this section, there shall be paid to the Secretary of State for the use of the State the same fees as are payable by corporations not in reorganization upon the filing of like certificates, agreements, reports or other papers.

§ 327. Stockholder's Derivative Action; Allegation of Stock Ownership

In any derivative suit instituted by a stockholder of a corporation, it shall be averred in the complaint that the plaintiff was a stockholder of the corporation at the time of the transaction of which such stockholder ~~he~~ complains or that such stockholder's stock thereafter devolved upon such stockholder by operation of law.

§ 328. Effect of Liability of Corporation on Impairment of Certain Transactions

The liability of a corporation of this State, or the stockholders, directors or officers thereof, or the rights or remedies of the creditors thereof, or of persons doing or transacting business with the corporation, shall not in any way be lessened or impaired by the sale of its assets, or by the increase or decrease in the capital stock of the corporation, or by its merger or consolidation with one or more corporations or by any change or amendment in its certificate of incorporation.

§ 329. Defective Organization of Corporation as Defense

(a) No corporation of this State and no person sued by any such corporation shall be permitted to assert the want of legal organization as a defense to any claim.

(b) This section shall not be construed to prevent judicial inquiry into the regularity or validity of the organization of a corporation, or its lawful possession of any corporate power it may assert in any other suit or proceeding where its corporate existence or the power to exercise the corporate rights it asserts is challenged, and evidence tending to sustain the challenge shall be admissible in any such suit or proceeding.

§ 330. Usury; Pleading by Corporation

No corporation shall plead any statute against usury in any court of law or equity in any suit instituted to enforce the payment of any bond, note or other evidence of indebtedness issued or assumed by it.

§ 341. Law Applicable to Close Corporation

(a) This subchapter applies to all close corporations, as defined in section 342 of this title. Unless a corporation elects to become a close corporation under this subchapter in the manner prescribed in this subchapter, it shall be subject in all respects to the provisions of this chapter, except the provisions of this subchapter.

(b) All provisions of this chapter shall be applicable to all close corporations, as defined in section 342 of this title, except insofar as this subchapter otherwise provides.

§ 342. Close Corporation Defined; Contents of Certificate of Incorporation

(a) A close corporation is a corporation organized under this chapter whose certificate of incorporation contains the provisions required by section 102 of this title and, in addition, provides that:

(1) All of the corporation's issued stock of all classes, exclusive of treasury shares, shall be represented by certificates and shall be held of record by not more than a specified number of persons, not exceeding thirty; and

(2) All of the issued stock of all classes shall be subject to one or more of the restrictions on transfer permitted by section 202 of this title; and

(3) The corporation shall make no offering of any of its stock of any class which would constitute a "public offering" within the meaning of the United States Securities Act of 1933, as it may be amended from time to time.

(b) The certificate of incorporation of a close corporation may set forth the qualifications of stockholders, either by specifying classes of persons who shall be entitled to be holders of record of stock of any class, or by specifying classes of persons who shall not be entitled to be holders of stock of any class or both.

(c) For purposes of determining the number of holders of record of the stock of a close corporation, stock which is held in joint or common tenancy or by the entireties shall be treated as held by one stockholder.

§ 343. Formation of a Close Corporation

A close corporation shall be formed in accordance with sections 101, 102 and 103 of this title, except that:

(a) Its certificate of incorporation shall contain a heading stating the name of the corporation and that it is a close corporation, and

(b) Its certificate of incorporation shall contain the provisions required by section 342 of this title.

§ 344. Election of Existing Corporation to Become a Close Corporation

Any corporation organized under this chapter may become a close corporation under this subchapter by executing, acknowledging, *and* filing, in accordance with section 103 of this title, a certificate of amendment of its certificate of incorporation which shall contain a statement that it elects to become a close corporation, the provisions required by section 342 of this title to appear in the certificate of incorporation of a close corporation, and a heading stating the name of the corporation and that it is a close corporation. Such amendment shall be adopted in accordance with the requirements of section 241 or 242 of this title, except that it must be approved by a vote of the holders of record of at least two-thirds of the shares of each class of stock of the corporation which are outstanding.

§ 345. Limitations on Continuation of Close Corporation Status

A close corporation continues to be such and to be subject to this subchapter until:

(a) It files with the Secretary of State a certificate of amendment deleting from its certificate of incorporation the provisions required or permitted by section 342 of this title to be stated in the certificate of incorporation to qualify it as a close corporation, or

(b) Any one of the provisions or conditions required or permitted by section 342 of this title to be stated in a certificate of incorporation to qualify a corporation as a close corporation has in fact been breached and neither the corporation nor any of its stockholders takes the steps required by section 348 of this title to prevent such loss of status or to remedy such breach.

§ 346. Voluntary Termination of Close Corporation Status by Amendment of Certificate of Incorporation; Vote Required

(a) A corporation may voluntarily terminate its status as a close corporation and cease to be subject to this subchapter by amending its certificate of incorporation to delete therefrom the additional provisions required or permitted by section 342 of this title to be stated in the certificate of incorporation of a close corporation. Any such amendment shall be adopted and shall become effective in accordance with section 242 of this title, except that it must be approved by a vote of the holders of record of at least two-thirds of the shares of each class of stock of the corporation which are outstanding.

(b) The certificate of incorporation of a close corporation may provide that on any amendment to terminate its status as a close corporation, a vote greater than two-thirds or a vote of all shares of any class shall be required; and if the certificate of incorporation contains such a provision, that provision shall not be amended, repealed or modified by any vote less than that required to terminate the corporation's status as a close corporation.

§ 347. Issuance or Transfer of Stock of a Close Corporation in Breach of Qualifying Conditions

(a) If stock of a close corporation is issued or transferred to any person who is not entitled under any provision of the certificate of incorporation permitted by section 342(b) of this title to be a holder of record of stock of such corporation, and if the certificate for such stock conspicuously notes the qualifications of the persons entitled to be holders of record thereof, such person is conclusively presumed to have notice of the fact of such person's ~~his~~ ineligibility to be a stockholder.

(b) If the certificate of incorporation of a close corporation states the number of persons, not in excess of thirty, who are entitled to be holders of record of its stock, and if the certificate for such stock conspicuously states such number, and if the issuance or transfer of stock to any person would cause the stock to be held by more than such number of persons, the person to whom such stock is issued or transferred is conclusively presumed to have notice of this fact.

(c) If a stock certificate of any close corporation conspicuously notes the fact of a restriction on transfer of stock of the corporation, and the restriction is one which is permitted by section 202 of this title, the transferee of the stock is conclusively presumed to have notice of the fact that such person ~~he~~ has acquired stock in violation of the restriction, if such acquisition violates the restriction.

(d) Whenever any person to whom stock of a close corporation has been issued or transferred has, or is conclusively presumed under this section to have, notice either (i) that such person ~~he~~ is a person not eligible to be a holder of stock of the corporation, or (ii) that transfer of stock to such person ~~him~~ would cause the stock of the corporation to be held by more than the number of persons permitted by its certificate of incorporation to hold stock of the corporation, or (iii) that the transfer of stock is in violation of a restriction on transfer of stock, the corporation may, at its option, refuse to register transfer of the stock into the name of the transferee.

(e) The provisions of subsection (d) shall not be applicable if the transfer of stock, even though otherwise contrary to subsections (a), (b) or (c), has been consented to by all the stockholders of the close corporation, or if the close corporation has amended its certificate of incorporation in accordance with section 346 of this title.

(f) The term "transfer," as used in this section, is not limited to a transfer for value.

(g) The provisions of this section do not in any way impair any rights of a transferee regarding any right to rescind the transaction or to recover under any applicable warranty express or implied.

§ 348. Involuntary Termination of Close Corporation Status; Proceeding to Prevent Loss of Status

(a) If any event occurs as a result of which one or more of the provisions or conditions included in a close corporation's certificate of incorporation pursuant to section 342 of this title to qualify it as a close corporation has been breached, the corporation's status as a close corporation under this subchapter shall terminate unless

(1) within thirty days after the occurrence of the event, or within thirty days after the event has been discovered, whichever is later, the corporation files with the Secretary of State a certificate, executed and acknowledged in accordance with section 103 of this title, stating that a specified provision or condition included in its certificate of incorporation pursuant to section 342 of this title to qualify it as a close corporation has ceased to be applicable, and furnishes a copy of such certificate to each stockholder, and

(2) the corporation concurrently with the filing of such certificate takes such steps as are necessary to correct the situation which threatens its status as a close corporation, including, without limitation, the refusal to register the transfer of stock which has been wrongfully transferred as provided by section 347 of this title, or a proceeding under subsection (b) of this section.

(b) The Court of Chancery, upon the suit of the corporation or any stockholder, shall have jurisdiction to issue all orders necessary to prevent the corporation from losing its status as a close corporation, or to restore its status as a close corporation by enjoining or setting aside any act or threatened act on the part of the corporation or a stockholder which would be inconsistent with any of the provisions or conditions required or permitted by section 342 of this title to be stated in the certificate of incorporation of a close corporation, unless it is an act approved in accordance with section 346 of this title. The Court of Chancery may enjoin or set aside any transfer or threatened transfer of stock of a close corporation which is contrary to the terms of its certificate of incorporation or of any transfer restriction permitted by section 202 of this title, and may enjoin any public offering, as defined in section 342 of this title, or threatened public offering of stock of the close corporation.

§ 349. Corporate Option Where a Restriction on Transfer of a Security Is Held Invalid

If a restriction on transfer of a security of a close corporation is held not to be authorized by § 202 of this title, the corporation shall nevertheless have an option, for a period of 30 days after the judgment setting aside the restriction becomes final, to acquire the restricted security at a price which is agreed upon by the parties, or if no agreement is reached as to price, then at the fair value as determined by the Court of

Chancery. In order to determine fair value, the Court may appoint an appraiser to receive evidence and report to the Court such appraisers ~~his~~ findings and recommendation as to fair value.

§ 350. Agreements Restricting Discretion of Directors

A written agreement among the stockholders of a close corporation holding a majority of the outstanding stock entitled to vote, whether solely among themselves or with a party not a stockholder, is not invalid, as between the parties to the agreement, on the ground that it so relates to the conduct of the business and affairs of the corporation as to restrict or interfere with the discretion or powers of the board of directors. The effect of any such agreement shall be to relieve the directors and impose upon the stockholders who are parties to the agreement the liability for managerial acts or omissions which is imposed on directors to the extent and so long as the discretion or powers of the board in its management of corporate affairs is controlled by such agreement.

§ 351. Management by Stockholders

The certificate of incorporation of a close corporation may provide that the business of the corporation shall be managed by the stockholders of the corporation rather than by a board of directors. So long as this provision continues in effect,

(1) No meeting of stockholders need be called to elect directors;

(2) Unless the context clearly requires otherwise, the stockholders of the corporation shall be deemed to be directors for purposes of applying provisions of this chapter; and

(3) The stockholders of the corporation shall be subject to all liabilities of directors.

Such a provision may be inserted in the certificate of incorporation by amendment if all incorporators and subscribers or all holders of record of all of the outstanding stock, whether or not having voting power, authorize such a provision. An amendment to the certificate of incorporation to delete such a provision shall be adopted by a vote of the holders of a majority of all outstanding stock of the corporation, whether or not otherwise entitled to vote. If the certificate of incorporation contains a provision authorized by this section, the existence of such provision shall be noted conspicuously on the face or back of every stock certificate issued by such corporation.

§ 352. Appointment of Custodian for Close Corporation

(a) In addition to the provisions of section 226 of this title respecting the appointment of a custodian for any corporation, the Court of Chancery, upon application of any stockholder, may appoint one or more persons to be custodians, and, if the corporation is insolvent, to be receivers, of any close corporation when:

(1) Pursuant to section 351 of this title the business and affairs of the corporation are managed by the stockholders and they are so divided that the business of the corporation is suffering or is threatened with irreparable injury and any remedy with respect to such deadlock provided in the certificate of incorporation or by-laws or in any written agreement of the stockholders has failed; or

(2) The petitioning stockholder has the right to the dissolution of the corporation under a provision of the certificate of incorporation permitted by section 355 of this title.

(b) In lieu of appointing a custodian for a close corporation under this section or section 226 of this title the Court of Chancery may appoint a provisional director, whose powers and status shall be as provided in section 353 of this title if the Court determines that it would be in the best interest of the corporation. Such appointment shall not preclude any subsequent order of the Court appointing a custodian for such corporation.

§ 353. Appointment of a Provisional Director in Certain Cases

(a) Notwithstanding any contrary provision of the certificate of incorporation or the by-laws or agreement of the stockholders, the Court of Chancery may appoint a provisional director for a close corporation if the directors are so divided respecting the management of the corporation's business and affairs that the votes required for action by the board of directors cannot be obtained with the consequence that the business and affairs of the corporation can no longer be conducted to the advantage of the stockholders generally.

(b) An application for relief under this section must be filed (1) by at least one-half of the number of directors then in office, (2) by the holders of at least one-third of all stock then entitled to elect directors, or, (3) if there be more than one class of stock then entitled to elect one or more directors, by the holders of two-thirds of the stock of any such class; but the certificate of incorporation of a close corporation may provide that a lesser proportion of the directors or of the stockholders or of a class of stockholders may apply for relief under this section.

(c) A provisional director shall be an impartial person who is neither a stockholder nor a creditor of the corporation or of any subsidiary or affiliate of the corporation, and whose further qualifications, if any, may be determined by the Court of Chancery. A provisional director is not a receiver of the corporation and does not have the title and powers of a custodian or receiver appointed under sections 226 and 291 of this title. A provisional director shall have all the rights and powers of a duly elected director of the corporation, including the right to notice of and to vote at meetings of directors, until such time as such person ~~he~~ shall be removed by order of the Court of Chancery or by the holders of a majority of all shares then entitled to vote to elect directors or by the holders of two-thirds of the shares of that class of voting shares which filed the application for appointment of a provisional director. A provisional director's ~~His~~ compensation shall be determined by agreement between such person ~~him~~ and the corporation subject to approval of the Court of Chancery, which may fix such person's ~~his~~ compensation in the absence of agreement or in the event of disagreement between the provisional director and the corporation.

(d) Even though the requirements of subsection (b) of this section relating to the number of directors or stockholders who may petition for appointment of a provisional director are not satisfied, the Court of Chancery may nevertheless appoint a provisional director if permitted by subsection (b) of section 352 of this title.

§ 354. Operating Corporation as Partnership

No written agreement among stockholders of a close corporation, nor any provision of the certificate of incorporation or of the by-laws of the corporation, which agreement or provision relates to any phase of the affairs of such corporation, including but not limited to the management of its business or declaration and payment of dividends or other division of profits or the election of directors or officers or the employment of stockholders by the corporation or the arbitration of disputes, shall be invalid on the ground that it is an attempt by the parties to the agreement or by the stockholders of the corporation to treat the corporation as if it were a partnership or to arrange relations among the stockholders or between the stockholders and the corporation in a manner that would be appropriate only among partners.

§ 355. Stockholders' Option to Dissolve Corporation

(a) The certificate of incorporation of any close corporation may include a provision granting to any stockholder, or to the holders of any specified number or percentage of shares of any class of stock, an option to have the corporation dissolved at will or upon the occurrence of any specified event or contingency. Whenever any such option to dissolve is exercised, the stockholders exercising such option shall give written notice thereof to all other stockholders. After the expiration of 30 days following the sending of such notice, the dissolution of the corporation shall proceed as if the required number of stockholders having voting power had consented in writing to dissolution of the corporation as provided by section 228 of this title.

(b) If the certificate of incorporation as originally filed does not contain a provision authorized by subsection (a), the certificate may be amended to include such provision if adopted by the affirmative vote of the holders of all the outstanding stock, whether or not entitled to vote, unless the certificate of incorporation specifically authorizes such an amendment by a vote which shall be not less than two-thirds of all the outstanding stock whether or not entitled to vote.

(c) Each stock certificate in any corporation whose certificate of incorporation authorizes dissolution as permitted by this section shall conspicuously note on the face thereof the existence of the provision. Unless noted conspicuously on the face of the stock certificate, the provision is ineffective.

§ 356. Effect of This Subchapter on Other Laws

The provisions of this subchapter shall not be deemed to repeal any statute or rule of law which is or would be applicable to any corporation which is organized under the provisions of this chapter but is not a close corporation.

F. INDIANA BUSINESS CORPORATION LAW

Current through end of 1997 First Special Session

Contents

CHAPTER 42. CONTROL SHARE ACQUISITIONS

CHAPTER 42. CONTROL SHARE ACQUISITIONS

§ 23–1–42–1. "Control Shares" Defined

Sec. 1. As used in this chapter, "control shares" means shares that, except for this chapter, would have voting power with respect to shares of an issuing public corporation that, when added to all other shares of the issuing public corporation owned by a person or in respect to which that person may exercise or direct the exercise of voting power, would entitle that person, immediately after acquisition of the shares (directly or indirectly, alone or as a part of a group), to exercise or direct the exercise of the voting power of the issuing public corporation in the election of directors within any of the following ranges of voting power:

(1) One-fifth (1/5) or more but less than one-third (1/3) of all voting power.

(2) One-third (1/3) or more but less than a majority of all voting power.

(3) A majority or more of all voting power.

§ 23–1–42–2. "Control Share Acquisition" Defined

Sec. 2. (a) As used in this chapter, "control share acquisition" means the acquisition (directly or indirectly) by any person of ownership of, or the power to direct the exercise of voting power with respect to, issued and outstanding control shares.

(b) For purposes of this section, shares acquired within ninety (90) days or shares acquired pursuant to a plan to make a control share acquisition are considered to have been acquired in the same acquisition.

(c) For purposes of this section, a person who acquires shares in the ordinary course of business for the benefit of others in good faith and not for the purpose of circumventing this chapter has voting power only of shares in respect of which that person would be able to exercise or direct the exercise of votes without further instruction from others.

(d) The acquisition of any shares of an issuing public corporation does not constitute a control share acquisition if the acquisition is consummated in any of the following circumstances:

(1) Before January 8, 1986.

(2) Pursuant to a contract existing before January 8, 1986.

(3) Pursuant to the laws of descent and distribution.

(4) Pursuant to the satisfaction of a pledge or other security interest created in good faith and not for the purpose of circumventing this chapter.

(5) Pursuant to a merger or plan of share exchange effected in compliance with IC 23–1–40 if the issuing public corporation is a party to the agreement of merger or plan of share exchange.

(e) The acquisition of shares of an issuing public corporation in good faith and not for the purpose of circumventing this chapter by or from:

(1) any person whose voting rights had previously been authorized by shareholders in compliance with this chapter; or

(2) any person whose previous acquisition of shares of an issuing public corporation would have constituted a control share acquisition but for subsection (d); does not constitute a control share acquisition, unless the acquisition entitles any person (directly or indirectly, alone or as a part of a group) to exercise or direct the exercise of voting power of the corporation in the election of directors in excess of the range of the voting power otherwise authorized.

§ 23–1–42–3. "Interested Shares" Defined

Sec. 3. As used in this chapter, "interested shares" means the shares of an issuing public corporation in respect of which any of the following persons may exercise or direct the exercise of the voting power of the corporation in the election of directors:

(1) An acquiring person or member of a group with respect to a control share acquisition.

(2) Any officer of the issuing public corporation.

(3) Any employee of the issuing public corporation who is also a director of the corporation.

§ 23–1–42–4. "Issuing Public Corporation" Defined

Sec. 4. (a) As used in this chapter, "issuing public corporation" means a corporation that has:

(1) one hundred (100) or more shareholders;

(2) its principal place of business, its principal office, or substantial assets within Indiana; and

(3) either:

(A) more than ten percent (10%) of its shareholders resident in Indiana;

(B) more than ten percent (10%) of its shares owned by Indiana residents; or

(C) ten thousand (10,000) shareholders resident in Indiana.

(b) The residence of a shareholder is presumed to be the address appearing in the records of the corporation.

(c) Shares held by banks (except as trustee or guardian), brokers or nominees shall be disregarded for purposes of calculating the percentages or numbers described in this section.

§ 23–1–42–5. Voting Rights Under IC 23–1–42–9

Sec. 5. Unless the corporation's articles of incorporation or bylaws provide that this chapter does not apply to control share acquisitions of shares of the corporation before the control share acquisition, control shares of an issuing public corporation acquired in a control share acquisition have only such voting rights as are conferred by section 9 of this chapter.

§ 23–1–42–6. Acquiring Person Statement

Sec. 6. Any person who proposes to make or has made a control share acquisition may at the person's election deliver an acquiring person statement to the issuing public corporation at the issuing public corporation's principal office. The acquiring person statement must set forth all of the following:

(1) The identity of the acquiring person and each other member of any group of which the person is a part for purposes of determining control shares.

(2) A statement that the acquiring person statement is given pursuant to this chapter.

(3) The number of shares of the issuing public corporation owned (directly or indirectly) by the acquiring person and each other member of the group.

(4) The range of voting power under which the control share acquisition falls or would, if consummated, fall.

(5) If the control share acquisition has not taken place:

(A) a description in reasonable detail of the terms of the proposed control share acquisition; and

(B) representations of the acquiring person, together with a statement in reasonable detail of the facts upon which they are based, that the proposed control share acquisition, if consummated, will not be contrary to law, and that the acquiring person has the financial capacity to make the proposed control share acquisition.

§ 23–1–42–7. Special Meeting of Shareholders

Sec. 7. (a) If the acquiring person so requests at the time of delivery of an acquiring person statement and gives an undertaking to pay the corporation's expenses of a special meeting, within ten (10) days thereafter, the directors of the issuing public corporation shall call a special meeting of shareholders of the issuing public corporation for the purpose of considering the voting rights to be accorded the shares acquired or to be acquired in the control share acquisition.

(b) Unless the acquiring person agrees in writing to another date, the special meeting of shareholders shall be held within fifty (50) days after receipt by the issuing public corporation of the request.

(c) If no request is made, the voting rights to be accorded the shares acquired in the control share acquisition shall be presented to the next special or annual meeting of shareholders.

(d) If the acquiring person so requests in writing at the time of delivery of the acquiring person statement, the special meeting must not be held sooner than thirty (30) days after receipt by the issuing public corporation of the acquiring person statement.

§ 23–1–42–8. Notice

Sec. 8. (a) If a special meeting is requested, notice of the special meeting of shareholders shall be given as promptly as reasonably practicable by the issuing public corporation to all shareholders of record as of the record date set for the meeting, whether or not entitled to vote at the meeting.

(b) Notice of the special or annual shareholder meeting at which the voting rights are to be considered must include or be accompanied by both of the following:

(1) A copy of the acquiring person statement delivered to the issuing public corporation pursuant to this chapter.

(2) A statement by the board of directors of the corporation, authorized by its directors, of its position or recommendation, or that it is taking no position or making no recommendation, with respect to the proposed control share acquisition.

§ 23–1–42–9. Voting Rights of Acquired Control Shares; Resolution

Sec. 9. (a) Control shares acquired in a control share acquisition have the same voting rights as were accorded the shares before the control share acquisition only to the extent granted by resolution approved by the shareholders of the issuing public corporation.

(b) To be approved under this section, the resolution must be approved by:

(1) each voting group entitled to vote separately on the proposal by a majority of all the votes entitled to be cast by that voting group, with the holders of the outstanding shares of a class being entitled to vote as a separate voting group if the proposed control share acquisition would, if fully carried out, result in any of the changes described in IC 23–1–38–4(a); and

(2) each voting group entitled to vote separately on the proposal by a majority of all the votes entitled to be cast by that group, excluding all interested shares.

§ 23–1–42–10. Redemption of Acquired Control Shares

Sec. 10. (a) If authorized in a corporation's articles of incorporation or bylaws before a control share acquisition has occurred, control shares acquired in a control share acquisition with respect to which no acquiring person statement has been filed with the issuing public corporation may, at any time during the period ending sixty (60) days after the last acquisition of control shares by the acquiring person, be subject to redemption by the corporation at the fair value thereof pursuant to the procedures adopted by the corporation.

(b) Control shares acquired in a control share acquisition are not subject to redemption after an acquiring person statement has been filed unless the shares are not accorded full voting rights by the shareholders as provided in section 9 of this chapter.

§ 23–1–42–11. Dissenters' Rights; "Fair Value" Defined

Sec. 11. (a) Unless otherwise provided in a corporation's articles of incorporation or bylaws before a control share acquisition has occurred, in the event control shares acquired in a control share acquisition are accorded full voting rights and the acquiring person has acquired control shares with a majority or more of all voting power, all shareholders of the issuing public corporation have dissenters' rights as provided in this chapter.

(b) As soon as practicable after such events have occurred, the board of directors shall cause a notice to be sent to all shareholders of the corporation advising them of the facts and that they have dissenters' rights to receive the fair value of their shares pursuant to IC 23–1–44.

(c) As used in this section, "fair value" means a value not less than the highest price paid per share by the acquiring person in the control share acquisition.

G. MARYLAND GENERAL CORPORATION LAW

(Selected Sections)

Contents

SUBTITLE 6. SPECIAL VOTING REQUIREMENTS

SUBTITLE 6. SPECIAL VOTING REQUIREMENTS

§ 3–601. Definitions

(a) *In general.*—In this subtitle, the following words have the meanings indicated.

(b) *Affiliate.*—"Affiliate", including the term "affiliated person", means a person that directly, or indirectly through one or more intermediaries, controls, or is controlled by, or is under common control with, a specified person.

(c) *Associate.*—"Associate", when used to indicate a relationship with any person, means:

(1) Any corporation or organization (other than the corporation or a subsidiary of the corporation) of which such person is an officer, director, or partner or is, directly or indirectly, the beneficial owner of 10 percent or more of any class of equity securities;

(2) Any trust or other estate in which such person has a substantial beneficial interest or as to which such person serves as trustee or in a similar fiduciary capacity; and

(3) Any relative or spouse of such person, or any relative of such spouse, who has the same home as such person or who is a director or officer of the corporation or any of its affiliates.

(d) *Beneficial owner.*—"Beneficial owner", when used with respect to any voting stock, means a person:

(1) That, individually or with any of its affiliates or associates, beneficially owns voting stock, directly or indirectly; or

(2) That, individually or with any of its affiliates or associates, has:

(i) The right to acquire voting stock (whether such right is exercisable immediately or only after the passage of time), pursuant to any agreement, arrangement, or understanding or upon the exercise of conversion rights, exchange rights, warrants or options, or otherwise; or

(ii) The right to vote voting stock pursuant to any agreement, arrangement, or understanding; or

(3) That has any agreement, arrangement, or understanding for the purpose of acquiring, holding, voting, or disposing of voting stock with any other person that beneficially owns, or whose affiliates or associates beneficially own, directly or indirectly, such shares of voting stock.

(e) *Business combination.*—"Business combination" means:

(1) Unless the merger, consolidation, or share exchange does not alter the contract rights of the stock as expressly set forth in the charter or change or convert in whole or in part the outstanding shares of stock of the corporation, any merger, consolidation, or share exchange of the corporation or any subsidiary with (i) any interested stockholder or (ii) any other corporation (whether or not itself an interested stockholder) which is, or after the merger, consolidation, or share exchange would be, an affiliate of an interested stockholder that was an interested stockholder prior to the transaction;

(2) Any sale, lease, transfer, or other disposition, other than in the ordinary course of business or pursuant to a dividend or any other method affording substantially proportionate treatment to the holders of voting stock, in one transaction or a series of transactions in any 12-month period, to any interested stockholder or any affiliate of any interested stockholder (other than the corporation or any of its subsidiaries) of any assets of the corporation or any subsidiary having, measured at the time the transaction or transactions are approved by the board of directors of the corporation, an aggregate book value as of the end of the corporation's most recently ended fiscal quarter of 10 percent or more of the total market value of the outstanding stock of the corporation or of its net worth as of the end of its most recently ended fiscal quarter;

(3) The issuance or transfer by the corporation, or any subsidiary, in one transaction or a series of transactions, of any equity securities of the corporation or any subsidiary which have an aggregate market value of 5 percent or more of the total market value of the outstanding stock of the corporation to any interested stockholder or any affiliate of any interested stockholder (other than the corporation or any of its subsidiaries) except pursuant to the exercise of warrants or rights to purchase securities offered pro rata to all holders of the corporation's voting stock or any other method affording substantially proportionate treatment to the holders of voting stock;

(4) The adoption of any plan or proposal for the liquidation or dissolution of the corporation in which anything other than cash will be received by an interested stockholder or any affiliate of any interested stockholder;

(5) Any reclassification of securities (including any reverse stock split), or recapitalization of the corporation, or any merger, consolidation, or share exchange of the corporation with any of its subsidiaries which has the effect, directly or indirectly, in one transaction or a series of transactions, of increasing by 5 percent or more of the total number of outstanding shares, the proportionate amount of the outstanding shares of any class of equity securities of the corporation or any subsidiary which is directly or indirectly owned by any interested stockholder or any affiliate of any interested stockholder; or

(6) The receipt by any interested stockholder or any affiliate of any interested stockholder (other than the corporation or any of its subsidiaries) of the benefit, directly or indirectly (except proportionately as a stockholder), of any loan, advance, guarantee, pledge, or other financial assistance or any tax credit or other tax advantage provided by the corporation or any of its subsidiaries.

(f) *Common stock.*—"Common stock" means any stock other than preferred or preference stock.

(g) *Control.*—"Control", including the terms "controlling", "controlled by" and "under common control with", means the possession, directly or indirectly, of the power to direct or cause the direction of the management and policies of a person, whether through the ownership of voting securities, by contract, or otherwise, and the beneficial ownership of 10 percent or more of the votes entitled to be cast by a corporation's voting stock creates a presumption of control.

(h) *Corporation.*—"Corporation" includes a real estate investment trust as defined in Title 8 of this article.

(i) *Equity security.*—"Equity security" means:

(1) Any stock or similar security, certificate of interest, or participation in any profit sharing agreement, voting trust certificate, or certificate of deposit for an equity security;

(2) Any security convertible, with or without consideration, into an equity security, or any warrant or other security carrying any right to subscribe to or purchase an equity security; or

(3) Any put, call, straddle, or other option or privilege of buying an equity security from or selling an equity security to another without being bound to do so.

(j) *Interested stockholder.*—"Interested stockholder" means any person (other than the corporation or any subsidiary) that:

(1)(i) Is the beneficial owner, directly or indirectly, of 10 percent or more of the voting power of the outstanding voting stock of the corporation after the date on which the corporation had 100 or more beneficial owners of its stock; or

(ii) Is an affiliate or associate of the corporation and was the beneficial owner, directly or indirectly, of 10 percent or more of the voting power of the then outstanding stock of the corporation:

1. At anytime within the 2–year period immediately prior to the date in question; and

2. After the date on which the corporation had 100 or more beneficial owners of its stock.

(2) For the purpose of determining whether a person is an interested stockholder, the number of shares of voting stock deemed to be outstanding shall include shares deemed owned by the person through application of subsection (d) of this section but may not include any other shares of voting stock which may be issuable pursuant to any agreement, arrangement, or understanding, or upon exercise of conversion rights, warrants or options, or otherwise.

(k) *Market value.*—"Market value" means:

(1) In the case of stock, the highest closing sale price during the 30 day period immediately preceding the date in question of a share of such stock on the composite tape for New York Stock Exchange-listed stocks, or, if such stock is not quoted on the composite tape, on the New York Stock Exchange, or, if such stock is not listed on such Exchange, on the principal United States securities exchange registered under the Securities Exchange Act of 1934 on which such stock is listed, or, if such stock is not listed on any such exchange, the highest closing bid quotation with respect to a share of such stock during the 30 day period preceding the date in question on the National Association of Securities Dealers, Inc. automated quotations system or any system then in use, or, if no such quotations are available, the fair market value on the date in question of a share of such stock as determined by the board of directors of the corporation in good faith; and

(2) In the case of property other than cash or stock, the fair market value of such property on the date in question as determined by the board of directors of the corporation in good faith.

(*l*) *Subsidiary.*—"Subsidiary" means any corporation of which voting stock having a majority of the votes entitled to be cast is owned, directly or indirectly, by the corporation.

(m) *Voting stock.*—"Voting stock" means shares of capital stock of a corporation entitled to vote generally in the election of directors.

(n) *Original articles of incorporation.*—"Original articles of incorporation" means:

(1) Articles of incorporation as originally filed or as amended in accordance with § 2-603 of this article; and

(2) Articles of incorporation as amended or restated by a corporation meeting the requirements of § 3-603(e)(1)(i), (ii), or (iv) of this subtitle, without regard to the voting requirements of § 3-603 (e)(1)(iii) of this subtitle.

§ 3-602. Business Combinations—In General

(a) *Prohibited between corporation and interested stockholder or affiliate.*—Unless an exemption under § 3-603(c), (d), or (e) of this subtitle applies, a corporation may not engage in any business combination with any interested stockholder or any affiliate of the interested stockholder for a period of 5 years following the most recent date on which the interested stockholder became an interested stockholder.

(b) *Approval of directors and stockholders.*—Unless an exemption under § 3-603 of this subtitle applies, in addition to any vote otherwise required by law or the charter of the corporation, a business combination that is not prohibited by subsection (a) of this section shall be recommended by the board of directors and approved by the affirmative vote of at least:

(1) 80 percent of the votes entitled to be cast by outstanding shares of voting stock of the corporation, voting together as a single voting group; and

(2) Two-thirds of the votes entitled to be cast by holders of voting stock other than voting stock held by the interested stockholder who will (or whose affiliate will) be a party to the business combination or by an affiliate or associate of the interested stockholder, voting together as a single voting group.

§ 3-603. Same—Exemptions

(a) *Definitions applicable to subsection (b).*—For purposes of this section:

(1) "Announcement date" means the first general public announcement of the proposal or intention to make a proposal of the business combination or its first communication generally to stockholders of the corporation, whichever is earlier;

(2) "Determination date" means the most recent date on which the interested stockholder became an interested stockholder; and

(3) "Valuation date" means:

(i) For a business combination voted upon by stockholders, the latter of the day prior to the date of the stockholders' vote or the day 20 days prior to the consummation of the business combination; and

(ii) For a business combination not voted upon by stockholders, the date of the consummation of the business combination.

(b) *Exemption from § 3–602—In general.*—The vote required by § 3–602(b) of this subtitle does not apply to a business combination as defined in § 3–601(e)(1) of this subtitle if each of the following conditions is met:

(1) The aggregate amount of the cash and the market value as of the valuation date of consideration other than cash to be received per share by holders of common stock in such business combination is at least equal to the highest of the following:

(i) The highest per share price (including any brokerage commissions, transfer taxes and soliciting dealers' fees) paid by the interested stockholder for any shares of common stock of the same class or series acquired by it within the 5–year period immediately prior to the announcement date of the proposal of the business combination, plus an amount equal to interest compounded annually from the earliest date on which the highest per share acquisition price was paid through the valuation date at the rate for 1–year United States Treasury obligations from time to time in effect, less the aggregate amount of any cash dividends paid and the market value of any dividends paid in other than cash, per share of common stock from the earliest date through the valuation date, up to the amount of the interest; or

(ii) The highest per share price (including any brokerage commissions, transfer taxes and soliciting dealers' fees) paid by the interested stockholder for any shares of common stock of the same class or series acquired by it on, or within the 5–year period immediately before, the determination date, plus an amount equal to interest compounded annually from the earliest date on which the highest per share acquisition price was paid through the valuation date at the rate for 1–year United States Treasury obligations from time to time in effect, less the aggregate amount of any cash dividends paid and the market value of any dividends paid in other than cash, per share of common stock from the earliest date through the valuation date, up to the amount of the interest; or

(iii) The market value per share of common stock of the same class or series on the announcement date, plus an amount equal to interest compounded annually from that date through the valuation date at the rate for 1–year United States Treasury obligations from time to time in effect, less the aggregate amount of any cash dividends paid and the market value of any dividends paid in other than cash, per share of common stock from that date through the valuation date, up to the amount of the interest; or

(iv) The market value per share of common stock of the same class or series on the determination date, plus an amount equal to interest compounded annually from that date through the valuation date at the rate for 1–year United States Treasury obligations from time to time in effect, less the aggregate amount of any cash dividends paid and the market value of any dividends paid in other than cash, per share of common stock from that date through the valuation date, up to the amount of the interest; or

(v) The price per share equal to the market value per share of common stock of the same class or series on the announcement date or on the determination date, whichever is higher, multiplied by the fraction of:

1. The highest per share price (including any brokerage commissions, transfer taxes and soliciting dealers' fees) paid by the interested stockholder for any shares of common stock of the same class or series acquired by it within the 5–year period immediately prior to the announcement date, over

2. The market value per share of common stock of the same class or series on the first day in such 5–year period on which the interested stockholder acquired any shares of common stock.

(2) The aggregate amount of the cash and the market value as of the valuation date of consideration other than cash to be received per share by holders of shares of any class or series of outstanding stock other than common stock in the business combination is at least equal to the highest of the following (whether or not the interested stockholder has previously acquired any shares of the particular class or series of stock):

(i) The highest per share price (including any brokerage commissions, transfer taxes and soliciting dealers' fees) paid by the interested stockholder for any shares of such class or series of stock acquired by it within the 5–year period immediately prior to the announcement date of the proposal of the business combination, plus an amount equal to interest compounded annually from the earliest date on which the highest per share acquisition price was paid through the valuation date at the rate for 1–year United States Treasury obligations from time to time in effect, less the aggregate amount of any cash dividends paid and the market value of any dividends paid in other than cash, per share of the class or series of stock from the earliest date through the valuation date, up to the amount of the interest; or

(ii) The highest per share price (including any brokerage commissions, transfer taxes and soliciting dealers' fees) paid by the interested stockholder for any shares of such class or series of stock acquired by it on, or within the 5-year period immediately prior to, the determination date, plus an amount equal to interest compounded annually from the earliest date on which the highest per share acquisition price was paid through the valuation date at the rate for 1-year United States Treasury obligations from time to time in effect, less the aggregate amount of any cash dividends paid and the market value of any dividends paid in other than cash, per share of the class or series of stock from the earliest date through the valuation date, up to the amount of the interest; or

(iii) The highest preferential amount per share to which the holders of shares of such class or series of stock are entitled in the event of any voluntary or involuntary liquidation, dissolution or winding up of the corporation; or

(iv) The market value per share of such class or series of stock on the announcement date, plus an amount equal to interest compounded annually from that date through the valuation date at the rate for 1-year United States Treasury obligations from time to time in effect, less the aggregate amount of any cash dividends paid and the market value of any dividends paid in other than cash, per share of the class or series of stock from that date through the valuation date, up to the amount of the interest; or

(v) The market value per share of such class or series of stock on the determination date, plus an amount equal to interest compounded annually from that date through the valuation date at the rate for 1-year United States Treasury obligations from time to time in effect, less the aggregate amount of any cash dividends paid and the market value of any dividends paid in other than cash, per share of the class or series of stock from that date through the valuation date, up to the amount of the interest; or

(vi) The price per share equal to the market value per share of such class or series of stock on the announcement date or on the determination date, whichever is higher, multiplied by the fraction of:

1. The highest per share price (including any brokerage commissions, transfer taxes and soliciting dealers' fees) paid by the interested stockholder for any shares of any

class of voting stock acquired by it within the 5-year period immediately prior to the announcement date, over

2. The market value per share of the same class of voting stock on the first day in such 5-year period on which the interested stockholder acquired any shares of the same class of voting stock.

(3) The consideration to be received by holders of any class or series of outstanding stock is to be in cash or in the same form as the interested stockholder has previously paid for shares of the same class or series of stock. If the interested stockholder has paid for shares of any class or series of stock with varying forms of consideration, the form of consideration for such class or series of stock shall be either cash or the form used to acquire the largest number of shares of such class or series of stock previously acquired by it.

(4)(i) After the determination date and prior to the consummation of such business combination:

1. There shall have been no failure to declare and pay at the regular date therefor any full periodic dividends (whether or not cumulative) on any outstanding preferred stock of the corporation;

2. There shall have been:

A. No reduction in the annual rate of dividends paid on any class or series of stock of the corporation that is not preferred stock (except as necessary to reflect any subdivision of the stock); and

B. An increase in such annual rate of dividends as necessary to reflect any reclassification (including any reverse stock split), recapitalization, reorganization or any similar transaction which has the effect of reducing the number of outstanding shares of the stock; and

3. The interested stockholder did not become the beneficial owner of any additional shares of stock of the corporation except as part of the transaction which resulted in such interested stockholder becoming an interested stockholder or by virtue of proportionate stock splits or stock dividends.

(ii) The provisions of sub-paragraphs 1. and 2. of subparagraph (i) do not apply if no interested stockholder or an affiliate or associate of the interested stockholder voted as a director of the corporation in a manner inconsistent with such sub-subparagraphs and the interested stockholder, within 10 days after any act or failure to act inconsistent with such sub-subparagraphs, notifies the board of directors of the corporation in writing that the interested stockholder disapproves thereof and requests in good faith that the board of directors rectify such act or failure to act.

(c) *Same—Resolution of board of directors.*—(1) Whether or not such business combinations are authorized or consummated in whole or in part after July 1, 1983 or after the determination date, the provisions of § 3-602 of this subtitle do not apply to business combinations that specifically, generally, or generally by types, as to specifically identified or unidentified existing or future interested stockholders or their affiliates, have been approved or exempted therefrom, in whole or in part, by resolution of the board of directors of the corporation:

(i) Prior to September 1, 1983 or such earlier date as may be irrevocably established by resolution of the board of directors; or

(ii) If involving transactions with a particular interested stockholder or its existing or future affiliates, at any time prior to the most recent time that the interested stockholder became an interested stockholder.

(2) Unless by its terms a resolution adopted under this subsection is made irrevocable, it may be altered or repealed by the board of directors, but this shall not affect any business combinations that have been consummated, or are the subject of an existing agreement entered into, prior to the alteration or repeal.

(d) *Same—Exception where board of directors elects to be bound.*—(1) Unless the charter or bylaws of the corporation specifically provides otherwise, the provisions of § 3-602 of this subtitle do not apply to business combinations of a corporation that, on July 1, 1983, had an existing interested stockholder, whether a business combination is with the existing stockholder or with any other person that becomes an interested stockholder after July 1, 1983, or their present or future affiliates, unless, at any time after July 1, 1983, the board of directors of the corporation elects by resolution to be subject, in whole or in part, specifically, generally, or generally by types, as to specifically identified or unidentified interested stockholders, to the provisions of § 3-602 of this subtitle.

(2) The charter or bylaws of the corporation may provide that if the board of directors adopts a resolution under paragraph (1) of this subsection the resolution shall be subject to approval of the stockholders in the manner and by the vote specified in the charter or the bylaws.

(3) An election under this subsection may be added to but may not be altered or repealed except by a charter amendment adopted by a vote of stockholders meeting the requirements of subsection (e)(1)(iii) of this section.

(4) If a corporation elects under this subsection to be included within the provisions of this subtitle generally, without qualification or limitation, it shall file with the Department articles supplementary

including a copy of the resolution making the election and a statement describing the manner in which the resolution was adopted. The articles supplementary shall be executed in the manner required by title 1 of this article. The articles supplementary constitute articles supplementary under section 1-101(e)(2) of this article, but do not constitute an amendment to the charter.

(e) *Same—Inapplicability to certain business combinations.*—(1) Unless the charter of the corporation provides otherwise, the provisions of § 3-602 of this subtitle do not apply to any business combination of:

(i) A close corporation as defined in § 4-101(b) of this article;

(ii) A corporation having fewer than 100 beneficial owners of its stock;

(iii) A corporation whose original articles of incorporation have a provision, or whose stockholders adopt a charter amendment after June 30, 1983 by a vote of at least 80 percent of the votes entitled to be cast by outstanding shares of voting stock of the corporation, voting together as a single voting group, and two-thirds of the votes entitled to be cast by persons (if any) who are not interested stockholders of the corporation or affiliates or associates of interested stockholders, voting together as a single voting group, expressly electing not to be governed by the provisions of § 3-602 of this subtitle in whole or in part, or in either case as to business combinations specifically, generally, or generally by types, or as to identified or unidentified existing or future interested stockholders or their affiliates, provided that, other than in the case of the original articles of incorporation, an amendment may not be effective until 18 months after the vote of stockholders and may not apply to any business combination of the corporation with an interested stockholder (or any affiliate of the interested stockholder) who became an interested stockholder on or before the date of the vote;

(iv) A corporation company registered under the Investment Company Act of 1940 as an open end investment company; or

(v) A corporation registered under the Investment Company Act of 1940 as a closed end investment company unless its board of directors adopts a resolution to be subject to § 3-602 of this subtitle on or after June 1, 2000, provided that the resolution shall not be effective with respect to a business combination with any person who has become an interested stockholder before the time that the resolution is adopted; or

(vi) A corporation with an interested stockholder that became an interested stockholder inadvertently, if the interested stockholder:

1. As soon as practicable (but not more than 10 days after the interested stockholder knew or should have known

it had become an interested stockholder) divests itself of a sufficient amount of the voting stock of the corporation so that it no longer is the beneficial owner, directly or indirectly, of 10 percent or more of the outstanding voting stock of the corporation; and

2. Would not at any time within the 5–year period preceding the announcement date with respect to the business combination have been an interested stockholder except by inadvertence.

(2) For purposes of paragraph (1)(ii) of this subsection, all stockholders of a corporation that have executed an agreement to which the corporation is an executing party governing the purchase and sale of stock of the corporation or a voting trust agreement governing stock of the corporation shall be considered a single beneficial owner of the stock covered by the agreement.

(f) *Business combinations of corporation having § 2–104(b)(5) charter provision.*—A business combination of a corporation that has a charter provision permitted by § 2–104(b)(5) of this article is subject to the voting requirements of § 3–602 of this subtitle unless one of the requirements or exemptions of subsections (b), (c), (d), or (e) of this section have been met.

H. NEW YORK BUSINESS CORPORATION LAW

(Selected Sections)

Contents

ARTICLE 5. CORPORATE FINANCE

ARTICLE 6. SHAREHOLDERS

ARTICLE 7. DIRECTORS AND OFFICERS

ARTICLE 5. CORPORATE FINANCE

§ 504. Consideration and Payment for Shares

(a) Consideration for the issue of shares shall consist of money or other property, tangible or intangible; labor or services actually received by or performed for the corporation or for its benefit or in its formation or reorganization; a binding obligation to pay the purchase price or the subscription price in cash or other property; a binding obligation to perform services having an agreed value or a combination thereof. In the absence of fraud in the transaction, the judgment of the board or shareholders, as the case may be, as to the value of the consideration received for shares shall be conclusive.

[(b). Repealed.]

(c) Shares with par value may be issued for such consideration, not less than the par value thereof, as is fixed from time to time by the board.

(d) Shares without par value may be issued for such consideration as is fixed from time to time by the board unless the certificate of incorporation reserves to the shareholders the right to fix the consideration. If such right is reserved as to any shares, a vote of the shareholders shall either fix the consideration to be received for the shares or authorize the board to fix such consideration.

(e) Treasury shares may be disposed of by a corporation on such terms and conditions as are fixed from time to time by the board.

(f) Upon distribution of authorized but unissued shares to shareholders, that part of the surplus of a corporation which is concurrently transferred to stated capital shall be the consideration for the issue of such shares.

(g) In the event of a conversion of bonds or shares into shares, or in the event of an exchange of bonds or shares for shares, with or without par value, the consideration for the shares so issued in exchange or conversion shall be the sum of (1) either the principal sum of, and accrued interest on, the bonds so exchanged or converted, or the stated capital then represented by the shares so exchanged or converted, plus (2) any additional consideration paid to the corporation for the new shares, plus (3) any stated capital not theretofore allocated to any designated class or series which is thereupon allocated to the new shares, plus (4) any surplus thereupon transferred to stated capital and allocated to the new shares.

(h) Certificates for shares may not be issued until the amount of the consideration therefor determined to be stated capital pursuant to section 506 (Determination of stated capital) has been paid in the form of cash, services rendered, personal or real property or a combination thereof and consideration for the balance (if any) complying with paragraph (a) of this section has been provided, except as provided in paragraphs (e) and (f) of section 505 (Rights and options to purchase shares; issue of rights and options to directors, officers and employees).

(i) When the consideration for shares has been provided in compliance with paragraph (h) of this section, the subscriber shall be entitled to all the rights and privileges of a holder of such shares and to a certificate representing his shares, and such shares shall be fully paid and nonassessable.

(j) Notwithstanding that such shares may be fully paid and nonassessable, the corporation may place in escrow shares issued for a binding obligation to pay cash or other property or to perform future services, or make other arrangements to restrict the transfer of the shares, and may credit distributions in respect of the shares against the obligation, until the obligation is performed. If the obligation is not performed in whole or in part, the corporation may pursue such remedies as are provided in the instrument evidencing the obligation or a related agreement or under law.

§ 505. Rights and Options to Purchase Shares; Issue of Rights and Options to Directors, Officers and Employees

(a)(1) Except as otherwise provided in this section or in the certificate of incorporation, a corporation may create and issue, whether or not in connection with the issue and sale of any of its shares or bonds, rights or options entitling the holders thereof to purchase from the corporation, upon such consideration, terms and conditions as may be fixed by the board, shares of any class or series, whether authorized but unissued shares, treasury shares or shares to be purchased or acquired or assets of the corporation.

(2)(i) In the case of a domestic corporation that has a class of voting stock registered with the Securities and Exchange Commission pursuant to section twelve of the Exchange Act, the terms and conditions of such rights or options may include, without limitation, restrictions or conditions that preclude or limit the exercise, transfer or receipt of such rights or options by an interested shareholder or any transferee of any such interested shareholder or that invalidate or void such rights or options held by any such interested shareholder or any such transferee. For the purposes of this subparagraph, the terms "resident domestic corporation", "voting stock", "Exchange Act" and "interested shareholder" shall have the same meanings as set forth in section nine hundred twelve of this chapter.

(ii) Determinations of the board of directors whether to impose, enforce or waive or otherwise render ineffective such limitations or conditions as are permitted by clause (i) of this subparagraph shall be subject to judicial review in an appropriate proceeding in which the courts formulate or apply appropriate standards in order to insure that such limitations or conditions are imposed, enforced or waived in the best long-term interests and short-term interests of the corporation and its shareholders considering, without limitation, the prospects for potential growth, development, productivity and profitability of the corporation.

(b) The consideration for shares to be purchased under any such right or option shall comply with the requirements of section 504 (Consideration and payment for shares).

(c) The terms and conditions of such rights or options, including the time or times at or within which and the price or prices at which they may be exercised and any limitations upon transferability, shall be set forth or incorporated by reference in the instrument or instruments evidencing such rights or options.

(d) The issue of such rights or options to one or more directors, officers or employees of the corporation or a subsidiary or affiliate thereof, as an incentive to service or continued service with the corporation, a subsidiary or affiliate thereof, or to a trustee on behalf of such directors, officers or employees, shall be authorized as required by the policies of all stock exchanges or automated quotation systems on which the corporation's shares are listed or authorized for trading, or if the corporation's shares are not so listed or authorized, by a majority of the votes cast at a meeting of shareholders by the holders of shares entitled to vote thereon, or authorized by and consistent with a plan adopted by such vote of shareholders. If, under the certificate of incorporation, there are preemptive rights to any of the shares to be thus subject to rights or options to purchase, either such issue or such plan, if any shall also be approved by the vote or written consent of the holders of a majority of the shares entitled to exercise preemptive rights with respect to such shares and such vote or written consent shall operate to release the preemptive rights with respect thereto of the holders of all the shares that were entitled to exercise such preemptive rights.

In the absence of preemptive rights, nothing in this paragraph shall require shareholder approval for the issuance of rights or options to purchase shares of the corporation in substitution for, or upon the assumption of, rights or options issued by another corporation, if such substitution or assumption is in connection with such other corporation's merger or consolidation with, or the acquisition of its shares or all or part of its assets by, the corporation or its subsidiary.

(e) A plan adopted by the shareholders for the issue of rights or options to directors, officers or employees shall include the material terms and conditions upon which such rights or options are to be issued, such as, but without limitation thereof, any restrictions on the number of shares that eligible individuals may have the right or option to purchase, the method of administering the plan, the terms and conditions of payment for shares in full or in installments, the issue of certificates for shares to be paid for in installments, any limitations upon the transferability of such shares and the voting and dividend rights to which the holders of such shares may be entitled, though the full amount of the consideration therefor has not been paid; provided that under this section no certificate for shares shall be delivered to a shareholder, prior to full payment therefor, unless the fact that the shares are partly paid is noted conspicuously on the face or back of such certificate.

(f) If there is shareholder approval for the issue of rights or options to individual directors, officers or employees, but not under an approved plan under paragraph (e), the terms and conditions of issue set forth in paragraph (e) shall be permissible except that the grantees of such rights or options shall not be granted voting or dividend rights until the consideration for the shares to which they are entitled under such rights or options has been fully paid.

(g) If there is shareholder approval for the issue of rights and options, such approval may provide that the board is authorized by certificate of amendment under section 805 (Certificate of amendment; contents) to increase the authorized shares of any class or series to such number as will be sufficient, when added to the previously authorized but unissued shares of such class or series, to satisfy any such rights or options entitling the holders thereof to purchase from the corporation authorized but unissued shares of such class or series.

(h) In the absence of fraud in the transaction, the judgment of the board shall be conclusive as to the adequacy of the consideration, tangible or intangible, received or to be received by the corporation for the issue of rights or options for the purchase from the corporation of its shares.

(i) The provisions of this section are inapplicable to the rights of the holders of convertible shares or bonds to acquire shares upon the exercise of conversion privileges under section 519 (Convertible shares and bonds).

§ 510. Dividends or Other Distributions in Cash or Property

(a) A corporation may declare and pay dividends, or make other distributions in cash or its bonds or its property, including the shares or bonds of other corporations, on its outstanding shares, except when currently the corporation is insolvent or would thereby be made insolvent, or when the declaration, payment or distribution would be contrary to any restrictions contained in the certificate of incorporation.

(b) Dividends may be declared or paid and other distributions may be made out of surplus only, so that the net assets of the corporation remaining after such declaration, payment or distribution shall at least equal the amount of its stated capital; except that a corporation engaged in the exploitation of natural resources or other wasting assets, including patents, or formed primarily for the liquidation of specific assets, may declare and pay dividends or make other distributions in excess of its surplus, computed after taking due account of depletion and amortization to the extent that the cost of the wasting or specific assets has been recovered by depletion reserves, amortization or sale, if the net assets remaining after such dividends or distributions are sufficient to cover the liquidation preferences of shares having such preferences in involuntary liquidation.

§ 513. Purchase, Redemption and Certain Other Transactions by a Corporation With Respect to Its Own Shares

(a) Notwithstanding any authority contained in the certificate of incorporation, the shares of a corporation may not be purchased by the corporation, or, if redeemable, convertible or exchangeable shares, may not be redeemed, converted, or exchanged; in each case into cash, other property, indebtedness or other securities of the corporation (other than shares of the corporation and rights to acquire such shares) if the corporation is insolvent or would thereby be made insolvent. Shares may be purchased or redeemed only out of surplus.

(b) When its redeemable, convertible or exchangeable shares are purchased by the corporation within the period during which such shares may be redeemed, converted or exchanged at the option of the corporation, the purchase price thereof shall not exceed the applicable redemption, conversation or exchange price stated in the certificate of incorporation. Upon a redemption, conversation or exchange, the amount payable by the corporation for shares having a cumulative preference on dividends may include the stated redemption, conversation or exchange price plus accrued dividends to the next dividend date following the date of redemption, conversation or exchange of such shares.

(c) No domestic corporation which is subject to the provisions of section nine hundred twelve of this chapter shall purchase or agree to purchase more than ten percent of the stock of the corporation from a shareholder for more than the market value thereof unless such purchase or agreement to purchase is approved by the affirmative vote of the board of directors and a majority of the votes of all outstanding shares entitled to vote thereon at a meeting of shareholders unless the certificate of incorporation requires a greater percentage of the votes of the outstanding shares to approve.

The provisions of this paragraph shall not apply when the corporation offers to purchase shares from all holders of stock or for stock which the holder has been the beneficial owner of for more than two years.

The terms "stock", "beneficial owner", and "market value" shall be as defined in section nine hundred twelve of this chapter.

§ 514. Agreements for Purchase by a Corporation of Its Own Shares

(a) An agreement for the purchase by a corporation of its own shares shall be enforceable by the shareholder and the corporation to the extent such purchase is permitted at the time of purchase by section 513 (Purchase or redemption by a corporation of its own shares).

(b) The possibility that a corporation may not be able to purchase its shares under section 513 shall not be a ground for denying to either party specific performance of an agreement for the purchase by a corporation of its own shares, if at the time for performance the corporation can purchase all or part of such shares under section 513.

ARTICLE 6. SHAREHOLDERS

§ 601. By–Laws

(a) The initial by-laws of a corporation shall be adopted by its incorporator or incorporators at the organization meeting. Thereafter, subject to section 613 (Limitations on right to vote), by-laws may be adopted, amended or repealed by a majority of the votes cast by the shares at the time entitled to vote in the election of any directors. When so provided in the certificate of incorporation or a by-law adopted by the shareholders, by-laws may also be adopted, amended or repealed by the board by such vote as may be therein specified, which may be greater than the vote otherwise prescribed by this chapter, but any by-law adopted by the board may be amended or repealed by the shareholders entitled to vote thereon as herein provided. Any reference in this chapter to a "by-law adopted by the shareholders" shall include a by-law adopted by the incorporator or incorporators.

(b) The by-laws may contain any provision relating to the business of the corporation, the conduct of its affairs, its rights or powers or the rights or powers of its shareholders, directors or officers, not inconsistent with this chapter or any other statute of this state or the certificate of incorporation.

§ 609. Proxies

(a) Every shareholder entitled to vote at a meeting of shareholders or to express consent or dissent without a meeting may authorize another person or persons to act for him by proxy.

(b) No proxy shall be valid after the expiration of eleven months from the date thereof unless otherwise provided in the proxy. Every proxy shall be recoverable at the pleasure of the shareholder executing it, except as otherwise provided in this section.

(c) The authority of the holder of a proxy to act shall not be revoked by the incompetence or death of the shareholder who executed the proxy unless, before the authority is exercised, written notice of an adjudication of such incompetence or of such death is received by the corporate officer responsible for maintaining the list of shareholders.

(d) Except when other provision shall have been made by written agreement between the parties, the record holder of shares which he holds as pledgee or otherwise as security or which belong to another, shall issue to the pledgor or to such owner of such shares, upon demand therefor and payment of necessary expenses thereof, a proxy to vote or take other action thereon.

(e) A shareholder shall not sell his vote or issue a proxy to vote to any person for any sum of money or anything of value, except as authorized in this section and section 620 (Agreements as to voting; provision in certificate of incorporation as to control of directors); provided, however, that this paragraph shall not apply to votes, proxies, or consents given by holders of preferred shares in connection with a proxy or consent solicitation made on identical terms to all holders of shares of the same class or series and remaining open for acceptance for at least twenty business days.

(f) A proxy which is entitled "irrevocable proxy" and which states that it is irrevocable, is irrevocable when it is held by any of the following or a nominee of any of the following:

(1) A pledgee;

(2) A person who has purchased or agreed to purchase the shares;

(3) A creditor or creditors of the corporation who extend or continue credit to the corporation in consideration of the proxy if the proxy states that it was given in consideration of such extension or continuation of credit, the amount thereof, and the name of the person extending or continuing credit;

(4) A person who has contracted to perform services as an officer of the corporation, if a proxy is required by the contract of employment, if the proxy states that it was given in consideration of such contract of employment, the name of the employee and the period of employment contracted for;

(5) A person designated by or under an agreement under paragraph (a) of section 620.

(g) Notwithstanding a provision in a proxy, stating that it is irrevocable, the proxy becomes revocable after the pledge is redeemed, or the debt of the corporation is paid, or the period of employment provided for in the contract of employment has terminated, or the agreement under paragraph (a) of section 620 has terminated; and, in a case provided for in subparagraphs (f)(3) or (4), becomes revocable three years after the date of the proxy or at the end of the period, if any, specified therein, whichever period is less, unless the period of irrevocability is renewed from time to time by the execution of a new irrevocable proxy as provided in this section. This paragraph does not affect the duration of a proxy under paragraph (b).

(h) A proxy may be revoked, notwithstanding a provision making it irrevocable, by a purchaser of shares without knowledge of the existence of the provision unless the existence of the proxy and its irrevocability is noted conspicuously on the face or back of the certificate representing such shares.

(i) Without limiting the manner in which a shareholder may authorize another person or persons to act for him as proxy pursuant to paragraph (a) of this section, the following shall constitute a valid means by which a shareholder may grant such authority.

(1) A shareholder may execute a writing authorizing another person or persons to act from him as proxy. Execution may be accomplished by the shareholder or the shareholder's authorized officer, director, employee or agent signing such writing or causing his or her signature to be affixed to such writing by any reasonable means including, but not limited to, by facsimile signature.

(2) A shareholder may authorize another person or persons to act for the shareholder as proxy by transmitting or authorizing the transmission of a telegram, cablegram or other means of electronic transmission to the person who will be the holder of the proxy or to a proxy solicitation firm, proxy support service organization or like agent duly authorized by the person who will be the holder of the proxy to receive such transmission, provided that any such telegram, cablegram or other means of electronic transmission must either set forth or be submitted with information from which it can be reasonably determined that the telegram, cablegram or other electronic transmission was authorized by the shareholder. If it is determined that such telegrams, cablegrams or other electronic transmissions are valid, the inspectors or, if there are no inspectors, such other persons making that determination shall specify the nature of the information upon which they relied.

(j) Any copy, facsimile telecommunication or other reliable reproduction of the writing or transmission created pursuant to paragraph (i) of this section may be substituted or used in lieu of the original writing or transmission for any and all purposes for which the original writing or transmission could be used, provided that such copy, facsimile telecommunication or other reproduction shall be a complete reproduction of the entire original writing or transmission.

§ 616. Greater Requirement as to Quorum and Vote of Shareholders

(a) The certificate of incorporation may contain provisions specifying either or both of the following:

(1) That the proportion of votes of shares, or the proportion of votes of shares of any class or series thereof, the holders of which shall be present in person or by proxy at any meeting of shareholders, including

a special meeting for election of directors under section 603 (Special meeting for election of directors), in order to constitute a quorum for the transaction of any business or of any specified item of business, including amendments to the certificate of incorporation, shall be greater than the proportion prescribed by this chapter in the absence of such provision.

(2) That the proportion of votes of shares, or votes of shares of a particular class or series of shares, that shall be necessary at any meeting of shareholders for the transaction of any business or of any specified item of business, including amendments to the certificate of incorporation, shall be greater than the proportion prescribed by this chapter in the absence of such provision.

(b) An amendment of the certificate of incorporation which changes or strikes out a provision permitted by this section, shall be authorized at a meeting of shareholders by two-thirds of the votes of the shares entitled to vote thereon, or of such greater proportion of votes of shares, or votes of shares of a particular class or series of shares, as may be provided specifically in the certificate of incorporation for changing or striking out a provision permitted by this section.

(c) If the certificate of incorporation of any corporation contains a provision authorized by this section, the existence of such provision shall be noted conspicuously on the face or back of every certificate for shares issued by such corporation, except that this requirement shall not apply to any corporation having any class of any equity security registered pursuant to Section twelve of the Securities Exchange Act of 1934, as amended.

§ 620. Agreements as to Voting; Provision in Certificate of Incorporation as to Control of Directors

(a) An agreement between two or more shareholders, if in writing and signed by the parties thereto, may provide that in exercising any voting rights, the shares held by them shall be voted as therein provided, or as they may agree, or as determined in accordance with a procedure agreed upon by them.

(b) A provision in the certificate of incorporation otherwise prohibited by law because it improperly restricts the board in its management of the business of the corporation, or improperly transfers to one or more shareholders or to one or more persons or corporations to be selected by him or them, all or any part of such management otherwise within the authority of the board under this chapter, shall nevertheless be valid:

(1) If all the incorporators or holders of record of all outstanding shares, whether or not having voting power, have authorized such provision in the certificate of incorporation or an amendment thereof; and

(2) If, subsequent to the adoption of such provision, shares are transferred or issued only to persons who had knowledge or notice thereof or consented in writing to such provision.

(c) A provision authorized by paragraph (b) shall be valid only so long as no shares of the corporation are listed on a national securities exchange or regularly quoted in an over-the-counter market by one or more members of a national or affiliated securities association.

(d)(1) Except as provided in paragraph (e), an amendment to strike out a provision authorized by paragraph (b) shall be authorized at a meeting of shareholders by

(A) (i) for any corporation in existence on the effective date of subparagraph (2) of this paragraph, two-thirds of the votes of the shares entitled to vote thereon and (ii) for any corporation in existence on the effective date of this clause the certificate of incorporation of which expressly provides such and for any corporation incorporated after the effective date of subparagraph (2) of this paragraph, a majority of the votes of the shares entitled to vote thereon or

(B) in either case, by such greater proportion of votes of shares as may be required by the certificate of incorporation for that purpose.

(2) Any corporation may adopt an amendment of the certificate of incorporation in accordance with the applicable clause or subclause of subparagraph (1) of this paragraph to provide that any further amendment of the certificate of incorporation that strikes out a provision authorized by paragraph (b) of this section shall be authorized at a meeting of the shareholders by a specified proportion of votes of the shares, or votes of a particular class or series of shares, entitled to vote thereon, provided that such proportion may not be less than a majority.

(e) Alternatively, if a provision authorized by paragraph (b) shall have ceased to be valid under this section, the board may authorize a certificate of amendment under section 805 (Certificate of amendment; contents) striking out such provision. Such certificate shall set forth the event by reason of which the provision ceased to be valid.

(f) The effect of any such provision authorized by paragraph (b) shall be to relieve the directors and impose upon the shareholders authorizing the same or consenting thereto the liability for managerial acts or omissions that is imposed on directors by this chapter to the extent that and so long as the discretion or powers of the board in its management of corporate affairs is controlled by any such provision.

(g) If the certificate of incorporation of any corporation contains a provision authorized by paragraph (b), the existence of such provision shall be noted conspicuously on the face or back of every certificate for shares issued by such corporation.

§ 622. Preemptive Rights

(a) As used in this section, the term:

(1) "Unlimited dividend rights" means the right without limitation as to amount either to all or to a share of the balance of current or liquidating dividends after the payment of dividends on any shares entitled to a preference.

(2) "Equity shares" means shares of any class, whether or not preferred as to dividends or assets, which have unlimited dividend rights.

(3) "Voting rights" means the right to vote for the election of one or more directors, excluding a right so to vote which is dependent on the happening of an event specified in the certificate of incorporation which would change the voting rights of any class of shares.

(4) "Voting shares" means shares of any class which have voting rights, but does not include bonds on which voting rights are conferred under section 518 (Corporate bonds).

(5) "Preemptive right" means the right to purchase shares or other securities to be issued or subjected to rights or options to purchase, as such right is defined in this section.

(b)(1) With respect to any corporation incorporated prior to the effective date of subparagraph (2) of this paragraph, except as otherwise provided in the certificate of incorporation, and except as provided in this section, the holders of equity shares of any class, in case of the proposed issuance by the corporation of, or the proposed granting by the corporation of rights or options to purchase, its equity shares of any class or any shares or other securities convertible into or carrying rights or options to purchase its equity shares of any class, shall, if the issuance of the equity shares proposed to be issued or issuable upon exercise of such rights or options or upon conversion of such other securities would adversely affect the unlimited dividend rights of such holders, have the right during a reasonable time and on reasonable conditions, both to be fixed by the board, to purchase such shares or other securities in such proportions as shall be determined as provided in this section.

(2) With respect to any corporation incorporated on or after the effective date of this subparagraph, the holders of such shares shall not have any preemptive right, except as otherwise expressly provided in the certificate of incorporation.

(c) Except as otherwise provided in the certificate of incorporation, and except as provided in this section, the holders of voting shares of any class, having any preemptive right under this paragraph on the date immediately prior to the effective date of subparagraph (2) of paragraph (b) of this section, in case of the proposed issuance by the corporation of, or the proposed granting by the corporation of rights or options to purchase, its voting shares of any class or any shares or other securities convertible into or carrying rights or options to purchase its voting shares of any class, shall, if the issuance of the voting shares proposed to be issued or issuable upon exercise of such rights or options or upon conversion of such other securities would adversely affect the voting rights of such holders, have the right during a reasonable time and on reasonable conditions, both to be fixed by the board, to purchase such shares or other securities in such proportions as shall be determined as provided in this section.

(d) The preemptive right provided for in paragraphs (b) and (c) shall entitle shareholders having such rights to purchase the shares or other securities to be offered or optioned for sale as nearly as practicable in such proportions as would, if such preemptive right were exercised, preserve the relative unlimited dividend rights and voting rights of such holders and at a price or prices not less favorable than the price or prices at which such shares or other securities are proposed to be offered for sale to others, without deduction of such reasonable expenses of and compensation for the sale, underwriting or purchase of such shares or other securities by underwriters or dealers as may lawfully be paid by the corporation. In case each of the shares entitling the holders thereof to preemptive rights does not confer the same unlimited dividend right or voting right, the board shall apportion the shares or other securities to be offered or optioned for sale among the shareholders having preemptive rights to purchase them in such proportions as in the opinion of the board shall preserve as far as practicable the relative unlimited dividend rights and voting rights of the holders at the time of such offering. The apportionment made by the board shall, in the absence of fraud or bad faith, be binding upon all shareholders.

(e) Unless otherwise provided in the certificate of incorporation, shares or other securities offered for sale or subjected to rights or options to purchase shall not be subject to preemptive rights under paragraph (b) or (c) of this section if they:

(1) Are to be issued by the board to effect a merger or consolidation or offered or subjected to rights or options for consideration other than cash;

(2) Are to be issued or subjected to rights or options under paragraph (d) of section 505 (Rights and options to purchase shares; issue of rights and options to directors, officers and employees);

(3) Are to be issued to satisfy conversion or option rights theretofore granted by the corporation;

(4) Are treasury shares;

(5) Are part of the shares or other securities of the corporation authorized in its original certificate of incorporation and are issued, sold or optioned within two years from the date of filing such certificate; or

(6) Are to be issued under a plan of reorganization approved in a proceeding under any applicable act of congress relating to reorganization or corporations.

(f) Shareholders of record entitled to preemptive rights on the record date fixed by the board under section 604 (Fixing record date), or, if no record date is fixed, then on the record date determined under section 604, and no others shall be entitled to the right defined in this section.

(g) The board shall cause to be given to each shareholder entitled to purchase shares or other securities in accordance with this section, a notice directed to him in the manner provided in section 605 (Notice of meetings of shareholders) setting forth the time within which and the terms and conditions upon which the shareholder may purchase such shares or other securities and also the apportionment made of the right to purchase among the shareholders entitled to preemptive rights. Such notice shall be given personally or by mail at least fifteen days prior to the expiration of the period during which the shareholder shall have the right to purchase. All shareholders entitled to preemptive rights to whom notice shall have been given as aforesaid shall be deemed conclusively to have had a reasonable time in which to exercise their preemptive rights.

(h) Shares or other securities which have been offered to shareholders having preemptive rights to purchase and which have not been purchased by them within the time fixed by the board may thereafter, for a period of not exceeding one year following the expiration of the time during which shareholders might have exercised such preemptive rights, be issued, sold or subjected to rights or options to any other person or persons at a price, without deduction of such reasonable expenses of and compensation for the sale, underwriting or purchase of such shares by underwriters or dealers as may lawfully be paid by the corporation, not less than that at which they were offered to such shareholders. Any such shares or other securities not so issued, sold or subjected to rights or options to others during such one year period shall thereafter again be subject to the preemptive rights of shareholders.

(i) Except as otherwise provided in the certificate of incorporation and except as provided in this section, no holder of any shares of any class shall as such holder have any preemptive right to purchase any other shares or securities of any class which at any time may be sold or offered for sale by the corporation. Unless otherwise provided in the certificate of incorporation, holders of bonds on which voting rights are conferred under section 518 shall have no preemptive rights.

§ 624. Books and Records; Right of Inspection, Prima Facie Evidence

(a) Each corporation shall keep correct and complete books and records of account and shall keep minutes of the proceedings of its shareholders, board and executive committee, if any, and shall keep at the office of the corporation in this state or at the office of its transfer agent or registrar in this state, a record containing the names and addresses of all shareholders, the number and class of shares held by each and the dates when they respectively became the owners of record thereof. Any of the foregoing books, minutes or records may be in written form or in any other form capable of being converted into written form within a reasonable time.

(b) Any person who shall have been a shareholder of record of a corporation upon at least five days' written demand shall have the right to examine in person or by agent or attorney, during usual business hours, its minutes of the proceedings of its shareholders and record of shareholders and to make extracts therefrom for any purpose reasonably related to such person's interest as a shareholder. Holders of voting trust certificates representing shares of the corporation shall be regarded as shareholders for the purpose of this section. Any such agent or attorney shall be authorized in a writing that satisfies the requirements of a writing under paragraph (b) of section 609 (Proxies). A corporation requested to provide information pursuant to this paragraph shall make available such information in written form and in any other format in which such information is maintained by the corporation and shall not be required to provide such information in any other format. If a request made pursuant to this paragraph includes a request to furnish information regarding beneficial owners, the corporation shall make available such information in its possession regarding beneficial owners as is provided to the corporation by a registered broker or dealer or a bank, association or other entity that exercises fiduciary powers in connection with the forwarding of information to such owners. The corporation shall not be required to obtain information about beneficial owners not in its possession.

(c) An inspection authorized by paragraph (b) may be denied to such shareholder or other person upon his refusal to furnish to the corporation, its transfer agent or registrar an affidavit that such inspection is not desired for a purpose which is in the interest of a business or object other than the business of the corporation and that he has not within five years sold or offered for sale any list of shareholders of any corporation of any type or kind, whether or not formed under the laws of this state, or aided or abetted any person in procuring any such record of shareholders for any such purpose.

(d) Upon refusal by the corporation or by an officer or agent of the corporation to permit an inspection of the minutes of the proceedings of its shareholders or of the record of shareholders as herein provided, the person making the demand for inspection may apply to the supreme court in the judicial district where the office of the corporation is located, upon such notice as the court may direct, for an order directing the corporation, its officer or agent to show cause why an order should not be granted permitting such inspection by the applicant. Upon the return day of the order to show cause, the court shall hear the parties summarily, by affidavit or otherwise, and if it appears that the applicant is qualified and entitled to such inspection, the court shall grant an order compelling such inspection and awarding such further relief as to the court may seem just and proper.

(e) Upon the written request of any shareholder, the corporation shall give or mail to such shareholder an annual balance sheet and profit and loss statement for the preceding fiscal year, and, if any interim balance sheet or profit and loss statement has been distributed to its shareholders or otherwise made available to the public, the most recent such interim balance sheet or profit and loss statement. The corporation shall be allowed a reasonable time to prepare such annual balance sheet and profit and loss statement.

(f) Nothing herein contained shall impair the power of courts to compel the production for examination of the books and records of a corporation.

(g) The books and records specified in paragraph (a) shall be prima facie evidence of the facts therein stated in favor of the plaintiff in any action or special proceeding against such corporation or any of its officers, directors or shareholders.

§ 625. Infant Shareholders and Bondholders

(a) A corporation may treat an infant who holds shares or bonds of such corporation as having capacity to receive and to empower others to receive dividends, interest, principal and other payments and distributions, to vote or express consent or dissent, in person or by proxy, and to make elections and exercise rights relating to such shares or bonds, unless, in the case of shares, the corporate officer responsible for maintaining the list of shareholders or the transfer agent of the corporation or, in the case of bonds, the treasurer or paying officer or agent has received written notice that such holder is an infant.

(b) An infant holder of shares or bonds of a corporation who has received or empowered others to receive payments or distributions, voted or expressed consent or dissent, or made an election or exercised a right relating thereto, shall have no right thereafter to disaffirm or avoid, as against the corporation, any such act on his part, unless prior to such receipt, vote, consent, dissent, election or exercise, as to shares, the corporate officer responsible for maintaining the list of shareholders or its transfer agent or, in the case of bonds, the treasurer or paying officer had received written notice that such holder was an infant.

(c) This section does not limit any other statute which authorizes any corporation to deal with an infant or limits the right of an infant to disaffirm his acts.

§ 626. Shareholders' Derivative Action Brought in the Right of the Corporation to Procure a Judgment in Its Favor

This section and Business Corporation Law §§ 627, 706, and 720 are popularly known as the "Coudert–Mitchell Laws."

(a) An action may be brought in the right of a domestic or foreign corporation to procure a judgment in its favor, by a holder of shares or of voting trust certificates of the corporation or of a beneficial interest in such shares or certificates.

(b) In any such action, it shall be made to appear that the plaintiff is such a holder at the time of bringing the action and that he was such a holder at the time of the transaction of which he complains, or that his shares or his interest therein devolved upon him by operation of law.

(c) In any such action, the complaint shall set forth with particularity the efforts of the plaintiff to secure the initiation of such action by the board or the reasons for not making such effort.

(d) Such action shall not be discontinued, compromised or settled, without the approval of the court having jurisdiction of the action. If the court shall determine that the interests of the shareholders or any class or classes thereof will be substantially affected by such discontinuance, compromise, or settlement, the court, in its discretion, may direct that notice, by publication or otherwise, shall be given to the shareholders or class or classes thereof whose interests it determines will be so affected; if notice is so directed to be given, the court may determine which one or more of the parties to the action shall bear the expense of giving the same, in such amount as the court shall determine and find to be reasonable in the circumstances, and the amount of such expense shall be awarded as special costs of the action and recoverable in the same manner as statutory taxable costs.

(e) If the action on behalf of the corporation was successful, in whole or in part, or if anything was received by the plaintiff or plaintiffs or a claimant or claimants as the result of a judgment, compromise or settlement of an action or claim, the court may award the plaintiff or plaintiffs, claimant or claimants, reasonable expenses, including reasonable attorney's fees, and shall direct him or them to account to the corporation for the remainder of the proceeds so received by him or them. This paragraph shall not apply to any judgment rendered for the benefit of injured shareholders only and limited to a recovery of the loss or damage sustained by them.

§ 627. Security for Expenses in Shareholders' Derivative Action Brought in the Right of the Corporation to Procure a Judgment in Its Favor

In any action specified in section 626 (Shareholders' derivative action brought in the right of the corporation to procure a judgment in its favor), unless the plaintiff or plaintiffs hold five percent or more of any class of the outstanding shares or hold voting trust certificates or a beneficial interest in shares representing five percent or more of any class of such shares, or the shares, voting trust certificates and beneficial interest of such plaintiff or plaintiffs have a fair value in excess of fifty thousand dollars, the corporation in whose right such action is brought shall be entitled at any stage of the proceedings before final judgment to require the plaintiff or plaintiffs to give security for the reasonable expenses, including attorney's fees, which may be incurred by it in connection with such action and by the other parties defendant in connection therewith for which the corporation may become liable under this chapter, under any contract or otherwise under law, to which the corporation shall have recourse in such amount as the court having jurisdiction of such action shall determine upon the termination of such action. The amount of such security may thereafter from time to time be increased or decreased in the discretion of the court having jurisdiction of such action upon showing that the security provided has or may become inadequate or excessive.

§ 630. Liability of Shareholders for Wages Due to Laborers, Servants or Employees

(a) The ten largest shareholders, as determined by the fair value of their beneficial interest as of the beginning of the period during which the unpaid services referred to in this section are performed, of every corporation (other than an investment company registered as such under an act of congress entitled "Investment Company Act of 1940"), no shares of which are listed on a national securities exchange or regularly quoted in an over-the-counter market by one or more members of a national or an affiliated securities association, shall jointly and severally be personally liable for all debts, wages or salaries due and owing to any of its laborers, servants or employees other than contractors, for services performed by them for such corporation. Before such laborer, servant or employee shall charge such shareholder for such services, he shall give notice in writing to such shareholder that he intends to hold him liable under this section. Such notice shall be given within one hundred and eighty days after termination of such services, except that if, within such period, the laborer, servant or employee demands an examination of the record of shareholders under paragraph (b) of section 624 (Books and records; right of inspection, prima facie evidence), such notice may be given within sixty days after he has been given the opportunity to examine the record of shareholders. An action to enforce such liability shall be commenced within ninety days after the return of an execution unsatisfied against the corporation upon a judgment recovered against it for such services.

(b) For the purposes of this section, wages or salaries shall mean all compensation and benefits payable by an employer to or for the account of the employee for personal services rendered by such employee. These shall specifically include but not be limited to salaries, overtime, vacation, holiday and severance pay; employer contributions to or payments of insurance or welfare benefits; employer contributions to pension or annuity funds; and any other moneys properly due or payable for services rendered by such employee.

(c) A shareholder who has paid more than his pro rata share under this section shall be entitled to contribution pro rata from the other shareholders liable under this section with respect to the excess so paid, over and above his pro rata share, and may sue them jointly or severally or any number of them to recover the amount due from them. Such recovery may be had in a separate action. As used in this paragraph, "pro rata" means in proportion to beneficial share interest. Before a shareholder may claim contribution from other shareholders under this paragraph, he shall, unless they have been given notice by a laborer, servant or employee under paragraph (a), give them notice in writing that he intends to hold them so liable to him. Such notice shall be given by him within twenty days after the date that notice was given to him by a laborer, servant or employee under paragraph (a).

ARTICLE 7. DIRECTORS AND OFFICERS

§ 709. Greater Requirement as to Quorum and Vote of Directors

(a) The certificate of incorporation may contain provisions specifying either or both of the following:

(1) That the proportion of directors that shall constitute a quorum for the transaction of business or of any specified item of business shall be greater than the proportion prescribed by this chapter in the absence of such provision.

(2) That the proportion of votes of directors that shall be necessary for the transaction of business or of any specified item of business shall be greater than the proportion prescribed by this chapter in the absence of such provision.

(b)(1) An amendment of the certificate of incorporation which changes or strikes out a provision permitted by this section shall be authorized at a meeting of shareholders by

(A) (i) for any corporation in existence on the effective date of subparagraph (2) of this paragraph, two-thirds of the votes of all outstanding shares entitled to vote thereon, and (ii) for any corporation in existence on the effective date of this clause the certificate of incorporation of which expressly provides such and for any corporation incorporated after the effective date of subparagraph (2) of this paragraph, a majority of the votes of all outstanding shares entitled to vote thereon or

(B) in either case, such greater proportion of votes of shares, or votes of a class or series of shares, as may be provided specifically in the certificate of incorporation for changing or striking out a provision permitted by this section.

(2) Any corporation may adopt an amendment of the certificate of incorporation in accordance with any applicable clause or subclause of subparagraph (1) of this paragraph to provide that any further amendment of the certificate of incorporation that changes or strikes out a provision permitted by this section shall be authorized at a meeting of the shareholders by a specified proportion of the votes of the shares, or particular class or series of shares, entitled to vote thereon, provided that such proportion may not be less than a majority.

§ 713. Interested Directors

(a) No contract or other transaction between a corporation and one or more of its directors, or between a corporation and any other corporation, firm, association or other entity in which one or more of its directors are directors or officers, or have a substantial financial interest, shall be either void or voidable for this reason alone or by reason alone that such director or directors are present at the meeting of the board, or of a committee thereof, which approves such contract or transaction, or that his or their votes are counted for such purpose:

(1) If the material facts as to such director's interest in such contract or transaction and as to any such common directorship, officership or financial interest are disclosed in good faith or known to the board or committee, and the board or committee approves such contract or transaction by a vote sufficient for such purpose without counting the vote of such interested director or, if the votes of the disinterested directors are insufficient to constitute an act of the board as defined in section 708 (Action by the board), by unanimous vote of the disinterested directors; or

(2) If the material facts as to such director's interest in such contract or transaction and as to any such common directorship, officership or financial interest are disclosed in good faith or known to the shareholders entitled to vote thereon, and such contract or transaction is approved by vote of such shareholders.

(b) If a contract or other transaction between a corporation and one or more of its directors, or between a corporation and any other corporation, firm, association or other entity in which one or more of its directors are directors or officers, or have a substantial financial interest, is not approved in accordance with paragraph (a), the corporation may avoid the contract or transaction unless the party or parties thereto shall establish affirmatively that the contract or transaction was fair and reasonable as to the corporation at the time it was approved by the board, a committee or the shareholders.

(c) Common or interested directors may be counted in determining the presence of a quorum at a meeting of the board or of a committee which approves such contract or transaction.

(d) The certificate of incorporation may contain additional restrictions on contracts or transactions between a corporation and its directors and may provide that contracts or transactions in violation of such restrictions shall be void or voidable by the corporation.

(e) Unless otherwise provided in the certificate of incorporation or the by-laws, the board shall have authority to fix the compensation of directors for services in any capacity.

§ 715. Officers

(a) The board may elect or appoint a president, one or more vice-presidents, a secretary and a treasurer, and such other officers as it may determine, or as may be provided in the by-laws.

(b) The certificate of incorporation may provide that all officers or that specified officers shall be elected by the shareholders instead of by the board.

(c) Unless otherwise provided in the certificate of incorporation or the by-laws, all officers shall be elected or appointed to hold office until the meeting of the board following the next annual meeting of shareholders or, in the case of officers elected by the shareholders, until the next annual meeting of shareholders.

(d) Each officer shall hold office for the term for which he is elected or appointed, and until his successor has been elected or appointed and qualified.

(e) Any two or more offices may be held by the same person. When all of the issued and outstanding stock of the corporation is owned by one person, such person may hold all or any combination of offices.

(f) The board may require any officer to give security for the faithful performance of his duties.

(g) All officers as between themselves and the corporation shall have such authority and perform such duties in the management of the corporation as may be provided in the by-laws or, to the extent not so provided, by the board.

(h) An officer shall perform his duties as an officer in good faith and with that degree of care which an ordinarily prudent person in a like position would use under similar circumstances. In performing his duties, an officer shall be entitled to rely on information, opinions, reports or statements including financial statements and other financial data, in each case prepared or presented by:

(1) one or more other officers or employees of the corporation or of any other corporation of which at least fifty percentum of the outstand-

ing shares of stock entitling the holders thereof to vote for the election of directors is owned directly or indirectly by the corporation, whom the officer believes to be reliable and competent in the matters presented, or

(2) counsel, public accountants or other persons as to matters which the officer believes to be within such person's professional or expert competence, so long as in so relying he shall be acting in good faith and with such degree of care, but he shall not be considered to be acting in good faith if he has knowledge concerning the matter in question that would cause such reliance to be unwarranted. A person who so performs his duties shall have no liability by reason of being or having been an officer of the corporation.

§ 716. Removal of Officers

(a) Any officer elected or appointed by the board may be removed by the board with or without cause. An officer elected by the shareholders may be removed, with or without cause, only by vote of the shareholders, but his authority to act as an officer may be suspended by the board for cause.

(b) The removal of an officer without cause shall be without prejudice to his contract rights, if any. The election or appointment of an officer shall not of itself create contract rights.

(c) An action to procure a judgment removing an officer for cause may be brought by the attorney-general or by ten percent of the votes of the outstanding shares, whether or not entitled to vote. The court may bar from re-election or reappointment any officer so removed for a period fixed by the court.

§ 717. Duty of Directors

(a) A director shall perform his duties as a director, including his duties as a member of any committee of the board upon which he may serve, in good faith and with that degree of care which an ordinarily prudent person in a like position would use under similar circumstances. In performing his duties, a director shall be entitled to rely on information, opinions, reports or statements including financial statements and other financial data, in each case prepared or presented by:

(1) one or more officers or employees of the corporation or of any other corporation of which at least fifty percentum of the outstanding shares of stock entitling the holders thereof to vote for the election of directors is owned directly or indirectly by the corporation, whom the director believes to be reliable and competent in the matters presented,

(2) counsel, public accountants or other persons as to matters which the director believes to be within such person's professional or expert competence, or

(3) a committee of the board upon which he does not serve, duly designated in accordance with a provision of the certificate of incorporation or the by-laws, as to matters within its designated authority, which committee the director believes to merit confidence, so long as in so relying he shall be acting in good faith and with such degree of care, but he shall not be considered to be acting in good faith if he has knowledge concerning the matter in question that would cause such reliance to be unwarranted. A person who so performs his duties shall have no liability by reason of being or having been a director of the corporation.

(b) In taking action, including, without limitation, action which may involve or relate to a change or potential change in the control of the corporation, a director shall be entitled to consider, without limitation, (1) both the long-term and the short-term interests of the corporation and its shareholders and (2) the effects that the corporation's actions may have in the short-term or in the long-term upon any of the following:

(i) the prospects for potential growth, development, productivity and profitability of the corporation;

(ii) the corporation's current employees;

(iii) the corporation's retired employees and other beneficiaries receiving or entitled to receive retirement, welfare or similar benefits from or pursuant to any plan sponsored, or agreement entered into, by the corporation;

(iv) the corporation's customers and creditors; and

(v) the ability of the corporation to provide, as a going concern, goods, services, employment opportunities and employment benefits and otherwise to contribute to the communities in which it does business.

Nothing in this paragraph shall create any duties owed by any director to any person or entity to consider or afford any particular weight to any of the foregoing or abrogate any duty of the directors, either statutory or recognized by common law or court decisions.

For purposes of this paragraph, "control" shall mean the possession, directly or indirectly, of the power to direct or cause the direction of the management and policies of the corporation, whether through the ownership of voting stock, by contract, or otherwise.

§ 719. Liability of Directors in Certain Cases

(a) Directors of a corporation who vote for or concur in any of the following corporate actions shall be jointly and severally liable to the corporation for the benefit of its creditors or shareholders, to the extent of any injury suffered by such persons, respectively, as a result of such action:

(1) The declaration of any dividend or other distribution to the extent that it is contrary to the provisions of paragraphs (a) and (b) of section 510 (Dividends or other distributions in cash or property).

(2) The purchase of the shares of the corporation to the extent that it is contrary to the provisions of section 513 (Purchase or redemption by a corporation of its own shares).

(3) The distribution of assets to shareholders after dissolution of the corporation without paying or adequately providing for all known liabilities of the corporation, excluding any claims not filed by creditors within the time limit set in a notice given to creditors under articles 10 (Non-judicial dissolution) or 11 (Judicial dissolution).

(4) The making of any loan contrary to section 714 (Loans to directors).

(b) A director who is present at a meeting of the board, or any committee thereof, when action specified in paragraph (a) is taken shall be presumed to have concurred in the action unless his dissent thereto shall be entered in the minutes of the meeting, or unless he shall submit his written dissent to the person acting as the secretary of the meeting before the adjournment thereof, or shall deliver or send by registered mail such dissent to the secretary of the corporation promptly after the adjournment of the meeting. Such right to dissent shall not apply to a director who voted in favor of such action. A director who is absent from a meeting of the board, or any committee thereof, when such action is taken shall be presumed to have concurred in the action unless he shall deliver or send by registered mail his dissent thereto to the secretary of the corporation or shall cause such dissent to be filed with the minutes of the proceedings of the board or committee within a reasonable time after learning of such action.

(c) Any director against whom a claim is successfully asserted under this section shall be entitled to contribution from the other directors who voted for or concurred in the action upon which the claim is asserted.

(d) Directors against whom a claim is successfully asserted under this section shall be entitled, to the extent of the amounts paid by them to the corporation as a result of such claims:

(1) Upon payment to the corporation of any amount of an improper dividend or distribution, to be subrogated to the rights of the corporation against shareholders who received such dividend or distribution with knowledge of facts indicating that it was not authorized by section 510, in proportion to the amounts received by them respectively.

(2) Upon payment to the corporation of any amount of the purchase price of an improper purchase of shares, to have the corporation rescind such purchase of shares and recover for their benefit, but at their expense, the amount of such purchase price from any seller who sold

such shares with knowledge of facts indicating that such purchase of shares by the corporation was not authorized by section 513.

(3) Upon payment to the corporation of the claim of any creditor by reason of a violation of subparagraph (a)(3), to be subrogated to the rights of the corporation against shareholders who received an improper distribution of assets.

(4) Upon payment to the corporation of the amount of any loan made contrary to section 714, to be subrogated to the rights of the corporation against a director who received the improper loan.

(e) A director shall not be liable under this section if, in the circumstances, he performed his duty to the corporation under section 717.

(f) This section shall not affect any liability otherwise imposed by law upon any director.

§ 720. Action Against Directors and Officers for Misconduct

(a) An action may be brought against one or more directors or officers of a corporation to procure a judgment for the following relief:

(1) To compel the defendant to account for his official conduct in the following cases:

(A) The neglect of, or failure to perform, or other violation of his duties in the management and disposition of corporate assets committed to his charge.

(B) The acquisition by himself, transfer to others, loss or waste of corporate assets due to any neglect of, or failure to perform, or other violation of his duties.

(2) To set aside an unlawful conveyance, assignment or transfer of corporate assets, where the transferee knew of its unlawfulness.

(3) To enjoin a proposed unlawful conveyance, assignment or transfer of corporate assets, where there is sufficient evidence that it will be made.

(b) An action may be brought for the relief provided in this section, and in paragraph (a) of section 719 (Liability of directors in certain cases) by a corporation, or a receiver, trustee in bankruptcy, officer, director or judgment creditor thereof, or, under section 626 (Shareholders' derivative action brought in the right of the corporation to procure a judgment in its favor), by a shareholder, voting trust certificate holder, or the owner of a beneficial interest in shares thereof.

(c) This section shall not affect any liability otherwise imposed by law upon any director or officer.

§ 721. Nonexclusivity of Statutory Provisions for Indemnification of Directors and Officers

The indemnification and advancement of expenses granted pursuant to, or provided by, this article shall not be deemed exclusive of any other rights to which a director or officer seeking indemnification or advancement of expenses may be entitled, whether contained in the certificate of incorporation or the by-laws or, when authorized by such certificate of incorporation or by-laws, (i) a resolution of shareholders, (ii) a resolution of directors, or (iii) an agreement providing for such indemnification, provided that no indemnification may be made to or on behalf of any director or officer if a judgment or other final adjudication adverse to the director or officer establishes that his acts were committed in bad faith or were the result of active and deliberate dishonesty and were material to the cause of action so adjudicated, or that he personally gained in fact a financial profit or other advantage to which he was not legally entitled. Nothing contained in this article shall affect any rights to indemnification to which corporate personnel other than directors and officers may be entitled by contract or otherwise under law.

§ 722. Authorization for Indemnification of Directors and Officers

(a) A corporation may indemnify any person made, or threatened to be made, a party to an action or proceeding (other than one by or in the right of the corporation to procure a judgment in its favor), whether civil or criminal, including an action by or in the right of any other corporation of any type or kind, domestic or foreign, or any partnership, joint venture, trust, employee benefit plan or other enterprise, which any director or officer of the corporation served in any capacity at the request of the corporation, by reason of the fact that he, his testator or intestate, was a director or officer of the corporation, or served such other corporation, partnership, joint venture, trust, employee benefit plan or other enterprise in any capacity, against judgments, fines, amounts paid in settlement and reasonable expenses, including attorneys' fees actually and necessarily incurred as a result of such action or proceeding, or any appeal therein, if such director or officer acted, in good faith, for a purpose which he reasonably believed to be in, or, in the case of service for any other corporation or any partnership, joint venture, trust, employee benefit plan or other enterprise, not opposed to, the best interests of the corporation and, in criminal actions or proceedings, in addition, had no reasonable cause to believe that his conduct was unlawful.

(b) The termination of any such civil or criminal action or proceeding by judgment, settlement, conviction or upon a plea of nolo contendere, or its equivalent, shall not in itself create a presumption that any such director or officer did not act, in good faith, for a purpose which he reasonably believed to be in, or, in the case of service for any other corporation or any partnership, joint venture, trust, employee benefit plan or other enterprise, not opposed to, the best interests of the corporation or that he had reasonable cause to believe that his conduct was unlawful.

(c) A corporation may indemnify any person made, or threatened to be made, a party to an action by or in the right of the corporation to procure a judgment in its favor by reason of the fact that he, his testator or intestate, is or was a director or officer of the corporation, or is or was serving at the request of the corporation as a director or officer of any other corporation of any type or kind, domestic or foreign, of any partnership, joint venture, trust, employee benefit plan or other enterprise, against amounts paid in settlement and reasonable expenses, including attorneys' fees, actually and necessarily incurred by him in connection with the defense or settlement of such action, or in connection with an appeal therein, if such director or officer acted, in good faith, for a purpose which he reasonably believed to be in, or, in the case of service for any other corporation or any partnership, joint venture, trust, employee benefit plan or other enterprise, not opposed to, the best interests of the corporation, except that no indemnification under this paragraph shall be made in respect of (1) a threatened action, or a pending action which is settled or otherwise disposed of, or (2) any claim, issue or matter as to which such person shall have been adjudged to be liable to the corporation, unless and only to the extent that the court in which the action was brought, or, if no action was brought, any court of competent jurisdiction, determines upon application that, in view of all the circumstances of the case, the person is fairly and reasonably entitled to indemnity for such portion of the settlement amount and expenses as the court deems proper.

(d) For the purpose of this section, a corporation shall be deemed to have requested a person to serve an employee benefit plan where the performance by such person of his duties to the corporation also imposes duties on, or otherwise involves services by, such person to the plan or participants or beneficiaries of the plan; excise taxes assessed on a person with respect to an employee benefit plan pursuant to applicable law shall be considered fines; and action taken or omitted by a person with respect to an employee benefit plan in the performance of such person's duties for a purpose reasonably believed by such person to be in the interest of the participants and beneficiaries of the plan shall be deemed to be for a purpose which is not opposed to the best interests of the corporation.

§ 723. Payment of Indemnification Other Than by Court Award

(a) A person who has been successful, on the merits or otherwise, in the defense of a civil or criminal action or proceeding of the character described in section 722 shall be entitled to indemnification as authorized in such section.

(b) Except as provided in paragraph (a), any indemnification under section 722 or otherwise permitted by section 721, unless ordered by a court under section 724 (Indemnification of directors and officers by a court), shall be made by the corporation, only if authorized in the specific case:

(1) By the board acting by a quorum consisting of directors who are not parties to such action or proceeding upon a finding that the director or officer has met the standard of conduct set forth in section 722 or established pursuant to section 721, as the case may be, or,

(2) If a quorum under subparagraph (1) is not obtainable or, even if obtainable, a quorum of disinterested directors so directs;

(A) By the board upon the opinion in writing of independent legal counsel that indemnification is proper in the circumstances because the applicable standard of conduct set forth in such sections has been met by such director or officer, or

(B) By the shareholders upon a finding that the director or officer has met the applicable standard of conduct set forth in such sections.

(c) Expenses incurred in defending a civil or criminal action or proceeding may be paid by the corporation in advance of the final disposition of such action or proceeding upon receipt of an undertaking by or on behalf of such director or officer to repay such amount as, and to the extent, required by paragraph (a) of section 725.

§ 724. Indemnification of Directors and Officers by a Court

(a) Notwithstanding the failure of a corporation to provide indemnification, and despite any contrary resolution of the board or of the shareholders in the specific case under section 723 (Payment of indemnification other than by court award), indemnification shall be awarded by a court to the extent authorized under section 722 (Authorization for indemnification of directors and officers), and paragraph (a) of section 723. Application therefor may be made, in every case, either:

(1) In the civil action or proceeding in which the expenses were incurred or other amounts were paid, or

(2) To the supreme court in a separate proceeding, in which case the application shall set forth the disposition of any previous application made to any court for the same or similar relief and also reasonable cause for the failure to make application for such relief in the action or proceeding in which the expenses were incurred or other amounts were paid.

(b) The application shall be made in such manner and form as may be required by the applicable rules of court or, in the absence thereof, by direction of a court to which it is made. Such application shall be upon notice to the corporation. The court may also direct that notice be given at the expense of the corporation to the shareholders and such other persons as it may designate in such manner as it may require.

(c) Where indemnification is sought by judicial action, the court may allow a person such reasonable expenses, including attorneys' fees, during the pendency of the litigation as are necessary in connection with his defense therein, if the court shall find that the defendant has by his pleadings or during the course of the litigation raised genuine issues of fact or law.

§ 725. Other Provisions Affecting Indemnification of Directors and Officers

(a) All expenses incurred in defending a civil or criminal action or proceeding which are advanced by the corporation under paragraph (c) of section 723 (Payment of indemnification other than by court award) or allowed by a court under paragraph (c) of section 724 (Indemnification of directors and officers by a court) shall be repaid in case the person receiving such advancement or allowance is ultimately found, under the procedure set forth in this article, not to be entitled to indemnification or, where indemnification is granted, to the extent the expenses so advanced by the corporation or allowed by the court exceed the indemnification to which he is entitled.

(b) No indemnification, advancement or allowance shall be made under this article in any circumstance where it appears:

(1) That the indemnification would be inconsistent with the law of the jurisdiction of incorporation of a foreign corporation which prohibits or otherwise limits such indemnification;

(2) That the indemnification would be inconsistent with a provision of the certificate of incorporation, a by-law, a resolution of the board or of the shareholders, an agreement or other proper corporate action, in effect at the time of the accrual of the alleged cause of action asserted in the threatened or pending action or proceeding in which the expenses were incurred or other amounts were paid, which prohibits or otherwise limits indemnification; or

(3) If there has been a settlement approved by the court, that the indemnification would be inconsistent with any condition with respect to indemnification expressly imposed by the court in approving the settlement.

(c) If any expenses or other amounts are paid by way of indemnification, otherwise than by court order or action by the shareholders, the corporation shall, not later than the next annual meeting of shareholders unless such meeting is held within three months from the date of such payment, and, in any event, within fifteen months from the date of such payment, mail to its shareholders of record at the time entitled to vote for the election of directors a statement specifying the persons paid, the amounts paid, and the nature and status at the time of such payment of the litigation or threatened litigation.

(d) If any action with respect to indemnification of directors and officers is taken by way of amendment of the by-laws, resolution of directors, or by agreement, then the corporation shall, not later than the next annual meeting of shareholders, unless such meeting is held within three months from the date of such action, and, in any event, within fifteen months from the date of such action, mail to its shareholders of record at the time entitled to vote for the election of directors a statement specifying the action taken.

(e) Any notification required to be made pursuant to the foregoing paragraph (c) or (d) of this section by any domestic mutual insurer shall be satisfied by compliance with the corresponding provisions o section one thousand two hundred sixteen off the insurance law.

(f) The provisions of this article relating to indemnification of directors and officers and insurance therefor shall apply to domestic corporations and foreign corporations doing business in this state, except as provided in section 1320 (Exemption from certain provisions).

§ 726. Insurance for Indemnification of Directors and Officers

(a) Subject to paragraph (b), a corporation shall have power to purchase and maintain insurance:

(1) To indemnify the corporation for any obligation which it incurs as a result of the indemnification of directors and officers under the provisions of this article, and

(2) To indemnify directors and officers in instances in which they may be indemnified by the corporation under the provisions of this article, and

(3) To indemnify directors and officers in instances in which they may not otherwise be indemnified by the corporation under the provisions of this article provided the contract of insurance covering such directors and officers provides, in a manner acceptable to the superintendent of insurance, for a retention amount and for co-insurance.

(b) No insurance under paragraph (a) may provide for any payment, other than cost of defense, to or on behalf of any director or officer:

(1) if a judgment or other final adjudication adverse to the insured director or officer establishes that his acts of active and deliberate dishonesty were material to the cause of action so adjudicated, or that he personally gained in fact a financial profit or other advantage to which he was not legally entitled, or

(2) in relation to any risk the insurance of which is prohibited under the insurance law of this state.

(c) Insurance under any or all subparagraphs of paragraph (a) may be included in a single contract or supplement thereto. Retrospective rated contracts are prohibited.

(d) The corporation shall, within the time and to the persons provided in paragraph (c) of section 725 (Other provisions affecting indemnification of directors or officers), mail a statement in respect of any insurance it has purchased or renewed under this section, specifying the insurance carrier, date of the contract, cost of the insurance, corporate positions insured, and a statement explaining all sums, not previously reported in a statement to shareholders, paid under any indemnification insurance contract.

(e) This section is the public policy of this state to spread the risk of corporate management, notwithstanding any other general or special law of this state or of any other jurisdiction including the federal government.

ARTICLE 9. MERGER OR CONSOLIDATION; GUARANTEE; DISPOSITION OF ASSETS; SHARE EXCHANGES

§ 912. Requirements Relating to Certain Business Combinations

(a) For the purposes of this section:

(1) "Affiliate" means a person that directly, or indirectly through one or more intermediaries, controls, or is controlled by, or is under common control with, a specified person.

(2) "Announcement date", when used in reference to any business combination, means the date of the first public announcement of the final, definitive proposal for such business combination.

(3) "Associate", when used to indicate a relationship with any person, means (A) any corporation or organization of which such person is an officer or partner or is, directly or indirectly, the beneficial owner of ten percent or more of any class of voting stock, (B) any trust or other estate in which such person has a substantial beneficial interest or as to which such person serves as trustee or in a similar fiduciary capacity, and (C) any relative or spouse of such person, or any relative of such spouse, who has the same home as such person.

(4) "Beneficial owner", when used with respect to any stock, means a person:

(A) that, individually or with or through any of its affiliates or associates, beneficially owns such stock, directly or indirectly; or

(B) that, individually or with or through any of its affiliates or associates, has (i) the right to acquire such stock (whether such right is exercisable immediately or only after the passage of time), pursuant to any agreement, arrangement or understanding (whether or not in writing), or upon the exercise of conversion rights, exchange rights, warrants or options, or otherwise; provided, however, that a person shall not be deemed the beneficial owner of stock tendered pursuant to a tender or exchange offer made by such person or any of such person's affiliates or associates until such tendered stock is accepted for purchase or exchange; or (ii) the right to vote such stock pursuant to any agreement, arrangement or understanding (whether or not in writing); provided, however, that a person shall not be deemed the beneficial owner of any stock under this item if the agreement, arrangement or understanding to vote such stock (X) arises solely from a revocable proxy or consent given in response to a proxy or consent solicitation made in accordance with the applicable rules and regulations under the Exchange Act and (Y) is not then reportable on a Schedule 13D under the Exchange Act (or any comparable or successor report); or

(C) that has any agreement, arrangement or understanding (whether or not in writing), for the purpose of acquiring, holding, voting (except voting pursuant to a revocable proxy or consent as described in item (ii) of clause (B) of this subparagraph), or disposing of such stock with any other person that beneficially owns; or whose affiliates or associates beneficially own, directly or indirectly, such stock.

(5) "Business combination", when used in reference to any domestic corporation and any interested shareholder of such corporation, means:

(A) any merger or consolidation of such corporation or any subsidiary of such corporation with (i) such interested shareholder or (ii) any other corporation (whether or not itself an interested shareholder of such corporation) which is, or after such merger or consolidation would be, an affiliate or associate of such interested shareholder;

(B) any sale, lease, exchange, mortgage, pledge, transfer or other disposition (in one transaction or a series of transactions) to or with such interested shareholder or any affiliate or associate of such interested shareholder of assets of such corporation or any subsidiary of such corporation (i) having an aggregate market value equal to ten percent or more of the aggregate market value of all the assets, determined on a consolidated basis, of such corporation, (ii) having an aggregate market value equal to ten percent or more of the aggregate market value of all the outstanding stock of such corporation, or (iii) representing ten percent or more of the earning power or net income, determined on a consolidated basis, of such corporation;

(C) the issuance or transfer by such corporation or any subsidiary of such corporation (in one transaction or a series of transactions) of any stock of such corporation or any subsidiary of such corporation which has an aggregate market value equal to five percent or more of the aggregate market value of all the outstanding stock of such corporation to such interested shareholder or any affiliate or associate of such interested shareholder except pursuant to the exercise of warrants or rights to purchase stock offered, or a dividend or distribution paid or made, pro rata to all shareholders of such corporation;

(D) the adoption of any plan or proposal for the liquidation or dissolution of such corporation proposed by, or pursuant to any agreement, arrangement or understanding (whether or not in writing) with, such interested shareholder or any affiliate or associate of such interested shareholder;

(E) any reclassification of securities (including, without limitation, any stock split, stock dividend, or other distribution of stock in respect of stock, or any reverse stock split), or recapitalization of such corporation, or any merger or consolidation of such corporation with any subsidiary of such corporation, or any other transaction (whether or not with or into or otherwise involving such interested shareholder), proposed by, or pursuant to any agreement, arrangement or understanding (whether or not in writing) with, such interested shareholder or any affiliate or associate of such interested shareholder, which has the effect, directly or indirectly, of increasing the proportionate share of the outstanding shares of any class or series of voting stock or securities convertible into voting stock of such corporation or any subsidiary of such corporation which is directly or indirectly owned by such interested shareholder or any affiliate or associate of such interested shareholder, except as a result of immaterial changes due to fractional share adjustments; or

(F) any receipt by such interested shareholder or any affiliate or associate of such interested shareholder of the benefit, directly or indirectly (except proportionately as a shareholder of such corporation) of any loans, advances, guarantees, pledges or other financial assistance or any tax credits or other tax advantages provided by or through such corporation.

(6) "Common stock" means any stock other than preferred stock.

(7) "Consummation date", with respect to any business combination, means the date of consummation of such business combination, or, in the case of a business combination as to which a shareholder vote is taken, the later of the business day prior to the vote or twenty days prior to the date of consummation of such business combination.

(8) "Control", including the terms "controlling", "controlled by" and "under common control with", means the possession, directly or indirectly, or the power to direct or cause the direction of the management and policies of a person, whether through the ownership of voting stock, by contract, or otherwise. A person's beneficial ownership of ten percent or more of a corporation's outstanding voting stock shall create a presumption that such person has control of such corporation. Notwithstanding the foregoing, a person shall not be deemed to have control of a corporation if such person holds voting stock, in good faith and not for the purpose of circumventing this section, as an agent, bank, broker,

nominee, custodian or trustee for one or more beneficial owners who do not individually or as a group have control of such corporation.

(9) "Exchange Act" means the Act of Congress known as the Securities Exchange Act of 1934, as the same has been or hereafter may be amended from time to time.

(10) "Interested shareholder", when used in reference to any domestic corporation, means any person (other than such corporation or any subsidiary of such corporation) that

(A)(i) is the beneficial owner, directly or indirectly, of twenty percent or more of the outstanding voting stock of such corporation; or

(ii) is an affiliate or associate of such corporation and at any time within the five-year period immediately prior to the date in question was the beneficial owner, directly or indirectly, of twenty percent or more of the then outstanding voting stock of such corporation; provided that

(B) for the purpose of determining whether a person is an interested shareholder, the number of shares of voting stock of such corporation deemed to be outstanding shall include shares deemed to be beneficially owned by the person through application of subparagraph four of this paragraph but shall not include any other unissued shares of voting stock of such corporation which may be issuable pursuant to any agreement, arrangement or understanding, or upon exercise of conversion rights, warrants or options, or otherwise.

(11) "Market value", when used in reference to stock or property of any domestic corporation, means:

(A) in the case of stock, the highest closing sale price during the thirty-day period immediately preceding the date in question of a share of such stock on the composite tape for New York stock exchange-listed stocks, or, if such stock is not quoted on such composite tape or if such stock is not listed on such exchange, on the principal United States securities exchange registered under the Exchange Act on which such stock is listed, or, if such stock is not listed on any such exchange, the highest closing bid quotation with respect to a share of such stock during the thirty-day period preceding the date in question on the National Association of Securities Dealers, Inc. Automated Quotations System or any system then in use, or if no such quotations are available, the fair market value on the date in question of a share of such stock as determined by the board of directors of such resident domestic corporation in good faith; and

(B) in the case of property other than cash or stock, the fair market value of such property on the date in question as determined by the board of directors of such corporation in good faith.

(12) "Preferred stock" means any class or series of stock of a domestic corporation which under the by-laws or certificate of incorporation of such corporation is entitled to receive payment of dividends

prior to any payment of dividends on some other class or series of stock, or is entitled in the event of any voluntary liquidation, dissolution or winding up of the corporation to receive payment or distribution of a preferential amount before any payments or distributions are received by some other class or series of stock.

* * *

(14) "Stock" means:

(A) any stock or similar security, any certificate of interest, any participation in any profit sharing agreement, any voting trust certificate, or any certificate of deposit for stock; and

(B) any security convertible, with or without consideration, into stock, or any warrant, call or other option or privilege of buying stock without being bound to do so, or any other security carrying any right to acquire, subscribe to or purchase stock.

(15) "Stock acquisition date", with respect to any person and any domestic corporation, means the date that such person first becomes an interested shareholder of such corporation.

(16) "Subsidiary" of any person means any other corporation of which a majority of the voting stock is owned, directly or indirectly, by such person.

(17) "Voting stock" means shares of capital stock of a corporation entitled to vote generally in the election of directors.

(b) Notwithstanding anything to the contrary contained in this chapter (except the provisions of paragraph (d) of this section), no domestic corporation shall engage in any business combination with any interested shareholder of such corporation for a period of five years following such interested shareholder's stock acquisition date unless such business combination or the purchase of stock made by such interested shareholder on such interested shareholder's stock acquisition date is approved by the board of directors of such corporation prior to such interested shareholder's stock acquisition date. If a good faith proposal is made in writing to the board of directors of such corporation regarding a business combination, the board of directors shall respond, in writing, within thirty days or such shorter period, if any, as may be required by the Exchange Act, setting forth its reasons for its decision regarding such proposal. If a good faith proposal to purchase stock is made in writing to the board of directors of such corporation, the board of directors, unless it responds affirmatively in writing within thirty days or such shorter period, if any, as may be required by the Exchange Act, shall be deemed to have disapproved such stock purchase.

(c) Notwithstanding anything to the contrary contained in this chapter (except the provisions of paragraphs (b) and (d) of this section), no domestic corporation shall engage at any time in any business combination with any interested shareholder of such corporation other than a business combination specified in any one of subparagraph (1), (2) or (3):

(1) A business combination approved by the board of directors of such corporation prior to such interested shareholder's stock acquisition date, or where the purchase of stock made by such interested shareholder on such interested shareholder's stock acquisition date had been approved by the board of directors of such corporation prior to such interested shareholder's stock acquisition date.

(2) A business combination approved by the affirmative vote of the holders of a majority of the outstanding voting stock not beneficially owned by such interested shareholder or any affiliate or associate of such interested shareholder at a meeting called for such purpose no earlier than five years after such interested shareholder's stock acquisition date.

(3) A business combination that meets all of the following conditions:

(A) The aggregate amount of the cash and the market value as of the consummation date of consideration other than cash to be received per share by holders of outstanding shares of common stock of such corporation in such business combination is at least equal to the higher of the following:

(i) the highest per share price paid by such interested shareholder at a time when he was the beneficial owner, directly or indirectly, of five percent or more of the outstanding voting stock of such corporation, for any shares of common stock of the same class or series acquired by it (X) within the five-year period immediately prior to the announcement date with respect to such business combination, or (Y) within the five-year period immediately prior to, or in, the transaction in which such interested shareholder became an interested shareholder, whichever is higher; plus, in either case, interest compounded annually from the earliest date on which such highest per share acquisition price was paid through the consummation date at the rate for one-year United States treasury obligations from time to time in effect; less the aggregate amount of any cash dividends paid, and the market value of any dividends paid other than in cash, per share of common stock since such earliest date, up to the amount of such interest; and

(ii) the market value per share of common stock on the announcement date with respect to such business combination or on such interested shareholder's stock acquisition date, whichever is higher; plus interest compounded annually from such date through the consummation date at the rate for one-year United States treasury obligations from time to time in effect; less the aggregate amount of any cash dividends paid, and the market value of any dividends paid other than in cash, per share of common stock since such date, up to the amount of such interest.

(B) The aggregate amount of the cash and the market value as of the consummation date of consideration other than cash to be received per share by holders of outstanding shares of any class or series of stock, other than common stock, of such corporation is at least equal to the highest of the following (whether or not such interested shareholder has previously acquired any shares of such class or series of stock):

(i) the highest per share price paid by such interested shareholder at a time when he was the beneficial owner, directly or indirectly, of five percent or more of the outstanding voting stock of such corporation, for any shares of such class or series of stock acquired by it (X) within the five-year period immediately prior to the announcement date with respect to such business combination, or (Y) within the five-year period immediately prior to, or in, the transaction in which such interested shareholder became an interested shareholder, whichever is higher; plus, in either case, interest compounded annually from the earliest date on which such highest per share acquisition price was paid through the consummation date at the rate for one-year United States treasury obligations from time to time in effect; less the aggregate amount of any cash dividends paid, and the market value of any dividends paid other than in cash, per share of such class or series of stock since such earliest date, up to the amount of such interest;

(ii) the highest preferential amount per share to which the holders of shares of such class or series of stock are entitled in the event of any voluntary liquidation, dissolution or winding up of such corporation, plus the aggregate amount of any dividends declared or due as to which such holders are entitled prior to payment of dividends on some other class or series of stock (unless the aggregate amount of such dividends is included in such preferential amount); and

(iii) the market value per share of such class or series of stock on the announcement date with respect to such business combination or on such interested shareholder's stock acquisition date, whichever is higher; plus interest compounded annually from such date through the consummation date at the rate for one-year United States treasury obligations from time to time in effect; less the aggregate amount of any cash dividends paid, and the market value of any dividends paid other than in cash, per share of such class or series of stock since such date, up to the amount of such interest.

(C) The consideration to be received by holders of a particular class or series of outstanding stock (including common stock) of such corporation in such business combination is in cash or in the same form as the interested shareholder has used to acquire the largest number of shares of such class or series of stock previously acquired by it, and such consideration shall be distributed promptly.

(D) The holders of all outstanding shares of stock of such corporation not beneficially owned by such interested shareholder immediately prior to the consummation of such business combination are entitled to receive in such business combination cash or other consideration for such shares in compliance with clauses (A), (B) and (C) of this subparagraph.

(E) After such interested shareholder's stock acquisition date and prior to the consummation date with respect to such business combination, such interested shareholder has not become the beneficial owner of any additional shares of voting stock of such corporation except:

(i) as part of the transaction which resulted in such interested shareholder becoming an interested shareholder;

(ii) by virtue of proportionate stock splits, stock dividends or other distributions of stock in respect of stock not constituting a business combination under clause (E) of subparagraph five of paragraph (a) of this section;

(iii) through a business combination meeting all of the conditions of paragraph (b) of this section and this paragraph; or

(iv) through purchase by such interested shareholder at any price which, if such price had been paid in an otherwise permissible business combination the announcement date and consummation date of which were the date of such purchase, would have satisfied the requirements of clauses (A), (B) and (C) of this subparagraph.

(d) The provisions of this section shall not apply:

(1) to any business combination of a domestic corporation that does not have a class of voting stock registered with the Securities and Exchange Commission pursuant to section twelve of the Exchange Act, unless the certificate of incorporation provides otherwise; or

(2) to any business combination of a domestic corporation whose certificate of incorporation has been amended to provide that such corporation shall be subject to the provisions of this section, which did not have a class of voting stock registered with the Securities and Exchange Commission pursuant to section twelve of the Exchange Act on the effective date of such amendment, and which is a business combination with an interested shareholder whose stock acquisition date is prior to the effective date of such amendment; or

(3) to any business combination of a domestic corporation (i) the original certificate of incorporation of which contains a provision expressly electing not to be governed by this section, or (ii) which adopts an amendment to such corporation's by-laws prior to March thirty-first, nineteen hundred eighty-six, expressly electing not to be governed by this section, or (iii) which adopts an amendment to such corporation's by-laws, approved by the affirmative vote of a majority of votes of the outstanding voting stock of such corporation, excluding the voting stock of interested shareholders and their affiliates and associates, expressly electing not to be governed by this section, provided that such amend-

ment to the by-laws shall not be effective until eighteen months after such vote of such corporation's shareholders and shall not apply to any business combination of such corporation with an interested shareholder whose stock acquisition date is on or prior to the effective date of such amendment; or

(4) to any business combination of a domestic corporation with an interested shareholder of such corporation which became an interested shareholder inadvertently, if such interested shareholder (i) as soon as practicable, divests itself of a sufficient amount of the voting stock of such corporation so that it no longer is the beneficial owner, directly or indirectly, of twenty percent or more of the outstanding voting stock of such corporation, and (ii) would not at any time within the five-year period preceding the announcement date with respect to such business combination have been an interested shareholder but for such inadvertent acquisition.

(5) to any business combination with an interested shareholder who was the beneficial owner, directly or indirectly, or five percent or more of the outstanding voting stock of such resident domestic corporation on October thirtieth, nineteen hundred eighty-five, and remained so to such interested shareholder's stock acquisition date.

ARTICLE 10. NON–JUDICIAL DISSOLUTION

§ 1002. Dissolution Under Provision in Certificate of Incorporation

(a) The certificate of incorporation may contain a provision that any shareholder, or the holders of any specified number or proportion of shares or votes of shares, or of any specified number or proportion of shares or votes of shares of any class or series thereof, may require the dissolution of the corporation at will or upon the occurrence of a specified event. If the certificate of incorporation contains such a provision, a certificate of dissolution under section 1003 (Certificate of dissolution; contents) may be signed, verified and delivered to the department of state as provided in section 104 (Certificate; requirements, signing, filing, effectiveness) when authorized by a holder or holders of the number or proportion of shares or votes of shares specified in such provision, given in such manner as may be specified therein, or if no manner is specified therein, when authorized on written consent signed by such holder or holders; or such certificate may be signed, verified and delivered to the department by such holder or holders or by such of them as are designated by them.

(b) An amendment of the certificate of incorporation which adds a provision permitted by this section, or which changes or strikes out such a provision, shall be authorized at a meeting of shareholders by vote of all outstanding shares, whether or not otherwise entitled to vote on any amendment, or of such lesser proportion of shares and of such class or series of shares, but not less than a majority of all outstanding shares entitled to vote on any amendment, as may be provided specifically in the certificate of incorporation for adding, changing or striking out a provision permitted by this section.

(c) If the certificate of incorporation of any corporation contains a provision authorized by this section, the existence of such provision shall be noted conspicuously on the face or back of every certificate for shares issued by such corporation.

ARTICLE 11. JUDICIAL DISSOLUTION

§ 1104. Petition in Case of Deadlock Among Directors or Shareholders

This section is popularly known as the "deadlock act."

(a) Except otherwise provided in the certificate of incorporation under section 613 (Limitations on right to vote), the holders of shares representing one-half of the votes of all outstanding shares of a corporation entitled to vote in an election of directors may present a petition for dissolution on one or more of the following grounds:

(1) That the directors are so divided respecting the management of the corporation's affairs that the votes required for action by the board cannot be obtained.

(2) That the shareholders are so divided that the votes required for the election of directors cannot be obtained.

(3) That there is internal dissension and two or more factions of shareholders are so divided that dissolution would be beneficial to the shareholders.

(b) If the certificate of incorporation provides that the proportion of votes required for action by the board, or the proportion of votes of shareholders required for election of directors, shall be greater than that otherwise required by this chapter, such a petition may be presented by the holders of shares representing more than one-third of the votes of all outstanding shares entitled to vote on non-judicial dissolution under section 1001 (Authorization of dissolution).

(c) Notwithstanding any provision in the certificate of incorporation, any holder of shares entitled to vote at an election of directors of a corporation, may present a petition for its dissolution on the ground that the shareholders are so divided that they have failed, for a period which includes at least two consecutive annual meeting dates, to elect successors to directors whose terms have expired or would have expired upon the election and qualification of their successors.

§ 1104–a. Petition for Judicial Dissolution Under Special Circumstances

(a) The holders of shares representing twenty percent or more of the votes of all outstanding shares of a corporation, other than a corporation registered as an investment company under an act of congress entitled "Investment Company Act of 1940", no shares of which are listed on a national securities exchange or regularly quoted in an over-the-counter market by one or more members of a national or an affiliated securities association, entitled to vote in an election of directors may present a petition of dissolution on one or more of the following grounds:

(1) The directors or those in control of the corporation have been guilty of illegal, fraudulent or oppressive actions toward the complaining shareholders;

(2) The property or assets of the corporation are being looted, wasted, or diverted for non-corporate purposes by its directors, officers or those in control of the corporation.

(b) The court, in determining whether to proceed with involuntary dissolution pursuant to this section, shall take into account:

(1) Whether liquidation of the corporation is the only feasible means whereby the petitioners may reasonably expect to obtain a fair return on their investment; and

(2) Whether liquidation of the corporation is reasonably necessary for the protection of the rights and interests of any substantial number of shareholders or of the petitioners.

(c) In addition to all other disclosure requirements, the directors or those in control of the corporation, no later than thirty days after the filing of a petition hereunder, shall make available for inspection and copying to the petitioners under reasonable working conditions the corporate financial books and records for the three preceding years.

(d) The court may order stock valuations be adjusted and may provide for a surcharge upon the directors or those in control of the corporation upon a finding of wilful or reckless dissipation or transfer of assets or corporate property without just or adequate compensation therefor.

§ 1111. Judgment or Final Order of Dissolution

(a) In an action or special proceeding under this article if, in the court's discretion, it shall appear that the corporation should be dissolved, it shall make a judgment or final order dissolving the corporation.

(b) In making its decision, the court shall take into consideration the following criteria:

(1) In an action brought by the attorney-general, the interest of the public is of paramount importance.

(2) In a special proceeding brought by directors or shareholders, the benefit to the shareholders of a dissolution is of paramount importance.

(3) In a special proceeding brought under section 1104 (Petition in case of deadlock among directors or shareholders) or section 1104–a (Petition for judicial dissolution under special circumstances) dissolution is not to be denied merely because it is found that the corporate business has been or could be conducted at a profit.

(c) If the judgment or final order shall provide for a dissolution of the corporation, the court may, in its discretion, provide therein for the distribution of the property of the corporation to those entitled thereto according to their respective rights.

(d) The clerk of the court or such other person as the court may direct shall transmit certified copies of the judgment or final order of dissolution to the department of state and to the clerk of the county in which the office of the corporation was located at the date of the judgment or order. Upon filing by the department of state, the corporation shall be dissolved.

(e) The corporation shall promptly thereafter transmit a certified copy of the judgment or final order to the clerk of each other county in which its certificate of incorporation was filed.

§ 1118. Purchase of Petitioner's Shares; Valuation

(a) In any proceeding brought pursuant to section eleven hundred four-a of this chapter, any other shareholder or shareholders or the corporation may, at any time within ninety days after the filing of such petition or at such later time as the court in its discretion may allow, elect to purchase the shares owned by the petitioners at their fair value and upon such terms and conditions as may be approved by the court, including the conditions of paragraph (c) herein. An election pursuant to this section shall be irrevocable unless the court, in its discretion, for just and equitable considerations, determines that such election be revocable.

(b) If one or more shareholders or the corporation elect to purchase the shares owned by the petitioner but are unable to agree with the petitioner upon the fair value of such shares, the court, upon the application of such prospective purchaser or purchasers or the petitioner, may stay the proceedings brought pursuant to section 1104–a of this chapter and determine the fair value of the petitioner's shares as of the day prior to the date on which such petition was filed, exclusive of any element of value arising from such filing but giving effect to any adjustment or surcharge found to be appropriate in the proceeding under section 1104–a of this chapter. In determining the fair value of the petitioner's shares, the court, in its discretion, may award interest from the date the petition is filed to the date of payment for the petitioner's share at an equitable rate upon judicially determined fair value of his shares.

(c) In connection with any election to purchase pursuant to this section:

(1) If such election is made beyond ninety days after the filing of the petition, and the court allows such petition, the court, in its discretion, may award the petitioner his reasonable expenses incurred in the proceeding prior to such election, including reasonable attorneys' fees;

(2) The court, in its discretion, may require, at any time prior to the actual purchase of petitioner's shares, the posting of a bond or other acceptable security in an amount sufficient to secure petitioner for the fair value of his shares.

ARTICLE 13. FOREIGN CORPORATIONS

§ 1317. Liabilities of Directors and Officers of Foreign Corporations

(a) Except as otherwise provided in this chapter, the directors and officers of a foreign corporation doing business in this state are subject, to the same extent as directors and officers of a domestic corporation, to the provisions of:

(1) Section 719 (Liability of directors in certain cases) except subparagraph (a)(3) thereof, and

(2) Section 720 (Action against directors and officers for misconduct.)

(b) Any liability imposed by paragraph (a) may be enforced in, and such relief granted by, the courts in this state, in the same manner as in the case of a domestic corporation.

§ 1318. Liability of Foreign Corporations for Failure to Disclose Required Information

A foreign corporation doing business in this state shall, in the same manner as a domestic corporation, disclose to its shareholders of record who are residents of this state the information required under paragraph (c) of section 510 (Dividends or other distributions in cash or property), paragraphs (f) and (g) of section 511 (Share distributions and changes), paragraph (d) of section 515 (Reacquired shares), paragraph (c) of section 516 (Reduction of stated capital in certain cases), and shall be liable as provided in section 520 (Liability for failure to disclose required information) for failure to comply in good faith with these requirements.

§ 1319. Applicability of Other Provisions

(a) In addition to articles 1 (Short title; definitions; application; certificates; miscellaneous) and 3 (Corporate name and service of process) and the other sections of article 13, the following provisions, to the extent provided therein, shall apply to a foreign corporation doing business in this state, its directors, officers and shareholders:

(1) Section 623 (Procedure to enforce shareholder's right to receive payment for shares).

(2) Section 626 (Shareholders' derivative action brought in the right of the corporation to procure a judgment in its favor).

(3) Section 627 (Security for expenses in shareholders' derivative action brought in the right of the corporation to procure a judgment in its favor).

(4) Section 721 (Exclusivity of statutory provisions for indemnification of directors and officers) through 727 (Insurance for indemnification of directors and officers), inclusive.

(5) Section 808 (Reorganization under act of congress).

(6) Section 907 (Merger or consolidation of domestic and foreign corporations).

§ 1320. Exemption From Certain Provisions

(a) Notwithstanding any other provision of this chapter, a foreign corporation doing business in this state which is authorized under this article, its directors, officers and shareholders, shall be exempt from the provisions of paragraph (e) of section 1316 (Voting trust records), subparagraph (a)(1) of section 1317 (Liabilities of directors and officers of foreign corporations), section 1318 (Liability of foreign corporations for failure to disclose required information) and subparagraph (a)(4) of section 1319 (Applicability of other provisions) if when such provision would otherwise apply:

(1) Shares of such corporation were listed on a national securities exchange, or

(2) Less than one-half of the total of its business income for the preceding three fiscal years, or such portion thereof as the foreign corporation was in existence, was allocable to this state for franchise tax purposes under the tax law.

I. PENNSYLVANIA BUSINESS CORPORATION LAW

(Selected Sections)

Contents

SUBCHAPTER B. FIDUCIARY DUTY

SUBCHAPTER C. DIRECTORS AND OFFICERS

SUBCHAPTER E. CONTROL TRANSACTIONS

SUBCHAPTER F. BUSINESS COMBINATIONS

SUBCHAPTER G. CONTROL–SHARE ACQUISITIONS

SUBCHAPTER B. FIDUCIARY DUTY

§ 1711. Alternative Provisions

(a) General rule.—Section 1716 (relating to alternative standard) shall not be applicable to any business corporation to which section 1715 (relating to exercise of powers generally) is applicable.

(b) Exceptions.—Section 1715 shall be applicable to:

(1) Any registered corporation described in section 2502(1)(i) (relating to registered corporation status), except a corporation:

(i) the bylaws of which explicitly provide that section 1715 or corresponding provisions of prior law shall not be applicable to the corporation by amendment adopted by the board of directors on or before July 26, 1990, in the case of a corporation that was a registered corporation described in section 2502(1)(i) on April 27, 1990; or

(ii) in any other case, the articles of which explicitly provide that section 1715 or corresponding provisions of prior law shall not be applicable to the corporation by a provision included in the original articles, or by an articles amendment adopted on or before 90 days after the corporation first becomes a registered corporation described in section 2502(1)(i).

(2) Any registered corporation described solely in section 2502(1)(ii), except a corporation:

(i) the bylaws of which explicitly provide that section 1715 or corresponding provisions of prior law shall not be applicable to the corporation by amendment adopted by the board of directors on or before April 27, 1991, in the case of a corporation that was a registered corporation described solely in section 2502(1)(ii) on April 27, 1990; or

(ii) in any other case, the articles of which explicitly provide that section 1715 or corresponding provisions of prior law shall not be applicable to the corporation by a provision included in the original articles, or by an articles amendment adopted on or before one year after the corporation first becomes a registered corporation described in section 2502(1)(ii).

(3) Any business corporation that is not a registered corporation described in section 2502(1), except a corporation:

(i) the bylaws of which explicitly provide that section 1715 or corresponding provisions of prior law shall not be applicable to the corporation by amendment adopted by the board of directors on or before April 27, 1991, in the case of a corporation that was a business corporation on April 27, 1990; or

(ii) in any other case, the articles of which explicitly provide that section 1715 or corresponding provisions of prior law shall not be applicable to the corporation by a provision included in the original articles, or by an articles amendment adopted on or before one year after the corporation first becomes a business corporation.

(c) Transitional provision.—A provision of the articles or bylaws adopted pursuant to section 511(b) (relating to alternative provisions) at a time when the corporation was not a business corporation that provides that section 515 (relating to exercise of powers generally) or corresponding provisions of prior law shall not be applicable to the corporation shall be deemed to provide that section 1715 shall not be applicable to the corporation.

§ 1712. Standard of Care and Justifiable Reliance

(a) Directors.—A director of a business corporation shall stand in a fiduciary relation to the corporation and shall perform his duties as a director, including his duties as a member of any committee of the board upon which he may serve, in good faith, in a manner he reasonably believes to be in the best interests of the corporation and with such care, including reasonable inquiry, skill and diligence, as a person of ordinary prudence would use under similar circumstances. In performing his duties, a director shall be entitled to rely in good faith on information, opinions, reports or statements, including financial statements and other financial data, in each case prepared or presented by any of the following:

(1) One or more officers or employees of the corporation whom the director reasonably believes to be reliable and competent in the matters presented.

(2) Counsel, public accountants or other persons as to matters which the director reasonably believes to be within the professional or expert competence of such person.

(3) A committee of the board upon which he does not serve, duly designated in accordance with law, as to matters within its designated authority, which committee the director reasonably believes to merit confidence.

(b) Effect of actual knowledge.—A director shall not be considered to be acting in good faith if he has knowledge concerning the matter in question that would cause his reliance to be unwarranted.

(c) Officers.—Except as otherwise provided in the bylaws, an officer shall perform his duties as an officer in good faith, in a manner he reasonably believes to be in the best interests of the corporation and with such care, including reasonable inquiry, skill and diligence, as a person of ordinary prudence would use under similar circumstances. A person who so performs his duties shall not be liable by reason of having been an officer of the corporation.

§ 1713. Personal Liability of Directors

(a) General rule.—If a bylaw adopted by the shareholders of a business corporation so provides, a director shall not be personally liable, as such, for monetary damages for any action taken unless:

(1) the director has breached or failed to perform the duties of his office under this subchapter; and

(2) the breach or failure to perform constitutes self-dealing, willful misconduct or recklessness.

(b) Exceptions.—Subsection (a) shall not apply to:

(1) the responsibility or liability of a director pursuant to any criminal statute; or

(2) the liability of a director for the payment of taxes pursuant to Federal, State or local law.

(c) Cross reference.—See 42 Pa.C.S. § 8332.5 (relating to corporate representatives).

§ 1714. Notation of Dissent

A director of a business corporation who is present at a meeting of its board of directors, or of a committee of the board, at which action on any corporate matter is taken on which the director is generally competent to act, shall be presumed to have assented to the action taken unless his dissent is entered in the minutes of the meeting or unless he files his written dissent to the action with the secretary of the meeting before the adjournment thereof or transmits the dissent in writing to the secretary of the corporation immediately after the adjournment of the meeting. The right to dissent shall not apply to a director who voted in favor of the action. Nothing in this subchapter shall bar a director from asserting that minutes of the meeting incorrectly omitted his dissent if, promptly upon receipt of a copy of such minutes, he notifies the secretary, in writing, of the asserted omission or inaccuracy.

§ 1715. Exercise of Powers Generally

(a) General rule.—In discharging the duties of their respective positions, the board of directors, committees of the board and individual directors of a business corporation may, in considering the best interests of the corporation, consider to the extent they deem appropriate:

(1) The effects of any action upon any or all groups affected by such action, including shareholders, employees, suppliers, customers and creditors of the corporation, and upon communities in which offices or other establishments of the corporation are located.

(2) The short-term and long-term interests of the corporation, including benefits that may accrue to the corporation from its long-term plans and the possibility that these interests may be best served by the continued independence of the corporation.

(3) The resources, intent and conduct (past, stated and potential) of any person seeking to acquire control of the corporation.

(4) All other pertinent factors.

(b) Consideration of interests and factors.—The board of directors, committees of the board and individual directors shall not be required, in considering the best interests of the corporation or the effects of any action, to regard any corporate interest or the interests of any particular group affected by such action as a dominant or controlling interest or factor. The consideration of interests and factors in the manner described in this subsection and in subsection (a) shall not constitute a violation of section 1712 (relating to standard of care and justifiable reliance).

(c) Specific applications.—In exercising the powers vested in the corporation, including, without limitation, those powers pursuant to section 1502 (relating to general powers), and in no way limiting the discretion of the board of directors, committees of the board and individual directors pursuant to subsections (a) and (b), the fiduciary duty of directors shall not be deemed to require them:

(1) to redeem any rights under, or to modify or render inapplicable, any shareholder rights plan, including, but not limited to, a plan adopted pursuant or made subject to section 2513 (relating to disparate treatment of certain persons);

(2) to render inapplicable, or make determinations under, the provisions of Subchapter E of Chapter 25 (relating to control transactions), Subchapter F of Chapter 25 (relating to business combinations), Subchapter G of Chapter 25 (relating to control-share acquisitions) or Subchapter H of Chapter 25 (relating to disgorgement by certain controlling shareholders following attempts to acquire control) or under any other provision of this title relating to or affecting acquisitions or potential or proposed acquisitions of control; or

(3) to act as the board of directors, a committee of the board or an individual director solely because of the effect such action might have on an acquisition or potential or proposed acquisition of control of the corporation or the consideration that might be offered or paid to shareholders in such an acquisition.

(d) Presumption.—Absent breach of fiduciary duty, lack of good faith or self-dealing, any act as the board of directors, a committee of the board or an individual director shall be presumed to be in the best interests of the corporation. In assessing whether the standard set forth in section 1712 has been satisfied, there shall not be any greater obligation to justify, or higher burden of proof with respect to, any act as the board of directors, any committee of the board or any individual director relating to or affecting an acquisition or potential or proposed acquisition of control of the corporation than is applied to any other act as a board of directors, any committee of the board or any individual director. Notwithstanding the preceding provisions of this subsection, any act as the board of directors, a committee of the board or an individual director relating to or affecting an acquisition or potential or proposed acquisition of control to which a majority of the disinterested directors shall have assented shall be presumed to satisfy the standard set forth in section 1712, unless it is proven by clear and convincing evidence that the disinterested directors did not assent to such act in good faith after reasonable investigation.

(e) Definition.—The term "disinterested director" as used in subsection (d) and for no other purpose means:

(1) A director of the corporation other than:

(i) A director who has a direct or indirect financial or other interest in the person acquiring or seeking to acquire control of the corporation or who is an affiliate or associate, as defined in section 2552 (relating to definitions), of, or was nominated or designated as a director by, a person acquiring or seeking to acquire control of the corporation.

(ii) Depending on the specific facts surrounding the director and the act under consideration, an officer or employee or former officer or employee of the corporation.

(2) A person shall not be deemed to be other than a disinterested director solely by reason of any or all of the following:

(i) The ownership by the director of shares of the corporation.

(ii) The receipt as a holder of any class or series of any distribution made to all owners of shares of that class or series.

(iii) The receipt by the director of director's fees or other consideration as a director.

(iv) Any interest the director may have in retaining the status or position of director.

(v) The former business or employment relationship of the director with the corporation.

(vi) Receiving or having the right to receive retirement or deferred compensation from the corporation due to service as a director, officer or employee.

(f) Cross reference.—See section 1711 (relating to alternative provisions).

§ 1716. Alternative Standard

(a) General rule.—In discharging the duties of their respective positions, the board of directors, committees of the board and individual directors of a business corporation may, in considering the best interests of the corporation, consider the effects of any action upon employees, upon suppliers and customers of the corporation and upon communities in which offices or other establishments of the corporation are located, and all other pertinent factors. The consideration of those factors shall not constitute a violation of section 1712 (relating to standard of care and justifiable reliance).

(b) Presumption.—Absent breach of fiduciary duty, lack of good faith or self-dealing, actions taken as a director shall be presumed to be in the best interests of the corporation.

(c) Cross reference.—See section 1711 (relating to alternative provisions).

§ 1717. Limitation on Standing

The duty of the board of directors, committees of the board and individual directors under section 1712 (relating to standard of care and justifiable reliance) is solely to the business corporation and may be enforced directly by the corporation or may be enforced by a shareholder, as such, by an action in the right of the corporation, and may not be enforced directly by a shareholder or by any other person or group. Notwithstanding the preceding sentence, sections 1715(a) and (b) (relating to exercise of powers generally) and 1716(a) (relating to alternative standard) do not impose upon the board of directors, committees of the board and individual directors, any legal or equitable duties, obligations or liabilities or create any right or cause of action against, or basis for standing to sue, the board of directors, committees of the board and individual directors.

SUBCHAPTER C. DIRECTORS AND OFFICERS

§ 1721. Board of Directors

Unless otherwise provided by statute or in a bylaw adopted by the shareholders, all powers enumerated in section 1502 (relating to general powers) and elsewhere in this subpart or otherwise vested by law in a business corporation shall be exercised by or under the authority of, and the business and affairs of every business corporation shall be managed under the direction of, a board of directors. If any such provision is made in the bylaws, the powers and duties conferred or imposed upon the board of directors by this subpart shall be exercised or performed to such extent and by such person or persons as shall be provided in the bylaws. Persons upon whom the liabilities of directors are imposed by this section shall to that extent be entitled to the rights and immunities conferred by or pursuant to this part and other provisions of law upon directors of a corporation.

SUBCHAPTER E. CONTROL TRANSACTIONS

§ 2541. Application and Effect of Subchapter

(a) General rule.—Except as otherwise provided in this section, this subchapter shall apply to a registered corporation unless:

(1) The registered corporation is one described in section 2502(1)(ii) or (2) (relating to registered corporation status):

(2)(i) the bylaws, by amendment adopted either:

(A) by March 23, 1984; or

(B) on or after March 23, 1988, and on or before June 21, 1988; and, in either event, not subsequently rescinded by an article amendment, explicitly provide that this subchapter shall not be applicable to the corporation in the case of a corporation which on June 21, 1988, did not have outstanding one or more classes or series of preference shares entitled, upon the occurrence of a default in the payment of dividends or another similar contingency, to elect a majority of the members of the board of directors;

(ii) a bylaw adopted on or before June 21, 1988, by a corporation excluded from the scope of this paragraph by the restriction of subparagraph (i) relating to certain outstanding preference shares shall be ineffective unless ratified under paragraph (3);

(3) the bylaws of which explicitly provide that this subchapter shall not be applicable to the corporation by amendment ratified by the board of directors on or after (in printing this act in the Laws of Pennsylvania and the Pennsylvania Consolidated Statutes, the Legislative Reference Bureau shall insert here, in lieu of this statement, the date which is the date of enactment of this amendatory act) and on or before (in printing this act in the Laws of Pennsylvania and the Pennsylvania Consolidated Statutes, the Legislative Reference Bureau shall insert here, in lieu of this statement, the date which is 90 days after the date of enactment of this amendatory act) in the case of a corporation:

(i) which on June 21, 1988, had outstanding one or more classes or series of preference shares entitled, upon the occurrence of a default in the payment of dividends or another similar contingency, to elect a majority of the members of the board of directors; and

(ii) the bylaws of which on that date contained a provision described in paragraph (2); or

(4) The articles explicitly provide that this subchapter shall not be applicable to the corporation by a provision included in the original articles, by an article amendment adopted prior to the date of the control transaction and prior to or on March 23, 1988, pursuant to the procedures then applicable to the corporation, or by an articles amendment adopted prior to the date of the control transaction and subsequent to March 23, 1988, pursuant to both:

(i) The procedures then applicable to the corporation; and

(ii) Unless such proposed amendment has been approved by the board of directors of the corporation, in which event this subparagraph shall not be applicable, the affirmative vote of the shareholders entitled to cast at least 80% of the votes which all shareholders are entitled to cast thereon.

A reference in the articles or bylaws to former section 910 (relating to right of shareholders to receive payment for shares following a control transaction) of the act of May 5, 1933 (P.L. 364, No. 106), known as the Business Corporation Law of 1933, shall be deemed a reference to this subchapter for the purposes of this section. See section 101(c) (relating to references to prior statutes).

(b) Inadvertent transactions.—This subchapter shall not apply to any person or group that inadvertently becomes a controlling person or group if that controlling person or group, as soon as practicable, divests itself of a sufficient amount of its voting shares so that it is no longer a controlling person or group.

(c) Certain subsidiaries.—This subchapter shall not apply to any corporation that on December 23, 1983, was a subsidiary of any other corporation.

§ 2542. Definitions

The following words and phrases when used in this subchapter shall have the meanings given to them in this section unless the context clearly indicates otherwise:

"Control transaction." The acquisition by a person or group of the status of a controlling person or group.

"Controlling person or group." A controlling person or group as defined in section 2543 (relating to controlling person or group).

"Fair value." A value not less than the highest price paid per share by the controlling person or group at any time during the 90–day period ending on and including the date of the control transaction plus an increment representing any value, including, without limitation, any proportion of any value payable for acquisition of control of the corporation, that may not be reflected in such price.

"Partial payment amount." The amount per share specified in section 2545(c)(2) (relating to contents of notice).

"Subsidiary." Any corporation as to which any other corporation has or has the right to acquire, directly or indirectly, through the exercise of all warrants, options and rights and the conversion of all convertible securities, whether issued or granted by the subsidiary or otherwise, voting power over voting shares of the subsidiary that would entitle the holders thereof to cast in excess of 50% of the votes that all shareholders would be entitled to cast in the election of directors of such subsidiary, except that a subsidiary will not be deemed to cease being a subsidiary as long as such corporation remains a controlling person or group within the meaning of this subchapter.

"Voting shares." The term shall have the meaning specified in section 2552 (relating to definitions).

§ 2543. Controlling Person or Group

(a) General rule.—For the purpose of this subchapter, a "controlling person or group" means a person who has, or a group of persons acting in concert that has, voting power over voting shares of the registered corporation that would entitle the holders thereof to cast at least 20% of the votes that all shareholders would be entitled to cast in an election of directors of the corporation.

(b) Exceptions generally.—Notwithstanding subsection (a):

(1) A person or group which would otherwise be a controlling person or group within the meaning of this section shall not be deemed a controlling person or group unless, subsequent to the later of March 23, 1988, or the date this subchapter becomes applicable to a corporation by bylaw or article amendment or otherwise, that person or group increases the percentage of outstanding voting shares of the corporation over which it has voting power to in excess of the percentage of outstanding voting shares of the corporation over which that person or group had voting power on such later date, and to at least the amount specified in subsection (a), as the result of forming or enlarging a group or acquiring, by purchase, voting power over voting shares of the corporation.

(2) No person or group shall be deemed to be a controlling person or group at any particular time if voting power over any of the following voting shares is required to be counted at such time in order to meet the 20% minimum:

(i) Shares which have been held continuously by a natural person since January 1, 1983, and which are held by such natural person at such time.

(ii) Shares which are held at such time by any natural person or trust, estate, foundation or other similar entity to the extent the shares were acquired solely by gift, inheritance, bequest, devise or other testamentary distribution or series of these transactions, directly or indirectly, from a natural person who had acquired the shares prior to January 1, 1983.

(iii) Shares which were acquired pursuant to a stock split, stock dividend, reclassification or similar recapitalization with respect to shares described under this paragraph that have been held continuously since their issuance by the corporation by the natural person or entity that acquired them from the corporation or that were acquired, directly or indirectly, from such natural person or entity, solely pursuant to a transaction or series of transactions described in subparagraph (ii), and that are held at such time by a natural person or entity described in subparagraph (ii).

(iv) Control shares as defined in section 2562 (relating to definitions) which have not yet been accorded voting rights pursuant to section 2564(a) (relating to voting rights of shares acquired in a control-share acquisition).

(v) Shares, the voting rights of which are attributable to a person under subsection (d) if:

(A) the person acquired the option or conversion right directly from or made the contract, arrangement or understanding or has the relationship directly with the corporation; and

(B) the person does not at the particular time own or otherwise effectively possess the voting rights of the shares.

(vi) Shares acquired directly from the corporation or an affiliate or associate, as defined in section 2552 (relating to definitions), of the corporation by a person engaged in business as an underwriter of securities who acquires the shares through his participation in good faith in a firm commitment underwriting registered under the Securities Act of 1933.

(3) In determining whether a person or group is or would be a controlling person or group at any particular time, there shall be disregarded voting power arising from a contingent right of the holders of one or more classes or series of preference shares to elect one or more members of the board of directors upon or during the continuation of a default in the payment of dividends on such shares or another similar contingency.

(c) Certain record holders.—A person shall not be a controlling person under subsection (a) if the person holds voting power, in good faith and not for the purpose of circumventing this subchapter, as an agent, bank, broker, nominee or trustee for one or more beneficial owners who do not individually or, if they are a group acting in concert, as a group have the voting power specified in subsection (a), or who are not deemed a controlling person or group under subsection (b).

(d) Existence of voting power.—For the purposes of this subchapter, a person has voting power over a voting share if the person has or shares, directly or indirectly, through any option, contract, arrangement, understanding, conversion right or relationship, or by acting jointly or in concert or otherwise, the power to vote, or to direct the voting of, the voting share.

§ 2544. Right of Shareholders to Receive Payment for Shares

Any holder of voting shares of a registered corporation that becomes the subject of a control transaction who shall object to the transaction shall be entitled to the rights and remedies provided in this subchapter.

§ 2545. Notice to Shareholders

(a) General rule.—Prompt notice that a control transaction has occurred shall be given by the controlling person or group to:

(1) Each shareholder of record of the registered corporation holding voting shares.

(2) To the court, accompanied by a petition to the court praying that the fair value of the voting shares of the corporation be determined

pursuant to section 2547 (relating to valuation procedures) if the court should receive pursuant to section 2547 certificates from shareholders of the corporation or an equivalent request for transfer of uncertificated securities.

(b) Obligations of the corporation.—If the controlling person or group so requests, the corporation shall, at the option of the corporation and at the expense of the person or group, either furnish a list of all such shareholders to the person or group or mail the notice to all such shareholders.

(c) Contents of notice.—The notice shall state that:

(1) All shareholders are entitled to demand that they be paid the fair value of their shares.

(2) The minimum value the shareholder can receive under this subchapter is the highest price paid per share by the controlling person or group within the 90–day period ending on and including the date of the control transaction, and stating that value.

(3) If the shareholder believes the fair value of his shares is higher, that this subchapter provides an appraisal procedure for determining the fair value of such shares, specifying the name of the court and its address and the caption of the petition referenced in subsection (a)(2), and stating that the information is provided for the possible use by the shareholder in electing to proceed with a court-appointed appraiser under section 2547. There shall be included in, or enclosed with, the notice a copy of this subchapter.

(d) Optional procedure.—The controlling person or group may, at its option, supply with the notice referenced in subsection (c) a form for the shareholder to demand payment of the partial payment amount directly from the controlling person or group without utilizing the court-appointed appraiser procedure of section 2547, requiring the shareholder to state the number and class or series, if any, of the shares owned by him, and stating where the payment demand must be sent and the procedures to be followed.

§ 2546. Shareholder Demand for Fair Value

(a) General rule.—after the occurrence of the control transaction, any holder of voting shares of the registered corporation may, prior to or within a reasonable time after the notice required by section 2545 (relating to notice to shareholders) is given, which time period may be specified in the notice, make written demand on the controlling person or group for payment of the amount provided in subsection (c) with respect to the voting shares of the corporation held by the shareholder, and the controlling person or group shall be required to pay that amount to the shareholder pursuant to the procedures specified in section 2547 (relating to valuation procedures).

(b) Contents of demand.—The demand of the shareholder shall state the number and class or series, if any, of the shares owned by him with respect to which the demand is made.

(c) Measure of value.—A shareholder making written demand under this section shall be entitled to receive cash for each of his shares in an amount equal to the fair value of each voting share as of the date on which the control transaction occurs, taking into account all relevant factors, including an increment representing a proportion of any value payable for acquisition of control of the corporation.

(d) Purchases independent of subchapter.—The provisions of this subchapter shall not preclude a controlling person or group subject to this subchapter from offering, whether in the notice required by section 2545 or otherwise, to purchase voting shares of the corporation at a price other than that provided in subsection (c), and the provisions of this subchapter shall not preclude any shareholder from agreeing to sell his voting shares at that or any other price to any person.

§ 2547. Valuation Procedures

(a) General rule.—If, within 45 days (or such other time period, if any, as required by applicable law) after the date of the notice required by section 2545 (relating to notice to shareholders), or, if such notice was not provided prior to the date of the written demand by the shareholder under section 2546 (relating to shareholder demand for fair value), then within 45 days (or such other time period, if any, required by applicable law) of the date of such written demand, the controlling person or group and the shareholder are unable to agree on the fair value of the shares or on a binding procedure to determine the fair value of the shares, then each shareholder who is unable to agree on both the fair value and on such a procedure with the controlling person or group and who so desires to obtain the rights and remedies provided in this subchapter shall, no later than 30 days after the expiration of the applicable 45–day or other period, surrender to the court certificates representing any of the shares that are certificated shares, duly endorsed for transfer to the controlling person or group, or cause any uncertificated shares to be transferred to the court as escrow agent under subsection (c) with a notice stating that the certificates or uncertificated shares are being surrendered or transferred, as the case may be, in connection with the petition referenced in section 2545 or, if no petition has theretofore been filed, the shareholder may file a petition within the 30–day period in the court praying that the fair value (as defined in this subchapter) of the shares be determined.

(b) Effect of failure to give notice and surrender certificates.—Any shareholder who does not so give notice and surrender any certificates or cause uncertificated shares to be transferred within such time period shall have no further right to receive, with respect to shares the certificates of which were not so surrendered or the uncertificated shares which were not so transferred under this section, payment under this subchapter from the controlling person or group with respect to the control transaction giving rise to the rights of the shareholder under this subchapter.

(c) Escrow and notice.—The court shall hold the certificates surrendered and the uncertificated shares transferred to it in escrow for, and shall promptly, following the expiration of the time period during which the certificates may be surrendered and the uncertificated shares transferred, provide a notice to the controlling person or group of the number of shares so surrendered or transferred.

(d) Partial payment for shares.—The controlling person or group shall then make a partial payment for the shares so surrendered or transferred to the court, within ten business days of receipt of the notice from the court, at a per-share price equal to the partial payment amount. The court shall then make payment as soon as practicable, but in any event within ten business days, to the shareholders who so surrender or transfer their shares to the court of the appropriate per-share amount received from the controlling person or group.

(e) Appointment of appraiser.—Upon receipt of any share certificate surrendered or uncertificated share transferred under this section, the court shall, as soon as practicable but in any event within 30 days, appoint an appraiser with experience in appraising share values of companies of like nature to the registered corporation to determine the fair value of the shares.

(f) Appraisal procedure.—The appraiser so appointed by the court shall, as soon as reasonably practicable, determine the fair value of the shares subject to its appraisal and the appropriate market rate of interest on the amount then owed by the controlling person or group to the holders of the shares. The determination of any appraiser so appointed by the court shall be final and binding on both the controlling person or group and all shareholders who so surrendered their share certificates or transferred their shares to the court, except that the determination of the appraiser shall be subject to review to the extent and within the time provided or prescribed by law in the case of other appointed judicial officers. See 42 Pa.C.S. §§ 5105(a)(3) (relating to right to appellate review) and 5571(b) (relating to appeals generally).

(g) Supplemental payment.—Any amount owed, together with interest, as determined pursuant to the appraisal procedures of this section shall be payable by the controlling person or group after it is so determined and upon and concurrently with the delivery or transfer to the controlling person or group by the court (which shall make delivery of the certificate or certificates surrendered or the uncertificated shares transferred to it to the controlling person or group as soon as practicable but in any event within ten business days after the final determination of the amount owed) of the certificate or certificates representing shares surrendered or the uncertified shares transferred to the court, and the court shall then make payment, as soon as practicable but in any event within ten business days after receipt of payment from the controlling person or group, to the shareholders who so surrendered or transferred their shares to the court of the appropriate per-share amount received from the controlling person or group.

(h) Voting and dividend rights during appraisal proceedings.—Shareholders who surrender their shares to the court pursuant to this section shall retain the right to vote their shares and receive dividends or other distributions thereon until the court receives payment in full for each of the shares so surrendered or transferred of the partial payment amount (and, thereafter, the controlling person or group shall be entitled to vote such shares and receive dividends or other distributions thereon). The fair value (as determined by the appraiser) of any dividends or other distributions so received by the shareholders shall be subtracted from any amount owing to such shareholders under this section.

(i) Powers of the court.—The court may appoint such agents, including the transfer agent of the corporation, or any other institution, to hold the share certificates so surrendered and the shares surrendered or transferred under this section, to effect any necessary change in record ownership of the shares after the payment by the controlling person or group to the court of the amount specified in subsection (h), to receive and disburse dividends or other distributions, to provide notices to shareholders and to take such other actions as the court determines are appropriate to effect the purposes of this subchapter.

(j) Costs and expenses.—The costs and expenses of any appraiser or other agents appointed by the court shall be assessed against the controlling person or group. The costs and expenses of any other procedure to determine fair value shall be paid as agreed to by the parties agreeing to the procedure.

(k) Jurisdiction exclusive.—The jurisdiction of the court under this subchapter is plenary and exclusive and the controlling person or group and all shareholders who so surrendered or transferred their shares to the court shall be made a party to the proceeding as in an action against their shares.

(*l*) Duty of corporation.—The corporation shall comply with requests for information, which may be submitted pursuant to procedures maintaining the confidentiality of the information, made by the court or the appraiser selected by the court. If any of the shares of the corporation are not represented by certificates, the transfer, escrow or retransfer of those shares contemplated by this section shall be registered by the corporation, which shall give the written notice required by section 1528(f) (relating to uncertificated shares) to the transferring shareholder, the court and the controlling shareholder or group, as appropriate in the circumstances.

(m) Payment under optional procedure.—Any amount agreed upon between the parties or determined pursuant to the procedure agreed upon between the parties shall be payable by the controlling person or group after it is agreed upon or determined and upon and concurrently with the delivery of any certificate or certificates representing such shares or the transfer of any uncertificated shares to the controlling person or group by the shareholder.

(n) Title to shares.—Upon full payment by the controlling person or group of the amount owed to the shareholder or to the court, as appropriate, the shareholder shall cease to have any interest in the shares.

§ 2548. Coordination With Control Transaction

(a) General rule.—A person or group that proposes to engage in a control transaction may comply with the requirements of this subchapter in connection with the control transaction, and the effectiveness of the rights afforded in this subchapter to shareholders may be conditioned upon the consummation of the control transaction.

(b) Notice.—The person or group shall give prompt written notice of the satisfaction of any such condition to each shareholder who has made demand as provided in this subchapter.

SUBCHAPTER F. BUSINESS COMBINATIONS

§ 2551. Application and Effect of Subchapter

(a) General rule.—Except as otherwise provided in this section, this subchapter shall apply to every registered corporation.

(b) Exceptions.—The provisions of this subchapter shall not apply to any business combination:

(1) Of a registered corporation described in section 2502(1)(ii) or (2) (relating to registered corporation status).

(2) Of a corporation whose articles have been amended to provide that the corporation shall be subject to the provisions of this subchapter, which was not a registered corporation described in section 2502(1)(i) on the effective date of such amendment, and which is a business combination with an interested shareholder whose share acquisition date is prior to the effective date of such amendment.

(3) Of a corporation:

(i) The bylaws of which, by amendment adopted by June 21, 1988, and not subsequently rescinded either by an article amendment or by a bylaw amendment approved by at least 85% of the whole board of directors, explicitly provide that this subchapter shall not be applicable to the corporation; or

(ii) The articles of which explicitly provide that this subchapter shall not be applicable to the corporation by a provision included in the original articles, or by an article amendment adopted pursuant to both:

(A) The procedures then applicable to the corporation; and

(B) The affirmative vote of the holders, other than interested shareholders and their affiliates and associates, of shares entitling the holders to cast a majority of the votes that all shareholders would be entitled to cast in an election of directors of the corporation, excluding the voting shares of interested shareholders and their affiliates and associates, expressly electing not to be governed by this subchapter.

The amendment to the articles shall not be effective until 18 months after the vote of the shareholders of the corporation and shall not apply to any business combination of the corporation with an interested shareholder whose share acquisition date is on or prior to the effective date of the amendment.

(4) Of a corporation with an interested shareholder of the corporation which became an interested shareholder inadvertently, if the interested shareholder:

(i) As soon as practicable, divests itself of a sufficient amount of the voting shares of the corporation so that it no longer is the beneficial owner, directly or indirectly, of shares entitling the person to cast at least 20% of the votes that all shareholders would be entitled to cast in an election of directors of the corporation; and

(ii) Would not at any time within the five-year period preceding the announcement date with respect to the business combination have been an interested shareholder but for such inadvertent acquisition.

(5) With an interested shareholder who was the beneficial owner, directly or indirectly, of shares entitling the person to cast at least 15% of the votes that all shareholders would be entitled to cast in an election of directors of the corporation on March 23, 1988, and remains so to the share acquisition date of the interested shareholder.

(6) Of a corporation that on March 23, 1988, was a subsidiary of any other corporation. A corporation that was a subsidiary on such date will not be deemed to cease being a subsidiary as long as the other corporation remains a controlling person or group of the subsidiary within the meaning of subchapter E (relating to control transactions). A reference in the articles or bylaws to former section 911 (relating to requirements relating to certain business combinations) of the act of May 5, 1933 (P.L. 364, No. 106), known as the business corporation law of 1933, shall be deemed a reference to this subchapter for the purposes of this section. See section 101(c) (relating to references to prior statutes).

(c) Continued applicability.—A registered corporation that is organized under the laws of this commonwealth shall not cease to be subject to this subchapter by reason of events occurring or actions taken while the corporation is subject to the provisions of this subchapter. See section 4146 (relating to provisions applicable to all foreign corporations).

§ 2552. Definitions

The following words and phrases when used in this subchapter shall have the meanings given to them in this section unless the context clearly indicates otherwise:

"Affiliate." A person that directly, or indirectly through one or more intermediaries, controls, or is controlled by, or is under common control with, a specified person.

"Announcement date." When used in reference to any business combination, the date of the first public announcement of the final, definitive proposal for such business combination.

"Associate." When used to indicate a relationship with any person:

(1) Any corporation or organization of which such person is an officer, director or partner or is, directly or indirectly, the beneficial owner of shares entitling that person to cast at least 10% of the votes that all shareholders would be entitled to cast in an election of directors of the corporation or organization;

(2) Any trust or other estate in which such person has a substantial beneficial interest or as to which such person serves as trustee or in a similar fiduciary capacity; and

(3) Any relative or spouse of such person, or any relative of the spouse, who has the same home as such person.

"Beneficial owner." When used with respect to any shares, a person:

(1) That, individually or with or through any of its affiliates or associates, beneficially owns such shares, directly or indirectly:

(2) That, individually or with or through any of its affiliates or associates, has:

(i) The right to acquire such shares (whether the right is exercisable immediately or only after the passage of time), pursuant to any agreement, arrangement or understanding (whether or not in writing), or upon the exercise of conversion rights, exchange rights, warrants or options, or otherwise, except that a person shall not be deemed the beneficial owner of shares tendered pursuant to a tender or exchange offer made by such person or the affiliates or associates of any such person until the tendered shares are accepted for purchase or exchange; or

(ii) The right to vote such shares pursuant to any agreement, arrangement or understanding (whether or not in writing), except that a person shall not be deemed the beneficial owner of any shares under this subparagraph if the agreement, arrangement or understanding to vote such shares:

(A) Arises solely from a revocable proxy or consent given in response to a proxy or consent solicitation made in accordance with the applicable rules and regulations under the Exchange Act; and

(B) Is not then reportable on a schedule 13D under the Exchange Act (or any comparable or successor report); or

(3) That has any agreement, arrangement or understanding (whether or not in writing), for the purpose of acquiring, holding, voting (except voting pursuant to a revocable proxy or consent as described in paragraph (2)(II)), or disposing of such shares with any other person that beneficially owns, or whose affiliates or associates beneficially own, directly or indirectly, such shares.

"Business combination." A business combination as defined in section 2554 (relating to business combination).

"Common shares." Any shares other than preferred shares.

"Consummation date." With respect to any business combination, the date of consummation of the business combination, or, in the case of a business combination as to which a shareholder vote is taken, the later of the business day prior to the vote or 20 days prior to the date of consummation of such business combination.

"Control," "controlling," "controlled by" or "under common control with." The possession, directly or indirectly, of the power to direct or cause the direction of the management and policies of a person, whether through the ownership of voting shares, by contract, or otherwise. A person's beneficial ownership of shares entitling that person to cast at least 10% of the votes that all shareholders would be entitled to cast in an election of directors of the corporation shall create a presumption that such person has control of the corporation. Notwithstanding the foregoing, a person shall not be deemed to have control of a corporation if such person holds voting shares, in good faith and not for the purpose of circumventing this subchapter, as an agent, bank, broker, nominee, custodian or trustee for one or more beneficial owners who do not individually or as a group have control of the corporation.

"Interested shareholder." An interested shareholder as defined in section 2553 (relating to interested shareholder).

"Market value." When used in reference to shares or property of any corporation:

(1) In the case of shares, the highest closing sale price during the 30–day period immediately preceding the date in question of the share

on the composite tape for New York Stock Exchange-listed shares, or, if the shares are not quoted on the composite tape or if the shares are not listed on the exchange, on the principal United States securities exchange registered under the Exchange Act, on which such shares are listed, or, if the shares are not listed on any such exchange, the highest closing bid quotation with respect to the share during the 30–day period preceding the date in question on the National Association of Securities Dealers, Inc. Automated Quotations System or any system then in use, or if no quotations are available, the fair market value on the date in question of the share as determined by the board of directors of the corporation in good faith.

(2) In the case of property other than cash or shares, the fair market value of the property on the date in question as determined by the board of directors of the corporation in good faith.

"Preferred shares." Any class or series of shares of a corporation which, under the bylaws or articles of the corporation, is entitled to receive payment of dividends prior to any payment of dividends on some other class or series of shares, or is entitled in the event of any voluntary liquidation, dissolution or winding up of the corporation to receive payment or distribution of a preferential amount before any payments or distributions are received by some other class or series of shares.

"Share acquisition date." With respect to any person and any registered corporation, the date that such person first becomes an interested shareholder of such corporation.

"Shares." (1) Any shares or similar security, any certificate of interest, any participation in any profit-sharing agreement, any voting trust certificate, or any certificate of deposit for shares.

(2) Any security convertible, with or without consideration, into shares, or any option right, conversion right or privilege of buying shares without being bound to do so, or any other security carrying any right to acquire, subscribe to or purchase shares.

"Subsidiary." Any corporation as to which any other corporation is the beneficial owner, directly or indirectly, of shares of the first corporation that would entitle the other corporation to cast in excess of 50% of the votes that all shareholders would be entitled to cast in the election of directors of the first corporation.

"Voting shares." Shares of a corporation entitled to vote generally in the election of directors.

§ 2553. Interested Shareholder

(a) General rule.—The term "interested shareholder," when used in reference to any registered corporation, means any person (other than the corporation or any subsidiary of the corporation) that:

(1) Is the beneficial owner, directly or indirectly, of shares entitling that person to cast at least 20% of the votes that all shareholders would be entitled to cast in an election of directors of the corporation; or

(2) Is an affiliate or associate of such corporation and at any time within the five-year period immediately prior to the date in question was the beneficial owner, directly or indirectly, of shares entitling that person to cast at least 20% of the votes that all shareholders would be entitled to cast in an election of directors of the corporation.

(b) Exception.—For the purpose of determining whether a person is an interested shareholder:

(1) The number of votes that would be entitled to be cast in an election of directors of the corporation shall be calculated by including shares deemed to be beneficially owned by the person through application of the definition of "beneficial owner" in section 2552 (relating to definitions), but excluding any other unissued shares of such corporation which may be issuable pursuant to any agreement, arrangement or understanding, or upon exercise of conversion or option rights, or otherwise; and

(2) There shall be excluded from the beneficial ownership of the interested shareholder any:

(i) Shares which have been held continuously by a natural person since January 1, 1983, and which are then held by that natural person;

(ii) Shares which are then held by any natural person or trust, estate, foundation or other similar entity to the extent such shares were acquired solely by gift, inheritance, bequest, devise or other testamentary distribution or series of those transactions, directly or indirectly, from a natural person who had acquired such shares prior to January 1, 1983; or

(iii) Shares which were acquired pursuant to a stock split, stock dividend, reclassification or similar recapitalization with respect to shares described under this paragraph that have been held continuously since their issuance by the corporation by the natural person or entity that acquired them from the corporation, or that were acquired, directly or indirectly, from the natural person or entity, solely pursuant to a transaction or series of transactions described in subparagraph (ii), and that are then held by a natural person or entity described in subparagraph (ii).

§ 2554. Business Combination

The term "business combination," when used in reference to any registered corporation and any interested shareholder of the corporation, means any of the following:

(1) A merger, consolidation, share exchange or division of the corporation or any subsidiary of the corporation:

(i) with the interested shareholder; or

(ii) with, involving or resulting in any other corporation (whether or not itself an interested shareholder of the registered corporation) which is, or after the merger, consolidation, share exchange or division would be, an affiliate or associate of the interested shareholder.

(2) A sale, lease, exchange, mortgage, pledge, transfer or other disposition (in one transaction or a series of transactions) to or with the interested shareholders or any affiliate or associate of such interested shareholder of assets of the corporation or any subsidiary of the corporation:

(i) Having an aggregate market value equal to 10% or more of the aggregate market value of all the assets, determined on a consolidated basis, of such corporation;

(ii) Having an aggregate market value equal to 10% or more of the aggregate market value of all the outstanding shares of such corporation; or

(iii) Representing 10% or more of the earning power or net income, determined on a consolidated basis, of such corporation.

(3) The issuance or transfer by the corporation or any subsidiary of the corporation (in one transaction or a series of transactions) of any shares of such corporation or any subsidiary of such corporation which has an aggregate market value equal to 5% or more of the aggregate market value of all the outstanding shares of the corporation to the interested shareholder or any affiliate or associate of such interested shareholder except pursuant to the exercise of option rights to purchase shares, or pursuant to the conversion of securities having conversion rights, offered, or a dividend or distribution paid or made, pro rata to all shareholders of the corporation.

(4) The adoption of any plan or proposal for the liquidation or dissolution of the corporation proposed by, or pursuant to, any agreement, arrangement or understanding (whether or not in writing) with the interested shareholder or any affiliate or associate of such interested shareholder.

(5) A reclassification of securities (including, without limitation, any split of shares, dividend of shares, or other distribution of shares in respect of shares, or any reverse split of shares), or recapitalization of the corporation, or any merger or consolidation of the corporation with any subsidiary of the corporation, or any other transaction (whether or not with or into or otherwise involving the interested shareholder), proposed by, or pursuant to, any agreement, arrangement or understanding (whether or not in writing) with the interested shareholder or any affiliate or associate of the interested shareholder, which has the effect, directly or indirectly, of increasing the proportionate share of the outstanding shares of any class or series of voting shares or securities

convertible into voting shares of the corporation or any subsidiary of the corporation which is, directly or indirectly, owned by the interested shareholder or any affiliate or associate of the interested shareholder, except as a result of immaterial changes due to fractional share adjustments.

(6) The receipt by the interested shareholder or any affiliate or associate of the interested shareholder of the benefit, directly or indirectly (except proportionately as a shareholder of such corporation), of any loans, advances, guarantees, pledges or other financial assistance or any tax credits or other tax advantages provided by or through the corporation.

§ 2555. Requirements Relating to Certain Business Combinations

Notwithstanding anything to the contrary contained in this subpart (except the provisions of section 2551 (relating to application and effect of subchapter)), a registered corporation shall not engage at any time in any business combination with any interested shareholder of the corporation other than:

(1) A business combination approved by the board of directors of the corporation prior to the interested shareholder's share acquisition date, or where the purchase of shares made by the interested shareholder on the interested shareholder's share acquisition date had been approved by the board of directors of the corporation prior to the interested shareholder's share acquisition date.

(2) A business combination approved:

(i) By the affirmative vote of the holders of shares entitling such holders to cast a majority of the votes that all shareholders would be entitled to cast in an election of directors of the corporation, not including any voting shares beneficially owned by the interested shareholder or any affiliate or associate of such interested shareholder, at a meeting called for such purpose no earlier than three months after the interested shareholder became, and if at the time of the meeting the interested shareholder is, the beneficial owner, directly or indirectly, of shares entitling the interested shareholder to cast at least 80% of the votes that all shareholders would be entitled to cast in an election of directors of the corporation, and if the business combination satisfies all the conditions of section 2556 (relating to certain minimum conditions); or

(ii) By the affirmative vote of all of the holders of all of the outstanding common shares.

(3) A business combination approved by the affirmative vote of the holders of shares entitling such holders to cast a majority of the votes that all shareholders would be entitled to cast in an election of directors

of the corporation, not including any voting shares beneficially owned by the interested shareholder or any affiliate or associate of the interested shareholder, at a meeting called for such purpose no earlier than five years after the interested shareholder's share acquisition date.

(4) A business combination approved at a shareholders' meeting called for such purpose no earlier than five years after the interested shareholder's share acquisition date that meets all of the conditions of section 2556.

§ 2556. Certain Minimum Conditions

A business combination conforming to section 2555(2)(I) or (4) (relating to requirements relating to certain business combinations) shall meet all of the following conditions:

(1) The aggregate amount of the cash and the market value as of the consummation date of consideration other than cash to be received per share by holders of outstanding common shares of such registered corporation in the business combination is at least equal to the higher of the following:

(i) The highest per share price paid by the interested shareholder at a time when the shareholder was the beneficial owner, directly or indirectly, of shares entitling that person to cast at least 5% of the votes that all shareholders would be entitled to cast in an election of directors of the corporation, for any common shares of the same class or series acquired by it:

(A) Within the five-year period immediately prior to the announcement date with respect to such business combination; or

(B) Within the five-year period immediately prior to, or in, the transaction in which the interested shareholder became an interested shareholder;

whichever is higher; plus, in either case, interest compounded annually from the earliest date on which the highest per-share acquisition price was paid through the consummation date at the rate for one-year United States treasury obligations from time to time in effect; less the aggregate amount of any cash dividends paid, and the market value of any dividends paid other than in cash, per common share since such earliest date, up to the amount of the interest.

(ii) The market value per common share on the announcement date with respect to the business combination or on the interested shareholder's share acquisition date, whichever is higher; plus interest compounded annually from such date through the consummation date at the rate for one-year United States treasury obligations from time to time in effect; less the aggregate amount of any cash dividends paid, and the market value of any dividends paid other than in cash, per common share since such date, up to the amount of the interest.

(2) The aggregate amount of the cash and the market value as of the consummation date of consideration other than cash to be received per share by holders of outstanding shares of any class or series of shares, other than common shares, of the corporation is at least equal to the highest of the following (whether or not the interested shareholder has previously acquired any shares of such class or series of shares):

(i) The highest per-share price paid by the interested shareholder at a time when the shareholder was the beneficial owner, directly or indirectly, of shares entitling that person to cast at least 5% of the votes that all shareholders would be entitled to cast in an election of directors of such corporation, for any shares of such class or series of shares acquired by it;

(A) Within the five-year period immediately prior to the announcement date with respect to the business combination; or

(B) Within the five-year period immediately prior to, or in, the transaction in which the interested shareholder became an interested shareholder;

whichever is higher; plus, in either case, interest compounded annually from the earliest date on which the highest per-share acquisition price was paid through the consummation date at the rate for one-year United States treasury obligations from time to time in effect; less the aggregate amount of any cash dividends paid, and the market value of any dividends paid other than in cash, per share of such class or series of shares since such earliest date, up to the amount of the interest.

(ii) The highest preferential amount per share to which the holders of shares of such class or series of shares are entitled in the event of any voluntary liquidation, dissolution or winding up of the corporation, plus the aggregate amount of any dividends declared or due as to which such holders are entitled prior to payment of dividends on some other class or series of shares (unless the aggregate amount of the dividends is included in such preferential amount).

(iii) The market value per share of such class or series of shares on the announcement date with respect to the business combination or on the interested shareholder's share acquisition date, whichever is higher; plus interest compounded annually from such date through the consummation date at the rate for one-year United States treasury obligations from time to time in effect; less the aggregate amount of any cash dividends paid and the market value of any dividends paid other than in cash, per share of such class or series of shares since such date, up to the amount of the interest.

(3) The consideration to be received by holders of a particular class or series of outstanding shares (including common shares) of the corporation in the business combination is in cash or in the same form as the

interested shareholder has used to acquire the largest number of shares of such class or series of shares previously acquired by it, and the consideration shall be distributed promptly.

(4) The holders of all outstanding shares of the corporation not beneficially owned by the interested shareholder immediately prior to the consummation of the business combination are entitled to receive in the business combination cash or other consideration for such shares in compliance with paragraphs (1), (2) and (3).

(5) After the interested shareholder's share acquisition date and prior to the consummation date with respect to the business combination, the interested shareholder has not become the beneficial owner of any additional voting shares of such corporation except:

(i) As part of the transaction which resulted in such interested shareholder becoming an interested shareholder;

(ii) By virtue of proportionate splits of shares, share dividends or other distributions of shares in respect of shares not constituting a business combination as defined in this subchapter;

(iii) Through a business combination meeting all of the conditions of section 2555(1), (2), (3) or (4);

(iv) Through purchase by the interested shareholder at any price which, if the price had been paid in an otherwise permissible business combination the announcement date and consummation date of which were the date of such purchase, would have satisfied the requirements of paragraphs (1), (2) and (3); or

(v) Through purchase required by and pursuant to the provisions of, and at no less than the fair value (including interest to the date of payment) as determined by a court-appointed appraiser under section 2547 (relating to valuation procedures) or, if such fair value was not then so determined, then at a price that would satisfy the conditions in subparagraph (iv).

SUBCHAPTER G. CONTROL–SHARE ACQUISITIONS

§ 2561. Application and Effect of Subchapter

(a) General rule.—Except as otherwise provided in this section, this subchapter shall apply to every registered corporation.

(b) Exceptions.—This subchapter shall not apply to any control-share acquisition:

(1) Of a registered corporation described in section 2502(1)(ii) or (2) (relating to registered corporation status).

(2) Of a corporation:

(i)(A) the bylaws of which explicitly provide that this subchapter shall not be applicable to the corporation by amendment adopted by the board of directors on or before July 26, 1990, in the case of a corporation:

(I) which on April 27, 1990, was a registered corporation described in section 2502(1)(i); and

(II) did not on that date have outstanding one or more classes or series of preference shares entitled, upon the occurrence of a default in the payment of dividends or another similar contingency, to elect a majority of the members of the board of directors;

(B) a bylaw adopted on or before July 26, 1990, by a corporation excluded from the scope of this subparagraph by clause (A)(II) shall be ineffective unless ratified under subparagraph (ii);

(ii) the bylaws of which explicitly provide that this subchapter shall not be applicable to the corporation by amendment ratified by the board of directors on or after (in printing this act in the Laws of Pennsylvania and the Pennsylvania Consolidated Statutes, the Legislative Reference Bureau shall insert here, in lieu of this statement, the date which is the date of enactment of this amendatory act) and on or before (in printing this act in the Laws of Pennsylvania and the Pennsylvania Consolidated Statutes, the Legislative Reference Bureau shall insert here, in lieu of this statement, the date which is 90 days after the date of enactment of this amendatory act) in the case of a corporation:

(A) which on April 27, 1990, was a registered corporation described in section 2502(1)(i);

(B) which on that date had outstanding one or more classes or series of preference shares entitled, upon the occurrence of a default in the payment of dividends or another similar contingency, to elect a majority of the members of the board of directors; and

(C) the bylaws of which on that date contained a provision described in subparagraph (i); or

(iii) in any other case, the articles of which explicitly provide that this subchapter shall not be applicable to the corporation by a provision included in the original articles, or by an articles amendment adopted at any time while it is a corporation other than a registered corporation described in section 2502(1)(i) or on or before 90 days after the corporation first becomes a registered corporation described in section 2502(1)(i).

(3) Consummated before October 17, 1989.

(4) Consummated pursuant to contractual rights or obligations existing before:

(i) October 17, 1989, in the case of a corporation which was a registered corporation described in section 2502(1)(i) on that date; or

(ii) in any other case, the date this subchapter becomes applicable to the corporation.

(5) Consummated:

(i) Pursuant to a gift, devise, bequest or otherwise through the laws of inheritance or descent.

(ii) By a settlor to a trustee under the terms of a family, testamentary or charitable trust.

(iii) By a trustee to a trust beneficiary or a trustee to a successor trustee under the terms of, or the addition, withdrawal or demise of a beneficiary or beneficiaries of, a family, testamentary or charitable trust.

(iv) Pursuant to the appointment of a guardian or custodian.

(v) Pursuant to a transfer from one spouse to another by reason of separation or divorce or pursuant to community property laws or other similar laws of any jurisdiction.

(vi) Pursuant to the satisfaction of a pledge or other security interest created in good faith and not for the purpose of circumventing this subchapter.

(vii) Pursuant to a merger, consolidation or plan of share exchange effected in compliance with the provisions of this chapter if the corporation is a party to the agreement of merger, consolidation or plan of share exchange.

(viii) Pursuant to a transfer from a person who beneficially owns voting shares of the corporation that would entitle the holder thereof to cast at least 20% of the votes that all shareholders would be entitled to cast in an election of directors of the corporation and who acquired beneficial ownership of such shares prior to October 17, 1989.

(ix) By the corporation or any of its subsidiaries.

(x) By any savings, stock ownership, stock option or other benefit plan of the corporation or any of its subsidiaries, or by any fiduciary with respect to any such plan when acting in such capacity.

(xi) By a person engaged in business as an underwriter of securities who acquires the shares directly from the corporation or an affiliate or associate of the corporation through his participation in good faith in a firm commitment underwriting registered under the Securities Act of 1933.

(xii) Or commenced by a person who first became an acquiring person:

(A) after April 27, 1990; and

(B)(I) at a time when this subchapter was or is not applicable to the corporation; or

(II) on or before ten business days after the first public announcement by the corporation that this subchapter is applicable to the corporation, if this subchapter was not applicable to the corporation on July 27, 1990.

(c) Effect of distributions.—For purposes of this subchapter, voting shares of a corporation acquired by a holder as a result of a stock split, stock dividend or other similar distribution by a corporation of voting shares issued by the corporation and not involving a sale of such voting shares shall be deemed to have been acquired by the holder in the same transaction (at the same time, in the same manner and from the same person) in which the holder acquired the shares with respect to which such voting shares were subsequently distributed by the corporation.

(d) Status of certain shares and effect of formation of group on status.—(1) No share over which voting power, or of which beneficial ownership, was or is acquired by the acquiring person in or in connection with a control-share acquisition described in subsection (b) shall be deemed to be a control share.

(2) In the case of affiliate, disinterested or existing shares, the acquisition of a beneficial ownership interest in a voting share by a group shall not, by itself, affect the status of an affiliate, disinterested or existing share, as such, if and so long as the person who had beneficial ownership of the share immediately prior to the acquisition of the beneficial ownership interest in the share by the group (or a direct or indirect transferee from the person to the extent such shares were acquired by the transferee solely pursuant to a transfer or series of transfers under subsection (b)(5)(i) through (vi)):

(i) is a participant in the group; and

(ii) continues to have at least the same voting and dispositive power over the share as the person had immediately prior to the acquisition of the beneficial ownership interest in the share by the group.

(3) Voting shares which are beneficially owned by a person described in paragraph (1), (2) or (3) of the definition of "affiliate shares" in section 2562 (relating to definitions) shall continue to be deemed affiliate shares, notwithstanding paragraph (2) of this subsection or the fact that such shares are also beneficially owned by a group.

(4) No share of a corporation over which voting power, or of which beneficial ownership, was or is acquired by the acquiring person after April 27, 1990, at a time when this subchapter was or is not applicable to the corporation shall be deemed to be a control share.

(e) Application of duties.—The duty of the board of directors, committees of the board and individual directors under section 2565 (relating to procedure for establishing voting rights of control shares) is solely to the corporation and may be enforced directly by the corporation or may be enforced by a shareholder, as such, by an action in the right of the corporation, and may not be enforced directly by a shareholder or by any other person or group.

§ 2562. Definitions

The following words and phrases when used in this subchapter shall have the meanings given to them in this section unless the context clearly indicates otherwise:

"Acquiring person." A person who makes or proposes to make a control-share acquisition. Two or more persons acting in concert, whether or not pursuant to an express agreement, arrangement, relationship or understanding, including as a partnership, limited partnership, syndicate, or through any means of affiliation whether or not formally organized, for the purpose of acquiring, holding, voting or disposing of shares of a registered corporation, shall also constitute a person for the purposes of this subchapter. A person, together with its affiliates and associates, shall constitute a person for the purposes of this subchapter.

"Affiliate," "associate" and "beneficial owner." The terms shall have the meanings specified in section 2552 (relating to definitions). The corporation may adopt reasonable provisions to evidence beneficial ownership, specifically including requirements that holders of voting shares of the corporation provide verified statements evidencing beneficial ownership and attesting to the date of acquisition thereof.

"Affiliate shares." All voting shares of a corporation beneficially owned by:

(1) an acquiring person;

(2) executive officers or directors who are also officers (including executive officers); or

(3) employee stock plans in which employee participants do not have, under the terms of the plan, the right to direct confidentially the manner in which shares held by the plan for the benefit of the employee will be voted in connection with the consideration of the voting rights to be accorded control shares.

The term does not include existing shares beneficially owned by executive officers or directors who are also officers (including executive officers) if the shares are shares described in paragraph (2) of the definition of "existing shares" that were beneficially owned continuously by the same person or entity described in such paragraph since January 1, 1988, or are shares described in paragraph (3) of that definition that were acquired with respect to such existing shares.

"Control." The term shall have the meaning specified in section 2573 (relating to definitions).

"Control-share acquisition." An acquisition, directly or indirectly, by any person of voting power over voting shares of a corporation that, but for this subchapter, would, when added to all voting power of the person over other voting shares of the corporation (exclusive of voting power of the person with respect to existing shares of the corporation), entitle the person to cast or direct the casting of such a percentage of the votes for the first time with respect to any of the following ranges that all shareholders would be entitled to cast in an election of directors of the corporation:

(1) at least 20% but less than 33⅓%;

(2) at least 33⅓ but less than 50%; or

(3) 50% or more.

"Control shares." Those voting shares of a corporation that, upon acquisition of voting power over such shares by an acquiring person, would result in a control-share acquisition. Voting shares beneficially owned by an acquiring person shall also be deemed to be control shares where such beneficial ownership was acquired by the acquiring person:

(1) within 180 days of the day the person makes a control-share acquisition; or

(2) with the intention of making a control-share acquisition.

"Disinterested shares." All voting shares of a corporation that are not affiliate shares and that were beneficially owned by the same holder (or a direct or indirect transferee from the holder to the extent such shares were acquired by the transferee solely pursuant to a transfer or series of transfers under section 2561(b)(5)(i) through (vi) (relating to application and effect of subchapter)) continuously during the period from:

(1) the last to occur of the following dates:

(i) 12 months preceding the record date described in paragraph (2);

(ii) five business days prior to the date on which there is first publicly disclosed or caused to be disclosed information that there is a person (including the acquiring person) who intends to engage or may seek to engage in a control-share acquisition or that there is a person (including the acquiring person) who has acquired shares as part of, or with the intent of making, a control-share acquisition, as determined by the board of directors of the corporation in good faith considering all the evidence that the board deems to be relevant to such determination, including, without limitation, media reports, share trading volume and changes in share prices; or

(iii)(A) October 17, 1989, in the case of a corporation which was a registered corporation on that date; or

(B) in any other case, the date this subchapter becomes applicable to the corporation; through

(2) the record date established pursuant to section 2565(c) (relating to notice and record date).

"Executive officer." When used with reference to a corporation, the president, any vice-president in charge of a principal business unit, division or function (such as sales, administration or finance), any other officer who performs a policy-making function or any other person who performs similar policy-making functions. Executive officers of subsidiaries shall be deemed executive officers of the corporation if they perform such policy-making functions for the corporation.

"Existing shares."

(1) Voting shares which have been beneficially owned continuously by the same natural person since January 1, 1988.

(2) Voting shares which are beneficially owned by any natural person or trust, estate, foundation or other similar entity to the extent the voting shares were acquired solely by gift, inheritance, bequest, devise or other testamentary distribution or series of these transactions, directly or indirectly, from a natural person who had beneficially owned the voting shares prior to January 1, 1988.

(3) Voting shares which were acquired pursuant to a stock split, stock dividend, or other similar distribution described in section 2561(c) (relating to effect of distributions) with respect to existing shares that have been beneficially owned continuously since their issuance by the corporation by the natural person or entity that acquired them from the corporation or that were acquired, directly or indirectly, from such natural person or entity, solely pursuant to a transaction or series of transactions described in paragraph (2), and that are held at such time by a natural person or entity described in paragraph (2).

"Proxy." Includes any proxy, consent or authorization.

"Proxy solicitation" or "Solicitation of proxies." Includes any solicitation of a proxy, including a solicitation of a revocable proxy of the nature and under the circumstances described in section 2563(b)(3) (relating to acquiring person safe harbor).

"Publicly disclosed or caused to be disclosed." Includes, but is not limited to, any disclosure (whether or not required by law) that becomes public made by a person:

(1) with the intent or expectation that such disclosure become public; or

(2) to another where the disclosing person knows, or reasonably should have known, that the receiving person was not under an obligation to refrain from making such disclosure, directly or indirectly, to the public and such receiving person does make such disclosure, directly or indirectly, to the public.

"Voting shares." The term shall have the meaning specified in section 2552 (relating to definitions).

§ 2563. Acquiring Person Safe Harbor

(a) Nonparticipant.—For the purposes of this subchapter, a person shall not be deemed an acquiring person, absent significant other activities indicating that a person should be deemed an acquiring person, by reason of voting or giving a proxy or consent as a shareholder of the corporation if the person is one who:

(1) did not acquire any voting shares of the corporation with the purpose of changing or influencing control of the corporation, seeking to acquire control of the corporation or influencing the outcome of a vote of shareholders under section 2564 (relating to voting rights of shares acquired in a control-share acquisition) or in connection with or as a participant in any agreement, arrangement, relationship, understanding or otherwise having any such purpose;

(2) if the control-share acquisition were consummated, would not be a person that has control over the corporation and will not receive, directly or indirectly, any consideration from a person that has control over the corporation other than consideration offered proportionately to all holders of voting shares of the corporation; and

(3) if a proxy or consent is given, executes a revocable proxy or consent given without consideration in response to a proxy or consent solicitation made in accordance with the applicable rules and regulations under the Exchange Act under circumstances not then reportable on Schedule 13D under the Exchange Act (or any comparable or successor report) by the person who gave the proxy or consent.

(b) Certain holders.—For the purpose of this subchapter, a person shall not be deemed an acquiring person if such person holds voting power within any of the ranges specified in the definition of "control-share acquisition":

(1) in good faith and not for the purpose of circumventing this subchapter, as an agent, bank, broker, nominee or trustee for one or more beneficial owners who do not individually or, if they are a group acting in concert, as a group have the voting power specified in any of the ranges in the definition of "control-share acquisition";

(2) in connection with the solicitation of proxies or consents by or on behalf of the corporation in connection with shareholder meetings or actions of the corporation;

(3) as a result of the solicitation of revocable proxies or consents with respect to voting shares if such proxies or consents both:

(i) are given without consideration in response to a proxy or consent solicitation made in accordance with the applicable rules and regulations under the Exchange Act; and

(ii) do not empower the holder thereof, whether or not this power is shared with any other person, to vote such shares except on the specific matters described in such proxy or consent and in accordance with the instructions of the giver of such proxy or consent; or

(4) to the extent of voting power arising from a contingent right of the holders of one or more classes or series of preference shares to elect one or more members of the board of directors upon or during the continuation of a default in the payment of dividends on such shares or another similar contingency.

§ 2564. Voting Rights of Shares Acquired in a Control–Share Acquisition

(a) General rule.—Control shares shall not have any voting rights unless a resolution approved by a vote of shareholders of the registered corporation at an annual or special meeting of shareholders pursuant to this subchapter restores to the control shares the same voting rights as other shares of the same class or series with respect to elections of directors and all other matters coming before the shareholders. Any such resolution may be approved only by the affirmative vote of the holders of a majority of the voting power entitled to vote in two separate votes as follows:

(1) all the disinterested shares of the corporation; and

(2) all voting shares of the corporation.

(b) Lapse of voting rights.—Voting rights accorded by approval of a resolution of shareholders shall lapse and be lost if any proposed control-share acquisition which is the subject of the shareholder approval is not consummated within 90 days after shareholder approval is obtained.

(c) Restoration of voting rights.—Any control shares that do not have voting rights accorded to them by approval of a resolution of shareholders as provided by subsection (a) or the voting rights of which lapse pursuant to subsection (b) shall regain such voting rights on transfer to a person other than the acquiring person or any affiliate or associate of the acquiring person (or direct or indirect transferee from the acquiring person or such affiliate or associate solely pursuant to a transfer or series of transfers under section 2561(b)(5)(i) through (vi) (relating to application and effect of subchapter)) unless such shares shall constitute control shares of the other person, in which case the voting rights of those shares shall again be subject to this subchapter.

§ 2565. Procedure for Establishing Voting Rights of Control Shares

(a) Special meeting.—A special meeting of the shareholders of a registered corporation shall be called by the board of directors of the corporation for the purpose of considering the voting rights to be accorded to the control shares if an acquiring person:

(1) files an information statement fully conforming to section 2566 (relating to information statement of acquiring person);

(2) makes a request in writing for a special meeting of the shareholders at the time of delivery of the information statement;

(3) makes a control-share acquisition or a bona fide written offer to make a control-share acquisition; and

(4) gives a written undertaking at the time of delivery of the information statement to pay or reimburse the corporation for the expenses of a special meeting of the shareholders.

The special meeting requested by the acquiring person shall be held on the date set by the board of directors of the corporation, but in no event later than 50 days after the receipt of the information statement by the corporation, unless the corporation and the acquiring person mutually agree to a later date. If the acquiring person so requests in writing at the time of delivery of the information statement to the corporation, the special meeting shall not be held sooner than 30 days after receipt by the corporation of the complete information statement.

(b) Special meeting not requested.—If the acquiring person complies with subsections (a)(1) and (3), but no request for a special meeting is made or no written undertaking to pay or reimburse the expenses of the meeting is given, the issue of the voting rights to be accorded to control shares shall be submitted to the shareholders at the next annual or special meeting of the shareholders of which notice had not been given prior to the receipt of such information statement, unless the matter of the voting rights becomes moot.

(c) Notice and record date.—The notice of any annual or special meeting at which the issue of the voting rights to be accorded the control shares shall be submitted to shareholders shall be given at least ten days prior to the date named for the meeting and shall be accompanied by:

(1) A copy of the information statement of the acquiring person.

(2) A copy of any amendment of such information statement previously delivered to the corporation at least seven days prior to the date on which such notice is given.

(3) A statement disclosing whether the board of directors of the corporation recommends approval of, expresses no opinion and remains neutral toward, recommends rejection of, or is unable to take a position with respect to according voting rights to control shares. In determining the position that it shall take with respect to according voting rights to control shares, including to express no opinion and remain neutral or to be unable to take a position with respect to such issue, the board of directors shall specifically consider, in addition to any other factors it deems appropriate, the effect of according voting rights to control shares upon the interests of employees and of communities in which offices or other establishments of the corporation are located.

(4) Any other matter required by this subchapter to be incorporated into or to accompany the notice of meeting of shareholders or that the corporation elects to include with such notice.

Only shareholders of record on the date determined by the board of directors in accordance with the provisions of section 1763 (relating to determination of shareholders of record) shall be entitled to notice of and to vote at the meeting to consider the voting rights to be accorded to control shares.

(d) Special meeting or submission of issue at annual or special meeting not required.—Notwithstanding subsections (a) and (b), the corporation is not required to call a special meeting of shareholders or otherwise present the issue of the voting rights to be accorded to the control shares at any annual or special meeting of shareholders unless:

(1) the acquiring person delivers to the corporation a complete information statement pursuant to section 2566; and

(2) at the time of delivery of such information statement, the acquiring person has:

(i) entered into a definitive financing agreement or agreements (which shall not include best efforts, highly confident or similar undertakings but which may have the usual and customary conditions including conditions requiring that the control-share acquisition be consummated and that the control shares be accorded voting rights) with one or more financial institutions or other persons having the necessary financial capacity as determined by the board of directors of the corporation in good faith to provide for any amounts of financing of the control-share acquisition not to be provided by the acquiring person; and

(ii) delivered a copy of such agreements to the corporation.

§ 2566. Information Statement of Acquiring Person

(a) Delivery of information statement.—An acquiring person may deliver to the registered corporation at its principal executive office an information statement which shall contain all of the following:

(1) The identity of the acquiring person and the identity of each affiliate and associate of the acquiring person.

(2) A statement that the information statement is being provided under this section.

(3) The number and class or series of voting shares and of any other security of the corporation beneficially owned, directly or indirectly, prior to the control-share acquisition and at the time of the filing of this statement by the acquiring person.

(4) The number and class or series of voting shares of the corporation acquired or proposed to be acquired pursuant to the control-share acquisition by the acquiring person and specification of the following

ranges of votes that the acquiring person could cast or direct the casting of relative to all the votes that would be entitled to be cast in an election of directors of the corporation that the acquiring person in good faith believes would result from consummation of the control-share acquisition:

(i) At least 20% but less than 33⅓%.

(ii) At least 33⅓% but less than 50%.

(iii) 50% or more.

(5) The terms of the control-share acquisition or proposed control-share acquisition, including:

(i) The source of moneys or other consideration and the material terms of the financial arrangements for the control-share acquisition and the plans of the acquiring person for meeting its debt-service and repayment obligations with respect to any such financing.

(ii) A statement identifying any pension fund of the acquiring person or of the corporation which is a source or proposed source of money or other consideration for the control-share acquisition, proposed control-share acquisition or the acquisition of any control shares and the amount of such money or other consideration which has been or is proposed to be used, directly or indirectly, in the financing of such acquisition.

(6) Plans or proposals of the acquiring person with regard to the corporation, including plans or proposals under consideration to:

(i) Enter into a business combination or combinations involving the corporation.

(ii) Liquidate or dissolve the corporation.

(iii) Permanently or temporarily shut down any plant, facility or establishment, or substantial part thereof, of the corporation, or sell any such plant, facility or establishment, or substantial part thereof, to any other person.

(iv) Otherwise sell all or a material part of the assets of, or merge, consolidate, divide or exchange the shares of the corporation to or with any other person.

(v) Transfer a material portion of the work, operations or business activities of any plant, facility or establishment of the corporation to a different location or to a plant, facility or establishment owned, as of the date the information statement is delivered, by any other person.

(vi) Change materially the management or policies of employment of the corporation or the policies of the corporation with respect to labor relations matters, including, but not limited to, the recognition of or negotiations with any labor organization representing employees of the corporation and the administration of collective bargaining agreements between the corporation and any such organization.

(vii) Change materially the charitable or community involvement or contributions or policies, programs or practices relating thereto of the corporation.

(viii) Change materially the relationship with suppliers or customers of, or the communities in which there are operations of, the corporation.

(ix) Make any other material change in the business, corporate structure, management or personnel of the corporation.

(7) The funding or other provisions the acquiring person intends to make with respect to all retiree insurance and employee benefit plan obligations.

(8) Any other facts that would be substantially likely to affect the decision of a shareholder with respect to voting on the control-share acquisition pursuant to section 2564 (relating to voting rights of shares acquired in a control-share acquisition).

(b) Amendment of information statement.—If any material change occurs in the facts set forth in the information statement, including any material increase or decrease in the number of voting shares of the corporation acquired or proposed to be acquired by the acquiring person, the acquiring person shall promptly deliver, to the corporation at its principal executive office, an amendment to the information statement fully explaining such material change.

§ 2567. Redemption

Unless prohibited by the terms of the articles of a registered corporation in effect before a control-share acquisition has occurred, the corporation may redeem all control shares from the acquiring person at the average of the high and low sales price of shares of the same class and series as such prices are specified on a national securities exchange, national quotation system or similar quotation listing service on the date the corporation provides notice to the acquiring person of the call for redemption:

(1) at any time within 24 months after the date on which the acquiring person consummates a control-share acquisition, if the acquiring person does not, within 30 days after consummation of the control-share acquisition, properly request that the issue of voting rights to be accorded control shares be presented to the shareholders under section 2565(a) or (b) (relating to procedure for establishing voting rights of control shares); and

(2) at any time within 24 months after the issue of voting rights to be accorded such shares is submitted to the shareholders pursuant to section 2565(a) or (b); and

(i) such voting rights are not accorded pursuant to section 2564(a) (relating to voting rights of shares acquired in control-share acquisition); or

(ii) such voting rights are accorded and subsequently lapse pursuant to section 2564(b) (relating to lapse of voting rights).

§ 2568. Board Determinations

All determinations made by the board of directors of the registered corporation under this subchapter shall be presumed to be correct unless shown by clear and convincing evidence that the determination was not made by the directors in good faith after reasonable investigation or was clearly erroneous.

SUBCHAPTER H. DISGORGEMENT BY CERTAIN CONTROLLING SHAREHOLDERS FOLLOWING ATTEMPTS TO ACQUIRE CONTROL

§ 2571. Application and Effect of Subchapter

(a) General rule.—Except as otherwise provided in this section, this subchapter shall apply to every registered corporation.

(b) Exceptions.—This subchapter shall not apply to any transfer of an equity security:

(1) Of a registered corporation described in section 2502(1)(ii) or (2) (relating to registered corporation status).

(2) Of a corporation:

(i)(A) the bylaws of which explicitly provide that this subchapter shall not be applicable to the corporation by amendment adopted by the board of directors on or before July 26, 1990, in the case of a corporation:

(I) which on April 27, 1990, was a registered corporation described in section 2502(1)(i); and

(II) did not on that date have outstanding one or more classes or series of preference shares entitled, upon the occurrence of a default in the payment of dividends or another similar contingency, to elect a majority of the members of the board of directors;

(B) a bylaw adopted on or before July 26, 1990, by a corporation excluded from the scope of this subparagraph by clause (A)(II) shall be ineffective unless ratified under subparagraph (ii);

(ii) the bylaws of which explicitly provide that this subchapter shall not be applicable to the corporation by amendment ratified by the board of directors on or after (in printing this act in the Laws of Pennsylvania and the Pennsylvania Consolidated Statutes, the Legislative Reference Bureau shall insert here, in lieu of this statement, the date which is the date of enactment of this amendatory act) and on or before (in printing this act in the Laws of Pennsylvania and the Pennsylvania Consolidated Statutes, the Legislative Reference Bureau shall insert here, in lieu of this statement, the date which is 90 days after the date of enactment of this amendatory act) in the case of a corporation:

(A) which on April 27, 1990, was a registered corporation described in section 2502(1)(i):

(B) which on that date had outstanding one or more classes or series of preference shares entitled, upon the occurrence of a default in the payment of dividends or another similar contingency, to elect a majority of the members of the board of directors; and

(C) the bylaws of which on that date contained a provision described in subparagraph (i); or

(iii) in any other case, the articles of which explicitly provide that this subchapter shall not be applicable to the corporation by a provision included in the original articles, or by an articles amendment adopted at any time while it is a corporation other than a registered corporation described in section 2502(1)(i) or on or before 90 days after the corporation first becomes a registered corporation described in section 2502(1)(i).

(3) Consummated before October 17, 1989, if both the acquisition and disposition of each equity security were consummated before October 17, 1989.

(4) Consummated by a person or group who first became a controlling person or group prior to:

(i) October 17, 1989, if such person or group does not after such date commence a tender or exchange offer for or proxy solicitation with respect to voting shares of the corporation, in the case of a corporation which was a registered corporation described in section 2502(1)(i) on that date; or

(ii) in any other case, the date this subchapter becomes applicable to the corporation.

(5) Constituting:

(i) In the case of a person or group that, as of October 17, 1989, beneficially owned shares entitling the person or group to cast at least 20% of the votes that all shareholders would be entitled to cast in an election of directors of the corporation:

(A) The disposition of equity securities of the corporation by the person or group.

(B) Subsequent dispositions of any or all equity securities of the corporation disposed of by the person or group where such subsequent dispositions are effected by the direct purchaser of the securities from the person or group if as a result of the acquisition by the purchaser of the securities disposed of by the person or group, the purchaser, immediately following the acquisition, is entitled to cast at least 20% of the votes that all shareholders would be entitled to cast in an election of directors of the corporation.

(ii) The transfer of the beneficial ownership of the equity security by:

(A) Gift, devise, bequest or otherwise through the laws of inheritance or descent.

(B) A settlor to a trustee under the terms of a family, testamentary or charitable trust.

(C) A trustee to a trust beneficiary or a trustee to a successor trustee under the terms of a family, testamentary or charitable trust.

(iii) The addition, withdrawal or demise of a beneficiary or beneficiaries of a family, testamentary or charitable trust.

(iv) The appointment of a guardian or custodian with respect to the equity security.

(v) The transfer of the beneficial ownership of the equity security from one spouse to another by reason of separation or divorce or pursuant to community property laws or other similar laws of any jurisdiction.

(vi) The transfer of record or the transfer of a beneficial interest or interests in the equity security where the circumstances surrounding the transfer clearly demonstrate that no material change in beneficial ownership has occurred.

(6) Consummated by:

(i) The corporation or any of its subsidiaries.

(ii) Any savings, stock ownership, stock option or other benefit plan of the corporation or any of its subsidiaries, or any fiduciary with respect to any such plan when acting in such capacity, or by any participant in any such plan with respect to any equity security acquired pursuant to any such plan or any equity security acquired as a result of the exercise or conversion of any equity security (specifically including any options, warrants or rights) issued to such participant by the corporation pursuant to any such plan.

(iii) A person engaged in business as an underwriter of securities who acquires the equity securities directly from the corporation or an affiliate or associate, as defined in section 2552 (relating to definitions), of the corporation through his participation in good faith in a firm commitment underwriting registered under the Securities Act of 1933.

(7)(i) where the acquisition of the equity security has been approved by a resolution adopted prior to the acquisition of the equity security; or

(ii) where the disposition of the equity security has been approved by a resolution adopted prior to the disposition of the equity security if the equity security at the time of the adoption of the resolution is beneficially owned by a person or group that is or was a controlling person or group with respect to the corporation and is in control of the corporation if:

> the resolution in either subparagraph (i) or (ii) is approved by the board of directors and ratified by the affirmative vote of the shareholders entitled to cast at least a majority of the votes which all shareholders are entitled to cast thereon and identifies the specific person or group that proposes such acquisition or disposition, the specific purpose of such acquisition or disposition and the specific number of equity securities that are proposed to be acquired or disposed of by such person or group.

(8) Acquired at any time by a person or group who first became a controlling person or group:

(i) after April 27, 1990; and

(ii)(A) at a time when this subchapter was or is not applicable to the corporation; or

(B) on or before ten business days after the first public announcement by the corporation that this subchapter is applicable to the corporation, if this subchapter was not applicable to the corporation on July 27, 1990.

(c) Effect of distributions.—For purposes of this subchapter, equity securities acquired by a holder as a result of a stock split, stock dividend or other similar distribution by a corporation of equity securities issued by the corporation not involving a sale of the securities shall be deemed to have been acquired by the holder in the same transaction (at the same time, in the same manner and from the same person) in which the holder acquired the existing equity security with respect to which the equity securities were subsequently distributed by the corporation.

(d) Formation of group.—For the purposes of this subchapter, if there is no change in the beneficial ownership of an equity security held by a person, then the formation of or participation in a group involving the person shall not be deemed to constitute an acquisition of the beneficial ownership of such equity security by the group.

§ 2572. Policy and Purpose

(a) General rule.—The purpose of this subchapter is to protect certain registered corporations and legitimate interests of various groups related to such corporations from certain manipulative and coercive actions. Specifically, this subchapter seeks to:

(1) Protect registered corporations from being exposed to and paying "greenmail."

(2) Promote a stable relationship among the various parties involved in registered corporations, including the public whose confidence in the future of a corporation tends to be undermined when a corporation is put "in play."

(3) Ensure that speculators who put registered corporations "in play" do not misappropriate corporate values for themselves at the expense of the corporation and groups affected by corporate actions.

(4) Discourage such speculators from putting registered corporations "in play" through any means, including, but not limited to, offering to purchase at least 20% of the voting shares of the corporation or threatening to wage or waging a proxy contest in connection with or as a means toward or part of a plan to acquire control of the corporation, with the effect of reaping short-term speculative profits.

Moreover, this subchapter recognizes the right and obligation of the Commonwealth to regulate and protect the corporations it creates from abuses resulting from the application of its own laws affecting generally corporate governance and particularly director obligations, mergers and related matters. Such laws, and the obligations imposed on directors or others thereunder, should not be the vehicles by which registered corporations are manipulated in certain instances for the purpose of obtaining short-term profits.

(b) Limitations.—The purpose of this subchapter is not to affect legitimate shareholder activity that does not involve putting a corporation "in play" or involve seeking to acquire control of the corporation. Specifically, the purpose of this subchapter is not to:

(1) curtail proxy contests on matters properly submitted for shareholder action under applicable State or other law, including, but not limited to, certain elections of directors, corporate governance matters such as cumulative voting or staggered boards, or other corporate matters such as environmental issues or conducting business in a particular country, if, in any such instance, such proxy contest is not utilized in connection with or as a means toward or part of a plan to put the corporation "in play" or to seek to acquire control of the corporation; or

(2) affect the solicitation of proxies or consents by or on behalf of the corporation in connection with shareholder meetings or actions of the corporation.

§ 2573. Definitions

The following words and phrases when used in this subchapter shall have the meanings given to them in this section unless the context clearly indicates otherwise:

"Beneficial owner." The term shall have the meaning specified in section 2552 (relating to definitions).

"Control." The power, whether or not exercised, to direct or cause the direction of the management and policies of a person, whether through the ownership of voting shares, by contract or otherwise.

"Controlling person or group."

(1)(i) A person or group who has acquired, offered to acquire or, directly or indirectly, publicly disclosed or caused to be disclosed (other than for the purpose of circumventing the intent of this subchapter) the intention of acquiring voting power over voting shares of a registered corporation that would entitle the holder thereof to cast at least 20% of the votes that all shareholders would be entitled to cast in an election of directors of the corporation; or

(ii) a person or group who has otherwise, directly or indirectly, publicly disclosed or caused to be disclosed (other than for the purposes of circumventing the intent of this subchapter) that it may seek to acquire control of a corporation through any means.

(2) Two or more persons acting in concert, whether or not pursuant to an express agreement, arrangement, relationship or understanding, including a partnership, limited partnership, syndicate, or through any means of affiliation whether or not formally organized, for the purpose of acquiring, holding, voting or disposing of equity securities of a corporation shall be deemed a group for purposes of this subchapter. Notwithstanding any other provision of this subchapter to the contrary, and regardless of whether a group has been deemed to acquire beneficial ownership of an equity security under this subchapter, each person who participates in a group, where such group is a controlling person or group as defined in this subchapter, shall also be deemed to be a controlling person or group for the purposes of this subchapter, and a direct or indirect transferee solely pursuant to a transfer or series of transfers under section 2571(b)(5)(ii) through (vi) (relating to application and effect of subchapter) of an equity security acquired from any person or group that is or becomes a controlling person or group, shall be deemed, with respect to such equity security, to be acting in concert with the controlling person or group, and shall be deemed to have acquired such equity security in the same transaction (at the same time, in the same manner and from the same person) as its acquisition by the controlling person or group.

"Equity security." Any security, including all shares, stock or similar security, and any security convertible into (with or without additional consideration) or exercisable for any such shares, stock or similar security, or carrying any warrant, right or option to subscribe to or purchase such shares, stock or similar security or any such warrant, right, option or similar instrument.

"Exchange Act." The term shall have the meaning specified in section 2552 (relating to definitions).

"Profit." The positive value, if any, of the difference between:

(1) the consideration received from the disposition of equity securities less only the usual and customary broker's commissions actually paid in connection with such disposition; and

(2) the consideration actually paid for the acquisition of such equity securities plus only the usual and customary broker's commissions actually paid in connection with such acquisition.

"Proxy." Includes any proxy, consent or authorization.

"Proxy solicitation" or "solicitation of proxies." Includes any solicitation of a proxy, including a solicitation of a revocable proxy of the nature and under the circumstances described in section 2573.1(b)(3) (relating to controlling person or group safe harbor).

"Publicly disclosed or caused to be disclosed." The term shall have the meaning specified in section 2562 (relating to definitions).

"Transfer." Acquisition or disposition.

"Voting shares." The term shall have the meaning specified in section 2552 (relating to definitions).

§ 2574. Controlling Person or Group Safe Harbor

(a) Nonparticipant.—For the purpose of this subchapter, a person or group shall not be deemed a controlling person or group, absent significant other activities indicating that a person or group should be deemed a controlling person or group, by reason of voting or giving a proxy or consent as a shareholder of the corporation if the person or group is one who or which:

(1) did not acquire any voting shares of the corporation with the purpose of changing or influencing control of the corporation or seeking to acquire control of the corporation or in connection with or as a participant in any agreement, arrangement, relationship, understanding or otherwise having any such purpose;

(2) if control were acquired, would not be a person or group or a participant in a group that has control over the corporation and will not receive, directly or indirectly, any consideration from a person or group that has control over the corporation other than consideration offered proportionately to all holders of voting shares of the corporation; and

(3) if a proxy or consent is given, executes a revocable proxy or consent given without consideration in response to a proxy or consent solicitation made in accordance with the applicable rules and regulations under the Exchange Act under circumstances not then reportable on Schedule 13D under the Exchange Act (or any comparable or successor report) by the person or group who gave the proxy or consent.

(b) Certain holders.—For the purpose of this subchapter, a person or group shall not be deemed a controlling person or group under subparagraph (1)(i) of the definition of "controlling person or group" in section 2573 (relating to definitions) if such person or group holds voting power:

(1) in good faith and not for the purpose of circumventing this subchapter, as an agent, bank, broker, nominee or trustee for one or more beneficial owners who do not individually or, if they are a group acting in concert, as a group have the voting power specified in subparagraph (1)(i) of the definition of "controlling person or group" in section 2573;

(2) in connection with the solicitation of proxies or consents by or on behalf of the corporation in connection with shareholder meetings or actions of the corporation; or

(3) in the amount specified in subparagraph (1)(i) of the definition of "controlling person or group" in section 2573 as a result of the solicitation of revocable proxies or consents with respect to voting shares if such proxies or consents both:

(i) are given without consideration in response to a proxy or consent solicitation made in accordance with the applicable rules and regulations under the exchange act; and

(ii) do not empower the holder thereof, whether or not this power is shared with any other person, to vote such shares except on the specific matters described in such proxy or consent and in accordance with the instructions of the giver of such proxy or consent.

(c) Preference shares.—In determining whether a person or group would be a controlling person or group within the meaning of this subchapter, there shall be disregarded voting power, and the seeking to acquire control of a corporation to the extent based upon voting power arising from a contingent right of the holders of one or more classes or series of preference shares to elect one or more members of the board of directors upon or during the continuation of a default in the payment of dividends on such shares or another similar contingency.

§ 2575. Ownership by Corporation of Profits Resulting From Certain Transactions

Any profit realized by any person or group who is or was a controlling person or group with respect to a registered corporation from the disposition of any equity security of the corporation to any person (including under Subchapter E (relating to control transactions) or otherwise), including, without limitation, to the corporation (including under Subchapter G (relating to control-share acquisitions) or otherwise) or to another member of the controlling person or group, shall belong to and be recoverable by the corporation where the profit is realized by such person or group:

(1) from the disposition of the equity security within 18 months after the person or group obtained the status of a controlling person or group; and

(2) the equity security had been acquired by the controlling person or group within 24 months prior to or 18 months subsequent to the obtaining by the person or group of the status of a controlling person or group.

Any transfer by a controlling person or group of the ownership of any equity security may be suspended on the books of the corporation, and certificates representing such securities may be duly-legended, to enforce the rights of the corporation under this subchapter.

§ 2576. Enforcement Actions

(a) Venue.—Actions to recover any profit due under this subchapter may be commenced in any court of competent jurisdiction by the registered corporation issuing the equity security or by any holder of any equity security of corporation in the name and on behalf of the corporation if the corporation fails or refuses to bring the action within 60 days after written request by a holder or shall fail to prosecute the action diligently. If a judgment requiring the payment of any such profits is entered, the party bringing such action shall recover all costs, including reasonable attorney fees, incurred in connection with enforcement of this subchapter.

(b) Jurisdiction.—By engaging in the activities necessary to become a controlling person or group and thereby becoming a controlling person or group, the person or group and all persons participating in the group consent to personal jurisdiction in the courts of this Commonwealth for enforcement of this subchapter. Courts of this Commonwealth may exercise personal jurisdiction over any controlling person or group in actions to enforce this subchapter. The terms of this section shall be supplementary to the provisions of 42 Pa.C.S. §§ 5301 (relating to persons) through 5322 (relating to bases of personal jurisdiction over persons outside this Commonwealth) and, for the purpose of this section, 42 Pa.C.S. § 5322(7)(iv) shall be deemed to include a controlling person or group as defined in section 2573 (relating to definitions). Service of process may be made upon such persons outside this Commonwealth in accordance with the procedures specified by 42 Pa.C.S. § 5323 (relating to service of process on persons outside this Commonwealth).

(c) Limitation.—Any action to enforce this subchapter shall be brought within two years from the date any profit recoverable by the corporation was realized.

SUBCHAPTER I. SEVERANCE COMPENSATION FOR EMPLOYEES TERMINATED FOLLOWING CERTAIN CONTROL-SHARE ACQUISITIONS

§ 2581. Definitions

The following words and phrases when used in this subchapter shall have the meanings given to them in this section unless the context clearly indicates otherwise:

"Acquiring person." The term shall have the meaning specified in section 2562 (relating to definitions).

"Control-share acquisition." The term shall have the meaning specified in section 2562.

"Control-share approval."

(1) The occurrence of both:

(i) a control-share acquisition to which Subchapter G (relating to control-share acquisitions) applies with respect to a registered corporation described in section 2502(1)(i) (relating to registered corporation status) by an acquiring person; and

(ii) the according by such registered corporation of voting rights pursuant to section 2564(a) (relating to voting rights of shares acquired in a control-share acquisition) in connection with such control-share acquisition to control shares of the acquiring person.

(2) The term shall also include a control-share acquisition effected by an acquiring person, other than a control-share acquisition described in section 2561(b)(3), (4) or (5) (other than subparagraph 2561(b)(5)(vii)) (relating to application and effect of subchapter) if the control-share acquisition:

(1)(A) occurs primarily in response to the actions of another acquiring person where Subchapter G (relating to control-share acquisitions) applies to a control-share acquisition or proposed control-share acquisition by such other acquiring person; and

(B) either:

(I) pursuant to an agreement or plan described in section 2561(b)(5)(vii);

(II) after adoption of an amendment to the articles of the registered corporation pursuant to section 2561(b)(2)(iii); or

(III) after reincorporation of the registered corporation in another jurisdiction:

if the agreement or plan is approved or the amendment or reincorporation is adopted by the board of directors of the corporation during the period commencing after the satisfaction by such other acquiring person of the requirements of section 2565(a) or (b) (relating to procedure for establishing voting rights of control shares) and ending 90 days after the date such issue is voted on by the shareholders, is withdrawn from consideration or becomes moot; or

(ii) is consummated in any manner by a person who satisfied, within two years prior to such acquisition, the requirements of section 2565(a) or (b).

"Control shares." The term shall have the meaning specified in section 2562.

"Eligible employee." Any employee of a registered corporation (or any subsidiary thereof) if:

(1) the registered corporation was the subject of a control-share approval;

(2) the employee was an employee of such corporation (or any subsidiary thereof) within 90 days before or on the day of the control-share approval and had been so employed for at least two years prior thereto; and

(3) the employment of the employee is in this Commonwealth.

"Employee." Any person lawfully employed by an employer.

"Employment in this Commonwealth."

(1) The entire service of an employee, performed inside and outside of this Commonwealth, if the service is localized in this Commonwealth.

(2) Service shall be deemed to be localized in this Commonwealth if:

(i) the service is performed entirely inside this Commonwealth; or

(ii) the service is performed both inside and outside of this Commonwealth but the service performed outside of this Commonwealth is incidental to the service of the employee inside this Commonwealth, as where such service is temporary or transitory in nature or consists of isolated transactions.

(3) Employment in this Commonwealth shall also include service of the employee, performed inside and outside of this Commonwealth, if the service is not localized in any state, but some of the service is performed in this Commonwealth, and:

(i) the base of operations of the employee is in this Commonwealth;

(ii) there is no base of operations, and the place from which such service is directed or controlled is in this Commonwealth; or

(iii) the base of operations of the employee or place from which such service is directed or controlled is not in any state in which some part of the service is performed, but the residence of the employee is in this Commonwealth.

"Minimum severance amount." With respect to an eligible employee, the weekly compensation of the employee multiplied by the number of the completed years of service of the employee, up to a maximum of 26 times the weekly compensation of the employee.

"Subsidiary." The term shall have the meaning specified in section 2552 (relating to definitions).

"Termination of employment." The layoff of at least six months, or the involuntary termination of an employee, except that any employee employed in a business operation who is continued or employed or offered employment (within 60 days) by the purchaser of such business operation, on substantially the same terms (including geographic location) as those pursuant to which the employee was employed in such business operation, shall not be deemed to have been laid off or involuntarily terminated for the purposes of this subchapter by such transfer of employment to the purchaser, but the purchaser shall make the lump-sum payment under this subchapter in the event of a layoff of at least six months or the involuntary termination of the employee within the period specified in section 2582 (relating to severance compensation).

"Weekly compensation." The average regular weekly compensation of an employee based on normal schedule of hours in effect for such employee over the last three months preceding the control-share approval.

"Year of service." Each full year during which the employee has been employed by the employer.

§ 2582. Severance Compensation

(a) General rule.—Any eligible employee whose employment is terminated, other than for willful misconduct connected with the work of the employee, within 90 days before the control-share approval with respect to the registered corporation if such termination was pursuant to an agreement, arrangement or understanding, whether formal or informal, with the acquiring person whose control shares were accorded voting rights in connection with such control-share approval or within 24 calendar months after the control-share approval with respect to the registered corporation shall receive a one-time, lump-sum payment from the employer equal to:

(1) the minimum severance amount with respect to the employee; less

(2) any payments made to the employee by the employer due to termination of employment, whether pursuant to any contract, policy, plan or otherwise, but not including any final wage payments to the employee or payments to the employee under pension, savings, retirement or similar plans.

(b) Limitation.—If the amount specified in subsection (a)(2) is at least equal to the amount specified in subsection (a)(1), no payment shall be required to be made under this subchapter.

(c) Due date of payment.—Severance compensation under this subchapter to eligible employees shall be made within one regular pay period after the last day of work of the employee, in the case of a layoff known at such time to be at least six months or an involuntary termination, and in all other cases within 30 days after the eligible employee first becomes entitled to compensation under this subchapter.

§ 2583. Enforcement and Remedies

(a) Notice.—Within 30 days of the control-share approval, the employer shall provide written notice to each eligible employee and to the collective bargaining representative, if any, of the rights of eligible employees under this subchapter.

(b) Remedies.—In the event any eligible employee is denied a lump-sum payment in violation of this subchapter, or the employer fails to provide the notice required by subsection (a), the employee on his or her own behalf or on behalf of other employees similarly situated, or the collective bargaining representative, if any, on the behalf of the employee, may, in addition to all other remedies available at law or in equity, bring an action to remedy such violation. In any such action, the court may order such equitable or legal relief as it deems just and proper.

(c) Civil penalty.—In the case of violations of subsection (a), the court may order the employer to pay to each employee who was subject to a termination of employment and entitled to severance compensation under this subchapter a civil penalty not to exceed $75 per day for each business day that notice was not provided to such employee.

(d) Successor liability.—The rights under this subchapter of any individual who was an eligible employee at the time of the control-share approval shall vest at that time, and in any action based on a violation of this subchapter, recovery may be secured against:

(1) a merged, consolidated or resulting domestic or foreign corporation or other successor employer; or

(2) the corporation after its status as a registered corporation has terminated; notwithstanding any provision of law to the contrary.

SUBCHAPTER J. BUSINESS COMBINATION TRANSACTIONS—LABOR CONTRACTS

§ 2585. Application and Effect of Subchapter

(a) General rule.—Except as otherwise provided in this section, this subchapter shall apply to every business combination transaction relating to a business operation if such business operation was owned by a registered corporation (or any subsidiary thereof) at the time of a control-share approval with respect to the corporation (regardless of the fact, if such be the case, that such operation after the control-share approval is owned by the registered corporation or any other person).

(b) Exceptions.—This subchapter shall not apply to:

(1) Any business combination transaction occurring more than five years after the control-share approval of the registered corporation.

(2) Any business operation located other than in this Commonwealth.

§ 2586. Definitions

The following words and phrases when used in this subchapter shall have the meanings given to them in this section unless the context clearly indicates otherwise:

"Business combination transaction." Any merger or consolidation, sale, lease, exchange or other disposition, in one transaction or a series of transactions, whether affecting all or substantially all the property and assets, including its good will, of the business operation that is the subject of the labor contract referred to in section 2587 (relating to labor contracts preserved in business combination transactions) or any transfer of a controlling interest in such business operation.

"Control-share approval." The term shall have the meaning specified in section 2581 (relating to definitions).

"Covered labor contract." Any labor contract if such contract:

(1) covers persons engaged in employment in this Commonwealth;

(2) was negotiated by a labor organization or by a collective bargaining agent or other representative;

(3) relates to a business operation that was owned by the registered corporation (or any subsidiary thereof) at the time of the control-share approval with respect to such corporation; and

(4) was in effect and covered such business operation and such employees at the time of such control-share approval.

"Employee" and "employment in this Commonwealth." The terms shall have the meanings specified in section 2581.

"Subsidiary." The term shall have the meaning specified in section 2552 (relating to definitions).

§ 2587. Labor Contracts Preserved in Business Combination Transactions

No business combination transaction shall result in the termination or impairment of the provisions of any covered labor contract, and the contract shall continue in effect pursuant to its terms until it is terminated pursuant to any termination provision contained therein, or until otherwise agreed upon by the parties to such contract or their successors.

§ 2588. Civil Remedies

(a) General rule.—In the event that an employee is denied or fails to receive wages, benefits or wage supplements or suffers any contractual loss as a result of a violation of this subchapter, the employee on his or her own behalf or on behalf of other employees similarly situated, or the labor organization or collective bargaining agent party to the labor contract, may, in addition to all other remedies available at law or in equity, bring an action in any court of competent jurisdiction to recover such wages, benefits, wage supplements or contractual losses and to enjoin the violation of this subchapter.

(b) Successor liability.—The rights under this subchapter of any employee at the time of the control-share approval shall vest at that time, and in any action based on a violation of this subchapter, recovery may be secured against:

(1) a merged, consolidated or resulting domestic or foreign corporation or other successor employer; or

(2) the corporation after its status as a registered corporation has terminated;

notwithstanding any provision of law to the contrary.

J. WYOMING MANAGEMENT STABILITY ACT

(Selected Sections)

Contents

ARTICLE 2. BONDHOLDER PROTECTION PROVISIONS

ARTICLE 2. BONDHOLDER PROTECTION PROVISIONS

§ 17–18–201. Protection Provisions; Applicability; Defined

(a) A qualified corporation may, if its articles of incorporation authorize it to utilize the bondholder protection provisions of this act, utilize any of the provisions set forth in subsection (b) of this section. These protections shall apply only to bonds, debentures or other debt instruments whose original aggregate value at maturity is equal to or greater than five million dollars ($5,000,000.00) and whose original term is two (2) years or greater. Any number of bondholder protection provisions may be in effect at any time.

(b) A qualified corporation may provide bondholder protection by requiring any or all of the following:

(i) Bondholder approval of the replacement of more than twenty-four percent (24%) of the directors in any twelve (12) month period. The filling of vacancies created by the death or resignation of directors shall not be counted against the twenty-four percent (24%) limit provided that those vacancies are filled by nominees of the board of directors. If more than twenty-four percent (24%) of the directors are to be replaced, the approval of holders of a majority of the bonds shall be obtained in writing at the meeting where the directors are to be replaced or no more than thirty (30) days prior to the meeting. The consent of the bondholders shall be obtained to exceeding the twenty-four percent (24%) limit rather than to the individual directors to be replaced. If consent is denied, which directors are to be replaced shall be determined by the relative number of votes for each director by shares entitled to vote;

(ii) Bondholder consent to any merger or acquisition which the corporation may be subject to or which the corporation may make, subject to the following:

(A) The notice of bondholder protection shall specify the size of merger or acquisition at or above which the bondholder consent is required. The size may vary depending on whether the company is the acquiring party or is being acquired. In a merger the relative memberships on the board of directors of the surviving corporation may be used to determine whether or not bondholder consent is required;

(B) The term acquisition shall be deemed to include the purchase of more than a specified percentage of the shares entitled to vote for directors by a person or combination of persons under common ownership or control or acting in concert. If a person or combination of persons acquires more than the specified percentage of shares, they shall be entitled to vote only the specified percentage until bondholder consent is acquired. The specified percentage shall be set in the notice of bondholder protection and shall not be less than ten percent (10%);

(C) The bondholder consent shall be to a specific merger or acquisition rather than the general concept of mergers and acquisitions.

(iii) Bondholder consent to the sale or disposal of certain assets, or assets exceeding a certain percentage of the corporation's total assets, or assets exceeding a set total value or any combination of these factors. The specifics of what requires bondholder consent shall be set forth in the notice of bondholder protection. Disposal of assets shall be construed to include the disposition of the assets to the shareholders either directly or through distribution of shares in a new or subsidiary corporation;

(iv) Bondholder consent to the acquisition of debt above a specified percentage of total assets, a specified percentage of the net worth of the corporation, a specific amount, or any combination of these factors. The consent may be required generally or may be required only if the debt is to be used to pay for a merger or acquisition or a distribution to shareholders. The notice of bondholder protection shall specify the conditions under which bondholder consent is required.

§ 17–18–202. Bondholder Protection Provision; Adoption Requirements; Revocation

(a) The corporation utilizes a bondholder protection provision by adopting and filing with the secretary of state a notice of bondholder protection as provided in this section.

(b) The notice of bondholder protection shall specify the percentage of bondholders whose consent is required for any action on that protection. The percentage may be different for different purposes. The percentage shall not be less than fifty percent (50%) nor greater than ninety percent (90%). The percentage shall be a percentage of the value at maturity of the bonds or other debt instruments issued and outstanding.

(c) Notices of bondholder protection shall be approved by the corporation in the same manner as changes in corporate bylaws except that the articles of incorporation may specify a different manner of approval. The notices shall be filed with the trustee or transfer agent, if any, for the bonds and with the secretary of state. The notice filed with the secretary of state shall be accompanied by the administrative fee specified by regulation to recover the administrative costs of the state of Wyoming. The notice shall be effective as of the date of filing with the secretary of state. The corporation shall send to each known bondholder by first class mail either the full notice of bondholder protection or a summary of the notice and information as to how the full notice may be obtained from the company. This notice to the bondholders shall be given no later than the due date of the first interest payment due more than thirty (30) days after the bondholder protection notice is filed with the secretary of state and may be included with the mailing of the interest payment.

(d) Bondholder protections may be revoked by the corporation in the same manner that notices of bondholder protection are issued and filed except that the revocation is effective as of a date specified in the notice filed with the secretary of state. The effective date shall be at least two (2) years and not more than six (6) years after filing the notice of revocation with the secretary of state.

§ 17–18–203. Bondholder Protection Provision; Amendments

(a) At any time any amendment may be made to the bondholder protection provisions with the consent of the percentage of bondholders required for action as stated in the notice of bondholder protection. Such an amendment shall be effective upon filing the bondholder's consent and notice of amendment with the secretary of state. However, the effective date shall be specified in the notice and shall be at least two (2) years and not more than six (6) years after filing the bondholder's consent and notice of the amendment with the secretary of state for amendments which:

(i) Change the time period for revocations to be effective;

(ii) Decrease the percentage of bondholders required for approval of an action;

(iii) Eliminate the requirement of bondholder approval for a specific action; or

(iv) Otherwise decrease the protection available to bondholders.

(b) The bondholder's consent shall be in writing signed by the bondholder or his lawful agent or trustee. Unless otherwise specified in W.S. 17–18–201 through 17–18–206 the consent is valid until revoked by the bondholder. The sale of the bond or debt instrument by the bondholder revokes the consent effective upon notification of the corporation or transfer agent of the sale.

§ 17-18-204. Limitations of the Bondholder Protection Provisions

(a) Nothing in the bondholder protection provisions shall be construed or applied to abridge or prohibit any contract, covenant or restriction made between any corporation and its bondholders, or any holder of any other debt instrument provided the contract, covenant or restriction would be lawful in the absence of W.S. 17-18-201 through 17-18-206. Unless specifically prohibited by prior contract any eligible corporation may extend to the holders of any bond or debt instrument described in W.S. 17-18-201(a) the opportunity to receive any bondholder protection provisions. If a corporation represents to potential purchasers of bonds in any prospectus or other written advice to potential purchasers that it has extended or intends to extend any bondholder protection provisions, it shall also state in the same document that the protections may be revoked as provided by W.S. 17-18-201 through 17-18-206.

(b) Protections under W.S. 17-18-201 through 17-18-206 shall be extended uniformly to all holders of the same class of bond or debt instrument but need not be extended uniformly to all classes of bonds or debt instruments.

§ 17-18-205. Bondholder Definition

The term bondholder shall include the owners of any debt instrument to which bondholder protections are extended.

§ 17-18-206. Additional Bondholder Protection Provisions Allowed

Any other bondholder protection provisions may be provided in the notice of bondholder protection, and shall be valid unless inconsistent with the provisions of W.S. 17-18-201 through 17-18-206 or other law.

K. MODEL [STATE] CONTROL SHARE STATUTE

Adopted effective April 22, 1988; amended and effective September 14, 1989

SYNOPSIS OF MODEL [STATE] CONTROL SHARE ACT AND SUMMARY OF PRINCIPAL DIFFERENCES BETWEEN MODEL ACT AND INDIANA STATUTE

The attached Model [State] Control Share Act ("Model Act" or "Act") has been drafted by a Joint Committee comprised of members of the Tender Offer Regulation Committee of the North American Securities Administrators Association and members of the State Regulation of Securities Committee of the American Bar Association. The Act is based upon the Indiana control share statute declared constitutional by the United States Supreme Court in CTS Corp. v. Dynamics Corp. Some 29 states, including Delaware, have amended their business corporation acts to include provisions governing takeovers, of which approximately 15 are of the control share variety.

The Model Act, like the Indiana statute, applies only to domestic corporations that meet specific criteria relating to minimum number or percentage of resident shares or shareholders. Jurisdiction attaches within 12 months after the effective date of the Act unless the corporation, by vote of its shareholders, determines to opt out of the Act's coverage. However, unlike the Indiana statute, in order that a corporation be automatically covered by the Model Act, it must be a corporation that has its securities registered under sec. 12 of the Securities Exchange Act of 1934 or subject to sec. 15(d) of that Act. The Model Act does not require the economic nexus criteria present in the Indiana and other statutes, such as principal place of business, substantial assets and number of employees. (See Section 3(g).)

Corporations that are not automatically covered by the Act may opt into coverage. However, unlike the Indiana statute, the Model Act provides certain eligibility criteria that an opting-in corporation must satisfy—namely, a minimum of 100 shareholders of record and at least one of the shareholder nexus criteria relating to resident shares or shareholders. (See Section 2(b).)

The Model Act requires that action to opt in or out of the Act be pursuant to the procedure for amending a corporation's articles—by shareholder vote in addition to a board of directors' resolution. The comparable Indiana procedures can be implemented through bylaw changes requiring only board action. (See Sections 2(b) and 4 (Intro).)

The cornerstone of the Model Act (and the Indiana statute) is a section providing that if a person acquires shares of a corporation to which the Act applies in excess of certain thresholds of voting power—

one-fifth (20%), one-third (33⅓%) and a majority (over 50%)—such shares have no voting power unless restored by vote of holders of a majority of the "non-interested shares" of the corporation. Although the Model Act's definition of "control shares," as well as the three voting control ranges, are the same as the Indiana statute, the Model Act (unlike the Indiana statute) does not affect the voting rights of shares representing up to 20% of all voting power, as well as additional shares acquired within a range of voting power for which shareholder approval has already been obtained. (See Sections 3(e)3I and 4(b) and (c).)

The Model Act does not cover acquisitions by persons who acquire shares for the benefit of others in the ordinary course of business (e.g., brokers and nominees), so long as such acquisition is made in good faith and not for the purpose of circumventing the Act. In addition, the Act excludes from the definition of "control share acquisition" the acquisition of shares in any of the following eleven circumstances:

1. Acquisition at a time when the corporation was not subject to the Act;

2. Acquisition pursuant to a contract entered into at a time when the corporation was not subject to the Act;

3. Acquisition by inheritance;

*4. Acquisition by inter vivos gift;

*5. Acquisition by transfer among family members or persons under direct common control;

6. Acquisition by a pledge or other security interest;

7. Acquisition by reason of a merger or plan of consolidation or share exchange, if the corporation is a party to such transactions;

8. Acquisition from another person where the Act would otherwise be invoked, provided that the person acquiring such shares does not thereby increase his or her voting power to a next higher threshold, and so long as there is only one such transfer;

*9. Acquisition of additional shares within the range of voting power for which approval has already been granted, or where the range was achieved through an excluded transaction;

*10. Where the corporation itself causes an increase in the person's voting power; and

*11. Pursuant to the solicitation of proxies.

(* indicates a Model Act exclusion that is not found in the Indiana statute.)

Not included in the Model Act is the Indiana statute's exclusion for the acquisition from another person of control shares that had been granted voting rights following a shareholder's vote.

The shareholder vote approval procedure under Section 5 of the Model Act is comparable to the approval procedure in the Indiana statute. To obtain approval, the acquiring person must deliver a disclosure statement that, among other things, identifies the person, states the number of shares directly or indirectly owned and the dates and prices at which such shares were acquired, and represents that the acquisition was lawful and that the person has the financial capacity to make it. A special meeting of shareholders then must be called within 10 days after delivery of the disclosure statement and must be held not less than 30 days nor more than 50 days after receipt of the request for the meeting. These time periods are meant to coordinate with the 60–day period after which tendering shareholders must be granted withdrawal rights under the federal takeover regulatory scheme in the Williams Act. In determining which shareholders may vote whether to accord voting rights to control shares, interested persons such as the acquiring person and officers and employee-directors of the corporation are excluded. (See Section 3(f).)

The Model Act includes the following provisions regarding the shareholder vote approval procedure which are not present in the Indiana statute: (i) a requirement that an acquiring person must publish in the newspaper, as well as deliver to the corporation, the disclosure statement (Section 5(a)); (ii) any proxy must be solicited separately from any offer to purchase shares of the corporation (Section 5(f)); and (iii) if the shareholders reject a resolution to accord voting rights for control shares, the resolution may be presented again for subsequent shareholder votes at special and annual shareholder meetings (Section 5(c)).

Unlike the Indiana statute that requires two separate majority vote approvals in order for voting rights to be restored to control shares, the Model Act provides for only one shareholder vote—a majority of all voting power, excluding "interested shares." (See Section 5(g).) If a person does not receive shareholder approval for restoring voting power to his or her control shares, the person has no voting power for shares above the threshold for which approval is required. Restoration of voting power other than by shareholder vote can occur in the following situations specified in Section 4(d) of the Model Act, neither of which is provided for under the Indiana statute: (i) where actions by the corporation cause the holder's ownership level to cross thresholds; and (ii) where control shares are transferred to a person whose percentage shareholdings will not exceed 20%.

The bracketed language in Section 4(d) providing for restoration of voting power following a three-year holding period is an item regarding which the Joint Committee was unable to reach a consensus. Consequently, public comments on this item are especially requested.

Remaining differences between the Model Act and the Indiana statute are: (i) the Model Act deals with competing bids, a subject Indiana has not addressed (see Section 5(h)); (ii) the Model Act requires the purchase at a fair price of all remaining shares by an affiliate of the corporation that has acquired a majority of the corporation's voting shares within one year after the corporation opted out of the Act (see Section 6); and (iii) the Model Act does not include the provisions contained in the Indiana statute relating to redemption by the corporation of acquired control shares and shareholder dissent and appraisal rights. (See the Additional Commentary at the end of the Public Discussion Draft.)

Summary of Principal Differences Between
Model Act and Indiana Statute

Definition of "Issuing Public Corporation". See Section 3(g)

—To be automatically covered by the Model Act definition, the corporation must be a "public" corporation in terms of having its securities registered under section 12 of the Securities Exchange Act of 1934 or being subject to section 15(d) of that Act. The Model Act definition does not contain the economic (as opposed to shareholder) nexus criteria present in the Indiana statute of principal place of business, substantial assets and number of employees.

Minimum eligibility criteria for a corporation to "opt-in". See Section 2(b)

—To elect to be covered by the Act, a domestic corporation must have at least 100 shareholders of record and satisfy at least one of the shareholder nexus criteria in subpar. 3(g)(1)B.

"Opt-in" and "Opt-out" Procedures. See Sections 2(b) and 4 (Intro.)

—The Model Act requires that such actions take place using the procedure for amending a corporation's articles—which necessitates a shareholder vote in addition to a board of directors' resolution. The Indiana statute opt-in and opt-out procedures can be implemented by by-law changes that require only board action.

Acquisition of Shares Up To and Between Ranges of Voting Control. See Sections 3(e)3I and (4)(b) and (c)

—Although the Model Act's definition of "Control Shares" as well as the 3 voting control ranges are the same as the Indiana statute, the Model Act (unlike the Indiana statute) accords voting rights for shares representing up to 20% of all voting power, as well as for additional shares acquired within a range of voting power for which shareholder approval had already been obtained.

Exclusions From the Definition of "Control Share Acquisition". See Sections 3(e)3A to K

—Exclusions in the Model Act that are not in the Indiana statute include: (i) acquisitions pursuant to an inter vivos gift; (ii) acquisitions pursuant to a transfer among immediate family members or persons under direct common control; (iii) acquisitions of additional shares within the same ranges of voting power either the person received approval for or the range the person is in as a result of shares acquired in an excluded transaction; (iv) "passive threshold crossing" situations; (v) proxy solicitations.

—Not contained in the Model Act is the Indiana statute exclusion for the acquisition from another person of control shares that had been granted voting rights following a shareholder's vote.

Shareholder Vote on Restoration of Voting Rights for Control Shares. See Section 5(g)

—Unlike the Indiana statute that requires two separate majority votes, the Model Act provides for only one shareholder vote—a majority of all voting power, excluding "interested shares".

Restoration of Voting Power Other than By Shareholder Vote. See Section 4(d)

—Model Act restoration provisions not contained in the Indiana statute include: (i) where actions by the corporation cause a person's ownership levels to cross thresholds; (ii) where control shares are transferred to someone whose percentage shareholdings will not exceed 20%. The bracketed language in Section 4(d) providing for restoration of voting power following a 3–year holding period is an item regarding which the Joint Committee was unable to reach a consensus. Consequently, public comments on this item are especially requested.

Shareholder Vote Approval Procedure. See Section 5

—The Model Act contains the following provisions not present in the Indiana statute: (i) a requirement that an acquiring person must publish in the newspaper, as well as deliver to the corporation, the disclosure statement (Section 5(a)); (ii) any proxy must be solicited separately from any offer to purchase shares of the corporation (Section 5(f)); if shareholders reject a resolution to accord voting rights for control shares, the resolution may be presented again for subsequent shareholder votes at special and annual shareholder meetings.

Competing Control Share Acquisition. See Section 5(h)

—The Model Act contains a specific section dealing with the competing bid situation which is not treated in the Indiana statute.

Special Minority Shareholder Rights. See Section 6

—The Model Act contains a provision not present in the Indiana statute that attempts to prevent abuses where a corporation has opted out of the Act and an affiliate of the corporation acquires a majority or more of the voting shares of the corporation within one year of the vote to opt-out.

Redemption of Acquired Control Shares and Dissent and Appraisal Rights

—The Model Act does not include provisions on these two subjects which are treated in the Indiana statute. See the Additional Commentary at the end of the Public Discussion Draft.

Article______

[STATE] CONTROL SHARE ACT

PRELIMINARY STATEMENT

This model statute and official comments ("Model Act" or "Act") is intended as a guide for states wishing to enact or amend a control share acquisition act. The Model Act was drafted by a joint committee ("Joint Committee") composed of members of the North American Securities Administrators Association ("NASAA") and members of the American Bar Association Committee on State Regulation of Securities ("ABA Committee"). Subsequent to the March 29, 1988 date, the Act was adopted by NASAA at its 1988 Spring Conference by vote of its member jurisdictions. The ABA Committee has not to date acted on or approved the Act. The Joint Committee adopted amendments to Sections 2 and 5 of the Model Act, effective August 1, 1989. The Joint Committee members have made no recommendation as to the desirability of this legislation for any particular state.

The need for this kind of Model Act resulted from the growing number of states considering control share acquisition legislation following the Supreme Court decision in CTS Corp. v. Dynamics Corp., ___ U.S. ___, 107 S.Ct. 1637 (1987) ("CTS"). In *CTS,* the Supreme Court held that the Indiana Control Share Acquisition Chapter ("Indiana Act") was neither preempted by federal law nor invalid as burdening interstate commerce. Indiana's law is intended to provide independent shareholders of domestic corporations meeting certain criteria the power to vote collectively on a proposed change of corporate control, by deciding whether to accord voting rights to shares held or to be acquired in excess of certain percentages. The purpose of the Joint Committee was to provide a uniform statute that comes within the constitutional limitations laid down by the Supreme Court in *CTS* and responds to the perceived need to modify or clarify certain provisions of the Indiana Act.

To improve the usefulness of the Model Act, Official Comments were prepared for each provision and specifically approved by the Joint Committee. The Official Comments describe the substantive decisions made in the drafting of each provision and further explain the meaning and purpose of the provision. The Model Act generally utilizes the statutory drafting principles set forth in *Drafting Rules for Uniform or Model Acts* promulgated by the National Conference of Commissioners on Uniform State Laws.

In drafting the Model Act, the Joint Committee departed from the Indiana statute only for good reason. In addition, the Joint Committee attempted to adhere to four requirements which emerged from the *CTS* decision. First, state tender offer regulation must not conflict with the federal policy "implicit in the Williams Act ... that independent shareholders faced with tender offers often are at a disadvantage" and require protection "from the coercive aspects of some tender offers." 107 S.Ct. at 1646. Second, state tender offer regulation may allow "*shareholders* to evaluate the fairness of the offer collectively" but should not "allow the state government to interpose its views of fairness between willing buyers and sellers of shares of the target company." 107 S.Ct. at 1646 (emphasis in original). Third, state tender offer regulation must "not give either management or the offeror an advantage in communicating with the shareholders about the impending offer." 107 S.Ct. at 1646. Fourth, state regulation may not impose " '*unreasonable* delay' "upon a tender offer. 107 S.Ct. at 1647 (emphasis in original).

The Supreme Court recognized in *CTS* that there is some room for state legislation regulating tender offers which "furthers the federal policy of investor protection" and is calculated to protect legitimate state interests. 107 S.Ct. at 1647. The Joint Committee did not consider it to be within its province, in drafting the Model Act, to resolve all tender offer abuses and problems that states may legitimately address or to take a position on the underlying policy issue of the desirability of state takeover regulation. Rather, the Committee sought only to draft a model control share act that (i) could serve as a guide for states considering enactment or amendment of such legislation, (ii) would withstand constitutional scrutiny and (iii) would be reasonably consistent with the existing framework of state corporation law and practice.

Section 1. **Citation.** This Article is known and may be cited as the [State] Control Share Act.

Section 2. **Application.**

(a) This Article applies to all issuing public corporations in existence on and after the effective date of this Article ... [revisor inserts date].

COMMENTARY TO SUBSECTION 2(a)

Coverage under this Act is invoked automatically with respect to those domestic corporations that meet the definitional criteria of "issuing public corporation" set forth in subsection 3(g). The voting power of a corporation's shares becomes subject to these provisions immediately upon effectiveness of the Act, unless the corporation takes the prescribed action to avoid coverage. The original March 29, 1988 form of this Section established a 12–month delayed effectiveness of the Act for the purpose of providing time for those corporations that wished to reject the statute's automatic coverage and take the "opt-out" opportunity presented in Section 4, without having to call a special shareholders meeting. However, as a result of U.S. Securities and Exchange Commission Rule 19c–4 under the Securities Exchange Act of 1934 (enacted subsequent to the March 29, 1988 completion of the Model Act) the subsection was amended by the Joint Committee effective August 1, 1989, whereby the 12–month delayed effectiveness language was eliminated and replaced with the immediate-effectiveness-upon-enactment language. The substitution was necessary to eliminate the adverse delisting-from-trading consequences that otherwise might flow to a publicly traded company under the SEC rule in circumstances where a corporation acts affirmatively to opt-into coverage of a control share statute.

(b) A domestic corporation that is not an issuing public corporation but that has one hundred (100) or more shareholders of record and meets one of the requirements set forth in subparagraph 3(g)(1)B, or an issuing public corporation to which this Article does not apply, may elect to be subject to this Article as an issuing public corporation by amending its articles of incorporation to provide that this Article shall apply to the corporation as of a specified date and filing the amendment in the [Office of the Secretary of State or other appropriate state office] on or before such date.

COMMENTARY TO SUBSECTION 2(b)

This subsection provides a procedure for domestic corporations that are not automatically covered by the Act because they do not have all the elements of an "issuing public corporation" to invoke the Act's coverage by an amendment to their articles of incorporation. Such "opt-in" also may be utilized both by an issuing public corporation that wishes coverage to begin immediately (prior to the expiration of the 12–month delay period), and by a corporation that previously opted out. Only about six of the existing state control share statutes provide an opt-in procedure.

This subsection also establishes eligibility criteria for a corporation that does not automatically qualify as an issuing public corporation. To elect coverage under the Act, a domestic corporation must have at least 100 shareholders of record and satisfy at least one of the three requirements listed in subparagraph 3(g)(1)B. That subparagraph—part of the definition of "issuing public corporation"—sets forth alternative criteria relating to the number (10,000) or percentage (10%) of resident shareholders, or the percentage (10%) of shares held by residents of the state.

The procedure to opt into the Act is that prescribed under the state business corporation law for amending a corporation's articles of incorporation—typically a board of directors resolution followed by a shareholder vote—and parallels the procedure to opt-out of the Act's application. The Joint Committee chose this approach, as opposed to an amendment to the corporation's bylaws (which can be accomplished by board action without shareholder involvement, and which some state control share statutes permit), because the Committee believes this opt-in procedure is an important corporate action that should require approval by a majority vote of shareholders. Paragraph 2(b) requires that, if the opt-in amendment to the corporation's articles is approved, it must be filed timely at the Office of the Secretary of State or other appropriate state office so as to provide public record and notice that the corporation is covered by the Act.

Section 3. **Definitions.** As used in this Article,

(a) "Acquiring person" means a person who makes or proposes to make, or persons acting as a "group" as defined in sec. 13(d)(3) of the Securities Exchange Act of 1934 who make or propose to make, a control share acquisition; but "acquiring person" does not include the issuing public corporation.

COMMENTARY TO SUBSECTION 3(a)

The Model Act's definition of "acquiring person" is new. Although the term is not found in the Indiana statute, the Joint Committee found it useful, particularly with its reference to Section 13(d)(3) of the federal Securities Exchange Act of 1934 ("1934 Act") dealing with the "group" concept. Thus, wherever "acquiring person" appears in the Act, any group (partnership, syndicate or other aggregation of persons acting in concert) is implicated.

(b) "Affiliate" means a person who directly or indirectly controls the corporation. "Control," means the possession, direct or indirect, of the power to direct or cause the direction of the management and policies of the corporation, whether through the ownership of voting securities, by contract, or otherwise. A person's beneficial ownership of ten percent or more of the voting power of a corporation's outstanding shares entitled to vote in the election of directors (except a person holding voting power in good faith as an agent, bank, broker, nominee, custodian or trustee for one or more beneficial owners who do not individually or as a group control the corporation) creates a presumption that the person controls the corporation.

COMMENTARY TO SUBSECTION 3(b)

The defined term is used several times in the Act to refer to persons who have an influential role in the direction of corporate management and policies, particularly with respect to the voting process. It is taken from the familiar definitions of "affiliate" and "control" found in Rule 405 under the Securities Act of 1933 ("1933 Act"), but is narrowed to suit the limited purpose to which it is put in the Act.

(c) "All voting power" means the aggregate voting power that the shareholders of an issuing public corporation would have in the election of directors, except for this Article.

COMMENTARY TO SUBSECTION 3(c)

This definition of "all voting power" likewise is unique to the Model Act. The phrase means the aggregate voting power that shareholders of all classes of the stock of the issuing public corporation would have in the election of directors, but for the application of the Act. The principal use of the definition is in subsection 5(g), which describes the shareholder vote taken for the purpose of determining whether or not voting power will be accorded to the shares that are the subject of a control share acquisition.

(d) "Control shares" means issued and outstanding shares of an issuing public corporation that, except for this Article, would have voting power when added to all other shares of the issuing public corporation owned of record or beneficially by an acquiring person or in respect to which that acquiring person may exercise or direct the exercise of voting power, that would entitle the acquiring person, immediately after acquisition of the shares (directly or indirectly), to exercise or direct the exercise of the voting power of the issuing public corporation in the election of directors within any of the following ranges of voting power:

(1) One-fifth (⅕) or more but less than one-third (⅓) of all voting power;

(2) One-third (⅓) or more but less than a majority of all voting power; or

(3) A majority or more of all voting power.

COMMENTARY TO SUBSECTION 3(d)

Although the definition of "control shares" in the Model Act is the same in all material respects as the definition in the Indiana statute (as well as most other state control share laws), the Model Act uses the definition somewhat differently. "Control shares" are equity securities of an issuing public corporation that, were it not for the Act, would permit the acquiring person voting power in the election of corporate directors in excess of any of the three thresholds specified—one-fifth, one-third or a majority. The reason for the triple threshold, according to the drafting commentary to the Indiana control share statute, is that: (i) 20% is the level of ownership at which, under equity accounting rules, a corporation may report the results of its investment in another corporation as a line item on its financial statements; (ii) 33% is generally recognized as a sufficient block of shares to constitute effective control for most, if not all, practical purposes where a public corporation's shareholders are generally dispersed; and (iii) a majority or more of voting power comprises literal control.

As used in the Model Act, "control shares" are all shares owned of record or beneficially by the acquiring person (including shares acquired in separate purchases over an extended period of time) that, when added to all other holdings of the acquiring person, entitle the acquiring person to exercise voting power in excess of one or more of the three specified thresholds of voting power. There is a difference between the Model Act and the Indiana statute with respect to the treatment of voting rights for control shares representing less than 20% of all voting power, and for control shares acquired within a range of voting power for which approval has already been obtained. See Commentary to subsections 4(b) and (c). Thus, while the Indiana statute and most of the other state control share laws emphasize the concept of the acquisition, the Model Act's focus is on the control shares themselves—the means of exercising control. The other statutes attempt to identify the transaction constituting the control share acquisition, and then sterilize shares involved in that transaction. For purposes of the Model Act, however, it does not matter which shares were involved in the control share acquisition transaction (so long as such a transaction occurred) and which shares were previously held. The consequence with respect to the voting rights of both kinds of shares is the same.

The definition provides that it is a person's actual ability to control the voting power over the requisite percentage of shares—and not merely record ownership—that is the key to determining whether the shares are "control shares." The definition includes both shares "owned of record or beneficially by an acquiring person" (covering the right to acquire the shares) and shares "in respect to which that acquiring person may exercise or direct the exercise of voting power." Additionally, the acquisition of control shares comes under the statute whether it occurs "directly or indirectly." Because the term "acquiring person" is defined to include a "group," an acquisition either by one person alone or by two or more persons acting cooperatively or in concert is covered. The reference to voting power "in the election of directors" is intended to deal with the situation in which the voting power of certain series or classes of a corporation's stock may be limited to specific issues. It is only voting power in electing the company's directors that is considered in the definition of "control shares."

(e)(1) "Control share acquisition" means acquisition by any person of ownership of, or the power to direct the exercise of voting power with respect to, control shares.

COMMENTARY TO SUBSECTION 3(e)(1)

Paragraph 3(e)(1) defines the phrase "control share acquisition" with language that is nearly identical to that contained in the other state control share statutes enacted to date—with the exception that the Model Act language does not include a provision establishing a conclusive presumption that shares acquired during any 90–day period are deemed to have been acquired in the same acquisition. This device for identifying the transaction (or series of transactions) that constitutes a control share acquisition is unnecessary here because the Act affects the voting rights only of control shares held in excess of the applicable percentage. Identification of the transaction in which the control shares were acquired is irrelevant. Thus, the Act allows more certainty than other state statutes in determining whether and when a control share acquisition has taken place.

(2) A person who acquires shares in the ordinary course of business for the benefit of others in good faith and not for the purpose of

circumventing this Article has not made a control share acquisition of shares in respect of which that person is not able to exercise or direct the exercise of votes without further instruction from others.

COMMENTARY TO SUBSECTION 3(e)(2)

Paragraph 3(e)(2) excludes from the definition of "control share acquisition" acquisitions made by persons, such as brokers or nominees, who acquire shares for the benefit of others in the ordinary course of business, so long as (i) the acquisition is made "in good faith and not for the purpose of circumventing" the Act, and (ii) the acquiror is not "able to exercise or direct the exercise of votes without further instruction from others" (typically, the beneficial owner). This type of provision is present in the Indiana law and in 10 of the other state control share statutes. The exclusion is designed to avoid application of the Act where, as part of normal commercial practices, record ownership of shares may be in the name of a broker or other nominee, but where actual voting power with respect to those shares is held by the broker's customer or the nominee's principal. If, however, voting power for such shares is not subject to such further instruction or direction from beneficial owners, but rather may be exercised independently by the broker or nominee, the exclusion does not apply. Moreover, the exclusion cannot be used to circumvent the chapter—such as where a broker's purchases for clients are in fact being made in concert with, and as part of an effort to assist, an acquiring person's plans to obtain effective voting control.

(3) The acquisition of any control shares does not constitute a control share acquisition if the acquisition is made in good faith and not for the purpose of circumventing this Article in any of the following circumstances:

COMMENTARY TO SUBSECTION 3(e)(3)

Paragraph 3(e)(3) contains eleven express exclusions from the definition of control share acquisition. There is considerable consistency among the states that have enacted control share statutes as to what transactions should not invoke the statutes' voting rights limitations and procedures. The exclusions generally cover: (i) transactions that, as a practical matter, do not carry the threat of a corporate takeover; (ii) transactions as to which director and collective shareholder approval are already required by another corporate law procedure; and (iii) transactions as to which equitable considerations argue against application of the Act. Each of the acquisitions described must be "made in good faith and not for the purpose of circumventing" the Act in order to qualify for the exclusion.

A. At a time when the corporation was not subject to this Article.

B. Pursuant to a contract entered into at a time when the corporation was not subject to this Article.

COMMENTARY TO SUBSECTION 3(e)(3)A and B

Subparagraphs 3(e)(3)A and B exclude share acquisitions that are made, or that result from a contract entered into at a time when the Act does not apply to the corporation. For constitutional and essential fairness reasons, the statute's provisions affecting control share voting power should only cover acquisitions (and contracts for acquisitions) which occur when the corporation is subject to the Act. Investors, then, can take it into consideration as they make their investment decisions. Conversely, acquisitions occurring, or contracts to acquire entered into, at a time when the corporation was not subject to the Act (either because the acquisition occurred before the effective date of the Act or because the corporation did not satisfy the definitional criteria of an issuing public corporation or had opted out) are excluded, even if subsequent events trigger application of the Act.

C. Pursuant to the laws of descent and distribution [citation, if desired].

COMMENTARY TO SUBSECTION 3(e)(3)C

Subparagraph 3(e)(3)C excludes shares acquired pursuant to the laws of descent and distribution. This is an exclusion contained in one form or another in all of the existing state control share statutes, and is based on the rationale that the acquisition of shares in such circumstances almost never alters the basic pattern of concentration of voting power in a corporation.

D. By a donee under an *inter vivos* gift.

COMMENTARY TO SUBSECTION 3(e)(3)D

Subparagraph 3(e)(3)D excludes shares acquired by a donee under an *inter vivos* gift. The exclusion is present in several of the state control share statutes, although not the Indiana statute. The Joint Committee regards this exclusion as having a similar rationale to that of the previous subparagraph. An *inter vivos* gift—from one living person to another—does not typically involve a change in the factors affecting corporate control. It most closely resembles (except that there is no death involved) a grantor or testator pursuant to a will or otherwise transferring shares without consideration. The effect on the corporation and its other shareholders is ordinarily nil. Of course, the "good faith" and "circumvention" language of the introductory clause apply to prevent the abuse of this exclusion.

E. Pursuant to a transfer between or among immediate family members, or between or among persons under direct common control. An "immediate family member" is any relative or spouse of a person, or any relative of such spouse, who has the same home as such person.

COMMENTARY TO SUBSECTION 3(e)(3)E

Subparagraph 3(e)(3)E is an exclusion found only in the Model Act covering transfers between or among immediate family members, or between or among individuals or entities under direct common control. Control is typically presumed upon beneficial ownership of ten percent or more of voting power. Immediate family members, as well as commonly controlled persons, almost certainly will be included in the definition of "acquiring person" by virtue of the "group" concept, and such a transfer does not change the control balance in the corporation. In other words, separate shareholdings by immediate family members or persons commonly controlled, in all circumstances contemplated by the Joint Committee, will be aggregated for purposes of determining whether a control share acquisition has occurred or will occur. Transfers between and among these individuals or entities have little or no effect. The definition of "immediate family member" comes from the definition of "associate" in Rule 14a–1 under the 1934 Act.

F. Pursuant to the satisfaction of a pledge or other security interest.

COMMENTARY TO SUBSECTION 3(e)(3)F

Subparagraph 3(e)(3)F provides an exclusion for shares acquired in satisfaction of a pledge or security interest, again with the "good faith" and lack of circumvention motivation. This exclusion is described in the commentary to the Indiana statute as being necessary and appropriate because such pledges will normally be made by one or a relatively small number of shareholders who already own shares within one of the ranges of voting power covered by the Act, and foreclosure of the pledge will normally affect no fundamental change in the pattern or the concentration of voting power. All existing state control share laws contain a form of this exclusion.

G. Pursuant to a merger or plan of consolidation or share exchange effected in compliance with [citation], if the issuing public corporation is a party to the agreement of merger or plan of consolidation or share exchange.

COMMENTARY TO SUBSECTION 3(e)(3)G

Subparagraph 3(e)(3)G excludes a transaction in which the control shares are acquired pursuant to a merger, consolidation or share exchange where an issuing public corporation is a party to the agreement. Present in all state control share statutes enacted to date, this provision is based on the premise that a share acquisition using such methods will either already have been approved by shareholders or would meet one of the statutory exceptions to the shareholder approval process (such as short-form mergers and parent-subsidiary mergers). The Model Act exclusion also specifically includes consolidations, not contained in the Indiana statute (although present in certain of the other states' statutes), inasmuch as a consolidation is similar in all relevant respects to a merger or share exchange.

H. From any person whose previous acquisition of control shares would have constituted a control share acquisition but for this paragraph 3(e)(3) (other than this subparagraph 3(e)(3)H), provided the acquisition does not result in the acquiring person holding voting power within a higher range of voting power than that of the person from whom the control shares were acquired.

COMMENTARY TO SUBSECTION 3(e)(3)H

Subparagraph 3(e)(3)H accords an exclusion for the acquisition of shares from any person whose previous acquisition would have been a control share acquisition but for application of paragraph 3(e)(3) (that is, this paragraph containing the exclusions). This "previous exclusion" provision is included in most of the other state control share statutes. The parenthetical language is new, however, and prevents the use of this exclusion in more than one transfer. The Joint Committee believes there to be little justification in allowing this exclusion to apply indefinitely to a block of control shares where the transaction in which the block is acquired does not itself qualify for an exclusion. Also new is the language limiting the exclusion to transfers that do not result in a higher (unapproved) range of voting power. (See subsection 4(c).) "Range of voting power" refers to the categories established in subsection 3(d).

I. Acquisition by a person of additional shares within the range of voting power for which such person has received approval pursuant to Section 5 or within the range of voting power resulting from shares acquired in a transaction described in this paragraph 3(e)(3).

COMMENTARY TO SUBSECTION 3(e)(3)I

Subparagraph 3(e)(3)I is a provision unique to the Model Act, but may simply make explicit what is implicit in other control share statutes. It accords an exclusion to the acquisition by a person of additional shares within the range of voting power for which such person has already received stockholder approval, and within the range of voting power enjoyed by someone who acquired shares in a transaction excluded from the definition of "control share acquisition" under these subparagraphs. Again, "range of voting power" refers to the categories described in subsection 3(d). As an example of the application of this provision, all of the shares acquired by a legatee of 22 percent of the outstanding stock of an issuing public corporation who then purchases in the market an additional ten percent, retain their full voting rights by virtue of subparagraph 3(e)(3)C (with respect to the 22 percent) and subparagraph 3(e)(3)I (with respect to the ten percent). The acquisition of another 2 percent, however, bringing the total to 34 percent, would constitute a control share acquisition and, under subsection 4(c), those shares that provide voting power of 33½ percent and more would be sterilized.

J. An increase in voting power resulting from any action taken by the issuing public corporation, provided the person whose voting power is thereby affected is not an affiliate of the corporation.

COMMENTARY TO SUBSECTION 3(e)(3)J

Subparagraph 3(e)(3)J is another exclusion that has no counterpart in existing statutes. It covers what might be considered "passive threshold crossing" situations. This occurs where, by reason of actions taken by the issuing public corporation, the subject shareholder's voting power is changed to an extent that it exceeds a control threshold. The Joint Committee feels an express exclusion is appropriate for this situation, in that an increase in voting power that results from acts of the corporation—*e.g.*, a redemption of shares, changes in share voting rights or capital structure, etc.—where the person holding shares whose voting power is affected thereby does not control the corporation's actions, should not constitute a "control share acquisition."

K. Pursuant to the solicitation of proxies subject to Regulation 14A under the Securities Exchange Act of 1934 or [citation to applicable state corporation statute].

COMMENTARY TO SUBSECTION 3(e)(3)K

Subparagraph 3(e)(3)K is an exclusion drafted by the Joint Committee to clarify that proxy solicitations are excluded from coverage of the Act. The exclusion refers to proxy solicitations both by 1934 Act reporting companies and by non–1934 Act companies that choose to be subject to the Model Act. Without such an exclusion, ordinary proxy solicitations would regularly result in a control share acquisition by the soliciting person in acquiring the power to direct the exercise of voting power of 20% or more. Proxy contests, while certainly having implications for corporate control, do not present the same threats to shareholder well-being that share acquisitions do.

Several other exclusions from the definition of control share acquisition that are contained in various of the existing state control share laws have not been included in the Model Act. Specifically, an exclusion for issuer benefit plans (as defined) was not adopted, in that management often is in a position to control the vote of those shares. Nor was the Joint Committee convinced of the need for an exclusion for resales by securities brokers or underwriters, which is found in several of the statutes. Finally, an exclusion covering acquisitions of control shares directly from the corporation is viewed by the Joint Committee as unduly favoring management and evidencing a "business protectionism" motivation, particularly since it can be used as a first step in a management buyout series of transactions.

Perhaps the most significant difference between the Model Act and the Indiana statute with respect to exclusions is that the Model Act does not contain an exclusion for the acquisition from another person of control shares as to which shareholders previously granted voting rights pursuant to the Act. It was the Joint Committee's determination not to include such an exclusion on the basis that the purposes of a control share statute have more to do with the identity, characteristics and plans of the specific acquiring person than with the block of stock. Accordingly, shareholders acting collectively should determine whether the new acquiring person should be allowed voting rights, based upon information contained in the disclosure statement and other facts brought to the shareholders' attention. An undisclosed transferee of such person, who did not receive approval from the shareholders for the voting rights of the block of control shares, may be as objectionable to the shareholders as the prior control shareholder was unobjectionable. Further, even though the absence of a "previous approval" exclusion may restrict somewhat the holder's ability to alienate control shares that have become, in all respects, the same as all other shares of the corporation by virtue of the shareholder approval process, such person still has an opportunity under the Act to sell blocks that will not be denied voting rights (up to 20% of a corporation's shares to a person who holds no other shares), thus reducing the hardship involved in owning a large block of control shares.

(f) "Interested shares" means the shares of an issuing public corporation in respect of which any of the following persons may exercise or direct the exercise, as of the applicable record date, of the voting power of the corporation in the election of directors, other than solely by the authority of a revocable proxy:

(1) The acquiring person.

(2) Any officer of the issuing public corporation.

(3) Any employee of the issuing public corporation who is also a director of the corporation.

COMMENTARY TO SUBSECTION 3(f)

The concept of "interested shares" is used in the Act for the purpose of identifying which shares will be permitted to vote on whether an acquiring person's control shares will be accorded voting rights, and is largely unrelated to the concept of "control shares." Even control shares that have been accorded voting rights pursuant to the procedures herein are voteless "interested shares" in a shareholder vote on a subsequent control share acquisition by the holder. The language of the definition, and the three categories of persons covered, are virtually identical to most existing state control share acts (with the exception of Wisconsin, which has only one threshold at one-fifth (⅕) beyond which voting power is diminished by 90%, and which permits all persons to vote all of their shares on the voting rights resolution).

"Interested shares" under the Model Act are those owned, or the voting power of which is exercised or directed, by (i) the acquiring person; (ii) any officer of the issuing public corporation; and (iii) any employee of the issuing public corporation who is also a director of the corporation. The Joint Committee considered suggestions to expand the definition to include holders of 10% or more of the stock and outside directors, but was not persuaded of the need to disenfranchise either of these categories. The "direct the exercise" language is intended to cover situations involving beneficial ownership and ownership by immediate family members and commonly controlled persons, as well as entities (such as employee stock option plans and voting trusts) a majority of the trustees of which are persons described in this subsection.

The major premise underlying the "interested share" concept is that the right to approve the exercise of control of an issuing public corporation should rest with owners of the corporation whose interest in the decision is *solely* as a pretransaction shareholder. As is pointed out in the Indiana commentary, the acquiring person's interest in the control share vote is obvious, and the interest of officers and "inside" directors is in preserving corporate positions which might be threatened by an acquisition. Thus, the shares held by these persons are "interested shares." The U.S. Supreme Court's decision in the *CTS* case specifically held that the Indiana statute's definition of "interested shares" was consistent with that statute's shareholder protection purposes in that it disqualified both the acquiror and inside management of the target corporation from voting on whether to grant voting rights to the acquiror's control shares. Moreover, this is one of the ways the Model Act "protects the independent shareholder against both of the contending parties ... further[ing] a basic purpose of the Williams

Act, 'plac[ing] investors on an equal footing with the takeover bidder [citations omitted]'." 107 S.Ct. 1645.

The Model Act's definition deals with two additional items: It clarifies the point in time at which the determination is made as to whether shares are "interested shares"—the record date. Most state statutes may be read as implying that this determination is made as of the meeting date. Also, the definition excludes from the category of "interested shares" those voted solely under the authority of a revocable proxy. This proviso appears necessary to permit management and the acquiring person to solicit proxies in connection with the meeting without thereby sterilizing those shares for the critical vote.

(g)(1) "Issuing public corporation" means a domestic corporation that has

A. any securities registered under section 12 or is subject to section 15(d) of the Securities Exchange Act of 1934; and

B. either

(i) more than ten percent (10%) of its shareholders resident in [state];

(ii) more than ten percent (10%) of its shares owned by [state] residents; or

(iii) ten thousand (10,000) shareholders resident in [state].

(2) The residence of a shareholder is presumed to be the address appearing in the records of the corporation.

(3) Shares held by banks (except as trustee or guardian), brokers or nominees are disregarded for purposes of calculating the percentages and numbers in this subsection 3(g).

COMMENTARY TO SUBSECTION 3(g)

Paragraph 3(g)(1) defines which corporations are "issuing public corporations" subject to the Act. While the Model Act follows certain of the definitional provisions of the Indiana statute, the definition in the Act differs in several significant respects.

As an initial matter, the company must be a domestic corporation, which is to say that it is subject to the state business corporation statute under which the Model Act will be adopted. Whereas the Indiana statute and the majority of the other state control share statutes restrict coverage to corporations chartered in those states, several states that enacted control share statutes after the *CTS* decision (Oklahoma, North Carolina, Massachusetts, Florida and Arizona) include within the coverage of their laws nondomiciled corporations with a strong economic nexus to the state. The emergence of post-*CTS* state control share laws that extended applicability to nondomestic corporations has resulted in vigorous calls for state preemption by some members of Congress and others, on the grounds that such laws would result in a "balkanization" of state takeover regulation. Where nondomestic corporations can be regulated by a state's control share statute, it is argued, a takeover offer for a particular corporation can be subject to the laws of more than one state involving conflicting requirements and procedures and making compliance with all of the applicable laws impossible.

In the *CTS* decision, the Supreme Court concluded that the Indiana Act did not create the risk of inconsistent state regulation, stating: "The Indiana Act poses no such problem. So long as each State regulates voting rights only in the corporations it has created, each corporation will be subject to the law of only one state. No principle of corporation law and practice is more firmly established than a state's authority to regulate domestic corporations, including the authority to define the voting rights of shareholders." 107 S.Ct. 1649.

In November 1987, the constitutionality of a state control share statute that sought to cover nondomestic corporations was addressed by a federal district court in *TLX Acquisition Corp. v. Telex Corporation* (No. CIV–87–2056–R; WD Okla. Nov. 3, 1987). In its decision, the court concluded that the Oklahoma control share statute, insofar as it sought to cover nondomestic corporations, was unconstitutional under the Commerce Clause. The result in the *TLX* case may have been predicted from the *CTS* decision in which the Supreme Court stated: "We agree that Indiana has no interest in protecting nonresident shareholders of nonresident corporations." 107 S.Ct. 1651.

It remains unclear from the language of *CTS* whether additional nexus criteria—beyond the requirement of being a domestic corporation—are necessary to ensure the Commerce Clause constitutionality of a control share statute, or are only "make weight" items. Clearly, the inclusion of these additional nexus criteria creates a possibility that some publicly held corporations will not automatically qualify as issuing public corporations in *any* Model Act states. Moreover, these tests are rarely accurate in revealing the true extent of home-state shareholdings, due to the prevalence of beneficial (nominee) ownership. Some Joint Committee members would prefer to eliminate all shareholder nexus criteria. However, the Committee determined that it is appropriate to include the resident shareholders and resident share tests in the Act because of the *CTS* language which indicated that the shareholder nexus criteria reinforced the Indiana Law's constitutionality for Commerce Clause purposes. The court stated at 107 S.Ct. 1652: "Moreover, unlike the Illinois statute invalidated in *MITE,* the Indiana Act applies only to corporations that have a substantial number of shareholders in Indiana. Thus, every application of the Indiana Act will affect a substantial number of Indiana residents, whom Indiana indisputably has an interest in protecting."

Thus, the Model Act definition in subparagraph 3(g)(1)B, contains the identical three alternative criteria used in the Indiana statute requiring either: (i) more than 10% of the corporation's shareholders resident in the state; (ii) more than 10% of the corporation's shares held by state residents; or (iii) 10,000 resident shareholders.

One of the substantive changes from the Indiana statute's definition which was made by the Joint Committee has to do with economic (as opposed to shareholder) nexus criteria. As a matter of policy, the Committee determined that factors relating to principal place of business, substantial assets and number of employees—criteria that are present in most of the state control share statutes enacted to date—should not be included in the Model Act. The principal reason for the Committee's decision was that those factors smack of local business protectionism, an objective that the Joint Committee sought to avoid. Moreover, the presence of such criteria raise[s] Commerce Clause questions which, after *CTS,* can be avoided by applying the Act with reference only to the residency of the corporation and its shareholders.

The second major departure in the Model Act from the Indiana definition is the Joint Committee's decision to base automatic eligibility under the Act as an "issuing public corporation" on the domestic corporation's status as a reporting company under the federal 1934 Act. The Committee regards the Act as a safeguard for the rights of stockholders primarily of "public" companies, and not for those of close corporations and corporations with relatively few investors. Typically, companies with a small number of shareholders have a more personal relationship with them, and those stockholders often are more active in monitoring and even participating in, the affairs of the corporation. The 1934 Act's standard for delineating between a public company and one that might be regarded as "private" is commonly understood and easy to apply. Private companies are given the authority, however, to choose to be treated by the Act like a public company. Accordingly, subparagraph 3(g)(1)A provides that the definition covers only corporations that have securities registered under Section 12 of the 1934 Act or are subject to Section 15(d) of the 1934 Act. These companies are automatically "issuing public corporations" unless they opt out. Reference was not included to companies under Section 12(b)(2)(G) of the 1934 Act (insurance companies), although states enacting a control share statute that wish to extend automatic coverage eligibility to such companies can do so by adding the phrase "or exempted from registration by s. 12(g)(2)(G) of that Act" at the appropriate place. The Joint Committee recognizes that many companies in regulated industries (*e.g.,* banks, utilities, communications firms, etc.) are subject to special change of control requirements that may or may not be consistent with the Act's theme.

Paragraph 3(g)(2) follows language present in most of the state control share laws, including Indiana's, establishing a conclusive presumption for purposes of determining whether a corporation meets any of the three alternative "residency" requirements in subparagraph 3(g)(1)B: For pragmatic reasons it is presumed that a shareholder's residence is the address appearing in the records of the corporation, although the Committee acknowledges that this residency test is far from perfect. Such language is also consistent with provisions in most state business corporation laws prescribing where written notice to shareholders is to be directed.

Subparagraph 3(g)(3) is also patterned after comparable provisions in other state statutes. It provides that shares held by banks (except as trustee or guardian), brokers or nominees are disregarded for purposes of calculating the percentages or numbers of shareholders in the determination of whether a corporation is an "issuing public corporation" subject to the Act. The effect of this rather arbitrary rule is to prevent what would otherwise be the case for most publicly held companies with large percentages of their stock held in "street name"—that is, New York residency for the predominance of their shares and shareholders.

(h) "Person" means any individual, corporation, partnership, unincorporated association or other entity.

COMMENTARY TO SUBSECTION 3(h)

Subsection 3(h) defines "person" consistent with the standard definitional language in most state business corporation laws to mean "any individual, corporation, partnership, unincorporated association or other entity."

Section 4. **Voting Rights of Control Shares.** Unless otherwise provided in the articles of incorporation before either a control share acquisition occurs or a disclosure statement is delivered, control shares that are the subject of a control share acquisition have only such voting rights as are accorded under this Section 4.

COMMENTARY TO SECTION 4

The heart of this Model Control Share Act is Section 4, which has the effect of reducing or eliminating entirely the voting power of control shares acquired in a control share acquisition unless those voting rights are restored pursuant to a procedure involving a shareholder vote. The shareholders thus are given a collective role in determining whether a newly-acquired or to-be-acquired concentration of shares of an issuing public corporation will be permitted any influence in the governance of that corporation. As a practical matter, it forces the acquiring person to (1) negotiate with the corporation's board of directors regarding a proposed change of control; or (2) persuade the corporation's shareholders (by making a sufficiently favorable offer or otherwise) to approve the acquiring person's voting power. Such a result tends to reduce the coercive aspects of a hostile tender offer, while furthering the philosophical rationale for this statute of permitting pretransaction shareholders of the corporation to deal with the acquiring person collectively. Also, it is presumed that such an effect will encourage more equitable distribution of the control premium.

The section begins with an express "opt-out" clause permitting a corporation that would otherwise be subject to the voting rights limitations of the statute, through amendment to its articles of incorporation (by the ordinary means provided in the corporate law), to make this Article inapplicable. Such action must be taken prior to the time a control share acquisition occurs or a disclosure statement is delivered to avoid implicating the "opt-out" decision in the control share voting procedure. Most of the existing state control share laws (all but Hawaii and North Carolina) include opt-out provisions, although some of these permit an opt-out by amendment to the bylaws rather than the corporate charter. The Joint Committee believes that the decision whether this statute will or will not apply to the corporation should be made by the shareholders. See also Section 6 and Commentary thereto.

(a) Subject to subsections (b)-(d) of this Section 4, the voting power of control shares having voting power of one-fifth (1/5) or more of all voting power is reduced to zero unless the shareholders of the issuing public corporation approve a resolution pursuant to the procedure set forth in Section 5 according the shares the same voting rights as they had before they became control shares.

COMMENTARY TO SUBSECTION 4(a)

This is the operative subsection of the statute. It clarifies an ambiguity found in a number of the state statutes, including Indiana's, as to exactly what happens to the voting rights of control shares in a control share acquisition. Some of the statutes, cryptically, state that such control shares "have only such voting rights as are conferred" by this chapter. The Model Act makes absolutely clear that, except as otherwise provided in the Act, such shares have *no* voting rights, unless they are approved by the disinterested shareholders.

(b) Except as provided in subsection 5(g), the voting power of control shares representing voting power of less than one-fifth (⅕) of all voting power is not affected by this Article.

COMMENTARY TO SUBSECTION 4(b)

The Joint Committee chose a different approach to sterilization of control shares from that found in the Indiana statute and most other state control share laws. Rather than reducing to zero the voting rights of the shares acquired in a transaction (or series of transactions within 90 days) that carries the acquiring person over the control share threshold, leaving the earlier acquired shares with full voting rights, this subsection provides that the voting power of all shares up to 20 percent is not affected by this Article.* Thus, for example, an acquiring person under the Indiana statute who, for reasons that are entirely immaterial to the purposes of the statute, goes from 13 percent to 21 percent shareholdings within the applicable 90–day period, loses the voting power of all shares except the previously acquired 13 percent; the result for the same shareholder under the Model Act is the loss of voting power for only the last one percent. The Joint Committee believes there is very little utility in trying to identify the transaction that takes an acquiring person over the threshold and to sterilize the shares involved in that transaction. Under the Model Act, the voting power of control shares representing voting power of less than 20 percent may be exercised, except (as the introductory phrase cautions) in connection with the approval vote.

* Ohio is the oldest of the state control statutes and, in concept, served as the original model. The major difference between the Ohio law and those that followed, however, is that Ohio actually prevents the acquisition of control shares, and not just the exercise of their voting rights, unless the shareholders grant approval. This prohibition against the purchase of shares regarded as conveying control was at the heart of the court's decision in *Fleet Aerospace Corp. v. Holderman,* 796 F.2d 135 (6th Cir., 1986) holding the Ohio statute to be an unconstitutional interference with interstate commerce. The Sixth Circuit Court of Appeals is now reviewing its decision in light of *CTS.*

(c) If control shares of the acquiring person previously have been accorded (pursuant to the procedure set forth in Section 5) the same voting rights they had before they became control shares, or if such control shares were acquired in a transaction excluded from the definition of "control share acquisition," then only the voting power of control shares acquired in a subsequent control share acquisition by such acquiring person within a higher range of voting power shall be reduced to zero.

COMMENTARY TO SUBSECTION 4(c)

Another ambiguity the Model Act attempts to correct is whether the voting power of control shares, once restored in accordance with the shareholder vote procedure, may be again eliminated by a subsequent control share acquisition. This subsection provides that once control shares have been accorded by shareholder vote the same voting rights they had before they were originally sterilized, or if such control shares were acquired in an excluded transaction, the shares retain those voting rights even when the acquiring person exceeds another control share threshold. Thus, the shareholder approval granted with respect to the voting rights of a 26 percent holder applies up to 33⅓ percent, and it is only the voting power of shares in excess of that next threshold that is then reduced to zero. Similarly, shares acquired in an inter vivos gift of 39 percent and the acquisition by the donee of up to another 11 percent retain their voting rights, even if their owner acquires additional shares beyond the majority threshold. It is only the voting rights of shares in excess of that majority threshold that are sterilized. See subparagraph 3(e)(3)I.

(d) The voting rights of control shares are restored to those accorded such shares prior to the control share acquisition in any of the following circumstances: (1) if, by reason of subsequent issuances of shares or other transactions by the issuing public corporation, the voting power of those control shares is reduced to a range of voting power for which approval has been granted or is not required; or (2) upon transfer to a person other than an acquiring person; or [(3) the expiration of three years after the date of a vote of shareholders pursuant to Section 5 failing to approve the resolution according voting rights to those control shares].

COMMENTARY TO SUBSECTION 4(d)

In addition to the shareholder approval procedure as provided under Section 5 of the Model Act, the statute permits the restoration of voting power of control shares in the following circumstances: (1) Where the issuing public corporation engages in a transaction, such as the issuance of additional shares, causing the voting power of control shares to be reduced to a lower range of voting power for which shareholder approval has already been granted, or for which no approval is necessary (i.e., less than 20 percent); or (2) where the control shares are transferred to someone whose percentage of shareholdings will not exceed 20 percent; or [(3) three years have expired after a shareholder vote failing to approve the voting rights resolution with respect to those shares].

The rationale for the first of these provisions is that the issuing public corporation is entirely responsible for taking the action that reduced the voting power of control shares to noncontrol level. Indeed, if someone else were to acquire the same resulting percentage, no control share acquisition would have occurred. The second provision merely makes explicit what probably is evident anyway: Shares that constituted control shares in the hands of an acquiring person become shares with ordinary voting rights in the hands of someone who has not made and does not propose to make a control share acquisition. The third provision is entirely new. It is intended to deflect criticisms voiced as to other control share statutes to the effect that perpetual sterilization of control shares is inequitable and confiscatory.

The bracketed language in the text of subsection 4(d) reflects the Joint Committee's inability to reach a clear consensus on whether voting rights of control shares should be restored after some period of time, even where the vote of disinterested shareholders to do so has failed to gain approval. Those who favor automatic restoration after three years point to the hardship and fundamental unfairness of perpetual sterilization of the shares, noting that three years is long enough to eliminate the coercion and abuses that can accompany partial tenders and other fractional acquisitions of control. Those who do not favor the provision argue that restoration of voting rights after three years without approval of disinterested shareholders is inconsistent with the statute's fundamental purpose, and would discourage other offers during the three-year waiting period. In any event, because the Act does not affect the voting rights of control shares up to 20 percent (subsection 4(b)), acquisition of 81 percent of the outstanding stock provides voting control notwithstanding the sterilization—for three years or forever—of the remaining 61 percent, since 19.9 percent then becomes an absolute majority of the shares still capable of voting. Because the Committee was divided on this issue, it was decided to include the proposal in bracketed form. Jurisdictions considering adopting the Model Act must reach their own decision on this issue.

Section 5. **Approval Procedure**

(a) Any acquiring person who proposes to make a control share acquisition may, and any acquiring person who has made a control share acquisition shall, publish in a newspaper of general circulation and deliver to the issuing public corporation at its principal office a disclosure statement. To be regarded as a disclosure statement, the document must set forth all of the following:

(1) The identity of the acquiring person;

(2) A statement that the disclosure statement is delivered pursuant to this Article;

(3) The number of shares of the issuing public corporation owned (directly or indirectly) by the acquiring person, the acquisition dates and the prices at which such shares were acquired;

(4) The voting power to which the acquiring person, except for Section 4, would be entitled;

(5) A form of the resolution to be considered by the shareholders hereunder; and

(6) If the control share acquisition has not yet occurred

A. a description in reasonable detail of the terms of the proposed control share acquisition; and

B. representations of the acquiring person, together with a statement in reasonable detail of the facts upon which they are based, that the proposed control share acquisition, if consummated, will not be contrary to law, and that the acquiring person has the financial capacity to make the proposed control share acquisition.

COMMENTARY TO SUBSECTION 5(a)

Section 5 follows very closely the procedure for approval of voting rights of control shares found in the Indiana statute and many of the other state laws. The Joint Committee has made few substantive changes, although certain procedural problems and ambiguities of the Indiana law have been dealt with.

The procedure begins with the publication and delivery to the issuing public corporation of a "disclosure statement" by an acquiring person. Unlike the comparable Indiana provision, in order to set the shareholder voting procedures in motion, this is made a mandatory procedure on the part of any acquiring person who has made a control share acquisition, and is optional on the part of a person who proposes to make a control share acquisition. Of course, an acquiring person who has acquired no shares but proposes to do so, and who does not publish and deliver a disclosure statement, does not invoke the shareholder voting procedures. The publication requirement (which is not found in the Indiana law) is designed to prevent an acquiring person who proposes to make, but who has not yet made, a control share acquisition from initiating the shareholder voting procedure without cost or serious consequence to the acquiring person. Such action might otherwise be employed simply to put the company "in play" without any real intent to follow through with the control share acquisition. The publication requirement is intended to invoke Rule 14d–2(b) under the 1934 Act which deems a public announcement of this type to constitute the commencement of a tender offer for purposes of Section 14(d) of the 1934 Act. The subsection goes on to identify the information (which is virtually the same as in the Indiana statute) that must be included in the disclosure statement. If the document does not contain all such information, it is not regarded as a disclosure statement and does not trigger the procedure that follows receipt of a disclosure statement. But, unlike the Indiana statute, failure to file a disclosure statement does not establish a redemption right on the part of the corporation. More generally, failures of compliance with the procedures established in this section of the Act can be remedied like any other breach of statutory corporate law—by resort to the courts.

(b) If the directors of the issuing public corporation so order, or if the acquiring person so requests at the time of delivery of a disclosure statement and gives an undertaking to pay the issuing public corporation's expenses in connection therewith, a special meeting of shareholders of the issuing public corporation must be called within ten (10) days after delivery of the disclosure statement for the purpose of considering the resolution relating to the voting rights to be accorded the shares acquired or to be acquired in the control share acquisition. Unless both the acquiring person and the issuing public corporation agree in writing to another date, the special meeting of shareholders must be held not sooner than thirty (30) days nor later than fifty (50) days after receipt by the issuing public corporation of the request or order for a special meeting.

COMMENTARY TO SUBSECTION 5(b)

Delivery of a valid disclosure statement begins the shareholder voting procedure. A special meeting of shareholders for the purpose of considering a resolution according voting rights to the control shares must be called within ten days if either the acquiring person so requests when delivering its disclosure statement (provided an undertaking is given by the acquiring person to pay the costs of the meeting), or if the directors of the issuing public corporation so order. The Joint Committee feels that the latter procedure, probably available under most state business corporation statutes anyway, ought to be explicitly applicable in these circumstances. The timing of the special meeting is designed to coordinate with time periods prescribed under the federal Williams Act, in particular, the special meeting must be held within 50 days of the request, unless otherwise agreed by the company and acquiring person, in order to fall within the 60–day period after which tendering shareholders must be granted withdrawal rights under Section 14(d)(5) of the 1934 Act. The 30–day minimum period, applicable unless otherwise agreed, permits sufficient time for the solicitation of proxies and other tasks necessary to prepare for and conduct the meeting.

Both the procedural and timing aspects of this subsection are structured to be consistent with the Indiana Act's provisions, regarding which the *CTS* decision observed: "Unlike the *MITE* statute, the Indiana Act does not give either management or the offeror an advantage in communicating with the shareholders about the impending offer. The Act also does not impose an indefinite delay on tender offers." 107 S.Ct. 1646.

(c) If no special meeting of shareholders is called pursuant to subsection 5(b), the resolution relating to the voting rights to be accorded the shares acquired in the control share acquisition must be presented to the next special or annual meeting of shareholders.

COMMENTARY TO SUBSECTION 5(c)

In the absence of a request for a special shareholders meeting by the acquiring person, the directors need not call such a meeting and the voting rights resolution will be presented at the next annual shareholders meeting or special meeting called for any purpose. This assures that the issue will be considered by shareholders at the next opportunity, whether or not the acquiring person wants the process to move more slowly. Control share voting rights that are approved at one meeting cannot be affected by a subsequent vote, except as provided in subsection 5(h) involving competing control share acquisitions.

(d) If a special meeting is called, notice of the special meeting of shareholders must be given as promptly as reasonably practicable by the issuing public corporation to all shareholders of record as of the record date set for the meeting. If the special meeting was requested by the acquiring person, the directors shall set the record date on a date not later than 15 days after the request was received by the issuing public corporation.

COMMENTARY TO SUBSECTION 5(d)

Notice of a special shareholders meeting must be given promptly after the meeting is called. The record date will be established on a date not later than 15 days after the request for a special meeting was received. This is the date for determination of whether shares constitute "interested shares" under subsection 3(f). It may be in the interests of the issuing public corporation to set an earlier record date, however, in order to try to reduce the drift of shares into the hands of arbitrageurs and other takeover speculators whose vote in the approval process may be dictated solely by short-term considerations. The 15–day period is intended to facilitate, if necessary, the beneficial owner inquiry provided for in Rule 14a–13 under the 1934 Act.

(e) Notice of the special meeting, or the annual meeting if no special meeting is called, must include or be accompanied by

(1) A copy of the disclosure statement;

(2) A statement by the board of directors of its position or recommendation, or that it is taking no position or making no recommendation, with respect to the resolution contained in the disclosure statement; and

(3) A description of any dissent and appraisal rights or any redemption procedure that may accompany or result from the vote of shareholders.

COMMENTARY TO SUBSECTION 5(e)

The notice of the special meeting must include, in addition to a copy of the acquiring person's disclosure statement and a position statement of the board of directors, a description of any dissent and appraisal rights or any redemption procedure that may accompany of result from the shareholder vote. Although the Joint Committee determined not to include in the Model Act either of the latter provisions for the reasons hereinafter discussed (*see* "ADDITIONAL COMMENTARY"), some states may choose nevertheless to insert dissent and appraisal rights and/or a redemption procedure or may apply general corporate law procedures to this transaction. And if they do, these provisions ought to be described in the notice. Of course, if the issuing public corporation is subject to the proxy requirements of Regulation 14A (which will usually be the case), the shareholders will receive considerably more information.

(f) Any other provisions of this Article notwithstanding, a proxy relating to a meeting of shareholders to be held pursuant to this Section 5 must be solicited separately from the offer to purchase or solicitation of an offer to sell shares of the issuing public corporation.

COMMENTARY TO SUBSECTION 5(f)

One criticism of the Indiana statute and other state control share acquisition laws involves the strategy of soliciting revocable proxies along with a tender of the shares in the tender offer. The acquiring person's acquisition of proxies from shareholders of record who tender has the effect of undermining the basic premise of the statute—that is, facilitating a collective decision by the pre-transaction shareholders on a change of control. Subsection 3(f) excludes from the definition of "interested shares" shares in respect of which voting power may be exercised or directed solely by the authority of a revocable proxy. This is to avoid the unintended consequence of requiring all shareholders to attend in person the meeting of shareholders, in order to prevent disenfranchisement of their shares by giving their proxy to an officer or director of the issuing public corporation. If proxies are to be solicited for purposes of the approval vote, therefore, both the acquiring person and the issuing public corporation will be on equal footing in having to make a separate solicitation.

(g) All votes cast at the meeting for or against the resolution contained in the disclosure statement must be identified as non-interested shares. To be approved, the resolution must receive the affirmative votes of a majority of all voting power, excluding all interested shares. If the resolution is not approved, the acquiring person not sooner than six months thereafter, may present a new resolution for a vote of shareholders in accordance with this Section 5 at any subsequent shareholders meeting as long as the voting power of the control shares described in the resolution is reduced.

COMMENTARY TO SUBSECTION 5(g)

This subsection sets forth the vote that must be obtained to approve a resolution granting voting rights to control shares. Unlike Indiana's statute, which requires two separate majority votes in circumstances in which the control share acquisition would effectuate changes in classes of shares, the Model Act calls for one affirmative majority vote in all cases. The sole voting requirement is a majority of all voting power, excluding all shares owned by the acquiring person or any officer or director/employee of the issuing public corporation. The Joint Committee considered and rejected the inclusion of the second shareholder vote requirement provided for in the Indiana Act (consisting of a majority of *all* voting power—that is, all shares authorized to vote in the election of directors by whomever owned). The Committee concluded that such a requirement would give undue weight to management votes and effectively require the acquiring person to purchase the control shares, rather than use a conditional tender offer. Thus, the Joint Committee believes it appropriate to determine, by the single vote provided for in subsection 5(g), the sentiments of shareholders of the issuing public corporation who are "disinterested" in the transaction, in the sense that neither the voting rights of their shares nor their position with the company will be affected by the vote.

The vote of disinterested shareholders to determine whether voting rights will be accorded control shares is the heart of the Indiana Act which provided the shareholder protection rationale for upholding its constitutionality in the *CTS* case. The Court, contrasting the Indiana Act with the Illinois statute struck down in *MITE,* stated "... [T]he statute now before the Court protects the independent shareholder against both of the contending parties. Thus, the Act furthers a basic purpose of the Williams Act, 'plac[ing] investors on an equal footing with the takeover bidder,'" [citations omitted]. 107 S.Ct. 1645. The Court went on to state: "The Indiana Act operates on the assumption, implicit in the Williams Act, that independent shareholders faced with tender offers often are at a disadvantage. By allowing such shareholders to vote as a group, the Act protects them from the coercive aspects of some tender offers." 107 S.Ct. 1646.

The theme of collective decision-making on a change of control was repeated in the *CTS* decision at 107 S.Ct. 1651 where the court stated: "The primary purpose of the Act is to protect the shareholders of Indiana corporations. It does this by affording shareholders, when a takeover offer is made, an opportunity to decide collectively whether the resulting change in voting control of the corporation, as they perceive it, would be desirable."

Several states have added additional requirements to the approval of voting rights for control shares (or even convening the shareholders meeting to vote on the proposition) that the Joint Committee considered and rejected for the Model Act. Four states (Arizona, Hawaii, Minnesota and Ohio) mandate the consummation of the control share acquisition within a specified period of time following the approval vote, or else the vote becomes void. Two of these states (Arizona and Minnesota) also require that the acquiring person must have definitive financing arrangements in place at the time the disclosure statement is delivered or no special meeting of shareholders is called. The Joint Committee was not convinced of the benefits of these provisions and did not include them.

The last sentence of the subsection was added to mitigate the punitive effects of a negative vote. This provision, unique to the Model Act, permits a new voting resolution to be presented to the shareholders again, but not sooner than six months after the resolution was defeated. The Joint Committee feels this procedure accommodates changed circumstances and provides fairness to the acquiring person.

(h)(1) For purposes of this subsection 5(h), "competing control share acquisition" means a control share acquisition or proposed control share acquisition that is the subject of a disclosure statement delivered to the issuing public corporation under subsection 5(a) not less than 25 days prior to the scheduled annual or special meeting date which has been or is required to be established under subsection 5(g) with respect to a pending control share acquisition.

(2) In the event that a competing control share acquisition is made or proposed, the issuing public corporation shall, at the option of the acquiring person making the competing control share acquisition, call for

a vote of shareholders to consider the resolution relating to the voting rights of the competing control share acquisition at the same meeting as has been or is to be called to consider the voting rights of the pending control share acquisition. In the event the acquiring person making the competing control share acquisition does not elect in writing to have the resolution relating to the voting rights of the competing control share acquisition considered at the same meeting, any vote shall be held as provided in subsection 5(c) except that in such case no vote may be called on the competing control share acquisition prior to the earlier of the vote on the resolution relating to voting rights of the pending control share acquisition or 51 days after receipt by the issuing public corporation of the request for a meeting by the acquiring person making the pending control share acquisition.

(3) If more than one resolution relating to a control share acquisition is to be considered at any meeting or at meetings scheduled for or occurring on the same day, all such resolutions relating to the voting rights of acquiring persons shall be considered by shareholders in the order in which the initial disclosure statements relating to such control share acquisitions were delivered to the issuing public corporation. However, no resolution approved by shareholders shall become effective until midnight of the date on which the respective shareholder approval occurs.

(4) If resolutions relating to two or more control share acquisitions are subject to shareholder vote under subsection 5(g), shares held by an acquiring person are considered interested shares only for purposes of a vote on a resolution relating to a control share acquisition by that same acquiring person.

COMMENTARY TO SUBSECTION 5(h)

The procedure under this subsection is designed to deal with a "competing control share acquisition"—meaning a control share acquisition that invokes the shareholder voting procedure of an issuing public corporation before the voting rights of control shares that are the subject of a prior control share acquisition have been restored. This subsection was repealed and recreated by the Joint Committee, effective August 1, 1989, based on an analysis and draft language contained in a comment letter submitted in connection with the Chicago Bar Association's evaluation in early 1989 of proposed takeover-related legislation in Illinois. The revised provision removes a delay feature that was contained in the original version of the subsection and provides a mechanism for simultaneous consideration of multiple competing bids. Under the revised provision, once a competing control share acquisition is interjected, shareholders are given the right to vote on resolutions relating to all acquisition proposals at the same meeting, provided that any competing bid is the subject of a disclosure statement delivered to the issuing public corporation not less than 25 days prior to the scheduled date of the meeting on the pending control share acquisition.

If a bidder does not meet the 25 day deadline (thus not meeting the competing bid definitional criteria), or if the 25 day deadline is met but the competing bidder elects in writing not to have its bid considered at the same meeting, no shareholder vote can be called regarding the subsequent competing bid until after the vote on the pending control share acquisition. Then if a resolution relating to a pending control share acquisition receives the requisite shareholder vote to grant full voting rights, actions with respect to a subsequent competing control share acquisition have no effect on the prior control shares (which had been granted full voting rights).

The language in paragraph (3) provides that multiple resolutions considered at the same meeting or separate meetings on the same day become effective simultaneously and that any procedural or timing machinations which may be attempted (adjourned meetings, late night meetings to cause the votes to occur on separate calendar days, etc.) cannot be used to cause the second acquiring person's resolution to become effective first, unless the first acquiring person's resolution has been defeated.

Under the language in paragraph (4), where two or more unconsummated control share acquisitions are pending, the shares of an acquiring person are not "interested shares" except with respect to the vote to restore that acquiring person's voting rights. They are sterilized, however, at a 20 percent or greater level.

(i) All provisions of [the state business corporations act] that are not inconsistent with the procedures set forth in this Section 5 shall apply to the meeting of shareholders of the issuing public corporation.

COMMENTARY TO SUBSECTION 5(i)

It is intended that nonconflicting provisions of the state business corporation act will apply, in addition to the procedures set forth in this Section 5, to the meeting of shareholders of the issuing public corporation.

Section 6. **Special Minority Shareholder Rights**

(a) This section applies to all transactions that, but for subparagraphs 3(e)(3)A and B, would be control share acquisitions in which

(1) The acquiring person is or includes an affiliate of the issuing public corporation;

(2) The corporation has, by a provision in its articles of incorporation adopted within the prior 12 months, elected not to be subject to this Article; and

(3) The acquiring person has acquired a majority or more of all voting power.

(b) Within 30 days after a control share acquisition subject to subsection 6(a) occurs, the acquiring person must make a written offer to purchase the shares of each remaining shareholder at a price at least equal to the highest price at which the control shares were acquired by the acquiring person within the 12 months immediately preceding the offer.

COMMENTARY TO SECTION 6

This section, which is not found in other state control share statutes, is intended to prevent abuses of the opt-out procedure in Section 4. It was prompted by the Joint Committee's concern that those who control an issuing public corporation can deny disinterested shareholders the protections afforded by this Act and circumvent the requirement for a vote of disinterested shares by bringing about a shareholders' vote to opt out of the Act as the first step of a control share acquisition. Without such a provision in the Act, management would have the power, given its influential role in the corporate voting process, to accomplish through an amendment to the articles of incorporation that which it could not accomplish through a vote of the disinterested shareholders. Particularly where management already holds substantial voting power, the amendment to the articles opting out could be effected over the opposition of a majority of the disinterested shares. This result not only would frustrate the central purpose of the Act, it might also be viewed as giving management an unfair advantage over other potential acquirors.

To address this problem, Section 6 requires that if an affiliate of the corporation—one who controls the management and policies, such as officers and directors—alone or with others, acquires a majority or more of the voting shares within one year of a vote to opt out of the Act, the acquiring person must offer to purchase all the remaining shares at a price no lower than the highest price paid for the acquired shares by the acquiring person during the past year. The Joint Committee believes this approach safeguards the rights of disinterested shareholders without depriving the corporation of the flexibility to opt out of the Act for what might be legitimate reasons.

Section 7. **Severability.** The provisions of this Article are severable. If any provision is invalid, or if its application to any person or circumstance is invalid, such invalidity shall not affect other provisions or applications which can be given effect without the invalid provision or application.

ADDITIONAL COMMENTARY

Redemption of Acquired Control Shares. The Model Act does not provide for the redemption of control shares by the issuing public corporation. The Indiana law permits such mandatory redemption, if authorized in the corporation's articles of incorporation or bylaws before the occurrence of the control share acquisition, within 60 days after the last acquisition of any control shares by the acquiring person if no disclosure statement has been delivered to the corporation. The Model Act, unlike the Indiana Act, makes the delivery of a disclosure statement mandatory where a control share acquisition has occurred. Thus, the Joint Committee determined that this provision is not necessary within the framework of the Model Act to influence an acquiring person to deliver a disclosure statement and, in fact, is meaningless in that context.

Furthermore, the Indiana statute, along with those of 11 other states, permits mandatory redemption by the issuing public corporation, if authorized in the corporation's articles of incorporation or bylaws before the occurrence of the control share acquisition, of control shares which are not accorded full voting rights by the shareholders. The Joint Committee again rejected this procedure, in that a mandatory redemption provision of this kind may be regarded as providing a statutory basis for "greenmail" or "redemption premium" payments from the corporation to the acquirer which could be ethically undesirable, financially burdensome to the corporation and discriminatory to the shareholders. Alternatively, a low redemption price could be set by the corporation, for example disregarding all recent market price increases, which could be unfair or even punitive to the acquiring person, notwithstanding that the acquiring person would know, in advance, of the possibility of mandatory redemption at a price to be determined by the corporation.

Further, if the restoration provision of paragraph 4(d)(3) is adopted, acquired control shares will regain full voting rights within a three-year period under the Act. Thus mandatory redemption under such circumstances is unnecessary, and is inconsistent with that provision.

Dissent and Appraisal Rights. The Model Act does not provide any special dissenters' rights. Indiana and nine other states offer dissent and appraisal rights under which dissenting shareholders may receive "fair value" for their shares which is not less than the highest price per share paid by the acquiring person in the control share acquisition. The Indiana statute's special dissenters' rights are available, unless the issuing public corporation's articles of incorporation or bylaws provide to the contrary prior to the acquisition, if the acquiring person's control shares give it a majority or more of all voting power. Payment of the aggregate amount of such "fair value" may be an unreasonable and burdensome financial obligation on the corporation to the detriment of both the corporation and its continuing shareholders. In addition, such special dissenters' rights are not necessary to protect shareholders from a newly dominant shareholder, since the disinterested shareholders, in voting to return full voting power to the acquirer, already will have had an opportunity to protect themselves through collective action, as envisioned by the Supreme Court in the *CTS* decision.

Notwithstanding the absence or presence of a special dissenters' rights provision in the Model Act, the corporation law of many jurisdictions, including Indiana, normally provides dissenters' rights of general applicability. These statutory procedures usually permit shareholders who register a dissent to certain transactions that are subject to shareholder vote to receive the "fair value" of their shares, but without the special definition of "fair value" that is contained in the Indiana control share statute's special dissenters' rights provision. Whether such general dissenters' rights provisions would apply to a control share acquisition vote, and how those rights would be enforced, is a matter for determination on a state-by-state basis. In any event the Model Act would not affect the normal operation of any state's corporation law in this regard, and general dissenters' rights would be available to the extent that the state deems such rights appropriate.

L. CORPORATION FORMS

Table of Forms

---

1. ILLINOIS FORMS

A. Secretary of State Form Articles of Incorporation

[See page 652 & 653 for forms)

Form **BCA-2.10**	**ARTICLES OF INCORPORATION**	
(Rev. Jan. 1999) Jesse White Secretary of State Department of Business Services Springfield, IL 62756 http://www.sos.state.il.us	This space for use by Secretary of State	**SUBMIT IN DUPLICATE!**
Payment must be made by certified check, cashier's check, Illinois attorney's check, Illinois C.P.A.'s check or money order, payable to "Secretary of State."		**This space for use by Secretary of State** Date Franchise Tax $ Filing Fee $ Approved:

1. CORPORATE NAME: ______________________________

(The corporate name must contain the word "corporation", "company", "incorporated," "limited" or an abbreviation thereof.)

2. Initial Registered Agent: ______________________________
First Name *Middle Initial* *Last name*

Initial Registered Office: ______________________________
Number *Street* *Suite #*

IL
City *County* *Zip Code*

3. Purpose or purposes for which the corporation is organized:
(If not sufficient space to cover this point, add one or more sheets of this size.)

tony and all lawful purposes for which corporations may be organized pursuant to the Business Corporation Act of 1983 of the State of Illinois.

4. Paragraph 1: Authorized Shares, Issued Shares and Consideration Received:

Class	Par Value per Share	Number of Shares Authorized	Number of Shares Proposed to be Issued	Consideration to be Received Therefor
	$			$
				TOTAL = $

Paragraph 2: The preferences, qualifications, limitations, restrictions and special or relative rights in respect of the shares of each class are:
(If not sufficient space to cover this point, add one or more sheets of this size.)

(over)

ARTICLES OF INCORPORATION

5. OPTIONAL: (a) Number of directors constituting the initial board of directors of the corporation: ________.
(b) Names and addresses of the persons who are to serve as directors until the first annual meeting of shareholders or until their successors are elected and qualify:

Name	Residential Address	City, State, ZIP

6. OPTIONAL: (a) It is estimated that the value of all property to be owned by the corporation for the following year wherever located will be: $ ________
(b) It is estimated that the value of the property to be located within the State of Illinois during the following year will be: $ ________
(c) It is estimated that the gross amount of business that will be transacted by the corporation during the following year will be: $ ________
(d) It is estimated that the gross amount of business that will be transacted from places of business in the State of Illinois during the following year will be: $ ________

7. OPTIONAL: *OTHER PROVISIONS*
Attach a separate sheet of this size for any other provision to be included in the Articles of Incorporation, e.g., authorizing preemptive rights, denying cumulative voting, regulating internal affairs, voting majority requirements, fixing a duration other than perpetual, etc.

8. **NAME(S) & ADDRESS(ES) OF INCORPORATOR(S)**

The undersigned incorporator(s) hereby declare(s), under penalties of perjury, that the statements made in the foregoing Articles of Incorporation are true.

Dated ________________________, ______
(Month & Day) *Year*

Signature and Name	Address
1. ________________ *Signature*	1. ________________ *Street*
________________ *(Type or Print Name)*	________________ *City/Town* *State* *ZIP Code*
2. ________________ *Signature*	2. ________________ *Street*
________________ *(Type or Print Name)*	________________ *City/Town* *State* *ZIP Code*
3. ________________ *Signature*	3. ________________ *Street*
________________ *(Type or Print Name)*	________________ *City/Town* *State* *ZIP Code*

(Signatures must be in **BLACK INK** on original document. Carbon copy, photocopy or rubber stamp signatures may only be used on conformed copies.)
NOTE: If a corporation acts as incorporator, the name of the corporation and the state of incorporation shall be shown and the execution shall be by its president or vice president and verified by him, and attested by its secretary or assistant secretary.

FEE SCHEDULE

- The initial franchise tax is assessed at the rate of 15/100 of 1 percent ($1.50 per $1,000) on the paid-in capital represented in this state, with a minimum of $25.
- The filing fee is $75.
- The **minimum total due** (franchise tax + filing fee) is **$100.**
(Applies when the Consideration to be Received as set forth in Item 4 does not exceed $16,667)
- The Department of Business Services in Springfield will provide assistance in calculating the total fees if necessary.
Illinois Secretary of State Springfield, IL 62756
Department of Business Services Telephone (217) 782-9522 or 782-9523

C-162.20

B. KATTEN MUCHIN ZAVIS & ROSENMAN FORM ARTICLES OF INCORPORATION*

Additional Provisions

ARTICLE 4.

Authorization To Board Of Directors To Issue Preferred Shares Or Special Classes In Series. The preferred shares authorized in paragraph 1 of this Fourth Article ("Preferred Shares") may be issued from time to time in one or more series with such distinctive serial designations and

(a) may have such voting powers, full or limited, or may be without voting powers and may have such sinking fund provisions;

(b) may be subject to redemption at such time or times and at such prices;

(c) may be entitled to receive such dividends (which may be cumulative or non-cumulative) at such rate or rates, on such conditions, and at such times, and payable in preference to, or in such relation to, the dividends payable on any other class or classes or series of shares;

(d) may have such rights and preferences upon dissolution of, or upon any distribution of the assets of, the corporation;

(e) may be made convertible into, or exchangeable for, shares of any other class or classes or of any other series of the same or any other class or classes or series of shares of the corporation, at such price or prices or at such rates of exchange, and with such adjustments; and

(f) shall have such other designations, preferences and relative, participating, optional of other special rights, and qualifications, limitations or restrictions thereof,

as shall be permitted by statute and hereafter be stated and expressed in the resolution or resolutions providing for the issue of such Preferred Shares from time to time adopted by the board of directors pursuant to authority so to do which is hereby vested in the board of directors.

ARTICLE 7.

(A) The shareholders shall have no preemptive rights to acquire unissued shares of the corporation, or securities of the corporation convertible into or carrying a right to subscribe to or acquire shares.

[*The shareholders shall have preemptive rights to acquire unissued shares of the corporation and securities of the corporation convertible into or carrying a right to subscribe to or acquire shares.*]*

* Thanks to Herbert S. Wander, Esq., a member of Katten Muchin Zavis & Rosenman, for furnishing the Illinois Form Articles of Incorporation and By-Laws.

* Alternative provisions are shown in brackets.

(B) The power to make, alter, amend or repeal the by-laws of the corporation shall be reserved to the shareholders.

(C) No shareholder shall have cumulative voting rights in elections for directors.

(D) Each of the following matters when submitted to shareholder vote pursuant to the requirements of the Business Corporation Act of 1983, as amended from time to time, or any successor statute, shall require for its adoption, approval or authorization, as the case may be, the affirmative vote of the holders of at least a majority of the total outstanding shares entitled to vote on the matter and, if applicable, the affirmative vote of the holders of at least a majority of the outstanding shares of each class or series of shares entitled to vote as a class on the matter:

(i) a proposed amendment to these Articles of Incorporation.

(ii) a plan of merger, consolidation or exchange.

(iii) a sale, lease, exchange, or other disposition of all, or substantially all, the property and assets, with or without the good will, of the corporation, if not made in the usual and regular course of business, and the determination of, or authorization of the board of directors to determine, any or all of the terms and conditions thereof and the consideration to be received by the corporation therefor.

(iv) a resolution to voluntarily dissolve the corporation.

[*(v) (insert clause only if preemptive rights are granted in Section A) the consideration for, and the terms and conditions of, the issuance and sale of shares of the corporation to its employees or to the employees of any subsidiary corporation without first offering the same to the shareholders of the corporation.*]

(E) No director of the corporation shall be liable to the corporation or its shareholders for monetary damages for breach of fiduciary duty as a director, except for liability

(i) for any breach of the director's duty of loyalty to the corporation or its shareholders,

(ii) for acts and omissions not in good faith or that involve intentional misconduct or a knowing violation of law,

(iii) under Section 8.65 of the Business Corporation Act of the State of Illinois or any successor provision, or

(iv) for any transaction from which the director derived an improper personal benefit.

Any repeal or modification of this paragraph hall not adversely affect any right or protection of a director of the corporation existing under these articles of incorporation with respect to any act or omission occurring prior to such repeal or modification.

[*The personal liability of the directors of the corporation is eliminated to the fullest extent permitted by the Business Corporation Act.*]

(F) The corporation shall, to the fullest extent permitted by the provisions of the Business Corporation Act, indemnify any and all persons whom it shall have power to indemnify.

Drafting Notes to Article Seven

1. *Amendment of Articles of Incorporation.* Unless otherwise provided in the Articles, a two-thirds shareholder vote is required for amendment of the Articles. The Articles may provide for amendment by simple majority or any higher percentage up to 100%. The Form Articles provide for amendment by simple majority. BCA 10.20 compare with RMBCA 10.03.

2. *Organic Acts (merger, consolidation, share exchange, sale, lease or exchange of assets, dissolution)* (BCA 11.20, 11.60, 12.15, compare with RMBCA 11.04, 12.01). Unless otherwise provided in the Articles, a two-thirds shareholder vote is required for approval of any of these actions. The Articles may provide that these acts require approval by a simple majority or any higher percentage up to 100%. The Form Articles provide for approval by simple majority.

3. *By-Law Amendment* (BCA 2.25 compare with RMBCA 10.20). Unless otherwise provided in the Articles, the shareholders or the Board of Directors may amend the By–Laws. The Articles may, however, reserve to the shareholders the power to amend the By–Laws. The Form Articles will normally be silent on this point. However, an alternative provision reserving such right to the shareholders is provided in the Form Articles and in Article IX of the Form By–Laws.

4. *Cumulative Voting* (BCA 7.40 compare with RMBCA 7.21, 7.28). Unless otherwise provided in the Articles, shareholders have cumulative voting rights. The Form Articles deny cumulative voting rights.

5. *Preemptive Rights* (BCA 6.50 compare with RMBCA 6.30). Unless otherwise provided in the Articles, shareholders have no preemptive rights. Nevertheless, for purpose of reference, the normal Form Articles will specifically deny shareholders' preemptive rights. However, an alternative provision granting preemptive rights to shareholders is provided in the Form Articles. If this alternative is selected, unless otherwise provided in the Articles, a two-thirds shareholder vote is required to sell the corporation's stock to its employees free of preemptive rights. The Form Articles set forth an alternative provision requiring approval by a simple majority to effect such sales.

6. *Reacquired Shares* (BCA 9.05(b)). Under the original version of the BCA, corporations were no longer allowed to create treasury shares. The right to do so has been amended back into the BCA (effective 1/1/94), and Illinois corporations can once again create treasury shares.

Unless otherwise provided in the Articles, reacquired shares become treasury shares until canceled, at which time, they become authorized but unissued shares. The Articles may, however, provide that such shares shall not be reissued, in which event such shares are canceled and the number of authorized shares is reduced by the number of such canceled shares. The Form Articles do not provide for cancellation of reacquired shares.

7. *Special Shareholders' Meetings* (BCA 7.05 compare with RMBCA 7.02). Special shareholders' meetings may be called by the President, the Board of Directors, or the holders of one-fifth of the outstanding shares or by such other persons as may be provided in the Articles or the By–Laws. Neither the Form Articles nor the standard By–Laws prepared by our office ("Form By–Laws") provide for the calling of special shareholders' meetings by any additional persons (Form By–Laws, Section 2.2).

8. *Shareholder Quorum and Shareholder Action* (BCA 7.60). The Articles may provide for a quorum of shares not less than one-third up to 100% or shareholder action by supermajority vote up to 100%. No such provision is made in the Form Articles. The Form By–Laws provide for a quorum of a majority and action by a majority of the quorum (Form By–Laws, Section 2.7).

9. *Staggered Board* (BCA 8.10(e) compare with RMBCA 8.06). If the Board of Directors consists of six or more members, the Articles or the By–Laws may provide for a staggered Board. Neither the Form Articles nor the Form By–Laws provide for a staggered Board.

10. *Director Quorum and Director Action* (BCA 8.15 compare with RMBCA 8.24). The Articles or the By–Laws may provide for a superquorum of Directors up to 100% or the vote of a supermajority of Directors up to 100%. The Form Articles have no such provision, and the Form By–Laws provide for a quorum of a majority and action by a majority of the quorum (Form By–Laws, Sections 3.6 and 3.7).

C. KATTEN MUCHIN ZAVIS & ROSENMAN FORM BY-LAWS

ARTICLE 1. OFFICES

SECTION 1.1. *Registered Office.* The corporation shall continuously maintain in the State of Illinois a registered office and a registered agent whose office is identical with such registered office.

SECTION 1.2. *Other Offices.* The corporation may also have other offices and places of business within or without the State of Illinois.

ARTICLE 2. SHAREHOLDERS

SECTION 2.1. *Annual Meeting.* An annual meeting of the shareholders for the purpose of electing directors and for the transaction of such other business as may come before the meeting shall be held on the ___ in ___ of each year, unless the board of directors, not less than ten (10) days prior to any such fixed annual meeting date, designates another date for such annual meeting, in which event the annual meeting of shareholders for that year shall be held on the date so designated. If the day fixed for the annual meeting shall be a Saturday, Sunday or legal holiday, such meeting shall be held on the next succeeding business day.

SECTION 2.2. *Special Meetings.* Special meetings of the shareholders may be called either by the chief executive officer of the corporation, by the board of directors or by the holders of not less than one-fifth of all the outstanding shares entitled to vote on the matter for which the meeting is called. Special meetings of the shareholders shall be called by the chief executive officer of the corporation at the request in writing of any one or more shareholders owning at least one-fifth of all the outstanding shares entitled to vote on the matter for which the meeting is called. Any such request shall state the purpose or purposes of the proposed meeting.

SECTION 2.3. *Place of Meetings.* The board of directors may designate any place as the place of meeting for any annual meeting or for any special meeting called by the board of directors. If no designation is made, or if a special meeting is otherwise called, the place of meeting shall be the corporation's principal place of business.

SECTION 2.4. *Notice of Meetings.* Written notice stating the place, date and hour of the meeting, and, in the case of a special meeting, the purpose or purposes for which the meeting is called, shall be delivered not less than ten (10) nor more than sixty (60) days before the date of the meeting, or in the case of a merger, consolidation, share exchange, or dissolution, or a sale, lease or exchange of assets, not less than twenty (20) nor more than sixty (60) days before the date of the meeting, either personally or by mail, by or at the direction of the chief executive officer, the secretary, or the officer or persons calling the meeting, to each shareholder of record entitled to vote at such meeting. If mailed, such notice shall be deemed to be delivered when deposited in the United

States mail, addressed to the shareholder at his address as it appears on the records of the corporation, with postage thereon prepaid. When a meeting is adjourned to another time or place, notice need not be given of the adjourned meeting if the time and place thereof are announced at the meeting at which the adjournment is taken.

SECTION 2.5. *Fixing of Record Date.* For the purpose of determining shareholders entitled to notice of or to vote at any meeting of shareholders, or shareholders entitled to receive payment of any dividend, or in order to make a determination of shareholders for any other proper purpose, the board of directors of the corporation may fix in advance a date as the record date for any such determination of shareholders, such date in any case to be not more than sixty (60) days and, for a meeting of shareholders, not less than ten (10) days, or in the case of a merger, consolidation, share exchange, dissolution or sale, lease or exchange of assets, not less than twenty (20) days, immediately preceding the date of such meeting. If no record date is fixed for the determination of shareholders entitled to notice of or to vote at a meeting of shareholders, or shareholders entitled to receive payment of a dividend, the record date for such determination of shareholders shall be the date on which notice of the meeting is mailed or the date on which the resolution of the board of directors declaring such dividend is adopted, as the case may be. When a determination of shareholders entitled to vote at any meeting of shareholders has been made as provided in this Section, such determination shall apply to any adjournment thereof

SECTION 2.6. *Voting Lists.* Within twenty (20) days after the record date for a meeting of shareholders or ten (10) days before such meeting, whichever is earlier, the officer or agent having charge of the transfer books for shares of the corporation shall make a complete list of the shareholders entitled to vote at such meeting, arranged in alphabetical order, showing the address of and the number of shares registered in the name of the shareholder. For a period often (10) days prior to such meeting, such list shall be kept on file at the registered office of the corporation and shall be open to inspection by any shareholder, and to copying at the shareholder's expense, at any time during usual business hours. Such list shall also be produced and kept open at the time and place of the meeting and may be inspected by any shareholder during the whole time of the meeting. The original share ledger or transfer book, or a duplicate thereof kept in the State of Illinois, shall be prima facie evidence as to the shareholders who are entitled to examine such list, share ledger or transfer book or to vote at any meeting of shareholders.

SECTION 2.7. *Quorum; Vote Required.* A majority of the outstanding shares of the corporation entitled to vote on a matter, represented in person or by proxy, shall constitute a quorum for consideration of such matter at a meeting of shareholders; provided that if less than a majority of the outstanding shares are represented at said meeting, a majority of the shares so represented may adjourn the meeting at any time without further notice. If a quorum is present, all elections shall be determined by plurality vote, and, with respect to all other matters, the affirmative vote of the majority of the shares represented at the meeting and entitled to vote on a matter shall be the act of the shareholders, unless the vote of a greater number or voting by classes is required by the Business Corporation Act of 1983 or the Articles of Incorporation. At any adjourned meeting at which a quorum is present, any business may be transacted which might have been transacted at the original meeting. A quorum which is present to organize a meeting shall not be broken by the subsequent withdrawal of one or more shareholders.

SECTION 2.8. Manner of Acting and Electronic Participation. Unless specifically prohibited by the articles of incorporation or by-laws, the shareholders may participate in and act at any meeting of the shareholders through the use of a conference telephone or interactive technology, including, but not limited to electronic transmission, internet usage, or remote communication, by means of which all persons participating in the meeting can communicate with each other. Participation in such meeting shall constitute attendance and presence in person at the meeting of the person or persons so participating.

SECTION 2.9. *Proxies.* Each shareholder entitled to vote at a meeting of shareholders or to express consent to corporate action in writing without a meeting may authorize another person or persons to act for him or her by proxy, but no such proxy shall be valid after the expiration of 11 months from the date thereof unless otherwise provided in the proxy. Each proxy shall be in writing executed by the shareholder giving the proxy or by his or her duly authorized attorney. Unless and until voted, every proxy shall be revocable at the pleasure of the person who executed it or of that person's legal representatives or assigns, except in those cases where an irrevocable proxy permitted by statute has been given.

SECTION 2.10. *Voting of Shares.* Each outstanding share entitled to vote on a matter submitted to vote at a meeting of shareholders shall be entitled to one vote upon each such matter. [*Cumulative Voting Provision—In all elections for directors, every shareholder shall have the right to vote the number of shares owned by such shareholder for as many persons as there are directors to be elected, or to cumulate such votes and give one candidate as many votes as shall equal the number of directors multiplied by the number of such shares, or to distribute such cumulative votes in any proportion among any number of candidates.*]

SECTION 2.11. *Voting of Shares By Certain Holders.* Shares of the corporation held by the corporation in a fiduciary capacity may be voted and shall be counted in determining the total number of outstanding shares entitled to vote at any given time.

Shares registered in the name of another corporation, domestic or foreign, may be voted by any officer, agent, proxy or other legal representative authorized to vote such shares under the law of incorporation of such corporation. The corporation may treat the president or other person holding the position of chief executive officer of such other corporation as authorized to vote such shares, together with any other person indicated and any other holder of an office indicated by the corporate shareholder to the corporation as a person or an officer authorized to vote such shares. Such persons and officers indicated shall be registered by the corporation on the transfer books for shares and included in any voting list prepared in accordance with Section 2.6 of these by-laws.

Shares registered in the name of a deceased person, a minor ward or a person under legal disability, may be voted by his or her administrator, executor, or court appointed guardian, either in person or by proxy, without a transfer of such shares into the name of such administrator, executor, or court appointed guardian. Shares registered in the name of a trustee may be voted by him or her, either in person or by proxy.

Shares registered in the name of a receiver may be voted by such receiver, and shares held by or under the control of a receiver may be voted by such receiver, without the transfer thereof into his or her name if authority so to do is contained in an appropriate order of the court by which such receiver was appointed.

A shareholder whose shares are pledged shall be entitled to vote such shares until the shares have been transferred into the name of the pledgee, and thereafter the pledgee shall be entitled to vote the shares so transferred.

SECTION 2.12. *Inspectors.* At any meeting of shareholders, the presiding officer may, or upon the request of any shareholder shall, appoint one or more persons as inspectors for such meeting.

Such inspectors shall ascertain and report the number of shares represented at the meeting, based upon their determination of the validity and effect of proxies, shall count all votes and report the results and shall do such other acts as are proper to conduct the election and voting with impartiality and fairness to all the shareholders.

Each report of an inspector shall be in writing and signed by him or by a majority of them if there be more than one inspector acting at such meeting. If there is more than one inspector, the report of a majority shall be the report of the inspectors. The report of the inspector or inspectors on the number of shares represented at the meeting and the results of the voting shall be prima facie evidence thereof.

SECTION 2.13. *Informal Action by Shareholders.* Any action required to be taken at any annual or special meeting of the shareholders, or any other action which may be taken at a meeting of the shareholders, may be taken without a meeting and without a vote, if a consent in writing, setting forth the action so taken, shall be signed (a) by the holders of outstanding shares having not less than the minimum number of votes that would be necessary to authorize or take such action at a meeting at which all shares entitled to vote thereon were present and voting, or (b) by all of the shareholders entitled to vote with respect to the subject matter thereof. If such consent is signed by less than all of the shareholders entitled to vote, then such consent shall become effective only if at least five (5) days prior to the execution of the consent notice in writing is delivered to all shareholders entitled to vote with respect to the matter thereof, and after the effective date of the consent, prompt notice of the taking of the corporation action without a meeting by less than unanimous written consent shall be given in writing to those shareholders who have not consented in writing.

SECTION 2.14. *Voting by Ballot.* Voting on any question or in any election may be by voice unless the presiding officer shall order, or any shareholder shall demand, that voting be by ballot.

ARTICLE 3. DIRECTORS

SECTION 3.1. *General Powers.* The business and affairs of the corporation shall be managed by or under the direction of the board of directors.

SECTION 3.2. *Number, Election, Tenure and Qualifications.* The number of directors of the corporation shall be ____. The number of directors may be increased or decreased from time to time by amendment of this, but no decrease shall have the effect of shortening the term of any incumbent director. *[The number of directors shall be not less than ___ nor more than ___ as fixed or changed from time to time, within the minimum and maximum, by the directors or the shareholders without further amendment of this, but no decrease shall have the effect of shortening the term of any incumbent director.]* The terms of all directors shall expire at the next annual shareholders' meeting following their election. The term of a director elected to fill a vacancy shall expire at the next annual shareholders' meeting at which his or her predecessor's term would have expired. The term of a director elected as a result of an increase in the number of directors shall expire at the next annual shareholders' meeting. Despite the expiration of a director's term, he or she shall continue to serve until the next meeting of shareholders at which he or she is re-elected or a successor or replacement director is elected. Directors need not be residents of the State of Illinois or shareholders of the corporation.

SECTION 3.3. *Regular Meetings.* A regular meeting of the board of directors shall be held without notice other than this by-law, immediately after the annual meeting of shareholders. The board of directors may provide, by resolution, the time and place for the holding of additional regular meetings without notice other than such resolution.

SECTION 3.4. *Special Meetings.* Special meetings of the board of directors may be called by or at the request of the chief executive officer of the corporation upon such notice as he or she deems appropriate or by or at the request of any one or more directors upon giving at least two (2) days notice to each director, either personally or by mail, facsimile, Telex or telegram. The person or persons authorized to call special meetings of the board of directors may fix any place as the place for holding any such special meeting called by them.

SECTION 3.5. *Notice.* If notice of any special meeting is mailed, such notice shall be deemed to be delivered on the second business day after the date on which it is deposited in the United States mail so addressed, with postage thereon prepaid. If notice be given by facsimile, Telex or telegram, such notice shall be deemed to be delivered on the date such facsimile, Telex or telegram is transmitted. The attendance of a director at any meeting shall constitute a waiver of notice of such meeting, except where a director attends a meeting for the express purpose of objecting to the transaction of any business because the meeting is not lawfully called or convened. Neither the business to be transacted at, nor the purpose of, any special meeting of the board of directors need be specified in the notice or waiver of notice of such meeting.

SECTION 3.6. *Quorum.* A majority of the number of directors fixed by these by-laws *[A majority of the directors then in office]* shall constitute a quorum for the transaction of business at any meeting of the board of directors, provided that if less than a majority of such number of directors is present at a meeting, a majority of the directors present may adjourn the meeting at any time without further notice.

SECTION 3.7. *Manner of Acting.* Unless the act of a greater number is required by statute, the Articles of Incorporation, or other provisions of these by-laws, the act of majority of the directors present at a meeting of the board of directors at which a quorum is present shall be the act of the board of directors.

Unless specifically prohibited by the Articles of Incorporation, members of the board of directors or of any committee of the board of directors may participate in and act at any meeting of such board or committee through the use of a conference telephone or other communications equipment by means of which all persons participating in the meeting can hear each other. Participation in such meeting shall constitute attendance and presence in person at the meeting of the person or persons so participating.

SECTION 3.8. *Vacancies.* Any vacancy occurring in the board of directors and any directorship to be filled by reason of an increase in the number of directors, arising between meetings of shareholders, may be filled [*by election at an animal meeting or at a special meeting of shareholders called for that purpose] [by appointment by the board of directors.*] A director appointed to fill a vacancy shall serve until the next meeting of shareholders at which directors are to be elected.

SECTION 3.9. *Informal Action by Directors.* Unless specifically prohibited by the Articles of Incorporation or by other provisions of these by-laws, any action required to be taken at a meeting of the board of directors, or any other action which may be taken at a meeting of the board of directors, or of any committee thereof, may be taken without a meeting if a consent in writing, setting forth the action so taken, shall be signed by all the directors entitled to vote with respect to the subject matter thereof, or by all the members of such committee, as the case may be. Any such consent signed by all the directors or all the members of the committee shall have the same effect as a unanimous vote at a meeting of directors at which a quorum was present, and may be stated as such in any document filed with the Secretary of State of the State of Illinois or with anyone else.

SECTION 3.10. *Compensation.* The board of directors, by the affirmative vote of a majority of the directors then in office, and irrespective of any personal interest of any of its members, shall have authority to establish reasonable compensation of all directors for services to the corporation as directors, officers, or otherwise. By resolution of the board of directors, the directors may be paid their expenses, if any, of attendance at each meeting of the board. No such payment previously mentioned in this shall preclude any director from serving the corporation in any other capacity and receiving compensation therefor.

SECTION 3.11. *Presumption of Assent.* A director of the corporation who is present at a meeting of the board of directors at which action on any corporate matter is taken shall be conclusively presumed to have assented to the action taken unless his or her dissent shall be entered in the minutes of the meeting or unless he or she files his or her written dissent to such action with the person acting as the secretary of the meeting before the adjournment thereof or forwards such dissent by registered or certified mail to the secretary of the corporation immediately after the adjournment of the meeting. Such right to dissent shall not apply to a director who voted in favor of such action.

SECTION 3.12. *Committees.* A majority of the directors fixed by these by-laws *[A majority of the directors then in office]* may, by resolution, create one or more committees and appoint members of the board to serve on any one or more of such committees. Each committee shall have two or more members who shall serve at the pleasure of the board. A majority of any committee shall constitute a quorum and a majority of a quorum is necessary for committee action. To the extent provided by the board of directors in such resolution, each committee shall have and exercise all of the authority of the board of directors in the management of the corporation, except that a committee may not: authorize distributions; approve or recommend to shareholders any act required by statute to be approved by shareholders; fill vacancies on the board or on any of its committees; elect or remove officers or fix the compensation of any member of the committee; adopt, amend or repeal the by-laws; approve a plan of merger not requiring shareholder approval; authorize or approve the reacquisition of shares, except according to a general formula or method prescribed by the board; authorize or approve the issuance or sale, or contract for sale, of shares or determine the designation and relative rights, preferences, and limitations of a series of shares, except that the board may direct a committee to fix the specific terms of issuance, sale or contract for sale of shares, or the number of shares to be allocated to particular employees under an employee benefit plan; or amend, alter, repeal, or take action inconsistent with any resolution or action of the board of directors when the resolution or action of the board of directors provides by its terms that it shall not be amended, altered or repealed by action of a committee. Vacancies in the membership of any committee shall be filled by the board of directors. Each committee shall keep regular minutes of its proceedings and report the same to the board when required. A committee may act by unanimous consent in writing without a meeting and, subject to action by the board of directors, each committee, by a majority vote of its members, shall determine the time and place of meetings and the notice therefor.

SECTION 3.13. *Resignation of Directors.* A director may resign at any time by giving written notice to the board of directors, its chairman, if any, or to the chief executive officer or secretary of the corporation. A resignation shall be effective when the notice is given unless the notice specifies a future date. The pending vacancy may be filled before the effective date, but the successor shall not take office until the effective date.

SECTION 3.14. *Removal of Directors.* One or more of the directors may be removed, with or without cause, at a meeting of shareholders by the affirmative vote of the holders of a majority of the outstanding shares then entitled to vote at an election of directors, except that no director shall be removed at a meeting of shareholders unless the notice of such meeting shall state that a purpose of the meeting is to vote upon the removal of one or more directors named in the notice, and then only the named director or directors may be removed at such meeting. [*If less than the entire board is to be removed, no director may be removed, with or without cause, if the votes cast against his or her removal would be sufficient to elect him or her if then cumulatively voted at an election of the entire board of directors.*] If a director has been elected by a class or series of shares, he or she may be removed only by the shareholders of that class or series.

ARTICLE 4. OFFICERS

SECTION 4.1. *Executive Officers.* The executive officers of the corporation shall be a president, a treasurer and a secretary. The corporation may also have one or more vice presidents, in which case each vice president shall also be an executive officer. Two or more offices may be held by the same person [*except the offices of president and secretary*].

The executive officers of the corporation shall be elected annually by the board of directors at its first meeting following the meeting of shareholders at which the board was elected.

[____. *Executive Officers. The executive officers of the corporation shall be a chairman of the board, a president, a treasurer and a secretary. The corporation may also have one or more vice presidents, in which case each vice president shall also be an executive officer. Two or more offices may be held by the same person,* [*but no officer shall execute, acknowledge or verify any instrument in more than one capacity*]. *The executive officers of the corporation shall be elected annually by the board of directors at its first meeting following the meeting of shareholders at which the board was elected.*]

SECTION 4.2. *Other Officers and Agents.* The board of directors may also elect a chairman of the board from among the directors and may elect one or more assistant vice presidents, assistant treasurers and assistant secretaries, and such other officers and agents as the board may at any time or from time to time determine to be advisable.

[____. *Other Officers and Agents. The board of directors may also elect one or more assistant vice presidents, assistant treasurers and assistant secretaries, and such other officers and agents as the board may at any time or from time to time determine to be advisable.*]

SECTION 4.3. *Tenure; Resignation; Removal; Vacancies.* Each officer of the corporation shall hold office until his successor is elected or appointed or until his earlier displacement from office by resignation, removal or otherwise; provided, that if the term of office of any officer elected or appointed pursuant to 4.2 of these by-laws shall have been fixed by the board of directors, he shall cease to hold such office no later than the date of expiration of such term, regardless of whether any other person shall have been elected or appointed to succeed him. Any officer may resign by written notice to the corporation and may be removed for cause or without cause by the board of directors whenever in its judgment the best interests of the corporation will be served thereby; provided, that any such removal shall be without prejudice to the contract rights, if any, of the officer so removed. Election or appointment of an officer or agent shall not of itself create contract rights. If the office of any officer becomes vacant for any reason, the vacancy may be filled by the board of directors.

SECTION 4.4. *Compensation.* The compensation of all officers of the corporation shall be fixed by the board of directors. No officer shall be prevented from receiving compensation by reason that he is also a director of the corporation.

SECTION 4.5. *Authority and Duties.* All officers and agents of the corporation, as between themselves and the corporation, shall have such express authority and perform such duties in the management of the property and affairs of the corporation as is provided in these by-laws, or, to the extent not provided, as may be determined by resolution of the board of directors not inconsistent with these by-laws. All officers and agents of the corporation shall also have such implied authority as recognized by the common law from time to time.

SECTION 4.6. *The Chairman of the Board.* The chairman of the board, if there be a chairman, shall preside at all meetings of the shareholders and directors, and he shall have such other powers and duties as the board of directors may from time to time prescribe.

[___. *The Chairman of the Board. The chairman of the board shall be the chief executive officer of the corporation. He shall preside at all meetings of the shareholders and the directors. He shall have general and active management of the business of the corporation, shall see to it that all resolutions and orders of the board of directors are carried into effect, and, in connection therewith, shall be authorized to delegate to the president and the other executive officers such of his powers and duties as chairman of the board at such times and in such manner as he may deem to be advisable. Except where by law or by order of the board of directors the signature of the president is required, the chairman of the board shall have the same power as the president to execute instruments on behalf of the corporation.*]

SECTION 4.7. *The President.* The president shall be the chief executive officer of the corporation. He shall have general and active management of the business of the corporation, shall see to it that all resolutions and orders of the board of directors are carried into effect, and in connection therewith, shall be authorized to delegate to the chairman of the board, if any, and the other executive officers of the corporation such of his powers and duties as president at such times and in such manner as he may deem to be advisable. In the absence or disability of the chairman of the board, or if there be no chairman, he shall preside at all meetings of the shareholders and the directors.

[___. *The President. The president shall be the chief operating officer of the corporation, and its executive officer next in authority to the chairman of the board. He shall assist the chairman of the board in the management of the business of the corporation, and, in the absence or disability of the chairman, he shall preside at all meetings of the shareholders and the directors, and exercise the other powers and perform the other duties of the chairman or designate the executive officers of the corporation by whom such other powers shall be exercised and other duties performed; and he shall have such other powers and duties as the board of directors may from time to time prescribe.*]

SECTION 4.8. *The Vice Presidents.* The vice president, if any, or, if there be more than one, the vice presidents, shall assist the *[chairman of the board and the]* president in the management of the business of the corporation and the implementation of resolutions and orders of the board of directors at such times and in such manner as the chief executive officer may deem to be advisable. If there be more than one vice president, the board of directors may designate one of them as executive vice president, in which case he shall be first in order of seniority after the president, and may also grant to others such titles as shall be descriptive of their respective functions or indicative of their relative seniority. The vice president, or, if there be more than one, the vice presidents in the order of their seniority as indicated by their titles or as otherwise determined by the board of directors, shall, in the absence or disability of the president, exercise the powers and perform the duties of president; and he or they shall have such other powers and duties as the board of directors or the chief executive officer may from time to time prescribe.

SECTION 4.9. *The Assistant Vice Presidents.* The assistant vice president, if any, or, if there be more than one, the assistant vice presidents, shall perform such duties as the board of directors or the chief executive officer may from time to time prescribe.

SECTION 4.10. *The Treasurer.* The treasurer shall have the care and custody of the corporate funds, and other valuable effects, including securities, and shall keep full and accurate accounts of receipts and disbursements in books belonging to the corporation and shall deposit all moneys and other valuable effects in the name and to the credit of the corporation in such depositories as may be designated by the board of directors. The treasurer shall disburse the funds of the corporation as may be ordered by the board of directors, taking proper vouchers for such disbursements, and shall render to *[the chairman of the board,]* the president and the board of directors, at meetings or whenever they may require it, an account of all his transactions as treasurer and of the financial condition of the corporation. If required by the board of directors, the treasurer shall give the corporation a bond for such term, in such sum and with such surety or sureties as shall be satisfactory to the board for the faithful performance of the duties of his office and for the restoration to the corporation, in case of his death, resignation, retirement or removal from office, of all books, papers, vouchers, money and other property of whatever kind in his possession or under his control belonging to the corporation.

SECTION 4.11. *The Assistant Treasurers.* The assistant treasurer, if any, or, if there be more than one, the assistant treasurers, in the order determined by the board of directors or by the chief executive officer, shall, in the absence or disability of the treasurer, exercise the powers and perform the duties of the treasurer; and he or they shall perform such other duties as the board of directors or the chief executive officer may from time to time prescribe.

SECTION 4.12. *The Secretary.* The secretary shall attend all meetings of the shareholders and of the board of directors and shall record the minutes of all proceedings taken at such meetings, or maintain all documents evidencing corporate actions taken by written consent of the shareholders or of the board of directors, in a book to be kept for that purpose; and he shall perform like duties for any committee of the board of directors when required. He shall have the authority to certify the by-laws, resolutions of the shareholders and board of directors and committees thereof, and other documents of the corporation as true and correct copies thereof. He shall see to it that all notices of meetings of the shareholders and of special meetings of the board of directors are duly given in accordance with these by-laws or as required by statute. He shall be the custodian of the seal, if any, of the corporation, and, when authorized by the board of directors, he shall cause the corporate seal, if any, to be affixed to any document requiring it, and, when so affixed, attested by his signature as secretary or by the signature of an assistant secretary; and he shall perform such other duties as the board of directors or the chief executive officer may from time to time prescribe.

SECTION 4.13. *The Assistant Secretaries.* The assistant secretary, if any, or, if there be more than one, the assistant secretaries, in the order determined by the board of directors or by the chief executive officer, shall, in the absence or disability of the secretary, exercise the powers and perform the duties of the secretary; and he or they shall perform such other duties as the board of directors or the chief executive officer may from time to time prescribe.

ARTICLE 5. CERTIFICATES FOR SHARES AND THEIR TRANSFER

SECTION 5.1. *Certificates.* The issued shares of the corporation shall be represented by certificates. The certificates shall be in such form as shall be determined by the board of directors, and shall be numbered and entered in the books of the corporation as they are issued. Each certificate shall exhibit the registered holder's name and the number and class of shares, and the designation of any series, that it evidences, shall set forth such other statements as may be required by statute, and shall be signed by *[the chairman of the board, the president] [the chief executive officer]* or a vice president and by the treasurer or an assistant treasurer or by the secretary or an assistant secretary, any or all of whose signatures may be facsimile if such certificate is countersigned by a transfer agent or registered by a registrar. In case any one or more of the officers who have signed or whose facsimile signatures appear on any such certificate shall cease to be such officer or officers of the corporation, or an officer of the transfer agent or registrar, before such certificate is issued and delivered, it may nonetheless be issued and delivered with the same effect as if such officer or officers had continued in office.

SECTION 5.2. *Lost Certificates.* The board of directors may direct that a new share certificate or certificates be issued in place of any certificate or certificates theretofore issued by the corporation which have been mutilated or which are alleged to have been lost, stolen or destroyed, upon presentation of each such mutilated certificate or the making by the person claiming any such certificate to have been lost, stolen or destroyed of an affidavit as to the facts and circumstances of the loss, theft or destruction thereof. The board of directors, in its discretion and as a condition precedent to the issuance of any new certificate, may require, or by resolution may delegate to the chief executive officer the power in his discretion to require from time to time, the owner of any certificate alleged to have been lost, stolen or destroyed, or his legal representative, to furnish the corporation with a bond, in such sum and with such surety or sureties as the board or the chief executive officer, as the case may be, may direct, as indemnity against any claim that may be made against the corporation in respect of such lost, stolen or destroyed certificate.

SECTION 5.3. *Registration of Transfer.* Upon surrender to the corporation or any transfer agent of the corporation of a certificate for shares duly endorsed or accompanied by proper evidence of succession, assignment or authority to transfer, the corporation shall issue or cause its transfer agent to issue a new certificate to the person entitled thereto, cancel the old certificate and record the transaction upon its books.

ARTICLE 6. WAIVER OF NOTICE

Whenever any notice is required to be given under the provisions of these by-laws, the Articles of Incorporation, or under the provisions of the Business Corporation Act of 1983, a waiver thereof in writing, signed by the person or persons entitled to such notice, whether before or after the time stated therein, shall be deemed equivalent to the giving of such notice. Attendance by a person at any meeting shall constitute waiver of notice thereof unless at the meeting such person objects to the holding of the meeting because proper notice was not given.

ARTICLE 7. INDEMNIFICATION

The corporation shall indemnify (a) any person who was or is a party or is threatened to be made a party to any threatened, pending or completed action or suit by or in the right of the corporation to procure a judgment in its favor by reason of the fact that such person is or was a director, officer, employee or agent of the corporation or is or was serving at the request of the corporation as a director, officer, employee or agent of another corporation, partnership, joint venture, trust or other enterprise, against expenses (including attorneys' fees) actually and reasonably incurred by such person in connection with the defense or settlement of such action or suit, and (b) any person who was or is a party or is threatened to be made a party to any threatened, pending or completed action, suit or proceeding, whether civil, criminal, administrative or investigative (other than an action by or in the right of the corporation) by reason of the fact that he is or was a director, officer, employee or agent of the corporation, or who is or was serving at the request of the corporation as a director, officer, employee or agent of another corporation, partnership, joint venture, trust or other enterprise, against expenses (including attorneys' fees), judgments, fines and amounts paid in settlement actually and reasonably incurred by him in connection with any such action, suit or proceeding, in each case to the fullest extent permissible under subs (a) through (f) and (h) through (k) of Section 8.75 of the Business Corporation Act of 1983, as amended from time to time, or the indemnification provisions of any successor statute. If the corporation pays indemnity or makes an advance of expenses to a director, officer, employee or agent, the corporation shall report the indemnification or advance in writing to the shareholders with or before the notice of the next shareholders meeting.

ARTICLE 8. GENERAL PROVISIONS

SECTION 8.1. *Contracts.* The board of directors may authorize any officer or officers, agent or agents, to enter into any contract or execute and deliver any instrument in the name of and on behalf of the corporation, and such authority may be general or confined to specific instances.

SECTION 8.2. *Loans.* No loans shall be contracted on behalf of the corporation and no evidences of indebtedness shall be issued in its name unless authorized by a resolution of the board of directors. Such authority may be general or confined to specific instances.

SECTION 8.3. *Checks, Drafts, Etc.* All checks, drafts or other orders for the payment of money, notes or other evidences of indebtedness issued in the name of the corporation, shall be signed by such officer or officers, agent or agents of the corporation and in such manner as shall from time to time be determined by resolution of the board of directors.

SECTION 8.4. *Deposits.* All funds of the corporation not otherwise employed shall be deposited from time to time to the credit of the corporation in such banks, trust companies or other depositories as the board of directors may select.

SECTION 8.5. *Fiscal Year.* The fiscal year of the corporation shall be fixed by resolution of the board of directors.

SECTION 8.6. *Dividends.* The board of directors may from time to time declare, and the corporation may pay, dividends on its outstanding shares in the manner and upon the terms and conditions provided by law or the Articles of Incorporation.

SECTION 8.7. *Seal.* The corporation may have, but shall not be required to have, a corporate seal as shall be determined by the secretary of the corporation in his discretion. If a corporate seal is obtained, the seal shall contain the name of the corporation and the words "Corporate Seal, Illinois", and the use thereof shall be determined from time to time by the officer or officers executing and delivering instruments on behalf of the corporation, provided that the affixing of a corporate seal to an instrument shall not give the instrument additional force or effect or change the construction thereof. The seal, if any, may be used by causing it or a facsimile thereof to be impressed or affixed or in any other manner reproduced.

SECTION 8.8. *Registered Shareholders.* Except as otherwise required by law, the corporation shall be entitled to recognize a person registered on its books as the holder of shares as the sole owner of such shares for all purposes, and shall not be bound to recognize any equitable or legal claim to or interest in such shares on the part of any person other than such registered holder, regardless of whether it shall have knowledge or notice of any such claim or interest. Without limiting the generality of the foregoing, the corporation shall be entitled to recognize the exclusive right of a person whose holding of shares is so registered on its books as of any record date fixed or determined pursuant to Section 2.5 of these by-laws to be treated as the sole owner of such shares for the purpose for which such record date was so fixed or determined.

SECTION 8.9. *Voting of Securities of Other Corporations.* In the event that the corporation shall at any time or from time to time own and have power to vote any securities (including but not limited to shares of stock) of any other issuer, they shall be voted by such person or persons, to such extent and in such manner, as may be determined by the board of directors.

SECTION 8.10. *Construction.* The headings in these by-laws are for purposes of reference only and shall not be considered in construing these by-laws. As used herein, the neuter gender shall also denote the masculine and feminine, and the masculine gender shall also denote the feminine and neuter.

ARTICLE 9. AMENDMENTS

These by-laws may be made, altered, amended or repealed by the shareholders or the board of directors, but no by-law adopted by the shareholders may be altered, amended or repealed by the board of directors.

[*These by-laws may only be altered, amended or repealed by the shareholders of the corporation.*]

Drafting Notes

1. *Annual Shareholders' Meeting Date* (BCA 7.05 compare with RMBCA 7.01). The standard By–Laws prepared by our office ("Form By–Laws") contain a blank for the annual shareholders' meeting date. The Board of Directors may, however, designate an alternative date (Form By–Laws, Section 2.1).
2. *Number of Directors* (BCA 8.10 compare with RMBCA 8.03). The Board of Directors may consist of one Director, regardless of the

number of shareholders. The By–Laws may also fix a range for the number of Directors provided that the maximum number does not exceed the minimum number by more than five. The Form By–Laws contain alternative provisions for (a) a fixed number, and (b) a range. Depending on which alternative is chosen, appropriate deletions will be required respecting the bracketed provisions in Sections 3.2, 3.6 and 3.12 of the Form By–Laws.

3. *Vacancies* (BCA 8.30 compare with RMBCA 8.10). Unless another method for filling vacancies is provided in the By–Laws, vacancies may be filled by the shareholders or the Board of Directors. Alternative methods for filling vacancies are provided in the Form By–Laws (Form By–Laws, Section 3.8). The norm (for closely-held corporations) is for vacancies to be filled by the shareholders.

4. *Officers* (BCA 8.50 compare with RMBCA 8.41). The Form By–Laws provide for executive officers who are a President (chief executive officer), a Treasurer and a Secretary, with provisions for election of one or more Vice Presidents, as executive officers, a Chairman of the Board and one or more Assistant Vice Presidents, Assistant Treasurers and Assistant Secretaries (Form By–Laws, Article IV). In addition, the Form By–Laws contain alternative provisions for a Chairman of the Board to be elected as the chief executive officer, with the President as the chief operating officer. See bracketed Sections 4.1, 4.2, 4.6 and 4.7 and the bracketed provisions in Sections 4.8 and 4.10. The Form By–Laws do not provide for the further alternatives for a Chairman as the chief operating officer and the President as the chief executive officer.

5. Please note that the Form By–Laws give you the option of providing that no two offices may be held by the same person. Illinois law no longer requires that this be true, but in certain circumstances, you may want to include this provision.

6. *Cumulative Voting* (BCA 7.40 compare with RMBCA 7.21, 7.28). The Form Articles deny cumulative voting (See Checklist of Considerations in Drafting Illinois Articles of Incorporation). However, if a corporation has cumulative voting, the bracketed provisions in Sections 2.9 and 3.14 of the Form By–Laws should be retained; otherwise, such provisions must be deleted.

7. *Special Directors' Meeting* (BCA 8.25 compare with RMBCA 8.20). The Form By–Laws provide that a special meeting of the board of directors may be called by or at the request of the chief executive officer of the corporation or any one or more directors (Form By–Laws, Section 3.4). The persons authorized to call special meetings of the board of directors may be changed to fit the particular needs of the corporation. A corporation which has a large number of directors may consider requiring the request of more than one director in order to call such a meeting.

2. DELAWARE FORMS

A. MORRIS, NICHOLS, ARSHT & TUNNELL FORM CERTIFICATE OF INCORPORATION*

CERTIFICATE OF INCORPORATION OF NE WCO, INC.

***FIRST*:** The name of the corporation is Newco, Inc. (hereinafter referred to as the "Corporation").

***SECOND*:** The address of the registered office of the Corporation in the State of Delaware is Corporation Trust Center, 1209 Orange Street, in the City of Wilmington, County of New Castle. The name of the registered agent of the Corporation at that address is The Corporation Trust Company.

***THIRD*:** The purpose of the Corporation is to engage in any lawful act or activity for which a corporation may be organized under the Delaware General Corporation Law.

***FOURTH*:** A. The total number of shares of all classes of stock which the Corporation shall have authority to issue is ______ (______), consisting of ______ (___) shares of Common Stock, par value one cent ($.01) per share (the "Common Stock") and ______ (___) shares of Preferred Stock, par value one cent ($01) per share (the "Preferred Stock").

B. The board of directors is authorized, subject to any limitations prescribed by law, to provide for the issuance of shares of Preferred Stock in series, and by filing a certificate pursuant to the applicable law of the State of Delaware (such certificate being hereinafter referred to as a "Preferred Stock Designation"), to establish from time to time the number of shares to be included in each such series, and to fix the designation, powers, preferences, and rights of the shares of each such series and any qualifications, limitations or restrictions thereof. The number of authorized shares of Preferred Stock may be increased or decreased (but not below the number of shares thereof then outstanding) by the affirmative vote of the holders of a majority of the Common Stock, without a vote of the holders of the Preferred Stock, or of any series thereof, unless a vote of any such holders is required pursuant to the terms of any Preferred Stock Designation.

C. Each outstanding share of Common Stock shall entitle the holder thereof to one vote on each matter properly submitted to the stockholders of the Corporation for their vote; *provided, however*, that, except as otherwise required by law, holders of Common Stock shall not be entitled to vote on any amendment to this Certificate of Incorporation

* Thanks to Frederick H. Alexander, a member of Morris, Nichols, Arsht & Tunnell, for furnishing the Delaware Form Certificate of Incorporation and By-Laws.

(including any Certificate of Designations relating to any series of Preferred Stock) that relates solely to the terms of one or more outstanding series of Preferred Stock if the holders of such affected series are entitled, either separately or together as a class with the holders of one or more other such series, to vote thereon by law or pursuant to this Certificate of Incorporation (including any Certificate of Designations relating to any series of Preferred Stock).

FIFTH: The following provisions are inserted for the management of the business and the conduct of the affairs of the Corporation, and for further definition, limitation and regulation of the powers of the Corporation and of its directors and stockholders:

A. The business and affairs of the Corporation shall be managed by or under the direction of the board of directors. In addition to the powers and authority expressly conferred upon them by statute or by this Certificate of Incorporation or the by-laws of the Corporation, the directors are hereby empowered to exercise all such powers and do all such acts and things as may be exercised or done by the Corporation.

B. The directors of the Corporation need not be elected by written ballot unless the by-laws so provide.

C. Any action required or permitted to be taken by the stockholders of the Corporation must be effected at a duly called annual or special meeting of stockholders of the Corporation and may not be effected by any consent in writing by such stockholders.

D. Special meetings of stockholders of the Corporation may be called only by the Chairman of the Board or the President or by the board of directors acting pursuant to a resolution adopted by a majority of the Whole Board. For purposes of this Certificate of Incorporation, the term "Whole Board" shall mean the total number of authorized directors whether or not there exist any vacancies in previously authorized directorships.

SIXTH: A. Subject to the rights of the holders of any series of Preferred Stock to elect additional directors under specified circumstances, the number of directors shall be fixed from time to time exclusively by the board of directors pursuant to a resolution adopted by a majority of the Whole Board. The directors, other than those who may be elected by the holders of any series of Preferred Stock under specified circumstances, shall be divided into three classes, with the term of office of the first class to expire at the Corporation's first annual meeting of stockholders, the term of office of the second class to expire at the Corporation's second annual meeting of stockholders and the term of office of the third class to expire at the Corporation's third annual meeting of stockholders, with each director to hold office until his or her successor shall have been duly elected and qualified. At each annual meeting of stockholders, directors elected to succeed those directors whose terms expire shall be elected for a term of office to expire at the third succeeding annual meeting of stockholders after their election, with each director to hold office until his or her successor shall have been duly elected and qualified.

B. Subject to the rights of the holders of any series of Preferred Stock then outstanding, newly created directorships resulting from any increase in the authorized number of directors or any vacancies in the board of directors resulting from death, resignation, retirement, disqualification, removal from office or other cause shall, unless otherwise required by law or by resolution of the board of directors, be filled only by a majority vote of the directors then in office, though less than a quorum (and not by stockholders), and directors so chosen shall serve for a term expiring at the annual meeting of stockholders at which the term of office of the class to which they have been chosen expires or until such director's successor shall have been duly elected and qualified. No decrease in the authorized number of directors shall shorten the term of any incumbent director.

C. Advance notice of stockholder nominations for the election of directors and of business to be brought by stockholders before any meeting of the stockholders of the Corporation shall be given in the manner provided in the by-laws of the Corporation.

D. Subject to the rights of the holders of any series of Preferred Stock then outstanding, any director, or the entire board of directors, may be removed from office at any time, but only for cause and only by the affirmative vote of the holders of at least ___ percent (___%) of the voting power of all of the then-outstanding shares of capital stock of the Corporation entitled to vote generally in the election of directors, voting together as a single class.

SEVENTH: The board of directors is expressly empowered to adopt, amend or repeal by-laws of the Corporation. Any adoption, amendment or repeal of the by-laws of the Corporation by the board of directors shall require the approval of a majority of the Whole Board. The stockholders shall also have power to adopt, amend or repeal the by-laws of the Corporation; provided, however, that, in addition to any vote of the holders of any class or series of stock of the Corporation required by law or by this Certificate of Incorporation, the affirmative vote of the holders of at least ___ percent (___%) of the voting power of all of the then-outstanding shares of the capital stock of the Corporation entitled to vote generally in the election of directors, voting together as a single class, shall be required to adopt, amend or repeal any provision of the by-laws of the Corporation.

EIGHTH: A director of the Corporation shall not be personally liable to the Corporation or its stockholders for monetary damages for breach of fiduciary duty as a director, except for liability (i) for any breach of the director's duty of loyalty to the Corporation or its stockholders, (ii) for acts or omissions not in good faith or which involve intentional misconduct or a knowing violation of law, (iii) under Section 174 of the Delaware General Corporation Law, or (iv) for any transaction from which the director derived an improper personal benefit. If the Delaware General Corporation Law is amended to authorize corporate action further eliminating or limiting the personal liability of directors, then the liability of a director of the Corporation shall be eliminated or limited to the fullest extent permitted by the Delaware General Corporation Law, as so amended.

Any repeal or modification of the foregoing paragraph by the stockholders of the Corporation shall not adversely affect any right or protection of a director of the Corporation existing at the time of such repeal or modification.

NINTH: The Corporation reserves the right to amend or repeal any provision contained in this Certificate of Incorporation in the manner prescribed by the laws of the State of Delaware and all rights conferred upon stockholders are granted subject to this reservation; provided, however, that, notwithstanding any other provision of this Certificate of Incorporation or any provision of law that might otherwise permit a lesser vote or no vote, but in addition to any vote of the holders of any class or series of the stock of this corporation required by law or by this Certificate of Incorporation, the affirmative vote of the holders of at least ___ percent (___%) of the voting power of all of the then-outstanding shares of the capital stock of the Corporation entitled to vote generally in the election of Directors, voting together as a single class, shall be required to amend or repeal this Article NINTH, Sections C or D of Article FIFTH, Article SIXTH, Article SEVENTH, or Article EIGHTH.

TENTH: The incorporator is _______, whose mailing address is _______.

I, THE UNDERSIGNED, being the incorporator, for the purpose of forming a corporation under the laws of the State of Delaware do make, file and record this Certificate of Incorporation, do certify that the facts herein stated are true, and, accordingly, have hereto set my hand this ___ day of _______, 2002.

signature

ARTICLE ___ CONTINUING DIRECTOR PROVISION

The board of directors is expressly authorized to cause the Corporation to issue rights pursuant to Section 157 of the Delaware General Corporation Law and, in that connection, to enter into any agreements necessary or convenient for such issuance [*,and to enter into other agreements necessary and convenient to the conduct of the business of the corporation.*] Any such agreement may include provisions limiting, in certain circumstances, the ability of the board of directors of the Corporation to redeem the securities issued pursuant thereto or to take other action thereunder or in connection therewith unless there is a specified number or percentage of Continuing Directors then in office. Pursuant to Section 141(a) of the Delaware General Corporation Law, the Continuing Directors shall have the power and authority to make all decisions and determinations, and exercise or perform such other acts, that any such agreement provides that such Continuing Directors shall make, exercise or perform. For purposes of this Article ___ and any such agreement, the term, "Continuing Directors," shall mean (1) those directors who were members of the board of directors of the Corporation at the time the Corporation entered into such agreement and any director who subsequently becomes a member of the board of directors, if such director's nomination for election to the board of directors is recommended or approved by the majority vote of the Continuing Directors then in office and (2) such other members of the board of directors, if any, designated in, or in the manner provided in, such agreement as Continuing Directors.

If the continuing director provision is adopted, the Section 102(b)(7) provision of the corporation should be amended to add: All references in this Article ___ to a director shall also be deemed to refer to any such director acting in his or her capacity as a Continuing Director.

B. MORRIS, NICHOLS, ARSHT & TUNNELL FORM BY-LAWS

BY-LAWS OF NEWCO, INC.

ARTICLE I–STOCKHOLDERS

Section 1. Annual Meeting.

(1) An annual meeting of the stockholders, for the election of directors to succeed those whose terms expire and for the transaction of such other business as may properly come before the meeting, shall be held at such place, on such date, and at such time as the Board of Directors shall each year fix, which date shall be within thirteen (13) months of the last annual meeting of stockholders.

(2) Nominations of persons for election to the Board of Directors and the proposal of business to be transacted by the stockholders may be made at an annual meeting of stockholders (a) pursuant to the Corporation's notice with respect to such meeting, (b) by or at the direction of the Board of Directors or (c) by any stockholder of record of the Corporation who was a stockholder of record at the time of the giving of the notice provided for in the following paragraph, who is entitled to vote at the meeting and who has complied with the notice procedures set forth in this section.

(3) For nominations or other business to be properly brought before an annual meeting by a stockholder pursuant to clause (c) of the foregoing paragraph, (1) the stockholder must have given timely notice thereof in writing to the Secretary of the Corporation, (2) such business must be a proper matter for stockholder action under the General Corporation Law of the State of Delaware, (3) if the stockholder, or the beneficial owner on whose behalf any such proposal or nomination is made, has provided the Corporation with a Solicitation Notice, as that term is defined in subclause (c)(iii) of this paragraph, such stockholder or beneficial owner must, in the case of a proposal, have delivered a proxy statement and form of proxy to holders of at least the percentage of the Corporation's voting shares required under applicable law to carry any such proposal, or, in the case of a nomination or nominations, have delivered a proxy statement and form of proxy to holders of a percentage of the Corporation's voting shares reasonably believed by such stockholder or beneficial holder to be sufficient to elect the nominee or nominees proposed to be nominated by such stockholder, and must, in either case, have included in such materials the Solicitation Notice and (4) if no Solicitation Notice relating thereto has been timely provided pursuant to this section, the stockholder or beneficial owner proposing such business or nomination must not have solicited a number of proxies sufficient to have required the delivery of such a Solicitation Notice under this section. To be timely, a stockholder's notice shall be delivered to the Secretary at the principal executive offices of the Corporation not less than 45 or more than 75 days prior to the first anniversary (the

"Anniversary") of the date on which the Corporation first mailed its proxy materials for the preceding year's annual meeting of stockholders; provided, however, that if the date of the annual meeting is advanced more than 30 days prior to or delayed by more than 30 days after the anniversary of the preceding year's annual meeting, notice by the stockholder to be timely must be so delivered not later than the close of business on the later of (i) the 90th day prior to such annual meeting or (ii) the 10th day following the day on which public announcement of the date of such meeting is first made. Such stockholder's notice shall set forth (a) as to each person whom the stockholder proposes to nominate for election or reelection as a director all information relating to such person as would be required to be disclosed in solicitations of proxies for the election of such nominees as directors pursuant to Regulation 14A under the Securities Exchange Act of 1934, as amended (the "Exchange Act"), and such person's written consent to serve as a director if elected; (b) as to any other business that the stockholder proposes to bring before the meeting, a brief description of such business, the reasons for conducting such business at the meeting and any material interest in such business of such stockholder and the beneficial owner, if any, on whose behalf the proposal is made; (c) as to the stockholder giving the notice and the beneficial owner, if any, on whose behalf the nomination or proposal is made (i) the name and address of such stockholder, as they appear on the Corporation's books, and of such beneficial owner, (ii) the class and number of shares of the Corporation that are owned beneficially and of record by such stockholder and such beneficial owner, and (iii) whether either such stockholder or beneficial owner intends to deliver a proxy statement and form of proxy to holders of, in the case of a proposal, at least the percentage of the Corporation's voting shares required under applicable law to carry the proposal or, in the case of a nomination or nominations, a sufficient number of holders of the Corporation's voting shares to elect such nominee or nominees (an affirmative statement of such intent, a "Solicitation Notice").

(4) Notwithstanding anything in the second sentence of the third paragraph of this Section 1 to the contrary, in the event that the number of directors to be elected to the Board of Directors is increased and there is no public announcement naming all of the nominees for director or specifying the size of the increased Board of Directors made by the Corporation at least 55 days prior to the Anniversary, a stockholder's notice required by this Bylaw shall also be considered timely, but only with respect to nominees for any new positions created by such increase, if it shall be delivered to the Secretary at the principal executive offices of the Corporation not later than the close of business on the 10th day following the day on which such public announcement is first made by the Corporation.

(5) Only persons nominated in accordance with the procedures set forth in this Section 1 shall be eligible to serve as directors and only such

business shall be conducted at an annual meeting of stockholders as shall have been brought before the meeting in accordance with the procedures set forth in this section. The chairman of the meeting shall have the power and the duty to determine whether a nomination or any business proposed to be brought before the meeting has been made in accordance with the procedures set forth in these By-Laws and, if any proposed nomination or business is not in compliance with these By-Laws, to declare that such defectively proposed business or nomination shall not be presented for stockholder action at the meeting and shall be disregarded.

(6) For purposes of these By-Laws, "public announcement" shall mean disclosure in a press release reported by the Dow Jones News Service, Associated Press or a comparable national news service or in a document publicly filed by the Corporation with the Securities and Exchange Commission pursuant to Section 13, 14 or 15(d) of the Exchange Act.

(7) Notwithstanding the foregoing provisions of this Section 1, a stockholder shall also comply with all applicable requirements of the Exchange Act and the rules and regulations thereunder with respect to matters set forth in this Section 1. Nothing in this Section 1 shall be deemed to affect any rights of stockholders to request inclusion of proposals in the Corporation's proxy statement pursuant to Rule 14a-8 under the Exchange Act.

Section 2. Special Meetings.

(1) Special meetings of the stockholders, other than those required by statute, may be called at any time by the Chairman of the Board or the President or by the Board of Directors acting pursuant to a resolution adopted by a majority of the Whole Board. For purposes of these By-Laws, the term "Whole Board" shall mean the total number of authorized directors whether or not there exist any vacancies in previously authorized directorships. The Board of Directors may postpone or reschedule any previously scheduled special meeting.

(2) Only such business shall be conducted at a special meeting of stockholders as shall have been brought before the meeting pursuant to the Corporation's notice of meeting. Nominations of persons for election to the Board of Directors may be made at a special meeting of stockholders at which directors are to be elected pursuant to the Corporation's notice of meeting (a) by or at the direction of the Board of Directors or (b) by any stockholder of record of the Corporation who is a stockholder of record at the time of giving of notice provided for in this paragraph, who shall be entitled to vote at the meeting and who complies with the notice procedures set forth in Section 1 of this Article I. Nominations by stockholders of persons for election to the Board of Directors may be made at such a special meeting of stockholders if the stockholder's notice

required by the third paragraph of Section 1 of this Article I shall be delivered to the Secretary at the principal executive offices of the Corporation not later than the close of business on the later of the 90th day prior to such special meeting or the 10th day following the day on which public announcement is first made of the date of the special meeting and of the nominees proposed by the Board of Directors to be elected at such meeting.

(3) Notwithstanding the foregoing provisions of this Section 2, a stockholder shall also comply with all applicable requirements of the Exchange Act and the rules and regulations thereunder with respect to matters set forth in this Section 2. Nothing in this Section 2 shall be deemed to affect any rights of stockholders to request inclusion of proposals in the Corporation's proxy statement pursuant to Rule 14a–8 under the Exchange Act.

Section 3. Notice of Meetings.

(1) Notice of the place, if any, date, and time of all meetings of the stockholders, and the means of remote communications, if any, by which stockholders and proxyholders may be deemed to be present in person and vote at such meeting, shall be given, not less than ten (10) nor more than sixty (60) days before the date on which the meeting is to be held, to each stockholder entitled to vote at such meeting, except as otherwise provided herein or required by law (meaning, here and hereinafter, as required from time to time by the Delaware General Corporation Law or the Certificate of Incorporation of the Corporation).

(2) When a meeting is adjourned to another time or place, notice need not be given of the adjourned meeting if the time and place, if any, thereof, and the means of remote communications, if any, by which stockholders and proxyholders may be deemed to be present in person and vote at such adjourned meeting are announced at the meeting at which the adjournment is taken; provided, however, that if the date of any adjourned meeting is more than thirty (30) days after the date for which the meeting was originally noticed, or if a new record date is fixed for the adjourned meeting, notice of the place, if any, date, and time of the adjourned meeting and the means of remote communications, if any, by which stockholders and proxyholders may be deemed to be present in person and vote at such adjourned meeting, shall be given in conformity herewith. At any adjourned meeting, any business may be transacted which might have been transacted at the original meeting.

Section 4. Quorum.

(1) At any meeting of the stockholders, the holders of a majority of all of the shares of the stock entitled to vote at the meeting, present in person or by proxy, shall constitute a quorum for all purposes, unless or except to the extent that the presence of a larger number may be

required by law. Where a separate vote by a class or classes or series is required, a majority of the shares of such class or classes or series present in person or represented by proxy shall constitute a quorum entitled to take action with respect to that vote on that matter.

(2) If a quorum shall fail to attend any meeting, the chairman of the meeting may adjourn the meeting to another place, if any, date, or time.

Section 5. Organization.

Such person as the Board of Directors may have designated or, in the absence of such a person, the Chairman of the Board or, in his or her absence, the President of the Corporation or, in his or her absence, such person as may be chosen by the holders of a majority of the shares entitled to vote who are present, in person or by proxy, shall call to order any meeting of the stockholders and act as chairman of the meeting. In the absence of the Secretary of the Corporation, the secretary of the meeting shall be such person as the chairman of the meeting appoints.

Section 6. Conduct of Business.

The chairman of any meeting of stockholders shall determine the order of business and the procedure at the meeting, including such regulation of the manner of voting and the conduct of discussion as seem to him or her in order. The chairman shall have the power to adjourn the meeting to another place, if any, date and time. The date and time of the opening and closing of the polls for each matter upon which the stockholders will vote at the meeting shall be announced at the meeting.

Section 7. Proxies and Voting.

(1) At any meeting of the stockholders, every stockholder entitled to vote may vote in person or by proxy authorized by an instrument in writing or by a transmission permitted by law filed in accordance with the procedure established for the meeting. Any copy, facsimile telecommunication or other reliable reproduction of the writing or transmission created pursuant to this paragraph may be substituted or used in lieu of the original writing or transmission for any and all purposes for which the original writing or transmission could be used, provided that such copy, facsimile telecommunication or other reproduction shall be a complete reproduction of the entire original writing or transmission.

(2) The Corporation may, and to the extent required by law, shall, in advance of any meeting of stockholders, appoint one or more inspectors to act at the meeting and make a written report thereof. The Corporation may designate one or more alternate inspectors to replace any inspector who fails to act. If no inspector or alternate is able to act at a meeting of stockholders, the person presiding at the meeting may, and to the extent required by law, shall, appoint one or more inspectors to act at the meeting. Each inspector, before entering upon the discharge

of his or her duties, shall take and sign an oath faithfully to execute the duties of inspector with strict impartiality and according to the best of his or her ability. Every vote taken by ballots shall be counted by a duly appointed inspector or inspectors.

(3) All elections shall be determined by a plurality of the votes cast, and except as otherwise required by law, all other matters shall be determined by a majority of the votes cast affirmatively or negatively.

Section 8. Stock List.

(1) A complete list of stockholders entitled to vote at any meeting of stockholders, arranged in alphabetical order for each class of stock and showing the address of each such stockholder and the number of shares registered in his or her name, shall be open to the examination of any such stockholder for a period of at least 10 days prior to the meeting in the manner provided by law.

(2) The stock list shall also be open to the examination of any stockholder during the whole time of the meeting as provided by law. This list shall presumptively determine the identity of the stockholders entitled to vote at the meeting and the number of shares held by each of them.

ARTICLE II—BOARD OF DIRECTORS

Section 1. Number, Election and Term of Directors.

Subject to the rights of the holders of any series of preferred stock to elect directors under specified circumstances, the number of directors shall be fixed from time to time exclusively by the Board of Directors pursuant to a resolution adopted by a majority of the Whole Board. The directors, other than those who may be elected by the holders of any series of preferred stock under specified circumstances, shall be divided, with respect to the time for which they severally hold office, into three classes with the term of office of the first class to expire at the Corporation's first annual meeting of stockholders, the term of office of the second class to expire at the Corporation's second annual meeting of stockholders and the term of office of the third class to expire at the Corporation's third annual meeting of stockholders, with each director to hold office until his or her successor shall have been duly elected and qualified. At each annual meeting of stockholders, commencing with the first annual meeting, (i) directors elected to succeed those directors whose terms then expire shall be elected for a term of office to expire at the third succeeding annual meeting of stockholders after their election, with each director to hold office until his or her successor shall have been duly elected and qualified, and (ii) if authorized by a resolution of the Board of Directors, directors may be elected to fill any vacancy on the Board of Directors, regardless of how such vacancy shall have been created.

Section 2. Newly Created Directorships and Vacancies.

Subject to the rights of the holders of any series of preferred stock then outstanding, newly created directorships resulting from any increase in the authorized number of directors or any vacancies in the Board of Directors resulting from death, resignation, retirement, disqualification, removal from office or other cause shall, unless otherwise required by law or by resolution of the Board of Directors, be filled only by a majority vote of the directors then in office, though less than a quorum (and not by stockholders), and directors so chosen shall serve for a term expiring at the annual meeting of stockholders at which the term of office of the class to which they have been elected expires or until such director's successor shall have been duly elected and qualified. No decrease in the number of authorized directors shall shorten the term of any incumbent director.

Section 3. Regular Meetings.

Regular meetings of the Board of Directors shall be held at such place or places, on such date or dates, and at such time or times as shall have been established by the Board of Directors and publicized among all directors. A notice of each regular meeting shall not be required.

Section 4. Special Meetings.

Special meetings of the Board of Directors may be called by the Chairman of the Board, the President or by a majority of the Whole Board and shall be held at such place, on such date, and at such time as they or he or she shall fix. Notice of the place, date, and time of each such special meeting shall be given to each director by whom it is not waived by mailing written notice not less than five (5) days before the meeting or by telephone or by telegraphing or telexing or by facsimile or electronic transmission of the same not less than twenty-four (24) hours before the meeting. Unless otherwise indicated in the notice thereof, any and all business may be transacted at a special meeting.

Section 5. Quorum.

At any meeting of the Board of Directors, a majority of the total number of the Whole Board shall constitute a quorum for all purposes. If a quorum shall fail to attend any meeting, a majority of those present may adjourn the meeting to another place, date, or time, without further notice or waiver thereof.

Section 6. Participation in Meetings By Conference Telephone.

Members of the Board of Directors, or of any committee thereof, may participate in a meeting of such Board of Directors or committee by means of conference telephone or other communications equipment by means of which all persons participating in the meeting can hear each other and such participation shall constitute presence in person at such meeting.

Section 7. Conduct of Business.

At any meeting of the Board of Directors, business shall be transacted in such order and manner as the Board of Directors may from time to time determine, and all matters shall be determined by the vote of a majority of the directors present, except as otherwise provided herein or required by law. Action may be taken by the Board of Directors without a meeting if all members thereof consent thereto in writing or by electronic transmission, and the writing or writings or electronic transmission or transmissions are filed with the minutes of proceedings of the Board of Directors. Such filing shall be in paper form if the minutes are maintained in paper form and shall be in electronic form if the minutes are maintained in electronic form.

Section 8. Compensation of Directors.

Unless otherwise restricted by the certificate of incorporation, the Board of Directors shall have the authority to fix the compensation of the directors. The directors may be paid their expenses, if any, of attendance at each meeting of the Board of Directors and may be paid a fixed sum for attendance at each meeting of the Board of Directors or paid a stated salary or paid other compensation as director. No such payment shall preclude any director from serving the Corporation in any other capacity and receiving compensation therefor. Members of special or standing committees may be allowed compensation for attending committee meetings.

ARTICLE III–COMMITTEES

Section 1. Committees of the Board of Directors.

The Board of Directors may from time to time designate committees of the Board of Directors, with such lawfully delegable powers and duties as it thereby confers, to serve at the pleasure of the Board of Directors and shall, for those committees and any others provided for herein, elect a director or directors to serve as the member or members, designating, if it desires, other directors as alternate members who may replace any absent or disqualified member at any meeting of the committee. In the absence or disqualification of any member of any committee and any alternate member in his or her place, the member or members of the committee present at the meeting and not disqualified from voting, whether or not he or she or they constitute a quorum, may by unanimous vote appoint another member of the Board of Directors to act at the meeting in the place of the absent or disqualified member.

Section 2. Conduct of Business.

Each committee may determine the procedural rules for meeting and conducting its business and shall act in accordance therewith, except as otherwise provided herein or required by law. Adequate provision shall be made for notice to members of all meetings; one-third (1/3) of the members shall constitute a quorum unless the committee shall consist of one (1) or two (2) members, in which event one (1) member shall constitute a quorum; and all matters shall be determined by a majority vote of the members present. Action may be taken by any committee without a meeting if all members thereof consent thereto in writing or by electronic transmission, and the writing or writings or electronic transmission or transmissions are filed with the minutes of the proceedings of such committee. Such filing shall be in paper form if the minutes are maintained in paper form and shall be in electronic form if the minutes are maintained in electronic form.

ARTICLE IV–OFFICERS

Section 1. Generally.

The officers of the Corporation shall consist of a Chairman of the Board, a President, one or more Vice Presidents, a Secretary, a Treasurer and such other officers as may from time to time be appointed by the Board of Directors. Officers shall be elected by the Board of Directors, which shall consider that subject at its first meeting after every annual meeting of stockholders. Each officer shall hold office until his or her successor is elected and qualified or until his or her earlier resignation or removal. Any number of offices may be held by the same person. The salaries of officers elected by the Board of Directors shall be fixed from time to time by the Board of Directors or by such officers as may be designated by resolution of the Board of Directors.

Section 2. Chairman of the Board.

The Chairman of the Board shall be the chief executive officer of the Corporation. Subject to the provisions of these By-laws and to the direction of the Board of Directors, he or she shall have the responsibility for the general management and control of the business and affairs of the Corporation and shall perform all duties and have all powers which are commonly incident to the office of chief executive or which are delegated to him or her by the Board of Directors. He or she shall have power to sign all stock certificates, contracts and other instruments of the Corporation which are authorized and shall have general supervision and direction of all of the other officers, employees and agents of the Corporation.

Section 3. President.

The President shall be the chief operating officer of the Corporation. He or she shall have general responsibility for the management and control of the operations of the Corporation and shall perform all duties and have all powers which are commonly incident to the office of chief operating officer or which are delegated to him or her by the Board of Directors. Subject to the direction of the Board of Directors and the Chairman of the Board, the President shall have power to sign all stock certificates, contracts and other instruments of the Corporation which are authorized and shall have general supervision of all of the other officers (other than the Chairman of the Board or any Vice Chairman), employees and agents of the Corporation.

Section 4. Vice President.

Each Vice President shall have such powers and duties as may be delegated to him or her by the Board of Directors. One (1) Vice President shall be designated by the Board of Directors to perform the duties and exercise the powers of the President in the event of the President's absence or disability.

Section 5. Treasurer.

The Treasurer shall have the responsibility for maintaining the financial records of the Corporation. He or she shall make such disbursements of the funds of the Corporation as are authorized and shall render from time to time an account of all such transactions and of the financial condition of the Corporation. The Treasurer shall also perform such other duties as the Board of Directors may from time to time prescribe.

Section 6. Secretary.

The Secretary shall issue all authorized notices for, and shall keep minutes of, all meetings of the stockholders and the Board of Directors. He or she shall have charge of the corporate books and shall perform such other duties as the Board of Directors may from time to time prescribe.

Section 7. Delegation of Authority.

The Board of Directors may from time to time delegate the powers or duties of any officer to any other officers or agents, notwithstanding any provision hereof.

Section 8. Removal.

Any officer of the Corporation may be removed at any time, with or without cause, by the Board of Directors.

Section 9. Action with Respect to Securities of Other Corporations.

Unless otherwise directed by the Board of Directors, the President or any officer of the Corporation authorized by the President shall have power to vote and otherwise act on behalf of the Corporation, in person or by proxy, at any meeting of stockholders of or with respect to any action of stockholders of any other Corporation in which this Corporation may hold securities and otherwise to exercise any and all rights and powers which this Corporation may possess by reason of its ownership of securities in such other Corporation.

ARTICLE V—STOCK

Section 1. Certificates of Stock.

Each stockholder shall be entitled to a certificate signed by, or in the name of the Corporation by, the President or a Vice President, and by the Secretary or an Assistant Secretary, or the Treasurer or an Assistant Treasurer, certifying the number of shares owned by him or her. Any or all of the signatures on the certificate may be by facsimile.

Section 2. Transfers of Stock.

Transfers of stock shall be made only upon the transfer books of the Corporation kept at an office of the Corporation or by transfer agents designated to transfer shares of the stock of the Corporation. Except where a certificate is issued in accordance with Section 4 of Article V of these By-laws, an outstanding certificate for the number of shares involved shall be surrendered for cancellation before a new certificate is issued therefor.

Section 3. Record Date.

(1) In order that the Corporation may determine the stockholders entitled to notice of or to vote at any meeting of stockholders, or to receive payment of any dividend or other distribution or allotment of any rights or to exercise any rights in respect of any change, conversion or exchange of stock or for the purpose of any other lawful action, the Board of Directors may, except as otherwise required by law, fix a record date, which record date shall not precede the date on which the resolution fixing the record date is adopted and which record date shall not be more than sixty (60) nor less than ten (10) days before the date of any meeting of stockholders, nor more than sixty (60) days prior to the time for such other action as hereinbefore described; provided, however, that

if no record date is fixed by the Board of Directors, the record date for determining stockholders entitled to notice of or to vote at a meeting of stockholders shall be at the close of business on the day next preceding the day on which notice is given or, if notice is waived, at the close of business on the day next preceding the day on which the meeting is held, and, for determining stockholders entitled to receive payment of any dividend or other distribution or allotment of rights or to exercise any rights of change, conversion or exchange of stock or for any other purpose, the record date shall be at the close of business on the day on which the Board of Directors adopts a resolution relating thereto.

(2) A determination of stockholders of record entitled to notice of or to vote at a meeting of stockholders shall apply to any adjournment of the meeting; provided, however, that the Board of Directors may fix a new record date for the adjourned meeting.

Section 4. Lost, Stolen or Destroyed Certificates.

In the event of the loss, theft or destruction of any certificate of stock, another may be issued in its place pursuant to such regulations as the Board of Directors may establish concerning proof of such loss, theft or destruction and concerning the giving of a satisfactory bond or bonds of indemnity.

Section 5. Regulations.

The issue, transfer, conversion and registration of certificates of stock shall be governed by such other regulations as the Board of Directors may establish.

ARTICLE VI—NOTICES

Section 1. Notices.

If mailed, notice to stockholders shall be deemed given when deposited in the mail, postage prepaid, directed to the stockholder at such stockholder's address as it appears on the records of the Corporation. Without limiting the manner by which notice otherwise may be given effectively to stockholders, any notice to stockholders may be given by electronic transmission in the manner provided in Section 232 of the Delaware General Corporation Law.

Section 2. Waivers.

A written waiver of any notice, signed by a stockholder or director, or waiver by electronic transmission by such person, whether given before or after the time of the event for which notice is to be given, shall be deemed equivalent to the notice required to be given to such person. Neither the business nor the purpose of any meeting need be specified in such a waiver. Attendance at any meeting shall constitute waiver of notice except attendance for the sole purpose of objecting to the timeliness of notice.

ARTICLE VII—MISCELLANEOUS

Section 1. Facsimile Signatures.

In addition to the provisions for use of facsimile signatures elsewhere specifically authorized in these By-laws, facsimile signatures of any officer or officers of the Corporation may be used whenever and as authorized by the Board of Directors or a committee thereof.

Section 2. Corporate Seal.

The Board of Directors may provide a suitable seal, containing the name of the Corporation, which seal shall be in the charge of the Secretary. If and when so directed by the Board of Directors or a committee thereof; duplicates of the seal may be kept and used by the Treasurer or by an Assistant Secretary or Assistant Treasurer.

Section 3. Reliance upon Books, Reports and Records.

Each director, each member of any committee designated by the Board of Directors, and each officer of the Corporation shall, in the performance of his or her duties, be fully protected in relying in good faith upon the books of account or other records of the Corporation and upon such information, opinions, reports or statements presented to the Corporation by any of its officers or employees, or committees of the Board of Directors so designated, or by any other person as to matters which such director or committee member reasonably believes are within such other person's professional or expert competence and who has been selected with reasonable care by or on behalf of the Corporation.

Section 4. Fiscal Year.

The fiscal year of the Corporation shall be as fixed by the Board of Directors.

Section 5. Time Periods.

In applying any provision of these By-laws which requires that an act be done or not be done a specified number of days prior to an event or that an act be done during a period of a specified number of days prior to an event, calendar days shall be used, the day of the doing of the act shall be excluded, and the day of the event shall be included.

ARTICLE VIII—INDEMNIFICATION OF DIRECTORS AND OFFICERS

Section 1. Right to Indemnification.

Each person who was or is made a party or is threatened to be made a party to or is otherwise involved in any action, suit or proceeding, whether civil, criminal, administrative or investigative (hereinafter a "proceeding"), by reason of the fact that he or she is or was a director or an officer of the Corporation or is or was serving at the request of the Corporation as a director, officer or trustee of another corporation or of a partnership, joint venture, trust or other enterprise, including service with respect to an employee benefit plan (hereinafter an "indemnitee"), whether the basis of such proceeding is alleged action in an official capacity as a director, officer or trustee or in any other capacity while serving as a director, officer or trustee, shall be indemnified and held harmless by the Corporation to the fullest extent authorized by the Delaware General Corporation Law, as the same exists or may hereafter be amended (but, in the case of any such amendment, only to the extent that such amendment permits the Corporation to provide broader indemnification rights than such law permitted the Corporation to provide prior to such amendment), against all expense, liability and loss (including attorneys' fees, judgments, fines, ERISA excise taxes or penalties and amounts paid in settlement) reasonably incurred or suffered by such indemnitee in connection therewith; provided, however, that, except as provided in Section 3 of this Article VIII with respect to proceedings to enforce rights to indemnification, the Corporation shall indemnify any such indemnitee in connection with a proceeding (or part thereof) initiated by such indemnitee only if such proceeding (or part thereof) was authorized by the Board of Directors of the Corporation.

Section 2. Right to Advancement of Expenses.

In addition to the right to indemnification conferred in Section 1 of this Article VIII, an indemnitee shall also have the right to be paid by the Corporation the expenses (including attorney's fees) incurred in defending any such proceeding in advance of its final disposition (hereinafter an "advancement of expenses"); provided, however, that, if the Delaware General Corporation Law requires, an advancement of expenses incurred by an indemnitee in his or her capacity as a director or officer (and not in any other capacity in which service was or is rendered by such indemnitee, including, without limitation, service to an employee benefit plan) shall be made only upon delivery to the Corporation of an undertaking (hereinafter an "undertaking"), by or on behalf of such indemnitee, to repay all amounts so advanced if it shall ultimately be determined by final judicial decision from which there is no further right to appeal (hereinafter a "final adjudication") that such indemnitee is not entitled to be indemnified for such expenses under this Section 2 or otherwise.

Section 3. Right of Indemnitee to Bring Suit.

If a claim under Section 1 or 2 of this Article VIII is not paid in full by the Corporation within sixty (60) days after a written claim has been received by the Corporation, except in the case of a claim for an advancement of expenses, in which case the applicable period shall be twenty (20) days, the indemnitee may at any time thereafter bring suit against the Corporation to recover the unpaid amount of the claim. If successful in whole or in part in any such suit, or in a suit brought by the Corporation to recover an advancement of expenses pursuant to the terms of an undertaking, the indemnitee shall be entitled to be paid also the expense of prosecuting or defending such suit. In (i) any suit brought by the indemnitee to enforce a right to indemnification hereunder (but not in a suit brought by the indemnitee to enforce a right to an advancement of expenses) it shall be a defense that, and (ii) in any suit brought by the Corporation to recover an advancement of expenses pursuant to the terms of an undertaking, the Corporation shall be entitled to recover such expenses upon a final adjudication that, the indemnitee has not met any applicable standard for indemnification set forth in the Delaware General Corporation Law. Neither the failure of the Corporation (including its directors who are not parties to such action, a committee of such directors, independent legal counsel, or its stockholders) to have made a determination prior to the commencement of such suit that indemnification of the indemnitee is proper in the circumstances because the indemnitee has met the applicable standard of conduct set forth in the Delaware General Corporation Law, nor an actual determination by the Corporation (including its directors who are not parties to such action, a committee of such directors, independent legal counsel, or its stockholders) that the indemnitee has not met such applicable standard of conduct, shall create a presumption that the indemnitee has not met the applicable standard of conduct or, in the case of such a suit brought by the indemnitee, be a defense to such suit. In any suit brought by the indemnitee to enforce a right to indemnification or to an advancement of expenses hereunder, or brought by the Corporation to recover an advancement of expenses pursuant to the terms of an undertaking, the burden of proving that the indemnitee is not entitled to be indemnified, or to such advancement of expenses, under this Article VIII or otherwise shall be on the Corporation.

Section 4. Non-Exclusivity of Rights.

The rights to indemnification and to the advancement of expenses conferred in this Article VIII shall not be exclusive of any other right which any person may have or hereafter acquire under any statute, the Corporation's Certificate of Incorporation, By-laws, agreement, vote of stockholders or directors or otherwise.

Section 5. Insurance.

The Corporation may maintain insurance, at its expense, to protect itself and any director, officer, employee or agent of the Corporation or another corporation, partnership, joint venture, trust or other enterprise against any expense, liability or loss, whether or not the Corporation would have the power to indemnify such person against such expense, liability or loss under the Delaware General Corporation Law.

Section 6. Indemnification of Employees and Agents of the Corporation.

The Corporation may, to the extent authorized from time to time by the Board of Directors, grant rights to indemnification and to the advancement of expenses to any employee or agent of the Corporation to the fullest extent of the provisions of this Article with respect to the indemnification and advancement of expenses of directors and officers of the Corporation.

Section 7. Nature of Rights.

The rights conferred upon indemnitees in this Article VIII shall be contract rights and such rights shall continue as to an indemnitee who has ceased to be a director, officer or trustee and shall inure to the benefit of the indemnitee's heirs, executors and administrators. Any amendment, alteration or repeal of this Article VIII that adversely affects any right of an indemnitee or its successors shall be prospective only and shall not limit or eliminate any such right with respect to any proceeding involving any occurrence or alleged occurrence of any action or omission to act that took place prior to such amendment or repeal.

ARTICLE IX—AMENDMENTS

In furtherance and not in limitation of the powers conferred by law, the Board of Directors is expressly authorized to adopt, amend and repeal these By–Laws subject to the power of the holders of capital stock of the Corporation to adopt, amend or repeal the By–Laws; provided, however, that, with respect to the power of holders of capital stock to adopt, amend and repeal By–Laws of the Corporation, notwithstanding any other provision of these By–Laws or any provision of law which might otherwise permit a lesser vote or no vote, but in addition to any affirmative vote of the holders of any particular class or series of the capital stock of the Corporation required by law, these By–Laws or any preferred stock, the affirmative vote of the holders of at least ______ percent of the voting power of all of the then-outstanding shares entitled to vote generally in the election of directors, voting together as a single class, shall be required to adopt, amend or repeal any provision of these By–Laws.

3. BAKER & MCKENZIE/RICHARDS, LAYTON & FINGER POISON PILL DOCUMENTS

Date:	March ___, 2002
To:	The Board of Directors of XYZ, Inc.
Re:	Stockholder Rights Plan

We have been asked to advise the Board of Directors of XYZ, Inc. (the "Company") in connection with the possible implementation of a stockholder rights plan ("Rights Plan"). We believe the Board of Directors should consider adopting such a plan for the following reasons: First, the Company may be considered an attractive target for an unsolicited takeover proposal. The price of the Company's common stock has declined from a 52-week high of $___ to a recent trading range of $___. The current trading prices do not reflect the prospective impact of certain of the Company's initiatives, such as the implementation of expense controls, the anticipated roll-out of new product lines, and the benefits of increased research and development expenditures. Management anticipates the benefits of the initiatives to drop to the bottom line and eventually lead to increased gross revenues. Second, in light of the declines this year in stock prices, approximately 140 companies adopted stockholder rights plans during the first half of 2001, an increase, according to Thompson Financial Securities Data, of 45% over the same period in 2000. Additionally, investment bankers view such plans as low cost insurance for takeover protections in today's environment of plunging stock prices. A properly designed Rights Plan will assist the Board of Directors in establishing a "level playing field" for negotiations with prospective acquirors. Consequently, we believe that the Board of Directors should consider the adoption of a stockholder rights plan as an important component of its stockholder protection strategy.

An effectively implemented, properly designed Rights Plan gives the Board of Directors a powerful tool to deal with a prospective acquiror to make certain that any proposed transaction is, in the Board's view, in the best interest of the Company and its stockholders. While a Rights Plan will not, and is not intended to, prohibit a person from initiating or completing an acquisition of the Company, it is intended to strengthen the ability of the Board of Directors to fulfill its fiduciary duties to take actions which are in the best interests of stockholders.

In connection with any decision with respect to the Company's adoption of a Rights Plan, we recommend that the Board consider the documents attached hereto. These documents consist of the following:

1. Overview Memorandum;
2. Questions and Answers Regarding the Rights Plan;

3. Summary of the Terms of the Proposed Rights Plan;
4. Summary of Financial Accounting and Tax Consequences;
5. Illustration of Dilution;
6. Form of Letter to Stockholders; and
7. Form of Press Release.

If, after consideration of the materials included with this memorandum, the Board wishes to proceed with the possible implementation of a Rights Plan, we advise the Board to obtain the advice and counsel of its financial advisors regarding, among other things, the current mergers and acquisitions environment and the effect on the price of the Company's common stock as a result of the implementation of a Rights Plan. We would also then provide the Board with a copy of the proposed Rights Plan.

OVERVIEW

We believe it is appropriate for XYZ, Inc. (the "Company") to consider whether to adopt a stockholder rights plan (a "Rights Plan"). An effectively implemented, properly designed Rights Plan gives the Board of Directors a powerful tool to deal with a prospective acquiror to make certain that any proposed transaction is, in the Board's view, in the best interests of the Company and its stockholders. The first Rights Plan was adopted by Crown Zellerbach Corporation in July 1984. Today, more than 2,300 Rights Plans are currently in effect.

A Rights Plan is designed to deter certain types of takeover tactics and to otherwise encourage third parties interested in acquiring a company to negotiate with its Board of Directors. In particular, a Rights Plan is intended to help (i) reduce the risk of coercive two-tiered, front-end loaded or partial offers which may not offer fair value to all stockholders; (ii) mitigate against market accumulators who through open market and/or private purchases may achieve a position of substantial influence or control without paying to selling or remaining stockholders a fair control premium; (iii) deter market accumulators who are simply interested in putting the Company "into play"; and (iv) preserve the Board of Directors' bargaining power and flexibility to deal with third-party acquirors and to otherwise seek to maximize values for all stockholders.

While a Rights Plan will not, and is not intended to, insulate the Company from all takeover attempts, it is intended to strengthen the ability of the Board of Directors to fulfill its fiduciary duties to take actions which are in the best interests of stockholders. Thus, for example, the Rights Plan should help substantially in deterring attempts to take over the Company on terms which are determined by the Board of Directors not to be acceptable. A Rights Plan, however, is not designed to deter a proxy contest or a fair offer for the whole Company. Also, a

Rights Plan may have little effect on a bidder which is well financed and prepared to pay a fair price for all shares in cash.

This memorandum discusses legal and financial considerations relating to the adoption of a Rights Plan, and also briefly describes the terms of a Rights Plan which we recommend for consideration. Tab 3 hereto contains a summary of the terms of the plan we would recommend that the Board consider.

DISCUSSION

I. *General Considerations*

Board adoption. A Rights Plan may be authorized and implemented by Board action without any stockholder vote. Following the adoption of a Rights Plan, a press release would be issued and a letter describing the plan would be sent to stockholders. Copies of proposed forms of press release and letter to stockholders are attached at Tab 7 and Tab 6, respectively.

Modification by Board. As more fully described in the section below entitled "Basic Terms," the Board is given substantial flexibility to amend the Rights Plan. In addition, the rights may be redeemed for nominal consideration prior to their becoming irrevocable.

Reasons for adopting a Rights Plan. Stockholder Rights Plans are basically designed to deter unfair takeover tactics and otherwise to encourage third parties interested in acquiring a company to negotiate with its Board of Directors. In particular, Rights Plans similar to the plan recommended for consideration by the Company are intended to put the Board of Directors in a better position in dealing with the types of activities and tactics described in clauses (i) through (iv) in the second paragraph under "Overview" above.

Standards and procedures. In connection with considering the adoption of a Rights Plan, the Board of Directors should follow certain standards and procedures, including, among others:

1. The Board should consider the perceived threats to the Company and its stockholders of coercive or unfair offers and accumulation programs;
2. The Rights Plan should be tailored so that it is reasonable in relation to the threats posed. Rights Plans should not be designed to bar an offer which the Board deems beneficial to stockholders;
3. The Board should receive advice from its legal and financial advisors concerning the current takeover environment, particularly circumstances peculiar to the Company and its industry, the financial and market impact of adoption of a Rights Plan, and the legality of the plan under applicable Delaware law;

4. The Board should be provided with and review the documents constituting the particular Rights Plan under consideration and a reasonable summary (as included herein) thereof;
5. The Board's legal and financial advisors should discuss with the Board the plan's terms, purposes and effects, and the factors relevant to its adoption. The Board's independent directors should be actively involved; and
6. Sufficient time for full review and informed decision-making should be taken.

Financial and tax effects. The adoption of a Rights Plan should have no impact on earnings per share and should not otherwise affect the financial statements of the Company until the rights trade separately and are "in the money."

The distribution of rights pursuant to a Rights Plan should not be taxable to the Company or to stockholders. However, stockholders may, depending upon the circumstances, recognize taxable income in the event that the rights become exercisable for common stock (or other consideration) of the Company or for common stock of the acquiring company. The Company's redemption of the rights also will be a taxable event to stockholders. A memorandum describing certain financial accounting and tax consequences of the adoption of a Rights Plan is included under Tab 4.

II. *Basic Terms*

The following is a general description of the stockholder Rights Plan which we recommend for consideration by the Company's Board. However, the terms of this Rights Plan can be varied to address any specific concerns that the Company or its Board may have. Set forth under "Common Variations" below are summaries of certain common provisions that other companies have included in their Rights Plans.

To implement the Rights Plan, the Board of Directors would authorize a dividend to all holders of the Company's common stock of one "right" for each share of common stock outstanding (the "Common Stock"). Each right would initially entitle its registered holder to purchase from the Company a fraction of a share of a new series of preferred stock of the Company (which is intended to be essentially the economic equivalent of the Common Stock), at an initial price intended to reflect the long-term trading value of a share of Common Stock over the term of the plan (the "Purchase Price"). Premiums over current market used by other companies have generally been in the 300–500% range, but the Purchase Price selected for the Company should be specifically determined based on advice from the Company's financial advisors.

Until a person acquires beneficial ownership of 15% or more of the outstanding Common Stock (thereby becoming an "Acquiring Person") or commences a tender offer that would result in his owning 15% or more of the outstanding Common Stock, the rights (i) are evidenced by the Common Stock certificates, (ii) may be transferred with and only with the Common Stock and (iii) are not exercisable. Upon the occurrence of any such events the rights become exercisable and separate certificates are distributed to the holders of record of the Common Stock; thereafter, the Common Stock and the rights trade separately.

The rights expire after a period of time from the date of issuance, unless earlier redeemed by the Company (as described below). We recommend 10 years as the term of the rights. The Board of Directors of the Company generally may redeem the rights at a nominal price (*i.e.*, $0.001 per right) until someone becomes an Acquiring Person.

If any person becomes an Acquiring Person, each holder of a right (other than the Acquiring Person and its affiliates and associates) thereafter has the right to receive, upon exercise of the right at the Purchase Price, Common Stock (or, under certain circumstances, a combination of cash, Common Stock, other securities or other assets) having a value of two times such Purchase Price.

If anyone becomes an Acquiring Person and the Company then (i) engages in a merger or other business combination transaction with another person in which the Common Stock are changed or exchanged, or (ii) sells or transfers 50% or more of its assets or earning power to another person or persons, each right (other than rights of the Acquiring Person and its affiliates and associates, which will have become void) thereafter entitles the holder of such right to receive, upon exercise of the right at the Purchase Price, Common Stock of such other person (or, in certain circumstances, of an affiliate of such other person) having a value of two times such Purchase Price.

At any time after any person becomes an Acquiring Person and prior to the earlier of one of the events described in clause (i) or (ii) in the previous paragraph or the acquisition by any person of 50% or more of the outstanding Common Stock, the Board of Directors may exchange the rights (other than rights held by the Acquiring Person and its affiliates or associates, which will have become void), in whole or in part, for Common Stock (or fractional shares of preferred stock having essentially equivalent rights, preferences and privileges) having a value per right equal to the difference between the value of the Common Stock receivable upon exercise of the right and the Purchase Price.

Until a right is exercised, holders have no stockholder rights (such as voting rights or rights to receive dividends). The terms of the rights, other than the redemption price, may be amended by the Board of Directors in any manner as long as the rights are redeemable. Thereafter, the terms of the rights may be amended in any manner, as long as the amendment does not adversely affect the interests of holders of rights.

III. *Common Variations*

Although most modern Rights Plans contain the provisions described under "Basic Terms" above, a number of variations have developed. Set forth below is a general discussion of two of the most common variations.

Many Rights Plans contain provisions that provide that a person does not become an "Acquiring Person" by acquiring beneficial ownership of 15% or more of the outstanding Common Stock if such person acquires such stock pursuant to a "Permitted Offer." Permitted Offer is often defined to mean a tender or exchange offer for all outstanding Common Stock at a price and on terms determined by the Board to be fair to stockholders and otherwise in the best interest of the Company and its stockholders. Sometimes, "Permitted Offer" is even more broadly defined to include the acquisition of shares pursuant to any transaction approved by the Board of Directors. Although these provisions may appear sensible, they are unnecessary in most modern Rights Plans for two reasons. First, many Rights Plans, including the one we recommend, provide that the Board of Directors can amend the Rights Plan in any respect, other than to change the redemption price, at any time prior to the time an Acquiring Person becomes such. Second, since the redemption price of the rights is generally a nominal amount (*i.e.*, $.001 per right), the Board can redeem the rights if and when it believes an acquisition transaction is in the best interests of the Company and its stockholders.

Some Rights Plans also have a so-called "back-door" redemption clause, which allows the Board to redeem the rights after an Acquiring Person has become such. The advocates of this provision believe that it gives the Board more room to negotiate with a hostile acquiror. On the other hand, the inclusion of such a provision creates an incentive for an aggressive acquiror to cross the triggering threshold, thereby forcing the Board, and not the acquiror, to make the final decision on whether or not the rights will dilute the acquiror. For this reason, our recommended Rights Plan does not include such a "back-door" redemption clause.

CONCLUSION

In summary, a Rights Plan is a flexible vehicle by which a company, by considering a variety of different structures, options and variations and by tailoring the plan to address the Company's individual needs and objectives, can provide significant protection to its stockholders. We recommend that XYZ, Inc. consider the adoption of a Rights Plan as an important component of its stockholder protection strategy.

QUESTIONS AND ANSWERS ABOUT STOCKHOLDER RIGHTS PLANS

1. *What is the purpose of a Stockholder Rights Plan?*

A stockholder rights plan ("Rights Plan") is designed to deter certain types of takeover tactics and to otherwise encourage third parties interested in acquiring the Company to negotiate with its Board of Directors. In particular, a Rights Plan is intended to help (i) reduce the risk of coercive two-tiered, front-end loaded or partial offers which may not offer fair value to all stockholders; (ii) mitigate against market accumulators who through open market and/or private purchases may achieve a position of substantial influence or control without paying to selling or remaining stockholders a fair control premium; (iii) deter market accumulators who are simply interested in putting the Company "into play"; and (iv) preserve the Board of Directors' bargaining power and flexibility to deal with third-party acquirors and to otherwise seek to maximize values for all stockholders.

While a Rights Plan will not, and is not intended, to insulate the Company from all takeovers, it is intended to strengthen the ability of the Board of Directors to fulfill its fiduciary duties to take actions which are in the best interests of stockholders. Thus, for example, the Rights Plan should help substantially in deterring attempts to take over the Company on terms which are determined by the Board of Directors not to be acceptable. A Rights Plan, however, is not designed to deter a proxy contest or a fair offer for the whole Company. Also, a Rights Plan may have little effect on a bidder which is well financed and prepared to pay a fair price for all shares in cash.

A Rights Plan is intended to achieve these goals by confronting a potential acquiror of the Company's common stock (the "Common Stock") with the possibility that the Company's stockholders will be able to dilute substantially the acquiror's equity interest by exercising "Rights" (which are issued under the Rights Plan) to buy additional stock in the Company—*or in certain cases, stock of the acquiror*—at a substantial discount.

2. *How many companies have Rights Plans?*

Since the first Rights Plan was adopted by Crown Zellerbach Corporation in July 1984, such plans have become commonplace in Delaware. Today, more than 2,300 Rights Plans are currently in effect. Many Fortune 500 companies have adopted Rights Plans. In addition, there is not a single state that does not permit their adoption.

3. *Why have so many companies considered the adoption of Rights Plans?*

In November 1985, the Delaware Supreme Court upheld a Rights Plan adopted by Household International as a legitimate action taken by a Board of Directors to protect its stockholders from coercive takeover tactics. In addition, a number of courts and state legislatures have recognized the potential benefits that a Rights Plan offers to assist a board of directors in protecting the best interests of all stockholders.

4. *How does the Board of Directors go about implementing a Rights Plan?*

If the Board of Directors, after fully considering a Rights Plan with the advice and the assistance of its legal and financial advisors, determines that the Rights Plan is in the best interests of the Company and its stockholders, the Board would declare a dividend distribution of one Right for each outstanding share of the Company's Common Stock. Each Right initially would be attached to each share of Common Stock and would entitle the holder of such Right to purchase 1/1000th of a share of a new series of preferred stock at a price which is designed to reflect the projected long-term value of the Company's Common Stock over the term of the Plan (*e.g.*, typically 3 to 5 times the current market price of the Common Stock when the Rights Plan is adopted). One one-thousandth of a share of preferred stock is intended to be the economic equivalent of one share of Common Stock. However, upon the occurrence of a "Flip-in" or "Flip-over" Event (described below), each Right would become the right to purchase Common Stock of the Company or, in certain circumstances, the acquiring person, at a substantial discount.

5. *Why are shares of preferred stock rather than Common Stock used in the Rights Plan?*

Although the dividend, liquidation, voting and other rights of the preferred stock are designed so that each 1/1000th of a share of preferred stock would have rights similar to one share of Common Stock, preferred stock is used so that the Company's authorized Common Stock could be used for other purposes and would not have to be reserved for issuance upon exercise of the Rights. In addition, since each full share of preferred stock is sufficient to cover the exercise of 1000 Rights, many fewer shares of preferred stock would have to be reserved.

6. *Will the adoption of a Rights Plan affect earnings per share or be a taxable event?*

Since the purchase price under the Rights greatly exceeds the market price of the Common Stock, the adoption of the Rights Plan should not be dilutive and should not affect reported earnings per share. In addition, the distribution of the Rights should not be a taxable event for either the Company or the stockholders receiving the Rights.

7. *When do the Rights first become exercisable?*

At the time the Rights Plan is adopted, the Rights are neither exercisable nor traded separately from the Common Stock. In fact, at the time of adoption of the Rights Plan, the Common Stock certificates represent both the outstanding Common Stock and the outstanding Rights.

The Rights will detach from the Common Stock (that is, Rights Certificates will be distributed and will trade separately) and become exercisable shortly after (i) any person or group acquires beneficial ownership of 15% or more of the outstanding Common Stock or (ii) any person or group commences a tender or exchange offer which would result in that person or group beneficially owning 15% or more of the outstanding Common Stock. The date on which the Rights detach is referred to as the Distribution Date.

8. *Is it likely that many Rights would be exercised following the Distribution Date?*

Until such time as the market price of the Common Stock rises above the exercise price of the Rights, it is highly unlikely that any holder of Rights would exercise such Rights. However, if a "Flip-in Event" or a "Flip-over Event" (described below) were to occur, the Rights would become valuable and entitle the holder to purchase Common Stock of the Company or common stock of the acquiror, as the case may be, at a substantial discount.

9. *What are the "Flip-in" or "Flip-over" events and what rights are created by the occurrence of such events?*

Flip-in Events - A Flip-in Event would be deemed to have occurred if any person becomes the beneficial owner of more than a specified percentage of the outstanding Common Stock (*i.e.*, 15%).

Upon the occurrence of a Flip-in Event, each holder of a Right, other than Rights held by an Acquiring Person, will thereafter be entitled to purchase Common Stock of the Company (or in certain circumstances cash, property or other securities of the Company) with a value at the time of such Flip-in Event of two times the then exercise price of the Rights. Since an Acquiring Person will not be entitled to exercise its Rights following the occurrence of a Flip-in Event, its equity interest in the Company would be substantially diluted.

Flip-over Events - A Flip-over Event will be deemed to have occurred if following the acquisition of 15% or more of the Common Stock by any person:

(i) the Company is acquired in a merger or other business combination;

(ii) the Company is the continuing or surviving corporation in a merger in which all or part of the Common Stock is exchanged for stock, cash or other property; or

(iii) 50% or more of the Company's assets or earning power is sold or otherwise transferred in one transaction or a series of related transactions.

The Flip-over Events are designed to avoid circumvention of the Flip-in rights and to make any second-step transaction economically prohibitive and thereby deter two-tiered or partial offers. Upon the occurrence of a Flip-over Event, each Right would entitle its holder to purchase common stock of the acquiring person with a value of twice the then exercise price of the Rights.

10. *When do the Rights expire?*

Unless redeemed or exchanged earlier by the Company, the Rights would expire ten years from the date of issuance. The ten year period has been selected by most companies to provide a meaningful period of protection.

11. *May the Board of Directors redeem the Rights and at what price?*

In general, the Board of Directors may redeem the Rights at any time prior to the time some person or group acquires beneficial ownership of, or announces its intention to commence, or commences, a tender or exchange offer with respect to, 15% or more of the outstanding Common Stock. The redemption price is $0.001 per Right.

In addition to the stated period for redemption, at any time prior to the date on which the Rights would otherwise become nonredeemable, the Board of Directors may amend the Rights Plan to extend the period for redemption.

12. *Under what circumstances might the Board of Directors wish to redeem the Rights?*

As described earlier, the Rights Plan is intended to enable the Board of Directors to respond to unsolicited acquisition proposals in a manner which is in the best interests of the Company and its stockholders. Accordingly, if there is a proposed takeover which the Board deems advantageous, the Board would be in a position to redeem the outstanding Rights at a nominal consideration. In addition, it is always possible that the circumstances relating to a particular unsolicited takeover and/or future developments in the takeover area, including future judicial decisions, might suggest at some future time that a Board of Directors consider the desirability of redeeming the outstanding Rights.

13. *Will the Board of Directors be able to amend the provisions of the Rights once the Rights Plan has been adopted?*

The Rights Plan provides the Board with significant flexibility to amend the terms of the Rights Plan. For so long as the Rights are redeemable, the Board may, without the approval of any holder of Rights, supplement or amend any provision of the Rights Plan other than to change the redemption price. At any time when the rights are not redeemable, the Board may amend the Rights Plan in any manner that does not adversely affect the holders of Rights.

14. *May additional Rights be issued after the date the Rights Plan is adopted, including in connection with Common Stock issuances upon the exercise of stock options and convertible security conversions?*

Prior to the Distribution Date, all Common Stock issued by the Company would have Rights attached.

After the Distribution Date, in general, the Company would issue Rights in connection with the Common Stock issued upon the exercise of stock options or under any employee plan or arrangement, or upon the exercise, conversion or exchange of securities issued by the Company prior to the Distribution Date.

15. *Where will the Rights be traded?*

Since the Rights prior to the Distribution Date are deemed to be represented by the Common Stock certificates, the Rights will initially be listed and traded on the same exchanges on which the Common Stock are listed and traded. However, prior to the Distribution Date, there will be no separate trading market for the Rights.

16. *What will happen if the Company does not have sufficient Common Stock to issue following the occurrence of either a "Flip-in" or a "Flip-over" event?*

The Rights Plan provides that, following a "Flip-in" event, the Company would be required to reduce the purchase price or to substitute, if necessary, cash, preferred stock, debt securities or other property with a value equal to the Common Stock which would otherwise be issuable.

This should not be a problem following a "Flip-over" event since, under the terms of the Rights Plan, the Company may not engage in a transaction (*e.g.*, a merger) constituting a "Flip-over" event unless the acquiring person has sufficient common stock authorized to permit the full exercise of the Rights.

17. *What impact would the adoption of the Rights Plan have on the Business Judgment Rule and future actions of the Board under the Plan?*

Following the adoption of the Rights Plan, the Board of Directors would of course continue to be required to exercise its duties with due care and loyalty and would continue to act as fiduciaries for the Company's stockholders. In this regard, it should be noted that future decisions with respect to a redemption of the Rights, like all other decisions in the takeover area, may prove difficult. In addition, although the business judgment rule should apply to all future decisions (including redemption) it is possible that a court in reviewing all the facts and circumstances (including the existence of a Rights Plan) may subject a Board's decision to greater scrutiny.

18. *Are there any disadvantages to adopting a Rights Plan?*

The primary disadvantage would be that, if and when the Rights became nonredeemable, the Company would lose flexibility in engaging in transactions qualifying as "Flip-over" events. Even though this is a disadvantage, it is necessary to achieve the deterrent effect of the Rights Plan. In addition, a number of institutional investors have submitted stockholder proposals requesting that the Rights Plans be redeemed or submitted to a stockholder vote.

19. *Why do some stockholders oppose Rights Plans*?

Opponents of Rights Plans have asserted that the effect of a Rights Plan is to usurp the right of stockholders to consider third party offers for their shares. Opponents also assert that the primary motivation in adopting Rights Plans is entrenchment of management.

SUMMARY OF THE TERMS OF THE PROPOSED RIGHTS PLAN

20. *Effectiveness*. The Rights Plan shall be effective as of the date of the Rights Agreement for all shares of the Company's common stock (the "Common Stock") outstanding on the established Record Date and for all Common Stock issued prior to the earliest of the Distribution Date (as defined below), the redemption of the Rights, the exchange of the Rights or the expiration of the Rights. In addition, in certain limited circumstances, Rights may be issued with respect to shares of Common Stock issued after the Distribution Date.

21. *Right Certificates*. Right Certificates shall be distributed to stockholders as soon as practicable after the Distribution Date. Until the Distribution Date, Rights shall be evidenced by certificates for Common Stock.

22. *Term*. The rights will expire on the tenth anniversary of the date of the Rights Agreement unless earlier redeemed or exchanged by the Company as provided below.

23. *Exercisability*. Initially, the Rights will not be exercisable. The Rights shall become exercisable upon the earlier of (i) the tenth calendar day after the first public announcement that a person or group (other than the Company, any of its subsidiaries or any employee stock plan of the Company), together with its affiliates and associates, has acquired, or obtained the right to acquire, beneficial ownership of 15% or more of the outstanding Common Stock (such person or group being called an "Acquiring Person"), or (ii) the tenth business day after the commencement of, or first public announcement of an intention to commence, a tender or exchange offer which would result in a person or group obtaining beneficial ownership of 15% or more of the outstanding Common Stock (the earlier of such dates being called the "Distribution Date"). The timing of the Distribution Date is in some cases subject to extension by the Board of Directors. After the Distribution Date, the Rights shall be exercisable by the registered holders of the Right Certifi-

cates. Each Right shall be exercisable for 1/1000th of a share of Series A Junior Participating Preferred Stock (the "Series A Preferred Stock") (as described below), subject to adjustment. The exercise price with respect to each Right shall be $____, subject to adjustment.

24. *Detachability*. Prior to the Distribution Date, the Rights shall be transferable only with the related Common Stock certificates and shall automatically be transferred with such certificates. After the Distribution Date, the Rights shall be separately transferable, and the Company will provide Right Certificates to all holders of Common Stock.

25. *Terms of Series A Preferred Stock*. The terms of the Series A Preferred Stock have been designed so that each 1/1000th of a share of Series A Preferred Stock will have economic attributes (*i.e.*, participation in dividends and liquidation and voting rights) substantially equivalent to one whole share of the Common Stock of the Company. In addition, the Series A Preferred Stock have certain minimum dividend and liquidation preferences. See Exhibit A for a more detailed description of the Series A Preferred Stock.

26. *The Flip–In Provision*. In the event that a person becomes an Acquiring Person (a "Flip–In Event"), the holder of each Right (other than the Acquiring Person, its affiliates and associates and certain transferees thereof) will thereafter have the right to receive, upon exercise thereof, for the exercise price, in lieu of shares of Series A Preferred Stock, that number of Common Stock which at the time of such transaction would have a market value of twice the exercise price. The Company may at its option substitute 1/1000ths of a share of Series A Preferred Stock for some or all of the Common Stock so issuable. In the event there is insufficient Common Stock to permit exercise in full of Rights, the Company must issue shares of Series A Preferred Stock, cash, property or other securities of the Company with an aggregate value equal to twice the exercise price. Upon the occurrence of any such Flip–In Event, any Rights that are owned by an Acquiring Person, its affiliates and certain transferees thereof shall become null and void.

27. *The Flip–Over Provision*. In the event that, from and after a Flip–In Event, (a) the Company is acquired in a merger or other business combination, (b) the Company is the continuing or surviving corporation in a merger in which all or part of the Company's Common Stock is exchanged for stock, cash or other property, or (c) 50% or more of the Company's assets, or assets accounting for 50% or more of its net income, are sold, leased, exchanged or otherwise transferred (in one or more transactions), proper provision shall be made so that each holder of a Right (other than the Acquiring Person, its affiliates and associates and certain transferees thereof whose Rights became void) shall thereafter have the right to receive, upon the exercise thereof, for the exercise price, that number of shares of common stock of the acquiring company

which at the time of such transaction would have a market value of twice the exercise price.

28. *Redemption.* The Rights are redeemable by the Board of Directors at a redemption price of $.001 per Right (the "Redemption Price") any time prior to the earlier of (i) the time that an Acquiring Person becomes such, or (ii) the expiration date. Immediately upon the action of the Board electing to redeem the Rights, and without any further action and without any notice, the right to exercise the Rights will terminate and the only right of the holders of Rights will be to receive the Redemption Price.

29. *Exchange.* At any time after a Flip–In Event, but prior to a Flip–Over Event or the time that any person becomes the beneficial owner of 50% or more of the outstanding Common Stock, the Board may exchange each Right for a number of shares of Common Stock (or fractional shares of Series A Preferred Stock or similar securities) having a value equal to the difference between the market value of the shares of Common Stock receivable upon exercise of the Right and the exercise price of the Right.

30. *Amendment.* For so long as the Rights are redeemable, the Company may, without the approval of any holder of the Rights, supplement or amend any provision of the Rights Agreement. At any time when the Rights are not redeemable, the Company may amend the Rights in any manner that does not adversely affect the holders of Rights. In no event may any supplement or amendment be made which changes the Redemption Price.

31. *Voting.* The holder of a Right, as such, will have no rights as a stockholder of the Company, including, without limitation, the right to vote or to receive dividends.

EXHIBIT A

DESCRIPTION OF SERIES A JUNIOR PARTICIPATING PREFERRED STOCK

32. *Designation, Par Value, and Ranking.* The Company will be authorized to issue shares of Series A Junior Participating Preferred Stock, par value $.001 per share ("Series A Preferred Stock"). The Series A Preferred Stock has the following features.

33. *Dividends.* The holders of Series A Preferred Stock are entitled to receive quarterly cumulative dividends in an amount per share equal to the greater of $10.00 or 1000 times the dividends declared on the Common Stock since the preceding quarterly dividend payment date, or with respect to the first quarterly dividend payment date, since the date of issuance. Noncash dividends are payable in kind in a per share amount equal to 1000 times any noncash dividends paid per share of Common Stock.

34. *Voting Rights*. Holders of Series A Preferred Stock are entitled to vote on each matter on which holders of Common Stock are entitled to vote, and shall have 1000 votes per share.

35. *Certain Restrictions*. Whenever quarterly dividends or distributions on the Series A Preferred Stock are in arrears, the Company's right to declare or pay dividends or other distributions on or to redeem or purchase any shares of stock ranking junior to or on a parity with the Series A Preferred Stock is subject to certain restrictions.

36. *Liquidation Rights*. Upon any liquidation, dissolution or winding up of the Corporation, whether voluntary or involuntary, the holders of shares of Series A Preferred Stock will be entitled to receive, before any distribution is made to holders of shares of Common Stock or any other stock ranking junior to the Series A Preferred Stock, a minimum of $1000 per share, plus an amount equal to any accrued dividends and distribution thereon whether or not declared, to the date of payment, and will be entitled to an aggregate payment of 1000 times the amount per share distributed to the holders of Common Stock.

37. *Redemption*. The shares of Series A Preferred Stock are not subject to redemption by the Company.

38. *Amalgamation, Merger, etc*. In the event of an amalgamation, merger or similar transaction in which the Common Stock are exchanged for or converted into other securities, cash or any other property, the shares of Series A Preferred Stock will be similarly exchanged or converted in an amount per share equal to 1000 times the amount per share of securities, cash or other property into which each share of Common Stock is changed or converted.

39. *Adjustment of Participation Rights*. In the event that, after the date of the Rights Agreement, a dividend in Common Stock is paid on the Common Stock, or the Common Stock is subdivided or combined, then the rights of the Series A Preferred Stock with respect to voting and participation in dividends, liquidation and merger consideration will automatically be adjusted proportionately.

40. *Rank*. The Series A Preferred Stock will rank senior to the Common Stock and, unless otherwise provided, junior to all future series of preferred stock.

FINANCIAL ACCOUNTING AND TAX CONSEQUENCES

Financial Accounting Consequences:

- No income statement impact unless and until the Rights become exercisable and are "in the money."
- Adoption of a Plan should have no balance sheet impact.
- Pooling considerations should no longer be relevant in light of the approval in June 2001 by the Financial Accounting Standards Board

("FASB") of its statements mandating the use of the purchase method of accounting for all business combinations commenced after June 30, 2001.

- The price paid to redeem Rights will be a charge to equity.
- Exercise of Rights and exchange of Rights for Common Stock will be treated as a capital transaction.

Tax Considerations:

- Distribution of Rights should not result in taxable income to the distributee or to the Company.
- When the Rights subsequently separate but are still "out of the money," there still should not be any taxable income to the distributee or the Company.
- If and when the Rights "flip-in" to the Company's Common Stock, it is again likely that there will not be any taxable event to the holder or the Company (although there is some possibility of taxability to holders of Rights if the "flip-in" can be linked to dividends received by the holders of the Company's Common Stock within three years of either side of the "flip-in" event). In addition, the "flip-in" could be taxable to holders of Rights if the Company has outstanding convertible securities with anti-dilution provisions which do not completely adjust for the "flip-in" of the Rights. In either case, the IRS could argue that the "flip-in" constitutes a taxable dividend to holders of Rights under the stock dividend rules of § 305 of the I.R.C. It also is possible that the "flip-in" event may be construed as a taxable exchange of a warrant to buy preferred stock (if the Rights were initially exercisable for preferred stock) for a warrant to buy Common Stock.
- If the Rights "flip-over" and become exercisable for Common Stock of the Acquiror, the holder would recognize a taxable gain (capital gain if the Right and the underlying stock are held as capital assets) equal to the difference between the holder' s basis in the Right and the fair market value of the "new" Right.
- If the Company redeems the Rights prior to the time the Rights separate from the Company's Common Stock, the payment of the redemption price to Stockholders will in all likelihood be dividend income. If the Company redeems the Rights after the time the Rights separate from the Common Stock, it is not entirely clear whether the payment of the redemption price to holders of Rights will be taxable to holders of Rights as capital gain or ordinary income but, in any event, should not be dividend income.
- The Internal Revenue Service has ruled privately that Rights do not constitute "other property" or "boot" for purposes of the reorganization provisions of the Internal Revenue Code. Thus, the fact that

Rights are to be issued with the Company's Common Stock as part of an acquisition by the Company should not restrict the Company' s ability to consummate those forms of tax-free reorganizations that do not permit boot.

ILLUSTRATION OF DILUTION

The following hypothetical example illustrates the "economic hurt" or "poison" inherent in the Rights Plan.

Assume the Company has 1,000 shares outstanding and a person purchases 15% or more of the outstanding shares, thereby becoming an "Acquiring Person" and triggering the "flip-in." Assume further the market price of the Company's Common Stock is $1 per share and the exercise price of the Rights is $4 per share.

Dilution in Voting. If all stockholders other than the Acquiring Person (whose Rights become void if there is a "flip-in") exercised their Rights, the Acquiring Person's voting power would be diluted down from 15% (*i.e.*, 150 shares owned out of 1,000 shares outstanding) to 1.92% (*i.e.*, 150 shares owned out of 7,800 shares outstanding).

The 7,800 shares outstanding assumes that stockholders exercise all their rights by paying $4 in cash for each Right. Such an exercise of Rights would, after the "flip-in", entitle all stockholders (other than an Acquiring Person) to purchase 8 shares of stock for each Right. That is, they are entitled to use the $4 exercise price to purchase shares equal to $8 in value. This would result in the issuance of 6,800 additional shares (850 Rights times 8 shares per Right). Since there were already 1,000 shares outstanding the new total outstanding becomes 7,800 shares.

Economic Dilution. In the same example described above, the economic dilution for the Acquiring Person is quite substantial (assuming the Acquiring Person's stock was worth $1 per share—*i.e.*, the market value immediately before the "flip-in" occurs), the Acquiring Person's shares fall in value by approximately 43.6% (from $1 per share to $0.564 per share).

This results from the following hypothetical analysis. Assume that the aggregate market value of the Company was $1,000 immediately before the "flip-in" (*i.e.*, 1,000 shares at $1 per share). The issuance of 6,800 additional shares upon exercise of the 850 Rights held by all stockholders other than the Acquiring Person added $3,400 in cash to the value of the Company (*i.e.*, 850 Rights times $4 per Right). This would increase the total value of the Company to $4,400, which results in a hypothetical value of $0.564 for each of the 7,800 outstanding shares.

FORM OF LETTER TO STOCKHOLDERS

_______ ___, 2002

Dear XYZ, Inc. Stockholder:

The Board of Directors has announced the adoption of a Stockholder Rights Plan. This letter describes the Plan and explains our reasons for adopting it. Also, we are enclosing a document entitled "Summary of Rights to Purchase Common Stock Shares of XYZ, Inc." which provides more detailed information about the Rights Plan, and we urge you to read it carefully.

The Plan is intended to protect your interests in the event XYZ, Inc. ("Company") is confronted with an unsolicited takeover attempt or certain types of unfair takeover tactics. Specifically, the Plan contains provisions designed to deter a gradual accumulation of shares in the open market, a partial or two-tiered tender offer that does not treat all stockholders equally, the acquisition in the open market or otherwise of shares constituting control without offering fair value to all stockholders, or other abusive takeover tactics which the Board believes are not in the best interests of the Company's stockholders. These tactics unfairly pressure stockholders, squeeze them out of their investment without giving them any real choice, and deprive them of the full value of their shares.

A large number of other companies have Rights Plans similar to the one we have adopted. We consider the Rights Plan to be the best available means of protecting your right to retain your equity investment in Company and the full value of that investment, while not foreclosing a fair acquisition bid for the Company.

The Plan is not intended to prevent a takeover of the Company and will not do so. The mere declaration of the rights dividend should not affect any prospective offeror willing to make an all cash offer at a full and fair price or willing to negotiate with the Board of Directors, and will not interfere with a merger or other business combination transaction approved by your Board of Directors.

Prior to adopting the Rights Plan, the Board of Directors was concerned that a person or company could acquire control of the Company without paying a fair premium for control and without offering a fair price to all stockholders, and that, if a competitor acquired control of the Company, the competitor would have a conflict of interest with respect to the Company and could use any acquired influence over or control of the Company to the detriment of the other stockholders of the Company. The Board believes that such results would not be in the best interests of all stockholders.

The Rights may be redeemed by the Company at $0.001 per Right up to the time any person or group has acquired 15% or more of the Company's shares, and thus they should not interfere with any merger or other business combination approved by the Board of Directors.

Issuance of the Rights does not in any way weaken the financial strength of the Company or interfere with its business plan. The issuance of the Rights has no dilutive effect, will not affect reported earnings per share, is not taxable to the Company or to you, and will not change the way in which you can currently trade the Company's shares. As explained in detail below, the Rights will only be exercisable if and when an event occurs which triggers their effectiveness. They will then operate to protect you against being deprived of your right to share in the full measure of the Company's long-term potential.

The Board was aware when it acted that some people have advanced arguments that securities of the type we are issuing deter legitimate acquisition proposals. We carefully considered these views and concluded that the arguments are speculative and do not justify leaving stockholders without this protection against unfair treatment by an acquiror—who, after all, is seeking his own company's advantage, not yours. The Board believes that the Rights represent a sound and reasonable means of addressing the complex issues of corporate policy created by the current takeover environment.

The Rights will be issued to stockholders of record on ______ ___, 2002, and will expire in ten years. Initially, the Rights will not be exercisable, certificates will not be sent to you, and the Rights will automatically trade with the Common Stock. However, ten days after a person or group either acquires 15% or more of the Company's Common Stock or commences a tender or exchange offer that would result in such person or group owning 15% or more of the outstanding shares (even if no purchases actually occur), the Rights will become exercisable and separate certificates representing the Rights will be distributed. We expect that the Rights will begin to trade independently from the Common Stock at that time. At no time will the Rights have any voting power.

Each Right initially will entitle the holder thereof to buy from the Company one unit of a share of preferred stock for $______. If, however, any person acquires 15% or more of the Company's Common Stock, each Right not owned by such 15%-or-more stockholder would become exercisable for the number of Common Stock of the Company (or in certain circumstances cash, property or other securities) having at that time a market value of two times the then current exercise price of the Right. If the Company is acquired in a merger or other business combination, or sells 50% or more of its assets or earning power to another person, at any time after a person acquires 15% or more of the Company's Common Stock, the Rights will entitle the holder thereof to buy a number of Common Stock of the acquiring company having a market value of twice the then current exercise price of each Right.

At any time after a person acquires 15% or more of the Company's Common Stock and prior to the earlier of the time (i) the Company is acquired in a merger or other business combination, (ii) the Company is the continuing or surviving corporation in a merger and all or part of the Company's Common Stock is exchanged for stock, cash or other property, or (iii) the Company sells 50% or more of its assets or earning power to another person, the Company may exchange each Right (other than Rights owned by a 15% or more stockholder which shall have become void) for a number of Common Stock of the Company (or in certain circumstances preferred stock of the Company) having a value equal to the difference between the market value of the Common Stock receivable upon exercise of the Right and the exercise price of the Right.

While, as noted above, the distribution of the Rights will not be taxable to you or the Company, stockholders may, depending upon the circumstances, recognize taxable income when the Rights become exercisable.

Maximizing long-term stockholder value is the major goal of the Company's management and Board of Directors.

Sincerely,

Chairman of the Board

FOR IMMEDIATE RELEASE CONTACT:
_______ 2002

XYZ, INC. ADOPTS
STOCKHOLDER RIGHTS PLAN

New York, New York—XYZ, Inc. ("XYZ") announced today that on _______, 2002, its Board of Directors adopted a Stockholder Rights Plan in which rights will be distributed as a dividend at the rate of one Right for each share of common stock, par value $0.001 per share, of XYZ (the "Common Stock") held by stockholders of record as of the close of business on _______ ___, 2002. The Rights Plan is designed to deter certain types of unfair takeover tactics and to prevent an acquiror from gaining control of XYZ without offering a fair price to all of XYZ's stockholders. The Rights will expire on _______, 2011.

Each Right initially will entitle stockholders to buy one one-thousandth of a share of Series A Junior Participating Preferred Stock Shares of XYZ, for $_______. The Rights will be exercisable only if a person or group acquires beneficial ownership of 15% or more of XYZ's Common Stock or commences a tender or exchange offer upon consummation of which such person or group would beneficially own 15% or more of XYZ's Common Stock.

If any person becomes the beneficial owner of 15% or more of XYZ's Common Stock, then each Right not owned by the 15%-or-more stockholder or related parties will entitle its holder to purchase, at the Right's then current exercise price, shares of XYZ's Common Stock (or in certain circumstances, cash, property, or other securities) having a value of twice the Right's then current exercise price. In addition, if after any person has become a 15%-or-more stockholder, XYZ is involved in a merger or other business combination transaction with another person in which XYZ does not survive or in which its Common Stock is changed or exchanged, or sells 50% or more of its assets or earning power to another person, each Right not owned by the 15%-or-more stockholder or related parties will entitle its holder to purchase, at the Right's then current exercise price, shares of common stock of such other person having a value of twice the Right's then current exercise price.

At any time after a person acquires 15% or more of XYZ's Common Stock and prior to the earlier of the time (i) XYZ is involved in a merger or other business combination transaction with another person in which XYZ does not survive or in which its Common Stock is changed or exchanged, (ii) XYZ is the continuing or surviving corporation in a merger and all or part of its Common Stock is exchanged for stock, cash or other property, or (iii) XYZ sells 50% or more of its assets or earning power to another person, XYZ may exchange each Right (other than Rights owned by the 15%-or-more stockholder which shall have become void) for a number of shares of Common Stock of XYZ (or in certain circumstances shares of preferred stock of XYZ) having a value equal to the difference between the market value of the shares of Common Stock receivable upon exercise of the Rights and the exercise price of the Right.

XYZ will generally be entitled to redeem the Rights at $0.001 per Right at any time until a 15% position has been acquired.

Details of the Stockholder Rights Plan are outlined in a letter which will be mailed to all stockholders.

About XYZ (www.XYZ.com)

[description of XYZ business]

The statements in this release regarding projected results are preliminary and "forward-looking statements" within the meaning of the Private Securities Litigation Reform Act of 1995. In addition, this report contains other forward-looking statements including statements regarding the Company's or third parties' expectations, predictions, views, opportunities, plans, strategies, beliefs, and statements of similar effect. The forward-looking statements in this report are subject to a variety of risks and uncertainties. Actual results could differ materially. Factors that could cause actual results to differ include but are not limited to the following: [description of factors].

4. PROXY STATEMENT, MERCK & CO.

Table of Contents

PROXY STATEMENT

Raymond V. Gilmartin
Chairman, President & Chief
Executive Officer

Merck & Co., Inc.

One Merck Drive
P.O. Box 100
Whitehouse Station, NJ 08889–0100

March 20, 2003

Dear Stockholders:

It is my pleasure to invite you to Merck's 2003 Annual Meeting of Stockholders. We will hold the meeting on Tuesday, April 22, 2003, at 2:00 p.m., in the Edward Nash Theatre at Raritan Valley Community College, Route 28 and Lamington Road, North Branch, New Jersey. During the Annual Meeting, we will discuss each item of business described in the Notice of Annual Meeting and Proxy Statement and give a report on the Company's business operations. There will also be time for questions.

This booklet includes the Notice of Annual Meeting and Proxy Statement. The Proxy Statement provides information about Merck in addition to describing the business we will conduct at the meeting.

We hope you will be able to attend the Annual Meeting. Whether or not you expect to attend, please vote your shares using any of the following methods: vote by telephone or the Internet, as described in the instructions you receive; sign and date the proxy card or voting instruction card and return it in the prepaid envelope; or vote in person at the meeting.

Sincerely,

PROXY STATEMENT

Notice of Annual Meeting of Stockholders

April 22, 2003

To the Stockholders:

The stockholders of Merck & Co., Inc. will hold their Annual Meeting on Tuesday, April 22, 2003, at 2:00 p.m., in the Edward Nash Theatre at Raritan Valley Community College, Route 28 and Lamington Road, North Branch, New Jersey. The purposes of the meeting are to:

- elect five directors for terms ending in 2006;
- consider and act upon a proposal to ratify the appointment of PricewaterhouseCoopers LLP as the Company's independent public accountants for 2003;
- consider and act upon a proposal to adopt the 2003 Incentive Stock Plan;
- consider and act upon a stockholder proposal concerning annual election of directors;
- consider and act upon a stockholder proposal concerning director nominees;
- consider and act upon a stockholder proposal concerning extension of prescription drug patents;
- consider and act upon a stockholder proposal concerning ethical and social performance of the Company; and
- transact such other business as may properly come before the meeting.

Only stockholders listed on the Company's records at the close of business on March 7, 2003 are entitled to vote.

By order of the Board of Directors,

Celia A. Colbert

Vice President, Secretary and
Assistant General Counsel

March 20, 2003

Merck & Co., Inc.
P. O. Box 100
Whitehouse Station, New Jersey 08889–0100
(908) 423–1000

March 20, 2003

Proxy Statement

QUESTIONS AND ANSWERS ABOUT THE ANNUAL MEETING AND VOTING

Q: Why did I receive this proxy statement?

A: The Board of Directors is soliciting your proxy to vote at the Annual Meeting because you are a stockholder at the close of business on March 7, 2003, the record date, and are entitled to vote at the meeting.

This proxy statement and 2002 annual report, along with either a proxy card or a voting instruction card, are being mailed to stockholders beginning March 20, 2003. The proxy statement summarizes the information you need to know to vote at the Annual Meeting. You do not need to attend the Annual Meeting to vote your shares.

Q: What is the difference between holding shares as a stockholder of record and as a beneficial owner?

A: If your shares are registered directly in your name with Merck's transfer agent, Wells Fargo Bank Minnesota, N.A., you are considered, with respect to those shares, the 'stockholder of record.? The proxy statement, annual report and proxy card have been sent directly to you by Merck.

If your shares are held in a stock brokerage account or by a bank or other nominee, you are considered the "beneficial owner" of shares held in street name. The proxy statement and annual report have been forwarded to you by your broker, bank or nominee who is considered, with respect to those shares, the stockholder of record. As the beneficial owner, you have the right to direct your broker, bank or nominee how to vote your shares by using the voting instruction card included in the mailing or by following their instructions for voting by telephone or the Internet.

Q: What is "householding" and how does it affect me?

A: Merck has adopted the process called "householding" for mailing the annual report and proxy statement in order to reduce printing costs and postage fees. Householding means that stockholders who share the same last name and address will receive only one copy of the annual report and proxy statement, unless we receive contrary instructions from any stockholder at that address. Merck will continue to mail a proxy card to each stockholder of record.

If you prefer to receive multiple copies of the proxy statement and annual report at the same address, additional copies will be provided to you promptly upon request. If you are a stockholder of record, you may contact us by writing to Merck Stockholder Services, P.O. Box 100, Whitehouse Station, NJ 08889–0100 or by calling our toll-free number 1–800–613–2104. Eligible stockholders of record receiving multiple copies of the annual report and proxy statement can request householding by contacting Merck in the same manner.

If you are a beneficial owner, you may request additional copies of the proxy statement and annual report or you may request householding by notifying your broker, bank or nominee.

Q. Can I access the proxy statement and annual report on the Internet instead of receiving paper copies?

A: This proxy statement and the 2002 annual report are located on Merck's web site. Most stockholders can access future proxy statements and annual reports on the Internet instead of receiving paper copies in the mail.

If you are a stockholder of record, you can choose this option by marking the appropriate box on your proxy card or by following the instructions if you vote by telephone or the Internet. If you choose to access future proxy statements and annual reports on the Internet, you will receive a proxy card in the mail next year with instructions containing the Internet address for those materials. Your choice will remain in effect until you advise us otherwise.

If you are a beneficial owner, please refer to the information provided by your broker, bank or nominee for instructions on how to elect to access future proxy statements and annual reports on the Internet. Most beneficial owners who elect electronic access will receive an e-mail message next year containing the Internet address for access to the proxy statement and annual report.

Q: What am I voting on?

A:

- Election of five directors: Mr. Lawrence A. Bossidy, Dr. Johnnetta B. Cole, Mr. William B. Harrison, Jr., Dr. William N. Kelley and Dr. Heidi G. Miller;
- Ratification of the appointment of PricewaterhouseCoopers LLP as independent public accountants for 2003; and
- Adoption of the 2003 Incentive Stock Plan.

The Board recommends a vote **FOR** each of the nominees to the Board of Directors and **FOR** the ratification of the appointment of PricewaterhouseCoopers LLP as independent public accountants for 2003 and adoption of the 2003 Incentive Stock Plan.

You will also vote on the following stockholder proposals:

- a proposal concerning annual election of directors;
- a proposal concerning director nominees;
- a proposal concerning extension of prescription drug patents; and
- a proposal concerning ethical and social performance of the Company.

The Board recommends a vote **AGAINST** the stockholder proposals.

Q: What is the voting requirement to elect the directors and to approve each of the proposals?

A: In the election of directors, the five persons receiving the highest number of affirmative votes will be elected. The ratification of the appointment of PricewaterhouseCoopers LLP as independent public accountants, adoption of the 2003 Incentive Stock Plan and approval of the stockholder proposals each require the affirmative vote of a majority of the votes cast. If you are present or represented by proxy at the Annual Meeting and you abstain, your abstention, as well as broker non-votes, are not counted as votes cast on any matter to which they relate.

Q: How many votes do I have?

A: You are entitled to one vote for each share of Common Stock that you hold, except for the election of directors. Because you may cumulate your votes in the election of directors, you are entitled to as many votes as equal the number of shares held by you at the close of business on the record date, multiplied by the number of directors to be elected.

Q: How do I cumulate my votes in the election of directors?

A: In connection with the cumulative voting feature for the election of directors, you are entitled to as many votes as equal the number of shares held by you at the close of business on the record date, multiplied by the number of directors to be elected. You may cast all of your votes for a single nominee or apportion your votes among any two or more nominees. For example, when five directors are to be elected, a holder of 100 shares may cast 500 votes for a single nominee, apportion 100 votes to each of five nominees or apportion 500 votes in any other manner by so noting in the space provided on the proxy card. Beneficial owners should contact their broker, bank or nominee to cumulate votes for directors. The cumulative voting feature for the election of directors is also available by voting in person at the Annual Meeting; it is not available by telephone or the Internet.

You may withhold votes from any or all nominees. Except for the votes that stockholders of record withhold from any or all nominees, the persons named in the proxy card will vote such proxy **FOR** and, if necessary, will exercise their cumulative voting rights to elect the nominees as directors of the Company.

Q: How do I vote?

A: You may vote using any of the following methods:

- *Proxy card or voting instruction card.* Be sure to sign and date the card and return it in the prepaid envelope. If you are a stockholder of record and you return your signed proxy card but do not indicate your voting preferences, the persons named in the proxy card will vote **FOR** the election of directors, the ratification of the appointment of PricewaterhouseCoopers LLP as independent public accountants for 2003 and adoption of the 2003 Incentive Stock Plan and **AGAINST** the stockholder proposals on your behalf.
- *By telephone or the Internet.* The telephone and Internet voting procedures established by Merck for stockholders of record are designed to authenticate your identity, to allow you to give your voting instructions and to confirm that these instructions have been properly recorded.

  The availability of telephone and Internet voting for beneficial owners will depend on the voting processes of your broker, bank or nominee. Therefore, we recommend that you follow the voting instructions in the materials you receive.
- *In person at the Annual Meeting.* All stockholders may vote in person at the Annual Meeting. You may also be represented by another person at the meeting by executing a proper proxy designating that person. If you are a beneficial owner of shares, you must obtain a legal proxy from your broker, bank or nominee and present it to the inspectors of election with your ballot when you vote at the meeting.

Q: What can I do if I change my mind after I vote my shares?

A: If you are a stockholder of record, you may revoke your proxy at any time before it is voted at the Annual Meeting by:

- sending written notice of revocation to the Secretary of the Company;
- submitting a new, proper proxy by telephone, Internet or paper ballot, after the date of the revoked proxy; or
- attending the Annual Meeting and voting in person.

If you are a beneficial owner of shares, you may submit new voting instructions by contacting your broker, bank or nominee. You may also vote in person at the Annual Meeting if you obtain a legal proxy as described in the answer to the previous question.

Q: Who will count the vote?

A: Representatives of IVS Associates, Inc. will tabulate the votes and act as inspectors of election.

Q: What shares are included on the proxy card?

A: The shares on your proxy card represent shares registered in your name as well as shares in the Merck Stock Investment Plan. However, the proxy card does not include shares held for participants in the Merck & Co., Inc. Employee Savings and Security Plan, Merck & Co., Inc. Employee Stock Purchase and Savings Plan, Hubbard ISA LLC Employee Savings Plan, Medco Health Solutions, Inc. 401(k) Savings Plan, Merck Puerto Rico Employee Savings and Security Plan, Merck Frosst Canada Inc. Stock Purchase Plan ("Merck Frosst Plan"), MSD Employee Share Ownership Plan and Merial 401(k) Savings Plan ("Merial Plan"). Instead, these participants will receive from plan trustees separate voting instruction cards covering these shares. If voting instructions are not received from participants in the Merck Frosst Plan, the plan trustee will vote the shares in accordance with the recommendations of the Board of Directors. If voting instructions are not received from participants in the Merial Plan, the plan trustee will vote the shares in the same proportion as it votes shares for which voting instructions are received. Trustees for the other plans will not vote shares for which no voting instructions are received from plan participants.

Q: What constitutes a quorum?

A: As of the record date, 2,244,349,140 shares of Merck Common Stock were issued and outstanding. A majority of the outstanding shares, present or represented by proxy, constitutes a quorum for the purpose of adopting proposals at the Annual Meeting. If you submit a properly executed proxy, then you will be considered part of the quorum.

Q: Who can attend the Annual Meeting?

A: All stockholders as of the record date may attend the Annual Meeting but must have an admission ticket. If you are a stockholder of record, the ticket attached to the proxy card will admit you and one guest. If you are a beneficial owner, you may request a ticket by writing to the Office of the Secretary, WS 3AB–05, Merck & Co., Inc., P.O. Box 100, Whitehouse Station, New Jersey 08889–0100 or by faxing your request to 908–735–1224. You must provide evidence of your ownership of shares with your ticket request, which you can obtain from your broker, bank or nominee. We encourage you or your broker to fax your ticket request and proof of ownership in order to avoid any mail delays.

Q: Are there any stockholders who own more than 5 percent of the Company's shares?

A: According to a filing made with the Securities and Exchange Commission on February 13, 2003, Fidelity, through its funds, subsidiaries and institutional accounts, owns approximately 5.4 percent of the Company's outstanding Common Stock. See "Security Ownership of Certain Beneficial Owners and Management" on page 15 for more information.

Q: When are the stockholder proposals due for the 2004 Annual Meeting?

A: In order to be considered for inclusion in next year's proxy statement, stockholder proposals must be submitted in writing by November 21, 2003 to Celia A. Colbert, Vice President, Secretary and Assistant General Counsel, WS 3A–65, Merck & Co., Inc., One Merck Drive, Whitehouse Station, NJ 08889–0100.

If you notify us after February 4, 2004 of an intent to present a proposal at the Company's 2004 Annual Meeting, we will have the right to exercise discretionary voting authority with respect to such proposal, if presented at the meeting, without including information regarding such proposal in our proxy materials.

Q: What happens if a nominee for director is unable to serve as a director?

A: If any of the nominees becomes unavailable for election, which we do not expect, votes will be cast for such substitute nominee or nominees as may be designated by the Board of Directors, unless the Board of Directors reduces the number of directors.

Q: How much did this proxy solicitation cost?

A: Georgeson Shareholder Communications, Inc. has been hired by the Company to assist in the distribution of proxy materials and solicitation of votes for $22,000, plus reasonable out-of-pocket expenses. Employees, officers and directors of the Company may also solicit proxies. We will reimburse brokerage houses and other custodians, nominees and fiduciaries for their reasonable out-of-pocket expenses for forwarding proxy and solicitation material to the owners of Common Stock.

Q: What is the Company's Web address?

A: The Merck home page is *www.merck.com*. You may also go directly to *www.merck.com/about/corporategovernance* for the following information:

- Policies of the Board—a statement of Merck's corporate governance principles; and
- Merck Board Committee Charters—Audit Committee, Committee on Corporate Governance, and Compensation and Benefits Committee.

PROXY STATEMENT

1. ELECTION OF DIRECTORS

Five directors are to be elected by stockholders at the Annual Meeting for three-year terms expiring in 2006. The Board's nominees are Mr. Lawrence A. Bossidy, Dr. Johnnetta B. Cole, Mr. William B. Harrison, Jr., Dr. William N. Kelley and Dr. Heidi G. Miller. All candidates have previously been elected by stockholders. Mr. Niall FitzGerald and Dr. Edward M. Scolnick resigned from the Board effective October 18, 2002 and December 31, 2002, respectively. After the election of five directors at the Annual Meeting, the Company will have eleven directors, including the six continuing directors whose present terms extend beyond the meeting. Information on the nominees and continuing directors follows.

Name, Age and Year First Elected Director	Business Experience and Other Directorships or Significant Affiliations

Nominees

For terms expiring in 2006

Lawrence A. Bossidy
Age—68
1992

Retired; Chairman (July 2001 to June 2002), Chief Executive Officer (July 2001 to February 2002) (also Chairman and Chief Executive Officer from December 1999 to April 2000), Honeywell International Inc.; Chairman and Chief Executive Officer, AlliedSignal, Inc. (1991 to 1999)

Director, J.P. Morgan Chase & Co. and Berkshire Hills Bancorp, Inc.; Member, The Business Council and The Business Roundtable

Johnnetta B. Cole, Ph.D.
Age—66
1994

President, Bennett College since July 2002; Presidential Distinguished Professor, Emory University (September 1998 through August 2001); President, Spelman College (1987 to June 1997)

Director, Coca-Cola Enterprises; Fellow, American Academy of Arts and Sciences and American Anthropological Association; Member, Council on Foreign Relations and National Council of Negro Women; Trustee, The Carter Center

William B. Harrison, Jr.
Age—59
1999

Chairman and Chief Executive Officer (since December 2001), President and Chief Executive Officer (January to December 2001), J.P. Morgan Chase & Co. (financial services); Chairman and Chief Executive Officer (January through December 2000), President and Chief Executive Officer (June through December 1999), Vice Chairman (1991 to December 1999), The Chase Manhattan Corporation

Director, New York Stock Exchange, Inc.; Member, The Business Council, The Business Roundtable, The Financial Services Forum and The Financial Services Roundtable

Professor of Medicine, Biochemistry and Biophysics, University of Pennsylvania School of Medicine since February 2000; Chief Executive Officer, University of Pennsylvania Health System, Dean of the School of Medicine and Executive Vice President, University of Pennsylvania (1989 to February 2000)

Director, Beckman Coulter, Inc. and GenVec, Inc.; Fellow, American Academy of Arts and Sciences; Master, American College of Physicians; Member, American Philosophical Society and Institute of Medicine of the National Academy of Sciences; Trustee, Emory University

William N. Kelley, M.D.
Age—63
1992

Executive Vice President (since March 2002) and Chief Financial Officer (since May 2002), Bank One Corporation; Vice Chairman, Marsh Inc. (January 2001 to March 2002); Senior Executive Vice President, Chief Financial Officer and Director, Priceline.com (February to November 2000); Chief Financial Officer, Citigroup (1998 to 2000)

Director, General Mills, Inc.; Trustee, Princeton University and NYU Medical School

Heidi G. Miller, Ph.D.
Age—49
2000

Directors Whose Terms Expire in 2004

President, The Andrew W. Mellon Foundation (philanthropic foundation) for more than five years

Director, American Express Company; Member, Board of Overseers, Teachers Insurance and Annuity Association of America-College Retirement Equities Fund

William G. Bowen, Ph.D.
Age—69
1986

President, SBC Communications, Inc. (diversified telecommunications) since December 2001; Vice Chairman, Evercore Capital Partners L.P. (January to November 2001); Chairman, Vice President Albert Gore's 2000 presidential election campaign (June to December 2000); Secretary of Commerce (January 1997 to June 2000)

Director, Joffrey Ballet; Trustee, Loyola University

William M. Daley
Age—54
2002

Elkins Professor (since 1984) and Chairman (since 1996), Department of Molecular Biology, Princeton University; Investigator, Howard Hughes Medical Institute (1989 to 1999)

Director, Cell Genesys, Inc.; Fellow, American Academy of Arts and Sciences; Member, American Academy of Microbiology and National Academy of Sciences and its Institute of Medicine

Thomas E. Shenk, Ph.D.
Age—56
2001

Directors Whose Terms Expire in 2005

Chairman of the Board, President and Chief Executive Officer of the Company for more than five years

Director, General Mills, Inc., Microsoft Corporation and Public Service Enterprise Group; President, International Federation of Pharmaceutical Manufacturers Associations; Executive Committee, Council on Competitiveness and Pharmaceutical Research and Manufacturers of America; Member, The Business Council and The Business Roundtable

Raymond V. Gilmartin
Age—62
1994

Chairman (since June 2000) and Chief Executive Officer (since September 1999), Fiduciary Trust Company International (global asset management services); Vice Chairman, Franklin Resources, Inc. (since January 2001); President, Fiduciary Trust Company International (1994 to 2000)

Director, Fortune Brands, Inc.; Trustee, American Ballet Theatre Foundation, The Andrew W. Mellon Foundation, The Conference Board, Cultural Institutions Retirement Systems, Howard Hughes Medical Institute, The Mayo Foundation, Teagle Foundation and Vassar College

Anne M. Tatlock
Age—63
2000

Professor of Medicine and Professor of Health Care Policy, Harvard Medical School since January 2003; President (April 1997 through December 2002) and Chief Executive Officer (July 1996 through December 2002), Partners HealthCare System, Inc.

Director, Charles River Laboratories, Inc. and Federal Reserve Bank of Boston; Fellow, American Academy of Arts and Sciences; Master, American College of Physicians; Member, Institute of Medicine of the National Academy of Sciences; Trustee, Boston Museum of Science, Cornell University, The Commonwealth Fund and WGBH Public Television

Samuel O. Thier, M.D.
Age—65
1994

Board Committees

The Board of Directors has six standing committees: Audit Committee, Committee on Corporate Governance, Compensation and Benefits Committee, Executive Committee, Finance Committee, and Committee on Public Policy and Social Responsibility. Members of the individual committees are named below:

Audit	Committee on Corporate Governance	Compensation and Benefits	Executive	Finance	Committee on Public Policy and Social Responsibility
L. A. Bossidy	L. A. Bossidy	L. A. Bossidy(*)	L. A. Bossidy	J. B. Cole	W. G. Bowen
H. G. Miller (*)	W. G. Bowen (*)	W. G. Bowen	W. G. Bowen	H. G. Miller	J. B. Cole
T. E. Shenk	W. N. Kelley	J. B. Cole	R. V. Gilmartin (*)	A. M. Tatlock (*)	W. M. Daley
S. O. Thier	A. M. Tatlock	W. N. Kelley	S. O. Thier		T. E. Shenk
	S. O. Thier				S. O. Thier (*)

(*) Chairperson

The Audit Committee, which is comprised of independent directors, is governed by a Board approved charter that contains, among other things, the Committee's membership requirements and responsibilities. The Audit Committee oversees the Company's accounting, financial reporting process, internal controls and audits, and consults with management, the internal auditors and the independent public accountants on, among other items, matters related to the annual audit, the published financial statements and the accounting principles applied. As part of its duties, the Audit Committee appoints, evaluates and retains the Company's independent public accountants. It also maintains direct responsibility for the compensation, termination and oversight of the Company's independent public accountants and evaluates the independent public accountants' qualifications, performance and independence. The Audit Committee approves all services provided to the Company by the independent public accountants and reviews all non-attest services to ensure they are permitted under current law. The Committee also monitors compliance with the Foreign Corrupt Practices Act and the Company's policies on ethical business practices and reports on these items to the Board. The Audit Committee will establish policies and procedures for the pre-approval of services provided by the independent public accountants. Further, the Audit Committee will establish procedures for the receipt, retention and treatment, on a confidential basis, of complaints received by the Company, including the Board and the Audit Committee, regarding accounting, internal accounting controls or auditing matters, and the confidential, anonymous submissions by employees of concerns regarding questionable accounting or auditing matters. The Audit Committee's Report is included on page 28 of this proxy statement. The Audit Committee Charter is set forth in Appendix A to this proxy statement and is available on the Company's website.

Financial Expert on Audit Committee: The Board has determined that Dr. Miller, who currently is the Executive Vice President and Chief Financial Officer of Bank One Corporation, and who previously was the chief financial officer for three different public companies, is the audit committee financial expert. The Board made a qualitative assessment of Dr. Miller's level of knowledge and experience based on a number of factors, including her formal education and experience as chief financial officer for reporting companies.

The Committee on Corporate Governance, formerly the Committee on Directors, which is comprised of independent directors, considers and makes recommendations on matters related to the practices, policies and procedures of the Board and takes a leadership role in shaping the corporate governance of the Company. As part of its duties, the Committee assesses the size, structure and composition of the Board and Board committees, coordinates evaluation of Board performance and reviews Board compensation. The Committee also acts as a screening and nominating committee for candidates considered for election to the Board. In this capacity it concerns itself with the composition of the Board with respect to depth of experience, balance of professional interests, required expertise and other factors, and evaluates prospective nominees identified by the Committee on its own initiative or referred to it by other Board members, management, stockholders or external sources. A stockholder may recommend a person as a nominee for director by writing to the Secretary of the Company. Recommendations must be received by January 23, 2004 and must comply with the procedures set forth in the Company's By–Laws in order to be considered at the 2004 Annual Meeting. The Committee on Corporate Governance Charter is available on the Company's website.

The Compensation and Benefits Committee, which is comprised of independent directors, consults generally with management on matters concerning executive compensation and on pension, savings and welfare benefit plans where Board or stockholder action is contemplated with respect to the adoption of or amendments to such plans. It makes recommendations to the Board of Directors on compensation generally, executive officer salaries, bonus awards and stock option grants, special awards and supplemental compensation. The Committee makes recommendations on organization, succession, the election of officers, consultantships and similar matters where Board approval is required. It also administers the Company's Executive Incentive Plan, Base Salary Deferral Plan, Deferral Program and Incentive Stock Plan and appoints and monitors the Management Pension Investment Committee. The Compensation and Benefits Committee Charter is available on the Company's website.

The Executive Committee acts for the Board of Directors when formal Board action is required between meetings in connection with matters already approved in principle by the full Board or to fulfill the formal duties of the Board.

The Finance Committee, which is comprised of independent directors, considers and makes recommendations on matters related to the financial affairs and policies of the Company, including capital structure issues, dividend policy, investment and debt policies, asset and portfolio management and financial transactions, as necessary.

The Committee on Public Policy and Social Responsibility, which is comprised of independent directors, advises the Board of Directors and management on Company policies and practices that pertain to the Company's responsibilities as a global corporate citizen, its obligations as a pharmaceutical company whose products and services affect health and quality of life around the world, and its commitment to high standards of ethics and integrity. It reviews social, political and economic trends that affect the Company's business; reviews the positions and strategies that the Company pursues to influence public policy; monitors and evaluates the Company's corporate citizenship programs and activities; and reviews legislative, regulatory, privacy and other matters that could impact the Company's stockholders, customers, employees and communities in which it operates.

Board and Board Committee Meetings

In 2002, the Board of Directors met nine times. Board committees met as follows during 2002: Committee on Corporate Governance, nine times; Audit Committee, seven times; Compensation and Benefits Committee, three times; Committee on Public Policy and Social Responsibility, twice; and Finance Committee, once. No meetings of the Executive Committee were held in 2002. All incumbent directors attended at least 75 percent of the meetings of the Board and of the committees on which they served.

Non-management directors will meet without management in three or more executive sessions to be scheduled in 2003. The Chairpersons of the Audit Committee, the Committee on Corporate Governance, and the Compensation and Benefits Committee will each preside over at least one executive session.

Compensation Committee Interlocks and Insider Participation

Lawrence A. Bossidy, William G. Bowen, Johnnetta B. Cole and William N. Kelley served on the Compensation and Benefits Committee during 2002. There were no Compensation and Benefits Committee interlocks or insider (employee) participation during 2002.

Independence of Directors

The Board of Directors has determined that to be considered independent, an outside director may not have a direct or indirect material relationship with the Company. A material relationship is one which impairs or inhibits—or has the potential to impair or inhibit—a director's exercise of critical and disinterested judgment on behalf of the Company and its stockholders. In determining whether a material relationship exists, the Board considers, for example, the sales or charitable contributions between Merck and an entity with which a director is affiliated (as an executive officer, partner or substantial stockholder) and whether a director is a former employee of the Company. The Board consults with the Company's counsel to ensure that the Board's determinations are consistent with all relevant securities and other laws and regulations regarding the definition of "independent director," including those set forth in pertinent listing standards of the New York Stock Exchange as in effect from time to time. The Committee on Corporate Governance reviews the Board's approach to determining director independence periodically and recommends changes as appropriate for consideration and approval by the full Board.

Consistent with these considerations, the Board affirmatively has determined that all directors are independent directors except Mr. Gilmartin, who is a Company employee.

Relationships with Outside Firms

William B. Harrison, Jr. is a director of the Company and in 2002 was the Chairman and Chief Executive Officer of J.P. Morgan Chase & Co., which provided financial advisory, commercial and investment banking services to the Company during 2002.

Anne M. Tatlock is a director of the Company and in 2002 was the investment manager for certain customer accounts at Fiduciary Trust Company International. Those accounts may, at times, hold shares of Merck Common Stock. However, Ms. Tatlock has divested all voting and/or investment power over any shares of Merck Common Stock held in those accounts and she disclaims beneficial ownership of any such shares.

Board's Role in Strategic Planning

The Board of Directors has the legal responsibility for overseeing the affairs of the Company and, thus, an obligation to keep informed about the Company's business and strategies. This involvement enables the Board to provide guidance to management in formulating and developing plans and to exercise independently its decision-making authority on matters of importance to the Company. Acting as a full Board and through the Board's six standing committees (Audit, Committee on Corporate Governance, Compensation and Benefits, Executive, Finance, and Committee on Public Policy and Social Responsibility), the Board is fully involved in the Company's strategic planning process.

Each year, typically in the summer, senior management sets aside a specific period to develop, discuss and refine the Company's long-range operating plan and overall corporate strategy. Strategic areas of importance include basic research and clinical development, global marketing and sales, manufacturing strategy, capability and capacity, and the public and political environments that affect the Company's business and operations. Specific operating priorities are developed to effectuate the Company's long-range plan. Some of the priorities are short-term in focus; others are based on longer-term planning horizons. Senior management reviews the conclusions reached at its summer meeting with the Board at an extended meeting that usually occurs in the fall. This meeting is focused on corporate strategy and involves both management presentations and input from the Board regarding the assumptions, priorities and strategies that will form the basis for management's operating plans and strategies.

At subsequent Board meetings, the Board continues to substantively review the Company's progress against its strategic plans and to exercise oversight and decision-making authority regarding strategic areas of importance and associated funding authorizations. For example, the Board typically reviews the Company's overall annual performance at its November meeting and considers the following year's operating budget and capital plan in December. The Board at its February meeting usually finalizes specific criteria against which the Company's performance will be evaluated for that year. In addition, Board meetings held throughout the year target specific strategies (for example, basic research) and critical areas (for example, U.S. healthcare public policy issues) for extended, focused Board input and discussion.

The role that the Board plays is inextricably linked to the development and review of the Company's strategic plan. Through these procedures, the Board, consistent with good corporate governance, encourages the long-term success of the Company by exercising sound and independent business judgment on the strategic issues that are important to the Company's business.

Compensation of Directors

Each director who is not a Company employee is compensated for services as a director by an annual retainer of $45,000 and a meeting fee of $1,200 for each Board and Committee meeting attended. In addition, Chairpersons of the Audit Committee, Committee on Corporate Governance, Compensation and Benefits Committee, Finance Committee, and Committee on Public Policy and Social Responsibility are compensated for such services by an annual retainer of $5,000. A director who is a Company employee does not receive any compensation for service as a director. The Company reimburses all directors for travel and other necessary business expenses incurred in the performance of their services for the Company and extends coverage to them under the Company's travel accident and directors' and officers' indemnity insurance policies. Directors are also eligible to participate in The Merck Company Foundation Matching Gift Program. The maximum gift total for a participant in the Program is $10,000 in any calendar year.

Under the Merck & Co., Inc. Plan for Deferred Payment of Directors' Compensation ("Plan for Deferred Payment of Directors' Compensation"), each director may elect to defer all or a portion of cash compensation from retainers and meeting fees. Any amount so deferred is, at the director's election, valued as if invested in any of 22 investment measures, including the Company's Common Stock, and is payable in cash in installments or as a lump sum on or after termination of service as a director. In addition to the compensation described above, on the first Friday following the Annual Meeting of Stockholders, each director receives a credit to his/her Merck Common Stock account under the Plan for Deferred Payment of Directors' Compensation of an amount equal to the value of one-third of the annual cash retainer.

In 1996, the Retirement Plan for the Directors of Merck & Co., Inc. (the "Directors' Retirement Plan") (which excludes current or former employees of the Company) was discontinued for directors who join the Board after December 31, 1995. Directors at the time of the change elected to either continue to accrue benefits under the Directors' Retirement Plan or, in lieu of accruing benefits under the Directors' Retirement Plan, receive additional compensation to be deferred in accordance with the terms of the Plan for Deferred Payment of Directors' Compensation. Eligible directors who elected not to accrue additional retirement benefits under the Directors' Retirement Plan will receive at retirement a pension benefit based on the amount of service accrued as of March 31, 1997. No current director is accruing a benefit under the Directors' Retirement Plan.

Under the Non–Employee Directors Stock Option Plan adopted by stockholders in 2001 (the "2001 Non–Employee Directors Stock Option Plan"), on the first Friday following the Company's Annual Meeting of Stockholders, non-employee directors each receive an option to purchase 5,000 shares of Merck Common Stock. The options issued since April 2002 become exercisable in equal installments on the first, second and third anniversaries of the grant date. Options issued prior to April 2002 become exercisable five years from the grant date and all options expire ten years from the grant date. The exercise price of the options is the average of the high and low prices of the Company's Common Stock on the grant date as quoted on the New York Stock Exchange. The exercise price is payable in cash at the time the stock options are exercised. In addition, the 2001 Non–Employee Directors Stock Option Plan and the prior plans, the 1996 Non–Employee Directors Stock Option Plan and the Non–Employee Directors Stock Option Plan, allow directors under certain circumstances to transfer stock options to members of their immediate family, family partnerships and family trusts.

Stock ownership guidelines for directors are set forth in the Policies of the Board, which are available on the Company's website. A target ownership level of 5,000 shares is to be achieved by each director within five years of joining the Board or as soon thereafter as practical. Shares held in the Merck Common Stock account under the Plan for Deferred Payment of Directors' Compensation are included in the target goal.

Security Ownership of Certain Beneficial Owners and Management

The table below reflects the number of shares beneficially owned by (a) each director and nominee for director of the Company; (b) each executive officer of the Company named in the Summary Compensation Table; (c) all directors, nominees and executive officers as a group; and (d) each person or group owning more than 5 percent of the outstanding shares of Merck Common Stock. Unless otherwise noted, the information is stated as of December 31, 2002 and the beneficial owners exercise sole voting and/or investment power over their shares.

Name of Beneficial Owner	Company Common Stock Shares Owned (a)	Right to Acquire Ownership Under Options Exercisable Within 60 Days	Percent of Class
Raymond V. Gilmartin	268,996(b)(c)	2,526,666	*
Lawrence A. Bossidy	38,330	10,000	*
William G. Bowen	38,831(b)(c)	—	*
Johnnetta B. Cole	7,354	4,400	*
William M. Daley	1,314(c)	—	*
William B. Harrison, Jr.	5,032	—	*
William N. Kelley	21,016	10,000	*
Heidi G. Miller	4,879(b)(c)	—	*
Thomas E. Shenk	3,016	—	*
Anne M. Tatlock	4,784(c)	—	*
Samuel O. Thier	5,215	—	*
David W. Anstice	125,466(b)	703,333	*
Judy C. Lewent	204,974	755,600	*
Edward M. Scolnick	250,455(b)	666,666	*
Per Wold-Olsen	106,849	606,933	*
All Directors, Nominees and Executive Officers as a Group	1,202,591(b)	7,286,552	*
FMR Corp.(d)	121,513,312	—	5.411%

(a) Includes equivalent shares of Common Stock held by the Trustee of the Merck & Co., Inc. Employee Savings and Security Plan for the accounts of individuals as follows: Mr. Gilmartin—5,521 shares, Mr. Anstice—4,249 shares, Ms. Lewent—5,658 shares, Dr. Scolnick—3,875 shares, Mr. Wold-Olsen—6,153 shares, and all directors and executive officers as a group—59,464 shares. Also includes shares of phantom Common Stock held in the Plan for Deferred Payment of Directors' Compensation or in the Merck & Co., Inc. Deferral Program as follows: Mr. Gilmartin—85,966 shares, Mr. Bossidy—8,330 shares, Dr. Bowen—6,266 shares, Dr. Cole—6,894 shares, Mr. Daley—1,125 shares, Mr. Harrison—3,632 shares, Dr. Kelley—19,316 shares, Dr. Miller—2,279 shares, Dr. Shenk—2,016 shares, Ms. Tatlock—3,841 shares, Dr. Thier—5,195 shares, Mr. Anstice—6,240 shares, Ms. Lewent—8,404 shares, and all directors and executive officers as a group—178,796 shares.

(b) Excludes shares of Common Stock held by family members in which beneficial ownership is disclaimed by the individuals as follows: Mr. Gilmartin—23,200 shares, Dr. Miller—5,000 shares, Mr. Anstice—539 shares, Dr. Scolnick—28,000 shares, and all directors and executive officers as a group—82,054 shares. Excludes 1,800 shares held by a trust of which Dr. Bowen is a trustee and in which he disclaims beneficial ownership. Excludes 23,335 shares beneficially held by a family limited partnership in a trust for the benefit of Mr. Gilmartin's family; Mr. Gilmartin disclaims beneficial ownership in the trust of which his spouse is a trustee.

(c) Includes shares of Common Stock in which the beneficial owners share voting and/or investment power as follows: 132,235 shares held by Mr. Gilmartin in a family limited partnership, 5,600 shares held by Dr. Bowen's spouse, 189 shares held in a trust for Mr. Daley's spouse, 600 shares held in custodial accounts for Dr. Miller's minor children, and 543 shares held by Ms. Tatlock's spouse.

(d) All information regarding FMR Corp. ("Fidelity") and its affiliates is based on information disclosed in a Schedule 13G (the "Fidelity Filing") filed with the Securities and Exchange Commission on February 13, 2003 by Fidelity, Edward C. Johnson 3rd and Abigail P. Johnson, whose business address is 82 Devonshire Street, Boston, MA 02109. According to the Fidelity Filing, through their ownership of voting common stock and the execution of a shareholders' voting agreement, members of the Johnson family may be deemed under the Investment Company Act of 1940 to form a controlling group with respect to Fidelity.

According to the Fidelity Filing, of the 121,513,312 shares of Merck Common Stock owned by Fidelity, Fidelity has the sole power to vote or direct the vote with respect to 11,045,231 shares and does not share voting power with respect to any other shares. According to the Fidelity Filing, neither Fidelity nor Edward C. Johnson 3rd has the sole power to vote or direct the voting of shares owned directly by the Fidelity funds, which power resides with the funds' Boards of Trustees. Various persons have the right to receive or the power to direct the receipt of dividends from, or the proceeds from the sale of, shares. No one person's interest in the shares of Merck Common Stock is more than 5 percent of the total outstanding shares.

* Less than 1 percent of the Company's outstanding shares of Common Stock.

Compensation and Benefits Committee Report on Executive Compensation

The Compensation and Benefits Committee of the Board (the "Committee") approves compensation objectives and policies for all employees and sets compensation for the Company's executive officers, including the individuals named in the Summary Compensation Table.

The Committee is comprised entirely of independent directors.

Objectives and Policies

The Committee seeks to ensure that:

- rewards are closely linked to Company-wide, division, area, team and individual performance;
- the interests of the Company's employees are aligned with those of its stockholders through potential stock ownership; and
- compensation and benefits are set at levels that enable the Company to attract and retain the high-quality employees it needs.

The Committee applies these objectives and policies through the broad and deep availability of both performance-based cash incentives and stock option grants.

Further, consistent with the long-term focus inherent within the Company's R & D-based pharmaceutical business, it is the policy of the Committee to make a high proportion of executive officer compensation dependent on long-term performance and on enhancing stockholder value.

The Company employs a formal system for developing measures of executive officer performance and for evaluating performance.

Provided that other compensation objectives are met, it is the Committee's intention that executive officer compensation be deductible for federal income tax purposes.

Total Compensation

Total compensation for executive officers comprises both short-term and longer-term elements. The short-term elements are base salary and bonus awards under the stockholder-approved Executive Incentive Plan ("EIP"). The longer-term element is stock option grants under the stockholder-approved Incentive Stock Plan ("ISP").

Comparisons of total compensation (including the above-stated elements) are made within the healthcare industry by reference to U.S.—headquartered companies. In 2002, other leading healthcare companies included Abbott Laboratories, Bristol–Myers Squibb, Johnson & Johnson, Eli Lilly, Pfizer, Pharmacia, Schering–Plough and Wyeth. Companies headquartered outside the United States are generally excluded from this comparison since executive officers of such companies typically reside in the country where their company is based and compensation practices differ. The Committee also considers broader industry information that it judges to be appropriate.

Base Salary

Executive officer base salaries are based on level of position within the Company and individual contribution, with reference to base salary levels of U.S.-based executives at other leading healthcare companies.

Bonus Awards

The Committee aims to provide performance-based cash incentive opportunities broadly and deeply throughout the organization.

Executive officer bonus targets are based on level of position within the Company and individual contribution, with reference to levels of bonus and total cash compensation (base salary plus bonus) of U.S.-based executives at other leading healthcare companies.

Individual bonus awards are determined with reference to Company-wide, division, area, team and individual performance for the previous fiscal year, based on a wide range of measures that permit comparisons with competitors' performance and internal targets set before the start of each fiscal year. Performance measures for 2002 covered operational, strategic and human resources areas. Approximately 70 percent of the objectives were based on quantitative measures of performance. The operational measures were earnings per share growth and sales growth compared to other leading healthcare companies (AstraZeneca, Bristol–Myers Squibb, GlaxoSmithKline, Johnson & Johnson, Eli Lilly, Novartis, Pfizer, Pharmacia, Roche Holding, Schering–Plough and Wyeth) and the change in the Company's return on operating assets versus the prior year. The Company used the same high standards for earnings per share growth, sales growth and return on operating assets that have been applied in prior years, notwithstanding that 2002 would be a "transition year" (as communicated to stockholders in December 2001), with financial results significantly impacted by patent expirations. The strategic measures refer primarily to the Company's communicated goal of being a top-tier growth company by continuing a strong commitment to research and preserving profitability through continuing productivity improvements in manufacturing. The human resources measures refer to teamwork and respect for the individual. These were assessed through a review of Company achievements in (a) building organizational capability with respect to performance management, succession planning and employee development, and leadership development, and (b) fostering a productive and diverse work environment through diversity initiatives, ethics and stewardship training, and implementation of action plans addressing results of a recent worldwide employee opinion survey. The Company met its performance objectives in 2002 with respect to strategic and human resources measures; however, the operating performance was below long-term growth objectives. In addition to Company-wide measures of performance, the Committee considered those performance factors particular to each executive officer (i.e., the performance of the division or area for which such officer had management responsibility and individual managerial accomplishments).

The Committee judged that executive officer bonus awards for 2002 were consistent with the level of accomplishment and appropriately reflected Company performance, including earnings per share growth, sales growth, return on operating assets and progress in research, manufacturing productivity and the management of human resources. The Committee relied heavily, but not exclusively, on these measures. It exercised judgment and discretion in light of these measures and in view of the Company's compensation objectives and policies described above to determine overall bonus funds and individual bonus awards.

Stock Options

Within the total number of shares authorized by stockholders, the Committee aims to provide stock option grants broadly and deeply throughout the organization.

Executive officer stock option grants are based on level of position within the Company and potential for individual contribution, with reference to levels of stock options and total direct compensation (total cash compensation plus stock options) of U.S.-based executives at other leading healthcare companies. The Committee also considers stock option grants previously made. As with the determination of base salaries and bonus awards, the Committee exercises judgment and discretion in view of the above criteria and its general policies. The exercise price of stock option grants is set at fair market value on grant date. Subject to the terms applicable to such grants, the stock options granted to executive officers in 2002 become exercisable in equal installments on the first, second and third anniversaries of the grant date and expire ten years from the grant date. Stock options previously granted to, and currently held by, executive officers could be first exercised five years from the grant date. The Company's long-term performance ultimately determines the value of stock options, since gains from stock option exercises are entirely dependent on the long-term growth of the Company's stock price.

The Committee expects the Chief Executive Officer and other executive officers named in the Summary Compensation Table to hold Merck Common Stock in an amount representing a multiple of base salary. For the Chief Executive Officer, the multiple is ten; for the other executive officers, the multiple is five. The Committee further expects that, until such multiples are reached, the Chief Executive Officer and the other executive officers hold a proportion of shares that may be purchased from the net gain on stock option exercise, after deducting exercise price, taxes and transaction costs. For the Chief Executive Officer, the proportion is 70 percent; for the other executive officers, the proportion is 60 percent.

Compensation of the Chief Executive Officer

Mr. Gilmartin's compensation in 2002, including base salary, bonus award and stock option grant, was determined within the same framework established for all executive officers of the Company.

Effective March 1, 2002, Mr. Gilmartin's base salary was increased to $1,500,000 from $1,400,004.

Mr. Gilmartin's bonus award was $1,500,000 for 2002, the same amount as for 2001. The award was determined in light of the Company performance measures of earnings per share growth, sales growth, return on operating assets and continuing progress in research, manufacturing productivity and the management of human resources. As stated previously, the Company met its performance objectives in 2002 with respect to strategic and human resources measures; however, the operating performance was below long-term growth objectives.

On March 1, 2002, Mr. Gilmartin was granted a stock option to purchase 500,000 shares of Merck Common Stock at the exercise price of $62.15. The exercise price of the stock option was set at fair market value on the grant date. Subject to the terms applicable to his grant, the stock option becomes exercisable in equal installments on the first, second and third anniversaries of the grant date and expires ten years from the grant date. Stock options previously granted to, and currently held by, Mr. Gilmartin could be first exercised five years from the grant date.

The Committee exercised its judgment and discretion in determining the level of each element of compensation, individually and in aggregate, for Mr. Gilmartin in 2002.

Compensation Analyses and Reviews

The Company periodically retains an outside compensation consultant to compare base salary and incentive compensation programs for the Company's executive officers with those of other leading healthcare companies and leading industrial companies to ensure that they are appropriate to the Company's objectives. The Committee exercises judgment and discretion in the information it reviews and the analyses it considers. In addition, the Committee itself has retained an outside compensation consultant to independently advise the Committee, as requested, on compensation objectives and policies for all employees and the setting of executive officer compensation.

Compensation and Benefits Committee

Lawrence A. Bossidy

Chairperson

William G. Bowen   Johnnetta B. Cole

William N. Kelley

Summary Compensation Table

The following table summarizes compensation earned in 2002, 2001 and 2000 by the Chief Executive Officer and the four other most highly paid individuals who were executive officers at the end of 2002.

		Annual Compensation			Long-Term Compensation			
					Awards		Payouts	
Name and Principal Position	Year	Salary ($)	Bonus ($)	Other Annual Compensation ($)	Restricted Stock Awards ($)	Securities Underlying Options/SARs(a) (#)	LTIP Payouts ($)	All Other Compensation ($)
Raymond V. Gilmartin	2002	$1,483,334	$1,500,000	—	—	500,000	$ —	$9,000 (b)
Chairman of the Board,	2001	1,383,338	1,500,000	—	—	500,000	—	7,650 (b)
President and Chief	2000	1,283,340	1,700,000	—	—	400,000	—	7,650 (b)
Executive Officer							—	
Edward M. Scolnick*	2002	854,170	800,000	—	—	200,000	—	4,500 (b)
Executive Vice-President,	2001	820,000	825,000	—	—	200,000	—	3,825 (b)
Science and Technology	2000	790,000	860,000	—	—	200,000	—	3,825 (b)
and President, Merck Research Laboratories								
Judy C. Lewent*	2002	607,500	585,000	—	—	150,000	—	9,000 (b)
Executive Vice President	2001	563,334	600,000	—	—	150,000	—	7,650 (b)
and Chief Financial Officer	2000	525,838	600,000	—	—	130,000	—	7,650 (b)
David W. Anstice*	2002	586,670	520,000	—	—	130,000	—	9,000 (b)
President, The Americas	2001	563,334	500,000	—	—	150,000	—	7,650 (b)
and U.S. Human Health	2000	526,670	600,000	—	—	130,000	—	7,650 (b)
Per Wold-Olsen	2002	554,170	540,000	—	—	130,000	—	9,000 (b)
President, Human Health—	2001	520,834	540,000	—	—	130,000	—	7,650 (b)
Europe, Middle East &	2000	495,838	515,000	—	—	130,000	—	7,650 (b)
Africa								

(a) No stock appreciation rights were granted to the executive officers named in the Summary Compensation Table.

(b) Company contribution to the Merck & Co., Inc. Employee Savings and Security Plan.

* As of January 1, 2003, Dr. Scolnick's title is President Emeritus, Merck Research Laboratories; Ms. Lewent's title is Executive Vice President, Chief Financial Officer and President, Human Health Asia; and Mr. Anstice's title is President, Human Health.

The following table provides information on stock options granted in 2002 to each of the Company's executive officers named in the Summary Compensation Table and stock options granted to all employees as a group. The table also shows the hypothetical gains that would exist for the options at the end of their ten-year terms for the executive officers named in the Summary Compensation Table and for all employees as a group (assuming their options had ten-year terms) at assumed compound rates of stock appreciation of 5 percent and 10 percent. The actual future value of the options will depend on the market value of the Company's Common Stock. All option exercise prices are based on fair market value on the date of grant.

Option/SAR Grants In Last Fiscal Year

	Individual Grants(a)					Potential Realizable Value at Assumed Annual Rates of Stock Price Appreciation For Option Term (b)		
Name	Date of Grant	Number of Securities Underlyin g Options/ SARs Granted (#)	Percent of Total Options/ SARs Granted To Employee s in Fiscal Year	Exercis e or Base Price ($/Sh)	Expiratio n Date	0%($)	5%($)	10%($)
Raymond V. Gilmartin	3/01/02	500,000	1.32 %	$62.15	2/29/12	—	$ 19,542,901	$ 49,525,547
Edward M. Scolnick	3/01/02	200,000	0.53 %	62.15	2/29/12	—	7,817,160	19,810,219
Judy C. Lewent	3/01/02	150,000	0.40 %	62.15	2/29/12	—	5,862,870	14,857,664
David W. Anstice	3/01/02	130,000	0.34 %	62.15	2/29/12	—	5,081,154	12,876,642
Per Wold-Olsen	3/01/02	130,000	0.34 %	62.15	2/29/12	—	5,081,154	12,876,642
All Employees as a Group	(c)	37,796,557	100.00 %	(c)	(c)	—	$ 1,454,194,709(d)	$3,685,214,907(d)

	0%	5%	10%
Total potential stock price appreciation from March 1, 2002 to February 29, 2012 for all stockholders at assumed rates of stock price appreciation(e)	—	$88,767,546,200	$224,954,390,503
Potential actual realizable value of options granted to all employees, assuming ten-year option terms, as a percentage of total potential stock price appreciation from March 1, 2002 to February 29, 2012 for all stockholders at assumed rates of stock price appreciation	—	1.64%	1.64%

(a) Options granted under the ISP to the Company's executive officers named in the Summary Compensation Table become exercisable in equal installments on the first, second and third anniversaries of the grant date and include a transferable stock option feature that allows the transfer of stock options to immediate family members, family partnerships and family trusts. The Company did not issue stock appreciation rights in 2002 to any of the executive officers named in the Summary Compensation Table.

(b) These amounts, based on assumed appreciation rates of 0 percent and the 5 percent and 10 percent rates prescribed by the Securities and Exchange Commission rules, are not intended to forecast possible future appreciation, if any, of the Company's stock price.

(c) Options were granted under the ISP throughout 2002 with various vesting schedules and expiration dates through the year 2012. The average exercise price of all options granted to employees in 2002 is $61.1776.

(d) No gain to the optionees is possible without an increase in stock price, which will benefit all stockholders.

(e) Based on a price of $62.15 on March 1, 2002, and a total of 2,271,094,459 shares of Merck Common Stock outstanding on February 28, 2002.

The following table shows the number of shares acquired on exercise of stock options and the aggregate gains realized on exercise in 2002 by the Company's executive officers named in the Summary Compensation Table. The table also shows the number of shares covered by exercisable and unexercisable options held by such executives on December 31, 2002 and the aggregate gains that would have been realized had these options been exercised on December 31, 2002, even though these options were not exercised and the unexercisable options could not have been exercised on December 31, 2002.

Aggregated Option/SAR Exercises in Last Fiscal Year and FY-End Option/SAR Values

Name	Shares Acquired On Exercise (#)	Value Realized (a) ($)	Number of Securities Underlying Unexercised Options/SARs at FY-End (#)		Value of Unexercised In-The-Money Options/ SARs at Fiscal Year-End (b) ($)	
			Exercisable	Unexercisable	Exercisable	Unexercisable
Raymond V. Gilmartin	—	$ —	2,010,000	2,150,000	$63,721,100	$0.00
Edward M. Scolnick	—	—	400,000	985,000	6,356,500	0.00
Judy C. Lewent	138,000	4,741,084	565,600	730,000	14,935,741	0.00
David W. Anstice	—	—	520,000	680,000	12,000,950	0.00
Per Wold-Olsen	—	—	423,600	660,000	10,965,808	0.00

(a) Market value on the date of exercise of shares covered by options exercised, less option exercise price.

(b) Market value of shares covered by in-the-money options on December 31, 2002 less option exercise price. Options are in-the-money if the market value of the shares covered by the options is greater than the option exercise price.

The "Long–Term Incentive Plans—Awards in Last Fiscal Year" table is not included because the Company did not make any long-term incentive plan awards during 2002.

Equity Compensation Plan Information

The following table summarizes information about the options, warrants and rights and other equity compensation under the Company's equity plans as of December 31, 2002. The table does not include information about the proposed 2003 Incentive Stock Plan or about tax qualified plans such as the Merck & Co., Inc. Employee Savings and Security Plan.

Plan Category	Number of securities to be issued upon exercise of outstanding options, warrants and rights (a)	Weighted-average exercise price of outstanding options, warrants and rights (b)	Number of securities remaining available for future issuance under equity compensation plans (excluding securities reflected in column (a)) (c)
Equity compensation plans approved by security holders (1)	213,935,906 (2)	$59.65	45,882,396 (2)
Equity compensation plans not approved by security holders (3) (4)	— (5)(6)	— (5)(6)	290,807 (5)
Total	213,935,906	$59.65	46,173,203

(1) Includes options to purchase shares of Company common stock and other rights under the following stockholder-approved plans: the 1991 Incentive Stock Plan, the 1996 Incentive Stock Plan, the 2001 Incentive Stock Plan, the Non-Employee Directors Stock Option Plan, the 1996 Non-Employee Directors Stock Option Plan and the 2001 Non-Employee Directors Stock Option Plan.

(2) Excludes approximately 944,268 shares of phantom stock deferred under the Merck & Co., Inc. Deferral Program. As of December 31, 2002, no shares were reserved for future issuance. Beginning January 1, 2003, one-tenth of 1 percent of the outstanding shares of Merck Common Stock on the last business day of the preceding calendar year plus any shares authorized under the Deferral Program and the Executive Incentive Plan in previous years but not issued are reserved for future issuance. The actual amount of shares to be issued prospectively equals the amount participants elect to defer from payouts under the Company's various incentive programs such as the Executive Incentive Plan.

(3) Includes options, warrants or rights under the Merck-Medco 2001 Employee Stock Purchase Plan, which is described more fully below, and the Plan for Deferred Payment of Directors' Compensation.

(4) The table does not include information for equity compensation plans and options and other warrants and rights assumed by the Company in connection with mergers and acquisitions and pursuant to which there remain outstanding options or other warrants or rights (collectively, "Assumed Plans"), which include the following: Medco Containment Services, Inc. 1991 Class C Non-Qualified Stock Option Plan; Medical Marketing Group, Inc. 1991 Special Non-Qualified Stock Option Plan; Systemed, Inc. 1993 Employee Stock Option Plan; SIBIA Neurosciences, Inc. 1996 Equity Incentive Plan; Provantage Health Services, Inc. 1996 Stock Incentive Plan; Rosetta Inpharmatics, Inc. 1997 Stock Plan; Rosetta Inpharmatics, Inc. 2000 Stock Plan; and Rosetta Inpharmatics, Inc. 2000 Directors' Stock Option Plan. A total of 4,320,559 shares of Merck Common Stock may be purchased under the Assumed Plans, at a weighted average exercise price of $16.293. No further grants may be made under any Assumed Plan. The table also excludes the Medco Health Solutions, Inc. Stock Incentive Plan, which will issue shares of Medco Health Solutions, Inc. and not shares of Merck Common Stock, if and when it becomes effective.

(5) Excludes approximately 121,997 shares of phantom Common Stock held in the Plan for Deferred Payment of Directors' Compensation. No shares are reserved under the plan for the future because all amounts are payable in cash, no shares of Merck Common Stock have been purchased or earmarked under this plan, and participants do not have any rights of stockholders with respect to account balances in this plan. The Plan for Deferred Payment of Directors' Compensation is described more fully on page 14 under "Compensation of Directors." Also excludes a total of 11,337 shares of restricted stock that were issued in connection with the exercise of certain unvested options under the Rosetta Inpharmatics, Inc. 1997 Stock Plan.

(6) Excludes shares to be issued under the Merck-Medco 2001 Employee Stock Purchase Plan (the "ESPP") because the number of shares and weighted average exercise price cannot be determined. Under the ESPP, eligible participants contribute a percentage of base pay for an offering period of one fiscal quarter of Medco Health Solutions, Inc. as described more fully below. The aggregate contributions are used to purchase shares of Merck Common Stock at 85 percent of market value determined as of the last day of the offering period. Participants are not obligated to retain the shares for any period and may cease contributing to the plan at any time. As of December 31, 2002, approximately 3,100 participants with an average base pay of $57,570 elected to contribute approximately 6.4 percent of base pay for the quarter that began December 28, 2002 and ends March 28, 2003.

Description of Non-Stockholder Approved Equity Plans

The material features of equity plans of the Company and its subsidiaries that have not been approved by the Company's stockholders are as follows:

Merck-Medco 2001 Employee Stock Purchase Plan—The Merck-Medco 2001 Employee Stock Purchase Plan (the "ESPP") permits some of Medco Health Solutions, Inc.'s full-time employees who earn less than $120,000 base pay per year to purchase shares of Merck Common Stock at 85 percent of the fair market value through accumulated payroll deductions during consecutive three-month plan offerings, coincident with the fiscal quarters of Medco Health Solutions, Inc., which uses a 52—53-week fiscal year. Each employee may use up to 10 percent of gross pay for these purchases, although the fair market value of the shares purchased may not exceed $25,000 per person for any calendar year. Initially, 800,000 shares of Merck Common Stock were reserved for issuance. The ESPP will terminate automatically at the earliest of (a) December 2004, (b) when the maximum number of shares has been purchased or (c) when terminated at the discretion of the board of directors of Medco Health Solutions, Inc. Shares purchased under the ESPP are not eligible for the tax treatment provided under Section 423 of the Internal Revenue Code of 1986, as amended.

Annual Benefits Payable Under Merck & Co., Inc. Retirement Plans

Annual benefits payable under the Retirement Plan for Salaried Employees of Merck & Co., Inc. and the Merck & Co., Inc. Supplemental Retirement Plan are based on a formula which (1) multiplies (a) the participant's final average compensation (as defined in the plans) by (b) a multiplier of 2 percent for years of-credited service (as defined in the plans) earned prior to July 1, 1995 and a multiplier of 1.6 percent for years of credited service earned after that date (total credited service not to exceed 35 years) and then (2) subtracts 1.6 percent of the participant's Social Security benefits multiplied by years of credited service (as defined in the plans), not to exceed 50 percent of the primary Social Security benefit.

The following tables show the estimated annual benefits payable using the 1.6 percent and 2 percent multipliers, respectively, under the Retirement Plan for Salaried Employees and the Supplemental Retirement Plan at age 65 to persons in specified compensation and years-of-service classifications, based on a straight-life annuity form of retirement income and without regard to the Social Security offset. Annual benefits payable under the plans can be estimated by adding the years of service earned prior to July 1, 1995 (Table 2) to those which could be earned after that date (Table 1).

Pension Plan Tables

Table 1: 1.6% Formula

Remuneration (Average Pension Compensation During Highest Five Consecutive Years in the Last Ten Years Before Retirement)	Years of Service (Estimated Annual Retirement Benefits For Years of Credited Service Shown Below)(a)				
	15	20	25	30	35
$ 800,000	$192,000	$ 256,000	$ 320,000	$ 384,000	$ 448,000
1,000,000	240,000	320,000	400,000	480,000	560,000
1,200,000	288,000	384,000	480,000	576,000	672,000
1,400,000	336,000	448,000	560,000	672,000	784,000
1,600,000	384,000	512,000	640,000	768,000	896,000
1,800,000	432,000	576,000	720,000	864,000	1,008,000
2,000,000	480,000	640,000	800,000	960,000	1,120,000
2,200,000	528,000	704,000	880,000	1,056,000	1,232,000
2,400,000	576,000	768,000	960,000	1,152,000	1,344,000
2,600,000	624,000	832,000	1,040,000	1,248,000	1,456,000
2,800,000	672,000	896,000	1,120,000	1,344,000	1,568,000
3,000,000	720,000	960,000	1,200,000	1,440,000	1,680,000
3,200,000	768,000	1,024,000	1,280,000	1,536,000	1,792,000
3,400,000	816,000	1,088,000	1,360,000	1,632,000	1,904,000
3,600,000	864,000	1,152,000	1,440,000	1,728,000	2,016,000
3,800,000	912,000	1,216,000	1,520,000	1,824,000	2,128,000

Table 2: 2% Formula(b)

Remuneration (Average Pension Compensation During Highest Five Consecutive Years in the Last Ten Years Before Retirement)	Years of Service (Estimated Annual Retirement Benefits for Years of Credited Service Shown Below)(a)			
	10	15	20	25
$ 800,000	$160,000	$ 240,000	$ 320,000	$ 400,000
1,000,000	200,000	300,000	400,000	500,000
1,200,000	240,000	360,000	480,000	600,000
1,400,000	280,000	420,000	560,000	700,000
1,600,000	320,000	480,000	640,000	800,000
1,800,000	360,000	540,000	720,000	900,000
2,000,000	400,000	600,000	800,000	1,000,000
2,200,000	440,000	660,000	880,000	1,100,000
2,400,000	480,000	720,000	960,000	1,200,000
2,600,000	520,000	780,000	1,040,000	1,300,000
2,800,000	560,000	840,000	1,120,000	1,400,000
3,000,000	600,000	900,000	1,200,000	1,500,000
3,200,000	640,000	960,000	1,280,000	1,600,000
3,400,000	680,000	1,020,000	1,360,000	1,700,000
3,600,000	720,000	1,080,000	1,440,000	1,800,000
3,800,000	760,000	1,140,000	1,520,000	1,900,000

(a) Benefits shown above are exclusive of the Social Security offset provided for by the benefit formula.

(b) Credited service is shown for the years specified to approximate the actual years of credited service earned prior to July 1, 1995 (at the 2 percent multiplier) by the executive officers named in the Summary Compensation Table other than Mr. Gilmartin. Mr. Gilmartin earned 1.0 year prior to July 1, 1995.

Under the Retirement Plan for Salaried Employees and the Supplemental Retirement Plan, years of credited service as of July 1, 1995, and as of December 31, 2002—which takes into account credited service both before and after July 1, 1995—are, respectively: Dr. Scolnick—13 years and 20.5 years; Ms. Lewent—15 years and 22.5 years; Mr. Anstice—20.5 years and 28 years; Mr. Wold-Olsen—21.5 years and 29 years. In addition, if these individuals retire from service with the Company at age 65 and with less than 35 years of actual credited service, pursuant to the enhanced pension provision of the Supplemental Retirement Plan applicable to *bona fide* executives, described in greater detail below, they will receive an additional month of credited service for each month of actual credited service prior to January 1, 1995 up to an aggregate total of 35 years of credited service. As of July 1, 1995 and December 31, 2002, Mr. Gilmartin had 1.0 and 8.5 years, respectively, of actual credited service in the Retirement Plan for Salaried Employees and the Supplemental Retirement Plan. Pursuant to an employment agreement that was in effect from June 9, 1994 until October 31, 1999, Mr. Gilmartin was credited with 28 years of credited service under the Supplemental Retirement Plan and the multiplier to be used in the formula for benefit calculation will be 1.6 percent. Benefits payable under the Company plans will be net of retirement benefits payable by Mr. Gilmartin's former employer.

For purposes of the Retirement Plan for Salaried Employees and the Supplemental Retirement Plan, pension compensation for a particular year, as used for the calculation of retirement benefits, includes salaries and annual EIP bonus awards received during the year. Pension compensation for 2002 differs from compensation reported in the Summary Compensation Table in that pension compensation includes the annual EIP bonus awards received in 2002 for services in 2001 rather than the EIP bonus awards received in 2003 for services in 2002. Pension compensation in 2002 was $2,983,334 for Mr. Gilmartin, $1,679,170 for Dr. Scolnick, $1,207,500 for Ms. Lewent, $1,086,670 for Mr. Anstice and $1,094,170 for Mr. Wold-Olsen.

The Supplemental Retirement Plan is an unfunded plan providing benefits to participants in certain retirement plans (the "primary plans") maintained by the Company and its subsidiaries as follows: (1) benefits not payable by the primary plans because of the limitations on benefits stipulated by the Internal Revenue Code, (2) benefits not payable by the primary plans because of the exclusion of deferred compensation from the benefit formulas of those plans ("supplemental benefit"), (3) a minimum annual aggregate benefit under this plan and the primary plans of $50,000 on a straight-life annuity basis for the incumbents at time of actual retirement in positions designated as *bona fide* executive or high policymaking under the Company's Corporate Policy on Executive Retirement (which includes all the named executive officers in the Summary Compensation Table), reduced in the event of retirement or death prior to normal retirement date and (4) for employees who, prior to January 1, 1995, were determined by the Company to have occupied *bona fide* executive or high policymaking positions and who do not have 35 years of credited service, an enhanced benefit payable upon retirement from active service at age 65 (unless the Compensation and Benefits Committee of the Board consents to payment upon early retirement, death or disability prior to age 65). The enhanced benefit is an amount calculated under the benefit formula in the primary plan using one additional month of credited service for each month of credited service accrued prior to January 1, 1995, during, or prior to attainment of, the designated position (up to the 35-year total) less (1) the minimum benefit, where applicable, or the supplemental benefit, (2) the primary plan benefit and (3) any retirement benefit payable from a plan not sponsored by the Company. The Supplemental Retirement Plan was amended as of January 1, 1995 to eliminate prospectively the enhanced benefit except for certain grandfathered participants. In general, other terms and conditions of benefit payments are determined by reference to the provisions of the primary plans.

Employment Contracts

Dr. Edward M. Scolnick and the Company agreed that as of January 1, 2003, he will serve as President Emeritus, Merck Research Laboratories ("MRL") and in that capacity will engage in scientific research in the Company's West Point, Pennsylvania facilities. Under that agreement and in connection with that assignment, as of the end of business on December 31, 2002, Dr. Scolnick voluntarily relinquished the following responsibilities, which he previously performed: Executive Vice President, Science and Technology; President, MRL; member of Merck's Management Committee; member of MRL's Research Management Committee; member of the Merck Board of Directors and the boards of certain Merck affiliates; and member of any other Company committee on which he was then serving.

Pursuant to that agreement, beginning January 1, 2003, Dr. Scolnick's base salary is $50,000 per month and he is eligible to participate in the various employee benefit plans that cover the Company's salaried employees, except that he is not eligible to receive incentive bonuses for award years after 2002 or stock option grants. The Company will allow Dr. Scolnick reasonable use of its corporate aircraft (if otherwise available) to attend conferences and external board meetings while he is a Company employee.

The agreement provides that upon termination of his employment, Dr. Scolnick will be treated as a retiree for purposes of Company retirement, savings, benefit and stock option plans. Furthermore, under the Supplemental Retirement Plan, final average compensation will not be less than it would have been had Dr. Scolnick's employment terminated on December 31, 2002. If the Company terminates Dr. Scolnick's employment for a reason other than cause prior to his 70th birthday, the Company will provide a one-time grant of $2 million to the academic institution of his choosing to enable him to set up and maintain a research laboratory, provided Dr. Scolnick executes a release and waiver of claims and a noncompete/nonsolicitation agreement and does not violate his conditions of employment. If such termination occurs prior to Dr. Scolnick's 64th birthday, the Company will take whatever steps may be necessary to provide that Dr. Scolnick will have not fewer than 35 years of credited service under the Supplemental Retirement Plan.

Indebtedness of Management

Dr. Douglas A. Greene, Executive Vice President, Clinical Sciences and Product Development, who joined the Company and became an executive officer in May 2000, received a loan from the Company in connection with his relocation. During 2002, the largest aggregate amount outstanding under the loan was $350,000 and as of March 3, 2003, the loan was no longer outstanding. The loan from the Company was interest free. Dr. Greene's designation as an executive officer of the Company ceased during 2002 and his employment with the Company terminated January 13, 2003.

Dr. Peter S. Kim, President, MRL, who joined the Company and became an executive officer in February 2001, also received an interest-free loan from the Company in connection with his relocation. During 2002, the largest aggregate amount outstanding under the loan was $475,000 and as of March 3, 2003, $350,000 was still outstanding.

The loans were made to Dr. Greene and Dr. Kim prior to the effective date of the prohibition of loans to executive officers under the Sarbanes–Oxley Act of 2002, and are grandfathered under such Act.

Performance Graph

The following graph compares the cumulative total stockholder return (stock price appreciation plus reinvested dividends) on the Company's Common Stock with the cumulative total return (including reinvested dividends) of the Dow Jones Pharmaceutical Index—United States Owned Companies (?DJPI?) and the Standard & Poor's 500 Index ("S & P 500 Index") for the five years ended December 31, 2002. Amounts below have been rounded to the nearest dollar or percent.

Comparison of Five-Year Cumulative Total Return*
Merck & Co., Inc., Dow Jones Pharmaceutical Index and S&P 500 Index

	End of Period Value	2002/1997 CAGR**
Merck	$117	3 %
DJPI	124	4
S&P 500	97	-1

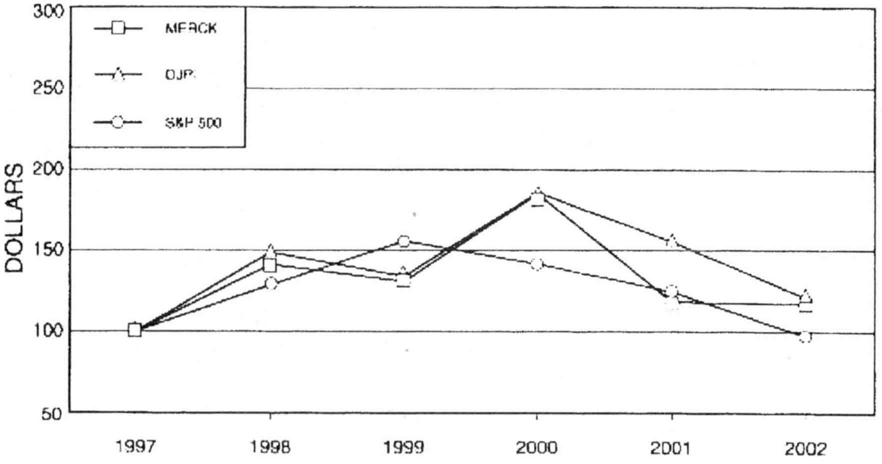

	1997	1998	1999	2000	2001	2002
MERCK	100.00	141.28	130.67	184.96	118.40	117.01
DJPI	100.00	148.67	133.94	185.78	155.22	123.59
S&P 500	100.00	128.58	155.63	141.46	124.66	97.08

Audit Committee

The Audit Committee's Report for 2002 follows.

Audit Committee's Report

The Board of Directors and the Audit Committee dismissed Arthur Andersen LLP as the Company's independent public accountants in February 2002 and engaged PricewaterhouseCoopers LLP to serve as the Company's independent public accountants for the fiscal year 2002. The Audit Committee, comprised of independent directors, met with the independent public accountants, management and internal auditors to assure that all were carrying out their respective responsibilities. The Audit Committee discussed with and received a letter from the independent public accountants confirming their independence. Both the independent public accountants and the internal auditors had full access to the Committee, including regular meetings without management present.

The Audit Committee met with the independent public accountants to discuss their fees and the scope and results of their audit work, including the adequacy of internal controls and the quality of financial reporting. The Committee also discussed with the independent public accountants their judgments regarding the quality and acceptability of the Company's accounting principles, the clarity of its disclosures and the degree of aggressiveness or conservatism of its accounting principles and underlying estimates. The Audit Committee reviewed and discussed the audited financial statements with management and recommended to the Board of Directors that these financial statements be included in the Company's Form 10–K filing with the Securities and Exchange Commission.

Audit Committee

Heidi G. Miller
Chairperson

Lawrence A. Bossidy

Thomas E. Shenk

Samuel O. Thier

As part of its duties, the Audit Committee also considered whether the provision of services other than audit services during fiscal year 2002 by PricewaterhouseCoopers LLP, the Company's independent public accountants for that period, is compatible with maintaining the accountants' independence. See All Other Fees below.

Fees for all services provided by PricewaterhouseCoopers LLP for fiscal year 2002 are as follows:

Audit Fees

Fees for services provided by PricewaterhouseCoopers LLP related to the 2002 annual financial statement audit and reviews of quarterly financial statements filed in the reports on Form 10–Q approximated $5.2 million.

Financial Information Systems Design and Implementation Fees

No services were provided by PricewaterhouseCoopers LLP in 2002 in connection with financial information systems design and implementation.

All Other Fees

Audit-Related Fees: Fees for audit-related services provided by PricewaterhouseCoopers LLP, primarily associated with Medco Health Solutions, Inc.'s Form S–1 registration statements, statutory audits and employee benefit plan audits, approximated $5.2 million.

***Tax Fees*: Fees for tax compliance approximated $0.50 million.**

Other: Fees for other services approximated $0.60 million.

Change in Independent Public Accountants

On February 26, 2002, the Board of Directors and its Audit Committee dismissed Arthur Andersen LLP as the Company's independent public accountants and engaged PricewaterhouseCoopers LLP to serve as the Company's independent public accountants for the fiscal year 2002. The appointment of PricewaterhouseCoopers LLP was ratified by stockholders at the Company's 2002 Annual Meeting of Stockholders.

Arthur Andersen's reports on the Company's consolidated financial statements for each of the years ended 2001 and 2000 did not contain an adverse opinion or disclaimer of opinion, nor were they qualified or modified as to uncertainty, audit scope or accounting principles.

During the years ended December 31, 2001 and 2000 and through March 21, 2002, there were no disagreements with Arthur Andersen on any matter of accounting principle or practice, financial statement disclosure, or auditing scope or procedure which, if not resolved to Arthur Andersen's satisfaction, would have caused them to make reference to the subject matter in connection with their report on the Company's consolidated financial statements for such years; and there were no reportable events as defined in Item 304(a)(*l*)(v) of Regulation S–K.

The Company provided Arthur Andersen with a copy of the foregoing disclosures. A copy of Arthur Andersen's letter, dated March 21, 2002, stating its agreement with such statements, is incorporated by reference to Exhibit 16 filed with the Annual Report on Form 10–K for the fiscal year ended December 31, 2001.

During the years ended December 31, 2001 and 2000 and through the date of the Board's decision, the Company did not consult PricewaterhouseCoopers with respect to the application of accounting principles to a specified transaction, either completed or proposed, or the type of audit opinion that might be rendered on the Company's consolidated financial statements, or any other matters or reportable events as set forth in Items 304(a)(2)(i) and (ii) of Regulation S–K.

2. RATIFICATION OF APPOINTMENT OF INDEPENDENT PUBLIC ACCOUNTANTS

The Audit Committee, comprised of independent members of the Board, has appointed PricewaterhouseCoopers LLP as independent public accountants of the Company with respect to its operations for the year 2003, subject to ratification by the holders of Common Stock of the Company. In taking this action, the Audit Committee considered carefully PricewaterhouseCoopers LLP's performance for the Company in that capacity since its retention in 2002, its independence with respect to the services to be performed and its general reputation for adherence to professional auditing standards. Representatives of PricewaterhouseCoopers LLP will be present at the Annual Meeting to make a statement if they desire to do so. They will also be available to answer appropriate questions from stockholders.

Because the members of the Audit Committee value stockholders' views on the Company's independent public accountants, there will be presented at the Annual Meeting a proposal for the ratification of the appointment of PricewaterhouseCoopers LLP. The Audit Committee believes ratification is advisable and in the best interests of the stockholders. If the appointment of PricewaterhouseCoopers LLP is not ratified, the matter of the appointment of independent public accountants will be considered by the Audit Committee.

The Audit Committee of the Board of Directors recommends a vote FOR this proposal.

3. ADOPTION OF THE 2003 INCENTIVE STOCK PLAN

There will be presented to the meeting a proposal to adopt the 2003 Incentive Stock Plan (the "Plan"). The Plan will replace the 2001 Incentive Stock Plan which, by its terms, expires on December 31, 2003. The Board of Directors believes stock options and other stock-based incentives play an important role in retaining the services of outstanding personnel and in encouraging such employees to have a greater financial investment in the Company (although the Plan does not necessarily require them to hold for investment the stock received under the Plan). The Board of Directors has approved the 2003 Incentive Stock Plan and directed that it be submitted to stockholders for approval.

The proposed Plan is set forth in Appendix B. Primary aspects of the proposed Plan are as follows:

General Information

Plan Administration. The Plan is administered by the Compensation and Benefits Committee of the Board of Directors, which is comprised of non-employee Directors, none of whom may receive any awards under the Plan (the "Committee"). The Committee establishes the terms and conditions of awards granted under the Plan, subject to certain limitations in the Plan. The Committee may delegate to the chief executive officer or other executive officers of the Company certain authority under the Plan, including the authority to grant awards to eligible employees who are not officers subject to Section 16 of the Securities

Exchange Act of 1934. As of December 31, 2002, there are approximately 89,800 individuals eligible to participate in the Plan, including approximately 15,300 Medco Health Solutions, Inc. employees.

Eligible Employees. The Committee may grant incentive stock options within the meaning of the Internal Revenue Code of 1986, nonqualified stock options, stock appreciation rights, performance share awards and restricted stock grants to regular employees of the Company, its subsidiaries, joint ventures, joint venture partners or affiliates who are designated by the Committee. No employee may receive grants under this Plan in any given year which, singly or in the aggregate, cover more than 3 million shares of Merck Common Stock.

Shares Available. The aggregate number of shares of Merck Common Stock that may be issued or transferred to grantees under the Plan shall not exceed 115 million shares plus shares granted but subsequently forfeited under the 2001 Incentive Stock Plan. If there is a stock split, stock dividend or other relevant change affecting the Company's shares, appropriate adjustments will be made in the number of shares that may be issued or transferred in the future and in the number of shares and price of all outstanding grants made before such event. If shares under a grant are not issued or transferred, those shares would again be available for inclusion in future grants. Payment of cash in lieu of shares would be considered an issuance or transfer of the shares. On March 3, 2003, the closing price of Merck Common Stock on the New York Stock Exchange was $52.49.

Grants Under the Plan

Stock Options. The Committee may grant options qualifying as incentive stock options under the Internal Revenue Code of 1986, other statutory stock options and nonqualified stock options. The term of an option shall be fixed by the Committee, but shall not exceed ten years. In the case of death of an optionee, under some circumstances, an option may extend for eleven years. The option price shall not be less than the fair market value of Merck Common Stock on the date of grant.

Stock Appreciation Rights. The Committee may grant stock appreciation rights ("SARs") either singly or in combination with an underlying stock option under the Plan. The term of a SAR shall be fixed by the Committee. SARs entitle the grantee to receive the same economic value that would have been derived from exercise of an option. Payment may be made in cash, in shares or a combination of both at the discretion of the Committee. If a SAR granted in combination with an underlying stock option is exercised, the right under the underlying option to purchase shares would terminate.

Performance Share Awards. The Committee may grant Performance Share Awards under which payment may be made in shares of Merck Common Stock, a combination of shares and cash or cash if the performance of the Company or any subsidiary, division, affiliate or joint venture of the Company selected by the Committee meets certain goals established by the Committee during an award period. The Committee would determine the goals, the length of an award period, the maximum payment value of an award and the minimum performance required before a payment would be made. The Committee may revise the goals and the computation of payment at any time to account for unforeseen events which occur during an award period and which have a substantial effect on the performance of the Company, subsidiary or division. In order to receive payment, a grantee must remain in the employ of the Company until the completion of the award period, except that the Committee may provide complete or partial exceptions to that requirement as it deems equitable.

Restricted Stock Grants. The Committee may also award shares under a Restricted Stock Grant. The grant would set forth a restriction period during which the grantee must remain in the employ of the Company in order to retain the shares under grant. If the grantee's employment terminates during the period, the grant would terminate and the grantee would be required to return the shares to the Company. However, the Committee may provide complete or partial exceptions to this requirement as it deems equitable. The grantee could not dispose of the shares prior to the expiration of the restriction period. During this period, the grantee would be entitled to vote the shares and, at the discretion of the Committee, receive dividends. Each certificate would bear a legend giving notice of the restrictions in the grant.

Other Share–Based Awards. The Committee also may grant shares of Merck Common Stock ("Share Awards") on the terms and conditions it determines in its discretion. Share Awards may be in addition to, or in lieu of, cash or other compensation due the grantee. Restricted Stock, Performance Share Awards and Share Awards may not exceed, in the aggregate, 12 million shares of Merck Common Stock.

U.S. Federal Income Tax Consequences

Following is an explanation of the U.S. federal income tax consequences for grantees who are subject to tax in the United States.

Stock Options. The grant of an incentive stock option or a nonqualified stock option would not result in income for the grantee or a deduction for the Company.

The exercise of a nonqualified stock option would result in ordinary income for the grantee and a deduction for the Company measured by the difference between the option price and the fair market value of the shares received at the time of exercise. Income tax withholding would be required.

The exercise of an incentive stock option would not result in income for the grantee if the grantee (i) does not dispose of the shares within two years after the date of grant or one year after the transfer of shares upon exercise and (ii) is an employee of the Company or a subsidiary of the Company from the date of grant and through and until three months before the exercise date. If these requirements are met, the basis of the shares upon later disposition would be the option price. Any gain will be taxed to the employee as long-term capital gain and the Company would not be entitled to a deduction. The excess of the market value on the exercise date over the option price is an item of tax preference, potentially subject to the alternative minimum tax.

If the grantee disposes of the shares prior to the expiration of either of the holding periods, the grantee would recognize ordinary income and the Company would be entitled to a deduction equal to the lesser of the fair market value of the shares on the exercise date minus the option price or the amount realized on disposition minus the option price. Any gain in excess of the ordinary income portion would be taxable as long-term or short-term capital gain.

SARs and Performance Share Awards. The grant of a SAR or a Performance Share Award would not result in income for the grantee or a deduction for the Company. Upon the exercise of a SAR or the receipt of shares or cash under a Performance Share Award, the grantee would recognize ordinary income and the Company would be entitled to a deduction measured by the fair market value of the shares plus any cash received. Income tax withholding would be required.

Restricted Stock Grants. The grant of Restricted Stock should not result in income for the grantee or in a deduction for the Company for federal income tax purposes, assuming the shares transferred are subject to restrictions resulting in a "substantial risk of forfeiture" as intended by the Company. If there are no such restrictions, the grantee would recognize ordinary income upon receipt of the shares. Any dividends paid to the grantee while the stock remained subject to restriction would be treated as compensation for federal income tax purposes. At the time the restrictions lapse, the grantee would receive ordinary income and the Company would be entitled to a deduction measured by the fair market value of the shares at the time of lapse. Income tax withholding would be required.

Share Awards. If Share Awards are in the nature of shares of Merck Common Stock (as opposed to phantom stock), they generally would be taxable as ordinary income equal to the aggregate of their fair market value when the grant is not subject to a substantial risk of forfeiture. If in the form of phantom stock, Share Awards generally would be taxable as ordinary income equal to the aggregate of their fair market value when convertible to cash or shares that are not subject to a substantial risk of forfeiture. In all events, the Company would be entitled to a deduction for the amount included in the grantee's income.

Other Information

If approved by Company stockholders, the Plan will be effective May 1, 2003 and will terminate on April 30, 2013, unless terminated earlier by the Board of Directors or extended by the Board with the approval of the stockholders. The Board may amend the Plan as it deems advisable but, if the Securities Exchange Act of 1934 requires the Company to obtain stockholder approval, then such approval will be sought. Unless approved by stockholders or as specifically otherwise required by the Plan (for example, in the case of a stock split), no adjustments or reduction of the exercise price of any outstanding incentive may be made in the event of a decline in stock price, either by reducing the exercise price of outstanding incentives or by cancelling outstanding incentives in connection with regranting incentives at a lower price to the same individual. Options are not assignable or transferable except for limited circumstances upon a grantee's death, or pursuant to rules that may be adopted by the Committee. The Committee may establish rules and procedures to permit a grantee to defer recognition of income or gain for incentives under the Plan.

Employees who will participate in the Plan in the future and the amounts of their allotments are to be determined by the Committee subject to any restrictions outlined above. Since no such determinations have yet been made, it is not possible to state the terms of any individual options which may be issued under the Plan or the names or positions of, or respective amounts of the allotment to, any individuals who may participate.

The Board of Directors recommends a vote FOR this proposal.

4. STOCKHOLDER PROPOSAL CONCERNING ANNUAL ELECTION OF DIRECTORS

Mrs. Evelyn Y. Davis, Watergate Office Building, 2600 Virginia Avenue N.W., Suite 215, Washington, D.C. 20037, owner of 450 shares of Common Stock of the Company, has given notice that she intends to present for action at the Annual Meeting the following resolution:

"RESOLVED: That the stockholders of Merck recommend that the Board of Directors take the necessary steps to reinstate the election of directors ANNUALLY, instead of the stagger system which was recently adopted.

"REASONS: Until recently, directors of Merck were elected annually by all shareholders.

"The great majority of New York Stock Exchange listed corporations elect all their directors each year.

"This insures that ALL directors will be more accountable to ALL shareholders each year and to a certain extent prevents the self-perpetuation of the Board.

"Last year the owners of 843,947,121 shares, representing approximately 62.6% of shares voting, voted FOR this proposal.

"If you AGREE, please mark your proxy FOR this resolution."

Board of Directors' Statement in Opposition to the Resolution

The Merck Board believes that the staggered system for electing directors helps assure continuity and stability of the Company's business strategies and policies and reinforces the Company's commitment to its long-term point of view rather than encouraging excessive focus on short-term goals. This benefit is particularly important to a research-based organization such as Merck, where product development often takes many years. Moreover, the Board does not believe that directors who serve three-year terms are any less accountable for short-term results than directors who serve a series of one-year terms. The Company's short-and long-term results demonstrate the commitment of our directors to achieving the Company's goals. The Board also values the wisdom and insight that comes with the institutional knowledge of its directors.

In the event of any unfriendly or unsolicited proposal to take over or restructure the Company, the staggered system would permit the Company time to negotiate with the sponsor, to consider alternative proposals and to assure that stockholder value is maximized. The Board appreciates that the sustained size and strength of the Company's market capitalization make takeover concerns less relevant to Merck than to certain other companies. However, our research continues to show that smaller institutions and individual stockholders, important constituencies to the Company, find the types of protections we outlined particularly valuable.

We think it is important to note that our full Board considers the merits of each stockholder proposal that will come before stockholders. In addition, because of the important corporate governance issues raised by a proposal calling for the annual election of directors, the Board's Committee on Corporate Governance reviews the proposal separately to ensure that it receives a complete assessment. Our system of Committee and full Board review of this issue has been in place for several years.

Stockholder resolutions calling for the annual election of directors have received support from a majority of the voting shares over the last several years. Those proposals were recommendations that the Board take the necessary steps to reinstate the annual election of directors. The steps necessary to eliminate the classified board are adoption of an amendment to the Company's Certificate of Incorporation by the Board and then approval of the amendment by the affirmative vote of 80 percent of the shares entitled to vote. The Company's classified system for electing directors was approved by the Board and adopted by the Company's stockholders in 1985 by an affirmative vote of 79 percent.

The Board does not take lightly any majority vote received on a stockholder proposal, particularly one raising important corporate governance concerns. It continues to evaluate this issue regularly; however, the Board currently believes that this proposal is not in the best interests of the Company or its stockholders.

The Board of Directors recommends a vote AGAINST this proposal.

5. STOCKHOLDER PROPOSAL CONCERNING DIRECTOR NOMINEES

Mr. Morris Scheffler, 59 Flower Road, Valley Stream, NY 11581, owner of 1,231 shares of Common Stock of the Company, has given notice that he intends to present for action at the Annual Meeting the following resolution:

> "RESOLVED: That there be 2 nominees for each new member of the Board of Directors. That a brief resume of their background, experience and stockholdings in the Corporation be delineated. This should make the Board less beholden to the Management and more attuned to the needs of the owners, the employees and the customers of the corporation.
>
> "REASONS: "Corporate democracy" has become an oxymoron. "Crony capitalism" is a more appropriate term. Directors are "selected" by incumbent directors and management. Stockholders, the true owners of the corporation are allowed to vote for the directors anointed by the hierarchy. This is analogous to the "free" elections in many dictatorships. You either voted for the dictator or did not vote. There was no alternative. In our "corporate democracy" you either vote for, against or withhold your vote but there are no alternative directors to vote for. Corporate directors take office unopposed and answer only to fellow directors and not to the owners of the corporation, the stockholders."

Board of Directors' Statement in Opposition to the Resolution

The Board believes the proposal, which requires that the Company nominate two nominees for each new member of the Board, is not in the best interests of the Company or its stockholders.

The Board's Committee on Corporate Governance, which is comprised entirely of independent directors, acts as a screening and nominating committee for candidates to be considered for election to the Board. In this capacity, the Committee considers a nominee's depth of experience, balance of professional interests, required expertise and other factors. The Committee strives to obtain the single most qualified individual for each opening on the Board of Directors, taking into account the strengths and expertise of other Board members at the time. The Board believes that each candidate nominated for stockholder consideration is fully qualified to serve on the Board. Accordingly, the Board believes that doubling the number of candidates to be considered by the stockholders will simply make the process more time consuming and less efficient. It would not have a positive impact on the composition or independence of the Board and would likely result in confusion on the part of stockholders.

In addition, any stockholder who wishes to recommend a person as a director nominee may do so by contacting the Secretary of the Company. The process a stockholder must follow is set forth on pages 11–12 of this proxy statement, in the paragraph describing the Committee on Corporate Governance and its nominating function. Thus, stockholders have a clear opportunity to participate in the nomination of Board members.

The Board believes the Company's current nominating process has achieved a well balanced, diverse and independent Board of Directors, and the changes required by the proposal are unnecessary and not in the best interests of the Company or its stockholders.

The Board of Directors recommends a vote AGAINST this proposal.

6. STOCKHOLDER PROPOSAL CONCERNING EXTENSION OF PRESCRIPTION DRUG PATENTS

The Province of St. Joseph of the Capuchin Order, 1015 North Ninth Street, Milwaukee, WI 53233, owner of 200 shares of Common Stock of the Company, and 20 co-proponents, whose names, addresses and shareholdings will be furnished by the Company upon receiving an oral or written request from a stockholder addressed to the Secretary of the Company, have given notice that they intend to present for action at the Annual Meeting the following resolution:

> "BE IT RESOLVED: "Shareholders request the Board of Directors to develop ethical criteria for the extension of patents on prescription drugs and to issue a report on the implications of such criteria. The Report, prepared at reasonable cost and omitting proprietary information, will be made available to all shareholders by September 2003.
>
> ---
>
> "We believe that every person has the right of access to health care; access to needed health care services and products is essential to human development and well-being.
>
> "Advances in pharmaceutical products play a significant role in countering disease and enhancing human health; approved generic pharmaceuticals, lower in cost but equally effective alternatives to brand names, expand access to needed treatments.
>
> "A National Institute for Health Care Management Study, May 2002, found that:

• Two-thirds of drugs approved by the FDA (1989–2000) were modified or identical versions of existing drugs—"me too" products.

• The percentage of new innovative drugs is decreasing.

• Modified medicines were often more expensive than older medicines, even where the FDA had found that they offered no significant advantages.

"There has been much publicity about excessive marketing of 'me-too' drugs and about strategies to extend patents on brand name pharmaceuticals. Changing a small aspect of a patented drug, suing generic companies or paying generic companies not to market their pharmaceuticals have been called 'devious tactics' by critics and 'gaming the patent system' by the chair of the Federal Trade Commission. Such actions harm a pharmaceutical company's image and affect shareholder value.

"The net result of such actions is not new innovative treatments or cures but:

• Lost cost savings for consumers, including health plans and providers;

• Lost public image when a company appears to renege on the original patent agreement;

• Lost value for shareholders when short term financial gain is chosen over long term value;

• Diminution in the number of truly innovative pharmaceutical products.

"Our Company's CEO has publicly stated that he believes that inappropriately delaying generic drugs is not beneficial for business, the consumer, or the health care system because generics play an important role in keeping down the rate of increase in drug costs. They also free up resources for health plans and providers to be able to afford truly new and innovative drugs which companies bring to market. 'We will not engage in any practices simply to delay the arrival of a generic to the market,' stated Mr. Gilmartin.

"We commend our CEO for his public statement and call upon our Company to take the next leadership steps on the important issue of patents.

"We believe that the requested policy and implementation report would be beneficial to health care consumers and shareholders, and would enhance our Company's image of transparency and accountability.

"Please vote *for* this proposal."

Board of Directors' Statement in Opposition to the Resolution

The Board of Directors recommends against adoption of the proposal. The Board and management of the Company believe that the Company has pursued the protection of its intellectual property in a manner that is in the interests of patients, health care payers and stockholders. As acknowledged by the proponents, Merck management has stated clearly that, while Merck will vigorously defend its patents, it will not pursue baseless legal or other remedies designed merely to delay the entry of generic medicines. The Board believes that taking such actions would be inconsistent with the long-term interests of stockholders.

Further, the issue of alleged unjustified actions to extend patents has been the subject of extensive recent study by the U.S. Federal Trade Commission. In its July 2002 report, Generic Drug Entry Prior to Patent Restoration, the FTC made a series of recommendations to address what it found were eight examples of situations between 1992 and 2000 where pharmaceutical companies had used a provision of the Drug Price Competition and Patent Restoration Act of 1984 (commonly known as the Hatch–Waxman law) to delay generic drug entry in a manner that the FTC found did not enhance competition. None of the cited examples involved a Merck product. In October 2002, President Bush proposed a regulation that would address the main recommendation of the FTC to remedy a flaw the FTC identified in this provision of the Hatch–Waxman law.

Given these facts, the Board believes that the expenditure of Company resources to prepare the proposed "ethical criteria for the extension of patents" would not assist the Company in managing its intellectual property. Instead, management will continue to pursue the policies cited favorably by the proponents.

The Board of Directors recommends a vote AGAINST this proposal.

7. STOCKHOLDER PROPOSAL CONCERNING ETHICAL AND SOCIAL PERFORMANCE OF THE COMPANY

Human Life International, 4 Family Life, Front Royal, VA 22630, owner of 128 shares of Common Stock of the Company, has given notice that it intends to present for action at the Annual Meeting the following resolution:

> "WHEREAS, Merck's Statement on Values says, 'Our business is preserving and improving human life. All of our actions must be measured by our success in achieving this goal. We are committed to the highest standards of ethics and integrity.'
>
> "WHEREAS, we believe Merck has violated its basic Statement on Values because of our Company's use of cell-culture lines from aborted humans.

"BE IT RESOLVED: The Board of Directors appoint a special committee of the Board, consisting solely of independent Board members, to review ways to link executive compensation with the Company's ethical and social performance, and in particular, with Merck's Statement on Values, and to report to the shareholders the results of the review. This report may omit confidential information and be prepared at reasonable cost."

Board of Directors' Statement in Opposition to the Resolution

The Board of Directors agrees that corporate conduct is inseparable from the conduct of individual employees in the performance of their work. Every Merck employee is responsible for adhering to business practices that are in accordance with the letter and spirit of applicable laws and with ethical principles that reflect the highest standards of corporate and individual behavior.

The Board notes that in May 1995, the Company established the Office of Ethics to help protect and promote the Company's high ethical standards on a worldwide basis by developing and overseeing global initiatives designed to deter illegal, unethical and improper behavior related to the Company's business. The Office also serves as an additional channel for the receipt and investigation of reports of unethical practices and for the investigation and resolution of internal complaints involving the management and fair treatment of employees.

The Company's unwavering commitment to high ethical standards applies to every aspect of its business, including its policies and practices related to use of cell culture lines, as it discovers, develops, manufactures and markets a broad range of innovative products to improve human and animal health.

The proposal seeks to have the Company appoint a committee made up of independent directors to review ways to link compensation with the Company's ethical and social performance. The Compensation and Benefits Committee of the Board, which is comprised entirely of independent directors, establishes compensation objectives and policies for all employees and sets compensation for the Company's executive officers. In evaluating performance and setting executive compensation, the Committee considers the Company's leadership principles which, among other things, are intended to support actions that reflect a high degree of integrity and ethics. In addition, the Committee on Public Policy and Social Responsibility, which also is comprised entirely of independent directors, monitors and evaluates factors that impact the ethical and social performance of the Company. In particular, it advises the Board of Directors and management on Company policies and practices that pertain to the Company's responsibilities as a global corporate citizen, its special obligations as a pharmaceutical company whose products and services affect health and quality of life around the world, and its commitment to the highest standards of ethics and integrity in all its dealings.

For these reasons, the Board of Directors feels that the proposal is unnecessary and contrary to the interests of the Company and its stockholders.

The Board of Directors recommends a vote AGAINST this proposal.

SECTION 16(a) BENEFICIAL OWNERSHIP REPORTING COMPLIANCE

Section 16(a) of the Securities Exchange Act of 1934 requires the Company's officers and directors, and persons who own more than 10 percent of a registered class of the Company's equity securities, to file reports of ownership and changes in ownership of such securities with the Securities and Exchange Commission and the New York Stock Exchange. Officers, directors and greater than 10–percent beneficial owners are required by applicable regulations to furnish the Company with copies of all Section 16(a) forms they file. We are not aware of any beneficial owner of more than 10 percent of our Common Stock.

Based solely upon a review of the copies of the forms furnished to the Company, or written representations from certain reporting persons that no Forms 5 were required, we believe that all filing requirements applicable to our officers and directors were complied with during the 2002 fiscal year.

OTHER MATTERS

The Board of Directors is not aware of any other matters to come before the meeting. However, if any other matters properly come before the meeting, it is the intention of the persons named in the enclosed proxy to vote said proxy in accordance with their judgment in such matters.

MERK & CO., INC.

March 20, 2003

Appendix A

AUDIT COMMITTEE CHARTER

Effective February 25, 2003, the Committee is comprised solely of independent directors, to serve at the pleasure of the Board.

MEMBERS

Heidi G. Miller, Chairperson*
Lawrence A. Bossidy
Thomas E. Shenk
Samuel O. Thier

The Chairperson of the Committee or, if not present, the senior outside Director present shall preside at all meetings of the Committee and provide an oral report to the Board on each meeting. The Committee shall hold a minimum of four meetings annually. The Company shall provide the Committee with adequate staff support and resources to discharge its responsibilities. The Committee may engage independent legal counsel and other advisors as the Committee deems advisable to carry out its responsibilities. The Company shall provide the Committee with full funding to engage the Company's independent public accountants as well as to retain independent counsel and other advisors for the Committee.

The Committee shall meet privately with the internal auditors and the independent public accountants at least quarterly and whenever else the Committee deems advisable. The Committee shall ensure that the independent public accountants are ultimately accountable to the Committee and the Board. The Committee's performance shall be evaluated annually by the Committee.

The Controller of the Company is the Secretary of the Committee. Minutes of each meeting will be prepared by the Secretary and submitted to Committee members for approval at the next meeting.

MEMBERSHIP REQUIREMENTS

The Committee must be comprised of at least three directors, each of whom is independent and "financially literate," and at least one of whom is an "audit committee financial expert," as such terms are defined in applicable New York Stock Exchange (NYSE) and Securities and Exchange Commission (SEC) rules and regulations.

Committee members may not simultaneously serve on the audit committee of more than three public companies, including the Company, unless the Board determines that such simultaneous service does not impair efficacy of Board service.

* Member is an "audit committee financial expert" as that term is defined in Item 401 of Regulation S–K promulgated by the SEC and she

is "independent of management" as that term is defined in Item 7(d)(3)(iv) of Schedule 14A promulgated by the SEC.

PURPOSE

1. Assist in the Board oversight of:
   - The integrity of the Company's financial statements.
   - The Company's compliance with legal and regulatory requirements.
   - The independent public accountants' qualifications and independence.
   - The performance of the Company's internal audit function and the independent public accountants.
   - The accounting and financial reporting processes of the Company and its audits.
2. Prepare the Audit Committee report for inclusion in the proxy statement as required by the SEC.

DUTIES AND RESPONSIBILITIES

1. Appoint, evaluate, and retain the Company's independent public accountants. Maintain direct responsibility for termination, compensation and oversight of the Company's independent public accountants (including the resolution of disagreements between management and the independent public accountants regarding financial reporting). The Company's independent public accountants shall report directly to the Committee.
2. Approve all services provided to the Company by the independent public accountants and review all non-attest services to ensure they are permitted under current law and regulation. Alternatively, establish policies and procedures for the pre-approval of services provided by the independent public accountants in a manner that complies with current federal securities laws and NYSE regulations.
3. Oversee the Company's accounting, financial reporting process, internal controls and audits. Consult with management, the internal auditors and the independent public accountants on matters related to the annual audit plan, audit procedures applied, audit and nonaudit fees, status of federal tax returns and related reserves, the published financial statements, the accounting principles applied, and any material changes thereto. Meet with the independent public accountants and internal auditors to discuss the results of their examinations.
4. Review at least annually a report of the independent public accountants describing their internal control procedures, material issues raised by such review and certain inquiries or investigations by

governmental or professional authorities, and all relationships between the independent public accountants and the Company. After reviewing the foregoing report and the independent public accountants' work, the Committee shall evaluate the independent public accountants' qualifications, performance and independence, including a review and evaluation of the lead partner of the independent public accountants.

5. Receive and review any other reports from the independent public accountants that are required under Generally Accepted Auditing Standards, other standards governing the independent public accountants or by the federal securities laws or NYSE.
6. Discuss the annual audited financial statements and quarterly statements, including Management's Discussion and Analysis, with management and the independent public accountants.
7. Discuss with management earnings press releases and financial information and earnings guidance provided to analysts and rating agencies. Review for compliance with regulations governing the use of non-Generally Accepted Accounting Principles financial measures and related disclosure requirements.
8. Engage independent legal, accounting and other advisors, as the Committee determines necessary to carry out their duties, and obtain appropriate funding from the Company, as determined by the Committee, for compensating such advisors.
9. Discuss policies with respect to risk assessment and management.
10. Meet separately with management, internal auditors and independent public accountants on a periodic basis.
11. Review with the independent public accountants any audit issues and management's response.
12. Set clear policies for the Company's hiring of employees or former employees of the independent public accountants.
13. Report regularly to the Board of Directors.
14. Review any significant issues concerning litigation and contingencies with management, counsel and the independent public accountants.
15. Review the insurance program of the Company and make recommendations to the Board on insurance policy.
16. Monitor compliance with the Foreign Corrupt Practices Act and the Company's policies on ethical business practices and report on the same to the Board.
17. Establish procedures for the receipt, retention and treatment, on a confidential basis, of complaints received by the Company, including the Board and the Audit Committee, regarding accounting,

internal accounting controls or auditing matters, and the confidential, anonymous submissions by employees of concerns regarding questionable accounting or auditing matters.

18. Review and reassess the adequacy of the Committee charter annually and make changes as appropriate.

19. Review and evaluate the performance of the Committee and its members annually.

QUORUM

For the transaction of business at any meeting of the Committee, two members shall constitute a quorum.

Appendix B

MERCK & CO., INC.
2003 INCENTIVE STOCK PLAN
(Effective May 1, 2003)

1. Purpose

The 2003 Incentive Stock Plan (the "Plan"), effective May 1, 2003, is established to encourage employees of Merck & Co., Inc. (the "Company"), its subsidiaries, its affiliates and its joint ventures to acquire Common Stock in the Company ("Common Stock"). It is believed that the Plan will serve the interests of the Company and its stockholders because it allows employees to have a greater personal financial interest in the Company through ownership of, or the right to acquire its Common Stock, which in turn will stimulate employees' efforts on the Company's behalf, and maintain and strengthen their desire to remain with the Company. It is believed that the Plan also will assist in the recruitment of employees.

2. Administration

The Plan shall be administered by the Compensation and Benefits Committee of the Board of Directors of the Company (the "Committee"). A Director of the Company may serve on the Committee only if he or she (i) is a "Non–Employee Director" for purposes of Rule 16b–3 under the Securities Exchange Act of 1934, as amended (the "Exchange Act", and (ii) satisfies the requirements of an "outside director" for purposes of Section 162(m) of the Internal Revenue Code (the "Code"). The Committee shall be responsible for the administration of the Plan including, without limitation, determining which Eligible Employees receive Incentives, the types of Incentives they receive under the Plan, the number of shares covered by Incentives granted under the Plan, and the other terms and conditions of such Incentives. Determinations by the Committee under the Plan including, without limitation, determinations of the Eligible Employees, the form, amount and timing of Incentives, the terms and provisions of Incentives and the writings evidencing Incentives, need not be uniform and may be made selectively among Eligible Employees who receive, or are eligible to receive, Incentives hereunder, whether or not such Eligible Employees are similarly situated.

The Committee shall have the responsibility of construing and interpreting the Plan, including the right to construe disputed or doubtful Plan provisions, and of establishing, amending and construing such rules and regulations as it may deem necessary or desirable for the proper administration of the Plan. Any decision or action taken or to be taken by the Committee, arising out of or in connection with the construction, administration, interpretation and effect of the Plan and of its rules and regulations, shall, to the maximum extent permitted by applicable law, be within its absolute discretion (except as otherwise specifically provided herein) and shall be final, binding and conclusive upon the Company, all Eligible Employees and any person claiming under or through any Eligible Employee.

The Committee, as permitted by applicable state law, may delegate any or all of its power and authority hereunder to the Chief Executive Officer or such other senior member of management as the Committee deems appropriate; provided, however, that the Committee may not delegate its authority with regard to any matter or action affecting an officer subject to Section 16 of the Exchange Act and that no such delegation shall be made in the case of Incentives intended to be qualified under Section 162(m) of the Code.

For the purpose of this section and all subsequent sections, the Plan shall be deemed to include this Plan and any comparable sub-plans established by subsidiaries which, in the aggregate, shall constitute one Plan governed by the terms set forth herein.

3. Eligibility

(a) **Employees.** Regular full-time and part-time employees employed by the Company, its parent, if any, or its subsidiaries, its affiliates and its joint ventures, including officers, whether or not directors of the Company, and employees of a joint venture partner or affiliate of the Company who provide services to the joint venture with such partner or affiliate (each such person, an "Employee"), shall be eligible to participate in the Plan if designated by the Committee ("Eligible Employees").

(b) **Non-employees.** The term "Employee" shall not include any of the following (collectively, "Excluded Persons"): a director who is not an employee or an officer; a person who is an independent contractor, or agrees or has agreed that he/she is an independent contractor; a person who has any agreement or understanding with the Company, or any of its affiliates or joint venture partners that he/she is not an employee or an Eligible Employee, even if he/she previously had been an employee or Eligible Employee; a person who is employed by a temporary or other employment agency, regardless of the amount of control, supervision or training provided by the Company or its affiliates; or a "leased employee" as defined under Section 414 (n) of the Code. An Excluded Person is not an Eligible Employee and cannot receive Incentives even if a court, agency or other authority rules that he/she is a common-law employee of the Company or its affiliates.

(c) **No Right To Continued Employment.** Nothing in the Plan shall interfere with or limit in any way the right of the Company, its parent, its subsidiaries, its affiliates or its joint ventures to terminate the employment of any participant at any time, nor confer upon any participant the right to continue in the employ of the Company, its parent, its subsidiaries, its affiliates or its joint ventures. No Eligible Employee shall have a right to receive an Incentive or any other benefit under this Plan or having been granted an Incentive or other benefit, to receive any additional Incentive or other benefit. Neither the award of an Incentive nor any benefits arising under such Incentives shall constitute an employment contract with the Company, its parent, its subsidiaries, its affiliates or its joint ventures, and accordingly, this Plan and the benefits hereunder may be terminated at any time in the sole and exclusive discretion of the Company without giving rise to liability on the part of the Company, its parent, its subsidiaries, its affiliates or its joint ventures for severance. Except as may be otherwise specifically stated in any other employee benefit plan, policy or program, neither any Incentive under this Plan nor any amount realized from any such Incentive shall be treated as compensation for any purposes of calculating an employee's benefit under any such plan, policy or program.

4. Term of the Plan

This Plan shall be effective as of May 1, 2003, subject to the approval of the Plan by the affirmative vote of the stockholders of the Company entitled to vote thereon at the time of such approval. No Incentive shall be granted under the Plan after April 30, 2013, but the term and exercise of Incentives granted theretofore may extend beyond that date.

5. Incentives

Incentives under the Plan may be granted in any one or a combination of (a) Incentive Stock Options, (b) Nonqualified Stock Options, (c) Stock Appreciation Rights, (d) Restricted Stock Grants, (e) Performance Shares, (f) Share Awards and (g) Phantom Stock Awards (collectively "Incentives"). All Incentives shall be subject to the terms and conditions set forth herein and to such other terms and conditions as may be established by the Committee.

6. Shares Available for Incentives

(a) **Shares Available.** Subject to the provisions of Section 6(c), the maximum number of shares of Common Stock of the Company that may be issued under the Plan is 115 million. Any shares under this Plan or under the predecessor Incentive Stock Plans that are not purchased or awarded under an Incentive that has lapsed, expired, terminated or been canceled, may be used for the further grant of Incentives under the Plan. Incentives and similar awards issued by an entity that is merged into or with the Company, acquired by the Company or otherwise involved in a similar corporate transaction with the Company are not considered issued under this Plan. Shares under this Plan may be delivered by the Company from its authorized but unissued shares of Common Stock or from issued and reacquired Common Stock held as treasury stock, or both. In no event shall fractional shares of Common Stock be issued under the Plan.

(b) **Limit on an Individual's Incentives.** In any calendar year, no Eligible Employee may receive (i) Incentives covering more than 3 million shares of the Company's Common Stock (such number of shares shall be adjusted in accordance with Section 6(c)), or (ii) any Incentive if such person owns more than 10 percent of the stock of the Company within the meaning of Section 422 of the Code, or (iii) any Incentive Stock Option, as defined in Section 422 of the Code, that would result in such person receiving a grant of Incentive Stock Options for stock that would have an aggregate fair market value in excess of $100,000, determined as of the time that the Incentive Stock Option is granted, that would be exercisable for the first time by such person during any calendar year.

(c) **Adjustment of Shares.** In the event of a reorganization, recapitalization, stock split, stock dividend, combination of shares, merger, consolidation, rights offering, spin off, split off, split up or other event identified by the Committee, the Committee shall make such adjustments, if any, as it may deem appropriate in (i) the number and kind of shares authorized for issuance under the Plan, (ii) the number and kind of shares subject to outstanding Incentives, (iii) the option price of Stock Options and (iv) the fair market value of Stock Appreciation Rights, provided that fractions of a share will be rounded down to the nearest whole share (other than for Incentive Stock Options). Any such determination shall be final, binding and conclusive on all parties.

7. Stock Options

The Committee may grant options qualifying as Incentive Stock Options as defined in Section 422 of the Code, and options other than Incentive Stock Options ("Nonqualified Options") (collectively "Stock Options"). Such Stock Options shall be subject to the following terms and conditions and such other terms and conditions as the Committee may prescribe:

(a) **Stock Option Price.** The option price per share with respect to each Stock Option shall be determined by the Committee, but shall not be less than 100 percent of the fair market value of the Common Stock on the date the Stock Option is granted, as determined by the Committee.

(b) **Period of Stock Option.** The period of each Stock Option shall be fixed by the Committee, provided that the period for all Stock Options shall not exceed ten years from the grant, provided further, however, that, in the event of the death of an Optionee prior to the expiration of a Nonqualified Option, such Nonqualified Option may, if the Committee so determines, be exercisable for up to eleven years from the date of the grant. The Committee may, subsequent to the granting of any Stock Option, extend the term thereof, but in no event shall the extended term exceed ten years from the original grant date.

(c) **Exercise of Stock Option and Payment Therefore.** No shares shall be issued until full payment of the option price has been made. The option price may be paid in cash or, if the Committee determines, in shares of Common Stock or a combination of cash and shares of Common Stock. If the Committee approves the use of shares of Common Stock as a payment method, the Committee shall establish such conditions as it deems appropriate for the use of Common Stock to exercise a Stock Option. Stock Options awarded under the Plan shall be exercised through such procedure or program as the Committee may establish or define from time to time, which may include a designated broker that must be used in exercising such Stock Options. The Committee may establish rules and procedures to permit an optionholder to defer recognition of gain upon the exercise of a Stock Option.

(d) **First Exercisable Date**. The Committee shall determine how and when shares covered by a Stock Option may be purchased. The Committee may establish waiting periods, the dates on which Stock Options become exercisable or "vested" and, subject to paragraph (b) of this section, exercise periods. The Committee may accelerate the exercisability of any Stock Option or portion thereof.

(e) **Termination of Employment.** Unless determined otherwise by the Committee, upon the termination of a Stock Option grantee's employment (for any reason other than gross misconduct), Stock Option privileges shall be limited to the shares that were immediately exercisable at the date of such termination. The Committee, however, in its discretion, may provide that any Stock Options outstanding but not yet exercisable upon the termination of a Stock Option grantee's employment may become exercisable in accordance with a schedule determined by the Committee. Such Stock Option privileges shall expire unless exercised within such period of time after the date of termination of employment as may be established by the Committee, but in no event later than the expiration date of the Stock Option.

(f) **Termination Due to Misconduct**. If a Stock Option grantee's employment is terminated for gross misconduct, as determined by the Company, all rights under the Stock Option shall expire upon the date of such termination.

(g) **Limits on Incentive Stock Options**. Except as may otherwise be permitted by the Code, an Eligible Employee may not receive a grant of Incentive Stock Options for stock that would have an aggregate fair market value in excess of $100,000 (or such other amount as the Internal Revenue Service may decide from time to time), determined as of the time that the Incentive Stock Option is granted, that would be exercisable for the first time by such person during any calendar year.

8. Stock Appreciation Rights

The Committee may, in its discretion, grant a right to receive the appreciation in the fair market value of shares of Common Stock ("Stock Appreciation Right") either singly or in combination with an underlying Stock Option granted hereunder. Such Stock Appreciation Right shall be subject to the following terms and conditions and such other terms and conditions as the Committee may prescribe:

(a) **Time and Period of Grant.** If a Stock Appreciation Right is granted with respect to an underlying Stock Option, it may be granted at the time of the Stock Option grant or at any time thereafter but prior to the expiration of the Stock Option grant. If a Stock Appreciation Right is granted with respect to an underlying Stock Option, at the time the Stock Appreciation Right is granted the Committee may limit the exercise period for such Stock Appreciation Right, before and after which period no Stock Appreciation Right shall attach to the underlying Stock Option. In no event shall the exercise period for a Stock Appreciation Right granted with respect to an underlying Stock Option exceed the exercise period for such Stock Option. If a Stock Appreciation Right is granted without an underlying Stock Option, the period for exercise of the Stock Appreciation Right shall be set by the Committee.

(b) **Value of Stock Appreciation Right.** If a Stock Appreciation Right is granted with respect to an underlying Stock Option, the grantee will be entitled to surrender the Stock Option which is then exercisable and receive in exchange therefor an amount equal to the excess of the fair market value of the Common Stock on the date the election to surrender is received by the Company in accordance with exercise procedures established by the Company over the Stock Option price (the "Spread") multiplied by the number of shares covered by the Stock Option which is surrendered. If a Stock Appreciation Right is granted without an underlying Stock Option, the grantee will receive upon exercise of the Stock Appreciation Right an amount equal to the excess of the fair market value of the Common Stock on the date the election to surrender such Stock Appreciation Right is received by the Company in accordance with exercise procedures established by the Company over the fair market value of the Common Stock on the date of grant multiplied by the number of shares covered by the grant of the Stock Appreciation Right. Notwithstanding the foregoing, in its sole discretion the Committee at the time it grants a Stock Appreciation Right may provide that the Spread covered by such Stock Appreciation Right may not exceed a specified amount.

(c) **Payment of Stock Appreciation Right.** Payment of a Stock Appreciation Right shall be in the form of shares of Common Stock, cash or any combination of shares and cash. The form of payment upon exercise of such a right shall be determined by the Committee either at the time of grant of the Stock Appreciation Right or at the time of exercise of the Stock Appreciation Right.

9. Performance Share Awards

The Committee may grant awards under which payment may be made in shares of Common Stock, cash or any combination of shares and cash if the performance of the Company or its parent or any subsidiary, division, affiliate or joint venture of the Company selected by the Committee during the Award Period meets certain goals established by the Committee ("Performance Share Awards"). Such Performance Share Awards shall be subject to the following terms and conditions and such other terms and conditions as the Committee may prescribe:

(a) **Award Period and Performance Goals.** The Committee shall determine and include in a Performance Share Award grant the period of time for which a Performance Share Award is made ("Award Period"). The Committee also shall establish performance objectives ("Performance Goals") to be met by the Company, its parent, subsidiary, division, affiliate or joint venture of the Company during the Award Period as a condition to payment of the Performance Share Award. The Performance Goals may include share price, pre-tax profits, earnings per share, return on stockholders' equity, return on assets, sales, net income or any combination of the foregoing or, solely for an Award not intended to constitute "performance-based compensation" under Section 162(m) of the Code, any other financial or other measurement established by the Committee. The Performance Goals may include minimum and optimum objectives or a single set of objectives.

(b) **Payment of Performance Share Awards.** The Committee shall establish the method of calculating the amount of payment to be made under a Performance Share Award if the Performance Goals are met, including the fixing of a maximum payment. The Performance Share Award shall be expressed in terms of shares of Common Stock and referred to as "Performance Shares." After the completion of an Award Period, the performance of the Company, its parent, subsidiary, division, affiliate or joint venture of the Company shall be measured against the Performance Goals, and the Committee shall determine, in accordance with the terms of such Performance Share Award, whether all, none or any portion of a Performance Share Award shall be paid. The Committee, in its discretion, may elect to make payment in shares of Common Stock, cash or a combination of shares and cash. Any cash payment shall be based on the fair market value of Performance Shares on, or as soon as practicable prior to, the date of payment. The Committee may establish rules and procedures to permit a grantee to defer recognition of income upon the attainment of a Performance Share Award.

(c) **Revision of Performance Goals.** As to any Award not intended to constitute "performance-based compensation" under Section 162(m) of the Code, at any time prior to the end of an Award Period, the Committee may revise the Performance Goals and the computation of payment if unforeseen events occur which have a substantial effect on the performance of the Company, its parent, subsidiary, division, affiliate or joint venture of the Company and which, in the judgment of the Committee, make the application of the Performance Goals unfair unless a revision is made.

(d) **Requirement of Employment.** A grantee of a Performance Share Award must remain in the employ of the Company, its parent, subsidiary, affiliate or joint venture until the completion of the Award Period in order to be entitled to payment under the Performance Share Award; provided that the Committee may, in its discretion, provide for a full or partial payment where such an exception is deemed equitable.

(e) **Dividends.** The Committee may, in its discretion, at the time of the granting of a Performance Share Award, provide that any dividends declared on the Common Stock during the Award Period, and which would have been paid with respect to Performance Shares had they been owned by a grantee, be (i) paid to the grantee, or (ii) accumulated for the benefit of the grantee and used to increase the number of Performance Shares of the grantee.

(f) **Limit on Performance Share Awards.** Incentives granted as Performance Share Awards under this section, Restricted Stock Grants under Section 10 and Other Share Based Awards under Section 11 shall not exceed, in the aggregate, 12 million shares of Common Stock (such number of shares shall be adjusted in accordance with Section 6(c)).

10. Restricted Stock Grants

The Committee may award shares of Common Stock to an Eligible Employee, which shares shall be subject to the following terms and conditions and such other terms and conditions as the Committee may prescribe ("Restricted Stock Grant"):

(a) **Requirement of Employment.** A grantee of a Restricted Stock Grant must remain in the employment of the Company during a period designated by the Committee ("Restriction Period") in order to retain the shares under the Restricted Stock Grant. If the grantee leaves the employment of the Company prior to the end of the Restriction Period, the Restricted Stock Grant shall terminate and the shares of Common Stock shall be returned immediately to the Company provided that the Committee may, at the time of the grant, provide for the employment restriction to lapse with respect to a portion or portions of the Restricted Stock Grant at different times during the Restriction Period. The Committee may, in its discretion, also provide for such complete or partial exceptions to the employment restriction as it deems equitable.

(b) **Restrictions on Transfer and Legend on Stock Certificates.** During the Restriction Period, the grantee may not sell, assign, transfer, pledge or otherwise dispose of the shares of Common Stock. Each certificate for shares of Common Stock issued hereunder shall contain a legend giving appropriate notice of the restrictions in the grant.

(c) **Escrow Agreement.** The Committee may require the grantee to enter into an escrow agreement providing that the certificates representing the Restricted Stock Grant will remain in the physical custody of an escrow holder until all restrictions are removed or expire.

(d) **Lapse of Restrictions.** All restrictions imposed under the Restricted Stock Grant shall lapse upon the expiration of the Restriction Period if the conditions as to employment set forth above have been met. The grantee shall then be entitled to have the legend removed from the certificates. The Committee may establish rules and procedures to permit a grantee to defer recognition of income upon the expiration of the Restriction Period.

(e) **Dividends.** The Committee shall, in its discretion, at the time of the Restricted Stock Grant, provide that any dividends declared on the Common Stock during the Restriction Period shall either be (i) paid to the grantee, or (ii) accumulated for the benefit of the grantee and paid to the grantee only after the expiration of the Restriction Period.

(f) **Performance Goals.** The Committee may designate whether any Restricted Stock Grant is intended to be "performance-based compensation" as that term is used in Section 162(m) of the Code. Any such Restricted Stock Grant designated to be "performance-based compensation" shall be conditioned on the achievement of one or more Performance Goals (as defined in Section 9(a)), to the extent required by Section 162(m).

(g) **Limit on Restricted Stock Grant.** Incentives granted as Restricted Stock Grants under this section, Performance Share Awards under Section 9 and Other Share Based Awards under Section 11 shall not exceed, in the aggregate, 12 million shares of Common Stock (such number of shares shall be adjusted in accordance with Section 6(c)).

11. Other Share–Based Awards

The Committee may grant an award of shares of common stock (a "Share Award") to any Eligible Employee on such terms and conditions as the Committee may determine in its sole discretion. Share Awards may be made as additional compensation for services rendered by the Eligible Employee or may be in lieu of cash or other compensation to which the Eligible Employee is entitled from the Company. Incentives granted as Share Based Awards under this section, Performance Share Awards under Section 9 and Restricted Stock Grants under Section 10 shall not exceed, in the aggregate, 12 million shares of Common Stock (such number of shares shall be adjusted in accordance with Section 6(c)).

12. Transferability

Each Incentive Stock Option granted under the Plan shall not be transferable other than by will or the laws of descent and distribution; each other Incentive granted under the Plan will not be transferable or assignable by the recipient, and may not be made subject to execution, attachment or similar procedures, other than by will or the laws of descent and distribution or as determined by the Committee in accordance with regulations promulgated under the Securities Exchange Act of 1934, or any other applicable law or regulation. Notwithstanding the foregoing, the Committee, in its discretion, may adopt rules permitting the transfer, solely as gifts during the grantee's lifetime, of Stock Options (other than Incentive Stock Options) to members of a grantee's immediate family or to trusts, family partnerships or similar entities for the benefit of such immediate family members. For this purpose, immediate family member means the grantee's spouse, parent, child, stepchild, grandchild and the spouses of such family members. The terms of a Stock Option shall be final, binding and conclusive upon the beneficiaries, executors, administrators, heirs and successors of the grantee.

13. Discontinuance or Amendment of the Plan

The Board of Directors may discontinue the Plan at any time and may from time to time amend or revise the terms of the Plan as permitted by applicable statutes, except that it may not, without the consent of the grantees affected, revoke or alter, in a manner unfavorable to the grantees of any Incentives hereunder, any Incentives then outstanding, nor may the Board amend the Plan without stockholder approval where the absence of such approval would cause the Plan to fail to comply with Rule 16b–3 under the Exchange Act, or any other requirement of applicable law or regulation. Unless approved by the Company's stockholders or as otherwise specifically provided under this Plan, no adjustments or reduction of the exercise price of any outstanding Incentives shall be made in the event of a decline in stock price, either by reducing the exercise price of outstanding Incentives or through cancellation of outstanding Incentives in connection with regranting of Incentives at a lower price to the same individual.

14. No Limitation on Compensation

Nothing in the Plan shall be construed to limit the right of the Company to establish other plans or to pay compensation to its employees, in cash or property, in a manner which is not expressly authorized under the Plan.

15. No Constraint on Corporate Action

Nothing in the Plan shall be construed (i) to limit, impair or otherwise affect the Company's right or power to make adjustments, reclassifications, reorganizations or changes of its capital or business structure, or to merge or consolidate, or dissolve, liquidate, sell or transfer all or any part of its business or assets, or (ii) except as provided in Section 13, to limit the right or power of the Company, its parent, or any subsidiary, affiliate or joint venture to take any action which such entity deems to be necessary or appropriate.

16. Withholding Taxes

The Company shall be entitled to deduct from any payment under the Plan, regardless of the form of such payment, the amount of all applicable income and employment taxes required by law to be withheld with respect to such payment or may require the Eligible Employee to pay to it such tax prior to and as a condition of the making of such payment. In accordance with any applicable administrative guidelines it establishes, the Committee may allow an Eligible Employee to pay the amount of taxes required by law to be withheld from an Incentive by withholding from any payment of Common Stock due as a result of such Incentive, or by permitting the Eligible Employee to deliver to the Company, shares of Common Stock having a fair market value, as determined by the Committee, equal to the amount of such required withholding taxes.

17. Compliance with Section 16

With respect to Eligible Employees subject to Section 16 of the Exchange Act ("Section 16 Officers"), transactions under the Plan are intended to comply with all applicable conditions of Rule 16b–3 or its successor under the Exchange Act. To the extent that compliance with any Plan provision applicable solely to the Section 16 Officers is not required in order to bring a transaction by such Section 16 Officer into compliance with Rule 16b–3, it shall be deemed null and void as to such transaction, to the extent permitted by law and deemed advisable by the Committee and its delegees. To the extent any provision of the Plan or action by the Plan administrators involving such Section 16 Officers is deemed not to comply with an applicable condition of Rule 16b–3, it shall be deemed null and void as to such Section 16 Officers, to the extent permitted by law and deemed advisable by the Plan administrators.

18. Use of Proceeds

The proceeds received by the Company from the sale of stock under the Plan shall be added to the general funds of the Company and shall be used for such corporate purposes as the Board of Directors shall direct.

19. Governing Law

The Plan, and all agreements hereunder, shall be construed in accordance with and governed by the laws of the State of New Jersey without giving effect to the principles of conflicts of laws.

20. Offset and Suspension of Exercise

Anything to the contrary in the Plan notwithstanding, the Plan administrators may (i) offset any Incentive by amounts reasonably believed to be owed to the Company by the grantee and (ii) disallow an Incentive to be exercised or otherwise payable during a time when the Company is investigating reasonably reliable allegations of gross misconduct by the grantee.

5. FORM OF PROXY, MERCK & CO.

MERCK

YOUR VOTE IS IMPORTANT
VOTE BY TELEPHONE / INTERNET
24 HOURS A DAY, 7 DAYS A WEEK

VOTE BY PHONE: **Call TOLL-FREE: 1-888-297-9639**

- Use any touch-tone telephone.
- Have your proxy card ready.
- Enter your Control Number located in the box below.
- Follow the simple recorded instructions.

VOTE BY INTERNET: ***The Web Address is:*** **http://www.proxyvoting.com/merck**

- Go to the web address listed above.
- Have your proxy card ready.
- Enter your Control Number located in the box below.
- Follow the simple instructions that appear on your computer screen.

IF YOU VOTE BY TELEPHONE OR BY INTERNET, DO NOT MAIL THE PROXY CARD. YOUR TELEPHONE OR INTERNET VOTE AUTHORIZES THE NAMED PROXIES TO VOTE YOUR SHARES IN THE SAME MANNER AS IF YOU VOTED YOUR PROXY CARD EXCEPT FOR THE CUMULATIVE VOTING FEATURE APPLICABLE TO THE ELECTION OF DIRECTORS, WHICH IS ONLY AVAILABLE BY VOTING THE PROXY CARD. THE TELEPHONE AND INTERNET VOTING FACILITIES WILL CLOSE AT 12:01 A.M. ON APRIL 22, 2003.

CONTROL NUMBER FOR TELEPHONE / INTERNET VOTING

SPECIMEN

▼ **DETACH PROXY CARD HERE IF YOU ARE NOT VOTING BY TELEPHONE OR BY INTERNET** ▼

The Board of Directors recommends a vote FOR Items 1, 2 and 3.

1. Election of Directors – The Board of Directors recommends a vote FOR the nominees listed below:

Nominees: 01 – Lawrence A. Bossidy* 02 – Johnnetta B. Cole*
03 – William B. Harrison, Jr.* 04 – William N. Kelley*
05 – Heidi G. Miller*

*Term expiring 2006

FOR all nominees listed	**WITHHOLD AUTHORITY** to vote for all nominees listed	**EXCEPTIONS**
☐	☐	☐

To withhold authority to vote for any individual nominee, mark the "Exceptions" box and write that nominee's name in the space provided below.

Exceptions ______________________________

To cumulate votes as to a particular nominee(s) as explained in the Proxy Statement, indicate the name(s) and the number of votes to be given to such nominee(s).

Cumulate ______________________________

	FOR	AGAINST	ABSTAIN
2. Ratification of the Appointment of Independent Public Accountants	☐	☐	☐
3. Adoption of the 2003 Incentive Stock Plan	☐	☐	☐

The Board of Directors recommends a vote AGAINST Items 4, 5, 6 and 7.

	FOR	AGAINST	ABSTAIN
4. *Stockholder Proposal Concerning Annual Election of Directors*	☐	☐	☐
5. *Stockholder Proposal Concerning Director Nominees*	☐	☐	☐
6. *Stockholder Proposal Concerning Extension of Prescription Drug Patents*	☐	☐	☐
7. *Stockholder Proposal Concerning Ethical and Social Performance of the Company*	☐	☐	☐

Proxy Card

I plan to attend the Annual Meeting. ☐

I would like to access future Proxy Statements and Annual Reports electronically (as described in the enclosed document). ☐

Please sign exactly as name or names appear on this Proxy Card. When signing as attorney, executor, administrator, trustee, custodian or guardian, give full title. If there is more than one named stockholder, all should sign unless evidence of authority to sign on behalf of others is attached.

Dated: ______________________________

____
Signature of Stockholder

____
Signature of Stockholder

Please complete, sign, date and return the Proxy Card promptly using the enclosed envelope.

II. PARTNERSHIPS

A. UNIFORM PARTNERSHIP ACT

1914 ACT

GENERAL NOTES

See, also, Uniform Partnership Act (1997), supra.

Contents & Prefatory Notes

PART I. PRELIMINARY PROVISIONS

Commissioners' Prefatory Note

The subject of a uniform law on partnership was taken up by the Conference of Commissioners on Uniform State Laws in 1902, and the Committee on Commercial Law was instructed to employ an expert and prepare a draft to be submitted to the next annual Conference. (See Am.Bar Assn.Report for 1902, p. 477.) At the meeting in 1903 the committee reported that it had secured the services of James Barr Ames, Dean of the Law School of Harvard University, as expert to draft the act. (See Am.Bar Assn.Report for 1903, p. 501.)

In 1905 the Committee on Commercial Law reported progress on this subject, and a resolution was passed by the Conference, directing that a draft be prepared upon the mercantile theory. (See Am.Bar Assn.Reports, 1905, pp. 731–738.) And in 1909 the committee reported that it had in its hands a draft of an act on this subject, which draft was recommitted to the committee for revision and amendment, with directions to report to the next Conference for discussion and action. (See Report, C.U.S.L., 1906, p. 40.)

In 1907 the matter was brought before the Conference and postponed until the 1908 meeting. (See Report, C.U.S.L., 1907, p. 93.) In 1908 the matter was discussed by the Conference. (See Am.Bar Assn.Reports, 1908, pp. 983, 1048.) And in 1909 the Second Tentative Draft of the Partnership Act was introduced and discussed. (See p. 1081 of Am.Bar Assn.Reports for 1909.)

In 1910 the committee reported that on account of the death of Dean Ames no progress had been made, but that Dr. Wm. Draper Lewis, then Dean and now Professor of Law at the Law School of the University of Pennsylvania, and Mr. James B. Lichtenberger, of the Philadelphia Bar, had prepared a draft of a partnership act on the so-called entity idea, with the aid of the various drafts and notes of Dean Ames, and that they had also submitted a draft of a proposed uniform act, embodying the theory that a partnership is an aggregate of individuals associated in business, which is that at present accepted in nearly all the states of the Union. (See Report C.U.S.L., 1910, p. 142.) Dean Lewis expressed his belief that with certain modifications the aggregate or common law theory should be adopted. A resolution was passed by the Conference that any action that might have theretofore been adopted by it, tending to limit the Committee on Commercial Law in its consideration of the partnership law to what is known as the entity theory, be rescinded and that the committee be allowed and directed to consider the subject of partnership at large as though no such resolution had been adopted by the Conference. (See p. 52.)

In the fall of 1910 the committee invited to a Conference, held in Philadelphia, all the teachers of, and writers on, partnerships, besides several other lawyers known to have made a special study of the subject. There was a large attendance. For two days the members of the committee and their guests discussed the theory on which the proposed act should be drawn. At the conclusion of the discussion the experts present recommended that the act be drawn on the aggregate or common law theory, with the modification that the partners be treated as owners of partnership property holding by a special tenancy which should be called tenancy in partnership. (See section 25 of the act recommended.) Accordingly, at the meeting of the Conference in the summer of 1911, the committee reported that, after hearing the discussion of experts, it had voted that Dean Lewis be requested to prepare a draft of a partnership act on the so-called common law theory. (See Report, C.U.S.L., 1911, p. 149.)

The committee reported another draft of the act to the Conference at its session in 1912, drawn on the aggregate or common law theory, with the modification referred to. At this session the Conference spent several days in the discussion of the act, again referring it to the Committee on Commercial Law for their further consideration. (See Report, C.U.S.L., 1912, p. 67.)

PARTNERSHIPS

The Committee on Commercial Law held a meeting in New York on March 29, 1913, and took up the draft of the act referred back to it by the Conference, and after careful consideration of the amendments suggested by the Conference, prepared their seventh draft, which was, at their annual session in the summer of 1913, submitted to the Conference. The Conference again spent several days in discussing the act and again referred it to the Committee on Commercial Law, this time mainly for protection in form.

The Committee on Commercial Law assembled in the City of New York, September 21, 1914, and had before them a new draft of the act, which had been carefully prepared by Dr. Wm. Draper Lewis with valuable suggestions submitted by Charles E. Shepard, Esq., one of the commissioners from the State of Washington, and others interested in the subject. The committee reported the Eighth Draft to the Conference which, on October 14, 1914, passed a resolution recommending the act for adoption to the legislatures of all the States.

Uniformity of the law of partnerships is constantly becoming more important, as the number of firms increases which not only carry on business in more than one state, but have among the members residents of different states.

It is however, proper here to emphasize the fact that there are other reasons, in addition to the advantages which will result from uniformity, for the adoption of the act now issued by the Commissioners. There is probably no other subject connected with our business law in which a greater number of instances can be found where, in matters of almost daily occurrence, the law is uncertain. This uncertainty is due, not only to conflict between the decisions of different states, but more to the general lack of consistency in legal theory. In several of the sections, but especially in those which relate to the rights of the partner and his separate creditors in partnership property, and to the rights of firm creditors where the personnel of the partnership has been changed without liquidation of partnership affairs, there exists an almost hopeless confusion of theory and practice, making the actual administration of the law difficult and often inequitable.

Another difficulty of the present partnership law is the scarcity of authority on matters of considerable importance in the daily conduct and in the winding up of partnership affairs. In any one state it is often impossible to find an authority on a matter of comparatively frequent occurrence, while not infrequently an exhaustive research of the reports of the decisions of all the states and the federal courts fails to reveal a single authority throwing light on the question. The existence of a statute stating in detail the rights of the partners inter se during the carrying on of the partnership business, and on the winding up of partnership affairs, will be a real practical advantage of moment to the business world.

The notes which are printed in connection with this edition of the Act were prepared by Dr. Wm. Draper Lewis, the draftsman. They are designed to point out the few changes in the law which the adoption of the act will effect, and the many confusions and uncertainties which it will end.

WALTER GEORGE SMITH

Chairman, Committee on Commercial Law

PART I. PRELIMINARY PROVISIONS

§ 1. Name of Act

This act may be cited as Uniform Partnership Act.

§ 2. Definition of Terms

In this act, "Court" includes every court and judge having jurisdiction in the case.

"Business" includes every trade, occupation, or profession.

"Person" includes individuals, partnerships, corporations, and other associations.

"Bankrupt" includes bankrupt under the Federal Bankruptcy Act or insolvent under any state insolvent act.

"Conveyance" includes every assignment, lease, mortgage, or encumbrance.

"Real property" includes land and any interest or estate in land.

§ 3. Interpretation of Knowledge and Notice

(1) A person has "knowledge" of a fact within the meaning of this act not only when he has actual knowledge thereof, but also when he has knowledge of such other facts as in the circumstances shows bad faith.

(2) A person has "notice" of a fact within the meaning of this act when the person who claims the benefit of the notice:

(a) States the fact to such person, or

(b) Delivers through the mail, or by other means of communication, a written statement of the fact to such person or to a proper person at his place of business or residence.

§ 4. Rules of Construction

(1) The rule that statutes in derogation of the common law are to be strictly construed shall have no application to this act.

(2) The law of estoppel shall apply under this act.

(3) The law of agency shall apply under this act.

(4) This act shall be so interpreted and construed as to effect its general purpose to make uniform the law of those states which enact it.

(5) This act shall not be construed so as to impair the obligations of any contract existing when the act goes into effect, nor to affect any action or proceedings begun or right accrued before this act takes effect.

§ 5. Rules for Cases Not Provided for in This Act

In any case not provided for in this act the rules of law and equity, including the law merchant, shall govern.

PART II. NATURE OF A PARTNERSHIP

§ 6. Partnership Defined

(1) A partnership is an association of two or more persons to carry on as co-owners a business for profit.

(2) But any association formed under any other statute of this state, or any statute adopted by authority, other than the authority of this state, is not a partnership under this act, unless such association would have been a partnership in this state prior to the adoption of this act; but this act shall apply to limited partnerships except in so far as the statutes relating to such partnerships are inconsistent herewith.

§ 7. Rules for Determining the Existence of a Partnership

In determining whether a partnership exists, these rules shall apply:

(1) Except as provided by section 16 persons who are not partners as to each other are not partners as to third persons.

(2) Joint tenancy, tenancy in common, tenancy by the entireties, joint property, common property, or part ownership does not of itself establish a partnership, whether such co-owners do or do not share any profits made by the use of the property.

(3) The sharing of gross returns does not of itself establish a partnership, whether or not the persons sharing them have a joint or common right or interest in any property from which the returns are derived.

(4) The receipt by a person of a share of the profits of a business is prima facie evidence that he is a partner in the business, but no such inference shall be drawn if such profits were received in payment:

(a) As a debt by installments or otherwise,

(b) As wages of an employee or rent to a landlord,

(c) As an annuity to a widow or representative of a deceased partner,

(d) As interest on a loan, though the amount of payment vary with the profits of the business,

(e) As the consideration for the sale of a good-will of a business or other property by installments or otherwise.

§ 8. Partnership Property

(1) All property originally brought into the partnership stock or subsequently acquired by purchase or otherwise, on account of the partnership, is partnership property.

(2) Unless the contrary intention appears, property acquired with partnership funds is partnership property.

(3) Any estate in real property may be acquired in the partnership name. Title so acquired can be conveyed only in the partnership name.

(4) A conveyance to a partnership in the partnership name, though without words of inheritance, passes the entire estate of the grantor unless a contrary intent appears.

PART III. RELATIONS OF PARTNERS TO PERSONS DEALING WITH THE PARTNERSHIP

§ 9. Partner Agent of Partnership as to Partnership Business

(1) Every partner is an agent of the partnership for the purpose of its business, and the act of every partner, including the execution in the partnership name of any instrument, for apparently carrying on in the usual way the business of the partnership of which he is a member binds the partnership, unless the partner so acting has in fact no authority to act for the partnership in the particular matter, and the person with whom he is dealing has knowledge of the fact that he has no such authority.

(2) An act of a partner which is not apparently for the carrying on of the business of the partnership in the usual way does not bind the partnership unless authorized by the other partners.

(3) Unless authorized by the other partners or unless they have abandoned the business, one or more but less than all the partners have no authority to:

(a) Assign the partnership property in trust for creditors or on the assignee's promise to pay the debts of the partnership,

(b) Dispose of the good-will of the business,

(c) Do any other act which would make it impossible to carry on the ordinary business of a partnership,

(d) Confess a judgment,

(e) Submit a partnership claim or liability to arbitration or reference.

(4) No act of a partner in contravention of a restriction on authority shall bind the partnership to persons having knowledge of the restriction.

§ 10. Conveyance of Real Property of the Partnership

(1) Where title to real property is in the partnership name, any partner may convey title to such property by a conveyance executed in the partnership name; but the partnership may recover such property unless the partner's act binds the partnership under the provisions of paragraph (1) of section 9, or unless such property has been conveyed by the grantee or a person claiming through such grantee to a holder for value without knowledge that the partner, in making the conveyance, has exceeded his authority.

(2) Where title to real property is in the name of the partnership, a conveyance executed by a partner, in his own name, passes the equitable interest of the partnership, provided the act is one within the authority of the partner under the provisions of paragraph (1) of section 9.

(3) Where title to real property is in the name of one or more but not all the partners, and the record does not disclose the right of the partnership, the partners in whose name the title stands may convey title to such property, but the partnership may recover such property if the partners' act does not bind the partnership under the provisions of paragraph (1) of section 9, unless the purchaser or his assignee, is a holder for value, without knowledge.

(4) Where the title to real property is in the name of one or more or all the partners, or in a third person in trust for the partnership, a conveyance executed by a partner in the partnership name, or in his own name, passes the equitable interest of the partnership, provided the act is one within the authority of the partner under the provisions of paragraph (1) of section 9.

(5) Where the title to real property is in the names of all the partners a conveyance executed by all the partners passes all their rights in such property.

§ 11. Partnership Bound by Admission of Partner

An admission or representation made by any partner concerning partnership affairs within the scope of his authority as conferred by this act is evidence against the partnership.

§ 12. Partnership Charged With Knowledge of or Notice to Partner

Notice to any partner of any matter relating to partnership affairs, and the knowledge of the partner acting in the particular matter, acquired while a partner or then present to his mind, and the knowledge of any other partner who reasonably could and should have communicated it to the acting partner, operate as notice to or knowledge of the partnership, except in the case of a fraud on the partnership committed by or with the consent of that partner.

§ 13. Partnership Bound by Partner's Wrongful Act

Where, by any wrongful act or omission of any partner acting in the ordinary course of the business of the partnership or with the authority of his co-partners, loss or injury is caused to any person, not being a partner in the partnership, or any penalty is incurred, the partnership is liable therefor to the same extent as the partner so acting or omitting to act.

§ 14. Partnership Bound by Partner's Breach of Trust

The partnership is bound to make good the loss:

(a) Where one partner acting within the scope of his apparent authority receives money or property of a third person and misapplies it; and

(b) Where the partnership in the course of its business receives money or property of a third person and the money or property so received is misapplied by any partner while it is in the custody of the partnership.

§ 15. Nature of Partner's Liability

All partners are liable

(a) Jointly and severally for everything chargeable to the partnership under sections 13 and 14.

(b) Jointly for all other debts and obligations of the partnership; but any partner may enter into a separate obligation to perform a partnership contract.

§ 16. Partner by Estoppel

(1) When a person, by words spoken or written or by conduct, represents himself, or consents to another representing him to any one, as a partner in an existing partnership or with one or more persons not actual partners, he is liable to any such person to whom such representation has been made, who has, on the faith of such representation, given credit to the actual or apparent partnership, and if he has made such representation or consented to its being made in a public manner he is liable to such person, whether the representation has or has not been made or communicated to such person so giving credit by or with the knowledge of the apparent partner making the representation or consenting to its being made.

(a) When a partnership liability results, he is liable as though he were an actual member of the partnership.

(b) When no partnership liability results, he is liable jointly with the other persons, if any, so consenting to the contract or representation as to incur liability, otherwise separately.

(2) When a person has been thus represented to be a partner in an existing partnership, or with one or more persons not actual partners, he is an agent of the persons consenting to such representation to bind them to the same extent and in the same manner as though he were a partner in fact, with respect to persons who rely upon the representation. Where all the members of the existing partnership consent to the representation, a partnership act or obligation results; but in all other cases it is the joint act or obligation of the person acting and the persons consenting to the representation.

§ 17. Liability of Incoming Partner

A person admitted as a partner into an existing partnership is liable for all the obligations of the partnership arising before his admission as though he had been a partner when such obligations were incurred, except that this liability shall be satisfied only out of partnership property.

PART IV. RELATIONS OF PARTNERS TO ONE ANOTHER

§ 18. Rules Determining Rights and Duties of Partners

The rights and duties of the partners in relation to the partnership shall be determined, subject to any agreement between them, by the following rules:

(a) Each partner shall be repaid his contributions, whether by way of capital or advances to the partnership property and share equally in the profits and surplus remaining after all liabilities, including those to partners, are satisfied; and must contribute towards the losses, whether of capital or otherwise, sustained by the partnership according to his share in the profits.

(b) The partnership must indemnify every partner in respect of payments made and personal liabilities reasonably incurred by him in the ordinary and proper conduct of its business, or for the preservation of its business or property.

(c) A partner, who in aid of the partnership makes any payment or advance beyond the amount of capital which he agreed to contribute, shall be paid interest from the date of the payment or advance.

(d) A partner shall receive interest on the capital contributed by him only from the date when repayment should be made.

(e) All partners have equal rights in the management and conduct of the partnership business.

(f) No partner is entitled to remuneration for acting in the partnership business, except that a surviving partner is entitled to reasonable compensation for his services in winding up the partnership affairs.

(g) No person can become a member of a partnership without the consent of all the partners.

(h) Any difference arising as to ordinary matters connected with the partnership business may be decided by a majority of the partners; but no act in contravention of any agreement between the partners may be done rightfully without the consent of all the partners.

§ 19. Partnership Books

The partnership books shall be kept, subject to any agreement between the partners, at the principal place of business of the partnership, and every partner shall at all times have access to and may inspect and copy any of them.

§ 20. Duty of Partners to Render Information

Partners shall render on demand true and full information of all things affecting the partnership to any partner or the legal representative of any deceased partner or partner under legal disability.

§ 21. Partner Accountable as a Fiduciary

(1) Every partner must account to the partnership for any benefit, and hold as trustee for it any profits derived by him without the consent of the other partners from any transaction connected with the formation, conduct, or liquidation of the partnership or from any use by him of its property.

(2) This section applies also to the representatives of a deceased partner engaged in the liquidation of the affairs of the partnership as the personal representatives of the last surviving partner.

§ 22. Right to an Account

Any partner shall have the right to a formal account as to partnership affairs:

(a) If he is wrongfully excluded from the partnership business or possession of its property by his co-partners,

(b) If the right exists under the terms of any agreement,

(c) As provided by section 21,

(d) Whenever other circumstances render it just and reasonable.

§ 23. Continuation of Partnership Beyond Fixed Term

(1) When a partnership for a fixed term or particular undertaking is continued after the termination of such term or particular undertaking without any express agreement, the rights and duties of the partners remain the same as they were at such termination, so far as is consistent with a partnership at will.

(2) A continuation of the business by the partners or such of them as habitually acted therein during the term, without any settlement or liquidation of the partnership affairs, is prima facie evidence of a continuation of the partnership.

PART V. PROPERTY RIGHTS OF A PARTNER

§ 24. Extent of Property Rights of a Partner

The property rights of a partner are (1) his rights in specific partnership property, (2) his interest in the partnership, and (3) his right to participate in the management.

§ 25. Nature of a Partner's Right in Specific Partnership Property

(1) A partner is co-owner with his partners of specific partnership property holding as a tenant in partnership.

(2) The incidents of this tenancy are such that:

(a) A partner, subject to the provisions of this act and to any agreement between the partners, has an equal right with his partners to possess specific partnership property for partnership purposes; but he has no right to possess such property for any other purpose without the consent of his partners.

(b) A partner's right in specific partnership property is not assignable except in connection with the assignment of rights of all the partners in the same property.

(c) A partner's right in specific partnership property is not subject to attachment or execution, except on a claim against the partnership. When partnership property is attached for a partnership debt the partners, or any of them, or the representatives of a deceased partner, cannot claim any right under the homestead or exemption laws.

(d) On the death of a partner his right in specific partnership property vests in the surviving partner or partners, except where the deceased was the last surviving partner, when his right in such property vests in his legal representative. Such surviving partner or partners, or the legal representative of the last surviving partner, has no right to possess the partnership property for any but a partnership purpose.

(e) A partner's right in specific partnership property is not subject to dower, curtesy, or allowances to widows, heirs, or next of kin.

§ 26. Nature of Partner's Interest in the Partnership

A partner's interest in the partnership is his share of the profits and surplus, and the same is personal property.

§ 27. Assignment of Partner's Interest

(1) A conveyance by a partner of his interest in the partnership does not of itself dissolve the partnership, nor, as against the other partners in the absence of agreement, entitle the assignee, during the continuance of the partnership, to interfere in the management or administration of the partnership business or affairs, or to require any information or account of partnership transactions, or to inspect the partnership books; but it merely entitles the assignee to receive in accordance with his contract the profits to which the assigning partner would otherwise be entitled.

(2) In case of a dissolution of the partnership, the assignee is entitled to receive his assignor's interest and may require an account from the date only of the last account agreed to by all the partners.

§ 28. Partner's Interest Subject to Charging Order

(1) On due application to a competent court by any judgment creditor of a partner, the court which entered the judgment, order, or decree, or any other court, may charge the interest of the debtor partner with payment of the unsatisfied amount of such judgment debt with interest thereon; and may then or later appoint a receiver of his share of the profits, and of any other money due or to fall due to him in respect of the partnership, and make all other orders, directions, accounts and inquiries which the debtor partner might have made, or which the circumstances of the case may require.

(2) The interest charged may be redeemed at any time before foreclosure, or in case of a sale being directed by the court may be purchased without thereby causing a dissolution:

(a) With separate property, by any one or more of the partners, or

(b) With partnership property, by any one or more of the partners with the consent of all the partners whose interests are not so charged or sold.

(3) Nothing in this act shall be held to deprive a partner of his right, if any, under the exemption laws, as regards his interest in the partnership.

PART VI. DISSOLUTION AND WINDING UP

§ 29. Dissolution Defined

The dissolution of a partnership is the change in the relation of the partners caused by any partner ceasing to be associated in the carrying on as distinguished from the winding up of the business.

§ 30. Partnership Not Terminated by Dissolution

On dissolution the partnership is not terminated, but continues until the winding up of partnership affairs is completed.

§ 31. Causes of Dissolution

Dissolution is caused:

(1) Without violation of the agreement between the partners,

(a) By the termination of the definite term or particular undertaking specified in the agreement,

(b) By the express will of any partner when no definite term or particular undertaking is specified,

(c) By the express will of all the partners who have not assigned their interests or suffered them to be charged for their separate debts, either before or after the termination of any specified term or particular undertaking,

(d) By the expulsion of any partner from the business bona fide in accordance with such a power conferred by the agreement between the partners;

(2) In contravention of the agreement between the partners, where the circumstances do not permit a dissolution under any other provision of this section, by the express will of any partner at any time;

(3) By any event which makes it unlawful for the business of the partnership to be carried on or for the members to carry it on in partnership;

(4) By the death of any partner;

(5) By the bankruptcy of any partner or the partnership;

(6) By decree of court under section 32.

§ 32. Dissolution by Decree of Court

(1) On application by or for a partner the court shall decree a dissolution whenever:

(a) A partner has been declared a lunatic in any judicial proceeding or is shown to be of unsound mind,

(b) A partner becomes in any other way incapable of performing his part of the partnership contract,

(c) A partner has been guilty of such conduct as tends to affect prejudicially the carrying on of the business,

(d) A partner wilfully or persistently commits a breach of the partnership agreement, or otherwise so conducts himself in matters relating to the partnership business that it is not reasonably practicable to carry on the business in partnership with him,

(e) The business of the partnership can only be carried on at a loss,

(f) Other circumstances render a dissolution equitable.

(2) On the application of the purchaser of a partner's interest under sections 28 or 29 [should read 27 or 28];

(a) After the termination of the specified term or particular undertaking,

(b) At any time if the partnership was a partnership at will when the interest was assigned or when the charging order was issued.

§ 33. General Effect of Dissolution on Authority of Partner

Except so far as may be necessary to wind up partnership affairs or to complete transactions begun but not then finished, dissolution terminates all authority of any partner to act for the partnership,

(1) With respect to the partners,

(a) When the dissolution is not by the act, bankruptcy or death of a partner; or

(b) When the dissolution is by such act, bankruptcy or death of a partner, in cases where section 34 so requires.

(2) With respect to persons not partners, as declared in section 35.

§ 34. Rights of Partner to Contribution From Co-partners After Dissolution

Where the dissolution is caused by the act, death or bankruptcy of a partner, each partner is liable to his co-partners for his share of any liability created by any partner acting for the partnership as if the partnership had not been dissolved unless

(a) The dissolution being by act of any partner, the partner acting for the partnership had knowledge of the dissolution, or

(b) The dissolution being by the death or bankruptcy of a partner, the partner acting for the partnership had knowledge or notice of the death or bankruptcy.

§ 35. Power of Partner to Bind Partnership to Third Persons After Dissolution

(1) After dissolution a partner can bind the partnership except as provided in Paragraph (3).

(a) By any act appropriate for winding up partnership affairs or completing transactions unfinished at dissolution;

(b) By any transaction which would bind the partnership if dissolution had not taken place, provided the other party to the transaction

(I) Had extended credit to the partnership prior to dissolution and had no knowledge or notice of the dissolution; or

(II) Though he had not so extended credit, had nevertheless known of the partnership prior to dissolution, and, having no knowledge or notice of dissolution, the fact of dissolution had not been advertised in a newspaper of general circulation in the place (or in each place if more than one) at which the partnership business was regularly carried on.

(2) The liability of a partner under Paragraph (1b) shall be satisfied out of partnership assets alone when such partner had been prior to dissolution

(a) Unknown as a partner to the person with whom the contract is made; and

(b) So far unknown and inactive in partnership affairs that the business reputation of the partnership could not be said to have been in any degree due to his connection with it.

(3) The partnership is in no case bound by any act of a partner after dissolution

(a) Where the partnership is dissolved because it is unlawful to carry on the business, unless the act is appropriate for winding up partnership affairs; or

(b) Where the partner has become bankrupt; or

(c) Where the partner has no authority to wind up partnership affairs; except by a transaction with one who

(I) Had extended credit to the partnership prior to dissolution and had no knowledge or notice of his want of authority; or

(II) Had not extended credit to the partnership prior to dissolution, and, having no knowledge or notice of his want of authority, the fact of his want of authority has not been advertised in the manner provided for advertising the fact of dissolution in Paragraph (1b II).

(4) Nothing in this section shall affect the liability under Section 16 of any person who after dissolution represents himself or consents to

another representing him as a partner in a partnership engaged in carrying on business.

§ 36. Effect of Dissolution on Partner's Existing Liability

(1) The dissolution of the partnership does not of itself discharge the existing liability of any partner.

(2) A partner is discharged from any existing liability upon dissolution of the partnership by an agreement to that effect between himself, the partnership creditor and the person or partnership continuing the business; and such agreement may be inferred from the course of dealing between the creditor having knowledge of the dissolution and the person or partnership continuing the business.

(3) Where a person agrees to assume the existing obligations of a dissolved partnership, the partners whose obligations have been assumed shall be discharged from any liability to any creditor of the partnership who, knowing of the agreement, consents to a material alteration in the nature or time of payment of such obligations.

(4) The individual property of a deceased partner shall be liable for all obligations of the partnership incurred while he was a partner but subject to the prior payment of his separate debts.

§ 37. Right to Wind Up

Unless otherwise agreed the partners who have not wrongfully dissolved the partnership or the legal representative of the last surviving partner, not bankrupt, has the right to wind up the partnership affairs; provided, however, that any partner, his legal representative or his assignee, upon cause shown, may obtain winding up by the court.

§ 38. Rights of Partners to Application of Partnership Property

(1) When dissolution is caused in any way, except in contravention of the partnership agreement, each partner, as against his co-partners and all persons claiming through them in respect of their interests in the partnership, unless otherwise agreed, may have the partnership property applied to discharge its liabilities, and the surplus applied to pay in cash the net amount owing to the respective partners. But if dissolution is caused by expulsion of a partner, bona fide under the partnership agreement and if the expelled partner is discharged from all partnership liabilities, either by payment or agreement under section 36(2), he shall receive in cash only the net amount due him from the partnership.

(2) When dissolution is caused in contravention of the partnership agreement the rights of the partners shall be as follows:

(a) Each partner who has not caused dissolution wrongfully shall have,

I. All the rights specified in paragraph (1) of this section, and

II. The right, as against each partner who has caused the dissolution wrongfully, to damages for breach of the agreement.

(b) The partners who have not caused the dissolution wrongfully, if they all desire to continue the business in the same name, either by themselves or jointly with others, may do so, during the agreed term for the partnership and for that purpose may possess the partnership property, provided they secure the payment by bond approved by the court, or pay to any partner who has caused the dissolution wrongfully, the value of his interest in the partnership at the dissolution, less any damages recoverable under clause (2a II) of this section, and in like manner indemnify him against all present or future partnership liabilities.

(c) A partner who has caused the dissolution wrongfully shall have:

I. If the business is not continued under the provisions of paragraph (2b) all the rights of a partner under paragraph (1), subject to clause (2a II), of this section,

II. If the business is continued under paragraph (2b) of this section the right as against his co-partners and all claiming through them in respect of their interests in the partnership, to have the value of his interest in the partnership, less any damages caused to his co-partners by the dissolution, ascertained and paid to him in cash, or the payment secured by bond approved by the court, and to be released from all existing liabilities of the partnership; but in ascertaining the value of the partner's interest the value of the good-will of the business shall not be considered.

§ 39. Rights Where Partnership Is Dissolved for Fraud or Misrepresentation

Where a partnership contract is rescinded on the ground of the fraud or misrepresentation of one of the parties thereto, the party entitled to rescind is, without prejudice to any other right, entitled,

(a) To a lien on, or a right of retention of, the surplus of the partnership property after satisfying the partnership liabilities to third persons for any sum of money paid by him for the purchase of an interest in the partnership and for any capital or advances contributed by him; and

(b) To stand, after all liabilities to third persons have been satisfied, in the place of the creditors of the partnership for any payments made by him in respect of the partnership liabilities; and

(c) To be indemnified by the person guilty of the fraud or making the representation against all debts and liabilities of the partnership.

§ 40. Rules for Distribution

In settling accounts between the partners after dissolution, the following rules shall be observed, subject to any agreement to the contrary:

(a) The assets of the partnership are:

I. The partnership property,

II. The contributions of the partners necessary for the payment of all the liabilities specified in clause (b) of this paragraph.

(b) The liabilities of the partnership shall rank in order of payment, as follows:

I. Those owing to creditors other than partners,

II. Those owing to partners other than for capital and profits,

III. Those owing to partners in respect of capital,

IV. Those owing to partners in respect of profits.

(c) The assets shall be applied in the order of their declaration in clause (a) of this paragraph to the satisfaction of the liabilities.

(d) The partners shall contribute, as provided by section 18(a) the amount necessary to satisfy the liabilities; but if any, but not all, of the partners are insolvent, or, not being subject to process, refuse to contribute, the other partners shall contribute their share of the liabilities, and, in the relative proportions in which they share the profits, the additional amount necessary to pay the liabilities.

(e) An assignee for the benefit of creditors or any person appointed by the court shall have the right to enforce the contributions specified in clause (d) of this paragraph.

(f) Any partner or his legal representative shall have the right to enforce the contributions specified in clause (d) of this paragraph, to the extent of the amount which he has paid in excess of his share of the liability.

(g) The individual property of a deceased partner shall be liable for the contributions specified in clause (d) of this paragraph.

(h) When partnership property and the individual properties of the partners are in possession of a court for distribution, partnership creditors shall have priority on partnership property and separate creditors on individual property, saving the rights of lien or secured creditors as heretofore.

(i) Where a partner has become bankrupt or his estate is insolvent the claims against his separate property shall rank in the following order:

I. Those owing to separate creditors,

II. Those owing to partnership creditors,

III. Those owing to partners by way of contribution.

§ 41. Liability of Persons Continuing the Business in Certain Cases

(1) When any new partner is admitted into an existing partnership, or when any partner retires and assigns (or the representative of the deceased partner assigns) his rights in partnership property to two or more of the partners, or to one or more of the partners and one or more third persons, if the business is continued without liquidation of the partnership affairs, creditors of the first or dissolved partnership are also creditors of the partnership so continuing the business.

(2) When all but one partner retire and assign (or the representative of a deceased partner assigns) their rights in partnership property to the remaining partner, who continues the business without liquidation of partnership affairs, either alone or with others, creditors of the dissolved partnership are also creditors of the person or partnership so continuing the business.

(3) When any partner retires or dies and the business of the dissolved partnership is continued as set forth in paragraphs (1) and (2) of this section, with the consent of the retired partners or the representative of the deceased partner, but without any assignment of his right in partnership property, rights of creditors of the dissolved partnership and of the creditors of the person or partnership continuing the business shall be as if such assignment had been made.

(4) When all the partners or their representatives assign their rights in partnership property to one or more third persons who promise to pay the debts and who continue the business of the dissolved partnership, creditors of the dissolved partnership are also creditors of the person or partnership continuing the business.

(5) When any partner wrongfully causes a dissolution and the remaining partners continue the business under the provisions of section 38(2b), either alone or with others, and without liquidation of the partnership affairs, creditors of the dissolved partnership are also creditors of the person or partnership continuing the business.

(6) When a partner is expelled and the remaining partners continue the business either alone or with others, without liquidation of the partnership affairs, creditors of the dissolved partnership are also creditors of the person or partnership continuing the business.

(7) The liability of a third person becoming a partner in the partnership continuing the business, under this section, to the creditors of the dissolved partnership shall be satisfied out of partnership property only.

(8) When the business of a partnership after dissolution is continued under any conditions set forth in this section the creditors of the dissolved partnership, as against the separate creditors of the retiring or

deceased partner or the representative of the deceased partner, have a prior right to any claim of the retired partner or the representative of the deceased partner against the person or partnership continuing the business, on account of the retired or deceased partner's interest in the dissolved partnership or on account of any consideration promised for such interest or for his right in partnership property.

(9) Nothing in this section shall be held to modify any right of creditors to set aside any assignment on the ground of fraud.

(10) The use by the person or partnership continuing the business of the partnership name, or the name of a deceased partner as part thereof, shall not of itself make the individual property of the deceased partner liable for any debts contracted by such person or partnership.

§ 42. Rights of Retiring or Estate of Deceased Partner When the Business Is Continued

When any partner retires or dies, and the business is continued under any of the conditions set forth in section 41(1, 2, 3, 5, 6), or section 38(2b) without any settlement of accounts as between him or his estate and the person or partnership continuing the business, unless otherwise agreed, he or his legal representative as against such person or partnership may have the value of his interest at the date of dissolution ascertained, and shall receive as an ordinary creditor an amount equal to the value of his interest in the dissolved partnership with interest, or, at his option or at the option of his legal representative, in lieu of interest, the profits attributable to the use of his right in the property of the dissolved partnership; provided that the creditors of the dissolved partnership as against the separate creditors, or the representative of the retired or deceased partner, shall have priority on any claim arising under this section, as provided by section 41(8) of this act.

§ 43. Accrual of Actions

The right to an account of his interest shall accrue to any partner, or his legal representative, as against the winding up partners or the surviving partners or the person or partnership continuing the business, at the date of dissolution, in the absence of any agreement to the contrary.

PART VII. MISCELLANEOUS PROVISIONS

§ 44. When Act Takes Effect

This act shall take effect on the ______ day of ______ two thousand one hundred and ______.

§ 45. Legislation Repealed

All acts or parts of acts inconsistent with this act are hereby repealed.

B. UNIFORM PARTNERSHIP ACT (1997)

1997 ACT

See, also, the Uniform Partnership Act as originally adopted in 1914, post.

Contents

ARTICLE 1

GENERAL PROVISIONS

ARTICLE 2

NATURE OF PARTNERSHIP

ARTICLE 3

RELATIONS OF PARTNERS TO PERSONS DEALING WITH PARTNERSHIP

ARTICLE 4

RELATIONS OF PARTNERS TO EACH OTHER AND TO PARTNERSHIP

ARTICLE 1. GENERAL PROVISIONS

§ 101. Definitions.

In this [Act]:

(1) "Business" includes every trade, occupation, and profession.

(2) "Debtor in bankruptcy" means a person who is the subject of:

(i) an order for relief under Title 11 of the United States Code or a comparable order under a successor statute of general application; or

(ii) a comparable order under federal, state, or foreign law governing insolvency.

(3) "Distribution" means a transfer of money or other property from a partnership to a partner in the partner's capacity as a partner or to the partner's transferee.

(4) "Foreign limited liability partnership" means a partnership that:

(i) is formed under laws other than the laws of this State; and

(ii) has the status of a limited liability partnership under those laws.

(5) "Limited liability partnership" means a partnership that has filed a statement of qualification under Section 1001 and does not have a similar statement in effect in any other jurisdiction.

(6) "Partnership" means an association of two or more persons to carry on as co-owners a business for profit formed under Section 202, predecessor law, or comparable law of another jurisdiction.

(7) "Partnership agreement" means the agreement, whether written, oral, or implied, among the partners concerning the partnership, including amendments to the partnership agreement.

(8) "Partnership at will" means a partnership in which the partners have not agreed to remain partners until the expiration of a definite term or the completion of a particular undertaking.

(9) "Partnership interest" or "partner's interest in the partnership" means all of a partner's interests in the partnership, including the partner's transferable interest and all management and other rights.

(10) "Person" means an individual, corporation, business trust, estate, trust, partnership, association, joint venture, government, governmental subdivision, agency, or instrumentality, or any other legal or commercial entity.

(11) "Property" means all property, real, personal, or mixed, tangible or intangible, or any interest therein.

(12) "State" means a State of the United States, the District of Columbia, the Commonwealth of Puerto Rico, or any territory or insular possession subject to the jurisdiction of the United States.

(13) "Statement" means a statement of partnership authority under Section 303, a statement of denial under Section 304, a statement of dissociation under Section 704, a statement of dissolution under Section 805, a statement of merger under Section 907, or an amendment or cancellation of any of the foregoing.

(14) "Transfer" includes an assignment, conveyance, lease, mortgage, deed, and encumbrance.

§ 102. Knowledge and Notice.

(a) A person knows a fact if the person has actual knowledge of it.

(b) A person has notice of a fact if the person:

(1) knows of it;

(2) has received a notification of it; or

(3) has reason to know it exists from all of the facts known to the person at the time in question.

(c) A person notifies or gives a notification to another by taking steps reasonably required to inform the other person in ordinary course, whether or not the other person learns of it.

(d) A person receives a notification when the notification:

(1) comes to the person's attention; or

(2) is duly delivered at the person's place of business or at any other place held out by the person as a place for receiving communications.

(e) Except as otherwise provided in subsection (f), a person other than an individual knows, has notice, or receives a notification of a fact for purposes of a particular transaction when the individual conducting the transaction knows, has notice, or receives a notification of the fact, or in any event when the fact would have been brought to the individual's attention if the person had exercised reasonable diligence. The person exercises reasonable diligence if it maintains reasonable routines for communicating significant information to the individual conducting the transaction and there is reasonable compliance with the routines. Reasonable diligence does not require an individual acting for the person to communicate information unless the communication is part of the individual's regular duties or the individual has reason to know of the transaction and that the transaction would be materially affected by the information.

(f) A partner's knowledge, notice, or receipt of a notification of a fact relating to the partnership is effective immediately as knowledge by, notice to, or receipt of a notification by the partnership, except in the case of a fraud on the partnership committed by or with the consent of that partner.

§ 103. Effect of Partnership Agreement; Nonwaivable Provisions.

(a) Except as otherwise provided in subsection (b), relations among the partners and between the partners and the partnership are governed by the partnership agreement. To the extent the partnership agreement does not otherwise provide, this [Act] governs relations among the partners and between the partners and the partnership.

(b) The partnership agreement may not:

(1) vary the rights and duties under Section 105 except to eliminate the duty to provide copies of statements to all of the partners;

(2) unreasonably restrict the right of access to books and records under Section 403(b);

(3) eliminate the duty of loyalty under Section 404(b) or 603(b)(3), but:

(i) the partnership agreement may identify specific types or categories of activities that do not violate the duty of loyalty, if not manifestly unreasonable; or

(ii) all of the partners or a number or percentage specified in the partnership agreement may authorize or ratify, after full disclosure of all material facts, a specific act or transaction that otherwise would violate the duty of loyalty;

(4) unreasonably reduce the duty of care under Section 404(c) or 603(b)(3);

(5) eliminate the obligation of good faith and fair dealing under Section 404(d), but the partnership agreement may prescribe the standards by which the performance of the obligation is to be measured, if the standards are not manifestly unreasonable;

(6) vary the power to dissociate as a partner under Section 602(a), except to require the notice under Section 601(1) to be in writing;

(7) vary the right of a court to expel a partner in the events specified in Section 601(5);

(8) vary the requirement to wind up the partnership business in cases specified in Section 801(4), (5), or (6); or

(9) vary the law applicable to a limited liability partnership under Section 106(b); or

(10) restrict rights of third parties under this [Act].

§ 104. Supplemental Principles of Law.

(a) Unless displaced by particular provisions of this [Act], the principles of law and equity supplement this [Act].

(b) If an obligation to pay interest arises under this [Act] and the rate is not specified, the rate is that specified in [applicable statute].

§ 105. Execution, Filing, and Recording of Statements.

(a) A statement may be filed in the office of [the Secretary of State]. A certified copy of a statement that is filed in an office in another state may be filed in the office of [the Secretary of State]. Either filing has the effect provided in this [Act] with respect to partnership property located in or transactions that occur in this State.

(b) A certified copy of a statement that has been filed in the office of the [Secretary of State] and recorded in the office for recording transfers of real property has the effect provided for recorded statements in this [Act]. A recorded statement that is not a certified copy of a statement filed in the office of the [Secretary of State] does not have the effect provided for recorded statements in this [Act].

(c) A statement filed by a partnership must be executed by at least two partners. Other statements must be executed by a partner or other person authorized by this [Act]. An individual who executes a statement as, or on behalf of, a partner or other person named as a partner in a statement shall personally declare under penalty of perjury that the contents of the statement are accurate.

(d) A person authorized by this [Act] to file a statement may amend or cancel the statement by filing an amendment or cancellation that names the partnership, identifies the statement, and states the substance of the amendment or cancellation.

(e) A person who files a statement pursuant to this section shall promptly send a copy of the statement to every nonfiling partner and to any other person named as a partner in the statement. Failure to send a copy of a statement to a partner or other person does not limit the effectiveness of the statement as to a person not a partner.

(f) The [Secretary of State] may collect a fee for filing or providing a certified copy of a statement. The [officer responsible for] recording transfers of real property may collect a fee for recording a statement.

§ 106. Law Governing Internal Relations.

(a) Except as otherwise provided in subsection (b), the law of a jurisdiction in which a partnership has its chief executive office governs relations among the partners and between the partners and the partnership.

(b) The law of this State governs relations among the partners and between the partners and the partnership and the liability of partners for an obligation of a limited liability partnership.

§ 107. Partnership Subject to Amendment or Repeal of [Act].

A partnership governed by this [Act] is subject to any amendment to or repeal of this [Act].

ARTICLE 2. NATURE OF PARTNERSHIP

§ 201. Partnership as Entity.

(a) A partnership is an entity distinct from its partners.

(b) A limited liability partnership continues to be the same entity that existed before the filing of a statement of qualification under Section 1001.

§ 202. Formation of Partnership.

(a) Except as otherwise provided in subsection (b), the association of two or more persons to carry on as co-owners a business for profit forms a partnership, whether or not the persons intend to form a partnership.

(b) An association formed under a statute other than this [Act], a predecessor statute, or a comparable statute of another jurisdiction is not a partnership under this [Act].

(c) In determining whether a partnership is formed, the following rules apply:

(1) Joint tenancy, tenancy in common, tenancy by the entireties, joint property, common property, or part ownership does not by itself establish a partnership, even if the co-owners share profits made by the use of the property.

(2) The sharing of gross returns does not by itself establish a partnership, even if the persons sharing them have a joint or common right or interest in property from which the returns are derived.

(3) A person who receives a share of the profits of a business is presumed to be a partner in the business, unless the profits were received in payment:

(i) of a debt by installments or otherwise;

(ii) for services as an independent contractor or of wages or other compensation to an employee;

(iii) of rent;

(iv) of an annuity or other retirement benefit to a beneficiary, representative, or designee of a deceased or retired partner;

(v) of interest or other charge on a loan, even if the amount of payment varies with the profits of the business, including a direct or indirect present or future ownership of the collateral, or rights to income, proceeds, or increase in value derived from the collateral; or

(vi) for the sale of the goodwill of a business or other property by installments or otherwise.

§ 203. Partnership Property.

Property acquired by a partnership is property of the partnership and not of the partners individually.

§ 204. When Property Is Partnership Property.

(a) Property is partnership property if acquired in the name of:

(1) the partnership; or

(2) one or more partners with an indication in the instrument transferring title to the property of the person's capacity as a partner or of the existence of a partnership but without an indication of the name of the partnership.

(b) Property is acquired in the name of the partnership by a transfer to:

(1) the partnership in its name; or

(2) one or more partners in their capacity as partners in the partnership, if the name of the partnership is indicated in the instrument transferring title to the property.

(c) Property is presumed to be partnership property if purchased with partnership assets, even if not acquired in the name of the partnership or of one or more partners with an indication in the instrument transferring title to the property of the person's capacity as a partner or of the existence of a partnership.

(d) Property acquired in the name of one or more of the partners, without an indication in the instrument transferring title to the property of the person's capacity as a partner or of the existence of a partnership and without use of partnership assets, is presumed to be separate property, even if used for partnership purposes.

ARTICLE 3. RELATIONS OF PARTNERS TO PERSONS DEALING WITH PARTNERSHIP

§ 301. Partner Agent of Partnership.

Subject to the effect of a statement of partnership authority under Section 303:

(1) Each partner is an agent of the partnership for the purpose of its business. An act of a partner, including the execution of an instrument in the partnership name, for apparently carrying on in the ordinary course the partnership business or business of the kind carried on by the partnership binds the partnership, unless the partner had no authority to act for the partnership in the particular matter and the person with whom the partner is dealing knew or has received a notification that the partner lacked authority.

(2) An act of a partner which is not apparently for carrying on in the ordinary course the partnership business or business of the kind carried on by the partnership binds the partnership only if the act was authorized by the other partners.

§ 302. Transfer of Partnership Property.

(a) Partnership property may be transferred as follows:

(1) Subject to the effect of a statement of partnership authority under Section 303, partnership property held in the name of the partnership may be transferred by an instrument of transfer executed by a partner in the partnership name.

(2) Partnership property held in the name of one or more partners with an indication in the instrument transferring the property to them of their capacity as partners or of the existence of a partnership, but without an indication of the name of the partnership, may be transferred by an instrument of transfer executed by the persons in whose name the property is held.

(3) Partnership property held in the name of one or more persons other than the partnership, without an indication in the instrument transferring the property to them of their capacity as partners or of the existence of a partnership, may be transferred by

an instrument of transfer executed by the persons in whose name the property is held.

(b) A partnership may recover partnership property from a transferee only if it proves that execution of the instrument of initial transfer did not bind the partnership under Section 301 and:

(1) as to a subsequent transferee who gave value for property transferred under subsection (a)(1) and (2), proves that the subsequent transferee knew or had received a notification that the person who executed the instrument of initial transfer lacked authority to bind the partnership; or

(2) as to a transferee who gave value for property transferred under subsection (a)(3), proves that the transferee knew or had received a notification that the property was partnership property and that the person who executed the instrument of initial transfer lacked authority to bind the partnership.

(c) A partnership may not recover partnership property from a subsequent transferee if the partnership would not have been entitled to recover the property, under subsection (b), from any earlier transferee of the property.

(d) If a person holds all of the partners' interests in the partnership, all of the partnership property vests in that person. The person may execute a document in the name of the partnership to evidence vesting of the property in that person and may file or record the document.

§ 303. Statement of Partnership Authority.

(a) A partnership may file a statement of partnership authority, which:

(1) must include:

(i) the name of the partnership;

(ii) the street address of its chief executive office and of one office in this State, if there is one;

(iii) the names and mailing addresses of all of the partners or of an agent appointed and maintained by the partnership for the purpose of subsection (b); and

(iv) the names of the partners authorized to execute an instrument transferring real property held in the name of the partnership; and

(2) may state the authority, or limitations on the authority, of some or all of the partners to enter into other transactions on behalf of the partnership and any other matter.

(b) If a statement of partnership authority names an agent, the agent shall maintain a list of the names and mailing addresses of all of the partners and make it available to any person on request for good cause shown.

(c) If a filed statement of partnership authority is executed pursuant to Section 105(c) and states the name of the partnership but does not contain all of the other information required by subsection (a), the statement nevertheless operates with respect to a person not a partner as provided in subsections (d) and (e).

(d) Except as otherwise provided in subsection (g), a filed statement of partnership authority supplements the authority of a partner to enter into transactions on behalf of the partnership as follows:

(1) Except for transfers of real property, a grant of authority contained in a filed statement of partnership authority is conclusive in favor of a person who gives value without knowledge to the contrary, so long as and to the extent that a limitation on that authority is not then contained in another filed statement. A filed cancellation of a limitation on authority revives the previous grant of authority.

(2) A grant of authority to transfer real property held in the name of the partnership contained in a certified copy of a filed statement of partnership authority recorded in the office for recording transfers of that real property is conclusive in favor of a person who gives value without knowledge to the contrary, so long as and to the extent that a certified copy of a filed statement containing a limitation on that authority is not then of record in the office for recording transfers of that real property. The recording in the office for recording transfers of that real property of a certified copy of a filed cancellation of a limitation on authority revives the previous grant of authority.

(e) A person not a partner is deemed to know of a limitation on the authority of a partner to transfer real property held in the name of the partnership if a certified copy of the filed statement containing the limitation on authority is of record in the office for recording transfers of that real property.

(f) Except as otherwise provided in subsections (d) and (e) and Sections 704 and 805, a person not a partner is not deemed to know of a limitation on the authority of a partner merely because the limitation is contained in a filed statement.

(g) Unless earlier canceled, a filed statement of partnership authority is canceled by operation of law five years after the date on which the statement, or the most recent amendment, was filed with the [Secretary of State].

§ 304. Statement of Denial.

A partner or other person named as a partner in a filed statement of partnership authority or in a list maintained by an agent pursuant to

Section 303(b) may file a statement of denial stating the name of the partnership and the fact that is being denied, which may include denial of a person's authority or status as a partner. A statement of denial is a limitation on authority as provided in Section 303(d) and (e).

§ 305. Partnership Liable for Partner's Actionable Conduct.

(a) A partnership is liable for loss or injury caused to a person, or for a penalty incurred, as a result of a wrongful act or omission, or other actionable conduct, of a partner acting in the ordinary course of business of the partnership or with authority of the partnership.

(b) If, in the course of the partnership's business or while acting with authority of the partnership, a partner receives or causes the partnership to receive money or property of a person not a partner, and the money or property is misapplied by a partner, the partnership is liable for the loss.

§ 306. Partner's Liability.

(a) Except as otherwise provided in subsections (b) and (c), all partners are liable jointly and severally for all obligations of the partnership unless otherwise agreed by the claimant or provided by law.

(b) A person admitted as a partner into an existing partnership is not personally liable for any partnership obligation incurred before the person's admission as a partner.

(c) An obligation of a partnership incurred while the partnership is a limited liability partnership whether arising in contract, tort, or otherwise, is solely the obligation of the partnership. A partner is not personally liable, directly or indirectly, by way of contribution or otherwise, for such an obligation solely by reason of being or so acting as a partner. This subsection applies notwithstanding anything inconsistent in the partnership agreement that existed immediately before the vote required to become a limited liability partnership under Section 1001(b).

§ 307. Actions by and Against Partnership and Partners.

(a) A partnership may sue and be sued in the name of the partnership.

(b) An action may be brought against the partnership and, to the extent not inconsistent with Section 306, any or all of the partners in the same action or in separate actions.

(c) A judgment against a partnership is not by itself a judgment against a partner. A judgment against a partnership may not be satisfied from a partner's assets unless there is also a judgment against the partner.

(d) A judgment creditor of a partner may not levy execution against the assets of the partner to satisfy a judgment based on a claim against the partnership unless the partner is personally liable for the claim under Section 306 and:

(1) a judgment based on the same claim has been obtained against the partnership and a writ of execution on the judgment has been returned unsatisfied in whole or in part;

(2) the partnership is a debtor in bankruptcy;

(3) the partner has agreed that the creditor need not exhaust partnership assets;

(4) a court grants permission to the judgment creditor to levy execution against the assets of a partner based on a finding that partnership assets subject to execution are clearly insufficient to satisfy the judgment, that exhaustion of partnership assets is excessively burdensome, or that the grant of permission is an appropriate exercise of the court's equitable powers; or

(5) liability is imposed on the partner by law or contract independent of the existence of the partnership.

(e) This section applies to any partnership liability or obligation resulting from a representation by a partner or purported partner under Section 308.

§ 308. Liability of Purported Partner.

(a) If a person, by words or conduct, purports to be a partner, or consents to being represented by another as a partner, in a partnership or with one or more persons not partners, the purported partner is liable to a person to whom the representation is made, if that person, relying on the representation, enters into a transaction with the actual or purported partnership. If the representation, either by the purported partner or by a person with the purported partner's consent, is made in a public manner, the purported partner is liable to a person who relies upon the purported partnership even if the purported partner is not aware of being held out as a partner to the claimant. If partnership liability results, the purported partner is liable with respect to that liability as if the purported partner were a partner. If no partnership liability results, the purported partner is liable with respect to that liability jointly and severally with any other person consenting to the representation.

(b) If a person is thus represented to be a partner in an existing partnership, or with one or more persons not partners, the purported partner is an agent of persons consenting to the representation to bind them to the same extent and in the same manner as if the purported partner were a partner, with respect to persons who enter into transactions in reliance upon the representation. If all of the partners of the existing partnership consent to the representation, a partnership act or obligation results. If fewer than all of the partners of the existing partnership consent to the representation, the person acting and the partners consenting to the representation are jointly and severally liable.

(c) A person is not liable as a partner merely because the person is named by another in a statement of partnership authority.

(d) A person does not continue to be liable as a partner merely because of a failure to file a statement of dissociation or to amend a statement of partnership authority to indicate the partner's dissociation from the partnership.

(e) Except as otherwise provided in subsections (a) and (b), persons who are not partners as to each other are not liable as partners to other persons.

ARTICLE 4. RELATIONS OF PARTNERS TO EACH OTHER AND TO PARTNERSHIP

§ 401. Partner's Rights and Duties.

(a) Each partner is deemed to have an account that is:

(1) credited with an amount equal to the money plus the value of any other property, net of the amount of any liabilities, the partner contributes to the partnership and the partner's share of the partnership profits; and

(2) charged with an amount equal to the money plus the value of any other property, net of the amount of any liabilities, distributed by the partnership to the partner and the partner's share of the partnership losses.

(b) Each partner is entitled to an equal share of the partnership profits and is chargeable with a share of the partnership losses in proportion to the partner's share of the profits.

(c) A partnership shall reimburse a partner for payments made and indemnify a partner for liabilities incurred by the partner in the ordinary course of the business of the partnership or for the preservation of its business or property.

(d) A partnership shall reimburse a partner for an advance to the partnership beyond the amount of capital the partner agreed to contribute.

(e) A payment or advance made by a partner which gives rise to a partnership obligation under subsection (c) or (d) constitutes a loan to the partnership which accrues interest from the date of the payment or advance.

(f) Each partner has equal rights in the management and conduct of the partnership business.

(g) A partner may use or possess partnership property only on behalf of the partnership.

(h) A partner is not entitled to remuneration for services performed for the partnership, except for reasonable compensation for services rendered in winding up the business of the partnership.

(i) A person may become a partner only with the consent of all of the partners.

(j) A difference arising as to a matter in the ordinary course of business of a partnership may be decided by a majority of the partners. An act outside the ordinary course of business of a partnership and an amendment to the partnership agreement may be undertaken only with the consent of all of the partners.

(k) This section does not affect the obligations of a partnership to other persons under Section 301.

§ 402. Distributions in Kind.

A partner has no right to receive, and may not be required to accept, a distribution in kind.

§ 403. Partner's Rights and Duties With Respect to Information.

(a) A partnership shall keep its books and records, if any, at its chief executive office.

(b) A partnership shall provide partners and their agents and attorneys access to its books and records. It shall provide former partners and their agents and attorneys access to books and records pertaining to the period during which they were partners. The right of access provides the opportunity to inspect and copy books and records during ordinary business hours. A partnership may impose a reasonable charge, covering the costs of labor and material, for copies of documents furnished.

(c) Each partner and the partnership shall furnish to a partner, and the legal representative of a deceased partner or partner under legal disability:

(1) without demand, any information concerning the partnership's business and affairs reasonably required for the proper exercise of the partner's rights and duties under the partnership agreement of this [Act]; and

(2) on demand, any other information concerning the partnership's business and affairs, except to the extent the demand or the information demanded is unreasonable or otherwise improper under the circumstances.

§ 404. General Standards of Partner's Conduct.

(a) The only fiduciary duties a partner owes to the partnership and the other partners are the duty of loyalty and the duty of care set forth in subsections (b) and (c).

(b) A partner's duty of loyalty to the partnership and the other partners is limited to the following:

(1) to account to the partnership and hold as trustee for it any property, profit, or benefit derived by the partner in the conduct and winding up of the partnership business or derived from a use by the partner of partnership property, including the appropriation of a partnership opportunity;

(2) to refrain from dealing with the partnership in the conduct or winding up of the partnership business as or on behalf of a party having an interest adverse to the partnership; and

(3) to refrain from competing with the partnership in the conduct of the partnership business before the dissolution of the partnership.

(c) A partner's duty of care to the partnership and the other partners in the conduct and winding up of the partnership business is limited to refraining from engaging in grossly negligent or reckless conduct, intentional misconduct, or a knowing violation of law.

(d) A partner shall discharge the duties to the partnership and the other partners under this [Act] or under the partnership agreement and exercise any rights consistently with the obligation of good faith and fair dealing.

(e) A partner does not violate a duty or obligation under this [Act] or under the partnership agreement merely because the partner's conduct furthers the partner's own interest.

(f) A partner may lend money to and transact other business with the partnership, and as to each loan or transaction, the rights and obligations of a partner are the same as those of a person who is not a partner, subject to other applicable law.

(g) This section applies to a person winding up the partnership business as the personal or legal representative of the last surviving partner as if the person were a partner.

§ 405. Actions by Partnership and Partners.

(a) A partnership may maintain an action against a partner for a breach of the partnership agreement, or for the violation of a duty to the partnership, causing harm to the partnership.

(b) A partner may maintain an action against the partnership or another partner for legal or equitable relief, with or without an accounting as to partnership business, to:

(1) enforce the partner's rights under the partnership agreement;

(2) enforce the partner's rights under this [Act], including:

(i) the partner's rights under Sections 401, 403, or 404;

(ii) the partner's right on dissociation to have the partner's interest in the partnership purchased pursuant to Section 701 or enforce any other right under Article 6 or 7; or

(iii) the partner's right to compel a dissolution and winding up of the partnership business under Section 801 or enforce any other right under Article 8; or

(3) enforce the rights and otherwise protect the interests of the partner, including rights and interests arising independently of the partnership relationship.

(c) The accrual of, and any time limitation on, a right of action for a remedy under this section is governed by other law. A right to an accounting upon a dissolution and winding up does not revive a claim barred by law.

§ 406. Continuation of Partnership Beyond Definite Term or Particular Undertaking.

(a) If a partnership for a definite term or particular undertaking is continued, without an express agreement, after the expiration of the term or completion of the undertaking, the rights and duties of the partners remain the same as they were at the expiration or completion, so far as is consistent with a partnership at will.

(b) If the partners, or those of them who habitually acted in the business during the term or undertaking, continue the business without any settlement or liquidation of the partnership, they are presumed to have agreed that the business will continue.

ARTICLE 5. TRANSFEREES AND CREDITORS OF PARTNER

§ 501. Partner Not Co-owner of Partnership Property.

A partner is not a co-owner of partnership property and has no interest in partnership property which can be transferred, either voluntarily or involuntarily.

§ 502. Partner's Transferable Interest in Partnership.

The only transferable interest of a partner in the partnership is the partner's share of the profits and losses of the partnership and the partner's right to receive distributions. The interest is personal property.

§ 503. Transfer of Partner's Transferable Interest.

(a) A transfer, in whole or in part, of a partner's transferable interest in the partnership:

(1) is permissible;

(2) does not by itself cause the partner's dissociation or a dissolution and winding up of the partnership business; and

(3) does not, as against the other partners or the partnership, entitle the transferee, during the continuance of the partnership, to participate in the management or conduct of the partnership business, to require access to information concerning or an account of partnership transactions, or to inspect or copy the partnership books or records.

(b) A transferee of a partner's transferable interest in the partnership has a right:

(1) to receive, in accordance with the transfer, distributions to which the transferor would otherwise be entitled;

(2) to receive upon the dissolution and winding up of the partnership business, in accordance with the transfer, the net amount otherwise distributable to the transferor; and

(3) to seek under Section 801(6) a judicial determination that it is equitable to wind up the partnership business.

(c) In a dissolution and winding up, a transferee is entitled to an account of partnership transactions only from the date of the latest account agreed to by all of the partners.

(d) Upon transfer, the transferor retains the rights and duties of a partner other than the interest in distributions transferred.

(e) A partnership need not give effect to a transferee's rights under this section until it has notice of the transfer.

(f) A transfer of a partner's transferable interest in the partnership in violation of a restriction on transfer contained in the partnership agreement is ineffective as to a person having notice of the restriction at the time of transfer.

§ 504. Partner's Transferable Interest Subject to Charging Order.

(a) On application by a judgment creditor of a partner or of a partner's transferee, a court having jurisdiction may charge the transferable interest of the debtor partner or transferee to satisfy the judgment. The court may appoint a receiver of the debtor's share of the distributions due or to become due to the debtor in respect of the partnership and make all other orders, directions, accounts, and inquiries the debtor might have made or which the circumstances of the case may require.

(b) A charging order constitutes a lien on the judgment debtor's transferable interest in the partnership. The court may order a foreclosure of the interest subject to the charging order at any time. The purchaser at the foreclosure sale has the rights of a transferee.

(c) At any time before foreclosure, an interest charged may be redeemed:

(1) by the judgment debtor;

(2) with property other than partnership property, by one or more of the other partners; or

(3) with partnership property, by one or more of the other partners with the consent of all of the partners whose interests are not so charged.

(d) This [Act] does not deprive a partner of a right under exemption laws with respect to the partner's interest in the partnership.

(e) This section provides the exclusive remedy by which a judgment creditor of a partner or partner's transferee may satisfy a judgment out of the judgment debtor's transferable interest in the partnership.

ARTICLE 6. PARTNER'S DISSOCIATION

§ 601. Events Causing Partner's Dissociation.

A partner is dissociated from a partnership upon the occurrence of any of the following events:

(1) the partnership's having notice of the partner's express will to withdraw as a partner or on a later date specified by the partner;

(2) an event agreed to in the partnership agreement as causing the partner's dissociation;

(3) the partner's expulsion pursuant to the partnership agreement;

(4) the partner's expulsion by the unanimous vote of the other partners if:

(i) it is unlawful to carry on the partnership business with that partner;

(ii) there has been a transfer of all or substantially all of that partner's transferable interest in the partnership, other than a transfer for security purposes, or a court order charging the partner's interest, which has not been foreclosed;

(iii) within 90 days after the partnership notifies a corporate partner that it will be expelled because it has filed a certificate of dissolution or the equivalent, its charter has been revoked, or its right to conduct business has been suspended by the jurisdiction of its incorporation, there is no revocation of the certificate of dissolution or no reinstatement of its charter or its right to conduct business; or

(iv) a partnership that is a partner has been dissolved and its business is being wound up;

(5) on application by the partnership or another partner, the partner's expulsion by judicial determination because:

(i) the partner engaged in wrongful conduct that adversely and materially affected the partnership business;

(ii) the partner willfully or persistently committed a material breach of the partnership agreement or of a duty owed to the partnership or the other partners under Section 404; or

(iii) the partner engaged in conduct relating to the partnership business which makes it not reasonably practicable to carry on the business in partnership with the partner;

(6) the partner's:

(i) becoming a debtor in bankruptcy;

(ii) executing an assignment for the benefit of creditors;

(iii) seeking, consenting to, or acquiescing in the appointment of a trustee, receiver, or liquidator of that partner or of all or substantially all of that partner's property; or

(iv) failing, within 90 days after the appointment, to have vacated or stayed the appointment of a trustee, receiver, or liquidator of the partner or of all or substantially all of the partner's property obtained without the partner's consent or acquiescence, or failing within 90 days after the expiration of a stay to have the appointment vacated;

(7) in the case of a partner who is an individual:

(i) the partner's death;

(ii) the appointment of a guardian or general conservator for the partner; or

(iii) a judicial determination that the partner has otherwise become incapable of performing the partner's duties under the partnership agreement;

(8) in the case of a partner that is a trust or is acting as a partner by virtue of being a trustee of a trust, distribution of the trust's entire transferable interest in the partnership, but not merely by reason of the substitution of a successor trustee;

(9) in the case of a partner that is an estate or is acting as a partner by virtue of being a personal representative of an estate, distribution of the estate's entire transferable interest in the partnership, but not merely by reason of the substitution of a successor personal representative; or

(10) termination of a partner who is not an individual, partnership, corporation, trust, or estate.

§ 602. Partner's Power to Dissociate; Wrongful Dissociation.

(a) A partner has the power to dissociate at any time, rightfully or wrongfully, by express will pursuant to Section 601(1).

(b) A partner's dissociation is wrongful only if:

(1) it is in breach of an express provision of the partnership agreement; or

(2) in the case of a partnership for a definite term or particular undertaking, before the expiration of the term or the completion of the undertaking:

(i) the partner withdraws by express will, unless the withdrawal follows within 90 days after another partner's dissociation by death or otherwise under Section 601(6) through (10) or wrongful dissociation under this subsection;

(ii) the partner is expelled by judicial determination under Section 601(5); or

(iii) the partner is dissociated by becoming a debtor in bankruptcy; or

(iv) in the case of a partner who is not an individual, trust other than a business trust, or estate, the partner is expelled or otherwise dissociated because it willfully dissolved or terminated.

(c) A partner who wrongfully dissociates is liable to the partnership and to the other partners for damages caused by the dissociation. The liability is in addition to any other obligation of the partner to the partnership or to the other partners.

§ 603. Effect of Partner's Dissociation.

(a) If a partner's dissociation results in a dissolution and winding up of the partnership business, Article 8 applies; otherwise, Article 7 applies.

(b) Upon a partner's dissociation:

(1) the partner's right to participate in the management and conduct of the partnership business terminates, except as otherwise provided in Section 803;

(2) the partner's duty of loyalty under Section 404(b)(3) terminates; and

(3) the partner's duty of loyalty under Section 404(b)(1) and (2) and duty of care under Section 404(c) continue only with regard to matters arising or events occurring before the partner's dissociation, unless the partner participates in winding up the partnership's business pursuant to Section 803.

ARTICLE 7. PARTNER'S DISSOCIATION WHEN BUSINESS NOT WOUND UP

§ 701. Purchase of Dissociated Partner's Interest.

(a) If a partner is dissociated from a partnership without resulting in a dissolution and winding up of the partnership business under Section 801, the partnership shall cause the dissociated partner's interest in the partnership to be purchased for a buyout price determined pursuant to subsection (b).

(b) The buyout price of a dissociated partner's interest is the amount that would have been distributable to the dissociating partner under Section 807(b) if, on the date of dissociation, the assets of the partnership were sold at a price equal to the greater of the liquidation value or the value based on a sale of the entire business as a going concern without the dissociated partner and the partnership were wound up as of that date. Interest must be paid from the date of dissociation to the date of payment.

(c) Damages for wrongful dissociation under Section 602(b), and all other amounts owing, whether or not presently due, from the dissociated partner to the partnership, must be offset against the buyout price. Interest must be paid from the date the amount owed becomes due to the date of payment.

(d) A partnership shall indemnify a dissociated partner whose interest is being purchased against all partnership liabilities, whether incurred before or after the dissociation, except liabilities incurred by an act of the dissociated partner under Section 702.

(e) If no agreement for the purchase of a dissociated partner's interest is reached within 120 days after a written demand for payment, the partnership shall pay, or cause to be paid, in cash to the dissociated partner the amount the partnership estimates to be the buyout price and accrued interest, reduced by any offsets and accrued interest under subsection (c).

(f) If a deferred payment is authorized under subsection (h), the partnership may tender a written offer to pay the amount it estimates to be the buyout price and accrued interest, reduced by any offsets under subsection (c), stating the time of payment, the amount and type of security for payment, and the other terms and conditions of the obligation.

(g) The payment or tender required by subsection (e) or (f) must be accompanied by the following:

(1) a statement of partnership assets and liabilities as of the date of dissociation;

(2) the latest available partnership balance sheet and income statement, if any;

(3) an explanation of how the estimated amount of the payment was calculated; and

(4) written notice that the payment is in full satisfaction of the obligation to purchase unless, within 120 days after the written notice, the dissociated partner commences an action to determine the buyout price, any offsets under subsection (c), or other terms of the obligation to purchase.

(h) A partner who wrongfully dissociates before the expiration of a definite term or the completion of a particular undertaking is not entitled to payment of any portion of the buyout price until the expiration of the term or completion of the undertaking, unless the partner establishes to the satisfaction of the court that earlier payment will not cause undue hardship to the business of the partnership. A deferred payment must be adequately secured and bear interest.

(i) A dissociated partner may maintain an action against the partnership, pursuant to Section 405(b)(2)(ii), to determine the buyout price of that partner's interest, any offsets under subsection (c), or other terms of the obligation to purchase. The action must be commenced within 120 days after the partnership has tendered payment or an offer to pay or within one year after written demand for payment if no payment or offer to pay is tendered. The court shall determine the buyout price of the dissociated partner's interest, any offset due under subsection (c), and accrued interest, and enter judgment for any additional payment or refund. If deferred payment is authorized under subsection (h), the court shall also determine the security for payment and other terms of the obligation to purchase. The court may assess reasonable attorney's fees and the fees and expenses of appraisers or other experts for a party to the action, in amounts the court finds equitable, against a party that the court finds acted arbitrarily, vexatiously, or not in good faith. The finding may be based on the partnership's failure to tender payment or an offer to pay or to comply with subsection (g).

§ 702. Dissociated Partner's Power to Bind and Liability to Partnership.

(a) For two years after a partner dissociates without resulting in a dissolution and winding up of the partnership business, the partnership, including a surviving partnership under [Article] 9, is bound by an act of the dissociated partner which would have bound the partnership under Section 301 before dissociation only if at the time of entering into the transaction the other party:

(1) reasonably believed that the dissociated partner was then a partner;

(2) did not have notice of the partner's dissociation; and

(3) is not deemed to have had knowledge under Section 303(e) or notice under Section 704(c).

(b) A dissociated partner is liable to the partnership for any damage caused to the partnership arising from an obligation incurred by the dissociated partner after dissociation for which the partnership is liable under subsection (a).

§ 703. Dissociated Partner's Liability to Other Persons.

(a) A partner's dissociation does not of itself discharge the partner's liability for a partnership obligation incurred before dissociation. A dissociated partner is not liable for a partnership obligation incurred after dissociation, except as otherwise provided in subsection (b).

(b) A partner who dissociates without resulting in a dissolution and winding up of the partnership business is liable as a partner to the other party in a transaction entered into by the partnership, or a surviving partnership under Article 9, within two years after the partner's dissociation, only if the partner is liable for the obligation under Section 306 and at the time of entering into the transaction the other party:

(1) reasonably believed that the dissociated partner was then a partner;

(2) did not have notice of the partner's dissociation; and

(3) is not deemed to have had knowledge under Section 303(e) or notice under Section 704(c).

(c) By agreement with the partnership creditor and the partners continuing the business, a dissociated partner may be released from liability for a partnership obligation.

(d) A dissociated partner is released from liability for a partnership obligation if a partnership creditor, with notice of the partner's dissociation but without the partner's consent, agrees to a material alteration in the nature or time of payment of a partnership obligation.

§ 704. Statement of Dissociation.

(a) A dissociated partner or the partnership may file a statement of dissociation stating the name of the partnership and that the partner is dissociated from the partnership.

(b) A statement of dissociation is a limitation on the authority of a dissociated partner for the purposes of Section 303(d) and (e).

(c) For the purposes of Sections 702(a)(3) and 703(b)(3), a person not a partner is deemed to have notice of the dissociation 90 days after the statement of dissociation is filed.

§ 705. Continued Use of Partnership Name.

Continued use of a partnership name, or a dissociated partner's name as part thereof, by partners continuing the business does not of itself make the dissociated partner liable for an obligation of the partners or the partnership continuing the business.

ARTICLE 8. WINDING UP PARTNERSHIP BUSINESS

§ 801. Events Causing Dissolution and Winding up of Partnership Business.

A partnership is dissolved, and its business must be wound up, only upon the occurrence of any of the following events:

(1) in a partnership at will, the partnership's having notice from a partner, other than a partner who is dissociated under Section 601(2) through (10), of that partner's express will to withdraw as a partner, or on a later date specified by the partner;

(2) in a partnership for a definite term or particular undertaking:

(i) within 90 days after a partner's dissociation by death or otherwise under Section 601(6) through (10) or wrongful dissociation under Section 602(b), the express will of at least half of the remaining partners to wind up the partnership business, for which purpose a partner's rightful dissociation pursuant to Section 602(b)(2)(i) constitutes the expression of that partner's will to wind up the partnership business.

(ii) the express will of all of the partners to wind up the partnership business; or

(iii) the expiration of the term or the completion of the undertaking;

(3) an event agreed to in the partnership agreement resulting in the winding up of the partnership business;

(4) an event that makes it unlawful for all or substantially all of the business of the partnership to be continued, but a cure of illegality within 90 days after notice to the partnership of the event is effective retroactively to the date of the event for purposes of this section;

(5) on application by a partner, a judicial determination that:

(i) the economic purpose of the partnership is likely to be unreasonably frustrated;

(ii) another partner has engaged in conduct relating to the partnership business which makes it not reasonably practicable to carry on the business in partnership with that partner; or

(iii) it is not otherwise reasonably practicable to carry on the partnership business in conformity with the partnership agreement; or

(6) on application by a transferee of a partner's transferable interest, a judicial determination that it is equitable to wind up the partnership business:

(i) after the expiration of the term or completion of the undertaking, if the partnership was for a definite term or particular undertaking at the time of the transfer or entry of the charging order that gave rise to the transfer; or

(ii) at any time, if the partnership was a partnership at will at the time of the transfer or entry of the charging order that gave rise to the transfer.

§ 802. Partnership Continues After Dissolution.

(a) Subject to subsection (b), a partnership continues after dissolution only for the purpose of winding up its business. The partnership is terminated when the winding up of its business is completed.

(b) At any time after the dissolution of a partnership and before the winding up of its business is completed, all of the partners, including any dissociating partner other than a wrongfully dissociating partner, may waive the right to have the partnership's business wound up and the partnership terminated. In that event:

(1) the partnership resumes carrying on its business as if dissolution had never occurred, and any liability incurred by the partnership or a partner after the dissolution and before the waiver is determined as if dissolution had never occurred; and

(2) the rights of a third party accruing under Section 804(1) or arising out of conduct in reliance on the dissolution before the third party knew or received a notification of the waiver may not be adversely affected.

§ 803. Right to Wind up Partnership Business.

(a) After dissolution, a partner who has not wrongfully dissociated may participate in winding up the partnership's business, but on application of any partner, partner's legal representative, or transferee, the [designate the appropriate court], for good cause shown, may order judicial supervision of the winding up.

(b) The legal representative of the last surviving partner may wind up a partnership's business.

(c) A person winding up a partnership's business may preserve the partnership business or property as a going concern for a reasonable time, prosecute and defend actions and proceedings, whether civil, criminal, or administrative, settle and close the partnership's business, dispose of and transfer the partnership's property, discharge the partnership's liabilities, distribute the assets of the partnership pursuant to Section 807, settle disputes by mediation or arbitration, and perform other necessary acts.

§ 804. Partner's Power to Bind Partnership After Dissolution.

Subject to Section 805, a partnership is bound by a partner's act after dissolution that:

(1) is appropriate for winding up the partnership business; or

(2) would have bound the partnership under Section 301 before dissolution, if the other party to the transaction did not have notice of the dissolution.

§ 805. Statement of Dissolution.

(a) After dissolution, a partner who has not wrongfully dissociated may file a statement of dissolution stating the name of the partnership and that the partnership has dissolved and is winding up its business.

(b) A statement of dissolution cancels a filed statement of partnership authority for the purposes of Section 303(d) and is a limitation on authority for the purposes of Section 303(e).

(c) For the purposes of Sections 301 and 804, a person not a partner is deemed to have notice of the dissolution and the limitation on the partners' authority as a result of the statement of dissolution 90 days after it is filed.

(d) After filing and, if appropriate, recording a statement of dissolution, a dissolved partnership may file and, if appropriate, record a statement of partnership authority which will operate with respect to a person not a partner as provided in Section 303(d) and (e) in any transaction, whether or not the transaction is appropriate for winding up the partnership business.

§ 806. Partner's Liability to Other Partners After Dissolution.

(a) Except as otherwise provided in subsection (b) and Section 306, after dissolution a partner is liable to the other partners for the partner's share of any partnership liability incurred under Section 804.

(b) A partner who, with knowledge of the dissolution, incurs a partnership liability under Section 804(2) by an act that is not appropriate for winding up the partnership business is liable to the partnership for any damage caused to the partnership arising from the liability.

§ 807. Settlement of Accounts and Contributions Among Partners.

(a) In winding up a partnership's business, the assets of the partnership, including the contributions of the partners required by this section, must be applied to discharge its obligations to creditors, including, to the extent permitted by law, partners who are creditors. Any surplus must be applied to pay in cash the net amount distributable to partners in accordance with their right to distributions under subsection (b).

(b) Each partner is entitled to a settlement of all partnership accounts upon winding up the partnership business. In settling accounts among the partners, the profits and losses that result from the liquidation of the partnership assets must be credited and charged to the partners' accounts. The partnership shall make a distribution to a partner in an amount equal to any excess of the credits over the charges in the partner's account. A partner shall contribute to the partnership an amount equal to any excess of the charges over the credits in the partner's account but excluding from the calculation charges attributable to an obligation for which the partner is not personally liable under Section 306.

(c) If a partner fails to contribute the full amount required under subsection (b), all of the other partners shall contribute, in the proportions in which those partners share partnership losses, the additional amount necessary to satisfy the partnership obligations for which they are personally liable under Section 306. A partner or partner's legal representative may recover from the other partners any contributions the partner makes to the extent the amount contributed exceeds that partner's share of the partnership obligations for which the partner is personally liable under Section 306.

(d) After the settlement of accounts, each partner shall contribute, in the proportion in which the partner shares partnership losses, the amount necessary to satisfy partnership obligations that were not known at the time of the settlement and for which the partner is personally liable under Section 306.

(e) The estate of a deceased partner is liable for the partner's obligation to contribute to the partnership.

(f) An assignee for the benefit of creditors of a partnership or a partner, or a person appointed by a court to represent creditors of a partnership or a partner, may enforce a partner's obligation to contribute to the partnership.

ARTICLE 9. CONVERSIONS AND MERGERS

§ 901. Definitions

In this article:

(1) "General partner" means a partner in a partnership and a general partner in a limited partnership.

(2) "Limited partner" means a limited partner in a limited partnership.

(3) "Limited partnership" means a limited partnership created under the [State Limited Partnership Act], predecessor law, or comparable law of another jurisdiction.

(4) "Partner" includes both a general partner and a limited partner.

§ 902. Conversion of Partnership to Limited Partnership.

(a) A partnership may be converted to a limited partnership pursuant to this section.

(b) The terms and conditions of a conversion of a partnership to a limited partnership must be approved by all of the partners or by a number or percentage specified for conversion in the partnership agreement.

(c) After the conversion is approved by the partners, the partnership shall file a certificate of limited partnership in the jurisdiction in which the limited partnership is to be formed. The certificate must include:

(1) a statement that the partnership was converted to a limited partnership from a partnership;

(2) its former name; and

(3) a statement of the number of votes cast by the partners for and against the conversion and, if the vote is less than unanimous, the number or percentage required to approve the conversion under the partnership agreement.

(d) The conversion takes effect when the certificate of limited partnership is filed or at any later date specified in the certificate.

(e) A general partner who becomes a limited partner as a result of the conversion remains liable as a general partner for an obligation incurred by the partnership before the conversion takes effect. If the other party to a transaction with the limited partnership reasonably believes when entering the transaction that the limited partner is a general partner, the limited partner is liable for an obligation incurred by the limited partnership within 90 days after the conversion takes effect. The limited partner's liability for all other obligations of the limited partnership incurred after the conversion takes effect is that of a limited partner as provided in the [State Limited Partnership Act].

§ 903. Conversion of Limited Partnership to Partnership.

(a) A limited partnership may be converted to a partnership pursuant to this section.

(b) Notwithstanding a provision to the contrary in a limited partnership agreement, the terms and conditions of a conversion of a limited partnership to a partnership must be approved by all of the partners.

(c) After the conversion is approved by the partners, the limited partnership shall cancel its certificate of limited partnership.

(d) The conversion takes effect when the certificate of limited partnership is canceled.

(e) A limited partner who becomes a general partner as a result of the conversion remains liable only as a limited partner for an obligation incurred by the limited partnership before the conversion takes effect. Except as otherwise provided in Section 306, the partner is liable as a general partner for an obligation of the partnership incurred after the conversion takes effect.

§ 904. Effect of Conversion; Entity Unchanged.

(a) A partnership or limited partnership that has been converted pursuant to this article is for all purposes the same entity that existed before the conversion.

(b) When a conversion takes effect:

(1) all property owned by the converting partnership or limited partnership remains vested in the converted entity;

(2) all obligations of the converting partnership or limited partnership continue as obligations of the converted entity; and

(3) an action or proceeding pending against the converting partnership or limited partnership may be continued as if the conversion had not occurred.

§ 905. Merger of Partnerships.

(a) Pursuant to a plan of merger approved as provided in subsection (c), a partnership may be merged with one or more partnerships or limited partnerships.

(b) The plan of merger must set forth:

(1) the name of each partnership or limited partnership that is a party to the merger;

(2) the name of the surviving entity into which the other partnerships or limited partnerships will merge;

(3) whether the surviving entity is a partnership or a limited partnership and the status of each partner;

(4) the terms and conditions of the merger;

(5) the manner and basis of converting the interests of each party to the merger into interests or obligations of the surviving entity, or into money or other property in whole or part; and

(6) the street address of the surviving entity's chief executive office.

(c) The plan of merger must be approved:

(1) in the case of a partnership that is a party to the merger, by all of the partners, or a number or percentage specified for merger in the partnership agreement; and

(2) in the case of a limited partnership that is a party to the merger, by the vote required for approval of a merger by the law of the State or foreign jurisdiction in which the limited partnership is organized and, in the absence of such a specifically applicable law, by all of the partners, notwithstanding a provision to the contrary in the partnership agreement.

(d) After a plan of merger is approved and before the merger takes effect, the plan may be amended or abandoned as provided in the plan.

(e) The merger takes effect on the later of:

(1) the approval of the plan of merger by all parties to the merger, as provided in subsection (c);

(2) the filing of all documents required by law to be filed as a condition to the effectiveness of the merger; or

(3) any effective date specified in the plan of merger.

§ 906. Effect of Merger.

(a) When a merger takes effect:

(1) the separate existence of every partnership or limited partnership that is a party to the merger, other than the surviving entity, ceases;

(2) all property owned by each of the merged partnerships or limited partnerships vests in the surviving entity;

(3) all obligations of every partnership or limited partnership that is a party to the merger become the obligations of the surviving entity; and

(4) an action or proceeding pending against a partnership or limited partnership that is a party to the merger may be continued as if the merger had not occurred, or the surviving entity may be substituted as a party to the action or proceeding.

(b) The [Secretary of State] of this State is the agent for service of process in an action or proceeding against a surviving foreign partnership or limited partnership to enforce an obligation of a domestic partnership or limited partnership that is a party to a merger. The surviving entity shall promptly notify the [Secretary of State] of the mailing address of its chief executive office and of any change of address. Upon receipt of process, the [Secretary of State] shall mail a copy of the process to the surviving foreign partnership or limited partnership.

(c) A partner of the surviving partnership or limited partnership is liable for:

(1) all obligations of a party to the merger for which the partner was personally liable before the merger;

(2) all other obligations of the surviving entity incurred before the merger by a party to the merger, but those obligations may be satisfied only out of property of the entity; and

(3) all obligations of the surviving entity incurred after the merger takes effect, but those obligations may be satisfied only out of property of the entity if the partner is a limited partner.

(d) If the obligations incurred before the merger by a party to the merger are not satisfied out of the property of the surviving partnership or limited partnership, the general partners of that party immediately before the effective date of the merger shall contribute the amount necessary to satisfy that party's obligations to the surviving entity, in the manner provided in Section 807 or in the Limited Partnership Act of the jurisdiction in which the party was formed, as the case may be, as if the merged party were dissolved.

(e) A partner of a party to a merger who does not become a partner of the surviving partnership or limited partnership is dissociated from the entity, of which that partner was a partner, as of the date the merger takes effect. The surviving entity shall cause the partner's interest in the entity to be purchased under Section 701 or another statute specifically applicable to that partner's interest with respect to a merger. The surviving entity is bound under Section 702 by an act of a general partner dissociated under this subsection, and the partner is liable under Section 703 for transactions entered into by the surviving entity after the merger takes effect.

§ 907. Statement of Merger.

(a) After a merger, the surviving partnership or limited partnership may file a statement that one or more partnerships or limited partnerships have merged into the surviving entity.

(b) A statement of merger must contain:

(1) the name of each partnership or limited partnership that is a party to the merger;

(2) the name of the surviving entity into which the other partnerships or limited partnership were merged;

(3) the street address of the surviving entity's chief executive office and of an office in this State, if any; and

(4) whether the surviving entity is a partnership or a limited partnership.

(c) Except as otherwise provided in subsection (d), for the purposes of Section 302, property of the surviving partnership or limited partnership which before the merger was held in the name of another party to the merger is property held in the name of the surviving entity upon filing a statement of merger.

(d) For the purposes of Section 302, real property of the surviving partnership or limited partnership which before the merger was held in the name of another party to the merger is property held in the name of the surviving entity upon recording a certified copy of the statement of merger in the office for recording transfers of that real property.

(e) A filed and, if appropriate, recorded statement of merger, executed and declared to be accurate pursuant to Section 105(c), stating the name of a partnership or limited partnership that is a party to the merger in whose name property was held before the merger and the name of the surviving entity, but not containing all of the other information required by subsection (b), operates with respect to the partnerships or limited partnerships named to the extent provided in subsections (c) and (d).

§ 908. Nonexclusive.

This [article] is not exclusive. Partnerships or limited partnerships may be converted or merged in any other manner provided by law.

ARTICLE 10. LIMITED LIABILITY PARTNERSHIP

§ 1001. Statement of Qualification.

(a) A partnership may become a limited liability partnership pursuant to this section.

(b) The terms and conditions on which a partnership becomes a limited liability partnership must be approved by the vote necessary to amend the partnership agreement except, in the case of a partnership agreement that expressly considers obligations to contribute to the partnership, the vote necessary to amend those provisions.

(c) After the approval required by subsection (b), a partnership may become a limited liability partnership by filing a statement of qualification. The statement must contain:

(1) The name of the partnership:

(2) the street address of the partnership's chief executive office and, if different, the street address of an office in this State, if any;

(3) if the partnership does not have an office in this State, the name and street address of the partnership's agent for service of process;

(4) a statement that the partnership elects to be a limited liability partnership; and

(5) a deferred effective date, if any.

(d) The agent of a limited liability partnership for service of process must be an individual who is a resident of this State or other person authorized to do business in this State.

(e) The status of a partnership as a limited liability partnership is effective on the later of the filing of the statement or a date specified in the statement. The status remains effective, regardless of changes in the partnership, until it is canceled pursuant to Section 105(d) or revoked pursuant to Section 1003.

(f) The status of a partnership as a limited liability partnership and the liability of its partners is not affected by errors or later changes in the information required to be contained in the statement of qualification under subsection (c).

(g) The filing of a statement of qualification establishes that a partnership has satisfied all conditions precedent to the qualification of the partnership as a limited liability partnership.

(h) An amendment or cancellation of a statement of qualification is effective when it is filed or on a deferred effective date specified in the amendment or cancellation.

§ 1002. Name.

The name of a limited liability partnership must end with "Registered Limited Liability Partnership," "Limited Liability Partnership," "R.L.L.P.," "L.L.P," "RLLP," or "LLP."

§ 1003. Annual Report.

(a) A limited liability partnership, and a foreign limited liability partnership authorized to transact business in this State, shall file an annual report in the office of the [Secretary of State] which contains:

(1) the name of the limited liability partnership and the State or other jurisdiction under whose laws the foreign limited liability partnership is formed;

(2) the street address of the partnership's chief executive office and, if different, the street address of an office in this State, if any; and

(3) if the partnership does not have an office in this State, the name and street address of the partnership's current agent for service of process.

(b) An annual report must be filed between [January 1 and April 1] of each year following the calendar year in which a partnership files a statement of qualification or a foreign partnership becomes authorized to transact business in this State.

(c) The [Secretary of State] may administratively revoke the statement of qualification of a partnership that fails to file an annual report when due or to pay the required filing fee. The [Secretary of State] shall provide the partnership at least 60 days' written notice of intent to revoke the statement. The notice must be mailed to the partnership at its chief executive office set forth in the last filed statement of qualification or annual report. The notice must specify the annual report that has not been filed, the fee that has not been paid, and the effective date o the revocation. The revocation is not effective if the annual report is filed and the fee is paid before the effective date of the revocation.

(d) A revocation under subsection (c) only affects a partnership's status as a limited liability partnership and is not an event of dissolution of the partnership.

(e) A partnership whose statement of qualification has been revoked may apply to the [Secretary of State] for reinstatement within two years after the effective date of the revocation. The application must state:

(1) the name of the partnership and the effective date of the revocation; and

(2) that the ground for revocation either did not exist or has been corrected.

(f) A reinstatement under subsection (e) relates back to and takes effect as of the effective date of the revocation, and the partnership's status as a limited liability partnership continues as if the revocation had never occurred.

ARTICLE 11. FOREIGN LIMITED LIABILITY PARTNERSHIP

§ 1101. Law Governing Foreign Limited Liability Partnership.

(a) The law under which a foreign limited liability partnership is formed govern relations among the partners and between the partners and the partnership and the liability of partners for obligations of the partnership.

(b) a foreign limited liability partnership may not be denied a statement of foreign qualification by reason of any difference between the laws under which the partnership was formed and the laws of this State.

(c) A statement of foreign qualification does not authorize a foreign limited liability partnership to engage in any business or exercise any power that a partnership may not engage in or exercise in this State as a limited liability partnership.

§ 1102. Statement of Foreign Qualification.

(a) Before transaction business in this State, a foreign limited liability partnership must file a statement of foreign qualification. The statement must contain:

(1) the name of the foreign limited liability partnership which satisfies the requirements of the State or other jurisdiction under whose law it is formed and ends with "Registered Limited Liability Partnership," "Limited Liability Partnership," "R.L.L.P.", "L.L.P.," "RLLP," or "LLP";

(2) the street address of the partnership's chief executive office and, if different, the street address of an office of the partnership in this State, if any;

(3) if there is no office of the partnership in this State, the name and street address of the partnership's agent for service of process; and

(4) a deferred effective date, if any.

(b) The agent of a foreign limited liability company for service of process must be an individual who is a resident of this State or other person authorized to do business in this State.

(c) The status of a partnership as a foreign limited liability partnership is effective on the later of the filing of the statement of foreign qualification or a date specified in the statement. The status remains effective, regardless of changes in the partnership, until it is canceled pursuant to Section 105(d) or revoked pursuant to Section 1003.

(d) An amendment or cancellation of a statement of foreign qualification is effective when it is filed or on a deferred effective date specified in the amendment or cancellation.

§ 1103. Effect of Failure to Qualify.

(a) A foreign limited liability partnership transaction business in this State may not maintain an action or proceeding in this State unless it has in effect a statement of foreign qualification.

(b) The failure or a foreign limited liability partnership to have in effect a statement of foreign qualification does not impair the validity of a contract or act of the foreign limited liability partnership or preclude it from defending an action or proceeding in this State.

(c) A limitation on personal liability of a partner is not waived solely by transacting business in this State without a statement of foreign qualification.

(d) If a foreign limited liability partnership transacts business in this State without a statement of foreign qualification, the [Secretary of State] is its agent for service of process with respect to a right of action arising out of the transaction of business in this State.

§ 1104. Activities Not Constituting Transacting Business.

(a) Activities of a foreign limited liability partnership which do not constitute transacting business for the purpose of this [article] include:

(1) maintaining, defending, or settling an action or proceeding;

(2) holding meeting of its partners or carrying on any other activity concerning its internal affairs;

(3) maintaining bank accounts;

(4) maintaining offices or agencies for the transfer, exchange, and registration of the partnership's own securities or maintaining trustees or depositories with respect to those securities;

(5) selling through independent contractors;

(6) soliciting or obtaining orders, whether by mail or through employees or agents or otherwise, if the orders require acceptance outside this State before they become contracts;

(7) creating or acquiring indebtedness, with or without a mortgage, or other security interest in property;

(8) collecting debts or foreclosing mortgages or other security interests in property securing the debts, and holding, protecting, and maintaining property so acquired;

(9) conducting an isolated transaction that is completed within 30 days and is not one in the course of similar transactions; and

(10) transacting business in interstate commerce.

(b) For purposes of this [article], the ownership in this State of income-producing real property or tangible personal property, other than property excluded under subsection (a), constitutes transacting business in this State.

(c) This section does not apply in determining the contacts or activities that may subject a foreign limited liability partnership to service of process, taxation, or regulation under any other law of this State.

§ 1105. Action by [Attorney General].

The [Attorney General] may maintain an action to restrain a foreign limited liability partnership from transacting business in this State in violation of this [article].

§ 1201. Uniformity of Application and Construction.

This [Act] shall be applied and construed to effectuate its general purpose to make uniform the law with respect to the subject of this [Act] among States enacting it.

§ 1202. Short Title.

This [Act] may be cited as the Uniform Partnership Act (1997) (~~1994~~).

§ 1203. Severability Clause.

If any provision of this [Act] or its application to any person or circumstance is held invalid, the invalidity does not affect other provisions or applications of this [Act] which can be given effect without the invalid provision or application, and to this end the provisions of this [Act] are severable.

§ 1204. Effective Date.

This [Act] takes effect....

§ 1205. Repeals.

Effective January 1, 199__, the following acts and parts of acts are repealed: [the State Partnership Act as amended and in effect immediately before the effective date of this [Act]].

§ 1206. Applicability.

(a) Before January 1, 199__, this [Act] governs only a partnership formed:

(1) after the effective date of this [Act], except a partnership that is continuing the business of a dissolved partnership under [Section 41 of the superceded Uniform Partnership Act]; and

(2) before the effective date of this [Act], that elects, as provided by subsection (c), to be governed by this [Act].

(b) On and after January 1, 199__, this [Act] governs all partnerships.

(c) Before January 1, 199__, a partnership voluntarily may elect, in the manner provided in its partnership agreement or by law for amending the partnership agreement, to be governed by this [Act]. The provisions of this [Act] relating to the liability of the partnership's partners to third parties apply to limit those partners' liability to a third party who had done business with the partnership within one year before the partnership's election to be governed by this [Act], only if the third party knows or has received a notification of the partnership's election to be governed by this [Act].

§ 1207. Savings Clause.

This [Act] does not affect an action or proceeding commenced or right accrued before this [Act] takes effect.

§ 1208. Effective Date.

These [Amendments] take effect ....

§ 1209. Repeals.

Effective January 1, 199__, the following acts and parts of acts are repealed: [the Limited Liability Partnership X amendments to the State Partnership Act as amended and in effect immediately before the effective date of these [Amendments]].

§ 1210. Applicability.

(a) Before January 1, 199__, these [Amendments] govern only a limited liability partnership formed:

(1) on or after the effective date of these [Amendments], unless that partnership is continuing the business of a dissolved limited liability partnership; and

(2) before the effective date of these [Amendments], that elects, as provided by subsection (c), to be governed by these [Amendments].

(b) On and after January 1, 199__, these [Amendments] govern all partnerships.

(c) Before January 1, 199__, a partnership voluntarily may elect, in the manner provided in its partnership agreement or by law for amending the partnership agreement, to be governed by these [Amendments]. The provisions of these [Amendments] relating to the liability of the partnership's partners to third parties apply to limit those partner' liability to a third party who had done business with the partnership within one year before the partnership's election to be governed by these [Amendments], only if the third party knows or has received a notification of the partnership's election to be governed by these [Amendments].

(d)The existing provisions for execution and filing a statement of qualification of a limited liability partnership continue until either the limited liability partnership elects to have this [Act] apply or January 1, 199__.

§ 1211. Savings Clause.

These [Amendments] do not affect an action or proceeding commenced or right accrued before these [Amendments] take effect.

C. UNIFORM LIMITED PARTNERSHIP ACT

1916 ACT

See, also, Revised Uniform Limited Partnership Act of 1976 with the 1985 amendments, supra.

Contents

Official Comment

The business reason for the adoption of acts making provisions for limited or special partners is that men in business often desire to secure capital from others. There are at least three classes of contracts which can be made with those from whom the capital is secured: One, the ordinary loan on interest; another, the loan where the lender, in lieu of interest, takes a share in the profits of the business; third, those cases in which the person advancing the capital secures, besides a share in the profits, some measure of control over the business.

At first, in the absence of statutes the courts, both in this country and in England, assumed that one who is interested in a business is bound by its obligations, carrying the application of this principle so far, that a contract where the only evidence of interest was a share in the profits made one who supposed himself a lender, and who was probably unknown to the creditors at the times they extended their credits, unlimitedly liable as a partner for the obligations of those actually conducting the business.

Later decisions have much modified the earlier cases. The lender who takes a share in the profits, except possibly in one or two of our jurisdictions, does not by reason of that fact run a risk of being held as a partner. If, however, his contract falls within the third class mentioned, and he has any measure of control over the business, he at once runs serious risk of being held liable for the debts of the business as a partner; the risk increasing as he increases the amount of his control.

The first Limited Partnership Act was adopted by New York in 1822; the other commercial states, during the ensuing 30 years, following her example. Most of the statutes follow the language of the New York statute with little material alteration. These statutes were adopted, and to a considerable degree interpreted by the courts, during that period when it was generally held that any interest in a business should make the person holding the interest liable for its obligations. As a result the courts usually assume in the interpretation of these statutes two principles as fundamental.

First: That a limited (or as he is also called a special) partner is a partner in all respects like any other partner, except that to obtain the privilege of a limitation on his liability, he has conformed to the statutory requirements in respect to filing a certificate and refraining from participation in the conduct of the business.

Second: The limited partner, on any failure to follow the requirements in regard to the certificate or any participation in the conduct of his business, loses his privilege of limited liability and becomes, as far as those dealing with the business are concerned, in all respects a partner.

The courts in thus interpreting the statutes, although they made an American partnership with limited members something very different from the French Societe en Commandite from which the idea of the original statutes was derived, unquestionably carried out the intent of those responsible for their adoption. This is shown by the very wording of the statutes themselves. For instance, all the statutes require that all partners, limited and general, shall sign the certificate, and nearly all state that: "If any false statement be made in such certificate all the persons interested in such partnership shall be liable for all the engagements thereof as general partners."

The practical result of the spirit shown in the language and in the interpretation of existing statutes, coupled with the fact that a man may now lend money to a partnership and take a share in the profits in lieu of interest without running serious danger of becoming bound for partnership obligations, has, to a very great extent, deprived the existing statutory provisions for limited partners of any practical usefulness. Indeed, apparently their use is largely confined to associations in which those who conduct the business have not more than one limited partner.

One of the causes forcing business into the corporate form, in spite of the fact that the corporate form is ill suited to many business conditions, is the failure of the existing limited partnership acts to meet the desire of the owners of a business to secure necessary capital under the existing limited partnership form of business association.

The draft herewith submitted proceeds on the following assumptions:

First: No public policy requires a person who contributes to the capital of a business, acquires an interest in the profits, and some degree of control over the conduct of the business, to become bound for the obligations of the business; provided creditors have no reason to believe at the times their credits were extended that such person was so bound.

Second: That persons in business should be able, while remaining themselves liable without limit for the obligations contracted in its conduct, to associate with themselves others who contribute to the capital and acquire rights of ownership, provided that such contributors do not compete with creditors for the assets of the partnership.

The attempt to carry out these ideas has led to the incorporation into the draft submitted of certain features, not found in, or differing from, existing limited partnership acts.

First: In the draft the person who contributes the capital, though in accordance with custom called a limited partner, is not in any sense a partner. He is, however, a member of the association (see Sec. 1.).

Second: As limited partners are not partners securing limited liability by filing a certificate, the association is formed when substantial compliance, in good faith, is had with the requirements for a certificate (Sec. 2(2)). This provision eliminates the difficulties which arise from the recognition of de facto associations, made necessary by the assumption that the association is not formed unless a strict compliance with the requirements of the act is had.

Third: The limited partner not being in any sense a principal in the business, failure to comply with the requirements of the act in respect to the certificate, while it may result in the nonformation of the association, does not make him a partner or liable as such. The exact nature of his ability in such cases is set forth in Sec. 11.

Fourth: The limited partner, while not as such in any sense a partner, may become a partner as any person not a member of the association may become a partner; and, becoming a partner, may nevertheless retain his rights as limited partner; this last provision enabling the entire capital embraced in the business to be divided between the limited partners, all the general partners being also limited partners (Sec. 12).

Fifth: The limited partner is not debarred from loaning money or transacting other business with the partnership as any other nonmember; provided he does not, in respect to such transactions, accept from the partnership collateral security, or receive from any partner or the partnership any payment, conveyance, or release from liability, if at the time the assets of the partnership are not sufficient to discharge its obligations to persons not general or limited partners. (Sec. 13).

Sixth: The substitution of a person as limited partner in place of an existing limited partner, or the withdrawal of a limited partner, or the addition of new limited partners, does not necessarily dissolve the association (Secs. 8, 16(2b)); no limited partner, however, can withdraw his contribution until all liabilities to creditors are paid (Sec. 16(1a)).

Seventh: As limited partners are not principals in transactions of the partnership, their liability, except for known false statements in the certificate (Sec. 6), is to the partnership, not to creditors of the partnership (Sec. 17). The general partners cannot, however, waive any liability of the limited partners to the prejudice of such creditors (Sec. 17(3)).

§ 1. Limited Partnership Defined

A limited partnership is a partnership formed by two or more persons under the provisions of Section 2, having as members one or more general partners and one or more limited partners. The limited partners as such shall not be bound by the obligations of the partnership.

§ 2. Formation

(1) Two or more persons desiring to form a limited partnership shall

(a) Sign and swear to a certificate, which shall state

I. The name of the partnership,

II. The character of the business,

III. The location of the principal place of business,

IV. The name and place of residence of each member; general and limited partners being respectively designated,

V. The term for which the partnership is to exist,

VI. The amount of cash and a description of and the agreed value of the other property contributed by each limited partner,

VII. The additional contributions, if any, agreed to be made by each limited partner and the times at which or events on the happening of which they shall be made,

VIII. The time, if agreed upon, when the contribution of each limited partner is to be returned,

IX. The share of the profits or the other compensation by way of income which each limited partner shall receive by reason of his contribution,

X. The right, if given, of a limited partner to substitute an assignee as contributor in his place, and the terms and conditions of the substitution,

XI. The right, if given, of the partners to admit additional limited partners,

XII. The right, if given, of one or more of the limited partners to priority over other limited partners, as to contributions or as to compensation by way of income, and the nature of such priority,

XIII. The right, if given, of the remaining general partner or partners to continue the business on the death, retirement or insanity of a general partner, and

XIV. The right, if given, of a limited partner to demand and receive property other than cash in return for his contribution.

(b) File for record the certificate in the office of [here designate the proper office].

(2) A limited partnership is formed if there has been substantial compliance in good faith with the requirements of paragraph (1).

§ 3. Business Which May Be Carried On

A limited partnership may carry on any business which a partnership without limited partners may carry on, except [here designate the business to be prohibited].

§ 4. Character of Limited Partner's Contribution

The contributions of a limited partner may be cash or other property, but not services.

§ 5. A Name Not to Contain Surname of Limited Partner; Exceptions

(1) The surname of a limited partner shall not appear in the partnership name, unless

(a) It is also the surname of a general partner, or

(b) Prior to the time when the limited partner became such the business had been carried on under a name in which his surname appeared.

(2) A limited partner whose name appears in a partnership name contrary to the provisions of paragraph (1) is liable as a general partner to partnership creditors who extend credit to the partnership without actual knowledge that he is not a general partner.

§ 6. Liability for False Statements in Certificate

If the certificate contains a false statement, one who suffers loss by reliance on such statement may hold liable any party to the certificate who knew the statement to be false.

(a) At the time he signed the certificate, or

(b) Subsequently, but within a sufficient time before the statement was relied upon to enable him to cancel or amend the certificate, or to file a petition for its cancellation or amendment as provided in Section 25(3).

§ 7. Limited Partner Not Liable to Creditors

A limited partner shall not become liable as a general partner unless, in addition to the exercise of his rights and powers as a limited partner, he takes part in the control of the business.

§ 8. Admission of Additional Limited Partners

After the formation of a limited partnership, additional limited partners may be admitted upon filing an amendment to the original certificate in accordance with the requirements of Section 25.

§ 9. Rights, Powers and Liabilities of a General Partner

(1) A general partner shall have all the rights and powers and be subject to all the restrictions and liabilities of a partner in a partnership without limited partners, except that without the written consent or ratification of the specific act by all the limited partners, a general partner or all of the general partners have no authority to

(a) Do any act in contravention of the certificate,

(b) Do any act which would make it impossible to carry on the ordinary business of the partnership,

(c) Confess a judgment against the partnership,

(d) Possess partnership property, or assign their rights in specific partnership property, for other than a partnership purpose,

(e) Admit a person as a general partner,

(f) Admit a person as a limited partner, unless the right so to do is given in the certificate,

(g) Continue the business with partnership property on the death, retirement or insanity of a general partner, unless the right so to do is given in the certificate.

§ 10. Rights of a Limited Partner

(1) A limited partner shall have the same rights as a general partner to

(a) Have the partnership books kept at the principal place of business of the partnership, and at all times to inspect and copy any of them.

(b) Have on demand true and full information of all things affecting the partnership, and a formal account of partnership affairs whenever circumstances render it just and reasonable, and

(c) Have dissolution and winding up by decree of court.

(2) A limited partner shall have the right to receive a share of the profits or other compensation by way of income, and to the return of his contribution as provided in Sections 15 and 16.

§ 11. Status of Person Erroneously Believing Himself a Limited Partner

A person who has contributed to the capital of a business conducted by a person or partnership erroneously believing that he has become a limited partner in a limited partnership, is not, by reason of his exercise of the rights of a limited partner, a general partner with the person or in the partnership carrying on the business, or bound by the obligations of such person or partnership; provided that on ascertaining the mistake he promptly renounces his interest in the profits of the business, or other compensation by way of income.

§ 12. One Person Both General and Limited Partner

(1) A person may be a general partner and a limited partner in the same partnership at the same time.

(2) A person who is a general, and also at the same time a limited partner, shall have all the rights and powers and be subject to all the restrictions of a general partner; except that, in respect to his contribution, he shall have the rights against the other members which he would have had if he were not also a general partner.

§ 13. Loans and Other Business Transactions With Limited Partner

(1) A limited partner also may loan money to and transact other business with the partnership, and, unless he is also a general partner, receive on account of resulting claims against the partnership, with general creditors, a pro rata share of the assets. No limited partner shall in respect to any such claim

(a) Receive or hold as collateral security any partnership property, or

(b) Receive from a general partner or the partnership any payment, conveyance, or release from liability, if at the time the assets of the partnership are not sufficient to discharge partnership liabilities to persons not claiming as general or limited partners,

(2) The receiving of collateral security, or a payment, conveyance, or release in violation of the provisions of paragraph (1) is a fraud on the creditors of the partnership.

§ 14. Relation of Limited Partners Inter Se

Where there are several limited partners the members may agree that one or more of the limited partners shall have a priority over other limited partners as to the return of their contributions, as to their compensation by way of income, or as to any other matter. If such an agreement is made it shall be stated in the certificate, and in the absence of such a statement all the limited partners shall stand upon equal footing.

§ 15. Compensation of Limited Partner

A limited partner may receive from the partnership the share of the profits or the compensation by way of income stipulated for in the certificate; provided, that after such payment is made, whether from the property of the partnership or that of a general partner, the partnership assets are in excess of all liabilities of the partnership except liabilities to limited partners on account of their contributions and to general partners.

§ 16. Withdrawal or Reduction of Limited Partner's Contribution

(1) A limited partner shall not receive from a general partner or out of partnership property any part of his contribution until

(a) All liabilities of the partnership, except liabilities to general partners and to limited partners on account of their contributions, have been paid or there remains property of the partnership sufficient to pay them,

(b) The consent of all members is had, unless the return of the contribution may be rightfully demanded under the provisions of paragraph (2), and

(c) The certificate is cancelled or so amended as to set forth the withdrawal or reduction.

(2) Subject to the provisions of paragraph (1) a limited partner may rightfully demand the return of his contribution

(a) On the dissolution of a partnership, or

(b) When the date specified in the certificate for its return has arrived, or

(c) After he has given six months' notice in writing to all other members, if no time is specified in the certificate either for the return of the contribution or for the dissolution of the partnership,

(3) In the absence of any statement in the certificate to the contrary or the consent of all members, a limited partner, irrespective of the nature of his contribution, has only the right to demand and receive cash in return for his contribution.

(4) A limited partner may have the partnership dissolved and its affairs wound up when

(a) He rightfully but unsuccessfully demands the return of his contribution, or

(b) The other liabilities of the partnership have not been paid, or the partnership property is insufficient for their payment as required by paragraph (1a) and the limited partner would otherwise be entitled to the return of his contribution.

§ 17. Liability of Limited Partner to Partnership

(1) A limited partner is liable to the partnership

(a) For the difference between his contribution as actually made and that stated in the certificate as having been made, and

(b) For any unpaid contribution which he agreed in the certificate to make in the future at the time and on the conditions stated in the certificate.

(2) A limited partner holds as trustee for the partnership

(a) Specific property stated in the certificate as contributed by him, but which was not contributed or which has been wrongfully returned, and

(b) Money or other property wrongfully paid or conveyed to him on account of his contribution.

(3) The liabilities of a limited partner as set forth in this section can be waived or compromised only by the consent of all members; but a waiver or compromise shall not affect the right of a creditor of a partnership who extended credit or whose claim arose after the filing and before a cancellation or amendment of the certificate, to enforce such liabilities.

(4) When a contributor has rightfully received the return in whole or in part of the capital of his contribution, he is nevertheless liable to the partnership for any sum, not in excess of such return with interest, necessary to discharge its liabilities to all creditors who extended credit or whose claims arose before such return.

§ 18. Nature of Limited Partner's Interest in Partnership

A limited partner's interest in the partnership is personal property.

§ 19. Assignment of Limited Partner's Interest

(1) A limited partner's interest is assignable.

(2) A substituted limited partner is a person admitted to all the rights of a limited partner who has died or has assigned his interest in a partnership.

(3) An assignee, who does not become a substituted limited partner, has no right to require any information or account of the partnership transactions or to inspect the partnership books; he is only entitled to receive the share of the profits or other compensation by way of income, or the return of his contribution, to which his assignor would otherwise be entitled.

(4) An assignee shall have the right to become a substituted limited partner if all the members (except the assignor) consent thereto or if the assignor, being thereunto empowered by the certificate, gives the assignee that right.

(5) An assignee becomes a substituted limited partner when the certificate is appropriately amended in accordance with Section 25.

(6) The substituted limited partner has all the rights and powers, and is subject to all the restrictions and liabilities of his assignor, except those liabilities of which he was ignorant at the time he became a limited partner and which could not be ascertained from the certificate.

(7) The substitution of the assignee as a limited partner does not release the assignor from liability to the partnership under Sections 6 and 17.

§ 20. Effect of Retirement, Death or Insanity of a General Partner

The retirement, death or insanity of a general partner dissolves the partnership, unless the business is continued by the remaining general partners

(a) Under a right so to do stated in the certificate, or

(b) With the consent of all members.

§ 21. Death of Limited Partner

(1) On the death of a limited partner his executor or administrator shall have all the rights of a limited partner for the purpose of settling his estate, and such power as the deceased had to constitute his assignee a substituted limited partner.

(2) The estate of a deceased limited partner shall be liable for all his liabilities as a limited partner.

§ 22. Rights of Creditors of Limited Partner

(1) On due application to a court of competent jurisdiction by any judgment creditor of a limited partner, the court may charge the interest of the indebted limited partner with payment of the unsatisfied amount of the judgment debt; and may appoint a receiver, and make all other orders, directions, and inquiries which the circumstances of the case may require.

In those states where a creditor on beginning an action can attach debts due the defendant before he has obtained a judgment against the defendant it is recommended that paragraph (1) of this section read as follows:

On due application to a court of competent jurisdiction by any creditor of a limited partner, the court may charge the interest of the indebted limited partner with payment of the unsatisfied amount of such claim; and may appoint a receiver, and make all other orders, directions, and inquiries which the circumstances of the case may require.

(2) The interest may be redeemed with the separate property of any general partner, but may not be redeemed with partnership property.

(3) The remedies conferred by paragraph (1) shall not be deemed exclusive of others which may exist.

(4) Nothing in this act shall be held to deprive a limited partner of his statutory exemption.

§ 23. Distribution of Assets

(1) In settling accounts after dissolution the liabilities of the partnership shall be entitled to payment in the following order:

(a) Those to creditors, in the order of priority as provided by law, except those to limited partners on account of their contributions, and to general partners,

(b) Those to limited partners in respect to their share of the profits and other compensation by way of income on their contributions,

(c) Those to limited partners in respect to the capital of their contributions,

(d) Those to general partners other than for capital and profits,

(e) Those to general partners in respect to profits,

(f) Those to general partners in respect to capital.

(2) Subject to any statement in the certificate or to subsequent agreement, limited partners share in the partnership assets in respect to their claims for capital, and in respect to their claims for profits or for compensation by way of income on their contributions respectively, in proportion to the respective amounts of such claims.

§ 24. When Certificate Shall Be Cancelled or Amended

(1) The certificate shall be cancelled when the partnership is dissolved or all limited partners cease to be such.

(2) A certificate shall be amended when

(a) There is a change in the name of the partnership or in the amount or character of the contribution of any limited partner,

(b) A person is substituted as a limited partner,

(c) An additional limited partner is admitted,

(d) A person is admitted as a general partner,

(e) A general partner retires, dies or becomes insane, and the business is continued under Section 20,

(f) There is a change in the character of the business of the partnership,

(g) There is a false or erroneous statement in the certificate,

(h) There is a change in the time as stated in the certificate for the dissolution of the partnership or for the return of a contribution,

(i) A time is fixed for the dissolution of the partnership, or the return of a contribution, no time having been specified in the certificate, or

(j) The members desire to make a change in any other statement in the certificate in order that it shall accurately represent the agreement between them.

§ 25. Requirements for Amendment and for Cancellation of Certificate

(1) The writing to amend a certificate shall

(a) Conform to the requirements of Section 2(1a) as far as necessary to set forth clearly the change in the certificate which it is desired to make, and

(b) Be signed and sworn to by all members, and an amendment substituting a limited partner or adding a limited or general partner shall be signed also by the member to be substituted or added, and when a limited partner is to be substituted, the amendment shall also be signed by the assigning limited partner.

(2) The writing to cancel a certificate shall be signed by all members.

(3) A person desiring the cancellation or amendment of a certificate, if any person designated in paragraphs (1) and (2) as a person who must execute the writing refuses to do so, may petition the [here designate the proper court] to direct a cancellation or amendment thereof.

(4) If the court finds that the petitioner has a right to have the writing executed by a person who refuses to do so, it shall order the [here designate the responsible official in the office designated in Section 2] in the office where the certificate is recorded to record the cancellation or amendment of the certificate; and where the certificate is to be amended, the court shall also cause to be filed for record in said office a certified copy of its decree setting forth the amendment.

(5) A certificate is amended or cancelled when there is filed for record in the office [here designate the office designated in Section 2] where the certificate is recorded

(a) A writing in accordance with the provisions of paragraph (1), or (2) or

(b) A certified copy of the order of court in accordance with the provisions of paragraph (4).

(6) After the certificate is duly amended in accordance with this section, the amended certificate shall thereafter be for all purposes the certificate provided for by this act.

§ 26. Parties to Actions

A contributor, unless he is a general partner, is not a proper party to proceedings by or against a partnership, except where the object is to enforce a limited partner's right against or liability to the partnership.

§ 27. Name of Act

This act may be cited as The Uniform Limited Partnership Act.

§ 28. Rules of Construction

(1) The rule that statutes in derogation of the common law are to be strictly construed shall have no application to this act.

(2) This act shall be so interpreted and construed as to effect its general purpose to make uniform the law of those states which enact it.

(3) This act shall not be so construed as to impair the obligations of any contract existing when the act goes into effect, nor to affect any action or proceedings begun or right accrued before this act takes effect.

§ 29. Rules for Cases Not Provided for in This Act

In any case not provided for in this act the rules of law and equity, including the law merchant, shall govern.

§ 30. Provisions for Existing Limited Partnerships

(1) A limited partnership formed under any statute of this state prior to the adoption of this act, may become a limited partnership under this act by complying with the provisions of Section 2; provided the certificate sets forth

(a) The amount of the original contribution of each limited partner, and the time when the contribution was made, and

(b) That the property of the partnership exceeds the amount sufficient to discharge its liabilities to persons not claiming as general or limited partners by an amount greater than the sum of the contributions of its limited partners.

(2) A limited partnership formed under any statute of this state prior to the adoption of this act, until or unless it becomes a limited partnership under this act, shall continue to be governed by the provisions of [here insert proper reference to the existing limited partnership act or acts], except that such partnership shall not be renewed unless so provided in the original agreement.

§ 31. Act (Acts) Repealed

Except as affecting existing limited partnerships to the extent set forth in Section 30, the act (acts) of [here designate the existing limited partnership act or acts] is (are) hereby repealed.

Editorial Note: In states which have adopted the 1976 Revised Uniform Limited Partnership Act, the provisions as to effective date and applicability should be carefully checked. In most states adopting said act, the provisions of the 1916 Limited Partnership Act still have some applicability.

D. REVISED UNIFORM LIMITED PARTNERSHIP ACT (1976) WITH THE 1985 AMENDMENTS

(The 1985 Amendments are indicated by Underscore and Strikeout)

See, also, original Uniform Limited Partnership Act of 1916, infra.

Contents

ARTICLE 1. GENERAL PROVISIONS

ARTICLE 2. FORMATION; CERTIFICATE OF LIMITED PARTNERSHIP

ARTICLE 3. LIMITED PARTNERS

ARTICLE 4. GENERAL PARTNERS

ARTICLE 5. FINANCE

ARTICLE 6. DISTRIBUTIONS AND WITHDRAWAL

Historical Note

The Revised Uniform Limited Partnership Act was approved by the National Conference of Commissioners on Uniform State Laws in 1976. It supersedes the original Uniform Limited Partnership Act approved by the National Conference in 1916.

In 1985 the National Conference initially approved a separate new Uniform Limited Partnership Act (1985). Subsequently, however, the National Conference determined that the separate new act should be eliminated and that the changes made in that act should instead be incorporated into the existing Revised Uniform Limited Partnership Act of 1976. Accordingly, the changes made in the Uniform Limited Partnership Act (1985) have been incorporated into the 1976 Act together with revised prefatory note and comments.

PREFATORY NOTE

In 1976, the National Conference of Commissioners on Uniform State Laws adopted the first revision of the Uniform Limited Partnership Act, originally promulgated in 1916. The 1976 Act was intended to modernize the prior uniform law while retaining the special character of limited partnerships as compared with corporations. The draftsman of a limited partnership agreement has a degree of flexibility in defining the relations among the partners that is not available in the corporate form. Moreover, the relationship among partners is consensual, and under some circumstances may require a general partner to seek approval of the other partners (sometimes unanimous approval) under circumstances that corporate management would find unthinkable. The limited partnership was not intended to be an alternative in all cases where the corporate form is undesirable for tax or other reasons, and the 1976 Act was not intended to make it so. The 1976 Act clarified many ambiguities and filled interstices in the 1916 Act by adding more detailed language and mechanics. In addition, it effected some important substantive changes from the prior uniform law.

The Uniform Limited Partnership Act (1976) with the 1985 Amendments (the 1985 Act) follows the 1976 Act very closely in most respects. It makes almost no change in the basic structure of the 1976 Act. It does, however, differ from the 1976 Act in certain significant respects for the purpose of more effectively modernizing, improving and establishing uniformity in the law of limited partnerships. The 1985 Act accomplishes this without impairing the basic philosophy or values underlying the 1976 Act, by incorporating into the structure, framework and text of the 1976 Act the best and most important improvements that have emerged in the limited partnership acts enacted recently by certain states. Most of those improvements were considered by the draftsmen of the 1976 Act but were not included in it because of uncertainties as to the possible consequences of such inclusion under applicable Federal income tax laws. Those uncertainties have since been resolved satisfactorily, and no impediment to incorporating them in the 1985 Act remains at this time.

Article 1 provides a list of all of the definitions used in the Act, integrates the use of limited partnership names with corporate names and provides for an office and agent for service of process in the state of organization. All of these provisions were innovations in the 1976 Act and were carried over from the 1976 Act to the 1985 Act. Article 2 collects in one place all provisions dealing with execution and filing of certificates of limited partnership and certificates of amendment and cancellation. When adopted in 1976, Articles 1 and 2 reflected an important change in the prior statutory scheme: recognition that the basic document in any partnership, including a limited partnership, is the partnership agreement. The certificate of limited partnership is not a constitutive document (except in the sense that it is a statutory prerequisite to creation of the limited partnership), and merely reflects the most basic matters as to which government officials, creditors and others dealing or considering dealing with the partnership should be put on notice. This principle is further implemented by the 1985 Act's elimination of the requirement, carried from the original 1916 Act into the 1976 Act, that the certificate of limited partnership set out the name, address and capital contribution of each limited partner and certain other details relating to the operation of the partnership and the respective rights of the partners. The former requirement served no significant practical purpose while it imposed on limited partnerships (particularly those having large numbers of partners or doing business in more than one state) inordinate administrative and logistical burdens and expenses connected with filing and amending their certificates of limited partnership. Many of the other changes made by the 1985 Act merely reflect the elimination of that requirement.

Article 3 deals with the single most difficult issue facing lawyers who use the limited partnership form of organization: the powers and potential liabilities of limited partners. Section 303 lists a number of activities in which a limited partner may engage without being held to have so significantly participated in the control of the business that he acquires the liability of a general partner. Moreover, it goes on to confine the liability of a limited partner who merely participates in control to situations in which persons who actually know of that participation in control are misled thereby to their detriment into reasonably believing the limited partner to be a general partner. This "detrimental reliance" test, together with an expansion of the "laundry list" of specific activities in which limited partners may participate without incurring liability, are among the principal innovations in the 1985 Act.

The provisions relating to general partners are collected in Article 4. It differs little from the corresponding article in the 1976 Act, except that some of the 1976 Act's references to the certificate of limited partnership have been changed to refer instead to the partnership agreement. This is in recognition of the principle that the limited partnership agreement, not the certificate of limited partnership, is the primary constitutive, organizational and governing document of a limited partnership. Article 5, dealing with finance, differs in some important respects from Article 5 of the 1976 Act, which itself made some important changes from the 1916 Act. The 1976 Act explicitly permitted contributions to the partnership to be made in the form of the contribution of services and promises to contribute cash, property or services, and provided that those who failed to perform promised services were required, in the absence of an agreement to the contrary, to pay the value of the services as stated in the certificate of limited partnership. These important innovations of the 1976 Act are retained in substance in the 1985 Act. However, the 1985 Act substitutes the partnership agreement and the records of the limited partnership for the certificate of limited partnership as the place such agreements are to be set out and such information is to be kept.

Article 6 of the 1976 Act, dealing with distributions and with the withdrawal of partners from the partnership, made a number of changes from the 1916 Act. For example, Section 608 created a statute of limitations applicable to the right of a limited partnership to recover all or part of a contribution that had been returned to a limited partner, whether to satisfy creditors or otherwise. The 1985 Act retains these features of the 1976 Act without substantive change.

In both the 1976 and the 1985 Acts, the assignability of partnership interests is dealt with in considerable detail in Article 7, and the provisions relating to dissolution appear in Article 8. Article 8 of the 1976 Act established a new standard for seeking judicial dissolution of a limited partnership, which standard is carried forward into the 1985 Act.

Article 9 of the 1976 and 1985 Acts deals with one of the thorniest questions for those who operate limited partnerships in more than one state, i.e., the status of the partnership in a state other than the state of its organization. Neither case law under the 1916 Act nor administrative practice made it clear which state's law governed the partnership or whether, in that other state, the limited partners continued to possess limited liability. Article 9 of the 1976 Act dealt with this problem by providing for registration of foreign limited partnerships and specifying choice-of-law rules. Article 9 of the 1985 Act retains all of those basic provisions and innovations of the 1976 Act.

Article 10 of the 1976 Act represented another significant innovation, by authorizing derivative actions to be brought by limited partners. The 1916 Act failed to address this entire concept. Article 10 of the 1985 Act clarifies certain provisions of the 1976 Act but does not make any substantive changes in the corresponding provisions of the 1976 Act.

Finally, Article 11 sets out a number of miscellaneous provisions, not the least of which are those dealing with the application of the new statute to limited partnerships in existence at the time of its enactment. Those provisions in the 1976 Act were expanded upon by the 1985 Act to give greater deference to the possible expectations, some of which may have constitutionally protected status, of partners in such limited partnerships concerning the continuing applicability to their partnerships of the law in effect when they were organized.

Caveat

Editorial Note: In states which have adopted the 1976 Revised Uniform Limited Partnership Act, the provisions as to effective date and applicability should be carefully checked. In most states adopting said act, the provisions of the 1916 Limited Partnership Act still have some applicability.

ARTICLE 1. GENERAL PROVISIONS

§ 101. Definitions

As used in this [Act], unless the context otherwise requires:

(1) "Certificate of limited partnership" means the certificate referred to in Section 201, and the certificate as amended or restated.

(2) "Contribution" means any cash, property, services rendered, or a promissory note or other binding obligation to contribute cash or property or to perform services, which a partner contributes to a limited partnership in his capacity as a partner.

(3) "Event of withdrawal of a general partner" means an event that causes a person to cease to be a general partner as provided in Section 402.

(4) "Foreign limited partnership" means a partnership formed under the laws of any state other than this State and having as partners one or more general partners and one or more limited partners.

(5) "General partner" means a person who has been admitted to a limited partnership as a general partner in accordance with the partnership agreement and named in the certificate of limited partnership as a general partner.

(6) "Limited partner" means a person who has been admitted to a limited partnership as a limited partner in accordance with the partnership agreement.

(7) "Limited partnership" and "domestic limited partnership" mean a partnership formed by two or more persons under the laws of this State and having one or more general partners and one or more limited partners.

(8) "Partner" means a limited or general partner.

(9) "Partnership agreement" means any valid agreement, written or oral, of the partners as to the affairs of a limited partnership and the conduct of its business.

(10) "Partnership interest" means a partner's share of the profits and losses of a limited partnership and the right to receive distributions of partnership assets.

(11) "Person" means a natural person, partnership, limited partnership (domestic or foreign), trust, estate, association, or corporation.

(12) "State" means a state, territory, or possession of the United States, the District of Columbia, or the Commonwealth of Puerto Rico.

COMMENT

The definitions in this section clarify a number of uncertainties in the law existing prior to the 1976 Act, and also make certain changes in such prior law. The 1985 Act makes very few additional changes in Section 101.

Contribution: this definition makes it clear that a present contribution of services and a promise to make a future payment of cash, contribution of property or performance of services are permissible forms for a contribution. Section 502 of the 1985 Act provides that a limited partner's promise to make a contribution is enforceable only when set out in a writing signed by the limited partner. (This result is not dissimilar from that under the 1976 Act, which required all promises of future contributions to be described in the certificate of limited partnership, which was to be signed by, among others, the partners making such promises.) The property or services contributed presently or promised to be contributed in the future must be accorded a value in the partnership agreement or the partnership records required to be kept pursuant to Section 105, and, in the case of a promise, that value may determine the liability of a partner who fails to honor his agreement (Section 502). Section 3 of the 1916 Act did not permit a limited partner's contribution to be in the form of services, although the inhibition did not apply to general partners.

Foreign limited partnership: the Act only deals with foreign limited partnerships formed under the laws of another "state" of the United States (see subdivision 12 of Section 101), and any adopting state that desires to deal by statute with the status of entities formed under the laws of foreign countries must make appropriate changes throughout the Act. The exclusion of such entities from the Act was not intended to suggest that their "limited partners" should not be accorded limited liability by the courts of a state adopting the Act. That question would be resolved by the choice-of-law rules of the forum state.

General partner: this definition recognizes the separate functions of the partnership agreement and the certificate of limited partnership. The partnership agreement establishes the basic grant of management power to the persons named as general partners; but because of the passive rule played by the limited partners, the separate, formal step of memorializing that grant of power in the certificate of limited partnership has been preserved to emphasize its importance and to provide notice of the identity of the partnership's general partners to persons dealing with the partnership.

Limited partner: unlike the definition of general partners, this definition provides for admission of limited partners through the partnership agreement alone and does not require identification of any limited partner in the certificate of limited partnership (Section 201). Under the 1916 and the 1976 Acts, being named as a limited partner in the certificate of limited partnership was a statutory requirement and, in most if not all cases, probably also a prerequisite to limited partner status. By eliminating the requirement that the certificate of limited partnership contain the name, address and capital contribution of each limited partner, the 1985 Act all but eliminates any risk that a person intended to be a limited partner may be exposed to liability as a general partner as a result of the inadvertent omission of any of that information from the certificate of limited partnership, and also dispenses with the need to amend the certificate of limited partnership upon the admission or withdrawal of, transfer of an interest by, or change in the address or capital contribution of, any limited partner.

Partnership agreement: the 1916 Act did not refer to the partnership agreement, assuming that all important matters affecting limited partners would be set forth in the certificate of limited partnership. Under modern practice, however, it has been common for the partners to enter into a comprehensive partnership agreement, only part of which was required to be included or summarized in the certificate of limited partnership. As reflected in Section 201 of the 1985 Act, the certificate of limited partnership is confined principally to matters respecting the partnership itself and the identity of general partners and other important issues are left to the partnership agreement. Most of the information formerly provided by, but no longer required to be included in, the certificate of limited partnership is now required to be kept in the partnership records (Section 105).

Partnership interest: this definition first appeared in the 1976 Act and is intended to define what it is that is transferred when a partnership interest is assigned.

§ 102. Name

The name of each limited partnership as set forth in its certificate of limited partnership:

(1) shall contain without abbreviation the words "limited partnership";

(2) may not contain the name of a limited partner unless (i) it is also the name of a general partner or the corporate name of a corporate general partner, or (ii) the business of the limited partnership had been carried on under that name before the admission of that limited partner;

(3) may not be the same as, or deceptively similar to, the name of any corporation or limited partnership organized under the laws of this State or licensed or registered as a foreign corporation or limited partnership in this State; and

(4) may not contain the following words [here insert prohibited words].

COMMENT

Subdivision (2) of Section 102 has been carried over from Section 5 of the 1916 Act with certain editorial changes. The remainder of Section 102 first appeared in the 1976 Act and primarily reflects the intention to integrate the registration of limited partnership names with that of corporate names. Accordingly, Section 201 provides for central, State-wide filing of certificates of limited partnership, and subdivisions (3) and (4) of Section 102 contain standards to be applied by the filing officer in determining whether the certificate should be filed. Subdivision (1) requires that the proper name of a limited partnership contain the words "limited partnership" in full. Subdivision (3) of the 1976 Act has been deleted, to reflect the deletion from Section 201 of any requirement that the certificate of limited partnership describe the partnership's purposes or the character of its business.

§ 103. Reservation of Name

(a) The exclusive right to the use of a name may be reserved by:

(1) any person intending to organize a limited partnership under this [Act] and to adopt that name;

(2) any domestic limited partnership or any foreign limited partnership registered in this State which, in either case, intends to adopt that name;

(3) any foreign limited partnership intending to register in this State and adopt that name; and

(4) any person intending to organize a foreign limited partnership and intending to have it register in this State and adopt that name.

(b) The reservation shall be made by filing with the Secretary of State an application, executed by the applicant, to reserve a specified name. If the Secretary of State finds that the name is available for use by a domestic or foreign limited partnership, he [or she] shall reserve the name for the exclusive use of the applicant for a period of 120 days. Once having so reserved a name, the same applicant may not again reserve the same name until more than 60 days after the expiration of the last 120–day period for which that applicant reserved that name. The right to the exclusive use of a reserved name may be transferred to any other person by filing in the office of the Secretary of State a notice of the transfer, executed by the applicant for whom the name was reserved and specifying the name and address of the transferee.

COMMENT

Section 103 first appeared in the 1976 Act. The 1916 Act did not provide for registration of names.

§ 104. Specified Office and Agent

Each limited partnership shall continuously maintain in this State:

(1) an office, which may but need not be a place of its business in this State, at which shall be kept the records required by Section 105 to be maintained; and

(2) an agent for service of process on the limited partnership, which agent must be an individual resident of this State, a domestic corporation, or a foreign corporation authorized to do business in this State.

COMMENT

Section 104 first appeared in the 1976 Act. It requires that a limited partnership have certain minimum contacts with its State of organization, i.e., an office at which the constitutive documents and basic financial information is kept and an agent for service of process.

§ 105. Records to Be Kept

(a) Each limited partnership shall keep at the office referred to in Section 104(1) the following:

(1) a current list of the full name and last known business address of each partner, separately identifying the general partners (in alphabetical order) and the limited partners (in alphabetical order);

(2) a copy of the certificate of limited partnership and all certificates of amendment thereto, together with executed copies of any powers of attorney pursuant to which any certificate has been executed;

(3) copies of the limited partnership's federal, state and local income tax returns and reports, if any, for the three most recent years;

(4) copies of any then effective written partnership agreements and of any financial statements of the limited partnership for the three most recent years; and

(5) unless contained in a written partnership agreement, a writing setting out:

(i) the amount of cash and a description and statement of the agreed value of the other property or services contributed by each partner and which each partner has agreed to contribute;

(ii) the times at which or events on the happening of which any additional contributions agreed to be made by each partner are to be made;

(iii) any right of a partner to receive, or of a general partner to make, distributions to a partner which include a return of all or any part of the partner's contribution; and

(iv) any events upon the happening of which the limited partnership is to be dissolved and its affairs wound up.

(b) Records kept under this section are subject to inspection and copying at the reasonable request and at the expense of any partner during ordinary business hours.

COMMENT

Section 105 first appeared in the 1976 Act. In view of the passive nature of the limited partner's position, it has been widely felt that limited partners are entitled to access to certain basic documents and information, including the certificate of limited partnership, any partnership agreement and a writing setting out certain important matters which, under the 1916 and 1976 Acts, were required to be set out in the certificate of limited partnership. In view of the great diversity among limited partnerships, it was thought inappropriate to require a standard form of financial report, and Section 105 does no more than require retention of tax returns and any other financial statements that are prepared. The names and addresses of general partners are made available to the general public in the certificate of limited partnership.

§ 106. Nature of Business

A limited partnership may carry on any business that a partnership without limited partners may carry on except [here designate prohibited activities].

COMMENT

Section 106 is identical to Section 3 of the 1916 Act. Many states require that certain regulated industries, such as banking, may be carried on only by entities organized pursuant to special statutes, and it is contemplated that the prohibited activities would be confined to the matters covered by those statutes.

§ 107. Business Transactions of Partner With Partnership

Except as provided in the partnership agreement, a partner may lend money to and transact other business with the limited partnership and, subject to other applicable law, has the same rights and obligations with respect thereto as a person who is not a partner.

COMMENT

Section 107 makes a number of important changes in Section 13 of the 1916 Act. Section 13, in effect, created a special fraudulent conveyance provision applicable to the making of secured loans by limited partners and the repayment by limited partnerships of loans from limited partners. Section 107 leaves that question to a state's general fraudulent conveyance statute. In addition, Section 107 eliminates the prohibition in Section 13 against a general partner's sharing pro rata with general creditors in the case of an unsecured loan. Of course, other doctrines developed under bankruptcy and insolvency laws may require the subordination of loans by partners under appropriate circumstances.

ARTICLE 2. FORMATION; CERTIFICATE OF LIMITED PARTNERSHIP

§ 201. Certificate of Limited Partnership

(a) In order to form a limited partnership, a certificate of limited partnership must be executed and filed in the office of the Secretary of State. The certificate shall set forth:

(1) the name of the limited partnership;

(2) the address of the office and the name and address of the agent for service of process required to be maintained by Section 104;

(3) the name and the business address of each general partner;

(4) the latest date upon which the limited partnership is to dissolve; and

(5) any other matters the general partners determine to include therein.

(b) A limited partnership is formed at the time of the filing of the certificate of limited partnership in the office of the Secretary of State or at any later time specified in the certificate of limited partnership if, in either case, there has been substantial compliance with the requirements of this section.

COMMENT

The 1985 Act requires far fewer matters to be set forth in the certificate of limited partnership than did Section 2 of the 1916 Act and Section 201 of the 1976 Act. This is in recognition of the fact that the partnership agreement, not the certificate of limited partnership, has become the authoritative and comprehensive document for most limited partnerships, and that creditors and potential creditors of the partnership do and should refer to the partnership agreement and to other information furnished to them directly by the partnership and by others, not to the certificate of limited partnership, to obtain facts concerning the capital and finances of the partnership and other matters of concern. Subparagraph (b), which is based upon the 1916 Act, has been retained to make it clear that existence of the limited partnership depends only upon compliance with this section. Its continued existence is not dependent upon compliance with other provisions of this Act.

§ 202. Amendment to Certificate

(a) A certificate of limited partnership is amended by filing a certificate of amendment thereto in the office of the Secretary of State. The certificate shall set forth:

(1) the name of the limited partnership;

(2) the date of filing the certificate; and

(3) the amendment to the certificate.

(b) Within 30 days after the happening of any of the following events, an amendment to a certificate of limited partnership reflecting the occurrence of the event or events shall be filed:

(1) the admission of a new general partner;

(2) the withdrawal of a general partner; or

(3) the continuation of the business under Section 801 after an event of withdrawal of a general partner.

(c) A general partner who becomes aware that any statement in a certificate of limited partnership was false when made or that any arrangements or other facts described have changed, making the certificate inaccurate in any respect, shall promptly amend the certificate.

(d) A certificate of limited partnership may be amended at any time for any other proper purpose the general partners determine.

(e) No person has any liability because an amendment to a certificate of limited partnership has not been filed to reflect the occurrence of any event referred to in subsection (b) of this section if the amendment is filed within the 30–day period specified in subsection (b).

(f) A restated certificate of limited partnership may be executed and filed in the same manner as a certificate of amendment.

COMMENT

Section 202 of the 1976 Act made substantial changes in Section 24 of the 1916 Act. Further changes in this section are made by the 1985 Act. Paragraph (b) lists the basic events—the addition or withdrawal of a general partner—that are so central to the function of the certificate of limited partnership that they require prompt amendment. With the elimination of the requirement that the certificate of limited partnership include the names of all limited partners and the amount and character of all capital contributions, the requirement of the 1916 and 1976 Acts that the certificate be amended upon the admission or withdrawal of limited partners or on any change in the partnership capital must also be eliminated. This change should greatly reduce the frequency and complexity of amendments to the certificate of limited partnership. Paragraph (c) makes it clear, as it was not clear under Section 24(2)(g) of the 1916 Act, that the certificate of limited partnership is intended to be an accurate description of the facts to which it relates at all times and does not speak merely as of the date it is executed.

Paragraph (e) provides a "safe harbor" against claims of creditors or others who assert that they have been misled by the failure to amend the certificate of limited partnership to reflect changes in any of the important facts referred to in paragraph (b); if the certificate of limited partnership is amended within 30 days of the occurrence of the event, no creditor or other person can recover for damages sustained during the interim. Additional protection is afforded by the provisions of Section 304. The elimination of the requirement that the certificate of limited partnership identify all limited partners and their respective capital contributions may have rendered paragraph (e) an obsolete and unnecessary vestige. The principal, if not the sole, purpose of paragraph (e) in the 1976 Act was to protect limited partners newly admitted to a partnership from being held liable as general partners when an amendment to the certificate identifying them as limited partners and describing their contributions was not filed contemporaneously with their admission to the partnership. Such liability cannot arise under the 1985 Act because such information is not required to be stated in the certificate. Nevertheless, the 1985 Act retains paragraph (e) because it is protective of partners, shielding them from liability to the extent its provisions apply, and does not create or impose any liability.

Paragraph (f) is added in the 1985 Act to provide explicit statutory recognition of the common practice of restating an amended certificate of limited partnership. While a limited partnership seeking to amend its certificate of limited partnership may do so by recording a restated certificate which incorporates the amendment, that is by no means the only purpose or function of a restated certificate, which may be filed for the sole purpose of restating in a single integrated instrument all the provisions of a limited partnership's certificate of limited partnership which are then in effect.

§ 203. Cancellation of Certificate

A certificate of limited partnership shall be cancelled upon the dissolution and the commencement of winding up of the partnership or at any other time there are no limited partners. A certificate of cancellation shall be filed in the office of the Secretary of State and set forth:

(1) the name of the limited partnership;

(2) the date of filing of its certificate of limited partnership;

(3) the reason for filing the certificate of cancellation;

(4) the effective date (which shall be a date certain) of cancellation if it is not to be effective upon the filing of the certificate; and

(5) any other information the general partners filing the certificate determine.

COMMENT

Section 203 changes Section 24 of the 1916 Act by making it clear that the certificate of cancellation should be filed upon the commencement of winding up of the limited partnership. Section 24 provided for cancellation "when the partnership is dissolved".

§ 204. Execution of Certificates

(a) Each certificate required by this Article to be filed in the office of the Secretary of State shall be executed in the following manner:

(1) an original certificate of limited partnership must be signed by all general partners;

(2) a certificate of amendment must be signed by at least one general partner and by each other general partner designated in the certificate as a new general partner; and

(3) a certificate of cancellation must be signed by all general partners.

(b) Any person may sign a certificate by an attorney-in-fact, but a power of attorney to sign a certificate relating to the admission of a general partner must specifically describe the admission.

(c) The execution of a certificate by a general partner constitutes an affirmation under the penalties of perjury that the facts stated therein are true.

COMMENT

Section 204 collects in one place the formal requirements for the execution of certificates which were set forth in Sections 2 and 25 of the 1916 Act. Those sections required that each certificate be signed by all partners, and there developed an unnecessarily cumbersome practice of having each limited partner sign powers of attorney to authorize the general partners to execute certificates of amendment on their behalf. The 1976 Act, while simplifying the execution requirements, nevertheless required that an original certificate of limited partnership be signed by all partners and a certificate of amendment by all new partners being admitted to the limited partnership. However the certificate of limited partnership is no longer required to include the name or capital contribution of any limited partner. Therefore, while the 1985 Act still requires all general partners to sign the original certificate of limited partnership, no limited partner is required to sign any certificate. Certificates of amendment are required to be signed by only one general partner, and all general partners must sign certificates of cancellation. The requirement in the 1916 Act that all certificates be sworn was deleted in the 1976 and 1985 Acts as potentially an unfair trap for the unwary (see, e.g., Wisniewski v. Johnson, 223 Va. 141, 286 S.E.2d 223 [1982]); in its place, paragraph (c) now provides, as a matter of law, that the execution of a certificate by a general partner subjects him to the penalties of perjury for inaccuracies in the certificate.

§ 205. Execution by Judicial Act

If a person required by Section 204 to execute any certificate fails or refuses to do so, any other person who is adversely affected by the failure or refusal may petition the [designate the appropriate court] to direct the execution of the certificate. If the court finds that it is proper for the certificate to be executed and that any person so designated has failed or refused to execute the certificate, it shall order the Secretary of State to record an appropriate certificate.

COMMENT

Section 205 of the 1976 Act changed subdivisions (3) and (4) of Section 25 of the 1916 Act by confining the persons who have standing to seek judicial intervention to partners and to those assignees who were adversely affected by the failure or refusal of the appropriate persons to file a certificate of amendment or cancellation. Section 205 of the 1985 Act reverses that restriction, and provides that any person adversely affected by a failure or refusal to file any certificate (not only a certificate of cancellation or amendment) has standing to seek judicial intervention.

§ 206. Filing in Office of Secretary of State

(a) Two signed copies of the certificate of limited partnership and of any certificates of amendment or cancellation (or of any judicial decree of amendment or cancellation) shall be delivered to the Secretary of State. A person who executes a certificate as an agent or fiduciary need not exhibit evidence of his [or her] authority as a prerequisite to filing. Unless the Secretary of State finds that any certificate does not conform to law, upon receipt of all filing fees required by law he [or she] shall:

(1) endorse on each duplicate original the word "Filed" and the day, month, and year of the filing thereof;

(2) file one duplicate original in his [or her] office; and

(3) return the other duplicate original to the person who filed it or his [or her] representative.

(b) Upon the filing of a certificate of amendment (or judicial decree of amendment) in the office of the Secretary of State, the certificate of limited partnership shall be amended as set forth therein, and upon the effective date of a certificate of cancellation (or a judicial decree thereof), the certificate of limited partnership is cancelled.

COMMENT

Section 206 first appeared in the 1976 Act. In addition to providing mechanics for the central filing system, the second sentence of this section does away with the requirement, formerly imposed by some local filing officers, that persons who have executed certificates under a power of attorney exhibit executed copies of the power of attorney itself. Paragraph (b) changes subdivision (5) of Section 25 of the 1916 Act by providing that certificates of cancellation are effective upon their effective date under Section 203.

§ 207. Liability for False Statement in Certificate

If any certificate of limited partnership or certificate of amendment or cancellation contains a false statement, one who suffers loss by reliance on the statement may recover damages for the loss from:

(1) any person who executes the certificate, or causes another to execute it on his behalf, and knew, and any general partner who knew or should have known, the statement to be false at the time the certificate was executed; and

(2) any general partner who thereafter knows or should have known that any arrangement or other fact described in the certificate has changed, making the statement inaccurate in any respect within a sufficient time before the statement was relied upon reasonably to have enabled that general partner to cancel or amend the certificate, or to file a petition for its cancellation or amendment under Section 205.

COMMENT

Section 207 changes Section 6 of the 1916 Act by providing explicitly for the liability of persons who sign a certificate as agent under a power of attorney and by confining the obligation to amend a certificate of limited partnership in light of future events to general partners.

§ 208. Scope of Notice

The fact that a certificate of limited partnership is on file in the office of the Secretary of State is notice that the partnership is a limited partnership and the persons designated therein as general partners are general partners, but it is not notice of any other fact.

COMMENT

Section 208 first appeared in the 1976 Act, and referred to the certificate's providing constructive notice of the status as limited partners of those so identified therein. The 1985 Act's deletion of any requirement that the certificate name limited partners requires that Section 208 be modified accordingly.

By stating that the filing of a certificate of limited partnership only results in notice of the general liability of the general partners, Section 208 obviates the concern that third parties may be held to have notice of special provisions set forth in the certificate. While this section is designed to preserve by implication the limited liability of limited partners, the implicit protection provided is not intended to change any liability of a limited partner which may be created by his action or inaction under the laws of estoppel, agency, fraud or the like.

§ 209. Delivery of Certificates to Limited Partners

Upon the return by the Secretary of State pursuant to Section 206 of a certificate marked "Filed," the general partners shall promptly deliver or mail a copy of the certificate of limited partnership and each certificate of amendment or cancellation to each limited partner unless the partnership agreement provides otherwise.

COMMENT

This section first appeared in the 1976 Act.

ARTICLE 3. LIMITED PARTNERS

§ 301. Admission of Limited Partners

(a) A person becomes a limited partner:

(1) at the time the limited partnership is formed; or

(2) at any later time specified in the records of the limited partnership for becoming a limited partner.

(b) After the filing of a limited partnership's original certificate of limited partnership, a person may be admitted as an additional limited partner:

(1) in the case of a person acquiring a partnership interest directly from the limited partnership, upon compliance with the partnership agreement or, if the partnership agreement does not so provide, upon the written consent of all partners; and

(2) in the case of an assignee of a partnership interest of a partner who has the power, as provided in Section 704, to grant the assignee the right to become a limited partner, upon the exercise of that power and compliance with any conditions limiting the grant or exercise of the power.

COMMENT

Section 301(a) is new; no counterpart was found in the 1916 or 1976 Acts. This section imposes on the partnership an obligation to maintain in its records the date each limited partner becomes a limited partner. Under the 1976 Act, one could not become a limited partner until an appropriate certificate reflecting his status as such was filed with the Secretary of State. Because the 1985 Act eliminates the need to name limited partners in the certificate of limited partnership, an alternative mechanism had to be established to evidence the fact and date of a limited partner's admission. The partnership records required to be maintained under Section 105 now serve that function, subject to the limitation that no person may become a limited partner before the partnership is formed (Section 201(b)).

Subdivision (1) of Section 301(b) adds to Section 8 of the 1916 Act an explicit recognition of the fact that unanimous consent of all partners is required for admission of new limited partners unless the partnership agreement provides otherwise. Subdivision (2) is derived from Section 19 of the 1916 Act but abandons the former terminology of "substituted limited partner".

§ 302. Voting

Subject to Section 303, the partnership agreement may grant to all or a specified group of the limited partners the right to vote (on a per capita or other basis) upon any matter.

COMMENT

Section 302 first appeared in the 1976 Act, and must be read together with subdivision (b)(6) of Section 303. Although the 1916 Act did not speak specifically of the voting powers of limited partners, it was not uncommon for partnership agreements to grant such powers to limited partners. Section 302 is designed only to make it clear that the partnership agreement may grant such power to limited partners. If such powers are granted to limited partners beyond the "safe harbor" of subdivisions (6) or (8) of Section 303(b), a court may (but of course need not) hold that, under the circumstances, the limited partners have participated in "control of the business" within the meaning of Section 303(a). Section 303(c) makes clear that the exercise of powers beyond the ambit of Section 303(b) is not ipso facto to be taken as taking part in the control of the business.

§ 303. Liability to Third Parties

(a) Except as provided in subsection (d), a limited partner is not liable for the obligations of a limited partnership unless he [or she] is also a general partner or, in addition to the exercise of his [or her] rights and powers as a limited partner, he [or she] participates in the control of the business. However, if the limited partner participates in the control of the business, he [or she] is liable only to persons who transact business with the limited partnership reasonably believing, based upon the limited partner's conduct, that the limited partner is a general partner.

(b) A limited partner does not participate in the control of the business within the meaning of subsection (a) solely by doing one or more of the following:

(1) being a contractor for or an agent or employee of the limited partnership or of a general partner or being an officer, director, or shareholder of a general partner that is a corporation;

(2) consulting with and advising a general partner with respect to the business of the limited partnership;

(3) acting as surety for the limited partnership or guaranteeing or assuming one or more specific obligations of the limited partnership;

(4) taking any action required or permitted by law to bring or pursue a derivative action in the right of the limited partnership;

(5) requesting or attending a meeting of partners;

(6) proposing, approving, or disapproving, by voting or otherwise, one or more of the following matters:

(i) the dissolution and winding up of the limited partnership;

(ii) the sale, exchange, lease, mortgage, pledge, or other transfer of all or substantially all of the assets of the limited partnership;

(iii) the incurrence of indebtedness by the limited partnership other than in the ordinary course of its business;

(iv) a change in the nature of the business;

(v) the admission or removal of a general partner;

(vi) the admission or removal of a limited partner;

(vii) a transaction involving an actual or potential conflict of interest between a general partner and the limited partnership or the limited partners;

(viii) an amendment to the partnership agreement or certificate of limited partnership; or

(ix) matters related to the business of the limited partnership not otherwise enumerated in this subsection (b), which the partnership agreement states in writing may be subject to the approval or disapproval of limited partners;

(7) winding up the limited partnership pursuant to Section 803; or

(8) exercising any right or power permitted to limited partners under this [Act] and not specifically enumerated in this subsection (b).

(c) The enumeration in subsection (b) does not mean that the possession or exercise of any other powers by a limited partner constitutes participation by him [or her] in the business of the limited partnership.

(d) A limited partner who knowingly permits his [or her] name to be used in the name of the limited partnership, except under circumstances permitted by Section 102(2), is liable to creditors who extend credit to the limited partnership without actual knowledge that the limited partner is not a general partner.

COMMENT

Section 303 makes several important changes in Section 7 of the 1916 Act. The first sentence of Section 303(a) differs from the text of Section 7 of the 1916 Act in that it speaks of participating (rather than taking part) in the control of the business; this was done for the sake of consistency with the second sentence of Section 303(a), not to change the meaning of the text. It is intended that judicial decisions interpreting the phrase "takes part in the control of the business" under the prior uniform law will remain applicable to the extent that a different result is not called for by other provisions of Section 303 and other provisions of the Act. The second sentence of Section 303(a) reflects a wholly new concept in the 1976 Act that has been further modified in the 1985 Act. It was adopted partly because of the difficulty of determining when the "control" line has been overstepped, but also (and more importantly) because of a determination that it is not sound public policy to hold a limited partner who is not also a general partner liable for the obligations of the partnership except to persons who have done business with the limited partnership reasonably believing based on the limited partner's conduct, that he is a general partner. Paragraph (b) is intended to provide a "safe harbor" by enumerating certain activities which a limited partner may carry on for the partnership without being deemed to have taken part in control of the business. This "safe harbor" list has been expanded beyond that set out in the 1976 Act to reflect case law and statutory developments and more clearly to assure that limited partners are not subjected to general liability where such liability is inappropriate. Paragraph (d) is derived from Section 5 of the 1916 Act, but adds as a condition to the limited partner's liability the requirement that a limited partner must have knowingly permitted his name to be used in the name of the limited partnership.

§ 304. Person Erroneously Believing Himself [or Herself] Limited Partner

(a) Except as provided in subsection (b), a person who makes a contribution to a business enterprise and erroneously but in good faith believes that he [or she] has become a limited partner in the enterprise is not a general partner in the enterprise and is not bound by its obligations by reason of making the contribution, receiving distributions from the enterprise, or exercising any rights of a limited partner, if, on ascertaining the mistake, he [or she]:

(1) causes an appropriate certificate of limited partnership or a certificate of amendment to be executed and filed; or

(2) withdraws from future equity participation in the enterprise by executing and filing in the office of the Secretary of State a certificate declaring withdrawal under this section.

(b) A person who makes a contribution of the kind described in subsection (a) is liable as a general partner to any third party who transacts business with the enterprise (i) before the person withdraws and an appropriate certificate is filed to show withdrawal, or (ii) before an appropriate certificate is filed to show that he [or she] is not a general partner, but in either case only if the third party actually believed in good faith that the person was a general partner at the time of the transaction.

COMMENT

Section 304 is derived from Section 11 of the 1916 Act. The "good faith" requirement has been added in the first sentence of Section 304(a). The provisions of subdivision (2) of Section 304(a) are intended to clarify an ambiguity in the prior law by providing that a person who chooses to withdraw from the enterprise in order to protect himself from liability is not required to renounce any of his then current interest in the enterprise so long as he has no further participation as an equity participant. Paragraph (b) preserves the liability of the equity participant prior to withdrawal by such person from the limited partnership or amendment to the certificate demonstrating that such person is not a general partner to any third party who has transacted business with the person believing in good faith that he was a general partner.

Evidence strongly suggests that Section 11 of the 1916 Act and Section 304 of the 1976 Act were rarely used, and one might expect that Section 304 of the 1985 Act may never have to be used. Section 11 of the 1916 Act and Section 304 of the 1976 Act could have been used by a person who invested in a limited partnership believing he would be a limited partner but who was not identified as a limited partner in the certificate of limited partnership. However, because the 1985 Act does not require limited partners to be named in the certificate, the only situation to which Section 304 would now appear to be applicable is one in which a person intending to be a limited partner was erroneously identified as a general partner in the certificate.

§ 305. Information

Each limited partner has the right to:

(1) inspect and copy any of the partnership records required to be maintained by Section 105; and

(2) obtain from the general partners from time to time upon reasonable demand (i) true and full information regarding the state of the business and financial condition of the limited partnership, (ii) promptly after becoming available, a copy of the limited partnership's federal, state, and local income tax returns for each year, and (iii) other information regarding the affairs of the limited partnership as is just and reasonable.

COMMENT

Section 305 changes and restates the rights of limited partners to information about the partnership formerly provided by Section 10 of the 1916 Act. Its importance has increased as a result of the 1985 Act's substituting the records of the partnership for the certificate of limited partnership as the place where certain categories of information are to be kept.

Section 305, which should be read together with Section 105(b), provides a mechanism for limited partners to obtain information about the partnership useful to them in making decisions concerning the partnership and their investments in it. Its purpose is not to provide a mechanism for competitors of the partnership or others having interests or agendas adverse to the partnership's to subvert the partnership's business. It is assumed that courts will protect limited partnerships from abuses and attempts to misuse Section 305 for improper purposes.

ARTICLE 4. GENERAL PARTNERS

§ 401. Admission of Additional General Partners

After the filing of a limited partnership's original certificate of limited partnership, additional general partners may be admitted as provided in writing in the partnership agreement or, if the partnership agreement does not provide in writing for the admission of additional general partners, with the written consent of all partners.

COMMENT

Section 401 is derived from, but represents a significant departure from, Section 9(1)(e) of the 1916 Act and Section 401 of the 1976 Act, which required, as a condition to the admission of an additional general partner, that all limited partners consent and that such consent specifically identify the general partner involved. Section 401 of the 1985 Act provides that the written partnership agreement determines the procedure for authorizing the admission of additional general partners, and that the written consent of all partners is required only when the partnership agreement fails to address the question.

§ 402. Events of Withdrawal

Except as approved by the specific written consent of all partners at the time, a person ceases to be a general partner of a limited partnership upon the happening of any of the following events:

(1) the general partner withdraws from the limited partnership as provided in Section 602;

(2) the general partner ceases to be a member of the limited partnership as provided in Section 702;

(3) the general partner is removed as a general partner in accordance with the partnership agreement;

(4) unless otherwise provided in writing in the partnership agreement, the general partner: (i) makes an assignment for the benefit of creditors; (ii) files a voluntary petition in bankruptcy; (iii) is adjudicated a bankrupt or insolvent; (iv) files a petition or answer seeking for himself [or herself] any reorganization, arrangement, composition, readjustment, liquidation, dissolution, or similar relief under any statute, law, or regulation; (v) files an answer or other pleading admitting or failing to contest the material allegations of a petition filed against him

[or her] in any proceeding of this nature; or (vi) seeks, consents to, or acquiesces in the appointment of a trustee, receiver, or liquidator of the general partner or of all or any substantial part of his [or her] properties;

(5) unless otherwise provided in writing in the partnership agreement, [120] days after the commencement of any proceeding against the general partner seeking reorganization, arrangement, composition, readjustment, liquidation, dissolution, or similar relief under any statute, law, or regulation, the proceeding has not been dismissed, or if within [90] days after the appointment without his [or her] consent or acquiescence of a trustee, receiver, or liquidator of the general partner or of all or any substantial part of his [or her] properties, the appointment is not vacated or stayed or within [90] days after the expiration of any such stay, the appointment is not vacated;

(6) in the case of a general partner who is a natural person,

(i) his [or her] death; or

(ii) the entry of an order by a court of competent jurisdiction adjudicating him [or her] incompetent to manage his [or her] person or his [or her] estate;

(7) in the case of a general partner who is acting as a general partner by virtue of being a trustee of a trust, the termination of the trust (but not merely the substitution of a new trustee);

(8) in the case of a general partner that is a separate partnership, the dissolution and commencement of winding up of the separate partnership;

(9) in the case of a general partner that is a corporation, the filing of a certificate of dissolution, or its equivalent, for the corporation or the revocation of its charter; or

(10) in the case of an estate, the distribution by the fiduciary of the estate's entire interest in the partnership.

COMMENT

Section 402 expands considerably the provisions of Section 20 of the 1916 Act, which provided for dissolution in the event of the retirement, death or insanity of a general partner. Subdivisions (1), (2) and (3) recognize that the general partner's agency relationship is terminable at will, although it may result in a breach of the partnership agreement giving rise to an action for damages. Subdivisions (4) and (5) reflect a judgment that, unless the limited partners agree otherwise, they ought to have the power to rid themselves of a general partner who is in such dire financial straits that he is the subject of proceedings under the National Bankruptcy Code or a similar provision of law. Subdivisions (6) through (10) simply elaborate on the notion of death in the case of a general partner who is not a natural person. Subdivisions (4) and (5) differ from their counterparts in the 1976 Act, reflecting the policy underlying the 1985 revision of Section 201, that the partnership agreement, not the certificate of limited partnership, is the appropriate document for setting out most provisions relating to the respective powers, rights and obligations of the partners inter se. Although the partnership agreement need not be written, the 1985 Act provides that, to protect the partners from fraud, these and certain other particularly significant provisions must be set out in a written partnership agreement to be effective for the purposes described in the Act.

§ 403. General Powers and Liabilities

(a) Except as provided in this [Act] or in the partnership agreement, a general partner of a limited partnership has the rights and powers and is subject to the restrictions of a partner in a partnership without limited partners.

(b) Except as provided in this [Act], a general partner of a limited partnership has the liabilities of a partner in a partnership without limited partners to persons other than the partnership and the other partners. Except as provided in this [Act] or in the partnership agreement, a general partner of a limited partnership has the liabilities of a partner in a partnership without limited partners to the partnership and to the other partners.

COMMENT

Section 403 is derived from Section 9(1) of the 1916 Act.

§ 404. Contributions by General Partner

A general partner of a limited partnership may make contributions to the partnership and share in the profits and losses of, and in distributions from, the limited partnership as a general partner. A general partner also may make contributions to and share in profits, losses, and distributions as a limited partner. A person who is both a general partner and a limited partner has the rights and powers, and is subject to the restrictions and liabilities, of a general partner and, except as provided in the partnership agreement, also has the powers, and is subject to the restrictions, of a limited partner to the extent of his [or her] participation in the partnership as a limited partner.

COMMENT

Section 404 is derived from Section 12 of the 1916 Act and makes clear that the partnership agreement may provide that a general partner who is also a limited partner may exercise all of the powers of a limited partner.

§ 405. Voting

The partnership agreement may grant to all or certain identified general partners the right to vote (on a per capita or any other basis), separately or with all or any class of the limited partners, on any matter.

COMMENT

Section 405 first appeared in the 1976 Act and is intended to make it clear that the Act does not require that the limited partners have any right to vote on matters as a separate class.

ARTICLE 5. FINANCE

§ 501. Form of Contribution

The contribution of a partner may be in cash, property, or services rendered, or a promissory note or other obligation to contribute cash or property or to perform services.

COMMENT

As noted in the comment to Section 101, the explicit permission to make contributions of services expands Section 4 of the 1916 Act.

§ 502. Liability for Contribution

(a) A promise by a limited partner to contribute to the limited partnership is not enforceable unless set out in a writing signed by the limited partner.

(b) Except as provided in the partnership agreement, a partner is obligated to the limited partnership to perform any enforceable promise to contribute cash or property or to perform services, even if he [or she] is unable to perform because of death, disability, or any other reason. If a partner does not make the required contribution of property or services, he [or she] is obligated at the option of the limited partnership to contribute cash equal to that portion of the value, as stated in the partnership records required to be kept pursuant to Section 105, of the stated contribution which has not been made.

(c) Unless otherwise provided in the partnership agreement, the obligation of a partner to make a contribution or return money or other property paid or distributed in violation of this [Act] may be compromised only by consent of all partners. Notwithstanding the compromise, a creditor of a limited partnership who extends credit, or, otherwise acts in reliance on that obligation after the partner signs a writing which reflects the obligation and before the amendment or cancellation thereof to reflect the compromise may enforce the original obligation.

COMMENT

Section 502(a) is new; it had no counterpart in the 1916 or 1976 Acts. Because, unlike the prior uniform acts, the 1985 Act does not require that promises to contribute cash, property or services be described in the limited partnership certificate, to protect against fraud it requires instead that such important promises be in a signed writing.

Although Section 17(1) of the 1916 Act required a partner to fulfill his promise to make contributions, the addition of contributions in the form of a promise to render services means that a partner who is unable to perform those services because of death or disability as well as because of an intentional default is required to pay the cash value of the services unless the partnership agreement provides otherwise.

Subdivision (c) is derived from, but expands upon, Section 17(3) of the 1916 Act.

§ 503. Sharing of Profits and Losses

The profits and losses of a limited partnership shall be allocated among the partners, and among classes of partners, in the manner provided in writing in the partnership agreement. If the partnership agreement does not so provide in writing, profits and losses shall be allocated on the basis of the value, as stated in the partnership records required to be kept pursuant to Section 105, of the contributions made by each partner to the extent they have been received by the partnership and have not been returned.

COMMENT

Section 503 first appeared in the 1976 Act. The 1916 Act did not provide the basis on which partners would share profits and losses in the absence of agreement. The 1985 Act differs from its counterpart in the 1976 Act by requiring that, to be effective, the partnership agreement provisions concerning allocation of profits and losses be in writing, and by its reference to records required to be kept pursuant to Section 105, the latter reflecting the 1985 changes in Section 201.

§ 504. Sharing of Distributions

Distributions of cash or other assets of a limited partnership shall be allocated among the partners and among classes of partners in the manner provided in writing in the partnership agreement. If the partnership agreement does not so provide in writing, distributions shall be made on the basis of the value, as stated in the partnership records required to be kept pursuant to Section 105, of the contributions made by each partner to the extent they have been received by the partnership and have not been returned.

COMMENT

Section 504 first appeared in the 1976 Act. The 1916 Act did not provide the basis on which partners would share distributions in the absence of agreement. Section 504 also differs from its counterpart in the 1976 Act by requiring that, to be effective, the partnership agreement provisions concerning allocation of distributions be in writing, and in its reference to records required to be kept pursuant to Section 105, the latter reflecting the 1985 changes in Section 201. This section also recognizes that partners may choose to share in distributions on a basis different from that on which they share in profits and losses.

ARTICLE 6. DISTRIBUTIONS AND WITHDRAWAL

§ 601. Interim Distributions

Except as provided in this Article, a partner is entitled to receive distributions from a limited partnership before his [or her] withdrawal from the limited partnership and before the dissolution and winding up thereof to the extent and at the times or upon the happening of the events specified in the partnership agreement.

COMMENT

Section 601 first appeared in the 1976 Act. The 1976 Act provisions have been modified to reflect the 1985 changes made in Section 201.

§ 602. Withdrawal of General Partner

A general partner may withdraw from a limited partnership at any time by giving written notice to the other partners, but if the withdrawal violates the partnership agreement, the limited partnership may recover from the withdrawing general partner damages for breach of the partnership agreement and offset the damages against the amount otherwise distributable to him [or her].

COMMENT

Section 602 first appeared in the 1976 Act, but is generally derived from Section 38 of the Uniform Partnership Act.

§ 603. Withdrawal of Limited Partner

A limited partner may withdraw from a limited partnership at the time or upon the happening of events specified in writing in the partnership agreement. If the agreement does not specify in writing the time or the events upon the happening of which a limited partner may withdraw or a definite time for the dissolution and winding up of the limited partnership, a limited partner may withdraw upon not less than six months' prior written notice to each general partner at his [or her] address on the books of the limited partnership at its office in this State.

COMMENT

Section 603 is derived from Section 16 of the 1916 Act. The 1976 Act provision has been modified to reflect the 1985 changes made in Section 201. This section additionally reflects the policy determination, also embodied in certain other sections of the 1985 Act, that to avoid fraud, agreements concerning certain matters of substantial importance to the partners will be enforceable only if in writing. If the partnership agreement does provide, in writing, whether a limited partner may withdraw and, if he may, when and on what terms and conditions, those provisions will control.

§ 604. Distribution Upon Withdrawal

Except as provided in this Article, upon withdrawal any withdrawing partner is entitled to receive any distribution to which he [or she] is entitled under the partnership agreement and, if not otherwise provided in the agreement, he [or she] is entitled to receive, within a reasonable time after withdrawal, the fair value of his [or her] interest in the limited partnership as of the date of withdrawal based upon his [or her] right to share in distributions from the limited partnership.

COMMENT

Section 604 first appeared in the 1976 Act. It fixes the distributive share of a withdrawing partner in the absence of an agreement among the partners.

§ 605. Distribution in Kind

Except as provided in writing in the partnership agreement, a partner, regardless of the nature of his [or her] contribution, has no right to demand and receive any distribution from a limited partnership in any form other than cash. Except as provided in writing in the partnership agreement, a partner may not be compelled to accept a distribution of any asset in kind from a limited partnership to the extent that the percentage of the asset distributed to him [or her] exceeds a percentage of that asset which is equal to the percentage in which he [or she] shares in distributions from the limited partnership.

COMMENT

The first sentence of Section 605 is derived from Section 16(3) of the 1916 Act; it also differs from its counterpart in the 1976 Act, reflecting the 1985 changes made in Section 201. The second sentence first appeared in the 1976 Act, and is intended to protect a limited partner (and the remaining partners) against a distribution in kind of more than his share of particular assets.

§ 606. Right to Distribution

At the time a partner becomes entitled to receive a distribution, he [or she] has the status of, and is entitled to all remedies available to, a creditor of the limited partnership with respect to the distribution.

COMMENT

Section 606 first appeared in the 1976 Act, and is intended to make it clear that the right of a partner to receive a distribution, as between the partners, is not subject to the equity risks of the enterprise. On the other hand, since partners entitled to distributions have creditor status, there did not seem to be a need for the extraordinary remedy of Section 16(4)(a) of the 1916 Act, which granted a limited partner the right to seek dissolution of the partnership if he was unsuccessful in demanding the return of his contribution. It is more appropriate for the partner to simply sue as an ordinary creditor and obtain a judgment.

§ 607. Limitations on Distribution

A partner may not receive a distribution from a limited partnership to the extent that, after giving effect to the distribution, all liabilities of the limited partnership, other than liabilities to partners on account of their partnership interests, exceed the fair value of the partnership assets.

COMMENT

Section 607 is derived from Section 16(1)(a) of the 1916 Act.

§ 608. Liability Upon Return of Contribution

(a) If a partner has received the return of any part of his [or her] contribution without violation of the partnership agreement or this [Act], he [or she] is liable to the limited partnership for a period of one year thereafter for the amount of the returned contribution, but only to the extent necessary to discharge the limited partnership's liabilities to creditors who extended credit to the limited partnership during the period the contribution was held by the partnership.

(b) If a partner has received the return of any part of his [or her] contribution in violation of the partnership agreement or this [Act], he [or she] is liable to the limited partnership for a period of six years thereafter for the amount of the contribution wrongfully returned.

(c) A partner receives a return of his [or her] contribution to the extent that a distribution to him [or her] reduces his [or her] share of the fair value of the net assets of the limited partnership below the value, as set forth in the partnership records required to be kept pursuant to Section 105, of his contribution which has not been distributed to him [or her].

COMMENT

Paragraph (a) is derived from Section 17(4) of the 1916 Act, but the one year statute of limitations has been added. Paragraph (b) is derived from Section 17(2)(b) of the 1916 Act but, again, a statute of limitations has been added.

Paragraph (c) first appeared in the 1976 Act. The provisions of former Section 17(2) that referred to the partner holding as "trustee" any money or specific property wrongfully returned to him have been eliminated. Paragraph (c) in the 1985 Act also differs from its counterpart in the 1976 Act to reflect the 1985 changes made in Sections 201 and 105.

ARTICLE 7. ASSIGNMENT OF PARTNERSHIP INTERESTS

§ 701. Nature of Partnership Interest

A partnership interest is personal property.

COMMENT

This section is derived from Section 18 of the 1916 Act.

§ 702. Assignment of Partnership Interest

Except as provided in the partnership agreement, a partnership interest is assignable in whole or in part. An assignment of a partnership interest does not dissolve a limited partnership or entitle the assignee to become or to exercise any rights of a partner. An assignment entitles the assignee to receive, to the extent assigned, only the distribution to which the assignor would be entitled. Except as provided in the partnership agreement, a partner ceases to be a partner upon assignment of all his [or her] partnership interest.

COMMENT

Section 19(1) of the 1916 Act provided simply that "a limited partner's interest is assignable", raising a question whether any limitations on the right of assignment were permitted. While the first sentence of Section 702 recognizes that the power to assign may be restricted in the partnership agreement, there was no intention to affect in any way the usual rules regarding restraints on alienation of personal property. The second and third sentences of Section 702 are derived from Section 19(3) of the 1916 Act. The last sentence first appeared in the 1976 Act.

§ 703. Rights of Creditor

On application to a court of competent jurisdiction by any judgment creditor of a partner, the court may charge the partnership interest of the partner with payment of the unsatisfied amount of the judgment with interest. To the extent so charged, the judgment creditor has only the rights of an assignee of the partnership interest. This [Act] does not deprive any partner of the benefit of any exemption laws applicable to his [or her] partnership interest.

COMMENT

Section 703 is derived from Section 22 of the 1916 Act but has not carried over some provisions that were thought to be superfluous. For example, references in Section 22(1) to specific remedies have been omitted, as has a prohibition in Section 22(2) against discharge of the lien with partnership property. Ordinary rules governing the remedies available to a creditor and the fiduciary obligations of general partners will determine those matters.

§ 704. Right of Assignee to Become Limited Partner

(a) An assignee of a partnership interest, including an assignee of a general partner, may become a limited partner if and to the extent that (i) the assignor gives the assignee that right in accordance with authority described in the partnership agreement, or (ii) all other partners consent.

(b) An assignee who has become a limited partner has, to the extent assigned, the rights and powers, and is subject to the restrictions and liabilities, of a limited partner under the partnership agreement and this [Act]. An assignee who becomes a limited partner also is liable for the obligations of his [or her] assignor to make and return contributions as provided in Articles 5 and 6. However, the assignee is not obligated for liabilities unknown to the assignee at the time he [or she] became a limited partner.

(c) If an assignee of a partnership interest becomes a limited partner, the assignor is not released from his [or her] liability to the limited partnership under Sections 207 and 502.

COMMENT

Section 704 is derived from Section 19 of the 1916 Act, but paragraph (b) defines more narrowly than Section 19 the obligations of the assignor that are automatically assumed by the assignee. Section 704 of the 1985 Act also differs from the 1976 Act to reflect the 1985 changes made in Section 201.

§ 705. Power of Estate of Deceased or Incompetent Partner

If a partner who is an individual dies or a court of competent jurisdiction adjudges him [or her] to be incompetent to manage his [or her] person or his [or her] property, the partner's executor, administrator, guardian, conservator, or other legal representative may exercise all of the partner's rights for the purpose of settling his [or her] estate or administering his [or her] property, including any power the partner had to give an assignee the right to become a limited partner. If a partner is a corporation, trust, or other entity and is dissolved or terminated, the powers of that partner may be exercised by its legal representative or successor.

COMMENT

Section 705 is derived from Section 21(1) of the 1916 Act. Former Section 21(2), making a deceased limited partner's estate liable for his liabilities as a limited partner was deleted as superfluous, with no intention of changing the liability of the estate.

ARTICLE 8. DISSOLUTION

§ 801. Nonjudicial Dissolution

A limited partnership is dissolved and its affairs shall be wound up upon the happening of the first to occur of the following:

(1) at the time specified in the certificate of limited partnership;

(2) upon the happening of events specified in writing in the partnership agreement;

(3) written consent of all partners;

(4) an event of withdrawal of a general partner unless at the time there is at least one other general partner and the written provisions of the partnership agreement permit the business of the limited partnership to be carried on by the remaining general partner and that partner

does so, but the limited partnership is not dissolved and is not required to be wound up by reason of any event of withdrawal if, within 90 days after the withdrawal, all partners agree in writing to continue the business of the limited partnership and to the appointment of one or more additional general partners if necessary or desired; or

(5) entry of a decree of judicial dissolution under Section 802.

COMMENT

Section 801 merely collects in one place all of the events causing dissolution. Paragraph (3) is derived from Sections 9(1)(g) and 20 of the 1916 Act, but adds the 90–day grace period. Section 801 also differs from its counterpart in the 1976 Act to reflect the 1985 changes made in Section 201.

§ 802. Judicial Dissolution

On application by or for a partner the [designate the appropriate court] court may decree dissolution of a limited partnership whenever it is not reasonably practicable to carry on the business in conformity with the partnership agreement.

COMMENT

Section 802 first appeared in the 1976 Act.

§ 803. Winding Up

Except as provided in the partnership agreement, the general partners who have not wrongfully dissolved a limited partnership or, if none, the limited partners, may wind up the limited partnership's affairs; but the [designate the appropriate court] court may wind up the limited partnership's affairs upon application of any partner, his [or her] legal representative, or assignee.

COMMENT

Section 803 first appeared in the 1976 Act, and is derived in part from Section 37 of the Uniform Partnership Act.

§ 804. Distribution of Assets

Upon the winding up of a limited partnership, the assets shall be distributed as follows:

(1) to creditors, including partners who are creditors, to the extent permitted by law, in satisfaction of liabilities of the limited partnership other than liabilities for distributions to partners under Section 601 or 604;

(2) except as provided in the partnership agreement, to partners and former partners in satisfaction of liabilities for distributions under Section 601 or 604; and

(3) except as provided in the partnership agreement, to partners first for the return of their contributions and secondly respecting their partnership interests, in the proportions in which the partners share in distributions.

COMMENT

Section 804 revises Section 23 of the 1916 Act by providing that (1) to the extent partners are also creditors, other than in respect of their interests in the partnership, they share with other creditors, (2) once the partnership's obligation to make a distribution accrues, it must be paid before any other distributions of an "equity" nature are made, and (3) general and limited partners rank on the same level except as otherwise provided in the partnership agreement.

ARTICLE 9. FOREIGN LIMITED PARTNERSHIPS

§ 901. Law Governing

Subject to the Constitution of this State, (i) the laws of the state under which a foreign limited partnership is organized govern its organization and internal affairs and the liability of its limited partners, and (ii) a foreign limited partnership may not be denied registration by reason of any difference between those laws and the laws of this State.

COMMENT

Section 901 first appeared in the 1976 Act.

§ 902. Registration

Before transacting business in this State, a foreign limited partnership shall register with the Secretary of State. In order to register, a foreign limited partnership shall submit to the Secretary of State, in duplicate, an application for registration as a foreign limited partnership, signed and sworn to by a general partner and setting forth:

(1) the name of the foreign limited partnership and, if different, the name under which it proposes to register and transact business in this State;

(2) the State and date of its formation;

(3) the name and address of any agent for service of process on the foreign limited partnership whom the foreign limited partnership elects to appoint; the agent must be an individual resident of this State, a domestic corporation, or a foreign corporation having a place of business in, and authorized to do business in, this State;

(4) a statement that the Secretary of State is appointed the agent of the foreign limited partnership for service of process if no agent has been appointed under paragraph (3) or, if appointed, the agent's authority has been revoked or if the agent cannot be found or served with the exercise of reasonable diligence;

(5) the address of the office required to be maintained in the state of its organization by the laws of that state or, if not so required, of the principal office of the foreign limited partnership;

(6) the name and business address of each general partner; and

(7) the address of the office at which is kept a list of the names and addresses of the limited partners and their capital contributions, together with an undertaking by the foreign limited partnership to keep those records until the foreign limited partnership's registration in this State is cancelled or withdrawn.

COMMENT

Section 902 first appeared in the 1976 Act. It was thought that requiring a full copy of the certificate of limited partnership and all amendments thereto to be filed in each state in which the partnership does business would impose an unreasonable burden on interstate limited partnerships and that the information Section 902 required to be filed would be sufficient to tell interested persons where they could write to obtain copies of those basic documents. Subdivision (3) of the 1976 Act has been omitted, and subdivisions (6) and (7) differ from their counterparts in the 1976 Act, to conform these provisions relating to the registration of foreign limited partnerships to the corresponding changes made by the Act in the provisions relating to domestic limited partnerships. The requirement that an application for registration be sworn to by a general partner is simply intended to produce the same result as is provided for in Section 204(c) with respect to certificates of domestic limited partnerships; the acceptance and endorsement by the Secretary of State (or equivalent authority) of an application which was not sworn by a general partner should be deemed a mere technical and insubstantial shortcoming, and should not result in the limited partners' being subjected to general liability for the obligations of the foreign limited partnership (See Section 907(c)).

§ 903. Issuance of Registration

(a) If the Secretary of State finds that an application for registration conforms to law and all requisite fees have been paid, he [or she] shall:

(1) endorse on the application the word "Filed", and the month, day, and year of the filing thereof;

(2) file in his [or her] office a duplicate original of the application; and

(3) issue a certificate of registration to transact business in this State.

(b) The certificate of registration, together with a duplicate original of the application, shall be returned to the person who filed the application or his [or her] representative.

COMMENT

Section 903 first appeared in the 1976 Act.

§ 904. Name

A foreign limited partnership may register with the Secretary of State under any name, whether or not it is the name under which it is registered in its state of organization, that includes without abbreviation the words "limited partnership" and that could be registered by a domestic limited partnership.

COMMENT

Section 904 first appeared in the 1976 Act.

§ 905. Changes and Amendments

If any statement in the application for registration of a foreign limited partnership was false when made or any arrangements or other facts described have changed, making the application inaccurate in any respect, the foreign limited partnership shall promptly file in the office of the Secretary of State a certificate, signed and sworn to by a general partner, correcting such statement.

COMMENT

Section 905 first appeared in the 1976 Act. It corresponds to the provisions of Section 202(c) relating to domestic limited partnerships.

§ 906. Cancellation of Registration

A foreign limited partnership may cancel its registration by filing with the Secretary of State a certificate of cancellation signed and sworn to by a general partner. A cancellation does not terminate the authority of the Secretary of State to accept service of process on the foreign limited partnership with respect to [claims for relief] [causes of action] arising out of the transactions of business in this State.

COMMENT

Section 906 first appeared in the 1976 Act.

§ 907. Transaction of Business Without Registration

(a) A foreign limited partnership transacting business in this State may not maintain any action, suit, or proceeding in any court of this State until it has registered in this State.

(b) The failure of a foreign limited partnership to register in this State does not impair the validity of any contract or act of the foreign limited partnership or prevent the foreign limited partnership from defending any action, suit, or proceeding in any court of this State.

(c) A limited partner of a foreign limited partnership is not liable as a general partner of the foreign limited partnership solely by reason of having transacted business in this State without registration.

(d) A foreign limited partnership, by transacting business in this State without registration, appoints the Secretary of State as its agent for service of process with respect to [claims for relief] [causes of action] arising out of the transaction of business in this State.

COMMENT

Section 907 first appeared in the 1976 Act.

§ 908. Action by [Appropriate Official]

The [designate the appropriate official] may bring an action to restrain a foreign limited partnership from transacting business in this State in violation of this Article.

COMMENT

Section 908 first appeared in the 1976 Act.

ARTICLE 10. DERIVATIVE ACTIONS

§ 1001. Right of Action

A limited partner may bring an action in the right of a limited partnership to recover a judgment in its favor if general partners with authority to do so have refused to bring the action or if an effort to cause those general partners to bring the action is not likely to succeed.

COMMENT

Section 1001 first appeared in the 1976 Act.

§ 1002. Proper Plaintiff

In a derivative action, the plaintiff must be a partner at the time of bringing the action and (i) must have been a partner at the time of the transaction of which he [or she] complains or (ii) his [or her] status as a partner must have devolved upon him by operation of law or pursuant to the terms of the partnership agreement from a person who was a partner at the time of the transaction.

COMMENT

Section 1002 first appeared in the 1976 Act.

§ 1003. Pleading

In a derivative action, the complaint shall set forth with particularity the effort of the plaintiff to secure initiation of the action by a general partner or the reasons for not making the effort.

COMMENT

Section 1003 first appeared in the 1976 Act.

§ 1004. Expenses

If a derivative action is successful, in whole or in part, or if anything is received by the plaintiff as a result of a judgment, compromise, or settlement of an action or claim, the court may award the plaintiff reasonable expenses, including reasonable attorney's fees, and shall direct him [or her] to remit to the limited partnership the remainder of those proceeds received by him [or her].

COMMENT

Section 1004 first appeared in the 1976 Act.

ARTICLE 11. MISCELLANEOUS

§ 1101. Construction and Application

This [Act] shall be so applied and construed to effectuate its general purpose to make uniform the law with respect to the subject of this [Act] among states enacting it.

COMMENT

Because the principles set out in Sections 28(1) and 29 of the 1916 Act have become so universally established, it was felt that the 1976 and 1985 Acts need not contain express provisions to the same effect. However, it is intended that the principles enunciated in those provisions of the 1916 Act also apply to this Act.

§ 1102. Short Title

This [Act] may be cited as the Uniform Limited Partnership Act.

§ 1103. Severability

If any provision of this [Act] or its application to any person or circumstance is held invalid, the invalidity does not affect other provisions or applications of the [Act] which can be given effect without the invalid provision or application, and to this end the provisions of this [Act] are severable.

§ 1104. Effective Date, Extended Effective Date and Repeal

Except as set forth below, the effective date of this [Act] is ______ and the following acts [list existing limited partnership acts] are hereby repealed:

(1) The existing provisions for execution and filing of certificates of limited partnerships and amendments thereunder and cancellations thereof continue in effect until [specify time required to create central filing system], the extended effective date, and Sections 102, 103, 104, 105, 201, 202, 203, 204 and 206 are not effective until the extended effective date.

(2) Section 402, specifying the conditions under which a general partner ceases to be a member of a limited partnership, is not effective until the extended effective date, and the applicable provisions of existing law continue to govern until the extended effective date.

(3) Sections 501, 502 and 608 apply only to contributions and distributions made after the effective date of this [Act].

(4) Section 704 applies only to assignments made after the effective date of this [Act].

(5) Article 9, dealing with registration of foreign limited partnerships, is not effective until the extended effective date.

(6) Unless otherwise agreed by the partners, the applicable provisions of existing law governing allocation of profits and losses (rather than the provisions of Section 503), distributions to a withdrawing partner (rather than the provisions of Section 604), and distribution of assets upon the winding up of a limited partnership (rather than the provisions of Section 804) govern limited partnerships formed before the effective date of this [Act].

COMMENT

Subdivisions (6) and (7) did not appear in Section 1104 of the 1976 Act. They are included in the 1985 Act to ensure that the application of the Act to limited partnerships formed and existing before the Act becomes effective would not violate constitutional prohibitions against the impairment of contracts.

§ 1105. Rules for Cases Not Provided for in This [Act]

In any case not provided for in this [Act] the provisions of the Uniform Partnership Act govern.

COMMENT

The result provided for in Section 1105 would obtain even in its absence in a jurisdiction which had adopted the Uniform Partnership Act, by operation of Section 6 of that act.

§ 1106. Savings Clause

The repeal of any statutory provision by this [Act] does not impair, or otherwise affect, the organization or the continued existence of a limited partnership existing at the effective date of this [Act], nor does the repeal of any existing statutory provision by this [Act] impair any contract or affect any right accrued before the effective date of this [Act].

COMMENT

Section 1106 did not appear in the 1976 Act. It is included in the 1985 Act to ensure that the application of the Act to limited partnerships formed and existing before the Act becomes effective would not violate constitutional prohibitions against the impairment of contracts.

E. DELAWARE REVISED UNIFORM PARTNERSHIP ACT

[REGISTERED LIMITED LIABILITY PARTNERSHIP]

Contents

SUBCHAPTER I. GENERAL PROVISIONS

SUBCHAPTER II. NATURE OF PARTNERSHIP

SUBCHAPTER III. RELATIONS OF PARTNERS TO PERSONS DEALING WITH PARTNERSHIP

SUBCHAPTER IV. RELATIONS OF PARTNERS TO EACH OTHER AND TO PARTNERSHIP

SUBCHAPTER X. LIMITED LIABILITY PARTNERSHIP

SUBCHAPTER XI. FOREIGN LIMITED LIABILITY PARTNERSHIP

SUBCHAPTER I. GENERAL PROVISIONS

§ 15–101. Definitions.

As used in this chapter unless the context otherwise requires:

(1) "Business" includes every trade, occupation and profession, the holding or ownership of property and any other activity for profit.

(2) "Certificate" means a certificate of conversion to partnership under § 15–901 of this title, a certificate of conversion to a non-Delaware entity under § 15–903 of this title, a certificate of merger or consolidation under § 15–902 of this title, a certificate of partnership domestication under § 15–904 of this title, a certificate of transfer and a certificate of transfer and continuance under § 15–905 of this title, a certificate of correction and a corrected certificate under § 15–118 of this title, and a certificate of termination of a certificate with a future effective date or time and a certificate of amendment of a certificate with a future effective date or time under § 15–105(i) of this title.

(3) "Debtor in bankruptcy" means a person who is the subject of:

(i) an order for relief under Title 11 of the United States Code or a comparable order under a successor statute of general application; or

(ii) a comparable order under State of Delaware federal, state or foreign law governing insolvency.

(4) "Distribution" means a transfer of money or other property from a partnership to a partner in the partner's capacity as a partner or to a transferee of all or a part of a partner's economic interest.

(5) "Domestic Partnership" means an association of two or more persons formed under § 15–202 of this title or predecessor law to carry on any lawful business, purpose or activity.

(6) "Economic interest" means a partner's share of the profits and losses of a partnership and the partner's right to receive distributions.

(7) "Foreign limited liability partnership" means a partnership that:

(i) is formed under laws other than the laws of the State of Delaware; and

(ii) has the status of a limited liability partnership under those laws.

(8) "Limited liability partnership" means a partnership that has filed a statement of qualification under § 15–1001 of this title and does not have a similar statement in effect in any other jurisdiction.

(9) "Liquidating Trustee" means a person, other than a partner, carrying out the winding up of a partnership.

(10) "Partner" means a person who has been admitted to a partnership as a partner of the partnership.

(11) "Partnership" means an association of two or more persons formed under § 15–202 of this title, predecessor law or comparable law of another jurisdiction to carry on any business, purpose or activity.

(12) "Partnership agreement" means the agreement, whether written, oral or implied, among the partners concerning the partnership, including amendments to the partnership agreement. A partnership is not required to execute its partnership agreement. A partnership is bound by its partnership agreement whether or not the partnership executes the partnership agreement.

(13) "Partnership at will" means a partnership that is not a partnership for a definite term or particular undertaking.

(14) "Partnership for a definite term or particular undertaking" means a partnership in which the partners have agreed to remain partners until the expiration of a definite term or the completion of a particular undertaking.

(15) "Partnership interest" or "partner's interest in the partnership" means all of a partner's interests in the partnership, including the partner's economic interest and all management and other rights.

(16) "Person" means a natural person, partnership, limited partnership, trust, estate, limited liability company, association, corporation, custodian, nominee or any other individual or entity in its own or any representative capacity, in each case, whether domestic or foreign.

(17) "Property" means all property, real, personal or mixed, tangible or intangible, or any interest therein.

(18) "State" means the District of Columbia or the Commonwealth of Puerto Rico or any state, territory, possession or other jurisdiction of the United States other than the State of Delaware.

(19) "Statement" means a statement of partnership existence under § 15–303 of this title, a statement of denial under § 15–304 of this title, a statement of dissociation under § 15–704 of this title, a statement of dissolution under § 15–805 of this title, a statement of qualification under § 15–1001 of this title, a statement of foreign qualification under § 15–1102 of this title, and an amendment or cancellation of any of the foregoing under § 15–105 of this title and a statement of correction and a corrected statement under § 15–118 of this title.

(20) "Transfer" includes an assignment, conveyance, lease, mortgage, deed, and encumbrance.

§ 15–102. Knowledge and notice.

(a) A person knows a fact if the person has actual knowledge of it.

(b) A person has notice of a fact:

(1) if the person knows of it;

(2) if the person has received a notification of it;

(3) if the person has reason to know it exists from all of the facts known to the person at the time in question; or

(4) by reason of a filing or recording of a statement or certificate to the extent provided by and subject to the limitations set forth in this chapter.

(c) A person notifies or gives a notification to another by taking steps reasonably required to inform the other person in the ordinary course, whether or not the other person obtains knowledge of it.

(d) A person receives a notification when the notification:

(1) comes to the person's attention; or

(2) is received at the person's place of business or at any other place held out by the person as a place for receiving communications.

(e) Except as otherwise provided in subsection (f), a person other than an individual knows, has notice, or receives a notification of a fact for purposes of a particular transaction when the individual conducting the transaction knows, has notice, or receives a notification of the fact, or in any event when the fact would have been brought to the individual's attention if the person had exercised reasonable diligence. The person exercises reasonable diligence if it maintains reasonable routines for communicating significant information to the individual conducting the transaction and there is reasonable compliance with the routines. Reasonable diligence does not require an individual acting for the person to communicate information unless the communication is part of the individual's regular duties or the individual has reason to know of the transaction and that the transaction would be materially affected by the information.

(f) A partner's knowledge, notice or receipt of a notification of a fact relating to the partnership is effective immediately as knowledge by, notice to or receipt of a notification by the partnership, except in the case of a fraud on the partnership committed by or with the consent of that partner.

§ 15–103. Effect of partnership agreement; nonwaivable provisions.

(a) Except as otherwise provided in subsection (b), relations among the partners and between the partners and the partnership are governed by the partnership agreement. To the extent the partnership agreement does not otherwise provide, this chapter governs relations among the partners and between the partners and the partnership.

(b) The partnership agreement may not:

(1) Vary the rights and duties under Section 15–105 except to eliminate the duty to provide copies of statements to all of the partners;

(2) Restrict a partner's rights to obtain information as provided in § 15-403 of this title, except as permitted by § 15-403(f) of this title;

(3) Eliminate the obligation of good faith and fair dealing under Section 15-404(d), but the partnership agreement may restrict the obligation or prescribe the standards by which the performance of the obligation is to be measured;

(4) Vary the power to dissociate as a partner under Section 15-602(a), except to require the notice under Section 15-601(1) to be in writing;

(5) Vary the right of a court to expel a partner in the events specified in Section 15-601(5);

(6) Vary the requirement to wind up the partnership business in cases specified in Section 15-801(4), (5) or (6); or

(7) Vary the law applicable to a limited liability partnership under Section 15-106(b).

(c) Notwithstanding anything to the contrary contained in this section, §§ 15-201, 15-203 and 15-501 of this title may be modified only to the extent provided in a statement of partnership existence and in a partnership agreement.

(d) It is the policy of this chapter to give maximum effect to the principle of freedom of contract and to the enforceability of partnership agreements.

(e) A partner or another person shall not be liable to the partnership or the other partners or another person that is a party to or otherwise bound by a partnership agreement for the partner's or other person's good faith reliance on the provisions of the partnership agreement.

§ 15-108. Name of partnership.

(a) The name of a partnership: (i) may contain the name of a partner and (ii) may contain the following words: "Company," "Association," "Club," "Foundation," "Fund," "Institute," "Society," "Union," "Syndicate," "Trust" (or abbreviations of like import).

(b) The name of a limited liability partnership shall contain as the last words or letters of its name the words "Limited Liability Partnership," the abbreviation "L.L.P." or the designation "LLP."

(c) The name of a partnership to be included in the statement of partnership existence, statement of qualification or statement of foreign qualification filed by such partnership must be such as to distinguish it upon the records of the Secretary of State from the name on such records of any corporation, partnership (including a limited liability partnership), limited partnership (including a limited liability limited partnership), business trust or limited liability company organized under the laws of the State of Delaware and reserved, registered, formed or organized with the Secretary of State or qualified to do business and registered as a foreign corporation, foreign limited liability partnership, foreign limited partnership, foreign business trust or foreign limited liability company in the State of Delaware; provided, however, that a partnership may be registered under any name which is not such as to distinguish it upon the records of the Secretary of State from the name of any domestic or foreign corporation, partnership (including a limited liability partnership), limited partnership (including a limited liability limited partnership), business trust or limited liability company reserved or registered under the laws of the State of Delaware with the written consent of the other corporation, partnership (including a limited liability partnership), limited partnership (including a limited liability limited partnership), business trust or limited liability company, which written consent shall be filed with the Secretary of State.

§ 15-110. Indemnification.

Subject to such standards and restrictions, if any, as are set forth in its partnership agreement, a partnership may, and shall have the power to, indemnify and hold harmless any partner or other person from and against any and all claims and demands whatsoever.

§ 15-120. Contractual appraisal rights.

A partnership agreement or an agreement of merger or consolidation may provide that contractual appraisal rights with respect to a partnership interest or another interest in a partnership shall be available for any class or group of partners or partnership interests in connection with any amendment of a partnership agreement, any merger or consolidation in which the partnership is a constituent party to the merger or consolidation, any conversion of the partnership to another business form, any transfer to or domestication in any jurisdiction by the partnership, or the sale of all or substantially all of the partnership's assets. The Court of Chancery shall have jurisdiction to hear and determine any matter relating to any such appraisal rights.

§ 15-121. Contested matters relating to partners; contested votes.

(a) Upon application of any partner of a partnership which is formed under the laws of the State of Delaware or doing business in the State of Delaware, the Court of Chancery may hear and determine the validity of any admission, election, appointment or dissociation of a partner of the partnership, and the right of any person to become or continue to be a partner of the partnership, and to that end make such order or decree in any such case as may be just and proper, with power to enforce the production of any books, papers and records relating to the issue. In any such application, the partnership shall be named as a party, and service of copies of the application upon the partnership shall be deemed to be service upon the partnership and upon the person or persons whose right to be a partner is contested and upon the person or persons, if any, claiming to be a partner or claiming the right to be a partner; and the person upon whom service is made shall forward immediately a copy of the application to the partnership and to the person or persons whose right to be a partner is contested and to the person or persons, if any, claiming to be a partner or the right to be a partner, in a postpaid, sealed, registered letter addressed to such partnership and such person or persons at their post-office addresses last known to the person upon whom service is made or furnished to the person upon whom service is made by the applicant partner. The Court may make such order respecting further or other notice of such application as it deems proper under the circumstances.

(b) Upon application of any partner of a partnership which is formed under the laws of the State of Delaware or doing business in the State of Delaware, the Court of Chancery may hear and determine the result of any vote of partners upon matters as to which the partners of the partnership, or any class or group of partners, have the right to vote pursuant to the partnership agreement or other agreement or this chapter (other than the admission, election, appointment or dissociation of partners). In any such application, the partnership shall be named as a party, and service of the application upon the person upon whom service is made shall be deemed to be service upon the partnership, and no other party need be joined in order for the Court to adjudicate the result of the vote. The Court may make such order respecting further or other notice of such application as it deems proper under the circumstances.

(c) Nothing herein contained limits or affects the right to serve process in any other manner now or hereafter provided by law. This section is an extension of and not a limitation upon the right otherwise existing of service of legal process upon nonresidents.

SUBCHAPTER II. NATURE OF PARTNERSHIP

§ 15–201. Partnership as entity.

(a) A partnership is a separate legal entity which is an entity distinct from its partners unless otherwise provided in a statement of partnership existence and in a partnership agreement.

(b) A limited liability partnership continues to be the same entity that existed before the filing of a statement of qualification under Section 15–1001.

§ 15-205. Admission without contribution or partnership interest.

Each person to be admitted as a partner to a partnership formed under either § 15-202(a)(i) or § 15-202(a)(ii) of this title may be admitted as a partner and may receive a partnership interest in the partnership without making a contribution or being obligated to make a contribution to the partnership. Each person to be admitted as a partner to a partnership formed under either § 15-202(a)(i) or § 15-202(a)(ii) of this title may be admitted as a partner without acquiring an economic interest in the partnership. Nothing contained in this section shall affect a partner's liability under § 15-306 of this title.

§ 15-206. Form of contribution.

The contribution of a partner may be in cash, property or services rendered, or a promissory note or other obligation to contribute cash or property or to perform services.

§ 15-207. Liability for contribution.

(a) A partner is obligated to the partnership to perform any promise to contribute cash or property or to perform services, even if the partner is unable to perform because of death, disability or any other reason. If a partner does not make the required contribution of property or services, the partner is obligated at the option of the partnership to contribute cash equal to that portion of the value of the contribution that has not been made. The foregoing option shall be in addition to, and not in lieu of, any other rights, including the right to specific performance, that the partnership may have against such partner under the partnership agreement or applicable law.

(b) A partnership agreement may provide that the partnership interest of any partner who fails to make any contribution that the partner is obligated to make shall be subject to specified penalties for, or specified consequences of, such failure. Such penalty or consequence may take the form of reducing or eliminating the defaulting partner's interest in the partnership, subordinating the partner's partnership interest to that of nondefaulting partners, a forced sale of the partner's partnership interest, forfeiture of the partner's partnership interest, the lending by other partners of the amount necessary to meet the partner's commitment, a fixing of the value of the partner's partnership interest by appraisal or by formula and redemption or sale of the partner's partnership interest at such value, or other penalty or consequence.

SUBCHAPTER III. RELATIONS OF PARTNERS TO PERSONS DEALING WITH PARTNERSHIP

§ 15–301. Partner agent of partnership.

Subject to the effect of a statement of partnership existence under Section 15–303:

(1) Each partner is an agent of the partnership for the purpose of its business, purposes or activities. An act of a partner, including the execution of an instrument in the partnership name, for apparently carrying on in the ordinary course the partnership's business, purposes or activities or business, purposes or activities of the kind carried on by the partnership binds the partnership, unless the partner had no authority to act for the partnership in the particular matter and the person with whom the partner was dealing had notice that the partner lacked authority.

(2) An act of a partner which is not apparently for carrying on in the ordinary course the partnership's business, purposes or activities or business, purposes or activities of the kind carried on by the partnership binds the partnership only if the act was authorized by the other partners.

§ 15–305. Partnership liable for partner's actionable conduct.

(a) A partnership is liable for loss or injury caused to a person, or for a penalty incurred, as a result of a wrongful act or omission, or other actionable conduct, of a partner acting in the ordinary course of business of the partnership or with authority of the partnership.

(b) If, in the course of the partnership's business or while acting with authority of the partnership, a partner receives or causes the partnership to receive money or property of a person not a partner, and the money or property is misapplied by a partner, the partnership is liable for the loss.

§ 15–306. Partner's liability.

(a) Except as otherwise provided in subsections (b) and (c), all partners are liable jointly and severally for all obligations of the partnership unless otherwise agreed by the claimant or provided by law.

(b) A person admitted as a partner into an existing partnership is not personally liable for any obligation of the partnership incurred before the person's admission as a partner.

(c) An obligation of a partnership incurred while the partnership is a limited liability partnership, whether arising in contract, tort or otherwise, is solely the obligation of the partnership. A partner is not personally liable, directly or indirectly, by way of indemnification, contribution, assessment or otherwise, for such an obligation solely by reason of being or so acting as a partner.

(d) The ability of an attorney-at-law, admitted to the practice of law in the State of Delaware, to practice law in a limited liability partnership, shall be determined by the Rules of the Supreme Court of the State of Delaware.

(e) Notwithstanding the provisions of subsection (c) of this section, under a partnership agreement or under another agreement, a partner may agree to be personally liable, directly or indirectly, by way of indemnification, contribution, assessment or otherwise, for any or all of the obligations of the partnership incurred while the partnership is a limited liability partnership.

§ 15-308. Liability of purported partner.

(a) If a person, by words or conduct, purports to be a partner, or consents to being represented by another as a partner, in a partnership or with one or more persons not partners, the purported partner is liable to a person to whom the representation is made, if that person, relying on the representation, enters into a transaction with the actual or purported partnership. If the representation, either by the purported partner or by a person with the purported partner's consent, is made in a public manner, the purported partner is liable to a person who relies upon the purported partnership even if the purported partner is not aware of being held out as a partner to the claimant. If a partnership obligation results, the purported partner is liable with respect to that obligation as if the purported partner were a partner. If no partnership obligation results, the purported partner is liable with respect to that obligation jointly and severally with any other person consenting to the representation. In the case of a limited liability partnership, a person's liability under Section 15-308(a) is subject to Section 15-306 as if the person were a partner in the limited liability partnership.

(b) If a person is thus represented to be a partner in an existing partnership, or with one or more persons not partners, the purported partner is an agent of persons consenting to the representation to bind them to the same extent and in the same manner as if the purported partner were a partner, with respect to persons who enter into transactions in reliance upon the representation. If all of the partners of the existing partnership consent to the representation, a partnership act or obligation results. If fewer than all of the partners of the existing partnership consent to the representation, the person acting and the partners consenting to the representation are jointly and severally liable.

(c) A person is not liable as a partner merely because the person is named by another in a statement of partnership existence.

(d) A person does not continue to be liable as a partner merely because of a failure to file a statement of dissociation or to amend a statement of partnership existence to indicate the partner's dissociation from the partnership.

(e) Except as otherwise provided in subsections (a) and (b), persons who are not partners as to each other are not liable as partners to other persons.

SUBCHAPTER IV. RELATIONS OF PARTNERS TO EACH OTHER AND TO PARTNERSHIP

§ 15–403. Partner's rights and duties with respect to information.

(a) Each partner and the partnership shall provide partners, former partners and the legal representative of a deceased partner or partner under a legal disability and their agents and attorneys, access to the books and records of the partnership and other information concerning the partnership's business and affairs (in the case of former partners, only with respect to the period during which they were partners) upon reasonable demand, for any purpose reasonably related to the partner's interest as a partner in the partnership. The right of access shall include access to:

(1) True and full information regarding the status of the business and financial condition of the partnership;

(2) Promptly after becoming available, a copy of the partnership's federal, state and local income tax returns for each year;

(3) A current list of the name and last known business, residence or mailing address of each partner;

(4) A copy of any statement and written partnership agreement and all amendments thereto, together with executed copies of any written powers of attorney pursuant to which the statement or the partnership agreement and any amendments thereto have been executed;

(5) True and full information regarding the amount of cash and a description and statement of the agreed value of any other property or services contributed by each partner and which each partner has agreed to contribute in the future, and the date on which each partner became a partner; and

(6) Other information regarding the affairs of the partnership as is just and reasonable.

The right of access includes the right to examine and make extracts from books and records and other information concerning the partnership's business and affairs. The partnership agreement may provide for, and in the absence of such provision in the partnership agreement, the partnership or the partner from whom access is sought may impose, reasonable standards (including standards governing what information and documents are to be furnished at what time and location and at whose expense) with respect to exercise of the right of access.

(b) A partnership agreement may provide that the partnership shall have the right to keep confidential from partners for such period of time as the partnership deems reasonable, any information which the partnership reasonably believes to be in the nature of trade secrets or other information the disclosure of which the partnership in good faith believes is not in the best interest of the partnership or could damage the partnership or its business or affairs or which the partnership is required by law or by agreement with a third party to keep confidential.

(c) A partnership and its partners may maintain the books and records and other information concerning the partnership in other than a written form if such form is capable of conversion into written form within a reasonable time.

(d) Any demand by a partner under this section shall be in writing and shall state the purpose of such demand.

(e) Any action to enforce any right arising under this section shall be brought in the Court of Chancery. If the partnership or a partner refuses to permit access as described in subsection (a)(3) of this section or does not reply to a demand that has been made within 5 business days after the demand has been made, the demanding partner, former partner, or legal representative of a deceased partner or partner under a legal disability may apply to the Court of Chancery for an order to compel such disclosure. The Court of Chancery is hereby vested with exclusive jurisdiction to determine whether or not the person making the demand is entitled to the books and records or other information concerning the partnership's business and affairs sought. The Court of Chancery may summarily order the partnership or partner to permit the demanding partner, former partner or legal representative of a deceased partner or partner under a legal disability and their agents and attorneys to provide access to the information described in subsection (a)(3) of this section and to make copies or extracts therefrom; or the Court of Chancery may summarily order the partnership or partner to furnish to the demanding partner, former partner or legal representative of a deceased partner or partner under a legal disability and their agents and attorneys the information described in subsection (a)(3) of this section on the condition that the partner, former partner or legal representative of a deceased partner or partner under a legal disability first pay to the partnership or to the partner from whom access is sought the reasonable cost of obtaining and furnishing such information and on such other conditions as the Court of Chancery deems appropriate. When a demanding partner, former partner or legal representative of a deceased partner or partner under a legal disability seeks to obtain access to information described in subsection (a)(3) of this section, the demanding partner, former partner or legal representative of a deceased partner or partner under a legal disability shall first establish (1) that the demanding partner, former partner or legal representative of a deceased partner or partner under a legal disability has complied with the provisions of this section respecting the form and manner of making demand for obtaining access to such information and (2) that the information the demanding partner, former partner or legal representative of a deceased partner or partner under a legal disability seeks is reasonably related to the partner's interest as a partner in the partnership. The Court of Chancery may, in its discretion, prescribe any limitations or conditions with reference to the access to information, or award such other or further relief as the Court of Chancery may deem just and proper. The Court of Chancery may order books, documents and records, pertinent extracts therefrom, or duly authenticated copies thereof, to be brought within the State of Delaware and kept in the State of Delaware upon such terms and conditions as the order may prescribe.

(f) The rights of a partner to obtain information as provided in this section may be restricted in an original partnership agreement or in any subsequent amendment approved or adopted by all of the partners and in compliance with any applicable requirements of the partnership agreement.

§ 15–404. General standards of partner's conduct.

(a) The only fiduciary duties a partner owes to the partnership and the other partners are the duty of loyalty and the duty of care set forth in subsections (b) and (c).

(b) A partner's duty of loyalty to the partnership and the other partners is limited to the following:

(1) to account to the partnership and hold as trustee for it any property, profit or benefit derived by the partner in the conduct or winding up of the partnership business or affairs or derived from a use by the partner of partnership property, including the appropriation of a partnership opportunity;

(2) to refrain from dealing with the partnership in the conduct or winding up of the partnership business or affairs as or on behalf of a party having an interest adverse to the partnership; and

(3) to refrain from competing with the partnership in the conduct of the partnership business or affairs before the dissolution of the partnership.

(c) A partner's duty of care to the partnership and the other partners in the conduct and winding up of the partnership business or affairs is limited to refraining from engaging in grossly negligent or reckless conduct, intentional misconduct, or a knowing violation of law.

(d) A partner shall discharge the duties to the partnership and the other partners under this chapter or under the partnership agreement and exercise any rights consistently with the obligation of good faith and fair dealing.

(e) A partner does not violate a duty or obligation under this chapter or under the partnership agreement solely because the partner's conduct furthers the partner's own interest.

(f) A partner may lend money to, borrow money from, act as a surety, guarantor or endorser for, guarantee or assume 1 or more specific obligations of, provide collateral for and transact other business with, the partnership and, subject to other applicable law, has the same rights and obligations with respect thereto as a person who is not a partner.

(g) This section applies to a person winding up the partnership business or affairs as the personal or legal representative of the last surviving partner as if the person were a partner.

§ 15–405. Actions by partnership and partners; derivative actions.

(a) A partnership may maintain an action against a partner for a breach of the partnership agreement, or for the violation of a duty to the partnership, causing harm to the partnership.

(b) A partner may maintain an action against the partnership or another partner for legal or equitable relief, with or without an accounting as to partnership business, to:

(1) enforce the partner's rights under the partnership agreement;

(2) enforce the partner's rights under this chapter, including:

(i) the partner's rights under Sections 15–401, 15–403 or 15–404;

(ii) the partner's right on dissociation to have the partner's interest in the partnership purchased pursuant to Section 15–701 or enforce any other right under Subchapter VI or VII; or

(iii) the partner's right to compel a dissolution and winding up of the partnership business under Section 15–801 or enforce any other right under Subchapter VIII; or

(3) enforce the rights and otherwise protect the interests of the partner, including rights and interests arising independently of the partnership relationship.

(c) The accrual of, and any time limitation on, a right of action for a remedy under this section is governed by other law. A right to an accounting upon a dissolution and winding up does not revive a claim barred by law.

(d) A partner may bring a derivative action in the Court of Chancery in the right of a partnership to recover a judgment in the partnership's favor.

(e) In a derivative action, the plaintiff must be a partner at the time of bringing the action and:

(1) At the time of the transaction of which the partner complains; or

(2) The partner's status as a partner had devolved upon the partner by operation of law or pursuant to the terms of the partnership agreement from a person who was a partner at the time of the transaction.

(f) In a derivative action, the complaint shall set forth with particularity the effort, if any, of the plaintiff to secure initiation of the action by the partnership or the reason for not making the effort.

(g) If a derivative action is successful, in whole or in part, as a result of a judgment, compromise or settlement of any such action, the court may award the plaintiff reasonable expenses, including reasonable attorney's fees, from any recovery in any such action or from a partnership.

SUBCHAPTER X. LIMITED LIABILITY PARTNERSHIP

§ 15–1001. Statement of qualification.

(a) A partnership may become a limited liability partnership pursuant to this section.

(b) The terms and conditions on which a partnership becomes a limited liability partnership must be approved by the vote necessary to amend the partnership agreement except, in the case of a partnership agreement that expressly considers obligations to contribute to the partnership, the vote necessary to amend those provisions.

(c) After the approval required by subsection (b), a partnership may become a limited liability partnership by filing a statement of qualification. The statement of qualification must contain:

(1) the name of the partnership;

(2) the address of the registered office and the name and address of the registered agent for service of process required to be maintained by Section 15–111 of this chapter;

(3) the number of partners of the partnership;

(4) a statement that the partnership elects to be a limited liability partnership; and

(5) the future effective date or time (which shall be a date or time certain) of the statement of qualification if it is not to be effective upon the filing of the statement of qualification.

(d) The status of a partnership as a limited liability partnership is effective on the later of the filing of the statement of qualification or a future effective date or time specified in the statement of qualification. The status as a limited liability partnership remains effective, regardless of changes in the partnership, until it is canceled pursuant to Section 15–105(d) of this chapter or revoked pursuant to Section 15–1003 of this chapter.

(e) A partnership is a limited liability partnership if there has been substantial compliance with the requirements of this subchapter. The status of a partnership as a limited liability partnership and the liability of its partners is not affected by errors or later changes in the information required to be contained in the statement of qualification under subsection (c).

(f) The filing of a statement of qualification establishes that a partnership has satisfied all conditions precedent to the qualification of the partnership as a limited liability partnership.

(g) An amendment or cancellation of a statement of qualification is effective when it is filed or on a future effective date or time specified in the amendment or cancellation.

(h) If a person is included in the number of partners of a limited liability partnership set forth in a statement of qualification, a statement of foreign qualification or an annual report, the inclusion of such person shall not be admissible as evidence in any action, suit or proceeding, whether civil, criminal, administrative or investigative, for the purpose of determining whether such person is liable as a partner of such limited liability partnership. The status of a partnership as a limited liability partnership and the liability of a partner of such limited liability partnership shall not be adversely affected if the number of partners stated in a statement of qualification, a statement of foreign qualification or an annual report is erroneously stated provided that the statement of qualification, the statement of foreign qualification or the annual report was filed in good faith.

(i) Notwithstanding anything in this chapter to the contrary, a domestic partnership having, or that, but for its election in accordance with Section 15–1206(c) of this Chapter, would have had, on December 31, 2001, the status of a registered limited liability partnership under predecessor law, shall have the status of a limited liability partnership under this chapter as of January 1, 2002, and, to the extent such partnership has not filed a statement of qualification pursuant to this section, the latest application or renewal application filed by such partnership under such predecessor law shall constitute a statement of qualification filed under this section.

SUBCHAPTER XI. FOREIGN LIMITED LIABILITY PARTNERSHIP

§ 15–1101. Law governing foreign limited liability partnership.

(a) The law under which a foreign limited liability partnership is formed governs relations among the partners and between the partners and the partnership and the liability of partners for obligations of the partnership.

(b) A foreign limited liability partnership may not be denied a statement of foreign qualification by reason of any difference between the law under which the partnership was formed and the law of the State of Delaware.

(c) A statement of foreign qualification does not authorize a foreign limited liability partnership to engage in any business or exercise any power that a partnership may not engage in or exercise in the State of Delaware as a limited liability partnership.

F. PARTNERSHIP FORMS

1. GENERAL PARTNERSHIP AGREEMENT

THIS GENERAL PARTNERSHIP AGREEMENT dated as of the ______ day of ______ 2002, by and between ______ and ______.

WHEREAS, the parties hereto, on this date, have agreed to form a general partnership; and

WHEREAS, the parties hereto, by this writing, desire to define the relative rights, duties and liabilities of the Partners in connection with such partnership.

NOW, THEREFORE, in consideration of the premises and the mutual promises hereinafter contained, the Partners hereby associate themselves and agree to form and do form a general partnership pursuant to the provisions of the Minnesota Uniform Partnership Act, Minnesota Statutes, Chapter 323, as amended, and the rights and liabilities of the Partners shall be as provided and set forth herein except as herein otherwise expressly provided.

ARTICLE 1. DEFINITIONS

1.1) *Definitions.* Unless the context otherwise requires, when used in this Agreement, the terms listed in this Section shall have the following meanings:

(a) "Assignment" means any sale, pledge, transfer, gift or other disposition, whether voluntary or by operation of law.

(b) "Code" means the Internal Revenue Code of 1986, as amended from time to time, or corresponding provisions of subsequent laws.

(c) "Partnership" means the ______ Partnership.

(d) "Partnership Accountants" means such firm of accountants as may be selected by the Partners to prepare and/or audit the books of account of the Partnership.

(e) "Partnership Interest" means the interest in the Partnership acquired and owned by each Partner.

(f) "Person" means any individual, partnership, corporation, trust, joint venture or association.

(g) "Prime Rate of Interest" means the prime rate of interest announced from time to time by Norwest Bank Minnesota, National Association.

(h) "Property" means the real property in ______ County, Minnesota, legally described on Exhibit A attached hereto, together with all buildings and improvements constructed or located on such real property, all fixtures located in such buildings or on such real estate, and all easements and rights benefitting or appurtenant to such buildings or real property, all of which is subject to a contract for deed.

ARTICLE 2. NAME, OFFICE, AND TERM

2.1) *Name of Partnership.* The name of the Partnership shall be ______.

2.2) *Principal Place of Business.* The office and principal place of business of the Partnership shall be ______ or such other place as the Partners shall, from time to time, determine.

2.3) *Term.* This Partnership shall commence as of the date hereof and shall continue for 40 years, unless sooner dissolved pursuant to the provisions of this Agreement or by operation of law.

ARTICLE 3. POWERS AND PURPOSES

3.1) *Purpose.* The business purpose of the Partnership shall be to own and manage the Property. The Partnership may conduct other business activities only as the Partners may agree from time to time.

3.2) *Power of the Partnership.* The Partnership shall have the power to do any and all things necessary or desirable in the conduct of such business to the same extent and as fully as a natural person doing business as a sole proprietor, including, but not limited to, the power to borrow such funds (and to secure same by mortgage, deed of trust, collateral or otherwise) and to enter into such contracts (including a contract for deed) and to execute such instruments as may be necessary or appropriate to accomplish its business purpose.

ARTICLE 4. PARTNERS

4.1) *Partners.* The Partners of the Partnership shall be ______.

ARTICLE 5. CONTRIBUTIONS

5.1) *Partnership Interests.* ______ and ______ shall each have a 50% interest in the capital, income, profits, and assets of the Partnership. Such percentage interest is the Partner's "Percentage Interest" in the Partnership. Any changes to the Partners' Percentage Interest shall be reflected in an amendment to this Agreement.

5.2) *Initial Capital Contributions.* ______ and ______ will make an initial contribution to the capital of the Partnership in consideration for their Partnership Interests of their rights, title and interest in the Property, which ______ and ______ hereby acknowledge is owned 50% by ______ and 50% by ______.

5.3) *Additional Contributions.* The Partners agree to make additional contributions to the Partnership as follows:

(a) *Required Contributions.* Each Partner agrees to make additional capital contributions to the Partnership so as to equally share the holding costs of the Property and the out-of-pocket administrative and operating expenses of the Partnership. All such additional contributions shall be in proportion to the Partners' Percentage Interests, and all such contributions which are not in proportion to the Partners' Percentage Interests shall be deemed a loan to the Partnership and shall be repaid by the Partnership as set forth in Section 5.7. Any Partner who does not make such additional contributions within 90 days after the mailing of written notice of demand by the Partner who made such contribution shall be personally indebted to the Partnership for the amount of additional contributions not made, plus interest from the date of demand at the rate set forth in Section 5.7, and plus and costs of collection, including attorneys' fees. The Partnership may exercise any and all remedies available to it at law or equity to enforce such obligation. Without limiting any other remedies available to the Partnership, the amount of such obligation, including interest and costs, may be offset by the Partnership against any amount payable to the defaulting Partner as a distribution or upon such Partner's separation from the Partnership.

(b) *Voluntary Contributions.* The Partners shall make such additional capital contributions to the Partnership as the Partners agree upon from time to time. All such additional contributions shall be in proportion to the Partners' Percentage Interests, and all such additional contributions which are not made in proportion to the Partners' Percentage Interests shall be deemed a loan to the Partnership and shall be repaid by the Partnership as set forth in Section 5.7.

5.4) *Capital Accounts.* A separate capital account shall be maintained for each Partner and shall consist of such Partner's initial capital contribution to the Partnership. Each Partner's capital account shall be increased by (i) such Partner's share of Partnership income which is credited to capital, if any, and (ii) such Partner's additional capital contributions to the Partnership, if any. Each Partner's capital account shall be reduced by (i) distributions in reduction of capital, and (ii) such Partner's share of Partnership losses which are charged to capital. Capital accounts shall be maintained at all times in the same proportions as the Partner's Percentage Interests. Revaluation of Partnership capital may be made from time to time appropriate to the maintenance of such proportions.

5.5) *No Interest on Capital Contribution.* No interest shall be paid on the capital contributions of the Partners or upon any undrawn profits of any Partner which are credited to such Partner's capital account.

5.6) *Withdrawal of Capital Contributions.* A Partner shall not be entitled to withdraw any part of its capital contribution or to receive repayment of such Partner's capital contribution or to receive any distribution from the Partnership except as specifically provided herein. All distributions from the Partnership to the Partners shall be made in proportion to the Partners' respective Percentage Interests. To the extent any distribution to or withdrawal by a Partner in the capacity as a Partner is not so made, it shall be deemed a loan which such Partner is obligated to repay on demand at such rate as set forth in Section 5.7.

5.7) *Loans to Partnership.* Subject to the approval of all the Partners, any Partner may make loans to the Partnership from time to time for Partnership business. No such loan shall be treated as a contribution to the capital of the Partnership for any purposes hereunder, nor entitle such Partner to any increase in such Partner's share of the net income and loss of and cash distributions from the Partnership. The Partnership shall be obligated to such Partner for the amount of any such loans together with interest at an annual rate equal to 2% over the Prime Rate of Interest. The principal and interest on any loans to the Partnership pursuant to this Section shall be repaid before any distributions or cash or property to the Partners. No Partner shall have any obligation to make any such loan to the Partnership.

ARTICLE 6. RIGHTS, POWERS, AND OBLIGATIONS OF PARTNERS

6.1) *Management.* Except as otherwise specifically provided in this Agreement, all Partnership decisions shall be made by the agreement of all of the Partners, but nothing in this Agreement shall be construed to prohibit or limit the authority of any Partner to transact any business for the Partnership which has been so authorized. Each Partner's voice in management shall be proportionate to such Partner's Percentage Interest. The Partners (acting solely and exclusively as provided in this Article) shall manage the affairs of the Partnership in a prudent and businesslike fashion, and shall use their best efforts to carry out the purposes and character of the business of the Partnership. Each Partner shall devote such of its time as it deems necessary to the management of the business of the Partnership, to the extent such management is entrusted to such Partner under the terms of this Section, and neither Partner shall be compensated for services to the Partnership, except to the extent specifically authorized by the Partners from time to time.

6.2) *Managing Partner.* Notwithstanding the provisions of Section 6.1 or any other provision in this Agreement, the Partners may elect a Managing Partner who shall have the authority and power to take the following actions relating to the day-to-day operations of the Partnership: (i) deposit all receipts received by or on behalf of the Partnership; (ii) pay expenses and other obligations of the Partnership incurred in the ordinary course of business; (iii) perform such other actions specifically directed in this Agreement; and (iv) perform such other actions as may be directed by the Partners from time to time. The Partners choose ______ as the initial Managing Partner.

6.3) *Dealings Between Partnership and Partners.* The Partnership may contract or otherwise deal with a Partner or any affiliate of a Partner including loans to the Partnership (secured or unsecured), or the purchase or sale of property or services. In any such transaction between the Partnership and a Partner or such Partner's affiliates, the agreement shall be in writing and approved by unanimous consent of the Partners, and compensation paid or promised shall be reasonable and compensation for goods or services shall be paid only for goods or services actually furnished.

6.4) *Responsibilities to Partnership.* The Partners may have other business interests and may engage in any similar or other business or trade, profession, or employment whatsoever, including business interests relating to the development, construction, sale, syndication, operation, and disposition of commercial real estate projects.

6.5) *Restrictions in Operations.* No Partner shall make or endorse any note for the Partnership, or procure money or incur any debt for the Partnership, nor discount, assign, sell, transfer or pledge any significant assets of the Partnership, except as authorized by both Partners.

6.6) *Execution of Documents.* Any deed, mortgage, bill of sale, lease, or other instrument purporting to convey or encumber assets of the Partnership in whole or in part, or any other instrument on behalf of the Partnership, shall be signed by both Partners on behalf of the Partnership except as otherwise agreed by the Partners.

6.7) *Admission of Additional Partners.* Additional persons may be admitted to the Partnership as additional or substituted Partners upon the agreement of the Partners at such time, for such contributions, and upon such other terms and conditions as they may agree.

6.8) *Meetings.* A meeting of the Partners may be called by either Partner upon giving any form of actual notice, orally or in writing. The presence of both Partners shall constitute a quorum at any meeting and waiver of notice.

ARTICLE 7. ACCOUNTING, RECORDS, AND REPORTS

7.1) *Fiscal Year.* The Partnership's fiscal year for financial reporting and for federal income tax purposes shall be the calendar year.

7.2) *Records and Accounting.* At all times during the existence of the Partnership, the Managing Partner shall keep or cause to be kept books and records of accounts utilizing the method of accounting selected by the Partners for federal income tax purposes which shall be adequate and appropriate for the Partnership's business, and in which each transaction of the Partnership shall be entered fully and accurately.

Such books of account shall include such separate and additional accounts for each Partner as shall be necessary to reflect accurately the rights and interests of the respective Partners and shall specifically reflect the name, address, and interest held by each Partner for the purpose of determining recipients of cash contributions, reports and notices. All such books and records shall be maintained at the above-described principal place of business of the Partnership.

7.3) *Bank Accounts.* The Partnership bank account, in the name of the Partnership, shall be maintained by the Partnership, and all Partnership monies received by the Partnership shall be deposited in said bank account and may be withdrawn by check signed by such persons as the Partners decide.

7.4) *Right of Inspection: Lists of Partners.* One copy of the books of account described in Section 7.2, together with a copy of this Agreement and other relevant agreements and any amendments thereto, and one copy of every document relating to the ownership of, and condition of title to, the Property shall at all times be maintained at the office of the Partnership, and each Partner or his duly authorized representatives shall have access to and the right to inspect and copy them during normal business hours.

7.5) *Reports to Partners.*

(a) *Annual Reports.* The Managing Partner shall cause to be prepared within 75 days after the close of each fiscal year a report containing an unaudited cash flow statement, and an operating statement reflecting income and disbursements.

(b) *Financial Statements—Review.* If requested by any Partner, but not more than once per year, the Partners shall cause reviewed financial statements of the Partnership to be prepared by the Partnership Accountants with an opinion expressed therein. Such review shall be performed at the Partnership's expense.

7.6) *Tax Returns.* The Managing partner shall prepare or cause to be prepared by the Partnership Accountants and shall file on or before the due date (or any extension thereof any federal, state or local tax returns required to be filed by the Partnership. The Partners shall cause the Partnership to pay any taxes payable by the Partnership. The Partners shall also prepare or cause to be prepared by such Partnership Accountants an unaudited statement of each Partner's share of the Partnership's income, gains, losses, deductions and credits for use in the preparation of such Partner's tax returns for such fiscal year, as well as an estimate of such Partner's share of the Partnership's taxable losses or gains for the succeeding fiscal year for use in the preparation of its declaration of estimated federal income tax. ______ shall be the Tax Matters Partner ("TMP") as defined in Code Section 6231(a)(7), for purposes of Code Sections 6221 to 6233; provided, ______ shall provide all of the Partners with any and all notices received from any taxing authorities and shall not respond to any such notices nor settle any tax dispute without the approval and consent of the Partners. The designation of ______ as TMP shall be made in the first Partnership tax return of the Partnership.

7.7) *Section 754 Election.* Upon receipt of the written request of a Partner, the successor-in-interest of a Partner, or of the executors, administrators or legal representatives of a Partner, the Partners shall file on behalf of the Partnership an election under Section 754 of the Code permitting an adjustment to basis under Sections 734 and 743 of the Code.

ARTICLE 8. ALLOCATIONS AND DISTRIBUTIONS

8.1) *Allocation of Income.* The Partners agree that, both for income tax purposes (except as otherwise specifically provided in this Article 3) and for financial purposes, net income or loss, and all items of income, gain or receipt, and all items of loss, deduction and credit of the Partnership shall be allocated between the Partners in accordance with the Partners' respective Percentage Interests.

8.2) *Tax Basis.* For income tax purposes, income, gain, loss and deduction with respect to property contributed to the Partnership by a Partner shall be shared among Partners so as to take account of the variation, if any, between the basis of the property to the Partnership and its fair market value at the time of contribution in the manner provided in Section 704(c) of the Code, as amended.

8.3) *Distributions of Cash.* The "Cash Of The Partnership Available For Distribution" as herein defined shall be distributed at least quarterly to the Partners (or assignees of Partnership Interests), in the same ratio as such Partners or assignees shared in the allocation of income or loss pursuant to Section 8.1 above. Subject to Section 5.7, the Cash Of The Partnership Available For Distribution shall be that cash received by the Partnership from all sources, including from any refinancing of the Property, less cash disbursements of every kind, and less such reserves for accrued expenses and working capital requirements as the Partners in their reasonable discretion may from time to time set aside. Notwithstanding the foregoing, liquidating distributions upon dissolution of the Partnership shall be made in accordance with Section 10.3 hereof. All distributions from the Partnership to the Partners shall be made in proportion to the Partners' Percentage Interests.

8.4) *Allocation Between Assignor and Assignee.* In the case of an effective Assignment by a Partner of part or all of its Partnership Interest during any fiscal year, the taxable income or loss allocable to such Partnership Interest in respect to such fiscal year shall be allocated between the assignor and the assignee in proportion to the number of months during such fiscal year that each was the holder of such

Partnership Interest, determined by reference to the date the Assignment thereof became effective.

8.5) *Sharing Liabilities.* The Partners agree that any economic losses sustained by them as a result of their status as Partners of the Partnership, and any liabilities or damages they may suffer or incur as a result, except as shall result from the wrongful or unauthorized acts of a Partner, shall be shared between them in accordance with their Percentage Interests.

8.6) *General Compliance with Section 704(b).* The capital accounts being maintained for the Partners and the allocations of Partnership items in Section 8.1 are intended to comply with Section 704(b) of the Code and applicable Treasury Regulations promulgated thereunder. If the partners determine that the manner in which such accounts are being maintained or such allocations are being made need to be modified to comply with the requirements of Section 704(b) of the Code and the applicable Treasury Regulations, the Partners may alter the method of maintaining such accounts and making such allocations and, if necessary, amend the Agreement accordingly; provided, any alteration in the method of maintaining such accounts and making such allocations and any amendment to the Agreement shall not materially alter the economic agreement among the Partners.

ARTICLE 9. ASSIGNMENT OF PARTNERSHIP INTERESTS

9.1 *Prohibition of Voluntary Sale or Assignment.* Except as otherwise provided herein, during the term of the Partnership, no Partner shall voluntarily sell, assign, transfer, set over, mortgage, pledge, hypothecate, or otherwise dispose of such Partner's Partnership Interest, in whole or in part, in the Partnership without the express written consent of the other Partner. Consent may be withheld for any reason or for no reason at all. Consent may also be conditioned upon any factors which the Partners deem necessary or desirable. No purported assignment of a Partnership Interest in violation of this Section 9.1(a) shall be valid or effective, and the Partnership may refuse to recognize any such purported assignment for any purpose.

ARTICLE 10. SEPARATION, DISSOLUTION, AND LIQUIDATION

10.1) *Separation of a Partner with Continuation of the Partnership.*

(a) The following events are referred to as an "involuntary transfer" of a Partner's (the "Assigning Partner") Partnership Interest:

(i) Death of a Partner,

(ii) Bankruptcy or insolvency of a Partner, or

(iii) Other involuntary transfer or assignment of a Partner's interest in the Partnership, including a transfer through levy, garnishment or foreclosure sale.

In the event of an involuntary transfer of an Assigning Partner's Partnership Interest as described above, the Partnership shall not for that reason dissolve or terminate but shall continue on the same terms and conditions herein provided as an existing Partnership if the other Partner (the "Remaining Partner") continues the business of the otherwise dissolved Partnership pursuant to Minnesota Statutes, Chapter 323. The transferee of the Assigning Partner's Partnership Interest, including a judgment creditor, representative of the estate or the heirs of the deceased Partner, or the trustee in bankruptcy or other representative of the bankrupt Partner, shall succeed to the Partnership Interest of the Assigning Partner, subject to all the liabilities and obligations of the Assigning Partner under this Agreement, and shall be deemed an assignee of the Partnership Interest of such partner in accordance with the provisions of the Uniform Partnership Act, and shall have such power as the Assigning Partner possessed to assign such Partnership Interest. Except as provided below, such creditor, personal representative or trustee shall not have the right to be substituted as a Partner but shall be entitled, as though it were a Partner, to receive distributions of cash and to be credited or debited with allocations of income or loss in the manner provided herein and to receive reports, but shall have no other rights of a Partner, and the consent of such creditor, personal representative or trustee shall not be required to approve any action of the Partnership. Notwithstanding the foregoing, upon the death of the Assigning Partner, the personal representative or beneficiary of the Assigning Partner's Partnership Interest shall have an option to become a Partner of the Partnership by delivering written notice of such exercise to the Remaining Partner, and, if the option is so exercised, such personal representative or beneficiary shall become a Partner of the Partnership with all of the rights and obligations of a Partner. Upon the request of the Remaining Partner, such personal representative or beneficiary shall execute such documents as may be requested to reflect his or her status as a Partner, including documents evidencing the assumption of liability for Partnership obligations. If the Remaining Partner does not elect to continue the business of the Partnership, then the affairs of the Partnership shall be wound up and terminated as provided in Sections 10.4 through 10.7 hereof.

(b) For purposes of ______'s existing bankruptcy case, the provisions of this Section 10.1 shall not become effective unless the case is converted to a case under Chapter 7 of the Bankruptcy Code or a Chapter 11 trustee is duly appointed by order of the Court.

10.2) *Events Resulting in a Wrongful Dissolution of the Partnership.* The Partnership shall be considered dissolved if any Partner (or assignee thereof) unilaterally (i) withdraws from the Partnership, or (ii) otherwise attempts to end such Partner's affiliation with the Partnership or terminates the Partnership (including seeking a judicial decree pursuant to Minn. Stat. § 323.31), excluding those events specifically addressed in Section 10.1. Any Partner (or assignee thereof) that causes one of the events described in clauses (i) or (ii) above to occur shall be considered to have retired from the Partnership (and is referred to herein as the "Retiring Partner") wrongfully and thereby caused the wrongful dissolution of the Partnership. In the event of such a dissolution, the other Partner (the "Remaining Partner") shall be solely entitled to continue the business of the Partnership. If the Remaining Partner elects to continue the business of the Partnership, the Remaining Partner shall execute an agreement agreeing to hold the Retiring Partner harmless from any liabilities of the Partnership. The Retiring Partner shall accept this hold-harmless agreement in full satisfaction of such Retiring Partner's Partnership Interest.

If the Remaining Partner does not elect to continue the business of the Partnership, then the affairs of the Partnership shall be wound up and the Partnership terminated as provided in Sections 10.4 through 10.7 hereof. Notwithstanding the preceding sentence, the amount to which the Retiring Partner is entitled upon winding-up and termination shall be reduced by any damages caused by the wrongful dissolution of the Partnership.

10.3) *Events Resulting in the Non–Wrongful Dissolution of the Partnership.* The Partnership shall be dissolved upon the happening of any of the following events:

(a) The sale or other disposition of all of the assets of the Partnership, except in the case of an installment sale of all of the assets of the Partnership, in which event the Partnership shall continue until the final installment payment; or

(b) The approval of all Partners; or

(c) The occurrence of any event which makes it unlawful for the business of the Partnership to be carried on or for the Partners to do it in a Partnership.

In the event of a non-wrongful dissolution, the business of the Partnership shall be wound up and terminated as provided in Sections 10.4 and 10.7 below.

10.4) *Final Statements.* Upon dissolution of the Partnership pursuant to Section 10.3 (or Sections 10. 1 or 10.2 in the event the Remaining Partner does not elect to continue the business), and again upon the completion of liquidation, statements shall be prepared by the Partnership's Accountants and furnished to the Partners and assignees of

Partnership Interests. The statements furnished upon dissolution shall list the assets and liabilities of the Partnership, and the statement furnished upon completion of liquidation shall describe the disposition of the assets, the payment of or provision for liabilities, and the application of any remaining cash.

10.5) *Liquidation.* Upon the dissolution of the Partnership pursuant to Section 10.3 (or Sections 10.1 or 10.2 in the event the Remaining Partner does not elect to continue the business), the Partners or the person required by law to wind up the Partnership's affairs shall reduce the assets of the Partnership to cash. The partners shall continue to share net income or losses during liquidation in accordance with Section 8.1. Proceeds shall be applied in the following order of priority, after taking into account all capital account adjustments for the Partnership's taxable year during which such liquidation occurs, unless a court of appropriate jurisdiction should rule otherwise:

(a) to the payment of liabilities and obligations of the Partnership (excluding liabilities and other obligations to the Partners) and the expenses of liquidation;

(b) to the establishment of such reserves as the partners or such person may reasonably deem necessary for any contingent liabilities and obligations of the Partnership for such period as the Partners or such person shall deem advisable for the purpose of disbursing the reserves in payment of such liabilities or obligations and, at the expiration of such period, the balance of such reserves, if any, shall be distributed as hereinafter provided;

(c) to the repayment of any loans or advances that may have been made by any of the Partners or any affiliates thereof to the Partnership;

(d) the balance of such proceeds, if any, shall be distributed to the Partners and assignees of Partnership Interests pro rata in accordance with their respective Percentage Interests.

10.6) *Distribution in Kind.* If it does not appear to be in the best interest of the Partners that certain Partnership assets be converted into cash, and if an equitable pro rate distribution can be made, Partnership assets may be distributed in kind upon the approval of all of the Partners.

10.7) *Distribution in Event of Dissolution.* A Partner shall not be entitled to demand or to receive any Partnership property other than cash, and such Partner shall not be entitled to any distribution in dissolution of the Partnership until all liabilities owed by such partner to the Partnership have been paid and until any unpaid contributions to the Partnership owing by such Partner have been contributed.

ARTICLE 11. IMPLEMENTATION PROVISIONS

11.1) *Conveyance to Partnership.* Simultaneous with the execution of this Agreement, ______ shall quit claim the Property to the Partnership, subject to the contract for deed. The Partners shall respectively be solely responsible for correcting any title matter affecting the Property which were caused by the action or inaction of the respective Partners.

11.2) *State Deed Tax.* The Partners shall be equally responsible for any State Deed Tax or other transfer and recording fees in connection with the conveyance of the Property to the Partnership.

ARTICLE 12. MISCELLANEOUS

12.1) *Amendments.* This Agreement may be amended only by a writing signed by all Partners.

12.2) *Binding Effect.* This Partnership Agreement shall bind and inure to the benefit of the parties hereto and their respective heirs, representatives, successors and assigns.

12.3) *Separability.* In the event of any conflict between a provision of this Agreement and any provision of the Uniform Partnership Act not subject to variation by this Agreement, the provisions of the Uniform Partnership Act shall govern. If one or more of the provisions of this Agreement or any application thereof shall be invalid, illegal or unenforceable in any respect, the validity, legality and enforceability of the remaining provisions and any other application thereof shall in no way be affected or impaired.

12.4) *Counterparts.* This Agreement may be executed in counterparts, all of which taken together shall constitute a single Agreement, or by the execution of a separate agreement under the terms of which the person executing such separate agreement specifically undertakes to be bound by the terms, provisions and agreements of this Agreement.

12.5) *Applicable Law.* All questions relating to the execution, validity, performance and interpretation of this Partnership Agreement shall be governed by the laws of the State of Minnesota.

12.6) *Notices.* All notices provided for herein shall be in writing and shall be sent by first-class prepaid registered or certified mail to the Partnership at the Partnership's principal office and to the Partners at their respective address or, with respect to any Partner, to such other address regarding which the Partnership have been notified in writing. Upon a written request sent to the Partnership's principal office, a complete list of all Partners' names and addresses will be furnished to any Partner. The initial address of ______ is as follows:

____

____

____

with a copy to:

____

____

____

____

The initial address of _______ is as follows:

____

____

____

with a copy to:

____

____

____

IN WITNESS WHEREOF, the parties hereto have executed this _______ General Partnership Agreement effective as of the day and year first above written.

____

____

2. LIMITED PARTNERSHIP AGREEMENT

Table of Contents

Agreement of Limited Partnership of [*Name*] Limited Partnership

A [*State*] Limited Partnership

THIS AGREEMENT OF LIMITED PARTNERSHIP is made as of the day of ______, [*Year*], by and between [*Name*], as General Partner, and [*Name*], [*Name*], and such other Limited Partners as may be added pursuant to the terms hereof as Limited Partners.

ARTICLE I. GENERAL PROVISIONS INFORMATION FOR CERTIFICATE

1.1 Formation of the Partnership. The General Partner and the Limited Partners hereby agree to form a limited partnership under the Act. The General Partner shall from time to time execute or cause to be executed all such certificates and other documents, and do or cause to be done all such filings, recordings, publishings, and other acts as the General Partner may deem necessary or appropriate to comply with the requirements of law for the formation and operation of the Partnership in all jurisdictions in which the Partnership shall desire to conduct business. The Partnership shall at all times be governed by the Act.

1.2 Name of the Partnership. The name of the Partnership is [*Name*], or such other name as shall be selected from time to time by the General Partner upon written notice to the Limited Partners.

1.3 Purpose. The purpose of the Partnership shall be to [*Describe*].

1.4 Office of the Partnership. The office of the Partnership required by the Revised Uniform Limited Partnership Act § 104 (RULPA) shall be located at [*Address*], or such other place or places in the state of [*State*] as the General Partner may from time to time designate by notice to the Limited Partners. In addition, the Partnership may maintain such other offices as the General Partner deems advisable.

1.5 Term. As provided in the Act, the formation of the Partnership shall occur upon the filing of a Certificate in the office of the Secretary [*of State*]. The Partnership shall continue until [*Date*], unless sooner dissolved and terminated upon the occurrence of any of the following events:

(a) The passage of ninety (90) days after the dissolution, merger, death, withdrawal, or adjudication of incompetency or bankruptcy of the last remaining General Partner, unless all of the Limited Partners consent in writing to continue the business of the Partnership pursuant to § 7.1;

(b) The sale, transfer, or other disposition of all or substantially all of the Partnership's assets as permitted by this Agreement; or

(c) The vote of the Majority of the Limited Partners to dissolve the Partnership;

provided, however, the Partnership shall not dissolve upon the dissolution, merger, withdrawal, death, or adjudication of incompetency or bankruptcy of less than all of the General Partners. The remaining General Partner hereby expressly agrees to continue the Partnership.

1.6 General Partner. The name and place of business of the General Partner is as follows: [*Describe*].

1.7 Amendment to Certificate of Limited Partnership. The General Partner shall cause an amendment to the Certificate to be filed in the office of the Secretary whenever the name of the Partnership is changed, the street address of the office of the Partnership required by RULPA § 104 is changed, the name or address of the General Partner is changed, an additional general partner is admitted to the Partnership, the address or name of the agent for service of process is changed, business is continued under RULPA § 801 after an event of withdrawal of a general partner, the date upon which the Partnership is to dissolve is changed, or a false or erroneous material statement has been discovered in the Certificate or any amendment thereto. The General Partner shall cause any amendment to the Certificate to be filed in the office of the Secretary. In addition, the General Partner shall take any other action that may be required or advisable to maintain the Partnership as a limited partnership existing under the Act.

1.8 Agent for Service of Process. The name and address of the agent for service of process of the Partnership shall be: [*Name, Address*].

ARTICLE II. DEFINITIONS

Unless otherwise expressly provided herein or unless the context otherwise requires, the terms with initial capital letters in this Partnership Agreement shall be defined as follows:

2.1 "Act" shall mean the [*State*] Revised Uniform Limited Partnership Act, codified at ______.

2.2 "Adjusted Capital Contribution" shall mean, with respect to each Partner as of a given date, such Partner's Capital Contribution pursuant to §§ 3.1 or 3.2 reduced by all Distributions made to such Partner or predecessor pursuant to § 4.1.1(a) and (b) prior to such date.

2.3 "Affiliate" shall mean any person or entity that directly, or indirectly through one or more intermediaries, controls or is controlled by, or is under common control with another person or entity.

2.4 "Agreement" shall mean this Agreement of Limited Partnership.

2.5 "Capital Account" shall mean the capital account to be maintained for each of the General Partners and each of the Limited Partners, which:

(a) Shall be increased by:

(1) The amount of money actually or deemed contributed by such Partner to the Partnership;

(2) The fair market value of the property contributed by such Partner to the Partnership (net of liabilities securing such contributed property that the Partnership is considered to assume or take subject to under IRC § 752); and

(3) Allocations to such Partner of Partnership income and gain (or items thereof), including income and gain exempt from tax and income and gain described in Treasury Reg. § 1.704–1(b)(2)(iv)(g), but excluding income and gain described in Reg. § 1.704–1(b)(4)(i); and

(b) Shall be decreased by:

(1) The amount of money distributed to such Partner by the Partnership;

(2) The fair market value of property distributed to such Partner by the Partnership (net of liabilities securing such distributed property that such Partner is considered to assume or take subject to under IRC § 752);

(3) Allocations to such Partner of expenditures of partnerships of the type described in IRC § 705(a)(2)(B); and

(4) Allocations of Partnership loss and deduction (or item thereof), including loss and deduction described in Reg. § 1.704–

1(b)(2)(iv)(g), but excluding items described in (b)(3) above and loss or deduction described in Reg. § 1.704–1(b)(4)(i) or (iii); and

(c) Shall be otherwise adjusted in accordance with the additional rules set forth in Reg. § 1.704–1(b)(2)(iv). For purposes of this Agreement, a Partner who has more than one interest in the Partnership shall have a single Capital Account that reflects all such interests, regardless of the class of interests owned by such Partner (e.g., general or limited) and regardless of the time or manner in which such interests were acquired. It is the intent of the Partnership that the Capital Accounts of all Partners be determined and maintained in accordance with the principles of Reg. § 1.704–1(b) at all times throughout the full term of the Partnership.

2.6 "Capital Contribution" shall mean, with respect to each Partner, the amount contributed by such Partner to the capital of the Partnership as described in §§ 3.1 or 3.2.

2.7 "Certificate" shall mean the certificate of limited partnership and any amendment thereto described in § 1.7.

2.8 "Code" shall mean the Internal Revenue Code of 2002, as amended, or any corresponding provisions of succeeding law.

2.9 "Distributable Cash" shall mean, with respect to any fiscal period, all cash receipts received by the Partnership from operations in the ordinary course of business including, without limitation, income from invested Reserves, but after deducting Operating Cash Expenses, debt service, commitment fees, loan broker fees, and other payments made in connection with any loan to the Partnership or other loan secured by a lien on Partnership assets, capital expenditures of the Partnership, and amounts set aside for the creation or addition to Reserves. Distributable Cash does not include Capital Contributions.

2.10 "Distributions" shall refer to cash or to other property, from any source, distributed to the Limited Partners and the General Partners by the Partnership, but shall not include any payments to the General Partners made under the provisions of §§ 5.2 or 5.3.

2.11 "General Partner" shall mean [*Name*] or any other Person who may become a substitute or additional General Partner and who is elected or admitted hereto as a General Partner pursuant to the terms of this Agreement. Reference to a General Partner shall be to any one of the General Partners.

2.12 "Interest" shall mean the entire ownership interest of a Partner in the Partnership at a particular time, including the right of such Partner to any and all benefits to which a Partner may be entitled as provided in this Agreement, together with the obligations of such Partner to comply with all the terms and provisions of this Agreement.

2.13 "Limited Partner" shall refer to any Person who is admitted to the Partnership as a limited partner. Reference to a "Limited Partner" shall be to any one of the Limited Partners.

2.14 "Majority of the Limited Partners" shall mean the vote of Limited Partners who own, in the aggregate, more than 50% of the total outstanding Limited Partners' Interests. Each Limited Partner shall have a number of votes equal to the percentage described in § 4.2(c)(3).

2.15 "Operating Cash Expenses" shall mean, with respect to any fiscal period, the amount of cash disbursed in the ordinary course of operations of the Partnership during such period, including, without limitation, all cash expenses, such as legal and accounting fees, insurance premiums, taxes, and repair and maintenance expenses. Operating Cash Expenses shall not include expenditures paid out of Reserves.

2.16 "Partners" shall refer collectively to the General Partners and the Limited Partners, and reference to a "Partner" shall be to any one of the Partners.

2.17 "Partnership" shall refer to [*Name*], the partnership governed by this Agreement.

2.18 "Person" shall mean any individual, partnership, corporation, trust, or other entity.

2.19 "Refinancing" shall mean any refinancing or borrowing by the Partnership, secured by the Partnership's assets other than borrowings in the approximate amount of [*Dollars*] initially made to finance the Partnership.

2.20 "Reserves" shall mean, with respect to any fiscal period, funds set aside or amounts allocated during such period to reserves which may be maintained by the Partnership for working capital and to pay taxes, insurance, debt service, or other costs or expenses of the Partnership.

2.21 "Sale" means any transaction (other than the receipt of Capital Contributions) of the Partnership not in the ordinary course of business, including, without limitation, sales (including condemnations), exchanges, or other dispositions of real or personal property, recoveries of damage awards, and insurance proceeds (other than business interruption insurance proceeds), but excluding any Refinancing.

2.22 "Sale or Refinancing Proceeds," "Sale Proceeds," or **"Refinancing Proceeds"** as the context requires, means all cash receipts of the Partnership arising from a Sale or Refinancing, less the following:

(a) The amount necessary for the payment of all debts and obligations of the Partnership related to the particular Sale or Refinancing;

(b) The amount appropriate to provide Reserves to pay taxes, insurance, debt service, repairs, replacements or renewals, or other costs or expenses of the Partnership (including costs of improvements or additions in connection with the property).

2.23 "Substituted Limited Partner" shall mean the entity or individual to whom a Limited Partner has transferred all or a portion of its Interest under Article VII.

2.24 "Terminated Partner" means any General Partner who dies, becomes legally incapacitated, dissolves, is removed, or becomes bankrupt, and any Limited Partner who withdraws under the provisions of § 7.7.

2.25 "Treasury Regulations" shall mean the Regulations promulgated under the Code, as amended, including corresponding provisions of succeeding Regulations.

ARTICLE III. CAPITAL CONTRIBUTIONS

3.1 Limited Partners. The Limited Partners have made Capital Contributions to the Partnership in the following amounts:

__________________ __________________ __________________

__________________ __________________ __________________

Receipt of such Capital Contributions is hereby acknowledged. No Limited Partner shall be required to make any additional Capital Contributions to the Partnership.

3.2 General Partner.

(a) *Initial Capital Contribution.* The General Partner has made a Capital Contribution to the Partnership in the amount of [*Dollars*].

(b) *Additional Capital Contributions.* The General Partner shall contribute in cash to the Partnership any amounts necessary or appropriate for the Partnership to pay, when due, any costs, expenses, or liabilities of the Partnership to the extent such costs or expenses are in excess of the cash receipts of the Partnership.

3.3 Interest. No Partner shall be entitled to receive interest on its Capital Contribution or Capital Account balance.

ARTICLE IV. ALLOCATION OF DISTRIBUTIONS, INCOME, LOSSES, AND OTHER ITEMS AMONG THE PARTNERS

4.1 Distributions to the Partners.

4.1.1 Cash Distributions.

(a) *From Operations.* Distributable Cash will be paid to the Partners in accordance with the percentage specified in § 4.2(c).

(b) *From Certain Sales or Refinancing Proceeds.* Distributions of Sale or Refinancing Proceeds other than in liquidation or Sale of all or substantially all Partnership property shall be made to the Partners in accordance with the following:

(i) First, to the Partners in accordance with their Adjusted Capital Contributions.

(ii) Second, to the Partners in accordance with the percentage specified in § 4.2(c).

(c) *In Liquidation.* Notwithstanding § 4.1.1(a) or (b), Distributions in liquidation of the Partnership and Sale Proceeds from the Sale of all or substantially all Partnership property shall be made to each Partner in the ratio that the positive Capital Account of each Partner, after adjustment for income or loss recognized by the Partnership in connection with such Sale and/or liquidation, bears to the sum of the positive Capital Accounts of all Partners (after such adjustment).

4.1.2 Distributions in Kind. Non-cash assets, if any, shall be distributed in a manner that reflects how cash proceeds from the Sale of such assets for fair market value would have been distributed (after any unrealized gain or loss attributable to such non-cash assets has been allocated among the Partners in accordance with § 4.2).

4.1.3 Deficit Balance. In the event of such Sale referred to in § 4.1.1(b) or of a liquidation as defined in Reg. § 1.704–1(b)(2)(ii)(g), the General Partner shall be required to contribute to the capital of the Partnership within the time period specified in § 4.1.4(b) an amount equal to the total of the negative balance in the General Partner's Capital Account, if any.

4.1.4 Timing.

(a) The General Partner will make Distributions (other than Distributions in liquidation) for a calendar quarter, if any, within [*Number*] days of the end of such quarter to Partners of record as of that date, and such Distributions shall be deemed made as of the last day of such calendar quarter for all purposes. Distributions will be made without regard to Capital Accounts (except for Distributions pursuant to § 4.1.1(c)) or the number of days during the quarter that a person is a Partner.

(b) The time and method of distributions described in § 4.1.1(c) and the deficit balance payment described in § 4.1.3 shall comply with Reg. § 1.704–1(b) or, as necessary, with any similar Regulations promulgated in the future, or if no such regulations apply, as soon as possible.

4.2 Allocation of Income and Losses.

(a) *Allocation of Income.* Except as provided in § 4.2(c), income and income exempt from federal income tax for each fiscal year of the Partnership shall be allocated as follows:

(i) General Partner ____________%
(ii) Limited Partners ____________%
____%

(b) *Allocation of Losses.* Except as set forth in § 4.2(c) below, losses and expenditures not deductible in computing federal income tax for each fiscal year of the Partnership shall be allocated as follows:

(i) General Partner ____________%
(ii) Limited Partners ____________%
____%

provided, however, in no event shall losses be allocated to any Limited Partner in an amount that would cause any deficit to his or her Capital Account to exceed zero. Any such losses shall be allocated to the General Partner.

(c) *Allocation of Gain on Sale or Disposition of Partnership Property.* Notwithstanding § 4.2(a), the gain from the Sale or disposition of all or substantially all of the property of the Partnership as computed for federal income tax purposes shall be allocated in the following manner and priority:

(1) If any Partners have a deficit in their Capital Accounts, the gain shall be allocated among such Partners in the proportion which such deficits bear to each other until no Partner has a deficit in its Capital Account;

(2) Second, to the Partners until the sum of the positive balance in each Partner's Capital Account equals the Adjusted Capital Contribution of such Partner;

(3) Thereafter, to the Partners in accordance with the percentages specified below:

(i) General Partner ____________%
(ii) Limited Partners ____________%
____%

(d) *Qualified Income Offset.* Notwithstanding anything contained herein to the contrary, if a Limited Partner unexpectedly receives an adjustment, allocation, or distribution described in Reg. § 1.704–1(b)(2)(ii)(d)(4), (5), and (6) that reduces its Capital Account balance below zero (computed after making all Capital Account adjustments for such fiscal year, debiting, as of the end of such fiscal year, adjustments, allocations, and distributions described in such clauses (4), (5) and (6) and crediting any amounts such Partner is obligated to restore or is deemed to be obligated to restore pursuant to the penultimate sentence of Reg. § 1.704–1(b)(4)(iv)(f)), then income of the Partnership shall be first allocated to such Limited Partners with deficit Capital Account balances in an amount and manner sufficient to eliminate such deficit balances as quickly as possible. This provision is intended to comply with Reg. § 1.704–1(b)(2)(ii) and shall be so interpreted and applied. Any allocation of income or gain pursuant to this § 4.2(d) shall be taken into account in computing subsequent allocations of income or gain pursuant to Article IV so that the net amount of income and gain allocated to the Partners, to the extent possible, equals the amounts that would have been allocated if no allocations under § 4.2(d) had occurred.

4.3 Determination of Income; Adjustments.

4.3.1 Computation of Income and Loss. The income and loss of the Partnership shall be determined at the end of each fiscal year of the Partnership and at such other time as the General Partner shall determine. Except as provided in § 4.3.2, the income and loss of the Partnership shall be determined and calculated in accordance with federal income tax rules and principles.

4.3.2 Adjustments to Income and Loss. For purposes of computing income or loss on the disposition of a Partnership asset or for purposes of determining the cost recovery, depreciation, or amortization deduction with respect to any asset, the Partnership shall use such asset's book value determined in accordance with Reg. § 1.704–1(b). Consequently, each asset's book value shall be equal to its adjusted basis for federal income tax purposes except as follows:

(a) The initial book value of any asset contributed by a Partner to the Partnership shall be the gross fair market value of such asset;

(b) The book value of all Partnership assets shall be adjusted to equal their respective gross fair market values, as determined by the General Partner as of the following times: (1) the acquisition of an additional Interest in the Partnership by new or existing Partner in exchange for more than a *de minimis* capital contribution; (2) the distributions by the Partnership to a Partner of more than a *de minimis* amount of the Partnership property other than money; (3) the termination of the Partnership for federal income tax purposes pursuant to the IRC § 708(b)(1)(B); and (4) the liquidation of any Partner's Interest in the Partnership;

(c) If the book value of an asset has been determined pursuant to this § 4.3, such book value shall thereafter be used, and shall thereafter be adjusted by depreciation or amortization, if any, taken into account with respect to such asset, for purposes of computing income or loss.

4.4 Tax Allocations: IRC § 704(c). In accordance with IRC § 704(c) and the Treasury Regulations thereunder, income, gain, loss, and deduction with respect to any property contributed to the capital of the Partnership shall, solely for tax purposes, be allocated among the Partners so as to take account of any variation between the adjusted basis of such property to the Partnership for federal income tax purposes and its initial book value computed in accordance with § 4.3.2(a).

In the event the book value of any Partnership property is adjusted pursuant to § 4.3.2(b), subsequent allocations of income, gain, loss, and deduction with respect to such asset shall take account of any variation between the adjusted basis of such asset for federal income tax purposes and its book value in the same manner as IRC § 704(c) and the Treasury Regulations thereunder.

Subject to the restrictions set forth in § 9.5 below, any elections or other decisions relating to such allocations shall be made by the General Partner in any manner that reasonably reflects the purpose and intention of this Agreement. Allocations pursuant to this § 4.4 are solely for purposes of federal, state, and local taxes and shall not affect, or in any way be taken into account in computing, any Partner's Capital Account or share of income or loss, or distributions pursuant to any provision of this Agreement.

4.5 Allocation Between Assignor and Assignee. The portion of the income or losses of the Partnership for any fiscal year of the Partnership during which an Interest is assigned by a Partner (or by an Assignee or successor in Interest to a Partner), that is allocable with respect to such Interest, shall be apportioned between the assignor and the assignee of the Interest on the basis of actual performance of the Partnership during the months of the fiscal year that each is the owner thereof. The Partnership shall determine the portion of its income or loss attributable to each half-month of the fiscal year using a half-month convention and employing a reasonable interim closing of the books method.

ARTICLE V. RIGHTS AND DUTIES OF THE GENERAL PARTNER

5.1 Management and Control. The General Partner shall have exclusive management and control of the business of the Partnership, and all decisions regarding the management and affairs of the Partnership shall be made by the General Partner. The General Partner shall have all the rights and powers of a general partner as provided in the Act and as otherwise provided by law. The signature or other action of the General Partner acting as such shall be the signature or other action of the Partnership. Except as otherwise expressly provided in this Agreement, the General Partner is hereby granted the right, power, and authority to do on behalf of the Partnership all things which, in its sole judgment, are necessary, proper, or desirable to carry out the aforementioned duties and responsibilities, including but not limited to the right, power, and authority from time to time to do those things specified elsewhere in this Agreement and the following:

(a) To spend the capital and revenues of the Partnership in the furtherance of the business of the Partnership;

(b) To acquire, improve, manage, charter, operate, sell, transfer, exchange, encumber, pledge, and dispose of any real or personal property of the Partnership;

(c) To cause the Partnership to reimburse the General Partner for reasonable out-of-pocket expenses actually incurred by the General Partner in connection with the Partnership's business, including, but not limited to, any expense incurred in the organization of the Partnership or in connection with the offer and/or sale of Interests;

(d) Employ and dismiss from employment any and all employees, agents, independent contractors, attorneys, and accountants, including Affiliates of the General Partner;

(e) To enter into such agreements, contracts, and similar arrangements as the General Partner deems necessary or appropriate to accomplish the purposes of the Partnership;

(f) To borrow money on a secured or unsecured basis from individuals, banks, and other lending institutions in order to finance or refinance Partnership assets, to meet other Partnership obligations, to provide Partnership working capital, and for any other Partnership purpose; to execute promissory notes, deeds of trust, and assignments of Partnership property and such other security instruments as a lender of funds may require to secure repayment of such borrowing; to change, substitute, or amend such borrowing as, in its judgment, is in the best interest of the Partnership, and to execute any and all documents which may be required by the bank or other financial institution or other source to establish an escrow, trust agreement, or trust account with the bank, institution, or other source for the receipt of funds, sale proceeds, and other payments and the disbursements thereof to service such loan(s);

(g) To borrow monies from the General Partner or any Affiliate of the General Partner, for use by the Partnership in its operations, the aggregate amount of which shall become an obligation of the Partnership to the General Partner or such Affiliate, and shall be repaid with interest (at an annual rate not to exceed [*Percent*], not to exceed maximum rates under applicable usury laws) to the General Partner or such Affiliate out of gross receipts of the Partnership before any cash distributions to the Partners, with no prepayment charge or penalty permitted on such a loan, and such amounts shall constitute a loan by the General Partner or the Affiliate to the Partnership and not a Capital Contribution;

(h) To lend monies to any [*person/Affiliate of the Partnership/General Partner/Affiliate of a General Partner*] for [*any purpose(s) related to the Partnership's operations and investments*] upon any terms and conditions, provided that the same shall:

(1) As to loans secured by first liens on real estate and fixtures, not be (i) for an amount in excess of [*Percent*] of fair market value; (ii) based on a rate less than the then Applicable Federal Rate; or (iii) for a period of longer than [*Number*] years.

(2) As to loans secured by tangible personal property and accounts receivable less than [*Number*] days overdue, not be (i) for an amount in excess of [*Percent*] of fair market value; (ii) based on a rate less than the then Applicable Federal Rate; or (iii) for a period of longer than [*Number*] years.

(3) As to other loans, not be

(i) for an amount in excess of [*Percent*] of fair market value;

(ii) based on a rate less than the then Applicable Federal Rate; or

(iii) for a period of longer than [*Number*] years.

(i) To purchase at the expense of the Partnership such liability, casualty, property, and other insurance as the General Partner in its sole discretion deems advisable to protect the partnership's assets against loss or claims of any nature; provided however, the General Partner shall not be liable to the Partnership or to other Partners for failure to purchase any insurance or if coverage should prove inadequate;

(j) To the extent that funds of the Partnership are, in the General Partner's judgment, not required for the conduct of the Partnership's business, temporarily invest the excess funds in the manner set forth in § 10.2;

(k) Sue and be sued, complain, defend, settle, or compromise with respect to any claim in favor of or against the Partnership, in the name and on behalf of the Partnership;

(*l*) Prosecute and protect and defend or cause to be protected and defended all patents, patent rights, trade names, trademarks, and service marks, and all applications with respect thereto that may be held by the Partnership;

(m) Enter into, execute, amend, supplement, acknowledge, and deliver any and all contracts, agreements, licenses, or other instruments necessary, proper, or desirable to carry out the purposes of the Partnership; and

(n) Determine that any cash receipts of the Partnership shall be added to Distributable Cash.

5.2 Compensation; Reimbursement. The General Partner shall receive [*Describe*] compensation for performing its duties as General Partner under this Agreement. This provision shall not affect the General Partner's rights to receive its share of Distribution of Partnership funds as set forth in Article IV or § 8.3, or to receive reimbursement for amounts expended as set forth in § 5.1(c), or to receive compensation or other payments pursuant to contracts entered into as provided in § 5.3.

5.3 Contracts With the General Partner or Its Affiliates.

5.3.1 Contracts. Subject to the conditions set forth in § 5.3.2, the General Partner may, on behalf of the Partnership, enter into contracts with itself or any of the General Partner's Affiliates.

5.3.2 Conditions. Any agreements, contracts, and arrangements between the Partnership and the General Partner or any of its Affiliates whereby the General Partner or its Affiliates shall loan money or render any services to or from the Partnership or sell or lease goods to or from the Partnership, other than those described in the Offering Memorandum, shall be subject to the following conditions:

(a) The compensation, price, or fee paid to the General Partner or any such Affiliate must be comparable and competitive with the compensation, price, or fee of any other Person who is rendering comparable services or selling or leasing comparable goods or borrowing or lending money which could reasonably be made available to the Partnership and shall be on competitive terms;

(b) Any such agreements, contracts, and arrangements shall be embodied in a written contract which describes the subject matter thereof and all compensation to be paid therefor; and

(c) Any such agreements, contracts, and arrangements must be approved by a majority vote of the Limited Partners.

5.3.3 Financing. The General Partner or its Affiliates may purchase property in its own name, and assume loans in connection therewith, and hold title thereto for the purpose of facilitating the acquisition of such property or the borrowing of money or obtaining financing for the Partnership if purchased for the Partnership for a price no greater than the cost of such property to the General Partner or such Affiliate, and provided there is no difference in the interest rates on the loans secured by the property at the time acquired by the General Partner or such Affiliate and the time acquired by the Partnership, nor any other benefit arising out of such transaction to the General Partner or such Affiliate apart from compensation otherwise permitted by this Agreement.

5.3.4 Validity. The validity of any transaction, agreement, or payment involving the Partnership and the General Partner or any Affiliate of the General Partner otherwise permitted by the terms of this Agreement shall not be affected by reason of the relationship between the Partnership and the General Partner or such Affiliate of the General Partner.

5.4 Right of Public to Rely on Authority of General Partner. Any person dealing with the Partnership or the General Partner may rely upon a certificate signed by the General Partner as to (a) the identity of any General Partner or Limited Partner hereof; (b) the existence or nonexistence of any fact or facts which constitute a condition precedent to acts by the General Partner or in any other manner germane to the affairs of the Partnership; (c) the persons who are authorized to execute and deliver any instrument or document of the Partnership; or (d) any act or failure to act by the Partnership or as to any other matter whatsoever involving the Partnership or any Partner.

5.5 Obligations of the General Partner. The General Partner shall:

(a) Devote to the Partnership and apply to the accomplishment of Partnership purposes so much of its time and attention as in its judgment is reasonably necessary to manage properly the affairs of the Partnership; *provided, however,* the General Partner is at all times specifically permitted to engage in any other business ventures and activities including such activities as may be deemed to be in competition with the Partnership and any conflict of interest which may result shall be resolved by the General Partner using its best business judgment;

(b) Cause the Partnership to have workmen's compensation, employer's liability, public liability, and property damage insurance in amounts required by law or believed by the General Partner to be adequate, whichever is greater;

(c) Maintain a Capital Account for each Partner;

(d) Cause the Partnership to carry out the obligations of the Partnership;

(e) Keep or cause to be kept the books and records required by § 9.1; and

(f) Prepare and deliver or cause to be prepared and delivered the reports required by § § 9.2 and 9.3.

5.6 Good Faith. The General Partner shall manage and control the affairs of the Partnership to the best of its ability, and the General Partner shall use its best efforts to carry out the purposes of the Partnership for the benefit of all the Partners. In exercising its powers, the General Partner recognizes its fiduciary responsibilities to the Partnership. The General Partner shall have fiduciary responsibility for the safekeeping and use of all funds and assets of the Partnership, whether or not in its immediate possession and control. The General Partner shall not employ, or permit another to employ, such funds or assets in any manner except for the exclusive benefit of the Partnership.

5.7 Liability; Indemnification. In carrying out its duties and exercising its powers pursuant to this Agreement, the General Partner shall exercise reasonable skill, care, and business judgment. Neither the General Partner nor any of its agents shall be liable to the Partnership or the other Partners for any act or omission based upon errors of judgment, negligence, or other fault in connection with the business or affairs of the Partnership so long as the Person against whom liability is asserted acted in good faith on behalf of the Partnership and in a manner reasonably believed by such Person to be within the scope of his or her authority under this Agreement and in the best interests of the Partnership but only if such action or failure to act does not constitute gross negligence or willful misconduct. The Partnership agrees to indemnify the General Partner and its agents to the fullest extent permitted by law and to save and hold it and them harmless from and with respect to all (i) fees, costs, and expenses incurred in connection with or resulting from any claim, action, or demand against the General Partner, the Partnership, or any of the agents of either of them that arise out of or in any way relate to the Partnership, its properties, business, or affairs; and (ii) such claims, actions, and demands and any losses or damages resulting from such claims, actions, and demands, including amounts paid in settlement or compromise (if recommended by attorneys for the Partnership) of any such claim, action, or demand; *provided, however,* that this indemnification shall apply only so long as the person against whom a claim, action, or demand is asserted has acted in good faith on behalf of the Partnership or the General Partner and in a manner reasonably believed by such person to be within the scope of his or her authority under this Agreement and in the best interests of the Partnership, but only if such action or failure to act does not constitute gross negligence or willful misconduct. The termination of any action, suit, or proceeding by judgment, order, settlement, or upon a plea of *nolo contendere* or its equivalent, shall not of itself create a presumption that any person acted with gross negligence or willful misconduct.

5.8 Dissenting Limited Partners. The Limited Partners are aware that the terms of this Agreement permit certain amendments of the Agreement to be effective and certain other actions to be taken or omitted by or with respect to the Partnership, in each case with the approval of less than all of the Limited Partners. Each Limited Partner agrees that the General Partner, with full power of substitution, is hereby authorized and empowered to execute, acknowledge, make, swear to, verify, consent to, deliver, record, file, and/or publish, for and in the behalf, in the name, place, and stead of each such undersigned Limited Partner, any and all instruments and documents which may be necessary or appropriate to permit such amendment to be lawfully made or action lawfully taken or omitted, regardless of whether such Limited Partner has approved such amendment or action.

ARTICLE VI. TERMINATION OF A GENERAL PARTNER

6.1 Death, Legal Incapacity, Dissolution, Removal, or Bankruptcy. The General Partner may *not* voluntarily withdraw as General Partner. Upon the death, legal incapacity, dissolution, removal, or bankruptcy of a General Partner, all of such Partner's rights and powers as a General Partner shall be terminated, except for any accrued rights to be compensated under § 5.2 and its rights under § 6.3, and such person shall cease to be a General Partner. Any of the remaining General Partners, if there are any, shall have the right to continue the business of the Partnership.

6.2 Removal of a General Partner. A majority of the Limited Partners may remove the General Partner. Written notice of such determination setting forth the effective date of such removal shall be served upon the General Partner, and as of the effective date, shall terminate all of such person's rights and powers as a General Partner. The Limited Partners may, at any time prior to the closing, revoke a notice of removal issued pursuant to this § 6.2. In that event, the Partnership shall not be obliged to purchase the Interest of the removed General Partner, and the Limited Partners shall reimburse the Partnership and the removed General Partner for any out-of-pocket costs incurred by the Partnership or the removed General Partner in obtaining the appraisal.

6.3 Interest of Terminated General Partner. In the event of the death, legal incapacity, dissolution, removal, or bankruptcy of a General Partner and if the business of the Partnership is not continued, then the Partnership shall be liquidated and terminated and the Partnership assets distributed in accordance with Article IV. Upon the death, legal incapacity, dissolution, removal, or bankruptcy of a General Partner and if the business of the Partnership is continued, then the Partnership shall purchase the Terminated Partner's Interest as follows:

(a) *Price.* The purchase price for the Interest of the Terminated Partner shall be the fair market value of its Interest as determined herein. If the Partnership and the Terminated Partner (or its successor in interest) cannot agree on such fair market value within 90 days of the terminating event, an appraisal of the fair market value of the Partnership's assets shall be made by the procedure described in § 6.3(b). Promptly following completion of the appraisal, the Capital Accounts of the Partners shall be adjusted as if all assets of the Partnership had been sold or disposed of for an amount equal to the Appraised Market Value, determined according to § 6.3(b), and the resulting income or loss allocated pursuant to Article VIII. The fair market value for the Interest of the Terminated Partner will then be the positive balance, if any, of the Terminated Partner's Capital Account, as adjusted.

(b) *Appraisal Procedure.* The Terminated Partner (or its successor in interest) and the Partnership shall each engage and pay an appraiser to appraise the fair market value of the Partnership's assets based on an assumed all-cash sale of the assets as of the date of the terminating event. The Partnership's appraiser shall be that appraiser receiving the most votes from the Limited Partners pursuant to a meeting held, or other action taken by, the Limited Partners in accordance with Article XII. An average of the value established by the Terminated Partner's appraiser and the value established by the Partnership's appraiser shall be taken as the appraised market value of the Partnership's assets (the "Appraised Market Value").

(c) *Terms.* The purchase of the Terminated Partner's interest shall close within [*Number*] days after submission of the appraisers' written reports. The purchase price shall be paid in cash at closing, and the Terminated Partner shall assign and convey its Interest to the Partnership. The Partnership may, at its option, pay 25% of the applicable purchase price in cash at closing and the balance in three equal annual installments of principal and interest with interest at [*Percent*] per annum, commencing one year after closing.

6.4 Indemnity. A Terminated Partner shall be indemnified by all of the remaining Partners from any Partnership liabilities except to the extent any such liabilities arose prior to such purchase and sale of the selling Partner's interest and were not taken into account in determining the amount the Terminated Partner would receive pursuant to § 6.3(a) or arise subsequent to such purchase and sale and result from the negligence or misconduct of the selling Partner.

6.5 Termination of Executory Contracts With the General Partner or Affiliates. Upon removal of a General Partner, all executory contracts between the Partnership and the terminating General Partner or any Affiliate thereof (unless such Affiliate is also an Affiliate of a continuing General Partner) may be terminated by the Partnership effective upon 60 days' prior written notice of such termination to the party so terminated. The terminating General Partner or any Affiliate (unless such Affiliate is also an Affiliate of a continuing General Partner) thereof may also terminate and cancel any such executory contract effective upon 60 days' prior written notice of such termination and cancellation given to the Partnership.

ARTICLE VII. RIGHTS AND OBLIGATIONS OF LIMITED PARTNERS

7.1 No Participation in Management. No Limited Partner (other than the General Partner in case it is also a Limited Partner) shall take part in the management of the Partnership's business, transact any business in the Partnership's name, or have the power to sign documents or otherwise bind the Partnership. The Limited Partners shall, however, have the power to vote upon the following Partnership matters:

(a) Termination of the Partnership, in accordance with § 1.5(a) and (c);

(b) Amendment of the Agreement of Limited Partnership, in accordance with § 11.1;

(c) Removal of the General Partner, in accordance with § 6.2;

(d) Continuation of the Partnership after the resignation, removal, dissolution, or bankruptcy of the General Partner, in accordance with § 6.3(a);

(e) Approval of agreements, contracts, and arrangements between the Partnership and the General Partner or any of its Affiliates, in accordance with § 5.3.2(c);

(f) Audit of the balance sheet accompanying an annual report, in accordance with § 9.2(d).

7.2 Limitation of Liability. Pursuant to the Act, no Limited Partner shall have any personal liability whatever in his or her capacity as a Limited Partner for the debts of the Partnership or any of its losses beyond the amount contributed by him or her to the capital of the Partnership as set forth in § 3.1.

7.3 Transfer of a Limited Partner's Interest.

7.3.1 Requirements. Subject to any restrictions on transferability required by law or contained elsewhere in this Agreement, a Limited Partner may assign in writing his or her Interest, provided:

(a) The assignee meets all of the requirements applicable to a Substituted Limited Partner and consents in writing in form satisfactory to the General Partner to be bound by the terms of this Agreement;

(b) The General Partner consents in writing to the assignment, which consent shall be withheld only if such assignment does not comply with § 7.3.1(a) or if such assignment is to a tax-exempt entity, or if such assignment would jeopardize the status of the Partnership as a partnership for federal income tax purposes, would cause the Partnership to be terminated under IRC § 708, or would violate, or cause the Partnership to violate, any applicable law or governmental rule or regulation, including without limitation, any applicable federal or state securities law; and

(c) if requested by the General Partner, an opinion from counsel for the Partnership is delivered to the General Partner stating that, in the opinion of said counsel, such assignment would not jeopardize the status of the Partnership as a partnership for federal income tax purposes, and would not violate, nor cause the Partnership to violate, any applicable law or governmental rule or regulation, including without limitation, any applicable federal or state securities law.

By executing this Agreement, each Limited Partner shall be deemed to have consented to any assignment consented to by the General Partner. Anything herein to the contrary notwithstanding, in no event shall an assignment be made to a minor (except in trust or pursuant to the Uniform Gifts to Minors Act) or to an incompetent.

7.3.2 Limited Liability. Each Limited Partner agrees that he or she will, upon request of the General Partner, execute such certificates or other documents and perform such acts as the General Partner deems appropriate after an assignment of that Limited Partner's Interest to preserve the limited liability status of the Partnership under the laws of the jurisdictions in which the Partnership is doing business. For purposes of this Section, any transfer of any Interest in the Partnership, whether voluntary or by operation of law, shall be considered an assignment.

7.3.3 Invalid Assignments. Any purported assignment of any Interest in the Partnership which is not made in compliance with this Agreement is hereby declared to be null and void and of no force or effect whatsoever.

7.3.4 Payment of Expenses. Each Limited Partner agrees that he or she will, prior to the time the General Partner consents to an assignment of any Interest by that Limited Partner, pay all reasonable expenses, including attorneys' fees, incurred by the Partnership in connection with such assignment.

7.3.5 Compliance with Applicable Statutes. Each of the Limited Partners, by executing this Agreement, hereby covenants and agrees that he or she will not, in any event, sell or distribute any Interest unless, in the opinion of counsel to the assignee (which counsel and opinion shall be satisfactory to counsel for the General Partner), such Interest may be legally sold or distributed in compliance with then-applicable federal and state statutes.

7.3.6 Rights of Assignor. Anything herein to the contrary notwithstanding, both the Partnership and the General Partner shall be entitled to treat the assignor of an Interest as the absolute owner thereof in all respects, and shall incur no liability for Distributions made in good faith to him or her, until such time as a written assignment that conforms to the requirements of this Article VII has been received by the Partnership and accepted by the General Partner.

7.4 Substituted Limited Partner.

7.4.1 Admission as Limited Partner—Consent by General Partner. The General Partner may, but need not, in its sole discretion, permit an assignee or transferee of the Interest of a Limited Partner to be and become a Substituted Limited Partner in the Partnership entitled to all the rights and benefits under this Agreement of the transferor or assignor of such Interest; but no such assignee or transferee shall be or become a Substituted Limited Partner unless and until the General Partner in writing consents to the admission of such Person as a Substituted Limited Partner, which consent may be withheld in the absolute discretion of the General Partner. The Partners hereby consent and agree to such admission of a Substituted Limited Partner by the General Partner.

7.4.2 Documents and Expenses. Each substituted Limited Partner, as a condition to his or her admission as a Limited Partner, shall execute and acknowledge such instruments, in form and substance satisfactory to the General Partner, as the General Partner shall deem necessary or desirable to effectuate such admission and to confirm the agreement of the Substituted Limited Partner to be bound by all the terms and provisions of this Agreement with respect to the Interest acquired. All reasonable expenses, including attorneys' fees, incurred by the Partnership in this connection shall be borne by such Substituted Limited Partner.

7.4.3 Agreement Binding. Any Person who is admitted to the Partnership as a Substituted Limited Partner shall be subject to and bound by all the provisions of this Agreement as if originally a party to this Agreement.

7.4.4 Voting Rights. Unless and until an assignee of an Interest in the Partnership becomes a Substituted Limited Partner, such assignee shall not be entitled to vote with respect to such Interest.

7.4.5 Effective Date. The effective date of admission of a Substituted Limited Partner shall be the date designated by the General Partner in writing to the Substituted Limited Partner, which shall not be later than the first day of the month next following the date upon which the General Partner has given its written consent to such substitution.

7.5 Indemnification and Terms of Admission. Each Limited Partner shall indemnify and hold harmless the Partnership, the General Partner, and every Limited Partner against any claim, action, suit, or proceeding, whether civil, criminal, administrative, or investigative, by reason of or arising from any actual or alleged misrepresentation or misstatement of facts or omission to state facts by such Limited Partner in connection with the admission of a Substituted Limited Partner to the Partnership, against expenses for which the Partnership or such other Person has not otherwise been reimbursed (including attorneys' fees, judgments, fines, and amounts paid in settlement) actually and reasonably incurred by him or her in connection with such action, suit or proceeding.

7.6 Death or Incapacity of Limited Partner. The death, legal incapacity, bankruptcy, or dissolution of a Limited Partner shall not cause a dissolution of the Partnership, but the rights of such Limited Partner to share in the Income or Loss of the Partnership and to receive Distributions shall, on the occurrence of such an event, devolve on his or her personal representative, or in the event of the death of one whose Partnership Interest is held in joint tenancy, pass to the surviving joint tenants, subject to the terms and conditions of this Agreement. However, in no event shall such personal representative become a Substituted Limited Partner solely by reason of such capacity. The estate of the Limited Partner shall be liable for all the obligations of the deceased or incapacitated Limited Partner.

7.7 Withdrawal of Partner. A Limited Partner shall have the right to withdraw upon 30 days' notice to the Partnership, thereby becoming a Terminated Partner. The Partnership shall purchase the Terminated Partner's Interest under the terms provided in § 6.3(a), (b) and (c). The Terminated Partner shall be indemnified in accordance with § 6.4.

ARTICLE VIII. DISSOLUTION AND TERMINATION

8.1 Assumption of Agreements. No vote by the Partners to dissolve the Partnership pursuant to § 1.5(c) shall be effective unless, prior to or concurrently with such vote, there shall have been established procedures for the assumption of the Partnership's obligations under the agreements in force immediately prior to such vote regarding dissolution, and there shall have been an irrevocable appointment of an agent who shall be empowered to give and receive notices, reports, and payments under such agreements and hold and exercise such other powers as are necessary to permit all other parties to such agreements to deal with such agent as if the agent were the sole owner of the Partnership's interest, which procedures are agreed to in writing by each of the other parties to such agreements.

8.2 Dissolution. The Partnership shall be dissolved upon the occurrence of any of the events identified in § 1.5. No Partner shall have the right to dissolve or terminate the Partnership for any reason other than as set forth in § 1.5 *or to withdraw voluntarily from the Partnership* other than as set forth in § 7.7, or to partition any property of the Partnership.

8.3 Distribution Upon Dissolution or Liquidation. Upon dissolution of the Partnership, the affairs of the Partnership shall be wound up and all of its debts and liabilities discharged in the order of priority as provided by law. If the Partnership is dissolved and wound up or is "liquidated" within the meaning of Reg. § 1.704–1(b)(2)(ii)(g), distributions shall be made in accordance with § 4.1.1(c). Each such distributee shall receive his or her share of the assets in cash or in kind, and the proportion of such share that is received in cash may vary, all as the General Partner in its sole discretion may decide.

8.4 Allocation of Income and Losses in Liquidation. Income and losses of the Partnership following the date of dissolution, including but not limited to income and losses upon the sale of all or substantially all of the Partnership assets, shall be determined in accordance with the provisions of § 4.3, and shall be credited or charged to the Capital Accounts of the Partners in the same manner as income and loss of the Partnership would have been credited or charged if there were no dissolution and liquidation.

8.5 Winding Up. The winding up of the affairs of the Partnership and the distribution of its assets shall be conducted exclusively by the General Partner, or if none, the Limited Partners who are hereby authorized to do all acts authorized by law for these purposes. Without limiting the generality of the foregoing, the General Partner, or if none, the Limited Partners, in carrying out such winding up and distribution, shall have full power and authority to sell all or any of the Partnership assets or to distribute the same in kind to the Partners subject to § 4.1.2. Any assets distributed in kind shall be subject to all operating agreements or other agreements relating thereto which shall survive the termination of the Partnership.

8.6 Cancellation. Upon compliance with the foregoing distribution plan, the General Partner, or if none, the Limited Partners, shall file a Certificate of Cancellation and the Partnership shall cease to exist.

ARTICLE IX. BOOKS, RECORDS, AND REPORTS

9.1 Books and Records. The General Partner shall keep at the Partnership's office the following Partnership documents required by RULPA § 104:

(a) A current list of the full name and last known business or residence address of each Partner, together with the capital contribution of each Partner;

(b) A copy of the Certificate and all amendments thereto, and executed copies of any powers of attorney pursuant to which any certificate has been executed;

(c) Copies of the Partnership's federal, state, and local income tax or information returns and reports, if any, for the six (6) most recent taxable years;

(d) Copies of this original Agreement and all Amendments to the Agreement;

(e) Financial statements of the Partnership for the six (6) most recent fiscal years; and

(f) The Partnership's books and records for at least the current and past three (3) fiscal years.

9.2 Delivery to Limited Partner and Inspection.

(a) Upon the request of a Limited Partner, the General Partner shall promptly deliver to the requesting Limited Partner, at the expense of the Partnership, a copy of the information required to be maintained by § 9.1(a), (b) or (d).

(b) Each Limited Partner has the right, upon reasonable request, to do each of the following:

(i) Inspect and copy during normal business hours any of the Partnership records required to be maintained by § 9.1; and

(ii) Obtain from the General Partner, promptly after becoming available, a copy of the Partnership's federal, state, and local income tax or information returns for each year.

(c) The General Partner shall send to each Partner within 90 days after the end of each taxable year the information necessary for the Partner to complete its federal and state income tax or information returns.

(d) Within 120 days after the end of each fiscal year, the General Partner shall provide each Partner with an annual report containing

(1) a balance sheet as of the end of such fiscal year and statements of income or loss, Partners' equity, cash flow, and changes in financial position for such fiscal year which may, at the option of the General Partner, or will, upon request of a Majority of the Limited Partners, be audited;

(2) a statement describing the amount of all fees, compensation, and distributions paid by the Partnership for such fiscal year to the General Partner or any Affiliate of the General Partner;

(3) a statement of changes in Partners' Capital Accounts; and

(4) a report of the activities of the Partnership during such fiscal year.

(e) The General Partner shall, at the expense of the Partnership, prepare and file with appropriate state authorities and the SEC all reports required to be filed by the Partnership by the respective state's securities laws or said Commission, as the case may be.

9.3 Tax Returns. The General Partner, at the Partnership's expense, shall cause to be prepared tax returns for the Partnership and shall further cause such returns to be timely filed with the appropriate authorities.

9.4 Designation of Tax Matters Partner. The General Partner is hereby designated as the "Tax Matters Partner" under IRC § 6231(a)(7), to manage administrative tax proceedings conducted at the Partnership level by the Internal Revenue Service with respect to Partnership matters. Any Partner has the right to participate in such administrative proceedings relating to the determination of partnership items at the Partnership level. Expenses of such administrative proceedings undertaken by the Tax Matters Partner will be paid for out of Partnership assets. Each other Partner who elects to participate in such proceedings will be responsible for any expenses incurred by such Partner in connection with such participation. Further, the cost of any adjustments to a Partner and the cost of any resulting audits or adjustments of a Partner's tax return will be borne solely by the affected Partner.

9.5 Tax Elections. The General Partner shall have the authority to cause the Partnership to make any election required or permitted to be made for income tax purposes if the General Partner determines, in its sole judgment, that such election is in the best interests of the Partnership. Notwithstanding the foregoing, the General Partner may cause the Partnership to make, in accordance with IRC § 754 (1954), as amended (the "Code"), a timely election to adjust the basis of the Partnership property as described in IRC §§ 734 and 743 in the sole discretion of the General Partner.

ARTICLE X. FISCAL AFFAIRS

10.1 Fiscal Year. The fiscal year of the Partnership shall be [*Describe*].

10.2 Partnership Funds. The funds of the Partnership shall be deposited in such bank account or accounts, or invested in such interest-bearing or non-interest-bearing investments, including, without limitation, checking and savings accounts, certificates of deposit, and time or demand deposits in commercial banks, banker's acceptances, securities issued by money market mutual funds, savings and loan association deposits, U.S. government securities and securities guaranteed by U.S. government agencies, as the General Partner shall, in its sole discretion, determine. Such funds shall not be commingled with funds of any other person. Withdrawals therefrom shall be made upon such signatures as the General Partner may designate.

10.3 Accounting Decisions. All decisions as to accounting principles, except as specifically provided to the contrary herein, shall be made by the General Partner.

10.4 Loans by the Partnership to the General Partner or Others. The Partnership shall not make any loans to the General Partner or to any other persons, except for purchase-money financing in connection with the sale of Partnership assets.

ARTICLE XI. AMENDMENTS OF PARTNERSHIP DOCUMENTS

11.1 Amendments in General. Except as otherwise provided in this Agreement, this Agreement may be amended with the consent of the General Partner and by a majority vote of the Limited Partners.

11.2 Amendments Without Consent of Limited Partners. In addition to any amendments otherwise authorized herein, amendments may be made to this Agreement from time to time by the General Partner, without the consent of any of the Limited Partners: (i) to add to the duties or obligations of the General Partner or to surrender any right or power granted to the General Partner herein, for the benefit of the Limited Partners; (ii) to correct any error or resolve any ambiguity in or inconsistency among any of the provisions hereof, or to make any other provision with respect to matters or questions arising under this Agreement that is not inconsistent with the provisions of this Agreement; (iii) to delete or add any provision of this Agreement required to be so deleted or added by any state securities commission or similar governmental authority for the benefit or protection of the Limited Partners; and (iv) to add to or change the name of the Partnership.

11.3 Amendments Needing Consent of Affected Partners. Notwithstanding §§ 11.1 and 11.2, without the consent of the Partner or Partners to be adversely affected by an amendment to this Agreement, this Agreement may not be amended to (i) convert a Limited Partner's interest into a General Partner's interest; (ii) modify the limited liability of a Limited Partner; (iii) alter the interest of a Partner in income, gain, losses, deductions, credits, and Distributions; (iv) increase, add, or alter any obligation of any Partner; or (v) alter any provisions of Article IV or VI or this § 11.3.

11.4 Amendments After Change of Law. This Agreement and any other Partnership documents may be amended, if necessary, by the General Partner without the consent of the Limited Partners if there occurs any change that permits or requires an amendment of this Agreement under the Act or of any other Partnership document under applicable law, so long as no Partner is adversely affected (or consent is given by such Partner).

11.5 Limited Partners' Execution of Amendments. The Limited Partners hereby agree to execute an amendment to this Agreement whenever the execution of an amendment to this Agreement is requested by the General Partner and such amendment has been approved as required herein, and they agree to execute such other instruments and documents and to perform such other acts, as may be required to comply with the Act for the valid formation and existence of the Partnership as a limited partnership thereunder, whenever the execution or performance thereof shall be requested by the General Partner, all within 10 days after the request by the General Partner. In the event that any of the provisions of any such amendment to this Agreement shall be inconsistent with any of the provisions of this Agreement (if they are different documents), the provisions of this Agreement shall govern and control as among the parties.

ARTICLE XII. MEETING AND VOTING RIGHTS

12.1 Notice of Meeting of Limited Partners.

12.1.1 Requirements for Calling Meeting. Upon the written request of holders of [*Percent*] or more of the Interests of the Limited Partners, the General Partner shall call a meeting of the Limited Partners. Notice of such meeting shall be given within thirty (30) days after, and the meeting shall be held within sixty (60) days after receipt of such request. The General Partner may also call a meeting of the Limited Partners on its own initiative by giving notice of such meeting not less than fourteen (14) and not more than sixty (60) days prior to the meeting. Any such notice shall state time, place, and, briefly, the purpose of the meeting, which shall be held at a reasonable time and place. Any Limited Partner may obtain a list of the names, addresses, and Interest owned by each Limited Partner upon written request to the General Partner. If a meeting is adjourned to another time or place, and if an announcement of the adjournment of time or place is made at the meeting, it shall not be necessary to give notice of the adjourned meeting. No notice of the time, place, or purpose of any meeting of Limited Partners need be given to any Limited Partner who attends in person or is represented by proxy, except for a Limited Partner attending a meeting for the express purpose of objecting at the beginning of the meeting to the transaction of any business on the ground that the meeting is not lawfully called or convened, or to any Limited Partner entitled to such notice who, in a writing executed and filed with the records of the meeting, either before or after the time thereof, waives such notice.

12.1.2 Record Date. For the purpose of determining the Limited Partners entitled to notice of, or to vote at, any meeting of the Limited Partners, or any adjournment or postponement thereof, or to vote by written consent without a meeting, the General Partner or the Limited Partners requesting such meeting or vote may fix, in advance, a date as the record date for any such determination of Limited Partners. Such date shall not be more than sixty (60) days nor less than ten (10) days before any such meeting or submission of a matter to the Limited Partners for a vote by written consent. If no record date is fixed for such determination of Limited Partners, the date on which notice of the meeting or submission of the matter to the Limited Partners for a vote by written consent is mailed should be the record date for such determination of Limited Partners.

12.2 Voting Rights and Procedure.

12.2.1 Voting Percentage. Each Limited Partner is entitled to a number of votes equal to the percentage described in § 4.2(c)(3).

12.2.2 Quorum. A Majority of the Limited Partners shall constitute a quorum at any meeting of the Partners.

12.2.3 Proxies. Each Limited Partner may authorize any person or persons to act for him or her by proxy with respect to any matter in which a Limited Partner is entitled to participate whether by waiving notice of any meeting or voting or participating at a meeting. Every proxy must be signed by the Limited Partner. No proxy shall be valid after the expiration of twelve (12) months from the date thereof unless otherwise provided in the proxy. Every proxy shall be revocable at the pleasure of the Limited Partner executing it, but the Partnership may rely on any properly executed proxy delivered to it until it receives written notice from the Limited Partner in question that said proxy has been revoked.

12.2.4 Action Taken Without Meeting. Any matter for which the approval or consent of the Limited Partners is required or for which the Limited Partners are authorized to take action under this Agreement or under applicable law may be approved or action may be taken by the Limited Partners without a meeting and shall be as valid and effective as action taken by the Limited Partners at a meeting assembled, if written consents to such action by the Limited Partners are signed by the Limited Partners owning Interests constituting in the aggregate the Interest required to approve or otherwise authorize such action and such written consents are delivered to the General Partner.

12.2.5 Attendance. Personal presence of the Limited Partners shall not be required at any meeting, provided an effective written consent to or rejection of the action proposed to be taken at such meeting is submitted to the General Partner. Attendance by a Limited Partner and voting in person at any meeting shall revoke any written consents or rejections of such Limited Partner submitted with respect to action proposed to be taken at such meeting.

12.2.6 Conduct of Meeting. At each meeting of Limited Partners, the Limited Partners present or represented by proxy, by majority vote, may adopt such rules not inconsistent with the Agreement for the conduct of such meeting as they shall deem appropriate.

ARTICLE XIII. POWER OF ATTORNEY

13.1 Power of Attorney.

13.1.1 General Partner. The Limited Partners, by their execution hereof, jointly and severally hereby make, constitute, and appoint the General Partner as their true and lawful agent and attorney-in-fact, with full power of substitutions, in their name, place, and stead to make, execute, sign, acknowledge, swear by, record, and file on behalf of them and on behalf of the Partnership (i) all certificates and other instruments deemed advisable by the General Partner to permit the Partnership to become or to continue as a limited partnership or partnership wherein the Limited Partners have limited liability in the jurisdiction where the Partnership may be doing business; (ii) all instruments that affect a change or modification of the Partnership in accordance with this Agreement, including without limitation the substitution of assignees as Substituted Limited Partners pursuant to § 7.4; (iii) all conveyances and other instruments deemed advisable by the General Partner to effect the dissolution and termination of the Partnership; (iv) all fictitious or assumed name certificates required or permitted to be filed on behalf of the Partnership; and (v) all other instruments which may be required or permitted by law to be filed on behalf of the Partnership.

13.1.2 In General. The foregoing power of attorney:

(a) Is coupled with an interest and shall be irrevocable and survive the death or incapacity of each Limited Partner;

(b) May be exercised by the General Partner either by signing separately as attorney-in-fact for each Limited Partner or, after listing all of the Limited Partners executing an instrument, by a signature acting as attorney-in-fact for all of them; and

(c) Shall survive the delivery of an assignment by a Limited Partner of his or her Interest; except that, where the assignee of the Interest of such Limited Partner has been approved by the General Partner for admission to the Partnership as a Substituted Limited Partner, the power of attorney of the assignor shall survive the delivery of such assignment for the sole purpose of enabling the General Partner to execute, acknowledge, and file any instrument necessary to effect such substitution.

13.1.3 Other Instruments. Each Limited Partner shall execute and deliver to the General Partner, within five days after receipt of the General Partner's request therefor, such further designation, powers-of-attorney, and other instruments as the General Partner deems necessary.

13.1.4 Termination of Appointment. The appointment of the General Partner as attorney-in-fact pursuant to this power of attorney automatically shall terminate as to such entity or person at such time as it ceases to be the General Partner and from such time shall be effective only as to the substituted General Partner designated or elected pursuant to this Agreement.

ARTICLE XIV. MISCELLANEOUS

14.1 Notices. Any notice, offer, consent, or other communication required or permitted to be given or made hereunder shall be in writing and shall be deemed to have been sufficiently given or made when delivered personally to the party (or an officer of the party) to whom the same is directed, or (except in the event of a mail strike) five days after being mailed by first-class mail, postage prepaid, if to the Partnership, to the offices described in § 1.4, or if to a Partner, to the address set forth on Schedule A. Any Partner may change his or her address for the purpose of this Article by giving notice of such change to the Partnership, such change to become effective on the tenth (10th) day after such notice is given.

14.2 Governing Law; Successors; Severability. This Agreement shall be governed by the laws of the State of [*State*] as such laws are applied by [*State*] courts to agreements entered into and to be performed in [*State*] by and between residents of [*State*], and shall, subject to the restrictions on transferability set forth herein, bind and inure to the benefit of the heirs, executors, personal representatives, successors, and assigns of the parties hereto. If any provision of this Agreement shall be held to be invalid, the remainder of this Agreement shall not be affected thereby.

14.3 Entire Agreement. This Agreement constitutes the entire agreement between the parties; it supersedes any prior agreement or understanding among them, oral or written, all of which are hereby cancelled. This Agreement may not be modified or amended other than pursuant to Article XI.

14.4 Headings, etc. The headings in this Agreement are inserted for convenience of reference only and shall not affect interpretation of this Agreement. Wherever from the context it appears appropriate, each term stated in either the singular or the plural shall include the singular and the plural, and the pronouns stated in either the masculine or the neuter gender shall include the masculine, the feminine, and the neuter.

14.5 No Waiver. The failure of any Partner to seek redress for violation, or to insist on strict performance of any covenant or condition of this Agreement shall not prevent a subsequent act which would have constituted a violation from having the effect of an original violation.

14.6 Counterparts. This Agreement may be executed in several counterparts, each of which shall be deemed an original but all of which shall constitute one and the same instrument.

14.7 Other Business Ventures. Any Partner, or any shareholder, director, employee, Affiliate, or other Person holding a legal or beneficial interest in any entity which is a Partner, may engage in or possess an interest in other business ventures of every nature and description, independently or with others, whether such ventures are competitive with the Partnership or otherwise; neither the Partnership nor the Partners shall have any right by virtue of this Agreement in or to such independent ventures or to the income or profits derived therefrom.

14.8 Venue. In the event that any suit is brought arising out of or in connection with this Agreement, the parties consent to the jurisdiction of, and agree that sole venue will lie in the state and federal courts located in [*Describe*].

14.9 Further Assurance. The Limited Partners will execute and deliver such further instruments and do such further acts and things as may be required to carry out the intent and purpose of this Agreement.

14.10 Creditors. None of the provisions of this Agreement shall be for the benefit of or enforceable by any of the creditors of the Partnership or Partners.

14.11 Remedies. The rights and remedies of the Partners hereunder shall not be mutually exclusive, and the exercise of any right to which a Partner is entitled shall not preclude the exercise of any other right he or she may have.

14.12 Authority. Each individual executing this Agreement on behalf of a partnership, corporation, or other entity warrants that he or she is authorized to do so and that this Agreement will constitute the legally binding obligation of the entity which such person represents.

IN WITNESS WHEREOF, the parties have executed this Agreement as of the date first above written.

General Partner:	Limited Partner:
______________________________	______________________________
By: ___________________________	By: ___________________________
Its ___________________________	Its ___________________________

[ATTACH SCHEDULE A. PARTNERS' ADDRESSES FOR NOTICE]

3. PROTOTYPE PARTNERSHIP AGREEMENT FOR A LIMITED LIABILITY PARTNERSHIP FORMED UNDER THE UNIFORM PARTNERSHIP ACT (1997)

AGREEMENT OF PARTNERSHIP[1] OF ____________________, LLP,

a [state] limited liability partnership

This PARTNERSHIP AGREEMENT of ______, LLP (the "Partnership"), is entered into and shall be effective as of the Effective Date (as hereafter defined) by and among the persons who execute this Agreement as Partners.

RECITALS

A. ______, ______, and ______ have agreed to create and become the partners (collectively with any other person who becomes a party to this Agreement, the "Partners") of a partnership to be known as ______, LLP (the "Partnership") in the State; and

B. ______, ______, and ______ have determined to qualify the Partnership as a limited liability partnership.

Now, therefore, for good and valuable consideration, the receipt and sufficiency of which are hereby acknowledged, and in consideration of the mutual covenants herein contained, the Partners agree as follows:

ARTICLE I. DEFINITIONS

For purposes of this Partnership Agreement, the following definitions shall apply:

"Act" shall mean the Uniform Partnership Act of [insert name of State in which statement of qualification will be filed].

"All of the Partners" shall mean all of the Partners at the time that the action is to be taken.

"Available Cash" shall mean the amount of cash of the Partnership that is in excess of the amount determined by the Managing Partners to be necessary for current expenses of the Partnership and a reserve for future expenses, capital expenditures, and other needs of the Partnership.

1. Drafted by the Subcommittee on the Prototype Limited Liability Partnership Agreement. Formed under the Uniform Partnership Act (1997), Committee on Partnerships and Unincorporated Business Organizations, Section of Business Law, American Bar Association. 58 Bus. Law. 689 (2003).

"Bankruptcy Code" means the federal Bankruptcy Code and the bankruptcy and insolvency statutes of any state, as amended.

"Breaching Partner" shall have the meaning set forth in Article 17.

"Business" shall have the meaning set forth in Article 6.

"Capital Account" shall mean each Partner's capital account as maintained pursuant to Article 13.

"Code" shall mean the Internal Revenue Code of 1986, as it may be amended from time to time.

"Consent," when applied to an action of the Partners, shall mean consent expressed at a meeting of the Partners, in writing without a meeting, or by some Partners at a meeting and by some Partners in writing.

"Dissociated Partner" shall mean (i) the Partner whose Withdrawal, Expulsion or other event (other than death or permanent disability resulting in the appointment of a legal representative) causes his or her Dissociation or (ii) the legal representative of a Partner whose death or permanent disability has resulted in the Partner's Dissociation.

"Dissociation" ("Dissociate") shall mean the Withdrawal, Expulsion, permanent disability, or death of a Partner or any other event that causes a person to cease to be a Partner.

"Dissociation Amount" shall mean, in the case of any Dissociated Partner, the amount of a Dissociated Partner's Capital Account determined through the Dissociation Date.

"Dissociation Date" shall mean, in the case of any Dissociated Partner, the date of the event resulting in the Partner's Dissociation.

"Effective Date" shall mean, the date upon which the statement of qualification of a limited liability partnership is filed with the [secretary of state] of the State.

"Expulsion" ("Expel" or "Expelled") shall mean a Partner's Dissociation as provided in Sections 15.3 and 21.1.

"Expelled Partner" shall mean the Partner who has been Expelled.

"Indemnified Partner" shall mean each Partner and Dissociated Partner entitled to indemnification by the Partnership pursuant to Article 20.

"Majority of the Partners" shall mean more than one half of the Partners (determined Per Capita) at the time that the action is to be taken.

"Managing Partners" means ______, ______, and ______, and any successor managing partner appointed by the Partners pursuant to Section 8.2 and 8.3.

"Other Partners" has the meaning set forth in Section 12.3.

"Partner" shall mean each individual or entity executing this Agreement as a Partner or subsequently admitted as a Partner and who is not a Dissociated Partner.

"Partnership" shall mean ______, LLP.

"Partnership Agreement" shall mean this Agreement as amended from time to time.

"Per Capita" shall mean, with respect to any action or obligation, a percentage, determined by dividing one by the number of Partners at the time the action is to be taken.

"Registration Period" shall mean the period during which the Partnership is a limited liability partnership within the meaning of the Act.

"Retirement Age" shall mean ______.

"State" shall mean the State/Commonwealth of ______.

"Transfer" shall mean an assignment, conveyance, encumbrance, exchange, pledge, hypothecation, lease, mortgage, sale or other disposition for consideration, or gift or other disposition for no consideration, whether voluntary, involuntary, by operation of law or otherwise.

"Two–Thirds of the Partners" shall mean 66 2/3% of All the Partners (determined Per Capita) except that in the case of Expulsion of a Partner, the Partner whose Expulsion is under consideration shall not be counted in determining All the Partners.

"Withdrawal" ("Withdraw") shall mean a Partner's Dissociation as a result of the Partner's act as provided in Section 15.2.

"Withdrawn Partner" shall mean the Partner whose Withdrawal causes his or her Dissociation.

ARTICLE 2. NAME AND PLACE OF BUSINESS

Section 2.1. Name. The activities and business of the Partnership shall be conducted under the name of ______, LLP and under such variations of this name as may be necessary to comply with the laws of other states within which the Partnership may do business or make investments, and such trade names as the Partnership may select.

Section 2.2. Place of Business. The principal place of business and chief executive office of the Partnership shall be in the City of ______, County of ______, State of ______, but additional places of business may be located elsewhere.

Section 2.3. Address. The mailing address of the Partnership shall be as follows:

ARTICLE 3. FORMATION, EFFECTIVENESS, AND TERM

Section 3.1. Formation of Partnership. The Partners (i) have formed a general partnership, (ii) have immediately thereafter unanimously voted to qualify as a limited liability partnership under the Act and authorized the filing of a statement of qualification, and (iii) have immediately after that vote declared this Agreement to be effective immediately after the said unanimous vote to qualify as a limited liability partnership. Before the filing and acceptance of the statement of qualification, the Partners have agreed and hereby confirm that no Partner has the authority to act on behalf of or bind the Partnership except for the execution and filing of the statement of qualification.

Section 3.2. Effectiveness. All provisions of this Partnership Agreement are effective immediately upon the Effective Date.

Section 3.3. Existence. The existence of the Partnership shall commence upon the Effective Date and shall continue until terminated and wound up pursuant to this Partnership Agreement or by law.

Section 3.4. Disclosure by Each Partner of Information at Time of Partnership Formation. Each Partner represents and warrants to the Partnership and each other Partner that, at the time of becoming a Partner, the Partner has disclosed any information reasonably related to their admission as a Partner that is material to that admission, and that no Partner is failing to disclose any information related thereto.

ARTICLE 4. AGREEMENT TO BE BOUND

Except as provided in this Partnership Agreement, the Act and the laws of [insert name of state in which statement of registration is filed] shall govern the internal affairs of the Partnership including the relationship of the Partners among themselves and the relationship between the Partners and the Partnership.

ARTICLE 5. QUALIFICATION AS A LIMITED LIABILITY PARTNERSHIP

Section 5.1. Agreement to Qualify. The Partnership shall be a limited liability partnership as that term is described in the Act, and the Managing Partners are authorized to execute a statement of qualification of a limited liability partnership or such other documents as may be required in order to qualify the Partnership in any jurisdiction which the Managing Partners deem appropriate.

Section 5.2. Authorization to Execute Statements. The Managing Partners are authorized to execute any statement of authority, annual report, statement of foreign qualification, revocation of a statement of qualification as a limited liability partnership, or other filing required or authorized to be filed by the Act, and pay appropriate fees therefore necessary or convenient to the Partnership's status as a limited liability partnership.

ARTICLE 6. BUSINESS AND PURPOSE OF THE PARTNERSHIP

The purpose of the Partnership is to engage in the business of ______ (the "Business"), and, except as otherwise provided in this Partnership Agreement, the Partnership shall not engage in any other activity or business. The Partnership shall have the powers to do such things as are incidental, proper or necessary to the operation of the Business, and to the carrying out of the objects, purposes, powers and privileges herein granted with respect to the Business, as well as to exercise all those powers conferred on partnerships organized under the Act, together with all other rights bestowed upon partnerships generally under the laws of the State, all with respect to the Business.

ARTICLE 7. OTHER BUSINESS OF THE PARTNERSHIP

The Business of the Partnership may include holding interests in other partnerships, limited liability companies, corporations, and other business entities engaging in business activities, but only if unanimously approved by the Partners.

ARTICLE 8. MANAGEMENT OF THE PARTNERSHIP

Section 8.1. Management of the Partnership. The day-to-day business affairs of the Partnership shall be managed by the Managing Partners. Except to the extent that this Partnership Agreement requires that an action be taken with the Consent of the Partners, the Managing Partners shall have the authority to make all decisions and take all actions necessary to conduct the business of the Partnership.

Section 8.2. Managing Partners. There shall be [three] Managing Partners, [one-third] of whom shall be elected at each annual meeting of the Partners.

Section 8.3. Removal of Managing Partners. By the Consent of a Majority of Partners, the Partners may, with or without cause, remove a Managing Partner at any time and name and appoint a successor Managing Partner.

Section 8.4. Statement of Authority. The Managing Partners shall file or cause to be filed such statements of authority as shall be appropriate for filing under the Act, including the timely amendment of all previously filed statements of authority.

ARTICLE 9. MATTERS REQUIRING CONSENT OF PARTNERS

Section 9.1. Items Requiring Consent of All of the Partners. The following actions may not be taken without the Consent of All of the Partners:

i. Amendment of the Partnership Agreement;

ii. Increase in the principal amount of any indebtedness guaranteed by the Partners;

iii. Mergers with or into other partnerships, corporations, limited liability companies, or other business entities;

iv. Except as required by the Act, dissolution of the Partnership;

v. Sale of all or substantially all assets of the Partnership; and

vi. Conversion of the Partnership into another form of business entity.

Section 9.2. Items Requiring Consent of Two–Thirds of the Partners. The following actions may not be taken without the Consent of Two–Thirds of the Partners:

i. Admission of any person, including a transferee, as a new Partner;

ii. Amendment (subject to Section 12.1) or waiver of a Partner's obligation to make a capital contribution;

iii. Admission of a transferee as a Partner; and

iv. Expulsion of a Partner.

Section 9.3. Items Requiring Consent of a Majority of the Partners. The following actions may not be taken without the Consent of a Majority of the Partners:

i. Creation or expansion of Partnership debt in excess of $_______;

ii. Purchase or sale of real estate;

iii. Entering into or modifying the lease of the Partnership's office facilities;

iv. Establishing new offices of the Partnership; and

v. Removal of a Managing Partner as provided on Section 8.3.

vi. Initiation of an action on behalf of the Partnership against any Partner or Dissociated Partner.

ARTICLE 10. MEETINGS AND ELECTION OF MANAGING PARTNERS

Section 10.1. Regular Meetings. Regular meetings of the Partners shall be held no less frequently than quarterly at such time and place determined by the Managing Partners. The first regular meeting of the Partners each calendar year shall be the annual meeting of the Partners.

Section 10.2. Special Meetings. Special meetings shall be called by the Managing Partners at the request of any ___ (___) or more of the Partners.

Section 10.3. Notice of Meetings. Partners shall be given notice orally, in writing or by electronic mail of any meeting and, to the extent known, the matters to be discussed at the meeting, but no defect in notice shall cause the action taken at such a meeting to be invalid.

Section 10.4. Election of Managing Partners. Each Partner shall have one (1) vote for each Managing Partner to be elected.

ARTICLE 11. AUTHORITY OF PARTNERS

Section 11.1. Authority on Behalf of the Partnership. No Partner shall have the right to hold himself or herself out as an agent of the Partnership in any business or activity other than the Business described in Articles 6 and 7.

Section 11.2. No Authority on Behalf of Other Partners. No Partner shall have the right to hold himself or herself out as an agent of any other Partner.

ARTICLE 12. PARTNERS' CONTRIBUTION TO THE PARTNERSHIP, GUARANTEE OF PARTNERSHIP OBLIGATIONS, AND LIABILITY FOR PARTNERSHIP OBLIGATIONS

Section 12.1. Partners' Obligation to Contribute in General. Except as expressly set forth in this Article 12, no Partner or Dissociated Partner shall have any obligation to contribute to the Partnership. The obligations to contribute as set forth in this Article 12 are solely for the benefit of the Partners and Dissociated Partners. No creditor of the Partnership or any other person shall have any right to rely upon or enforce any contribution obligation contained in this Agreement. The Partners reserve the right to amend or waive any contribution obligation of any Partner with or without consideration at any time, but no Partner's obligation to contribute shall be increased without that Partner's express written consent.

Section 12.2. Initial Contributions. Each Partner shall contribute $______ in cash which represents each Partner's share of the necessary start-up capital for the Partnership.

Section 12.3. Guarantees and Contributions. At the request of the Managing Partners, each Partner agrees to execute his or her personal guarantee of any indebtedness of the Partnership not to exceed $______. The Managing Partners shall attempt to structure the guarantee in such a manner as to limit each Partner's guarantee to that Partner's Per Capita share of the indebtedness. In the event any Partner is required to make any payment with respect to such indebtedness, the Partnership shall indemnify that Partner for all amounts paid or incurred with respect to such indebtedness. In the event any Partner (the "Paying Partner") is obligated to make a guaranty payment in excess of the Paying Partner's Per Capita share of the indebtedness, each other Partner (an "Other Partner") shall be obligated to pay over to the Paying Partner in an amount equal to the Other Partner's Per Capita share of the excess of the amount paid by the Paying Partner over the Paying Partner's Per Capita share of the indebtedness.

Section 12.4. Contribution and Indemnification with Respect to Obligations Incurred by the Partnership at a Time Other than During the Qualification Period. Each Partner agrees to contribute an amount equal to that Partner's Per Capita share of the excess of (i) the amount that the Partnership is obligated to pay in Indemnification under Article 20 to an Indemnified Partner on account of a liability or obligation of the Partnership that was incurred at a time while the Partnership is not a limited liability partnership over (ii) the amount paid or reimbursed to the Indemnified Partner by the Partnership and under policies of insurance carried by the Partnership.

Section 12.5. Obligation of Partner or Dissociated Partner to Contribute to the Partnership. Any Partner or Dissociated Partner whose actions have contributed to the creation of a liability or obligation of the Partnership with respect to which that Partner or Dissociated Partner would not be entitled to indemnification under Article 20 shall contribute an amount sufficient to indemnify the Partnership against all costs, obligations, and liabilities of the Partnership arising from such actions (including the obligation to indemnify any other Indemnified Partner) except to the extent that obligation or liability is paid or reimbursed under a policy of insurance carried by the Partnership.

Section 12.6. Liability for Partnership Obligations. Except as specifically provided in this Agreement, in accordance with section 306(c) of the Act, no Partner shall be personally liable or accountable, directly or indirectly (including by way of indemnification, contribution, assessment or otherwise), for debts, obligations and liabilities of, or chargeable to, the Partnership, or another Partner or Partners, whether arising in tort, contract or otherwise, solely by reason of being a Partner or acting (or omitting to act) in such capacity, which such debts, obligations and liabilities occur, are incurred or are assumed while the Partnership is a limited liability partnership.

Section 12.7. Contribution and Indemnity Obligations Controlling Regardless of Liability Protection. The obligation to contribute under this Article 12 shall continue notwithstanding the qualification of the Partnership as a limited liability partnership and notwithstanding Section 12.6 of this Agreement.

ARTICLE 13. CAPITAL ACCOUNTS

Section 13.1. Account. An individual Capital Account shall be established and maintained for each Partner. Each Partner's Capital

Account (a) shall be increased by (i) the amount of money and net value of property contributed to the Partnership and (ii) the Partner's allocable share of income and gain allocated pursuant to this Partnership Agreement, and (b) shall be decreased by (i) the amount of money and fair market value of property distributed to that Partner and (ii) that Partner's allocable share of deductions and loss allocated pursuant to this Partnership Agreement. To the extent a Partner has a deficit Capital Account, [the Partner will be allocated items as income and the other Partners will be allocated income in such a manner as to eliminate the deficit as quickly as possible] [the Partner will not be entitled to distributions until the deficit is eliminated]. Except to the extent provided in Article 12, no Partner will have an obligation to restore a deficit Capital Account.

Section 13.2. Adjustments to Account. The assets of the Partnership shall be revalued to their respective fair market value (and the amount of adjustment in the value shall be treated as gain or loss and allocated to the Capital Accounts of the Partners as provided in Article 15) upon a contribution of money, property [or services] in exchange for an interest in the Partnership, a distribution of money or property to a Partner in full or partial liquidation of the Partner's interest in the Partnership, or the liquidation of the Partnership. The Capital Accounts shall not be so adjusted on the Dissociation of a Partner. For purposes of making adjustments pursuant to this Section 13.2, the gross fair market values of Partnership assets shall be determined as follows: (i) accounts receivable shall be valued at ___ percent (___%) of face amount and (ii) all other assets shall be valued at their respective fair market values prior to the event causing such adjustment.

ARTICLE 14. SHARING OF DISTRIBUTIONS AND ALLOCATIONS OF PROFITS AND LOSSES

Section 14.1. Distribution of Available Cash. The Available Cash of the Partnership shall be distributed not less frequently than monthly [in the proportions determined by the Managing Partners]. All distributions which, when made, exceed the recipient Partner's basis in his or her interest in the Partnership shall be considered advances or drawings against the Partner's share of taxable income or gain. To the extent it is determined at the end of the Partnership year that the recipient Partner has not been allocated taxable income or gain that equals or exceeds the total of such advances or drawings for such Partnership year, the recipient Partner shall be obligated to recontribute any such advances or draws to the Partnership in the amount by which such advance(s) or drawing(s) exceed such Partner's basis in his or her interest in the Partnership as of the last day of the Partnership's tax year, taking into account any and all increases or decreases in basis of such Partner's interest in the Partnership from the time(s) of any such advance(s) or drawing(s).

Section 14.2. Allocations of Losses. Losses, deductions, and credits of the Partnership shall be allocated to the Partners in proportion to their Capital Accounts.

Section 14.3. Allocations of Profits. Profits, gains, and income of the Partnership shall be allocated:

i. First, to the Partners who have been allocated losses and deductions of the Partnership until they have been allocated profits, gain, and income equal to the losses and deductions so allocated;

ii. Second, to the Partners in the same proportions as Available Cash is distributed during the same Partnership year.

Section 14.4. [Tax Clauses].

ARTICLE 15. DISSOCIATION OF PARTNERS

Section 15.1. Effect of Dissociation. The Dissociation of a Partner shall neither result in the dissolution of the Partnership nor require the winding up of the Partnership business, and the rights of the Dissociated Partner and remaining Partners shall be determined under this Partnership Agreement.

Section 15.2. Withdrawal of a Partner. A Partner may withdraw from the Partnership at any time upon notice in writing, addressed to the Managing Partners. Unless otherwise mutually agreed between the Partnership (acting as determined by the Managing Partners) and the withdrawing Partner, the withdrawing Partner shall cease to be a Partner and shall be Dissociated from the Partnership upon delivery of the notice of withdrawal.

Section 15.3. Expulsion of a Partner. The Partnership may expel a Partner upon the Consent of Two–Thirds of the Partners. Such Expulsion shall be effective regardless of whether the Expulsion is for cause or otherwise. Upon Expulsion, the Partner shall be Dissociated from the Partnership.

Section 15.4. Death or Permanent Disability of a Partner or Assignment of a Partner's Interest. A Partner shall cease to be a Partner and shall be dissociated from the Partnership on the Partner's death, permanent disability, or upon any purported Transfer of all or any portion of the Partner's interest in the Partnership whether voluntary, involuntary, or by operation of law.

Section 15.5. Termination of Entity Partners. Absent the consent of Two-Thirds of the Partners, a Partner who is not an individual shall cease to be a Partner and shall be Dissociated from the Partnership upon:

(1) the Transfer of any ownership interest in the entity Partner;

(2) the earlier of its dissolution or termination or the winding up of its business; or

(3) the distribution or attempted transfer of the interest in the Partnership.

ARTICLE 16. RIGHTS OF DISSOCIATED PARTNERS

Section 16.1. Payments to Deceased Partners, Partners Who Become Permanently Disabled and Partners Who Dissociate After Retirement Age. Any Dissociated Partner whose Dissociation is the result of the Dissociated Partner's death or permanent disability or who otherwise Dissociates for any reason after reaching Retirement Age, shall be entitled to receive an amount equal to the Dissociation Amount to be paid without interest in four equal installments, the first to be paid on or before thirty (30) days after the end of the calendar year in which the Dissociation occurs, with the remaining payments to be made on or before the first, second and third anniversaries of the Dissociation Date of the Dissociated Partner.

Section 16.2. Payments to Other Dissociated Partners. Any Dissociated Partner not described in subsection 16.1 shall be entitled to receive an amount equal to seventy percent (70%) of the Dissociation Amount to be paid without interest in ten equal annual installments commencing on the first anniversary of the Dissociation Date for the Dissociated Partner.

Section 16.3. Payments Reduced for Amounts Owing from Dissociated Partners. The payments due to Dissociated Partners under this Article 16 may be reduced for amounts owing by the Dissociating Partner to the Partnership, including any damages owing as a result of any breach of this Partnership Agreement.

Section 16.4. Tax Treatment of Payments to Dissociated Partners. Payments to Dissociated Partners under this Article 16 shall be treated as paid for the Dissociated Partner's interest in Partnership property other than property described in Code section 736(b)(2).

Section 16.5. Interest in Partnership Assets. No Dissociated Partner shall have any interest in any accounts receivable, rights of the Partnership to receive or collect cash, or other specific assets of the Partnership.

Section 16.6. Rights and Duties of Dissociated Partner Under the Partnership Agreement. Except with respect to provisions concerning contribution and indemnification and rights to payments under this Article 16, a Dissociated Partner shall cease to have rights and duties under this Partnership Agreement as of the Dissociation Date.

ARTICLE 17. CONSEQUENCES OF VIOLATION OF COVENANTS

If a Partner breaches any provision of this Partnership Agreement (a "Breaching Partner"), then, in addition to all other rights and remedies available to the Partnership, the Breaching Partner shall be liable in damages, without requirement of a prior accounting, to the Partnership for all costs and liabilities that the Partnership or any Partner may incur as a result of such breach, including reasonable attorneys' fees incurred in connection with the breach and in connection with recovery of damages from the Breaching Partner. The Partnership may apply any distributions otherwise payable to the Breaching Partner to satisfy any claims it may have against the Breaching Partner.

ARTICLE 18. DUTIES OF PARTNERS TO THE PARTNERSHIP

Section 18.1. Fiduciary Duties of the Partners (Generally). The only fiduciary duties a Partner owes to the Partnership and the other Partners are the duty of loyalty and the duty of care set forth in Sections 18.2 and 18.3.

Section 18.2. Duty of Loyalty. A Partner's duty of loyalty to the Partnership and the other Partners is limited to the following:

(i) to account to the Partnership and hold as trustee for it any property, profit, or benefit derived by the Partner in the conduct and winding up of the Partnership business or derived from a use by the Partner of Partnership property, including the appropriation of a Partnership opportunity;

(ii) to refrain from dealing with the Partnership in the conduct or winding up of the Partnership business as or on behalf of a party having an interest adverse to the Partnership; and

(iii) to refrain from competing with the Partnership in the conduct of the Partnership business before the dissolution of the Partnership.

Section 18.3. Duty of Care. A Partner's duty of care to the Partnership and the other Partners in the conduct and winding up of the Partnership business is limited to refraining from engaging in grossly negligent or reckless conduct, intentional misconduct, or a knowing violation of law.

Section 18.4. Obligation of Good Faith and Fair Dealing. A Partner shall discharge the duties to the Partnership and the other Partners under this Partnership Agreement and the Act and exercise any rights consistently with the obligation of good faith and fair dealing.

Section 18.5. Furtherance of Partner's Own Interests. A Partner does not violate a duty or obligation under this Partnership Agreement or the Act merely because the Partner's conduct furthers the Partner's own interest.

Section 18.6. Transacting Business with the Partnership. A Partner may lend money to and transact other business with the Partnership, and as to each loan or transaction the rights and obligations of the

Partner are the same as those of a person who is not a Partner, subject to other applicable law.

Section 18.7. Time Devoted to Partnership Business; Competing with the Partnership. Each Partner agrees that he or she will devote substantially full time to the Partnership Business until he or she Dissociates. In addition, prior to Dissociation, each Partner agrees that he or she shall not compete with the Partnership and that he or she shall offer all matters that might constitute opportunities for the Partnership to the Partnership.

Section 18.8. Confidentiality of Partnership Information. Each Partner agrees to maintain all business information with respect to the Partnership in confidence, and agrees not to use or disclose any business information, trade secrets, processes, or confidences of the Partnership in competition with the Partnership. This obligation of confidentiality shall survive the Dissociation of any Partner.

Section 18.9. Standards of Conduct in Winding Up Partnership. This Article 18 applies to a person winding up the Partnership business as the personal or legal representative of the last surviving Partner as if the person were a Partner.

Section 18.10. Modification of Standards of the Act. Except as expressly set forth herein, the Partners agree to be bound by RUPA section 404.

Section 18.11. Partnership Books and Records.

(i) The Partnership shall provide to each Partner during ordinary business hours access to its books and records for the purpose of copying and inspecting them.

(ii) The Partnership shall provide to each former Partner during ordinary business hours access to its books and records pertaining to the period during which they were partners for the purpose of copying and inspecting them.

(iii) The rights of inspection and copying provided in subsections (i) and (ii) above may be exercised by the agents and attorneys of a partner or former partner.

(iv) The Partnership may impose a reasonable charge, as determined by the managing Partners, covering the costs of labor and material, for copies of books and records furnished.

Section 18.12. Obligation of Partnership and Other Partners to Provide Information. The Partnership and each Partner are obligated to furnish to a Partner, and to the legal representative of a deceased Partner or a Partner under legal disability:

(i) without demand, any information concerning the Partnership's business and affairs reasonably required for the proper exercise of the Partner's rights and duties under the Partnership Agreement or RUPA; and

(ii) on demand, any other information concerning the Partnership's business and affairs, except to the extent the demand or the information demanded is unreasonable or otherwise improper under the circumstances.

ARTICLE 19. TITLE TO PROPERTY

All real and personal property of the Partnership shall be owned by the Partnership as an entity. No Partner shall have any ownership interest in the Partnership property in his or her own individual name or right.

ARTICLE 20. INDEMNIFICATION

The Partnership shall indemnify each Partner and Dissociated Partner (an "Indemnified Partner") with respect to any Partnership debt, obligation, or liability of, or chargeable to, the Partnership or such Indemnified Partner, whether arising in tort, contract, or otherwise, which such debts, obligations, and liabilities occur, are incurred, or are assumed in the course of the Partnership's Business and in accordance with the provisions of this Partnership Agreement. Notwithstanding the foregoing sentence, no Partner or Dissociated Partner shall be entitled to indemnification for any Partnership obligation resulting from the Indemnified Partner's grossly negligent or reckless conduct, intentional misconduct, or knowing violation of the law, except to the extent such obligation or liability is paid or reimbursed under a policy of insurance carried by the Partnership.

ARTICLE 21. RESTRICTIONS ON TRANSFER; NEW PARTNERS

Section 21.1 Nature of Partnership Interest. Each Partner's interest in the Partnership shall be personal property for all purposes.

Section 21.2. No Transfer. A Partner may not directly or indirectly Transfer the Partner's interest in the Partnership, nor shall a Partner permit the Partner's interest in the Partnership to be directly or indirectly Transferred. An attempted Transfer of a Partner's interest in the Partnership shall not render the transferee a Partner without the Consent of Two–Thirds of the Partners, but shall result in the transferee having only those rights stated in section 503(b) of the Act.

Section 21.3. New Partners. No person shall become a Partner except with the Consent of Two–Thirds of the Partners and upon execution of this Partnership Agreement.

ARTICLE 22. DISSOLUTION

Section 22.1. Events of Dissolution. The Partnership shall be dissolved and its affairs wound up upon the occurrence of any of the following events:

(a) The written consent of All of the Partners;

(b) The sale, transfer or assignment of all or substantially all of the assets of the Partnership;

(c) (i) The adjudication of the Partnership as insolvent within the meaning of insolvency in either bankruptcy or equity proceedings; (ii) the filing of an involuntary petition in bankruptcy against the Partnership (which is not dismissed within ninety (90) days); (iii) the filing against the Partnership of a petition for reorganization under the Bankruptcy Code (which is not dismissed within ninety (90) days); (iv) a general assignment by the Partnership for the benefit of creditors; (v) the voluntary claim (by the Partnership) that it is insolvent under any provision(s) of the Bankruptcy Code; or (vi) the appointment for the Partnership of a temporary or permanent receiver, trustee, custodian, or sequestration and such receiver, trustee, custodian, or sequestration is not dismissed within ninety (90) days; or

(d) As otherwise required by the Act.

Section 22.2. Winding Up of Partnership Affairs. In the event of the dissolution of the Partnership for any reason, the Managing Partners shall proceed promptly to wind up the affairs of and liquidate the assets of the Partnership and shall without delay file a statement of dissolution. Except as otherwise provided in this Partnership Agreement, by the Act, or other applicable law, the Partners shall continue to share distributions and tax allocations during the period of liquidation in the same manner as before the dissolution.

Section 22.3. Liquidating Distributions. After paying or providing for the payment of all debts or liabilities and obligations of the Partnership and all expenses of liquidation, the proceeds of the liquidation and any other assets of the Partnership shall be distributed to or for the benefit of the Partners in accordance with the Partners' positive Capital Accounts.

Section 22.4. Termination. Upon completion of the winding up of the affairs of the Partnership and the distribution of all Partnership assets, the Partnership shall terminate, and the Managing Partners shall thereupon execute and file such additional statements of dissolution and any and all other documents required to effectuate the dissolution and termination of the Partnership.

ARTICLE 23. GENERAL PROVISIONS

Section 23.1. Amendment. This Partnership Agreement may not be amended, modified, altered, or changed in any respect whatsoever, except by a further Partnership Agreement in writing, duly executed by all of the Partners.

Section 23.2. Binding on Heirs, Successors, and Assigns. Except as provided herein to the contrary, this Partnership Agreement shall be binding upon and inure to the benefit of the parties signatory hereto (as well as to all future parties who are admitted as Partners in this Partnership), their respective spouses, heirs, executors, legal representatives, and permitted successors and assigns.

Section 23.3. Books and Records. The Partnership's books and records, together with all of the documents and papers pertaining to the business of the Partnership, shall be kept at the chief executive offices of the Partnership, and at all reasonable times shall be open to the inspection of, and may be copied and excerpts taken therefrom by, any Partner or his or her authorized representative for any proper purpose. The books and records of the Partnership shall be kept on a calendar-year basis in accordance with the method of accounting required for federal income tax purposes, consistently applied, and shall reflect all Partnership transactions and be appropriate and adequate for the Partnership Business.

Section 23.4. Construction. This Partnership Agreement, including the recitals, which are an integral part of this Agreement, shall be construed in its entirety according to its plain meaning. The parties hereby agree that this Partnership Agreement shall be construed as an agreement negotiated at arm's length between equally sophisticated business-persons, each represented and advised by separate counsel of each party's choosing. This Partnership Agreement shall not, therefore, be construed against the party who provided or drafted all or any portion of this Partnership Agreement.

Section 23.5. Counterparts. Any number of counterparts of this Partnership Agreement may be executed, and each such counterpart shall be deemed to be an original instrument, but all such counterparts together shall constitute but one agreement.

Section 23.6. Further Actions. Each party hereto agrees to do all acts and things and to make, execute, and deliver such written instruments as shall from time to time be reasonably required to carry out the terms and provisions of this Partnership Agreement.

Section 23.7. Notices. All notices under this Partnership Agreement shall be in writing and shall be served upon the other parties at the addresses set forth in the books and records of the Partnership.

Section 23.8. Severability. If any provision of this Partnership Agreement shall be found by a court of competent jurisdiction to be illegal, in conflict with any law of the State, or otherwise unenforceable, the validity and enforceability of the remaining provisions shall not be affected, and the rights and obligations of the parties shall be construed and enforced as if this Partnership Agreement did not contain the particular provision found to be illegal, invalid, or otherwise unenforceable.

Section 23.9. Situs. It is the intention of the Partners that the laws of the State should govern the validity of this Partnership Agreement, the construction of its terms, the interpretation of the rights and duties of the Partners and other matters.

Section 23.10. Waiver. No consent to, or waiver of, express or implied by a Partner or the Partnership, or the breach or default by any Partner in the performance of his or her obligations under this Agreement shall be deemed or construed to be a consent to or waiver of any other breach or default.

Section 23.11. Dispute Resolution.

Section 23.12. Entire Agreement. This Partnership Agreement constitutes the entire agreement between the Partners and supersedes all prior agreements, representations, warranties, statements, promises, and understandings (whether oral or written) with respect to the subject matter hereof.

IN WITNESS WHEREOF, the Partners have executed this Partnership Agreement as of ______, ______, ______.

[Names and signatures of all partners]

Schedule 1

Schedule of Capital Contributions (name of partner, amount of contribution, and date of contribution).

____

Name of Partner Address Amount of Contribution Date of Contribution

____

____

____

EXHIBIT A. STATEMENT OF QUALIFICATION

This Statement of Qualification, made and effective this the ______ day of ______, 20___, provides as follows:

1. The partnership as to which this Statement of Qualification applies is designated: [name of partnership] (the "Partnership").

2. The street address of chief executive office of the Partnership is [street address of chief executive office].

3. The street address of one office of the Partnership in this State, if there is one, is [street address of office in State].

4. If there is no office in this State listed under 2 or 3 above, the name and street address of the Partnership's registered office and agent for service of process is: [name and street address of agent for service of process].

5. The partnership elects to be a limited liability partnership.

6. This Statement of Qualification shall have the following deferred effective date: ______.

The undersigned personally declare that the contents of this statement are accurate.

[partnership name]

______ By: [name of signer], General Partner

______ By: [name of signer], General Partner

EXHIBIT B. STATEMENT OF FOREIGN QUALIFICATION

This Statement of Foreign Qualification, made and effective this the ______ day of ______, 20___, provides as follows:

1. The partnership as to which this Statement of Foreign Qualification applies is designated: [name of partnership] (the "Partnership").

2. The street address of chief executive office of the Partnership is [street address of chief executive office].

3. The street address of one office of the Partnership in this State, if there is one, is [street address of office in State].

4. If there is no office in this State listed under 2 or 3 above, the name and street address of the Partnership's registered office and agent for service of process is: [name and street address of agent for service of process].

5. This Statement of Qualification shall have the following deferred effective date: ______.

The undersigned personally declares that the contents of this statement are accurate.

[partnership name]

______ By: [name of signer], General Partner

______ By: [name of signer], General Partner

EXHIBIT C. STATEMENT OF PARTNERSHIP AUTHORITY

This Statement of Partnership Authority, made and effective this the ______ day of ______, 20___, provides as follows:

1. The partnership as to which this Statement of Partnership Authority applies is designed: [name of partnership] (the "Partnership").

2. The street address of chief executive office of the Partnership is [street address of chief executive office].

3. The street address of one office of the Partnership in this State, if there is one, is [street address of office in State].

4. The names and mailing addresses of all of the partners are: [names and mailing addresses of all partners].

—or—

The name and mailing address of an agent appointed and maintained by the partnership for the purpose of [RUPA section 303(b)] is [name and mailing address of agent].

5. The names of partners authorized to execute an instrument transferring real property held in the name of the partnership are: [names of authorized partners].

6. The following partners have the additional indicated authority: [describe additional authority to enter into transactions other than the transfer of real estate or to undertake other matters].

7. The following partners are subject to the indicated limitations on their authority: [describe limitations on authority to enter into transactions other than the transfer of real estate or to undertake other matters].

The undersigned personally declare under penalty of perjury that the contents of the statement are accurate.

_______ By: [name of signer], General Partner

_______ By: [name of signer], General Partner

EXHIBIT D. STATEMENT OF DISSOLUTION

Notice is hereby given that the partnership doing business under the name of _______ has dissolved and is winding up its business.

The undersigned is a partner in said partnership who has not wrongfully dissociated.

The undersigned personally declares under penalty of perjury that the contents of this Statement of Dissolution are accurate.

____

[name of signer]

III. LIMITED LIABILITY COMPANIES

A. UNIFORM LIMITED LIABILITY COMPANY ACT (1995)

Commissioners' Prefatory Note

Borrowing from abroad, Wyoming initiated a national movement in 1977 by enacting this country's first limited liability company act. The movement started slowly as the Internal Revenue Service took more than ten years to announce finally that a Wyoming limited liability company would be taxed like a partnership. Since that time, every State has adopted or is considering its own distinct limited liability company act, many of which have already been amended one or more times.

The allure of the limited liability company is its unique ability to bring together in a single business organization the best features of all other business forms—properly structured, its owners obtain both a corporate-styled liability shield and the pass-through tax benefits of a partnership. General and limited partnerships do not offer their partners a corporate-styled liability shield. Corporations, including those having made a Subchapter S election, do not offer their shareholders all the pass-through tax benefits of a partnership. All state limited liability company acts contain provisions for a liability shield and partnership tax status.

Despite these two common themes, state limited liability company acts display a dazzling array of diversity. Multistate activities of businesses are widespread. Recognition of out-of-state limited liability companies varies. Unfortunately, this lack of uniformity manifests itself in basic but fundamentally important questions, such as: may a company be formed and operated by only one owner; may it be formed for purposes other than to make a profit; whether owners have the power and right to withdraw from a company and receive a distribution of the fair value of their interests; who has the apparent authority to bind the company and the limits of that authority; what are the fiduciary duties of owners and managers to a company and each other; how are the rights to manage a company allocated among its owners and managers; do the owners have the right to sue a company and its other owners in their own right as well as derivatively on behalf of the company; may general and limited partnerships be converted to limited liability companies and may limited liability companies merge with other limited liability companies and other business organizations; what is the law governing foreign limited liability companies; and are any or all of these and other rules simply default rules that may be modified by agreement or are they non-waivable.

Practitioners and entrepreneurs struggle to understand the law governing limited liability companies organized in their own State and to understand the burgeoning law of other States. Simple questions concerning where to organize are increasingly complex. Since most state limited liability company acts are in their infancy, little if any interpretative case law exists. Even when case law develops, it will have limited precedential value because of the diversity of the state acts.

Accordingly, uniform legislation in this area of the law appeared to have become urgent.

After a Study Committee appointed by the National Conference of Commissioners in late 1991 recommended that a comprehensive project be undertaken, the Conference appointed a Drafting Committee which worked on a Uniform Limited Liability Company Act (ULLCA) from early 1992 until its adoption by the Conference at its Annual Meeting in August 1994. The Drafting Committee was assisted by a blue ribbon panel of national experts and other interested and affected parties and organizations. Many, if not all, of those assisting the Committee brought substantial experience from drafting limited liability company legislation in their own States. Many are also authors of leading treatises and articles in the field. Those represented in the drafting process included an American Bar Association (ABA) liaison, four advisors representing the three separate ABA Sections of Business Law, Taxation, and Real Property, Trust and Probate, the United States Treasury Department, the Internal Revenue Service, and many observers representing several other organizations, including the California Bar Association, the New York City Bar Association, the American College of Real Estate Lawyers, the National Association of Certified Public Accountants, the National Association of Secretaries of State, the Chicago and Lawyers Title Companies, the American Land Title Association, and several university law and business school faculty members.

The Committee met nine times and engaged in numerous national telephonic conferences to discuss policies, review over fifteen drafts, evaluate legal developments and consider comments by our many knowledgeable advisers and observers, as well as an ABA subcommittee's earlier work on a prototype. In examining virtually every aspect of each state limited liability company act, the Committee maintained a single policy vision—to draft a flexible act with a comprehensive set of default rules designed to substitute as the essence of the bargain for small entrepreneurs and others.

This Act is flexible in the sense that the vast majority of its provisions may be modified by the owners in a private agreement. To simplify, those non-waivable provisions are set forth in a single subsection. Helped thereby, sophisticated parties will negotiate their own deal with the benefit of counsel.

The Committee also recognized that small entrepreneurs without the benefit of counsel should also have access to the Act. To that end, the great bulk of the Act sets forth default rules designed to operate a limited liability company without sophisticated agreements and to recognize that members may also modify the default rules by oral agreements defined in part by their own conduct. Uniquely, the Act combines two simple default structures which depend upon the presence of designations in the articles of organization. All default rules under the Act flow from these two designations.

First, unless the articles reflect that a limited liability company is a term company and the duration of that term, the company will be an at-will company. Generally, an at-will company dissolves more easily than a term company and its owners may demand a payment of the fair value of their interests at any time. Owners of a term company must generally wait until the expiration of the term to obtain the value of their interests. Secondly, unless the articles reflect that a company will be managed by managers, the company will be managed by its members. This designation controls whether the members or managers have apparent agency authority, management authority, the nature of fiduciary duties in the company, and important dissolution characteristics.

In January of 1995 the Executive Committee of the Conference adopted an amendment to harmonize the Act with new and important Internal Revenue Service announcements, and the amendment was ratified by the National Conference at its Annual Meeting in August of 1995. The amendment modifies the Act's dissolution provision.

The adoption of ULLCA will provide much needed consistency among the States, with flexible default rules, and multistate recognition of limited liability on the part of company owners. It will also promote the development of precedential case law.

Contents

ARTICLE 1. GENERAL PROVISIONS

ARTICLE 2. ORGANIZATION

ARTICLE 1. GENERAL PROVISIONS

SECTION 101. DEFINITIONS

In this [Act]:

(1) "Articles of organization" means initial, amended, and restated articles of organization and articles of merger. In the case of a foreign limited liability company, the term includes all records serving a similar function required to be filed in the office of the [Secretary of State] or other official having custody of company records in the State or country under whose law it is organized.

(2) "At-will company" means a limited liability company other than a term company.

(3) "Business" includes every trade, occupation, profession, and other lawful purpose, whether or not carried on for profit.

(4) "Debtor in bankruptcy" means a person who is the subject of an order for relief under Title 11 of the United States Code or a comparable order under a successor statute of general application or a comparable order under federal, state, or foreign law governing insolvency.

(5) "Distribution" means a transfer of money, property, or other benefit from a limited liability company to a member in the member's capacity as a member or to a transferee of the member's distributional interest.

(6) "Distributional interest" means all of a member's interest in distributions by the limited liability company.

(7) "Entity" means a person other than an individual.

(8) "Foreign limited liability company" means an unincorporated entity organized under laws other than the laws of this State which afford limited liability to its owners comparable to the liability under Section 303 and is not required to obtain a certificate of authority to transact business under any law of this State other than this [Act].

(9) "Limited liability company" means a limited liability company organized under this [Act].

(10) "Manager" means a person, whether or not a member of a manager-managed company, who is vested with authority under Section 301.

(11) "Manager-managed company" means a limited liability company which is so designated in its articles of organization.

(12) "Member-managed company" means a limited liability company other than a manager-managed company.

(13) "Operating agreement" means the agreement under Section 103 concerning the relations among the members, managers, and limited liability company. The term includes amendments to the agreement.

(14) "Person" means an individual, corporation, business trust, estate, trust, partnership, limited liability company, association, joint venture, government, governmental subdivision, agency, or instrumentality, or any other legal or commercial entity.

(15) "Principal office" means the office, whether or not in this State, where the principal executive office of a domestic or foreign limited liability company is located.

(16) "Record" means information that is inscribed on a tangible medium or that is stored in an electronic or other medium and is retrievable in perceivable form.

(17) "Sign" means to identify a record by means of a signature, mark, or other symbol, with intent to authenticate it.

(18) "State" means a State of the United States, the District of Columbia, the Commonwealth of Puerto Rico, or any territory or insular possession subject to the jurisdiction of the United States.

(19) "Term company" means a limited liability company in which its members have agreed to remain members until the expiration of a term specified in the articles of organization.

(20) "Transfer" includes an assignment, conveyance, deed, bill of sale, lease, mortgage, security interest, encumbrance, and gift.

Comment

Uniform Limited Liability Company Act ("ULLCA") definitions, like the rest of the Act, are a blend of terms and concepts derived from the Uniform Partnership Act ("UPA"), the Uniform Partnership Act (1994) ("UPA 1994", also previously known as the Revised Uniform Partnership Act or "RUPA"), the Revised Uniform Limited Partnership Act ("RULPA"), the Uniform Commercial Code ("UCC"), and the Model Business Corporation Act ("MBCA"), or their revisions from time to time; some are tailored specially for this Act.

"Business." A limited liability company may be organized to engage in an activity either for or not for profit. The extent to which contributions to a nonprofit company may be deductible for Federal income tax purposes is determined by federal law. Other state law determines the extent of exemptions from state and local income and property taxes.

"Debtor in bankruptcy." The filing of a voluntary petition operates immediately as an "order for relief." See Sections 601(7)(i) and 602(b)(2)(iii).

"Distribution." This term includes all sources of a member's distributions including the member's capital contributions, undistributed profits, and residual interest in the assets of the company after all claims, including those of third parties and debts to members, have been paid.

"Distributional interest." The term does not include a member's broader rights to participate in the management of the company. See Comments to Article 5.

"Foreign limited liability company." The term is not restricted to companies formed in the United States.

"Manager." The rules of agency apply to limited liability companies. Therefore, managers may designate agents with whatever titles, qualifications, and responsibilities they desire. For example, managers may designate an agent as "President."

"Manager-managed company." The term includes only a company designated as such in the articles of organization. In a manager-managed company agency authority is vested exclusively in one or more managers and not in the members. See Sections 101(10) (manager), 203(a)(6) (articles designation), and 301(b) (agency authority of members and managers).

"Member-managed limited liability company." The term includes every company not designated as "manager-managed" under Section 203(a)(6) in its articles of organization.

"Operating agreement." This agreement may be oral. Members may agree upon the extent to which their relationships are to be governed by writings.

"Principal office." The address of the principal office must be set forth in the annual report required under Section 211(a)(3).

"Record." This Act is the first Uniform Act promulgated with a definition of this term. The definition brings this Act in conformity with the present state of technology and accommodates prospective future technology in the communication and storage of information other than by human memory. Modern methods of communicating and storing information employed in commercial practices are no longer confined to physical documents.

The term includes any writing. A record need not be permanent or indestructible, but an oral or other unwritten communication must be stored or preserved on some medium to qualify as a record. Information that has not been retained other than through human memory does not qualify as a record. A record may be signed or may be created without the knowledge or intent of a particular person. Other law must be consulted to determine admissibility in evidence, the applicability of statute of frauds, and other questions regarding the use of records. Under Section 206(a), electronic filings may be permitted and even encouraged.

SECTION 102. KNOWLEDGE AND NOTICE

(a) A person knows a fact if the person has actual knowledge of it.

(b) A person has notice of a fact if the person:

(1) knows the fact;

(2) has received a notification of the fact; or

(3) has reason to know the fact exists from all of the facts known to the person at the time in question.

(c) A person notifies or gives a notification of a fact to another by taking steps reasonably required to inform the other person in ordinary course, whether or not the other person knows the fact.

(d) A person receives a notification when the notification:

(1) comes to the person's attention; or

(2) is duly delivered at the person's place of business or at any other place held out by the person as a place for receiving communications.

(e) An entity knows, has notice, or receives a notification of a fact for purposes of a particular transaction when the individual conducting the transaction for the entity knows, has notice, or receives a notification of the fact, or in any event when the fact would have been brought to the individual's attention had the entity exercised reasonable diligence. An entity exercises reasonable diligence if it maintains reasonable routines for communicating significant information to the individual conducting the transaction for the entity and there is reasonable compliance with the routines. Reasonable diligence does not require an individual acting for the entity to communicate information unless the communication is part of the individual's regular duties or the individual has reason to know of the transaction and that the transaction would be materially affected by the information.

Comment

Knowledge requires cognitive awareness of a fact, whereas notice is based on a lesser degree of awareness. The Act imposes constructive knowledge under limited circumstances. See Comments to Sections 301(c), 703, and 704.

SECTION 103. EFFECT OF OPERATING AGREEMENT; NON-WAIVABLE PROVISIONS

(a) Except as otherwise provided in subsection (b), all members of a limited liability company may enter into an operating agreement, which need not be in writing, to regulate the affairs of the company and the conduct of its business, and to govern relations among the members, managers, and company. To the extent the operating agreement does not otherwise provide, this [Act] governs relations among the members, managers, and company.

(b) The operating agreement may not:

(1) unreasonably restrict a right to information or access to records under Section 408;

(2) eliminate the duty of loyalty under Section 409(b) or 603(b)(3), but the agreement may:

(i) identify specific types or categories of activities that do not violate the duty of loyalty, if not manifestly unreasonable; and

(ii) specify the number or percentage of members or disinterested managers that may authorize or ratify, after full disclosure of all material facts, a specific act or transaction that otherwise would violate the duty of loyalty;

(3) unreasonably reduce the duty of care under Section 409(c) or 603(b)(3);

(4) eliminate the obligation of good faith and fair dealing under Section 409(d), but the operating agreement may determine the standards by which the performance of the obligation is to be measured, if the standards are not manifestly unreasonable;

(5) vary the right to expel a member in an event specified in Section 601(6);

(6) vary the requirement to wind up the limited liability company's business in a case specified in Section 801(3) or (4); or

(7) restrict rights of a person, other than a manager, member, and transferee of a member's distributional interest, under this [Act].

Comment

The operating agreement is the essential contract that governs the affairs of a limited liability company. Since it is binding on all members, amendments must be approved by all members unless otherwise provided in the agreement. Although many agreements will be in writing, the agreement and any amendments may be oral or may be in the form of a record. Course of dealing, course of performance and usage of trade are relevant to determine the meaning of the agreement unless the agreement provides that all amendments must be in writing.

This section makes clear that the only matters an operating agreement may not control are specified in subsection (b). Accordingly, an operating agreement may modify or eliminate any rule specified in any section of this Act except matters specified in subsection (b). To the extent not otherwise mentioned in subsection (b), every section of this Act is simply a default rule, regardless of whether the language of the section appears to be otherwise mandatory. This approach eliminates the necessity of repeating the phrase "unless otherwise agreed" in each section and its commentary.

Under subsection (b)(1), an operating agreement may not unreasonably restrict the right to information or access to any records under Section 408. This does not create an independent obligation beyond Section 408 to maintain any specific records. Under subsections (b)(2) to (4), an irreducible core of fiduciary responsibilities survive any contrary provision in the operating agreement. Subsection (b)(2)(i) authorizes an operating agreement to modify, but not eliminate, the three specific duties of loyalty set forth in Section 409(b)(1) to (3) provided the modification itself is not manifestly unreasonable, a question of fact.

Subsection (b)(2)(ii) preserves the common law right of the members to authorize future or ratify past violations of the duty of loyalty provided there has been a full disclosure of all material facts. The authorization or ratification must be unanimous unless otherwise provided in an operating agreement, because the authorization or ratification itself constitutes an amendment to the agreement. The authorization or ratification of specific past or future conduct may sanction conduct that would have been manifestly unreasonable under subsection (b)(2)(i).

SECTION 104. SUPPLEMENTAL PRINCIPLES OF LAW

(a) Unless displaced by particular provisions of this [Act], the principles of law and equity supplement this [Act].

(b) If an obligation to pay interest arises under this [Act] and the rate is not specified, the rate is that specified in [applicable statute].

Comment

Supplementary principles include, but are not limited to, the law of agency, estoppel, law merchant, and all other principles listed in UCC Section 1–103, including the law relative to the capacity to contract, fraud, misrepresentation, duress, coercion, mistake, bankruptcy, and other validating and invalidating clauses. Other principles such as those mentioned in UCC Section 1–205 (Course of Dealing and Usage of Trade) apply as well as course of performance. As with UPA 1994 Section 104, upon which this provision is based, no substantive change from either the UPA or the UCC is intended. Section 104(b) establishes the applicable rate of interest in the absence of an agreement among the members.

SECTION 105. NAME

(a) The name of a limited liability company must contain "limited liability company" or "limited company" or the abbreviation "L.L.C.", "LLC", "L.C.", or "LC". "Limited" may be abbreviated as "Ltd.", and "company" may be abbreviated as "Co.".

(b) Except as authorized by subsections (c) and (d), the name of a limited liability company must be distinguishable upon the records of the [Secretary of State] from:

(1) the name of any corporation, limited partnership, or company incorporated, organized or authorized to transact business, in this State;

(2) a name reserved or registered under Section 106 or 107;

(3) a fictitious name approved under Section 1005 for a foreign company authorized to transact business in this State because its real name is unavailable.

(c) A limited liability company may apply to the [Secretary of State] for authorization to use a name that is not distinguishable upon the records of the [Secretary of State] from one or more of the names described in subsection (b). The [Secretary of State] shall authorize use of the name applied for if:

(1) the present user, registrant, or owner of a reserved name consents to the use in a record and submits an undertaking in form satisfactory to the [Secretary of State] to change the name to a name that is distinguishable upon the records of the [Secretary of State] from the name applied for; or

(2) the applicant delivers to the [Secretary of State] a certified copy of the final judgment of a court of competent jurisdiction establishing the applicant's right to use the name applied for in this State.

(d) A limited liability company may use the name, including a fictitious name, of another domestic or foreign company which is used in this State if the other company is organized or authorized to transact business in this State and the company proposing to use the name has:

(1) merged with the other company;

(2) been formed by reorganization with the other company; or

(3) acquired substantially all of the assets, including the name, of the other company.

SECTION 106. RESERVED NAME

(a) A person may reserve the exclusive use of the name of a limited liability company, including a fictitious name for a foreign company whose name is not available, by delivering an application to the [Secretary of State] for filing. The application must set forth the name and address of the applicant and the name proposed to be reserved. If the [Secretary of State] finds that the name applied for is available, it must be reserved for the applicant's exclusive use for a nonrenewable 120–day period.

(b) The owner of a name reserved for a limited liability company may transfer the reservation to another person by delivering to the [Secretary of State] a signed notice of the transfer which states the name and address of the transferee.

Comment

A foreign limited liability company that is not presently authorized to transact business in the State may reserve a fictitious name for a nonrenewable 120–day period. When its actual name is available, a company will generally register that name under Section 107 because the registration is valid for a year and may be extended indefinitely.

SECTION 107. REGISTERED NAME

(a) A foreign limited liability company may register its name subject to the requirements of Section 1005, if the name is distinguishable upon the records of the [Secretary of State] from names that are not available under Section 105(b).

(b) A foreign limited liability company registers its name, or its name with any addition required by Section 1005, by delivering to the [Secretary of State] for filing an application:

(1) setting forth its name, or its name with any addition required by Section 1005, the State or country and date of its organization, and a brief description of the nature of the business in which it is engaged; and

(2) accompanied by a certificate of existence, or a record of similar import, from the State or country of organization.

(c) A foreign limited liability company whose registration is effective may renew it for successive years by delivering for filing in the office of the [Secretary of State] a renewal application complying with subsection (b) between October 1 and December 31 of the preceding year. The renewal application renews the registration for the following calendar year.

(d) A foreign limited liability company whose registration is effective may qualify as a foreign company under its name or consent in writing to the use of its name by a limited liability company later organized under this [Act] or by another foreign company later authorized to transact business in this State. The registered name terminates when the limited liability company is organized or the foreign company qualifies or consents to the qualification of another foreign company under the registered name.

SECTION 108. DESIGNATED OFFICE AND AGENT FOR SERVICE OF PROCESS

(a) A limited liability company and a foreign limited liability company authorized to do business in this State shall designate and continuously maintain in this State:

(1) an office, which need not be a place of its business in this State; and

(2) an agent and street address of the agent for service of process on the company.

(b) An agent must be an individual resident of this State, a domestic corporation, another limited liability company, or a foreign corporation or foreign company authorized to do business in this State.

Comment

Limited liability companies organized under Section 202 or authorized to transact business under Section 1004 are required to designate and continuously maintain an office in the State. Although the designated office need not be a place of business, it most often will be the only place of business of the company. The company must also designate an agent for service of process within the State and the agent's street address. The agent's address need not be the same as the company's designated office address. The initial office and agent designations must be set forth in the articles of organization, including the address of the designated office. See Section 203(a)(2) to (3). The current office and agent designations must be set forth in the company's annual report. See Section 211(a)(2). See also Section 109 (procedure for changing the office or agent designations), Section 110 (procedure for an agent to resign), and Section 111(b) (the filing officer is the service agent for the company if it fails to maintain its own service agent).

SECTION 109. CHANGE OF DESIGNATED OFFICE OR AGENT FOR SERVICE OF PROCESS

A limited liability company may change its designated office or agent for service of process by delivering to the [Secretary of State] for filing a statement of change which sets forth:

(1) the name of the company;

(2) the street address of its current designated office;

(3) if the current designated office is to be changed, the street address of the new designated office;

(4) the name and address of its current agent for service of process; and

(5) if the current agent for service of process or street address of that agent is to be changed, the new address or the name and street address of the new agent for service of process.

SECTION 110. RESIGNATION OF AGENT FOR SERVICE OF PROCESS

(a) An agent for service of process of a limited liability company may resign by delivering to the [Secretary of State] for filing a record of the statement of resignation.

(b) After filing a statement of resignation, the [Secretary of State] shall mail a copy to the designated office and another copy to the limited liability company at its principal office.

(c) An agency is terminated on the 31st day after the statement is filed in the office of the [Secretary of State].

SECTION 111. SERVICE OF PROCESS

(a) An agent for service of process appointed by a limited liability company or a foreign limited liability company is an agent of the company for service of any process, notice, or demand required or permitted by law to be served upon the company.

(b) If a limited liability company or foreign limited liability company fails to appoint or maintain an agent for service of process in this State or the agent for service of process cannot with reasonable diligence be found at the agent's address, the [Secretary of State] is an agent of the company upon whom process, notice, or demand may be served.

(c) Service of any process, notice, or demand on the [Secretary of State] may be made by delivering to and leaving with the [Secretary of State], the [Assistant Secretary of State], or clerk having charge of the limited liability company department of the [Secretary of State's] office duplicate copies of the process, notice, or demand. If the process, notice, or demand is served on the [Secretary of State], the [Secretary of State] shall forward one of the copies by registered or certified mail, return receipt requested, to the company at its designated office. Service is effected under this subsection at the earliest of:

(1) the date the company receives the process, notice, or demand;

(2) the date shown on the return receipt, if signed on behalf of the company; or

(3) five days after its deposit in the mail, if mailed postpaid and correctly addressed.

(d) The [Secretary of State] shall keep a record of all processes, notices, and demands served pursuant to this section and record the time of and the action taken regarding the service.

(e) This section does not affect the right to serve process, notice, or demand in any manner otherwise provided by law.

Comment

Service of process on a limited liability company and a foreign company authorized to transact business in the State must be made on the company's agent for service of process whose name and address should be on file with the filing office. If for any reason a company fails to appoint or maintain an agent for service of process or the agent cannot be found with reasonable diligence at the agent's address, the filing officer will be deemed the proper agent.

SECTION 112. NATURE OF BUSINESS AND POWERS

(a) A limited liability company may be organized under this [Act] for any lawful purpose, subject to any law of this State governing or regulating business.

(b) Unless its articles of organization provide otherwise, a limited liability company has the same powers as an individual to do all things necessary or convenient to carry on its business or affairs, including power to:

(1) sue and be sued, and defend in its name;

(2) purchase, receive, lease, or otherwise acquire, and own, hold, improve, use, and otherwise deal with real or personal property, or any legal or equitable interest in property, wherever located;

(3) sell, convey, mortgage, grant a security interest in, lease, exchange, and otherwise encumber or dispose of all or any part of its property;

(4) purchase, receive, subscribe for, or otherwise acquire, own, hold, vote, use, sell, mortgage, lend, grant a security interest in, or otherwise dispose of and deal in and with, shares or other interests in or obligations of any other entity;

(5) make contracts and guarantees, incur liabilities, borrow money, issue its notes, bonds, and other obligations, which may be convertible into or include the option to purchase other securities of the limited liability company, and secure any of its obligations by a mortgage on or a security interest in any of its property, franchises, or income;

(6) lend money, invest and reinvest its funds, and receive and hold real and personal property as security for repayment;

(7) be a promoter, partner, member, associate, or manager of any partnership, joint venture, trust, or other entity;

(8) conduct its business, locate offices, and exercise the powers granted by this [Act] within or without this State;

(9) elect managers and appoint officers, employees, and agents of the limited liability company, define their duties, fix their compensation, and lend them money and credit;

(10) pay pensions and establish pension plans, pension trusts, profit sharing plans, bonus plans, option plans, and benefit or incentive plans for any or all of its current or former members, managers, officers, employees, and agents;

(11) make donations for the public welfare or for charitable, scientific, or educational purposes; and

(12) make payments or donations, or do any other act, not inconsistent with law, that furthers the business of the limited liability company.

Comment

A limited liability company may be organized for any lawful purpose unless the State has specifically prohibited a company from engaging in a specific activity. For example, many States require that certain regulated industries, such as banking and insurance, be conducted only by organizations that meet the special requirements. Also, many States impose restrictions on activities in which a limited liability company may engage. For example, the practice of certain professionals is often subject to special conditions.

A limited liability company has the power to engage in and perform important and necessary acts related to its operation and function. A company's power to enter into a transaction is distinguishable from the authority of an agent to enter into the transaction. See Section 301 (agency rules).

ARTICLE 2. ORGANIZATION

SECTION 201. LIMITED LIABILITY COMPANY AS LEGAL ENTITY

A limited liability company is a legal entity distinct from its members.

Comment

A limited liability company is legally distinct from its members who are not normally liable for the debts, obligations, and liabilities of the company. See Section 303. Accordingly, members are not proper parties to suits against the company unless an object of the proceeding is to enforce members' rights against the company or to enforce their liability to the company.

SECTION 202. ORGANIZATION

(a) One or more persons may organize a limited liability company, consisting of one or more members, by delivering articles of organization to the office of the [Secretary of State] for filing.

(b) Unless a delayed effective date is specified, the existence of a limited liability company begins when the articles of organization are filed.

(c) The filing of the articles of organization by the [Secretary of State] is conclusive proof that the organizers satisfied all conditions precedent to the creation of a limited liability company.

Comment

Any person may organize a limited liability company by performing the ministerial act of signing and filing the articles of organization. The person need not be a member. As a matter of flexibility, a company may be organized and operated with only one member to enable sole proprietors to obtain the benefit of a liability shield. The effect of organizing or operating a company with one member on the Federal tax classification of the company is determined by federal law.

The existence of a company begins when the articles are filed. Therefore, the filing of the articles of organization is conclusive as to the existence of the limited liability shield for persons who enter into transactions on behalf of the company. Until the articles are filed, a firm is not organized under this Act and is not a "limited liability company" as defined in Section 101(9). In that case, the parties' relationships are not governed by this Act unless they have expressed a contractual intent to be bound by the provisions of the Act. Third parties would also not be governed by the provisions of this Act unless they have expressed a contractual intent to extend a limited liability shield to the members of the would-be limited liability company.

SECTION 203. ARTICLES OF ORGANIZATION

(a) Articles of organization of a limited liability company must set forth:

(1) the name of the company;

(2) the address of the initial designated office;

(3) the name and street address of the initial agent for service of process;

(4) the name and address of each organizer;

(5) whether the company is to be a term company and, if so, the term specified;

(6) whether the company is to be manager-managed, and, if so, the name and address of each initial manager; and

(7) whether one or more of the members of the company are to be liable for its debts and obligations under Section 303(c).

(b) Articles of organization of a limited liability company may set forth:

(1) provisions permitted to be set forth in an operating agreement; or

(2) other matters not inconsistent with law.

(c) Articles of organization of a limited liability company may not vary the non-waivable provisions of Section 103(b). As to all other matters, if any provision of an operating agreement is inconsistent with the articles of organization:

(1) the operating agreement controls as to managers, members, and members' transferees; and

(2) the articles of organization control as to persons, other than managers, members and their transferees, who reasonably rely on the articles to their detriment.

Comment

The articles serve primarily a notice function and generally do not reflect the substantive agreement of the members regarding the business affairs of the company. Those matters are generally reserved for an operating agreement which may be unwritten. Under Section 203(b), the articles may contain provisions permitted to be set forth in an operating agreement. Where the articles and operating agreement conflict, the operating agreement controls as to members but the articles control as to third parties. The articles may also contain any other matter not inconsistent with law. The most important is a Section 301(c) limitation on the authority of a member or manager to transfer interests in the company's real property.

A company will be at-will unless it is designated as a term company and the duration of its term is specified in its articles under Section 203(a)(5). The duration of a term company may be specified in any manner which sets forth a specific and final date for the dissolution of the company. For example, the period specified may be in the form of "50 years from the date of filing of the articles" or "the period ending on January 1, 2020." Mere specification of a particular undertaking of an uncertain business duration is not sufficient unless the particular undertaking is within a longer fixed period. An example of this type of designation would include "2020 or until the building is completed, whichever occurs first." When the specified period is incorrectly specified, the company will be an at-will company. Notwithstanding the correct specification of a term in the articles, a company will be an at-will company among the members under Section 203(c)(1) if an operating agreement so provides. A term company that continues after the expiration of its term specified in its articles will also be an at-will company.

A term company possesses several important default rule characteristics that differentiate it dramatically from an at-will company. An operating agreement may alter any of these rules. Any dissociation of an at-will member dissolves a member-managed company unless a specified percentage of the remaining members agree to continue the business of the company. Before the expiration of its term, only specified dissociation events (excluding voluntary withdrawal) of a term member will dissolve a member-managed company unless a specified percentage of the remaining members agree to continue the business of the company. See Comments to Sections 601 and 801(b)(3). Also, even if the dissociation of an at-will member does not result in a dissolution of a member-managed company, the dissociated member is entitled to have the company purchase that member's interest for its fair value. Unless the company earlier dissolves, a term member must generally await the expiration of the agreed term to withdraw the fair value of the interest. See Comments to Section 701(a).

A company will be member-managed unless it is designated as manager-managed under Section 203(a)(6). Absent further designation in the articles, a company will be a member-managed at-will company. The designation of a limited liability company as either member-or manager-managed is important because it defines who are agents and have the apparent authority to bind the company under Section 301 and determines whether the dissociation of members who are not managers will threaten dissolution of the company. In a member-managed company, the members have the agency authority to bind the company. In a manager-managed company only the managers have that authority. The effect of the agency structure of a company on the Federal tax classification of the company is determined by federal law. The agency designation relates only to agency and does not preclude members of a manager-managed company from participating in the actual management of company business. See Comments to Section 404(b).

In a member-managed company, the dissociation of any member will cause the company to dissolve unless a specified percentage of the remaining members agree to continue the business of the company. In a manager-managed company, only the dissociation of any member who is also a manager threatens dissolution of the company. Only where there are no members who are also managers will the dissociation of members who are not managers threaten dissolution of a manager-managed company. See Comments to Section 801.

SECTION 204. AMENDMENT OR RESTATEMENT OF ARTICLES OF ORGANIZATION

(a) Articles of organization of a limited liability company may be amended at any time by delivering articles of amendment to the [Secretary of State] for filing. The articles of amendment must set forth the:

(1) name of the limited liability company;

(2) date of filing of the articles of organization; and

(3) amendment to the articles.

(b) A limited liability company may restate its articles of organization at any time. Restated articles of organization must be signed and filed in the same manner as articles of amendment. Restated articles of organization must be designated as such in the heading and state in the heading or in an introductory paragraph the limited liability company's present name and, if it has been changed, all of its former names and the date of the filing of its initial articles of organization.

Comment

An amendment to the articles requires the consent of all the members unless an operating agreement provides for a lesser number. See Section 404(c)(3).

SECTION 205. SIGNING OF RECORDS

(a) Except as otherwise provided in this [Act], a record to be filed by or on behalf of a limited liability company in the office of the [Secretary of State] must be signed in the name of the company by a:

(1) manager of a manager-managed company;

(2) member of a member-managed company;

(3) person organizing the company, if the company has not been formed; or

(4) fiduciary, if the company is in the hands of a receiver, trustee, or other court-appointed fiduciary.

(b) A record signed under subsection (a) must state adjacent to the signature the name and capacity of the signer.

(c) Any person may sign a record to be filed under subsection (a) by an attorney-in-fact. Powers of attorney relating to the signing of records to be filed under subsection (a) by an attorney-in-fact need not be filed in the office of the [Secretary of State] as evidence of authority by the person filing but must be retained by the company.

Comment

Both a writing and a record may be signed. An electronic record is signed when a person adds a name to the record with the intention to authenticate the record. See Sections 101(16) ("record" definition) and 101(17) ("signed" definition).

Other provisions of this Act also provide for the filing of records with the filing office but do not require signing by the persons specified in clauses (1) to (3). Those specific sections prevail.

SECTION 206. FILING IN OFFICE OF [SECRETARY OF STATE]

(a) Articles of organization or any other record authorized to be filed under this [Act] must be in a medium permitted by the [Secretary of State] and must be delivered to the office of the [Secretary of State]. Unless the [Secretary of State] determines that a record fails to comply as to form with the filing requirements of this [Act], and if all filing fees have been paid, the [Secretary of State] shall file the record and send a receipt for the record and the fees to the limited liability company or its representative.

(b) Upon request and payment of a fee, the [Secretary of State] shall send to the requester a certified copy of the requested record.

(c) Except as otherwise provided in subsection (d) and Section 207(c), a record accepted for filing by the [Secretary of State] is effective:

(1) at the time of filing on the date it is filed, as evidenced by the [Secretary of State's] date and time endorsement on the original record; or

(2) at the time specified in the record as its effective time on the date it is filed.

(d) A record may specify a delayed effective time and date, and if it does so the record becomes effective at the time and date specified. If a delayed effective date but no time is specified, the record is effective at the close of business on that date. If a delayed effective date is later than the 90th day after the record is filed, the record is effective on the 90th day.

Comment

The definition and use of the term "record" permits filings with the filing office under this Act to conform to technological advances that have been adopted by the filing office. However, since Section 206(a) provides that the filing "must be in a medium permitted by the [Secretary of State]", the Act simply conforms to filing changes as they are adopted.

SECTION 207. CORRECTING FILED RECORD

(a) A limited liability company or foreign limited liability company may correct a record filed by the [Secretary of State] if the record contains a false or erroneous statement or was defectively signed.

(b) A record is corrected:

(1) by preparing articles of correction that:

(i) describe the record, including its filing date, or attach a copy of it to the articles of correction;

(ii) specify the incorrect statement and the reason it is incorrect or the manner in which the signing was defective; and

(iii) correct the incorrect statement or defective signing; and

(2) by delivering the corrected record to the [Secretary of State] for filing.

(c) Articles of correction are effective retroactively on the effective date of the record they correct except as to persons relying on the uncorrected record and adversely affected by the correction. As to those persons, articles of correction are effective when filed.

SECTION 208. CERTIFICATE OF EXISTENCE OR AUTHORIZATION

(a) A person may request the [Secretary of State] to furnish a certificate of existence for a limited liability company or a certificate of authorization for a foreign limited liability company.

(b) A certificate of existence for a limited liability company must set forth:

(1) the company's name;

(2) that it is duly organized under the laws of this State, the date of organization, whether its duration is at-will or for a specified term, and, if the latter, the period specified;

(3) if payment is reflected in the records of the [Secretary of State] and if nonpayment affects the existence of the company, that all fees, taxes, and penalties owed to this State have been paid;

(4) whether its most recent annual report required by Section 211 has been filed with the [Secretary of State];

(5) that articles of termination have not been filed; and

(6) other facts of record in the office of the [Secretary of State] which may be requested by the applicant.

(c) A certificate of authorization for a foreign limited liability company must set forth:

(1) the company's name used in this State;

(2) that it is authorized to transact business in this State;

(3) if payment is reflected in the records of the [Secretary of State] and if nonpayment affects the authorization of the company, that all fees, taxes, and penalties owed to this State have been paid;

(4) whether its most recent annual report required by Section 211 has been filed with the [Secretary of State];

(5) that a certificate of cancellation has not been filed; and

(6) other facts of record in the office of the [Secretary of State] which may be requested by the applicant.

(d) Subject to any qualification stated in the certificate, a certificate of existence or authorization issued by the [Secretary of State] may be relied upon as conclusive evidence that the domestic or foreign limited liability company is in existence or is authorized to transact business in this State.

SECTION 209. LIABILITY FOR FALSE STATEMENT IN FILED RECORD

If a record authorized or required to be filed under this [Act] contains a false statement, one who suffers loss by reliance on the statement may recover damages for the loss from a person who signed the record or caused another to sign it on the person's behalf and knew the statement to be false at the time the record was signed.

SECTION 210. FILING BY JUDICIAL ACT

If a person required by Section 205 to sign any record fails or refuses to do so, any other person who is adversely affected by the failure or refusal may petition the [designate the appropriate court] to direct the signing of the record. If the court finds that it is proper for the record to be signed and that a person so designated has failed or refused to sign the record, it shall order the [Secretary of State] to sign and file an appropriate record.

SECTION 211. ANNUAL REPORT FOR [SECRETARY OF STATE]

(a) A limited liability company, and a foreign limited liability company authorized to transact business in this State, shall deliver to the [Secretary of State] for filing an annual report that sets forth:

(1) the name of the company and the State or country under whose law it is organized;

(2) the address of its designated office and the name and address of its agent for service of process in this State;

(3) the address of its principal office; and

(4) the names and business addresses of any managers.

(b) Information in an annual report must be current as of the date the annual report is signed on behalf of the limited liability company.

(c) The first annual report must be delivered to the [Secretary of State] between [January 1 and April 1] of the year following the calendar year in which a limited liability company was organized or a foreign company was authorized to transact business. Subsequent annual reports must be delivered to the [Secretary of State] between [January 1 and April 1] of the ensuing calendar years.

(d) If an annual report does not contain the information required in subsection (a), the [Secretary of State] shall promptly notify the reporting limited liability company or foreign limited liability company and return the report to it for correction. If the report is corrected to contain the information required in subsection (a) and delivered to the [Secretary of State] within 30 days after the effective date of the notice, it is timely filed.

Comment

Failure to deliver the annual report within 60 days after its due date is a primary ground for administrative dissolution of the company under Section 809. See Comments to Sections 809 to 812.

ARTICLE 3. RELATIONS OF MEMBERS AND MANAGERS TO PERSONS DEALING WITH LIMITED LIABILITY COMPANY

SECTION 301. AGENCY OF MEMBERS AND MANAGERS

(a) Subject to subsections (b) and (c):

(1) Each member is an agent of the limited liability company for the purpose of its business, and an act of a member, including the signing of an instrument in the company's name, for apparently carrying on in the ordinary course the company's business or business of the kind carried on by the company binds the company, unless the member had no authority to act for the company in the particular matter and the person with whom the member was dealing knew or had notice that the member lacked authority.

(2) An act of a member which is not apparently for carrying on in the ordinary course the company's business or business of the

kind carried on by the company binds the company only if the act was authorized by the other members.

(b) Subject to subsection (c), in a manager-managed company:

(1) A member is not an agent of the company for the purpose of its business solely by reason of being a member. Each manager is an agent of the company for the purpose of its business, and an act of a manager, including the signing of an instrument in the company's name, for apparently carrying on in the ordinary course the company's business or business of the kind carried on by the company binds the company, unless the manager had no authority to act for the company in the particular matter and the person with whom the manager was dealing knew or had notice that the manager lacked authority.

(2) An act of a manager which is not apparently for carrying on in the ordinary course the company's business or business of the kind carried on by the company binds the company only if the act was authorized under Section 404.

(c) Unless the articles of organization limit their authority, any member of a member-managed company or manager of a manager-managed company may sign and deliver any instrument transferring or affecting the company's interest in real property. The instrument is conclusive in favor of a person who gives value without knowledge of the lack of the authority of the person signing and delivering the instrument.

Comment

Members of a member-managed and managers of manager-managed company, as agents of the firm, have the apparent authority to bind a company to third parties. Members of a manager-managed company are not as such agents of the firm and do not have the apparent authority, as members, to bind a company. Members and managers with apparent authority possess actual authority by implication unless the actual authority is restricted in an operating agreement. Apparent authority extends to acts for carrying on in the ordinary course the company's business and business of the kind carried on by the company. Acts beyond this scope bind the company only where supported by actual authority created before the act or ratified after the act.

Ordinarily, restrictions on authority in an operating agreement do not affect the apparent authority of members and managers to bind the company to third parties without notice of the restriction. However, the restriction may make a member or manager's conduct wrongful and create liability to the company for the breach. This rule is subject to three important exceptions. First, under Section 301(c), a limitation reflected in the articles of organization on the authority of any member or manager to sign and deliver an instrument affecting an interest in company real property is effective when filed, even to persons without knowledge of the agent's lack of authority. The effect of such a limitation on authority on the Federal tax classification of the company is determined by federal law. Secondly, under Section 703, a dissociated member's apparent authority terminates two years after dissociation, even to persons without knowledge of the dissociation. Thirdly, under Section 704, a dissociated member's apparent authority may be terminated earlier than the two years by filing a statement of dissociation. The statement is effective 90 days after filing, even to persons without knowledge of the filing. Together, these three provisions provide constructive knowledge to the world of the lack of apparent authority of an agent to bind the company.

SECTION 302. LIMITED LIABILITY COMPANY LIABLE FOR MEMBER'S OR MANAGER'S ACTIONABLE CONDUCT

A limited liability company is liable for loss or injury caused to a person, or for a penalty incurred, as a result of a wrongful act or omission, or other actionable conduct, of a member or manager acting in the ordinary course of business of the company or with authority of the company.

Comment

Since a member of a manager-managed company is not as such an agent, the acts of the member are not imputed to the company unless the member is acting under actual or apparent authority created by circumstances other than membership status.

SECTION 303. LIABILITY OF MEMBERS AND MANAGERS

(a) Except as otherwise provided in subsection (c), the debts, obligations, and liabilities of a limited liability company, whether arising in contract, tort, or otherwise, are solely the debts, obligations, and liabilities of the company. A member or manager is not personally liable for a debt, obligation, or liability of the company solely by reason of being or acting as a member or manager.

(b) The failure of a limited liability company to observe the usual company formalities or requirements relating to the exercise of its company powers or management of its business is not a ground for imposing personal liability on the members or managers for liabilities of the company.

(c) All or specified members of a limited liability company are liable in their capacity as members for all or specified debts, obligations, or liabilities of the company if:

(1) a provision to that effect is contained in the articles of organization; and

(2) a member so liable has consented in writing to the adoption of the provision or to be bound by the provision.

Comment

A member or manager, as an agent of the company, is not liable for the debts, obligations, and liabilities of the company simply because of the agency. A member or manager is responsible for acts or omissions to the extent those acts or omissions would be actionable in contract or tort against the member or manager if that person were acting in an individual capacity. Where a member or manager delegates or assigns the authority or duty to exercise appropriate company functions, the member or manager is ordinarily not personally liable for the acts or omissions of the officer, employee, or agent if the member or manager has complied with the duty of care set forth in Section 409(c).

Under Section 303(c), the usual liability shield may be waived, in whole or in part, provided the waiver is reflected in the articles of organization and the member has consented in writing to be bound by the waiver. The importance and unusual nature of the waiver consent requires that the consent be evidenced by a writing and not merely an unwritten record. See Comments to Section 205. The effect of a waiver on the Federal tax classification of the company is determined by federal law.

ARTICLE 4. RELATIONS OF MEMBERS TO EACH OTHER AND TO LIMITED LIABILITY COMPANY

SECTION 401. FORM OF CONTRIBUTION

A contribution of a member of a limited liability company may consist of tangible or intangible property or other benefit to the company, including money, promissory notes, services performed, or other agreements to contribute cash or property, or contracts for services to be performed.

Comment

Unless otherwise provided in an operating agreement, admission of a member and the nature and valuation of a would-be member's contribution are matters requiring the consent of all of the other members. See Section 404(c)(7). An agreement to contribute to a company is controlled by the operating agreement and therefore may not be created or modified without amending that agreement through the unanimous consent of all the members, including the member to be bound by the new contribution terms. See 404(c)(1).

SECTION 402. MEMBER'S LIABILITY FOR CONTRIBUTIONS

(a) A member's obligation to contribute money, property, or other benefit to, or to perform services for, a limited liability company is not excused by the member's death, disability, or other inability to perform personally. If a member does not make the required contribution of property or services, the member is obligated at the option of the company to contribute money equal to the value of that portion of the stated contribution which has not been made.

(b) A creditor of a limited liability company who extends credit or otherwise acts in reliance on an obligation described in subsection (a), and without notice of any compromise under Section 404(c)(5), may enforce the original obligation.

Comment

An obligation need not be in writing to be enforceable. Given the informality of some companies, a writing requirement may frustrate reasonable expectations of members based on a clear oral agreement. Obligations may be compromised with the consent of all of the members under Section 404(c)(5), but the compromise is generally effective only among the consenting members. Company creditors are bound by the compromise only as provided in Section 402(b).

SECTION 403. MEMBER'S AND MANAGER'S RIGHTS TO PAYMENTS AND REIMBURSEMENT

(a) A limited liability company shall reimburse a member or manager for payments made and indemnify a member or manager for liabilities incurred by the member or manager in the ordinary course of the business of the company or for the preservation of its business or property.

(b) A limited liability company shall reimburse a member for an advance to the company beyond the amount of contribution the member agreed to make.

(c) A payment or advance made by a member which gives rise to an obligation of a limited liability company under subsection (a) or (b) constitutes a loan to the company upon which interest accrues from the date of the payment or advance.

(d) A member is not entitled to remuneration for services performed for a limited liability company, except for reasonable compensation for services rendered in winding up the business of the company.

Comment

The presence of a liability shield will ordinarily prevent a member or manager from incurring personal liability on behalf of the company in the ordinary course of the company's business. Where a member of a member-managed or a manager of a manager-managed company incurs such liabilities, Section 403(a) provides that the company must indemnify the member or manager where that person acted in the ordinary course of the company's business or the preservation of its property. A member or manager is therefore entitled to indemnification only if the act was within the member or manager's actual authority. A member or manager is therefore not entitled to indemnification for conduct that violates the duty of care set forth in Section 409(c) or for tortuous conduct against a third party. Since members of a manager-managed company do not possess the apparent authority to bind the company, it would be more unusual for such a member to incur a liability for indemnification in the ordinary course of the company's business.

SECTION 404. MANAGEMENT OF LIMITED LIABILITY COMPANY

(a) In a member-managed company:

(1) each member has equal rights in the management and conduct of the company's business; and

(2) except as otherwise provided in subsection (c), any matter relating to the business of the company may be decided by a majority of the members.

(b) In a manager-managed company:

(1) each manager has equal rights in the management and conduct of the company's business;

(2) except as otherwise provided in subsection (c), any matter relating to the business of the company may be exclusively decided by the manager or, if there is more than one manager, by a majority of the managers; and

(3) a manager:

(i) must be designated, appointed, elected, removed, or replaced by a vote, approval, or consent of a majority of the members; and

(ii) holds office until a successor has been elected and qualified, unless the manager sooner resigns or is removed.

(c) The only matters of a member or manager-managed company's business requiring the consent of all of the members are:

(1) the amendment of the operating agreement under Section 103;

(2) the authorization or ratification of acts or transactions under Section 103(b)(2)(ii) which would otherwise violate the duty of loyalty;

(3) an amendment to the articles of organization under Section 204;

(4) the compromise of an obligation to make a contribution under Section 402(b);

(5) the compromise, as among members, of an obligation of a member to make a contribution or return money or other property paid or distributed in violation of this [Act];

(6) the making of interim distributions under Section 405(a), including the redemption of an interest;

(7) the admission of a new member;

(8) the use of the company's property to redeem an interest subject to a charging order;

(9) the consent to dissolve the company under Section 801(b)(2);

(10) a waiver of the right to have the company's business wound up and the company terminated under Section 802(b);

(11) the consent of members to merge with another entity under Section 904(c)(1); and

(12) the sale, lease, exchange, or other disposal of all, or substantially all, of the company's property with or without goodwill.

(d) Action requiring the consent of members or managers under this [Act] may be taken without a meeting.

(e) A member or manager may appoint a proxy to vote or otherwise act for the member or manager by signing an appointment instrument, either personally or by the member's or manager's attorney-in-fact.

Comment

In a member-managed company, each member has equal rights in the management and conduct of the company's business unless otherwise provided in an operating agreement. For example, an operating agreement may allocate voting rights based upon capital contributions rather than the subsection (a) per capita rule. Also, member disputes as to any matter relating to the company's business may be resolved by a majority of the members unless the matter relates to a matter specified either in subsection (c) (unanimous consent required) or in Section 801(b)(3)(i) (special consent required). Regardless of how the members allocate management rights, each member is an agent of the company with the apparent authority to bind the company in the ordinary course of its business. See Comments to Section 301(a). A member's right to participate in management terminates upon dissociation. See Section 603(b)(1).

In a manager-managed company, the members, unless also managers, have no rights in the management and conduct of the company's business unless otherwise provided in an operating agreement. If there is more than one manager, manager disputes as to any matter relating to the company's business may be resolved by a majority of the managers unless the matter relates to a matter specified either in subsection (c) (unanimous member consent required) or Section 801(b)(3)(i) (special consent required). Managers must be designated, appointed, or elected by a majority of the members. A manager need not be a member and is an agent of the company with the apparent authority to bind the company in the ordinary course of its business. See Sections 101(10) and 301(b).

To promote clarity and certainty, subsection (c) specifies those exclusive matters requiring the unanimous consent of the members, whether the company is member-or manager-managed. For example, interim distributions, including redemptions, may not be made without the unanimous consent of all the members. Unless otherwise agreed, all other company matters are to be determined under the majority of members or managers rules of subsections (a) and (b).

SECTION 405. SHARING OF AND RIGHT TO DISTRIBUTIONS

(a) Any distributions made by a limited liability company before its dissolution and winding up must be in equal shares.

(b) A member has no right to receive, and may not be required to accept, a distribution in kind.

(c) If a member becomes entitled to receive a distribution, the member has the status of, and is entitled to all remedies available to, a creditor of the limited liability company with respect to the distribution.

Comment

Recognizing the informality of many limited liability companies, this section creates a simple default rule regarding interim distributions. Any interim distributions made must be in equal shares and approved by all members. See Section 404(c)(6). The rule assumes that: profits will be shared equally; some distributions will constitute a return of contributions that should be shared equally rather than a distribution of profits; and property contributors should have the right to veto any distribution that threatens their return of contributions on liquidation. In the simple case where the members make equal contributions of property or equal contributions of services, those assumptions avoid the necessity of maintaining a complex capital account or determining profits. Where some members contribute services and others property, the unanimous vote necessary to approve interim distributions protects against unwanted distributions of contributions to service contributors. Consistently, Section 408(a) does not require the company to maintain a separate account for each member, the Act does not contain a default rule for allocating profits and losses, and Section 806(b) requires that liquidating distributions to members be made in equal shares after the return of contributions not previously returned. See Comments to Section 806(b).

Section 405(c) governs distributions declared or made when the company was solvent. Section 406 governs distributions declared or made when the company is insolvent.

SECTION 406. LIMITATIONS ON DISTRIBUTIONS

(a) A distribution may not be made if:

(1) the limited liability company would not be able to pay its debts as they become due in the ordinary course of business; or

(2) the company's total assets would be less than the sum of its total liabilities plus the amount that would be needed, if the company were to be dissolved, wound up, and terminated at the time of the distribution, to satisfy the preferential rights upon dissolution, winding up, and termination of members whose preferential rights are superior to those receiving the distribution.

(b) A limited liability company may base a determination that a distribution is not prohibited under subsection (a) on financial statements prepared on the basis of accounting practices and principles that are reasonable in the circumstances or on a fair valuation or other method that is reasonable in the circumstances.

(c) Except as otherwise provided in subsection (e), the effect of a distribution under subsection (a) is measured:

(1) in the case of distribution by purchase, redemption, or other acquisition of a distributional interest in a limited liability company, as of the date money or other property is transferred or debt incurred by the company; and

(2) in all other cases, as of the date the:

(i) distribution is authorized if the payment occurs within 120 days after the date of authorization; or

(ii) payment is made if it occurs more than 120 days after the date of authorization.

(d) A limited liability company's indebtedness to a member incurred by reason of a distribution made in accordance with this section is at parity with the company's indebtedness to its general, unsecured creditors.

(e) Indebtedness of a limited liability company, including indebtedness issued in connection with or as part of a distribution, is not considered a liability for purposes of determinations under subsection (a) if its terms provide that payment of principal and interest are made only if and to the extent that payment of a distribution to members could then be made under this section. If the indebtedness is issued as a distribution, each payment of principal or interest on the indebtedness is treated as a distribution, the effect of which is measured on the date the payment is made.

Comment

This section establishes the validity of company distributions, which in turn determines the potential liability of members and managers for improper distributions under Section 407. Distributions are improper if the company is insolvent under subsection (a) at the time the distribution is measured under subsection (c). In recognition of the informality of many limited liability companies, the solvency determination under subsection (b) may be made on the basis of a fair valuation or other method reasonable under the circumstances.

The application of the equity insolvency and balance sheet tests present special problems in the context of the purchase, redemption, or other acquisition of a company's distributional interests. Special rules establish the time of measurement of such transfers. Under Section 406(c)(1), the time for measuring the effect of a distribution to purchase a distributional interest is the date of payment. The company may make payment either by transferring property or incurring a debt to transfer property in the future. In the latter case, subsection (c)(1) establishes a clear rule that the legality of the distribution is tested when the debt is actually incurred, not later when the debt is actually paid. Under Section 406(e), indebtedness is not considered a liability for purposes of subsection (a) if the terms of the indebtedness itself provide that payments can be made only if and to the extent that a payment of a distribution could then be made under this section. The effect makes the holder of the indebtedness junior to all other creditors but senior to members in their capacity as members.

SECTION 407. LIABILITY FOR UNLAWFUL DISTRIBUTIONS

(a) A member of a member-managed company or a member or manager of a manager-managed company who votes for or assents to a distribution made in violation of Section 406, the articles of organization, or the operating agreement is personally liable to the company for the amount of the distribution which exceeds the amount that could have been distributed without violating Section 406, the articles of organization, or the operating agreement if it is established that the member or manager did not perform the member's or manager's duties in compliance with Section 409.

(b) A member of a manager-managed company who knew a distribution was made in violation of Section 406, the articles of organization, or the operating agreement is personally liable to the company, but only to the extent that the distribution received by the member exceeded the amount that could have been properly paid under Section 406.

(c) A member or manager against whom an action is brought under this section may implead in the action all:

(1) other members or managers who voted for or assented to the distribution in violation of subsection (a) and may compel contribution from them; and

(2) members who received a distribution in violation of subsection (b) and may compel contribution from the member in the amount received in violation of subsection (b).

(d) A proceeding under this section is barred unless it is commenced within two years after the distribution.

Comment

Whenever members or managers fail to meet the standards of conduct of Section 409 and vote for or assent to an unlawful distribution, they are personally liable to the company for the portion of the distribution that exceeds the maximum amount that could have been lawfully distributed. The recovery remedy under this section extends only to the company, not the company's creditors. Under subsection (a), members and managers are not liable for an unlawful distribution provided their vote in favor of the distribution satisfies the duty of care of Section 409(c).

Subsection (a) creates personal liability in favor of the company against members or managers who approve an unlawful distribution for the entire amount of a distribution that could not be lawfully distributed. Subsection (b) creates personal liability against only members who knowingly received the unlawful distribution, but only in the amount measured by the portion of the actual distribution received that was not lawfully made. Members who both vote for or assent to an unlawful distribution and receive a portion or all of the distribution will be liable, at the election of the company, under either but not both subsections.

A member or manager who is liable under subsection (a) may seek contribution under subsection (c)(1) from other members and managers who also voted for or assented to the same distribution and may also seek recoupment under subsection (c)(2) from members who received the distribution, but only if they accepted the payments knowing they were unlawful.

The two-year statute of limitations of subsection (d) is measured from the date of the distribution. The date of the distribution is determined under Section 406(c).

SECTION 408. MEMBER'S RIGHT TO INFORMATION

(a) A limited liability company shall provide members and their agents and attorneys access to its records, if any, at the company's principal office or other reasonable locations specified in the operating agreement. The company shall provide former members and their agents and attorneys access for proper purposes to records pertaining to the period during which they were members. The right of access provides the opportunity to inspect and copy records during ordinary business hours. The company may impose a reasonable charge, limited to the costs of labor and material, for copies of records furnished.

(b) A limited liability company shall furnish to a member, and to the legal representative of a deceased member or member under legal disability:

(1) without demand, information concerning the company's business or affairs reasonably required for the proper exercise of the member's rights and performance of the member's duties under the operating agreement or this [Act]; and

(2) on demand, other information concerning the company's business or affairs, except to the extent the demand or the information demanded is unreasonable or otherwise improper under the circumstances.

(c) A member has the right upon written demand given to the limited liability company to obtain at the company's expense a copy of any written operating agreement.

Comment

Recognizing the informality of many limited liability companies, subsection (a) does not require a company to maintain any records. In general, a company should maintain records necessary to enable members to determine their share of profits and losses and their rights on dissociation. If inadequate records are maintained to determine those and other critical rights, a member may maintain an action for an accounting under Section 410(a). Normally, a company will maintain at least records required by state or federal authorities regarding tax and other filings.

The obligation to furnish access includes the obligation to insure that all records, if any, are accessible in intelligible form. For example, a company that switches computer systems has an obligation either to convert the records from the old system or retain at least one computer capable of accessing the records from the old system.

The right to inspect and copy records maintained is not conditioned on a member or former member's purpose or motive. However, an abuse of the access and copy right may create a remedy in favor of the other members as a violation of the requesting member or former member's obligation of good faith and fair dealing. See Section 409(d).

Although a company is not required to maintain any records under subsection (a), it is nevertheless subject to a disclosure duty to furnish specified information under subsection (b)(1). A company must therefore furnish to members, without demand, information reasonably needed for members to exercise their rights and duties as members. A member's exercise of these duties justifies an unqualified right of access to the company's records. The member's right to company records may not be unreasonably restricted by the operating agreement. See Section 103(b)(1).

SECTION 409. GENERAL STANDARDS OF MEMBER'S AND MANAGER'S CONDUCT

(a) The only fiduciary duties a member owes to a member-managed company and its other members are the duty of loyalty and the duty of care imposed by subsections (b) and (c).

(b) A member's duty of loyalty to a member-managed company and its other members is limited to the following:

(1) to account to the company and to hold as trustee for it any property, profit, or benefit derived by the member in the conduct or winding up of the company's business or derived from a use by the member of the company's property, including the appropriation of a company's opportunity;

(2) to refrain from dealing with the company in the conduct or winding up of the company's business as or on behalf of a party having an interest adverse to the company; and

(3) to refrain from competing with the company in the conduct of the company's business before the dissolution of the company.

(c) A member's duty of care to a member-managed company and its other members in the conduct of and winding up of the company's business is limited to refraining from engaging in grossly negligent or reckless conduct, intentional misconduct, or a knowing violation of law.

(d) A member shall discharge the duties to a member-managed company and its other members under this [Act] or under the operating agreement and exercise any rights consistently with the obligation of good faith and fair dealing.

(e) A member of a member-managed company does not violate a duty or obligation under this [Act] or under the operating agreement merely because the member's conduct furthers the member's own interest.

(f) A member of a member-managed company may lend money to and transact other business with the company. As to each loan or transaction, the rights and obligations of the member are the same as those of a person who is not a member, subject to other applicable law.

(g) This section applies to a person winding up the limited liability company's business as the personal or legal representative of the last surviving member as if the person were a member.

(h) In a manager-managed company:

(1) a member who is not also a manager owes no duties to the company or to the other members solely by reason of being a member;

(2) a manager is held to the same standards of conduct prescribed for members in subsections (b) through (f);

(3) a member who pursuant to the operating agreement exercises some or all of the rights of a manager in the management and conduct of the company's business is held to the standards of conduct in subsections (b) through (f) to the extent that the member exercises the managerial authority vested in a manager by this [Act]; and

(4) a manager is relieved of liability imposed by law for violation of the standards prescribed by subsections (b) through (f) to the extent of the managerial authority delegated to the members by the operating agreement.

Comment

Under subsections (a), (c), and (h), members and managers, and their delegates, owe to the company and to the other members and managers only the fiduciary duties of loyalty and care set forth in subsections (b) and (c) and the obligation of good faith and fair dealing set forth in subsection (d). An operating agreement may not waive or eliminate the duties or obligation, but may, if not manifestly unreasonable, identify activities and determine standards for measuring the performance of them. See Section 103(b)(2) to (4).

Upon a member's dissociation, the duty to account for personal profits under subsection (b)(1), the duty to refrain from acting as or representing adverse interests under subsection (b)(2), and the duty of care under subsection (c) are limited to those derived from matters arising or events occurring before the dissociation unless the member participates in winding up the company's business. Also, the duty not to compete terminates upon dissociation. See Section 603(b)(3) and (b)(2). However, a dissociated member is not free to use confidential company information after dissociation. For example, a dissociated member of a company may immediately compete with the company for new clients but must exercise care in completing on-going client transactions and must account to the company for any fees from the old clients on account of those transactions. Subsection (c) adopts a gross negligence standard for the duty of care, the standard actually used in most partnerships and corporations.

Subsection (b)(2) prohibits a member from acting adversely or representing an adverse party to the company. The rule is based on agency principles and seeks to avoid the conflict of opposing interests in the mind of the member agent whose duty is to act for the benefit of the principal company. As reflected in subsection (f), the rule does not prohibit the member from dealing with the company other than as an adversary. A member may generally deal with the company under subsection (f) when the transaction is approved by the company.

Subsection (e) makes clear that a member does not violate the obligation of good faith under subsection (d) merely because the member's conduct furthers that member's own interest. For example, a member's refusal to vote for an interim distribution because of negative tax implications to that member does not violate that member's obligation of good faith to the other members. Likewise, a member may vote against a proposal by the company to open a shopping center that would directly compete with another shopping center in which the member owns an interest.

SECTION 410. ACTIONS BY MEMBERS

(a) A member may maintain an action against a limited liability company or another member for legal or equitable relief, with or without an accounting as to the company's business, to enforce:

(1) the member's rights under the operating agreement;

(2) the member's rights under this [Act]; and

(3) the rights and otherwise protect the interests of the member, including rights and interests arising independently of the member's relationship to the company.

(b) The accrual, and any time limited for the assertion, of a right of action for a remedy under this section is governed by other law. A right to an accounting upon a dissolution and winding up does not revive a claim barred by law.

Comment

During the existence of the company, members have under this section access to the courts to resolve claims against the company and other members, leaving broad judicial discretion to fashion appropriate legal remedies. A member pursues only that member's claim against the company or another member under this section. Article 11 governs a member's derivative pursuit of a claim on behalf of the company.

A member may recover against the company and the other members under subsection (a)(3) for personal injuries or damage to the member's property caused by another member. One member's negligence is therefore not imputed to bar another member's action.

SECTION 411. CONTINUATION OF TERM COMPANY AFTER EXPIRATION OF SPECIFIED TERM

(a) If a term company is continued after the expiration of the specified term, the rights and duties of the members and managers remain the same as they were at the expiration of the term except to the extent inconsistent with rights and duties of members and managers of an at-will company.

(b) If the members in a member-managed company or the managers in a manager-managed company continue the business without any winding up of the business of the company, it continues as an at-will company.

Comment

A term company will generally dissolve upon the expiration of its term unless either its articles are amended before the expiration of the original specified term to provide for an additional specified term or the members or managers simply continue the company as an at-will company under this section. Amendment of the articles specifying an additional term requires the unanimous consent of the members. See Section 404(c)(3). Therefore, any member has the right to block the amendment. Absent an amendment to the articles, a company may only be continued under subsection (b) as an at-will company. The decision to continue a term company as an at-will company does not require the unanimous consent of the members and is treated as an ordinary business matter with disputes resolved by a simple majority vote of either the members or managers. See Section 404. In that case, subsection (b) provides that the members' conduct amends or becomes part of an operating agreement to "continue" the company as an at-will company. The amendment to the operating agreement does not alter the rights of creditors who suffer detrimental reliance because the company does not liquidate after the expiration of its specified term. See Section 203(c)(2).

Preexisting operating-agreement provisions continue to control the relationship of the members under subsection (a) except to the extent inconsistent with the rights and duties of members of an at-will company with an operating agreement containing the same provisions. However, the members could agree in advance that, if the company's business continues after the expiration of its specified term, the company continues as a company with a new specified term or that the provisions of its operating agreement survive the expiration of the specified term.

ARTICLE 5. TRANSFEREES AND CREDITORS OF MEMBER

SECTION 501. MEMBER'S DISTRIBUTIONAL INTEREST

(a) A member is not a co-owner of, and has no transferable interest in, property of a limited liability company.

(b) A distributional interest in a limited liability company is personal property and, subject to Sections 502 and 503, may be transferred in whole or in part.

(c) An operating agreement may provide that a distributional interest may be evidenced by a certificate of the interest issued by the limited liability company and, subject to Section 503, may also provide for the transfer of any interest represented by the certificate.

Comment

Members have no property interest in property owned by a limited liability company. A distributional interest is personal property and is defined under Section 101(6) as a member's interest in distributions only and does not include the member's broader rights to participate in management under Section 404 and to inspect company records under Section 408.

Under Section 405(a), distributions are allocated in equal shares unless otherwise provided in an operating agreement. Whenever it is desirable to allocate distributions in proportion to contributions rather than per capita, certification may be useful to reduce valuation issues. The effect of certification on the Federal tax classification of the company is determined by federal law.

SECTION 502. TRANSFER OF DISTRIBUTIONAL INTEREST

A transfer of a distributional interest does not entitle the transferee to become or to exercise any rights of a member. A transfer entitles the transferee to receive, to the extent transferred, only the distributions to which the transferor would be entitled.

Comment

Under Sections 501(b) and 502, the only interest a member may freely transfer is that member's distributional interest. A member's transfer of part, all, or substantially all of a distributional interest will threaten the dissolution of the company under Section 801(b)(3)(i) only if the transfer constitutes an event of dissociation. See Section 601(3). Member dissociation has defined dissolution consequences under Section 801(b)(3)(i) depending upon whether the company is an at-will or term company and whether it is member-or manager-managed. Only the transfer of all or substantially all of a member's distributional interest constitutes or may constitute a member dissociation. A transfer of less than substantially all of a member's distributional interest is not an event of dissociation. A member ceases to be a member upon the transfer of all that member's distributional interest and that transfer is also an event of dissociation under Section 601(3). Relating the event of dissociation to the member's transfer of all of the member's distributional interest avoids the need for the company to track potential future dissociation events associated with a member no longer financially interested in the company. Also, all the remaining members may expel a member upon the transfer of "substantially all" the member's distributional interest. The expulsion is an event of dissociation under Section 601(5)(ii).

SECTION 503. RIGHTS OF TRANSFEREE

(a) A transferee of a distributional interest may become a member of a limited liability company if and to the extent that the transferor gives the transferee the right in accordance with authority described in the operating agreement or all other members consent.

(b) A transferee who has become a member, to the extent transferred, has the rights and powers, and is subject to the restrictions and liabilities, of a member under the operating agreement of a limited liability company and this [Act]. A transferee who becomes a member also is liable for the transferor member's obligations to make contributions under Section 402 and for obligations under Section 407 to return unlawful distributions, but the transferee is not obligated for the transferor member's liabilities unknown to the transferee at the time the transferee becomes a member.

(c) Whether or not a transferee of a distributional interest becomes a member under subsection (a), the transferor is not released from liability to the limited liability company under the operating agreement or this [Act].

(d) A transferee who does not become a member is not entitled to participate in the management or conduct of the limited liability company's business, require access to information concerning the company's transactions, or inspect or copy any of the company's records.

(e) A transferee who does not become a member is entitled to:

(1) receive, in accordance with the transfer, distributions to which the transferor would otherwise be entitled;

(2) receive, upon dissolution and winding up of the limited liability company's business:

(i) in accordance with the transfer, the net amount otherwise distributable to the transferor;

(ii) a statement of account only from the date of the latest statement of account agreed to by all the members;

(3) seek under Section 801(5) a judicial determination that it is equitable to dissolve and wind up the company's business.

(f) A limited liability company need not give effect to a transfer until it has notice of the transfer.

Comment

The only interest a member may freely transfer is the member's distributional interest. A transferee may acquire the remaining rights of a member only by being admitted as a member of the company by all of the remaining members. The effect of these default rules and any modifications on the Federal tax classification of the company is determined by federal law.

A transferee not admitted as a member is not entitled to participate in management, require access to information, or inspect or copy company records. The only rights of a transferee are to receive the distributions the transferor would otherwise be entitled, receive a limited statement of account, and seek a judicial dissolution under Section 801(b)(6).

Subsection (e) sets forth the rights of a transferee of an existing member. Although the rights of a dissociated member to participate in the future management of the company parallel the rights of a transferee, a dissociated member retains additional rights that accrued from that person's membership such as the right to enforce Article 7 purchase rights. See and compare Sections 603(b)(1) and 801(b)(5) and Comments.

SECTION 504. RIGHTS OF CREDITOR

(a) On application by a judgment creditor of a member of a limited liability company or of a member's transferee, a court having jurisdiction may charge the distributional interest of the judgment debtor to satisfy the judgment. The court may appoint a receiver of the share of the distributions due or to become due to the judgment debtor and make all other orders, directions, accounts, and inquiries the judgment debtor might have made or which the circumstances may require to give effect to the charging order.

(b) A charging order constitutes a lien on the judgment debtor's distributional interest. The court may order a foreclosure of a lien on a distributional interest subject to the charging order at any time. A purchaser at the foreclosure sale has the rights of a transferee.

(c) At any time before foreclosure, a distributional interest in a limited liability company which is charged may be redeemed:

(1) by the judgment debtor;

(2) with property other than the company's property, by one or more of the other members; or

(3) with the company's property, but only if permitted by the operating agreement.

(d) This [Act] does not affect a member's right under exemption laws with respect to the member's distributional interest in a limited liability company.

(e) This section provides the exclusive remedy by which a judgment creditor of a member or a transferee may satisfy a judgment out of the judgment debtor's distributional interest in a limited liability company.

Comment

A charging order is the only remedy by which a judgment creditor of a member or a member's transferee may reach the distributional interest of a member or member's transferee. Under Section 503(e), the distributional interest of a member or transferee is limited to the member's right to receive distributions from the company and to seek judicial liquidation of the company.

ARTICLE 6. MEMBER'S DISSOCIATION

SECTION 601. EVENTS CAUSING MEMBER'S DISSOCIATION

A member is dissociated from a limited liability company upon the occurrence of any of the following events:

(1) the company's having notice of the member's express will to withdraw upon the date of notice or on a later date specified by the member;

(2) an event agreed to in the operating agreement as causing the member's dissociation;

(3) upon transfer of all of a member's distributional interest, other than a transfer for security purposes or a court order charging the member's distributional interest which has not been foreclosed;

(4) the member's expulsion pursuant to the operating agreement;

(5) the member's expulsion by unanimous vote of the other members if:

(i) it is unlawful to carry on the company's business with the member;

(ii) there has been a transfer of substantially all of the member's distributional interest, other than a transfer for security purposes or a court order charging the member's distributional interest which has not been foreclosed;

(iii) within 90 days after the company notifies a corporate member that it will be expelled because it has filed a certificate of dissolution or the equivalent, its charter has been revoked, or its right to conduct business has been suspended by the jurisdiction of its incorporation, the member fails to obtain a revocation of the certificate of dissolution or a reinstatement of its charter or its right to conduct business; or

(iv) a partnership or a limited liability company that is a member has been dissolved and its business is being wound up;

(61) on application by the company or another member, the member's expulsion by judicial determination because the member:

(i) engaged in wrongful conduct that adversely and materially affected the company's business;

(ii) willfully or persistently committed a material breach of the operating agreement or of a duty owed to the company or the other members under Section 409; or

(iii) engaged in conduct relating to the company's business which makes it not reasonably practicable to carry on the business with the member;

(7) the member's:

(i) becoming a debtor in bankruptcy;

(ii) executing an assignment for the benefit of creditors;

(iii) seeking, consenting to, or acquiescing in the appointment of a trustee, receiver, or liquidator of the member or of all or substantially all of the member's property; or

(iv) failing, within 90 days after the appointment, to have vacated or stayed the appointment of a trustee, receiver, or liquidator of the member or of all or substantially all of the member's property obtained without the member's consent or acquiescence, or failing within 90 days after the expiration of a stay to have the appointment vacated;

(8) in the case of a member who is an individual:

(i) the member's death;

(ii) the appointment of a guardian or general conservator for the member; or

(iii) a judicial determination that the member has otherwise become incapable of performing the member's duties under the operating agreement;

(9) in the case of a member that is a trust or is acting as a member by virtue of being a trustee of a trust, distribution of the trust's entire rights to receive distributions from the company, but not merely by reason of the substitution of a successor trustee;

(10) in the case of a member that is an estate or is acting as a member by virtue of being a personal representative of an estate, distribution of the estate's entire rights to receive distributions from the company, but not merely the substitution of a successor personal representative; or

(11) termination of the existence of a member if the member is not an individual, estate, or trust other than a business trust.

Comment

The term "dissociation" refers to the change in the relationships among the dissociated member, the company and the other members caused by a member's ceasing to be associated in the carrying on of the company's business. Member dissociation for any reason from a member-managed at-will company will cause a dissolution of the company under Section 801(b)(3) unless a specified percentage of the remaining members agree to continue the business of the company. If the dissociation does not dissolve the company, the dissociated member's distributional interest must be immediately purchased by the company under Article 7. Member dissociation from a member-managed term company, but only for the reasons specified in paragraphs (7) to (11), will cause a dissolution of the company under Section 801(b)(3) unless a specified percentage of the remaining members agree to continue the business of the company. Member dissociations specified in paragraphs (1) to (6) do not threaten dissolution under Section 801(b)(3) of a member-managed term company. If the dissociation does not dissolve the company, it is not required to purchase the dissociated member's distributional interest until the expiration of the specified term that existed on the date of the member's dissociation. If an at-will company or a term company is manager-managed, only the dissociation of a member who is also a manager or, if there is none, any member specified above threatens dissolution. The effect on the Federal tax classification of the company creating a member-manager with a minimal interest in the company is determined by federal law.

A member may be expelled from the company under paragraph (5)(ii) by the unanimous vote of the other members upon a transfer of "substantially all" of the member's distributional interest other than for a transfer as security for a loan. A transfer of "all" of the member's distributional interest is an event of dissociation under paragraph (3).

Although a member is dissociated upon death, the effect of the dissociation where the company does not dissolve depends upon whether the company is at-will or term and whether manager-managed. Only the decedent's distributional interest transfers to the decedent's estate which does not acquire the decedent member's management rights. See Section 603(b)(1). Unless otherwise agreed, if the company was at-will, the estate's distributional interest must be purchased by the company at fair value determined at the date of death. However, if a term company, the estate and its transferees continue only as the owner of the distributional interest with no management rights until the expiration of the specified term that existed on the date of death. At the expiration of that term, the company must purchase the interest of a dissociated member if the company continues for an additional term by amending its articles or simply continues as an at-will company. See Sections 411 and 701(a)(2) and Comments. Before that time, the estate and its transferees have the right to make application for a judicial dissolution of the company under Section 801(b)(5) as successors in interest to a dissociated member. See Comments to Sections 801, 411, and 701. Where the members have allocated management rights on the basis of contributions rather than simply the number of members, a member's death will result in a transfer of management rights to the remaining members on a proportionate basis. This transfer of rights may be avoided by a provision in an operating agreement extending the Section 701(a)(1) at-will purchase right to a decedent member of a term company.

SECTION 602. MEMBER'S POWER TO DISSOCIATE; WRONGFUL DISSOCIATION

(a) Unless otherwise provided in the operating agreement, a member has the power to dissociate from a limited liability company at any time, rightfully or wrongfully, by express will pursuant to Section 601(1).

(b) If the operating agreement has not eliminated a member's power to dissociate, the member's dissociation from a limited liability company is wrongful only if:

(1) it is in breach of an express provision of the agreement; or

(2) before the expiration of the specified term of a term company:

(i) the member withdraws by express will;

(ii) the member is expelled by judicial determination under Section 601(6);

(iii) the member is dissociated by becoming a debtor in bankruptcy; or

(iv) in the case of a member who is not an individual, trust other than a business trust, or estate, the member is expelled or otherwise dissociated because it willfully dissolved or terminated its existence.

(c) A member who wrongfully dissociates from a limited liability company is liable to the company and to the other members for damages caused by the dissociation. The liability is in addition to any other obligation of the member to the company or to the other members.

(d) If a limited liability company does not dissolve and wind up its business as a result of a member's wrongful dissociation under subsection (b), damages sustained by the company for the wrongful dissociation must be offset against distributions otherwise due the member after the dissociation.

Comment

A member has the power to withdraw from both an at-will company and a term company although the effects of the withdrawal are remarkably different. See Comments to Section 601. At a minimum, the exercise of a power to withdraw enables members to terminate their continuing duties of loyalty and care. See Section 603(b)(2) to (3).

A member's power to withdraw by express will may be eliminated by an operating agreement. The effect of a such a provision on the Federal tax classification of the company is determined by federal law. An operating agreement may eliminate a member's power to withdraw by express will to promote the business continuity of an at-will company by removing the threat of dissolution and to eliminate the member's right to force the company to purchase the member's distributional interest. See Sections 801(b)(3) and 701(a)(1). However, such a member retains the ability to seek a judicial dissolution of the company. See Section 801(b)(5).

If a member's power to withdraw by express will is not eliminated in an operating agreement, the withdrawal may nevertheless be made wrongful under subsection (b). All dissociations, including withdrawal by express will, may be made wrongful under subsection (b)(1) in both an at-will and term company by the inclusion of a provision in an operating agreement. Even where an operating agreement does not eliminate the power to withdraw by express will or make any dissociation wrongful, the dissociation of a member of a term company for the reasons specified under subsection (b)(2) is wrongful. The member is liable to the company and other members for damages caused by a wrongful dissociation under subsection (c) and, under subsection (d), the damages may be offset against all distributions otherwise due the member after the dissociation. Section 701(f) provides a similar rule permitting damages for wrongful dissociation to be offset against any company purchase of the member's distributional interest.

SECTION 603. EFFECT OF MEMBER'S DISSOCIATION

(a) Upon a member's dissociation:

(1) in an at-will company, the company must cause the dissociated member's distributional interest to be purchased under [Article] 7; and

(2) in a term company:

(i) if the company dissolves and winds up its business on or before the expiration of its specified term, [Article] 8 applies to determine the dissociated member's rights to distributions; and

(ii) if the company does not dissolve and wind up its business on or before the expiration of its specified term, the company must cause the dissociated member's distributional interest to be purchased under [Article] 7 on the date of the expiration of the term specified at the time of the member's dissociation.

(b) Upon a member's dissociation from a limited liability company:

(1) the member's right to participate in the management and conduct of the company's business terminates, except as otherwise provided in Section 803, and the member ceases to be a member and is treated the same as a transferee of a member;

(2) the member's duty of loyalty under Section 409(b)(3) terminates; and

(3) the member's duty of loyalty under Section 409(b)(1) and (2) and duty of care under Section 409(c) continue only with regard to matters arising and events occurring before the member's dissociation, unless the member participates in winding up the company's business pursuant to Section 803.

Comment

Dissociation from an at-will company that does not dissolve the company causes the dissociated member's distributional interest to be immediately purchased under Article 7. See Comments to Sections 602 and 603. Dissociation from a term company that does not dissolve the company does not cause the dissociated member's distributional interest to be purchased under Article 7 until the expiration of the specified term that existed on the date of dissociation.

Subsection (b)(1) provides that a dissociated member forfeits the right to participate in the future conduct of the company's business. Dissociation does not however forfeit that member's right to enforce the Article 7 rights that accrue by reason of the dissociation. Similarly, where dissociation occurs by death, the decedent member's successors in interest may enforce that member's Article 7 rights. See and compare Comments to Section 503(e).

Dissociation terminates the member's right to participate in management, including the member's actual authority to act for the company under Section 301, and begins the two-year period after which a member's apparent authority conclusively ends. See Comments to Section 703. Dissociation also terminates a member's continuing duties of loyalty and care, except with regard to continuing transactions, to the company and other members unless the member participates in winding up the company's business. See Comments to Section 409.

ARTICLE 7. MEMBER'S DISSOCIATION WHEN BUSINESS NOT WOUND UP

SECTION 701. COMPANY PURCHASE OF DISTRIBUTIONAL INTEREST

(a) A limited liability company shall purchase a distributional interest of a:

(1) member of an at-will company for its fair value determined as of the date of the member's dissociation if the member's dissociation does not result in a dissolution and winding up of the company's business under Section 801; or

(2) member of a term company for its fair value determined as of the date of the expiration of the specified term that existed on the date of the member's dissociation if the expiration of the specified term does not result in a dissolution and winding up of the company's business under Section 801.

(b) A limited liability company must deliver a purchase offer to the dissociated member whose distributional interest is entitled to be purchased not later than 30 days after the date determined under subsection (a). The purchase offer must be accompanied by:

(1) a statement of the company's assets and liabilities as of the date determined under subsection (a);

(2) the latest available balance sheet and income statement, if any; and

(3) an explanation of how the estimated amount of the payment was calculated.

(c) If the price and other terms of a purchase of a distributional interest are fixed or are to be determined by the operating agreement, the price and terms so fixed or determined govern the purchase unless the purchaser defaults. If a default occurs, the dissociated member is entitled to commence a proceeding to have the company dissolved under Section 801(4)(iv).

(d) If an agreement to purchase the distributional interest is not made within 120 days after the date determined under subsection (a), the dissociated member, within another 120 days, may commence a proceeding against the limited liability company to enforce the purchase. The company at its expense shall notify in writing all of the remaining members, and any other person the court directs, of the commencement of the proceeding. The jurisdiction of the court in which the proceeding is commenced under this subsection is plenary and exclusive.

(e) The court shall determine the fair value of the distributional interest in accordance with the standards set forth in Section 702 together with the terms for the purchase. Upon making these determinations, the court shall order the limited liability company to purchase or cause the purchase of the interest.

(f) Damages for wrongful dissociation under Section 602(b), and all other amounts owing, whether or not currently due, from the dissociated member to a limited liability company, must be offset against the purchase price.

Comment

This section sets forth default rules regarding an otherwise mandatory company purchase of a distributional interest. Even though a dissociated member's rights to participate in the future management of the company are equivalent to those of a transferee of a member, the dissociation does not forfeit that member's right to enforce the Article 7 purchase right. Similarly, if the dissociation occurs by reason of death, the decedent member's successors in interest may enforce the Article 7 rights. See Comments to Sections 503(e) and 603(b)(1).

An at-will company must purchase a dissociated member's distributional interest under subsection (a)(1) when that member's dissociation does not result in a dissolution of the company. The purchase price is equal to the fair value of the interest determined as of the date of dissociation. Any damages for wrongful dissociation must be offset against the purchase price.

Dissociation from a term company does not require an immediate purchase of the member's interest but certain types of dissociation may cause the dissolution of the company. See Section 801(b)(3). A term company must only purchase the dissociated member's distributional interest under subsection (a)(2) on the expiration of the specified term that existed on the date of the member's dissociation. The purchase price is equal to the fair value of the interest determined as of the date of the expiration of that specified term. Any damages for wrongful dissociation must be offset against the purchase price.

The valuation dates differ between subsections (a)(1) and (a)(2) purchases. The former is valued on the date of member dissociation whereas the latter is valued on the date of the expiration of the specified term that existed on the date of dissociation. A subsection (a)(2) dissociated member therefore assumes the risk of loss between the date of dissociation and the expiration of the then stated specified term. See Comments to Section 801 (dissociated member may file application to dissolve company under Section 801(b)(6)).

The default valuation standard is fair value. See Comments to Section 702. An operating agreement may fix a method or formula for determining the purchase price and the terms of payment. The purchase right may be modified. For example, an operating agreement may eliminate a member's power to withdraw from an at-will company which narrows the dissociation events contemplated under subsection (a)(1). See Comments to Section 602(a). However, a provision in an operating agreement providing for complete forfeiture of the purchase right may be unenforceable where the power to dissociate has not also been eliminated. See Section 104(a).

The company must deliver a purchase offer to the dissociated member within 30 days after the date determined under subsection (a). The offer must be accompanied by information designed to enable the dissociated member to evaluate the fairness of the offer. The subsection (b)(3) explanation of how the offer price was calculated need not be elaborate. For example, a mere statement of the basis of the calculation, such as "book value," may be sufficient.

The company and the dissociated member must reach an agreement on the purchase price and terms within 120 days after the date determined under subsection (a). Otherwise, the dissociated member may file suit within another 120 days to enforce the purchase under subsection (d). The court will then determine the fair value and terms of purchase under subsection (e). See Section 702. The member's lawsuit is not available under subsection (c) if the parties have previously agreed to price and terms in an operating agreement.

SECTION 702. COURT ACTION TO DETERMINE FAIR VALUE OF DISTRIBUTIONAL INTEREST

(a) In an action brought to determine the fair value of a distributional interest in a limited liability company, the court shall:

(1) determine the fair value of the interest, considering among other relevant evidence the going concern value of the company, any agreement among some or all of the members fixing the price or specifying a formula for determining value of distributional interests for any other purpose, the recommendations of any appraiser appointed by the court, and any legal constraints on the company's ability to purchase the interest;

(2) specify the terms of the purchase, including, if appropriate, terms for installment payments, subordination of the purchase obligation to the rights of the company's other creditors, security for a

deferred purchase price, and a covenant not to compete or other restriction on a dissociated member; and

(3) require the dissociated member to deliver an assignment of the interest to the purchaser upon receipt of the purchase price or the first installment of the purchase price.

(b) After the dissociated member delivers the assignment, the dissociated member has no further claim against the company, its members, officers, or managers, if any, other than a claim to any unpaid balance of the purchase price and a claim under any agreement with the company or the remaining members that is not terminated by the court.

(c) If the purchase is not completed in accordance with the specified terms, the company is to be dissolved upon application under Section 801(b)(5)(iv). If a limited liability company is so dissolved, the dissociated member has the same rights and priorities in the company's assets as if the sale had not been ordered.

(d) If the court finds that a party to the proceeding acted arbitrarily, vexatiously, or not in good faith, it may award one or more other parties their reasonable expenses, including attorney's fees and the expenses of appraisers or other experts, incurred in the proceeding. The finding may be based on the company's failure to make an offer to pay or to comply with Section 701(b).

(e) Interest must be paid on the amount awarded from the date determined under Section 701(a) to the date of payment.

Comment

The default valuation standard is fair value. Under this broad standard, a court is free to determine the fair value of a distributional interest on a fair market, liquidation, or any other method deemed appropriate under the circumstances. A fair market value standard is not used because it is too narrow, often inappropriate, and assumes a fact not contemplated by this section—a willing buyer and a willing seller.

The court has discretion under subsection (a)(2) to include in its order any conditions the court deems necessary to safeguard the interests of the company and the dissociated member or transferee. The discretion may be based on the financial and other needs of the parties.

If the purchase is not consummated or the purchaser defaults, the dissociated member or transferee may make application for dissolution of the company under subsection (c). The court may deny the petition for good cause but the proceeding affords the company an opportunity to be heard on the matter and avoid dissolution. See Comments to Section 801(b)(5).

The power of the court to award all costs and attorney's fees incurred in the suit under subsection (d) is an incentive for both parties to act in good faith. See Section 701(c).

SECTION 703. DISSOCIATED MEMBER'S POWER TO BIND LIMITED LIABILITY COMPANY

For two years after a member dissociates without the dissociation resulting in a dissolution and winding up of a limited liability company's business, the company, including a surviving company under [Article] 9, is bound by an act of the dissociated member which would have bound the company under Section 301 before dissociation only if at the time of entering into the transaction the other party:

(1) reasonably believed that the dissociated member was then a member;

(2) did not have notice of the member's dissociation; and

(3) is not deemed to have had notice under Section 704.

Comment

A dissociated member of a member-managed company does not have actual authority to act for the company. See Section 603(b)(1). Under Section 301(a), a dissociated member of a member-managed company has apparent authority to bind the company in ordinary course transactions except as to persons who knew or had notice of the dissociation. This section modifies that rule by requiring the person to show reasonable reliance on the member's status as a member provided a Section 704 statement has not been filed within the previous 90 days. See also Section 804 (power to bind after dissolution).

SECTION 704. STATEMENT OF DISSOCIATION

(a) A dissociated member or a limited liability company may file in the office of the [Secretary of State] a statement of dissociation stating the name of the company and that the member is dissociated from the company.

(b) For the purposes of Sections 301 and 703, a person not a member is deemed to have notice of the dissociation 90 days after the statement of dissociation is filed.

ARTICLE 8. WINDING UP COMPANY'S BUSINESS

SECTION 801. EVENTS CAUSING DISSOLUTION AND WINDING UP OF COMPANY'S BUSINESS

A limited liability company is dissolved, and its business must be wound up, upon the occurrence of any of the following events:

(1) an event specified in the operating agreement;

(2) consent of the number or percentage of members specified in the operating agreement;

(3) an event that makes it unlawful for all or substantially all of the business of the company to be continued, but any cure of

illegality within 90 days after notice to the company of the event is effective retroactively to the date of the event for purposes of this section;

(4) on application by a member or a dissociated member, upon entry of a judicial decree that:

(i) the economic purpose of the company is likely to be unreasonably frustrated;

(ii) another member has engaged in conduct relating to the company's business that makes it not reasonably practicable to carry on the company's business with that member;

(iii) it is not otherwise reasonably practicable to carry on the company's business in conformity with the articles of organization and the operating agreement;

(iv) the company failed to purchase the petitioner's distributional interest as required by Section 701; or

(v) the managers or members in control of the company have acted, are acting, or will act in a manner that is illegal, oppressive, fraudulent, or unfairly prejudicial to the petitioner; or

(5) on application by a transferee of a member's interest, a judicial determination that it is equitable to wind up the company's business:

(i) after the expiration of the specified term, if the company was for a specified term at the time the applicant became a transferee by member dissociation, transfer, or entry of a charging order that gave rise to the transfer; or

(ii) at any time, if the company was at will at the time the applicant became a transferee by member dissociation, transfer, or entry of a charging order that gave rise to the transfer.

Comment

The dissolution rules of this section are mostly default rules and may be modified by an operating agreement. However, an operating agreement may not modify or eliminate the dissolution events specified in subsection (b)(4) (illegal business) or subsection (b)(5) (member application). See Section 103(b)(6).

The relationship between member dissociation and company dissolution is set forth under subsection (b)(3). In order for member dissociation to cause the dissolution of a company, the dissociation must be recognized as one that triggers a dissolution vote and a specified percentage of the remaining members must fail to agree within 90 days after the dissociation to avoid dissolution under subsection (b)(3)(i). See Comments to Section 601. The means of voting and standard for avoiding dissolution may be modified in an operating agreement and would constitute a "right to continue" recognized under subsection (b)(3)(ii). The effect on the Federal tax classification of the company altering the specified percentage vote is determined by federal law.

Decision-making under this Act is normally by a majority in number of the members or managers for ordinary matters and unanimity for specified extraordinary matters. See Section 404(a) to (c). The majority of members holding requisite distributions rights varies this rule and is used only in subsection (b)(3)(i). Under this Act, distributions are shared on a per capita basis. See Comments to Section 405. Therefore, under the default rule, a majority in number would also be a majority of members holding requisite distributions rights unless the company has in excess of one hundred members.

A member or dissociated member whose interest is not required to be purchased by the company under Section 701 may make application under subsection (b)(5) for the involuntary dissolution of both an at-will company and a term company. A transferee may make application under subsection (b)(6). A transferee's application right, but not that of a member or dissociated member, may be modified by an operating agreement. See Section 103(b)(6). A dissociated member is not treated as a transferee for purposes of an application under subsections (b)(5) and (b)(6). See Section 603(b)(1). For example, this affords reasonable protection to a dissociated member of a term company to make application under subsection (b)(5) before the expiration of the term that existed at the time of dissociation. For purposes of a subsection (b)(5) application, a dissociated member includes a successor in interest, e.g., surviving spouse. See Comments to Section 601.

In the case of applications under subsections (b)(5) and (b)(6), the applicant has the burden of proving either the existence of one or more of the circumstances listed under subsection (b)(5) or that it is equitable to wind up the company's business under subsection (b)(6). Proof of the existence of one or more of the circumstances in subsection (b)(5), may be the basis of a subsection (b)(6) application. Even where the burden of proof is met, the court has the discretion to order relief other than the dissolution of the company. Examples include an accounting, a declaratory judgment, a distribution, the purchase of the distributional interest of the applicant or another member, or the appointment of a receiver. See Section 410.

A court has the discretion to dissolve a company under subsection (b)(5)(i) when the company has a very poor financial record that is not likely to improve. In this instance, dissolution is an alternative to placing the company in bankruptcy. A court may dissolve a company under subsections (b)(5)(ii), (b)(5)(iii), and (b)(5)(iv) for serious and protracted misconduct by one or more members. Subsection (b)(5)(v) provides a specific remedy for an improper squeeze-out of a member.

In determining whether and what type of relief to order under subsections (b)(5) and (b)(6) involuntary dissolution suits, a court should take into account other rights and remedies of the applicant. For example, a court should not grant involuntary dissolution of an at-will company if the applicant member has the right to dissociate and force the company to purchase that member's distributional interest under Sections 701 and 702. In other cases, involuntary dissolution or some other remedy such as a buy-out might be appropriate where, for example, one or more members have (i) engaged in fraudulent or unconscionable conduct, (ii) improperly expelled a member seeking an unfair advantage of a provision in an operating agreement that provides for a significantly lower price on expulsion than would be payable in the event of voluntary dissociation, or (iii) engaged in serious misconduct and the applicant member is a member of a term company and would not have a right to have the company purchase that member's distributional interest upon dissociation until the expiration of the company's specified term.

SECTION 802. LIMITED LIABILITY COMPANY CONTINUES AFTER DISSOLUTION

(a) Subject to subsection (b), a limited liability company continues after dissolution only for the purpose of winding up its business.

(b) At any time after the dissolution of a limited liability company and before the winding up of its business is completed, the members, including a dissociated member whose dissociation caused the dissolution, may unanimously waive the right to have the company's business wound up and the company terminated. In that case:

(1) the limited liability company resumes carrying on its business as if dissolution had never occurred and any liability incurred by the company or a member after the dissolution and before the waiver is determined as if the dissolution had never occurred; and

(2) the rights of a third party accruing under Section 804(a) or arising out of conduct in reliance on the dissolution before the third party knew or received a notification of the waiver are not adversely affected.

Comment

The liability shield continues in effect for the winding up period because the legal existence of the company continues under subsection (a). The company is terminated on the filing of articles of termination. See Section 805.

SECTION 803. RIGHT TO WIND UP LIMITED LIABILITY COMPANY'S BUSINESS

(a) After dissolution, a member who has not wrongfully dissociated may participate in winding up a limited liability company's business, but on application of any member, member's legal representative, or transferee, the [designate the appropriate court], for good cause shown, may order judicial supervision of the winding up.

(b) A legal representative of the last surviving member may wind up a limited liability company's business.

(c) A person winding up a limited liability company's business may preserve the company's business or property as a going concern for a reasonable time, prosecute and defend actions and proceedings, whether civil, criminal, or administrative, settle and close the company's business, dispose of and transfer the company's property, discharge the company's liabilities, distribute the assets of the company pursuant to Section 806, settle disputes by mediation or arbitration, and perform other necessary acts.

SECTION 804. MEMBER'S OR MANAGER'S POWER AND LIABILITY AS AGENT AFTER DISSOLUTION

(a) A limited liability company is bound by a member's or manager's act after dissolution that:

(1) is appropriate for winding up the company's business; or

(2) would have bound the company under Section 301 before dissolution, if the other party to the transaction did not have notice of the dissolution.

(b) A member or manager who, with knowledge of the dissolution, subjects a limited liability company to liability by an act that is not appropriate for winding up the company's business is liable to the company for any damage caused to the company arising from the liability.

Comment

After dissolution, members and managers continue to have the authority to bind the company that they had prior to dissolution provided that the third party did not have notice of the dissolution. See Section 102(b) (notice defined). Otherwise, they have only the authority appropriate for winding up the company's business. See Section 703 (agency power of member after dissociation).

SECTION 805. ARTICLES OF TERMINATION

(a) At any time after dissolution and winding up, a limited liability company may terminate its existence by filing with the [Secretary of State] articles of termination stating:

(1) the name of the company;

(2) the date of the dissolution; and

(3) that the company's business has been wound up and the legal existence of the company has been terminated.

(b) The existence of a limited liability company is terminated upon the filing of the articles of termination, or upon a later effective date, if specified in the articles of termination.

Comment

The termination of legal existence also terminates the company's liability shield. See Comments to Section 802 (liability shield continues in effect during winding up). It also ends the company's responsibility to file an annual report. See Section 211.

SECTION 806. DISTRIBUTION OF ASSETS IN WINDING UP LIMITED LIABILITY COMPANY'S BUSINESS

(a) In winding up a limited liability company's business, the assets of the company must be applied to discharge its obligations to creditors, including members who are creditors. Any surplus must be applied to pay in money the net amount distributable to members in accordance with their right to distributions under subsection (b).

(b) Each member is entitled to a distribution upon the winding up of the limited liability company's business consisting of a return of all contributions which have not previously been returned and a distribution of any remainder in equal shares.

SECTION 807. KNOWN CLAIMS AGAINST DISSOLVED LIMITED LIABILITY COMPANY

(a) A dissolved limited liability company may dispose of the known claims against it by following the procedure described in this section.

(b) A dissolved limited liability company shall notify its known claimants in writing of the dissolution. The notice must:

(1) specify the information required to be included in a claim;

(2) provide a mailing address where the claim is to be sent;

(3) state the deadline for receipt of the claim, which may not be less than 120 days after the date the written notice is received by the claimant; and

(4) state that the claim will be barred if not received by the deadline.

(c) A claim against a dissolved limited liability company is barred if the requirements of subsection (b) are met, and:

(1) the claim is not received by the specified deadline; or

(2) in the case of a claim that is timely received but rejected by the dissolved company, the claimant does not commence a proceeding to enforce the claim within 90 days after the receipt of the notice of the rejection.

(d) For purposes of this section, "claim" does not include a contingent liability or a claim based on an event occurring after the effective date of dissolution.

Comment

A known claim will be barred when the company provides written notice to a claimant that a claim must be filed with the company no later than at least 120 days after receipt of the written notice and the claimant fails to file the claim. If the claim is timely received but is rejected by the company, the claim is nevertheless barred unless the claimant files suit to enforce the claim within 90 days after the receipt of the notice of rejection. A claim described in subsection (d) is not a "known" claim and is governed by Section 808. This section does not extend any other applicable statutes of limitation. See Section 104. Depending on the management of the company, members or managers must discharge or make provision for discharging all of the company's known liabilities before distributing the remaining assets to the members. See Sections 806(a), 406, and 407.

SECTION 808. OTHER CLAIMS AGAINST DISSOLVED LIMITED LIABILITY COMPANY

(a) A dissolved limited liability company may publish notice of its dissolution and request persons having claims against the company to present them in accordance with the notice.

(b) The notice must:

(1) be published at least once in a newspaper of general circulation in the [county] in which the dissolved limited liability company's principal office is located or, if none in this State, in which its designated office is or was last located;

(2) describe the information required to be contained in a claim and provide a mailing address where the claim is to be sent; and

(3) state that a claim against the limited liability company is barred unless a proceeding to enforce the claim is commenced within five years after publication of the notice.

(c) If a dissolved limited liability company publishes a notice in accordance with subsection (b), the claim of each of the following claimants is barred unless the claimant commences a proceeding to enforce the claim against the dissolved company within five years after the publication date of the notice:

(1) a claimant who did not receive written notice under Section 807;

(2) a claimant whose claim was timely sent to the dissolved company but not acted on; and

(3) a claimant whose claim is contingent or based on an event occurring after the effective date of dissolution.

(d) A claim not barred under this section may be enforced:

(1) against the dissolved limited liability company, to the extent of its undistributed assets; or

(2) if the assets have been distributed in liquidation, against a member of the dissolved company to the extent of the member's proportionate share of the claim or the company's assets distributed to the member in liquidation, whichever is less, but a member's total

liability for all claims under this section may not exceed the total amount of assets distributed to the member.

Comment

An unknown claim will be barred when the company publishes notice requesting claimants to file claims with the company and stating that claims will be barred unless the claimant files suit to enforce the claim within five years after the date of publication. The procedure also bars known claims where the claimant either did not receive written notice described in Section 807 or received notice, mailed a claim, but the company did not act on the claim.

Depending on the management of the company, members or managers must discharge or make provision for discharging all of the company's known liabilities before distributing the remaining assets to the members. See Comment to Section 807. This section does not contemplate that a company will postpone member distributions until all unknown claims are barred under this section. In appropriate cases, the company may purchase insurance or set aside funds permitting a distribution of the remaining assets. Where winding up distributions have been made to members, subsection (d)(2) authorizes recovery against those members. However, a claimant's recovery against a member is limited to the lesser of the member's proportionate share of the claim or the amount received in the distribution. This section does not extend any other applicable statutes of limitation. See Section 104.

SECTION 809. GROUNDS FOR ADMINISTRATIVE DISSOLUTION

The [Secretary of State] may commence a proceeding to dissolve a limited liability company administratively if the company does not:

(1) pay any fees, taxes, or penalties imposed by this [Act] or other law within 60 days after they are due; or

(2) deliver its annual report to the [Secretary of State] within 60 days after it is due.

Comment

Administrative dissolution is an effective enforcement mechanism for a variety of statutory obligations under this Act and it avoids the more expensive judicial dissolution process. When applicable, administrative dissolution avoids wasteful attempts to compel compliance by a company abandoned by its members.

SECTION 810. PROCEDURE FOR AND EFFECT OF ADMINISTRATIVE DISSOLUTION

(a) If the [Secretary of State] determines that a ground exists for administratively dissolving a limited liability company, the [Secretary of State] shall enter a record of the determination and serve the company with a copy of the record.

(b) If the company does not correct each ground for dissolution or demonstrate to the reasonable satisfaction of the [Secretary of State] that each ground determined by the [Secretary of State] does not exist within 60 days after service of the notice, the [Secretary of State] shall administratively dissolve the company by signing a certification of the dissolution that recites the ground for dissolution and its effective date. The [Secretary of State] shall file the original of the certificate and serve the company with a copy of the certificate.

(c) A company administratively dissolved continues its existence but may carry on only business necessary to wind up and liquidate its business and affairs under Section 802 and to notify claimants under Sections 807 and 808.

(d) The administrative dissolution of a company does not terminate the authority of its agent for service of process.

Comment

A company's failure to comply with a ground for administrative dissolution may simply occur because of oversight. Therefore, subsections (a) and (b) set forth a mandatory notice by the filing officer to the company of the ground for dissolution and a 60 day grace period for correcting the ground.

SECTION 811. REINSTATEMENT FOLLOWING ADMINISTRATIVE DISSOLUTION

(a) A limited liability company administratively dissolved may apply to the [Secretary of State] for reinstatement within two years after the effective date of dissolution. The application must:

(1) recite the name of the company and the effective date of its administrative dissolution;

(2) state that the ground for dissolution either did not exist or have been eliminated;

(3) state that the company's name satisfies the requirements of Section 105; and

(4) contain a certificate from the [taxing authority] reciting that all taxes owed by the company have been paid.

(b) If the [Secretary of State] determines that the application contains the information required by subsection (a) and that the information is correct, the [Secretary of State] shall cancel the certificate of dissolution and prepare a certificate of reinstatement that recites this determination and the effective date of reinstatement, file the original of the certificate, and serve the company with a copy of the certificate.

(c) When reinstatement is effective, it relates back to and takes effect as of the effective date of the administrative dissolution and the company may resume its business as if the administrative dissolution had never occurred.

SECTION 812. APPEAL FROM DENIAL OF REINSTATEMENT

(a) If the [Secretary of State] denies a limited liability company's application for reinstatement following administrative dissolution, the [Secretary of State] shall serve the company with a record that explains the reason or reasons for denial.

(b) The company may appeal the denial of reinstatement to the [name appropriate] court within 30 days after service of the notice of denial is perfected. The company appeals by petitioning the court to set aside the dissolution and attaching to the petition copies of the [Secretary of State's] certificate of dissolution, the company's application for reinstatement, and the [Secretary of State's] notice of denial.

(c) The court may summarily order the [Secretary of State] to reinstate the dissolved company or may take other action the court considers appropriate.

(d) The court's final decision may be appealed as in other civil proceedings.

ARTICLE 9. CONVERSIONS AND MERGERS

SECTION 901. DEFINITIONS

In this [article]:

(1) "Corporation" means a corporation under [the State Corporation Act], a predecessor law, or comparable law of another jurisdiction.

(2) "General partner" means a partner in a partnership and a general partner in a limited partnership.

(3) "Limited partner" means a limited partner in a limited partnership.

(4) "Limited partnership" means a limited partnership created under [the State Limited Partnership Act], a predecessor law, or comparable law of another jurisdiction.

(5) "Partner" includes a general partner and a limited partner.

(6) "Partnership" means a general partnership under [the State Partnership Act], a predecessor law, or comparable law of another jurisdiction.

(7) "Partnership agreement" means an agreement among the partners concerning the partnership or limited partnership.

(8) "Shareholder" means a shareholder in a corporation.

Comment

Section 907 makes clear that the provisions of Article 9 are not mandatory. Therefore, a partnership or a limited liability company may convert or merge in any other manner provided by law. However, if the requirements of Article 9 are followed, the conversion or merger is legally valid. Article 9 is not restricted to domestic business entities.

SECTION 902. CONVERSION OF PARTNERSHIP OR LIMITED PARTNERSHIP TO LIMITED LIABILITY COMPANY

(a) A partnership or limited partnership may be converted to a limited liability company pursuant to this section.

(b) The terms and conditions of a conversion of a partnership or limited partnership to a limited liability company must be approved by all of the partners or by a number or percentage of the partners required for conversion in the partnership agreement.

(c) An agreement of conversion must set forth the terms and conditions of the conversion of the interests of partners of a partnership or of a limited partnership, as the case may be, into interests in the converted limited liability company or the cash or other consideration to be paid or delivered as a result of the conversion of the interests of the partners, or a combination thereof.

(d) After a conversion is approved under subsection (b), the partnership or limited partnership shall file articles of organization in the office of the [Secretary of State] which satisfy the requirements of Section 203 and contain:

(1) a statement that the partnership or limited partnership was converted to a limited liability company from a partnership or limited partnership, as the case may be;

(2) its former name;

(3) a statement of the number of votes cast by the partners entitled to vote for and against the conversion and, if the vote is less than unanimous, the number or percentage required to approve the conversion under subsection (b); and

(4) in the case of a limited partnership, a statement that the certificate of limited partnership is to be canceled as of the date the conversion took effect.

(e) In the case of a limited partnership, the filing of articles of organization under subsection (d) cancels its certificate of limited partnership as of the date the conversion took effect.

(f) A conversion takes effect when the articles of organization are filed in the office of the [Secretary of State] or at any later date specified in the articles of organization.

(g) A general partner who becomes a member of a limited liability company as a result of a conversion remains liable as a partner for an obligation incurred by the partnership or limited partnership before the conversion takes effect.

(h) A general partner's liability for all obligations of the limited liability company incurred after the conversion takes effect is that of a member of the company. A limited partner who becomes a member as a result of a conversion remains liable only to the extent the limited partner was liable for an obligation incurred by the limited partnership before the conversion takes effect.

Comment

Subsection (b) makes clear that the terms and conditions of the conversion of a general or limited partnership to a limited liability company must be approved by all of the partners unless the partnership agreement specifies otherwise.

SECTION 903. EFFECT OF CONVERSION; ENTITY UNCHANGED

(a) A partnership or limited partnership that has been converted pursuant to this [article] is for all purposes the same entity that existed before the conversion.

(b) When a conversion takes effect:

(1) all property owned by the converting partnership or limited partnership vests in the limited liability company;

(2) all debts, liabilities, and other obligations of the converting partnership or limited partnership continue as obligations of the limited liability company;

(3) an action or proceeding pending by or against the converting partnership or limited partnership may be continued as if the conversion had not occurred;

(4) except as prohibited by other law, all of the rights, privileges, immunities, powers, and purposes of the converting partnership or limited partnership vest in the limited liability company; and

(5) except as otherwise provided in the agreement of conversion under Section 902(c), all of the partners of the converting partnership continue as members of the limited liability company.

Comment

A conversion is not a conveyance or transfer and does not give rise to claims of reverter or impairment of title based on a prohibited conveyance or transfer. Under subsection (b)(1), title to all partnership property, including real estate, vests in the limited liability company as a matter of law without reversion or impairment.

SECTION 904. MERGER OF ENTITIES

(a) Pursuant to a plan of merger approved under subsection (c), a limited liability company may be merged with or into one or more limited liability companies, foreign limited liability companies, corporations, foreign corporations, partnerships, foreign partnerships, limited partnerships, foreign limited partnerships, or other domestic or foreign entities.

(b) A plan of merger must set forth:

(1) the name of each entity that is a party to the merger;

(2) the name of the surviving entity into which the other entities will merge;

(3) the type of organization of the surviving entity;

(4) the terms and conditions of the merger;

(5) the manner and basis for converting the interests of each party to the merger into interests or obligations of the surviving entity, or into money or other property in whole or in part; and

(6) the street address of the surviving entity's principal place of business.

(c) A plan of merger must be approved:

(1) in the case of a limited liability company that is a party to the merger, by all of the members or by a number or percentage of members specified in the operating agreement;

(2) in the case of a foreign limited liability company that is a party to the merger, by the vote required for approval of a merger by the law of the State or foreign jurisdiction in which the foreign limited liability company is organized;

(3) in the case of a partnership or domestic limited partnership that is a party to the merger, by the vote required for approval of a conversion under Section 902(b); and

(4) in the case of any other entities that are parties to the merger, by the vote required for approval of a merger by the law of this State or of the State or foreign jurisdiction in which the entity is organized and, in the absence of such a requirement, by all the owners of interests in the entity.

(d) After a plan of merger is approved and before the merger takes effect, the plan may be amended or abandoned as provided in the plan.

(e) The merger is effective upon the filing of the articles of merger with the [Secretary of State], or at such later date as the articles may provide.

Comment

This section sets forth a "safe harbor" for cross-entity mergers of limited liability companies with both domestic and foreign: corporations, general and limited partnerships, and other limited liability companies. Subsection (c) makes clear that the terms and conditions of the plan of merger must be approved by all of the partners unless applicable state law specifies otherwise for the merger.

SECTION 905. ARTICLES OF MERGER

(a) After approval of the plan of merger under Section 904(c), unless the merger is abandoned under Section 904(d), articles of merger must be signed on behalf of each limited liability company and other entity that is a party to the merger and delivered to the [Secretary of State] for filing. The articles must set forth:

(1) the name and jurisdiction of formation or organization of each of the limited liability companies and other entities that are parties to the merger;

(2) for each limited liability company that is to merge, the date its articles of organization were filed with the [Secretary of State];

(3) that a plan of merger has been approved and signed by each limited liability company and other entity that is to merge;

(4) the name and address of the surviving limited liability company or other surviving entity;

(5) the effective date of the merger;

(6) if a limited liability company is the surviving entity, such changes in its articles of organization as are necessary by reason of the merger;

(7) if a party to a merger is a foreign limited liability company, the jurisdiction and date of filing of its initial articles of organization and the date when its application for authority was filed by the [Secretary of State] or, if an application has not been filed, a statement to that effect; and

(8) if the surviving entity is not a limited liability company, an agreement that the surviving entity may be served with process in this State and is subject to liability in any action or proceeding for the enforcement of any liability or obligation of any limited liability company previously subject to suit in this State which is to merge, and for the enforcement, as provided in this [Act], of the right of members of any limited liability company to receive payment for their interest against the surviving entity.

(b) If a foreign limited liability company is the surviving entity of a merger, it may not do business in this State until an application for that authority is filed with the [Secretary of State].

(c) The surviving limited liability company or other entity shall furnish a copy of the plan of merger, on request and without cost, to any member of any limited liability company or any person holding an interest in any other entity that is to merge.

(d) Articles of merger operate as an amendment to the limited liability company's articles of organization.

SECTION 906. EFFECT OF MERGER

(a) When a merger takes effect:

(1) the separate existence of each limited liability company and other entity that is a party to the merger, other than the surviving entity, terminates;

(2) all property owned by each of the limited liability companies and other entities that are party to the merger vests in the surviving entity;

(3) all debts, liabilities, and other obligations of each limited liability company and other entity that is party to the merger become the obligations of the surviving entity;

(4) an action or proceeding pending by or against a limited liability company or other party to a merger may be continued as if the merger had not occurred or the surviving entity may be substituted as a party to the action or proceeding; and

(5) except as prohibited by other law, all the rights, privileges, immunities, powers, and purposes of every limited liability company and other entity that is a party to a merger vest in the surviving entity.

(b) The [Secretary of State] is an agent for service of process in an action or proceeding against the surviving foreign entity to enforce an obligation of any party to a merger if the surviving foreign entity fails to appoint or maintain an agent designated for service of process in this State or the agent for service of process cannot with reasonable diligence be found at the designated office. Upon receipt of process, the [Secretary of State] shall send a copy of the process by registered or certified mail, return receipt requested, to the surviving entity at the address set forth in the articles of merger. Service is effected under this subsection at the earliest of:

(1) the date the company receives the process, notice, or demand;

(2) the date shown on the return receipt, if signed on behalf of the company; or

(3) five days after its deposit in the mail, if mailed postpaid and correctly addressed.

(c) A member of the surviving limited liability company is liable for all obligations of a party to the merger for which the member was personally liable before the merger.

(d) Unless otherwise agreed, a merger of a limited liability company that is not the surviving entity in the merger does not require the limited liability company to wind up its business under this [Act] or pay its liabilities and distribute its assets pursuant to this [Act].

(e) Articles of merger serve as articles of dissolution for a limited liability company that is not the surviving entity in the merger.

SECTION 907. [ARTICLE] NOT EXCLUSIVE

This [article] does not preclude an entity from being converted or merged under other law.

ARTICLE 10. FOREIGN LIMITED LIABILITY COMPANIES

SECTION 1001. LAW GOVERNING FOREIGN LIMITED LIABILITY COMPANIES

(a) The laws of the State or other jurisdiction under which a foreign limited liability company is organized govern its organization and internal affairs and the liability of its managers, members, and their transferees.

(b) A foreign limited liability company may not be denied a certificate of authority by reason of any difference between the laws of another jurisdiction under which the foreign company is organized and the laws of this State.

(c) A certificate of authority does not authorize a foreign limited liability company to engage in any business or exercise any power that a limited liability company may not engage in or exercise in this State.

Comment

The law where a foreign limited liability company is organized, rather than this Act, governs that company's internal affairs and the liability of its owners. Accordingly, any difference between the laws of the foreign jurisdiction and this Act will not constitute grounds for denial of a certificate of authority to transact business in this State. However, a foreign limited liability company transacting business in this State by virtue of a certificate of authority is limited to the business and powers that a limited liability company may lawfully pursue and exercise under Section 112.

SECTION 1002. APPLICATION FOR CERTIFICATE OF AUTHORITY

(a) A foreign limited liability company may apply for a certificate of authority to transact business in this State by delivering an application to the [Secretary of State] for filing. The application must set forth:

(1) the name of the foreign company or, if its name is unavailable for use in this State, a name that satisfies the requirements of Section 1005;

(2) the name of the State or country under whose law it is organized;

(3) the street address of its principal office;

(4) the address of its initial designated office in this State;

(5) the name and street address of its initial agent for service of process in this State;

(6) whether the duration of the company is for a specified term and, if so, the period specified;

(7) whether the company is manager-managed, and, if so, the name and address of each initial manager; and

(8) whether the members of the company are to be liable for its debts and obligations under a provision similar to Section 303(c).

(b) A foreign limited liability company shall deliver with the completed application a certificate of existence or a record of similar import authenticated by the secretary of state or other official having custody of company records in the State or country under whose law it is organized.

Comment

As with articles of organization, the application must be signed and filed with the filing office. See Sections 105, 107 (name registration), 205, 206, 209 (liability for false statements), and 1005.

SECTION 1003. ACTIVITIES NOT CONSTITUTING TRANSACTING BUSINESS

(a) Activities of a foreign limited liability company that do not constitute transacting business in this State within the meaning of this [article] include:

(1) maintaining, defending, or settling an action or proceeding;

(2) holding meetings of its members or managers or carrying on any other activity concerning its internal affairs;

(3) maintaining bank accounts;

(4) maintaining offices or agencies for the transfer, exchange, and registration of the foreign company's own securities or maintaining trustees or depositories with respect to those securities;

(5) selling through independent contractors;

(6) soliciting or obtaining orders, whether by mail or through employees or agents or otherwise, if the orders require acceptance outside this State before they become contracts;

(7) creating or acquiring indebtedness, mortgages, or security interests in real or personal property;

(8) securing or collecting debts or enforcing mortgages or other security interests in property securing the debts, and holding, protecting, and maintaining property so acquired;

(9) conducting an isolated transaction that is completed within 30 days and is not one in the course of similar transactions of a like manner; and

(10) transacting business in interstate commerce.

(b) For purposes of this [article], the ownership in this State of income-producing real property or tangible personal property, other than property excluded under subsection (a), constitutes transacting business in this State.

(c) This section does not apply in determining the contacts or activities that may subject a foreign limited liability company to service of process, taxation, or regulation under any other law of this State.

SECTION 1004. ISSUANCE OF CERTIFICATE OF AUTHORITY

Unless the [Secretary of State] determines that an application for a certificate of authority fails to comply as to form with the filing requirements of this [Act], the [Secretary of State], upon payment of all filing fees, shall file the application and send a receipt for it and the fees to the limited liability company or its representative.

SECTION 1005. NAME OF FOREIGN LIMITED LIABILITY COMPANY

(a) If the name of a foreign limited liability company does not satisfy the requirements of Section 105, the company, to obtain or maintain a certificate of authority to transact business in this State, must use a fictitious name to transact business in this State if its real name is unavailable and it delivers to the [Secretary of State] for filing a copy of the resolution of its managers, in the case of a manager-managed company, or of its members, in the case of a member-managed company, adopting the fictitious name.

(b) Except as authorized by subsections (c) and (d), the name, including a fictitious name to be used to transact business in this State, of a foreign limited liability company must be distinguishable upon the records of the [Secretary of State] from:

(1) the name of any corporation, limited partnership, or company incorporated, organized, or authorized to transact business in this State;

(2) a name reserved or registered under Section 106 or 107; and

(3) the fictitious name of another foreign limited liability company authorized to transact business in this State.

(c) A foreign limited liability company may apply to the [Secretary of State] for authority to use in this State a name that is not distinguishable upon the records of the [Secretary of State] from a name described in subsection (b). The [Secretary of State] shall authorize use of the name applied for if:

(1) the present user, registrant, or owner of a reserved name consents to the use in a record and submits an undertaking in form satisfactory to the [Secretary of State] to change its name to a name that is distinguishable upon the records of the [Secretary of State] from the name of the foreign applying limited liability company; or

(2) the applicant delivers to the [Secretary of State] a certified copy of a final judgment of a court establishing the applicant's right to use the name applied for in this State.

(d) A foreign limited liability company may use in this State the name, including the fictitious name, of another domestic or foreign entity that is used in this State if the other entity is incorporated, organized, or authorized to transact business in this State and the foreign limited liability company:

(1) has merged with the other entity;

(2) has been formed by reorganization of the other entity; or

(3) has acquired all or substantially all of the assets, including the name, of the other entity.

(e) If a foreign limited liability company authorized to transact business in this State changes its name to one that does not satisfy the requirements of Section 105, it may not transact business in this State under the name as changed until it adopts a name satisfying the requirements of Section 105 and obtains an amended certificate of authority.

SECTION 1006. REVOCATION OF CERTIFICATE OF AUTHORITY

(a) A certificate of authority of a foreign limited liability company to transact business in this State may be revoked by the [Secretary of State] in the manner provided in subsection (b) if:

(1) the company fails to:

(i) pay any fees, taxes, and penalties owed to this State;

(ii) deliver its annual report required under Section 211 to the [Secretary of State] within 60 days after it is due;

(iii) appoint and maintain an agent for service of process as required by this [article]; or

(iv) file a statement of a change in the name or business address of the agent as required by this [article]; or

(2) a misrepresentation has been made of any material matter in any application, report, affidavit, or other record submitted by the company pursuant to this [article].

(b) The [Secretary of State] may not revoke a certificate of authority of a foreign limited liability company unless the [Secretary of State] sends the company notice of the revocation, at least 60 days before its effective date, by a record addressed to its agent for service of process in this State, or if the company fails to appoint and maintain a proper agent in this State, addressed to the office required to be maintained by Section 108. The notice must specify the cause for the revocation of the certificate of authority. The authority of the company to transact business in this State ceases on the effective date of the revocation unless the foreign limited liability company cures the failure before that date.

SECTION 1007. CANCELLATION OF AUTHORITY

A foreign limited liability company may cancel its authority to transact business in this State by filing in the office of the [Secretary of State] a certificate of cancellation. Cancellation does not terminate the authority of the [Secretary of State] to accept service of process on the company for [claims for relief] arising out of the transactions of business in this State.

SECTION 1008. EFFECT OF FAILURE TO OBTAIN CERTIFICATE OF AUTHORITY

(a) A foreign limited liability company transacting business in this State may not maintain an action or proceeding in this State unless it has a certificate of authority to transact business in this State.

(b) The failure of a foreign limited liability company to have a certificate of authority to transact business in this State does not impair the validity of a contract or act of the company or prevent the foreign limited liability company from defending an action or proceeding in this State.

(c) Limitations on personal liability of managers, members, and their transferees are not waived solely by transacting business in this State without a certificate of authority.

(d) If a foreign limited liability company transacts business in this State without a certificate of authority, it appoints the [Secretary of

State] as its agent for service of process for [claims for relief] arising out of the transaction of business in this State.

SECTION 1009. ACTION BY [ATTORNEY GENERAL]

The [Attorney General] may maintain an action to restrain a foreign limited liability company from transacting business in this State in violation of this [article].

ARTICLE 11. DERIVATIVE ACTIONS

SECTION 1101. RIGHT OF ACTION

A member of a limited liability company may maintain an action in the right of the company if the members or managers having authority to do so have refused to commence the action or an effort to cause those members or managers to commence the action is not likely to succeed.

Comment

A member may bring an action on behalf of the company when the members or managers having the authority to pursue the company recovery refuse to do so or an effort to cause them to pursue the recovery is not likely to succeed. See Comments to Section 411(a) (personal action of member against company or another member).

SECTION 1102. PROPER PLAINTIFF

In a derivative action for a limited liability company, the plaintiff must be a member of the company when the action is commenced; and:

(1) must have been a member at the time of the transaction of which the plaintiff complains; or

(2) the plaintiff's status as a member must have devolved upon the plaintiff by operation of law or pursuant to the terms of the operating agreement from a person who was a member at the time of the transaction.

SECTION 1103. PLEADING

In a derivative action for a limited liability company, the complaint must set forth with particularity the effort of the plaintiff to secure initiation of the action by a member or manager or the reasons for not making the effort.

Comment

There is no obligation of the company or its members or managers to respond to a member demand to bring an action to pursue a company recovery.

However, if a company later decides to commence the demanded action or assume control of the derivative litigation, the member's right to commence or control the proceeding ordinarily ends.

SECTION 1104. EXPENSES

If a derivative action for a limited liability company is successful, in whole or in part, or if anything is received by the plaintiff as a result of a judgment, compromise, or settlement of an action or claim, the court may award the plaintiff reasonable expenses, including reasonable attorney's fees, and shall direct the plaintiff to remit to the limited liability company the remainder of the proceeds received.

ARTICLE 12. MISCELLANEOUS PROVISIONS

SECTION 1201. UNIFORMITY OF APPLICATION AND CONSTRUCTION

This [Act] shall be applied and construed to effectuate its general purpose to make uniform the law with respect to the subject of this [Act] among States enacting it.

SECTION 1202. SHORT TITLE

This [Act] may be cited as the Uniform Limited Liability Company Act (1995).

SECTION 1203. SEVERABILITY CLAUSE

If any provision of this [Act] or its application to any person or circumstance is held invalid, the invalidity does not affect other provisions or applications of this [Act] which can be given effect without the invalid provision or application, and to this end the provisions of this [Act] are severable.

SECTION 1204. EFFECTIVE DATE

This [Act] takes effect [________].

SECTION 1205. TRANSITIONAL PROVISIONS

(a) Before January 1, 199__, this [Act] governs only a limited liability company organized:

(1) after the effective date of this [Act], unless the company is continuing the business of a dissolved limited liability company under [Section of the existing Limited Liability Company Act]; and

(2) before the effective date of this [Act], which elects, as provided by subsection (c), to be governed by this [Act].

(b) On and after January 1, 199__, this [Act] governs all limited liability companies.

(c) Before January 1, 199__, a limited liability company voluntarily may elect, in the manner provided in its operating agreement or by law for amending the operating agreement, to be governed by this [Act].

Comment

Under subsection (a)(1), the application of the Act is mandatory for all companies formed after the effective date of the Act determined under Section 1204. Under subsection (a)(2), the application of the Act is permissive, by election under subsection (c), for existing companies for a period of time specified in subsection (b) after which application becomes mandatory. This affords existing companies and their members an opportunity to consider the changes effected by this Act and to amend their operating agreements, if appropriate. If no election is made, the Act becomes effective after the period specified in subsection (b). The period specified by adopting States may vary, but a period of five years is a common period in similar cases.

SECTION 1206. SAVINGS CLAUSE

This [Act] does not affect an action or proceeding commenced or right accrued before the effective date of this [Act].

B. DELAWARE LIMITED LIABILITY COMPANY ACT

Table of Contents

Subchapter I. General Provisions

§ 18-101. Definitions

As used in this chapter unless the context otherwise requires:

(1) "Bankruptcy" means an event that causes a person to cease to be a member as provided in § 18-304 of this title.

(2) "Certificate of formation" means the certificate referred to in s 18-201 of this title, and the certificate as amended.

(3) "Contribution" means any cash, property, services rendered or a promissory note or other obligation to contribute cash or property or to perform services, which a person contributes to a limited liability company in his capacity as a member.

* * *

(5) "Knowledge" means a person's actual knowledge of a fact, rather than the person's constructive knowledge of the fact.

(6) "Limited liability company" and "domestic limited liability company" means a limited liability company formed under the laws of the State of Delaware and having 1 or more members.

(7) "Limited liability company agreement" means any agreement (whether referred to as a limited liability company agreement, operating agreement or otherwise), written or oral, of the member or members as to the affairs of a limited liability company and the conduct of its business. A limited liability company is not required to execute its limited liability company agreement. A limited liability company is bound by its limited liability company agreement whether or not the limited liability company executes the limited liability company agreement. A limited liability company agreement of a limited liability company having only 1 member shall not be unenforceable by reason of there being only 1 person who is a party to the limited liability company agreement. A written limited liability company agreement or another written agreement or writing:

a. May provide that a person shall be admitted as a member of a limited liability company, or shall become an assignee of a limited liability company interest or other rights or powers of a member to the extent assigned, and shall become bound by the limited liability company agreement:

1. If such person (or a representative authorized by such person orally, in writing or by other action such as payment for a limited liability company interest) executes the limited liability company agreement or any other writing evidencing the intent of such person to become a member or assignee; or

2. Without such execution, if such person (or a representative authorized by such person orally, in writing or by other action such as payment for a limited liability company interest) complies with the conditions for becoming a member or assignee as set forth in the limited liability company agreement or any other writing; and

b. Shall not be unenforceable by reason of its not having been signed by a person being admitted as a member or becoming an assignee as provided in subparagraph a. of this paragraph, or by reason of its having been signed by a representative as provided in this chapter.

(8) "Limited liability company interest" means a member's share of the profits and losses of a limited liability company and a member's right to receive distributions of the limited liability company's assets.

(9) "Liquidating trustee" means a person carrying out the winding up of a limited liability company.

(10) "Manager" means a person who is named as a manager of a limited liability company in, or designated as a manager of a limited liability company pursuant to, a limited liability company agreement or similar instrument under which the limited liability company is formed.

(11) "Member" means a person who has been admitted to a limited liability company as a member as provided in § 18–301 of this title or, in the case of a foreign limited liability company, in accordance with the laws of the state or foreign country or other foreign jurisdiction under which the foreign limited liability company is organized.

(12) "Person" means a natural person, partnership (whether general or limited and whether domestic or foreign), limited liability company, foreign limited liability company, trust, estate, association, corporation, custodian, nominee or any other individual or entity in its own or any representative capacity.

(13) "Personal representative" means, as to a natural person, the executor, administrator, guardian, conservator or other legal representative thereof and, as to a person other than a natural person, the legal representative or successor thereof.

(14) "State" means the District of Columbia or the Commonwealth of Puerto Rico or any state, territory, possession or other jurisdiction of the United States other than the State of Delaware.

§ 18–102. Name Set Forth in Certificate

The name of each limited liability company as set forth in its certificate of formation:

(1) Shall contain the words "Limited Liability Company" or the abbreviation "L.L.C." or the designation "LLC";

(2) May contain the name of a member or manager;

(3) Must be such as to distinguish it upon the records in the office of the Secretary of State from the name of any corporation, limited partnership, business trust, limited liability partnership or limited liability company reserved, registered, formed or organized under the laws of the State of Delaware or qualified to do business or registered as a foreign corporation, foreign limited partnership or foreign limited liability company in the State of Delaware; provided, however, that a limited liability company may register under any name which is not such as to distinguish it upon the records in the office of the Secretary of State from the name of any domestic or foreign corporation, limited partnership, business trust, limited liability partnership or limited liability company reserved, registered, formed or organized under the laws of the State of Delaware with the written consent of the other corporation, limited partnership, business trust, limited liability partnership or limited liability company, which written consent shall be filed with the Secretary of State; and

(4) May contain the following words: "Company", "Association", "Club", "Foundation", "Fund", "Institute", "Society", "Union", "Syndicate", "Limited" or "Trust" (or abbreviations of like import).

§ 18–103. Reservation of Name

(a) The exclusive right to the use of a name may be reserved by:

(1) Any person intending to organize a limited liability company under this chapter and to adopt that name;

(2) Any domestic limited liability company or any foreign limited liability company registered in the State of Delaware which, in either case, proposes to change its name;

(3) Any foreign limited liability company intending to register in the State of Delaware and adopt that name; and

(4) Any person intending to organize a foreign limited liability company and intending to have it register in the State of Delaware and adopt that name.

(b) The reservation of a specified name shall be made by filing with the Secretary of State an application, executed by the applicant, specifying the name to be reserved and the name and address of the applicant. If the Secretary of State finds that the name is available for use by a domestic or foreign limited liability company, he shall reserve the name for the exclusive use of the applicant for a period of 120-days. Once having so reserved a name, the same applicant may again reserve the same name for successive 120 day periods. The right to the exclusive use of a reserved name may be transferred to any other person by filing in the Office of the Secretary of State a notice of the transfer, executed by the applicant for whom the name was reserved, specifying the name to be transferred and the name and address of the transferee. The reservation of a specified name may be cancelled by filing with the Secretary of State a notice of cancellation, executed by the applicant or transferee, specifying the name reservation to be cancelled and the name and address of the applicant or transferee. Unless the Secretary of State finds that any application, notice of transfer, or notice of cancellation filed with the Secretary of State as required by this subsection does not conform to law, upon receipt of all filing fees required by law the Secretary shall prepare and return to the person who filed such instrument a copy of the filed instrument with a notation thereon of the action taken by the Secretary of State.

* * *

§ 18-104. Registered Office; Registered Agent

(a) Each limited liability company shall have and maintain in the State of Delaware:

(1) A registered office, which may but need not be a place of its business in the State of Delaware; and

(2) A registered agent for service of process on the limited liability company, which agent may be either an individual resident of the State of Delaware whose business office is identical with the limited liability company's registered office, or a domestic corporation, or a domestic limited partnership, or a domestic limited liability company, or a domestic business trust, or a foreign corporation, or a foreign limited partnership, or a foreign limited liability company authorized to do business in the State of Delaware having a business office identical with such registered office, which is generally open during normal business hours to accept service of process and otherwise perform the functions of a registered agent, or the limited liability company itself.

* * *

§ 18-106. Nature of Business Permitted; Powers

(a) A limited liability company may carry on any lawful business, purpose or activity, whether or not for profit, with the exception of the business of granting policies of insurance, or assuming insurance risks or banking as defined in § 126 of Title 8.

(b) A limited liability company shall possess and may exercise all the powers and privileges granted by this chapter or by any other law or by its limited liability company agreement, together with any powers incidental thereto, including such powers and privileges as are necessary or convenient to the conduct, promotion or attainment of the business, purposes or activities of the limited liability company.

(c) Notwithstanding any provision of this chapter to the contrary, without limiting the general powers enumerated in subsection (b) above, a limited liability company shall, subject to such standards and restrictions, if any, as are set forth in its limited liability company agreement, have the power and authority to make contracts of guaranty and suretyship, and enter interest interest rate, basis, currency, hedge or other swap agreements, or cap, floor, put, call, option, exchange or collar agreements, derivative agreements or other agreements similar to any of the foregoing.

§ 18–107. Business Transactions of Member or Manager With the Limited Liability Company

Except as provided in a limited liability company agreement, a member or manager may lend money to, borrow money from, act as a surety, guarantor or endorser for, guarantee or assume 1 or more obligations of, provide collateral for, and transact other business with, a limited liability company and, subject to other applicable law, has the same rights and obligations with respect to any such matter as a person who is not a member or manager.

§ 18–108. Indemnification

Subject to such standards and restrictions, if any, as are set forth in its limited liability company agreement, a limited liability company may, and shall have the power to, indemnify and hold harmless any member or manager or other person from and against any and all claims and demands whatsoever.

* * *

Subchapter II. Formation; Certificate of Formation

§ 18–201. Certificate of Formation

(a) In order to form a limited liability company, 1 or more authorized persons must execute a certificate of formation. The certificate of formation shall be filed in the Office of the Secretary of State and set forth:

(1) The name of the limited liability company;

(2) The address of the registered office and the name and address of the registered agent for service of process required to be maintained by § 18–104 of this chapter; and

(3) Any other matters the members determine to include therein.

(b) A limited liability company is formed at the time of the filing of the initial certificate of formation in the Office of the Secretary of State or at any later date or time specified in the certificate of formation if, in either case, there has been substantial compliance with the requirements of this section. A limited liability company formed under this chapter shall be a separate legal entity, the existence of which as a separate legal entity shall continue until cancellation of the limited liability company's certificate of formation.

* * *

§ 18-202. Amendment to Certificate of Formation

(a) A certificate of formation is amended by filing a certificate of amendment thereto in the Office of the Secretary of State. The certificate of amendment shall set forth:

(1) The name of the limited liability company; and

(2) The amendment to the certificate of formation.

(b) A manager or, if there is no manager, then any member who becomes aware that any statement in a certificate of formation was false when made, or that any matter described has changed making the certificate of formation false in any material respect, shall promptly amend the certificate of formation.

(c) A certificate of formation may be amended at any time for any other proper purpose.

(d) Unless otherwise provided in this chapter or unless a later effective date or time (which shall be a date or time certain) is provided for in the certificate of amendment, a certificate of amendment shall be effective at the time of its filing with the Secretary of State.

§ 18-203. Cancellation of Certificate

A certificate of formation shall be cancelled upon the dissolution and the completion of winding up of a limited liability company, or as provided in § 18-104(d) or § 18-1108 of this chapter, or upon the filing of a certificate of merger or consolidation if the limited liability company is not the surviving or resulting entity in a merger or consolidation. A certificate of cancellation shall be filed in the office of the Secretary of State to accomplish the cancellation of a certificate of formation upon the dissolution and the completion of winding up of a limited liability company and shall set forth:

(1) The name of the limited liability company;

(2) The date of filing of its certificate of formation;

(3) The future effective date or time (which shall be a date or time certain) of cancellation if it is not to be effective upon the filing of the certificate; and

(4) Any other information the person filing the certificate of cancellation determines.

§ 18–204. Execution

(a) Each certificate required by this subchapter to be filed in the Office of the Secretary of State shall be executed by 1 or more authorized persons.

(b) Unless otherwise provided in a limited liability company agreement, any person may sign any certificate or amendment thereof or enter into a limited liability company agreement or amendment thereof by an agent, including an attorney-in-fact. An authorization, including a power of attorney, to sign any certificate or amendment thereof or to enter into a limited liability company agreement or amendment thereof need not be in writing, need not be sworn to, verified or acknowledged, and need not be filed in the Office of the Secretary of State, but if in writing, must be retained by the limited liability company.

(c) The execution of a certificate by an authorized person constitutes an oath or affirmation, under the penalties of perjury in the third degree, that, to the best of the authorized person's knowledge and belief, the facts stated therein are true.

* * *

§ 18–206. Filing

(a) The original signed copy of the certificate of formation and of any certificates of amendment, correction, amendment of a certificate of merger or consolidation, termination of a merger or consolidation or cancellation (or of any judicial decree of amendment or cancellation), and of any certificate of merger or consolidation, any restated certificate, any certificate of conversion to limited liability company, any certificate of transfer, any certificate of transfer and continuance, any certificate of limited liability company domestication, and of any certificate of revival shall be delivered to the Secretary of State. A person who executes a certificate as an agent or fiduciary need not exhibit evidence of that person's authority as a prerequisite to filing. Any signature on any certificate authorized to be filed with the Secretary of State under any provision of this chapter may be a facsimile, a conformed signature or an electronically transmitted signature. Unless the Secretary of State finds that any certificate does not conform to law, upon receipt of all filing fees required by law the Secretary of State shall:

(1) Certify that the certificate of formation, the certificate of amendment, the certificate of correction, the certificate of amendment of a

certificate of merger or consolidation, the certificate of termination of a merger or consolidation, the certificate of cancellation (or of any judicial decree of amendment or cancellation), the certificate of merger or consolidation, the restated certificate, the certificate of conversion to limited liability company, the certificate of transfer, the certificate of transfer and continuance, the certificate of limited liability company domestication or the certificate of revival has been filed in the Secretary of State's office by endorsing upon the original certificate the word "Filed," and the date and hour of the filing. This endorsement is conclusive of the date and time of its filing in the absence of actual fraud;

(2) File and index the endorsed certificate;

(3) Prepare and return to the person who filed it or that person's representative a copy of the original signed instrument, similarly endorsed, and shall certify such copy as a true copy of the original signed instrument; and

(4) Enter such information from the certificate as the Secretary of State deems appropriate into the Delaware Corporation Information System or any system which is a successor thereto in the office of the Secretary of State, and such information shall be permanently maintained as a public record. A copy of each certificate shall be permanently maintained on optical disk or by other suitable medium.

(b) Upon the filing of a certificate of amendment (or judicial decree of amendment), certificate of correction or restated certificate in the office of the Secretary of State, or upon the future effective date or time of a certificate of amendment (or judicial decree thereof) or restated certificate, as provided for therein, the certificate of formation shall be amended or restated as set forth therein. Upon the filing of a certificate of cancellation (or a judicial decree thereof), or a certificate of merger or consolidation which acts as a certificate of cancellation or a certificate of transfer, or upon the future effective date or time of a certificate of cancellation (or a judicial decree thereof) or of a certificate of merger or consolidation which acts as a certificate of cancellation or a certificate of transfer, as provided for therein, or as specified in § 18–104(d) of this title, the certificate of formation is cancelled. Upon the filing of a certificate of limited liability company domestication or upon the future effective date or time of a certificate of limited liability company domestication, the entity filing the certificate of limited liability company domestication is domesticated as a limited liability company with the effect provided in § 18–212 of this title. Upon the filing of a certificate of conversion to limited liability company or upon the future effective date or time of a certificate of conversion to limited liability company, the entity filing the certificate of conversion to limited liability company is converted to a limited liability company with the effect provided in § 18–214 of this title. Upon the filing of a certificate of amendment of a certificate of merger or consolidation, the certificate of merger or consolidation identified in the certificate of amendment of a certificate of merger or consolidation is amended. Upon the filing of a certificate of termination of a merger or consolidation, the certificate of merger or consolidation identified in the certificate of termination of a merger or consolidation is terminated. Upon the filing of a certificate of revival, the limited liability company is revived with the effect provided in § 18–1109 of this title.

* * *

§ 18–209. Merger and Consolidation

(a) As used in this section, "other business entity" means a corporation, or a business trust or association, a real estate investment trust, a common-law trust, or any other unincorporated business, including a partnership (whether general (including a limited liability partnership) or limited (including a limited liability partnership)), and a foreign limited liability company, but excluding a domestic limited liability company.

(b) Pursuant to an agreement of merger or consolidation, 1 or more domestic limited liability companies may merge or consolidate with or into 1 or more domestic limited liability companies or 1 or more other business entities formed or organized under the laws of the State of Delaware or any other state or the United States or any foreign country or other foreign jurisdiction, or any combination thereof, with such domestic limited liability companies or other business entity as the agreement shall provide being the surviving or resulting domestic limited liability companies or other business entity. Unless otherwise provided in the limited liability company agreement, a merger or consolidation shall be approved by each domestic limited liability company which is to merge or consolidate by the members or, if there is more than one class or group of members, then by each class or group of members, in either case, by members who own more than 50 percent of the then current percentage or other interest in the profits of the domestic limited liability company owned by all of the members or by the members in each class or group, as appropriate. In connection with a merger or consolidation hereunder, rights or securities of, or interests in, a domestic limited liability company or other business entity which is a constituent party to the merger or consolidation may be exchanged for or converted into cash, property, rights or securities of, or interests in, the surviving or resulting domestic limited liability company or other business entity or, in addition to or in lieu thereof, may be exchanged for or converted into cash, property, rights or securities of, or interests in, a domestic limited liability company or other business entity which is not the surviving or resulting limited liability company or other business entity in the merger or consolidation. Notwithstanding prior approval, an agreement of merger or consolidation may be terminated or amended pursuant to a provision for such termination or amendment contained in the agreement of merger or consolidation.

(c) If a domestic limited liability company is merging or consolidating under this section, the domestic limited liability company or other business entity surviving or resulting in or from the merger or consolidation shall file a certificate of merger or consolidation in the office of the Secretary of State. The certificate of merger or consolidation shall state:

(1) The name and jurisdiction of formation or organization of each of the domestic limited liability companies or other business entities which is to merge or consolidate;

(2) That an agreement of merger or consolidation has been approved and executed by each of the domestic limited liability companies or other business entities which is to merge or consolidate;

(3) The name of the surviving or resulting domestic limited liability company or other business entity;

(4) The future effective date or time (which shall be a date or time certain) of the merger or consolidation if it is not to be effective upon the filing of the certificate of merger or consolidation;

(5) That the agreement of merger or consolidation is on file at a place of business of the surviving or resulting domestic limited liability company or other business entity, and shall state the address thereof;

(6) That a copy of the agreement of merger or consolidation will be furnished by the surviving or resulting domestic limited liability company or other business entity, on request and without cost, to any member of any domestic limited liability company or any person holding an interest in any other business entity which is to merge or consolidate;

* * *

(e) A certificate of merger or consolidation shall act as a certificate of cancellation for a domestic limited liability company which is not the surviving or resulting entity in the merger or consolidation. Whenever this section requires the filing of a certificate of merger or consolidation, such requirement shall be deemed satisfied by the filing of an agreement of merger or consolidation containing the information required by this section to be set forth in the certificate of merger or consolidation.

(f) An agreement of merger or consolidation approved in accordance with subsection (b) of this section may: (1) Effect any amendment to the limited liability company agreement or (2) Effect the adoption of a new limited liability company agreement, for a limited liability company if it is the surviving or resulting limited liability company in the merger or consolidation. Any amendment to a limited liability company agreement or adoption of a new limited liability company agreement made pursuant to the foregoing sentence shall be effective at the effective time or date of the merger or consolidation. The provisions of this subsection shall not be construed to limit the accomplishment of a merger or of any of the matters referred to herein by any other means provided for in a limited liability company agreement or other agreement or as otherwise permitted by law, including that the limited liability company agreement of any constituent limited liability company to the merger or consolidation (including a limited liability company formed for the purpose of consummating a merger or consolidation) shall be the limited liability company agreement of the surviving or resulting limited liability company.

(g) When any merger or consolidation shall have become effective under this section, for all purposes of the laws of the State of Delaware, all of the rights, privileges and powers of each of the domestic limited liability companies and other business entities that have merged or consolidated, and all property, real, personal and mixed, and all debts due to any of said domestic limited liability companies and other business entities, as well as all other things and causes of action belonging to each of such domestic limited liability companies and other business entities, shall be vested in the surviving or resulting domestic limited liability company or other business entity, and shall thereafter be the property of the surviving or resulting domestic limited liability company or other business entity as they were of each of the domestic limited liability companies and other business entities that have merged or consolidated, and the title to any real property vested by deed or otherwise, under the laws of the State of Delaware, in any of such domestic limited liability companies and other business entities, shall not revert or be in any way impaired by reason of this chapter; but all rights of creditors and all liens upon any property of any of said domestic limited liability companies and other business entities shall be preserved unimpaired, and all debts, liabilities and duties of each of the said domestic limited liability companies and other business entities that have merged or consolidated shall thenceforth attach to the surviving or resulting domestic limited liability company or other business entity, and may be enforced against it to the same extent as if said debts, liabilities and duties had been incurred or contracted by it. Unless otherwise agreed, a merger or consolidation of a domestic limited liability company, including a domestic limited liability company which is not the surviving or resulting entity in the merger or consolidation, shall not require such domestic limited liability company to wind up its affairs under § 18-803 of this chapter or pay its liabilities and distribute its assets under § 18-804 of this chapter.

Subchapter III. Members

§ 18-301. Admission of Members

(a) In connection with the formation of a limited liability company, a person is admitted as a member of the limited liability company upon the later to occur of:

(1) The formation of the limited liability company; or

(2) The time provided in and upon compliance with the limited liability company agreement or, if the limited liability company agreement does not so provide, when the person's admission is reflected in the records of the limited liability company.

(b) After the formation of a limited liability company, a person is admitted as a member of the limited liability company:

(1) In the case of a person who is not an assignee of a limited liability company interest, including a person acquiring a limited liability company interest directly from the limited liability company and a person to be admitted as a member of the limited liability company without acquiring a limited liability company interest in the limited liability company at the time provided in and upon compliance with the limited liability company agreement or, if the limited liability company agreement does not so provide, upon the consent of all members and when the person's admission is reflected in the records of the limited liability company;

(2) In the case of an assignee of a limited liability company interest, as provided in § 18-704(a) of this title and at the time provided in and upon compliance with the limited liability company agreement or, if the limited liability company agreement does not so provide, when any such person's permitted admission is reflected in the records of the limited liability company; or

(3) Unless otherwise provided in an agreement of merger or consolidation, in the case of a person acquiring a limited liability company interest in a surviving or resulting limited liability company pursuant to a merger or consolidation approved in accordance with § 18-209(b) of this title, at the time provided in and upon compliance with the limited liability company agreement of the surviving or resulting limited liability company.

(c) In connection with the domestication of a non-United States entity (as defined in § 18-212 of this title) as a limited liability company in the State of Delaware in accordance with § 18-212 of this title or the conversion of an other entity (as defined in § 18-214 of this title) to a domestic limited liability company in accordance with § 18-214 of this title, a person is admitted as a member of the limited liability company at the time provided in and upon compliance with the limited liability company agreement.

(d) A person may be admitted to a limited liability company as a member of the limited liability company and may receive a limited liability company interest in the limited liability company without making a contribution or being obligated to make a contribution to the limited liability company. Unless otherwise provided in a limited liability company agreement, a person may be admitted to a limited liability company as a member of the limited liability company without acquiring a limited liability company interest in the limited liability company. Unless otherwise provided in a limited liability company agreement, a person may be admitted as the sole member of a limited liability company without making a contribution or being obligated to make a contribution to the limited liability company or without acquiring a limited liability company interest in the limited liability company.

(e) Unless otherwise provided in a limited liability company agreement or another agreement, a member shall have no preemptive right to subscribe to any additional issue of limited liability company interests or another interest in a liability company.

§ 18–302. Classes and Voting

(a) A limited liability company agreement may provide for classes or groups of members having such relative rights, powers and duties as the limited liability company agreement may provide, and may make provision for the future creation in the manner provided in the limited liability company agreement of additional classes or groups of members having such relative rights, powers and duties as may from time to time be established, including rights, powers and duties senior to existing classes and groups of members. A limited liability company agreement may provide for the taking of an action, including the amendment of the limited liability company agreement, without the vote or approval of any member or class or group of members, including an action to create under the provisions of the limited liability company agreement a class or group of limited liability company interests that was not previously outstanding. A limited liability company agreement may provide that any member or class or group of members shall have no voting rights.

(b) A limited liability company agreement may grant to all or certain identified members or a specified class or group of the members the right to vote separately or with all or any class or group of the members or managers, on any matter. Voting by members may be on a per capita, number, financial interest, class, group or any other basis.

(c) A limited liability company agreement may set forth provisions relating to notice of the time, place or purpose of any meeting at which any matter is to be voted on by any members, waiver of any such notice, action by consent without a meeting, the establishment of a record date, quorum requirements, voting in person or by proxy, or any other matter with respect to the exercise of any such right to vote.

(d) Unless otherwise provided in a limited liability company agreement, on any matter that is to be voted on by members, the members may take such action without a meeting, without prior notice and without a vote if a consent or consents in writing, setting forth the action so taken, shall be signed by the members having not less than the minimum number of votes that would be necessary to authorize or take such action at a meeting at which all members in the limited liability company entitled to vote thereon were present and voted. Unless otherwise provided in a limited liability company agreement, on any matter that is to be voted on by members, the members may vote in person or by proxy.

§ 18–303. Liability to Third Parties

(a) Except as otherwise provided by this chapter, the debts, obligations and liabilities of a limited liability company, whether arising in contract, tort or otherwise, shall be solely the debts, obligations and liabilities of the limited liability company, and no member or manager of a limited liability company shall be obligated personally for any such debt, obligation or liability of the limited liability company solely by reason of being a member or acting as a manager of the limited liability company.

(b) Notwithstanding the provisions of subsection (a) of this section, under a limited liability company agreement or under another agreement, a member or manager may agree to be obligated personally for any or all of the debts, obligations and liabilities of the limited liability company.

§ 18–304. Events of Bankruptcy

A person ceases to be a member of a limited liability company upon the happening of any of the following events:

(1) Unless otherwise provided in a limited liability company agreement, or with the written consent of all members, a member:

(a) Makes an assignment for the benefit of creditors;

(b) Files a voluntary petition in bankruptcy;

(c) Is adjudged a bankrupt or insolvent, or has entered against the member an order for relief, in any bankruptcy or insolvency proceeding;

(d) Files a petition or answer seeking for the member any reorganization, arrangement, composition, readjustment, liquidation, dissolution or similar relief under any statute, law or regulation;

(e) Files an answer or other pleading admitting or failing to contest the material allegations of a petition filed against the member in any proceeding of this nature;

(f) Seeks, consents to or acquiesces in the appointment of a trustee, receiver or liquidator of the member or of all or any substantial part of the member's properties; or

(2) Unless otherwise provided in a limited liability company agreement, or with the written consent of all members, 120 days after the commencement of any proceeding against the member seeking reorganization, arrangement, composition, readjustment, liquidation, dissolution or similar relief under any statute, law or regulation, if the proceeding

has not been dismissed, or if within 90 days after the appointment without the member's consent or acquiescence of a trustee, receiver or liquidator of the member or of all or any substantial part of the member's properties, the appointment is not vacated or stayed, or within 90 days after the expiration of any such stay, the appointment is not vacated.

§ 18–305. Access to and Confidentiality of Information; Records

(a) Each member of a limited liability company has the right, subject to such reasonable standards (including standards governing what information and documents are to be furnished at what time and location and at whose expense) as may be set forth in a limited liability company agreement or otherwise established by the manager or, if there is no manager, then by the members, to obtain from the limited liability company from time to time upon reasonable demand for any purpose reasonably related to the member's interest as a member of the limited liability company:

(1) True and full information regarding the status of the business and financial condition of the limited liability company;

(2) Promptly after becoming available, a copy of the limited liability company's federal, state and local income tax returns for each year;

(3) A current list of the name and last known business, residence or mailing address of each member and manager;

(4) A copy of any written limited liability company agreement and certificate of formation and all amendments thereto, together with executed copies of any written powers of attorney pursuant to which the limited liability company agreement and any certificate and all amendments thereto have been executed;

(5) True and full information regarding the amount of cash and a description and statement of the agreed value of any other property or services contributed by each member and which each member has agreed to contribute in the future, and the date on which each became a member; and

(6) Other information regarding the affairs of the limited liability company as is just and reasonable.

(b) Each manager shall have the right to examine all of the information described in (a) of this section for a purpose reasonably related to his position as a manager.

(c) The manager of a limited liability company shall have the right to keep confidential from the members, for such period of time as the manager deems reasonable, any information which the manager reasonably believes to be in the nature of trade secrets or other information the disclosure of which the manager in good faith believes is not in the best interest of the limited liability company or could damage the limited liability company or its business or which the limited liability company is required by law or by agreement with a third party to keep confidential.

(d) A limited liability company may maintain its records in other than a written form if such form is capable of conversion into written form within a reasonable time.

(e) Any demand by a member under this section shall be in writing and shall state the purpose of such demand.

(f) Any action to enforce any right arising under this section shall be brought in the Court of Chancery. If the limited liability company refuses to permit a member to obtain or a manager to examine the information described in subsection (a)(3) of this section or does not reply to the demand that has been made within 5 business days after the demand has been made, the demanding member or manager may apply to the Court of Chancery for an order to compel such disclosure. The Court of Chancery is hereby vested with exclusive jurisdiction to determine whether or not the person seeking such information is entitled to the information sought. The Court of Chancery may summarily order the limited liability company to permit the demanding member to obtain or manager to examine the information described in subsection (a)(3) of this section and to make copies or abstracts therefrom, or the Court of Chancery may summarily order the limited liability company to furnish to the demanding member or manager the information described in subsection (a)(3) of this section on the condition that the demanding member or manager first pay to the limited liability company the reasonable cost of obtaining and furnishing such information and on such other conditions as the Court of Chancery deems appropriate. When a demanding member seeks to obtain or a manager seeks to examine the information described in subsection (a)(3) of this section, the demanding member or manager shall first establish (1) that the demanding member or manager has complied with the provisions of this section respecting the form and manner of making demand for obtaining or examining of such information, and (2) that the information the demanding member or manager seeks is reasonably related to the member's interest as a member or the manager's position as a manager, as the case may be. The Court of Chancery may, in its discretion, prescribe any limitations or conditions with reference to the obtaining or examining of information, or award such other or further relief as the Court of Chancery may deem just and proper. The Court of Chancery may order books, documents and records, pertinent extracts therefrom, or duly authenticated copies thereof, to be brought within the State of Delaware and kept in the State of Delaware upon such terms and conditions as the order may prescribe.

§ 18-306. Remedies for Breach of Limited Liability Company Agreement by Member

A limited liability company agreement may provide that: (1) A member who fails to perform in accordance with, or to comply with the terms and conditions of, the limited liability company agreement shall be subject to specified penalties or specified consequences; and (2) At the time or upon the happening of events specified in the limited liability company agreement, a member shall be subject to specified penalties or specified consequences.

Subchapter IV. Managers

§ 18–401. Admission of Managers

A person may be named or designated as a manager of the limited liability company as provided in § 18–101(10) of this title.

§ 18–402. Management of Limited Liability Company

Unless otherwise provided in a limited liability company agreement, the management of a limited liability company shall be vested in its members in proportion to the then current percentage or other interest of members in the profits of the limited liability company owned by all of the members, the decision of members owning more than 50 percent of the said percentage or other interest in the profits controlling; provided however, that if a limited liability company agreement provides for the management, in whole or in part, of a limited liability company by a manager, the management of the limited liability company, to the extent so provided, shall be vested in the manager who shall be chosen in the manner provided in the limited liability company agreement. The manager shall also hold the offices and have the responsibilities accorded to him by the members and set forth in a limited liability company agreement. Subject to § 18–602 of this title, a manager shall cease to be a manager as provided in a limited liability company agreement. A limited liability company may have more than 1 manager. Unless otherwise provided in a limited liability company agreement, each member and manager has the authority to bind the limited liability company.

§ 18–403. Contributions by a Manager

A manager of a limited liability company may make contributions to the limited liability company and share in the profits and losses of, and in distributions from, the limited liability company as a member. A person who is both a manager and a member has the rights and powers, and is subject to the restrictions and liabilities, of a manager and, except as provided in a limited liability company agreement, also has the rights and powers, and is subject to the restrictions and liabilities, of a member to the extent of his participation in the limited liability company as a member.

§ 18–404. Classes and Voting

(a) A limited liability company agreement may provide for classes or groups of managers having such relative rights, powers and duties as the limited liability company agreement may provide, and may make provision for the future creation in the manner provided in the limited liability company agreement of additional classes or groups of managers having such relative rights, powers and duties as may from time to time be established, including rights, powers and duties senior to existing classes and groups of managers. A limited liability company agreement may provide for the taking of an action, including the amendment of the limited liability company agreement, without the vote or approval of any manager or class or group of managers, including an action to create under the provisions of the limited liability company agreement a class or group of limited liability company interests that was not previously outstanding.

(b) A limited liability company agreement may grant to all or certain identified managers or a specified class or group of the managers the right to vote, separately or with all or any class or group of managers or members, on any matter. Voting by managers may be on a per capita, number, financial interest, class, group or any other basis.

(c) A limited liability company agreement may set forth provisions relating to notice of the time, place or purpose of any meeting at which any matter is to be voted on by any manager or class or group of managers, waiver of any such notice, action by consent without a meeting, the establishment of a record date, quorum requirements, voting in person or by proxy, or any other matter with respect to the exercise of any such right to vote.

(d) Unless otherwise provided in a limited liability company agreement, on any matter that is to be voted on by managers, the managers may take such action without a meeting, without prior notice and without a vote if a consent or consents in writing, setting forth the action so taken, shall be signed by the managers having not less than the minimum number of votes that would be necessary to authorize or take such action at a meeting at which all managers entitled to vote thereon were present and voted. Unless otherwise provided in a limited liability company agreement, on any matter that is to be voted on by managers, the managers may vote in person or by proxy.

§ 18–405. Remedies for Breach of Limited Liability Company Agreement by Manager

A limited liability company agreement may provide that: (1) A manager who fails to perform in accordance with, or to comply with the terms and conditions of, the limited liability company agreement shall be subject to specified penalties or specified consequences; and (2) At the time or upon the happening of events specified in the limited liability company agreement, a manager shall be subject to specified penalties or specified consequences.

§ 18–406. Reliance on Reports and Information by Member or Manager

A member or manager of a limited liability company shall be fully protected in relying in good faith upon the records of the limited liability company and upon such information, opinions, reports or statements presented to the limited liability company by any of its other managers, members, officers, employees, or committees of the limited liability company, or by any other person, as to matters the member or manager reasonably believes are within such other person's professional or expert competence and who has been selected with reasonable care by or on behalf of the limited liability company, including information, opinions, reports or statements as to the value and amount of the assets, liabilities, profits or losses of the limited liability company or any other facts pertinent to the existence and amount of assets from which distributions to members might properly be paid.

Unless otherwise provided in the limited liability company agreement, a member or manager of a limited liability company has the power and authority to delegate to 1 or more other persons the member's or manager's, as the case may be, rights and powers to manage and control the business and affairs of the limited liability company, including to delegate to agents, officers and employees of a member or manager or the limited liability company, and to delegate by a management agreement or another agreement with, or otherwise to, other persons. Unless otherwise provided in the limited liability company agreement, such delegation by a member or manager of a limited liability company shall not cause the member or manager to cease to be a member or manager, as the case may be, of the limited liability company.

Subchapter V. Finance

§ 18–501. Form of Contribution

The contribution of a member to a limited liability company may be in cash, property or services rendered, or a promissory note or other obligation to contribute cash or property or to perform services.

§ 18–502. Liability for Contribution

(a) Except as provided in a limited liability company agreement, a member is obligated to a limited liability company to perform any promise to contribute cash or property or to perform services, even if he is unable to perform because of death, disability or any other reason. If a member does not make the required contribution of property or services, the member is obligated at the option of the limited liability company to contribute cash equal to that portion of the agreed value (as stated in the records of the limited liability company) of the contribution that has not been made. The foregoing option shall be in addition to, and not in lieu of, any other rights, including the right to specific performance, that the limited liability company may have against such member under the limited liability company agreement or applicable law.

(b) Unless otherwise provided in a limited liability company agreement, the obligation of a member to make a contribution or return money or other property paid or distributed in violation of this chapter may be compromised only by consent of all the members. Notwithstanding the compromise, a creditor of a limited liability company who extends credit, after the entering into of a limited liability company agreement or an amendment thereto which, in either case, reflects the obligation, and before the amendment thereof to reflect the compromise, may enforce the original obligation to the extent that, in extending credit, the creditor reasonably relied on the obligation of a member to make a contribution or return. A conditional obligation of a member to make a contribution or return money or other property to a limited liability company may not be enforced unless the conditions of the obligation have been satisfied or waived as to or by such member. Conditional obligations include contributions payable upon a discretionary call of a limited liability company prior to the time the call occurs.

(c) A limited liability company agreement may provide that the interest of any member who fails to make any contribution that the member is obligated to make shall be subject to specified penalties for, or specified consequences of, such failure. Such penalty or consequence may take the form of reducing or eliminating the defaulting member's proportionate interest in a limited liability company, subordinating the member's limited liability company interest to that of nondefaulting members, a forced sale of that limited liability company interest, forfeiture of his or her limited liability company interest, the lending by other members of the amount necessary to meet the defaulting member's commitment, a fixing of the value of his or her limited liability company interest by appraisal or by formula and redemption or sale of the limited liability company interest at such value, or other penalty or consequence.

§ 18-503. Allocation of Profits and Losses

The profits and losses of a limited liability company shall be allocated among the members, and among classes or groups of members, in the manner provided in a limited liability company agreement. If the limited liability company agreement does not so provide, profits and losses shall be allocated on the basis of the agreed value (as stated in the records of the limited liability company) of the contributions made by each member to the extent they have been received by the limited liability company and have not been returned.

§ 18-504. Allocation of Distributions

Distributions of cash or other assets of a limited liability company shall be allocated among the members, and among classes or groups of members, in the manner provided in a limited liability company agreement. If the limited liability company agreement does not so provide, distributions shall be made on the basis of the agreed value (as stated in the records of the limited liability company) of the contributions made by each member to the extent they have been received by the limited liability company and have not been returned.

§ 18–505. Defense of Usury Not Available

No obligation of a member or manager of a limited liability company to the limited liability company arising under the limited liability company agreement or a separate agreement or writing, and no note, instrument or other writing evidencing any such obligation of a member or manager, shall be subject to the defense of usury, and no member or manager shall interpose the defense of usury with respect to any such obligation in any action.

Subchapter VI. Distributions and Resignation

§ 18–601. Interim Distributions

Except as provided in this subchapter, to the extent and at the times or upon the happening of the events specified in a limited liability company agreement, a member is entitled to receive from a limited liability company distributions before the member's resignation from the limited liability company and before the dissolution and winding up thereof.

§ 18–602. Resignation of Manager

A manager may resign as a manager of a limited liability company at the time or upon the happening of events specified in a limited liability company agreement and in accordance with the limited liability company agreement. A limited liability company agreement may provide that a manager shall not have the right to resign as a manager of a limited liability company. Notwithstanding that a limited liability company agreement provides that a manager does not have the right to resign as a manager of a limited liability company, a manager may resign as a manager of a limited liability company at any time by giving written notice to the members and other managers. If the resignation of a manager violates a limited liability company agreement, in addition to any remedies otherwise available under applicable law, a limited liability company may recover from the resigning manager damages for breach of the limited liability company agreement and offset the damages against the amount otherwise distributable to the resigning manager.

§ 18–603. Resignation of Member

A member may resign from a limited liability company only at the time or upon the happening of events specified in a limited liability company agreement and in accordance with the limited liability company agreement. Notwithstanding anything to the contrary under applicable law, unless a limited liability company agreement provides otherwise, a member may not resign from a limited liability company prior to the dissolution and winding up of the limited liability company. Notwithstanding anything to the contrary under applicable law, a limited liability company agreement may provide that a limited liability company interest may not be assigned prior to the dissolution and winding up of the limited liability company.

Unless otherwise provided in a limited liability company agreement, a limited liability company whose original certificate of formation was filed with the Secretary of State and effective on or prior to July 31, 1996, shall continue to be governed by this section as in effect on July 31, 1996, and shall not be governed by this section.

§ 18-604. Distribution Upon Resignation

Except as provided in this subchapter, upon resignation any resigning member is entitled to receive any distribution to which such member is entitled under a limited liability company agreement and, if not otherwise provided in a limited liability company agreement, such member is entitled to receive, within a reasonable time after resignation, the fair value of such member's limited liability company interest as of the date of resignation based upon such member's right to share in distributions from the limited liability company.

§ 18-605. Distribution in Kind

Except as provided in a limited liability company agreement, a member, regardless of the nature of the member's contribution, has no right to demand and receive any distribution from a limited liability company in any form other than cash. Except as provided in a limited liability company agreement, a member may not be compelled to accept a distribution of any asset in kind from a limited liability company to the extent that the percentage of the asset distributed to him exceeds a percentage of that asset which is equal to the percentage in which the member shares in distributions from the limited liability company. Except as provided in the limited liability company agreement, a member may be compelled to accept a distribution of any asset in kind from a limited liability company to the extent that the percentage of the asset distributed is equal to a percentage of that asset which is equal to the percentage in which the member shares in distributions from the limited liability company.

§ 18-606. Right to Distribution

Subject to §§ 18-607 and 18-804 of this chapter, and unless otherwise provided in a limited liability company agreement, at the time a member becomes entitled to receive a distribution, the member has the status of, and is entitled to all remedies available to, a creditor of a limited liability company with respect to the distribution. A limited liability company agreement may provide for the establishment of a record date with respect to allocations and distributions by a limited liability company.

§ 18–607. Limitations on Distribution

(a) A limited liability company shall not make a distribution to a member to the extent that at the time of the distribution, after giving effect to the distribution, all liabilities of the limited liability company, other than liabilities to members on account of their limited liability company interests and liabilities for which the recourse of creditors is limited to specified property of the limited liability company, exceed the fair value of the assets of the limited liability company, except that the fair value of property that is subject to a liability for which the recourse of creditors is limited shall be included in the assets of the limited liability company only to the extent that the fair value of that property exceeds that liability. For purposes of this subsection (a), the term "distribution" shall not include amounts constituting reasonable compensation for present or past services or reasonable payments made in the ordinary course of business pursuant to a bona fide retirement plan or other benefits program.

(b) A member who receives a distribution in violation of subsection (a) of this section, and who knew at the time of the distribution that the distribution violated subsection (a) of this section, shall be liable to a limited liability company for the amount of the distribution. A member who receives a distribution in violation of subsection (a) of this section, and who did not know at the time of the distribution that the distribution violated subsection (a) of this section, shall not be liable for the amount of the distribution. Subject to subsection (c) of this section, this subsection shall not affect any obligation or liability of a member under an agreement or other applicable law for the amount of a distribution.

(c) Unless otherwise agreed, a member who receives a distribution from a limited liability company shall have no liability under this chapter or other applicable law for the amount of the distribution after the expiration of three years from the date of the distribution unless an action to recover the distribution from such member is commenced prior to the expiration of the said three year period and an adjudication of liability against such member is made in the said action.

Subchapter VII. Assignment of Limited Liability Company Interests

§ 18–701. Nature of Limited Liability Company Interest

A limited liability company interest is personal property. A member has no interest in specific limited liability company property.

§ 18–702. Assignment of Limited Liability Company Interest

(a) A limited liability company interest is assignable in whole or in part except as provided in a limited liability company agreement. The assignee of a member's limited liability company interest shall have no right to participate in the management of the business and affairs of a limited liability company except as provided in a limited liability company agreement and upon:

(1) The approval of all of the members of the limited liability company other than the member assigning his limited liability company interest; or

(2) Compliance with any procedure provided for in the limited liability company agreement.

(b) Unless otherwise provided in a limited liability company agreement:

(1) An assignment of a limited liability company interest does not entitle the assignee to become or to exercise any rights or powers of a member;

(2) An assignment of a limited liability company interest entitles the assignee to share in such profits and losses, to receive such distribution or distributions, and to receive such allocation of income, gain, loss, deduction, or credit or similar item to which the assignor was entitled, to the extent assigned; and

(3) A member ceases to be a member and to have the power to exercise any rights or powers of a member upon assignment of all of the member's limited liability company interest. Unless otherwise provided in a limited liability company agreement, the pledge of, or granting of a security interest, lien or other encumbrance in or against, any or all of the limited liability company interest of a member shall not cause the member to cease to be a member or to have the power to exercise any rights or powers of a member.

(c) A limited liability company agreement may provide that a member's interest in a limited liability company may be evidenced by a certificate of limited liability company interest issued by the limited liability company.

(d) Unless otherwise provided in a limited liability company agreement and except to the extent assumed by agreement, until an assignee of a limited liability company interest becomes a member, the assignee shall have no liability as a member solely as a result of the assignment.

(e) Unless otherwise provided in the limited liability company agreement, a limited liability company may acquire, by purchase, redemption or otherwise, any limited liability company interest or other interest of a member or manager in the limited liability company. Unless otherwise provided in the limited liability company agreement, any such interest so acquired by the limited liability company shall be deemed canceled.

18–703. Member's Limited Liability Company Interest Subject to Charging Order

(a) On application by a judgment creditor of a member or of a member's assignee, a court having jurisdiction may charge the limited liability company interest of the judgment debtor to satisfy the judgment. The court may appoint a receiver of the share of the distributions due or to become due to the judgment debtor in respect of the limited liability company which receiver shall have only the rights of an assignee, and the court may make all other orders, directions, accounts and inquiries the judgment debtor might have made or which the circumstances of the case may require.

(b) A charging order constitutes a lien on the judgment debtor's limited liability company interest. The court may order a foreclosure of the limited liability company interest subject to the charging order at any time. The purchaser at the foreclosure sale has only the rights of an assignee.

(c) Unless otherwise provided in a limited liability company agreement, at any time before foreclosure, a limited liability company interest charged may be redeemed:

(1) by the judgment debtor;

(2) with property other than limited liability company property, by one or more of the other members; or

(3) by the limited liability company with the consent of all of the members whose interests are not so charged.(d) This chapter does not deprive a member of a right under exemption laws with respect to the member's limited liability company interest.

(e) This section provides the exclusive remedy by which a judgment creditor of a member or member's assignee may satisfy a judgment out of the judgment debtor's limited liability company interest.

(f) No creditor of a member shall have any right to obtain possession of, or otherwise exercise legal or equitable remedies with respect to, the property of the limited liability company.

§ 18–704. Right of Assignee to Become Member

(a) An assignee of a limited liability company interest may become a member as provided in a limited liability company agreement and upon:

(1) The approval of all of the members of the limited liability company other than the member assigning his limited liability company interest; or

(2) Compliance with any procedure provided for in the limited liability company agreement.

(b) An assignee who has become a member has, to the extent assigned, the rights and powers, and is subject to the restrictions and liabilities, of a member under a limited liability company agreement and this chapter. Notwithstanding the foregoing, unless otherwise provided in a limited liability company agreement, an assignee who becomes a member is liable for the obligations of the assignor to make contributions as provided in § 18–502 of this title, but shall not be liable for the obligations of the assignor under subchapter VI of this title. However, the assignee is not obligated for liabilities, including the obligations of the assignor to make contributions as provided in § 18–502 of this title, unknown to the assignee at the time the assignee became a member and which could not be ascertained from a limited liability company agreement.

(c) Whether or not an assignee of a limited liability company interest becomes a member, the assignor is not released from his liability to a limited liability company under subchapters V and VI of this chapter.

§ 18–705. Powers of Estate of Deceased or Incompetent Member

If a member who is an individual dies or a court of competent jurisdiction adjudges the member to be incompetent to manage the member's person or property, the member's personal representative may exercise all of the member's rights for the purpose of settling the member's estate or administering the member's property, including any power under a limited liability company agreement of an assignee to become a member. If a member is a corporation, trust or other entity and is dissolved or terminated, the powers of that member may be exercised by its personal representative.

Subchapter VIII. Dissolution

§ 18–801. Dissolution

(a) A limited liability company is dissolved and its affairs shall be wound up upon the first to occur of the following:

(1) At the time specified in a limited liability company agreement, but if no such time is set forth in the limited liability company agree-

ment, then the limited liability company shall have a perpetual existence;

(2) Upon the happening of events specified in a limited liability company agreement;

(3) Unless otherwise provided in a limited liability company agreement, upon the affirmative vote or written consent of the members of the limited liability company or, if there is more than 1 class or group of members, then by each class or group of members, in either case, by members who own more than two-thirds of the then-current percentage or other interest in the profits of the limited liability company owned by all of the members or by the members in each class or group, as appropriate;

(4) At any time there are no members; provided, that the limited liability company is not dissolved and is not required to be wound up if:

a. Unless otherwise provided in a limited liability company agreement, within 90 days or such other period as is provided for in the limited liability company agreement after the occurrence of the event that terminated the continued membership of the last remaining member, the personal representative of the last remaining member agrees in writing to continue the limited liability company and to the admission of the personal representative of such member or its nominee or designee to the limited liability company as a member, effective as of the occurrence of the event that terminated the continued membership of the last remaining member; provided, that a limited liability company agreement may provide that the personal representative of the last remaining member shall be obligated to agree in writing to continue the limited liability company and to the admission of the personal representative of such member or its nominee or designee to the limited liability company as a member, effective as of the occurrence of the event that terminated the continued membership of the last remaining member, or

b. A member is admitted to the limited liability company in the manner provided for in the limited liability company agreement, effective as of the occurrence of the event that terminated the continued membership of the last remaining member, within 90 days or such other period as is provided for in the limited liability company agreement after the occurrence of the event that terminated the continued membership of the last remaining member, pursuant to a provision of the limited liability company agreement that specifically provides for the admission of a member to the limited liability company after there is no longer a remaining member of the limited liability company.

(5) The entry of a decree of judicial dissolution under § 18–802 of this title.

(b) Unless otherwise provided in a limited liability company agreement, the death, retirement, resignation, expulsion, bankruptcy or dissolution of any member or the occurrence of any other event that terminates the continued membership of any member shall not cause the limited liability company to be dissolved or its affairs to be wound up, and upon the occurrence of any such event, the limited liability company shall be continued without dissolution.

§ 18-802. Judicial Dissolution

On application by or for a member or manager the Court of Chancery may decree dissolution of a limited liability company whenever it is not reasonably practicable to carry on the business in conformity with a limited liability company agreement.

§ 18-803. Winding Up

(a) Unless otherwise provided in a limited liability company agreement, a manager who has not wrongfully dissolved a limited liability company or, if none, the members or a person approved by the members or, if there is more than one class or group of members, then by each class or group of members, in either case, by members who own more than 50 percent of the then current percentage or other interest in the profits of the limited liability company owned by all of the members or by the members in each class or group, as appropriate, may wind up the limited liability company's affairs; but the Court of Chancery, upon cause shown, may wind up the limited liability company's affairs upon application of any member or manager, the member's or manager's personal representative or assignee, and in connection therewith, may appoint a liquidating trustee.

(b) Upon dissolution of a limited liability company and until the filing of a certificate of cancellation as provided in § 18-203 of this title, the persons winding up the limited liability company's affairs may, in the name of, and for and on behalf of, the limited liability company, prosecute and defend suits, whether civil, criminal or administrative, gradually settle and close the limited liability company's business, dispose of and convey the limited liability company's property, discharge or make reasonable provision for the limited liability company's liabilities, and distribute to the members any remaining assets of the limited liability company, all without affecting the liability of members and managers and without imposing liability on a liquidating trustee.

§ 18-804. Distribution of Assets

(a) Upon the winding up of a limited liability company, the assets shall be distributed as follows:

(1) To creditors, including members and managers who are creditors, to the extent otherwise permitted by law, in satisfaction of liabili-

ties of the limited liability company (whether by payment or the making of reasonable provision for payment thereof) other than liabilities for which reasonable provision for payment has been made and liabilities for distributions to members and former members under § 18-601 or § 18-604 of this title;

(2) Unless otherwise provided in a limited liability company agreement, to members and former members in satisfaction of liabilities for distributions under § 18-601 or § 18-604 of this title; and

(3) Unless otherwise provided in a limited liability company agreement, to members first for the return of their contributions and second respecting their limited liability company interests, in the proportions in which the members share in distributions.

(b) A limited liability company which has dissolved:

(1) Shall pay or make reasonable provision to pay all claims and obligations, including all contingent, conditional or unmatured contractual claims, known to the limited liability company;

(2) Shall make such provision as will be reasonably likely to be sufficient to provide compensation for any claim against the limited liability company which is the subject of a pending action, suit or proceeding to which the limited liability company is a party; and

(3) Shall make such provision as will be reasonably likely to be sufficient to provide compensation for claims that have not been made known to the limited liability company or that have not arisen but that, based on facts known to the limited liability company, are likely to arise or to become known to the limited liability company within 10 years after the date of dissolution. If there are sufficient assets, such claims and obligations shall be paid in full and any such provision for payment made shall be made in full. If there are insufficient assets, such claims and obligations shall be paid or provided for according to their priority and, among claims of equal priority, ratably to the extent of assets available therefor. Unless otherwise provided in the limited liability company agreement, any remaining assets shall be distributed as provided in this chapter. Any liquidating trustee winding up a limited liability company's affairs who has complied with this section shall not be personally liable to the claimants of the dissolved limited liability company by reason of such person's actions in winding up the limited liability company.

(c) A member who receives a distribution in violation of subsection (a) of this section, and who knew at the time of the distribution that the distribution violated subsection (a) of this section, shall be liable to the limited liability company for the amount of the distribution. For purposes of the immediately preceding sentence, the term "distribution" shall not include amounts constituting reasonable compensation for present or past services or reasonable payments made in the ordinary course of business pursuant to a bona fide retirement plan or other benefits program. A member who receives a distribution in violation of subsection (a) of this section, and who did not know at the time of the distribution that the distribution violated subsection (a) of this section, shall not be liable for the amount of the distribution. Subject to subsection (d) of this section, this subsection shall not affect any obligation or liability of a member under an agreement or other applicable law for the amount of a distribution.

(d) Unless otherwise agreed, a member who receives a distribution from a limited liability company to which this section applies shall have no liability under this chapter or other applicable law for the amount of the distribution after the expiration of 3 years from the date of the distribution unless an action to recover the distribution from such member is commenced prior to the expiration of the said 3–year period and an adjudication of liability against such member is made in the said action.

(e) Section 18–607 of this title shall not apply to a distribution to which this section applies.

* * *

C. LIMITED LIABILITY COMPANY FORMS

Table of Contents

SHAW PITTMAN LLP FORM OPERATING AGREEMENT FOR DELAWARE LIMITED LIABILITY CORPORATION*

OPERATING AGREEMENT OF XYZ PARTNERS, L.L.C.

THIS OPERATING AGREEMENT (the "Agreement") of XYZ Partners, L.L.C., a Delaware limited liability company (the "Company"), is made as of ______ ("Effective Date") by and among the Company and the Members (as defined below).

RECITALS:

WHEREAS, the Members desire to enter into this Agreement to provide for the operation and management of the Company.

NOW, THEREFORE, in consideration of the mutual covenants and agreements herein contained and other good and valuable consideration, the receipt and sufficiency of which are hereby acknowledged, the parties agree as follows:

SECTION 1

Formation and Purpose

1.1 Formation

1.1.1 The Members, by execution of this Agreement, form the Company as a limited liability company under and pursuant

* Thanks to Jack Lewis, Esq., a member of Shaw Pittman LLP for providing this Form Operating Agreement.

to the Delaware Limited Liability Company Act (the "Act"). For that purpose, the Members have caused the Company's Certificate of Formation to be executed and filed with the Secretary of State of the State of Delaware.

1.1.2 Each Member adopts this Agreement as the Operating Agreement of the Company, pursuant to the Act.

1.2 Subscription for Membership Interests

1.2.1 Each Member agrees to his status as a Member and subscribes for the acquisition of a Membership Interest, upon the terms and conditions set forth in this Agreement.

1.3 Name

The name of the Company is XYZ Partners, L.L.C. All Company business must be conducted in the name of the Company or such other names that comply with applicable law as the Board of Managers may select from time to time.

1.4 Governing Law

This Agreement and all issues regarding the rights and obligations of the Members, the construction, enforcement and interpretation hereof, and the formation, administration and termination of the Company shall be governed by the provisions of the Act and other applicable laws of the State of Delaware without reference to conflict of laws principles.

1.5 Purposes

The Company has been formed for the purposes of transacting any and all lawful business for which limited liability companies may be organized under the Act, and it is specifically contemplated that the activity of the Company shall consist solely of providing, through its Members, services under the Consulting Services Agreements, and such other activities as the Board of Managers shall have unanimously determined to be joint endeavors of the Members in which each Member will share equally in the resulting income and expense.

1.6 Foreign Qualification Governmental Filings

Prior to the Company's conducting business in any jurisdiction other than the State of Delaware, the Board of Managers, or Officers, if any, shall cause the Company to comply with all requirements necessary to qualify the Company as a foreign limited liability company in such jurisdiction. The Board of Managers, or Officers, if any shall execute, acknowledge, swear to and deliver all certificates and other instruments conforming to this Agreement that are necessary or appropriate to qualify, or, as appropriate, to continue or terminate such qualification of, the Company as a foreign limited liability company in all such jurisdictions in which the Company may conduct business.

SECTION 2

Definitions

2.1 Definitions

2.1.1 "Act" means the Delaware Limited Liability Company Act, as amended from time to time.

2.1.2 "Code" means the Internal Revenue Code of 1986, as amended, and any successor statute.

2.1.3 "Company" means XYZ Partners, L.L.C.

2.1.4 "Consulting Services Agreement" means, with respect to each of John Smith and Jane Jones, that certain Consulting Services Agreement dated ______, among such person, as named consultant thereunder, and ABC, Inc.

2.1.5 "Debt Instrument" means a promissory note or installment contractual obligation.

2.1.6 "Managers" means the individual(s) designated as Managers of the Company from time to time in accordance with the provisions of Section 4.1.1.

2.1.7 "Members" means those persons identified on *Exhibit A*, as such exhibit may be amended from time to time.

2.1.8 "Membership Interest" shall have the meaning ascribed to it in Section 3.1.2.

2.1.9 "Net Cash Flow" shall have the meaning ascribed to it in Section 6.1.1.

2.1.10 "Net Contributions" shall mean the amount of any capital contributions made by a Member.

2.1.11 "Officers" shall have the meaning ascribed to it in Section 4.1.1(b).

2.1.12 "Transfer" shall have the meaning ascribed to it in Section 9.2.1.

2.2 Other Terms

Other terms used in this Agreement are defined in the context in which they are used and shall have the meanings there indicated.

SECTION 3

Status, Rights and Obligations of Members

3.1 Members

3.1.1 *Members*. The names of the Members of the Company and the notice address of each such Member are set forth on *Exhibit A* attached hereto.

3.1.2 *Membership Interests*. The Members agree that each Member's percentage of ownership interest in the Company (hereinafter referred to as a "Membership Interest") shall be as set forth on *Exhibit A*, as it may be amended from time to time pursuant to this Agreement.

3.2 Voting

Members shall vote in relative proportion to their respective Membership Interests. Any action requiring a vote, consent or approval of a "majority of the Members" shall be authorized if Members holding more than fifty percent (50%) of the outstanding Membership Interests entitled to vote, vote for, consent to or approve of, such action.

3.3 Meetings of Members

3.3.1 *Meetings*. Meetings of Members shall be held at such date, time and place as the Board of Managers may fix from time to time. Meetings of the Members may be called by the Board of Managers or by any Manager for the purpose of addressing any matters on which the Members may vote.

3.3.2 *Notice*. Written notice of a meeting of Members shall be sent or otherwise given to each Member not less than ten (10) nor more than sixty (60) days before the date of the meeting. The notice shall specify the place, date and hour of the meeting and the general nature of the business to be transacted. Notice of any meeting of Members shall be given in the manner prescribed by Section 10.4 hereof.

3.4 Action Without Meeting

Any action required or permitted to be taken at a meeting of the Members may be taken without a meeting if the action is approved by a majority of the Members. Each such action without a meeting shall be evidenced by one or more written consents to be filed with the Company's records. Such action shall be effective as of the date specified in the written consent(s). Prompt notice of the taking of such action without a meeting by less than unanimous written approval shall be given to those Members who have not approved of such action in writing.

3.5 Restricted Activities

3.5.1 *Use of Company Information.* Each Member covenants and agrees with the Company and the other Members that, except on behalf of the Company and as authorized by the Company, it will not use or permit others to use, disclose or divulge to others, copy or reproduce or remove from the custody and control of the Company any information relating to or used in the business and operations of the Company whether in written or unwritten form or in a form produced or stored by any magnetic, electrical or mechanical means or process, that is confidential information or a trade secret of the Company.

3.5.2 *Other Business Ventures.* Each Member may engage in or possess any interest in any other business of any nature and description, independently or with others, and neither the Company nor the other Members shall have any rights in or to any such independent venture or the income or profits derived therefrom.

3.6 No Preemptive Rights.

No Member shall have any preemptive, preferential or other similar right with respect to

(i) additional capital contributions or loans to the Company; or

(ii) the issuance or sale of any Membership Interests by the Company.

SECTION 4

Management of the Company

4.1 Management by Board of Managers

4.1.1 *Appointment and Replacement of Managers; Officers.*

(a) *Number; Election.* The operation of the Company shall be managed by, and the responsibility for managing the business and affairs of the Company shall be delegated to, a Board of Managers consisting of not more than five (5) managers (as defined in Section 8–101 of the Act) (each a "Manager") appointed by a majority of the Members, each of whom shall be a natural person but who does not need to be a Member. The initial Managers of the Company shall be John Smith and Jane Jones.

(b) *Officers.* The responsibility for managing the business and affairs of the Company may be delegated by the Board of Managers to such other persons as may be appointed by the Board of Managers. The Board of Managers of the Company may, from time to time as they deem advisable, appoint officers of the Company (the "Officers") and assign in writing titles (including, without limitation, President, Vice President, Secretary and Treasurer) to any such person. Unless the Board of Managers decides otherwise, if the title is one commonly used for officers of a business corporation formed under the Delaware General Corporation Law, the assignment of such title shall constitute the delegation to such person of the authorities and duties that are normally associated with that office. Any delegation pursuant to this Section 4 may be revoked at any time by the Board of Managers.

(c) *Term; Resignation; Removal.* Each Manager shall hold office until his successor is elected and qualified or until his earlier resignation or removal. Any Manager may resign at any time upon written notice to the Company. Any Manager may be removed, with or without cause, by the vote of a majority of the Members.

(d) *Filling of Vacancies.* Vacancies resulting from any increase in the authorized number of Managers and any vacancies on the Board of Managers resulting from death, resignation, disqualification, removal or other cause shall be filled by the affirmative vote of a majority of the remaining Managers, and the Managers so chosen shall hold office until the next annual election and until their successors are duly elected and shall qualify, or until their earlier resignation or removal.

4.1.2 *General Authority of the Board of Managers.*

(a) Except to the extent that the approval of the Members (or Members holding a specified proportion of interests) is otherwise required by this Agreement or the Act, and subject to the conditions and limitations set forth elsewhere in this Section 4, the Board of Managers shall have full, complete and exclusive discretion to manage and control the business of the Company in furtherance of the purposes for which the Company is formed. The Board of Managers shall exercise its best efforts to promote and protect the interests of the Company and shall devote such time and attention as is reasonably necessary and appropriate to discharge such obligations.

(b) In furtherance and not in limitation of the foregoing grant of authority, the Board of Managers (including any delegated Officer) is empowered on behalf of the Company to negotiate, execute and deliver such agreements, instruments, deeds, certificates and other documents as the Board of Managers deem necessary and appropriate in the Board of Managers' discretion to effect the purposes and interests of the Company.

(c) All decisions made for and on behalf of the Company by the Board of Managers shall be binding upon the Company. No person dealing with the Company shall be required to determine the authority of the Board of Managers or any Officer to enter into any undertaking on behalf of the Company, nor to determine any fact or circumstance bearing upon the existence of such authority; *provided, however*, that nothing herein shall extinguish, limit, or condition the liability of the Board of Managers or any Officer to the Members to discharge their obligations in accordance with this Agreement and the Act.

4.1.3 *Meetings of the Board of Managers.*

(a) *Place of Meetings.* The Board of Managers of the Company may hold meetings, both regular and special, either within or outside the State of Delaware.

(b) *Regular Meetings.* Regular meetings of the Board of Managers may be held without other notice at such time and at such place as shall from time to time be determined by the Board of Managers.

(c) *Special Meetings.* Special meetings of the Board of Managers may be called by any Manager or the President of the Company (if a President has been designated), on one day's notice to each Manager, either personally or by mail, facsimile, telegram or express courier.

(d) *Quorum; Vote Required for Action.* At all meetings of the Board of Managers, a majority of the total number of Managers then in office shall constitute a quorum for the transaction of business and the act of a majority of the Managers present at any meeting at which there is a quorum shall be the act of the Board of Managers, except as may be otherwise specifically provided herein or in the Certificate of Formation. If a quorum shall not be present at any meeting of the Board of Managers, the Managers present may adjourn the meeting from time to time, without notice other than announcement at the meeting of the time and place of the adjourned meeting, until a quorum shall be present.

(e) *Participation By Conference Telephone.* Managers may participate in a meeting of the Board of Managers by means of conference telephone or similar communications equipment by means of which all persons participating in the meeting can hear each other, and participation in a meeting pursuant to this subsection shall constitute presence in person at such meeting.

(f) *Action Without Meeting*. Any action required or permitted to be taken at any meeting of the Board of Managers may be taken without a meeting, if a majority of the Managers then in office consent thereto in writing, and the writing or writings are filed with the minutes of proceedings of the Board of Managers.

4.1.4 *Limitations Upon Managers' Authority.*

(a) Without first obtaining the unanimous written consent of the Members, the Board of Managers shall not:

(i) Do any act in contravention of this Agreement;

(ii) Do any act (other than a sale of all or any part of the assets of the Company) that would make it impossible to carry on the ordinary business of the Company;

(iii) Admit a person as a Member of the Company other than in accordance with the terms of this Agreement; or

(iv) Require any Member to contribute to the capital of the Company except as expressly provided in this Agreement.

(b) The foregoing limitations are in addition to, and do not supersede any other limitations or prohibitions expressly imposed upon the Managers under this Agreement or by the Act.

4.1.5 *Reimbursement.*

All expenses incurred with respect to the organization, operation and management of the Company shall be borne by the Company. The Managers shall be entitled to reimbursement from the Company for direct expenses allocable to the organization, operation and management of the Company.

4.3 Managers and Affiliates Dealing With the Company

The Board of Managers may appoint, employ, contract or otherwise deal with any person, including persons with whom a Manager is affiliated, and persons in which a Manager has a financial interest, for transacting Company business, including any acts or services for the Company as the Managers may approve; *provided, however*, that fees or other payments and terms of any contract with such parties shall not be in excess of prevailing competitive rates for such transactions.

SECTION 5

Capital Contributions and Financial Obligations of Members

5.1 Initial Capital Contributions

Contemporaneously with the execution of this Agreement, each Member shall make the initial cash capital contribution set opposite such Member's name in *Exhibit A*. Such capital shall be used by the Company to fund the operations of the Company and pay the expenses thereof. In addition, each Member shall, by execution of this Agreement, be deemed to have contributed to the Company all of such Member's right to receive payments under sections 4 and 5 of such Member's Consulting Services Agreement, and so much of section 8 of such agreement as may be relevant to Losses (within the meaning of such section) that are treated by the Members as incurred by the Company. After such contribution of rights, the Members shall be considered to receive any such payments under the Consulting Services Agreements as an agent of the Company, and consistent therewith shall pay over, assign to, or account to the Company for all such payments received thereunder. Such rights shall, at the time of contribution, be considered to have fair market value of zero, and no amount shall be reflected in such Member's capital account by reason of the contribution of such rights.

5.2 Additional Contributions

5.2.1 The Board of Managers may arrange for the provision of such additional funds as are deemed necessary to conduct Company business. Such additional funds may be raised by loans to the Company from outside sources, or by loans or capital contributions to the Company from one or more Members.

5.2.2 No Member shall be required to make any additional capital contributions to the Company, unless all the Members have agreed in writing that such capital contribution is or may be required on certain conditions.

5.3 No Interest Upon Capital Contributions

No Member shall be entitled to be paid interest by the Company on his capital contributions.

5.4 Return of Capital Contributions

No Member shall be entitled to withdraw any part of his capital contributions or his capital account or to receive any distribution from the Company, except as specifically provided in this Agreement. Except as otherwise provided herein, there shall be no obligation to return to any Member or withdrawn Member any part of such Member's capital contributions to the Company for so long as the Company continues in existence.

5.5 Loans Not to be Treated as Capital Contributions

Loans or advances by any Member to the Company shall not be considered capital contributions and shall not increase the capital account balance of the lending or advancing Member.

5.6 No Loans Required.

Except as provided in this Agreement, no Member shall be required under any circumstances to contribute or lend any money or property to the Company, except to the extent that such Member has agreed to do so in writing.

5.7 No Third Party Beneficiaries.

The provisions of this Agreement relating to the financial obligations of Members are not intended to be for the benefit of any creditor or other person (except Members) to whom any debts, liabilities or obligations are owed by (or who otherwise has any claim against) the Company or any of the Members; and, except for Members, no creditor or other person shall obtain any right under any of such provisions or shall by reason of any of such provisions make any claim with respect to any debt, liability or obligation (or otherwise) against the Company or any of the Members.

SECTION 6

Distributions of Cash and Property

6.1 Distribution of Net Cash Flow and Mandatory Tax Distributions

6.1.1 *Net Cash Flow Defined.* The term "Net Cash Flow" for a fiscal year of the Company shall mean:

(a) All cash receipts as shown on the books of the Company (excluding, however, capital contributions from Members and net proceeds to the Company from the sale or the disposition of substantially all of the Company's assets), reduced by cash disbursements for Company purposes including interest and principal upon loans, and all cash reserves set aside by the Board of Managers that the Board of Managers deem necessary or appropriate to accomplish the Company business; *plus*

(b) Any other funds, including amounts previously set aside as reserves by the Board of Managers, deemed available by the Board of Managers for distribution as Net Cash Flow.

6.1.2 *Priority of Distribution*. Subject to Section 6.1.3, the Board of Managers shall determine what portion of the Net Cash Flow of the Company for a fiscal year shall be paid to Members as a distribution; provided that such distribution shall be paid out to the Members *pro rata* in accordance with their respective Membership Interests. The Board of Managers shall determine the timing of when such distributions shall be made to the Members.

6.1.3 *Mandatory Distributions for Taxes*. With respect to any fiscal year in which the Company has net income allocable to the Members in accordance with Section 7.2.2, the Board of Managers shall cause the Company to distribute to each Member pursuant to Section 6.1.2 an amount equal to not less than fifty percent (50%) of the net income so allocated to such Member with respect to such fiscal year; provided however, that in no event shall a distribution be required under this Section 6.1.3 in excess of the Company's Net Cash Flow for such fiscal year. Distributions required under this section 6.1.3 shall be made not later than the April 1 following the close of such fiscal year.

6.2 Distribution of the Proceeds of Dissolution

If the Company dissolves, the net proceeds of dissolution, including any accompanying sale of Company assets, shall be distributed in the following order of priority:

(a) First, toward the satisfaction of all outstanding debts and other obligations of the Company, including Members who are creditors.

(b) Then, *pro rata* among those Members with positive capital account balances, in proportion to their respective capital account balances, after adjustments for distributions under Sections 6.1 and tax allocations for the current fiscal year.

6.3 Distribution of Debt Instruments

6.3.1 In the event the Company sells any of its assets and all or a portion of the sales price is paid by a Debt Instrument, if such sale occurs in conjunction with the dissolution of the Company, all interest and principal received by the Company shall be treated as net proceeds of dissolution, and shall be distributed in accordance with Section 6.2 hereof.

6.3.2 In the event the Company holds a Debt Instrument as described in Section 6.3.1 and the Company either is dissolved in conjunction with the sale that gave rise to such Debt Instrument or dissolves prior to payment in full of such Debt Instrument, the Board of Managers shall assign such

Debt Instrument to a trustee who shall collect all sums that may become due and payable under the Debt Instrument, who shall have the power and authority to act to enforce all rights of the holder of such Debt Instrument and who shall distribute such sums pursuant to the formula described in Section 6.2.

6.4 Distributions in Kind

6.4.1 No Member shall be entitled to demand and receive distributions other than in cash form, except for the distribution of rights under such Member's Consulting Services Agreement contemplated by Section 6.4.2 of this Agreement . .

6.4.2 If any Company assets are distributed in kind, such assets shall be distributed to each Member, provided that, to the maximum extent possible, the rights of the Company to receive payments with respect to services, reimbursements or indemnification, under a Member's Consulting Services Agreement, to the extent arising after the event causing the Company's dissolution, shall be distributed to such Member. The amount by which the fair market value of any property to be distributed in kind to the Members exceeds or is less than the tax basis of such property shall, to the extent not otherwise recognized by the Company, be taken into account for purposes of allocation of gain or loss and distributions of proceeds to the Members under this Section 6 as if the property had been sold by the Company for its fair market value on the date of the distribution and the proceeds distributed. The fair market value of any property to be distributed in kind to the Members shall be determined by the Board of Managers in their reasonable discretion, except that any to be distributed in kind to the Members shall be valued as follows:

(a) If the securities are then traded on a national securities exchange, the NASDAQ National Market System (or a similar national quotation system) or the NASDAQ SmallCap Market, then the value shall be deemed to be the average of the closing prices of the securities on such exchange or system over the 30–day period ending three (3) days prior to the distribution; and

(b) If the securities are actively traded over-the-counter, then the value shall be deemed to be the average of the closing bid prices over the 30–day period ending three (3) days prior to the distribution; and

(c) If there is no active public trading market for the securities, then the value shall be the fair market value thereof, as determined in the reasonable discretion of the Board of Managers.

(d) Rights under any Member's Consulting Services Agreement distributed pursuant to Section 6.4.2, to the extent relating to payments for services or reimbursements for expenses or indemnifiable losses attributable to periods after the event causing the Company's distribution of such rights, shall be considered to have a fair market value of zero.

SECTION 7

Federal and State Tax Matters

7.1 Maintenance of Members' Capital Accounts

With respect to each Member, a separate "capital account" for such Member shall be established and maintained throughout the full term of the Company in accordance with applicable Treasury Regulations that must be complied with in order for the allocations of taxable profits and losses provided in this Agreement to have "economic effect" under applicable Treasury Regulations.

7.2 Allocations of Profits and Losses of the Company

Subject to Section 7.3 below, the Company's net income or loss for a fiscal year, computed in accordance with Treasury Regulations section 1.704–1(b)(2)(iv), shall be allocated among the Members for each fiscal year as follows:

7.2.1 *Net Loss.* The net loss (other than from a sale or disposition of all or substantially all of the Company's assets), if any, for a fiscal year of the Company shall be allocated to the Members in accordance with their respective Membership Interests.

7.2.2 *Net Income.* The net income (other than from a sale or disposition of all or substantially all of the Company's assets), if any, for a fiscal year of the Company shall be allocated to the Members in accordance with their respective Membership Interests.

7.2.3 *Net Loss from Sale of All or Substantially All of the Company Assets.* The net loss from a sale or other disposition of all or substantially all of the Company assets shall be allocated among the Members as follows:

(a) First, to the Members, if any, having positive capital account balances in excess of their Net Contributions amounts in proportion to such excess positive balances, until the balance in each such Member's capital account equals the amount of such Member's Net Contributions, or, if there is insufficient loss to accomplish this result, to cause such excess positive balances to be in the same ratio as the Members' respective Membership Interests;

(b) Second, to the Members, if any, having positive capital account balances, in proportion to such positive balances, until the balances in their capital accounts equal zero; and

(c) Thereafter, to the Members in accordance with their respective Membership Interests.

7.2.4 *Net Income from Sale of All or Substantially All of the Company Assets*. The net income from a sale or other disposition of all or substantially all of the Company assets shall be allocated among the Members as follows:

(a) First, to the Members, if any, having negative capital account balances, in proportion to such negative balances, until the balances in their capital accounts equal zero;

(b) Second, to the extent any Member has a positive capital account balance that is less than the amount of such Member's Net Contributions, to each such Member, in the amounts necessary, and in the ratio of such amounts, to cause the positive capital account balance of each such Member to be equal to the amount of such Member's Net Contributions;

(c) Third, to the Members in the amounts necessary, and in the ratio of such amounts, to cause their positive capital account balances in excess of the amounts of their respective Net Contributions to be in the same ratio as their respective Membership Interests; and

(d) Thereafter, to the Members in accordance with their respective Membership Interests.

7.3 Special Tax Allocations

Notwithstanding anything to the contrary contained above in Section 7.2:

7.3.1 The Company shall comply with Treasury Regulation Section 1.704–2 with respect to the allocation of deductions and minimum gain relating to nonrecourse debts of the Company.

7.3.2 No Member shall be allocated a net loss that would cause or increase a deficit balance in his capital account in excess of any actual or deemed obligation of such Member to restore deficits (as defined in Treasury Regulation Section 1.704–1(b)(2)(ii)(c)). If any Member shall receive with respect to the Company an adjustment, allocation or distribution in the nature described in Treasury Regulation Section 1.704–1(b)(2)(ii)(d)(4)-(6) that causes or increases a deficit in such Member's capital account, such Member shall be allocated items of income and gain in an amount and manner as will eliminate such deficit balance as quickly as possible. It is intended that this Section 8.3.2 shall constitute a "qualified income offset" within the meaning of Treasury Regulation Section 1.704–1(b)(2)(ii)(d)(3).

7.3.3 Any allocations required pursuant to Section 7.3.2 shall be taken into account in allocating net income and net loss pursuant to Section 7.2 above so that, to the extent possible, the net amount of such allocations shall be equal to the net amount that would have been allocated to each Member if the allocations pursuant to Section 7.3.2 had not occurred.

7.3.4 Any portion of any income, gain, loss or deduction with respect to property contributed to the Company by a Member (or revalued pursuant to Treasury Regulation section 1.704–1(b)(2)(iv)(f) shall be allocated among the Members in accordance with Code Section 704(c) and Treasury Regulation Section 1.704–3 so as to take account of the variation, if any, between the adjusted tax basis of such property to the Company and its fair market value at the time of the contributions.

7.3.5 In the event of the Transfer of all or any part of a Membership Interest (in accordance with the provisions of this Agreement) at any time other than the end of a fiscal year, the share of income or loss (in respect of the Membership Interest so transferred) shall be allocated between the transferor and the transferee in the same ratio as the number of days in such fiscal year before and after such Transfer. The provisions of this Section 7.3.5 shall not apply to any income or loss attributable to the sale or other disposition of all or substantially all of the Company assets, or to other extraordinary non-recurring items. Such income and loss shall be allocated to the owner of the Membership Interest as of the date of closing of the sale or other disposition, or, with respect to other extraordinary non-recurring items, the date the income is realized or the loss is incurred, as the case may be.

7.4 Tax Year and Accounting Matters

The taxable year of the Company shall be the calendar year. The Company shall adopt such methods of accounting, and file its tax returns on the methods of accounting, as determined by the Board of Managers upon the advice of the certified public accounting firm servicing the books and records of the Company.

7.5 Tax Matters Partner

Jane Jones shall be the "Tax Matters Partner" for federal income tax purposes. All costs and expenses incurred by the Tax Matters Partner in performing her duties as such (including legal and accounting fees) shall be borne by the Company.

7.6 Tax Elections

The Tax Matters Partner, in the exercise of his reasonable discretion, may cause the Company to make or revoke all tax elections provided for under the Code.

SECTION 8

Term and Termination of the Company

8.1 Term of the Company

The term of the Company commenced upon the filing of the Certificate of Formation, and shall continue until dissolved and terminated in accordance with this Agreement.

8.2 Events of Termination

The Company shall be dissolved upon the occurrence of any of the following events:

8.2.1 The unanimous written consent of the Members to dissolve and terminate the Company;

8.2.2 The sale, transfer or assignment of substantially all the assets of the Company;

8.2.3 Unless waived by unanimous written consent of the Members, the termination or amendment of any Member's Consulting Services Agreement affecting the payments to be made thereafter pursuant to sections 4, 5 or 8 of such agreement, unless such termination or amendment shall simultaneously and identically apply to every Member's Consulting Services Agreement;

8.2.4 The death, resignation, retirement, expulsion, bankruptcy or dissolution of a Member or occurrence of any other event that terminates the continued membership of a Member in the Company;

8.2.5 Entry of a decree of judicial dissolution; or

8.2.6 As otherwise required by Delaware law.

8.3 Conclusion of Affairs

In the event of the dissolution of the Company for any reason, the Board of Managers shall proceed promptly to wind up the affairs of and liquidate the Company. Except as otherwise provided in this Agreement, the Members shall continue to share distributions and tax allocations during the period of liquidation in the same manner as before the dissolution. The Board of Managers shall have reasonable discretion to determine the time, manner and terms of any sale or sales of Company property pursuant to such liquidation having due regard to the activity and the condition and relevant market and general financial and economic conditions and consistent with their fiduciary obligations to the Members.

8.4 Liquidating Distributions

After paying or providing for the payment of all debts or liabilities of the Company and all expenses of liquidation, and subject to the right of the Board of Managers to set up such reserves as they may deem reasonably necessary for any contingent or unforeseen liabilities or obligations of the Company, the proceeds of the liquidation and any other assets of the Company shall be distributed to or for the benefit of the Members in accordance with this Agreement. The Board of Managers shall have the right to distribute assets in kind, valued at the then fair market value of such assets (as determined in accordance with Section 6.4.2), as a liquidating distribution to the Members.

8.5 Termination

Within a reasonable time following the completion of the liquidation of the Company, the Board of Managers shall supply to each of the Members a statement that shall set forth the assets and the liabilities of the Company as of the date of complete liquidation and each Member's portion of the distributions pursuant to this Agreement. Upon completion of the liquidation of the Company and the distribution of all Company assets, the Company shall terminate and the Board of Managers shall have the authority to execute and file with the Delaware Secretary of State a Certificate of Cancellation of the Company, as well as any and all other documents required to effectuate the dissolution and termination of the Company.

SECTION 9

Admission, Transfers, Addition, Substitution, and Withdrawal of Members

9.1 Admission

A new Member may be admitted to membership in the Company through the issuance by the Company of a Membership Interest directly to such new Member upon the unanimous written consent of the Members.

9.2 Restrictions on Transfers

9.2.1 Membership Interests (including "economic interest") may be assigned, sold, gifted, pledged, encumbered, mortgaged or otherwise transferred (a "Transfer") in whole or in part only upon the written consent of a majority of the Members; provided that no such Transfer shall be made unless the Company shall have been offered, and such offer remains unaccepted for 20 days, the opportunity to purchase such Member's Membership Interest at a price and on terms no less favorable than those of such proposed Transfer. 9.2.2 Unless waived by the Board of Managers, a Membership Interest shall not be Transferred in the absence of an opinion of counsel, satisfactory to the Board of Managers, that the transfer of the Membership Interest is exempt from the registration requirements under the Securities Act of 1933, as amended, or any applicable state securities laws.

9.3 Admission of Substituted or Additional Members

9.3.1 No person not a Member on the date of this Agreement shall become a Member hereunder under any of the provisions hereof unless such person shall expressly assume and agree to be bound by all of the terms and conditions of this Agreement. Each such person shall also cause to be delivered to the Company, at his, her or its sole cost and expense such documents or instruments as may be required in the discretion of the Board of Managers in order to effect such person's admission as an additional Member. Upon compliance with all provisions hereof applicable to such person becoming a Member, the Board of Managers are authorized to execute and deliver such amendments hereto as are necessary to constitute such person or entity a Member of the Company. Any transferee of a Membership Interest that has not been admitted as a substituted Member shall be an "assignee," entitled only to allocations of net profits, net losses and other tax items of the Company and to distributions from the Company, and shall not be entitled to vote or participate in the affairs and management of the Company.

9.3.2 A Member who has Transferred his Membership Interest shall cease to be a Member upon Transfer of the Member's entire Membership Interest and thereafter shall have no further powers, rights or privileges as a Member hereunder, but shall, unless otherwise relieved of such obligations by agreement of all the other Members or by operation of law, remain liable for all obligations and duties as a Member related to the time during which he was a Member.

9.3.3 The Company, each Member and any other person or persons having business with the Company need deal only with Members who are admitted as Members of the Company, and they shall not be required to deal with any other person by reason of a Transfer by a Member, except as otherwise provided in this Agreement. In the absence of the written consent provided in Section 9.2.1, any payment to an assigning Member shall acquit the Company and the Managers of all liability to any other persons who may be interested in such payment by reason of a Transfer by such Member.

9.3.4 No person shall have a perfected lien or security interest in a Membership Interest unless the creation of such interest is in accord with the provisions of this Agreement and the Company is notified of such interest and provided a copy of all documentation with respect thereto, including financing statements, prior to execution and filing.

9.3.5 Any Transfer not in accord with this Agreement shall be void.

9.3.6 Each Member agrees not to Transfer all or any part of his Membership Interest (or take or omit any action, that could result in a deemed Transfer) if such Transfer (either considered alone or in the aggregate with prior Transfers by other Members) would result in the Company being treated as a "publicly traded partnership" under Code Section 7704.

9.4 No Right to Withdraw

No Member shall have any right to voluntarily resign or otherwise withdraw from the Company without the unanimous written consent of the Members.

9.5 Effect of Withdrawal

On and as of the effective date of a Member's withdrawal from the Company under the provisions of this Agreement, such former Member shall cease to have any Membership Interest or any management or other rights, status or privileges of a Member, but such former Member shall not be released or discharged from any of the obligations of a Member under the provisions of this Agreement, unless agreed to and evidenced by the unanimous written consent of the Members.

SECTION 10

Administrative Provisions

10.1 Principal Office

10.1.1 The initial principal place of business and principal office of the Company shall be at ______. The Company may relocate the principal office and principal place of business and have such additional offices as the Managers may deem advisable.

101.2 The Managers shall have the power, on behalf of the Company, to designate, where required, a registered agent (or other agent for receipt of service of process) in each state or other jurisdiction in which the Company transacts business and to designate, to the extent required, an office, place of business or mailing address, within or without that state or other jurisdiction.

10.2 Bank Accounts

10.2.1 Funds of the Company shall be deposited in an account or accounts of a type, in form and name and in a bank(s) or other financial institution(s) that are participants in federal insurance programs as selected by the Board of Managers. The Board of Managers shall arrange for the appropriate conduct of such accounts. Funds may be withdrawn from such accounts only for bona fide and legitimate Company purposes and may from time to time be invested in such short-term securities, money market funds, certificates of deposit or other liquid assets as the Board of Managers deem appropriate.

10.2.2 The Members acknowledge that the Board of Managers may maintain Company funds in accounts, money market funds, certificates of deposit, other liquid assets in excess of the insurance provided by the Federal Deposit Insurance Corporation or other depository insurance institutions and that the Board of Managers shall not be accountable or liable for any loss of such funds resulting from failure or insolvency of the depository institution.

10.3 Books and Records

10.3.1 At all times during the term of the Company, the Board of Managers shall keep, or cause to be kept, full and faithful books of account, records and supporting documents, which shall reflect, completely, accurately and in reasonable detail, each transaction of the Company (including, without limitation, transactions with the Managers or affiliates). The books of account shall be maintained and tax returns prepared and filed in the method of accounting determined by the Board of Managers. The books of account, records and all documents and other writings of the Company shall be kept and maintained at the principal office of the Company. Each Member or his designated representative shall, upon reasonable notice to the Board of Managers, have access to such financial books, records and documents during reasonable business hours and may inspect and make copies of any of them at his own expense.

10.3.2 The Board of Managers shall cause the Company to keep at its principal office the following:

(a) A current list of the full name and last known business address of each Member, in alphabetical order;

(b) A copy of the Certificate of Formation and all articles of amendment and certificates of amendment thereto;

(c) Copies of the Company's federal, state and local income tax returns and reports, if any, for the three (3) most recent years; and

(d) Copies of this Agreement, as it may be amended, and of any financial statements of the Company for the three (3) most recent years.

10.4 Notices

All notices required or permitted hereunder shall be in writing and shall be deemed effectively given: (a) upon personal delivery to the party to be notified, (b) when sent by confirmed facsimile if sent during normal business hours of the recipient, if not, then on the next business day, (c) five (5) days after having been sent by registered or certified mail, return receipt requested, postage prepaid, or (d) one (1) business day after deposit with a nationally recognized overnight courier, specifying next day delivery, with written verification of receipt. All communications shall be sent to the Company at the address as set forth in Section 10.1.1 and to a Member at the Member's address set forth on *Exhibit A* attached hereto or at such other address as the Company or a Member may designate by ten (10) days" advance written notice to the other parties hereto.

SECTION 11

Indemnification and Limitation of Liability

11.1 Indemnification of Members and Managers

Except as provided in Section 11.3, every person who was or is a party or who is threatened to be made a party to any pending, completed, or impending action, suit, or proceeding of any kind, whether civil, criminal, administrative, arbitrative or investigative (whether or not by or in the right of the Company) by reason of (i) being or having been a Manager, Officer or Member of the Company; (ii) being or having been a member, manager, partner, officer, or director of any other entity at the request of the Company; or (iii) serving or having served in a representative capacity for the Company in connection with any partnership, joint venture, committee, trust, employee benefit plan or other enterprise, shall be indemnified by the Company against all expenses (including reasonable attorney fees), judgments, fines, penalties, awards, costs, amounts paid in settlement and liabilities of all kinds, actually incurred by him incidental to or resulting from such action, suit, or proceeding to the fullest extent permitted under the Act, without limiting any other indemnification rights to which he otherwise may be entitled. The Company may, but shall not be required to, purchase insurance on behalf of such person against liability asserted against or incurred by such person in his capacity as a Manager, Officer or Member whether or not the Company would have authority to indemnify him against the same liability under the provisions of this Section 11.1 or the Act.

11.2 Liability Limitation

Except as provided in Section 11.3, no Member or Manager shall have liability to the Company or other Members for monetary damages resulting from a single transaction, occurrence or isolated course of conduct.

11.3 Qualification of Indemnification

The indemnification rights and limitations on liabilities set forth in Sections 11.1 and 11.2 shall not apply to claims based upon gross negligence, any willful misconduct or intentional breach of the terms of this Agreement, or knowing violations of criminal law or any federal or state securities law, nor shall such indemnification rights preclude the Company or any Member from recovery for any loss or damage otherwise covered under any insurance policy or fidelity bonding. Nothing herein shall be deemed to prohibit or limit the Company's right to pay, or obtain insurance covering, the costs (including attorney fees) to defend an indemnitee, Member, Officer or Manager against any such claims, subject to a full reservation of rights to reimbursement in the event of a final adjudication adverse to such indemnitee, Member, Officer or Manager.

11.4 Advances for Expenses

Expenses (including reasonable attorney fees) incurred by or in respect of any such person in connection with any such action, suit or proceeding, whether civil, criminal, administrative, arbitrative or investigative, may be paid by the Company in advance of the final disposition thereof upon receipt of an undertaking by or on behalf of such person to repay such amount, unless it shall ultimately be determined that he is entitled to be indemnified by the Company, in which case reimbursement shall not be required.

11.5 Elimination of Liability

The Members acknowledge, agree and desire that, except as set forth in Section 11.3, the liability of any Member, Officer or Manager to the Company or to any of the other Members shall be eliminated, to the maximum extent possible, pursuant to the Act. The provisions of this Section 11 are in addition to, and not in substitution for, any other right to indemnity to which any person who is or may be indemnified by or pursuant to this Section 11 may otherwise be entitled, and to the powers otherwise accorded by law to the Company to indemnify any such person and to purchase and maintain insurance on behalf of any such person against any liability asserted against or incurred by him in any capacity referred to in this Section 11 or arising from his status as serving or having served in any such capacity (whether or not the Company would have the power to indemnify against such liability).

11.6 No Retroactive Effect of Amendment

No amendment or repeal of this Section 11 shall limit or eliminate the right to indemnification provided hereunder with respect to acts or omissions occurring before such amendment or repeal.

SECTION 12

Miscellaneous Provisions

12.1 Entire Agreement

This Agreement, including the exhibits attached hereto and incorporated herein by reference, constitutes the entire agreement of the Members with respect to the matters covered herein. This Agreement supersedes all prior agreements and oral understandings among the Members with respect to such matters.

12.2 Amendment; Form of Company

12.2.1 Except as provided by law or otherwise set forth herein, this Agreement may only be modified or amended by the written consent of a majority of the Members; *provided, however*, that *Exhibit A* hereto may be amended from time to time by the Board of Managers to the extent required to accurately reflect the then current status of the information contained thereon.

12.2.2 Without first obtaining the written consent of a majority of the Members, the Board of Managers shall not change or reorganize the Company into any other legal form.

12.3 Severability

Each provision of this Agreement shall be considered severable and if for any reason any provision or provisions hereof are determined to be invalid and contrary to existing or future law, such provision shall be deemed to be restated to reflect as nearly as possible the original intentions of the parties to this Agreement in accordance with applicable law. The remainder of this Agreement shall remain in full force and effect.

12.4 Successors

Except as expressly otherwise provided herein, this Agreement is binding upon, and inures to the benefit of, the parties hereto and their respective heirs, executors, administrators, personal and legal representatives, successors and assigns.

12.5 Counterparts

This Agreement may be executed in any number of counterparts, each of which shall be an original, but all of which together shall constitute one instrument, binding upon all parties hereto, notwithstanding that all such parties may not have executed the same counterpart.

IN WITNESS WHEREOF, the parties have executed this Agreement to be effective as of the Effective Date.

MEMBERS:

____

John Smith

____

Jane Jones

EXHIBIT A

Name	Address	Membership Interest	Capital Contribution
John Smith	____________ ____________	50%	$1,000
Jane Jones	____________ ____________	50%	$1,000
TOTAL		100%	$2,000

IV. FEDERAL SECURITIES LAW

A. SECURITIES ACT OF 1933

(Selected Sections)

15 U.S.C.A. §§ 77a et seq.

Contents

TITLE I

Short Title

Section 1. This subchapter may be cited as the "Securities Act of 1933."

Section 2. (a) *Definitions.* When used in this title, unless the context otherwise requires—

(1) The term "security" means any note, stock, treasury stock, bond, debenture, evidence of indebtedness, certificate of interest or participation in any profit-sharing agreement, collateral-trust certificate, preorganization certificate or subscription, transferable share, investment contract, voting-trust certificate, certificate of deposit for a security, fractional undivided interest in oil, gas, or other mineral rights, any put, call, straddle, option, or privilege on any security, certificate of deposit, or group or index of securities (including any interest therein or based on the value thereof), or any put, call, straddle, option, or privilege entered into on a national securities exchange relating to foreign currency, or, in general, any interest or instrument commonly known as a "security," or any certificate of interest or participation in, temporary or interim certificate for, receipt for, guarantee of, or warrant or right to subscribe to or purchase, any of the foregoing.

(2) The term "person" means an individual, a corporation, a partnership, an association, a joint-stock company, a trust, any unincorporated organization, or a government or political subdivision thereof. As used in this paragraph the term "trust" shall include only a trust where the interest or interests of the beneficiary or beneficiaries are evidenced by a security.

(3) The term "sale" or "sell" shall include every contract of sale or disposition of a security or interest in a security, for value. The term "offer to sell", "offer for sale", or "offer" shall include every attempt or offer to dispose of, or solicitation of an offer to buy, a security or interest in a security, for value. The terms defined in this paragraph and the term "offer to buy" as used in subsection (c) of section 5 shall not include preliminary negotiations or agreements between an issuer (or any person directly or indirectly controlling or controlled by an issuer, or under direct or indirect common control with an issuer) and any underwriter or among underwriters who are or are to be in privity of contract with an issuer (or any person directly or indirectly controlling or controlled by an issuer, or under direct or indirect common control with an issuer). Any security given or delivered with, or as a bonus on account of, any purchase of securities or any other thing, shall be conclusively presumed to constitute a part of the subject of such purchase and to have been offered and sold for value. The issue or transfer of a right or privilege, when originally issued or transferred with a security, giving the holder of such security the right to convert such security into another security of the same issuer or of another person, or giving a right to subscribe to another security of the same issuer or of another person, which right cannot be exercised until some future date, shall not be deemed to be an offer or sale of such other security; but the issue or transfer of such other security upon the exercise of such right of conversion or subscription shall be deemed a sale of such other security.

(4) The term "issuer" means every person who issues or proposes to issue any security; except that with respect to certificates of deposit, voting-trust certificates, or collateral-trust certificates, or with respect to certificates of interest or shares in an unincorporated investment trust not having a board of directors (or persons performing similar functions) or of the fixed, restricted management, or unit type, the term "issuer" means the person or persons performing the acts and assuming the duties of depositor or manager pursuant to the provisions of the trust or other agreement or instrument under which such securities are issued; except that in the case of an unincorporated association which provides by its articles for limited liability of any or all of its members, or in the case of a trust, committee, or other legal entity, the trustees or members thereof shall not be individually liable as issuers of any security issued by the association, trust, committee, or other legal entity; except that with respect to equipment-trust certificates or like securities, the term "issuer" means the person by whom the equipment or property is or is to be used; and except that with respect to fractional undivided interests in oil, gas, or other mineral rights, the term "issuer" means the owner of any such right or of any interest in such right (whether whole or fractional) who creates fractional interests therein for the purpose of public offerings.

(5) The term "Commission" means the Securities and Exchange Commission.

(6) The term "Territory" means Puerto Rico, the Virgin Islands, and the insular possessions of the United States.

(7) The term "interstate commerce" means trade or commerce in securities or any transportation or communication relating thereto among the several States or between the District of Columbia or any Territory of the United States and any State or other Territory, or between any foreign country and any State, Territory, or the District of Columbia, or within the District of Columbia.

(8) The term "registration statement" means the statement provided for in section 6, and includes any amendment thereto and any report, document, or memorandum filed as part of such statement or incorporated therein by reference.

(9) The term "write" or "written" shall include printed, lithographed, or any means of graphic communication.

(10) The term "prospectus" means any prospectus, notice, circular, advertisement, letter, or communication, written or by radio or television, which offers any security for sale or confirms the sale of any security; except that (a) a communication sent or given after the effective date of the registration

statement (other than a prospectus permitted under subsection (b) of section 10) shall not be deemed a prospectus if it is proved that prior to or at the same time with such communication a written prospectus meeting the requirements of subsection (a) of section 10 at the time of such communication was sent or given to the person to whom the communication was made, and (b) a notice, circular, advertisement, letter, or communication in respect of a security shall not be deemed to be a prospectus if it states from whom a written prospectus meeting the requirements of section 10 may be obtained and, in addition, does no more than identify the security, state the price thereof, state by whom orders will be executed, and contain such other information as the Commission, by rules or regulations deemed necessary or appropriate in the public interest and for the protection of investors, and subject to such terms and conditions as may be prescribed therein, may permit.

(11) The term "underwriter" means any person who has purchased from an issuer with a view to, or offers or sells for an issuer in connection with, the distribution of any security, or participates or has a direct or indirect participation in any such undertaking, or participates or has a participation in the direct or indirect underwriting of any such undertaking; but such term shall not include a person whose interest is limited to a commission from an underwriter or dealer not in excess of the usual and customary distributors' or sellers' commission. As used in this paragraph the term "issuer" shall include, in addition to an issuer, any person directly or indirectly controlling or controlled by the issuer, or any person under direct or indirect common control with the issuer.

(12) The term "dealer" means any person who engages either for all or part of his time, directly or indirectly, as agent, broker, or principal, in the business of offering, buying, selling, or otherwise dealing or trading in securities issued by another person.

(13) The term "insurance company" means a company which is organized as an insurance company, whose primary and predominant business activity is the writing of insurance or the reinsuring of risks underwritten by insurance companies, and which is subject to supervision by the insurance commissioner, or a similar official or agency of a State or territory or the District of Columbia; or any receiver or similar official or any liquidating agent for such company, in his capacity as such.

(14) The term "separate account" means an account established and maintained by an insurance company pursuant to the laws of any State or territory of the United States, the District of Columbia, or of Canada or any province thereof, under which income, gains and losses, whether or not realized, from assets allocated to such account, are, in accordance with the applicable contract, credited to or charged against such account without regard to other income, gains or losses of the insurance company.

(15) The term "accredited investor" shall mean—

(i) a bank as defined in section 3(a)(2) whether acting in its individual or fiduciary capacity; an insurance company as defined in paragraph 13 of this subsection; an investment company registered under the Investment Company Act of 1940 or a business development company as defined in section 2(a)(48) of that Act; a Small Business Investment Company licensed by the Small Business Administration; or an employee benefit plan, including an individual retirement account, which is subject to the provisions of the Employee Retirement Income Security Act of 1974, if the investment decision is made by a plan fiduciary, as defined in section 3(21) of such Act, which is either a bank, insurance company, or registered investment adviser; or

(ii) any person who, on the basis of such factors as financial sophistication, net worth, knowledge, and experience in financial matters, or amount of assets under management qualifies as an accredited investor under rules and regulations which the Commission shall prescribe.

(b) *Consideration of promotion of efficiency, competition, and capital formation.*

Whenever pursuant to this title the Commission is engaged in rulemaking and is required to consider or determine whether an action is necessary or appropriate in the public interest, the Commission shall also consider, in addition to the protection of investors, whether the action will promote efficiency, competition, and capital formation.

Classes of Securities Under This Subchapter

Section 3. (a) *Exempted securities.* Except as hereinafter expressly provided, the provisions of this title shall not apply to any of the following classes of securities:

(1) Reserved.

(2) Any security issued or guaranteed by the United States or any territory thereof, or by the District of Columbia, or by any State of the United States, or by any political subdivision of a State or Territory, or by any public instrumentality of one or more States or Territories, or by any person controlled or supervised by and acting as an instrumentality of the Government of the United States pursuant to authority granted by the Congress of the United States; or any certificate of deposit for any of the foregoing; or any security issued or guaranteed by any bank; or any security issued by or representing an interest in or a direct obligation of a Federal Reserve bank; is amended by inserting "or any interest or participation in any common trust fund or similar fund that is excluded" from the definition of the term "investment company" under section 3(c)(3) of the Investment Company Act of 1940; or any security which is an industrial development bond (as defined in section 103(c)(2) of the Internal Revenue Code of 1954) the interest on which is excludable from gross income under section 103(a)(1) of such Code if, by reason of the application of paragraph (4) or (6) of section 103(c) of such Code (determined as if paragraphs (4)(A), (5), and (7) were not included in such section 103(c)), paragraph (1) of such section 103(c) does not apply to such security; or any interest or participation in a single trust fund, or in a collective trust fund maintained by a bank, or any security arising out of a contract issued by an insurance company, which interest, participation, or security is issued in connection with (A) a stock bonus, pension, or profit-sharing plan which meets the requirements for qualification under section 401 of the Internal Revenue Code of 1954, (B) an annuity plan which meets the requirements for the deduction of the employer's contributions under section 404(a)(2) of such Code, or (C) a governmental plan as defined in section 414(d) of such Code which has been established by an employer for the exclusive benefit of its employees or their beneficiaries for the purpose of distributing to such employees or their beneficiaries the corpus and income of the funds accumulated under such plan, if under such plan it is impossible, prior to the satisfaction of all liabilities with respect to such employees and their beneficiaries, for any part of the corpus or income to be used for, or diverted to, purposes other than the exclusive benefit of such employees or their beneficiaries, other than any plan described in clause (A), (B), or (C) of this paragraph (i) the contributions under which are held in a single trust fund or in a separate account maintained by an insurance company for a single employer and under which an amount in excess of the employer's contribution is allocated to the purchase of securities (other than interests or participations in the trust or separate account itself) issued by the employer or any company directly or indirectly controlling, controlled by, or under common control with the employer, (ii) which covers employees some or all of whom are employees within the meaning of section 401(c)(1) of such Code, or (iii) which is a plan funded by an annuity contract described in section 403(b) of such Code. The Commission, by rules and regulations or order, shall exempt from the provisions of section 5 of this title any interest or participation issued in connection with a stock bonus, pension, profit-sharing, or annuity plan which covers employees some or all of whom are employees within the meaning of section 401(c)(1) of the Internal Revenue Code of 1954, if and to the extent that the Commission determines this to be necessary or appropriate in the public interest and consistent with the protection of investors and the purposes fairly intended by the policy and provisions of this title. For the purposes of this paragraph, a security issued or guaranteed by a bank shall not include any interest or participation in any collective trust fund maintained by a bank; and the term "bank" means any national bank, or any banking institution organized under the laws of any State, territory, or the District of Columbia, the business of which is substantially confined to banking and is supervised by the State or territorial banking commission or similar official; except that in the case of a common trust fund or similar fund, or a collective trust fund, the term "bank" has the same meaning as in the Investment Company Act of 1940.

(3) Any note, draft, bill of exchange, or bankers' acceptance which arises out of a current transaction or the proceeds of which have been or are to be used for current transactions, and which has a maturity at the time of issuance of not exceeding nine months, exclusive of days of grace, or any renewal thereof the maturity of which is likewise limited;

(4) Any security issued by a person organized and operated exclusively for religious, educational, benevolent, fraternal, charitable, or reformatory purposes and not for pecuniary profit, and no part of the net earnings of which inures to the benefit of any person, private stockholder, or individual; or any security of a fund that is excluded from the definition of an investment company under section 3(c)(10)(B) of the Investment Company Act of 1940;

(5) Any security issued (A) by a savings and loan association, building and loan association, cooperative bank, homestead association, or similar institution, which is supervised and examined by State or Federal authority having supervision over any such institution; or (B) by (i) a farmer's cooperative organization exempt from tax under section 521 of the Internal Revenue Code of 1954, (ii) a corporation described in section 501(c)(16) of such Code and exempt from tax under section 501(a) of such Code, or (iii) a corporation described in section 501(c)(2) of such Code which is exempt from tax under section 501(a) of such Code and is organized for the exclusive purpose of holding title to property, collecting income therefrom, and turning over the entire amount thereof, less expenses, to an organization or corporation described in clause (i) or (ii);

(6) Any interest in a railroad equipment trust. For purposes of this paragraph "interest in a railroad equipment trust" means any interest in an equipment trust, lease, conditional sales contract or other similar arrangement entered into, issued, assumed, guaranteed by, or for the benefit of, a common carrier to finance the acquisition of rolling stock, including motive power;

(7) Certificates issued by a receiver or by a trustee or debtor in possession in a case under title 11 of the United States Code, with the approval of the court;

(8) Any insurance or endowment policy or annuity contract or optional annuity contract, issued by a corporation subject to the supervision of the insurance commissioner, bank commissioner, or any agency or officer performing like functions, of any State or Territory of the United States or the District of Columbia;

(9) Except with respect to a security exchanged in a case under title 11 of the United States Code, any security exchanged by the issuer with its existing security holders exclusively where no commission or other remuneration is paid or given directly or indirectly for soliciting such exchange;

(10) Except with respect to a security exchanged in a case under title 11 of the United States Code, any security which is issued in exchange for one or more bona fide outstanding securities, claims or property interests, or partly in such exchange and partly for cash, where the terms and conditions of such issuance and exchange are approved, after a hearing upon the fairness of such terms and conditions at which all persons to whom it is proposed to issue securities in such exchange shall have the right to appear, by any court, or by any official or agency of the United States, or by any State or Territorial banking or insurance commission or other governmental authority expressly authorized by law to grant such approval;

(11) Any security which is a part of an issue offered and sold only to persons resident within a single State or Territory, where the issuer of such security is a person resident and doing business within, or, if a corporation, incorporated by and doing business within, such State or Territory.

(12) Any equity security issued in connection with the acquisition by a holding company of a bank under section 3(a) of the Bank Holding Company Act of 1956 or a savings association under section 10(e) of the Homeowner's Loan Act, if—

(A) the acquisition occurs solely as part of a reorganization in which security holders exchange their shares of a bank or savings association for shares of a newly formed holding company with no significant assets other than securities of the bank or savings association and the existing subsidiaries of the bank or savings association;

(B) the security holders receive, after that reorganization, substantially the same proportional share interests in the holding company as they held in the bank or savings association, except for nominal changes in shareholders' interests resulting from lawful elimination of fractional interests and the exercise of dissenting shareholders' rights under State or Federal law;

(C) the rights and interests of security holders in the holding company are substantially the same as those in the bank or savings association prior to the transaction, other than as may be required by law; and

(D) the holding company has substantially the same assets and liabilities, on a consolidated basis, as the bank or savings association had prior to the transaction.

For purposes of this paragraph, the term "savings association" means a savings association (as defined in section 3(b) of the Federal Insurance Deposit Act) the deposits of which are insured by the Federal Deposit Insurance Corporation.

(13) Any security issued by or any interest or participation in any church plan, company or account that is excluded from the definition of an investment company under section 3(c)(14) of the Investment Company Act of 1940.

(b) *Additional exemptions.* The Commission may from time to time by its rules and regulations, and subject to such terms and conditions as may be prescribed therein, add any class of securities to the securities exempted as provided in this section, if it finds that the enforcement of this title with respect to such securities is not necessary in the public interest and for the protection of investors by reason of the small amount involved or the limited character of the public offering; but no issue of securities shall be exempted under this subsection where the aggregate amount at which such issue is offered to the public exceeds $5,000,000.

(c) *Securities issued by small investment company.* The Commission may from time to time by its rules and regulations and subject to such terms and conditions as may be prescribed therein, add to the securities exempted as provided in this section any class of securities issued by a small business investment company under the Small Business Investment Act of 1958 if it finds, having regard to the purposes of that Act, that the enforcement of this Act with respect to such securities is not necessary in the public interest and for the protection of investors.

Exempted Transactions

Section 4. The provisions of section 5 shall not apply to—

(1) transactions by any person other than an issuer, underwriter, or dealer.

(2) transactions by an issuer not involving any public offering.

(3) transactions by a dealer (including an underwriter no longer acting as an underwriter in respect of the security involved in such transaction), except—

(A) transactions taking place prior to the expiration of forty days after the first date upon which the security was bona fide offered to the public by the issuer or by or through an underwriter,

(B) transactions in a security as to which a registration statement has been filed taking place prior to the expiration of forty days after the effective date of such registration statement or prior to the expiration of forty days after the first date upon which the security was bona fide offered to the public by the issuer or by or through an underwriter after such effective date, whichever is later (excluding in the computation of such forty days any time during which a stop order issued under section 8 is in effect as to the security), or such shorter period as the Commission may specify by rules and regulations or order, and

(C) transactions as to securities constituting the whole or a part of an unsold allotment to or subscription by such dealer as a participant in the distribution of such securities by the issuer or by or through an underwriter.

With respect to transactions referred to in clause (B), if securities of the issuer have not previously been sold pursuant to an earlier effective registration statement the applicable period, instead of forty days, shall be ninety days, or such shorter period as the Commission may specify by rules and regulations or order.

(4) brokers' transactions executed upon customers' orders on any exchange or in the over-the-counter market but not the solicitation of such orders.

(5)(A) Transactions involving offers or sales of one or more promissory notes directly secured by a first lien on a single parcel of real estate upon which is located a dwelling or other residential or commercial structure, and participation interests in such notes—

(i) where such securities are originated by a savings and loan association, savings bank, commercial bank, or similar banking institution which is supervised and examined by a Federal or State authority, and are offered and sold subject to the following conditions:

(a) the minimum aggregate sales price per purchaser shall not be less than $250,000;

(b) the purchaser shall pay cash either at the time of the sale or within sixty days thereof; and

(c) each purchaser shall buy for his own account only; or

(ii) where such securities are originated by a mortgagee approved by the Secretary of Housing and Urban Development pursuant to sections 203 and 211 of the National Housing Act, and are offered or sold subject to the three conditions specified in subparagraph (A)(i) to any institution described in such subparagraph or to any insurance company subject to the supervision of the insurance commissioner, or any agency or officer performing like function, of any State or Territory of the United States or the District of Columbia, or the Federal Home Loan Mortgage Corporation, the Federal National Mortgage Association, or the Government National Mortgage Association.

(B) Transactions between any of the entities described in subparagraph (A)(i) or (A)(ii) hereof involving non-assignable contracts to buy or sell the foregoing securities which are to be completed within two years, where the seller of the foregoing securities pursuant to any such contract is one of the parties described in subparagraph (A)(i) or (A)(ii) who may originate such securities and the purchaser of such securities pursuant to any such contract is any institution described in subparagraph (A)(i) or any insurance company described in subparagraph (A)(ii), the Federal Home Loan Mortgage Corporation, Federal National Mortgage Association, or the Government National Mortgage Association and where the foregoing securities are subject to the three conditions for sale set forth in subparagraphs (A)(i)(a) through (c).

(C) The exemption provided by subparagraphs (A) and (B) hereof shall not apply to resales of the securities acquired pursuant thereto, unless each of the conditions for sale contained in subparagraphs (A)(i)(a) through (c) are satisfied.

(6) transactions involving offers or sales by an issuer solely to one or more accredited investors, if the aggregate offering price of an issue of securities offered in reliance on this paragraph does not exceed the amount allowed under section 3(b) of this title, if there is no advertising or public solicitation in connection with the transaction by the issuer or anyone acting on the issuer's behalf, and if the issuer files such notice with the Commission as the Commission shall prescribe.

Prohibitions Relating to Interstate Commerce and the Mails

Section 5. (a) *Sale or delivery after sale of unregistered securities.* Unless a registration statement is in effect as to a security, it shall be unlawful for any person, directly or indirectly—

(1) to make use of any means or instruments of transportation or communication in interstate commerce or of the mails to sell such security through the use or medium of any prospectus or otherwise; or

(2) to carry or cause to be carried through the mails or in interstate commerce, by any means or instruments of transportation, any such security for the purpose of sale or for delivery after sale.

(b) *Necessity of prospectus meeting requirements of section 10 of this title.* It shall be unlawful for any person, directly or indirectly—

(1) to make use of any means or instruments of transportation or communication in interstate commerce or of the mails to carry or transmit any prospectus relating to any security with respect to which a registration statement has been filed under this title, unless such prospectus meets the requirements of section 10; or

(2) to carry or cause to be carried through the mails or in interstate commerce any such security for the purpose of sale or for delivery after sale, unless accompanied or preceded by a prospectus that meets the requirements of subsection (a) of section 10.

(c) *Necessity of filing registration statement.* It shall be unlawful for any person, directly or indirectly, to make use of any means or instruments of transportation or communication in interstate commerce or of the mails to offer to sell or offer to buy through the use or medium of any prospectus or otherwise any security, unless a registration statement has been filed as to such security, or while the registration statement is the subject of a refusal order or stop order or (prior to the effective date of the registration statement) any public proceeding or examination under section 8.

Registration of Securities and Signing of Registration Statement

Section 6. (a) *Method of registration.* Any security may be registered with the Commission under the terms and conditions hereinafter provided, by filing a registration statement in triplicate, at least one of which shall be signed by each issuer, its principal executive officer or officers, its principal financial officer, its comptroller or principal accounting officer, and the majority of its board of directors or persons performing similar functions (or, if there is no board of directors or persons performing similar functions, by the majority of the persons or board having the power of management of the issuer), and in case the issuer is a foreign or Territorial person by its duly authorized representative in the United States; except that when such registration statement relates to a security issued by a foreign government, or political subdivision thereof, it need be signed only by the underwriter of such security. Signatures of all such persons when written on the said registration statements shall be presumed to have been so written by authority of the person whose signature is so affixed and the burden of proof, in the event such authority shall be denied, shall be upon the party denying the same. The affixing of any signature without the authority of the purported signer shall constitute a violation of this title. A registration statement shall be deemed effective only as to the securities specified therein as proposed to be offered.

(b) *Registration fee*

(1) Recovery of cost of services

The Commission shall, in accordance with this subsection, collect registration fees that are designed to recover the costs to the government of the securities registration process, and costs related to such process, including enforcement activities, policy and rulemaking activities, administration, legal services, and international regulatory activities.

(2) Fee payment required

At the time of filing a registration statement, the applicant shall pay to the Commission a fee that shall be equal to the sum of the amounts (if any) determined under the rates established by paragraphs (3) and (4). The Commission shall publish in the Federal Register notices of the fee rates applicable under this section for each fiscal year.

(3) General revenue fees

The rate determined under this paragraph is a rate equal to $200 per $1,000,000 of the maximum aggregate price at which such securities are proposed to be offered, except that during fiscal year 2007 and any succeeding fiscal year such rate is equal to $67 per $1,000,000 of the maximum aggregate price at which such securities are proposed to be offered. Fees collected during any fiscal year pursuant to this paragraph shall be deposited and credited as general revenues of the Treasury.

(4) Offsetting collection fees

(A) In general

Except as provided in subparagraphs (B) and (C), the rate determined under this paragraph is a rate equal to the following amount per $1,000,000 of the maximum aggregate price at which such securities are proposed to be offered:

(i) $95 during fiscal year 1998;

(ii) $78 during fiscal year 1999;

(iii) $64 during fiscal year 2000;

(iv) $50 during fiscal year 2001;

(v) $39 during fiscal year 2002;

(vi) $28 during fiscal year 2003;

(vii) $9 during fiscal year 2004;

(viii) $5 during fiscal year 2005; and

(ix) $0 during fiscal year 2006 or any succeeding fiscal year.

(B) Limitation; deposit

Except as provided in subparagraph (C), no amounts shall be collected pursuant to this paragraph (4) for any fiscal year except to the extent provided in advance in appropriations Acts. Fees collected during any fiscal year pursuant to this paragraph shall be deposited and credited as offsetting collections in accordance with appropriations Acts.

(C) Lapse of appropriations

If on the first day of a fiscal year a regular appropriation to the Commission has not been enacted, the Commission shall continue to collect fees (as offsetting collections) under this paragraph at the rate in effect during the preceding fiscal year, until such a regular appropriation is enacted.

(5) Pro rata application of rates

The rates required by this subsection shall be applied pro rata to amounts and balances equal to less than $1,000,000.

(c) *Time registration effective.* The filing with the Commission of a registration statement, or of an amendment to a registration statement, shall be deemed to have taken place upon the receipt thereof, but the filing of a registration statement shall not be deemed to have taken place unless it is accompanied by a United States postal money order or a certified bank check or cash for the amount of the fee required under subsection (b).

(d) *Information available to public.* The information contained in or filed with any registration statement shall be made available to the public under such regulations as the Commission may prescribe, and copies thereof, photostatic or otherwise, shall be furnished to every applicant at such reasonable charge as the Commission may prescribe.

Information Required in Registration Statement

Section 7. (a) The registration statement, when relating to a security other than a security issued by a foreign government, or political subdivision thereof, shall contain the information, and be accompanied by the documents specified in Schedule A, and when relating to a security issued by a foreign government, or political subdivision thereof, shall contain the information, and be accompanied by the documents, specified in Schedule B; except that the Commission may by rules or regulations provide that any such information or document need not be included in respect of any class of issuers or securities if it finds that the requirement of such information or document is inapplicable to such class and that disclosure fully adequate for the protection of investors is otherwise required to be included within the registration statement. If any accountant, engineer, or appraiser, or any person whose profession gives authority to a statement made by him, is named as having prepared or certified any part of the registration statement, or is named as having prepared or certified a report or valuation for use in connection with the registration statement, the written consent of such person shall be filed with the registration statement. If any such person is named as having prepared or certified a report or valuation (other than a public official document or statement) which is used in connection with the registration statement, but is not named as having prepared or certified such report or valuation for use in connection with the registration statement, the written consent of such person shall be filed with the registration statement unless the Commission dispenses with such filing as impracticable or as involving undue hardship on the person filing the registration statement. Any such registration statement shall contain such other information, and be accompanied by such other documents, as the Commission may by rules or regulations require as being necessary or appropriate in the public interest or for the protection of investors.

(b)(1) The Commission shall prescribe special rules with respect to registration statements filed by any issuer that is a blank check company. Such rules may, as the Commission determines necessary or appropriate in the public interest or for the protection of investors—

(A) require such issuers to provide timely disclosure, prior to or after such statement becomes effective under section 8, of (i) information regarding the company to be acquired and the specific application of the proceeds of the offering, or (ii) additional information necessary to prevent such statement from being misleading;

(B) place limitations on the use of such proceeds and the distribution of securities by such issuer until the disclosures required under subparagraph (A) have been made; and

(C) provide a right of rescission to shareholders of such securities.

(2) The Commission may, as it determines consistent with the public interest and the protection of investors, by rule or order exempt any issuer or class of issuers from the rules prescribed under paragraph (1).

(3) For purposes of paragraph (1) of this subsection, the term "blank check company" means any

development stage company that is issuing a penny stock (within the meaning of section 3(a)(51) of this title) and that—

(A) has no specific business plan or purpose; or

(B) has indicated that its business plan is to merge with an unidentified company or companies.

Taking Effect of Registration Statements and Amendments Thereto

Section 8. (a) *Effective date of registration statement.* Except as hereinafter provided, the effective date of a registration statement shall be the twentieth day after the filing thereof or such earlier date as the Commission may determine, having due regard to the adequacy of the information respecting the issuer theretofore available to the public, to the facility with which the nature of the securities to be registered, their relationship to the capital structure of the issuer and the rights of holders thereof can be understood, and to the public interest and the protection of investors. If any amendment to any such statement is filed prior to the effective date of such statement, the registration statement shall be deemed to have been filed when such amendment was filed; except that an amendment filed with the consent of the Commission, prior to the effective date of the registration statement, or filed pursuant to an order of the Commission, shall be treated as a part of the registration statement.

(b) *Incomplete or inaccurate registration statement.* If it appears to the Commission that a registration statement is on its face incomplete or inaccurate in any material respect, the Commission may, after notice by personal service or the sending of confirmed telegraphic notice not later than ten days after the filing of the registration statement, and opportunity for hearing (at a time fixed by the Commission) within ten days after such notice by personal service or the sending of such telegraphic notice, issue an order prior to the effective date of registration refusing to permit such statement to become effective until it has been amended in accordance with such order. When such statement has been amended in accordance with such order the Commission shall so declare and the registration shall become effective at the time provided in subsection (a) or upon the date of such declaration, whichever date is the later.

(c) *Effective date of amendment to registration statement.* An amendment filed after the effective date of the registration statement, if such amendment, upon its face, appears to the Commission not to be incomplete or inaccurate in any material respect, shall become effective on such date as the Commission may determine, having due regard to the public interest and the protection of investors.

(d) *Untrue statements or omissions in registration statement.* If it appears to the Commission at any time that the registration statement includes any untrue statement of a material fact or omits to state any material fact required to be stated therein or necessary to make the statements therein not misleading, the Commission may, after notice by personal service or the sending of confirmed telegraphic notice, and after opportunity for hearing (at a time fixed by the Commission) within fifteen days after such notice by personal service or the sending of such telegraphic notice, issue a stop order suspending the effectiveness of the registration statement. When such statement has been amended in accordance with such stop order the Commission shall so declare and thereupon the stop order shall cease to be effective.

(e) *Examination for issuance of stop order.* The Commission is empowered to make an examination in any case in order to determine whether a stop order should issue under subsection (d) of this section. In making such examination the Commission or any officer or officers designated by it shall have access to and may demand the production of any books and papers of, and may administer oaths and affirmations to and examine, the issuer, underwriter, or any other person, in respect of any matter relevant to the examination, and may, in its discretion, require the production of a balance sheet exhibiting the assets and liabilities of the issuer, or its income statement, or both, to be certified to by a public or certified accountant approved by the Commission. If the issuer or underwriter shall fail to cooperate, or shall obstruct or refuse to permit the making of an examination, such conduct shall be proper ground for the issuance of a stop order.

(f) *Notice requirements.* Any notice required under this section shall be sent to or served on the issuer, or, in case of a foreign government or political subdivision thereof, to or on the underwriter, or, in the case of a foreign or Territorial person, to or on its duly authorized representative in the United

States named in the registration statement, properly directed in each case of telegraphic notice to the address given in such statement.

Cease-and-Desist Proceedings

Section 8A. (a) *Authority of the Commission.* If the Commission finds, after notice and opportunity for hearing, that any person is violating, has violated, or is about to violate any provision of this subchapter, or any rule or regulation thereunder, the Commission may publish its findings and enter an order requiring such person, and any other person that is, was, or would be a cause of the violation, due to an act or omission the person knew or should have known would contribute to such violation, to cease and desist from committing or causing such violation and any future violation of the same provision, rule or regulation. Such order may, in addition to requiring a person to cease and desist from committing or causing a violation, require such person to comply, or to take steps to effect compliance, with such provision, rule, or regulation, upon such terms and conditions and within such time as the Commission may specify in such order. Any such order may, as the Commission deems appropriate, require future compliance or steps to effect future compliance, either permanently or for such period of time as the Commission may specify, with such provision, rule, or regulation with respect to any security, any issuer, or any other person.

(b) *Hearing.* The notice instituting proceedings pursuant to subsection (a) shall fix a hearing date not earlier than 30 days nor later than 60 days after service of the notice unless an earlier or a later date is set by the Commission with the consent of any respondent so served.

(c) *Temporary Order.* (1) In general. Whenever the Commission determines that the alleged violation or threatened violation specified in the notice instituting proceedings pursuant to subsection (a) of this section, or the continuation thereof, is likely to result in significant dissipation or conversion of assets, significant harm to investors, or substantial harm to the public interest, including, but not limited to, losses to the Securities Investor Protection Corporation, prior to the completion of the proceedings, the Commission may enter a temporary order requiring the respondent to cease and desist from the violation or threatened violation and to take such action to prevent the violation or threatened violation and to prevent dissipation or conversion of assets, significant harm to investors, or substantial harm to the public interest as the Commission deems appropriate pending completion of such proceeding. Such an order shall be entered only after notice and opportunity for a hearing, unless the Commission determines that notice and hearing prior to entry would be impracticable or contrary to the public interest. A temporary order shall become effective upon service upon the respondent and, unless set aside, limited, or suspended by the Commission or a court of competent jurisdiction, shall remain effective and enforceable pending the completion of the proceedings.

(2) Applicability. This subsection shall apply only to a respondent that acts, or, at the time of the alleged misconduct acted, as a broker, dealer, investment adviser, investment company, municipal securities dealer, government securities broker, government securities dealer, or transfer agent, or is, or was at the time of the alleged misconduct, an associated person of, or a person seeking to become associated with, any of the foregoing.

(d) *Review of temporary orders.* (1) Commission review. At any time after the respondent has been served with a temporary cease-and-desist order pursuant to subsection (c) of this section, the respondent may apply to the Commission to have the order set aside, limited, or suspended. If the respondent has been served with a temporary cease-and-desist order entered without a prior Commission hearing, the respondent may, within 10 days after the date on which the order was served, request a hearing on such application and the Commission shall hold a hearing and render a decision on such application at the earliest possible time.

(2) Judicial review. Within—

(A) 10 days after the date the respondent was served with a temporary cease-and-desist order entered with a prior Commission hearing, or

(B) 10 days after the Commission renders a decision on an application and hearing under paragraph (1), with respect to any temporary cease-and-desist order entered without a prior Commission hearing, the respondent may apply to the United States district court for the district in which the respondent resides or has its principal place of business, or for the District of Columbia, for an order setting aside, limiting, or suspending the effectiveness or enforcement of the order, and the court shall have jurisdiction to enter such an order. A respondent served with a temporary cease-and-desist order entered without a prior Commission hearing may not apply to the court except after hearing and decision by the Commission on the respondent's application under paragraph (1) of this subsection.

(3) No automatic stay of temporary order. The commencement of proceedings under paragraph (2) of this subsection shall not, unless specifically ordered by the court, operate as a stay of the Commission's order.

(4) Exclusive review. Section 9(a) of this title shall not apply to a temporary order entered pursuant to this section.

(e) *Authority to enter an order requiring an accounting and disgorgement.* In any cease-and-desist proceeding under subsection (a) of this section, the Commission may enter an order requiring accounting and disgorgement, including reasonable interest. The Commission is authorized to adopt rules, regulations, and orders concerning payments to investors, rates of interest, periods of accrual, and such other matters as it deems appropriate to implement this subsection.

(f) *Authority of the Commission to Prohibit Persons from Serving as Officers or Directors.* In any cease-and-desist proceeding under subsection (a), the Commission may issue an order to prohibit, conditionally or unconditionally, and permanently or for such period of time as it shall determine, any person who has violated section 17(a)(1) or the rules or regulations thereunder, from acting as an officer or director of any issuer that has a class of securities registered pursuant to section 12 of the Securities Exchange Act of 1934, or that is required to file reports pursuant to section 15(d) of that Act, if the conduct of that person demonstrates unfitness to serve as an officer or director of any such issuer.

Court Review of Orders

Section 9. (a) Any person aggrieved by an order of the Commission may obtain a review of such order in the court of appeals of the United States, within any circuit wherein such person resides or has his principal place of business, or in the United States Court of Appeals for the District of Columbia, by filing in such Court, within sixty days after the entry of such order, a written petition praying that the order of the Commission be modified or be set aside in whole or in part. A copy of such petition shall be forthwith transmitted by the clerk of the court to the Commission, and thereupon the Commission shall file in the court the record upon which the order complained of was entered, as provided in section 2112 of title 28. No objection to the order of the Commission shall be considered by the court unless such objection shall have been urged before the Commission. The finding of the Commission as to the facts, if supported by evidence, shall be conclusive. If either party shall apply to the court for leave to adduce additional evidence, and shall show to the satisfaction of the court that such additional evidence is material and that there were reasonable grounds for failure to adduce such evidence in the hearing before the Commission, the court may order such additional evidence to be taken before the Commission and to be adduced upon the hearing in such manner and upon such terms and conditions as to the court may seem proper. The Commission may modify its findings as to the facts, by reason of the additional evidence so taken, and it shall file such modified or new findings, which, if supported by evidence, shall be conclusive, and its recommendation, if any, for the modification or setting aside of the original order. The jurisdiction of the court shall be exclusive and its judgment and decree, affirming, modifying, or setting aside, in whole or in part, any order of the Commission, shall be final, subject to review by the Supreme Court of the United States upon certiorari or certification as provided in section 1254 of title 28.

(b) The commencement of proceedings under subsection (a) of this section shall not, unless specifically ordered by the court, operate as a stay of the Commission's order.

Information Required in Prospectus

Section 10. (a) *Information in registration statement; documents not required.* Except to the extent otherwise permitted or required pursuant to this subsection or subsections (c), (d), or (e) of this section—

(1) a prospectus relating to a security other than a security issued by a foreign government or political subdivision thereof, shall contain the in-

formation contained in the registration statement, but it need not include the documents referred to in paragraphs (28) to (32), inclusive, of Schedule A;

(2) a prospectus relating to a security issued by a foreign government or political subdivision thereof shall contain the information contained in the registration statement, but it need not include the documents referred to in paragraphs (13) and (14) of Schedule B;

(3) notwithstanding the provisions of paragraphs (1) and (2) of this subsection when a prospectus is used more than nine months after the effective date of the registration statement, the information contained therein shall be as of a date not more than sixteen months prior to such use, so far as such information is known to the user of such prospectus or can be furnished by such user without unreasonable effort or expense;

(4) there may be omitted from any prospectus any of the information required under this subsection (a) which the Commission may by rules or regulations designate as not being necessary or appropriate in the public interest or for the protection of investors.

(b) *Summarizations and omissions allowed by rules and regulations.* In addition to the prospectus permitted or required in subsection (a) of this section, the Commission shall by rules or regulations deemed necessary or appropriate in the public interest or for the protection of investors permit the use of a prospectus for the purposes of subsection (b)(1) of section 5 of this title which omits in part or summarizes information in the prospectus specified in subsection (a) of this section. A prospectus permitted under this subsection shall, except to the extent the Commission by rules or regulations deemed necessary or appropriate in the public interest or for the protection of investors otherwise provides, be filed as part of the registration statement but shall not be deemed a part of such registration statement for the purposes of section 11 of this title. The Commission may at any time issue an order preventing or suspending the use of a prospectus permitted under this subsection, if it has reason to believe that such prospectus has not been filed (if required to be filed as part of the registration statement) or includes any untrue statement of a material fact or omits to state any material fact required to be stated therein or necessary to make the statements therein, in the light of the circumstances under which such prospectus is or is to be used, not misleading. Upon issuance of an order under this subsection, the Commission shall give notice of the issuance of such order and opportunity for hearing by personal service or the sending of confirmed telegraphic notice. The Commission shall vacate or modify the order at any time for good cause or if such prospectus has been filed or amended in accordance with such order.

(c) *Additional information required by rules and regulations.* Any prospectus shall contain such other information as the Commission may by rules or regulations require as being necessary or appropriate in the public interest or for the protection of investors.

(d) *Classification of prospectuses.* In the exercise of its powers under subsections (a), (b), or (c) of this section, the Commission shall have authority to classify prospectuses according to the nature and circumstances of their use or the nature of the security, issue, issuer, or otherwise, and, by rules and regulations and subject to such terms and conditions as it shall specify therein, to prescribe as to each class the form and contents which it may find appropriate and consistent with the public interest and the protection of investors.

(e) *Information in conspicuous part of prospectus.* The statements or information required to be included in a prospectus by or under authority of subsections (a), (b), (c), or (d) of this section, when written, shall be placed in a conspicuous part of the prospectus and, except as otherwise permitted by rules or regulations, in type as large as that used generally in the body of the prospectus.

(f) *Prospectus consisting of radio or television broadcast.* In any case where a prospectus consists of a radio or television broadcast, copies thereof shall be filed with the Commission under such rules and regulations as it shall prescribe. The Commission may by rules and regulations require the filing with it of forms and prospectuses used in connection with the offer or sale of securities registered under this title.

Civil Liabilities on Account of False Registration Statement

Section 11. (a) *Persons possessing cause of action, persons liable.* In case any part of the registration statement, when such part became effective, contained an untrue statement of a material fact or omitted to state a material fact required to be stated therein or necessary to make the statements therein not misleading, any person acquiring such security (unless it is proved that at the time of such acquisition he knew of such untruth or omission) may, either at law or in equity, in any court of competent jurisdiction, sue—

(1) every person who signed the registration statement;

(2) every person who was a director of (or person performing similar functions) or partner in the issuer at the time of the filing of the part of the registration statement with respect to which his liability is asserted;

(3) every person who, with his consent, is named in the registration statement as being or about to become a director, person performing similar functions, or partner;

(4) every accountant, engineer, or appraiser, or any person whose profession gives authority to a statement made by him, who has with his consent been named as having prepared or certified any part of the registration statement, or as having prepared or certified any report or valuation which is used in connection with the registration statement, with respect to the statement in such registration statement, report, or valuation, which purports to have been prepared or certified by him;

(5) every underwriter with respect to such security.

If such person acquired the security after the issuer has made generally available to its security holders an earning statement covering a period of at least twelve months beginning after the effective date of the registration statement, then the right of recovery under this subsection shall be conditioned on proof that such person acquired the security relying upon such untrue statement in the registration statement or relying upon the registration statement and not knowing of such omission, but such reliance may be established without proof of the reading of the registration statement by such person.

(b) *Persons exempt from liability upon proof of issues.* Notwithstanding the provisions of subsection (a) no person, other than the issuer, shall be liable as provided therein who shall sustain the burden of proof—

(1) that before the effective date of the part of the registration statement with respect to which his liability is asserted (A) he had resigned from or had taken such steps as are permitted by law to resign from, or ceased or refused to act in, every office, capacity, or relationship in which he was described in the registration statement as acting or agreeing to act, and (B) he had advised the Commission and the issuer in writing that he had taken such action and that he would not be responsible for such part of the registration statement; or

(2) that if such part of the registration statement became effective without his knowledge, upon becoming aware of such fact he forthwith acted and advised the Commission, in accordance with paragraph (1), and, in addition, gave reasonable public notice that such part of the registration statement had become effective without his knowledge; or

(3) that (A) as regards any part of the registration statement not purporting to be made on the authority of an expert, and not purporting to be a copy of or extract from a report or valuation of an expert, and not purporting to be made on the authority of a public official document or statement, he had, after reasonable investigation, reasonable ground to believe and did believe, at the time such part of the registration statement became effective, that the statements therein were true and that there was no omission to state a material fact required to be stated therein or necessary to make the statements therein not misleading; and (B) as regards any part of the registration statement purporting to be made upon his authority as an expert or purporting to be a copy of or extract from a report or valuation of himself as an expert, (i) he had, after reasonable investigation, reasonable ground to believe and did believe, at the time such part of the registration statement became effective, that the statements therein were true and that there was no omission to state a material fact required to be stated therein or necessary to make the statements therein not misleading, or (ii) such part of the registration statement did not fairly represent his statement as an expert or was not a fair copy of or extract from his report or valuation as an

expert; and (C) as regards any part of the registration statement purporting to be made on the authority of an expert (other than himself) or purporting to be a copy of or extract from a report or valuation of an expert (other than himself), he had no reasonable ground to believe and did not believe, at the time such part of the registration statement became effective, that the statements therein were untrue or that there was an omission to state a material fact required to be stated therein or necessary to make the statements therein not misleading, or that such part of the registration statement did not fairly represent the statement of the expert or was not a fair copy of or extract from the report or valuation of the expert; and (D) as regards any part of the registration statement purporting to be a statement made by an official person or purporting to be a copy of or extract from a public official document, he had no reasonable ground to believe and did not believe, at the time such part of the registration statement became effective, that the statements therein were untrue, or that there was an omission to state a material fact required to be stated therein or necessary to make the statements therein not misleading, or that such part of the registration statement did not fairly represent the statement made by the official person or was not a fair copy of or extract from the public official document.

(c) *Standard of reasonableness.* In determining, for the purpose of paragraph (3) of subsection (b) of this section, what constitutes reasonable investigation and reasonable ground for belief, the standard of reasonableness shall be that required of a prudent man in the management of his own property.

(d) *Effective date of registration statement with regard to underwriters.* If any person becomes an underwriter with respect to the security after the part of the registration statement with respect to which his liability is asserted has become effective, then for the purposes of paragraph (3) of subsection (b) of this section such part of the registration statement shall be considered as having become effective with respect to such person as of the time when he became an underwriter.

(e) *Measure of damages; undertaking for payment of costs.* The suit authorized under subsection (a) may be to recover such damages as shall represent the difference between the amount paid for the security (not exceeding the price at which the security was offered to the public) and (1) the value thereof as of the time such suit was brought, or (2) the price at which such security shall have been disposed of in the market before suit, or (3) the price at which such security shall have been disposed of after suit but before judgment if such damages shall be less than the damages representing the difference between the amount paid for the security (not exceeding the price at which the security was offered to the public) and the value thereof as of the time such suit was brought: Provided, That if the defendant proves that any portion or all of such damages represents other than the depreciation in value of such security resulting from such part of the registration statement, with respect to which his liability is asserted, not being true or omitting to state a material fact required to be stated therein or necessary to make the statements therein not misleading, such portion of or all such damages shall not be recoverable. In no event shall any underwriter (unless such underwriter shall have knowingly received from the issuer for acting as an underwriter some benefit, directly or indirectly, in which all other underwriters similarly situated did not share in proportion to their respective interests in the underwriting) be liable in any suit or as a consequence of suits authorized under subsection (a) for damages in excess of the total price at which the securities underwritten by him and distributed to the public were offered to the public. In any suit under this or any other section of this title the court may, in its discretion, require an undertaking for the payment of the costs of such suit, including reasonable attorney's fees, and if judgment shall be rendered against a party litigant, upon the motion of the other party litigant, such costs may be assessed in favor of such party litigant (whether or not such undertaking has been required) if the court believes the suit or the defense to have been without merit, in an amount sufficient to reimburse him for the reasonable expenses incurred by him, in connection with such suit, such costs to be taxed in the manner usually provided for taxing of costs in the court in which the suit was heard.

(f) *Joint and several liability.* (1) Except as provided in paragraph (2), all or any one or more of the persons specified in subsection (a) shall be jointly and severally liable, and every person who becomes liable to make any payment under this section may recover contribution as in cases of contract from any person who, if sued separately, would have been liable to make the same payment, unless the person who has become liable was, and the other was not, guilty of fraudulent misrepresentation.

(2)(A) The liability of an outside director under subsection (e) of this section shall be determined in accordance with 21D(f) of the Securities Exchange Act of 1934.

(B) For purposes of this paragraph, the term "outside director" shall have the meaning given such term by rule or regulation of the Commission.

(g) *Offering price to public as maximum amount recoverable.* In no case shall the amount recoverable under this section exceed the price at which the security was offered to the public.

Civil Liabilities Arising in Connection With Prospectuses and Communications

Section 12. (a) In general. Any person who—

(1) offers or sells a security in violation of section 5, or

(2) offers or sells a security (whether or not exempted by the provisions of section 3, other than paragraph (2) of subsection (a) thereof), by the use of any means or instruments of transportation or communication in interstate commerce or of the mails, by means of a prospectus or oral communication, which includes an untrue statement of a material fact or omits to state a material fact necessary in order to make the statements, in the light of the circumstances under which they were made, not misleading (the purchaser not knowing of such untruth or omission), and who shall not sustain the burden of proof that he did not know, and in the exercise of reasonable care could not have known, of such untruth or omission,

shall be liable, subject to subsection (b), to the person purchasing such security from him, who may sue either at law or in equity in any court of competent jurisdiction, to recover the consideration paid for such security with interest thereon, less the amount of any income received thereon, upon the tender of such security, or for damages if he no longer owns the security.

Limitation of Actions

Section 13. No action shall be maintained to enforce any liability created under section 11 or section 12(a)(2) unless brought within one year after the discovery of the untrue statement or the omission, or after such discovery should have been made by the exercise of reasonable diligence, or, if the action is to enforce a liability created under section 12(a)(1), unless brought within one year after the violation upon which it is based. In no event shall any such action be brought to enforce a liability created under section 11 or section 12(a)(1) more than three years after the security was bona fide offered to the public, or under section 12(a)(2) more than three years after the sale.

Contrary Stipulations Void

Section 14. Any condition, stipulation, or provision binding any person acquiring any security to waive compliance with any provision of this title or of the rules and regulations of the Commission shall be void.

Liability of Controlling Persons

Section 15. Every person who, by or through stock ownership, agency, or otherwise, or who, pursuant to or in connection with an agreement or understanding with one or more other persons by or through stock ownership, agency, or otherwise, controls any person liable under section 11 or 12, shall also be liable jointly and severally with and to the same extent as such controlled person to any person to whom such controlled person is liable, unless the controlling person had no knowledge of or reasonable ground to believe in the existence of the facts by reason of which the liability of the controlled person is alleged to exist.

Fraudulent Interstate Transactions

Section 17. *Use of interstate commerce for purpose of fraud or deceit.* (a) It shall be unlawful for any person in the offer or sale of any securities by the use of any means or instruments of transportation or communication in interstate commerce or by the use of the mails, directly or indirectly—

(1) to employ any device, scheme, or artifice to defraud, or

(2) to obtain money or property by means of any untrue statement of a material fact or any

omission to state a material fact necessary in order to make the statements made, in the light of the circumstances under which they were made, not misleading, or

(3) to engage in any transaction, practice, or course of business which operates or would operate as a fraud or deceit upon the purchaser.

(b) *Use of interstate commerce for purposes of offering for sale.* It shall be unlawful for any person, by the use of any means or instruments of transportation or communication in interstate commerce or by the use of the mails, to publish, give publicity to, or circulate any notice, circular, advertisement, newspaper, article, letter, investment service, or communication which, though not purporting to offer a security for sale, describes such security for a consideration received or to be received, directly or indirectly, from an issuer, underwriter, or dealer, without fully disclosing the receipt, whether past or prospective, of such consideration and the amount thereof.

(c) *Exemptions of section 3 not applicable to this section.* The exemptions provided in section 3 shall not apply to the provisions of this section.

Exemption From State Regulation of Securities Offerings

Section 18. (a) Scope of exemption

Except as otherwise provided in this section, no law, rule, regulation, or order, or other administrative action of any State or any political subdivision thereof—

(1) requiring, or with respect to, registration or qualification of securities, or registration or qualification of securities transactions, shall directly or indirectly apply to a security that—

(A) is a covered security; or

(B) will be a covered security upon completion of the transaction;

(2) shall directly or indirectly prohibit, limit, or impose any conditions upon the use of—

(A) with respect to a covered security described in subsection (b) of this section, any offering document that is prepared by or on behalf of the issuer; or

(B) any proxy statement, report to shareholders, or other disclosure document relating to a covered security or the issuer thereof that is required to be and is filed with the Commission or any national securities organization registered under section 15A of the Securities Exchange Act of 1934, except that this subparagraph does not apply to the laws, rules, regulations, or orders, or other administrative actions of the State of incorporation of the issuer; or

(3) shall directly or indirectly prohibit, limit, or impose conditions, based on the merits of such offering or issuer, upon the offer or sale of any security described in paragraph (1).

(b) Covered securities

For purposes of this section, the following are covered securities:

(1) Exclusive Federal registration of nationally traded securities.

A security is a covered security if such security is—

(A) listed, or authorized for listing, on the New York Stock Exchange or the American Stock Exchange, or listed or authorized for listing on the National Market System of the NASDAQ Stock Market (or any successor to such entities);

(B) listed, or authorized for listing, on a national securities exchange (or tier or segment thereof) that has listing standards that the Commission determines by rule (on its own initiative or on the basis of a petition) are substantially similar to the listing standards applicable to securities described in subparagraph (A); or

(C) is a security of the same issuer that is equal in seniority or that is a senior security to a security described in subparagraph (A) or (B).

(2) Exclusive Federal registration of investment companies.

A security is a covered security if such security is a security issued by an investment company that is registered, or that has filed a registration statement, under the Investment Company Act of 1940.

(3) Sales to qualified purchasers.

A security is a covered security with respect to the offer or sale of the security to qualified purchasers, as defined by the Commission by rule. In prescribing such rule, the Commission may define the term "qualified purchaser" differently with respect to different categories of securities, consistent with the public interest and the protection of investors.

(4) Exemption in connection with certain exempt offerings.

A security is a covered security with respect to a transaction that is exempt from registration under this title pursuant to—

(A) paragraph (1) or (3) of section 77d of this title, and the issuer of such security files reports with the Commission pursuant to section 78m or 78o(d) of the Securities Exchange Act of 1934;

(B) section 77d(4) of this title;

(C) section 77c(a) of this title, other than the offer or sale of a security that is exempt from such registration pursuant to paragraph (4),(10) or (11) of such section, except that a municipal security that is exempt from such registration pursuant to paragraph (2) of such section is not a covered security with respect to the offer or sale of such security in the State in which the issuer of such security is located; or

(D) Commission rules or regulations issued under section 77d(2) of this title, except that this subparagraph does not prohibit a State from imposing notice filing requirements that are substantially similar to those required by rule or regulation under section 77d(2) of this title that are in effect on September 1, 1996.

(c) Preservation of authority

(1) Fraud authority

Consistent with this section, the securities commission (or any agency or officer performing like functions) of any State shall retain jurisdiction under the laws of such State to investigate and bring enforcement actions with respect to fraud or deceit, or unlawful conduct by a broker or dealer, in connection with securities or securities transactions.

(2) Preservation of filing requirements

(A) Notice filings permitted.

Nothing in this section prohibits the securities commission (or any agency or office performing like functions) of any State from requiring the filing of any document filed with the Commission pursuant to this title, together with annual or periodic reports of the value of securities sold or offered to be sold to persons located in the State (if such sales data is not included in documents filed with the Commission), solely for notice purposes and the assessment of any fee, together with a consent to service of process and any required fee.

(B) Preservation of fees.

(i) In general.

Until otherwise provided by law, rule, regulation, or order, or other administrative action of any State, or any political subdivision thereof, adopted after October 11, 1996, filing or registration fees with respect to securities or securities transactions shall continue to be collected in amounts determined pursuant to State law as in effect on the day before such date.

(ii) Schedule.

The fees required by this subparagraph shall be paid, and all necessary supporting data on sales or offers for sales required under subparagraph (A), shall be reported on the same schedule as would have been applicable had the issuer not relied on the exemption provided in subsection (a) of this section.

(C) Availability of preemption contingent on payment of fees.

(i) In general.

During the period beginning on October 11, 1996, and ending 3 years after October 11, 1996, the securities commission (or any agency or office performing like functions) of any State may require the registration of securities issued by any issuer who refuses to pay the fees required by subparagraph (B).

(ii) Delays.

For purposes of this subparagraph, delays in payment of fees or underpayments of fees that are promptly remedied shall not constitute a refusal to pay fees.

(D) Fees not permitted on listed securities.

Notwithstanding subparagraphs (A), (B), and (C), no filing or fee may be required with respect to any security that is a covered security pursuant to subsection (b)(1) of this section, or will be such a covered security upon completion of the transaction, or is a security of the same issuer that is equal in seniority or that is a senior security to a security that is a covered security pursuant to subsection (b)(1) of this section.

(3) Enforcement of requirements

Nothing in this section shall prohibit the securities commission (or any agency or office performing like functions) of any State from suspending the offer or sale of securities within such State as a result of the failure to submit any filing or fee required under law and permitted under this section.

(d) Definitions

For purposes of this section, the following definitions shall apply:

(1) Offering document.

The term "offering document"—

(A) has the meaning given the term "prospectus" in section 2(a)(10) of this title, but without regard to the provisions of subparagraphs (a) and (b) of that section; and

(B) includes a communication that is not deemed to offer a security pursuant to a rule of the Commission.

(2) Prepared by or on behalf of the issuer.

Not later than 6 months after the date of enactment of the National Securities Markets Improvements Act of 1996, (October 11, 1996) the Commission shall, by rule, define the term "prepared by or on behalf of the issuer" for purposes of this section.

(3) State.

The term "State" has the same meaning as in section 78c of the Securities Exchange Act of 1954.

(4) Senior security.

The term "senior security" means any bond, debenture, note, or similar obligation or instrument constituting a security and evidencing indebtedness, and any stock of a class having priority over any other class as to distribution of assets or payment of dividends.

Special Powers of Commission

Section 19. (a) *[Rules and regulations; general matters; registration statements, prospectuses, and definitions; effective date; good faith compliance; forms.]* The Commission shall have authority from time to time to make, amend, and rescind such rules and regulations as may be necessary to carry out the provisions of this title, including rules and regulations governing registration statements and prospectuses for various classes of securities and issuers, and defining accounting, technical, and trade terms used in this title. Among other things, the Commission shall have authority, for the purposes of this title, to prescribe the form or forms in which required information shall be set forth, the items or details to be shown in the balance sheet and earning statement, and the methods to be followed in the preparation of accounts, in the appraisal or valuation of assets and liabilities, in the determination of depreciation and depletion, in the differentiation of recurring and nonrecurring income, in the differentiation of investment and operating income, and in the preparation, where the Commission deems it necessary or desirable, of consolidated balance sheets or income accounts of any person directly or indirectly controlling or controlled by the issuer, or any person under direct or indirect common control with the issuer. The rules and regulations of the Commission shall be effective upon publication in the manner which the Commission shall prescribe. No provision of this title imposing any liability shall apply to any act done or omitted in good faith in conformity with any rule or regulation of the Commission, notwithstanding that such rule or regulation may, after such act or omission, be amended or rescinded or be determined by judicial or other authority to be invalid for any reason.

(b) Recognition of Accounting Standards. (1) *In General.* In carrying out its authority under subsection (a) and under section 13(b) of the Securities Exchange Act of 1934, the Commission may recognize, as 'generally accepted' for purposes of the securities laws, any accounting principles established by a standard setting body

(A) that

(i) is organized as a private entity;

(ii) has, for administrative and operational purposes, a board of trustees (or equivalent body) serving in the public interest, the majority of whom are not, concurrent with their service on such board, and have not been during the 2-year period preceding such service, associated persons of any registered public accounting firm;

(iii) is funded as provided in section 109 of the Sarbanes-Oxley Act of 2002;

(iv) has adopted procedures to ensure prompt consideration, by majority vote of its members, of changes to accounting principles necessary to reflect emerging accounting issues and changing business practices; and

(v) considers, in adopting accounting principles, the need to keep standards current in order to reflect changes in the business environment, the extent to which international convergence on high quality accounting standards is necessary or appropriate in the public interest and for the protection of investors; and

(B) that the Commission determines has the capacity to assist the Commission in fulfilling the requirements of subsection (a) and section 13(b) of the Securities Exchange Act of 1934, because, at a minimum, the standard setting body is capable of improving the accuracy and effectiveness of financial reporting and the protection of investors under the securities laws.

(2) *Annual Report.* A standard setting body described in paragraph (1) shall submit an annual report to the Commission and the public, containing audited financial statements of that standard setting body.

(c) *Investigations; evidence; geographical limits.* For the purpose of all investigations which, in the opinion of the Commission, are necessary and proper for the enforcement of this title, any member of the Commission or any officer or officers designated by it are empowered to administer oaths and affirmations, subpena witnesses, take evidence, and require the production of any books, papers, or other documents which the Commission deems relevant or material to the inquiry. Such attendance of witnesses and the production of such documentary evidence may be required from any place in the United States or any Territory at any designated place of hearing.

(d) *Federal-State cooperation in securities matters; areas of cooperation; annual conferences and other meetings; authorization of appropriations.* (1) The Commission is authorized to cooperate with any association composed of duly constituted representatives of State governments whose primary assignment is the regulation of the securities business within those States, and which, in the judgment of the Commission, could assist in effectuating greater uniformity in Federal-State securities matters. The Commission shall, at its discretion, cooperate, coordinate, and share information with such an association for the purposes of carrying out the policies and projects set forth in paragraphs (2) and (3).

(2) It is the declared policy of this subsection that there should be greater Federal and State cooperation in securities matters, including—

(A) maximum effectiveness of regulation,

(B) maximum uniformity in Federal and State regulatory standards,

(C) minimum interference with the business of capital formation, and

(D) a substantial reduction in costs and paperwork to diminish the burdens of raising investment capital (particularly by small business) and to diminish the costs of the administration of the Government programs involved.

(3) The purpose of this subsection is to engender cooperation between the Commission, any such association of State securities officials, and other duly constituted securities associations in the following areas:

(A) the sharing of information regarding the registration or exemption of securities issues applied for in the various States;

(B) the development and maintenance of uniform securities forms and procedures; and

(C) the development of a uniform exemption from registration for small issuers which can be agreed upon among several States or between the States and the Federal Government. The Commission shall have the authority to adopt such an exemption as agreed upon for Federal purposes.

Nothing in this Act shall be construed as authorizing preemption of State law.

(4) In order to carry out these policies and purposes, the Commission shall conduct an annual conference as well as such other meetings as are deemed necessary, to which representatives from such securities associations, securities self-regulatory organizations, agencies, and private organizations involved in capital formation shall be invited to participate.

(5) For fiscal year 1982, and for each of the three succeeding fiscal years, there are authorized to be appropriated such amounts as may be necessary and appropriate to carry out the policies, provisions, and purposes of this subsection. Any sums so appropriated shall remain available until expended.

(6) Notwithstanding any other provision of law, neither the Commission nor any other person shall be required to establish any procedures not specifically required by the securities laws, as that term is defined in section 3(a)(47) of the Securities Exchange Act of 1934, or by chapter 5 of title 5, United States Code, in connection with cooperation, coordination, or consultation with—

(A) any association referred to in paragraph (1) or (3) or any conference or meeting referred to in paragraph (4), while such association, conference, or meeting is carrying out activities in furtherance of the provisions of this subsection; or

(B) any forum, agency, or organization, or group referred to in section 503 of the Small Business Investment Incentive Act of 1980, while such forum, agency, organization, or group is carrying out activities in furtherance of the provisions of such section 503.

As used in this paragraph, the terms "association", "conference", "meeting", "forum", "agency", "organization", and "group" include any committee, subgroup, or representative of such entities.

Jurisdiction of Offenses and Suits

Section 22. (a) Federal and State courts; venue; service of process; review; removal; costs.

The district courts of the United States and United States courts of any Territory shall have jurisdiction of offenses and violations under this title and under the rules and regulations promulgated by the Commission in respect thereto, and concurrent with State and Territorial courts except as provided in section 16 with respect to covered class actions, of all suits in equity and actions at law brought to enforce any liability or duty created by this title. Any such suit or action may be brought in the district wherein the defendant is found or is an inhabitant or transacts business, or in the district where the offer or sale took place, if the defendant participated therein, and process in such cases may be served in any other district of which the defendant is an inhabitant or wherever the defendant may be found. Judgments and decrees so rendered shall be subject to review as provided in sections 1254, 1291, 1292, and 1294 of title 28, United States Code. Except as provided in section 16(c),no case arising under this title and brought in any State court of competent jurisdiction shall be removed to any court of the United States. No costs shall be assessed for or against the Commission in any proceeding under this title brought by or against it in the Supreme Court or such other courts.

(b) Contumacy or refusal to obey subpoena; contempt.

In case of contumacy or refusal to obey a subpena issued to any person, any of the said United States courts, within the jurisdiction of which said person guilty of contumacy or refusal to obey is found or resides, upon application by the Commission may issue to such person an order requiring such person to appear before the Commission, or one of its examiners designated by it, there to produce documentary evidence if so ordered, or there to give evidence touching the matter in question; and any failure to obey such order of the court may be punished by said court as a contempt thereof.

SCHEDULE OF INFORMATION REQUIRED IN REGISTRATION STATEMENT

Schedule A

(1) The name under which the issuer is doing or intends to do business;

(2) the name of the State or other sovereign power under which the issuer is organized;

(3) the location of the issuer's principal business office, and if the issuer is a foreign or territorial person, the name and address of its agent in the United States authorized to receive notice;

(4) the names and addresses of the directors or persons performing similar functions, and the chief executive, financial and accounting officers, chosen or to be chosen if the issuer be a corporation, association, trust, or other entity; of all partners, if the issuer be a partnership; and of the issuer, if the issuer be an individual; and of the promoters in the case of a business to be formed, or formed within two years prior to the filing of the registration statement;

(5) the names and addresses of the underwriters;

(6) the names and addresses of all persons, if any, owning of record or beneficially, if known, more than 10 per centum of any class of stock of the issuer, or more than 10 per centum in the aggregate of the outstanding stock of the issuer as of a date within twenty days prior to the filing of the registration statement;

(7) the amount of securities of the issuer held by any person specified in paragraphs (4), (5), and (6) of this schedule, as of a date within twenty days prior to the filing of the registration statement, and, if possible, as of one year prior thereto, and the amount of the securities, for which the registration statement is filed, to which such persons have indicated their intention to subscribe;

(8) the general character of the business actually transacted or to be transacted by the issuer;

(9) a statement of the capitalization of the issuer, including the authorized and outstanding amounts of its capital stock and the proportion thereof paid up, the number and classes of shares in which such capital stock is divided, par value thereof, or if it has no par value, the stated or assigned value thereof, a description of the respective voting rights, preferences, conversion and exchange rights, rights to dividends, profits, or capital of each class, with respect to each other class, including the retirement and liquidation rights or values thereof;

(10) a statement of the securities, if any, covered by options outstanding or to be created in connection with the security to be offered, together with the names and addresses of all persons, if any, to be allotted more than 10 per centum in the aggregate of such options;

(11) the amount of capital stock of each class issued or included in the shares of stock to be offered;

(12) the amount of the funded debt outstanding and to be created by the security to be offered, with a brief description of the date, maturity, and character of such debt, rate of interest, character of amortization provisions, and the security, if any, therefor. If substitution of any security is permissible, a summarized statement of the conditions under which such substitution is permitted. If substitution is permissible without notice, a specific statement to that effect;

(13) the specific purposes in detail and the approximate amounts to be devoted to such purposes, so far as determinable, for which the security to be offered is to supply funds, and if the funds are to be raised in part from other sources, the amounts thereof and the sources thereof, shall be stated;

(14) the remuneration, paid or estimated to be paid, by the issuer or its predecessor, directly or indirectly, during the past year and ensuing year, to (a) the directors or persons performing similar functions, and (b) its officers and other persons, naming them wherever such remuneration exceeded $25,000 during any such year;

(15) the estimated net proceeds to be derived from the security to be offered;

(16) the price at which it is proposed that the security shall be offered to the public or the method by which such price is computed and any variation therefrom at which any portion of such security is proposed to be offered to any persons or classes of persons, other than the underwriters, naming them or specifying the class. A variation in price may be proposed prior to the date of the public offering of the security, but the Commission shall immediately be notified of such variation;

(17) all commissions or discounts paid or to be paid, directly or indirectly, by the issuer to the underwriters in respect of the sale of the security to be offered. Commissions shall include all cash, securities, contracts, or anything else of value, paid, to be set aside, disposed of, or understandings with or for the benefit of any other persons in which any underwriter is interested, made, in connection with the sale of such security. A commission paid or to be paid in connection with the sale of such security by a person in which the issuer has an interest or which is controlled or directed by, or under common control with, the issuer shall be deemed to have

been paid by the issuer. Where any such commission is paid the amount of such commission paid to each underwriter shall be stated;

(18) the amount or estimated amounts, itemized in reasonable detail, of expenses, other than commissions specified in paragraph (17) of this schedule, incurred or borne by or for the account of the issuer in connection with the sale of the security to be offered or properly chargeable thereto, including legal, engineering, certification, authentication, and other charges;

(19) the net proceeds derived from any security sold by the issuer during the two years preceding the filing of the registration statement, the price at which such security was offered to the public, and the names of the principal underwriters of such security;

(20) any amount paid within two years preceding the filing of the registration statement or intended to be paid to any promoter and the consideration for any such payment;

(21) the names and addresses of the vendors and the purchase price of any property, or goodwill, acquired or to be acquired, not in the ordinary course of business, which is to be defrayed in whole or in part from the proceeds of the security to be offered, the amount of any commission payable to any person in connection with such acquisition, and the name or names of such person or persons, together with any expense incurred or to be incurred in connection with such acquisition, including the cost of borrowing money to finance such acquisition;

(22) full particulars of the nature and extent of the interest, if any, of every director, principal executive officer, and of every stockholder holding more than 10 per centum of any class of stock or more than 10 per centum in the aggregate of the stock of the issuer, in any property acquired, not in the ordinary course of business of the issuer, within two years preceding the filing of the registration statement or proposed to be acquired at such date;

(23) the names and addresses of counsel who have passed on the legality of the issue;

(24) dates of and parties to, and the general effect concisely stated of every material contract made, not in the ordinary course of business, which contract is to be executed in whole or in part at or after the filing of the registration statement or which contract has been made not more than two years before such filing. Any management contract or contract providing for special bonuses or profit-sharing arrangements, and every material patent or contract for a material patent right, and every contract by or with a public utility company or an affiliate thereof, providing for the giving or receiving of technical or financial advice or service (if such contract may involve a charge to any party thereto at a rate in excess of $2,500 per year in cash or securities or anything else of value), shall be deemed a material contract;

(25) a balance sheet as of a date not more than ninety days prior to the date of the filing of the registration statement showing all of the assets of the issuer, the nature and cost thereof, whenever determinable, in such detail and in such form as the Commission shall prescribe (with intangible items segregated), including any loan in excess of $20,000 to any officer, director, stockholder or person directly or indirectly controlling or controlled by the issuer, or person under direct or indirect common control with the issuer. All the liabilities of the issuer in such detail and such form as the Commission shall prescribe, including surplus of the issuer showing how and from what sources such surplus was created, all as of a date not more than ninety days prior to the filing of the registration statement. If such statement be not certified by an independent public or certified accountant, in addition to the balance sheet required to be submitted under this schedule, a similar detailed balance sheet of the assets and liabilities of the issuer, certified by an independent public or certified accountant, of a date not more than one year prior to the filing of the registration statement, shall be submitted;

(26) a profit and loss statement of the issuer showing earnings and income, the nature and source thereof, and the expenses and fixed charges in such detail and such form as the Commission shall prescribe for the latest fiscal year for which such statement is available and for the two preceding fiscal years, year by year, or, if such issuer has been in actual business for less than three years, then for such time as the issuer has been in actual business, year by year. If the date of the filing of the registration statement is more than six months after the close of the last fiscal year, a statement from such closing date to the latest practicable date.

Such statement shall show what the practice of the issuer has been during the three years or lesser period as to the character of the charges, dividends or other distributions made against its various surplus accounts, and as to depreciation, depletion, and maintenance charges, in such detail and form as the Commission shall prescribe, and if stock dividends or avails from the sale of rights have been credited to income, they shall be shown separately with a statement of the basis upon which the credit is computed. Such statement shall also differentiate between any recurring and nonrecurring income and between any investment and operating income. Such statement shall be certified by an independent public or certified accountant;

(27) if the proceeds, or any part of the proceeds, of the security to be issued is to be applied directly or indirectly to the purchase of any business, a profit and loss statement of such business certified by an independent public or certified accountant, meeting the requirements of paragraph (26) of this schedule, for the three preceding fiscal years, together with a balance sheet, similarly certified, of such business, meeting the requirements of paragraph (25) of this schedule of a date not more than ninety days prior to the filing of the registration statement or at the date such business was acquired by the issuer if the business was acquired by the issuer more than ninety days prior to the filing of the registration statement;

(28) a copy of any agreement or agreements (or, if identical agreements are used, the forms thereof) made with any underwriter, including all contracts and agreements referred to in paragraph (17) of this schedule;

(29) a copy of the opinion or opinions of counsel in respect to the legality of the issue, with a translation of such opinion, when necessary, into the English language;

(30) a copy of all material contracts referred to in paragraph (24) of this schedule, but no disclosure shall be required of any portion of any such contract if the Commission determines that disclosure of such portion would impair the value of the contract and would not be necessary for the protection of the investors;

(31) unless previously filed and registered under the provisions of this title, and brought up to date, (a) a copy of its articles of incorporation, with all amendments thereof and of its existing bylaws or instruments corresponding thereto, whatever the name, if the issuer be a corporation; (b) copy of all instruments by which the trust is created or declared, if the issuer is a trust; (c) a copy of its articles of partnership or association and all other papers pertaining to its organization, if the issuer is a partnership, unincorporated association, joint-stock company, or any other form of organization; and

(32) a copy of the underlying agreements or indentures affecting any stock, bonds, or debentures offered or to be offered.

In case of certificates of deposit, voting trust certificates, collateral trust certificates, certificates of interest or shares in unincorporated investment trusts, equipment trust certificates, interim or other receipts for certificates, and like securities, the Commission shall establish rules and regulations requiring the submission of information of a like character applicable to such cases, together with such other information as it may deem appropriate and necessary regarding the character, financial or otherwise, of the actual issuer of the securities and/or the person performing the acts and assuming the duties of depositor or manager.

Schedule B

(1) Name of borrowing government or subdivision thereof;

(2) specific purposes in detail and the approximate amounts to be devoted to such purposes, so far as determinable, for which the security to be offered is to supply funds, and if the funds are to be raised in part from other sources, the amounts thereof and the sources thereof, shall be stated;

(3) the amount of the funded debt and the estimated amount of the floating debt outstanding and to be created by the security to be offered, excluding intergovernmental debt, and a brief description of the date, maturity, character of such debt, rate of interest, character of amortization provisions, and the security, if any, therefor. If substitution of any security is permissible, a statement of the conditions under which such substitution is permitted. If substitution is permissible without notice, a specific statement to that effect;

(4) whether or not the issuer or its predecessor has, within a period of twenty years prior to the filing of the registration statement, defaulted on the principal or interest of any external security, excluding intergovernmental debt, and, if so, the date, amount, and circumstances of such default, and the terms of the succeeding arrangement, if any;

(5) the receipts, classified by source, and the expenditures, classified by purpose, in such detail and form as the Commission shall prescribe for the latest fiscal year for which such information is available and the two preceding fiscal years, year by year;

(6) the names and addresses of the underwriters;

(7) the name and address of its authorized agent, if any, in the United States;

(8) the estimated net proceeds to be derived from the sale in the United States of the security to be offered;

(9) the price at which it is proposed that the security shall be offered in the United States to the public or the method by which such price is computed. A variation in price may be proposed prior to the date of the public offering of the security, but the Commission shall immediately be notified of such variation;

(10) all commissions paid or to be paid, directly or indirectly, by the issuer to the underwriters in respect of the sale of the security to be offered. Commissions shall include all cash, securities, contracts, or anything else of value, paid, to be set aside, disposed of, or understandings with or for the benefit of any other persons in which the underwriter is interested, made, in connection with the sale of such security. Where any such commission is paid, the amount of such commission paid to each underwriter shall be stated;

(11) the amount or estimated amounts, itemized in reasonable detail, of expenses, other than the commissions specified in paragraph (10) of this schedule, incurred or borne by or for the account of the issuer in connection with the sale of the security to be offered or properly chargeable thereto, including legal, engineering, certification, and other charges;

(12) the names and addresses of counsel who have passed upon the legality of the issue;

(13) a copy of any agreement or agreements made with any underwriter governing the sale of the security within the United States; and

(14) an agreement of the issuer to furnish a copy of the opinion or opinions of counsel in respect to the legality of the issue, with a translation, where necessary, into the English language. Such opinion shall set out in full all laws, decrees, ordinances, or other acts of Government under which the issue of such security has been authorized.

B. SECURITIES EXCHANGE ACT OF 1934

(Selected Sections)

15 U.S.C.A. §§ 78a et seq.

TITLE I—REGULATION OF SECURITIES EXCHANGES

Contents

FOREIGN CORRUPT PRACTICES ACT AMENDMENTS OF 1988

TITLE I—REGULATION OF SECURITIES EXCHANGES

Short Title

Section 1. This chapter may be cited as the Securities Exchange Act of 1934.

Necessity for Regulation

Section 2. For the reasons hereinafter enumerated, transactions in securities as commonly conducted upon securities exchanges and over-the-counter markets are affected with a national public interest which makes it necessary to provide for regulation and control of such transactions and of practices and matters related thereto, including transactions by officers, directors, and principal security holders, to require appropriate reports, to remove impediments to and perfect the mechanisms of a national market system for securities and a national system for the clearance and settlement of securities transactions and the safeguarding of securities and funds related thereto, and to impose requirements necessary to make such regulation and control reasonably complete and effective, in order to protect interstate commerce, the national credit, the Federal taxing power, to protect and make more effective the national banking system and Federal Reserve System, and to insure the maintenance of fair and honest markets in such transactions:

(1) Such transactions (a) are carried on in large volume by the public generally and in large part originate outside the States in which the exchanges and over-the-counter markets are located and/or are effected by means of the mails and instrumentalities of interstate commerce; (b) constitute an important part of the current of interstate commerce; (c) involve in large part the securities of issuers engaged in interstate commerce; (d) involve the use of credit, directly affect the financing of trade, industry, and transportation in interstate commerce, and directly affect and influence the volume of interstate commerce; and affect the national credit.

(2) The prices established and offered in such transactions are generally disseminated and quoted throughout the United States and foreign countries and constitute a basis for determining and establishing the prices at which securities are bought and sold, the amount of certain taxes owing to the United States and to the several States by owners, buyers, and sellers of securities, and the value of collateral for bank loans.

(3) Frequently the prices of securities on such exchanges and markets are susceptible to manipulation and control, and the dissemination of such prices gives rise to excessive speculation, resulting in sudden and unreasonable fluctuations in the prices of securities which (a) cause alternately unreasonable expansion and unreasonable contraction of the volume of credit available for trade, transportation, and industry in interstate commerce, (b) hinder the proper appraisal of the value of securities and thus prevent a fair calculation of taxes owing to the United States and to the several States by owners, buyers, and sellers of securities, and (c) prevent the fair valuation of collateral for bank loans and/or obstruct the effective operation of the national banking system and Federal Reserve System.

(4) National emergencies, which produce widespread unemployment and the dislocation of trade, transportation, and industry, and which burden interstate commerce and adversely affect the general welfare, are precipitated, intensified, and prolonged by manipulation and sudden and unreasonable fluctuations of security prices and by excessive speculation on such exchanges and markets, and to meet such emergencies the Federal Government is put to such great expense as to burden the national credit.

Definitions and Application of Title

Section 3. (a) When used in this title, unless the context otherwise requires—

(1) The term "exchange" means any organization, association, or group of persons, whether incorporated or unincorporated, which constitutes, maintains, or provides a market place or facilities for bringing together purchasers and sellers of securities or for otherwise performing with respect to securities the functions commonly performed by a stock exchange as that term is generally under-

stood, and includes the market place and the market facilities maintained by such exchange.

(2) The term "facility" when used with respect to an exchange includes its premises, tangible or intangible property whether on the premises or not, any right to the use of such premises or property or any service thereof for the purpose of effecting or reporting a transaction on an exchange (including, among other things, any system of communication to or from the exchange, by ticker or otherwise, maintained by or with the consent of the exchange), and any right of the exchange to the use of any property or service.

(3)(A) The term "member" when used with respect to a national securities exchange means (i) any natural person permitted to effect transactions on the floor of the exchange without the services of another person acting as broker, (ii) any registered broker or dealer with which such a natural person is associated, (iii) any registered broker or dealer permitted to designate as a representative such a natural person, and (iv) any other registered broker or dealer which agrees to be regulated by such exchange and with respect to which the exchange undertakes to enforce compliance with the provisions of this title, the rules and regulations thereunder, and its own rules. For purposes of sections 6(b)(1), 6(b)(4), 6(b)(6), 6(b)(7), 6(d), 17(d), 19(d), 19(e), 19(g), 19(h), and 21 of this title, the term "member" when used with respect to a national securities exchange also means, to the extent of the rules of the exchange specified by the Commission, any person required by the Commission to comply with such rules pursuant to section 6(f) of this title.

(B) The term "member" when used with respect to a registered securities association means any broker or dealer who agrees to be regulated by such association and with respect to whom the association undertakes to enforce compliance with the provisions of this title, the rules and regulations thereunder, and its own rules.

(4) The term "broker" means any person engaged in the business of effecting transactions in securities for the account of others, but does not include a bank.

(5) The term "dealer" means any person engaged in the business of buying and selling securities for his own account, through a broker or otherwise, but does not include a bank, or any person insofar as he buys or sells securities for his own account, either individually or in some fiduciary capacity, but not as a part of a regular business.

(6) The term "bank" means (A) a banking institution organized under the laws of the United States, (B) a member bank of the Federal Reserve System, (C) any other banking institution, whether incorporated or not, doing business under the laws of any State or of the United States, a substantial portion of the business of which consists of receiving deposits or exercising a fiduciary power similar to those permitted to national banks under the authority of the Comptroller of the Currency pursuant to the first section of Public Law 87–722 (12 U.S.C. 92a), and which is supervised and examined by State or Federal authority having supervision over banks, and which is not operated for the purpose of evading the provisions of this title, and (D) a receiver, conservator, or other liquidating agent of any institution or firm included in clauses (A), (B), or (C) of this paragraph.

(7) The term "director" means any director of a corporation or any person performing similar functions with respect to any organization, whether incorporated or unincorporated.

(8) The term "issuer" means any person who issues or proposes to issue any securities; except that with respect to certificates of deposit for securities, voting-trust certificates, or collateral-trust certificates, or with respect to certificates of interest or shares in an unincorporated investment trust not having a board of directors or of the fixed, restricted management, or unit type, the term "issuer" means the person or persons performing the acts and assuming the duties of depositor or manager pursuant to the provisions of the trust or other agreement or instrument under which such securities are issued; and except that with respect to equipment-trust certificates or like securities, the term "issuer" means the person by whom the equipment or property is, or is to be, used.

(9) The term "person" means a natural person, company, government, or political subdivision, agency, or instrumentality of a government.

(10) The term "security" means any note, stock, treasury stock, bond, debenture, certificate of interest or participation in any profit-sharing agreement or in any oil, gas, or other mineral royalty or lease, any collateral-trust certificate, preorganization cer-

tificate or subscription, transferable share, investment contract, voting-trust certificate, certificate of deposit for a security, any put, call, straddle, option, derivative or privilege on any security, certificate of deposit, or group or index of securities (including any interest therein or based on the value thereof), or any put, call, straddle, option, or privilege entered into on a national securities exchange relating to foreign currency, or in general, any instrument commonly known as a "security"; or any certificate of interest or participation in, temporary or interim certificate for, receipt for, or warrant or right to subscribe to or purchase, any of the foregoing; but shall not include currency or any note, draft, bill of exchange, or banker's acceptance which has a maturity at the time of issuance of not exceeding nine months, exclusive of days of grace, or any renewal thereof the maturity of which is likewise limited.

(11) The term "equity security" means any stock or similar security; or any security convertible, with or without consideration, into such a security; or carrying any warrant or right to subscribe to or purchase such a security; or any such warrant or right; or any other security which the Commission shall deem to be of similar nature and consider necessary or appropriate, by such rules and regulations as it may prescribe in the public interest or for the protection of investors, to treat as an equity security.

(12)(A) The term "exempted security" or "exempted securities" includes—

(i) government securities, as defined in paragraph (42) of this subsection;

(ii) municipal securities, as defined in paragraph (29) of this subsection;

(iii) any interest or participation in any common trust fund or similar fund that is excluded from the definition of the term "investment company" under section 3(c)(3) of the Investment Company Act of 1940;

(iv) any interest or participation in a single trust fund, or a collective trust fund maintained by a bank, or any security arising out of a contract issued by an insurance company, which interest, participation, or security is issued in connection with a qualified plan as defined in subparagraph (C) of this paragraph;

(v) any security issued by or any interest or participation in any pooled income fund, collective trust fund, collective investment fund, or similar fund that is excluded from the definition of an investment company under section 3(c)(10)(B) of the Investment Company Act of 1940;

(vi) solely for purposes of section 78l, 78m, 78n, and 78p of this title, any security issued by or any interest or participation in any church plan, company, or account that is excluded from the definition of an investment company under section 80a–3(c)(14) of the Investment Company Act of 1940; and

(vii) such other securities (which may include, among others, unregistered securities, the market in which is predominantly intrastate) as the Commission may, by such rules and regulations as it deems consistent with the public interest and the protection of investors, either unconditionally or upon specified terms and conditions or for stated periods, exempt from the operation of any one or more provisions of this title which by their terms do not apply to an "exempted security" or to "exempted securities".

(B)(i) Notwithstanding subparagraph (A)(i) of this paragraph, government securities shall not be deemed to be "exempted securities" for the purposes of section 17A of this title.

(ii) Notwithstanding subparagraph (A)(ii) of this paragraph, municipal securities shall not be deemed to be 'exempted securities' for the purposes of sections 15 and 17A of this title.

(C) For purposes of subparagraph (A)(iv) of this paragraph, the term "qualified plan" means (i) a stock bonus, pension, or profit-sharing plan which meets the requirements for qualification under section 401 of the Internal Revenue Code of 1954, (ii) an annuity plan which meets the requirements for the deduction of the employer's contribution under section 404(a)(2) of such Code, or (iii) a governmental plan as defined in section 414(d) of such Code which has been established by an employer for the exclusive benefit of its employees or their beneficiaries for the purpose of distributing to such employees or their beneficiaries the corpus and income of the funds accumulated under such plan, if under such plan it is impossible, prior to the satisfaction of all liabilities with respect to such employees and their beneficiaries, for any part of the corpus or income to be used for, or diverted to, purposes other than the exclusive benefit of such employees or their beneficiaries, other than any plan described in clause (i), (ii), or (iii) of this subparagraph which (I) covers employees some or all of whom are employees within the meaning of section 401(c) of such Code, or (II) is a plan funded by an annuity contract described in section 403(b) of such Code.

(13) The terms "buy" and "purchase" each include any contract to buy, purchase, or otherwise acquire.

(14) The terms "sale" and "sell" each include any contract to sell or otherwise dispose of.

(15) The term "Commission" means the Securities and Exchange Commission established by section 4 of this title.

(16) The term "State" means any State of the United States, the District of Columbia, Puerto Rico, the Virgin Islands, or any other possession of the United States.

(17) The term "interstate commerce" means trade, commerce, transportation, or communication among the several States, or between any foreign country and any State, or between any State and any place or ship outside thereof. The term includes intrastate use of (A) any facility of a national securities exchange or of a telephone or other interstate means of communication, or (B) any other interstate instrumentality.

(18) The term "person associated with a broker or dealer" or "associated person of a broker or dealer" means any partner, officer, director, or branch manager of such broker or dealer (or any person occupying a similar status or performing similar functions), or any person directly or indirectly controlling, controlled by, or under common control with such broker or dealer, or any employee of such broker or dealer, except that any person associated with a broker or dealer whose functions are solely clerical or ministerial shall not be included in the meaning of such term for purposes of section 15(b) of this title (other than paragraph (6) thereof).

(19) The terms "investment company," "affiliated person," "insurance company," "separate account", and "company" have the same meanings as in the Investment Company Act of 1940.

(20) The terms "investment adviser" and "underwriter" have the same meanings as in the Investment Advisers Act of 1940.

* * *

(26) The term "self-regulatory organization" means any national securities exchange, registered securities association, or registered clearing agency, or (solely for purposes of sections 19(b), 19(c), and 23(b) of this title) the Municipal Securities Rulemaking Board established by section 15B of this title.

* * *

(38) The term "market maker" means any specialist permitted to act as a dealer, any dealer acting in the capacity of block positioner, and any dealer who, with respect to a security, holds himself out (by entering quotations in an inter-dealer communications system or otherwise) as being willing to buy and sell such security for his own account on a regular or continuous basis.

(39) A person is subject to a "statutory disqualification" with respect to membership or participation in, or association with a member of, a self-regulatory organization, if such person—

(A) has been and is expelled or suspended from membership or participation in, or barred or suspended from being associated with a member of, any self-regulatory organization, foreign equivalent of a self-regulatory organization, foreign or international securities exchange, contract market designated pursuant to section 5 of the Commodity Exchange Act, or any substantially equivalent foreign statute or regulation or futures associates registered under section 17 of such Act, or any substantially foreign statute or regulation or has been and is denied trading privileges on any such contract market or foreign equivalent;

(B) is subject to—

(i) an order of the Commission, other appropriate regulatory agency, or foreign financial regulatory authority—

(I) denying, suspending for a period not exceeding 12 months, or revoking his registration as a broker, dealer, municipal securities dealer, government securities broker, or government securities dealer or limiting his activities as a foreign person performing a function substantially equivalent to any of the above; or

(II) barring or suspending for a period not exceeding 12 months his being associated with a broker, dealer, municipal securities dealer, government securities broker, government securities dealer, or foreign person performing a function substantially equivalent to any of the above;

(ii) an order of the Commodity Futures Trading Commission denying, suspending, or revoking his registration under the Commodity Exchange Act; or

(iii) an order by a foreign financial regulatory authority denying, suspending, or revoking the person's authority to engage in transactions in contracts of sale of a commodity for future delivery or other instruments traded on or subject to the rules of a contract market, board of trade, or foreign equivalent thereof;

(C) by his conduct while associated with a broker, dealer, municipal securities dealer, government securities broker, or government securities dealer, or while associated with an entity or person required to be registered under the Commodity Exchange Act, has been found to be a cause of any effective suspension, expulsion, or order of the character described in subparagraph (A) or (B) of this paragraph, and in entering such a suspension, expulsion, or order, the Commission, an appropriate regulatory agency, or any such self-regulatory organization shall have jurisdiction to find whether or not any person was a cause thereof;

(D) by his conduct while associated with any broker, dealer, municipal securities dealer, government securities broker, government securities dealer, or any other entity engaged in transactions in securities, or while associated with an entity engaged in transactions in contracts of sale of a commodity for future delivery or other instruments traded on or subject to the rules of a contract market, board of trade, or foreign equivalent thereof, has been found to be a cause of any effective suspension, expulsion, or order by a foreign or international securities exchange or foreign financial regulatory authority empowered by a foreign government to administer or enforce its laws relating to financial transactions as described in subparagraphs (A) or (B) of this paragraph;

(E) has associated with him any person who is known, or in the exercise of reasonable care should be known, to him to be a person described by subparagraph (A), (B), (C) or (D) of this paragraph; or

(F) has committed or omitted any act, or is subject to an order or finding, enumerated in subparagraph (D), (E), (G) or (H) of paragraph (4) of section 15(b) of this title, has been convicted of any offense specified in subparagraph (B) of such paragraph (4) or any other felony within ten years of the date of the filing of an application for membership or participation in, or to become associated with a member of, such self-regulatory organization, is enjoined from any action, conduct, or practice specified in subparagraph (C) of such paragraph (4), has willfully made or caused to be made in any application for membership or participation in, or to become associated with a member of, a self-regulatory organization, report required to be filed with a self-regulatory organization, or proceeding before a self-regulatory organization, any statement which was at the time, and in the light of the circumstances under which it was made, false or misleading with respect to any material fact, or has omitted to state in any such application, report, or proceeding any material fact which is required to be stated therein.

* * *

(50) The term "foreign securities authority" means any foreign government, or any governmental body or regulatory organization empowered by a foreign government to administer or enforce its laws as they relate to securities matters.

* * *

(b) *Power to define technical, trade, accounting and other terms.* The Commission and the Board of Governors of the Federal Reserve System, as to matters within their respective jurisdictions, shall have power by rules and regulations to define technical, trade, accounting, and other terms used in this title, consistently with the provisions and purposes of this title.

* * *

(58) The term "audit committee" means—

(A) a committee (or equivalent body) established by and amongst the board of directors of an issuer for the purpose of overseeing the accounting and financial reporting processes of the issuer and audits of the financial statements of the issuer; and

(B) if no such committee exists with respect to an issuer, the entire board of directors of the issuer.

(59) The term "registered public accounting firm" has the same meaning as in section 2 of the Sarbanes–Oxley Act of 2002.

Securities and Exchange Commission

Section 4. (a) *Establishment; members; terms of office.* There is hereby established a Securities and Exchange Commission (hereinafter referred to as the "Commission") to be composed of five commissioners to be appointed by the President by and with the advice and consent of the Senate. Not more than three of such commissioners shall be members of the same political party, and in making appointments members of different political parties shall be appointed alternately as nearly as may be practicable. No commissioner shall engage in any other business, vocation, or employment than that of serving as commissioner, nor shall any commissioner participate, directly or indirectly, in any stock-market operations or transactions of a character subject to regulation by the Commission pursuant to this title. Each Commissioner shall hold office for a term of five years and until his successor is appointed and has qualified, except that he shall not so continue to serve beyond the expiration of the next session of Congress subsequent to the expiration of said fixed term of office, and except (1) any Commissioner appointed to fill a vacancy occurring prior to the expiration of the term for which his predecessor was appointed shall be appointed for the remainder of such term, and (2) the terms of office of the Commissioners first taking office after the enactment of this title shall expire as designated by the President at the time of nomination, one at the end of one year, one at the end of two years, one at the end of three years, one at the end of four years, and one at the end of five years, after the date of the enactment of this title.

* * *

Delegation of Functions by Commission

Section 4A. (a) *Authorization; functions delegable; eligible persons; application of other laws.* In addition to its existing authority, the Securities and Exchange Commission shall have the authority to delegate, by published order or rule, any of its functions to a division of the Commission, an individual Commissioner, an administrative law judge, or an employee or employee board, including functions with respect to hearing, determining, ordering, certifying, reporting, or otherwise acting as to any work, business, or matter. Nothing in this section shall be deemed to supersede the provisions of section 556(b) of title 5, or to authorize the delegation of the function of rule-making as defined in subchapter II of chapter 5 of title 5, United States Code, with reference to general rules as distinguished from rules of particular applicability, or of the making of any rule pursuant to section 19(c) of this title.

(b) *Right of review; procedure.* With respect to the delegation of any of its functions, as provided in subsection (a) of this section, the Commission shall retain a discretionary right to review the action of any such division of the Commission, individual Commissioner, administrative law judge, employee, or employee board, upon its own initiative or upon petition of a party to or intervenor in such action, within such time and in such manner as the Commission by rule shall prescribe. The vote of one member of the Commission shall be sufficient to bring any such action before the Commission for review. A person or party shall be entitled to review by the Commission if he or it is adversely affected by action at a delegated level which (1) denies any request for action pursuant to section 8(a) or section 8(c) of the Securities Act of 1933 or the first sentence of section 12(d) of this title; (2) suspends trading in a security pursuant to section 12(k) of this title; or (3) is pursuant to any provision of this title in a case of adjudication, as defined in section 551 of title 5, United States Code, not required by this title to be determined on the record after notice and opportunity for hearing (except to the extent there is involved a matter described in section 554(a)(1) through (6) of such title 5).

(c) *Finality of delegated actions.* If the right to exercise such review is declined, or if no such review is sought within the time stated in the rules promulgated by the Commission, then the action of any such division of the Commission, individual Commissioner, administrative law judge, employee, or employee board, shall, for all purposes, including appeal or review thereof, be deemed the action of the Commission.

Transfer of Functions With Respect to Assignment of Personnel to Chairman

Section 4B. In addition to the functions transferred by the provisions of Reorganization Plan Numbered 10 of 1950 (64 Stat. 1265), there are hereby transferred from the Commission to the Chairman of the Commission the functions of the Commission with respect to the assignment of Commission personnel, including Commissioners, to perform such functions as may have been delegated by the Commission to the Commission personnel, including Commissioners, pursuant to section 4A of this title.

Appearance and Practice Before the Commission

Section 4C. (a) *Authority to Censure.* The Commission may censure any person, or deny, temporarily or permanently, to any person the privilege of appearing or practicing before the Commission in any way, if that person is found by the Commission, after notice and opportunity for hearing in the matter

(1) not to possess the requisite qualifications to represent others;

(2) to be lacking in character or integrity, or to have engaged in unethical or improper professional conduct; or

(3) to have willfully violated, or willfully aided and abetted the violation of, any provision of the securities laws or the rules and regulations issued thereunder.

(b) *Definition.* With respect to any registered public accounting firm or associated person, for purposes of this section, the term 'improper professional conduct' means—

(1) intentional or knowing conduct, including reckless conduct, that results in a violation of applicable professional standards; and

(2) negligent conduct in the form of—

(A) a single instance of highly unreasonable conduct that results in a violation of applicable professional standards in circumstances in which the registered public accounting firm or associated person knows, or should know, that heightened scrutiny is warranted; or

(B) repeated instances of unreasonable conduct, each resulting in a violation of applicable professional standards, that indicate a lack of competence to practice before the Commission.

Transactions on Unregistered Exchanges

Section 5. It shall be unlawful for any broker, dealer, or exchange, directly or indirectly, to make use of the mails or any means or instrumentality of interstate commerce for the purpose of using any facility of an exchange within or subject to the jurisdiction of the United States to effect any transaction in a security, or to report any such transaction, unless such exchange (1) is registered as a national securities exchange under section 6 of this title, or (2) is exempted from such registration upon application by the exchange because, in the opinion of the commission, by reason of the limited volume of transactions effected on such exchange, it is not practicable and not necessary or appropriate in the public interest or for the protection of investors to require such registration.

National Securities Exchanges

Section 6. (a) *Registration; application.* An exchange may be registered as a national securities exchange under the terms and conditions hereinafter provided in this section and in accordance with the provisions of section 19(a) of this title, by filing with the Commission an application for registration in such form as the Commission, by rule, may prescribe containing the rules of the exchange and such other information and documents as the Commission, by rule, may prescribe as necessary or appropriate in the public interest or for the protection of investors.

(b) *Determination by Commission requisite to registration of applicant as national securities exchange.* An exchange shall not be registered as a national securities exchange unless the Commission determines that—

(1) Such exchange is so organized and has the capacity to be able to carry out the purposes of this title and to comply, and (subject to any rule or order of the Commission pursuant to section 17(d) or 19(g)(2) of this title) to enforce compliance by its members and persons associated with its members, with the provisions of this title, the rules and regulations thereunder, and the rules of the exchange.

(2) Subject to the provisions of subsection (c) of this section, the rules of the exchange provide that any registered broker or dealer or natural person associated with a registered broker or dealer may become a member of such exchange and any person may become associated with a member thereof.

(3) The rules of the exchange assure a fair representation of its members in the selection of its directors and administration of its affairs and provide that one or more directors shall be representative of issuers and investors and not be associated with a member of the exchange, broker, or dealer.

(4) The rules of the exchange provide for the equitable allocation of reasonable dues, fees, and other charges among its members and issuers and other persons using its facilities.

(5) The rules of the exchange are designed to prevent fraudulent and manipulative acts and practices, to promote just and equitable principles of trade, to foster cooperation and coordination with persons engaged in regulating, clearing, settling, processing information with respect to, and facilitating transactions in securities, to remove impediments to and perfect the mechanism of a free and open market and a national market system, and, in general, to protect investors and the public interest; and are not designed to permit unfair discrimination between customers, issuers, brokers, or dealers, or to regulate by virtue of any authority conferred by this title matters not related to the purposes of this title or the administration of the exchange.

(6) The rules of the exchange provide that (subject to any rule or order of the Commission pursuant to section 17(d) or 19(g)(2) of this title) its members and persons associated with its members shall be appropriately disciplined for violation of the provisions of this title, the rules or regulations thereunder, or the rules of the exchange, by expulsion, suspension, limitation of activities, functions, and operations, fine, censure, being suspended or barred from being associated with a member, or any other fitting sanction.

(7) The rules of the exchange are in accordance with the provisions of subsection (d) of this section, and in general, provide a fair procedure for the disciplining of members and persons associated with members, the denial of membership to any person seeking membership therein, the barring of any person from becoming associated with a member thereof, and the prohibition or limitation by the exchange of any person with respect to access to services offered by the exchange or a member thereof.

(8) The rules of the exchange do not impose any burden on competition not necessary or appropriate in furtherance of the purposes of this title.

(9) The rules of the exchange prohibit the listing of any security issued in a limited partnership rollup transaction (as such term is defined in paragraphs (4) and (5) of section 14(h) of this title), unless such transaction was conducted in accordance with procedures designed to protect the rights of limited partners, including—

(A) the right of dissenting limited partners to one of the following:

(i) an appraisal and compensation;

(ii) retention of a security under substantially the same terms and conditions as the original issue;

(iii) approval of the limited partnership rollup transaction by not less than 75 percent of the outstanding securities of each of the participating limited partnerships;

(iv) the use of a committee of limited partners that is independent, as determined in accordance with rules prescribed by the exchange, of the general partner or sponsor, that has been approved by a majority of the outstanding units of each of the participating limited partnerships, and that has such authority as is necessary to protect the interest of limited partners, including the authority to hire independent advisors, to negotiate with the general partner or sponsor on behalf of the limited partners, and to make a recommendation to the limited partners with respect to the proposed transaction; or

(v) other comparable rights that are prescribed by rule by the exchange and that are designed to protect dissenting limited partners;

(B) the right not to have their voting power unfairly reduced or abridged;

(C) the right not to bear an unfair portion of the costs of a proposed limited partnership rollup transaction that is rejected; and

(D) restrictions on the conversion of contingent interests or fees into non-contingent interests or fees and restrictions on the receipt of a non-contingent equity interest in exchange for fees for services which have not yet been provided.

As used in this paragraph, the term "dissenting limited partner" means a person who, on the date on which soliciting material is mailed to investors, is a holder of a beneficial interest in a limited partnership that is the subject of a limited partnership rollup transaction, and who casts a vote against the transaction and complies with procedures established by the exchange, except that for purposes of an exchange or tender offer, such person shall file an objection in writing under the rules of the exchange during the period during which the offer is outstanding.

(c) *Denial of membership in national exchanges; denial of association with member; conditions; limitation of membership.* (1) A national securities exchange shall deny membership to (A) any person, other than a natural person, which is not a registered broker or dealer or (B) any natural person who is not, or is not associated with, a registered broker or dealer.

(2) A national securities exchange may, and in cases in which the Commission, by order, directs as necessary or appropriate in the public interest or for the protection shall, deny membership to any registered broker or dealer or natural person associated with a registered broker or dealer, and bar from becoming associated with a member any person, who is subject to a statutory disqualification. * * *

* * *

(d) *Discipline of national securities exchange members and persons associated with members; summary proceedings.* (1) In any proceeding by a national securities exchange to determine whether a member or person associated with a member should be disciplined (other than a summary proceeding pursuant to paragraph (3) of this subsection), the exchange shall bring specific charges, notify such member or person of, and give him an opportunity to defend against, such charges, and keep a record. * * *

* * *

(e) *Commissions, allowances, discounts and other fees.* (1) On and after the date of enactment of the Securities Acts Amendments of 1975, no national securities exchange may impose any schedule or fix rates of commissions, allowances, discounts, or other fees to be charged by its members: * * *

* * *

(f) *Compliance of nonmembers with exchange rules.* The Commission, by rule or order, as it deems necessary or appropriate in the public interest and for the protection of investors, to maintain fair and orderly markets, or to assure equal regulation, may require—

(1) any person not a member or a designated representative of a member of a national securities exchange effecting transactions on such exchange without the services of another person acting as a broker, or

(2) any broker or dealer not a member of a national securities exchange effecting transactions on such exchange on a regular basis,

to comply with such rules of such exchange as the Commission may specify.

(g) *Authority to adopt rules relating to transactions in derivatives.* A national securities exchange may adopt and implement rules applicable to members of such exchange, and material associated persons that have filed notice or are required to file notice under section 15D(a)(1)(B) of this title and that are associated with members for which the exchange is the designated examining authority, who engage in transactions in derivatives—

(1) to enforce compliance with applicable provisions of this title and the rules and regulations thereunder;

(2) to provide that any such person shall be appropriately disciplined for violations of applicable provisions of this title and the rules and regulations thereunder;

(3) to provide for reasonable inspection and examination of the books and records of any such person;

(4) to prevent fraudulent and manipulative acts and practices;

(5) to promote just and equitable principles of trade; and

(6) to require the establishment of, and adherence to, appropriate internal controls structures.

Manipulation of Security Prices

Section 9. (a) *Transactions relating to purchase or sale of security.* It shall be unlawful for any person, directly or indirectly, by the use of the mails or any means or instrumentality of interstate commerce, or of any facility of any national securities exchange, or for any member of a national securities exchange—

(1) For the purpose of creating a false or misleading appearance of active trading in any security registered on a national securities exchange, or a false or misleading appearance with respect to the market for any such security, (A) to effect any transaction in such security which involves no change in the beneficial ownership thereof, or (B) to enter an order or orders for the purchase of such security with the knowledge that an order or orders of substantially the same size, at substantially the same time and at substantially the same price, for the sale of any such security, has been or will be entered by or for the same or different parties, or (C) to enter any order or orders for the sale of any such security with the knowledge that an order or orders of substantially the same size, at substantially the same time, and at substantially the same price, for the purchase of such security, has been or will be entered by or for the same or different parties.

(2) To effect, alone or with one or more other persons, a series of transactions in any security registered on a national securities exchange creating actual or apparent active trading in such security or raising or depressing the price of such security, for the purpose of inducing the purchase or sale of such security by others.

(3) If a dealer or broker, or other person selling or offering for sale or purchasing or offering to purchase the security, to induce the purchase or sale of any security registered on a national securities exchange by the circulation or dissemination in the ordinary course of business of information to the effect that the price of any such security will or is likely to rise or fall because of market operations of any one or more persons conducted for the purpose of raising or depressing the prices of such security.

(4) If a dealer or broker, or other person selling or offering for sale or purchasing or offering to purchase the security, to make, regarding any security registered on a national securities exchange, for the purpose of inducing the purchase or sale of such security, any statement which was at the time and in the light of the circumstances under which it was made, false or misleading with respect to any material fact, and which he knew or had reasonable ground to believe was so false or misleading.

(5) For a consideration, received directly or indirectly from a dealer or broker, or other person selling or offering for sale or purchasing or offering to purchase the security, to induce the purchase or sale of any security registered on a national securities exchange by the circulation or dissemination of information to the effect that the price of any such security will or is likely to rise or fall because of the market operations of any one or more persons conducted for the purpose of raising or depressing the price of such security.

(6) To effect either alone or with one or more other persons any series of transactions for the purchase and/or sale of any security registered on a national securities exchange for the purpose of pegging, fixing, or stabilizing the price of such security in contravention of such rules and regulations as the Commission may prescribe as necessary or appropriate in the public interest or for the protection of investors.

(b) *Transactions relating to puts, calls, straddles or options.* It shall be unlawful for any person to effect, by use of any facility of a national securities exchange, in contravention of such rules and regulations as the Commission may prescribe as necessary or appropriate in the public interest or for the protection of investors—

(1) any transaction in connection with any security whereby any party to such transaction acquires any put, call, straddle, or other option or

privilege of buying the security from or selling the security to another without being bound to do so; or

(2) any transaction in connection with any security with relation to which he has, directly or indirectly, any interest in any such put, call, straddle, option, or privilege; or

(3) any transaction in any security for the account of any person who he has reason to believe has, and who actually has, directly or indirectly, any interest in any such put, call, straddle, option, or privilege with relation to such security.

(c) *Endorsement or guarantee of puts, calls, straddles or options.* It shall be unlawful for any member of a national securities exchange directly or indirectly to endorse or guarantee the performance of any put, call, straddle, option, or privilege in relation to any security registered on a national securities exchange, in contravention of such rules and regulations as the Commission may prescribe as necessary or appropriate in the public interest or for the protection of investors.

(d) *Registered warrant, right, or convertible security not included in put, call, straddle, or any registered warrant, right, or convertible security.* The terms "put", "call", "straddle", "option", or "privilege" as used in this section shall not include any registered warrant, right, or convertible security.

(e) *Persons liable; suits at law or in equity.* Any person who willfully participates in any act or transaction in violation of subsection (a), (b), or (c) of this section, shall be liable to any person who shall purchase or sell any security at a price which was affected by such act or transaction, and the person so injured may sue in law or in equity in any court of competent jurisdiction to recover the damages sustained as a result of any such act or transaction. In any such suit the court may, in its discretion, require an undertaking for the payment of the costs of such suit, and assess reasonable costs, including reasonable attorneys' fees, against either party litigant. Every person who becomes liable to make any payment under this subsection may recover contribution as in cases of contract from any person who, if joined in the original suit, would have been liable to make the same payment. No action shall be maintained to enforce any liability created under this section, unless brought within one year after the discovery of the facts constituting the violation and within three years after such violation.

(f) The provisions of subsection (a) shall not apply to an exempted security.

(g) *Authority of Commission.* Notwithstanding any other provision of law, the Commission shall have the authority to regulate the trading of any put, call, straddle, option, or privilege on any security, certificate of deposit, or group or index of securities (including any interest therein or based on the value thereof), or any put, call, straddle, option, or privilege entered into on a national securities exchange relating to foreign currency (but not, with respect to any of the foregoing, an option on a contract for future delivery).

(h) *Limitations on practices that affect market volatility.* It shall be unlawful for any person, by the use of the mails or any means or instrumentality of interstate commerce or of any facility of any national securities exchange, to use or employ any act or practice in connection with the purchase or sale of any equity security in contravention of such rules or regulations as the Commission may adopt, consistent with the public interest, the protection of investors, and the maintenance of fair and orderly markets—

(1) to prescribe means reasonably designed to prevent manipulation of price levels of the equity securities market or a substantial segment thereof; and

(2) to prohibit or constrain, during periods of extraordinary market volatility, any trading practice in connection with the purchase or sale of equity securities that the Commission determines (A) has previously contributed significantly to extraordinary levels of volatility that have threatened the maintenance of fair and orderly markets; and (B) is reasonably certain to engender such levels of volatility if not prohibited or constrained.

In adopting rules under paragraph (2), the Commission shall, consistent with the purposes of this subsection, minimize the impact on the normal operations of the market and a natural person's freedom to buy or sell any equity security.

Manipulative and Deceptive Devices

Section 10. It shall be unlawful for any person, directly or indirectly, by the use of any means or instrumentality of interstate commerce or of the mails, or of any facility of any national securities exchange—

(a) To effect a short sale, or to use or employ any stop-loss order in connection with the purchase or sale, of any security registered on a national securities exchange, in contravention of such rules and regulations as the Commission may prescribe as necessary or appropriate in the public interest or for the protection of investors.

(b) To use or employ, in connection with the purchase or sale of any security registered on a national securities exchange or any security not so registered, any manipulative or deceptive device or contrivance in contravention of such rules and regulations as the Commission may prescribe as necessary or appropriate in the public interest or for the protection of investors.

Audit Requirements

Section 10A. (a) *In general.* Each audit required pursuant to this chapter of the financial statements of an issuer by a registered public accounting firm shall include, in accordance with generally accepted auditing standards, as may be modified or supplemented from time to time by the Commission—

(1) procedures designed to provide reasonable assurance of detecting illegal acts that would have a direct and material effect on the determination of financial statement amounts;

(2) procedures designed to identify related party transactions that are material to the financial statements or otherwise require disclosure therein; and

(3) an evaluation of whether there is substantial doubt about the ability of the issuer to continue as a going concern during the ensuing fiscal year.

(b) *Required response to audit discoveries.* (1) Investigation and report to management. If, in the course of conducting an audit pursuant to this chapter to which subsection (a) of this section applies, the registered public accounting firm detects or otherwise becomes aware of information indicating that an illegal act (whether or not perceived to have a material effect on the financial statements of the issuer) has or may have occurred, the firm shall, in accordance with generally accepted auditing standards, as may be modified or supplemented from time to time by the Commission—

(A)(i) determine whether it is likely that an illegal act has occurred; and (ii) if so, determine and consider the possible effect of the illegal act on the financial statements of the issuer, including any contingent monetary effects, such as fines, penalties, and damages; and

(B) as soon as practicable, inform the appropriate level of the management of the issuer and assure that the audit committee of the issuer, or the board of directors of the issuer in the absence of such a committee, is adequately informed with respect to illegal acts that have been detected or have otherwise come to the attention of such firm in the course of the audit, unless the illegal act is clearly inconsequential.

(2) Response to failure to take remedial action. If, after determining that the audit committee of the board of directors of the issuer, or the board of directors of the issuer in the absence of an audit committee, is adequately informed with respect to illegal acts that have been detected or have otherwise come to the attention of the firm in the course of the audit of such firm, the registered public accounting firm concludes that—

(A) the illegal act has a material effect on the financial statements of the issuer;

(B) the senior management has not taken, and the board of directors has not caused senior management to take, timely and appropriate remedial actions with respect to the illegal act; and

(C) the failure to take remedial action is reasonably expected to warrant departure from a standard report of the auditor, when made, or warrant resignation from the audit engagement;

the registered public accounting firm shall, as soon as practicable, directly report its conclusions to the board of directors.

(3) Notice to Commission; response to failure to notify. An issuer whose board of directors receives a report under paragraph (2) shall inform the Commission by notice not later than 1 business day after the receipt of such report and shall

furnish the registered public accounting firm making such report with a copy of the notice furnished to the Commission. If the registered public accounting firm fails to receive a copy of the notice before the expiration of the required 1–business-day period, the registered public accounting firm shall—

(A) resign from the engagement; or

(B) furnish to the Commission a copy of its report (or the documentation of any oral report given) not later than 1 business day following such failure to receive notice.

(4) Report after resignation. If a registered public accounting firm resigns from an engagement under paragraph (3)(A), the firm shall, not later than 1 business day following the failure by the issuer to notify the Commission under paragraph (3), furnish to the Commission a copy of the report of the firm (or the documentation of any oral report given).

(c) *Auditor liability limitation.* No registered public accounting firm shall be liable in a private action for any finding, conclusion, or statement expressed in a report made pursuant to paragraph (3) or (4) of subsection (b) of this section, including any rule promulgated pursuant thereto.

(d) *Civil penalties in cease-and-desist proceedings.* If the Commission finds, after notice and opportunity for hearing in a proceeding instituted pursuant to section 78u–3 of this title, that a registered public accounting firm has willfully violated paragraph (3) or (4) of subsection (b) of this section, the Commission may, in addition to entering an order under section 78u–3 of this title, impose a civil penalty against the registered public accounting firm and any other person that the Commission finds was a cause of such violation. The determination to impose a civil penalty and the amount of the penalty shall be governed by the standards set forth in section 78u–2 of this title.

(e) *Preservation of existing authority.* Except as provided in subsection (d) of this section, nothing in this section shall be held to limit or otherwise affect the authority of the Commission under this chapter.

(f) *Definitions.* As used in this section, the term "illegal act" means an act or omission that violates any law, or any rule or regulation having the force of law.

As used in this section, the term "issuer" means an issuer (as defined in section 78c of this title), the securities of which are registered under section 78l of this title, or that is required to file reports pursuant to section 78o(d) of this title, or that files or has filed a registration statement that has not yet become effective under the Securities Act of 1933 (15 U.S.C. 77a et seq.), and that it has not withdrawn.

(g) *Prohibited activities.* Except as provided in subsection (h) of this section, it shall be unlawful for a registered public accounting firm (and any associated person of that firm, to the extent determined appropriate by the Commission) that performs for any issuer any audit required by this chapter or the rules of the Commission under this chapter or, beginning 180 days after the date of commencement of the operations of the Public Company Accounting Oversight Board established under section 7211 of this title (in this section referred to as the "Board"), the rules of the Board, to provide to that issuer, contemporaneously with the audit, any non-audit service, including—

(1) bookkeeping or other services related to the accounting records or financial statements of the audit client;

(2) financial information systems design and implementation;

(3) appraisal or valuation services, fairness opinions, or contribution-in-kind reports;

(4) actuarial services;

(5) internal audit outsourcing services;

(6) management functions or human resources;

(7) broker or dealer, investment adviser, or investment banking services;

(8) legal services and expert services unrelated to the audit; and

(9) any other service that the Board determines, by regulation, is impermissible.

(h) *Preapproval required for non-audit services.* A registered public accounting firm may engage in any non-audit service, including tax services, that is not described in any of paragraphs (1) through (9) of subsection (g) of this section for an audit client, only if the activity is approved in advance by the audit committee of the issuer, in accordance with subsection (i) of this section.

(i) *Preapproval requirements.* (1) In general.

(A) Audit committee action. All auditing services (which may entail providing comfort letters in connection with securities underwritings or statutory audits required for insurance companies for purposes of State law) and non-audit services, other than as provided in subparagraph (B), provided to an issuer by the auditor of the issuer shall be preapproved by the audit committee of the issuer.

(B) De minimis exception. The preapproval requirement under subparagraph (A) is waived with respect to the provision of non-audit services for an issuer, if—

(i) the aggregate amount of all such non-audit services provided to the issuer constitutes not more than 5 percent of the total amount of revenues paid by the issuer to its auditor during the fiscal year in which the nonaudit services are provided;

(ii) such services were not recognized by the issuer at the time of the engagement to be non-audit services; and

(iii) such services are promptly brought to the attention of the audit committee of the issuer and approved prior to the completion of the audit by the audit committee or by 1 or more members of the audit committee who are members of the board of directors to whom authority to grant such approvals has been delegated by the audit committee.

(2) Disclosure to investors. Approval by an audit committee of an issuer under this subsection of a non-audit service to be performed by the auditor of the issuer shall be disclosed to investors in periodic reports required by section 78m(a) of this title.

(3) Delegation authority. The audit committee of an issuer may delegate to 1 or more designated members of the audit committee who are independent directors of the board of directors, the authority to grant preapprovals required by this subsection. The decisions of any member to whom authority is delegated under this paragraph to preapprove an activity under this subsection shall be presented to the full audit committee at each of its scheduled meetings.

(4) Approval of audit services for other purposes. In carrying out its duties under subsection (m)(2) of this section, if the audit committee of an issuer approves an audit service within the scope of the engagement of the auditor, such audit service shall be deemed to have been preapproved for purposes of this subsection.

(j) *Audit partner rotation.* It shall be unlawful for a registered public accounting firm to provide audit services to an issuer if the lead (or coordinating) audit partner (having primary responsibility for the audit), or the audit partner responsible for reviewing the audit, has performed audit services for that issuer in each of the 5 previous fiscal years of that issuer.

(k) *Reports to audit committees.* Each registered public accounting firm that performs for any issuer any audit required by this chapter shall timely report to the audit committee of the issuer—

(1) all critical accounting policies and practices to be used;

(2) all alternative treatments of financial information within generally accepted accounting principles that have been discussed with management officials of the issuer, ramifications of the use of such alternative disclosures and treatments, and the treatment preferred by the registered public accounting firm; and

(3) other material written communications between the registered public accounting firm and the management of the issuer, such as any management letter or schedule of unadjusted differences.

(*l*) *Conflicts of interest.* It shall be unlawful for a registered public accounting firm to perform for an issuer any audit service required by this chapter, if a chief executive officer, controller, chief financial officer, chief accounting officer, or any person serving in an equivalent position for the issuer, was employed by that registered independent public accounting firm and participated in any capacity in the audit of that issuer during the 1-year period preceding the date of the initiation of the audit.

(m) *Standards relating to audit committees.* (1) Commission rules.

(A) In general. Effective not later than 270 days after the date of enactment of this subsection, the Commission shall, by rule, direct the national securities exchanges and national securities associations to prohibit the listing of any security of an issuer that is not in compliance with the requirements of any portion of paragraphs (2) through (6).

(B) Opportunity to cure defects. The rules of the Commission under subparagraph (A) shall provide for appropriate procedures for an issuer to have an opportunity to cure any defects that would be the basis for a prohibition under subparagraph (A), before the imposition of such prohibition.

(2) Responsibilities relating to registered public accounting firms. The audit committee of each issuer, in its capacity as a committee of the board of directors, shall be directly responsible for the appointment, compensation, and oversight of the work of any registered public accounting firm employed by that issuer (including resolution of disagreements between management and the auditor regarding financial reporting) for the purpose of preparing or issuing an audit report or related work, and each such registered public accounting firm shall report directly to the audit committee.

(3) Independence.

(A) In general. Each member of the audit committee of the issuer shall be a member of the board of directors of the issuer, and shall otherwise be independent.

(B) Criteria. In order to be considered to be independent for purposes of this paragraph, a member of an audit committee of an issuer may not, other than in his or her capacity as a member of the audit committee, the board of directors, or any other board committee—

(i) accept any consulting, advisory, or other compensatory fee from the issuer; or

(ii) be an affiliated person of the issuer or any subsidiary thereof.

(C) Exemption authority. The Commission may exempt from the requirements of subparagraph (B) a particular relationship with respect to audit committee members, as the Commission determines appropriate in light of the circumstances.

(4) Complaints. Each audit committee shall establish procedures for—

(A) the receipt, retention, and treatment of complaints received by the issuer regarding accounting, internal accounting controls, or auditing matters; and

(B) the confidential, anonymous submission by employees of the issuer of concerns regarding questionable accounting or auditing matters.

(5) Authority to engage advisers. Each audit committee shall have the authority to engage independent counsel and other advisers, as it determines necessary to carry out its duties.

(6) Funding. Each issuer shall provide for appropriate funding, as determined by the audit committee, in its capacity as a committee of the board of directors, for payment of compensation—

(A) to the registered public accounting firm employed by the issuer for the purpose of rendering or issuing an audit report; and

(B) to any advisers employed by the audit committee under paragraph (5).

Registration Requirements for Securities

Section 12. (a) *General requirement of registration.* It shall be unlawful for any member, broker, or dealer to effect any transaction in any security (other than an exempted security) on a national securities exchange unless a registration is effective as to such security for such exchange in accordance with the provisions of this title and the rules and regulations thereunder.

(b) *Procedure for registration; information.* A security may be registered on a national securities exchange by the issuer filing an application with the exchange (and filing with the Commission such duplicate originals thereof as the Commission may require), which application shall contain—

(1) Such information, in such detail, as to the issuer and any person directly or indirectly controlling or controlled by, or under direct or indirect common control with, the issuer, and any guarantor of the security as to principal or interest or both, as the Commission may by rules and regulations re-

quire, as necessary or appropriate in the public interest or for the protection of investors, in respect of the following:

(A) the organization, financial structure and nature of the business;

(B) the terms, position, rights, and privileges of the different classes of securities outstanding;

(C) the terms on which their securities are to be, and during the preceding three years have been, offered to the public or otherwise;

(D) the directors, officers, and underwriters, and each security holder of record holding more than 10 per centum of any class of any equity security of the issuer (other than an exempted security), their remuneration and their interests in the securities of, and their material contracts with, the issuer and any person directly or indirectly controlling or controlled by, or under direct or indirect common control with, the issuer;

(E) remuneration to others than directors and officers exceeding $20,000 per annum;

(F) bonus and profit-sharing arrangements;

(G) management and service contracts;

(H) options existing or to be created in respect of their securities;

(I) material contracts, not made in the ordinary course of business, which are to be executed in whole or in part at or after the filing of the application or which were made not more than 2 years before such filing, and every material patent or contract for a material patent right shall be deemed a material contract;

(J) balance sheets for not more than the three preceding fiscal years, certified if required by the rules and regulations of the Commission by a registered public accounting firm;

(K) profit and loss statements for not more than the three preceding fiscal years, certified if required by the rules and regulations of the Commission by a registered public accounting firm; and

(L) any further financial statements which the Commission may deem necessary or appropriate for the protection of investors.

(2) Such copies of articles of incorporation, bylaws, trust indentures, or corresponding documents by whatever name known, underwriting arrangements, and other similar documents of, and voting trust agreements with respect to, the issuer and any person directly or indirectly controlling or controlled by, or under direct or indirect common control with, the issuer as the Commission may require as necessary or appropriate for the proper protection of investors and to insure fair dealing in the security.

(3) Such copies of material contracts, referred to in paragraph (1)(I) above, as the Commission may require as necessary or appropriate for the proper protection of investors and to insure fair dealing in the security.

(c) *Additional or alternative information.* If in the judgment of the Commission any information required under subsection (b) is inapplicable to any specified class or classes of issuers, the Commission shall require in lieu thereof the submission of such other information of comparable character as it may deem applicable to such class of issuers.

(d) *Effective date of registration; withdrawal of registration.* If the exchange authorities certify to the Commission that the security has been approved by the exchange for listing and registration, the registration shall become effective thirty days after the receipt of such certification by the Commission or within such shorter period of time as the Commission may determine. A security registered with a national securities exchange may be withdrawn or stricken from listing and registration in accordance with the rules of the exchange and, upon such terms as the Commission may deem necessary to impose for the protection of investors, upon application by the issuer or the exchange to the Commission; whereupon the issuer shall be relieved from further compliance with the provisions of this section and section 13 of this title and any rules or regulations under such sections as to the securities so withdrawn or stricken. An unissued security may be registered only in accordance with such rules and regulations as the Commission may prescribe as necessary or appropriate in the public interest or for the protection of investors.

* * *

(f) *Unlisted trading privileges for security originally listed on another national exchange.* (1)(A) Notwithstanding the preceding subsections of this section, any national securities exchange, in accordance with the requirements of this subsection and the rules hereunder, may extend unlisted trading privileges to—

(i) any security that is listed and registered on a national securities exchange, subject to subparagraph (B); and

(ii) any security that is otherwise registered pursuant to this section, or that would be required to be so registered except for the exemption from registration provided in subparagraph (B) or (G) of subsection (g)(2) of this section, subject to subparagraph (E) of this paragraph.

(B) A national securities exchange may not extend unlisted trading privileges to a security described in subparagraph (A)(i) during such interval, if any, after the commencement of an initial public offering of such security, as is or may be required pursuant to subparagraph (C).

(C) Not later than 180 days after October 22, 1994, the Commission shall prescribe, by rule or regulation, the duration of the interval referred to in subparagraph (B), if any, as the Commission determines to be necessary or appropriate for the maintenance of fair and orderly markets, the protection of investors and the public interest, or otherwise in furtherance of the purposes of this chapter. Until the earlier of the effective date of such rule or regulation or 240 days after October 22, 1994, such interval shall begin at the opening of trading on the day on which such security commences trading on the national securities exchange with which such security is registered and end at the conclusion of the next day of trading.

(D) The Commission may prescribe, by rule or regulation such additional procedures or requirements for extending unlisted trading privileges to any security as the Commission deems necessary or appropriate for the maintenance of fair and orderly markets, the protection of investors and the public interest, or otherwise in furtherance of the purposes of this title.

(E) No extension of unlisted trading privileges to securities described in subparagraph (A)(ii) may occur except pursuant to a rule, regulation, or order of the Commission approving such extension or extensions. In promulgating such rule or regulation or in issuing such order, the Commission—

(i) shall find that such extension or extensions of unlisted trading privileges is consistent with the maintenance of fair and orderly markets, the protection of investors and the public interest, and otherwise in furtherance of the purposes of this title;

(ii) shall take account of the public trading activity in such securities, the character of such trading, the impact of such extension on the existing markets for such securities, and the desirability of removing impediments to and the progress that has been made toward the development of a national market system; and

(iii) shall not permit a national securities exchange to extend unlisted trading privileges to such securities if any rule of such national securities exchange would unreasonably impair the ability of a dealer to solicit or effect transactions in such securities for its own account, or would unreasonably restrict competition among dealers in such securities or between such dealers acting in the capacity of market makers who are specialists and such dealers who are not specialists.

(F) An exchange may continue to extend unlisted trading privileges in accordance with this paragraph only if the exchange and the subject security continue to satisfy the requirements for eligibility under this paragraph, including any rules and regulations issued by the Commission pursuant to this paragraph, except that unlisted trading privileges may continue with regard to securities which had been admitted on such exchange prior to July 1, 1964, notwithstanding the failure to satisfy such requirements. If unlisted trading privileges in a security are discontinued pursuant to this subparagraph, the exchange shall cease trading in that security, unless the exchange and the subject security thereafter satisfy the requirements of this paragraph and the rules issued hereunder.

(G) For purposes of this paragraph—

(i) a security is the subject of an initial public offering if—

(I) the offering of the subject security is registered under the Securities Act of 1933; and

(II) the issuer of the security, immediately prior to filing the registration statement with respect to the offering, was not subject to the reporting requirements of section 13 or 15(d) of this title; and

(ii) an initial public offering of such security commences at the opening of trading on the day on which such security commences trading on the national securities exchange with which such security is registered.

(2)(A) At any time within 60 days of commencement of trading on an exchange of a security pursuant to unlisted trading privileges, the Commission may summarily suspend such unlisted trading privileges on the exchange. Such suspension shall not be reviewable under section 25 of this title and shall not be deemed to be a final agency action for purposes of section 704 of Title 5. Upon such suspension—

(i) the exchange shall cease trading in the security by the close of business on the date of such suspension, or at such time as the Commission may prescribe by rule or order for the maintenance of fair and orderly markets, the protection of investors and the public interest, or otherwise in furtherance of the purposes of this title; and

(ii) if the exchange seeks to extend unlisted trading privileges to the security, the exchange shall file an application to reinstate its ability to do so with the Commission pursuant to such procedures as the Commission may prescribe by rule or order for the maintenance of fair and orderly markets, the protection of investors and the public interest, or otherwise in furtherance of the purposes of this chapter.

(B) A suspension under subparagraph (A) shall remain in effect until the Commission, by order, grants approval of an application to reinstate, as described in subparagraph (A)(ii).

(C) A suspension under subparagraph (A) shall not affect the validity or force of an extension of unlisted trading privileges in effect prior to such suspension.

(D) The Commission shall not approve an application by a national securities exchange to reinstate its ability to extend unlisted trading privileges to a security unless the Commission finds, after notice and opportunity for hearing, that the extension of unlisted trading privileges pursuant to such application is consistent with the maintenance of fair and orderly markets, the protection of investors and the public interest, and otherwise in furtherance of the purposes of this chapter. If the application is made to reinstate unlisted trading privileges to a security described in paragraph (1)(A)(ii), the Commission—

(i) shall take account of the public trading activity in such security, the character of such trading, the impact of such extension on the existing markets for such a security, and the desirability of removing impediments to and the progress that has been made toward the development of a national market system; and

(ii) shall not grant any such application if any rule of the national securities exchange making application under this subsection would unreasonably impair the ability of a dealer to solicit or effect transactions in such security for its own account, or would unreasonably restrict competition among dealers in such security or between such dealers acting in the capacity of marketmakers who are specialists and such dealers who are not specialists.

(3) Notwithstanding paragraph (2), the Commission shall by rules and regulations suspend unlisted trading privileges in whole or in part for any or all classes of securities for a period not exceeding twelve months, if it deems such suspension necessary or appropriate in the public interest or for the protection of investors or to prevent evasion of the purposes of this title.

(4) On the application of the issuer of any security for which unlisted trading privileges on any exchange have been continued or extended pursuant to this subsection, or of any broker or dealer who makes or creates a market for such security, or of any other person having a bona fide interest in the question of termination or suspension of such unlisted trading privileges, or on its own motion, the Commission shall by order terminate, or suspend for a period not exceeding twelve months, such unlisted trading privileges for such security if the Commission finds, after appropriate notice and opportunity for hearing, that such termination or suspension is necessary or appropriate in the public interest or for the protection of investors.

(5) In any proceeding under this subsection in which appropriate notice and opportunity for hearing are required, notice of not less than ten days to the applicant in such proceeding, to the issuer of the security involved, to the exchange which is

seeking to continue or extend or has continued or extended unlisted trading privileges for such security, and to the exchange, if any, on which such security is listed and registered, shall be deemed adequate notice, and any broker or dealer who makes or creates a market for such security, and any other person having a bona fide interest in such proceeding, shall upon application be entitled to be heard.

(6) Any security for which unlisted trading privileges are continued or extended pursuant to this subsection shall be deemed to be registered on a national securities exchange within the meaning of this chapter. The powers and duties of the Commission under this chapter shall be applicable to the rules of an exchange in respect of any such security. The Commission may, by such rules and regulations as it deems necessary or appropriate in the public interest or for the protection of investors, either unconditionally or upon specified terms and conditions, or for stated periods, exempt such securities from the operation of any provision of section 13, 14, 15 of this title.

* * *

(g) *Registration of securities by issuer; exemptions.* (1) Every issuer which is engaged in interstate commerce, or in a business affecting interstate commerce, or whose securities are traded by use of the mails or any means or instrumentality of interstate commerce shall—

(A) within one hundred and twenty days after the last day of its first fiscal year ended after the effective date of this subsection on which the issuer has total assets exceeding $1,000,000 and a class of equity security (other than an exempted security) held of record by seven hundred and fifty or more persons; and

(B) within one hundred and twenty days after the last day of its first fiscal year ended after two years from the effective date of this subsection on which the issuer has total assets exceeding $1,000,000 and a class of equity security (other than an exempted security) held of record by five hundred or more but less than seven hundred and fifty persons,

register such security by filing with the Commission a registration statement (and such copies thereof as the Commission may require) with respect to such security containing such information and documents as the Commission may specify comparable to that which is required in an application to register a security pursuant to subsection (b) of this section. Each such registration statement shall become effective sixty days after filing with the Commission or within such shorter period as the Commission may direct. Until such registration statement becomes effective it shall not be deemed filed for the purposes of section 18 of this title. Any issuer may register any class of equity security not required to be registered by filing a registration statement pursuant to the provisions of this paragraph. The Commission is authorized to extend the date upon which any issuer or class of issuers is required to register a security pursuant to the provisions of this paragraph.

(2) The provisions of this subsection shall not apply in respect of—

(A) any security listed and registered on a national securities exchange.

(B) any security issued by an investment company registered pursuant to section 8 of the Investment Company Act of 1940.

(C) any security, other than permanent stock, guaranty stock, permanent reserve stock, or any similar certificate evidencing nonwithdrawable capital, issued by a savings and loan association, building and loan association, cooperative bank, homestead association, or similar institution, which is supervised and examined by State or Federal authority having supervision over any such institution.

(D) any security of an issuer organized and operated exclusively for religious, educational, benevolent, fraternal, charitable, or reformatory purposes and not for pecuniary profit, and no part of the net earnings of which inures to the benefit of any private shareholder or individual; or any security of a fund that is excluded from the definition of an investment company under section 80a–3(c)(10)(B) of the Investment Company Act of 1940.

(E) any security of an issuer which is a "cooperative association" as defined in the Agricultural Marketing Act, approved June 15, 1929, as amended, or a federation of such cooperative associations, if such federation possesses no greater powers or purposes than cooperative associations so defined.

(F) any security issued by a mutual or cooperative organization which supplies a commodity or service primarily for the benefit of its members and operates not for pecuniary profit, but only if the security is part of a class issuable only to persons who purchase commodities or services from the issuer, the security is transferable only to a successor in interest or occupancy of premises serviced or to be served by the issuer, and no dividends are payable to the holder of the security.

(G) any security issued by an insurance company if all of the following conditions are met:

(i) Such insurance company is required to and does file an annual statement with the Commissioner of Insurance (or other officer or agency performing a similar function) of its domiciliary State, and such annual statement conforms to that prescribed by the National Association of Insurance Commissioners or in the determination of such State commissioner, officer or agency substantially conforms to that so prescribed.

(ii) Such insurance company is subject to regulation by its domiciliary State of proxies, consents, or authorizations in respect of securities issued by such company and such regulation conforms to that prescribed by the National Association of Insurance Commissioners.

(iii) After July 1, 1966, the purchase and sales of securities issued by such insurance company by beneficial owners, directors, or officers of such company are subject to regulation (including reporting) by its domiciliary State substantially in the manner provided in section 16 of this title.

(H) any interest or participation in any collective trust funds maintained by a bank or in a separate account maintained by an insurance company which interest or participation is issued in connection with (i) a stock-bonus, pension, or profit-sharing plan which meets the requirements for qualification under section 401 of the Internal Revenue Code of 1954, or (ii) an annuity plan which meets the requirements for deduction of the employer's contribution under section 404(a)(2) of such Code.

(3) The Commission may by rules or regulations or, on its own motion, after notice and opportunity for hearing, by order, exempt from this subsection any security of a foreign issuer, including any certificate of deposit for such a security, if the Commission finds that such exemption is in the public interest and is consistent with the protection of investors.

(4) Registration of any class of security pursuant to this subsection shall be terminated ninety days, or such shorter period as the Commission may determine, after the issuer files a certification with the Commission that the number of holders of record of such class of security is reduced to less than three hundred persons.

* * *

(h) *Exemption by rules and regulations from certain provisions of section.* The Commission may by rules and regulations, or upon application of an interested person, by order, after notice and opportunity for hearing, exempt in whole or in part any issuer or class of issuers from the provisions of subsection (g) of this section or from section 13, 14, or 15(d), or may exempt from section 16 any officer, director, or beneficial owner of securities of any issuer, any security of which is required to be registered pursuant to subsection (g) hereof, upon such terms and conditions and for such period as it deems necessary or appropriate, if the Commission finds, by reason of the number of public investors, amount of trading interest in the securities, the nature and extent of the activities of the issuer, income or assets of the issuer or otherwise, that such action is not inconsistent with the public interest or the protection of investors.

* * *

(i) *Securities issued by banks.* In respect of any securities issued by banks the deposits of which are insured in accordance with the Federal Deposit Insurance Act or institutions the accounts of which are insured by the Federal Savings and Loan Insurance Corporation, the powers, functions, and duties vested in the Commission to administer and enforce sections 10A(m), 12, 13, 14(a), 14(c), 14(d), 14(f), and 16 of this Act, and sections 302, 303, 304, 306, 401(b), 404, 406, and 407 of the Sarbanes–Oxley Act of 2002, (1) with respect to national banks and banks operating under the Code of Law for the District of Columbia are vested in the Comptroller of the Currency, (2) with respect to all other member banks of the Federal Reserve System are vested in the Board of Governors of the Federal Reserve System, (3) with respect to all other insured banks are vested in the Federal Deposit Insurance Corporation, and (4) with respect to savings associations the accounts of which are insured by the Federal Deposit Insurance Corporation are vested in the Office of Thrift Supervision. The Comptroller of the Currency, the Board of Governors of the Federal Reserve System, the Federal Deposit Insurance Corporation, and the Office of Thrift Supervision shall have the power to make such rules and regulations as may be necessary for the execution of the functions vested in them as provided in this subsection. In carrying out their responsibilities under this subsection, the agencies named in the first sentence of this subsection shall issue substantially similar regulations to regulations and rules issued by the Commission under sections 10A(m), 12, 13, 14(a), 14(c), 14(d), 14(f), and 16 of this Act, and sections 302, 303, 304, 306, 401(b), 404, 406, and 407 of the Sarbanes–Oxley Act of 2002, unless they find that implementation of substantially similar regulations with respect to insured banks and insured institutions are not necessary or appropriate in the public interest or for protection of investors, and publish such findings, and the detailed reasons therefor, in the Federal Register. Such regulations of the above-named agencies, or the reasons for failure to publish such substantially similar regulations to those of the Commission, shall be published in the Federal Register within 120 days of the date of enactment of this subsection, and, thereafter, within 60 days of any changes made by the Commission in its relevant regulations and rules.

(j) *Denial, suspension, or revocation of registration; notice and hearing.* The Commission is authorized, by order, as it deems necessary or appropriate for the protection of investors to deny, to suspend the effective date of, to suspend for a period not exceeding twelve months, or to revoke the registration of a security, if the Commission finds, on the record after notice and opportunity for hearing, that the issuer of such security has failed to comply with any provision of this title or the rules and regulations thereunder. No member of a national securities exchange, broker, or dealer shall make use of the mails or any means or instrumentality of interstate commerce to effect any transaction in, or to induce the purchase or sale of, any security the registration of which has been and is suspended or revoked pursuant to the preceding sentence.

(k) *Trading suspensions; emergency authority.* (1) If in its opinion the public interest and the protection of investors so require, the Commission is authorized by order—

(A) summarily to suspend trading in any security (other than an exempted security) for a period not exceeding 10 business days, and

(B) summarily to suspend all trading on any national securities exchange or otherwise, in securities other than exempted securities, for a period not exceeding 90 calendar days.

The action described in subparagraph (B) shall not take effect unless the Commission notifies the President of its decision and the President notifies the Commission that the President does not disapprove of such decision.

(2) *Emergency orders.* (A) The Commission, in an emergency, may by order summarily take such action to alter, supplement, suspend, or impose requirements or restrictions with respect to any matter or action subject to regulation by the Commission or a self-regulatory organization under this title, as the Commission determines is necessary in the public interest and for the protection of investors—

(i) to maintain or restore fair and orderly securities markets (other than markets in exempted securities); or

(ii) to ensure prompt, accurate, and safe clearance and settlement of transactions in securities (other than exempted securities).

(B) An order of the Commission under this paragraph (2) shall continue in effect for the period specified by the Commission, and may be extended, except that in no event shall the Commission's action continue in effect for more than 10 business days, including extensions. In exercising its authority under this paragraph, the Commission shall not be required to comply with the provisions of section 553 of title 5, United States Code, or with the provisions of section 19(c) of this title.

(3) *Termination of emergency actions by President.* The President may direct that action taken by

the Commission under paragraph (1)(B) or paragraph (2) of this subsection shall not continue in effect.

(4) No member of a national securities exchange, broker, or dealer shall make use of the mails or any means or instrumentality of interstate commerce to effect any transaction in, or to induce the purchase or sale of, any security in contravention of an order of the Commission under this subsection unless such order has been stayed, modified, or set aside as provided in paragraph (5) of this subsection or has ceased to be effective upon direction of the President as provided in paragraph (3).

(5) An order of the Commission pursuant to this subsection shall be subject to review only as provided in section 25(a) of this title. Review shall be based on an examination of all the information before the Commission at the time such order was issued. The reviewing court shall not enter a stay, writ of mandamus, or similar relief unless the court finds, after notice and hearing before a panel of the court, that the Commission's action is arbitrary, capricious, an abuse of discretion, or otherwise not in accordance with law.

(6) For purposes of this subsection, the term "emergency" means a major market disturbance characterized by or constituting—

(A) sudden and excessive fluctuations of securities prices generally, or a substantial threat thereof, that threaten fair and orderly markets, or

(B) a substantial disruption of the safe or efficient operation of the national system for clearance and settlement of securities, or a substantial threat thereof.

(*l*) *Issuance of any security in contravention of rules and regulations; application to annuity contracts and variable life policies.* It shall be unlawful for an issuer, any class of whose securities is registered pursuant to this section or would be required to be so registered except for the exemption from registration provided by subsection (g)(2)(B) or (g)(2)(G) of this section, by the use of any means or instrumentality of interstate commerce, or of the mails, to issue, either originally or upon transfer, any of such securities in a form or with a format which contravenes such rules and regulations as the Commission may prescribe as necessary or appropriate for the prompt and accurate clearance and settlement of transactions in securities. The provisions of this subsection shall not apply to variable annuity contracts or variable life policies issued by an insurance company or its separate accounts.

Periodical and Other Reports

Section 13. (a) *Reports by issuer of security; contents.* Every issuer of a security registered pursuant to section 12 of this title shall file with the Commission, in accordance with such rules and regulations as the Commission may prescribe as necessary or appropriate for the proper protection of investors and to insure fair dealing in the security—

(1) such information and documents (and such copies thereof) as the Commission shall require to keep reasonably current the information and documents required to be included in or filed with an application or registration statement filed pursuant to section 12, except that the Commission may not require the filing of any material contract wholly executed before July 1, 1962.

(2) such annual reports (and such copies thereof), certified if required by the rules and regulations of the Commission by independent public accountants, and such quarterly reports (and such copies thereof), as the Commission may prescribe.

Every issuer of a security registered on a national securities exchange shall also file a duplicate original of such information, documents, and reports with the exchange.

(b) *Form of report; books, records, and internal accounting; derivatives.* (1) The Commission may prescribe, in regard to reports made pursuant to this title, the form or forms in which the required information shall be set forth, the items or details to be shown in the balance sheet and the earning statement, and the methods to be followed in the preparation of reports, in the appraisal or valuation of assets and liabilities, in the determination of depreciation and depletion, in the differentiation of recurring and nonrecurring income, in the differentiation of investment and operating income, and in the preparation, where the Commission deems it necessary or desirable, of separate and/or consolidated balance sheets or income accounts of any person directly or indirectly controlling or controlled by the issuer, or any person under direct or indirect common control with the issuer; but in the case of the reports of any person whose methods of accounting are prescribed under the provisions of any law of the United States, or any rule or regulation thereunder, the rules and regulations of the Commission with respect to reports shall not be inconsistent with the requirements imposed by such law or rule or regulation in respect of the same subject matter (except that such rules and regulations of the Commission may be inconsistent with such requirements to the extent that the Commission determines that the public interest or the protection of investors so requires).

(2) Every issuer which has a class of securities registered pursuant to section 12 of this title and every issuer which is required to file reports pursuant to section 15(d) of this title shall—

(A) make and keep books, records, and accounts, which, in reasonable detail, accurately and fairly reflect the transactions and dispositions of the assets of the issuer;

(B) devise and maintain a system of internal accounting controls sufficient to provide reasonable assurances that—

(i) transactions are executed in accordance with management's general or specific authorization;

(ii) transactions are recorded as necessary (I) to permit preparation of financial statements in conformity with generally accepted accounting principles or any other criteria applicable to such statements, and (II) to maintain accountability for assets;

(iii) access to assets is permitted only in accordance with management's general or specific authorization; and

(iv) the recorded accountability for assets is compared with the existing assets at reasonable intervals and appropriate action is taken with respect to any differences; and

(C) notwithstanding any other provision of law, pay the allocable share of such issuer of a reasonable annual accounting support fee or fees, determined in accordance with section 109 of the Sarbanes–Oxley Act of 2002.

(3)(A) With respect to matters concerning the national security of the United States, no duty or liability under paragraph (2) of this subsection shall be imposed upon any person acting in cooperation with the head of any Federal department or agency responsible for such matters if such act in cooperation with such head of a department or agency was done upon the specific, written directive of the head of such department or agency pursuant to Presidential authority to issue such directives. Each directive issued under this paragraph shall set forth the specific facts and circumstances with respect to which the provisions of this paragraph are to be invoked. Each such directive shall, unless renewed in writing, expire one year after the date of issuance.

(B) Each head of a Federal department or agency of the United States who issues a directive pursuant to this paragraph shall maintain a complete file of all such directives and shall, on October 1 of each year, transmit a summary of matters covered by such directives in force at any time during the previous year to the Permanent Select Committee on Intelligence of the House of Representatives and the Select Committee on Intelligence of the Senate.

(4) No criminal liability shall be imposed for failing to comply with the requirements of paragraph (2) of this subsection except as provided in paragraph (5) of this subsection.

(5) No person shall knowingly circumvent or knowingly fail to implement a system of internal accounting controls or knowingly falsify any book, record, or account described in paragraph (2).

(6) Where an issuer which has a class of securities registered pursuant to section 12 of this title or an issuer which is required to file reports pursuant to section 15(d) of this title holds 50 per centum or less of the voting power with respect to a domestic or foreign firm, the provisions of paragraph (2) require only that the issuer proceed in good faith to use its influence, to the extent reasonable under the issuer's circumstances, to cause such domestic or foreign firm to devise and maintain a system of internal accounting controls consistent with paragraph (2). Such circumstances include the relative degree of the issuer's ownership of the domestic or foreign firm and the laws and practices governing the business operations of the country in which such firm is located. An issuer which demonstrates good faith efforts to use such influence shall be conclusively presumed to have complied with the requirements of paragraph (2).

(7) For the purpose of paragraph (2) of this subsection, the terms "reasonable assurances" and "reasonable detail" mean such level of detail and degree of assurance as would satisfy prudent officials in the conduct of their own affairs.

(c) *Alternative reports.* If in the judgment of the Commission any report required under subsection (a) is inapplicable to any specified class or classes of issuers, the Commission shall require in lieu thereof the submission of such reports of comparable character as it may deem applicable to such class or classes of issuers.

(d) *Reports by persons acquiring more than five per centum of certain classes of securities.* (1) Any person who, after acquiring directly or indirectly the beneficial ownership of any equity security of a class which is registered pursuant to section 12 of this title, or any equity security of an insurance company which would have been required to be so registered except for the exemption contained in section 12(g)(2)(G) of this title, or any equity security issued by a closed-end investment company registered under the Investment Company Act of 1940 or any equity security issued by a Native Corporation pursuant to Section 37(d)(6) of the Alaska Naive Claims Settlement Act, is directly or indirectly the beneficial owner of more than 5 per centum of such class shall, within ten days after such acquisition, send to the issuer of the security at its principal executive office, by registered or certified mail, send to each exchange where the security is traded, and file with the Commission, a statement containing such of the following information, and such additional information, as the Commission may by rules and regulations prescribe as necessary or appropriate in the public interest or for the protection of investors—

(A) the background, and identity, residence, and citizenship of, and the nature of such beneficial ownership by, such person and all other persons by whom or on whose behalf the purchases have been or are to be effected;

(B) the source and amount of the funds or other consideration used or to be used in making the purchases, and if any part of the purchase price or proposed purchase price is represented or is to be represented by funds or other consideration borrowed or otherwise obtained for the purpose of acquiring, holding, or trading such security, a description of the transaction and the names of the parties thereto, except that where a source of funds is a loan made in the ordinary course of business by a bank, as defined in section 3(a)(6) of this title, if the person filing such statement so requests, the name of the bank shall not be made available to the public;

(C) if the purpose of the purchases or prospective purchases is to acquire control of the business of the issuer of the securities, any plans or proposals which such persons may have to liquidate such issuer, to sell its assets to or merge it with any other persons, or to make any other major change in its business or corporate structure;

(D) the number of shares of such security which are beneficially owned, and the number of shares concerning which there is a right to acquire, directly or indirectly, by (i) such person, and (ii) by each associate of such person, giving the name and address of each such associate; and

(E) information as to any contracts, arrangements, or understandings with any person with respect to any securities of the issuer, including but not limited to transfer of any of the securities, joint ventures, loan or option arrangements, puts or calls, guaranties of loans, guaranties against loss or guaranties of profits, division of losses or profits, or the giving or withholding of proxies, naming the persons with whom such contracts, arrangements, or understandings have been entered into, and giving the details thereof.

(2) If any material change occurs in the facts set forth in the statements to the issuer and the exchange, and in the statement filed with the Commission, an amendment shall be transmitted to the issuer and the exchange and shall be filed with the Commission, in accordance with such rules and regulations as the Commission may prescribe as necessary or appropriate in the public interest or for the protection of investors.

(3) When two or more persons act as a partnership, limited partnership, syndicate, or other group for the purpose of acquiring, holding, or disposing of securities of an issuer, such syndicate or group shall be deemed a "person" for the purposes of this subsection.

(4) In determining, for purposes of this subsection, any percentage of a class of any security, such

class shall be deemed to consist of the amount of the outstanding securities of such class, exclusive of any securities of such class held by or for the account of the issuer or a subsidiary of the issuer.

(5) The Commission, by rule or regulation or by order, may permit any person to file in lieu of the statement required by paragraph (1) of this subsection or the rules and regulations thereunder, a notice stating the name of such person, the number of shares of any equity securities subject to paragraph (1) which are owned by him, the date of their acquisition and such other information as the Commission may specify, if it appears to the Commission that such securities were acquired by such person in the ordinary course of his business and were not acquired for the purpose of and do not have the effect of changing or influencing the control of the issuer nor in connection with or as a participant in any transaction having such purpose or effect.

(6) The provisions of this subsection shall not apply to—

(A) any acquisition or offer to acquire securities made or proposed to be made by means of a registration statement under the Securities Act of 1933;

(B) any acquisition of the beneficial ownership of a security which, together with all other acquisitions by the same person of securities of the same class during the preceding twelve months, does not exceed 2 per centum of that class;

(C) any acquisition of an equity security by the issuer of such security;

(D) any acquisition or proposed acquisition of a security which the Commission, by rules or regulations or by order, shall exempt from the provisions of this subsection as not entered into for the purpose of, and not having the effect of, changing or influencing the control of the issuer or otherwise as not comprehended within the purposes of this subsection.

(e) *Purchase of securities by issuer.* (1) It shall be unlawful for an issuer which has a class of equity securities registered pursuant to section 12 of this title, or which is a closed-end investment company registered under the Investment Company Act of 1940, to purchase any equity security issued by it if such purchase is in contravention of such rules and regulations as the Commission, in the public interest or for the protection of investors, may adopt (A) to define acts and practices which are fraudulent, deceptive, or manipulative, and (B) to prescribe means reasonably designed to prevent such acts and practices. Such rules and regulations may require such issuer to provide holders of equity securities of such class with such information relating to the reasons for such purchase, the source of funds, the number of shares to be purchased, the price to be paid for such securities, the method of purchase, and such additional information, as the Commission deems necessary or appropriate in the public interest or for the protection of investors, or which the Commission deems to be material to a determination whether such security should be sold.

(2) For the purpose of this subsection, a purchase by or for the issuer or any person controlling, controlled by, or under common control with the issuer, or a purchase subject to control of the issuer or any such person, shall be deemed to be a purchase by the issuer. The Commission shall have power to make rules and regulations implementing this paragraph in the public interest and for the protection of investors, including exemptive rules and regulations covering situations in which the Commission deems it unnecessary or inappropriate that a purchase of the type described in this paragraph shall be deemed to be a purchase by the issuer for purposes of some or all of the provisions of paragraph (1) of this subsection.

(3) At the time of filing such statement as the Commission may require by rule pursuant to paragraph (1) of this subsection, the person making the filing shall pay to the Commission a fee of 1/50 of 1 per centum of the value of securities proposed to be purchased. The fee shall be reduced with respect to securities in an amount equal to any fee paid with respect to any securities issued in connection with the proposed transaction under section 6(b) of the Securities Act of 1933, or the fee paid under that section shall be reduced in an amount equal to the fee paid to the Commission in connection with such transaction under this paragraph.

(f) *Reports by institutional investment managers.* (1) Every institutional investment manager which uses the mails, or any means or instrumentality of interstate commerce in the course of its business as an institutional investment manager and which exercises investment discretion with respect to accounts holding equity securities of a class described in section 13(d)(1) of this title having an aggregate fair market value on the last trading day in any of the preceding twelve months of at least $100,000,000 or such lesser amount (but in no case less than $10,000,000) as the Commission, by rule, may determine, shall file reports with the Commission in such form, for such periods, and at such times after the end of such periods as the Commission, by rule, may prescribe, but in no event shall such reports be filed for periods longer than one year or shorter than one quarter. Such reports shall include for each such equity security held on the last day of the reporting period by accounts (in aggregate or by type as the Commission, by rule, may prescribe) with respect to which the institutional investment manager exercises investment discretion (other than securities held in amounts which the Commission, by rule, determines to be insignificant for purposes of this subsection), the name of the issuer and the title, class, CUSIP number, number of shares or principal amount, and aggregate fair market value of each such security. Such reports may also include for accounts (in aggregate or by type) with respect to which the institutional investment manager exercises investment discretion such of the following information as the Commission, by rule, prescribes—

(A) the name of the issuer and the title, class, CUSIP number, number of shares or principal amount, and aggregate fair market value or cost or amortized cost of each other security (other than an exempted security) held on the last day of the reporting period by such accounts;

(B) the aggregate fair market value or cost or amortized cost of exempted securities (in aggregate or by class) held on the last day of the reporting period by such accounts;

(C) the number of shares of each equity security of a class described in section 13(d)(1) of this title held on the last day of the reporting period by such accounts with respect to which the institutional investment manager possesses sole or shared authority to exercise the voting rights evidenced by such securities;

(D) the aggregate purchases and aggregate sales during the reporting period of each security (other than an exempted security) effected by or for such accounts; and

(E) with respect to any transaction or series of transactions having a market value of at least $500,000 or such other amount as the Commission, by rule, may determine, effected during the reporting period by or for such accounts in any equity security of a class described in section 13(d)(1) of this title—

(i) the name of the issuer and the title, class, and CUSIP number of the security;

(ii) the number of shares or principal amount of the security involved in the transaction;

(iii) whether the transaction was a purchase or sale;

(iv) the per share price or prices at which the transaction was effected;

(v) the date or dates of the transaction;

(vi) the date or dates of the settlement of the transaction;

(vii) the broker or dealer through whom the transaction was effected;

(viii) the market or markets in which the transaction was effected; and

(ix) such other related information as the Commission, by rule, may prescribe.

* * *

(5)(A) For purposes of this subsection the term "institutional investment manager" includes any person, other than a natural person, investing in or buying and selling securities for its own account, and any person exercising investment discretion with respect to the account of any other person.

* * *

(g) *Statement of equity security ownership.* (1) Any person who is directly or indirectly the beneficial owner of more than 5 per centum of any security of a class described in subsection (d)(1) of this section shall send to the issuer of the security and shall file with the Commission a statement setting forth, in such form and at such time as the Commission may, by rule, prescribe—

(A) such person's identity, residence, and citizenship; and

(B) the number and description of the shares in which such person has an interest and the nature of such interest.

(2) If any material change occurs in the facts set forth in the statement sent to the issuer and filed with the Commission, an amendment shall be transmitted to the issuer and shall be filed with the Commission, in accordance with such rules and regulations as the Commission may prescribe as necessary or appropriate in the public interest or for the protection of investors.

(3) When two or more persons act as a partnership, limited partnership, syndicate, or other group for the purpose of acquiring, holding, or disposing of securities of an issuer, such syndicate or group shall be deemed a "person" for the purposes of this subsection.

(4) In determining, for purposes of this subsection, any percentage of a class of any security, such class shall be deemed to consist of the amount of the outstanding securities of such class, exclusive of any securities of such class held by or for the account of the issuer or a subsidiary of the issuer.

(5) In exercising its authority under this subsection, the Commission shall take such steps as it deems necessary or appropriate in the public interest or for the protection of investors (A) to achieve centralized reporting of information regarding ownership, (B) to avoid unnecessarily duplicative reporting by and minimize the compliance burden on persons required to report, and (C) to tabulate and promptly make available the information contained in any report filed pursuant to this subsection in a manner which will, in the view of the Commission, maximize the usefulness of the information to other Federal and State agencies and the public.

(6) The Commission may, by rule or order, exempt, in whole or in part, any person or class of persons from any or all of the reporting requirements of this subsection as it deems necessary or appropriate in the public interest or for the protection of investors.

(h) *Large trade reporting.* (1) For the purpose of monitoring the impact on the securities markets of securities transactions involving a substantial volume or a large fair market value or exercise value and for the purpose of otherwise assisting the Commission in the enforcement of this title, each large trader shall—

(A) provide such information to the Commission as the Commission may by rule or regulation prescribe as necessary or appropriate, identifying such large trader and all accounts in or through which such large trader effects such transactions; and

(B) identify, in accordance with such rules or regulations as the Commission may prescribe as necessary or appropriate, to any registered broker or dealer by or through whom such large trader directly or indirectly effects securities transactions, such large trader and all accounts directly or indirectly maintained with such broker or dealer by such large trader in or through which such transactions are effected.

(2) Every registered broker or dealer shall make and keep for prescribed periods such records as the Commission by rule or regulation prescribes as necessary or appropriate in the public interest, for the protection of investors, or otherwise in furtherance of the purposes of this title, with respect to securities transactions that equal or exceed the reporting activity level effected directly or indirectly by or through such registered broker or dealer of or for any person that such broker or dealer knows is a large trader, or any person that such broker or dealer has reason to know is [a] large trader on the basis of transactions in securities effected by or through such broker or dealer. Such records shall be available for reporting to the Commission, or any self-regulatory organization that the Commission shall designate to receive such reports, on the morning of the day following the day the transactions were effected, and shall be reported to the Commission or a self-regulatory organization designated by the Commission immediately upon request by the Commission or such a self-regulatory organization. Such records and reports shall be in a format and transmitted in a manner prescribed by the Commission (including, but not limited to, machine readable form).

(3) The Commission may prescribe rules or regulations governing the manner in which transactions and accounts shall be aggregated for the purpose of this subsection, including aggregation on the basis of common ownership or control.

(4) All records required to be made and kept by registered brokers and dealers pursuant to this sub-

section with respect to transactions effected by large traders are subject at any time, or from time to time, to such reasonable periodic, special, or other examinations by representatives of the Commission as the Commission deems necessary or appropriate in the public interest, for the protection of investors, or otherwise in furtherance of the purposes of this title.

(5) In exercising its authority under this subsection, the Commission shall take into account—

(A) existing reporting systems;

(B) the costs associated with maintaining information with respect to transactions effected by large traders and reporting such information to the Commission or self-regulatory organizations; and

(C) the relationship between the United States and international securities markets.

(6) The Commission, by rule, regulation, or order, consistent with the purposes of this title, may exempt any person or class of persons or any transaction or class of transactions, either conditionally or upon specified terms and conditions or for stated periods, from the operation of this subsection, and the rules and regulations thereunder.

(7) Authority of Commission to limit disclosure of information

Notwithstanding any other provision of law, the Commission shall not be compelled to disclose any information required to be kept or reported under this subsection. Nothing in this subsection shall authorize the Commission to withhold information from Congress, or prevent the Commission from complying with a request for information from any other Federal department or agency requesting information for purposes within the scope of its jurisdiction, or complying with an order of a court of the United States in an action brought by the United States or the Commission. For purposes of section 552 of Title 5, United States Code, this subsection shall be considered a statute described in subsection (b)(3)(B) of such section 552.

(8) Definitions

For purposes of this subsection—

(A) the term "large trader" means every person who, for his own account or an account for which he exercises investment discretion, effects transactions for the purchase or sale of any publicly traded security or securities by use of any means or instrumentality of interstate commerce or of the mails, or of any facility of a national securities exchange, directly or indirectly by or through a registered broker or dealer in an aggregate amount equal to or in excess of the identifying activity level;

(B) the term "publicly traded security" means any equity security (including an option on individual equity securities, and an option on a group or index of such securities) listed, or admitted to unlisted trading privileges, on a national securities exchange, or quoted in an automated interdealer quotation system;

(C) the term "identifying activity level" means transactions in publicly traded securities at or above a level of volume, fair market value, or exercise value as shall be fixed from time to time by the Commission by rule or regulation, specifying the time interval during which such transactions shall be aggregated;

(D) the term "reporting activity level" means transactions in publicly traded securities at or above a level of volume, fair market value, or exercise value as shall be fixed from time to time by the Commission by rule, regulation, or order, specifying the time interval during which such transactions shall be aggregated; and

(E) the term "person" has the meaning given in section 3(a)(9) of this title and also includes two or more persons acting as a partnership, limited partnership, syndicate, or other group, but does not include a foreign central bank.

(i) *Accuracy of Financial Reports.* Each financial report that contains financial statements, and that is required to be prepared in accordance with (or reconciled to) generally accepted accounting principles under this title and filed with the Commission shall reflect all material correcting adjustments that have been identified by a registered public accounting firm in accordance with generally accepted accounting principles and the rules and regulations of the Commission.

(j) *Off-Balance Sheet Transactions.* Not later than 180 days after the date of enactment of the Sarbanes–Oxley Act of 2002, the Commission shall issue final rules providing that each annual and quarterly financial report required to be filed with the Commission shall disclose all material off-balance sheet transactions, arrangements, obligations (including contingent obligations), and other relationships of the issuer with unconsolidated entities or other persons, that may have a material current or future effect on financial condition, changes in financial condition, results of operations, liquidity, capital expenditures, capital resources, or significant components of revenues or expenses.

(k) *Prohibition on Personal Loans to Executives.*(1) *In General.*—It shall be unlawful for any issuer (as defined in section 2 of the Sarbanes–Oxley Act of 2002), directly or indirectly, including through any subsidiary, to extend or maintain credit, to arrange for the extension of credit, or to renew an extension of credit, in the form of a personal loan to or for any director or executive officer (or equivalent thereof) of that issuer. An extension of credit maintained by the issuer on the date of enactment of this subsection shall not be subject to the provisions of this subsection, provided that there is no material modification to any term of any such extension of credit or any renewal of any such extension of credit on or after that date of enactment.

(2) *Limitation.*—Paragraph (1) does not preclude any home improvement and manufactured home loans (as that term is defined in section 5 of the Home Owners' Loan Act (12 U.S.C. 1464)), consumer credit (as defined in section 103 of the Truth in Lending Act (15 U.S.C. 1602)), or any extension of credit under an open end credit plan (as defined in section 103 of the Truth in Lending Act (15 U.S.C. 1602)), or a charge card (as defined in section 127(c)(4)(e) of the Truth in Lending Act (15 U.S.C. 1637(c)(4)(e)), or any extension of credit by a broker or dealer registered under section 15 of this title to an employee of that broker or dealer to buy, trade, or carry securities, that is permitted under rules or regulations of the Board of Governors of the Federal Reserve System pursuant to section 7 of this title (other than an extension of credit that would be used to purchase the stock of that issuer), that is—

(A) made or provided in the ordinary course of the consumer credit business of such issuer;

(B) of a type that is generally made available by such issuer to the public; and

(C) made by such issuer on market terms, or terms that are no more favorable than those offered by the issuer to the general public for such extensions of credit.

(3) *Rule of Construction for Certain Loans.*—Paragraph (1) does not apply to any loan made or maintained by an insured depository institution (as defined in section 3 of the Federal Deposit Insurance Act (12 U.S.C. 1813)), if the loan is subject to the insider lending restrictions of section 22(h) of the Federal Reserve Act (12 U.S.C. 375b).

(*l*) *Real Time Issuer Disclosures.* Each issuer reporting under section 13(a) or 15(d) shall disclose to the public on a rapid and current basis such additional information concerning material changes in the financial condition or operations of the issuer, in plain English, which may include trend and qualitative information and graphic presentations, as the Commission determines, by rule, is necessary or useful for the protection of investors and in the public interest.

Proxies

Section 14. (a) *Solicitation of proxies in violation of rules and regulations.* It shall be unlawful for any person, by the use of the mails or by any means or instrumentality of interstate commerce or of any facility of a national securities exchange or otherwise, in contravention of such rules and regulations as the Commission may prescribe as necessary or appropriate in the public interest or for the protection of investors, to solicit or to permit the use of his name to solicit any proxy or consent or authorization in respect of any security (other than an exempted security) registered pursuant to section 12 of this title.

(b) *Giving or refraining from giving proxy in respect of any security carried for account of customer.* (1) It shall be unlawful for any member of a national securities exchange, or any broker or dealer registered under this title, or any bank, association, or other entity that exercises fiduciary powers, in contravention of such rules and regulations as the Commission may prescribe as necessary or appropriate in the public interest or for the protection of investors, to give, or to refrain from giving a proxy, consent, authorization, or information statement in respect of any security registered pursuant to section 12 of this title, or any security issued by an investment company registered under the Investment Company Act of 1940 and carried for the account of a customer.

(2) With respect to banks, the rules and regulations prescribed by the Commission under paragraph (1) shall not require the disclosure of the names of beneficial owners of securities in an account held by the bank on the date of enactment of this paragraph unless the beneficial owner consents to the disclosure. The provisions of this paragraph shall not apply in the case of a bank which the Commission finds has not made a good faith effort to obtain such consent from such beneficial owners.

(c) *Information to holders of record prior to annual or other meeting.* Unless proxies, consents, or authorizations in respect of a security registered pursuant to section 12 of this title, or any security issued by an investment company registered under the Investment Company Act of 1940 are solicited by or on behalf of the management of the issuer from the holders of record of such security in accordance with the rules and regulations prescribed under subsection (a) of this section, prior to any annual or other meeting of the holders of such security, such issuer shall, in accordance with rules and regulations prescribed by the Commission, file with the Commission and transmit to all holders of record of such security information substantially equivalent to the information which would be required to be transmitted if a solicitation were made, but no information shall be required to be filed or transmitted pursuant to this subsection before July 1, 1964.

(d) *Tender offer by owner of more than five per centum of class of securities; exceptions.* (1) It shall be unlawful for any person, directly or indirectly, by use of the mails or by any means or instrumentality of interstate commerce or of any facility of a national securities exchange or otherwise, to make a tender offer for, or a request or invitation for tenders of, any class of any equity security which is registered pursuant to section 12 of this title, or any equity security of an insurance company which would have been required to be so registered except for the exemption contained in section 12(g)(2)(G) of this title, or any equity security issued by a closed-end investment company registered under the Investment Company Act of 1940, if, after consummation thereof, such person would, directly or indirectly, be the beneficial owner of more than 5 per centum of such class, unless at the time copies of the offer or request or invitation are first published or sent or given to security holders such person has filed with the Commission a statement containing such of the information specified in section 13(d) of this title, and such additional information as the Commission may by rules and regulations prescribe as necessary or appropriate in the public interest or for the protection of investors. All requests or invitations for tenders or advertisements making a tender offer or requesting or inviting tenders of such a security shall be filed as a part of such statement and shall contain such of the information contained in such statement as the Commission may by rules and regulations prescribe. Copies of any additional material soliciting or requesting such tender offers subsequent to the initial solicitation or request shall contain such information as the Commission may by rules and regulations prescribe as necessary or appropriate in the public interest or for the protection of investors, and shall be filed with the Commission not later than the time copies of such material are first published or sent or given to security holders. Copies of all statements, in the form in which such material is furnished to security holders and the Commission, shall be sent to the issuer not later than the date such material is first published or sent or given to any security holders.

(2) When two or more persons act as a partnership, limited partnership, syndicate, or other group for the purpose of acquiring, holding, or disposing of securities of an issuer, such syndicate or group shall be deemed a "person" for purposes of this subsection.

(3) In determining, for purposes of this subsection, any percentage of a class of any security, such class shall be deemed to consist of the amount of the outstanding securities of such class, exclusive of any securities of such class held by or for the account of the issuer or a subsidiary of the issuer.

(4) Any solicitation or recommendation to the holders of such a security to accept or reject a tender offer or request or invitation for tenders shall be made in accordance with such rules and regulations as the Commission may prescribe as necessary or appropriate in the public interest or for the protection of investors.

(5) Securities deposited pursuant to a tender offer or request or invitation for tenders may be withdrawn by or on behalf of the depositor at any time until the expiration of seven days after the time definitive copies of the offer or request or invitation are first published or sent or given to security holders, and at any time after sixty days from the date of the original tender offer or request or invitation, except as the Commission may otherwise prescribe by rules, regulations, or order as necessary or appropriate in the public interest or for the protection of investors.

(6) Where any person makes a tender offer, or request or invitation for tenders, for less than all the outstanding equity securities of a class, and where a greater number of securities is deposited pursuant thereto within ten days after copies of the offer or request or invitation are first published or sent or given to security holders than such person is bound or willing to take up and pay for, the securities taken up shall be taken up as nearly as may be pro rata, disregarding fractions, according to the number of securities deposited by each depositor. The provisions of this subsection shall also apply to securities deposited within ten days after notice of an increase in the consideration offered to security holders, as described in paragraph (7), is first published or sent or given to security holders.

(7) Where any person varies the terms of a tender offer or request or invitation for tenders before the expiration thereof by increasing the consideration offered to holders of such securities, such person shall pay the increased consideration to each security holder whose securities are taken up and paid for pursuant to the tender offer or request or invitation for tenders whether or not such securities have been taken up by such person before the variation of the tender offer or request or invitation.

(8) The provisions of this subsection shall not apply to any offer for, or request or invitation for tenders of, any security—

(A) if the acquisition of such security, together with all other acquisitions by the same person of securities of the same class during the preceding twelve months, would not exceed 2 per centum of that class;

(B) by the issuer of such security; or

(C) which the Commission, by rules or regulations or by order, shall exempt from the provisions of this subsection as not entered into for the purpose of, and not having the effect of, changing or influencing the control of the issuer or otherwise as not comprehended within the purposes of this subsection.

(e) *Untrue statement of material fact or omission of fact with respect to tender offer.* It shall be unlawful for any person to make any untrue statement of a material fact or omit to state any material fact necessary in order to make the statements made, in the light of the circumstances under which they are made, not misleading, or to engage in any fraudulent, deceptive, or manipulative acts or practices, in connection with any tender offer or request or invitation for tenders, or any solicitation of security holders in opposition to or in favor of any such offer, request, or invitation. The Commission shall, for the purposes of this subsection, by rules and regulations define, and prescribe means reasonably designed to prevent, such acts and practices as are fraudulent, deceptive, or manipulative.

(f) *Election or designation of majority of directors of issuer by owner of more than five per centum of class of securities at other than meeting of security holders.* If, pursuant to any arrangement or understanding with the person or persons acquiring securities in a transaction subject to subsection (d) of this section or subsection (d) of section 13 of this title, any persons are to be elected or designated as directors of the issuer, otherwise than at a meeting of security holders, and the persons so elected or designated will constitute a majority of the directors of the issuer, then, prior to the time any such person takes office as a director, and in accordance with rules and regulations prescribed by the Commission, the issuer shall file with the Commission, and transmit to all holders of record of securities of the issuer who would be entitled to vote at a meeting for election of directors, information substantially equivalent to the information which would be required by subsection (a) or (c) of this section to be transmitted if such person or persons were nominees for election as directors at a meeting of such security holders.

* * *

Directors, Officers, and Principal Stockholders

Section 16. (a) *Disclosures Required.* (1) *Directors, Officers, and Principal Stockholders Required to File.* Every person who is directly or indirectly the beneficial owner of more than 10 percent of any class of any equity security (other than an exempted security) which is registered pursuant to section 12, or who is a director or an officer of the issuer of such security, shall file the statements required by this subsection with the Commission (and, if such security is registered on a national securities exchange, also with the exchange).

(2) *Time of Filing.* The statements required by this subsection shall be filed—

(A) at the time of the registration of such security on a national securities exchange or by the effective date of a registration statement filed pursuant to section 12(g);

(B) within 10 days after he or she becomes such beneficial owner, director, or officer;

(C) if there has been a change in such ownership, or if such person shall have purchased or sold a security-based swap agreement (as defined in section 206(b) of the Gramm–Leach–Bliley Act) involving such equity security, before the end of the second business day following the day on which the subject transaction has been executed, or at such other time as the Commission shall establish, by rule, in any case in which the Commission determines that such 2–day period is not feasible.

(3) *Contents of Statements.* A statement filed—

(A) under subparagraph (A) or (B) of paragraph (2) shall contain a statement of the amount of all equity securities of such issuer of which the filing person is the beneficial owner; and

(B) under subparagraph (C) of such paragraph shall indicate ownership by the filing person at the date of filing, any such changes in such ownership, and such purchases and sales of the security-based swap agreements as have occurred since the most recent such filing under such subparagraph.

(4) *Electronic Filing and Availability.* Beginning not later than 1 year after the date of enactment of the Sarbanes–Oxley Act of 2002—

(A) a statement filed under subparagraph (C) of paragraph (2) shall be filed electronically;

(B) the Commission shall provide each such statement on a publicly accessible Internet site not later than the end of the business day following that filing; and

(C) the issuer (if the issuer maintains a corporate website) shall provide that statement on that corporate website, not later than the end of the business day following that filing.

(b) *Profits from purchase and sale of security within six months.* For the purpose of preventing the unfair use of information which may have been obtained by such beneficial owner, director, or officer by reason of his relationship to the issuer, any profit realized by him from any purchase and sale, or any sale and purchase, of any equity security of such issuer (other than an exempted security) within any period of less than six months, unless such security was acquired in good faith in connection with a debt previously contracted, shall inure to and be recoverable by the issuer, irrespective of any intention on the part of such beneficial owner, director, or officer in entering into such transaction of holding the security purchased or of not repurchasing the security sold for a period exceeding six months. Suit to recover such profit may be instituted at law or in equity in any court of competent jurisdiction by the issuer, or by the owner of any security of the issuer in the name and in behalf of the issuer if the issuer shall fail or refuse to bring such suit within sixty days after request or shall fail diligently to prosecute the same thereafter; but no such suit shall be brought more than two years after the date such profit was realized. This subsection shall not be construed to cover any transaction where such beneficial owner was not such both at the time of the purchase and sale, or the sale and purchase, of the security involved, or any transaction or transactions which the Commission by rules and regulations may exempt as not comprehended within the purpose of this subsection.

(c) *Conditions for sale of security by beneficial owner, director, or officer.* It shall be unlawful for any such beneficial owner, director, or officer, directly or indirectly, to sell any equity security of such issuer (other than an exempted security), if the person selling the security or his principal (1) does not own the security sold, or (2) if owning the security, does not deliver it against such sale within twenty days thereafter, or does not within five days after such sale deposit it in the mails or other usual channels of transportation; but no person shall be deemed to have violated this subsection if he proves that notwithstanding the exercise of good faith he was unable to make such delivery or deposit within such time, or that to do so would cause undue inconvenience or expense.

(d) *Securities held in investment account, transactions in ordinary course of business and establishment of primary or secondary market.* The provisions of subsection (b) of this section shall not apply to any purchase and sale, or sale and purchase, and the provisions of subsection (c) of this section shall not apply to any sale, of an equity security not then or theretofore held by him in an investment account, by a dealer in the ordinary course of his business and incident to the establishment or maintenance by him of a primary or secondary market (otherwise than on a national securities exchange or an exchange exempted from registration under section 5 of this title) for such security. The Commission may, by such rules and regulations as it deems necessary or appropriate in the public interest, define and prescribe terms and conditions with respect to securities held in an investment account and transactions made in the ordinary course of business and incident to the establishment or maintenance of a primary or secondary market.

(e) *Application of section to foreign or domestic arbitrage transactions.* The provisions of this section shall not apply to foreign or domestic arbitrage transactions unless made in contravention of such rules and regulations as the Commission may adopt in order to carry out the purposes of this section.

Records and Reports

Section 17. (a) *Rules and regulations.* (1) Every national securities exchange, member thereof, broker or dealer who transacts a business in securities through the medium of any such member, registered securities association, registered broker or dealer, registered municipal securities dealer, registered securities information processor, registered transfer agent, and registered clearing agency and the Municipal Securities Rulemaking Board shall make and keep for prescribed periods such records, furnish such copies thereof, and make and disseminate such reports as the Commission, by rule, prescribes as necessary or appropriate in the public interest, for the protection of investors, or otherwise in furtherance of the purposes of this title.

(2) Every registered clearing agency shall also make and keep for prescribed periods such records, furnish such copies thereof, and make and disseminate such reports, as the appropriate regulatory agency for such clearing agency, by rule, prescribes as necessary or appropriate for the safeguarding of securities and funds in the custody or control of such clearing agency or for which it is responsible.

(3) Every registered transfer agent shall also make and keep for prescribed periods such records, furnish such copies thereof, and make such reports as the appropriate regulatory agency for such transfer agent, by rule, prescribes as necessary or appropriate in furtherance of the purposes of section 17A of this title.

(b) *Examination of records; notice; avoidance of duplication and undue regulatory burden.* All records of persons described in subsection (a) of this section are subject at any time, or from time to time, to such reasonable periodic, special, or other examinations by representatives of the Commission and the appropriate regulatory agency for such persons as the Commission or the appropriate regulatory agency for such persons deems necessary or appropriate in the public interest, for the protection of investors, or otherwise in furtherance of the purposes of this title: Provided, however, That the Commission shall, prior to conducting any such examination of a registered clearing agency, registered transfer agent, or registered municipal securities dealer for which it is not the appropriate regulatory agency, give notice to the appropriate regulatory agency for such clearing agency, transfer agent, or municipal securities dealer of such proposed examination and consult with such appropriate regulatory agency concerning the feasibility and desirability of coordinating such examination with examinations conducted by such appropriate regulatory agency with a view to avoiding unnecessary regulatory duplication or undue regulatory burdens for such clearing agency, transfer agent, or municipal securities dealer. Nothing in the proviso to the preceding sentence shall be construed to impair or limit (other than by the requirement of prior consultation) the power of the Commission under this subsection to examine any clearing agency, transfer agent, or municipal securities dealer or to affect in any way the power of the Commission under any other provision of this title or otherwise to inspect, examine, or investigate any such clearing agency, transfer agent, or municipal securities dealer.

(c) *Copies of reports filed with other regulatory agencies.*

(1) Every clearing agency, transfer agent, and municipal securities dealer for which the Commission is not the appropriate regulatory agency shall (A) file with the appropriate regulatory agency for such clearing agency, transfer agent, or municipal securities dealer a copy of any application, notice, proposal, report, or document filed with the Commission by reason of its being a clearing agency, transfer agent, or municipal securities dealer and (B) file with the Commission a copy of any application, notice, proposal, report, or document filed with such appropriate regulatory agency by reason of its being a clearing agency, transfer agent, or municipal securities dealer. The Municipal Securities Rulemaking Board shall file with each agency enumerated in section 3(a)(34)(A) of this title copies of every proposed rule change filed with the Commission pursuant to section 19(b) of this title.

(2) The appropriate regulatory agency for a clearing agency, transfer agent, or municipal securities dealer for which the Commission is not the appropriate regulatory agency shall file with the Commission notice of the commencement of any proceeding and a copy of any order entered by such appropriate regulatory agency against any clearing agency, transfer agent, municipal securities dealer, or person associated with a transfer agent or municipal securities dealer, and the Commission shall file with such appropriate regulatory agency, if any, notice of the commencement of any proceeding and a copy of any order entered by the Commission against the clearing agency, transfer agent, or municipal securities dealer, or against any person associated with a transfer agent or municipal securities dealer for which the agency is the appropriate regulatory agency.

(3) The Commission and the appropriate regulatory agency for a clearing agency, transfer agent, or municipal securities dealer for which the Commission is not the appropriate regulatory agency shall each notify the other and make a report of any examination conducted by it of such clearing agency, transfer agent, or municipal securities dealer, and, upon request, furnish to the other a copy of such report and any data supplied to it in connection with such examination.

(4) The Commission or the appropriate regulatory agency may specify that documents required to be filed pursuant to this subsection with the Commission or such agency, respectively, may be retained by the originating clearing agency, transfer agent, or municipal securities dealer, or filed with another appropriate regulatory agency. The Commission or the appropriate regulatory agency (as the case may be) making such a specification shall continue to have access to the document on request.

(d) *Self-regulatory organizations.*

(1) The Commission, by rule or order, as it deems necessary or appropriate in the public interest and for the protection of investors, to foster cooperation and coordination among self-regulatory organizations, or to remove impediments to and foster the development of a national market system and national system for the clearance and settlement of securities transactions, may—

(A) with respect to any person who is a member of or participant in more than one self-regulatory organization, relieve any such self-regulatory organization of any responsibility under this title (i) to receive regulatory reports from such person, (ii) to examine such person for compliance, or to enforce compliance by such person, with specified provisions of this title, the rules and regulations thereunder, and its own rules, or (iii) to carry out other specified regulatory functions with respect to such person, and

(B) allocate among self-regulatory organizations the authority to adopt rules with respect to matters as to which, in the absence of such allocation, such self-regulatory organizations share authority under this title.

In making any such rule or entering any such order, the Commission shall take into consideration the regulatory capabilities and procedures of the self-regulatory organizations, availability of staff, convenience of location, unnecessary regulatory duplication, and such other factors as the Commission may consider germane to the protection of investors, cooperation and coordination among self-regulatory organizations, and the development of a national market system and a national system for the clearance and settlement of securities transactions. The Commission, by rule or order, as it deems necessary or appropriate in the public interest and for the protection of investors, may require any self-regulatory organization relieved of any responsibility pursuant to this paragraph, and any person with respect to whom such responsibility relates, to take such steps as are specified in any such rule or order to notify customers of, and persons doing business with, such person of the limited nature of such self-regulatory organization's responsibility for such person's acts, practices, and course of business.

(2) A self-regulatory organization shall furnish copies of any report of examination of any person who is a member of or a participant in such self-regulatory organization to any other self-regulatory organization of which such person is a member or in which such person is a participant upon the request of such person, such other self-regulatory organization, or the Commission.

(e) *Balance sheet and income statement; other financial statements and information.*

(1) (A) Every registered broker or dealer shall annually file with the Commission a balance sheet and income statement certified by a registered public accounting firm prepared on a calendar or fiscal year basis, and such other financial statements (which shall, as the Commission specifies, be certified) and information concerning its financial condition as the Commission, by rule may prescribe as necessary or appropriate in the public interest or for the protection of investors.

(B) Every registered broker and dealer shall annually send to its customers its certified balance sheet and such other financial statements and information concerning its financial condition as the Commission, by rule, may prescribe pursuant to subsection (a) of this section.

(C) The Commission, by rule or order, may conditionally or unconditionally exempt any registered broker or dealer, or class of such brokers or dealers, from any provision of this paragraph if the Commission determines that such exemption is consistent with the public interest and the protection of investors.

(2) The Commission, by rule, as it deems necessary or appropriate in the public interest or for the protection of investors, may prescribe the form and content of financial statements filed pursuant to this title and the accounting principles and accounting standards used in their preparation.

(f) *Missing, lost, counterfeit, and stolen securities.*

(1) Every national securities exchange, member thereof, registered securities association, broker, dealer, municipal securities dealer, government securities broker, government securities dealer, registered transfer agent, registered clearing agency, participant therein, member of the Federal Reserve System, and bank whose deposits are insured by the Federal Deposit Insurance Corporation shall—

(A) report to the Commission or other person designated by the Commission and, in the case of securities issued pursuant to chapter 31 of title 31, United States Code, to the Secretary of the Treasury such information about missing, lost, counterfeit, or stolen securities, in such form and within such time as the Commission, by rule, determines is necessary or appropriate in the public interest or for the protection of investors; such information shall be available on request for a reasonable fee, to any such exchange, member, association, broker, dealer, municipal securities dealer, transfer agent, clearing agency, participant, member of the Federal Reserve System, or insured bank, and such other persons as the Commission, by rule, designates; and

(B) make such inquiry with respect to information reported pursuant to this subsection as the Commission, by rule, prescribes as necessary or appropriate in the public interest or for the protection of investors, to determine whether securities in their custody or control, for which they are responsible, or in which they are effecting, clearing, or settling a transaction have been reported as missing, lost, counterfeit, or stolen.

(2) Every member of a national securities exchange, broker, dealer, registered transfer agent, and registered clearing agency, shall require that each of its partners, directors, officers, and employees be fingerprinted and shall submit such fingerprints, or cause the same to be submitted, to the Attorney General of the United States for identification and appropriate processing. The Commission, by rule, may exempt from the provisions of this paragraph upon specified terms, conditions, and periods, any class of partners, directors, officers, or employees of any such member, broker, dealer,

transfer agent, or clearing agency, if the Commission finds that such action is not inconsistent with the public interest or the protection of investors. Notwithstanding any other provision of law, in providing identification and processing functions, the Attorney General shall provide the Commission and self-regulatory organizations designated by the Commission with access to all criminal history record information.

(3) (A) In order to carry out the authority under paragraph (1) above, the Commission or its designee may enter into agreement with the Attorney General to use the facilities of the National Crime Information Center ("NCIC") to receive, store, and disseminate information in regard to missing, lost, counterfeit, or stolen securities and to permit direct inquiry access to NCIC's file on such securities for the financial community.

(B) In order to carry out the authority under paragraph (1) of this subsection, the Commission or its designee and the Secretary of the Treasury shall enter into an agreement whereby the Commission or its designee will receive, store, and disseminate information in the possession, and which comes into the possession, of the Department of the Treasury in regard to missing, lost, counterfeit, or stolen securities.

(4) In regard to paragraphs (1), (2), and (3), above insofar as such paragraphs apply to any bank or member of the Federal Reserve System, the Commission may delegate its authority to:

(A) the Comptroller of the Currency as to national banks and banks operating under the Code of Law for the District of Columbia;

(B) the Federal Reserve Board [Board of Governors of the Federal Reserve System] in regard to any member of the Federal Reserve System which is not a national bank or a bank operating under the Code of Law for the District of Columbia; and

(C) the Federal Deposit Insurance Corporation for any State bank which is insured by the Federal Deposit Insurance Corporation but which is not a member of the Federal Reserve System.

(5) The Commission shall encourage the insurance industry to require their insured to report expeditiously instances of missing, lost, counterfeit, or stolen securities to the Commission or to such other person as the Commission may, by rule, designate to receive such information.

(g) *Persons extending credit.* Any broker, dealer, or other person extending credit who is subject to the rules and regulations prescribed by the Board of Governors of the Federal Reserve System pursuant to this title shall make such reports to the Board as it may require as necessary or appropriate to enable it to perform the functions conferred upon it by this title. If any such broker, dealer, or other person shall fail to make any such report or fail to furnish full information therein, or, if in the judgment of the Board it is otherwise necessary, such broker, dealer, or other person shall permit such inspections to be made by the Board with respect to the business operations of such broker, dealer, or other person as the Board may deem necessary to enable it to obtain the required information.

(h) *Risk assessment for holding company systems.*

(1) Obligations to obtain, maintain, and report information. Every person who is (A) a registered broker or dealer, or (B) a registered municipal securities dealer for which the Commission is the appropriate regulatory agency, shall obtain such information and make and keep such records as the Commission by rule prescribes concerning the registered person's policies, procedures, or systems for monitoring and controlling financial and operational risks to it resulting from the activities of any of its associated persons, other than a natural person. Such records may be required to describe each of the financial and securities activities conducted by, and the customary sources of capital and funding of, those of its associated persons whose business activities are reasonably likely to have a material impact on the financial or operational condition of such registered person, including its net capital, its liquidity, or its ability to conduct or finance its operations. The Commission, by rule, may require reports of such information to be filed with the Commission no more frequently than quarterly.

(2) Authority to require additional information. If, as a result of adverse market conditions or based on reports provided to the Commission pursuant to paragraph (1) of this subsection or other available information, the Commission reasonably concludes that it has concerns regarding the financial or operational condition of (A) any registered broker or dealer, or (B) any registered municipal securities

dealer, government securities broker, or government securities dealer for which the Commission is the appropriate regulatory agency, the Commission may require the registered person to make reports concerning the financial and securities activities of any of such person's associated persons, other than a natural person, whose business activities are reasonably likely to have a material impact on the financial or operational condition of such registered person. The Commission, in requiring reports pursuant to this paragraph, shall specify the information required, the period for which it is required, the time and date on which the information must be furnished, and whether the information is to be furnished directly to the Commission or to a self-regulatory organization with primary responsibility for examining the registered person's financial and operational condition.

(3) Reporting by holding companies and other material associated persons—Every person, other than a natural person, who is associated with (A) a registered broker or dealer, or (B) a registered municipal securities dealer for which the Commission is the appropriate regulatory agency, and whose business activities are reasonably likely to have a material impact on the financial or operational condition of such registered person, including its net capital, its liquidity, or its ability to conduct or finance its operations, shall make such reports concerning the associated person's policies, procedures, or systems for monitoring and controlling the financial and operation risks to the registered person and its associated persons as the Commission, by rule, prescribes. Such reports may be required to describe, without limitation, each of the associated person's financial and securities activities, and customary sources of capital and funding. The Commission, by rule, may require such reports to be filed with the Commission no more frequently than quarterly.

(4) Recordkeeping by holding companies and other material associated persons—All persons subject to the reporting requirements under paragraph (3) of this subsection shall keep and maintain such records as are necessary to permit the Commission to verify the information contained in reports filed with the Commission pursuant to paragraph (3).

(5) Examination of holding companies and other material associated persons-All records of persons subject to the reporting requirements contained in paragraph (3) of this subsection are subject at any time, or from time to time, to such reasonable periodic, special, or other examinations by representatives of the Commission as the Commission deems necessary or appropriate to verify the information contained in reports filed with the Commission pursuant to paragraph (3).

(6) Use of alternative reports by registered persons and their holding companies and other material associated persons—The Commission, insofar as it determines is consistent with the purposes of this title, shall permit persons subject to the reporting requirements of paragraphs (1), (2), and (3) of this subsection, to use reports otherwise created and maintained to meet the reporting requirements of those paragraphs.

(7) Special provisions with respect to associated persons subject to Federal banking agency regulation. (A) Cooperation in implementation. In developing and implementing reporting requirements pursuant to paragraphs (1) and (3) of this subsection with respect to associated persons subject to examination by or reporting requirements of a Federal banking agency, the Commission shall consult with and consider the views of each such Federal banking agency. If a Federal banking agency comments in writing on a proposed rule of the Commission under this subsection that has been published for comment, the Commission shall respond in writing to such written comment before adopting the proposed rule. The Commission shall, at the request of the Federal banking agency, publish such comment and response in the Federal Register at the time of publishing the adopted rule.

(B) Use of banking agency reports. A registered broker, dealer, or municipal securities dealer shall be in compliance with any recordkeeping or reporting requirement adopted pursuant to paragraphs (1) and (3) of this subsection concerning an associated person that is subject to examination by or reporting requirements of a Federal banking agency if such broker, dealer, or municipal securities dealer utilizes for such recordkeeping or reporting requirement copies of reports filed by the associated person with the Federal banking agency pursuant to section 5211 of the Revised Statutes, section 9 of the Federal Reserve Act, section 7(a) of the Federal Deposit Insurance Act, section 10(b) of the Home Owners' Loan Act, or section 8 of the Bank Holding Company Act of 1956. The Commission may, however, by rule adopted pursuant to paragraphs (1) and (3), require any broker, dealer, or municipal securities dealer filing such reports with the Commission to obtain, maintain, or report supplemental information if the Commission makes an explicit finding that such supplemental information is necessary to inform the Commission regarding potential risks to such broker, dealer, or municipal securities dealer. Prior to requiring any such supplemental information, the Commission shall first request the Federal banking agency to expand its reporting requirements to include such information.

(C) Procedure for requiring additional information. Prior to making a request pursuant to paragraph (2) of this subsection for information with respect to an associated person that is subject to examination by or reporting requirements of a Federal banking agency, the Commission shall—

(i) notify such agency of the information required with respect to such associated person; and

(ii) consult with such agency to determine whether the information required is available from such agency and for other purposes, unless the Commission determines that any delay resulting from such consultation would be inconsistent with ensuring the financial and operational condition of the broker, dealer, municipal securities dealer, government securities broker, or government securities dealer or the stability or integrity of the securities markets.

(D) Exclusion for examination reports. Nothing in this subsection shall be construed to permit the Commission to require any registered broker or dealer, or any registered municipal securities dealer, government securities broker, or government securities dealer for which the Commission is the appropriate regulatory agency, to obtain, maintain, or furnish any examination report of any Federal banking agency or any supervisory recommendations or analysis contained therein.

(E) Confidentiality of information provided. No information provided to or obtained by the Commission from any Federal banking agency pursuant to a request by the Commission under subparagraph (C) of this paragraph regarding any associated person which is subject to examination by or reporting requirements of a Federal banking agency may be disclosed to any other person (other than a self-regulatory organization), without the prior written approval of the Federal banking agency. Nothing in this subsection shall authorize the Commission to withhold information from Congress, or prevent the Commission from complying with a request for information from any other Federal department or agency requesting the information for purposes within the scope of its jurisdiction, or complying with an order of a court of the United States in an action brought by the United States or the Commission.

(F) Notice to banking agencies concerning financial and operational condition concerns. The Commission shall notify the Federal banking agency of any concerns of the Commission regarding significant financial or operational risks resulting from the activities of any registered broker or dealer, or any registered municipal securities dealer, government securities broker, or government securities dealer for which the Commission is the appropriate regulatory agency, to any associated person thereof which is subject to examination by or reporting requirements of the Federal banking agency.

(G) Definition. For purposes of this paragraph, the term "Federal banking agency" shall have the same meaning as the term "appropriate Federal bank agency" in section 3(q) of the Federal Deposit Insurance Act.

(8) Exemptions. The Commission by rule or order may exempt any person or class of persons, under such terms and conditions and for such periods as the Commission shall provide in such rule or order, from the provisions of this subsection, and the rules thereunder. In granting such exemptions, the Commission shall consider, among other factors—

(A) whether information of the type required under this subsection is available from a supervisory agency (as defined in section 1101(6) of the Right to Financial Privacy Act of 1978), a State insurance commission or similar State agency, the Commodity Futures Trading Commission, or a similar foreign regulator;

(B) the primary business of any associated person;

(C) the nature and extent of domestic or foreign regulation of the associated person's activities;

(D) the nature and extent of the registered person's securities activities; and

(E) with respect to the registered person and its associated persons, on a consolidated basis, the amount and proportion of assets devoted to, and revenues derived from, activities in the United States securities markets.

(9) Authority to limit disclosure of information. Notwithstanding any other provision of law, the Commission shall not be compelled to disclose any information required to be reported under this subsection, or any information supplied to the Commission by any domestic or foreign regulatory agency that relates to the financial or operational condition of any associated person of a registered broker, dealer, government securities broker, government securities dealer, or municipal securities dealer. Nothing in this subsection shall authorize the Commission to withhold information from Congress, or prevent the Commission from complying with a request for information from any other Federal department or agency requesting the information for purposes within the scope of its jurisdiction, or complying with an order of a court of the United States in an action brought by the United States or the Commission. For purposes of section 552 of title 5, United States Code, this subsection shall be considered a statute described in subsection (b)(3)(B) of such section 552. In prescribing regulations to carry out the requirements of this subsection, the Commission shall designate information described in or obtained pursuant to subparagraph (B) or (C) of paragraph (3) of this subsection as confidential information for purposes of section 24(b)(2) of this title.

(i) *Investment bank holding companies.*

(1) Elective supervision of an investment bank holding company not having a bank or savings association affiliate.

(A) In general. An investment bank holding company that is not—

(i) an affiliate of an insured bank (other than an institution described in subparagraph (D), (F), or (G) of section 2(c)(2), or held under section 4(f), of the Bank Holding Company Act of 1956), or a savings association;

(ii) a foreign bank, foreign company, or company that is described in section 8(a) of the International Banking Act of 1978; or

(iii) a foreign bank that controls, directly or indirectly, a corporation chartered under section 25A of the Federal Reserve Act, may elect to become supervised by filing with the Commission a notice of intention to become supervised, pursuant to subparagraph (B) of this paragraph. Any investment bank holding company filing such a notice shall be supervised in accordance with this section and comply with the rules promulgated by the Commission applicable to supervised investment bank holding companies.

(B) Notification of status as a supervised investment bank holding company. An investment bank holding company that elects under subparagraph (A) to become supervised by the Commission shall file with the Commission a written notice of intention to become supervised by the Commission in such form and containing such information and documents concerning such investment bank holding company as the Commission, by rule, may prescribe as necessary or appropriate in furtherance of the purposes of this section. Unless the Commission finds that such supervision is not necessary or appropriate in furtherance of the purposes of this section, such supervision shall become effective 45 days after the date of receipt of such written notice by the Commission or within such shorter time period as the Commission, by rule or order, may determine.

(2) Election not to be supervised by the commission as an investment bank holding company.

(A) Voluntary withdrawal. A supervised investment bank holding company that is supervised pursuant to paragraph (1) may, upon such terms and conditions as the Commission deems necessary or appropriate, elect not to be supervised by the Commission by filing a written notice of withdrawal from Commission supervision. Such notice shall not become effective until 1 year after receipt by the Commission, or such shorter or longer period as the Commission deems necessary or appropriate to ensure effective supervision of the material risks to the supervised investment bank holding company and to the affiliated broker or dealer, or to prevent evasion of the purposes of this section.

(B) Discontinuation of commission supervision. If the Commission finds that any supervised investment bank holding company that is supervised pursuant to paragraph (1) is no longer in existence or has ceased to be an investment bank holding company, or if the Commission finds that continued supervision of such a supervised investment bank holding company is not consistent with the purposes of this section, the Commission may discontinue the supervision pursuant to a rule or order, if any, promulgated by the Commission under this section.

(3) Supervision of investment bank holding companies.

(A) Recordkeeping and reporting.

(i) In general. Every supervised investment bank holding company and each affiliate thereof shall make and keep for prescribed periods such records, furnish copies thereof, and make such reports, as the Commission may require by rule, in order to keep the Commission informed as to-

(I) the company's or affiliate's activities, financial condition, policies, systems for monitoring and controlling financial and operational risks, and transactions and relationships between any broker or dealer affiliate of the supervised investment bank holding company; and

(II) the extent to which the company or affiliate has complied with the provisions of this Act and regulations prescribed and orders issued under this Act.

(ii) Form and contents. Such records and reports shall be prepared in such form and according to such specifications (including certification by a registered public accounting firm), as the Commission may require and shall be provided promptly at any time upon request by the Commission. Such records and reports may include—

(I) a balance sheet and income statement;

(II) an assessment of the consolidated capital of the supervised investment bank holding company;

(III) an independent auditor's report attesting to the supervised investment bank holding company's compliance with its internal risk management and internal control objectives; and

(IV) reports concerning the extent to which the company or affiliate has complied with the provisions of this title and any regulations prescribed and orders issued under this title.

(B) Use of existing reports.

(i) In general. The Commission shall, to the fullest extent possible, accept reports in fulfillment of the requirements under this paragraph that the supervised investment bank holding company or its affiliates have been required to provide to another appropriate regulatory agency or self-regulatory organization.

(ii) Availability. A supervised investment bank holding company or an affiliate of such company shall provide to the Commission, at the request of the Commission, any report referred to in clause (i).

(C) Examination authority.

(i) Focus of examination authority. The Commission may make examinations of any supervised investment bank holding company and any affiliate of such company in order to—

(I) inform the Commission regarding—

(aa) the nature of the operations and financial condition of the supervised investment bank holding company and its affiliates;

(bb) the financial and operational risks within the supervised investment bank holding company that may affect any broker or dealer controlled by such supervised investment bank holding company; and

(cc) the systems of the supervised investment bank holding company and its affiliates for monitoring and controlling those risks; and

(II) monitor compliance with the provisions of this subsection, provisions governing transactions and relationships between any broker or dealer affiliated with the supervised investment bank holding company and any of the company's other affiliates, and applicable provisions of subchapter II of chapter 53, title 31, United States Code (commonly referred to as the "Bank Secrecy Act") and regulations thereunder.

(ii) Restricted focus of examinations. The Commission shall limit the focus and scope of any examination of a supervised investment bank holding company to—

(I) the company; and

(II) any affiliate of the company that, because of its size, condition, or activities, the nature or size of the transactions between such affiliate and any affiliated broker or dealer, or the centralization of functions within the holding company system, could, in the discretion of the Commission, have a materially adverse effect on the operational or financial condition of the broker or dealer.

(iii) Deference to other examinations. For purposes of this subparagraph, the Commission shall, to the fullest extent possible, use the reports of examination of an institution described in subparagraph (D), (F), or (G) of section 2(c)(2), or held under section 4(f), of the Bank Holding Company Act of 1956 made by the appropriate regulatory agency, or of a licensed insurance company made by the appropriate State insurance regulator.

(4) Functional regulation of banking and insurance activities of supervised investment bank holding companies. The Commission shall defer to—

(A) the appropriate regulatory agency with regard to all interpretations of, and the enforcement of, applicable banking laws relating to the activities, conduct, ownership, and operations of banks, and institutions described in subparagraph (D), (F), and (G) of section 2(c)(2), or held under section 4(f), of the Bank Holding Company Act of 1956; and

(B) the appropriate State insurance regulators with regard to all interpretations of, and the enforcement of, applicable State insurance laws relating to the activities, conduct, and operations of insurance companies and insurance agents.

(5) Definitions. For purposes of this subsection:

(A) The term "investment bank holding company" means—

(i) any person other than a natural person that owns or controls one or more brokers or dealers; and

(ii) the associated persons of the investment bank holding company.

(B) The term "supervised investment bank holding company" means any investment bank holding company that is supervised by the Commission pursuant to this subsection.

(C) The terms "affiliate", "bank", "bank holding company", "company", "control", and "savings association" have the same meanings as given in section 2 of the Bank Holding Company Act of 1956.

(D) The term "insured bank" has the same meaning as given in section 3 of the Federal Deposit Insurance Act.

(E) The term "foreign bank" has the same meaning as given in section 1(b)(7) of the International Banking Act of 1978.

(F) The terms "person associated with an investment bank holding company" and "associated person of an investment bank holding company" mean any person directly or indirectly controlling, controlled by, or under common control with, an investment bank holding company.

(j) *Authority to limit disclosure of information.* Notwithstanding any other provision of law, the Commission shall not be compelled to disclose any information required to be reported under subsection (h) or (i) or any information supplied to the Commission by any domestic or foreign regulatory agency that relates to the financial or operational condition of any associated person of a broker or dealer, investment bank holding company, or any affiliate of an investment bank holding company. Nothing in this subsection shall authorize the Commission to withhold information from Congress, or prevent the Commission from complying with a request for information from any other Federal department or agency or any self-regulatory organization requesting the information for purposes within the scope of its jurisdiction, or complying with an order of a court of the United States in an action brought by the United States or the Commission. For purposes of section 552 of title 5, United States Code, this subsection shall be considered a statute described in subsection (b)(3)(B) of such section 552. In prescribing regulations to carry out the requirements of this subsection, the Commission shall designate information described in or obtained pursuant to subparagraphs (A), (B), and (C) of subsection (i)(5) as confidential information for purposes of section 24(b)(2) of this title.

(k) *Coordination of examining authorities.*

(1) Elimination of duplication. The Commission and the examining authorities, through cooperation and coordination of examination and oversight activities, shall eliminate any unnecessary and burdensome duplication in the examination process.

(2) Coordination of examinations. The Commission and the examining authorities shall share such information, including reports of examinations, customer complaint information, and other nonpublic regulatory information, as appropriate to foster a coordinated approach to regulatory oversight of bro-

kers and dealers that are subject to examination by more than one examining authority.

(3) Examinations for cause. At any time, any examining authority may conduct an examination for cause of any broker or dealer subject to its jurisdiction.

(4) Confidentiality.

(A) In general. Section 24 shall apply to the sharing of information in accordance with this subsection. The Commission shall take appropriate action under section 24(c) to ensure that such information is not inappropriately disclosed.

(B) Appropriate disclosure not prohibited. Nothing in this paragraph authorizes the Commission or any examining authority to withhold information from the Congress, or prevent the Commission or any examining authority from complying with a request for information from any other Federal department or agency requesting the information for purposes within the scope of its jurisdiction, or complying with an order of a court of the United States in an action brought by the United States or the Commission.

(5) Definition. For purposes of this subsection, the term "examining authority" means a self-regulatory organization registered with the Commission under this title (other than a registered clearing agency) with the authority to examine, inspect, and otherwise oversee the activities of a registered broker or dealer.

Liability for Misleading Statements

Section 18. (a) *Persons liable; persons entitled to recover; defense of good faith; suit at law or in equity; costs, etc.* Any person who shall make or cause to be made any statement in any application, report, or document filed pursuant to this title or any rule or regulation thereunder or any undertaking contained in a registration statement as provided in subsection (d) of section 15 of this title, which statement was at the time and in the light of the circumstances under which it was made false or misleading with respect to any material fact, shall be liable to any person (not knowing that such statement was false or misleading) who, in reliance upon such statement, shall have purchased or sold a security at a price which was affected by such statement, for damages caused by such reliance, unless the person sued shall prove that he acted in good faith and had no knowledge that such statement was false or misleading. A person seeking to enforce such liability may sue at law or in equity in any court of competent jurisdiction. In any such suit the court may, in its discretion, require an undertaking for the payment of the costs of such suit, and assess reasonable costs, including reasonable attorneys' fees, against either party litigant.

(b) *Contribution.* Every person who becomes liable to make payment under this section may recover contribution as in cases of contact from any person who, if joined in the original suit, would have been liable to make the same payment.

(c) *Periods of limitations.* No action shall be maintained to enforce any liability created under this section unless brought within one year after the discovery of the facts constituting the cause of action and within three years after such cause of action accrued.

Liability of Controlling Persons and Persons Who Aid and Abet Violations

Section 20. (a) *Joint and several liability; good faith defense.* Every person who, directly or indirectly, controls any person liable under any provision of this title or of any rule or regulation thereunder shall also be liable jointly and severally with and to the same extent as such controlled person to any person to whom such controlled person is liable, unless the controlling person acted in good faith and did not directly or indirectly induce the act or acts constituting the violation or cause of action.

(b) *Unlawful activity through or by means of any other person.* It shall be unlawful for any person, directly or indirectly, to do any act or thing which it would be unlawful for such person to do under the provisions of this title or any rule or regulation thereunder through or by means of any other person.

(c) *Hindering, delaying or obstructing making or filing of any document, report or information.* It shall be unlawful for any director or officer of, or any owner of any securities issued by, any issuer required to file any document, report, or information under this title or any rule or regulation thereunder without just cause to hinder, delay, or obstruct the making or filing of any such document, report, or information.

(d) *Liability for trading in securities while in possession of material nonpublic information.* Wherever communicating, or purchasing or selling a security while in possession of, material nonpublic information would violate, or result in liability to any purchaser or seller of the security under any provision of this title, or any rule or regulation thereunder, such conduct in connection with a purchase or sale of a put, call, straddle, option, or privilege with respect to such security or with respect to a group or index of securities including such security, shall also violate and result in comparable liability to any purchaser or seller of that security under such provision, rule, or regulation.

(e) *Prosecution of persons who aid and abet violations.* For purposes of any action brought by the Commission under paragraph (1) or (3) of section 21(d) of this title, any person that knowingly provides substantial assistance to another person in violation of a provision of this chapter, or of any rule or regulation issued under this chapter, shall be deemed to be in violation of such provision to the same extent as the person to whom such assistance is provided.

Liability to Contemporaneous Traders for Insider Trading

Section 20A. (a) *Private rights of action based on contemporaneous trading.* Any person who violates any provision of this title or the rules or regulations thereunder by purchasing or selling a security while in possession of material, nonpublic information shall be liable in an action in any court of competent jurisdiction to any person who, contemporaneously with the purchase or sale of securities that is the subject of such violation, has purchased (where such violation is based on a sale of securities) or sold (where such violation is based on a purchase of securities) securities of the same class.

(b) *Limitations on liability.* (1) The total amount of damages imposed under subsection (a) shall not exceed the profit gained or loss avoided in the transaction or transactions that are the subject of the violation.

(2) The total amount of damages imposed against any person under subsection (a) shall be diminished by the amounts, if any, that such person may be required to disgorge, pursuant to a court order obtained at the instance of the Commission, in a proceeding brought under section 21(d) of this title relating to the same transaction or transactions.

(3) No person shall be liable under this section solely by reason of employing another person who is liable under this section, but the liability of a controlling person under this section shall be subject to section 20(a) of this title.

(4) No action may be brought under this section more than 5 years after the date of the last transaction that is the subject of the violation.

(c) *Joint and several liability for communicating.* Any person who violates any provision of this title or the rules or regulations thereunder by communicating material, nonpublic information shall be jointly and severally liable under subsection (a) with, and to the same extent as, any person or persons liable under subsection (a) to whom the communication was directed.

(d) *Authority not to restrict other express or implied rights of action.* Nothing in this section shall be construed to limit or condition the right of any person to bring an action to enforce a requirement of this title or the availability of any cause of action implied from a provision of this title.

(e) *Provisions not to affect public prosecutions.* This section shall not be construed to bar or limit in any manner any action by the Commission or the Attorney General under any other provision of this title, nor shall it bar or limit in any manner any action to recover penalties, or to seek any other order regarding penalties.

Investigations and Actions

Section 21. (a) *Authority and discretion of Commission to investigate violations.* (1) The Commission may, in its discretion, make such investigations as it deems necessary to determine whether any person has violated, is violating, or is about to violate any provision of this title, the rules or regulations thereunder, the rules of a national securities exchange or registered securities association of which such person is a member or a person associated with a member, the rules of a registered clearing agency in which such person is a participant, the rules of the Public Company Accounting Oversight Board, of which such person is a registered public accounting firm or a person associated with such a firm, or the rules of the Municipal Securities Rulemaking Board, and may require or permit any person to file with it a statement in writing, under oath or otherwise as the Commission shall determine, as to all the facts and circumstances concerning the matter to be investigated. The Commission is authorized in its discretion, to publish information concerning any such violations, and to investigate any facts, conditions, practices, or matters which it may deem necessary or proper to aid in the enforcement of such provisions, in the prescribing of rules and regulations under this chapter, or in securing information to serve as a basis for recommending further legislation concerning the matters to which this chapter relates.

(2) On request from a foreign securities authority, the Commission may provide assistance in accordance with this paragraph if the requesting authority states that the requesting authority is conducting an investigation which it deems necessary to determine whether any person has violated, is violating, or is about to violate any laws or rules relating to securities matters that the requesting authority administers or enforces. The Commission may, in its discretion, conduct such investigation as the Commission deems necessary to collect information and evidence pertinent to the request for assistance. Such assistance may be provided without regard to whether the facts stated in the request would also constitute a violation of the laws of the United States. In deciding whether to provide such assistance, the Commission shall consider whether (A) the requesting authority has agreed to provide reciprocal assistance in securities matters to the Commission; and (B) compliance with the request would prejudice the public interest of the United States.

(b) *Attendance of witnesses; production of records.* For the purpose of any such investigation, or any other proceeding under this chapter, any member of the Commission or any officer designated by it is empowered to administer oaths and affirmations, subpena witnesses, compel their attendance, take evidence, and require the production of any books, papers, correspondence, memoranda, or other records which the Commission deems relevant or material to the inquiry. Such attendance of witnesses and the production of any such records may be required from any place in the United States or any State at any designated place of hearing.

(c) *Judicial enforcement of investigative power of commission; refusal to obey subpoena; criminal sanctions.* In case of contumacy by, or refusal to obey a subpena issued to, any person, the Commission may invoke the aid of any court of the United States within the jurisdiction of which such investigation or proceeding is carried on, or where such person resides or carries on business, in requiring the attendance and testimony of witnesses and the production of books, papers, correspondence, memoranda, and other records. And such court may issue an order requiring such person to appear before the Commission or member or officer designated by the Commission, there to produce records, if so ordered, or to give testimony touching the matter under investigation or in question; and any failure to obey such order of the court may be punished by such court as a contempt thereof. All process in any such case may be served in the judicial district whereof such person is an inhabitant or wherever he may be found. Any person who shall, without just cause, fail or refuse to attend and testify or to answer any lawful inquiry or to produce books, papers, correspondence, memoranda, and other records, if in his power so to do, in obedience to the subpena of the Commission, shall be guilty of a misdemeanor and, upon conviction, shall be subject to a fine of not more than $1,000 or to imprisonment for a term of not more than one year, or both.

(d) *Injunction proceedings; criminal proceedings.* (1) Whenever it shall appear to the Commission that any person is engaged or is about to engage in acts or practices constituting a violation of any provision of this chapter, the rules or regulations thereunder, the rules of a national securities exchange or registered securities association of which such person is a member or a person associated with a member, the rules of a registered clearing agency in which such person is a participant, the rules of the Public Company Accounting Oversight Board, of which such person is a registered public accounting firm or a person associated with such a firm, or the rules of the Municipal Securities Rulemaking Board, it may in its discretion bring an action in the proper district court of the United States, the United States District Court for the District of Columbia, or the United States courts of any territory or other place subject to the jurisdiction of the United States, to enjoin such acts or practices, and upon a proper showing a permanent or temporary injunction or restraining order shall be granted without bond. The Commission may transmit such evidence as may be available concerning such acts or practices as may constitute a violation of any provision of this chapter or the rules or regulations thereunder to the Attorney General, who may, in his discretion, institute the necessary criminal proceedings under this chapter.

(2) In any proceeding under paragraph (1) of this subsection, the court may prohibit, conditionally or unconditionally, and permanently or for such period of time as it shall determine, any person who violated section 10(b) of this chapter or the rules or regulations thereunder from acting as an officer or director of any issuer that has a class of securities registered pursuant to section 12 of this title or that is required to file reports pursuant to section 15(d) of this title if the person's conduct demonstrates unfitness to serve as an officer or director of any such issuer.

(3)(A) *Authority of Commission.* Whenever it shall appear to the Commission that any person has violated any provision of this title, the rules or regulations thereunder, or a cease-and-desist order entered by the Commission pursuant to section 21C of this chapter, other than by committing a violation subject to a penalty pursuant to section 21A of this title, the Commission may bring an action in a United States district court to seek, and the court shall have jurisdiction to impose, upon a proper showing, a civil penalty to be paid by the person who committed such violation.

(B)(i) *First Tier.* The amount of the penalty shall be determined by the court in light of the facts and circumstances. For each violation, the amount of the penalty shall not exceed the greater of (I) $5,000 for a natural person or $50,000 for any other person, or (II) the gross amount of pecuniary gain to such defendant as a result of the violation.

(ii) *Second Tier.* Notwithstanding clause (i), the amount of penalty for each such violation shall not exceed the greater of (I) $50,000 for a natural person or $250,000 for any other person, or (II) the gross amount of pecuniary gain to such defendant as a result of the violation, if the violation described in subparagraph (A) involved fraud, deceit, manipulation, or deliberate or reckless disregard of a regulatory requirement.

(iii) *Third Tier.* Notwithstanding clauses (i) and (ii), the amount of penalty for each such violation shall not exceed the greater of (I) $100,000 for a natural person or $500,000 for any other person, or (II) the gross amount of pecuniary gain to such defendant as a result of the violation, if—

(aa) the violation described in subparagraph (A) involved fraud, deceit, manipulation, or deliberate or reckless disregard of a regulatory requirement; and

(bb) such violation directly or indirectly resulted in substantial losses or created a significant risk of substantial losses to other persons.

(iv) *Internet–related violations*—In any case in which the Internet or other interactive computer service (as defined in section 35B) is used as part of the act or omission resulting in a violation referred to in subparagraph (A), the amount of the penalty provided for in this subparagraph shall be doubled.

(C)(i) A penalty imposed under this section shall be payable into the Treasury of the United States except as otherwise provided in section 308 of the Sarbanes–Oxley Act of 2002.

(ii) If a person upon whom such a penalty is imposed shall fail to pay such penalty within the time prescribed in the court's order, the Commission may refer the matter to the Attorney General who shall recover such penalty by action in the appropriate United States district court.

(iii) The actions authorized by this paragraph may be brought in addition to any other action that the Commission or the Attorney General is entitled to bring.

(iv) For purposes of section 27 of this title, action under this paragraph shall be actions to enforce a liability or a duty created by this title.

(D) In an action to enforce a cease-and-desist order entered by the Commission pursuant to section 21C, each separate violation of such order shall be a separate offense, except that in the case of a violation through a continuing failure to comply with the order, each day of the failure to comply shall be deemed a separate offense.

(4) *Prohibition of attorney's fees paid from Commission disgorgement funds.* Except as otherwise ordered by the court upon motion by the Commission, or, in the case of an administrative action, as otherwise ordered by the Commission, funds disgorged as the result of an action brought by the Commission in Federal court, or as a result of any Commission administrative action, shall not be dis-

tributed as payment for attorney's fees or expenses incurred by private parties seeking distribution of the disgorged funds.

(5) *Equitable Relief.* In any action or proceeding brought or instituted by the Commission under any provision of the securities laws, the Commission may seek, and any Federal court may grant, any equitable relief that may be appropriate or necessary for the benefit of investors.

(6) *Authority of a Court to Prohibit Persons from Participating in an Offering of Penny Stock.* (A) *In General.* In any proceeding under paragraph (1) against any person participating in, or, at the time of the alleged misconduct who was participating in, an offering of penny stock, the court may prohibit that person from participating in an offering of penny stock, conditionally or unconditionally, and permanently or for such period of time as the court shall determine.

(B) *Definition.* For purposes of this paragraph, the term "person participating in an offering of penny stock" includes any person engaging in activities with a broker, dealer, or issuer for purposes of issuing, trading, or inducing or attempting to induce the purchase or sale of, any penny stock. The Commission may, by rule or regulation, define such term to include other activities, and may, by rule, regulation, or order, exempt any person or class of persons, in whole or in part, conditionally or unconditionally, from inclusion in such term.

(e) *Mandamus.* Upon application of the Commission the district courts of the United States, and the United States courts of any territory or other place subject to the jurisdiction of the United States shall have jurisdiction to issue writs of mandamus, injunctions, and orders commanding (1) any person to comply with the provisions of this chapter, the rules, regulations, and orders thereunder, the rules of a national securities exchange or registered securities association of which such person is a member or person associated with a member, the rules of a registered clearing agency in which such person is a participant, the rules of the Public Company Accounting Oversight Board, of which such person is a registered public accounting firm or a person associated with such a firm, the rules of the Municipal Securities Rulemaking Board, or any undertaking contained in a registration statement as provided in subsection (d) of section 15 of this chapter, (2) any national securities exchange or registered securities association to enforce compliance by its members and persons associated with its members with the provisions of this chapter, the rules, regulations, and orders thereunder, and the rules of such exchange or association, or (3) any registered clearing agency to enforce compliance by its participants with the provisions of the rules of such clearing agency.

(f) *Rules of self-regulatory organizations.* Notwithstanding any other provision of this chapter, the Commission shall not bring any action pursuant to subsection (d) or (e) of this section against any person for violation of, or to command compliance with, the rules of a self-regulatory organization or the Public Company Accounting Oversight Board unless it appears to the Commission that (1) such self-regulatory organization or the Public Company Accounting Oversight Board is unable or unwilling to take appropriate action against such person in the public interest and for the protection of investors, or (2) such action is otherwise necessary or appropriate in the public interest or for the protection of investors.

(g) *Consolidation of actions, consent of commission.* Notwithstanding the provisions of section 1407(a) of title 28, United States Code, or any other provision of law, no action for equitable relief instituted by the Commission pursuant to the securities laws shall be consolidated or coordinated with other actions not brought by the Commission, even though such other actions may involve common questions of fact, unless such consolidation is consented to by the Commission.

(h) *Access to records.* (1) The Right to Financial Privacy Act of 1978 shall apply with respect to the Commission, except as otherwise provided in this subsection.

(2) Notwithstanding section 1105 or 1107 of the Right to Financial Privacy Act of 1978, the Commission may have access to and obtain copies of, or the information contained in financial records of a customer from a financial institution without prior notice to the customer upon an ex parte showing to an appropriate United States district court that the Commission seeks such financial records pursuant to a subpena issued in conformity with the requirements of section 19(b) of the Securities Act of 1933, section 21(b) of the Securities Exchange Act of

1934, section 18(c) of the Public Utility Holding Company Act of 1935, section 42(b) of the Investment Company Act of 1940, or section 209(b) of the Investment Advisers Act of 1940, and that the Commission has reason to believe that—

(A) delay in obtaining access to such financial records, or the required notice, will result in—

(i) flight from prosecution;

(ii) destruction of or tampering with evidence;

(iii) transfer of assets or records outside the territorial limits of the United States;

(iv) improper conversion of investor assets; or

(v) impeding the ability of the Commission to identify or trace the source or disposition of funds involved in any securities transaction;

(B) such financial records are necessary to identify or trace the record or beneficial ownership interest in any security;

(C) the acts, practices or course of conduct under investigation involve—

(i) the dissemination of materially false or misleading information concerning any security, issuer, or market, or the failure to make disclosures required under the securities laws, which remain uncorrected; or

(ii) a financial loss to investors or other persons protected under the securities laws which remains substantially uncompensated; or

(D) the acts, practices or course of conduct under investigation—

(i) involve significant financial speculation in securities; or

(ii) endanger the stability of any financial or investment intermediary.

* * *

Civil Penalties for Insider Trading

Section 21A. (a) *Authority to impose civil penalties.* (1) Judicial actions by commission authorized. Whenever it shall appear to the Commission that any person has violated any provision of this chapter or the rules or regulations thereunder by purchasing or selling a security while in possession of material, nonpublic information in, or has violated any such provision by communicating such information in connection with, a transaction on or through the facilities of a national securities exchange or from or through a broker or dealer, and which is not part of a public offering by an issuer of securities other than standardized options, the Commission—

(A) may bring an action in a United States district court to seek and the court shall have jurisdiction to impose, a civil penalty to be paid by the person who committed such violation; and

(B) may, subject to subsection (b)(1) bring an action in a United States district court to seek, and the court shall have jurisdiction to impose, a civil penalty to be paid by a person who, at the time of the violation directly or indirectly controlled the person who committed such violation.

(2) The amount of the penalty which may be imposed on the person who committed such violation shall be determined by the court in light of the fact and circumstances, but shall not exceed three times the profit gained or loss avoided as a result of such unlawful purchase, sale, or communication.

(3) The amount of the penalty which may be imposed on any person who, at the time of the violation, directly or indirectly controlled the person who committed such violation, shall be determined by the court in light of the facts and circumstances, but shall not exceed the greater of $1,000,000, or three times the amount of the profit gained or loss avoided as a result of such controlled person's violation. If such controlled person's violation was a violation by communication, the profit gained or loss avoided as a result of the violation shall, for purposes of this paragraph only, be deemed to be limited to the profit gained or loss avoided by the person or persons to whom the controlled person directed such communication.

(b) *Limitations on liability.* (1) No controlling person shall be subject to a penalty under subsection (a)(1)(B) of this section unless the Commission establishes that—

(A) such controlling person knew or recklessly disregarded the fact that such controlled person was likely to engage in the act or acts constituting the violation and failed to take appropriate steps to prevent such act or acts before they occurred; or

(B) such controlling person knowingly or recklessly failed to establish, maintain, or enforce any policy or procedure required under section 15(f) of this title or section 80b–4a of this title and such failure substantially contributed to or permitted the occurrence of the act or acts constituting the violation.

(2) No person shall be subject to a penalty under subsection (a) solely by reason of employing another person who is subject to a penalty under such subsection, unless such employing person is liable as a controlling person under paragraph (1) of this subsection. Section 20(a) of this title shall not apply to actions under subsection (a) of this section.

(c) *Authority of Commission.* The Commission, by such rules, regulations, and orders as it considers necessary or appropriate in the public interest or for the protection of investors, may exempt, in whole or in part, either unconditionally or upon specific terms and conditions, any person or transaction or class of persons or transactions from this section.

(d) *Procedures for collection.* (1) A penalty imposed under this section shall (subject to subsection (e) of this section) be payable into the Treasury of the United States except as otherwise provided in section 308 of the Sarbanes–Oxley Act of 2002.

(2) If a person upon whom such a penalty is imposed shall fail to pay such penalty within the time prescribed in the court's order, the Commission may refer the matter to the Attorney General who shall recover such penalty by action in the appropriate United States district court.

(3) The actions authorized by this section may be brought in addition to any other actions that the Commission or the Attorney General are entitled to bring.

(4) For purposes of section 27 of this title, actions under this section shall be actions to enforce a liability or a duty created by this chapter.

(5) No action may be brought under this section more than 5 years after the date of the purchase or sale. This section shall not be construed to bar or limit in any manner any action by the Commission or the Attorney General under any other provision of this chapter, nor shall it bar or limit in any manner any action to recover penalties, or to seek any other order regarding penalties, imposed in an action commenced within 5 years of such transaction.

(e) *Authority to award bounties to informants.* Notwithstanding the provisions of subsection (d)(1) of this section, there shall be paid from amounts imposed as a penalty under this section and recovered by the Commission or the Attorney General, such sums, not to exceed 10 percent of such amounts, as the Commission deems appropriate, to the person or persons who provide information leading to the imposition of such penalty. Any determinations under this subsection, including whether, to whom, or in what amount to make payments, shall be in the sole discretion of the Commission, except that no such payment shall be made to any member, officer, or employee of any appropriate regulatory agency, the Department of Justice, or a self-regulatory organization. Any such determination shall be final and not subject to judicial review.

(f) *Definition.* For purposes of this section, "profit gained" or "loss avoided" is the difference between the purchase or sale price of the security and the value of that security as measured by the trading price of the security a reasonable period after public dissemination of the nonpublic information.

Civil Remedies in Administrative Proceedings

Section 21B. (a) *Commission authority to assess money penalties.* In any proceeding instituted pursuant to sections 15(b)(4), 15(b)(6), 15D, 15E, or 17A of this title against any person, the Commission or the appropriate regulatory agency may impose a civil penalty if it finds, on the record after notice and opportunity for hearing that such person—

(1) has willfully violated any provision of the Securities Act of 1933, the Investment Company Act of 1940, the Investment Advisers Act of 1940, or this chapter, or the rules or regulations thereunder, or the rules of the Municipal Securities Rulemaking Board;

(2) has willfully aided, abetted, counseled, commanded, induced, or procured such a violation by any other person;

(3) has willfully made or caused to be made in any application for registration or report required

to be filed with the Commission or with any other appropriate regulatory agency under this chapter, or in any proceeding before the Commission with respect to registration, any statement which was, at the time and in the light of the circumstances under which it was made, false or misleading with respect to any material fact, or has omitted to state in any such application or report any material fact which is required to be stated therein; or

* * *

(b) *Maximum amount of penalty.* (1) The maximum amount of penalty for each act or omission described in subsection (a) shall be $5,000 for a natural person or $50,000 for any other person.

(2) Notwithstanding paragraph (1), the maximum amount of penalty for each such act or omission shall be $50,000 for a natural person or $250,000 for any other person if the act or omission described in subsection (a) involved fraud, deceit, manipulation, or deliberate or reckless disregard of a regulatory requirement.

(3) Notwithstanding paragraphs (1) and (2), the maximum amount of penalty for each such act or omission shall be $100,000 for a natural person or $500,000 for any other person if—

(A) The act or omission described in subsection (a) of this section involved fraud, deceit, manipulation, or deliberate or reckless disregard of a regulatory requirement; and

(B) such act or omission directly or indirectly resulted in substantial losses or created a significant risk of substantial losses to other persons or resulted in substantial pecuniary gain to the person who committed the act or omission.

(4) *Internet-related violations.* In any case in which the Internet or other interactive computer service (as defined in section 35B) is used as part of the act or omission resulting in a violation referred to in subsection (a), the amount of the penalty provided for in this subsection shall be doubled.

(c) *Determination of public interest.* In considering under this section whether a penalty is in the public interest, the Commission or the appropriate regulatory agency may consider—

(1) whether the act or omission for which such penalty is assessed involved fraud, deceit, manipulation, or deliberate or reckless disregard of a regulatory requirement;

(2) the harm to other persons resulting either directly or indirectly from such act or omission;

(3) the extent to which any person was unjustly enriched, taking into account any restitution made to persons injured by such behavior;

(4) whether such person previously has been found by the Commission, another appropriate regulatory agency, or a self-regulatory organization to have violated the Federal securities laws, State securities laws, or the rules of a self-regulatory organization, has been enjoined by a court of competent jurisdiction from violations of such laws or rules, or has been convicted by a court of competent jurisdiction of violations of such laws or any felony or misdemeanor described in section 15(b)(4)(B) of this title;

(5) the need to deter such person and other persons from committing such acts or omissions; and

(6) such other matters as justice may require.

(d) *Evidence concerning the ability to pay.* In any proceeding in which the Commission or the appropriate regulatory agency may impose a penalty under this section, a respondent may present evidence of the respondent's ability to pay such penalty. The Commission or the appropriate regulatory agency may, in its discretion, consider such evidence in determining whether such penalty is in the public interest. Such evidence may relate to the extent of such person's ability to continue in business and the collectability of a penalty, taking into account any other claims of the United States or third parties upon such person's assets and the amount of such person's assets.

(e) *Authority to enter an order requiring an accounting and disgorgement.* In any proceeding in which the Commission or the appropriate regulatory agency may impose a penalty under this section, the Commission or the appropriate regulatory agency may enter an order requiring accounting and disgorgement, including reasonable interest. The Commission is authorized to adopt rules, regulations, and orders concerning payments to investors, rates of interest, periods of accrual, and such other matters as it deems appropriate to implement this subsection.

Cease-and-Desist Proceedings

Section 21C. (a) *Authority of the Commission.* If the Commission finds, after notice and opportunity for hearing, that any person is violating, has violated, or is about to violate any provision of this chapter, or any rule or regulation thereunder, the Commission may publish its findings and enter an order requiring such person, and any other person that is, was, or would be a cause of the violation, due to an act or omission the person knew or should have known would contribute to such violation, to cease and desist from committing or causing such violation and any future violation of the same provision, rule, or regulation. Such order may, in addition to requiring a person to cease and desist from committing or causing a violation, require such person to comply, or to take steps to effect compliance, with such provision, rule, or regulation, upon such terms and conditions and within such time as the Commission may specify in such order. Any such order may, as the Commission deems appropriate, require future compliance or steps to effect future compliance, either permanently or for such period of time as the Commission may specify, with such provision, rule, or regulation with respect to any security, any issuer, or any other person.

(b) *Hearing.* The notice instituting proceedings pursuant to subsection (a) of this section shall fix a hearing date not earlier than 30 days nor later than 60 days after service of the notice unless an earlier or a later date is set by the Commission with the consent of any respondent so served.

(c) *Temporary order.* (1) Whenever the Commission determines that the alleged violation or threatened violation specified in the notice instituting proceedings pursuant to subsection (a) of this section, or the continuation thereof, is likely to result in significant dissipation or conversion of assets, significant harm to investors, or substantial harm to the public interest, including, but not limited to, losses to the Securities Investor Protection Corporation, prior to the completion of the proceedings, the Commission may enter a temporary order requiring the respondent to cease and desist from the violation or threatened violation and to take such action to prevent the violation or threatened violation and to prevent dissipation or conversion of assets, significant harm to investors, or substantial harm to the public interest as the Commission deems appropriate pending completion of such proceedings. Such an order shall be entered only after notice and opportunity for a hearing, unless the Commission determines that notice and hearing prior to entry would be impracticable or contrary to the public interest. A temporary order shall become effective upon service upon the respondent and, unless set aside, limited, or suspended by the Commission or a court of competent jurisdiction, shall remain effective and enforceable pending the completion of the proceedings.

(2) Paragraph 1 shall apply only to a respondent that acts, or, at the time of the alleged misconduct acted, as a broker, dealer, investment adviser, investment company, municipal securities dealer, government securities broker, government securities dealer, registered public accounting firm (as defined in section 2 of the Sarbanes-Oxley Act of 2002), or transfer agent, or is, or was at the time of the alleged misconduct, an associated person of, or a person seeking to become associated with, any of the foregoing.

(3) *Temporary Freeze.* (A) *in General.* (i) *Issuance of Temporary Order.* Whenever, during the course of a lawful investigation involving possible violations of the Federal securities laws by an issuer of publicly traded securities or any of its directors, officers, partners, controlling persons, agents, or employees, it shall appear to the Commission that it is likely that the issuer will make extraordinary payments (whether compensation or otherwise) to any of the foregoing persons, the Commission may petition a Federal district court for a temporary order requiring the issuer to escrow, subject to court supervision, those payments in an interest-bearing account for 45 days.

(ii) *Standard.* A temporary order shall be entered under clause (i), only after notice and opportunity for a hearing, unless the court determines that notice and hearing prior to entry of the order would be impracticable or contrary to the public interest.

(iii) *Effective Period.* A temporary order issued under clause (i) shall—

(I) become effective immediately;

(II) be served upon the parties subject to it; and

(III) unless set aside, limited or suspended by a court of competent jurisdiction, shall remain effective and enforceable for 45 days.

(iv) Extensions Authorized.—The effective period of an order under this subparagraph may be extended by the court upon good cause shown for not longer than 45 additional days, provided that the combined period of the order shall not exceed 90 days.

(B) *Process on Determination of Violations.*

(i) *Violations Charged.*—If the issuer or other person described in subparagraph (A) is charged with any violation of the Federal securities laws before the expiration of the effective period of a temporary order under subparagraph (A) (including any applicable extension period), the order shall remain in effect, subject to court approval, until the conclusion of any legal proceedings related thereto, and the affected issuer or other person, shall have the right to petition the court for review of the order.

(ii) *Violations Not Charged.* If the issuer or other person described in subparagraph (A) is not charged with any violation of the Federal securities laws before the expiration of the effective period of a temporary order under subparagraph (A) (including any applicable extension period), the escrow shall terminate at the expiration of the 45-day effective period (or the expiration of any extension period, as applicable), and the disputed payments (with accrued interest) shall be returned to the issuer or other affected person.

(d) *Review of temporary orders.* (1) At any time after the respondent has been served with a temporary cease-and-desist order pursuant to subsection (c) of this section, the respondent may apply to the Commission to have the order set aside, limited, or suspended. If the respondent has been served with a temporary cease-and-desist order entered without a prior Commission hearing, the respondent may, within 10 days after the date on which the order was served, request a hearing on such application and the Commission shall hold a hearing and render a decision on such application at the earliest possible time.

(2) Within—

(A) 10 days after the date the respondent was served with a temporary cease-and-desist order entered with a prior Commission hearing, or

(B) 10 days after the Commission renders a decision on an application and hearing under paragraph (1), with respect to any temporary cease-and-desist order entered without a prior Commission hearing,

the respondent may apply to the United States district court for the district in which the respondent resides or has its principal place of business, or for the District of Columbia, for an order setting aside, limiting, or suspending the effectiveness or enforcement of the order, and the court shall have jurisdiction to enter such an order. A respondent served with a temporary cease-and-desist order entered without a prior Commission hearing may not apply to the court except after hearing and decision by the Commission on the respondent's application under paragraph (1) of this subsection.

(3) The commencement of proceedings under paragraph (2) of this subsection shall not, unless specifically ordered by the court, operate as a stay of the Commission's order.

(4) Section 25 of this title shall not apply to a temporary order entered pursuant to this section.

(e) *Authority to enter an order requiring an accounting and disgorgement.* In any cease-and-desist proceeding under subsection (a) of this section, the Commission may enter an order requiring accounting and disgorgement, including reasonable interest. The Commission is authorized to adopt rules, regulations, and orders concerning payments to investors, rates of interest, periods of accrual, and such other matters as it deems appropriate to implement this subsection.

(f) *Authority of the Commission to Prohibit Persons from Serving as Officers or Directors.* In any cease-and-desist proceeding under subsection (a), the Commission may issue an order to prohibit, conditionally or unconditionally, and permanently or for such period of time as it shall determine, any person who has violated section 10(b) or the rules or regulations thereunder, from acting as an officer or director of any issuer that has a class of securities registered pursuant to section 12, or that is required to file reports pursuant to section 15(d), if the conduct of that person demonstrates unfitness to serve as an officer or director of any such issuer.

Private Securities Litigation

Section 21D. (a) Private class actions

(1) In general

The provisions of this subsection shall apply in each private action arising under this chapter that is brought as a plaintiff class action pursuant to the Federal Rules of Civil Procedure.

(2) Certification filed with complaint

(A) In general

Each plaintiff seeking to serve as a representative party on behalf of a class shall provide a sworn certification, which shall be personally signed by such plaintiff and filed with the complaint, that—

(i) states that the plaintiff has reviewed the complaint and authorized its filing;

(ii) states that the plaintiff did not purchase the security that is the subject of the complaint at the direction of plaintiff's counsel or in order to participate in any private action arising under this chapter;

(iii) states that the plaintiff is willing to serve as a representative party on behalf of a class, including providing testimony at deposition and trial, if necessary;

(iv) sets forth all of the transactions of the plaintiff in the security that is the subject of the complaint during the class period specified in the complaint;

(v) identifies any other action under this chapter, filed during the 3-year period preceding the date on which the certification is signed by the plaintiff, in which the plaintiff has sought to serve as a representative party on behalf of a class; and

(vi) states that the plaintiff will not accept any payment for serving as a representative party on behalf of a class beyond the plaintiff's pro rata share of any recovery, except as ordered or approved by the court in accordance with paragraph (4).

(B) Nonwaiver of attorney-client privilege

The certification filed pursuant to subparagraph (A) shall not be construed to be a waiver of the attorney-client privilege.

(3) Appointment of lead plaintiff

(A) Early notice to class members

(i) In general

Not later than 20 days after the date on which the complaint is filed, the plaintiff or plaintiffs shall cause to be published, in a widely circulated national business-oriented publication or wire service, a notice advising members of the purported plaintiff class—

(I) of the pendency of the action, the claims asserted therein, and the purported class period; and

(II) that, not later than 60 days after the date on which the notice is published, any member of the purported class may move the court to serve as lead plaintiff of the purported class.

(ii) Multiple actions

If more than one action on behalf of a class asserting substantially the same claim or claims arising under this chapter is filed, only the plaintiff or plaintiffs in the first filed action shall be required to cause notice to be published in accordance with clause (i).

(iii) Additional notices may be required under Federal Rules

Notice required under clause (i) shall be in addition to any notice required pursuant to the Federal Rules of Civil Procedure.

(B) Appointment of lead plaintiff

(i) In general

Not later than 90 days after the date on which a notice is published under subparagraph (A)(i), the court shall consider any motion made by a purported class member in response to the notice, including any motion by a class member who is not individually named as a plaintiff in the complaint or complaints, and shall appoint as lead plaintiff the member or members of the purported plaintiff class that the court determines to be most capable of adequately representing the interests of class members (hereafter in this paragraph referred to as the "most adequate plaintiff") in accordance with this subparagraph.

(ii) Consolidated actions

If more than one action on behalf of a class asserting substantially the same claim or claims arising under this chapter has been filed, and any party has sought to consolidate those actions for pretrial purposes or for trial, the court shall not make the determination required by clause (i) until after the decision on the motion to consolidate is rendered. As soon as practicable after such decision is rendered, the court shall appoint the most adequate plaintiff as lead plaintiff for the consolidated actions in accordance with this paragraph.

(iii) Rebuttable presumption

(I) In general

Subject to subclause (II), for purposes of clause (i), the court shall adopt a presumption that the most adequate plaintiff in any private action arising under this chapter is the person or group of persons that—

(aa) has either filed the complaint or made a motion in response to a notice under subparagraph (A)(i);

(bb) in the determination of the court, has the largest financial interest in the relief sought by the class; and

(cc) otherwise satisfies the requirements of Rule 23 of the Federal Rules of Civil Procedure.

(II) Rebuttal evidence

The presumption described in subclause (I) may be rebutted only upon proof by a member of the purported plaintiff class that the presumptively most adequate plaintiff—

(aa) will not fairly and adequately protect the interests of the class; or

(bb) is subject to unique defenses that render such plaintiff incapable of adequately representing the class.

(iv) Discovery

For purposes of this subparagraph, discovery relating to whether a member or members of the purported plaintiff class is the most adequate plaintiff may be conducted by a plaintiff only if the plaintiff first demonstrates a reasonable basis for a finding that the presumptively most adequate plaintiff is incapable of adequately representing the class.

(v) Selection of lead counsel

The most adequate plaintiff shall, subject to the approval of the court, select and retain counsel to represent the class.

(vi) Restrictions on professional plaintiffs

Except as the court may otherwise permit, consistent with the purposes of this section, a person may be a lead plaintiff, or an officer, director, or fiduciary of a lead plaintiff, in no more than 5 securities class actions brought as plaintiff class actions pursuant to the Federal Rules of Civil Procedure during any 3–year period.

(4) Recovery by plaintiffs

The share of any final judgment or of any settlement that is awarded to a representative party serving on behalf of a class shall be equal, on a per share basis, to the portion of the final judgment or settlement awarded to all other members of the class. Nothing in this paragraph shall be construed to limit the award of reasonable costs and expenses (including lost wages) directly relating to the representation of the class to any representative party serving on behalf of a class.

(5) Restrictions on settlements under seal

The terms and provisions of any settlement agreement of a class action shall not be filed under seal, except that on motion of any party to the settlement, the court may order filing under seal for those portions of a settlement agreement as to which good cause is shown for such filing under seal. For purposes of this paragraph, good cause shall exist only if publication of a term or provision of a settlement agreement would cause direct and substantial harm to any party.

(6) Restrictions on payment of attorneys' fees and expenses

Total attorneys' fees and expenses awarded by the court to counsel for the plaintiff class shall not exceed a reasonable percentage of the amount of any damages and prejudgment interest actually paid to the class.

(7) Disclosure of settlement terms to class members

Any proposed or final settlement agreement that is published or otherwise disseminated to the class shall include each of the following statements, along with a cover page summarizing the information contained in such statements:

(A) Statement of plaintiff recovery

The amount of the settlement proposed to be distributed to the parties to the action, determined in the aggregate and on an average per share basis.

(B) Statement of potential outcome of case

(i) Agreement on amount of damages

If the settling parties agree on the average amount of damages per share that would be recoverable if the plaintiff prevailed on each claim alleged under this chapter, a statement concerning the average amount of such potential damages per share.

(ii) Disagreement on amount of damages

If the parties do not agree on the average amount of damages per share that would be recoverable if the plaintiff prevailed on each claim alleged under this chapter, a statement from each settling party concerning the issue or issues on which the parties disagree.

(iii) Inadmissibility for certain purposes

A statement made in accordance with clause (i) or (ii) concerning the amount of damages shall not be admissible in any Federal or State judicial action or administrative proceeding, other than an action or proceeding arising out of such statement.

(C) Statement of attorneys' fees or costs sought

If any of the settling parties or their counsel intend to apply to the court for an award of attorneys' fees or costs from any fund established as part of the settlement, a statement indicating which parties or counsel intend to make such an application, the amount of fees and costs that will be sought (including the amount of such fees and costs determined on an average per share basis), and a brief explanation supporting the fees and costs sought. Such information shall be clearly summarized on the cover page of any notice to a party of any proposed or final settlement agreement.

(D) Identification of lawyers' representatives

The name, telephone number, and address of one or more representatives of counsel for the plaintiff class who will be reasonably available to answer questions from class members concerning any matter contained in any notice of settlement published or otherwise disseminated to the class.

(E) Reasons for settlement

A brief statement explaining the reasons why the parties are proposing the settlement.

(F) Other information

Such other information as may be required by the court.

(8) Security for payment of costs in class actions

In any private action arising under this chapter that is certified as a class action pursuant to the Federal Rules of Civil Procedure, the court may require an undertaking from the attorneys for the plaintiff class, the plaintiff class, or both, or from the attorneys for the defendant, the defendant, or both, in such proportions and at such times as the court determines are just and equitable, for the payment of fees and expenses that may be awarded under this subsection.

(9) Attorney conflict of interest

If a plaintiff class is represented by an attorney who directly owns or otherwise has a beneficial interest in the securities that are the subject of the litigation, the court shall make a determination of whether such ownership or other interest constitutes a conflict of interest sufficient to disqualify the attorney from representing the plaintiff class.

(b) Requirements for securities fraud actions

(1) Misleading statements and omissions

In any private action arising under this chapter in which the plaintiff alleges that the defendant—

(A) made an untrue statement of a material fact; or

(B) omitted to state a material fact necessary in order to make the statements made, in the light of the circumstances in which they were made, not misleading;

the complaint shall specify each statement alleged to have been misleading, the reason or reasons why the statement is misleading, and, if an allegation regarding the statement or omission is made on information and belief, the complaint shall state with particularity all facts on which that belief is formed.

(2) Required state of mind

In any private action arising under this chapter in which the plaintiff may recover money damages only on proof that the defendant acted with a particular state of mind, the complaint shall, with respect to each act or omission alleged to violate this chapter, state with particularity facts giving rise to a strong inference that the defendant acted with the required state of mind.

(3) Motion to dismiss; stay of discovery

(A) Dismissal for failure to meet pleading requirements

In any private action arising under this chapter, the court shall, on the motion of any defendant, dismiss the complaint if the requirements of paragraphs (1) and (2) are not met.

(B) Stay of discovery

In any private action arising under this chapter, all discovery and other proceedings shall be stayed during the pendency of any motion to dismiss, unless the court finds upon the motion of any party that particularized discovery is necessary to preserve evidence or to prevent undue prejudice to that party.

(C) Preservation of evidence

(i) In general

During the pendency of any stay of discovery pursuant to this paragraph, unless otherwise ordered by the court, any party to the action with actual notice of the allegations contained in the complaint shall treat all documents, data compilations (including electronically recorded or stored data), and tangible objects that are in the custody or control of such person and that are relevant to the allegations, as if they were the subject of a continuing request for production of documents from an opposing party under the Federal Rules of Civil Procedure.

(ii) Sanction for willful violation

A party aggrieved by the willful failure of an opposing party to comply with clause (i) may apply to the court for an order awarding appropriate sanctions.

(D) Circumvention of stay of discovery

Upon a proper showing, a court may stay discovery proceedings in any private action in a State court, as necessary in aid of its jurisdiction, or to protect or effectuate its judgments, in an action subject to a stay of discovery pursuant to this paragraph.

(4) Loss causation

In any private action arising under this chapter, the plaintiff shall have the burden of proving that the act or omission of the defendant alleged to violate this chapter caused the loss for which the plaintiff seeks to recover damages.

(c) Sanctions for abusive litigation

(1) Mandatory review by court

In any private action arising under this chapter, upon final adjudication of the action, the court shall include in the record specific findings regarding compliance by each party and each attorney representing any party with each requirement of Rule 11(b) of the Federal Rules of Civil Procedure as to any complaint, responsive pleading, or dispositive motion.

(2) Mandatory sanctions

If the court makes a finding under paragraph (1) that a party or attorney violated any requirement of Rule 11(b) of the Federal Rules of Civil Procedure as to any complaint, responsive pleading, or dispositive motion, the court shall impose sanctions on such party or attorney in accordance with Rule 11 of the Federal Rules of Civil Procedure. Prior to making a finding that any party or attorney has violated Rule 11 of the Federal Rules of Civil Procedure, the court shall give such party or attorney notice and an opportunity to respond.

(3) Presumption in favor of attorneys' fees and costs

(A) In general

Subject to subparagraphs (B) and (C), for purposes of paragraph (2), the court shall adopt a presumption that the appropriate sanction—

(i) for failure of any responsive pleading or dispositive motion to comply with any requirement of Rule 11(b) of the Federal Rules of Civil Procedure is an award to the opposing party of the reasonable attorneys' fees and other expenses incurred as a direct result of the violation; and

(ii) for substantial failure of any complaint to comply with any requirement of Rule 11(b) of the Federal Rules of Civil Procedure is an award to the opposing party of the reasonable attorneys' fees and other expenses incurred in the action.

(B) Rebuttal evidence

The presumption described in subparagraph (A) may be rebutted only upon proof by the party or attorney against whom sanctions are to be imposed that—

(i) the award of attorneys' fees and other expenses will impose an unreasonable burden on that party or attorney and would be unjust, and the failure to make such an award would not impose a greater burden on the party in whose favor sanctions are to be imposed; or

(ii) the violation of Rule 11(b) of the Federal Rules of Civil Procedure was de minimis.

(C) Sanctions

If the party or attorney against whom sanctions are to be imposed meets its burden under subparagraph (B), the court shall award the sanctions that the court deems appropriate pursuant to Rule 11 of the Federal Rules of Civil Procedure.

(d) Defendant's right to written interrogatories

In any private action arising under this chapter in which the plaintiff may recover money damages, the court shall, when requested by a defendant, submit to the jury a written interrogatory on the issue of each such defendant's state of mind at the time the alleged violation occurred.

(e) Limitation on damages

(1) In general

Except as provided in paragraph (2), in any private action arising under this chapter in which the plaintiff seeks to establish damages by reference to the market price of a security, the award of damages to the plaintiff shall not exceed the difference between the purchase or sale price paid or received, as appropriate, by the plaintiff for the subject security and the mean trading price of that security during the 90–day period beginning on the date on which the information correcting the misstatement or omission that is the basis for the action is disseminated to the market.

(2) Exception

In any private action arising under this chapter in which the plaintiff seeks to establish damages by reference to the market price of a security, if the plaintiff sells or repurchases the subject security prior to the expiration of the 90–day period described in paragraph (1), the plaintiff's damages shall not exceed the difference between the purchase or sale price paid or received, as appropriate, by the plaintiff for the security and the mean trading price of the security during the period beginning immediately after dissemination of information correcting the misstatement or omission and ending on the date on which the plaintiff sells or repurchases the security.

(3) Definition

For purposes of this subsection, the "mean trading price" of a security shall be an average of the daily trading price of that security, determined as of the close of the market each day during the 90–day period referred to in paragraph (1).

(f) Proportionate liability

(1) Applicability

Nothing in this subsection shall be construed to create, affect, or in any manner modify, the standard for liability associated with any action arising under the securities laws.

(2) Liability for damages

(A) Joint and several liability

Any covered person against whom a final judgment is entered in a private action shall be liable for damages jointly and severally only if the trier of fact specifically determines that such covered person knowingly committed a violation of the securities laws.

(B) Proportionate liability

(i) In general

Except as provided in subparagraph (A), a covered person against whom a final judgment is entered in a private action shall be liable solely for the portion of the judgment that corresponds to the percentage of responsibility of that covered person, as determined under paragraph (3).

(ii) Recovery by and costs of covered person

In any case in which a contractual relationship permits, a covered person that prevails in any private action may recover the attorney's fees and costs of that covered person in connection with the action.

(3) Determination of responsibility

(A) In general

In any private action, the court shall instruct the jury to answer special interrogatories, or if there is no jury, shall make findings, with respect to each covered person and each of the other persons claimed by any of the parties to have caused or contributed to the loss incurred by the plaintiff, including persons who have entered into settlements with the plaintiff or plaintiffs, concerning—

(i) whether such person violated the securities laws;

(ii) the percentage of responsibility of such person, measured as a percentage of the total fault of all persons who caused or contributed to the loss incurred by the plaintiff; and

(iii) whether such person knowingly committed a violation of the securities laws.

(B) Contents of special interrogatories or findings

The responses to interrogatories, or findings, as appropriate, under subparagraph (A) shall specify the total amount of damages that the plaintiff is entitled to recover and the percentage of responsibility of each covered person found to have caused or contributed to the loss incurred by the plaintiff or plaintiffs.

(C) Factors for consideration

In determining the percentage of responsibility under this paragraph, the trier of fact shall consider—

(i) the nature of the conduct of each covered person found to have caused or contributed to the loss incurred by the plaintiff or plaintiffs; and

(ii) the nature and extent of the causal relationship between the conduct of each such person and the damages incurred by the plaintiff or plaintiffs.

(4) Uncollectible share

(A) In general

Notwithstanding paragraph (2)(B), upon motion made not later than 6 months after a final judgment is entered in any private action, the court determines that all or part of the share of the judgment of the covered person is not collectible against that covered person, and is also not collectible against a covered person described in paragraph (2)(A), each covered person described in paragraph (2)(B) shall be liable for the uncollectible share as follows:

(i) Percentage of net worth

Each covered person shall be jointly and severally liable for the uncollectible share if the plaintiff establishes that—

(I) the plaintiff is an individual whose recoverable damages under the final judgment are equal to more than 10 percent of the net worth of the plaintiff; and

(II) the net worth of the plaintiff is equal to less than $200,000.

(ii) Other plaintiffs

With respect to any plaintiff not described in subclauses (I) and (II) of clause (i), each covered person shall be liable for the uncollectible share in proportion to the percentage of responsibility of that covered person, except that the total liability of a covered person under this clause may not exceed 50 percent of the proportionate share of that covered person, as determined under paragraph (3)(B).

(iii) Net worth

For purposes of this subparagraph, net worth shall be determined as of the date immediately preceding the date of the purchase or sale (as applicable) by the plaintiff of the security that is the subject of the action, and shall be equal to the fair market value of assets, minus liabilities, including the net value of the investments of the plaintiff in real and personal property (including personal residences).

(B) Overall limit

In no case shall the total payments required pursuant to subparagraph (A) exceed the amount of the uncollectible share.

(C) Covered persons subject to contribution

A covered person against whom judgment is not collectible shall be subject to contribution and to any continuing liability to the plaintiff on the judgment.

(5) Right of contribution

To the extent that a covered person is required to make an additional payment pursuant to paragraph (4), that covered person may recover contribution—

(A) from the covered person originally liable to make the payment;

(B) from any covered person liable jointly and severally pursuant to paragraph (2)(A);

(C) from any covered person held proportionately liable pursuant to this paragraph who is liable to make the same payment and has paid less than his or her proportionate share of that payment; or

(D) from any other person responsible for the conduct giving rise to the payment that would have been liable to make the same payment.

(6) Nondisclosure to jury

The standard for allocation of damages under paragraphs (2) and (3) and the procedure for reallocation of uncollectible shares under paragraph (4) shall not be disclosed to members of the jury.

(7) Settlement discharge

(A) In general

A covered person who settles any private action at any time before final verdict or judgment shall be discharged from all claims for contribution brought by other persons. Upon entry of the settlement by the court, the court shall enter a bar order constituting the final discharge of all obligations to the plaintiff of the settling covered person arising out of the action. The order shall bar all future claims for contribution arising out of the action—

(i) by any person against the settling covered person; and

(ii) by the settling covered person against any person, other than a person whose liability has been extinguished by the settlement of the settling covered person.

(B) Reduction

If a covered person enters into a settlement with the plaintiff prior to final verdict or judgment, the verdict or judgment shall be reduced by the greater of—

(i) an amount that corresponds to the percentage of responsibility of that covered person; or

(ii) the amount paid to the plaintiff by that covered person.

(8) Contribution

A covered person who becomes jointly and severally liable for damages in any private action may recover contribution from any other person who, if joined in the original action, would have been liable for the same damages. A claim for contribution shall be determined based on the percentage of responsibility of the claimant and of each person against whom a claim for contribution is made.

(9) Statute of limitations for contribution

In any private action determining liability, an action for contribution shall be brought not later than 6 months after the entry of a final, nonappealable judgment in the action, except that an action for contribution brought by a covered person who was required to make an additional payment pursuant to paragraph (4) may be brought not later than 6 months after the date on which such payment was made.

(10) Definitions

For purposes of this subsection—

(A) a covered person "knowingly commits a violation of the securities laws"—

(i) with respect to an action that is based on an untrue statement of material fact or omission of a material fact necessary to make the statement not misleading, if—

(I) that covered person makes an untrue statement of a material fact, with actual knowledge that the representation is false, or omits to state a fact necessary in order to make the statement made not misleading, with actual knowledge that, as a result of the omission, one of the material representations of the covered person is false; and

(II) persons are likely to reasonably rely on that misrepresentation or omission; and

(ii) with respect to an action that is based on any conduct that is not described in clause (i), if that covered person engages in that conduct with actual knowledge of the facts and circumstances that make the conduct of that covered person a violation of the securities laws;

(B) reckless conduct by a covered person shall not be construed to constitute a knowing commission of a violation of the securities laws by that covered person;

(C) the term "covered person" means—

(i) a defendant in any private action arising under this chapter; or

(ii) a defendant in any private action arising under section 77k of this title, who is an outside director of the issuer of the securities that are the subject of the action; and

(D) the term "outside director" shall have the meaning given such term by rule or regulation of the Commission.

Application of Safe Harbor for Forward-Looking Statements

Section 21E. (a) Applicability

This section shall apply only to a forward-looking statement made by—

(1) an issuer that, at the time that the statement is made, is subject to the reporting requirements of section 78m(a) or 78o(d) of this title;

(2) a person acting on behalf of such issuer;

(3) an outside reviewer retained by such issuer making a statement on behalf of such issuer; or

(4) an underwriter, with respect to information provided by such issuer or information derived from information provided by such issuer.

(b) Exclusions

Except to the extent otherwise specifically provided by rule, regulation, or order of the Commission, this section shall not apply to a forward-looking statement—

(1) that is made with respect to the business or operations of the issuer, if the issuer—

(A) during the 3-year period preceding the date on which the statement was first made—

(i) was convicted of any felony or misdemeanor described in clauses (i) through (iv) of section 78o(b)(4)(B) of this title; or

(ii) has been made the subject of a judicial or administrative decree or order arising out of a governmental action that—

(I) prohibits future violations of the antifraud provisions of the securities laws;

(II) requires that the issuer cease and desist from violating the antifraud provisions of the securities laws; or

(III) determines that the issuer violated the antifraud provisions of the securities laws;

(B) makes the forward-looking statement in connection with an offering of securities by a blank check company;

(C) issues penny stock;

(D) makes the forward-looking statement in connection with a rollup transaction; or

(E) makes the forward-looking statement in connection with a going private transaction; or

(2) that is—

(A) included in a financial statement prepared in accordance with generally accepted accounting principles;

(B) contained in a registration statement of, or otherwise issued by, an investment company;

(C) made in connection with a tender offer;

(D) made in connection with an initial public offering;

(E) made in connection with an offering by, or relating to the operations of, a partnership, limited liability company, or a direct participation investment program; or

(F) made in a disclosure of beneficial ownership in a report required to be filed with the Commission pursuant to section 78m(d) of this title.

(c) Safe Harbor

(1) In general

Except as provided in subsection (b) of this section, in any private action arising under this chapter that is based on an untrue statement of a material fact or omission of a material fact necessary to make the statement not misleading, a person referred to in subsection (a) of this section shall not be liable with respect to any forward-looking statement, whether written or oral, if and to the extent that—

(A) the forward-looking statement is—

(i) identified as a forward-looking statement, and is accompanied by meaningful cautionary statements identifying important factors that could cause actual results to differ materially from those in the forward-looking statement; or

(ii) immaterial; or

(B) the plaintiff fails to prove that the forward-looking statement—

(i) if made by a natural person, was made with actual knowledge by that person that the statement was false or misleading; or

(ii) if made by a business entity; was—

(I) made by or with the approval of an executive officer of that entity; and

(II) made or approved by such officer with actual knowledge by that officer that the statement was false or misleading.

(2) Oral forward-looking statements

In the case of an oral forward-looking statement made by an issuer that is subject to the reporting requirements of section 78m(a) or 78o(d) of this title, or by a person acting on behalf of such issuer, the requirement set forth in paragraph (1)(A) shall be deemed to be satisfied—

(A) if the oral forward-looking statement is accompanied by a cautionary statement—

(i) that the particular oral statement is a forward-looking statement; and

(ii) that the actual results might differ materially from those projected in the forward-looking statement; and

(B) if—

(i) the oral forward-looking statement is accompanied by an oral statement that additional information concerning factors that could cause actual results to materially differ from those in the forward-looking statement is contained in a readily available written document, or portion thereof;

(ii) the accompanying oral statement referred to in clause (i) identifies the document, or portion thereof, that contains the additional information about those factors relating to the forward-looking statement; and

(iii) the information contained in that written document is a cautionary statement that satisfies the standard established in paragraph (1)(A).

(3) Availability

Any document filed with the Commission or generally disseminated shall be deemed to be readily available for purposes of paragraph (2).

(4) Effect on other safe harbors

The exemption provided for in paragraph (1) shall be in addition to any exemption that the Commission may establish by rule or regulation under subsection (g) of this section.

(d) Duty to update

Nothing in this section shall impose upon any person a duty to update a forward-looking statement.

(e) Dispositive motion

On any motion to dismiss based upon subsection (c)(1) of this section, the court shall consider any statement cited in the complaint and any cautionary statement accompanying the forward-looking statement, which are not subject to material dispute, cited by the defendant.

(f) Stay pending decision on motion

In any private action arising under this chapter, the court shall stay discovery (other than discovery that is specifically directed to the applicability of the exemption provided for in this section) during the pendency of any motion by a defendant for summary judgment that is based on the grounds that—

(1) the statement or omission upon which the complaint is based is a forward-looking statement within the meaning of this section; and

(2) the exemption provided for in this section precludes a claim for relief.

(g) Exemption authority

In addition to the exemptions provided for in this section, the Commission may, by rule or regulation, provide exemptions from or under any provision of this chapter, including with respect to liability that is based on a statement or that is based on projections or other forward-looking information, if and to the extent that any such exemption is consistent with the public interest and the protection of investors, as determined by the Commission.

(h) Effect on other authority of Commission

Nothing in this section limits, either expressly or by implication, the authority of the Commission to exercise similar authority or to adopt similar rules and regulations with respect to forward-looking statements under any other statute under which the Commission exercises rulemaking authority.

(i) Definitions

For purposes of this section, the following definitions shall apply:

(1) Forward-looking statement

The term "forward-looking statement" means—

(A) a statement containing a projection of revenues, income (including income loss), earnings (including earnings loss) per share, capital expenditures, dividends, capital structure, or other financial items;

(B) a statement of the plans and objectives of management for future operations, including plans or objectives relating to the products or services of the issuer;

(C) a statement of future economic performance, including any such statement contained in a discussion and analysis of financial condition by the management or in the results of operations included pursuant to the rules and regulations of the Commission;

(D) any statement of the assumptions underlying or relating to any statement described in subparagraph (A), (B), or (C);

(E) any report issued by an outside reviewer retained by an issuer, to the extent that the report assesses a forward-looking statement made by the issuer; or

(F) a statement containing a projection or estimate of such other items as may be specified by rule or regulation of the Commission.

(2) Investment company

The term "investment company" has the same meaning as in section 80a–3(a) of this title.

(3) Going private transaction

The term "going private transaction" has the meaning given that term under the rules or regulations of the Commission issued pursuant to section 78m(e) of this title.

(4) Person acting on behalf of an issuer

The term "person acting on behalf of an issuer" means any officer, director, or employee of such issuer.

(5) Other terms

The terms "blank check company", "roll-up transaction", "partnership", "limited liability company", "executive officer of an entity" and "direct participation investment program", have the meanings given those terms by rule or regulation of the Commission.

Unlawful Representations

Section 26. No action or failure to act by the Commission or the Board of Governors of the Federal Reserve System, in the administration of this chapter shall be construed to mean that the particular authority has in any way passed upon the merits of, or given approval to, any security or any transaction or transactions therein, nor shall such action or failure to act with regard to any statement or report filed with or examined by such authority pursuant to this chapter or rules and regulations thereunder, be deemed a finding by such authority that such statement or report is true and accurate on its face or that it is not false or misleading. It shall be unlawful to make, or cause to be made, to any prospective purchaser or seller of a security any representation that any such action or failure to act by any such authority is to be so construed or has such effect.

Jurisdiction of Offenses and Suits

Section 27. The district courts of the United States and the United States courts of any Territory or other place subject to the jurisdiction of the United States shall have exclusive jurisdiction of violations of this chapter or the rules and regulations thereunder, and of all suits in equity and actions at law brought to enforce any liability or duty created by this chapter or the rules and regulations thereunder. Any criminal proceeding may be brought in the district wherein any act or transaction constituting the violation occurred. Any suit or action to enforce any liability or duty created by this chapter or rules and regulations thereunder, or enjoin any violation of such chapter or rules and regulations, may be brought in any such district or in the district wherein the defendant is found or is an inhabitant or transacts business, and process in such cases may be served in any other district of which the defendant is an inhabitant or wherever the defendant may be found. Judgments and decrees so rendered shall be subject to review as provided in sections 1254, 1291, 1292, and 1294 of title 28, United Stated Code. No costs shall be assessed for or against the Commission in any proceeding under this chapter brought by or against it in the Supreme Court or such other courts.

Special Provision Relating to Statute of Limitations on Private Cause of Action

Section 27A. (a) *Effect on pending causes of action.* The limitation period for any private civil action implied under section 10(b) of this title that was commenced on or before June 19, 1991, shall be the limitation period provided by the laws applicable in the jurisdiction, including principles of retroactivity, as such laws existed on June 19, 1991.

(b) *Effect on dismissed causes of action.* Any private civil action implied under section 10(b) of this title that was commenced on or before June 19, 1991—

(1) which was dismissed as time barred subsequent to June 19, 1991, and

(2) which would have been timely filed under the limitation period provided by the laws applicable in the jurisdiction, including principles of retroactivity, as such laws existed on June 19, 1991,

shall be reinstated on motion by the plaintiff not later than 60 days after December 19, 1991.

Effect on Existing Law

Section 28. (a) *Addition of rights and remedies; recovery of actual damages; State securities commissions.* Except as provided in subsection (f), the rights and remedies provided by this chapter shall be in addition to any and all other rights and remedies that may exist at law or in equity; but no person permitted to maintain a suit for damages under the provisions of this chapter shall recover, through satisfaction of judgment in one or more actions, a total amount in excess of his actual damages on account of the act complained of. Except as otherwise specifically provided in this chapter, nothing in this chapter shall affect the jurisdiction of the securities commission (or any agency or officer performing like functions) of any State over any security or any person insofar as it does not conflict with the provisions of this chapter or the rules and regulations thereunder. No State law which prohibits or regulates the making or promoting of wagering or gaming contracts, or the operation of "bucket shops" or other similar or related activities, shall invalidate any put, call, straddle, option, privilege, or other security, or apply to any activity which is incidental or related to the offer, purchase, sale, exercise, settlement, or closeout of any such instrument, if such instrument is traded pursuant to rules and regulations of a self-regulatory organization that are filed with the Commission pursuant to section 78s(b) of this title.

(b) *Modification of disciplinary procedures.* Nothing in this chapter shall be construed to modify existing law with regard to the binding effect (1) on any member of or participant in any self-regulatory organization of any action taken by the authorities of such organization to settle disputes between its members or participants, (2) on any municipal securities dealer or municipal securities broker of any action taken pursuant to a procedure established by the Municipal Securities Rulemaking Board to settle disputes between municipal securities dealers and municipal securities brokers, or (3) of any action described in paragraph (1) or (2) on any person who has agreed to be bound thereby.

(c) *Continuing validity of disciplinary sanctions.* The stay, setting aside, or modification pursuant to section 19(e) of this title of any disciplinary sanction imposed by a self-regulatory organization on a member thereof, person associated with a member, or participant therein, shall not affect the validity or force of any action taken as a result of such sanction by the self-regulatory organization prior to such stay, setting aside, or modification: Provided, That such action is not inconsistent with the provisions of this chapter or the rules or regulations thereunder. The rights of any person acting in good faith which arise out of any such action shall not be affected in any way by such stay, setting aside, or modification.

(d) *Physical location of facilities of registered clearing agencies or registered transfer agents not to subject changes in beneficial or record ownership of securities to State or local taxes.* No State or political subdivision thereof shall impose any tax on any change in beneficial or record ownership of securities effected through the facilities of a registered clearing agency or registered transfer agent or any nominee thereof or custodian therefor or upon the delivery or transfer of securities to or through or receipt from such agency or agent or any nominee thereof or custodian therefor, unless such change in beneficial or record ownership or such transfer or delivery or receipt would otherwise be taxable by such State or political subdivision if the facilities of such registered clearing agency, registered transfer agent, or any nominee thereof or custodian therefor were not physically located in the taxing State or political subdivision. No State or political subdivision thereof shall impose any tax on securities which are deposited in or retained by a registered clearing agency, registered transfer agent, or any nominee thereof or custodian therefor, unless such securities would otherwise be taxable by such State or political subdivision if the facilities of such registered clearing agency, registered transfer agent, or any nominee thereof or custodian therefor were not physically located in the taxing State or political subdivision.

(e) *Exchanges broker and dealer commissions; brokerage and research services.* (1) No person using the mails, or any means or instrumentality of interstate commerce, in the exercise of investment discretion with respect to an account shall be deemed to have acted unlawfully or to have breached a fiduciary duty under State or Federal law unless expressly provided to the contrary by a law enacted by the Congress or any State subsequent to June 4, 1975 solely by reason of his having caused the account to pay a member of an exchange, broker, or dealer an amount of commission for effecting a securities transaction in excess of the amount of commission another member of an exchange, broker, or dealer would have charged for effecting that transaction, if such person determined in good faith that such amount of commission was reasonable in relation to the value of the brokerage and research services provided by such member, broker, or dealer, viewed in terms of either that particular transaction or his overall responsibilities with respect to the accounts as to which he exercises investment discretion. This subsection is exclusive and plenary insofar as conduct is covered by the foregoing, unless otherwise expressly provided by contract: Provided, however, That nothing in this subsection shall be construed to impair or limit the power of the Commission under any other provision of this chapter or otherwise.

(2) A person exercising investment discretion with respect to an account shall make such disclosure of his policies and practices with respect to commissions that will be paid for effecting securities transactions, at such times and in such manner, as the appropriate regulatory agency, by rule, may prescribe as necessary or appropriate in the public interest or for the protection of investors.

(3) For purposes of this subsection a person provides brokerage and research services insofar as he—

(A) furnishes advice, either directly or through publications or writings, as to the value of securities, the advisability of investing in, purchasing, or selling securities, and the availability of securities or purchasers or sellers of securities;

(B) furnishes analyses and reports concerning issuers, industries, securities, economic factors and trends, portfolio strategy, and the performance of accounts; or

(C) effects securities transactions and performs functions incidental thereto (such as clearance, settlement, and custody) or required in connection therewith by rules of the Commission or a self-regulatory organization of which such person is a member or person associated with a member or in which such person is a participant.

(f) *Limitations on remedies.*—

(1) CLASS ACTION LIMITATIONS.—No covered class action based upon the statutory or common law of any State or subdivision thereof may be maintained in any State or Federal court by any private party alleging—

(A) a misrepresentation or omission of a material fact in connection with the purchase or sale of a covered security; or

(B) that the defendant used or employed any manipulative or deceptive device or contrivance in connection with the purchase or sale of a covered security.

(2) REMOVAL OF COVERED CLASS ACTIONS.—Any covered class action brought in any State court involving a covered security, as set forth in paragraph (1), shall be removable to the Federal district court for the district in which the action is pending, and shall be subject to paragraph (1).

(3) PRESERVATION OF CERTAIN ACTIONS—

(A) ACTIONS UNDER STATE LAW OF STATE OF INCORPORATION.—

(i) ACTIONS PRESERVED.—Notwithstanding paragraph (1) or (2), a covered class action described in clause (ii) of this subparagraph that is based upon the statutory or common law of the State in which the issuer is incorporated (in the case of a corporation) or organized (in the case of any other entity) may be maintained in a State or Federal court by a private party.

(ii) PERMISSIBLE ACTIONS.—A covered class action is described in this clause if it involves—

(I) the purchase or sale of securities by the issuer or an affiliate of the issuer exclusively from or to holders of equity securities of the issuer; or

(II) any recommendation, position, or other communication with respect to the sale of securities of an issuer that—

(aa) is made by or on behalf of the issuer or an affiliate of the issuer to holders of equity securities of the issuer; and

(bb) concerns decisions of such equity holders with respect to voting their securities, acting in response to a tender or exchange offer, or exercising dissenters' or appraisal rights.

(B) STATE ACTIONS.—

(i) IN GENERAL.—Notwithstanding any other provision of this subsection, nothing in this subsection may be construed to preclude a State or political subdivision thereof or a State pension plan from bringing an action involving a covered security on its own behalf, or as a member of a class comprised solely of other States, political subdivisions, or State pension plans that are named plaintiffs, and that have authorized participation, in such action.

(ii) STATE PENSION PLAN DEFINED.—For purposes of this subparagraph, the term "State pension plan" means a pension plan established and maintained for its employees by the government of a State or political subdivision thereof, or by any agency or instrumentality thereof.

(C) ACTIONS UNDER CONTRACTUAL AGREEMENTS BETWEEN ISSUERS AND INDENTURE TRUSTEES.—Notwithstanding paragraph (1) or (2), a covered class action that seeks to enforce a contractual agreement between an issuer and an indenture trustee may be maintained in a State or Federal court by a party to the agreement or a successor to such party.

(D) REMAND OF REMOVED ACTIONS.—In an action that has been removed from a

State court pursuant to paragraph (2), if the Federal court determines that the action may be maintained in State court pursuant to this subsection, the Federal court shall remand such action to such State court.

(4) PRESERVATION OF STATE JURISDICTION.—The securities commission (or any agency or office performing like functions) of any State shall retain jurisdiction under the laws of such State to investigate and bring enforcement actions.

(5) DEFINITIONS.—For purposes of this subsection, the following definitions shall apply:

(A) AFFILIATE OF THE ISSUER.—The term "affiliate of the issuer" means a person that directly or indirectly, through one or more intermediaries, controls or is controlled by or is under common control with, the issuer.

(B) COVERED CLASS ACTION.—The term "covered class action" means—

(i) any single lawsuit in which—

(I) damages are sought on behalf of more than 50 persons or prospective class members, and questions of law or fact common to those persons or members of the prospective class, without reference to issues of individualized reliance on an alleged misstatement or omission, predominate over any questions affecting only individual persons or members; or

(II) one or more named parties seek to recover damages on a representative basis on behalf of themselves and other unnamed parties similarly situated, and questions of law or fact common to those persons or members of the prospective class predominate over any questions affecting only individual persons or members; or

(ii) any group of lawsuits filed in or pending in the same court and involving common questions of law or fact, in which—

(I) damages are sought on behalf of more than 50 persons; and

(II) the lawsuits are joined, consolidated, or otherwise proceed as a single action for any purpose.

(C) EXCEPTION FOR DERIVATIVE ACTIONS.—Notwithstanding subparagraph (B), the term 'covered class action' does not include an exclusively derivative action brought by one or more shareholders on behalf of a corporation.

(D) COUNTING OF CERTAIN CLASS MEMBERS.—For purposes of this paragraph, a corporation, investment company, pension plan, partnership, or other entity, shall be treated as one person or prospective class member, but only if the entity is not established for the purpose of participating in the action.

(E) COVERED SECURITY.—The term "covered security" means a security that satisfies the standards for a covered security specified in paragraph (1) or (2) of section 18(b) of this title, at the time during which it is alleged that the misrepresentation, omission, or manipulative or deceptive conduct occurred, except that such term shall not include any debt security that is exempt from registration under the Securities Act of 1933 pursuant to rules issued by the Commission under section 4(2) of that Act.

(F) RULE OF CONSTRUCTION.—Nothing in this paragraph shall be construed to affect the discretion of a State court in determining whether actions filed in such court should be joined, consolidated, or otherwise allowed to proceed as a single action.

Validity of Contracts

Section 29. (a) *Waiver provisions.* Any condition, stipulation, or provision binding any person to waive compliance with any provision of this chapter or of any rule or regulation thereunder, or of any rule of an exchange required thereby shall be void.

(b) *Contract provisions in violation of chapter.* Every contract made in violation of any provision of this chapter or of any rule or regulation thereunder, and every contract (including any contract for listing a security on an exchange) heretofore or hereafter made the performance of which involves the violation of, or the continuance of any relationship or practice in violation of, any provision of this title or any rule or regulation thereunder, shall be void (1) as regards the rights of any person who, in violation of any such provision, rule, or regulation, shall have made or engaged in the performance of any such contract, and (2) as regards the rights of any person who, not being a party to such contract, shall have acquired any right thereunder with actual knowledge of the facts by reason of which the making or performance of such contract was in violation of any such provision, rule, or regulation: *Provided,* (A) That no contract shall be void by reason of this subsection because of any violation of any rule or regulation prescribed pursuant to paragraph (3) of subsection (c) of section 15 of this title, and (B) that no contract shall be deemed to be void by reason of this subsection in any action maintained in reliance upon this subsection, by any person to or for whom any broker or dealer sells, or from or for whom any broker or dealer purchases, a security in violation of any rule or regulation prescribed pursuant to paragraph (1) or (2) of subsection (c) of section 15 of this title, unless such action is brought within one year after the discovery that such sale or purchase involves such violation and within three years after such violation. The Commission may, in a rule or regulation prescribed pursuant to such paragraph (2) of such section 78o(c) of this title, designate such rule or regulation, or portion thereof, as a rule or regulation, or portion thereof, a contract in violation of which shall not be void by reason of this subsection.

(c) *Validity of loans; extensions of credit, and creation of liens; actual knowledge of violation.* Nothing in this chapter shall be construed (1) to affect the validity of any loan or extension of credit (or any extension or renewal thereof) made or of any lien created prior or subsequent to the enactment of this chapter, unless at the time of the making of such loan or extension of credit (or extension or renewal thereof) or the creating of such lien, the person making such loan or extension of credit (or extension or renewal thereof) or acquiring such lien shall have actual knowledge of facts by reason of which the making of such loan or extension of credit (or extension or renewal thereof) or the acquisition of such lien is a violation of the provisions of this title or any rule or regulation thereunder, or (2) to afford a defense to the collection of any debt or obligation or the enforcement of any lien by any person who shall have acquired such debt, obligation, or lien in good faith for value and without actual knowledge of the violation of any provision of this title or any rule or regulation thereunder affecting the legality of such debt, obligation, or lien.

Prohibited Foreign Trade Practices by Issuers

Section 30A. (a) *Prohibition.* It shall be unlawful for any issuer which has a class of securities registered pursuant to section 12 of this title or which is required to file reports under section 15(d) of this title, or for any officer, director, employee, or agent of such issuer or any stockholder thereof acting on behalf of such issuer, to make use of the mails or any means or instrumentality of interstate commerce corruptly in furtherance of an offer, payment, promise to pay, or authorization of the payment of any money, or offer, gift, promise to give, or authorization of the giving of anything of value to—

(1) any foreign official for purposes of—

(A)(i) influencing any act or decision of such foreign official in his official capacity, or (ii) inducing such foreign official to do or omit to do any act in violation of the lawful duty of such official, or (iii) securing any improper advantage; or

(B) inducing such foreign official to use his influence with a foreign government or instrumentality thereof to affect or influence any act or decision of such government or instrumentality,

in order to assist such domestic concern in obtaining or retaining business for or with, or directing business to, any person;

(2) any foreign political party or official thereof or any candidate for foreign political office for purposes of—

(A)(i) influencing any act or decision of such party, official, or candidate in its or his official capacity, or (ii) inducing such party, official, or candidate to do or omit to do an act in violation of the lawful duty of such party, official, or candidate, (iii) securing any improper advantage; or

(B) inducing such party, official, or candidate to use its or his influence with a foreign government or instrumentality thereof to affect or influence any act or decision of such government or instrumentality, in order to assist such issuer in obtaining or retaining business for or with, or directing business to, any person; or

(3) any person, while knowing that all or a portion of such money or thing of value will be offered, given, or promised, directly or indirectly, to any foreign official, to any foreign political party or official thereof, or to any candidate for foreign political office, for purposes of—

(A)(i) influencing any act or decision of such foreign official, political party, party official, or candidate in his or its official capacity, or (ii) inducing such foreign official, political party, party official, or candidate to do or omit to do any act in violation of the lawful duty of such foreign official, political party, party official, or candidate, or (iii) securing any improper advantage; or

(B) inducing such foreign official, political party, party official, or candidate to use his or its influence with a foreign government or instrumentality thereof to affect or influence any act or decision of such government or instrumentality,

in order to assist such issuer in obtaining or retaining business for or with, or directing business to, any person.

(b) *Exception for routine governmental action.* Subsection (a) shall not apply to any facilitating or expediting payment to a foreign official, political party, or party official the purpose of which is to expedite or to secure the performance of a routine governmental action by a foreign official, political party, or party official.

(c) *Affirmative defenses.* It shall be an affirmative defense to actions under subsection (a) or (g) of this section that—

(1) the payment, gift, offer, or promise of anything of value that was made, was lawful under the written laws and regulations of the foreign official's, political party's, party official's, or candidate's country; or

(2) the payment, gift, offer, or promise of anything of value that was made, was a reasonable and bona fide expenditure, such as travel and lodging expenses, incurred by or on behalf of a foreign official, party, party official, or candidate and was directly related to—

(A) the promotion, demonstration, or explanation of products or services; or

(B) the execution or performance of a contract with a foreign government or agency thereof.

(d) *Guidelines by the Attorney General.* Not later than one year after August 23, 1988, the Attorney General, after consultation with the Commission, the Secretary of Commerce, the United States Trade Representative, the Secretary of State, and the Secretary of the Treasury, and after obtaining the views of all interested persons through public notice and comment procedures, shall determine to what extent compliance with this section would be enhanced and the business community would be assisted by further clarification of the preceding provisions of this section and may, based on such determination and to the extent necessary and appropriate, issue—

(1) guidelines describing specific types of conduct, associated with common types of export sales arrangements and business contracts, which for purposes of the Department of Justice's present enforcement policy, the Attorney General determines would be in conformance with the preceding provisions of this section; and

(2) general precautionary procedures which issuers may use on a voluntary basis to conform their conduct to the Department of Justice's present enforcement policy regarding the preceding provisions of this section.

The Attorney General shall issue the guidelines and procedures referred to in the preceding sentence in accordance with the provisions of subchapter II of chapter 5 of Title 5 and those guidelines and procedures shall be subject to the provisions of chapter 7 of that title.

(e) *Opinions of the Attorney General.* (1) The Attorney General, after consultation with appropriate departments and agencies of the United States and after obtaining the views of all interested persons through public notice and comment procedures, shall establish a procedure to provide responses to specific inquiries by issuers concerning conformance of their conduct with the Department of Justice's present enforcement policy regarding the preceding provisions of this section. The Attorney General shall, within 30 days after receiving such a request, issue an opinion in response to that request. The opinion shall state whether or not certain specified prospective conduct would, for purposes of the Department of Justice's present enforcement policy, violate the preceding provisions of this section. Additional requests for opinions may be filed with the Attorney General regarding other specified prospective conduct that is beyond the scope of conduct specified in previous requests. In any action brought under the applicable provisions of this section, there shall be a rebuttable presumption that conduct, which is specified in a request by an issuer and for which the Attorney General has issued an opinion that such conduct is in conformity with the Department of Justice's present enforcement policy, is in compliance with the preceding provisions of this section. Such a presumption may be rebutted by a preponderance of the evidence. In considering the presumption for purposes of this paragraph, a court shall weigh all relevant factors, including but not limited to whether the information submitted to the Attorney General was accurate and complete and whether it was within the scope of the conduct specified in any request received by the Attorney General. The Attorney General shall establish the procedures required by this paragraph in accordance with the provisions of subchapter II of chapter 5 of Title 5 and that procedure shall be subject to the provisions of chapter 7 of that title.

(2) Any document or other material which is provided to, received by, or prepared in the Department of Justice or any other department or agency of the United States in connection with a request by an issuer under the procedure established under paragraph (1), shall be exempt from disclosure under section 552 of title 5, United States Code, and shall not, except with the consent of the issuer, be made publicly available, regardless of whether the Attorney General responds to such a request or the issuer withdraws such request before receiving a response.

(3) Any issuer who has made a request to the Attorney General under paragraph (1) may withdraw such request prior to the time the Attorney General issues an opinion in response to such request. Any request so withdrawn shall have no force or effect.

(4) The Attorney General shall, to the maximum extent practicable, provide timely guidance concerning the Department of Justice's present enforcement policy with respect to the preceding provisions of this section to potential exporters and small businesses that are unable to obtain specialized counsel on issuers that are unable to obtain specialized counsel on issues pertaining to such provisions. Such guidance shall be limited to responses to requests under paragraph (1) concerning conformity of specified prospective conduct with the Department of Justice's present enforcement policy regarding the preceding provisions of this section and general explanations of compliance responsibilities and of potential liabilities under the preceding provisions of this section.

(f) *Definitions.* For purposes of this section:

(1) (A) The term "foreign official" means any officer or employee of a foreign government or any department, agency, or instrumentality thereof, or any person acting in an official capacity for or on behalf of any such government or department, agency, or instrumentality or for or on behalf of any such public international organization.

(B) For purposes of subparagraph (A), the term "public international organization" means—

(i) an organization that is designated by Executive order pursuant to section 1 of the International Organizations Immunities Act *(22 U.S.C. 288)*; or

(ii) any other international organization that is designated by the President by Executive order for the purposes of this section, effective as of the date of publication of such order in the Federal Register.

(2)(A) A person's state of mind is "knowing" with respect to conduct, a circumstance, or a result if—

(i) such person is aware that such person is engaging in such conduct, that such circumstance exists, or that such result is substantially certain to occur; or

(ii) such person has a firm belief that such circumstance exists or that such result is substantially certain to occur.

(B) When knowledge of the existence of a particular circumstance is required for an offense, such knowledge is established if a person is aware of a high probability of the existence of such circumstance, unless the person actually believes that such circumstance does not exist.

(3)(A) The term "routine governmental action" means only an action which is ordinarily and commonly performed by a foreign official in—

(i) obtaining permits, licenses, or other official documents to qualify a person to do business in a foreign country;

(ii) processing governmental papers, such as visas and work orders;

(iii) providing police protection, mail pick-up and delivery, or scheduling inspections associated with contract performance or inspections related to transit of goods across country;

(iv) providing phone service, power and water supply, loading and unloading cargo, or protecting perishable products or commodities from deterioration; or

(v) actions of a similar nature.

(B) The term "routine governmental action" does not include any decision by a foreign official whether, or on what terms, to award new business to or to continue business with a particular party, or any action taken by a foreign official involved in the decisionmaking process to encourage a decision to award new business to or continue business with a particular party.

(g) *Alternative jurisdiction.*

(1) It shall also be unlawful for any issuer organized under the laws of the United States, or a State, territory, possession, or commonwealth of the United States or a political subdivision thereof and which has a class of securities registered pursuant to section 78l of this title or which is required to file reports under section 78o(d) of this title, or for any United States person that is an officer, director, employee, or agent of such issuer or a stockholder thereof acting on behalf of such issuer, to corruptly do any act outside the United States in furtherance of an offer, payment, promise to pay, or authorization of the payment of any money, or offer, gift, promise to give, or authorization of the giving of anything of value to any of the persons or entities set forth in paragraphs (1), (2), and (3) of subsection (a) of this section for the purposes set forth therein, irrespective of whether such issuer or such officer, director, employee, agent, or stockholder makes use of the mails or any means or instrumentality of interstate commerce in furtherance of such offer, gift, payment, promise, or authorization.

(2) As used in this subsection, the term "United States person" means a national of the United States (as defined in section 101 of the Immigration and Nationality Act (*8 U.S.C. 1101*)) or any corporation, partnership, association, joint-stock company, business trust, unincorporated organization, or sole proprietorship organized under the laws of the United States or any State, territory, possession, or commonwealth of the United States, or any political subdivision thereof.

Penalties

Section 32. (a) *Willful violations; false and misleading statements.* Any person who willfully violates any provision of this chapter (other than section 30A of this title), or any rule or regulation thereunder the violation of which is made unlawful or the observance of which is required under the terms of this title, or any person who willfully and knowingly makes, or causes to be made, any statement in any application, report, or document required to be filed under this title or any rule or regulation thereunder or any undertaking contained in a registration statement as provided in subsection (d) of section 15 of this title or by any self-regulatory organization in connection with an application for membership or participation therein or to become associated with a member thereof, which statement was false or misleading with respect to any material fact, shall upon conviction be fined not more than $5,000,000 or imprisoned not more than 20 years, or both, except that when such person is a person other than a natural person, a fine not exceeding $25,000,000 may be imposed; but no person shall be subject to imprisonment under this section for the violation of any rule or regulation if he proves that he had no knowledge of such rule or regulation.

(b) *Failure to file information, documents, or reports.* Any issuer which fails to file information, documents, or reports required to be filed under subsection (d) of section 15 of this title or any rule or regulation thereunder shall forfeit to the United States the sum of $100 for each and every day such failure to file shall continue. Such forfeiture, which shall be in lieu of any criminal penalty for such failure to file which might be deemed to arise under subsection (a) of this section, shall be payable into the Treasury of the United States and shall be recoverable in a civil suit in the name of the United States.

(c) *Violations by issuers, officers, directors, stockholders, employees, or agents of issuers.* (1)(A) Any issuer that violates section 30A(a) or (g) of this title shall be fined not more than $2,000,000.

(B) Any issuer that violates section 30A(a) or (g) of this title shall be subject to a civil penalty of not more than $10,000 imposed in an action brought by the Commission.

(A) Any officer, director, employee, or agent of an issuer, or stockholder acting on behalf of such issuer, who willfully violates subsection (a) or (g) of section 78dd–1 of this title shall be fined not more than $100,000, or imprisoned not more than 5 years, or both.

(B) Any officer, director, employee, or agent of an issuer, or stockholder acting on behalf of such issuer, who violates subsection (a) or (g) of section 78dd–1 of this title shall be subject to a civil penalty of not more than $10,000 imposed in an action brought by the Commission.

(3) Whenever a fine is imposed under paragraph (2) upon any officer, director, employee, agent, or stockholder of an issuer, such fine may not be paid, directly or indirectly, by such issuer.

FOREIGN CORRUPT PRACTICES ACT AMENDMENTS OF 1988

Prohibited Foreign Trade Practices by Domestic Concerns

Section 104. (a) *Prohibition.* It shall be unlawful for any domestic concern, other than an issuer which is subject to section 30A of the Securities Exchange Act of 1934, or for any officer, director, employee, or agent of such domestic concern or any stockholder thereof acting on behalf of such domestic concern, to make use of the mails or any means or instrumentality of interstate commerce corruptly in furtherance of an offer, payment, promise to pay, or authorization of the payment of any money, or offer, gift, promise to give, or authorization of the giving of anything of value to—

(1) any foreign official for purposes of—

(A)(i) influencing any act or decision of such foreign official in his official capacity, or (ii) inducing such foreign official to do or omit to do any act in violation of the lawful duty of such official, or (iii) securing any improper advantage; or

(B) inducing such foreign official to use his influence with a foreign government or instrumentality thereof to affect or influence any act or decision of such government or instrumentality,

in order to assist such domestic concern in obtaining or retaining business for or with, or directing business to, any person;

(2) any foreign political party or official thereof or any candidate for foreign political office for purposes of—

(A)(i) influencing any act or decision of such party, official, or candidate in its or his official capacity, or (ii) inducing such party, official, or candidate to do or omit to do an act in violation of the lawful duty of such party, official, or candidate, or (iii) securing any improper advantage; or

(B) inducing such party, official, or candidate to use its or his influence with a foreign government or instrumentality thereof to affect or influence any act or decision of such government or instrumentality,

in order to assist such domestic concern in obtaining or retaining business for or with, or directing business to, any person; or

(3) any person, while knowing that all or a portion of such money or thing of value will be offered, given, or promised, directly or indirectly, to any foreign official, to any foreign political party or official thereof, or to any candidate for foreign political office, for purposes of—

(A)(i) influencing any act or decision of such foreign official, political party, party official, or candidate in his or its official capacity, or (ii) inducing such foreign official, political party, party official, or candidate to do or omit to do any act in violation of the lawful duty of such foreign official, political party, party official, or candidate, or (iii) securing any improper advantage; or

(B) inducing such foreign official, political party, party official, or candidate to use his or its influence with a foreign government or instrumentality thereof to affect or influence any act or decision of such government or instrumentality,

in order to assist such domestic concern in obtaining or retaining business for or with, or directing business to, any person.

(b) *Exception for routine governmental action.* Subsections (a) and (i) of this section shall not apply to any facilitating or expediting payment to a foreign official, political party, or party official the purpose of which is to expedite or to secure the performance of a routine governmental action by a foreign official, political party, or party official.

(c) *Affirmative defenses.* It shall be an affirmative defense to actions under subsection (a) or (i) of this section that—

(1) the payment, gift, offer, or promise of anything of value that was made, was lawful under the written laws and regulations of the foreign official's, political party's, party official's, or candidate's country; or

(2) the payment, gift, offer, or promise of anything of value that was made, was a reasonable and bona fide expenditure, such as travel and lodging expenses, incurred by or on behalf of a foreign official, party, party official, or candidate and was directly related to—

(A) the promotion, demonstration, or explanation of products or services; or

(B) the execution or performance of a contract with a foreign government or agency thereof.

(d) *Injunctive relief.* (1) When it appears to the Attorney General that any domestic concern to which this section applies, or officer, director, employee, agent, or stockholder thereof, is engaged, or about to engage, in any act or practice constituting a violation of subsection (a) or (i) of this section, the Attorney General may, in his discretion, bring a civil action in an appropriate district court of the United States to enjoin such act or practice, and upon a proper showing, a permanent injunction or a temporary restraining order shall be granted without bond.

(2) For the purpose of any civil investigation which, in the opinion of the Attorney General, is necessary and proper to enforce this section, the Attorney General or his designee are empowered to administer oaths and affirmations, subpoena witnesses, take evidence, and require the production of any books, papers, or other documents which the Attorney General deems relevant or material to such investigation. The attendance of witnesses and the production of documentary evidence may be required from any place in the United States, or any territory, possession, or commonwealth of the United States, at any designated place of hearing.

(3) In case of contumacy by, or refusal to obey a subpoena issued to, any person, the Attorney General may invoke the aid of any court of the United States within the jurisdiction of which such investigation or proceeding is carried on, or where such person resides or carries on business, in requiring the attendance and testimony of witnesses and the production of books, papers, or other documents. Any such court may issue an order requiring such person to appear before the Attorney General or his designee, there to produce records, if so ordered, or to give testimony touching the matter under investigation. Any failure to obey such order of the court may be punished by such court as a contempt thereof. All process in any such case may be served in the judicial district in which such person resides or may be found. The Attorney General may make such rules relating to civil investigations as may be necessary or appropriate to implement the provisions of this subsection.

(e) *Guidelines by the Attorney General.* Not later than 6 months after August 23, 1988, the Attorney General, after consultation with the Securities and Exchange Commission, the Secretary of Commerce, the United States Trade Representative, the Secretary of State, and the Secretary of the Treasury, and after obtaining the views of all interested persons through public notice and comment procedures, shall determine to what extent compliance with this section would be enhanced and the business community would be assisted by further clarification of the preceding provisions of this section and may, based on such determination and to the extent necessary and appropriate, issue—

(1) guidelines describing specific types of conduct, associated with common types of export sales arrangements and business contracts, which for purposes of the Department of Justice's present enforcement policy, the Attorney General de-

termines would be in conformance with the preceding provisions of this section; and

(2) general precautionary procedures which domestic concerns may use on a voluntary basis to conform their conduct to the Department of Justice's present enforcement policy regarding the preceding provisions of this section.

The Attorney General shall issue the guidelines and procedures referred to in the preceding sentence in accordance with the provisions of subchapter II of chapter 5 of Title 5 and those guidelines and procedures shall be subject to the provisions of chapter 7 of that title.

(f) *Opinions of the Attorney General.* (1) The Attorney General, after consultation with appropriate departments and agencies of the United States and after obtaining the views of all interested persons through public notice and comment procedures, shall establish a procedure to provide responses to specific inquiries by domestic concerns concerning conformance of their conduct with the Department of Justice's present enforcement policy regarding the preceding provisions of this section. The Attorney General shall, within 30 days after receiving such a request, issue an opinion in response to that request. The opinion shall state whether or not certain specified prospective conduct would, for purposes of the Department of Justice's present enforcement policy, violate the preceding provisions of this section. Additional requests for opinions may be filed with the Attorney General regarding other specified prospective conduct that is beyond the scope of conduct specified in previous requests. In any action brought under the applicable provisions of this section, there shall be a rebuttable presumption that conduct, which is specified in a request by a domestic concern and for which the Attorney General has issued an opinion that such conduct is in conformity with the Department of Justice's present enforcement policy, is in compliance with the preceding provisions of this section. Such a presumption may be rebutted by a preponderance of the evidence. In considering the presumption for purposes of this paragraph, a court shall weigh all relevant factors, including but not limited to whether the information submitted to the Attorney General was accurate and complete and whether it was within the scope of the conduct specified in any request received by the Attorney General. The Attorney General shall establish the procedure required by this paragraph in accordance with the provisions of subchapter II of chapter 5 of title 5 and that procedure shall be subject to the provisions of chapter 7 of that title.

(2) Any document or other material which is provided to, received by, or prepared in the Department of Justice or any other department or agency of the United States in connection with a request by a domestic concern under the procedure established under paragraph (1), shall be exempt from disclosure under section 552 of title 5, United States Code, and shall not, except with the consent of the domestic concern, be made publicly available, regardless of whether the Attorney General responds to such a request or the domestic concern withdraws such request before receiving a response.

(3) Any domestic concern who has made a request to the Attorney General under paragraph (1) may withdraw such request prior to the time the Attorney General issues an opinion in response to such request. Any request so withdrawn shall have no force or effect.

(4) The Attorney General shall, to the maximum extent practicable, provide timely guidance concerning the Department of Justice's present enforcement policy with respect to the preceding provisions of this section to potential exporters and small businesses that are unable to obtain specialized counsel on issues pertaining to such provisions. Such guidance shall be limited to responses to requests under paragraph (1) concerning conformity of specified prospective conduct with the Department of Justice's present enforcement policy regarding the preceding provisions of this section and general explanations of compliance responsibilities and of potential liabilities under the preceding provisions of this section.

(g) *Penalties.* (1)(A) Any domestic concern that violates subsection (a) or (i) or this section shall be fined not more than $2,000,000.

(B) Any domestic concern that violates subsection (a) or (i) of this section shall be subject to a civil penalty of not more than $10,000 imposed in an action brought by the Attorney General.

(A) Any natural person that is an officer, director, employee, or agent of a domestic concern, or stockholder acting on behalf of such domestic concern, who willfully violates subsection (a) or (i) of this section shall be fined not more than $100,000 or imprisoned not more than 5 years, or both.

(B) Any natural person that is an officer, director, employee, or agent of a domestic concern, or stockholder acting on behalf of such domestic concern, who violates subsection (a) or (i) of this section shall be subject to a civil penalty of not more than $10,000 imposed in an action brought by the Attorney General.

(3) Whenever a fine is imposed under paragraph (2) upon any officer, director, employee, agent, or stockholder of a domestic concern, such fine may not be paid, directly or indirectly, by such domestic concern.

(h) *Definitions.* For purposes of this section:

(1) The term "domestic concern" means—

(A) any individual who is a citizen, national, or resident of the United States; and

(B) any corporation, partnership, association, joint-stock company, business trust, unincorporated organization, or sole proprietorship which has its principal place of business in the United States, or which is organized under the laws of a State of the United States or a territory, possession, or commonwealth of the United States.

(2)(A) The term "foreign official" means any officer or employee of a foreign government or any department, agency, or instrumentality thereof, or any person acting in an official capacity for or on behalf of any such government or department, agency, or instrumentality or for or on behalf of any such public international organization.

(B) For purposes of subparagraph (A), the term "public international organization" means—

(i) an organization that is designated by Executive order pursuant to section 1 of the International Organizations Immunities Act (*22 U.S.C. 288*); or

(ii) any other international organization that is designated by the President by Executive order for the purposes of this section, effective as of the date of publication of such order in the Federal Register.

(3)(A) A person's state of mind is "knowing" with respect to conduct, a circumstance, or a result if—

(i) such person is aware that such person is engaging in such conduct, that such circumstance exists, or that such result is substantially certain to occur; or

(ii) such person has a firm belief that such circumstance exists or that such result is substantially certain to occur.

(B) When knowledge of the existence of a particular circumstance is required for an offense, such knowledge is established if a person is aware of a high probability of the existence of such circumstance, unless the person actually believes that such circumstance does not exist.

(4)(A) The term "routine governmental action" means only an action which is ordinarily and commonly performed by a foreign official in—

(i) obtaining permits, licenses, or other official documents to qualify a person to do business in a foreign country;

(ii) processing governmental papers, such as visas and work orders;

(iii) providing police protection, mail pick-up and delivery, or scheduling inspections associated with contract performance or inspections related to transit of goods across country;

(iv) providing phone service, power and water supply, loading and unloading cargo, or protecting perishable products or commodities from deterioration; or

(v) actions of a similar nature.

(B) The term "routine governmental action" does not include any decision by a foreign official whether, or on what terms, to award new business to or to continue business with a particular party, or any action taken by a foreign official involved in the decision-making process to encourage a decision to award new business to or continue business with a particular party.

(5) The term "interstate commerce" means trade, commerce, transportation, or communication among the several States, or between any foreign country and any State or between any State and any place or ship outside thereof, and such term includes the intrastate use of—

(A) a telephone or other interstate means of communication, or

(B) any other interstate instrumentality.

(i) Alternative jurisdiction

(1) It shall also be unlawful for any United States person to corruptly do any act outside the United States in furtherance of an offer, payment, promise to pay, or authorization of the payment of any money, or offer, gift, promise to give, or authorization of the giving of anything of value to any of the persons or entities set forth in paragraphs (1), (2), and (3) of subsection (a), for the purposes set forth therein, irrespective of whether such United States person makes use of the mails or any means or instrumentality of interstate commerce in furtherance of such offer, gift, payment, promise, or authorization.

(2) As used in this subsection, the term "United States person" means a national of the United States (as defined in section 101 of the Immigration and Nationality Act (*8 U.S.C. 1101*)) or any corporation, partnership, association, joint-stock company, business trust, unincorporated organization, or sole proprietorship organized under the laws of the United States or any State, territory, possession, or commonwealth of the United States, or any political subdivision thereof.

C. RULES UNDER SECURITIES ACT OF 1933

(Selected)

Contents

GENERAL

GENERAL

Rule 134. Communications Not Deemed a Prospectus

The term "prospectus" as defined in Section 2(10) of the Act shall not include a notice, circular, advertisement, letter, or other communication published or transmitted to any person after a registration statement has been filed if it contains only the statements required or permitted to be included therein by the following provisions of this section:

(a) Such communication may include any one or more of the following items of information, which need not follow the numerical sequence of this paragraph:

(1) the name of the issuer of the security;

(2) the full title of the security and the amount being offered;

(3) a brief indication of the general type of business of the issuer, limited to the following:

(i) in the case of a manufacturing company, the general type of manufacturing and the principal products or classes of products manufactured;

(ii) in the case of a public utility company, the general type of services rendered and a brief indication of the area served;

* * *

(iv) in the case of any other type of company, a corresponding statement;

(4) the price of the security, or if the price is not known, the method of its determination or the probable price range as specified by the issuer or the managing underwriter;

(5) in the case of a debt security with a fixed (non-contingent) interest provision, the yield or, if the yield is not known, the probable yield range, as specified by the issuer or the managing underwriter;

(6) the name and address of the sender of the communication and the fact that he is participating, or expects to participate, in the distribution of the security;

(7) the names of the managing underwriters;

(8) the approximate date upon which it is anticipated the proposed sale to the public will commence;

(9) whether, in the opinion of counsel, the security is a legal investment for savings banks, fiduciaries, insurance companies, or similar investors under the laws of any State or Territory or the District of Columbia;

(10) whether, in the opinion of counsel, the security is exempt from specified taxes, or the extent to which the issuer has agreed to pay any tax with respect to the security or measured by the income therefrom;

(11) whether the security is being offered through rights issued to security holders, and, if so, the class of securities the holders of which will be entitled to subscribe, the subscription ratio, the actual or proposed record date, the date upon which the rights were issued or are expected to be issued, the actual or anticipated date upon which they will expire, and the approximate subscription price, or any of the foregoing;

(12) any statement or legend required by any state law or administrative authority.

* * *

(14)(i) With respect to any class of debt securities, any class of convertible debt securities or any class of preferred stock, the security rating or ratings assigned to the class of securities by any nationally recognized statistical rating organization and the name or names of the nationally recognized statistical rating organization(s) which assigned such rating(s).

(ii) For the purpose of paragraph 14(a)(i) of this section, the term "nationally recognized statistical rating organization" shall have the same meaning as used in Rule 15c3–1(c)(2)(vi)(F) under the Securities Exchange Act of 1934.

* * *

(b) Except as provided in paragraph (c) of this section every communication used pursuant to this section shall contain the following:

(1) if the registration statement has not yet become effective, the following statement:

"A registration statement relating to these securities has been filed with the Securities and Exchange Commission but has not yet become effective. These securities may not be sold nor may offers to buy be accepted prior to the time the registration statement becomes effective. This (communication) shall not constitute an offer to sell or the solicitation of an offer to buy nor shall there be any sale of these securities in any State in which such offer, solicitation or sale would be unlawful prior to registration or qualification under the securities laws of any such State."

(2) a statement whether the security is being offered in connection with a distribution by the issuer or by a security holder, or both, and whether the issue represents new financing or refunding or both; and

(3) the name and address of a person or persons from whom a written prospectus meeting the requirements of Section 10 of the Act may be obtained.

(c) Any of the statements or information specified in paragraph (b) may, but need not, be contained in a communication: (i) which does no more than state from whom a written prospectus meeting the requirements of Section 10 of the Act may be obtained, identify the security, state the price thereof and state by whom orders will be executed; or (ii) which is accompanied or preceded by a prospectus or a summary prospectus which meets the requirements of Section 10 of the Act at the date of such preliminary communication.

(d) A communication sent or delivered to any person pursuant to this rule which is accompanied or preceded by a prospectus which meets the requirements of Section 10 of the Act at the date of such communication, may solicit from the recipient of the communication an offer to buy the security or request the recipient to indicate, upon an enclosed or attached coupon or card, or in some other manner, whether he might be interested in the security, if the communication contains substantially the following statement:

"No offer to buy the securities can be accepted and no part of the purchase price can be received until the registration statement has become effective, and any such offer may be withdrawn or revoked, without obligation or commitment of any kind, at any time prior to notice of its acceptance given after the effective date. An indication of interest in response to this advertisement will involve no obligation or commitment of any kind."

Provided, that such statement need not be included in such a communication to a dealer if the communication refers to a prior communication to the dealer, with respect to the same security, in which the statement was included.

(e) In the case of an investment company registered under the Investment Company Act of 1940 that holds itself out as a "money market fund," a communication used under this section shall contain the disclosure required by section 230.482(a)(7).

Rule 135. Notice of Proposed Registered Offerings

(a) When notice is not an offer. For purposes of section 5 of the Act only, an issuer or a selling security holder (and any person acting on behalf of either of them) that publishes through any medium a notice of a proposed offering to be registered under the Act will not be deemed to offer its securities for sale through that notice if:

(1) Legend. The notice includes a statement to the effect that it does not constitute an offer of any securities for sale; and

(2) Limited notice content. The notice otherwise includes no more than the following information:

(i) The name of the issuer;

(ii) The title, amount and basic terms of the securities offered;

(iii) The amount of the offering, if any, to be made by selling security holders;

(iv) The anticipated timing of the offering;

(v) A brief statement of the manner and the purpose of the offering, without naming the underwriters;

(vi) Whether the issuer is directing its offering to only a particular class of purchasers;

(vii) Any statements or legends required by the laws of any state or foreign country or administrative authority; and

(viii) In the following offerings, the notice may contain additional information, as follows:

(A) Rights offering. In a rights offering to existing security holders:

(1) The class of security holders eligible to subscribe;

(2) The subscription ratio and expected subscription price;

(3) The proposed record date;

(4) The anticipated issuance date of the rights; and

(5) The subscription period or expiration date of the rights offering.

(B) Offering to employees. In an offering to employees of the issuer or an affiliated company:

(1) The name of the employer;

(2) The class of employees being offered the securities;

(3) The offering price; and

(4) The duration of the offering period.

(C) Exchange offer. In an exchange offer:

(1) The basic terms of the exchange offer;

(2) The name of the subject company;

(3) The subject class of securities sought in the exchange offer.

(D) Rule 145(a) offering. In a Rule 145(a) offering:

(1) The name of the person whose assets are to be sold in exchange for the securities to be offered;

(2) The names of any other parties to the transaction;

(3) A brief description of the business of the parties to the transaction;

(4) The date, time and place of the meeting of security holders to vote on or consent to the transaction; and

(5) A brief description of the transaction and the basic terms of the transaction.

(b) Corrections of misstatements about the offering. A person that publishes a notice in reliance on this section may issue a notice that contains no more information than is necessary to correct inaccuracies published about the proposed offering.

Note to Rule 135: Communications under this section relating to business combination transactions must be filed as required by Rule 425(b).

* * *

Rule 137. Definition of "Offers", "Participates", or "Participation" in Section 2(11) in Relation to Certain Publications by Persons Independent of Participants in a Distribution

The terms "offers", "participates", or "participation" in Section 2(11) shall not be deemed to apply to the publication or distribution of information, opinions or recommendations with respect to the securities of a registrant which is required to file reports pursuant to Section 13 or 15(d) of the Securities Exchange Act of 1934 and has filed or proposes to file a registration statement under the Securities Act of 1933 if—

(a) such information, opinions and recommendations are published and distributed in the regular course of its business by a dealer which is not and does not propose to be a participant in the distribution of the security to which the registration statement relates; and

(b) such dealer receives no consideration, directly or indirectly, in connection with the publication and distribution of such information, opinions or recommendations from the registrant, a selling security holder or any participant in the distribution or any other person interested in the securities to which the registration statement relates, and such information, opinions or recommendations are not published or distributed pursuant to any arrangement or understanding, direct or indirect, with such issuer, underwriter, dealer or selling security holder; provided, however, that nothing herein shall forbid payment of the regular subscription or purchase price of the document or other written communication in which such information, opinions or recommendations appear.

Rule 138. Definition of "Offer for Sale" and "Offer to Sell" in Sections 2(10) and 5(c) in Relation to Certain Publications

(a) Where a registrant which meets the requirements of paragraph (c)(1), (c)(2) or (c)(3) of this section proposes to file, has filed or has an effective registration statement under the Act relating solely to a nonconvertible debt security or to a nonconvertible, nonparticipating preferred stock, publication or distribution in the regular course of its business by a broker or dealer of information, opinions or recommendations relating solely to common stock or to debt or preferred stock convertible into common stock of such issuer shall not be deemed to constitute an offer for sale or offer to sell the security to which such registration statement relates for purposes of sections 2(10) and 5(c) of the Act, even though such broker or dealer is or will be a participant in the distribution of the security to which such registration statement relates.

(b) Where a registrant which meets the requirements of paragraph (c)(1), (c)(2) or (c)(3) of this section proposes to file, has filed or has an effective registration statement under the Act relating solely to common stock or to debt or preferred stock convertible into common stock, the publication or distribution in the regular course of its business by a broker or dealer of information, opinions or recommendations relating solely to a nonconvertible debt security, or to a nonconvertible nonparticipating preferred stock shall not be deemed to constitute an offer for sale or offer to sell the security to which such registration statement relates for purposes of sections 2(10) and 5(c) of the Act, even though such broker or dealer is or will be a participant in the distribution of the security to which such registration statement relates.

(c)(1) The registrant meets all of the conditions for the use of Form S–2 or Form F–2;

(2) The registrant meets the registrant requirements of Form S–3 or Form F–3; or

(3) The registrant is a foreign private issuer which meets all the registrant requirements of Form F–3, other than the reporting history provisions of paragraph A.1. and A.2.(a) of General Instruction I of such form, and meets the minimum float or investment grade securities provisions of either paragraph B.1. or B.2. of General Instruction I. of such form and the registrant's securities have been traded for a period of at least 12 months on a designated offshore securities market, as defined in Rule 902(a).

Instruction to Rule 138.

When a registration statement relates to securities which are being registered for an offering to be made on a continuous or delayed basis pursuant to Rule 415(a)(1)(x) under the Act and the securities which are being registered include classes of securities which are specified in both paragraphs (a) and (b) of this section on either an allocated or unallocated basis, a broker or dealer may nonetheless rely on:

1. Paragraph (a) of this section when the offering in which such broker or dealer is or will be a participant relates solely to classes of securities specified in paragraph (a) of this section, and

2. Paragraph (b) of this section when the offering in which such broker or dealer is or will be a participant relates solely to classes of securities specified in paragraph (b) of this section.

Rule 139. Definition of "Offer for Sale" and "Offer to Sell" in Sections 2(10) and 5(c) in Relation to Certain Publications

Where a registrant which is required to file reports pursuant to section 13 or 15(d) of the Securities Exchange Act of 1934 or which is a foreign private issuer meeting the conditions of paragraph (a)(2) of this section proposes to file, has filed or has an effective registration statement under the Securities Act of 1933 relating to its securities, the publication or distribution by a broker or dealer of information, an opinion or a recommendation with respect to the registrant or any class of its securities shall not be deemed to constitute an offer for sale or offer to sell the securities registered or proposed to be registered for purposes of sections 2(10) and 5(c) of the Act, even though such broker or dealer is or will be a participant in the distribution of such securities, if the conditions of paragraph (a) or (b) have been met:

(a)(1) The registrant meets the registrant requirements of Form S–3 or Form F–3 and the minimum float or investment grade securities provisions of either paragraph (B)(1) or (2) of General Instruction I of the respective form and such information, opinion or recommendation is contained in a publication which is distributed with reasonable regularity in the normal course of business; or

(2) The registrant is a foreign private issuer that meets all the registrant requirements of Form F–3 (s 239.33 of this chapter), other than the reporting history provisions of paragraphs A.1. and A.2.(a) of General Instruction I of such form, and meets the minimum float or investment grade securities provisions of either paragraph B.1. or B.2. of General Instruction I of such form, and the registrant's securities have been traded for a period of at least 12 months on a designated offshore securities market, as defined in s 230.902(a), and such information, opinion or recommendation is contained in a publication which is distributed with reasonable regularity in the normal course of business.

(b)(1) Such information, opinion or recommendation is contained in a publication which:

(i) Is distributed with reasonable regularity in the normal course of business and

(ii) Includes similar information, opinions or recommendations with respect to a substantial number of companies in the registrant's industry or sub-industry, or contains a comprehensive list of securities currently recommended by such broker or dealer;

(2) Such information, opinion or recommendation is given no materially greater space or prominence in such publication than that given to other securities or registrants; and

(3) An opinion or recommendation as favorable or more favorable as to the registrant or any class of its securities was published by the broker or dealer in the last publication of such broker or

dealer addressing the registrant or its securities prior to the commencement of participation in the distribution.

Instructions to Rule 139.

1. For purposes of paragraph (a), a research report has not been distributed with "reasonable regularity" if it contains information, an opinion, or a recommendation concerning a company with respect to which a broker or dealer currently is not publishing research.

2. Where projections of a registrant's sales or earnings are included, the publication must comply with the following in order to meet paragraphs (b)(1) and (b)(3).

A. The projections must have been published previously on a regular basis in order for the publication to meet paragraph (b)(1)(i);

B. The projections must be included with respect to either a substantial number of companies in the registrant's industry or sub-industry or all companies in a comprehensive list which is contained in the publication, and must cover the same periods with respect to such companies as with respect to the registrant, in order to meet the requirements of paragraph (b)(1)(ii); and

C. Because projections constitute opinions within the meaning of the Rule, they must come within paragraph (b)(3).

* * *

Rule 144. Persons Deemed Not to Be Engaged in a Distribution and Therefore Not Underwriters

Preliminary Note to Rule 144

Rule 144 is designed to implement the fundamental purposes of the Act, as expressed in its preamble, "To provide full and fair disclosure of the character of the securities sold in interstate commerce and through the mails, and to prevent fraud in the sale thereof ... " The rule is designed to prohibit the creation of public markets in securities of issuers concerning which adequate current information is not available to the public. At the same time, where adequate current information concerning the issuer is available to the public, the rule permits the public sale in ordinary trading transactions of limited amounts of securities owned by persons controlling, controlled by or under common control with the issuer and by persons who have acquired restricted securities of the issuer.

Certain basic principles are essential to an understanding of the requirement of registration in the Act:

1. If any person utilizes the jurisdictional means to sell any non-exempt security to any other person, the security must be registered unless a statutory exemption can be found for the transaction.

2. In addition to the exemptions found in Section 3, four exemptions applicable to transactions in securities are contained in Section 4. Three of these Section 4 exemptions are clearly not available to anyone acting as an "underwriter" of securities. (The fourth, found in Section 4(4), is available only to those who act as brokers under certain limited circumstances.) An understanding of the term "underwriter" is therefore important to anyone who wishes to determine whether or not an exemption from registration is available for his sale of securities.

The term underwriter is broadly defined in Section 2(11) of the Act to mean any person who has purchased from an issuer with a view to, or offers or sells for an issuer in connection with, the distribution of any security, or participates or has a direct or indirect participation in any such undertaking, or participates or has a participation in the direct or indirect underwriting of any such undertaking. The interpretation of this definition has traditionally focused on the words "with a view to" in the phrase "purchased from an issuer with a view to ... distribution." Thus, an investment banking firm which arranges with an issuer for the public sale of its securities is clearly an "underwriter" under that Section. Individual investors who are not professionals in the securities business may also be "underwriters" within the meaning of that term as used in the Act if they act as links in a chain of transactions through which securities move from an issuer to the public. Since it is difficult to ascertain the mental state of the purchaser at the time of his acquisition, subsequent acts and circumstances have been considered to determine whether such person took with a view to distribution at the time of his acquisition. Emphasis has been placed on factors such as the length of time the person has held the securities and whether there has been an unforeseeable change in circumstances of the holder. Experience has shown, however, that reliance upon such factors as the above has not assured adequate protection of investors through the maintenance of informed trading markets and has led to uncertainty in the application of the registration provisions of the Act.

It should be noted that the statutory language of Section 2(11) is in the disjunctive. Thus, it is insufficient to conclude that a person is not an underwriter solely because he did not purchase securities from an issuer with a view to their distribution. It must also be established that the person is not offering or selling for an issuer in connection with the distribution of the securities, does not participate or have a direct or indirect participation in any such undertaking, and does not participate or have a participation in the direct or indirect underwriting of such an undertaking.

In determining when a person is deemed not to be engaged in a distribution several factors must be considered.

First, the purpose and underlying policy of the Act to protect investors requires that there be adequate current information concerning the issuer, whether the resales of securities by persons result in a distribution or are effected in trading transactions. Accordingly, the availability of the rule is conditioned on the existence of adequate current public information.

Secondly, a holding period prior to resale is essential, among other reasons, to assure that those persons who buy under a claim of a Section 4(2) exemption have assumed the economic risks of investment, and therefore are not acting as conduits for sale to the public of unregistered securities, directly or indirectly, on behalf of an issuer. It should be noted that there is nothing in Section 2(11) which places a time limit on a person's status as an underwriter. The public has the same need for protection afforded by registration whether the securities are distributed shortly after their purchase or after a considerable length of time.

A third factor, which must be considered in determining what is deemed not to constitute a "distribution," is the impact of the particular transaction or transactions on the trading markets. Section 4(1) was intended to exempt only routine trading transactions between individual investors with respect to securities already issued and not to exempt distributions by issuers or acts of other individuals who engage in steps necessary to such distributions. Therefore, a person reselling securities under Section 4(1) of the Act must sell the securities in such limited quantities and in such a manner as not to disrupt the trading markets. The larger the amount of securities involved, the more likely it is that such resales may involve methods of offering and amounts of compensation usually associated with a distribution rather than routine trading transactions. Thus, solicitation of buy orders or the payment of extra compensation are not permitted by the rule.

In summary, if the sale in question is made in accordance with *all* of the provisions of the rule, as set forth below, any person who sells restricted securities shall be deemed not to be engaged in a distribution of such securities and therefore not an underwriter thereof. The rule also provides that any person who sells restricted or other securities on behalf of a person in a control relationship with the issuer shall be deemed not to be engaged in a distribution of such securities and therefore not to be an underwriter thereof, if the sale is made in accordance with *all* the conditions of the rule.

Rule 144

(a) *Definitions.* The following definitions shall apply for the purposes of this rule.

(1) An "affiliate" of an issuer is a person that directly, or indirectly through one or more intermediaries, controls, or is controlled by, or is under common control with, such issuer.

(2) The term "person" when used with reference to a person for whose account securities are to be sold in reliance upon this rule includes, in addition to such person, all of the following persons:

(i) Any relative or spouse of such person, or any relative of such spouse, any one of whom has the same home as such person;

(ii) Any trust or estate in which such person or any of the persons specified in paragraph (a)(2)(i) of this section collectively own ten percent or more of the total beneficial interest or of which any of such persons serve as trustee, executor or in any similar capacity; and

(iii) Any corporation or other organization (other than the issuer) in which such person or any of the persons specified in paragraph (a)(2)(i) of this section are the beneficial owners collectively of ten percent or more of any class of equity securities or ten percent or more of the equity interest.

(3) The term "restricted securities" means:

(i) securities acquired directly or indirectly from the issuer, or from an affiliate of the issuer, in a transaction or chain of transactions not involving any public offering;

(ii) securities acquired from the issuer that are subject to the resale limitations of § 230.502(d) under Regulation D or §§ 230.701(c);

(iii) securities acquired in a transaction or chain of transactions meeting the requirements of Rule 144A;

(iv) securities acquired from the issuer in a transaction subject to the conditions of Regulation CE;

(v) equity securities of domestic issuers acquired in a transaction or chain of transactions subject to the conditions of Rule 901 or Rule 903 under Regulation S (Rule 901 through Rule 905, and Preliminary Notes).

(vi) Securities acquired in a transaction made under § 230.801 to the same extent and proportion that the securities held by the security holder of the class with respect to which the rights offering was made were as of the record date for the rights offering "restricted securities" within the meaning of this paragraph (a)(3); and

(vii) Securities acquired in a transaction made under § 230.802 to the same extent and proportion that the securities that were tendered or exchanged in the exchange offer or business combination were "restricted securities" within the meaning of this paragraph (a)(3).

(b) *Conditions to be Met.* Any affiliate or other person who sells restricted securities of an issuer for his own account, or any person who sells restricted or any other securities for the account of an affiliate of the issuer of such securities, shall be deemed not to be engaged in a distribution of such securities and therefore not to be an underwriter thereof within the meaning of Section 2(11) of the Act if all of the conditions of this rule are met.

(c) *Current Public Information.* There shall be available adequate current public information with respect to the issuer of the securities. Such information shall be deemed to be available only if either of the following conditions is met:

(1) *Filing of Reports.* The issuer has securities registered pursuant to Section 12 of the Securities Exchange Act of 1934, has been subject to the reporting requirements of Section 13 of that Act for a period of at least 90 days immediately preceding the sale of the securities and has filed all the reports required to be filed thereunder during the 12 months preceding such sale (or for such shorter period that the issuer was required to file such reports); or has securities registered pursuant to the Securities Act of 1933, has been subject to the reporting requirements of Section 15(d) of the Securities Exchange Act of 1934 for a period of at least 90 days immediately preceding the sale of the securities and has filed all the reports required to be filed thereunder during the 12 months preceding such sale (or for such shorter period that the issuer was required to file such reports). The person for whose account the securities are to be sold shall be entitled to rely upon a statement in whichever is the most recent report, quarterly or annual, required to be filed and filed by the issuer that such issuer has filed all reports required to be filed by Section 13 or 15(d) of the Securities Exchange Act of 1934 during the preceding 12 months (or for such shorter period that the issuer was required to file such reports) and has been subject to such filing requirements for the past 90 days, unless he knows or has reason to believe that the issuer has not complied with such requirements. Such person shall also be entitled to rely upon a written statement from the issuer that it has complied with such reporting requirements unless he knows or has reason to believe that the issuer has not complied with such requirements.

(2) *Other Public Information.* If the issuer is not subject to Section 13 or 15(d) of the Securities Exchange Act of 1934, there is publicly available the information concerning the issuer specified in paragraph (a)(5)(i) to (xiv), inclusive, and paragraph (a)(5)(xvi) of Rule 15c2–11 under that Act or, if the

issuer is an insurance company, the information specified in Section 12(g)(2)(G)(i) of that Act.

(d) *Holding Period for Restricted Securities.* If the securities sold are restricted securities, the following provisions apply:

(1) *General rule.* A minimum of one year must elapse between the later of the date of the acquisition of the securities from the issuer or from an affiliate of the issuer, and any resale of such securities in reliance on this section for the account of either the acquiror or any subsequent holder of those securities. If the acquiror takes the securities by purchase, the one-year period shall not begin until the full purchase price or other consideration is paid or given by the person acquiring the securities from the issuer or from an affiliate of the issuer.

(2) *Promissory Notes, Other Obligations or Installment Contracts.* Giving the issuer or affiliate of the issuer from whom the securities were purchased a promissory note or other obligation to pay the purchase price, or entering into an installment purchase contract with such seller, shall not be deemed full payment of the purchase price unless the promissory note, obligation or contract:

(i) provides for full recourse against the purchaser of the securities;

(ii) is secured by collateral, other than the securities purchased, having a fair market value at least equal to the purchase price of the securities purchased; and

(iii) shall have been discharged by payment in full prior to the sale of the securities.

(3) *Determination of Holding Period.* The following provisions shall apply for the purpose of determining the period securities have been held:

(i) *Stock Dividends, Splits and Recapitalizations.* Securities acquired from the issuer as a dividend or pursuant to a stock split, reverse split or recapitalization shall be deemed to have been acquired at the same time as the securities on which the dividend or, if more than one, the initial dividend was paid, the securities involved in the split or reverse split, or the securities surrendered in connection with the recapitalization;

(ii) *Conversions.* If the securities sold were acquired from the issuer for a consideration consisting solely of other securities of the same issuer surrendered for conversion, the securities so acquired shall be deemed to have been acquired at the same time as the securities surrendered for conversion;

(iii) *Contingent Issuance of Securities.* Securities acquired as a contingent payment of the purchase price of an equity interest in a business, or the assets of a business, sold to the issuer or an affiliate of the issuer shall be deemed to have been acquired at the time of such sale if the issuer or affiliate was then committed to issue the securities subject only to conditions other than the payment of further consideration for such securities. An agreement entered into in connection with any such purchase to remain in the employment of, or not to compete with, the issuer or affiliate or the rendering of services pursuant to such agreement shall not be deemed to be the payment of further consideration for such securities.

(iv) *Pledged Securities.* Securities which are bona fide pledged by an affiliate of the issuer when sold by the pledgee, or by a purchaser, after a default in the obligation secured by the pledge, shall be deemed to have been acquired when they were acquired by the pledgor, except that if the securities were pledged without recourse they shall be deemed to have been acquired by the pledgee at the time of the pledge or by the purchaser at the time of purchase.

(v) *Gifts of Securities.* Securities acquired from an affiliate of the issuer by gift shall be deemed to have been acquired by the donee when they were acquired by the donor.

(vi) *Trusts.* Where a trust settlor is an affiliate of the issuer, securities acquired from the settlor by the trust, or acquired from the trust by the beneficiaries thereof, shall be deemed to have been acquired when such securities were acquired by the settlor.

(vii) *Estates.* Where a deceased person was an affiliate of the issuer, securities held by the estate of such person or acquired from such estate by the beneficiaries thereof shall be deemed to have been acquired when they were acquired by the deceased person, except that no holding period is required if the estate is not an affiliate of the issuer or if the securities are sold by a beneficiary of the estate who is not such an affiliate.

NOTE: While there is no holding period or amount limitation for estates and beneficiaries thereof which are not affiliates of the issuer, paragraphs (c), (h) and (i) of the rule apply to securities sold by such persons in reliance upon the rule.

(viii) *Rule 145(a) transactions.* The holding period for securities acquired in a transaction specified in Rule 145(a) shall be deemed to commence on the date the securities were acquired by the purchaser in such transaction. This provision shall not apply, however, to a transaction effected solely for the purpose of forming a holding company.

(e) *Limitation on Amount of Securities Sold.* Except as hereinafter provided, the amount of securities which may be sold in reliance upon this rule shall be determined as follows:

(1) *Sales by Affiliates.* If restricted or other securities are sold for the account of an affiliate of the issuer, the amount of securities sold, together with all sales of restricted and other securities of the same class for the account of such person within the preceding three months, shall not exceed the greater of (i) one percent of the shares or other units of the class outstanding as shown by the most recent report or statement published by the issuer, or (ii) the average weekly volume of trading in such securities reported on all national securities exchanges and/or reported through the automated quotation system of a registered securities association during the four calendar weeks preceding the filing of the notice required by paragraph (h), or, if no such notice is required, the date of receipt of the order to execute the transaction by the broker or the date of execution of the transaction directly with a market maker, or (iii) the average weekly volume of trading in such securities reported through the consolidated transaction reporting system contemplated by Rule 11Aa3–1 under the Securities Exchange Act of 1934 during the four-week period specified in subdivision (ii) of this subparagraph.

(2) *Sales by Persons Other Than Affiliates.* The amount of restricted securities sold for the account of any person other than an affiliate of the issuer, together with all other sales of restricted securities of the same class for the account of such person within the preceding three months, shall not exceed the amount specified in paragraphs (e)(1)(i), (1)(ii) or (1)(iii) of this section, whichever is applicable, unless the conditions in paragraph (k) of this rule are satisfied.

(3) *Determination of Amount.* For the purpose of determining the amount of securities specified in paragraphs (e)(1) and (2) of this rule, the following provisions shall apply:

(i) Where both convertible securities and securities of the class into which they are convertible are sold, the amount of convertible securities sold shall be deemed to be the amount of securities of the class into which they are convertible for the purpose of determining the aggregate amount of securities of both classes sold;

(ii) The amount of securities sold for the account of a pledgee thereof, or for the account of a purchaser of the pledged securities, during any period of three months within one year after a default in the obligation secured by the pledge, and the amount of securities sold during the same three-month period for the account of the pledgor shall not exceed, in the aggregate, the amount specified in subparagraph (1) or (2) of this paragraph, whichever is applicable;

(iii) The amount of securities sold for the account of a donee thereof during any period of three months within one year after the donation, and the amount of securities sold during the same three-month period for the account of the donor, shall not exceed, in the aggregate, the amount specified in subparagraph (1) or (2) of this paragraph, whichever is applicable;

(iv) Where securities were acquired by a trust from the settlor of the trust, the amount of such securities sold for the account of the trust during any period of three months within one year after the acquisition of the securities by the trust, and the amount of securities sold during the same three-month period for the account of the settlor, shall not exceed, in the aggregate, the amount specified in subparagraph (1) or (2) of this paragraph, whichever is applicable;

(v) The amount of securities sold for the account of the estate of a deceased person, or for the account of a beneficiary of such estate, during any period of three months and the amount of securities sold during the same period for the account of the deceased person prior to his death shall not exceed, in the aggregate, the amount specified in subparagraph (1) or (2) of this paragraph, whichever is applicable, *Provided,* That no limitation on amount shall apply if the estate or beneficiary thereof is not an affiliate of the issuer;

(vi) When two or more affiliates or other persons agree to act in concert for the purpose of selling securities of an issuer, all securities of the same class sold for the account of all such persons during any period of three months shall be aggregated for the purpose of determining the limitation on the amount of securities sold;

(vii) The following sales of securities need not be included in determining the amount of securities sold in reliance upon this section; securities sold pursuant to an effective registration statement under the Act; securities sold pursuant to an exemption provided by Regulation A under the Act; securities sold in a transaction exempt pursuant to Section 4 of the Act and not involving any public offering; and securities sold offshore pursuant to Regulation S under the Act.

(f) *Manner of Sale.* The securities shall be sold in "brokers' transactions" within the meaning of section 4(4) of the Act or in transactions directly with a "market maker," as that term is defined in section 3(a)(38) of the Securities Exchange Act of 1934, and the person selling the securities shall not (1) solicit or arrange for the solicitation of orders to buy the securities in anticipation of or in connection with such transaction, or (2) make any payment in connection with the offer or sale of the securities to any person other than the broker who executes the order to sell the securities. The requirements of this paragraph, however, shall not apply to securities sold for the account of the estate of a deceased person or for the account of a beneficiary of such estate provided the estate or beneficiary thereof is not an affiliate of the issuer; nor shall they apply to securities sold for the account of any person other than an affiliate of the issuer, provided the conditions of paragraph (k) of this rule are satisfied.

(g) *Brokers' Transactions.* The term "brokers' transactions" in Section 4(4) of the Act shall for the purposes of this rule be deemed to include transactions by a broker in which such broker—

(1) does no more than execute the order or orders to sell the securities as agent for the person for whose account the securities are sold; and receives no more than the usual and customary broker's commission;

(2) neither solicits nor arranges for the solicitation of customers' orders to buy the securities in anticipation of or in connection with the transaction; provided, that the foregoing shall not preclude *(i)* inquiries by the broker of other brokers or dealers who have indicated an interest in the securities within the preceding 60 days, *(ii)* inquiries by the broker of his customers who have indicated an unsolicited bona fide interest in the securities within the preceding 10 business days; or *(iii)* the publication by the broker of bid and ask quotations for the security in an inter-dealer quotation system provided that such quotations are incident to the maintenance of a bona fide inter-dealer market for the security for the broker's own account and that the broker has published bona fide bid and ask quotations for the security in an inter-dealer quotation system on each of at least twelve days within the preceding thirty calendar days with no more than four business days in succession without such two-way quotations;

Note to Subparagraph (g)(2)(ii): The broker should obtain and retain in his files written evidence of indications of bona fide unsolicited interest by his customers in the securities at the time such indications are received.

(3) after reasonable inquiry is not aware of circumstances indicating that the person for whose account the securities are sold is an underwriter with respect to the securities or that the transaction is a part of a distribution of securities of the issuer. Without limiting the foregoing, the broker shall be deemed to be aware of any facts or statements contained in the notice required by paragraph (h) below.

Notes. 1. The broker, for his own protection, should obtain and retain in his files a copy of the notice required by paragraph (h).

2. The reasonable inquiry required by paragraph (g)(3) above should include, but not necessarily be limited to, inquiry as to the following matters:

a. The length of time the securities have been held by the person for whose account they are to be sold. If practicable, the inquiry should include physical inspection of the securities;

b. The nature of the transaction in which the securities were acquired by such person;

c. The amount of securities of the same class sold during the past six months by all persons whose sales are required to be taken into consideration pursuant to paragraph (e) above;

d. Whether such person intends to sell additional securities of the same class through any other means;

e. Whether such person has solicited or made any arrangement for the solicitation of buy orders in connection with the proposed sale of securities;

f. Whether such person has made any payment to any other person in connection with the proposed sale of the securities; and

g. The number of shares or other units of the class outstanding, or the relevant trading volume.

(h) *Notice of Proposed Sale.* If the amount of securities to be sold in reliance upon the rule during any period of three months exceeds 500 shares or other units or has an aggregate sale price in excess of $10,000, three copies of a notice on Form 144 shall be filed with the Commission at its principal office in Washington, D.C.; and if such securities are admitted to trading on any national securities exchange, one copy of such notice shall also be transmitted to the principal exchange on which such securities are so admitted. The Form 144 shall be signed by the person for whose account the securities are to be sold and shall be transmitted for filing concurrently with either the placing with a broker of an order to execute a sale of securities in reliance upon this rule or the execution directly with a market maker of such a sale. Neither the filing of such notice nor the failure of the Commission to comment thereon shall be deemed to preclude the Commission from taking any action it deems necessary or appropriate with respect to the sale of the securities referred to in such notice. The requirements of this paragraph, however, shall not apply to securities sold for the account of any person other than an affiliate of the issuer, provided the conditions of paragraph (k) of this rule are satisfied.

(i) *Bona Fide Intention to Sell.* The person filing the notice required by paragraph (h) shall have a bona fide intention to sell the securities referred to therein within a reasonable time after the filing of such notice.

(j) *Non-exclusive Rule.* Although this rule provides a means for reselling restricted securities and securities held by affiliates without registration, it is not the exclusive means for reselling such securities in that manner. Therefore, it does not eliminate or otherwise affect the availability of any exemption for resales under the Securities Act that a person or entity may be able to rely upon.

(k) *Termination of Certain Restrictions on Sales of Restricted Securities by Persons Other Than Affiliates.* The requirements of paragraphs (c), (e), (f) and (h) of this rule shall not apply to restricted securities sold for the account of a person who is not an affiliate of the issuer at the time of the sale and has not been an affiliate during the preceding three months, provided a period of at least two years has elapsed since the later of the date the securities were acquired from the issuer or from an affiliate of the issuer. In computing the two-year period for purposes of this provision, reference should be made to paragraph (d) of this section.

Rule 144A. Private Resales of Securities to Institutions

Preliminary Notes to Rule 144A

1. This section relates solely to the application of Section 5 of the Act and not to antifraud or other provisions of the federal securities laws.

2. Attempted compliance with this section does not act as an exclusive election; any seller hereunder may also claim the availability of any other applicable exemption from the registration requirements of the Act.

3. In view of the objective of this section and the policies underlying the Act, this section is not available with respect to any transaction or series of transactions that, although in technical compliance with this section, is part of a plan or scheme to evade the registration provisions of the Act. In such cases, registration under the Act is required.

4. Nothing in this section obviates the need for any issuer or any other person to comply with the

securities registration or broker-dealer registration requirements of the Securities Exchange Act of 1934 (the "Exchange Act"), whenever such requirements are applicable.

5. Nothing in this section obviates the need for any person to comply with any applicable state law relating to the offer or sale of securities.

6. Securities acquired in a transaction made pursuant to the provisions of this section are deemed to be "restricted securities" within the meaning of § 230.144(a)(3) of this chapter.

7. The fact that purchasers of securities from the issuer thereof may purchase such securities with a view to reselling such securities pursuant to this section will not affect the availability to such issuer of an exemption under Section 4(2) of the Act, or Regulation D under the Act, from the registration requirements of the Act.

(a) *Definitions*

(1) For purposes of this section, "qualified institutional buyer" shall mean:

(i) Any of the following entities, acting for its own account or the accounts of other qualified institutional buyers, that in the aggregate owns and invests on a discretionary basis at least $100 million in securities of issuers that are not affiliated with the entity:

(A) Any *insurance company* as defined in Section 2(13) of the Act;

* * *

(B) Any *investment company* registered under the Investment Company Act or any *business development company* as defined in Section 2(a)(48) of that Act;

(C) Any *Small Business Investment Company* licensed by the U.S. Small Business Administration under Section 301(c) or (d) of the Small Business Investment Act of 1958;

(D) Any *plan* established and maintained by a state, its political subdivisions, or any agency or instrumentality of a state or its political subdivisions, for the benefit of its employees;

(E) Any *employee benefit plan* within the meaning of Title I of the Employee Retirement Income Security Act of 1974;

(F) Any *trust fund* whose trustee is a bank or trust company and whose participants are exclusively plans of the types identified in paragraph (a)(1)(i)(D) or (E) of this section, except trust funds that include as participants individual retirement accounts or H.R. 10 plans.

(G) Any *business development company* as defined in Section 202(a)(22) of the Investment Advisers Act of 1940;

(H) Any organization described in Section 501(c)(3) of the Internal Revenue Code, corporation (other than a bank as defined in Section 3(a)(2) of the Act or a savings and loan association or other institution referenced in Section 3(a)(5)(A) of the Act or a foreign bank or savings and loan association or equivalent institution), partnership, or Massachusetts or similar business trust; and

(I) Any *investment adviser* registered under the Investment Advisers Act.

(ii) Any *dealer* registered pursuant to Section 15 of the Exchange Act, acting for its own account or the accounts of other qualified institutional buyers, that in the aggregate owns and invests on a discretionary basis at least $10 million of securities of issuers that are not affiliated with the dealer, *provided that* securities constituting the whole or a part of an unsold allotment to or subscription by a dealer as a participant in a public offering shall not be deemed to be owned by such dealer;

(iii) Any *dealer* registered pursuant to Section 15 of the Exchange Act acting in a riskless principal transaction on behalf of a qualified institutional buyer;

NOTE: A registered dealer may act as agent, on a non-discretionary basis, in a transaction with a qualified institutional buyer without itself having to be a qualified institutional buyer.

(iv) Any investment company registered under the Investment Company Act, acting for its own account or for the accounts of other qualified institutional buyers, that is part of a family of investment companies which own in the aggregate at least $100 million in securities of issuers, other than issuers that are affiliated with the investment company or are part of such family of investment companies. "Family of investment companies" means any two or more investment companies registered under the Investment Company Act, except for a unit investment trust whose assets consist solely of shares of one or more registered investment companies, that have the same investment adviser (or, in the case of unit investment trusts, the same depositor), *provided that,* for purposes of this section:

(A) each series of a series company (as defined in Rule 18f–2 under the Investment Company Act) shall be deemed to be a separate investment company; and

(B) investment companies shall be deemed to have the same adviser (or depositor) if their advisers (or depositors) are majority-owned subsidiaries of the same parent, or if one investment company's adviser (or depositor) is a majority-owned subsidiary of the other investment company's adviser (or depositor);

(v) Any entity, all of the equity owners of which are qualified institutional buyers, acting for its own account or the accounts of other qualified institutional buyers; and

(vi) Any *bank* as defined in Section 3(a)(2) of the Act, any savings and loan association or other institution as referenced in Section 3(a)(5)(A) of the Act, *or* any foreign bank or savings and loan association or equivalent institution, acting for its own account or the accounts of other qualified institutional buyers, that in the aggregate owns and invests on a discretionary basis at least $100 million in securities of issuers that are not affiliated with it and that has an audited net worth of at least $25 million as demonstrated in its latest annual financial statements, as of a date not more than 16 months preceding the date of sale under the Rule in the case of a U.S. bank or savings and loan association, and not more than 18 months preceding such date of sale for a foreign bank or savings and loan association or equivalent institution.

(2) In determining the aggregate amount of securities owned and invested on a discretionary basis by an entity, the following instruments and interests shall be excluded: bank deposit notes and certificates of deposit; loan participations; repurchase agreements; securities owned but subject to a repurchase agreement; and currency, interest rate and commodity swaps.

(3) The aggregate value of securities owned and invested on a discretionary basis by an entity shall be the cost of such securities, except where the entity reports its securities holdings in its financial statements on the basis of their market value, and no current information with respect to the cost of those securities has been published. In the latter event, the securities may be valued at market for purposes of this section.

(4) In determining the aggregate amount of securities owned by an entity and invested on a discretionary basis, securities owned by subsidiaries of the entity that are consolidated with the entity in its financial statements prepared in accordance with generally accepted accounting principles may be included if the investments of such subsidiaries are managed under the direction of the entity, except that, unless the entity is a reporting company under Section 13 or 15(d) of the Exchange Act, securities owned by such subsidiaries may not be included if the entity itself is a majority-owned subsidiary that would be included in the consolidated financial statements of another enterprise.

(5) For purposes of this section, "riskless principal transaction" means a transaction in which a dealer buys a security from any person and makes a simultaneous offsetting sale of such security to a qualified institutional buyer, including another dealer acting as riskless principal for a qualified institutional buyer.

(6) For purposes of this section, "effective conversion premium" means the amount, expressed as a percentage of the security's conversion value, by which the price at issuance of a convertible security exceeds its conversion value.

(7) For purposes of this section, "effective exercise premium" means the amount, expressed as a percentage of the warrant's exercise value, by which the sum of the price at issuance and the exercise price of a warrant exceeds its exercise value.

(b) *Sales by Persons other than Issuers or Dealers.* Any person, other than the issuer or a dealer, who offers or sells securities in compliance with the conditions set forth in paragraph (d) of this section shall be deemed not to be engaged in a distribution of such securities and therefore not to be an underwriter of such securities within the meaning of Sections 2(11) and 4(1) of the Act.

(c) *Sales by Dealers.* Any dealer who offers or sells securities in compliance with the conditions set forth in paragraph (d) of this section shall be deemed not to be a participant in a distribution of such securities within the meaning of Section 4(3)(C) of the Act and not to be an underwriter of such securities within the meaning of Section 2(11) of the Act, and such securities shall be deemed not to have been offered to the public within the meaning of Section 4(3)(A) of the Act.

(d) *Conditions to be Met.* To qualify for exemption under this section, an offer or sale must meet the following conditions:

(1) The securities are offered or sold only to a qualified institutional buyer or to an offeree or purchaser that the seller and any person acting on behalf of the seller reasonably believe is a qualified institutional buyer. In determining whether a prospective purchaser is a qualified institutional buyer, the seller and any person acting on its behalf shall be entitled to rely upon the following non-exclusive methods of establishing the prospective purchaser's ownership and discretionary investments of securities:

(i) The prospective purchaser's most recent publicly available financial statements, *provided that* such statements present the information as of a date within 16 months preceding the date of sale of securities under this section in the case of a U.S. purchaser and within 18 months preceding such date of sale for a foreign purchaser;

(ii) The most recent publicly available information appearing in documents filed by the prospective purchaser with the Commission or another United States federal, state, or local governmental agency or self-regulatory organization, or with a foreign governmental agency or self-regulatory organization, *provided that* any such information is as of a date within 16 months preceding the date of sale of securities under this section in the case of a U.S. purchaser and within 18 months preceding such date of sale for a foreign purchaser;

(iii) The most recent publicly available information appearing in a recognized securities manual, *provided that* such information is as of a date within 16 months preceding the date of sale of securities under this section in the case of a U.S. purchaser and within 18 months preceding such date of sale for a foreign purchaser; or

(iv) A certification by the chief financial officer, a person fulfilling an equivalent function, or other executive officer of the purchaser, specifying the amount of securities owned and invested on a discretionary basis by the purchaser as of a specific date on or since the close of the purchaser's most recent fiscal year, or, in the case of a purchaser that is a member of a family of investment companies, a certification by an executive officer of the investment adviser specifying the amount of securities owned by the family of investment companies as of a specific date on or since the close of the purchaser's most recent fiscal year;

(2) The seller and any person acting on its behalf takes reasonable steps to ensure that the purchaser is aware that the seller may rely on the exemption from the provisions of Section 5 of the Act provided by this section;

(3) The securities offered or sold:

(i) Were not, when issued, of the same class as securities listed on a national securities exchange registered under Section 6 of the Exchange Act or quoted in a U.S. automated inter-dealer quotation system; *Provided,* that securities that are convertible or exchangeable into securities so listed or quoted at the time of issuance and that had an effective conversion premium of less than 10 percent, shall be treated as securities of the class into which they are convertible or exchangeable; and that warrants that may be exercised for securities so listed or quoted at the time of issuance, for a period of less than 3 years from the date of issuance, or that had an effective exercise premium of less than 10 percent, shall be treated as securities of the class to be issued upon exercise; and *provided further* that the Commission may from time to time, taking into account then-existing market practices, designate additional securities and classes of securities that will not be deemed of the same class as securities listed on a national securities exchange or quoted in a U.S. automated inter-dealer quotation system; and

(ii) Are not securities of an open-end investment company, unit investment trust or face-amount certificate company that is or is required to be registered under Section 8 of the Investment Company Act; and

(4)(i) In the case of securities of an issuer that is neither subject to Section 13 or 15(d) of the Exchange Act, nor exempt from reporting pursuant to Rule 12g3–2(b) under the Exchange Act, nor a foreign government as defined in Rule 405 eligible to register securities under Schedule B of the Act, the holder and a prospective purchaser designated by the holder have the right to obtain from the issuer, upon request of the holder, and the prospective purchaser has received from the issuer, the seller, or a person acting on either of their behalf, at or prior to the time of sale, upon such prospective purchaser's request to the holder or the issuer, the following information (which shall be reasonably current in relation to the date of resale under this section): a very brief statement of the nature of the business of the issuer and the products and services it offers; and the issuer's most recent balance sheet and profit and loss and retained earnings statements, and similar financial statements for such part of the two preceding fiscal years as the issuer has been in operation (the financial statements should be audited to the extent reasonably available).

(ii) The requirement that the information be "reasonably current" will be presumed to be satisfied if:

(A) The balance sheet is as of a date less than 16 months before the date of resale, the statements of profit and loss and retained earnings are for the 12 months preceding the date of such balance sheet, and if such balance sheet is not as of a date less than 6 months before the date of resale, it shall be accompanied by additional statements of profit and loss and retained earnings for the period from the date of such balance sheet to a date less than 6 months before the date of resale; and

(B) The statement of the nature of the issuer's business and its products and services offered is as of a date within 12 months prior to the date of resale; or

(C) With regard to foreign private issuers, the required information meets the timing requirements of the issuer's home country or principal trading markets.

(e) Offers and sales of securities pursuant to this section shall be deemed not to affect the availability of any exemption or safe harbor relating to any previous or subsequent offer or sale of such securities by the issuer or any prior or subsequent holder thereof.

Rule 145. Reclassifications of Securities, Mergers, Consolidations and Acquisitions of Assets

Preliminary Note to Rule 145

Rule 145 is designed to make available the protection provided by registration under the Securities Act of 1933, as amended (Act), to persons who are offered securities in a business combination of the type described in subparagraphs (a)(1), (2), and (3) of the Rule. The thrust of the Rule is that an "offer", "offer to sell", "offer for sale", or "sale" occurs when there is submitted to security holders a plan or agreement pursuant to which such holders are required to elect, on the basis of what is in substance a new investment decision, whether to accept a new or different security in exchange for their existing security. Rule 145 embodies the Commission's determination that such transactions are subject to the registration requirements of the Act, and that the previously existing "no-sale" theory of Rule 133 is no longer consistent with the statutory purposes of the Act.

Transactions for which statutory exemptions under the Act, including those contained in Sections 3(a)(9), 3(a)(10), 3(a)(11), and 4(2), are otherwise available are not affected by Rule 145.

Rule 145

Note 1: Reference is made to Rule 153A, describing the prospectus delivery required in a transaction of the type referred to in Rule 145.

Note 2: A reclassification of securities covered by Rule 145 would be exempt from registration pursuant to Sections 3(a)(9) or 3(a)(11) of the Act if the conditions of either of these sections are satisfied.

(a) *Transactions Within the Rule.* An "offer", "offer to sell", "offer for sale" or "sale" shall be deemed to be involved, within the meaning of Section 2(3) of the Act, so far as the security holders of a corporation or other person are concerned where, pursuant to statutory provisions of the jurisdiction under which such corporation or other person is organized, or pursuant to provisions contained in its certificate of incorporation or similar controlling instruments, or otherwise, there is submitted for the vote or consent of such security holders a plan or agreement for—

(1) *Reclassifications.* A reclassification of securities of such corporation or other person, other than a stock split, reverse stock split, or change in par value, which involves the substitution of a security for another security;

(2) *Mergers or Consolidations.* A statutory merger or consolidation or similar plan of acquisition in which securities of such corporation or other person held by such security holders will become or be exchanged for securities of any other person, except where the sole purpose of the transaction is to change an issuer's domicile; or

(3) *Transfers of Assets.* A transfer of assets of such corporation or other person, to another person in consideration of the issuance of securities of such other person or any of its affiliates, if:

(i)(A) such plan or agreement provides for dissolution of the corporation or other person whose security holders are voting or consenting; or

(ii)(B) such plan or agreement provides for a pro rata or similar distribution of such securities to the security holders voting or consenting; or

(iii)(C) the board of directors or similar representatives of such corporation or other person, adopts resolutions relative to (A) or (B) above within one year after the taking of such vote or consent; or

(iv)(D) the transfer of assets is a part of a preexisting plan for distribution of such securities, notwithstanding (A), (B) or (C), above.

(b) *Communications before a Registration Statement is filed.* Communications made in connection with or relating to a transaction described in paragraph (a) of this section that will be registered under the Act may be made under § 230.135, § 230.165 or § 230.166.

(c) *Persons and Parties Deemed to be Underwriters.* For purposes of this rule, any party to any transaction specified in paragraph (a), other than the issuer, or any person who is an affiliate of such party at the time any such transaction is submitted for vote or consent, who publicly offers or sells securities of the issuer acquired in connection with any such transaction, shall be deemed to be engaged in a distribution and therefore to be an underwriter thereof within the meaning of Section 2(11) of the Act. The term "party" as used in this paragraph (c) shall mean the corporations, business entities, or other persons, other than the issuer, whose assets or capital structure are affected by the transactions specified in paragraph (a).

(d) *Resale provisions for persons and parties deemed underwriters.* Notwithstanding the provisions of paragraph (c), a person or party specified therein shall not be deemed to be engaged in a distribution and therefore not to be an underwriter of registered securities acquired in a transaction specified in paragraph (a) of this section if:

(1) Such securities are sold by such person or party in accordance with the provisions of paragraphs (c), (e), (f) and (g) of Rule 144;

(2) Such person or party is not an affiliate of the issuer, and a period of at least one year, as determined in accordance with paragraph (d) of § 230.144, has elapsed since the date the securities were acquired from the issuer in such transaction, and the issuer meets the requirements of paragraph (c) of § 230.144; or

(3) Such person or party is not, and has not been for at least three months, an affiliate of the issuer, and a period of at least two years, as determined in accordance with paragraph (d) of § 230.144, has elapsed since the date the securities were acquired from the issuer in such transaction.

(e) *Definition of "Person".* The term "person" as used in paragraphs (c) and (d) of this rule, when used with reference to a person for whose account securities are to be sold, shall have the same meaning as the definition of that term in paragraph (a)(2) of Rule 144 under the Act.

Rule 147. "Part of an Issue," "Person Resident," and "Doing Business Within" for Purposes of Section 3(a)(11)

Preliminary Notes

1. This rule shall not raise any presumption that the exemption provided by Section 3(a)(11) of

the Act is not available for transactions by an issuer which do not satisfy all of the provisions of the rule.

2. Nothing in this rule obviates the need for compliance with any state law relating to the offer and sale of the securities.

3. Section 5 of the Act requires that all securities offered by the use of the mails or by any means or instruments of transportation or communication in interstate commerce be registered with the Commission. Congress, however, provided certain exemptions in the Act from such registration provisions where there was no practical need for registration or where the benefits of registration were too remote. Among those exemptions is that provided by Section 3(a)(11) of the Act for transactions in "any security which is a part of an issue offered and sold only to persons resident within a single State or Territory, where the issuer of such security is a person resident and doing business within * * * such State or Territory." The legislative history of that Section suggests that the exemption was intended to apply only to issues genuinely local in character, which in reality represent local financing by local industries, carried out through local investment. Rule 147 is intended to provide more objective standards upon which responsible local businessmen intending to raise capital from local sources may rely in claiming the section 3(a)(11) exemption.

All of the terms and conditions of the rule must be satisfied in order for the rule to be available. These are: (i) That the issuer be a resident of and doing business within the state or territory in which all offers and sales are made; and (ii) that no part of the issue be offered or sold to non-residents within the period of time specified in the rule. For purposes of the rule the definition of "issuer" in section 2(4) of the Act shall apply.

All offers, offers to sell, offers for sale, and sales which are part of the same issue must meet all of the conditions of Rule 147 for the rule to be available. The determination whether offers, offers to sell, offers for sale and sales of securities are part of the same issue (i.e., are deemed to be "integrated") will continue to be a question of fact and will depend on the particular circumstances. See Securities Act of 1933 Release No. 4434 (December 6, 1961)(26 FR 9158). Securities Act Release No. 4434 indicated that in determining whether offers and sales should be regarded as part of the same issue and thus should be integrated any one or more of the following factors may be determinative:

(i) Are the offerings part of a single plan of financing;

(ii) Do the offerings involve issuance of the same class of securities;

(iii) Are the offerings made at or about the same time;

(iv) Is the same type of consideration to be received; and

(v) Are the offerings made for the same general purpose.

Subparagraph (b)(2) of the rule, however, is designed to provide certainty to the extent feasible by identifying certain types of offers and sales of securities which will be deemed not part of an issue, for purposes of the rule only.

Persons claiming the availability of the rule have the burden of proving that they have satisfied all of its provisions. However, the rule does not establish exclusive standards for complying with the Section 3(a)(11) exemption. The exemption would also be available if the issuer satisfied the standards set forth in relevant administrative and judicial interpretations at the time of the offering but the issuer would have the burden of proving the availability of the exemption. Rule 147 relates to transactions exempted from the registration requirements of Section 5 of the Act by section 3(a)(11). Neither the rule nor section 3(a)(11) provides an exemption from the registration requirements of section 12(g) of the Securities Exchange Act of 1934, the anti-fraud provisions of the federal securities laws, the civil liability provisions of section 12(2) of the Act or other provisions of the federal securities laws.

Finally, in view of the objectives of the rule and the purposes and policies underlying the Act, the rule shall not be available to any person with respect to any offering which, although in technical compliance with the rule, is part of a plan or scheme by such person to make interstate offers or sales of securities. In such cases registration pursuant to the Act is required.

4. The rule provides an exemption for offers and sales by the issuer only. It is not available for offers or sales of securities by other persons. Section

3(a)(11) of the Act has been interpreted to permit offers and sales by persons controlling the issuer, if the exemption provided by that section would have been available to the issuer at the time of the offering. See Securities Act Release No. 4434. Controlling persons who want to offer or sell securities pursuant to section 3(a)(11) may continue to do so in accordance with applicable judicial and administrative interpretations.

(a) *Transactions Covered.*

Offers, offers to sell, offers for sale and sales by an issuer of its securities made in accordance with all of the terms and conditions of this rule shall be deemed to be part of an issue offered and sold only to persons resident and doing business within such state or territory, within the meaning of Section 3(a)(11) of the Act.

(b) *Part of an Issue.*

(1) For purposes of this rule, all securities of the issuer which are part of an issue shall be offered, offered for sale or sold in accordance with all of the terms and conditions of this rule.

(2) For purposes of this rule only, an issue shall be deemed not to include offers, offers to sell, offers for sale or sales of securities of the issuer pursuant to the exemptions provided by Section 3 or Section 4(2) of the Act or pursuant to a registration statement filed under the Act, that take place prior to the six month period immediately preceding or after the six month period immediately following any offers, offers for sale or sales pursuant to this rule, *provided that*, there are during either of said six month periods no offers, offers for sale or sales of securities by or for the issuer of the same or similar class as those offered, offered for sale or sold pursuant to the rule.

NOTE: In the even that securities of the same or similar class as those offered pursuant to the rule are offered, offered for sale or sold less than six months prior to or subsequent to any offer, offer for sale or sale pursuant to this rule, see Preliminary Note 3 hereof, as to which offers, offers to sell, offers for sale, or sales are part of an issue.

(c) *Nature of the Issuer.*

The issuer of the securities shall at the time of any offers and the sales be a person resident and doing business within the state or territory in which all of the offers, offers to sell, offers for sale and sales are made.

(1) The issuer shall be deemed to be a resident of the state or territory in which:

(i) it is incorporated or organized, if a corporation, limited partnership, trust or other form of business organization that is organized under state or territorial law;

(ii) its principal office is located, if a general partnership or other form of business organization that is not organized under any state or territorial law;

(iii) his principal residence is located, if an individual.

(2) The issuer shall be deemed to be doing business within a state or territory if:

(i) the issuer derived at least 80% of its gross revenues and those of its subsidiaries on a consolidated basis;

(A) for its most recent fiscal year, if the first offer of any part of the issue is made during the first six months of the issuer's current fiscal year; or

(B) for the first six months of its current fiscal year or during the twelve month fiscal period ending with such six month period, if the first offer of any part of the issue is made during the last six months of the issuer's current fiscal year

from the operation of a business or of real property located in or from the rendering of services within such state or territory; provided, however, that this provision does not apply to any issuer which has not had gross revenues in excess of $5,000 from the sale of products or services or other conduct of its business for its most recent twelve month fiscal period; and

(ii) the issuer had at the end of its most recent semi-annual fiscal period prior to the first offer of any part of the issue, at least 80 percent of its assets and those of its subsidiaries on a consolidated basis located within such state or territory;

(iii) the issuer intends to use and uses at least 80% of the net proceeds to the issuer from sales made pursuant to this rule in connection with the operation of a business or of real property, the purchase of real property located in, or the rendering of services within such state or territory; and

(iv) the principal office of the issuer is located within such state or territory.

(d) *Offerees and Purchasers: Person Resident.*

Offers, offers to sell, offers for sale and sales of securities that are part of an issue shall be made only to persons resident within the state or territory of which the issuer is a resident. For purposes of determining the residence of offerees and purchasers:

(1) A corporation, partnership, trust or other form of business organization shall be deemed to be a resident of a state or territory if, at the time of the offer and sale to it, it has its principal office within such state or territory.

(2) An individual shall be deemed to be a resident of a state or territory if such individual has, at the time of the offer and sale to him, his principal residence in the state or territory.

(3) A corporation, partnership, trust or other form of business organization which is organized for the specific purpose of acquiring part of an issue offered pursuant to this rule shall be deemed not to be a resident of a state or territory unless all of the beneficial owners of such organization are residents of such state or territory.

(e) *Limitation of Resales.*

During the period in which securities that are part of an issue are being offered and sold by the issuer, and for a period of nine months from the date of the last sale by the issuer of such securities, all resales of any part of the issue, by any person, shall be made only to persons resident within such state or territory.

NOTES: 1. In the case of convertible securities resales of either the convertible security, or if it is converted, the underlying security, could be made during the period described in paragraph (e) only to persons resident within such state or territory. For purposes of this rule a conversion in reliance on Section 3(a)(9) of the Act does not begin a new period.

2. Dealers must satisfy the requirements of Rule 15c2–11 under the Securities Exchange Act of 1934 prior to publishing any quotation for a security, or submitting any quotation for publication, in any quotation medium.

(f) *Precautions Against Interstate Offers and Sales.*

(1) The issuer shall, in connection with any securities sold by it pursuant to this rule:

(i) place a legend on the certificate or other document evidencing the security stating that the securities have not been registered under the Act and setting forth the limitations on resale contained in paragraph (e);

(ii) issue stop transfer instructions to the issuer's transfer agent, if any, with respect to the securities, or, if the issuer transfers its own securities, make a notation in the appropriate records of the issuer; and

(iii) obtain a written representation from each purchaser as to his residence.

(2) The issuer shall, in connection with the issuance of new certificates for any of the securities that are part of the same issue that are presented for transfer during the time period specified in paragraph (e), take the steps required by subsections (f)(1)(i) and (ii).

(3) The issuer shall, in connection with any offers, offers to sell, offers for sale or sales by it pursuant to this rule, disclose, in writing, the limitations on resale contained in paragraph (e) and the provisions of subsections (f)(1)(i) and (ii) and subparagraph (f)(2).

* * *

Rule 149. Definition of "Exchanged" in Section 3(a)(9), for Certain Transactions

The term "exchanged" in section 3(a)(9) shall be deemed to include the issuance of a security in consideration of the surrender by the existing security holders of the issuer, of outstanding securities of the issuer, notwithstanding the fact that the surrender of the outstanding securities may be required by the terms of the plan of exchange to be accompanied by such payment in cash by the security holder as may be necessary to effect an equitable adjustment, in respect of dividends or interest paid or payable on the securities involved in the exchange, as between such security holder and other security holders of the same class accepting the offer of exchange.

Rule 150. Definition of "Commission or Other Remuneration" in Section 3(a)(9), for Certain Transactions

The term "commission or other remuneration" in Section 3(a)(9) shall not include payments made by the issuer, directly or indirectly, to its security holders in connection with an exchange of securities for outstanding securities, when such payments are part of the terms of the offer of exchange.

* * *

Rule 152. Definition of "Transactions by an Issuer Not Involving Any Public Offering" in Section 4(2), for Certain Transactions

The phrase "transactions by an issuer not involving any public offering" in Section 4(2) shall be deemed to apply to transactions not involving any public offering at the time of said transactions although subsequently thereto the issuer decides to make a public offering and/or files a registration statement.

Rule 155. Integration of Abandoned Offerings

Preliminary Note to Rule 155

Compliance with paragraph (b) or (c) of this section provides a non-exclusive safe harbor from integration of private and registered offerings. Because of the objectives of Rule 155 and the policies underlying the Act, Rule 155 is not available to any issuer for any transaction or series of transactions that, although in technical compliance with the rule, is part of a plan or scheme to evade the registration requirements of the Act.

(a) Definition of terms. For the purposes of this section only, a private offering means an unregistered offering of securities that is exempt from registration under Section 4(2) or 4(6) of the Act (15 U.S.C. 77d(2) and 77d(6)) or Rule 506 of Regulation D (§ 230.506).

(b) Abandoned private offering followed by a registered offering. A private offering of securities will not be considered part of an offering for which the issuer later files a registration statement if:

(1) No securities were sold in the private offering;

(2) The issuer and any person(s) acting on its behalf terminate all offering activity in the private offering before the issuer files the registration statement;

(3) The Section 10(a) final prospectus and any Section 10 preliminary prospectus used in the registered offering disclose information about the abandoned private offering, including:

(i) The size and nature of the private offering;

(ii) The date on which the issuer abandoned the private offering;

(iii) That any offers to buy or indications of interest given in the private offering were rejected or otherwise not accepted; and

(iv) That the prospectus delivered in the registered offering supersedes any offering materials used in the private offering; and

(4) The issuer does not file the registration statement until at least 30 calendar days after termination of all offering activity in the private offering, unless the issuer and any person acting on its behalf offered securities in the private offering only to persons who were (or who the issuer reasonably believes were):

(i) Accredited investors (as that term is defined in § 230.501(a)); or

(ii) Persons who satisfy the knowledge and experience standard of § 230.506(b)(2)(ii).

(c) Abandoned registered offering followed by a private offering. An offering for which the issuer filed a registration statement will not be considered part of a later commenced private offering if:

(1) No securities were sold in the registered offering;

(2) The issuer withdraws the registration statement under § 230.477;

(3) Neither the issuer nor any person acting on the issuer's behalf commences the private offering earlier than 30 calendar days after the effective date of withdrawal of the registration statement under § 230.477;

(4) The issuer notifies each offeree in the private offering that:

(i) The offering is not registered under the Act;

(ii) The securities will be "restricted securities" (as that term is defined in § 230.144(a)(3)) and may not be resold unless they are registered under the Act or an exemption from registration is available;

(iii) Purchasers in the private offering do not have the protection of Section 11 of the Act (15 U.S.C. 77k); and

(iv) A registration statement for the abandoned offering was filed and withdrawn, specifying the effective date of the withdrawal; and

(5) Any disclosure document used in the private offering discloses any changes in the issuer's business or financial condition that occurred after the issuer filed the registration statement that are material to the investment decision in the private offering.

Rule 175. Liability for Certain Statements by Issuers

(a) A statement within the coverage of paragraph (b) below which is made by or on behalf of an issuer or by an outside reviewer retained by the issuer shall be deemed not to be a fraudulent statement (as defined in paragraph (d) below), unless it is shown that such statement was made or reaffirmed without a reasonable basis or was disclosed other than in good faith.

(b) This rule applies to the following statements:

(1) A forward-looking statement (as defined in paragraph (c) of this section) made in a document filed with the Commission, in Part I of a quarterly report on Form 10–Q and Form 10–QSB, § 249.308a of this chapter, or in an annual report to shareholders meeting the requirements of Rules 14a–3(b) and (c) or 14c–3(a) and (b) under the Securities Exchange Act of 1934, a statement reaffirming such forward-looking statement subsequent to the date the document was filed or the annual report was made publicly available, or a forward-looking statement made prior to the date the document was filed or the date the annual report was publicly available if such statement is reaffirmed in a filed document, in Part I of a quarterly report on Form 10–Q and Form 10–QSB, or in an annual report made publicly available within a reasonable time after the making of such forward-looking statement; Provided, That (i) At the time such statements are made or reaffirmed, either the issuer is subject to the reporting requirements of section 13(a) or 15(d) of the Securities Exchange Act of 1934 and has complied with the requirements of Rule 13a–1 or 15d–1 thereunder, if applicable, to file its most recent annual report on Form 10–K and Form 10–KSB, Form 20–F, or Form 40–F; or, if the issuer is not subject to the reporting requirements of section 13(a) or 15(d) of the Securities Exchange Act of 1934, the statements are made in a registration statement filed under the Securities Act of 1933, offering statement, or solicitation of interest written document or broadcast script under Regulation A or pursuant to section 12(b) or (g) of the Securities Exchange Act of 1934, and (ii) The statements are not made by or on behalf of an issuer that is an investment company registered under the Investment Company Act of 1940; and

(2) Information which is disclosed in a document filed with the Commission, in Part I of a quarterly report on Form 10–Q and Form 10–QSB (§ 249.308a of this chapter) or in an annual report to shareholders meeting the requirements of Rules 14a–3(b) and (c) or 14c–3(a) and (b) under the Securities Exchange Act of 1934 (§§ 240.14a–3(b) and (c) or 240.14a–3(a) and (b) of this chapter) and which relates to (i) the effects of changing prices on the business enterprise, presented voluntarily or pursuant to Item 303 of Regulation S–K (§ 229.303 of this chapter) or Regulation S–B (§ 228.303 of this chapter) Management's Discussion and Analysis of Financial Condition and Results of Operations, or Item 5 of Form 20–F, Operating and Financial Review and Prospects, (§ 249.220f of this chapter) "Management's discussion and analysis of financial condition and results of operations," or Item 302 of Regulation S–K (§ 229.302 of this chapter), "Supplementary financial information," or Rule 3–20(c) of Regulation S–X (§ 210.3–20(c) of this chapter), or (ii) the value of proved oil and gas reserves (such as a standardized measure of discounted future net cash flows relating to proved oil and gas reserves as set forth in paragraphs 30–34 of Statement of Financial Accounting Standards No. 69) presented voluntarily or pursuant to Item 302 of Regulation S–K (§ 229.302 of this chapter).

(c) For the purpose of this rule the term "forward looking statement" shall mean and shall be limited to:

(1) A statement containing a projection of revenues, income (loss), earnings (loss) per share,

capital expenditures, dividends, capital structure or other financial items;

(2) A statement of management's plans and objectives for future operations;

(3) A statement of future economic performance contained in management's discussion and analysis of financial condition and results of operations included pursuant to Item 303 of Regulation S–K (§ 229.303 of this chapter) or Item 5 of Form 20–F; or

(4) Disclosed statements of the assumptions underlying or relating to any of the statements described in (1), (2) or (3) above.

(d) For the purpose of this rule the term "fraudulent statement" shall mean a statement which is an untrue statement of a material fact, a statement false or misleading with respect to any material fact, an omission to state a material fact necessary to make a statement not misleading, or which constitutes the employment of a manipulative, deceptive, or fraudulent device, contrivance, scheme, transaction, act, practice, course of business, or an artifice to defraud, as those terms are used in the Securities Act of 1933 or the rules or regulations promulgated thereunder.

Rule 176. Circumstances Affecting the Determination of What Constitutes Reasonable Investigation and Reasonable Grounds for Belief Under Section 11 of the Securities Act

In determining whether or not the conduct of a person constitutes a reasonable investigation or a reasonable ground for belief meeting the standard set forth in section 11(c), relevant circumstances include, with respect to a person other than the issuer:

(a) The type of issuer;

(b) The type of security;

(c) The type of person;

(d) The office held when the person is an officer;

(e) The presence or absence of another relationship to the issuer when the person is a director or proposed director;

(f) Reasonable reliance on officers, employees, and others whose duties should have given them knowledge of the particular facts (in the light of the functions and responsibilities of the particular person with respect to the issuer and the filing);

(g) When the person is an underwriter, the type of underwriting arrangement, the role of the particular person as an underwriter and the availability of information with respect to the registrant; and

(h) Whether, with respect to a fact or document incorporated by reference, the particular person had any responsibility for the fact or document at the time of the filing from which it was incorporated.

* * *

REGULATION A—CONDITIONAL SMALL ISSUES EXEMPTION

Rule 251. Scope of Exemption

A public offer or sale of securities that meets the following terms and conditions shall be exempt under section 3(b) from the registration requirements of the Securities Act of 1933 (the "Securities Act"):

(a) *Issuer.* The issuer of the securities:

(1) is an entity organized under the laws of the United States or Canada, or any State, Province, Territory or possession thereof, or the District of Columbia, with its principal place of business in the United States or Canada;

(2) is not subject to section 13 or 15(d) of the Securities Exchange Act of 1934 (the "Exchange Act") immediately before the offering;

(3) is not a development stage company that either has no specific business plan or purpose, or has indicated that its business plan is to merge with an unidentified company or companies;

(4) is not an investment company registered or required to be registered under the Investment Company Act of 1940;

(5) is not issuing fractional undivided interests in oil or gas rights as defined in Rule 300, or a similar interest in other mineral rights; and

(6) is not disqualified because of Rule 262.

(b) *Aggregate Offering Price.* The sum of all cash and other consideration to be received for the securities ("aggregate offering price") shall not exceed $5,000,000, including no more than $1,500,000 offered by all selling security holders, less the aggregate offering price for all securities sold within the twelve months before the start of and during the offering of securities in reliance upon Regulation A. No affiliate resales are permitted if the issuer has not had net income from continuing operations in at least one of its last two fiscal years.

NOTE: Where a mixture of cash and non-cash consideration is to be received, the aggregate offering price shall be based on the price at which the securities are offered for cash. Any portion of the aggregate offering price attributable to cash received in a foreign currency shall be translated into United States currency at a currency exchange rate in effect on or at a reasonable time prior to the date of the sale of the securities. If securities are not offered for cash, the aggregate offering price shall be based on the value of the consideration as established by bona fide sales of that consideration made within a reasonable time, or, in the absence of sales, on the fair value as determined by an accepted standard. Valuations of non-cash consideration must be reasonable at the time made.

(c) *Integration with Other Offerings.* Offers and sales made in reliance on this Regulation A will not be integrated with:

(1) prior offers or sales of securities; or

(2) subsequent offers or sales of securities that are:

(i) registered under the Securities Act, except as provided in Rule 254(d);

(ii) made in reliance on Rule 701;

(iii) made pursuant to an employee benefit plan;

(iv) made in reliance on Regulation S; or

(v) made more than six months after the completion of the Regulation A offering.

NOTE: If the issuer offers or sells securities for which the safe harbor rules are unavailable, such offers and sales still may not be integrated with the Regulation A offering, depending on the particular facts and circumstances.

(d) *Offering Conditions.*

(1) *Offers.*

(i) Except as allowed by Rule 254, no offer of securities shall be made unless a Form 1–A offering statement has been filed with the Commission.

(ii) After the Form 1–A offering statement has been filed:

(A) oral offers may be made;

(B) written offers under Rule 255 may be made;

(C) printed advertisements may be published or radio or television broadcasts made, if they state from whom a Preliminary Offering Circular or Final Offering Circular may be obtained, and contain no more than the following information:

(*1*) the name of the issuer of the security;

(*2*) the title of the security, the amount being offered and the per unit offering price to the public;

(*3*) the general type of the issuer's business; and

(*4*) a brief statement as to the general character and location of its property.

(iii) after the Form 1–A offering statement has been qualified, other written offers may be made, but only if accompanied with or preceded by a Final Offering Circular.

(2) *Sales.*

(i) No sale of securities shall be made until:

(A) the Form 1–A offering statement has been qualified;

(B) a Preliminary Offering Circular or Final Offering Circular is furnished to the prospective purchaser at least 48 hours prior to the mailing of the confirmation of sale to that person; and

(C) a Final Offering Circular is delivered to the purchaser with the confirmation of sale, unless it has been delivered to that person at an earlier time.

(ii) Sales by a dealer (including an underwriter no longer acting in that capacity for the security involved in such transaction) that take place within 90 days after the qualification of the Regulation A offering statement may be made only if the dealer delivers a copy of the current offering circular to the purchaser before or with the confirmation of sale. The issuer or underwriter of the offering shall provide requesting dealers with reasonable quantities of the offering circular for this purpose.

(3) *Continuous or delayed offerings.* Continuous or delayed offerings may be made under this Regulation A if permitted by Rule 415.

Rule 252. Offering Statement

(a) *Documents to be Included.* The offering statement consists of the facing sheet of Form 1–A, the contents required by the form and any other material information necessary to make the required statements, in the light of the circumstances under which they are made, not misleading.

(b) *Paper, printing, language and pagination.* The requirements for offering statements are the same as those specified in Rule 403 for registration statements under the Act.

(c) *Confidential treatment.* A request for confidential treatment may be made under Rule 406 for information required to be filed * * *.

(d) *Signatures.* The issuer, its Chief Executive Officer, Chief Financial Officer, a majority of the members of its board of directors or other governing body, and each selling security holder shall sign the offering statement. If a signature is by a person on behalf of any other person, evidence of authority to sign shall be filed, except where an executive officer signs for the issuer. * * * If the issuer is a limited partnership, a majority of the board of directors of any corporate general partner also shall sign.

(e) *Number of copies and where to file.* Seven copies of the offering statement, at least one of which is manually signed, shall be filed with the Commission's main office in Washington, D.C.

(f) [Reserved]

(g) *Qualification.* (1) If there is no delaying notation as permitted by paragraph (g)(2) of this section or suspension proceeding under Rule 258, an offering statement is qualified without Commission action on the 20th calendar day after its filing.

(2) An offering statement containing the following notation can be qualified only by order of the Commission, unless such notation is removed prior to Commission action as described in paragraph (g)(3) of this section:

> This offering statement shall only be qualified upon order of the Commission, unless a subsequent amendment is filed indicating the intention to become qualified by operation of the terms of Regulation A.

(3) The delaying notation specified in paragraph (g)(2) of this section can be removed only by an amendment to the offering statement that contains the following language:

> This offering statement shall become qualified on the 20th calendar day following the filing of this amendment.

(h) Amendments.

(1) If any information in the offering statement is amended, an amendment, signed in the same manner as the initial filing, shall be filed. Seven copies of every amendment shall be filed with the Commission's Main Office in Wash. D.C.

(2) An amendment to include a delaying notation pursuant to paragraph (g)(2) or to remove one pursuant to paragraph (g)(3) of this section after the initial filing of an offering statement may be made by telegram or letter or facsimile transmission. Each such telegraphic amendment shall be confirmed in writing within a reasonable time by filing a signed copy. Such confirmation shall not be deemed an amendment.

Rule 253. Offering Circular

(a) *Contents.* An offering circular shall include the narrative and financial information required by Form 1–A.

(b) *Presentation of Information.* (1) Information in the offering circular shall be presented in a clear, concise and understandable manner and in a type size that is easily readable. Repetition of information should be avoided; cross-referencing of information within the document is permitted.

(2) Where an offering circular is distributed through an electronic medium, issuers may satisfy legibility requirements applicable to printed documents by presenting all required information in a format readily communicated to investors.

(c) *Date.* An offering circular shall be dated approximately as of the date of the qualification of the offering statement of which it is a part.

(d) *Cover page legend.* The cover page of every offering circular shall display the following statement in capital letters printed in boldfaced type at least as large as that used generally in the body of such offering circular:

THE UNITED STATES SECURITIES AND EXCHANGE COMMISSION DOES NOT PASS UPON THE MERITS OF OR GIVE ITS APPROVAL TO ANY SECURITIES OFFERED OR THE TERMS OF THE OFFERING, NOR DOES IT PASS UPON THE ACCURACY OR COMPLETENESS OF ANY OFFERING CIRCULAR OR OFFERED SELLING LITERATURE. THESE SECURITIES ARE OFFERED PURSUANT TO AN EXEMPTION FROM REGISTRATION WITH THE COMMISSION; HOWEVER, THE COMMISSION HAS NOT MADE AN INDEPENDENT DETERMINATION THAT THE SECURITIES OFFERED HEREUNDER ARE EXEMPT FROM REGISTRATION.

(e) *Revisions.* (1) An offering circular shall be revised during the course of an offering whenever the information it contains has become false or misleading in light of existing circumstances, material developments have occurred, or there has been a fundamental change in the information initially presented.

(2) An offering circular for a continuous offering shall be updated to include, among other things, updated financial statements, 12 months after the date the offering statement was qualified.

(3) Every revised or updated offering circular shall be filed as an amendment to the offering statement and requalified in accordance with Rule 252.

Rule 254. Solicitation of Interest Document for Use Prior to an Offering Statement

(a) An issuer may publish or deliver to prospective purchasers a written document or make scripted radio or television broadcasts to determine whether there is any interest in a contemplated securities offering. Following submission of the written document or script of the broadcast to the Commission, as required by paragraph (b) of this section, oral communications with prospective investors and other broadcasts are permitted. The written documents, broadcasts and oral communications are each subject to the antifraud provisions of the federal securities laws. No solicitation or acceptance of money or other consideration, nor of any commitment, binding or otherwise, from any prospective investor is permitted. No sale may be made until qualification of the offering statement.

(b) While not a condition to any exemption pursuant to this section:

(1) On or before the date of its first use, the issuer shall submit a copy of any written document or the script of any broadcast with the Commission's main office in Washington, D.C. (*Attention:* Office of Small Business Policy). The document or broadcast script shall either contain or be accompanied by the name and telephone number of a person able to answer questions about the document or the broadcast.

NOTE: Only solicitation of interest material that contains substantive changes from or additions to previously submitted material needs to be submitted.

(2) The written document or script of the broadcast shall:

(i) state that no money or other consideration is being solicited, and if sent in response, will not be accepted;

(ii) state that no sales of the securities will be made or commitment to purchase accepted until delivery of an offering circular that includes complete information about the issuer and the offering;

(iii) state that an indication of interest made by a prospective investor involves no obligation or commitment of any kind; and

(iv) identify the chief executive officer of the issuer and briefly and in general its business and products.

(3) Solicitations of interest pursuant to this provision may not be made after the filing of an offering statement.

(4) Sales may not be made until 20 calendar days after the last publication or delivery of the document or radio or television broadcast.

(c) Any written document under this section may include a coupon, returnable to the issuer indicating interest in a potential offering, revealing the name, address and telephone number of the prospective investor.

(d) Where an issuer has a bona fide change of intention and decides to register an offering after using the process permitted by this section without having filed the offering statement prescribed by Rule 252, the Regulation A exemption for offers made in reliance upon this section will not be subject to integration with the registered offering, if at least 30 calendar days have elapsed between the last solicitation of interest and the filing of the registration statement with the Commission, and all solicitation of interest documents have been submitted to the Commission. With respect to integration with other offerings, see Rule 251(c).

(e) Written solicitation of interest materials submitted to the Commission and otherwise in compliance with this section shall not be deemed to be a prospectus as defined in Section 2(10) of the Securities Act.

Rule 255. Preliminary Offering Circulars

(a) Prior to qualification of the required offering statement, but after its filing, a written offer of securities may be made if it meets the following requirements:

(1) The outside front cover page of the material bears the caption "Preliminary Offering Circular," the date of issuance, and the following statement, which shall run along the left hand margin of the page and be printed perpendicular to the text, in boldfaced type at least as large as that used generally in the body of such offering circular:

> An offering statement pursuant to Regulation A relating to these securities has been filed with the Securities and Exchange Commission.
>
> Information contained in this Preliminary Offering Circular is subject to completion or amendment. These securities may not be sold nor may offers to buy be accepted prior to the time an offering circular which is not designated as a Preliminary Offering Circular is delivered and the offering statement filed with the Commission becomes qualified. This Preliminary Offering Circular shall not constitute an offer to sell or the solicitation of an offer to buy nor shall there be any sales of these securities in any state in which such offer, solicitation or sale would be unlawful prior to registration or qualification under the laws of any such state.

(2) The Preliminary Offering Circular contains substantially the information required in an offering circular by Form 1–A, except that information with respect to offering price, underwriting discounts or commissions, discounts or commissions to dealers, amount of proceeds, conversion rates, call prices, or other matters dependent upon the offering price may be omitted. The outside front cover page of the Preliminary Offering Circular shall include a bona fide estimate of the range of the maximum offering price and maximum number of shares or other units of securities to be offered or a bona fide estimate of the principal amount of debt securities to be offered.

(3) The material is filed as a part of the offering statement.

(b) If a Preliminary Offering Circular is inaccurate or inadequate in any material respect, a revised Preliminary Offering Circular or a complete Offering Circular shall be furnished to all persons to whom securities are to be sold at least 48 hours prior to the mailing of any confirmation of sale to such persons, or shall be sent to such persons under such circumstances that it would normally be received by them 48 hours prior to receipt of confirmation of the sale.

Rule 256. Filing of Sales Material

While not a condition to an exemption pursuant to this provision, seven copies of any advertisement or written communication, or the script of any radio or television broadcast, shall be filed with the main office of the Commission in Wash. D.C.

NOTE: Only sales material that contains substantive changes from or additions from previously filed material needs to be filed.

Rule 257. Reports of Sales and Use of Proceeds

While not a condition to an exemption pursuant to this provision, the issuer and/or each selling security holder shall file seven copies of a report concerning sales and use of proceeds on Form 2–A, or other form prescribed with the main office of the Commission in Washington, D.C. This report shall be filed at the following times:

(a) every six months after the qualification of the offering statement or any amendment until substantially all the proceeds have been applied; and

(b) within 30 calendar days after the termination, completion or final sale of securities in the offering, or the application of the proceeds from the offering, whichever is the latest event. This report should be labelled the final report. For purposes of this section, the temporary investment of proceeds pending final application shall not constitute application of the proceeds.

Rule 258. Suspension of the Exemption

(a) The Commission may at any time enter an order temporarily suspending a Regulation A exemption if it has reason to believe that:

(1) no exemption is available or any of the terms, conditions or requirements of the Regulation have not been complied with, including failures to provide the Commission a copy of the document or broadcast script under Rule 254, to file any sales material as required by Rule 256 or report as required by Rule 257;

(2) the offering statement, any sales or solicitation of interest material contains any untrue statement of a material fact or omits to state a material fact necessary in order to make the statements made, in light of the circumstances under which they are made, not misleading;

(3) the offering is being made or would be made in violation of section 17 of the Securities Act;

(4) an event has occurred after the filing of the offering statement which would have rendered the exemption hereunder unavailable if it had occurred prior to such filing;

(5) any person specified in paragraph (a) of Rule 262 has been indicted for any crime or offense of the character specified in paragraph (a)(3) of Rule 262, or any proceeding has been initiated for the purpose of enjoining any such person from engaging in or continuing any conduct or practice of the character specified in paragraph (a)(4) of Rule 262;

(6) any person specified in paragraph (b) of Rule 262 has been indicted for any crime or offense of the character specified in paragraph (b)(1) of Rule 262, or any proceeding has been initiated for the purpose of enjoining any such person from engaging in or continuing any conduct or practice of the character specified in paragraph (b)(2) of Rule 262; or

(7) the issuer or any promoter, officer, director or underwriter has failed to cooperate, or has obstructed or refused to permit the making of an investigation by the Commission in connection with any offering made or proposed to be made in reliance on Regulation A.

(b) Upon the entry of an order under paragraph (a) of this section, the Commission will promptly give notice to the issuer, any underwriter and any selling security holder:

(1) that such order has been entered, together with a brief statement of the reasons for the entry of the order; and

(2) that the Commission upon receipt of a written request within 30 calendar days after the entry of the order, will within 20 calendar days after receiving the request, order a hearing at a place to be designated by the Commission.

(c) If no hearing is requested and none is ordered by the Commission, an order entered under paragraph (a) of this section shall become permanent on the 30th calendar day after its entry and shall remain in effect unless or until it is modified or vacated by the Commission. Where a hearing is requested or is ordered by the Commission, the Commission will, after notice of and opportunity for such hearing, either vacate the order or enter an order permanently suspending the exemption.

(d) The Commission may, at any time after notice of and opportunity for hearing, enter an order permanently suspending the exemption for any reason upon which it could have entered a temporary suspension order under paragraph (a) of this section. Any such order shall remain in effect until vacated by the Commission.

(e) All notices required by this section shall be given by personal service, registered or certified mail to the addresses given by the issuer, any underwriter and any selling security holder in the offering statement.

Rule 259. Withdrawal or Abandonment of Offering Statements

(a) If none of the securities which are the subject of an offering statement have been sold and such offering statement is not the subject of a proceeding under Rule 258, the offering statement may be withdrawn with the Commission's consent. The application for withdrawal shall state the reason the offering statement is to be withdrawn, shall be signed by an authorized representative of the issuer and shall be provided to the main office in Washington, D.C.

(b) When an offering statement has been on file with the Commission for nine months without amendment and has not become qualified, the Commission may, in its discretion, proceed in the following manner to determine whether such offering statement has been abandoned by the issuer. If the offering statement has been amended, the 9–month period shall be computed from the date of the latest amendment.

(1) Notice will be sent to the issuer, and to any counsel for the issuer named in the offering statement, by registered or certified mail, return receipt requested, addressed to the most recent addresses for the issuer and issuer's counsel as reflected in the offering statement. Such notice will inform the issuer and issuer's counsel that the offering statement or amendments thereto is out of date and must be either amended to comply with applicable requirements of Regulation A or be withdrawn within 30 calendar days after the notice.

(2) If the issuer or issuer's counsel fail to respond to such notice by filing a substantive amendment or withdrawing the offering statement or does not furnish a satisfactory explanation as to why the issuer has not done so within 30 calendar days, the Commission may declare the offering statement abandoned.

Rule 260. Insignificant Deviations From a Term, Condition or Requirement of Regulation A

(a) A failure to comply with a term, condition or requirement of Regulation A will not result in the loss of the exemption from the requirements of section 5 of the Securities Act for any offer or sale to a particular individual or entity, if the person relying on the exemption establishes:

(1) the failure to comply did not pertain to a term, condition or requirement directly intended to protect that particular individual or entity;

(2) the failure to comply was insignificant with respect to the offering as a whole, provided that any failure to comply with paragraphs (a), (b), (d)(1) and (3) of Rule 251 shall be deemed to be significant to the offering as a whole; and

(3) a good faith and reasonable attempt was made to comply with all applicable terms, conditions and requirements of Regulation A.

(b) A transaction made in reliance upon Regulation A shall comply with all applicable terms, conditions and requirements of the regulation, where an exemption is established only through reliance upon paragraph (a) of this section, the failure to comply shall nonetheless be actionable by the Commission under section 20 of the Act.

(c) This provision provides no relief or protection from a proceeding under Rule 258.

Rule 261. Definitions

As used in this Regulation A, all terms have the same meanings as in Rule 405, except that all references to "registrant" in those definitions shall refer to the issuer of the securities to be offered and sold under Regulation A. In addition, these terms have the following meanings:

(a) *Final Offering Circular*—The current offering circular contained in a qualified offering statement;

(b) *Preliminary Offering Circular*—The offering circular described in Rule 255(a).

Rule 262. Disqualification Provisions

Unless, upon a showing of good cause and without prejudice to any other action by the Commission, the Commission determines that it is not necessary under the circumstances that the exemption provided by this Regulation A be denied, the exemption shall not be available for the offer or sale of securities, if:

(a) the issuer, any of its predecessors or any affiliated issuer:

(1) has filed a registration statement which is the subject of any pending proceeding or examination under section 8 of the Act, or has been the subject of any refusal order or stop order thereunder within 5 years prior to the filing of the offering statement required by Rule 252;

(2) is subject to any pending proceeding under Rule 258 or any similar section adopted under section 3(b) of the Securities Act, or to an order entered thereunder within 5 years prior to the filing of such offering statement;

(3) has been convicted within 5 years prior to the filing of such offering statement of any felony or misdemeanor in connection with the purchase or sale of any security or involving the making of any false filing with the Commission;

(4) is subject to any order, judgment, or decree of any court of competent jurisdiction temporarily or preliminarily restraining or enjoining, or is subject to any order, judgment or decree of any court of competent jurisdiction, entered within 5 years prior to the filing of such offering statement, permanently restraining or enjoining, such person from engaging in or continuing any conduct or practice in connection with the purchase or sale of any security or involving the making of any false filing with the Commission; or

(5) is subject to a United States Postal Service false representation order entered under 39 U.S.C. § 3005 within 5 years prior to the filing of the offering statement, or is subject to a temporary restraining order or preliminary injunction entered under 39 U.S.C. § 3007 with respect to conduct alleged to have violated 39 U.S.C. § 3005. The entry of an order, judgment or decree against any affiliated entity before the affiliation with the issuer arose, if the affiliated entity is not in control of the issuer and if the affiliated entity and the issuer are not under the common control of a third party who was in control of the affiliated entity at the time of such entry does not come within the purview of this paragraph (a) of this section.

(b) any director, officer or general partner of the issuer, beneficial owner of 10 percent or more of any class of its equity securities, any promoter of the issuer presently connected with it in any capacity, any underwriter of the securities to be offered, or any partner, director or officer of any such underwriter:

(1) has been convicted within 10 years prior to the filing of the offering statement required by Rule 252 of any felony or misdemeanor in connection with the purchase or sale of any security, involving the making of a false filing with the Commission, or arising out of the conduct of the business of an underwriter, broker, dealer, municipal securities dealer, or investment adviser;

(2) is subject to any order, judgment, or decree of any court of competent jurisdiction temporarily or preliminarily enjoining or restraining, or is subject to any order, judgment, or decree of any court of competent jurisdiction, entered within 5 years prior to the filing of such offering statement, permanently enjoining or restraining such person from engaging in or continuing any conduct or practice in connection with the purchase or sale of any security, involving the making of a false filing with the Commission, or arising out of the conduct of the business of an underwriter, broker, dealer, municipal securities dealer, or investment adviser;

(3) is subject to an order of the Commission entered pursuant to section 15(b), 15B(a), or 15B(c) of the Exchange Act, or section 203(e) or (f) of the Investment Advisers Act of 1940;

(4) is suspended or expelled from membership in, or suspended or barred from association with a member of, a national securities exchange registered under section 6 of the Exchange Act or a national securities association registered under section 15A of the Exchange Act for any act or omission to act constituting conduct inconsistent with just and equitable principles of trade; or

(5) is subject to a United States Postal Service false representation order entered under 39 U.S.C. § 3005 within 5 years prior to the filing of the offering statement required by Rule 252, or is subject to a restraining order or preliminary injunction entered under 39 U.S.C. § 3007 with respect to conduct alleged to have violated 39 U.S.C. § 3005.

(c) any underwriter of such securities was an underwriter or was named as an underwriter of any securities:

(1) covered by any registration statement which is the subject of any pending proceeding or examination under section 8 of the Act, or is the subject of any refusal order or stop order entered thereunder within 5 years prior to the filing of the offering statement required by Rule 252; or

(2) covered by any filing which is subject to any pending proceeding under Rule 258 or any similar rule adopted under section 3(b) of the Securities Act, or to an order entered thereunder within 5 years prior to the filing of such offering statement.

Rule 263. Consent to Service of Process

(a) If the issuer is not organized under the laws of any of the states of or the United States of America, it shall at the time of filing the offering statement required by Rule 252, furnish to the Commission a written irrevocable consent and power of attorney on Form F–X.

(b) Any change to the name or address of the agent for service of the issuer shall be communicated promptly to the Commission through amendment of the requisite form and referencing the file number of the relevant offering statement.

REGULATION C—REGISTRATION

Rule 400. Application of Regulation C

The rules contained in this regulation shall govern every registration of securities under the Act, except that any provision in a form, or an item of Regulation S–K referred to in such form, covering the same subject matter as any such rule shall be controlling unless otherwise specifically provided herein.

General Requirements

* * *

Rule 404. Preparation of Registration Statement

(a) A registration statement shall consist of the facing sheet of the applicable form; a prospectus containing the information called for by Part I of such form; the information, list of exhibits, undertakings and signatures required to be set forth in Part II of such form; financial statements and schedules; exhibits; any other information or documents filed as part of the registration statement; and all documents or information incorporated by reference in the foregoing (whether or not required to be filed).

(b) All general instructions, instructions to items of the form, and instructions as to financial statements, exhibits, or prospectuses are to be omitted from the registration statement in all cases.

(c) The prospectus shall contain the information called for by all of the items of Part I of the applicable form, except that unless otherwise specified, no reference need be made to inapplicable items, and negative answers to any item in Part I may be omitted. A copy of the prospectus may be filed as a part of the registration statement in lieu of furnishing the information in item-and-answer form. Wherever a copy of the prospectus is filed in lieu of information in item-and-answer form, the text of the items of the form is to be omitted from the registration statement, as well as from the prospectus, except to the extent provided in paragraph (d) of this rule.

* * *

Rule 405. Definitions of Terms

Unless the context otherwise requires, all terms used in this regulation, or in the forms for registration have the same meanings as in the Act and in the general rules and regulations. In addition, the following definitions apply, unless the context otherwise requires:

Affiliate. An "affiliate" of, or person "affiliated" with, a specified person, is a person that directly, or indirectly through one or more intermediaries, controls or is controlled by, or is under common control with, the person specified.

Amount. The term "amount," when used in regard to securities, means the principal amount if relating to evidences of indebtedness, the number of shares if relating to shares, and the number of units if relating to any other kind of security.

Associate. The term "associate," when used to indicate a relationship with any person, means (1) a corporation or organization (other than the registrant or a majority-owned subsidiary of the registrant) of which such person is an officer or partner or is, directly or indirectly, the beneficial owner of 10 percent or more of any class of equity securities, (2) any trust or other estate in which such person has a substantial beneficial interest or as to which such person serves as trustee or in a similar capacity, and (3) any relative or spouse of such person, or any relative of such spouse, who has the same home as such person or who is a director or officer of the registrant or any of its parents or subsidiaries.

Business development company. The term "business development company" refers to a company which has elected to be regulated as a business development company under sections 55 through 65 of the Investment Company Act of 1940.

Certified. The term "certified," when used in regard to financial statements, means examined and reported upon with an opinion expressed by an independent public or certified public accountant.

Charter. The term "charter" includes articles of incorporation, declarations of trust, articles of association or partnership, or any similar instrument, as amended, affecting (either with or without filing with any governmental agency) the organization or creation of an incorporated or unincorporated person.

Common equity. The term "common equity" means any class of common stock or an equivalent interest, including but not limited to a unit of beneficial interest in a trust or a limited partnership interest.

Commission. The term "Commission" means the Securities and Exchange Commission.

Control. The term "control" (including the terms "controlling," "controlled by" and "under common control with") means the possession, direct or indirect, of the power to direct or cause the direction of the management and policies of a person, whether through the ownership of voting securities, by contract, or otherwise.

Director. The term "director" means any director of a corporation or any person performing similar functions with respect to any organization whether incorporated or unincorporated.

* * *

Employee. The term "employee" does not include a director, trustee, or officer.

Employee benefit plan. The term "employee benefit plan" means any written purchase, savings, option, bonus, appreciation, profit sharing, thrift, incentive, pension or similar plan solely for employees, directors, general partners, trustees (where the registrant is a business trust), officers, or consultants or advisors. However, consultants or advisors may participate in an employee benefit plan only if:

(1) They are natural persons;

(2) They provide bona fide services to the registrant; and

(3) The services are not in connection with the offer or sale of securities in a capital-raising transaction, and do not directly or indirectly promote or maintain a market for the registrant's securities.

Equity security. The term "equity security" means any stock or similar security, certificate of interest or participation in any profit sharing agreement, preorganization certificate or subscription, transferable share, voting trust certificate or certificate of deposit for an equity security, limited partnership interest, interest in a joint venture, or certificate of interest in a business trust; or any security convertible, with or without consideration into such a security, or carrying any warrant or right to subscribe to or purchase such a security; or any such warrant or right; or any put, call, straddle, or other option or privilege of buying such a security from or selling such a security to another without being bound to do so.

Executive officer. The term "executive officer," when used with reference to a registrant, means its president, any vice president of the registrant in charge of a principal business unit, division or function (such as sales, administration or finance), any other officer who performs a policy making function or any other person who performs similar policy making functions for the registrant. Executive officers of subsidiaries may be deemed executive officers of the registrant if they perform such policy making functions for the registrant.

Fiscal year. The term "fiscal year" means the annual accounting period or, if no closing date has been adopted, the calendar year ending on December 31.

* * *

Material. The term "material," when used to qualify a requirement for the furnishing of information as to any subject, limits the information required to those matters to which there is a substantial likelihood that a reasonable investor would attach importance in determining whether to purchase the security registered.

Officer. The term "officer" means a president, vice president, secretary, treasurer or principal financial officer, comptroller or principal accounting officer, and any person routinely performing corresponding functions with respect to any organization whether incorporated or unincorporated.

Parent. A "parent" of a specified person is an affiliate controlling such person directly, or indirectly through one or more intermediaries.

Predecessor. The term "predecessor" means a person the major portion of the business and assets of which another person acquired in a single succession, or in a series of related successions in each of which the acquiring person acquired the major portion of the business and assets of the acquired person.

Principal underwriter. The term "principal underwriter" means an underwriter in privity of contract with the issuer of the securities as to which he is underwriter, the term "issuer" having the meaning given in sections 2(4) and 2(11) of the Act.

Promoter. (1) The term "promoter" includes—

(i) Any person who, acting alone or in conjunction with one or more other persons, directly or indirectly takes initiative in founding and organizing the business or enterprise of an issuer; or

(ii) Any person who, in connection with the founding and organizing of the business or enterprise of an issuer, directly or indirectly receives in consideration of services or property, or both services and property, 10 percent or more of any class of securities of the issuer or 10 percent or more of the proceeds from the sale of any class of such securities. However, a person who receives such securities or proceeds either solely as underwriting commissions or solely in consideration of property shall not be deemed a promoter within the meaning of this paragraph if such person does not otherwise take part in founding and organizing the enterprise.

(2) All persons coming within the definition of "promoter" in paragraph (1) of this definition may be referred to as "founders" or "organizers" or by another term provided that such term is reasonably descriptive of those persons' activities with respect to the issuer.

Prospectus. Unless otherwise specified or the context otherwise requires, the term "prospectus" means a prospectus meeting the requirements of section 10(a) of the Act.

Registrant. The term "registrant" means the issuer of the securities for which the registration statement is filed.

Share. The term "share" means a share of stock in a corporation or unit of interest in an unincorporated person.

* * *

Succession. The term "succession" means the direct acquisition of the assets comprising a going business, whether by merger, consolidation, purchase, or other direct transfer. The term does not include the acquisition of control of a business unless followed by the direct acquisition of its assets. The terms "succeed" and "successor" have meanings correlative to the foregoing.

* * *

Voting securities. The term "voting securities" means securities the holders of which are presently entitled to vote for the election of directors.

* * *

Rule 408. Additional Information

In addition to the information expressly required to be included in a registration statement, there shall be added such further material information, if any, as may be necessary to make the required statements, in the light of the circumstances under which they are made, not misleading.

Rule 415. Delayed or Continuous Offering and Sale of Securities

(a) Securities may be registered for an offering to be made on a continuous or delayed basis in the future. *Provided,* That—

(1) The registration statement pertains only to:

(i) Securities which are to be offered or sold solely by or on behalf of a person or persons other than the registrant, a subsidiary of the registrant or a person of which the registrant is a subsidiary;

(ii) Securities which are to be offered and sold pursuant to a dividend or interest reinvestment plan or an employee benefit plan of the registrant;

(iii) Securities which are to be issued upon the exercise of outstanding options, warrants or rights;

(iv) Securities which are to be issued upon conversion of other outstanding securities;

(v) Securities which are pledged as collateral;

(vi) Securities which are registered on Form F–6;

(vii) Mortgage related securities, including such securities as mortgage backed debt and mortgage participation or pass through certificates;

(viii) Securities which are to be issued in connection with business combination transactions;

(ix) Securities the offering of which will be commenced promptly, will be made on a continuous basis and may continue for a period in excess of 30 days from the date of initial effectiveness; or

(x) Securities registered (or qualified to be registered) on Form S–3 or Form F–3 which are to be offered and sold on a continuous or delayed basis by or on behalf of the registrant, a subsidiary of the registrant or a person of which the registrant is a subsidiary.

(xi) Shares of common stock which are to be offered and sold on a delayed or continuous basis by or on behalf of a registered closed-end management investment company or business development company that makes periodic repurchase offers pursuant to s 270.23c–3 of this chapter.

(2) Securities in paragraphs (a)(1)(viii) through (x) may only be registered in an amount which, at the time the registration statement becomes effective, is reasonably expected to be offered and sold within two years from the initial effective date of the registration.

(3) The registrant furnishes the undertakings required by Item 512(a) of Regulation S–K (s 229.512 of this chapter).

(4) In the case of a registration statement pertaining to an at the market offering of equity securities by or on behalf of the registrant:

(i) The offering comes within paragraph (a)(1)(x); (ii) where voting stock is registered, the amount of securities registered for such purposes must not exceed 10% of the aggregate market value of the registrant's outstanding voting stock held by non-affiliates of the registrant (calculated as of a date within 60 days prior to the date of filing); (iii) the securities must be sold through an underwriter or underwriters, acting as principal(s) or as agent(s) for the registrant; and (iv) the underwriter or underwriters must be named in the prospectus which is part of the registration statement. As used in this paragraph, the term "at the market offering" means an offering of securities into an existing trading market for outstanding shares of the same class at other than a fixed price on or through the facilities of a national securities exchange or to or through a market maker otherwise than on an exchange.

(b) This section shall not apply to any registration statement pertaining to securities issued by a face-amount certificate company or redeemable securities issued by an open-end management company or unit investment trust under the Investment Company Act of 1940 or any registration statement filed by any foreign government or political subdivision thereof.

FORM AND CONTENTS OF PROSPECTUSES

Rule 421. Presentation of Information in Prospectuses

(a) The information required in a prospectus need not follow the order of the items or other requirements in the form. Such information shall not, however, be set forth in such fashion as to obscure any of the required information or any information necessary to keep the required information from being incomplete or misleading. Where an item requires information to be given in a prospectus in tabular form it shall be given in substantially the tabular form specified in the item.

(b) You must present the information in a prospectus in a clear, concise and understandable manner. You must prepare the prospectus using the following standards:

(1) Present information in clear, concise sections, paragraphs, and sentences. Whenever possible, use short, explanatory sentences and bullet lists;

(2) Use descriptive headings and subheadings;

(3) Avoid frequent reliance on glossaries or defined terms as the primary means of explaining information in the prospectus. Define terms in a glossary or other section of the document only if the meaning is unclear from the context. Use a glossary only if it facilitates understanding of the disclosure; and

(4) Avoid legal and highly technical business terminology.

Note to Rule 421(b):

In drafting the disclosure to comply with this section, you should avoid the following:

1. Legalistic or overly complex presentations that make the substance of the disclosure difficult to understand;

2. Vague "boilerplate" explanations that are imprecise and readily subject to different interpretations;

3. Complex information copied directly from legal documents without any clear and concise explanation of the provision(s); and

4. Disclosure repeated in different sections of the document that increases the size of the document but does not enhance the quality of the information.

* * *

Rule 430. Prospectus for Use Prior to Effective Date

(a) A form of prospectus filed as a part of the registration statement shall be deemed to meet the requirements of section 10 of the Act for the purpose of section 5(b)(1) thereof prior to the effective date of the registration statement, provided such form of prospectus contains substantially the information required by the Act and the rules and regulations thereunder to be included in a prospectus meeting the requirements of section 10(a) of the Act for the securities being registered, or contains substantially that information except for the omission of information with respect to the offering price, underwriting discounts or commissions, discounts or commissions to dealers, amount of proceeds, conversion rates, call prices, or other matters dependent upon the offering price. Every such form of prospectus shall be deemed to have been filed as a part of the registration statement for the purpose of section 7 of the Act.

(b) A form of prospectus filed as part of a registration statement on Form N–1A (s 239.15A and s 274.11A of this chapter), Form N–2 (s 239.14 and s 274.11a–1 of this chapter), Form N–3 (s 239.17a and s 274.11b of this chapter), or Form N–4 (s 239.17b and s 274.11c of this chapter) shall be deemed to meet the requirements of Section 10 of the Act for the purpose of Section 5(b)(1) thereof prior to the effective date of the registration statement, provided that:

(1) Such form of prospectus meets the requirements of paragraph (a) of this section; and

(2) Such registration statement contains a form of Statement of Additional Information that is made available to persons receiving such prospectus upon written or oral request, and without charge, unless the form of prospectus contains the information otherwise required to be disclosed in the form of Statement of Additional Information. Every such form of prospectus shall be deemed to have been filed as part of the registration statement for the purpose of section 7 of the Act.

* * *

Rule 431. Summary Prospectuses

(a) A summary prospectus prepared and filed (except a summary prospectus filed by an open-end management investment company registered under the Investment Company Act of 1940) as part of a registration statement in accordance with this section shall be deemed to be a prospectus permitted under section 10(b) of the Act (15 U.S.C. 77j(b)) for the purpose of section 5(b)(1) of the Act (15 U.S.C. 77e(b)(1)) if the form used for registration of the securities to be offered provides for the use of a summary prospectus * * *.

(b) A summary prospectus shall contain the information specified in the instructions as to summary prospectuses in the form used for registration of the securities to be offered. Such prospectus may include any other information the substance of which is contained in the registration statement except as otherwise specifically provided in the instructions as to summary prospectuses in the form used for registration. It shall not include any information the substance of which is not contained in the registration statement except that a summary prospectus may contain any information specified in Rule 134(a). No reference need be made to inapplicable terms and negative answers to any item of the form may be omitted.

(c) All information included in a summary prospectus, other than the statement required by paragraph (e) of this section, may be expressed in such condensed or summarized form as may be appropriate in the light of the circumstances under which the prospectus is to be used. The information need not follow the numerical sequence of the items of the form used for registration. Every summary prospectus shall be dated approximately as of the date of its first use.

* * *

Rule 432. Additional Information Required to be Included in Prospectuses Relating to Tender Offers

Notwithstanding the provisions of any form for the registration of securities under the Act, any prospectus relating to securities to be offered in connection with a tender offer for, or a request or invitation for tenders of, securities subject to either § 240.13e–4 or section 14(d) of the Securities Exchange Act of 1934 must include all of the information required by § 240.13e–4(d)(1) or § 240.14d–6(d)(1) of this chapter, as applicable, in all tender offers, requests or invitations that are published, sent or given to the holders of such securities.

* * *

Rule 460. Distribution of Preliminary Prospectus

(a) Pursuant to the statutory requirement that the Commission in ruling upon requests for acceleration of the effective date of a registration statement shall have due regard to the adequacy of the information respecting the issuer theretofore available to the public, the Commission may consider whether the persons making the offering have taken reasonable steps to make the information contained in the registration statement conveniently available to underwriters and dealers who it is reasonably anticipated will be invited to participate in the distribution of the security to be offered or sold.

(b)(1) As a minimum, reasonable steps to make the information conveniently available would involve the distribution, to each underwriter and dealer who it is reasonably anticipated will be invited to participate in the distribution of the security, a reasonable time in advance of the anticipated effective date of the registration statement, of as many copies of the proposed form of preliminary prospectus permitted by Rule 430 as appears to be reasonable to secure adequate distribution of the preliminary prospectus.

* * *

(c) The granting of acceleration will not be conditioned upon

(1) The distribution of a preliminary prospectus in any state where such distribution would be illegal; or

(2) The distribution of a preliminary prospectus (i) in the case of a registration statement relating solely to securities to be offered at competitive bidding, provided the undertaking in Item 512(d)(1) of Regulation S–K is included in the registration statement and distribution of prospectuses pursuant to such undertaking is made prior to the publication or distribution of the invitation for bids, or (ii) in the case of a registration statement relating to a security issued by a face-amount certificate company or a redeemable security issued by an open-end management company or unit investment trust if any other security of the same class is currently being offered or sold, pursuant to an effective registration statement by the issuer or by or through an underwriter, or (iii) in the case of an offering of subscription rights unless it is contemplated that the distribution will be made through dealers and the underwriters intend to make the offering during the stockholders' subscription period, in which case copies of the preliminary prospectus must be distributed to dealers prior to the effective date of the registration statement in the same fashion as is required in the case of other offerings through underwriters, or (iv) in the case of a registration statement pertaining to a security to be offered pursuant to an exchange offer or transaction described in Rule 145.

Rule 461. Acceleration of Effective Date

(a) Requests for acceleration of the effective date of a registration statement shall be made in writing by the registrant and the managing underwriters of the proposed issue, or, if there are no managing underwriters, by the principal underwriters of the proposed issue, and shall state the date upon which it is desired that the registration statement shall become effective. Such requests may be made in writing or orally, provided that, if an oral request is to be made, a letter indicating that fact and stating that the registrant and the managing or principal underwriters are aware of their obligations under the Act must accompany the registration statement for a pre-effective amendment thereto at the time of filing with the Commission. Written requests may be sent to the Commission by facsimile transmission. If, by reason of the expected arrangements in connection with the offering, it is to be requested that the registration statement shall become effective at a particular hour of the day, the Commission must be advised to that effect not later than the second business day before the day which it is desired that the registration statement shall become effective. A person's request for acceleration will be considered confirmation of such person's awareness of the person's obligations under the Act. Not later than the time of filing the last amendment prior to the effective date of the registration statement, the registrant shall inform the Commission as to whether or not the amount of compensation to be allowed or paid to the underwriters and any other arrangements among the registrant, the underwriters and other broker-dealers participating in the distribution, as described in the registration statement, have been reviewed to the extent required by the National Association of Securities Dealers, Inc. and such Association has issued a statement expressing no objections to the compensation and other arrangements.

(b) Having due regard to the adequacy of information respecting the registrant theretofore available to the public, to the facility with which the nature of the securities to be registered, their relationship to the capital structure of the registrant issuer and the rights of holders thereof can be understood, and to the public interest and the protection of investors, as provided in section 8(a) of the Act, it is the general policy of the Commission, upon request, as provided in paragraph (a) of this section, to permit acceleration of the effective date of the registration statement as soon as possible after the filing of appropriate amendments, if any. In determining the date on which a registration statement shall become effective, the following are included in the situations in which the Commission considers that the statutory standards of section 8(a) may not be met and may refuse to accelerate the effective date:

(1) Where there has not been a bona fide effort to make the prospectus reasonably concise, readable, and in compliance with the plain English requirements of Rule 421(d) of Regulation C (17 CFR 230.421(d)) in order to facilitate an understanding of the information in the prospectus.

(2) Where the form of preliminary prospectus, which has been distributed by the issuer or underwriter, is found to be inaccurate or inadequate in any material respect, until the Commission has received satisfactory assurance that appropriate correcting material has been sent to all underwriters and dealers who received such preliminary prospectus or prospectuses in quantity sufficient for their information and the information of others to whom the inaccurate or inadequate material was sent.

(3) Where the Commission is currently making an investigation of the issuer, a person controlling the issuer, or one of the underwriters, if any, of the securities to be offered, pursuant to any of the Acts administered by the Commission.

(4) Where one or more of the underwriters, although firmly committed to purchase securities covered by the registration statement, is subject to and does not meet the financial responsibility requirements of Rule 15c3–1 under the Securities Exchange Act of 1934. For the purposes of this paragraph underwriters will be deemed to be firmly committed even though the obligation to purchase is subject to the usual conditions as to receipt of opinions of counsel, accountants, etc., the accuracy of warranties or representations, the happening of calamities or the occurrence of other events the determination of which is not expressed to be in the sole or absolute discretion of the underwriters.

(5) Where there have been transactions in securities of the registrant by persons connected with or proposed to be connected with the offering which may have artificially affected or may artificially affect the market price of the security being offered.

(6) Where the amount of compensation to be allowed or paid to the underwriters and any other arrangements among the registrant, the underwriters and other broker-dealers participating in the distribution, as described in the registration statement, if required to be reviewed by the National Association of Securities Dealers, Inc. (NASD), have

been reviewed by the NASD and the NASD has not issued a statement expressing no objections to the compensation and other arrangements.

(7) Where, in the case of a significant secondary offering at the market, the registrant, selling security holders and underwriters have not taken sufficient measures to insure compliance with Regulation M (§§ 242.100 through 242.105 of this chapter).

(c) Insurance against liabilities arising under the Act, whether the cost of insurance is borne by the registrant, the insured or some other person, will not be considered a bar to acceleration, unless the registrant is a registered investment company or a business development company and the cost of such insurance is borne by other than an insured officer or director of the registrant. In the case of such a registrant, the Commission may refuse to accelerate the effective date of the registration statement when the registrant is organized or administered pursuant to any instrument (including a contract for insurance against liabilities arising under the Act) that protects or purports to protect any director or officer of the company against any liability to the company or its security holders to which he or she would otherwise be subject by reason of willful misfeasance, bad faith, gross negligence or reckless disregard of the duties involved in the conduct of his or her office.

* * *

AMENDMENTS; WITHDRAWALS

Rule 473. Delaying Amendments

(a) An amendment in the following form filed with a registration statement, or as an amendment to a registration statement which has not become effective, shall be deemed, for the purpose of section 8(a) of the Act, to be filed on such date or dates as may be necessary to delay the effective date of such registration statement (1) until the registrant shall file a further amendment which specifically states as provided in paragraph (b) of this rule that such registration statement shall thereafter become effective in accordance with section 8(a) of the Act, or (2) until the registration statement shall become effective on such date as the Commission, acting pursuant to section 8(a), may determine:

"The registrant hereby amends this registration statement on such date or dates as may be necessary to delay its effective date until the registrant shall file a further amendment which specifically states that this registration statement shall thereafter become effective in accordance with section 8(a) of the Securities Act of 1933 or until the registration statement shall become effective on such date as the Commission acting pursuant to said section 8(a), may determine."

(b) An amendment which for the purpose of paragraph (a)(1) of this section specifically states that a registration statement shall thereafter become effective in accordance with section 8(a) of the Act, shall be in the following form:

"This registration statement shall hereafter become effective in accordance with the provisions of section 8(a) of the Securities Act of 1933."

(c) An amendment pursuant to paragraph (a) of this rule which is filed with a registration statement shall be set forth on the facing page thereof following the calculation of the registration fee. Any such amendment filed after the filing of the registration statement, any amendment altering the proposed date of public sale of the securities being registered, or any amendment filed pursuant to paragraph (b) of this rule may be made by telegram, letter, or facsimile transmission. Each such telegraphic amendment shall be confirmed in writing within a reasonable time by the filing of a signed copy of the amendment. Such confirmation shall not be deemed an amendment.

(d) No amendments pursuant to paragraph (a) of this section may be filed with a registration statement on Form F–7, F–8 or F–80; on Form F–9 or F–10 relating to an offering being made contemporaneously in the United States and the registrant's home jurisdiction; on Form S–8; on Form S–3, F–2 or F–3 relating to a dividend or interest reinvestment plan; or on Form S–4 complying with General Instruction G of that Form.

* * *

REGULATION D—LIMITED OFFERINGS

Preliminary Notes

1. The following rules relate to transactions exempted from the registration requirements of section 5 of the Securities Act of 1933 (the "Act"). Such transactions are not exempt from the antifraud, civil liability, or other provisions of the federal securities laws. Issuers are reminded of their obligation to provide such further material information, if any, as may be necessary to make the information required under this regulation, in light of the circumstances under which it is furnished, not misleading.

2. Nothing in these rules obviates the need to comply with any applicable state law relating to the offer and sale of securities. Regulation D is intended to be a basic element in a uniform system of federal-state limited offering exemptions consistent with the provisions of sections 18 and 19(c) of the Act. In those states that have adopted Regulation D, or any version of Regulation D, special attention should be directed to the applicable state laws and regulations, including those relating to registration of persons who receive remuneration in connection with the offer and sale of securities, to disqualification of issuers and other persons associated with offerings based on state administrative orders or judgments, and to requirements for filings of notices of sales.

3. Attempted compliance with any rule in Regulation D does not act as an exclusive election; the issuer can also claim the availability of any other applicable exemption. For instance, an issuer's failure to satisfy all the terms and conditions of Rule 506 shall not raise any presumption that the exemption provided by section 4(2) of the Act is not available.

4. These rules are available only to the issuer of the securities and not to any affiliate of that issuer or to any other person for resales of the issuer's securities. The rules provide an exemption only for the transactions in which the securities are offered or sold by the issuer, not for the securities themselves.

5. These rules may be used for business combinations that involve sales by virtue of Rule 145(a) or otherwise.

6. In view of the objectives of these rules and the policies underlying the Act, Regulation D is not available to any issuer for any transaction or chain of transactions that, although in technical compliance with these rules, is part of a plan or scheme to evade the registration provisions of the Act. In such cases, registration under the Act is required.

7. Securities offered and sold outside the United States in accordance with Regulation S need not be registered under the Act. See Release No. 33–6863. Regulation S may be relied upon for such offers and sales even if coincident offers and sales are made in accordance with Regulation D inside the United States. Thus, for example, persons who are offered and sold securities in accordance with Regulation S would not be counted in the calculation of the number of purchasers under Regulation D. Similarly, proceeds from such sales would not be included in the aggregate offering price. The provisions of this note, however, do not apply if the issuer elects to rely solely on Regulation D for offers or sales to persons made outside the United States.

Rule 501. Definitions and Terms Used in Regulation D

As used in Regulation D, the following terms shall have the meaning indicated:

(a) *Accredited investor.* "Accredited investor" shall mean any person who comes within any of the following categories, or who the issuer reasonably believes comes within any of the following categories, at the time of the sale of the securities to that person:

(1) Any bank as defined in section 3(a)(2) of the Act, or any savings and loan association or other institution as defined in section 3(a)(5)(A) of the Act whether acting in its individual or fiduciary capacity; any broker or dealer registered pursuant to section 15 of the Securities Exchange Act of 1934; insurance company as defined in section 2(13) of the Act; investment company registered under the Investment Company Act of 1940 or a business development company as defined in section 2(a)(48) of that Act; Small Business Investment Company licensed by the U.S. Small Business Administration under section 301(c) or (d) of the Small Business

Investment Act of 1958; any plan established and maintained by a state, its political subdivisions, or any agency or instrumentality of a state or its political subdivisions for the benefit of its employees, if such plan has total assets in excess of $5,000,000; employee benefit plan within the meaning of the Employee Retirement Income Security Act of 1974 if the investment decision is made by a plan fiduciary, as defined in section 3(21) of such Act, which is either a bank, savings and loan association, insurance company, or registered investment adviser, or if the employee benefit plan has total assets in excess of $5,000,000 or, if a self-directed plan, with investment decisions made solely by persons that are accredited investors;

(2) Any private business development company as defined in section 202(a)(22) of the Investment Advisers Act of 1940;

(3) Any organization described in Section 501(c)(3) of the Internal Revenue Code, corporation, Massachusetts or similar business trust, or partnership, not formed for the specific purpose of acquiring the securities offered, with total assets in excess of $5,000,000;

(4) Any director, executive officer, or general partner of the issuer of the securities being offered or sold, or any director, executive officer, or general partner of a general partner of that issuer;

(5) Any natural person whose individual net worth, or joint net worth with that person's spouse, at the time of his purchase exceeds $1,000,000;

(6) Any natural person who had an individual income in excess of $200,000 in each of the two most recent years or joint income with that person's spouse in excess of $300,000 in each of those years and has a reasonable expectation of reaching the same income level in the current year;

(7) Any trust, with total assets in excess of $5,000,000, not formed for the specific purpose of acquiring the securities offered, whose purchase is directed by a sophisticated person as described in § 230.506(b)(2)(ii); and

(8) Any entity in which all of the equity owners are accredited investors.

(b) *Affiliate.* An "affiliate" of, or person "affiliated" with, a specified person shall mean a person that directly, or indirectly through one or more intermediaries, controls or is controlled by, or is under common control with, the person specified.

(c) *Aggregate offering price.* "Aggregate offering price" shall mean the sum of all cash, services, property, notes, cancellation of debt, or other consideration to be received by an issuer for issuance of its securities. Where securities are being offered for both cash and non-cash consideration, the aggregate offering price shall be based on the price at which the securities are offered for cash. Any portion of the aggregate offering price attributable to cash received in a foreign currency shall be translated into United States currency at the currency exchange rate in effect at a reasonable time prior to or on the date of the sale of the securities. If securities are not offered for cash, the aggregate offering price shall be based on the value of the consideration as established by bona fide sales of that consideration made within a reasonable time, or, in the absence of sales, on the fair value as determined by an accepted standard. Such valuations of non-cash consideration must be reasonable at the time made.

(d) *Business combination.* "Business combination" shall mean any transaction of the type specified in paragraph (a) of Rule 145 under the Act and any transaction involving the acquisition by one issuer, in exchange for all or a part of its own or its parent's stock, of stock of another issuer if, immediately after the acquisition, the acquiring issuer has control of the other issuer (whether or not it had control before the acquisition).

(e) *Calculation of number of purchasers.* For purposes of calculating the number of purchasers under Rule 505(b) and Rule 506(b) only, the following shall apply:

(1) The following purchasers shall be excluded:

(i) Any relative, spouse or relative of the spouse of a purchaser who has the same principal residence as the purchaser;

(ii) Any trust or estate in which a purchaser and any of the persons related to him as specified in paragraph (e)(1)(i) or (e)(1)(iii) of Rule 501 collectively have more than 50 percent of the beneficial interest (excluding contingent interests);

(iii) Any corporation or other organization of which a purchaser and any of the persons related to him as specified in paragraph (e)(1)(i) or (e)(1)(ii) of Rule 501 collectively are beneficial owners of more than 50 percent of the equity securities (excluding directors' qualifying shares) or equity interests; and

(iv) Any accredited investor.

(2) A corporation, partnership or other entity shall be counted as one purchaser. If, however, that entity is organized for the specific purpose of acquiring the securities offered and is not an accredited investor under paragraph (a)(8) of Rule 501, then each beneficial owner of equity securities or equity interests in the entity shall count as a separate purchaser for all provisions of Regulation D, except as to the extent provided in subdivision (1) of this paragraph (e).

(3) A non-contributory employee benefit plan within the meaning of Title I of the Employee Retirement Income Security Act of 1974 shall be counted as one purchaser where the trustee makes all investment decisions for the plan.

(f) *Executive officer.* "Executive officer" shall mean the president, any vice president in charge of a principal business unit, division or function (such as sales, administration or finance), any other officer who performs a policy making function, or any other person who performs similar policy making functions for the issuer. Executive officers of subsidiaries may be deemed executive officers of the issuer if they perform such policy making functions for the issuer.

(g) *Issuer.* The definition of the term "issuer" in section 2(4) of the Act shall apply, except that in the case of a proceeding under the Federal Bankruptcy Code, the trustee or debtor in possession shall be considered the issuer in an offering under a plan of reorganization, if the securities are to be issued under the plan.

(h) *Purchaser representative.* "Purchaser representative" shall mean any person who satisfies all of the following conditions or who the issuer reasonably believes satisfies all of the following conditions:

(1) Is not an affiliate, director, officer or other employee of the issuer, or beneficial owner of 10 percent or more of any class of the equity securities or 10 percent or more of the equity interest in the issuer, except where the purchaser is:

(i) A relative of the purchaser representative by blood, marriage or adoption and not more remote than a first cousin;

(ii) A trust or estate in which the purchaser representative and any persons related to him as specified in paragraph (h)(1)(i) or (h)(1)(iii) of Rule 501 collectively have more than 50 percent of the beneficial interest (excluding contingent interest) or of which the purchaser representative serves as trustee, executor, or in any similar capacity; or

(iii) A corporation or other organization of which the purchaser representative and any persons related to him as specified in paragraph (h)(1)(i) or (h)(1)(ii) of Rule 501 collectively are the beneficial owners of more than 50 percent of the equity securities (excluding directors' qualifying shares) or equity interests;

(2) Has such knowledge and experience in financial and business matters that he is capable of evaluating, alone, or together with other purchaser representatives of the purchaser, or together with the purchaser, the merits and risks of the prospective investment;

(3) Is acknowledged by the purchaser in writing, during the course of the transaction, to be his purchaser representative in connection with evaluating the merits and risks of the prospective investment; and

(4) Discloses to the purchaser in writing prior to the sale of securities to that purchaser any material relationship between himself or his affiliates and the issuer or its affiliates that then exists, that is mutually understood to be contemplated, or that has existed at any time during the previous two years, and any compensation received or to be received as a result of such relationship.

Note 1: A person acting as a purchaser representative should consider the applicability of the registration and antifraud provisions relating to brokers and dealers under the Securities Exchange Act of 1934 ("Exchange Act") and relating to investment advisers under the Investment Advisers Act of 1940.

Note 2: The acknowledgment required by paragraph (h)(3) and the disclosure required by paragraph (h)(4) of Rule 501 must be made with specific reference to each prospective investment.

Advance blanket acknowledgment, such as for "all securities transactions" or "all private placements," is not sufficient.

Note 3: Disclosure of any material relationships between the purchaser representative or his affiliates and the issuer or its affiliates does not relieve the purchaser representative of his obligation to act in the interest of the purchaser.

Rule 502. General Conditions to be Met

The following conditions shall be applicable to offers and sales made under Regulation D (Rules 501–508):

(a) *Integration.* All sales that are part of the same Regulation D offering must meet all of the terms and conditions of Regulation D. Offers and sales that are made more than six months before the start of a Regulation D offering or are made more than six months after completion of a Regulation D offering will not be considered part of that Regulation D offering, so long as during those six month periods there are no offers or sales of securities by or for the issuer that are of the same or a similar class as those offered or sold under Regulation D, other than those offers or sales of securities under an employee benefit plan as defined in Rule 405 under the Act.

Note: The term "offering" is not defined in the Act or in Regulation D. If the issuer offers or sells securities for which the safe harbor rule in paragraph (a) of Rule 502 is unavailable, the determination as to whether separate sales of securities are part of the same offering (*i.e.* are considered "integrated") depends on the particular facts and circumstances. Generally, transactions otherwise meeting the requirements of an exemption will not be integrated with simultaneous offerings being made outside the United States in compliance with Regulation S.

The following factors should be considered in determining whether offers and sales should be integrated for purposes of the exemptions under Regulation D:

(a) Whether the sales are part of a single plan of financing;

(b) Whether the sales involve issuance of the same class of securities;

(c) Whether the sales have been made at or about the same time;

(d) Whether the same type of consideration is received; and

(e) Whether the sales are made for the same general purpose. *See* Release No. 33–4552 (November 6, 1962).

(b) *Information requirements.*

(1) *When information must be furnished.*

If the issuer sells securities under Rule 505 or Rule 506 to any purchaser that is not an accredited investor, the issuer shall furnish the information specified in paragraph (b)(2) of this section to such purchaser a reasonable time prior to sale. The issuer is not required to furnish the specified information to purchasers when it sells securities under Rule 504(a), or to any accredited investor.

Note: When an issuer provides information to investors pursuant to paragraph (b)(1), it should consider providing such information to accredited investors as well, in view of the anti-fraud provisions of the federal securities laws.

(2) *Type of information to be furnished.*

(i) If the issuer is not subject to the reporting requirements of section 13 or 15(d) of the Exchange Act, at a reasonable time prior to the sale of securities, the issuer shall furnish the following information, to the extent material to an understanding of the issuer, its business, and the securities being offered:

(A) *Non-financial statement information.* If the issuer is eligible to use Regulation A, the same kind of information as would be required in Part II of Form 1–A. If the issuer is not eligible to use Regulation A, the same kind of information as required in Part I of a registration statement filed under the Securities Act on the form that the issuer would be entitled to use.

(B) *Financial statement information. (1) Offering up to $2,000,000.* The information required in Item 310 of Regulation S–B, except that only the issuer's balance sheet, which shall be dated within 120 days of the start of the offering, must be audited.

(2) Offerings up to $7,500,000. The financial statement information required in Form SB–2. If

an issuer, other than a limited partnership, cannot obtain audited financial statements without unreasonable effort or expense, then only the issuer's balance sheet, which shall be dated within 120 days of the start of the offering, must be audited. If the issuer is a limited partnership and cannot obtain the required financial statements without unreasonable effort or expense, it may furnish financial statements that have been prepared on the basis of Federal income tax requirements and examined and reported on in accordance with generally accepted auditing standards by an independent public or certified accountant.

(3) Offerings over $7,500,000. The financial statement as would be required in a registration statement filed under the Act on the form that the issuer would be entitled to use. If an issuer, other than a limited partnership, cannot obtain audited financial statements without unreasonable effort or expense, then only the issuer's balance sheet, which shall be dated within 120 days of the start of the offering, must be audited. If the issuer is a limited partnership and cannot obtain the required financial statements without unreasonable effort or expense, it may furnish financial statements that have been prepared on the basis of Federal income tax requirements and examined and reported on in accordance with generally accepted auditing standards by an independent public or certified accountant.

(C) If the issuer is a foreign private issuer eligible to use Form 20–F, the issuer shall disclose the same kind of information required to be included in a registration statement filed under the Act on the form that the issuer would be entitled to use. The financial statements need be certified only to the extent required by paragraph (b)(2)(i)(B)(*1*), (*2*) or (*3*) of this section, as appropriate.

(ii) If the issuer is subject to the reporting requirements of section 13 or 15(d) of the Exchange Act, at a reasonable time prior to the sale of securities the issuer shall furnish the information specified in paragraph (b)(2)(ii)(A) or (b)(2)(ii)(B), and in either event the information specified in paragraph (b)(2)(ii)(C) of Rule 502:

(A) The issuer's annual report to shareholders for the most recent fiscal year, if such annual report meets the requirements of Rule 14a–3 or Rule 14c–3 under the Exchange Act, the definitive proxy statement filed in connection with that annual report, and, if requested by the purchaser in writing, a copy of the issuer's most recent Form 10–K and Form 10–KSB under the Exchange Act.

(B) The information contained in an annual report on Form 10–K or 10–KSB under the Exchange Act or in a registration statement on Form S–1, SB–1, SB–2 or Form S–11, or Form S–18 under the Act or on Form 10 or Form 10–SB under the Exchange Act, whichever filing is the most recent required to be filed.

(C) The information contained in any reports or documents required to be filed by the issuer under sections 13(a), 14(a), 14(c), and 15(d) of the Exchange Act since the distribution or filing of the report or registration statement specified in paragraph (A) or (B), and a brief description of the securities being offered, the use of the proceeds from the offering, and any material changes in the issuer's affairs that are not disclosed in the documents furnished.

(D) If the issuer is a foreign private issuer, the issuer may provide in lieu of the information specified in paragraph (b)(2)(ii)(A) or (B) of this section, the information contained in its most recent filing on Form 20–F or Form F–1.

(iii) Exhibits required to be filed with the Commission as part of a registration statement or report, other than an annual report to shareholders or parts of that report incorporated by reference in a Form 10–K and Form 10–KSB report, need not be furnished to each purchaser that is not an accredited investor if the contents of the material exhibits are identified and such exhibits are made available to the purchaser upon his written request, a reasonable time prior to his purchase.

(iv) At a reasonable time prior to the sale material of securities to any purchaser that is not an accredited investor in a transaction under Rule 505 or Rule 506, the issuer shall furnish the purchaser a brief description in writing of any written information concerning the offering that has been provided by the issuer to any accredited investor but not previously delivered to such unaccredited purchaser. The issuer shall furnish any portion or all of this information to the purchaser, upon his written request a reasonable time prior to his purchase.

(v) The issuer shall also make available to each purchaser at a reasonable time prior to his purchase of securities in a transaction under Rule 505 or Rule 506 the opportunity to ask questions and receive answers concerning the terms and conditions of the offering and to obtain any additional information which the issuer possesses or can acquire without unreasonable effort or expense that is necessary to verify the accuracy of information furnished under paragraph (b)(2)(i) or (ii) of Rule 502.

(vi) For business combinations or exchange offers, in addition to information required by Form S–4, the issuer shall provide to each purchaser at the time the plan is submitted to security holders, or, with an exchange, during the course of the transaction and prior to sale, written information about any terms or arrangements of the proposed transactions that are materially different from those for all other security holders. For purposes of this subsection, an issuer which is not subject to the reporting requirements of section 13 or 15(d) of the Exchange Act may satisfy the requirements of Part I.B. or C. of Form S–4 by compliance with paragraph (b)(2)(i) of Rule 502.

(vii) At a reasonable time prior to the sale of securities to any purchaser that is not an accredited investor in a transaction under Rule 505 or Rule 506, the issuer shall advise the purchaser of the limitations on resale in the manner contained in paragraph (d)(2) of this section. Such disclosure may be contained in other materials required to be provided by this paragraph.

(c) *Limitation on manner of offering.* Except as provided in Rule 504(b)(1), neither the issuer nor any person acting on its behalf shall offer or sell the securities by any form of general solicitation or general advertising, including, but not limited to, the following:

(1) Any advertisement, article, notice or other communication published in any newspaper, magazine, or similar media or broadcast over television or radio; and

(2) Any seminar or meeting whose attendees have been invited by any general solicitation or general advertising.

Provided, however, that publication by an issuer of a notice in accordance with § 230.135c shall not be deemed to constitute general solicitation or general advertising for purposes of this section; provided further, that, if the requirements of § 230.135e are satisfied, providing any journalist with access to press conferences held outside of the United States, to meetings with issuer or selling security holder representatives conducted outside of the United States, or to written press-related materials released outside of the United States, at or in which a present or proposed offering of securities is discussed, will not be deemed to constitute general solicitation or general advertising for purposes of this section.

(d) *Limitations on resale.* Except as provided in Rule 504(b)(1), securities acquired in a transaction under Regulation D shall have the status of securities acquired in a transaction under section 4(2) of the Act and cannot be resold without registration under the Act or an exemption therefrom. The issuer shall exercise reasonable care to assure that the purchasers of the securities are not underwriters within the meaning of section 2(11) of the Act, which reasonable care may be demonstrated by the following:

(1) Reasonable inquiry to determine if the purchaser is acquiring the securities for himself or for other persons;

(2) Written disclosure to each purchaser prior to sale that the securities have not been registered under the Act and, therefore, cannot be resold unless they are registered under the Act or unless an exemption from registration is available; and

(3) Placement of a legend on the certificate or other document that evidences the securities stating that the securities have not been registered under the Act and setting forth or referring to the restrictions on transferability and sale of the securities.

While taking these actions will establish the requisite reasonable care, it is not the exclusive method to demonstrate such care. Other actions by the issuer may satisfy this provision. In addition, Rule 502(b)(2)(vii) require the delivery of written disclosure of the limitations on resale to investors in certain instances.

Rule 503. Filing of Notice of Sales

(a) An issuer offering or selling securities in reliance on Rule 504, 505 or 506 shall file with the

Commission five copies of a notice on Form D no later than 15 days after the first sale of securities.

(b) One copy of every notice on Form D shall be manually signed by a person duly authorized by the issuer.

(c) If sales are made under Rule 505, the notice shall contain an undertaking by the issuer to furnish to the Commission, upon the written request of its staff, the information furnished by the issuer under Rule 502(b)(2) to any purchaser that is not an accredited investor.

(d) Amendments to notices filed under paragraph (a) of Rule 503 need only report the issuer's name and the information required by Part C and any material change in the facts from those set forth in Parts A and B.

(e) A notice on Form D shall be considered filed with the Commission under paragraph (a) of Rule 503:

(1) As of the date on which it is received at the Commission's principal office in Washington, D.C.; or

(2) As of the date on which the notice is mailed by means of United States registered or certified mail to the Commission's principal office in Washington, D.C., if the notice is delivered to such office after the date on which it is required to be filed.

Rule 504. Exemption for Limited Offerings and Sales of Securities Not Exceeding $1,000,000

(a) *Exemption.* Offers and sales of securities that satisfy the conditions in paragraph (b) of this Rule 504 by an issuer that is not:

(1) subject to the reporting requirements of section 13 or 15(d) of the Exchange Act;

(2) an investment company; or

(3) a development stage company that either has no specific business plan or purpose or has indicated that its business plan is to engage in a merger or acquisition with an unidentified company or companies, or other entity or person, shall be exempt from the provision of section 5 of the Act under section 3(b) of the Act.

(b)(1) *General conditions.* To qualify for exemption under this § 230.504, offers and sales must satisfy the terms and conditions of §§ 230.501 and 230.502(a), (c) and (d), except that the provisions of § 230.502(c) and (d) will not apply to offers and sales of securities under this § 230.504 that are made:

(i) Exclusively in one or more states that provide for the registration of the securities, and require the public filing and delivery to investors of a substantive disclosure document before sale, and are made in accordance with those state provisions;

(ii) In one or more states that have no provision for the registration of the securities or the public filing or delivery of a disclosure document before sale, if the securities have been registered in at least one state that provides for such registration, public filing and delivery before sale, offers and sales are made in that state in accordance with such provisions, and the disclosure document is delivered before sale to all purchasers (including those in the states that have no such procedure); or

(iii) Exclusively according to state law exemptions from registration that permit general solicitation and general advertising so long as sales are made only to "accredited investors" as defined in § 230.501(a).

(2) The aggregate offering price for an offering of securities under this Rule 504, as defined in Rule 501(c), shall not exceed $1,000,000, less the aggregate offering price for all securities sold within the twelve months before the start of and during the offering of securities under this Rule 504, in reliance on any exemption under section 3(b), or in violation of section 5(a) of the Securities Act.

NOTE 1: The calculation of the aggregate offering price is illustrated as follows:

If an issuer sold $900,000 on June 1, 1987 under this Rule 504 and an additional $4,100,000 on December 1, 1987 under § 230.505, the issuer could not sell any of its securities under this Rule 504 until December 1, 1988. Until then the issuer must count the December 1, 1987 sale towards the $1,000,000 limit within the preceding twelve months.

NOTE 2: If a transaction under Rule 504 fails to meet the limitation on the aggregate offering price, it does not affect the availability of this Rule 504 for the other transactions considered in applying such limitation. For example, if an issuer sold $1,000,000 worth of its securities on January 1, 1988 under this Rule 504 and an additional $500,000 worth on July 1, 1988, this Rule 504 would not be available for the later sale, but would still be applicable to the January 1, 1988 sale.

Rule 505. Exemption for Limited Offers and Sales of Securities Not Exceeding $5,000,000

(a) *Exemption.* Offers and sales of securities that satisfy the conditions in paragraph (b) of Rule 505 by an issuer that is not an investment company shall be exempt from the provisions of section 5 of the Act under section 3(b) of the Act.

(b) *Conditions to be met—(1) General Conditions.* To qualify for exemption under this section, offers and sales must satisfy the terms and conditions of Rules 501 and 502.

(2) *Specific conditions.*

(i) *Limitation on aggregate offering price.* The aggregate offering price for an offering of securities under Rule 505, as defined in Rule 501(c), shall not exceed $5,000,000, less the aggregate offering price for all securities sold within the twelve months before the start of and during the offering of securities under Rule 505 in reliance on any exemption under section 3(b) of the Act or in violation of section 5(a) of the Act.

Note: The calculation of the aggregate offering price is illustrated as follows:

Example 1. If an issuer sold $2,000,000 of its securities on June 1, 1982 under Rule 505 and an additional $1,000,000 on September 1, 1982, the issuer would be permitted to sell only $2,000,000 more under this § 230.505 until June 1, 1983. Until that date the issuer must count both prior sales towards the $5,000,000 limit. However, if the issuer made its third sale on June 1, 1983, the issuer could then sell $4,000,000 of its securities because the June 1, 1982 sale would not be within the preceding twelve months.

Example 2. If an issuer sold $500,000 of its securities on June 1, 1982 under Rule 504 and an additional $4,500,000 on December 1, 1982 under Rule 505, then the issuer could not sell any of its securities under Rule 505 until June 1, 1983. At that time it could sell an additional $500,000 of its securities.

(ii) *Limitation on number of purchasers.* There are no more than or the issuer reasonably believes that there are no more than 35 purchasers of securities from the issuer in any offering under this section.

Note: See Rule 501(e) for the calculation of the number of purchasers and Rule 502(a) for what may or may not constitute an offering under this section.

(iii) *Disqualifications.* No exemption under Rule 505 shall be available for the securities of any issuer described in Rule 262 of Regulation A, except that for purposes of Rule 505 only:

(A) The term "filing of the notification required by Rule 252" as used in Rule 262(a), (b) and (c) shall mean the first sale of securities under Rule 505;

(B) The term "underwriter" as used in Rule 262(b) and (c) shall mean a person that has been or will be paid directly or indirectly remuneration for solicitation of purchasers in connection with sales of securities under Rule 505; and

(C) Paragraph (b)(2)(iii) of Rule 505 shall not apply to any issuer if the Commission determines, upon a showing of good cause, that it is not necessary under the circumstances that the exemption be denied. Any such determination shall be without prejudice to any other action by the Commission in any other proceeding or matter with respect to the issuer or any other person.

Rule 506. Exemption for Limited Offers and Sales Without Regard to Dollar Amount of Offering

(a) *Exemption.* Offers and sales of securities by an issuer that satisfy the conditions in paragraph (b) of Rule 506 shall be deemed to be transactions not involving any public offering within the meaning of section 4(2) of the Act.

(b) *Conditions to be met.*

(1) *General conditions.* To qualify for exemption under Rule 506, offers and sales must satisfy all the terms and conditions of Rules 501 and 502.

(2) *Specific conditions.*

(i) *Limitation on number of purchasers.* There are no more than or the issuer reasonably believes that there are no more than 35 purchasers of securities from the issuer in any offering under this section.

Note: See Rule 501(e) for the calculation of the number of purchasers and Rule 502(a) for what may or may not constitute an offering under Rule 506.

(ii) *Nature of purchasers.* Each purchaser who is not an accredited investor either alone or with his purchaser representative(s) has such knowledge and experience in financial and business matters that he is capable of evaluating the merits and risks of the prospective investment, or the issuer reasonably believes immediately prior to making any sale that such purchaser comes within this description.

Rule 507. Disqualifying Provision Relating to Exemptions Under Rules 504, 505 and 506

(a) No exemption under Rules 504, 505 or 506 shall be available for an issuer if such issuer, any of its predecessors or affiliates have been subject to any order, judgment, or decree of any court of competent jurisdiction temporarily, preliminary or permanently enjoining such person for failure to comply with Rule 503.

(b) Paragraph (a) of this section shall not apply if the Commission determines, upon a showing of good cause, that it is not necessary under the circumstances that the exemption be denied.

Rule 508. Insignificant Deviations From a Term, Condition or Requirement of Regulation D

(a) A failure to comply with a term, condition or requirement of Rules 504, 505 or 506 will not result in the loss of the exemption from the requirements of section 5 of the Act for any offer or sale to a particular individual or entity, if the person relying on the exemption shows:

(1) the failure to comply did not pertain to a term, condition or requirement directly intended to protect that particular individual or entity; and

(2) the failure to comply was insignificant with respect to the offering as a whole, provided that any failure to comply with paragraph (c) of Rule 502, paragraph (b)(2) of Rule 504, paragraphs (b)(2)(i) and (ii) of Rule 505 and paragraph (b)(2)(i) of Rule 506 shall be deemed to be significant to the offering as a whole; and

(3) a good faith and reasonable attempt was made to comply with all applicable terms, conditions and requirements of Rules 504, 505 or 506.

(b) A transaction made in reliance on Rule 504, 505 or 506 shall comply with all applicable terms, conditions and requirements of Regulation D. Where an exemption is established only through reliance upon paragraph (a) of this section, the failure to comply shall nonetheless be actionable by the Commission under section 20 of the Act.

D. RULES UNDER SECURITIES EXCHANGE ACT OF 1934

(Selected)

Contents

DEFINITIONS

Rule 3b–2. Definition of "Officer"

The term "officer" means a president, vice president, secretary, treasury or principal financial officer, comptroller or principal accounting officer, and any person routinely performing corresponding functions with respect to any organization whether incorporated or unincorporated.

MANIPULATION AND DECEPTION

Rule 10b–5. Employment of Manipulative and Deceptive Devices

It shall be unlawful for any person, directly or indirectly, by the use of any means or instrumentality of interstate commerce, or of the mails, or of any facility of any national securities exchange,

(a) to employ any device, scheme, or artifice to defraud,

(b) to make any untrue statement of a material fact or to omit to state a material fact necessary in order to make the statements made, in the light of the circumstances under which they were made, not misleading, or

(c) to engage in any act, practice, or course of business which operates or would operate as a fraud or deceit upon any person,

in connection with the purchase or sale of any security.

Rule 10b5–1. Trading "On the Basis of" Material Nonpublic Information in Insider Trading Cases

Preliminary Note to Rule 10b5–1

This provision defines when a purchase or sale constitutes trading "on the basis of" material nonpublic information in insider trading cases brought under Section 10(b) of the Act and Rule 10b–5 thereunder. The law of insider trading is otherwise defined by judicial opinions construing Rule 10b–5, and Rule 10b5–1 does not modify the scope of insider trading law in any other respect.

(a) General. The "manipulative and deceptive devices" prohibited by Section 10(b) of the Act (15 U.S.C. 78j) and § 240.10b–5 thereunder include, among other things, the purchase or sale of a security of any issuer, on the basis of material nonpublic information about that security or issuer, in breach of a duty of trust or confidence that is owed directly, indirectly, or derivatively, to the issuer of that security or the shareholders of that issuer, or to any other person who is the source of the material nonpublic information.

(b) Definition of "on the basis of." Subject to the affirmative defenses in paragraph (c) of this section, a purchase or sale of a security of an issuer is "on the basis of" material nonpublic information about that security or issuer if the person making the purchase or sale was aware of the material nonpublic information when the person made the purchase or sale.

(c) Affirmative defenses.

(1)(i) Subject to paragraph (c)(1)(ii) of this section, a person's purchase or sale is not "on the basis of" material nonpublic information if the person making the purchase or sale demonstrates that:

(A) before becoming aware of the information, the person had:

(1) entered into a binding contract to purchase or sell the security,

(2) instructed another person to purchase or sell the security for the instructing person's account, or

(3) adopted a written plan for trading securities;

(B) the contract, instruction, or plan described in paragraph (c)(1)(i)(A) of this Section:

(1) specified the amount of securities to be purchased or sold and the price at which and the date on which the securities were to be purchased or sold;

(2) included a written formula or algorithm, or computer program, for determining the amount of securities to be purchased or sold and the price at which and the date on which the securities were to be purchased or sold; or

(3) did not permit the person to exercise any subsequent influence over how, when, or whether to effect purchases or sales; provided, in addition, that any other person who, pursuant to the contract, instruction, or plan, did exercise such influence must not have been aware of the material nonpublic information when doing so; and

(C) the purchase or sale that occurred was pursuant to the contract, instruction, or plan. A purchase or sale is not "pursuant to a contract, instruction, or plan" if, among other things, the person who entered into the contract, instruction, or plan altered or deviated from the contract, instruction, or plan to purchase or sell securities (whether by changing the amount, price, or timing of the purchase or sale), or entered into or altered a corresponding or hedging transaction or position with respect to those securities.

(ii) Paragraph (c)(1)(i) of this section is applicable only when the contract, instruction, or plan to purchase or sell securities was given or entered into in good faith and not as part of a plan or scheme to evade the prohibitions of this section.

(iii) This paragraph (c)(1)(iii) defines certain terms as used in paragraph (c)of this Section.

(A) Amount. "Amount" means either a specified number of shares or other securities or a specified dollar value of securities.

(B) Price. "Price" means the market price on a particular date or a limit price, or a particular dollar price.

(C) Date. "Date" means, in the case of a market order, the specific day of the year on which the order is to be executed (or as soon thereafter as is practicable under ordinary principles of best execution). "Date" means, in the case of a limit order, a day of the year on which the limit order is in force.

(2) A person other than a natural person also may demonstrate that a purchase or sale of securities is not "on the basis of" material nonpublic information if the person demonstrates that:

(i) The individual making the investment decision on behalf of the person to purchase or sell the securities was not aware of the information; and

(ii) The person had implemented reasonable policies and procedures, taking into consideration the nature of the person's business, to ensure that individuals making investment decisions would not violate the laws prohibiting trading on the basis of material nonpublic information. These policies and procedures may include those that restrict any purchase, sale, and causing any purchase or sale of any security as to which the person has material nonpublic information, or those that prevent such individuals from becoming aware of such information.

Rule 10b5–2. Duties of Trust or Confidence in Misappropriation Insider Trading Cases

Preliminary Note to Rule 10b5–2:

This section provides a non-exclusive definition of circumstances in which a person has a duty of trust or confidence for purposes of the "misappropriation" theory of insider trading under Section 10(b) of the Act and Rule 10b–5. The law of insider trading is otherwise defined by judicial opinions construing Rule 10b–5, and Rule10b5–2 does not modify the scope of insider trading law in any other respect.

(a) Scope of Rule. This section shall apply to any violation of Section 10(b)of the Act (15 U.S.C. 78j(b)) and § 240.10b–5 thereunder that is based on the purchase or sale of securities on the basis of, or the communication of, material nonpublic information misappropriated in breach of a duty of trust or confidence.

(b) Enumerated "duties of trust or confidence." For purposes of this section, a "duty of trust or confidence" exists in the following circumstances, among others:

(1) Whenever a person agrees to maintain information in confidence;

(2) Whenever the person communicating the material nonpublic information and the person to whom it is communicated have a history, pattern, or practice of sharing confidences, such that the recipient of the information knows or reasonably should know that the person communicating the material nonpublic information expects that the recipient will maintain its confidentiality; or

(3) Whenever a person receives or obtains material nonpublic information from his or her spouse, parent, child, or sibling; provided, however, that the person receiving or obtaining the information may demonstrate that no duty of trust or confidence existed with respect to the information, by establishing that he or she neither knew nor reasonably should have known that the person who was the source of the information expected that the person would keep the information confidential, because of the parties' history, pattern, or practice of sharing and maintaining confidences, and because there was no agreement or understanding to maintain the confidentiality of the information.

Rule 10b–18. Purchases of Certain Equity Securities by the Issuer and Others

(a) *Definitions.* Unless the context otherwise requires, all terms used in this section shall have the same meaning as in the Act. In addition, unless the context otherwise requires, the following definitions shall apply:

(1) The term "affiliate" means any person that directly or indirectly controls, is controlled by, or is under common control with, the issuer;

(2) The term "affiliated purchaser" means

(i) A person acting in concert with the issuer for the purpose of acquiring the issuer's securities; or

(ii) An affiliate who, directly or indirectly, controls the issuer's purchases of such securities, whose purchases are controlled by the issuer or whose purchases are under common control with those of the issuer;

Provided, however, That the term "affiliated purchaser" shall not include a broker, dealer, or other person solely by reason of his making Rule 10b–18 bids or effecting Rule 10b–18 purchases on behalf of the issuer and for its account and shall not include an officer or director of the issuer solely by reason of his participation in the decision to authorize Rule 10b–18 bids or Rule 10b–18 purchases by or on behalf of the issuer;

(3) The term "Rule 10b–18 purchase" means a purchase of common stock of an issuer by or for the issuer or any affiliated purchaser of the issuer, but does not include any purchase of such stock

(i) Effected during the restricted period specified in § 242.102 of this chapter during a distribution ((as defined in § 242.100) of this chapter) of such common stock, or during a distribution for which such common stock is a reference security, by the issuer or any of its affiliated purchasers;

(ii) Effected by or for an issuer plan by an agent independent of the issuer;

(iii) If it is a fractional interest in a security, evidenced by a script certificate, order form, or similar document;

(iv) Pursuant to a merger, acquisition, or similar transaction involving a recapitalization;

(v) Which is subject to Rule 13e–1 under the Act;

(vi) Pursuant to a tender offer that is subject to Rule 13e–4 under the Act or specifically excepted therefrom;

(vii) Pursuant to a tender offer that is subject to Section 14(d) of the Act and the rules and regulations thereunder.

(4) The term "Rule 10b–18 bid" means

(i) A bid for securities that, if accepted, or

(ii) A limit order to purchase securities that, if executed would result in a Rule 10b–18 purchase;

(5) The term plan has the meaning contained in § 242.100 of this chapter;

(6) The term agent independent of the issuer has the meaning contained in § 242.100 of this chapter;

(7) The term "consolidated system" means the consolidated transaction reporting system contemplated by Rule 11Aa3–1;

(8) The term "reported security" means any security as to which last sale information is reported in the consolidated system;

(9) The term "exchange traded security" means any security, except a reported security, that it listed, or admitted to unlisted trading privileges, on a national securities exchange;

(10) The term "NASDAQ security" means any security, except a reported security, as to which bid and offer quotations are reported in the automated quotation system ("NASDAQ") operated by the National Association of Securities Dealers, Inc. ("NASD");

(11) The term "trading volume" means

(i) With respect to a reported security, the average daily trading volume for the security reported in the consolidated system in the four calendar weeks preceding the week in which the Rule 10b–18 purchase is to be effected or the Rule 10b–18 bid is to be made;

(ii) With respect to an exchange traded security, the average of the aggregate daily trading volume, including the daily trading volume reported on all exchanges on which the security is traded and, if such security is also a NASDAQ security, the daily trading volume for such security made available by the NASD, for the four calendar weeks preceding the week in which the Rule 10b–18 purchase is to be effected or the Rule 10b–18 bid is to be made;

(iii) With respect to a NASDAQ security that is not an exchange traded security, the average daily trading volume for such security made available by the NASD for the four calendar weeks preceding the week in which the Rule 10b–18 purchase is to be effected or the Rule 10b–18 bid is to be made;

Provided, however, That such trading volume under paragraph (a)(11)(i), (ii) and (iii) shall not include any Rule 10b–18 purchase of a block by or for the issuer or any affiliated purchaser of the issuer;

(12) The term "purchase price" means the price paid per share

(i) For a reported security, or an exchange traded security on a national securities exchange, exclusive of any commission paid to a broker acting as agent, or commission equivalent, mark-up, or differential paid to a dealer;

(ii) For a NASDAQ security, or a security that is not a reported security or a NASDAQ security, otherwise than on a national securities exchange, inclusive of any commission equivalent, mark-up, or differential paid to a dealer;

(13) The term "round lot" means 100 shares or other customary unit of trading for a security;

(14) The term "block" means a quantity of stock that either

(i) Has a purchase price of $200,000 or more; or

(ii) Is at least 5,000 shares and has a purchase price of at least $50,000; or

(iii) Is at least 20 round lots of the security and totals 150 percent or more of the trading volume for that security or, in the event that trading volume data are unavailable, is at least 20 round lots of the security and totals at least one-tenth of one percent (.001) of the outstanding shares of the security, exclusive of any shares owned by any affiliate;

Provided, however, That a block under paragraph (a)(14)(i), (ii) and (iii) shall not include any amount that a broker or a dealer, acting as principal, has accumulated for the purpose of sale or resale to the issuer or to any affiliated purchaser of the issuer if the issuer or such affiliated purchaser knows or has reason to know that such amount was accumulated for such purpose, nor shall it include any amount that a broker or dealer has sold short to the issuer or to any affiliated purchaser of the issuer if the issuer or such affiliated purchaser knows or has reason to know that the sale was a short sale.

(15) The term market-wide trading suspension means either:

(i) A market-wide trading halt imposed pursuant to the rules of a national securities exchange or a registered national securities association, in response to a market-wide decline during a single trading session; or

(ii) A market-wide trading suspension ordered by the Commission pursuant to Section 12(k) of the Act, *15 U.S.C. 78l(k).*

(b) *Conditions to be met.*

In connection with a Rule 10b–18 purchase, or with a Rule 10b–18 bid that is made by the use of any means or instrumentality of interstate commerce or of the mails, or of any facility of any national securities exchange, an issuer, or an affiliated purchaser of the issuer, shall not be deemed to have violated Section 9(a)(2) of the Act or Rule 10b–5 under the Act, solely by reason of the time or price at which its Rule 10b–18 bids or Rule 10b–18 purchases are made or the amount of such bids or purchases or the number of brokers or dealers used in connection with such bids or purchases if the issuer or affiliated purchaser of the issuer

(1) (*One broker or dealer*) Effects all Rule 10b–18 purchases from or through only one broker on any single day, or, if a broker is not used, with only one dealer on a single day, and makes or causes to be made all Rule 10b–18 bids to or through only one broker on any single day, or, if a broker is not used, to only one dealer on a single day; *Provided, however,* That

(i) This paragraph (b)(1) shall not apply to Rule 10b–18 purchases which are not solicited by or on behalf of the issuer or affiliated purchaser; and

(ii) Where Rule 10b–18 purchases or Rule 10b–18 bids are made by or on behalf of more than one affiliated purchaser of the issuer (or the issuer and one or more of its affiliated purchasers) on a single day, this paragraph (b)(1) shall apply to all such bids and purchases in the aggregate; and

(2) (*Time of purchases*) Effects all Rule 10b–18 purchases from or through a broker or dealer

(i) In a reported security, (A) such that the purchaser would not constitute the opening transaction in the security reported in the consolidated system; and (B) if the principal market of such security is an exchange, at a time other than during the one-half hour before the scheduled close of trading on the principal market; and (C) if the purchase is to be made on an exchange, at a time other than during the one-half hour before the scheduled close of trading on the national securities exchange on which the purchase is to be made; and (D) if the purchase is to be made otherwise than on a national securities exchange, at a time other than during the one-half hour before the termination of the period in which last sale prices are reported in the consolidated system;

(ii) In any exchange traded security, on any national securities exchange, (A) such that the Rule 10b–18 purchase would not constitute the opening transaction in the security on such exchange; and (B) at a time other than during the one-half hour before the schedule close of trading on the exchange;

(iii) In any NASDAQ security, otherwise than on a national securities exchange, if a current independent bid quotation for the security is reported in Level 2 of NASDAQ; and

(3) (*Price of purchases*) Effects all Rule 10b–18 purchases from or through a broker or dealer at a purchase price, or makes or causes to be made all Rule 10b–18 bids to or through a broker or dealer at a price

(i) For a reported security, that is not higher than the published bid, as that term is defined in Rule 11Ac1–1(a)(9) under the Act, that is the highest current independent published bid or the last independent sale price reported in the consolidated system, whichever is higher;

(ii) On a national securities exchange, for an exchange traded security, that is not higher than the current independent bid quotation or the last independent sale price on that exchange, whichever is higher;

(iii) Otherwise than on a national securities exchange for a NASDAQ security, that is not higher than the lowest current independent offer quotation reported in Level 2 of NASDAQ; or

(iv) Otherwise than on a national securities exchange, for a security that is not a reported security or a NASD security, that is not higher than the lowest current independent offer quotation, determined on the basis of reasonable inquiry; and

(4) (*Volume of purchases*) Effects from or through a broker or dealer all Rule 10b–18 purchases other than block purchases

(i) Of a reported security, an exchange traded security or a NASDAQ security, in an amount that, when added to the amounts of all other Rule 10b–18 purchases, other than block purchases, from or through a broker or dealer effected by or for the issuer or any affiliated purchaser of the issuer on that day, does not exceed the higher of (A) one round lot or (B) the number of round lots closest to 25 percent of the trading volume for the security;

(ii) Of any other security, in an amount that (A) when added to the amounts of all other Rule 10b–18 purchases, other than block purchases, from or through a broker or dealer effected by or for the issuer or any affiliated purchaser of the issuer on that day, does not exceed one round lot or (B) when added to the amounts of all other Rule 10b–18 purchases other than block purchases from or through a broker or dealer effected by or for the issuer or any affiliated purchaser of the issuer during the day and the preceding five business days, does not exceed 1/20th of one percent (0.0005) of the outstanding shares of the security, exclusive of shares known to be owned beneficially by affiliates.

(c) *Conditions following a market-wide trading suspension.* The conditions of paragraph (b) of this section shall apply in connection with a Rule 10b–18 bid or a Rule 10b–18 purchase effected during a trading session following the termination of a market-wide trading suspension, except that the time of purchase condition in paragraph (b)(2) of this section shall not apply, either:

(1) From the reopening of trading until the scheduled close of trading; or

(2) At the opening of trading on the next trading day, if a market-wide trading suspension is in effect at the scheduled close of a trading session.

(d) No presumption shall arise that an issuer or affiliated purchaser of an issuer has violated Sections 9(a)(2) or 10(b) of the Act or Rule 10b–5 under the Act if the Rule 10b–18 bids or Rule 10b–18 purchases of such issuer or affiliated purchaser do not meet the conditions specified in paragraphs (b) or (c) of this section.

Rule 10A–2. Auditor Independence

It shall be unlawful for an auditor not to be independent under Rule 2–01(c)(2)(iii)(B), (c)(4), (c)(6), (c)(7), and Rule 2–07.

Rule 10A–3. Listing Standards Relating to Audit Committees

(a) Pursuant to section 10A(m) of the Act and section 3 of the Sarbanes–Oxley Act of 2002:

(1) *National securities exchanges.* The rules of each national securities exchange registered pursuant to section 6 of the Act must, in accordance with the provisions of this section, prohibit the initial or continued listing of any security of an issuer that is not in compliance with the requirements of any portion of paragraph (b) or (c) of this section.

(2) *National securities associations.* The rules of each national securities association registered pursuant to section 15A of the Act must, in accordance with the provisions of this section, prohibit the initial or continued listing in an automated inter-dealer quotation system of any security of an issuer that is not in compliance with the requirements of any portion of paragraph (b) or (c) of this section.

(3) *Opportunity to cure defects.* The rules required by paragraphs (a)(1) and (a)(2) of this section must provide for appropriate procedures for a listed issuer to have an opportunity to cure any defects that would be the basis for a prohibition under paragraph (a) of this section, before the imposition of such prohibition. Such rules also may provide that if a member of an audit committee ceases to be independent in accordance with the requirements of this section for reasons outside the member's reasonable control, that person, with notice by the issuer to the applicable national securities exchange or national securities association, may remain an audit committee member of the listed issuer until the earlier of the next annual shareholders meeting of the listed issuer or one year from the occurrence of the event that caused the member to be no longer independent.

(4) *Notification of noncompliance.* The rules required by paragraphs (a)(1) and (a)(2) of this section must include a requirement that a listed issuer must notify the applicable national securities exchange or national securities association promptly after an executive officer of the listed issuer becomes aware of any material noncompliance by the listed issuer with the requirements of this section.

(5) *Implementation.* (i) The rules of each national securities exchange or national securities association meeting the requirements of this section must

be operative, and listed issuers must be in compliance with those rules, by the following dates:

(A) July 31, 2005 for foreign private issuers and small business issuers (as defined in Rule 12b–2); and

(B) For all other listed issuers, the earlier of the listed issuer's first annual shareholders meeting after January 15, 2004, or October 31, 2004.

(ii) Each national securities exchange and national securities association must provide to the Commission, no later than July 15, 2003, proposed rules or rule amendments that comply with this section.

(iii) Each national securities exchange and national securities association must have final rules or rule amendments that comply with this section approved by the Commission no later than December 1, 2003.

(b) *Required standards.* (1) *Independence.* (i) Each member of the audit committee must be a member of the board of directors of the listed issuer, and must otherwise be independent; provided that, where a listed issuer is one of two dual holding companies, those companies may designate one audit committee for both companies so long as each member of the audit committee is a member of the board of directors of at least one of such dual holding companies.

(ii) *Independence requirements for non-investment company issuers.* In order to be considered to be independent for purposes of this paragraph (b)(1), a member of an audit committee of a listed issuer that is not an investment company may not, other than in his or her capacity as a member of the audit committee, the board of directors, or any other board committee:

(A) Accept directly or indirectly any consulting, advisory, or other compensatory fee from the issuer or any subsidiary thereof, provided that, unless the rules of the national securities exchange or national securities association provide otherwise, compensatory fees do not include the receipt of fixed amounts of compensation under a retirement plan (including deferred compensation) for prior service with the listed issuer (provided that such compensation is not contingent in any way on continued service); or

(B) Be an affiliated person of the issuer or any subsidiary thereof.

(iii) *Independence requirements for investment company issuers.* In order to be considered to be independent for purposes of this paragraph (b)(1), a member of an audit committee of a listed issuer that is an investment company may not, other than in his or her capacity as a member of the audit committee, the board of directors, or any other board committee:

(A) Accept directly or indirectly any consulting, advisory, or other compensatory fee from the issuer or any subsidiary thereof, provided that, unless the rules of the national securities exchange or national securities association provide otherwise, compensatory fees do not include the receipt of fixed amounts of compensation under a retirement plan (including deferred compensation) for prior service with the listed issuer (provided that such compensation is not contingent in any way on continued service); or

(B) Be an "interested person" of the issuer as defined in section 2(a)(19) of the Investment Company Act of 1940.

(iv) *Exemptions from the independence requirements.* (A) For an issuer listing securities pursuant to a registration statement under section 12 of the Act, or for an issuer that has a registration statement under the Securities Act of 1933 covering an initial public offering of securities to be listed by the issuer, where in each case the listed issuer was not, immediately prior to the effective date of such registration statement, required to file reports with the Commission pursuant to section 13(a) or 15(d) of the Act:

(1) All but one of the members of the listed issuer's audit committee may be exempt from the independence requirements of paragraph (b)(1)(ii) of this section for 90 days from the date of effectiveness of such registration statement; and

(2) A minority of the members of the listed issuer's audit committee may be exempt from the independence requirements of paragraph (b)(1)(ii) of this section for one year from the date of effectiveness of such registration statement.

(B) An audit committee member that sits on the board of directors of a listed issuer and an affiliate of the listed issuer is exempt from the requirements of paragraph (b)(1)(ii)(B) of this section if the member, except for being a director on each such board of directors, otherwise meets the independence requirements of paragraph (b)(1)(ii) of this section for each such entity, including the receipt of only ordinary-course compensation for serving as a member of the board of directors, audit committee or any other board committee of each such entity.

(C) An employee of a foreign private issuer who is not an executive officer of the foreign private issuer is exempt from the requirements of paragraph (b)(1)(ii) of this section if the employee is elected or named to the board of directors or audit committee of the foreign private issuer pursuant to the issuer's governing law or documents, an employee collective bargaining or similar agreement or other home country legal or listing requirements.

(D) An audit committee member of a foreign private issuer may be exempt from the requirements of paragraph (b)(1)(ii)(B) of this section if that member meets the following requirements:

(1) The member is an affiliate of the foreign private issuer or a representative of such an affiliate;

(2) The member has only observer status on, and is not a voting member or the chair of, the audit committee; and

(3) Neither the member nor the affiliate is an executive officer of the foreign private issuer.

(E) An audit committee member of a foreign private issuer may be exempt from the requirements of paragraph (b)(1)(ii)(B) of this section if that member meets the following requirements:

(1) The member is a representative or designee of a foreign government or foreign governmental entity that is an affiliate of the foreign private issuer; and

(2) The member is not an executive officer of the foreign private issuer.

(F) In addition to paragraphs (b)(1)(iv)(A) through (E) of this section, the Commission may exempt from the requirements of paragraphs (b)(1)(ii) or (b)(1)(iii) of this section a particular relationship with respect to audit committee members, as the Commission determines appropriate in light of the circumstances.

(2) *Responsibilities relating to registered public accounting firms.* The audit committee of each listed issuer, in its capacity as a committee of the board of directors, must be directly responsible for the appointment, compensation, retention and oversight of the work of any registered public accounting firm engaged (including resolution of disagreements between management and the auditor regarding financial reporting) for the purpose of preparing or issuing an audit report or performing other audit, review or attest services for the listed issuer, and each such registered public accounting firm must report directly to the audit committee.

(3) *Complaints.* Each audit committee must establish procedures for:

(i) The receipt, retention, and treatment of complaints received by the listed issuer regarding accounting, internal accounting controls, or auditing matters; and

(ii) The confidential, anonymous submission by employees of the listed issuer of concerns regarding questionable accounting or auditing matters.

(4) *Authority to engage advisers.* Each audit committee must have the authority to engage independent counsel and other advisers, as it determines necessary to carry out its duties.

(5) *Funding.* Each listed issuer must provide for appropriate funding, as determined by the audit committee, in its capacity as a committee of the board of directors, for payment of:

(i) Compensation to any registered public accounting firm engaged for the purpose of preparing or issuing an audit report or performing other audit, review or attest services for the listed issuer;

(ii) Compensation to any advisers employed by the audit committee under paragraph (b)(4) of this section; and

(iii) Ordinary administrative expenses of the audit committee that are necessary or appropriate in carrying out its duties.

(c) *General exemptions.*

(1) At any time when an issuer has a class of securities that is listed on a national securities exchange or national securities association subject to the requirements of this section, the listing of other classes of securities of the listed issuer on a national securities exchange or national securities association is not subject to the requirements of this section.

(2) At any time when an issuer has a class of common equity securities (or similar securities) that is listed on a national securities exchange or national securities association subject to the requirements of this section, the listing of classes of securities of a direct or indirect consolidated subsidiary or an at least 50% beneficially owned subsidiary of the issuer (except classes of equity securities, other than non-convertible, non-participating preferred securities, of such subsidiary) is not subject to the requirements of this section.

(3) The listing of securities of a foreign private issuer is not subject to the requirements of paragraphs (b)(1) through (b)(5) of this section if the foreign private issuer meets the following requirements:

(i) The foreign private issuer has a board of auditors (or similar body), or has statutory auditors, established and selected pursuant to home country legal or listing provisions expressly requiring or permitting such a board or similar body;

(ii) The board or body, or statutory auditors is required under home country legal or listing requirements to be either:

(A) Separate from the board of directors; or

(B) Composed of one or more members of the board of directors and one or more members that are not also members of the board of directors;

(iii) The board or body, or statutory auditors, are not elected by management of such issuer and no executive officer of the foreign private issuer is a member of such board or body, or statutory auditors;

(iv) Home country legal or listing provisions set forth or provide for standards for the independence of such board or body, or statutory auditors, from the foreign private issuer or the management of such issuer;

(v) Such board or body, or statutory auditors, in accordance with any applicable home country legal or listing requirements or the issuer's governing documents, are responsible, to the extent permitted by law, for the appointment, retention and oversight of the work of any registered public accounting firm engaged (including, to the extent permitted by law, the resolution of disagreements between management and the auditor regarding financial reporting) for the purpose of preparing or issuing an audit report or performing other audit, review or attest services for the issuer; and

(vi) The audit committee requirements of paragraphs (b)(3), (b)(4) and (b)(5) of this section apply to such board or body, or statutory auditors, to the extent permitted by law.

(4) The listing of a security futures product cleared by a clearing agency that is registered pursuant to section 17A of the Act or that is exempt from the registration requirements of section 17A pursuant to paragraph (b)(7)(A) of such section is not subject to the requirements of this section.

(5) The listing of a standardized option, as defined in Rule 9b–1(a)(4), issued by a clearing agency that is registered pursuant to section 17A of the Act is not subject to the requirements of this section.

(6) The listing of securities of the following listed issuers are not subject to the requirements of this section:

(i) Asset–Backed Issuers (as defined in Rule 13a–14(g) and Rule 15d–14(g));

(ii) Unit investment trusts (as defined in Section 4(2) of the Investment Company Act of 1940); and

(iii) Foreign governments (as defined in Rule 3b–4(a)).

(7) The listing of securities of a listed issuer is not subject to the requirements of this section if:

(i) The listed issuer, as reflected in the applicable listing application, is organized as a trust or other unincorporated association that does not have a board of directors or persons acting in a similar capacity; and

(ii) The activities of the listed issuer that is described in paragraph (c)(7)(i) of this section are limited to passively owning or holding (as well as administering and distributing amounts in respect of) securities, rights, collateral or other assets on behalf of or for the benefit of the holders of the listed securities.

(d) *Disclosure*. Any listed issuer availing itself of an exemption from the independence standards contained in paragraph (b)(1)(iv) of this section (except paragraph (b)(1)(iv)(B) of this section), the general exemption contained in paragraph (c)(3) of this section or the last sentence of paragraph (a)(3) of this section, must:

(1) Disclose its reliance on the exemption and its assessment of whether, and if so, how, such reliance would materially adversely affect the ability of the audit committee to act independently and to satisfy the other requirements of this section in any proxy or information statement for a meeting of shareholders at which directors are elected that is filed with the Commission pursuant to the requirements of section 14 of the Act; and

(2) Disclose the information specified in paragraph (d)(1) of this section in, or incorporate such information by reference from such proxy or information statement filed with the Commission into, its annual report filed with the Commission pursuant to the requirements of section 13(a) or 15(d) of the Act.

(e) *Definitions*. Unless the context otherwise requires, all terms used in this section have the same meaning as in the Act. In addition, unless the context otherwise requires, the following definitions apply for purposes of this section:

(1)(i) The term *affiliate* of, or a person *affiliated* with, a specified person, means a person that directly, or indirectly through one or more intermediaries, controls, or is controlled by, or is under common control with, the person specified.

(ii)(A) A person will be deemed not to be in control of a specified person for purposes of this section if the person:

(1) Is not the beneficial owner, directly or indirectly, of more than 10% of any class of voting equity securities of the specified person; and

(2) Is not an executive officer of the specified person.

(B) Paragraph (e)(1)(ii)(A) of this section only creates a safe harbor position that a person does not control a specified person. The existence of the safe harbor does not create a presumption in any way that a person exceeding the ownership requirement in paragraph (e)(1)(ii)(A)(*1*) of this section controls or is otherwise an affiliate of a specified person.

(iii) The following will be deemed to be affiliates:

(A) An executive officer of an affiliate;

(B) A director who also is an employee of an affiliate;

(C) A general partner of an affiliate; and

(D) A managing member of an affiliate.

(iv) For purposes of paragraph (e)(1)(i) of this section, dual holding companies will not be deemed to be affiliates of or persons affiliated with each other by virtue of their dual holding company arrangements with each other, including where directors of one dual holding company are also directors of the other dual holding company, or where directors of one or both dual holding companies are also directors of the businesses jointly controlled, directly or indirectly, by the dual holding companies (and, in each case, receive only ordinary-course compensation for serving as a member of the board of directors, audit committee or any other board committee of the dual holding companies or any entity that is jointly controlled, directly or indirectly, by the dual holding companies).

(2) In the case of foreign private issuers with a two-tier board system, the term *board of directors* means the supervisory or non-management board.

(3) In the case of a listed issuer that is a limited partnership or limited liability company where such entity does not have a board of directors or equivalent body, the term *board of directors* means the board of directors of the managing general partner, managing member or equivalent body.

(4) The term *control* (including the terms *controlling*, *controlled by* and under *common control with*) means the possession, direct or indirect, of the power to direct or cause the direction of the management and policies of a person, whether through the ownership of voting securities, by contract, or otherwise.

(5) The term *dual holding companies* means two foreign private issuers that:

(i) Are organized in different national jurisdictions;

(ii) Collectively own and supervise the management of one or more businesses which are conducted as a single economic enterprise; and

(iii) Do not conduct any business other than collectively owning and supervising such businesses and activities reasonably incidental thereto.

(6) The term *executive officer* has the meaning set forth in Rule 3b–7.

(7) The term *foreign private issuer* has the meaning set forth in Rule 3b–4(c).

(8) The term *indirect* acceptance by a member of an audit committee of any consulting, advisory or other compensatory fee includes acceptance of such a fee by a spouse, a minor child or stepchild or a child or stepchild sharing a home with the member or by an entity in which such member is a partner, member, an officer such as a managing director occupying a comparable position or executive officer, or occupies a similar position (except limited partners, non-managing members and those occupying similar positions who, in each case, have no active role in providing services to the entity) and which provides accounting, consulting, legal, investment banking or financial advisory services to the issuer or any subsidiary of the issuer.

(9) The terms *listed* and *listing* refer to securities listed on a national securities exchange or listed in an automated inter-dealer quotation system of a national securities association or to issuers of such securities.

Instructions to Rule 10A–3

1. The requirements in paragraphs (b)(2) through (b)(5), (c)(3)(v) and (c)(3)(vi) of this section do not conflict with, and do not affect the application of, any requirement or ability under a listed issuer's governing law or documents or other home country legal or listing provisions that requires or permits shareholders to ultimately vote on, approve or ratify such requirements. The requirements instead relate to the assignment of responsibility as between the audit committee and management. In such an instance, however, if the listed issuer provides a recommendation or nomination regarding such responsibilities to shareholders, the audit committee of the listed issuer, or body performing similar functions, must be responsible for making the recommendation or nomination.

2. The requirements in paragraphs (b)(2) through (b)(5), (c)(3)(v), (c)(3)(vi) and Instruction 1 of this section do not conflict with any legal or listing requirement in a listed issuer's home jurisdiction that prohibits the full board of directors from delegating such responsibilities to the listed issuer's audit committee or limits the degree of such delegation. In that case, the audit committee, or body performing similar functions, must be granted such responsibilities, which can include advisory powers, with respect to such matters to the extent permitted by law, including submitting nominations or recommendations to the full board.

3. The requirements in paragraphs (b)(2) through (b)(5), (c)(3)(v) and (c)(3)(vi) of this section do not conflict with any legal or listing requirement in a listed issuer's home jurisdiction that vests such responsibilities with a government entity or tribunal. In that case, the audit committee, or body performing similar functions, must be granted such responsibilities, which can include advisory powers, with respect to such matters to the extent permitted by law.

4. For purposes of this section, the determination of a person's beneficial ownership must be made in accordance with Rule 13d–3.

REGISTRATION AND REPORTING

Rule 12b–2. Definitions

Unless the context otherwise requires, the following terms, when used in the rules contained in this regulation or in Regulation 13A or 15D or in the forms for statements and reports filed pursuant to sections 12, 13 or 15(d) of the act, shall have the respective meanings indicated in this rule:

Accelerated filer. (1) The term "accelerated filer" means an issuer after it first meets the following conditions as of the end of its fiscal year:

(i) The aggregate market value of the voting and non-voting common equity held by non-affiliates of the issuer is $75 million or more;

(ii) The issuer has been subject to the requirements of Section 13(a) or 15(d) of the Act for a period of at least twelve calendar months;

(iii) The issuer has filed at least one annual report pursuant to Section 13(a) or 15(d) of the Act; and

(iv) The issuer is not eligible to use Forms 10–KSB and 10–QSB for its annual and quarterly reports.

NOTE to paragraph (1): The aggregate market value of the issuer's outstanding voting and non-voting common equity shall be computed by use of the price at which the common equity was last sold, or the average of the bid and asked prices of such common equity, in the principal market for such common equity, as of the last business day of the issuer's most recently completed second fiscal quarter.

(2) Entering and Exiting Accelerated Filer Status. (i) The determination for whether a non-accelerated filer becomes an accelerated filer as of the end of the issuer's fiscal year governs the annual report to be filed for that fiscal year, the quarterly and annual reports to be filed for the subsequent fiscal year and all annual and quarterly reports to be filed thereafter while the issuer remains an accelerated filer.

(ii) Once an issuer becomes an accelerated filer, it will remain an accelerated filer unless the issuer becomes eligible to use Forms 10–KSB and 10–QSB for its annual and quarterly reports. In that case, the issuer will not become an accelerated filer again unless it subsequently meets the conditions in paragraph (1) of this definition.

* * *

REGISTRATION OF SECURITIES

Rule 12g–1. Exemption From Section 12(g)

An issuer shall be exempt from the requirement to register any class of equity securities pursuant to section 12(g)(1) if on the last day of its most recent fiscal year the issuer had total assets not exceeding $10 million and, with respect to a foreign private issuer, such securities were not quoted in an automated inter-dealer quotation system.

REPORTS OF ISSUERS

Rule 13a–1. Requirement of Annual Reports

Every issuer having securities registered pursuant to Section 12 of the Act shall file an annual report on the appropriate form authorized or prescribed therefor for each fiscal year after the last full fiscal year for which financial statements were filed in its registration statement. Annual reports shall be filed within the period specified in the appropriate form.

* * *

Rule 13a–11. Current Reports on Form 8–K

(a) * * * [E]very registrant subject to Rule 13a–1 shall file a current report on Form 8–K within the period specified in that form, unless substantially the same information as that required by Form 8–K has been previously reported by the registrant.

Rule 13a–13. Quarterly Reports on Form 10–Q and Form 1–QSB

(a) * * * [E]very issuer which has securities registered pursuant to Section 12 of the Act and is required to file annual reports pursuant to Section 13 of the Act and has filed or intends to file such reports on Form 10–K and Form 10–KSB, * * * shall file a quarterly report on Form 10–Q and Form 10–KSB, within the period specified in General Instruction A.1. to that form for each of the first three fiscal quarters of each fiscal year of the issuer, commencing with the first fiscal quarter following the most recent fiscal year for which full financial statements were included in the registration statement, or, if the registration statement included financial statements for an interim period subsequent to the most recent fiscal year and meeting the requirements of Article 10 of Regulation S–X, for the first fiscal quarter subsequent to the quarter reported upon in the registration statement. The first quarterly report of the issuer shall be filed either within 45 days after the effective date of the registration statement or on or before the date on which such report would have been required to be filed if the issuer had been required to file reports on Form 10–Q and Form 10–QSB as of its last fiscal quarter, whichever is later.

* * *

Rule 13a–14. Certification of Disclosure in Annual and Quarterly Reports

(a) Each report, including transition reports, filed on Form 10–Q, Form 10–QSB, Form 10–K, Form 10–KSB, Form 20–F or Form 40–F under section 13(a) of the Act (15 U.S.C. 78m(a)), other than a report filed by an Asset–Backed Issuer (as defined in paragraph (g) of this section), must include a certification containing the information set forth in paragraph (b) of this section in the form specified in the report. Each principal executive officer or officers and principal financial officer or officers of the issuer, or persons performing similar functions, at the time of filing of the report must sign the certification.

(b) The certification included in each report specified in paragraph (a) of this section must be in the form specified in the report and consist of a statement of the certifying officer that:

(1) He or she has reviewed the report being filed;

(2) Based on his or her knowledge, the report does not contain any untrue statement of a material fact or omit to state a material fact necessary to make the statements made, in light of the circumstances under which such statements were made, not misleading with respect to the period covered by the report;

(3) Based on his or her knowledge, the financial statements, and other financial information included in the report, fairly present in all material respects the financial condition, results of operations and cash flows of the issuer as of, and for, the periods presented in the report;

(4) He or she and the other certifying officers are responsible for establishing and maintaining disclosure controls and procedures (as such term is defined in paragraph (c) of this section) for the issuer and have:

(i) Designed such disclosure controls and procedures to ensure that material information relating to the issuer, including its consolidated subsidiaries, is made known to them by others within those entities, particularly during the period in which the periodic reports are being prepared;

(ii) Evaluated the effectiveness of the issuer's disclosure controls and procedures as of a date within 90 days prior to the filing date of the report (''Evaluation Date''); and

(iii) Presented in the report their conclusions about the effectiveness of the disclosure controls and procedures based on their evaluation as of the Evaluation Date;

(5) He or she and the other certifying officers have disclosed, based on their most recent evaluation, to the issuer's auditors and the audit committee of the board of directors (or persons fulfilling the equivalent function):

(i) All significant deficiencies in the design or operation of internal controls which could adversely affect the issuer's ability to record, process, summarize and report financial data and have identified for the issuer's auditors any material weaknesses in internal controls; and

(ii) Any fraud, whether or not material, that involves management or other employees who have a significant role in the issuer's internal controls; and

(6) He or she and the other certifying officers have indicated in the report whether or not there were significant changes in internal controls or in other factors that could significantly affect internal controls subsequent to the date of their most recent evaluation, including any corrective actions with regard to significant deficiencies and material weaknesses.

(c) For purposes of this section and Rule 13a–15 of this chapter, the term ''disclosure controls and procedures'' means controls and other procedures of an issuer that are designed to ensure that information required to be disclosed by the issuer in the reports that it files or submits under the Act is recorded, processed, summarized and reported, within the time periods specified in the Commission's rules and forms. Disclosure controls and procedures include, without limitation, controls and procedures designed to ensure that information required to be disclosed by an issuer in the reports that it files or submits under the Act is accumulated and communicated to the issuer's management, including its principal executive officer or officers and principal financial officer or officers, or persons performing similar functions, as appropriate to allow timely decisions regarding required disclosure.

(d) A person required to provide the certification specified in paragraph (a) of this section may not have the certification signed on his or her behalf pursuant to a power of attorney or other form of confirming authority.

(e) Each annual report filed by an Asset–Backed Issuer (as defined in paragraph (g) of this section) under section 13(a) of the Act) must include a certification addressing the following items:

(1) Review by the certifying officer of the annual report and other reports containing distribution information for the period covered by the annual report;

(2) The absence in these reports, to the best of the certifying officer's knowledge, of any untrue statement of material fact or omission of a material fact necessary to make the statements made, in light of the circumstances under which such statements were made, not misleading;

(3) The inclusion in these reports, to the best of the certifying officer's knowledge, of the financial information required to be provided to the trustee under the governing documents of the issuer; and

(4) Compliance by the servicer with its servicing obligations and minimum servicing standards.

(f) With respect to Asset–Backed Issuers, the certification required by paragraph (e) of this section must be signed by the trustee of the trust (if the trustee signs the annual report) or the senior officer in charge of securitization of the depositor (if the depositor signs the annual report). Alternatively, the senior officer in charge of the servicing function of the master servicer (or entity performing the equivalent functions) may sign the certification.

(g) For purposes of this section, the term Asset–Backed Issuer means any issuer whose reporting obligation results from the registration of securities it issued that are primarily serviced by the cash flows of a discrete pool of receivables or other financial assets, either fixed or revolving, that by their terms convert into cash within a finite time period plus any rights or other assets designed to assure the servicing or timely distribution of proceeds to security holders.

Rule 13a–15. Issuer's Disclosure Controls and Procedures Related to Preparation of Required Reports

(a) Every issuer that has a class of securities registered pursuant to section 12 of the Act, other than an Asset–Backed Issuer (as defined in Rule 13a–14(g) of this chapter), a small business investment company registered on Form N–5, or a unit investment trust as defined by Section 4(2) of the Investment Company Act of 1940, must maintain disclosure controls and procedures (as defined in Rule 13a–14(c) of this chapter).

(b) Within the 90–day period prior to the filing date of each report requiring certification under Rule 13a–14 and Rule 30a–2 of this chapter, an evaluation must be carried out under the supervision and with the participation of the issuer's management, including the issuer's principal executive officer or officers and principal financial officer or officers, or persons performing similar functions, of the effectiveness of the design and operation of the issuer's disclosure controls and procedures.

REPORTS BY BENEFICIAL OWNERS

Rule 13d–1. Filing of Schedules 13D and 13G

(a) Any person who, after acquiring directly or indirectly the beneficial ownership of any equity security of a class which is specified in paragraph (i) of this section, is directly or indirectly the beneficial owner of more than 5 percent of the class shall, within 10 days after the acquisition, file with the Commission, a statement containing the information required by Schedule 13D.

(b)(1) A person who would otherwise be obligated under paragraph (a) of this section to file a statement on Schedule 13D may, in lieu thereof, file with the Commission, a short form statement on Schedule 13G. *Provided,* That:

(i) Such person has acquired such securities in the ordinary course of his business and not with the purpose nor with the effect of changing or influencing the control of the issuer, nor in connection with or as a participant in any transaction having such purpose or effect, including any transaction subject to Rule 13d–3(b);

* * *

(2) The Schedule 13G filed pursuant to paragraph (b)(1) of this section shall be filed within 45 days after the end of the calendar year in which the person became obligated under paragraph (b)(1) of this section to report the person's beneficial ownership as of the last day of the calendar year, Provided, That it shall not be necessary to file a Schedule 13G unless the percentage of the class of equity security specified in paragraph (i) of this section beneficially owned as of the end of the calendar year is more than five percent; However, if the person's direct or indirect beneficial ownership exceeds 10 percent of the class of equity securities prior to the end of the calendar year, the initial Schedule 13G shall be filed within 10 days after the end of the first month in which the person's direct or indirect beneficial ownership exceeds 10 percent of the class of equity securities, computed as of the last day of the month.

* * *

Rule 13d–2. Filing of Amendments to Schedule 13D or 13G

(a) Schedule 13D—If any material change occurs in the facts set forth in the Schedule 13D required by Rule 13d–1a, including, but not limited to, any material increase or decrease in the percentage of the class beneficially owned, the person or persons who were required to file the statement shall promptly file or cause to be filed with the Commission an amendment disclosing that change. An acquisition or disposition of beneficial ownership of securities in an amount equal to one percent or more of the class of securities shall be deemed "material" for purposes of this section; acquisitions or dispositions of less than those amounts may be material, depending upon the facts and circumstances.

* * *

Rule 13d–3. Determination of Beneficial Owner

(a) For the purposes of section 13(d) and 13(g) of the Act a beneficial owner of a security includes any person who, directly or indirectly, through any contract, arrangement, understanding, relationship, or otherwise has or shares:

(1) *Voting power* which includes the power to vote, or to direct the voting of, such security; and/or

(2) *Investment power* which includes the power to dispose, or to direct the disposition, of such security.

(b) Any person who, directly or indirectly, creates or uses a trust, proxy, power of attorney, pooling arrangement or any other contract, arrangement, or device with the purpose or effect of divesting such person of beneficial ownership of a security or preventing the vesting of such beneficial ownership as part of a plan or scheme to evade the reporting requirements of section 13(d) or 13(g) of the Act shall be deemed for purposes of such section to be the beneficial owner of such security.

(c) All securities of the same class beneficially owned by a person, regardless of the form which such beneficial ownership takes, shall be aggregated in calculating the number of shares beneficially owned by such person.

(d) Notwithstanding the provisions of paragraphs (a) and (c) of this rule:

(1)(i) A person shall be deemed to be the beneficial owner of a security, subject to the provisions of paragraph (b) of this rule, if that person has the right to acquire beneficial ownership of such security, as defined in Rule 13d–3(a), within sixty days, including but not limited to any right acquired: (A) through the exercise of any option, warrant or right; (B) through the conversion of a security; (C) pursuant to the power to revoke a trust, discretionary account, or similar arrangement; or (D) pursuant to the automatic termination of a trust, discretionary account or similar arrangement; provided, however, any person who acquires a security or power specified in paragraphs (A), (B) or (C), above, with the purpose or effect of changing or influencing the control of the issuer, or in connection with or as a participant in any transaction having such purpose or effect, immediately upon such acquisition shall be deemed to be the beneficial owner of the securities which may be acquired through the exercise or conversion of such security or power. Any securities not outstanding which are subject to such options, warrants, rights or conversion privileges shall be deemed to be outstanding for the purpose of computing the percentage of outstanding securities of the class owned by such person but shall not be deemed to be outstanding for the purpose of computing the percentage of the class by any other person.

(ii) Paragraph (d)(1)(i) of this section remains applicable for the purpose of determining the obligation to file with respect to the underlying security even though the option, warrant, right or convertible security is of a class of equity security, as defined in Rule 13d–1(i), and may therefore give rise to a separate obligation to file.

(2) A member of a national securities exchange shall not be deemed to be a beneficial owner of securities held directly or indirectly by it on behalf of another person solely because such member is the record holder of such securities and, pursuant to the rules of such exchange, may direct the vote of such securities, without instruction, on other than contested matters or matters that may affect substantially the rights or privileges of the holders of the securities to be voted, but is otherwise precluded by the rules of such exchange from voting without instruction.

(3) A person who in the ordinary course of business is a pledgee of securities under a written pledge agreement shall not be deemed to be the beneficial owner of such pledged securities until the pledgee has taken all formal steps necessary which are required to declare a default and determines that the power to vote or to direct the vote or to dispose or to direct the disposition of such pledged securities will be exercised, provided that:

(i) The pledgee agreement is bona fide and was not entered into with the purpose nor with the effect of changing or influencing the control of the issuer, nor in connection with any transaction having such purpose or effect, including any transaction subject to Rule 13d–3(b);

(ii) The pledgee is a person specified in Rule 13d–1(b)(ii), including persons meeting the conditions set forth in paragraph (G) thereof; and

(iii) The pledgee agreement, prior to default, does not grant to the pledgee:

(A) The power to vote or to direct the vote of the pledged securities; or

(B) The power to dispose or direct the disposition of the pledged securities, other than the grant of such power(s) pursuant to a pledge agreement under which credit is extended subject to Regulation T and in which the pledgee is a broker or dealer registered under section 15 of the Act.

(4) A person engaged in business as an underwriter of securities who acquires securities through his participation in good faith in a firm commitment underwriting registered under the Securities Act of 1933 shall not be deemed to be the beneficial owner of such securities until the expiration of forty days after the date of such acquisition.

Rule 13d–4. Disclaimer of Beneficial Ownership

Any person may expressly declare in any statement filed that the filing of such statement shall not be construed as an admission that such person is, for the purposes of section 13(d), or 13(g) of the Act, the beneficial owner of any securities covered by the statement.

Rule 13d–5. Acquisition of Securities

(a) A person who becomes a beneficial owner of securities shall be deemed to have acquired such securities for purposes of section 13(d)(1) of the Act, whether such acquisition was through purchase or otherwise. However, executors or administrators of a decedent's estate generally will be presumed not to have acquired beneficial ownership of the securities in the decedent's estate until such time as such executors or administrators are qualified under local law to perform their duties.

(b)(1) When two or more persons agree to act together for the purpose of acquiring, holding, voting or disposing of equity securities of an issuer, the group formed thereby shall be deemed to have acquired beneficial ownership, for purposes of sections 13(d) and 13(g) of the Act, as of the date of such agreement, of all equity securities of that issuer beneficially owned by any such persons.

(2) Notwithstanding the previous paragraph, a group shall be deemed not to have acquired any equity securities beneficially owned by the other members of the group solely by virtue of their concerted actions relating to the purchase of equity securities directly from an issuer in a transaction not involving a public offering: *Provided,* That:

(i) All the members of the group are persons specified in Rule 13d–1(b)(1)(ii);

(ii) The purchase is in the ordinary course of each member's business and not with the purpose nor with the effect of changing or influencing control of the issuer, nor in connection with or as a participant in any transaction having such purpose or effect, including any transaction subject to Rule 13d-3(b);

(iii) There is no agreement among, or between any members of the group to act together with respect to the issuer or its securities except for the purpose of facilitating the specific purchase involved; and

(iv) The only actions among or between any members of the group with respect to the issuer or its securities subsequent to the closing date of the non-public offering are those which are necessary to conclude ministerial matters directly related to the completion of the offer or sale of the securities.

Rule 13d-6. Exemption of Certain Acquisitions

The acquisition of securities of an issuer by a person who, prior to such acquisition, was a beneficial owner of more than five percent of the outstanding securities of the same class as those acquired shall be exempt from section 13(d) of the Act: *Provided,* That:

(a) The acquisition is made pursuant to preemptive subscription right in an offering made to all holders of securities of the class to which the preemptive subscription rights pertain;

(b) Such person does not acquire additional securities except through the exercise of his pro rata share of the preemptive subscription rights; and

(c) The acquisition is duly reported if required, pursuant to section 16(a) of the Act and the rules and regulations thereunder.

Rule 13d-7. Dissemination

One copy of the Schedule filed pursuant to Rule 13d-1 and Rule 13d-2 shall be sent to the issuer of the security at its principal executive office, by registered or certified mail. A copy of Schedules filed pursuant to Rule 13d-1(a) and Rule 13d-2(a) shall also be sent to each national securities exchange where the security is traded.

REPURCHASES BY ISSUERS

Rule 13e-1. Purchase of Securities by the Issuer During a Third-Party Tender Offer

An issuer that has received notice that it is the subject of a tender offer made under Section 14(d)(1) of the Act, that has commenced under Rule 14d-2 must not purchase any of its equity securities during the tender offer unless the issuer first:

(a) Files a statement with the Commission containing the following information:

(1) The title and number of securities to be purchased;

(2) The names of the persons or classes of persons from whom the issuer will purchase the securities;

(3) The name of any exchange, inter-dealer quotation system or any other market on or through which the securities will be purchased;

(4) The purpose of the purchase;

(5) Whether the issuer will retire the securities, hold the securities in its treasury, or dispose of the securities. If the issuer intends to dispose of the securities, describe how it intends to do so; and

(6) The source and amount of funds or other consideration to be used to make the purchase. If the issuer borrows any funds or other consideration to make the purchase or enters any agreement for the purpose of acquiring, holding, or trading the securities, describe the transaction and agreement and identify the parties; and

(b) Pays the fee required by Rule 0-11 when it files the initial statement.

(c) This section does not apply to periodic repurchases in connection with an employee benefit plan or other similar plan of the issuer so long as the purchases are made in the ordinary course and not in response to the tender offer.

Instruction to Rule 13e-1:

File eight copies if paper filing is permitted.

Rule 13e-3. Going Private Transactions by Certain Issuers or Their Affiliates

(a) *Definitions.* Unless indicated otherwise or the context requires, all terms used in this section and in Schedule 13E-3 shall have the same meaning as in the Act or elsewhere in the General Rules and Regulations thereunder. In addition, the following definitions apply:

(1) An "affiliate" of an issuer is a person that directly or indirectly through one or more intermediaries controls, is controlled by, or is under common control with such issuer. For the purposes of this section only, a person who is not an affiliate of an issuer at the commencement of such person's tender offer for a class of equity securities of such issuer will not be deemed an affiliate of such issuer prior to the stated termination of such tender offer and any extensions thereof;

(2) The term "purchase" means any acquisition for value including, but not limited to, (i) any acquisition pursuant to the dissolution of an issuer subsequent to the sale or other disposition of substantially all the assets of such issuer to its affiliate, (ii) any acquisition pursuant to a merger, (iii) any acquisition of fractional interests in connection with a reverse stock split, and (iv) any acquisition subject to the control of an issuer or an affiliate of such issuer;

(3) A "Rule 13e-3 transaction" is any transaction or series of transactions involving one or more of the transactions described in paragraph (a)(3)(i) of this section which has either a reasonable likelihood or a purpose of producing, either directly or indirectly, any of the effects described in paragraph (a)(3)(ii) of this section;

(i) The transactions referred to in paragraph (a)(3) of this section are:

(A) A purchase of any equity security by the issuer of such security or by an affiliate of such issuer;

(B) A tender offer for or request or invitation for tenders of any equity security made by the issuer of such class of securities or by an affiliate of such issuer; or

(C) A solicitation subject to Regulation 14A of any proxy, consent or authorization of, or a distribution subject to Regulation 14C of information statements to, any equity security holder by the issuer of the class of securities or by an affiliate of such issuer, in connection with: a merger, consolidation, reclassification, recapitalization, reorganization or similar corporate transaction of an issuer or between an issuer (or its subsidiaries) and its affiliate; a sale of substantially all the assets of an issuer to its affiliate or group of affiliates; or a reverse stock split of any class of equity securities of the issuer involving the purchase of fractional interests.

(ii) The effects referred to in paragraph (a)(3) of this section are:

(A) Causing any class of equity securities of the issuer which is subject to Section 12(g) or Section 15(d) of the Act to be held of record by less than 300 persons; or

(B) Causing any class of equity securities of the issuer which is either listed on a national securities exchange or authorized to be quoted in an inter-dealer quotation system of a registered national securities association to be neither listed on any national securities exchange nor authorized to be quoted on an inter-dealer quotation system of any registered national securities association.

(4) An "unaffiliated security holder" is any security holder of an equity security subject to a Rule 13e-3 transaction who is not an affiliate of the issuer of such security.

(b) *Application of Section to an Issuer (or an Affiliate of Such Issuer) Subject to Section 12 of the Act.*

(1) It shall be a fraudulent, deceptive or manipulative act or practice, in connection with a Rule 13e-3 transaction, for an issuer which has a class of equity securities registered pursuant to Section 12 of the Act or which is a closed-end investment company registered under the Investment Company Act of 1940, or an affiliate of such issuer, directly or indirectly.

(i) To employ any device, scheme or artifice to defraud any person;

(ii) To make any untrue statement of a material fact or to omit to state a material fact necessary in order to make the statements made, in light of the circumstances under which they were made, not misleading; or

(iii) To engage in any act, practice or course of business which operates or would operate as a fraud or deceit upon any person.

(2) As a means reasonably designed to prevent fraudulent, deceptive or manipulative acts or practices in connection with any Rule 13e–3 transaction, it shall be unlawful for an issuer which has a class of equity securities registered pursuant to Section 12 of the Act, or an affiliate of such issuer, to engage, directly or indirectly, in a Rule 13e–3 transaction unless:

(i) Such issuer or affiliate complies with the requirements of paragraphs (d), (e) and (f) of this Section; and

(ii) The Rule 13e–3 transaction is not in violation of paragraph (b)(1) of this section.

(c) *Application of Section to an Issuer (or an Affiliate of Such Issuer) Subject to Section 15(d) of the Act.*

(1) It shall be unlawful as a fraudulent, deceptive or manipulative act or practice for an issuer which is required to file periodic reports pursuant to Section 15(d) of the Act, or an affiliate of such issuer, to engage, directly or indirectly, in a Rule 13e–3 transaction unless such issuer or affiliate complies with the requirements of paragraphs (d), (e) and (f) of this section.

(2) An issuer or affiliate which is subject to paragraph (c)(1) of this section and which is soliciting proxies or distributing information statements in connection with a transaction described in paragraph (a)(3)(i)(A) of this section may elect to use the timing procedures for conducting a solicitation subject to Regulation 14A or a distribution subject to Regulation 14C in complying with paragraphs (d), (e) and (f) of this section, *provided that* if an election is made, such solicitation or distribution is conducted in accordance with the requirements of the respective regulations, including the filing of preliminary copies of soliciting materials or an information statement at the time specified in Regulation 14A or 14C, respectively.

(d) *Material Required to be Filed.*

The issuer or affiliate engaging in a Rule 13e–3 transaction must file with the Commission:

(1) A Schedule 13E–3 (§ 240.13e–100), including all exhibits;

(2) An amendment to Schedule 13E–3 reporting promptly any material changes in the information set forth in the schedule previously filed; and

(3) A final amendment to Schedule 13E–3 reporting promptly the results of the Rule 13e–3 transaction.

(e) *Disclosure of Certain Information.*

(1) In addition to disclosing the information required by any other applicable rule or regulation under the federal securities laws, the issuer or affiliate engaging in a § 240.13e–3 transaction must disclose to security holders of the class that is the subject of the transaction, as specified in paragraph (f) of this section, the following:

(i) The information required by Item 1 of Schedule 13E–3 (§ 240.13e–100) (Summary Term Sheet);

(ii) The information required by Items 7, 8 and 9 of Schedule 13E–3, which must be prominently disclosed in a "Special Factors" section in the front of the disclosure document;

(iii) A prominent legend on the outside front cover page that indicates that neither the Securities and Exchange Commission nor any state securities commission has: approved or disapproved of the transaction; passed upon the merits or fairness of the transaction; or passed upon the adequacy or accuracy of the disclosure in the document. The legend also must make it clear that any representation to the contrary is a criminal offense;

(iv) The information concerning appraisal rights required by § 229.1016(f) of this chapter; and

(v) The information required by the remaining items of Schedule 13E–3, except for § 229.1016 of this chapter (exhibits), or a fair and adequate summary of the information.

Instructions to paragraph (e)(1):

1. If the Rule 13e–3 transaction also is subject to Regulation 14A (§§ 240.14a–1 through 240.14b–2) or 14C (§§ 240.14c–1 through 240.14c–101), the registration provisions and rules of the Securities Act of 1933, Regulation 14D or § 240.13e–4, the information required by paragraph (e)(1) of this section must be combined with the proxy statement, information statement, prospectus or tender offer material sent or given to security holders.

2. If the Rule 13e–3 transaction involves a registered securities offering, the legend required by § 229.501(b)(7) of this chapter must be combined with the legend required by paragraph (e)(1)(iii) of this section.

3. The required legend must be written in clear, plain language.

(2) If there is any material change in the information previously disclosed to security holders, the issuer or affiliate must disclose the change promptly to security holders as specified in paragraph (f)(1)(iii) of this section.

(f) *Dissemination of disclosure.* (1) If the Rule 13e–3 transaction involves a purchase as described in paragraph (a)(3)(i)(A) of this section or a vote, consent, authorization, or distribution of information statements as described in paragraph (a)(3)(i)(C) of this section, the issuer or affiliate engaging in the Rule 13e–3 transaction shall:

(i) Provide the information required by paragraph (e) of this section: (A) in accordance with the provisions of any applicable federal or state law, but in no event later than 20 days prior to: any such purchase; any such vote, consent or authorization; or with respect to the distribution of information statements, the meeting date, or if corporate action is to be taken by means of the written authorization or consent of security holders, the earliest date on which corporate action may be taken, *Provided, however,* That if the purchase subject to this section is pursuant to a tender offer excepted from Rule 13e–4 by paragraph (g)(5) of Rule 13e–4, the information required by paragraph (e) of this section shall be disseminated in accordance with paragraph (e) of Rule 13e–4 no later than 10 business days prior to any purchase pursuant to such tender offer, (B) to each person who is a record holder of a class of equity security subject to the Rule 13e–3 transaction as of a date not more than 20 days prior to the date of dissemination of such information.

(ii) If the issuer or affiliate knows that securities of the class of securities subject to the Rule 13e–3 transaction are held of record by a broker, dealer, bank or voting trustee or their nominees, such issuer or affiliate shall (unless Rule 14a–3(d) or 14c–7 is applicable) furnish the number of copies of the information required by paragraph (e) of this section that are requested by such persons (pursuant to inquiries by or on behalf of the issuer or affiliate), instruct such persons to forward such information to the beneficial owners of such securities in a timely manner and undertake to pay the reasonable expenses incurred by such persons in forwarding such information; and

(iii) Promptly disseminate disclosure of material changes to the information required by paragraph (d) of this section in a manner reasonably calculated to inform security holders.

(2) If the Rule 13e–3 transaction is a tender offer or a request or invitation for tenders of equity securities which is subject to Regulation 14D or Rule 13e–4, the tender offer containing the information required by paragraph (e) of this section, and any material change with respect thereto, shall be published, sent or given in accordance with Regulation 14D or Rule 13e–4, respectively, to security holders of the class of securities being sought by the issuer or affiliate.

(g) *Exceptions.* This section shall not apply to:

(1) Any Rule 13e–3 transaction by or on behalf of a person which occurs within one year of the date of termination of a tender offer in which such person was the bidder and became an affiliate of the issuer as a result of such tender offer *provided* that the consideration offered to unaffiliated security holders in such Rule 13e–3 transaction is at least equal to the highest consideration offered during such tender offer and *provided further* that:

(i) If such tender offer was made for any or all securities of a class of the issuer;

(A) Such tender offer fully disclosed such person's intention to engage in a Rule 13e–3 transaction, the form and effect of such transaction and, to the extent known, the proposed terms thereof; and

(B) Such Rule 13e–3 transaction is substantially similar to that described in such tender offer; or

(ii) If such tender offer was made for less than all the securities of a class of the issuer:

(A) Such tender offer fully disclosed a plan of merger, a plan of liquidation or a similar binding agreement between such person and the issuer with respect to a Rule 13e–3 transaction; and

(B) Such Rule 13e–3 transaction occurs pursuant to the plan of merger, plan of liquidation or similar binding agreement disclosed in the bidder's tender offer.

(2) Any Rule 13e–3 transaction in which the security holders are offered or receive only an equity security *provided* That:

(i) such equity security has substantially the same rights as the equity security which is the subject of the Rule 13e–3 transaction including, but not limited to, voting, dividends, redemption and liquidation rights except that this requirement shall be deemed to be satisfied if unaffiliated security holders are offered common stock;

(ii) such equity security is registered pursuant to section 12 of the Act or reports are required to be filed by the issuer thereof pursuant to section 15(d) of the Act; and

(iii) if the security which is the subject of the Rule 13e–3 transaction was either listed on a national securities exchange or authorized to be quoted in an inter-dealer quotation system of a registered national securities association, such equity security is either listed on a national securities exchange or authorized to be quoted in an inter-dealer quotation system of a registered national securities association.

(3) Transactions by a holding company registered under the Public Utility Holding Company Act of 1935 in compliance with the provisions of that Act;

(4) Redemptions, calls or similar purchases of an equity security by an issuer pursuant to specific provisions set forth in the instrument(s) creating or governing that class of equity securities; or

(5) Any solicitation by an issuer with respect to a plan of reorganization under Chapter XI of the Bankruptcy Act, as amended, if made after the entry of an order approving such plan pursuant to section 1125(b) of that Act and after, or concurrently with, the transmittal of information concerning such plan as required by section 1125(b) of the Act.

(6) Any tender offer or business combination made in compliance with § 230.802 of this chapter, Rule 13e–4(h)(8) or Rule 14d–1(c).

Rule 13e–4. Tender Offers by Issuers

(a) *Definitions.* Unless the context otherwise requires, all terms used in this section and in Schedule TO shall have the same meaning as in the Act or elsewhere in the General Rules and Regulations thereunder. In addition, the following definitions shall apply:

(1) The term "issuer" means any issuer which has a class of equity security registered pursuant to section 12 of the Act, or which is required to file periodic reports pursuant to section 15(d) of the Act, or which is a closed-end investment company registered under the Investment Company Act of 1940.

(2) The term "issuer tender offer" refers to a tender offer for, or a request or invitation for tenders of, any class of equity security, made by the issuer of such class of equity security or by an affiliate of such issuer.

(3) As used in this section and in Schedule TO, the term "business day" means any day, other than Saturday, Sunday or a federal holiday, and shall consist of the time period from 12:01 a.m. through 12:00 midnight Eastern Time. In computing any time period under this Rule or Schedule 13E–4, the date of the event that begins the running of such time period shall be included *except that* if such event occurs on other than a business day such period shall begin to run on and shall include the first business day thereafter.

(4) The term commencement means 12:01 a.m. on the date that the issuer or affiliate has first published, sent or given the means to tender to security holders. For purposes of this section, the means to tender includes the transmittal form or a statement regarding how the transmittal form may be obtained.

(5) The term "termination" means the date after which securities may not be tendered pursuant to an issuer tender offer.

(6) The term "security holders" means holders of record and beneficial owners of securities of the class of equity security which is the subject of an issuer tender offer.

(7) The term "security position listing" means, with respect to the securities of any issuer held by a registered clearing agency in the name of the clearing agency or its nominee, a list of those participants in the clearing agency on whose behalf the clearing agency holds the issuer's securities and of the participants' respective positions in such securities as of a specified date.

(b) *Filing, disclosure and dissemination.* As soon as practicable on the date of commencement of the issuer tender offer, the issuer or affiliate making the issuer tender offer must comply with:

(1) The filing requirements of paragraph (c)(2) of this section;

(2) The disclosure requirements of paragraph (d)(1) of this section; and

(3) The dissemination requirements of paragraph (e) of this section.

(c) *Material Required to be Filed.* The issuer or affiliate making the issuer tender offer must file with the Commission:

(1) All written communications made by the issuer or affiliate relating to the issuer tender offer, from and including the first public announcement, as soon as practicable on the date of the communication;

(2) A Schedule TO (§ 240.14d–100), including all exhibits;

(3) An amendment to Schedule TO (§ 240.14d–100) reporting promptly any material changes in the information set forth in the schedule previously filed; and

(4) A final amendment to Schedule TO (§ 240.14d–100) reporting promptly the results of the issuer tender offer.

Instructions to Rule 13e–4(c):

1. Pre-commencement communications must be filed under cover of Schedule TO (§ 240.14d–100) and the box on the cover page of the schedule must be marked.

2. Any communications made in connection with an exchange offer registered under the Securities Act of 1933 need only be filed under § 230.425 of this chapter and will be deemed filed under this section.

3. Each pre-commencement written communication must include a prominent legend in clear, plain language advising security holders to read the tender offer statement when it is available because it contains important information. The legend also must advise investors that they can get the tender offer statement and other filed documents for free at the Commission's web site and explain which documents are free from the issuer.

4. See §§ 230.135, 230.165 and 230.166 of this chapter for pre-commencement communications made in connection with registered exchange offers.

5. "Public announcement" is any oral or written communication by the issuer, affiliate or any person authorized to act on their behalf that is reasonably designed to, or has the effect of, informing the public or security holders in general about the issuer tender offer.

(d) *Disclosure of tender offer information to security holders.*

(1) The issuer or affiliate making the issuer tender offer must disclose, in a manner prescribed by paragraph (e)(1) of this section, the following:

(i) The information required by Item 1 of Schedule TO (§ 240.14d–100) (summary term sheet); and

(ii) The information required by the remaining items of Schedule TO for issuer tender offers, except for Item 12 (exhibits), or a fair and adequate summary of the information.

(2) If there are any material changes in the information previously disclosed to security holders, the issuer or affiliate must disclose the changes promptly to security holders in a manner specified in paragraph (e)(3) of this section.

(3) If the issuer or affiliate disseminates the issuer tender offer by means of summary publication as described in paragraph (e)(1)(iii) of this section, the summary advertisement must not include a transmittal letter that would permit security holders to tender securities sought in the offer and must disclose at least the following information:

(i) The identity of the issuer or affiliate making the issuer tender offer;

(ii) The information required by § 229.1004(a)(1) and § 229.1006(a) of this chapter;

(iii) Instructions on how security holders can obtain promptly a copy of the statement required by paragraph (d)(1) of this section, at the issuer or affiliate's expense; and

(iv) A statement that the information contained in the statement required by paragraph (d)(1) of this section is incorporated by reference.

(e) *Dissemination of Tender Offers to Security Holders.*

An issuer tender offer will be deemed to be published, sent or given to security holders if the issuer or affiliate making the issuer tender offer complies fully with one or more of the methods described in this section.

(1) For issuer tender offers in which the consideration offered consists solely of cash and/or securities exempt from registration under section 3 of the Securities Act of 1933 *(15 U.S.C. 77c)*:

(i) *Dissemination of cash issuer tender offers by long-form publication:*

By making adequate publication in a newspaper or newspapers, on the date of commencement of the issuer tender offer, of the information required by paragraph (d)(1) of this section.

(ii) *Dissemination of any issuer tender offer by use of stockholder and other lists:*

(A) By mailing or otherwise furnishing a statement containing the information required by paragraph (d)(1) of this section to each security holder whose name appears on the most recent stockholder list of the issuer;

(B) By contacting each participant on the most recent security position listing of any clearing agency within the possession or access of the issuer or affiliate making the tender offer, and making inquiry of each such participant as to the approximate number of beneficial owners of the securities sought in the offer are held by the participant;

(C) By furnishing to each such participant a sufficient number of copies of the statement required by paragraph (d)(1) of this section for transmittal to the beneficial owners; and

(D) By agreeing to reimburse promptly each such participant for reasonable expenses incurred by it in forwarding such statement to the beneficial owners.

(iii) *Dissemination of certain cash issuer tender offers by summary publication:*

(A) If the issuer tender offer is not subject to Rule 13e–3, by making adequate publication in a newspaper or newspapers, on the date of commencement of the issuer tender offer, of a summary advertisement containing the information required by paragraph (d)(3) of this section; and

(B) By mailing or otherwise furnishing promptly the statement required by paragraph (d)(1) of this section and a transmittal letter to any security holder who requests either a copy of such statement or a transmittal letter.

Instructions to paragraph (e)(1):

For purposes of paragraphs (e)(1)(i) and (e)(1)(iii) of this section, adequate publication of the issuer tender offer may require publication in a newspaper with a national circulation, a newspaper with metropolitan or regional circulation, or a combination of the two, depending upon the facts and circumstances involved.

(2) For tender offers in which the consideration consists solely or partially of securities registered under the Securities Act of 1933, a registration statement containing all of the required information, including pricing information, has been filed and a preliminary prospectus or a prospectus that meets the requirements of Section 10(a) of the Securities Act (15 U.S.C. (*15 U.S.C. 77j*(a)), including a letter of transmittal, is delivered to security holders. However, for going-private transactions (as defined by Rule 13e–3) and roll-up transactions (as described by Item 901 of Regulation S–K (§ 229.901 of this chapter)), a registration statement registering the securities to be offered must have become effective and only a prospectus that meets the requirements of Section 10(a) of the Securities Act may be delivered to security holders on the date of commencement.

Instructions to paragraph (e)(2):

1. If the prospectus is being delivered by mail, mailing on the date of commencement is sufficient.

2. A preliminary prospectus used under this section may not omit information under § 230.430 or § 230.430A of this chapter.

3. If a preliminary prospectus is used under this section and the issuer must disseminate material changes, the tender offer must remain open for the period specified in paragraph (e)(3) of this section.

4. If a preliminary prospectus is used under this section, tenders may be requested in accordance with § 230.162(a) of this chapter.

(3) If a material change occurs in the information published, sent or given to security holders, the issuer or affiliate must disseminate promptly disclosure of the change in a manner reasonably calculated to inform security holders of the change. In a

registered securities offer where the issuer or affiliate disseminates the preliminary prospectus as permitted by paragraph (e)(2) of this section, the offer must remain open from the date that material changes to the tender offer materials are disseminated to security holders, as follows:

(i) Five business days for a prospectus supplement containing a material change other than price or share levels;

(ii) Ten business days for a prospectus supplement containing a change in price, the amount of securities sought, the dealer's soliciting fee, or other similarly significant change;

(iii) Ten business days for a prospectus supplement included as part of a post-effective amendment; and

(iv) Twenty business days for a revised prospectus when the initial prospectus was materially deficient.

(f) *Manner of Making Tender Offer.*

(1) The issuer tender offer, unless withdrawn, shall remain open until the expiration of:

(i) At least twenty business days from its commencement; and

(ii) At least ten business days from the date that notice of an increase or decrease in the percentage of the class of securities being sought or the consideration offered or the dealer's soliciting fee to be given is first published, sent or given to security holders.

Provided, however, That, for purposes of this paragraph, the acceptance for payment by the issuer or affiliate of an additional amount of securities not to exceed two percent of the class of securities that is the subject of the tender offer shall not be deemed to be an increase. For purposes of this paragraph, the percentage of a class of securities shall be calculated in accordance with section 14(d)(3) of the Act.

(2) The issuer or affiliate making the issuer tender offer shall permit securities tendered pursuant to the issuer tender offer to be withdrawn:

(i) At any time during the period such issuer tender offer remains open; and

(ii) If not yet accepted for payment, after the expiration of forty business days from the commencement of the issuer tender offer.

(3) If the issuer or affiliate makes a tender offer for less than all of the outstanding equity securities of a class, and if a greater number of securities is tendered pursuant thereto then the issuer or affiliate is bound or willing to take up and pay for, the securities taken up and paid for shall be taken up and paid for as nearly as may be pro rata, disregarding fractions, according to the number of securities tendered by each security holder during the period such offer remains open; *Provided, however,* That this provision shall not prohibit the issuer or affiliate making the issuer tender offer from:

(i) accepting all securities tendered by persons who own, beneficially or of record, an aggregate of not more than a specified number which is less than one hundred shares of such security and who tender all their securities, before prorating securities tendered by others; or

(ii) accepting by lot securities tendered by security holders who tender all securities held by them and who, when tendering their securities, elect to have either all or none or at least a minimum amount or none accepted, if the issuer or affiliate first accepts all securities tendered by security holders who do not so elect;

(4) In the event the issuer or affiliate making the issuer tender offer increases the consideration offered after the issuer tender offer has commenced, such issuer or affiliate shall pay such increased consideration to all security holders whose tendered securities are accepted for payment by such issuer or affiliate.

(5) The issuer or affiliate making the tender offer shall either pay the consideration offered, or return the tendered securities, promptly after the termination or withdrawal of the tender offer.

(6) Until the expiration of at least ten business days after the date of termination of the issuer tender offer, neither the issuer nor any affiliate shall make any purchases, otherwise than pursuant to the tender offer, of:

(i) any security which is the subject of the issuer tender offer, or any security of the same class and series, or any right to purchase any such securities; and

(ii) in the case of an issuer tender offer which is an exchange offer any security being offered pursuant to such exchange offer, or any security of the same class and series, or any right to purchase any such security.

(7) The time periods for the minimum offering periods pursuant to this section shall be computed on a concurrent as opposed to a consecutive basis.

(8) No issuer or affiliate shall make a tender offer unless:

(i) The tender offer is open to all security holders of the class of securities subject to the tender offer; and

(ii) The consideration paid to any security holder pursuant to the tender offer is the highest consideration paid to any other security holder during such tender offer.

(9) Paragraph (f)(8)(i) of this rule shall not:

(i) Affect dissemination under paragraph (e) of this rule; or

(ii) Prohibit an issuer or affiliate from making a tender offer excluding all security holders in a state where the issuer or affiliate is prohibited from making the tender offer by administrative or judicial action pursuant to a state statute after a good faith effort by the issuer or affiliate to comply with such statute.

(10) Paragraph (f)(8)(ii) of this rule shall not prohibit the offer of more than one type of consideration in a tender offer, provided that:

(i) Security holders are afforded equal right to elect among each of the types of consideration offered; and

(ii) The highest consideration of each type paid to any security holder is paid to any other security holder receiving that type of consideration.

(11) If the offer and sale of securities constituting consideration offered in an issuer tender offer is prohibited by the appropriate authority of a state after a good faith effort by the issuer or affiliate to register or qualify the offer and sale of such securities in such state:

(i) The issuer or affiliate may offer security holders in such state an alternative form of consideration; and

(ii) Paragraph (f)(10) of this rule shall not operate to require the issuer or affiliate to offer or pay the alternative form of consideration to security holders in any other state.

* * *

(h) This rule shall not apply to:

(1) Calls or redemptions of any security in accordance with the terms and conditions of its governing instruments;

(2) Offers to purchase securities evidenced by a scrip certificate, order form or similar document which represents a fractional interest in a share of stock or similar security;

(3) Offers to purchase securities pursuant to a statutory procedure for the purchase of dissenting security holders' securities;

(4) Any tender offer which is subject to section 14(d) of the Act;

(5) Offers to purchase from security holders who own as of a specified date prior to the announcement of the offer an aggregate of not more than a specified number of shares that is less than one hundred: *Provided however,* That: (i) the offer complies with paragraph (f)(8)(i) of this rule with respect to security holders who own a number of shares equal to or less than the specified number of shares, except that an issuer can elect to exclude participants in a plan as that term is defined in § 242.100 of this chapter, or to exclude security holders who do not own their shares as of a specified date determined by the issuer; and (ii) the offer complies with paragraph (f)(8)(ii) of this rule or the consideration paid pursuant to the offer is determined on the basis of a uniformly applied formula based on the market price of the subject security;

(6) An issuer tender offer made solely to effect a rescission offer: *Provided, however,* That the offer is registered under the Securities Act of 1933, and the consideration is equal to the price paid by each security holder, plus legal interest if the issuer elects to or is required to pay legal interest; or

(7) Offers by closed-end management investment companies to repurchase equity securities pursuant to Rule 23c–3 of this chapter; or

(8) *Cross-border tender offers (Tier I).* Any issuer tender offer (including any exchange offer) where the issuer is a foreign private issuer as defined in Rule 3b–4 if the following conditions are satisfied.

(i) Except in the case of an issuer tender offer which is commenced during the pendency of a tender offer made by a third party in reliance on Rule 14d–1(c), U.S. holders do not hold more than 10 percent of the class of securities sought in the offer (as determined under Instruction 2 to paragraph (h)(8) and paragraph (i) of this section); and

(ii) The issuer or affiliate must permit U.S. holders to participate in the offer on terms at least as favorable as those offered any other holder of the same class of securities that is the subject of the offer; however:

(A) Registered exchange offers. If the issuer or affiliate offers securities registered under the Securities Act of 1933 (*15 U.S.C. 77a* et seq.), the issuer or affiliate need not extend the offer to security holders in those states or jurisdictions that prohibit the offer or sale of the securities after the issuer or affiliate has made a good faith effort to register or qualify the offer and sale of securities in that state or jurisdiction, except that the issuer or affiliate must offer the same cash alternative to security holders in any such state or jurisdiction that it has offered to security holders in any other state or jurisdiction.

(B) Exempt exchange offers. If the issuer or affiliate offers securities exempt from registration under § 230.802 of this chapter, the issuer or affiliate need not extend the offer to security holders in those states or jurisdictions that require registration or qualification, except that the issuer or affiliate must offer the same cash alternative to security holders in any such state or jurisdiction that it has offered to security holders in any other state or jurisdiction.

(C) Cash only consideration. The issuer or affiliate may offer U.S. holders cash only consideration for the tender of the subject securities, notwithstanding the fact that the issuer or affiliate is offering security holders outside the United States a consideration that consists in whole or in part of securities of the issuer or affiliate, if the issuer or affiliate has a reasonable basis for believing that the amount of cash is substantially equivalent to the value of the consideration offered to non-U.S. holders, and either of the following conditions are satisfied:

(1) The offered security is a "margin security" within the meaning of Regulation T (*12 CFR 220.2*) and the issuer or affiliate undertakes to provide, upon the request of any U.S. holder or the Commission staff, the closing price and daily trading volume of the security on the principal trading market for the security as of the last trading day of each of the six months preceding the announcement of the offer and each of the trading days thereafter; or

(2) If the offered security is not a "margin security" within the meaning of Regulation T (*12 CFR 220.2*), the issuer or affiliate undertakes to provide, upon the request of any U.S. holder or the Commission staff, an opinion of an independent expert stating that the cash consideration offered to U.S. holders is substantially equivalent to the value of the consideration offered security holders outside the United States.

(D) Disparate tax treatment. If the issuer or affiliate offers "loan notes" solely to offer sellers tax advantages not available in the United States and these notes are neither listed on any organized securities market nor registered under the Securities Act of 1933 (*15 U.S.C. 77a* et seq.), the loan notes need not be offered to U.S. holders.

(iii) Informational documents.

(A) If the issuer or affiliate publishes or otherwise disseminates an informational document to the holders of the securities in connection with the issuer tender offer (including any exchange offer), the issuer or affiliate must furnish that informational document, including any amendments thereto, in English, to the Commission on Form CB (§ 249.480 of this chapter) by the first business day after publication or dissemination. If the issuer or affiliate is a foreign company, it must also file a Form F–X (§ 239.42 of this chapter) with the Commission at the same time as the submission of Form CB to appoint an agent for service in the United States.

(B) The issuer or affiliate must disseminate any informational document to U.S. holders, including any amendments thereto, in English, on a comparable basis to that provided to security holders in the home jurisdiction.

(C) If the issuer or affiliate disseminates by publication in its home jurisdiction, the issuer or affiliate must publish the information in the United States in a manner reasonably calculated to inform U.S. holders of the offer.

(iv) An investment company registered or required to be registered under the Investment Company Act of 1940 (*15 U.S.C. 80a–1* et seq.), other than a registered closed-end investment company, may not use this paragraph (h)(8); or

(9) Any other transaction or transactions, if the Commission, upon written request or upon its own motion, exempts such transaction or transactions, either unconditionally, or on specified terms and conditions, as not constituting a fraudulent, deceptive or manipulative act or practice comprehended within the purpose of this section.

(i) *Cross-border tender offers (Tier II).* Any issuer tender offer (including any exchange offer) that meets the conditions in paragraph (i)(1) of this section shall be entitled to the exemptive relief specified in paragraph (i)(2) of this section provided that such issuer tender offer complies with all the requirements of this section other than those for which an exemption has been specifically provided in paragraph (i)(2) of this section:

(1) Conditions.

(i) The issuer is a foreign private issuer as defined in Rule 3b–4 and is not an investment company registered or required to be registered under the Investment Company Act of 1940 (*15 U.S.C. 80a–1* et seq.), other than a registered closed-end investment company; and

(ii) Except in the case of an issuer tender offer which is commenced during the pendency of a tender offer made by a third party in reliance on Rule 14d–1(d), U.S. holders do not hold more than 40 percent of the class of securities sought in the offer (as determined under Instruction 2 to paragraphs (h)(8) and (i) of this section).

(2) Exemptions. The issuer tender offer shall comply with all requirements of this section other than the following:

(i) Equal treatment—loan notes. If the issuer or affiliate offers loan notes solely to offer sellers tax advantages not available in the United States and these notes are neither listed on any organized securities market nor registered under the Securities Act (*15 U.S.C. 77a* et seq.), the loan notes need not be offered to U.S. holders, notwithstanding paragraph (f)(8) and (h)(9) of this section.

(ii) Equal treatment—separate U.S. and foreign offers. Notwithstanding the provisions of paragraph (f)(8) of this section, an issuer or affiliate conducting an issuer tender offer meeting the conditions of paragraph (i)(1) of this section may separate the offer into two offers: One offer made only to U.S. holders and another offer made only to non-U.S. holders. The offer to U.S. holders must be made on terms at least as favorable as those offered any other holder of the same class of securities that is the subject of the tender offer.

(iii) Notice of extensions. Notice of extensions made in accordance with the requirements of the home jurisdiction law or practice will satisfy the requirements of Rule 14e–1(d).

(iv) Prompt payment. Payment made in accordance with the requirements of the home jurisdiction law or practice will satisfy the requirements of Rule 14e–1(c).

Instructions to paragraph (h)(8) and (i) of this section:

1. Home jurisdiction means both the jurisdiction of the issuer's incorporation, organization or chartering and the principal foreign market where the issuer's securities are listed or quoted.

2. U.S. holder means any security holder resident in the United States. To determine the percentage of outstanding securities held by U.S. holders:

i. Calculate the U.S. ownership as of 30 days before the commencement of the issuer tender offer;

ii. Include securities underlying American Depositary Shares convertible or exchangeable into the securities that are the subject of the tender offer when calculating the number of subject securities outstanding, as well as the number held by U.S. holders. Exclude from the calculations other types of securities that are convertible or exchangeable into the securities that are the subject of the tender offer, such as warrants, options and convertible securities. Exclude from those calculations securities held by persons who hold more than 10 percent of the subject securities;

iii. Use the method of calculating record ownership in Rule 12g3–2(a), except that your inquiry as to the amount of securities represented by accounts of customers resident in the United States may be limited to brokers, dealers, banks and other nominees located in the United States, your jurisdiction of incorporation, and the jurisdiction that is the primary trading market for the subject securities, if different than your jurisdiction of incorporation;

iv. If, after reasonable inquiry, you are unable to obtain information about the amount of securities represented by accounts of customers resident in the United States, you may assume, for purposes of this definition, that the customers are residents of the jurisdiction in which the nominee has its principal place of business; and

v. Count securities as beneficially owned by residents of the United States as reported on reports of beneficial ownership that are provided to you or publicly filed and based on information otherwise provided to you.

3. United States. United States means the United States of America, its territories and possessions, any State of the United States, and the District of Columbia.

4. The exemptions provided by paragraphs (h)(8) and (i) of this section are not available for any securities transaction or series of transactions that technically complies with paragraph (h)(8) or (i) of this section but are part of a plan or scheme to evade the provisions of this section.

(j)(1) It shall be a fraudulent, deceptive or manipulative act or practice, in connection with an issuer tender offer, for an issuer or an affiliate of such issuer, in connection with an issuer tender offer:

(i) To employ any device, scheme or artifice to defraud any person;

(ii) To make any untrue statement of a material fact or to omit to state a material fact necessary in order to make the statements made, in the light of the circumstances under which they were made, not misleading; or

(iii) To engage in any act, practice or course of business which operates or would operate as a fraud or deceit upon any person.

(2) As a means reasonably designed to prevent fraudulent, deceptive or manipulative acts or practices in connection with any issuer tender offer, it shall be unlawful for an issuer or an affiliate of such issuer to make an issuer tender offer unless:

(i) Such issuer or affiliate complies with the requirements of paragraphs (b), (c), (d), (e) and (f) of this section; and

(ii) The issuer tender offer is not in violation of paragraph (j)(1) of this section

REPORTS BY INSTITUTIONAL MANAGERS

Rule 13f-1. Reporting by Institutional Investment Managers of Information With Respect to Accounts Over Which They Exercise Investment Discretion

(a)(1) Every institutional investment manager which exercises investment discretion with respect to accounts holding section 13(f) securities, as defined in paragraph (c) of this section, having an aggregate fair market value on the last trading day of any month of any calendar year of at least $100,000,000 shall file a report on Form 13F with the Commission within 45 days after the last day of such calendar year and within 45 days after the last day of each of the first three calendar quarters of the subsequent calendar year.

(2) An amendment to a Form 13F (§ 249.325 of this chapter) report, other than one reporting only holdings that were not previously reported in a public filing for the same period, must set forth the complete text of the Form 13F. Amendments must be numbered sequentially.

(b) For the purposes of this rule, "investment discretion" has the meaning set forth in section 3(a)(35) of the Act. An institutional investment manager shall also be deemed to exercise "investment discretion" with respect to all accounts over which any person under its control exercises investment discretion.

(c) For purposes of this rule "section 13(f) securities" shall mean equity securities of a class described in section 13(d)(1) of the Act that are admitted to trading on a national securities exchange or quoted on the automated quotation system of a registered securities association. In determining what classes of securities are section 13(f) securities, an institutional investment manager may rely on the most recent list of such securities published by the Commission pursuant to section 13(f)(3) of the Act. Only securities of a class on such list shall be counted in determining whether an institutional investment manager must file a report under this rule and only those securities shall be reported in such report. Where a person controls the issuer of a class of equity securities which are "section 13(f) securities" as defined in this rule, those securities shall not be deemed to be "section 13(f) securities" with respect to the controlling person, provided that such person does not otherwise exercise investment discretion with respect to accounts with fair market value of at least $100,000,000 within the meaning of paragraph (a) of this section.

* * *

SOLICITATION OF PROXIES

Rule 14a–1. Definitions

Unless the context otherwise requires, all terms used in this regulation have the same meanings as in the Act or elsewhere in the General Rules and Regulations thereunder. In addition, the following definitions apply unless the context otherwise requires:

(a) *Associate.* The term "associate" used to indicate a relationship with any person, means (1) any corporation or organization (other than the issuer or a majority owned subsidiary of the issuer) of which such person is an officer or partner or is, directly or indirectly, the beneficial owner of 10 percent or more of any class of equity securities, (2) any trust or other estate in which such person has a substantial beneficial interest or as to which such person serves as trustee or in a similar fiduciary capacity, and (3) any relative or spouse of such person, or any relative of such spouse, who has the same home as such person or who is a director or officer of the issuer or any of its parents or subsidiaries.

(b) *Employee benefit plan.* For purposes of Rules 14a–13, 14b–1 and 14b–2, the term "employee benefit plan" means any purchase, savings, option, bonus, appreciation, profit sharing, thrift, incentive, pension or similar plan primarily for employees, directors, trustees or officers.

(c) *Entity that exercises fiduciary powers.* The term "entity that exercises fiduciary powers" means any entity that holds securities in nominee name or otherwise on behalf of a beneficial owner but does not include a clearing agency registered pursuant to section 17A of the Act or a broker or a dealer.

(d) *Exempt employee benefit plan securities.* For purposes of Rules 14a–13, 14b–1 and 14b–2, the term "exempt employee benefit plan securities" means: (1) securities of the registrant held by an employee benefit plan, as defined in paragraph (b) of this section, where such plan is established by the registrant; or (2) if notice regarding the current solicitation has been given pursuant to Rule 14a–13(a)(1)(ii)(C) or if notice regarding the current request for a list of names, addresses and securities positions of beneficial owners has been given pursuant to Rule 14a–13(b)(3), securities of the registrant held by an employee benefit plan, as defined in paragraph (b) of this section, where such plan is established by an affiliate of the registrant.

(e) *Last fiscal year.* The term "last fiscal year" of the registrant means the last fiscal year of the registrant ending prior to the date of the meeting for which proxies are to be solicited or if the solicitation involves written authorizations or consents in lieu of a meeting, the earliest date they may be used to effect corporate action.

(f) *Proxy.* The term "proxy" includes every proxy, consent or authorization within the meaning of section 14(a) of the Act. The consent or authorization may take the form of failure to object or to dissent.

(g) *Proxy statement.* The term "proxy statement" means the statement required by Rule 14a–3(a) whether or not contained in a single document.

(h) *Record date.* The term "record date" means the date as of which the record holders of securities entitled to vote at a meeting or by written consent or authorization shall be determined.

(i) *Record holder.* For purposes of Rules 14a–13, 14b–1 and 14b–2, the term "record holder" means any broker, dealer, voting trustee, bank, association or other entity that exercises fiduciary powers which holds securities of record in nominee name or otherwise or as a participant in a clearing agency registered pursuant to section 17A of the Act.

(j) *Registrant.* The term "registrant" means the issuer of the securities in respect of which proxies are to be solicited.

(k) *Respondent bank.* For purposes of Rules 14a–13, 14b–1 and 14b–2, the term "respondent bank" means any bank, association or other entity that exercises fiduciary powers which holds securities on behalf of beneficial owners and deposits such securities for safekeeping with another bank, association or other entity that exercises fiduciary powers.

(*l*) *Solicitation.* (1) The terms "solicit" and "solicitation" include:

(i) Any request for a proxy whether or not accompanied by or included in a form of proxy;

(ii) Any request to execute or not to execute, or to revoke, a proxy; or

(iii) The furnishing of a form of proxy or other communication to security holders under circumstances reasonably calculated to result in the procurement, withholding or revocation of a proxy.

(2) The terms do not apply, however, to:

(i) The furnishing of a form of proxy to a security holder upon the unsolicited request of such security holder;

(ii) The performance by the registrant of acts required by Rule 14a–7;

(iii) The performance by any person of ministerial acts on behalf of a person soliciting a proxy; or

(iv) A communication by a security holder who does not otherwise engage in a proxy solicitation (other than a solicitation exempt under Rule 14a–2) stating how the security holder intends to vote and the reasons therefor, provided that the communication:

(A) is made by means of speeches in public forums, press releases, published or broadcast opinions, statements, or advertisements appearing in a broadcast media, or newspaper, magazine or other bona fide publication disseminated on a regular basis,

(B) is directed to persons to whom the security holder owes a fiduciary duty in connection with the voting of securities of a registrant held by the security holder, or

(C) is made in response to unsolicited requests for additional information with respect to a prior communication by the security holder made pursuant to this paragraph (*l*)(2)(iv).

Rule 14a–2. Solicitations to Which Rules 14a–3 to 14a–15 Apply

Rules 14a–3 to 14a–15 except as specified, apply to every solicitation of a proxy with respect to securities registered pursuant to section 12 of the Act, whether or not trading in such securities has been suspended. To the extent specified below, certain of these sections also apply to roll-up transactions that do not involve an entity with securities registered pursuant to Section 12 of the Act.

(a) Rule 14a–15 does not apply to the following:

(1) Any solicitation by a person in respect to securities carried in his name or in the name of his nominee (otherwise than as voting trustee) or held in his custody, if such person—

(i) Receives no commission or remuneration for such solicitation, directly or indirectly, other than reimbursement of reasonable expenses.

(ii) Furnishes promptly to the person solicited (or such person's household in accordance with Rule 14a–3(e)(1)) a copy of all soliciting material with respect to the same subject matter or meeting received from all persons who shall furnish copies thereof for such purpose and who shall, if requested, defray the reasonable expenses to be incurred in forwarding such material, and

(iii) In addition, does no more than impartially instruct the person solicited to forward a proxy to the person, if any, to whom the person solicited desires to give a proxy, or impartially request from the person solicited instructions as to the authority to be conferred by the proxy and state that a proxy will be given if no instructions are received by a certain date.

(2) Any solicitation by a person in respect of securities of which he is the beneficial owner;

(3) Any solicitation involved in the offer and sale of securities registered under the Securities Act of 1933: *Provided,* That this paragraph shall not apply to securities to be issued in any transaction of the character specified in paragraph (a) of Rule 145 under that Act;

(4) Any solicitation with respect to a plan of reorganization under Chapter 11 of the Bankruptcy Reform Act of 1978, as amended, if made after the entry of an order approving the written disclosure statement concerning a plan of reorganization pur-

suant to section 1125 of said Act and after, or concurrently with, the transmittal of such disclosure statement as required by section 1125 of said Act;

(5) Any solicitation which is subject to Rule 62 under the Public Utility Holding Company Act of 1935; and

(6) Any solicitation through the medium of a newspaper advertisement which informs security holders of a source from which they may obtain copies of a proxy statement, form of proxy and any other soliciting material and does no more than (i) name the registrant, (ii) state the reason for the advertisement, and (iii) identify the proposal or proposals to be acted upon by security holders.

(b) Rules 14a–3 to 14a–6 (other than 1400–6(g), 14a–8, and Rules 14a–10) to 14a–15 do not apply to the following:

(1) Any solicitation by or on behalf of any person who does not, at any time during such solicitation, seek directly or indirectly, either on its own or another's behalf, the power to act as proxy for a security holder and does not furnish or otherwise request, or act on behalf of a person who furnishes or requests, a form of revocation, abstention, consent or authorization. *Provided, however,* that the exemption set forth in this paragraph shall not apply to:

(i) the registrant or an affiliate or associate of the registrant (other than an officer or director or any person serving in a similar capacity);

(ii) an officer or director of the registrant or any person serving in a similar capacity engaging in a solicitation financed directly or indirectly by the registrant;

(iii) an officer, director, affiliate or associate of a person that is ineligible to rely on the exemption set forth in this paragraph (other than persons specified in paragraph (b)(1)(i) of this section), or any person serving in a similar capacity;

(iv) any nominee for whose election as a director proxies are solicited;

(v) any person soliciting in opposition to a merger, recapitalization, reorganization, sale of assets or other extraordinary transaction recommended or approved by the board of directors of the registrant who is proposing or intends to propose an alternative transaction to which such person or one of its affiliates is a party;

(vi) any person who is required to report beneficial ownership of the registrant's equity securities on a Schedule 13D, unless such person has filed a Schedule 13D and has not disclosed pursuant to Item 4 thereto an intent, or reserved the right, to engage in a control transaction, or any contested solicitation for the election of directors;

(vii) any person who receives compensation from an ineligible person directly related to the solicitation of proxies, other than pursuant to Rule 14a–13;

(viii) where the registrant is an investment company registered under the Investment Company Act of 1940, an "interested person" of that investment company, as that term is defined in Section 2(a)(19) of the Investment Company Act;

(ix) any person who, because of a substantial interest in the subject matter of the solicitation, is likely to receive a benefit from a successful solicitation that would not be shared pro rata by all other holders of the same class of securities, other than a benefit arising from the person's employment with the registrant; and

(x) any person acting on behalf of any of the foregoing.

(2) Any solicitation made otherwise than on behalf of the registrant where the total number of persons solicited is not more than ten; and

(3) The furnishing of proxy voting advice by any person (the "advisor") to any other person with whom the advisor has a business relationship, if:

(i) The advisor renders financial advice in the ordinary course of his business;

(ii) The advisor discloses to the recipient of the advice any significant relationship with the registrant or any of its affiliates, or a security holder proponent of the matter on which advice is given, as well as any material interests of the advisor in such matter.

(iii) The advisor receives no special commission or remuneration for furnishing the proxy voting advice from any person other than a recipient of the advice and other persons who receive similar advice under this subsection; and

(iv) The proxy voting advice is not furnished on behalf of any person soliciting proxies or on behalf of a participant in an election subject to the provisions of Rule 14a–11; and

(4) Any solicitation in connection with a roll-up transaction as defined in Item 901(c) of Regulation S–K in which the holder of a security that is the subject of a proposed roll-up transaction engages in preliminary communications with other holders of securities that are the subject of the same limited partnership roll-up transaction for the purpose of determining whether to solicit proxies, consents, or authorizations in opposition to the proposed limited partnership roll-up transaction; provided, however, that:

(i) This exemption shall not apply to a security holder who is an affiliate of the registrant or general partner or sponsor; and

(ii) This exemption shall not apply to a holder of five percent (5%) or more of the outstanding securities of a class that is the subject of the proposed roll-up transaction who engages in the business of buying and selling limited partnership interests in the secondary market unless that holder discloses to the persons to whom the communications are made such ownership interest and any relations of the holder to the parties of the transaction or to the transaction itself, as required by Rule 14a–6(n)(1) and specified in the Notice of Exempt Preliminary Roll-up Communication. If the communication is oral, this disclosure may be provided to the security holder orally. Whether the communication is written or oral, the notice required by Rule14a–6(n) and Rule 14a–104 shall be furnished to the Commission.

Rule 14a–3. Information to Be Furnished to Security Holders

(a) No solicitation subject to this regulation shall be made unless each person solicited is concurrently furnished or has previously been furnished with a written proxy statement containing the information specified in Schedule 14A or with a preliminary or definitive written proxy statement included in a registration statement filed under the Securities Act of 1933 on Form S–4 or F–4 or N–14 and containing the information specified in such Form.

(b) If the solicitation is made on behalf of the registrant, other than an investment company registered under the Investment Company Act of 1940, and relates to an annual (or special meeting in lieu of the annual) meeting of security holders, or written consent in lieu of such meeting, at which directors are to be elected, each proxy statement furnished pursuant to paragraph (a) of this section shall be accompanied or preceded by an annual report to security holders as follows:

* * *

(1) The report shall include, for the registrant and its subsidiaries consolidated, audited balance sheets as of the end of the two most recent fiscal years and audited statements of income and cash flows for each of the three most recent fiscal years prepared in accordance with Regulation S–X, except that the provisions of Article 3 (other than §§ 3–03(e), 3–04 and 3–20) and Article 11 shall not apply. Any financial statement schedules or exhibits or separate financial statements which may otherwise be required in filings with the Commission may be omitted.

* * *

(2)(i) Financial statements and notes thereto shall be presented in roman type at least as large and as legible as 10–point modern type. If necessary for convenient presentation, the financial statements may be in roman type as large and as legible as 8–point modern type. All type shall be leaded at least 2–point.

(ii) Where the annual report to security holders is delivered through an electronic medium, issuers may satisfy legibility requirements applicable to printed documents, such as type size and font, by presenting all required information in a format readily communicated to investors.

(3) The report shall contain the supplementary financial information required by Item 302 of Regulation S–K.

(4) The report shall contain information concerning changes in and disagreements with accountants on accounting and financial disclosure required by Item 304 of Regulation S–K.

(5)(i) The report shall contain the selected financial data required by Item 301 of Regulation S–K.

(ii) The report shall contain management's discussion and analysis of financial condition and results of operations required by Item 303 of Regulation S–K or, if applicable, a plan of operation required by Item 303(a) of Regulation S–B.

(iii) The report shall contain the quantitative and qualitative disclosures about market risk required by Item 305 of Regulation S–K (§ 229.305 of this chapter).

(6) The report shall contain a brief description of the business done by the registrant and its subsidiaries during the most recent fiscal year which will, in the opinion of management, indicate the general nature and scope of the business of the registrant and its subsidiaries.

(7) The report shall contain information relating to the registrant's industry segments, classes of similar products or services, foreign and domestic operations and export sales required by paragraphs (b), (c)(1)(i) and (d) of Item 101 of Regulation S–K.

(8) The report shall identify each of the registrant's directors and executive officers, and shall indicate the principal occupation or employment of each such person and the name and principal business of any organization by which such person is employed.

(9) The report shall contain the market price of and dividends on the registrant's common equity and related security holder matters required by Item 201 of Regulation S–K.

(10) The registrant's proxy statement, or the report, shall contain an undertaking in bold face or otherwise reasonably prominent type to provide without charge to each person solicited, upon the written request of any such person, a copy of the registrant's annual report on Form 10–K and Form 10–KSB including the financial statements and the financial statement schedules, required to be filed with the Commission pursuant to Rule 13a–1 under the Act for the registrant's most recent fiscal year, and shall indicate the name and address (including title or department) of the person to whom such a written request is to be directed. In the discretion of management, a registrant need not undertake to furnish without charge copies of all exhibits to its Form 10–K and Form 10–KSB provided that the copy of the annual report on Form 10–K and Form 10–KSB furnished without charge to requesting security holders is accompanied by a list briefly describing all the exhibits not contained therein and indicating that the registrant will furnish any exhibit upon the payment of a specified reasonable fee which fee shall be limited to the registrant's reasonable expenses in furnishing such exhibit. If the registrant's annual report to security holders complies with all of the disclosure requirements of Form 10–K and Form 10–KSB and is filed with the Commission in satisfaction of its Form 10–K and Form 10–KSB filing requirements, such registrant need not furnish a separate Form 10–K and Form 10–KSB to security holders who receive a copy of such annual report.

Note: Pursuant to the undertaking required by paragraph (b)(10) of this rule, a registrant shall furnish a copy of its annual report on Form 10–K and Form 10–KSB to a beneficial owner of its securities upon receipt of a written request from such person. Each request must set forth a good faith representation that, as of the record date for the solicitation requiring the furnishing of the annual report to security holders pursuant to paragraph (b) of this section, the person making the request was a beneficial owner of securities entitled to vote.

(11) Subject to the foregoing requirements, the report may be in any form deemed suitable by management and the information required by paragraphs (b)(5) to (b)(10) of this rule may be presented in an appendix or other separate section of the report, provided that the attention of security holders is called to such presentation.

Note: Registrants are encouraged to utilize tables, schedules, charts, and graphic illustrations to present financial information in an understandable manner. Any presentation of financial information must be consistent with the data in the financial statements contained in the report and, if appropriate, should refer to relevant portions of the financial statements and notes thereto.

(12) [Reserved]

(13) Paragraph (b) of this section shall not apply, however, to solicitations made on behalf of the registrant before the financial statements are available if a solicitation is being made at the same time in opposition to the registrant and if the registrant's proxy statement includes an undertaking in bold face type to furnish such annual report to all persons being solicited at least 20 calendar days before the date of the meeting or, if the solicitation refers to a written consent or authorization in lieu

of a meeting, at least 20 calendar days prior to the earliest date on which it may be used to effect corporate action.

(c) Seven copies of the report sent to security holders pursuant to this rule shall be mailed to the Commission, solely for its information, not later than the date on which such report is first sent or given to security holders or the date on which preliminary copies, or definitive copies, if preliminary filing was not required, of solicitation material are filed with the Commission pursuant to Rule 14a-6, whichever date is later. The report is not deemed to be "soliciting material" or to be "filed" with the Commission or subject to this regulation otherwise than as provided in this Rule, or to the liabilities of section 18 of the Act, except to the extent that the registrant specifically requests that it be treated as a part of the proxy soliciting material or incorporates it in the proxy statement or other filed report by reference.

(d) An annual report to security holders prepared on an integrated basis pursuant to General Instruction H to Form 10-K and Form 10-KSB may also be submitted in satisfaction of this rule. When filed as the annual report on Form 10-K and Form 10-KSB, responses to the Items of that form are subject to section 18 of the Act notwithstanding paragraph (c) of this section.

(e)(1)(i) A registrant will be considered to have delivered an annual report to security holders of record who share an address if:

(A) The registrant delivers one annual report or proxy statement, as applicable, to the shared address;

(B) The registrant addresses the annual report or proxy statement, as applicable, to the security holders as a group (for example, "ABC Fund [or Corporation] Security Holders," "Jane Doe and Household," "The Smith Family"), to each of the security holders individually (for example, "John Doe and Richard Jones") or to the security holders in a form to which each of the security holders has consented in writing;

Note to paragraph (e)(1)(i)(B):

Unless the company addresses the annual report or proxy statement to the security holders as a group or to each of the security holders individually, it must obtain, from each security holder to be included in the householded group, a separate affirmative written consent to the specific form of address the company will use.

(C) The security holders consent, in accordance with paragraph (e)(1)(ii) of this section, to delivery of one annual report or proxy statement, as applicable;

(D) With respect to delivery of the proxy statement, the registrant delivers, together with or subsequent to delivery of the proxy statement, a separate proxy card for each security holder at the shared address; and

(E) The registrant includes an undertaking in the proxy statement to deliver promptly upon written or oral request a separate copy of the annual report or proxy statement, as applicable, to a security holder at a shared address to which a single copy of the document was delivered.

(ii) Consent.

(A) Affirmative written consent. Each security holder must affirmatively consent, in writing, to delivery of one annual report or proxy statement, as applicable. A security holder's affirmative written consent will only be considered valid if the security holder has been informed of:

(1) The duration of the consent;

(2) The specific types of documents to which the consent will apply;

(3) The procedures the security holder must follow to revoke consent; and

(4) The registrant's obligation to begin sending individual copies to a security holder within thirty days after the security holder revokes consent.

(B) Implied consent. The registrant need not obtain affirmative written consent from a security holder for purposes of paragraph (e)(1)(ii)(A) of this section if all of the following conditions are met:

(1) The security holder has the same last name as the other security holders at the shared address or the registrant reasonably believes that the security holders are members of the same family;

(2) The registrant has sent the security holder a notice at least 60 days before the registrant begins to rely on this section concerning delivery of annual reports and proxy statements to that security holder. The notice must:

(i) Be a separate written document;

(ii) State that only one annual report or proxy statement, as applicable, will be delivered to the shared address unless the registrant receives contrary instructions;

(iii) Include a toll-free telephone number, or be accompanied by a reply form that is pre-addressed with postage provided, that the security holder can use to notify the registrant that the security holder wishes to receive a separate annual report or proxy statement;

(iv) State the duration of the consent;

(v) Explain how a security holder can revoke consent;

(vi) State that the registrant will begin sending individual copies to a security holder within thirty days after the security holder revokes consent; and

(vii) Contain the following prominent statement, or similar clear and understandable statement, in bold-face type: "Important Notice Regarding Delivery of Security Holder Documents." This statement also must appear on the envelope in which the notice is delivered. Alternatively, if the notice is delivered separately from other communications to security holders, this statement may appear either on the notice or on the envelope in which the notice is delivered.

Note to paragraph (e)(1)(ii)(B)(2):

The notice should be written in plain English. See § 230.421(d)(2) of this chapter for a discussion of plain English principles.

(3) The registrant has not received the reply form or other notification indicating that the security holder wishes to continue to receive an individual copy of the annual report or proxy statement, as applicable, within 60 days after the registrant sent the notice; and

(4) The registrant delivers the document to a post office box or residential street address.

Note to paragraph (e)(1)(ii)(B)(4):

The registrant can assume that a street address is residential unless the registrant has information that indicates the street address is a business.

(iii) Revocation of consent. If a security holder, orally or in writing, revokes consent to delivery of one annual report or proxy statement to a shared address, the registrant must begin sending individual copies to that security holder within 30 days after the registrant receives revocation of the security holder's consent.

(iv) Definition of address. Unless otherwise indicated, for purposes of this section, address means a street address, a post office box number, an electronic mail address, a facsimile telephone number or other similar destination to which paper or electronic documents are delivered, unless otherwise provided in this section. If the registrant has reason to believe that the address is a street address of a multi-unit building, the address must include the unit number.

Note to paragraph (e)(1).

A person other than the registrant making a proxy solicitation may deliver a single proxy statement to security holders of record or beneficial owners who have separate accounts and share an address if: (a) the registrant or intermediary has followed the procedures in this section; and (b) the registrant or intermediary makes available the shared address information to the person in accordance with Rule 14a–7(a)(2)(i) and (ii).

(2) Notwithstanding paragraphs (a) and (b) of this section, unless state law requires otherwise, a registrant is not required to send an annual report or proxy statement to a security holder if:

(i) An annual report and a proxy statement for two consecutive annual meetings; or

(ii) All, and at least two, payments (if sent by first class mail) of dividends or interest on securities, or dividend reinvestment confirmations, during a twelve month period, have been mailed to such security holder's address and have been returned as undeliverable. If any such security holder delivers or causes to be delivered to the registrant written notice setting forth his then current address for security holder communications purposes, the registrant's obligation to deliver an annual report or a proxy statement under this section is reinstated.

(f) The provisions of paragraph (a) of this section shall not apply to a communication made by means of speeches in public forums, press releases, published or broadcast opinions, statements, or advertisements appearing in a broadcast media, newspaper, magazine or other bona fide publication disseminated on a regular basis, provided that:

(1) no form of proxy, consent or authorization or means to execute the same is provided to a security holder in connection with the communication; and

(2) at the time the communication is made, a definitive proxy statement is on file with the Commission pursuant to Rule 14a–6(b).

Rule 14a–4. Requirements as to Proxy

(a) The form of proxy (1) shall indicate in bold-face type whether or not the proxy is solicited on behalf of the registrant's board of directors or, if provided other than by a majority of the board of directors, shall indicate in bold-face type on whose behalf the solicitation is made; (2) shall provide a specifically designated blank space for dating the proxy card; and (3) shall identify clearly and impartially each separate matter intended to be acted upon, whether or not related to or conditioned on the approval of other matters, and whether proposed by the registrant or by security holders. No reference need be made, however, to proposals as to which discretionary authority is conferred pursuant to paragraph (c) of this section.

Note to paragraph (a)(3) (electronic filers): Electronic filers shall satisfy the filing requirements of Rule 14a–6(a) or (b) with respect to the form of proxy by filing the form of proxy as an appendix at the end of the proxy statement. Forms of proxy shall not be filed as exhibits or separate documents within an electronic submission.

(b)(1) Means shall be provided in the form of proxy whereby the person solicited is afforded an opportunity to specify by boxes a choice between approval or disapproval of, or abstention with respect to each separate matter referred to therein as intended to be acted upon, other than elections to office. A proxy may confer discretionary authority with respect to matters as to which a choice is not specified by the security holder provided that the form of proxy states in bold-face type how it is intended to vote the shares represented by the proxy in each such case.

(2) A form of proxy which provides for the election of directors shall set forth the names of persons nominated for election as directors. Such form of proxy shall clearly provide any of the following means for security holders to withhold authority to vote for each nominee:

(i) a box opposite the name of each nominee which may be marked to indicate that authority to vote for such nominee is withheld; or

(ii) an instruction in bold-face type which indicates that the security holder may withhold authority to vote for any nominee by lining through or otherwise striking out the name of any nominee; or

(iii) designated blank spaces in which the shareholder may enter the names of nominees with respect to whom the shareholder chooses to withhold authority to vote; or

(iv) any other similar means, provided that clear instructions are furnished indicting how the shareholder may withhold authority to vote for any nominee.

Such form of proxy also may provide a means for the security holder to grant authority to vote for the nominees set forth, as a group, provided that there is a similar means for the security holder to withhold authority to vote for such group of nominees. Any such form of proxy which is executed by the security holder in such manner as not to withhold authority to vote for the election of any nominee shall be deemed to grant such authority, provided that the form of proxy so states in bold-face type.

Instructions. 1. Paragraph (2) does not apply in the case of a merger, consolidation or other plan if the election of directors is an integral part of the plan.

2. If applicable state law gives legal effect to votes cast against a nominee, then in lieu of, or in addition to, providing a means for security holders to withhold authority to vote, the issuer should provide a similar means for security holders to vote against each nominee.

(c) A proxy may confer discretionary authority to vote with respect to any of the following matters:

(1) For an annual meeting of shareholders, if the registrant did not have notice of the matter at least 45 days before the date on which the registrant first mailed its proxy materials for the prior year's annual meeting of shareholders (or date specified by an advance notice provision), and a specific statement to that effect is made in the proxy statement or form of proxy. If during the prior year the registrant did not hold an annual meeting, or if the date of the meeting has changed more than 30 days from

the prior year, then notice must not have been received a reasonable time before the registrant mails its proxy materials for the current year.

(2) In the case in which the registrant has received timely notice in connection with an annual meeting of shareholders (as determined under paragraph (c)(1) of this section), if the registrant includes, in the proxy statement, advice on the nature of the matter and how the registrant intends to exercise its discretion to vote on each matter. However, even if the registrant includes this information in its proxy statement, it may not exercise discretionary voting authority on a particular proposal if the proponent:

(i) Provides the registrant with a written statement, within the time-frame determined under paragraph (c)(1) of this section, that the proponent intends to deliver a proxy statement and form of proxy to holders of at least the percentage of the company's voting shares required under applicable law to carry the proposal;

(ii) Includes the same statement in its proxy materials filed under Rule 14a-6; and

(iii) Immediately after soliciting the percentage of shareholders required to carry the proposal, provides the registrant with a statement from any solicitor or other person with knowledge that the necessary steps have been taken to deliver a proxy statement and form of proxy to holders of at least the percentage of the company's voting shares required under applicable law to carry the proposal.

(3) For solicitations other than for annual meetings or for solicitations by persons other than the registrant, matters which the persons making the solicitation do not know, a reasonable time before the solicitation, are to be presented at the meeting, if a specific statement to that effect is made in the proxy statement or form of proxy.

(4) Approval of the minutes of the prior meeting if such approval does not amount to ratification of the action taken at that meeting;

(5) The election of any person to any office for which a bona fide nominee is named in the proxy statement and such nominee is unable to serve or for good cause will not serve.

(6) Any proposal omitted from the proxy statement and form of proxy pursuant to Rules 14a-8 or 14a-9.

(7) Matters incident to the conduct of the meeting.

(d) No proxy shall confer authority (1) to vote for the election of any person to any office for which a bona fide nominee is not named in the proxy statement, (2) to vote at any annual meeting other than the next annual meeting (or any adjournment thereof) to be held after the date on which the proxy statement and form of proxy are first sent or given to security holders, (3) to vote with respect to more than one meeting (and any adjournment thereof) or more than one consent solicitation or (4) to consent to or authorize any action other than the action proposed to be taken in the proxy statement, or matters referred to in paragraph (c) of this rule. A person shall not be deemed to be a bona fide nominee and he shall not be named as such unless he has consented to being named in the proxy statement and to serve if elected. *Provided, however,* that nothing in Rule 14a-4 shall prevent any person soliciting in support of nominees who, if elected, would constitute a minority of the board of directors, from seeking authority to vote for nominees named in the registrant's proxy statement, so long as the soliciting party:

(i) seeks authority to vote in the aggregate for the number of director positions then subject to election;

(ii) represents that it will vote for all the registrant nominees, other than those registrant nominees specified by the soliciting party;

(iii) provides the security holder an opportunity to withhold authority with respect to any other registrant nominee by writing the name of that nominee on the form of proxy; and

(iv) states on the form of proxy and in the proxy statement that there is no assurance that the registrant's nominees will serve if elected with any of the soliciting party's nominees.

(e) The proxy statement or form of proxy shall provide, subject to reasonable specified conditions, that the shares represented by the proxy will be voted and that where the person solicited specifies by means of a ballot provided pursuant to paragraph (b) a choice with respect to any matter to be acted upon, the shares will be voted in accordance with the specifications so made.

(f) No person conducting a solicitation subject to this regulation shall deliver a form of proxy, consent or authorization to any security holder unless the security holder concurrently receives, or has previously received, a definitive proxy statement that has been filed with, or mailed for filing to, the Commission pursuant to Rule 14a–6(b).

Rule 14a–5. Presentation of Information in Proxy Statement

(a) The information included in the proxy statement shall be clearly presented and the statements made shall be divided into groups according to subject matter and the various groups of statements shall be preceded by appropriate headings. The order of items and sub-items in the schedule need not be followed. Where practicable and appropriate, the information shall be presented in tabular form. All amounts shall be stated in figures. Information required by more than one applicable item need not be repeated. No statement need be made in response to any item or sub-item which is inapplicable.

(b) Any information required to be included in the proxy statement as to terms of securities or other subject matter which from a standpoint of practical necessity must be determined in the future may be stated in terms of present knowledge and intention. To the extent practicable, the authority to be conferred concerning each such matter shall be confined within limits reasonably related to the need for discretionary authority. Subject to the foregoing, information which is not known to the persons on whose behalf the solicitation is to be made and which it is not reasonably within the power of such persons to ascertain or procure may be omitted, if a brief statement of the circumstances rendering such information unavailable is made.

(c) Any information contained in any other proxy soliciting material which has been furnished to each person solicited in connection with the same meeting or subject matter may be omitted from the proxy statement, if a clear reference is made to the particular document containing such information.

(d)(1) All printed proxy statements shall be in roman type at least as large and as legible as 10–point modern type, except that to the extent necessary for convenient presentation financial statements and other tabular data, but not the notes thereto, may be in roman type at least as large and as legible as 8–point modern type. All such type shall be leaded at least 2 points.

(2) Where a proxy statement is delivered through an electronic medium, issuers may satisfy legibility requirements applicable to printed documents, such as type size and font, by presenting all required information in a format readily communicated to investors.

(e) All proxy statements shall disclose, under an appropriate caption, the following dates:

(1) The deadline for submitting shareholder proposals for inclusion in the registrant's proxy statement and form of proxy for the registrant's next annual meeting, calculated in the manner provided in Rule 14a–8(e) (Question 5); and

(2) The date after which notice of a shareholder proposal submitted outside the processes of Rule 14a–8 is considered untimely, either calculated in the manner provided by Rule 14a–4(c)(1) or as established by the registrant's advance notice provision, if any, authorized by applicable state law.

(f) If the date of the next annual meeting is subsequently advanced or delayed by more than 30 calendar days from the date of the annual meeting to which the proxy statement relates, the registrant shall, in a timely manner, inform shareholders of such change, and the new dates referred to in paragraphs (e)(1) and (e)(2) of this section, by including a notice, under Item 5, in its earliest possible quarterly report on Form 10–Q (§ 249.308a of this chapter) or Form 10–QSB (§ 249.308b of this chapter), or, in the case of investment companies, in a shareholder report under § 270.30d–1 of this chapter under the Investment Company Act of 1940, or, if impracticable, any means reasonably calculated to inform shareholders.

Rule 14a–6. Filing Requirements

(a) *Preliminary proxy statement.* Five preliminary copies of the proxy statement and form of proxy shall be filed with the Commission at least 10 calendar days prior to the date definitive copies of such material are first sent or given to security holders, or such shorter period prior to that date as the Commission may authorize upon a showing of good cause thereunder. A registrant, however, shall not file with the Commission a preliminary proxy statement, form of proxy or other soliciting material to be furnished to security holders concurrently therewith if the solicitation relates to an annual (or special meeting in lieu of the annual) meeting, or for an investment company registered under the Investment Company Act of 1940, or a business development company, if the solicitation relates to any meeting of security holders at which the only matters to be acted upon are: (1) the election of directors; (2) the election, approval or ratification of accountant(s); (3) a security holder proposal included pursuant to Rule 14a–8; (4) The approval or ratification of a plan as defined in paragraph (a)(7)(ii) of Item 402 of Regulation S–K (§ 229.402(a)(7)(ii) of this chapter) or amendments to such a plan; (5) with respect to an investment company registered under the Investment Company Act of 1940 or a business development company, a proposal to continue, without change, any advisory or other contract or agreement that previously has been the subject of a proxy solicitation for which proxy material was filed with the Commission pursuant to this rule; and/or (6) with respect to an open-end investment company registered under the Investment Company Act of 1940, a proposal to increase the number of shares authorized to be issued. This exclusion from filing preliminary proxy material does not apply if the registrant comments upon or refers to a solicitation in opposition in connection with the meeting in its proxy material.

Note 1: The filing of revised material does not recommence the ten day time period unless the revised material contains material revisions or material new proposal(s) that constitute a fundamental change in the proxy material.

Note 2: The official responsible for the preparation of the proxy material should make every effort to verify the accuracy and completeness of the information required by the applicable rules. The preliminary material should be filed with the Commission at the earliest practicable date.

Note 3. Solicitation in Opposition: For purposes of the exclusion from filing preliminary proxy material, a "solicitation in opposition" includes: (a) any solicitation opposing a proposal supported by the registrant; and (b) any solicitation supporting a proposal that the registrant does not expressly support, other than a security holder proposal included in the registrant's proxy material pursuant to Rule 14a–8. The inclusion of a security holder proposal in the registrant's proxy material pursuant to Rule 14a–8 does not constitute a "solicitation in opposition," even if the registrant opposes the proposal and/or includes a statement in opposition to the proposal.

Note 4: A registrant that is filing proxy material in preliminary form only because the registrant has commented on or referred to a solicitation in opposition should indicate that fact in a transmittal letter when filing the preliminary material with the Commission.

(b) *Definitive proxy statement and other soliciting materials.* Eight definitive copies of the proxy statement, form of proxy and all other soliciting material, in the form in which such material is furnished to security holders, shall be filed with, or mailed for filing to, the Commission not later than the date such material is first sent or given to any security holders. Three copies of such material shall at the same time be filed with, or mailed for filing to, each national securities exchange upon which any class of securities of the registrant is listed and registered.

(c) *Personal solicitation materials.* If the solicitation is to be made in whole or in part by personal solicitation, eight copies of all written instructions or other material which discusses or reviews, or comments upon the merits of, any matter to be acted upon and which is furnished to the persons making the actual solicitation for their use directly or indirectly in connection with the solicitation shall be filed with, or mailed for filing to, the Commission by the person on whose behalf the solicitation is made not later than the date any such material is first sent or given to such individuals.

(d) *Release dates.* All preliminary proxy statements and forms of proxy filed pursuant to paragraph (a) of this section shall be accompanied by a statement of the date on which definitive copies thereof filed pursuant to paragraph (b) of this section are intended to be released to security holders. All definitive material filed pursuant to paragraph (b) of this section shall be accompanied by a statement of the date on which copies of such material have been released to security holders, or, if not released, the date on which copies thereof are intended to be released. All material filed pursuant to paragraph (c) of this section shall be accompanied by a statement of the date on which copies thereof were released to the individual who will make the actual solicitation or if not released, the date on which copies thereof are intended to be released.

(e)(1) *Public Availability of Information.* All copies of preliminary proxy statements and forms of proxy filed pursuant to paragraph (a) of this section shall be clearly marked "Preliminary Copies," and shall be deemed immediately available for public inspection unless confidential treatment is obtained pursuant to paragraph (e)(2) of this section.

(2) *Confidential Treatment.* If action is to be taken with respect to any matter specified in Item 14 of Schedule 14A, all copies of the preliminary proxy statement and form of proxy filed pursuant to paragraph (a) of this section shall be for the information of the Commission only and shall not be deemed available for public inspection until filed with the Commission in definitive form, provided that:

(i) the proxy statement does not relate to a matter or proposal subject to Rule 13e–3 * * *;

(ii) Neither the parties to the transaction nor any persons authorized to act on their behalf have made any public communications relating to the transaction except for statements where the content is limited to the information specified in § 230.135 of this chapter; and

(iii) the filed material is marked "Confidential, For Use of the Commission Only." In any and all cases, such material may be disclosed to any department or agency of the United States Government and to the Congress, and the Commission may make such inquiries or investigation in regard to the material as may be necessary for an adequate review thereof by the Commission.

Instruction to paragraph (e)(2): If communications are made publicly that go beyond the information specified in § 230.135 of this chapter, the preliminary proxy materials must be re-filed promptly with the Commission as public materials.

(f) *Communications not required to be filed.* Copies of replies to inquiries from security holders requesting further information and copies of communications which do no more than request that forms of proxy theretofore solicited be signed and returned need not be filed pursuant to this rule.

(g) *Solicitations subject to Rule 14a–2(b)(1).*

(1) Any person who:

(i) engages in a solicitation pursuant to Rule 14a–2(b)(1), and

(ii) at the commencement of that solicitation owns beneficially securities of the class which is the subject of the solicitation with a market value of over $5 million, shall furnish or mail to the Commission, not later than three days after the date this written solicitation is first sent or given to any security holder, five copies of a statement containing the information specified in the Notice of Exempt Solicitation which statement shall attach as an exhibit all written soliciting materials. Five copies of an amendment to such statement shall be furnished or mailed to the Commission, in connection with dissemination of any additional communications, not later than three days after the date the additional material is first sent or given to any security holder. Three copies of the Notice of Exempt Proxy Solicitation and amendments thereto shall, at the same time the materials are furnished or mailed to the Commission, be furnished or led to each national securities exchange upon which any class of securities of the registrant is listed and registered.

(2) Notwithstanding paragraph (g)(1) of this section, no such submission need be made with respect to oral solicitations (other than with respect to scripts used in connection with such oral solicitations), speeches delivered in a public forum, press releases, published or broadcast opinions, statements, and advertisements appearing in a broadcast media, or a newspaper, magazine or other bona fide publication disseminated on a regular basis.

(h) *Revised material.* Where any proxy statement, form of proxy or other material filed pursuant to this rule is amended or revised, two of the copies of such amended or revised material filed pursuant to this rule * * * shall be marked to indicate clearly and precisely the changes effected therein. If the amendment or revision alters the text of the material the changes in such text shall be indicated by means of underscoring or in some other appropriate manner.

(i) *Fees.* At the time of filing the proxy solicitation material, the persons upon whose behalf the solicitation is made, other than investment companies registered under the Investment Company Act of 1940, shall pay to the Commission the following applicable fee:

(1) For preliminary proxy material involving acquisitions, mergers, spinoffs, consolidations or proposed sales or other dispositions of substantially all the assets of the company, a fee established in accordance with Rule 0-11 (§ 240.0-11 of this chapter) shall be paid. No refund shall be given.

(2) For all other proxy submissions and submissions made pursuant to Rule 14a-6(g), no fee shall be required.

(1) Any proxy statement, form of proxy or other soliciting material required to be filed by this section that also is either

(i) Included in a registration statement filed under the Securities Act of 1933 on Forms S-4 (§ 239.25 of this chapter), F-4 (§ 239.34 of this chapter) or N-14 (§ 239.23 of this chapter); or

(ii) Filed under § 230.424, § 230.425 or § 230.497 of this chapter is required to be filed only under the Securities Act, and is deemed filed under this section.

(2) Under paragraph (j)(1) of this section, the fee required by paragraph (i) of this section need not be paid.

(k) *Computing time periods.* In computing time periods beginning with the filing date specified in Regulation 14A, the filing date shall be counted as the first day of the time period and midnight of the last day shall constitute the end of the specified time period.

* * *

Rule 14a-7. Obligations of Registrants to Provide a List of, or Mail Soliciting Material to, Security Holders

(a) If the registrant has made or intends to make a proxy solicitation in connection with a security holder meeting or action by consent or authorization, upon the written request by any record or beneficial holder of securities of the class entitled to vote at the meeting or to execute a consent or authorization to provide a list of security holders or to mail the requesting security holder's materials, regardless of whether the request references this section, the registrant shall:

(1) deliver to the requesting security holder within five business days after receipt of the request:

(i) notification as to whether the registrant has elected to mail the security holder's soliciting materials or provide a security holder list if the election under paragraph (b) is to be made by the registrant;

(ii) a statement of the approximate number of record holders and beneficial holders, separated by type of holder and class, owning securities in the same class or classes as holders which have been or are to be solicited on management's behalf, or any more limited group of such holders designated by the security holder if available or retrievable under the registrant's or its transfer agent's security holder data systems; and

(iii) the estimated cost of mailing a proxy statement, form of proxy or other communication to such holders, including to the extent known or reasonably available, the estimated costs of any bank, broker, and similar person through whom the registrant has solicited or intends to solicit beneficial owners in connection with the security holder meeting or action.

(2) perform the acts set forth in either paragraphs (a)(2)(i) or (a)(2)(ii) of this section, at the registrant's or requesting security holder's option, as specified in paragraph (b) of this section:

(i) Mail copies of any proxy statement, form of proxy or other soliciting material furnished by the security holder to the record holders, including banks, brokers, and similar entities, designated by the security holder. A sufficient number of copies must be mailed to the banks, brokers, and similar entities for distribution to all beneficial owners designated by the security holder. If the registrant has received affirmative written or implied consent to deliver a single proxy statement to security holders at a shared address in accordance with the procedures in Rule 14a-3(e)(1), a single copy of the proxy statement furnished by the security holder shall be mailed to that address. The registrant shall mail the security holder material with reasonable promptness after tender of the material to be mailed, envelopes or other containers therefor, postage or payment for postage and other reasonable expenses of effecting such mailing. The registrant shall not be responsible for the content of the material; or

(ii) Deliver the following information to the requesting security holder within five business days of receipt of the request: a reasonably current list of the names, addresses and security positions of the record holders, including banks, brokers and similar entities holding securities in the same class or classes as holders which have been or are to be solicited on management's behalf, or any more limited group of such holders designated by the security holder if available or retrievable under the registrant's or its transfer agent's security holder data systems; the most recent list of names, addresses and security positions of beneficial owners as specified in Rule 14a–13(b), in the possession, or which subsequently comes into the possession, of the registrant; and the names of security holders at a shared address that have consented to delivery of a single copy of proxy materials to a shared address, if the registrant has received written or implied consent in accordance with Rule 14a–3(e)(1). All security holder list information shall be in the form requested by the security holder to the extent that such form is available to the registrant without undue burden or expense. The registrant shall furnish the security holder with updated record holder information on a daily basis or, if not available on a daily basis, at the shortest reasonable intervals, provided, however, the registrant need not provide beneficial or record holder information more current than the record date for the meeting or action.

(b)(1) The requesting security holder shall have the options set forth in paragraph (a)(2) of this section, and the registrant shall have corresponding obligations, if the registrant or general partner or sponsor is soliciting or intends to solicit with respect to:

(i) A proposal that is subject to Rule 13e–3;

* * *

(2) With respect to all other requests pursuant to this section, the registrant shall have the option to either mail the security holder's material or furnish the security holder list as set forth in this section.

(c) At the time of a list request, the security holder making the request shall:

(1) if holding the registrant's securities through a nominee, provide the registrant with a statement by the nominee or other independent third party, or a copy of a current filing made with the Commission and furnished to the registrant, confirming such holder's beneficial ownership; and

(2) provide the registrant with an affidavit, declaration, affirmation or other similar document provided for under applicable state law identifying the proposal or other corporate action that will be the subject of the security holder's solicitation or communication and attesting that:

(i) the security holder will not use the list information for any purpose other than to solicit security holders with respect to the same meeting or action by consent or authorization for which the registrant is soliciting or intends to solicit or to communicate with security holders with respect to a solicitation commenced by the registrant; and

(ii) the security holder will not disclose such information to any person other than a beneficial owner for whom the request was made and an employee or agent to the extent necessary to effectuate the communication or solicitation.

(d) The security holder shall not use the information furnished by the registrant pursuant to paragraph (a)(2)(ii) of this section for any purpose other than to solicit security holders with respect to the same meeting or action by consent or authorization for which the registrant is soliciting or intends to solicit or to communicate with security holders with respect to a solicitation commenced by the registrant; or disclose such information to any person other than an employee, agent, or beneficial owner for whom a request was made to the extent necessary to effectuate the communication or solicitation. The security holder shall return the information provided pursuant to paragraph (a)(2)(ii) of this section and shall not retain any copies thereof or of any information derived from such information after the termination of the solicitation.

(e) The security holder shall reimburse the reasonable expenses incurred by the registrant in performing the acts requested pursuant to paragraph (a) of this section.

Notes to Rule 14a–7.

1. Reasonably prompt methods of distribution to security holders may be used instead of mailing. If an alternative distribution method is chosen, the costs of that method should be considered where necessary rather than the costs of mailing.

2. When providing the information required by Rule 14a–7(a)(1)(ii), if the registrant has re-

ceived affirmative written or implied consent to delivery of a single copy of proxy materials to a shared address in accordance with Rule 14a–3(e)(1), it shall exclude from the number of record holders those to whom it does not have to deliver a separate proxy statement.

Rule 14a–8. Shareholder Proposals

This section addresses when a company must include a shareholder's proposal in its proxy statement and identify the proposal in its form of proxy when the company holds an annual or special meeting of shareholders. In summary, in order to have your shareholder proposal included on a company's proxy card, and included along with any supporting statement in its proxy statement, you must be eligible and follow certain procedures. Under a few specific circumstances, the company is permitted to exclude your proposal, but only after submitting its reasons to the Commission. We structured this section in a question-and-answer format so that it is easier to understand. The references to "you" are to a shareholder seeking to submit the proposal.

(a) Question 1: What is a proposal? A shareholder proposal is your recommendation or requirement that the company and/or its board of directors take action, which you intend to present at a meeting of the company's shareholders. Your proposal should state as clearly as possible the course of action that you believe the company should follow. If your proposal is placed on the company's proxy card, the company must also provide in the form of proxy means for shareholders to specify by boxes a choice between approval or disapproval, or abstention. Unless otherwise indicated, the word "proposal" as used in this section refers both to your proposal, and to your corresponding statement in support of your proposal (if any).

(b) Question 2: Who is eligible to submit a proposal, and how do I demonstrate to the company that I am eligible?

(1) In order to be eligible to submit a proposal, you must have continuously held at least $2,000 in market value, or 1%, of the company's securities entitled to be voted on the proposal at the meeting for at least one year by the date you submit the proposal. You must continue to hold those securities through the date of the meeting.

(2) If you are the registered holder of your securities, which means that your name appears in the company's records as a shareholder, the company can verify your eligibility on its own, although you will still have to provide the company with a written statement that you intend to continue to hold the securities through the date of the meeting of shareholders. However, if like many shareholders you are not a registered holder, the company likely does not know that you are a shareholder, or how many shares you own. In this case, at the time you submit your proposal, you must prove your eligibility to the company in one of two ways:

(i) The first way is to submit to the company a written statement from the "record" holder of your securities (usually a broker or bank) verifying that, at the time you submitted your proposal, you continuously held the securities for at least one year. You must also include your own written statement that you intend to continue to hold the securities through the date of the meeting of shareholders; or

(ii) The second way to prove ownership applies only if you have filed a Schedule 13D (§ 240.13d–101), Schedule 13G (§ 240.13d–102), Form 3 (§ 249.103 of this chapter), Form 4 (§ 249.104 of this chapter) and/or Form 5 (§ 249.105 of this chapter), or amendments to those documents or updated forms, reflecting your ownership of the shares as of or before the date on which the one-year eligibility period begins. If you have filed one of these documents with the SEC, you may demonstrate your eligibility by submitting to the company:

(A) A copy of the schedule and/or form, and any subsequent amendments reporting a change in your ownership level;

(B) Your written statement that you continuously held the required number of shares for the one-year period as of the date of the statement; and

(C) Your written statement that you intend to continue ownership of the shares through the date of the company's annual or special meeting.

(c) Question 3: How many proposals may I submit? Each shareholder may submit no more than one proposal to a company for a particular shareholders' meeting.

(d) Question 4: How long can my proposal be? The proposal, including any accompanying supporting statement, may not exceed 500 words.

(e) Question 5: What is the deadline for submitting a proposal?

(1) If you are submitting your proposal for the company's annual meeting, you can in most cases find the deadline in last year's proxy statement. However, if the company did not hold an annual meeting last year, or has changed the date of its meeting for this year more than 30 days from last year's meeting, you can usually find the deadline in one of the company's quarterly reports on Form 10–Q (§ 249.308a of this chapter) or 10–QSB (§ 249.308b of this chapter), or in shareholder reports of investment companies under § 270.30d–1 of this chapter of the Investment Company Act of 1940. In order to avoid controversy, shareholders should submit their proposals by means, including electronic means, that permit them to prove the date of delivery.

(2) The deadline is calculated in the following manner if the proposal is submitted for a regularly scheduled annual meeting. The proposal must be received at the company's principal executive offices not less than 120 calendar days before the date of the company's proxy statement released to shareholders in connection with the previous year's annual meeting. However, if the company did not hold an annual meeting the previous year, or if the date of this year's annual meeting has been changed by more than 30 days from the date of the previous year's meeting, then the deadline is a reasonable time before the company begins to print and mail its proxy materials.

(3) If you are submitting your proposal for a meeting of shareholders other than a regularly scheduled annual meeting, the deadline is a reasonable time before the company begins to print and mail its proxy materials.

(f) Question 6: What if I fail to follow one of the eligibility or procedural requirements explained in answers to Questions 1 through 4 of this section?

(1) The company may exclude your proposal, but only after it has notified you of the problem, and you have failed adequately to correct it. Within 14 calendar days of receiving your proposal, the company must notify you in writing of any procedural or eligibility deficiencies, as well as of the time frame for your response. Your response must be postmarked, or transmitted electronically, no later than 14 days from the date you received the company's notification. A company need not provide you such notice of a deficiency if the deficiency cannot be remedied, such as if you fail to submit a proposal by the company's properly determined deadline. If the company intends to exclude the proposal, it will later have to make a submission under Rule 14a–8 and provide you with a copy under Question 10 below, Rule 14a–8(j).

(2) If you fail in your promise to hold the required number of securities through the date of the meeting of shareholders, then the company will be permitted to exclude all of your proposals from its proxy materials for any meeting held in the following two calendar years.

(g) Question 7: Who has the burden of persuading the Commission or its staff that my proposal can be excluded? Except as otherwise noted, the burden is on the company to demonstrate that it is entitled to exclude a proposal.

(h) Question 8: Must I appear personally at the shareholders' meeting to present the proposal?

(1) Either you, or your representative who is qualified under state law to present the proposal on your behalf, must attend the meeting to present the proposal. Whether you attend the meeting yourself or send a qualified representative to the meeting in your place, you should make sure that you, or your representative, follow the proper state law procedures for attending the meeting and/or presenting your proposal.

(2) If the company holds its shareholder meeting in whole or in part via electronic media, and the company permits you or your representative to present your proposal via such media, then you may appear through electronic media rather than traveling to the meeting to appear in person.

(3) If you or your qualified representative fail to appear and present the proposal, without good cause, the company will be permitted to exclude all of your proposals from its proxy materials for any meetings held in the following two calendar years.

(i) Question 9: If I have complied with the procedural requirements, on what other bases may a company rely to exclude my proposal?

(1) Improper under state law: If the proposal is not a proper subject for action by shareholders

under the laws of the jurisdiction of the company's organization;

Note to paragraph (i)(1): Depending on the subject matter, some proposals are not considered proper under state law if they would be binding on the company if approved by shareholders. In our experience, most proposals that are cast as recommendations or requests that the board of directors take specified action are proper under state law. Accordingly, we will assume that a proposal drafted as a recommendation or suggestion is proper unless the company demonstrates otherwise.

(2) Violation of law: If the proposal would, if implemented, cause the company to violate any state, federal, or foreign law to which it is subject;

Note to paragraph (i)(2): We will not apply this basis for exclusion to permit exclusion of a proposal on grounds that it would violate foreign law if compliance with the foreign law would result in a violation of any state or federal law.

(3) Violation of proxy rules: If the proposal or supporting statement is contrary to any of the Commission's proxy rules, including Rule 14a–9, which prohibits materially false or misleading statements in proxy soliciting materials;

(4) Personal grievance; special interest: If the proposal relates to the redress of a personal claim or grievance against the company or any other person, or if it is designed to result in a benefit to you, or to further a personal interest, which is not shared by the other shareholders at large;

(5) Relevance: If the proposal relates to operations which account for less than 5 percent of the company's total assets at the end of its most recent fiscal year, and for less than 5 percent of its net earnings and gross sales for its most recent fiscal year, and is not otherwise significantly related to the company's business;

(6) Absence of power/authority: If the company would lack the power or authority to implement the proposal;

(7) Management functions: If the proposal deals with a matter relating to the company's ordinary business operations;

(8) Relates to election: If the proposal relates to an election for membership on the company's board of directors or analogous governing body;

(9) Conflicts with company's proposal: If the proposal directly conflicts with one of the company's own proposals to be submitted to shareholders at the same meeting;

Note to paragraph (i)(9): A company's submission to the Commission under this section should specify the points of conflict with the company's proposal.

(10) Substantially implemented: If the company has already substantially implemented the proposal;

(11) Duplication: If the proposal substantially duplicates another proposal previously submitted to the company by another proponent that will be included in the company's proxy materials for the same meeting;

(12) Resubmissions: If the proposal deals with substantially the same subject matter as another proposal or proposals that has or have been previously included in the company's proxy materials within the preceding 5 calendar years, a company may exclude it from its proxy materials for any meeting held within 3 calendar years of the last time it was included if the proposal received:

(i) Less than 3% of the vote if proposed once within the preceding 5 calendar years;

(ii) Less than 6% of the vote on its last submission to shareholders if proposed twice previously within the preceding 5 calendar years; or

(iii) Less than 10% of the vote on its last submission to shareholders if proposed three times or more previously within the preceding 5 calendar years; and

(13) Specific amount of dividends: If the proposal relates to specific amounts of cash or stock dividends.

(j) Question 10: What procedures must the company follow if it intends to exclude my proposal?

(1) If the company intends to exclude a proposal from its proxy materials, it must file its reasons with the Commission no later than 80 calendar days before it files its definitive proxy statement and form of proxy with the Commission. The company must simultaneously provide you with a copy of its submission. The Commission staff may permit the company to make its submission later than 80 days before the company files its definitive proxy statement and form of proxy, if the company demonstrates good cause for missing the deadline.

(2) The company must file six paper copies of the following:

(i) The proposal;

(ii) An explanation of why the company believes that it may exclude the proposal, which should, if possible, refer to the most recent applicable authority, such as prior Division letters issued under the rule; and

(iii) A supporting opinion of counsel when such reasons are based on matters of state or foreign law.

(k) Question 11: May I submit my own statement to the Commission responding to the company's arguments?

Yes, you may submit a response, but it is not required. You should try to submit any response to us, with a copy to the company, as soon as possible after the company makes its submission. This way, the Commission staff will have time to consider fully your submission before it issues its response. You should submit six paper copies of your response.

(*l*) Question 12: If the company includes my shareholder proposal in its proxy materials, what information about me must it include along with the proposal itself?

(1) The company's proxy statement must include your name and address, as well as the number of the company's voting securities that you hold. However, instead of providing that information, the company may instead include a statement that it will provide the information to shareholders promptly upon receiving an oral or written request.

(2) The company is not responsible for the contents of your proposal or supporting statement.

(m) Question 13: What can I do if the company includes in its proxy statement reasons why it believes shareholders should not vote in favor of my proposal, and I disagree with some of its statements?

(1) The company may elect to include in its proxy statement reasons why it believes shareholders should vote against your proposal. The company is allowed to make arguments reflecting its own point of view, just as you may express your own point of view in your proposal's supporting statement.

(2) However, if you believe that the company's opposition to your proposal contains materially false or misleading statements that may violate our anti-fraud rule, Rule 14a–9, you should promptly send to the Commission staff and the company a letter explaining the reasons for your view, along with a copy of the company's statements opposing your proposal. To the extent possible, your letter should include specific factual information demonstrating the inaccuracy of the company's claims. Time permitting, you may wish to try to work out your differences with the company by yourself before contacting the Commission staff.

(3) We require the company to send you a copy of its statements opposing your proposal before it mails its proxy materials, so that you may bring to our attention any materially false or misleading statements, under the following timeframes:

(i) If our no-action response requires that you make revisions to your proposal or supporting statement as a condition to requiring the company to include it in its proxy materials, then the company must provide you with a copy of its opposition statements no later than 5 calendar days after the company receives a copy of your revised proposal; or

(ii) In all other cases, the company must provide you with a copy of its opposition statements no later than 30 calendar days before its files definitive copies of its proxy statement and form of proxy under Rule 14a–6.

Rule 14a–9. False or Misleading Statements

(*a*) No solicitation subject to this regulation shall be made by means of any proxy statement, form of proxy, notice of meeting or other communication, written or oral, containing any statement which, at the time and in the light of the circumstances under which it is made, is false or misleading with respect to any material fact, or which omits to state any material fact necessary in order to make the statements therein not false or misleading or necessary to correct any statement in any earlier communication with respect to the solicitation of a proxy for the same meeting or subject matter which has become false or misleading.

(*b*) The fact that a proxy statement, form of proxy or other soliciting material has been filed with or examined by the Commission shall not be deemed a finding by the Commission that such material is accurate or complete or not false or misleading, or that the Commission has passed upon the merits of or approved any statement contained therein or any matter to be acted upon by security holders. No representation contrary to the foregoing shall be made.

Note. The following are some examples of what, depending upon particular facts and circumstances, may be misleading within the meaning of this section:

(a) Predictions as to specific future market values.

(b) Material which directly or indirectly impugns character, integrity or personal reputation, or directly or indirectly makes charges concerning improper, illegal or immoral conduct or associations, without factual foundation.

(c) Failure to so identify a proxy statement, form of proxy and other soliciting material as to clearly distinguish it from the soliciting material of any other person or persons soliciting for the same meeting or subject matter.

(d) Claims made prior to a meeting regarding the results of a solicitation.

* * *

Rule 14a-10. Prohibition of Certain Solicitations

No person making a solicitation which is subject to Rules 14a-1 to 14a-10 shall solicit:

(a) any undated or post-dated proxy, or

(b) any proxy which provides that it shall be deemed to be dated as of any date subsequent to the date on which it is signed by the security holder.

Rule 14a-11. Special Provisions Applicable to Election Contests

Removed and Reserved effective November 10, 1999.

Rule 14a-12. Solicitation Before Furnishing a Proxy Statement

(a) Notwithstanding the provisions of Rule 14a-3(a), a solicitation may be made before furnishing security holders with a proxy statement meeting the requirements of Rule 14a-3(a) if:

(1) Each written communication includes:

(i) The identity of the participants in the solicitation (as defined in Instruction 3 to Item 4 of Schedule 14A (Rule 14a-101)) and a description of their direct or indirect interests, by security holdings or otherwise, or a prominent legend in clear, plain language advising security holders where they can obtain that information; and

(ii) A prominent legend in clear, plain language advising security holders to read the proxy statement when it is available because it contains important information. The legend also must explain to investors that they can get the proxy statement, and any other relevant documents, for free at the Commission's web site and describe which documents are available free from the participants; and

(2) A definitive proxy statement meeting the requirements of Rule 14a-3(a) is sent or given to security holders solicited in reliance on this section before or at the same time as the forms of proxy, consent or authorization are furnished to or requested from security holders.

(b) Any soliciting material published, sent or given to security holders in accordance with paragraph (a) of this section must be filed with the Commission no later than the date the material is first published, sent or given to security holders. Three copies of the material must at the same time be filed with, or mailed for filing to, each national securities exchange upon which any class of securities of the registrant is listed and registered. The soliciting material must include a cover page in the form set forth in Schedule 14A (Rule 14a-101) and the appropriate box on the cover page must be marked. Soliciting material in connection with a registered offering is required to be filed only under Rule 424 or Rule 425 of this chapter, and will be deemed filed under this section.

(c) Solicitations by any person or group of persons for the purpose of opposing a solicitation subject to this regulation by any other person or group of persons with respect to the election or removal of directors at any annual or special meeting of security holders also are subject to the following provisions:

(1) Application of this rule to annual report. Notwithstanding the provisions of Rule 14a-3(b) and (c), any portion of the annual report referred to in Rule 14a-3(b) that comments upon or refers to any solicitation subject to this rule, or to any participant in the solicitation, other than the solicitation by the management, must be filed with the Commission as proxy material subject to this regulation. This must be filed in electronic format unless an exemption is available under Rules 201 or 202 of Regulation S-T (§ 232.201 or § 232.202 of this chapter).

(2) Use of reprints or reproductions. In any solicitation subject to this Rule 14a-12(c), soliciting material that includes, in whole or part, any reprints or reproductions of any previously published material must:

(i) State the name of the author and publication, the date of prior publication, and identify any person who is quoted without being named in the previously published material.

(ii) Except in the case of a public or official document or statement, state whether or not the consent of the author and publication has been obtained to the use of the previously published material as proxy soliciting material.

(iii) If any participant using the previously published material, or anyone on his or her behalf, paid, directly or indirectly, for the preparation or prior publication of the previously published material, or has made or proposes to make any payments or give any other consideration in connection with the publication or republication of the material, state the circumstances.

Instructions to Rule 14a-12

1. If paper filing is permitted, file eight copies of the soliciting material with the Commission, except that only three copies of the material specified by Rule 14a-12(c)(1) need be filed.

2. Any communications made under this section after the definitive proxy statement is on file but before it is disseminated also must specify that the proxy statement is publicly available and the anticipated date of dissemination.

Rule 14a-13. Obligation of Registrants in Communicating With Beneficial Owners

(a) If the registrant knows that securities of any class entitled to vote at a meeting (or by written consents or authorizations if no meeting is held) with respect to which the registrant intends to solicit proxies, consents or authorizations are held of record by a broker, dealer, voting trustee, bank, association, or other entity that exercises fiduciary powers in nominee name or otherwise, the registrant shall:

(1) By first class mail or other equally prompt means: (i) inquire of each such record holder: (A) whether other persons are the beneficial owners of such securities and if so, the number of copies of the proxy and other soliciting material necessary to supply such material to such beneficial owners; (B) in the case of an annual (or special meeting in lieu of the annual) meeting, or written consents in lieu of such meeting, at which directors are to be elected, the number of copies of the annual report to security holders necessary to supply such report to beneficial owners to whom such reports are to be distributed by such record holder or its nominee and not by the registrant; and (C) if the record holder has an obligation under Rule 14b-1(b)(3) or Rule 14b-2(b)(4)(ii) and (iii), whether an agent has been designated to act on its behalf in fulfilling such obligation and, if so, the name and address of such agent; and (D) whether it holds the registrant's securities on behalf of any respondent bank and, if so, the name and address of each such respondent bank; and (ii) indicate to each such record holder: (A) whether the registrant, pursuant to paragraph (c) of this section, intends to distribute the annual report to security holders to beneficial owners of its securities whose names, addresses and securities positions are disclosed pursuant to Rule 14b-1(b)(3) and Rule 14b-2(b)(4)(ii) and (iii); (B) the record date; and (C) at the option of the registrant, any employee benefit plan established by an affiliate of the registrant that holds securities of the registrant that the registrant elects to treat as exempt employee benefit plan securities;

(2) Upon receipt of a record holder's or respondent bank's response indicating, pursuant to Rule 14b-2(b)(1)(i), the names and addresses of its respondent banks, within one business day after the date such response is received, make an inquiry of and give notification to each such respondent bank in the same manner required by paragraph (a)(1) of this section; *Provided, however,* the inquiry re-

quired by paragraphs (a)(1) and (a)(2) of this section shall not cover beneficial owners of exempt employee benefit plan securities;

(3) Make the inquiry required by paragraph (a)(1) of this section at least 20 business days prior to the record date of the meeting of security holders, or (i) if such inquiry is impracticable 20 business days prior to the record date of a special meeting, as many days before the record date of such meeting as is practicable or, (ii) if consents or authorizations are solicited, and such inquiry is impracticable 20 business days before the earliest date on which they may be used to effect corporate action, as many days before that date as is practicable, or (iii) at such later time as the rules of a national securities exchange on which the class of securities in question is listed may permit for good cause shown; *Provided, however,* that if a record holder or respondent bank has informed the registrant that a designated office(s) or department(s) is to receive such inquiries, the inquiry shall be made to such designated office(s) or department(s); and

(4) Supply, in a timely manner, each record holder and respondent bank of whom the inquiries required by paragraphs (a)(1) and (a)(2) of this section are made with copies of the proxy, other proxy soliciting material, and/or the annual report to security holders, in such quantities, assembled in such form and at such place(s), as the record holder or respondent bank may reasonably request in order to send such material to each beneficial owner of securities who is to be furnished with such material by the record holder or respondent bank; and

(5) Upon the request of any record holder or respondent bank that is supplied with proxy soliciting material and/or annual reports to security holders pursuant to paragraph (a)(4) of this section, pay its reasonable expenses for completing the mailing of such material to beneficial owners.

Note 1: If the registrant's list of security holders indicates that some of its securities are registered in the name of a clearing agency registered pursuant to Section 17A of the Act (e.g., "Cede & Co.," nominee for the Depository Trust Company), the registrant shall make appropriate inquiry of the clearing agency and thereafter of the participants in such clearing agency who may hold on behalf of a beneficial owner or respondent bank, and shall comply with the above paragraph with respect to any such participant (*see* Rule 14a–1(i)).

Note 2: The attention of registrants is called to the fact that each broker, dealer, bank, association and other entity that exercises fiduciary powers has an obligation pursuant to Rules 14b–1(b) and 14b–2(b) (except as provided therein with respect to employee benefit plan securities held in nominee name) and, with respect to brokers and dealers, applicable self-regulatory organization requirements to obtain and forward, within the time periods prescribed therein, (a) proxies (or in lieu thereof requests for voting instructions) and proxy soliciting materials to beneficial owners on whose behalf it holds securities, and (b) annual reports to security holders to beneficial owners on whose behalf it holds securities, unless the registrant has notified the record holder or respondent bank that it has assumed responsibility to mail such material to beneficial owners whose names, addresses and securities positions are disclosed pursuant to Rule 14b–1(b)(3) and Rule 14b–2(b)(4)(ii) and (iii).

Note 3: The attention of registrants is called to the fact that registrants have an obligation, pursuant to paragraph (d) of this section, to cause proxies (or in lieu thereof requests for voting instructions), proxy soliciting material and annual reports to security holders to be furnished, in a timely manner, to beneficial owners of exempt employee benefit plan securities.

(b) Any registrant requesting pursuant to Rule 14b–1(b)(3) and Rule 14b–2(b)(4)(ii) and (iii) a list of names, addresses and securities positions of beneficial owners of its securities who either have consented or have not objected to disclosure of such information shall:

(1) By first class mail or other equally prompt means, inquire of each record holder and each respondent bank identified to the registrant pursuant to Rule 14b–2(b)(4)(i) whether such record holder or respondent bank holds the registrant's securities on behalf of any respondent banks and, if so, the name and address of each such respondent bank;

(2) Request such list to be compiled as of a date no earlier than five business days after the date the registrant's request is received by the record holder or respondent bank; *Provided, however,* that if the record holder or respondent bank has informed the registrant that a designated office(s) or depart-

ment(s) is to receive such requests, the request shall be made to such designated office(s) or department(s);

(3) Make such request to the following persons that hold the registrant's securities on behalf of beneficial owners: all brokers, dealers, banks, associations and other entities that exercise fiduciary powers; *Provided, however,* such request shall not cover beneficial owners of exempt employee benefit plan securities as defined in Rule 14a-1(d)(1); and, at the option of the registrant, such request may give notice of any employee benefit plan established by an affiliate of the registrant that holds securities of the registrant that the registrant elects to treat as exempt employee benefit plan securities;

(4) Use the information furnished in response to such request exclusively for purposes of corporate communications; and

(5) Upon the request of any record holder or respondent bank to whom such request is made, pay the reasonable expenses, both direct and indirect, of providing beneficial owner information.

Note: A registrant will be deemed to have satisfied its obligations under paragraph (b) of this section by requesting consenting and non-objecting beneficial owner lists from a designated agent acting on behalf of the record holder or respondent bank and paying to that designated agent the reasonable expenses of providing the beneficial owner information.

(c) A registrant, at its option, may mail its annual report to security holders to the beneficial owners whose identifying information is provided by record holders and respondent banks, pursuant to Rule 14b-1(b)(3) and Rule 14b-2(b)(4)(ii) and (iii) provided that such registrant notifies the record holders and respondent banks, at the time it makes the inquiry required by paragraph (a) of this section, that the registrant will mail the annual report to security holders to the beneficial owners so identified.

(d) If a registrant solicits proxies, consents or authorizations from record holders and respondent banks who hold securities on behalf of beneficial owners, the registrant shall cause proxies (or in lieu thereof requests for voting instructions), proxy soliciting material and annual reports to security holders to be furnished, in a timely manner, to beneficial owners of exempt employee benefit plan securities.

Rule 14b-1. Obligation of Registered Brokers and Dealers in Connection With the Prompt Forwarding of Certain Communications to Beneficial Owners

(a) *Definitions.* Unless the context otherwise requires, all terms used in this section shall have the same meanings as in the Act and, with respect to proxy soliciting material, as in Rule 14a-1 thereunder and, with respect to information statements, as in Rule 14c-1 thereunder. In addition, as used in this section, the term "registrant" means:

(1) The issuer of a class of securities registered pursuant to Section 12 of the Act; or

(2) An investment company registered under the Investment Company Act of 1940.

(b) *Dissemination and beneficial owner information requirements.* A broker or dealer registered under Section 15 of the Act shall comply with the following requirements for disseminating certain communications to beneficial owners and providing beneficial owner information to registrants.

(1) The broker or dealer shall respond, by first class mail or other equally prompt means, directly to the registrant no later than seven business days after the date it receives an inquiry made in accordance with Rule 14a-13(a) or Rule 14c-7(a) by indicating, by means of a search card or otherwise:

(i) The approximate number of customers of the broker or dealer who are beneficial owners of the registrant's securities that are held of record by the broker, dealer, or its nominee;

(ii) The number of customers of the broker or dealer who are beneficial owners of the registrant's securities who have objected to disclosure of their names, addresses, and securities positions if the registrant has indicated, pursuant to Rule 14a-13(a)(1)(ii)(A) or Rule 14c-7(a)(1)(ii)(A), that it will distribute the annual report to security holders to beneficial owners of its securities whose names, addresses and securities positions are disclosed pursuant to paragraph (b)(3) of this section; and

(iii) The identity of the designated agent of the broker or dealer, if any, acting on its behalf in fulfilling its obligations under paragraph (b)(3) of this section; *Provided, however,* that if the broker or dealer has informed the registrant that a designated office(s) or department(s) is to receive such inquiries, receipt for purposes of paragraph (b)(1) of this section shall mean receipt by such designated office(s) or department(s).

(2) The broker or dealer shall, upon receipt of the proxy, other proxy soliciting material, information statement, and/or annual reports to security holders, forward such materials to its customers who are beneficial owners of the registrant's securities no later than five business days after receipt of the proxy material, information statement or annual reports.

Note to paragraph (b)(2):

At the request of a registrant, or on its own initiative so long as the registrant does not object, a broker or dealer may, but is not required to deliver one annual report, proxy statement or information statement to more than one beneficial owner sharing an address if the requirements set forth in Rule 14a–3(e)(1) (with respect to annual reports and proxy statements) and Rule 14c–3(c) (with respect to annual reports and information statements) applicable to registrants, with the exception of Rule 14a–3(e)(1)(i)(E), are satisfied instead by the broker or dealer.

(3) The broker or dealer shall, through its agent or directly:

(i) Provide the registrant, upon the registrant's request, with the names, addresses, and securities positions, compiled as of a date specified in the registrant's request which is no earlier than five business days after the date the registrant's request is received, of its customers who are beneficial owners of the registrant's securities and who have not objected to disclosure of such information; *Provided, however,* that if the broker or dealer has informed the registrant that a designated office(s) or department(s) is to receive such requests, receipt shall mean receipt by such designated office(s) or department(s); and

(ii) Transmit the data specified in paragraph (b)(3)(i) of this section to the registrant no later than five business days after the record date or other date specified by the registrant.

Note 1: Where a broker or dealer employs a designated agent to act on its behalf in performing the obligations imposed on the broker or dealer by paragraph (b)(3) of this section, the five business day time period for determining the date as of which the beneficial owner information is to be compiled is calculated from the date the designated agent receives the registrant's request. In complying with the registrant's request for beneficial owner information under paragraph (b)(3) of this section, a broker or dealer need only supply the registrant with the names, addresses, and securities positions of non-objecting beneficial owners.

Note 2: If a broker or dealer receives a registrant's request less than five business days before the requested compilation date, it must provide a list compiled as of a date that is no more than five business days after receipt and transmit the list within five business days after the compilation date.

(c) *Exceptions to dissemination and beneficial owner information requirements.* A broker or dealer registered under Section 15 of the Act shall be subject to the following with respect to its dissemination and beneficial owner information requirements.

(1) With regard to beneficial owners of exempt employee benefit plan securities, the broker or dealer shall:

(i) Not include information in its response pursuant to paragraph (b)(1) of this section or forward proxies (or in lieu thereof requests for voting instructions), proxy soliciting material, information statements, or annual reports to security holders pursuant to paragraph (b)(2) of this section to such beneficial owners; and

(ii) Not include in its response, pursuant to paragraph (b)(3) of this section, data concerning such beneficial owners.

(2) A broker or dealer need not satisfy:

(i) Its obligations under paragraphs (b)(2) and (b)(3) of this section if a registrant does not provide assurance of reimbursement of the broker's or dealer's reasonable expenses, both direct and indirect, incurred in connection with performing the obligations imposed by paragraphs (b)(2) and (b)(3) of this section; or

(ii) Its obligation under paragraph (b)(2) of this section to forward annual reports to non-objecting beneficial owners identified by the broker or dealer, through its agent or directly, pursuant to paragraph (b)(3) of this section if the registrant notifies the broker or dealer pursuant to Rule 14a–13(c) or Rule 14c–7(c) that the registrant will mail the annual report to such non-objecting beneficial owners identified by the broker or dealer and delivered in a list to the registrant pursuant to paragraph (b)(3) of this section.

(3) In its response pursuant to paragraph (b)(1) of this section, a broker or dealer shall not include information about annual reports, proxy statements or information statements that will not be delivered to security holders sharing an address because of the broker or dealer's reliance on the procedures referred to in the Note to paragraph (b)(2) of this section.

* * *

Rule 14b–2. Obligation of Banks, Associations and Other Entities That Exercise Fiduciary Powers in Connection With the Prompt Forwarding of Certain Communications to Beneficial Owners

(a) *Definitions.* Unless the context otherwise requires, all terms used in this section shall have the same meanings as in the Act and, with respect to proxy soliciting material, as in Rule 14a–1 thereunder and, with respect to information statements, as in Rule 14c–1 thereunder. In addition, as used in this section, the following terms shall apply:

(1) The term "bank" means a bank, association, or other entity that exercises fiduciary powers.

(2) The term "beneficial owner" includes any person who has or shares, pursuant to an instrument, agreement, or otherwise, the power to vote, or to direct the voting of a security.

Note 1: If more than one person shares voting power, the provisions of the instrument creating that voting power shall govern with respect to whether consent to disclosure of beneficial owner information has been given.

Note 2: If more than one person shares voting power or if the instrument creating that voting power provides that such power shall be exercised by different persons depending on the nature of the corporate action involved, all persons entitled to exercise such power shall be deemed beneficial owners; *Provided, however,* that only one such beneficial owner need be designated among the beneficial owners to receive proxies or requests for voting instructions, other proxy soliciting material, information statements, and/or annual reports to security holders, if the person so designated assumes the obligation to disseminate, in a timely manner, such materials to the other beneficial owners.

(3) The term "registrant" means:

(i) The issuer of a class of securities registered pursuant to Section 12 of the Act; or

(ii) An investment company registered under the Investment Company Act of 1940.

(b) *Dissemination and beneficial owner information requirements.* A bank shall comply with the following requirements for disseminating certain communications to beneficial owners and providing beneficial owner information to registrants.

(1) The bank shall:

(i) Respond, by first class mail or other equally prompt means, directly to the registrant, no later than one business day after the date it receives an inquiry made in accordance with Rule 14a–13(a) or Rule 14c–7(a) by indicating the name and address of each of its respondent banks that holds the registrant's securities on behalf of beneficial owners, if any; and

(ii) Respond, by first class mail or other equally prompt means, directly to the registrant no later than seven business days after the date it receives an inquiry made in accordance with Rule 14a–13(a) or Rule 14c–7(a) by indicating, by means of a search card or otherwise:

(A) The approximate number of customers of the bank who are beneficial owners of the registrant's securities that are held of record by the bank or its nominee;

(B) If the registrant has indicated, pursuant to Rule 14a–13(a)(1)(ii)(A) or Rule 14c–7(a)(1)(ii)(A), that it will distribute the annual report to security holders to beneficial owners of its securities whose names, addresses, and securities positions are disclosed pursuant to paragraphs (b)(4)(ii) and (iii) of this section:

(1) With respect to customer accounts opened on or before December 28, 1986, the number of beneficial owners of the registrant's securities who have affirmatively consented to disclosure of their names, addresses, and securities positions; and

(2) With respect to customer accounts opened after December 28, 1986, the number of beneficial owners of the registrant's securities who have not objected to disclosure of their names, addresses, and securities positions; and

(C) The identity of its designated agent, if any, acting on its behalf in fulfilling its obligations under paragraphs (b)(4)(ii) and (iii) of this section;

Provided, however, that, if the bank or respondent bank has informed the registrant that a designated office(s) or department(s) is to receive such inquiries, receipt for purposes of paragraphs (b)(1)(i) and (ii) of this section shall mean receipt by such designated office(s) or department(s).

(2) Where proxies are solicited, the bank shall, within five business days after the record date:

(i) Execute an omnibus proxy, including a power of substitution, in favor of its respondent banks and forward such proxy to the registrant; and

(ii) Furnish a notice to each respondent bank in whose favor an omnibus proxy has been executed that it has executed such a proxy, including a power of substitution, in its favor pursuant to paragraph (b)(2)(i) of this section.

(3) Upon receipt of the proxy, other proxy soliciting material, information statement, and/or annual reports to security holders, the bank shall forward such materials to each beneficial owner on whose behalf it holds securities, no later than five business days after the date it receives such material and, where a proxy is solicited, the bank shall forward, with the other proxy soliciting material and/or the annual report, either:

(i) A properly executed proxy:

(A) indicating the number of securities held for such beneficial owner;

(B) bearing the beneficial owner's account number or other form of identification, together with instructions as to the procedures to vote the securities;

(C) briefly stating which other proxies, if any, are required to permit securities to be voted under the terms of the instrument creating that voting power or applicable state law; and

(D) being accompanied by an envelope addressed to the registrant or its agent, if not provided by the registrant; or

(ii) A request for voting instructions (for which registrant's form of proxy may be used and which shall be voted by the record holder bank or respondent bank in accordance with the instructions received), together with an envelope addressed to the record holder bank or respondent bank.

Note to paragraph (b)(3):

At the request of a registrant, or on its own initiative so long as the registrant does not object, a bank may, but is not required to, deliver one annual report, proxy statement or information statement to more than one beneficial owner sharing an address if the requirements set forth in Rule 14a–3(e)(1) (with respect to annual reports and proxy statements) and Rule 14c–3(c) (with respect to annual reports and information statements) applicable to registrants, with the exception of Rule 14a–3(e)(1)(i)(E), are satisfied instead by the bank.

(4) The bank shall:

(i) Respond, by first class mail or other equally prompt means, directly to the registrant no later than one business day after the date it receives an inquiry made in accordance with Rule 14a–13(b)(1) or Rule 14c–7(b)(1) by indicating the name and address of each of its respondent banks that holds the registrant's securities on behalf of beneficial owners, if any;

(ii) Through its agent or directly, provide the registrant, upon the registrant's request, and within the time specified in paragraph (b)(4)(iii) of this section, with the names, addresses, and securities position, compiled as of a date specified in the registrant's request which is no earlier than five business days after the date the registrant's request is received, of:

(A) With respect to customer accounts opened on or before December 28, 1986, beneficial owners of the registrant's securities on whose behalf it holds securities who have consented affirmatively to disclosure of such information, subject to paragraph (b)(5) of this section; and

(B) With respect to customer accounts opened after December 28, 1986, beneficial owners of the registrant's securities on whose behalf it holds securities who have not objected to disclosure of such information;

Provided, however, that if the record holder bank or respondent bank has informed the registrant that a designated office(s) or department(s) is to receive such requests, receipt for purposes of paragraphs (b)(4)(i) and (ii) of this section shall mean receipt by such designated office(s) or department(s); and

(iii) Through its agent or directly, transmit the data specified in paragraph (b)(4)(ii) of this section to the registrant no later than five business days after the date specified by the registrant.

Note 1: Where a record holder bank or respondent bank employs a designated agent to act on its behalf in performing the obligations imposed on it by paragraphs (b)(4)(ii) and (iii) of this section, the five business day time period for determining the date as of which the beneficial owner information is to be compiled is calculated from the date the designated agent receives the registrant's request. In complying with the registrant's request for beneficial owner information under paragraphs (b)(4)(ii) and (iii) of this section, a record holder bank or respondent bank need only supply the registrant with the names, addresses and securities positions of affirmatively consenting and non-objecting beneficial owners.

Note 2: If a record holder bank or respondent bank receives a registrant's request less than five business days before the requested compilation date, it must provide a list compiled as of a date that is no more than five business days after receipt and transmit the list within five business days after the compilation date.

(5) For customer accounts opened on or before December 28, 1986, unless the bank has made a good faith effort to obtain affirmative consent to disclosure of beneficial owner information pursuant to paragraph (b)(4)(ii) of this section, the bank shall provide such information as to beneficial owners who do not object to disclosure of such information. A good faith effort to obtain affirmative consent to disclosure of beneficial owner information shall include, but shall not be limited to, making an inquiry:

(i) Phrased in neutral language, explaining the purpose of the disclosure and the limitations on the registrant's use thereof;

(ii) Either in at least one mailing separate from other account mailings or in repeated mailings; and

(iii) In a mailing that includes a return card, postage paid enclosure.

(c) *Exceptions to dissemination and beneficial owner information requirements.* The bank shall be subject to the following with respect to its dissemination and beneficial owner requirements.

(1) With regard to beneficial owners of exempt employee benefit plan securities, the bank shall not:

(i) Include information in its response pursuant to paragraph (b)(1) of this section; or forward proxies (or in lieu thereof requests for voting instructions), proxy soliciting material, information statements, or annual reports to security holders pursuant to paragraph (b)(3) of this section to such beneficial owners; or

(ii) Include in its response pursuant to paragraphs (b)(4) and (b)(5) of this section data concerning such beneficial owners.

(2) The bank need not satisfy:

(i) Its obligations under paragraphs (b)(2), (b)(3), and (b)(4) of this section if a registrant does not provide assurance of reimbursement of its reasonable expenses, both direct and indirect, incurred in connection with performing the obligations imposed by paragraphs (b)(2), (b)(3), and (b)(4) of this section; or

(ii) Its obligation under paragraph (b)(3) of this section to forward annual reports to consenting and non-objecting beneficial owners identified pursuant to paragraphs (b)(4)(ii) and (iii) of this section if the registrant notifies the record holder bank or respondent bank, pursuant to Rule 14a–13(c) or Rule 14c–7(c), that the registrant will mail the annual report to beneficial owners whose names, addresses and securities positions are disclosed pursuant to paragraphs (b)(4)(ii) and (iii) of this section.

(3) For the purposes of determining the fees which may be charged to registrants pursuant to Rule 14a–13(b)(5), Rule 14c–7(a)(5), and paragraph (c)(2) of this section for performing obligations under paragraphs (b)(2), (b)(3), and (b)(4) of this section: an amount no greater than that permitted to be charged by brokers or dealers for reimbursement of their reasonable expenses, both direct and indirect, incurred in connection with performing the obligations imposed by paragraphs (b)(2) and (b)(3) of Rule 14b–1, shall be deemed to be reasonable.

(4) In its response pursuant to paragraph (b)(1)(ii)(A) of this section, a bank shall not include information about annual reports, proxy statements or information statements that will not be delivered to security holders sharing an address because of the bank's reliance on the procedures referred to in the Note to paragraph (b)(3) of this section.

TENDER OFFERS

Rule 14d–1. Scope of and Definitions Applicable to Regulations 14D and 14E

(a) *Scope.* Regulation 14D (Rules 14d–1 through 14d–101) shall apply to any tender offer which is subject to section 14(d)(1) of the Act, including, but not limited to, any tender offer for securities of a class described in that section which is made by an affiliate of the issuer of such class. Regulation 14E (Rules 14e–1 and 14e–2) shall apply to a tender offer for securities (other than exempted securities) unless otherwise noted therein.

* * *

(g) *Definitions.* Unless the context otherwise requires, all terms used in Regulation 14D and Regulation 14E have the same meaning as in the Act and in Rule 12b–2 promulgated thereunder. In addition, for purposes of sections 14(d) and 14(e) of the Act and Regulations 14D and 14E, the following definitions apply:

(1) The term beneficial owner shall have the same meaning as that set forth in Rule 13d–3: Provided, however, That, except with respect to Rule 14d–3 and Rule 14d–9(d), the term shall not include a person who does not have or share investment power or who is deemed to be a beneficial owner by virtue of Rule 13d–3(d)(1)(§ 240.13d–3(d)(1));

(2) The term "bidder" means any person who makes a tender offer or on whose behalf a tender offer is made: *Provided, however,* That the term does not include an issuer which makes a tender offer for securities of any class of which it is the issuer;

(3) The term "business day" means any day, other than Saturday, Sunday or a federal holiday, and shall consist of the time period from 12:01 a.m. through 12:00 midnight Eastern time. In computing any time period under section 14(d)(5) of section 14(d)(6) of the Act or under Regulation 14D or Regulation 14E, the date of the event which begins the running of such time period shall be included *except that* if such event occurs on other than a business day such period shall begin to run on and shall include the first business day thereafter; and

(4) The term initial offering period means the period from the time the offer commences until all minimum time periods, including extensions, required by Regulations 14D (§§ 240.14d–1 through 240.14d–103) and 14E (§§ 240.14e–1 through 240.14e–8) have been satisfied and all conditions to the offer have been satisfied or waived within these time periods.

(5) The term "security holders" means holders of record and beneficial owners of securities which are the subject of a tender offer;

(6) The term "security position listing" means, with respect to securities of any issuer held by a registered clearing agency in the name of the clearing agency or its nominee, a list of those participants in the clearing agency on whose behalf the clearing agency holds the issuer's securities and of the participants' respective positions in such securities as of a specified date.

(7) The term subject company means any issuer of securities which are sought by a bidder pursuant to a tender offer;

(8) The term subsequent offering period means the period immediately following the initial offering period meeting the conditions specified in Rule 14d–11.

(9) The term "tender offer material" means:

(i) The bidder's formal offer, including all the material terms and conditions of the tender offer and all amendments thereto;

(ii) The related transmittal letter (whereby securities of the subject company which are sought in the tender offer may be transmitted to the bidder or its depositary) and all amendments thereto; and

(iii) Press releases, advertisements, letters and other documents published by the bidder or sent or given by the bidder to security holders which, directly or indirectly, solicit, invite or request tenders of the securities being sought in the tender offer;

(h) *Signatures*. Where the Act or the rules thereunder, including paragraphs (a) and (c) of this section, require a document filed with or furnished to the Commission to be signed, such document shall be manually signed, or signed using either typed signatures or duplicated or facsimile versions of manual signatures. Where typed, duplicated or facsimile signatures are used, each signatory to the filing shall manually sign a signature page or other document authenticating, acknowledging or otherwise adopting his or her signature that appears in the filing. Such document shall be executed before or at the time the filing is made and shall be retained by the registrant for a period of five years. Upon request, the registrant shall furnish to the Commission or its staff a copy of any or all documents retained pursuant to this section.

Rule 14d-2. Date of Commencement of a Tender Offer

(a) Date of commencement. A bidder will have commenced its tender offer for purposes of section 14(d) of the Act (*15 U.S.C. 78n*) and the rules under that section at 12:01 a.m. on the date when the bidder has first published, sent or given the means to tender to security holders. For purposes of this section, the means to tender includes the transmittal form or a statement regarding how the transmittal form may be obtained.

(b) Pre-commencement communications. A communication by the bidder will not be deemed to constitute commencement of a tender offer if:

(1) It does not include the means for security holders to tender their shares into the offer; and

(2) All written communications relating to the tender offer, from and including the first public announcement, are filed under cover of Schedule TO (§ 240.14d-100) with the Commission no later than the date of the communication. The bidder also must deliver to the subject company and any other bidder for the same class of securities the first communication relating to the transaction that is filed, or required to be filed, with the Commission.

Instructions to paragraph (b)(2)

1. The box on the front of Schedule TO indicating that the filing contains pre-commencement communications must be checked.

2. Any communications made in connection with an exchange offer registered under the Securities Act of 1933 need only be filed under § 230.425 of this chapter and will be deemed filed under this section.

3. Each pre-commencement written communication must include a prominent legend in clear, plain language advising security holders to read the tender offer statement when it is available because it contains important information. The legend also must advise investors that they can get the tender offer statement and other filed documents for free at the Commission's web site and explain which documents are free from the offeror.

4. See §§ 230.135, 230.165 and 230.166 of this chapter for pre-commencement communications made in connection with registered exchange offers.

5. "Public announcement" is any oral or written communication by the bidder, or any person authorized to act on the bidder's behalf, that is reasonably designed to, or has the effect of, informing the public or security holders in general about the tender offer.

(c) Filing and other obligations triggered by commencement. As soon as practicable on the date of commencement, a bidder must comply with the filing requirements of Rule 14d-3(a), the dissemination requirements of Rule 14d-4(a) or (b), and the disclosure requirements of Rule 14d-6(a).

Rule 14d-3. Filing and Transmission of Tender Offer Statement

(a) *Filing and transmittal.* No bidder shall make a tender offer if, after consummation thereof, such bidder would be the beneficial owner of more than 5 percent of the class of the subject company's securities for which the tender offer is made, unless as soon as practicable on the date of the commencement of the tender offer such bidder:

(1) Files with the Commission a Tender Offer Statement on Schedule TO, including all exhibits thereto;

(2) Hand delivers a copy of such Schedule TO, including all exhibits thereto:

(i) To the subject company at its principal executive office; and

(ii) To any other bidder, which has filed a Schedule TO with the Commission relating to a tender offer which has not yet terminated for the same class of securities of the subject company, at such bidder's principal executive office or at the address of the person authorized to receive notices and communications (which is disclosed on the cover sheet of such other bidder's Schedule TO);

(3) Gives telephonic notice of the information required by Rule 14d–6(e)(2)(i) and (ii) and mails by means of first class mail a copy of such Schedule TO, including all exhibits thereto:

(i) To each national securities exchange where such class of the subject company's securities is registered and listed for trading (which may be based upon information contained in the subject company's most recent Annual Report on Form 10–K and Form 10–KSB filed with the Commission unless the bidder has reason to believe that such information is not current) which telephonic notice shall be made when practicable prior to the opening of each such exchange; and

(ii) To the National Association of Securities Dealers, Inc. ("NASD") if such class of the subject company's securities is authorized for quotation in the NASDAQ interdealer quotation system.

(b) *Post-commencement amendments and additional materials.* The bidder making the tender offer must file with Commission:

(1) An amendment to Schedule TO (§ 240.14d–100) reporting promptly any material changes in the information set forth in the schedule previously filed and including copies of any additional tender offer materials as exhibits; and

(2) A final amendment to Schedule TO (§ 240.14d–100) reporting promptly the results of the tender offer.

Instruction to paragraph (b): A copy of any additional tender offer materials or amendment filed under this section must be sent promptly to the subject company and to any exchange and/or NASD, as required by paragraph (a) of this section, but in no event later than the date the materials are first published, sent or given to security holders.

(c) *Certain announcements.* Notwithstanding the provisions of paragraph (b) of this section, if the additional tender offer material or an amendment to Schedule 14D–1 discloses only the number of shares deposited to date, and/or announces an extension of the time during which shares may be tendered, then the bidder may file such tender offer material or amendment and send a copy of such tender offer material or amendment to the subject company, any exchange and/or the NASD, as required by paragraph (a) of this section, promptly after the date such tender offer material is first published or sent or given to security holders.

Rule 14d–4. Dissemination of Certain Tender Offers

As soon as practicable on the date of commencement of a tender offer, the bidder must publish, send or give the disclosure required by Rule 14d–6 to security holders of the class of securities that is the subject of the offer, by complying with all of the requirements of any of the following:

(a) Cash tender offers and exempt securities offers. For tender offers in which the consideration consists solely of cash and/or securities exempt from registration under section 3 of the Securities Act of 1933:

(1) *Long-form publication.* The bidder makes adequate publication in a newspaper or newspapers of long-form publication of the tender offer.

(2) *Summary publication.* (i) If the tender offer is not subject to Rule 13e–3, the bidder makes adequate publication in a newspaper or newspapers of a summary advertisement of the tender offer; and

(ii) Mails by first class mail or otherwise furnishes with reasonable promptness the bidder's tender offer materials to any security holder who requests such tender offer materials pursuant to the summary advertisement or otherwise.

(3) *Use of stockholder lists and security position listings.* Any bidder using stockholder lists and se-

curity position listings pursuant to Rule 14d–5 shall comply with paragraphs (a)(1) or (a)(2) of this section on or prior to the date of the bidder's request for such lists or listing pursuant to Rule 14d–5(a).

(b) Registered securities offers. For tender offers in which the consideration consists solely or partially of securities registered under the Securities Act of 1933, a registration statement containing all of the required information, including pricing information, has been filed and a preliminary prospectus or a prospectus that meets the requirements of section 10(a) of the Securities Act, including a letter of transmittal, is delivered to security holders. However, for going-private transactions (as defined by § 240.13e–3) and roll-up transactions (as described by Item 901 of Regulation S–K), a registration statement registering the securities to be offered must have become effective and only a prospectus that meets the requirements of section 10(a) of the Securities Act may be delivered to security holders on the date of commencement.

Instructions to paragraph (b)

1. If the prospectus is being delivered by mail, mailing on the date of commencement is sufficient.

2. A preliminary prospectus used under this section may not omit information under § 230.430 or § 230.430A of this chapter.

3. If a preliminary prospectus is used under this section and the bidder must disseminate material changes, the tender offer must remain open for the period specified in paragraph (d)(2) of this section.

4. If a preliminary prospectus is used under this section, tenders may be requested in accordance with § 230.162(a) of this chapter.

(c) *Adequate publication.* Depending on the facts and circumstances involved, adequate publication of a tender offer pursuant to this section may require publication in a newspaper with a national circulation or may only require publication in a newspaper with metropolitan or regional circulation or may require publication in a combination thereof: *Provided, however,* That publication in all editions of a daily newspaper with a national circulation shall be deemed to constitute adequate publication.

(d) *Publication of changes.* (1) If a tender offer has been published or sent or given to security holders by one or more of the methods enumerated in this section, a material change in the information published or sent or given to security holders shall be promptly disseminated to security holders in a manner reasonably designed to inform security holders of such change; *Provided, however,* That if the bidder has elected pursuant to Rule 14d–5(f)(1) of this section to require the subject company to disseminate amendments disclosing material changes to the tender offer materials pursuant to Rule 14d–5, the bidder shall disseminate material changes in the information published or sent or given to security holders at least pursuant to Rule 14d–5.

(2) In a registered securities offer where the bidder disseminates the preliminary prospectus as permitted by paragraph (b) of this section, the offer must remain open from the date that material changes to the tender offer materials are disseminated to security holders, as follows:

(i) Five business days for a prospectus supplement containing a material change other than price or share levels;

(ii) Ten business days for a prospectus supplement containing a change in price, the amount of securities sought, the dealer's soliciting fee, or other similarly significant change;

(iii) Ten business days for a prospectus supplement included as part of a post-effective amendment; and

(iv) Twenty business days for a revised prospectus when the initial prospectus was materially deficient.

Rule 14d–5. Dissemination of Certain Tender Offers by the Use of Stockholder Lists and Security Position Listings

(a) *Obligations of the subject company.* Upon receipt by a subject company at its principal executive offices of a bidder's written request, meeting the requirements of paragraph (e) of this section, the subject company shall comply with the following sub-paragraphs.

(1) The subject company shall notify promptly transfer agents and any other person who will assist the subject company in complying with the requirements of this section of the receipt by the subject

company of a request by a bidder pursuant to this section.

(2) The subject company shall promptly ascertain whether the most recently prepared stockholder list, written or otherwise, within the access of the subject company was prepared as of a date earlier than ten business days before the date of the bidder's request and, if so, the subject company shall promptly prepare or cause to be prepared a stockholder list as of the most recent practicable date which shall not be more than ten business days before the date of the bidder's request.

(3) The subject company shall make an election to comply and shall comply with all of the provisions of either paragraph (b) or paragraph (c) of this section. The subject company's election once made shall not be modified or revoked during the bidder's tender offer and extensions thereof.

(4) No later than the second business day after the date of the bidder's request, the subject company shall orally notify the bidder, which notification shall be confirmed in writing, of the subject company's election made pursuant to paragraph (a)(3) of this section. Such notification shall indicate (i) the approximate number of security holders of the class of securities being sought by the bidder and, (ii) if the subject company elects to comply with paragraph (b) of this section, appropriate information concerning the location for delivery of the bidder's tender offer materials and the approximate direct costs incidental to the mailing to security holders of the bidder's tender offer materials computed in accordance with paragraph (g)(2) of this section.

(b) *Mailing of tender offer materials by the subject company.* A subject company which elects pursuant to paragraph (a)(3) of this section to comply with the provisions of this paragraph shall perform the acts prescribed by the following subparagraphs.

(1) The subject company shall promptly contact each participant named on the most recent security position listing of any clearing agency within the access of the subject company and make inquiry of each such participant as to the approximate number of beneficial owners of the subject company securities being sought in the tender offer held by each such participant.

(2) No later than the third business day after delivery of the bidder's tender offer materials pursuant to paragraph (g)(1) of this section, the subject company shall begin to mail or cause to be mailed by means of first class mail a copy of the bidder's tender offer materials to each person whose name appears as a record holder of the class of securities for which the offer is made on the most recent stockholder list referred to in paragraph (a)(2) of this section. The subject company shall use its best efforts to complete the mailing in a timely manner but in no event shall such mailing be completed in a substantially greater period of time than the subject company would complete a mailing to security holders of its own materials relating to the tender offer.

(3) No later than the third business day after the delivery of the bidder's tender offer materials pursuant to paragraph (g)(1) of this section, the subject company shall begin to transmit or cause to be transmitted a sufficient number of sets of the bidder's tender offer materials to the participants named on the security position listings described in paragraph (b)(1) of this section. The subject company shall use its best efforts to complete the transmittal in a timely manner, but in no event shall such transmittal be completed in a substantially greater period of time than the subject company would complete a transmittal to such participants pursuant to security position listings of clearing agencies of its own material relating to the tender offer.

(4) The subject company shall promptly give oral notification to the bidder, which notification shall be confirmed in writing, of the commencement of the mailing pursuant to paragraph (b)(2) of this section and of the transmittal pursuant to paragraph (b)(3) of this section.

(5) During the tender offer and any extension thereof the subject company shall use reasonable efforts to update the stockholder list and shall mail or cause to be mailed promptly following each update a copy of the bidder's tender offer materials (to the extent sufficient sets of such materials have been furnished by the bidder) to each person who has become a record holder since the later of (i) the date of preparation of the most recent stockholder list referred to in paragraph (a)(2) of this section or (ii) the last preceding update.

(6) If the bidder has elected pursuant to paragraph (f)(1) of this section to require the subject company to disseminate amendments disclosing material changes to the tender offer materials pursu-

ant to this section, the subject company, promptly following delivery of each such amendment, shall mail or cause to be mailed a copy of each such amendment to each record holder whose name appears on the shareholder list described in paragraphs (a)(2) and (b)(5) of this section and shall transmit or cause to be transmitted sufficient copies of such amendment to each participant named on security position listings who received sets of the bidder's tender offer materials pursuant to paragraph (b)(3) of this section.

(7) The subject company shall not include any communication other than the bidder's tender offer materials or amendments thereto in the envelopes or other containers furnished by the bidder.

(8) Promptly following the termination of the tender offer, the subject company shall reimburse the bidder the excess, if any, of the amounts advanced pursuant to paragraph (f)(3)(iii) over the direct cost incidental to compliance by the subject company and its agents in performing the acts required by this section computed in accordance with paragraph (g)(2) of this section.

(c) *Delivery of stockholder lists and security position listings.* A subject company which elects pursuant to paragraph (a)(3) of this section to comply with the provisions of this paragraph shall perform the acts prescribed by the following subparagraphs.

(1) No later than the third business day after the date of the bidder's request, the subject company shall furnish to the bidder at the subject company's principal executive office a copy of the names and addresses of the record holders on the most recent stockholder list referred to in paragraph (a)(2) of this section; the names and addresses of participants identified on the most recent security position listing of any clearing agency that is within the access of the subject company; and the most recent list of names, addresses and security positions of beneficial owners as specified in Rule 14a–13(b), in the possession of the subject company, or that subsequently comes into its possession. All security holder list information must be in the format requested by the bidder to the extent the format is available to the subject company without undue burden or expense.

(2) If the bidder has elected pursuant to paragraph (f)(1) of this section to require the subject company to disseminate amendments disclosing material changes to the tender offer materials, the subject company shall update the stockholder list by furnishing the bidder with the name and address of each record holder named on the stockholder list, and not previously furnished to the bidder, promptly after such information becomes available to the subject company during the tender offer and any extensions thereof.

(d) *Liability of subject company and others.* Neither the subject company nor any affiliate or agent of the subject company nor any clearing agency shall be:

(1) Deemed to have made a solicitation or recommendation respecting the tender offer within the meaning of section 14(d)(4) based solely upon the compliance or noncompliance by the subject company or any affiliate or agent of the subject company with one or more requirements of this section;

(2) Liable under any provision of the Federal securities laws to the bidder or to any security holder based solely upon the inaccuracy of the current names or addresses on the stockholder list or security position listing, unless such inaccuracy results from a lack of reasonable care on the part of the subject company or any affiliate or agent of the subject company;

(3) Deemed to be an "underwriter" within the meaning of section (2)(11) of the Securities Act of 1933 for any purpose of that Act or any rule or regulation promulgated thereunder based solely upon the compliance or noncompliance by the subject company or any affiliate or agent of the subject company with one or more of the requirements of this section;

(4) Liable under any provision of the Federal securities laws for the disclosure in the bidder's tender offer materials, including any amendment thereto, based solely upon the compliance or noncompliance by the subject company or any affiliate or agent of the subject company with one or more of the requirements of this section.

(e) *Content of the bidder's request.* The bidder's written request referred to in paragraph (a) of this section shall include the following:

(1) The identity of the bidder;

(2) The title of the class of securities which is the subject of the bidder's tender offer;

(3) A statement that the bidder is making a request to the subject company pursuant to paragraph (a) of this section for the use of the stockholder list and security position listings for the purpose of disseminating a tender offer to security holders;

(4) A statement that the bidder is aware of and will comply with the provisions of paragraph (f) of this section;

(5) A statement as to whether or not it has elected pursuant to paragraph (f)(1) of this section to disseminate amendments disclosing material changes to the tender offer materials pursuant to this section; and

(6) The name, address and telephone number of the person whom the subject company shall contact pursuant to paragraph (a)(4) of this section.

(f) *Obligations of the bidder.* Any bidder who requests that a subject company comply with the provisions of paragraph (a) of this section shall comply with the following subparagraphs:

(1) The bidder shall make an election whether or not to require the subject company to disseminate amendments disclosing material changes to the tender offer materials pursuant to this section, which election shall be included in the request referred to in paragraph (a) of this section and shall not be revocable by the bidder during the tender offer and extensions thereof.

(2) With respect to a tender offer subject to section 14(d)(1) of the Act in which the consideration consists solely of cash and/or securities exempt from registration under section 3 of the Securities Act of 1933, the bidder shall comply with the requirements of Rule 14d–4(a)(3).

(3) If the subject company elects to comply with paragraph (b) of this section,

(i) The bidder shall promptly deliver the tender offer materials after receipt of the notification from the subject company as provided in paragraph (a)(4) of this section;

(ii) The bidder shall promptly notify the subject company of any amendment to the bidder's tender offer materials requiring compliance by the subject company with paragraph (b)(6) of this section and shall promptly deliver such amendment to the subject company pursuant to paragraph (g)(1) of this section;

(iii) The bidder shall advance to the subject company an amount equal to the approximate cost of conducting mailings to security holders computed in accordance with paragraph (g)(2) of this section;

(iv) The bidder shall promptly reimburse the subject company for the direct costs incidental to compliance by the subject company and its agents in performing the acts required by this section computed in accordance with paragraph (g)(2) of this section which are in excess of the amount advanced pursuant to paragraph (f)(2)(iii) of this section; and

(v) The bidder shall mail by means of first class mail or otherwise furnish with reasonable promptness the tender offer materials to any security holder who requests such materials.

(4) If the subject company elects to comply with paragraph (c) of this section,

(i) The subject company shall use the stockholder list and security position listings furnished to the bidder pursuant to paragraph (c) of this section exclusively in the dissemination of tender offer materials to security holders in connection with the bidder's tender offer and extensions thereof;

(ii) The bidder shall return the stockholder lists and security position listings furnished to the bidder pursuant to paragraph (c) of this section promptly after the termination of the bidder's tender offer;

(iii) The bidder shall accept, handle and return the stockholder lists and security position listings furnished to the bidder pursuant to paragraph (c) of this section to the subject company on a confidential basis;

(iv) The bidder shall not retain any stockholder list or security position listing furnished by the subject company pursuant to paragraph (c) of this section, or any copy thereof, nor retain any information derived from any such list or listing or copy thereof after the termination of the bidder's tender offer;

(v) The bidder shall mail by means of first class mail, at its own expense, a copy of its tender offer materials to each person whose identity appears on the stockholder list as furnished and updated by the subject company pursuant to paragraphs (c)(1) and (c)(2) of this section;

(vi) The bidder shall contact the participants named on the security position listing of any clearing agency, make inquiry of each participant as to the approximate number of sets of tender offer materials required by each such participant, and furnish, at its own expense, sufficient sets of tender offer materials and any amendment thereto to each such participant for subsequent transmission to the beneficial owners of the securities being sought by the bidder;

(vii) The bidder shall mail by means of first class mail or otherwise furnish with reasonable promptness the tender offer materials to any security holder who requests such materials; and

(viii) The bidder shall promptly reimburse the subject company for direct costs incidental to compliance by the subject company and its agents in performing the acts required by this section computed in accordance with paragraph (g)(2) of this section.

(g) *Delivery of materials, computation of direct costs.*

(1) Whenever the bidder is required to deliver tender offer materials or amendments to tender offer materials, the bidder shall deliver to the subject company at the location specified by the subject company in its notice given pursuant to paragraph (a)(4) of this section a number of sets of the materials or of the amendment, as the case may be, at least equal to the approximate number of security holders specified by the subject company in such notice, together with appropriate envelopes or other containers therefor: *Provided, however,* That such delivery shall be deemed not to have been made unless the bidder has complied with paragraph (f)(3)(iii) of this section at the time the materials or amendments, as the case may be, are delivered.

(2) The approximate direct cost of mailing the bidder's tender offer materials shall be computed by adding (i) the direct cost incidental to the mailing of the subject company's last annual report to shareholders (excluding employee time), less the costs of preparation and printing of the report, and postage, plus (ii) the amount of first class postage required to mail the bidder's tender offer materials. The approximate direct costs incidental to the mailing of the amendments to the bidder's tender offer materials shall be computed by adding (iii) the estimated direct costs of preparing mailing labels, of updating shareholder lists and of third party handling charges plus (iv) the amount of first class postage required to mail the bidder's amendment. Direct costs incidental to the mailing of the bidder's tender offer materials and amendments thereto when finally computed may include all reasonable charges paid by the subject company to third parties for supplies or services, including costs attendant to preparing shareholder lists, mailing labels, handling the bidder's materials, contacting participants named on security position listings and for postage, but shall exclude indirect costs, such as employee time which is devoted to either contesting or supporting the tender offer on behalf of the subject company. The final billing for direct costs shall be accompanied by an appropriate accounting in reasonable detail.

Note to Rule 14d–5. Reasonably prompt methods of distribution to security holders may be used instead of mailing. If alternative methods are chosen, the approximate direct costs of distribution shall be computed by adding the estimated direct costs of preparing the document for distribution through the chosen medium (including updating of shareholder lists) plus the estimated reasonable cost of distribution through that medium. Direct costs incidental to the distribution of tender offer materials and amendments thereto may include all reasonable charges paid by the subject company to third parties for supplies or services, including costs attendant to preparing shareholder lists, handling the bidder's materials, and contacting participants named on security position listings, but shall not include indirect costs, such as employee time which is devoted to either contesting or supporting the tender offer on behalf of the subject company.

Rule 14d–6. Disclosure Requirements With Respect to Tender Offers

(a) *Information required on date of commencement.*

(1) *Long-form publication.* If a tender offer is published, sent or given to security holders on the date of commencement by means of long-form publication pursuant to Rule 14d–4(a)(1), such long-form publication shall include the information required by paragraph (d)(1) of this section.

(2) *Summary publication.* If a tender offer is published, sent or given to security holders on the date of commencement by means of summary publication pursuant to Rule 14d–4(a)(2),

(i) The summary advertisement shall contain and shall be limited to, the information required by paragraph (d)(2) of this section; and

(ii) The tender offer materials furnished by the bidder upon the request of any security holder shall include the information required by paragraph (d)(1) of this section.

(3) *Use of stockholder lists and security position listings.* If a tender offer is published or sent or given to security holders on the date of commencement by the use of stockholder lists and security position listings pursuant to Rule 14d–4(a)(3),

(i) The summary advertisement must contain at least the information required by paragraph (d)(2) of this section; and

(ii) The tender offer materials transmitted to security holders pursuant to such lists and security position listings and furnished by the bidder upon the request of any security holder shall include the information required by paragraph (d)(1) of this section.

(4) *Other tender offers.* If a tender offer is published or sent or given to security holders other than pursuant to Rule 14d–4(a), the tender offer materials which are published or sent or given to security holders on the date of commencement of such offer shall include the information required by paragraph (d)(1) of this section.

(b) *Information required in other tender offer materials published after commencement.* Except for tender offer materials described in paragraphs (a)(2)(ii) and (a)(3)(ii) of this section, additional tender offer materials published, sent or given to security holders after commencement must include:

(1) The identities of the bidder and subject company;

(2) The amount and class of securities being sought;

(3) The type and amount of consideration being offered; and

(4) The scheduled expiration date of the tender offer, whether the tender offer may be extended and, if so, the procedures for extension of the tender offer.

Instruction to paragraph (b): If the additional tender offer materials are summary advertisements, they also must include the information required by paragraphs (d)(2)(v) of this section.

(c) *Material changes.* A material change in the information published or sent or given to security holders shall be promptly disclosed to security holders in additional tender offer materials.

(d) *Information to be included.*

(1) Tender offer materials other than summary publication. The following information is required by paragraphs (a)(1), (a)(2)(ii), (a)(3)(ii) and (a)(4) of this section:

(i) The information required by Item 1 of Schedule TO (Summary Term Sheet); and

(ii) The information required by the remaining items of Schedule TO for third-party tender offers, except for Item 12 (exhibits) of Schedule TO, or a fair and adequate summary of the information.

(2) Summary Publication. The following information is required in a summary advertisement under paragraphs (a)(2)(i) and (a)(3)(i) of this section:

(i) The identity of the bidder and the subject company;

(ii) The information required by Item 1004(a)(1) of Regulation M–A;

(iii) If the tender offer is for less than all of the outstanding securities of a class of equity securities, a statement as to whether the purpose or one of the purposes of the tender offer is to acquire or influence control of the business of the subject company;

(iv) A statement that the information required by paragraph (d)(1) of this section is incorporated by reference into the summary advertisement;

(v) Appropriate instructions as to how security holders may obtain promptly, at the bidder's expense, the bidder's tender offer materials; and

(vi) In a tender offer published or sent or given to security holders by use of stockholder lists and security position listings under Rule 14d–4(a)(3), a statement that a request is being made for such lists and listings. The summary publication also must state that tender offer materials will be mailed to record holders and will be furnished to brokers, banks and similar persons whose name appears or whose nominee appears on the list of security holders or, if applicable, who are listed as participants in a clearing agency's security position listing for subsequent transmittal to beneficial owners of such securities. If the list furnished to the bidder also included beneficial owners pursuant to Rule 14d–5(c)(1) and tender offer materials will be mailed directly to beneficial holders, include a statement to that effect.

(3) No transmittal letter. Neither the initial summary advertisement nor any subsequent summary advertisement may include a transmittal letter (the letter furnished to security holders for transmission of securities sought in the tender offer) or any amendment to the transmittal letter.

Rule 14d–7. Additional Withdrawal Rights

(a) *Rights.* (1) In addition to the provisions of Rule 14(d)(5) of the Act, any person who has deposited securities pursuant to a tender offer has the right to withdraw any such securities during the period such offer, request or invitation remains open.

(2) Exemption during subsequent offering period. Notwithstanding the provisions of section 14(d)(5) of the Act (*15 U.S.C. 78n(d)(5)*) and paragraph (a) of this section, the bidder need not offer withdrawal rights during a subsequent offering period.

(b) *Notice of withdrawal.* Notice of withdrawal pursuant to this section shall be deemed to be timely upon the receipt by the bidder's depositary of a written notice of withdrawal specifying the name(s) of the tendering stockholder(s), the number or amount of the securities to be withdrawn and the name(s) in which the certificate(s) is (are) registered, if different from that of the tendering security holder(s). A bidder may impose other reasonable requirements, including certificate numbers and a signed request for withdrawal accompanied by a signature guarantee, as conditions precedent to the physical release of withdrawn securities.

Rule 14d–8. Exemption From Statutory Pro Rata Requirement

Notwithstanding the pro rata provisions of Section 14(d)(6) of the Act, if any person makes a tender offer or request or invitation for tenders, for less than all of the outstanding equity securities of a class, and if a greater number of securities are deposited pursuant thereto than such person is bound or willing to take up and pay for, the securities taken up and paid for shall be taken up and paid for as nearly as may be pro rata, disregarding fractions, according to the number of securities deposited by each depositor during the period such offer, request or invitation remains open.

Rule 14d–9. Solicitation/Recommendation Statements With Respect to Certain Tender Offers

(a) *Pre-commencement communications.* A communication by a person described in paragraph (e) of this section with respect to a tender offer will not be deemed to constitute a recommendation or solicitation under this section if:

(1) The tender offer has not commenced under Rule 14d–2; and

(2) The communication is filed under cover of Schedule 14D–9 with the Commission no later than the date of the communication.

Instructions to paragraph (a)(2):

1. The box on the front of Schedule 14D–9 indicating that the filing contains pre-commencement communications must be checked.

2. Any communications made in connection with an exchange offer registered under the Securities Act of 1933 need only be filed under § 230.425 of this chapter and will be deemed filed under this section.

3. Each pre-commencement written communication must include a prominent legend in clear, plain language advising security holders to read the company's solicitation/recommendation statement when it is available because it contains important information. The legend also must advise investors that they can get the recommendation and other filed documents for free at the Commission's web site and explain which documents are free from the filer.

4. See §§ 230.135, 230.165 and 230.166 of this chapter for pre-commencement communications made in connection with registered exchange offers.

(b) *Post-commencement communications.* After commencement by a bidder under Rule 14d–2, no solicitation or recommendation to security holders may be made by any person described in paragraph (e) of this section with respect to a tender offer for such securities unless as soon as practicable on the date such solicitation or recommendation is first published or sent or given to security holders such person complies with the following:

(1) Such person shall file with the Commission eight copies of a Tender Offer Solicitation/Recommendation Statement on Schedule 14D–9, including all exhibits thereto; and

(2) If such person is either the subject company or an affiliate of the subject company,

(i) Such person shall hand deliver a copy of the Schedule 14D–9 to the bidder at its principal office or at the address of the person authorized to receive notices and communications (which is set forth on the cover sheet of the bidder's Schedule TO) filed with the Commission; and

(ii) Such person shall give telephonic notice (which notice to the extent possible shall be given prior to the opening of the market) of the information required by Items 1003(d) and 1012(a) of Regulation M–A and shall mail a copy of the Schedule to each national securities exchange where the class of securities is registered and listed for trading and, if the class is authorized for quotation in the NASDAQ interdealer quotation system, to the National Association of Securities Dealers, Inc. ("NASD").

(3) If such person is neither the subject company nor an affiliate of the subject company,

(i) Such person shall mail a copy of the schedule to the bidder at its principal office or at the address of the person authorized to receive notices and communications (which is set forth on the cover sheet of the bidder's Schedule TO filed with the Commission); and

(ii) Such person shall mail a copy of the Schedule to the subject company at its principal office.

(c) *Amendments.* If any material change occurs in the information set forth in the Schedule 14D–9 required by this section, the person who filed such Schedule 14D–9 shall:

(1) File with the Commission eight copies of an amendment on Schedule 14D–9 disclosing such change promptly, but not later than the date such material is first published, sent or given to security holders; and

(2) Promptly deliver copies and give notice of the amendment in the same manner as that specified in paragraph (b)(2) or paragraph (b)(3) of this section, whichever is applicable; and

(3) Promptly disclose and disseminate such change in a manner reasonably designed to inform security holders of such change.

(d) *Information required in solicitation or recommendation.* Any solicitation or recommendation to holders of a class of securities referred to in section 14(d)(1) of the Act with respect to a tender offer for such securities shall include the name of the person making such solicitation or recommendation and the information required by Items 1 through 8 of Schedule 14D–9 or a fair and adequate summary thereof: *Provided, however,* That such solicitation or recommendation may omit any of such information previously furnished to security holders of such class of securities by such person with respect to such tender offer.

(e) *Applicability*

(1) Except as is provided in paragraphs (e)(2) and (f) of this section, this section shall only apply to the following persons:

(i) The subject company, any director, officer, employee, affiliate or subsidiary of the subject company;

(ii) Any record holder or beneficial owner of any security issued by the subject company, by the bidder, or by any affiliate of either the subject company or the bidder; and

(iii) Any person who makes a solicitation or recommendation to security holders on behalf of any of the foregoing or on behalf of the bidder other than by means of a solicitation or recommendation to security holders which has been filed with the Commission pursuant to this section or Rule 14d–3.

(2) Notwithstanding paragraph (e)(1) of this section, this section shall not apply to the following persons:

(i) A bidder who has filed a Schedule TO pursuant to Rule 14d–3;

(ii) Attorneys, banks, brokers, fiduciaries or investment advisers who are not participating in a tender offer in more than a ministerial capacity and who furnish information and/or advice regarding such tender offer to their customers or clients on the unsolicited request of such customers or clients or solely pursuant to a contract or a relationship providing for advice to the customer or client to whom the information and/or advice is given.

(iii) Any person specified in paragraph (e)(1) of this section if:

(A) The subject company is the subject of a tender offer conducted under Rule 14d–1(c);

(B) Any person specified in paragraph (e)(1) of this section furnishes to the Commission on Form CB (§ 249.480 of this chapter) the entire informational document it publishes or otherwise disseminates to holders of the class of securities in connection with the tender offer no later than the next business day after publication or dissemination;

(C) Any person specified in paragraph (e)(1) of this section disseminates any informational document to U.S. holders, including any amendments thereto, in English, on a comparable basis to that provided to security holders in the issuer's home jurisdiction; and

(D) Any person specified in paragraph (e)(1) of this section disseminates by publication in its home jurisdiction, such person must publish the information in the United States in a manner reasonably calculated to inform U.S. security holders of the offer.

(f) *Stop-look-and-listen communication.* This section shall not apply to the subject company with respect to a communication by the subject company to its security holders which only:

(1) Identifies the tender offer by the bidder;

(2) States that such tender offer is under consideration by the subject company's board of directors and/or management;

(3) States that on or before a specified date (which shall be no later than 10 business days from the date of commencement of such tender offer) the subject company will advise such security holders of (i) whether the subject company recommends acceptance or rejection of such tender offer; expresses no opinion and remains neutral toward such tender offer; or is unable to take a position with respect to such tender offer and (ii) the reason(s) for the position taken by the subject company with respect to the tender offer (including the inability to take a position); and

(4) Requests such security holders to defer making a determination whether to accept or reject such tender offer until they have been advised of the subject company's position with respect thereto pursuant to paragraph (f)(3) of this section.

(g) *Statement of management's position.* A statement by the subject company of its position with respect to a tender offer which is required to be published or sent or given to security holders pursuant to Rule 14e–2 shall be deemed to constitute a solicitation or recommendation within the meaning of this section and section 14(f)(4) of the Act.

Rule 14d–10. Equal Treatment of Security Holders

(a) No bidder shall make a tender offer unless:

(1) The tender offer is open to all security holders of the class of securities subject to the tender offer; and

(2) The consideration paid to any security holder pursuant to the tender offer is the highest consideration paid to any other security holder during such tender offer.

(b) Paragraph (a)(1) of this section shall not:

(1) Affect dissemination under Rule 14d–4 (§ 240.14d–4); or

(2) Prohibit a bidder from making a tender offer excluding all security holders in a state where the bidder is prohibited from making the tender offer by administrative or judicial action pursuant to a state statute after a good faith effort by the bidder to comply with such statute.

(c) Paragraph (a)(2) of this section shall not prohibit the offer of more than one type of consideration in a tender offer, provided that:

(1) Security holders are afforded equal right to elect among each of the types of consideration offered; and

(2) The highest consideration of each type paid to any security holder is paid to any other security holder receiving that type of consideration.

(d) If the offer and sale of securities constituting consideration offered in a tender offer is prohibited by the appropriate authority of a state after a good faith effort by the bidder to register or qualify the offer and sale of such securities in such state:

(1) The bidder may offer security holders in such state an alternative form of consideration; and

(2) Paragraph (c) of this section shall not operate to require the bidder to offer or pay the alternative form of consideration to security holders in any other state.

(e) This section shall not apply to any tender offer with respect to which the Commission, upon written request or upon its own motion, either unconditionally or on specified terms and conditions, determines that compliance with this section is not necessary or appropriate in the public interest or for the protection of investors.

Rule 14e-1. Unlawful Tender Offer Practices

As a means reasonably designed to prevent fraudulent, deceptive or manipulative acts or practices within the meaning of section 14(e) of the Act, no person who makes a tender offer shall:

(a) Hold such tender offer open for less than twenty business days from the date such tender offer is first published or sent or given to security holders; provided, however, that if the tender offer involves a roll-up transaction as defined in Item 901(c) of Regulation S-K and the securities being offered are registered (or authorized to be registered) on Form S-4 or Form F-4, the offer shall not be open for less than sixty calendar days from the date the tender offer is first published or sent to security holders;

(b) Increase or decrease the percentage of the class of securities being sought or the consideration offered or the dealer's soliciting fee to be given in a tender offer unless such tender remains open for at least ten business days from the date that notice of such increase or decrease is first published or sent or given to security holders:

Provided, however, That, for purposes of this paragraph, the acceptance for payment by the bidder of an additional amount of securities not to exceed two percent of the class of securities that is the subject of the tender offer shall not be deemed to be an increase. For purposes of this paragraph, the percentage of a class of securities shall be calculated in accordance with Rule 14(d)(3) of the Act.

(c) Fail to pay the consideration offered or return the securities deposited by or on behalf of security holders promptly after the termination or withdrawal of a tender offer. This paragraph does not prohibit a bidder electing to offer a subsequent offering period under Rule 14d-11 from paying for securities during the subsequent offering period in accordance with that section.

(d) Extend the length of a tender offer without issuing a notice of such extension by press release or other public announcement, which notice shall include disclosure of the approximate number of securities deposited to date and shall be issued no later than the earlier of (i) 9:00 a.m. Eastern time, on the next business day after the scheduled expiration date of the offer or (ii), if the class of securities which is the subject of the tender offer is registered on one or more national securities exchanges, the first opening of any one of such exchanges on the next business day after the scheduled expiration date of the offer.

(e) The periods of time required by paragraphs (a) and (b) of this section shall be tolled for any period during which the bidder has failed to file in electronic format, absent a hardship exemption (§§ 232.201 and 232.202 of this chapter), the Schedule 14D-1 Tender Offer Statement (§ 240.14d-100 of this chapter), any tender offer material specified in paragraph (a) of Item 11 of that Schedule, and any amendments thereto. If such documents were filed in paper pursuant to a hardship exemption (see § 232.201 and § 232.202(d) of this chapter), the minimum offering periods shall be tolled for any period during which a required confirming electronic copy of such Schedule and tender offer material is delinquent.

Rule 14e-2. Position of Subject Company With Respect to a Tender Offer

(a) *Position of subject company.* As a means reasonably designed to prevent fraudulent, deceptive or manipulative acts or practices within the meaning of section 14(e) of the Act, the subject company, no later than 10 business days from the date the tender offer is first published or sent or given, shall publish, send or give to security holders a statement disclosing that the subject company:

(1) Recommends acceptance or rejection of the bidder's tender offer;

(2) Expresses no opinion and is remaining neutral toward the bidder's tender offer; or

(3) Is unable to take a position with respect to the bidder's tender offer.

(b) *Material change.* If any material change occurs in the disclosure required by paragraph (a) of this section, the subject company shall promptly publish, send or give a statement disclosing such material change to security holders.

* * *

Rule 14e-3. Transactions in Securities on the Basis of Material, Nonpublic Information in the Context of Tender Offers

(a) If any person has taken a substantial step or steps to commence, or has commenced, a tender offer (the "offering person"), it shall constitute a fraudulent, deceptive or manipulative act or practice within the meaning of section 14(e) of the Act for any other person who is in possession of material information relating to such tender offer which information he knows or has reason to know is nonpublic and which he knows or has reason to know has been acquired directly or indirectly from (1) the offering person, (2) the issuer of the securities sought or to be sought by such tender offer, or (3) any officer, director, partner or employee or any other person acting on behalf of the offering person or such issuer, to purchase or sell or cause to be purchased or sold any of such securities or any securities convertible into or exchangeable for any such securities or any option or right to obtain or to dispose of any of the foregoing securities, unless within a reasonable time prior to any purchase or sale such information and its source are publicly disclosed by press release or otherwise.

(b) A person other than a natural person shall not violate paragraph (a) of this section if such person shows that:

(1) The individual(s) making the investment decision on behalf of such person to purchase or sell any security described in paragraph (a) or to cause any such security to be purchased or sold by or on behalf of others did not know the material, nonpublic information; and

(2) Such person had implemented one or a combination of policies and procedures, reasonable under the circumstances, taking into consideration the nature of the person's business, to ensure that individual(s) making investment decision(s) would not violate paragraph (a), which policies and procedures may include, but are not limited to, (i) those which restrict any purchase, sale and causing any purchase and sale of any such security or (ii) those which prevent such individual(s) from knowing such information.

(c) Notwithstanding anything in paragraph (a) to the contrary, the following transactions shall not be violations of paragraph (a) of this section:

(1) Purchase(s) of any security described in paragraph (a) by a broker or by another agent on behalf of an offering person; or

(2) Sale(s) by any person of any security described in paragraph (a) to the offering person.

(d)(1) As a means reasonably designed to prevent fraudulent, deceptive or manipulative acts or practices within the meaning of section 14(e) of the Act, it shall be unlawful for any person described in paragraph (d)(2) of this section to communicate material, nonpublic information relating to a tender offer to any other person under circumstances in which it is reasonably foreseeable that such communication is likely to result in a violation of this section except that this paragraph shall not apply to a communication made in good faith,

(i) To the officers, directors, partners or employees of the offering person, to its advisors or to other persons, involved in the planning, financing, preparation or execution of such tender offer;

(ii) To the issuer whose securities are sought or to be sought by such tender offer, to its officers, directors, partners, employees or advisors or to other persons, involved in the planning, financing, preparation or execution of the activities of the issuer with respect to such tender offer; or

(iii) To any person pursuant to a requirement of any statute or rule or regulation promulgated thereunder.

(2) The persons referred to in paragraph (d)(1) of this section are:

(i) The offering person or its officers, directors, partners, employees or advisors;

(ii) The issuer of the securities sought or to be sought by such tender offer or its officers, directors, partners, employees or advisors;

(iii) Anyone acting on behalf of the persons in paragraph (d)(2)(i) or the issuer or persons in paragraph (d)(2)(ii); and

(iv) Any person in possession of material information relating to a tender offer which information he knows or has reason to know is nonpublic and which he knows or has reason to know has been acquired directly or indirectly from any of the above.

Rule 14e–4. Prohibited Transactions in Connection With Partial Tender Offers

(a) Definitions. For purposes of this section:

(1) The amount of a person's "net long position" in a subject security shall equal the excess, if any, of such person's "long position" over such person's "short position." For the purposes of determining the net long position as of the end of the proration period and for tendering concurrently to two or more partial tender offers, securities that have been tendered in accordance with the Rule and not withdrawn are deemed to be part of the person's long position.

(i) Such person's "long position," is the amount of subject securities that such person:

(A) or his agent has title to or would have title to but for having lent such securities; or

(B) has purchased, or has entered into an unconditional contract, binding on both parties thereto, to purchase but has not yet received; or

(C) has exercised a standardized call option for; or

(D) has converted, exchanged, or exercised an equivalent security for; or

(E) is entitled to receive upon conversion, exchange, or exercise of an equivalent security.

(ii) Such person's "short position," is the amount of subject securities or subject securities underlying equivalent securities that such person:

(A) has sold, or has entered into an unconditional contract, binding on both parties thereto, to sell; or

(B) has borrowed; or

(C) has written a non-standardized call option, or granted any other right pursuant to which his shares may be tendered by another person; or

(D) is obligated to deliver upon exercise of a standardized option sold on or after the date that a tender offer is first publicly announced or otherwise made known by the bidder to holders of the security to be acquired, if the exercise price of such option is lower than the highest tender offer price or stated amount of the consideration offered for the subject security. For the purpose of this paragraph, if one or more tender offers for the same security are ongoing on such date, the announcement date shall be that of the first announced offer.

(2) The term "equivalent security" means (i) any security (including any option, warrant, or other right to purchase the subject security), issued by the person whose securities are the subject of the offer, that is immediately convertible into, or exchangeable or exercisable for, a subject security, or (ii) any other right or option (other than a standardized call option) that entitles the holder thereto to acquire a subject security, but only if the holder thereof reasonably believes that the maker or writer of the right or option has title to and possession of the subject security and upon exercise will promptly deliver the subject security.

(3) The term "subject security" means a security that is the subject of any tender offer or request or invitation for tenders.

(4) For purposes of this rule, a person shall be deemed to "tender" a security if he (i) delivers a subject security pursuant to an offer, (ii) causes such delivery to be made, (iii) guarantees delivery of a subject security pursuant to a tender offer, (iv) causes a guarantee of such delivery to be given by another person, or (v) uses any other method by which acceptance of a tender offer may be made.

(5) The term "partial tender offer" means a tender offer or request or invitation for tenders for less

than all of the outstanding securities subject to the offer in which tenders are accepted either by lot or on a pro rata basis for a specified period, or a tender offer for all of the outstanding shares that offers a choice of consideration in which tenders for different forms of consideration may be accepted either by lot or on a pro rata basis for a specified period.

(6) The term "standardized call option" means any call option that is traded on an exchange, or for which quotation information is disseminated in an electronic interdealer quotation system of a registered national securities association.

(b) It shall be unlawful for any person acting alone or in concert with others, directly or indirectly, to tender any subject security in a partial tender offer:

(1) For his own account unless at the time of tender, and at the end of the proration period or period during which securities are accepted by lot (including any extensions thereof), he has a net long position equal to or greater than the amount tendered in (i) the subject security and will deliver or cause to be delivered such security for the purpose of tender to the person making the offer within the period specified in the offer, or (ii) an equivalent security and, upon the acceptance of his tender will acquire the subject security by conversion, exchange, or exercise of such equivalent security to the extent required by the terms of the offer, and will deliver or cause to be delivered the subject security so acquired for the purpose of tender to the person making the offer within the period specified in the offer; or

(2) For the account of another person unless the person making the tender (i) possesses the subject security or an equivalent security, or (ii) has a reasonable belief that, upon information furnished by the person on whose behalf the tender is made, such person owns the subject security or an equivalent security and will promptly deliver the subject security or such equivalent security for the purpose of tender to the person making the tender.

(c) This rule shall not prohibit any transaction or transactions which the Commission, upon written request or upon its own motion, exempts, either unconditionally or on specified terms and conditions.

Rule 14f-1. Change in Majority of Directors

If, pursuant to any arrangement or understanding with the person or persons acquiring securities in a transaction subject to sections 13(d) or 14(d) of the Act, any persons are to be elected or designated as directors of the issuer, otherwise than at a meeting of security holders, and the persons so elected or designated will constitute a majority of the directors of the issuer, then, not less than 10 days prior to the date any such person takes office as a director, or such shorter period prior to that date as the Commission may authorize upon a showing of good cause therefor, the issuer shall file with the Commission and transmit to all holders of record of securities of the issuer who would be entitled to vote at a meeting for election of directors, information substantially equivalent to the information which would be required by Items 6(a), (d), (e), and (f), 7, and 8 of Schedule 14A of Regulation 14A to be transmitted if such person or persons were nominees for election as directors at a meeting of such security holders. Eight copies of such information shall be filed with the Commission.

OVER-THE-COUNTER MARKETS

Rule 15c-2-8. Delivery of Prospectus

(a) It shall constitute a deceptive act or practice, as those terms are used in Section 15(c)(2) of the Act, for a broker or dealer to participate in a distribution of securities with respect to which a registration statement has been filed under the Securities Act of 1933 unless he complies with the requirements set forth in paragraphs (b) through (g) below. For the purposes of this rule a broker or dealer participating in the distribution shall mean any underwriter and any member or proposed member of the selling group.

(b) In connection with an issue of securities, the issuer of which has not previously been required to file reports pursuant to sections 13(a) or 15(d) of the Securities Exchange Act of 1934, unless such issuer has been exempted from the requirement to file reports thereunder pursuant to section 12(h) of the Act, such broker or dealer shall deliver a copy of the preliminary prospectus to any person who is expected to receive a confirmation of sale at least 48 hours prior to the mailing of such confirmation.

(c) Such broker or dealer shall take reasonable steps to furnish to any person who makes written request for a preliminary prospectus between the filing date and a reasonable time prior to the effective date of the registration statement to which such prospectus relates, a copy of the latest preliminary prospectus on file with the Commission. Reasonable steps shall include receiving an undertaking by the managing underwriter or underwriters to mail such copy to the address given in the requests.

(d) Such broker or dealer shall take reasonable steps to comply promptly with the written request of any person for a copy of the final prospectus relating to such securities during the period between the effective date of the registration statement and the later of either the termination of such distribution, or the expiration of the applicable 40 or 90 day period under Section 4(3) of the Securities Act of 1933. Reasonable steps shall include receiving an undertaking by the managing underwriter or underwriters to mail such copy to the address given in the requests. (The 40–day and 90–day periods referred to above shall be deemed to apply for purposes of this rule irrespective of the provisions of paragraph (b) and (d) of Rule 174 under the Securities Act of 1934).

(e) Such broker or dealer shall take reasonable steps (i) to make available a copy of the preliminary prospectus relating to such securities to each of his associated persons who is expected, prior to the effective date, to solicit customers' orders for such securities before the making of any such solicitation by such associated persons and (ii) to make available to each such associated person a copy of any amended preliminary prospectus promptly after the filing thereof.

(f) Such broker or dealer shall take reasonable steps to make available a copy of the final prospectus relating to such securities to each of his associated persons who is expected, after the effective date, to solicit customers' orders for such securities prior to the making of any such solicitation by such associated persons, unless a preliminary prospectus which is substantially the same as the final prospectus except for matters relating to the price of the stock has been so made available.

(g) If the broker or dealer is a managing underwriter of such distribution, he shall take reasonable steps to see to it that all other brokers or dealers participating in such distribution are promptly furnished with sufficient copies, as requested by them, of each preliminary prospectus, each amended preliminary prospectus and the final prospectus to enable them to comply with paragraphs (b), (c), (d) and (e) above.

(h) If the broker or dealer is a managing underwriter of such distribution, he shall take reasonable steps to see that any broker or dealer participating in the distribution or trading in the registered security is furnished reasonable quantities of the final prospectus relating to such securities, as requested by him, in order to enable him to comply with the prospectus delivery requirements of Section 5(b)(1) and (2) of the Securities Act of 1933.

(i) This rule shall not require the furnishing of prospectuses in any state where such furnishing would be unlawful under the laws of such state; provided, however, that this provision is not to be construed to relieve a broker-dealer from complying with the requirements of Section 5(b)(1) and (2) of the Securities Act of 1933.

(j) For purposes of this section, the term preliminary prospectus shall include the term prospectus subject to completion as used in Rule 434(a), and the term final prospectus shall include the term Section 10(a) prospectus as used in Rule 434(a).

Rule 15c-2-11. Initiation or Resumption of Quotations Without Specified Information

Preliminary Note:

Brokers and dealers may wish to refer to Securities Exchange Act Release No. 29094 (April 17, 1991), for a discussion of procedures for gathering and reviewing the information required by this rule and the requirement that a broker or dealer have a reasonable basis for believing that the information is accurate and obtained from reliable sources.

(a) As a means reasonably designed to prevent fraudulent, deceptive, or manipulative acts or practices, it shall be unlawful for a broker or dealer to publish any quotation for a security or, directly or indirectly, to submit any such quotation for publication, in any quotation medium (as defined in this section) unless such broker or dealer has in its records the documents and information required by this paragraph (for purposes of this section, "paragraph (a) information"), and, based upon a review of the paragraph (a) information together with any other documents and information required by paragraph (b) of this section, has a reasonable basis under the circumstances for believing that the paragraph (a) information is accurate in all material respects, and that the sources of the paragraph (a) information are reliable. The information required pursuant to this paragraph is:

(1) A copy of the prospectus specified by section 10(a) of the Securities Act of 1933 for an issuer that has filed a registration statement under the Securities Act of 1933, other than a registration statement on Form F–6, which became effective less than 90 calendar days prior to the day on which such broker or dealer publishes or submits the quotation to the quotation medium, *Provided* That such registration statement has not thereafter been the subject of a stop order which is still in effect when the quotation is published or submitted; or

(2) A copy of the offering circular provided for under Regulation A under the Securities Act of 1933 for an issuer that has filed a notification under Regulation A which became effective less than 40 calendar days prior to the day on which such broker or dealer publishes or submits the quotation to the quotation medium, *Provided* That the offering circular provided for under Regulation A has not thereafter become the subject of a suspension order which is still in effect when the quotation is published or submitted; or

(3) A copy of the issuer's most recent annual report filed pursuant to Section 13 or 15(d) of the Act or a copy of the annual statement referred to in Section 12(g)(2)(G)(i) of the Act, in the case of an issuer required to file reports pursuant to Section 13 or 15(d) of the Act or an issuer of a security covered by section 12(g)(2)(B) or (G) of the Act, together with any quarterly and current reports that have been filed under the provisions of the Act by the issuer after such annual report or annual statement; *Provided, however,* That until such issuer has filed its first annual report pursuant to Section 13 or 15(d) of the Act or annual statement referred to in Section 12(g)(2)(G)(i) of the Act, the broker or dealer has in its records a copy of the prospectus specified by Section 10(a) of the Securities Act of 1933 included in a registration statement filed by the issuer under the Securities Act of 1933, other than a registration statement on Form F–6, that became effective within the prior 16 months or a copy of any registration statement filed by the issuer under Section 12 of the Act that became effective within the prior 16 months, together with any quarterly and current reports filed thereafter under section 13 or 15(d) of the Act; and *Provided Further* That the broker or dealer has a reasonable basis under the circumstances for believing that the issuer is current in filing annual, quarterly, and current reports filed pursuant to section 13 or 15(d) of the Act, or, in the case of an insurance company exempted from section 12(g) of the Act by reason of section 12(g)(2)(G) thereof, the annual statement referred in section 12(g)(2)(G)(i) of the Act; or

(4) The information furnished to the Commission pursuant to Rule 12g3–2(b) since the beginning of the issuer's last fiscal year, in the case of an issuer exempt from Section 12(g) of the Act by reason of compliance with the provisions of Rule 12g3–2(b), which information the broker or dealer shall make reasonably available upon request to any person expressing an interest in a proposed transaction in the security with such broker or dealer; or

(5) The following information, which shall be reasonably current in relation to the day the quotation is submitted and which the broker or dealer shall make reasonably available upon request to any person expressing an interest in a proposed transaction in the security with such broker or dealer:

(i) the exact name of the issuer and its predecessor (if any);

(ii) the address of its principal executive offices;

(iii) the state of incorporation, if it is a corporation;

(iv) the exact title and class of the security;

(v) the par or stated value of the security;

(vi) the number of shares or total amount of the securities outstanding as of the end of the issuer's most recent fiscal year;

(vii) the name and address of the transfer agent;

(viii) the nature of the issuer's business;

(ix) the nature of products or services offered;

(x) the nature and extent of the issuer's facilities;

(xi) the name of the chief executive officer and members of the board of directors;

(xii) the issuer's most recent balance sheet and profit and loss and retained earnings statements;

(xiii) similar financial information for such part of the two preceding fiscal years as the issuer or its predecessor has been in existence;

(xiv) whether the broker or dealer or any associated person is affiliated, directly or indirectly with the issuer;

(xv) whether the quotation is being published or submitted on behalf of any other broker or dealer, and, if so, the name of such broker or dealer; and,

(xvi) whether the quotation is being submitted or published directly or indirectly on behalf of the issuer, or any director, officer or any person, directly or indirectly the beneficial owner of more than 10 per cent of the outstanding units or shares of any equity security of the issuer, and, if so, the name of such person, and the basis for any exemption under the federal securities laws for any sales of such securities on behalf of such person.

If such information is made available to others upon request pursuant to this paragraph, such delivery, unless otherwise represented, shall not constitute a representation by such broker or dealer that such information is accurate, but shall constitute a representation by such broker or dealer that the information is reasonably current in relation to the day the quotation is submitted, that the broker or dealer has a reasonable basis under the circumstances for believing the information is accurate in all material respects, and that the information was obtained from sources which the broker or dealer has a reasonable basis for believing are reliable. This paragraph (a)(5) shall not apply to any security of an issuer included in paragraph (a)(3) of this section unless a report or statement of such issuer described in paragraph (a)(3) of this section is not reasonably available to the broker or dealer. A report or statement of an issuer described in paragraph (a)(3) of this section shall be "reasonably available" when such report or statement is filed with the Commission.

(b) With respect to any security the quotation of which is within the provisions of this section, the broker or dealer submitting or publishing such quotation shall have in its records the following documents and information:

(1) A record of the circumstances involved in the submission of publication of such quotation, including the identity of the person or persons for whom the quotation is being submitted or published and any information regarding the transactions provided to the broker or dealer by such person or persons;

(2) A copy of any trading suspension order issued by the Commission pursuant to Section 12(k) of the Act respecting any securities of the issuer or its predecessor (if any) during the 12 months preceding the date of the publication or submission of the quotation, or a copy of the public release issued by the Commission announcing such trading suspension order; and

(3) A copy or a written record of any other material information (including adverse information) regarding the issuer which comes to the broker's or dealer's knowledge or possession before the publication or submission of the quotation.

(c) The broker or dealer shall preserve the documents and information required under paragraphs (a) and (b) of this section for a period of not less than three years, the first two years in an easily accessible place.

(d)(1) For any security of an issuer included in paragraph (a)(5) of this section, the broker or dealer submitting the quotation shall furnish to the interdealer quotation system (as defined in paragraph (e)(2) of this section), in such form as such system shall prescribe, at least 3 business days before the quotation is published or submitted, the information regarding the security and the issuer which such broker or dealer is required to maintain pursuant to said paragraph (a)(5) of this section.

(2) For any security of an issuer included in paragraph (a)(3) of this section, (i) a broker-dealer shall be in compliance with the requirement to obtain current reports filed by the issuer if the broker-dealer obtains all current reports filed with the Commission by the issuer as of a date up to five business days in advance of the earlier of the date of submission of the quotation to the quotation medium and the date of submission of paragraph (a)

information pursuant to Schedule H of the By–Laws of the National Association of Securities Dealers, Inc.; and (ii) a broker-dealer shall be in compliance with the requirements to obtain the annual, quarterly, and current reports filed by the issuer, if the broker-dealer has made arrangements to receive all such reports when filed by the issuer and it has regularly received reports from the issuer on a timely basis, unless the broker-dealer has a reasonable basis under the circumstances for believing that the issuer has failed to file a required report or has filed a report but has not sent it to the broker-dealer.

(e) For purposes of this rule:

(1) "Quotation medium" shall mean any "inter-dealer quotation system" or any publication or electronic communications network or other device which is used by brokers or dealers to make known to others their interest in transactions in any security, including offers to buy or sell at a stated price or otherwise, or invitations of offers to buy or sell.

(2) "Inter-dealer quotation system" shall mean any system of general circulation to brokers or dealers which regularly disseminates quotations of identified brokers or dealers.

(3) Except as otherwise specified in this rule, "quotation" shall mean any bid or offer at a specified price with respect to a security, or any indication of interest by a broker or dealer in receiving bids or offers from others for a security, or any indication by a broker or dealer that he wishes to advertise his general interest in buying or selling a particular security.

(4) "Issuer," in the case of quotations represented by American Depositary Receipts, shall mean the issuer of the deposited shares represented by such American Depositary Receipts.

(f) The provisions of this rule shall not apply to:

(1) The publication or submission of a quotation respecting a security admitted to trading on a national securities exchange and which is traded on such an exchange on the same day as, or on the business day next preceding, the day the quotation is published or submitted.

(2) The publication or submission by a broker or dealer, solely on behalf of a customer (other than a person acting as or for a dealer), of a quotation that represents the customer's indication of interest and does not involve the solicitation of the customer's interest; *Provided, however,* That this paragraph (f)(2) shall not apply to a quotation consisting of both a bid and an offer, each of which is at a specified price, unless the quotation medium specifically identifies the quotation as representing such an unsolicited customer interest.

(3)(i) The publication or submission, in an interdealer quotation system that specifically identifies as such unsolicited customer indications of interest of the kind described in paragraph (f)(2) of this section, of a quotation respecting a security which has been the subject of quotations (exclusive of any identified customer interests) in such a system on each of at least 12 days within the previous 30 calendar days, with no more than 4 business days in succession without a quotation; or

(ii) The publication or submission, in an interdealer quotation system that does not so identify any such unsolicited customer indications of interest, of a quotation respecting a security which has been the subject of both bid and ask quotations in an interdealer quotation system at specified prices on each of at least 12 days within the previous 30 calendar days, with no more than 4 business days in succession without such a two-way quotation;

(iii) A dealer acting in the capacity of market maker, as defined in section 3(a)(38) of the Act, that has published or submitted a quotation respecting a security in an interdealer quotation system and such quotation has qualified for an exception provided in this paragraph (f)(3), may continue to publish or submit quotations for such security in the interdealer quotation system without compliance with this section unless and until such dealer ceases to submit or publish a quotation or ceases to act in the capacity of market maker respecting such security.

* * *

(5) The publication or submission of a quotation respecting a security that is authorized for quotation in the NASDAQ system (as defined in Rule 11Ac1–2(a)(3) of this chapter), and such

authorization is not suspended, terminated, or prohibited.

(g) The requirement in subparagraph (a)(5) that the information with respect to the issuer be "reasonably current" will be presumed to be satisfied, unless the broker or dealer has information to the contrary, if:

(1) the balance sheet is as of a date less than 16 months before the publication or submission of the quotation, the statements of profit and loss and retained earnings are for the 12 months preceding the date of such balance sheet, and if such balance sheet is not as of a date less than 6 months before the publication or submission of the quotation, it shall be accompanied by additional statements of profit and loss and retained earnings for the period from the date of such balance sheet to a date less than 6 months before the publication or submission of the quotation.

(2) other information regarding the issuer specified in subparagraph (a)(5) is as of a date within 12 months prior to the publication or submission of the quotation.

(h) This rule shall not prohibit any publication or submission of any quotation if the Commission, upon written request or upon its own motion, exempts such quotation either unconditionally or on specific terms and conditions, as not constituting a fraudulent, manipulative or deceptive practice comprehended within the purpose of this rule.

REPORTS OF DIRECTORS, OFFICERS, AND PRINCIPAL SHAREHOLDERS

Rule 16a-1. Definition of Terms

Terms defined in this Rule shall apply solely to Section 16 of the Act and the rules thereunder. These terms shall not be limited to Section 16(a) of the Act but also shall apply to all other subsections under Section 16 of the Act.

(a) The term "beneficial owner" shall have the following applications:

(1) Solely for purposes of determining whether a person is a beneficial owner of more than ten percent of any class of equity securities registered pursuant to Section 12 of the Act, the term "beneficial owner" shall mean any person who is deemed a beneficial owner pursuant to Section 13(d) of the Act and the rules thereunder; *provided, however,* that the following institutions or persons shall not be deemed the beneficial owner of securities of such class held for the benefit of third parties or in customer or fiduciary accounts in the ordinary course of business (or in the case of an employee benefit plan specified in subparagraph (vi) below, of securities of such class allocated to plan participants where participants have voting power) as long as such shares are acquired by such institutions or persons without the purpose or effect of changing or influencing control of the issuer or engaging in any arrangement subject to Rule 13d-3(b):

(i) A broker or dealer registered under Section 15 of the Act;

(ii) A bank as defined in Section 3(a)(6) of the Act;

(iii) An insurance company as defined in Section 3(a)(19) of the Act;

(iv) An investment company registered under Section 8 of the Investment Company Act of 1940;

(v) Any person registered as an investment adviser registered under Section 203 of the Investment Advisers Act of 1940 or under the laws of any State.

(vi) An employee benefit plan as defined in Section 3(3) of the Employee Retirement Income Security Act of 1974, as amended, 29 U.S.C. 1001 et seq. ("ERISA") that is subject to the provisions of ERISA, or any such plan that is not subject to ERISA that is maintained primarily for the benefit of the employees of a state or local government or instrumentality, or an endowment fund;

(vii) A parent holding company or control person, provided the aggregate amount held directly by the parent or control person, and directly and indirectly by their subsidiaries or affiliates that are not persons specified in paragraphs (a)(1)(i) through (ix), does not exceed one percent of the securities of the subject class;

(viii) A savings association as defined in Section 3(b) of the Federal Deposit Insurance Act (12 U.S.C. 1813);

(ix) A church plan that is excluded from the definition of an investment company under section 3(c)(14) of the Investment Company Act of 1940; and

(x) A group, provided that all the members are persons specified in Rule 16a–1(a)(1)(i) through (ix).

Note to paragraph (a). Pursuant to this section, a person deemed a beneficial owner of more than ten percent of any class of equity securities registered under Section 12 of the Act would file a Form 3, but the securities holdings disclosed on Form 3, and changes in beneficial ownership reported on subsequent Forms 4 or 5, would be determined by the definition of "beneficial owner" in paragraph (a)(2) of this section.

(2) Other than for purposes of determining whether a person is a beneficial owner of more than ten percent of any class of equity securities registered under Section 12 of the Act, the term "beneficial owner" shall mean any person who, directly or indirectly, through any contract, arrangement, understanding, relationship or otherwise, has or shares a direct or indirect pecuniary interest in the equity securities, subject to the following:

(i) The term "pecuniary interest" in any class of equity securities shall mean the opportunity, directly or indirectly, to profit or share in any profit derived from a transaction in the subject securities.

(ii) The term "indirect pecuniary interest" in any class of equity securities shall include, but not be limited to:

(A) securities held by members of a person's immediate family sharing the same household; provided, however, that the presumption of such beneficial ownership may be rebutted; see also Rule16a–1(a)(4);

(B) a general partner's proportionate interest in the portfolio securities held by a general or limited partnership. The general partner's proportionate interest, as evidenced by the partnership agreement in effect at the time of the transaction and the partnership's most recent financial statements, shall be the greater of:

(*1*) the general partner's share of the partnership's profits, including profits attributed to any limited partnership interests held by the general partner and any other interests in profits that arise from the purchase and sale of the partnership's portfolio securities; or

(*2*) the general partner's share of the partnership capital account, including the share attributable to any limited partnership interest held by the general partner.

(C) a performance-related fee, other than an asset-based fee, received by any broker, dealer, bank, insurance company, investment company, investment adviser, investment manager, trustee or person or entity performing a similar function; *provided, however,* that no pecuniary interest shall be present where:

(*1*) the performance-related fee, regardless of when payable, is calculated based upon net capital gains and/or net capital appreciation generated from the portfolio or from the fiduciary's overall performance over a period of one year or more; and

(*2*) equity securities of the issuer do not account for more than ten percent of the market value of the portfolio. A right to a nonperformance-related fee alone shall not represent a pecuniary interest in the securities;

(D) a person's right to dividends that is separated or separable from the underlying securities. Otherwise, a right to dividends alone shall not represent a pecuniary interest in the securities;

(E) a person's interest in securities held by a trust, as specified in Rule 16a–8(b); and

(F) a person's right to acquire equity securities through the exercise or conversion of any derivative security, whether or not presently exercisable.

(iii) A shareholder shall not be deemed to have a pecuniary interest in the portfolio securities held by a corporation or similar entity in which the person owns securities if the shareholder is not a controlling shareholder of the entity and does not have or share investment control over the entity's portfolio.

(3) Where more than one person subject to section 16 of the Act is deemed to be a beneficial owner of the same equity securities, all such persons must report as beneficial owners of the securities, either separately or jointly, as provided in Rule 16a–3(j). In such cases, the amount of short-swing profit

recoverable shall not be increased above the amount recoverable if there were only one beneficial owner.

(4) Any person filing a statement pursuant to Section 16(a) of the Act may state that the filing shall not be deemed an admission that such person is, for purposes of Section 16 of the Act or otherwise, the beneficial owner of any equity securities covered by the statement.

(5) The following interests are deemed not to confer beneficial ownership for purposes of Section 16 of the Act:

(i) Interests in portfolio securities held by any holding company registered under the Public Utility Holding Company Act of 1935;

(ii) Interests in portfolio securities held by any investment company registered under the Investment Company Act of 1940; and

(iii) Interests in securities comprising part of a broad-based, publicly traded market basket or index of stocks, approved for trading by the appropriate federal governmental authority.

(b) The term "call equivalent position" shall mean a derivative security position that increases in value as the value of the underlying equity increases, including, but not limited to, a long convertible security, a long call option, and a short put option position.

(c) The term "derivative securities" shall mean any option, warrant, convertible security, stock appreciation right, or similar right with an exercise or conversion privilege at a price related to an equity security, or similar securities with a value derived from the value of an equity security, but shall not include:

(1) rights of a pledgee of securities to sell the pledged securities;

(2) rights of all holders of a class of securities of an issuer to receive securities pro rata, or obligations to dispose of securities, as a result of a merger, exchange offer, or consolidation involving the issuer of the securities;

(3) rights or obligations to surrender a security, or have a security withheld, upon the receipt or exercise of a derivative security or the receipt or vesting of equity securities, in order to satisfy the exercise price or the tax withholding consequences of receipt, exercise, or vesting;

(4) interests in broad-based index options, broad-based index futures, and broad-based publicly traded market baskets of stocks approved for trading by the appropriate federal governmental authority;

(5) interests or rights to participate in employee benefit plans of the issuer;

(6) rights with an exercise or conversion privilege at a price that is not fixed; or

(7) options granted to an underwriter in a registered public offering for the purpose of satisfying over-allotments in such offering.

(d) The term "equity security of such issuer" shall mean any equity security or derivative security relating to an issuer, whether or not issued by that issuer.

(e) The term "immediate family" shall mean any child, stepchild, grandchild, parent, stepparent, grandparent, spouse, sibling, mother-in-law, father-in-law, son-in-law, daughter-in-law, brother-in-law, or sister-in-law, and shall include adoptive relationships.

(f) The term "officer" shall mean an issuer's president, principal financial officer, or principal accounting officer (or, if there is no such accounting officer, the controller), any vice-president of the issuer in charge of a principal business unit, division or function (such as sales, administration or finance), any other officer who performs a policy-making function, or any other person who performs similar policy-making functions for the issuer. Officers of the issuer's parent(s) or subsidiaries shall be deemed officers of the issuer if they perform such policy-making functions for the issuer. In addition, when the issuer is a limited partnership, officers or employees of the general partner(s) who perform policy-making functions for the limited partnership are deemed officers of the limited partnership. When the issuer is a trust, officers or employees of the trustee(s) who perform policy-making functions for the trust are deemed officers of the trust.

Note: "Policy-making function" is not intended to include policy-making functions that are not significant. If pursuant to Item 401(b) of Regulation S–K the issuer identifies a person as an "executive officer," it is presumed that the Board of Directors has made that judgment and that the persons so identified are the officers for purposes of Section 16 of the

Act, as are such other persons enumerated in this paragraph (f) but not in Item 401(b).

(g) The term "portfolio securities" shall mean all securities owned by an entity, other than securities issued by the entity.

(h) The term "put equivalent position" shall mean a derivative security position that increases in value as the value of the underlying equity decreases, including, but not limited to, a long put option and a short call option position.

Rule 16a-2. Persons and Transactions Subject to Section 16

Any person who is the beneficial owner, directly or indirectly, of more than ten percent of any class of equity securities ("ten percent beneficial owner") registered pursuant to Section 12 of the Act, any director or officer of the issuer of such securities, and any person specified in Section 17(a) of the Public Utility Holding Company Act of 1935 or Section 30(f) of the Investment Company Act of 1940, * * *, shall be subject to the provisions of Section 16 of the Act. The rules under Section 16 of the Act apply to any class of equity securities of an issuer whether or not registered under Section 12 of the Act. The rules under Section 16 of the Act also apply to non-equity securities as provided by the Public Utility Holding Company Act of 1935 and the Investment Company Act of 1940. With respect to transactions by persons subject to Section 16 of the Act:

(a) A transaction(s) carried out by a director or officer in the six months prior to the director or officer becoming subject to Section 16 of the Act shall be subject to Section 16 of the Act and reported on the first required Form 4 only if the transaction(s) occurred within six months of the transaction giving rise to the Form 4 filing obligation and the director or officer became subject to Section 16 of the Act solely as a result of the issuer registering a class of equity securities pursuant to Section 12 of the Act.

(b) A transaction(s) following the cessation of director or officer status shall be subject to section 16 of the Act only if:

(1) Executed within a period of less than six months of an opposite transaction subject to section 16(b) of the Act that occurred while that person was a director or officer; and

(2) Not otherwise exempted from section 16(b) of the Act pursuant to the provisions of this chapter. Note to Paragraph (b): For purposes of this paragraph, an acquisition and a disposition each shall be an opposite transaction with respect to the other.

(c) The transaction that results in a person becoming a ten percent beneficial owner is not subject to Section 16 of the Act unless the person otherwise is subject to Section 16 of the Act. A ten percent beneficial owner not otherwise subject to Section 16 of the Act must report only those transactions conducted while the beneficial owner of more than ten percent of a class of equity securities of the issuer registered pursuant to Section 12 of the Act.

(d)(1) Transactions by a person or entity shall be exempt from the provisions of Section 16 of the Act for the 12 months following appointment and qualification, to the extent such person or entity is acting as:

(i) Executor or administrator of the estate of a decedent;

(ii) Guardian or member of a committee for an incompetent;

(iii) Receiver, trustee in bankruptcy, assignee for the benefit of creditors, conservator, liquidating agent, or other similar person duly authorized by law to administer the estate or assets of another person; or

(iv) Fiduciary in a similar capacity.

(2) Transactions by such person or entity acting in a capacity specified in paragraph (d)(1) of this section after the period specified in that paragraph shall be subject to section 16 of the Act only where the estate, trust, or other entity is a beneficial owner of more than ten percent of any class of equity security registered pursuant to section 12 of the Act.

Rule 16a-3. Reporting Transactions and Holdings

(a) Initial statements of beneficial ownership of equity securities required by Section 16(a) of the Act shall be filed on Form 3. Statements of changes in beneficial ownership required by that Section shall be filed on Form 4. Annual statements shall be filed on Form 5. At the election of the reporting person, any transaction required to be reported on Form 5 may be reported on an earlier filed Form 4. All such statements shall be prepared and filed in accordance with the requirements of the applicable form.

(b) A person filing statements pursuant to Section 16(a) of the Act with respect to any class of equity securities registered pursuant to Section 12 of the Act need not file an additional statement on Form 3:

(1) When an additional class of equity securities of the same issuer becomes registered pursuant to Section 12 of the Act; or

(2) When such person assumes a different or an additional relationship to the same issuer (for example, when an officer becomes a director).

(c) Any issuer that has equity securities listed on more than one national securities exchange may designate one exchange as the only exchange with which reports pursuant to Section 16(a) of the Act need be filed. Such designation shall be made in writing and shall be filed with the Commission and with each national securities exchange on which any equity security of the issuer is listed at the time of such election. The reporting person's obligation to file reports with each national securities exchange on which any equity security of the issuer is listed shall be satisfied by filing with the exchange so designated.

(d) Any person required to file a statement with respect to securities of a single issuer under both Section 16(a) of the Act and either Section 17(a) of the Public Utility Holding Company Act of 1935 or Section 30(f) of the Investment Company Act of 1940 may file a single statement containing the required information, which will be deemed to be filed under both Acts.

(e) Any person required to file a statement under Section 16(a) of the Act shall, not later than the time the statement is transmitted for filing with the Commission, send or deliver a duplicate to the person designated by the issuer to receive such statements, or, in the absence of such a designation, to the issuer's corporate secretary or person performing equivalent functions.

(f)(1) A Form 5 shall be filed by every person who at any time during the issuer's fiscal year was subject to Section 16 of the Act with respect to such issuer, except as provided in paragraph (2) below. The Form shall be filed within 45 days after the issuer's fiscal year end, and shall disclose the following holdings and transactions not reported previously on Forms 3, 4 or 5:

(i) All transactions during the most recent fiscal year that were exempt from section 16(b) of the Act, except:

(A) Exercises and conversions of derivative securities exempt under either Rule 16b–3 or Rule 16b–6(b), and any transaction exempt under Rule 16b–3(d), Rule 16b–3(e), or Rule 16b–3(f) (these are required to be reported on Form 4);

(B) Transactions exempt from section 16(b) of the Act pursuant to Rule 16b–3(c), which shall be exempt from section 16(a) of the Act; and

(C) Transactions exempt from section 16(a) of the Act pursuant to another rule;

(ii) Transactions that constituted small acquisitions pursuant to Rule 16a–6(a);

(iii) all holdings and transactions that should have been reported during the most recent fiscal year, but were not; and

(iv) with respect to the first Form 5 requirement for a reporting person, all holdings and transactions that should have been reported in each of the issuer's last two fiscal years but were not, based on the reporting person's reasonable belief in good faith in the completeness and accuracy of the information.

(2) Notwithstanding the above, no Form 5 shall be required where all transactions otherwise required to be reported on the Form 5 have been reported before the due date of the Form 5.

Note: Persons no longer subject to Section 16 of the Act, but who were subject to the Section at any time during the issuer's fiscal year, must file a Form 5 unless paragraph (f)(2) is satisfied. See also Rule 16a–2(b) regarding the reporting obligations of persons ceasing to be officers or directors.

(g)(1) A Form 4 must be filed to report: all transactions not exempt from section 16(b) of the Act; all transactions exempt from section 16(b) of the Act pursuant to Rule 16b–3(d), Rule 16b–3(e), or Rule 16b–3(f); and all exercises and conversions of derivative securities, regardless of whether exempt from section 16(b) of the Act. Form 4 must be filed before the end of the second business day following the day on which the subject transaction has been executed.

(2) Solely for purposes of section 16(a)(2)(C) of the Act and paragraph (g)(1) of this section, the date on which the executing broker, dealer or plan administrator notifies the reporting person of the execution of the transaction is deemed the date of execution for a transaction where the following conditions are satisfied:

(i) the transaction is pursuant to a contract, instruction or written plan for the purchase or sale of equity securities of the issuer (as defined in Rule 16a–1(d)) that satisfies the affirmative defense conditions of Rule 10b5–1(c) of this chapter; and

(ii) the reporting person does not select the date of execution.

(3) Solely for purposes of section 16(a)(2)(C) of the Act and paragraph (g)(1) of this section, the date on which the plan administrator notifies the reporting person that the transaction has been executed is deemed the date of execution for a discretionary transaction (as defined in Rule 16b–3(b)(1)) for which the reporting person does not select the date of execution.

(4) In the case of the transactions described in paragraphs (g)(2) and (g)(3) of this section, if the notification date is later than the third business day following the trade date of the transaction, the date of execution is deemed to be the third business day following the trade date of the transaction.

(5) At the option of the reporting person, transactions that are reportable on Form 5 may be reported on Form 4, so long as the Form 4 is filed no later than the due date of the Form 5 on which the transaction is otherwise required to be reported.

(h) The date of filing with the Commission shall be the date of receipt by the Commission; *provided, however,* that a Form 3, 4, or 5 shall be deemed to have been timely filed if the filing person establishes that the Form had been transmitted timely to a third party company or governmental entity providing delivery services in the ordinary course of business, which guaranteed delivery of the filing to the Commission no later than the required filing date.

(i) *Signatures.* Where Section 16 of the Act, or the rules or forms thereunder, require a document filed with or furnished to the Commission to be signed, such document shall be manually signed, or signed using either typed signatures or duplicated or facsimile versions of manual signatures. Where typed, duplicated or facsimile signatures are used, each signatory to the filing shall manually sign a signature page or other document authenticating, acknowledging or otherwise adopting his or her signature that appears in the filing. Such document shall be executed before or at the time the filing is made and shall be retained by the filer for a period of five years. Upon request, the filer shall furnish to the Commission or its staff a copy of any or all documents retained pursuant to this section.

(j) Where more than one person subject to section 16 of the Act is deemed to be a beneficial owner of the same equity securities, all such persons must report as beneficial owners of the securities, either separately or jointly. Where persons in a group are deemed to be beneficial owners of equity securities pursuant to Rule 16a–1(a)(1) due to the aggregation of holdings, a single Form 3, 4 or 5 may be filed on behalf of all persons in the group. Joint and group filings must include all required information for each beneficial owner, and such filings must be signed by each beneficial owner, or on behalf of such owner by an authorized person.

Rule 16a–4. Derivative Securities

(a) For purposes of Section 16 of the Act, both derivative securities and the underlying securities to which they relate shall be deemed to be the same class of equity securities, *except that* the acquisition or disposition of any derivative security shall be separately reported.

(b) The exercise or conversion of a call equivalent position shall be reported on Form 4 and treated for reporting purposes as:

(1) A purchase of the underlying security; and

(2) A closing of the derivative security position.

(c) The exercise or conversion of a put equivalent position shall be reported on Form 4 and treated for reporting purposes as:

(1) A sale of the underlying security; and

(2) A closing of the derivative security position.

(d) The disposition or closing of a long derivative security position, as a result of cancellation or expiration, shall be exempt from section 16(a) of the Act if exempt from section 16(b) of the Act pursuant to Rule 16b–6(d).

Note to Rule 16a–4: A purchase or sale resulting from an exercise or conversion of a derivative security may be exempt from section 16(b) of the Act pursuant to Rule 16b–3 or Rule 16b–6(b).

Rule 16a–6. Small Acquisitions

(a) Any acquisition of an equity security or the right to acquire such securities, other than an acquisition from the issuer (including an employee benefit plan sponsored by the issuer), not exceeding $10,000 in market value shall be reported on Form 5, subject to the following conditions:

(1) Such acquisition, when aggregated with other acquisitions of securities of the same class (including securities underlying derivative securities, but excluding acquisitions exempted by rule from section 16(b) or previously reported on Form 4 or Form 5) within the prior six months, does not exceed a total of $10,000 in market value; and

(2) The person making the acquisition does not within six months thereafter make any disposition, other than by a transaction exempt from section 16(b) of the Act.

(b) If an acquisition no longer qualifies for the reporting deferral in paragraph (a) of this section, all such acquisitions that have not yet been reported must be reported on Form 4 before the end of the second business day following the day on which the conditions of paragraph (a) of this section are no longer met.

Rule 16a–7. Transactions Effected in Connection With a Distribution

(a) Any purchase and sale, or sale and purchase, of a security that is made in connection with the distribution of a substantial block of securities shall be exempt from the provisions of Section 16(a) of the Act, to the extent specified in this Rule, subject to the following conditions:

(1) The person effecting the transaction is engaged in the business of distributing securities and is participating in good faith, in the ordinary course of such business, in the distribution of such block of securities; and

(2) The security involved in the transaction is:

(i) part of such block of securities and is acquired by the person effecting the transaction, with a view to distribution thereof, from the issuer or other person on whose behalf such securities are being distributed or from a person who is participating in good faith in the distribution of such block of securities; or

(ii) a security purchased in good faith by or for the account of the person effecting the transaction for the purpose of stabilizing the market price of securities of the class being distributed or to cover an over-allotment or other short position created in connection with such distribution.

(b) Each person participating in the transaction must qualify on an individual basis for an exemption pursuant to this section.

Rule 16a–9. Stock Splits, Stock Dividends, and Pro Rata Rights

The following shall be exempt from Section 16 of the Act:

(a) The increase or decrease in the number of securities held as a result of a stock split or stock dividend applying equally to all securities of a class, including a stock dividend in which equity securities of a different issuer are distributed; and

(b) the acquisition of rights, such as shareholder or preemptive rights, pursuant to a pro rata grant to all holders of the same class of equity securities registered under Section 12 of the Act.

Note: The exercise or sale of a pro rata right shall be reported pursuant to Rule 16a–4 and the exercise shall be eligible for exemption from Section 16(b) of the Act pursuant to Rule 16b–6(b).

Rule 16a–10. Exemptions Under Section 16(a)

Except as provided in Rule 16a–6, any transaction exempted from the requirements of Section 16(a) of the Act, insofar as it is otherwise subject to the provisions of Section 16(b), shall be likewise exempt from Section 16(b) of the Act.

EXEMPTION OF CERTAIN TRANSACTIONS FROM SECTION 16(b)

Rule 16b–1. Transactions Approved by a Regulatory Authority

(a) Any purchase and sale, or sale and purchase, of a security shall be exempt from Section 16(b) of the Act, if the transaction is effected by an investment company registered under the Investment Company Act of 1940 and both the purchase and sale of such security have been exempted from the provisions of Section 17(a) of the Investment Company Act of 1940, by rule or order of the Commission.

(b) Any purchase and sale, or sale and purchase, of a security shall be exempt from the provisions of Section 16(b) of the Act if:

(1) the person effecting the transaction is either a holding company registered under the Public Utility Holding Company Act of 1935 or a subsidiary thereof; and

(2) both the purchase and the sale of the security have been approved or permitted by the Commission pursuant to the applicable provisions of that Act and the rules and regulations thereunder.

Rule 16b–3. Transactions Between Issuer and Its Officers and Directors

(a) *General.* A transaction between the issuer (including an employee benefit plan sponsored by the issuer) and an officer or director of the issuer that involves issuer equity securities shall be exempt from section 16(b) of the Act if the transaction satisfies the applicable conditions set forth in this section.

(b) *Definitions.*

(1) A Discretionary Transaction shall mean a transaction pursuant to an employee benefit plan that:

(i) Is at the volition of a plan participant;

(ii) Is not made in connection with the participant's death, disability, retirement or termination of employment;

(iii) Is not required to be made available to a plan participant pursuant to a provision of the Internal Revenue Code; and

(iv) Results in either an intra-plan transfer involving an issuer equity securities fund, or a cash distribution funded by a volitional disposition of an issuer equity security.

(2) An Excess Benefit Plan shall mean an employee benefit plan that is operated in conjunction with a Qualified Plan, and provides only the benefits or contributions that would be provided under a Qualified Plan but for any benefit or contribution limitations set forth in the Internal Revenue Code of 1986, or any successor provisions thereof.

(3)(i) A Non–Employee Director shall mean a director who:

(A) Is not currently an officer (as defined in Rule 16a–1(f)) of the issuer or a parent or subsidiary of the issuer, or otherwise currently employed by the issuer or a parent or subsidiary of the issuer;

(B) Does not receive compensation, either directly or indirectly, from the issuer or a parent or subsidiary of the issuer, for services rendered as a consultant or in any capacity other than as a director, except for an amount that does not exceed the dollar amount for which disclosure would be required pursuant to § 229.404(a) of this chapter;

(C) Does not possess an interest in any other transaction for which disclosure would be required pursuant to § 229.404(a) of this chapter; and

(D) Is not engaged in a business relationship for which disclosure would be required pursuant to § 229.404(b) of this chapter.

(ii) Notwithstanding paragraph (b)(3)(i) of this section, a Non–Employee Director of a closed-end investment company shall mean a director who is not an "interested person" of the issuer, as that term is defined in Section 2(a)(19) of the Investment Company Act of 1940.

(4) A Qualified Plan shall mean an employee benefit plan that satisfies the coverage and participation requirements of sections 410 and 401(a)(26) of the Internal Revenue Code of 1986, or any successor provisions thereof.

(5) A Stock Purchase Plan shall mean an employee benefit plan that satisfies the coverage and participation requirements of sections 423(b)(3) and 423(b)(5), or section 410, of the Internal Revenue Code of 1986, or any successor provisions thereof.

(c) *Tax-conditioned plans.* Any transaction (other than a Discretionary Transaction) pursuant to a Qualified Plan, an Excess Benefit Plan, or a Stock Purchase Plan shall be exempt without condition.

(d) *Grants, awards and other acquisitions from the issuer.* Any transaction involving a grant, award or other acquisition from the issuer (other than a Discretionary Transaction) shall be exempt if:

(1) The transaction is approved by the board of directors of the issuer, or a committee of the board of directors that is composed solely of two or more Non–Employee Directors;

(2) The transaction is approved or ratified, in compliance with section 14 of the Act, by either: the affirmative votes of the holders of a majority of the securities of the issuer present, or represented, and entitled to vote at a meeting duly held in accordance with the applicable laws of the state or other jurisdiction in which the issuer is incorporated; or the written consent of the holders of a majority of the securities of the issuer entitled to vote; provided that such ratification occurs no later than the date of the next annual meeting of shareholders; or

(3) The issuer equity securities so acquired are held by the officer or director for a period of six months following the date of such acquisition, provided that this condition shall be satisfied with respect to a derivative security if at least six months elapse from the date of acquisition of the derivative security to the date of disposition of the derivative security (other than upon exercise or conversion) or its underlying equity security.

(e) Dispositions to the issuer. Any transaction involving the disposition to the issuer of issuer equity securities (other than a Discretionary Transaction) shall be exempt, provided that the terms of such disposition are approved in advance in the manner prescribed by either paragraph (d)(1) or paragraph (d)(2) of this section.

(f) Discretionary Transactions. A Discretionary Transaction shall be exempt only if effected pursuant to an election made at least six months following the date of the most recent election, with respect to any plan of the issuer, that effected a Discretionary Transaction that was:

(1) An acquisition, if the transaction to be exempted would be a disposition; or

(2) A disposition, if the transaction to be exempted would be an acquisition.

Notes to Rule 16b–3

Note (1): The exercise or conversion of a derivative security that does not satisfy the conditions of this section is eligible for exemption from section 16(b) of the Act to the extent that the conditions of Rule 16b–6(b) are satisfied.

Note (2): Section 16(a) reporting requirements applicable to transactions exempt pursuant to this section are set forth in Rule 16a–3(f) and (g) and Rule 16a–4.

Note (3): The approval conditions of paragraphs (d)(1), (d)(2) and (e) of this section require the approval of each specific transaction, and are not satisfied by approval of a plan in its entirety except for the approval of a plan pursuant to which the terms and conditions of each transaction are fixed in advance, such as a formula plan. Where the terms of a subsequent transaction (such as the exercise price of an option, or the provision of an exercise or tax withholding right) are provided for in a transaction as initially approved pursuant to paragraphs (d)(1), (d)(2) or (e), such subsequent transaction shall not require further specific approval.

Rule 16b–6. Derivative Securities

(a) The establishment of or increase in a call equivalent position or liquidation of or decrease in a put equivalent position shall be deemed a purchase of the underlying security for purposes of Section 16(b) of the Act, and the establishment of or increase in a put equivalent position or liquidation of or decrease in a call equivalent position shall be deemed a sale of the underlying securities for purposes of Section 16(b) of the Act; *provided, however,* that if the increase or decrease occurs as a result of the fixing of the exercise price of a right initially issued without a fixed price, where the date the price is fixed is not known in advance and is outside the control of the recipient, the increase or decrease shall be exempt from Section 16(b) of the Act with respect to any offsetting transaction within the six months prior to the date the price is fixed.

(b) The closing of a derivative security position as a result of its exercise or conversion shall be exempt from the operation of Section 16(b) of the Act, and the acquisition of underlying securities at a fixed exercise price due to the exercise or conversion of a call equivalent position or the disposition of underlying securities at a fixed exercise price due to the exercise of a put equivalent position shall be exempt from the operation of Section 16(b) of the Act; *provided, however,* that the acquisition of underlying securities from the exercise of an out-of-the-money option, warrant, or right shall not be exempt unless the exercise is necessary to comport with the sequential exercise provisions of the Internal Revenue Code (26 U.S.C. § 422A).

Note to Paragraph (b): The exercise or conversion of a derivative security that does not satisfy the conditions of this section is eligible for exemption from section 16(b) of the Act to the extent that the conditions of Rule 16b–3 are satisfied.

(c) In determining the short-swing profit recoverable pursuant to Section 16(b) of the Act from transactions involving the purchase and sale or sale and purchase of derivative and other securities, the following rules apply:

(1) Short-swing profits in transactions involving the purchase and sale or sale and purchase of derivative securities that have identical characteristics (*e.g.,* purchases and sales of call options of the same strike price and expiration date, or purchases and sales of the same series of convertible debentures) shall be measured by the actual prices paid or received in the short-swing transactions.

(2) Short-swing profits in transactions involving the purchase and sale or sale and purchase of derivative securities having different characteristics but related to the same underlying security (*e.g.,* the purchase of a call option and the sale of a convertible debenture) or derivative securities and underlying securities shall not exceed the difference in price of the underlying security on the date of purchase or sale and the date of sale or purchase. Such profits may be measured by calculating the short-swing profits that would have been realized had the subject transactions involved purchases and sales solely of the derivative security that was purchased or solely of the derivative security that was sold, valued as of the time of the matching purchase or sale, and calculated for the lesser of the number of underlying securities actually purchased or sold.

(d) Upon cancellation or expiration of an option within six months of the writing of the option, any profit derived from writing the option shall be recoverable under Section 16(b) of the Act. The profit shall not exceed the premium received for writing the option. The disposition or closing of a long derivative security position, as a result of cancellation or expiration, shall be exempt from Section 16(b) of the Act where no value is received from the cancellation or expiration.

Rule 16b–7. Mergers, Reclassifications, and Consolidations

(a) The following transactions shall be exempt from the provisions of Section 16(b) of the Act:

(1) The acquisition of a security of a company, pursuant to a merger or consolidation, in exchange for a security of a company which, prior to the merger or consolidation, owned 85 percent or more of either

(i) the equity securities of all other companies involved in the merger or consolidation, or in the case of a consolidation, the resulting company; or

(ii) the combined assets of all the companies involved in the merger or consolidation, computed according to their book values prior to the merger or consolidation as determined by reference to their most recent available financial statements for a 12 month period prior to the merger or consolidation, or such shorter time as the company has been in existence.

(2) The disposition of a security, pursuant to a merger or consolidation, of a company which, prior to the merger or consolidation, owned 85 percent or more of either

(i) the equity securities of all other companies involved in the merger or consolidation or, in the case of a consolidation, the resulting company; or

(ii) the combined assets of all the companies undergoing merger or consolidation, computed according to their book values prior to the merger or consolidation as determined by reference to their most recent available financial statements for a 12 month period prior to the merger or consolidation.

(b) A merger within the meaning of this section shall include the sale or purchase of substantially all the assets of one company by another in exchange for equity securities which are then distributed to the security holders of the company that sold its assets.

(c) Notwithstanding the foregoing, if a person subject to Section 16 of the Act makes any non-exempt purchase of a security in any company involved in the merger or consolidation and any non-exempt sale of a security in any company involved in the merger or consolidation within any period of less than six months during which the merger or consolidation took place, the exemption provided by this Rule shall be unavailable to the extent of such purchase and sale.

E. REGULATION S–T—GENERAL RULES AND REGULATIONS FOR ELECTRONIC FILINGS

(Selected)

Contents

ELECTRONIC FILING REQUIREMENTS

Item 100. Persons and entities subject to mandated electronic filing.

The following persons or entities shall be subject to the electronic filing requirements of this [regulation]:

(a) Registrants whose filings are subject to review by the Division of Corporation Finance;

(b) Registrants whose filings are subject to review by the Division of Investment Management; and

(c) Any party (including natural persons) that files a document jointly with, or as a third party filer with respect to, a registrant that is subject to mandated electronic filing requirements.

Item 101. Mandated Electronic Submissions and Exceptions

(a) Mandated electronic submissions.

(1) The following filings, including any related correspondence and supplemental information, except as otherwise provided, shall be submitted in electronic format:

(i) Registration statements and prospectuses filed pursuant to the Securities Act or registration statements filed pursuant to Sections 12(b) or 12(g) of the Exchange Act;

(ii) Statements and applications filed with the Commission pursuant to the Trust Indenture Act, other than applications for exemptive relief filed pursuant to section 304 and section 310 of that Act;

(iii) Statements, reports and schedules filed with the Commission pursuant to section 13, 14, or 15(d) of the Exchange Act, and proxy materials required to be furnished for the information of the Commission in connection with annual reports on Form 10–K or Form 10–KSB filed pursuant to section 15(d) of the Exchange Act;

Item 103. Liability for Transmission Errors or Omissions in Documents Filed Via EDGAR

An electronic filer shall not be subject to the liability and anti-fraud provisions of the federal securities laws with respect to an error or omission in an electronic filing resulting solely from electronic transmission errors beyond the control of the filer, where the filer corrects the error or omission by the filing of an amendment in electronic format as soon as reasonably practicable after the electronic filer becomes aware of the error or omission.

F. FORMS UNDER SECURITIES ACT OF 1933

(Selected)

Contents

FORM S–1

Registration Statement Under the Securities Act of 1933

* * *

GENERAL INSTRUCTIONS

I. Eligibility Requirements for Use of Form S–1

This Form shall be used for the registration under the Securities Act of 1933 ("Securities Act") of securities of all registrants for which no other form is authorized or prescribed, except that this Form shall not be used for securities of foreign governments or political sub-divisions thereof.

II. Application of General Rules and Regulations

A. Attention is directed to the General Rules and Regulations under the Securities Act, particularly those comprising Regulation C thereunder. That Regulation contains general requirements regarding the preparation and filing of the registration statement.

B. Attention is directed to Regulation S–K for the requirements applicable to the content of the nonfinancial statement portions of registration statements under the Securities Act. Where this Form directs the registrant to furnish information required by Regulation S–K and the item of Regulation S–K so provides, information need only be furnished to the extent appropriate.

III. Exchange Offers

If any of the securities being registered are to be offered in exchange for securities of any other issuer the prospectus shall also include the information which would be required by Item 11 if the securities of such other issuer were registered on this Form. There shall also be included the information concerning such securities of such other issuer which would be called for by Item 9 if such securities were being registered. In connection with this instruction, reference is made to Rule 409.

IV. Roll-up Transactions

If the securities to be registered on this Form will be issued in a roll-up transaction as defined in Item 901(c) of Regulation S–K (17 CFR 229.901(c)), attention is directed to the requirements of Form S–4 applicable to roll-up transactions, including, but not limited to, General Instruction I.

V. Registration of Additional Securities

With respect to the registration of additional securities for an offering pursuant to Rule 462(b) under the Securities Act, the registrant may file a registration statement consisting only of the following: The facing page; a statement that the contents of the earlier registration statement, identified by file number, are incorporated by reference; required opinions and consents; the signature page; and any price-related information omitted from the earlier registration statement in reliance on Rule 430A that the registrant chooses to include in the new registration statement. The information contained in such a Rule 462(b) registration statement shall be deemed to be a part of the earlier registration statement as of the date of effectiveness of the Rule 462(b) registration statement. Any opinion or consent required in the Rule 462(b) registration statement may be incorporated by reference from the earlier registration statement with respect to the offering, if: (i) Such opinion or consent expressly provides for such incorporation; and (ii) such opinion relates to the securities registered pursuant to Rule 462(b). See Rule 411(c) and Rule 439(b) under the Securities Act.

PART I. INFORMATION REQUIRED IN PROSPECTUS

Item 1. Forepart of the Registration Statement and Outside Front Cover Page of Prospectus

Set forth in the forepart of the registration statement and on the outside front cover page of the prospectus the information required by Item 501 of Regulation S–K.

Item 2. Inside Front and Outside Back Cover Pages of Prospectus

Set forth on the inside front cover page of the prospectus or, where permitted, on the outside back cover page, the information required by Item 502 of Regulation S–K.

Item 3. Summary Information, Risk Factors and Ratio of Earnings to Fixed Charges

Furnish the information required by Item 503 of Regulation S–K.

Item 4. Use of Proceeds

Furnish the information required by Item 504 of Regulation S–K.

Item 5. Determination of Offering Price

Furnish the information required by Item 505 of Regulation S–K.

Item 6. Dilution

Furnish the information required by Item 506 of Regulation S–K.

Item 7. Selling Security Holders

Furnish the information required by Item 507 of Regulation S–K.

Item 8. Plan of Distribution

Furnish the information required by Item 508 of Regulation S–K.

Item 9. Description of Securities to be Registered

Furnish the information required by Item 202 of Regulation S–K.

Item 10. Interests of Named Experts and Counsel

Furnish the information required by Item 509 of Regulation S–K.

Item 11. Information With Respect to the Registrant

Furnish the following information with respect to the registrant:

(a) Information required by Item 101 of Regulation S–K, description of business;

(b) Information required by Item 102 of Regulation S–K, description of property;

(c) Information required by Item 103 of Regulation S–K, legal proceedings;

(d) Where common equity securities are being offered, information required by Item 201 of Regulation S–K, market price of and dividends on the registrant's common equity and related stockholder matters;

(e) Financial statements meeting the requirements of Regulation S–K.

(f) Information required by Item 301 of Regulation S–K, selected financial data;

(g) Information required by Item 302 of Regulation S–K, supplementary financial information;

(h) Information required by Item 303 of Regulation S–K, management's discussion and analysis of financial condition and results of operations;

(i) Information required by Item 304 of Regulation S–K, changes in and disagreements with accountants on accounting and financial disclosure;

(j) Information required by Item 305 of Regulation S–K (S29.305 of this chapter), quantitative and qualitative disclosures about market risk.

(k) Information required by Item 401 of Regulation S–K, directors and executive officers;

(*l*) Information required by Item 402 of Regulation S–K, executive compensation;

(m) Information required by Item 403 of Regulation S–K, security ownership of certain beneficial owners and management; and

(n) Information required by Item 404 of Regulation S–K, certain relationships and related transactions.

Item 12. Disclosure of Commission Position on Indemnification for Securities Act Liabilities

Furnish the information required by Item 510 of Regulation S–K.

PART II. INFORMATION NOT REQUIRED IN PROSPECTUS

Item 13. Other Expenses of Issuance and Distribution

Furnish the information required by Item 511 of Regulation S–K.

Item 14. Indemnification of Directors and Officers

Furnish the information required by Item 702 of Regulation S–K.

Item 15. Recent Sales of Unregistered Securities

Furnish the information required by Item 701 of Regulation S–K.

Item 16. Exhibits and Financial Statement Schedules

(a) Subject to the rules regarding incorporation by reference, furnish the exhibits as required by Item 601 of Regulation S–K.

(b) Furnish the financial statement schedules required by Regulation S–K and Item 11(e) of this Form. These schedules shall be lettered or numbered in the manner described for exhibits in paragraph (a).

Item 17. Undertakings

Furnish the undertakings required by Item 512 of Regulation S–K.

FORM S-3

Registration Statement Under the Securities Act of 1933

* * *

GENERAL INSTRUCTIONS

I. Eligibility Requirements for Use of Form S–3.

This form may be used by any registrant which meets the requirements of paragraph (a) of this section ("Registrant Requirements") for the registration of securities under the Securities Act of 1933 ("Securities Act") which are offered in any transaction specified in paragraph (b) of this section ("Transaction Requirements"), provided that the requirements applicable to the specified transaction are met. With respect to majority-owned subsidiaries, see paragraph (c) below. * * *

A. Registrant Requirements.

Registrants must meet the following conditions in order to use this Form for registration under the Securities Act of securities offered in the transactions specified in paragraph B. below:

1. The registrant is organized under the laws of the United States or any State or Territory or the District of Columbia and has its principal business operations in the United States or its territories.

2. The registrant has a class of securities registered pursuant to Section 12(b) of the Securities Exchange Act of 1934 ("Exchange Act") or a class of equity securities registered pursuant to Section 12(g) of the Exchange Act or is required to file reports pursuant to Section 15(d) of the Exchange Act.

3. The registrant: (a) has been subject to the requirements of Section 12 or 15(d) of the Exchange Act and has filed all the material required to be filed pursuant to Sections 13, 14 or 15(d) for a period of at least twelve calendar months immediately preceding the filing of the registration statement on this Form; and (b) has filed in a timely manner all reports required to be filed during the twelve calendar months and any portion of a month immediately preceding the filing of the registration statement and, if the registrant has used (during the twelve calendar months and any portion of a month immediately preceding the filing of the registration statement) Rule 12b–25(b) under the Exchange Act with respect to a report or a portion of a report, that report or portion thereof has actually been filed within the time period prescribed by the Rule.

* * *

5. Neither the registrant nor any of its consolidated or unconsolidated subsidiaries have, since the end of the last fiscal year for which certified financial statements of the registrant and its consolidated subsidiaries were included in a report filed pursuant to Section 13(a) or 15(d) of the Exchange Act: (a) failed to pay any dividend or sinking fund installment on preferred stock; or (b) defaulted (i) on any installment or installments on indebtedness for borrowed money, or (ii) on any rental on one or more long term leases, which defaults in the aggregate are material to the financial position of the registrant and its consolidated and unconsolidated subsidiaries, taken as a whole.

* * *

B. Transaction Requirements.

Security offerings meeting any of the following conditions and made by registrants meeting the Registrant Requirements specified in paragraph A, above may be registered on this Form:

1. Primary And Secondary Offerings By Certain Registrants. Securities to be offered for cash by or on behalf of a registrant, or outstanding securities to be offered for cash for the account of any person other than the registrant, including securities acquired by standby underwriters in connection with the call or redemption by the registrant of warrants or a class of convertible securities; *provided* that the aggregate market value of the voting stock held by non-affiliates of the registrant is $75 million or more.

Instructions. The aggregate market value of the registrant's outstanding voting stock shall be computed by use of the price at which the stock was last sold, or the average of the bid and asked prices of such stock, as of a date within 60 days prior to the date of filing. See the definition of "affiliate" in Securities Act Rule 405.

2. Primary Offerings of Certain Debt and Non-convertible Preferred Securities. Non-convertible securities to be offered for cash by or on behalf of a registrant, provided such securities are "investment grade securities," as defined below. A non-convertible debt or preferred security is an "investment grade security" if, at the time of effectiveness of the registration statement, at least one nationally recognized statistical rating organization (as that term is used in Rule 15c3–1(c)(2)(vi)(F) under the Securities Exchange Act of 1934) has rated the security in one of its generic rating categories which signifies investment grade; typically, the four highest rating categories (within which there may be sub-categories or gradations indicating relative standing) signify investment grade.

3. Transactions Involving Secondary Offerings. Outstanding securities to be offered for the account of any person other than the issuer, including securities acquired by standby underwriters in connection with the call or redemption by the issuer of warrants or a class of convertible securities, if securities of the same class are listed and registered on a national securities exchange or are quoted on the automated quotation system of a national securities association. * * * *

* * *

PART I. INFORMATION REQUIRED IN PROSPECTUS

Item 1. Forepart of the Registration Statement and Outside Front Cover Page of Prospectus.

Set forth in the forepart of the registration statement and on the outside front cover page of the prospectus the information required by Item 501 of Regulation S–K.

Item 2. Inside Front and Outside Back Cover Pages of Prospectus.

Set forth on the inside front cover page of the prospectus or, where permitted, on the outside back cover page, the information required by Item 502 of Regulation S–K.

Item 3. Summary Information, Risk Factors and Ratio of Earnings to Fixed Charges.

Furnish the information required by Item 503 of Regulation S–K.

Item 4. Use of Proceeds.

Furnish the information required by Item 504 of Regulation S–K.

Item 5. Determination of Offering Price.

Furnish the information required by Item 505 of Regulation S–K.

Item 6. Dilution.

Furnish the information required by Item 506 of Regulation S–K.

Item 7. Selling Security Holders.

Furnish the information required by Item 507 of Regulation S–K.

Item 8. Plan of Distribution.

Furnish the information required by Item 508 of Regulation S–K.

Item 9. Description of Securities to be Registered.

Furnish the information required by Item 202 of Regulation S–K unless capital stock is to be registered and securities of the same class are registered pursuant to Section 12 of the Exchange Act.

Item 10. Interests of Named Experts and Counsel.

Furnish the information required by Item 509 of Regulation S–K.

Item 11. Material Changes.

(a) Describe any and all material changes in the registrant's affairs which have occurred since the end of the latest fiscal year for which certified financial statements were included in the latest annual report to security holders and which have not been described in a report on Form 10–Q or Form 8–K filed under the Exchange Act.

(b) Include in the prospectus, if not incorporated by reference therein from the reports filed under the Exchange Act specified in Item 12(a), a proxy or information statement filed pursuant to Section 14 of the Exchange Act, or a prospectus previously filed pursuant to Rule 424(b) or (c) under the Securities Act or where no prospectus was required to be filed pursuant to Rule 424(b), the prospectus included in the registration statement at effectiveness, or a Form 8–K filed during either of the two preceding fiscal years; (i) information required by Rule 3–05 and Article 11 of Regulation S–X; (ii) restated financial statements prepared in accordance with Regulation S–X if there has been a change in accounting principles or a correction of an error where such change or correction requires a material retroactive restatement of financial statements; (iii) restated financial statements prepared in accordance with Regulation S–X where one or more business combinations accounted for by the pooling of interest method of accounting have been consummated subsequent to the most recent fiscal year and the acquired businesses, considered in the aggregate, are significant pursuant to Rule 11–01(b); or (iv) any financial information required because of a material disposition of assets outside the normal course of business.

Item 12. Incorporation of Certain Information by Reference.

(a) The documents listed in (1) and (2) below shall be specifically incorporated by reference into the prospectus, by means of a statement to that effect in the prospectus listing all such documents.

(1) the registrant's latest annual report on Form 10–K filed pursuant to Section 13(a) or 15(d) of the Exchange Act which contains financial statements for the registrant's latest fiscal year for which a Form 10–K was required to have been filed;

(2) all other reports filed pursuant to Section 13(a) or 15(d) of the Exchange Act since the end of the fiscal year covered by the annual report referred to in (1) above; and

(3) if capital stock is to be registered and securities of the same class are registered under Section 12, of the Exchange Act, the description of such class of securities which is contained in a registration statement filed under the Exchange Act, including any amendment or reports filed for the purpose of updating such description.

(b) The prospectus shall also state that all documents subsequently filed by the registrant pursuant to Sections 13(a), 13(c), 14 or 15(d) of the Exchange Act, prior to the termination of the offering, shall be deemed to be incorporated by reference into the prospectus.

(c)(1) You must state (i) that you will provide to each person, including any beneficial owner, to whom a prospectus is delivered, a copy of any or all of the information that has been incorporated by reference in the prospectus but not delivered with the prospectus;

(ii) that you will provide this information upon written or oral request;

(iii) that you will provide this information at no cost to the requester;

(iv) the name, address, and telephone number to which the request for this information must be made.

(2) You must (i) identify the reports and other information that you file with the SEC; and

(ii) state that the public may read and copy any materials you file with the SEC as the SEC's Public Reference Room at 450 Fifth Street, N.W., Washington, D.C. 20549. State that the public may obtain information on the operation of the Public Reference Room by calling the SEC at 1–800–SEC–0330. If you are an electronic filer, state that the SEC maintains an Internet site that contains reports, proxy and information statements, and other information regarding issuers that file electronically with the SEC and state the address of that site (http://www.sec.gov). You are encouraged to give your Internet address, if available.

Instruction. Attention is directed to Rule 439 regarding consent to use of material incorporated by reference.

Item 13. Disclosure of Commission Position on Indemnification for Securities Act Liabilities.

Furnish the information required by Item 510 of Regulation S–K.

PART II. INFORMATION NOT REQUIRED IN PROSPECTUS

Item 14. Other Expenses of Issuance and Distribution.

Furnish the information required by Item 511 of Regulation S–K.

Item 15. Indemnification of Directors and Officers.

Furnish the information required by Item 702 of Regulation S–K.

Item 16. Exhibits.

Subject to the rules regarding incorporation by reference, furnish the exhibits required by Item 601 of Regulation S–K.

Item 17. Undertakings.

Furnish the undertakings required by Item 512 of Regulation S–K.

FORM S-4

Registration Statement Under the Securities Act of 1933

* * *

GENERAL INSTRUCTIONS

A. Rule as to Use of Form S-4.

1. This Form may be used for registration under the Securities Act of 1933 ("Securities Act") of securities to be issued (1) in a transaction of the type specified in paragraph (a) of Rule 145; (2) in a merger in which the applicable state law would not require the solicitation of the votes or consents of all of the security holders of the company being acquired; (3) in an exchange offer for securities of the issuer or another entity; (4) in a public reoffering or resale of any such securities acquired pursuant to this registration statement; or (e) in more than one of the kinds of transaction listed in paragraphs (a) through (d) registered on one registration statement.

* * *

E. Compliance with Exchange Act Rules.

1. If a corporation or other person submits a proposal to its security holders entitled to vote on, or consent to, the transaction which the securities being registered are to be issued, and such person's submission to its security holders is subject to Regulation 14A or 14C under the Exchange Act, then the provisions of such Regulations shall apply in all respects to such person's submission, except that (a) the prospectus may be in the form of a proxy or information statement and may contain the information required by this Form in lieu of that required by Schedule 14A or 14C of Regulation 14A or 14C under the Exchange Act; and (b) copies of the preliminary and definitive proxy or information statement, form of proxy or other material filed as a part of the registration statement shall be deemed filed pursuant to such person's obligations under such Regulations.

2. If the proxy or information material sent to security holders is not subject to Regulation 14A or 14C, all such material shall be filed as a part of the registration statement at the time the statement is filed or as an amendment thereto prior to the use of such material.

3. If the transaction in which the securities being registered are to be issued is subject to Section 13(e), 14(d) or 14(e) of the Exchange Act, the provisions of those sections and the rules and regulations thereunder shall apply to the transaction in addition to the provisions of this Form.

* * *

PART I. INFORMATION REQUIRED IN THE PROSPECTUS

A. Information About The Transaction

Item 1. Forepart of Registration Statement and Outside Front Cover Page of Prospectus.

Set forth in the forepart of the registration statement and on the outside front cover page of the prospectus the information required by Item 501 of Regulation S-K.

Item 2. Inside Front and Outside Back Cover Pages of Prospectus.

Provide the information required by Item 502 of Regulation S-K. In addition, on the inside front cover page, you must state (1) that the prospectus incorporates important business and financial information about the company that is not included in or delivered with the document; and (2) that this information is available without charge to security holders upon written or oral request. Give the name, address, and telephone number to which security holders must make this request. In addition, you must state that to obtain timely delivery, security holders must request the information no later than five business days before the date they must make their investment decision. Specify the date by which security holders must request this information. You must highlight this statement by print type or otherwise.

Item 3. Risk Factors, Ratio of Earnings to Fixed Charges and Other Information.

Provide in the forepart of the prospectus a summary containing the information required by Item 503 of Regulation S-K and the following:

(a) The name, complete mailing address (including the Zip Code), and telephone number (including the area code) of the principal executive offices of the registrant and the company being acquired;

(b) A brief description of the general nature of the business conducted by the registrant and by the company being acquired;

(c) A brief description of the transaction in which the securities being registered are to be offered;

(d) The information required by Item 301 of Regulation S–K (§ 229.301 of this chapter) (selected financial data) for the registrant and the company being acquired. To the extent the information is required to be presented in the prospectus pursuant to Items 12, 14, 16 or 17, it need not be repeated pursuant to this Item.

(e) If material, the information required by Item 301 of Regulation S–K for the registrant on a pro forma basis, giving effect to the transaction. To the extent the information is required to be presented in the prospectus pursuant to Items 12 or 14, it need not be repeated pursuant to this Item.

(f) In comparative columnar form, historical and pro forma per share data of the registrant and historical and equivalent pro forma per share data of the company being acquired for the following items:

(1) book value per share as of the date financial data is presented pursuant to Item 301 of Regulation S–K (§ 229.301 of this chapter) (selected financial data);

(2) cash dividends declared per share for the periods for which financial data is presented pursuant to Item 301 of Regulation S–K (§ 229.301 of this chapter) (selected financial data);

(3) income (loss) per share from continuing operations for the periods for which financial data is presented pursuant to Item 301 of Regulation S–K (§ 229.301 of this chapter) (selected financial data).

Instruction to paragraphs (e) and (f).

For a business combination accounted for as a purchase, the financial information required by paragraphs (e) and (f) shall be presented only for the most recent fiscal year and interim period. For a business combination accounted for as a pooling, the financial information required by paragraphs (e) and (f) (except for information with regard to book value) shall be presented for the most recent three fiscal years and interim period. For a business combination accounted for as a pooling, information with regard to book value shall be presented as of the end of the most recent fiscal year and interim period. Equivalent pro forma per share amounts shall be calculated by multiplying the pro forma income (loss) per share before non-recurring charges or credits directly attributable to the transaction, pro forma book value per share, and the pro forma dividends per share of the registrant by the exchange ratio so that the per share amounts are equated to the respective values for one share of the company being acquired.

(g) With respect to the registrant and the company being acquired, a brief statement comparing the percentage of outstanding shares entitled to vote held by directors, executive officers and their affiliates and the vote required for approval of the proposed transaction;

(h) A statement as to whether any federal or state regulatory requirements must be complied with or approval must be obtained in connection with the transaction, and if so, the status of such compliance or approval;

(i) A statement about whether or not dissenters' rights of appraisal exist, including a cross-reference to the information provided pursuant to Item 18 or 19 of this Form; and

(j) A brief statement about the tax consequences of the transaction, or if appropriate, consisting of a cross-reference to the information provided pursuant to Item 4 of this Form.

(k) A brief statement about the tax consequences of the transaction, or if appropriate, consisting of a cross-reference to the information provided pursuant to Item 4 of this Form.

Item 4. Terms of the Transaction.

(a) Furnish a summary of the material features of the proposed transaction. The summary shall include, where applicable:

(1) A brief summary of the terms of the acquisition agreement;

(2) The reasons of the registrant and of the company being acquired for engaging in the transaction;

(3) The information required by Item 202 of Regulation S-K, description of registrant's securities, unless: (i) the registrant would meet the requirements for use of Form S-3 and elects to furnish information pursuant to Item 10, (ii) capital stock is to be registered and (iii) securities of the same class are registered under Section 12 of the Exchange Act and (i) listed for trading or admitted to unlisted trading privileges on a national securities exchange; or (ii) are securities for which bid and offer quotations are reported in an automated quotations system operated by a national securities association;

(4) An explanation of any material differences between the rights of security holders of the company being acquired and the rights of holders of the securities being offered;

(5) A brief statement as to the accounting treatment of the transaction; and

(6) The federal income tax consequences of the transaction.

(b) If a report, opinion or appraisal materially relating to the transaction has been received from an outside party, and such report, opinion or appraisal is referred to in the prospectus, furnish the same information as would be required by Item 9(b)(1) through (6) of Schedule 13E-3.

(c) Incorporate the acquisition agreement by reference into the prospectus by means of a statement to that effect.

Item 5. Pro Forma Financial Information.

Furnish financial information required by Article 11 of Regulation S-X with respect to this transaction.

* * *

Item 6. Material Contacts with the Company Being Acquired.

Describe any past, present or proposed material contracts, arrangements, understandings, relationships, negotiations or transactions during the periods for which financial statements are presented or incorporated by reference pursuant to Part I.B. or C. of this Form between the company being acquired or its affiliates and the registrant or its affiliates, such as those concerning: a merger, consolidation or acquisition; a tender offer or other acquisition of securities; an election of directors; or a sale or other transfer of a material amount of assets.

Item 7. Additional Information Required for Reoffering by Persons and Parties Deemed to Be Underwriters.

If any of the securities are to be reoffered to the public by any person or party who is deemed to be an underwriter thereof, furnish the following information in the prospectus, at the time it is being used for the reoffer of the securities to the extent it is not already furnished therein:

(a) The information required by Item 507 of Regulation S-K, selling security holders; and

(b) Information with respect to the consummation of the transaction pursuant to which the securities were acquired and any material change in the registrant's affairs subsequent to the transaction.

Item 8. Interests of Named Experts and Counsel.

Furnish the information required by Item 509 of Regulation S-K.

Item 9. Disclosure of Commission Position on Indemnification for Securities Act Liabilities.

Furnish the information required by Item 510 of Regulation S-K.

B. Information About The Registrant

Item 10. Information with Respect to S-3 Registrants.

If the registrant meets the requirements for use of Form S-3 and elects to furnish information in accordance with the provisions of this Item, furnish information as required below:

(a) Describe any and all material changes in the registrant's affairs that have occurred since the end of the latest fiscal year for which audited financial statements were included in the latest annual report to security holders and that have not been described in a report on Form 10-Q and Form 10-QSB or Form 8-K filed under the Exchange Act.

* * *

Item 11. Incorporation of Certain Information by Reference.

If the registrant meets the requirements of Form S–3 and elects to furnish information in accordance with the provisions of Item 10 of this Form:

(a) Incorporate by reference into the prospectus, by means of a statement to that effect listing all documents so incorporated, the documents listed in paragraphs (1), (2) and, if applicable, (3) below.

(1) The registrant's latest annual report on Form 10–K and Form 10–KSB filed pursuant to Section 13(a) or 15(d) of the Exchange Act which contains financial statements for the registrant's latest fiscal year for which a Form 10–K was required to be filed;

(2) All other reports filed pursuant to Section 13(a) or 15(d) of the Exchange Act since the end of the fiscal year covered by the annual report referred to in Item 11(a)(1) of this Form;

(3) If capital stock is to be registered and securities of the same class are registered under Section 12 of the Exchange Act and: (i) listed for trading or admitted to unlisted trading privileges on a national securities exchange; or (ii) are securities for which bid and offer quotations are reported in an automated quotations system operated by a national securities association, the description of such class of securities which is contained in a registration statement filed under the Exchange Act, including any amendment or reports filed for the purpose of updating such description.

(b) The prospectus also shall state that all documents subsequently filed by the registrant pursuant to Sections 13(a), 13(c), 14 or 15(d) of the Exchange Act, prior to one of the following dates, whichever is applicable, shall be deemed to be incorporated by reference into the prospectus:

(1) If a meeting of security holders is to be held, the date on which such meeting is held;

(2) If a meeting of security holders is not to be held, the date on which the transaction is consummated;

(3) If securities of the registrant are being offered in exchange for securities of any other issuer, the date the offering is terminated; or

(4) If securities are being offered in a reoffering or resale of securities acquired pursuant to this registration statement, the date the reoffering is terminated.

Instruction. Attention is directed to Rule 439 regarding consent to the use of material incorporated by reference.

(c) You must (1) identify the reports and other information that you file with the SEC; and

(2) state that the public may read and copy any materials you file with the SEC at the SEC's Public Reference Room at 450 Fifth Street, N.W., Washington, D.C. 20549. State that the public may obtain information on the operation of the Public Reference Room by calling the SEC at 1–800–SEC–0330. If you an electronic filer, state that the SEC maintains an Internet site that contains reports, proxy and information statements, and other information regarding issuers that file electronically with the SEC and state the address of that site (http://www.sec.gov). You are encouraged to give your Internet address, if available.

Item 12. Information with Respect to S–2 or S–3 Registrants.

If the registrant meets the requirements for use of Form S–2 or S–3 and elects to comply with this Item, furnish the information required by either paragraph (a) or (b) of this Item. * * *

(a) If the registrant elects to deliver this prospectus together with its latest annual report to security holders, which at the time of original preparation met the requirements of either Rule 14a–3 or 14c–3, or a complete and legible facsimile of its latest annual report to security holders:

(1) Indicate that the prospectus is accompanied by either a copy of the registrant's latest Form 10–K or Form 10–KSB or a copy of the registrant's latest annual report to security holders, whichever the registrant elects to deliver pursuant to paragraph (a) of this Item.

(2) Provide financial and other information with respect to the registrant in the form required by Part I of Form 10–Q as of the end of the most recent fiscal quarter which ended after the end of the last fiscal year * * *

(4) Describe any and all material changes in the registrant's affairs that have occurred since the end of the latest fiscal year * * *

(b) If the registrant does not elect to deliver its latest Form 10-K or Form 10-KSB or its latest annual report to security holders:

(1) Furnish a brief description of the business done by the registrant and its subsidiaries during the most recent fiscal year as required by Rule 14a-3 to be included in an annual report to security holders. The description also should take into account changes in the registrant's business that have occurred between the end of the latest fiscal year and the effective date of the registration statement.

(2) Include financial statements and information as required by Rule 14a-3(b)(1) (240.14a-3(b)(1) of this chapter) to be included in an annual report to security holders.

* * *

(3) Furnish the information required by the following:

(i) Item 101(b), (c)(1)(i) and (d) of Regulation S-K, industry segments, classes of similar products or services, foreign and domestic operations and export sales;

(ii) where common equity securities are being offered, Item 201 of Regulation S-K, market price of and dividends on the registrant's common equity and related stockholder matters;

(iii) Item 301 or Regulation S-K, selected financial data;

(iv) Item 302 of Regulation S-K, supplementary financial information;

(v) Item 303 of Regulation S-K, management's discussion and analysis of financial condition and results of operations;

(vi) Item 304 of Regulation S-K, changes in and disagreements with accountants on accounting and financial disclosure; and

(vii) Item 305 of Regulation S-K, quantitative and qualitative disclosures about market risk.

(c) The registrant shall furnish the information required by paragraph (b) of this Item if:

(1) the registrant was required to make a material retroactive restatement of financial statements because of

(i) a change in accounting principles; or

(ii) a correction of an error; or

(iii) a consummation of one or more business combinations accounted for by the pooling of interest method of accounting was effected subsequent to the most recent fiscal year and the acquired business considered in the aggregate meet the test of a significant subsidiary; or

(2) the registrant engaged in a material disposition of assets outside of the normal course of business; and

(3) such restatement of financial statements or disposition of assets was not reflected in the registrant's latest annual report to security holders and/or its latest Form 10-K or Form 10-KSB filed pursuant to Sections 13(a) or 15(d) of the Exchange Act.

Item 13. Incorporation of Certain Information by Reference.

If the registrant meets the requirements of Form S-2 or S-3 and elects to furnish information in accordance with the provisions of Item 12 of this Form:

(a) Incorporate by reference into the prospectus, by means of a statement to that effect in the prospectus listing all documents so incorporated, the documents listed in paragraphs (1) and (2) of this Item * * *

(b) The registrant also may state, if it so chooses, that specifically described portions of its annual or quarterly report to security holders, other than those portions required to be incorporated by reference pursuant to paragraphs (a)(3) and (4) of this Item, are not part of the registration statement. In such case, the description of portions that are not incorporated by reference or that are excluded shall be made with clarity and in reasonable detail.

(c) *Electronic filings.* Electronic filers electing to deliver and incorporate by reference all, or any portion, of the quarterly or annual report to security holders pursuant to this Item shall file as an exhibit such quarterly or annual report to security holders, or such portion thereof that is incorporated by reference, in electronic format.

(d) You must (1) identify the reports and other information that you file with the SEC; and

(2) state that the public may read and copy any materials you file with the SEC at the SEC's Public

Reference Room at 450 Fifth Street, N.W., Washington, D.C. 20549. State that the public may obtain information on the operation of the Public Reference Room by calling the SEC at 1–800–SEC–0330. If you are an electronic filer, state that the SEC maintains an Internet site that contains reports, proxy and information statements, and other information regarding issuers that file electronically with the SEC and state the address of that site (http://www.sec.gov). You are encouraged to give your Internet address, if available.

Item 14. Information with Respect to Registrants Other Than S–3 or S–2 Registrants.

If the registrant does not meet the requirements for use of Form S–2 or S–3, or otherwise elects to comply with this Item in lieu of Item 10 or 12, furnish the information required by:

(a) Item 101 of Regulation S–K, description of business;

(b) Item 102 of Regulation S–K, description of property;

(c) Item 103 of Regulation S–K, legal proceedings;

(d) Where common equity securities are being issued, Item 201 of Regulation S–K, market price of and dividends on the registrant's common equity and related stockholder matters;

(e) Financial statements meeting the requirements of Regulation S–X, (schedules required by Regulation S–X shall be filed as "Financial Statement Schedules" pursuant to Item 21 of this Form), as well as financial information required by Rule 3–05 and Article 11 of Regulation S–X with respect to transactions other than that pursuant to which the securities being registered are to be issued;

(f) Item 301 of Regulation S–K, selected financial data;

(g) Item 302 of Regulation S–K, supplementary financial information;

(h) Item 303 of Regulation S–K management's discussion and analysis of financial condition and results of operations;

(i) Item 304 of Regulation S–K, changes in and disagreements with accountants on accounting and financial disclosure; and

(j) Item 305 of Regulation S–K, quantitative and qualitative disclosures about market risk.

C. Information About The Company Being Acquired

Item 15. Information with Respect to S–3 Companies.

If the company being acquired meets the requirements for use of Form S–3 and compliance with this Item is elected, furnish the information that would be required by Items 10 and 11 of this Form if securities of such company were being registered.

Item 16. Information with Respect to S–2 or S–3 Companies.

If the company being acquired meets the requirements for use of Form S–2 or S–3 and compliance with this Item is elected, furnish the information that would be required by Items 12 and 13 of this Form if securities of such company were being registered.

Item 17. Information with Respect to Companies Other Than S–3 or S–2 Companies.

If the company being acquired does not meet the requirements for use of Form S–2 or S–3, or compliance with this Item is otherwise elected in lieu of Item 15 or 16, furnish the information required by paragraph (a) or (b) of this Item, whichever is applicable.

(a) If the company being acquired is subject to the reporting requirements of Section 13(a) or 15(d) of the Exchange Act, or compliance with this subparagraph in lieu of subparagraph (b) of this Item is selected, furnish the information that would be required by Item 14 of this Form if the securities of such company were being registered; * * *

(b) If the company being acquired is not subject to the reporting requirements of either Section 13(a) or 15(d) of the Exchange Act; or, because of Section 12(i) of the Exchange Act, has not furnished an annual report to security holders pursuant to Rule 14a–3 or Rule 14c–3 for its latest fiscal year; furnish the information that would be required by the following if securities of such company were being registered:

(1) a brief description of the business done by the company which indicates the general nature and scope of the business;

(2) Item 201 of Regulation S-K, market price of and dividends on the registrant's common equity and related stockholder matters;

(3) Item 301 of Regulation S-K, selected financial data;

(4) Item 302 of Regulation S-K, supplementary financial information;

(5) Item 303 of Regulation S-K, management's discussion and analysis of financial condition and results of operations;

(6) Item 304(b) of Regulation S-K, changes in and disagreements with accountants on accounting and financial disclosure;

(7) financial statements as would be required in an annual report sent to security holders pursuant to Rules 14a-3(b)(1) and (b)(2), if an annual report was required.

(7) If the registrant's security holders are not voting, the transaction is not a roll-up transaction (as described by Item 901 of Regulation S-K (§ 229.901 of this chapter)), and:

(i) the company being acquired is significant to the registrant in excess of the 20% level as determined under § 210.3-05(b)(2), provide financial statements of the company being acquired for the latest fiscal year in conformity with GAAP. In addition, if the company being acquired has provided its security holders with financial statements prepared in conformity with GAAP for either or both of the two fiscal years before the latest fiscal year, provide the financial statements for those years; or

(ii) the company being acquired is significant to the registrant at or below the 20% level, no financial information (including pro forma and comparative per share information) for the company being acquired need be provided.

Instructions:

(1) The financial statements required by this paragraph for the latest fiscal year need be audited only to the extent practicable. The financial statements for the fiscal years before the latest fiscal year need not be audited if they were not previously audited.

(2) If the financial statements required by this paragraph are prepared on the basis of a comprehensive body of accounting principles other than U.S. GAAP, provide reconciliation to U.S. GAAP in accordance with Item 17 of Form 20-F (§ 249.220f of this chapter) unless a reconciliation is unavailable or not obtainable without unreasonable cost or expense. At a minimum, provide a narrative description of all material variations in accounting principles, practices and methods used in preparing the non-U.S. GAAP financial statements from those accepted in the U.S. when the financial statements are prepared on a basis other than U.S. GAAP.

(3) If this Form is used to register resales to the public by any person who is deemed an underwriter within the meaning of Rule 145(c) (§ 230.145(c) of this chapter) with respect to the securities being reoffered, the financial statements must be audited for the fiscal years required to be presented under paragraph (b)(2) of Rule 3-05 of Regulation S-X (17 CFR 210.3-05(b)(2)).

(4) In determining the significance of an acquisition for purposes of this paragraph, apply the tests prescribed in Rule 1-02(w) (§ 210.1-02(w) of this chapter).

* * *

(8) The quarterly financial and other information as would have been required had the company being acquired been required to file Part I of Form 10-Q and Form 10-QSB for the most recent quarter for which such a report would have been on file at the time the registration statement becomes effective or for a period ending as of a more recent date.

* * *

(10) Item 305 of Regulation S-K, quantitative and qualitative disclosures about market risk.

D. Voting and Management Information

Item 18. Information if Proxies, Consents or Authorizations are to be Solicited.

(a) If proxies, consents or authorizations are to be solicited, furnish the following information, except as provided by paragraph (b) of this Item:

(1) The information required by Item 1 of Schedule 14A, date, time and place information;

(2) The information required by Item 2 of Schedule 14A, revocability of proxy;

(3) The information required by Item 3 of Schedule 14A, dissenters' rights of appraisal;

(4) The information required by Item 4 of Schedule 14A, persons making the solicitation;

(5) With respect to both the registrant and the company being acquired, the information required by:

(i) Item 5 of Schedule 14A, interest of certain persons in matters to be acted upon; and

(ii) Item 6 of Schedule 14A, voting securities and principal holders thereof;

(6) The information required by Item 21 of Schedule 14A, vote required for approval; and

(7) With respect to each person who will serve as a director or an executive officer of the surviving or acquiring company, the information required by:

(i) Item 401 of Regulation S–K, directors and executive officers;

(ii) Item 402 of Regulation S–K, executive compensation; and

(iii) Item 404 of Regulation S–K, certain relationships and related transactions.

(b) If the registrant or the company being acquired meets the requirements for use of Form S–2 or S–3, any information required by paragraphs (a)(5)(ii) and (7) of this Item with respect to such company may be incorporated by reference from its latest annual report on Form 10–K and Form 10–KSB.

Item 19. Information if Proxies, Consents or Authorizations are not to be Solicited or in an Exchange Offer.

(a) If the transaction is an exchange offer or if proxies, consents or authorizations are not to be solicited, furnish the following information, except as provided by paragraph (c) of this Item:

(1) The information required by Item 2 of Schedule 14C, statement that proxies are not to be solicited;

(2) The date, time and place of the meeting of security holders, unless such information is otherwise disclosed in material furnished to security holders with the prospectus;

(3) The information required by Item 3 of Schedule 14A, dissenters' rights of appraisal;

(4) With respect to both the registrant and the company being acquired, a brief description of any material interest, direct or indirect, by the security holdings or otherwise, of affiliates of the registrant and of the company being acquired, in the proposed transactions;

Instruction.

This subparagraph shall not apply to any interest arising from the ownership of securities of the registrant where the security of the registrant where the security holder receives no extra or special benefit not shared on a pro rata basis by all other holders of the same class.

(5) With respect to both the registrant and the company being acquired, the information required by Item 6 of Schedule 14A, voting securities and principal holders thereof;

(6) The information required by Item 21 of Schedule 14A, vote required for approval; and

(7) With respect to each person who will serve as a director or an executive officer of the surviving or acquiring company, the information required by:

(i) Item 401 of Regulation S–K, directors and executive officers;

(ii) Item 402 of Regulation S–K, executive compensation; and

(iii) Item 404 of Regulation S–K, certain relationships and related transactions.

(b) If the transaction is an exchange offer, furnish the information required by paragraphs (a)(4), (a)(5), (a)(6) and (a)(7) of this Item, except as provided by paragraph (c) of this Item.

(c) If the registrant or the company being acquired meets the requirements for use of Form S–2 or S–3, any information required by paragraphs (a)(5) and (7) of this Item with respect to such company may be incorporated by reference from its latest annual report on Form 10–K and Form 10–KSB.

PART II. INFORMATION NOT REQUIRED IN PROSPECTUS

Item 20. Indemnification of Directors and Officers.

Furnish the information required by Item 702 of Regulation S–K.

Item 21. Exhibits and Financial Statement Schedules.

(a) Subject to the rules regarding incorporation by reference, furnish the exhibits as required by Item 601 of Regulation S–K.

* * *

FORM SB-1

Registration Statement Under the Securities Act of 1933

GENERAL INSTRUCTIONS

A. Use of Form and Place of Filing

1. (a) A "small business issuer," defined in Rule 405 of the Securities Act of 1933 (the "Securities Act") may use this form to register up to $10,000,000 of securities to be sold for cash, if they have not registered more than $10,000,000 in securities offerings in any continuous 12–month period, including the transaction being registered. In calculating the $10,000,000 ceiling, issuers should include all offerings which were registered under the Securities Act, other than any amounts registered on Form S–8.

(b) A small business issuer may use this form until it (1) registers more than $10 million under the Securities Act in any continuous 12–month period (other than securities registered on Form S–8), (2) elects to file on a non-transitional disclosure document (other than the proxy statement disclosure in Schedule 14A), or (3) no longer meets the definition of small business issuer. Non-transitional disclosure documents include: (1) Securities Act registration statement forms other than Forms SB–1, S–3 (if the issuer incorporates by reference transitional Exchange Act reports), S–8 and S–4 (if the issuer relies upon the transitional disclosure format in that form); (2) Exchange Act periodic reporting Forms 10–K and 10–Q; (3) Exchange Act registration statement Form 10; and (4) reports or registration statements on Forms 10–KSB, 10–QSB or 10–SB which do not use the transitional disclosure document format. A reporting company may not return to the transitional disclosure forms.

2. The small business issuer shall file the registration statement in the Washington, D.C. office.

3. If the small business issuer is a reporting company or a holding company of a bank (see the definition of "bank" in section 12(i) of the Securities Exchange Act of 1934), it should file the registration statement in the Commission's Washington D.C. headquarters.

B. General Requirements

1. In preparing a registration statement on this Form, reference should be made to the General Rules and Regulations under the Securities Act, particularly Regulation C which sets forth requirements for the preparation and filing of a registration statement such as paper type and size.

2. Issuers registering securities for the first time should be aware of Form SR and Rule 463 under the Securities Act concerning sales of registered securities and the use of proceeds. First-time issuers also should be aware of Exchange Act Rule 15c2–8 which requires broker-dealers to deliver a prospectus 48 hours before a sale of securities can be confirmed.

3. Issuers engaged in real estate, oil and gas or mining activities should consult the Industry Guides in Item 801 of Regulation S–K: Real estate companies also should refer to Item 13 [Investment Policies of Registrant], Item 14 [Description of Real Estate], and Item 15 [Operating Data] of Form S–11.

C. Preparation and Filing of the Registration Statement

Part I of this form, which relates to the content of certain information about the issuer, provides several alternative disclosure formats. The registrant may elect any of these alternative formats.

D. Financial Statement Requirements

Regardless of the disclosure model used, all registrants shall provide the financial statements required by Part F/S of this Form SB–1.

E. Composition of Prospectus

The information required by Part I and Part F/S of this regulation statement shall comprise the prospectus.

F. Cover Page of Registration Statement

Issuers electing Alternative 1 should furnish the information required by Item 501 of Regulation S–B in lieu of the information required by Alternative 1 with respect to the cover page of the registration statement. Issuers electing Alternative 2 should furnish the information required by Item 501 of Regulation S–B in lieu of the information required by Item 1 of Alternative 2.

G. Canadian Issuer—Consent of Service

Canadian issuers eligible to use this Form should file as an exhibit to this registration statement a written irrevocable consent and power of attorney on Form F–X.

H. Registration of Additional Securities

With respect to the registration of additional securities for an offering pursuant to Rule 462(b) under the Securities Act, the registrant may file a registration statement consisting only of the following: The facing page; a statement that the contents of the earlier registration statement, identified by file number, are incorporated by reference; required opinions and consents; the signature page; and any price-related information omitted from the earlier registration statement in reliance on Rule 430A that the registrant chooses to include in the new registration statement. The information contained in such a Rule 462(b) registration statement shall be deemed to be a part of the earlier registration statement as of the date of effectiveness of the Rule 462(b) registration statement. Any opinion or consent required in the Rule 462(b) registration statement may be incorporated by reference from the earlier registration statement with respect to the offering, if: (i) Such opinion or consent expressly provides for such incorporation; and (ii) such opinion relates to the securities registered pursuant to Rule 462(b). See Rule 411(c) and Rule 439(b) under the Securities Act.

PART I—NARRATIVE INFORMATION REQUIRED IN PROSPECTUS

Alternative 1

Corporate issuers may elect to furnish the information required by Model A of Form 1–A, as well as the following information.

Item 1. Inside Front and Outside Back Cover Pages of Prospectus.

Furnish the information required by Item 502 of Regulation S–B.

Item 2. Significant Parties.

List the full names and business and residential addresses, as applicable, for the following persons:

(1) the issuer's directors;

(2) the issuer's officers;

(3) the issuer's general partners;

(4) record owners of 5 percent or more of any class of the issuer's equity securities;

(5) beneficial owners of 5 percent or more of any class of the issuer's equity securities;

(6) promoters of the issuer;

(7) affiliates of the issuer;

(8) counsel to the issuer with respect to the proposed offering;

(9) each underwriter with respect to the proposed offering;

(10) the underwriter's directors;

(11) the underwriter's officers;

(12) the underwriter's general partners; and

(13) counsel to the underwriter.

Item 3. Relationship with Issuer of Experts Named in Registration Statement.

Furnish the information required by Item 509 of Regulation S–B, if applicable.

Item 4. Selling Security Holders.

Furnish the information required by Item 507 of Regulation S–B, if applicable.

Item 5. Changes in and Disagreements with Accountants.

Furnish the information required by Item 304 of Regulation S–B, if applicable.

Item 6. Disclosure of Commission position on Indemnification for Securities Act Liabilities.

Furnish the information required by Item 510 of Regulation S–B.

Alternative 2

Any issuer may elect to furnish the information required by Model B of Part II of Form 1–A, as well as the following information.

Item 1. Inside Front and Outside Back Cover Pages of Prospectus.

Furnish the information required by Item 502 of Regulation S–B.

Item 2. Significant Parties.

List the full names and business and residential addresses, as applicable, for the following persons:

(1) the issuer's directors;

(2) the issuer's officers;

(3) the issuer's general partners;

(4) record owners of 5 percent or more of any class of the issuer's equity securities;

(5) beneficial owners of 5 percent or more of any class of the issuer's equity securities;

(6) promoters of the issuer;

(7) affiliates of the issuer;

(8) counsel to the issuer with respect to the proposed offering;

(9) each underwriter with respect to the proposed offering;

(10) the underwriter's directors;

(11) the underwriter's officers;

(12) the underwriter's general partners; and

(13) counsel to the underwriter.

Item 3. Relationship with Issuer of Experts Named in Registration Statement.

Furnish the information required by Item 509 of Regulation S–B, if applicable.

Item 4. Legal Proceedings.

Furnish the information required by Item 103 of Regulation S–B.

Item 5. Changes in and Disagreements with Accountants.

Furnish the information required by Item 304 of Regulation S–B is applicable.

Item 6. Disclosure of Commission Position on Indemnification for Securities Act Liabilities.

Furnish the information required by Item 510 of Regulation S–B.

PART F/S—FINANCIAL INFORMATION REQUIRED IN PROSPECTUS

Furnish the information required by Item 310 of Regulation S–B.

PART II—INFORMATION NOT REQUIRED IN PROSPECTUS

Item 1. Indemnification of Directors and Officers.

Furnish the information required by Item 702 of Regulation S–B.

Item 2. Other Expenses of Issuance and Distribution.

Furnish the information required by Item 511 of Regulation S–B.

Item 3. Undertakings.

Furnish the undertakings required by Item 512 of Regulation S–B.

Item 4. Unregistered Securities Issued or Sold Within One Year.

(a) As to any unregistered securities issued by the issuer or any of its predecessors or affiliated issuers within one year prior to the filing of this Form SB–1, state:

(1) the name of such issuer;

(2) the title and amount of securities issued;

(3) the aggregate offering price or other consideration for which they were issued and the basis for computing the amount thereof;

(4) the names and identities of the persons to whom the securities were issued.

(b) As to any unregistered securities of the issuer or any of its predecessors or affiliated issuers which were sold within one year prior to the filing of this Form SB–1 by or for the account of any person who at the time was a director, officer, promoter or principal security holder of the issuer of such securities, or was an underwriter of any securities of such issuer, furnish the information specified in subsections (1) through (4) of paragraph (a).

(c) Indicate the section of the Securities Act or Commission rule or regulation relied upon for exemption from the registration requirements of such Act and state briefly the facts relied upon for such exemption.

Item 5. Index to Exhibits.

(a) An index to the exhibits should be presented.

(b) Each exhibit should be listed in the exhibit index according to the number assigned to it in Part III of Form 1–A or Item 6, below.

(c) The index to exhibits should identify the location of the exhibit under the sequential page numbering system for this Form SB–1.

(d) where exhibits are incorporated by reference, the reference shall be made in the index of exhibits.

Instructions:

1. Any document or part thereof filed with the Commission pursuant to any Act administered by the Commission may, subject to the limitations of Rule 24 of the Commission's Rules of Practice, be incorporated by reference as an exhibit to any registration statement.

2. If any modification has occurred in the text of any document incorporated by reference since the filing thereof, the issuer shall file with the reference a statement containing the text of such modification and the date thereof.

3. Procedurally, the techniques specified in Rule 411(d) of Regulation C shall be followed.

Item 6. Description of Exhibits.

As appropriate, the issuer should file as exhibits those documents required to be filed under Part III of Form 1–A. Part III of Form 1–A lists 10 exhibits. The registrant also shall file:

(11) *Opinion re legality*—An opinion of counsel as to the legality of the securities covered by the Registration Statement, indicating whether they will, when sold, be legally issued, fully paid and non-assessable, and if debt securities, whether they will be binding obligations of the issuer.

(12) *Additional exhibits*—Any additional exhibits which the issuer may wish to file, which shall be so marked as to indicate clearly the subject matters to which they refer.

(13) *Form F–X*—Canadian issuers shall file a written irrevocable consent and power of attorney on Form F–X.

* * *

FORM SB–2

Registration Statement Under the Securities Act of 1933

Form SB–2 is available to any small business issuer to raise any dollar amount of funds in cash. It may be used for repeat offerings as long as the issuer continues to meet the definition of "small business issuer" under Regulation S–B. Regulation S–B is intended solely at small businesses.

G. FORMS AND SCHEDULES UNDER SECURITIES EXCHANGE ACT OF 1934

(Selected)

FORM 8–K

CURRENT REPORT

Pursuant to Section 13 or 15(d) of the Securities Exchange Act of 1934

* * *

GENERAL INSTRUCTIONS

A. Rule as to Use of Form 8–K.

Form 8–K shall be used for current reports under Section 13 or 15(d) of the Securities Exchange Act of 1934, filed pursuant to Rule 13a–11 or Rule 15d–11, and for reports of nonpublic information required to be disclosed by Regulation FD (17 CFR 243.100 and 243.101).

B. Events to be Reported and Time for Filing of Reports.

1. A report on this form is required to be filed upon the occurrence of any one or more of the events specified in Items 1–4, 6 and 10 of this form. A report of an event specified in Items 1–3 is to be filed within 15 calendar days after the occurrence of the event. A report of an event specified in Item 4, 6 or 10 is to be filed within 5 business days after the occurrence of the event; if the event occurs on a Saturday, Sunday, or holiday on which the Commission is not open for business then the 5 business day period shall begin to run on and include the first business day thereafter. A report on this form pursuant to Item 8 is required to be filed within 15 calendar days after the date on which the registrant makes the determination to use a fiscal year end different from that used in its most recent filing with the Commission. A registrant either furnishing a report on this form under Item 9 or electing to file a report on this form under Item 5 solely to satisfy its obligations under Regulation FD must furnish such report or make such filing in accordance with the requirements of Rule 100(a) of Regulation FD). A report on this form pursuant to Item 11 is required to be filed not later than the date prescribed for transmission of the notice to directors and executive officers required by Rule 104(b)(2) of Regulation BTR.

2. The information in a report furnished pursuant to Item 9 shall not be deemed to be "filed" for the purposes of Section 18 of the Exchange Act or otherwise subject to the liabilities of that section, except if the registrant specifically states that the

information is to be considered "filed" under the Exchange Act or incorporates it by reference into a filing under the Securities Act or the Exchange Act.

3. If substantially the same information as that required by this form has been previously reported by the registrant, an additional report of the information on this form need not be made. The term "previously reported" is defined in Rule 12b–2.

4. When considering current reporting on this form, particularly of other events of material importance pursuant to Item 5 and of information pursuant to Item 9, registrants should have due regard for the accuracy, completeness and currency of the information in registration statements filed under the Securities Act of 1933 which incorporate by reference information in reports filed pursuant to the Securities Exchange Act of 1934, including reports on this form.

5. A registrant's report under Item 5 or Item 9 will not be deemed an admission as to the materiality of any information in the report that is required to be disclosed solely by Regulation FD.

6. A report on this form is required to be furnished upon the occurrence of any of the events specified in Item 12 of this form. A report of an event specified in Item 12 is to be furnished within 5 business days after the occurrence of the event; if the event occurs on a Saturday, Sunday or holiday on which the Commission is not open for business, the 5 business day period shall begin to run on and include the first business day thereafter. The information in a report furnished pursuant to Item 12 shall not be deemed to be "filed" for purposes of Section 18 of the Exchange Act or otherwise subject to the liability of that section, except if the registrant specifically states that the information is to be considered "filed" under the Exchange Act or incorporates it by reference into a filing under the Securities Act or the Exchange Act.

* * *

F. Incorporation by Reference.

If the registrant makes available to its stockholders or otherwise publishes, within the period prescribed for filing the report, a press release or other document or statement containing information meeting some or all of the requirements of this form, the information called for may be incorporated by reference to such published document or statement, in answer or partial answer to any item or items of this form, provided copies thereof are filed as an exhibit to the report on this form.

INFORMATION TO BE INCLUDED IN THE REPORT

Item 1. Changes in Control of Registrant.

(a) If, to the knowledge of management, a change in control of the registrant has occurred, state the name of the person(s) who acquired such control; the amount and the source of the consideration used by such person(s); the basis of the control; the date and a description of the transaction(s) which resulted in the change in control; the percentage of voting securities of the registrant now beneficially owned directly or indirectly by the person(s) who acquired control; and the identity of the person(s) from whom control was assumed. If the source of all or any part of the consideration used is a loan made in the ordinary course of business by a bank as defined by Section 3(a)(6) of the Act, the identity of such bank shall be omitted provided a request for confidentiality has been made pursuant to Section 13(d)(1)(B) of the Act by the person(s) who acquired control. In lieu thereof, the material shall indicate that disclosure of the identity of the bank has been so omitted and filed separately with the Commission.

Instructions. 1. State the terms of any loans or pledges obtained by the new control group for the purpose of acquiring control, and the names of the lenders or pledgees.

2. Any arrangements or understandings among members of both the former and new control groups and their associates with respect to election of directors or other matters should be described.

(b) Furnish the information required by Item 403(c) of Regulation S–K.

Item 2. Acquisition or Disposition of Assets.

If the registrant or any of its majority-owned subsidiaries has acquired or disposed of a significant amount of assets, otherwise than in the ordinary course of business, furnish the following information:

(a) The date and manner of acquisition or disposition and a brief description of the assets involved, the nature and amount of consideration given or received therefor, the principle followed in determining the amount of such consideration, the identity of the persons from whom the assets were acquired or to whom they were sold and the nature of any material relationship between such persons and the registrant or any of its affiliates, any director or officer of the registrant, or any associate of such director or officer. If the transaction being reported is an acquisition, identify the source(s) of the funds used unless all or any part of the consideration used is a loan made in the ordinary course of business by a bank as defined by Section 3(a)(6) of the Act in which the identity of such bank shall be omitted provided a request for confidentiality has been made pursuant to Section 13(d)(1)(B) of the Act. In lieu thereof, the material shall indicate that the identity of the bank has been so omitted and filed separately with the Commission.

(b) If any assets so acquired by the registrant or its subsidiaries constituted plant, equipment or other physical property, state the nature of the business in which the assets were used by the persons from whom acquired and whether the registrant intends to continue such use or intends to devote the assets to other purposes, indicating such other purposes.

* * *

Item 3. Bankruptcy or Receivership.

(a) If a receiver, fiscal agent or similar officer has been appointed for a registrant or its parent, in a proceeding under the Bankruptcy Act or in any other proceeding under State or Federal law in which a court or governmental agency has assumed jurisdiction over substantially all of the assets or business of the registrant or its parent, or if such jurisdiction has been assumed by leaving the existing directors and officers in possession but subject to the supervision and orders of a court or governmental body, identify the proceeding, the court or governmental body, the date jurisdiction was assumed, the identity of the receiver, fiscal agent or similar officer and the date of his appointment.

* * *

Item 4. Changes in Registrant's Certifying Accountant.

(a) If an independent accountant who was previously engaged as the principal accountant to audit the registrant's financial statements, or an independent accountant upon whom the principal accountant expressed reliance in its report regarding a significant subsidiary, resigns (or indicates it declines to stand for re-election after the completion of the current audit) or is dismissed, then provide the information required by Item 304(a)(1), including compliance with Item 304(a)(3), of Regulation S–K, and the related instructions to Item 304.

(b) If a new independent accountant has been engaged as either the principal accountant to audit the registrant's financial statements or as an independent accountant on whom the principal accountant has expressed, or is expected to express, reliance in its report regarding a significant subsidiary, then provide the information required by Item 304(a)(2), of Regulation S–K.

Instruction. The resignation or dismissal of an independent accountant, or its declination to stand for re-election, is a reportable event separate from the engagement of a new independent accountant. On some occasions two reports on Form 8–K will be required for a single change in accountants, the first on the resignation (or declination to stand for re-election) or dismissal of the former accountant and the second when the new accountant is engaged. Information required in the second Form 8–K in such situations need not be provided to the extent it has been previously reported in the first such Form 8–K.

Item 5. Other Events and Regulation FD Disclosure.

The registrant may, at its option, report under this item any events, with respect to which information is not otherwise called for by this form, that the registrant deems of importance to security holders. The registrant may, at its option, file a report under this item disclosing the nonpublic information required to be disclosed by Regulation FD.

Item 6. Resignations of Registrant's Directors.

(a) If a director has resigned or declined to stand for re-election to the board of directors since the date of the last annual meeting of shareholders because of a disagreement with the registrant on any matter relating to the registrant's operations, policies or practices, and if the director has furnished the registrant with a letter describing such disagreement and requesting that the matter be disclosed, the registrant shall state the date of such resignation or declination to stand for re-election and summarize the director's description of the disagreement.

(b) If the registrant believes that the description provided by the director is incorrect or incomplete, it may include a brief statement presenting its views of the disagreement.

(c) The registrant shall file a copy of the director's letter as an exhibit with all copies of the Form 8–K required to be filed pursuant to general Instruction E.

* * *

Item 9. Regulation FD Disclosure.

Unless filed under Item 5, report under this item only information the registrant elects to disclose through Form 8–K pursuant to Regulation FD.

Item 10. Amendments to the Registrant's Code of Ethics, or Waiver of a Provision of the Code of Ethics.

(a) The registrant must briefly describe the nature of any amendment to a provision of its code of ethics that applies to the registrant's principal executive officer, principal financial officer, principal accounting officer or controller, or persons performing similar functions and that relates to any element of the code of ethics definition enumerated in Item 406(b) of Regulations S–K and S–B.

(b) If the registrant has granted a waiver, including an implicit waiver, from a provision of the code of ethics to one of these officers or persons that relates to one or more of the items set forth in Item 406(b) of Regulations S–K and S–B of this chapter), the registrant must briefly describe the nature of the waiver, the name of the person to whom the waiver was granted, and the date of the waiver.

(c) The registrant does not need to provide any information pursuant to this Item if it discloses the required information on its Internet website within five business days following the date of the amendment or waiver and the registrant has disclosed in its most recently filed annual report its Internet address and intention to provide disclosure in this manner. If the registrant elects to disclose the information required by this Item through its website, such information must remain available on the website for at least a 12–month period. Following the 12–month period, the registrant must retain the information for a period of not less than five years. Upon request, the registrant must furnish to the Commission or its staff a copy of any or all information retained pursuant to this requirement.

Instructions. 1. The registrant does not need to disclose technical, administrative or other non-substantive amendments to its code of ethics.

2. For purposes of this Item:

a. The term "waiver" means the approval by the registrant of a material departure from a provision of the code of ethics; and

b. The term "implicit waiver" means the registrant's failure to take action within a reasonable period of time regarding a material departure from a provision of the code of ethics that has been made known to an executive officer, as defined in Rule 3b–7, of the registrant.

Item 11. Temporary Suspension of Trading Under Registrant's Employee Benefit Plans.

Not later than the date prescribed for transmission of the notice required by Rule 104(b)(2) of Regulation BTR of this chapter), provide the information specified in Rule 104(b) of this chapter and the date the registrant received the notice required by section 101(i)(2)(E) of the Employment Retirement Income Security Act of 1974).

Item 12. Results of Operations and Financial Condition

(a) If a registrant, or any person acting on its behalf, makes any public announcement or release (including any update of an earlier announcement or release) disclosing material non-public information regarding the registrant's results of operations or financial condition for a completed quarterly or annual fiscal period, the registrant shall briefly identify the announcement or release and include the text of that announcement or release as an exhibit;

(b) A Form 8-K is not required to be furnished to the Commission under this Item 12 in the case of disclosure of material non-public information that is disclosed orally, telephonically, by webcast, by broadcast, or by similar means if:

(1) The information is provided as part of a presentation that is complementary to, and initially occurs within 48 hours after, a related, written announcement or release that has been furnished on Form 8-K pursuant to this Item 12 prior to the presentation;

(2) The presentation is broadly accessible to the public by dial-in conference call, by webcast, by broadcast, or by similar means;

(3) The financial and other statistical information contained in the presentation is provided on the registrant's web site, together with any information that would be required under Rule 100 of Regulation G; and

(4) The presentation was announced by a widely disseminated press release, that included instructions as to when and how to access the presentation and the location on the registrant's web site where the information would be available.

FORM 10-K

Annual Report Pursuant to Section 13 or 15(d) of the Securities Exchange Act of 1934

GENERAL INSTRUCTIONS

A. Rule as to Use of Form 10-K.

(1) This form shall be used for annual reports pursuant to Sections 13 or 15(d) of the Securities Exchange Act of 1934 for which no other form is prescribed. This form also shall be used for transition reports filed pursuant to Section 13 or 15(d) of the Securities Exchange Act of 1934.

(2) Annual reports on this form shall be filed within the following period:

(a) For accelerated filers (as defined in Rule 12b-2 of this chapter):

(i) 90 days after the end of the fiscal year covered by the report for fiscal years ending on or after December 15, 2002 and before December 15, 2003;

(ii) 75 days after the end of the fiscal year covered by the report for fiscal years ending on or after December 15, 2003 and before December 15, 2004; and

(iii) 60 days after the end of the fiscal year covered by the report for fiscal years ending on or after December 15, 2004; and

(b) 90 days after the end of the fiscal year covered by the report for all other registrants.

* * *

D. Signature and Filing of Report.

(1) Three complete copies of the report, including financial statements, financial statement schedules, exhibits, and all other papers and documents filed as a part thereof, and five additional copies which need not include exhibits, shall be filed with the Commission. At least one complete copy of the report, including financial statements, financial statement schedules, exhibits, and all other papers and documents filed as a part thereof, shall be filed with each exchange on which any class of securities of the registrant is registered. At least one complete copy of the report filed with the Commission and one such copy filed with each exchange shall be manually signed. Copies not manually signed shall bear typed or printed signatures.

(2)(a) The report must be signed by the registrant, and on behalf of the registrant by its principal executive officer or officers (who also must provide the certification required by Rule 13a-14 or Rule 15d-14 exactly as specified in this form), its principal financial officer or officers (who also must provide the certification required by Rule 13a-14 or Rule 15d-14 exactly as specified in this form), its controller or principal accounting officer, and by at least the majority of the board of directors or persons performing similar functions. Where the registrant is a limited partnership, the report must be signed by the majority of the board of directors of any corporate general partner who signs the report.

* * *

G. Information to be Incorporated by Reference.

(1) Attention is directed to Rule 12b–23 which provides for the incorporation by reference of information contained in certain documents in answer or partial answer to any item of a report.

(2) The information called for by Parts I and II of this Form (Items 1 through 9 or any portion thereof) may, at the registrant's option, be incorporated by reference from the registrant's annual report to security holders furnished to the Commission pursuant to Rule 14a–3(b) or Rule 14c–3(c) or from the registrant's annual report to security holders, even if not furnished to the Commission pursuant to Rule 14a–3(b) or Rule 14c–3(a), provided such annual report contains the information required by Rule 14a–3.

Note 1: In order to fulfill the requirements of Part I of Form 10–K, the incorporated portion of the annual report to security holders must contain the information required by Items 1–3 of Form 10–K, to the extent applicable.

Note 2. If any information required by Part I or Part II is incorporated by reference into an electronic format document from the annual report to security holders as provided in General Instruction G, any portion of the annual report to security holders incorporated by reference shall be filed as an exhibit in electronic format, as required by *Item 601(b)(13)* of Regulation S–K.

(3) The information called for by Part III (Items 10, 11, 12 and 13) shall be incorporated by reference from the registrant's definitive proxy statement (filed or to be filed pursuant to Regulation 14A) or definitive information statement (filed or to be filed pursuant to Regulation 14C) which involves the election of directors, if such definitive proxy statement or information statement is filed with the Commission not later than 120 days after the end of the fiscal year covered by the Form 10–K. However, if such definitive proxy or information statement is not filed with the Commission in the 120–day period or is not required to be filed with the Commission by virtue of Rule 3a12–3(b) under the Exchange Act, the Items comprising the Part III information must be filed as part of the Form 10–K, or as an amendment to the Form 10–K under cover of Form 8, not later than the end of the 120–day period. It should be noted that the information regarding executive officers required by Item 401 of Regulation S–K may be included in Part I of Form 10–K under an appropriate caption. See Instruction 3 to Item 401(b) of Regulation S–K.

* * *

H. Integrated Reports to Security Holders.

Annual reports to security holders may be combined with the required information of Form 10–K and will be suitable for filing with the Commission if the following conditions are satisfied:

(1) The combined report contains full and complete answers to all items required by Form 10–K. When responses to a certain item of required disclosure are separated within the combined report, an appropriate cross-reference should be made. If the information required by Part III of Form 10–K is omitted by virtue of General Instruction G, a definitive proxy or information statement shall be filed.

(2) The cover page and the required signatures are included. As appropriate, a cross-reference sheet should be filed indicating the location of information required by the items of the Form.

* * *

PART I

[See General Instruction G(2).]

Item 1. Business.

Furnish the information required by Item 101 of Regulation S–K except that the discussion of the development of the registrant's business need only include developments since the beginning of the fiscal year for which this report is filed.

Item 2. Properties.

Furnish the information required by Item 102 of Regulation S–K.

Item 3. Legal Proceedings.

(a) Furnish the information required by Item 103 of Regulation S–K.

(b) As to any proceeding that was terminated during the fourth quarter of the fiscal year covered by this report, furnish information similar to that required by Item 103 of Regulation S–K, including the date of termination and a description of the disposition thereof with respect to the registrant and its subsidiaries.

Item 4. Submission of Matters to a Vote of Security Holders.

If any matter was submitted during the fourth quarter of the fiscal year covered by this report to a vote of security holders, through the solicitation of proxies or otherwise, furnish the following information:

(a) The date of the meeting and whether it was an annual or special meeting.

(b) If the meeting involved the election of directors, the name of each director elected at the meeting and the name of each other director whose term of office as a director continued after the meeting.

(c) A brief description of each other matter voted upon at the meeting and state the number of votes cast for, against or withheld, as well as the number of abstentions and broker nonvotes, as to each matter, including a separate tabulation with respect to each nominee for office.

(d) A description of the terms of any settlement between the registrant and any other participant (as defined in Rule 14a–11 of Regulation 14A under the Act) terminating any solicitation subject to Rule 14a–11, including the cost or anticipated cost to the registrant.

Instructions:

1. If any matter has been submitted to a vote of security holders otherwise than at a meeting of such security holders, corresponding information with respect to such submission shall be furnished. The solicitation of any authorization or consent (other than a proxy to vote at a stockholders' meeting) with respect to any matter shall be deemed a submission of such matter to a vote of security holders within the meaning of this item.

2. Paragraph (a) need be answered only if paragraph (b) or (c) is required to be answered.

3. Paragraph (b) need not be answered if (i) proxies for the meeting were solicited pursuant to Regulation 14A under the Act, (ii) there was no solicitation in opposition to the management's nominees as listed in the proxy statement, and (iii) all of such nominees were elected. If the registrant did not solicit proxies and the board of directors as previously reported to the Commission was re-elected in its entirety, a statement to that effect in answer to paragraph (b) will suffice as an answer thereto.

4. Paragraph (c) need not be answered for all matters voted upon at the meeting, including both contested and uncontested elections of directors.

5. If the registrant has furnished to its security holders proxy soliciting material containing the information called for by paragraph (d), the paragraph may be answered by reference to the information contained in such material.

(a) Furnish the information required by *Item 201* of Regulation S–K (§ 229.201 of this chapter) and *Item 701* of Regulation S–K (§ 229.701 of this chapter) as to all equity securities of the registrant sold by the registrant during the period covered by the report that were not registered under the Securities Act other than unregistered sales made in reliance on Regulation S. Provided that if the Item 701 information previously has been included in a Quarterly Report on *Form 10–Q* or *10–QSB* (§ 249.308a or 249.308b of this chapter) it need not be furnished.

(b) If required pursuant to *Rule 463* (17 CFR 230.463) of the Securities Act of 1933, furnish the information required by Item 701(f) of Regulation S–K (§ 229.701(f) of this chapter).

6. If the registrant has published a report containing all of the information called for by this item, the item may be answered by a reference to the information contained in such report.

PART II

[See General Instruction G(2).]

Item 5. Market for Registrant's Common Equity and Related Stockholder Matters.

(a) Furnish the information required by *Item 201* of Regulation S–K (§ 229.201 of this chapter) and

Item 701 of Regulation S–K (§ 229.701 of this chapter) as to all equity securities of the registrant sold by the registrant during the period covered by the report that were not registered under the Securities Act other than unregistered sales made in reliance on Regulation S. Provided that if the Item 701 information previously has been included in a Quarterly Report on *Form 10–Q* or *10–QSB* (§ 249.308a or 249.308b of this chapter) it need not be furnished.

(b) If required pursuant to *Rule 463* (17 CFR 230.463) of the Securities Act of 1933, furnish the information required by Item 701 (f) of Regulation S–K (§ 229.701(f) of this chapter).

Item 6. Selected Financial Data.

Furnish the information required by Item 301 of Regulation S–K.

Item 7. Management's Discussion and Analysis of Financial Condition and Results of Operation.

Furnish the information required by Item 303 of Regulation S–K.

Item 7A. Quantitative and Qualitative Disclosures About Market Risk.

Furnish the information required by Item 305 of Regulation S–K.

Item 8. Financial Statements and Supplementary Data.

Furnish financial statements meeting the requirements of Regulation S–X, except § 210.3–05 and Article 11 thereof, and the supplementary financial information required by Item 302 of Regulation S–K. Financial statements of the registrant and its subsidiaries consolidated [as required by Rule 14a–3(b)] shall be filed under this item. Other financial statements and schedules required under Regulation S–X may be filed as "Financial Statement Schedules" pursuant to Item 13, Exhibits, Financial Statement Schedules, and Reports on Form 8–K, of this Form.

* * *

Item 9. Disagreements on Accounting and Financial Disclosure.

Furnish the information required by Item 304 of Regulation S–K.

PART III

[See General Instruction G(3).]

Item 10. Directors and Executive Officers of the Registrant.

Furnish the information required by Items 401, 405 and 406 of Regulation S–K.

* * *

Item 12. Security Ownership of Certain Beneficial Owners and Management.

Furnish the information required by Item 403 of Regulation S–K.

Item 13. Certain Relationships and Related Transactions.

Furnish the information required by Item 404 of Regulation S–K.

Item 14. Controls and Procedures.

Furnish the information required by Item 307 of Regulation S–K.

PART IV

Item 15. Exhibits, Financial Statement Schedules, and Reports on Form 8–K.

(a) List the following documents filed as a part of the report:

1. All financial statements.

2. Those financial statement schedules required to be filed by Item 8 of this Form, and by paragraph (b) below.

3. Those exhibits required by Item 601 of Regulation S–K and by paragraph (c) below. Identify in the list each management contract or compensation plan or arrangement required to be filed as an exhibit to this form pursuant to Item 14(c) of this report

* * *

(c) Registrants shall file, as exhibits to this Form, the exhibits required by Item 601 of Regulation S–K.

* * *

Item 16. Principal Accountant Fees and Services.

Furnish the information required by Item 9(e) of Schedule 14A.

(1) Disclose, under the caption *Audit Fees*, the aggregate fees billed for each of the last two fiscal years for professional services rendered by the principal accountant for the audit of the registrant's annual financial statements and review of financial statements included in the registrant's Form 10–Q or 10–QSB or services that are normally provided by the accountant in connection with statutory and regulatory filings or engagements for those fiscal years.

(2) Disclose, under the caption *Audit-Related Fees*, the aggregate fees billed in each of the last two fiscal years for assurance and related services by the principal accountant that are reasonably related to the performance of the audit or review of the registrant's financial statements and are not reported under Item 9(e)(1) of Schedule 14A. Registrants shall describe the nature of the services comprising the fees disclosed under this category.

(3) Disclose, under the caption *Tax Fees*, the aggregate fees billed in each of the last two fiscal years for professional services rendered by the principal accountant for tax compliance, tax advice, and tax planning. Registrants shall describe the nature of the services comprising the fees disclosed under this category.

(4) Disclose, under the caption *All Other Fees*, the aggregate fees billed in each of the last two fiscal years for products and services provided by the principal accountant, other than the services reported in Items 9(e)(1) through 9(e)(3) of Schedule 14A. Registrants shall describe the nature of the services comprising the fees disclosed under this category.

(5)(i) Disclose the audit committee's pre-approval policies and procedures described in paragraph (c)(7)(i) of Rule 2–01 of Regulation S–X.

(ii) Disclose the percentage of services described in each of Items 9(e)(2) through 9(e)(4) of Schedule 14A that were approved by the audit committee pursuant to paragraph (c)(7)(i)(C) of Rule 2–01 of Regulation S–X.

(6) If greater than 50 percent, disclose the percentage of hours expended on the principal accountant's engagement to audit the registrant's financial statements for the most recent fiscal year that were attributed to work performed by persons other than the principal accountant's full-time, permanent employees.

Instruction to Item 16.

A registrant that is an Asset–Backed Issuer (as defined in Rule 13a–14(g) and Rule 15d–14(g) of this chapter) is not required to disclose the information required by this Item.

CERTIFICATIONS*

I, [identify the certifying individual], certify that:

1. I have reviewed this annual report on Form 10–K of [identify registrant];

2. Based on my knowledge, this annual report does not contain any untrue statement of a material fact or omit to state a material fact necessary to make the statements made, in light of the circumstances under which such statements were made, not misleading with respect to the period covered by this annual report;

3. Based on my knowledge, the financial statements, and other financial information included in this annual report, fairly present in all material respects the financial condition, results of operations and cash flows of the registrant as of, and for, the periods presented in this annual report;

4. The registrant's other certifying officers and I are responsible for establishing and maintaining disclosure controls and procedures (as defined in Exchange Act Rules 13a–14 and 15d–14) for the registrant and have:

a) designed such disclosure controls and procedures to ensure that material information relating to the registrant, including its consolidated subsidiaries, is made known to us by others within those entities, particularly during the period in which this annual report is being prepared;

b) evaluated the effectiveness of the registrant's disclosure controls and procedures as of a date within 90 days prior to the filing date of this annual report (the "Evaluation Date"); and

c) presented in this annual report our conclusions about the effectiveness of the disclosure controls and procedures based on our evaluation as of the Evaluation Date;

5. The registrant's other certifying officers and I have disclosed, based on our most recent evaluation, to the registrant's auditors and the audit committee of registrant's board of directors (or persons performing the equivalent functions):

a) all significant deficiencies in the design or operation of internal controls which could adversely affect the registrant's ability to record, process, summarize and report financial data and have identified for the registrant's auditors any material weaknesses in internal controls; and

b) any fraud, whether or not material, that involves management or other employees who have a significant role in the registrant's internal controls; and

6. The registrant's other certifying officers and I have indicated in this annual report whether there were significant changes in internal controls or in other factors that could significantly affect internal controls subsequent to the date of our most recent evaluation, including any corrective actions with regard to significant deficiencies and material weaknesses.

Date: ______

____

[Signature]
[Title]

* Provide a separate certification for each principal executive officer and principal financial officer of the registrant. See Rules 13a–14 and 15d–14. The required certification must be in the exact form set forth above.

FORM 10–Q

For Quarterly Reports Under Section 13 or 15(d) of the Securities Exchange Act of 1934

GENERAL INSTRUCTIONS

A. Rule as to Use of Form 10–Q.

1. Form 10–Q shall be used for quarterly reports under Section 13 or 15(d) of the Securities Exchange Act of 1934), filed pursuant to Rule 13a–13 or Rule 15d–13. A quarterly report on this form pursuant to Rule 13a–13 or Rule 15d–13 shall be filed within the following period after the end of each of the first three fiscal quarters of each fiscal year, but no report need be filed for the fourth quarter of any fiscal year:

a. For accelerated filers:

(i) 45 days after the end of the fiscal quarter for fiscal years ending on or after December 15, 2002 and before December 15, 2004;

(ii) 40 days after the end of the fiscal quarter for fiscal years ending on or after December 15, 2004 and before December 15, 2005; and

(iii) 35 days after the end of the fiscal quarter for fiscal years ending on or after December 15, 2005; and

b. 45 days after the end of the fiscal quarter for all other issuers.

* * *

E. Integrated Reports to Security Holders.

Quarterly reports to security holders may be combined with the required information of Form 10–Q and will be suitable for filing with the Commission if the following conditions are satisfied:

1. The combined report contains full and complete answers to all items required by Part I of this form. When responses to a certain item of required disclosure are separated within the combined report, an appropriate cross-reference should be made.

2. If not included in the combined report, the cover page, appropriate responses to Part II, and the required signatures shall be included in the Form 10–Q. Additionally, as appropriate, a cross-reference sheet should be filed indicating the location of information required by the items of the form.

3. If an electronic filer files any portion of a quarterly report to security holders in combination with the required information of Form 10–Q, as provided in this instruction, only such portions filed in satisfaction of the Form 10–Q requirements shall be filed in electronic format.

F. Filed Status of Information Presented.

1. Pursuant to Rule 13a–13(d) and Rule 15d–13(d), the information presented in satisfaction of the requirements of Items 1, 2 and 3 of Part I of this form, whether included directly in a report on this form, incorporated therein by reference from a report, document or statement filed as an exhibit to Part I of this form pursuant to Instruction D(1) above, included in an integrated report pursuant to Instruction E above, or contained in a statement regarding computation of per share earnings or a letter regarding a change in accounting principles filed as an exhibit to Part I pursuant to Item 601 of Regulation S–K, except as provided by Instruction F(2) below, shall not be deemed filed for the purpose of Section 18 of the Act or otherwise subject to the liabilities of that section of the Act but shall be subject to the other provisions of the Act.

2. Information presented in satisfaction of the requirements of this form other than those of Items (1), (2), and (3) of Part I shall be deemed filed for the purpose of Section 18 of the Act; except that, where information presented in response to Item (1) or (2) of Part I (or as an exhibit thereto) is also used to satisfy Part II requirements through incorporation by reference, only that portion of Part I (or exhibit thereto) consisting of the information required by Part II shall be deemed so filed.

G. Signature and Filing of Report.

If the report is filed in paper pursuant to a hardship exemption from electronic filing (see Item 201 *et seq.* of Regulation S–T, three complete copies of the report, including any financial statements, exhibits or other papers or documents filed as a part thereof, and five additional copies which need not include exhibits must be filed with the Commission. At least one complete copy of the report, including any financial statements, exhibits or other papers or documents filed as a part thereof, must be filed with each exchange on which any class of securities of the registrant is registered. At least one complete copy of the report filed with the Commission and one such copy filed with each exchange must be manually signed on the registrant's behalf by a duly authorized officer of the registrant and by the principal financial or chief accounting officer of the registrant. (See Rule 12b–11(d).) Copies not manually signed must bear typed or printed signatures. In the case where the principal executive officer, principal financial officer or chief accounting officer is also duly authorized to sign on behalf of the registrant, one signature is acceptable provided that the registrant clearly indicates the dual responsibilities of the signatory. In addition, each principal executive officer and principal financial officer of the registrant must provide the certification required by Rule 13a–14 (or Rule 15d–14 (exactly as specified in this form.

H. Omission of Information by Certain Wholly–Owned Subsidiaries.

If on the date of the filing of its report on Form 10–Q, the registrant meets the conditions specified in paragraph (1) below, then such registrant may omit the information called for in the items specified in paragraph (2) below.

1. Conditions for availability of the relief specified in paragraph (2) below:

a. All of the registrant's equity securities are owned, either directly or indirectly, by a single person which is a reporting company under the Act and which has filed all the material required to be filed pursuant to Section 13, 14 or 15(d) thereof, as applicable;

b. During the preceding thirty-six calendar months and any subsequent period of days, there has not been any material default in the payment of principal, interest, a sinking or purchase fund installment, or any other material default not cured within thirty days, with respect to any indebtedness of the registrant or its subsidiaries, and there has not been any material default in the payment of rentals under material long-term leases; and

c. There is prominently set forth, on the cover page of the Form 10–Q, a statement that the registrant meets the conditions set forth in General Instruction H(1)(a) and (b) of Form 10–Q and is therefore filing this form with the reduced disclosure format.

2. Registrants meeting the conditions specified in paragraph (1) above are entitled to the following relief:

a. Such registrants may omit the information called for by Item 2 of Part I, Management's Discussion and Analysis of Financial Condition and Results of Operations, provided that the registrant includes in the Form 10–Q a management's narrative analysis of the results of operations explaining the reasons for material changes in the amount of revenue and expense items between the most recent fiscal year-to-date period presented and the corresponding year-to-date period in the preceding fiscal year. Explanations of material changes should include, but not be limited to, changes in the various elements which determine revenue and expense levels such as unit sales volume, prices charged and paid, production levels, production cost variances, labor costs and discretionary spending programs. In addition, the analysis should include an explanation of the effect of any changes in accounting principles and practices or method of application that have a material effect on net income as reported.

b. Such registrants may omit the information called for in the following Part II Items: Item 2, Changes in Securities; Item 3, Defaults Upon Senior Securities; and Item 4, Submission of Matters to a Vote of Security Holders.

c. Such registrants may omit the information called for by Item 3 of Part I, Quantitative and Qualitative Disclosures About Market Risk.

PART I. FINANCIAL INFORMATION

Item 1. Financial Statements.

Provide the information required by Rule 10–01 of Regulation S–X.

Item 2. Management's Discussion and Analysis of Financial Condition and Results of Operations.

Furnish the information required by Item 303 of Regulation S–K.

Item 3. Quantitative and Qualitative Disclosures about market risk.

Furnish the information required by Item 305 of Reg. S–K.

Item 4. Controls and Procedures.

Furnish the information required by Item 307 of Regulation S–K.

PART II. OTHER INFORMATION

* * *

Item 1. Legal Proceedings.

Furnish the information required by Item 103 of Regulation S–K. As to such proceedings which have been terminated during the period covered by the report, provide similar information, including the date of termination and a description of the disposition thereof with respect to the registrant and its subsidiaries.

Instruction. A legal proceeding need only be reported in the 10–Q filed for the quarter in which it first became a reportable event and in subsequent quarters in which there have been material developments. Subsequent Form 10–Q filings in the same fiscal year in which a legal proceeding or a material development is reported should reference any previous reports in that year.

Item 2. Changes in Securities.

(a) If the constituent instruments defining the rights of the holders of any class of registered securities have been materially modified, give the title of the class of securities involved and state briefly the general effect of such modification upon the rights of holders of such securities.

(b) If the rights evidenced by any class of registered securities have been materially limited or qualified by the issuance or modification of any other class of securities, state briefly the general effect of the issuance or modification of such other class of securities upon the rights of the holders of the registered securities.

(c) Furnish the information required by Item 701 of Regulation S–K as to all equity securities of the registrant sold by the registrant during the period covered by the report that were not registered under the Securities Act.

(d) If required pursuant to *Rule 463* (17 CFR 230.463) of the Securities Act of 1933, furnish the information required by *Item 701(f)* of Regulation S–K (§ 229.701(f) of this chapter).

Instruction. Working capital restrictions and other limitations upon the payment of dividends are to be reported hereunder.

Item 3. Defaults upon Senior Securities.

(a) If there has been any material default in the payment of principal, interest, a sinking or purchase fund installment, or any other material default not cured within 30 days, with respect to any indebtedness of the registrant or any of its significant subsidiaries exceeding 5 percent of the total assets of the registrant and its consolidated subsidiaries, identify the indebtedness and state the nature of the default. In the case of such a default in the payment of principal, interest, or a sinking or purchase fund installment, state the amount of the default and the total arrearage on the date of filing this report.

Instruction. This paragraph refers only to events which have become defaults under the governing instruments, *i.e.,* after the expiration of any period of grace and compliance with any notice requirements.

(b) If any material arrearage in the payment of dividends has occurred or if there has been any other material delinquency not cured within 30 days, with respect to any class of preferred stock of the registrant which is registered or which ranks prior to any class of registered securities, or with respect to any class of preferred stock of any significant subsidiary of the registrant, give the title of the class and state the nature of the arrearage or delinquency. In the case of an arrearage in the payment of dividends, state the amount and the total arrearage on the date of filing this report.

Instruction. Item 3 need not be answered as to any default or arrearage with respect to any class of securities all of which is held by, or for the account of, the registrant or its totally held subsidiaries.

Item 4. Submission of Matters to a Vote of Security Holders.

If any matter has been submitted to a vote of security holders during the period covered by this report, through the solicitation of proxies or otherwise, furnish the following information:

(a) The date of the meeting and whether it was an annual or special meeting.

(b) If the meeting involved the election of directors, state the name of each director elected at the meeting and the name of each other director whose term of office as a director continued after the meeting.

(c) A brief description of each other matter voted upon at the meeting and state the number of votes cast for, against or withheld, as well as the number of abstentions and broker nonvotes, as to each such matter, including a separate tabulation with respect to each nominee for office.

(d) Describe the terms of any settlement between the registrant and any other participant (as defined in Rule 14a–11 of Regulation 14A under the Act) terminating any solicitation subject to Rule 14a–11, including the cost or anticipated cost to the registrant.

Instructions. 1. If any matter has been submitted to a vote of security holders otherwise than at a meeting of such security holders, corresponding information with respect to such submission shall be furnished. The solicitation of any authorization or consent (other than a proxy to vote at a stockholders' meeting) with respect to any matter shall be deemed a submission of such matter to a vote of security holders within the meaning of this item.

2. Paragraph (a) need be answered only if paragraph (b) or (c) is required to be answered.

3. Paragraph (b) need not be answered if (i) proxies for the meeting were solicited pursuant to Regulation 14 under the Act, (ii) there was no solicitation in opposition to the management's nominees as listed in the proxy statement, and (iii) all of such nominees were elected. If the registrant did not solicit proxies and the board of directors as previously reported to the Commission was re-elected in its entirety, a statement to that effect in answer to paragraph (b) will suffice as an answer thereto.

4. Paragraph (c) must be answered for all matters voted upon at the meeting, including both contested and uncontested elections of directors.

5. If the registrant has furnished to its security holders proxy soliciting material containing the information called for by paragraph (d), the paragraph may be answered by reference to the information contained in such material.

6. If the registrant has published a report containing all of the information called for by this item, the item may be answered by a reference to the information contained in such report.

Item 5. Other Information.

The registrant may, at its option, report under this item any information, not previously reported in a report on Form 8–K, with respect to which information is not otherwise called for by this form. If disclosure of such information is made under this item, it need not be repeated in a report on Form 8–K which would otherwise be required to be filed with respect to such information or in a subsequent report on Form 10–Q.

Item 6. Exhibits and Reports on Form 8–K.

(a) Furnish the exhibits required by Item 601 of Regulation S–K.

(b) Reports on Form 8–K. State whether any reports on Form 8–K have been filed during the quarter for which this report is filed, listing the items reported, any financial statements filed, and the dates of any such reports.

CERTIFICATIONS*

I, [identify the certifying individual], certify that:

1. I have reviewed this quarterly report on Form 10–Q of [identify registrant];

2. Based on my knowledge, this quarterly report does not contain any untrue statement of a material fact or omit to state a material fact necessary to make the statements made, in light of the circumstances under which such statements were made, not misleading with respect to the period covered by this quarterly report;

3. Based on my knowledge, the financial statements, and other financial information included in this quarterly report, fairly present in all material respects the financial condition, results of operations and cash flows of the registrant as of, and for, the periods presented in this quarterly report;

4. The registrant's other certifying officers and I are responsible for establishing and maintaining disclosure controls and procedures (as defined in Exchange Act Rules 13a–14 and 15d–14) for the registrant and we have:

a) designed such disclosure controls and procedures to ensure that material information relating to the registrant, including its consolidated subsidiaries, is made known to us by others within those entities, particularly during the period in which this quarterly report is being prepared;

b) evaluated the effectiveness of the registrant's disclosure controls and procedures as of a date within 90 days prior to the filing date of this quarterly report (the "Evaluation Date"); and

c) presented in this quarterly report our conclusions about the effectiveness of the disclosure controls and procedures based on our evaluation as of the Evaluation Date;

5. The registrant's other certifying officers and I have disclosed, based on our most recent evaluation, to the registrant's auditors and the audit committee of registrant's board of directors (or persons performing the equivalent function):

a) all significant deficiencies in the design or operation of internal controls which could adversely affect the registrant's ability to record, process, summarize and report financial data and have identified for the registrant's auditors any material weaknesses in internal controls; and

b) any fraud, whether or not material, that involves management or other employees who have a significant role in the registrant's internal controls; and

6. The registrant's other certifying officers and I have indicated in this quarterly report whether or not there were significant changes in internal controls or in other factors that could significantly affect internal controls subsequent to the date of our most recent evaluation, including any corrective actions with regard to significant deficiencies and material weaknesses.

Date: ______

____

[Signature]
[Title]

* Provide a separate certification for each principal executive officer and principal financial officer of the registrant. See Rules 13a–14 and 15d–14. The required certification must be in the exact form set forth above.

SCHEDULE 13D

Information to be Included in Statements Filed Pursuant to Rule 13d–1(a) and Amendments Thereto Filed Pursuant to Rule 13d–2(a)

* * *

Item 1. Security and Issuer.

State the title of the class of equity securities to which this statement relates and the name and address of the principal executive offices of the issuer of such securities.

Item 2. Identity and Background.

If the person filing this statement or any person enumerated in Instruction C of this statement is a corporation, general partnership, limited partnership, syndicate or other group of persons, state its name, the state or other place of its organization, its principal business, the address of its principal business, the address of its principal office and the information required by (d) and (e) of this Item. If the person filing this statement or any person enumerated in Instruction C is a natural person, provide the information specified in (a) through (f) of this Item with respect to such person(s).

(a) Name;

(b) Residence or business address;

(c) Present principal occupation or employment and the name, principal business and address of any corporation or other organization in which such employment is conducted;

(d) Whether or not, during the last five years, such person has been convicted in a criminal proceeding (excluding traffic violations or similar misdemeanors) and, if so, give the dates, nature of conviction, name and location of court, any penalty imposed, or other disposition of the case;

(e) Whether or not, during the last five years, such person was a party to a civil proceeding of a judicial or administrative body of competent jurisdiction and as a result of such proceeding was or is subject to a judgment, decree or final order enjoining future violations of, or prohibiting or mandating activities subject to, federal or state securities laws or finding any violation with respect to such laws; and, if so, identify and describe such proceedings and summarize the terms of such judgment, decree or final order; and

(f) Citizenship.

Item 3. Source and Amount of Funds or Other Consideration.

State the source and the amount of funds or other consideration used or to be used in making the purchases, and if any part of the purchase price is or will be represented by funds or other consideration borrowed or otherwise obtained for the purpose of acquiring, holding, trading or voting the securities, a description of the transaction and the names of the parties thereto. Where material, such information should also be provided with respect to prior acquisitions not previously reported pursuant to this regulation. If the source of all or any part of the funds is a loan made in the ordinary course of business by a bank, as defined in Section 3(a)(6) of the Act, the name of the bank shall not be made available to the public if the person at the time of filing the statement so requests in writing and files such request, naming such bank, with the Secretary of the Commission. If the securities were acquired other than by purchase, describe the method of acquisition.

Item 4. Purpose of Transaction.

State the purpose or purposes of the acquisition of securities of the issuer. Describe any plans or proposals which the reporting persons may have which relate to or would result in:

(a) The acquisition by any person of additional securities of the issuer, or the disposition of securities of the issuer;

(b) An extraordinary corporate transaction, such as a merger, reorganization or liquidation, involving the issuer or any of its subsidiaries;

(c) A sale or transfer of a material amount of assets of the issuer or any of its subsidiaries;

(d) Any change in the present board of directors or management of the issuer, including any plans or proposals to change the number or term of directors or to fill any existing vacancies on the board;

(e) Any material change in the present capitalization or dividend policy of the issuer;

(f) Any other material change in the issuer's business or corporate structure, including but not limited to, if the issuer is a registered closed-end investment company, any plans or proposals to make any changes in its investment policy for which a vote is required by section 13 of the Investment Company Act of 1940;

(g) Changes in the issuer's charter, bylaws or instruments corresponding thereto or other actions which may impede the acquisition of control of the issuer by any person:

(h) Causing a class of securities of the issuer to be delisted from a national securities exchange or to cease to be authorized to be quoted in an inter-dealer quotation system of a registered national securities association;

(i) A class of equity securities of the issuer becoming eligible for termination of registration pursuant to Section 12(g)(4) of the Act; or

(j) Any action similar to any of those enumerated above.

Item 5. Interest in Securities of the Issuer.

(a) State the aggregate number and percentage of the class of securities identified pursuant to Item 1 (which may be based on the number of securities outstanding as contained in the most recently available filing with the Commission by the issuer unless the filing person has reason to believe such information is not current) beneficially owned (identifying those shares which there is a right to acquire) by each person named in Item 2. The above mentioned information should also be furnished with respect to persons who, together with any of the persons named in Item 2, comprise a group within the meaning of Section 13(d)(3) of the Act;

(b) For each person named in response to paragraph (a), indicate the number of shares as to which there is sole power to vote or to direct the vote, shared power to vote or to direct the vote, sole power to dispose or to direct the disposition, or shared power to dispose or to direct the disposition. Provide the applicable information required by Item 2 with respect to each person with whom the power to vote or to direct the vote or to dispose or direct the disposition is shared;

(c) Describe any transactions in the class of securities reported on that were effected during the past sixty days or since the most recent filing on Schedule 13D, whichever is less, by the persons named in response to paragraph (a).

Instruction. The description of a transaction required by Item 5(c) shall include, but not necessarily be limited to: (1) the identity of the person covered by Item 5(c) who effected the transaction; (2) the date of the transaction; (3) the amount of securities involved; (4) the price per share or unit; and (5) where and how the transaction was effected.

(d) If any other person is known to have the right to receive or the power to direct the receipt of dividends from, or the proceeds from the sale of, such securities, a statement to that effect should be included in response to this item and, if such interest relates to more than five percent of the class, such person should be identified. A listing of the shareholders of an investment company registered under the Investment Company Act of 1940 or the beneficiaries of an employee benefit plan, pension fund or endowment fund is not required.

(e) If applicable, state the date on which the reporting person ceased to be the beneficial owner of more than five percent of the class of securities.

Instruction. For computations regarding securities which represent a right to acquire an underlying security, see Rule 13d–3(d)(1) and the note thereto.

Item 6. Contracts, Arrangements, Understandings or Relationships With Respect to Securities of the Issuer.

Describe any contracts, arrangements, understandings or relationships (legal or otherwise) among the persons named in Item 2 and between such persons and any person with respect to any securities of the issuer, including but not limited to transfer or voting of any of the securities, finder's fees, joint ventures, loan or option arrangements, put or calls, guarantees of profits, division of profits or loss, or the giving or withholding of proxies, naming the persons with whom such contracts, arrangements, understandings or relationships have been entered into. Include such information for any of the securities that are pledged or otherwise subject to a contingency the occurrence of which would give another person voting power or investment power over such securities except that disclosure of standard default and similar provisions contained in loan agreements need not be included.

Item 7. Material to be Filed as Exhibits.

The following shall be filed as exhibits: copies of written agreements relating to the filing of joint acquisition statements as required by Rule 13d–1(K) and copies of all written agreements, contracts, arrangements, understandings, plans or proposals relating to (1) the borrowing of funds to finance the acquisition as disclosed in Item 3; (2) the acquisition of issuer control, liquidation, sale of assets, merger, or change in business or corporate structure or any other matter as disclosed in Item 4; and (3) the transfer or voting of the securities, finder's fees, joint ventures, options, puts, calls, guarantees of loans, guarantees against loss or of profit, or the giving or withholding of any proxy as disclosed in Item 6.

SCHEDULE 13E–3

Transaction Statement Pursuant to Section 13(e) and Rule 13e–3

* * *

GENERAL INSTRUCTIONS

A. File eight copies of the statement, including all exhibits, with the Commission if paper filing is permitted.

B. This filing must be accompanied by a fee payable to the Commission as required by § 240.0–11(b).

C. If the statement is filed by a general or limited partnership, syndicate or other group, the information called for by Items 3, 5, 6, 10 and 11 must be given with respect to: (i) Each partner of the general partnership; (ii) each partner who is, or functions as, a general partner of the limited partnership; (iii) each member of the syndicate or group; and (iv) each person controlling the partner or member. If the statement is filed by a corporation or if a person referred to in (i), (ii), (iii) or (iv) of this Instruction is a corporation, the information called for by the items specified above must be given with respect to: (a) Each executive officer and director of the corporation; (b) each person controlling the corporation; and (c) each executive officer and director of any corporation or other person ultimately in control of the corporation.

D. Depending on the type of Rule 13e–3 transaction, this statement shall be filed with the Commission:

1. Concurrently with the filing of "Preliminary Copies" of soliciting materials or an information statement pursuant to Regulations 14A or 14C under the Act;

2. Concurrently with the filing of a registration statement under the Securities Act of 1933;

3. As soon as practicable on the date a tender offer is first published, sent or given to security holders; or

4. At least 30 days prior to any purchase of any securities of the class of securities subject to the Rule 13e–3 transaction, if the transaction does not involve a solicitation, an information statement, the registration of securities or a tender offer, as described in 1, 2 or 3 of this Instruction.

5. If the Rule 13e–3 transaction involves a series of transactions, the issuer or affiliate shall file this statement at the time indicated in 1–4 of this general instruction for the first transaction of such series and shall promptly amend this schedule with respect to each subsequent transaction in such series.

* * *

Item 1. Summary Term Sheet. Furnish the information required by *Item 1001* of Regulation M–A (§ 229.1001 of this chapter) unless information is disclosed to security holders in a prospectus that meets the requirements of *§ 230.421(d)* of this chapter.

Item 2. Subject Company Information. Furnish the information required by *Item 1002* of Regulation M–A (§ 229.1002 of this chapter).

Item 3. Identity and Background of Filing Person. Furnish the information required by *Item 1003(a) through (c)* of Regulation M–A (§ 229.1003 of this chapter).

Item 4. Terms of the Transaction. Furnish the information required by *Item 1004(a) and (c) through (f)* of Regulation M–A (§ 229.1004 of this chapter).

Item 5. Past Contacts, Transactions, Negotiations and Agreements. Furnish the information required by *Item 1005(a) through (c) and (e)* of Regulation M–A (§ 229.1005 of this chapter).

Item 6. Purposes of the Transaction and Plans or Proposals. Furnish the information required by *Item 1006(b) and (c)(1) through (8)* of Regulation M–A (§ 229.1006 of this chapter).

Instruction to Item 6: In providing the information specified in Item 1006(c) for this item, discuss any activities or transactions that would occur after the *Rule 13e–3* transaction.

Item 7. Purposes, Alternatives, Reasons and Effects. Furnish the information required by *Item 1013* of Regulation M–A (§ 229.1013 of this chapter).

Item 8. Fairness of the Transaction. Furnish the information required by *Item 1014* of Regulation M–A (§ 229.1014 of this chapter).

Item 9. Reports, Opinions, Appraisals and Negotiations. Furnish the information required by *Item 1015* of Regulation M–A (§ 229.1015 of this chapter).

Item 10. Source and Amounts of Funds or Other Consideration. Furnish the information required by *Item 1007* of Regulation M–A (§ 229.1007 of this chapter).

Item 11. Interest in Securities of the Subject Company. Furnish the information required by *Item 1008* of Regulation M–A (§ 229.1008 of this chapter).

Item 12. The Solicitation or Recommendation. Furnish the information required by *Item 1012(d) and (e)* of Regulation M–A (§ 229.1012 of this chapter).

Item 13. Financial Statements. Furnish the information required by *Item 1010(a) through (b)* of Regulation M–A (§ 229.1010 of this chapter) for the issuer of the subject class of securities.

Instructions to Item 13:

1. The disclosure materials disseminated to security holders may contain the summarized financial information required by Item 1010(c) of Regulation M–A (§ 229.1010 of this chapter) instead of the financial information required by Item 1010(a) and (b). In that case, the financial information required by Item 1010(a) and (b) of Regulation M–A must be disclosed directly or incorporated by reference in the statement. If summarized financial information is disseminated to security holders, include appropriate instructions on how more complete financial information can be obtained. If the summarized financial information is prepared on the basis of a comprehensive body of accounting principles other than U.S. GAAP, the summarized financial information must be accompanied by a reconciliation as described in Instruction 2.

2. If the financial statements required by this Item are prepared on the basis of a comprehensive body of accounting principles other than U.S. GAAP, provide a reconciliation to U.S. GAAP in accordance with Item 17 of *Form 20–F* (§ 249.220f of this chapter).

3. The filing person may incorporate by reference financial statements contained in any document filed with the Commission, solely for the purposes of this schedule, if: (a) the financial statements substantially meet the requirements of this Item; (b) an express statement is made that the financial statements are incorporated by reference; (c) the matter incorporated by reference is clearly identified by page, paragraph, caption or otherwise; and (d) if the matter incorporated by reference is not filed with this Schedule, an indication is made where the information may be inspected and copies obtained. Financial statements that are required to be presented in comparative form for two or more fiscal years or periods may not be incorporated by reference unless the material incorporated by reference includes the entire period for which the comparative data is required to be given. See General Instruction F to this Schedule.

Item 14. Persons/Assets, Retained, Employed, Compensated or Used. Furnish the information required by *Item 1009* of Regulation M–A (§ 229.1009 of this chapter).

Item 15. Additional Information. Furnish the information required by *Item 1011(b)* of Regulation M–A (§ 229.1011 of this chapter).

Item 16. Exhibits. File as an exhibit to the Schedule all documents specified in *Item 1016(a) through (d), (f) and (g)* of Regulation M–A (§ 229.1016 of this chapter).

* * *

SCHEDULE 14A

Information Required in Proxy Statement

* * *

Notes. A. Where any item calls for information with respect to any matter to be acted upon and such matter involves other matters with respect to which information is called for by other items of this schedule, the information called for by such other items shall also be given. For example, where a solicitation of security holders is for the purpose of approving the authorization of additional securities which are to be used to acquire another specified company, and the registrants' security holders will not have a separate opportunity to vote upon the transaction, the solicitation to authorize the securities is also a solicitation with respect to the acquisition. Under those facts, information required by Items 11, 13, and 14 shall be furnished.

B. Where any item calls for information with respect to any matter to be acted upon at the meeting, such item need be answered in the registrant's soliciting material only with respect to proposals to be made by or on behalf of the registrant.

C. Except as otherwise specifically provided, where any item calls for information for a specified period in regard to directors, officers or other persons holding specified positions or relationships, the information shall be given in regard to any person who held any of the specified positions or relationships at any time during the period. However, information need not be included for any portion of the period during which such person did not hold any such position or relationship provided a statement to that effect is made.

* * *

Item 1. Date, Time and Place Information

(a) State the date, time and place of the meeting of security holders, and the complete mailing address, including ZIP Code, of the principal executive offices of the registrant, unless such information is otherwise disclosed in material furnished to security holders with or preceding the proxy statement. If action is to be taken by written consent, state the date by which consents are to be submitted if state law requires that such a date be specified or if the person soliciting intends to set a date.

(b) On the first page of the proxy statement, as delivered to security holders, state the approximate date on which the proxy statement and form of proxy are first sent or given to security holders.

(c) Furnish the information required to be in the proxy statement by Rule 14a–5(e).

Item 2. Revocability of Proxy

State whether or not the person giving the proxy has the power to revoke it. If the right of revocation before the proxy is exercised is limited or is subject to compliance with any formal procedure, briefly describe such limitation or procedure.

Item 3. Dissenters' Rights of Appraisal

Outline briefly the rights of appraisal or similar rights of dissenters with respect to any matter to be acted upon and indicate any statutory procedure required to be followed by dissenting security holders in order to perfect such rights. Where such rights may be exercised only within a limited time after the date of adoption of a proposal, the filing of a charter amendment or other similar act, state whether the persons solicited will be notified of such date.

Instruction 1. Indicate whether a security holder's failure to vote against a proposal will constitute a waiver of his appraisal or similar rights and whether a vote against a proposal will be deemed to satisfy any notice requirements under State law with respect to appraisal rights. If the State law is unclear, state what position will be taken in regard to these matters.

Instruction 2. Open-end investment companies registered under the Investment Company Act of 1940 are not required to respond to this item.

Item 4. Persons Making the Solicitation.

(a) *Solicitations not subject to Rule 14a–12(c).* (1) If the solicitation is made by the registrant, so state. Give the name of any director of the registrant who has informed the issuer in writing that he intends to oppose any action intended to be taken by the registrant and indicate the action which he intends to oppose.

(2) If the solicitation is made otherwise than by the registrant, so state and give the names of the participants in the solicitation, as defined in paragraphs (a)(iii), (iv), (v) and (vi) of Instruction 3 to this item.

(3) If the solicitation is to be made otherwise than by the use of the mails, describe the methods to be employed. If the solicitation is to be made by specially engaged employees or paid solicitors, state (i) the material features of any contract or arrangement for such solicitation and identify the parties, and (ii) the cost or anticipated cost thereof.

(4) State the names of the persons by whom the cost of solicitation has been or will be borne, directly or indirectly.

(b) *Solicitations subject to Rule 14a–12(c).* (1) State by whom the solicitation is made and describe the methods employed and to be employed to solicit security holders.

(2) If regular employees of the registrant or any other participant in a solicitation have been or are to be employed to solicit security holders, describe the class or classes of employees to be so employed, and the manner and nature of their employment for such purpose.

(3) If specially engaged employees, representatives or other persons have been or are to be employed to solicit security holders, state (i) the material features of any contract or arrangement for such solicitation and identify the parties (ii) the cost or anticipated cost thereof, and (iii) the approximate number of such employees or employees of any other person (naming such other person) who will solicit security holders.

(4) State the total amount estimated to be spent and the total expenditures to date for, in furtherance of, or in connection with the solicitation of security holders.

(5) State by whom the cost of the solicitation will be borne. If such cost to be borne initially by any person other than the registrant, state whether reimbursement will be sought from the registrant, and, if so, whether the question of such reimbursement will be submitted to a vote of security holders.

(6) If any such solicitation is terminated pursuant to a settlement between the registrant and any other participant in such solicitation, describe the terms of such settlement, including the cost or anticipated cost thereof to the registrant.

Instructions. 1. With respect to solicitations subject to Rule 14a–12(c), costs and expenditures within the meaning of this item 3 shall include fees for attorneys, accountants, public relations or financial advisers, solicitors, advertising, printing, transportation, litigation and other costs incidental to the solicitation, except that the registrant may exclude the amount of such costs represented by the amount normally expended for a solicitation for an election of directors in the absence of a contest, and costs represented by salaries and wages of regular employees and officers, provided a statement to the effect is included in the proxy statement.

2. The information required pursuant to paragraph (b)(6) of this item should be included in any amended or revised proxy statement or other soliciting materials relating to the same meeting or subject matter furnished to security holders by the registrant subsequent to the date of settlement.

3. For purposes of this Item 4 and Item 5 of this Schedule 14A: (a) The terms "participant" and "participant in a solicitation" include the following:

(i) the registrant;

(ii) any director of the registrant, and any nominee for whose election as a director proxies are solicited;

(iii) any committee or group which solicits proxies, any member of such committee or group, and any person whether or not named as a member who, acting alone or with one or more other persons, directly or indirectly takes the initiative, or engages, in organizing, directing, or arranging for the financing of any such committee or group;

(iv) any person who finances or joins with another to finance the solicitation of proxies, except persons who contribute not more than $500 and who are not otherwise participants;

(v) any person who lends money or furnishes credit or enters into any other arrangements, pursuant to any contract or understanding with a participant, for the purpose of financing or otherwise inducing the purchase, sale, holding or voting of securities of the registrant by any participant or other persons, in support of or in opposition to a participant; except that such terms do not include a bank, broker or dealer who, in the ordinary course of business, lends money or executes orders for the purchase or sale of securities and who is not otherwise a participant; and

(vi) any person who solicits proxies.

(b) The terms "participant" and "participant in a solicitation" do not include:

(i) any person or organization retained or employed by a participant to solicit security holders and whose activities are limited to the duties required to be performed in the course of such employment;

(ii) any person who merely transmits proxy soliciting material or performs other ministerial or clerical duties;

(iii) any person employed by a participant in the capacity of attorney, accountant, or advertising, public relations or financial adviser, and whose activities are limited to the duties required to be performed in the course of such employment;

(iv) any person regularly employed as an officer or employee of the registrant or any of its subsidiaries who is not otherwise a participant; or

(v) any officer or director of, or any person regularly employed by, any other participant, if such officer, director or employee is not otherwise a participant.

Item 5. Interest of Certain Persons in Matters to be Acted Upon

(a) *Solicitations not subject to Rule 14a–11.* Describe briefly any substantial interest, direct or indirect, by security holdings or otherwise, of each of the following persons in any matter to be acted upon, other than elections to office:

(1) If the solicitation is made on behalf of registrant, each person who has been a director or officer of the registrant at any time since the beginning of the last fiscal year.

(2) If the solicitation is made otherwise than on behalf of registrant, each participant in the solicitation, as defined in paragraphs (a)(iii), (iv), (v) and (vi) of Instruction 3 to Item 4 of this Schedule 14A.

(3) Each nominee for election as a director of the registrant.

(4) Each associate of the foregoing persons.

Instruction. Except in the case of a solicitation subject to this regulation made in opposition to another solicitation subject to this regulation, this sub-item (a) shall not apply to any interest arising from the ownership of securities of the registrant where the security holder receives no extra or special benefit not shared on a pro rata basis by all other holders of the same class.

(b) *Solicitation subject to Rule 14a–12(c).*

(1) Describe briefly any substantial interest, direct or indirect, by security holdings or otherwise, of each participant as defined in paragraphs (a)(ii), (iii), (iv), (v) and (vi) of Instruction 3 to Item 4 of this Schedule 14A, in any matter to be acted upon at the meeting, and include with respect to each participant the following information, or a fair and accurate summary thereof:

(i) Name and business address of the participant.

(ii) The participant's present principal occupation or employment and the name, principal business and address of any corporation or other organization in which such employment is carried on.

(iii) State whether or not, during the past ten years, the participant has been convicted in a criminal proceeding (excluding traffic violations or similar misdemeanors) and, if so, give dates, nature of conviction, name and location of court, and penalty imposed or other disposition of the case. A negative answer need not be included in the proxy statement or other soliciting material.

(iv) State the amount of each class of securities of the registrant which the participant owns beneficially, directly or indirectly.

(v) State the amount of each class of securities of the registrant which the participant owns of record but not beneficially.

(vi) State with respect to all securities of the registrant purchased or sold within the past two years, the dates on which they were purchased or sold and the amount purchased or sold on each date.

(vii) If any part of the purchase price or market value of any of the shares specified in paragraph (b)(1)(vi) of this Item is represented by funds borrowed or otherwise obtained for the purpose of acquiring or holding such securities, so state and indicate the amount of the indebtedness as of the latest practicable date. If such funds were borrowed or obtained otherwise than pursuant to a margin account or bank loan in the regular course of business of a bank, broker or dealer, briefly describe the transaction, and state the names of the parties.

(viii) State whether or not the participant is, or was within the past year, a party to any contract, arrangements or understandings with any person with respect to any securities of the registrant, including, but not limited to joint ventures, loan or option arrangements, puts or calls, guarantees against loss or guarantees of profit, division of losses or profits, or the giving or withholding of proxies. If so, name the parties to such contracts, arrangements or understandings and give the details thereof.

(ix) State the amount of securities of the registrant owned beneficially, directly or indirectly, by each of the participant's associates and the name and address of each such associate.

(x) State the amount of each class of securities of any parent or subsidiary of the registrant which the participant owns beneficially, directly or indirectly.

(xi) Furnish for the participant and associates of the participant the information required by Item 404(a) of Regulation S–K.

(xii) State whether or not the participant or any associates of the participant have any arrangement or understanding with any person—

(A) with respect to any future employment by the registrant or its affiliates; or

(B) with respect to any future transactions to which the registrant or any of its affiliates will or may be a party.

If so, describe such arrangement or understanding and state the names of the parties thereto.

(2) With respect to any person, other than a director or executive officer of the registrant acting solely in that capacity, who is a party to an arrangement or understanding pursuant to which a nominee for election as director is proposed to be elected, describe any substantial interest, direct or indirect, by security holdings or otherwise, that such person has in any matter to be acted upon at the meeting, and furnish the information called for by paragraphs (b)(1)(xi) and (xii) of this Item.

Instruction: For purposes of this Item 5, beneficial ownership shall be determined in accordance with Rule 13d–3 under the Act.

Item 6. Voting Securities and Principal Holders Thereof.

(a) State as to each class of voting securities of the registrant entitled to be voted at the meeting, the number of shares outstanding and the number of votes to which each class is entitled.

(b) State the record date, if any, with respect to this solicitation. If the right to vote or give consent is not to be determined, in whole or in part, by reference to a record date, indicate the criteria for the determination of security holders entitled to vote or give consent.

(c) If action is to be taken with respect to the election of directors and if the persons solicited have cumulative voting rights: (1) Make a statement that they have such rights, (2) briefly describe such rights, (3) state briefly the conditions precedent to the exercise thereof, and (4) if discretionary authority to cumulate votes is solicited, so indicate.

(d) Furnish the information required by Item 403(a) of Regulation S–K to the extent known by the persons on whose behalf the solicitation is made.

(e) If, to the knowledge of the persons on whose behalf the solicitation is made, a change in control of the registrant has occurred since the beginning of its last fiscal year, state the name of the person(s) who acquired such control, the amount and the source of the consideration used by such person or persons; the basis of the control, the date and a description of the transaction(s) which resulted in the change of control and the percentage of voting securities of the registrant now beneficially owned directly or indirectly by the person(s) who acquired control; and the identity of the person(s) from whom control was assumed. If the source of all or any part of the consideration used is a loan made in the ordinary course of business by a bank as defined by section 3(a)(6) of the Act, the identity of such bank shall be omitted provided a request for confidentiality has been made pursuant to section 13(d)(1)(B) of the Act by the person(s) who acquired control. In lieu thereof, the material shall indicate that the identity of the bank has been so omitted and filed separately with the Commission.

Instructions. 1. State the terms of any loans or pledges obtained by the new control group for the purpose of acquiring control, and the names of the lenders or pledgees. 2. Any arrangements or understandings among members of both the former and new control groups and their associates with respect to election of directors or other matters should be described.

Item 7. Directors and Executive Officers

If action is to be taken with respect to election of directors, furnish the following information, in tabular form to the extent practicable. However, if the solicitation is made on behalf of persons other than the registrant, the information required need be furnished only as to nominees of the persons making the solicitation.

(a) The information required by Instruction 4 to Item 103 of Regulation S–K with respect to directors and executive officers.

(b) The information required by Items 401, 404(a) and (c), and 405 of Regulation S–K.

(c) The information required by Item 404(b) of Regulation S–K.

(d)(1) State whether or not the registrant has standing audit, nominating and compensation committees of the Board of Directors, or committees performing similar functions. If the registrant has such committees, however designated, identify each committee member, state the number of committee meetings held by each such committee during the last fiscal year and describe briefly the functions performed by such committees. Such disclosure need not be provided to the extent it is duplicative of disclosure provided in accordance with Item 401(i) of Regulation S–K (§ 229.401(i) of this chapter).

(2) If the registrant has a nominating or similar committee, state whether the committee will consider nominees recommended by security holders and, if so, describe the procedures to be followed by security holders in submitting such recommendations.

(3) If the registrant has an audit committee:

(i) Provide the information required by Item 306 of Regulation S–K.

(ii) State whether the registrant's Board of Directors has adopted a written charter for the audit committee.

(iii) Include a copy of the written charter, if any, as an appendix to the registrant's proxy statement, unless a copy has been included as an appendix to the registrant's proxy statement within the registrant's past three fiscal years.

(iv)(A) If the registrant is a listed issuer, as defined in Rule 10A–3:

(1) Disclose whether the members of the audit committee are independent, as independence for audit committee members is defined in the listing standards applicable to the listed issuer. If the registrant does not have a separately designated audit committee, or committee performing similar functions, the registrant must provide the disclosure with respect to all members of its board of directors.

(2) If the listed issuer's board of directors determines, in accordance with the listing standards applicable to the listed issuer, to appoint a director to the audit committee who is not independent (apart from the requirements in Rule 10A–3) because of exceptional or limited or similar circumstances, disclose the nature of the relationship that makes that individual not independent and the reasons for the board of directors' determination.

(B) If the registrant, including a small business issuer, is not a listed issuer, disclose whether the registrant has an audit committee established in accordance with section 3(a)(58)(A) of the Act) and, if so, whether the members of the committee are independent. In determining whether a member is independent, the registrant must use a definition for audit committee member independence of a national securities exchange registered pursuant to section 6(a) of the Act) or a national securities association registered pursuant to section 15A(a) of the Act) that has been approved by the Commission (as such definition may be modified or supplemented), and state which definition was used. Whichever definition is chosen must be applied consistently to all members of the audit committee.

(v) The information required by paragraph (d)(3) of this Item shall not be deemed to be "soliciting material," or to be "filed" with the Commission or subject to Regulation 14A or 14C other than as provided in this Item, or to the liabilities of section 18 of the Exchange Act except to the extent that the registrant specifically requests that the information be treated as soliciting material or specifically incorporates it by reference into a document filed under the Securities Act or the Exchange Act. Such information will not be deemed to be incorporated by reference into any filing under the Securities Act or the Exchange Act, except to the extent that the registrant specifically incorporates it by reference.

(vi) The disclosure required by this paragraph (d)(3) need only be provided one time during any fiscal year.

(vii) Investment companies registered under the Investment Company Act of 1940, other than closed-end investment companies, need not provide the information required by this paragraph (d)(3).

(e) In lieu of paragraphs (a) through (d)(2) of this Item, investment companies registered under the Investment Company Act of 1940 must furnish the information required by Item 22(b) of this Schedule 14A.

(f) State the total number of meetings of the board of directors (including regularly scheduled and special meetings) which were held during the last full fiscal year. Name each incumbent director who during the last full fiscal year attended fewer than 75 percent of the aggregate of (1) the total number of meetings of the board of directors (held during the period for which he has been a director) and (2) the total number of meetings held by all committees of the board on which he served (during the periods that he served).

(g) If a director has resigned or declined to stand for re-election to the board of directors since the date of the last annual meeting of shareholders because of a disagreement with the issuer on any matter relating to the issuer's operations, policies or practices, and if the director has furnished the issuer with a letter describing such disagreement and requesting that the matter be disclosed, the issuer shall state the date of resignation or declination to stand for re-election and summarize the director's description of the disagreement.

If the registrant believes that the description provided by the director is incorrect or incomplete, it may include a brief statement presenting its views of the disagreement.

Item 8. Compensation of Directors and Executive Officers

(See Note C at the beginning of Schedule 14A.)

Furnish the information required by *Item 402* (§ 229.402 of this chapter) of Regulation S–K if action is to be taken with regard to:

(a) the election of directors;

(b) any bonus, profit sharing or other compensation plan, contract or arrangement in which any director, nominee for election as a director, or executive officer of the registrant will participate;

(c) any pension or retirement plan in which any such person will participate; or

(d) the granting or extension to any such person of any options, warrants or rights to purchase any securities, other than warrants or rights issued to security holders as such, on a pro rata basis.

However, if the solicitation is made on behalf of persons other than the registrant, the information required need be furnished only as to nominees of the persons making the solicitation and associates of such nominees. In the case of investment companies registered under the Investment Company Act of 1940 and registrants that have elected to be regulated as business development companies, furnish the information required by Item 22(b)(6) of this Schedule.

Instruction. If an otherwise reportable compensation plan became subject to such requirements because of an acquisition or merger and, within one year of the acquisition or merger, such plan was terminated for purposes of prospective eligibility, the registrant may furnish a description of its obligation to the designated individuals pursuant to the compensation plan. Such description may be furnished in lieu of a description of the compensation plan in the proxy statement.

Item 9. Independent Public Accountants

If the solicitation is made on behalf of the registrant and relates to (1) the annual (or special meeting in lieu of annual) meeting of security holders at which directors are to be elected, or a solicitation of consents or authorizations in lieu of such meeting or (2) the election, approval or ratification of the registrant's accountant, furnish the following information describing the registrant's relationship with its independent public accountant:

(a) The name of the principal accountant selected or being recommended to security holders for election approval or ratification for the current year. If no accountant has been selected or recommended, so state and briefly describe the reasons therefor.

(b) The name of the principal accountant for the fiscal year most recently completed if different from the accountant selected or recommended for the current year or if no accountant has yet been selected or recommended for the current year.

(c) The proxy statement shall indicate (1) whether or not representatives of the principal accountant for the current year and for the most recently completed fiscal year are expected to be present at the security holders' meeting, (2) whether or not they will have the opportunity to make a statement if they desire to do so and (3) whether or not such representatives are expected to be available to respond to appropriate questions.

(d) If during the registrant's two most recent fiscal years or any subsequent interim period, (1) an independent accountant who was previously engaged as the principal accountant to audit the registrant's financial statements, or an independent accountant on whom the principal accountant expressed reliance in its report regarding a significant subsidiary, has resigned (or indicated it has declined to stand for re-election after the completion of the current audit) or was dismissed, or (2) a new independent accountant has been engaged as either the principal accountant to audit the registrant's financial statements or as an independent accountant on whom the principal accountant has expressed or is expected to express reliance in its report regarding a significant subsidiary, then, notwithstanding any previous disclosure, provide the information required by Item 304(a) of Regulation S–K.

(e)(1) Disclose, under the caption Audit Fees, the aggregate fees billed for each of the last two fiscal years for professional services rendered by the principal accountant for the audit of the registrant's annual financial statements and review of financial statements included in the registrant's Form 10–Q or 10–QSB or services that are normally provided by the accountant in connection with statutory and regulatory filings or engagements for those fiscal years.

(2) Disclose, under the caption Audit–Related Fees, the aggregate fees billed in each of the last two fiscal years for assurance and related services by the principal accountant that are reasonably related to the performance of the audit or review of the registrant's financial statements and are not reported under paragraph (e)(1) of this section. Registrants shall describe the nature of the services comprising the fees disclosed under this category.

(3) Disclose, under the caption Tax Fees, the aggregate fees billed in each of the last two fiscal years for professional services rendered by the principal accountant for tax compliance, tax advice, and tax planning. Registrants shall describe the nature of the services comprising the fees disclosed under this category.

(4) Disclose, under the caption All Other Fees, the aggregate fees billed in each of the last two fiscal years for products and services provided by the principal accountant, other than the services reported in paragraphs (e)(1) through (e)(3) of this section. Registrants shall describe the nature of the services comprising the fees disclosed under this category.

(5)(i) Disclose the audit committee's pre-approval policies and procedures described in Rule 2–01(c)(7)(i).

(ii) Disclose the percentage of services described in each of paragraphs (e)(2) through (e)(4) of this section that were approved by the audit committee pursuant to Rule 2–01(c)(7)(i)(C).

(6) If greater than 50 percent, disclose the percentage of hours expended on the principal accountant's engagement to audit the registrant's financial statements for the most recent fiscal year that were attributed to work performed by persons other than the principal accountant's full-time, permanent employees.

(7) If the registrant is an investment company, disclose the aggregate non-audit fees billed by the registrant's accountant for services rendered to the registrant, and to the registrant's investment adviser (not including any subadviser whose role is primarily portfolio management and is subcontracted with or overseen by another investment adviser), and any entity controlling, controlled by, or under common control with the adviser that provides ongoing services to the registrant for each of the last two fiscal years of the registrant. (8) If the registrant is an investment company, disclose whether the audit committee of the board of directors has considered whether the provision of non-audit services that were rendered to the registrant's investment adviser (not including any subadviser whose role is primarily portfolio management and is subcontracted with or overseen by another investment adviser), and any entity controlling, controlled by, or under common control with the investment adviser that provides ongoing services to the registrant that were not pre-approved pursuant to Rule 2–01(c)(7)(ii) is compatible with maintaining the principal accountant's independence.

(8) If the registrant is an investment company, disclose whether the audit committee of the board of directors has considered whether the provision of non-audit services that were rendered to the registrant's investment adviser (not including any subadviser whose role is primarily portfolio management and is subcontracted with or overseen by another investment adviser), and any entity controlling, controlled by, or under common control with the investment adviser that provides ongoing services to the registrant that were not pre-approved pursuant to Rule 2–01(c)(7)(ii) is compatible with maintaining the principal accountant's independence.

Item 10. Compensation Plans

If action is to be taken with respect to any plan pursuant to which cash or noncash compensation may be paid or distributed, furnish the following information:

(a) *Plans Subject to Securityholder Action.*

(1) Describe briefly the material features of the plan being acted upon, identify each class of persons who will be eligible to participate therein, indicate the approximate number of persons in each such class and state the basis of such participation.

(2)(i) In the tabular format specified below, disclose the benefits or amounts that will be received by or allocated to each of the following under the plan being acted upon, if such benefits or amounts are determinable:

NEW PLAN BENEFITS

	Plan Name	
Name and Position	Dollar Value ($)	Number of Units
CEO		
#A		
#B		
#C		
#D		
Executive Group		
Non–Executive Officer Group		
Non–Executive Officer Employee Group		

(ii) The table required by paragraph (a)(2)(i) of this Item shall provide information as to the following persons:

(A) Each person (stating name and position) specified in paragraph (a)(3) of Item 402 of Regulation S–K;

Instruction: In the case of investment companies registered under the Investment Company Act of 1940, furnish the information for Compensated Persons as defined in Item 22(b)(6) of this Schedule in lieu of the persons specified in paragraph (a)(3) of

Item 402 of Regulation S–K (§ 229.402(a)(3) of this chapter).

(B) All current executive officers as a group;

(C) All current directors who are not executive officers as a group; and

(D) All employees, including all current officers who are not executive officers, as a group.

Instruction to New Plan Benefits Table.

Additional columns should be added for each plan with respect to which securityholder action is to be taken.

(iii) If the benefits or amounts specified in paragraph (a)(2)(i) of this Item are not determinable, state the benefits or amounts which would have been received by or allocated to each of the following for the last completed fiscal year if the plan had been in effect, if such benefits or amounts may be determined in the table specified in paragraph (a)(2)(i) of this Item:

(A) Each person (stating name and position) specified in paragraph (a)(3) of Item 402 of Regulation S–K;

(B) All current executive officers as a group;

(C) All current directors who are not executive officers as a group; and

(D) All Employees, including all current officers who are not executive officers, as a group.

(3) If the plan to be acted upon can be amended, otherwise than by a vote of securityholders to increase the cost thereof to the registrant or to alter the allocation of the benefits as between the persons and groups specified in paragraph (2)(a) of this item, state the nature of the amendments which can be so made.

(b) *Additional Information Regarding Specific Plans Subject to Securityholder Action.*

(1) With respect to any pension or retirement plan submitted for securityholder action, state:

(i) The approximate total amount necessary to fund the plan with respect to past services, the period over which such amount is to be paid and the estimated annual payments necessary to pay the total amount over such period; and

(ii) The estimated annual payment to be made with respect to current services. In the case of a pension or retirement plan, information called for by paragraph (a)(2) of this Item may be furnished in the format specified by paragraph (f)(1) of Item 402 of Regulation S–K.

Instruction. In the case of investment companies registered under the Investment Company Act of 1940, refer to instruction 4 in Item 22(b)(6)(ii) of this Schedule in lieu of paragraph (f)(1) of Item 402 of Regulation S–K (§ 229.402(f)(1) of this chapter).

(2)(i) With respect to any specific grant of or any plan containing options, warrants or rights submitted for security holder action, state:

(A) The title and amount of securities underlying such options, warrants or rights;

(B) The prices, expiration dates and other material conditions upon which the options, warrants or rights may be exercised;

(C) The consideration received or to be received by the registrant or subsidiary for the granting or extension of the options, warrants or rights;

(D) The market value of the securities underlying the options, warrants or rights as of the latest practicable date; and

(E) In the case of options, the federal income tax consequences of the issuance and exercise of such options to the recipient and the registrant; and

(ii) State separately the amount of such options received or to be received by the following persons if such benefits or amounts are determinable:

(A) Each person (stating name and position) specified in paragraph (a)(3) of Item 402 of Regulation S–K;

(B) All current executive officers as a group;

(C) All current directors who are not executive officers as a group;

(D) Each nominee for election as a director;

(E) Each associate of any of such directors, executive officer or nominees;

(F) Each other person who received or is to receive 5 percent of such options, warrants or rights; and

(G) All employees, including all current officers who are not executive officers, as a group.

Instructions

1. The term "plan" as used in this Item means any plan as defined in paragraph (a)(7)(ii) of Item 402 of Regulation S–K.

2. If action is to be taken with respect to a material amendment or modification of an existing plan, the item shall be answered with respect to the plan as proposed to be amended or modified and shall indicate any material differences from the existing plan.

3. If the plan to be acted upon is set forth in a written document, three copies thereof shall be filed with the Commission at the time copies of the proxy statement and form of proxy are filed pursuant to paragraph (a) or (b) of Rule 14a–6. Electronic filers shall file with the Commission a copy of such written plan document in electronic format as an appendix to the proxy statement. It need not be provided to security holders unless it is part of the proxy statement.

4. Paragraphs (b)(2)(ii) does not apply to warrants or rights to be issued to security holders as such on a pro rata basis.

5. The Commission should be informed, as supplemental information, when the proxy statement is first filed, as to when the options, warrants, or rights and the shares called for thereby will be registered under the Securities Act or, if such registration is not contemplated, the section of the Securities Act or rule of the Commission under which exemption from such registration is claimed and the facts relied upon to make the exemption available.

Item 11. Authorization or Issuance of Securities Otherwise Than for Exchange

If action is to be taken with respect to the authorization or issuance of any securities otherwise than for exchange for outstanding securities of the issuer, furnish the following information:

(a) State the title and amount of securities to be authorized or issued.

(b) Furnish the information required by Item 202 of Regulation S–K. If the terms of the securities cannot be stated or estimated with respect to any or all of the securities to be authorized, because no offering thereof is contemplated in the proximate future, and if no further authorization by security holders for the issuance thereof is to be obtained, it should be stated that the terms of the securities to be authorized, including dividend or interest rates, conversion prices, voting rights, redemption prices, maturity dates, and similar matters will be determined by the board of directors. If the securities are additional shares of common stock of a class outstanding, the description may be omitted except for a statement of the preemptive rights, if any. Where the statutory provisions with respect to preemptive rights are so indefinite or complex that they cannot be stated in summarized form, it will suffice to make a statement in the form of an opinion of counsel as to the existence and extent of such rights.

(c) Describe briefly the transaction in which the securities are to be issued, including a statement as to (1) the nature and approximate amount of consideration received or to be received by the registrant, and (2) the approximate amount devoted to each purpose so far as determinable for which the net proceeds have been or are to be used. If it is impracticable to describe the transaction in which the securities are to be issued, state the reason, indicate the purpose of the authorization of the securities, and state whether further authorization for the issuance of the securities by a vote of security holders will be solicited prior to such issuance.

(d) If the securities are to be issued otherwise than in a general public offering for cash, state the reasons for the proposed authorization or issuance and the general effect thereof upon the rights of existing security holders.

(e) Furnish the information required by Item 13(a) of this schedule.

Item 12. Modification or Exchange of Securities

If action is to be taken with respect to the modification of any class of securities of the registrant, or the issuance or authorization for issuance of securities of the registrant in exchange for outstanding securities of the registrant, furnish the following information:

(a) If outstanding securities are to be modified, state the title and amount thereof. If securities are to be issued in exchange for outstanding securities, state the title and amount of securities to be so issued, the title and amount of outstanding securities to be exchanged therefor and the basis of the exchange.

(b) Describe any material differences between the outstanding securities and the modified or new securities in respect of any of the matters concerning which information would be required in the description of the securities in Item 202 of Regulation S–K.

(c) State the reasons for the proposed modification or exchange and the general effect thereof upon the rights of existing security holders.

(d) Furnish a brief statement as to arrears in dividends or as to defaults in principal or interest in respect to the outstanding securities which are to be modified or exchanged and such other information as may be appropriate in the particular case to disclose adequately the nature and effect of the proposed action.

(e) Outline briefly any other material features of the proposed modification or exchange. If the plan of proposed action is set forth in a written document, file copies thereof with the Commission in accordance with Rule 14a–8.

(f) Furnish the information required by Item 13(a) of this schedule.

Instruction. If the existing security is presently listed and registered on a national securities exchange, state whether the registrant to apply for listing and registration of the new or reclassified security on such exchange or any other exchange. If the registrant does not intend to make such application, state the effect of the termination of such listing and registration.

Item 13. Financial and Other Information

(*See* Notes D and E at the beginning of this Schedule.)

(a) Information required. If action is to be taken with respect to any matter specified in Item 11 or 12, furnish the following information:

(1) Financial statements meeting the requirements of Regulation S–X, including financial information required by Rule 3–05 and Article 11 of Regulation S–X with respect to transactions other than that pursuant to which action is to be taken as described in this proxy statement;

(2) Item 302 of Regulation S–K, supplementary financial information;

(3) Item 303 of Regulation S–K, management's discussion and analysis of financial condition and results of operations;

(4) Item 304 of Regulation S–K, changes in and disagreements with accountants on accounting and financial disclosure; and

(5) Item 305 of Regulation S–K, quantitative and qualitative disclosures about market risk; and

(6) A statement as to whether or not representatives of the principal accountants for the current year and for the most recently completed fiscal year:

(i) are expected to be present at the security holders' meeting;

(ii) will have the opportunity to make a statement if they desire to do so; and

(iii) are expected to be available to respond to appropriate questions.

(b) Incorporation by reference. The information required pursuant to paragraph (a) of this Item may be incorporated by reference into the proxy statement as follows:

(1) S–3 registrants. If the registrant meets the requirements of Form S–3 (*see* Note E of this Schedule), it may incorporate by reference to previously-filed documents any of the information required by paragraph (a) of this Item, provided that the requirements of paragraph (c) are met. When the registrant meets the requirements of Form S–3 and has elected to furnish the required information by incorporation by reference, the registrant may elect to update the information so incorporated by reference to information in subsequently-filed documents.

(2) All registrants. The registrant may incorporate by reference any of the information required by paragraph (a) of this Item, provided that the information is contained in an annual report to security holders or a previously-filed statement or report, such report or statement is delivered to security holders with the proxy statement and the requirements of paragraph (c) are met.

(c) Certain conditions applicable to incorporation by reference. Registrants eligible to incorporate by reference into the proxy statement the information required by paragraph (a) of this Item in the man-

ner specified by paragraphs (b)(1) and (b)(2) may do so only if:

(1) the information is not required to be included in the proxy statement pursuant to the requirement of another Item;

(2) the proxy statement identifies on the last page(s) the information incorporated by reference; and

(3) the material incorporated by reference substantially meets the requirements of this Item or the appropriate portions of this Item.

Instructions to Item 13. 1. Notwithstanding the provisions of this Item, any or all of the information required by paragraph (a) of this Item, not material for the exercise of prudent judgment in regard to the matter to be acted upon may be omitted. In the usual case the information is deemed material to the exercise of prudent judgment where the matter to be acted upon is the authorization or issuance of a material amount of senior securities, but the information is not deemed material where the matter to be acted upon is the authorization or issuance of common stock, otherwise than in an exchange, merger, consolidation, acquisition or similar transaction, the authorization of preferred stock without present intent to issue or the authorization of preferred stock for issuance for cash in an amount constituting fair value.

2. In order to facilitate compliance with Rule 2–02(a) of Regulation S–X, one copy of the definitive proxy statement filed with the Commission shall include a manually signed copy of the accountant's report. If the financial statements are incorporated by reference, a manually signed copy of the accountant's report shall be filed with the definitive proxy statement.

3. Notwithstanding the provisions of Regulation S–X, no schedules other than those prepared in accordance with Rules 12–15, 12–28 and 12–29 (or, for management investment companies, Rules 12–12 through 12–14) of that regulation need be furnished in the proxy statement.

4. Unless registered on a national securities exchange or otherwise required to furnish such information, registered investment companies need not furnish the information required by paragraphs (a)(2) or (3) of this Item.

5. If the registrant submits preliminary proxy material incorporating by reference financial statements required by this Item, the registrant should furnish a draft of the financial statements if the document from which they are incorporated has not been filed with or furnished to the Commission.

6. A registered investment company need not comply with Items (a)(2), (a)(3), and (a)(5) of this Item 13.

Item 14. Mergers, Consolidations, Acquisitions and Similar Matters

Instructions to Item 14.

1. In transactions in which the consideration offered to security holders consists wholly or in part of securities registered under the Securities Act of 1933, furnish the information required by Form S–4 (§ 239.25 of this chapter), Form F–4 (§ 239.34 of this chapter), or Form N–14 (§ 239.23 of this chapter), as applicable, instead of this Item. Only a Form S–4, Form F–4, or Form N–14 must be filed in accordance with § 240.14a–6(j).

2. (a) In transactions in which the consideration offered to security holders consists wholly of cash, the information required by paragraph (c)(1) of this Item for the acquiring company need not be provided unless the information is material to an informed voting decision (*e.g.*, the security holders of the target company are voting and financing is not assured).

(b) Additionally, if only the security holders of the target company are voting:

i. The financial information in paragraphs (b)(8)—(11) of this Item for the acquiring company and the target need not be provided; and

ii. The information in paragraph (c)(2) of this Item for the target company need not be provided. If, however, the transaction is a going-private transaction (as defined by § 240.13e–3), then the information required by paragraph (c)(2) of this Item must be provided and to the extent that the going-private rules require the information specified in paragraph (b)(8)—(b)(11) of this Item, that information must be provided as well.

3. In transactions in which the consideration offered to security holders consists wholly of securities exempt from registration under the Securities Act of 1933 or a combination of exempt securities

and cash, information about the acquiring company required by paragraph (c)(1) of this Item need not be provided if only the security holders of the acquiring company are voting, unless the information is material to an informed voting decision. If only the security holders of the target company are voting, information about the target company in paragraph (c)(2) of this Item need not be provided. However, the information required by paragraph (c)(2) of this Item must be provided if the transaction is a going-private (as defined by § 240.13e–3) or roll-up (as described by Item 901 of Regulation S–K (§ 229.901 of this chapter)) transaction.

4. The information required by paragraphs (b)(8)—(11) and (c) need not be provided if the plan being voted on involves only the acquiring company and one or more of its totally held subsidiaries and does not involve a liquidation or a spin-off.

5. To facilitate compliance with Rule 2–02(a) of Regulation S–X (§ 210.2–02(a) of this chapter) (technical requirements relating to accountants' reports), one copy of the definitive proxy statement filed with the Commission must include a signed copy of the accountant's report. If the financial statements are incorporated by reference, a signed copy of the accountant's report must be filed with the definitive proxy statement. Signatures may be typed if the document is filed electronically on EDGAR. *See* Rule 302 of Regulation S–T (§ 232.302 of this chapter).

6. Notwithstanding the provisions of Regulation S–X, no schedules other than those prepared in accordance with § 210.12–15, § 210.12–28 and § 210.12–29 of this chapter (or, for management investment companies, §§ 210.12–12 through 210.12–14 of this chapter) of that regulation need be furnished in the proxy statement.

7. If the preliminary proxy material incorporates by reference financial statements required by this Item, a draft of the financial statements must be furnished to the Commission staff upon request if the document from which they are incorporated has not been filed with or furnished to the Commission.

(a) *Applicability.*

If action is to be taken with respect to any of the following transactions, provide the information required by this Item:

(1) A merger or consolidation;

(2) An acquisition of securities of another person;

(3) An acquisition of any other going business or the assets of a going business;

(4) A sale or other transfer of all or any substantial part of assets; or

(5) A liquidation or dissolution.

(b) *Transaction information.*

Provide the following information for each of the parties to the transaction unless otherwise specified:

(1) *Summary term sheet.* The information required by Item 1001 of Regulation M–A (§ 229.1001 of this chapter).

(2) *Contact information.* The name, complete mailing address and telephone number of the principal executive offices.

(3) *Business conducted.* A brief description of the general nature of the business conducted.

(4) *Terms of the transaction.* The information required by *Item 1004(a)(2)* of Regulation M–A (§ 229.1004 of this chapter).

(5) *Regulatory approvals.* A statement as to whether any federal or state regulatory requirements must be complied with or approval must be obtained in connection with the transaction and, if so, the status of the compliance or approval.

(6) *Reports, opinions, appraisals.* If a report, opinion or appraisal materially relating to the transaction has been received from an outside party, and is referred to in the proxy statement, furnish the information required by *Item 1015(b)* of Regulation M–A (§ 229.1015 of this chapter).

(7) *Past contacts, transactions or negotiations.* The information required by Items *1005(b)* and *1011(a)(1)* of Regulation M–A (§ 229.1005 of this chapter and § 229.1011 of this chapter), for the parties to the transaction and their affiliates during the periods for which financial statements are presented or incorporated by reference under this Item.

(8) *Selected financial data.* The selected financial data required by *Item 301* of Regulation S–K (§ 229.301 of this chapter).

(9) *Pro forma selected financial data.* If material, the information required by Item 301 of Regulation

S–K (§ 229.301 of this chapter) for the acquiring company, showing the pro forma effect of the transaction.

(10) *Pro forma information.* In a table designed to facilitate comparison, historical and pro forma per share data of the acquiring company and historical and equivalent pro forma per share data of the target company for the following Items:

(i) Book value per share as of the date financial data is presented pursuant to Item 301 of Regulation S–K (§ 229.301 of this chapter);

(ii) Cash dividends declared per share for the periods for which financial data is presented pursuant to Item 301 of Regulation S–K (§ 229.301 of this chapter); and

(iii) Income (loss) per share from continuing operations for the periods for which financial data is presented pursuant to Item 301 of Regulation S–K (§ 229.301 of this chapter).

Instructions to paragraphs (b)(8), (b)(9) and (b)(10):

1. For a business combination accounted for as a purchase, present the financial information required by paragraphs (b)(9) and (b)(10) only for the most recent fiscal year and interim period. 2. For a business combination accounted for as a pooling, present the financial information required by paragraphs (b)(9) and (b)(10) (except for information with regard to book value) for the most recent three fiscal years and interim period. For purposes of these paragraphs, book value information need only be provided for the most recent balance sheet date.

Calculate the equivalent pro forma per share amounts for one share of the company being acquired by multiplying the exchange ratio times each of:

(i) The pro forma income (loss) per share before non-recurring charges or credits directly attributable to the transaction;

(ii) The pro forma book value per share; and

(iii) The pro forma dividends per share of the acquiring company.

3. Unless registered on a national securities exchange or otherwise required to furnish such information, registered investment companies need not furnish the information required by paragraphs (b)(8) and (b)(9) of this Item.

(11) *Financial information.* If material, financial information required by *Article 11* of Regulation S–X (§§ 210.10–01 through 229.11–03 of this chapter) with respect to this transaction.

Instructions to paragraph (b)(11):

1. Present any Article 11 information required with respect to transactions other than those being voted upon (where not incorporated by reference) together with the pro forma information relating to the transaction being voted upon. In presenting this information, you must clearly distinguish between the transaction being voted upon and any other transaction.

2. If current pro forma financial information with respect to all other transactions is incorporated by reference, you need only present the pro forma effect of this transaction.

(c) *Information about the parties to the transaction.*

(1) *Acquiring company.* Furnish the information required by Part B (Registrant Information) of Form S–4 (§ 239.25 of this chapter) or Form F–4 (§ 239.34 of this chapter), as applicable, for the acquiring company. However, financial statements need only be presented for the latest two fiscal years and interim periods.

(2) *Acquired company.* Furnish the information required by Part C (Information with Respect to the Company Being Acquired) of Form S–4 (§ 239.25 of this chapter) or Form F–4 (§ 239.34 of this chapter), as applicable.

(d) *Information about parties to the transaction: registered investment companies and business development companies.*

If the acquiring company or the acquired company is an investment company registered under the Investment Company Act of 1940 or a business development company as defined by Section 2(a)(48) of the Investment Company Act of 1940, provide the following information for that company instead of the information specified by paragraph (c) of this Item:

(1) Information required by *Item 101* of Regulation S–K (§ 229.101 of this chapter), description of business;

(2) Information required by *Item 102* of Regulation S–K (§ 229.102 of this chapter), description of property;

(3) Information required by *Item 103* of Regulation S–K (§ 229.103 of this chapter), legal proceedings;

(4) Information required by *Item 201* of Regulation S–K (§ 229.201 of this chapter), market price of and dividends on the registrant's common equity and related stockholder matters;

(5) Financial statements meeting the requirements of *Regulation S–X*, including financial information required by *Rule 3-05* and *Article 11* of Regulation S–X (§ 210.3–05 and § 210.11–01 through § 210.11–03 of this chapter) with respect to transactions other than that as to which action is to be taken as described in this proxy statement;

(6) Information required by *Item 301* of Regulation S–K (§ 229.301 of this chapter), selected financial data;

(7) Information required by *Item 302* of Regulation S–K (§ 229.302 of this chapter), supplementary financial information;

(8) Information required by *Item 303* of Regulation S–K (§ 229.303 of this chapter), management's discussion and analysis of financial condition and results of operations; and

(9) Information required by *Item 304* of Regulation S–K (§ 229.304 of this chapter), changes in and disagreements with accountants on accounting and financial disclosure.

Instruction to paragraph (d) of Item 14: Unless registered on a national securities exchange or otherwise required to furnish such information, registered investment companies need not furnish the information required by paragraphs (d)(6), (d)(7) and (d)(8) of this Item.

(e) *Incorporation by reference.*

(1) The information required by paragraph (c) of this section may be incorporated by reference into the proxy statement to the same extent as would be permitted by Form S–4 (§ 239.25 of this chapter) or Form F–4 (§ 239.34 of this chapter), as applicable.

(2) Alternatively, the registrant may incorporate by reference into the proxy statement the information required by paragraph (c) of this Item if it is contained in an annual report sent to security holders in accordance with § 240.14a–3 of this chapter with respect to the same meeting or solicitation of consents or authorizations that the proxy statement relates to and the information substantially meets the disclosure requirements of Item 14 or Item 17 of Form S–4 (§ 239.25 of this chapter) or Form F–4 (§ 239.34 of this chapter), as applicable.

Item 15. Acquisition or Disposition of Property

If action is to be taken with respect to the acquisition or disposition of any property, furnish the following information:

(a) Describe briefly the general character and location of the property.

(b) State the nature and amount of consideration to be paid or received by the registrant or any subsidiary. To the extent practicable, outline briefly the facts bearing upon the question of the fairness of the consideration.

(c) State the name and address of the transferer or transferee, as the case may be and the nature of any material relationship of such person to the registrant or any affiliate of the registrant.

(d) Outline briefly any other material features of the contract or transaction.

Item 16. Restatement of Accounts

If action is to be taken with respect to the restatement of any asset, capital, or surplus account of the registrant, furnish the following information:

(a) State the nature of the restatement and the date as of which it is to be effective.

(b) Outline briefly the reasons for the restatement and for the selection of the particular effective date.

(c) State the name and amount of each account (including any reserve accounts) affected by the restatement and the effect of the restatement thereon. Tabular presentation of the amounts shall be made when appropriate, particularly in the case of recapitalizations.

(d) To the extent practicable, state whether and the extent, if any, to which, the restatement will, as of the date thereof, alter the amount available for distribution to the holders of equity securities.

Item 17. Action with Respect to Reports

If action is to be taken with respect to any report of the registrant or of its directors, officers or committees or any minutes of meeting of its stockholders, furnish the following information:

(a) State whether or not such action is to constitute approval or disapproval of any of the matters referred to in such reports or minutes.

(b) Identify each of such matters which it is intended will be approved or disapproved, and furnish the information required by the appropriate item or items of this schedule with respect to each such matter.

Item 18. Matters Not Required to be Submitted

If action is to be taken with respect to any matter which is not required to be submitted to a vote of security holders, state the nature of such matter, the reasons for submitting it to a vote of security holders and what action is intended to be taken by the registrant in the event of a negative vote on the matter by the security holders.

Item 19. Amendment of Charter, Bylaws or Other Documents

If action is to be taken with respect to any amendment of the registrant's charter, bylaws or other documents as to which information is not required above, state briefly the reasons for and the general effect of such amendment.

Instructions. 1. Where the matter to be acted upon is the classification of directors, state whether vacancies which occur during the year may be filled by the board of directors to serve only until the next annual meeting or may be so filled for the remainder of the full term.

2. Attention is directed to the discussion of disclosure regarding anti-takeover and similar proposals in Release No. 34–15230 (Oct. 13, 1978).

Item 20. Other Proposed Action

If action is to be taken on any matter not specifically referred to above, describe briefly the substance of each such matter in substantially the same degree of detail as is required by Items 5 to 19, inclusive, above, and with respect to investment companies registered under the Inv. Company Act of 1940, Item 22 of this schedule.

Item 21. Voting Procedures

As to each matter which is to be submitted to a vote of security holders, furnish the following information:

(a) State the vote required for approval or election, other than for the approval of auditors.

(b) Disclose the method by which votes will be counted, including the treatment and effect of abstentions and brokers non-votes under applicable state law as well as registrant charter and by-law provisions.

* * *

Item 23. Delivery of documents to security holders sharing an address.

If one annual report or proxy statement is being delivered to two or more security holders who share an address in accordance with § 240.14a–3(e)(1), furnish the following information:

(a) State that only one annual report or proxy statement, as applicable, is being delivered to multiple security holders sharing an address unless the registrant has received contrary instructions from one or more of the security holders;

(b) Undertake to deliver promptly upon written or oral request a separate copy of the annual report or proxy statement, as applicable, to a security holder at a shared address to which a single copy of the documents was delivered and provide instructions as to how a security holder can notify the registrant that the security holder wishes to receive a separate copy of an annual report or proxy statement, as applicable;

(c) Provide the phone number and mailing address to which a security holder can direct a notification to the registrant that the security holder wishes to receive a separate annual report or proxy statement, as applicable, in the future; and

(d) Provide instructions how security holders sharing an address can request delivery of a single copy of annual reports or proxy statements if they are receiving multiple copies of annual reports or proxy statements.

SCHEDULE TO

Tender Offer Statement Under Section 14(d)(1) or 13(e)(1) of the Securities Exchange Act of 1934

Securities and Exchange Commission,

Washington, D.C. 20549

Schedule TO

Tender Offer Statement under Section 14(d)(1) or 13(e)(1) of the Securities Exchange Act of 1934

(Amendment No. ___)

____

(Name of Subject Company (issuer))

____

(Names of Filing Persons (identifying status as offeror, issuer or other person))

____

(Title of Class of Securities)

____

(CUSIP Number of Class of Securities)

(Name, address, and telephone numbers of person authorized to receive notices and communications on behalf of filing persons)

Calculation of Filing Fee

Transaction valuation[1] Amount of filing fee

[ ] Check the box if any part of the fee is offset as provided by Rule 0–11(a)(2) and identify the filing with which the offsetting fee was previously paid. Identify the previous filing by registration statement number, or the Form or Schedule and the date of its filing.

Amount Previously Paid: ______________________

Form or Registration No.: ______________________

Filing Party: ______________________

Date Filed: ______________________

[ ] Check the box if the filing relates solely to preliminary communications made before the commencement of a tender offer.

Check the appropriate boxes below to designate any transactions to which the statement relates:

[ ] third-party tender offer subject to Rule 14d–1.

[ ] issuer tender offer subject to Rule 13e–4.

[ ] going-private transaction subject to Rule 13e–3.

[ ] amendment to Schedule 13D under Rule 13d–2.

Check the following box if the filing is a final amendment reporting the results of the tender offer: [ ]

General Instructions:

A. File eight copies of the statement, including all exhibits, with the Commission if paper filing is permitted.

B. This filing must be accompanied by a fee payable to the Commission as required by § 240.0–11.

C. If the statement is filed by a general or limited partnership, syndicate or other group, the information called for by Items 3 and 5–8 for a third-party tender offer and Items 5–8 for an issuer tender offer must be given with respect to: (i) Each partner of the general partnership; (ii) each partner who is, or functions as, a general partner of the limited partnership; (iii) each member of the syndicate or group; and (iv) each person controlling the partner or member. If the statement is filed by a corporation or if a person referred to in (i), (ii), (iii) or (iv) of this Instruction is a corporation, the information called for by the items specified above must be given with respect to: (a) Each executive officer and director of the corporation; (b) each person controlling the corporation; and (c) each executive officer and director of any corporation or other person ultimately in control of the corporation.

D. If the filing contains only preliminary communications made before the commencement of a tender offer, no signature or filing fee is required. The filer need not respond to the items in the schedule. Any pre-commencement communications that are filed under cover of this schedule need not be incorporated by reference into the schedule.

E. If an item is inapplicable or the answer is in the negative, so state. The statement published, sent or

1. Set forth the amount on which the filing fee is calculated and state how it was determined.

given to security holders may omit negative and not applicable responses. If the schedule includes any information that is not published, sent or given to security holders, provide that information or specifically incorporate it by reference under the appropriate item number and heading in the schedule. Do not recite the text of disclosure requirements in the schedule or any document published, sent or given to security holders. Indicate clearly the coverage of the requirements without referring to the text of the items.

F. Information contained in exhibits to the statement may be incorporated by reference in answer or partial answer to any item unless it would render the answer misleading, incomplete, unclear or confusing. A copy of any information that is incorporated by reference or a copy of the pertinent pages of a document containing the information must be submitted with this statement as an exhibit, unless it was previously filed with the Commission electronically on EDGAR. If an exhibit contains information responding to more than one item in the schedule, all information in that exhibit may be incorporated by reference once in response to the several items in the schedule for which it provides an answer. Information incorporated by reference is deemed filed with the Commission for all purposes of the Act.

G. A filing person may amend its previously filed Schedule 13D (§ 240.13d–101) on Schedule TO (§ 240.14d–100) if the appropriate box on the cover page is checked to indicate a combined filing and the information called for by the fourteen disclosure items on the cover page of Schedule 13D (§ 240.13d–101) is provided on the cover page of the combined filing with respect to each filing person.

H. The final amendment required by § 240.14d–3(b)(2) and § 240.13e–4(c)(4) will satisfy the reporting requirements of section 13(d) of the Act with respect to all securities acquired by the offeror in the tender offer.

I. Amendments disclosing a material change in the information set forth in this statement may omit any information previously disclosed in this statement.

J. If the tender offer disclosed on this statement involves a going-private transaction, a combined Schedule TO (§ 240.14d–100) and Schedule 13E–3 (§ 240.13e–100) may be filed with the Commission under cover of Schedule TO. The Rule 13e–3 box on the cover page of the Schedule TO must be checked to indicate a combined filing. All information called for by both schedules must be provided except that Items 1—3, 5, 8 and 9 of Schedule TO may be omitted to the extent those items call for information that duplicates the item requirements in Schedule 13E–3.

K. For purposes of this statement, the following definitions apply:

(1) The term offeror means any person who makes a tender offer or on whose behalf a tender offer is made;

(2) The term issuer tender offer has the same meaning as in Rule 13e–4(a)(2); and

(3) The term third-party tender offer means a tender offer that is not an issuer tender offer.

Special Instructions for Complying With Schedule TO

Under Sections 13(e), 14(d) and 23 of the Act and the rules and regulations of the Act, the Commission is authorized to solicit the information required to be supplied by this schedule.

Disclosure of the information specified in this schedule is mandatory, except for I.R.S. identification numbers, disclosure of which is voluntary. The information will be used for the primary purpose of disclosing tender offer and going-private transactions. This statement will be made a matter of public record. Therefore, any information given will be available for inspection by any member of the public.

Because of the public nature of the information, the Commission can use it for a variety of purposes, including referral to other governmental authorities or securities self-regulatory organizations for investigatory purposes or in connection with litigation involving the Federal securities laws or other civil, criminal or regulatory statutes or provisions. I.R.S. identification numbers, if furnished, will assist the Commission in identifying security holders and, therefore, in promptly processing tender offer and going-private statements.

Failure to disclose the information required by this schedule, except for I.R.S. identification numbers, may result in civil or criminal action against the persons involved for violation of the Federal securities laws and rules.

SCHEDULE TO

Item 1. Summary Term Sheet

Furnish the information required by Item 1001 of Regulation M–A (§ 229.1001 of this chapter) unless information is disclosed to security holders in a prospectus that meets the requirements of § 230.421(d) of this chapter.

Item 2. Subject Company Information

Furnish the information required by Item 1002(a) through (c) of Regulation M–A (§ 229.1002 of this chapter).

Item 3. Identity and Background of Filing Person

Furnish the information required by Item 1003(a) through (c) of Regulation M–A (§ 229.1003 of this chapter) for a third-party tender offer and the information required by Item 1003(a) of Regulation M–A (§ 229.1003 of this chapter) for an issuer tender offer.

Item 4. Terms of the Transaction

Furnish the information required by Item 1004(a) of Regulation M–A (§ 229.1004 of this chapter) for a third-party tender offer and the information required by Item 1004(a) through (b) of Regulation M–A (§ 229.1004 of this chapter) for an issuer tender offer.

Item 5. Past Contacts, Transactions, Negotiations and Agreements

Furnish the information required by Item 1005(a) and (b) of Regulation M–A (§ 229.1005 of this chapter) for a third-party tender offer and the information required by Item 1005(e) of Regulation M–A (§ 229.1005) for an issuer tender offer.

Item 6. Purposes of the Transaction and Plans or Proposals

Furnish the information required by Item 1006(a) and (c)(1) through (7) of Regulation M–A (§ 229.1006 of this chapter) for a third-party tender offer and the information required by Item 1006(a) through (c) of Regulation M–A (§ 229.1006 of this chapter) for an issuer tender offer.

Item 7. Source and Amount of Funds or Other Consideration

Furnish the information required by Item 1007(a), (b) and (d) of Regulation M–A (§ 229.1007 of this chapter).

Item 8. Interest in Securities of the Subject Company

Furnish the information required by Item 1008 of Regulation M–A (§ 229.1008 of this chapter).

Item 9. Persons/Assets, Retained, Employed, Compensated or Used

Furnish the information required by Item 1009(a) of Regulation M–A (§ 229.1009 of this chapter).

Item 10. Financial Statements

If material, furnish the information required by Item 1010(a) and (b) of Regulation M–A (§ 229.1010 of this chapter) for the issuer in an issuer tender offer and for the offeror in a third-party tender offer.

Instructions to Item 10:

1. Financial statements must be provided when the offeror's financial condition is material to security holder's decision whether to sell, tender or hold the securities sought. The facts and circumstances of a tender offer, particularly the terms of the tender offer, may influence a determination as to whether financial statements are material, and thus required to be disclosed.

2. Financial statements are not considered material when: (a) The consideration offered consists solely of cash; (b) the offer is not subject to any financing condition; and either: (c) the offeror is a public reporting company under Section 13(a) or 15(d) of the Act that files reports electronically on EDGAR, or (d) the offer is for all outstanding securities of the subject class. Financial information may be required, however, in a two-tier transaction. See Instruction 5 below.

3. The filing person may incorporate by reference financial statements contained in any document filed with the Commission, solely for the purposes of this schedule, if: (a) The financial statements substantially meet the requirements of this item; (b) an express statement is made that the financial statements are incorporated by reference; (c) the information incorporated by reference is clearly identified by page, paragraph, caption or otherwise; and (d) if the information incorporated by reference is not filed with this schedule, an indication is made

where the information may be inspected and copies obtained. Financial statements that are required to be presented in comparative form for two or more fiscal years or periods may not be incorporated by reference unless the material incorporated by reference includes the entire period for which the comparative data is required to be given. See General Instruction F to this schedule.

4. If the offeror in a third-party tender offer is a natural person, and such person's financial information is material, disclose the net worth of the offeror. If the offeror's net worth is derived from material amounts of assets that are not readily marketable or there are material guarantees and contingencies, disclose the nature and approximate amount of the individual's net worth that consists of illiquid assets and the magnitude of any guarantees or contingencies that may negatively affect the natural person's net worth.

5. Pro forma financial information is required in a negotiated third-party cash tender offer when securities are intended to be offered in a subsequent merger or other transaction in which remaining target securities are acquired and the acquisition of the subject company is significant to the offeror under § 210.11–01(b)(1) of this chapter. The offeror must disclose the financial information specified in Item 3(f) and Item 5 of Form S–4 (§ 239.25 of this chapter) in the schedule filed with the Commission, but may furnish only the summary financial information specified in Item 3(d), (e) and (f) of Form S–4 in the disclosure document sent to security holders. If pro forma financial information is required by this instruction, the historical financial statements specified in Item 1010 of Regulation M–A (§ 229.1010 of this chapter) are required for the bidder.

6. The disclosure materials disseminated to security holders may contain the summarized financial information specified by Item 1010(c) of Regulation M–A (§ 229.1010 of this chapter) instead of the financial information required by Item 1010(a) and (b). In that case, the financial information required by Item 1010(a) and (b) of Regulation M–A must be disclosed in the statement. If summarized financial information is disseminated to security holders, include appropriate instructions on how more complete financial information can be obtained. If the summarized financial information is prepared on the basis of a comprehensive body of accounting principles other than U.S. GAAP, the summarized financial information must be accompanied by a reconciliation as described in Instruction 8 of this Item.

7. If the offeror is not subject to the periodic reporting requirements of the Act, the financial statements required by this Item need not be audited if audited financial statements are not available or obtainable without unreasonable cost or expense. Make a statement to that effect and the reasons for their unavailability.

8. If the financial statements required by this Item are prepared on the basis of a comprehensive body of accounting principles other than U.S. GAAP, provide a reconciliation to U.S. GAAP in accordance with Item 17 of Form 20–F (§ 249.220f of this chapter), unless a reconciliation is unavailable or not obtainable without unreasonable cost or expense. At a minimum, however, when financial statements are prepared on a basis other than U.S. GAAP, a narrative description of all material variations in accounting principles, practices and methods used in preparing the non-U.S. GAAP financial statements from those accepted in the U.S. must be presented.

Item 11. Additional Information

Furnish the information required by Item 1011 of Regulation M–A (§ 229.1011 of this chapter).

Item 12. Exhibits

File as an exhibit to the Schedule all documents specified by Item 1016 (a), (b), (d), (g) and (h) of Regulation M–A (§ 229.1016 of this chapter).

Item 13. Information Required by Schedule 13E–3

If the Schedule TO is combined with Schedule 13E–3 (§ 240.13e–100), set forth the information required by Schedule 13E–3 that is not included or covered by the items in Schedule TO.

Signature. After due inquiry and to the best of my knowledge and belief, I certify that the information set forth in this statement is true, complete and correct.

____

(Signature)

____

(Name and title)

____

(Date)

Instruction to Signature: The statement must be signed by the filing person or that person's authorized representative. If the statement is signed on behalf of a person by an authorized representative (other than an executive officer of a corporation or general partner of a partnership), evidence of the representative's authority to sign on behalf of the person must be filed with the statement. The name and any title of each person who signs the statement must be typed or printed beneath the signature. See §§ 240.12b–11 and 240.14d–1(f) with respect to signature requirements.

SCHEDULE 14D–9

Solicitation/Recommendation Statement Pursuant to Section 14(d)(4) of the Securities Exchange Act of 1934

* * *

GENERAL INSTRUCTIONS

A. File eight copies of the statement, including all exhibits, with the Commission if paper filing is permitted.

B. If the filing contains only preliminary communications made before the commencement of a tender offer, no signature is required. The filer need not respond to the items in the schedule. Any precommencement communications that are filed under cover of this schedule need not be incorporated by reference into the schedule.

C. If an item is inapplicable or the answer is in the negative, so state. The statement published, sent or given to security holders may omit negative and not applicable responses. If the schedule includes any information that is not published, sent or given to security holders, provide that information or specifically incorporate it by reference under the appropriate item number and heading in the schedule. Do not recite the text of disclosure requirements in the schedule or any document published, sent or given to security holders. Indicate clearly the coverage of the requirements without referring to the text of the items.

D. Information contained in exhibits to the statement may be incorporated by reference in answer or partial answer to any item unless it would render the answer misleading, incomplete, unclear or confusing. A copy of any information that is incorporated by reference or a copy of the pertinent pages of a document containing the information must be submitted with this statement as an exhibit, unless it was previously filed with the Commission electronically on EDGAR. If an exhibit contains information responding to more than one item in the schedule, all information in that exhibit may be incorporated by reference once in response to the several items in the schedule for which it provides an answer. Information incorporated by reference is deemed filed with the Commission for all purposes of the Act.

E. Amendments disclosing a material change in the information set forth in this statement may omit any information previously disclosed in this statement.

Item 1. Subject Company Information. Furnish the information required by *Item 1002(a) and (b) of Regulation M–A* (§ 229.1002 of this chapter).

Item 2. Identity and Background of Filing Person. Furnish the information required by *Item 1003(a) and (d) of Regulation M–A* (§ 229.1003 of this chapter).

Item 3. Past Contacts, Transactions, Negotiations and Agreements. Furnish the information required by *Item 1005(d) of Regulation M–A* (§ 229.1005 of this chapter).

Item 4. The Solicitation or Recommendation. Furnish the information required by *Item 1012(a) through (c) of Regulation M–A* (§ 229.1012 of this chapter).

Item 5. Person/Assets, Retained, Employed, Compensated or Used. Furnish the information required by *Item 1009(a) of Regulation M–A* (§ 229.1009 of this chapter).

Item 6. Interest in Securities of the Subject Company. Furnish the information required by

Item 1008(b) of Regulation M–A (§ 229.1008 of this chapter).

Item 7. Purposes of the Transaction and Plans or Proposals. Furnish the information required by *Item 1006(d) of Regulation M–A* (§ 229.1006 of this chapter).

Item 8. Additional Information. Furnish the information required by *Item 1011(b) of Regulation M–A* (§ 229.1011 of this chapter).

Item 9. Exhibits. File as an exhibit to the Schedule all documents specified by *Item 1016(a), (e) and (g) of Regulation M–A* (§ 229.1016 of this chapter).

H. REGULATION S–K

(Selected)

* * *

Item 303. Management's Discussion and Analysis of Financial Condition and Results of Operations

(a) *Full fiscal years.* Discuss registrant's financial condition, changes in financial condition and results of operations. The discussion shall provide information as specified in paragraphs (a)(1) through (5) of this Item and also shall provide such other information that the registrant believes to be necessary to an understanding of its financial condition, changes in financial condition and results of operations. Discussions of liquidity and capital resources may be combined whenever the two topics are interrelated. Where in the registrant's judgment a discussion of segment information or of other subdivisions of the registrant's business would be appropriate to an understanding of such business, the discussion shall focus on each relevant, reportable segment or other subdivision of the business and on the registrant as a whole.

(1) *Liquidity.* Identify any known trends or any known demands, commitments, events or uncertainties that will result in or that are reasonably likely to result in the registrant's liquidity increasing or decreasing in any material way. If a material deficiency is identified, indicate the course of action that the registrant has taken or proposes to take to remedy the deficiency. Also identify and separately describe internal and external sources of liquidity, and briefly discuss any material unused sources of liquid assets.

(2) *Capital resources.* (i) Describe the registrant's material commitments for capital expenditures as of the end of the latest fiscal period, and indicate the general purpose of such commitments and the anticipated source of funds needed to fulfill such commitments.

(ii) Describe any known material trends, favorable or unfavorable, in the registrant's capital resources. Indicate any expected material changes in the mix and relative cost of such resources. The discussion shall consider changes between equity, debt and any off-balance sheet financing arrangements.

(3) *Results of operations.* (i) Describe any unusual or infrequent events or transactions or any significant economic changes that materially affected the amount of reported income from continuing operations and, in each case, indicate the extent to which income was so affected. In addition, describe any other significant components of revenues or expenses that, in the registrant's judgment, should be described in order to understand the registrant's results of operations.

(ii) Describe any known trends or uncertainties that have had or that the registrant reasonably expects will have a material favorable or unfavorable impact on net sales or revenues or income from continuing operations. If the registrant knows of events that will cause a material change in the relationship between costs and revenues (such as known future increases in costs of labor or materials or price increases or inventory adjustments), the change in the relationship shall be disclosed.

(iii) To the extent that the financial statements disclose material increases in net sales or revenues, provide a narrative discussion of the extent to which such increases are attributable to increases in prices or to increases in the volume or amount of goods or services being sold or to the introduction of new products or services.

(iv) For the three most recent fiscal years of the registrant, or for those fiscal years in which the registrant has been engaged in business, whichever period is shortest, discuss the impact of inflation and changing prices on the registrant's net sales and revenues and on income from continuing operations.

(4) *Off-balance sheet arrangements.* (i) In a separately-captioned section, discuss the registrant's off-balance sheet arrangements that have or are reasonably likely to have a current or future effect on the registrant's financial condition, changes in financial condition, revenues or expenses, results of operations, liquidity, capital expenditures or capital resources that is material to investors. The disclosure shall include the items specified in paragraphs (a)(4)(i)(A), (B), (C) and (D) of this Item to the extent necessary to an understanding of such arrangements and effect and shall also include such other information that the registrant believes is necessary for such an understanding.

(A) The nature and business purpose to the registrant of such off-balance sheet arrangements;

(B) The importance to the registrant of such off-balance sheet arrangements in respect of its liquidity, capital resources, market risk support, credit risk support or other benefits;

(C) The amounts of revenues, expenses and cash flows of the registrant arising from such arrangements; the nature and amounts of any interests retained, securities issued and other indebtedness incurred by the registrant in connection with such arrangements; and the nature and amounts of any other obligations or liabilities (including contingent obligations or liabilities) of the registrant arising from such arrangements that are or are reasonably likely to become material and the triggering events or circumstances that could cause them to arise; and

(D) Any known event, demand, commitment, trend or uncertainty that will result in or is reasonably likely to result in the termination, or material reduction in availability to the registrant, of its off-balance sheet arrangements that provide material benefits to it, and the course of action that the registrant has taken or proposes to take in response to any such circumstances.

(ii) As used in this paragraph (a)(4), the term off-balance sheet arrangement means any transaction, agreement or other contractual arrangement to which an entity unconsolidated with the registrant is a party, under which the registrant has:

(A) Any obligation under a guarantee contract that has any of the characteristics identified in paragraph 3 of FASB Interpretation No. 45, Guarantor's Accounting and Disclosure Requirements for Guarantees, Including Indirect Guarantees of Indebtedness of Others (November 2002) ("FIN 45"), as may be modified or supplemented, and that is not excluded from the initial recognition and measurement provisions of FIN 45 pursuant to paragraphs 6 or 7 of that Interpretation;

(B) A retained or contingent interest in assets transferred to an unconsolidated entity or similar arrangement that serves as credit, liquidity or market risk support to such entity for such assets;

(C) Any obligation, including a contingent obligation, under a contract that would be accounted for as a derivative instrument, except that it is both indexed to the registrant's own stock and classified in stockholders' equity in the registrant's statement of financial position, and therefore excluded from the scope of FASB Statement of Financial Accounting Standards No. 133, Accounting for Derivative Instruments and Hedging Activities (June 1998), pursuant to paragraph 11(a) of that Statement, as may be modified or supplemented; or

(D) Any obligation, including a contingent obligation, arising out of a variable interest (as referenced in FASB Interpretation No. 46, Consolidation of Variable Interest Entities (January 2003), as may be modified or supplemented) in an unconsolidated entity that is held by, and material to, the registrant, where such entity provides financing, liquidity, market risk or credit risk support to, or engages in leasing, hedging or research and development services with, the registrant.

(5) Tabular disclosure of contractual obligations. (i) In a tabular format, provide the information specified in this paragraph (a)(5) as of the latest fiscal year end balance sheet date with respect to the registrant's known contractual obligations specified in the table that follows this paragraph (a)(5)(i). The registrant shall provide amounts, aggregated by type of contractual obligation. The registrant may disaggregate the specified categories of contractual obligations using other categories suitable to its business, but the presentation must include all of the obligations of the registrant that fall within the specified categories. A presentation covering at least the periods specified shall be included. The tabular presentation may be accompanied by footnotes to describe provisions that create, increase or accelerate obligations, or other pertinent data to the extent necessary for an understanding of the timing and amount of the registrant's specified contractual obligations.

	Payments due by period				
Contractual obligations	Total	Less than 1 year	1–3 years	3–5 years	More than 5 years
[Long–Term Debt Obligations]					
[Capital Lease Obligations]					
[Operating Lease Obligations]					
[Purchase Obligations]					
[Other Long–Term Liabilities Reflected on the Registrant's Balance Sheet under GAAP]					
Total					

(ii) Definitions: The following definitions apply to this paragraph (a)(5):

(A) Long–Term Debt Obligation means a payment obligation under long-term borrowings referenced in FASB Statement of Financial Accounting Standards No. 47 Disclosure of Long–Term Obligations (March 1981), as may be modified or supplemented.

(B) Capital Lease Obligation means a payment obligation under a lease classified as a capital lease pursuant to FASB Statement of Financial Accounting Standards No. 13 Accounting for Leases (November 1976), as may be modified or supplemented.

(C) Operating Lease Obligation means a payment obligation under a lease classified as an operating lease and disclosed pursuant to FASB Statement of Financial Accounting Standards No. 13 Accounting for Leases (November 1976), as may be modified or supplemented.

(D) Purchase Obligation means an agreement to purchase goods or services that is enforceable and legally binding on the registrant that specifies all significant terms, including: fixed or minimum quantities to be purchased; fixed, minimum or variable price provisions; and the approximate timing of the transaction.

Instructions to Paragraph 303(a).

1. The registrant's discussion and analysis shall be of the financial statements and of other statistical data that the registrant believes will enhance a reader's understanding of its financial condition, changes in financial condition and results of operations. Generally, the discussion shall cover the three year period covered by the financial statements and shall use year-to-year comparisons or any other formats that in the registrant's judgment enhance a reader's understanding. However, where trend information is relevant, reference to the five year selected financial data appearing pursuant to Item 301 of Regulation S–K may be necessary.

2. The purpose of the discussion and analysis shall be to provide to investors and other users information relevant to an assessment of the financial condition and results of operations of the registrant as determined by evaluating the amounts and

certainty of cash flows from operations and from outside sources.

3. The discussion and analysis shall focus specifically on material events and uncertainties known to management that would cause reported financial information not to be necessarily indicative of future operating results or of future financial condition. This would include descriptions and amounts of (A) matters that would have an impact on future operations and have not had an impact in the past, and (B) matters that have had an impact on reported operations and are not expected to have an impact upon future operations.

* * *

5. The term "liquidity" as used in this Item refers to the ability of an enterprise to generate adequate amounts of cash to meet the enterprise's needs for cash. Except where it is otherwise clear from the discussion, the registrant shall indicate those balance sheet conditions or income or cash flow items which the registrant believes may be indicators of its liquidity condition. Liquidity generally shall be discussed on both a long-term and short-term basis. The issue of liquidity shall be discussed in the context of the registrant's own business or businesses. For example a discussion of working capital may be appropriate for certain manufacturing, industrial or related operations but might be inappropriate for a bank or public utility.

* * *

7. Any forward-looking information supplied is expressly covered by the safe harbor rule for projections. See Rule 175 under the Securities Act, Rule 3b–6 under the Exchange Act and Securities Act Release No. 6084 (June 25, 1979).

Instructions to Paragraph 303(a)(4):

1. No obligation to make disclosure under paragraph (a)(4) of this Item shall arise in respect of an off-balance sheet arrangement until a definitive agreement that is unconditionally binding or subject only to customary closing conditions exists or, if there is no such agreement, when settlement of the transaction occurs.

2. Registrants should aggregate off-balance sheet arrangements in groups or categories that provide material information in an efficient and understandable manner and should avoid repetition and disclosure of immaterial information. Effects that are common or similar with respect to a number of off-balance sheet arrangements must be analyzed in the aggregate to the extent the aggregation increases understanding. Distinctions in arrangements and their effects must be discussed to the extent the information is material, but the discussion should avoid repetition and disclosure of immaterial information.

3. For purposes of paragraph (a)(4) of this Item only, contingent liabilities arising out of litigation, arbitration or regulatory actions are not considered to be off-balance sheet arrangements.

4. Generally, the disclosure required by paragraph (a)(4) shall cover the most recent fiscal year. However, the discussion should address changes from the previous year where such discussion is necessary to an understanding of the disclosure.

5. In satisfying the requirements of paragraph (a)(4) of this Item, the discussion of off-balance sheet arrangements need not repeat information provided in the footnotes to the financial statements, provided that such discussion clearly cross-references to specific information in the relevant footnotes and integrates the substance of the footnotes into such discussion in a manner designed to inform readers of the significance of the information that is not included within the body of such discussion.

(b) *Interim periods.* If interim period financial statements are included or are required to be included by Article 3 of Regulation S–X, a management's discussion and analysis of the financial condition and results of operations shall be provided so as to enable the reader to assess material changes in financial condition and results of operations between the periods specified in paragraphs (b) (1) and (2) of this Item. The discussion and analysis shall include a discussion of material changes in those items specifically listed in paragraph (a) of this Item, except that the impact of inflation and changing prices on operations for interim periods need not be addressed.

(1) Material changes in financial condition. Discuss any material changes in financial condition from the end of the preceding fiscal year to the date of the most recent interim balance sheet provided. If the interim financial statements include an inter-

im balance sheet as of the corresponding interim date of the preceding fiscal year, any material changes in financial condition from that date to the date of the most recent interim balance sheet provided also shall be discussed. If discussions of changes from both the end and the corresponding interim date of the preceding fiscal year are required, the discussions may be combined at the discretion of the registrant.

(2) Material changes in results of operations. Discuss any material changes in the registrant's results of operations with respect to the most recent fiscal year-to-date period for which an income statement is provided and the corresponding year-to-date period of the preceding fiscal year. If the registrant is required to or has elected to provide an income statement for the most recent fiscal quarter, such discussion also shall cover material changes with respect to that fiscal quarter and the corresponding fiscal quarter in the preceding fiscal year. In addition, if the registrant has elected to provide an income statement for the twelve-month period ended as of the date of the most recent interim balance sheet provided, the discussion also shall cover material changes with respect to that twelve-month period and the twelve-month period ended as of the corresponding interim balance sheet date of the preceding fiscal year. Notwithstanding the above, if for purposes of a registration statement a registrant subject to paragraph (b) of Rule 3–03 of Regulation S–X provides a statement of income for the twelve-month period ended as of the date of the most recent interim balance sheet provided in lieu of the interim income statements otherwise required, the discussion of material changes in that twelve-month period will be in respect to the preceding fiscal year rather than the corresponding preceding period.

Instructions to Paragraph (b) of Item 303.

1. If interim financial statements are presented together with financial statements for full fiscal years, the discussion of the interim financial information shall be prepared pursuant to this paragraph (b) and the discussion of the full fiscal year's information shall be prepared pursuant to paragraph (a) of this Item. Such discussions may be combined.

2. In preparing the discussion and analysis required by this paragraph (b), the registrant may presume that users of the interim financial information have read or have access to the discussion and analysis required by paragraph (a) for the preceding fiscal year.

3. The discussion and analysis required by this paragraph (b) is required to focus only on material changes. Where the interim financial statements reveal material changes from period to period in one or more significant line items, the causes for the changes shall be described if they have not already been disclosed: Provided, however, That if the causes for a change in one line item also relate to other line items, no repetition is required. Registrants need not recite the amounts of changes from period to period which are readily computable from the financial statements. The discussion shall not merely repeat numerical data contained in the financial statements. The information provided shall include that which is available to the registrant without undue effort or expense and which does not clearly appear in the registrant's condensed interim financial statements.

4. The registrant's discussion of material changes in results of operations shall identify any significant elements of the registrant's income or loss from continuing operations which do not arise from or are not necessarily representative of the registrant's ongoing business.

5. The registrant shall discuss any seasonal aspects of its business which have had a material effect upon its financial condition or results of operation.

6. Any forward-looking information supplied is expressly covered by the safe harbor rule for projections. See Rule 175 under the Securities Act, Rule 3b–6 under the Exchange Act and Securities Act Release No. 6084 (June 25, 1979).

7. The registrant is not required to include the table required by paragraph (a)(5) of this Item for interim periods. Instead, the registrant should disclose material changes outside the ordinary course of the registrant's business in the specified contractual obligations during the interim period.

(c) *Safe harbor.* (1) The safe harbor provided in section 27A of the Securities Act of 1933 and section 21E of the Securities Exchange Act of 1934 ("statutory safe harbors") shall apply to forward-looking information provided pursuant to paragraphs (a)(4) and (5) of this Item, provided that the disclosure is made by: an issuer; a person acting on behalf of the issuer; an outside reviewer retained by the issuer making a statement on behalf of the issuer; or an underwriter, with respect to information provided by the issuer or information derived from information provided by the issuer.

(2) For purposes of paragraph (c) of this Item only:

(i) All information required by paragraphs (a)(4) and (5) of this Item is deemed to be a forward looking statement as that term is defined in the statutory safe harbors, except for historical facts.

(ii) With respect to paragraph (a)(4) of this Item, the meaningful cautionary statements element of the statutory safe harbors will be satisfied if a registrant satisfies all requirements of that same paragraph (a)(4) of this Item.

* * *

Item 307. Controls and Procedures.

(a) *Evaluation of disclosure controls and procedures.* Disclose the conclusions of the registrant's principal executive officer or officers and principal financial officer or officers, or persons performing similar functions, about the effectiveness of the registrant's disclosure controls and procedures (as defined in Rules 13a–14(c) and 15d–14(c)) based on their evaluation of these controls and procedures as of a date within 90 days of the filing date of the quarterly or annual report that includes the disclosure required by this paragraph.

(b) *Changes in internal controls.* Disclose whether or not there were significant changes in the registrant's internal controls or in other factors that could significantly affect these controls subsequent to the date of their evaluation, including any corrective actions with regard to significant deficiencies and material weaknesses.

(c) *Asset-Backed Issuers.* A registrant that is an Asset–Backed Issuer (as defined in Rule 13a–14(g) and Rule 15d–14(g)) is not required to disclose the information required by this Item.

Item 401. Directors, executive officers, promoters and control persons.

* * *

(h) *Audit committee financial expert.* (1)(i) Disclose that the registrant's board of directors has determined that the registrant either:

(A) Has at least one audit committee financial expert serving on its audit committee; or

(B) Does not have an audit committee financial expert serving on its audit committee.

(ii) If the registrant provides the disclosure required by paragraph(h)(1)(i)(A) of this Item, it must disclose the name of the audit committee financial expert and whether that person is independent, as that term is used in Item 7(d)(3)(iv) of Schedule 14A under the Exchange Act.

(iii) If the registrant provides the disclosure required by paragraph(h)(1)(i)(B) of this Item, it must explain why it does not have an audit committee financial expert.

(i) *Identification of the audit committee.* (1) If you meet the following requirements, provide the disclosure in paragraph (i)(2) of this section:

(i) You are a listed issuer, as defined in Rule 10A–3 of this chapter;

(ii) You are filing either an annual report on Form 10–K or 10–KSB, or a proxy statement or information statement pursuant to the Exchange Act if action is to be taken with respect to the election of directors; and

(iii) You are neither:

(A) A subsidiary of another listed issuer that is relying on the exemption in Rule 10A–3(c)(2) of this chapter; nor

(B) Relying on any of the exemptions in Rule 10A–3(c)(4) through (c)(7) of this chapter.

(2)(i) State whether or not the registrant has a separately-designated standing audit committee established in accordance with section 3(a)(58)(A) of the Exchange Act), or a committee performing similar functions. If the registrant has such a committee, however designated, identify each committee member. If the entire board of directors is acting as the registrant's audit committee as specified in section 3(a)(58)(B) of the Exchange Act, so state.

(ii) If applicable, provide the disclosure required by Rule 10A–3(d) of this chapter regarding an exemption from the listing standards for audit committees.

Item 402. Executive Compensation

(a) *General.*

(1) *Treatment of Specific Types of Issuers.*

(i) *Small Business Issuers.* A registrant that qualifies as "small business issuer," as defined by Item 10(a)(1) of Regulation S-B, will be deemed to comply with this item if it provides the information required by paragraph (b) (Summary Compensation Table), paragraphs (c)(1) and (c)(2)(i)–(v) (Option/SAR Grants Table), paragraph (d) (Aggregated Option/SAR Exercise and Fiscal Year-End Option/SAR Value Table), paragraph (e) (Long-Term Incentive Plan Awards Table), paragraph (g) (Compensation of Directors), paragraph (h) (Employment Contracts, Termination of Employment and Change in Control Arrangements) and paragraph (i)(1) and (2) (Report on Repricing of Options/SARs) of this item.

Text of subsection (a)(1)(ii) effective Sept.30, 2000.

(ii) *Foreign private issuers.* A foreign private issuer will be deemed to comply with this item if it provides the information required by Items 6.B. and 6.E.2. of Form 20-F (*17 CFR 249.220f*), with more detailed information provided if otherwise made publicly available.

(2) *All Compensation Covered.* This item requires clear, concise and understandable disclosure of all plan and non-plan compensation awarded to, earned by, or paid to the named executive officers designated under paragraph (a)(3) of this item, and directors covered by paragraph (g) of this item by any person for all services rendered in all capacities to the registrant and its subsidiaries, unless otherwise specified in this item. Except as provided by paragraph (a)(5) of this item, all such compensation shall be reported pursuant to this item, even if also called for by another requirement, including transactions between the registrant and a third party where the primary purpose of the transaction is to furnish compensation to any such named executive officer or director. No item reported as compensation for one fiscal year need be reported as compensation for a subsequent fiscal year.

(3) *Persons Covered.* Disclosure shall be provided pursuant to this item for each of the following (the "named executive officers"):

(i) all individuals serving as the registrant's chief executive officer or acting in a similar capacity during the last completed fiscal year ("CEO"), regardless of compensation level;

(ii) the registrant's four most highly compensated executive officers other than the CEO who were serving as executive officers at the end of the last completed fiscal year; and

(iii) up to two additional individuals for whom disclosure would have been provided pursuant to paragraph (a)(3)(ii) of this item but for the fact that the individual was not serving as an executive officer of the registrant at the end of the last completed fiscal year.

Instructions to Item 402(a)(3).

1. *Determination of Most Highly Compensated Executive Officers.* The determination as to which executive officers are most highly compensated shall be made by reference to total annual salary and bonus for the last completed fiscal year (as required to be disclosed pursuant to paragraph (b)(2)(iii)(A) and (B) of this item), but including the dollar value of salary or bonus amounts forgone pursuant to Instruction 3 to paragraph (b)(2)(iii)(A) and (B) of this item, *provided, however,* that no disclosure need be provided for any executive officer, other than the CEO, whose total annual salary and bonus, as so determined, does not exceed $100,000.

2. *Inclusion of Executive Officer of Subsidiary.* It may be appropriate in certain circumstances for a registrant to include an executive officer of a subsidiary in the disclosure required by this item. *See* Rule 3b-7 under the Exchange Act.

3. *Exclusion of Executive Officer due to Unusual or Overseas Compensation.* It may be appropriate in limited circumstances for a registrant not to include in the disclosure required by this item an individual, other than its CEO, who is one of the registrant's most highly compensated executive officers. Among the factors that should be considered in determining not to name an individual are: (a) the distribution or accrual of an unusually large amount of cash compensation (such as a bonus or commission) that is not part of a recurring arrangement and is unlikely to continue; and (b) the payment of amounts of cash compensation relating to overseas assignments that may be attributed predominantly to such assignments.

(4) *Information for Full Fiscal Year.* If the CEO served in that capacity during part of a fiscal year with respect to which information is required information should be provided as to all of his or her compensation for the full fiscal year. If a named executive officer (other than the CEO) served as an executive officer of the registrant (whether or not in the same position) during any part of a fiscal year with respect to which information is required, information shall be provided as to all compensation of that individual for the full fiscal year.

(5) *Transactions With Third Parties Reported under Item 404.* This item includes transactions between the registrant and a third party where the primary purpose of the transaction is to furnish compensation to a named executive officer. No information need be given in response to any paragraph of this item, other than paragraph (j), as to any such third-party transaction if the transaction has been reported in response to Item 404 of Regulation S–K.

(6) *Omission of Table or Column.* A table or column may be omitted, if there has been no compensation awarded to, earned by or paid to any of the named executives required to be reported in that table or column in any fiscal year covered by that table.

(7) *Definitions.* For purposes of this item:

(i) The term "stock appreciation rights" ("SARs") refers to SARs payable in cash or stock, including SARs payable in cash or stock at the election of the registrant or a named executive officer.

(ii) The term "plan" includes, but is not limited to, the following: any plan, contract, authorization or arrangement, whether or not set forth in any formal documents, pursuant to which the following may be received: cash, stock, restricted stock or restricted stock units, phantom stock, stock options, SARs, stock options in tandem with SARs, warrants, convertible securities, performance units and performance shares, and similar instruments. A plan may be applicable to one person. Registrants may omit information regarding group life, health, hospitalization, medical reimbursement or relocation plans that do not discriminate in scope, terms or operation, in favor of executive officers or directors of the registrant and that are available generally to all salaried employees.

(iii) The term "long-term incentive plan" means any plan providing compensation intended to serve as incentive for performance to occur over a period longer than one fiscal year, whether such performance is measured by reference to financial performance of the registrant or an affiliate, the registrant's stock price, or any other measure, but excluding restricted stock, stock option and SAR plans.

(8) *Location of Specified Information.* The information required by paragraphs (i), (k) and (*l*) of this item need not be provided in any filings other than a registrant proxy or information statement relating to an annual meeting of security holders at which directors are to be elected (or special meeting or written consents in lieu of such meeting). Such information will not be deemed to be incorporated by reference into any filing under the Securities Act or the Exchange Act, except to the extent that the registrant specifically incorporates it by reference.

(9) *Liability for Specified Information.* The information required by paragraphs (k) and (*l*) of this item shall not be deemed to be "soliciting material" or to be "filed" with the Commission or subject to Regulations 14A or 14C, other than as provided in this item, or to the liabilities of Section 18 of the Exchange Act, except to the extent that the registrant specifically requests that such information be treated as soliciting material or specifically incorporates it by reference into a filing under the Securities Act or the Exchange Act.

(b) *Summary Compensation Table.* (1) *General.* The information specified in paragraph (b)(2) of this item, concerning the compensation of the named executive officers for each of the registrant's last three completed fiscal years, shall be provided in a Summary Compensation Table, in the tabular format specified below.

SUMMARY COMPENSATION TABLE

					Long Term Compensation			
		Annual Compensation			Awards		Payouts	
(a)	(b)	(c)	(d)	(e)	(f)	(g)	(h)	(i)
Name and Principal Position	Year	Salary ($)	Bonus ($)	Other Annual Compensation ($)	Restricted Stock Award(s) ($)	Securities Underlying Options/ SARs (#)	LTIP Payouts ($)	Compensation ($)
CEO	____							
	____							
	____							
A	____							
	____							
	____							
B	____							
	____							
	____							
C	____							
	____							
	____							
D	____							
	____							
	____							

(2) The Table shall include:

(i) The name and principal position of the executive officer (column (a));

(ii) Fiscal year covered (column (b));

(iii) Annual compensation (columns (c), (d) and (e)), including:

(A) The dollar value of base salary (cash and non-cash) earned by the named executive officer during the fiscal year covered (column (c));

(B) The dollar value of bonus (cash and non-cash) earned by the named executive officer during the fiscal year covered (column (d)); and

Instructions to Item 402(b)(2)(iii)(A) and (B).

1. Amounts deferred at the election of a named executive officer, whether pursuant to a plan established under Section 401(k) of the Internal Revenue Code, or otherwise, shall be included in the salary column (column (c)) or bonus column (column (d)), as appropriate, for the fiscal year in which earned. If the amount of salary or bonus earned in a given fiscal year is not calculable through the latest practicable date, that fact must be disclosed in a footnote and such amount must be disclosed in the subsequent fiscal year in the appropriate column for the fiscal year in which earned.

2. For stock or any other form of non-cash compensation, disclose the fair market value at the time the compensation is awarded, earned or paid.

3. Registrants need not include in the salary column (column (c)) or bonus column (column (d)) any amount of salary or bonus forgone at the election of a named executive officer pursuant to a registrant program under which stock, stock-based or other forms of non-cash compensation may be received by a named executive in lieu of a portion of annual compensation earned in a covered fiscal year. However, the receipt of any such form of non-cash compensation in lieu of salary or bonus earned for a covered fiscal year must be disclosed in the appropriate column of the Table corresponding to that fiscal year (i.e.), restricted stock awards (column (f)); options or SARs (column (g)); all other compensation (column (i)), or, if made pursuant to a long-term incentive plan and therefore not reporta-

ble at grant in the Summary Compensation Table, a footnote must be added to the salary or bonus column so disclosing and referring to the Long–Term Incentive Plan Table (required by paragraph (e) of this item) where the award is reported.

(C) The dollar value of other annual compensation not properly categorized as salary or bonus, as follows (column (e)):

(*1*) Perquisites and other personal benefits, securities or property, unless the aggregate amount of such compensation is the lesser of either $50,000 or 10% of the total of annual salary and bonus reported for the named executive officer in columns (c) and (d);

(*2*) Above-market or preferential earnings on restricted stock, options, SARs or deferred compensation paid during the fiscal year or payable during that period but deferred at the election of the named executive officer;

(*3*) Earnings on long-term incentive plan compensation paid during the fiscal year or payable during that period but deferred at the election of the named executive officer;

(*4*) Amounts reimbursed during the fiscal year for the payment of taxes; and

(*5*) The dollar value of the difference between the price paid by a named executive officer for any security of the registrant or its subsidiaries purchased from the registrant or its subsidiaries (through deferral of salary or bonus, or otherwise), and the fair market value of such security at the date of purchase, unless that discount is available generally, either to all security holders or to all salaried employees of the registrant.

Instructions to Item 402(b)(2)(iii)(C).

1. Each perquisite or other personal benefit exceeding 25% of the total perquisites and other personal benefits reported for a named executive officer must be identified by type and amount in a footnote or accompanying narrative discussion to column (e).

2. Perquisites and other personal benefits shall be valued on the basis of the aggregate incremental cost to the registrant and its subsidiaries.

3. Interest on deferred or long-term compensation is above-market only if the rate of interest exceeds 120% of the applicable federal long-term rate, with compounding (as prescribed under Section 1274(d) of the Internal Revenue Code) at the rate that corresponds most closely to the rate under the registrant's plan at the time the interest rate or formula is set. In the event of a discretionary reset of the interest rate, the requisite calculation must be made on the basis of the interest rate at the time of such reset, rather than when originally established. Only the above-market portion of the interest must be included. If the applicable interest rates vary depending upon conditions such as a minimum period of continued service, the reported amount should be calculated assuming satisfaction of all conditions to receiving interest at the highest rate.

4. Dividends (and dividend equivalents) on restricted stock, options, SARs or deferred compensation denominated in stock ("deferred stock") are preferential only if earned at a rate higher than dividends on the registrant's common stock. Only the preferential portion of the dividends or equivalents must be included.

(iv) Long-term compensation (columns (f), (g) and (h)), including:

(A) The dollar value (net of any consideration paid by the named executive officer) of any award of restricted stock, including share units (calculated by multiplying the closing market price of the registrant's unrestricted stock on the date of grant by the number of shares awarded) (column (f));

(B) The sum of the number of securities underlying stock options granted, with or without tandem SARs, and the number of freestanding SARs (column (g)); and

(C) The dollar value of all payouts pursuant to long-term incentive plans ("LTIPs") as defined in paragraph (a)(7)(iii) of this item (column (h)).

Instructions to Item 402(b)(2)(iv).

1. Awards of restricted stock that are subject to performance-based conditions on vesting, in addition to lapse of time and/or continued service with the registrant or a subsidiary, may be reported as LTIP awards pursuant to paragraph (e) of this item instead of in column (f). If this approach is selected, once the restricted stock vests, it must be reported as an LTIP payout in column (h).

2. The registrant shall, in a footnote to the Summary Compensation Table (appended to column (f), if included), disclose:

a. The number and value of the aggregate restricted stock holdings at the end of the last completed fiscal year. The value shall be calculated in the manner specified in paragraph (b)(2)(iv)(A) of this item using the value of the registrant's shares at the end of the last completed fiscal year;

b. For any restricted stock award reported in the Summary Compensation Table that will vest, in whole or in part, in under three years from the date of grant, the total number of shares awarded and the vesting schedule; and

c. Whether dividends will be paid on the restricted stock reported in column (f).

3. If at any time during the last completed fiscal year, the registrant has adjusted or amended the exercise price of stock options or freestanding SARs previously awarded to a named executive officer, whether through amendment, cancellation or replacement grants, or any other means ("repriced"), the registrant shall include the number of options or freestanding SARs so repriced as Stock Options/SARs granted and required to be reported in column (g).

4. If any specified performance target, goal or condition to payout was waived with respect to any amount included in LTIP payouts reported in column (h), the registrant shall so state in a footnote to column (h).

(v) All other compensation for the covered fiscal year that the registrant could not properly report in any other column of the Summary Compensation Table (column (i)). Any compensation reported in this column for the last completed fiscal year shall be identified and quantified in a footnote. Such compensation shall include, but not be limited to:

(A) The amount paid, payable or accrued to any named executive officer pursuant to a plan or arrangement in connection with:

(*1*) the resignation, retirement or any other termination of such executive officer's employment with the registrant and its subsidiaries; or

(*2*) a change in control of the registrant or a change in the executive officer's responsibilities following such a change in control;

(B) The dollar value of above-market or preferential amounts earned on restricted stock, options, SARs or deferred compensation during the fiscal year, or calculated with respect to that period, except that if such amounts are paid during the period, or payable during the period but deferred at the election of a named executive officer, this information shall be reported as Other Annual Compensation in column (e). *See* Instructions 3 and 4 to paragraph 402(b)(2)(iii)(C) of this item;

(C) The dollar value of amounts earned on long-term incentive plan compensation during the fiscal year, or calculated with respect to that period, except that if such amounts are paid during that period, or payable during that period at the election of the named executive officer, this information shall be reported as Other Annual Compensation in column (e);

(D) Annual registrant contributions or other allocations to vested and unvested defined contribution plans; and

(E) The dollar value of any insurance premiums paid by, or on behalf of, the registrant during the covered fiscal year with respect to term life insurance for the benefit of a named executive officer, and, if there is any arrangement or understanding, whether formal or informal, that such executive officer has or will receive or be allocated an interest in any cash surrender value under the insurance policy, either:

(*1*) The full dollar value of the remainder of the premiums paid by, or on behalf of, the registrant; or

(*2*) If the premiums will be refunded to the registrant on termination of the policy, the dollar value of the benefit to the executive officer of the remainder of the premium paid by, or on behalf of, the registrant during the fiscal year. The benefit shall be determined for the period, projected on an actuarial basis, between payment of the premium and the refund.

Instructions to Item 402(b)(2)(v).

1. LTIP awards and amounts received on exercise of options and SARs need not be reported as All Other Compensation in column (i).

2. Information relating to defined benefit and actuarial plans should not be reported pursuant to paragraph (b) of this item, but instead should be reported pursuant to paragraph (f) of this item.

3. Where alternative methods of reporting are available under paragraph (b)(2)(v)(E) of this item, the same method should be used for each of the

named executive officers. If the registrant chooses to change methods from one year to the next, that fact, and the reason therefor, should be disclosed in a footnote to column (i).

Instruction to Item 402(b).

Information with respect to fiscal years prior to the last completed fiscal year will not be required if the registrant was not a reporting company pursuant to Section 13(a) or 15(d) of the Exchange Act at any time during that year, except that the registrant will be required to provide information for any such year if that information previously was required to be provided in response to a Commission filing requirement.

(c) *Option/SAR Grants Table.*

(1) The information specified in paragraph (c)(2) of this item, concerning individual grants of stock options (whether or not in tandem with SARs), and freestanding SARs made during the last completed fiscal year to each of the named executive officers shall be provided in the tabular format specified below:

Option/SAR Grants in Last Fiscal Year

	Individual Grants				Potential Realizable Value at Assumed Annual Rates of Stock Price Appreciation for Optional Term		Alternative to (f) and (g): Grant Date Value
(a)	(b)	(c)	(d)	(e)	(f)	(g)	(h)
Name	Number of Securities Under-Op- tions/ lying Options/ SARs Granted (#)	% of Total SARs Granted to Employees in Fiscal Year	Exercise or Base Price ($/Sh)	Expiration Date	5% ($)	10% ($)	Grant Date Present Value $
CEO							
A							
B							
C							
D							

(2) The Table shall include, with respect to each grant:

(i) The name of the executive officer (column (a));

(ii) Number of securities underlying option/SARs granted (column (b));

(iii) The percent the grant represents of total options and SARs granted to employees during the fiscal year (column (c));

(iv) The per-share exercise or base price of the options or SARs granted (column (d)). If such exercise or base price is less than the market price of the underlying security on the date of grant, a separate, adjoining column shall be added showing market price on the date of grant;

(v) The expiration date of the options or SARs (column (e)); and

(vi) Either (A) the potential realizable value of each grant of options or freestanding SARs or (B) the present value of each grant, as follows:

(A) The potential realizable value of each grant of options or freestanding SARs, assuming that the market price of the underlying security appreciates in value from the date of grant to the end of the option or SAR term, at the following annualized rates:

(*1*) 5% (column (f));

(*2*) 10% (column (g)); and

(*3*) If the exercise or base price was below the market price of the underlying security at the date of grant, provide an additional column labeled 0%, to show the value at grant-date market price; or

(B) The present value of the grant at the date of grant, under any option pricing model (alternative column (f)).

Instructions to Item 402(c).

1. If more than one grant of options and/or freestanding SARs was made to a named executive officer during the last completed fiscal year, a separate line should be used to provide disclosure of each such grant. However, multiple grants during a single fiscal year may be aggregated where each grant was made at the same exercise and/or base price and has the same expiration date, and the same performance vesting thresholds, if any. A single grant consisting of options and/or freestanding SARs shall be reported as separate grants with respect to each tranche with a different exercise and/or base price, performance vesting threshold, or expiration date.

2. Options or freestanding SARs granted in connection with an option repricing transaction shall be reported in this table. *See* Instruction 3 to paragraph (b)(2)(iv) of this item.

3. Any material term of the grant, including but not limited to the date of exercisability, the number of SARs, performance units or other instruments granted in tandem with options, a performance-based condition to exercisability, a reload feature, or a tax-reimbursement feature, shall be footnoted.

4. If the exercise or base price is adjustable over the term of any option or freestanding SAR in accordance with any prescribed standard or formula, including but not limited to an index or premium price provision, describe the following, either by footnote to column (c) or in narrative accompanying the Table: (a) the standard of formula; and (b) any constant assumption made by the registrant regarding any adjustment to the exercise price in calculating the potential option or SAR value.

5. If any provision of a grant (other than an antidilution provision) could cause the exercise price to be lowered, registrants must clearly and fully disclose these provisions and their potential consequences either by a footnote or accompanying textual narrative.

6. In determining the grant-date market or base price of the security underlying options or freestanding SARs, the registrant may use either the closing market price per share of the security, or any other formula prescribed for the security.

7. The potential realizable dollar value of a grant (columns (f) and (g)) shall be the product of: (a) the difference between: (1) the product of the per-share market price at the time of the grant and the sum of 1 plus the adjusted stock price appreciation rate (the assumed rate of appreciation compounded annually over the term of the option or SAR); and (ii) the per-share exercise price of the option or SAR; and (b) the number of securities underlying the grant at fiscal year-end.

8. Registrants may add one or more separate columns using the formula prescribed in Instruction 7 to paragraph (c) of this item, to reflect the following:

a. the registrant's historic rate of appreciation over a period equivalent to the term of such options and/or SARs;

b. 0% appreciation, where the exercise or base price was equal to or greater than the market price of the underlying securities on the date of grant; and

c. N% appreciation, the percentage appreciation by which the exercise or base price exceeded the market price at grant. Where the grant included multiple tranches with exercise or base prices exceeding the market price of the underlying security by varying degrees, include an additional column for each additional tranche.

9. Where the registrant chooses to use the grant-date valuation alternative specified in paragraph (c)(2)(vi)(B) of this item, the valuation shall be footnoted to describe the valuation method used. Where the registrant has used a variation of the Black–Scholes or binomial option pricing model, the description shall identify the use of such pricing model and describe the assumptions used relating to the expected volatility, risk-free rate of return, dividend yield and time of exercise. Any adjustments for non-transferability or risk of forfeiture also shall be disclosed. In the event another valuation method is used, the registrant is required to describe the methodology as well as any material assumptions.

(d) *Aggregated Option/SAR Exercises and Fiscal Year–End Option/SAR Value Table.*

(1) The information specified in paragraph (d)(2) of this item, concerning each exercise of stock options (or tandem SARs) and freestanding SARs during the last completed fiscal year by each of the named executive officers and the fiscal year-end value of unexercised options and SARs, shall be provided on an aggregated basis in the tabular format specified below:

Aggregated Option/SAR Exercises in Last Fiscal Year
and FY–End Option/SAR Values

(a)	(b)	(c)	(d)	(e)
			Number of Securities Underlying Unexercised Options/SARs at FY–End (#)	Value of Unexercised In-the-Money Options/SARs at FY–End ($)
Name	Shares Acquired on Exercise (#)	Value Realized ($)	Exercisable/ Unexercisable	Exercisable/ Unexercisable
CEO				
A				
B				
C				
D				

(2) The table shall include:

(i) The name of the executive officer (column (a));

(ii) The number of shares received upon exercise, or, if no shares were received, the number of securities with respect to which the options or SARs were exercised (column (b));

(iii) The aggregate dollar value realized upon exercise (column (c));

(iv) The total number of securities underlying unexercised options and SARs held at the end of the last completed fiscal year, separately identifying the exercisable and unexercisable options and SARs (column (d)); and

(v) The aggregate dollar value of in-the-money, unexercised options and SARs held at the end of the fiscal year, separately identifying the exercisable and unexercisable options and SARs (column (e)).

Instructions to Item 402(d)(2).

1. Options or freestanding SARs are in-the-money if the fair market value of the underlying securities exceeds the exercise or base price of the option or SAR. The dollar values in columns (c) and (e) are calculated by determining the difference between the fair market value of the securities underlying the options or SARs and the exercise or base price of the options or SARs at exercise or fiscal year-end, respectively.

2. In calculating the dollar value realized upon exercise (column (c)), the value of any related payment or other consideration provided (or to be provided) by the registrant to or on behalf of a named executive officer, whether in payment of the exercise price or related taxes, shall not be included. Payments by the registrant in reimbursement of tax obligations incurred by a named executive officer are required to be disclosed in accordance with paragraph (b)(2)(iii)(C)(4) of this item.

(e) *Long–Term Incentive Plan ("LTIP") Awards Table.*

(1) The information specified in paragraph (e)(2) of this item, regarding each award made to a named executive officer in the last completed fiscal year under any LTIP, shall be provided in the tabular format specified below:

Long–Term Incentive Plans—Awards in Last Fiscal Year

(a)	(b)	(c)	(d)	(e)	(f)
			Estimated Future Payouts under Non–Stock Price–Based Plans		
Name	Number of Shares, Units or Other Rights (#)	Performance or Other Period Until Maturation or Payout	Threshold ($or #)	Target ($or #)	Maximum ($or #)
CEO					
A					
B					
C					
D					

(2) The Table shall include:

(i) The name of the executive officer (column (a));

(ii) The number of shares, units or other rights awarded under any LTIP, and, if applicable, the number of shares underlying any such unit or right (column (b));

(iii) The performance or other time period until payout or maturation of the award (column (c)); and

(iv) For plans not based on stock price, the dollar value of the estimated payout, the number of shares to be awarded as the payout or a range of estimated payouts denominated in dollars or number of shares under the award (threshold, target and maximum amount) (columns (d) through (f)).

Instructions to Item 402(e).

1. For purposes of this paragraph, the term "long-term incentive plan" or "LTIP" shall be defined in accordance with paragraph (a)(7)(iii) of this item.

2. Describe in a footnote or in narrative text accompanying this table the material terms of any award, including a general description of the formula or criteria to be applied in determining the amounts payable. Registrants are not required to disclose any factor, criterion or performance-related or other condition to payout or maturation of a particular award that involves confidential commercial or business information, disclosure of which would adversely affect the registrant's competitive position.

3. Separate disclosure shall be provided in the Table for each award made to a named executive officer, accompanied by the information specified in Instruction 2 to this paragraph. If awards are made to a named executive officer during the fiscal year under more than one plan, identify the particular plan under which each such award was made.

4. For column (d), "threshold" refers to the minimum amount payable for a certain level of performance under the plan. For column (e), "target" refers to the amount payable if the specified performance target(s) are reached. For column (f), "maximum" refers to the maximum payout possible under the plan.

5. In column (e), registrants must provide a representative amount based on the previous fiscal year's performance if the target award is not determinable.

6. A tandem grant of two instruments, only one of which is pursuant to a LTIP, need be reported only in the table applicable to the other instrument. For example, an option granted in tandem with a performance share would be reported only as an option grant, with the tandem feature noted.

(f) *Defined Benefit or Actuarial Plan Disclosure.*

(1) *Pension Plan Table.*

(i) For any defined benefit or actuarial plan under which benefits are determined primarily by final compensation (or average final compensation) and years of service, provide a separate Pension Plan Table showing estimated annual benefits payable upon retirement (including amounts attributable to any defined benefit supplementary or excess pension award plans) in specified compensation and years of service classifications in the format specified below.

PENSION PLAN TABLE

	Years of Service				
Remuneration	15	20	25	30	35
125,000					
150,000					
175,000					
200,000					
225,000					
250,000					
300,000					
400,000					
450,000					
500,000					

(ii) Immediately following the Table, the registrant shall disclose:

(A) The compensation covered by the plan(s), including the relationship of such covered compensation to the annual compensation reported in the Summary Compensation Table required by paragraph (b)(2)(iii) of this item, and state the current compensation covered by the plan for any named executive officer whose covered compensation differs substantially (by more than 10%) from that set forth in the annual compensation columns of the Summary Compensation Table;

(B) The estimated credited years of service for each of the named executive officers; and

(C) A statement as to the basis upon which benefits are computed (e.g., straight-life annuity amounts), and whether or not the benefits listed in the Pension Plan Table are subject to any deduction for Social Security or other offset amounts.

(2) *Alternative Pension Plan Disclosure.* For any defined benefit or actuarial plan under which benefits are not determined primarily by final compensation (or average final compensation) and years of service, the registrant shall state in narrative form:

(i) The formula by which benefits are determined; and

(ii) The estimated annual benefits payable upon retirement at normal retirement age for each of the named executive officers.

Instructions to Item 402(f).

1. *Pension Levels.* Compensation set forth in the Pension Plan Table pursuant to paragraph (f)(1)(i) of this item shall allow for reasonable increases in existing compensation levels; alternatively, registrants may present as the highest compensation level in the Pension Plan Table an amount equal to 120% of the amount of covered compensation of the most highly compensated individual named in the Summary Compensation Table required by paragraph (b)(2) of this item.

2. *Normal Retirement Age.* The term "normal retirement age" means normal retirement age as defined in a pension or similar plan or, if not defined therein, the earliest time at which a participant may retire without any benefit reduction due to age.

(g) *Compensation of Directors.*

(1) *Standard Arrangements.* Describe any standard arrangements, stating amounts, pursuant to which directors of the registrant are compensated for any services provided as a director, including any additional amounts payable for committee participation or special assignments.

(2) *Other Arrangements.* Describe any other arrangements pursuant to which any director of the registrant was compensated during the registrant's last completed fiscal year for any service provided as a director, stating the amount paid and the name of the director.

Instruction to Item 402(g)(2).

The information required by paragraph (g)(2) of this item shall include any arrangement, including consulting contracts, entered into in consideration of the director's service on the board. The material terms of any such arrangement shall be included.

(h) *Employment Contracts and Termination of Employment and Change-in-Control Arrangements.* Describe the terms and conditions of each of the following contracts or arrangements:

(1) Any employment contract between the registrant and a named executive officer; and

(2) Any compensatory plan or arrangement, including payments to be received from the registrant, with respect to a named executive officer, if such plan or arrangement results or will result from the resignation, retirement or any other termination of such executive officer's employment with the registrant and its subsidiaries or from a change-in-control of the registrant or a change in the named executive officer's responsibilities following a change-in-control and the amount involved, includ-

ing all periodic payments or installments, exceeds $100,000.

(i) *Report on Repricing of Options/SARs.* (1) If at any time during the last completed fiscal year, the registrant, while a reporting company pursuant to Section 13(a) or 15(d) of the Exchange Act, has adjusted or amended the exercise price of stock options or SARs previously awarded to any of the named executive officers, whether through amendment, cancellation or replacement grants, or any other means ("repriced"), the registrant shall provide the information specified in paragraphs (i)(2) and (i)(3) of this item.

(2) The compensation committee (or other board committee performing equivalent functions or, in the absence of any such committee, the entire board of directors) shall explain in reasonable detail any such repricing of options and/or SARs held by a named executive officer in the last completed fiscal year, as well as the basis for each such repricing.

(3)(i) The information specified in paragraph (i)(3)(*ii*) of this item, concerning all such repricings of options and SARs held by *any* executive officer during the last ten completed fiscal years, shall be provided in the tabular format specified below:

Ten–Year Option/SAR Repricings

(a) Name	(b) Date	(c) Number of Securities Underlying Options/ SARs Repriced or Amended (#)	(d) Market Price of Stock at Time of Repricing or Amendment ($)	(e) Exercise Price at Time of Repricing or Amendment ($)	(f) New Exercise Price ($)	(g) Length of Original Option Term Remaining at Date of Repricing or *Amendment*

(ii) The Table shall include, with respect to each repricing:

(A) The name and position of the executive officer (column (a));

(B) The date of each repricing (column (b));

(C) The number of securities underlying replacement or amended options or SARs (column (c));

(D) The per-share market price of the underlying security at the time of repricing (column (d));

(E) The original exercise price or base price of the cancelled or amended option or SAR (column (e));

(F) The per-share exercise price of base price of the replacement option or SAR (column (f)); and

(G) The amount of time remaining before the replaced or amended option or SAR would have expired (column (g)).

Instructions to Item 402(i).

1. The required report shall be made over the name of each member of the registrant's compensation committee, or other board committee performing equivalent functions or, in the absence of any such committee, the entire board of directors.

2. A replacement grant is any grant of options or SARs reasonably related to any prior or potential option or SAR cancellation, whether by an exchange or existing options or SARs for options or SARs with new terms; the grant of new options or SARs in tandem with previously granted options or SARs that will operate to cancel the previously granted options or SARs upon exercise; repricing of previously granted options or SARs; or otherwise. If a corresponding original grant was canceled in a prior year, information about such grant nevertheless must be disclosed pursuant to this paragraph.

3. If the replacement grant is not made at the current market price, describe the terms of the grant in a footnote or accompanying textual narrative.

4. This paragraph shall not apply to any repricing occurring through the operation of:

a. a plan formula or mechanism that results in the periodic adjustment of the option or SAR exercise or base price;

b. a plan antidilution provision; or

c. a recapitalization or similar transaction equally affecting all holders of the class of securities underlying the options or SARs.

5. Information required by paragraph (i)(3) of this item shall not be provided for any repricing effected before the registrant became a reporting company pursuant to Section 13(a) or 15(d) of the Exchange Act.

(j) *Additional Information with Respect to Compensation Committee Interlocks and Insider Participation in Compensation Decisions.* Under the caption "Compensation Committee Interlocks and Insider Participation,"

(1) The registrant shall identify each person who served as a member of the compensation committee of the registrant's board of directors (or board committee performing equivalent functions) during the last completed fiscal year, indicating each committee member who:

(i) was, during the fiscal year, an officer or employee of the registrant or any of its subsidiaries;

(ii) was formerly an officer of the registrant or any of its subsidiaries; or

(iii) had any relationship requiring disclosure by the registrant under any paragraph of Item 404 of Regulation S–K. In this event, the disclosure required by Item 404 shall accompany such identification.

(2) If the registrant has no compensation committee (or other board committee performing equivalent functions), the registrant shall identify each officer and employee of the registrant or any of its subsidiaries, and any former officer of the registrant or any of its subsidiaries, who, during the last completed fiscal year, participated in deliberations of the registrant's board of directors concerning executive officer compensation.

(3) The registrant shall describe any of the following relationships that existed during the last completed fiscal year:

(i) an executive officer of the registrant served as a member of the compensation committee (or other board committee performing equivalent functions or, in the absence of any such committee, the entire board of directors) of another entity, one of whose executive officers served on the compensation committee (or other board committee performing equivalent functions or, in the absence of any such committee, the entire board of directors) of the registrant;

(ii) an executive officer of the registrant served as a director of another entity, one of whose executive officers served on the compensation committee (or other board committee performing equivalent functions or, in the absence of any such committee, the entire board of directors) of the registrant; and

(iii) an executive officer of the registrant served as a member of the compensation committee (or other board committee performing equivalent functions or, in the absence of any such committee, the entire board of directors) of another entity, one of whose executive officers served as a director of the registrant.

(4) Disclosure required under paragraph (j)(3) of this item regarding any compensation committee member or other director of the registrant who also served as an executive officer of another entity shall be accompanied by the disclosure called for by Item 404 with respect to that person.

Instruction to Item 402(j).

For purposes of this paragraph, the term "entity" shall not include an entity exempt from tax under Section 501(c)(3) of the Internal Revenue Code.

(k) *Board Compensation Committee Report on Executive Compensation.*

(1) Disclosure of the compensation committee's compensation policies applicable to the registrant's executive officers (including the named executive officers), including the specific relationship of corporate performance to executive compensation, is required with respect to compensation reported for the last completed fiscal year.

(2) Discussion is required of the compensation committee's bases for the CEO's compensation reported for the last completed fiscal year, including the factors and criteria upon which the CEO's compensation was based. The committee shall include a specific discussion of the relationship of the registrant's performance to the CEO's compensation for the last completed fiscal year, describing each measure of the registrant's performance, whether qualitative or quantitative, on which the CEO's compensation was based.

(3) The required disclosure shall be made over the name of each member of the registrant's com-

pensation committee (or, in the absence of a compensation committee, the board committee performing equivalent functions or the entire board of directors). If the board of directors modified or rejected in any material way any action or recommendation by such committee with respect to such decision in the last completed fiscal year, the disclosure must so indicate and explain the reasons for the board's actions, and be made over the names of all members of the board.

Instructions to Item 402(k).

1. Boilerplate language should be avoided in describing factors and criteria underlying awards or payments of executive compensation in the statement required.

2. Registrants are not required to disclose target levels with respect to specific quantitative or qualitative performance-related factors considered by the committee (or board), or any factors or criteria involving confidential commercial or business information, the disclosure of which would have an adverse effect on the registrant.

(*l*) *Performance Graph.*

(1) Provide a line graph comparing the yearly percentage change in the registrant's cumulative total shareholder return on a class of common stock registered under Section 12 of the Exchange Act (as measured by dividing (i) the sum of (A) the cumulative amount of dividends for the measurement period, assuming dividend reinvestment, and (B) the difference between the registrant's share price at the end and the beginning of the measurement period; by (ii) the share price at the beginning of the measurement period) with

(i) the cumulative total return of a board equity market index assuming reinvestment of dividends, that includes companies whose equity securities are traded on the same exchange or NASDAQ market or are of comparable market capitalization; *provided, however,* that if the registrant is a company within the Standard & Poor's 500 Stock Index, the registrant must use that index; and

(ii) the cumulative total return, assuming reinvestment of dividends, of:

(A) a published industry or line-of-business index;

(B) peer issuer(s) selected in good faith. If the registrant does not select its peer issuer(s) on an industry or line-of-business basis, the registrant shall disclose the basis for its selection; or

(C) issuer(s) with similar market capitalization(s), but only if the registrant does not use a published industry or line-of-business index and does not believe it can reasonably identify a peer group. If the registrant uses this alternative, the graph shall be accompanied by a statement of the reasons for this selection.

(2) For purposes of paragraph (*l*)(1) of this item, the term "measurement period" shall be the period beginning at the "measurement point" established by the market close on the last trading day before the beginning of the registrant's fifth preceding fiscal year, through and including the end of the registrant's last completed fiscal year. If the class of securities has been registered under section 12 of the Exchange Act for a shorter period of time, the period covered by the comparison may correspond to that time period.

(3) For purposes of paragraph (*l*)(1)(ii)(A) of this item, the term "published industry or line-of-business index" means any index that is prepared by a party other than the registrant or an affiliate and is accessible to the registrant's security holders; provided, however, that registrants may use an index prepared by the registrant or affiliate if such index is widely recognized and used.

(4) If the registrant selects a different index from an index used for the immediately preceding fiscal year, explain the reason(s) for this change and also compare the registrant's total return with that of both the newly selected index and the index used in the immediately preceding fiscal year.

Instructions to Item 402(l).

1. In preparing the required graphic comparisons, the registrant should:

a. use, to the extent feasible, comparable methods of presentation and assumptions for the total return calculations required by paragraph (*l*)(1) of this item; *provided, however,* that if the registrant constructs its own peer group index under paragraph (*l*)(1)(ii)(B), the same methodology must be used in calculating both the registrant's total return and that on the peer group index; and

b. assume the reinvestment of dividends into additional shares of the same class of equity securities at the frequency with which dividends are paid on such securities during the applicable fiscal year.

2. In constructing the graph:

(a) The closing price at the measurement point must be converted into a fixed investment, stated in dollars, in the registrant's stock (or in the stocks represented by a given index), with cumulative returns for each subsequent fiscal year measured as a change from that investment; and

(b) Each fiscal year should be plotted with points showing the cumulative total return as of that point. The value of the investment as of each point plotted on a given return line is the number of shares held at that point multiplied by then-prevailing share price.

3. The registrant is required to present information for the registrant's last five fiscal years, and may choose to graph a longer period; but the measurement point, however, shall remain the same.

4. Registrants may include comparisons using performance measures in addition to total return, such as return on average common shareholders' equity, so long as the registrant's compensation committee (or other board committee performing equivalent functions or, in the absence of any such committee, the entire board of directors) describes the link between that measure and the level of executive compensation in the statement required by paragraph (k) of this Item.

5. If the registrant uses a peer issuer(s) comparison or comparison with issuer(s) with similar market capitalizations, the identity of those issuers must be disclosed and the returns of each component issuer of the group must be weighted according to the respective issuer's stock market capitalization at the beginning of each period for which a return is indicated.

* * *

Item 406. Code of Ethics

(a) Disclose whether the registrant has adopted a code of ethics that applies to the registrant's principal executive officer, principal financial officer, principal accounting officer or controller, or persons performing similar functions. If the registrant has not adopted such a code of ethics, explain why it has not done so.

(b) For purposes of this Item 406, the term code of ethics means written standards that are reasonably designed to deter wrongdoing and to promote:

(1) Honest and ethical conduct, including the ethical handling of actual or apparent conflicts of interest between personal and professional relationships;

(2) Full, fair, accurate, timely, and understandable disclosure in reports and documents that a registrant files with, or submits to, the Commission and in other public communications made by the registrant;

(3) Compliance with applicable governmental laws, rules and regulations;

(4) The prompt internal reporting of violations of the code to an appropriate person or persons identified in the code; and

(5) Accountability for adherence to the code.

(c) The registrant must:

(1) File with the Commission a copy of its code of ethics that applies to the registrant's principal executive officer, principal financial officer, principal accounting officer or controller, or persons performing similar functions, as an exhibit to its annual report;

(2) Post the text of such code of ethics on its Internet website and disclose, in its annual report, its Internet address and the fact that it has posted such code of ethics on its Internet website; or

(3) Undertake in its annual report filed with the Commission to provide to any person without charge, upon request, a copy of such code of ethics and explain the manner in which such request may be made.

(d) If the registrant intends to satisfy the disclosure requirement under Item 10 of Form 8-K regarding an amendment to, or a waiver from, a provision of its code of ethics that applies to the registrant's principal executive officer, principal financial officer, principal accounting officer or controller, or persons performing similar functions and that relates to any element of the code of ethics definition enumerated in paragraph (b) of this Item by posting such information on its Internet website, disclose the registrant's Internet address and such intention.

Instructions to Item 406.

* * *

2. If a registrant elects to satisfy paragraph (c) of this Item by posting its code of ethics on its website pursuant to paragraph (c)(2), the code of ethics must remain accessible on its website for as long as the registrant remains subject to the requirements of this Item and chooses to comply with this Item by posting its code on its website pursuant to paragraph (c)(2).

* * *

Item 504. Use of Proceeds

State the principal purposes for which the net proceeds to the registrant from the securities to be offered are intended to be used and the approximate amount intended to be used for each such purpose. Where registrant has no current specific plan for the proceeds, or a significant portion thereof, the registrant shall so state and discuss the principal reasons for the offering.

Instructions to Item 504.

* * *

6. Where the registrant indicates that the proceeds may, or will, be used to finance acquisitions of other businesses, the identity of such businesses, if known, or, if not known, the nature of the businesses to be sought, the status of any negotiations with respect to the acquisition, and a brief description of such business shall be included. Where, however, pro forma financial statements reflecting such acquisition are not required by Regulation S–X to be included, in the registration statement, the possible terms of any transaction, the identification of the parties thereto or the nature of the business sought need not be disclosed, to the extent that the registrant reasonably determines that public disclosure of such information would jeopardize the acquisition. Where Regulation S–X would require financial statements of the business to be acquired to be included, the description of the business to be acquired shall be more detailed.

7. The registrant may reserve the right to change the use of proceeds, provided that such reservation is due to certain contingencies that are discussed specifically and the alternatives to such use in that event are indicated.

*

I. REGULATION FD

Rule 100. General Rule Regarding Selective Disclosure.

(a) Whenever an issuer, or any person acting on its behalf, discloses any material nonpublic information regarding that issuer or its securities to any person described in paragraph (b)(1) of this section, the issuer shall make public disclosure of that information as provided in Rule 101(e):

(1) Simultaneously, in the case of an intentional disclosure; and

(2) Promptly, in the case of a non-intentional disclosure.

(b)(1) Except as provided in paragraph (b)(2) of this section, paragraph (a) of this section shall apply to a disclosure made to any person outside the issuer:

(i) Who is a broker or dealer, or a person associated with a broker or dealer, as those terms are defined in Section 3(a) of the Securities Exchange Act of 1934 (15 U.S.C. 78c(a));

(ii) Who is an investment adviser, as that term is defined in Section 202(a)(11) of the Investment Advisers Act of 1940 (15 U.S.C. 80b–2(a)(11)); an institutional investment manager, as that term is defined in Section 13(f)(5) of the Securities Exchange Act of 1934 (15 U.S.C. 78m(f)(5)), that filed a report on Form 13F (17 CFR 249.325) with the Commission for the most recent quarter ended prior to the date of the disclosure; or a person associated with either of the foregoing. For purposes of this paragraph, a "person associated with an investment adviser or institutional investment manager" has the meaning set forth in Section 202(a)(17) of the Investment Advisers Act of 1940 (15 U.S.C. 80b–2(a)(17)), assuming for these purposes that an institutional investment manager is an investment adviser;

(iii) Who is an investment company, as defined in Section 3 of the Investment Company Act of 1940 (15 U.S.C. 80a–3), or who would be an investment company but for Section 3(c)(1) (15 U.S.C. 80a–3(c)(1)) or Section 3(c)(7) (15 U.S.C. 80a–3(c)(7)) thereof, or an affiliated person of either of the foregoing. For purposes of this paragraph, "affiliated person" means only those persons described in Section 2(a)(3)(C), (D), (E), and (F) of the Investment Company Act of 1940 (15 U.S.C. 80a–2(a)(3)(C), (D), (E), and (F)), assuming for these purposes that a person who would be an investment company but for Section 3(c)(1) (15 U.S.C. 80a–3(c)(1)) or Section 3(c)(7) (15 U.S.C. 80a–3(c)(7)) of the Investment Company Act of 1940 is an investment company; or

(iv) Who is a holder of the issuer's securities, under circumstances in which it is reasonably foreseeable that the person will purchase or sell the issuer's securities on the basis of the information.

(2) Paragraph (a) of this section shall not apply to a disclosure made:

(i) To a person who owes a duty of trust or confidence to the issuer (such as an attorney, investment banker, or accountant);

(ii) To a person who expressly agrees to maintain the disclosed information in confidence;

(iii) To an entity whose primary business is the issuance of credit ratings, provided the information is disclosed solely for the purpose of developing a credit rating and the entity's ratings are publicly available; or

(iv) In connection with a securities offering registered under the Securities Act, other than an offering of the type described in any of Rule 415(a)(1)(i)–(vi) (§ 230.415(a)(1)(i)–(vi) of this chapter).

Rule 101. Definitions.

This section defines certain terms as used in Regulation FD (§§ 243.100–243.103).

(a) Intentional. A selective disclosure of material nonpublic information is "intentional" when the person making the disclosure either knows, or is reckless in not knowing, that the information he or she is communicating is both material and nonpublic.

(b) Issuer. An "issuer" subject to this regulation is one that has a class of securities registered under Section 12 of the Securities Exchange Act of 1934 (15 U.S.C. 78l), or is required to file reports under Section 15(d) of the Securities Exchange Act of 1934 (15 U.S.C. 78o(d)), including any closed-end investment company (as defined in Section 5(a)(2) of the Investment Company Act of 1940) (15 U.S.C. 80a–5(a)(2)), but not including any other investment company or any foreign government or foreign private issuer, as those terms are defined in Rule 405 under the Securities Act (§ 230.405 of this chapter).

(c) Person acting on behalf of an issuer. "Person acting on behalf of an issuer" means any senior official of the issuer (or, in the case of a closed-end investment company, a senior official of the issuer's investment adviser), or any other officer, employee, or agent of an issuer who regularly communicates with any person described in Rule 100(b)(1)(i), (ii), or (iii), or with holders of the issuer's securities. An officer, director, employee, or agent of an issuer who discloses material nonpublic information in breach of a duty of trust or confidence to the issuer shall not be considered to be acting on behalf of the issuer.

(d) Promptly. "Promptly" means as soon as reasonably practicable (but in no event after the later of 24 hours or the commencement of the next day's trading on the New York Stock Exchange) after a senior official of the issuer (or, in the case of a closed-end investment company, a senior official of the issuer's investment adviser) learns that there has been a non-intentional disclosure by the issuer or person acting on behalf of the issuer of information that the senior official knows, or is reckless in not knowing, is both material and nonpublic.

(e) Public disclosure.

(1) Except as provided in paragraph (e)(2) of this section, an issuer shall make the "public disclosure" of information required by Rule 100(a) by furnishing to or filing with the Commission a Form 8–K (17 CFR 249.308) disclosing that information.

(2) An issuer shall be exempt from the requirement to furnish or file a Form 8–K if it instead disseminates the information through another method (or combination of methods) of disclosure that is reasonably designed to provide broad, non-exclusionary distribution of the information to the public.

(f) Senior official. "Senior official" means any director, executive officer (as defined in § 240.3b–7 of this chapter), investor relations or public relations officer, or other person with similar functions.

(g) Securities offering. For purposes of Rule 100(b)(2)(iv):

(1) Underwritten offerings. A securities offering that is underwritten commences when the issuer reaches an understanding with the broker-dealer that is to act as managing underwriter and continues until the later of the end of the period during which a dealer must deliver a prospectus or the sale of the securities (unless the offering is sooner terminated);

(2) Non-underwritten offerings. A securities offering that is not underwritten:

(i) If covered by Rule 415(a)(1)(x) (§ 230.415(a)(1)(x) of this chapter), commences when the issuer makes its first bona fide offer in a takedown of securities and continues until the later of the end of the period during which each dealer must deliver a prospectus or the sale of the securities in that takedown (unless the takedown is sooner terminated);

(ii) If a business combination as defined in Rule 165(f)(1) (§ 230.165(f)(1) of this chapter), commences when the first public announcement of the transaction is made and continues until the completion of the vote or the expiration of the tender offer, as applicable (unless the transaction is sooner terminated);

(iii) If an offering other than those specified in paragraphs (a) and (b) of this section, commences when the issuer files a registration statement and continues until the later of the end of the period during which each dealer must deliver a prospectus or the sale of the securities (unless the offering is sooner terminated).

Rule 102. No Effect on Antifraud Liability.

No failure to make a public disclosure required solely by Section 100 shall be deemed to be a violation of Rule 10b–5 (17 CFR 240.10b–5) under the Securities Exchange Act.

Rule 103. No Effect on Exchange Act Reporting Status.

A failure to make a public disclosure required solely by Rule100 shall not affect whether:

(a) For purposes of Forms S–2 (17 CFR 239.12), S–3 (17 CFR 239.13) and S–8 (17 CFR 239.16b) under the Securities Act, an issuer is deemed to have filed all the material required to be filed pursuant to Section 13 or 15(d) of the Securities Exchange Act of 1934 (15 U.S.C. 78m or 78o(d)) or, where applicable, has made those filings in a timely manner; or

(b) There is adequate current public information about the issuer for purposes of § 230.144(c) of this chapter (Rule 144(c)).

J. REGULATION M–A

Contents

Item 1000. Definitions.

The following definitions apply to the terms used in Regulation M–A (§§ 229.1000 through 229.1016), unless specified otherwise:

(a) *Associate* has the same meaning as in § 240.12b–2 of this chapter;

(b) *Instruction C* means General Instruction C to Schedule 13E–3 (§ 240.13e–100 of this chapter) and General Instruction C to Schedule TO (§ 240.14d–100 of this chapter);

(c) *Issuer tender offer* has the same meaning as in § 240.13e–4(a)(2) of this chapter;

(d) *Offeror* means any person who makes a tender offer or on whose behalf a tender offer is made;

(e) *Rule 13e–3 transaction* has the same meaning as in § 240.13e–3(a)(3) of this chapter;

(f) *Subject company* means the company or entity whose securities are sought to be acquired in the transaction (*e.g.*, the target), or that is otherwise the subject of the transaction;

(g) *Subject securities* means the securities or class of securities that are sought to be acquired in the transaction or that are otherwise the subject of the transaction; and

(h) *Third-party tender offer* means a tender offer that is not an issuer tender offer.

Item 1001. Summary term sheet.

Summary term sheet. Provide security holders with a summary term sheet that is written in plain English. The summary term sheet must briefly describe in bullet point format the most material terms of the proposed transaction. The summary term sheet must provide security holders with sufficient information to understand the essential features and significance of the proposed transaction. The bullet points must cross-reference a more detailed discussion contained in the disclosure document that is disseminated to security holders.

Instructions to Item 1001:

1. The summary term sheet must not recite all information contained in the disclosure document that will be provided to security holders. The summary term sheet is intended to serve as an overview of all material matters that are presented in the accompanying documents provided to security holders.
2. The summary term sheet must begin on the first or second page of the disclosure document provided to security holders.
3. Refer to Rule 421(b) and (d) of Regulation C of the Securities Act (§ 230.421 of this chapter) for a description of plain English disclosure.

Item 1002. Subject company information.

(a) *Name and address.* State the name of the subject company (or the issuer in the case of an issuer tender offer), and the address and telephone number of its principal executive offices.

(b) *Securities.* State the exact title and number of shares outstanding of the subject class of equity securities as of the most recent practicable date. This may be based upon information in the most recently available filing with the Commission by the subject company unless the filing person has more current information.

(c) *Trading market and price.* Identify the principal market in which the subject securities are traded and state the high and low sales prices for the subject securities in the principal market (or, if there is no principal market, the range of high and low bid quotations and the source of the quotations) for each quarter during the past two years. If there is no established trading market for the securities (except for limited or sporadic quotations), so state.

(d) *Dividends.* State the frequency and amount of any dividends paid during the past two years with respect to the subject securities. Briefly describe any restriction on the subject company's current or future ability to pay dividends. If the filing person is not the subject company, furnish this information to the extent known after making reasonable inquiry.

(e) *Prior public offerings.* If the filing person has made an underwritten public offering of the subject securities for cash during the past three years that was registered under the Securities Act of 1933 or exempt from registration under Regulation A (§ 230.251 through § 230.263 of this chapter), state the date of the offering, the amount of securities offered, the offering price per share (adjusted for stock splits, stock dividends, etc. as appropriate) and the aggregate proceeds received by the filing person.

(f) *Prior stock purchases.* If the filing person purchased any subject securities during the past two years, state the amount of the securities purchased, the range of prices paid and the average purchase price for each quarter during that period. Affiliates need not give information for purchases made before becoming an affiliate.

Item 1003. Identity and background of filing person.

(a) *Name and address.* State the name, business address and business telephone number of each filing person. Also state the name and address of each person specified in Instruction C to the schedule (except for Schedule 14D–9 (§ 240.14d–101 of this chapter)). If the filing person is an affiliate of the subject company, state the nature of the affiliation. If the filing person is the subject company, so state.

(b) *Business and background of entities.* If any filing person (other than the subject company) or any person specified in Instruction C to the schedule is not a natural person, state the person's principal business, state or other place of organization, and the information required by paragraphs (c)(3) and (c)(4) of this section for each person.

(c) *Business and background of natural persons.* If any filing person or any person specified in Instruction C to the schedule is a natural person, provide the following information for each person:

(1) Current principal occupation or employment and the name, principal business and address of any corporation or other organization in which the employment or occupation is conducted;

(2) Material occupations, positions, offices or employment during the past five years, giving the starting and ending dates of each and the name, principal business and address of any corporation or other organization in which the occupation, position, office or employment was carried on;

(3) A statement whether or not the person was convicted in a criminal proceeding during the past five years (excluding traffic violations or similar misdemeanors). If the person was convicted, describe the criminal proceeding, including the dates, nature of conviction, name and location of court, and penalty imposed or other disposition of the case;

(4) A statement whether or not the person was a party to any judicial or administrative proceeding during the past five years (except for matters that were dismissed without sanction or settlement) that resulted in a judgment, decree or final order enjoining the person from future violations of, or prohibiting activities subject to, federal or state securities laws, or a finding of any violation of federal or state securities laws. Describe the proceeding, including a summary of the terms of the judgment, decree or final order; and

(5) Country of citizenship.

(d) *Tender offer.* Identify the tender offer and the class of securities to which the offer relates, the name of the offeror and its address (which may be based on the offeror's Schedule TO (§ 240.14d–100 of this chapter) filed with the Commission).

Instruction to Item 1003: If the filing person is making information relating to the transaction available on the Internet, state the address where the information can be found.

Item 1004. Terms of the transaction.

(a) *Material terms*. State the material terms of the transaction.

(1) *Tender offers*. In the case of a tender offer, the information must include:

(i) The total number and class of securities sought in the offer;

(ii) The type and amount of consideration offered to security holders;

(iii) The scheduled expiration date;

(iv) Whether a subsequent offering period will be available, if the transaction is a third-party tender offer;

(v) Whether the offer may be extended, and if so, how it could be extended;

(vi) The dates before and after which security holders may withdraw securities tendered in the offer;

(vii) The procedures for tendering and withdrawing securities;

(viii) The manner in which securities will be accepted for payment;

(ix) If the offer is for less than all securities of a class, the periods for accepting securities on a pro rata basis and the offeror's present intentions in the event that the offer is oversubscribed;

(x) An explanation of any material differences in the rights of security holders as a result of the transaction, if material;

(xi) A brief statement as to the accounting treatment of the transaction, if material; and

(xii) The federal income tax consequences of the transaction, if material.

(2) *Mergers or Similar Transactions*. In the case of a merger or similar transaction, the information must include:

(i) A brief description of the transaction;

(ii) The consideration offered to security holders;

(iii) The reasons for engaging in the transaction;

(iv) The vote required for approval of the transaction;

(v) An explanation of any material differences in the rights of security holders as a result of the transaction, if material;

(vi) A brief statement as to the accounting treatment of the transaction, if material; and

(vii) The federal income tax consequences of the transaction, if material.

Instruction to Item 1004(a): If the consideration offered includes securities exempt from registration under the Securities Act of 1933, provide a description of the securities that complies with Item 202 of Regulation S–K (§ 229.202). This description is not required if the issuer of the securities meets the requirements of General Instructions I.A, I.B.1 or I.B.2, as applicable, or I.C. of Form S–3 (§ 239.13 of this chapter) and elects to furnish information by incorporation by reference; only capital stock is to be issued; and securities of the same class are registered under section 12 of the Exchange Act and either are listed for trading or admitted to unlisted trading privileges on a national securities exchange; or are securities for which bid and offer quotations are reported in an automated quotations system operated by a national securities association.

(b) *Purchases*. State whether any securities are to be purchased from any officer, director or affiliate of the subject company and provide the details of each transaction.

(c) *Different terms*. Describe any term or arrangement in the Rule 13e–3 transaction that treats any subject security holders differently from other subject security holders.

(d) *Appraisal rights*. State whether or not dissenting security holders are entitled to any appraisal rights. If so, summarize the appraisal rights. If there are no appraisal rights available under state law for security holders who object to the transaction, briefly outline any other rights that may be available to security holders under the law.

(e) *Provisions for unaffiliated security holders*. Describe any provision made by the filing person in connection with the transaction to grant unaffiliated security holders access to the corporate files of the filing person or to obtain counsel or appraisal services at the expense of the filing person. If none, so state.

(f) *Eligibility for listing or trading*. If the transaction involves the offer of securities of the filing person in exchange for equity securities held by unaffiliated security holders of the subject company, describe whether or not the filing person will take steps to assure that the securities offered are or will be eligible for trading on an automated quotations system operated by a national securities association.

Item 1005. Past contacts, transactions, negotiations and agreements.

(a) *Transactions*. Briefly state the nature and approximate dollar amount of any transaction, other than those described in paragraphs (b) or (c) of this section, that occurred during the past two years, between the filing person (including any person specified in Instruction C of the schedule) and;

(1) The subject company or any of its affiliates that are not natural persons if the aggregate value of the transactions is more than one percent of the subject company's consolidated revenues for:

(i) The fiscal year when the transaction occurred; or

(ii) The past portion of the current fiscal year, if the transaction occurred in the current year; and

Instruction to Item 1005(a)(1): The information required by this Item may be based on information in the subject company's most recent filing with the Commission, unless the filing person has reason to believe the information is not accurate.

(2) Any executive officer, director or affiliate of the subject company that is a natural person if the aggregate value of the transaction or series of similar transactions with that person exceeds $60,000.

(b) *Significant corporate events.* Describe any negotiations, transactions or material contacts during the past two years between the filing person (including subsidiaries of the filing person and any person specified in Instruction C of the schedule) and the subject company or its affiliates concerning any:

(1) Merger;

(2) Consolidation;

(3) Acquisition;

(4) Tender offer for or other acquisition of any class of the subject company's securities;

(5) Election of the subject company's directors; or

(6) Sale or other transfer of a material amount of assets of the subject company.

(c) *Negotiations or contacts.* Describe any negotiations or material contacts concerning the matters referred to in paragraph (b) of this section during the past two years between:

(1) Any affiliates of the subject company; or

(2) The subject company or any of its affiliates and any person not affiliated with the subject company who would have a direct interest in such matters.

Instruction to paragraphs (b) and (c) of Item 1005: Identify the person who initiated the contacts or negotiations.

(d) *Conflicts of interest.* If material, describe any agreement, arrangement or understanding and any actual or potential conflict of interest between the filing person or its affiliates and:

(1) The subject company, its executive officers, directors or affiliates; or

(2) The offeror, its executive officers, directors or affiliates.

Instruction to Item 1005(d): If the filing person is the subject company, no disclosure called for by this paragraph is required in the document disseminated to security holders, so long as substantially the same information was filed with the Commission previously and disclosed in a proxy statement, report or other communication sent to security holders by the subject company in the past year. The document disseminated to security holders, however, must refer specifically to the discussion in the proxy statement, report or other communication that was sent to security holders previously. The information also must be filed as an exhibit to the schedule.

(e) *Agreements involving the subject company's securities.* Describe any agreement, arrangement, or understanding, whether or not legally enforceable, between the filing person (including any person specified in Instruction C of the schedule) and any other person with respect to any securities of the subject company. Name all persons that are a party to the agreements, arrangements, or understandings and describe all material provisions.

Instructions to Item 1005(e):

1. The information required by this Item includes: the transfer or voting of securities, joint ventures, loan or option arrangements, puts or calls, guarantees of loans, guarantees against loss, or the giving or withholding of proxies, consents or authorizations.

2. Include information for any securities that are pledged or otherwise subject to a contingency, the occurrence of which would give another person the power to direct the voting or disposition of the subject securities. No disclosure, however, is required about standard default and similar provisions contained in loan agreements.

Item 1006. Purposes of the transaction and plans or proposals.

(a) *Purposes*. State the purposes of the transaction.

(b) *Use of securities acquired*. Indicate whether the securities acquired in the transaction will be retained, retired, held in treasury, or otherwise disposed of.

(c) *Plans*. Describe any plans, proposals or negotiations that relate to or would result in:

(1) Any extraordinary transaction, such as a merger, reorganization or liquidation, involving the subject company or any of its subsidiaries;

(2) Any purchase, sale or transfer of a material amount of assets of the subject company or any of its subsidiaries;

(3) Any material change in the present dividend rate or policy, or indebtedness or capitalization of the subject company;

(4) Any change in the present board of directors or management of the subject company, including, but not limited to, any plans or proposals to change the number or the term of directors or to fill any existing vacancies on the board or to change any material term of the employment contract of any executive officer;

(5) Any other material change in the subject company's corporate structure or business, including, if the subject company is a registered closed-end investment company, any plans or proposals to make any changes in its investment policy for which a vote would be required by Section 13 of the Investment Company Act of 1940 (15 U.S.C. 80a–13);

(6) Any class of equity securities of the subject company to be delisted from a national securities exchange or cease to be authorized to be quoted in an automated quotations system operated by a national securities association;

(7) Any class of equity securities of the subject company becoming eligible for termination of registration under Section 12(g)(4) of the Act (15 U.S.C. 78l);

(8) The suspension of the subject company's obligation to file reports under Section 15(d) of the Act (15 U.S.C. 78o);

(9) The acquisition by any person of additional securities of the subject company, or the disposition of securities of the subject company; or

(10) Any changes in the subject company's charter, bylaws or other governing instruments or other actions that could impede the acquisition of control of the subject company.

(d) *Subject company negotiations*. If the filing person is the subject company:

(1) State whether or not that person is undertaking or engaged in any negotiations in response to the tender offer that relate to:

(i) A tender offer or other acquisition of the subject company's securities by the filing person, any of its subsidiaries, or any other person; or

(ii) Any of the matters referred to in paragraphs (c)(1) through (c)(3) of this section; and

(2) Describe any transaction, board resolution, agreement in principle, or signed contract that is entered into in response to the tender offer that relates to one or more of the matters referred to in paragraph (d)(1) of this section.

Instruction to Item 1006(d)(1): If an agreement in principle has not been reached at the time of filing, no disclosure under paragraph (d)(1) of this section is required of the possible terms of or the parties to the transaction if in the opinion of the board of directors of the subject company disclosure would jeopardize continuation of the negotiations. In that case, disclosure indicating that negotiations are being undertaken or are underway and are in the preliminary stages is sufficient.

Item 1007. Source and amount of funds or other consideration.

(a) *Source of funds*. State the specific sources and total amount of funds or other consideration to be used in the transaction. If the transaction involves a tender offer, disclose the amount of funds or other consideration required to purchase the maximum amount of securities sought in the offer.

(b) *Conditions*. State any material conditions to the financing discussed in response to paragraph (a) of this section. Disclose any alternative financing arrangements or alternative financing plans in the event the primary financing plans fall through. If none, so state.

(c) *Expenses*. Furnish a reasonably itemized statement of all expenses incurred or estimated to be incurred in connection with the transaction including, but not limited to, filing, legal, accounting and appraisal fees, solicitation expenses and printing costs and state whether or not the subject company has paid or will be responsible for paying any or all expenses.

(d) *Borrowed funds*. If all or any part of the funds or other consideration required is, or is expected, to be borrowed, directly or indirectly, for the purpose of the transaction:

(1) Provide a summary of each loan agreement or arrangement containing the identity of the parties, the term, the collateral, the stated and effective interest rates, and any other material terms or conditions of the loan; and

(2) Briefly describe any plans or arrangements to finance or repay the loan, or, if no plans or arrangements have been made, so state.

Instruction to Item 1007(d): If the transaction is a third-party tender offer and the source of all or any part of the funds used in the transaction is to come from a loan made in the ordinary course of business by a bank as defined by Section 3(a)(6) of the Act (15 U.S.C. 78c), the name of the bank will not be made available to the public if the filing person so requests in writing and files the request, naming the bank, with the Secretary of the Commission.

Item 1008. Interest in securities of the subject company.

(a) *Securities ownership.* State the aggregate number and percentage of subject securities that are beneficially owned by each person named in response to Item 1003 of Regulation M–A (§ 229.1003) and by each associate and majority-owned subsidiary of those persons. Give the name and address of any associate or subsidiary.

Instructions to Item 1008(a):

1. For purposes of this section, beneficial ownership is determined in accordance with Rule 13d–3 (§ 240.13d–3 of this chapter) under the Exchange Act. Identify the shares that the person has a right to acquire.

2. The information required by this section may be based on the number of outstanding securities disclosed in the subject company's most recently available filing with the Commission, unless the filing person has more current information.

3. The information required by this section with respect to officers, directors and associates of the subject company must be given to the extent known after making reasonable inquiry.

(b) *Securities transactions.* Describe any transaction in the subject securities during the past 60 days. The description of transactions required must include, but not necessarily be limited to:

(1) The identity of the persons specified in the Instruction to this section who effected the transaction;

(2) The date of the transaction;

(3) The amount of securities involved;

(4) The price per share; and

(5) Where and how the transaction was effected.

Instructions to Item 1008(b):

1. Provide the required transaction information for the following persons:

(a) The filing person (for all schedules);

(b) Any person named in Instruction C of the schedule and any associate or majority-owned subsidiary of the issuer or filing person (for all schedules except Schedule 14D–9 (§ 240.14d–101 of this chapter));

(c) Any executive officer, director, affiliate or subsidiary of the filing person (for Schedule 14D–9 (§ 240.14d–101 of this chapter);

(d) The issuer and any executive officer or director of any subsidiary of the issuer or filing person (for an issuer tender offer on Schedule TO (§ 240.14d–100 of this chapter)); and

(e) The issuer and any pension, profit-sharing or similar plan of the issuer or affiliate filing the schedule (for a going-private transaction on Schedule 13E–3 (§ 240.13e–100 of this chapter)).

2. Provide the information required by this Item if it is available to the filing person at the time the statement is initially filed with the Commission. If the information is not initially available, it must be obtained and filed with the Commission promptly, but in no event later than three business days after the date of the initial filing, and if material, disclosed in a manner reasonably designed to inform security holders. The procedure specified by this instruction is provided to maintain the confidentiality of information in order to avoid possible misuse of inside information.

Item 1009. Persons/assets, retained, employed, compensated or used.

(a) *Solicitations or recommendations.* Identify all persons and classes of persons that are directly or indirectly employed, retained, or to be compensated to make solicitations or recommendations in connection with the transaction. Provide a summary of all material terms of employment, retainer or other arrangement for compensation.

(b) *Employees and corporate assets.* Identify any officer, class of employees or corporate assets of the subject company that has been or will be employed or used by the filing person in connection with the transaction. Describe the purpose for their employment or use.

Instruction to Item 1009(b): Provide all information required by this Item except for the information required by paragraph (a) of this section and Item 1007 of Regulation M–A (§ 229.1007).

Item 1010. Financial statements.

(a) *Financial information.* Furnish the following financial information:

(1) Audited financial statements for the two fiscal years required to be filed with the company's most recent annual report under Sections 13 and 15(d) of the Exchange Act (15 U.S.C. 78m; 15 U.S.C. 78o);

(2) Unaudited balance sheets, comparative year-to-date income statements and related earnings per share data, statements of cash flows, and comprehensive income required to be included in the company's most recent quarterly report filed under the Exchange Act;

(3) Ratio of earnings to fixed charges, computed in a manner consistent with Item 503(d) of Regulation S–K (§ 229.503(d)), for the two most recent fiscal years and the interim periods provided under paragraph (a)(2) of this section; and

(4) Book value per share as of the date of the most recent balance sheet presented.

(b) *Pro forma information.* If material, furnish pro forma information disclosing the effect of the transaction on:

(1) The company's balance sheet as of the date of the most recent balance sheet presented under paragraph (a) of this section;

(2) The company's statement of income, earnings per share, and ratio of earnings to fixed charges for the most recent fiscal year and the latest interim period provided under paragraph (a)(2) of this section; and

(3) The company's book value per share as of the date of the most recent balance sheet presented under paragraph (a) of this section.

(c) *Summary Information.* Furnish a fair and adequate summary of the information specified in paragraphs (a) and (b) of this section for the same periods specified. A fair and adequate summary includes:

(1) The summarized financial information specified in § 210.1–02(bb)(1) of this chapter;

(2) Income per common share from continuing operations (basic and diluted, if applicable);

(3) Net income per common share (basic and diluted, if applicable);

(4) Ratio of earnings to fixed charges, computed in a manner consistent with Item 503(d) of Regulation S–K (§ 229.503(d));

(5) Book value per share as of the date of the most recent balance sheet; and

(6) If material, pro forma data for the summarized financial information specified in paragraph (c)(1) through (c)(5) of this section disclosing the effect of the transaction.

Item 1011. Additional information.

(a) *Agreements, regulatory requirements and legal proceedings*. If material to a security holder's decision whether to sell, tender or hold the securities sought in the tender offer, furnish the following information:

(1) Any present or proposed material agreement, arrangement, understanding or relationship between the offeror or any of its executive officers, directors, controlling persons or subsidiaries and the subject company or any of its executive officers, directors, controlling persons or subsidiaries (other than any agreement, arrangement or understanding disclosed under any other sections of Regulation M–A (§§ 229.1000 through 229.1016));

Instruction to paragraph (a)(1): In an issuer tender offer disclose any material agreement, arrangement, understanding or relationship between the offeror and any of its executive officers, directors, controlling persons or subsidiaries.

(2) To the extent known by the offeror after reasonable investigation, the applicable regulatory requirements which must be complied with or approvals which must be obtained in connection with the tender offer;

(3) The applicability of any anti-trust laws;

(4) The applicability of margin requirements under Section 7 of the Act (15 U.S.C. 78g) and the applicable regulations; and

(5) Any material pending legal proceedings relating to the tender offer, including the name and location of the court or agency in which the proceedings are pending, the date instituted, the principal parties, and a brief summary of the proceedings and the relief sought.

Instruction to Item 1011(a)(5): A copy of any document relating to a major development (such as pleadings, an answer, complaint, temporary restraining order, injunction, opinion, judgment or order) in a material pending legal proceeding must be furnished promptly to the Commission staff on a supplemental basis.

(b) *Other material information*. Furnish such additional material information, if any, as may be necessary to make the required statements, in light of the circumstances under which they are made, not materially misleading.

Item 1012. The solicitation or recommendation.

(a) *Solicitation or recommendation*. State the nature of the solicitation or the recommendation. If this statement relates to a recommendation, state whether the filing person is advising holders of the subject securities to accept or reject the tender offer or to take other action with respect to the tender offer and, if so, describe the other action recommended. If the filing person is the subject company and is not making a recommendation, state whether the subject company is expressing no opinion and is remaining neutral toward the tender offer or is unable to take a position with respect to the tender offer.

(b) *Reasons*. State the reasons for the position (including the inability to take a position) stated in paragraph (a) of this section. Conclusory statements such as "The tender offer is in the best interests of shareholders" are not considered sufficient disclosure.

(c) *Intent to tender*. To the extent known by the filing person after making reasonable inquiry, state whether the filing person or any executive officer, director, affiliate or subsidiary of the filing person currently intends to tender, sell or hold the subject securities that are held of record or beneficially owned by that person.

(d) *Intent to tender or vote in a going-private transaction*. To the extent known by the filing person after making reasonable inquiry, state whether or not any executive officer, director or affiliate of the issuer (or any person specified in Instruction C to the schedule) currently intends to tender or sell subject securities owned or held by that person and/or how each person currently intends to vote subject securities, including any securities the person has proxy authority for. State the reasons for the intended action.

Instruction to Item 1012(d): Provide the information required by this section if it is available to the filing person at the time the statement is initially filed with the Commission. If the information is not available, it must be filed with the Commission promptly, but in no event later than three business days after the date of the initial filing, and if material, disclosed in a manner reasonably designed to inform security holders.

(e) *Recommendations of others*. To the extent known by the filing person after making reasonable inquiry, state whether or not any person specified in paragraph (d) of this section has made a recommendation either in support of or opposed to the transaction and the reasons for the recommendation.

Item 1013. Purposes, alternatives, reasons and effects in a going-private transaction.

(a) *Purposes*. State the purposes for the Rule 13e–3 transaction.

(b) *Alternatives.* If the subject company or affiliate considered alternative means to accomplish the stated purposes, briefly describe the alternatives and state the reasons for their rejection.

(c) *Reasons.* State the reasons for the structure of the Rule 13e–3 transaction and for undertaking the transaction at this time.

(d) *Effects.* Describe the effects of the Rule 13e–3 transaction on the subject company, its affiliates and unaffiliated security holders, including the federal tax consequences of the transaction.

Instructions to Item 1013:

1. Conclusory statements will not be considered sufficient disclosure in response to this section.

2. The description required by paragraph (d) of this section must include a reasonably detailed discussion of both the benefits and detriments of the Rule 13e–3 transaction to the subject company, its affiliates and unaffiliated security holders. The benefits and detriments of the Rule 13e–3 transaction must be quantified to the extent practicable.

3. If this statement is filed by an affiliate of the subject company, the description required by paragraph (d) of this section must include, but not be limited to, the effect of the Rule 13e–3 transaction on the affiliate's interest in the net book value and net earnings of the subject company in terms of both dollar amounts and percentages.

Item 1014. Fairness of the going-private transaction.

(a) *Fairness.* State whether the subject company or affiliate filing the statement reasonably believes that the Rule 13e–3 transaction is fair or unfair to unaffiliated security holders. If any director dissented to or abstained from voting on the Rule 13e–3 transaction, identify the director, and indicate, if known, after making reasonable inquiry, the reasons for the dissent or abstention.

(b) *Factors considered in determining fairness.* Discuss in reasonable detail the material factors upon which the belief stated in paragraph (a) of this section is based and, to the extent practicable, the weight assigned to each factor. The discussion must include an analysis of the extent, if any, to which the filing person's beliefs are based on the factors described in Instruction 2 of this section, paragraphs (c), (d) and (e) of this section and Item 1015 of Regulation M–A (§ 229.1015).

(c) *Approval of security holders.* State whether or not the transaction is structured so that approval of at least a majority of unaffiliated security holders is required.

(d) *Unaffiliated representative.* State whether or not a majority of directors who are not employees of the subject company has retained an unaffiliated representative to act solely on behalf of unaffiliated security holders for purposes of negotiating the terms of the Rule 13e–3 transaction and/or preparing a report concerning the fairness of the transaction.

(e) *Approval of directors.* State whether or not the Rule 13e–3 transaction was approved by a majority of the directors of the subject company who are not employees of the subject company.

(f) *Other offers.* If any offer of the type described in paragraph (viii) of Instruction 2 to this section has been received, describe the offer and state the reasons for its rejection.

Instructions to Item 1014:

1. A statement that the issuer or affiliate has no reasonable belief as to the fairness of the Rule 13e–3 transaction to unaffiliated security holders will not be considered sufficient disclosure in response to paragraph (a) of this section.

2. The factors that are important in determining the fairness of a transaction to unaffiliated security holders and the weight, if any, that should be given to them in a particular context will vary. Normally such factors will include, among others, those referred to in paragraphs (c), (d) and (e) of this section and whether the consideration offered to unaffiliated security holders constitutes fair value in relation to:

(i) Current market prices;

(ii) Historical market prices;

(iii) Net book value;

(iv) Going concern value;

(v) Liquidation value;

(vi) Purchase prices paid in previous purchases disclosed in response to Item 1002(f) of Regulation M–A (§ 229.1002(f));

(vii) Any report, opinion, or appraisal described in Item 1015 of Regulation M–A (§ 229.1015); and

(viii) Firm offers of which the subject company or affiliate is aware made by any unaffiliated person, other than the filing persons, during the past two years for:

(A) The merger or consolidation of the subject company with or into another company, or *vice versa*;

(B) The sale or other transfer of all or any substantial part of the assets of the subject company; or

(C) A purchase of the subject company's securities that would enable the holder to exercise control of the subject company.

3. Conclusory statements, such as "The Rule 13e–3 transaction is fair to unaffiliated security holders in relation to net book value, going concern value and future prospects of the issuer" will not be considered sufficient disclosure in response to paragraph (b) of this section.

Item 1015. Reports, opinions, appraisals and negotiations.

(a) *Report, opinion or appraisal.* State whether or not the subject company or affiliate has received any report, opinion (other than an opinion of counsel) or appraisal from an outside party that is materially related to the Rule 13e–3 transaction, including, but not limited to: any report, opinion or appraisal relating to the consideration or the fairness of the consideration to be offered to security holders or the fairness of the transaction to the issuer or affiliate or to security holders who are not affiliates.

(b) *Preparer and summary of the report, opinion or appraisal.* For each report, opinion or appraisal described in response to paragraph (a) of this section or any negotiation or report described in response to Item 1014(d) of Regulation M–A (§ 229.1014) or Item 14(b)(6) of Schedule 14A (§ 240.14a–101 of this chapter) concerning the terms of the transaction:

(1) Identify the outside party and/or unaffiliated representative;

(2) Briefly describe the qualifications of the outside party and/or unaffiliated representative;

(3) Describe the method of selection of the outside party and/or unaffiliated representative;

(4) Describe any material relationship that existed during the past two years or is mutually understood to be contemplated and any compensation received or to be received as a result of the relationship between:

(i) The outside party, its affiliates, and/or unaffiliated representative; and

(ii) The subject company or its affiliates;

(5) If the report, opinion or appraisal relates to the fairness of the consideration, state whether the subject company or affiliate determined the amount of consideration to be paid or whether the outside party recommended the amount of consideration to be paid; and

(6) Furnish a summary concerning the negotiation, report, opinion or appraisal. The summary must include, but need not be limited to, the procedures followed; the findings and recommendations; the bases for and methods of arriving at such findings and recommendations; instructions received from the subject company or affiliate; and any limitation imposed by the subject company or affiliate on the scope of the investigation.

Instruction to Item 1015(b): The information called for by paragraphs (b)(1), (2) and (3) of this section must be given with respect to the firm that provides the report, opinion or appraisal rather than the employees of the firm that prepared the report.

(c) *Availability of documents.* Furnish a statement to the effect that the report, opinion or appraisal will be made available for inspection and copying at the principal executive offices of the subject company or affiliate during its regular business hours by any interested equity security holder of the subject company or representative who has been so designated in writing. This statement also may provide that a copy of the report, opinion or appraisal will be transmitted by the subject company or affiliate to any interested equity security holder of the subject company or representative who has been so designated in writing upon written request and at the expense of the requesting security holder.

Item 1016. Exhibits.

File as an exhibit to the schedule:

(a) Any disclosure materials furnished to security holders by or on behalf of the filing person, including:

(1) Tender offer materials (including transmittal letter);

(2) Solicitation or recommendation (including those referred to in Item 1012 of Regulation M–A (§ 229.1012));

(3) Going-private disclosure document;

(4) Prospectus used in connection with an exchange offer where securities are registered under the Securities Act of 1933; and

(5) Any other disclosure materials;

(b) Any loan agreement referred to in response to Item 1007(d) of Regulation M–A (§ 229.1007(d));

Instruction to Item 1016(b): If the filing relates to a third-party tender offer and a request is made under Item 1007(d) of Regulation M–A (§ 229.1007(d)), the identity of the bank providing financing may be omitted from the loan agreement filed as an exhibit.

(c) Any report, opinion or appraisal referred to in response to Item 1014(d) or Item 1015 of Regulation M–A (§ 229.1014(d) or § 229.1015);

(d) Any document setting forth the terms of any agreement, arrangement, understanding or relationship referred to in response to Item 1005(e) or Item 1011(a)(1) of Regulation M–A (§ 229.1005(e) or § 229.1011(a)(1));

(e) Any agreement, arrangement or understanding referred to in response to § 229.1005(d), or the pertinent portions of any proxy statement, report or other communication containing the disclosure required by Item 1005(d) of Regulation M–A (§ 229.1005(d));

(f) A detailed statement describing security holders' appraisal rights and the procedures for exercising those appraisal rights referred to in response to Item 1004(d) of Regulation M–A (§ 229.1004(d));

(g) Any written instruction, form or other material that is furnished to persons making an oral solicitation or recommendation by or on behalf of the filing person for their use directly or indirectly in connection with the transaction; and

(h) Any written opinion prepared by legal counsel at the filing person's request and communicated to the filing person pertaining to the tax consequences of the transaction. Exhibit Table to Item 1016 of Regulation M–A.

K. REGULATION BTR—BLACKOUT TRADING RESTRICTION

Contents

Item 100. Definitions.

As used in Regulation BTR, unless the context otherwise requires:

(a) The term "acquired in connection with service or employment as a director or executive officer," when applied to a director or executive officer, means that he or she acquired, directly or indirectly, an equity security:

(1) At a time when he or she was a director or executive officer, under a compensatory plan, contract, authorization or arrangement, including, but not limited to, an option, warrants or rights plan, a pension, retirement or deferred compensation plan or a bonus, incentive or profit-sharing plan (whether or not set forth in any formal plan document), including a compensatory plan, contract, authorization or arrangement with a parent, subsidiary or affiliate;

(2) At a time when he or she was a director or executive officer, as a result of any transaction or business relationship described in paragraph (a) or (b) of Item 404 of Regulation S–K or, in the case of a foreign private issuer, Item 7.B of Form 20–F (but without application of the disclosure thresholds of such provisions), to the extent that he or she has a pecuniary interest (as defined in paragraph (*l*) of this section) in the equity securities;

(3) At a time when he or she was a director or executive officer, as directors' qualifying shares or other securities that he or she must hold to satisfy minimum ownership requirements or guidelines for directors or executive officers;

(4) Prior to becoming, or while, a director or executive officer where the equity security was acquired as a direct or indirect inducement to service or employment as a director or executive officer; or

(5) Prior to becoming, or while, a director or executive officer where the equity security was received as a result of a business combination in respect of an equity security of an entity involved in the business combination that he or she had acquired in connection with service or employment as a director or executive officer of such entity.

(b) Except as provided in [Item] 102, the term "blackout period":

(1) With respect to the equity securities of any issuer (other than a foreign private issuer), means any period of more than three consecutive business days during which the ability to purchase, sell or otherwise acquire or transfer an interest in any equity security of such issuer held in an individual account plan is temporarily suspended by the issuer or by a fiduciary of the plan with respect to not fewer than 50% of the participants or beneficiaries located in the United States and its territories and possessions under all individual account plans (as defined in paragraph (j) of this section) maintained by the issuer that permit participants or beneficiaries to acquire or hold equity securities of the issuer;

(2) With respect to the equity securities of any foreign private issuer (as defined in [Item] 3b–4(c) of this chapter), means any period of more than three consecutive business days during which both:

(i) The conditions of paragraph (b)(1) of this section are met; and

(ii) (A) The number of participants and beneficiaries located in the United States and its territories and possessions subject to the temporary suspension exceeds 15% of the total number of employees of the issuer and its consolidated subsidiaries; or

(B) More than 50,000 participants and beneficiaries located in the United States and its territories and possessions are subject to the temporary suspension.

(3) In determining the individual account plans (as defined in paragraph (j) of this section) maintained by an issuer for purposes of this paragraph (b):

(i) The rules under section 414(b), (c), (m) and (*o*) of the Internal Revenue Code are to be applied; and

(ii) An individual account plan that is maintained outside of the United States primarily for the benefit of persons substantially all of whom are nonresident aliens (within the meaning of section 104(b)(4) of the Employee Retirement Income Security Act of 1974) is not to be considered.

(4) In determining the number of participants and beneficiaries in an individual account plan (as defined in paragraph (j) of this section) maintained by an issuer:

(i) The determination may be made as of any date within the 12–month period preceding the beginning date of the temporary suspension in question; provided that if there has been a significant change in the number of participants or beneficiaries in an individual account plan since the date selected, the determination for such plan must be made as of the most recent practicable date that reflects such change; and

(ii) The determination may be made without regard to overlapping plan participation.

(c) (1) The term "director" has, except as provided in paragraph (c)(2) of this section, the meaning set forth in section 3(a)(7) of the Exchange Act.

(2) In the case of a foreign private issuer, the term director means an individual within the definition set forth in section 3(a)(7) of the Exchange Act who is a management employee of the issuer.

(d) The term "derivative security" has the meaning set forth in [Item]16a–1(c) of this chapter.

(e) The term "equity security" has the meaning set forth in section 3(a)(11) of the Exchange Act and [Item] 3a11–1 of this chapter.

(f) The term "equity security" of the issuer means any equity security or derivative security relating to an issuer, whether or not issued by that issuer.

(g) The term "Exchange Act" means the Securities Exchange Act of 1934.

(h) (1) The term "executive officer" has, except as provided in paragraph (h)(2) of this section, the meaning set forth in [Item]16a–1(f) of this chapter.

(2) In the case of a foreign private issuer, the term executive officer means the principal executive officer or officers, the principal financial officer or officers and the principal accounting officer or officers of the issuer.

(i) The term "exempt security" has the meaning set forth in section 3(a)(12) of the Exchange Act.

(j) The term "individual account plan" means a pension plan which provides for an individual account for each participant and for benefits based solely upon the amount contributed to the participant's account, and any income, expenses, gains and losses, and any forfeitures of accounts of other participants which may be allocated to such participant's account, except that such term does not include a one-participant retirement plan (within the meaning of section 101(i)(8)(B) of the Employee Retirement Income Security Act of 1974), nor does it include a pension plan in which participation is limited to directors of the issuer.

(k) The term "issuer" means an issuer (as defined in section 3(a)(8) of the Exchange Act), the securities of which are registered under section 12 of the Exchange Act or that is required to file reports under section 15(d) of the Exchange Act or that files or has filed a registration statement that has not yet become effective under the Securities Act of 1933 and that it has not withdrawn.

(*l*) The term "pecuniary interest" has the meaning set forth in [Item]16a–1(a)(2)(i) of this chapter and the term indirect pecuniary interest has the meaning set forth in [Item]16a–1(a)(2)(ii) of this chapter. Section 16a–1(a)(2)(iii) of this chapter also shall apply to determine pecuniary interest for purposes of this regulation.

Item 101. Prohibition of insider trading during pension fund blackout periods.

(a) Except to the extent otherwise provided in paragraph (c) of this section, it is unlawful under section 306(a)(1) of the Sarbanes–Oxley Act of 2002 for any director or executive officer of an issuer of any equity security (other than an exempt security), directly or indirectly, to purchase, sell or otherwise acquire or transfer any equity security of the issuer (other than an exempt security) during any blackout period with respect to such equity security, if such director or executive officer acquires or previously acquired such equity security in connection with his or her service or employment as a director or executive officer.

(b) For purposes of section 306(a)(1) of the Sarbanes–Oxley Act of 2002, any sale or other transfer of an equity security of the issuer during a blackout period will be treated as a transaction involving an equity security "acquired in connection with service or employment as a director or executive officer" (as defined in [Item]100(a)) to the extent that the director or executive officer has a pecuniary interest (as defined in [Item]100(*l*)) in such equity security, unless the director or executive officer establishes by specific identification of securities that the transaction did not involve an equity security "acquired in connection with service or employment as a director or executive officer." To establish that the equity security was not so acquired, a director or executive officer must identify the source of the equity securities and demonstrate that he or she has utilized the same specific identification for any purpose related to the transaction (such as tax reporting and any applicable disclosure and reporting requirements).

(c) The following transactions are exempt from section 306(a)(1) of the Sarbanes–Oxley Act of 2002:

(1) Any acquisition of equity securities resulting from the reinvestment of dividends in, or interest on, equity securities of the same issuer if the acquisition is made pursuant to a plan providing for the regular reinvestment of dividends or interest and the plan provides for broad-based participation, does not discriminate in favor of employees of the issuer and operates on substantially the same terms for all plan participants;

(2) Any purchase or sale of equity securities of the issuer pursuant to a contract, instruction or written plan entered into by the director or executive officer that satisfies the affirmative defense conditions of § 240.10b5–1(c) of this chapter; provided that the director or executive officer did not enter into or modify the contract, instruction or written plan during the blackout period in question, or while aware of the actual or approximate beginning or ending dates of that blackout period (whether or not the director or executive officer received notice of the blackout period as required by Section 306(a)(6) of the Sarbanes–Oxley Act of 2002).

(3) Any purchase or sale of equity securities, other than a Discretionary Transaction (as defined in [Item]16b–3(b)(1) of this chapter), pursuant to a Qualified Plan (as defined in [Item]16b–3(b)(4) of this chapter), an Excess Benefit Plan (as defined in [Item]16b–3(b)(2) of this chapter) or a Stock Purchase Plan (as defined in [Item]16b–3(b)(5) of this chapter) (or, in the case of a foreign private issuer, pursuant to an employee benefit plan that either (i) has been approved by the taxing authority of a foreign jurisdiction, or (ii) is eligible for preferential treatment under the tax laws of a foreign jurisdiction because the plan provides for broad-based employee participation); provided that a Discretionary Transaction that meets the conditions of paragraph (c)(2) of this section also shall be exempt;

(4) Any grant or award of an option, stock appreciation right or other equity compensation pursuant to a plan that, by its terms:

(i) Permits directors or executive officers to receive grants or awards; and

(ii) Either:

(A) States the amount and price of securities to be awarded to designated directors and executive officers or categories of directors and executive officers (though not necessarily to others who may participate in the plan) and specifies the timing of awards to directors and executive officers; or

(B) Sets forth a formula that determines the amount, price and timing, using objective criteria (such as earnings of the issuer, value of the securities, years of service, job classification, and compensation levels);

(5) Any exercise, conversion or termination of a derivative security that the director or executive officer did not write or acquire during the blackout period (as defined in [Item]100(b)) in question, or while aware of the actual or approximate beginning or ending dates of that blackout period (whether or not the director or executive officer received notice of the blackout period as required by Section 306(a)(6) of the Sarbanes–Oxley Act of 2002); and either:

(i) The derivative security, by its terms, may be exercised, converted or terminated only on a fixed date, with no discretionary provision for earlier exercise, conversion or termination; or

(ii) The derivative security is exercised, converted or terminated by a counterparty and the director or executive officer does not exercise any influence on the counterparty with respect to whether or when to exercise, convert or terminate the derivative security;

(6) Any acquisition or disposition of equity securities involving a bona fide gift or a transfer by will or the laws of descent and distribution;

(7) Any acquisition or disposition of equity securities pursuant to a domestic relations order, as defined in the Internal Revenue Code or Title I of the Employment Retirement Income Security Act of 1974, or the rules thereunder;

(8) Any sale or other disposition of equity securities compelled by the laws or other requirements of an applicable jurisdiction;

(9) Any acquisition or disposition of equity securities in connection with a merger, acquisition, divestiture or similar transaction occurring by operation of law; and

(10) The increase or decrease in the number of equity securities held as a result of a stock split or stock dividend applying equally to all securities of that class, including a stock dividend in which equity securities of a different issuer are distributed; and the acquisition of rights, such as shareholder or pre-emptive rights, pursuant to a pro rata grant to all holders of the same class of equity securities.

Item 102. Exceptions to definition of blackout period.

The term "blackout period," as defined in [Item] 100(b), does not include:

(a) A regularly scheduled period in which participants and beneficiaries may not purchase, sell or otherwise acquire or transfer an interest in any equity security of an issuer, if a description of such period, including its frequency and duration and the plan transactions to be suspended or otherwise affected, is:

(1) Incorporated into the individual account plan or included in the documents or instruments under which the plan operates; and

(2) Disclosed to an employee before he or she formally enrolls, or within 30 days following formal enrollment, as a participant under the individual account plan or within 30 days after the adoption of an amendment to the plan. For purposes of this paragraph (a)(2), the disclosure may be provided in any graphic form that is reasonably accessible to the employee; or

(b) Any trading suspension described in [Item] 100(b) that is imposed in connection with a corporate merger, acquisition, divestiture or similar transaction involving the plan or plan sponsor, the principal purpose of which is to permit persons affiliated with the acquired or divested entity to become participants or beneficiaries, or to cease to be participants or beneficiaries, in an individual account plan; provided that the persons who become participants or beneficiaries in an individual account plan are not able to participate in the same class of equity securities after the merger, acquisition, divestiture or similar transaction as before the transaction.

Item 103. Issuer right of recovery; right of action by equity security owner.

(a) Recovery of profits. Section 306(a)(2) of the Sarbanes–Oxley Act of 2002 provides that any profit realized by a director or executive officer from any purchase, sale or other acquisition or transfer of any equity security of an issuer in violation of section 306(a)(1) of that Act will inure to and be recoverable by the issuer, regardless of any intention on the part of the director or executive officer in entering into the transaction.

(b) Actions to recover profit. Section 306(a)(2) of the Sarbanes–Oxley Act of 2002 provides that an action to recover profit may be instituted at law or in equity in any court of competent jurisdiction by the issuer, or by the owner of any equity security of the issuer in the name and on behalf of the issuer if the issuer fails or refuses to bring such action within 60 days after the date of request, or fails diligently to prosecute the action thereafter, except that no such suit may be brought more than two years after the date on which such profit was realized.

(c) Measurement of profit.

(1) In determining the profit recoverable in an action undertaken pursuant to section 306(a)(2) of the Sarbanes–Oxley Act of 2002 from a transaction that involves a purchase, sale or other acquisition or transfer (other than a grant, exercise, conversion or termination of a derivative security) in violation of section 306(a)(1) of that Act of an equity security of an issuer that is registered pursuant to section 12(b) or 12(g) of the Exchange Act and listed on a national securities exchange or listed in an automated inter-dealer quotation system of a national securities association, profit (including any loss avoided) may be measured by comparing the difference between the amount paid or received for the equity security on the date of the transaction during the blackout period and the average market price of the equity security calculated over the first three trading days after the ending date of the blackout period.

(2) In determining the profit recoverable in an action undertaken pursuant to section 306(a)(2) of the Sarbanes–Oxley Act of 2002 from a transaction that is not described in paragraph (c)(1) of this section, profit (including any loss avoided) may be measured in a manner that is consistent

with the objective of identifying the amount of any gain realized or loss avoided by a director or executive officer as a result of a transaction taking place in violation of section 306(a)(1) of that Act during the blackout period as opposed to taking place outside of such blackout period.

(3) The terms of this section do not limit in any respect the authority of the Commission to seek or determine remedies as the result of a transaction taking place in violation of section 306(a)(1) of the Sarbanes–Oxley Act.

Item 104. Notice.

(a) In any case in which a director or executive officer is subject to section 306(a)(1) of the Sarbanes–Oxley Act of 2002 in connection with a blackout period (as defined in [Item]100(b)) with respect to any equity security, the issuer of the equity security must timely notify each director or officer and the Commission of the blackout period.

(b) For purposes of this section:

(1) The notice must include:

(i) The reason or reasons for the blackout period;

(ii) A description of the plan transactions to be suspended during, or otherwise affected by, the blackout period;

(iii) A description of the class of equity securities subject to the blackout period;

(iv) The length of the blackout period by reference to:

(A) The actual or expected beginning date and ending date of the blackout period; or

(B) The calendar week during which the blackout period is expected to begin and the calendar week during which the blackout period is expected to end, provided that the notice to directors and executive officers describes how, during such week or weeks, a director or executive officer may obtain, without charge, information as to whether the blackout period has begun or ended; and provided further that the notice to the Commission describes how, during the blackout period and for a period of two years after the ending date of the blackout period, a security holder or other interested person may obtain, without charge, the actual beginning and ending dates of the blackout period.

(C) For purposes of this paragraph (b)(1)(iv), a calendar week means a seven-day period beginning on Sunday and ending on Saturday; and

(v) The name, address and telephone number of the person designated by the issuer to respond to inquiries about the blackout period, or, in the absence of such a designation, the issuer's human resources director or person performing equivalent functions.

(2) (i) Notice to an affected director or executive officer will be considered timely if the notice described in paragraph (b)(1) of this section is provided (in graphic form that is reasonably accessible to the recipient):

(A) No later than five business days after the issuer receives the notice required by section 101(i)(2)(E) of the Employment Retirement Income Security Act of 1974; or

(B) If no such notice is received by the issuer, a date that is at least 15 calendar days before the actual or expected beginning date of the blackout period.

(ii) Notwithstanding paragraph (b)(2)(i) of this section, the requirement to give advance notice will not apply in any case in which the inability to provide advance notice of the blackout period is due to events that were unforeseeable to, or circumstances that were beyond the reasonable control of, the issuer, and the issuer reasonably so determines in writing. Determinations described in the preceding sentence must be dated and signed by an authorized representative of the issuer. In any case in which this exception to the advance notice requirement applies, the issuer must provide the notice described in paragraph (b)(1) of this section, as well as a copy of the written determination, to all affected directors and executive officers as soon as reasonably practicable.

(iii) If there is a subsequent change in the beginning or ending dates of the blackout period as provided in the notice to directors and executive officers under paragraph (b)(2)(i) of this section, an issuer must provide directors and executive officers with an updated notice explaining the reasons for the change in the date or dates and identifying all material changes in the information contained in the prior notice. The updated notice is required to be provided as soon as reasonably practicable, unless such notice in advance of the termination of a blackout period is impracticable.

(3) Notice to the Commission will be considered timely if:

(i) The issuer, except as provided in paragraph (b)(3)(ii) of this section, files a current report on Form 8–K within the time prescribed for filing the report under the instructions for the form; or

(ii) In the case of a foreign private issuer (as defined in [Item]3b–4(c) of this chapter), the issuer includes the information set forth in paragraph (b)(1) of this section in the first annual report on Form 20–F or 40–F required to be filed after the receipt of the notice of a blackout period required by 29 CFR 2520.101–3(c) within the time prescribed for filing the report under the instructions for the form or in an earlier filed report on Form 6–K.

(iii) If there is a subsequent change in the beginning or ending dates of the blackout period as provided in the notice to the Commission under paragraph (b)(3)(i) of this section, an issuer must file a current report on Form 8–K containing the updated beginning or ending dates of the blackout period, explaining the reasons for the change in the date or dates and identifying all material changes in the information contained in the prior report. The updated notice is required to be provided as soon as reasonably practicable.

L. SECURITIES LITIGATION UNIFORM STANDARDS ACT OF 1998

Contents

An Act to amend the Securities Act of 1933 and the Securities Exchange Act of 1934 to limit the conduct of securities class actions under State law, and for other purposes.

SEC. 1. SHORT TITLE.

This Act may be cited as the "Securities Litigation Uniform Standards Act of 1998".

SEC. 2. FINDINGS.

The Congress finds that—

(1) the Private Securities Litigation Reform Act of 1995 sought to prevent abuses in private securities fraud lawsuits;

(2) since enactment of that legislation, considerable evidence has been presented to Congress that a number of securities class action lawsuits have shifted from Federal to State courts;

(3) this shift has prevented that Act from fully achieving its objectives;

(4) State securities regulation is of continuing importance, together with Federal regulation of securities, to protect investors and promote strong financial markets; and

(5) in order to prevent certain State private securities class action lawsuits alleging fraud from being used to frustrate the objectives of the Private Securities Litigation Reform Act of 1995, it is appropriate to enact national standards for securities class action lawsuits involving nationally traded securities, while preserving the appropriate enforcement powers of State securities regulators and not changing the current treatment of individual lawsuits.

TITLE I—SECURITIES LITIGATION UNIFORM STANDARDS

SEC. 101. LIMITATION ON REMEDIES.

(a) AMENDMENTS TO THE SECURITIES ACT OF 1933.—

(1) AMENDMENT.—Section 16 of the Securities Act of 1933 (15 U.S.C. 77p) is amended to read as follows:

"SEC. 16. ADDITIONAL REMEDIES; LIMITATION ON REMEDIES.

"(a) REMEDIES ADDITIONAL.—Except as provided in subsection (b), the rights and remedies provided by this title shall be in addition to any and all other rights and remedies that may exist at law or in equity.

"(b) CLASS ACTION LIMITATIONS.—No covered class action based upon the statutory or common law of any State or subdivision thereof may be maintained in any State or Federal court by any private party alleging—

"(1) an untrue statement or omission of a material fact in connection with the purchase or sale of a covered security; or

"(2) that the defendant used or employed any manipulative or deceptive device or contrivance in connection with the purchase or sale of a covered security.

"(c) REMOVAL OF COVERED CLASS ACTIONS.—Any covered class action brought in any State court involving a covered security, as set forth in subsection (b), shall be removable to the Federal district court for the district in which the action is pending, and shall be subject to subsection (b).

"(d) PRESERVATION OF CERTAIN ACTIONS.—

"(1) ACTIONS UNDER STATE LAW OF STATE OF INCORPORATION.—

"(A) ACTIONS PRESERVED.—Notwithstanding subsection (b) or (c), a covered class action described in subparagraph (B) of this paragraph that is based upon the statutory or common law of the State in which the issuer is incorporated (in the case of a corporation) or organized (in the case of any other entity) may be maintained in a State or Federal court by a private party.

"(B) PERMISSIBLE ACTIONS.—A covered class action is described in this subparagraph if it involves—

"(i) the purchase or sale of securities by the issuer or an affiliate of the issuer exclusively from or to holders of equity securities of the issuer; or

"(ii) any recommendation, position, or other communication with respect to the sale of securities of the issuer that—

"(I) is made by or on behalf of the issuer or an affiliate of the issuer to holders of equity securities of the issuer; and

"(II) concerns decisions of those equity holders with respect to voting their securities, acting in response to a tender or exchange offer, or exercising dissenters'' or appraisal rights.

"(2) STATE ACTIONS.—

"(A) IN GENERAL.—Notwithstanding any other provision of this section, nothing in this section may be construed to preclude a State or political subdivision thereof or a State pension plan from bringing an action involving a covered security on its own behalf, or as a member of a class comprised solely of other States, political subdivisions, or State pension plans that are named plaintiffs, and that have authorized participation, in such action.

"(B) STATE PENSION PLAN DEFINED.—For purposes of this paragraph, the term 'State pension plan' means a pension plan established and maintained for its employees by the government of the State or political subdivision thereof, or by any agency or instrumentality thereof.

"(3) ACTIONS UNDER CONTRACTUAL AGREEMENTS BETWEEN ISSUERS AND INDENTURE TRUSTEES.—Notwithstanding subsection (b) or (c), a covered class action that seeks to enforce a contractual agreement between an issuer and an indenture trustee may be maintained in a State or Federal court by a party to the agreement or a successor to such party.

"(4) REMAND OF REMOVED ACTIONS.—In an action that has been removed from a State court pursuant to subsection (c), if the Federal court determines that the action may be maintained in State court pursuant to this subsection, the Federal court shall remand such action to such State court.

"(e) PRESERVATION OF STATE JURISDICTION.—The securities commission (or any agency or office performing like functions) of any State shall retain jurisdiction under the laws of such State to investigate and bring enforcement actions.

"(f) DEFINITIONS.—For purposes of this section, the following definitions shall apply:

"(1) AFFILIATE OF THE ISSUER.—The term 'affiliate of the issuer' means a person that directly or indirectly, through one or more intermediaries, controls or is controlled by or is under common control with, the issuer.

"(2) COVERED CLASS ACTION—

"(A) IN GENERAL.—The term 'covered class action' means—

"(i) any single lawsuit in which—

"(I) damages are sought on behalf of more than 50 persons or prospective class members, and questions of law or fact common to those persons or members of the prospective class, without reference to issues of individualized reliance on an alleged misstatement or omission, predominate over any questions affecting only individual persons or members; or

"(II) one or more named parties seek to recover damages on a representative basis on behalf of themselves and other unnamed parties similarly situated, and questions of law or fact common to those persons or members of the prospective class predominate over any questions affecting only individual persons or members; or

"(ii) any group of lawsuits filed in or pending in the same court and involving common questions of law or fact, in which—

"(I) damages are sought on behalf of more than 50 persons; and

"(II) the lawsuits are joined, consolidated, or otherwise proceed as a single action for any purpose.

"(B) EXCEPTION FOR DERIVATIVE ACTIONS.—Notwithstanding subparagraph (A), the term 'covered class action' does not include an exclusively derivative action brought by one or more shareholders on behalf of a corporation.

"(C) COUNTING OF CERTAIN CLASS MEMBERS.—For purposes of this paragraph, a corporation, investment company, pension plan, partnership, or other entity, shall be treated as one person or prospective class member, but only if the entity is not established for the purpose of participating in the action.

"(D) RULE OF CONSTRUCTION.—Nothing in this paragraph shall be construed to affect the discretion of a State court in determining whether actions filed in such court should be joined, consolidated, or otherwise allowed to proceed as a single action.

"(3) COVERED SECURITY.—The term 'covered security' means a security that satisfies the standards for a covered security specified in paragraph (1) or (2) of section 18(b) at the time during which it is alleged that the misrepresentation, omission, or manipulative or deceptive conduct occurred, except that such term shall not include any debt security that is exempt from registration under this title pursuant to rules issued by the Commission under section 4(2).".

(2) CIRCUMVENTION OF STAY OF DISCOVERY.—Section 27(b) of the Securities Act of 1933 (15 U.S.C. 77z–1(b)) is amended by inserting after paragraph (3) the following new paragraph:

"(4) CIRCUMVENTION OF STAY OF DISCOVERY.—Upon a proper showing, a court may stay discovery proceedings in any private action in a State court as necessary in aid of its jurisdiction, or to protect or effectuate its judgments, in an action subject to a stay of discovery pursuant to this subsection.".

(3) CONFORMING AMENDMENTS.—Section 22(a) of the Securities Act of 1933 (15 U.S.C. 77v(a)) is amended—

(A) by inserting "except as provided in section 16 with respect to covered class actions," after "Territorial courts,"; and

(B) by striking "No case" and inserting"Except as provided in section 16(c), no case".

(b) AMENDMENTS TO THE SECURITIES EXCHANGE ACT OF 1934—

(1) AMENDMENT.—Section 28 of the Securities Exchange Act of 1934 (15 U.S.C. 78bb) is amended—

(A) in subsection (a), by striking "The rights and remedies" and inserting "Except as provided in subsection (f), the rights and remedies"; and

(B) by adding at the end the following new subsection:

"(f) LIMITATIONS ON REMEDIES.—

on thereof may be maintained in any State or Federal court by any private party alleging—

"(A) a misrepresentation or omission of a material fact in connection with the purchase or sale of a covered security; or

"(B) that the defendant used or employed any manipulative or deceptive device or contrivance in connection with the purchase or sale of a covered security.

"(2) REMOVAL OF COVERED CLASS ACTIONS.—Any covered class action brought in any State court involving a covered security, as set forth in paragraph (1), shall be removable to the Federal district court for the district in which the action is pending, and shall be subject to paragraph (1).

"(3) PRESERVATION OF CERTAIN ACTIONS—

"(A) ACTIONS UNDER STATE LAW OF STATE INCORPORATION.—

"(i) ACTIONS PRESERVED.—Notwithstanding paragraph (1) or (2), a covered class action described in clause (ii) of this subparagraph that is based upon the statutory or common law of the State in which the issuer is incorporated (in the case of a corporation) or organized (in the case of any other entity) may be maintained in a State or Federal court by a private party.

"(ii) PERMISSIBLE ACTIONS.—A covered class action is described in this clause if it involves—

"(I) the purchase or sale of securities by the issuer or an affiliate of the issuer exclusively from or to holders of equity securities of the issuer; or

"(II) any recommendation, position, or other communication with respect to the sale of securities of an issuer that—

"(aa) is made by or on behalf of the issuer or an affiliate of the issuer to holders of equity securities of the issuer; and

"(bb) concerns decisions of such equity holders with respect to voting their securities, acting in response to a tender or exchange offer, or exercising dissenters' or appraisal rights.

"(B) STATE ACTIONS.—

"(i) IN GENERAL.—Notwithstanding any other provision of this subsection, nothing in this subsection may be construed to preclude a State or political subdivision thereof or a State pension plan from bringing an action involving a covered security on its own behalf, or as a member of a class comprised solely of other States, political subdivisions, or State pension plans that are named plaintiffs, and that have authorized participation, in such action.

"(ii) STATE PENSION PLAN DEFINED.—For purposes of this subparagraph, the term 'State pension plan' means a pension plan established and maintained for its employees by the government of a State or political subdivision thereof, or by any agency or instrumentality thereof.

"(C) ACTIONS UNDER CONTRACTUAL AGREEMENTS BETWEEN ISSUERS AND INDENTURE TRUSTEES.—Notwithstanding paragraph (1) or (2), a covered class action that seeks to enforce a contractual agreement between an issuer and an indenture trustee may be maintained in a State or Federal court by a party to the agreement or a successor to such party.

"(D) REMAND OF REMOVED ACTIONS.—In an action that has been removed from a State court pursuant to paragraph (2), if the Federal court determines that the action may be maintained in State court pursuant to this subsection, the Federal court shall remand such action to such State court.

"(4) PRESERVATION OF STATE JURISDICTION.—The securities commission (or any agency or office performing like functions) of any State shall retain jurisdiction under the laws of such State to investigate and bring enforcement actions.

"(5) DEFINITIONS.—For purposes of this subsection, the following definitions shall apply:

"(A) AFFILIATE OF THE ISSUER.—The term 'affiliate of the issuer' means a person that directly or indirectly, through one or more intermediaries, controls or is controlled by or is under common control with, the issuer.

"(B) COVERED CLASS ACTION.—The term 'covered class action' means—

"(i) any single lawsuit in which—

"(I) damages are sought on behalf of more than 50 persons or prospective class members, and questions of law or fact common to those persons or members of the prospective class, without reference to issues of individualized reliance on an alleged misstatement or omission, predominate over any questions affecting only individual persons or members; or

"(II) one or more named parties seek to recover damages on a representative basis on behalf of themselves and other unnamed parties similarly situated, and questions of law or fact common to those persons or members of the prospective class predominate over any questions affecting only individual persons or members; or

"(ii) any group of lawsuits filed in or pending in the same court and involving common questions of law or fact, in which—

"(I) damages are sought on behalf of more than 50 persons; and

"(II) the lawsuits are joined, consolidated, or otherwise proceed as a single action for any purpose.

"(C) EXCEPTION FOR DERIVATIVE ACTIONS.—Notwithstanding subparagraph (B), the term 'covered class action' does not include an exclusively derivative action brought by one or more shareholders on behalf of a corporation.

"(D) COUNTING OF CERTAIN CLASS MEMBERS.—For purposes of this paragraph, a corporation, investment company, pension plan, partnership, or other entity, shall be treated as one person or prospective class member, but only if the entity is not established for the purpose of participating in the action.

"(E) COVERED SECURITY.—The term 'covered security' means a security that satisfies the standards for a covered security specified in paragraph (1) or (2) of section 18(b) of the Securities Act of 1933, at the time during which it is alleged that the misrepresentation, omission, or manipulative or deceptive conduct occurred, except that such term shall not include any debt security that is exempt from registration under the Securities Act of 1933 pursuant to rules issued by the Commission under section 4(2) of that Act.

"(F) RULE OF CONSTRUCTION.—Nothing in this paragraph shall be construed to affect the discretion of a State court in determining whether actions filed in such court should be joined, consolidated, or otherwise allowed to proceed as a single action.".

(2) CIRCUMVENTION OF STAY OF DISCOVERY.—Section 21D(b)(3) of the Securities Exchange Act of 1934 (15 U.S.C. 78u–4(b)(3)) is amended by adding at the end the following new subparagraph:

"(D) CIRCUMVENTION OF STAY OF DISCOVERY.—Upon a proper showing, a court may stay discovery proceedings in any private action in a State court, as necessary in aid of its jurisdiction, or to protect or effectuate its judgments, in an action subject to a stay of discovery pursuant to this paragraph.".

(c) APPLICABILITY.—The amendments made by this section shall not affect or apply to any action commenced before and pending on the date of enactment of this Act.

SEC. 102. PROMOTION OF RECIPROCAL SUBPOENA ENFORCEMENT.

(a) COMMISSION ACTION.—The Securities and Exchange Commission, in consultation with State securities commissions (or any agencies or offices performing like functions), shall seek to encourage the adoption of State laws providing for reciprocal enforcement by State securities commissions of subpoenas issued by another State securities commission seeking to compel persons to attend, testify in, or produce documents or records in connection with an action or investigation by a State securities commission of an alleged violation of State securities laws.

(b) REPORT.—Not later than 24 months after the date of enactment of this Act, the Securities and Exchange Commission (hereafter in this section referred to as the "Commission") shall submit a report to the Congress—

(1) identifying the States that have adopted laws described in subsection (a);

(2) describing the actions undertaken by the Commission and State securities commissions to promote the adoption of such laws; and

(3) identifying any further actions that the Commission recommends for such purposes.

M. SARBANES–OXLEY ACT OF 2002

Pub. L. No. 107–204

(codified as amended in scattered sections of 15 U.S.C.)

An Act To protect investors by improving the accuracy and reliability of corporate disclosures made pursuant to the securities laws, and for other purposes.

Be it enacted by the Senate and House of Representatives of the United States of America in Congress assembled,

Contents

Sec.

TITLE IV—ENHANCED FINANCIAL DISCLOSURES

TITLE V—ANALYST CONFLICTS OF INTEREST

TITLE VI—COMMISSION RESOURCES AND AUTHORITY

TITLE VII—STUDIES AND REPORTS

TITLE VIII—CORPORATE AND CRIMINAL FRAUD ACCOUNTABILITY

TITLE IX—WHITE–COLLAR CRIME PENALTY ENHANCEMENTS

SEC. 1. SHORT TITLE; TABLE OF CONTENTS.

* * *

SEC. 2. DEFINITIONS.

(a) IN GENERAL.—In this Act, the following definitions shall apply:

(1) APPROPRIATE STATE REGULATORY AUTHORITY.—The term "appropriate State regulatory authority" means the State agency or other authority responsible for the licensure or other regulation of the practice of accounting in the State or States having jurisdiction over a registered public accounting firm or associated person thereof, with respect to the matter in question.

(2) AUDIT.—The term "audit" means an examination of the financial statements of any issuer by an independent public accounting firm in accordance with the rules of the Board or the Commission (or, for the period preceding the adoption of applicable rules of the Board under section 103, in accordance with then-applicable generally accepted auditing and related standards for such purposes), for the purpose of expressing an opinion on such statements.

(3) AUDIT COMMITTEE.—The term "audit committee" means—

(A) a committee (or equivalent body) established by and amongst the board of directors of an issuer for the purpose of overseeing the accounting and financial reporting processes of the issuer and audits of the financial statements of the issuer; and

(B) if no such committee exists with respect to an issuer, the entire board of directors of the issuer.

(4) AUDIT REPORT.—The term "audit report" means a document or other record—

(A) prepared following an audit performed for purposes of compliance by an issuer with the requirements of the securities laws; and

(B) in which a public accounting firm either—

(i) sets forth the opinion of that firm regarding a financial statement, report, or other document; or

(ii) asserts that no such opinion can be expressed.

(5) BOARD.—The term "Board" means the Public Company Accounting Oversight Board established under section 101.

(6) COMMISSION.—The term "Commission" means the Securities and Exchange Commission.

(7) ISSUER.—The term "issuer" means an issuer (as defined in section 3 of the Securities Exchange Act of 1934 (15 U.S.C. 78c)), the securities of which are registered under section 12 of that Act (15 U.S.C. 78l), or that is required to file reports under section 15(d) (15 U.S.C. 78o(d)), or that files or has filed a registration statement that has not yet become effective under the Securities Act of 1933 (15 U.S.C. 77a et seq.), and that it has not withdrawn.

(8) NON–AUDIT SERVICES.—The term "non-audit services" means any professional services provided to an issuer by a registered public accounting firm, other than those provided to an issuer in connection with an audit or a review of the financial statements of an issuer.

(9) PERSON ASSOCIATED WITH A PUBLIC ACCOUNTING FIRM.—

(A) IN GENERAL.—The terms "person associated with a public accounting firm" (or with a "registered public accounting firm") and "associated person of a public accounting firm" (or of a "registered public accounting firm") mean any individual proprietor, partner, shareholder, principal, accountant, or other professional employee of a public accounting firm, or any other independent contractor or entity that, in connection with the preparation or issuance of any audit report—

(i) shares in the profits of, or receives compensation in any other form from, that firm; or

(ii) participates as agent or otherwise on behalf of such accounting firm in any activity of that firm.

(B) EXEMPTION AUTHORITY.—The Board may, by rule, exempt persons engaged only in ministerial tasks from the definition in subparagraph (A), to the extent that the Board determines that any such exemption is consistent with the purposes of this Act, the public interest, or the protection of investors.

(10) PROFESSIONAL STANDARDS.—The term "professional standards" means—

(A) accounting principles that are—

(i) established by the standard setting body described in section 19(b) of the Securities Act of 1933, as amended by this Act, or prescribed by the Commission under section 19(a) of that Act (15 U.S.C. 17a(s)) or section 13(b) of the Securities Exchange Act of 1934 (15 U.S.C. 78a(m)); and

(ii) relevant to audit reports for particular issuers, or dealt with in the quality control system of a particular registered public accounting firm; and

(B) auditing standards, standards for attestation engagements, quality control policies and procedures, ethical and competency standards, and independence standards (including rules implementing title II) that the Board or the Commission determines—

(i) relate to the preparation or issuance of audit reports for issuers; and

(ii) are established or adopted by the Board under section 103(a), or are promulgated as rules of the Commission.

(11) PUBLIC ACCOUNTING FIRM.—The term "public accounting firm" means—

(A) a proprietorship, partnership, incorporated association, corporation, limited liability company, limited liability partnership, or other legal entity that is engaged in the practice of public accounting or preparing or issuing audit reports; and

(B) to the extent so designated by the rules of the Board, any associated person of any entity described in subparagraph (A).

(12) REGISTERED PUBLIC ACCOUNTING FIRM.—The term "registered public accounting firm" means a public accounting firm registered with the Board in accordance with this Act.

(13) RULES OF THE BOARD.—The term "rules of the Board" means the bylaws and rules of the Board (as submitted to, and approved, modified, or amended by the Commission, in accordance with section 107), and those stated policies, practices, and interpretations of the Board that the Commission, by rule, may deem to be rules of the Board, as necessary or appropriate in the public interest or for the protection of investors.

(14) SECURITY.—The term "security" has the same meaning as in section 3(a) of the Securities Exchange Act of 1934 (15 U.S.C. 78c(a)).

(15) SECURITIES LAWS.—The term "securities laws" means the provisions of law referred to in section 3(a)(47) of the Securities Exchange Act of 1934 (15 U.S.C. 78c(a)(47)), as amended by this Act, and includes the rules, regulations, and orders issued by the Commission thereunder.

(16) STATE.—The term "State" means any State of the United States, the District of Columbia, Puerto Rico, the Virgin Islands, or any other territory or possession of the United States.

(b) CONFORMING AMENDMENT.—Section 3(a)(47) of the Securities Exchange Act of 1934 (15 U.S.C. 78c(a)(47)) is amended by inserting "the Sarbanes–Oxley Act of 2002," before "the Public".

SEC. 3. COMMISSION RULES AND ENFORCEMENT.

(a) REGULATORY ACTION.—The Commission shall promulgate such rules and regulations, as may be necessary or appropriate in the public interest or for the protection of investors, and in furtherance of this Act.

(b) ENFORCEMENT.—

(1) IN GENERAL.—A violation by any person of this Act, any rule or regulation of the Commission issued under this Act, or any rule of the Board shall be treated for all purposes in the same manner as a violation of the Securities Exchange Act of 1934 (15 U.S.C. 78a et seq.) or the rules and regulations issued thereunder, consistent with the provisions of this Act, and any such person shall be subject to the same penalties, and to the same extent, as for a violation of that Act or such rules or regulations.

(2) INVESTIGATIONS, INJUNCTIONS, AND PROSECUTION OF OFFENSES.—Section 21 of the Securities Exchange Act of 1934 (15 U.S.C. 78u) is amended—

(A) in subsection (a)(1), by inserting "the rules of the Public Company Accounting Oversight Board, of which such person is a registered public accounting firm or a person associated with such a firm," after "is a participant,";

(B) in subsection (d)(1), by inserting "the rules of the Public Company Accounting Oversight Board, of which such person is a registered public accounting firm or a person associated with such a firm," after "is a participant,";

(C) in subsection (e), by inserting "the rules of the Public Company Accounting Oversight Board, of which such person is a registered public accounting firm or a person associated with such a firm," after "is a participant,"; and

(D) in subsection (f), by inserting "or the Public Company Accounting Oversight Board" after "self-regulatory organization" each place that term appears.

(3) CEASE–AND–DESIST PROCEEDINGS.—Section 21C(c)(2) of the Securities Exchange Act of 1934 (15 U.S.C. 78u–3(c)(2)) is amended by inserting "registered public accounting firm (as defined in section 2 of the Sarbanes-Oxley Act of 2002)," after "government securities dealer,".

(4) ENFORCEMENT BY FEDERAL BANKING AGENCIES.—Section 12(i) of the Securities Exchange Act of 1934 (15 U.S.C. 78l(i)) is amended by—

(A) striking "sections 12," each place it appears and inserting "sections 10A(m), 12,"; and

(B) striking "and 16," each place it appears and inserting "and 16 of this Act, and sections 302, 303, 304, 306, 401(b), 404, 406, and 407 of the Sarbanes–Oxley Act of 2002,".

(c) EFFECT ON COMMISSION AUTHORITY.—Nothing in this Act or the rules of the Board shall be construed to impair or limit—

(1) the authority of the Commission to regulate the accounting profession, accounting firms, or persons associated with such firms for purposes of enforcement of the securities laws;

(2) the authority of the Commission to set standards for accounting or auditing practices or auditor independence, derived from other provisions of the securities laws or the rules or regulations thereunder, for purposes of the preparation and issuance of any audit report, or otherwise under applicable law; or

(3) the ability of the Commission to take, on the initiative of the Commission, legal, administrative, or disciplinary action against any registered public accounting firm or any associated person thereof.

TITLE I—PUBLIC COMPANY ACCOUNTING OVERSIGHT BOARD

SEC. 101. ESTABLISHMENT; ADMINISTRATIVE PROVISIONS.

(a) ESTABLISHMENT OF BOARD.—There is established the Public Company Accounting Oversight Board, to oversee the audit of public companies that are subject to the securities laws, and related matters, in order to protect the interests of investors and further the public interest in the preparation of informative, accurate, and independent audit reports for companies the securities of which are sold to, and held by and for, public investors. The Board shall be a body corporate, operate as a nonprofit corporation, and have succession until dissolved by an Act of Congress.

(b) STATUS.—The Board shall not be an agency or establishment of the United States Government, and, except as otherwise provided in this Act, shall be subject to, and have all the powers conferred upon a nonprofit corporation by, the District of Columbia Nonprofit Corporation Act. No member or person employed by, or agent for, the Board shall be deemed to be an officer or employee of or agent for the Federal Government by reason of such service.

(c) DUTIES OF THE BOARD.—The Board shall, subject to action by the Commission under section 107, and once a determination is made by the Commission under subsection (d) of this section—

(1) register public accounting firms that prepare audit reports for issuers, in accordance with section 102;

(2) establish or adopt, or both, by rule, auditing, quality control, ethics, independence, and other standards relating to the preparation of audit reports for issuers, in accordance with section 103;

(3) conduct inspections of registered public accounting firms, in accordance with section 104 and the rules of the Board;

(4) conduct investigations and disciplinary proceedings concerning, and impose appropriate sanctions where justified upon, registered public accounting firms and associated persons of such firms, in accordance with section 105;

(5) perform such other duties or functions as the Board (or the Commission, by rule or order) determines are necessary or appropriate to promote high professional standards among, and improve the quality of audit services offered by, registered public accounting firms and associated persons thereof, or otherwise to carry out this Act, in order to protect investors, or to further the public interest;

(6) enforce compliance with this Act, the rules of the Board, professional standards, and the securities laws relating to the preparation and issuance of audit reports and the obligations and liabilities of accountants with respect thereto, by registered public accounting firms and associated persons thereof; and

(7) set the budget and manage the operations of the Board and the staff of the Board.

(d) COMMISSION DETERMINATION.—The members of the Board shall take such action (including hiring of staff, proposal of rules, and adoption of initial and transitional auditing and other professional standards) as may be necessary or appropriate to enable the Commission to determine, not later than 270 days after the date of enactment of this Act, that the Board is so organized and has the capacity to carry out the requirements of this title, and to enforce compliance with this title by registered public accounting firms and associated persons thereof. The Commission shall be responsible, prior to the appointment of the Board, for the planning for the establishment and administrative transition to the Board's operation.

(e) BOARD MEMBERSHIP.—

(1) COMPOSITION.—The Board shall have 5 members, appointed from among prominent individuals of integrity and reputation who have a demonstrated commitment to the interests of investors and the public, and an understanding of the responsibilities for and nature of the financial disclosures required of issuers under the securities laws and the obligations of accountants with respect to the preparation and issuance of audit reports with respect to such disclosures.

(2) LIMITATION.—Two members, and only 2 members, of the Board shall be or have been certified public accountants pursuant to the laws of 1 or more States, provided that, if 1 of those 2 members is the chairperson, he or she may not have been a practicing certified public accountant for at least 5 years prior to his or her appointment to the Board.

(3) FULL-TIME INDEPENDENT SERVICE.—Each member of the Board shall serve on a full-time basis, and may not, concurrent with service on the Board, be employed by any other person or engage in any other professional or business activity. No member of the Board may share in any of the profits of, or receive payments from, a public accounting firm (or any other person, as determined by rule of the Commission), other than fixed continuing payments, subject to such conditions as the Commission may impose, under standard arrangements for the retirement of members of public accounting firms.

(4) APPOINTMENT OF BOARD MEMBERS.—

(A) INITIAL BOARD.—Not later than 90 days after the date of enactment of this Act, the Commission, after consultation with the Chairman of the Board of Governors of the Federal Reserve System and the Secretary of the Treasury, shall appoint the chairperson and other initial members of the Board, and shall designate a term of service for each.

(B) VACANCIES.—A vacancy on the Board shall not affect the powers of the Board, but shall be filled in the same manner as provided for appointments under this section.

(5) TERM OF SERVICE.—

(A) IN GENERAL.—The term of service of each Board member shall be 5 years, and until a successor is appointed, except that—

(i) the terms of office of the initial Board members (other than the chairperson) shall expire in annual increments, 1 on each of the first 4 anniversaries of the initial date of appointment; and

(ii) any Board member appointed to fill a vacancy occurring before the expiration of the term for which the predecessor was appointed shall be appointed only for the remainder of that term.

(B) TERM LIMITATION.—No person may serve as a member of the Board, or as chairperson of the Board, for more than 2 terms, whether or not such terms of service are consecutive.

(6) REMOVAL FROM OFFICE.—A member of the Board may be removed by the Commission from office, in accordance with section 107(d)(3), for good cause shown before the expiration of the term of that member.

(f) POWERS OF THE BOARD.—In addition to any authority granted to the Board otherwise in this Act, the Board shall have the power, subject to section 107—

(1) to sue and be sued, complain and defend, in its corporate name and through its own counsel, with the approval of the Commission, in any Federal, State, or other court;

(2) to conduct its operations and maintain offices, and to exercise all other rights and powers authorized by this Act, in any State, without regard to any qualification, licensing, or other provision of law in effect in such State (or a political subdivision thereof);

(3) to lease, purchase, accept gifts or donations of or otherwise acquire, improve, use, sell, exchange, or convey, all of or an interest in any property, wherever situated;

(4) to appoint such employees, accountants, attorneys, and other agents as may be necessary or appropriate, and to determine their qualifications, define their duties, and fix their salaries or other compensation (at a level that is comparable to private sector self-regulatory, accounting, technical, supervisory, or other staff or management positions);

(5) to allocate, assess, and collect accounting support fees established pursuant to section 109, for the Board, and other fees and charges imposed under this title; and

(6) to enter into contracts, execute instruments, incur liabilities, and do any and all other acts and things necessary, appropriate, or incidental to the conduct of its operations and the exercise of its obligations, rights, and powers imposed or granted by this title.

(g) RULES OF THE BOARD.—The rules of the Board shall, subject to the approval of the Commission—

(1) provide for the operation and administration of the Board, the exercise of its authority, and the performance of its responsibilities under this Act;

(2) permit, as the Board determines necessary or appropriate, delegation by the Board of any of its functions to an individual member or employee of the Board, or to a division of the Board, including functions with respect to hearing, determining, ordering, certifying, reporting, or otherwise acting as to any matter, except that—

(A) the Board shall retain a discretionary right to review any action pursuant to any such delegated function, upon its own motion;

(B) a person shall be entitled to a review by the Board with respect to any matter so delegated, and the decision of the Board upon such review shall be deemed to be the action of the Board for all purposes (including appeal or review thereof); and

(C) if the right to exercise a review described in subparagraph (A) is declined, or if no such review is sought within the time stated in the rules of the Board, then the action taken by the holder of such delegation shall for all purposes, including appeal or review thereof, be deemed to be the action of the Board;

(3) establish ethics rules and standards of conduct for Board members and staff, including a bar on practice before the Board (and the Commission, with respect to Board-related matters) of 1 year for former members of the Board, and appropriate periods (not to exceed 1 year) for former staff of the Board; and

(4) provide as otherwise required by this Act.

(h) ANNUAL REPORT TO THE COMMISSION.—The Board shall submit an annual report (including its audited financial statements) to the Commission, and the Commission shall transmit a copy of that report to the Committee on Banking, Housing, and Urban Affairs of the Senate, and the Committee on Financial Services of the House of Representatives, not later than 30 days after the date of receipt of that report by the Commission.

SEC. 102. REGISTRATION WITH THE BOARD.

(a) MANDATORY REGISTRATION.—Beginning 180 days after the date of the determination of the Commission under section 101(d), it shall be unlawful for any person that is not a registered public accounting firm to prepare or issue, or to participate in the preparation or issuance of, any audit report with respect to any issuer.

(b) APPLICATIONS FOR REGISTRATION.—

(1) FORM OF APPLICATION.—A public accounting firm shall use such form as the Board may prescribe, by rule, to apply for registration under this section.

(2) CONTENTS OF APPLICATIONS.—Each public accounting firm shall submit, as part of its application for registration, in such detail as the Board shall specify—

(A) the names of all issuers for which the firm prepared or issued audit reports during the immediately preceding calendar year, and for which the firm expects to prepare or issue audit reports during the current calendar year;

(B) the annual fees received by the firm from each such issuer for audit services, other accounting services, and non-audit services, respectively;

(C) such other current financial information for the most recently completed fiscal year of the firm as the Board may reasonably request;

(D) a statement of the quality control policies of the firm for its accounting and auditing practices;

(E) a list of all accountants associated with the firm who participate in or contribute to the preparation of audit reports, stating the license or certification number of each such person, as well as the State license numbers of the firm itself;

(F) information relating to criminal, civil, or administrative actions or disciplinary proceedings pending against the firm or any associated person of the firm in connection with any audit report;

(G) copies of any periodic or annual disclosure filed by an issuer with the Commission during the immediately preceding calendar year which discloses accounting disagreements between such issuer and the firm in connection with an audit report furnished or prepared by the firm for such issuer; and

(H) such other information as the rules of the Board or the Commission shall specify as necessary or appropriate in the public interest or for the protection of investors.

(3) CONSENTS.—Each application for registration under this subsection shall include—

(A) a consent executed by the public accounting firm to cooperation in and compliance with any request for testimony or the production of documents made by the Board in the furtherance of its authority and responsibilities under this title (and an agreement to secure and enforce similar consents from each of the associated persons of the public accounting firm as a condition of their continued employment by or other association with such firm); and

(B) a statement that such firm understands and agrees that cooperation and compliance, as described in the consent required by subparagraph (A), and the securing and enforcement of such consents from its associated persons, in accordance with the rules of the Board, shall be a condition to the continuing effectiveness of the registration of the firm with the Board.

(c) ACTION ON APPLICATIONS.—

(1) TIMING.—The Board shall approve a completed application for registration not later than 45 days after the date of receipt of the application, in accordance with the rules of the Board, unless the Board, prior to such date, issues a written notice of disapproval to, or requests more information from, the prospective registrant.

(2) TREATMENT.—A written notice of disapproval of a completed application under paragraph (1) for registration shall be treated as a disciplinary sanction for purposes of sections 105(d) and 107(c).

(d) PERIODIC REPORTS.—Each registered public accounting firm shall submit an annual report to the Board, and may be required to report more frequently, as necessary to update the information contained in its application for registration under this section, and to provide to the Board such additional information as the Board or the Commission may specify, in accordance with subsection (b)(2).

(e) PUBLIC AVAILABILITY.—Registration applications and annual reports required by this subsection, or such portions of such applications or reports as may be designated under rules of the Board, shall be made available for public inspection, subject to rules of the Board or the Commission, and to applicable laws relating to the confidentiality of proprietary, personal, or other information contained in such applications or reports, provided that, in all events, the Board shall protect from public disclosure information reasonably identified by the subject accounting firm as proprietary information.

(f) REGISTRATION AND ANNUAL FEES.—The Board shall assess and collect a registration fee and an annual fee from each registered public accounting firm, in amounts that are sufficient to recover the costs of processing and reviewing applications and annual reports.

SEC. 103. AUDITING, QUALITY CONTROL, AND INDEPENDENCE STANDARDS AND RULES.

(a) AUDITING, QUALITY CONTROL, AND ETHICS STANDARDS.—

(1) IN GENERAL.—The Board shall, by rule, establish, including, to the extent it determines appropriate, through adoption of standards proposed by 1 or more professional groups of accountants designated pursuant to paragraph (3)(A) or advisory groups convened pursuant to paragraph (4), and amend or otherwise modify or alter, such auditing and related attestation standards, such quality control standards, and such ethics standards to be used by registered public accounting firms in the preparation and issuance of audit reports, as required by this Act or the rules of the Commission, or as may be necessary or appropriate in the public interest or for the protection of investors.

(2) RULE REQUIREMENTS.—In carrying out paragraph (1), the Board—

(A) shall include in the auditing standards that it adopts, requirements that each registered public accounting firm shall—

(i) prepare, and maintain for a period of not less than 7 years, audit work papers, and other information related to any audit report, in sufficient detail to support the conclusions reached in such report;

(ii) provide a concurring or second partner review and approval of such audit report (and other related information), and concurring approval in its issuance, by a qualified person (as prescribed by the Board) associated with the public accounting firm, other than the person in charge of the audit, or by an independent reviewer (as prescribed by the Board); and

(iii) describe in each audit report the scope of the auditor's testing of the internal control structure and procedures of the issuer, required by section 404(b), and present (in such report or in a separate report)—

(I) the findings of the auditor from such testing;

(II) an evaluation of whether such internal control structure and procedures—

(aa) include maintenance of records that in reasonable detail accurately and fairly reflect the transactions and dispositions of the assets of the issuer;

(bb) provide reasonable assurance that transactions are recorded as necessary to permit preparation of financial statements in accordance with generally accepted accounting principles, and that receipts and expenditures of the issuer are being made only in accordance with authorizations of management and directors of the issuer; and

(III) a description, at a minimum, of material weaknesses in such internal controls, and of any material noncompliance found on the basis of such testing.

(B) shall include, in the quality control standards that it adopts with respect to the issuance of audit reports, requirements for every registered public accounting firm relating to—

(i) monitoring of professional ethics and independence from issuers on behalf of which the firm issues audit reports;

(ii) consultation within such firm on accounting and auditing questions;

(iii) supervision of audit work;

(iv) hiring, professional development, and advancement of personnel;

(v) the acceptance and continuation of engagements;

(vi) internal inspection; and

(vii) such other requirements as the Board may prescribe, subject to subsection (a)(1).

(3) AUTHORITY TO ADOPT OTHER STANDARDS.—

(A) IN GENERAL.—In carrying out this subsection, the Board—

(i) may adopt as its rules, subject to the terms of section 107, any portion of any statement of auditing standards or other professional standards that the Board determines satisfy the requirements of paragraph (1), and that were proposed by 1 or more professional groups of accountants that shall be designated or recognized by the Board, by rule, for such purpose, pursuant to this paragraph or 1 or more advisory groups convened pursuant to paragraph (4); and

(ii) notwithstanding clause (i), shall retain full authority to modify, supplement, revise, or subsequently amend, modify, or repeal, in whole or in part, any portion of any statement described in clause (i).

(B) INITIAL AND TRANSITIONAL STANDARDS.—The Board shall adopt standards described in subparagraph (A)(i) as initial or transitional standards, to the extent the Board determines necessary, prior to a determination of the Commission under section 101(d), and such standards shall be separately approved by the Commission at the time of that determination, without regard to the procedures required by section 107 that otherwise would apply to the approval of rules of the Board.

(4) ADVISORY GROUPS.—The Board shall convene, or authorize its staff to convene, such expert advisory groups as may be appropriate, which may include practicing accountants and other experts, as well as representatives of other interested groups, subject to such rules as the Board may prescribe to prevent conflicts of interest, to make recommendations concerning the content (including proposed drafts) of auditing, quality control, ethics, independence, or other standards required to be established under this section.

(b) INDEPENDENCE STANDARDS AND RULES.—The Board shall establish such rules as may be necessary or appropriate in the public interest or for the protection of investors, to implement, or as authorized under, title II of this Act.

(c) COOPERATION WITH DESIGNATED PROFESSIONAL GROUPS OF ACCOUNTANTS AND ADVISORY GROUPS.—

(1) IN GENERAL.—The Board shall cooperate on an ongoing basis with professional groups of accountants designated under subsection (a)(3)(A) and advisory groups convened under subsection (a)(4) in the examination of the need for changes in any standards subject to its authority under subsection (a), recommend issues for inclusion on the agendas of such designated professional groups of accountants or advisory groups, and take such other steps as it deems appropriate to increase the effectiveness of the standard setting process.

(2) BOARD RESPONSES.—The Board shall respond in a timely fashion to requests from designated professional groups of accountants and advisory groups referred to in paragraph (1) for any changes in standards over which the Board has authority.

(d) EVALUATION OF STANDARD SETTING PROCESS.—The Board shall include in the annual report required by section 101(h) the results of its standard setting responsibilities during the period to which the report relates, including a discussion of the work of the Board with any designated professional groups of accountants and advisory groups described in paragraphs (3)(A) and (4) of subsection (a), and its pending issues agenda for future standard setting projects.

SEC. 104. INSPECTIONS OF REGISTERED PUBLIC ACCOUNTING FIRMS.

(a) IN GENERAL.—The Board shall conduct a continuing program of inspections to assess the degree of compliance of each registered public accounting firm and associated persons of that firm with this Act, the rules of the Board, the rules of the Commission, or professional standards, in connection with its performance of audits, issuance of audit reports, and related matters involving issuers.

(b) INSPECTION FREQUENCY.—

(1) IN GENERAL.—Subject to paragraph (2), inspections required by this section shall be conducted—

(A) annually with respect to each registered public accounting firm that regularly provides audit reports for more than 100 issuers; and

(B) not less frequently than once every 3 years with respect to each registered public accounting firm that regularly provides audit reports for 100 or fewer issuers.

(2) ADJUSTMENTS TO SCHEDULES.—The Board may, by rule, adjust the inspection schedules set under paragraph (1) if the Board finds that different inspection schedules are consistent with the purposes of this Act, the public interest, and the protection of investors. The Board may conduct special inspections at the request of the Commission or upon its own motion.

(c) PROCEDURES.—The Board shall, in each inspection under this section, and in accordance with its rules for such inspections—

(1) identify any act or practice or omission to act by the registered public accounting firm, or by any associated person thereof, revealed by such inspection

that may be in violation of this Act, the rules of the Board, the rules of the Commission, the firm's own quality control policies, or professional standards;

(2) report any such act, practice, or omission, if appropriate, to the Commission and each appropriate State regulatory authority; and

(3) begin a formal investigation or take disciplinary action, if appropriate, with respect to any such violation, in accordance with this Act and the rules of the Board.

(d) CONDUCT OF INSPECTIONS.—In conducting an inspection of a registered public accounting firm under this section, the Board shall—

(1) inspect and review selected audit and review engagements of the firm (which may include audit engagements that are the subject of ongoing litigation or other controversy between the firm and 1 or more third parties), performed at various offices and by various associated persons of the firm, as selected by the Board;

(2) evaluate the sufficiency of the quality control system of the firm, and the manner of the documentation and communication of that system by the firm; and

(3) perform such other testing of the audit, supervisory, and quality control procedures of the firm as are necessary or appropriate in light of the purpose of the inspection and the responsibilities of the Board.

(e) RECORD RETENTION.—The rules of the Board may require the retention by registered public accounting firms for inspection purposes of records whose retention is not otherwise required by section 103 or the rules issued thereunder.

(f) PROCEDURES FOR REVIEW.—The rules of the Board shall provide a procedure for the review of and response to a draft inspection report by the registered public accounting firm under inspection. The Board shall take such action with respect to such response as it considers appropriate (including revising the draft report or continuing or supplementing its inspection activities before issuing a final report), but the text of any such response, appropriately redacted to protect information reasonably identified by the accounting firm as confidential, shall be attached to and made part of the inspection report.

(g) REPORT.—A written report of the findings of the Board for each inspection under this section, subject to subsection (h), shall be—

(1) transmitted, in appropriate detail, to the Commission and each appropriate State regulatory authority, accompanied by any letter or comments by the Board or the inspector, and any letter of response from the registered public accounting firm; and

(2) made available in appropriate detail to the public (subject to section 105(b)(5)(A), and to the protection of such confidential and proprietary information as the Board may determine to be appropriate, or as may be required by law), except that no portions of the inspection report that deal with criticisms of or potential defects in the quality control systems of the firm under inspection shall be made public if those criticisms or defects are addressed by the firm, to the satisfaction of the Board, not later than 12 months after the date of the inspection report.

(h) INTERIM COMMISSION REVIEW.—

(1) REVIEWABLE MATTERS.—A registered public accounting firm may seek review by the Commission, pursuant to such rules as the Commission shall promulgate, if the firm—

(A) has provided the Board with a response, pursuant to rules issued by the Board under subsection (f), to the substance of particular items in a draft inspection report, and disagrees with the assessments contained in any final report prepared by the Board following such response; or

(B) disagrees with the determination of the Board that criticisms or defects identified in an inspection report have not been addressed to the satisfaction of the Board within 12 months of the date of the inspection report, for purposes of subsection (g)(2).

(2) TREATMENT OF REVIEW.—Any decision of the Commission with respect to a review under paragraph (1) shall not be reviewable under section 25 of the Securities Exchange Act of 1934 (15 U.S.C. 78y), or deemed to be "final agency action" for purposes of section 704 of title 5, United States Code.

(3) TIMING.—Review under paragraph (1) may be sought during the 30-day period following the date of the event giving rise to the review under subparagraph (A) or (B) of paragraph (1).

SEC. 105. INVESTIGATIONS AND DISCIPLINARY PROCEEDINGS.

(a) IN GENERAL.—The Board shall establish, by rule, subject to the requirements of this section, fair procedures for the investigation and disciplining of registered public accounting firms and associated persons of such firms.

(b) INVESTIGATIONS.—

(1) AUTHORITY.—In accordance with the rules of the Board, the Board may conduct an investigation of any act or practice, or omission to act, by a registered public accounting firm, any associated person of such firm, or both, that may violate any provision of this Act, the rules of the Board, the provisions of the securities laws relating to the preparation and issuance of audit reports and the obligations and liabilities of accountants with respect thereto, including the rules of the Commission issued under this Act, or professional standards, regardless of how the act, practice, or omission is brought to the attention of the Board.

(2) TESTIMONY AND DOCUMENT PRODUCTION.—In addition to such other actions as the Board determines to be necessary or appropriate, the rules of the Board may—

(A) require the testimony of the firm or of any person associated with a registered public accounting firm, with respect to any matter that the Board considers relevant or material to an investigation;

(B) require the production of audit work papers and any other document or information in the possession of a registered public accounting firm or any associated person thereof, wherever domiciled, that the Board considers relevant or material to the investigation, and may inspect the books and records of such firm or associated person to verify the accuracy of any documents or information supplied;

(C) request the testimony of, and production of any document in the possession of, any other person, including any client of a registered public accounting firm that the Board considers relevant or material to an investigation under this section, with appropriate notice, subject to the needs of the investigation, as permitted under the rules of the Board; and

(D) provide for procedures to seek issuance by the Commission, in a manner established by the Commission, of a subpoena to require the testimony of, and production of any document in the possession of, any person, including any client of a registered public accounting firm, that the Board considers relevant or material to an investigation under this section.

(3) NONCOOPERATION WITH INVESTIGATIONS.—

(A) IN GENERAL.—If a registered public accounting firm or any associated person thereof refuses to testify, produce documents, or otherwise cooperate with the Board in connection with an investigation under this section, the Board may—

(i) suspend or bar such person from being associated with a registered public accounting firm, or require the registered public accounting firm to end such association;

(ii) suspend or revoke the registration of the public accounting firm; and

(iii) invoke such other lesser sanctions as the Board considers appropriate, and as specified by rule of the Board.

(B) PROCEDURE.—Any action taken by the Board under this paragraph shall be subject to the terms of section 107(c).

(4) COORDINATION AND REFERRAL OF INVESTIGATIONS.—

(A) COORDINATION.—The Board shall notify the Commission of any pending Board investigation involving a potential violation of the securities laws, and thereafter coordinate its work with the work of the Commission's Division of Enforcement, as necessary to protect an ongoing Commission investigation.

(B) REFERRAL.—The Board may refer an investigation under this section—

(i) to the Commission;

(ii) to any other Federal functional regulator (as defined in section 509 of the Gramm–Leach–Bliley Act (15 U.S.C. 6809)), in the case of an investigation that concerns an audit report for an institution that is subject to the jurisdiction of such regulator; and

(iii) at the direction of the Commission, to—

(I) the Attorney General of the United States;

(II) the attorney general of 1 or more States; and

(III) the appropriate State regulatory authority.

(5) USE OF DOCUMENTS.—

(A) CONFIDENTIALITY.—Except as provided in subparagraph (B), all documents and information prepared or received by or specifically for the

Board, and deliberations of the Board and its employees and agents, in connection with an inspection under section 104 or with an investigation under this section, shall be confidential and privileged as an evidentiary matter (and shall not be subject to civil discovery or other legal process) in any proceeding in any Federal or State court or administrative agency, and shall be exempt from disclosure, in the hands of an agency or establishment of the Federal Government, under the Freedom of Information Act (5 U.S.C. 552a), or otherwise, unless and until presented in connection with a public proceeding or released in accordance with subsection (c).

(B) AVAILABILITY TO GOVERNMENT AGENCIES.—Without the loss of its status as confidential and privileged in the hands of the Board, all information referred to in subparagraph (A) may—

(i) be made available to the Commission; and

(ii) in the discretion of the Board, when determined by the Board to be necessary to accomplish the purposes of this Act or to protect investors, be made available to—

(I) the Attorney General of the United States;

(II) the appropriate Federal functional regulator (as defined in section 509 of the Gramm–Leach–Bliley Act (15 U.S.C. 6809)), other than the Commission, with respect to an audit report for an institution subject to the jurisdiction of such regulator;

(III) State attorneys general in connection with any criminal investigation; and

(IV) any appropriate State regulatory authority,

each of which shall maintain such information as confidential and privileged.

(6) IMMUNITY.—Any employee of the Board engaged in carrying out an investigation under this Act shall be immune from any civil liability arising out of such investigation in the same manner and to the same extent as an employee of the Federal Government in similar circumstances.

(c) DISCIPLINARY PROCEDURES.—

(1) NOTIFICATION; RECORDKEEPING.—The rules of the Board shall provide that in any proceeding by the Board to determine whether a registered public accounting firm, or an associated person thereof, should be disciplined, the Board shall—

(A) bring specific charges with respect to the firm or associated person;

(B) notify such firm or associated person of, and provide to the firm or associated person an opportunity to defend against, such charges; and

(C) keep a record of the proceedings.

(2) PUBLIC HEARINGS.—Hearings under this section shall not be public, unless otherwise ordered by the Board for good cause shown, with the consent of the parties to such hearing.

(3) SUPPORTING STATEMENT.—A determination by the Board to impose a sanction under this subsection shall be supported by a statement setting forth—

(A) each act or practice in which the registered public accounting firm, or associated person, has engaged (or omitted to engage), or that forms a basis for all or a part of such sanction;

(B) the specific provision of this Act, the securities laws, the rules of the Board, or professional standards which the Board determines has been violated; and

(C) the sanction imposed, including a justification for that sanction.

(4) SANCTIONS.—If the Board finds, based on all of the facts and circumstances, that a registered public accounting firm or associated person thereof has engaged in any act or practice, or omitted to act, in violation of this Act, the rules of the Board, the provisions of the securities laws relating to the preparation and issuance of audit reports and the obligations and liabilities of accountants with respect thereto, including the rules of the Commission issued under this Act, or professional standards, the Board may impose such disciplinary or remedial sanctions as it determines appropriate, subject to applicable limitations under paragraph (5), including—

(A) temporary suspension or permanent revocation of registration under this title;

(B) temporary or permanent suspension or bar of a person from further association with any registered public accounting firm;

(C) temporary or permanent limitation on the activities, functions, or operations of such firm or person (other than in connection with required additional professional education or training);

(D) a civil money penalty for each such violation, in an amount equal to—

(i) not more than $100,000 for a natural person or $2,000,000 for any other person; and

(ii) in any case to which paragraph (5) applies, not more than $750,000 for a natural person or $15,000,000 for any other person;

(E) censure;

(F) required additional professional education or training; or

(G) any other appropriate sanction provided for in the rules of the Board.

(5) INTENTIONAL OR OTHER KNOWING CONDUCT.—The sanctions and penalties described in subparagraphs (A) through (C) and (D)(ii) of paragraph (4) shall only apply to—

(A) intentional or knowing conduct, including reckless conduct, that results in violation of the applicable statutory, regulatory, or professional standard; or

(B) repeated instances of negligent conduct, each resulting in a violation of the applicable statutory, regulatory, or professional standard.

(6) FAILURE TO SUPERVISE.—

(A) IN GENERAL.—The Board may impose sanctions under this section on a registered accounting firm or upon the supervisory personnel of such firm, if the Board finds that—

(i) the firm has failed reasonably to supervise an associated person, either as required by the rules of the Board relating to auditing or quality control standards, or otherwise, with a view to preventing violations of this Act, the rules of the Board, the provisions of the securities laws relating to the preparation and issuance of audit reports and the obligations and liabilities of accountants with respect thereto, including the rules of the Commission under this Act, or professional standards; and

(ii) such associated person commits a violation of this Act, or any of such rules, laws, or standards.

(B) RULE OF CONSTRUCTION.—No associated person of a registered public accounting firm shall be deemed to have failed reasonably to supervise any other person for purposes of subparagraph (A), if—

(i) there have been established in and for that firm procedures, and a system for applying such procedures, that comply with applicable rules of the Board and that would reasonably be expected to prevent and detect any such violation by such associated person; and

(ii) such person has reasonably discharged the duties and obligations incumbent upon that person by reason of such procedures and system, and had no reasonable cause to believe that such procedures and system were not being complied with.

(7) EFFECT OF SUSPENSION.—

(A) ASSOCIATION WITH A PUBLIC ACCOUNTING FIRM.—It shall be unlawful for any person that is suspended or barred from being associated with a registered public accounting firm under this subsection willfully to become or remain associated with any registered public accounting firm, or for any registered public accounting firm that knew, or, in the exercise of reasonable care should have known, of the suspension or bar, to permit such an association, without the consent of the Board or the Commission.

(B) ASSOCIATION WITH AN ISSUER.—It shall be unlawful for any person that is suspended or barred from being associated with an issuer under this subsection willfully to become or remain associated with any issuer in an accountancy or a financial management capacity, and for any issuer that knew, or in the exercise of reasonable care should have known, of such suspension or bar, to permit such an association, without the consent of the Board or the Commission.

(d) REPORTING OF SANCTIONS.—

(1) RECIPIENTS.—If the Board imposes a disciplinary sanction, in accordance with this section, the Board shall report the sanction to—

(A) the Commission;

(B) any appropriate State regulatory authority or any foreign accountancy licensing board with which such firm or person is licensed or certified; and

(C) the public (once any stay on the imposition of such sanction has been lifted).

(2) CONTENTS.—The information reported under paragraph (1) shall include—

(A) the name of the sanctioned person;

(B) a description of the sanction and the basis for its imposition; and

(C) such other information as the Board deems appropriate.

(e) STAY OF SANCTIONS.—

(1) IN GENERAL.—Application to the Commission for review, or the institution by the Commission of review, of any disciplinary action of the Board shall operate as a stay of any such disciplinary action, unless and until the Commission orders (summarily or after notice and opportunity for hearing on the question of a stay, which hearing may consist solely of the submission of affidavits or presentation of oral arguments) that no such stay shall continue to operate.

(2) EXPEDITED PROCEDURES.—The Commission shall establish for appropriate cases an expedited procedure for consideration and determination of the question of the duration of a stay pending review of any disciplinary action of the Board under this subsection.

SEC. 106. FOREIGN PUBLIC ACCOUNTING FIRMS.

(a) APPLICABILITY TO CERTAIN FOREIGN FIRMS.—

(1) IN GENERAL.—Any foreign public accounting firm that prepares or furnishes an audit report with respect to any issuer, shall be subject to this Act and the rules of the Board and the Commission issued under this Act, in the same manner and to the same extent as a public accounting firm that is organized and operates under the laws of the United States or any State, except that registration pursuant to section 102 shall not by itself provide a basis for subjecting such a foreign public accounting firm to the jurisdiction of the Federal or State courts, other than with respect to controversies between such firms and the Board.

(2) BOARD AUTHORITY.—The Board may, by rule, determine that a foreign public accounting firm (or a class of such firms) that does not issue audit reports nonetheless plays such a substantial role in the preparation and furnishing of such reports for particular issuers, that it is necessary or appropriate, in light of the purposes of this Act and in the public interest or for the protection of investors, that such firm (or class of firms) should be treated as a public accounting firm (or firms) for purposes of registration under, and oversight by the Board in accordance with, this title.

(b) PRODUCTION OF AUDIT WORKPAPERS.—

(1) CONSENT BY FOREIGN FIRMS.—If a foreign public accounting firm issues an opinion or otherwise performs material services upon which a registered public accounting firm relies in issuing all or part of any audit report or any opinion contained in an audit report, that foreign public accounting firm shall be deemed to have consented—

(A) to produce its audit workpapers for the Board or the Commission in connection with any investigation by either body with respect to that audit report; and

(B) to be subject to the jurisdiction of the courts of the United States for purposes of enforcement of any request for production of such workpapers.

(2) CONSENT BY DOMESTIC FIRMS.—A registered public accounting firm that relies upon the opinion of a foreign public accounting firm, as described in paragraph (1), shall be deemed—

(A) to have consented to supplying the audit workpapers of that foreign public accounting firm in response to a request for production by the Board or the Commission; and

(B) to have secured the agreement of that foreign public accounting firm to such production, as a condition of its reliance on the opinion of that foreign public accounting firm.

(c) EXEMPTION AUTHORITY.—The Commission, and the Board, subject to the approval of the Commission, may, by rule, regulation, or order, and as the Commission (or Board) determines necessary or appropriate in the public interest or for the protection of investors, either unconditionally or upon specified terms and conditions exempt any foreign public accounting firm, or any class of such firms, from any provision of this Act or the rules of the Board or the Commission issued under this Act.

(d) DEFINITION.—In this section, the term "foreign public accounting firm" means a public accounting firm that is organized and operates under the laws of a foreign government or political subdivision thereof.

SEC. 107. COMMISSION OVERSIGHT OF THE BOARD.

(a) GENERAL OVERSIGHT RESPONSIBILITY.—The Commission shall have oversight and enforcement authority over the Board, as provided in this Act. The provisions of section 17(a)(1) of the Securities Exchange Act of 1934 (15 U.S.C. 78q(a)(1)), and of section 17(b)(1) of the Securities Exchange Act of 1934 (15 U.S.C. 78q(b)(1)) shall apply to the Board as fully as if the Board were a "registered securities association" for purposes of those sections 17(a)(1) and 17(b)(1).

(b) RULES OF THE BOARD.—

(1) DEFINITION.—In this section, the term "proposed rule" means any proposed rule of the Board, and any modification of any such rule.

(2) PRIOR APPROVAL REQUIRED.—No rule of the Board shall become effective without prior approval of the Commission in accordance with this section, other than as provided in section 103(a)(3)(B) with respect to initial or transitional standards.

(3) APPROVAL CRITERIA.—The Commission shall approve a proposed rule, if it finds that the rule is consistent with the requirements of this Act and the securities laws, or is necessary or appropriate in the public interest or for the protection of investors.

(4) PROPOSED RULE PROCEDURES.—The provisions of paragraphs (1) through (3) of section 19(b) of the Securities Exchange Act of 1934 (15 U.S.C. 78s(b)) shall govern the proposed rules of the Board, as fully as if the Board were a "registered securities association" for purposes of that section 19(b), except that, for purposes of this paragraph—

(A) the phrase "consistent with the requirements of this title and the rules and regulations thereunder applicable to such organization" in section 19(b)(2) of that Act shall be deemed to read "consistent with the requirements of title I of the Sarbanes–Oxley Act of 2002, and the rules and regulations issued thereunder applicable to such organization, or as necessary or appropriate in the public interest or for the protection of investors"; and

(B) the phrase "otherwise in furtherance of the purposes of this title" in section 19(b)(3)(C) of that Act shall be deemed to read "otherwise in furtherance of the purposes of title I of the Sarbanes–Oxley Act of 2002".

(5) COMMISSION AUTHORITY TO AMEND RULES OF THE BOARD.—The provisions of section 19(c) of the Securities Exchange Act of 1934 (15 U.S.C. 78s(c)) shall govern the abrogation, deletion, or addition to portions of the rules of the Board by the Commission as fully as if the Board were a "registered securities association" for purposes of that section 19(c), except that the phrase "to conform its rules to the requirements of this title and the rules and regulations thereunder applicable to such organization, or otherwise in furtherance of the purposes of this title" in section 19(c) of that Act shall, for purposes of this paragraph, be deemed to read "to assure the fair administration of the Public Company Accounting Oversight Board, conform the rules promulgated by that Board to the requirements of title I of the Sarbanes–Oxley Act of 2002, or otherwise further the purposes of that Act, the securities laws, and the rules and regulations thereunder applicable to that Board".

(c) COMMISSION REVIEW OF DISCIPLINARY ACTION TAKEN BY THE BOARD.—

(1) NOTICE OF SANCTION.—The Board shall promptly file notice with the Commission of any final sanction on any registered public accounting firm or on any associated person thereof, in such form and containing such information as the Commission, by rule, may prescribe.

(2) REVIEW OF SANCTIONS.—The provisions of sections 19(d)(2) and 19(e)(1) of the Securities Exchange Act of 1934 (15 U.S.C. 78s (d)(2) and (e)(1)) shall govern the review by the Commission of final disciplinary sanctions imposed by the Board (including sanctions imposed under section 105(b)(3) of this Act for noncooperation in an investigation of the Board), as fully as if the Board were a self-regulatory organization and the Commission were the appropriate regulatory agency for such organization for purposes of those sections 19(d)(2) and 19(e)(1), except that, for purposes of this paragraph—

(A) section 105(e) of this Act (rather than that section 19(d)(2)) shall govern the extent to which application for, or institution by the Commission on its own motion of, review of any disciplinary action of the Board operates as a stay of such action;

(B) references in that section 19(e)(1) to "members" of such an organization shall be deemed to be references to registered public accounting firms;

(C) the phrase "consistent with the purposes of this title" in that section 19(e)(1) shall be deemed to read "consistent with the purposes of this title and title I of the Sarbanes–Oxley Act of 2002";

(D) references to rules of the Municipal Securities Rulemaking Board in that section 19(e)(1) shall not apply; and

(E) the reference to section 19(e)(2) of the Securities Exchange Act of 1934 shall refer instead to section 107(c)(3) of this Act.

(3) COMMISSION MODIFICATION AUTHORITY.—The Commission may enhance, modify, cancel, reduce, or require the remission of a sanction imposed by the Board upon a registered public accounting firm or associated person thereof, if the Commission, having due regard for the public interest and the protection of investors, finds, after a proceeding in accordance with this subsection, that the sanction—

(A) is not necessary or appropriate in furtherance of this Act or the securities laws; or

(B) is excessive, oppressive, inadequate, or otherwise not appropriate to the finding or the basis on which the sanction was imposed.

(d) CENSURE OF THE BOARD; OTHER SANCTIONS.—

(1) RESCISSION OF BOARD AUTHORITY.—The Commission, by rule, consistent with the public interest, the protection of investors, and the other purposes of this Act and the securities laws, may relieve the Board of any responsibility to enforce compliance with any provision of this Act, the securities laws, the rules of the Board, or professional standards.

(2) CENSURE OF THE BOARD; LIMITATIONS.—The Commission may, by order, as it determines necessary or appropriate in the public interest, for the protection of investors, or otherwise in furtherance of the purposes of this Act or the securities laws, censure or impose limitations upon the activities, functions, and operations of the Board, if the Commission finds, on the record, after notice and opportunity for a hearing, that the Board—

(A) has violated or is unable to comply with any provision of this Act, the rules of the Board, or the securities laws; or

(B) without reasonable justification or excuse, has failed to enforce compliance with any such provision or rule, or any professional standard by a registered public accounting firm or an associated person thereof.

(3) CENSURE OF BOARD MEMBERS; REMOVAL FROM OFFICE.—The Commission may, as necessary or appropriate in the public interest, for the protection of investors, or otherwise in furtherance of the purposes of this Act or the securities laws, remove from office or censure any member of the Board, if the Commission finds, on the record, after notice and opportunity for a hearing, that such member—

(A) has willfully violated any provision of this Act, the rules of the Board, or the securities laws;

(B) has willfully abused the authority of that member; or

(C) without reasonable justification or excuse, has failed to enforce compliance with any such provision or rule, or any professional standard by any registered public accounting firm or any associated person thereof.

SEC. 108. ACCOUNTING STANDARDS.

(a) AMENDMENT TO SECURITIES ACT OF 1933.—Section 19 of the Securities Act of 1933 (15 U.S.C. 77s) is amended—

(1) by redesignating subsections (b) and (c) as subsections (c) and (d), respectively; and

(2) by inserting after subsection (a) the following:

"(b) RECOGNITION OF ACCOUNTING STANDARDS.—

"(1) IN GENERAL.—In carrying out its authority under subsection (a) and under section 13(b) of the Securities Exchange Act of 1934, the Commission may recognize, as 'generally accepted' for purposes of the securities laws, any accounting principles established by a standard setting body—

"(A) that—

"(i) is organized as a private entity;

"(ii) has, for administrative and operational purposes, a board of trustees (or equivalent body) serving in the public interest, the majority of whom are not, concurrent with their service on such board, and have not been during the 2–year period preceding such service, associated persons of any registered public accounting firm;

"(iii) is funded as provided in section 109 of the Sarbanes–Oxley Act of 2002;

"(iv) has adopted procedures to ensure prompt consideration, by majority vote of its members, of changes to accounting principles necessary to reflect emerging accounting issues and changing business practices; and

"(v) considers, in adopting accounting principles, the need to keep standards current in order to reflect changes in the business environment, the extent to which international convergence on high quality accounting standards is necessary or appropriate in the public interest and for the protection of investors; and

"(B) that the Commission determines has the capacity to assist the Commission in fulfilling the requirements of subsection (a) and section 13(b) of the Securities Exchange Act of 1934, because, at a minimum, the standard setting body is capable of improving the accuracy and effectiveness of financial reporting and the protection of investors under the securities laws.

"(2) ANNUAL REPORT.—A standard setting body described in paragraph (1) shall submit an annual report to the Commission and the public, containing audited financial statements of that standard setting body.".

(b) COMMISSION AUTHORITY.—The Commission shall promulgate such rules and regulations to carry out section 19(b) of the Securities Act of 1933, as added by this section, as it deems necessary or appropriate in the public interest or for the protection of investors.

(c) NO EFFECT ON COMMISSION POWERS.—Nothing in this Act, including this section and the amendment made by this section, shall be construed to impair or limit the authority of the Commission to establish accounting principles or standards for purposes of enforcement of the securities laws.

(d) STUDY AND REPORT ON ADOPTING PRINCIPLES–BASED ACCOUNTING.—

(1) STUDY.—

(A) IN GENERAL.—The Commission shall conduct a study on the adoption by the United States financial reporting system of a principles-based accounting system.

(B) STUDY TOPICS.—The study required by subparagraph (A) shall include an examination of—

(i) the extent to which principles-based accounting and financial reporting exists in the United States;

(ii) the length of time required for change from a rules-based to a principles-based financial reporting system;

(iii) the feasibility of and proposed methods by which a principles-based system may be implemented; and

(iv) a thorough economic analysis of the implementation of a principles-based system.

(2) REPORT.—Not later than 1 year after the date of enactment of this Act, the Commission shall submit a report on the results of the study required by paragraph (1) to the Committee on Banking, Housing, and Urban Affairs of the Senate and the Committee on Financial Services of the House of Representatives.

SEC. 109. FUNDING.

(a) IN GENERAL.—The Board, and the standard setting body designated pursuant to section 19(b) of the Securities Act of 1933, as amended by section 108, shall be funded as provided in this section.

(b) ANNUAL BUDGETS.—The Board and the standard setting body referred to in subsection (a) shall each establish a budget for each fiscal year, which shall be reviewed and approved according to their respective internal procedures not less than 1 month prior to the commencement of the fiscal year to which the budget pertains (or at the beginning of the Board's first fiscal year, which may be a short fiscal year). The budget of the Board shall be subject to approval by the Commission. The budget for the first fiscal year of the Board shall be prepared and approved promptly following the appointment of the initial five Board members, to permit action by the Board of the organizational tasks contemplated by section 101(d).

(c) SOURCES AND USES OF FUNDS.—

(1) RECOVERABLE BUDGET EXPENSES.—The budget of the Board (reduced by any registration or annual fees received under section 102(e) for the year preceding the year for which the budget is being computed), and all of the budget of the standard setting body referred to in subsection (a), for each fiscal year of each of those 2 entities, shall be payable from annual accounting support fees, in accordance with subsections (d) and (e). Accounting support fees and other receipts of the Board and of such standard-setting body shall not be considered public monies of the United States.

(2) FUNDS GENERATED FROM THE COLLECTION OF MONETARY PENALTIES.—Subject to the availability in advance in an appropriations Act, and notwithstanding subsection (i), all funds collected by the Board as a result of the assessment of monetary penalties shall be used to fund a merit scholarship program for undergraduate and graduate students enrolled in accredited ac-

counting degree programs, which program is to be administered by the Board or by an entity or agent identified by the Board.

(d) ANNUAL ACCOUNTING SUPPORT FEE FOR THE BOARD.—

(1) ESTABLISHMENT OF FEE.—The Board shall establish, with the approval of the Commission, a reasonable annual accounting support fee (or a formula for the computation thereof), as may be necessary or appropriate to establish and maintain the Board. Such fee may also cover costs incurred in the Board's first fiscal year (which may be a short fiscal year), or may be levied separately with respect to such short fiscal year.

(2) ASSESSMENTS.—The rules of the Board under paragraph (1) shall provide for the equitable allocation, assessment, and collection by the Board (or an agent appointed by the Board) of the fee established under paragraph (1), among issuers, in accordance with subsection (g), allowing for differentiation among classes of issuers, as appropriate.

(e) ANNUAL ACCOUNTING SUPPORT FEE FOR STANDARD SETTING BODY.—The annual accounting support fee for the standard setting body referred to in subsection (a)—

(1) shall be allocated in accordance with subsection (g), and assessed and collected against each issuer, on behalf of the standard setting body, by 1 or more appropriate designated collection agents, as may be necessary or appropriate to pay for the budget and provide for the expenses of that standard setting body, and to provide for an independent, stable source of funding for such body, subject to review by the Commission; and

(2) may differentiate among different classes of issuers.

(f) LIMITATION ON FEE.—The amount of fees collected under this section for a fiscal year on behalf of the Board or the standards setting body, as the case may be, shall not exceed the recoverable budget expenses of the Board or body, respectively (which may include operating, capital, and accrued items), referred to in subsection (c)(1).

(g) ALLOCATION OF ACCOUNTING SUPPORT FEES AMONG ISSUERS.—Any amount due from issuers (or a particular class of issuers) under this section to fund the budget of the Board or the standard setting body referred to in subsection (a) shall be allocated among and payable by each issuer (or each issuer in a particular class, as applicable) in an amount equal to the total of such amount, multiplied by a fraction—

(1) the numerator of which is the average monthly equity market capitalization of the issuer for the 12-month period immediately preceding the beginning of the fiscal year to which such budget relates; and

(2) the denominator of which is the average monthly equity market capitalization of all such issuers for such 12-month period.

(h) CONFORMING AMENDMENTS.—Section 13(b)(2) of the Securities Exchange Act of 1934 (15 U.S.C. 78m(b)(2)) is amended—

(1) in subparagraph (A), by striking "and" at the end; and

(2) in subparagraph (B), by striking the period at the end and inserting the following: "; and "(C) notwithstanding any other provision of law, pay the allocable share of such issuer of a reasonable annual accounting support fee or

fees, determined in accordance with section 109 of the Sarbanes–Oxley Act of 2002.".

(i) RULE OF CONSTRUCTION.—Nothing in this section shall be construed to render either the Board, the standard setting body referred to in subsection (a), or both, subject to procedures in Congress to authorize or appropriate public funds, or to prevent such organization from utilizing additional sources of revenue for its activities, such as earnings from publication sales, provided that each additional source of revenue shall not jeopardize, in the judgment of the Commission, the actual and perceived independence of such organization.

(j) START–UP EXPENSES OF THE BOARD.—From the unexpended balances of the appropriations to the Commission for fiscal year 2003, the Secretary of the Treasury is authorized to advance to the Board not to exceed the amount necessary to cover the expenses of the Board during its first fiscal year (which may be a short fiscal year).

TITLE II—AUDITOR INDEPENDENCE

SEC. 201. SERVICES OUTSIDE THE SCOPE OF PRACTICE OF AUDITORS.

(a) PROHIBITED ACTIVITIES.—Section 10A of the Securities Exchange Act of 1934 (15 U.S.C. 78j–1) is amended by adding at the end the following:

"(g) PROHIBITED ACTIVITIES.—Except as provided in subsection (h), it shall be unlawful for a registered public accounting firm (and any associated person of that firm, to the extent determined appropriate by the Commission) that performs for any issuer any audit required by this title or the rules of the Commission under this title or, beginning 180 days after the date of commencement of the operations of the Public Company Accounting Oversight Board established under section 101 of the Sarbanes–Oxley Act of 2002 (in this section referred to as the 'Board'), the rules of the Board, to provide to that issuer, contemporaneously with the audit, any non-audit service, including—

"(1) bookkeeping or other services related to the accounting records or financial statements of the audit client;

"(2) financial information systems design and implementation;

"(3) appraisal or valuation services, fairness opinions, or contribution-in-kind reports;

"(4) actuarial services;

"(5) internal audit outsourcing services;

"(6) management functions or human resources;

"(7) broker or dealer, investment adviser, or investment banking services;

"(8) legal services and expert services unrelated to the audit; and

"(9) any other service that the Board determines, by regulation, is impermissible.

"(h) PREAPPROVAL REQUIRED FOR NON–AUDIT SERVICES.—A registered public accounting firm may engage in any non-audit service, including tax services, that is not described in any of paragraphs (1) through (9) of subsection (g) for an audit client, only if the activity is approved in advance by the audit committee of the issuer, in accordance with subsection (i).".

(b) EXEMPTION AUTHORITY.—The Board may, on a case by case basis, exempt any person, issuer, public accounting firm, or transaction from the prohibition on the provision of services under section 10A(g) of the Securities Exchange Act of 1934 (as added by this section), to the extent that such exemption is necessary or appropriate in the public interest and is consistent with the protection of investors, and subject to review by the Commission in the same manner as for rules of the Board under section 107.

SEC. 202. PREAPPROVAL REQUIREMENTS.

Section 10A of the Securities Exchange Act of 1934 (15 U.S.C. 78j–1), as amended by this Act, is amended by adding at the end the following:

"(i) PREAPPROVAL REQUIREMENTS.—

"(1) IN GENERAL.—

"(A) AUDIT COMMITTEE ACTION.—All auditing services (which may entail providing comfort letters in connection with securities underwritings or statutory audits required for insurance companies for purposes of State law) and non-audit services, other than as provided in subparagraph (B), provided to an issuer by the auditor of the issuer shall be preapproved by the audit committee of the issuer.

"(B) DE MINIMUS EXCEPTION.—The preapproval requirement under subparagraph (A) is waived with respect to the provision of non-audit services for an issuer, if—

"(i) the aggregate amount of all such non-audit services provided to the issuer constitutes not more than 5 percent of the total amount of revenues paid by the issuer to its auditor during the fiscal year in which the nonaudit services are provided;

"(ii) such services were not recognized by the issuer at the time of the engagement to be non-audit services; and

"(iii) such services are promptly brought to the attention of the audit committee of the issuer and approved prior to the completion of the audit by the audit committee or by 1 or more members of the audit committee who are members of the board of directors to whom authority to grant such approvals has been delegated by the audit committee.

"(2) DISCLOSURE TO INVESTORS.—Approval by an audit committee of an issuer under this subsection of a non-audit service to be performed by the auditor of the issuer shall be disclosed to investors in periodic reports required by section 13(a).

"(3) DELEGATION AUTHORITY.—The audit committee of an issuer may delegate to 1 or more designated members of the audit committee who are independent directors of the board of directors, the authority to grant preapprovals required by this subsection. The decisions of any member to whom authority is delegated under this paragraph to preapprove an activity under this subsection shall be presented to the full audit committee at each of its scheduled meetings.

"(4) APPROVAL OF AUDIT SERVICES FOR OTHER PURPOSES.—In carrying out its duties under subsection (m)(2), if the audit committee of an issuer approves an audit service within the scope of the engagement of the auditor, such audit service shall be deemed to have been preapproved for purposes of this subsection.".

SEC. 203. AUDIT PARTNER ROTATION.

Section 10A of the Securities Exchange Act of 1934 (15 U.S.C. 78j–1), as amended by this Act, is amended by adding at the end the following:

"(j) AUDIT PARTNER ROTATION.—It shall be unlawful for a registered public accounting firm to provide audit services to an issuer if the lead (or coordinating) audit partner (having primary responsibility for the audit), or the audit partner responsible for reviewing the audit, has performed audit services for that issuer in each of the 5 previous fiscal years of that issuer.".

SEC. 204. AUDITOR REPORTS TO AUDIT COMMITTEES.

Section 10A of the Securities Exchange Act of 1934 (15 U.S.C. 78j–1), as amended by this Act, is amended by adding at the end the following:

"(k) REPORTS TO AUDIT COMMITTEES.—Each registered public accounting firm that performs for any issuer any audit required by this title shall timely report to the audit committee of the issuer—

"(1) all critical accounting policies and practices to be used;

"(2) all alternative treatments of financial information within generally accepted accounting principles that have been discussed with management officials of the issuer, ramifications of the use of such alternative disclosures and treatments, and the treatment preferred by the registered public accounting firm; and

"(3) other material written communications between the registered public accounting firm and the management of the issuer, such as any management letter or schedule of unadjusted differences.".

SEC. 205. CONFORMING AMENDMENTS.

(a) DEFINITIONS.—Section 3(a) of the Securities Exchange Act of 1934 (15 U.S.C. 78c(a)) is amended by adding at the end the following:

"(58) AUDIT COMMITTEE.—The term 'audit committee' means—

"(A) a committee (or equivalent body) established by and amongst the board of directors of an issuer for the purpose of overseeing the accounting and financial reporting processes of the issuer and audits of the financial statements of the issuer; and

"(B) if no such committee exists with respect to an issuer, the entire board of directors of the issuer.

"(59) REGISTERED PUBLIC ACCOUNTING FIRM.—The term 'registered public accounting firm' has the same meaning as in section 2 of the Sarbanes–Oxley Act of 2002.".

(b) AUDITOR REQUIREMENTS.—Section 10A of the Securities Exchange Act of 1934 (15 U.S.C. 78j–1) is amended—

(1) by striking "an independent public accountant" each place that term appears and inserting "a registered public accounting firm";

(2) by striking "the independent public accountant" each place that term appears and inserting "the registered public accounting firm";

(3) in subsection (c), by striking "No independent public accountant" and inserting "No registered public accounting firm"; and

(4) in subsection (b)—

(A) by striking "the accountant" each place that term appears and inserting "the firm";

(B) by striking "such accountant" each place that term appears and inserting "such firm"; and

(C) in paragraph (4), by striking "the accountant's report" and inserting "the report of the firm".

(c) OTHER REFERENCES.—The Securities Exchange Act of 1934 (15 U.S.C. 78a et seq.) is amended—

(1) in section 12(b)(1) (15 U.S.C. 78l(b)(1)), by striking "independent public accountants" each place that term appears and inserting "a registered public accounting firm"; and

(2) in subsections (e) and (i) of section 17 (15 U.S.C. 78q), by striking "an independent public accountant" each place that term appears and inserting "a registered public accounting firm".

(d) CONFORMING AMENDMENT.—Section 10A(f) of the Securities Exchange Act of 1934 (15 U.S.C. 78k(f)) is amended—

(1) by striking "DEFINITION" and inserting "DEFINITIONS"; and

(2) by adding at the end the following: "As used in this section, the term 'issuer' means an issuer (as defined in section 3), the securities of which are registered under section 12, or that is required to file reports pursuant to section 15(d), or that files or has filed a registration statement that has not yet become effective under the Securities Act of 1933 (15 U.S.C. 77a et seq.), and that it has not withdrawn.".

SEC. 206. CONFLICTS OF INTEREST.

Section 10A of the Securities Exchange Act of 1934 (15 U.S.C. 78j–1), as amended by this Act, is amended by adding at the end the following:

"(*l*) CONFLICTS OF INTEREST.—It shall be unlawful for a registered public accounting firm to perform for an issuer any audit service required by this title, if a chief executive officer, controller, chief financial officer, chief accounting officer, or any person serving in an equivalent position for the issuer, was employed by that registered independent public accounting firm and participated in any capacity in the audit of that issuer during the 1–year period preceding the date of the initiation of the audit.''.

SEC. 207. STUDY OF MANDATORY ROTATION OF REGISTERED PUBLIC ACCOUNTING FIRMS.

(a) STUDY AND REVIEW REQUIRED.—The Comptroller General of the United States shall conduct a study and review of the potential effects of requiring the mandatory rotation of registered public accounting firms.

(b) REPORT REQUIRED.—Not later than 1 year after the date of enactment of this Act, the Comptroller General shall submit a report to the Committee on Banking, Housing, and Urban Affairs of the Senate and the Committee on Financial Services of the House of Representatives on the results of the study and review required by this section.

(c) DEFINITION.—For purposes of this section, the term ''mandatory rotation'' refers to the imposition of a limit on the period of years in which a particular registered public accounting firm may be the auditor of record for a particular issuer.

SEC. 208. COMMISSION AUTHORITY.

(a) COMMISSION REGULATIONS.—Not later than 180 days after the date of enactment of this Act, the Commission shall issue final regulations to carry out each of subsections (g) through (*l*) of section 10A of the Securities Exchange Act of 1934, as added by this title.

(b) AUDITOR INDEPENDENCE.—It shall be unlawful for any registered public accounting firm (or an associated person thereof, as applicable) to prepare or issue any audit report with respect to any issuer, if the firm or associated person engages in any activity with respect to that issuer prohibited by any of subsections (g) through (*l*) of section 10A of the Securities Exchange Act of 1934, as added by this title, or any rule or regulation of the Commission or of the Board issued thereunder.

SEC. 209. CONSIDERATIONS BY APPROPRIATE STATE REGULATORY AUTHORITIES.

In supervising nonregistered public accounting firms and their associated persons, appropriate State regulatory authorities should make an independent determination of the proper standards applicable, particularly taking into consideration the size and nature of the business of the accounting firms they supervise and the size and nature of the business of the clients of those firms. The standards applied by the Board under this Act should not be presumed to be applicable for purposes of this section for small and medium sized nonregistered public accounting firms.

TITLE III—CORPORATE RESPONSIBILITY

SEC. 301. PUBLIC COMPANY AUDIT COMMITTEES.

Section 10A of the Securities Exchange Act of 1934 (15 U.S.C. 78f) is amended by adding at the end the following:

''(m) STANDARDS RELATING TO AUDIT COMMITTEES.—

"(1) COMMISSION RULES.—

"(A) IN GENERAL.—Effective not later than 270 days after the date of enactment of this subsection, the Commission shall, by rule, direct the national securities exchanges and national securities associations to prohibit the listing of any security of an issuer that is not in compliance with the requirements of any portion of paragraphs (2) through (6).

"(B) OPPORTUNITY TO CURE DEFECTS.—The rules of the Commission under subparagraph (A) shall provide for appropriate procedures for an issuer to have an opportunity to cure any defects that would be the basis for a prohibition under subparagraph (A), before the imposition of such prohibition.

"(2) RESPONSIBILITIES RELATING TO REGISTERED PUBLIC ACCOUNTING FIRMS.—The audit committee of each issuer, in its capacity as a committee of the board of directors, shall be directly responsible for the appointment, compensation, and oversight of the work of any registered public accounting firm employed by that issuer (including resolution of disagreements between management and the auditor regarding financial reporting) for the purpose of preparing or issuing an audit report or related work, and each such registered public accounting firm shall report directly to the audit committee.

"(3) INDEPENDENCE.—

"(A) IN GENERAL.—Each member of the audit committee of the issuer shall be a member of the board of directors of the issuer, and shall otherwise be independent.

"(B) CRITERIA.—In order to be considered to be independent for purposes of this paragraph, a member of an audit committee of an issuer may not, other than in his or her capacity as a member of the audit committee, the board of directors, or any other board committee—

"(i) accept any consulting, advisory, or other compensatory fee from the issuer; or

"(ii) be an affiliated person of the issuer or any subsidiary thereof.

"(C) EXEMPTION AUTHORITY.—The Commission may exempt from the requirements of subparagraph (B) a particular relationship with respect to audit committee members, as the Commission determines appropriate in light of the circumstances.

"(4) COMPLAINTS.—Each audit committee shall establish procedures for—

"(A) the receipt, retention, and treatment of complaints received by the issuer regarding accounting, internal accounting controls, or auditing matters; and

"(B) the confidential, anonymous submission by employees of the issuer of concerns regarding questionable accounting or auditing matters.

"(5) AUTHORITY TO ENGAGE ADVISERS.—Each audit committee shall have the authority to engage independent counsel and other advisers, as it determines necessary to carry out its duties.

"(6) FUNDING.—Each issuer shall provide for appropriate funding, as determined by the audit committee, in its capacity as a committee of the board of directors, for payment of compensation—

"(A) to the registered public accounting firm employed by the issuer for the purpose of rendering or issuing an audit report; and

"(B) to any advisers employed by the audit committee under paragraph (5).".

SEC. 302. CORPORATE RESPONSIBILITY FOR FINANCIAL REPORTS.

(a) REGULATIONS REQUIRED.—The Commission shall, by rule, require, for each company filing periodic reports under section 13(a) or 15(d) of the Securities Exchange Act of 1934 (15 U.S.C. 78m, 78o(d)), that the principal executive officer or officers and the principal financial officer or officers, or persons performing similar functions, certify in each annual or quarterly report filed or submitted under either such section of such Act that—

(1) the signing officer has reviewed the report;

(2) based on the officer's knowledge, the report does not contain any untrue statement of a material fact or omit to state a material fact necessary in order to make the statements made, in light of the circumstances under which such statements were made, not misleading;

(3) based on such officer's knowledge, the financial statements, and other financial information included in the report, fairly present in all material respects the financial condition and results of operations of the issuer as of, and for, the periods presented in the report;

(4) the signing officers—

(A) are responsible for establishing and maintaining internal controls;

(B) have designed such internal controls to ensure that material information relating to the issuer and its consolidated subsidiaries is made known to such officers by others within those entities, particularly during the period in which the periodic reports are being prepared;

(C) have evaluated the effectiveness of the issuer's internal controls as of a date within 90 days prior to the report; and

(D) have presented in the report their conclusions about the effectiveness of their internal controls based on their evaluation as of that date;

(5) the signing officers have disclosed to the issuer's auditors and the audit committee of the board of directors (or persons fulfilling the equivalent function)—

(A) all significant deficiencies in the design or operation of internal controls which could adversely affect the issuer's ability to record, process, summarize, and report financial data and have identified for the issuer's auditors any material weaknesses in internal controls; and

(B) any fraud, whether or not material, that involves management or other employees who have a significant role in the issuer's internal controls; and

(6) the signing officers have indicated in the report whether or not there were significant changes in internal controls or in other factors that could significantly affect internal controls subsequent to the date of their evaluation, including any corrective actions with regard to significant deficiencies and material weaknesses.

(b) FOREIGN REINCORPORATIONS HAVE NO EFFECT.—Nothing in this section 302 shall be interpreted or applied in any way to allow any issuer to lessen the legal force of the statement required under this section 302, by an issuer having reincorporated or having engaged in any other transaction that resulted in the transfer of the corporate domicile or offices of the issuer from inside the United States to outside of the United States.

(c) DEADLINE.—The rules required by subsection (a) shall be effective not later than 30 days after the date of enactment of this Act.

SEC. 303. IMPROPER INFLUENCE ON CONDUCT OF AUDITS.

(a) RULES TO PROHIBIT.—It shall be unlawful, in contravention of such rules or regulations as the Commission shall prescribe as necessary and appropriate in the public interest or for the protection of investors, for any officer or director of an issuer, or any other person acting under the direction thereof, to take any action to fraudulently influence, coerce, manipulate, or mislead any independent public or certified accountant engaged in the performance of an audit of the financial statements of that issuer for the purpose of rendering such financial statements materially misleading.

(b) ENFORCEMENT.—In any civil proceeding, the Commission shall have exclusive authority to enforce this section and any rule or regulation issued under this section.

(c) NO PREEMPTION OF OTHER LAW.—The provisions of subsection (a) shall be in addition to, and shall not supersede or preempt, any other provision of law or any rule or regulation issued thereunder.

(d) DEADLINE FOR RULEMAKING.—The Commission shall—

(1) propose the rules or regulations required by this section, not later than 90 days after the date of enactment of this Act; and

(2) issue final rules or regulations required by this section, not later than 270 days after that date of enactment.

SEC. 304. FORFEITURE OF CERTAIN BONUSES AND PROFITS.

(a) ADDITIONAL COMPENSATION PRIOR TO NONCOMPLIANCE WITH COMMISSION FINANCIAL REPORTING REQUIREMENTS.—If an issuer is required to prepare an accounting restatement due to the material noncompliance of the issuer, as a result of misconduct, with any financial reporting requirement under the securities laws, the chief executive officer and chief financial officer of the issuer shall reimburse the issuer for—

(1) any bonus or other incentive-based or equity-based compensation received by that person from the issuer during the 12–month period following the first public issuance or filing with the Commission (whichever first occurs) of the financial document embodying such financial reporting requirement; and

(2) any profits realized from the sale of securities of the issuer during that 12–month period.

(b) COMMISSION EXEMPTION AUTHORITY.—The Commission may exempt any person from the application of subsection (a), as it deems necessary and appropriate.

SEC. 305. OFFICER AND DIRECTOR BARS AND PENALTIES.

(a) UNFITNESS STANDARD.—

(1) SECURITIES EXCHANGE ACT OF 1934.—Section 21(d)(2) of the Securities Exchange Act of 1934 (15 U.S.C. 78u(d)(2)) is amended by striking "substantial unfitness" and inserting "unfitness".

(2) SECURITIES ACT OF 1933.—Section 20(e) of the Securities Act of 1933 (15 U.S.C. 77t(e)) is amended by striking "substantial unfitness" and inserting "unfitness".

(b) EQUITABLE RELIEF.—Section 21(d) of the Securities Exchange Act of 1934 (15 U.S.C. 78u(d)) is amended by adding at the end the following:

"(5) EQUITABLE RELIEF.—In any action or proceeding brought or instituted by the Commission under any provision of the securities laws, the Commission may seek, and any Federal court may grant, any equitable relief that may be appropriate or necessary for the benefit of investors.".

SEC. 306. INSIDER TRADES DURING PENSION FUND BLACKOUT PERIODS.

(a) PROHIBITION OF INSIDER TRADING DURING PENSION FUND BLACKOUT PERIODS.—

(1) IN GENERAL.—Except to the extent otherwise provided by rule of the Commission pursuant to paragraph (3), it shall be unlawful for any director or executive officer of an issuer of any equity security (other than an exempted security), directly or indirectly, to purchase, sell, or otherwise acquire or transfer any equity security of the issuer (other than an exempted security) during any blackout period with respect to such equity security if such director or officer acquires such equity security in connection with his or her service or employment as a director or executive officer.

(2) REMEDY.—

(A) IN GENERAL.—Any profit realized by a director or executive officer referred to in paragraph (1) from any purchase, sale, or other acquisition or transfer in violation of this subsection shall inure to and be recoverable by the issuer, irrespective of any intention on the part of such director or executive officer in entering into the transaction.

(B) ACTIONS TO RECOVER PROFITS.—An action to recover profits in accordance with this subsection may be instituted at law or in equity in any court of competent jurisdiction by the issuer, or by the owner of any security of the issuer in the name and in behalf of the issuer if the issuer fails or refuses to bring such action within 60 days after the date of request, or fails diligently to prosecute the action thereafter, except that no such suit shall be brought more than 2 years after the date on which such profit was realized.

(3) RULEMAKING AUTHORIZED.—The Commission shall, in consultation with the Secretary of Labor, issue rules to clarify the application of this subsection and to prevent evasion thereof. Such rules shall provide for the application of the requirements of paragraph (1) with respect to entities treated as a single employer with respect to an issuer under section 414(b), (c), (m), or (*o*) of the Internal Revenue Code of 1986 to the extent necessary to clarify the application of such requirements and to prevent evasion thereof. Such rules may also provide for appropriate exceptions from the requirements of this subsection, including exceptions for purchases pursuant to an automatic dividend reinvestment program or purchases or sales made pursuant to an advance election.

(4) BLACKOUT PERIOD.—For purposes of this subsection, the term "blackout period", with respect to the equity securities of any issuer—

(A) means any period of more than 3 consecutive business days during which the ability of not fewer than 50 percent of the participants or beneficiaries under all individual account plans maintained by the issuer to purchase, sell, or otherwise acquire or transfer an interest in any equity of such issuer held in such an individual account plan is temporarily suspended by the issuer or by a fiduciary of the plan; and

(B) does not include, under regulations which shall be prescribed by the Commission—

(i) a regularly scheduled period in which the participants and beneficiaries may not purchase, sell, or otherwise acquire or transfer an interest in any equity of such issuer, if such period is—

(I) incorporated into the individual account plan; and

(II) timely disclosed to employees before becoming participants under the individual account plan or as a subsequent amendment to the plan; or

(ii) any suspension described in subparagraph (A) that is imposed solely in connection with persons becoming participants or beneficiaries, or ceasing to be participants or beneficiaries, in an individual account plan by reason of a corporate merger, acquisition, divestiture, or similar transaction involving the plan or plan sponsor.

(5) INDIVIDUAL ACCOUNT PLAN.—For purposes of this subsection, the term "individual account plan" has the meaning provided in section 3(34) of the Employee Retirement Income Security Act of 1974 (29 U.S. C. 1002(34), except that such term shall not include a one-participant retirement plan (within the meaning of section 101(i)(8)(B) of such Act (29 U.S.C. 1021(i)(8)(B))).

(6) NOTICE TO DIRECTORS, EXECUTIVE OFFICERS, AND THE COMMISSION.—In any case in which a director or executive officer is subject to the requirements of this subsection in connection with a blackout period (as defined in paragraph (4)) with respect to any equity securities, the issuer of such equity securities shall timely notify such director or officer and the Securities and Exchange Commission of such blackout period.

(b) NOTICE REQUIREMENTS TO PARTICIPANTS AND BENEFICIARIES UNDER ERISA.—

(1) IN GENERAL.—Section 101 of the Employee Retirement Income Security Act of 1974 (29 U.S.C. 1021) is amended by redesignating the second

subsection (h) as subsection (j), and by inserting after the first subsection (h) the following new subsection:

"(i) NOTICE OF BLACKOUT PERIODS TO PARTICIPANT OR BENEFICIARY UNDER INDIVIDUAL ACCOUNT PLAN.—

"(1) DUTIES OF PLAN ADMINISTRATOR.—In advance of the commencement of any blackout period with respect to an individual account plan, the plan administrator shall notify the plan participants and beneficiaries who are affected by such action in accordance with this subsection.

"(2) NOTICE REQUIREMENTS.—

"(A) IN GENERAL.—The notices described in paragraph (1) shall be written in a manner calculated to be understood by the average plan participant and shall include—

"(i) the reasons for the blackout period,

"(ii) an identification of the investments and other rights affected,

"(iii) the expected beginning date and length of the blackout period,

"(iv) in the case of investments affected, a statement that the participant or beneficiary should evaluate the appropriateness of their current investment decisions in light of their inability to direct or diversify assets credited to their accounts during the blackout period, and

"(v) such other matters as the Secretary may require by regulation.

"(B) NOTICE TO PARTICIPANTS AND BENEFICIARIES.—Except as otherwise provided in this subsection, notices described in paragraph (1) shall be furnished to all participants and beneficiaries under the plan to whom the blackout period applies at least 30 days in advance of the blackout period.

"(C) EXCEPTION TO 30–DAY NOTICE REQUIREMENT.—In any case in which—

"(i) a deferral of the blackout period would violate the requirements of subparagraph (A) or (B) of section 404(a)(1), and a fiduciary of the plan reasonably so determines in writing, or

"(ii) the inability to provide the 30–day advance notice is due to events that were unforeseeable or circumstances beyond the reasonable control of the plan administrator, and a fiduciary of the plan reasonably so determines in writing, subparagraph (B) shall not apply, and the notice shall be furnished to all participants and beneficiaries under the plan to whom the blackout period applies as soon as reasonably possible under the circumstances unless such a notice in advance of the termination of the blackout period is impracticable.

"(D) WRITTEN NOTICE.—The notice required to be provided under this subsection shall be in writing, except that such notice may be in electronic or other form to the extent that such form is reasonably accessible to the recipient.

"(E) NOTICE TO ISSUERS OF EMPLOYER SECURITIES SUBJECT TO BLACKOUT PERIOD.—In the case of any blackout period in connection with an individual account plan, the plan administrator shall provide timely notice of such blackout period to the issuer of any employer securities subject to such blackout period.

"(3) EXCEPTION FOR BLACKOUT PERIODS WITH LIMITED APPLICABILITY.—In any case in which the blackout period applies only to 1 or more participants or beneficiaries in connection with a merger, acquisition, divestiture, or similar transaction involving the plan or plan sponsor and occurs solely in connection with becoming or ceasing to be a participant or beneficiary under the plan by reason of such merger, acquisition, divestiture, or transaction, the requirement of this subsection that the notice be provided to all participants and beneficiaries shall be treated as met if the notice required under paragraph (1) is provided to such participants or beneficiaries to whom the blackout period applies as soon as reasonably practicable.

"(4) CHANGES IN LENGTH OF BLACKOUT PERIOD.—If, following the furnishing of the notice pursuant to this subsection, there is a change in the beginning date or length of the blackout period (specified in such notice pursuant to paragraph (2)(A)(iii)), the administrator shall provide affected participants and beneficiaries notice of the change as soon as reasonably practicable. In relation to the extended blackout period, such notice shall meet the requirements of paragraph (2)(D) and shall specify any material change in the matters referred to in clauses (i) through (v) of paragraph (2)(A).

"(5) REGULATORY EXCEPTIONS.—The Secretary may provide by regulation for additional exceptions to the requirements of this subsection which the Secretary determines are in the interests of participants and beneficiaries.

"(6) GUIDANCE AND MODEL NOTICES.—The Secretary shall issue guidance and model notices which meet the requirements of this subsection.

"(7) BLACKOUT PERIOD.—For purposes of this subsection—

"(A) IN GENERAL.—The term 'blackout period' means, in connection with an individual account plan, any period for which any ability of participants or beneficiaries under the plan, which is otherwise available under the terms of such plan, to direct or diversify assets credited to their accounts, to obtain loans from the plan, or to obtain distributions from the plan is temporarily suspended, limited, or restricted, if such suspension, limitation, or restriction is for any period of more than 3 consecutive business days.

"(B) EXCLUSIONS.—The term 'blackout period' does not include a suspension, limitation, or restriction—

"(i) which occurs by reason of the application of the securities laws (as defined in section 3(a)(47) of the Securities Exchange Act of 1934),

"(ii) which is a change to the plan which provides for a regularly scheduled suspension, limitation, or restriction which is disclosed to participants or beneficiaries through any summary of material modifications, any materials describing specific investment alternatives under the plan, or any changes thereto, or

"(iii) which applies only to 1 or more individuals, each of whom is the participant, an alternate payee (as defined in section 206(d)(3)(K)), or any other beneficiary pursuant to a qualified domestic relations order (as defined in section 206(d)(3)(B)(i)).

"(8) INDIVIDUAL ACCOUNT PLAN.—

"(A) IN GENERAL.—For purposes of this subsection, the term 'individual account plan' shall have the meaning provided such term in section 3(34), except that such term shall not include a one-participant retirement plan.

"(B) ONE-PARTICIPANT RETIREMENT PLAN.—For purposes of subparagraph (A), the term 'one-participant retirement plan' means a retirement plan that—

"(i) on the first day of the plan year—

"(I) covered only the employer (and the employer's spouse) and the employer owned the entire business (whether or not incorporated), or

"(II) covered only one or more partners (and their spouses) in a business partnership (including partners in an S or C corporation (as defined in section 1361(a) of the Internal Revenue Code of 1986)),

"(ii) meets the minimum coverage requirements of section 410(b) of the Internal Revenue Code of 1986 (as in effect on the date of the enactment of this paragraph) without being combined with any other plan of the business that covers the employees of the business,

"(iii) does not provide benefits to anyone except the employer (and the employer's spouse) or the partners (and their spouses),

"(iv) does not cover a business that is a member of an affiliated service group, a controlled group of corporations, or a group of businesses under common control, and

"(v) does not cover a business that leases employees.".

(2) ISSUANCE OF INITIAL GUIDANCE AND MODEL NOTICE.—The Secretary of Labor shall issue initial guidance and a model notice pursuant to section 101(i)(6) of the Employee Retirement Income Security Act of 1974 (as added by this subsection) not later than January 1, 2003. Not later than 75 days after the date of the enactment of this Act, the Secretary shall promulgate interim final rules necessary to carry out the amendments made by this subsection.

(3) CIVIL PENALTIES FOR FAILURE TO PROVIDE NOTICE.—Section 502 of such Act (29 U.S.C. 1132) is amended—

(A) in subsection (a)(6), by striking "(5), or (6)" and inserting "(5), (6), or (7)";

(B) by redesignating paragraph (7) of subsection (c) as paragraph (8); and

(C) by inserting after paragraph (6) of subsection (c) the following new paragraph:

"(7) The Secretary may assess a civil penalty against a plan administrator of up to $100 a day from the date of the plan administrator's failure or refusal to provide notice to participants and beneficiaries in accordance with section 101(i). For purposes of this paragraph, each violation with respect to any single participant or beneficiary shall be treated as a separate violation.''.

(3) PLAN AMENDMENTS.—If any amendment made by this subsection requires an amendment to any plan, such plan amendment shall not be required to be made before the first plan year beginning on or after the effective date of this section, if—

(A) during the period after such amendment made by this subsection takes effect and before such first plan year, the plan is operated in good faith compliance with the requirements of such amendment made by this subsection, and

(B) such plan amendment applies retroactively to the period after such amendment made by this subsection takes effect and before such first plan year.

(c) EFFECTIVE DATE.—The provisions of this section (including the amendments made thereby) shall take effect 180 days after the date of the enactment of this Act. Good faith compliance with the requirements of such provisions in advance of the issuance of applicable regulations thereunder shall be treated as compliance with such provisions.

SEC. 307. RULES OF PROFESSIONAL RESPONSIBILITY FOR ATTORNEYS.

Not later than 180 days after the date of enactment of this Act, the Commission shall issue rules, in the public interest and for the protection of investors, setting forth minimum standards of professional conduct for attorneys appearing and practicing before the Commission in any way in the representation of issuers, including a rule—

(1) requiring an attorney to report evidence of a material violation of securities law or breach of fiduciary duty or similar violation by the company or any agent thereof, to the chief legal counsel or the chief executive officer of the company (or the equivalent thereof); and

(2) if the counsel or officer does not appropriately respond to the evidence (adopting, as necessary, appropriate remedial measures or sanctions with respect to the violation), requiring the attorney to report the evidence to the audit committee of the board of directors of the issuer or to another committee of the board of directors comprised solely of directors not employed directly or indirectly by the issuer, or to the board of directors.

SEC. 308. FAIR FUNDS FOR INVESTORS.

(a) CIVIL PENALTIES ADDED TO DISGORGEMENT FUNDS FOR THE RELIEF OF VICTIMS.—If in any judicial or administrative action brought by the Commission under the securities laws (as such term is defined in section 3(a)(47) of the Securities Exchange Act of 1934 (15 U.S.C. 78c(a)(47)) the Commission obtains an order requiring disgorgement against any person for a violation of such laws or the rules or regulations thereunder, or such person agrees in settlement of any such action to such disgorgement, and the Commission also obtains pursuant to such laws a civil penalty against such person, the amount of such civil penalty shall, on the motion or at the direction of the Commission, be added to and become part of the disgorgement fund for the benefit of the victims of such violation.

(b) ACCEPTANCE OF ADDITIONAL DONATIONS.—The Commission is authorized to accept, hold, administer, and utilize gifts, bequests and devises of property, both real and personal, to the United States for a disgorgement fund described in subsection (a). Such gifts, bequests, and devises of money and proceeds from sales of other property received as gifts, bequests, or devises shall be deposited in the disgorgement fund and shall be available for allocation in accordance with subsection (a).

(c) STUDY REQUIRED.—

(1) SUBJECT OF STUDY.—The Commission shall review and analyze—

(A) enforcement actions by the Commission over the five years preceding the date of the enactment of this Act that have included proceedings to obtain civil penalties or disgorgements to identify areas where such proceedings may be utilized to efficiently, effectively, and fairly provide restitution for injured investors; and

(B) other methods to more efficiently, effectively, and fairly provide restitution to injured investors, including methods to improve the collection rates for civil penalties and disgorgements.

(2) REPORT REQUIRED.—The Commission shall report its findings to the Committee on Financial Services of the House of Representatives and the Committee on Banking, Housing, and Urban Affairs of the Senate within 180 days after of the date of the enactment of this Act, and shall use such findings to revise its rules and regulations as necessary. The report shall include a discussion of regulatory or legislative actions that are recommended or that may be necessary to address concerns identified in the study.

(d) CONFORMING AMENDMENTS.—Each of the following provisions is amended by inserting ", except as otherwise provided in section 308 of the Sarbanes–Oxley Act of 2002" after "Treasury of the United States":

(1) Section 21(d)(3)(C)(i) of the Securities Exchange Act of 1934 (15 U.S.C. 78u(d)(3)(C)(i)).

(2) Section 21A(d)(1) of such Act (15 U.S.C. 78u–1(d)(1)).

(3) Section 20(d)(3)(A) of the Securities Act of 1933 (15 U.S.C. 77t(d)(3)(A)).

(4) Section 42(e)(3)(A) of the Investment Company Act of 1940 (15 U.S.C. 80a-41(e)(3)(A)).

(5) Section 209(e)(3)(A) of the Investment Advisers Act of 1940 (15 U.S.C. 80b–9(e)(3)(A)).

(e) DEFINITION.—As used in this section, the term "disgorgement fund" means a fund established in any administrative or judicial proceeding described in subsection (a).

TITLE IV—ENHANCED FINANCIAL DISCLOSURES

SEC. 401. DISCLOSURES IN PERIODIC REPORTS.

(a) DISCLOSURES REQUIRED.—Section 13 of the Securities Exchange Act of 1934 (15 U.S.C. 78m) is amended by adding at the end the following:

"(i) ACCURACY OF FINANCIAL REPORTS.—Each financial report that contains financial statements, and that is required to be prepared in accordance with (or reconciled to) generally accepted accounting principles under this title and filed with the Commission shall reflect all material correcting adjustments that have been identified by a registered public accounting firm in accordance with generally accepted accounting principles and the rules and regulations of the Commission.

"(j) OFF–BALANCE SHEET TRANSACTIONS.—Not later than 180 days after the date of enactment of the Sarbanes–Oxley Act of 2002, the Commission shall issue final rules providing that each annual and quarterly financial report required to be filed with the Commission shall disclose all material off-balance sheet transactions, arrangements, obligations (including contingent obligations), and other relationships of the issuer with unconsolidated entities or other persons, that may have a material current or future effect on financial condition, changes in financial condition, results of operations, liquidity, capital expenditures, capital resources, or significant components of revenues or expenses.".

(b) COMMISSION RULES ON PRO FORMA FIGURES.—Not later than 180 days after the date of enactment of the Sarbanes–Oxley Act fo 2002, the Commission shall issue final rules providing that pro forma financial information included in any periodic or other report filed with the Commission pursuant to the securities laws, or in any public disclosure or press or other release, shall be presented in a manner that—

(1) does not contain an untrue statement of a material fact or omit to state a material fact necessary in order to make the pro forma financial information, in light of the circumstances under which it is presented, not misleading; and

(2) reconciles it with the financial condition and results of operations of the issuer under generally accepted accounting principles.

(c) STUDY AND REPORT ON SPECIAL PURPOSE ENTITIES.—

(1) STUDY REQUIRED.—The Commission shall, not later than 1 year after the effective date of adoption of off-balance sheet disclosure rules required by section 13(j) of the Securities Exchange Act of 1934, as added by this section, complete a study of filings by issuers and their disclosures to determine—

(A) the extent of off-balance sheet transactions, including assets, liabilities, leases, losses, and the use of special purpose entities; and

(B) whether generally accepted accounting rules result in financial statements of issuers reflecting the economics of such off-balance sheet transactions to investors in a transparent fashion.

(2) REPORT AND RECOMMENDATIONS.—Not later than 6 months after the date of completion of the study required by paragraph (1), the Commission shall submit a report to the President, the Committee on Banking, Housing, and Urban Affairs of the Senate, and the Committee on Financial Services of the House of Representatives, setting forth—

(A) the amount or an estimate of the amount of off-balance sheet transactions, including assets, liabilities, leases, and losses of, and the use of special purpose entities by, issuers filing periodic reports pursuant to section 13 or 15 of the Securities Exchange Act of 1934;

(B) the extent to which special purpose entities are used to facilitate off-balance sheet transactions;

(C) whether generally accepted accounting principles or the rules of the Commission result in financial statements of issuers reflecting the economics of such transactions to investors in a transparent fashion;

(D) whether generally accepted accounting principles specifically result in the consolidation of special purpose entities sponsored by an issuer in cases in which the issuer has the majority of the risks and rewards of the special purpose entity; and

(E) any recommendations of the Commission for improving the transparency and quality of reporting off-balance sheet transactions in the financial statements and disclosures required to be filed by an issuer with the Commission.

SEC. 402. ENHANCED CONFLICT OF INTEREST PROVISIONS.

(a) PROHIBITION ON PERSONAL LOANS TO EXECUTIVES.—Section 13 of the Securities Exchange Act of 1934 (15 U.S.C. 78m), as amended by this Act, is amended by adding at the end the following:

"(k) PROHIBITION ON PERSONAL LOANS TO EXECUTIVES.—

"(1) IN GENERAL.—It shall be unlawful for any issuer (as defined in section 2 of the Sarbanes–Oxley Act of 2002), directly or indirectly, including through any subsidiary, to extend or maintain credit, to arrange for the extension of credit, or to renew an extension of credit, in the form of a personal loan to or for any director or executive officer (or equivalent thereof) of that issuer. An extension of credit maintained by the issuer on the date of enactment of this subsection shall not be subject to the provisions of this subsection, provided that there is no material modification to any term of any such extension of credit or any renewal of any such extension of credit on or after that date of enactment.

"(2) LIMITATION.—Paragraph (1) does not preclude any home improvement and manufactured home loans (as that term is defined in section 5 of the Home Owners' Loan Act (12 U.S.C. 1464)), consumer credit (as defined in section 103 of the Truth in Lending Act (15 U.S.C. 1602)), or any extension of credit under an open end credit plan (as defined in section 103 of the Truth in Lending Act (15 U.S.C. 1602)), or a charge card (as defined in section 127(c)(4)(e) of the Truth in Lending Act (15 U.S.C. 1637(c)(4)(e)), or any extension of credit by a broker or dealer registered under section 15 of this title to an employee of that broker or dealer to buy, trade, or carry securities, that is permitted under rules or regulations of the Board of Governors of the Federal Reserve System pursuant to section 7 of this title (other than an extension of credit that would be used to purchase the stock of that issuer), that is—

"(A) made or provided in the ordinary course of the consumer credit business of such issuer;

"(B) of a type that is generally made available by such issuer to the public; and

"(C) made by such issuer on market terms, or terms that are no more favorable than those offered by the issuer to the general public for such extensions of credit.

"(3) RULE OF CONSTRUCTION FOR CERTAIN LOANS.—Paragraph (1) does not apply to any loan made or maintained by an insured depository institution (as defined in section 3 of the Federal Deposit Insurance Act (12 U.S.C. 1813)), if the loan is subject to the insider lending restrictions of section 22(h) of the Federal Reserve Act (12 U.S.C. 375b).".

SEC. 403. DISCLOSURES OF TRANSACTIONS INVOLVING MANAGEMENT AND PRINCIPAL STOCKHOLDERS.

(a) AMENDMENT.—Section 16 of the Securities Exchange Act of 1934 (15 U.S. C. 78p) is amended by striking the heading of such section and subsection (a) and inserting the following:

"SEC. 16. DIRECTORS, OFFICERS, AND PRINCIPAL STOCKHOLDERS.

"(a) DISCLOSURES REQUIRED.—

"(1) DIRECTORS, OFFICERS, AND PRINCIPAL STOCKHOLDERS REQUIRED TO FILE.—Every person who is directly or indirectly the beneficial owner of more than 10 percent of any class of any equity security (other than an exempted security) which is registered pursuant to section 12, or who is a director or an officer of the issuer of such security, shall file the statements required by this subsection with the Commission (and, if such security is registered on a national securities exchange, also with the exchange).

"(2) TIME OF FILING.—The statements required by this subsection shall be filed—

"(A) at the time of the registration of such security on a national securities exchange or by the effective date of a registration statement filed pursuant to section 12(g);

"(B) within 10 days after he or she becomes such beneficial owner, director, or officer;

"(C) if there has been a change in such ownership, or if such person shall have purchased or sold a security-based swap agreement (as defined in section 206(b) of the Gramm–Leach–Bliley Act (15 U.S.C. 78c note)) involving such equity security, before the end of the second business day following the day on which the subject transaction has been executed, or at such other time as the Commission shall establish, by rule, in any case in which the Commission determines that such 2–day period is not feasible.

"(3) CONTENTS OF STATEMENTS.—A statement filed—

"(A) under subparagraph (A) or (B) of paragraph (2) shall contain a statement of the amount of all equity securities of such issuer of which the filing person is the beneficial owner; and

"(B) under subparagraph (C) of such paragraph shall indicate ownership by the filing person at the date of filing, any such changes in such ownership, and such purchases and sales of the security-based swap agreements as have occurred since the most recent such filing under such subparagraph.

"(4) ELECTRONIC FILING AND AVAILABILITY.—Beginning not later than 1 year after the date of enactment of the Sarbanes–Oxley Act of 2002—

"(A) a statement filed under subparagraph (C) of paragraph (2) shall be filed electronically;

"(B) the Commission shall provide each such statement on a publicly accessible Internet site not later than the end of the business day following that filing; and

"(C) the issuer (if the issuer maintains a corporate website) shall provide that statement on that corporate website, not later than the end of the business day following that filing.".

(b) EFFECTIVE DATE.—The amendment made by this section shall be effective 30 days after the date of the enactment of this Act.

SEC. 404. MANAGEMENT ASSESSMENT OF INTERNAL CONTROLS.

(a) RULES REQUIRED.—The Commission shall prescribe rules requiring each annual report required by section 13(a) or 15(d) of the Securities Exchange Act of 1934 (15 U.S.C. 78m or 78o(d)) to contain an internal control report, which shall—

(1) state the responsibility of management for establishing and maintaining an adequate internal control structure and procedures for financial reporting; and

(2) contain an assessment, as of the end of the most recent fiscal year of the issuer, of the effectiveness of the internal control structure and procedures of the issuer for financial reporting.

(b) INTERNAL CONTROL EVALUATION AND REPORTING.—With respect to the internal control assessment required by subsection (a), each registered public accounting firm that prepares or issues the audit report for the issuer shall attest to, and report on, the assessment made by the management of the issuer. An attestation made under this subsection shall be made in accordance with standards for attestation engagements issued or adopted by the Board. Any such attestation shall not be the subject of a separate engagement.

SEC. 405. EXEMPTION.

Nothing in section 401, 402, or 404, the amendments made by those sections, or the rules of the Commission under those sections shall apply to any investment company registered under section 8 of the Investment Company Act of 1940 (15 U.S.C. 80a–8).

SEC. 406. CODE OF ETHICS FOR SENIOR FINANCIAL OFFICERS.

(a) CODE OF ETHICS DISCLOSURE.—The Commission shall issue rules to require each issuer, together with periodic reports required pursuant to section 13(a) or 15(d) of the Securities Exchange Act of 1934, to disclose whether or not, and if not, the reason therefor, such issuer has adopted a code of ethics for senior financial officers, applicable to its principal financial officer and comptroller or principal accounting officer, or persons performing similar functions.

(b) CHANGES IN CODES OF ETHICS.—The Commission shall revise its regulations concerning matters requiring prompt disclosure on Form 8–K (or any successor thereto) to require the immediate disclosure, by means of the filing of such form, dissemination by the Internet or by other electronic means, by any issuer of any change in or waiver of the code of ethics for senior financial officers.

(c) DEFINITION.—In this section, the term "code of ethics" means such standards as are reasonably necessary to promote—

(1) honest and ethical conduct, including the ethical handling of actual or apparent conflicts of interest between personal and professional relationships;

(2) full, fair, accurate, timely, and understandable disclosure in the periodic reports required to be filed by the issuer; and

(3) compliance with applicable governmental rules and regulations.

(d) DEADLINE FOR RULEMAKING.—The Commission shall—

(1) propose rules to implement this section, not later than 90 days after the date of enactment of this Act; and

(2) issue final rules to implement this section, not later than 180 days after that date of enactment.

SEC. 407. DISCLOSURE OF AUDIT COMMITTEE FINANCIAL EXPERT.

(a) RULES DEFINING "FINANCIAL EXPERT".—The Commission shall issue rules, as necessary or appropriate in the public interest and consistent with the protection of investors, to require each issuer, together with periodic reports required pursuant to sections 13(a) and 15(d) of the Securities Exchange Act of 1934, to disclose whether or not, and if not, the reasons therefor, the audit committee of that issuer is comprised of at least 1 member who is a financial expert, as such term is defined by the Commission.

(b) CONSIDERATIONS.—In defining the term "financial expert" for purposes of subsection (a), the Commission shall consider whether a person has, through education and experience as a public accountant or auditor or a principal financial officer, comptroller, or principal accounting officer of an issuer, or from a position involving the performance of similar functions—

(1) an understanding of generally accepted accounting principles and financial statements;

(2) experience in—

(A) the preparation or auditing of financial statements of generally comparable issuers; and

(B) the application of such principles in connection with the accounting for estimates, accruals, and reserves;

(3) experience with internal accounting controls; and

(4) an understanding of audit committee functions.

(c) DEADLINE FOR RULEMAKING.—The Commission shall—

(1) propose rules to implement this section, not later than 90 days after the date of enactment of this Act; and

(2) issue final rules to implement this section, not later than 180 days after that date of enactment.

SEC. 408. ENHANCED REVIEW OF PERIODIC DISCLOSURES BY ISSUERS.

(a) REGULAR AND SYSTEMATIC REVIEW.—The Commission shall review disclosures made by issuers reporting under section 13(a) of the Securities Exchange Act of 1934 (including reports filed on Form 10–K), and which have a class of securities listed on a national securities exchange or traded on an automated quotation facility of a national securities association, on a regular and systematic basis for the protection of investors. Such review shall include a review of an issuer's financial statement.

(b) REVIEW CRITERIA.—For purposes of scheduling the reviews required by subsection (a), the Commission shall consider, among other factors—

(1) issuers that have issued material restatements of financial results;

(2) issuers that experience significant volatility in their stock price as compared to other issuers;

(3) issuers with the largest market capitalization;

(4) emerging companies with disparities in price to earning ratios;

(5) issuers whose operations significantly affect any material sector of the economy; and

(6) any other factors that the Commission may consider relevant.

(c) MINIMUM REVIEW PERIOD.—In no event shall an issuer required to file reports under section 13(a) or 15(d) of the Securities Exchange Act of 1934 be reviewed under this section less frequently than once every 3 years.

SEC. 409. REAL TIME ISSUER DISCLOSURES.

Section 13 of the Securities Exchange Act of 1934 (15 U.S.C. 78m), as amended by this Act, is amended by adding at the end the following:

"(*l*) REAL TIME ISSUER DISCLOSURES.—Each issuer reporting under section 13(a) or 15(d) shall disclose to the public on a rapid and current basis such additional information concerning material changes in the financial condition or operations of the issuer, in plain English, which may include trend and qualitative information and graphic presentations, as the Commission determines, by rule, is necessary or useful for the protection of investors and in the public interest.".

TITLE V—ANALYST CONFLICTS OF INTEREST

SEC. 501. TREATMENT OF SECURITIES ANALYSTS BY REGISTERED SECURITIES ASSOCIATIONS AND NATIONAL SECURITIES EXCHANGES.

(a) RULES REGARDING SECURITIES ANALYSTS.—The Securities Exchange Act of 1934 (15 U.S.C. 78a et seq.) is amended by inserting after section 15C the following new section:

"SEC. 15D. SECURITIES ANALYSTS AND RESEARCH REPORTS.

"(a) ANALYST PROTECTIONS.—The Commission, or upon the authorization and direction of the Commission, a registered securities association or national securities exchange, shall have adopted, not later than 1 year after the date of enactment of this section, rules reasonably designed to address conflicts of interest that can arise when securities analysts recommend equity securities in research reports and public appearances, in order to improve the objectivity of research and provide investors with more useful and reliable information, including rules designed—

"(1) to foster greater public confidence in securities research, and to protect the objectivity and independence of securities analysts, by—

"(A) restricting the prepublication clearance or approval of research reports by persons employed by the broker or dealer who are engaged in investment banking activities, or persons not directly responsible for investment research, other than legal or compliance staff;

"(B) limiting the supervision and compensatory evaluation of securities analysts to officials employed by the broker or dealer who are not engaged in investment banking activities; and

"(C) requiring that a broker or dealer and persons employed by a broker or dealer who are involved with investment banking activities may not, directly or indirectly, retaliate against or threaten to retaliate against any securities analyst employed by that broker or dealer or its affiliates as a result of an adverse, negative, or otherwise unfavorable research report that may adversely affect the present or prospective investment banking relationship of the broker or dealer with the issuer that is the subject of the research report, except that such rules may not limit the authority of a broker or dealer to discipline a securities analyst for causes other than such research report in accordance with the policies and procedures of the firm;

"(2) to define periods during which brokers or dealers who have participated, or are to participate, in a public offering of securities as underwriters or dealers should not publish or otherwise distribute research reports relating to such securities or to the issuer of such securities;

"(3) to establish structural and institutional safeguards within registered brokers or dealers to assure that securities analysts are separated by appropriate informational partitions within the firm from the review, pressure, or oversight of those whose involvement in investment banking activities might potentially bias their judgment or supervision; and

"(4) to address such other issues as the Commission, or such association or exchange, determines appropriate.

"(b) DISCLOSURE.—The Commission, or upon the authorization and direction of the Commission, a registered securities association or national securities exchange, shall have adopted, not later than 1 year after the date of enactment of this section, rules reasonably designed to require each securities analyst to disclose in public appearances, and each registered broker or dealer to disclose in each research report, as applicable, conflicts of interest that are known or should have been known by the securities analyst or the broker or dealer, to exist at the time of the appearance or the date of distribution of the report, including—

"(1) the extent to which the securities analyst has debt or equity investments in the issuer that is the subject of the appearance or research report;

"(2) whether any compensation has been received by the registered broker or dealer, or any affiliate thereof, including the securities analyst, from the issuer that is the subject of the appearance or research report, subject to such exemptions as the Commission may determine appropriate and necessary to prevent disclosure by virtue of this paragraph of material non-public information regarding specific potential future investment banking transactions of such issuer, as is appropriate in the public interest and consistent with the protection of investors;

"(3) whether an issuer, the securities of which are recommended in the appearance or research report, currently is, or during the 1–year period preceding the date of the appearance or date of distribution of the report has been, a client of the registered broker or dealer, and if so, stating the types of services provided to the issuer;

"(4) whether the securities analyst received compensation with respect to a research report, based upon (among any other factors) the investment banking revenues (either generally or specifically earned from the issuer being analyzed) of the registered broker or dealer; and

"(5) such other disclosures of conflicts of interest that are material to investors, research analysts, or the broker or dealer as the Commission, or such association or exchange, determines appropriate.

"(c) DEFINITIONS.—In this section—

"(1) the term 'securities analyst' means any associated person of a registered broker or dealer that is principally responsible for, and any associated person who reports directly or indirectly to a securities analyst in connection with, the preparation of the substance of a research report, whether or not any such person has the job title of 'securities analyst'; and

"(2) the term 'research report' means a written or electronic communication that includes an analysis of equity securities of individual companies or industries, and that provides information reasonably sufficient upon which to base an investment decision.".

(b) ENFORCEMENT.—Section 21B(a) of the Securities Exchange Act of 1934 (15 U.S.C. 78u–2(a)) is amended by inserting "15D," before "15B".

(c) COMMISSION AUTHORITY.—The Commission may promulgate and amend its regulations, or direct a registered securities association or national securities exchange to promulgate and amend its rules, to carry out section 15D of the Securities Exchange Act of 1934, as added by this section, as is necessary for the protection of investors and in the public interest.

TITLE VI—COMMISSION RESOURCES AND AUTHORITY

SEC. 601. AUTHORIZATION OF APPROPRIATIONS.

Section 35 of the Securities Exchange Act of 1934 (15 U.S.C. 78kk) is amended to read as follows:

"SEC. 35. AUTHORIZATION OF APPROPRIATIONS.

"In addition to any other funds authorized to be appropriated to the Commission, there are authorized to be appropriated to carry out the functions, powers, and duties of the Commission, $776,000,000 for fiscal year 2003, of which—

"(1) $102,700,000 shall be available to fund additional compensation, including salaries and benefits, as authorized in the Investor and Capital Markets Fee Relief Act (Public Law 107–123; 115 Stat. 2390 et seq.);

"(2) $108,400,000 shall be available for information technology, security enhancements, and recovery and mitigation activities in light of the terrorist attacks of September 11, 2001; and

"(3) $98,000,000 shall be available to add not fewer than an additional 200 qualified professionals to provide enhanced oversight of auditors and audit services required by the Federal securities laws, and to improve Commission investigative and disciplinary efforts with respect to such auditors and services, as well as for additional professional support staff necessary to strengthen the programs of the Commission involving Full Disclosure and Prevention and Suppression of Fraud, risk management, industry technology review, compliance, inspections, examinations, market regulation, and investment management.".

SEC. 602. APPEARANCE AND PRACTICE BEFORE THE COMMISSION.

The Securities Exchange Act of 1934 (15 U.S.C. 78a et seq.) is amended by inserting after section 4B the following:

"SEC. 4C. APPEARANCE AND PRACTICE BEFORE THE COMMISSION.

"(a) AUTHORITY TO CENSURE.—The Commission may censure any person, or deny, temporarily or permanently, to any person the privilege of appearing or practicing before the Commission in any way, if that person is found by the Commission, after notice and opportunity for hearing in the matter—

"(1) not to possess the requisite qualifications to represent others;

"(2) to be lacking in character or integrity, or to have engaged in unethical or improper professional conduct; or

"(3) to have willfully violated, or willfully aided and abetted the violation of, any provision of the securities laws or the rules and regulations issued thereunder.

"(b) DEFINITION.—With respect to any registered public accounting firm or associated person, for purposes of this section, the term 'improper professional conduct' means—

"(1) intentional or knowing conduct, including reckless conduct, that results in a violation of applicable professional standards; and

"(2) negligent conduct in the form of—

"(A) a single instance of highly unreasonable conduct that results in a violation of applicable professional standards in circumstances in which the registered public accounting firm or associated person knows, or should know, that heightened scrutiny is warranted; or

"(B) repeated instances of unreasonable conduct, each resulting in a violation of applicable professional standards, that indicate a lack of competence to practice before the Commission.".

SEC. 603. FEDERAL COURT AUTHORITY TO IMPOSE PENNY STOCK BARS.

(a) Securities Exchange Act of 1934—Section 21(d) of the Securities Exchange Act of 1934 (15 U.S.C. 78u(d)), as amended by this Act, is amended by adding at the end the following:

"(6) AUTHORITY OF A COURT TO PROHIBIT PERSONS FROM PARTICIPATING IN AN OFFERING OF PENNY STOCK.—

"(A) IN GENERAL.—In any proceeding under paragraph (1) against any person participating in, or, at the time of the alleged misconduct who was participating in, an offering of penny stock, the court may prohibit that person from participating in an offering of penny stock, conditionally or unconditionally, and permanently or for such period of time as the court shall determine.

"(B) DEFINITION.—For purposes of this paragraph, the term 'person participating in an offering of penny stock' includes any person engaging in activities with a broker, dealer, or issuer for purposes of issuing, trading, or inducing or attempting to induce the purchase or sale of, any penny stock. The Commission may, by rule or regulation, define such term to include other activities, and may, by rule, regulation, or order, exempt any person or class of persons, in whole or in part, conditionally or unconditionally, from inclusion in such term.".

(b) Securities Act of 1933.—Section 20 of the Securities Act of 1933 (15 U.S.C. 77t) is amended by adding at the end the following:

"(g) AUTHORITY OF A COURT TO PROHIBIT PERSONS FROM PARTICIPATING IN AN OFFERING OF PENNY STOCK.—

"(1) IN GENERAL.—In any proceeding under subsection (a) against any person participating in, or, at the time of the alleged misconduct, who was participating in, an offering of penny stock, the court may prohibit that person from participating in an offering of penny stock, conditionally or unconditionally, and permanently or for such period of time as the court shall determine.

"(2) DEFINITION.—For purposes of this subsection, the term 'person participating in an offering of penny stock' includes any person engaging in activities with a broker, dealer, or issuer for purposes of issuing, trading, or inducing or attempting to induce the purchase or sale of, any penny stock. The Commission may, by rule or regulation, define such term to include other activities, and may, by rule, regulation, or order, exempt any person or class of persons, in whole or in part, conditionally or unconditionally, from inclusion in such term.".

SEC. 604. QUALIFICATIONS OF ASSOCIATED PERSONS OF BROKERS AND DEALERS.

(a) BROKERS AND DEALERS.—Section 15(b)(4) of the Securities Exchange Act of 1934 (15 U.S.C. 78o) is amended—

(1) by striking subparagraph (F) and inserting the following:

"(F) is subject to any order of the Commission barring or suspending the right of the person to be associated with a broker or dealer;"; and

(2) in subparagraph (G), by striking the period at the end and inserting the following: "; or

"(H) is subject to any final order of a State securities commission (or any agency or officer performing like functions), State authority that supervises or examines banks, savings associations, or credit unions, State insurance commission (or any agency or office performing like functions), an appropriate Federal banking agency (as defined in section 3 of the Federal Deposit Insurance Act (12 U.S.C. 1813(q))), or the National Credit Union Administration, that—

"(i) bars such person from association with an entity regulated by such commission, authority, agency, or officer, or from engaging in the business of securities, insurance, banking, savings association activities, or credit union activities; or

"(ii) constitutes a final order based on violations of any laws or regulations that prohibit fraudulent, manipulative, or deceptive conduct.".

(b) INVESTMENT ADVISERS.—Section 203(e) of the Investment Advisers Act of 1940 (15 U.S.C. 80b–3(e)) is amended—

(1) by striking paragraph (7) and inserting the following:

"(7) is subject to any order of the Commission barring or suspending the right of the person to be associated with an investment adviser;";

(2) in paragraph (8), by striking the period at the end and inserting "; or"; and

(3) by adding at the end the following:

"(9) is subject to any final order of a State securities commission (or any agency or officer performing like functions), State authority that supervises or examines banks, savings associations, or credit unions, State insurance commission (or any agency or office performing like functions), an appropriate Federal banking agency (as defined in section 3 of the Federal Deposit Insurance Act (12 U.S.C. 1813(q))), or the National Credit Union Administration, that—

"(A) bars such person from association with an entity regulated by such commission, authority, agency, or officer, or from engaging in the business of securities, insurance, banking, savings association activities, or credit union activities; or

"(B) constitutes a final order based on violations of any laws or regulations that prohibit fraudulent, manipulative, or deceptive conduct.".

(c) CONFORMING AMENDMENTS.—

(1) SECURITIES EXCHANGE ACT OF 1934.—The Securities Exchange Act of 1934 (15 U.S.C. 78a et seq.) is amended—

(A) in section 3(a)(39)(F) (15 U.S.C. 78c(a)(39)(F))—

(i) by striking "or (G)" and inserting "(H), or (G)"; and

(ii) by inserting ", or is subject to an order or finding," before "enumerated";

(B) in each of section 15(b)(6)(A)(i) (15 U.S.C. 78o(b)(6)(A)(i)), paragraphs (2) and (4) of section 15B(c) (15 U.S.C. 78o–4(c)), and subparagraphs (A) and (C) of section 15C(c)(1) (15 U.S.C. 78o–5(c)(1))—

(i) by striking "or (G)" each place that term appears and inserting "(H), or (G)"; and

(ii) by striking "or omission" each place that term appears, and inserting ", or is subject to an order or finding,"; and

(C) in each of paragraphs (3)(A) and (4)(C) of section 17A(c) (15 U.S.C. 78q–1(c))—

(i) by striking "or (G)" each place that term appears and inserting "(H), or (G)"; and

(ii) by inserting ", or is subject to an order or finding," before "enumerated" each place that term appears.

(2) INVESTMENT ADVISERS ACT OF 1940.—Section 203(f) of the Investment Advisers Act of 1940 (15 U.S.C. 80b–3(f)) is amended—

(A) by striking "or (8)" and inserting "(8), or (9)"; and

(B) by inserting "or (3)" after "paragraph (2)".

TITLE VII—STUDIES AND REPORTS

SEC. 701. GAO STUDY AND REPORT REGARDING CONSOLIDATION OF PUBLIC ACCOUNTING FIRMS.

(a) STUDY REQUIRED.—The Comptroller General of the United States shall conduct a study—

(1) to identify—

(A) the factors that have led to the consolidation of public accounting firms since 1989 and the consequent reduction in the number of firms capable of providing audit services to large national and multi-national business organizations that are subject to the securities laws;

(B) the present and future impact of the condition described in subparagraph (A) on capital formation and securities markets, both domestic and international; and

(C) solutions to any problems identified under subparagraph (B), including ways to increase competition and the number of firms capable of providing audit services to large national and multinational business organizations that are subject to the securities laws;

(2) of the problems, if any, faced by business organizations that have resulted from limited competition among public accounting firms, including—

(A) higher costs;

(B) lower quality of services;

(C) impairment of auditor independence; or

(D) lack of choice; and

(3) whether and to what extent Federal or State regulations impede competition among public accounting firms.

(b) CONSULTATION.—In planning and conducting the study under this section, the Comptroller General shall consult with—

(1) the Commission;

(2) the regulatory agencies that perform functions similar to the Commission within the other member countries of the Group of Seven Industrialized Nations;

(3) the Department of Justice; and

(4) any other public or private sector organization that the Comptroller General considers appropriate.

(c) REPORT REQUIRED.—Not later than 1 year after the date of enactment of this Act, the Comptroller General shall submit a report on the results of the study required by this section to the Committee on Banking, Housing, and Urban Affairs of the Senate and the Committee on Financial Services of the House of Representatives.

SEC. 702. COMMISSION STUDY AND REPORT REGARDING CREDIT RATING AGENCIES.

(a) STUDY REQUIRED.—

(1) IN GENERAL.—The Commission shall conduct a study of the role and function of credit rating agencies in the operation of the securities market.

(2) AREAS OF CONSIDERATION.—The study required by this subsection shall examine—

(A) the role of credit rating agencies in the evaluation of issuers of securities;

(B) the importance of that role to investors and the functioning of the securities markets;

(C) any impediments to the accurate appraisal by credit rating agencies of the financial resources and risks of issuers of securities;

(D) any barriers to entry into the business of acting as a credit rating agency, and any measures needed to remove such barriers;

(E) any measures which may be required to improve the dissemination of information concerning such resources and risks when credit rating agencies announce credit ratings; and

(F) any conflicts of interest in the operation of credit rating agencies and measures to prevent such conflicts or ameliorate the consequences of such conflicts.

(b) REPORT REQUIRED.—The Commission shall submit a report on the study required by subsection (a) to the President, the Committee on Financial

Services of the House of Representatives, and the Committee on Banking, Housing, and Urban Affairs of the Senate not later than 180 days after the date of enactment of this Act.

SEC. 703. STUDY AND REPORT ON VIOLATORS AND VIOLATIONS.

(a) STUDY.—The Commission shall conduct a study to determine, based upon information for the period from January 1, 1998, to December 31, 2001—

(1) the number of securities professionals, defined as public accountants, public accounting firms, investment bankers, investment advisers, brokers, dealers, attorneys, and other securities professionals practicing before the Commission—

(A) who have been found to have aided and abetted a violation of the Federal securities laws, including rules or regulations promulgated thereunder (collectively referred to in this section as "Federal securities laws"), but who have not been sanctioned, disciplined, or otherwise penalized as a primary violator in any administrative action or civil proceeding, including in any settlement of such an action or proceeding (referred to in this section as "aiders and abettors"); and

(B) who have been found to have been primary violators of the Federal securities laws;

(2) a description of the Federal securities laws violations committed by aiders and abettors and by primary violators, including—

(A) the specific provision of the Federal securities laws violated;

(B) the specific sanctions and penalties imposed upon such aiders and abettors and primary violators, including the amount of any monetary penalties assessed upon and collected from such persons;

(C) the occurrence of multiple violations by the same person or persons, either as an aider or abettor or as a primary violator; and

(D) whether, as to each such violator, disciplinary sanctions have been imposed, including any censure, suspension, temporary bar, or permanent bar to practice before the Commission; and

(3) the amount of disgorgement, restitution, or any other fines or payments that the Commission has assessed upon and collected from, aiders and abettors and from primary violators.

(b) REPORT.—A report based upon the study conducted pursuant to subsection (a) shall be submitted to the Committee on Banking, Housing, and Urban Affairs of the Senate, and the Committee on Financial Services of the House of Representatives not later than 6 months after the date of enactment of this Act.

SEC. 704. STUDY OF ENFORCEMENT ACTIONS.

(a) STUDY REQUIRED.—The Commission shall review and analyze all enforcement actions by the Commission involving violations of reporting requirements imposed under the securities laws, and restatements of financial statements, over the 5-year period preceding the date of enactment of this Act, to identify areas of reporting that are most susceptible to fraud, inappropriate manipulation, or inappropriate earnings management, such as revenue recognition and the accounting treatment of off-balance sheet special purpose entities.

(b) REPORT REQUIRED.—The Commission shall report its findings to the Committee on Financial Services of the House of Representatives and the Committee on Banking, Housing, and Urban Affairs of the Senate, not later than 180 days after the date of enactment of this Act, and shall use such findings to revise its rules and regulations, as necessary. The report shall include a discussion of regulatory or legislative steps that are recommended or that may be necessary to address concerns identified in the study.

SEC. 705. STUDY OF INVESTMENT BANKS.

(a) GAO STUDY.—The Comptroller General of the United States shall conduct a study on whether investment banks and financial advisers assisted public companies in manipulating their earnings and obfuscating their true financial condition. The study should address the rule of investment banks and financial advisers—

(1) in the collapse of the Enron Corporation, including with respect to the design and implementation of derivatives transactions, transactions involving special purpose vehicles, and other financial arrangements that may have had the effect of altering the company's reported financial statements in ways that obscured the true financial picture of the company;

(2) in the failure of Global Crossing, including with respect to transactions involving swaps of fiberoptic cable capacity, in the designing transactions that may have had the effect of altering the company's reported financial statements in ways that obscured the true financial picture of the company; and

(3) generally, in creating and marketing transactions which may have been designed solely to enable companies to manipulate revenue streams, obtain loans, or move liabilities off balance sheets without altering the economic and business risks faced by the companies or any other mechanism to obscure a company's financial picture.

(b) REPORT.—The Comptroller General shall report to Congress not later than 180 days after the date of enactment of this Act on the results of the study required by this section. The report shall include a discussion of regulatory or legislative steps that are recommended or that may be necessary to address concerns identified in the study.

TITLE VIII—CORPORATE AND CRIMINAL FRAUD ACCOUNTABILITY

SEC. 801. SHORT TITLE.

This title may be cited as the "Corporate and Criminal Fraud Accountability Act of 2002".

SEC. 802. CRIMINAL PENALTIES FOR ALTERING DOCUMENTS.

(a) IN GENERAL.—Chapter 73 of title 18, United States Code, is amended by adding at the end the following:

"§ 1519. Destruction, alteration, or falsification of records in Federal investigations and bankruptcy

'Whoever knowingly alters, destroys, mutilates, conceals, covers up, falsifies, or makes a false entry in any record, document, or tangible object with the intent to impede, obstruct, or influence the investigation or proper administration of any matter within the jurisdiction of any department or agency of the United States or any case filed under title 11, or in relation to or contemplation of any such matter or case, shall be fined under this title, imprisoned not more than 20 years, or both.

"§ 1520. Destruction of corporate audit records

"(a)(1) Any accountant who conducts an audit of an issuer of securities to which section 10A(a) of the Securities Exchange Act of 1934 (15 U.S.C. 78j-1(a)) applies, shall maintain all audit or review workpapers for a period of 5 years from the end of the fiscal period in which the audit or review was concluded.

"(2) The Securities and Exchange Commission shall promulgate, within 180 days, after adequate notice and an opportunity for comment, such rules and regulations, as are reasonably necessary, relating to the retention of relevant records such as workpapers, documents that form the basis of an audit or review, memoranda, correspondence, communications, other documents, and records (including electronic records) which are created, sent, or received in connection with an audit or review and contain conclusions, opinions, analyses, or financial data relating to such an audit or review, which is conducted by any accountant who conducts an audit of an issuer of securities to which section 10A(a) of the Securities Exchange Act of 1934 (15 U.S.C. 78j–1(a)) applies. The Commission may, from time to time, amend or supplement the rules and regulations that it is required to promulgate under this section, after adequate notice and an opportunity for comment, in order to ensure that such rules and regulations adequately comport with the purposes of this section.

"(b) Whoever knowingly and willfully violates subsection (a)(1), or any rule or regulation promulgated by the Securities and Exchange Commission under subsection (a)(2), shall be fined under this title, imprisoned not more than 10 years, or both.

"(c) Nothing in this section shall be deemed to diminish or relieve any person of any other duty or obligation imposed by Federal or State law or regulation to maintain, or refrain from destroying, any document.".

(b) CLERICAL AMENDMENT.—The table of sections at the beginning of chapter 73 of title 18, United States Code, is amended by adding at the end the following new items:

"1519. Destruction, alteration, or falsification of records in Federal investigations and bankruptcy.

"1520. Destruction of corporate audit records.".

SEC. 803. DEBTS NONDISCHARGEABLE IF INCURRED IN VIOLATION OF SECURITIES FRAUD LAWS.

Section 523(a) of title 11, United States Code, is amended—

(1) in paragraph (17), by striking "or" after the semicolon;

(2) in paragraph (18), by striking the period at the end and inserting "; or"; and

(3) by adding at the end, the following:

"(19) that—

"(A) is for—

"(i) the violation of any of the Federal securities laws (as that term is defined in section 3(a)(47) of the Securities Exchange Act of 1934), any of the State securities laws, or any regulation or order issued under such Federal or State securities laws; or

"(ii) common law fraud, deceit, or manipulation in connection with the purchase or sale of any security; and

"(B) results from—

"(i) any judgment, order, consent order, or decree entered in any Federal or State judicial or administrative proceeding;

"(ii) any settlement agreement entered into by the debtor; or

"(iii) any court or administrative order for any damages, fine, penalty, citation, restitutionary payment, disgorgement payment, attorney fee, cost, or other payment owed by the debtor.".

SEC. 804. STATUTE OF LIMITATIONS FOR SECURITIES FRAUD.

(a) IN GENERAL.—Section 1658 of title 28, United States Code, is amended—

(1) by inserting "(a)" before "Except"; and

(2) by adding at the end the following:

"(b) Notwithstanding subsection (a), a private right of action that involves a claim of fraud, deceit, manipulation, or contrivance in contravention of a regulatory requirement concerning the securities laws, as defined in section 3(a)(47) of the Securities Exchange Act of 1934 (15 U.S.C. 78c(a)(47)), may be brought not later than the earlier of—

"(1) 2 years after the discovery of the facts constituting the violation; or

"(2) 5 years after such violation.".

(b) EFFECTIVE DATE.—The limitations period provided by section 1658(b) of title 28, United States Code, as added by this section, shall apply to all proceedings addressed by this section that are commenced on or after the date of enactment of this Act.

(c) NO CREATION OF ACTIONS.—Nothing in this section shall create a new, private right of action.

SEC. 805. REVIEW OF FEDERAL SENTENCING GUIDELINES FOR OBSTRUCTION OF JUSTICE AND EXTENSIVE CRIMINAL FRAUD.

(a) ENHANCEMENT OF FRAUD AND OBSTRUCTION OF JUSTICE SENTENCES.—Pursuant to section 994 of title 28, United States Code, and in accordance with this section, the United States Sentencing Commission shall review and amend, as appropriate, the Federal Sentencing Guidelines and related policy statements to ensure that—

(1) the base offense level and existing enhancements contained in United States Sentencing Guideline 2J1.2 relating to obstruction of justice are sufficient to deter and punish that activity;

(2) the enhancements and specific offense characteristics relating to obstruction of justice are adequate in cases where—

(A) the destruction, alteration, or fabrication of evidence involves—

(i) a large amount of evidence, a large number of participants, or is otherwise extensive;

(ii) the selection of evidence that is particularly probative or essential to the investigation; or

(iii) more than minimal planning; or

(B) the offense involved abuse of a special skill or a position of trust;

(3) the guideline offense levels and enhancements for violations of section 1519 or 1520 of title 18, United States Code, as added by this title, are sufficient to deter and punish that activity;

(4) a specific offense characteristic enhancing sentencing is provided under United States Sentencing Guideline 2B1.1 (as in effect on the date of enactment of this Act) for a fraud offense that endangers the solvency or financial security of a substantial number of victims; and

(5) the guidelines that apply to organizations in United States Sentencing Guidelines, chapter 8, are sufficient to deter and punish organizational criminal misconduct.

(b) EMERGENCY AUTHORITY AND DEADLINE FOR COMMISSION ACTION.—The United States Sentencing Commission is requested to promulgate the guidelines or amendments provided for under this section as soon as practicable, and in any event not later than 180 days after the date of enactment of this Act, in accordance with the procedures set forth in section 219(a) of the Sentencing Reform Act of 1987, as though the authority under that Act had not expired.

SEC. 806. PROTECTION FOR EMPLOYEES OF PUBLICLY TRADED COMPANIES WHO PROVIDE EVIDENCE OF FRAUD.

(a) IN GENERAL.—Chapter 73 of title 18, United States Code, is amended by inserting after section 1514 the following:

"§ 1514A. Civil action to protect against retaliation in fraud cases

"(a) WHISTLEBLOWER PROTECTION FOR EMPLOYEES OF PUBLICLY TRADED COMPANIES.—No company with a class of securities registered under section 12 of the Securities Exchange Act of 1934 (15 U.S.C. 78l), or that is required to file reports under section 15(d) of the Securities Exchange Act of 1934 (15 U.S.C. 78o(d)), or any officer, employee, contractor, subcontractor, or agent of such company, may discharge, demote, suspend, threaten, harass, or in any other manner discriminate against an employee in the terms and conditions of employment because of any lawful act done by the employee—

"(1) to provide information, cause information to be provided, or otherwise assist in an investigation regarding any conduct which the employee reasonably believes constitutes a violation of section 1341, 1343, 1344, or 1348, any rule or regulation of the Securities and Exchange Commission, or any provision of Federal law relating to fraud against shareholders, when the information or assistance is provided to or the investigation is conducted by—

"(A) a Federal regulatory or law enforcement agency;

"(B) any Member of Congress or any committee of Congress; or

"(C) a person with supervisory authority over the employee (or such other person working for the employer who has the authority to investigate, discover, or terminate misconduct); or

"(2) to file, cause to be filed, testify, participate in, or otherwise assist in a proceeding filed or about to be filed (with any knowledge of the employer) relating to an alleged violation of section 1341, 1343, 1344, or 1348, any rule or regulation of the Securities and Exchange Commission, or any provision of Federal law relating to fraud against shareholders.

"(b) ENFORCEMENT ACTION.—

"(1) IN GENERAL.—A person who alleges discharge or other discrimination by any person in violation of subsection (a) may seek relief under subsection (c), by—

"(A) filing a complaint with the Secretary of Labor; or

"(B) if the Secretary has not issued a final decision within 180 days of the filing of the complaint and there is no showing that such delay is due to the bad faith of the claimant, bringing an action at law or equity for de novo review in the appropriate district court of the United States, which shall have jurisdiction over such an action without regard to the amount in controversy.

"(2) PROCEDURE.—

"(A) IN GENERAL.—An action under paragraph (1)(A) shall be governed under the rules and procedures set forth in section 42121(b) of title 49, United States Code.

"(B) EXCEPTION.—Notification made under section 42121(b)(1) of title 49, United States Code, shall be made to the person named in the complaint and to the employer.

"(C) BURDENS OF PROOF.—An action brought under paragraph (1)(B) shall be governed by the legal burdens of proof set forth in section 42121(b) of title 49, United States Code.

"(D) STATUTE OF LIMITATIONS.—An action under paragraph (1) shall be commenced not later than 90 days after the date on which the violation occurs.

"(c) REMEDIES.—

"(1) IN GENERAL.—An employee prevailing in any action under subsection (b)(1) shall be entitled to all relief necessary to make the employee whole.

"(2) COMPENSATORY DAMAGES.—Relief for any action under paragraph (1) shall include—

"(A) reinstatement with the same seniority status that the employee would have had, but for the discrimination;

"(B) the amount of back pay, with interest; and

"(C) compensation for any special damages sustained as a result of the discrimination, including litigation costs, expert witness fees, and reasonable attorney fees.

"(d) RIGHTS RETAINED BY EMPLOYEE.—Nothing in this section shall be deemed to diminish the rights, privileges, or remedies of any employee under any Federal or State law, or under any collective bargaining agreement.".

(b) CLERICAL AMENDMENT.—The table of sections at the beginning of chapter 73 of title 18, United States Code, is amended by inserting after the item relating to section 1514 the following new item:

"1514A. Civil action to protect against retaliation in fraud cases.".

SEC. 807. CRIMINAL PENALTIES FOR DEFRAUDING SHAREHOLDERS OF PUBLICLY TRADED COMPANIES.

(a) IN GENERAL.—Chapter 63 of title 18, United States Code, is amended by adding at the end the following:

"§ 1348. Securities fraud

"Whoever knowingly executes, or attempts to execute, a scheme or artifice—

"(1) to defraud any person in connection with any security of an issuer with a class of securities registered under section 12 of the Securities Exchange Act of 1934 (15 U.S.C. 78l) or that is required to file reports under section 15(d) of the Securities Exchange Act of 1934 (15 U.S.C. 78o(d)); or

"(2) to obtain, by means of false or fraudulent pretenses, representations, or promises, any money or property in connection with the purchase or sale of any security of an issuer with a class of securities registered under section 12 of the Securities Exchange Act of 1934 (15 U.S.C. 78l) or that is required to file reports under section 15(d) of the Securities Exchange Act of 1934 (15 U.S.C. 78o(d));

shall be fined under this title, or imprisoned not more than 25 years, or both.".

(b) CLERICAL AMENDMENT.—The table of sections at the beginning of chapter 63 of title 18, United States Code, is amended by adding at the end the following new item:

"1348. Securities fraud.".

TITLE IX—WHITE–COLLAR CRIME PENALTY ENHANCEMENTS

SEC. 901. SHORT TITLE.

This title may be cited as the "White–Collar Crime Penalty Enhancement Act of 2002".

SEC. 902. ATTEMPTS AND CONSPIRACIES TO COMMIT CRIMINAL FRAUD OFFENSES.

(a) IN GENERAL.—Chapter 63 of title 18, United States Code, is amended by inserting after section 1348 as added by this Act the following:

"§ 1349. Attempt and conspiracy

"Any person who attempts or conspires to commit any offense under this chapter shall be subject to the same penalties as those prescribed for the offense, the commission of which was the object of the attempt or conspiracy.

(b) CLERICAL AMENDMENT.—The table of sections at the beginning of chapter 63 of title 18, United States Code, is amended by adding at the end the following new item:

"1349. Attempt and conspiracy.".

SEC. 903. CRIMINAL PENALTIES FOR MAIL AND WIRE FRAUD.

(a) MAIL FRAUD.—Section 1341 of title 18, United States Code, is amended by striking "five" and inserting "20".

(b) WIRE FRAUD.—Section 1343 of title 18, United States Code, is amended by striking "five" and inserting "20".

SEC. 904. CRIMINAL PENALTIES FOR VIOLATIONS OF THE EMPLOYEE RETIREMENT INCOME SECURITY ACT OF 1974.

Section 501 of the Employee Retirement Income Security Act of 1974 (29 U.S.C. 1131) is amended—

(1) by striking "$5,000" and inserting "$100,000";

(2) by striking "one year" and inserting "10 years"; and

(3) by striking "$100,000" and inserting "$500,000".

SEC. 905. AMENDMENT TO SENTENCING GUIDELINES RELATING TO CERTAIN WHITE–COLLAR OFFENSES.

(a) DIRECTIVE TO THE UNITED STATES SENTENCING COMMISSION.—Pursuant to its authority under section 994(p) of title 18, United States Code, and in accordance with this section, the United States Sentencing Commission shall review and, as appropriate, amend the Federal Sentencing Guidelines and related policy statements to implement the provisions of this Act.

(b) REQUIREMENTS.—In carrying out this section, the Sentencing Commission shall—

(1) ensure that the sentencing guidelines and policy statements reflect the serious nature of the offenses and the penalties set forth in this Act, the growing incidence of serious fraud offenses which are identified above, and the need to modify the sentencing guidelines and policy statements to deter, prevent, and punish such offenses;

(2) consider the extent to which the guidelines and policy statements adequately address whether the guideline offense levels and enhancements for violations of the sections amended by this Act are sufficient to deter and punish

such offenses, and specifically, are adequate in view of the statutory increases in penalties contained in this Act;

(3) assure reasonable consistency with other relevant directives and sentencing guidelines;

(4) account for any additional aggravating or mitigating circumstances that might justify exceptions to the generally applicable sentencing ranges;

(5) make any necessary conforming changes to the sentencing guidelines; and

(6) assure that the guidelines adequately meet the purposes of sentencing, as set forth in section 3553(a)(2) of title 18, United States Code.

(c) EMERGENCY AUTHORITY AND DEADLINE FOR COMMISSION ACTION.—The United States Sentencing Commission is requested to promulgate the guidelines or amendments provided for under this section as soon as practicable, and in any event not later than 180 days after the date of enactment of this Act, in accordance with the procedures set forth in section 219(a) of the Sentencing Reform Act of 1987, as though the authority under that Act had not expired.

SEC. 906. CORPORATE RESPONSIBILITY FOR FINANCIAL REPORTS.

(a) IN GENERAL.—Chapter 63 of title 18, United States Code, is amended by inserting after section 1349, as created by this Act, the following:

"§ 1350. Failure of corporate officers to certify financial reports

"(a) CERTIFICATION OF PERIODIC FINANCIAL REPORTS.—Each periodic report containing financial statements filed by an issuer with the Securities Exchange Commission pursuant to section 13(a) or 15(d) of the Securities Exchange Act of 1934 (15 U.S.C. 78m(a)or 78o(d)) shall be accompanied by a written statement by the chief executive officer and chief financial officer (or equivalent thereof) of the issuer.

"(b) CONTENT.—The statement required under subsection (a) shall certify that the periodic report containing the financial statements fully complies with the requirements of section 13(a) or 15(d) of the Securities Exchange Act pf 1934 (15 U.S.C. 78m or 78o(d)) and that information contained in the periodic report fairly presents, in all material respects, the financial condition and results of operations of the issuer.

"(c) CRIMINAL PENALTIES.—Whoever—

"(1) certifies any statement as set forth in subsections (a) and (b) of this section knowing that the periodic report accompanying the statement does not comport with all the requirements set forth in this section shall be fined not more than $1,000,000 or imprisoned not more than 10 years, or both; or

"(2) willfully certifies any statement as set forth in subsections (a) and (b) of this section knowing that the periodic report accompanying the statement does not comport with all the requirements set forth in this section shall be fined not more than $5,000,000, or imprisoned not more than 20 years, or both.".

(b) CLERICAL AMENDMENT.—The table of sections at the beginning of chapter 63 of title 18, United States Code, is amended by adding at the end the following:

"1350. Failure of corporate officers to certify financial reports.".

TITLE X—CORPORATE TAX RETURNS

SEC. 1001. SENSE OF THE SENATE REGARDING THE SIGNING OF CORPORATE TAX RETURNS BY CHIEF EXECUTIVE OFFICERS.

It is the sense of the Senate that the Federal income tax return of a corporation should be signed by the chief executive officer of such corporation.

TITLE XI—CORPORATE FRAUD ACCOUNTABILITY

SEC. 1101. SHORT TITLE.

This title may be cited as the "Corporate Fraud Accountability Act of 2002".

SEC. 1102. TAMPERING WITH A RECORD OR OTHERWISE IMPEDING AN OFFICIAL PROCEEDING.

Section 1512 of title 18, United States Code, is amended—

(1) by redesignating subsections (c) through (i) as subsections (d) through (j), respectively; and

(2) by inserting after subsection (b) the following new subsection:

"(c) Whoever corruptly—

"(1) alters, destroys, mutilates, or conceals a record, document, or other object, or attempts to do so, with the intent to impair the object's integrity or availability for use in an official proceeding; or

"(2) otherwise obstructs, influences, or impedes any official proceeding, or attempts to do so,

shall be fined under this title or imprisoned not more than 20 years, or both.".

SEC. 1103. TEMPORARY FREEZE AUTHORITY FOR THE SECURITIES AND EXCHANGE COMMISSION.

(a) IN GENERAL.—Section 21C(c) of the Securities Exchange Act of 1934 (15 U.S.C. 78u–3(c)) is amended by adding at the end the following:

"(3) TEMPORARY FREEZE.—

"(A) IN GENERAL.—

"(i) ISSUANCE OF TEMPORARY ORDER.—Whenever, during the course of a lawful investigation involving possible violations of the Federal securities laws by an issuer of publicly traded securities or any of its directors, officers, partners, controlling persons, agents, or employees, it shall appear to the Commission that it is likely that the issuer will make extraordinary payments (whether compensation or otherwise) to any of the foregoing persons, the Commission may petition a Federal district court for a temporary order requiring the issuer to escrow, subject to court supervision, those payments in an interest-bearing account for 45 days.

"(ii) STANDARD.—A temporary order shall be entered under clause (i), only after notice and opportunity for a hearing, unless the court determines that notice and hearing prior to entry of the order would be impracticable or contrary to the public interest.

"(iii) EFFECTIVE PERIOD.—A temporary order issued under clause (i) shall—

"(I) become effective immediately;

"(II) be served upon the parties subject to it; and

"(III) unless set aside, limited or suspended by a court of competent jurisdiction, shall remain effective and enforceable for 45 days.

"(iv) EXTENSIONS AUTHORIZED.—The effective period of an order under this subparagraph may be extended by the court upon good cause shown for not longer than 45 additional days, provided that the combined period of the order shall not exceed 90 days.

"(B) PROCESS ON DETERMINATION OF VIOLATIONS.—

"(i) VIOLATIONS CHARGED.—If the issuer or other person described in subparagraph (A) is charged with any violation of the Federal securities laws before the expiration of the effective period of a temporary order under subparagraph (A) (including any applicable extension period), the order shall remain in effect, subject to court approval, until the conclusion of any legal proceedings related thereto, and the affected issuer or other person, shall have the right to petition the court for review of the order.

"(ii) VIOLATIONS NOT CHARGED.—If the issuer or other person described in subparagraph (A) is not charged with any violation of the Federal securities laws before the expiration of the effective period of a temporary order under subparagraph (A) (including any applicable extension period), the escrow shall terminate at the expiration of the 45–day effective period (or the expiration of any extension period, as applicable), and the disputed payments (with accrued interest) shall be returned to the issuer or other affected person.".

(b) TECHNICAL AMENDMENT.—Section 21C(c)(2) of the Securities Exchange Act of 1934 (15 U.S.C. 78u–3(c)(2)) is amended by striking "This" and inserting "paragraph (1)".

SEC. 1104. AMENDMENT TO THE FEDERAL SENTENCING GUIDELINES.

(a) REQUEST FOR IMMEDIATE CONSIDERATION BY THE UNITED STATES SENTENCING COMMISSION.—Pursuant to its authority under section 994(p) of title 28, United States Code, and in accordance with this section, the United States Sentencing Commission is requested to—

(1) promptly review the sentencing guidelines applicable to securities and accounting fraud and related offenses;

(2) expeditiously consider the promulgation of new sentencing guidelines or amendments to existing sentencing guidelines to provide an enhancement for officers or directors of publicly traded corporations who commit fraud and related offenses; and

(3) submit to Congress an explanation of actions taken by the Sentencing Commission pursuant to paragraph (2) and any additional policy recommendations the Sentencing Commission may have for combating offenses described in paragraph (1).

(b) CONSIDERATIONS IN REVIEW.—In carrying out this section, the Sentencing Commission is requested to—

(1) ensure that the sentencing guidelines and policy statements reflect the serious nature of securities, pension, and accounting fraud and the need for aggressive and appropriate law enforcement action to prevent such offenses;

(2) assure reasonable consistency with other relevant directives and with other guidelines;

(3) account for any aggravating or mitigating circumstances that might justify exceptions, including circumstances for which the sentencing guidelines currently provide sentencing enhancements;

(4) ensure that guideline offense levels and enhancements for an obstruction of justice offense are adequate in cases where documents or other physical evidence are actually destroyed or fabricated;

(5) ensure that the guideline offense levels and enhancements under United States Sentencing Guideline 2B1.1 (as in effect on the date of enactment of this Act) are sufficient for a fraud offense when the number of victims adversely involved is significantly greater than 50;

(6) make any necessary conforming changes to the sentencing guidelines; and

(7) assure that the guidelines adequately meet the purposes of sentencing as set forth in section 3553 (a)(2) of title 18, United States Code.

(c) EMERGENCY AUTHORITY AND DEADLINE FOR COMMISSION ACTION.—The United States Sentencing Commission is requested to promulgate the guidelines or amendments provided for under this section as soon as practicable, and in any event not later than the 180 days after the date of enactment of this Act, in accordance with the procedures sent forth in section 21(a) of the Sentencing Reform Act of 1987, as though the authority under that Act had not expired.

SEC. 1105. AUTHORITY OF THE COMMISSION TO PROHIBIT PERSONS FROM SERVING AS OFFICERS OR DIRECTORS.

(a) SECURITIES EXCHANGE ACT OF 1934.—Section 21C of the Securities Exchange Act of 1934 (15 U.S.C. 78u–3) is amended by adding at the end the following:

"(f) AUTHORITY OF THE COMMISSION TO PROHIBIT PERSONS FROM SERVING AS OFFICERS OR DIRECTORS.—In any cease-and-desist proceeding under subsection (a), the Commission may issue an order to prohibit, conditionally or unconditionally, and permanently or for such period of time as it shall determine, any person who has violated section 10(b) or the rules or regulations thereunder, from acting as an officer or director of any issuer that has a class of securities registered pursuant to section 12, or that is required to file reports pursuant to section 15(d), if the conduct of that person demonstrates unfitness to serve as an officer or director of any such issuer.''.

(b) SECURITIES ACT OF 1933.—Section 8A of the Securities Act of 1933 (15 U.S.C. 77h–1) is amended by adding at the end of the following:

"(f) AUTHORITY OF THE COMMISSION TO PROHIBIT PERSONS FROM SERVING AS OFFICERS OR DIRECTORS.—In any cease-and-desist proceeding under subsection (a), the Commission may issue an order to prohibit, conditionally or unconditionally, and permanently or for such period of time as it shall determine, any person who has violated section 17(a)(1) or the rules or regulations thereunder, from acting as an officer or director of any issuer that has a class of securities registered pursuant to section 12 of the Securities Exchange Act of 1934, or that is required to file reports pursuant to section 15(d) of that Act, if the conduct of that person demonstrates unfitness to serve as an officer or director of any such issuer.''.

SEC. 1106. INCREASED CRIMINAL PENALTIES UNDER SECURITIES EXCHANGE ACT OF 1934.

Section 32(a) of the Securities Exchange Act of 1934 (15 U.S.C. 78ff(a)) is amended—

(1) by striking "$1,000,000, or imprisoned not more than 10 years" and inserting "$5,000,000, or imprisoned not more than 20 years"; and

(2) by striking "$2,500,000" and inserting "$25,000,000".

SEC. 1107. RETALIATION AGAINST INFORMANTS.

(a) IN GENERAL.—Section 1513 of title 18, United States Code, is amended by adding at the end the following:

"(e) Whoever knowingly, with the intent to retaliate, takes any action harmful to any person, including interference with the lawful employment or livelihood of any person, for providing to a law enforcement officer any truthful information relating to the commission or possible commission of any Federal offense, shall be fined under this title or imprisoned not more than 10 years, or both.''.

Approved July 30, 2002.

N. APPEARANCE AND PRACTICE BEFORE THE COMMISSION

§ 201.102

* * *

(e) Suspension and disbarment.

(1) Generally. The Commission may censure a person or deny, temporarily or permanently, the privilege of appearing or practicing before it in any way to any person who is found by the Commission after notice and opportunity for hearing in the matter:

(i) Not to possess the requisite qualifications to represent others; or

(ii) To be lacking in character or integrity or to have engaged in unethical or improper professional conduct; or

(iii) To have willfully violated, or willfully aided and abetted the violation of any provision of the Federal securities laws or the rules and regulations thereunder.

(iv) With respect to persons licensed to practice as accountants, "improper professional conduct" under § 201.102(e)(1)(ii) means:

(A) Intentional or knowing conduct, including reckless conduct, that results in a violation of applicable professional standards; or

(B) Either of the following two types of negligent conduct:

(1) A single instance of highly unreasonable conduct that results in a violation of applicable professional standards in circumstances in which an accountant knows, or should know, that heightened scrutiny is warranted.

(2) Repeated instances of unreasonable conduct, each resulting in a violation of applicable professional standards, that indicate a lack of competence to practice before the Commission.

(2) Certain professionals and convicted persons. Any attorney who has been suspended or disbarred by a court of the United States or of any State; or any person whose license to practice as an accountant, engineer, or other professional or expert has been revoked or suspended in any State; or any person who has been convicted of a felony or a misdemeanor involving moral turpitude shall be forthwith suspended from appearing or practicing before the Commission. A disbarment, suspension, revocation or conviction within the meaning of this section shall be deemed to have occurred when the disbarring, suspending, revoking or convicting agency or tribunal enters its judgment or order, including a judgment or order on a plea of nolo contendere, regardless of whether an appeal of such judgment or order is pending or could be taken.

(3) Temporary suspensions. An order of temporary suspension shall become effective upon service on the respondent. No order of temporary suspension shall be entered by the Commission pursuant to paragraph (e)(3)(i) of this section more than 90 days after the date on which the final judgment or order entered in

a judicial or administrative proceeding described in paragraph (e)(3)(i)(A) or (e)(3)(i)(B) of this section has become effective, whether upon completion of review or appeal procedures or because further review or appeal procedures are no longer available.

(i) The Commission, with due regard to the public interest and without preliminary hearing, may, by order, temporarily suspend from appearing or practicing before it any attorney, accountant, engineer, or other professional or expert who has been by name:

(A) Permanently enjoined by any court of competent jurisdiction, by reason of his or her misconduct in an action brought by the Commission, from violating or aiding and abetting the violation of any provision of the Federal securities laws or of the rules and regulations thereunder; or

(B) Found by any court of competent jurisdiction in an action brought by the Commission to which he or she is a party or found by the Commission in any administrative proceeding to which he or she is a party to have violated (unless the violation was found not to have been willful) or aided and abetted the violation of any provision of the Federal securities laws or of the rules and regulations thereunder.

(ii) Any person temporarily suspended from appearing and practicing before the Commission in accordance with paragraph (e)(3)(i) of this section may, within 30 days after service upon him or her of the order of temporary suspension, petition the Commission to lift the temporary suspension. If no petition has been received by the Commission within 30 days after service of the order, the suspension shall become permanent.

(iii) Within 30 days after the filing of a petition in accordance with paragraph (e)(3)(ii) of this section, the Commission shall either lift the temporary suspension, or set the matter down for hearing at a time and place designated by the Commission, or both, and, after opportunity for hearing, may censure the petitioner or disqualify the petitioner from appearing or practicing before the Commission for a period of time or permanently. In every case in which the temporary suspension has not been lifted, every hearing held and other action taken pursuant to this paragraph (e)(3) shall be expedited in accordance with § 201.500. If the hearing is held before a hearing officer, the time limits set forth in § 201.531 will govern review of the hearing officer's initial decision.

(iv) In any hearing held on a petition filed in accordance with paragraph (e)(3)(ii) of this section, the staff of the Commission shall show either that the petitioner has been enjoined as described in paragraph (e)(3)(i)(A) of this section or that the petitioner has been found to have committed or aided and abetted violations as described in paragraph (e)(3)(i)(B) of this section and that showing, without more, may be the basis for censure or disqualification. Once that showing has been made, the burden shall be upon the petitioner to show cause why he or she should not be censured or temporarily or permanently disqualified from appearing and practicing before the Commission. In any such hearing, the petitioner may not contest any finding made against him or her or fact admitted by him or her in the judicial or administrative proceeding upon which the proceeding under this paragraph (e)(3) is predicated. A person who has consented to the entry of a permanent injunction as described in paragraph (e)(3)(i)(A) of this section without admitting the facts set forth in the complaint shall be presumed for all purposes under this paragraph (e)(3) to have been enjoined by reason of the misconduct alleged in the complaint.

(4) Filing of prior orders. Any person appearing or practicing before the Commission who has been the subject of an order, judgment, decree, or finding as set forth in paragraph (e)(3) of this section shall promptly file with the Secretary a copy thereof (together with any related opinion or statement of the agency or tribunal involved). Failure to file any such paper, order, judgment, decree or finding shall not impair the operation of any other provision of this section.

(5) Reinstatement.

(i) An application for reinstatement of a person permanently suspended or disqualified under paragraph (e)(1) or (e)(3) of this section may be made at any time, and the applicant may, in the Commission's discretion, be afforded a hearing; however, the suspension or disqualification shall continue unless and until the applicant has been reinstated by the Commission for good cause shown.

(ii) Any person suspended under paragraph (e)(2) of this section shall be reinstated by the Commission, upon appropriate application, if all the grounds for application of the provisions of that paragraph are subsequently removed by a reversal of the conviction or termination of the suspension, disbarment, or revocation. An application for reinstatement on any other grounds by any person suspended under paragraph (e)(2) of this section may be filed at any time and the applicant shall be accorded an opportunity for a hearing in the matter; however, such suspension shall continue unless and until the applicant has been reinstated by order of the Commission for good cause shown.

(6) Other proceedings not precluded. A proceeding brought under paragraph (e)(1), (e)(2) or (e)(3) of this section shall not preclude another proceeding brought under these same paragraphs.

(7) Public hearings. All hearings held under this paragraph (e) shall be public unless otherwise ordered by the Commission on its own motion or after considering the motion of a party.

O. STANDARDS OF PROFESSIONAL CONDUCT FOR ATTORNEYS APPEARING AND PRACTICING BEFORE THE COMMISSION IN THE REPRESENTATION OF AN ISSUER

Contents

Rule 205.1 Purpose and Scope

This part sets forth minimum standards of professional conduct for attorneys appearing and practicing before the Commission in the representation of an issuer. These standards supplement applicable standards of any jurisdiction where an attorney is admitted or practices and are not intended to limit the ability of any jurisdiction to impose additional obligations on an attorney not inconsistent with the application of this part. Where the standards of a state or other United States jurisdiction where an attorney is admitted or practices conflict with this part, this part shall govern.

Rule 205.2 Definitions

For purposes of this part, the following definitions apply:

(a) Appearing and practicing before the Commission:

(1) Means:

(i) Transacting any business with the Commission, including communications in any form;

(ii) Representing an issuer in a Commission administrative proceeding or in connection with any Commission investigation, inquiry, information request, or subpoena;

(iii) Providing advice in respect of the United States securities laws or the Commission's rules or regulations thereunder regarding any document that the attorney has notice will be filed with or submitted to, or incorporated into any document that will be filed with or submitted to, the Commission, including the provision of such advice in the context of preparing, or participating in the preparation of, any such document; or

(iv) Advising an issuer as to whether information or a statement, opinion, or other writing is required under the United States securities laws or the Commission's rules or regulations thereunder to be filed with or submitted to, or incorporated into any document that will be filed with or submitted to, the Commission; but

(2) Does not include an attorney who:

(i) Conducts the activities in paragraphs (a)(1)(i) through (a)(1)(iv) of this section other than in the context of providing legal services to an issuer with whom the attorney has an attorney-client relationship; or

(ii) Is a non-appearing foreign attorney.

(b) Appropriate response means a response to an attorney regarding reported evidence of a material violation as a result of which the attorney reasonably believes:

(1) That no material violation, as defined in paragraph (i) of this section, has occurred, is ongoing, or is about to occur;

(2) That the issuer has, as necessary, adopted appropriate remedial measures, including appropriate steps or sanctions to stop any material violations that are ongoing, to prevent any material violation that has yet to occur, and to remedy or otherwise appropriately address any material violation that has already occurred and to minimize the likelihood of its recurrence; or

(3) That the issuer, with the consent of the issuer's board of directors, a committee thereof to whom a report could be made pursuant to Rule 205.3(b)(3), or a qualified legal compliance committee, has retained or directed an attorney to review the reported evidence of a material violation and either:

(i) Has substantially implemented any remedial recommendations made by such attorney after a reasonable investigation and evaluation of the reported evidence; or

(ii) Has been advised that such attorney may, consistent with his or her professional obligations, assert a colorable defense on behalf of the issuer (or the issuer's officer, director, employee, or agent, as the case may be) in any investigation or judicial or administrative proceeding relating to the reported evidence of a material violation.

(c) Attorney means any person who is admitted, licensed, or otherwise qualified to practice law in any jurisdiction, domestic or foreign, or who holds himself or herself out as admitted, licensed, or otherwise qualified to practice law.

(d) Breach of fiduciary duty refers to any breach of fiduciary or similar duty to the issuer recognized under an applicable federal or state statute or at common law, including but not limited to misfeasance, nonfeasance, abdication of duty, abuse of trust, and approval of unlawful transactions.

(e) Evidence of a material violation means credible evidence, based upon which it would be unreasonable, under the circumstances, for a prudent and competent attorney not to conclude that it is reasonably likely that a material violation has occurred, is ongoing, or is about to occur.

(f) Foreign government issuer means a foreign issuer as defined in Rule 405 eligible to register securities on Schedule B of the Securities Act of 1933.

(g) In the representation of an issuer means providing legal services as an attorney for an issuer, regardless of whether the attorney is employed or retained by the issuer.

(h) Issuer means an issuer (as defined in section 3 of the Securities Exchange Act of 1934), the securities of which are registered under section 12 of that Act, or that is required to file reports under section 15(d) of that Act), or that files or has filed a registration statement that has not yet become effective under the Securities Act of 1933, and that it has not withdrawn, but does not include a foreign government issuer. For purposes of paragraphs (a) and (g) of this section, the term "issuer" includes any person controlled by an issuer, where an attorney provides legal services to such person on behalf of, or at the behest, or for the benefit of the issuer, regardless of whether the attorney is employed or retained by the issuer.

(i) Material violation means a material violation of an applicable United States federal or state securities law, a material breach of fiduciary duty arising under United States federal or state law, or a similar material violation of any United States federal or state law.

(j) Non-appearing foreign attorney means an attorney:

(1) Who is admitted to practice law in a jurisdiction outside the United States;

(2) Who does not hold himself or herself out as practicing, and does not give legal advice regarding, United States federal or state securities or other laws (except as provided in paragraph (j)(3)(ii) of this section); and

(3) Who:

(i) Conducts activities that would constitute appearing and practicing before the Commission only incidentally to, and in the ordinary course of, the practice of law in a jurisdiction outside the United States; or

(ii) Is appearing and practicing before the Commission only in consultation with counsel, other than a non-appearing foreign attorney, admitted or licensed to practice in a state or other United States jurisdiction.

(k) Qualified legal compliance committee means a committee of an issuer (which also may be an audit or other committee of the issuer) that:

(1) Consists of at least one member of the issuer's audit committee (or, if the issuer has no audit committee, one member from an equivalent committee of independent directors) and two or more members of the issuer's board of directors who are not employed, directly or indirectly, by the issuer and who are not, in the case of a registered investment company, "interested persons" as defined in section 2(a)(19) of the Investment Company Act of 1940;

(2) Has adopted written procedures for the confidential receipt, retention, and consideration of any report of evidence of a material violation under Rule 205.3;

(3) Has been duly established by the issuer's board of directors, with the authority and responsibility:

(i) To inform the issuer's chief legal officer and chief executive officer (or the equivalents thereof) of any report of evidence of a material violation (except in the circumstances described in Rule 205.3(b)(4));

(ii) To determine whether an investigation is necessary regarding any report of evidence of a material violation by the issuer, its officers, directors, employees or agents and, if it determines an investigation is necessary or appropriate, to:

(A) Notify the audit committee or the full board of directors;

(B) Initiate an investigation, which may be conducted either by the chief legal officer (or the equivalent thereof) or by outside attorneys; and

(C) Retain such additional expert personnel as the committee deems necessary; and

(iii) At the conclusion of any such investigation, to:

(A) Recommend, by majority vote, that the issuer implement an appropriate response to evidence of a material violation; and

(B) Inform the chief legal officer and the chief executive officer (or the equivalents thereof) and the board of directors of the results of any such investigation under this section and the appropriate remedial measures to be adopted; and

(4) Has the authority and responsibility, acting by majority vote, to take all other appropriate action, including the authority to notify the Commission in the event that the issuer fails in any material respect to implement an appropriate response that the qualified legal compliance committee has recommended the issuer to take.

(*l*) Reasonable or reasonably denotes, with respect to the actions of an attorney, conduct that would not be unreasonable for a prudent and competent attorney.

(m) Reasonably believes means that an attorney believes the matter in question and that the circumstances are such that the belief is not unreasonable.

(n) Report means to make known to directly, either in person, by telephone, by e-mail, electronically, or in writing.

Rule 205.3 Issuer as Client

(a) Representing an issuer. An attorney appearing and practicing before the Commission in the representation of an issuer owes his or her professional and ethical duties to the issuer as an organization. That the attorney may work with and advise the issuer's officers, directors, or employees in the course of representing the issuer does not make such individuals the attorney's clients.

(b) Duty to report evidence of a material violation.

(1) If an attorney, appearing and practicing before the Commission in the representation of an issuer, becomes aware of evidence of a material violation by the issuer or by any officer, director, employee, or agent of the issuer, the attorney shall report such evidence to the issuer's chief legal officer (or the equivalent thereof) or to both the issuer's chief legal officer and its chief executive officer (or the equivalents thereof) forthwith. By communicating such information to the issuer's officers or directors, an attorney does not reveal client confidences or secrets or privileged or otherwise protected information related to the attorney's representation of an issuer.

(2) The chief legal officer (or the equivalent thereof) shall cause such inquiry into the evidence of a material violation as he or she reasonably believes is appropriate to determine whether the material violation described in the report has occurred, is ongoing, or is about to occur. If the chief legal officer (or the equivalent thereof) determines no material violation has occurred, is ongoing, or is about to occur, he or she shall notify the reporting attorney and advise the reporting attorney of the basis for such determination. Unless the chief legal officer (or the equivalent thereof) reasonably believes that no material violation has occurred, is ongoing, or is about to occur, he or she shall take all reasonable steps to cause the

issuer to adopt an appropriate response, and shall advise the reporting attorney thereof. In lieu of causing an inquiry under this paragraph (b), a chief legal officer (or the equivalent thereof) may refer a report of evidence of a material violation to a qualified legal compliance committee under paragraph (c)(2) of this section if the issuer has duly established a qualified legal compliance committee prior to the report of evidence of a material violation.

(3) Unless an attorney who has made a report under paragraph (b)(1) of this section reasonably believes that the chief legal officer or the chief executive officer of the issuer (or the equivalent thereof) has provided an appropriate response within a reasonable time, the attorney shall report the evidence of a material violation to:

(i) The audit committee of the issuer's board of directors;

(ii) Another committee of the issuer's board of directors consisting solely of directors who are not employed, directly or indirectly, by the issuer and are not, in the case of a registered investment company, "interested persons" as defined in section 2(a)(19) of the Investment Company Act of 1940) (if the issuer's board of directors has no audit committee); or

(iii) The issuer's board of directors (if the issuer's board of directors has no committee consisting solely of directors who are not employed, directly or indirectly, by the issuer and are not, in the case of a registered investment company, "interested persons" as defined in section 2(a)(19) of the Investment Company Act of 1940).

(4) If an attorney reasonably believes that it would be futile to report evidence of a material violation to the issuer's chief legal officer and chief executive officer (or the equivalents thereof) under paragraph (b)(1) of this section, the attorney may report such evidence as provided under paragraph (b)(3) of this section.

(5) An attorney retained or directed by an issuer to investigate evidence of a material violation reported under paragraph (b)(1), (b)(3), or (b)(4) of this section shall be deemed to be appearing and practicing before the Commission. Directing or retaining an attorney to investigate reported evidence of a material violation does not relieve an officer or director of the issuer to whom such evidence has been reported under paragraph (b)(1), (b)(3), or (b)(4) of this section from a duty to respond to the reporting attorney.

(6) An attorney shall not have any obligation to report evidence of a material violation under this paragraph (b) if:

(i) The attorney was retained or directed by the issuer's chief legal officer (or the equivalent thereof) to investigate such evidence of a material violation and:

(A) The attorney reports the results of such investigation to the chief legal officer (or the equivalent thereof); and

(B) Except where the attorney and the chief legal officer (or the equivalent thereof) each reasonably believes that no material violation has occurred, is ongoing, or is about to occur, the chief legal officer (or the equivalent thereof) reports the results of the investigation to the issuer's board of directors, a committee thereof to whom a report could be made pursuant to paragraph (b)(3) of this section, or a qualified legal compliance committee; or

(ii) The attorney was retained or directed by the chief legal officer (or the equivalent thereof) to assert, consistent with his or her professional obligations, a colorable defense on behalf of the issuer (or the issuer's officer, director, employee, or agent, as the case may be) in any investigation or judicial or administrative proceeding relating to such evidence of a material violation, and the chief legal officer (or the equivalent thereof) provides reasonable and timely reports on the progress and outcome of such proceeding to the issuer's board of directors, a committee thereof to whom a report could be made pursuant to paragraph (b)(3) of this section, or a qualified legal compliance committee.

(7) An attorney shall not have any obligation to report evidence of a material violation under this paragraph (b) if such attorney was retained or directed by a qualified legal compliance committee:

(i) To investigate such evidence of a material violation; or

(ii) To assert, consistent with his or her professional obligations, a colorable defense on behalf of the issuer (or the issuer's officer, director, employee, or agent, as the case may be) in any investigation or judicial or administrative proceeding relating to such evidence of a material violation.

(8) An attorney who receives what he or she reasonably believes is an appropriate and timely response to a report he or she has made pursuant to paragraph (b)(1), (b)(3), or (b)(4) of this section need do nothing more under this section with respect to his or her report.

(9) An attorney who does not reasonably believe that the issuer has made an appropriate response within a reasonable time to the report or reports made pursuant to paragraph (b)(1), (b)(3), or (b)(4) of this section shall explain his or her reasons therefor to the chief legal officer (or the equivalent thereof), the chief executive officer (or the equivalent thereof), and directors to whom the attorney reported the evidence of a material violation pursuant to paragraph (b)(1), (b)(3), or (b)(4) of this section.

(10) An attorney formerly employed or retained by an issuer who has reported evidence of a material violation under this part and reasonably believes that he or she has been discharged for so doing may notify the issuer's board of directors or any committee thereof that he or she believes that he or she has been discharged for reporting evidence of a material violation under this section.

(c) Alternative reporting procedures for attorneys retained or employed by an issuer that has established a qualified legal compliance committee.

(1) If an attorney, appearing and practicing before the Commission in the representation of an issuer, becomes aware of evidence of a material violation by the issuer or by any officer, director, employee, or agent of the issuer, the attorney may, as an alternative to the reporting requirements of paragraph (b) of this section, report such evidence to a qualified legal compliance committee, if the issuer has previously formed such a committee. An attorney who reports evidence of a material violation to such a qualified legal compliance committee has satisfied his or her obligation to report such evidence and is not required to assess the issuer's response to the reported evidence of a material violation.

(2) A chief legal officer (or the equivalent thereof) may refer a report of evidence of a material violation to a previously established qualified legal compliance committee in lieu of causing an inquiry to be conducted under paragraph (b)(2) of this section. The chief legal officer (or the equivalent thereof) shall inform the reporting attorney that the report has been referred to a qualified legal compliance committee. Thereafter, pursuant to the requirements under Rule 205.2(k), the qualified legal compliance committee shall be responsible for responding to the evidence of a material violation reported to it under this paragraph (c).

(d) Issuer confidences.

(1) Any report under this section (or the contemporaneous record thereof) or any response thereto (or the contemporaneous record thereof) may be used by an attorney in connection with any investigation, proceeding, or litigation in which the attorney's compliance with this part is in issue.

(2) An attorney appearing and practicing before the Commission in the representation of an issuer may reveal to the Commission, without the issuer's consent, confidential information related to the representation to the extent the attorney reasonably believes necessary:

(i) To prevent the issuer from committing a material violation that is likely to cause substantial injury to the financial interest or property of the issuer or investors;

(ii) To prevent the issuer, in a Commission investigation or administrative proceeding from committing perjury, proscribed in 18 U.S.C. 1621; suborning perjury, proscribed in 18 U.S.C. 1622; or committing any act proscribed in 18 U.S.C. 1001 that is likely to perpetrate a fraud upon the Commission; or

(iii) To rectify the consequences of a material violation by the issuer that caused, or may cause, substantial injury to the financial interest or property of the issuer or investors in the furtherance of which the attorney's services were used.

Rule 205.4 Responsibilities of Supervisory Attorneys

(a) An attorney supervising or directing another attorney who is appearing and practicing before the Commission in the representation of an issuer is a supervisory attorney. An issuer's chief legal officer (or the equivalent thereof) is a supervisory attorney under this section.

(b) A supervisory attorney shall make reasonable efforts to ensure that a subordinate attorney, as defined in Rule 205.5(a), that he or she supervises or directs conforms to this part. To the extent a subordinate attorney appears and practices before the Commission in the representation of an issuer, that subordinate attorney's supervisory attorneys also appear and practice before the Commission.

(c) A supervisory attorney is responsible for complying with the reporting requirements in Rule 205.3 when a subordinate attorney has reported to the supervisory attorney evidence of a material violation.

(d) A supervisory attorney who has received a report of evidence of a material violation from a subordinate attorney under Rule 205.3 may report such evidence to the issuer's qualified legal compliance committee if the issuer has duly formed such a committee.

Rule 205.5 Responsibilities of a Subordinate Attorney

(a) An attorney who appears and practices before the Commission in the representation of an issuer on a matter under the supervision or direction of another attorney (other than under the direct supervision or direction of the issuer's chief legal officer (or the equivalent thereof)) is a subordinate attorney.

(b) A subordinate attorney shall comply with this part notwithstanding that the subordinate attorney acted at the direction of or under the supervision of another person.

(c) A subordinate attorney complies with Rule 205.3 if the subordinate attorney reports to his or her supervising attorney under Rule 205.3(b) evidence of a material violation of which the subordinate attorney has become aware in appearing and practicing before the Commission.

(d) A subordinate attorney may take the steps permitted or required by Rule 205.3(b) or (c) if the subordinate attorney reasonably believes that a supervisory attorney to whom he or she has reported evidence of a material violation under Rule 205.3(b) has failed to comply with Rule 205.3.

Rule 205.6 Sanctions and Discipline

(a) A violation of this part by any attorney appearing and practicing before

the Commission in the representation of an issuer shall subject such attorney to the civil penalties and remedies for a violation of the federal securities laws available to the Commission in an action brought by the Commission thereunder.

(b) An attorney appearing and practicing before the Commission who violates any provision of this part is subject to the disciplinary authority of the Commission, regardless of whether the attorney may also be subject to discipline for the same conduct in a jurisdiction where the attorney is admitted or practices. An administrative disciplinary proceeding initiated by the Commission for violation of this part may result in an attorney being censured, or being temporarily or permanently denied the privilege of appearing or practicing before the Commission.

(c) An attorney who complies in good faith with the provisions of this part shall not be subject to discipline or otherwise liable under inconsistent standards imposed by any state or other United States jurisdiction where the attorney is admitted or practices.

(d) An attorney practicing outside the United States shall not be required to comply with the requirements of this part to the extent that such compliance is prohibited by applicable foreign law.

Rule 205.7 No Private Right of Action.

(a) Nothing in this part is intended to, or does, create a private right of action against any attorney, law firm, or issuer based upon compliance or noncompliance with its provisions.

(b) Authority to enforce compliance with this part is vested exclusively in the Commission.

V. CORPORATE GOVERNANCE

A. NEW YORK STOCK EXCHANGE MANUAL, SELECTED PROVISIONS

202.00 MATERIAL INFORMATION

202.01 Internal Handling of Confidential Corporate Matters

Unusual market activity or a substantial price change has on occasion occurred in a company's securities shortly before the announcement of an important corporate action or development. Such incidents are extremely embarrassing and damaging to both the company and the Exchange since the public may quickly conclude that someone acted on the basis of inside information.

Negotiations leading to mergers and acquisitions, stock splits, the making of arrangements preparatory to an exchange or tender offer, changes in dividend rates or earnings, calls for redemption, and new contracts, products, or discoveries are the type of developments where the risk of untimely and inadvertent disclosure of corporate plans are most likely to occur. Frequently, these matters require extensive discussion and study by corporate officials before final decisions can be made. Accordingly, extreme care must be used in order to keep the information on a confidential basis.

Where it is possible to confine formal or informal discussions to a small group of the top management of the company or companies involved, and their individual confidential advisors where adequate security can be maintained, premature public announcement may properly be avoided. In this regard, the market action of a company's securities should be closely watched at a time when consideration is being given to important corporate matters. If unusual market activity should arise, the company should be prepared to make an immediate public announcement of the matter.

At some point it usually becomes necessary to involve other persons to conduct preliminary studies or assist in other preparations for contemplated transactions, e.g., business appraisals, tentative financing arrangements, attitude of large outside holders, availability of major blocks of stock, engineering studies and market analyses and surveys. Experience has shown that maintaining security at this point is virtually impossible. Accordingly, fairness requires that the company make an immediate public announcement as soon as disclosures relating to such important matters are made to outsiders.

The extent of the disclosures will depend upon the stage of discussions, studies, or negotiations. So far as possible, public statements should be definite as to price, ratio, timing and/or any other pertinent information necessary to permit a reasonable evaluation of the matter. As a minimum, they should include those disclosures made to outsiders. Where an initial announcement cannot be specific or complete, it will need to be supplemented from time to time as more definitive or different terms are discussed or determined.

Corporate employees, as well as directors and officers, should be regularly reminded as a matter of policy that they must not disclose confidential information they may receive in the course of their duties and must not attempt to take advantage of such information themselves.

In view of the importance of this matter and the potential difficulties involved, the Exchange suggests that a periodic review be made by each company of the manner in which confidential information is being handled within its own organization. A reminder notice of the company's policy to those in sensitive areas might also be helpful.

A sound corporate disclosure policy is essential to the maintenance of a fair and orderly securities market. It should minimize the occasions where the Exchange finds it necessary to temporarily halt trading in a security due to information leaks or rumors in connection with significant corporate transactions.

While the procedures are directed primarily at situations involving two or more companies, they are equally applicable to major corporate developments involving a single company.

202.02 Relationship Between Company Officials and Others

(A) Security Analysts, Institutional Investors, Etc.

Security analysts play an increasingly important role in the evaluation and interpretation of the financial affairs of listed companies.

Annual reports, quarterly reports, and interim releases cannot by their nature provide all of the financial and statistical data that should be available to the investing public. The Exchange recommends that companies observe an "open door" policy in their relations with security analysts, financial writers, shareholders, and others who have legitimate investment interest in the company's affairs.

A company should not give information to one inquirer which it would not give to another, nor should it reveal information it would not willingly give or has not given to the press for publication. Thus, for companies to give advance earnings, dividend, stock split, merger, or tender information to analysts, whether representing an institution, brokerage house, investment advisor, large shareholder, or anyone else, would clearly violate Exchange policy. On the other hand, it should not withhold information in which analysts or other members of the investment public have a warrantable interest.

If during the course of a discussion with analysts substantive material not previously published is disclosed, that material should be simultaneously released to the public. The various security analysts societies usually have a regular procedure to be followed where formal presentations are made. The company should follow these same precautions when dealing with groups of industry analysts in small or closed meetings.

. . .

202.03 Dealing With Rumors or Unusual Market Activity

The market activity of a company's securities should be closely watched at a time when consideration is being given to significant corporate matters. If rumors or unusual market activity indicate that information on impending developments has leaked out, a frank and explicit announcement is clearly required. If rumors are in fact false or inaccurate, they should be promptly denied or clarified. A statement to the effect that the company knows of no corporate developments to account for the unusual market activity can have a salutary effect. It is obvious that if such a public statement is contemplated, management should be checked prior to any public comment so as to avoid any embarrassment or potential criticism. If rumors are correct or there are developments, an immediate candid statement to the public as to the state of negotiations or of development of corporate plans in the rumored area must be made directly and openly. Such statements are essential despite the business inconvenience which may be caused and even though the matter may not as yet have been presented to the company's Board of Directors for consideration.

The Exchange recommends that its listed companies contact their Exchange representative if they become aware of rumors circulating about their company. Exchange Rule 435 provides that no member,

member organization or allied member shall circulate in any manner rumors of a sensational character which might reasonably be expected to affect market conditions on the Exchange. Information provided concerning rumors will be promptly investigated.

202.05 Timely Disclosure of Material News Developments

A listed company is expected to release quickly to the public any news or information which might reasonably be expected to materially affect the market for its securities. This is one of the most important and fundamental purposes of the listing agreement which the company enters into with the Exchange.

A listed company should also act promptly to dispel unfounded rumors which result in unusual market activity or price variations.

202.06 Procedure for Public Release of Information

Immediate Release Policy

The normal method of publication of important corporate data is by means of a press release. This may be either by telephone or in written form. Any release of information that could reasonably be expected to have an impact on the market for a company's securities should be given to the wire services and the press "For Immediate Release."

The spirit of the immediate release policy is not considered to be violated on weekends where a "Hold for Sunday or Monday A.M.'s" is used to obtain a broad public release of the news. This procedure facilitates the combination of a press release with a mailing to shareholders.

Annual and quarterly earnings, dividend announcements, mergers, acquisitions, tender offers, stock splits, major management changes, and any substantive items of unusual or non-recurrent nature are examples of news items that should be handled on an immediate release basis. News of major new products, contract awards, expansion plans, and discoveries very often fall into the same category. Unfavorable news should be reported as promptly and candidly as favorable news. Reluctance or unwillingness to release a negative story or an attempt to disguise unfavorable news endangers management's reputation for integrity. Changes in accounting methods to mask such occurrences can have a similar impact.

It should be a company's primary concern to assure that news will be handled in proper perspective. This necessitates appropriate restraint, good judgment, and careful adherence to the facts. Any projections of financial data, for instance, should be soundly based, appropriately qualified, conservative and factual. Excessive or misleading conservatism should be avoided. Likewise, the repetitive release of essentially the same information is not appropriate.

Few things are more damaging to a company's shareholder relations or to the general public's regard for a company's securities than information improperly withheld. On the other hand, a volume of press releases is not to be used since important items can become confused with trivia.

Premature announcements of new products whose commercial application cannot yet be realistically evaluated should be avoided, as should overly optimistic forecasts, exaggerated claims and unwarranted promises. Should subsequent developments indicate that performance will not match earlier projections, this too should be reported and explained.

Judgment must be exercised as to the timing of a public release on those corporate developments where the immediate release policy is not involved or where disclosure would endanger the company's goals or provide information helpful to a competitor. In these cases, the company should weigh the fairness to both present and potential shareholders who at any given moment may be considering buying or selling the company's stock.

. . .

Release to Newspapers and News Wire Services

(C) News which ought to be the subject of immediate publicity must be released by the fastest available means. The fastest available means may vary in individual cases and according to the time of day. Ordinarily, this requires a release to the public press by telephone, facsimile, or hand delivery, or some combination of such methods. Transmittal of such a release to the press solely by mail is not considered satisfactory. Similarly, release of such news exclusively to local press would not be sufficient for adequate and prompt disclosure to the investing public.

To insure adequate coverage, releases requiring immediate publicity should be given to Dow Jones & Company, Inc., Reuters Economic Services and Bloomberg Business News.

Companies are also encouraged to promptly distribute their releases to Associated Press and United Press International as well as to newspapers in New York City and in cities where the company is headquartered or has plants or other major facilities.

A copy of any press release which may significantly impact on trading should also be sent promptly to the attention of the company's Exchange representative, by facsimile.

. . .

Every news release should include the name and telephone number of a company official who will be available if a newspaper or news wire service desires to confirm or clarify the release.

303.00 CORPORATE GOVERNANCE STANDARDS

303.00 Corporate Governance Standards

In addition to the numerical listing standards, the Exchange has adopted certain corporate governance listing standards. These standards apply to all companies listing common stock on the Exchange. However, the Exchange does not apply a particular standard to a non-U.S. company if the company provides the Exchange with written certification from independent counsel of the company's country of domicile stating that the company's corporate governance practices comply with home country law and the rules of the principal securities market for the company's stock outside the United States.

303.01 Audit Committee

(A) Audit Committee Policy. Each company must have a qualified audit committee.

(B) Requirements for a Qualified Audit Committee.

(1) Formal Charter. The Board of Directors must adopt and approve a formal written charter for the audit committee. The audit committee must review and reassess the adequacy of the audit committee charter on an annual basis. The charter must specify the following:

(a) the scope of the audit committee's responsibilities and how it carries out those responsibilities, including structure, processes and membership requirements;

(b) that the outside auditor for the company is ultimately accountable to the Board of Directors and audit committee of the company, that the audit committee and Board of Directors have the ultimate authority and responsibility to select, evaluate and, where appropriate, replace the outside auditor (or to nominate the outside auditor to be proposed for shareholder approval in any proxy statement); and

(c) that the audit committee is responsible for ensuring that the outside auditor submits on a periodic basis to the audit committee a formal written statement delineating all relationships between the auditor and the company and that the audit committee is responsible for actively engaging in a dialogue with the outside auditor with respect to any disclosed relationships or services that may impact the objectivity and independence of the outside auditor and for recommending that the Board of Directors take appropriate action in response to the outside auditors' report to satisfy itself of the outside auditors' independence.

(2) Composition/Expertise Requirement of Audit Committee Members.

(a) Each audit committee shall consist of at least three directors, all of whom have no relationship to the company that may interfere with the exercise of their independence from management and the company ('Independent");

(b) Each member of the audit committee shall be financially literate, as such qualification is interpreted by the company's Board of Directors in its business judgment, or must become financially literate within a reasonable period of time after his or her appointment to the audit committee; and

(c) At least one member of the audit committee must have accounting or related financial management expertise, as the Board of Directors interprets such qualification in its business judgment.

(3) Independence Requirement of Audit Committee Members. In addition to the definition of Independent provided above in (2)(a), the following restrictions shall apply to every audit committee member:

(a) Employees. A director who is an employee (including non-employee executive officers) of the company or any of its affiliates may not serve on the audit committee until three years following the termination of his or her employment. In the event the employment relationship is with a former parent or predecessor of the company, the director could serve on the audit committee after three years following the termination of the relationship between the company and the former parent or predecessor.

(b) Business Relationship. A director (i) who is a partner, controlling shareholder, or executive officer of an organization that has a business relationship with the company, or (ii) who has a direct business relationship with the company (e.g., a consultant) may serve on the audit committee only if the company's Board of Directors determines in its business judgment that the relationship does not interfere with the director's exercise of independent judgment. In making a determination regarding the independence of a director pursuant to this paragraph, the Board of Directors should consider, among other things, the materiality of the relationship to the company, to the director, and, if applicable, to the organization with which the director is affiliated.

"Business relationships" can include commercial, industrial, banking, consulting, legal, accounting and other relationships. A director can have this relationship directly with the company, or the director can be a partner, officer or employee of an organization that has such a relationship. The director may serve on the audit committee without the above-referenced Board of Directors' determination after three years following the termination of, as applicable either (1) the relationship between the organization with which the director is affiliated and the company, (2) the relationship between the director and his or her partnership status, shareholder interest or executive officer position, or (3) the direct business relationship between the director and the company.

(c) Cross Compensation Committee Link. A director who is employed as an executive of another corporation where any of the company's executives serves on that corporation's compensation committee may not serve on the audit committee.

(d) Immediate Family. A director who is an Immediate Family member of an individual who is an executive officer of the company or any of its affiliates cannot serve on the audit committee until three years following the termination of such employment relationship. See para.303.02 for definition of "Immediate Family".

. . .

(Since 1956 the Exchange has required all domestic companies listing on the Exchange to have at least two outside directors on their boards.)

303.02 Application of Standards

(A) "Immediate Family" includes a person's spouse, parents, children, siblings, mothers-in-law and fathers-in-law, sons and daughters-in-law, brothers and sisters-in-law, and anyone (other than employees) who shares such person's home.

(B) "Affiliate" includes a subsidiary, sibling company, predecessor, parent company, or former parent company.

(C) Written Affirmation. As part of the initial listing process, and with respect to any subsequent changes to the composition of the audit committee, and otherwise approximately once each year, each company should provide the Exchange written confirmation regarding:

(1) any determination that the company's Board of Directors has made regarding the independence of directors pursuant to any of the subparagraphs above;

(2) the financial literacy of the audit committee members;

(3) the determination that at least one of the audit committee members has accounting or related financial management expertise; and

(4) the annual review and reassessment of the adequacy of the audit committee charter.

(D) Independence Requirement of Audit Committee Members. Notwithstanding the requirements of subparagraphs (3)(a) and (3)(d) of para. 303.01, one director who is no longer an employee or who is an Immediate Family member of a former executive officer of the company or its affiliates, but is not considered independent pursuant to these provisions due to the three-year restriction period, may be appointed, under exceptional and limited circumstances, to the audit committee if the company's board of directors determines in its business judgment that membership on the committee by the individual is required by the best interests of the corporation and its shareholders, and the company discloses, in the next annual proxy statement subsequent to such determination, the nature of the relationship and the reasons for that determination.

(E) "Officer" shall have the meaning specified in Rule 16a–1(f) under the Securities Exchange Act of 1934, or any successor rule.

(F) Initial Public Offering. Companies listing in conjunction with their initial public offering (including spin-offs and carve outs) will be required to have two qualified audit committee members in place within three months of listing and a third qualified member in place within twelve months of listing.

309.00 PURCHASES OF COMPANY STOCK BY DIRECTORS AND OFFICERS

309.00 Purchases of Company Stock by Directors and Officers

Many shareholders feel that directors and officers should have a meaningful investment in the companies they manage. The extent of this ownership, naturally, would vary in accordance with the financial circumstances of the persons involved. As shareholders themselves, directors are more likely to represent the viewpoint of other shareholders whose interests they are charged with protecting. Similarly, officers—the executive management group—may well perform more effectively with the incentive of stock options or a share in the equity ownership of the company.

The Exchange has encouraged the broadening of share ownership through stock option and employee stock purchase plans, especially those plans that include all or a large portion of the company's employees. The approval of shareholders has been a prerequisite of Exchange listing of new shares for the more limited key officer plans.

The widespread endorsement of director and officer share ownership brings with it questions that concern the timing of their stock transactions. When may a director or officer properly buy or sell shares of his company's stock? When is it appropriate to award stock options to key executives? There is no simple, uniform answer to these questions, but they do underscore the importance of a policy of adequate timely disclosure both for the benefit of the investing public and for the protection of management.

Competition requires that companies engage in active programs of research, development, and exploration. For many companies, more than half of today's sales represent new products or services invented, discovered, developed, or radically redesigned during the last ten years. Nevertheless, more experimental projects fail than result in salable and profitable products or services. Public disclosure at the earlier stages of new developments may be premature. In addition, competition and the best interest of the company and its shareholders may require a veil of secrecy around new developments before they reach the stage where public disclosure is appropriate. Still, hindsight is remarkably keen and the accusation can always be made that a purchase or sale of stock by a director was dictated by inside knowledge of a future favorable or unfavorable development.

Shareholders have indicated however that they want directors and officers to have a meaningful investment in the companies they manage. So, in the interest of promoting better shareholder relationships, some general rules under which corporate officials may properly buy or sell stock in their company may be helpful. One appropriate method of purchase might be a periodic investment program where the directors or officers make regular purchases under an established program administered by a broker and where the timing of purchases is outside the control of the individual. It would also seem appropriate for officials to buy or sell stock in their companies for a 30–day period commencing one week after the annual report has been mailed to shareholders and otherwise broadly circulated (provided, of course, that the annual report has adequately covered important corporate developments and that no new major undisclosed developments occur within that period).

Transactions may also be appropriate under the following circumstances, provided that prior to making a purchase or sale a director or officer contacts the chief executive officer of the company to be sure there are no important developments pending which need to be made public before an insider could properly participate in the market:

- Following a release of quarterly results, which includes adequate comment on new developments during the period. This timing of transactions might be even more appropriate where the report has been mailed to shareholders.
- Following the wide dissemination of information on the status of the company and current results. For example, transactions may be appropriate after a proxy statement or prospectus which gives such information in connection with a merger or new financing.

- At those times when there is relative stability in the company's operations and the market for its securities. Under these circumstances, timing of transactions may be relatively less important. Of course such periods of relative stability will vary greatly from time to time and will also depend to a large extent on the nature of the industry or the company.

Where a development of major importance is expected to reach the appropriate time for announcement within the next few months, transactions by directors and officers should be avoided.

Corporate officials should wait until after the release of earnings, dividends, or other important developments have appeared in the press before making a purchase or sale. This permits the news to be widely disseminated and negates the inference that officials had an inside advantage. Similarly, transactions just prior to important press releases should be avoided.

In granting stock options to directors and key officers, the same philosophy that relates to purchases and sales may well apply. Where an established pattern or formula is part of a plan specifically approved by shareholders, the question of timing may not arise. In taking up an option, the timing of a purchase is not usually critical as the price is set at the time the option is granted. The reasoning relating to stock options might also apply to employee stock purchase plans in which directors and officers may be entitled to participate.

The considerations that affect director and officer transactions in stock of their own company may be pertinent to transactions in the shares of other companies with which discussions of merger, acquisition, important contracts, etc., are being considered or carried on. The same considerations apply to the families or close associates of directors and officers who are often presumed to have preferential access to information. As far as the public is concerned, they also are insiders. While this assumption may be unjustified in many cases, it is a fact of life which those in positions of leadership and responsibility cannot ignore.

Some companies have adopted policies for the guidance of their personnel relating to transactions in the company's stock, as well as other areas where conflicts of interest could arise. Such policies can be very helpful to employees who have access to important confidential information, as well as to the directors and officers.

In the final analysis, directors and officers must be guided by a sense of fairness to all segments of the investing public.

Within the framework of any policies adopted by the company, the final decision with respect to securities transactions must rest with each director and officer. Each case must ultimately stand or fall on its own merits. No single rule could possibly cover all situations; nor should unnecessary restrictions be permitted to discourage shareholders among these business leaders who play such a vital role in the success of our system of free enterprise.

Particular attention is directed to Sections 10(b) and 16 of the Securities Exchange Act of 1934 and Rule 10b–5 thereunder.

312.00 SHAREHOLDER APPROVAL POLICY

312.01 Shareholders' Interest

Shareholders' interest and participation in corporate affairs has greatly increased. Management has responded by providing more extensive and frequent reports on matters of interest to investors. In addition, an increasing number of important corporate decisions are being referred to shareholders for their approval. This is especially true of transactions involving the issuance of additional securities.

Good business practice is frequently the controlling factor in the determination of management to submit a matter to shareholders for approval even though neither the law nor the company's charter makes such approvals necessary. The Exchange encourages this growth in corporate democracy. For example, due to the recent growth of officer and director equity—based compensation arrangements and the increased interest of shareholders in this area, companies may determine to submit stock option and similar plans to shareholders for approval, whether or not the Exchange requires such approval.

312.03 Shareholder Approval

Shareholder approval is a prerequisite to listing in four situations:

(a) Shareholder approval is required with respect to a stock option or purchase plan, or any other arrangement, pursuant to which officers or directors may acquire stock (collectively, a "Plan") except:

(1) for warrants or rights issued generally to security holders of the company;

(2) pursuant to a broadly-based Plan;

(3) where options or shares are to be issued to a person not previously employed by the company, as a material inducement to such person's entering into an employment contract with the company; or

(4) pursuant to a Plan that provides that (i) no single officer or director may acquire under the Plan more than one percent of the shares of the issuer's common stock outstanding at the time the Plan is adopted, and (ii) together with all Plans of the issuer (other than Plans for which shareholder approval is not required under subsections (1) to (3) above), does not authorize the issuance of more than five percent of the issuer's common stock outstanding at the time the Plan is adopted.

(b) Shareholder approval is required prior to the issuance of common stock, or of securities convertible into or exercisable for common stock, to:

(1) a director, officer or substantial security holder of the company (a "Related Party");

(2) a subsidiary, affiliate or other closely-related person of a Related Party; or

(3) any company or entity in which a Related Party has a substantial direct or indirect interest; if the number of shares of common stock to be issued, or if the number of shares of common stock into which the securities may be convertible or exercisable, exceeds either one percent of the number of shares of common stock or one percent of the voting power outstanding before the issuance.

However, if the Related Party involved in the transaction is classified as such solely because such person is a substantial security holder, and if the issuance relates to a sale of stock for cash at a price at least as great as each of the book and market value of the issuer's common stock, then shareholder approval will not be required unless the number of shares of common stock to be issued, or unless the number of shares of common stock into which the securities may be convertible or exercisable, exceeds either five percent of the number of shares of common stock or five percent of the voting power outstanding before the issuance.

(c) Shareholder approval is required prior to the issuance of common stock, or of securities

convertible into or exercisable for common stock, in any transaction or series of related transactions if:

(1) the common stock has, or will have upon issuance, voting power equal to or in excess of 20 percent of the voting power outstanding before the issuance of such stock or of securities convertible into or exercisable for common stock; or

(2) the number of shares of common stock to be issued is, or will be upon issuance, equal to or in excess of 20 percent of the number of shares of common stock outstanding before the issuance of the common stock or of securities convertible into or exercisable for common stock.

However, shareholder approval will not be required for any such issuance involving:

- any public offering for cash;
- any bona fide private financing, if such financing involves a sale of: common stock, for cash, at a price at least as great as each of the book and market value of the issuer's common stock; or

- securities convertible into or exercisable for common stock, for cash, if the conversion or exercise price is at least as great as each of the book and market value of the issuer's common stock.

(d) Shareholder approval is required prior to an issuance that will result in a change of control of the issuer.

312.04 For the Purpose of Para. 312.03

For the purpose of Para. 312.03:

(a) Shareholder approval is required if any of the subparagraphs (a), (b), (c) or (d) of Para. 312.03 require such approval, notwithstanding the fact that the transaction does not require approval under one or more of the other subparagraphs.

(b) Pursuant to subparagraphs (b) and (c) of Para. 312.03, shareholder approval is required for the issuance of securities convertible into or exercisable for common stock if the stock that can be issued upon conversion or exercise exceeds the applicable percentages. This is the case even if such convertible or exchangeable securities are not to be listed on the Exchange. The Exchange's policy regarding the need to apply to list common stock reserved for issuance on the conversion or the exercise of other securities is described in Para. 703.07.

(c) Only shares actually issued and outstanding (excluding treasury shares or shares held by a subsidiary) are to be used in making any calculation provided for in that paragraph. Unissued shares reserved for issuance upon conversion of securities or upon exercise of options or warrants will not be regarded as outstanding.

(d) An interest consisting of less than either five percent of the number of shares of common stock or five percent of the voting power outstanding of a company or entity shall not be considered a substantial interest or cause the holder of such an interest to be regarded as a substantial security holder.

(e) "Voting power outstanding" refers to the aggregate number of votes that may be cast by holders of those securities outstanding that entitle the holders thereof to vote generally on all matters submitted to the company's security holders for a vote.

(f) "Bona fide private financing" refers to a sale in which either:

- a registered broker-dealer purchases the securities from the issuer with a view to the private sale of such securities to one or more purchasers; or
- the issuer sells the securities to multiple purchasers, and no one such purchaser, or group of related purchasers, acquires, or has the right to acquire upon exercise or conversion of the securities, more than five percent of the shares of the issuer's common stock

or more than five percent of the issuer's voting power before the sale.

(g) "Officer" has the same meaning as defined by the Securities and Exchange Commission in Rule 16a–1(f) under the Securities Exchange Act of 1934, or any successor rule.

(h) A Plan is "broadly-based" if, pursuant to the terms of the Plan:

- at least a majority of the company's full-time employees in the United States, who are "exempt employees," as defined under Fair Labor Standards Act of 1938, are eligible to receive stock or options under the Plan; and
- at least a majority of the shares of stock or shares of stock underlying options awarded under the Plan during any three year period must be awarded to employees who are not officers or directors of the company.

312.05 Exceptions

Exceptions may be made to the shareholder approval policy in Para. 312.03 upon application to the Exchange when (1) the delay in securing stockholder approval would seriously jeopardize the financial viability of the enterprise and (2) reliance by the company on this exception is expressly approved by the Audit Committee of the Board.

A company relying on this exception must mail to all shareholders not later than 10 days before issuance of the securities a letter alerting them to its omission to seek the shareholder approval that would otherwise be required under the policy of the Exchange and indicating that the Audit Committee of the Board has expressly approved the exception.

313.00 VOTING RIGHTS

313.00 Voting Rights

(A) Voting Rights Policy. On May 5, 1994, the Exchange's Board of Directors voted to modify the Exchange's Voting Rights Policy, which had been based on former SEC Rule 19c–4. The Policy is more flexible than Rule 19c–4. Accordingly, the Exchange will continue to permit corporate actions or issuances by listed companies that would have been permitted under Rule 19c–4, as well as other actions or issuances that are not inconsistent with the new Policy. In evaluating such other actions or issuances, the Exchange will consider, among other things, the economics of such actions or issuances and the voting rights being granted. The Exchange's interpretations under the Policy will be flexible, recognizing that both the capital markets and the circumstances and needs of listed companies change over time. The text of the Exchange's Voting Rights Policy is as follows:

Voting rights of existing shareholders of publicly traded common stock registered under Section 12 of the Exchange Act cannot be disparately reduced or restricted through any corporate action or issuance. Examples of such corporate action or issuance include, but are not limited to, the adoption of time phased voting plans, the adoption of capped voting rights plans, the issuance of super voting stock, or the issuance of stock with voting rights less than the per share voting rights of the existing common stock through an exchange offer.

(B) Non–Voting Common Stock. The Exchange's voting rights policy permits the listing of the voting common stock of a company which also has outstanding a non-voting common stock as well as the listing of non-voting common stock. However, certain safeguards must be provided to holders of a listed non-voting common stock:

(1) Any class of non-voting common stock that is listed on the Exchange must meet all original listing standards. The rights of the holders of the non-voting common stock should, except for voting rights, be substantially the same as those of the holders of the company's voting common stock.

(2) The requirement that listed companies publish at least once a year and submit to shareholders an annual report (Para. 203.01) applies equally to holders of voting common stock and to holders of listed non-voting common stock.

(3) In addition, although the holders of shares of listed non-voting common stock are not entitled to vote generally on matters submitted for shareholder action, holders of any listed non-voting common stock must receive all communications, including proxy material, sent generally to the holders of the voting securities of the listed company.

(C) Preferred Stock, Minimum Voting Rights Required. Preferred stock, voting as a class, should have the right to elect a minimum of two directors upon default of the equivalent of six quarterly dividends. The right to elect directors should accrue regardless of whether defaulted dividends occurred in consecutive periods.

The right to elect directors should remain in effect until cumulative dividends have been paid in full or until non-cumulative dividends have been paid regularly for at least a year. The preferred stock quorum should be low enough to ensure that the right to elect directors can be exercised as soon as it accrues. In no event should the quorum exceed the percentage required for a quorum of the common stock required for the election of directors. The Exchange prefers that no quorum requirement be fixed in respect of the right of a preferred stock, voting as a class, to elect directors when dividends are in default.

The Exchange recommends that preferred stock should have minimum voting rights even if the preferred stock is not listed.

Increase in Authorized Amount or Creation of a Pari Passu Issue—

- An increase in the authorized amount of a class of preferred stock or the creation of a pari passu issue should be approved by a majority of the holders of the outstanding shares of the class or classes to be affected. The Board of Directors may increase the authorized amount of a series or create an additional series ranking pari passu without a vote by the existing series if shareholders authorized such action by the Board of Directors at the time the class of preferred stock was created.

Creation of a Senior Issue—

- Creation of a senior equity security should require approval of at least two-thirds of the outstanding preferred shares. The Board of Directors may create a senior series without a vote by the existing series if shareholders authorized such action by the Board of Directors at the time of the existing series of preferred stock was created.
- A vote by an existing class of preferred stock is not required for the creation of a senior issue if the existing class has previously received adequate notice of redemption to occur within 90 days. However, the vote of the existing class should not be denied if all or part of the existing issue is being retired with proceeds from the sale of the new stock.

Alteration of Existing Provisions—

- Approval by the holders of at least two-thirds of the outstanding shares of a preferred stock should be required for adoption of any charter or by-law amendment that would materially affect existing terms of the preferred stock.
- If all series of a class of preferred stock are not equally affected by the proposed changes, there should be a two-thirds approval of the class and a two-thirds approval of the series that will have a diminished status.
- The charter should not hinder the shareholders' right to alter the terms of a preferred stock by limiting modification to specific items, e.g., interest rate, redemption price.

SUPPLEMENTARY MATERIAL

.10 Companies with Dual Class Structures—

The restriction against the issuance of super voting stock is primarily intended to apply to the issuance of a new class of stock, and companies with existing dual class capital structures would generally be permitted to issue additional shares of the existing super voting stock without conflict with this Policy.

.20 Consultation with the Exchange—

Violation of the Exchange's Voting Rights Policy could result in the loss of an Issuer's Exchange market or public trading market. The Policy can apply to a variety of corporate actions and securities issuances, not just super voting or so-called "time phase" voting common stock. While the Policy will continue to permit actions previously permitted under Rule 19c–4, it is extremely important that listed companies communicate their intentions to their Exchange representatives as early as possible before taking any action or committing to take any action that may be inconsistent with the Policy. The Exchange urges listed companies not to assume, without first discussing the matter with the Exchange staff, that a particular issuance of common or preferred stock or the taking of some other corporate action will necessarily be consistent with the Policy. It is suggested that copies of preliminary proxy or other material concerning matters subject to the Policy be furnished to the Exchange for review prior to formal filing.

.40 Non–U.S. Companies—

The Exchange will accept any action or issuance relating to the voting rights structure of a non-U.S. company that is in compliance with the Exchange's requirements for domestic companies or that is not prohibited by the company's home country law.

B. PROPOSED CHANGES TO NEW YORK STOCK EXCHANGE CORPORATE GOVERNANCE STANDARDS

303.00 Corporate Governance Standards

Pending the implementation of the new corporate governance standards set forth in Section 303A infra, in accordance with the transition provisions adopted by the Exchange, the standards contained in this Section 303.00 will continue to apply.

303A*

General Application

Companies listed on the Exchange must comply with certain standards regarding corporate governance as codified in this Section 303A. Consistent with the NYSE's traditional approach, as well as the requirements of the Sarbanes–Oxley Act of 2002, certain provisions of Section 303A are applicable to some listed companies but not to others.

Equity Listings

Section 303(A) applies in full to all companies listing common equity securities, with the following exceptions:

Controlled Companies. A company of which more than 50% of the voting power is held by an individual, a group or another company need not comply with the requirements of Sections 303A(1), (4) or (5). A controlled company that chooses to take advantage of any or all of these exemptions must disclose in its annual meeting proxy that choice, that it is a controlled company and the basis for the determination. Controlled companies must comply with the remaining provisions of Section 303A.

Limited Partnerships and Companies in Bankruptcy. Due to their unique attributes, limited partnerships and companies in bankruptcy proceedings need not comply with the requirements of Sections 303A(1), (4) or (5). However, all limited partnerships (at the general partner level) and companies in bankruptcy proceedings must comply with the remaining provisions of Section 303A.

* Text of all proposed rules except Rule 303A(A)(8) filed at *Notice of Filing of Proposed Rule Change and Amendment No. 1 Thereto by the New York Stock Exchange, Inc. Relating to Corporate Governance*, SEC Release No. 34–47672; File No. SR–NYSE–2002–33, April 11, 2003, *available at* http://www.sec.gov/rules/sro/34-47672.htm. Rule 303A(A)(8) was filed with the SEC separately by the NYSE. *Notice of Filing of Proposed Rule Change by the New York Stock Exchange, Inc. Relating to Shareholder Approval of Equity Compensation Plans and the Voting of Proxies*, SEC Release No. 34–46620; File No. SR–NYSE–2002–46, October 8, 2002, *available at* http://www.sec.gov/rules/sro/34-46620.htm.

Closed-End Funds. The Exchange considers the significantly expanded standards and requirements provided for in Section 303A to be unnecessary for closed-end management companies given the pervasive federal regulation applicable to them. However, closed-end management companies must comply with the requirements set out in Sections 303A(6), (7) and (12)(b).

Other Entities. Section 303A does not apply to passive business organizations in the form of trusts (such as royalty trusts) or to derivatives and special purpose securities (such as those described in Sections 703.16, 703.19, 703.20 and 703.21).

Foreign Private Issuers. Listed companies that are foreign private issuers (as such term is defined in Rule 3b–4 under the Exchange Act) are permitted to follow home country practice in lieu of the provisions of this Section 303A, except that such companies are required to comply with the requirements of Sections 303A(6) (including the applicable commentary), (7)(a) and (c), (11) and (12)(b).

Preferred and Debt Listings

Section 303A does not generally apply to companies listing only preferred or debt securities on the Exchange. To the extent required by Rule 10A–3 under the Exchange Act, all companies listing only preferred or debt securities on the NYSE are required to comply with the requirements of Sections 303A(6) (including the applicable commentary), (7)(a) and (c), and (12)(b).

Effective Dates/Transition Periods

Companies that do not already have majority-independent boards will need time to recruit qualified independent directors, and companies with classified boards may need additional time to implement the new standards in a series of director elections. Accordingly, all listed companies will be required to comply with the standards in Sections 303A(1) and (2) no later than eighteen months following publication of SEC approval of these standards in the Federal Register. If a company has a classified board and a change would be required for a director who would not normally stand for election within the 18 month period, the company will have an additional year, or a total of 30 months after publication of SEC approval of Section 303A in the Federal Register, to effect the change in that director position.

Companies will have the same 18–month and 30–month periods described above to comply with the new qualification standards applicable to audit, nominating and compensation committee members. As a general matter, the existing audit committee requirements provided for in Section 303 continue to apply to NYSE listed companies pending the transition to the new rules.

Companies listing in conjunction with their initial public offering must comply within 24 months of listing. Companies listing upon transfer from another market have 24 months from the date of transfer in which to comply with any requirement to the extent the market on which they were listed did not have the same requirement. To the extent the other market has a substantially similar requirement but also had a transition period from the effective date of that market's rule, which period had not yet expired, the company will have at least as long a transition period as would have been available to it on the other market.

While the above time periods are needed to recruit directors, the Exchange believes that listed companies, IPOs and transfers can much more quickly implement the other requirements of Section 303A. The provision for a public reprimand letter set out in Section 303A(13) is effective upon publication of SEC approval of Section 303A in the Federal Register. The remaining requirements can also be implemented quickly. Accordingly, the following standards are effective six months from publication of SEC approval of Section 303A in the Federal Register:

- Executive sessions of non-management directors (subsection 3);
- Nomination and compensation committees with requisite charters (subsections 4 and 5);
- Audit committee with requisite charter (subsection 7);
- Corporate governance guidelines and code of business conduct and ethics (subsections 9 and 10);
- Foreign private issuer statement of significant differences from NYSE standards (subsection 11); and
- CEO certification of compliance with listing standards (subsection 12).

Once those six months are expired, we expect all newly listed companies, both IPOs and transfers, to have provided for these requirements by the time of listing on the Exchange.

1. Listed companies must have a majority of independent directors.

Commentary: Effective boards of directors exercise independent judgment in carrying out their responsibilities. Requiring a majority of independent directors will increase the quality of board oversight and lessen the possibility of damaging conflicts of interest.

2. In order to tighten the definition of "independent director" for purposes of these standards:

(a) No director qualifies as "independent" unless the board of directors affirmatively determines that the director has no material relationship with the listed company (either directly or as a partner, shareholder or officer of an organi-

zation that has a relationship with the company). Companies must disclose these determinations.

Commentary: It is not possible to anticipate, or explicitly to provide for, all circumstances that might signal potential conflicts of interest, or that might bear on the materiality of a director's relationship to a listed company. Accordingly, it is best that boards making "independence" determinations broadly consider all relevant facts and circumstances. In particular, when assessing the materiality of a director's relationship with the company, the board should consider the issue not merely from the standpoint of the director, but also from that of persons or organizations with which the director has an affiliation. Material relationships can include commercial, industrial, banking, consulting, legal, accounting, charitable and familial relationships, among others However, as the concern is independence from management, the Exchange does not view ownership of even a significant amount of stock, by itself, as a bar to an independence finding. Of course in no event can any current employee of the listed company be deemed independent of management.

The basis for a board determination that a relationship is not material must be disclosed in the company's annual proxy statement or, if the company does not file an annual proxy statement, in the company's annual report on Form 10–K filed with the SEC. In this regard, a board may adopt and disclose categorical standards to assist it in making determinations of independence and may make a general disclosure if a director meets these standards. Any determination of independence for a director who does not meet these standards must be specifically explained. A company must disclose any standard it adopts. It may then make the general statement that the independent directors meet the standards set by the board without detailing particular aspects of the immaterial relationships between individual directors and the company (except where there is a presumption of non-independence, as described in the commentary to Section 303A(2)(b)). In the event that a director with a business or other relationship that does not fit within the disclosed standards is determined to be independent, a board must disclose the basis for its determination in the manner described above. This approach provides investors with an adequate means of assessing the quality of a board's independence and its independence determinations while avoiding excessive disclosure of immaterial relationships.

(b) In addition:

(i) A director who receives, or whose immediate family member receives, more than $100,000 per year in direct compensation from the listed company, other than director and committee fees and pension or other forms of deferred compensation for prior service (provided such compensation is not contingent in any way on continued service), is presumed not to be independent until five

years after he or she ceases to receive more than $100,000 per year in such compensation.

Commentary: A listed company's board may negate this presumption with respect to a director if the board determines (and no independent director dissents) that, based upon the relevant facts and circumstances, such compensatory relationship is not material. Any affirmative determination of independence made by the board in these circumstances must be specifically explained in the listed company's proxy statement, or, if the company does not file a proxy statement, in the company's annual report filed on Form 10–K with the SEC, and cannot be covered by a categorical standard adopted in accordance with the commentary to Section 303A(2)(a). Compensation received by a director for former service as an interim Chairman or CEO does not need to be considered as a factor by a board in determining independence under this presumption. If a person who received more than $100,000 per year in direct compensation from a listed company dies or becomes incapacitated, the presumption of non-independence applicable to his or her immediate family members will cease immediately upon such death or determination of incapacity.

(ii) A director who is affiliated with or employed by, or whose immediate family member is affiliated with or employed in a professional capacity by, a present or former internal or external auditor of the company is not "independent" until five years after the end of either the affiliation or the auditing relationship.

(iii) A director who is employed, or whose immediate family member is employed, as an executive officer of another company where any of the listed company's present executives serves on that company's compensation committee is not "independent" until five years after the end of such service or the employment relationship.

(iv) A director who is an executive officer or an employee, or whose immediate family member is an executive officer, of another company (A) that accounts for at least 2% or $1 million, whichever is greater, of the listed company's consolidated gross revenues, or (B) for which the listed company accounts for at least 2% or $1 million, whichever is greater, of such other company's consolidated gross revenues, in each case is not "independent" until five years after falling below such threshold.

General Commentary to Section 303A(2)(b): An "immediate family member" includes a person's spouse, parents, children, siblings, mothers and fathers-in-law, sons and daughters-in-law, brothers and sisters-in-law, and anyone (other than domestic employees) who shares such person's home.

Transition Rule. During the five years immediately following [insert the effective date of this listing standard], each five year "look back" period referenced in sub-paragraphs (b)(i) through (b)(iv) shall instead be the period since [insert effective date of this listing standard]. For example, if a director received in excess of $100,000 per year in direct compensation from a listed company during the year prior to [insert effective date of this listing standard], there will be no required presumption that the director is not independent unless such compensatory relationship extended past [insert effective date of this listing standard].

3. **To empower non-management directors to serve as a more effective check on management, the non-management directors of each company must meet at regularly scheduled executive sessions without management.**

Commentary: To promote open discussion among the non-management directors, companies must schedule regular executive sessions in which those directors meet without management participation. "Non-management" directors are all those who are not company officers (as that term is defined in Rule 16a-1(f) under the Securities Act of 1933), and includes such directors who are not independent by virtue of a material relationship, former status or family membership, or for any other reason. Regular scheduling of such meetings is important not only to foster better communication among non-management directors, but also to prevent any negative inference from attaching to the calling of executive sessions. There need not be a single presiding director at all executive sessions of the non-management directors. If one director is chosen to preside at these meetings, his or her name must be disclosed in the annual proxy statement or, if the company does not file an annual proxy statement, in the company's annual report on Form 10-K filed with the SEC. Alternatively, a company may disclose the procedure by which a presiding director is selected for each executive session. For example, a company may wish to rotate the presiding position among the chairs of board committees. In order that interested parties may be able to make their concerns known to the non-management directors, a company must disclose a method for such parties to communicate directly and confidentially with the presiding director or with the non-management directors as a group. That method can follow the same process established for communications to the audit committee required by Section 303A(7)(c)(ii).

4. **(a) Listed companies must have a nominating/corporate governance committee composed entirely of independent directors.**

(b) The nominating/corporate governance committee must have a written charter that addresses:

(i) the committee's purpose—which, at minimum, must be to: identify individuals qualified to become board members, and to select, or to recommend that the board select, the director nominees for the next annual meeting of shareholders; and develop and recommend to the board a set of corporate governance principles applicable to the corporation;

(ii) the committee's goals and responsibilities—which must reflect, at minimum, the board's criteria for selecting new directors, and oversight of the evaluation of the board and management; and

(iii) an annual performance evaluation of the committee.

Commentary: A nominating/corporate governance committee is central to the effective functioning of the board. New director and board committee nominations are among a board's most important functions. Placing this responsibility in the hands of an independent nominating/corporate governance committee can enhance the independence and quality of nominees. The committee is also responsible for taking a leadership role in shaping the corporate governance of a corporation.

If a company is legally required by contract or otherwise to provide third parties with the ability to nominate directors (for example, preferred stock rights to elect directors upon a dividend default, shareholder agreements, and management agreements), the selection and nomination of such directors need not be subject to the nominating committee process.

The nominating/corporate governance committee charter should also address the following items: committee member qualifications; committee member appointment and removal; committee structure and operations (including authority to delegate to subcommittees); and committee reporting to the board. In addition, the charter should give the nominating/corporate governance committee sole authority to retain and terminate any search firm to be used to identify director candidates, including sole authority to approve the search firm's fees and other retention terms.

Boards may allocate the responsibilities of the nominating/corporate governance committee to committees of their own denomination, provided that the committees are composed entirely of independent directors. Any such committee must have a published committee charter. To avoid any confusion, note that the audit committee functions specified in Section 303A(7) may not be allocated to a different committee, other than as noted in the General Commentary to Section 303A(7).

5. (a) Listed companies must have a compensation committee composed entirely of independent directors.

(b) The compensation committee must have a written charter that addresses:

(i) the committee's purpose—which, at minimum, must be to discharge the board's responsibilities relating to compensation of the company's executives, and to produce an annual report on executive compensation for inclusion in the company's proxy statement, or, if the company does not file a proxy statement, in the company's annual report filed on Form 10–K with the SEC, in accordance with applicable rules and regulations;

(ii) the committee's duties and responsibilities—which, at minimum, must be to:

(A) review and approve corporate goals and objectives relevant to CEO compensation, evaluate the CEO's performance in light of those goals and objectives, and have sole authority to determine the CEO's compensation level based on this evaluation; and

(B) make recommendations to the board with respect to non-CEO compensation, incentive-compensation plans and equity-based plans; and

(iii) an annual performance evaluation of the compensation committee.

Commentary: In determining the long-term incentive component of CEO compensation, the committee should consider the company's performance and relative shareholder return, the value of similar incentive awards to CEOs at comparable companies, and the awards given to the listed company's CEO in past years. To avoid confusion, note that the compensation committee is not precluded from approving awards (with or without ratification of the board) as may be required to comply with applicable tax laws (i.e., Rule 162(m)).

The compensation committee charter should also address the following items: committee member qualifications; committee member appointment and removal; committee structure and operations (including authority to delegate to subcommittees); and committee reporting to the board.

Additionally, if a compensation consultant is to assist in the evaluation of director, CEO or senior executive compensation, the compensation committee charter should give that committee sole authority to retain and terminate the consulting firm, including sole authority to approve the firm's fees and other retention terms.

Boards may allocate the responsibilities of the compensation committee to committees of their own denomination, provided that the committees are composed entirely of independent directors. Any such committee must have a published committee charter. To avoid any confusion, note that the audit committee functions specified in Section 303A(7) may not be allocated to a different committee, other than as noted in the General Commentary to Section 303A(7).

6. Add to the "independence" requirement for audit committee membership the requirements of Rule 10A–3(b)(1) under the Exchange Act, subject to the exemptions provided for in Rule 10A–3(c).

Commentary Applicable to All Companies: While it is not the audit committee's responsibility to certify the company's financial statements or to guarantee the auditor's report, the committee stands at the crucial intersection of management, independent auditors, internal auditors and the board of directors. The Exchange supports additional directors' fees to compensate audit committee members for the significant time and effort they expend to fulfill their duties as audit committee members, but does not believe that any member of the audit committee should receive any compensation other than such director's fees from the company. If a director satisfies the definition of "independent director" set out in Section 303A(2), then his or her receipt of a pension or other form of deferred compensation from the company for prior service (provided such compensation is not contingent in any way on continued service) will not preclude him or her from satisfying the requirement that director's fees are the only form of compensation he or she receives from the company.

An audit committee member may receive his or her fee in cash and/or company stock or options or other in-kind consideration ordinarily available to directors, as well as all of the regular benefits that other directors receive. Because of the significantly greater commitment of audit committee members, they may receive reasonable compensation greater than that paid to the other directors (as may other directors for other committee work). Disallowed compensation for an audit committee member includes fees paid directly or indirectly for services as a consultant or a legal or financial advisor, regardless of the amount. Disallowed compensation also includes compensation paid to such a director's firm for such consulting or advisory services even if the director is not the actual service provider. Disallowed compensation is not intended to include ordinary compensation paid in another customer or supplier or other business relationship that the board has already determined to be immaterial for purposes of its basic director independence analysis. To avoid any confusion, note that this requirement pertains only to audit committee qualification and not to the independence determinations that the board must make for other directors.

Commentary Applicable to All Companies Other than Foreign Private Issuers: Each member of the committee must be financially literate, as such qualification is interpreted by the company's board in its business judgment, or must become financially literate within a reasonable period of time after his or her appointment to the audit committee. In addition, at least one member of the audit committee must have accounting or related financial management expertise, as the company's board interprets such qualification in its business judgment. A board may presume that a person who satisfies the definition of audit committee financial expert set out in Item 401(e) of Regulation S–K has accounting or related financial management expertise.

Because of the audit committee's demanding role and responsibilities, and the time commitment attendant to committee membership, each prospective audit committee member should evaluate carefully the existing demands on his or her time before accepting this important assignment. Additionally, if an audit committee member simultaneously serves on the audit committee of more than three public companies, and the listed company does not limit the number of audit committees on which its audit committee members serve, then in each case, the board must determine that such simultaneous service would not impair the ability of such member to effectively serve on the listed company's audit committee and disclose such determination in the annual proxy statement or, if the company does not file an annual proxy statement, in the company's annual report on Form 10–K filed with the SEC.

7. **(a) Each company is required to have a minimum three person audit committee composed entirely of independent directors that meet the requirements of Section 303A(6).**

   (b) The audit committee must have a written charter that addresses:

   (i) the committee's purpose—which, at minimum, must be to:

   (A) assist board oversight of (1) the integrity of the company's financial statements, (2) the company's compliance with legal and regulatory requirements, (3) the independent auditor's qualifications and independence, and (4) the performance of the company's internal audit function and independent auditors; and

   (B) prepare the report required by the SEC's proxy rules to be included in the company's annual proxy statement, or, if the company does not file a proxy statement, in the company's annual report filed on Form 10–K with the SEC;

(ii) the duties and responsibilities of the audit committee set out in Section 303A (7)(c) and (d); and

(iii) an annual performance evaluation of the audit committee.

(c) As required by Rule 10A–3(b)(2), (3), (4) and (5) of the Securities Exchange Act of 1934, and subject to the exemptions provided for in Rule 10A–3(c), the audit committee must:

(i) directly appoint, retain, compensate, evaluate and terminate the company's independent auditors;

Commentary: In connection with this requirement, the audit committee must have the sole authority to approve all audit engagement fees and terms, as well as all significant non-audit engagements with the independent auditors. In addition, the independent auditor must report directly to the audit committee. This requirement does not preclude the committee from obtaining the input of management, but these responsibilities may not be delegated to management. The audit committee must be directly responsible for oversight of the independent auditors, including resolution of disagreements between management and the independent auditor and pre-approval of all non-audit services.

(ii) establish procedures for the receipt, retention and treatment of complaints from listed company employees on accounting, internal accounting controls or auditing matters, as well as for confidential, anonymous submissions by listed company employees of concerns regarding questionable accounting or auditing matters;

(iii) obtain advice and assistance from outside legal, accounting or other advisors as the audit committee deems necessary to carry out its duties; and

Commentary: In the course of fulfilling its duties, the audit committee may wish to consult with independent counsel and other advisors. The audit committee must be empowered to retain and compensate these advisors without seeking board approval.

(iv) receive appropriate funding, as determined by the audit committee, from the listed company for payment of compensation to the outside legal, accounting or other advisors employed by the audit committee.

(d) In addition to the duties set out in Section 303(A)(7)(c), the duties of the audit committee must be, at a minimum, to:

(i) at least annually, obtain and review a report by the independent auditor describing: the firm's internal quality-control procedures; any material issues raised by the most recent internal quality-control review, or peer re-

view, of the firm, or by any inquiry or investigation by governmental or professional authorities, within the preceding five years, respecting one or more independent audits carried out by the firm, and any steps taken to deal with any such issues; and (to assess the auditor's independence) all relationships between the independent auditor and the company;

Commentary: After reviewing the foregoing report and the independent auditor's work throughout the year, the audit committee will be in a position to evaluate the auditor's qualifications, performance and independence. This evaluation should include the review and evaluation of the lead partner of the independent auditor. In making its evaluation, the audit committee should take into account the opinions of management and the company's internal auditors (or other personnel responsible for the internal audit function). In addition to assuring the regular rotation of the lead audit partner as required by law, the audit committee should further consider whether, in order to assure continuing auditor independence, there should be regular rotation of the audit firm itself. The audit committee should present its conclusions with respect to the independent auditor to the full board.

(ii) discuss the annual audited financial statements and quarterly financial statements with management and the independent auditor, including the company's disclosures under "Management's Discussion and Analysis of Financial Condition and Results of Operations;"

(iii) discuss earnings press releases, as well as financial information and earnings guidance provided to analysts and rating agencies;

Commentary: The audit committee's responsibility to discuss earnings releases as well as financial information and earnings guidance may be done generally (i.e., discussion of the types of information to be disclosed and the type of presentation to be made). The audit committee need not discuss in advance each earnings release or each instance in which a company may provide earnings guidance.

(iv) discuss policies with respect to risk assessment and risk management;

Commentary: While it is the job of the CEO and senior management to assess and manage the company's exposure to risk, the audit committee must discuss guidelines and policies to govern the process by which this is handled. The audit committee should discuss the company's major financial risk exposures and the steps management has taken to monitor and control such exposures. The audit committee is not required to be the sole body responsible for risk assessment and management, but, as stated above, the committee must discuss guidelines and policies to govern the process by which risk assessment and management is undertaken. Many companies, particularly financial companies, manage and assess their risk through mechanisms other than the audit committee. The processes these companies have in place should be reviewed in a general manner by the audit committee, but they need not be replaced by the audit committee.

(v) meet separately, periodically, with management, with internal auditors (or other personnel responsible for the internal audit function) and with independent auditors

Commentary: To perform its oversight functions most effectively, the audit committee must have the benefit of separate sessions with management, the independent auditors and those responsible for the internal audit function. As noted herein, all listed companies must have an internal audit function. These separate sessions may be more productive than joint sessions in surfacing issues warranting committee attention.

(vi) review with the independent auditor any audit problems or difficulties and management's response;

Commentary: The audit committee must regularly review with the independent auditor any difficulties the auditor encountered in the course of the audit work, including any restrictions on the scope of the independent auditor's activities or on access to requested information, and any significant disagreements with management. Among the items the audit committee may want to review with the auditor are: any accounting adjustments that were noted or proposed by the auditor but were "passed" (as immaterial or otherwise); any communications between the audit team and the audit firm's national office respecting auditing or accounting issues presented by the engagement; and any "management" or "internal control" letter issued, or proposed to be issued, by the audit firm to the company. The review should also include discussion of the responsibilities, budget and staffing of the company's internal audit function.

(vii) set clear hiring policies for employees or former employees of the independent auditors; and

Commentary: Employees or former employees of the independent auditor are often valuable additions to corporate management. Such individuals' familiarity with the business, and personal rapport with the employees, may be attractive qualities when filling a key opening. However, the audit committee should set hiring policies taking into account the pressures that may exist for auditors consciously or subconsciously seeking a job with the company they audit.

(viii) report regularly to the board of directors.

Commentary: The audit committee should review with the full board any issues that arise with respect to the quality or integrity of the company's financial statements, the company's compliance with legal or regulatory requirements, the performance and independence of the company's independent auditors, or the performance of the internal audit function.

General Commentary to Section 303A(7)(d): While the fundamental responsibility for the company's financial statements and disclosures rests with management and the independent auditor, the audit committee must review: (A) major issues regarding accounting principles and financial statement presentations, including any significant changes in the company's selection or application of accounting principles, and major issues as to the adequacy of the company's internal controls and any special audit steps adopted in light of material control deficiencies; (B) analyses prepared by management and/or the independent auditor setting forth significant financial reporting issues and judgments made in connection with the preparation of the financial statements, including analyses of the effects of alternative GAAP methods on the financial statements; (C) the effect of regulatory and accounting initiatives, as well as off-balance sheet structures, on the financial statements of the company; and (D) the type and presentation of information to be included in earnings press releases (paying particular attention to any use of "pro forma," or "adjusted" non-GAAP, information), as well as review any financial information and earnings guidance provided to analysts and rating agencies.

General Commentary to Section 303A(7): To avoid any confusion, note that the audit committee functions specified in Section 303A(7) are the sole responsibility of the audit committee and may not be allocated to a different committee.

(e) Each listed company must have an internal audit function.

Commentary: Listed companies must maintain an internal audit function to provide management and the audit committee with ongoing assessments of the company's risk management processes and system of internal control. A company may choose to outsource this function to a firm other than its independent auditor.

8. Shareholder Approval of Equity Compensation Plans and the Voting of Proxies *

To increase shareholder control over equity-compensation plans, shareholders must be given the opportunity to vote on all equity-compensation plans, except inducement awards, plans relating to mergers or acquisitions, and tax qualified and parallel nonqualified plans.

Commentary: Equity-compensation plans can help align shareholder and management interests, and equity-based awards have become very im-

* NYSE Rulemaking. Self-Regulatory Organizations; Notice of Filing of Proposed Rule Change by the New York Stock Exchange, Inc. Relating to Shareholder Approval of Equity Compensation Plans and the Voting of Proxies. (Release No. 34–46620; File No. SR–NYSE–2002–46) October 8, 2002. Available at http://www.sec.gov/rules/sro/34–46620.htm

portant components of employee compensation. In order to provide checks and balances on the process of earmarking shares to be used for equity-based awards, and to provide shareholders a voice regarding the resulting dilution, the Exchange requires that all equity-compensation plans, and any material revisions to the terms of such plans, be subject to stockholder approval.

For these purposes, a "material revision" would include, but not be limited to, a revision that: materially increases the number of shares available under the plan (other than an increase solely to reflect a reorganization, stock split, merger, spinoff or similar transaction); changes the types of awards available under the plan; materially expands the class of persons eligible to receive awards under or otherwise participate in the plan; materially extends the term of the plan; or materially changes the method of determining the strike price of options under the plan. In addition, if a plan contains a provision that prohibits repricing of options, any revision that deletes or limits the scope of such a provision will be considered a material revision for purposes of this rule. If a plan does not contain a provision that specifically permits repricing of options, the plan will be considered for this purpose as prohibiting repricing, and any actual repricing of options will be considered a material revision of the plan, even if the plan itself is not revised.

There are certain types of plans and awards, however, which are appropriately exempt from this shareholder approval requirement. Employment inducement awards—that is, grants of options or shares as a material inducement to such person's first becoming an employee of the issuer or any of its subsidiaries—will not be subject to shareholder approval under this rule. The Exchange recognizes the urgency that may attach to the granting of options and other equity-based compensation in the context of inducing a candidate to accept employment and the resulting impracticality of obtaining a shareholder vote in these situations.

In the case of corporate acquisitions and mergers, two exceptions are appropriate. First, shareholder approval will not be required to convert, replace or adjust outstanding options or other equity compensation awards to reflect the transaction. Second, shares available under certain plans acquired in corporate acquisitions and mergers may be used for certain post-transaction grants without further shareholder approval. This exception applies to situations where the party which is not a listed company following the transaction has shares available for grant under pre-existing plans that were previously approved by shareholders. These shares may be used for post-transaction grants of options and other equity awards by the listed company (after appropriate adjustment of the number of shares to reflect the transaction), either under the pre-existing plan or another plan, without further shareholder approval, so long as (1) the time during which those shares are available for grants is not extended beyond the period when they would have been available under the pre-existing plan, absent the transaction, and (2) such options and other awards are not granted to individuals who were employed by the granting company at the time the merger or acquisition was consummated. The Exchange would view a plan adopted in contemplation of the merger or acquisition transaction as not pre-existing for purposes of this exception. The NYSE believes that this exception is appropriate because it believes that it will not result in any increase in the aggregate potential dilution of the combined enterprise.

Because inducement awards and mergers or acquisitions are not routine occurrences, and are not likely to be abused, the Exchange considers these exceptions to be consistent with the fundamental policy involved in this standard.

Similarly, any plan intended to meet the requirements of Section 401(a) of the Internal Revenue Code (e.g., ESOPs), any parallel nonqualified plan and any plan intended to meet the requirements of Section 423 of the Internal Revenue Code is exempt from the shareholder approval requirement. Plans such as Section 401(a) plans and Section 423 plans are already regulated under the Internal Revenue Code and Treasury regulations. Section 423 plans, which are stock purchase plans under which an employee can purchase no more than $25,000 worth of stock per year at a plan-specified discount capped at 15%, are also required under the Internal Revenue Code to receive shareholder approval. While Section 401(a) plans and their parallel nonqualified plans are not required to be approved by shareholders, the shares issued under these plans must be "expensed" (i.e., treated as a compensation expense on the income statement) by the company issuing the shares. Equity compensation plans that would qualify for the exception described in this paragraph but for features necessary to comply with foreign tax law in the non-U.S. jurisdiction in which the employees covered by the plan reside, are also exempt from shareholder approval under this section.

In circumstances in which equity compensation plans and amendments thereto are not subject to shareholder approval, the plans and amendments still must be subject to the approval of the company's compensation committee or a majority of the company's independent directors.

This rule will be applicable to a plan adopted before the effective date of this rule only upon any subsequent material revision of the plan.

In addition, the Exchange will preclude its member organizations from giving a proxy to vote on equity compensation plans unless the beneficial owner of the shares has given voting instructions. This will be codified in proposed changes to NYSE Rule 452.

9. Listed companies must adopt and disclose corporate governance guidelines.

Commentary: No single set of guidelines would be appropriate for every company, but certain key areas of universal importance include director qualifications and responsibilities, responsibilities of key board committees, and director compensation. Given the importance of corporate governance, each listed company's website must include its corporate governance guidelines and the charters of its most important committees (including at least the audit, and if applicable, compensation and nominating committees). Each company's annual report must state that the foregoing information is available on its website, and that the information is available in print to any shareholder who requests it. Making this information publicly available should promote better investor understanding of the company's policies and procedures, as well as more conscientious adherence to them by directors and management.

The following subjects must be addressed in the corporate governance guidelines:

- **Director qualification standards.** These standards should, at minimum, reflect the independence requirements set forth in Sections 303A(1) and (2). Companies may also address other substantive qualification requirements, including policies limiting the number of boards on which a director may sit, and director tenure, retirement and succession.
- **Director responsibilities.** These responsibilities should clearly articulate what is expected from a director, including basic duties and responsibilities with respect to attendance at board meetings and advance review of meeting materials.
- **Director access to management and, as necessary and appropriate, independent advisors.**
- **Director compensation.** Director compensation guidelines should include general principles for determining the form and amount of director compensation (and for reviewing those principles, as appropriate). The board should be aware that questions as to directors' independence may be raised when directors' fees and emoluments exceed what is customary. Similar concerns may be raised when the company makes substantial charitable contributions to organizations in which a director is affiliated, or enters into consulting contracts with (or provides other indirect forms of compensation to) a director. The board should critically evaluate each of these matters when determining the form and amount of director compensation, and the independence of a director.
- **Director orientation and continuing education.**
- **Management succession.** Succession planning should include policies and principles for CEO selection and performance review, as well as policies regarding succession in the event of an emergency or the retirement of the CEO.

- **Annual performance evaluation of the board.** The board should conduct a self-evaluation at least annually to determine whether it and its committees are functioning effectively.

10. **Listed companies must adopt and disclose a code of business conduct and ethics for directors, officers and employees, and promptly disclose any waivers of the code for directors or executive officers.**

Commentary: No code of business conduct and ethics can replace the thoughtful behavior of an ethical director, officer or employee. However, such a code can focus the board and management on areas of ethical risk, provide guidance to personnel to help them recognize and deal with ethical issues, provide mechanisms to report unethical conduct, and help to foster a culture of honesty and accountability.

Each code of business conduct and ethics must require that any waiver of the code for executive officers or directors may be made only by the board or a board committee and must be promptly disclosed to shareholders. This disclosure requirement should inhibit casual and perhaps questionable waivers, and should help assure that, when warranted, a waiver is accompanied by appropriate controls designed to protect the company. It will also give shareholders the opportunity to evaluate the board's performance in granting waivers.

Each code of business conduct and ethics must also contain compliance standards and procedures that will facilitate the effective operation of the code. These standards should ensure the prompt and consistent action against violations of the code. Each listed company's website must include its code of business conduct and ethics. Each company's annual report must state that the foregoing information is available on its website, and that the information is available in print to any shareholder who requests it.

Each company may determine its own policies, but all listed companies should address the most important topics, including the following:

- **Conflicts of interest.** A "conflict of interest" occurs when an individual's private interest interferes in any way—or even appears to interfere—with the interests of the corporation as a whole. A conflict situation can arise when an employee, officer or director takes actions or has interests that may make it difficult to perform his or her company work objectively and effectively. Conflicts of interest also arise when an employee, officer or director, or a member of his or her family, receives improper personal benefits as a result of his or her position in the company. Loans to, or guarantees of obligations of, such persons are of special concern. The company should have a policy prohibiting such conflicts of interest, and providing a means for employees, officers and directors to communicate potential conflicts to the company.

- **Corporate opportunities.** Employees, officers and directors should be prohibited from (a) taking for themselves personally opportunities that are discovered through the use of corporate property, information or position; (b) using corporate property, information, or position for personal gain; and (c) competing with the company. Employees, officers and directors owe a duty to the company to advance its legitimate interests when the opportunity to do so arises.

- **Confidentiality.** Employees, officers and directors should maintain the confidentiality of information entrusted to them by the company or its customers, except when disclosure is authorized or legally mandated. Confidential information includes all non-public information that might be of use to competitors, or harmful to the company or its customers, if disclosed.

- **Fair dealing.** Each employee, officer and director should endeavor to deal fairly with the company's customers, suppliers, competitors and employees. None should take unfair advantage of anyone through manipulation, concealment, abuse of privileged information, misrepresentation of material facts, or any other unfair-dealing practice. Companies may write their codes in a manner that does not alter existing legal rights and obligations of companies and their employees, such as "at will" employment arrangements.

- **Protection and proper use of company assets.** All employees, officers and directors should protect the company's assets and ensure their efficient use. Theft, carelessness and waste have a direct impact on the company's profitability. All company assets should be used for legitimate business purposes.

- **Compliance with laws, rules and regulations (including insider trading laws).** The company should proactively promote compliance with laws, rules and regulations, including insider trading laws. Insider trading is both unethical and illegal, and should be dealt with decisively.

- **Encouraging the reporting of any illegal or unethical behavior.** The company should proactively promote ethical behavior. The company should encourage employees to talk to supervisors, managers or other appropriate personnel when in doubt about the best course of action in a particular situation. Additionally, employees should report violations of laws, rules, regulations or the code of business conduct to appropriate personnel. To encourage employees to report such violations, the company must ensure that employees know that the company will not allow retaliation for reports made in good faith.

11. Listed foreign private issuers must disclose any significant ways in which their corporate governance practices differ from those followed by domestic companies under NYSE listing standards.

Commentary: Foreign private issuers must make their U.S. investors aware of the significant ways in which their home-country practices differ from those followed by domestic companies under NYSE listing standards. However, foreign private issuers are not required to present a detailed, item-by-item analysis of these differences. Such a disclosure would be long and unnecessarily complicated. Moreover, this requirement is not intended to suggest that one country's corporate governance practices are better or more effective than another. The Exchange believes that U.S. shareholders should be aware of the significant ways that the governance of a listed foreign private issuer differs from that of a U.S. listed company. The Exchange underscores that what is required is a brief, general summary of the significant differences, not a cumbersome analysis.

Listed foreign private issuers may provide this disclosure either on their web site (provided it is in the English language and accessible from the United States) and/or in their annual report as distributed to shareholders in the United States in accordance with Sections 103.00 and 203.01 of the Listed Company Manual (again, in the English language). If the disclosure is only made available on the web site, the annual report shall so state and provide the web address at which the information may be obtained.

12. (a) Each listed company CEO must certify to the NYSE each year that he or she is not aware of any violation by the company of NYSE corporate governance listing standards.

Commentary: The CEO's annual certification to the NYSE that, as of the date of certification, he or she is unaware of any violation by the company of NYSE corporate governance listing standards will focus the CEO and senior management on the company's compliance with the listing standards. Both this certification to the NYSE, and any CEO/CFO certifications required to be filed with the SEC regarding the quality of the company's public disclosure, must be disclosed in the listed company's annual report to shareholders or, if the company does not prepare an annual report to shareholders, in the companies annual report on Form 10–K filed with the SEC.

(b) Each listed company CEO must promptly notify the NYSE after any executive officer of the listed company becomes aware of any material non-compliance with any applicable provisions of this Section 303(A).

13. The NYSE may issue a public reprimand letter to any listed company that violates a NYSE listing standard.

Commentary: Suspending trading in or delisting a company can be harmful to the very shareholders that the NYSE listing standards seek to protect; the NYSE must therefore use these measures sparingly and judiciously. For this reason it is appropriate for the NYSE to have the ability to apply a lesser sanction to deter companies from violating its corporate governance (or other) listing standards. Accordingly, the NYSE may issue a public reprimand letter to a company that it determines has violated a NYSE listing standard. For companies that repeatedly or flagrantly violate NYSE listing standards, suspension and delisting remain the ultimate penalties. For clarification, this lesser sanction is not intended for use in the case of companies that fall below the financial and other continued listing standards provided in Chapter 8 of the Listed Company Manual. The processes and procedures provided for in Chapter 8 govern the treatment of companies falling below those standards.

C. CORPORATE GOVERNANCE POLICIES

Contents

---

1. Governance Principles, General Electric Company*

The following principles have been approved by the board of directors and, along with the charters and key practices of the board committees, provide the framework for the governance of GE. The board recognizes that there is an on-going and energetic debate about corporate governance, and it will review these principles and other aspects of GE governance annually or more often if deemed necessary.

1. *Role of Board and Management.* GE's business is conducted by its employees, managers and officers, under the direction of the chief executive officer (CEO) and the oversight of the board, to enhance the long-term value of the company for its shareowners. The board of directors is elected by the shareowners to oversee management and to assure that the long-term interests of the shareowners are being served. Both the board of directors and management recognize that the long-term interests of shareowners are advanced by responsibly addressing the concerns of other stakeholders and interested parties including employees, recruits, customers, suppliers, GE communities, government officials and the public at large.

2. *Functions of Board.* The board of directors has 8 scheduled meetings a year at which it reviews and discusses reports by management on the performance of the company, its plans and prospects, as well as immediate issues facing the company. Directors are expected to attend all scheduled board and committee meetings. In addition to its general oversight of management, the board also performs a number of specific functions, including:

a. selecting, evaluating and compensating the CEO and overseeing CEO succession planning;

b. providing counsel and oversight on the selection, evaluation, development and compensation of senior management;

c. reviewing, approving and monitoring fundamental financial and business strategies and major corporate actions;

* *Available at http*://www.ge.com/en/spotlight/commitment/governance/governance_principles.htm

d. assessing major risks facing the company—and reviewing options for their mitigation; and

e. ensuring processes are in place for maintaining the integrity of the company—the integrity of the financial statements, the integrity of compliance with law and ethics, the integrity of relationships with customers and suppliers, and the integrity of relationships with other stakeholders.

3. *Qualifications.* Directors should possess the highest personal and professional ethics, integrity and values, and be committed to representing the long-term interests of the shareowners. They must also have an inquisitive and objective perspective, practical wisdom and mature judgment. We endeavor to have a board representing diverse experience at policy-making levels in business, government, education and technology, and in areas that are relevant to the company's global activities.

Directors must be willing to devote sufficient time to carrying out their duties and responsibilities effectively, and should be committed to serve on the board for an extended period of time. Directors should offer their resignation in the event of any significant change in their personal circumstances, including a change in their principal job responsibilities.

Directors who also serve as CEOs or in equivalent positions should not serve on more than two boards of public companies in addition to the GE board, and other directors should not serve on more than four other boards of public companies in addition to the GE board. Current positions in excess of these limits may be maintained unless the board determines that doing so would impair the director's service on the GE board.

The board does not believe that arbitrary term limits on directors' service are appropriate, nor does it believe that directors should expect to be renominated annually until they reach the mandatory retirement age. The board self-evaluation process described below will be an important determinant for board tenure. Directors will not be nominated for election to the board after their 73rd birthday, although the full board may nominate candidates over 73 for special circumstances.

4. *Independence of Directors.* A majority of the directors will be independent directors under the proposed New York Stock Exchange (NYSE) rules. The board has determined that 11 of GE's 17 directors are independent.

All future non-employee directors will be independent. GE will seek to have a minimum of ten independent directors at all times, and it is the board's goal that at least two-thirds of the directors will be independent under the NYSE guidelines. Directors who do not meet the NYSE's independence standards also make valuable contributions to the board and to the company by reason of their experience and wisdom.

To be considered independent under the proposed NYSE rules, the board must determine that a director does not have any direct or indirect material relationship with GE. The board has established the following guidelines to assist it in determining director independence in accordance with that proposed rule:

a. A director will not be independent if, within the preceding five years: (i) the director was employed by GE; (ii) an immediate family member of the director was employed by GE as an officer; (iii) the director was employed by or affiliated with GE's independent auditor; (iv) an immediate family member of the director was employed by GE's independent auditor as a partner, principal or manager; or (v) a GE executive officer was on the board of directors of a company which employed the GE director, or which employed an immediate family member of the director as an officer;

b. The following commercial or charitable relationships will not be considered to be material relationships that would impair a director's independence: (i) if a GE director is an executive officer of another company that does business with GE and the annual sales to, or purchases from, GE are less than one percent of the annual revenues of the company he or she serves as an executive officer; (ii) if a GE director is an executive officer of another company which is indebted to GE, or to which GE is indebted, and the total amount of either company's indebtedness to the other is less than one percent of the total consolidated assets of the company he or she serves as an executive officer; and (iii) if a GE director serves as an officer, director or trustee of a charitable organization, and GE's discretionary charitable contributions to the organization are less than one percent of that organization's total annual charitable receipts. (GE's automatic matching of employee charitable contributions will not be included in the amount of GE's contributions for this purpose.) The board will annually review all commercial and charitable relationships of directors. Whether directors meet these categorical independence tests will be reviewed and will be made public annually prior to their standing for re-election to the board.

c. The following 11 directors are independent under the foregoing guidelines: [Omitted]

d. For relationships not covered by the guidelines in subsection (b) above, the determination of whether the relationship is material or not, and therefore whether the director would be independent or not, shall be made by the directors who satisfy the independence guidelines set forth in subsections (a) and (b) above. For example, if a director is the CEO of a company that purchases products and services from GE that are more than one percent of that company's annual revenues, the independent directors could determine, after considering all of the relevant circumstances, whether such a relationship was material or immaterial, and whether the director would therefore be considered independent under the proposed NYSE rules. The company would explain in the next proxy statement the basis for any board determination that a relationship was immaterial despite the fact that it did not meet the categorical standards of immateriality set forth in subsection (b) above.

The company will not make any personal loans or extensions of credit to directors or executive officers, other than consumer loans or credit card services on terms offered to the general public. No director or family member may provide personal services for compensation to the company.

5. *Size of Board and Selection Process.*The directors are elected each year by the shareowners at the annual meeting of shareowners. Shareholders may propose nominees for consideration by the nominating and corporate governance committee by submitting the names and supporting information to: Secretary, General Electric Company, 3135 Easton Turnpike, Fairfield, CT 06828. The board proposes a slate of nominees to the shareowners for election to the board. The board also determines the number of directors on the board provided that there are at least 10. Between annual shareowner meetings, the board may elect directors to serve until the next annual meeting. The board believes that, given the size and breadth of GE and the need for diversity of board views, the size of the board should be in the range of 15 directors.

6. *Board Committees.* The board has established the following committees to assist the board in discharging its responsibilities: (i) audit; (ii) management development and compensation; (iii) nominating and corporate governance; and (iv) public responsibilities. The current charters and key practices of these committees are published on the GE website, and will be mailed to shareowners on written request. The committee chairs report the highlights of their meetings to the full board following each meeting of the respective committees. The committees occasionally hold meetings in conjunction with the full board. For example, it is the practice of the audit committee to meet in conjunction with the full board in February so that all directors may participate in the review of the annual financial statements for the prior year and financial plans for the current year.

7. *Independence of Committee Members.* In addition to the requirement that a majority of the board satisfy the independence standards discussed in section 4 above, members of the audit committee must also satisfy an additional NYSE independence requirement. Specifically, they may not directly or indirectly receive any compensation from the company other than their directors' compensation. As a matter of policy, the board will also apply this additional requirement to members of the management development and compensation committee and to members of the nominating and corporate governance committee.

8. ***Meetings of Non–Employee Directors.*** The board will have at least three regularly scheduled meetings a year for the non-employee directors without management present. The directors have determined that the chairman of the management development and compensation committee will preside at such meetings, and will serve as the presiding director in performing such other functions as the board may direct, including advising on the selection of committee chairs and advising management on the agenda for board meetings. The non-employee directors may meet without management present at such other times as determined by the presiding director.

9. ***Self-Evaluation.*** As described more fully in the key practices of the nominating and corporate governance committee, the board and each of the committees will perform an annual self-evaluation. Each November, the directors will be requested to provide their assessments of the effectiveness of the board and the committees on which they serve. The individual assessments will be organized and summarized by an independent corporate governance expert for discussion with the board and the committees in December.

10. ***Setting Board Agenda.*** The board shall be responsible for its agenda. At the December board meeting, the CEO will propose for the board's approval key issues of strategy, risk and integrity to be scheduled and discussed during the course of the next calendar year. Before that meeting, the board will be invited to offer its suggestions. As a result of this process, a schedule of major discussion items for the following year will be established. Prior to each board meeting, the CEO will discuss the other specific agenda items for the meeting with the presiding director. The CEO and the presiding director, or committee chair as appropriate, shall determine the nature and extent of information that shall be provided regularly to the directors before each scheduled board or committee meeting. Directors are urged to make suggestions for agenda items, or additional pre-meeting materials, to the CEO, the presiding director, or appropriate committee chair at any time.

11. ***Ethics and Conflicts of Interest.*** The board expects GE directors, as well as officers and employees, to act ethically at all times and to acknowledge their adherence to the policies comprising GE's code of conduct set forth in the company's integrity manual, The Spirit and Letter of Our Commitment. The board will not permit any waiver of any ethics policy for any director or executive officer. If an actual or potential conflict of interest arises for a director, the director shall promptly inform the CEO and the presiding director. If a significant conflict exists and cannot be resolved, the director should resign. All directors will recuse themselves from any discussion or decision affecting their personal, business or professional interests.The board shall resolve any conflict of interest question involving the CEO, a vice chairman or a senior vice president, and the CEO shall resolve any conflict of interest issue involving any other officer of the company.

12. *Reporting of Concerns to Non–Employee Directors or the Audit Committee.* Anyone who has a concern about GE's conduct, or about the company's accounting, internal accounting controls or auditing matters, may communicate that concern directly to the presiding director, to the non-employee directors, or to the audit committee. Such communications may be confidential or anonymous, and may be e-mailed, submitted in writing, or reported by phone to special addresses and a toll-free phone number that are published on the company's website. Concerns relating to accounting, internal controls, auditing or officer conduct shall be sent immediately to the presiding director and to the chair of the audit committee and will be simultaneously reviewed and addressed by GE's ombudsman in the same way that other concerns are addressed by the company. The status of all outstanding concerns addressed to the non-employee directors, the presiding director, or the audit committee will be reported to the presiding director and the chair of the audit committee on a quarterly basis. The presiding director, or the audit committee chair may direct that certain matters be presented to the audit committee or the full board and may direct special treatment, including the retention of outside advisors or counsel, for any concern addressed to them. The company's integrity manual prohibits any employee from retaliating or taking any adverse action against anyone for raising or helping to resolve an integrity concern.

13. *Compensation of Board.* The nominating and corporate governance committee shall have the responsibility for recommending to the board compensation and benefits for non-employee directors. In discharging this duty, the committee shall be guided by three goals: compensation should fairly pay directors for work required in a company of GE's size and scope; compensation should align directors' interests with the long-term interests of shareowners; and the structure of the compensation should be simple, transparent and easy for shareowners to understand. As discussed more fully in the key practices of the nominating and corporate governance committee, the committee believes these goals will be served by providing 40% of non-employee director compensation in cash and 60% in deferred stock units starting in 2003. At the end of each year, the nominating and corporate governance committee shall review non-employee director compensation and benefits.

14. *Succession Plan.* The board shall approve and maintain a succession plan for the CEO and senior executives, based upon recommendations from the management development and compensation committee.

15. *Annual Compensation Review of Senior Management.* The management development and compensation committee shall annually approve the goals and objectives for compensating the CEO. That committee shall evaluate the CEO's performance in light of these goals before setting the CEO's salary, bonus and other incentive and equity compensation. The committee shall also annually approve the compensation structure for the company's officers, and shall evaluate the performance of the company's senior executive officers before approving their salary, bonus and other incentive and equity compensation.

16. ***Access to Senior Management***. Non-employee directors are encouraged to contact senior managers of the company without senior corporate management present. To facilitate such contact, non-employee directors are expected to make two regularly scheduled visits to GE businesses a year without corporate management being present.

17. ***Access to Independent Advisors.*** The board and its committees shall have the right at any time to retain independent outside financial, legal or other advisors.

18. ***Director Orientation.*** The general counsel and the chief financial officer shall be responsible for providing an orientation for new directors, and for periodically providing materials or briefing sessions for all directors on subjects that would assist them in discharging their duties. Each new director shall, within six months of election to the board, spend a day at corporate headquarters for personal briefing by senior management on the company's strategic plans, its financial statements, and its key policies and practices.

2. The Walt Disney Company, Corporate Governance Guidelines*

Composition of the Board of Directors

The Certificate of Incorporation of the Corporation provides that the Board of Directors shall consist of not less than nine or more than 21 Directors, with the exact number being determined from time to time by resolution of the Board. The Board believes that a desirable target number of Directors is 12 to 15, allowing, however, for changing circumstances that may warrant a higher or lower number.

It is the policy of the Board of Directors that the Board at all times reflect the following characteristics.

Each Director shall at all times represent the interests of the shareholders of the Corporation.

Each Director shall at all times exhibit high standards of integrity, commitment and independence of thought and judgment.

Each Director shall dedicate sufficient time, energy and attention to ensure the diligent performance of their duties.

The Board shall meet the standards of independence from the Company and its management set forth under "Director Independence" below.

The Board shall encompass a range of talent, skill and expertise sufficient to provide sound and prudent guidance with respect to all of the Corporation's operations and interests.

The Board shall reflect the diversity of the Corporation's shareholders, employees, customers, guests and communities.

Functions of the Board of Directors

The responsibility of the Board of Directors is to supervise and direct the management of the Corporation in the interest and for the benefit of the Corporation's shareholders. To that end, the Board of Directors shall have the following duties:

(1) Overseeing the conduct of the Corporation's business to evaluate whether the business is being properly managed;

(2) Reviewing and, where appropriate, approving the Corporation's major financial objectives, plans and actions;

(3) Reviewing and, where appropriate, approving major changes in, and determinations of other major issues respecting, the appropriate auditing and accounting principles and practices to be used in the preparation of the Corporation's financial statements;

* As approved by the Board of Directors on December 3, 2002

(4) Assessing major risk factors relating to the Corporation and its performance, and reviewing measures to address and mitigate such risks;

(5) Regularly evaluating the performance and approving the compensation of the Chief Executive Officer and, with the advice of the Chief Executive Officer, regularly evaluating the performance of principal senior executives; and

(6) Planning for succession with respect to the position of Chief Executive Officer and monitoring management's succession planning for other key executives.

The Board of Directors has delegated to the Chief Executive Officer, working with the other executive officers of the Corporation and its affiliates, the authority and responsibility for managing the business of the Corporation in a manner consistent with the standards of the Corporation, and in accordance with any specific plans, instructions or directions of the Board.

The Chief Executive Officer shall seek the advice and, in appropriate situations, the approval of the Board with respect to extraordinary actions to be undertaken by the Corporation, including those that would make a significant change in the financial structure or control of the Corporation, the acquisition or disposition of any significant business or the entry of the Corporation into a major new line of business.

Director Independence

It is the policy of the Board of Directors that a substantial majority of the members of the Board be independent of the Corporation's management. For a Director to be deemed "independent," the Board shall affirmatively determine that the Director has no material relationship with the Corporation or its affiliates or any member of the senior management of the Corporation or his or her affiliates. This determination shall be disclosed in the proxy statement for each annual meeting of the Corporation's shareholders. In making this determination, the Board shall not deem a Director to be independent if he or she:

- is, or within the past five years has been, employed by the Corporation or any of its affiliates;
- is, or within the past five years has been, affiliated with or employed by a (present or former) auditor of the Corporation or any of its affiliates;
- currently participates, or within the past five years has participated, in an interlocking directorate in which an executive officer of the Corporation or any of its affiliates serves on the compensation committee of a company that concurrently employs the Director;
- is, or is a director, executive officer, general partner or significant equity holder (i.e., in excess of 10%) of an entity that is, a paid

adviser, paid consultant or paid provider of other professional services to the Corporation, any of its affiliates, any member of senior management or any affiliate of a member of senior management, if the amount of such payments has exceeded $60,000 during the current fiscal year of the Corporation;

- is a director, executive officer, general partner or significant equity holder (i.e., in excess of 10%) of a significant purchaser of goods or nonprofessional services from, or supplier of goods or nonprofessional services to, the Corporation or any of its affiliates;
- is affiliated with or employed by a tax-exempt entity that receives significant contributions (i.e., more than 3% of the annual contributions received by the entity or more than $200,000 in a single fiscal year, whichever amount is lower) from the Corporation, any of its affiliates, any member of senior management or any affiliate of a member of senior management; or
- is a member of the immediate family of any person who would not qualify as independent under the foregoing standards; provided, that employment of an immediate family member of a Director in a non-officer position shall not preclude the Board from determining that the Director is independent.

For purposes of these Guidelines, the terms:

- "affiliate" means any corporation or other entity that controls, is controlled by or is under common control with the Corporation, as evidenced by the power to elect a majority of the board of directors or comparable governing body of such entity; and
- "immediate family" means spouse, parents, children, siblings, mothers-and fathers-in-law, sons-and daughters-in-law, brothers-and sisters-in-law and anyone (other than employees) sharing a person's home.

The Board shall undertake an annual review of the independence of all non-employee Directors. In advance of the meeting at which this review occurs, each non-employee Director shall be asked to provide the Board with full information regarding the Director's business and other relationships with the Corporation and its affiliates and with senior management and their affiliates to enable the Board to evaluate the Director's independence.

Directors have an affirmative obligation to inform the Board of any material changes in their circumstances or relationships that may impact their designation by the Board as "independent." This obligation includes all business relationships between Directors and the Corporation and its affiliates or members of senior management and their affiliates, whether or not such business relationships are subject to the approval requirement set forth in the following provision.

Business Relationships with Directors

For the purpose of minimizing the risk of actual or perceived conflicts of interest (but without affecting any determination of Director independence pursuant to the preceding provisions), any monetary arrangement between a Director (including any member of a Director's immediate family) and the Corporation or any of its affiliates or members of senior management or their affiliates for goods or services shall be subject to approval by the Board of Directors as a whole. Such approval shall not be required where:

(a) the Director's sole interest in the arrangement is by virtue of his or her status as a director, executive officer and/or holder of a less than 10% equity interest (other than a general partnership interest) in an entity with which the Corporation or any of its affiliates has concluded such an arrangement; and

(b) the arrangement involves payments to or from the entity that constitute less than 5% of the entity's annual gross revenues; and

(c) the Director is not personally involved in (i) the negotiation and execution of the arrangement, (ii) performance of the services or provision of the goods or (iii) the monetary arrangement.

Stock Ownership by Directors

It is the policy of the Board that all Directors, consistent with their responsibilities to the shareholders of the Corporation as a whole, hold a significant equity interest in the Corporation. Toward this end, the Board expects that all Directors own, or acquire within three years of first becoming a Director, shares of common stock of the Corporation (including share units under the Corporation's 1997 Non–Employee Directors Stock and Deferred Compensation Plan, or any successor plan) having a market value of at least $100,000.

The Board recognizes that exceptions to this policy may be necessary or appropriate in individual cases, and may approve such exceptions from time to time as it deems appropriate in the interest of the Corporation's shareholders.

Board Leadership

The bylaws of the Corporation provide that the Chief Executive Officer of the Corporation shall serve as Chairman of the Board. The Board recognizes that there may be circumstances in the future that would lead it to separate these offices, but believes there is no reason to do so at this time.

The non-management Directors shall designate one non-management Director to serve as the Presiding Director to chair the Board's executive sessions. In addition, the Presiding Director shall advise the

Chairman of the Board and Committee Chairs with respect to agendas and information needs relating to Board and Committee meetings; provide advice with respect to the selection of Committee Chairs; and perform such other duties as the Board may from time to time delegate to assist the Board in the fulfillment of its responsibilities. The Presiding Director shall serve for such term as the Board shall determine. The identity of the Presiding Director shall be set forth in the proxy statement for the Corporation's annual meeting, together with a method for interested parties to communicate directly with the presiding Director or with the non-management Directors as a group.

Management Succession and Review

At least once a year, the Chief Executive Officer of the Corporation shall meet with the non-management Directors to discuss potential successors as Chief Executive Officer. The non-management Directors shall meet in executive session following such presentations to consider such discussions. The Chief Executive Officer shall also have in place at all times a confidential written procedure for the timely and efficient transfer of his or her responsibilities in the event of his or her sudden incapacitation or departure, including recommendations for longer-term succession arrangements. The Chief Executive Officer shall review this procedure periodically with the Governance and Nominating Committee.

The Chief Executive Officer shall also review periodically with the non-management Directors the performance of other key members of the senior management of the Corporation, as well as potential succession arrangements for such management members. Any waiver of the requirements of the Corporation's Standards of Business Conduct with respect to any such member of senior management shall be reported to, and be subject to the approval of, the Board of Directors.

Board Meetings

The Chairman, in consultation with the other members of the Board, shall determine the timing and length of the meetings of the Board. The Board expects that six regular meetings at appropriate intervals are in general desirable for the performance of the Board's responsibilities. In addition to regularly scheduled meetings, unscheduled Board meetings may be called upon appropriate notice at any time to address specific needs of the Corporation.

The Chairman shall establish the agenda for each Board meeting. Each Director shall be entitled to suggest the inclusion of items on the agenda, request the presence of or a report by any member of the Corporation's senior management, or at any Board meeting raise subjects that are not on the agenda for that meeting.

The agendas for Board meetings shall provide opportunities for the operating heads of the major businesses of the Corporation to make presentations to the Board during the course of the year. At one meeting each year the Board shall be presented the long-term strategic plan for the Corporation and the principal issues that the Corporation expects to face in the future. Sufficient time shall be allocated for this presentation to allow for questions by and full discussion with the members of the Board.

At least twice during each year, the Board shall meet in regularly scheduled executive session, without the participation of the Chief Executive Officer or other members of the Corporation's management to review matters concerning the relationship of the Board with the management Directors and other members of the Corporation's management and such other matters as the Presiding Director and participating Directors may deem appropriate. The Board shall not take formal actions at such sessions, although the participating Directors may make recommendations for consideration by the full Board. Additional executive sessions may be scheduled from time to time as determined by a majority of the non-management Directors in consultation with the Presiding Director and the Chairman of the Board.

Board Committees

Committees shall be established by the Board from time to time to facilitate and assist in the execution of the Board's responsibilities. Committees may be standing or ad hoc. Generally, a Committee shall be constituted to address issues that, because of their complexity, technical nature, level of detail, time requirements and/or sensitivity, cannot be adequately addressed within the normal agenda for Board meetings.

There are currently four standing committees:

Executive Committee

Audit Committee

Compensation Committee

Governance and Nominating Committee

Each Committee shall have a written charter of responsibilities, duties and authorities, which shall periodically be reviewed by the Board. Each Committee shall report to the full Board with respect to its activities, findings and recommendations after each meeting.

Each Committee shall have full power and authority, in consultation with the Chairman of the Board, to retain the services of such advisers and experts, including counsel, as the Committee deems necessary or appropriate with respect to specific matters within its purview.

Committee Membership

The Chairman of the Board, after consideration of the desires, experience and expertise of individual Directors, shall recommend to the Governance and Nominating Committee the assignment of Directors to

Committees, including the designation of Committee Chairs. The Governance and Nominating Committee shall review such recommendations and report to the Board thereon.

In acting upon such recommendation and report, the full Board shall give consideration to the following objectives:

- the target size of each Committee should be three to five members, unless circumstances call for an exception;
- Committee membership should be rotated, on a staggered basis, at five-year intervals, subject to any applicable legal, regulatory and stock exchange listing requirements; and
- Committee Chairs should also be rotated at reasonable intervals, taking into account any applicable legal, regulatory and stock exchange listing requirements.

The Audit, Compensation and Governance and Nominating Committees shall be composed entirely of independent Directors. The Executive Committee shall include the Chief Executive Officer of the Corporation. At least half of its members shall be independent Directors.

If any Director ceases to be independent under the standards set forth herein while serving on any Committee whose members must be independent, he or she shall promptly resign from that Committee.

Committee Meetings

Each Committee Chair, in consultation with the Chairman of the Board, shall establish agendas and set meetings at the frequency and length appropriate and necessary to carry out the Committee's responsibilities.

Any Director who is not a member of a particular Committee may attend any Committee meeting with the concurrence of the Committee Chair or a majority of the members of the Committee.

Board Materials

Directors shall receive information and data that are important to their understanding of the businesses of the Corporation, in writing, and in sufficient time to prepare for meetings. This material shall be as brief as possible while still providing the desired information; it shall be analytic as well as informational; and it shall include highlights and summaries whenever appropriate. Directors may request that the Chairman of the Board or appropriate members of senior management present to the Board information on specific topics relating to the Corporation and its operations.

Directors are encouraged to keep themselves informed with respect to the Corporation's affairs between Board meetings through direct individual contacts with members of the senior management of the

Corporation and its affiliates. The Secretary of the Corporation shall, whenever requested, assist in arranging and facilitating such contacts.

Board Conduct and Review

Members of the Board of Directors shall act at all times in accordance with the requirements of the Corporation's Standards of Business Conduct, which shall be applicable to each Director. This obligation shall at all times include, without limitation, strict adherence to the Corporation's policies with respect to conflicts of interest, confidentiality, protection of the Corporation's assets, ethical conduct in all business dealings and respect for and compliance with applicable law. Any waiver of the requirements of the Standards of Business Conduct with respect to any individual Director shall be reported to, and be subject to the approval of, the Board of Directors.

The Board shall conduct an annual review and evaluation of its conduct and performance based upon completion by all Directors of an evaluation form that includes, among other things, an assessment of (a) the Board's composition and independence; (b) the Board's access to and review of information from management, and the quality of such information; (c) the Board's responsiveness to shareholder concerns; (d) maintenance and implementation of the Corporation's standards of conduct; and (e) maintenance and implementation of these Guidelines. The review shall seek to identify specific areas, if any, in need of improvement or strengthening and shall culminate in a discussion by the full Board of the results and any actions to be taken. The Governance and Nominating Committee shall have responsibility for ensuring that the annual review and evaluation are carried out.

Selection of New Directors

The Board shall be responsible for selecting its own members. The Board delegates the screening process for new Directors to the Governance and Nominating Committee, with counsel from the Chairman of the Board.

In selecting new Directors, the Board shall give the highest priority to meeting the standards and qualifications set forth at the beginning of these Guidelines. In this connection, the Board shall seek candidates whose service on other boards will not adversely affect their ability to dedicate the requisite time to service on this Board. The Board believes that Directors who are full-time employees of other companies should not serve on more than three other public company boards at a time, and that Directors who are retired from active employment should not serve on more than six such boards. The Board may, however, make exceptions to this standard as it deems appropriate in the interest of the Corporation's shareholders.

The Company shall assist the Board by providing appropriate orientation programs for new Directors, which shall be designed both to familiarize new Directors with the full scope of the Company's businesses and key challenges and to assist new Directors in developing and maintaining skills necessary or appropriate for the performance of their responsibilities. The Board and the Company's management shall similarly work together to develop and implement appropriate continuing education programs for the same purposes.

The Board also recognizes that it is important for the Board to balance the benefits of continuity with the benefits of fresh viewpoints and experience. Therefore, each non-management Director shall submit to the Board a letter of resignation upon the occurrence of any of the following:

(a) Resignation or retirement from, or termination of, the Director's principal current employment, or other similarly material changes in professional occupation or association;

(b) Completion of twelve years of service as a member of the Board, and completion of each three years thereafter; and

(c) Reaching retirement age under the Company's retirement policy for Directors, which is 72 for all Directors other than former Chief Executive Officers of the Corporation, for whom the retirement age is 75.

In each instance, the Board shall be free to accept or reject the letter of resignation. The Board shall act promptly with respect to each such letter of resignation and shall promptly notify the Director concerned of its decision.

Social Responsibility

The Corporation has a responsibility to the communities in which it operates, as well as to its shareholders. To allow appropriate Board review and input, management shall prepare and present to the Board an annual review of the policies, practices and contributions made in fulfillment of the Corporation's social responsibilities. In addition, management shall report annually on its diversity efforts and the results thereof.

Implementation of the Guidelines

If the Board ascertains at any time that any of the Guidelines set forth herein are not in full force and effect, the Board shall take such action as it deem reasonably necessary to assure full compliance as promptly as practicable.

D. SHAREHOLDER PROPOSALS

Contents

---

1. Nondiscriminatory Employment Policy

Proxy Statement of CBRL Group, Inc.
November 26, 2002

* * *

SHAREHOLDER PROPOSAL*

Who is submitting this shareholder proposal?

The New York City Employees' Retirement System, Office of the Comptroller, 1 Centre Street, New York, New York 10007, has stated that it is the beneficial owner of 98,984 shares of our common stock and has informed us that it intends to present the proposal described below at the annual meeting.

What is the shareholder proposal?

> **Whereas,** in February, 1991 the management of CBRL Group, Inc. (formerly Cracker Barrel Old Country Stores) announced a policy of discrimination in employment against gay men and lesbians; and
>
> **Whereas,** although CBRL Group's management asserts that this discrimination policy has been rescinded, the company refused to rehire or compensate fired workers; and
>
> **Whereas,** employment discrimination on the basis of sexual orientation may deprive corporations of the services of productive employees, leading to less efficient corporate operations which in turn can have a negative impact on shareholder value;
>
> **RESOLVED,** shareholders request the Board of Directors to implement non-discriminatory policies relating to sexual orientation and

* This shareholder proposal received a 58% vote. 2003 Shareholder Proxy Season Overview: Social and Corporate Governance Resolution Trends, A Report from the Investor Responsibility Research Center (IRRC) and the Interfaith Center on Corporate Responsibility (ICCR), February 12, 2003, page 2, *available at* http:www.irrc.org.

to add explicit prohibitions against such discrimination to its corporate employment policy statement.

What does the Board recommend?

Our Board of Directors recommends that you vote **AGAINST** this proposal.

Why does our Board recommend voting against this proposal?

While our Board shares the proponent's interests in preventing discrimination in the workplace, our Board believes that our current policies and practices already achieve the objectives of this proposal. Despite the proponent's assertions, we do not dismiss gay and lesbian personnel on the basis of their sexual orientation. We hire men and women solely on the basis of their relevant qualifications, experience and performance capabilities and we are committed to keeping our workplaces free of all forms of discrimination. We do not obtain information with respect to sexual orientation, and we comply with applicable local, state and federal employment laws and adhere to equal employment hiring policies which require us to hire without regard to race, color, creed, age or gender. Our Board believes that any attempt to name all possible examples of prohibited discrimination other than those which are specifically prohibited by federal law would result in a long list that would only divert attention from the basic goal of a diverse and fully compliant workplace. Even more troubling is the fact that it would be impossible to list every group which has the potential to be discriminated against in some way. By listing only some such groups, other groups could be made to feel they were deliberately being excluded from our anti-discrimination policies.

Directly stated, we adhere to the letter and spirit of the law regarding non-discrimination in the workplace and seek to comply at all times with all applicable laws affecting hiring and employment. In fact, we desire to hire the broadest range of qualified and capable employees for all positions. Because we already adhere to such a broad policy and because many years ago Cracker Barrel Old Country Store, Inc. stated that it had no policy against gay or lesbian individuals, and rescinded any written statements which may have been regarded as establishing a discriminatory policy with respect to gay or lesbian individuals, our Board does not believe that a formal or written non-discrimination policy relating specifically and exclusively to sexual orientation is appropriate or necessary.

2. Executive Compensation Plan

Reebok International Ltd.

Proxy Statement for Annual Meeting of Shareholders

May 6, 2003

* * *

SHAREHOLDER PROPOSAL THAT THE BOARD OF DIRECTORS ADOPT AN EXECUTIVE COMPENSATION POLICY THAT ALL FUTURE STOCK OPTION GRANTS TO SENIOR EXECUTIVES SHALL BE PERFORMANCE–BASED.

The following proposal was submitted on behalf of the Sheet Metal Workers' National Pension Fund (“Sheet Metal Workers”), a shareholder of the company, by Matthew Benny Hernandez. Sheet Metal Workers has informed the Company that its address is 1750 New York Ave., N.W., 6th Floor, Washington, DC 20006, and that it is the owner of approximately 1,700 shares of the Company's Common stock.

“Resolved, that the shareholders of Reebok International (the "Company") request that the Board of Directors adopt an executive compensation policy that all future stock option grants to senior executives shall be performance-based. For the purposes of this resolution, a stock option is performance-based if the option exercise price is indexed or linked to an industry peer group stock performance index so that the options have value only to the extent that the Company's stock price performance exceeds the peer group performance level.”

Supporting Statement

“As long-term shareholders of the Company, we support executive compensation policies and practices that provide challenging performance objectives and serve to motivate executives to achieve long-term corporate value maximization goals. While salaries and bonuses compensate management for short-term results, the grant of stock and stock options has become the primary vehicle for focusing management on achieving long-term results. Unfortunately, stock option grants can and do often provide levels of compensation well beyond those merited. It has become abundantly clear that stock option grants without specific performance-based targets often reward executives for stock price increases due solely to a general stock market rise, rather than to extraordinary company performance.

Indexed stock options are options whose exercise price moves with an appropriate peer group index composed of a company's primary competitors. The resolution requests that the Company's Board ensure that future senior executive stock option plans link the options exercise price to an industry performance index associated with a peer group of companies selected by the Board, such as those companies used in the Company's proxy statement to compare 5 year stock price performance.

Implementing an indexed stock option plan would mean that our Company's participating executives would receive payouts only if the Company's stock price performance was better than that of the peer group average. By tying the exercise price to a market index, indexed options reward participating executives for outperforming the competition. Indexed options would have value when our Company's stock price rises in excess of its peer group average or declines less than its peer group average stock price decline. By downwardly adjusting the exercise price of the option during a downturn in the industry, indexed options remove pressure to reprice stock options. In short, superior performance would be rewarded.

At present, stock options granted by the Company are not indexed to peer group performance standards. As long-term owners, we feel strongly that our Company would benefit from the implementation of a stock option program that rewarded superior long-term corporate performance. In response to strong negative public and shareholder reactions to the excessive financial rewards provided executives by non-performance based option plans, a growing number of shareholder organizations, executive compensation experts, and companies are supporting the implementation of performance-based stock options plans such as that advocated in this resolution. We urge your support for this important governance reform."

Statement of Board of Directors Recommending A Vote Against This Shareholder Proposal

Reebok's Board and Management Development and Compensation Committee (the "Compensation Committee") strongly support the concept of performance-based compensation arrangements as a critical component of executive compensation. The Company's compensation approach for executives historically has emphasized incentive-based compensation over salary. However, for the reasons described below, the Board believes that adopting a policy of linking all future executive stock options to an industry peer group stock performance index would unduly restrict the Compensation Committee's choice among performance-based compensation arrangements, and therefore would not be in the best interests of Reebok's shareholders.

The Board of Directors believes that the Compensation Committee's approach already provides appropriate links between executive compensation and Reebok's performance and aligns the interests of executives with those of stockholders. The Committee is composed of four independent Directors. They use outside consulting firms to stay informed of developments in the design of compensation packages and to provide a benchmark to compare Reebok's total compensation package to companies with which Reebok competes for management talent to ensure the compensation is consistent with the philosophy. Very few major companies currently use indexed stock options as a form of performance-based compensation. If Reebok implemented an indexed stock option plan as called for in the shareholder proposal, its stock option program could compare less favorably to the programs of comparable companies, and Reebok could be at a disadvantage in relation to its competitors when it comes to recruiting and retaining the most qualified executives. To offset a less favorable stock option plan, Reebok might have to increase the cash portion of its executive compensation package, thereby reducing the connection between executive compensation and shareholder value, or increase the number of stock options granted, thereby increasing the dilutive effect upon existing shareholders' equity investments.

The Board believes that its current compensation program aligns the interests of executives with those of stockholders. Executives realize value from options when Reebok performance improves, which leads to an increase in the price of Reebok's common stock and benefits all stockholders. Alignment of the interests of executives with those of stockholders is less clear under an indexed stock option plan, particularly when the option price decreases with a decline in the market index. In this instance, an executive could benefit from a decline in the index while stockholders would not. As a consequence of the poor alignment of interests with stockholders generally, this indexed option mechanism is not widely used, particularly by those with whom Reebok competes for executive talent. If the industry as a whole does well, employees would not get the same benefits enjoyed by other shareholders, since exercise prices would rise with stock prices.

In addition, the Compensation Committee of the Board reviews, approves and oversees all of the policies under which compensation is paid to Reebok's executives. The Board believes that it is important to preserve the flexibility of its compensation program so that the Compensation Committee can choose incentives that best balance the variety of goals that Reebok seeks to pursue through its compensation arrangements. In choosing what type of performance-based compensation scheme to use for its executives, the Committee must consider a variety of factors, such as what goals the Board has established for management, tax consequences of various arrangements and competitive practice. The proposal would limit the Compensation Committee's flexibility by requiring that stock options be tied to a specific performance measure—a peer group stock performance index—in a specific way (by tying the exercise price, rather than amounts granted or the vesting schedules, to a performance measure). As the Board evaluates Reebok's operations and business goals, the Board believes that the Compensation Committee should have the flexibility to measure performance by criteria other than relative stock price performance and to tie options to these other criteria or to grant traditional fixed-price options and tie other forms of annual or long-term compensation to performance criteria that are varied from time to time, as Reebok's goals and challenges change.

The rules governing stock options are in constant flux and indexing the exercise price of stock options could have serious accounting consequences on Reebok's financial reporting. Accounting Principles Board Opinion No. 25 and FASB Interpretation No. 44 provide the accounting and financial reporting guidance for stock options. The measurement date for determining compensation costs for stock options is the first date on which are known both: (a) the number of shares that an individual employee is entitled to receive and (b) the option exercise price. If executives' stock options were indexed in accordance with the proposal, Reebok would have to re-measure the compensation cost related to these stock options at each quarterly financial reporting period and recognize that expense over the period the employee performs the related services. To the extent that the exercise price of a stock option is less than the fair market value of the stock option on the date of grant of the stock option, compensation arising from the exercise would not be based on future performance and the expense would have to be recognized on the date of grant. Current financial reporting requirements for stock options do not require the associated compensation expense to be included in net earnings if the exercise price equals or exceeds the underlying stock's fair market value on the date of grant. If the proposal were adopted, additional compensation expense might have to be recognized in the income statement arising from indexing stock options, which would negatively impact Reebok's reported financial performance as compared to other companies. The Board believes that the use of indexed options could depress and artificially add volatility to Reebok's earnings and would not be beneficial to stockholders' interests.

In sum, the Board believes that the current executive compensation policy aligns executive incentives with the long-term interests of its stockholders. The Board also believes that the stockholder proposal would undermine the long-term interests of the stockholders by adversely affecting Reebok's ability to attract and retain the most qualified executives needed to manage its business. The Board believes that the New York Stock Exchange's Proposed Governance Rules regarding Compensation Committees are designed to provide independent oversight of executive compensation while permitting the Committee to retain needed flexibility. In light of the proposed rules, the Board believes that the Committee should retain flexibility to make performance-based executive compensation decisions based on a review of all relevant information without imposing rigid, pre-set constraints called for in the proposal.

For the reasons outlined above, after appropriate consideration and upon recommendation of the Management Development and Compensation Committee, as well as after appropriate consideration by the Board of Directors, the Board recommends that shareholders vote AGAINST Proposal 2.

3. Annual Elections of Board of Directors

Reebok International Ltd.
Proxy Statement for Annual Meeting of Shareholders
May 6, 2003

* * *

SHAREHOLDER PROPOSAL THAT ALL MEMBERS OF THE BOARD OF DIRECTORS BE ELECTED ANNUALLY

The following proposal was submitted on behalf of the Connecticut Retirement Plans & Trust Fund ("CRPTF"), a shareholder of the company, by Denise L. Nappier, Treasurer of the State of Connecticut. CRPTF has informed the Company that its address is Office of the Treasurer, 55 Elm Street, Hartford, CT 06106–1773, and that it is the owner of approximately 36,650 shares of the Company's Common stock.

"RESOLVED: that the shareholders of Reebok International Ltd. urge the Board of Directors to take the necessary steps to eliminate the classification of the Board of Directors of the Company and to require that all Directors stand for election annually. The Board declassification shall be completed in a manner that does not affect the unexpired terms of Directors previously elected."

Supporting Statement

"We believe the election of directors is the most powerful way Reebok shareholders influence the strategic direction of our company. Currently, the Board is divided into three classes of three members each. Each class serves staggered three-year terms. Because of this structure, shareholders may only vote on roughly one-third of the directors each year.

The staggered term structure of Reebok's Board is not in the best interests of shareholders because it reduces accountability and is an unnecessary anti-takeover device. Shareholders should have the opportunity to vote on the performance of the entire Board of Directors each year. We feel that such annual accountability serves to keep directors closely focused on the performance of top executives and on increasing shareholder value. Annual election of all directors gives shareholders the power to either completely replace their Board, or replace a majority of directors, if a situation arises which warrants such drastic action.

We do not believe destaggering the Board of Reebok will be destabilizing to our company or impact the continuity of director service. Our directors, like the directors of the overwhelming majority of other public companies, are routinely elected with over 95% shareholder approval.

There are indications from studies that classified boards and other anti-takeover devices have an adverse impact on shareholder value. A 1991 study by Lilli Gordon of the Gordon Group and John Pound of

Harvard University found that companies with restrictive corporate governance structures, including those with classified boards, are "significantly less likely to exhibit outstanding long-term performance relative to their industry peers."

A growing number of shareholders appear to agree with our concerns. According to the Investor Responsibility Resource Center (IRRC), in 2002, a majority of shareholders supported shareholder proposals asking their boards to repeal classified board structures at 36 companies, including Great Lakes Chemical (79.4% support), Airborne (84.5% support), Goodyear Tire (74.4% support) and Starwood Hotels (77.8% support).

In addition, a binding board-sponsored resolution at Waste Management received 78.3% of the vote and was adopted. Great Lakes Chemical has announced they will place a binding resolution to declassify their board on its 2003 proxy ballot.

At the 2002 annual meeting of Reebok this resolution received the support of 54.1% of shareholders who voted on this resolution.

We believe that adoption of this proposal will be beneficial to the company and its shareholders."

Statement of Board of Directors Recommending A Vote Against This Shareholder Proposal

The Board of Directors believes that the present system of electing directors of the Company in three classes is in the best interests of the Company and its stockholders and should not be changed.

Importantly, Massachusetts law mandates the use of a staggered board for all publicly held Massachusetts corporations. Reebok is a Massachusetts corporation. The legislative history surrounding the enactment of this law demonstrates a clear preference for classified boards in the interest of public policy. The affirmative vote of two-thirds of the outstanding shares is required to opt out of the Massachusetts law and declassify the Board. The Board has and will continue to take into consideration the votes of the shareholders, but shareholder support for the proposal is not clear or overwhelming enough to override the public policy dictate of state law as evidenced by the voting results over the past few years. Only 41% of all outstanding shares at the 2002 meeting voted to declassify the Board and the proposal received only a slight majority of the votes cast. Moreover, none of the companies cited as examples in the supporting statement are Massachusetts corporations. The Board takes into consideration the public policy aspects of Massachusetts law and the wishes of all its constituents in its goal to increase shareholder value.

The Board believes that a classified board enhances continuity and stability in the Company's management and policies since a majority of the directors at any given time will have had a prior experience and familiarity with the business of the Company. This continuity and stability facilitates more effective long-term planning and is integral to increasing the Company's value to stockholders. Moreover, such continuity helps the Company attract and retain qualified individuals willing to commit the time and dedication necessary to understand the Company, its operations and competitive environment. A classified board offers important advantages to stockholders and is the preferred method of governance for the majority of Fortune 500 companies.

The Board is committed to corporate accountability and does not accept the proposition that a classified board insulates directors from responsibility. A classified board permits stockholders to annually change one-third of the directors and thereby substantially change the Board's composition and character. Corporate accountability depends on the selection of responsible and experienced individuals, not on whether they serve terms of one year or three. The independent Board Affairs Committee reviews the independence of directors and evaluates the contribution of individual directors and the Board's contribution as a whole on an annual basis. This Committee also reviews director nominations, recommends guidelines and criteria for Board membership, and has responsibility for other corporate governance issues.

Moreover, Reebok has a strong corporate governance position. The Board is presently comprised of ten directors, seven of which are independent, and only two of which are current employees. The Board has had a majority of independent directors for a number of years. In addition, the Company has added four new highly qualified and independent directors during the last two years. Those who have been up for election have been overwhelmingly approved by shareholders. This Board with its majority of independent directors complies with requirements of the Sarbanes–Oxley Act and the proposed NYSE rules that will not be effective for a few years.

The Company understands that the Board should be responsive to shareholders and has taken steps to assure corporate accountability through such measures as maintaining a majority of outside directors; and having only independent directors on the Audit Committee, the Management Development and Compensation Committee and the Board Affairs Committee. In order to align the interests of the Board members with those of shareholders, the Board has a policy mandating required levels of stock ownership by its Directors and requiring the deferral of at least 40% of an outside directors' annual retainer into Reebok Common Stock.

A classified board protects shareholders against potentially coercive takeover tactics, whereby a party attempts to acquire control on terms that do not offer the greatest value to all stockholders. Because a classified board prevents the immediate removal of directors, any person seeking to acquire control of the company is encouraged to negotiate with the Board. This ensures that the Board has sufficient time to develop and consider appropriate strategies, which enhance its ability to negotiate the best result for all stockholders.

Finally, shareholders should be aware that adoption of this proposal would not eliminate board classification and institute in its place the annual election of directors, but would merely constitute a recommendation by the stockholders that the Board consider enacting such a change. The affirmative vote of two-thirds of the outstanding shares or a vote of the directors is required to opt out of the Massachusetts law and declassify the Board.

For the reasons outlined above, after appropriate consideration and upon recommendation of the Board Affairs Committee, as well as after appropriate consideration by the Board of Directors, the Board recommends that shareholders vote AGAINST Proposal 3.

4. Separation of CEO Board and Chairman, Withdrawn Shareholder Proposal

Shareholder Proposal submitted by AFSCME for inclusion in Tenet Healthcare Corporation's Proxy Statement*

RESOLVED, that the shareholders of Tenet Healthcare Corporation ("Tenet") ask the board of directors to adopt a policy that the board's chairperson be an independent director who has not previously served as an officer of Tenet; provided that the policy should be implemented in a way that does not violate any existing contractual provision.

This proposal requests the board separate the roles of chairman and chief executive officer at Tenet. In our view it is important to take this action in light of the performance of the top officers of our company over the past year. From October to March 24, 2003 Tenet experienced a $17 billion loss in share value. We believe this loss has been caused by a series of revelations about company strategy and regulatory investigations which reveal deep problems with Tenet's monitoring and control systems.

Tenet's problems first surfaced last year when Federal agents raided the Company's Redding Medical Center in an investigation into unnecessary medical procedures. This was followed by revelations that the Company's management pursued a business strategy involving aggressive pricing, which led to Tenet receiving high levels of Medicare "outlier" payments and other reimbursements by third-party insurers.

Tenet came under fire for these practices from both patient advocates and government agencies and has now revised its billing practices. A January 9, 2003 editorial in the *Wall Street Journal* noted the damage that has been caused by these practices: "Tenet's mistake wasn't in getting what it could from Medicare loopholes, but that it didn't let shareholders know that the windfall couldn't last." Numerous lawsuits have been filed against the company, some of them alleging that Tenet failed to disclose how dependent it was on its aggressive pricing strategy.

The leadership of Tenet's Chairman and CEO Jeffrey Barbakow has been faulted during this crisis. He professed that he was unaware of the relationship between Tenet's aggressive pricing and its high levels of

* This proposal was submitted by American Federation of State, County, and Municipal Employees, AFL–CIO (AFSCME). "The pricing and disclosure problems as well as reports of government investigations that have come to light in the last six months have caused a $17 billion drop in Tenet's market value. We believe these problems are a result of inadequate monitoring and control at the highest levels of the company. A new structure must be implemented that will allow for greater board oversight if the company is to quickly regain the confidence of investors. We have asked the company to agree to implement our proposal or face a vote later this year," said AFSCME Pension Plan Chair Gerald W. McEntee. *AFSCME Employees Pension Plan Submits Shareholder Proposals at Tenet,* press release dated March 27, 2003, available at http://www.afscme.org. The proposal was later was withdrawn because Tenet agreed to implement changes without a shareholder vote.

Medicare "outlier" payments, firing his CFO and COO who were reportedly the architects of the strategy. Analyst David Woodyatt stated in a November 11, 2002 *Wall Street Journal* article that Mr. Barbakow " 'obviously fumbled the ball to some degree by not asking the right questions... You get into a situation where either he knew and didn't tell us, so you can't trust him, or he didn't know something he should have known.' "

Given the profound failures of the past and the challenges of the future it is clear in our view that our company would benefit from having the additional oversight an independent director would bring to the chairman's role. Although the board may work collaboratively with the CEO, we believe the tasks that lie ahead for the board have the potential to bring it into a more contentious relationship with management. There is a heightened risk now that our CEO's interests will conflict with the board's duty to direct and monitor the company's business and affairs.

We urge shareholders to vote *For* this proposal.

5. By–Law Amendment to Permit Nomination of Directors by Shareholders

A. Shareholder Proposal submitted by AFSCME for inclusion in Citigroup Incorporated's Proxy Statement (2003)

RESOLVED, pursuant to Article XXI of the Bylaws of Citigroup Inc. and section 109(a) of the Delaware General Corporation Law, the stockholders hereby amend the Bylaws to add the following Article III, section 12:

> "The Company shall include in its proxy materials for a meeting of stockholders the name, together with the Disclosure and Statement (both defined below), of any person nominated for election to the Company's board of directors by a stockholder or group thereof that satisfies the requirements of this section 12 (the "Nominating Stockholder"), and shall allow stockholders to vote with respect to such nominee on the Company's proxy card. Each Nominating Stockholder may nominate one candidate for election at a meeting.
>
> To be eligible to make a nomination, a Nominating Stockholder must:
>
> (a) beneficially own 3% or more of the Company's outstanding common stock;
>
> (b) provide written notice received by the Company's Secretary within the time period specified in the first paragraph of Article III, section 11; such notice shall contain (i) with respect to the nominee, (A) the information required by Items 5(b) and 7 of SEC Schedule 14A and (B) such nominee's consent to being named in the proxy statement and to serving as a director if elected; and (ii) with respect to the Nominating Stockholder, the participant information required by Item 5(b) of Schedule 14A (with separate disclosure for each stockholder in a proposing group) (all disclosure in this section 12(b) is referred to as the "Disclosure"); and
>
> (c) execute an undertaking that it agrees to (i) assume all liability arising out of any violation of law or regulation in connection with the Nominating Stockholder's communications with stockholders of the Company, including the Disclosure; (ii) to the extent it uses soliciting material other than the Company's proxy materials, comply with all laws and regulations relating thereto.
>
> In addition to the Disclosure, the Company shall include in its proxy materials a 500–word statement by the Nominating Stockholder in support of the nominee's candidacy (the "Statement"). The Board of Directors shall adopt a procedure for timely resolving disputes over whether the Disclosure and Statement comply with SEC rules, including Rule 14a–9."

SUPPORTING STATEMENT

Stockholders currently have no meaningful control over the process by which candidates are selected for election to company boards of directors. Citigroup's bylaws state that stockholders may suggest candidates, but there is no requirement that the candidates be placed on the ballot. Indeed, there is no indication in any of Citigroup's last five proxy statements that any stockholder nominee was considered.

We believe that direct access to the proxy for purposes of electing a director nominated by stockholders is the most effective mechanism for ensuring diverse opinions and independent oversight. The need for such oversight is especially acute now, we think, in light of the challenges Citigroup has faced this year, including a sagging stock price and multiple government investigations related to analyst independence and IPO allocations.

We urge shareholders to vote for this proposal.

B. SEC No–Action Letter on AFSCME's shareholder proposal*

January 31, 2003

Publicly Available April 14, 2003

Re: Citigroup Inc.

Incoming letter dated December 19, 2002

The proposal amends the bylaws to require that Citigroup include the name, along with certain disclosures and statements, of any person nominated for election to the board by a stockholder who beneficially owns 3% or more of Citigroup's outstanding stock.

There appears to be some basis for your view that Citigroup may exclude the proposal under rule 14a–8(i)(8), as relating to an election for membership on its board of directors. It appears that the proposal, rather than establishing procedures for nomination or qualification generally, would establish a procedure that may result in contested elections of directors. Accordingly, the Division will not recommend enforcement action to the Commission if Citigroup omits the first proposal from its proxy materials in reliance on rule 14a–8(i)(8). In reaching this position, we have not found it necessary to address the alternative bases for omission upon which Citigroup relies.

Sincerely,
Attorney–Advisor

* 2003 WL 1900802

VI. UNIFORM FRAUDULENT TRANSFER ACT (1984)

Contents

---

§ 1. Definitions.

As used in this [Act]:

(1) "Affiliate" means:

(i) a person who directly or indirectly owns, controls, or holds with power to vote, 20 percent or more of the outstanding voting securities of the debtor, other than a person who holds the securities,

(A) as a fiduciary or agent without sole discretionary power to vote the securities; or

(B) solely to secure a debt, if the person has not exercised the power to vote;

(ii) a corporation 20 percent or more of whose outstanding voting securities are directly or indirectly owned, controlled, or held with power to vote, by the debtor or a person who directly or indirectly owns, controls, or holds, with power to vote, 20 percent or more of the outstanding voting securities of the debtor, other than a person who holds the securities,

(A) as a fiduciary or agent without sole power to vote the securities; or

(B) solely to secure a debt, if the person has not in fact exercised the power to vote;

(iii) a person whose business is operated by the debtor under a lease or other agreement, or a person substantially all of whose assets are controlled by the debtor; or

(iv) a person who operates the debtor's business under a lease or other agreement or controls substantially all of the debtor's assets.

(2) "Asset" means property of a debtor, but the term does not include:

(i) property to the extent it is encumbered by a valid lien;

(ii) property to the extent it is generally exempt under nonbankruptcy law; or

(iii) an interest in property held in tenancy by the entireties to the extent it is not subject to process by a creditor holding a claim against only one tenant.

(3) "Claim" means a right to payment, whether or not the right is reduced to judgment, liquidated, unliquidated, fixed, contingent, matured, unmatured, disputed, undisputed, legal, equitable, secured, or unsecured.

(4) "Creditor" means a person who has a claim.

(5) "Debt" means liability on a claim.

(6) "Debtor" means a person who is liable on a claim.

(7) "Insider" includes:

(i) if the debtor is an individual,

(A) a relative of the debtor or of a general partner of the debtor;

(B) a partnership in which the debtor is a general partner;

(C) a general partner in a partnership described in clause (B); or

(D) a corporation of which the debtor is a director, officer, or person in control;

(ii) if the debtor is a corporation,

(A) a director of the debtor;

(B) an officer of the debtor;

(C) a person in control of the debtor;

(D) a partnership in which the debtor is a general partner;

(E) a general partner in a partnership described in clause (D); or

(F) a relative of a general partner, director, officer, or person in control of the debtor;

(iii) if the debtor is a partnership,

(A) a general partner in the debtor;

(B) a relative of a general partner in, a general partner of, or a person in control of the debtor;

(C) another partnership in which the debtor is a general partner;

(D) a general partner in a partnership described in clause (C); or

(E) a person in control of the debtor;

(iv) an affiliate, or an insider of an affiliate as if the affiliate were the debtor; and

(v) a managing agent of the debtor.

(8) "Lien" means a charge against or an interest in property to secure payment of a debt or performance of an obligation, and includes a security interest created by agreement, a judicial lien obtained by legal or equitable process or proceedings, a common-law lien, or a statutory lien.

(9) "Person" means an individual, partnership, corporation, association, organization, government or governmental subdivision or agency, business trust, estate, trust, or any other legal or commercial entity.

(10) "Property" means anything that may be the subject of ownership.

(11) "Relative" means an individual related by consanguinity within the third degree as determined by the common law, a spouse, or an individual related to a spouse within the third degree as so determined, and includes an individual in an adoptive relationship within the third degree.

(12) "Transfer" means every mode, direct or indirect, absolute or conditional, voluntary or involuntary, of disposing of or parting with an asset or an interest in an asset, and includes payment of money, release, lease, and creation of a lien or other encumbrance.

(13) "Valid lien" means a lien that is effective against the holder of a judicial lien subsequently obtained by legal or equitable process or proceedings.

§ 2. Insolvency

(a) A debtor is insolvent if the sum of the debtor's debts is greater than all of the debtor's assets at a fair valuation.

(b) A debtor who is generally not paying his [or her] debts as they become due is presumed to be insolvent.

(c) A partnership is insolvent under subsection (a) if the sum of the partnership's debts is greater than the aggregate, at a fair valuation, of all of the partnership's assets and the sum of the excess of the value of each general partner's nonpartnership assets over the partner's nonpartnership debts.

(d) Assets under this section do not include property that has been transferred, concealed, or removed with intent to hinder, delay, or defraud creditors or that has been transferred in a manner making the transfer voidable under this [Act].

(e) Debts under this section do not include an obligation to the extent it is secured by a valid lien on property of the debtor not included as an asset.

§ 3. Value

(a) Value is given for a transfer or an obligation if, in exchange for the transfer or obligation, property is transferred or an antecedent debt is secured or satisfied, but value does not include an unperformed promise made otherwise than in the ordinary course of the promisor's business to furnish support to the debtor or another person.

(b) For the purposes of Sections 4(a)(2) and 5, a person gives a reasonably equivalent value if the person acquires an interest of the debtor in an asset pursuant to a regularly conducted, noncollusive foreclosure sale or execution of a power of sale for the acquisition or disposition of the interest of the debtor upon default under a mortgage, deed of trust, or security agreement.

(c) A transfer is made for present value if the exchange between the debtor and the transferee is intended by them to be contemporaneous and is in fact substantially contemporaneous.

§ 4. Transfers Fraudulent as to Present and Future Creditors

(a) A transfer made or obligation incurred by a debtor is fraudulent as to a creditor, whether the creditor's claim arose before or after the transfer was made or the obligation was incurred, if the debtor made the transfer or incurred the obligation:

(1) with actual intent to hinder, delay, or defraud any creditor of the debtor; or

(2) without receiving a reasonably equivalent value in exchange for the transfer or obligation, and the debtor:

(i) was engaged or was about to engage in a business or a transaction for which the remaining assets of the debtor were unreasonably small in relation to the business or transaction; or

(ii) intended to incur, or believed or reasonably should have believed that he [or she] would incur, debts beyond his [or her] ability to pay as they became due.

(b) In determining actual intent under subsection (a)(1), consideration may be given, among other factors, to whether:

(1) the transfer or obligation was to an insider;

(2) the debtor retained possession or control of the property transferred after the transfer;

(3) the transfer or obligation was disclosed or concealed;

(4) before the transfer was made or obligation was incurred, the debtor had been sued or threatened with suit;

(5) the transfer was of substantially all the debtor's assets;

(6) the debtor absconded;

(7) the debtor removed or concealed assets;

(8) the value of the consideration received by the debtor was reasonably equivalent to the value of the asset transferred or the amount of the obligation incurred;

(9) the debtor was insolvent or became insolvent shortly after the transfer was made or the obligation was incurred;

(10) the transfer occurred shortly before or shortly after a substantial debt was incurred; and

(11) the debtor transferred the essential assets of the business to a lienor who transferred the assets to an insider of the debtor.

§ 5. Transfers Fraudulent as to Present Creditors

(a) A transfer made or obligation incurred by a debtor is fraudulent as to a creditor whose claim arose before the transfer was made or the obligation was incurred if the debtor made the transfer or incurred the obligation without receiving a reasonably equivalent value in exchange for the transfer or obligation and the debtor was insolvent at that time or the debtor became insolvent as a result of the transfer or obligation.

(b) A transfer made by a debtor is fraudulent as to a creditor whose claim arose before the transfer was made if the transfer was made to an insider for an antecedent debt, the debtor was insolvent at that time, and the insider had reasonable cause to believe that the debtor was insolvent.

§ 6. When Transfer Is Made or Obligation is Incurred

For the purposes of this [Act]:

(1) a transfer is made:

(i) with respect to an asset that is real property other than a fixture, but including the interest of a seller or purchaser under a contract for the sale of the asset, when the transfer is so far perfected that a good-faith purchaser of the asset from the debtor against whom applicable law permits the transfer to be perfected cannot acquire an interest in the asset that is superior to the interest of the transferee; and

(ii) with respect to an asset that is not real property or that is a fixture, when the transfer is so far perfected that a creditor on a simple contract cannot acquire a judicial lien otherwise than under this [Act] that is superior to the interest of the transferee;

(2) if applicable law permits the transfer to be perfected as provided in paragraph (1) and the transfer is not so perfected before the commencement of an action for relief under this [Act], the transfer is deemed made immediately before the commencement of the action;

(3) if applicable law does not permit the transfer to be perfected as provided in paragraph (1), the transfer is made when it becomes effective between the debtor and the transferee;

(4) a transfer is not made until the debtor has acquired rights in the asset transferred;

(5) an obligation is incurred:

(i) if oral, when it becomes effective between the parties; or

(ii) if evidenced by a writing, when the writing executed by the obligor is delivered to or for the benefit of the obligee.

§ 7. Remedies of Creditors

(a) In an action for relief against a transfer or obligation under this [Act], a creditor, subject to the limitations in Section 8, may obtain:

(1) avoidance of the transfer or obligation to the extent necessary to satisfy the creditor's claim;

[(2) an attachment or other provisional remedy against the asset transferred or other property of the transferee in accordance with the procedure prescribed by [ ];]

(3) subject to applicable principles of equity and in accordance with applicable rules of civil procedure,

(i) an injunction against further disposition by the debtor or a transferee, or both, of the asset transferred or of other property;

(ii) appointment of a receiver to take charge of the asset transferred or of other property of the transferee; or

(iii) any other relief the circumstances may require.

(b) If a creditor has obtained a judgment on a claim against the debtor, the creditor, if the court so orders, may levy execution on the asset transferred or its proceeds.

§ 8. Defenses, Liability, and Protection of Transferee

(a) A transfer or obligation is not voidable under Section 4(a)(1) against a person who took in good faith and for a reasonably equivalent value or against any subsequent transferee or obligee.

(b) Except as otherwise provided in this section, to the extent a transfer is voidable in an action by a creditor under Section 7(a)(1), the creditor may recover judgment for the value of the asset transferred, as adjusted under subsection (c), or the amount necessary to satisfy the creditor's claim, whichever is less. The judgment may be entered against:

(1) the first transferee of the asset or the person for whose benefit the transfer was made; or

(2) any subsequent transferee other than a good faith transferee who took for value or from any subsequent transferee.

(c) If the judgment under subsection (b) is based upon the value of the asset transferred, the judgment must be for an amount equal to the value of the asset at the time of the transfer, subject to adjustment as the equities may require.

(d) Notwithstanding voidability of a transfer or an obligation under this [Act], a good-faith transferee or obligee is entitled, to the extent of the value given the debtor for the transfer or obligation, to

(1) a lien on or a right to retain any interest in the asset transferred;

(2) enforcement of any obligation incurred; or

(3) a reduction in the amount of the liability on the judgment.

(e) A transfer is not voidable under Section 4(a)(2) or Section 5 if the transfer results from:

(1) termination of a lease upon default by the debtor when the termination is pursuant to the lease and applicable law; or

(2) enforcement of a security interest in compliance with Article 9 of the Uniform Commercial Code.

(f) A transfer is not voidable under Section 5(b):

(1) to the extent the insider gave new value to or for the benefit of the debtor after the transfer was made unless the new value was secured by a valid lien;

(2) if made in the ordinary course of business or financial affairs of the debtor and the insider; or

(3) if made pursuant to a good-faith effort to rehabilitate the debtor and the transfer secured present value given for that purpose as well as an antecedent debt of the debtor.

§ 9. Extinguishment of [Claim for Relief] [Cause of Action]

A [claim for relief] [cause of action] with respect to a fraudulent transfer or obligation under this [Act] is extinguished unless action is brought:

(a) under Section 4(a)(1), within 4 years after the transfer was made or the obligation was incurred or, if later, within one year after the transfer or obligation was or could reasonably have been discovered by the claimant;

(b) under Section 4(a)(2) or 5(a), within 4 years after the transfer was made or the obligation was incurred; or

(c) under Section 5(b), within one year after the transfer was made or the obligation was incurred.

§ 10. Supplementary Provisions

Unless displaced by the provisions of this [Act], the principles of law and equity, including the law merchant and the law relating to principal and agent, estoppel, laches, fraud, misrepresentation, duress, coercion, mistake, insolvency, or other validating or invalidating cause, supplement its provisions.

§ 11. Uniformity of Application and Construction

This [Act] shall be applied and construed to effectuate its general purpose to make uniform the law with respect to the subject of this [Act] among states enacting it.

§ 12. Short Title

This [Act] may be cited as the Uniform Fraudulent Transfer Act.

§ 13. Repeal

The following acts and all other acts and parts of acts inconsistent herewith are hereby repealed.

VII. AMERICAN BAR ASSOCIATION MODEL RULES OF PROFESSIONAL CONDUCT

Contents

Rule 1.2 Scope of Representation and Allocation of Authority Between Client and Lawyer

(a) Subject to paragraphs (c) and (d), a lawyer shall abide by a client's decisions concerning the objectives of representation and, as required by Rule 1.4, shall consult with the client as to the means by which they are to be pursued. A lawyer may take such action on behalf of the client as is impliedly authorized to carry out the representation. A lawyer shall abide by a client's decision whether to settle a matter. In a criminal case, the lawyer shall abide by the client's decision, after consultation with the lawyer, as to a plea to be entered, whether to waive jury trial and whether the client will testify.

(b) A lawyer's representation of a client, including representation by appointment, does not constitute an endorsement of the client's political, economic, social or moral views or activities.

(c) A lawyer may limit the scope of the representation if the limitation is reasonable under the circumstances and the client gives informed consent.

(d) A lawyer shall not counsel a client to engage, or assist a client, in conduct that the lawyer knows is criminal or fraudulent, but a lawyer may discuss the legal consequences of any proposed course of conduct with a client and may counsel or assist a client to make a good faith effort to determine the validity, scope, meaning or application of the law.

COMMENT

Allocation of Authority between Client and Lawyer

[1] Paragraph (a) confers upon the client the ultimate authority to determine the purposes to be served by legal representation, within the limits imposed

by law and the lawyer's professional obligations. The decisions specified in paragraph (a), such as whether to settle a civil matter, must also be made by the client. See Rule 1.4(a)(1) for the lawyer's duty to communicate with the client about such decisions. With respect to the means by which the client's objectives are to be pursued, the lawyer shall consult with the client as required by Rule 1.4(a)(2) and may take such action as is impliedly authorized to carry out the representation.

[2] On occasion, however, a lawyer and a client may disagree about the means to be used to accomplish the client's objectives. Clients normally defer to the special knowledge and skill of their lawyer with respect to the means to be used to accomplish their objectives, particularly with respect to technical, legal and tactical matters. Conversely, lawyers usually defer to the client regarding such questions as the expense to be incurred and concern for third persons who might be adversely affected. Because of the varied nature of the matters about which a lawyer and client might disagree and because the actions in question may implicate the interests of a tribunal or other persons, this Rule does not prescribe how such disagreements are to be resolved. Other law, however, may be applicable and should be consulted by the lawyer. The lawyer should also consult with the client and seek a mutually acceptable resolution of the disagreement. If such efforts are unavailing and the lawyer has a fundamental disagreement with the client, the lawyer may withdraw from the representation. See Rule 1.16(b)(4). Conversely, the client may resolve the disagreement by discharging the lawyer. See Rule 1.16(a)(3).

* * *

Criminal, Fraudulent and Prohibited Transactions

[9] Paragraph (d) prohibits a lawyer from knowingly counseling or assisting a client to commit a crime or fraud. This prohibition, however, does not preclude the lawyer from giving an honest opinion about the actual consequences that appear likely to result from a client's conduct. Nor does the fact that a client uses advice in a course of action that is criminal or fraudulent of itself make a lawyer a party to the course of action. There is a critical distinction between presenting an analysis of legal aspects of questionable conduct and recommending the means by which a crime or fraud might be committed with impunity.

[10] When the client's course of action has already begun and is continuing, the lawyer's responsibility is especially delicate. The lawyer is required to avoid assisting the client, for example, by drafting or delivering documents that the lawyer knows are fraudulent or by suggesting how the wrongdoing might be concealed. A lawyer may not continue assisting a client in conduct that the lawyer originally supposed was legally proper but then discovers is criminal or fraudulent. The lawyer must, therefore, withdraw from the representation of the client in the matter. See Rule 1.16(a). In some cases, withdrawal alone might be insufficient. It may be necessary for the lawyer to give notice of the fact of withdrawal and to disaffirm any opinion, document, affirmation or the like. See Rule 4.1.

[11] Where the client is a fiduciary, the lawyer may be charged with special obligations in dealings with a beneficiary.

[12] Paragraph (d) applies whether or not the defrauded party is a party to the transaction. Hence, a lawyer must not participate in a transaction to effectuate criminal or fraudulent avoidance of tax liability. Paragraph (d) does not preclude undertaking a criminal defense incident to a general retainer for legal services to a lawful enterprise. The last clause of paragraph (d) recognizes that determining the validity or interpretation of a statute or regulation may require a course of action involving disobedience of the statute or regulation or of the interpretation placed upon it by governmental authorities.

[13] If a lawyer comes to know or reasonably should know that a client expects assistance not permitted by the Rules of Professional Conduct or other law or if the lawyer intends to act contrary to the client's instructions, the lawyer must consult with the client regarding the limitations on the lawyer's conduct. See Rule 1.4(a)(5).

Rule 1.4 Communication

(a) A lawyer shall:

(1) promptly inform the client of any decision or circumstance with respect to which the client's informed consent, as defined in Rule 1.0(e), is required by these Rules;

(2) reasonably consult with the client about the means by which the client's objectives are to be accomplished;

(3) keep the client reasonably informed about the status of the matter;

(4) promptly comply with reasonable requests for information; and

(5) consult with the client about any relevant limitation on the lawyer's conduct when the lawyer knows that the client expects assistance not permitted by the Rules of Professional Conduct or other law.

(b) A lawyer shall explain a matter to the extent reasonably necessary to permit the client to make informed decisions regarding the representation.

COMMENT

* * *

Communicating with Client

[2] If these Rules require that a particular decision about the representation be made by the client, paragraph (a)(1) requires that the lawyer promptly consult with and secure the client's consent prior to taking action unless prior discussions with the client have resolved what action the client wants the lawyer to take. For example, a lawyer who receives from opposing counsel an offer of settlement in a civil controversy or a proffered plea bargain in a criminal case must promptly inform the client of its substance unless the client has previously

indicated that the proposal will be acceptable or unacceptable or has authorized the lawyer to accept or to reject the offer. See Rule 1.2(a).

[3] Paragraph (a)(2) requires the lawyer to reasonably consult with the client about the means to be used to accomplish the client's objectives. In some situations C depending on both the importance of the action under consideration and the feasibility of consulting with the client C this duty will require consultation prior to taking action. In other circumstances, such as during a trial when an immediate decision must be made, the exigency of the situation may require the lawyer to act without prior consultation. In such cases the lawyer must nonetheless act reasonably to inform the client of actions the lawyer has taken on the client's behalf. Additionally, paragraph (a)(3) requires that the lawyer keep the client reasonably informed about the status of the matter, such as significant developments affecting the timing or the substance of the representation.

Explaining Matters

[5] The client should have sufficient information to participate intelligently in decisions concerning the objectives of the representation and the means by which they are to be pursued, to the extent the client is willing and able to do so. Adequacy of communication depends in part on the kind of advice or assistance that is involved. For example, when there is time to explain a proposal made in a negotiation, the lawyer should review all important provisions with the client before proceeding to an agreement. In litigation a lawyer should explain the general strategy and prospects of success and ordinarily should consult the client on tactics that are likely to result in significant expense or to injure or coerce others. On the other hand, a lawyer ordinarily will not be expected to describe trial or negotiation strategy in detail. The guiding principle is that the lawyer should fulfill reasonable client expectations for information consistent with the duty to act in the client's best interests, and the client's overall requirements as to the character of representation. In certain circumstances, such as when a lawyer asks a client to consent to a representation affected by a conflict of interest, the client must give informed consent, as defined in Rule 1.0(e).

[6] Ordinarily, the information to be provided is that appropriate for a client who is a comprehending and responsible adult. However, fully informing the client according to this standard may be impracticable, for example, where the client is a child or suffers from diminished capacity. See Rule 1.14. When the client is an organization or group, it is often impossible or inappropriate to inform every one of its members about its legal affairs; ordinarily, the lawyer should address communications to the appropriate officials of the organization. See Rule 1.13. Where many routine matters are involved, a system of limited or occasional reporting may be arranged with the client.

Rule 1.6 Confidentiality of Information

(a) A lawyer shall not reveal information relating to the representation of a client unless the client gives informed consent, the disclosure is impliedly authorized in order to carry out the representation or the disclosure is permitted by paragraph (b).

(b) A lawyer may reveal information relating to the representation of a client to the extent the lawyer reasonably believes necessary:

(1) to prevent reasonably certain death or substantial bodily harm;

(2) to secure legal advice about the lawyer's compliance with these Rules;

(3) to establish a claim or defense on behalf of the lawyer in a controversy between the lawyer and the client, to establish a defense to a criminal charge or civil claim against the lawyer based upon conduct in which the client was involved, or to respond to allegations in any proceeding concerning the lawyer's representation of the client; or

(4) to comply with other law or a court order.

COMMENT

* * *

[2] A fundamental principle in the client-lawyer relationship is that, in the absence of the client's informed consent, the lawyer must not reveal information relating to the representation. See Rule 1.0(e) for the definition of informed consent. This contributes to the trust that is the hallmark of the client-lawyer relationship. The client is thereby encouraged to seek legal assistance and to communicate fully and frankly with the lawyer even as to embarrassing or legally damaging subject matter. The lawyer needs this information to represent the client effectively and, if necessary, to advise the client to refrain from wrongful conduct. Almost without exception, clients come to lawyers in order to determine their rights and what is, in the complex of laws and regulations, deemed to be legal and correct. Based upon experience, lawyers know that almost all clients follow the advice given, and the law is upheld.

[3] The principle of client-lawyer confidentiality is given effect by related bodies of law: the attorney-client privilege, the work product doctrine and the rule of confidentiality established in professional ethics. The attorney-client privilege and work-product doctrine apply in judicial and other proceedings in which a lawyer may be called as a witness or otherwise required to produce evidence concerning a client. The rule of client-lawyer confidentiality applies in situations other than those where evidence is sought from the lawyer through compulsion of law. The confidentiality rule, for example, applies not only to matters communicated in confidence by the client but also to all information relating to the representation, whatever its source. A lawyer may not disclose such information except as authorized or required by the Rules of Professional Conduct or other law. See also Scope.

[4] Paragraph (a) prohibits a lawyer from revealing information relating to the representation of a client. This prohibition also applies to disclosures by a lawyer that do not in themselves reveal protected information but could reasonably lead to the discovery of such information by a third person. A lawyer's use of a hypothetical to discuss issues relating to the representation is permissible so

long as there is no reasonable likelihood that the listener will be able to ascertain the identity of the client or the situation involved.

Authorized Disclosure

[5] Except to the extent that the client's instructions or special circumstances limit that authority, a lawyer is impliedly authorized to make disclosures about a client when appropriate in carrying out the representation. In some situations, for example, a lawyer may be impliedly authorized to admit a fact that cannot properly be disputed or to make a disclosure that facilitates a satisfactory conclusion to a matter. Lawyers in a firm may, in the course of the firm's practice, disclose to each other information relating to a client of the firm, unless the client has instructed that particular information be confined to specified lawyers.

Disclosure Adverse to Client

[6] Although the public interest is usually best served by a strict rule requiring lawyers to preserve the confidentiality of information relating to the representation of their clients, the confidentiality rule is subject to limited exceptions. Paragraph (b)(1) recognizes the overriding value of life and physical integrity and permits disclosure reasonably necessary to prevent reasonably certain death or substantial bodily harm. Such harm is reasonably certain to occur if it will be suffered imminently or if there is a present and substantial threat that a person will suffer such harm at a later date if the lawyer fails to take action necessary to eliminate the threat. Thus, a lawyer who knows that a client has accidentally discharged toxic waste into a town's water supply may reveal this information to the authorities if there is a present and substantial risk that a person who drinks the water will contract a life-threatening or debilitating disease and the lawyer's disclosure is necessary to eliminate the threat or reduce the number of victims.

* * *

[10] Other law may require that a lawyer disclose information about a client. Whether such a law supersedes Rule 1.6 is a question of law beyond the scope of these Rules. When disclosure of information relating to the representation appears to be required by other law, the lawyer must discuss the matter with the client to the extent required by Rule 1.4. If, however, the other law supersedes this Rule and requires disclosure, paragraph (b)(4) permits the lawyer to make such disclosures as are necessary to comply with the law.

[11] A lawyer may be ordered to reveal information relating to the representation of a client by a court or by another tribunal or governmental entity claiming authority pursuant to other law to compel the disclosure. Absent informed consent of the client to do otherwise, the lawyer should assert on behalf of the client all nonfrivolous claims that the order is not authorized by other law or that the information sought is protected against disclosure by the attorney-client privilege or other applicable law. In the event of an adverse ruling, the lawyer must consult with the client about the possibility of appeal to the extent required by Rule 1.4. Unless review is sought, however, paragraph (b)(4) permits the lawyer to comply with the court's order.

[12] Paragraph (b) permits disclosure only to the extent the lawyer reasonably believes the disclosure is necessary to accomplish one of the purposes specified. Where practicable, the lawyer should first seek to persuade the client to take suitable action to obviate the need for disclosure. In any case, a disclosure adverse to the client's interest should be no greater than the lawyer reasonably believes necessary to accomplish the purpose. If the disclosure will be made in connection with a judicial proceeding, the disclosure should be made in a manner that limits access to the information to the tribunal or other persons having a need to know it and appropriate protective orders or other arrangements should be sought by the lawyer to the fullest extent practicable.

* * *

Withdrawal

[14] If the lawyer's services will be used by the client in materially furthering a course of criminal or fraudulent conduct, the lawyer must withdraw, as stated in Rule 1.16(a)(1). After withdrawal the lawyer is required to refrain from making disclosure of the client's confidences, except as otherwise permitted by Rule 1.6. Neither this Rule nor Rule 1.8(b) nor Rule 1.16(d) prevents the lawyer from giving notice of the fact of withdrawal, and the lawyer may also withdraw or disaffirm any opinion, document, affirmation, or the like. Where the client is an organization, the lawyer may be in doubt whether contemplated conduct will actually be carried out by the organization. Where necessary to guide conduct in connection with this Rule, the lawyer may make inquiry within the organization as indicated in Rule 1.13(b).

Former Client

[17] The duty of confidentiality continues after the client-lawyer relationship has terminated. See Rule 1.9(c)(2). See Rule 1.9(c)(1) for the prohibition against using such information to the disadvantage of the former client.

Rule 1.7 Conflict of Interest: Current Clients

(a) Except as provided in paragraph (b), a lawyer shall not represent a client if the representation involves a concurrent conflict of interest. A concurrent conflict of interest exists if:

(1) the representation of one client will be directly adverse to another client; or

(2) there is a significant risk that the representation of one or more clients will be materially limited by the lawyer's responsibilities to another client, a former client or a third person or by a personal interest of the lawyer.

(b) Notwithstanding the existence of a concurrent conflict of interest under paragraph (a), a lawyer may represent a client if:

(1) the lawyer reasonably believes that the lawyer will be able to provide competent and diligent representation to each affected client;

(2) the representation is not prohibited by law;

(3) the representation does not involve the assertion of a claim by one client against another client represented by the lawyer in the same litigation or other proceeding before a tribunal; and

(4) each affected client gives informed consent, confirmed in writing.

COMMENT

General Principles

[1] Loyalty and independent judgment are essential elements in the lawyer's relationship to a client. Concurrent conflicts of interest can arise from the lawyer's responsibilities to another client, a former client or a third person or from the lawyer's own interests. For specific Rules regarding certain concurrent conflicts of interest, see Rule 1.8. For former client conflicts of interest, see Rule 1.9. For conflicts of interest involving prospective clients, see Rule 1.18. For definitions of "informed consent" and "confirmed in writing," see Rule 1.0(e) and (b).

[2] Resolution of a conflict of interest problem under this Rule requires the lawyer to: 1) clearly identify the client or clients; 2) determine whether a conflict of interest exists; 3) decide whether the representation may be undertaken despite the existence of a conflict, i.e., whether the conflict is consentable; and 4) if so, consult with the clients affected under paragraph (a) and obtain their informed consent, confirmed in writing. The clients affected under paragraph (a) include both of the clients referred to in paragraph (a)(1) and the one or more clients whose representation might be materially limited under paragraph (a)(2).

[3] A conflict of interest may exist before representation is undertaken, in which event the representation must be declined, unless the lawyer obtains the informed consent of each client under the conditions of paragraph (b). To determine whether a conflict of interest exists, a lawyer should adopt reasonable procedures, appropriate for the size and type of firm and practice, to determine in both litigation and non-litigation matters the persons and issues involved. See also Comment to Rule 5.1. Ignorance caused by a failure to institute such procedures will not excuse a lawyer's violation of this Rule. As to whether a client-lawyer relationship exists or, having once been established, is continuing, see Comment to Rule 1.3 and Scope.

[4] If a conflict arises after representation has been undertaken, the lawyer ordinarily must withdraw from the representation, unless the lawyer has obtained the informed consent of the client under the conditions of paragraph (b). See Rule 1.16. Where more than one client is involved, whether the lawyer may continue to represent any of the clients is determined both by the lawyer's ability to comply with duties owed to the former client and by the lawyer's ability to represent adequately the remaining client or clients, given the lawyer's duties to the former client. See Rule 1.9. See also Comments [5] and [29].

[5] Unforeseeable developments, such as changes in corporate and other organizational affiliations or the addition or realignment of parties in litigation, might create conflicts in the midst of a representation, as when a company sued by the lawyer on behalf of one client is bought by another client represented by the lawyer in an unrelated matter. Depending on the circumstances, the lawyer

may have the option to withdraw from one of the representations in order to avoid the conflict. The lawyer must seek court approval where necessary and take steps to minimize harm to the clients. See Rule 1.16. The lawyer must continue to protect the confidences of the client from whose representation the lawyer has withdrawn. See Rule 1.9(c).

Identifying Conflicts of Interest: Directly Adverse

[6] Loyalty to a current client prohibits undertaking representation directly adverse to that client without that client's informed consent. Thus, absent consent, a lawyer may not act as an advocate in one matter against a person the lawyer represents in some other matter, even when the matters are wholly unrelated. The client as to whom the representation is directly adverse is likely to feel betrayed, and the resulting damage to the client-lawyer relationship is likely to impair the lawyer's ability to represent the client effectively. In addition, the client on whose behalf the adverse representation is undertaken reasonably may fear that the lawyer will pursue that client's case less effectively out of deference to the other client, i.e., that the representation may be materially limited by the lawyer's interest in retaining the current client. Similarly, a directly adverse conflict may arise when a lawyer is required to cross-examine a client who appears as a witness in a lawsuit involving another client, as when the testimony will be damaging to the client who is represented in the lawsuit. On the other hand, simultaneous representation in unrelated matters of clients whose interests are only economically adverse, such as representation of competing economic enterprises in unrelated litigation, does not ordinarily constitute a conflict of interest and thus may not require consent of the respective clients.

[7] Directly adverse conflicts can also arise in transactional matters. For example, if a lawyer is asked to represent the seller of a business in negotiations with a buyer represented by the lawyer, not in the same transaction but in another, unrelated matter, the lawyer could not undertake the representation without the informed consent of each client.

Identifying Conflicts of Interest: Material Limitation

[8] Even where there is no direct adverseness, a conflict of interest exists if there is a significant risk that a lawyer's ability to consider, recommend or carry out an appropriate course of action for the client will be materially limited as a result of the lawyer's other responsibilities or interests. For example, a lawyer asked to represent several individuals seeking to form a joint venture is likely to be materially limited in the lawyer's ability to recommend or advocate all possible positions that each might take because of the lawyer's duty of loyalty to the others. The conflict in effect forecloses alternatives that would otherwise be available to the client. The mere possibility of subsequent harm does not itself require disclosure and consent. The critical questions are the likelihood that a difference in interests will eventuate and, if it does, whether it will materially interfere with the lawyer's independent professional judgment in considering alternatives or foreclose courses of action that reasonably should be pursued on behalf of the client.

Lawyer's Responsibilities to Former Clients and Other Third Persons

[9] In addition to conflicts with other current clients, a lawyer's duties of loyalty and independence may be materially limited by responsibilities to former clients under Rule 1.9 or by the lawyer's responsibilities to other persons, such as fiduciary duties arising from a lawyer's service as a trustee, executor or corporate director.

Personal Interest Conflicts

[10] The lawyer's own interests should not be permitted to have an adverse effect on representation of a client. For example, if the probity of a lawyer's own conduct in a transaction is in serious question, it may be difficult or impossible for the lawyer to give a client detached advice. Similarly, when a lawyer has discussions concerning possible employment with an opponent of the lawyer's client, or with a law firm representing the opponent, such discussions could materially limit the lawyer's representation of the client. In addition, a lawyer may not allow related business interests to affect representation, for example, by referring clients to an enterprise in which the lawyer has an undisclosed financial interest. See Rule 1.8 for specific Rules pertaining to a number of personal interest conflicts, including business transactions with clients. See also Rule 1.10 (personal interest conflicts under Rule 1.7 ordinarily are not imputed to other lawyers in a law firm).

* * *

Interest of Person Paying for a Lawyer's Service

[13] A lawyer may be paid from a source other than the client, including a co-client, if the client is informed of that fact and consents and the arrangement does not compromise the lawyer's duty of loyalty or independent judgment to the client. See Rule 1.8(f). If acceptance of the payment from any other source presents a significant risk that the lawyer's representation of the client will be materially limited by the lawyer's own interest in accommodating the person paying the lawyer's fee or by the lawyer's responsibilities to a payer who is also a co-client, then the lawyer must comply with the requirements of paragraph (b) before accepting the representation, including determining whether the conflict is consentable and, if so, that the client has adequate information about the material risks of the representation.

Prohibited Representations

[14] Ordinarily, clients may consent to representation notwithstanding a conflict. However, as indicated in paragraph (b), some conflicts are nonconsentable, meaning that the lawyer involved cannot properly ask for such agreement or provide representation on the basis of the client's consent. When the lawyer is representing more than one client, the question of consentability must be resolved as to each client.

[15] Consentability is typically determined by considering whether the interests of the clients will be adequately protected if the clients are permitted to give their informed consent to representation burdened by a conflict of interest. Thus, under paragraph (b)(1), representation is prohibited if in the circumstances the lawyer cannot reasonably conclude that the lawyer will be able to

provide competent and diligent representation. See Rule 1.1 (competence) and Rule 1.3 (diligence).

* * *

[17] Paragraph (b)(3) describes conflicts that are nonconsentable because of the institutional interest in vigorous development of each client's position when the clients are aligned directly against each other in the same litigation or other proceeding before a tribunal. Whether clients are aligned directly against each other within the meaning of this paragraph requires examination of the context of the proceeding. Although this paragraph does not preclude a lawyer's multiple representation of adverse parties to a mediation (because mediation is not a proceeding before a "tribunal" under Rule 1.0(m)), such representation may be precluded by paragraph (b)(1).

Informed Consent

[18] Informed consent requires that each affected client be aware of the relevant circumstances and of the material and reasonably foreseeable ways that the conflict could have adverse effects on the interests of that client. See Rule 1.0(e) (informed consent). The information required depends on the nature of the conflict and the nature of the risks involved. When representation of multiple clients in a single matter is undertaken, the information must include the implications of the common representation, including possible effects on loyalty, confidentiality and the attorney-client privilege and the advantages and risks involved. See Comments [30] and [31] (effect of common representation on confidentiality).

[19] Under some circumstances it may be impossible to make the disclosure necessary to obtain consent. For example, when the lawyer represents different clients in related matters and one of the clients refuses to consent to the disclosure necessary to permit the other client to make an informed decision, the lawyer cannot properly ask the latter to consent. In some cases the alternative to common representation can be that each party may have to obtain separate representation with the possibility of incurring additional costs. These costs, along with the benefits of securing separate representation, are factors that may be considered by the affected client in determining whether common representation is in the client's interests.

Consent Confirmed in Writing

[20] Paragraph (b) requires the lawyer to obtain the informed consent of the client, confirmed in writing. Such a writing may consist of a document executed by the client or one that the lawyer promptly records and transmits to the client following an oral consent. See Rule 1.0(b). See also Rule 1.0(n) (writing includes electronic transmission). If it is not feasible to obtain or transmit the writing at the time the client gives informed consent, then the lawyer must obtain or transmit it within a reasonable time thereafter. See Rule 1.0(b). The requirement of a writing does not supplant the need in most cases for the lawyer to talk with the client, to explain the risks and advantages, if any, of representation burdened with a conflict of interest, as well as reasonably available alternatives, and to afford the client a reasonable opportunity to consider the risks and alternatives and to raise questions and concerns. Rather, the writing is required in order to impress upon clients the seriousness of the decision the client is being

asked to make and to avoid disputes or ambiguities that might later occur in the absence of a writing.

Revoking Consent

[21] A client who has given consent to a conflict may revoke the consent and, like any other client, may terminate the lawyer's representation at any time. Whether revoking consent to the client's own representation precludes the lawyer from continuing to represent other clients depends on the circumstances, including the nature of the conflict, whether the client revoked consent because of a material change in circumstances, the reasonable expectations of the other client and whether material detriment to the other clients or the lawyer would result.

Consent to Future Conflict

[22] Whether a lawyer may properly request a client to waive conflicts that might arise in the future is subject to the test of paragraph (b). The effectiveness of such waivers is generally determined by the extent to which the client reasonably understands the material risks that the waiver entails. The more comprehensive the explanation of the types of future representations that might arise and the actual and reasonably foreseeable adverse consequences of those representations, the greater the likelihood that the client will have the requisite understanding. Thus, if the client agrees to consent to a particular type of conflict with which the client is already familiar, then the consent ordinarily will be effective with regard to that type of conflict. If the consent is general and open-ended, then the consent ordinarily will be ineffective, because it is not reasonably likely that the client will have understood the material risks involved. On the other hand, if the client is an experienced user of the legal services involved and is reasonably informed regarding the risk that a conflict may arise, such consent is more likely to be effective, particularly if, e.g., the client is independently represented by other counsel in giving consent and the consent is limited to future conflicts unrelated to the subject of the representation. In any case, advance consent cannot be effective if the circumstances that materialize in the future are such as would make the conflict nonconsentable under paragraph (b).

Conflicts in Litigation

* * *

[25] When a lawyer represents or seeks to represent a class of plaintiffs or defendants in a class-action lawsuit, unnamed members of the class are ordinarily not considered to be clients of the lawyer for purposes of applying paragraph (a)(1) of this Rule. Thus, the lawyer does not typically need to get the consent of such a person before representing a client suing the person in an unrelated matter. Similarly, a lawyer seeking to represent an opponent in a class action does not typically need the consent of an unnamed member of the class whom the lawyer represents in an unrelated matter.

Nonlitigation Conflicts

[26] Conflicts of interest under paragraphs (a)(1) and (a)(2) arise in contexts other than litigation. For a discussion of directly adverse conflicts in

transactional matters, see Comment [7]. Relevant factors in determining whether there is significant potential for material limitation include the duration and intimacy of the lawyer's relationship with the client or clients involved, the functions being performed by the lawyer, the likelihood that disagreements will arise and the likely prejudice to the client from the conflict. The question is often one of proximity and degree. See Comment [8].

* * *

[28] Whether a conflict is consentable depends on the circumstances. For example, a lawyer may not represent multiple parties to a negotiation whose interests are fundamentally antagonistic to each other, but common representation is permissible where the clients are generally aligned in interest even though there is some difference in interest among them. Thus, a lawyer may seek to establish or adjust a relationship between clients on an amicable and mutually advantageous basis; for example, in helping to organize a business in which two or more clients are entrepreneurs, working out the financial reorganization of an enterprise in which two or more clients have an interest or arranging a property distribution in settlement of an estate. The lawyer seeks to resolve potentially adverse interests by developing the parties' mutual interests. Otherwise, each party might have to obtain separate representation, with the possibility of incurring additional cost, complication or even litigation. Given these and other relevant factors, the clients may prefer that the lawyer act for all of them.

Special Considerations in Common Representation

[29] In considering whether to represent multiple clients in the same matter, a lawyer should be mindful that if the common representation fails because the potentially adverse interests cannot be reconciled, the result can be additional cost, embarrassment and recrimination. Ordinarily, the lawyer will be forced to withdraw from representing all of the clients if the common representation fails. In some situations, the risk of failure is so great that multiple representation is plainly impossible. For example, a lawyer cannot undertake common representation of clients where contentious litigation or negotiations between them are imminent or contemplated. Moreover, because the lawyer is required to be impartial between commonly represented clients, representation of multiple clients is improper when it is unlikely that impartiality can be maintained. Generally, if the relationship between the parties has already assumed antagonism, the possibility that the clients' interests can be adequately served by common representation is not very good. Other relevant factors are whether the lawyer subsequently will represent both parties on a continuing basis and whether the situation involves creating or terminating a relationship between the parties.

[30] A particularly important factor in determining the appropriateness of common representation is the effect on client-lawyer confidentiality and the attorney-client privilege. With regard to the attorney-client privilege, the prevailing rule is that, as between commonly represented clients, the privilege does not attach. Hence, it must be assumed that if litigation eventuates between the clients, the privilege will not protect any such communications, and the clients should be so advised.

[31] As to the duty of confidentiality, continued common representation will almost certainly be inadequate if one client asks the lawyer not to disclose to the other client information relevant to the common representation. This is so because the lawyer has an equal duty of loyalty to each client, and each client has the right to be informed of anything bearing on the representation that might affect that client's interests and the right to expect that the lawyer will use that information to that client's benefit. See Rule 1.4. The lawyer should, at the outset of the common representation and as part of the process of obtaining each client's informed consent, advise each client that information will be shared and that the lawyer will have to withdraw if one client decides that some matter material to the representation should be kept from the other. In limited circumstances, it may be appropriate for the lawyer to proceed with the representation when the clients have agreed, after being properly informed, that the lawyer will keep certain information confidential. For example, the lawyer may reasonably conclude that failure to disclose one client's trade secrets to another client will not adversely affect representation involving a joint venture between the clients and agree to keep that information confidential with the informed consent of both clients.

[32] When seeking to establish or adjust a relationship between clients, the lawyer should make clear that the lawyer's role is not that of partisanship normally expected in other circumstances and, thus, that the clients may be required to assume greater responsibility for decisions than when each client is separately represented. Any limitations on the scope of the representation made necessary as a result of the common representation should be fully explained to the clients at the outset of the representation. See Rule 1.2(c).

[33] Subject to the above limitations, each client in the common representation has the right to loyal and diligent representation and the protection of Rule 1.9 concerning the obligations to a former client. The client also has the right to discharge the lawyer as stated in Rule 1.16.

Organizational Clients

[34] A lawyer who represents a corporation or other organization does not, by virtue of that representation, necessarily represent any constituent or affiliated organization, such as a parent or subsidiary. See Rule 1.13(a). Thus, the lawyer for an organization is not barred from accepting representation adverse to an affiliate in an unrelated matter, unless the circumstances are such that the affiliate should also be considered a client of the lawyer, there is an understanding between the lawyer and the organizational client that the lawyer will avoid representation adverse to the client's affiliates, or the lawyer's obligations to either the organizational client or the new client are likely to limit materially the lawyer's representation of the other client.

[35] A lawyer for a corporation or other organization who is also a member of its board of directors should determine whether the responsibilities of the two roles may conflict. The lawyer may be called on to advise the corporation in matters involving actions of the directors. Consideration should be given to the frequency with which such situations may arise, the potential intensity of the conflict, the effect of the lawyer's resignation from the board and the possibility of the corporation's obtaining legal advice from another lawyer in such situations. If there is material risk that the dual role will compromise the lawyer's

independence of professional judgment, the lawyer should not serve as a director or should cease to act as the corporation's lawyer when conflicts of interest arise. The lawyer should advise the other members of the board that in some circumstances matters discussed at board meetings while the lawyer is present in the capacity of director might not be protected by the attorney-client privilege and that conflict of interest considerations might require the lawyer's recusal as a director or might require the lawyer and the lawyer's firm to decline representation of the corporation in a matter.

Rule 1.13 Organization as Client

(a) A lawyer employed or retained by an organization represents the organization acting through its duly authorized constituents.

(b) If a lawyer for an organization knows that an officer, employee or other person associated with the organization is engaged in action, intends to act or refuses to act in a matter related to the representation that is a violation of a legal obligation to the organization, or a violation of law which reasonably might be imputed to the organization, and is likely to result in substantial injury to the organization, the lawyer shall proceed as is reasonably necessary in the best interest of the organization. In determining how to proceed, the lawyer shall give due consideration to the seriousness of the violation and its consequences, the scope and nature of the lawyer's representation, the responsibility in the organization and the apparent motivation of the person involved, the policies of the organization concerning such matters and any other relevant considerations. Any measures taken shall be designed to minimize disruption of the organization and the risk of revealing information relating to the representation to persons outside the organization. Such measures may include among others:

(1) asking for reconsideration of the matter;

(2) advising that a separate legal opinion on the matter be sought for presentation to appropriate authority in the organization; and

(3) referring the matter to higher authority in the organization, including, if warranted by the seriousness of the matter, referral to the highest authority that can act on behalf of the organization as determined by applicable law.

(c) If, despite the lawyer's efforts in accordance with paragraph (b), the highest authority that can act on behalf of the organization insists upon action, or a refusal to act, that is clearly a violation of law and is likely to result in substantial injury to the organization, the lawyer may resign in accordance with Rule 1.16.

(d) In dealing with an organization's directors, officers, employees, members, shareholders or other constituents, a lawyer shall explain the identity of the client when the lawyer knows or reasonably should know that the organization's interests are adverse to those of the constituents with whom the lawyer is dealing.

(e) A lawyer representing an organization may also represent any of its directors, officers, employees, members, shareholders or other constituents, subject to the provisions of Rule 1.7. If the organization's consent to the dual representation is required by Rule 1.7, the consent shall be given by an appropriate official of the organization other than the individual who is to be represented, or by the shareholders.

COMMENT

The Entity as the Client

[1] An organizational client is a legal entity, but it cannot act except through its officers, directors, employees, shareholders and other constituents. Officers, directors, employees and shareholders are the constituents of the corporate organizational client. The duties defined in this Comment apply equally to unincorporated associations. "Other constituents" as used in this Comment means the positions equivalent to officers, directors, employees and shareholders held by persons acting for organizational clients that are not corporations.

[2] When one of the constituents of an organizational client communicates with the organization's lawyer in that person's organizational capacity, the communication is protected by Rule 1.6. Thus, by way of example, if an organizational client requests its lawyer to investigate allegations of wrongdoing, interviews made in the course of that investigation between the lawyer and the client's employees or other constituents are covered by Rule 1.6. This does not mean, however, that constituents of an organizational client are the clients of the lawyer. The lawyer may not disclose to such constituents information relating to the representation except for disclosures explicitly or impliedly authorized by the organizational client in order to carry out the representation or as otherwise permitted by Rule 1.6.

[3] When constituents of the organization make decisions for it, the decisions ordinarily must be accepted by the lawyer even if their utility or prudence is doubtful. Decisions concerning policy and operations, including ones entailing serious risk, are not as such in the lawyer's province. However, different considerations arise when the lawyer knows that the organization may be substantially injured by action of a constituent that is in violation of law. In such a circumstance, it may be reasonably necessary for the lawyer to ask the constituent to reconsider the matter. If that fails, or if the matter is of sufficient seriousness and importance to the organization, it may be reasonably necessary for the lawyer to take steps to have the matter reviewed by a higher authority in the organization. Clear justification should exist for seeking review over the head of the constituent normally responsible for it. The stated policy of the organization may define circumstances and prescribe channels for such review, and a lawyer should encourage the formulation of such a policy. Even in the absence of organization policy, however, the lawyer may have an obligation to refer a matter to higher authority, depending on the seriousness of the matter and whether the constituent in question has apparent motives to act at variance with the

organization's interest. Review by the chief executive officer or by the board of directors may be required when the matter is of importance commensurate with their authority. At some point it may be useful or essential to obtain an independent legal opinion.

[4] The organization's highest authority to whom a matter may be referred ordinarily will be the board of directors or similar governing body. However, applicable law may prescribe that under certain conditions the highest authority reposes elsewhere, for example, in the independent directors of a corporation.

Relation to Other Rules

[5] The authority and responsibility provided in this Rule are concurrent with the authority and responsibility provided in other Rules. In particular, this Rule does not limit or expand the lawyer's responsibility under Rule 1.6, 1.8, 1.16, 3.3 or 4.1. If the lawyer's services are being used by an organization to further a crime or fraud by the organization, Rule 1.2(d) can be applicable.

* * *

Clarifying the Lawyer's Role

[7] There are times when the organization's interest may be or become adverse to those of one or more of its constituents. In such circumstances the lawyer should advise any constituent, whose interest the lawyer finds adverse to that of the organization of the conflict or potential conflict of interest, that the lawyer cannot represent such constituent, and that such person may wish to obtain independent representation. Care must be taken to assure that the individual understands that, when there is such adversity of interest, the lawyer for the organization cannot provide legal representation for that constituent individual, and that discussions between the lawyer for the organization and the individual may not be privileged.

[8] Whether such a warning should be given by the lawyer for the organization to any constituent individual may turn on the facts of each case.

Dual Representation

[9] Paragraph (e) recognizes that a lawyer for an organization may also represent a principal officer or major shareholder.

Derivative Actions

[10] Under generally prevailing law, the shareholders or members of a corporation may bring suit to compel the directors to perform their legal obligations in the supervision of the organization. Members of unincorporated associations have essentially the same right. Such an action may be brought nominally by the organization, but usually is, in fact, a legal controversy over management of the organization.

[11] The question can arise whether counsel for the organization may defend such an action. The proposition that the organization is the lawyer's client does not alone resolve the issue. Most derivative actions are a normal incident of an organization's affairs, to be defended by the organization's lawyer like any other suit. However, if the claim involves serious charges of wrongdoing by those in control of the organization, a conflict may arise between the lawyer's

duty to the organization and the lawyer's relationship with the board. In those circumstances, Rule 1.7 governs who should represent the directors and the organization.

Rule 1.16 Declining or Terminating Representation

(a) Except as stated in paragraph (c), a lawyer shall not represent a client or, where representation has commenced, shall withdraw from the representation of a client if:

(1) the representation will result in violation of the rules of professional conduct or other law;

(2) the lawyer's physical or mental condition materially impairs the lawyer's ability to represent the client; or

(3) the lawyer is discharged.

(b) Except as stated in paragraph (c), a lawyer may withdraw from representing a client if:

(1) withdrawal can be accomplished without material adverse effect on the interests of the client;

(2) the client persists in a course of action involving the lawyer's services that the lawyer reasonably believes is criminal or fraudulent;

(3) the client has used the lawyer's services to perpetrate a crime or fraud;

(4) the client insists upon taking action that the lawyer considers repugnant or with which the lawyer has a fundamental disagreement;

(5) the client fails substantially to fulfill an obligation to the lawyer regarding the lawyer's services and has been given reasonable warning that the lawyer will withdraw unless the obligation is fulfilled;

(6) the representation will result in an unreasonable financial burden on the lawyer or has been rendered unreasonably difficult by the client; or

(7) other good cause for withdrawal exists.

(c) A lawyer must comply with applicable law requiring notice to or permission of a tribunal when terminating a representation. When ordered to do so by a tribunal, a lawyer shall continue representation notwithstanding good cause for terminating the representation.

(d) Upon termination of representation, a lawyer shall take steps to the extent reasonably practicable to protect a client's interests, such as giving reasonable notice to the client, allowing time for employment of other counsel, surrendering papers and property to which the client is entitled and refunding any advance payment of fee or expense that has not been earned or incurred. The lawyer may retain papers relating to the client to the extent permitted by other law.

COMMENT

[1] A lawyer should not accept representation in a matter unless it can be performed competently, promptly, without improper conflict of interest and to completion. Ordinarily, a representation in a matter is completed when the agreed-upon assistance has been concluded. See Rules 1.2(c) and 6.5. See also Rule 1.3, Comment [4].

Mandatory Withdrawal

[2] A lawyer ordinarily must decline or withdraw from representation if the client demands that the lawyer engage in conduct that is illegal or violates the Rules of Professional Conduct or other law. The lawyer is not obliged to decline or withdraw simply because the client suggests such a course of conduct; a client may make such a suggestion in the hope that a lawyer will not be constrained by a professional obligation.

* * *

Discharge

[4] A client has a right to discharge a lawyer at any time, with or without cause, subject to liability for payment for the lawyer's services. Where future dispute about the withdrawal may be anticipated, it may be advisable to prepare a written statement reciting the circumstances.

* * *

Optional Withdrawal

[7] A lawyer may withdraw from representation in some circumstances. The lawyer has the option to withdraw if it can be accomplished without material adverse effect on the client's interests. Withdrawal is also justified if the client persists in a course of action that the lawyer reasonably believes is criminal or fraudulent, for a lawyer is not required to be associated with such conduct even if the lawyer does not further it. Withdrawal is also permitted if the lawyer's services were misused in the past even if that would materially prejudice the client. The lawyer may also withdraw where the client insists on taking action that the lawyer considers repugnant or with which the lawyer has a fundamental disagreement.

* * *

Rule 2.1 Advisor

In representing a client, a lawyer shall exercise independent professional judgment and render candid advice. In rendering advice, a lawyer may refer not only to law but to other considerations such as moral, economic, social and political factors, that may be relevant to the client's situation.

COMMENT

Scope of Advice

[1] A client is entitled to straightforward advice expressing the lawyer's honest assessment. Legal advice often involves unpleasant facts and alternatives that a client may be disinclined to confront. In presenting advice, a lawyer endeavors to sustain the client's morale and may put advice in as acceptable a form as honesty permits. However, a lawyer should not be deterred from giving candid advice by the prospect that the advice will be unpalatable to the client.

[2] Advice couched in narrow legal terms may be of little value to a client, especially where practical considerations, such as cost or effects on other people, are predominant. Purely technical legal advice, therefore, can sometimes be inadequate. It is proper for a lawyer to refer to relevant moral and ethical considerations in giving advice. Although a lawyer is not a moral advisor as such, moral and ethical considerations impinge upon most legal questions and may decisively influence how the law will be applied.

[3] A client may expressly or impliedly ask the lawyer for purely technical advice. When such a request is made by a client experienced in legal matters, the lawyer may accept it at face value. When such a request is made by a client inexperienced in legal matters, however, the lawyer's responsibility as advisor may include indicating that more may be involved than strictly legal considerations.

* * *

Offering Advice

[5] In general, a lawyer is not expected to give advice until asked by the client. However, when a lawyer knows that a client proposes a course of action that is likely to result in substantial adverse legal consequences to the client, the lawyer's duty to the client under Rule 1.4 may require that the lawyer offer advice if the client's course of action is related to the representation. Similarly, when a matter is likely to involve litigation, it may be necessary under Rule 1.4 to inform the client of forms of dispute resolution that might constitute reasonable alternatives to litigation. A lawyer ordinarily has no duty to initiate investigation of a client's affairs or to give advice that the client has indicated is unwanted, but a lawyer may initiate advice to a client when doing so appears to be in the client's interest.

VIII. RESTATEMENT (SECOND) OF AGENCY

Contents

---

§ 1. Agency; Principal; Agent

(1) Agency is the fiduciary relation which results from the manifestation of consent by one person to another that the other shall act on his behalf and subject to his control, and consent by the other so to act.

(2) The one for whom action is to be taken is the principal.

(3) The one who is to act is the agent.

§ 2. Master; Servant; Independent Contractor

(1) A master is a principal who employs an agent to perform service in his affairs and who controls or has the right to control the physical conduct of the other in the performance of the service.

(2) A servant is an agent employed by a master to perform service in his affairs whose physical conduct in the performance of the service is controlled or is subject to the right to control by the master.

(3) An independent contractor is a person who contracts with another to do something for him but who is not controlled by the other nor subject to the other's right to control with respect to his physical conduct in the performance of the undertaking. He may or may not be an agent.

§ 5. Subagents and Subservants

(1) A subagent is a person appointed by an agent empowered to do so, to perform functions undertaken by the agent for the principal, but for whose conduct the agent agrees with the principal to be primarily responsible.

(2) A subservant is a person appointed by a servant empowered to do so, to perform functions undertaken by the servant for the master and subject to the control as to his physical conduct both by the master and by the servant, but for whose conduct the servant agrees with the principal to be primarily responsible.

§ 7. Authority

Authority is the power of the agent to affect the legal relations of the principal by acts done in accordance with the principal's manifestations of consent to him.

§ 8. Apparent Authority

Apparent authority is the power to affect the legal relations of another person by transactions with third persons, professedly as agent for the other, arising from and in accordance with the other's manifestations to such third persons.

§ 8A. Inherent Agency Power

Inherent agency power is a term used in the restatement of this subject to indicate the power of an agent which is derived not from authority, apparent authority or estoppel, but solely from the agency relation and exists for the protection of persons harmed by or dealing with a servant or other agent.

§ 8B. Estoppel—Change of Position

(1) A person who is not otherwise liable as a party to a transaction purported to be done on his account, is nevertheless subject to liability to persons who have changed their positions because of their belief that the transaction was entered into by or for him, if

(a) he intentionally or carelessly caused such belief, or

(b) knowing of such belief and that others might change their positions because of it, he did not take reasonable steps to notify them of the facts.

(2) An owner of property who represents to third persons that another is the owner of the property or who permits the other so to represent, or who realizes that third persons believe that another is the owner of the property, and that he could easily inform the third persons of the facts, is subject to the loss of the property if the other disposes of

it to third persons who, in ignorance of the facts, purchase the property or otherwise change their position with reference to it.

(3) Change of position, as the phrase is used in the restatement of this subject, indicates payment of money, expenditure of labor, suffering a loss or subjection to legal liability.

§ 26. Creation of Authority; General Rule

Except for the execution of instruments under seal or for the performance of transactions required by statute to be authorized in a particular way, authority to do an act can be created by written or spoken words or other conduct of the principal which, reasonably interpreted, causes the agent to believe that the principal desires him so to act on the principal's account.

§ 27. Creation of Apparent Authority: General Rule

Except for the execution of instruments under seal or for the conduct of transactions required by statute to be authorized in a particular way, apparent authority to do an act is created as to a third person by written or spoken words or any other conduct of the principal which, reasonably interpreted, causes the third person to believe that the principal consents to have the act done on his behalf by the person purporting to act for him.

§ 82. Ratification

Ratification is the affirmance by a person of a prior act which did not bind him but which was done or professedly done on his account, whereby the act, as to some or all persons, is given effect as if originally authorized by him.

§ 83. Affirmance

Affirmance is either

(a) a manifestation of an election by one on whose account an unauthorized act has been done to treat the act as authorized, or

(b) conduct by him justifiable only if there were such an election.

TOPIC 1. GENERAL PRINCIPLES

§ 140. Liability Based Upon Agency Principles

The liability of the principal to a third person upon a transaction conducted by an agent, or the transfer of his interests by an agent, may be based upon the fact that:

(a) the agent was authorized;

(b) the agent was apparently authorized; or

(c) the agent had a power arising from the agency relation and not dependent upon authority or apparent authority.

§ 143. Effect of Ratification

Upon ratification with knowledge of the material facts, the principal becomes responsible for contracts and conveyances made for him by one purporting to act on his account as if the transaction had been authorized, if there has been no supervening loss of capacity by the principal or change in the law which would render illegal the authorization or performance of such a transaction.

§ 219. When Master Is Liable for Torts of His Servants

(1) A master is subject to liability for the torts of his servants committed while acting in the scope of their employment.

(2) A master is not subject to liability for the torts of his servants acting outside the scope of their employment, unless:

(a) the master intended the conduct or the consequences, or

(b) the master was negligent or reckless, or

(c) the conduct violated a non-delegable duty of the master, or

(d) the servant purported to act or speak on behalf of the principal and there was reliance upon apparent authority, or he was aided in accomplishing the tort by the existence of the agency relation.

§ 220. Definition of Servant

(1) A servant is a person employed to perform services in the affairs of another and who with respect to the physical conduct in the performance of the services is subject to the other's control or right to control.

(2) In determining whether one acting for another is a servant or an independent contractor, the following matters of fact, among others, are considered:

(a) the extent of control which, by the agreement, the master may exercise over the details of the work;

(b) whether or not the one employed is engaged in a distinct occupation of business;

(c) the kind of occupation, with reference to whether, in the locality, the work is usually done under the direction of the employer or by a specialist without supervision;

(d) the skill required in the particular occupation;

(e) whether the employer or the workman supplies the instrumentalities, tools, and the place of work for the person doing the work;

(f) the length of time for which the person is employed;

(g) the method of payment, whether by the time or by the job;

(h) whether or not the work is a part of the regular business of the employer;

(i) whether or not the parties believe they are creating the relation of master and servant; and

(j) whether the principal is or is not in business.

§ 228. General Statement

(1) Conduct of a servant is within the scope of employment if, but only if:

(a) it is of the kind he is employed to perform;

(b) it occurs substantially within the authorized time and space limits;

(c) it is actuated, at least in part, by a purpose to serve the master, and

(d) if force is intentionally used by the servant against another, the use of force is not unexpectable by the master.

(2) Conduct of a servant is not within the scope of employment if it is different in kind from that authorized, far beyond the authorized time or space limits, or too little actuated by a purpose to serve the master.

§ 229. Kind of Conduct Within Scope of Employment

(1) To be within the scope of the employment, conduct must be of the same general nature as that authorized, or incidental to the conduct authorized.

(2) In determining whether or not the conduct, although not authorized, is nevertheless so similar to or incidental to the conduct authorized as to be within the scope of employment, the following matters of fact are to be considered:

(a) whether or not the act is one commonly done by such servants;

(b) the time, place and purpose of the act;

(c) the previous relations between the master and the servant;

(d) the extent to which the business of the master is apportioned between different servants;

(e) whether or not the act is outside the enterprise of the master or, if within the enterprise, has not been entrusted to any servant;

(f) whether or not the master has reason to expect that such an act will be done;

(g) the similarity in quality of the act done to the act authorized;

(h) whether or not the instrumentality by which the harm is done has been furnished by the master to the servant;

(i) the extent of departure from the normal method of accomplishing an authorized result; and

(j) whether or not the act is seriously criminal.

IX. FEDERAL RULES OF CIVIL PROCEDURE

Contents

Rule 23. Class Actions

(a) *Prerequisites to a class action.* One or more members of a class may sue or be sued as representative parties on behalf of all only if (1) the class is so numerous that joinder of all members is impracticable, (2) there are questions of law or fact common to the class, (3) the claims or defenses of the representative parties are typical of the claims or defenses of the class, and (4) the representative parties will fairly and adequately protect the interests of the class.

(b) *Class actions maintainable.* An action may be maintained as a class action if the prerequisites of subdivision (a) are satisfied, and in addition:

(1) the prosecution of separate actions by or against individual members of the class would create a risk of

(A) inconsistent or varying adjudications with respect to individual members of the class which would establish incompatible standards of conduct for the party opposing the class, or

(B) adjudications with respect to individual members of the class which would as a practical matter be dispositive of the interests of the other members not parties to the adjudications or substantially impair or impede their ability to protect their interests; or

(2) the party opposing the class has acted or refused to act on grounds generally applicable to the class, thereby making appropriate final injunctive relief or corresponding declaratory relief with respect to the class as a whole; or

(3) the court finds that the questions of law or fact common to the members of the class predominate over any questions affecting only individual members, and that a class action is superior to other available methods for the fair and efficient adjudication of the controversy. The matters pertinent to the findings include: (A) the interest of members of the class in individually controlling the prosecution or defense of separate actions; (B) the extent and nature of any litigation concerning the controversy already commenced by or against members of the class; (C) the desirability or undesirability of concentrating the litigation of the claims in the particular forum; (D) the difficulties likely to be encountered in the management of a class action.

(c) *Determination by order whether class action to be maintained; notice; judgment; actions conducted partially as class actions.*

(1) As soon as practicable after the commencement of an action brought as a class action, the court shall determine by order whether it is to be so maintained. An order under this subdivision may be conditional, and may be altered or amended before the decision on the merits.

(2) In any class action maintained under subdivision (b)(3), the court shall direct to the members of the class the best notice practicable under the circumstances, including individual notice to all members who can be identified through reasonable effort. The notice shall advise each member that (A) the court will exclude the member from the class if the member so requests by a specified date; (B) the judgment, whether favorable or not, will include all members who do not request exclusion; and (C) any member who does not request exclusion may, if the member desires, enter an appearance through counsel.

(3) The judgment in an action maintained as a class action under subdivision (b)(1) or (b)(2), whether or not favorable to the class, shall include and describe those whom the court finds to be members of the class. The judgment in an action maintained as a class action under subdivision

(b)(3), whether or not favorable to the class, shall include and specify or describe those to whom the notice provided in subdivision (c)(2) was directed, and who have not requested exclusion, and whom the court finds to be members of the class.

(4) When appropriate (A) an action may be brought or maintained as a class action with respect to particular issues, or (B) a class may be divided into subclasses and each subclass treated as a class, and the provisions of this rule shall then be construed and applied accordingly.

(d) *Orders in conduct of actions.* In the conduct of actions to which this rule applies, the court may make appropriate orders: (1) determining the course of proceedings or prescribing measures to prevent undue repetition or complication in the presentation of evidence or argument; (2) requiring, for the protection of the members of the class or otherwise for the fair conduct of the action, that notice be given in such manner as the court may direct to some or all of the members of any step in the action, or of the proposed extent of the judgment, or of the opportunity of members to signify whether they consider the representation fair and adequate, to intervene and present claims or defenses, or otherwise to come into the action; (3) imposing conditions on the representative parties or on intervenors; (4) requiring that the pleadings be amended to eliminate therefrom allegations as to representation of absent persons, and that the action proceed accordingly; (5) dealing with similar procedural matters. The orders may be combined with an order under Rule 16, and may be altered or amended as may be desirable from time to time.

(e) *Dismissal or compromise.* A class action shall not be dismissed or compromised without the approval of the court, and notice of the proposed dismissal or compromise shall be given to all members of the class in such manner as the court directs.

(f) *Appeals.* A court of appeals may in its discretion permit an appeal from an order of a district court granting or denying class action certification under this rule if application is made to it within ten days after entry of the order. An appeal does not stay proceedings in the district court unless the district judge or the court of appeals so orders.

Rule 23.1 Derivative Actions by Shareholders

In a derivative action brought by one or more shareholders or members to enforce a right of a corporation or of an unincorporated association, the corporation or association having failed to enforce a right which may properly be asserted by it, the complaint shall be verified and shall allege (1) that the plaintiff was a shareholder or member at the time of the transaction of which the plaintiff complains or that the plaintiff's share or membership thereafter devolved on the plaintiff by operation of law, and (2) that the action is not a collusive one to confer jurisdiction on a court of the United States which it would not otherwise have. The complaint shall also allege with particularity the efforts, if any, made by the plaintiff to obtain the action the plaintiff desires from the directors or comparable authority and, if necessary, from the shareholders or members, and the reasons for the plaintiff's failure to obtain the action or for not making the effort. The derivative action may not be maintained if it appears that the plaintiff does not fairly and adequately represent the interests of the shareholders or members similarly situated in enforcing the right of the corporation or association. The action shall not be dismissed or compromised without the approval of the court, and notice of the proposed dismissal or compromise shall be given to shareholders or members in such manner as the court directs.

X. DELAWARE CHANCERY COURT RULES

Contents

Rule 23. Class Actions

(a) Requisites to Class Action. One or more members of a class may sue or be sued as representative parties on behalf of all only if (1) the class is so numerous that joinder of all members is impracticable, (2) there are questions of law or fact common to the class, (3) the claims or defenses of the representative parties are typical of the claims or defenses of the class, and (4) the representative parties will fairly and adequately protect the interests of the class.

(b) Class Actions Maintainable. An action may be maintained as a class action if the prerequisites of paragraph (a) are satisfied, and in addition:

(1) The prosecution of separate actions by or against individual members of the class would create a risk of:

(A) Inconsistent or varying adjudications with respect to individual members of the class which would establish incompatible standards of conduct for the party opposing the class, or

(B) Adjudications with respect to individual members of the class which would as a practical matter be dispositive of the interests of the other members not parties to the adjudications or substantially impair or impede their ability to protect their interests; or

(2) The party opposing the class has acted or refused to act on grounds generally applicable to the class, thereby making appropriate final injunctive relief or corresponding declaratory relief with respect to the class as a whole; or

(3) The Court finds that the questions of law or fact common to the members of the class predominate over any questions affecting only individual members, and that a class action is superior to other available methods for the fair and efficient adjudication of the controversy. The matter pertinent to the findings include:

(A) The interest of members of the class in individually controlling the prosecution or defense of separate actions;

(B) The extent and nature of any litigation concerning the controversy already commenced by or against members of the class;

(C) The desirability or undesirability of concentrating the litigation of the claims in the particular forum;

(D) The difficulties likely to be encountered in the management of a class action.

(c) Determination by Order Whether Class Action to Be Maintained; Notice; Judgment; Actions Conducted Partially as Class Actions.

(1) As soon as practicable after the commencement of an action brought as a class action, the Court shall determine by order whether it is to be so maintained. An order under this paragraph may be conditional, and may be altered or amended before the decision on the merits.

(2) In any class action maintained under paragraph (b)(3), the Court shall direct to the members of the class the best notice practicable under the circumstances, including individual notice to all members who can be identified through reasonable effort. The notice shall advise each member that:

(A) The Court will exclude a member from the class if the member so requests by a specified date;

(B) The judgment, whether favorable or not, will include all members who do not request exclusion; and

(C) Any member who does not request exclusion may, if the member desires, enter an appearance through his counsel.

(3) The judgment in an action maintained as a class action under paragraph (b)(1) or (b)(2), whether or not favorable to the class, shall include and describe those whom the Court finds to be members of the class. The judgment in an action maintained as a class action under paragraph (b)(3), whether or not favorable to the class, shall include and specify or describe those to whom the notice provided in paragraph (c)(2) was directed, and who have not requested exclusion, and whom the Court finds to be members of the class.

(4) When appropriate (A) an action may be brought or maintained as a class action with respect to particular issues, or (B) a class may be divided into subclasses and each subclass treated as a class, and the provisions of this rule shall then be construed and applied accordingly.

(d) Orders in Conduct of Actions. In the conduct of actions to which this rule applies, the Court may make appropriate orders: (1) Determining the course of proceedings or prescribing measures to prevent undue repetition or complication in the presentation of evidence or argument; (2) requiring, for the protection of the members of the class or otherwise for the fair conduct of the action, that notice be given in such manner as the Court directs to some or all of the members of any step in the action, or of the proposed extent of the judgment, or of the opportunity of members to signify whether they consider the representation fair and adequate, to intervene and present claims or defenses, or otherwise to come into the action; (3) imposing conditions on the representative parties or on intervenors; (4) requiring that the pleadings be amended to eliminate therefrom allegations as to representation of absent persons, and that the action proceed accordingly; (5) dealing with similar procedural matters. The orders may be combined with an order under Rule 16, and may be altered or amended as may be desirable from time to time.

(e) Dismissal or Compromise. A class action shall not be dismissed or compromised without the approval of the Court, and notice by mail, publication or otherwise of the proposed dismissal or compromise shall be given to all members of the class in such manner as the Court directs; except that if the dismissal is to be without prejudice to the class or with prejudice to the plaintiff only, then such dismissal shall be ordered without notice thereof if there is a showing that no compensation in any form has passed directly or indirectly from any of the defendants to the plaintiff or plaintiff's attorney and that no promise to give any such compensation has been made.

Rule 23.1 Derivative Actions by Shareholders

In a derivative action brought by 1 or more shareholders or members to enforce a right of a corporation or of an unincorporated association, the corporation or association having failed to enforce a right which may properly be asserted by it, the complaint shall allege that the plaintiff was a shareholder or member at the time of the transaction of which the plaintiff complains or that the plaintiff's share or membership thereafter devolved on the plaintiff by operation of law. The complaint shall also allege with particularity the efforts, if any, made by the plaintiff to obtain the action the plaintiff desires from the directors or comparable authority and the reasons for the plaintiff's failure to obtain the action or for not making the effort. The action shall not be dismissed or compromised without the approval of the Court, and notice by mail, publication or otherwise of the proposed dismissal or compromise shall be given to shareholders or members in such manner as the Court directs; except that if the dismissal is to be without prejudice or with prejudice to the plaintiff only, then such dismissal shall be ordered without notice thereof if there is a showing that no compensation in any form has passed directly or indirectly from any of the defendants to the plaintiff or plaintiff's attorney and that no promise to give any such compensation has been made.

XI. INTERNAL REVENUE SERVICE "CHECK THE BOX" REGULATIONS

INTERNAL REVENUE SERVICE, DEPARTMENT OF TREASURY

(Selected Provisions)

26 C.F.R. §§ 301.7701 et. seq.

§ 301.7701–2 Business entities; definitions

(a) Business entities. For purposes of this section and § 301.7701–3, a business entity is any entity recognized for federal tax purposes (including an entity with a single owner that may be disregarded as an entity separate from its owner under § 301.7701–3) that is not properly classified as a trust under § 301.7701–4 or otherwise subject to special treatment under the Internal Revenue Code. A business entity with two or more members is classified for federal tax purposes as either a corporation or a partnership. A business entity with only one owner is classified as a corporation or is disregarded; if the entity is disregarded, its activities are treated in the same manner as a sole proprietorship, branch, or division of the owner.

(b) Corporations. For federal tax purposes, the term corporation means—

(1) A business entity organized under a Federal or State statute, or under a statute of a federally recognized Indian tribe, if the statute describes or refers to the entity as incorporated or as a corporation, body corporate, or body politic;

(2) An association (as determined under § 301.7701–3);

(3) A business entity organized under a State statute, if the statute describes or refers to the entity as a joint-stock company or joint-stock association;

(4) An insurance company;

(5) A State-chartered business entity conducting banking activities, if any of its deposits are insured under the Federal Deposit Insurance Act, as amended, 12 U.S.C. 1811 et seq., or a similar federal statute;

(6) A business entity wholly owned by a State or any political subdivision thereof;

(7) A business entity that is taxable as a corporation under a provision of the Internal Revenue Code other than section 7701(a)(3); and

(8) Certain foreign entities—(i) In general. Except as provided in paragraphs (b)(8)(ii) and (d) of this section, the following business entities formed in the following jurisdictions:

American Samoa, Corporation

Argentina, Sociedad Anonima

Australia, Public Limited Company

Austria, Aktiengesellschaft

Barbados, Limited Company

Belgium, Societe Anonyme

Belize, Public Limited Company

Bolivia, Sociedad Anonima

Brazil, Sociedade Anonima

Canada, Corporation and Company

Chile, Sociedad Anonima

People's Republic of China, Gufen Youxian Gongsi

Republic of China (Taiwan), Ku-fen Yu-hsien Kung-szu

Colombia, Sociedad Anonima

Costa Rica, Sociedad Anonima

Cyprus, Public Limited Company

Czech Republic, Akciova Spolecnost

Denmark, Aktieselskab

Ecuador, Sociedad Anonima or Compania Anonima

Egypt, Sharikat Al–Mossahamah

El Salvador, Sociedad Anonima

Finland, Osakeyhtio/Aktiebolag

France, Societe Anonyme
Germany, Aktiengesellschaft
Greece, Anonymos Etairia
Guam, Corporation
Guatemala, Sociedad Anonima
Guyana, Public Limited Company
Honduras, Sociedad Anonima
Hong Kong, Public Limited Company
Hungary, Reszvenytarsasag
Iceland, Hlutafelag
India, Public Limited Company
Indonesia, Perseroan Terbuka
Ireland, Public Limited Company
Israel, Public Limited Company
Italy, Societa per Azioni
Jamaica, Public Limited Company
Japan, Kabushiki Kaisha
Kazakstan, Ashyk Aktsionerlik Kogham
Republic of Korea, Chusik Hoesa
Liberia, Corporation
Luxembourg, Societe Anonyme
Malaysia, Berhad
Malta, Partnership Anonyme
Mexico, Sociedad Anonima
Morocco, Societe Anonyme
Netherlands, Naamloze Vennootschap
New Zealand, Limited Company
Nicaragua, Compania Anonima
Nigeria, Public Limited Company
Northern Mariana Islands, Corporation
Norway, Aksjeselskap
Pakistan, Public Limited Company
Panama, Sociedad Anonima
Paraguay, Sociedad Anonima
Peru, Sociedad Anonima
Philippines, Stock Corporation
Poland, Spolka Akcyjna
Portugal, Sociedade Anonima
Puerto Rico, Corporation
Romania, Societe pe Actiuni
Russia, Otkrytoye Aktsionernoy Obshchestvo
Saudi Arabia, Sharikat Al–Mossahamah
Singapore, Public Limited Company
Slovak Republic, Akciova Spolocnost
South Africa, Public Limited Company
Spain, Sociedad Anonima
Surinam, Naamloze Vennootschap
Sweden, Publika Aktiebolag
Switzerland, Aktiengesellschaft
Thailand, Borisat Chamkad (Mahachon)
Trinidad and Tobago, Public Limited Company
Tunisia, Societe Anonyme
Turkey, Anonim Sirket
Ukraine, Aktsionerne Tovaristvo Vidkritogo Tipu
United Kingdom, Public Limited Company
United States Virgin Islands, Corporation
Uruguay, Sociedad Anonima
Venezuela, Sociedad Anonima or Compania Anonima

(ii)(A) Exceptions in certain cases. The following entities will not be treated as corporations under paragraph (b)(8)(i) of this section:

(1) With regard to Canada, a Nova Scotia Unlimited Liability Company (or any other company or corporation all of whose owners have unlimited liability pursuant to federal or provincial law).

(2) With regard to India, a company deemed to be a public limited company solely by operation of Section 43A(1) (relating to corporate ownership of the company), section 43A(1A) (relating to annual average turnover), or section 43A(1B) (relating to ownership interests in other companies) of the Companies Act, 1956 (or any combination of these), provided that the organizational documents of such deemed public limited company continue to meet the requirements of section 3(1)(iii) of the Companies Act, 1956.

(3) With regard to Malasia, a Sendirian Berhad. (B) Inclusions in certain cases. With regard to Mexico,

the term Sociedad Anonima includes a Sociedad Anonima that chooses to apply the variable capital provision of Mexican corporate law (Sociedad Anonima de Capital Variable).

(iii) Public companies. With regard to Cyprus, Hong Kong, Jamaica, and Trinidad and Tobago, the term public limited company includes any limited company which is not a private limited company under the laws of those jurisdictions. In all other cases, where the term Public Limited Company is not defined, that term shall include any Limited Company defined as a public company under the corporate laws of the relevant jurisdiction.

(iv) Limited companies. Any reference to a limited company (whether public or private) in paragraph (b)(8)(i) of this section includes, as the case may be, companies limited by shares and companies limited by guarantee.

(v) Multilingual countries. Different linguistic renderings of the name of an entity listed in paragraph (b)(8)(i) of this section shall be disregarded. For example, an entity formed under the laws of Switzerland as a Societe Anonyme will be a corporation and treated in the same manner as an Aktiengesellschaft.

(c) Other business entities. For federal tax purposes—

(1) The term partnership means a business entity that is not a corporation under paragraph (b) of this section and that has at least two members.

(2) Wholly owned entities—(i) In general. A business entity that has a single owner and is not a corporation under paragraph (b) of this section is disregarded as an entity separate from its owner.

(ii) Special rule for certain business entities. If the single owner of a business entity is a bank (as defined in section 581), then the special rules applicable to banks will continue to apply to the single owner as if the wholly owned entity were a separate entity.

(d) Special rule for certain foreign business entities—(1) In general. Except as provided in paragraph (d)(3) of this section, a foreign business entity described in paragraph (b)(8)(i) of this section will not be treated as a corporation under paragraph (b)(8)(i) of this section if—

(i) The entity was in existence on May 8, 1996;

(ii) The entity's classification was relevant (as defined in § 301.7701-3(d)) on May 8, 1996;

(iii) No person (including the entity) for whom the entity's classification was relevant on May 8, 1996, treats the entity as a corporation for purposes of filing such person's federal income tax returns, information returns, and withholding documents for the taxable year including May 8, 1996;

(iv) Any change in the entity's claimed classification within the sixty months prior to May 8, 1996, occurred solely as a result of a change in the organizational documents of the entity, and the entity and all members of the entity recognized the federal tax consequences of any change in the entity's classification within the sixty months prior to May 8, 1996;

(v) A reasonable basis (within the meaning of section 6662) existed on May 8, 1996, for treating the entity as other than a corporation; and

(vi) Neither the entity nor any member was notified in writing on or before May 8, 1996, that the classification of the entity was under examination (in which case the entity's classification will be determined in the examination).

(2) Binding contract rule. If a foreign business entity described in paragraph (b)(8)(i) of this section is formed after May 8, 1996, pursuant to a written binding contract (including an accepted bid to develop a project) in effect on May 8, 1996, and all times thereafter, in which the parties agreed to engage (directly or indirectly) in an active and substantial business operation in the jurisdiction in which the entity is formed, paragraph (d)(1) of this section will be applied to that entity by substituting the date of the entity's formation for May 8, 1996.

(3) Termination of grandfather status—(i) In general. An entity that is not treated as a corporation under paragraph (b)(8)(i) of this section by reason of paragraph (d)(1) or (d)(2) of this section will be treated permanently as a corporation under paragraph (b)(8)(i) of this section from the earliest of:

(A) The effective date of an election to be treated as an association under § 301.7701-3;

(B) A termination of the partnership under section 708(b)(1)(B) (regarding sale or exchange of 50 percent or more of the total interest in an entity's capital or profits within a twelve month period); or

(C) A division of the partnership under section 708(b)(2)(B).

(ii) Special rule for certain entities. For purposes of paragraph (d)(2) of this section, paragraph (d)(3)(i)(B) of this section shall not apply if the sale or exchange of interests in the entity is to a related person (within the meaning of sections 267(b) and 707(b)) and occurs no later than twelve months after the date of the formation of the entity.

(e) Effective date. Except as otherwise provided in this paragraph (e), the rules of this section apply as of January 1, 1997. The reference to the Finnish, Maltese, and Norwegian entities in paragraph (b)(8)(i) of this section is applicable on November 29, 1999. The reference to the Trinidadian entity in paragraph (b)(8)(i) of this section applies to entities formed on or after November 29, 1999. Any Maltese or Norwegian entity that becomes an eligible entity as a result of paragraph (b)(8)(i) of this section in effect on November 29, 1999 may elect by February 14, 2000 to be classified for federal tax purposes as an entity other than a corporation retroactive to any period from and including January 1, 1997. Any Finnish entity that becomes an eligible entity as a result of paragraph (b)(8)(i) of this section in effect on November 29, 1999 may elect by February 14, 2000 to be classified for federal tax purposes as an entity other than a corporation retroactive to any period from and including September 1, 1997.

§ 301.7701-3 Classification of certain business entities

(a) In general. A business entity that is not classified as a corporation under § 301.7701-2(b)(1), (3), (4), (5), (6), (7), or (8) (an eligible entity) can elect its classification for federal tax purposes as provided in this section. An eligible entity with at least two members can elect to be classified as either an association (and thus a corporation under § 301.7701-2(b)(2)) or a partnership, and an eligible entity with a single owner can elect to be classified as an association or to be disregarded as an entity separate from its owner. Paragraph (b) of this section provides a default classification for an eligible entity that does not make an election. Thus, elections are necessary only when an eligible entity chooses to be classified initially as other than the default classification or when an eligible entity chooses to change its classification. An entity whose classification is determined under the default classification retains that classification (regardless of any changes in the members' liability that occurs at any time during the time that the entity's classification is relevant as defined in paragraph (d) of this section) until the entity makes an election to change that classification under paragraph (c)(1) of this section. Paragraph (c) of this section provides rules for making express elections. Paragraph (d) of this section provides special rules for foreign eligible entities. Paragraph (e) of this section provides special rules for classifying entities resulting from partnership terminations and divisions under section 708(b). Paragraph (f) of this section sets forth the effective date of this section and a special rule relating to prior periods.

(b) Classification of eligible entities that do not file an election—(1) Domestic eligible entities. **Except as provided in paragraph (b)(3) of this** section, unless the entity elects otherwise, a domestic eligible entity is—

(i) A partnership if it has two or more members; or

(ii) Disregarded as an entity separate from its owner if it has a single owner.

(2) Foreign eligible entities—(i) In general. Except as provided in paragraph (b)(3) of this section, unless the entity elects otherwise, a foreign eligible entity is—

(A) A partnership if it has two or more members and at least one member does not have limited liability;

(B) An association if all members have limited liability; or

(C) Disregarded as an entity separate from its owner if it has a single owner that does not have limited liability.

(ii) Definition of limited liability. For purposes of paragraph (b)(2)(i) of this section, a member of a foreign eligible entity has limited liability if the member has no personal liability for the debts of or claims against the entity by reason of being a member. This determination is based solely on the statute or law pursuant to which the entity is organized, except that if the underlying statute or law allows the entity to specify in its organizational documents whether the members will have limited liability, the organizational documents may also be relevant. For purposes of this section, a member has personal liability if the creditors of the entity may seek satisfaction of all or any portion of the debts or claims against the entity from the member as such. A member has personal liability for purposes of this paragraph even if the member makes an agreement under which another person (whether or not a member of the entity) assumes such liability or agrees to indemnify that member for any such liability.

(3) Existing eligible entities—(i) In general. Unless the entity elects otherwise, an eligible entity in existence prior to the effective date of this section will have the same classification that the entity claimed under §§ 301.7701-1 through 301.7701-3 as in effect on the date prior to the effective date of this section; except that if an eligible entity with a single owner claimed to be a partnership under those regulations, the entity will be disregarded as an entity separate from its owner under this paragraph (b)(3)(i). For special rules regarding the classification of such entities for periods prior to the effective date of this section, see paragraph (f)(2) of this section.

(ii) Special rules. For purposes of paragraph (b)(3)(i) of this section, a foreign eligible entity is treated as being in existence prior to the effective date of this section only if the entity's classification was relevant (as defined in paragraph (d) of this section) at any time during the sixty months prior to the effective date of this section. If an entity claimed different classifications prior to the effective date of this section, the entity's classification for purposes of paragraph (b)(3)(i) of this section is the last classification claimed by the entity. If a foreign eligible entity's classification is relevant prior to the effective date of this section, but no federal tax or information return is filed or the federal tax or information return does not indicate the classification of the entity, the entity's classification for the period prior to the effective date of this section is determined under the regulations in effect on the date prior to the effective date of this section.

(c) Elections—(1) Time and place for filing—(i) In general. Except as provided in paragraphs (c)(1)(iv) and (v) of this section, an eligible entity may elect to be classified other than as provided under paragraph (b) of this section, or to change its classification, by filing Form 8832, Entity Classification Election, with the service center designated on Form 8832. An election will not be accepted unless all of the information required by the form and instructions, including the taxpayer identifying number of the entity, is provided on Form 8832. See § 301.6109-1 for rules on applying for and displaying Employer Identification Numbers.

(ii) Further notification of elections. An eligible entity required to file a federal tax or information return for the taxable year for which an election is made under paragraph (c)(1)(i) of this section must attach a copy of its Form 8832 to its federal tax or information return for that year. If the entity is not required to file a return for that year, a copy of its Form 8832 must be attached to the federal income tax or information return of any direct or indirect owner of the entity for the taxable year of the owner that includes the date on which the election was effective. An indirect owner of the entity does not have to attach a copy of the Form 8832 to its return if an entity in which it has an interest is already filing a copy of the Form 8832 with its return. If an entity, or one of its direct or indirect owners, fails to attach a copy of a Form 8832 to its return as directed in this section, an otherwise valid election under paragraph (c)(1)(i) of this section will not be invalidated, but the non-filing party may be subject to penalties, including any applicable penalties if the federal tax or information returns are inconsistent with the entity's election under paragraph (c)(1)(i) of this section.

(iii) Effective date of election. An election made under paragraph (c)(1)(i) of this section will be effective on the date specified by the entity on Form 8832 or on the date filed if no such date is specified on the election form. The effective date specified on Form 8832 can not be more than 75 days prior to the date on which the election is filed and can not be more than 12 months after the date on which the election is filed. If an election specifies an effective date more than 75 days prior to the date on which the election is filed, it will be effective 75 days prior to the date it was filed. If an election specifies an effective date more than 12 months from the date on which the election is filed, it will be effective 12 months after the date it was filed. If an election specifies an effective date before January 1, 1997, it will be effective as of January 1, 1997. If a purchasing corporation makes an election under section 338 regarding an acquired subsidiary, an election under paragraph (c)(1)(i) of this section for the acquired subsidiary can be effective no earlier than the day after the acquisition date (within the meaning of section 338(h)(2)).

(iv) Limitation. If an eligible entity makes an election under paragraph (c)(1)(i) of this section to change its classification (other than an election made by an existing entity to change its classification as of the effective date of this section), the entity cannot change its classification by election again during the sixty months succeeding the effective date of the election. However, the Commissioner may permit the entity to change its classification by election within the sixty months if more than fifty percent of the ownership interests in the entity as of the effective date of the subsequent election are owned by persons that did not own any interests in the entity on the filing date or on the effective date of the entity's prior election. An election by a newly formed eligible entity that is effective on the date of formation is not considered a change for purposes of this paragraph (c)(1)(iv).

(v) Deemed elections—(A) Exempt organizations. An eligible entity that has been determined to be, or claims to be, exempt from taxation under section 501(a) is treated as having made an election under this section to be classified as an association. Such election will be effective as of the first day for which exemption is claimed or determined to apply, regardless of when the claim or determination is made, and will remain in effect unless an election is made under paragraph (c)(1)(i) of this section after the date the claim for exempt status is withdrawn or rejected or the date the determination of exempt status is revoked.

(B) Real estate investment trusts. An eligible entity that files an election under section 856(c)(1) to be treated as a real estate investment trust is treated as having made an election under this section to be classified as an association. Such election will be effective as of the first day the entity is treated as a real estate investment trust.

(vi) Examples. The following examples illustrate the rules of this paragraph (c)(1):

Example 1. On July 1, 1998, X, a domestic corporation, purchases a 10% interest in Y, an eligible entity formed under Country A law in 1990. The entity's classification was not relevant to any person for federal tax or information purposes prior to X's acquisition of an interest in Y. Thus, Y is not considered to be in existence on the effective date of this section for purposes of paragraph (b)(3) of this section. Under the applicable Country A statute, all members of Y have limited liability as defined in paragraph (b)(2)(ii) of this section. Accordingly, Y is classified as an association under paragraph (b)(2)(i)(B) of this section unless it elects under this paragraph (c) to be classified as a partnership. To be classified as a partnership as of July 1, 1998, Y must file a Form 8832 by September 14, 1998. See paragraph (c)(1)(i) of this section. Because an election cannot be effective more than 75 days prior to the date on which it is filed, if Y files its Form 8832 after September 14, 1998, it will be classified as an association from July 1, 1998, until the effective date of the election. In that case, it could not change its classification by election under this paragraph (c) during the sixty months succeeding the effective date of the election.

Example 2. (i) Z is an eligible entity formed under Country B law and is in existence on the effective date of this section within the meaning of paragraph (b)(3) of this section. Prior to the effective date of this section, Z claimed to be classified as an association. Unless Z files an election under this paragraph (c), it will continue to be classified as an association under paragraph (b)(3) of this section.

(ii) Z files a Form 8832 pursuant to this paragraph (c) to be classified as a partnership, effective as of the effective date of this section. Z can file an election to be classified as an association at any time thereafter, but then would not be permitted to change its classification by election during the sixty months succeeding the effective date of that subsequent election.

(2) Authorized signatures—(i) In general. An election made under paragraph (c)(1)(i) of this section must be signed by—

(A) Each member of the electing entity who is an owner at the time the election is filed; or

(B) Any officer, manager, or member of the electing entity who is authorized (under local law or the entity's organizational documents) to make the election and who represents to having such authorization under penalties of perjury.

(ii) Retroactive elections. For purposes of paragraph (c)(2)(i) of this section, if an election under paragraph (c)(1)(i) of this section is to be effective for any period prior to the time that it is filed, each person who was an owner between the date the election is to be effective and the date the election is filed, and who is not an owner at the time the election is filed, must also sign the election.

(iii) Changes in classification. For paragraph (c)(2)(i) of this section, if an election under paragraph (c)(1)(i) of this section is made to change the classification of an entity, each person who was an owner on the date that any transactions under paragraph (g) of this section are deemed to occur, and who is not an owner at the time the election is filed, must also sign the election. This paragraph (c)(2)(iii) applies to elections filed on or after November 29, 1999.

(d) Special rules for foreign eligible entities—(1) For purposes of this section, a foreign eligible entity's classification is relevant when its classification affects the liability of any person for federal tax or information purposes. For example, a foreign entity's classification would be relevant if U.S. income was paid to the entity and the determination by the withholding agent of the amount to be withheld under chapter 3 of the Internal Revenue Code (if any) would vary depending upon whether the entity is classified as a partnership or as an association. Thus, the classification might affect the documentation that the withholding agent must receive from the entity, the type of tax or information return to file, or how the return must be prepared. The date that the classification of a foreign eligible entity is relevant is the date an event occurs that creates an obligation to file a federal tax return, information return, or statement for which the classification of the entity must be determined. Thus, the classification of a foreign entity is relevant, for example, on the date that an interest in the entity is acquired which will require a U.S. person to file an information return on Form 5471.

(2) Special rule when classification is no longer relevant—If the classification of a foreign eligible entity which was previously relevant for federal tax purposes ceases to be relevant for sixty consecutive months, the entity's classification will initially be determined under the default classification when the classification of the foreign eligible entity again becomes relevant. The date that the classification of a foreign entity ceases to be relevant is the date an event occurs that causes the classification to no longer be relevant, or, if no event occurs in a taxable year that causes the classification to be relevant, then the date is the first day of that taxable year.

(e) Coordination with section 708(b). Except as provided in § 301.7701-2(d)(3) (regarding termination of grandfather status for certain foreign business entities), an entity resulting from a transaction described in section 708(b)(1)(B) (partnership termination due to sales or exchanges) or section 708(b)(2)(B) (partnership division) is a partnership.

(f) Changes in number of members of an entity—(1) **Associations**. The classification of an eligible entity as an association is not affected by any change in the number of members of the entity.

(2) **Partnerships and single member entities**. An eligible entity classified as a partnership becomes disregarded as an entity separate from its owner when the entity's membership is reduced to one member. A single member entity disregarded as an entity separate from its owner is classified as a partnership when the entity has more than one member. If an elective classification change under paragraph (c) of this section is effective at the same time as a membership change described in this paragraph (f)(2), the deemed transactions in paragraph (g) of this section resulting from the elective change preempt the transactions that would result from the change in membership.

(3) **Effect on sixty month limitation**. A change in the number of members of an entity does not result in the creation of a new entity for purposes of the sixty month limitation on elections under paragraph (c)(1)(iv) of this section.

(4) **Examples**. The following examples illustrate the application of this paragraph (f):

Example 1. A, a U.S. person, owns a domestic eligible entity that is disregarded as an entity separate from its owner.

On January 1, 1998, B, a U.S. person, buys a 50 percent interest in the entity from A. Under this paragraph (f), the entity is classified as a partnership when B acquires an interest in the entity. However, A and B elect to have the entity classified as an association effective on January 1, 1998. Thus, B is treated as buying shares of stock on January 1, 1998. (Under paragraph (c)(1)(iv) of this section, this election is treated as a change in classification so that the entity generally cannot change its classification by election again during the sixty months succeeding the effective date of the election.) Under paragraph (g)(1) of this section, A is treated as contributing the assets and liabilities of the entity to the newly formed association immediately before the close of December 31, 1997. Because A does not retain control of the association as required by section 351, A's contribution will be a taxable event. Therefore, under section 1012, the association will take a fair market value basis in the assets contributed by A, and A will have a fair market value basis in the stock received. A will have no additional gain upon the sale of stock to B, and B will have a cost basis in the stock purchased from A.

Example 2. (i) On April 1, 1998, A and B, U.S. persons, form X, a foreign eligible entity. X is treated as an association under the default provisions of paragraph (b)(2)(i) of this section, and X does not make an election to be classified as a partnership. A subsequently purchases all of B's interest in X.

(ii) Under paragraph (f)(1) of this section, X continues to be classified as an association. X, however, can subsequently elect to be disregarded as an entity separate from A. The sixty month limitation of paragraph (c)(1)(iv) of this section does not prevent X from making an election because X has not made a prior election under paragraph (c)(1)(i) of this section.

Example 3. (i) On April 1, 1998, A and B, U.S. persons, form X, a foreign eligible entity. X is treated as an association under the default provisions of paragraph (b)(2)(i) of this section, and X does not make an election to be classified as a partnership. On January 1, 1999, X elects to be classified as a partnership effective on that date. Under the sixty month limitation of paragraph (c)(1)(iv) of this section, X cannot elect to be classified as an association until January 1, 2004 (i.e., sixty months after the effective date of the election to be classified as a partnership).

(ii) On June 1, 2000, A purchases all of B's interest in X. After A's purchase of B's interest, X can no longer be classified as a partnership because X has only one member. Under paragraph (f)(2) of this section, X is disregarded as an entity separate from A when A becomes the only member of X. X, however, is not treated as a new entity for purposes of paragraph (c)(1)(iv) of this section. As a result, the sixty month limitation of paragraph (c)(1)(iv) of this section continues to apply to X, and X cannot elect to be classified as an association until January 1, 2004 (i.e., sixty months after January 1, 1999, the effective date of the election by X to be classified as a partnership).

(5) **Effective date**. This paragraph (f) applies as of November 29, 1999.

(g) **Elective changes in classification**—(1) **Deemed treatment of elective change**.—(i) *Partnership to association*. If an eligible entity classified as a partnership elects under paragraph (c)(1)(i) of this section to be classified as an association, the following is deemed to occur: The partnership contributes all of its assets and liabilities to the association in exchange for stock in the association, and immediately thereafter, the partnership liquidates by distributing the stock of the association to its partners.

(ii) *Association to partnership*. If an eligible entity classified as an association elects under paragraph (c)(1)(i) of this section to be classified as a partnership, the following is deemed to occur: The association distributes all of its assets and liabilities to its shareholders in liquidation of the association, and immediately thereafter, the shareholders contribute all of the distributed assets and liabilities to a newly formed partnership.

(iii) *Association to disregarded entity*. If an eligible entity classified as an association elects under paragraph (c)(1)(i) of this section to be disregarded as an entity separate from its owner, the following is deemed to occur: The association distributes all of its assets and liabilities to its single owner in liquidation of the association.

(iv) *Disregarded entity to an association*. If an eligible entity that is disregarded as an entity separate from its owner elects under paragraph (c)(1)(i) of this section to be classified as an association, the following is deemed to occur: The owner of the eligible entity contributes all of the assets and liabilities of the entity to the association in exchange for stock of the association.

(2) **Effect of elective changes**. The tax treatment of a change in the classification of an entity for federal tax purposes by election under paragraph (c)(1)(i) of this section is determined under all relevant provisions of the Internal Revenue Code and general principles of tax law, including the step transaction doctrine.

(3) **Timing of election**—(i) *In general.* An election under paragraph (c)(1)(i) of this section that changes the classification of an eligible entity for federal tax purposes is treated as occurring at the start of the day for which the election is effective. Any transactions that are deemed to occur under this paragraph (g) as a result of a change in classification are treated as occurring immediately before the close of the day before the election is effective. For example, if an election is made to change the classification of an entity from an association to a partnership effective on January 1, the deemed transactions specified in paragraph (g)(1)(ii) of this section (including the liquidation of the association) are treated as occurring immediately before the close of December 31 and must be reported by the owners of the entity on December 31. Thus, the last day of the association's taxable year will be December 31 and the first day of the partnership's taxable year will be January 1.

(ii) *Coordination with section 338 election.* A purchasing corporation that makes a qualified stock purchase of an eligible entity taxed as a corporation may make an election under section 338 regarding the acquisition if it satisfies the requirements for the election, and may also make an election to change the classification of the target corporation. If a taxpayer makes an election under section 338 regarding its acquisition of another entity taxable as a corporation and makes an election under paragraph (c) of this section for the acquired corporation (effective at the earliest possible date as provided by paragraph (c)(1)(iii) of this section), the transactions under paragraph (g) of this section are deemed to occur immediately after the deemed asset purchase by the new target corporation under section 338.

(iii) *Application to successive elections in tiered situations.* When elections under paragraph (c)(1)(i) of this section for a series of tiered entities are effective on the same date, the eligible entities may specify the order of the elections on Form 8832. If no order is specified for the elections, any transactions that are deemed to occur in this paragraph (g) as a result of the classification change will be treated as occurring first for the highest tier entity's classification change, then for the next highest tier entity's classification change, and so forth down the chain of entities until all the transactions under this paragraph (g) have occurred. For example, Parent, a corporation, wholly owns all of the interest of an eligible entity classified as an association (S1), which wholly owns another eligible entity classified as an association (S2), which wholly owns another eligible entity classified as an association (S3). Elections under paragraph (c)(1)(i) of this section are filed to classify S1, S2, and S3 each as disregarded as an entity separate from its owner effective on the same day. If no order is specified for the elections, the following transactions are deemed to occur under this paragraph (g) as a result of the elections, with each successive transaction occurring on the same day immediately after the preceding transaction S1 is treated as liquidating into Parent, then S2 is treated as liquidating into Parent, and finally S3 is treated as liquidating into Parent.

(4) **Effective date**. This paragraph (g) applies to elections that are filed on or after November 29, 1999. Taxpayers may apply this paragraph (g) retroactively to elections filed before November 29, 1999 if all taxpayers affected by the deemed transactions file consistently with this paragraph (g).

(h) **Effective date**—(1) **In general**. Except as otherwise provided in this section, the rules of this section are applicable as of January 1, 1997.

(2) **Prior treatment of existing entities**. In the case of a business entity that is not described in § 301.7701–2(b)(1), (3), (4), (5), (6), or (7), and that was in existence prior to January 1, 1997, the entity's claimed classification(s) will be respected for all periods prior to January 1, 1997, if—

(i) The entity had a reasonable basis (within the meaning of section 6662) for its claimed classification;

(ii) The entity and all members of the entity recognized the federal tax consequences of any change in the entity's classification within the sixty months prior to January 1, 1997; and

(iii) Neither the entity nor any member was notified in writing on or before May 8, 1996, that the classification of the entity was under examination (in which case the entity's classification will be determined in the examination).

*

XII. PRESENT AND FUTURE VALUE TABLES

Terminal Value of One Dollar at the End of *n* Years

Year	1%	2%	3%	4%	5%	6%	7%	8%	9%	10%
1	1.0100	1.0200	1.0300	1.0400	1.0500	1.0600	1.0700	1.0800	1.0900	1.1000
2	1.0201	1.0404	1.0609	1.0816	1.1025	1.1236	1.1449	1.1664	1.1881	1.2100
3	1.0303	1.0612	1.0927	1.1249	1.1576	1.1910	1.2250	1.2597	1.2950	1.3310
4	1.0406	1.0824	1.1255	1.1699	1.2155	1.2625	1.3108	1.3605	1.4116	1.4641
5	1.0510	1.1041	1.1593	1.2167	1.2763	1.3382	1.4026	1.4693	1.5386	1.6105
6	1.0615	1.1262	1.1941	1.2653	1.3401	1.4185	1.5077	1.5869	1.6771	1.7716
7	1.0721	1.1487	1.2299	1.3159	1.4071	1.5036	1.6058	1.7138	1.8280	1.9487
8	1.0829	1.1717	1.2668	1.3686	1.4775	1.5938	1.7182	1.8509	1.9926	2.1436
9	1.0937	1.1951	1.3048	1.4233	1.5513	1.6895	1.8385	1.9990	2.1719	2.3579
10	1.1046	1.2190	1.3439	1.4802	1.6289	1.7908	1.9672	2.1589	2.3674	2.5937
11	1.1157	1.2434	1.3842	1.5395	1.7103	1.8983	2.1049	2.3316	2.5804	2.8531
12	1.1268	1.2682	1.4258	1.6010	1.7959	2.0122	2.2522	2.5182	2.8127	3.1384
13	1.1381	1.2936	1.4685	1.6651	1.8856	2.1329	2.4098	2.7196	3.0658	3.4523
14	1.1495	1.3195	1.5126	1.7317	1.9799	2.2609	2.5785	2.9372	3.3417	3.7975
15	1.1610	1.3459	1.5580	1.8009	2.0789	2.3966	2.7590	3.1722	3.6425	4.1772
20	1.2202	1.4859	1.8061	2.1911	2.6533	3.2071	3.8697	4.6610	5.6044	6.7275
25	1.2824	1.6406	2.0938	2.6658	3.3864	4.2919	5.4274	6.8485	8.6231	10.835
50	1.6446	2.6916	4.3839	7.1067	11.467	18.420	29.457	46.902	74.358	117.39
100	2.7048	7.2446	19.219	50.505	131.50	339.30	867.71	2,199.8	5,529.0	13,780

Present Value of One Dollar Due at the End of *n* Years

n	1%	2%	3%	4%	5%	6%	7%	8%	9%	10%
1	.99010	.98039	.97007	.96154	.95238	.94340	.93458	.92593	.91743	.90909
2	.98030	.96117	.94260	.92456	.90703	.89000	.87344	.85734	.84168	.82645
3	.97059	.94232	.91514	.88900	.86384	.83962	.81630	.79383	.77218	.75131
4	.96098	.92385	.88849	.85480	.82270	.79209	.76290	.73503	.70843	.68301
5	.95147	.90573	.86261	.82193	.78353	.74726	.71299	.68058	.64993	.62092
6	.94204	.88797	.83748	.79031	.74622	.70496	.66634	.63017	.59627	.56447
7	.93272	.87056	.81309	.75992	.71068	.66506	.62275	.58349	.54703	.51316
8	.92348	.85349	.78941	.73069	.67684	.62741	.58201	.54027	.50187	.46651
9	.91434	.83675	.76642	.70259	.64461	.59190	.54393	.50025	.46043	.42410
10	.90529	.82035	.74409	.67556	.61391	.55839	.50835	.46319	.42241	.38554
11	.89632	.80426	.72242	.64958	.58468	.52679	.47509	.42888	.38753	.35049
12	.88745	.78849	.70138	.62460	.55684	.49697	.44401	.39711	.35553	.31863
13	.87866	.77303	.68095	.60057	.53032	.46884	.41496	.36770	.32618	.28966
14	.86996	.75787	.66112	.57747	.50507	.44230	.38782	.34046	.29925	.26333
15	.86135	.74301	.64186	.55526	.48102	.41726	.36245	.31524	.27454	.23939
16	.85282	.72845	.62317	.53391	.45811	.39365	.33873	.29189	.25187	.21763
17	.84438	.71416	.60502	.51337	.43630	.37136	.31657	.27027	.23107	.19784
18	.83602	.70016	.58739	.49363	.41552	.35034	.29586	.25025	.21199	.17986
19	.82774	.68643	.57029	.47464	.39573	.33051	.27651	.23171	.19449	.16351
20	.81954	.67297	.55367	.45639	.37689	.31180	.25842	.21455	.17843	.14864
21	.81143	.65978	.53755	.43883	.35894	.29415	.24151	.19866	.16370	.13513
22	.80340	.64684	.52189	.42195	.34185	.27750	.22571	.18394	.15018	.12285
23	.79544	.63416	.50669	.40573	.32557	.26180	.21095	.17031	.13778	.11168
24	.78757	.62172	.49193	.39012	.31007	.24698	.19715	.15770	.12640	.10153
25	.77977	.60958	.47760	.37512	.29530	.23300	.18425	.14602	.11597	.09230

PRESENT AND FUTURE VALUE TABLES

Present Value of One Dollar Per Year for *n* Years

Years	1%	2%	3%	4%	5%	6%	7%	8%	9%	10%
1	0.9901	0.9804	0.9709	0.9615	0.9524	0.9434	0.9346	0.9259	0.9174	0.9091
2	1.9704	1.9416	1.9135	1.8861	1.8594	1.8334	1.8080	1.7833	1.7591	1.7355
3	2.9410	2.8839	2.8286	2.7751	2.7232	2.6730	2.6243	2.5771	2.5313	2.4869
4	3.9020	3.8077	3.7171	3.6299	3.5460	3.4651	3.3872	3.3121	3.2397	3.1699
5	4.8534	4.7135	4.5797	4.4518	4.3295	4.2124	4.1002	3.9927	3.8897	3.7908
6	5.7955	5.6014	5.4172	5.2421	5.0757	4.9173	4.7665	4.6229	4.4859	4.3553
7	6.7282	6.4720	6.2303	6.0021	5.7864	5.5824	5.3893	5.2064	5.0330	4.8684
8	7.6517	7.3255	7.0197	6.7327	6.4632	6.2098	5.9713	5.7466	5.5348	5.3349
9	8.5660	8.1622	7.7861	7.4353	7.1078	6.8017	6.5152	6.2469	5.9952	5.7590
10	9.4713	8.9826	8.5302	8.1109	7.7217	7.3601	7.0236	6.7101	6.4177	6.1446
11	10.3676	9.7868	9.2526	8.7605	8.3064	7.8869	7.4987	7.1390	6.8052	6.4951
12	11.2551	10.5753	9.9540	9.3851	8.8633	8.3838	7.9427	7.5361	7.1607	6.8137
13	12.1337	11.3484	10.6350	9.9856	9.3936	8.8527	8.3577	7.9038	7.4869	7.1034
14	13.0037	12.1062	11.2961	10.5631	9.8986	9.2950	8.7455	8.2442	7.7862	7.3667
15	13.8651	12.8493	11.9379	11.1184	10.3797	9.7122	9.1079	8.5595	8.0607	7.6061
20	18.0456	16.3514	14.8775	13.5903	12.4622	11.4699	10.5940	9.8181	9.1285	8.5136
25	22.0232	19.5235	17.4131	15.6221	14.0939	12.7834	11.6536	10.6748	9.8226	9.0770
50	39.1961	31.4236	25.7298	21.4822	18.2559	15.7619	13.8007	12.2335	10.9617	9.9148
100	63.0289	43.0984	31.5989	24.5050	19.8479	16.6175	14.2693	12.4943	11.1091	9.9993

Assumption: Payment made at the end of each year.

†